THE NEW INTERPRETER'S™ BIBLE

IN TWELVE VOLUMES

VOLUME ONE

GENERAL ARTICLES ON
THE BIBLE

GENERAL ARTICLES ON
THE OLD TESTAMENT

THE BOOK OF
GENESIS

THE BOOK OF
EXODUS

THE BOOK OF
LEVITICUS

EDITORIAL BOARD

THE NEW INTERPRETER'S™ BIBLE

GENERAL ARTICLES
&
INTRODUCTION, COMMENTARY, & REFLECTIONS
FOR EACH BOOK OF THE BIBLE
INCLUDING
THE APOCRYPHAL / DEUTEROCANONICAL BOOKS
IN
TWELVE VOLUMES

VOLUME
I

ABINGDON PRESS
Nashville

THE NEW INTERPRETER'S BIBLE
VOLUME I

Copyright © 1994 by Abingdon Press

This book is printed on recycled, acid-free paper.

Library of Congress Cataloging-in-Publication Data

The New Interpreter's Bible: general articles & introduction,
    commentary, & reflections for each book of the Bible, including the
Apocryphal/Deuterocanical books.
        p. cm.
    Full texts and critical notes of the New International Version and
the New Revised Standard Version of the Bible in parallel columns.
        Includes bibliographical references.
        ISBN 0-687-27814-7 (v. 1: alk. paper)
        1. Bible—Commentaries. 2. Abingdon Press. I. Bible. English.
New International. 1994. II. Bible. English. New Revised
Standard. 1994.
BS491.2.N484   1994
220.7'7—dc20   94-21292
                                                                                      CIP

PUBLICATION STAFF
Editorial Director: Neil M. Alexander
Managing Editor: Michael E. Lawrence
Project Director: Jack A. Keller, Jr.
Assistant Editor: Eli D. Fisher, Jr.
Chief Copy Editor: Linda S. Allen
Art Director: Nancy R. Bozeman
Designer: J. S. Laughbaum
Copy Processing Manager: Sylvia S. Marlow
Composition Specialist: Kathy M. Harding
Publishing Systems Analyst: Glenn R. Hinton
Prepress Manager: William E. Gentry
Prepress Systems Technician: Thomas E. Mullins
Production Coordinator: Mary M. Johannes
Scheduling: Laurene M. Brazzell
        Helen M. Pouliot
Print Procurement Coordinator: David M. Sanders

94 95 96 97 98 99 00 01 02 03—10 9 8 7 6 5 4 3 2 1

MANUFACTURED IN THE UNITED STATES OF AMERICA

CONSULTANTS

NEIL M. ALEXANDER
Vice President/Editorial Director
Abingdon Press
Nashville, Tennessee

OWEN F. CAMPION
Associate Publisher
Our Sunday Visitor
Huntington, Indiana

MINERVA G. CARCAÑO
Minister-in-Charge
South Valley Cooperative Ministry
Albuquerque, New Mexico

V. L. DAUGHTERY, JR.
Pastor
Park Avenue United Methodist Church
Valdosta, Georgia

SHARON NEUFER EMSWILER
Pastor
First United Methodist Church
Rock Island, Illinois

JUAN G. FELICIANO
Pastor
Iglesia Metodista Unida–Kedzie Avenue
Chicago, Illinois

CELIA BREWER MARSHALL
Lecturer
University of North Carolina at Charlotte
Charlotte, North Carolina

NANCY C. MILLER-HERRON
Attorney and clergy member of the
    Tennessee Conference
The United Methodist Church
Dresden, Tennessee

ROBERT C. SCHNASE
Pastor
First United Methodist Church
McAllen, Texas

BILL SHERMAN
Pastor
Woodmont Baptist Church
Nashville, Tennessee

RODNEY T. SMOTHERS
Pastor
Central United Methodist Church
Atlanta, Georgia

WILLIAM D. WATLEY
Pastor
St. James African Methodist Episcopal Church
Newark, New Jersey

TALLULAH FISHER WILLIAMS
Pastor
Hartzell Memorial United Methodist Church
Chicago, Illinois

SUK-CHONG YU
Pastor
San Francisco Korean United Methodist Church
San Francisco, California

CONTRIBUTORS

ELIZABETH ACHTEMEIER
Adjunct Professor of Bible and Homiletics
Union Theological Seminary in Virginia
Richmond, Virginia
(Presbyterian Church [U.S.A.])
Joel

LESLIE C. ALLEN
Professor of Old Testament
Fuller Theological Seminary
Pasadena, California
(Baptist)
1 & 2 Chronicles

GARY A. ANDERSON
Associate Professor of Religious Studies
University of Virginia
Charlottesville, Virginia
(The Roman Catholic Church)
Introduction to Israelite Religion

DAVID L. BARTLETT
Lantz Professor of Preaching and
   Communication
The Divinity School
Yale University
New Haven, Connecticut
(American Baptist Churches in the U.S.A.)
1 Peter

ROBERT A. BENNETT
Professor of Old Testament
Episcopal Divinity School
Cambridge, Massachusetts
(The Episcopal Church)
Zephaniah

ADELE BERLIN
Professor of Hebrew and East Asian
   Languages and Literature
University of Maryland
College Park, Maryland
Introduction to Hebrew Poetry

BRUCE C. BIRCH
Professor of Old Testament
Wesley Theological Seminary
Washington, DC
(The United Methodist Church)
1 & 2 Samuel

PHYLLIS A. BIRD
Associate Professor of Old Testament
   Interpretation
Garrett-Evangelical Theological Seminary
Evanston, Illinois
(The United Methodist Church)
The Authority of the Bible

C. CLIFTON BLACK
Associate Professor of New Testament
Perkins School of Theology
Southern Methodist University
Dallas, Texas
(The United Methodist Church)
1, 2, & 3 John

JOSEPH BLENKINSOPP
John A. O'Brien Professor of Biblical Studies
Department of Theology
University of Notre Dame
Notre Dame, Indiana
(The Roman Catholic Church)
Introduction to the Pentateuch

M. EUGENE BORING
Professor of New Testament
Brite Divinity School
Texas Christian University
Fort Worth, Texas
(Christian Church [Disciples of Christ])
Matthew

WALTER BRUEGGEMANN
William Marcellus McPheeters Professor of Old Testament
Columbia Theological Seminary
Decatur, Georgia
(United Church of Christ)
Exodus

DAVID G. BUTTRICK
Professor of Homiletics and Liturgics
The Divinity School
Vanderbilt University
Nashville, Tennessee
(United Church of Christ)
The Use of the Bible in Preaching

RONALD E. CLEMENTS
Samuel Davidson Professor of Old Testament
King's College
University of London
London, England
(Baptist Union of Great Britain and Ireland)
Deuteronomy

RICHARD J. CLIFFORD
Professor of Old Testament
Weston School of Theology
Cambridge, Massachusetts
(The Roman Catholic Church)
Introduction to Wisdom Literature

JOHN J. COLLINS
Professor of Hebrew Bible
The Divinity School
University of Chicago
Chicago, Illinois
(The Roman Catholic Church)
Introduction to Early Jewish Religion

ROBERT B. COOTE
Professor of Old Testament
San Francisco Theological Seminary
San Anselmo, California
(Presbyterian Church [U.S.A.])
Joshua

FRED B. CRADDOCK
Bandy Distinguished Professor of Preaching and New Testament, Emeritus
Candler School of Theology
Emory University
Atlanta, Georgia
(Christian Church [Disciples of Christ])
Hebrews

TONI CRAVEN
Professor of Hebrew Bible
Brite Divinity School
Texas Christian University
Fort Worth, Texas
(The Roman Catholic Church)
Introduction to Narrative Literature

JAMES L. CRENSHAW
Robert L. Flowers Professor of Old Testament
The Divinity School
Duke University
Durham, North Carolina
(Baptist)
Sirach

KEITH R. CRIM
Pastor
New Concord Presbyterian Church
Concord, Virginia
(Presbyterian Church [U.S.A.])
Modern English Versions of the Bible

R. ALAN CULPEPPER
Professor of New Testament
Department of Religion
Baylor University
Waco, Texas
(Southern Baptist Convention)
Luke

KATHERYN PFISTERER DARR
Associate Professor of Hebrew Bible
The School of Theology
Boston University
Boston, Massachusetts
(The United Methodist Church)
Ezekiel

ROBERT DORAN
Professor of Religion
Amherst College
Amherst, Massachusetts
1 & 2 Maccabees

THOMAS B. DOZEMAN
Professor of Old Testament
United Theological Seminary
Dayton, Ohio
(Presbyterian Church [U.S.A.])
Numbers

JAMES D. G. DUNN
Lightfoot Professor of Divinity
Department of Theology
University of Durham
Durham, England
(The Methodist Church [Great Britain])
1 & 2 Timothy; Titus

ELDON JAY EPP
Harkness Professor of Biblical Literature
and Chairman of the Department of Religion
Case Western Reserve University
Cleveland, Ohio
(The Episcopal Church)
Ancient Texts and Versions of the New Testament

KATHLEEN ROBERTSON FARMER
Professor of Old Testament
United Theological Seminary
Dayton, Ohio
(The United Methodist Church)
Ruth

CAIN HOPE FELDER
Professor of New Testament Language
and Literature
The School of Divinity
Howard University
Washington, DC
(The United Methodist Church)
Philemon

TERENCE E. FRETHEIM
Professor of Old Testament
Luther Northwestern Theological Seminary
Saint Paul, Minnesota
(Evangelical Lutheran Church in America)
Genesis

FRANCISCO O. GARCÍA-TRETO
Professor of Religion and Chairman of the
Department of Religion
Trinity University
San Antonio, Texas
(Presbyterian Church [U.S.A.])
Nahum

CATHERINE GUNSALUS GONZÁLEZ
Professor of Church History
Columbia Theological Seminary
Decatur, Georgia
(Presbyterian Church [U.S.A.])
The Use of the Bible in Hymns, Liturgy, and Education

JUSTO L. GONZÁLEZ
Adjunct Professor of Church History
Columbia Theological Seminary
Decatur, Georgia
(The United Methodist Church)
How the Bible Has Been Interpreted in Christian Tradition

DONALD E. GOWAN
Robert Cleveland Holland Professor of Old
Testament
Pittsburgh Theological Seminary
Pittsburgh, Pennsylvania
(Presbyterian Church [U.S.A.])
Amos

JUDITH MARIE GUNDRY-VOLF
Assistant Professor of New Testament
Fuller Theological Seminary
Pasadena, California
(Presbyterian Church [U.S.A.])
Ephesians

DANIEL J. HARRINGTON
Professor of New Testament
Weston School of Theology
Cambridge, Massachusetts
(The Roman Catholic Church)
Introduction to the Canon

RICHARD B. HAYS
Associate Professor of New Testament
The Divinity School
Duke University
Durham, North Carolina
(The United Methodist Church)
Galatians

THEODORE HIEBERT
Assistant Professor of Hebrew Bible/Old
Testament
The Divinity School
Harvard University
Cambridge, Massachusetts
(Mennonite Church)
Habakkuk

CARL R. HOLLADAY
Professor of New Testament
Candler School of Theology
Emory University
Atlanta, Georgia
Contemporary Methods of Reading the Bible

MORNA D. HOOKER
Lady Margaret's Professor of Divinity
The Divinity School
University of Cambridge
Cambridge, England
(The Methodist Church [Great Britain])
Philippians

DAVID C. HOPKINS
Professor of Old Testament
Wesley Theological Seminary
Washington, DC
(United Church of Christ)
Life in Ancient Palestine

DENISE DOMBKOWSKI HOPKINS
Professor of Old Testament
Wesley Theological Seminary
Washington, DC
(United Church of Christ)
Judith

LUKE T. JOHNSON
Robert W. Woodruff Professor of New
Testament and Christian Origins
Candler School of Theology
Emory University
Atlanta, Georgia
(The Roman Catholic Church)
James

WALTER C. KAISER, JR.
Colman Mockler Distinguished Professor
of Old Testament
Gordon-Conwell Theological Seminary
South Hamilton, Massachusetts
(The Evangelical Free Church of America)
Leviticus

LEANDER E. KECK
Winkley Professor of Biblical Theology
The Divinity School
Yale University
New Haven, Connecticut
(Christian Church [Disciples of Christ])
Introduction to The New Interpreter's Bible

CHAN-HIE KIM
Professor of New Testament and Director of
Korean Studies
The School of Theology at Claremont
Claremont, California
(The United Methodist Church)
Reading the Bible as Asian Americans

RALPH W. KLEIN
Dean and Christ Seminary-Seminex Professor of
Old Testament
Lutheran School of Theology at Chicago
Chicago, Illinois
(Evangelical Lutheran Church in America)
Ezra; Nehemiah

MICHAEL KOLARCIK
Assistant Professor
Regis College
Toronto, Ontario
Canada
(The Roman Catholic Church)
Book of Wisdom

WILLIAM L. LANE
Paul T. Walls Professor of Wesleyan
and Biblical Studies
The School of Religion
Seattle Pacific University
Seattle, Washington
(Free Methodist Church of North America)
2 Corinthians

ANDREW T. LINCOLN
Department of Biblical Studies
University of Sheffield
Sheffield, England
(The Church of England)
Colossians

J. CLINTON MCCANN
Assistant Professor of Old Testament
Eden Theological Seminary
St. Louis, Missouri
(Presbyterian Church [U.S.A.])
Psalms

ABRAHAM J. MALHERBE
Buckingham Professor of New Testament
Criticism and Interpretation
The Divinity School
Yale University
New Haven, Connecticut
(Church of Christ)
*The Cultural Context of the New Testament:
The Greco-Roman World*

W. EUGENE MARCH
Arnold Black Rhodes Professor of Old
Testament
Louisville Presbyterian Theological Seminary
Louisville, Kentucky
(Presbyterian Church [U.S.A.])
Haggai

JAMES EARL MASSEY
Dean and Professor of Preaching
and Biblical Studies
The School of Theology
Anderson University
(Church of God [Anderson, Ind.])
*Reading the Bible from Particular Social
Locations: An Introduction;
Reading the Bible as African Americans*

J. MAXWELL MILLER
Professor of Old Testament
Candler School of Theology
Emory University
Atlanta, Georgia
(The United Methodist Church)
Introduction to the History of Ancient Israel

PATRICK D. MILLER
Charles T. Haley Professor of Old Testament
Theology
Princeton Theological Seminary
Princeton, New Jersey
(Presbyterian Church [U.S.A.])
Jeremiah

FREDERICK J. MURPHY
Associate Professor and Chair of the
Department of Religious Studies
College of the Holy Cross
Worcester, Massachusetts
(The Roman Catholic Church)
Introduction to Apocalyptic Literature

CAROL A. NEWSOM
Associate Professor of Old Testament
Candler School of Theology
Emory University
Atlanta, Georgia
(The Episcopal Church)
Job

GEORGE W. E. NICKELSBURG
Professor of Christian Origins and Early Judaism
School of Religion
University of Iowa
Iowa City, Iowa
(Evangelical Lutheran Church in America)
*The Jewish Context of the New
Testament*

IRENE NOWELL
Associate Professor of Religious Studies
Benedictine College
Atchison, Kansas
(The Roman Catholic Church)
Tobit

KATHLEEN M. O'CONNOR
Associate Professor of Biblical Studies
Maryknoll School of Theology
Maryknoll, New York
(The Roman Catholic Church)
Lamentations

GAIL R. O'DAY
Associate Professor of Biblical Preaching
Candler School of Theology
Emory University
Atlanta, Georgia
(United Church of Christ)
John

BEN C. OLLENBURGER
Associate Professor of Old Testament
Associated Mennonite Biblical Seminaries
Elkhart, Indiana
(Mennonite Church)
Zechariah

DENNIS T. OLSON
Assistant Professor of Old Testament
Princeton Theological Seminary
Princeton, New Jersey
(Evangelical Lutheran Church in America)
Judges

CAROLYN OSIEK
Professor of New Testament
Department of Biblical Languages
and Literature
Catholic Theological Union
Chicago, Illinois
(The Roman Catholic Church)
Reading the Bible as Women

SAMUEL PAGÁN
Regional Translation Coordinator for the United
Bible Societies
Miami, Florida
(Christian Church [Disciples of Christ])
Obadiah

SIMON B. PARKER
Associate Professor of Hebrew Bible and
Harrell F. Beck Scholar in Hebrew Scripture
The School of Theology
Boston University
Boston, Massachusetts
(The United Methodist Church)
*The Ancient Near Eastern Literary
Background of the Old Testament*

PHEME PERKINS
Professor of New Testament
Boston College
Chestnut Hill, Massachusetts
(The Roman Catholic Church)
Mark

DAVID L. PETERSEN
Professor of Old Testament
The Iliff School of Theology
Denver, Colorado
(Presbyterian Church [U.S.A.])
Introduction to Prophetic Literature

CHRISTOPHER C. ROWLAND
Dean Ireland's Professor of the Exegesis
of Holy Scripture
The Queen's College
Oxford, England
(The Church of England)
Revelation

ANTHONY J. SALDARINI
Professor of Biblical Studies
Boston College
Chestnut Hill, Massachusetts
(The Roman Catholic Church)
Baruch; Letter of Jeremiah

J. PAUL SAMPLEY
Professor of New Testament and
Christian Origins
The School of Theology and The Graduate Division
Boston University
Boston, Massachusetts
(The United Methodist Church)
1 Corinthians

JUDITH E. SANDERSON
Assistant Professor of Hebrew Bible
Department of Theology and Religious Studies
Seattle University
Seattle, Washington
*Ancient Texts and Versions of the Old
Testament*

EILEEN M. SCHULLER
Associate Professor
Department of Religious Studies
McMaster University
Hamilton, Ontario
Canada
(The Roman Catholic Church)
Malachi

FERNANDO F. SEGOVIA
Associate Professor of New Testament
and Early Christianity
The Divinity School
Vanderbilt University
Nashville, Tennessee
(The Roman Catholic Church)
Reading the Bible as Hispanic Americans

CHRISTOPHER R. SEITZ
Associate Professor of Old Testament
The Divinity School
Yale University
New Haven, Connecticut
(The Episcopal Church)
Isaiah 40–66

CHOON-LEONG SEOW
Associate Professor of Old Testament
Princeton Theological Seminary
Princeton, New Jersey
(Presbyterian Church [U.S.A.])
1 & 2 Kings

MICHAEL A. SIGNER
Abrams Professor of Jewish Thought and
Culture
Department of Theology
University of Notre Dame
Notre Dame, Indiana
*How the Bible Has Been Interpreted in
Jewish Tradition*

MOISÉS SILVA
Professor of New Testament
Westminster Theological Seminary
Philadelphia, Pennsylvania
(The Orthodox Presbyterian Church)
*Contemporary Theories of Biblical
Interpretation*

DANIEL J. SIMUNDSON
Professor of Old Testament and Dean of
Academic Affairs
Luther Northwestern Theological Seminary
Saint Paul, Minnesota
(Evangelical Lutheran Church in America)
Micah

ABRAHAM SMITH
Assistant Professor of New Testament
and Christian Origins
The School of Theology
Boston University
Boston, Massachusetts
(The National Baptist Convention, USA, Inc.)
1 & 2 Thessalonians

DANIEL L. SMITH-CHRISTOPHER
Associate Professor of Theological Studies
Department of Theology
Loyola Marymount University
Los Angeles, California
(The Society of Friends [Quaker])
*Daniel; Bel and the Dragon; Prayer of
Azariah; Susannah*

MARION L. SOARDS
Professor of New Testament Studies
Louisville Presbyterian Theological Seminary
Louisville, Kentucky
(Presbyterian Church [U.S.A.])
Acts

ROBERT C. TANNEHILL
Harold B. Williams Professor of Biblical Studies
Methodist Theological School in Ohio
Delaware, Ohio
(The United Methodist Church)
The Gospels and Narrative Literature

GEORGE E. TINKER
Associate Professor of Cross-Cultural Ministries
The Iliff School of Theology
Denver, Colorado
(Evangelical Lutheran Church in America)
Reading the Bible as Native Americans

W. SIBLEY TOWNER
The Reverend Archibald McFadyen Professor of
Biblical Interpretation
Union Theological Seminary in Virginia
Richmond, Virginia
(Presbyterian Church [U.S.A.])
Ecclesiastes

PHYLLIS TRIBLE
Baldwin Professor of Sacred Literature
Union Theological Seminary
New York, New York
Jonah

GENE M. TUCKER
Professor of Old Testament
Candler School of Theology
Emory University
Atlanta, Georgia
(The United Methodist Church)
Isaiah 1–39

CHRISTOPHER M. TUCKETT
Rylands Professor of Biblical Criticism
and Exegesis
Faculty of Theology
University of Manchester
Manchester, England
(The Church of England)
Jesus and the Gospels

RAYMOND C. VAN LEEUWEN
Professor of Religion and Theology
Calvin College
Grand Rapids, Michigan
(Christian Reformed Church in North America)
Proverbs

ROBERT W. WALL
Professor of Biblical Studies
The School of Religion
Seattle Pacific University
Seattle, Washington
(Free Methodist Church of North America)
Introduction to Epistolary Literature

DUANE F. WATSON
Associate Professor of New Testament Studies
Department of Religion and Philosophy
Malone College
Canton, Ohio
(The United Methodist Church)
2 Peter; Jude

RENITA J. WEEMS
Assistant Professor of Hebrew Bible
The Divinity School
Vanderbilt University
Nashville, Tennessee
(African Methodist Episcopal Church)
Song of Songs

SIDNIE A. WHITE
Assistant Professor of Religion
Department of Religion
Albright College
Reading, Pennsylvania
(The Episcopal Church)
Esther; Additions to Esther

VINCENT L. WIMBUSH
Professor of New Testament and
Christian Origins
Union Theological Seminary
New York, New York
(Progressive National Baptist Convention, Inc.)
*The Ecclesiastical Context of the New
Testament*

N. THOMAS WRIGHT
Lecturer in New Testament Studies
Fellow, Tutor, and Chaplain
Worcester College
Oxford, England
(The Church of England)
Romans

GALE A. YEE
Associate Professor of Old Testament
Department of Theology
University of Saint Thomas
Saint Paul, Minnesota
(The Roman Catholic Church)
Hosea

FEATURES OF
THE NEW INTERPRETER'S BIBLE

The general aim of *The New Interpreter's Bible* is to bring the best in contemporary biblical scholarship into the service of the church to enhance preaching, teaching, and study of the Scriptures. To accomplish that general aim, the design of *The New Interpreter's Bible* has been shaped by two controlling principles: (1) form serves function, and (2) maximize ease of use.

General articles provide the reader with concise, up-to-date, balanced introductions and assessments of selected topics. In most cases, a brief bibliography points the way to further exploration of a topic. Many of the general articles are placed in volumes 1 and 8, at the beginning of the coverage of the Old and New Testaments, respectively. Others have been inserted in those volumes where the reader will encounter the corresponding type of literature (e.g., "Introduction to Prophetic Literature" appears in Volume 6 alongside several of the prophetic books).

Coverage of each biblical book begins with an "Introduction" that acquaints the reader with the essential historical, sociocultural, literary, and theological issues necessary to understand the biblical book. A short bibliography and an outline of the biblical book are found at the end of each Introduction. The introductory sections are the only material in *The New Interpreter's Bible* printed in a single wide-column format.

The biblical text is divided into coherent and manageable primary units, which are located within larger sections of Scripture. At the opening discussion of any large section of Scripture, readers will often find material identified as "Overview," which includes remarks applicable to the large section of text. The primary unit of text may be as short as a few verses or as long as a chapter or more. This is the point at which the biblical text itself is reprinted in *The New Interpreter's Bible*. Dealing with Scripture in terms of these primary units allows discussion of important issues that are overlooked in a verse-by-verse treatment. Each scriptural unit is identified by text citation and a short title.

The full texts and critical notes of the New International Version and the New Revised Standard Version of the Bible are presented in parallel columns for quick reference. Since every translation is to some extent an interpretation as well, the inclusion of these two widely known and influential modern translations provides an easy comparison that in many cases will lead to a better understanding of a passage. Biblical passages are set in two-column format and placed in green tint-blocks to make it easy to recognize them at a glance. The NIV and NRSV material is clearly identified on each page on which the text appears.

Immediately following each biblical text is a section marked "Commentary," which provides an exegetical analysis informed by linguistic, text-critical, historical-critical, literary, social-scientific, and theological methods. The Commentary serves as a reliable, judicious guide through the text, pointing out the critical problems as well as key interpretive issues.

The exegetical approach is "text-centered." That is, the commentators focus primarily on the text in its final form rather than on (a) a meticulous rehearsal of problems of scholarship associated with a text, (b) a thorough reconstruction of the pre-history of the text, or (c) an exhaustive rehearsal of the text's interpretive history. Of course, some attention to scholarly problems, to the pre-history of a text, and to historic interpretations that have shaped streams of tradition is important in particular cases precisely in order to illumine the several levels of meaning in the final form of the text. But the *primary* focus is on the canonical text itself. Moreover, the Commentary not only describes pertinent aspects of the text, but also teaches the reader what to look for in the text so as to develop the reader's own capacity to analyze and interpret the text.

Commentary material runs serially for a few paragraphs or a few pages, depending on what is required by the biblical passage under discussion.

Commentary material is set in a two-column format. Occasional subheads appear in a bold green font. The next level of subdivisions appears as bold black fonts and a third level as black italic fonts. Footnotes are placed at the bottom of the column in which the superscripts appear.

Key words in Hebrew, Aramaic, or Greek are printed in the original-language font, accompanied by a transliteration and a translation or explanation.

Immediately following the Commentary, in most cases, is the section called "Reflections." A detailed exposition growing directly out of the discussion and issues dealt with in the Commentary, Reflections are geared specifically toward helping those who interpret Scripture in the life of the church by providing "handles" for grasping the significance of Scripture for faith and life today. Recognizing that the text has the capacity to shape the life of the Christian community, this section presents multiple possibilities for preaching and teaching in light of each biblical text. That is, instead of providing the preacher or teacher full illustrations, poems, outlines, and the like, the Reflections offer *several* trajectories of possible interpretation that connect with the situation of the contemporary listeners. Recognizing the power of Scripture to speak anew to diverse situations, not all of the suggested trajectories could be appropriated on any one occasion. Preachers and teachers want some specificity about the implications of the text, but not so much specificity that the work is done for them. The ideas in the Reflections are meant to stimulate the thought of preachers and teachers, not to replace it.

Three-quarter width colums distinguish Reflections materials from biblical text and Commentary.

Occasional maps, charts, and illustrations appear throughout the volumes at points where they are most likely to be immediately useful to the reader.

CONTENTS

VOLUME I

INTRODUCTION TO THE NEW INTERPRETER'S BIBLE

LEANDER E. KECK

The publication of *The Interpreter's Bible (IB),* beginning in 1951, was a significant event in the history of Christian publishing in North America, for as its General Editor (George A. Buttrick) observed, no commentary on the whole Bible had appeared in English for fifty years. Understandably, the *IB* quickly established itself as the commentary that one expected to find in the libraries of pastors and professors of Bible, churches, colleges, and seminaries. The sale of nearly three million volumes implies that it met a real need. Four decades later, its successor appears in quite different circumstances, yet is guided by the same vision: to provide a commentary on Scripture whose scholarly treatment of the ancient texts is of the highest order and whose exposition is useful to those who interpret the Bible today. To do in our time what our predecessors did in theirs requires *The New Interpreter's Bible (NIB)* to be a wholly new work for a largely new situation.

So much has changed in four decades that it is useful to recall the context in which the *IB* made its mark. To begin with, in some ways the circumstances in which the *NIB* appears are the reverse of those of its predecessor. In the 1950s, Americans, being recent victors in a titanic war, were confident that their future would be much better than their past if they but survived the threat of communism; in the 1990s, they have contempt for communism as a failed system, but many fear their own future. Then, Protestant Christianity was thriving but saw the Roman Catholic Church of Pius XII as a threat; today, after Vatican II, Protestants regard Catholics as colleagues, but some are anxious about the apparent stagnation of their own denominations. Then, neo-orthodoxy and Christian existentialism, which emphasized the deciding self, were ascendant, and it was widely assumed that real theologians were fluent in German; today, those theologies have been superseded by theologies of social change, and the drum beat of much theology has a Latin American rhythm. Further, in those days biblical theology insisted that whereas the Canaanite deities were nature gods, the God of Israel acts in history; nowadays, there is uncertainty about history but intense interest in ecology and God's concern for the earth. Then, critical biblical study was dominated by liberal Protestants who viewed Catholic scholarship as pre-critical and ignored conservative Protestant biblical study as virtually fundamentalist; today, although the historical-critical method (which has become more complex in the intervening years) is taken for granted by Catholic and evangelical scholars too, it is being criticized not only by the right but also by the left—by those who insist that the text must be approached as a literary work, as a work of art, irrespective of the author's intent or the circumstances in which he produced it.

In the 1950s, the newly translated Revised Standard Version created such fury that in some places it was burned ceremoniously, while in the 1990s the New Revised Standard Version creates hardly a ripple, being regarded by some as a rather cautious translation. In those days, Christians of all persuasions and ecclesial identities generally accorded the Bible normative status in matters of faith and ethics, and so looked to it for the answers to life's problems; by the nineties, however, many have concluded that the Bible's pervasive patriarchalism makes it the source more of the problem than of the solution.

Finally, when the *IB* appeared, the pool of potential contributors included very few women and African Americans, and no Asian Americans or Hispanic Americans. Because contributors to the *IB* included but one woman and one African American, it inevitably reflected the perspectives of white male liberal Protestants. The *NIB*, on the other hand, enlists the participation of a significant number of women and minority scholars. Given such changes, only a completely new commentary could relate perceptively the inherited Scripture to the unfolding present.

While the aim of the *NIB* is essentially the same as that of its predecessor, pursuing that aim effectively is now a much more complex task. In addition to the markedly changed situation in which the recent work is done, biblical study too has undergone important shifts. Indeed, it was not long before the limitations of the *IB*, especially of the commentary section as a whole, walled off from exposition, became apparent—not enough attention was given to the biblical text itself. More important, the commentary proper did not—and could not—lead naturally into the exposition, which, therefore, appeared as a parallel, independent interpretation. The *IB* intended to bridge the oft-lamented chasm between the investigation of the Bible in academe and the preaching and teaching of it in the churches, but its policy of assigning the commentary to a professional biblical scholar and the exposition to an accomplished preacher actually reinforced the gap between the professor's lectern and the preacher's pulpit. The most important difference between the *IB* and the *NIB* is apparent at just this point; the *NIB* has assigned both tasks to the same writer.

Nonetheless, while it is appropriate to distinguish historical and literary explanation of the text as a work of the past from reflection on its import in various situations today, it is also necessary to ground the latter in the former. The fact that most writers of the *NIB* are professional Bible scholars reflects the conviction that what effective and imaginative interpretation needs most is solid grounding in an explanation of the text that engages the religious and moral content of Scripture.

The *NIB*, in other words, reflects the changed understanding of exegesis that has occurred in North America since the 1950s. Today, hardly anyone would regard it as "a series of comments . . . like the 'notes' appended to a Shakespearean text," as George Buttrick explained in the *IB*. There is nothing mysterious about "exegesis." It is simply the Greek word ἐξήγησις (*exēgēsis*), which means "bringing out"—hence, bringing out the meaning.

The contributors to the *IB* dealt with the text as was common at the time (Muilenberg's commentary on Isaiah being an exception for its interest in rhetorical matters). Because historical criticism had not yet been accepted everywhere, college and seminary courses in Bible commonly devoted considerable time to demonstrating matters like the multiple sources of the Pentateuch or the existence of Q (a collection of Jesus' sayings used, apparently, in Matthew and Luke), and were more concerned to expound the leading ideas in biblical writings—e.g., social justice in Amos, the Spirit in John—than in analyzing carefully the texts as texts. Courses in the teachings of Jesus were common, but not in exegesis of a Gospel. German biblical scholarship was often regarded as "radical"—enough to arouse suspicion and encourage neglect.

Ironically, largely through closer acquaintance with German scholarship in the 1950s and 1960s, the current view of exegesis developed, abetted by the rise of biblical theology in North America. American professors on sabbatical, as well as a stream of graduate students, found that German biblical study was made fruitful by combining close analysis of the text (its composition, its use of earlier sources and traditions, its ideas' relation to comparable ones in the surrounding cultures) with engagement of theological issues, as posed by Karl Barth and Rudolf Bultmann in particular. Whereas Anglo-Saxon discussions of a biblical book often ended with a section on "The Permanent Religious Value of ____," in German lecture halls the exegesis of a passage exposed theological issues throughout. Moreover, German scholarship's attempt to recover the history of the traditions used by the biblical writers required careful attention to every detail in the text. Swiftly, such exegetical courses were introduced into theological education in America. The *NIB,* too, reflects the conviction that exegesis entails not only thorough literary and historical-critical analysis but also attention to the import of the theological and ethical content of the Bible for life and thought today.

Whereas the *IB* had the field to itself, the *NIB* appears at a time of numerous commentary series in English, each with its own character and focus, ranging from those intended to facilitate continuing research to those designed for group study and personal enrichment. The *NIB* is distinctive not only because it consistently attends to both critical exegesis and constructive interpretation, but also because it distinguishes the one from the other. The reader can, therefore, profit from seeing how careful attention to the text can open up possibilities for imaginative interpretation. Although the "Commentary" section is the larger part of the interpretive material, the "Reflections" section is by no means an appendage. For interpreters, the exegetical part is the essential means to the goal; at the same time, the reflections are more suggestive than definitive. In other words, the *NIB* regards exegesis and reflection as two foci in an ellipse.

This perspective is reflected not only in the selection of writers but also in the administrative structure created for the project. Of the eleven members of the Editorial Board, three have special responsibility for the "Reflections" parts of the *NIB;* one of them, as Senior Homiletics Editor, is also a member of the Executive Committee. This structure assures that at every level, from policy making to the selection of writers, to editorial oversight, the dual foci interact. Further, a Panel of Consultants has assisted the Editors by providing counsel with regard to general matters of style and readability, use of language, sensitivity to the understandings of those whose experiences have differed from that of white males, and the diverse needs of the anticipated range of the users of the *NIB.*

Given the remarkable variety of writings in the Bible, on the one hand, and the differing needs of readers, on the other, only a cadre of diverse writers can produce an appropriate commentary. Compared with the *IB,* the roster of writers in the *NIB* is far more diverse theologically (including evangelicals and moderates as well as liberals), confessionally (Roman Catholics as well as various Protestants participating), and demographically (African American, Asian American, Hispanic American, and Native American authors contributing). Of the ninety-seven contributors, twenty-two are women—a higher percentage than in the various guilds of Bible scholars. Each writer brings both professional competence and individual perspective, of which the theological, confessional, and demographic factors are a part. While writers have been encouraged to call attention to alternative interpretations as appropriate, they have not been expected to compile views or to forego their own freedom to use those methods and to advocate those construals of the text that they deem most sound and appropriate. In short, because each part of the *NIB* is written by an individual and not by a committee, the diversity and inclusiveness of the *NIB* appears in the work as a whole.

The most important reason for writing commentaries at all is that experience has shown that readers need help in understanding the biblical text. Precisely what is needed, however, depends partly on what is in the text and partly on what is in the reader, because both the Bible and its readers are conditioned by time and place. Since the writers of the *NIB* discuss the Bible's involvement in time and place, here it is useful to reflect on the reader of the Bible and its commentaries. One's time and place affect significantly what one sees and does not see in the text, the questions one brings to it, and what one expects from it. The needs of a pastor preparing to preach in a largely immigrant congregation, of a church school teacher in a barrio, and of a seminary student writing a term paper are not the same as those of a pastor getting ready to lead a Lenten Bible study in a suburban congregation. No commentary can do everything or meet the needs and expectations of everyone. While most commentary users will want information, exactly what information is desired varies greatly. Some readers will want help in understanding ancient ways of thinking, while others will look for aid in appreciating biblical ideas and assumptions they understand but find difficult to accept.

The need for information pertaining to the Bible—especially its religious and cultural contexts—has been ameliorated since the *IB* appeared, partly because of advances in research and partly because discoveries have enriched the fund of knowledge. For example, whereas an article in volume 12 of the *IB* informed the readers in a preliminary way about the Dead Sea Scrolls (discovered in 1947), today most of these texts have long been available in English. Moreover, today reference works such as *The Interpreter's Dictionary of the Bible* are readily available, as are various compilations of texts from the ancient Near East. Consequently, the general articles in the *NIB* that provide basic information have not only been kept to a minimum but are cast in a way that addresses the questions commentary users often ask.

Moreover, the *NIB* includes a number of articles that deal explicitly with matters of interpretation. The more inclusive the churches and other institutions become, on the one hand, and the more diversified the methods of biblical study become, on the other, the more important it is that interpreters of the Bible be alert to the inevitable pluralism in interpretation. While the historical-critical method remains foundational, the articles by Carl Holladay and Moisés Silva show that in recent years other ways of reading texts have come to supplement, and sometimes to compete with, the historical exegesis. By bringing such matters to the attention of the reader, the *NIB* helps the user to see his or her own interpretation in broader perspective, and tacitly invites one to expand the resources for understanding on which one relies. Above all, the articles dealing with aspects of interpretation encourage the user to see that "meaning" is a rich and complex experience, not simply a matter of finding the "right answer" to exegetical questions.

We would sell the Bible short were we to read it only to nourish what we already believe and think, or to support what we already do or avoid doing. The Bible also challenges us to alter our believing, thinking, and doing. Once this is granted, it becomes apparent that who, where, when, and what we are must not be allowed to govern our understanding of the Bible so effectively that the only challenge we experience from it is to be better at what we are already about. Alert readers have discovered repeatedly that the Bible has surprises for everyone. In the present context, this means that the one thing users of the *NIB*, however diverse they may be, have in common is the need to hear as accurately as possible what the text says (and does not say), and to grasp why it says it the way it says it. Otherwise, the

commentary is not a window through which one sees into the text (not unlike a window in an aquarium or in a glass-bottom boat), but a mirror reflecting who we already are. The purpose of all the various methods employed by the contributors, even if used in their respective theological, confessional, and demographic perspectives, is to assist the reader in meeting the text itself, though no method or combination of methods can guarantee that one hears it either as did those who heard it first or without distortion today. Neither what the Bible originally "meant" nor what it now "means"—to use an oversimplified contrast—occurs in a vacuum.

The Bible is not simply the passive recipient of multiple modes of study and interpretation, but repeatedly has demonstrated its capacity to interpret its readers by providing images, concepts, and perspectives whose interpretive power often exceeds the (usually) controlled interpretations of the interpreter. Just as writers and artists sometimes convey more than they intend (and sometimes less), so readers and viewers discern more than they expected. In other words, on the road of interpretation, the traffic moves in both directions. The *NIB* formalizes this by distinguishing "Commentary" from "Reflections," the former being the disciplined interrogation of the text, and the latter the opportunity for the text to talk back, so to speak. Of course, the reflection does not spring spontaneously or independently from either the text or the exegesis; it is no less the work of the commentator than the exegesis. Nonetheless, the two tasks, intimately related though they are, are distinguishable. As an exegete, the commentator's task is to pin down as precisely as possible the historical meaning(s) of the text; in the reflection the writer's task is to free the text so that it can assert itself, the reflection being an act of midwifery, which assists but does not control the birth of meaning. The reader who uses the *NIB* as a resource for his or her own interpretive work becomes a participant in the process and not a mere consumer of interpretations.

It was, of course, the church that, in a variety of ways and across considerable time, determined which writings are to be included and which are to be excluded. However, while all churches accept the same twenty-seven books as the New Testament (NT), the churches have not yet agreed on which ones constitute the Old Testament (OT). Many users of the *NIB* will, therefore, find Daniel Harrington's article on the canon particularly instructive, for in telling the story of the making of the Bible it also shows that there are, in fact, different "OTs" that reflect the decisions of the various churches. The Bible is not only about a particular history, but itself has a history. Every interpreter benefits from knowing that history.

The OT part of the *NIB* includes those books (and parts of books) commonly called the Apocrypha. These writings were included in the Greek version of the OT, used by the Greek-speaking early church but not part of the Hebrew Scriptures. When Jerome, a fourth-century Christian scholar, translated the Hebrew OT into Latin (Vulgate), he omitted these books (except for additions to Daniel and Esther), calling them "Apocrypha." Later, after Latin versions of these writings were added to the OT, the Council of Trent included them formally in the Roman Catholic canon. This was in response to Luther, who had assembled them into an "appendix" to the OT, commending them as useful, though not canonical. The Calvinist tradition went farther, omitting them altogether. The *NIB*, aiming to be useful to the whole Christian community, includes them. However, instead of sandwiching these books between the testaments—a practice that reflects no church's canon—the *NIB* simply has them stand alongside the book in which they appear in the Roman Catholic canon. Thus all users of the *NIB* have access to an OT more nearly like that used by the early church. The "Apocryphal" literature is immensely important for understanding the historical and religious contexts in which both early Judaism and early Greek-using Christianity emerged.

There exists also a considerable body of early Christian gospels, acts of various apostles, and epistles, some of which were probably written in late NT times. None of them is included in the *NIB* for the simple reason that these writings, sometimes mislabeled "NT Apocrypha," were never part of any church's canon. There are no "lost books of the Bible." The many writings from biblical times that were never included in the canons of either synagogue or church do not belong in a commentary on the Bible itself, despite their importance.

Evidence indicates that a significant percentage of the users of the original *IB* found it helpful to have two versions of the biblical text on the page before them. The *NIB*, therefore, continues this policy, but has replaced the RSV with the NRSV and the Author-

ized Version ("King James") with the New International Version (NIV), which is widely used, particularly in evangelical circles, as a complement to the KJV. Readers unable to use Hebrew and Greek will often find that comparing translations is a good way to identify exegetical problems, because major differences in translation reflect diverging understandings of the Hebrew or Greek; all translation is interpretation—something that all bilingual readers understand first hand.

The commentators, of course, based their work on the Greek and Hebrew texts. From time to time, they also comment on the translations printed, and thereby help the reader understand better the limits of all translations. Likewise, they sometimes find it necessary to comment on the wording of the standard printed Hebrew and Greek texts as well, thereby alerting the reader to the sometimes problematic nature of the textual tradition—a phenomenon that can be pursued in the two articles on ancient texts and versions.

Every form of the biblical text that one can read today reflects someone's (or some group's) best judgment about the correct wording of the text; even the manuscripts themselves have copyists' corrections. The assertion that the original manuscripts of the Bible (the "autographs") were free of all error remains an assertion without evidence, since every original manuscript disappeared centuries ago. These observations do not imply that the wording of the Bible is unreliable; quite the opposite is the case, given our abundant data. The point, rather, is that the reliability of the Hebrew and Greek texts is the outcome of painstakingly careful work. In short, the *NIB* makes it possible for every serious interpreter of the Bible to have a basic knowledge of the sort of book the Bible is and how it came to be what it is.

Twentieth-century scholarship has exposed the many ways in which the Bible as we have it, as well as the individual writings themselves and the materials they used, are deeply embedded in Israelite/early Jewish and early Christian communities. Likewise, it has become evident how much these communities owed to the cultures of which they were a part. Consequently, a historical understanding of the Bible requires attention to the cultural and religious history of Mediterranean and Near Eastern antiquity, as the relevant articles make clear. While there is a profound sense in which the

Bible is its own interpreter (often traceable by the influence of one writing on another, technically called "inter-textuality"), understanding the biblical literature in its original contexts entails attending also to the growing mass of nonbiblical materials, both literary (texts such as the book of Enoch or the Dead Sea Scrolls), and nonliterary (inscriptions, coins, archaeological evidence). No other book, when studied historically, opens so many doors to cultures and religions other than our own. This is not surprising, since the books of the Bible were written during a span of a thousand years and in a part of the world that was home to a succession of cultures. Again and again, the *NIB* makes the fruits of such study accessible to the interpreter where it matters most: understanding a biblical book or a passage in it.

Even though only a fraction of antiquity has been preserved and discovered, the amount of material deemed pertinent for biblical study has become so vast that one can easily be intimidated by the scope of historical-critical investigation. The scholarly study of the Bible *has* become complex, especially when literary and sociological/anthropological approaches are used in addition to the various dimensions of historical criticism. What must not be lost sight of, though, is this: Exegesis is really a matter of asking appropriate and fruitful questions in an orderly way. For example, it is helpful to ask at the outset what one needs to know in order to understand the passage (or book). In the case of stories about events, it is important to understand the story—its emphasis, point of view, etc.—before trying to understand the events it reports. It is even more important to remember that because the questions themselves are quite straightforward, everyone can ask them! This is why the readers of the *NIB* can develop their own exegetical skills by attending not only to what the commentator says but also to how he or she goes about the task.

The Bible, while enjoying a unique status in the church, does not belong to the church alone. In diverse ways it has become the key to a good deal of Western culture: art, music, political theory, and energies for social change. It has also been an important factor in resisting change and in legitimating patterns of power, wars, and ignorance posing as knowledge. Either way, the Bible accomplished

these things only through its interpreters. Which is to say that even today—or perhaps particularly today—interpretation matters because it has consequences; it is not simply a matter of taste. Indeed, the more authoritative the text, the more important its interpretation.

If the Christian community (all churches) has not agreed completely on which books are in the OT, it has not agreed on the nature and source of the Bible's authority either, and often there are wider differences among Protestants than between them and Roman Catholics on this subject. In order to express the unique authority of the Bible, most Christians continue to relate it to "the Word of God," many saying that the Bible *is* the Word of God, while others regard it as the instrument of God's Word, or the place where that Word is heard most penetratingly. Neither formulation is problem-free. If the former tends to objectify "the Word of God" (regarding the Word as a thing) in order to emphasize *what* one encounters in the Bible, the latter tends to subjectivize the Word in order to accent the encounter *experience* (regarding the Word as an event). Indeed, each way of putting the matter appears to be formulated with the dangers of the other in view. In any case, once one says that the Bible *is* God's Word, it is difficult not to say also that it is God's words; conversely, by differentiating the Word from its bearer, it becomes difficult to avoid absorbing the Word into the experience itself.

Given the diverse ways of understanding the relation of the Bible to God's Word, contributors to the *NIB* probably reflect as wide a range of views as its users. What deserves remembering is that exegetical questions cannot be settled by conclusions drawn from any view of the Bible's relation to God's Word, but only on the basis of public evidence and inferences from that evidence. The same must be said about the Bible's source of authority—its being inspired.

Fortunately, the most important thing to be said is also the most obvious—namely, that it is not what anyone says about the Bible that makes it authoritative but what the Bible says about God and human life before God. The Bible has its own way of commending itself to those whose careful reading opens understanding. The *NIB* will have fulfilled its purpose when it helps that happen.

INTRODUCTION TO THE CANON

DANIEL J. HARRINGTON, S.J.

In Christian theology the canon of Scripture refers to the list of sacred books that serves as the rule or norm of Christian faith and life. The word *canon* derives from the Greek κανών *kanōn* (Hebrew קנה *qāneh*), which means "reed" or "measuring stick."[1] One sense of *kanōn* was "ruler"—that by which straightness could be measured. The idea of measure in *canon* opened up the term to various metaphorical uses in literature, art, and music, as well as in commerce and in making chronological tables. The weapon known as the "cannon," from which a projectile was shot through a barrel, recaptured the primitive sense of "reed."

The notion of canon as rule or norm of faith and life predominated among Christian writers of the first three centuries CE. Paul invoked peace and mercy on "all who walk according to this *kanōn*" (Gal 6:16). Clement of Rome contrasted the "glorious and holy rule [*kanōn*] of our tradition" with empty and vain cares.[2] Clement of Alexandria urged Christians to live in accord with "the rule [*kanōn*] of faith" and "the rule [*kanōn*] of truth."[3] Likewise, Irenaeus spoke often about "the rule of truth" attested by Scripture and tradition but perverted by heretics.[4]

Despite the prominence of "canon" as rule or norm of faith and life, other Christian uses of *kanōn* are documented. Paul in 2 Cor 10:13-16 employed it to refer to the geographical limits placed by God on Paul's apostolic ministry. From about 300 CE onward, the plural *kanones* was used to designate the decrees or rules promulgated by church councils and synods. The plural *kanones* also referred to various lists or tables, such as those of the parallel passages in the Gospels compiled by Eusebius. The official list of clergy attached to a specific church was also known as a *kanōn,* according to the decrees of the Council of Nicea (Canons 16, 17, 19).

Only in the second half of the fourth century was *kanōn* and its derivatives applied to the list of books sacred to Christians. Athanasius refers to *Shepherd of Hermas* as not belonging to the canon. In his 39th Festal Letter (written at Easter 367), Athanasius distinguished the canonical books (*biblia kanonizomena*) from the apocryphal books. The Synod of Laodicea in 363 CE ruled that only "canonical" books should be read in the churches.

So by the end of the fourth century CE the two components of the Christian concept of "canon" came together: the canon as rule or norm of

---

1. Bruce M. Metzger, *The Canon of the New Testament: Its Origin, Development, and Significance* (Oxford: Clarendon, 1987) 289-93.

2. *1 Clement* 7:2.

3. *Stromata* 4.15.98; 6.15.124.

4. *Against Heresies 3.2.1; 3.11.1; etc.*

Christian faith and life, and the canon as the list of books sacred to Christians. Since the first component really concerns the authority of the Bible, the focus of this article will be on the canon as the list of sacred books. Nevertheless, the two issues cannot be entirely separated, as the sections on the history of the canon and the theological issues related to the canon will show. In fact, the genius (or the tragedy, depending on one's perspective) of the Christian theological tradition has been to join to the concept of "canon of Scripture" the idea of an authoritative list of sacred books, and its function as the norm or rule of faith and life.

THE SHAPE OF THE CANON(S) TODAY

All Christians today accept as the first part of the Christian canon of Scripture the books of the Hebrew Bible. The Jewish tradition has divided these books into three categories: Torah (Genesis, Exodus, Leviticus, Numbers, Deuteronomy), Prophets (Joshua, Judges, 1–2 Samuel, 1–2 Kings, Isaiah, Jeremiah, Ezekiel, Twelve Minor Prophets), and Writings (Psalms, Job, Proverbs, Ruth, Song of Songs, Ecclesiastes, Lamentations, Esther, Daniel, Ezra–Nehemiah, 1–2 Chronicles). The collection of twenty-four books is customarily called "Tanakh," an acronym derived from the first Hebrew letter of each category: תורה (*Tôrâ,* Law), נביאים (*Něbî'îm,* Prophets), and וכתובים (*Kětûbîm,* Writings).

The content of Protestant versions of the Old Testament (OT) corresponds to that of the Hebrew Bible. But the material is arranged differently (under the influence of the Septuagint) and divided into thirty-nine books. The "two-volume" historical books (1–2 Samuel, 1–2 Kings, 1–2 Chronicles, Ezra–Nehemiah) and the twelve Minor Prophets are counted as separate books. The thirty-nine books fall into four blocks: Law (Genesis–Deuteronomy), Historical Books (Joshua–Esther), Wisdom Books (Job–Song of Songs), and Prophets (Isaiah–Malachi).

Bibles published under Roman Catholic auspices contain all the books of the Hebrew Bible as well as seven more books—Tobit, Judith, 1–2 Maccabees, Wisdom, Sirach, and Baruch—and some additions to Esther and Daniel. These books were part of the manuscript traditions of the Greek (Septuagint) and Latin (Vulgate) Bibles. In Catholic Bibles, they are interspersed among the uncontested books of the Hebrew tradition, whereas Protestant Bibles that include them customarily place them as an appendix to the OT. The seven additional books are sometimes called "deuterocanonical," suggesting debate about their place in the canon (as opposed to the "protocanonical" books contained in the Hebrew Bible). They are also known as the Apocrypha ("hidden" or "secret" books), along with other works (3–4 Maccabees, Prayer of Manasseh, 1–2 Esdras) that are sometimes printed in Bibles but not reckoned as canonical Scripture by either Protestants or Catholics. The canons of Orthodox churches contain books over and above what appear in the Roman Catholic canon. The Greek Orthodox Church includes the books of the larger canon as well as 3 Maccabees and 2 Esdras. The Ethiopian Orthodox canon contains even more material (*1 Enoch, Jubilees,* pseudo-Josephus, etc.).

All Christians today share the same canon of twenty-seven New Testament (NT) books. The first division of the NT consists of the Gospels attributed to Matthew, Mark, Luke, and John, as well as the Acts of the Apostles (written by the author of Luke's Gospel). The thirteen epistles attributed to Paul are divided into two categories: nine written to communities (Romans, 1–2 Corinthians, Galatians, Ephesians, Philippians, Colossians, 1–2 Thessalonians) and four addressed to persons (1–2 Timothy, Titus, Philemon). Within these two categories, the letters are arranged by length, from longest to shortest (although Ephesians is slightly longer than Galatians). The Letter to the Hebrews comes next, probably because of its traditional connections to Paul (see Heb 13:22-25). It is followed by the seven "general" or "catholic" epistles: James, 1–2 Peter, 1–3 John, and Jude. Revelation, or the Apocalypse of John, concludes the NT canon.

THE HISTORY OF THE OT CANON

Two often repeated but very doubtful propositions have dominated discussion about the OT canon. The first proposition is that the list of books belonging to the canon of Hebrew Scriptures was fixed definitively at the Council, or Synod, of Jamnia (also called Yavneh) in the late first century CE. The second proposition is that Jews and Protestants follow the Palestinian canon, whereas Catholics (and Orthodox) follow the canon used in Alexandria. Attention to the problems associated with these two propositions can help to focus what we know (and do not know) about the history of the OT canon.[5]

Was the canon of Hebrew Scriptures really fixed definitively at the Council of Jamnia? Jamnia is the Greek name given to the place called Yavneh-yam in Hebrew, near the Mediterranean coast in Israel, not far from present-day Tel-Aviv. After the capture of Jerusalem and the destruction of its Temple in 70 CE by the Romans, Jamnia became the center of a restoration movement led by Rabban Yohanan ben Zakkai. This movement sought to reconstruct Judaism on the basis of biblical interpretation and the codification of traditions now that the Temple was fallen and the Jewish people no longer controlled their ancestral land. The school or movement begun by Yohanan ben Zakkai synthesized elements from the Pharisaic, scribal, and priestly movements before 70 CE and provided the foundations of what came to be known as the rabbinic movement.[6]

The problem associated with the term "Council of Jamnia" arises from applying later Christian understandings of terms like *council* or *synod* to first-century Judaism. The Jamnia/Yavneh movement was a school active in the late first and early second centuries CE. There was no single meeting (like a church synod or council) gathering Jewish scholars from all over Palestine and beyond to make decisions affecting all Jews. From the sources available to us, what took place at Jamnia were debates over traditions, and there is no indication that the resolutions of these debates were immediately accepted or taken to be definitive for all Judaism. In fact, the movement begun by Yohanan ben Zakkai is best viewed as a minority seeking to respond creatively to one of the greatest crises in Jewish history.

One of the traditions debated at Jamnia concerned which books "made the hands unclean." The ritual uncleanness of the hands and their purification is treated in the Mishnah's tractate *Yadayim*. In *m. Yad.* 3:5 we are told as a general principle: "All the Sacred Scriptures make the hands unclean." Therefore, after touching the scrolls containing the Scriptures, one is expected to wash one's hands. The reason for this belief and this practice remains somewhat mysterious to us: Was it magical thinking, a

way of instilling reverence, or something else? The Mishnah paragraph goes on to narrate a rabbinic debate about whether Ecclesiastes and/or Song of Songs makes the hands unclean. Unless they do, they would not count as sacred Scripture. The paragraph recounts the opinions of various rabbis on the matter and concludes that both books make the hands unclean, thus affirming their status as Scripture.

There were other debates among rabbis about the status of five biblical books. There were doubts about Ecclesiastes, presumably because of its negativism about life, and Song of Songs, presumably because of its eroticism when not interpreted allegorically. Likewise there were objections to Ezekiel because it contradicted the Torah at some points, Proverbs because of its internal contradictions, and Esther because its Hebrew text never mentions God. These debates are noted in rabbinic sources. But there is no indication that these were widespread objections (they seem in fact to be individual or minority views) or that the Council of Jamnia met in formal session to make decisions about what belonged on the list of canonical books.

In fact, the basic canon of Hebrew Scriptures was probably fixed long before the so-called Council of Jamnia, perhaps as early as the second century BCE.[7] Parts of the Torah (the first five books, also known as the Pentateuch) are acknowledged to be very ancient (hymns and legal materials). But the final form of the Torah most likely appeared in Israel's exile in Babylon, or shortly thereafter. Thus "the book of the Law" found in Josiah's time probably refers not to the Torah itself but perhaps to a code incorporated into the Torah in its editing process (see 2 Kgs 22:8-13). The mandate given by the Persian king to Ezra that he should govern the province "Beyond the River" according to the "wisdom of your God which is in your hand" (Ezra 7:25) may refer to the Torah that was newly edited in Babylon and may indicate its function as rule or norm for life in Israel. Yet there are too many uncertainties involved with this text (the date of Ezra's mission, whether the "wisdom" indeed refers to the Torah, whether the Torah was intended to be used as the Jewish law-code under the Persians) to put it forward as real proof for the canonical status of the Torah in the fifth or fourth centuries BCE.

---

5. F. F. Bruce, *The Canon of Scripture* (Downers Grove: Inter-Varsity, 1988).

6. Jacob Neusner, *Judaism: The Evidence of the Mishnah,* 2nd ed. (Atlanta: Scholars Press, 1988).

7. S. Z. Leiman, *The Canonization of Hebrew Scripture: The Talmudic and Midrashic Evidence* (Hamden, Conn.: Archon Books, 1976).

We are on surer ground (ironically) with the prologue to the noncanonical (for Jews and Protestants) book of Sirach (also known as Ecclesiasticus). The book was written in Hebrew at Jerusalem around 200 BCE by Jesus the Son of Sirach, son of Eleazar, of Jerusalem (50:27). It was translated into Greek by the author's grandson after he came to Egypt in 132 BCE. The Greek text is part of the wider (Catholic) canon, whereas the Hebrew original is not part of the Jewish-Protestant canon. In the prologue, Sirach's grandson describes his grandfather as having devoted himself to the "reading of the law and the prophets and the other books of our fathers." This mode of speaking suggests that by the mid-second century BCE there was a recognition of the classic threefold division of books and a belief that these books contained the traditional wisdom of Israel.

One aspect of the controversy that led to the Maccabean revolt in the 160s BCE was the attempt to substitute for the Torah another law-code and thus bring the Jews of the Land of Israel into line with other peoples of the Seleucid Empire. According to 1 Macc 1:56-57, measures were taken to destroy copies of the Torah and to punish those who retained them. After the revolt and victory of the Maccabees, Judas is said to have "collected all the books that had been lost on account of the war that had come upon us, and they are in our possession" (2 Macc 2:14). Thus Judas Maccabeus is supposed to have continued the process of collecting records and books that Nehemiah had undertaken. Some scholars take this description to indicate that in the second century BCE the Jewish people already had a clear idea of sacred Scriptures that were to be preserved in the capital city of the Jewish people.[8]

The evidence from the Qumran community neither affirms nor denies a second-century BCE date for the Hebrew canon. On the one hand, the Essenes (who founded this community probably out of disappointment at the course of the Maccabean revolt) read the books that we know as the Hebrew Scriptures. Manuscripts of all but the book of Esther have been found at Qumran. Whether its absence is due to the Essenes' objection to Esther because of its content or only because of historical accident is not clear. The Qumran community undertook regular study of the Hebrew Scriptures and made copies of them. They also produced biblical commentaries on the Prophets, designed to show how the "mysteries" of prophecies were being resolved in the life and history of their own community. They made anthologies of biblical texts on various topics. The Qumran Essenes were very much a "biblical" community, and the biblical manuscripts from Qumran have yielded valuable information about the textual history of the Hebrew Bible.

On the other hand, it is not at all clear whether and how the Qumran Essenes distinguished between canonical and noncanonical books. Besides biblical books, copies of community rules (*Manual of Discipline, Damascus Document*), hymnbooks (*Thanksgiving Hymns*), biblical commentaries (*Pesharim*), previously known and unknown Pseudepigrapha (*Jubilees, Genesis Apocryphon*), a battle plan for the eschatological conflict (*War Scroll*), and what some regard as an alternate version of the Torah in which God speaks the words of "Scripture" in the first person (*Temple Scroll*) have been found. The problem is that we do not know (nor does there seem to be any way of knowing) how the Qumran Essenes looked upon these books. Did they regard them as inferior, equal to, or even superior to what we know as canonical Scripture? Thus the Dead Sea discoveries prove only that the "canonical" books were very important to the Qumran Essenes. But they do not tell us whether, in fact, the Essenes had any idea of a "canon" of Scripture or to what books they may have accorded or denied canonical status.

Writing in the late first century CE (93–95) in response to the anti-Jewish slanders of Apion (an Alexandrian writer of the first century CE), Josephus contrasted the "myriads of inconsistent books" possessed by the Greeks with the twenty-two (and only twenty-two!) of the Hebrew Scriptures that contain the record of all time. He divided them into three categories: the five books of Moses, the thirteen books of the Prophets, and the remaining four books containing hymns to God and precepts for the conduct of human life.[9] Behind the number twenty-two (instead of twenty-four) may be a tradition associated with the number of letters in the Hebrew alphabet (twenty-two) and the related idea that all wisdom is present in Israel's Scriptures. To arrive at this

8. R. Beckwith, *The Old Testament Canon of the New Testament Church and Its Background in Early Judaism* (Grand Rapids: Eerdmans, 1986).

9. *Against Apion* 1:37-43.

number, Josephus (or his tradition) may have joined Ruth to Judges or Psalms, and Lamentations to Jeremiah. It is not necessary to assume that Josephus shared his rabbinic contemporaries' doubts about the canonical status of Ecclesiastes or Song of Songs.

The traditional number of twenty-four books appears in 4 Ezra 14:45-46, written in the late first or early second century CE. The text distinguishes between "the twenty-four books" that are to be made public and read by worthy and unworthy alike, and "the seventy that were written last" that are to be given to the wise among the people. This text is important because it differentiates between canonical and "apocryphal" ("hidden") books, and because it gives the traditional number of books constituting the Hebrew canon.

The twenty-four books are listed in a *baraita* (a tradition from 70–200 CE) in tractate *Baba Batra* of the Babylonian Talmud: the Torah (Genesis–Deuteronomy); the Prophets (Joshua, Judges, Samuel, Kings, Jeremiah, Ezekiel, Isaiah, the Twelve); and the Writings (Ruth, Psalms, Job, Proverbs, Ecclesiastes, Song of Songs, Lamentations, Daniel, Esther, Ezra, Chronicles). Note that in some cases (the places of Isaiah, Ruth, Song of Songs and Ecclesiastes, and Daniel and Esther) the order of books differs from what has become the traditional one. Since the books were written on multiple scrolls and not in one codex or leaf-book, like the Christian Bibles, the order of books was not very important.

From the Jewish sources we know that by the late first century CE there was a distinction between sacred or canonical books and other books. These books numbered twenty-four (or twenty-two) and were divided into three categories: Law, Prophets, and Writings. How these books came to be regarded as canonical among Jews is not entirely clear. This seems to have been a gradual development, perhaps beginning with the Torah (see Ezra 7:25-26), and gradually extended to the Prophets and Writings (prologue to Sirach) by or in the second century BCE (2 Macc 2:14). There is little evidence and no need for an official declaration by a "council" or "synod" at Jamnia/Yavneh regarding the number and content of canonical books. The debates about the status of certain books (Ecclesiastes, Song of Songs, Ezekiel, Proverbs, Esther) need not be taken to mean that there was widespread and serious doubt about their canonical character, at least to the extent that

they were in danger of being dropped from the canon in the first or second centuries.

The second doubtful proposition dominating discussion about the OT canon assumes that Jews in Alexandria had a wider canon of sacred books (including the seven "deuterocanonicals") and that early Christians simply took over that canon. But the real story is not so simple or straightforward.[10]

The Greek Bible has a long history. The delightful legend in the *Letter of Aristeas* and other sources that seventy(-two) translators working seventy(-two) days produced the same version conceals a complex process in which the various parts (probably the Torah first of all) of the Hebrew Bible were translated into Greek. The process probably began not long after the time of Alexander the Great and continued with various revisions (Theodotion and Aquila) into the second century CE. Although one purpose of the translation may have been to give access to the Jewish Scriptures to non-Jews, the primary beneficiaries were Greek-speaking Jews living outside the land of Israel.

The Greek Bible, or Septuagint (meaning "seventy" for the seventy[-two] translators of the Aristeas legend), was the Bible of the early Christians. While Jesus and the first Palestinian Christians probably did use the Hebrew Bible, as soon as Christianity moved beyond the land of Israel the Greek Septuagint became the church's Bible. However, there is evidence from Qumran of the use of the Greek Bible even within the boundaries of Palestine. Most NT writers quoted the Bible according to the Septuagint version. And very quickly the early Christian evangelists and apologists used the Septuagint as the quarry for their arguments to "prove" the truth of Christianity (e.g., by appealing to *parthenos* in the Septuagint of Isa 7:14 to base the virginal conception of Jesus on Scripture; see Matt 1:23).

Jews reacted to the Christian appropriation of the Septuagint in two ways. They responded defensively by arguing that the Hebrew Scriptures did not say what the Christians found in the Greek Bible (see Justin Martyr's *Dialogue with Trypho the Jew*). They also revised the Greek Bible to bring it more in line with the wording and textual tradition of the Hebrew original (the revisions ascribed to Theodotion and Aquila). A second line of response was simply to ignore the Greek text altogether and thus to hand

---

10. A. C. Sundberg, *The Old Testament in the Early Church* (Cambridge, Mass.: Harvard University Press, 1964).

it over to the Christians. The Greek Bible was a Jewish production. It was used extensively by Hellenistic-Jewish writers such as Philo of Alexandria and Flavius Josephus. Yet it has been kept in existence mainly by Christians. There are a few fragmentary manuscripts (some among the Dead Sea Scrolls) that can be identified as Jewish. But the vast bulk of evidence that we have for the Septuagint is Christian.

The Christian character of our evidence for the Septuagint makes talk about the wider canon of the Alexandrian Jews both circular and suspect. There is no sure way of knowing whether Alexandrian Jews had a clear idea of a biblical canon and what they may have included within it. What we do know is that some Christians (perhaps under Jewish influence) included in their canon some books beyond those customarily included in the Hebrew canon.

The evidence of the earliest full manuscripts of the Septuagint is surprisingly mixed.[11] The fourth-century Sinai manuscript contains Tobit, Judith, 1 and 4(!) Maccabees, Wisdom, and Sirach. But it does not have Exodus, Leviticus, and Deuteronomy, and is missing most of Joshua through Kingdoms.[12] The fourth-century Vatican manuscript does not include the books of Maccabees. The fifth-century Alexandrian manuscript contains the traditional "wider" canon (including the seven "deuterocanonicals") but suggests that *Psalms of Solomon* belongs somehow with the Scriptures.

The early Christian manuscripts of the Greek Bible and the early patristic evidence indicate that there was some fluidity regarding the status of the "deuterocanonical" books. Although the lists of OT books drawn up by Origen (185–254 CE) and Athanasius (367 CE) correspond to the Hebrew canon, in practice both writers used the "deuterocanonical" books. In the Latin West the position of those books within the canon of Scripture seems to have been firm from Tertullian (late 2nd and early 3rd cent.) onward. Thus Jerome's insistence in the late fourth century on a return to the Hebrew canon was controversial and regarded as something of an innovation. He was first to call the deuterocanonicals the "Apocrypha." He quoted from them and praised their ethical content, but did not regard them as part of the canon and argued that they may not be used for establishing doctrine.

Augustine (early 5th cent.) emerged as the defender of the wider canon (including Tobit, Judith, 1–2 Maccabees, Sirach, Wisdom, and Baruch). Various local councils followed Augustine. In fact, they were simply endorsing what had become the general consensus in the West and in large parts of the East. And this remained the basic situation up to the time of the Reformation. In general, the wider canon was accepted, but it seems to have made little doctrinal or practical difference; there may also have been pockets of resistance to it. Indeed, it became customary to include in Latin Bibles some works not held to be canonical at all: Prayer of Manasseh and 3–4 Esdras.[13]

When the Reformers embraced the principle of *sola scriptura* (Scripture alone), they raised anew the question of what constitutes sacred Scripture. Martin Luther had a particular doctrinal objection to 2 Macc 12:45-46, which was offered as the biblical ground for prayer on behalf of the dead and was thus involved in the controversy over indulgences. Luther criticized 2 Maccabees (and Esther) as containing "too much Judaism and pagan vice." He returned to Jerome's principle of "Hebrew truth": The OT consists of the books contained in the Hebrew canon. Nevertheless, Luther included the so-called Apocrypha in an appendix to his 1534 German translation. His practice set the pattern for many Protestant Bibles through the centuries; the "Apocrypha" are not interspersed among the uncontested books but are included in a separate section by themselves.

In response to Luther and other Reformers, the Council of Trent in 1546 set aside Jerome's distinction between "Hebrew truth" and the Apocrypha. It followed the tradition of the Latin Vulgate and adopted the wider canon, including the seven controversial books. It produced the first definitive list of OT books, and its decree is followed in Bibles prepared under Catholic auspices until this day.

So the matter is more complicated than saying that Protestants follow the Palestinian canon and Catholics follow the Alexandrian canon. The evidence we have for the wider canon is Christian.

---

11. See the discussions by Bruce and Beckwith. These books and Metzger's supply the full documentation for the history of the OT and NT canons.

12. The books of 1–2 Samuel and 1–2 Kings appear in the Septuagint as 1–4 Kingdoms.

13. Three Esdras = Esdras A in the LXX, consisting of 2 Chronicles 35–36, Ezra, and Nehemiah 7–8. Four Esdras consists of a Jewish apocalypse (chaps. 3–14) plus Christian material in chaps. 1–2 and 15–16, which are sometimes called 5 Ezra and 6 Ezra.

Christians may have borrowed the wider canon from Jews, but we cannot be certain about that, and still less about when and where the borrowing took place. What is certain is that there was some fluidity regarding the contents of the OT in early Christianity. The two decisive moments that led up to the present division among Christians are the debate between Jerome (for "Hebrew truth") and Augustine (for the wider and by then "traditional" canon of the Latin West), and the challenge by Luther and other Reformers to the Apocrypha and the response by the Council of Trent affirming the wider canon.

THE HISTORY OF THE NT CANON

The complexity and fluidity that marked the development of the OT canon were matched in the development of the NT canon.[14] The Bible of the earliest church, of course, was the Greek OT. It was studied carefully as a book about Jesus the Messiah, the place where the prophecies fulfilled by him could be found. It was also read publicly at church gatherings. There seems to have been no conscious movement in the early days of Christianity to produce a new collection of sacred books. Primitive Christianity focused on the person of Jesus, especially his death and resurrection. The OT supplied the necessary reading material when interpreted from the perspective of Christ and of promise and fulfillment.

By 200 CE, however, there was general acceptance in the churches of the core of what we call the NT canon, consisting of the four Gospels, Acts, Paul's epistles, 1 Peter, and 1 John. By the late fourth century the Greek and Latin churches for the most part had accepted the twenty-seven-book NT canon, used in churches ever since. What happened between the first days of the Christian movement and about 400 CE to bring about the now traditional NT canon?

The earliest NT writings—Paul's uncontested epistles (Romans, 1–2 Corinthians, Galatians, Philippians, 1 Thessalonians, Philemon) were all more or less responses to particular problems and situations in the mid-first-century churches of Asia Minor, Greece, and Italy. Yet these "occasional" writings were viewed as also having lasting value and significance for other churches. One response to this evaluation of Paul's letters was to collect them into a kind of anthology. Another response was to imitate Paul's style and language, and to bring them to bear on the problems of the late-first-century churches in the Mediterranean area. Some scholars see this response as the origin of the so-called deutero-pauline writings: Ephesians, Colossians, 2 Thessalonians, and the Pastorals (1–2 Timothy, Titus).[15] One theory is that Ephesians was originally prepared as the introduction to an early collection of Pauline letters and a kind of summary of Pauline thought for late-first-century Christians.[16] At any rate, by the late first or early second century the Pauline letters—both those seven undoubtedly composed by Paul and the six others ascribed to him—had been gathered in a corpus of Pauline texts. And with the Pauline collection came problems of interpretation, as 2 Pet 3:16 indicates: "There are some things in them hard to understand, which the ignorant and unstable twist to their own destruction, as they do the other scriptures" (NRSV).

Whereas Paul wrote first to bridge the geographical distance, the evangelists wrote to bridge the chronological distance separating Jesus' death and resurrection, on the one hand, and their readers on the other. One of Mark's several purposes in writing the first Gospel around 70 CE was to gather into an order and present in written form the available traditions about Jesus. Matthew and Luke, writing around 90 CE, independently followed Mark's biographical-theological outline and supplemented it with teachings from Q (the Sayings Source) and other sources. John, probably working independently from the Synoptic evangelists, put into order the traditions about Jesus that developed in the Johannine school and presented them in the framework of Jesus' public activity ("Book of Signs" = John 1–12) and his last days ("Book of Glory" = John 13–21). So by the end of the first century there were at least four full-scale collections of traditions about Jesus. Nevertheless, though these Gospels eventually became part of the same canon of Scripture and do in fact

---

14. See the full study by Metzger, *The Canon of the NT*. See also H. von Campenhausen, *The Formation of the Christian Bible* (Philadelphia: Fortress, 1972); and H. Y. Gamble, *The New Testament Canon: Its Making and Meaning* (Philadelphia: Fortress, 1985).

15. Scholarly opinion about the number of deutero-pauline writings is not unanimous; however, most agree that the Pastorals are deutero-pauline.

16. E. J. Goodspeed, *The Making of Ephesians* (Chicago: University of Chicago Press, 1933).

complement one another, there is no indication that the evangelists set out to produce their Gospels as "sacred Scriptures."

The other books of the NT were also composed in the late first century (70–100 CE). Acts was Luke's second volume, the companion to his story of Jesus. The letters ascribed to Peter, James, and Jude are analogous to Paul's letters, and probably circulated on the same basis. Hebrews has a vague relation to Paul (see Heb 13:22-25) and often was taken to be part of the Pauline corpus. The Johannine epistles and Revelation had obvious connections with the Fourth Gospel and the Johannine school.

The books of the NT were all composed by the beginning of the second century CE (though some scholars today push 2 Peter and the Pastorals well into the second century). But they still had not attained the status of "canon." The Christian writers of the early second century—the so-called Apostolic Fathers—allude to and even quote these writings (especially the Gospels and the Pauline writings). However, there is not yet an indication that these books represent a true canon—that is, a list of sacred books that serves as the rule or norm of Christian faith and life.

Two historical forces facilitated the development of a NT canon. One (Marcion) sought to make the canon too small. The other (Gnosticism and Montanism) tried to make the canon too large.

Marcion, a wealthy shipowner from Sinope (a seaport of Pontus along the Black Sea), was a member of the Christian community at Rome in the mid-second century. Marcion regarded Christ as the messenger of the Supreme God of goodness. This God was to be distinguished from the inferior God of justice, the creator and God of the Jews. Therefore, Marcion rejected the entire OT. He also believed that the apostles misunderstood the teaching of Christ. Thus his NT "canon" contained only ten letters attributed to Paul (the nine to communities, plus Philemon) and the Gospel of Luke (Paul's alleged companion in Acts). Even these books had first to be shorn of what Marcion judged to be "interpolations" (e.g., 2 Thess 1:6-8; Gal 3:16–4:6) that conflicted with his reading of Paul. The effect of Marcion's narrow canon would have been the complete rejection of Christianity's past in Judaism. And that was a step the churches at Rome and elsewhere were not willing to take.

From Montanism (a late 2nd-cent. sect) and Gnosticism (a broader religious movement in the 2nd and 3rd cents.) there was pressure to extend the limits of the list of "sacred books." These were different movements and had different histories. What they had in common, however, was an emphasis on revelations from above in the context of religious experiences. Both movements attracted followings in second-century Christianity and posed a threat to the kinds of Christianity that eventually coalesced into "orthodoxy."

The Gnostics in particular produced a substantial body of writings, as the Nag Hammadi Library, discovered in 1947 in Egypt, attests.[17] Although those documents are written in Coptic (a late dialect of Egyptian) and were copied in the late fourth century, many were composed in Greek in the second and third centuries. Some scholars even contend that parts (e.g., of the *Gospel of Thomas*) go back to the first century and antedate our canonical writings. Moreover, also in circulation were other "apocryphal" Gospels attributed to various apostles (Peter, Philip, Thomas, etc.) and groups (Ebionites, Nazarenes, Egyptians, etc.) as well as various Acts of Apostles (John, Peter, Paul, Andrew, etc.), Apocalypses (Peter, Fifth and Sixth Ezra, etc.), and Letters (to the Laodiceans, 3 Corinthians, etc.). Some of these started out as novels—innocent entertainment for an interested Christian public. But others, especially the gnostic writings, were intended to convey the fruit of religious experience and to teach about God, the world, and the human condition.

The problem facing the churches in the late second century was clear: How does one distinguish among the various Christian writings? Which ones are to be taken seriously? Which are to be read in the churches? On which can one base Christian doctrine?

The major operative criteria seem to have been orthodoxy of content, apostolic origin, and general acceptance by the churches.[18] The words *operative* and *seem* are important, because no one theologian systematized these criteria nor did any central institution (council, bishops, or pope) promulgate them. Rather, judging from the results, one can deduce that these three criteria guided the second- and

---

17. James M. Robinson, ed., *The Nag Hammadi Library in English,* 3rd ed. (San Francisco: Harper & Row, 1988).

18. See the discussions by Bruce in *The Canon of Scripture,* 255-69; and Metzger in *The Canon of the NT,* 251-54.

third-century church as it moved toward a basic canon of NT books.

"Orthodoxy" meant that a book had to be consistent with the basic doctrines already recognized as normative by churches. "Apostolicity" implies at least the presumption of apostolic authorship (John, Matthew, Paul, Jude, James, Peter) or association with an apostle (Mark with Peter, Luke with Paul). "Acceptance" indicates that these books were used in the churches and cited by reliable bishops and theologians. This combination of theological and historical criteria probably governed the complicated process by which the NT canon was established in its basic outline. What was included in that outline by the late second century can be known from the so-called Muratorian Canon.

The Muratorian Canon is named after its discoverer and editor, Ludovico Muratori. In 1740 Muratori published an eighth-century Latin manuscript consisting of eighty-five lines and providing comments on books included in and excluded from the NT canon. Almost all scholars date the original composition (whether in Latin or Greek) to the late second century.[19] Without being an authoritative or definitive document, the Muratorian Canon shows what books were accepted at Rome and what books were rejected. There are some surprising absences and the even more surprising presence of the book of Wisdom.

The first part of the Muratorian Canon is lost, but it clearly referred to the Gospels of Matthew and Mark. The next items are the Gospels of Luke and John, "the Acts of All the Apostles" (perhaps a way of excluding the apocryphal acts of particular apostles), Paul's letters to the churches and to individuals, the letter of Jude, two letters of John, Wisdom ("written by Solomon's friends in his honor"), and the apocalypses of John and Peter. The list acknowledges that the *Apocalypse of Peter* is contested by some ("which some of our people will not have to be read in church"). It rejects as infected with Marcion's heresy the alleged Pauline letters to the Laodiceans (probably not the one in Col 4:16) and the Alexandrians (probably not Hebrews). It also rejects *Shepherd of Hermas* as canonical, since it

19. But see A. C. Sundberg, "Canon Muratori: A Fourth-Century List," *Harvard Theological Review* 66 (1973) 1-41. See also G. M. Hahneman, *The Muratorian Fragment and the Development of the Canon* (Oxford: Clarendon, 1992), who argues for a fourth-century date. But P. Henne, "La Datation du *Canon* de Muratori," *Revue Biblique* 100 (1993) 54-75, rejects Sundberg's arguments and supports a second-century date.

was written "in the city of Rome quite recently, in our own times." It goes on to reject the writings of Arsinous, Valentinus, and so on before the manuscript breaks off. There is no mention of Hebrews, James, 1–2 Peter, and 3 John.

Writing in the early fourth century, Eusebius, bishop of Caesarea in Palestine, distinguished three kinds of books vying for recognition in the churches. Twenty-two books were "universally acknowledged": the four Gospels, Acts, the Pauline epistles (including Hebrews), 1 John, 1 Peter, and ("should it seem right") Revelation. The "disputed" books ("but recognized by the majority") were James, Jude, 2 Peter, and 2–3 John. The third category ("spurious") included books not recognized as canonical: *Acts of Paul, Shepherd of Hermas, Apocalypse of Peter, Barnabas, Teaching of the Apostles, Gospel of the Hebrews,* and ("should it seem right") Revelation.

These two lists—one from the West and the other from the East—show consensus regarding the main part of the canon and controversy regarding the edges (Hebrews, some catholic epistles, Revelation). The fourth-century Sinai manuscript contains all twenty-seven books (though in a peculiar order) plus *Barnabas* and part of *Shepherd of Hermas.* The fourth-century Vatican manuscript breaks off in the middle of Hebrews, before reaching Paul's letters to individuals and Revelation (the order of the books differed from what later became standard). The fifth-century Alexandrian manuscript included *1 Clement,* part of *2 Clement,* and (at one time) *Psalms of Solomon.* The early manuscripts confirm the evidence of the Muratorian and Eusebian lists that there was general agreement about most of the books but persistent "fuzziness" about the limits of the canon and the status of the books in the canon. The distinguished theologians of the fourth and early fifth centuries did much to clear up that "fuzziness."

In his festal letter of Easter 367 CE, Athanasius, bishop of Alexandria, listed the twenty-seven books that now make up our canon: four Gospels, Acts, seven catholic epistles, fourteen Pauline epistles (including Hebrews), and Revelation. He called them the "springs of salvation" (see Isa 12:3) and affirmed that "in these alone is the teaching of true religion proclaimed as good news; let no one add to these or take anything from them." Jerome included the same books on his list but elsewhere acknowledged that the "custom of the Latins" does not accept Hebrews, and the "churches of the Greeks" do not accept John's Apocalypse. Likewise, Augustine listed the same twenty-seven books but recognized that some books had not been accepted by all the churches. So by the late fourth and early fifth centuries there was growing consensus about the twenty-seven books as constituting the NT canon. Yet there was no official church pronouncement about the canon and no firm agreement at all about the order of books (which apparently was not regarded as important).

The Third Council of Carthage (397 CE), following the Council of Hippo (393 CE), resolved that nothing should be read in church under the name of the divine Scriptures except the canonical writings. The NT books are listed as follows: Gospels, Acts, thirteen Pauline epistles, Hebrews, 1–2 Peter, 1–3 John, James, Jude, and John's Apocalypse. However, the best manuscripts of Pope Innocent I's list (405 CE) seem to omit Hebrews.

Despite some persistent "fuzziness" about the edges of the canon (continuing up to this day in Eastern churches), it is fair to say that shortly after 400 CE the twenty-seven books of our present NT canon were recognized as sacred writings that can serve as the rule or norm of Christian faith and life.

The most important subsequent challenge to that consensus came from Martin Luther in the early sixteenth century. Luther had theological problems with four books: Hebrews, because it teaches no repentance for sinners after baptism; James, because it is an epistle of "straw"; Jude, because (according to Luther) it depends on 2 Peter and quotes apocryphal OT writings; and Revelation, because it lacked the proper prophetic and apostolic dimensions. Luther placed these four books at the end of his German translation of the NT, though he did not remove them from the Bible.

Underlying Luther's objections to these books was the theological principle that biblical books should be evaluated according to their success in "promoting" (treiben ["drive"] in German) Christ. The books that most successfully promote Christ (in Luther's opinion) are John's Gospel, Paul's letters to the Galatians and Romans, and 1 Peter (and perhaps also Ephesians and 1 John). Without denying the now traditional twenty-seven-book canon, Luther raised the issue of "the canon within the canon"; that is, some books are more important and thus more "canonical" because of their great theological value in promoting Christ.

At its fourth session (April 1546) the Council of Trent listed the twenty-seven "received" books of the NT. There was some debate about recognizing the historical distinction between the "acknowledged" and the "disputed" books, but not much came of this. What is important about the Council of Trent's action was that for the first time the content of the Bible was made an article of faith and confirmed with an anathema: "If anyone does not receive these books in their entirety, with all their parts . . . as sacred and canonical, and knowingly and willingly rejects the aforesaid traditions, let him be anathema."

The traditional canon of twenty-seven NT books was confirmed also in several Protestant confessions of faith: the French Confession of Faith (1559), the Belgic Confession (1561), the Thirty-Nine Articles issued by the Church of England (1563), and the Westminster Confession of Faith (1647). Thus the general agreement about the NT canon today among Catholics and Protestants.

THEOLOGICAL ISSUES

What we can and cannot know about the history of the canon of Scripture is relatively clear. The result is a general agreement among the Christian churches as to what constitutes sacred Scripture (apart from the question of the deuterocanonicals/Apocrypha). Nevertheless, associated with that history and consensus are some interesting theological problems.

Terminology. For Jews the Scriptures are "Tanakh" (Tôrâ, Něbîʾîm, Kětûbîm), the Hebrew acronym for the three main divisions of books. For English-speaking Jews, they are the "Hebrew Scriptures" or the "Jewish Scriptures."

The Christian Bible, however, is divided into two major parts, traditionally called the OT and the NT. In recent years biblical scholars, theologians, and ecumenists have questioned the value and accuracy of these traditional titles. To many "modern" people the adjective old can carry with it a pejorative connotation—something no longer useful and, therefore, to be thrown out or disregarded, in favor of what is more useful and valuable (the "new"). The word testament is used in English now mainly in legal contexts—one's last will and testament.

Another possible translation of the Greek noun διαθήκη *diathēkē,* besides "testament," is "covenant," which is by far a more central biblical concept (though not nearly as central as biblical theologians of the past have made it). But with Old and New Covenants comes the problem of the opposition between "old" and "new" as well as the failure to recognize that the Bible speaks of multiple covenants, or at least multiple renewals, of the one covenant. Adding to the confusion are the different values associated with "old" and "new." In antiquity, the "old" was good and the "new" had to prove its value. Today the "old" is obsolete and, therefore, disposable, whereas the "new" is at least advertised (therefore, widely accepted) as superior and destined to replace the "old."

This controversy about labeling the two parts of the Christian Bible is more than a debate about words.[20] It really concerns Christian attitudes toward the legacy of Israel: Is the OT to be jettisoned (as Marcion suggested), or to be kept as an essential part of Christian faith? If it is to be kept, how should it be used—as religious texts to be taken seriously in their own right, as preparation for the gospel, or as the necessary presupposition for understanding the NT?

Christians have proposed some substitute titles for OT and NT: Hebrew and Greek Scriptures, Jewish and Christian Scriptures, and First and Second/Other Testaments. These proposals, however, bear their own burdens. The terms *Hebrew* and *Jewish* can imply that Christians have ceded these books back to Jews, thus reviving Marcion's program. The Catholic canon contains some OT books surely composed in Greek (Wisdom, 2 Maccabees) and others whose only extant or best preserved versions are in Greek (1 Maccabees, Sirach, Judith, Tobit, Baruch). And "First" versus "Second" or "Other" is really a bland version of "Old" and "New," and carries with it the same basic set of problems. So until a more suitable substitute emerges, we will probably continue to talk about the OT and the NT. Nevertheless, we now recognize better the problematic nature of those labels.

The Canonical Text. The Council of Trent's decree about the canon of Scripture took as its criterion (at least in content) the Latin Vulgate. What was canonical in the Vulgate (the "common" Latin version) counted as Scripture. This meant that the seven deuterocanonical/apocryphal books were reckoned to be part of the canon for Catholics. Protestants followed Luther's lead in denying to these writings canonical status, in part at least because they were not in the Hebrew text. This famous controversy from the sixteenth century raises the prior question: Which text is the canonical one?

Both Catholics and Protestants today take as their norm the "original" Hebrew and Greek texts. But which is the original text? Textual critics have developed for both Testaments theories of local text-types: Palestinian, Samaritan, and Babylonian families for the Hebrew OT; and Alexandrian, Western, and Byzantine families for the Greek NT. These local groupings are much debated today. The point here is, however, that the Hebrew and Greek textual traditions are far from uniform in every respect.

Some parts of the Bible are now generally acknowledged *not* to have been originally part of the books with which they have been transmitted. Two well-known examples are the passage about the woman taken in adultery (John 7:53–8:11) and the compendium of resurrection appearances (Mark 16:9-20). Moreover, many books are acknowledged *not* to have been written by their traditional authors: Deuteronomy (by Moses), the Psalms (by David), James and Jude (by the Lord's brothers), the later "Pauline" writings, and so forth. One factor toward acceptance of these writings into the canon may well have been their traditional ascriptions. Do they, therefore, remain in the canon under false pretenses?[21]

Different text-types, later additions to books, and the phenomenon of pseudepigraphy (whereby books are attributed to famous people who didn't actually write them) raise interesting questions in connection with the canon of Scripture. However, the fundamental principle in these debates is that canonicity pertains to the document as the document of the faith-community.[22] It is not tied to a particular text-type or to one edition of the work or to the accuracy of what is said about its original circumstances. Most biblical scholars today would agree that textual criticism approaches (but may never reach) the original texts (also called "autographs"—written by the first author), that the history of transmission makes John 7:53–8:11

---

20. Norbert Lohfink, *The Covenant Never Revoked* (New York: Paulist, 1991).

21. D. G. Meade, *Pseudonymity and Canon* (Grand Rapids: Eerdmans, 1987).
22. Metzger, *The Canon of the NT,* 270.

and Mark 16:9-20 canonical (but not Johannine or Markan), and that the biblical Pseudepigrapha are fully canonical (though perhaps not composed by their alleged authors). There is no need for an obsessive or overly scrupulous attitude toward determining the exact text of the canonical Scriptures. The history of the canon indicates that a certain "fuzziness" has always been part of the process.

The Value of the Deuterocanonicals/Apocrypha. The seven additional books included in the Catholic OT are not very controversial today. They are customarily read in Catholic churches as Scripture but receive no special prominence. When included in Bibles produced under Protestant auspices they generally appear in a special section ("The Apocrypha"). Whether readers wish to regard them as canonical depends largely on personal decision and theological tradition. The inclusion of these books in *The New Interpreter's Bible* is indicative of the current inclusive attitude (as opposed to the exclusiveness of thirty or forty years ago).

The question remains, however: Do these books make a difference? Tobit and Judith are now understood as short stories or novellas (like Jonah and Esther). They are far more important as sources for post-exilic Jewish piety than as historical documents. Although hardly histories in the modern scientific sense, 1 and 2 Maccabees do supply a great deal of information about Palestinian Judaism in the second century BCE. Luther's objection to the alleged teaching about prayers for the dead in 2 Macc 12:44-45 no longer stirs much controversy. The text is regarded as the author's own peculiar interpretation of Judas Maccabeus's decision to send a sin-offering to the Jerusalem Temple on behalf of himself and his surviving colleagues in the light of the alleged idolatry committed by Jewish soldiers who fell in battle (see 2 Macc 12:39-43).

The book of Baruch is a kind of pastiche of words and phrases from the Hebrew Bible (especially Daniel 9, Job 28, and Isaiah 40–66). It provides reflections on the theological significance of Israel's exile in the sixth century BCE and the subsequent restoration to the land of Israel. The book of Sirach adds greatly (fifty-one chaps.) to the corpus of Wisdom literature in the Bible. Not all of its contributions, however, are welcome to readers today (especially its misogynistic statements, as in 42:9-14).

The book of Wisdom is probably the most signifi-

cant among the seven additional books. Written in Greek at Alexandria in the first century BCE in Solomon's persona, Wisdom blends the religious traditions of the Hebrew Bible with the language and conceptuality of Greek philosophy; for example, in talking about immortal (3:1-12) and even pre-existent souls (8:19-20), the cardinal virtues (8:7), the perishable body weighing down the soul (9:15), and divine providence (14:3). Moreover, Wisdom's depictions of the Suffering Righteous person (1:16–3:12), the pre-existent figure of Wisdom (7:22-30), and Wisdom's activity throughout the history of Israel (as in the exodus, according to 18:14-19) possess great christological significance. The presence of the book of Wisdom in the canon makes the Catholic Bible different from the Protestant Bible. Likewise, the presence of the NT books makes the Christian Bible different from the Jewish Bible. These differences need not be exaggerated or developed into matter for polemics (as they have been in the past). Yet they should be acknowledged.

Open or Closed? The longstanding debate between Catholics and Protestants about the limits of the OT canon raises a related question: May the churches add or subtract books from the canon of Scripture? The answer is that they may but probably will not and should not do so.[23]

The matter of adding books to the canon is sometimes brought up with regard to a modern spiritual classic such as Martin Luther King, Jr.'s, "Letter from a Birmingham Jail." The obvious objection is that, however inspiring and deeply theological King's letter may be, it has not been used and accepted by the churches for almost two thousand years, as the canonical books have been.

Perhaps the most intriguing case involves the discovery of ancient books. In the late 1940s there were two sensational discoveries of manuscripts roughly contemporary with the NT: the Jewish manuscripts that constitute the Dead Sea Scrolls, and the gnostic Christian codices from Nag Hammadi in Egypt. Some scholars argue that the *Gospel of Thomas,* discovered at Nag Hammadi, contains forms of Jesus' sayings that are older and more original than their parallels in the canonical Gospels.[24] Assuming that these scholars are correct (and there is much doubt about that), should we make the *Gospel of Thomas* part of the church's canon? Or suppose that the hypothetical collection of sayings known as Q (from the German *Quelle,* meaning "source") and used independently by Matthew and Luke in their editions of Mark were to be discovered whole and entire. Would Q be part of the canon? Or what if archaeologists were to discover Paul's "previous letter" (1 Cor 5:9) or his mysterious Letter to the Laodiceans (Col 4:16)? Would these documents become Scripture?

The basic principle in dealing with these ancient books would be the same as that applied in determining the case of modern works: the use and acceptance of these books within the churches. Before a council or a world-church body or a pope could decree these ancient but lost books to be canonical, there would have to develop some pattern of use and acceptance on the local level leading to a broad consensus. In other words, such books would have to recapitulate the process that the undoubtedly canonical books had already passed through. However, this is very unlikely to happen, precisely because the NT books of the canon share a common 1,600-year history apart from the other books. The more likely scenario is that Q or the "previous letter" or the Letter to the Laodiceans would be accepted not as canonical but rather as valuable witness to the early church's faith (such as *Didache, 1 Clement,* the letters of Ignatius, and so forth).

There have also been occasional proposals to omit books from the canon. Although he never omitted them, Luther did express doubts about the theological value of Hebrews, James, Jude, and Revelation. More daring modern theologians have come forward with proposals toward streamlining the canon in the alleged interests of ecumenism, or getting rid of the hierarchical-patriarchal thinking represented by the Pastorals, or doing away with the so-called "anti-Jewish" passages in John's Gospel, or purging the canon of the wild apocalypticism in Revelation. Such extreme proposals are worth considering, precisely because they force us to rethink the content of the biblical books and decide whether the complaints are justified. But it remains highly unlikely that anything will come of them, precisely because of the 1,600-year tradition of use and acceptance.

Canon Within the Canon. Although adding to or subtracting from the canon of Scripture seems unlikely and unwise, the churches have always placed more emphasis on some books than on others. There is a significant amount of theological diversity within the canon in both the OT (compare Ecclesiastes and Daniel on life after death) and the NT (compare Paul and James on faith and works). Indeed, there is so much diversity that according to some the canon has been the principle of disunity, not of unity, in the churches.[25] One can analyze the history of the church by looking at what books exercised the predominant influence in various traditions: Matthew and the Pastorals among Roman Catholics, Paul's letters (especially Galatians and Romans) among Protestants, the Johannine writings for the Eastern Orthodox, the early chapters of Acts for sectarians, and so forth. It is fair to say that every Christian group takes its stand on certain canonical books and ignores others.

Luther made this issue explicit by contending that some books (John, Galatians, Romans, 1 Peter) best promote Christ, and other books (Hebrews, James, Jude, Revelation) are theologically suspect or less useful. Luther's forthrightness on this matter has led to a debate about the propriety of acknowledging a "canon within the canon"; that is, whether there is a small core of allegedly superior books within the entire collection of canonical books.

There is a positive value to recognizing and admitting that various Christian groups have paid more attention to some biblical books than others. Such an exercise can contribute greatly to a kind of Christian unity, for one group can see that the other group also bases itself on the Scriptures. In this way the canon—despite, indeed because of, all its diversity—can help toward Christian unity.[26]

The problem comes with raising the "canon within the canon" to the level of a theological principle. Any list of "core" books is bound to be arbitrary and unbalanced. We might find ourselves repeating what Marcion tried to do by reducing the Scriptures to some Pauline letters and an expurgated version of Luke's Gospel. Even Luther's list, despite its theological sophistication, has the effect of muting certain voices within the canon. Should the church

25. Ernst Käsemann, "The Canon of the New Testament and the Unity of the Church," in *Essays on New Testament Themes* (London: SCM, 1964).
26. Oscar Cullmann, *Unity Through Diversity* (Philadelphia: Fortress, 1988).

ignore the plea for social justice and practical Christianity found in the letter of James? Should Revelation's reminder of the transitory character of earthly empires and its hope for a heavenly kingdom be kept from Christian people? Should the early church's struggle to develop adequate and effective social structures that is witnessed in the Pastorals be pushed aside?

There is much in the Bible that reflects the situation of a small group of people in the ancient Near East (Israel) or the position of a religious minority movement in the Greco-Roman world (the early church). There are materials (for example, the NT "household codes"—e.g., Eph 5:21–6:9; Col 3:18–4:1; and 1 Pet 2:13–3:12) that seem quaint or shocking or even monstrous to Westerners today. Yet these same texts can offer hope and encouragement and direction to some Christians (as in China) who find themselves in analogous minority settings.

The debate about the canon within the canon is stimulating intellectually and challenging theologically. But elevating it to a theological principle runs the risks of theological arbitrariness and of silencing voices that the church needs to hear.

Canon and Church. In matters of both history and theology there is an inextricable connection between the canon of Scripture and the church. The nature of this connection has in the past been the topic for debate and polemic. Catholics have often appealed to the gradual development of the biblical canon to show that the Bible is the church's book, since the individual books grew out of the church's experience and were declared canonical by the church. In this view the canon is the "authoritative collection of books." Protestants have argued that the books of the Bible provide the rule by which church life is to be guided and measured in all ages. The (divine) authority resides in the books, which proved themselves to be inspired and, therefore, authoritative. Thus the canon is the "collection of authoritative books."[27]

These traditional formulations of the issue of canon and church each contain some truth: The canon of Scripture is the church's book, and the canon functions as the norm of church life. The problem comes when one loses sight of the symbiotic relationship between canon and faith community. Christianity is not really a "religion of the book," nor

should it make the Bible into an icon (something to be admired but never touched). Just as in its historical development the canon of Scripture demanded a faith-community, so also in church life today the canon ought to actualize and guide the faith-community.

Vatican II's Constitution on Divine Revelation (*Dei verbum*) insisted that "Sacred Tradition, Sacred Scripture, and the Magisterium of the church are so connected and associated that one of them cannot stand without the others." This is a sound and balanced Catholic approach to a problem that every church faces in some form, though it leaves unresolved exactly how disputes are to be adjudicated. The conciliar statement is preceded by what surely must be applauded as an ecumenical breakthrough between Catholics and Protestants: "[The] Magisterium is not superior to the Word of God, but is its servant. It teaches only what has been handed on to it."[28]

Criticism of the Canon. The discovery of early Christian writings outside the canon of Scripture—the Nag Hammadi documents and the so-called NT Apocrypha—has led in some quarters to the questioning of the canon itself. Some of these documents may be older than books contained in the canon, or at least they may contain traditions that are more primitive and, therefore, more authentic than what appears in the canon.[29] Moreover, the church's canon represents a narrow selection of early Christian writings. The early Christian movement was far more diverse and even exotic than the traditional canon allows. The canon was shaped by representatives of one kind of Christianity and has served as an instrument of censorship and repression for 1,600 years—so some say.

One may agree or disagree with these criticisms on historical grounds. The evidence is ambiguous, with serious scholars on either side. In dealing with them on a theological level, however, it first is necessary to distinguish between study of the NT as a canonical document (by and for the faith-community) and research on Christian origins. The latter pursuit involves all the available resources, no matter what their origin or theological orthodoxy. The former pursuit focuses on those books that the faith-community has singled out as expressing accurately and properly what it believes. One cannot

27. Metzger, *The Canon of the NT,* 282-88.

28. *Dei verbum,* 10.
29. Koester, *Ancient Christian Gospels.*

divorce history and theology entirely, of course. But Christian origins and NT study are not precisely the same.

Early Christianity may well have been even more diverse than its scriptural canon indicates. The problem for us today is that we have no way to decide whether the piety represented in the Nag Hammadi documents or the NT Apocrypha was a lunatic fringe or a serious contender to what emerged as the mainstream of "orthodoxy." So the attempt to tie the NT canon to one movement among many stands or falls with the same historical undertaking. Given the literary and theological diversity with the canon, however, it is hard to imagine those twenty-seven books as expressing the ideology and political skill of one party among early Christians.

Canonical Criticism. One approach to Scripture that is prominent in biblical scholarship today is called canonical criticism. As formulated by Brevard Childs,[30] it is more a theological program than an exegetical method. The first task of the canonical critic is to describe the theological shape of the final canonical form of the biblical book. Thus the focus is on the book itself, not (at least primarily) on its pre-history or sources or parallels. The second task is to explore the theological significance of the canonical text for the community of faith not only in the past but also in the present and future. This step involves the history of interpretation as well as more obvious modes of actualization in preaching and teaching.

One does not have to subscribe entirely to Childs's program or follow him in all its details to recognize the merits of his proposal. Its focus on the present canonical text is sound on both literary and theological grounds. Its interest in the Bible as a collection of religious books is only appropriate to a work whose central theme is God's relationship to a people and, through Christ, to all peoples. Objections to Childs's program concern its lack of interest in historical issues and its fluid and ambiguous use of the word *canonical.*

Whatever the merit of the objections (and they are serious), the program of canonical criticism describes what Christian preachers and teachers do. Directed by the tradition of faith, they come to the canon of Scripture expecting to find in it guidance for their lives. They recognize the need first of all to understand the Scriptures on their own terms—with respect for their language, modes of communication, and content. Then reflecting on how the Scriptures have been used within the faith-community (Jewish and Christian), they try to discern what the text might be saying to their own social and/or personal situation. They seek to discover analogies between the experiences of the ancient faith community and those of faithful people today. They seek to show that the canonical Scriptures can and do illumine the lives even of those who live in different times and places. Born of preaching, canonical criticism is a preacher's method.

BIBLIOGRAPHY

Beckwith, R. *The Old Testament Canon of the New Testament Church and Its Background in Early Judaism.* Grand Rapids: Eerdmans, 1986.

Bruce, F. F. *The Canon of Scripture.* Downers Grove, Ill.: Inter-Varsity, 1988.

Metzger, B. M. *The Canon of the New Testament: Its Origin, Development, and Significance.* Oxford: Clarendon, 1987.

Sundberg, A. C. *The Old Testament in the Early Church.* Cambridge, Mass.: Harvard University Press, 1964.

von Campenhausen, H. *The Formation of the Christian Bible.* Philadelphia: Fortress, 1972.

30. B. Childs, *Introduction to the Old Testament as Scripture* (Philadelphia: Fortress, 1979); *The New Testament as Canon: An Introduction* (Philadelphia: Fortress, 1984).

MODERN ENGLISH VERSIONS OF THE BIBLE

KEITH R. CRIM

The enterprise of translating the Bible into English has continued to flourish, but there is still limited agreement concerning the theory of translation best suited to biblical literature. On the one hand are translations that retain wherever possible the word order and sentence structure of the original Hebrew, Aramaic, and Greek documents. These include the Revised Standard Version (RSV, NT 1946; OT and NT 1952; Deuterocanonical/Apocryphal books 1957), the New Revised Standard Version (NRSV, 1989), and the New International Version (NIV, NT 1973; OT and NT 1978). These versions display faithfulness in translation as faithfulness to the *form* of the original languages combined with necessary adjustments to the grammar and syntax of English. In form-centered translations, a pronoun is usually translated by a pronoun and a verb by a verb, even though there may be a more idiomatic way of expressing the meaning in English. Compare NRSV Judg 1:35, "The hand of the house of Joseph rested heavily on them," with the more idiomatic wording in the Revised English Bible (REB, 1989): "But the Joseph tribes increased their pressure on them."

By contrast, other translations give priority to the *content* and are willing to adjust the form to English usage. In addition to the REB, these include the Good News Bible (GNB, also known as Today's English Version, NT 1966; revised NT with OT 1976). At a more complex literary level, the Jewish Publication Society version, *Tanakh: The Sacred Scriptures* (TNK, 1985), combines a content-centered approach and sensitivity to literary form. TNK achieved both clarity and simplicity—e.g., Isa 26:3: "The confident mind You guard in safety,/ In safety because it trusts in You." Note the use of inclusive language. (*Tanakh* is a Hebrew acronym for the three divisions of the Hebrew Bible: תורה *Tôrâ,* the Five Books of Moses; נביאים *Nĕbî'îm,* the Prophets; and כתובים *Kĕtûbîm,* the Writings.)

Other versions have undergone revisions that mark a transition in the reverse direction—from content-centered to form-centered. In the 1970 edition of the New American Bible (NAB), precedence was given to content. In 1988 the NAB OT was reissued together with a significantly revised NT, giving greater attention to the form of the original languages. For example, Matt 5:18, "of this much I assure you," was replaced in the revision by "Amen, I say to you." Similar changes abound throughout the NT.

To a lesser extent, the New English Bible (NEB, 1970) is also more idiomatic than the version that replaced it, the Revised English Bible (REB, 1989). The REB, however, is the clearer of the two and uses inclusive language, although with less consistency than the NRSV.

The distinction between form-centered and content-centered involves many nuances and is only one measure of the differences among versions.

THE THREE STAGES OF BIBLE TRANSLATION

1. Because no original manuscripts of any of the books of the Bible are known to exist, and the ancient manuscripts that scholars use as the basis of translation differ widely at many points, a translation of the Bible begins with determining the text that is to be translated. In spite of the wide agreement among scholars on textual questions, examination of the notes in the margin of modern translations reveals that scholars still differ as to which manuscript is most accurate in a specific passage.

2. The next issue is the meaning of the text in its original language. Here there is a wider range of disagreement that involves the meaning of individual words, the meaning of those words in differing contexts, and the meaning of larger segments of text. Questions of the meaning of cultural features (What is an *Ephod* in Exod 28:4?), of the literary genres involved (Is this passage prose or poetry, and does that make any difference?), of doctrinal formulations (Does "righteousness" catch the right meaning in Rom 1:17*a*?), and a host of other issues must be dealt with in the course of completing a translation.

3. When these problems have been resolved, the translators must still grapple with the decisions of how to express the meaning in the target language. (Modern scholars work with translations of the Bible into many different languages and it is customary to speak of the "target language," or the "receptor language," because the same principles apply to any given language). Here the distinctive features of each version become evident, and the interest of the Bible-reading public is aroused. "Why did the translators say it this way?" they ask.

LEVELS OF COMPLEXITY

The traditional approach has been to make a translation simple or complex in keeping with the original form of the different parts of Scripture. But this approach is not centered on the needs of the Bible-reading public. In addition to the explosion of new Bible translations in Protestantism since World War II, the renewed interest in Bible translation in the Roman Catholic Church, inspired by the encyc-

lical *Divino afflante Spiritu* (September 30, 1943), resulted in unprecedented ecumenical cooperation in the translation and distribution of Scripture. One aspect of this cooperation has been special emphasis on joint translations by Catholics and Protestants, which make the Bible available to wide audiences around the world. Advances in linguistics and translation theory have made it possible to produce translations in less complex language without resorting to paraphrase. It is no longer adequate to have only one version of the Bible for most languages, but translations at different levels of language complexity are needed in order to reach increasingly large numbers of readers.

THE LURE OF ARCHAIC LANGUAGE

Because the language of the King James Bible and its successors is familiar to many, various recent translations have retained vocabulary and sentence structures handed down from the past—e.g., "The evil are ensnared by the transgression of their lips" (Prov 12:13 NRSV; cf. KJV). The basic question is whether priority should be given to expressing clearly the meaning of the Bible, or to approaching as nearly as possible the vocabulary, sentence structure, and idioms of the original languages of Scripture. These issues are often debated in terms of "faithfulness to Scripture," but in reality they involve complex questions of translation theory, beginning with a definition of what "faithfulness to Scripture" involves.

An important factor in making decisions in this area is the identity of the audience or audiences who will read and study a given version. For example, in the 1980s church leaders, both Protestant and Catholic, found that readers for whom English is a second language could benefit from an easier version than any then available. To meet this need, the United Bible Societies produced the NT of the *Bible for Today's Family* (Contemporary English Version [CEV], 1991) and began work on the OT as well.

The question of level of linguistic usage is not new. Martin Luther, in preparing his German translation of the Bible, went to the ordinary people of his day to observe the way in which they spoke, so that he could make the Bible easily understood. In linguistic terms, his focus was on the receptor language, how the message is best expressed with accuracy, clarity, and beauty, so that each reader can understand the message.

Even in the present day, however, the criterion for style in Bible translation may be closeness to the form of the original language. As a result, form and content, instead of being in harmony, may clash. In the book of Job, for example, the magnificent poetic passages are usually translated by maintaining the parallelism of the Hebrew lines, with the result that readers unaccustomed to reading long poetic passages easily become discouraged. That much parallelism, while effective in biblical Hebrew, is rare in English.

HARMONIZING FORM AND CONTENT

One proposal is that a Bible translation should be as literal as possible and as free as necessary. But by what standards does the translator determine what is "possible" and what is "necessary"? Possible for whom? Necessary to achieve what purpose? The real interests of the reader may not be considered at all.

To be sure, it is always possible to translate each occurrence of a given word in the original languages by repeatedly using the same word in the target language, even though the meaning of the word is different in each context. For example, σαρξ (sarx) is used in the NT in eight different meanings.[1] Both the RSV and the NRSV translate *sarx* contextually in four areas of meaning—e.g., "human parents," Heb 12:9 (RSV "earthly fathers"); "my own people," Rom 11:14 (RSV "fellow Jews"); "human standards," 1 Cor 1:26 (RSV, "worldy standards"); and "flesh," Rev 19:18, where "flesh" (i.e., "meat") is contextually correct in both the RSV and the NRSV. But in four other areas of meaning the RSV and the NRSV continue the traditional translation of *sarx* as "flesh" (e.g., 1 Tim 3:16; John 1:14; Gal 4:23; Heb 5:7). In these and many other passages, modern English versions differ in the way they interpret the meaning in different contexts.

DEALING WITH PRESUPPOSITIONS

Ideological considerations also play a role. The books and the scholarly papers written by Bible

1. J. P. Louw and E. A. Nida. *Greek-English Lexicon of the New Testament Based on Semantic Domains*. Vol. 1 (New York: United Bible Societies, 1988) xiv-xv.

translators make clear that there are often strong differences of opinion among members of any given translation committee. No one who has spent a lifetime defending a position wants to see his or her committee reject that position. In the case of one translation committee, the members were chosen because they had not yet written books that they would feel obliged to defend.

Moreover, the prevailing atmosphere of the religious communities and of the world they exist in may lead to new views of the translator's task. As American society became aware of the importance of eliminating sexual bias in much of contemporary English, there was an increasing demand for inclusive language. As a result, the revisers who prepared the NRSV adopted a style that was not gender specific when referring to human participants, while, where they deemed it necessary, retaining male language for the deity. Other translations have made less extensive changes to achieve the same purpose.

FROM THE REVISED STANDARD VERSION TO THE NEW REVISED STANDARD VERSION

As a lineal descendant of the King James Version and the American Standard Version of 1901, the Revised Standard Version (NT 1946; OT 1952) became the most widely read and studied modern English version of the Bible. A limited revision of the NT was published in 1971. In terms of the total picture of modern versions, however, the publication of the RSV marked the end of a period, rather than the beginning of a new period. After it was published, new discoveries of ancient manuscripts of the Bible, especially the Dead Sea Scrolls; the publication of competing versions; the demand for more contemporary language; and new advances in biblical interpretation, linguistics, and translation theory had by 1971 made it desirable to undertake a full revision of the RSV Bible. This revision was published in 1989 as the New Revised Standard Version (NRSV).

The National Council of Churches, as holder of the copyright, had directed that a revision be undertaken to make necessary changes "(1) in paragraph structure and punctuation; (2) in the elimination of archaisms while retaining the flavor of the Tyndale-King James Bible tradition; (3) in striving for greater accuracy, clarity, and euphony; and (4) in eliminating masculine-oriented language relating to people, so far as this could be done without distorting passages that reflect the historical situation of ancient patriarchal culture and society."[2] The general nature of the first three points is in marked contrast to the specific mandate in point 4.

Point 3 came to include extensive improvements in the interpretation of disputed passages and in establishing the text that served as the basis for the translation. Because of the commitment to maintaining continuity with the Tyndale-King James tradition, however, it proved impossible to make the translation as clear as most other contemporary translations. For many readers, the familiar language and style brought over from the traditional versions compensated for this loss.

Textual Basis. At the time the new revision was begun not all of the Dead Sea Scrolls had been made available to scholars, but the committee was given permission to study important fragments of the books of Samuel. From them significant emendations were made. These include a passage between 1 Sam 10:27 and 11:1, which was inserted into the translation without any verse number, and additions to 1:11 based on ancient Greek manuscripts and the Qumran material. These and other additions are identified in footnotes to the text. Other corrections were made on the basis of ancient versions in other languages and on conjectures made by scholars where the text seemed to have been corrupted in the process of transmission. For the translation of the New Testament, the committee followed the third and most recent edition of *The Greek New Testament,* published by the United Bible Societies. They also had access to the 4th edition, which had not yet been published when the NRSV Bible was released to the public.

Interpretation. On the basis of continuing philological and exegetical work since the publication of the RSV, the NRSV has changed the interpretation of many passages. Notable examples are found in many of the terms used in worship in Leviticus. For example, "peace offering" (3:1 and elsewhere) has been replaced by "sacrifice of well-being," following the wording used in the TNK. The familiar passage in Deut 33:27, "The eternal God is your dwelling place," is interpreted differently in the NRSV, "He

subdues the ancient gods,/ shatters the forces of old" (cf. REB and NAB). The TNK, the NIV, the GNB, and the NJB all retain the traditional interpretation. Other passages that were revised on the basis of continuing research include Isa 35:8; 63:8*b*-9; and 2 Esdr 10:27. In Gen 6:6; Amos 7:3; and elsewhere, instead of saying the Lord "repented" or "was sorry," the NRSV uses the translation "relented."

English Style and Wording. It was inevitable that archaic verb forms and pronouns would be eliminated from the NRSV, but whole sentences follow the same word order as the Greek or Hebrew. Compare NRSV 2 Kgs 12:20, "His servants arose, devised a conspiracy, and killed Joash," with the NIV rendering: "His officials conspired against him and assassinated him."

In the publicity for the NRSV, particular emphasis was placed on the use of inclusive language. A variety of devices was used to achieve this goal. In Matthew 5, the RSV's "men" is replaced by "people" (v. 11), by "no one" (v. 15), by "other" (vv. 16, 19), and by other appropriate expressions. The RSV 5:22—"every one who is angry with his brother"—contrasts with NRSV: "if you are angry with a brother or sister." Other examples from the NRSV include Jas 1:2 and 2:1, "brothers and sisters"; 1:9, "the believer"; 3:2, "is perfect"; Jer 31:30, "all shall die for their own sins . . . everyone who eats sour grapes. . . . " Although references to God and clearly patriarchal passages were not made inclusive, the NRSV has been more thorough in using inclusive language than any other English language translation.

THE NEW ENGLISH BIBLE AND THE REVISED ENGLISH BIBLE

The New English Bible (NEB, NT 1961; OT and NT 1970) was born in the fresh enthusiasm for modern translations of the Bible immediately following the end of World War II. The proposal for this translation was made in May 1949 by the General Assembly of the Church of Scotland. The response from other denominations and groups was enthusiastic, and the project became fully representative of the non-Roman Catholic bodies in the British Isles. Roman Catholic representatives later attended as observers. After the publication of the completed Bible in 1970, the committee was not dissolved, and

---

2. Bruce M. Metzger et al., *The Making of the New Revised Standard Version of the Bible* (Grand Rapids: Eerdmans, 1991).

the Roman Catholic Church entered into full membership and thus became involved in the translation of the Revised English Bible (REB, 1989).

The NEB was planned as a translation "in the language of the present day." To this end, the translators were free to abandon the grammatical constructions of the Hebrew, Aramaic, and Greek languages and to avoid the literal translation of idioms. The NT underwent moderate revision before being published together with the OT and the Deuterocanonical/Apocryphal books in 1970. In 1974, a mere four years later, the Joint Committee of the Churches, which was responsible for the translation, began efforts toward a major revision of the text. This revision was published in 1989 as the Revised English Bible. It was not a minor revision that touched up a few passages or incorporated a few new insights. Rather, far-ranging changes were made, so that while it is clear that the greater part of the text has survived, it is also clear that the distinctive nature of the NEB has been altered. Many of the changes are the result of reconsideration of the interpretations espoused by Professor Sir Godfrey Driver, convenor of the OT Panel of the NEB.

Throughout the REB, archaisms were abandoned and controversial interpretations were replaced by more traditional language. In addition, the revisers eliminated much of the male-oriented language, although not so thoroughly as did the NRSV. A comparison of Matt 16:25-26 in the REB ("Whoever wants to save his life will lose it . . . ") and the NRSV ("For those who want to save their life will lose it . . . ") illustrates the NRSV's consistent use of plural pronouns in general statements.

The NEB, with its single-column format and the verse numbers moved to the side of the page, looks much like an ordinary book. The REB has the familiar two-column format of most other current versions of the Bible, and the verse numbers are back in the text, rather than in the margin. Both features are a help in reading aloud in worship. Also, the reader is helped by the movement away from "donnish English," such as that found in NEB Heb 1:1-4, with long sentences and such words as *effulgence.*

Textual Basis. Especially in the OT of the NEB, the translators were free to make textual emendations on a case-by-case basis. Verses and words were eliminated, emended, or transposed. Psalm 41:9*b* was moved to 10*b* in both the NEB and the REB. In the NEB, Isa 5:24-25 was moved to a position between Isa 10:4 and 10:5, and the phrase "in the scroll of a book it is prescribed for me" in Ps 40:7*b* was omitted conjecturally, a decision not followed by the REB. These emendations illustrate some of the many changes from the NEB to the more traditional REB. One emendation in the NEB that the REB might well have abandoned but did not is found in Prov 12:12. R. Bullard points out that this emendation requires "repointing at least one word, rearranging the order of three words, and giving one word the meaning of a cognate root in Arabic."[3]

The NT uses an eclectic text. Matt 27:16-17 reads "Jesus Bar-Abbas" in both verses in the NEB and "Jesus Barabbas" in both verses in the REB. "Barabbas/Bar-Abbas" is not adopted in the GNB, the NIV, or the NAB; it is in the text with brackets in the NAB 2nd ed, and with a footnote in the NRSV; and it is included in footnotes in both the JB and NJB.

Interpretation. The preface to the REB is guarded in its statements, venturing only to say, "Moreover the widespread enthusiasm for The New English Bible has resulted in its being frequently used for reading aloud in public worship, the implications of which had not been fully anticipated by the translators." That is to say, when read aloud in a public gathering, the wording was at times shocking (e.g., Josh 15:18, an interpretation that was abandoned in the REB). In REB Cant 1:7 the woman is still "left picking lice," but in 2:3, 5 the apricots have yielded to the traditional apple. Throughout both Testaments, beginning with Gen 1:1-2, the REB chose more traditional wording and simpler syntax, with great gain in clarity.

English Style and Wording. The REB translators not only made such necessary changes as abandoning archaic pronouns and verb forms, but also found more natural semantic equivalents for proverbial sayings. An outstanding example is 1 Kgs 20:11, where the REB "The time for boasting is after the battle" replaces the NEB "The lame must not think himself a match for the nimble," which bears no similarity to the original. The revisers also corrected some lapses in the NEB: In Judg 3:21, Ehud no longer seems to commit harakiri, but plunges his sword into the belly of his enemy Eglon.

Several features that brought criticism on the NEB were also modified. The NEB's strange device of

---

3. R. Bullard, "The New English Bible," in *The Word of God: A Guide to English Versions of the Bible,* ed. Lloyd R. Bailey (Atlanta: John Knox, 1982) 54.

indenting lines of poetry in accordance with a theory of variations in line length was abandoned. Few readers knew what it meant, and it followed no principle of English poetry. Beginning with Gen 1:1-2 the REB again and again opted for more traditional interpretation and wording. Some readings in the NEB were changed in the REB, but not improved (e.g., 2 Sam 13:12). The NEB has Tamar say, "Do not behave like a beast," while REB translates, "Do not behave so infamously." Neither sounds like the words of a frightened woman.

THE NEW INTERNATIONAL VERSION

In 1965 a group of evangelical scholars representing the Christian Reformed Church and the National Association of Evangelicals met at Palos Heights, Illinois, to discuss the need for a new translation of the Bible into English. Although this was a period of intense concern for new translations, these scholars felt that none of the projects then under way would meet the needs of their constituency. As the preface to the NIV reports, they desired an accurate translation characterized by the clarity and literary quality that could meet a wide variety of purposes: "public and private reading, teaching, preaching, memorizing and liturgical use." They also wanted to preserve a continuity with the traditional language and form of the English Bible. Perhaps the most distinctive statement in the preface about the translation is that "the translators were united in their commitment to the authority and infallibility of the Bible as God's Word in written form."

They were charged with eliminating archaic pronouns and verb forms, modifying sentence structure, and showing sensitivity to the contextual meaning of words. All of these are concerns shared by the other major translations published subsequent to the RSV. The successful carrying out of this agenda has produced a Bible that, while more modern in these respects than RSV, still does not include a distinguishing feature of the NRSV—language that is not gender specific. Nevertheless, for large segments of the Bible-reading public the NIV is the version of choice.

Textual Basis. The translators made their decisions about textual problems in both the OT and the NT on the basis of standard textual principles. It is interesting to note, however, that while footnotes in the translation refer to the Dead Sea Scrolls, the LXX, and other versions, there is no mention of any decisions based on conjecture. A classic example of a textual problem is found in 1 Sam 13:1, where the Masoretic Text (MT) lacks a numeral for Saul's age when he became king, and says he reigned over Israel two years. The NIV corrects this to say that Saul came to the throne when he was thirty years old and that he reigned forty-two years. In a footnote, the NIV justifies the number forty-two by basing it on the "round number" (40) in Acts 13:21. Most translations would label both of these decisions in the NIV as conjecture. In the NT, rather than use any one modern Greek Testament as their basis, the translators decided each issue on its merits. A number of readings that are not generally accepted as authentic are given in footnotes (e.g., 1 John 5:7-8), thus providing help for readers accustomed to the KJV.

Interpretation. A careful reader will find many passages in which the NIV presents a meaning not universally accepted. Genesis 1:2 begins, "Now the earth was formless and empty," and a footnote to the word *was* reads "or possibly *became.*" This reflects a belief common in some evangelical Protestant circles that v. 1 refers to the creation at the dawn of time, a creation that included various ancient life forms that perished when that creation was destroyed, and many eons later the world was remade as described in Gen 1:2–2:3. Another of the principles followed was that the translation should "clearly reflect the unity and harmony of the Spirit-inspired Writings." The translation of Acts 2:27 is word for word the same as the quotation in Ps 16:10, and in both passages the words "Holy One" are capitalized. Isaiah 7:14 and Matt 1:23 are identical, except that Matthew reads "and they will call him," while in Isaiah we have "and will call him," where the subject is "the virgin." A note in the Isaiah passage cites the alternate readings "and he" or "and they." In many passages messianic references are implied by the use of capital letters; e.g., Psalm 2, "Anointed One," "One," "King," and "Son" (twice). As a whole, the NIV represents a solidly evangelical stance.

English Style and Wording. The translators have achieved a style that is generally clear and pleasant to read, and the style is close enough to that of the RSV and its predecessors to sound familiar to Protestant churchgoers. But great familiarity may not be a help in dealing with the large remnant of awkward expressions that have about them the ring of biblical language. Saul's command to the priest in 1 Sam 14:19 reads, "Withdraw your hand," leaving the reader to wonder where the priest had put his hand. Other awkward phrases pointed out by reviewers include the following "literal" translations from the Hebrew: "the firstfruits of all their manhood" (Ps 105:36); "anointing you with the oil of joy" (Ps 45:7 [Heb v 8]); "by your favor you exalt our horn" (Ps 89:17); and many other occurrences of the word *horn* as a metaphor for strength. Passages such as these fall short of the announced goal of "sensitivity to the contextual meaning of words."

The use of male-oriented language was not an issue for the translators. Thus far it does not seem to be an issue for readers of the NIV.

THE NEW AMERICAN BIBLE

The history of this Roman Catholic translation of the Bible reflects the changes in the Catholic Church since the Confraternity of Christian Doctrine (CCD) began a new translation into English in 1936. The first great change resulted from the encyclical *Divino afflante Spiritu* (1943), which approved translations from the original languages rather than from the Latin Vulgate. The second change was the acceptance of modern scholarly interpretation of the Bible and thus cooperation with non-Catholic scholars. The third was a change in the understanding of the nature of translation and the way modern linguistics can be utilized in translating the Bible.

Under the sponsorship of the CCD, the translation moved along traditional lines, following the original text in a literal manner with minimum adjustment to the structure of English. But as the work progressed there was greater concern to use more contemporary language, so that by the time the entire Bible was published in 1970 the NAB had a distinctly contemporary ring. In time, however, its limitations became apparent. Especially when the NAB was read in the liturgy, the need for a more traditional and formal version was recognized. To achieve this and other ends it was decided in 1978 to produce "a thorough revision of the New Testament to reflect advances in scholarship and to satisfy needs identified through pastoral experience." In

1986 this revision was published with the existing version of the OT.

There was widespread sentiment to make the NAB NT a "literal" translation. The General Introduction to the Catholic Study Bible (CSB, 1990), a study edition of the NAB, states that the NAB "takes its place alongside rigorously literal translations such as the Revised Standard Version." While the NAB NT in its present form is less "dynamic" than the 1970 edition, it is by no means as "rigorously literal" as the RSV or the NRSV, with their traditional language and involved sentence structures. In time the Catholic Church may rejoice that this is the case.

Another issue was that of inclusive language, and the NAB NT is careful to be inclusive in generic references to human beings. This is also done in the reading guides and reference articles in the CSB.

Finally, the CSB explicitly states that the use of such terms as "Palestine" and "Israel" in the NAB NT does not indicate any stance on modern political issues.

Textual Basis. In both the OT and the NT, the English text represents the mainstream of textual criticism. There are some special comments, however. A footnote to John 7:53–8:11 concludes with the statement, "The Catholic Church accepts this passage as canonical scripture." The longer ending to Mark follows v. 8, and in turn is followed by the shorter ending, in which the verses are numbered successively. The Freer Logion is translated in full in a footnote following the shorter endings to Mark. In preference to the MT of Psalms, the Hebrew text underlying the new Latin Psalter (*Liber Psalmorum*, 1944, 1945) was used. The Sinaiticus Greek recension was used in the translation of Tobit, and fragments in Hebrew and Aramaic were consulted. Judith, 2 Maccabees, and parts of Esther were translated from the Greek. The Dead Sea Scrolls were "consulted extensively," especially in 1 and 2 Samuel. Early editions of the OT contained notes identifying the changes made as a result. In the 1970 edition and the revised NT of 1986, footnotes in both Testaments identify textual issues and explain concisely how they were dealt with.

Since the OT has not been revised, problems noted earlier by reviewers remain. In Proverbs and in Job 28 and elsewhere a number of changes had been introduced in the order of verses, but these changes are no more convincing now than when they were first proposed. Psalm 2:11-12 reads "pay homage to him" rather than the traditional "kiss the Son," but is not emended to "kiss his feet" with RSV, NRSV, and others.

Interpretation. The notes and the translation itself are careful to emphasize the christological features of the OT and their fulfillment in the NT. Isaiah 7:14; 52:13–53:12; and many other passages are dealt with in notes that are specifically messianic in interpretation. The tone is irenic.

English Style and Wording. The goal of the translators of the second edition of the NT was to communicate to "ordinary educated people." "The editors have consequentially moved in the direction of a formal-equivalence approach to translation, matching the vocabulary, structure, and even word order of the original as closely as possible in the receptor language." The OT of the NAB was left at the original dynamic level.

The NT was further revised to achieve inclusive language and more dignity as suitable for liturgical use. The gain and the loss can be seen in Matt 10:11. The first edition reads smoothly: "Look for a worthy person in every town or village you come to and stay with him until you leave." The revised text reads, "Whatever town or village you enter, look for a worthy person in it, and stay there until you leave." The former has a slight advantage in natural style, but the latter has inclusive language. But did changing "Of this much I assure you" (Matt 5:18) to "Amen, I say to you" clarify the meaning or improve the style?

The poetry of the Psalms and of other poetic writings is printed in such a way as to show the parallelism of the Hebrew lines. The level of language is more formal than that of narrative passages, but there is a strength of expression appropriate to the various moods and genres.

TANAKH, THE HOLY SCRIPTURES

September 1962 saw the appearance of *The Torah,* the first section of the Jewish Scriptures, in a totally new translation into English under the sponsorship of the Jewish Publication Society (JPS). The second part of the Hebrew canon, *The Prophets,* appeared in a single volume in 1978, and *The Writings* in 1982. In the intervening years, JPS had issued a series of special publications containing one book each, and a single volume containing the "Five Scrolls and Jonah." This new version was generally known as the "Jewish Publication Society Translation" (JPS), but for the one-volume edition in 1988 it was decided to use the traditional acronym for the three divisions of the Hebrew Bible, *Tôrâ* (Law), *Nĕbî'îm* (Prophets), and *Kĕtûbîm,* (Writings), thus TNK, or *Tanakh—the Holy Scriptures.*

The translation was begun by a committee of seven: three biblical scholars, one representative of each of the three sections of organized Jewish religious life in the United States—Conservative, Reformed, and Orthodox, and a representative of the JPS. This committee translated the Torah, the Prophets, and the Five Scrolls (Song of Songs, Ruth, Lamentations, Ecclesiastes, and Esther). A second committee, organized later in the same manner, translated the remaining books of The Writings. Harry M. Orlinsky served throughout the project as Editor-in-Chief.

The style of the translation is at a high literary level, using a large vocabulary, mercifully free from colloquialisms and inappropriate expressions. There are lapses, however. Deuteronomy 31:16, e.g., reads, "You are soon to lie with your fathers," and Isa 40:31 contains either a paraphrase or a striking interpretation of the text: "But they who trust in the LORD shall renew their strength/As eagles grow new plumes." A note says this refers to a popular belief that eagles regain their youth when they molt.

After the first edition of the earliest volumes, some changes were made, which, while important in themselves, still did little to substantially alter the nature of the final text. For example, in the 1962 edition of *The Torah,* Gen 1:26 reads, "I will make man in My image, after My likeness," and the final edition reads, "Let us make man in our image, after our likeness."

Textual Basis. The title page identifies this as a translation "according to the traditional Hebrew text." More than any other English translation, TNK has lived up to that promise. This does not mean, however, that textual problems have been ignored. In the Torah and the Prophets textual notes are frequent. Many of them read, "Meaning of Heb. [Hebrew] uncertain," and this may be followed by "emendation yields," with a suggested alternate reading for the text. In other passages, the translators chose to follow the consonantal text (כתיב *kĕtîb*), or to cite the LXX or other ancient versions. For the books of Samuel, the evidence of the Dead Sea Scrolls was accepted in numerous passages. Frequent footnotes alert the reader to textual problems, as well as supplying information that is essential to an understanding of the text. Occasionally a note informs the reader that a verse or a part of a verse has been moved, or should be moved in order to clarify the meaning (e.g., Isa 22:7, 10).

The translators of the Writings, however, did not introduce emendations of the text (though the notes and emendations already made in the Five Scrolls before their committee started its work were retained) and they kept explanatory notes "to a minimum." They frequently give in a footnote the "literal" meaning, especially when that reading is traditional and well known. In some passages, they followed the *kĕtîb;* e.g., Job 13:15 ("He may well slay me; I may have no hope").

Interpretation. In his *Notes on the New Translation of the Torah* (1969), Orlinsky set a high standard for establishing the meaning of the language of Scripture, and for expressing that meaning contextually. Throughout the Bible the translators have found clear English expressions for Hebrew idioms that, when translated "literally," are misleading in that specific context. Usually when a traditional interpretation has been replaced, the "literal" meaning is given in a footnote, while the text contains the natural English equivalent (see Ps 56:5 "mortals" [lit. "flesh"]; Ps 38:5 [Eng. v. 4] "overwhelmed me" [lit. "gone over my head," in everyday English this would mean "too hard to understand"]). In numerous other cases a word was inserted in square brackets to make the meaning clear: Jer 20:10, "All my [supposed] friends." The traditional and literal translation "Virgin daughter of Zion" has long since been replaced throughout the TNK by "Fair Maiden Zion" or similar phrasing.

The translators dealt well with problems of polysemy—that is, cases in which a lexeme in Hebrew has a variety of meanings that cannot be expressed in a given target language [in this case, English] by any one lexeme and must, therefore, be translated in a variety of ways according to context, or the correct meaning will be missed. In the TNK the word צדקה (*ṣĕdāqâ*), for example, is translated as "merit" (Ps 106:31), or "just reward" (Ps 24:5), or "triumph" (Ps 98:2), or "victory" (Isa 46:12), or "truth" (Isa 45:23). It is useless to look for a single meaning that would fit all the occurrences of the lexical unit (word or idiom) or to ask what the "literal" meaning is.

English Style and Wording. The clear, elegant style makes reading the TNK a pleasure. From the outset the preponderance of parataxis in biblical Hebrew is overcome by the skillful use of subordinate clauses, and the choice of vocabulary provides appropriate variety. There is no attempt to adopt or mimic English poetic forms, and yet the poetic passages for the most part sound poetic, with a variety of moods expressed through both form and content (e.g., Job 12–14).

A few archaisms survive. In the first edition that notorious archaism "lest" is found in Exod 1:10, but has been replaced in the final edition by the appropriate modern expression "so that . . . not." In the Psalms it lives on in 2:12 and elsewhere.

GOOD NEWS BIBLE (TODAY'S ENGLISH VERSION)

From the late 1950s on, the United Bible Societies commissioned distinctively new translations of the Bible into a large number of languages, beginning with Spanish and English. These translations were based not only on current biblical scholarship, but also on modern linguistic principles, which enabled the translators to structure the language in such a way as to reach a wide range of readers while remaining faithful to the message. In 1966 the NT in English was published as *Good News for Modern Man,* followed by the publication of separate portions of the OT, and in 1976 by the OT and a revised NT, under the title *Good News Bible.*

The translators had been chosen for their experience in multi-lingual situations as well as for their scholarship, and the translation proved highly popular. Robert G. Bratcher, the translator of the NT, served as chair of the OT committee. The Deuterocanonical/Apocryphal books were published in 1979.

Textual Basis. For the NT the translation relied on the Greek text published by the United Bible Societies, and the Kittel *Biblia Hebraica* was generally followed for the OT. The translators preferred not to emend the text if there were solid scholarly reasons for retaining the traditional reading. Frequently a note refers to "one ancient translation" or "several ancient translations" to support a deviation from MT. Emendations are identified as "probable text," followed by a translation of the Hebrew. In

Song of Songs and Job, rubrics identify the speakers where the Hebrew text does not.

Interpretation. Here again the translators took a conservative approach. They rejected the policy of adopting "new meanings" based on cognates in Semitic languages and relied on linguistic evidence and on close observance of context as the best indicators of meaning. In many cases allusions that would have been clear to the original reader are obscure. For example, Isa 14:4b-21 falls into two distinct divisions. In 14:4 the king of Babylon is identified, but in 12-21 he is referred to as the morning star. For clarity of interpretation, the GNB identifies him as "King of Babylon, bright morning star," thus taking implicit information and making it explicit, much like identifying "The Great Emancipator" explicitly as Lincoln for someone not knowing American history. In v. 16 "those who see you" are those in Sheol with him, and the GNB clarifies the passage by identifying them as "the dead." The distinction between implicit information and paraphrase is that the former clarifies the meaning while adding no information not in the text itself.

The 1976 edition of the GNB endeavored to avoid male-oriented language, but a decade later it had become clear that further revision was desirable. In 1986 the American Bible Society Board of Managers approved the undertaking of a new edition of both Testaments that would be more sensitive to issues of gender. It was published in 1992.

English Style and Wording. The GNB based its approach to poetic sections, not on whether the Hebrew text can be read as if it were poetic, but on whether that type of matter is normally presented in poetic form in contemporary English. Many passages printed in English translations in lines and stanzas as if they were poetry are, according to their genre, really prose sermons or political threats. Printing them as poetry fails to alert the English reader to their true nature and thus distorts their meaning. Note that Mic 1:5-16 is printed as prose in the GNB, and 4:1-4 as poetry. Much of the Prophetic literature is more readily understood in English prose. Job (except the prologue and epilogue), Psalms, and Song of Songs are printed as poetry; Proverbs as prose aphorisms; and most of Ecclesiastes as prose. Particular care was taken to make the translation of Job and Song of Songs as poetical as possible without employing rhyme schemes and stanza structure.

Because the GNB was designed to reach readers unfamiliar with traditional biblical language, adjustments in vocabulary were made. In 2 Sam 7:16b, the GNB reads, "Your dynasty will never end." Romans 12:20 "coals of fire" (often read literally as abuse or torture) has become "make him burn with shame." Psalm 23:3, "for his name's sake" (often misheard as "namesake") becomes "as he has promised."

THE JERUSALEM BIBLE AND THE NEW JERUSALEM BIBLE

The Jerusalem Bible is one of several translations that were made into modern European languages on the basis of *La Bible de Jérusalem* (BJ, 1956), a modern French translation at a high literary level, prepared by the scholars of the Dominican Biblical School in Jerusalem. The popularity of the French version paved the way for a wide audience eager to have a similar work in English. As a result, The Jerusalem Bible (1966) was translated by a group of Roman Catholic scholars in the United Kingdom. Although the initial English draft of a few books was made from the French, that of the largest part of the OT was made from the original languages and compared with the French.

A thorough revision of the French BJ was published in 1973, and it was evident that the developments in biblical scholarship since the 1950s and increasing sophistication and experience in translation theory had made the French revision quite different from the JB. Clearly, a revision of the JB was called for. The New Jerusalem Bible (NJB), translated directly from the Hebrew, Greek, and Aramaic, was published in 1985. The general editor's foreword states, "Only where the text admits of more than one interpretation has the option chosen by the *Bible de Jérusalem* been followed, unless permission to adopt another view was granted by the editors of that work." This statement ties the English version closely to the French. As in the JB, the introductions to the various parts of the canon and the extensive notes have been translated directly from the French.

Although there have been paperback editions with abbreviated notes, the standard form in which the JB and the NJB have been published is a 9" x 6" hardcover book of 2,045 pages (JB) and 2,802 pages (NJB). The size, the scholarly notes, and the study aids clearly mark it as a study Bible, and the single-column format and the small type face limit its usefulness for public reading.

Textual Basis. The textual scholarship underlying these two editions is of the highest quality, and the decisions to emend were well based. Many of the earlier emendations were altered in the NJB. In Sam 30:17, for example, the NJB does not include the explanatory phrase "putting them under the ban," found in the JB. In both editions the passage on "lots" (1 Sam 14:41) is emended on the basis of the LXX, and the words "Isaac remained silent" (Gen 27:38) are added from the LXX. The NJB does not contain the words added to the NRSV after 1 Sam 10:27 on the basis of Q ms(s). The words "into one body," omitted from the JB in 1 Cor 12:13, were restored in the NJB.

Interpretation. In both editions the introductory essays to the various books are clear and pleasant to read, free of jargon and in the mainstream of contemporary scholarship. But the two sets of notes bear witness to the great advances in Catholic scholarship during those decades. For an example of the changes in interpretation between the JB and the NJB, consider the contrast between the first note on Genesis 14 in each version. The JB mentions "a document of great age which has been touched up to give greater prominence to Abraham . . . the incident is not improbable," and the NJB says, "a late imitation of the antique . . . historically impossible."

English Style and Wording. On almost every page the reader who compares the JB and the NJB can find examples of improvements in style and vocabulary. The revisers have taken a document of fine English prose and poetry and made it even better at many points. Two policies knowingly adopted,

however, worked against the ease of understanding. The general editor's foreword alerts us to the policy of regularly rendering "theological key concepts" by the same word. This may well work against clarity in dealing with multiple meanings. This is carried further to include "single terms or expressions" that had been rendered in a variety of ways. Going this one additional step means losing the variations of meaning from one context to another in the interests of verbal consistency. Translators ignore polysemy at their own risk.

The NJB abandoned the JB's unfortunate use of "holocaust," with its contemporary connotations, using instead the traditional "burnt offering" (Lev *passim*). The NJB continues the JB's practice of using the divine name Yahweh throughout.

In addition to the translations discussed in this article, there are others that find favor with readers. The differences among the many translations available today give clear evidence that different groups of readers want and need different translations. There is still no "perfect translation," but among the major translations, neither are there any without merit.

BIBLIOGRAPHY

Lewis, Jack P. *The English Bible from KJV to NIV: A History and Evaluation.* 2nd ed. Grand Rapids: Baker Book House, 1991. Includes extensive bibliography.

Metzger, Bruce M., Robert C. Dentan, and Walter Harrelson. *The Making of the New Revised Standard Version of the Bible.* Grand Rapids: Eerdmans, 1989.

Nida, Eugene A. *Toward a Science of Translating.* Leiden: E. G. Brill, 1964.

Orlinsky, H. M., and Robert G. Bratcher. *A History of Bible Translations and the North American Contribution.* Atlanta: Scholars Press, 1991.

THE AUTHORITY OF THE BIBLE

PHYLLIS A. BIRD

OUTLINE

INTRODUCTION

The Bible has always had special authority for Christians, but the nature and consequences of that authority have been understood in different ways during the Bible's long history of formation and use. Fundamental to all views, however, has been the belief that the Bible constitutes a privileged source of knowledge about the nature and will of God. Traditionally this understanding was expressed in terms of divine authorship or agency. Thus the Bible was, or contained, the "word of God."

Throughout most of the church's history, the Bible's authority was simply assumed. It required no defense or theory of origin and operation. In modern times, however, beginning around 1700, traditional beliefs and sources of authority came under attack from several quarters. The church's attempts to defend the credibility and authority of the Bible against these assaults gave rise during the following centuries to the doctrines of authority and inspiration that have shaped current belief. Today these theories are being reevaluated and reformulated in the light of new questions raised by a "postmodern" age.

This article considers the meaning of biblical authority for contemporary Christian faith. It adopts a historical approach, but is oriented to American debate in the final decade of the twentieth century. Although it is informed by American Protestant experience, it seeks to place the question in a global and ecumenical context. In narrowing its focus to Christian understanding, it recognizes that other faith traditions view the Bible, in whole or in part, as sacred literature, according it varying types and degrees of authority. It also acknowledges a special indebtedness to Judaism, as a community of origin in which the earliest Christian scriptures were formed, and as a continuing community of faith and scholarship. Nevertheless, the centrality of the witness to Christ in Christian understandings of Scripture gives distinctive shape and emphasis to Christian views of biblical authority.

Modern Debate. The subject of biblical authority has occupied a prominent place in the theological debates and church controversies of the twentieth century, especially in American Protestantism. During the latter half of the century, in particular, the question of authority has become the central theological issue relating to the Bible, especially within the evangelical or conservative wing of Protestantism.[1] As a result most recent literature on the subject has been shaped by the debate with and within evangelicalism. Discussion outside this orbit tends to be ignored or obscured, and issues of authority that are not framed in the dominant language of discourse tend to be neglected or misconstrued.[2]

Modern doctrines of biblical authority were formulated in response to the rise of new historical methods of interpretation (see below), and current debate among evangelicals and other conservatives remains focused on issues relating to historical criticism. But new challenges and new questions have arisen, outside and inside the old camps, and these are shifting the focus and terms of debate.

Within the old liberal wing of the church, a disposition to reject traditional authority, and suspect authority *per se,* is giving way to a new quest for identity and norms. In a context characterized by religious and cultural pluralism and loss of common social values, the Bible is being rediscovered; and its primacy as a source for faith and life is being reaffirmed.[3] In the Roman Catholic Church, official acceptance of historical-critical methods has fostered a rebirth of biblical scholarship and contributed to a broad ecumenical consensus concerning methods of exegesis. At the same time, theological interpretation in all churches has remained heavily determined by confessional tradition, frustrating earlier hopes of achieving theological consensus by means of a common Bible interpreted by common exegetical methods.[4] Ecclesial tradition has been exposed as a far more dominant factor in biblical interpretation than Protestants have generally admitted, reopening older questions about both the nature and the locus of authority for interpretation, and the relationship of the Bible to tradition.

Academic study of the Bible is also undergoing major change. Once dominant historical-critical methods are being attacked or eclipsed by literary, structuralist, and reader-oriented criticism. Some of the new methods appear to invite or employ older, pre-critical ways of viewing the text, thus by-passing the controversies surrounding historical-critical interpretation. But they raise new questions about norms of interpretation and authority for faith that do not permit simple reaffirmation of traditional views. Often their assumptions about the nature of the text, and the reader, conflict with traditional understandings of the Bible as sacred Scripture.

---

1. The term *evangelical* is used in this article to designate a broad segment of American Protestantism that understands itself as maintaining traditional or orthodox belief over against positions that are described variously as "liberal," "neo-orthodox," or "modernist." In this broad usage it includes groups that may be defined by others as "fundamentalist," as well as those who prefer the label "neo-evangelical." Conservatives or traditionalists outside the Reformed tradition are less likely to adopt the evangelical label, although they often share closely related views concerning the Bible and biblical authority. For the function of scriptural hermeneutics, and views of scriptural authority, in defining positions within evangelicalism, see Gerald T. Sheppard, "Biblical Hermeneutics: The Academic Language of Evangelical Identity," *USQR* 32 (1977) 81-94.

2. See, e.g., the critique of Rogers and McKim by Avery Dulles, "Scholasticism and the Church," *TToday* 38 (1981) 339, noting the omission of all Roman Catholic theologians since the Reformation.

3. See, e.g., the new United Methodist statement on the primacy of Scripture in "Theological Guidelines: Sources and Criteria," contained in the 1988 and 1992 *Book of Discipline,* and the recent study document issued by the United Church of Canada, entitled "The Authority and Interpretation of Scripture," Theology and Faith Committee, 1989 (review by A. M. Watts, *Touchstone,* May 1990).

4. Ellen Flesseman-van Leer, ed., *The Bible: Its Authority and Interpretation in the Ecumenical Movement,* Faith and Order Paper 99 (Geneva: World Council of Churches, 1980) 1-4.

Challenges to traditional conceptions and arguments concerning biblical authority are arising from other quarters as well, as voices excluded from earlier debate are heard. Those on the margins of the old centers of theological and ecclesiastical power remain suspicious of the relationship between the Bible and establishment theology (defined as "orthodoxy" or "traditional" faith). Many feminists, for example, find the concept as well as the claims of biblical authority problematic in light of their experience of the Bible as a weapon of patriarchy. African Americans bring another neglected perspective to the discussion, distinguished by a distinctive hermeneutic, shaped by experiences of slavery and racism and by a distinct cultural tradition. Different, but related, issues of authority are raised by other groups that have received the Bible from the hands of their oppressors or experienced it as an instrument in the suppression of their cultural heritage (e.g., indigenous peoples of the Americas). The question of biblical authority is also being raised in a fresh and urgent way by encounters with nonbiblical religions, not only in distant lands, but also in America's cities and suburbs.

Doctrines and Definitions. Traditional understanding of the Bible's authority was closely associated with notions of divine communication. The Bible was described as God's "Word," although relatively few of its actual words are represented as divine speech. In attempting to explain how human language could represent divine thought, early Jewish and Christian theologians appealed to the concept of *inspiration.* The idea was derived from a prophetic model, but was extended to writings and utterances of diverse origin and content. In its earliest use it was an inference from effect, a means of accounting for the acknowledged sacred character of certain writings, not a means of establishing their authority. And it described the (inspired) human agent, not the text. It soon developed into a means of asserting a variety of claims about the nature and content of the text itself, but it was not until the modern period that a fully articulated theory of inspiration was formulated or acquired the status of doctrine. In modern formulations, the doctrine of inspiration typically reverses the original order of reasoning; the inspiration imputed to the biblical

texts is now seen as proof of their divine origin and authority, and guarantor of their truth.[5]

Because the authority of the Bible has been so closely identified with the doctrine of inspiration in modern discussion, efforts to analyze or reassert the Bible's claims to authority often focus on this concept.[6] Recent attempts have been made to reformulate the notion of inspiration in a manner compatible with present knowledge of the origins of the canon and modern understandings of psychological and mental processes.[7] Nevertheless, the concept of inspiration remains a theory of agency that cannot in itself define or secure the authority of the Bible.[8]

Two other terms that are closely identified with claims of biblical authority are *inerrancy* and *infallibility.* Both represent modern attempts to spell out the implications of traditional belief in a new age confronted by new questions—in this case, questions about the veracity of biblical statements, occasioned by new knowledge and new canons of truth. Both seek to maintain ancient affirmations of the trustworthiness of Scripture as divine revelation, translating those affirmations into modern terms. Although the claims expressed by these two closely related concepts are considered by many as essential criteria of biblical authority, neither describes the full nature or scope of that authority, and both are second-order concepts, deriving their meaning from more fundamental affirmations (see below).

Debates over biblical authority tend to focus on particular attributes of the text and neglect the fundamentally relational character of all authority. Authority describes the power of one subject to influence another in such a way that a claim upon the other is established and acknowledged. The nature of the claim and the manner of its operation will vary with the subject and the relationship in which it is exercised, but it is not effected by assertion alone; it requires acknowledgment—

5. Richard F. Smith, "Inspiration and Inerrancy," in Raymond E. Brown et al., eds., *The Jerome Biblical Commentary* (Englewood Cliffs, N.J.: Prentice-Hall, 1968) 500-12; Paul J. Achtemeier, *The Inspiration of Scripture: Problems and Proposals,* Biblical Perspectives on Current Issues (Philadelphia: Westminster, 1980).

6. E.g., Robert Gnuse, *The Authority of the Bible: Theories of Inspiration, Revelation and the Canon of Scripture* (Mahwah, N.J.: Paulist, 1985) 14-65; Robert Johnston, *Evangelicals at an Impasse: Biblical Authority in Practice* (Atlanta: John Knox, 1979) 15-47; Luis Alonso-Schökel, *The Inspired Word: Scripture in the Light of Language and Literature* (New York: Herder and Herder, 1972) 58-73.

7. See esp. Gnuse, *Authority,* 105-36.

8. See Flesseman-van Leer, *The Bible,* 7.

through appropriate response.[9] Authority is not a possession, nor can it be freely created. It is a quality of a relationship that develops over time and involves an element of trust and trustworthiness. And it is always exercised within a community.[10]

Authority is contextual; it is always relative to particular situations and relationships. It is, therefore, highly varied, and variable, in its content, extent, and forms of expression. A given person, institution, or writing may exercise different types and degrees of authority in relation to different audiences, expectations, and needs. While some types of authority may be more generalized than others, such as the authority of a parent (in contrast, e.g., to that of a teacher), none is comprehensive—including the authority of the Bible. Although the authority of Scripture is understood to derive from God, the Bible itself has a particular and limited purpose in God's relationship to the church and the world, and its authority must be understood in relation to that purpose and those relationships. To equate the authority of the Bible with the authority of God is to fall into the sin of idolatry.

Much of the debate over the authority of the Bible concerns the nature of the authority, rather than the extent ("high" or "low"). What kind of book is this, and what kind of message, or communication, does it contain? To whom is it addressed, and under what conditions? Who or what determines appropriate expectations and responses?[11] Who may "rightly" interpret it, and according to what canons? How

does it stand in relation to other sources of authority, and how are conflicting claims to be adjudicated?

Underlying many of these questions is the issue of meaning. The Bible's authority is one of communication; it depends on understanding. When its message is no longer comprehended, or when its word is heard as false or irrelevant, its authority is jeopardized or annulled. That is the reason for the crisis of biblical authority that has characterized much of the modern period; a radically changed world and world view have rendered old ways of understanding the text unintelligible, objectionable, or simply inconsequential for many. Continued affirmation of the Bible's authority requires new ways of interpreting the text and appropriating its message. The question of biblical authority is inextricably bound up with the question of interpretation and hermeneutics. Thus some attention must be given in this article to key issues and episodes in the history of biblical interpretation that have particular bearing on the question of authority.

Two principles are crucial to assessing various interpretations and claims concerning the authority of the Bible, and to formulating a contemporary statement of its nature and consequences. (1) The Bible itself must be the primary source of any answer to the question of its nature and purpose, and any view of its message and authority must be consonant with its form—as an ordered collection of disparate writings. (2) The meaning and authority of the Bible cannot be determined apart from the community that created, transmitted, and interpreted it. Both principles require that any understanding of biblical authority must have a recognizable historical dimension, even when the question is limited to contemporary authority. Scripture comes to us as a word from the past and exhibits in its language and content a continuing link with that past. It serves first of all as an indispensable memory of the church. But it must also be heard as a contemporary word, since it witnesses to a God who is not bound to the past, but is active in the present, shaping the future. Thus the Bible's authority for the church also depends on its ability to speak an intelligible and credible word to the present generation.

These two functions of Scripture, as memory and present word, have corresponding forms of authority, which need not be formulated in identical terms and may change over time in relation to changing needs and world views. Any concept or claim of

---

9. Dictionary definitions are helpful in showing the wide variety of ways in which authority is exercised or expressed, e.g., through knowledge, prestige, and personal influence, as "weight of testimony" or "reliability of a source or witness" (*Webster's New World Dictionary of the American Language,* 2nd College Edition [New York: Prentice Hall, 1986]; and *The Concise Oxford Dictionary of Current English,* 6th ed. [Oxford: Clarendon, 1976]), but they tend to stress the power of the subject (e.g., *Webster's New World Dictionary* defines *authority* as "the power or right to make commands, enforce obedience, take actions, or make final decisions") and neglect the relationship in which it is exhibited. Authority is imputed to a subject from its effects on another subject, who obeys, follows, trusts, believes, etc.

10. Darrell Jodock, *The Church's Bible: Its Contemporary Authority* (Minneapolis: Fortress, 1989) 105-10.

11. The question of appropriate response, or use, is critical and often neglected, and it is the most difficult because it cannot be answered in purely formal terms. It concerns the way in which the Bible's authority functions in particular life situations, e.g., in ethical decisions (such as those relating to abortion, immigration, taxation, and the environment). In practice, the Bible as an authority for faith interacts with other authorities in complex ways that are not adequately represented by formal declarations or doctrines. See David Kelsey, *The Uses of Scripture in Recent Theology* (Philadelphia: Fortress, 1975) for one attempt to analyze how appeals to biblical authority function in the work of selected modern theologians. Cf. Johnston, *Evangelicals,* vii-viii, who laments the inability of evangelicals, all claiming a common belief in biblical authority, to agree on what this means in relation to many major issues of the day.

authority must be congruent, however, with the Bible's own internal witness to its nature and purposes. Theories of biblical authority that are to have credibility must honor the Bible's own word in its own world—which can never simply be equated with our own. The contribution of modern historical consciousness and modern historical study of the Bible is insistence that the integrity of the biblical witness not be compromised by denying or subordinating its historical character, hence its cultural particularity, to the demands of contemporary readers. The Bible's authority is intimately connected with its character as a bridge between the past and present activity of God.

SCRIPTURE IN ANCIENT ISRAEL

Scripture is the creation of a community[12] that recognizes certain writings as authoritative.[13] In the case of the Christian Bible, two communities were instrumental in shaping and defining the final corpus. What the church received from Israel and the synagogue had to be substantially reinterpreted in the light of the new revelation in Christ. Nevertheless, the Christian Bible remains in its most basic sense a Jewish Bible, in which the fundamental terms for the church's understanding of the divine presence that had broken into history and transformed its life were given to it by the community formed at Sinai. The people of the resurrection read their Bible as descendants and heirs of the people of the exodus.

The writings that the church describes as "holy Scripture" and "Word of God" comprise a diverse collection of documents composed over a period of more than a thousand years and attributed to many different authors. Thus any notion of divine authorship must reckon with the Bible's own internal witness to its complex human origins. The fundamental issue in the history of debate over biblical authority is the question of how to acknowledge and

relate the divine and the human nature of these writings.[14] Modern biblical and historical scholarship has enabled us to reconstruct much of the process by which our canon of Scriptures came into being, permitting us to see it as a historical product in a way that earlier generations could not. The Holy Book is seen once again as a collection (*ta biblia,* "the books," in its original Greek designation), but this time in a manner that relates individual writings more precisely to the situations in which they arose.

The books that comprise our biblical canon did not originate as "scripture" and, with notable exceptions, do not claim divine authorship or inspiration for themselves.[15] Within these books, however, are references to earlier writings for which divine authorship and authority are claimed. Thus New Testament (NT) writings frequently cite the Jewish scriptures, identifying their words as divine speech. Long before the Old Testament (OT) canon was closed or its writings completed, however, a concept of Scripture had come into being that would have an enduring effect on Jewish and Christian understandings of sacred writings.[16]

Deuteronomic Torah: The Authority of Sacred Law. The earliest datable reference to a written document whose words are identified, at least indirectly, as the words of God is found in the account of Josiah's reforms (c. 621 BCE). The "book" (or "document") discovered during the course of repairs to the Temple is identified more specifically as the "book of the law" (2 Kgs 22:11) and "book of the covenant" (2 Kgs 23:2). Although the narrative does not use the expression "law of God," it makes clear that the words read before the king were understood

---

12. *Community* is used here as a flexible term for any communal entity with a sense of common identity. It may at times correspond to an entire people, nation, or religious group and at other times represent a particular party, church, or subgroup. Both of the two major faith communities with which we will be concerned were at all times internally diverse, so that the concept of community does not imply unanimity. The same qualifications pertain to such collective designations as "Israel," "the church," "the synagogue," etc.

13. To say this is not to deny that it is also the product of inspired speakers and writers or that it is ultimately the work of God. It is, however, to focus on the necessary communal act of recognition, without which there would be no Scripture.

14. The doctrine of inspiration has been particularly useful and appealing, despite its inadequacies, because it provides a means for affirming the divine origin of what are clearly human writings (Gnuse, *Authority,* 14). Not until the modern period, however, was attention given to the question of *how* inspiration operated. See Richard F. Smith, "Inspiration and Inerrancy," in Brown et al., *The Jerome Biblical Commentary,* 505.

15. Exceptions in the OT are the book of Deuteronomy (1:1-3) and a number of the Minor Prophets whose superscriptions identify the contents of the book as "the word of the LORD" spoken or revealed to the prophet (Hos 1:1; Joel 1:1; Mic 1:1; Zeph 1:1; Mal 1:1). In the NT, only the book of Revelation (1:1-2) makes a comparable claim, placing itself in the OT prophetic tradition. In contrast, the letters of Paul are clearly pastoral writings that make no attempt to present themselves as divinely inspired writings.

16. Since the time of Origen, the two parts of the Christian Bible have been referred to as the OT and the NT. Several candidates to replace the confessional nomenclature with more neutral descriptive terminology have been suggested, e.g., "Hebrew Bible/Scriptures" or, less frequently, "First Testament." These necessary and useful attempts to find nondiscriminatory language do not, however, represent the customary or current use of either of the two faith communities involved. Since this article is concerned with the meaning of these writings precisely in their function as authoritative for faith, the traditional nomenclature has been retained.

as none other than Yahweh's words and that in failing to obey the "words of this book," Israel had disobeyed Yahweh's commands (23:13; cf. vv. 16, 19).

Both the language used to describe the book and the covenant-making that accompanies its reception link it with the book of Deuteronomy, whose central section (Deut 4:44–28:68) is introduced as "the law that Moses set before the Israelites" (4:44 NRSV), and more specifically as "the commandments of Yahweh" (4:2). According to Deut 4:13-14, the book contained the covenant stipulations declared to Israel by Yahweh at Horeb (Sinai) and expounded by Moses at Yahweh's charge.

Torah as Constitution. Deuteronomy is unique within the Hebrew Bible in its claims to embody a written deposition of authoritative law and as a book whose text is referred to elsewhere in the OT.[17] References to it abound in the "Deuteronomistic" exhortations and accusations of the books of Joshua and Kings, as well as various prophetic writings (e.g., Josh 1:7, 8; 1 Kgs 2:3; 2 Kgs 10:31; 17:34, 37; Jer 9:13; Amos 2:4). The collective term used to designate this body of writings is תורה *tôrâ,* traditionally rendered as "law," but etymologically identified with "teaching" or "instruction." In Deuteronomy's usage it refers to a body of stipulations having normative and prescriptive force, but it is not an umbrella term for every rule, decision, or enactment of Israelite legal authority.[18] It is more specifically covenantal law, the implementing legislation of the covenant made by God with Israel at Horeb.

This special sense of Deuteronomic torah as Israel's "constitution" was recognized by Josephus, who rendered it with the Greek term πολιτεία (*politeia,* "polity") rather than νομός (*nomos,* "law"/"lawcode"). Interpreting the Pentateuch for a Gentile audience in the first century CE, Josephus described the book of Deuteronomy as preserving the "divinely authorized and comprehensive 'polity' or national 'constitution' " that Moses had delivered to Israel, in both written and oral forms, in the final days of his life.[19] The torah of Deuteronomy sets forth the principles and policies of a "divinely authorized social order that Israel must implement to secure its collective political existence as the people of God."[20]

The notion of divinely issued decrees and commands contained in a written document and intended as a normative guide for a people bound to God by a covenant relationship is specific to Deuteronomy and the Deuteronomic "school," but it has played a foundational role in Jewish and Christian understandings of Scripture. It contains the essential notions of a communal document, which is to be appropriated individually and internally by each member of the community. It is a gift of God, the consequence of divine initiative in creating a new people. In its demands it reveals the character of its giver. It is both written and oral in nature and, therefore, not limited to the word once spoken. It is a word that always addresses a new generation, with demands for new covenant commitment.

The term *torah* was ultimately extended to the Pentateuch as a whole and with it the claims of divine origin and authority, as well as Mosaic "authorship." In that context "law" would come to have a broader meaning, and the Deuteronomic ordinances would find their place as the climactic word of a story of God's purposes and action from the creation of the world to the creation of Israel, a story to be continued on the other side of the Jordan. In that narrative context, the words of Moses spoken on the plains of Moab are for the new generation that will claim the promise and enter the land. The book of Deuteronomy is fully aware that the Israel it addresses no longer stands at Horeb. It recalls, and refashions, the words spoken at the mountain, so that they remain true to the character of the divine speaker and the changing historical circumstances of the audience.

The Two-Part Structure of Covenantal Law. Deuteronomy represents a critical stage in the transformation of tradition, but it was neither the beginning nor the end of the process. Behind Deuteronomy stands the covenant tradition of the older narrative sources of the Pentateuch; after it stand the later prescriptive collections of the Pentateuch and the body of oral and written decisions of the rabbis that continued to give instruction to Israel in ever-new circumstances of life. Within this continuing tradition one feature deserves special note, since it points to the essential combination of stability and flexibility in Israel's notion of "law" and scripture. Deuteronomy, like the older tradition on which it rests, is presented as a two-part composition, consisting of the Decalogue (Exod 20:2-17;

---

17. S. Dean McBride, Jr. "Polity of the Covenant People: The Book of Deuteronomy," *Int* 41 (1987) 231.
18. Ibid., 232-33.
19. Ibid., 229.
20. Ibid., 233.

Deut 5:6-21) followed by a diverse body of ordinances, or "rulings." While the Decalogue remains essentially unchanged, the collection of rulings is greatly expanded in Deuteronomy, not only by new and different cases, but also by interpretive and hortatory elaboration.

Two classes of divine commands are recognized in this arrangement. The "Ten Words" may be understood as statements of policy or basic norms that Deuteronomy insists were heard by Israel directly from the voice of God at Horeb and received on tablets written by the finger of God (Deut 4:12-13; 5:4, 22; 9:10). The "statutes and ordinances" may be understood as implementing legislation that Yahweh had charged Moses to teach to the Israelites for their observance in the land they are about to occupy (Deut 4:14; cf. 5:31). The distinction between the two classes involves differences of form, function, terminology, and historical setting—but not authority. Both are covenantal law and expressive of divine will, but the latter body is mediated and historically conditioned in a way that the former is not.

Deuteronomy's interpretation of the two-part structure of covenantal law employs both historical and theological arguments. The covenant made at Horeb must be reappropriated by every generation (Deut 5:3; 11:2-7). Its basic demands of loyalty and justice are unchanging; they are heard and stamped upon the mind as the direct address of God (4:10-13; 5:22-24), and their constancy is assured by memoranda on stone tablets. But changed and changing circumstances are reflected throughout the book and signaled by the constant refrain of "today" (Deut 5:1; 11:2, 8, 13, etc.). Deuteronomy's "today" is a dynamic concept and must be understood as such. The social and political circumstances reflected in the book clearly point to the seventh century BCE as the time of its composition, rather than the eleventh century of its narrative setting. To Hebrew readers of Josiah's day, the references to the "nations" and their practices would have been transparent allusions to religious and political relations of their own day.

Mediated Word. Deuteronomy contributes one further element of Israel's understanding of Scripture: the fundamental role of human mediation in divine communication. The divine law is spoken and expounded by Moses. But mediation implies contingency. At the heart of Israel's traditions concerning

God's revelation to Israel lies a tension between the absolute and unchanging nature of God and God's will for the covenant community, and the changing (historical) circumstances of life in which Israel must live out its covenant faithfulness. Both are acknowledged, and bound together, in the traditions of God's revelation in the wilderness—and Moses is the figure who unites them. All divinely authorized law or instruction in Israel was "Mosaic," identified with the formative period of Israel's life, located in the wilderness narrative. Yet the several collections of laws in the Pentateuch and the obvious accretions to the earlier laws clearly point to later times. The later laws do not replace the earlier ones, but stand side by side as witness to a continuing "Mosaic" function.

Torah in Post-Exilic Judaism. A century after Josiah's reforms, Mosaic *torah* figures prominently in another account of national renewal. Nehemiah 8 relates how Ezra, the priest and scribe, read from the "book of the law of Moses" (8:1) to an assembly of returned exiles at their request. The assembly comprised "both men and women and all who could hear with understanding" (8:2 NRSV), and the reading was accompanied by interpretation (8:7-8). Whether this is to be understood as translation (into the Aramaic vernacular) or exegesis (spelling out meanings and implications) is uncertain, but the narrative makes clear that the law was understood as both authoritative for the community and requiring interpretation by skilled experts. It also introduces us to a new religious title, "scribe" (8:1, 4, 9, 13), apparently designating a new class of scholars who study and expound the law (cf. Ezra 7:6, 21). The context of the reading (from a raised platform, with accompanying acts of homage and blessing) and the subsequent action by the heads of the ancestral houses (who gather on the following day to "study the words of the law") appear to reflect late practice associated with the synagogue, where public reading and private study were the central activities of religious life. But whatever the date, torah in this account has assumed a new place in communal life.

The book designated alternately as the "law of Moses" (8:1) and "law of God" (8:8, 18) appears to have been substantially identical with that read by Josiah to "all the people, both small and great" (2 Kgs 23:2 NRSV), although it may have been contained in a larger pentateuchal corpus. In both instances, it is understood to represent the authoritative word of God, binding on the community as a whole; but the meaning of the book has changed with the changing circumstances of the community.

Mosaic torah as defined by Deuteronomy contained directives for life, more specifically the life of the nation. It was communal in its orientation and political in its implications: The king was to meditate upon it and govern in accordance with its commands (Deut 17:18-20; cf. 2 Kgs 22:10-13; 23:1-3, 24); foreign alliances were to be rejected (Deut 7:1-2); and the fate and welfare of the nation depended on obedience to its commands (Deut 30:16-18; 2 Kgs 17:19; 22:23). But it also laid demands on *every* Israelite able to understand its commands (Deut 31:12; 2 Kgs 23:2; Neh 8:3, 12). It was to be read publicly before the entire assembly (Deut 31:10-12; cf. 2 Kgs 23:2; Neh 8:2) and to be an object of study and meditation (Deut 6:6-7; Neh 8:13). It was not simply policy for rulers or guidance for judges and cultic officials. Its primary audience was the covenant community, individually and collectively.

In the postexilic setting, the political dimensions of the law are absent, and the problem of foreign alliances is now a problem of marriage with foreigners (Neh 9:1-2; 10:28-30; Ezra 9–10; cf. Deut 7:3). A scribe of the law holds the book, and the people take the initiative, not the king. The community has been redefined as constituted by the reading and hearing of the word of God. Authority for governing the community is now invested in a book and its interpreters.

Implications for Christian Understanding of Scripture. All of these features of the understanding and use of Israel's earliest Scriptures have relevance for Christian understanding of the nature of Scripture and scriptural authority, and all have received confirmation in Christian doctrine and use. The fundamental affirmations of this tradition are that Scripture is both communal and individual in its address, and its authority must be realized at both levels. Understanding is necessary to assent, and understanding requires interpretation. Interpretation involves special knowledge and skill, but study and meditation are the obligation of all who are capable. The authoritative word is from the past, but is directed anew to each generation. Its message is heard differently in different contexts, requiring different responses. The word lays demands on its

hearers—for the ordering of community, family, and individual life—but it also provides the means to fulfill those demands. It is a means of grace, God's gift, in which the nature and will of the giver are revealed. Its purposes are life and well-being. If later interpretations of the "law" narrowed and perverted this understanding in frozen literalism and false contrasts with the "gospel," the Deuteronomic understanding of torah continued nevertheless to dominate the evolving corpus and conception of Scripture.

Expanding Torah: The Authority of Sacred Story. Varieties of Scripture. Although the law occupied a position of primacy in Israel's Scriptures, it was not the only form of sacred writing recognized as authoritative in Israel, nor the earliest composition. Before the "book of the law" had received its final form, other writings had come into existence that would ultimately form part of Israel's sacred canon.[21] Some were joined to the "book of the law" to form the Pentateuch. Others found their way into later collections of Hebrew scriptures, and some were lost, forgotten, or circulated outside the finally authorized canon. During the whole period of canon formation, new writings continued to be produced. The question of when these writings became "scripture," and for whom, is difficult to answer. Originally composed and cherished by particular groups within Israel, as the law itself, they served limited purposes related to particular institutions or occasions, and only gradually became part of a "national" literature. Outside the Pentateuch, they never formed a single unified corpus, but retained the character of a library, even in their final canonical form.[22]

The history of the growth of the canon, and of individual books within the canon, shows that the authority of the scriptures depends on the recognition of a community, but also that recognition may be accorded in a variety of ways for a variety of reasons. Before the individual writings were

21. The history of the Pentateuch is currently debated, both in respect to its component parts and the circumstances of its final composition. That it is a composite work, however, is recognized by the majority of scholars, who also acknowledge the separate character of Deuteronomy within the "Five Books." This article assumes the existence of early narrative traditions (J, E) employed in the construction of the larger work, along with smaller complexes of traditions of various sorts.
22. The view of canon formation presented here is essentially that of Lee Martin McDonald, *The Formation of the Christian Biblical Canon* (Nashville: Abingdon, 1988) 48-66. For a view that minimizes the differences among Jewish canons as well as between the Jewish and Christian OT canons, see Roger Beckwith, *The Old Testament Canon of the New Testament Church and Its Background in Early Judaism* (Grand Rapids: Eerdmans, 1985).

assembled into a body of "scripture," each had established its authority in respect to its own peculiar character and use: laws, to guide and govern the community; ancestral tales and historical narratives, to create and confirm a sense of identity and trace the activity of God in past experience and event; prophetic oracles, to illuminate God's action in the present and to warn; proverbs, to counsel; psalms, to direct prayer and praise; didactic tales, to instruct and encourage steadfastness. Similar distinctions of purpose and use, and consequently types of authority, characterize the NT writings.

The distinctive character and authority of the individual writings is maintained by continuing distinction of form and boundaries within the canonical collection. But the unity of the collection, however loose or variable, imposes a new demand on interpreters to relate the component parts to each other and to the new whole—and a corresponding new demand to reconceive the authority of the whole and its parts. The unified collection has a new locus, or loci, of interpretation—the synagogue and the church—and it is in relation to the new needs of these two new institutions that the authority of Scripture came to be defined. The shift to a new communal context of interpretation and use began with the liturgical reading of Scripture in the postexilic period, as evidenced by Nehemiah 8, but the move from Scripture to canon extended over centuries. Not until the end of the first century CE was there a definitive Jewish canon; the OT canon, together with the NT of the Christian Bible, was not fixed until the fourth century CE—without final unanimity. Thus even as collections of writings began to be formed for use by new religious bodies, the boundaries of the collections varied, reflecting differing theological emphases and interests and differing views of the authority of individual writings as well as criteria of authority.

The Narrative Setting of Israelite Law. Mosaic torah played a determinative role in Israelite understanding of Scripture, but in its present literary context, it is embedded in a narrative that is decisive for its interpretation. The Pentateuch presents an account of Israel's origins, set in the context of world history and looking to the occupation of a homeland in the mountains of Canaan. In various recensions, the underlying narrative attempted to comprehend, and defend, Israel's identity and vocation as the people of Yahweh and spell out the terms and consequences of that relationship. Thus history complemented law in revealing God's nature and purposes for Israel by supplying the story of divine initiative and action that had given birth to the nation and preserved it through various threats.[23]

Covenantal law had a narrative setting, which was finally fleshed out, from many sources, to comprise the present pentateuchal account. In this literary context, torah as divine instruction was extended from sacred law to sacred story. Within this context the words of the law are given a specific historical setting and purpose, appearing as the historically conditioned terms of a relationship set within God's overarching purposes and actions in the world. Fixed in time, Mosaic law opens the way to new teachings and new commands in relation to God's new actions in history. But it is also located outside of time and history. The place of revelation is the mountain of God, located in the wilderness, in a place apart. Mosaic law is isolated and magnified as the model of all subsequent teaching. Thus torah is both absolutized and historicized in its pentateuchal setting.

Prophetic Word and Prophetic Authority. The Pentateuch, as the first corpus of writings to acquire the shape and authority of canonical scripture, was composed of testimony to God's revelation in deed and word. So too was the second major section of the Jewish canon, comprising the historical books from Joshua through Kings together with the prophetic writings. Here, however, the divine word is mediated not by Moses, but by prophets. The Deuteronomists represented the prophets as continuing the Mosaic office (Deut 18:15, 17-20; cf. 34:10). In their construction, the word once spoken at Horeb is spoken anew to successive generations through the prophets, giving divine direction to a new age. In contrast to the word from the mountain, however, the prophetic word is timely, specific, and bound to the circumstances of its delivery—or so it would appear. As a divine word, however, it also had the potential of disclosing God's nature and will in a way that might instruct future generations as well. Ultimately, prophetic words, like Mosaic commands, were preserved in collections that were studied, expounded, and amplified.

The attempt to link the two forms of divine com-

23. See James A. Sanders, *From Sacred Story to Sacred Text: Canon as Paradigm* (Philadelphia: Fortress, 1987) 18-19, for a view that emphasizes the priority of story in the canonical process.

munication represented by prophecy and law is clearly a secondary effort. It is nevertheless instructive as an attempt to claim the authority of written torah for prophetic speech and at the same time to subordinate prophecy to Mosaic law. While the activity of prophets is attested from premonarchic to postexilic times, and prophetic speech may have been viewed by some as the primary and preferred form of divine communication, prophetic oracles do not appear to have been gathered into books until the eighth or seventh century BCE, the same period in which the Deuteronomic book of the law was being formed and promulgated; and they did not achieve the status of Scripture until the exile, at the earliest.

Prophetic speech in its primary setting was marked by directness and immediacy; it provided divine guidance for specific occasions and needs, solicited and unsolicited. And it carried the authority of divine speech; the prophet spoke in the divine first person, as God's messenger or as one possessed by God's Spirit. These very attributes, however, made the prophetic word a problematic source of divine guidance. It was sporadic, occasional, tied to passing events, and sometimes unavailable (Mic 3:7). It could not be obtained at will, and when it could, it was suspect (1 Kgs 22:5-7; Jer 23:16, 21-22, 25-32).

The question of authority in claims of divine communication is raised in its earliest and most acute form in relation to prophetic words. Conflicting messages (1 Kgs 22:5-28; Jer 28:1-17), predictions that failed (Jer 28:11; 29:18-19; cf. 2 Kgs 24:6), and lying or deluded prophets (Jer 23:16-32; cf. 1 Kgs 13:18; 22:19-23; Mic 3:5-8) are among the issues that attended prophecy, especially in the final years of the Judean state, a time in which the question of truth in prophetic pronouncements had come to have life-and-death significance. Who had the true word from God? By what signs could one recognize it? On these questions hung the fate of the nation—and the future of prophecy itself.[24]

24. See James A. Sanders, "Hermeneutic in True and False Prophecy," in *Canon and Authority: Essays in Old Testament Religion and Authority,* ed. George W. Coats and Burke O. Long (Philadelphia: Fortress, 1977) 24-41; James L. Crenshaw, *Prophetic Conflict,* BZAW 124 (Berlin: de Gruyter, 1971); Brevard S. Childs, *Old Testament Theology in a Canonical Context* (Philadelphia: Fortress, 1985) 133-44; and Gerald T. Sheppard, "True and False Prophecy within Scripture," in *Canon, Theology, and Old Testament Interpretation: Essays in Honor of Brevard S. Childs,* ed. Gene M. Tucker, David L. Petersen, and Robert R. Wilson (Philadelphia: Fortress, 1988) 262-82.

In this period, tests were formulated that have significance for contemporary debates. First, the truth of a word, and hence the assurance that it was a message from God and not simply an invention of the prophet's own mind or desire, could not be assured by any formula of speech or professional title. False messages, described as "lying" or "deceptive" words, were spoken by persons bearing the title "prophet" and introduced by the standard formula of introduction, "thus says the LORD" (Jer 28:1-5, 10-11; cf. 12-16). Attempts to distinguish true from false messages by the manner of reception or delivery are accorded limited credibility. "False prophets" (a term coined by the Greek translators, but unknown in Hebrew) are said to receive their messages through dreams or visions of their own heads, rather than by direct audition or access to the divine assembly (1 Kgs 22:19-23; Jer 23:16-32), or to "steal" one another's words (Jer 23:30). They may also be characterized by frenzied behavior (1 Kgs 18:26-27). But most of these criteria are not easily discernible, or may be applied to canonical prophets as well (Jer 29:26-27). Another effort to establish criteria of credibility was associated with signs, but this too was judged inadequate (Deut 13:1-5). In the final analysis, the truth of a word could be judged only by its content and by the vindication of time (Deut 18:21-22; Jer 28:9)—a criterion of little use to the hearer, who must decide immediately which word to follow.

If the message itself held the clues to its origins and truth, then the hearer's, or reader's, chief resource for assessing its claims was the faith tradition. For the Deuteronomists, this core of belief was embodied in the law given through Moses, and more particularly in the Decalogue and the first commandment. This was no strange word or new command, not difficult to obtain or comprehend, and not dependent on dreams or esoteric interpretations, but available to all (Deut 30:11-14). It was to be recited, bound to head and hand, written on the door post, and taught to the next generation (Deut 6:4-9). Nine centuries later, early Christian theologians would make a similar appeal to the "rule of faith" as the criterion for judging the claims of various writings to authoritative status in the church's Scriptures. Such appeals to tradition have their own pitfalls, however, tending to make past formulations and experience a norm rather than a guide for discerning the divine presence and will in new situations and new forms. The tension between prophecy and law characterizes the whole history of the canon and of the church.

The Writings: New Models and Meanings of Scripture and Authority. The Law and the Prophets formed the heart of the Jewish Scriptures, which the church inherited from Israel, but those Scriptures embraced a far more diverse collection of writings, whose boundaries were still in flux when the first Christian writings were being formed. The third section of the Hebrew canon, designated simply The Writings, was a loose assemblage of works that had for the most part arisen subsequent to the earlier collections or did not fit the recognized categories of form or content. It included a collection of sacred songs and prayers drawn from public worship and private devotion (Psalms) and a number of compositions from the world of wisdom, including a collection of maxims and instructions (Proverbs); a skeptic's monologue on the apparent meaninglessness of life (Qoheleth), and a dramatic poem on the justice of God explored through the dialogue of a sufferer with his would-be comforters (Job). Love songs (Song of Solomon), elegies (Lamentations), didactic novels and heroic tales (Ruth, Esther, Daniel [1–6, together with apocalyptic visions, 7–12]), and new historiographic writings (Ezra–Nehemiah, Chronicles) completed the collection that ultimately won the approval of Pharisaic Judaism. Other works contended for inclusion, however, and are cited as authoritative by Jewish writers in the first two centuries BCE and even as late as the fourth century CE, although the shorter canon was generally accepted after 90 CE.

The final segment of the Jewish canon involves a debate concerning the nature and scope of Scripture and the manner of divine revelation in which the emergence of Christianity as a distinct movement within sectarian Judaism played a critical role. The closing of the OT canon was precipitated by a crisis of identity in which two religious communities defined themselves, in part at least, by their differing uses of common scriptures and their eventual construction of distinct canons. The process was complex, especially in the first century CE, when both Judaism and Christianity were marked by great internal diversity, including diversity of views about the authority of Scripture and the canon of sacred books.[25] The final outcome of this internal and external debate was a contracted Jewish canon and an expanded Christian OT.

The third section of the Jewish canon is a miscellany, lacking any clear center or overarching conceptual framework. In Greek canon lists, these writings do not constitute a distinct unit, but are combined in varying order and arrangement with the prophetic and historical books, thus extending the category as well as the corpus of "the Prophets." This segment of Scripture has played an important role in a series of critical questions concerning definitions and boundaries of canon, scripture, church, and synagogue. It also contributes more specifically to the question of scriptural authority.

First, the diversity of the writings that completed the Jewish canon, even in its short version, extends the notion of Scripture to include works that cannot readily be interpreted as the record of divine speech or action, even when broadly defined as "sacred story." The authority of these books must rest on broader grounds, which cannot be identified by a single concept of origin or agency, but must be related to their function in shaping and sustaining community identity—a function that is also central to the earlier collections.[26] The concept of Scripture must be recast in relation to this broader corpus, as the collection of writings that informs and instructs Israel in its identity and vocation as the people of God. In myriad ways it tells Israel who it is, why it has been created and preserved ("chosen"), and what is expected of it.

It performs this function by means of multiple voices and genres. The internal diversity of the scriptures is magnified in the third division of the Hebrew canon, which preserves voices of conflict and dissent, defenders and critics of tradition, even religious skeptics. Thus it is the witness of a community in debate—a feature also discernible within the older canonical writings. Theological diversity and debate are a fundamental feature of both testaments, and any doctrine of biblical authority must be consonant with this aspect of its character.

The Scriptures are not simply multivocal, but historical in their essential nature. They grew—through accretion and selection. They were not handed down from heaven or created in a single

---

25. Rowan A. Greer, "The Christian Bible and Its Interpretation," Part Two in *Early Biblical Interpretation,* by James L. Kugel and Rowan A. Greer (Philadelphia: Westminster, 1986) 120-21.

26. See Kugel and Greer, *Early Biblical Interpretation,* 40-51, for a helpful attempt to discern the primary themes and motives in this diverse literature. Kugel suggests that many of the writings from the Restoration and its aftermath exhibit attempts to link current history and experience with a "canonical" past or "canonical" models (46).

moment, but are the product of a particular community and changing circumstances of life. They testify to the eternal out of their own historical and cultural particularity. Their authority is one of historical and historically conditioned writings. That is equally true of the Christian canon, which added a final chapter to the collected writings—but not to the history of dialogue and witness, which continued beyond the boundaries of the canon.

Canon and Authority. The formation of the Jewish canon as a bound collection of sacred writings was the final stage in the community's recognition of the authority of these works, a process that would be repeated in the church's formation of its own canon. The canon did not establish the authority of the writings, but acknowledged existing authority. And it did not contain all of the writings judged to be inspired, true, and profitable for knowledge of God and conduct of life, but only those deemed essential and having broad appeal within the community. The criteria for inclusion remain one of the most debated issues; what is essential to affirm here is that the canon represents a selection, based primarily on use.

Canon implies boundaries, which have significant consequences for interpretation and use. Different degrees or types of authority are accorded to works inside and outside canonical boundaries, as may be seen in differing Protestant and Catholic uses of the deuterocanonical/apocryphal writings. *Canon* does not, however, imply fixed or unchangeable boundaries. The Hebrew canon grew—and contracted—and differed according to the community of reference. The Pentateuch appears to have acquired the status and function of a canon for Second Temple Judaism, and a small prophetic "canon" may have been recognized by some Jewish circles as early as the exile.[27] In the century before the closing of the Jewish canon, however, Sadducees, Essenes, and Pharisees all had different canons, with the Sadducees recognizing only the Law of Moses as authoritative and the Essenes employing the widest selection of writings.

Canon is a function of political power as well as theological persuasion. The canons of both Judaism and Christianity reflect the views of the dominant parties—and the survivors. To the extent that canonical status was determined by use, it was weighted in favor of use by the largest or most prestigious cities, churches, and religious leaders. Modern historical scholarship has allowed us to see the losers and dissenters in earlier battles over the Bible and to recognize that early Judaism and Christianity were far more diverse than the later orthodoxy of each tradition has suggested.

The church inherited a canon of scriptures that was still in flux, in respect to both the number of books and the written text. From the evidence of first-century BCE and CE manuscripts, and from what can be reconstructed of the history of the OT text, it is clear that the notion of inspired and authoritative writings did not mean for the ancient guardians of those texts that the words themselves must remain unchanged—even where those words are represented explicitly, as in the prophetic writings, as the direct communication of God. Until the end of the first century CE, a dynamic understanding of divine communication in Scripture seems to have prevailed. This is exhibited in its early stages in redactional activity, evident in virtually all of the OT books: New understandings of the divine purpose and will were incorporated directly into the received scriptures. With the closing of the canon, however, that continuing interpretive effort had to take its place outside of the canon and alongside the received text in various types of commentaries.[28] Thus at the time the church was coming into existence, the concept of Scripture as the "Word of God" had not yet acquired the literal interpretation it received in the second century CE.

Scripture in the time of Christian origins also did not imply that all "canonical" writings had the same type or degree of authority. Within the Hebrew Scriptures a hierarchy of authority was recognized, which is discernible in NT citations. The Pentateuch had preeminence, as the earliest body of writings to achieve its final form and as a corpus identified with Mosaic teaching and authority. Prophecy had succeeded torah as the means of continuing revelation in the post-Mosaic age and had given rise to a second corpus of authoritative writings, which appears generally to have been accorded secondary status within early Judaism. By 200 BCE a relatively closed prophetic canon was recognized by the dominant group, which held that the period of prophecy had ceased.[29]

27. McDonald, *Formation*, 50.

28. Sanders, *Sacred Story*, 140; and *Torah and Canon* (Philadelphia: Fortress, 1972) xiv-xv.
29. Associated with the time of Ezra in 1 Macc 9:27; 4:45-46; Josephus, *Against Apion* 1.8.14; McDonald, *Formation*, 50-51.

For those holding this view, inspired and authoritative writing had also ceased. Those writings that were ultimately recognized as the third division of the Jewish canon had either to claim continuing inspiration or to establish their authority on other grounds. One attempt to formulate a criterion of authority that did not depend on the concept of prophetic inspiration is exhibited in the argument of "defiling the hands" that was used to assert the canonicity of certain contested works (Ecclesiastes and Song of Songs). The expression appears to refer to a quality of holiness recognized in the liturgical reading of Scripture, particularly the Law.[30] This was ultimately extended to the whole corpus of authorized scriptures, distinguishing them from other popular, but "noncanonical," writings, especially the so-called "hidden" or apocryphal works.[31] In seeking a term to describe writings that could not be included within the prophetic corpus, the creators of the three-part canon simply named them "the Writings" (in Greek, *hagiographa,* "Holy Writings"). In some circles of first-century Judaism, however, the concept of "inspired" or prophetic writing appears to have been extended to include all of the writings outside the Pentateuch (evidenced by LXX canon lists). Some believed that prophecy had not ceased, among them Christians who attempted to portray their movement as a revival of prophecy in the latter days.[32]

THE BIRTH OF THE CHRISTIAN BIBLE

Jewish and Christian Scriptures in the First Century CE. Christianity was born as a sectarian movement in first-century Judaism, and for a century at least some Christians continued to think of themselves as Jews. For all Christians in the formative period, "Scripture" was the Jewish Scriptures, whose authority and importance for the church's self-understanding are evidenced in the multitude of citations and allusions in early Christian writings. The center of the earliest Christian canon was the Law, and references to Scripture as a whole employ the two-part designation "the law and the prophets" (Matt 5:17; Luke 24:27; Acts 28:23). Only one NT reference suggests a three-part canon (Luke 24:44 [NRSV], referring to "the law of Moses, the prophets, and the psalms"). The notion of divine authorship and agency in the Scriptures can be seen in citations of OT passages that attribute the words directly to God or the Holy Spirit, without reference to the intermediary author, even where the OT lacks the rubric "says the LORD."[33] Little or no distinction of author or literary type is made; all words are understood as God's words and, therefore, as having equal authority.[34]

The church inherited a canon and a concept of Scripture, together with means of interpreting it. In developing its own distinctive hermeneutics, it adapted current Jewish theory and practice. Where the church differed from its parent faith in respect to a common Bible was primarily in the relative weight it attached to scriptural authority. For Christians, the primary focus of divine revelation was not Scripture, but Christ, to whom Scripture was understood to bear witness. Christian preaching ("the gospel") was the primary authority for faith in the first centuries, and Scripture was interpreted in its light.[35] Christians believed that God's purposes for Israel as revealed in the Scriptures had reached an end in Jesus. As a consequence, they sought to show how Scripture pointed to Christ. Scripture, as the authoritative word from the past, had a decisive role to play in confirming and interpreting the new revelatory event, but it had no meaning, or could not properly be understood, apart from that event (2 Cor 3:12-18). It was still the authoritative Word of God, but it no longer communicated salvation.[36] This orientation toward Christ as the center and

---

30. The precise origin and meaning of the expression are debated. See G. W. Anderson, "Canonical and Non-Canonical," in The Cambridge History of the Bible, vol. 1, *From the Beginnings to Jerome,* eds. P. R. Ackroyd and C. E. Evans (Cambridge: Cambridge University Press, 1970), 114. What is clear, however, is that this manner of designating authoritative Scripture rests on liturgical use, rather than on concepts of divine origin (inspiration). Liturgical orientation is also exhibited in the term rabbinic Judaism came to use for the Scriptures as a whole: מקרא *miqra',* "that which is read [aloud]." Judaism never employed the term *canon* (Greek κανών *kanōn,* "standard"), which Christians adopted in the fourth century CE to designate their authorized corpus of scriptures. (See ibid., 114, 134, 156).

31. Ibid., 134, 156.

32. McDonald, *Formation,* 53; cf. James Barr, *Holy Scripture: Canon, Authority, Criticism* (Philadelphia: Westminster, 1983) 55-56.

33. Henry M. Shires, *Finding the Old Testament in the New* (Philadelphia: Westminster, 1974) 21; cf. 62.

34. Thus, e.g., Psalms (the most frequently cited book) is used in the same way as Deuteronomy and Isaiah (the most frequently cited books of the Pentateuch and Prophets), although as literature it has an entirely different character. And while its words are typically identified with David, the Holy Spirit is understood to speak through them. See ibid., 126-27; see esp. 35-64 for analysis of varying uses of Scripture by different NT authors, as well as the extent of the corpus of sacred writings. See also Greer, "The Christian Bible and Its Interpretation," 126-54.

35. Greer, "The Christian Bible and Its Interpretation," 114.

36. Barr, *Holy Scripture* 14.

source of faith distinguished Christianity from the beginning and determined Christian understanding of Scripture, including the new Christian writings that would eventually stand alongside the OT canon. Christians, in contrast to Jews, were not primarily a people of the book.[37]

Christian use of Scripture shifted emphasis from God's activity in the past to God's activity in the present, a shift that affected the shape of the Christian OT and also the Jewish canon. Christians shared the belief of certain Jewish groups that the time of revelation was not past. In their conviction that the new age of the Spirit, predicted for the final days, had dawned, Christians were attracted to Jewish apocalyptic and messianic literature, which likewise expected a dramatic reappearance of divine activity in history. Christian use of these writings, as well as their "misuse" of the older canonical literature, seems to have been one factor behind the move by the dominant Jewish party to fix both the corpus and the text of the Jewish Scriptures at the end of the first century CE. The resulting canon admitted only one apocalyptic writing (Daniel) and no writings composed originally in Greek, apparently in reaction to the Christian adoption of the Septuagint (the Greek version of the Jewish Scriptures, produced in Alexandria).[38] Thus hermeneutics had a decisive influence on *which* books were considered authoritative as well as on *how* their authority was understood.

The Christian OT canon remained open for two more centuries, with continued, and ultimately unresolved, debate concerning some of the later writings, but a general preference for an expanded corpus based on the Septuagint.[39] Nevertheless, the main corpus of the OT had already attained such a degree of authority by the time Christians appropriated it as their own that no significant challenge was made against any individual book of the shorter Jewish canon. The real challenge to the authority of the Jewish Scriptures was directed to the corpus as a whole, and from that challenge the Christian Bible was born.

The Shape and Authority of the Christian Bible. The first century and a half of the church's life was marked by wide diversity of understanding and practice as different communities attempted in different ways to relate the new faith to its parent religion and to other religious and philosophical movements. The consensus that finally emerged charted a course between two extremes, represented on the one hand by Jewish Christians, who insisted on maintaining their Jewish heritage and denied the divinity of Christ, and on the other by Gnostic Christians, who depreciated the created order and the Jewish Scriptures and denied the full humanity of Christ.[40] By the mid-second century the primary challenge came from the Gnostics and Gnostic-influenced thinkers.

Marcion, a lay member of the Roman congregation who was heavily influenced by Gnostics and Paul, had come to believe that the Jewish Bible was incompatible with the gospel. Moreover, he argued, the God of the Jewish Scriptures was not the God of Jesus Christ, but a vengeful and changeable god, whose eye-for-eye morality was superseded by Jesus' ethic of love. Christ had not only rendered the law obsolete, but also revealed a new God. Marcion insisted that the church sever its Jewish roots completely, including the Jewish Scriptures; and he rejected attempts to hold on to these (in his view) outmoded and antithetical texts by such arbitrary methods of interpretation as allegory and typology. Establishing a counterchurch in 144 CE, he also proposed a counter Scripture. In place of the Jewish Scriptures, he proposed a canon of Christian writings consisting of an expurgated version of the Gospel of Luke (with all OT influences eliminated) and a freely edited collection of ten letters of Paul.[41]

The church ultimately rejected Marcion's theology and his canon, but in so doing it had to rethink its understanding of Scripture. In the end it reappropriated and reappraised the Jewish Scriptures in relation to a new collection of Christian Scriptures.

Christian Writings. Christian writings had begun to appear soon after the birth of the church, but they were intended to assist, not replace, oral proclamation, which was the authoritative form of the apostolic witness in the first century.[42] The circulation of

---

37. Greer, "The Christian Bible and Its Interpretation," 112, 114, 202; McDonald, *Formation,* 66.

38. McDonald, *Formation,* 61-62; cf. Karlfried Froehlich, trans. and ed., *Biblical Interpretation in the Early Church,* Sources of Early Christian Thought (Philadelphia: Fortress, 1984) 2-3.

39. See Albert C. Sundberg, "The Bible Canon and the Christian Doctrine of Inspiration," *Int* 29 (1975) 58-59; McDonald, *Formation,* 178.

40. Greer, "The Christian Bible and Its Interpretation," 116.

41. McDonald, *Formation,* 86-88; Froehlich, *Biblical Interpretation,* 10-11.

42. McDonald, *Formation,* 76-77.

written Gospels, referred to as "Memoirs of the Apostles," did not mean, however, that they were immediately treated as Scripture.[43] The creation and adoption of a canon of Christian Scriptures had multiple sources and motives. The death of the first witnesses and the delay of the parousia gave impetus to the recording of the oral tradition, as did the difficulty of certifying oral tradition. Apologetic motives played a role in the composition and use of some of the NT writings, as did the needs of community worship and instruction, and the need to communicate with a rapidly expanding church for which personal communication was no longer possible. Practical reasons dictated the composition of most of the writings.

The growth of the NT and final establishment of a closed authoritative canon paralleled in many ways the process by which the OT canon came into being. The sayings of Jesus were considered authoritative from the beginning and had the status of Scripture before they were recorded in any collection or Gospel. Citations of Jesus' words became frequent in the second century, typically coupled with OT citations, and often derived from written Gospels (mostly Matthew). Citations from NT epistles also appear in this period, though less frequently, and there is evidence that Paul's letters were being circulated among a number of churches in Asia Minor and beyond. There is also evidence of liturgical use of the Gospels for public reading in worship—alternating with the Prophets. Whatever the original purpose and occasion of these writings, when they were placed alongside the OT Scriptures in worship and in appeals to authoritative teaching, they functioned as Scripture, whether they were formally accorded this status or not.

The Twofold Canon. The NT canon was not finally fixed until the fourth century, but the principal and the core literature had been established by the time of Irenaeus (writing c. 170–180), who provided the nomenclature and the theory for uniting the two canons in a single Christian Bible. Irenaeus, who appears to have been the first to designate the two-part Scriptures as OT and NT, conceived of the history revealed in the two testaments as that of salvation in which the Hebrew

Scriptures had a positive role in preparing the Jewish people for Christ. The incarnate Word of God was the head of this history, uniting and summing up all in God, but present in it from the beginning, revealing God the Father in creation and in the whole history of Israel. The revelation of the Word as attested by the Scriptures occurred in stages, marked by four covenants (Adam, Noah, Moses, Christ), in which the form and content of the message were appropriate for the particular dispensation in which it was given. Consequently, each testament was necessary to this progressive revelation of the one God, with the OT providing an indispensable pedagogy for Christ.[44]

Irenaeus's main contribution to the developing Christian Bible was his recognition of the need for an authoritative collection of NT writings to represent the apostolic witness. He did not define the limits of the canon, but focused on the Gospels, which he saw as the primary source for the tradition held by the church. His insistence on a fourfold Gospel, rather than the selection of one (as Marcion's Luke or the Ebionites' Matthew) or a harmony (Tatian's *Diatessaron*), was based on use in the churches of his day. But his arguments (four were dictated by the four quarters of the world and the four winds[45]) are a reminder that the whole process of Scripture formation, including canonization, is stamped by finite and culturally determined human reasoning.

Irenaeus's effort to establish a Christian Bible was motivated by his concern to defend the Christian message from heresy. For him, the primary form of that message was the apostolic witness, entrusted to the church and guaranteed by the succession of bishops. Its key, and the true canon of the church, was the "canon [or "rule"] of faith" (*regula fidei*), a summary of the essential content of the apostolic preaching resident in the church. While not verbally fixed, Irenaeus's formulation of it corresponds closely to the content of the later creeds.[46] It represented the essential content of "the one faith" that "the church, though dispersed throughout the whole world . . . [had] received from the apostles and their disciples." It was with this canon that heresy was opposed, but it needed the fuller witness of the Scriptures.

43. Although the words of Christ were accorded Scripture-like authority from the beginning, there is disagreement among scholars about when in the second century that authority was extended to the books as a whole. See ibid., 74; Hans von Campenhausen, *The Formation of the Christian Bible* (Philadelphia: Fortress, 1972) 118-21.

44. Greer, "The Christian Bible and Its Interpretation," 155-57, 163-74.
45. Irenaeus, *Against Heresies* 3.11.8, 9.
46. Ibid., 1:10.1.

For Irenaeus, the rule of faith was the key that unlocked the Scriptures and the standard of truth by which all writings and teachings were to be judged, but it also depended on the Scriptures, deriving its categories of interpretation from them. Irenaeus likened the Scriptures to a mosaic, made up of many distinct passages, and the rule of faith to the "hypothesis" that enabled one to arrange the passages in the right order. Elsewhere he described the two as twin brothers whose message was in principle identical. For Irenaeus, Scripture and tradition could not be opposed or ranked; they needed each other and were mutually dependent.[47]

Irenaeus's understanding of Scripture and scriptural authority became the common property of Christian orthodoxy. It included a two-part canon, a hermeneutical principle derived from it and applied to it, and an authority structure capable of determining valid interpretations of Scripture. He also found a way of holding on to the Jewish Scriptures without resorting to allegory or other methods of interpretation that ignored their plain meaning and ancient context.

In his defense of the Jewish Scriptures as essential to Christian theology and authoritative for Christian faith, Irenaeus addressed a fundamental problem of all Scripture: its dual character as a word from the past, which is always to some degree alien and unrepeatable, and as a word for the present, informing and forming faith. With his view of progressive revelation and his concept of the educational purposes of past failings and punishment, Irenaeus was able to claim the continuing truth and revelatory power of the past while expressing a clear realization that elements in the ancient writings no longer represented the understanding of the community—and might even stand in opposition to it. That recognition is not new with Irenaeus, but is a constitutive feature of the whole process of scripture formation and transmission. What is new is the explicit recognition of a historical dimension: revelation as suited to the times and conditions under which it occurs. With this view of accommodation, both past and present are freed from the constraints of forced harmonization or unanimity of thought.

Criteria of Canonicity. The primary test for authority made by the early church was faithfulness in conveying the apostolic witness, which came to be formulated in terms of authorship. The under-

lying concern was to ground the church's faith in Jesus in reliable tradition. Yet the notion of reliable transmission of the Jesus tradition did not rest on historical connection alone. Neither Mark nor Luke could claim apostolic authorship, and the *Gospel of Thomas,* which did, was rejected—because its message did not conform to what the general church understood as apostolic teaching, even though some of its sayings may actually have originated with Christ. Thus the claim of apostolicity, which was eventually extended to the whole NT canon, was a claim about the content of the message, rather than the history of its origins.[48]

The notion of "orthodoxy" as a criterion of authority is even more strained. The church opted for a canon characterized by a plurality of theologies, because the church itself, from its earliest days, did not have a single unified theology. The unique contribution of Scripture, over against the rule of faith, was and is its irreducible pluralism, its articulation of the one faith in multiple voices—which requires prioritizing in the act of appropriation. The truth in the notion of orthodoxy as a criterion is that the recognized writings needed to lie within a general range of accepted belief.

Inspiration is the criterion most commonly cited by modern interpreters to explain the authority of the canonical writings, but without elaboration it is inadequate and misleading. All of the competing canons consisted of writings understood to be inspired, but writings that claimed no canonical status were also recognized as inspired. Thus inspiration was a necessary, but insufficient, criterion. Moreover, many noncanonical writings claimed inspiration, while few canonical writings did so. The Montanists, with their new scriptures, made the church wary of inspiration as a criterion, especially in the East, resulting in a neglect of prophetic literature—and suspicion of the book of Revelation as late as the fourth century.[49] The Montanist excesses illustrate an important feature, however, of general early Christian understanding of inspiration—namely, the belief that inspiration had not ceased

47. Greer, "The Christian Bible and Its Interpretation," 124, 157.

48. For a discussion of several criteria for a NT canon, see McDonald, *Formation,* 146-63.

49. Montanism was an enthusiastic revival movement that spread rapidly through the church in the late second century, emphasizing the imminent return of Christ and the new gift of the Spirit. The Montanists stressed the new revelation given by their prophets and set forth their visions in new apocalypses, claiming superior authority for the "New Prophecy of the Paraclete" over the former revelation. See von Campenhausen, *Formation,* 221-23.

with the canonical writings—and that it was a gift to the whole church, not simply a possession of certain writers.

In the final analysis, the formation of the NT canon and the Christian Bible closely paralleled the process for the OT Scriptures. Both rested ultimately on the recognition of a community through its use, but in neither case does this supply an adequate criterion of judgment. At the base of the recognition was the community's belief that these writings conveyed a true representation of God and of the saving acts that constituted the community, that they offered trustworthy guidance for the present, and more particularly that they served the needs of the community at the time of the closing of the canon. Thus truth in representing the tradition and suitability for meeting current needs were the twin tests of authority in the creation of the Christian Bible.

AUTHORITY IN THE WESTERN CHURCH

Wherever the question of biblical authority has been raised in the history of the canon, it has been linked to the question of meaning and the underlying question of purpose. For most of that history, belief in the Bible as a source of divine revelation and a guide to salvation was unchallenged, but it could be maintained only by hermeneutical means that enabled readers to discern the spiritual message in the human words. Modern critics of the Bible's primitive cosmology and ethics are not alone in finding much within the Scriptures incredible or offensive, and Marcion was not the first to expose the defects in the OT's portrait of God.

The Jewish philosopher and exegete Philo of Alexandria (c. 20 BCE–50 CE), recognized that the biblical stories were filled with "impossibilities," "impieties," and "absurdities" when read literally. But his Hellenistic understanding of inspiration, as affecting the production of the text itself, led him to seek a deeper spiritual meaning through the use of allegory—a method of interpretation developed by Greek exegetes as a means of discovering higher cosmological or ethical truths behind the ancient Greek mythical texts. He also found a rationale for the OT's anthropomorphic representations of God in the concept of accommodation. The anthropomorphisms, he argued, were an accommodation of God to human thought, enabling finite human minds to apprehend the infinitely great and unknowable God.[50]

The great Christian theologian and exegete of the early church, Origen of Alexandria (c.185–254 CE) built his own hermeneutical theory on these foundations. Origen found the model for God's condescending or accommodating to human weakness in the incarnation, which he saw as revealing God's manner of communication from the beginning. In Scripture, God had stooped to speak human language, which was like children's speech. Like a school teacher or a father, God adopted "baby talk" to lead his children according to their ability to comprehend. The means of communication, Origen argued, was suited to its purpose. The Bible was a book of salvation, not of human science; it suited God's salvific purposes, not the human search for knowledge. For Origen, Scripture was a guide for the soul in its ascent to its true home in the Platonic realm of spiritual reality. The "stumbling blocks" placed before the reader by the divine author were a sign of the Bible's higher purpose and an invitation to search it out. Origen's hermeneutical theory enabled readers to move from the limited literal sense of the text to the higher spiritual meaning, but it also lent itself to uncontrolled speculation, arbitrary equivalences, and even denial that the ancient writers had spoken for their own time at all.

In the fourth and fifth centuries a rival school arose in Antioch, challenging the excesses of Alexandrian spirituality. Antiochene exegesis drew upon a different pagan and Jewish philosophical heritage in its grammatical-historical approach to the text. Rabbinic exegesis, aimed at applying the text to practical questions, and a concern for history, textual criticism, and classical rhetoric provided the foundations for the Antiochene emphasis on the natural meaning of the text in its historical context. For John Chrysostom (c. 347–407), the principle of accommodation exemplified in the incarnation led to a focus on the humble text, rather than the lofty meanings spun out by philosophers. But he too

50. Froehlich, *Biblical Interpretation*, 6-7; Jack B. Rogers and Donald K. McKim, *The Authority and Interpretation of the Bible: An Historical Approach* (San Francisco: Harper & Row, 1979) 11-12, view the notion of accommodation as a key and constant feature of pre-modern exegetical theory, which was lost by Protestant orthodoxy and its heirs in their defense of the Bible against modern criticism. Their reconstruction of the historical understanding of biblical authority has been challenged on several grounds, especially in regard to the concept of inerrancy. See, e.g., John D. Woodbridge, *Biblical Authority: A Critique of the Rogers/McKim Proposal* (Grand Rapids: Zondervan, 1982). Nevertheless, it remains a useful historical survey.

recognized that some statements could not be understood literally and that mere literalism, with no concern for the divine purpose and character of the words, could easily result in "utter absurdity." Antiochene exegesis was also governed by a stronger emphasis on the apostolic tradition as a guide to interpretation.

Despite the differences between the two ancient exegetical schools, they shared a common belief that the primary purpose and content of Scripture was salvation and that whatever did not accord with that message was not authoritative. They also recognized a distinction of content and form, in which the form of the message represented a divine accommodation to human thought and speech. That meant that the literal meaning of the text, however incomprehensible or offensive, had a purpose in God's communication in the Scriptures and could not be dismissed entirely. Thus readers were able to acknowledge difficulties in the text without jeopardizing the fundamental authority of the Scriptures.

Elements of both Alexandrian and Antiochene exegesis combined in the hermeneutical theory of Augustine (354–430). He, like Origen, sought the higher meaning of the text by means of allegorical interpretation, but he also affirmed the root historical meaning, preferring to give both a literal and a spiritual meaning of the same text. This did not, however, affirm their equal value, but rather showed that the one prefigured the other. His preference for the spiritual meaning led at times to strained interpretations, but his exegesis was generally more restrained than Origen's because of his appeal to the rule of faith and the authority of the church in interpreting Scripture.

Augustine believed that the goal of Scripture was to induce love for God and neighbor and thus to order Christian life toward its heavenly home, but this love was to be found in its true form only in the church. Against various heretical sects who based their beliefs on private interpretations of Scripture, Augustine appealed to the authority of the church, declaring that he would "not believe the gospel except moved by the authority of the Catholic Church."[51] For Augustine, as for Irenaeus and Chrysostom, the rule of faith supplied the basic principles for interpreting Scripture and for resolving ambiguities.

Augustine developed a hermeneutical theory that became the foundation for exegesis throughout the Middle Ages. Recognizing four "senses" to be sought in every biblical book (if not every text), he brought together all of the major exegetical streams of the earlier period. Attention to the *literal* sense preserved the Antiochene tradition of grammatical-historical exegesis; the *allegorical* sense continued the tradition of typological interpretation; the *tropological* meaning made room for the moral message emphasized by Chrysostom and the rabbis; while the *anagogical* sense maintained the Alexandrian emphasis on the spiritual sense. Appeal to the fourfold sense of the text permitted the Bible to serve a variety of practical and speculative needs, as the foundation for doctrine and ethics and as a guide to the spiritual life. Recognition of multiple senses was an ideal solution to a problem inherent in the concept of Scripture as it had developed in Jewish and Christian tradition and in the character of the text. A clearly composite text of different types of material and levels of insight, divergent views, and conflicting statements was to be read as the authoritative record of God's self-disclosure and saving action in the past and as a present source of divine guidance. But the notion of multiple meanings also led to uncontrolled speculation and ecclesiastical control, which undermined the authority of Scripture while maintaining the principle of Scripture as norm.

The authority of the Bible, understood as the inspired and inerrant word of God, was maintained throughout the Middle Ages without formal challenge. Although Scholasticism[52] revived the question of the place of philosophy in apprehending divine truth, suggesting a role for reason alongside revelation, the greatest of the Scholastics, Thomas Aquinas (c. 1225–1274), gave precedence to Scripture in his magisterial synthesis of reason and faith. While he sought to secure a place for reason in leading to faith, he recognized the divinely revealed truths of Scripture as surpassing reason. The means of apprehending those truths, however, was through the literal sense of the text. In his concern to be scientific, Aquinas turned away from allegorical speculation to the grammatical-historical sense of the text, insisting that it must be the basis of all other meanings.

---

51. Augustine *Contra Epistolam Manichaei Fundamenti,* V. 6.

52. Scholasticism refers to the teaching that flourished in the schools of the eleventh through the fifteenth centuries. See Rogers and McKim, *Authority,* 36-48.

The Protestant Reformation. Luther. Where Luther differed from his medieval colleagues was not in asserting the authority of the Bible, but in denying the authority of the church and pope. Forced to acknowledge a conflict between the two authorities to which he had appealed, he chose Scripture. Luther's choice, and his view of opposing claims, widened a rift between the church and Scripture that had begun developing in the fourteenth century. Prior to that time Scripture and the tradition maintained in the church were understood to "co-inhere"; there could be no ultimate discrepancy between the two sources, because each derived authority from Christ, the living Word who spoke through both. In his earliest arguments, Luther still tried to hold on to the belief that church and Scripture spoke with a common voice. When he could no longer reconcile the two, however, he chose Scripture as the firmer foundation and surer guide. Although his view of alternative, and opposing, authorities had antecedents,[53] the political and theological crisis in the church of Luther's day made his appeal to *sola scriptura* ("Scripture alone") a revolutionary cry, whose echoes still resound in a fractured church.

Luther's attempt to reform the church of his day appealed to the Bible as the norm of faith and doctrine, setting it over against the church's teaching. As the primary and unchanging source of the gospel, it stood as witness against ecclesiastical perversions and served as a source of both judgment and renewal of the church. Moreover, it was accessible to every believer, or at least potentially so. Luther's opposition to the ecclesiastical establishment of his day was directed at its control not only of souls, but also of Scripture. The fanciful interpretations characteristic of medieval biblical exegesis served mainly, he believed, to obscure the meaning of the text, setting human invention in the place of the divine word. For Luther and his Reformed colleagues, the "plain" or literal (grammatical-historical) meaning, rather than the allegorical sense, conveyed the intention of the divine author—hence the true "spiritual" sense.

The Reformers' appeal to the Bible as the primary source and norm of faith and their understanding of Scripture as the self-interpreting word of God set Scripture over against, or at least alongside, the church and its teaching office as an independent, and privileged, source of authority. Thus the Reformation reversed the two interpretive principles of the preceding age, setting literal reading over spiritual or allegorical and the word of Scripture over the word of the church.

Luther never gave systematic formulation to his understanding of the authority and inspiration of the Bible. While he regarded both the book and the authors as inspired and referred to the Scriptures as the "Word of God," he never simply identified that word with the words of Scripture. Rather, the word of God was Christ; but like Christ, whose humanity Luther emphasized, God's Word in Scripture was incarnate, communicating the divine message in weak and imperfect human speech. The authority of the Bible for Luther came from the One to whom it bears witness, and must be confirmed in the heart of the believer. Thus it was both objective and subjective.[54]

Luther recognized the Bible as both a divine instrument and a human document—of decidedly uneven quality. The aim of exegesis, in his view, was to discern the gospel, contained in both testaments, and distinguish it from the Law. Those portions of Scripture that did not "urge" Christ were not worthy of belief. With this criterion of authority for faith, Luther boldly dismissed some Scripture as unworthy, including the books of Esther, James, and Revelation—yet he retained them in his canon, honoring tradition over his own discernment. He also reopened the question of the OT canon, which had never been formally settled, opting for the shorter canon of Jerome and Jewish orthodoxy.

Calvin. Calvin's understanding of Scripture was close to Luther's, but was given more systematic and theoretical expression in his theological writings and commentaries.[55] For Calvin, the key to the understanding and authority of Scripture was the activity of the Holy Spirit speaking in Scripture, but also prompting the heart and mind of the believer to recognition and assent. This "internal testimony of the Holy Spirit" is essential to the acknowledgment of Scripture as "the word of the Lord." The words themselves are merely the record of God's speaking

---

53. E.g., Henry of Ghent (d. 1293); see George H. Tavard, *Holy Writ or Holy Church: The Crisis of the Protestant Reformation* (New York: Harper and Bros., 1959) 22-79.

54. See B. A. Gerrish, "Biblical Authority and the Continental Reformation," *SJT* 10 (1957) 342-43; Rogers and McKim, *Authority*, 75-88.

55. See Rogers and McKim, *Authority*, 89-116; J. K. S. Reid, *The Authority of Scripture: A Study of Reformation and Post-Reformation Understanding of the Bible* (London: Methuen, 1957) 29-55.

and are not themselves either inspired or authoritative. The content of Scripture, apprehended through the internal action of the Spirit, is the word of salvation, but the words of Scripture in their human and historical meaning constitute the essential and sole access to that divine word.

Both Luther and Calvin gave new emphasis to the authority of Scripture, drawing on traditional views of the Bible as the inspired "word of God," but both emphasized the continuing activity of the divine speaker and the necessity of encounter with that speaker in the heart and mind of the believer. Consequently, the authority of Scripture could not be located exclusively either in the words themselves or in the historical authors. The two great Reformers had opened the door to a new understanding of the inspiration and authority of Scripture that had ancient roots and combined emphases on faith and reason that had tended to diverge in medieval exegesis. Their successors, however, fell back on the medieval underpinnings of the Reformers' thought, attempting to defend the Bible against the counterattack of the Roman Catholic Church and new critical forms of interpretation by means of a rigid theory of verbal inspiration. Protestant orthodoxy also extended and absolutized the claims of scriptural authority, vesting in the biblical text the authority previously given to tradition, philosophy, and ecclesiastical structures. By the seventeenth century, the Bible had become a compendium of fixed theological statements. Gradually a new apparatus of interpretation was imposed upon the text in which doctrine would again hold the key.

Roman Catholic and Protestant Proclamations and Praxis. Roman Catholic response to Protestant elevation of scriptural authority took a variety of forms, exhibited in the debate on Scripture that took place at the Council of Trent (1545–1563).[56] While all of the participants were intent on upholding the authority of the church against Protestant assaults, they differed on the mutual relations of the church and Scripture and the connection of each with revelation. The Council had to reconcile differences that ranged from "Scripture alone" to "the church alone," as well as the priority of "continuing revelation." The statement that was finally adopted affirmed two modes of revelation, declaring that the pure gospel was contained and handed on *in libris scriptis et sine scripto traditionibus,* "in written books and unwritten traditions," and that both were to be received and venerated *pari pietatis affectu ac reverentia,* "with equal feeling of piety and reverence."[57] The compromise displeased those who objected to placing tradition on the same level with Scripture, but by refusing to specify how each authority related to the other, it permitted a view of the priority of Scripture.

The mainstream of Roman Catholic thought interpreted the Tridentine declaration as affirming Scripture and tradition as "two sources" of revelation, in which the content of revelation was divided materially between the two. This interpretation has recently been called into question, but it stood for almost five centuries as the dominant view and "one of the most important points of controversial theology" directed against the Protestant doctrine of *sola scriptura.* The Council itself apparently rejected this interpretation when it removed the *partim . . . partim* from an earlier draft that had declared that the "truth [of the gospel] is contained partly (*partim*) in written books, partly (*partim*) in unwritten traditions."[58] Moreover it defined Scripture as *norma normans et non normata,* "the norm that governs, but is not governed," suggesting an understanding of Scripture as the norm for the traditions of the church, which appears close to the views of Protestant orthodoxy.[59]

Despite similarities in formal pronouncements and doctrines affirming the authority of Scripture, the Bible played a quite different role in Protestantism than in Roman Catholicism or the Eastern churches. The two branches of the Western church had different canons and different authoritative texts, and they differed markedly in their views of interpretive authority. Against Luther's preference for the Jewish OT canon favored by Jerome, the Council of Trent endorsed the longer canon drawn up at the council of Hippo (393 CE), declaring that all of the books of the OT and the NT, including the deuterocanonical/apocryphal books, were of equal authority. It also authorized the Latin Vulgate as the

56. See Tavard, *Holy Writ,* 196-209 for a detailed account of the debate, and 113-91 for the various positions taken in the preceding three decades.

57. H. J. Schroeder, *Canons and Decrees of the Council of Trent* (London: Herder, 1941) 17, 296.

58. See Tavard, *Holy Writ,* 202, 205, 208, 244-45.

59. See the Lutheran description of Scripture as *norma normans,* "the norm that governs," and the tradition or the confessions as the *norma normata,* "the norm that is governed [by Scripture]" (Book of Concord; see Gnuse, *Authority,* 8).

"authentic" edition for public reading, exposition, and disputation, in contrast to the Reformers' appeal to the original Hebrew and Greek. But the Council went beyond the establishment of an authoritative text and canon, attempting to secure authoritative interpretation as well. No interpretation should be considered valid, it decreed, which was "contrary to that sense which holy mother Church has held and now holds," for "it is her office to judge about the true sense and interpretation of Scripture."[60] This reassertion of the principle that Luther had opposed resulted in continuing ecclesiastical control of Roman Catholic biblical interpretation.

Protestants, following Luther, shifted authority for interpretation from the teaching office of the church to the individual conscience informed by the Holy Spirit.[61] Despite latent conflicts and unresolved tensions concerning the actual locus of authority for interpretation, Protestantism took a generally "democratic" approach, marked in some traditions by a strong populist emphasis.

The Bible also functioned in a quite different way in the congregational life and personal piety of Protestants. The symbolism of the word, read and expounded, at the center of the traditional Protestant service of worship points to a fundamentally different way of understanding scriptural authority than that of the traditional Roman Catholic mass. Similarly, the subordination of Scripture to the liturgy, or incorporation of Scripture into liturgy, in Orthodox practice signals a different disposition toward Scripture, even where common affirmations may be made concerning its authority for faith. Moreover, the Bible functions for many Protestants as the primary medium of communion with God, hence it plays a critical role in Protestants' experience of God—a major factor distinguishing Protestant and Catholic approaches to feminist theology.[62] The dominant image of evangelical Protestantism today is of a Bible-centered faith, and Protestants

in predominantly Roman Catholic or Orthodox countries typically identify themselves as "Bible believers." Whatever the accuracy of this claim, and implied contrast, it is an important witness to the authority accorded to the Bible by a major stream of the Reformation.[63]

In its practice, as well as its confessions, Protestantism centered its life on the Bible and looked to the Bible for guidance in all matters of belief and practice. As a consequence, the challenge to traditional understanding of the Bible and biblical authority occasioned by the Enlightenment had an especially traumatic and far-reaching effect on Protestantism. Although it eventually made an impact on Roman Catholicism, in the Modernist controversies of the late nineteenth and twentieth centuries, the ancient church remained intact, while the younger churches were shaken to their foundations, many sustaining irreparable breaches.

AUTHORITY IN AMERICA

Scenes of Battle: Setting the Stage. American Protestantism, together with its descendants around the globe, is characterized by a unique interest in the question of biblical authority, which arises from its peculiar history and distinguishes it from its European ancestors and confessional kin.[64] Both the shape of the church, with its multiple denominations and independent churches, and its theological discourse have been deeply marked by battles over the Bible, battles that are being replayed in many denominations today. The major battles were fought in the period between the 1880s and the 1920s and have their roots in the particular confluence of two streams of influence, Renaissance learning and Reformation piety, as they met on the American frontier. The history of their antecedents and earlier interactions in Europe is important for understanding the modern debate, but the constraints of this article limit consideration to a few key developments.

60. Schroeder, *Canons,* 19, 298; Thomas Aquinas Collins and Raymond E. Brown, "Church Pronouncements," in Brown et al., *The Jerome Biblical Commentary,* 627; cf. Gerrish, "Biblical Authority," 339.

61. Formally, the Protestant claim locates the authority in Scripture itself, speaking of the "self-interpreting word." In practice, however, authority rests with the individual interpreter and/or the faith community of the believer. Recent Protestant critique and ecumenical discussion have led to the recognition that the authority exercised by Protestant confessional groups closely resembles that formally claimed by the Roman Catholic *magisterium.*

62. Mary Ann Tolbert, "Protestant Feminists and the Bible: On the Horns of a Dilemma," in *The Pleasure of Her Text: Feminist Readings of the Biblical and Historical Texts,* ed. Alice Bach (Philadelphia: Trinity International, 1990) 11-12.

63. The distinction between Bible-centered and liturgy-centered worship is breaking down today as a result of liturgical changes occasioned by Vatican II and the growing phenomenon of communal exegesis in base communities.

64. An exception to the dominant Protestant pattern has been the African American church, which developed its own distinctive (counter) hermeneutics and in which biblical authority was not tied to textual or scientific claims. Trust in the message was combined with suspicion of its interpreters, ancient as well as modern.

The Doctrine of Inerrancy. Post-Reformation Protestantism, especially on the Continent, responded to the Roman Catholic Counter-Reformation by adopting its weapons, reverting to an older scholastic mode in attempting to systematize the work of the Reformers.[65] Fighting battles on several fronts, including battles with humanists and intra-Protestant disputes, both Lutheran and Reformed traditions developed confessions aimed at securing the faith, in which the doctrine of Scripture was the key article.[66] Theology, conceived as a science of systematically ordered truths, was grounded in Scripture, whose sufficiency and trustworthiness had to be defended. Viewed as a book of revealed truths, which together presented a comprehensive system of knowledge, the Bible's technical accuracy took on heightened importance, especially in the new intellectual climate created by the revolution in science and philosophy. The meaning and efficacy of Scripture came to depend on a conception of the Bible as verbally inspired and inerrant; and the work of the Holy Spirit was now conceived primarily as ensuring the Bible's accuracy, rather than as awakening faith in the believer.

In seventeenth-century Reformed scholasticism, inerrancy became the key claim on which the Bible's authority rested, a claim that directed interpretive efforts to resolving apparent conflicts in the text and focused attention on the form of the text—even including the Hebrew vowel points. Thus the Reformed theologian Francis Turretin (1632–87) argued:

We have always thought the truer and safer way to keep the authenticity of the original text safe and sound against the cavils of all profane persons and heretics whatever, and to put the principle of faith upon a sure and immovable basis, is that which holds the points to be of divine origin . . . and therefore, that the adversaries err who wish to impugn the authority of the Hebrew manuscript from the newness of the points.[67]

---

65. See Rogers and McKim, *Authority,* 147-261.

66. See ibid., 462-72 ("Appendix: Reformed Confessions on Scripture") for a useful collection of texts. The articles on Scripture commonly stand at the head of the confessions and tend to become progressively longer and more detailed, as illustrated by the Second Helvetic Confession of 1566 and the 1646 Confession of Faith of the Westminster Assembly of Divines (the Westminster Confession).

67. Cited by ibid., 180. Turretin was a key figure linking seventeenth-century Reformed theology in Europe to nineteenth-century theology in America. His textbook, *Institutio Theologiae Elencticae* (1674), dominated the theology of Princeton Seminary during its first century (1812–1912). In it, 355 pages were devoted to the doctrine of Scripture, which he believed to be the most important subject in theology (Rogers and McKim, *Authority,* xvii, 175-76).

These efforts at securing the authority of the Bible would later serve to undermine it as new historical and scientific data challenged the premises of the claims. The battle over inerrancy had its roots in the seventeenth century, but it did not break in full force until two centuries later.

Renaissance Scholarship. The Renaissance revival of classical learning brought with it a new interest in the study of the Bible and new linguistic and historical tools for the task. In contrast to the ecclesiastical exegesis of the Middle Ages, whose aims were theological and devotional, the new scholarship was primarily historical in its interest, broadly humanistic in character, and marked by a spirit of critical and open inquiry. Its focus on the literal and historical meaning of the text corresponded to the new Reformation emphasis; and many Protestant scholars welcomed the new learning with enthusiasm, viewing it as a means of recovering the original meaning of the ancient authors and freeing the Bible from dogmatic interpretation and ecclesiastical control. But the alliance was an uneasy one, and many within the church saw the new scholarship as a direct threat, not only to traditional interpretation of the Bible, but also to the Bible's authority as a source and norm of faith. Their apprehension was fueled by free thinkers, as well as others, openly hostile to the church, who saw in the new criticism a means to unmask religion and reject its supernatural claims by exposing the Bible's human character, crude expression, and fallibility.

The new biblical scholarship analyzed the Bible in the same manner and with the same tools that had been used to study classical literature, making comparisons of content, concepts, vocabulary, and style between different writings, both inside and outside the Bible. The results challenged traditional views of authorship and chronology, which had been the linchpins of a biblical history of salvation. Historical-critical scholarship transformed salvation history into "mere history"—and judged it historically false, or so it appeared to many. In its reconstruction of the history behind the texts, it resembled the old allegorical readings in finding the key to the "true" meaning of the text in a reality behind the text—only it reflected the new spirit of the times by seeking a historical explanation rather than a spiritual one.

For pious advocates, the new method liberated

the Bible from traditional dogmas of interpretation that had been imposed on the Scriptures and did not arise from the text itself. It allowed the Bible to speak in its own voice, or better, voices. Recognition of multiple authors and circumstances of composition made it possible to explain discrepancies and contradictions that had troubled exegetes from earliest times. It was no longer necessary to deny or disguise the discord by harmonizing readings. Many welcomed the new clarity and believed they could now hear the ancient authors' words as they had intended them, unobscured by intervening interpreters. One could now know, or hope to know, the historical Jesus behind the dogmatic portrait. After initial resistance, the new learning made rapid progress in the universities, especially in Germany.

Among most believers and ecclesiastical authorities, however, the new interpretation caused deep consternation. In its focus on the human words of Scripture and natural causality, it appeared to deny or exclude the notion of divine authorship and to leave no room for the action of the Holy Spirit. Whether directly or indirectly, it challenged traditional understandings of the authorship, inspiration, and authority of the Bible. It replaced a divine oracle with a collection of human words, robbing believers of the one sure foundation of faith and casting doubt on the wisdom of the past. At a time when Protestants had elevated the Bible to the position of supreme authority and infallible guide, critical scholarship appeared to many to have turned it into a babble of voices from an alien past without a clear and authoritative word for the present. A new scholarly elite had taken away the Bible so recently restored to the people.

Resistance took many forms and varied according to regional and confessional context, personal disposition, and education. For the broad base of believers, historical-critical scholarship was, and remains in much of the Christian world today, an esoteric science that has obscured the plain meaning of the text. The seeming alliance of Christian scholars with humanists of anti-ecclesiastical and even atheistic bent served to reinforce a latent suspicion of all critical scholarship, leaving a legacy of anti-intellectualism deeply embedded in some streams of Protestantism, in particular in American evangelicalism. The embrace of the new criticism by the Deists in England and its contribution to a radically atheistic rationalism in France led to ecclesiastical responses by both Protestants and Catholics that attempted to maintain the authority and traditional interpretation of the Bible by means of prescriptive confessions and declarations. Scripture was once again subordinated to the ruling authority of the church.

Protestant rhetoric invested supreme authority in the Bible but left unclear where authority for interpretation lay. One stream of the Reformation emphasized the individual conscience, illumined by the Holy Spirit, as the final interpreter, with the Bible as the ultimate source of truth. This emphasis on individual interpretation apart from, or in opposition to, church tradition encouraged fragmentation into new denominations and sects based on differing understandings of particular biblical teachings (e.g., baptism and sabbath observance). The mainstream of Lutheran and Reformed tradition, however, retained a strong sense of the church's teaching and disciplining authority, exercising that authority in attempts to demonstrate and defend the Bible's truth and primacy.

New Locus and Form of Authority. Protestant orthodoxy's attempt to control biblical interpretation was a response not merely to new interpretations that were deemed false and dangerous, but also to a new locus of interpretive activity—hence authority—that was largely outside of ecclesiastical control. The early and strong opposition of Roman Catholic and orthodox Protestant ecclesiastical authorities to the new biblical scholarship had the effect of branding it secular and forcing it into opposition to the church, or at least independence from it. Thus the church contributed to the autonomy of biblical criticism, freeing it from clerical supervision, but also severing its ties to the dogmatic tradition that continued to dominate private devotion and preaching. "Precritical" interpretation continued to be the norm long after critical study had become established in the university, and attempts to open the church's door to the ostracized criticism were hampered by its history of secular development.

It was not simply the secular character of the new biblical scholarship that created a problem of authority in the church, but the independence of the new discipline from dogmatic theology—and from the new "scientific" theology that had emerged from the old biblically oriented dogmatics. The new discipline of biblical studies raises a number of critical new questions concerning authority in biblical interpretation: What is the authority of biblical scholarship in its historical and literary judgments for theological construction and for the faith of believers? Are some methods of interpretation more valid, or more appropriate, than others for use of the Bible as a resource for faith? Are some excluded, and if so, on what grounds? What are the criteria for judging the adequacy or truth of the methods and results of modern critical study of the Bible, and who is qualified to make such judgments?

The questions raised for the church and for traditional belief by all forms of new knowledge and investigation, including biblical studies, are not easily answered. Appeal to old standards in response to new questions may actually serve to undermine the Bible's authority, since these are commonly formulated in propositional forms involving extrinsic norms (such as plenary verbal inspiration, Mosaic authorship, or concepts of historicity and facticity foreign to the biblical writers). Attempts to defend traditional understandings also tend to deny the essential character of Scripture as a bridge between the past and present action of God, by means of which God addresses new generations through words from the past. The expectation of hearing a word for today—hence a new word—is fundamental to the church's understanding of Scripture. This means, however, that the message for the present generation cannot simply be equated with the message spoken to the ancestors. The problem with both historical and dogmatic interpretations of Scripture is that they tend to fix as normative a single meaning at a single time, thereby missing the essential dynamic character of Scripture as the meeting place of past word with an ever-changing present. The word of God becomes imprisoned in the text rather than freed for fresh hearing and response.

Behind the Scenes: Roots of the Great Debate. The roots of the American debate lay in the German universities and the English and Scottish churches. General ecclesiastical resistance to the new criticism was first broken in Germany during the eighteenth and nineteenth centuries, where the relative freedom of the universities from church restraint provided an environment in which the new exploration could take place. But the universities were also the primary centers of theological debate and training of pastors, so that the new study had a significant impact on the church. The result was that Germany pioneered historical-critical study of the Scriptures—as an expression of faith, rather than doubt.

The Battle in Britain. England lagged behind the Continent in accepting a critical approach to the Bible. Ecclesiastical control of the universities and the early Deist controversy gave a different cast to the discussion, as did the Evangelical Revival, which largely ignored the questions raised by the rationalist critique. In Germany, discussion had focused on the problem of relating historical fact to religious truth, or dogma. German theologians responded by developing a science of interpretation (hermeneutics) that would enable movement from historical exegesis to contemporary faith within the framework of the church's traditional confession. In contrast, the English debate focused on the problem of science and faith, and more specifically on the conflict of reason and revelation as defined by early-eighteenth-century Deism.[68] This debate decisively affected the American understanding of the problem.

Deist denial of special divine action or communication in history and its insistence on a universe ruled by divinely instituted laws of nature as revealed by modern science left no room for revelation (identified with miracles) or prophecy and cast doubt on the credibility of the biblical "reports," and hence on the authority of the Bible. An overconfident young science, embraced by critical religious thinkers, forced the argument onto its ground. Defenders of Scripture were pressed into an uncritical stance and responded by asserting the infallibility and the scientific credibility of the Bible in all its statements. Biblical apologists attempted to give scientific proof for the Genesis account of creation, to find evidence of the deluge and Noah's ark, and to defend the Bible's chronology as well as its miracles. In this defense, however, the problems of literalism became ever more evident and the arguments more strained.

The publication in 1859 of Darwin's *On the Origin of Species* directly challenged the literalists' attempt to defend biblical cosmology with a six-day creation in 4004 BCE. Scientists and religious skeptics acclaimed the new theory, as did numerous theologians who saw it as generally supporting current studies on the Pentateuch (which had recognized a development of ideas exhibited in a

---

68. W. Neil, "The Criticism and Theological Use of the Bible, 1700–1950," chap. VII in *The Cambridge History of the Bible,* Vol. 3, The West from the Reformation to the Present Day, ed. S. L. Greenslade (Cambridge: Cambridge University Press, 1963) 251-79.

succession of "documents" discernible within the Pentateuch). But for those who linked the authority of the Bible to literal infallibility, it was a call to arms. In 1864 some 11,000 clergy signed the Oxford Declaration, aimed at countering the new "heresy" by denouncing all who denied that the whole Bible was the word of God. In the view of the signatories, Genesis said all there was to be known about origins; any other view was blasphemy.[69]

The victory, however, was short lived; within three decades, biblical faith had made peace with natural science through the mediation of devout but critical biblical scholars. Contributing factors were the broad support for Darwin's theory of evolution by the scientific and philosophical communities and the arguments of a new generation of biblical scholars influenced by German criticism, who insisted that the Bible should be treated on its own terms, not forced to fit the categories of modern science. The Bible was a book of religious testimony, they insisted, not a manual of science.[70]

New Awakening, New Science. In America, critical biblical study was a foreign import, which did not finally take root until the end of the nineteenth century—although it had been introduced almost a century earlier.[71] The early decades of the nineteenth century saw a new wave of revivalism sweep the country and establish itself on the frontier, giving rise to new denominations and sects and reshaping older ones. This movement, which determined the character and shape of American religion for the rest of the nineteenth century and much of the twentieth, elevated emotion as the sign of authentic religion and emphasized individual decision and simple propositional faith. The Bible figured prominently in the new religious wars over the "essential" content of faith, but the major battle over the Bible did not break until the end of the century.

Renewed contact with the intellectual world beyond America's shores after the disruption of the Civil War brought in rapid succession two new waves of assault on the thought world of most Americans, challenging a broad stratum of the population to come to terms with the scientific world view. Darwin's evolutionary theory had an impact in America similar to that in England, with public debate by national leaders and immediate general rejection. But its rapid acceptance in the scientific community and among the more broadly educated segments of the population led ultimately to wide acceptance of a critical scientific-historical world view. The crisis this caused for traditional religious views was profound and prolonged, however, because the religious regeneration that America had experienced in the New Awakening had been linked to a theological retreat into a rigidly anti-critical defense of "traditional doctrines." The key to the reintegration of the intellectual and religious worlds of devout, but thinking, Christians was critical biblical interpretation. Although its advance was marked by bitter resistance, heresy trials and church divisions, this time it had come to stay.

Inerrancy on Trial: Scholastic and Populist Defense. The Briggs Trial. Biblical criticism came to America in the latter part of the nineteenth century as a mature and established discipline, part of a broad influx of German learning. Many American biblical scholars embraced it eagerly, and conservatives rallied to meet them in battles that affected virtually every American denomination. None was more deeply torn than the Presbyterian Church, whose conflict was symbolized in the heresy trial of Charles Briggs.[72] At his inauguration in 1881 to the chair of Biblical Theology at Union Theological Seminary in New York, Briggs had defended historical criticism, characterizing the dogma of inerrancy as an attempt to "prop up divine authority by human authority." Such errors as historians find cannot destroy the authority of Scripture, he argued, which is from God. Moreover, he insisted, the claim of inerrancy is nowhere made by the Bible itself nor sanctioned by the creeds of the church.

The immediate target of Briggs's attack was an article in the *Presbyterian Review* (April 1881) by Princeton theologian A. A. Hodge and NT scholar Benjamin Warfield. In it they produced a classic statement of the doctrine of scriptural inerrancy.

---

69. Ibid., 257-63.

70. See ibid., 268-72, 279-82, 287-89.

71. Jerry Wayne Brown, *The Rise of Biblical Criticism in America 1800–1870: The New England Scholars* (Middletown, Conn.: Wesleyan University Press, 1969); summary treatment in Phyllis A. Bird, *The Bible as the Church's Book* (Philadelphia: Westminster, 1982) 59-61.

72. Debate over the authority of the Bible centered in the Reformed tradition as carried in this country primarily by the Presbyterian Church; hence our attention to this debate, which made front-page news at the time. The resulting polarization in that church, however, has affected most American denominations, especially those that define themselves as theologically conservative or have significant segments that do. Churches with strong liturgical traditions (Roman Catholic, Orthodox, Episcopalian), liberal orientation (Congregationalist/United Church of Christ), or charismatic emphasis (Pentecostals, until recently) have been less affected, or differently affected, by these debates. See below for the continuing debate.

According to them, the Scriptures not only contain the word of God, but are the word of God; hence all their elements and all their affirmations are absolutely errorless. Apparent inconsistencies and conflicts with other sources of information are due to imperfect copies of the now-lost originals ("autographs") or failure to realize the point of view of the author. In their view: "The historical faith of the Church has always been, that all the affirmations of Scripture of all kinds, whether of spiritual doctrine or duty, or of physical or historical fact, or of psychological or philosophical principle, are without any error, when the *ipsissima verba* of the original autographs are ascertained and interpreted in their natural and intended sense."[73]

This statement was adopted as the official position of the Presbyterian Church, and Briggs was suspended from the Presbyterian ministry on grounds of heresy—retaining his chair, however, as the seminary severed its denominational ties. The "Princeton theology" had won the battle of the Bible, at least for the time—but its time was measured. A half century later, biblical study at Princeton was taught with the same critical assumptions and the same methodologies as at Union. By the third decade of this century, a critical approach to the Bible was the norm in the seminaries of all of the older denominations, if not in the pew. And in the middle of the century the Roman Catholic Church, the only Western church that had officially condemned historical-critical study of the Bible, opened its doors to it and commended it as a pastoral tool. Today many evangelicals are also cautiously appropriating its methods and perspective. The shift in stance, which is still contested in significant segments of the church, came about as the church came to see the new scholarship as an ally, rather than an enemy, of faith.

The backbone of Presbyterian resistance in the twentieth century was the "Princeton Theology," an expression of post-Reformation scholasticism deriving from Turretin and the Westminster Confession.[74] Hodge contributed to this theology by shifting attention from the Confession to the Bible as the final authority for the system of theology presented therein. He also gave the first systematic treatment to the doctrine of inspiration. "Inspiration," he wrote, "was an influence of the Holy Spirit on the minds of certain select men, which rendered them the organs of God for infallible communication of his mind and will. They were in such a sense the organs of God, that what they said, God said."[75] Maintaining that this view was "the common doctrine of the Church" since the beginning, Hodge appeared unaware of the concept of accommodation common to the early church theologians and the Reformers.

The Princeton Theology linked the authority of Scripture to its inerrant words, treating the Bible as a repository of information on all manner of things, whose accuracy had to be defended by current standards.[76] Scripture was understood as divine speech in universally valid and universally intelligible form, in which historical and cultural contexts played an insignificant role. This frozen view of Scripture had widespread appeal, and continues to appeal to those who seek a changeless word in changing times. In America the last decades of the nineteenth century and the first decades of the twentieth century were times when the world was changing too fast for many. Current revival of the debates of that period is likewise a response to rapidly changing times and uncertain, or conflicting, values.

The Scopes Trial. A distinctive feature of the inerrantist debate in America has been the coupling of rationalistic scholasticism, as represented by the old Princeton school, with fundamentalist, and populist, anti-intellectualism.[77] These two strains within the inerrantist camp are symbolized by the two debates that galvanized opinion: the Briggs trial of 1891, featuring two eastern seminary professors, and the Scopes trial of 1925, featuring a frontier school teacher, represented by an atheist "big-city"

73. Cited by Rogers and McKim, *Authority,* 169.

74. To which all Princeton faculty were required to subscribe; Rogers and McKim, *Authority,* 200-203, 279-80, 357-58.

75. Charles Hodge, *Systematic Theology,* 3 vols. (Grand Rapids: Eerdmans, 1960) 1:154.

76. E.g., Hodge declared that "the Bible is to the theologian what nature is to the man of science. It is his store-house of facts; and his method of ascertaining what the Bible teaches, is the same as that which the natural philosopher adopts to ascertain what nature teaches" (*Systematic Theology,* 1:10).

77. Anti-intellectualism does not define fundamentalism, but represents a deep-seated and broad impulse in American religious consciousness. It does provide fertile ground, however, for fundamentalist arguments, as illustrated by Harold Lindsell in his widely read book *The Battle for the Bible* (Grand Rapids: Zondervan, 1970). In it, he attempted to win over the Southern Baptist Church to the inerrantist position by sounding the alarm against the critical biblical interpretation invading the seminaries. "Godly men through the ages," he argued, "have come to the Scriptures without advanced theological training and have been better interpreters and more spiritual leaders than many who have undergone the most rigorous theological training" (7). Lindsell's is not the first, nor the last, attempt to rally devout laity against the seminaries, or to control intellectual inquiry.

lawyer, and an evangelical populist politician. The latter trial was a key battle for fundamentalism, which had made inerrancy its touchstone. It provided a national forum for its cause, but also subjected it to a devastating media attack.[78]

Fundamentalism arose in the early decades of this century out of the old revivalist evangelicalism that had been the Protestant establishment in nineteenth-century America, but found itself increasingly challenged or eclipsed by the rise of new philosophies of life and new religious perspectives. Its primary target was the new liberal theology (later called "Modernism") that attempted to integrate the findings of science, biblical criticism, and historical studies and reformulate Christian doctrine in their light. Distrusting the new syntheses, traditional Protestants emphasized a simple Bible-centered theology, whose appeal was strengthened by the perplexing array of new alternatives. Between 1920 and 1925 the movement gave particular attention to the teaching of evolution in the public schools, culminating in the Scopes "monkey trial," which served as a public debate between Fundamentalism and Modernism.

John Scopes, a Tennessee biology teacher, was charged with violating a state law against the teaching of Darwinism in the public schools. He was defended by ACLU lawyer Clarence Darrow, whose primary aim was to ridicule and humiliate those who would bring such a charge. While Darrow's immediate target was the lawyer for the prosecution, the famous politician and orator William Jennings Bryan, he meant to discredit fundamentalists generally as well as the "stage of civilization" of the state of Tennessee.

Bryan, a lay preacher and ardent champion of social reform, had become obsessed with the question of evolution, because of the social Darwinism he identified with it. Opposing the notion that the strongest must prevail in society, he entered the fray, but allowed himself to be discredited when he attempted to defend the Bible's science. With the national media covering the debate, Darrow forced Bryan into an untenable literalist position; and although Darrow lost the case (later reversed on a technicality), he succeeded in portraying the fundamentalist position as intellectually untenable. Americans in the 1920s were generally enthusiastic believers in science, and that included many moderate Protestant conservatives, who quietly withdrew their support from the fundamentalist movement after 1925.

That did not mean the end of the movement, however, nor did it signal a general willingness to accord religious scholarship the same trust and awe as scientific expertise. Fundamentalism continued to thrive in local congregations, Bible schools, mission organizations, and through various media, and it remains a significant force today, although splintered into a number of factions. Distrust of biblical scholarship continues among a wide spectrum of believers who share Bryan's conviction that "the one beauty about the word of God is that it does not take an expert to understand it."[79]

CURRENT ISSUES AND OPTIONS

New Evangelicalism. Contemporary evangelicalism represents a complex phenomenon, whose diversity has been analyzed in a variety of ways.[80] Despite wide differences of theology and ecclesiology, evangelicals share a common emphasis on the final, or sole, authority of the Bible. In their emphasis on the primacy of Scripture, they understand themselves as maintaining the ancient faith of the church in the tradition of the Reformers, defending it against modern forms of perversion and erosion.

Within evangelicalism, differing theological positions are associated with differing ways of describing or appealing to the authority of the Bible.[81] Thus fundamentalists and other conservative evangelicals generally prefer the term *inerrancy* to describe their understanding, insisting that it is "the badge of evangelicalism."[82] The language of "inerrancy" emphasizes the necessary relationship between the accuracy of the words and the authority of the message, often extending the claims to historical and scientific statements as well as spiritual and moral teachings. An example of this position is provided by "The Chicago Statement on Biblical Inerrancy"

---

78. See Garry Wills, *Under God: Religion and American Politics* (New York: Simon and Schuster, 1990) 97-124, for a discerning analysis of the religiopolitical aspects of the trial.

79. Quoted by Wills, *Under God,* 112.
80. See George M. Marsden, *Understanding Fundamentalism and Evangelicalism* (Grand Rapids: Eerdmans, 1991); cf. Sheppard, "Hermeneutics," 82-83.
81. See Donald K. McKim, *The Bible in Theology and Preaching* (Nashville: Abingdon, 1994) 52-62, 76-86; Mark A. Noll, "Evangelicals and the Study of the Bible," chap. 9 in *Evangelicalism and Modern America,* ed. George Marsden (Grand Rapids: Eerdmans, 1984) 103-21; and Sheppard, "Hermeneutics," for evangelical views and uses of Scripture.
82. Lindsell, cited by McKim, *The Bible in Theology and Preaching,* 89; see Noll, "Inerrancy," for a survey of evangelical debate over the term.

(1979), which bears a close resemblance to the Hodge and Warfield statement.[83]

The "Chicago Statement" represents an attempt to reassert an older view of scriptural authority in the face of a new evangelicalism, which began to emerge in the 1940s and departed in various ways from its fundamentalist roots. Neo-evangelicalism represented a resurgence of evangelicalism in a postmodern milieu in which neither the old liberal nor fundamentalist positions seemed adequate. Arising from a stagnant and defensive fundamentalism, the new evangelicals rejected the separatism, sectarianism, and social conservatism of their once-vital parent. In their attempts to move evangelicalism into the mainstream of American society and religion, they have been drawn increasingly into the world of contemporary biblical scholarship. Thus new evangelicals commonly exhibit some degree of openness to modern, historically informed understandings of Scripture and doctrine and consequently reject efforts to bind Scripture to eighteenth- and nineteenth-century understandings of inspiration and truth.

While new evangelicals represent a considerable spectrum within evangelicalism and define their positions in different terms, most tend to prefer the language of "infallibility" to describe their confidence in Scripture as the authoritative word of God. They are no less committed than fundamentalists to upholding the authority of the Bible, but they understand its message and purpose differently—and thus operate with different hermeneutics. For new evangelicals, the purpose of Scripture is to "bring people to faith and salvation in Jesus Christ." It accomplishes this purpose as "a book that presents a gospel message of salvation received, interpreted, and handed over by men," not a timeless truth or idea. The authority of its message is established by the witness of the Holy Spirit, not by rational argument. Thus *inerrancy* is viewed as an inappropriate and misleading term for describing the basis of the Bible's claim to authority. As a book whose purposes are theological, rather than scientific or historical, its "complete trustworthiness and its ability to accomplish its purpose" is better affirmed, they believe, by the term *infallible.*[84]

Ecumenical Perspectives. The prominence of evangelicalism in the history of American religious life has meant that its preoccupation with the question of biblical authority has generally set the terms for addressing the subject. Ecumenical discussion fostered by the World Council of Churches and the contributions of a vigorous and theologically grounded Catholic biblical scholarship in the last half of this century have brought new perspectives and a broader horizon to the question, which is still largely neglected in most general treatments of the subject.[85] Ecumenical consideration of the place of the Bible in the churches' attempts to articulate their unity has led Protestants to acknowledge a much greater role of tradition in shaping doctrine and uses of Scripture than confessions generally admit. And although evangelicals have generally remained outside these discussions, a similar recognition has begun to emerge concerning the role of church and tradition in evangelical interpretation. What has been learned from ecumenical discussion is what the history of the Bible itself has taught us: The Bible is the creation of the church and reflects, as well as directs, the church's understanding in its continuing interpretation and use. Behind slogans of "Scripture alone" are the realities of community faith and doctrine, which have an inescapably particular, and therefore plural, character when viewed from the perspective of the church as a whole.[86]

While Protestants have gained new appreciation for the church and tradition in their understanding of Scripture and scriptural authority, Roman Catholics have elevated the place of Scripture within the church and redefined tradition. It is now widely believed that the traditional two-source theory misrepresented the Council of Trent, which held a more unified view of Scripture and tradition, and that its

---

83. The "Chicago Statement" is a nineteen-article statement defining the "biblical and historic position on the inerrancy of Scripture," formulated by the International Conference on Biblical Inerrancy, an ecumenical assembly that met in Chicago in 1978. Norman Geissler, who edited the papers from the conference, introduces the "Statement" by highlighting the connection with authority: The authority of Scripture is a key issue for the Christian Church in this and every age. . . . Recognition of the total truth and trustworthiness of Holy Scripture is essential to a full grasp and adequate confession of its authority (Norman L. Geisler, ed. *Inerrancy* [Grand Rapids: Zondervan, 1979] ix). In the statement, both "inerrancy" and "infallibility" are used to describe "the total truth and trustworthiness of Holy Scripture" (ibid., 493). See Articles XI, XII, and XIX.

84. McKim, *The Bible in Theology and Preaching,* 87-99.
85. Exceptions seem to depend on Roman Catholic contributors, exemplified by the final chapter in Gnuse, *Authority,* "Ecumenical Discussion: Scripture and Tradition," 113-21, and Avery Dulles, "Scripture: Recent Protestant and Catholic Views," *Theology Today* 37, 1 (April 1980) 7-26. Space is lacking in this article for an adequate review of the important series of consultations and documents sponsored by the World Council of Churches, in which both Roman Catholic and Orthodox views were represented, as well as a broad spectrum of Protestantism. See Flesseman-van Leer, *The Bible.*
86. Flesseman-van Leer, *The Bible,* 1-12.

equation of the two sources is unacceptable. In reinterpreting the Tridentine statement, Vatican II substituted "tradition" for "traditions," understanding it as a fluid and dynamic process, rather than a collection of beliefs, directives, etc. Tradition is described as "the presence of Christ in the faith of the Church manifesting itself anew for each generation. . . . [It] makes Scripture available and understandable to a changing and imperfect world where the biblical text must be reinterpreted."[87] This understanding has much in common with Protestant notions of the living Word and the Holy Spirit as the author and interpreter of Scripture. The main difference between converging Protestant and Roman Catholic views of Scripture remains authority for interpretation, with Protestants unwilling to hand this over to the church, and Catholics unwilling to entrust it to unqualified or unscrupulous exegetes.

At the same time that greater variety has been recognized in understanding and using the Bible, and hence variety in the ways its authority is conceived and actualized, a new and broad consensus has been achieved concerning the meaning of the Scriptures in their ancient contexts of origin.[88] This consensus spans confessional, and even religious, divisions, creating a new meeting place for biblical scholars—and a new set of questions for the churches. But it also contributes positively to reformulating the question of authority. Through its recognition of the irreducible plurality of perspectives and theologies within the Bible itself, modern biblical scholarship has occasioned a more dynamic conception of the Bible's message, a search for continuities rather than a center and acknowledgment of contextual factors in the communication of divine truth. It has thereby provided a bridge to the pluralistic and conflicted world of the present, in which the word of Scripture can carry the authority of the word of God only as it addresses individuals and communities in their specific needs, while simultaneously witnessing to the oneness of God, whose purposes are the redemption and *shalom* of the whole creation. Modern historical understanding of the Bible also suggests that the Bible's authority does not rest in its word alone, as declarative utterance or command, but in its nature as the witness of a community to the source of its life and the record of its continual struggle to comprehend the new thing God is doing in creation. Thus

the Bible presents itself as a book of questions as well as answers, and it has authority insofar as it compels us to engage those questions with our own experience.

Feminist Critique. As early Christians found much within the Jewish Scriptures morally and intellectually incompatible with their faith in Christ, so feminists today find much within the two-part canon morally offensive and incompatible with the message of the gospel as they have come to understand it. And as early Christians took different paths in responding to the perceived defect of the Scriptures, so too do feminists today.[89]

Those in the early church whose position would ultimately receive the stamp of orthodoxy insisted that the witness to God's activity in the ages prior to Christ was essential to Christian understanding. In order to retain that witness they developed various means of interpretation that subordinated, reinterpreted (by figurative and allegorical means), or dismissed as no longer relevant passages that appeared incompatible with later belief. A similar approach is taken by some feminists today. But the enterprise of recovering a liberating message from a sexist text involves a more radical assessment of the problem of Scripture, for it is apparent that the patriarchal and/or androcentric bias that feminists identify as a sinful betrayal or denial of the gospel is deeply embedded in the texts of both testaments—and also in the communities behind the texts.

Feminist theology shares in large measure the basic hermeneutical stance of other liberationist theologies, but it exhibits a stronger sense of disparity between the gospel as transmitted historically through Scripture, creeds, and church teaching and God's intention for humanity as discerned through the contemporary working of the Holy Spirit, in communities outside the church as well as within.[90]

87. Gnuse, *Authority,* 116.
88. Scholarly disputes generally remain within a common realm of discourse, however disparate the views; and they are not primarily governed by confessional differences.

89. See Katharine Doob Sakenfeld, "Feminist Perspectives on Bible and Theology: An Introduction to Selected Issues and Literature," *Int* 42 (1988) 5-18; Carolyn Osiek, "The Feminist and the Bible: Hermeneutical Alternatives," in *Feminist Perspectives on Biblical Scholarship,* ed. Adela Yarbro Collins (Chico, Calif.: Scholars Press, 1985); cf. McKim, *The Bible in Theology and Preaching,* 172-91.
90. Feminism is a complex movement uniting women inside and outside the church and in other religious bodies. Despite wide differences, most are united in condemning biblical patriarchy, and for many, including some feminist theologians and biblical scholars, this means rejecting the Bible's authority. Feminism is also characterized by an emphasis on the authority of experience, in particular, women's shared experience of oppression. Thus a key issue in feminist theology is the question of how this source of authority relates to the authority of the Bible and tradition. On the special problem of the Bible for Protestant feminists, see Mary Ann Tolbert, "Protestant Feminists and the Bible: On the Horns of a Dilemma," in *The Pleasure of Her Text: Feminist Readings of the Biblical and Historical Texts,* ed. Alice Bach (Philadelphia: Trinity International, 1990) 5-23. There is no single feminist theology, and affinities with liberation theologies are not claimed by all feminists.

For most feminists, in contrast to other liberationists, the record of the past contains no model for the future, no core of tradition untainted by patriarchy—although some find a message of equality in an original Jesus tradition, and in selected texts and traditions of both testaments when read with a feminist hermeneutic. Whether they acknowledge such a "subversive memory" in the text, feminists in general regard the memory of the past as recorded and brought into the present by Scripture as failure to grasp and actualize the will of God, rather than faithfulness. The Bible, they insist, presents a deficient and distorted witness to God's nature and purposes by virtue of its androcentrism.

Reaffirmations. Feminist critique represents the most radical form of the contemporary questioning of biblical authority, often extending to the notion of authority itself.[91] Any affirmation of the authority of Scripture today must take account of that critique, which requires clarification of what is essential to the claim. Different assessments and different formulations will be made according to the believer's experience, theology, and social or ecclesial context. The following is one attempt to reaffirm the authority of the Bible in light of feminist critique and modern biblical scholarship. It is not intended as a comprehensive statement, but as a concluding summary of the preceding arguments.

Feminist critique contributes two fundamental assertions that correlate closely with two essential affirmations of traditional understanding of the Bible and biblical authority. The first is the recognition of the pervasive androcentrism in the text and the culture, which serves as a needed reminder that Scripture is a human product and instrument and, therefore, culturally conditioned and limited—a feature of Scripture that has been affirmed in every age, even as every age has attempted to deny or minimize it. The Bible conveys the word of God, or becomes the word of God, only as fully human words, the record of human thought and experience. The

temptation in claiming divine authority for Scripture has always been to deny its fundamental human character. The offense of the Bible's androcentrism provides a needed reminder that its words and ideas, as our own, are culturally conditioned. It is also a reminder that the Bible is the record of a sinful people—fearful, shortsighted, rebellious, like ourselves—a record of betrayal as well as faithfulness to the revelation they had received. The authority of Scripture does not depend on infallible words or model behavior but in the ability of its words to confront readers with the story and the presence of a God who redeems sinners by assuming their weakness, and empowers the weak and the silent (or silenced) with visions and with speech.

The second assertion is the ground of the first: Feminist critique of androcentrism is rooted in the conviction that it is a perversion of the gospel, or of God's intention for creation. The condemnation points to continuing recognition of a norm within the tradition, and the Scriptures with which the tradition is bound. Feminist critique is rooted in the gospel, or in an ideal of full humanity that is consonant with the gospel. Whatever the ultimate origin of the shared sense of injustice over patriarchal structures of social organization and meaning, Christian feminists find resources of judgment and alternative vision in the gospel transmitted by the church and informed by the Scriptures. That affirmation, which is made in different ways by different feminist theologians, is evidence of the Bible's continuing authority, even where it is sharply limited or formally denied. And it is consonant with the traditional understanding of a norm within Scripture, interpreting and judging Scripture. The Bible's authority rests in its ability to confront readers or hearers with the gospel so that it is heard not merely as a historical word, but as a present assurance and demand.

The authority of the Bible is communal, requiring individual confirmation. It is, therefore, marked by inevitable tension and is always in the process of being reconstituted. Affirmation of biblical authority is indispensable to Christian identity and belief, but it does not compel assent to any particular interpretation of content—only hearing, with a disposition to hear a word from God. That predisposition to hearing is a sign of the Bible's authority. The Bible

---

91. Feminists are not alone in questioning or rejecting the concept of authority. Rejection of authority has commonly been associated with liberal theology and a modern critical spirit. The association of authority with hierarchical systems of social organization and value is, however, closely tied to feminist analysis of patriarchy. Much of feminist, as well as general, critique of authority falsely identifies it with authoritarianism. Authority can be expressed in forms of mutual respect and obligation and does not depend on hierarchical structures or arbitrary exercise of power. For a feminist attempt at reformulating the concept of authority, and debate over the usefulness or necessity of the concept, see Letty M. Russell, *Household of Freedom: Authority in Feminist Theology* (Philadelphia: Westminster, 1987).

comes to each reader or hearer with the church's commendation and testimony that God has spoken through its words and will continue to speak through them. For Christians, the Bible is not a neutral or unknown entity, however unknown its actual content; it bears credentials and a burden of expectations. But the authority that gives it a hearing can be retained only as it is reconfirmed through fresh encounter with the text and appropriation of its message. This reappropriation is both an individual and a communal task.

The Bible means different things to different people, but Christians are not free to construct their own meanings apart from the community that created and transmitted the Scriptures—however painful that relationship. The Bible is the church's book and never stands alone, despite Protestant declarations of *sola scriptura;* nor does it simply stand alongside tradition, as the traditional Catholic theory of two sources suggested. Rather, Scripture is both a product of tradition and a part of the church's ongoing tradition, and it cannot be interpreted as a document of faith apart from that context of communal interpretation and use. Communal authority does not demand consensus, but it does demand engagement. The Bible exercises no authority for those who cease to listen or to struggle with it. While the degree of dissent tolerated by communities and individuals varies widely, unanimity of belief is not a demand of biblical authority.

The Bible's authority is grounded in past experience, which is never sufficient for an ever-changing present.[92] The insufficiency of past formulations of belief as contained in Scripture, and tradition, is seen with particular clarity by feminists in their identification of the patriarchal stamp of all our inherited institutions and ideas. Feminist insistence that past understanding, however profound and essential to Christian identity, is not sufficient for the future exposes false bases of biblical authority. The reason why the Bible continues to exercise authority for successive generations in ever new situations is that it points beyond itself to God, whose purposes and nature are never fully or finally expressed in historical communications. Even in its function as memory, the Bible witnesses to a dynamic relationship at the heart of its testimony.

The Bible's authority derives from God, but it must be understood in terms appropriate to the medium in which it operates. The Bible comes to us as literature, a human, historical product combining memory, art, and reason in the attempts of a community to comprehend and confess its encounter with the divine. Its multivocal and multivalent witness comprises the testimony of more than a millennium, framed in different languages and idioms, in different political and cultural contexts. As the record of many voices, speaking in harmony and discord, its authority is exercised through the conversation, not by suppressing or harmonizing the multiple voices. The church is obliged by the form of its Scriptures to listen for the voice of God in the dialogue of a community. It acknowledges the authority of Book and Author by continuing that dialogue.

The Bible's authority does not rest in the infallibility of its statements, but in the truth of its witness to a creating and redeeming power, which can and must be known as a present reality. The Bible as the word of God in human words exhibits the cultural limits and sinful distortions of humanity in every age, witnessing thereby to the central affirmation of Christian faith that God is most fully and truly revealed in assuming this same human nature. The Bible shares the incarnational character of the One to whom it bears witness. It proclaims by its composition as well as its declarations that the Creator has chosen to be revealed in creation, even coming among us as one of us. But that manifestation does not exhaust or circumscribe the divine presence or power, and the word by which that action is recalled and re-presented is only the servant of the living Word. The words of God spoken to prophets and poets are essential to Christian faith and carry the authority of their Speaker, but the word of God cannot be contained in any document; nor can it be comprehended apart from the Word made flesh, which is both the center and the norm of Scripture.

92. This is not a denial of the sufficiency of Scripture to awaken faith or serve as a ground and norm of belief; it is, rather, recognition of the inadequacy of all past knowledge.

BIBLIOGRAPHY

Achtemeier, Paul J. *The Inspiration of Scripture: Problems and Proposals.* Biblical Perspectives on Current Issues. Philadelphia: Westminster, 1980. Not a discussion of authority *per se,* but an analysis of a key idea in theories of scriptural authority.

Barton, John. *People of the Book? The Authority of the Bible in Christianity.* Louisville: Westminster/John Knox, 1988. A reformulation of the meaning of biblical authority by a British biblical scholar in dialogue with fundamentalist views.

Flesseman-van Leer, Ellen, ed. *The Bible: Its Authority and Interpretation in the Ecumenical Movement.* Faith and Order Paper 99. Geneva: World Council of Churches, 1980. An analysis of issues identified in a series of ecumenical studies between 1949 and 1978.

Gnuse, Robert. *The Authority of the Bible: Theories of Inspiration, Revelation and the Canon of Scripture.* New York: Paulist, 1985. A Roman Catholic perspective by an American biblical scholar.

Jodock, Darrell. *The Church's Bible: Its Contemporary Authority.* Minneapolis: Fortress, 1989. A constructive Lutheran approach based on the collaboration of a historical theologian and a biblical scholar.

Rogers, Jack B., and Donald K. McKim. *The Authority of the Bible: An Historical Approach.* San Francisco: Harper & Row, 1979. An attempt to reclaim a Reformed tradition eclipsed by post-Reformation scholasticism.

HOW THE BIBLE HAS BEEN INTERPRETED IN JEWISH TRADITION

MICHAEL A. SIGNER

From the return of the community after the Babylonian exile in the sixth century BCE, the Bible and its interpretation played a central role in the life of the Jewish people. In Neh 8:1-8, Ezra reads from the book of the Law of God. He is surrounded by the priests who translate and interpret it to the people. These two activities of reading the word of God and making the divine message comprehensible so that it may be applied in the life of Israel provide the boundaries for all descriptions of biblical studies in Judaism. Generations of teachers and students have demonstrated concern for the sacred character of its words and their transmission. In addition, they have continually reinterpreted these words in the light of their contemporary milieu. This dynamic approach to the possibility of interpreting the word of God has provided Judaism with the opportunity for renewal throughout its history.

The term *Bible* is somewhat alien to Jewish religious discourse. Scripture is referred to as מקרא (*Miqrā'*, "what is read") or כתבי קודש (*Kitbê Qôdeš*, "sacred writings"). The most frequently used word is תורה (*Tôrâ*, "teaching"). When referring to the entire corpus of biblical books, Jews use the Hebrew acronym תנך (TNK), which represents the threefold division of the canon into תורה (*Tôrâ*, the Five Books of Moses), נביאים (*Nĕbî'îm*, Prophets—Joshua–2 Kings, Isaiah, Jeremiah, Ezekiel, and the Twelve Minor Prophets), and כתובים (*Kĕtûbîm*, Writings—Psalms, Proverbs, Job, Song of Songs, Ruth, Lamentations, Ecclesiastes, Esther, Daniel, Ezra, Nehemiah, and 1–2 Chronicles). This order of the books, which appears in the Babylonian Talmud tractate *Baba Batra* 14b, indicates that for Jews the canon of Scripture ends with a narration of the return of the Jewish community to its homeland by the order of Cyrus.

All three sections of Scripture are called "Torah" in an effort to maintain the unity within divine revelation. However, it is clear that the Five Books of Moses have, since antiquity, been understood as the most sacred. Passages from the Prophets or Writings are always interpreted to harmonize with the Pentateuch.

The scroll of the Pentateuch has been part of the liturgical life of the synagogue since the classical rabbinic period. There is a body of laws that govern the material to be used for writing, how it is sewn together, and how it is used during worship. By contrast, the prophetic books and hagiographa, which were written on scrolls during the Tannaitic and Amoraic periods (the first five hundred years of the Common Era), have been read from codices in the synagogues since the Middle Ages.

Torah is understood as the "Tree of Life" that provides a path for Jews to fulfill the will of their creator. Until the modern period, the task of interpretation was assumed by the Rabbis. Their exegesis was developed through many genres: *Midrash* (מדרש Homilies), *Perush* (פרוש Commentaries), *Piyyut* (פיוט religious poetry), Legal Codes and Responsa (responses to questions), and philosophical and mystical treatises. It would be fair to conclude that no genre of post-biblical Jewish literature is unrelated to the explication of Scripture.

At the core of Jewish scriptural interpretation is the conviction that the Hebrew language is sacred because it is identified with the divine speech. For this reason the Rabbis, as early as the second century CE, attempted to define the limits of interpretation. There were those who believed that every word or, indeed, every letter could form the basis for interpretation. These rabbis, whom we might call "maximalists," thought that even the decorations or crowns on the letters should be interpreted. In contrast, other rabbis thought that "Scripture speaks in human language." The position of the "minimalists" was that God had accommodated human beings, endowing them with reason, and had revealed Torah in terms that required a logical approach to exegesis. From their perspective, Scripture was subject to the same rules of interpretation as any language. Words could not be fragmented, or twisted out of context. The tension between "minimalist" and "maximalist" types of interpretation can be translated in two technical terms used throughout the history of Jewish exegesis: פשט (*Peshat,* or "plain meaning") and דרש (*Derash,* or "homiletical meaning"). In the medieval and modern periods, there has been a preference to claim that *Peshat* has represented the higher aim of Jewish interpretation. However, a survey of Jewish biblical exegesis indicates that *Derash* has been a constant impetus for creativity. It may be claimed that what was *Peshat* for one generation became *Derash* for the next. As a religious community, Jews sought to ground the reinterpretation of their traditions within the context of Scripture and its language. Therefore, both *Peshat* and *Derash* in dialectical tension provide vital elements for interpretation.

One can chart the most significant reformulations of Judaism throughout its history by noting the developments within scriptural interpretation. In each era there are three significant spheres of exegetical activity. The first is at the lexical or philological level. The ancient Rabbis and their successors were concerned with the interpretation of Scripture

so that it could be appreciated by the community. In the medieval and modern periods one can discern that translation of the Bible into the contemporary vernacular is a significant part of exegetical activity. The second area is a focus on the sequence or coherence of the biblical text. Innovations in grammar and syntax made this a particularly creative field of Jewish exegesis. This area brought contemporary concerns into tension with classical rabbinic explanations of Scripture so that *Peshat* and *Derash* could be harmonized. The third domain of exegetical reformulation concentrated on harmonizing the traditional concerns of Scripture with elements of contemporary culture. As philosophical or scientific developments in non-Jewish culture became the subject of controversy, the genre of biblical interpretation became a significant locus for Jewish self-expression and polemics about the boundaries of the secular world and sacred text.

THE CLASSICAL PERIOD

The Rabbis, who emerged as religious leaders after the destruction of the Temple in 70 CE, provided the lenses through which the Jewish people have viewed the biblical text. From their perspective, Moses received both a written and an oral Torah at Sinai. The latter was a complete revelation of all possible interpretations of the written document.

God said to Moses: "Write these things, for it is by means of these things that I have made a covenant with Israel." (Exod 34:27) When God was about to give the Torah, He recited it to Moses in proper order, Scriptures, Mishnah, Aggadah, and Talmud, for God spoke all these words (Exod 20:1), even the answers to questions which distinguished scholars in the future are destined to ask their teachers did God reveal to Moses![1]

The interpretations of the written law—while known to Moses—were to be "discovered" by subsequent generations of teachers who would make them known to their students. Torah study became the process for resolving the contradictions between the contemporary world of the interpreters and the written and oral law.

Rabbinic Judaism is, therefore, a religion of a dual canon constituted by written and oral Torah wherein the structure of Jewish interpretation since the beginning of the third century CE has been

1. *Tanhuma* Buber (1885), *Ki Tissa* 58b.

grounded on the presumption that revelation of both Torahs was simultaneous. The Rabbis simply worked out the revelation that had taken place at Sinai "in proper order." One rabbinic text interpreted Eccl 12:11, "The words of the Sages are like goads [*Kaddorbānot*] which are given from one shepherd" in the following way:

Rabbi Berechiah said: What is the meaning of "like goads" (כדרבנות *Kaddorbā̄nôt*)? It means כדר בנות *Kaddur Banot,* a girl's ball, which maidens toss in sport from one to another. So it is when the Sages enter the house of study, and are occupied with Torah. One says its meaning is this, and another says its meaning is that. One gives such an opinion; his fellow a different one. But they were all "given from one shepherd"—that is from Moses who received the teaching from God who is One and unique in the world.[2]

The "play" of rabbinic interpretation is evidenced in the document that the Rabbis considered fundamental to oral law, the Mishnah (משנה teaching or repetition). As the passage cited previously from Tanchuma indicates, Miqra and Mishnah constituted a single revelation. According to rabbinic tradition, Mishnah was compiled by Rabbi Judah the Patriarch, based on the oral traditions of his predecessors who were called "Tannaim." Some modern scholars have emphasized the independence of the Mishnah from the biblical text with respect to its formal structure and language. From the perspective of the history of Judaism, the Mishnah is a seminal document for all subsequent interpretations of Scripture regarding religious practice.

Moreover, it is possible to discern motifs congruent with the biblical canon within the six divisions סדרים (*Sedarim*) of the Mishnah.[3] Although the Mishnah has a complex textual tradition that indicates that there were various arrangements of its six divisions, there is a strong conjunction between the order in which the Sedarim were traditionally studied and biblical motifs from the creation of the world in Genesis through the eschatological themes of the restoration of the Temple.

The correlation of biblical and mishnaic themes commences in the first order, *Zeraim,* which focuses on appropriate times for acknowledging the divine through prayer, and on the holiness of the land of Israel through appropriate giving of tithes. This set of legal practices is linked to the pentateuchal

themes of Genesis and Deuteronomy, which focus on the creation of the earth, its seasons, and the role Israel has undertaken as the covenanted people of God. The next order, *Moed,* begins with a description of the sabbath laws and continues with explanations of the biblical festivals: Passover, Pentecost, and Tabernacles. This order develops the pentateuchal themes of how the people of Israel serve God both within and beyond the borders of the Land. *Neziqin* concentrates on laws of property and personal injury, while *Nashim* provides details on the legal procedure for marriage, divorce, and adulterous relationships. These Sedarim rooted solidly in the legislative sections of Exodus, Leviticus, and Deuteronomy, contribute a more profound characterization of the place of human interaction in the Jewish community.

From the idea of the earth and its creatures and their obligation to the divine, the Mishnah shifts ground to a discussion of how human beings ought to behave toward one another. In the remaining two Sedarim, which delineate the laws of *Qodashim* (Holy Things) and *Tohorot* (Purities), the Mishnah describes practices that relate to the Temple cult and priestly activities. Later generations of Rabbis would draw upon these orders for such practical issues as the ritual slaughter of animals for human consumption and other dietary laws, or the laws of women's menstrual purity. Even though many of the laws delineated in the Mishnah were no longer in practice since the Temple had been destroyed for more than a century, the Rabbis included them. This was most likely because of their hope that the Temple would be restored and the exile brought to a conclusion. One rabbinic tradition states, "Scholars who occupy themselves with the halakhot [laws] of the Temple are regarded by Scripture as if the Temple had been rebuilt in their time." The Mishnah thereby encompasses all scriptural concerns from the creation of the world to the hope for the coming of the messiah and the vindication of the people Israel.

The Mishnah indicates the centrality of Scripture in religious practice. Tractate *Berakhot* (Blessings) provides evidence that the Rabbis had fixed, "Hear O Israel, the Lord is our God, the Lord is One" (Deut 6:4) as a significant liturgical text that was recited in the evening and morning prayer together with other passages from the Torah. In tractate *Megilla* (Scroll) is a description of the appropriate Torah lections for the festivals and special sabbaths. Furthermore, the legal

2. *Pesiq. R.* 8a.
3. The six major divisions of the Mishnah comprise sixty-three tractates, each ranging from three to twenty-four chapters.

passages in Exodus 21–23 provide the basis for an elaborate conceptual scheme of torts and damages in tractates *Baba Qama, Baba Metzi'a,* and *Baba Batra.* The Rabbis traced their own legitimacy as divinely sanctioned interpreters of Torah in tractate *Abot.* Although there are profound formal differences between the Mishnah and Scripture, the two documents complement each other.

Mishnah provided the primary text of interpretation in the rabbinic academies in Palestine and Babylon from the third until the sixth or seventh centuries.[4] Those rabbinic expositions, called גמרא (Gemara), focus on the source of authority or reasoning within the Mishnah. Together the Mishnah and the Gemara constitute what the Rabbis called תלמוד ("Talmud"[5]). Two categories of interpretation develop in the Talmuds written in both Israel and Babylonia. One method, known as Halakha, focuses on the development of a body of ritual and civil legal practice for the Jewish community. Although the Gemara does not define a unified body of law, its dialectical arguments illustrate a variety of approaches to any single issue. In the Talmud many discussions of the Mishnaic text can be understood as the attempt to find the appropriate biblical warrant for the Mishnah. The second method, no less important, was the development of the Aggadah. In these passages the Rabbis allow their imagination to function freely, developing theological and ethical principles. Biblical narratives are developed to reveal the intention of obscure biblical texts, or passages the Rabbis found incompatible with their understanding of the texts. For example, the call of Hosea to marry a harlot (Hos 1:2) is introduced by the Rabbis in the form of a dialogue between the prophet and God. Hosea expresses anger and disappointment at the behavior of the people. He urges God to abandon them to the punishment of exile. God then decides that Hosea must discover for himself how profound God's bond with Israel might be, and orders him to marry a woman of harlotry (*Pesiq. R.* 87:a-b). Halakhah and Aggadah, though not specifically distinguished in the text of the Talmuds, parallel the legal and narrative unity of the Bible and thereby constitute the woof and warp of the oral

Torah. The Talmud became the primary text for Jewish religious life and praxis in Judaism.

The collection of biblical interpretations known as Midrash constitutes the other major genre of biblical interpretation from the classical period. The word *midrash* encompasses both a method of expounding the biblical text and a name for a collection of these discourses. Michael Fishbane has demonstrated that midrash draws upon techniques of interpretation already present in the biblical text itself.[6] Yet the collections of midrash as they have been transmitted by the tradition constitute a separate literary genre. Joseph Heinemann has argued that *midrash* derive from the homilies that were part of the religious life in the synagogue, which were sometimes called Bet Midrash (House of Study).[7]

Collections of midrash may have been composed as early as the third century, but most of them seem to originate from the fifth to the eighth centuries CE. In contrast to the Gemara on the Mishnah, which was composed in both Palestine and Babylon, midrashim appear to be the product of Jewish communities in Palestine. There are some remarkable parallels between the midrashim and patristic literature, both Greek and Syriac, in hermeneutical methods. Origen and Jerome both reveal an awareness of midrashic literature.

Midrashic literature moves in two main directions: creative historiography and creative philology. In creative histiography, the Rabbis fill out the biblical narrative by supplying details, identifying persons, and drawing anachronistic pictures of the living conditions of biblical characters. We may learn, for example, that Abraham's "fear" in Gen 15:1 is the result of his victory over the Canaanite kings in Genesis 14; or that Moses sat in the rabbinic academy listening to the discourses of Rabbi Akiba. Creative philology permits the Rabbis to make their own divisions of the words and sentences of the biblical text that lay before them. In this manner they discover that when Abraham celebrated the weaning of Isaac (ביום הגמל *běyôm higā mēl*), he was really giving a feast in honor of his circumcision on the eighth day (*bayom he + gimmel* [ה + ג] = 8).

Most introductions to rabbinic literature classify

---

4. These Rabbis were called Amoraim.

5. *Talmud,* as conventionally understood, can refer more broadly to a printed edition of either the Babylonian or Jerusalem Talmud, which may include other commentaries (particularly Rashi's), biblical references, and lexical notes in addition to the talmudic text.

6. Michael Fishbane, "Inner Biblical Exegesis: Types and Strategies of Interpretation in Ancient Israel," in *Midrash and Literature,* eds. Geoffrey H. Hartman and Sanford Budick (New Haven: Yale University Press, 1986) 19-37.

7. Joseph Heinemann, "The Nature of Aggadah," in Hartman and Budick, *Midrash and Literature,* 41-56.

midrash collections according to "Halakhic" or "Tannaitic" midrashim and "Exegetical" or "Homeletical" midrashim. The basis for the first category rests on the assumption that these collections relate to the earliest period of rabbinic activity, which was oriented toward deriving laws "Halakhah" directly from the biblical text (*Tanna* is the term rabbinic literature uses to describe the teachers mentioned in the Mishnah). The second category is organized according to either the feasts or the special sabbaths of the Jewish calendar. Scholars have questioned the assumptions supporting these classifications. Halakhic midrashim also contain large sections of Aggadah. The textual history of the exegetical and homiletical midrashim indicates that their present arrangement has been modified throughout their transmission.

The "Halakhic" midrashim form a continuous commentary on the Pentateuch from Exodus to Deuteronomy. *Mekhilta* comments on portions of Exodus and includes treatment of both legal and narrative passages. The rabbinic commentary on Leviticus is called *Sifra* and bears a close relationship to Mishnah, indicating that the laws of sacrifice may be derived directly from the Torah itself, without a process of abstraction or deductive reasoning employed by Mishnah. *Sifre* on Numbers elucidates both narrative and legal portions of the book, omitting Numbers 13–14 and 16–17. *Sifre* is also the name for the Halakhic midrash on Deuteronomy, which seems to have been exclusively a commentary on legal passages, with aggadic portions added later. The Halakhic midrashim are quoted in the Babylonian Talmud, and often have parallel passages in the homiletical midrashim.

The collections of midrashim considered homiletical are arranged under the title *Midrash Rabbah* ("The Great Midrash") on the Five Books of Moses and the five scrolls. They were composed at different periods and have distinct literary histories. What unites these collections is their formal similarity. They appear to be structured by the order of verses in the biblical text. Other homiletical midrashim such as *Pesikta d'Rav Kahana*, *Pesikta Rabbati,* and *Tanhuma* derive their structure from the special feasts and sabbaths of the Jewish calendar.

Some scholars believe that these midrashim may represent collections of homilies that were preached in the synagogues in Palestine. These sermons begin with a proem, or *Petihah,* which commences with a verse from the *Kĕtûbîm* (Writings) and is expounded with illustrative biblical texts or newly composed parables leading up to the verse from the weekly Torah reading. Scholars assert that the verses from the Prophets may represent the הפטרה (*Haftarah,* or prophetic lection), for that sabbath. The complexity of these proems (several proems may appear for a single verse), indicates that in Palestine synagogues divided the weekly reading of Torah over a three- to four-year cycle, as distinguished from Babylonia, where the Torah was divided into fifty-four portions and read in a single year.

After the proem, the rabbinic homily might expound several verses from the weekly portion. The sermon concludes with a חתימה (*Hãtîmâ,* or conclusion). The *Hatima* is formulated by reversing the order of the proem. Beginning with the verse from the weekly Torah portion, the midrash advances to verses from the Prophets. In these prophetic verses, the rabbinic voice disappears from the Midrash, and it appears that God alone is speaking directly to the audience. Comfort and consolation are the prophetic message of the *Hatima.* Often, the preacher contrasts the situation in "this world" with the "world to come," allowing the prophetic words to illuminate the bright and glorious future for the Jewish people.

Midrash as a literature encouraged the continuing dialogue between the Jewish people and their past as embedded in the biblical texts. It permitted the past to be eternally present when Jews gathered in the synagogue for study and prayer. James Kugel has expressed the power of Midrash in its relationship to Scripture.

In Midrash the Bible becomes a world unto itself. Midrashic exegesis is the way into that world; it does not seek to view present-day reality through biblical spectacles, neither to find referents of biblical prophecy in present-day happenings, nor to find referents to the daily life of the soul in biblical allegory. Instead it simply overwhelms the present; the Bible's time is important, while the present is not; and so it invites the reader to cross over into the enterable world of Scripture.[8]

God's revelation to Israel on Mt. Sinai (Exodus 19) is transformed from a moment of singularity for Israel into a universal revelation. In *Mekhilta,* the

---

8. James Kugel, "Two Introductions to Midrash," in *Midrash and Literature,* eds. Geoffrey H. Hartman and Sanford Budick (New Haven: Yale University Press, 1986) 90.

Rabbis claim that Torah was given in the wilderness and in fire and in water. Just as they are free to all the inhabitants of the world, so also the words of Torah are free to all. Israel freely chose to undertake the commandments after God offered them to all the other nations.[9] Midrash understands Israel's biblical history with its tragic exile through the text of Cant 1:5: "I am black but beautiful" (author trans.). Israel is darkened by the exile, but beautiful in the eyes of God. Midrash reveals the rabbinic imagination emboldened to reformulate the letters, sentences, and books of Scripture, merging the Jewish people in any era into the scriptural drama.

The Talmud and midrashim constitute the two principal genres of creative biblical interpretation during the classical period. However, during this era synagogue life with its weekly Torah and prophetic readings gave birth to yet another channel of interpretation. These public readings were accompanied by an Aramaic translation: the Targum. The principal Targum texts are the *Targum Onqelos, Yerusalmi, Neofiti on the Pentateuch,* and the *Targum of the Prophets.*

This practice of vernacular translation is attested in the Mishnah.[10] It was to be read after every verse of the lection from the Pentateuch and after every third verse of the reading from the Prophets. The Targums are not literal translations of the Hebrew, but often contain paraphrases or literary embellishments. One of their primary purposes seems to have been to harmonize the biblical text with rabbinic interpretation as expressed in the Talmud. The Rabbis' avoidance of biblical anthropomorphism is reflected in the Targum's rendition of "And God said," by the locution, "A word came from before the Lord." The *Targum to the Prophets* is characterized by aggadic expansion of the biblical text.

By the third century it was suggested that the Hebrew text of the weekly lection be read twice in Hebrew and once in Aramaic.[11] This practice has continued in some traditional Jewish communities into the modern period. In the Middle Ages, the Aramaic Targum was supplemented in Arabic-speaking lands by Saadia Gaon's translation. In Europe there were translations into Old French,

Judaeo-German, and Ladino (Judaeo-Spanish). This focus on the transmission of the biblical text to the people in their own vernacular symbolizes the effort to make the biblical lessons available to the people in the language they could understand.

Mishnah, Talmud, Midrash, and Targum constitute the classical texts of rabbinic biblical interpretation. As "classics" they engender a long tradition of interpretation themselves. Subsequent generations of Jewish literature draw upon the formal aspects of Talmud and Midrash to create their own expositions of Scripture. Two characteristics distinguish the compositions of the classical period. First, they are compilations rather than the work of a single author. They feature the traditions of all the Rabbis, rather than the work of any one of them. Second, they have a utopian and atemporal nature. The classic texts of the Rabbis do not emphasize the time or place when something happened. When the Mishnah narrates an incident about an individual, it begins with the words, "A story about. . . . " The transcendent presentation of time and space in these texts may have reinforced the Rabbis' estimation that written and oral Torah were the twin repositories of divine wisdom.

THE MEDIEVAL PERIOD

Jewish biblical studies in the medieval period begin with the division of the world of late antiquity into Islamic and Christian cultures. From the eighth and ninth centuries, focus on the Bible moves beyond the genres of Talmud, Midrash, and Targum into the development of commentary (*Perush*). Individual authors writing commentaries on individual books replace collective or pseudonymous authorship of anthologies. Each section of the canon—Torah, Prophets, Hagiographa—has its own history of exegesis. The preponderance of commentaries was written on the Pentateuch, but works from the Hagiographa, such as Psalms and Song of Songs, generated many works of interpretation.

In their writings, medieval exegetes maintain a reverential attitude toward the authority of the ancient Rabbis. They share with their forebears a belief in the simultaneous revelation of the written and oral Torah, and the obligation to carry on the task of eliciting their complementary nature. However, medieval authors reveal the exigencies of their own intellectual milieu. Toward that end, they

---

9. *Mekhilta Baḥodesh, Yitro* sec. 5.
10. *Meg.* 4:4.
11. *Ber.* 8a-b.

engage in arguments with one another, and in polemics with both Islamic and Christian scholars. Religious apologetics and controversy become a significant focus in medieval exegetical writings.

Despite the shared religious goal of expounding the biblical text, the study of the Bible by Jews during the medieval period was influenced by geographic and cultural factors. Jewish authors who lived in areas of Islamic culture in the East, North Africa, and Spain from the eighth until the fifteenth centuries developed a different approach to the Bible than those who resided in Europe during the same period. The assimilation of the linguistic and philosophical heritage of Hellenistic civilization by Arabic writers made a profound impression upon the Jews who lived among them. Appropriation of these disciplines extended to the fact that commentaries on Jewish sacred scripture were composed in Arabic by acknowledged rabbinic authorities. Ideas and concepts from these arabic commentaries would find their way into the Hebrew lexicon due to the efforts of the twelfth-century immigrants from Spain to Provence.

In European centers of Jewish learning, where the literature of biblical exegesis emerged only in the eleventh century, rabbinic Hebrew was utilized exclusively. Although philosophical speculation and interest in grammar and lexicography were by no means absent, the European Rabbis did not develop the technical vocabulary that their colleagues appropriated from Islamic culture. They did not write dictionaries or grammars of the Bible. They composed commentaries and collections of Midrash.

After the fifteenth century, Jewish biblical exegesis developed a greater sense of homogeneity. After their expulsion in 1492, Spanish Jews, known as Sephardim, had thoroughly assimilated the writings of the northern European Rabbis, called Ashkenazim. Jewish authors from the European centers moved eastward into Poland and the Ukraine. The language of biblical exegesis until this later medieval period was exclusively Hebrew. Much of the creative spirit in biblical studies moved from the genre of commentary (*Perush*) to homiletics (*Derush*). Important developments in the field of Jewish mystical literature, *Kabbalah,* have significant bearing on the language and thought of biblical exegesis.

The first major exegete of rabbinic Judaism in the medieval period was Saadia ben Joseph al-Fayyumi

(882–942). His intellectual activity was stimulated by a major challenge to the fundamental principle of rabbinic Judaism, that the oral Torah was divinely revealed to Moses at Mount Sinai and the Rabbis were its legitimate inheritors. After the rise of Islam in the seventh and eighth centuries, the studies of oral and written Torah continued in the rabbinic academies of the newly conquered lands. The heads of the Talmudic academies in Baghdad continued the activity of their predecessors, spreading the interpretation of rabbinic Judaism. Their efforts to consolidate the teachings of previous generations of Rabbis extended to written Torah. They canonized the *Targum of Onqelos* (Aramaic translation) and began to compose codes of law.

By the eighth century, however, some Jewish authors challenged the divine origin of the oral Torah, one of the primary assumptions of rabbinic Judaism. These theologians, who were later called Karaites, a name derived from Hebrew *Miqra,* or Scripture, insisted that divine revelation was to be found only in the Tanakh. The oral Torah was exclusively the creation of the Rabbis, lacking divine sanction. Therefore, Karaite exegetes claimed that all Jewish ritual practice must be derived exclusively from the text of Scripture based on rules of grammar and syntax. Karaite biblical hermeneutics led to religious practices that diverged from those of the Rabbis with respect to laws of sabbath, marriage, and diet. Commentaries by Karaite authors were written in Arabic on the Pentateuch, the Prophets, and the Hagiographa. These exegetical works focused on grammar and syntax, often challenging rabbinic interpretations that were founded on loose association with the biblical text itself.

Saadia ben Joseph's writings on the Bible represent a defense of the divinely revealed character of the Oral Torah as the only legitimate interpretation of written Torah. He promoted this justification of the rabbis by creating new genres in scriptural exegesis. At the lexical level, he wrote the first dictionary of the Hebrew Bible (HB), *Sefer HaEgron.* More important, he prepared a translation of the Hebrew Scripture into Arabic (*Tafsir*). Saadia demonstrated the importance of translation for biblical studies. His goal was to translate Scripture into the vernacular and make it comprehensible to Jews and non-Jews. This results in a translation that permits the reader to enter the textual world of the biblical context. He is determined always to transmit the sense of a passage, no matter how difficult it might be in the original. This requires him to translate according to context within the sentence. Often the use of the conjunction *and* is expanded into complex sentences with adverbial conjunctions or other subordinate clauses. These smooth and readable translations were based on Saadia's conclusion that one should translate according to the plain meaning except under specific circumstances, such as (a) when experience or sense data contradict the plain meaning; (b) when reason contradicts the plain meaning; (c) when two verses contradict each other; (d) when the written text contradicts the rabbinic tradition; (e) when Scripture uses anthropomorphism.

To accompany his translations, he wrote commentaries (*Sharkh*), sometimes in two versions, on the Pentateuch, Psalms, Proverbs, and Job. An introduction preceded each of these commentaries, focusing on the fundamental idea of the book and how this idea was coherent with its rhetorical form. In his insistence on the congruity of rhetorical form and theological content, we can see that the principles of translating the biblical text became the foundations for Saadia's introduction to his commentaries. The contents of Scripture are constituted through narratives about the past through which Jews are led to the service of God. In addition, Scripture provides promises that are validated only when they are fulfilled.

For Saadia, the Pentateuch focuses on the importance of educating humanity about its obligations to God. These obligations, or commandments, are formulated in three types of locutions. At times they are framed as a simple command that does not reveal its purpose. Commandments expressed in this manner provide an opportunity for obedience to the One who gave them. A second type of commandment is revealed together with its reward and punishment. In this formulation of commandment, Saadia discerns a higher level than the first, because we have a choice to obey or disobey. The most important formulation of divine commandment in the Pentateuch appears in the form of a narrative that reveals what happened to those who obeyed and experienced success, or those who disobeyed and were punished.

Improvement of the moral and spiritual character of the Jewish people constitutes the central theme of Saadia's investigations of the books in the Hagiographa. In his introduction to Proverbs, Saadia calls it the book of knowledge or wisdom. The central theme of the book is discerned in recognizing twelve topics and their opposites, which helps the reader to acquire wisdom or knowledge. The division of a biblical book into topics also provides the framework in his introduction to the book of Psalms. Saadia claimed that there were five basic forms of speech: direct address, interrogation, narrative, commandment or admonition, and prayer or petition. These five elementary forms yield eighteen rhetorical modes that constitute "the totality of edification." Saadia concludes that what is common to all forms of speech in Psalms is that they focus on commandment and prohibition, what humanity is obliged to do and what is prohibited. The book of Job provides an occasion for Saadia to explore the theme of theodicy. Human suffering ultimately serves a pedagogic purpose. In the speeches of Job's comforters, Saadia discerns two ways of understanding suffering. People suffer so that they might change their evil ways or as punishment for their sins. Saadia rejects these formulations, and argues that suffering comes as a test for the individual, who will be rewarded in the end. Each of Saadia's commentaries, in its introduction and exegesis of individual chapters, presents a coherent monograph on a specific theme.

Complementing his translation and exegetical works, Saadia wrote *The Book of Beliefs and Opinions*, a philosophical treatise presenting his theology of the coherence of scriptural revelation and rabbinic tradition of Judaism. Although the form of the book is entirely philosophical, the major themes within this treatise focus on Scripture: creation, commandment, reward, and punishment. Saadia asserted that scriptural revelation is entirely congruent with human reason when the latter is properly used. He argued that the report of reliable witnesses or tradition is a source of knowledge equivalent to what can be learned by the senses or through logical deduction.

The consistency of Saadia's views throughout the variety of genres makes him one of the most significant exegetes of the Bible in Judaism. His commentaries were well-known in Arabic-speaking Jewish communities. To those Jews who read only Hebrew, his commentaries were transmitted by quotations in the writings of Jewish exegetes in Spain.

Biblical studies continued in Spain. During the tenth and eleventh centuries, the authors wrote in Arabic. They drew upon the rich traditions of Arabic language, with its well-developed disciplines of philology, lexicography, and poetics. In addition, they were heir to the philosophical polemics and religious apologetics that had been developed in the eastern Mediterranean. Karaite exegesis presented a continuing challenge for these authors to justify rabbinic interpretation of Scripture.

In the tenth and eleventh centuries, a specialization in grammar and lexicography dominated the exegetical efforts of Jewish authors in Spain. They produced dictionaries and grammars of biblical texts. For example, Menahem ibn Saruq (c. 960) wrote a dictionary, while Jonah Ibn Janah (c. 950–1040) composed a systematic work on the Hebrew language, focusing on problems of metathesis (exchange of letters within a single word), syntax, and poetics. Biblical commentaries written during this period focus almost exclusively on linguistic problems.

Abraham ibn Ezra (1092–1167) wrote commentaries on almost all books of the Bible, often producing two recensions of a commentary to the same book. By his extensive quotation, Ibn Ezra transmitted much of the Arabic writings of his predecessors to audiences who read only Hebrew. Ibn Ezra subtly shifts from specialization in linguistic problems to the synthetic effort to apply the insights derived from philological study to the classical literature of the rabbis.

In his introduction to the commentary on the Pentateuch, Ibn Ezra describes his program for Scripture exegesis in comparison to other contemporary Jewish, Karaite, and Christian methods. He builds his method on the foundation of human reason. Reason, for Ibn Ezra, is the "angel" that mediates between God and humanity. Therefore, understanding any obscurity in Scripture commences with an investigation of its language, which is designed to accommodate human beings. This leads him to focus on the written text of Scripture as it had been transmitted by tradition, and limit the use of rabbinic exegesis that relied on changes in the orthography of the Hebrew text.

When the biblical text contradicts human experience, Ibn Ezra attempts to harmonize them. At times he relies on a solution that suggests that the chronological distance between scriptural language and the contemporary reader accounts for the difficulty. On other occasions he relies on metaphor to explain away these contradictions. For example, he maintained that God's request for Hosea to marry a harlot was in conflict with the pattern of divine behavior in the Bible, and that these passages could

be explained as occurring only in a vision. His insistence on the rational and historical basis for explaining what happened to biblical characters led him to deny the validity of narrations created by the Rabbis to explain the events in Scripture. For example, he cast doubt on Jeremiah's authorship of Lamentations, denying that it was the book burned by Jehoiakin.

Ibn Ezra did not argue for the exegete's complete reliance on historical and rational explication. Rabbinic tradition provided the only reliable guide to explain Jewish law. The lack of complete explanations for all the commandments in the Pentateuch was a clear indication that the oral Torah was required. In his introduction to the Pentateuch commentary, Ibn Ezra demonstrates that the lack of details for calculating the monthly and yearly calendar implies the necessity for further rabbinic elaboration. The use of grammar alone to explicate these scriptural passages would lead to erroneous interpretation were it not for the comprehensive rules for the calendar, which were provided by the Rabbis. The conclusions of the Rabbis could be set aside only if one could demonstrate that a legal decision was based on an opinion of one sage. In all other cases, Ibn Ezra's exegetical system insisted on the rigorous use of grammar within the framework of classical rabbinic literature.

We now turn from Ibn Ezra's mid-twelfth-century synthesis of the exegetical achievements of Jewry under Islamic culture to the developments within the northern European or Ashkenazi communities. Jewish scholars began to settle the areas in the Rhineland and present-day Alsace-Lorraine, and Champagne as early as the ninth century, emigrating from northern Italy. By the eleventh century, the first literary works of the Ashkenazi Rabbis emerge, focusing on the explication of the Talmud and the composition of liturgical poetry.

The Jews who inhabited these regions also seem to have been in contact with learned Christians who inquired about the meaning of passages in Hebrew Scriptures. In the late eleventh century, Gilbert Crispin, Abbot of Westminster, composed a "dialogue" with a learned Jew from Mainz about the interpretation of Scripture. The goal of the dialogue was to convince the Jewish interlocutor about the truth of Christianity. By contrast, Stephen Harding, Abbot of Citeaux, described a meeting at the abbey where Jews were invited to respond to his inquiries about the Hebrew basis for textual problems in the Vulgate. The contrast between his description of an intellectual encounter and the missionary spirit of Crispin's *Dialogus* provides the background to Jewish exegetical developments in Ashkenaz.

In the exegetical writings of Rabbi Solomon ben Isaac of Troyes (1040–1105), known as Rashi, the HB receives its classical Jewish garment. Having studied at the Rhineland academies, Rashi transmitted the accumulated learning of the Ashkenazi Rabbis to the soil of France. He was profoundly interested in explicating the complex dialectics of the Talmud into an orderly argument that students could follow. As one who composed liturgical poetry, Rashi was aware of the multiple meanings of biblical words when they were used in different semantic contexts.

In Rashi's exegetical framework, Scripture and the Rabbis constitute a single world. Therefore, one may derive the meaning of one from the other. His commentaries fuse rabbinic literature and the HB into a seamless text. At the same time, they insist upon discovering the *Peshuto shel Miqra,* bringing out the plain meaning of the biblical text in a narrative order that reduces the number of rabbinic midrashim relevant to a specific passage in Scripture.

Both the integrity of rabbinic interpretation and its defense in the presence of Christian argument shape Rashi's exegesis. His prefatory remarks to Gen 1:1 provide an excellent example of these concerns. Citing a passage from *Midrash Tanḥuma,* he raises the question of why the Pentateuch begins with the creation narrative rather than the mandate of the Passover (Exod 12:1) which was the "first commandment God gave to Israel." Rashi's response was grounded on a passage in Ps 111:6, which asserts that God declared his mighty acts to Israel, providing them with an inheritance among the nations. Thus if the nations of the world accused Israel of robbing the seven Canaanite nations of their territory, Israel could respond that all the earth belongs to God, who created it and gave it to whoever was upright from the divine perspective. By God's will it passed to the Canaanites, and by God's will it was given to Israel. The apologetic nature of this passage is patent. Rashi focuses on interpreting the creation narrative as an argument that the Pentateuch is not simply a book of divine mandates that regulate Israel's conduct, but the revelation of a covenant between God and the Jewish people.

The interpretation of the Song of Songs provided another opportunity for Rashi to present a hermeneutical framework grounded on the language of Scripture itself, but indicated that the rabbinic allegorical interpretation of the Canticle of God's love for Israel was correct. He asserted that Solomon had composed the Canticle through the power of the Holy Spirit to show that Israel would endure one exile after another, and would mourn for its former glory when it was God's chosen among all the nations. Israel would then recount God's merciful acts and her own misdeeds. Solomon composed this narrative on the example of a young widow who longs for her husband, recounting his youthful love for her. Her husband mourns for her, recalling her beauty and the powerful bonds of love between them, and says that her exile is not permanent and that he will return to her in the future. The commentary itself explicates both the narrative of the lovers and the stages in the relationship between God and Israel from the creation of the world until the end of Israel's exile in the messianic era.

Rashi's commentary on Psalms reveals his exegetical method of relocating passages, which the Rabbis interpreted in an eschatological manner, within the framework of the Bible itself. Psalm 2 had been interpreted as a description of the messianic battle at the end of history by the rabbis. Rashi repeats their explanation, but also provides a *Teshuba leMinim,* a refutation of the heretics. He asserts that the opening verses of the Psalm refer to 2 Sam 5:17, in which the Philistines gather to overthrow David, who had been crowned in Jerusalem. Rashi ascribes Ps 2:10-12 to the "Prophets of Israel" who rebuke the nations of the world to turn aside from their evil ways and obey God. This exegetical technique responds to Christian interpretation by a positive Jewish assertion that the passages in question contain a positive promise of the future redemption of Israel.

Rashi's younger colleague, Rabbi Joseph Kara, and scholars in the generation of Rashi's grandson, Rabbi Samuel ben Meir, continue to develop his exegetical techniques. Their search for the *Peshuto shel Miqra,* or plain meaning, often leads them to more intense focus on the biblical text, which, in turn, diminishes their effort to harmonize rabbinic interpretation with Scripture. Some of the rabbis, such as Rabbi Joseph of Orleans, engage in refutations of Christian typological interpretation.

The commentaries written by Christian scholars, such as Hugh, Richard, and Andrew at the Abbey of St. Victor in Paris, during the twelfth century reflect contact with the exegesis of Rashi and his disciples. Particularly in the exegesis written by Andrew of St. Victor one can discover "traditions of the Hebrews" in Latin translation that have direct parallels in the commentaries of Rashi, Rabbi Joseph Kara, and Rabbi Samuel ben Meir. It is remarkable that Andrew at times accepts these Jewish interpretations, preferring them to those of the Church Fathers or the writings of his own teachers. Andrew's pupil, Herbert of Bosham, who was part of the scholarly community of Thomas à Beckett, indicates a greater capacity for utilizing rabbinic literature in his own commentary on the psalter. Christian utilization of Rashi and his pupils continues into the writings of other scholars, such as the fourteenth-century Franciscan, Nicholas of Lyra.

Ashkenazi Rabbis of the thirteenth century turned their efforts toward a more dialectical study of the Bible. Rashi became their point of departure from the biblical text. They then use various passages from both Scripture and rabbinic literature to resolve the contradictions they discern behind Rashi's question. For example, they might dispute Rashi's argument in the introduction to his Torah commentary, mentioned above, that Exod 12:1 was the first commandment God gave to Israel. These Rabbis were known as *Tosafot,* "those who added." They did not compile independent commentaries on biblical books, but their interpretations were transmitted as parts of anthologies. In addition to compiling anthologies of *Tosafot* commentaries, these same scholars composed new anthologies of classical midrashim on the books of Scripture, such as the *Yalqut Shim'oni.*

The creativity in biblical studies among the Rabbis in northern Europe during the twelfth and thirteenth centuries had its parallel in Iberia and the Mediterranean world. However, the rise of the Reconquista from the north and the invasion of the intolerant Almohades from the south changed the intellectual atmosphere. Emigration meant that new centers of study would flourish in Egypt, Provence, and in the new Christian monarchies of Spain.

Moses Maimonides (1135–1205), known in most circles as a philosopher, did not write in the genre of biblical commentary. However, one could argue that the entire scope of his writings focuses on Scripture, providing various approaches for its proper interpretation. Moreover, subsequent generations of Jewish students of Scripture drew upon his writings as the basis for their own work.

The introduction to the *Commentary on the Mishnah,* written in Arabic, weaves both biblical text and rabbinic midrash into a coherent narrative of how the divine Word was transmitted from Moses through Aaron and the elders to the children of Israel. In his *Book of the Commandments,* Maimonides provides one of the first attempts to delineate precisely which of the scriptural admonitions constitute the rabbinically prescribed number of 613 positive and negative commandments. In the *Mishneh Torah,* the first effort to codify the written and oral Torah, Maimonides presents an accounting of how each category of Jewish law had developed from pre-scriptural times through the age of the rabbis.

Building a bridge between the God of Moses and Aristotle would seem to be the purpose of Maimonides' *Guide of the Perplexed.* However, the reconciliation between philosophical perspectives and Jewish revealed tradition shaped the *Guide* into a treatise on the hermeneutics of Scripture. Maimonides stated, "The first purpose of this Treatise is to explain the meaning of certain terms occurring in the books of Prophecy. [The] second purpose [is] the explanation of very obscure parables occurring in the books of the prophets but not explicitly identified as such."

Consistent with these purposes, the first part of the *Guide* provides a lexicon of biblical terms that are used with respect to God, and suggests how they might be understood. Part two offers an exposition of the nature of biblical prophecy with particular emphasis on the unique character of Moses. Maimonides concluded the *Guide* with a discussion on divine providence (which is presented as a commentary on the book of Job) and an examination of the character of divine legislation or commandments.

In Maimonides' hermeneutical system, all of the divine commandments had an inner meaning. With his emphasis on the significance of the "inner meaning" of Scripture, allegorical interpretation moves to the core of proper biblical exegesis and is not simply an apologetic embellishment. This approach to Scripture emphasizes the necessary connection between learning, moral perfection, and knowledge of God.

Provence and northern Spain inherited the linguistic and philosophical traditions of the previous generations as well as the challenge of Maimonides' synthesis of Aristotle with Judaism. Philosophical interpretation had to be defended against those Rabbis who argued that the divine Word as transmitted in written and oral Torah was sufficient. These rabbis asserted that too much allegorization would have led Maimonides to deny concepts such as creation *ex nihilo* or the resurrection of the dead. Turning the Torah into parables would undermine observance of the commandments; perhaps even worse, it would validate Christian claims to the true interpretation of Jewish Scripture.

The Kimchi family, Joseph (c. 1105–c. 1170) and his two sons, Moses (d. c. 1190) and David (c. 1160–c. 1235), moved to Narbonne from Spain and wrote commentaries on Scripture, responding to the rabbis who attacked philosophical and allegorical methods. Rabbi Joseph Kimchi composed *The Book of the Covenant* to defend Jewish interpretation of Scripture against Christian typological exegesis. The use of rationalism in this treatise demonstrates how philosophical methods could be used to support traditional rabbinic understanding of legal and prophetic passages. Rabbi David Kimchi, known as RaDaK, asserted that rationalist approaches to understanding the miracles in Scripture or prophecy were simply an extension of the original efforts of the classical Rabbis. Wherever possible, RaDaK argued that rigorous examination of biblical language yielded the most satisfactory explanations of figurative language. In addition, rational inquiry provided the best answers to Christian typological interpretations. For RaDaK, philosophy was one more weapon in Israel's arsenal for reclaiming the truth of its interpretation of Scripture despite its condition of exile. In his commentary on Jer 9:23, RaDaK asserts that Israel's covenant with God was the covenant of reason.

Let him that glories glory in this, that he understands and knows Me. Understanding God is understanding that He is one, eternal and noncorporeal, that He creates all and supervises all; that He manages the upper and lower worlds in wisdom. The knowledge of God is walking in His ways, performing mercy, justice and righteousness, as he performs with them.

The most extensive exegetical writings of the Kimchi family come from David. He wrote a systematic treatise on the textual criticism of the Bible, *Eṭ Sofer* (*The Scribe's Pen*), which describes manu-

script variants and the problems of the Massorah. In addition he wrote a grammar book, *Sefer Mikhlol* (*The Compendium*), containing both a dictionary and a description of Hebrew grammatical rules. He wrote commentaries on Genesis, all the Prophets, Psalms, Proverbs, and Chronicles. In addition, he wrote allegorical commentaries on the Garden of Eden, Cain and Abel, and the first chapter of Ezekiel. These commentaries reflect the approach developed by his father, and also by Abraham ibn Ezra, where rigorous philological analysis is combined with a rationalist approach. He maintains a strict division between the pursuit of plain meaning and homiletical meaning. However, he uses the Talmudic Aggadah to develop moral and ethical lessons.

Like his father, David Kimchi actively pursued polemics against Christian allegorical interpretations of the HB. Many of these polemical interpretations appear in his commentary on the book of Psalms. Many of David Kimchi's works were translated into Latin and were influential for Christian Hebraists in the sixteenth and seventeenth centuries.

Maimonides' emphasis on "inner meaning" of Scripture stimulated the growth of an alternative nonphilosophical method of biblical hermeneutics in both Provence and Spain during the twelfth and thirteenth centuries. This method of interpretation, known as *Kabbalah* ("received tradition"), was associated with esoteric traditions of the classical Rabbis. The Kabbalists asserted that Scripture had an inner meaning that was to be discovered through their theosophic teachings rather than by philosophical categories.

The teachers of these kabbalistic doctrines were well-known rabbinic authorities who wrote commentaries on the Talmud, produced codifications of Jewish law, and answered inquiries on how Jewish law should be practiced. In writing their treatises they drew upon the language of classical rabbinic midrash rather than philosophical language that was translated from Arabic into Hebrew. Their primary concerns were with a profound understanding of how God was manifest in the universe and how the observance of the commandments bound the Jewish people to the cosmos.

The key to kabbalistic systems was grounded in the axiom that Scripture was the language of God. Therefore, its words and letters were more than conventional means of communication. They represented a concentration of energy and express a wealth of meaning that could not be fully translated into human language.

Rabbi Moses ben Nachman (1194–1270), known as Nachmanides, wrote a commentary on the Pentateuch that is one of the first literary witnesses to the kabbalistic approach to Scripture. In his introduction, he argues that the "entire Torah consists of the names of God, and that the words we read can be divided in a very different way." Nachmanides suggested that the Torah was originally revealed as a continuous string of letters. Moses was then presented with the divisions of these words so that the text could be read as the commandments. However, he was also given an oral tradition that transmitted the esoteric reading of the text as a sequence of divine names. The reader of Scripture who had studied the esoteric tradition could have access to both levels of meaning. However, Nachmanides set his own task as an interpreter of the Torah according to the traditional modes of rabbinic plain meaning and Aggadah, drawing upon the commentaries of Rashi and Abraham ibn Ezra, and occasionally alluding to those passages that were pregnant with esoteric meaning.

By the end of the thirteenth century, Jewish biblical interpretation continued its role as the vehicle for expanding upon philosophical or kabbalistic themes. Levi ben Gershom (1288–1344) in Provence promoted his philosophical and ethical teachings in his biblical commentaries. Rabbi Bachya ben Asher of Saragossa wrote commentaries on the Pentateuch. Bachya ben Asher introduced a four-level division for the interpretation of scriptural verses: *peshat,* or "plain meaning"; *derash,* or "rabbinic aggadah"; *derekh hassekhel,* or "philosophical"; and *sod,* or "kabbalistic." Under Bachya ben Asher's influence, or perhaps from the surrounding Christian culture, the fourfold interpretation of Scripture, also known by the acronym פרדס (*pardēs*, "the garden"), became a popular schema for the composition of biblical commentaries after the fourteenth century.

The later medieval period, from the fifteenth through the eighteenth centuries, witnessed another development in biblical commentary. Marc Saperstein has demonstrated that the sermons delivered in synagogues were rewritten into commentaries on Scripture.[12] These "commentaries" became the literary vehicles for expanding on philosophical, kabbal-

istic, or moral themes. They provide a window into the theological concerns, ritual practices, and moral problems of the communities throughout the Jewish dispersion.

THE MODERN PERIOD

At the dawn of the modern era, the eighteenth century, Jewish society was fragmented into three geographical and cultural areas: Western Europe, Eastern Europe (the former kingdom of Poland, which had been divided between Russia and Austria-Hungary), and the Ottoman Empire. This division has significance for the study of the Bible, because it indicates the distance that modern Western European thought had to travel before entering all elements of Jewish society. As civil emancipation became a possibility for Jews in France and Germany, they were enjoined to consider seriously the possibilities offered by non-Jewish culture and society. Their co-religionists in Eastern Europe were not presented with the same political possibilities, but the importance of Western European thought was recognized. In the Ottoman Empire, Jewish religious thinkers would not contend with the challenges of modernity until the twentieth century.

Only in Western Europe, particularly in Germany, was the Bible perceived as a cultural bridge between Jews and non-Jews. Before the Western European Enlightenment, external cultural influences were either absorbed or integrated into Jewish biblical studies in an indirect manner. As we have seen, Jewish exegetes in the Middle Ages sometimes responded to Christian study of the HB with direct polemical attacks. In the modern period, Jewish students of the Bible entertain the philological and historical discoveries generated by Christian biblical scholars without hostility, and often as a stimulus to their own work. The extent of this cultural integration evoked a serious debate among the Jews because it demanded a sundering of the context for biblical studies from the oral Law. From the perspective of traditional rabbinic Judaism, this dichotomy between oral and written Law constituted heresy. Beyond the theological issue, many traditional Rabbis recognized that by using nontraditional Hebrew sources Jews would be led away from the Jewish community and Jewish observance. This ambivalence toward separating the HB from its connections with rabbinic literature characterizes Judaism from

---

12. Marc Saperstein, *Jewish Preaching: 1200–1800, An Anthology* (New Haven: Yale University Press, 1989) 5-26.

the eighteenth century through the modern period. It leads to a division into what we might call "biblical studies," which integrates the philological and historical insights with the heritage of pre-modern Jewry, and "biblical research," which focuses exclusively on the attempt to illuminate the HB within the context of its own world. Biblical research has absorbed Jews within the university community or within liberal seminaries. It has had an influence on the world of biblical studies through its work in translations.

Moses Mendelssohn (1729–86) presents the first example of the tension that modernity introduced for Jewish biblical studies. His desire was to produce a translation of the HB into elegant German and combine it with a commentary in Hebrew *(Biur)*. The primary purpose of this translation was to open the gateway to general culture for the Jewish community, and lead them toward an aesthetic outlook. He set about the task by gathering a group of like-minded scholars, assigning them commentaries. As the editor, Mendelssohn provided a unifying tone for both biblical translation and commentary.

In his introduction to the *Commentary on the Torah,* Mendelssohn asserted that his goal was to focus on the language and grammar of Scripture. This emphasis had been lost to Jewish biblical commentary since the thirteenth-century scholar Rabbi David Kimchi. Primarily this grammatical method allowed Mendelssohn to demonstrate the essential correctness of Jewish traditional explanation of Torah. Christian scholars, he claimed, did not "recognize the traditions of our Sages and do not keep the Massorah." Therefore, they are not bound by vowel points and accents. For them, the Jewish Scripture is just a "historical work." The sages, however, established the Massorah to preclude the need for conjecture. Jews cannot simply modify the text of the Torah "for a grammarian's conjecture." Mendelssohn presents a defense of traditional Jewish understanding of the Pentateuch by emphasizing its linguistic foundation.

The translation and commentary on Psalms permitted Mendelssohn greater latitude with respect to the aesthetics of biblical language. Here, Mendelssohn acknowledged his debt to Herder's *Vom Geist der ebraeischer Poesie* (1782–83) and R. Lowth's *De sacra poesi habraeroum* (1753). He focused on the parallelism of the psalms, hoping to

accustom the reader to the lyric poetry of the Jews without seeing the prophetic and mystical sides.

Mendelssohn and his colleagues seem to have reached their audience. Subscription lists indicate that Jews in Western European cities who were predisposed to assimilation into the larger society were not alone in purchasing them. Many Jews in smaller communities, particularly in Galicia, and the Eastern European Pale of settlement also supported the translation and commentary. This success met with condemnation from some of the leading Rabbis, such as Akiba Eger and Yehezkiel Landau. They attacked Mendelssohn's translations for making Hebrew subordinate to German and leading Jews into assimilation and apostasy.

The opening to Jewish students of the universities in Berlin, Jena, and Halle in the nineteenth century brought a new generation to the study of oriental languages. By the 1820s a Society for the Scientific Study of Judaism (*Wissenschaft des Judentums*) commenced publication on a critical examination of Jewish history and literature. The principal activity of the advocates of scientific study of Judaism was in post-biblical Hebrew literature or the oral Torah rather than the Bible. Those who advocated religious reform within Judaism focused their efforts on changing the liturgy or Jewish ritual laws. Scripture seemed to be beyond their interests.

However, by mid-century the idea of progress became very much a part of the ideology of the reformers. A platform promulgated by Rabbis in Frankfurt "recognized the possibility of unlimited progress in Mosaism." Inevitably, the reformers and advocates of *Wissenschaft des Judentums* began to react to the results of historical criticism by Christian scholars in their own writings. Rabbi Abraham Geiger (1810–79), founder of the Reform Rabbinical Seminary in Berlin, was the first scholar to incorporate the modern systematic study of biblical books into the program of *Wissenschaft des Judentums* and made it a part of his seminary curriculum. In his work on the History of the Text of the Hebrew Bible *(Urschrift und übersetzungen der Bibel in ihrer Abhängigkeit von der inneren Entwicklung des Judentums,* 1857), Geiger articulated the integration of historical-critical studies and Jewish theology. He argued that the history of the biblical text was linked to the history of the Jewish people; and it was possible to reconstruct the inner history of Israel's faith from the external history of the biblical text. What exegesis and midrash achieved at a later period was accomplished through manipulation of the biblical text. In this manner, Geiger constructed a coherent thesis that assumed a different Hebrew *Vorlage* behind the translations and versions, rather than ascribing them to copyists' errors. He associated the textual variants with the divergent social, political, and intellectual groups of Second Temple Judaism.

Geiger also wrote an *Introduction to Biblical Writings* (1871–73) in which he argued that the prophetic books form the nucleus of the Bible; that the Pentateuch was a later work composed from various sources and united by a single redactor; and that the historical experience of the exodus was limited to the tribes of Joseph. This introduction, derived from his course at the rabbinical seminary in Berlin, was consistent with Geiger's idea that the Prophets who proclaimed the centrality of ethical monotheism and Israel's universal mission constituted the core of the HB.

Reactions to the reformers' ideas about Scripture came from rabbis in both Eastern and Western Europe. Meir Loeb ben Jehiel Michael (1809–79), known by the acronym Malbim, wrote a commentary on the books of the HB, whose explicit purpose was to oppose the "rabbis, preachers and readers who butcher Judaism in their commentaries." Malbim asserted that the oral Torah was divinely revealed. Therefore, every word in the biblical text was necessary. More important for Malbim was that the sages of the Jewish tradition had utilized a linguistic approach since antiquity, which they called *Peshat*. Therefore, all interpretations of the rabbis were grounded on a linguistic foundation and were more authentic than the explanations offered by those Jews who used modern historical methods.

Malbim's attitude toward historical criticism was not completely shared by his Orthodox colleagues in Western European countries like Germany and Italy. They focused their arguments on efforts to tamper with the unity of the Pentateuch, while they were willing to utilize modern scholarly methods on the other parts of the HB. Samuel David Luzzatto (1800–65) in Padua translated the Pentateuch into Italian and wrote a Hebrew commentary, affirming a belief in the divinely revealed character of the Torah. It displays great reverence for Rashi and argues that one need not take Genesis literally, but may understand its narratives as model lessons for moral values. In his commentary on Isaiah, he was

less fideistic. He reviewed the arguments against the unity of Isaiah and rejected them purely on their merit. Luzzatto, however, found merit in the arguments that denied the Solomonic authorship of the book of Ecclesiastes.

In Frankfurt-am-Main, Samson Raphael Hirsch (1808–88) opposed any historical dimension in the analysis of the Pentateuch. His translation and commentary asserted that Torah, like nature, is a fact. No principle revealed in Torah may be denied, even when it is beyond the power of human understanding. The central principle of Torah is that it is beyond history, not contingent upon the will of society or any individual. In Hirsch's commentary on the Pentateuch and on Psalms, one may discern his use of allegory to advance his theological interpretation of Torah or Law as the eternal truth of Judaism. Hirsch's colleagues at the Hildesheimer Rabbinerseminar in Berlin were in complete solidarity with his views on the Pentateuch. However, they were more moderate in their view of the benefits that could be derived from modern scholarly methods. Rabbi Esriel Hildesheimer declared that "Bible commentary demanded investigation from a new point of view and required the use of valuable linguistic material." Rabbi David Zvi Hoffman wrote commentaries on Genesis, Leviticus, and Deuteronomy, attacking the Graf-Wellhausen hypothesis. He articulated the axiom of the divine revelation of Torah, asserting that the written Torah can be understood only in conjunction with the oral Law. Like Mendelssohn, he declared that the Masoretic Text (MT) and its vowel points were an inviolable integrity. From Hoffman's perspective, Scripture was the word of God in content as well as expression. Therefore, one could recognize only those aspects of modern scholarship that did not question its integrity or sanctity.

Another instructor at the Hildesheimer Rabbinerseminar, Rabbi Jakob Barth, utilized academic research to separate the authorship of Isaiah 40–66 from the rest of the book. In addition to his linguistic analysis, he also adduced proof from the Talmud (Tractate *B. Bat.* 15a) that some passages in Isaiah had been written by Hezekiah. Orthodox Jewish scholars would accept the results of historical explanations in biblical books outside the Pentateuch, especially when they could be justified by sacred rabbinic texts.

It is clear that intra-religious polemics and ideology had a definite impact on the acceptance of non-Jewish biblical studies in the Jewish community. Both Reform and Orthodox Jewish scholars were drawn into the debate about the theories developed by Old Testament (OT) scholars in the universities. In the early years of the twentieth century, Solomon Schechter, who had taught at Cambridge University and become a leader of Conservative Judaism, exposed a theological dimension of the Graf-Wellhausen documentary hypothesis. The post-exilic dating of the Priestly document with the "legalism" of its content was, in Schechter's words, grounded in the "Higher Antisemitism." Thus what proposed itself as "objective scholarship" was grounded in anti-Jewish apologetic. Schechter articulated the sentiments of even those Jews who did not object to historical studies, but who were highly suspicious of apologetics masked as scholarship.

Schechter's statement about biblical historical studies had broader implications for the Jewish tradition. It affirmed the gap that separated Christian scholars who read the HB from their Jewish counterparts. The statement also adumbrated radical changes that have taken place in the twentieth century Jewish community and shaped the way in which Jews interpret their Scripture. Among these changes we might specify the massive migration to America at the beginning of the century; the rise of Zionism as a movement of Jewish self-renewal; the Holocaust; and the founding of the state of Israel.

From the perspective of these changes in the Jewish community, it would seem appropriate to describe biblical interpretation in the twentieth century as oscillating between explaining the Bible only in its historical context and reassembling aspects of the rabbinic tradition. The academic environment of the university and liberal rabbinical seminary have stimulated work by Jewish scholars, who have contributed to the historical approach. Rabbis in both Europe and North America have written commentaries on the Pentateuch and other parts of the HB that are used in both synagogue worship and study programs. These commentaries, while presenting some of the results of historical research, emphasize the rabbinic tradition.

By 1894 the Jewish Publication Society of America (JPS) undertook a revision of an earlier translation by Rabbi Isaac Leeser (1853). The committee was chaired by Marcus Jastrow, a professor at Columbia University. The committee was reconstituted in 1907 with Max L. Margolis of Dropsie College serving as the principal translator. By 1917, the committee had approved the work of Margolis. The

JPS translation (1917) served as the principal text in American Jewish synagogues and institutions until 1955, when a committee for revision was constituted under the leadership of Harry M. Orlinsky, who taught at Hebrew Union College–Jewish Institute of Religion. Orlinsky's committee was composed of scholars who taught in seminaries and universities—E. A. Speiser (Pennsylvania) and H. L. Ginsberg (Jewish Theological Seminary of America)—and Rabbis B. J. Bamberger (Reform), Max Arzt (Conservative), H. Freedman (Orthodox). They completed their work on all three sections of the HB by 1979. The JPS committee's efforts reflect a "descriptive translation" that draws upon the rich background of ancient Near Eastern culture to produce a text accessible to the modern reader. Wherever possible, the translators attempt to reduce theological implications. Therefore, in Gen 1:2 the Hebrew רוח אלהים (*rûaḥ ʾĕlōhîm*) is translated as "a wind from God sweeping over the water." The reader becomes aware of passages that are difficult to translate by a notation indicating "translation uncertain."

Another significant effort in Jewish biblical translation was the collaboration by two Jewish scholars in Germany, Franz Rosenzweig (1886–1929) and Martin Buber (1878–1964). Their collaborative translation was motivated by their common project of a renewal of Jewish identity in Germany as well as by their individual theological and philosophical investigations. By the time of Rosenzweig's death in 1929, they had completed the Pentateuch; Buber continued the work in Germany until 1938, when he left for Israel. The translation was completed between 1950 and 1961.

The Buber-Rosenzweig translation has its foundation in Buber's philosophical assumption of the dialogue as a primary human way of knowing. The Bible is, in Hebrew, *Miqra,* "that which calls out or exclaims." It can be understood only by the reader who is to become a partner in the dialogue; one who expects the texts to be as relevant today as it was to previous generations. Poor translation, rather than historical criticism, threatened the relationship of the individual with Scripture. The scholarly task was to restore the original structure of the text that points to its underlying plan. Then the text could resume its perennial function of teaching.

Buber's approach was to discover the living unity of the text rather than atomizing it into a series of unrelated literary strands. By focusing on the particularities of biblical language and rhetoric, Buber and Rosenzweig sought to be faithful to its unique voice. In contrast to Mendelssohn's effort to elevate Hebrew to elegant German, they attempted to mold the German to the starkness of Hebrew.

In addition to his work of translation, Buber wrote a number of books on the history of ideas in Hebrew Scripture. A number of other academicians in Israel and the United States also contributed to this historical genre. Yehezkiel Kaufmann (1889–1965), Umberto Cassuto (1883–1951), and Joseph Klausner (1874–1965) wrote on the history of ancient Israelite religion. While they utilized the same historical methods as non-Jewish scholars, they advocated a reconstruction based on Jewish peoplehood and nationalism. The history of biblical research in Israeli and American universities reflects the dynamic relationship between the demands of a scholarly discipline and changing perspectives on the continuity between the biblical and rabbinic periods.

In shifting our perspective from the international academy to the synagogues in North America, it would be fair to conclude that most Jews have not been touched by the results of biblical studies. The cycle of weekly Torah and prophetic readings have provided Rabbis with opportunities to share their theological perspectives. The use of Scripture as a basis for moral and ethical exhortation is common to the homiletics of Orthodox, Conservative, and Reform Rabbis. To some extent the emphasis of Reform Judaism on the prophetic literature yielded an emphasis on issues of social justice. However, the renewal of ritual observance during the 1970s and 1980s among all philosophies of American Jewry required biblical commentaries that also promoted a retrieval of insights from the rabbinic and medieval periods. One can discern this integration of biblical studies with the insights of Jewish religious ideas in the commentaries of Nahum Sarna (b. 1923).[13]

Two commentaries on the Pentateuch that are currently used in North American synagogues reveal this tendency to balance modern and pre-modern perspectives. Rabbi J. H. Hertz (1872–1946), a graduate of the Jewish Theological Seminary of America and later Chief Rabbi of the United Hebrew Congregations of the British Commonwealth, completed a one-volume commentary on the Pentateuch

and Haftarah (Prophetic passages). Hertz presented his reader with a commentary that combined an emphasis on "plain meaning" with the insights from the best of Jewish and European culture. Dante and T. H. Huxley are quoted, together with Rashi and Nachmanides. There is a strong emphasis on moral and ethical issues. Hertz condemns social evils. He adopts the insights of Samson Raphael Hirsch and David Zvi Hoffman to indicate that the sacrifices prescribed in Leviticus are symbols of human gratitude and dependance upon God.

Hertz's commentary employs a strong apologetic attack on any attempt to suggest that Scripture and modern science contradict each other. However, any scholarly opinion that criticizes the unity of the Pentateuch or the antiquity of its sources receives lengthy rebuttal. These counterarguments are often presented in the supplementary notes appended to each book of the Pentateuch. The reader of the Hertz Pentateuch is, therefore, inured to any concept of historical development. The insights of Jews and non-Jews are presented to polish the image of the perfect revelation God gave to Moses at Mount Sinai.

A contrasting perspective on the nature of a commentary on the Pentateuch for the synagogue was presented by W. Gunther Plaut (b. 1912) and Bernard Bamberger (1904–80), both Rabbis of the Reform movement: *The Torah: A Modern Commentary*.[14] Plaut was the principal architect of the commentary, while Bamberger wrote the commentary on Leviticus.

Where Hertz was hostile to comparisons of the Pentateuch to its ancient Near Eastern background, Plaut invites them. Each book of the Pentateuch has an introduction written by William Hallo, summarizing the contributions of historical studies to a modern understanding of the Pentateuch. Hertz emphasizes the divine inspiration of the Pentateuch. Plaut's introduction argues that "the Torah is ancient Israel's distinctive reference of its search for God." It records the meeting of the human and the divine, the great moments of encounter. Therefore, the text is touched by an ineffable essence. For Plaut, "God is not the author of the text, the people are. God's voice may be heard through theirs if we listen with the human mind." Consistent with Reform Judaism's emphasis on personal autonomy in relig-

13. Nahum Sarna, *Understanding Genesis* (New York: Schocken, 1966); *Exploring Exodus* (New York: Schocken, 1991); and *Songs of the Heart: An Introduction to Psalms* (New York: Schocken, 1993).

14. W. Gunther Plaut and Bernard Bamberger, *The Torah: A Modern Commentary* (New York: Union of American Hebrew Congregations, 1991).

ious life, he asserts, "The Commentary is neither an apology for nor an endorsement of every passage. It will present the modern readers with tools for understanding and leave the option to them."[15]

The Plaut-Bamberger commentary carries out its plan to both educate and inspire the modern Jewish reader. Breaking with the traditional rabbinic divisions of the Pentateuch into the weekly portions read on the Sabbath, it is divided by literary units. Each unit contains a general introduction, followed by the Hebrew text and the JPS translation, with either Plaut's or Bamberger's philological notes. A discussion of theological and halakhic issues follows the text, translation, and notes. Each unit concludes with excerpts from Jewish and non-Jewish sources relating to the most significant themes. There is an emphasis on moral and ethical issues, but the relationship between the Pentateuch and Jewish law and practice are discussed without apology.

In concluding our survey of biblical interpretation within the Jewish tradition, it seems appropriate to retrieve the rabbinic image of Torah study as פרדס (Pardes, an orchard). Many Rabbis understood the letters of Pardes as an acronym describing hermeneutical approaches to the text: פשט (Peshat, plain meaning), רמז (Remez, allusion or allegory), דרש (Derash, homiletical), and סוד (Sod, mystical). By the end of the Middle Ages, Jewish interpreters of the Bible wrote their commentaries, offering systematic explanations of each verse according to its appropriate level. Each approach, however, was understood as a point of entry into the orchard of divine delights.

For the rabbis, medieval Jews, and even Jews of modernity to read Scripture in the synagogue or in private study is to enter the richness of the Jewish people's encounter with the divine. Michael Fishbane has indicated that interpretation of the divine Word has been an integral part of Jewish life even during the biblical period itself.[16] Given this perspective, one could argue that the fruits of modern biblical scholarship permit modern Jews to appreciate parts of the orchard that previously have been

obscured. Each generation of Jews has added to the beauty of the orchard. They have responded to the wisdom of an early rabbinic teacher who claimed, "Turn it, and turn it again, for everything is contained in it."

BIBLIOGRAPHY

Classical Period

Halivni, D. Weiss. *Midrash, Mishnah and Gemara: The Jewish Predilection for Justified Law.* Cambridge, Mass.: Harvard University Press, 1986. A discussion of the relationship between the written Torah and the literary expressions of oral Torah.

Neusner, J. *The Oral Torah: The Sacred Books in Judaism.* Atlanta: Scholars Press, 1991. Neusner examines the interrelationships between the documents that transmit rabbinic Judaism.

Strack, H. L., and G. Stemberger. *Introduction to the Talmud and Midrash.* Translated by M. Bockmuehl. Minneapolis: Fortress, 1992. This book provides an introduction to rabbinic literature, its genres and their histories with extensive bibliography.

Medieval Period

Bacher, W. "Biblical Exegesis," *The Jewish Encyclopedia* (1906) III:1962-1974. Bacher's article focuses on the linguistic emphasis of medieval Jewish exegetical writings.

Banitt, M. *Rashi: Interpreter of the Biblical Letter.* Tel Aviv: Chaim Rosenberg School of Jewish Studies, Tel Aviv University, 1985. Rashi's exegesis is examined within the context of medieval French culture.

Funkenstein, A. *Perceptions of Jewish History.* Berkeley: University of California Press, 1993. Funkenstein presents medieval Jewish exegesis in relationship to both Islamic and Christian civilizations.

Saperstein, M. *Jewish Preaching: 1200–1800.* New Haven: Yale University Press, 1989. The introduction provides a history of the relationship between biblical exegesis and Jewish preaching with comparisons to Christianity.

Talmage, F. "Keep Your Sons from Scripture: The Bible in Medieval Jewish Scholarship and Spirituality." In C. Thoma and M. Wyschograd, *Understanding Scripture: Explorations of Jewish and Christian Traditions of Interpretation.* Mahwah, N.J.: 1987, 81-101; and "Apples of Gold: The Inner Meaning of Sacred Texts in Medieval Judaism." In A. Green, ed. *Jewish Spirituality: From the Bible Through the Middle Ages.* New York: Crossroad, 1986, 313-55. These two essays by Talmage constitute an excellent introduction to the place of Scripture in medieval Judaism.

Walfish, B. *Esther in Medieval Garb: Jewish Interpretation of the Book of Esther in the Middle Ages.* Albany: State University of New York Press, 1993. This volume represents an innovative approach to the study of exegesis on a single book of Scripture.

Modern Period

Altmann, A. *Moses Mendelssohn: A Biographical Study.* Birmingham: University of Alabama Press, 1973. In chapter 5, Altmann provides an analysis of the intellectual and social milieu of Mendelssohn's translation.

Fishbane, M. *Garments of Torah.* Bloomington: Indiana University Press, 1989. Essays on ancient, medieval, and modern Jewish biblical hermeneutics emphasize elements of continuity within the Jewish tradition.

Ochs, P., ed. *The Return to Scripture in Judaism and Christianity: Essays in Postcritical Scriptural Interpretation.* Mahwah, N.Y.: Paulist, 1993. The efforts by Jewish scholars in modernity to reintegrate elements from the entire spectrum of Jewish interpretations are described.

Orlinsky, H. M. *Essays in Biblical Culture and Bible Translation.* New York: KTAV Publishing, 1974. A collection of articles that focus on modern Jewish approaches to exegesis and its practitioners.

---

15. Ibid., introduction.

16. Michael Fishbane, *Garments of Torah: Essays in Biblical Hermeneutics* (Bloomington: Indiana University Press, 1992).

HOW THE BIBLE HAS BEEN INTERPRETED IN CHRISTIAN TRADITION

JUSTO L. GONZÁLEZ

Christianity was born in the midst of a people who already possessed scriptures. Although the canon of the Hebrew Scriptures was not yet fixed, there was general agreement as to a basic list of books regarded as authoritative. From the very beginning, the early Christian community laid claim on these Hebrew Scriptures as its own. Eventually, there would be debates between Christians and Jews, as well as among Christians, about exactly which of these ancient books—if any—should be considered "Scripture." Yet even before such debates erupted it became clear that the vast majority of the people of Israel would not accept the Christian understanding of Hebrew Scripture. Christians claimed that Jesus of Nazareth, who had been crucified by order of the Roman Empire, was the Christ, the Messiah. Most Jews rejected that claim. Such divergent understandings of the Hebrew Scriptures forced Christians to interpret the texts anew, in order to show how they pointed to Jesus as the Messiah. Thus it is true, as Rowan Greer has said, that "basic to the task of the formative period is the transformation of the Hebrew Scriptures so that they may become a witness to Christ."[1]

On the other hand, Christians were not the first to face the task of interpreting the Hebrew Scriptures. On the contrary, from the very beginning the

people of Israel were constantly faced with the need to interpret the events of their history and the writings that spoke of them. When the Hebrew prophets looked at the exile and return from Babylon, they saw those events in the light of their ancestors' bondage in Egypt and their liberation from that bondage. Later, when they had to struggle against Syrian and Greek power, they saw that struggle in the light of both the exodus from Egypt and the return from exile. Thus the Hebrew Scripture that Christians claimed for themselves contained much of the history of its own interpretation—indeed, much of it was the record of that history.

The same is true of the part of the Bible that we now call the New Testament (NT). The writers of the NT did not consciously set out to write Christian scriptures parallel to those the church had in common with Israel. Rather, they interpreted the events of Jesus' life and of the life of the church, in the light of the ancient scriptures of Israel. In doing so, they provided the earliest Christian interpretations of the Bible, and these in turn came to form part of the Christian Bible—just as the prophets' interpretations of the exodus came to form part of the Hebrew Bible (HB).

This article deals only tangentially with NT interpretations of Hebrew Scriptures, centering attention on the history of Christian interpretation outside the

---

1. James L. Kugel and Rowan A. Greer, *Early Biblical Interpretation* (Philadelphia: Westminster, 1986) 111.

NT. Yet, it is important to remember that what we are retelling is not a history that began after the writing of the NT, or apart from it, but a history that actually continues the very process by which the entire Bible—Old Testament (OT) as well as NT—was written.

THE EARLY CHURCH

In a way, the most important and urgent question the early church had to face regarding biblical interpretation was that of the continuity or discontinuity between the Hebrew Scriptures and the Christian gospel. This was the major point at issue in the early conflict between Christianity and traditional Judaism, at least as the book of Acts depicts it. Brought before the Sanhedrin, first Peter and then Stephen claim that the death and resurrection of Jesus are the fulfillment of Hebrew Scripture, and that any who oppose Christian preaching are to be counted with those who in ancient times also opposed the will of God. This the leaders of the Sanhedrin cannot accept, and it is for that reason that Peter and John are flogged and Stephen is stoned. Two main points are at issue here: the resurrection of Jesus (or his glorification, for Stephen speaks of Jesus' being at the right hand of God, and not literally of his being resurrected) and the interpretation of Scripture. Clearly, the leaders of the Sanhedrin cannot accept the claim that Jesus has been raised from the dead. But closely tied to this is the fact that in order to accept such a claim they would also have to agree to a particular interpretation of Scripture; one that claims Jesus as indeed the Messiah announced by the prophets and anointed by God for the salvation of Israel. Thus the debate is not only about Jesus and his resurrection, but also about the meaning of Scripture. The first Christians—who are also Jews—claim that Jesus is the fulfillment of Scripture and that there is a clear continuity between the biblical tradition and their own teaching; the traditional Jews reject that claim, seeing a radical discontinuity between their Bible and what the Christians preach.

Even among Christians, however, the issue was not simple. It was not just a matter of reading through the entire OT and clearly seeing Jesus and his message in every line. As any preacher or Sunday school teacher knows, much in the OT is not easy to relate to the Christian message. There are commandments to annihilate entire cities, destroying everyone and everything in sight. There are instructions for worship and sacrifice that hardly seem relevant. There are lists of names that are not even interesting. What are Christians to do with all that, and many other similar materials?

A radical but rather simple solution was to reject the OT altogether. The most famous early Christian leader to take this position was Marcion. The son of a Christian bishop and a firm believer in Paul's message of grace, Marcion came to the conclusion that the god of the OT is not the same as the Father of Jesus Christ. It is not that the OT is false or is a human invention that passes for a divine word, but rather that it is the revelation of another god than that of the Christian gospel. Indeed, the good news according to Marcion is precisely that—far above the vindictive, jealous, punctilious god of the OT, who has made this world—there is the gracious, loving, forgiving God of Jesus and Paul, by whose grace we are forgiven.[2] Therefore, although the OT is trustworthy in the sense of being a true revelation of a truly existing god, it is not authoritative, since the one who is revealed in it is not the supreme, loving God of the gospel.

This interpretation of the OT and its contrast with the Christian message is based on a similar contrast between cosmology and soteriology—between Marcion's view of the world and his understanding of salvation. Marcion sees no good in the physical world, which to him is nothing but a prison in which spiritual reality—namely, human souls—is entrapped. The god of the OT, the merciless Jehovah, is also a god whose values are so twisted that after making this world he "saw that it was good." It is a god who grants spiritual significance to material things, and for that reason requires bloody sacrifices and burnt offerings. Jehovah's jealousy and vindictiveness is all of one piece with his having created this physical world, in which our souls are deceived and entrapped. In contrast to this god of creation stands the God of salvation, whose message is one of pure love and grace. This is the God of Jesus and of Paul, but certainly not of the OT, who therefore must be rejected, not as false, but as radically discontinuous with the gospel of Jesus Christ. Jehovah is the creator and thus the god of this world, but

2. For this reason, the subtitle of Harnack's classical work on Marcion is particularly appropriate: *The Gospel of the Foreign God.* A. von Harnack, *Marcion: Das Evangelium vom fremdem Gott* (Berlin: Akademie-Verlag, 1960).

above him stands the Father, the "foreign God" whose message Christians must proclaim.

Oddly enough, this manner of interpreting the OT and its relationship to the gospel, while having a strong anti-Jewish element, agrees with the Jewish claim that there is no real continuity between the Hebrew Scriptures and what Christians proclaim. Marcion and Judaism agree that Christianity and Judaism are different religions, so that one is not a legitimate outcome of the other. Their point of disagreement—and an all-important one—is which of the two is legitimate.

Marcion's views were not entirely original or unique, for others, particularly among the Gnostics, also disparaged the OT. Earlier in the second century, a certain Cerdo, who probably met Marcion in Rome c. 140, taught that the god of the OT is characterized by a sort of vindictive justice that is contrary to grace. The Ophites (from the Greek ὄφις *ophis,* "snake") made the serpent the hero of the creation story, who helps humankind advance from the ignorance to which the creator god had subjected them. Similar views were held by other Gnostic sects of which little is known, such as the Naasenes, the Cainites, and the Sethites.

The very number of people and sects holding to such negative views of the OT shows how attractive they were. That attraction is easy to understand; if one believes that the OT is the revelation of a different god, or of a power of evil, one is excused from the need to interpret it. All the difficulties disappear. It no longer matters that Jehovah ordered all the people in Jericho to be slaughtered, or that there are strange laws and rituals in Leviticus and Numbers, or that Jehovah boasts of being "a jealous God, punishing children for the iniquity of parents, to the third and the fourth generation of those who reject me." It is now possible to start anew, without any burdensome baggage of ancient scriptures.

This seemingly easy solution to the problem of OT interpretation, however, creates new problems. Marcion's strongest critic was Tertullian, who combined theological perspicacity with a keen sense of humor. Making fun of Marcion's dichotomy between creation and redemption, Tertullian complains that Marcion's God has not made even a miserable vegetable, while the supposedly inferior god was making and ruling all of this world. Where was Marcion's God all the while? Centuries later, Esnik of Colb, an Armenian who lived in the fifth

century, posed a similar question: "Why did the Stranger not take pity on mankind till twenty-nine generations were in Hell?"[3]

The point of such criticism should be clear: To deny all validity to the OT is to turn Christianity into a religion that has nothing to do with human history and to make its God a Johnny-come-lately whose supposed love for humanity is thereby implicitly denied. Furthermore, Marcion's "solution" was unacceptable to the vast majority of Christians for several other reasons. It denied the doctrine of creation and, by implication, of providence. By making the physical world evil, it tended to imply that the Savior could not have come in the flesh— Marcion himself appears to have denied the physical birth of Jesus. For similar reasons, such a view had difficulties with the doctrine of the final resurrection, so cherished by Christians. For all these reasons— and many others—the early church was not ready simply to discard the OT. It was precisely this decision to claim a body of Scripture written centuries earlier and under different circumstances that made it necessary for Christians to find ways to interpret the OT.

Before turning to that matter, however, it is necessary to point out another contribution Marcion made to the history of the Christian Bible and its interpretation: the very idea of a NT. From the beginning the Christian church had adopted the OT as Scripture. Although from an early date specifically Christian writings used as authoritative were in circulation—in particular the Gospels and the letters of Paul—apparently no one saw the need to compile and define a list of such specifically Christian Scriptures. It was Marcion who saw that need, made urgent for him by his rejection of the OT. If the OT is not revealed Scripture—or if it is the revealed Scripture of the wrong god—Christians are left without any scripture at all, unless they can take some of their earliest writings and declare them to have the authority of inspired scripture. This was precisely what Marcion did. Since he was convinced than no one had understood the gospel of grace as well as Paul, the Pauline epistles were the core of his canon. To this was added the Gospel of Luke, on the basis that it was written by Paul's faithful companion. Naturally, in order to be consistent, Marcion had to expunge from this canon all refer-

---

3. J. M. Schmid, *Marcion and His Influence,* trans. E. C. Blackman (London: SPCK, 1948) 76.

ences to the OT, which he declared to be Judaizing additions to the original text. The main point, however, is that, having rejected the entire OT, Marcion was forced to develop an alternative list of authoritative books, and thus offered the first canon of the NT.

In any case, the early church had to interpret the OT so as to relate it to the church's message and its own life. This process obviously started the very day the church was born, for initially all its members were Jews, who, therefore, sought to understand the events surrounding the life and death of Jesus, and their own life as a community, in terms of the Hebrew Scriptures. The entire NT stands as a witness to that process, for its various authors are constantly relating their message to the sacred texts of the Hebrew people. Sometimes the process and the issues it raises take center stage, as in Paul's letter to the Romans, where the issue is precisely how the message of Christianity relates to the revelation of God to Israel. Yet, even when this question does not appear at the very center of theological discourse, all the authors of the NT agree that there is a close relationship between the OT and the gospel they proclaim. On this matter, as on many others, the early church followed the lead of the NT writers.

Even after one has agreed that the OT, just as much as the NT, is Christian Scripture, the question remains: How is the OT to be interpreted so as to show and understand its relationship to the gospel? That was the central question of biblical interpretation for the first generations of Christians, and we will explore it in the next few paragraphs.

Before we tackle that exploration, however, it is important to remember that the early church posed and experienced this question very differently than we do today. To us, it seems quite obvious that the writer of Leviticus or Isaiah deals with questions of his time, very different from those of the early centuries of the Christian era or from those of our own time. Our tendency, therefore, is to begin by trying to understand the original meaning of a text, in its historic setting, and then ask how it relates to our setting—or even if it relates at all. That was not the attitude of the early church as it approached the OT—nor of any of the ancients, as they approached any authoritative text whatsoever. They took for granted that the text belonged to their community and referred to it, and from that premise moved on to explore what the text actually said to them.

Rowan Greer has expressed these contrasting approaches:

To the modern reader, early Christian interpretations of the Hebrew Scriptures appear to be transformations of the biblical text that alter its meaning. We tend to think of an original sense, understood historically, and to regard theological interpretation as a departure from the true meaning of the text. Nothing could be farther from the point of view of religious writers in late antiquity. Pagan, Jew, and Christian were united in assuming the general correlation of sacred texts with the beliefs and practices of religious communities. Scripture represented the authority for those beliefs and practices, but at the same time the religious convictions of the community unveiled the true meaning of Scripture. Far from supplying a new meaning, the transformations of sacred books disclosed their true significance.[4]

This point is crucial if we are to understand early Christian biblical interpretation. If we forget it, it may appear to us at times that the ancients are not taking the text seriously, but are interpreting it according to their convenience, without regard for its historical setting and original meaning. Were we to level such an accusation at them, we might be surprised to hear them respond that it is we who do not take the text seriously, for we seek to analyze it as an objective, lifeless reality, when in truth it is a living text, whose significance is precisely in its relationship to a living community of belief and practice.

Having raised that caveat, we may now explore the various manners in which early Christian writers interpreted the biblical text. In this regard, it has become customary among modern scholars to classify such interpretations according to three categories: prophecy, allegory, and typology. That classification is a valid tool, as long as one is not too rigid about it. Indeed, although the ancients did distinguish in theory among these three methods of biblical interpretation, in fact they often passed almost imperceptibly from one to the other, and no ancient Christian writer is entirely consistent in their use. Again, they were not as interested in the theory of biblical interpretation as they were in helping the community hear the word of Scripture. Therefore, when we today seek to systematize their hermeneutical principles and procedures, we must be careful lest we forget the living faith and the living community in which those principles and procedures were or were not applied.

4. Kugel and Greer, *Early Biblical Interpretation*, 126.

Prophecy. Let us look first at prophecy, which is the ancient method of biblical interpretations that modern readers will find less foreign, since it is often applied to this day. Although in the Bible a "prophet" is not necessarily nor primarily one who foretells the future, but rather one who speaks in the name of God, in most early Christian literature the term *prophecy* is already used, as it is today, in the sense of prediction. That is what is meant by most ancient Christian writers, and by modern historians of biblical interpretation, by a "prophetic" method of interpreting scripture. Briefly stated, this method sees in the words of an ancient text an announcement of something that would happen in the future—most commonly at the time of Christ, but also at the time in which the interpreter is living. This method is found throughout the NT, although not as often as one might think. (As we shall see further on, much of what we tend to read as prophecy may have been intended as typology.)

Prophecy is certainly a preferred method of reading the OT in the Gospel of Matthew, where the theme of the fulfillment of prophecy appears repeatedly. According to Matthew, the birth of Jesus "took place to fulfill what had been spoken by the Lord through the prophet" (Matt 1:22 NRSV), and the same is true of his birth in Bethlehem (Matt 2:5-6), the flight into Egypt (Matt 2:15), the slaughter of the innocents (Matt 2:17-18), the decision to settle in Nazareth (Matt 2:23), and a host of other events.

The same method was employed by other early Christian writers, both in the NT and outside of it. Very soon lists of prooftexts seem to have developed—what scholars call lists of Testimonia—for it is clear that different authors, some of whom do not seem to know each other's work, are quoting the same texts in a similar sequence. Whether such Testimonia were actual written lists of texts and their interpretation, or were transmitted orally through preaching and teaching—much as today's preachers borrow illustrations from each other—is not clear. The discovery of a Jewish list of testimonies at Qumran would seem to indicate that, even before the advent of Christianity, there were such written lists, some of them defending or promoting particular positions within Judaism, and that Christianity took up and adapted, if not the lists themselves, at least the practice of developing and employing such lists.

Prophecy had the decided advantage that it was a fairly simple and straightforward method of show-ing the continuity between the religion of Israel and Christianity. Significantly, early Christian writers used prophecy, so to speak, "in both directions": They used it, much as it still is used today in some circles, to argue that Jesus was indeed the Messiah and that, therefore, if Jews are to be true to their Scriptures, they must accept him as such. But it was also used against Marcion and others who denied the authority of the OT, in order to prove that the OT was indeed the word of God—if Isaiah, for instance, predicted the virgin birth, this proves that Isaiah must have been truly inspired.

One of the fullest ancient discussions on the interpretation of the OT as prophecy referring to Jesus and his followers is to be found in Justin Martyr's *Dialogue with Trypho*. In this work, Justin depicts himself as debating the meaning of the OT with a Jewish scholar. According to Justin:

> Sometimes He [the Holy Spirit] uttered words about what was to take place, as if it was then taking place, or had taken place. And unless those who read perceive this art, they will not be able to follow the words of the prophet as they ought. For example's sake, I shall repeat some prophetic passages, that you may understand what I say. When he speaks by Isaiah, "He was led as a sheep to the slaughter, and like a lamb before the shearer," He speaks as if the suffering had already taken place.[5]

Strictly speaking, this is what is meant by an interpretation of the OT as prophecy. Note that, according to Justin, the words in such prophetic utterances did not refer to either the prophet's own time or to the past, but rather to the future—and this is true even when they are in the present or the past tense. In this sense, then, a "prophecy" is a word or saying whose true meaning is not revealed until its fulfillment in a future event.

While this method of biblical interpretation proved to be a powerful tool for early Christian polemics, it clearly had its shortcomings. These are mainly two. The first is that, although this method makes sense of a number of passages, which then become favorite prooftexts, there are numerous other passages for whose interpretation it is utterly useless. Were we to read the entire OT, marking every single passage that could be considered prophetic by any stretch of the imagination, still most of the OT would remain unmarked. Lengthy legal and ceremonial sections, historical narratives, gene-

---

5. *Dialogue with Trypho* 114.1 (ANF, 1:256).

alogies, poetry, and other materials are part of the OT, but they cannot be interpreted as prophecy. What, then, do we do with such passages? Do we simply declare that, because they do not foretell the future, they are not part of God's revelation? Do we simply ignore them, declaring that they are no longer relevant? The reading of the OT as prophecy, although applicable to some passages, is useless for most others.

The second shortcoming of a reading of the OT as a series of prophecies is that it makes the authority and the applicability of the text depend on its fulfillment, and be limited to it. If what Justin says is true, and the Holy Spirit directly inspired a prophet to utter words that referred, not to the prophet's own time, but to events seven or eight centuries into the future, the clear implication is that the words themselves made no sense and had no value to the prophet, nor to all the intervening generations until their fulfillment. Taking Justin's example of Isa 53:7, if the "sheep led to the slaughter" is Jesus and none other, what meaning could these words possibly have had for the prophet and his contemporaries? What meaning could they have had for a devout Jew living in the fourth century BCE? Or one could illustrate this difficulty with an example of some of the modern interpretations of the book of Revelation. According to one of those interpretations, quite popular a few decades ago, the "beast" in Revelation whose number is 666 was none other than Soviet communism. Does that mean that this particular passage had no meaning for those first readers in Asia Minor to whom it was addressed? That it had no meaning for the many generations of Christians who have lived between the first and the twentieth centuries? That it had to wait for Stalin and communism in order to become significant for the church?

Allegory. Precisely such difficulties as these made other methods of biblical interpretation necessary. One of these other methods was allegory. Christians did not invent or create the allegorical method of interpretation, just as they were not the first to read the OT as a series of prophecies. On the contrary, allegorical interpretation of sacred and other ancient texts had been common practice in the Mediterranean basin long before the advent of Christianity. Among the Greeks and those who shared their cultural inheritance, it had become customary to interpret the ancient myths, particularly the poems of Homer and Hesiod, as allegories

referring to various virtues or to the truths expounded more systematically by later philosophers.[6]

The same procedure had become popular among Jews. Some of the material discovered in Qumran, as well as a number of rabbinic writings of the same period, already provide examples of allegorical interpretation of ancient texts. However, it was particularly in Alexandria that this method of biblical interpretation flourished among Jews who sought to show to their pagan neighbors that the Hebrew Scriptures were not as "barbaric" as might otherwise appear. Already in the second century BCE, a certain Aristobulos wrote an *Exegesis of the Law of Moses,* whose purpose was to demonstrate that "Moses" had stated in allegory the same truths that the Greek philosophers later expounded, and therefore that whatever there was of value in Greek philosophy had been taken from Jewish Scriptures. Along the same lines, Philo of Alexandria, who was roughly a contemporary of Jesus, wrote extensively on the true meaning of sacred scripture, interpreting it as a vast allegory, and thereby making it compatible with what he and his contemporaries considered the best of Greek philosophy.

Allegory thus had the advantage that it allowed exegetes to respond to those who objected that the biblical narratives were too crass and "unphilosophical." According to those who interpreted Scripture allegorically, in such cases the crassness resides not in the biblical text, but in the objection itself, which does not realize that the Bible speaks in a "spiritual" sense.

For who that has understanding will suppose that the first, and second, and third day, and the evening and the morning, existed without a sun, a moon, and stars? and that the first day was, as it were, also without a sky? And who is so foolish as to suppose that God, after the manner of a husbandman, planted a paradise in Eden, towards the east, and placed in it a tree of life, visible and palpable, so that one tasting of the fruit by the bodily teeth obtained life? and again, that one was a partaker of good and evil by masticating what was taken from a tree? And if God is said to walk in the paradise in the evening, and Adam to hide himself under a tree, I do not suppose that any one doubts that these things figuratively indicate certain mysteries, the history having taken place in appearance, and not literally.[7]

Probably the best way to communicate the essence of the allegorical method of biblical interpre-

6. On this point, see Robert M. Grant, *The Earliest Lives of Jesus* (London: SPCK, 1961) 45-46.
7. Origen, *De principiis,* 4, 1, 16 (ANF, 4:365).

tation is to examine the hermeneutical method of that master of allegorical interpretation who wrote those words, Origen of Alexandria. Numerous allegorical interpretations of various passages of the OT had been given by Christians before the time of Origen. At some point in the second century, the author of the so-called epistle of *Barnabas* made ample use of allegory—although not exclusively. Later, just before the time of Origen, Clement of Alexandria likewise provided a number of examples of such interpretations. But none of them equalled Origen, the great teacher who flourished in Alexandria early in the third century.

Origen approached Scripture as both a devout Christian and a Platonist. As a Christian, he was convinced that God spoke through the sacred text and that such speech demanded obedience. It is easy to underscore the freedom of interpretation that results from Origen's allegorical method so that one forgets that he was a true and faithful son of the church, ready to seek martyrdom at an early age and never teaching anything contrary to Christian tradition. On the other hand, as a Platonist, Origen yearned for eternal, immutable truth, the sort of truth that cannot be perceived by the senses, and he expected every text of Scripture to yield that sort of truth. He was also convinced that, just as the physical world points to spiritual realities, so also do the words of Scripture point to a deeper truth beyond their literal sense.

A parallelism between the tripartite composition of human beings and the meaning of Scripture stands behind Origen's theory of the triple sense of Scripture. According to him, a scriptural text usually has three meanings: a literal or physical meaning, a moral or psychic meaning, and a spiritual or intellectual meaning. The reference to the tripartite constitution of a human being, as body, soul, and spirit, is obvious. These various meanings are hierarchically ordered, just as body, soul, and spirit are hierarchically ordered. And, just as body, soul, and spirit are all God's creation, so also are all the various meanings of a text true and valid, although one should always seek the higher meanings.

This is at least the theory behind Origen's exegetical method. In truth, he seldom expounds a particular text according to its threefold meaning. On occasion, he declares that a text is clearly metaphorical, so that a strictly literal interpretation would be wrong. Such is the case, for instance, of John 15,

where Jesus speaks of himself as a vine. At other times, Origen grows enthusiastic with the manifold meanings he can discover in a text, so that rather than three he expounds four, five, or even more meanings. Most often, however, he simply elucidates two senses, the literal and the spiritual or allegorical. As R. P. C. Hanson, one of his foremost interpreters, has said, "On the whole the 'moral' sense plays no significant part in Origen's exegesis, not because he had no occasion to draw edifying or devotional lessons from the text of the Bible but because in the practical work of expounding Scripture he found it impossible to maintain the distinction between the 'moral' and the 'spiritual' sense, and the former became absorbed in the later."[8]

In any case, what is important for our purposes is that Origen usually approaches a biblical text seeking to discover a meaning hidden behind the obvious words, and couched in allegory. In this general approach, he was no innovator, for Jewish and Christian scholars alike had long found it expedient to interpret the difficult passages allegorically. The author of the so-called epistle of *Barnabas,* for instance, could make no sense of a literal interpretation of the prohibition of eating pork, and therefore declared that what this precept means is that believers must not associate with people who remember their Master only when they are in need, as pigs do when they are hungry.[9] Likewise, the commandment regarding circumcision referred to what Paul calls the "circumcision of the heart," and it was an evil angel that led Jews to take it literally.[10] What Origen did add to this approach, already quite common in his time, was the thorough and systematic manner in which he applied it.

To Origen, the entire Bible is an allegorical document, and its unity is such that the entire document must be used to interpret each of its parts. This is a rather common hermeneutical principle, often expressed in our days in statements like "The Bible is its best interpreter," or "A text must be read in the light of its context." When Origen applies this principle, however, what he means is that, since every word has a hidden meaning, one must search throughout the Bible in order to find that meaning. R. P. C. Hanson has collected a few of the hundreds

8. R. P. C. Hanson, *Allegory and Event: A Study of the Sources and Significance of Origen's Interpretation of Scripture* (London: SCM, 1959) 243.
9. *Barn.* 10.3.
10. *Barn.* 9.4-5.

of words to which Origen thus assigns an allegorical meaning:

"Horse" in the Bible usually means "voice"; "today" means "the present age"; "leaven" means "teaching"; "silver" and "trumpet" mean "word"; "clouds" . . . mean "holy ones"; "feet" mean "the counsel by which we tread the journey of life"; "well" means "the teaching of the Bible"; "linen" means "chastity"; "thighs" mean "beginning"; "unmixed wine" means "misfortune"; "bottle" means "body"; "secret" and "treasury" mean "the reason."[11]

A second hermeneutical principle to which Origen refers repeatedly is that "nothing is to be said of God that is unworthy of him." In practical terms, this means that any passage whose literal reading implies something unworthy of the Godhead must be interpreted only in a "spiritual" sense. Obviously, it also means that no allegorical interpretation must imply anything unworthy of the divine. Such "unworthiness," however, must be understood not only in the moral sense—God can do no evil—but also in the metaphysical. In this sense, anthropomorphisms, or any hint of change in the Godhead, must be rejected as unworthy of God.

Finally, a most important hermeneutical principle for Origen is that the interpreter must be subject to "the rule of faith." Scripture is to be interpreted within the community of faith, as that community's book, and not as a private hunting ground for the exegete. Origen's understanding of "the rule of faith" was rather wide; therefore, he felt free to speculate on such matters as the preexistence of souls and the existence of past and future worlds. Even so, he considers himself subject to "the rule of faith," and will not knowingly contradict it—on occasion he warns his readers that a particular interpretation, while not contradicting the doctrine of the church, goes beyond what that doctrine has established and must be taken as his own personal speculation.

Origen's understanding of the Bible as belonging to the church, and of his own task as an interpreter as bound by the rule of faith, is crucial. Without such restraints, Hanson's dictum would be true, that Origen "transforms the Bible into a divine crossword puzzle the solution to whose clues is locked in Origen's bosom."[12] Hanson is correct in that Origen never gives sufficient reason for coming to

such conclusions as *horse* means "voice," and that *linen* means "chastity." In that sense, it is true that the solution to the apparent puzzle of the meaning of Scripture is locked in Origen's bosom. What is not true, however, is that Origen is ready to interpret Scripture according to his own personal whim, as if he stands alone before the sacred text. On the contrary, he makes it very clear that the text belongs to the community and that it must be interpreted on that basis.

Even though Origen considered himself a faithful exponent of Christian truth, many of his contemporaries disagreed and considered him a heretic. After his death, some saw in his teachings the germ of a number of controversies and heretical doctrines that greatly distressed the life of the church. By the sixth century, many of his more extreme views—and some that he probably never held, but that were generally ascribed to him—had been officially condemned as heretical. Throughout that process, many people believed that the source—or at least the justification—of Origen's most outlandish views was his allegorical interpretation of Scripture, which allowed him to pour into the biblical text whatever doctrine he later wished to extract from it. For that reason and others, although allegorical interpretation continued to be quite common, it was distrusted.

Compared with prophecy, allegory had the advantage of being able to find meaning in any and all texts of Scripture, while prophecy served only to interpret those texts that could somehow be shown to be fulfilled in later events. On the other hand, it had the decided disadvantage of making the interpreter master of the text and its meaning, rather than vice versa. The methods also coincide in that the stress is on the *words* of the text, rather than in the events to which a text refers. It is important to stress this fact, for modern readers might be inclined to think that an allegorical interpretation makes the words of a text less important, when in fact the opposite is true. Since the sense of a text is to be found in the hidden meaning of its words, every word is of utmost importance. It is for this reason that Origen devoted so much effort to establishing the exact text of Scripture, as witnessed by his monumental Hexapla. It is also for this reason that, when two parallel texts differ, he feels constrained to consider them altogether different—as in the case of the Lord's Prayer, where Origen declares that the

11. Hanson, *Allegory and Event*, 247-48.
12. Ibid., 248.

two texts that appear in the Gospels refer to two separate occasions.

The main difference is that, while prophecy takes the words quite literally, allegory takes them as profound metaphors needing to be elucidated. Also, while prophecy usually looks to the fulfillment of a particular prediction in a particular event, allegory tends to relate the text not so much to events as to eternal and moral truths.

Typology. The third method of biblical interpretation that was current in the early church is typology. This method is discussed by Justin Martyr in the same text that has been partially quoted above, in which he compares and relates it to prophecy: "For the Holy Spirit sometimes brought about that something, which was the type of the future, should be done clearly; sometimes He uttered words about what was to take place, as if it was then taking place, or had taken place."[13]

In this brief passage, it is important to note the contrast Justin makes between "words" *(logoi)* and "types" *(typoi)*. The first refer to what we have called prophecy; there are words in the sacred text that refer to future events—particularly the events of the life of Christ and the birth of the church. In the "types," by contrast, what the Holy Spirit directs is not the actual words of the writer, but the events of which the writer speaks. Both point to the future, but in one case what points to the future is the text itself, and in the other it is the event of which the text speaks.

This may be clarified by means of some examples from Justin himself:

The mystery, then, of the lamb which God enjoined to be sacrificed as the Passover, was a type of Christ; with whose blood, in proportion to their faith in Him, they anoint their houses, i.e., themselves, who believe in Him.[14]

And the offering of fine flour, sirs, . . . which was prescribed to be present on behalf of those purified from leprosy, was a type of the bread of the Eucharist, the celebration of which our Lord Jesus Christ prescribed.[15]

Hence also Jacob . . . being himself a type of Christ, had married the two handmaids of his two free wives, and of them begat sons, for the purpose of indicating beforehand that Christ would receive even all those who amongst Japheth's race are descendants of Canaan, equally with the free, and would have the children as fellow-heirs.[16]

In these three quotations, Justin actually uses the word *type*. What he means by this is that there are past events and commandments ordained and ordered by God so as to point to a future event—most often to Jesus Christ and the Christian life. To a modern reader, such interpretations may seem as far-fetched as the most capricious of Origen's allegories. To the ancients, however, there was an important difference: While an allegorical interpretation does away with the historical meaning of the text, a typological interpretation sees the meaning in the earlier event itself, whose historicity it does not deny. Justin does not say that the Jews were not supposed to sacrifice the paschal lamb, or that to understand the passage in the OT as referring to an actual lamb is a misinterpretation. On the contrary, he asserts that God commanded that the paschal lamb be sacrificed, and that God did this in order to have that lamb point to Jesus and his sacrifice. This was what the ancients meant by "typology," and they often insisted that it was very different from a mere allegorical interpretation. In typology, the stress lies on the event itself—and not on the words—prefiguring other events. This was stated quite clearly by Irenaeus, bishop of Lyons late in the second century: "It is not by means of visions alone which were seen, and words which were proclaimed, but also in actual works, that He was beheld by the prophets, in order that through them He might prefigure and show forth future events beforehand."[17]

Although some of Justin's typological interpretations of events and commandments in the OT, as quoted above, may appear artificial and even capricious to most modern readers, they are in fact based on a coherent view of history. Justin does not believe that he is bringing to the text or to the biblical narrative an element foreign to it, but rather that he is uncovering the relationship of that narrative to the entire course of human history, ever since creation. For Justin, as for Irenaeus and other early Christians, the life, death, and resurrection of Jesus are not merely the result of historical circumstance. They are not even God's last-minute remedy to the human condition. They are, rather, the very goal of history, for which God had planned from the beginning and to which all of creation and all of history point. According to Irenaeus, the Word incarnate in

13. *Dialogue with Trypho* 114.1 (ANF, 1:256).
14. Ibid., 40.1 (ANF, 1:214).
15. Ibid., 41.1 (ANF, 1:215).
16. Ibid., 140.1 (ANF, 1:269).

17. *Adv. haer.* 4.20.12 (ANF, 1:492).

Jesus was the model that God used in creating Adam and Eve. And according to Justin, all of creation is patterned after the cross, which he sees in the shape of sails and ploughs, and even in the human body:

For consider all the things in the world, whether without this form they could be administered or have any community. For the sea is not traversed except that trophy which is called a sail abide safe in the ship; and the earth is not ploughed without it: diggers and mechanics do not do their work, except with tools that have this shape. And the human form differs from that of the irrational animals in nothing else than in its being erect and having the hands extended, and having on the face extending from the forehead what is called the nose, through which there is respiration for the living creature; and this shows no other form than that of the cross.[18]

Thus typology involves an entire view of history and of the gospel within it—as do also prophecy and allegory.[19] Allegory tends to look for eternal, perennial meanings in a text. Its interest lies, not in history, but in eternal truth. Therefore, it reads the text as a shadow or a sign of changeless realities beyond— much as Platonism looks at the physical, changing world as a shadow of the intellectual, changeless world. It is for this reason that "very often even when Origen defends the historical truth of a passage it appears to be quite unrelated to what he regards as its true meaning."[20] Prophecy focuses on the historical fulfillment of a text and in this sense places history closer to the center, but it still sees no meaning in history except as the occasion on which someone was guided by the Spirit to speak words relating to the future. Typology, however, goes beyond prophecy in that it focuses on events at both ends of the equation; it is a matter of events pointing to events. Although past events did point to Jesus Christ—or to the life of the church—they did have meaning in themselves, for they were part of God's guidance of history towards its goal.

Thus a single passage from the OT might be interpreted differently by Christians, while still relating it to their own situation. Take for instance the well-known passage from Isaiah 53:7: "He was led like a lamb to the slaughter, and as a sheep before her shearers is silent" (NIV). Interpreted propheti-

cally, this passage clearly refers to Jesus and to none other. Before the time of Jesus, it had no meaning or applicability, except in pointing to the future. After the time of Jesus, its only significance is in confirming that Jesus is indeed the one announced by the prophet. If one interprets it allegorically, one tries to find hidden meanings in words like *lamb* or *slaughter,* and one may come to the conclusion that the passage means, for instance, that true virtue, like a sheep, does not defend itself, but is willing to give of itself to others, as a sheep goes before the shearer in order to give up its wool, which will warm and comfort others. If one interprets the passage typologically, one will agree that the passage refers to Jesus, but that this is so because God has so ordered history that the just are repeatedly killed and persecuted for the redemption of others. On this basis, it is quite possible that the passage, although correctly applied to Jesus, originally referred to the prophet himself or to Israel or to a particular leader. Also, since history continues along the same pattern, it is also possible to apply the passage to ourselves without thereby denying that it refers primarily to Jesus; when the church suffers, the pattern of which the prophet spoke, and of which Jesus is the supreme instance, appears once again.

These three methods of biblical interpretation— prophecy, allegory, and typology—were widely used in the early church. Virtually every ancient Christian writer made use of prophecy, both because it was fairly simple and straightforward and because there was a tradition of such interpretation. Prophecy, however, did not apply to most of the OT; therefore, ancient Christians had recourse in varying degrees to both allegory and typology.

Of these two, the most common in the very early church seems to have been typology, which appears repeatedly in the NT. Paul employs it, for instance, when he refers to "the spiritual rock that followed them [the ancestors in the desert]" and then declares that "the rock was Christ" (1 Cor 10:4 NRSV). He also applies the same method, although he calls it an allegory, in Galatians 4, where he compares the son of the slave to the son of the free; he does not mean that those events narrated in Genesis did not actually take place or that their significance lies in some hidden meaning of the words themselves, but that the events were a prefiguring of the present situation of Christians. Even some passages that at first sight appear to be cases of prophetic interpreta-

18. Justin *I Apology,* 55.1 (ANF, 1:181).
19. This is a subject I have discussed elsewhere. See *Christian Thought Revisited: Three Types of Theology* (Nashville: Abingdon, 1989) 65-76.
20. M. F. Wiles, "Origen as Biblical Scholar," in *The Cambridge History of the Bible,* 3 vols. (Cambridge: University of Cambridge Press, 1963–70) 1:472.

tion could also be typological in nature. For instance, when Matthew declares that the flight into Egypt took place in order "to fulfill what had been spoken by the Lord through the prophet, 'Out of Egypt I have called my son' " (Matt 2:15 NRSV), does he mean that the words were exclusively prophetic in nature, with no reference to the Exodus, or does he mean that there is a typological relationship between Israel's flight to and return from Egypt, and similar events in the life of Jesus? Given the brevity of the text, it is impossible to tell.

In any case, typology continued to be the most generally employed method throughout the second century. The epistle of *Barnabas,* probably written in the middle of that century, and often quoted as a prime example of early allegorical interpretation, also makes ample use of typology. Jesus "was to offer in sacrifice for our sins the vessel of the Spirit, in order that the type established in Isaac when he was offered upon the altar might be fully accomplished."[21] And, "what do you suppose this to be a type of, that a command was given to Israel, that men of the greatest wickedness, should offer a heifer, and slay and burn it? . . . The calf is Jesus."[22] At about the same time, bishop Melito of Sardis wrote a paschal homily in which he declares of Jesus: "This is he who in Abel was slain, in Isaac was bound, who in Jacob dwelt in a strange land, who in Joseph was sold, who in Moses was cast out, in the lamb was sacrificed, and in David was hunted, in the prophets was dishonoured."[23] Other examples abound in the writings of other second-century writers, such as Justin, Theophilus of Antioch, Irenaeus, and Clement of Alexandria.

With Clement, however, and especially with Origen, Christian allegorical interpretation came to the foreground. It was in Alexandria that Philo had earlier proposed and developed an allegorical reading of the Hebrew Scriptures, which he used to show that they were compatible with the best of the Platonic tradition. Clement and Origen followed the same path, although now attempting to show the compatibility between Platonism and Christianity. Since Platonism sought eternal, changeless truths, it was that sort of truth that these Christian Platonists

also sought in Scripture, and they did so by means of allegorical interpretation.

In Origen himself, allegory showed both its versatility and its great dangers. Therefore, while many followed Origen's method of allegorical interpretation, others blamed Origen's "deviations" from Christian doctrine on that very method. In fact, however, even those who criticized the allegorism of the great Alexandrine would on occasion apply the same method. Such was the case, for instance, with Methodius of Olympus, one of Origen's most vocal critics late in the third century and early in the fourth, who nevertheless wrote several treatises whose hermeneutical method is very similar to Origen's. Others, such as Jerome and Augustine, were fascinated with the allegorical method at an early age, but later abandoned it—or at least tried to limit its more fanciful flights. In the preface to his *Commentary on Obadiah,* Jerome tells us that in his youth he wrote a small work (now lost) on that prophet, in which he interpreted the text allegorically. He bemoans having done so and offers this new commentary as a corrective. Augustine followed a similar path. He had been greatly aided by the allegorical interpretations of Ambrose, which showed him that the Bible was not as inelegant as his rhetorical training made it seem, nor as crude as the Manichees claimed. One of his earliest writings, *On Genesis Against the Manichees,* makes use of that insight, seeking to refute Manichean doctrine by means of an allegorical interpretation of Genesis. This, however, did not prove satisfactory, since the Manichees rejected all allegorical interpretation. When, years later, Augustine took up again the task of commenting on Genesis, he was much less inclined to interpret it allegorically. The very title of his last commentary on that book of the Bible, *De Genesi ad litteram* ("On Genesis, literally") shows this trend in his thought. This evolution in hermeneutical method was paralleled by a similar evolution in his theology. At first, immediately after his conversion, Augustine wrote a series of treatises in which the influence of Neoplatonism is so marked that some interpreters have even doubted that they can truly be called Christian. But later, particularly as his duties as a bishop and a teacher of the church forced him to hold more closely to traditional Christian doctrine and to avoid speculation that might lead others to err, Augustine was more inclined to pay closer attention to the biblical narrative, and to

---

21. *Barn.* 7 (ANF, 1:141).
22. *Barn.* 8 (ANF, 1:142).
23. *Hom.* 69, in *The Homily on the Passion by Bishop Melito of Sardis,* trans. Campbell Bonner (London: Christophers, 1940) 176.

the text embodying it, than to possible hidden meanings behind the text itself.

Both Jerome and Augustine spoke Latin and were brought up in the Latin-speaking West. Meanwhile, the leaders of the church in the Greek-speaking eastern half of the Roman Empire continued the ancient ways of interpreting Scripture, well aware of the differences and even tensions among various hermeneutical approaches. Gregory of Nyssa, for instance, was very much influenced by Origen, and repeatedly followed his lead in interpreting the Bible allegorically. In his treatise *On the Life of Moses,* Gregory follows Origen's principle of different levels of meaning in a text to the point of telling the entire story twice—first from a literal standpoint and then interpreting the entire life of Moses as a vast allegory referring to the mystical ascent of the soul to God. Gregory's older brother, Basil of Caesarea—commonly known as Basil the Great—followed a different course, pointing out the dangers of allegory and insisting on a literal and historical interpretation of the text. When, after Basil's death, Gregory decided to complete the work that his older brother had been composing on the six days of creation, he also decided quite consciously to avoid the allegorical interpretations he so loved and to be faithful to his brother's intent by not departing from the literal and historical meaning of the text.

The most consistent and coherent opposition to allegorical interpretation, however, came from the school of Antioch. This was a city where Christianity had flourished from an early date, if we are to believe the witness of Acts. It was also, according to the same witness, the place where the followers of Jesus were first called Christians. The church in that city had a very clear and strong sense of history, not only because its own history went back to NT times, but also because most of the events narrated in the Bible were purported to have taken place nearby. Traffic between Antioch and Palestine was constant. The Jewish population was numerous and was firmly connected to its historical roots in Palestine. As a result, Antiochene Christians were not as inclined as were the Alexandrines to think of "the Holy Land" as an allegorical way to refer to heaven.

As a result, Antiochene exegesis had long been suspicious of allegory. At least two of its earlier exponents, Paul of Samosata and Eustathius of Antioch, had been condemned as heretics, and in both cases Origenists played no small part. That system's last great teacher before the time of Constantine, Lucian of Antioch, was later credited with having been the real originator of Arianism—although that is a matter that scholars debate. What is certain is that Lucian was one of the ablest biblical scholars of his time, that his corrected text of the Septuagint (LXX) on the basis of the Hebrew original gained wide acceptance, and that he was adamantly opposed to allegorical interpretation. By the middle of the fourth century, the leading figure of this school was Diodore of Tarsus, most of whose works have unfortunately disappeared. We do know, however, that they consisted mainly of Bible commentaries, and that in them he insisted on a grammatical analysis of the text in order to reach its historical meaning, much as Lucian had done, and to reject allegory as a means of biblical interpretation—except in those cases in which the grammatical and literary analyses show that the historical meaning of the text itself is allegorical. Later, two of his disciples would become famous: the preacher John of Antioch, whom posterity has dubbed Chrysostom (the golden mouthed) and the biblical scholar and commentator Theodore of Mopsuestia, later known as "the Interpreter."

Although his knowledge of Hebrew appears to have been limited, Theodore of Mopsuestia was well aware that there were disagreements between the Hebrew text and the commonly accepted Greek translation—an awareness that had earlier led Lucian of Antioch to work on a corrected version of the LXX. In his writings it is clear that he is also aware that certain passages, and even entire books of the Bible, are much easier to accept as sacred Scripture if one is willing to allegorize them. A case in point is the Song of Songs, which many had come to interpret as a vast allegory regarding the love between the soul and God. Theodore read the text and came to the conclusion that it is an erotic love poem. Rather than interpret it allegorically, he would interpret it literally, and exclude it from the canon.

Unfortunately, Theodore's treatise *On Allegory and History* has been lost. All indications are that in it he attacked allegorical interpretation and expounded the theory behind typology. In any case, his extant works suffice to give us a clear idea of his own exegetical method, and perhaps even of its development during his own lifetime. In his commentary on Psalms, which seems to be one of his earliest works, he takes for granted that the one who speaks in the Psalms is always David, and that he does so as a prophet. While Theodore is aware that a number of psalms refer to events after David's time—which shows his historical perspicacity—this poses no major difficulty, for in such cases David was prophesying about events to come. One notable characteristic is that according to Theodore very few of these prophecies refer to Christ; most refer to events in the history of Israel, such as the Babylonian captivity or the struggles during the Maccabean period. Apparently, even at this early stage in his career, Theodore was already looking to the historical sense of a passage as the locus where its meaning is to be found.

This becomes even clearer in Theodore's *Commentary on the Book of the Twelve.* In general, Theodore places each of the minor prophets approximately in the historical setting in which modern scholars place them—except that he takes the story of Jonah as a historical account and seeks to relate it to the fall of Nineveh. Here, however, he departs from his assumption in the commentary on Psalms, that a prophet must speak about the future. On the contrary, most of the passages in the prophets refer to events in the prophet's own time, or shortly thereafter. He has no use for an interpretation that takes isolated verses or sayings from a prophet, and then decides that these sayings relate to Jesus, while others refer to Zerubbabel or to other events and people of the time. The prophets are speaking of their own time and to their own time. The only passages that are given a direct christological meaning are those that had long been defined as such by their use in the NT, and the last two verses in Malachi, where he sees an announcement of the coming of Elijah before the Second Coming of Jesus.

This manner of reading the prophets is grounded on Theodore's typological understanding of the way in which the OT relates to the NT and to the life of the church. He wishes to retain the relationship between the two testaments, and to affirm that the OT does have a message for the Christian church. But he is not willing to do this at the expense of the validity of OT passages within their own historical setting. Both prophecy—which he had earlier employed in interpreting the Psalms—and allegory—which he seems to have always rejected—fall short on this account; both make the OT relevant for Christians at the expense of denying its historical

relevance for Israel. "He firmly believes that the Law foreshadowed Christ. But at the same time, while he believes that all of God's revelation is summed up in Christ, he refuses to allow that the revelation God gives of Himself in the Old Testament is meaningless apart from Christ."[24]

This is the reason why Theodore rejects both allegory and prophecy: Both deny ultimate revelatory significance to the historical events of which the text speaks. He makes this point in attempting to respond to those who argued that Paul himself had used allegorical interpretation, for in Galatians 4 he says that the story of Sarah, Hagar, and their two sons is an allegory. Theodore responds that in this case Paul is not using the term *allegory* in the same sense in which allegorical interpreters use it. Paul is denying neither the reality nor the significance of the story of Hagar and Sarah; rather, he is comparing events of the past in which God was active with events of the present in which God is similarly active, which is the very essence of typology. Thus, although Paul calls it an allegory, his interpretation is typological.

THE MIDDLE AGES

Jerome died in 420, Theodore in 428, Augustine in 430. Not only were the great interpreters of Scripture dying, but so was the ancient world. Ten years before the death of Jerome, Rome was sacked by the Goths. Soon the entire western portion of the Roman Empire would be divided among several Germanic kingdoms. In the centuries that ensued, when civil disorder, foreign invasion, and economic chaos were common occurrences, most of the science and wisdom salvaged from antiquity took refuge in the church and its institutions, particularly monasteries. As a result, for centuries the Bible was read through monastic eyes.

This was no longer an age of avid research. It was a time when much of the historical and linguistic knowledge of the past was forgotten, and when, therefore, the kind of exegetical study that Theodore of Mopsuestia had modeled was no longer possible. The main source of philological and historical knowledge that these centuries employed, the *Etymologies* of Isidore of Seville, while compiling an

24. Rowan A. Greer, *Theodore of Mopsuestia: Exegete and Theologian* (Westminster: Faith Press, 1961) 107.

enormous amount of material, were often more fanciful than factual.

Medieval Monasticism. Reading the Bible through monastic eyes meant two things. It meant first of all that the Bible was usually interpreted as a call to monastic renunciation and contemplation. Gregory the Great, the main authority through whom the Middle Ages received the legacy of Christian antiquity, read the Bible primarily as a manual on morality and asceticism. During Gregory's time, and in the centuries immediately following, there was much less doctrinal and theological debate than there had been at the times of Origen or Augustine. Only in the ninth century, during the brief revival in learning brought about under the Carolingians, was there a measure of theological debate—and in those debates the Bible was indeed used as the main point of reference for correct doctrine. But by and large, Gregory and his successors for five centuries did not have to cope with significant theological dissent. Their struggle was more against the temptations of "the world"—and it was as an aide in that struggle that the Bible was most often read and interpreted. This, in addition to the lack of adequate tools for historical and linguistic research, meant that the most profitable and accessible way to interpret Scripture was as a vast moral allegory. Not only the Song of Songs, but also the stories of Moses, Job, and Ezekiel are in fact parables or metaphors referring to the soul's ascent to God and the many perils and temptations it finds along the way. Therefore, reading the Bible through monastic eyes first meant reading it allegorically, even when—as was the case with Gregory—one repeatedly denounced the dangers implicit in fanciful flights of allegorical interpretation.

Reading the Bible through monastic eyes also meant reading it in the context of prayer and worship. What one must always keep in mind is that such use is in itself a form of interpretation. A reading of Isaiah 53 on Good Friday, for instance, is already an interpretation of that passage, even if no further words of explanation are added—and, as the same reading is repeated in the same liturgical context year after year, the interpretation implied by that setting becomes normative. Medieval monasticism, centering its life as it usually did on communal worship, developed its own traditions of biblical interpretation. Sometimes these traditions were expressed in treatises on the use of the Bible in worship,

such as those of Bruno of Würzburg in the eleventh century; but most often they were tacitly accepted as the normative interpretation of particular texts. In any case, the influence of these traditions can be traced far beyond the confines of monasteries, for as theology and biblical interpretation found wider fields of activity, they continued much of the legacy they had received from monastic liturgical interpretation. (It has often been remarked, for instance, that Martin Luther interpreted the psalms christologically, as referring to Jesus. The reason why he did this, even long after leaving the monastery, is that when he was a monk he had grown accustomed to hearing and repeating particular psalms in specific settings of the liturgical year: Advent, Christmas, Good Friday, etc.)

The twelfth century brought about both a revival of monasticism and the beginnings of new conditions that would eventually lead to an alternative way of reading the Bible. The outstanding figure in the monastic revival was Bernard of Clairvaux, who brought the tradition of monastic biblical interpretation to its high point. Devoted as he was to the contemplation of the humanity of Christ, Bernard paid attention to the historical, literal meaning of the NT, particularly the Gospels. However, his main purpose in reading Scripture was not to inquire what the sacred text says in itself, or what it was intended to say when it was written, but to benefit the soul in its quest for union with Christ. Read in the context of the monastic community, the text could yield a variety of meanings, according to the needs of each soul. Since the goal of the reading of Scripture is not knowledge, but the love of God, every reading that leads to such love is true and faithful. It is precisely this spiritual purpose of union with Christ that gives Scripture its unity; therefore, Bernard and his followers felt quite free to interpret the Bible allegorically—particularly the OT, which must be read in such a way as to find Christ in every single page.

Thus, in spite of his deep respect for Scripture, Bernard could declare: "I no longer wish to listen to Moses, whom I find to be no more that a stutterer. Isaiah's lips are unclean. Jeremiah cannot speak, for he is but a child. Actually, all the prophets are mutes. Let me rather listen to Him of whom they speak."[25]

Cathedral Schools and Medieval Universities. On the other hand, the twelfth century saw a parallel

---

25. Bernard *Sermons on the Song of Songs* 2.2.

development that would soon lead to a different way of reading the Bible. With the growth of cities, cathedral schools began to rival monasteries as centers of learning, and a number of them eventually developed into universities. In these cathedral schools, and later in the universities, one read the Bible mainly as a source of knowledge and as a means of settling intellectual disagreements and disputes. The earlier centuries of the Middle Ages had been remarkably free of theological controversy; those that did arise were often mere repetition of debates that had taken place during the patristic period and thus often could be solved on the basis of patristic authority. The main opponents of most monastic readers of Scripture in the early Middle Ages were the devil, the flesh, and the world. It was as a shield against these opponents that such monks read the Bible, seeking guidance, inspiration, and wisdom. Beginning in the twelfth century, and flowering in the thirteenth, a new mood arose, particularly in the universities. Although the devil, the flesh, and the world were still considered the great enemies of the Christian life, the scholastics read the Bible as a source of knowledge and of arguments against those who disagreed with them. Thus once again, as had been the case during the great theological debates of the fourth and fifth centuries, the Bible tended to become the great arbiter in theological debate, rather than the guidebook leading the believer in the paths of faith and righteousness. One could say that while traditional monasticism read the Bible in quest of wisdom, the scholastics read it in quest of knowledge—although such contrasts should not be exaggerated, since most scholastics were also monks.

Since the cathedral schools were the forerunners of the great medieval universities, it is to them that one must look for the historical background of scholastic biblical interpretation. One of the main activities of such cathedral schools was the development, compilation, and transmission of glosses to the biblical text. The master of a cathedral school would gather bits of information from earlier writers, which might clarify (or amplify) the meaning of a text, and would write such bits between the lines or at the margin of the text itself. Sometimes, although not usually, he would also add his own views or brief comments. Copied down by students and others, such glossae circulated widely among scholars. Since by their very nature they were compila-

tions of previous wisdom, they influenced each other, so that the task of determining what comes from a particular master is almost impossible. Until the twelfth century, these various glossae were generally fragmentary, usually dealing with no more than a particular book or section of Scripture. Early in the twelfth century, however, Anselm of Laon, with the support and collaboration of several colleagues and students, set out to compile a gloss of the entire Bible. With constant addition and variation, this became known as the *Glossa ordinaria,* one of the main tools biblical scholars and commentators employed throughout the rest of the Middle Ages. Following its example and methodology, a number of these scholars produced fuller glosses on parts of Scripture, and these too became widely used. Most notable among them was the *Magna glosatura* of Peter Lombard on the Pauline epistles and the psalter, which was not quite as influential in later scholasticism as were his four books of *Sentences,* but it did influence the manner in which the rest of the Middle Ages read Paul's works. In any case, since such glosses were mostly compilations of earlier views, they did not add much to the interpretation of Scripture, except by establishing standard interpretations of particular texts.

Some of the masters of cathedral schools also produced commentaries on entire books of the Bible. By the middle of the twelfth century, there were numerous commentaries on most of the books of the Bible, and their number was growing rapidly. Greatly dependent on the glossae as they were, and written at a time when individual scholarship and authorship were not particularly prized, there is much repetition and similarity among these various commentaries. They were generally intended as an aid to preaching and teaching; therefore, their tone is often homiletical and hortatory.

It has been pointed out that one of the main difficulties the authors of these commentaries found was the ancient tradition that distinguished between a "literal" and a "spiritual" sense in Scripture.[26] By then, partly as a reaction to the excesses to which extreme allegorization could lead, it had become generally recognized that one should pay particular attention to the "literal" meaning of a text. This included not only grammatical commentary but also an exposition of the meaning of the text within its

26. Beryl Smalley, "The Bible in the Medieval Schools," in *The Cambridge History of the Bible,* 2:214-16.

original historical setting—to the degree that such was possible with the often scant knowledge of history that the Middle Ages possessed. Such "literal" meaning could not be bypassed in favor of the "spiritual." Nor should the two be confused. Therefore, the master was expected to give clear indication of when he was interpreting a text "literally" or "spiritually." The "spiritual" interpretation provided the master opportunity to apply the text to the religious and moral life, often by means of typology or of allegory. Most often, such spiritual interpretation was in truth a moral exposition, exhorting the student or the reader to greater effort in the pursuit of virtue.

The difficulty was that, while the early scholastic commentators felt compelled to follow the traditional distinction between the literal and the spiritual, they had no clear theological framework to guide them in the application or evaluation of that distinction. On the one hand, the "literal" sense must govern all interpretation and must never be ignored, while, on the other hand, the "spiritual" was considered to be more valuable, for it dealt with permanent truth rather than with transitory events or things. Thus the early scholastic commentators found themselves at an impasse produced by the unavoidable tensions between their insistence on the value of the "literal" sense and their reliance on a Platonic metaphysics and epistemology. To them, true knowledge must be the knowledge of eternal, changeless reality, and such knowledge does not come through the senses. At best, sense perception leads to a pale imitation of eternal truth. At the worst, it leads to self-deception. How then can the "literal" meaning of Scripture lead to the "spiritual"?

It was left to Thomas Aquinas to propose a way out of this impasse—which he conceived in terms of his own Aristotelian metaphysics and epistemology. Thomas believed that the senses played an important and necessary role in knowledge, which was based on the knowledge of concrete, historical reality. He was, therefore, quite ready to admit that the author of a biblical text could not know all that the text itself would later come to mean in God's providence, as history unfolded. That original meaning is the "literal" sense. It is normative and must never be abandoned or contradicted. Later interpreters, being in a relatively privileged position because they know later history, can and should interpret the text according to the meaning learned from that history and from their present circumstances. This is the "spiritual" meaning of the text. The use of a text in order to derive such "spiritual" meanings is quite legitimate and even necessary, for without it the text would remain in the past, and not directly apply to different circumstances. Yet only the "literal" meaning has final authority, in the sense that it requires acceptance by all and can thus serve as the basis for theological argument.

The literal sense was defined as the sacred writer's full original meaning. It included the whole message which he meant to convey at the prompting of his inspiration for the benefit of his public whether present or future. . . . The spiritual sense was defined as the meaning which God, the chief author of Scripture and of the events it describes, had put into sacred history. The sacred writers, who took part in it, could not understand a significance which had not yet been revealed. Their successors would discern it in the light of subsequent revelation. Thomas deduced from his premise that no argument could be drawn from the spiritual interpretation, but only from the literal. The spiritual could be used for edification of the faithful, but not for proof.

The Thomist definition gained general acceptance, hesitating at first in some quarters, but later carrying conviction. It disposed of the difficulties arising from metaphor and prophecy and focused interest on the writer's original meaning. It restricted the use of moralities in political propaganda, where they caused most muddle. . . . On the other hand, lecturers made free with Thomas's permission to use the spiritual senses for edification. What master would have cared to deprive his pupils of instruction in the technique of preaching? Allegories and moralities, no longer "higher" or "nobler," remained indispensable. They would last in exegesis just as long as the medieval sermon lasted.[27]

It was not only in commentaries, sermons, and glossae that the scholastics used the Bible. As has been indicated above, one of the characteristics of scholasticism was that it tended to read the Bible as a source of knowledge and theological argument, rather than as a book of edification, as was customary in traditional monasticism. The reading of Scripture in the context of theological debate, and as a source of knowledge and ammunition to be employed in such debates, was further stimulated by the scholastic method itself. The scholastic academic exercise *par excellence* was the *disputatio*. This usually dealt with a very specific question—for instance, "whether, as the eternal Word of God, the knowledge of Christ actually includes infinite objects."[28]

27. Ibid., 2:215-16.
28. St. Bonaventure *Quaestiones disputatae de scientia Christi*, q. 1.

The question itself was sometimes chosen in advance, and sometimes at the very beginning of the "disputation," depending on the nature of the exercise. There followed a process whereby those present—often including the public—were allowed to list arguments both for a positive and for a negative answer. These arguments, following the example of the glossae, usually consisted of brief quotations from Scripture, patristic literature, the philosophers, and other authorities. It was up to the teacher leading the exercise to come up with a solution that included not only his own answer, but also a response to all the objections raised in the previous section. The result was a literary structure that became characteristic of much scholastic theological literature: A question is posed, followed by two lists of arguments that seem to lead in contradictory directions, then by the author's answer to the question, and finally by a "solution" to each argument on the other side—a solution that cannot deny the authority of the texts quoted, but must interpret them in such a way as not to contradict the author's answer to the question.

As a result of such methodology, not only the Bible but all ancient authorities tended to be read and employed as sources for proof texts. There was no room for extended exegesis of a passage, nor for its use in edification, consolation, or moral exhortation. The quote would be brief and must be employed to prove a point. If there is any consideration of the context—which is seldom the case—this appears only in the author's "solution" to the objections, in which sometimes it is argued that, in its proper context, the text quoted has a different meaning.

Finally, in order to complete the picture of biblical interpretation during the Middle Ages, a word must be added regarding the pursuit of what today we would call "biblical scholarship," particularly with reference to the study of the original languages of Scripture. The commonly held notion that the Middle Ages had no interest in such matters must be corrected. It is true that most medieval theologians and scholars relied exclusively on the received text of the Vulgate (Vg), and that Hebrew and Greek were not part of the normal theological curriculum. Yet that is not the entire picture. Jerome was commonly regarded as a paradigm of biblical scholars, particularly since he had produced the Vg. And Jerome himself had made it quite clear that the task

of translation always involves interpretation. Therefore, the knowledge of the biblical languages, and of the customs and traditions that stand before them, was a common desire among medieval scholars, even though few attained such knowledge. Wherever anti-Semitic prejudice and violence did not preclude it, Christian scholars sought to learn from Jewish rabbis, not only the Hebrew language, but also the traditions and customs that might serve to illumine the meaning of the biblical text. This was particularly true in Spain, where centuries of social exchange among Jews, Christians, and Moslems had produced an openness that did not exist elsewhere in Europe—until, toward the end of the Middle Ages, Spain became as intolerant as the rest of Western Europe.

Nor is it true that medieval scholars were unaware of variants in the text of the Bible and in other ancient writings. In fact, there were lists of such variants and attempts at correcting various readings. What is true is that, lacking the printing press, and therefore a means to produce texts guaranteed to be identical, the task of spending long years of arduous work comparing manuscripts in order to establish a text, and then to entrust it to the same process of copying that had introduced the variants in the first place, seemed futile.

THE REFORMATION AND BEYOND

All of these currents were present in the sixteenth century. The traditional monastic reading of Scripture, as a source of wisdom and edification rather than of knowledge and doctrine, was typical of the monastic revival that centered in Spain around such figures as St. Teresa of Avila, St. John of the Cross, Fray Luis de León, and St. Ignatius of Loyola. Although all of them could on occasion make use of the Bible as a tool in controversy, their usual reading of the sacred text was as a guide for the life of monastic renunciation, rather than as a manual of theology.

Catholic Interpreters. The scholastic reading of Scripture, and even much of the scholastic method that was closely associated with it, continued in the work of a number of Catholic theologians, much of whose work was quite independent from anti-Protestant polemics, such as the great Dominican professor at Salamanca, Domingo Báñez (1528–1604). At the same university, another Dominican scholar,

Francisco de Vitoria (1492–1546) applied the traditional scholastic method to an entirely new theological problem in his lectures *On the Indians.* Thomas de Vio Cajetan (1468–1534), who became involved in the issues regarding the Protestant Reformation because he was papal legate to Germany when the Reformation erupted, developed much of his theology along traditional lines. His *Commentaries on the Summa,* published from 1507 to 1522, in general reflect the same exegetical and hermeneutical methods that Thomas Aquinas had developed.

As anti-Protestant polemics came to the foreground in Catholic theology, the scholastic method proved particularly useful. Here was a method whose characteristic reading of Scripture was doctrinal and polemical. In its traditional form, it had developed subtle distinctions and had even created disagreement and debate where there was none, for the very sake of its method. Now that some of the central doctrines of Christianity were debated, most traditional theologians sought to refute the reformers by means of a similar method. In the polemical writings of theologians like John Eck (1486–1543), James Hochstraten (1460–1527), and James Latomus (1475–1544), one can see the scholastic method of reading Scripture, now applied to the task of refuting the doctrines of Protestantism.

It was the thrust of anti-Protestant polemics that led the Council of Trent (1545–63) to its two major decisions regarding the Bible and its authority.[29] (The Council also defined the canon of Scripture, but this was not then at issue between Protestants and Catholics; in any case, all that it did in this respect was to ratify the decisions of the earlier Council of Florence.)

The most momentous declaration of Trent regarding Scripture had to do with its authority vis-à-vis the authority of tradition. In this regard, the Council decreed that on matters of faith and morals the books of Scripture were to be held "in equal devotion and reverence" with the tradition of the church. Almost one fourth of those present at the Council would have preferred the use of the word *similar* rather than *equal,* but they were outvoted. It also appears that most of those who voted for the final decree did not intend to say that tradition was an independent, or even a parallel, source of Christian doctrine, but

simply that Scripture should always be interpreted in agreement with it. In any case, this decree left its mark on Roman Catholic biblical interpretation, at least until Vatican II reopened the issue. This, however, did not mean that all was settled, for it is quite clear that there are many different and even contradictory elements in Christian tradition; thus there was still ample room for argument and disagreement. What it did mean was that the theological and hermeneutical debate would often turn away from Scripture to the issue of what tradition actually held—theologians who disagreed on the meaning of a biblical text were to settle their differences, not exclusively or even primarily by examining the text itself, but by searching the tradition. It was also unclear how far that tradition extended. Most Protestant theologians agreed on granting at least a measure of authority to the patristic tradition, as illumining the meaning of the biblical text. But the Council of Trent, and particularly its more extremist interpreters, understood by "tradition" all the teachings and declarations of the church and its teachers, including those of the medieval scholastics and even the present magisterium of the church.

The second momentous decision of the Council of Trent was its declaration that the Vg edition of Scripture was to be "taken as authentic in public readings, disputations, preaching, and exposition." The Council issued this decree as a response to those reformers who based some of their arguments on the original Greek and Hebrew texts of the Bible, and also to the proliferation of vernacular translations that seemed to undercut a number of doctrines based on the Vg. The mood of the more conservative elements in the Council was expressed by a Spanish cardinal who declared that vernacular translations were "mothers of heresy" and should, therefore, be forbidden—or at least limited to less dangerous books like Psalms and Acts. Although his extreme position did not win the day at Trent, soon many among the more conservative Catholics interpreted and applied the decrees of the Council along those lines.

Strictly speaking, the Council left much room for maneuvering: It did not determine which of the many variant Latin texts were to be regarded as authentic; it reaffirmed the authority of the Hebrew and Greek texts; and it neither precluded nor prohibited new translations. Yet, partially as a response to the concern of those who feared that vernacular

---

29. On Trent, its decisions, and how they were interpreted and applied, see F. J. Crehan, "The Bible in the Roman Catholic Church from Trent to the Present Day," in *The Cambridge History of the Bible,* 3:199-237.

translations would result in heresy, the Council ordered that such vernacular versions be published with explanatory notes. The main purpose of these notes was to ensure that the biblical text was interpreted according to the teachings of the church. (As a reaction to this policy, Protestant Bible societies developed their own policy to publish the Bible "without notes.") In practical terms, this conciliar decision tended to limit the freedom of biblical scholars and interpreters. As the Roman Catholic Church became more conservative, and its translations of the Bible into the various vernacular languages were based on the Vg instead of the original languages, Catholic believers throughout the world were placed at a decided disadvantage to Protestants.

This does not mean that biblical scholarship ceased. On the contrary, the quest for the original text and its meaning continued and even flourished after the end of the Middle Ages. The fall of Constantinople (1453) brought to Western Europe a flood of Greek manuscripts and scholars, which led to a revival in Greek studies in the West. The invention of the movable-type printing press made scholars increasingly aware of the degree to which manuscripts had been corrupted as they were copied and recopied, and for the first time provided the opportunity to produce multiple copies of an identical text. The result was a veritable flood of critical editions of ancient texts.

The scholar whose name has become indissolubly united with this movement is Erasmus of Rotterdam. He tended to read the Bible much as the earlier monastic tradition had done, as a source of wisdom and moral inspiration. Yet it was not his interpretation of the Bible, but his more scholarly work on its actual text, that proved to be most significant. His edition of the Greek NT, published in 1516, marked a new age in biblical scholarship. In 1520, a group of scholars at the university of Alcalá in Spain, under the direction of Cardinal Francisco Ximenes de Cisneros, published the Complutensian Polyglot Bible, which included texts in Hebrew, Greek, Aramaic, and Latin. Ximenes himself was aware of the impact such studies could have on theology, for on receiving the first volume of this Bible he declared that it "opens the sacred sources of our religion, from which will flow a theology much purer than any derived from less direct sources"[30]—a view that, had

it been professed a generation later, would have been declared to be heretical. Even after the anti-Protestant reaction had made statements such as Ximenes' questionable, Catholic scholars continued this tradition of biblical scholarship. In 1568–72, Benito Arias Montano, at the behest of Philip II, published in Antwerp a polyglot Bible that included texts in Hebrew, Greek, and Syriac as well as a literal Latin translation. In 1597, the sixteen volumes of Alfonso Salmerón's *Commentaries on the New Testament* were published posthumously; Salmerón was one of the original companions of Ignatius in the founding of the Jesuits. Although the seventeenth century did not see an equal production of Catholic biblical scholarship, the tradition continued until it once more came to the foreground in modern times.

Protestant Interpreters. All of these traditions of biblical scholarship and interpretation merged and took new forms in Martin Luther. As an Augustinian canon, he had learned and always continued to practice the medieval monastic tradition of reading Scripture for wisdom and edification. As a doctor and professor of Bible, he was well aware and made use of the scholarly and philological work of Erasmus and his medieval predecessors. As a reformer, he soon found himself involved in controversies that forced him to read Scripture as a source of doctrine and knowledge—although he never did this after the manner of the scholastics.

The study and interpretation of the Bible was one of Luther's paramount concerns even before the beginning of the Reformation. Luther's other main concern, which soon coalesced with his biblical interpretation, was the quest for redemption and its meaning. A modern scholar has correctly assessed the importance of biblical interpretation for Luther in declaring that "it was as a Biblical theologian that Luther understood himself and wanted others, both his friends and his enemies, to understand him. . . . It was as a Biblical theologian that he took up polemics. In fact, it was as a Biblical theologian that he became the Reformer."[31]

Although Luther has become famous for his principle of *sola scriptura,* it is important to note that for him the "Word of God" was much more than Scripture. According to the Bible itself, the Word of God is none other than God: "In the beginning was the Word, and the Word was with God, and the

---

30. Quoted by Conde de Cedillo, *El Cardenal Cisneros, Gobernador del Reino* (Madrid: Real Academia de la Historia, 1921–28) 1:195.

31. Jaroslav Pelikan, *Luther the Expositor,* companion volume to *Luther's Works* (St. Louis: Concordia, 1959) 46-47.

Word was God" (John 1:1 NRSV). Furthermore, the Word is God in action. When God speaks, God does. "God said, 'Let there be . . . ' and there was" (see Genesis 1). What this means is that God's Word, more than mere information that can be contained in a written page, is action—creative and redemptive action. This action comes to us primarily in Jesus Christ, and comes to us through history. Although Christ is also the cosmic Second Person of the Trinity, it is in his historical act of redemption, and in the community of the faithful, that we come to know him. Thus the Word of God comes to us primarily as an act of redemption—even though that Word has already been active in the world since the very act of creation. For these reasons, although Luther held great respect for the Bible, insisting on its primary and unique authority, for him the Bible is the Word of God in a derivative sense, because it contains the record of the actions of the Word of God on our behalf.

This provided Luther with an argument against those who declared that, since the church had determined the canon of Scripture, the church had authority over the Bible. It is also the reason why many of Luther's statements regarding Scripture prove so shocking to those who hold to biblical inerrancy. As to the first, Luther simply declared that it was not the church, but the gospel, that produced the Bible. All the church did was to recognize the gospel in certain books, and not in others. Ultimately, the gospel—the redemptive action of God— is above both the church and the Bible. For the same reason, those who hold fast to the inerrancy of Scripture, even at the expense of the gospel, are themselves in error, for they read the Bible as a book of information about the world and about God rather than as a book of gospel and redemption. "Luther recognized mistakes and inconsistencies in Scripture and treated them with lofty indifference because they did not touch the heart of the Gospel."[32] It is for this reason that he can declare that James is "an epistle of straw," for he cannot find the gospel in it. It is also for that reason that he feels free to apply the methods of scholarship to the biblical text, with no fear that it will thereby lose its authority.

When reading the Bible for edification, and even for non-polemical theological argument, Luther's reading is often typological, and may even lapse into allegory. Yet he also agreed with Thomas Aquinas that when it came to theological debate only the literal meaning should be employed. Hence, "Luther's insistence that in a theological controversy, where proof rather than mere illustration was needed, only the precise meaning of a Scriptural text was to be used. He did not mean that it was altogether illegitimate to use Scriptural passages for the illustration of a point analogous to their meaning. His sermons and commentaries abounded with instances of just such use, some of them skillful, others humorous. But he put such use of the Scriptures into the same category as allegory. It was legitimate for illumination, not for support."[33]

Calvin also insisted on the need to ascertain the historical meaning of a text. Given his humanistic and legal training, he did this much more consistently, and with a more critical approach, than Luther. "Calvin like Luther was quite ready to recognize manifest error in the New Testament, in a citation from the Old Testament and in matters of chronology."[34] From the humanists, he learned the need to establish the original text, and to read it in its historical context, before seeking to apply it to contemporary debates. From the tradition of legal scholarship, he learned the principle of accommodation: God's revelation, like human laws, was always given in a way suitable to its historical and human context.[35] It was the interpreter's task to clarify its meaning, both in its original setting and in the interpreter's own setting.

Some of the lesser figures of the Reformation did insist on the absolute inerrancy of Scripture. Andreas Osiander, for instance, sought to reconcile the diverse accounts of particular events in the various gospels by claiming that every account that differed from the others in any detail must refer to a different event.[36] Since the Lord's Prayer in Matthew is different from that in Luke, Jesus must have taught two different prayers. And, since the number of fishes, loaves, and leftover baskets are not the same in any two Gospel accounts, Jesus must have fed a different multitude in each of those accounts.

The literalism of the Anabaptists proved a greater challenge than that of Osiander and others like him,

32. R. H. Bainton, "The Bible in the Reformation," in *The Cambridge History of the Bible,* 3:12.

33. Pelikan, *Luther the Expositor,* 112.
34. Bainton, "The Bible," 13.
35. J. B. Rogers and D. K. McKim, *The Authority and Interpretation of the Bible: An Historical Approach* (New York: Harper & Row, 1979) 97-100.
36. Bainton, "The Bible," 13-14.

for it had serious political and ecclesiastical implications. While the various Anabaptist groups differed on many points of doctrine, they all tended to agree that the practices of the church in the NT ought to be followed to the letter. This included not only believers' baptism, which soon became the trademark of Anabaptists, but also the relationship between the church and society at large. In the NT, the church is a persecuted community. Most theologians in the sixteenth century held the traditional view that this was a matter of historical circumstance. Not so the Anabaptists, who held that when Christians are truly faithful they will necessarily be persecuted, because their views, values, and mores will clash with those of society at large. The reason why believers' baptism became so important was precisely that baptism was supposed to indicate a radical break with that society, and infants were incapable of making that decision. Infant baptism takes for granted that those who grow up in a Christian society will be Christians. The Anabaptists did not believe that there was such a thing as a Christian society. The NT speaks of a church that clashes with the world, and that is, therefore, part of the very nature of the church. To claim otherwise would be to declare the NT to be no longer valid for the church.

By the seventeenth century, much of the freshness of Luther and Calvin had been lost. Given the emphasis the great reformers had placed on Scripture, it was unavoidable that their followers would develop detailed theories as to its inspiration and authority. The Protestant scholastics of the seventeenth century insisted on the "full" and "verbal" inspiration of Scripture. Full inspiration means that everything in the Bible—even those things that the authors knew by natural means—is directly inspired by God. Paul knew by natural means about the money sent by the Philippians. But the Holy Spirit inspired what he wrote to them about it, just as the Holy Spirit inspired what he had to say about the meaning of the cross. Furthermore, the Spirit inspired the exact words the authors were to use, and this is what is meant by "verbal" inspiration. If one notes a difference in style between various authors, this is due to the Spirit's taking such differences into account, and dictating to each author different words according to what would have been the natural style of each. By the early eighteenth century, Lutheran theologian David Hollaz claimed that the vocalization points in the Masoretic text of the OT were just as inspired as the Sermon on the Mount. Similar developments took place among theologians of the Reformed tradition, where François Turretin (1623–87) declared that not only was the vocalization of the OT inspired, but also the Holy Spirit had kept later copies safe from all error.[37]

Partly as a reaction to scholasticism, a series of movements appeared, emphasizing the need for personal piety rather than strict, cold orthodoxy. Pietists, Moravians, Methodists, and many who participated in the Great Awakenings in the United States were all convinced that the Bible should be read primarily as a guide to Christian life and piety. Most of them were orthodox in their beliefs and did accept the authority of the Bible in doctrinal matters. For them, however, the main reason why Christians should read the Bible was not so much to discover and clarify obscure points of doctrine, but to illumine their own lives. In some ways, the approach of many a Methodist to the Bible was reminiscent of the approach of a medieval monk: The Bible should be read in a disciplined fashion, in a context of prayer and devotion, and with the purpose of improving the quality of one's discipleship.

Typical of this approach to Scripture are the words of John Wesley in the Preface to his *Explanatory Notes upon the Old Testament*:

If you desire to read the Scriptures in such a manner as may most effectually answer this end [of holiness], it would be advisable: (1) To set apart a little time, if you can, every morning and evening for that purpose. (2) At each time, if you have leisure, to read a chapter out of the Old, and one out of the New, Testament. . . . (3) To read this with a single eye, to know the whole will of God, and have a fixed resolution to do it. In order to do know his will, you should, (4) Have a constant eye to the analogy of faith. . . . (5) Serious and earnest prayer should be constantly used before we consult the oracles of God. . . . (6) It might also be of use, if, while we read, we were frequently to pause and examine ourselves by what we read.[38]

Historical-Critical Study. Meanwhile, an entirely different way of reading the Bible had also been developing. Hearkening back to the time of the Renaissance, there were those who applied to the

37. On the theory of biblical inspiration of Lutheran scholasticism, see J. L. González, *A History of Christian Thought*, 2nd ed., vol. 3 (Nashville: Abingdon, 1987) 261-63; on Turretin's, ibid., 276-77.
38. John Wesley, "Preface to the Old Testament," in *John Wesley's Commentary on the Bible: A One-Volume Condensation of His Explanatory Notes,* ed. G. Roger Schoenhals (Grand Rapids: Zondervan, 1990) 20.

biblical text principles of literary and historical criticism similar to those applied to other ancient writings. Erasmus and others sought to restore the text itself. As time passed and the restraints of orthodoxy were removed an increasing number of scholars urged a more rationalist approach to the sacred text. At first, their aim was to show that the teaching of the Bible is eminently rational. Eventually, however, many came to the conclusion that much of what the Bible says is contradicted by science. Others applied themselves to the study of the text itself and of its historical, literary, and cultural background. The posthumous publication of *Apology for the Rational Worshippers of God,* by H. R. Reimarus (1694–1767), shocked the intellectual world of Germany by raising questions about the historicity of the Bible, and by explaining away any miracles found in biblical accounts. By the nineteenth century, such positions had become relatively common. In 1835, D. F. Strauss published a *Life of Jesus,* in which he argued that what is important in the NT is not what it says about Jesus, but the essential truth to which it points: the ultimate oneness of God and humanity. Ernest Renan's *Life of Jesus* (1863), while less scholarly than Strauss's, had a wider impact, for "it was short, popular and sentimental."[39] Ever since, there has been a steady stream of publications, at both academic and scholarly levels exemplified by Strauss and at the more popular level of Renan, that have nurtured an ongoing discussion on the historical origins of biblical texts.

Since the early nineteenth century, much has been learned through the historical-critical method and its various byproducts. Today we know much more than ever before about the cultural, social, and linguistic background of the Bible. Cities long gone have been excavated. Lost languages have been recovered and have given us greater understanding of biblical Hebrew. Layers of composition in the text allow us to understand its significance at various points in its development. As part of the historical-critical enterprise, a number of methods were devised that have made a very significant contribution to our understanding of biblical texts.[40]

The historical-critical approach was not without its critics. In some cases, this method led scholars to postpone or ignore all questions regarding the use and authority of the Bible in the Christian community. In such cases, their work falls beyond the parameters of this essay, which deals precisely with such use and authority. On the other hand, many responded to the challenges raised by the historical-critical method by refusing to allow it a place in biblical studies. The Bible, they insisted, is a divine book, and is not subject to the scrutiny of such human methods. In response to the new methods and their findings, the more conservative gathered around the banner of the "fundamentals" of the Christian faith and brought the doctrine of biblical inerrancy to the fore. Thus the very advances of the historical-critical method evoked a reaction that tended to discount most of the achievements of that method.

The greatest challenges to the historical-critical method, however, did not come from its critics, but from those who employed that method in order to critique some of its earlier findings. As time passed, it became increasingly evident that much of what had passed for historical studies in the nineteenth century was in fact a projection of middle-class bourgeois perspectives, by which earlier times were judged and interpreted.[41] The most famous of the many works leading to this conclusion was Albert Schweitzer's *The Quest for the Historical Jesus,* which clearly showed that much of what supposedly objective scholars found in Jesus was a reflection of their own values and times. Thus the stage was set for the "balanced conservatism"[42] that has characterized biblical historical scholarship during most of the twentieth century.

This is not to say, however, that theologians could now ignore the findings of the historical-critical method. The great contribution of neo-orthodoxy in this respect, and of Karl Barth in particular, was precisely to show that the results of historical and literary criticism of the Bible can and should be incorporated into theology. Commenting on Barth's impact in this regard, Alan Richardson has sug-

39. W. Neil, "The Criticism and Theological Use of the Bible, 1700–1950," *The Cambridge History of the Bible,* 3:281.

40. See the article by C. R. Holladay, "Contemporary Methods of Reading the Bible," in this volume, in which he lists the following methods that have resulted from this approach to Scripture, or at least have been enhanced by it: textual criticism, source criticism, traditio-historical criticism, form criticism, redaction criticism, composition criticism, audience criticism, and canonical criticism.

41. "They could show . . . that such a picture of Jesus or of the OT prophets . . . told more about the ideals of bourgeois Christianity in the late nineteenth century than about the carpenter from Nazareth or the little man from Tekoa." (K. Stendahl, "Biblical Theology, Contemporary," in *The Interpreter's Dictionary of the Bible,* 4 vols. [Nashville: Abingdon, 1962], 1:418).

42. S. J. De Vries, "Biblical Criticism, History of," in ibid., 1:417.

gested: "It is Barth's demonstration of the fact that the historical-critical method is not necessarily bound up with the presuppositions of liberal theology which may well turn out to have been his most significant theological discovery."[43]

Barth's work, and his recognition of the results of historical inquiry into the Bible, gave new impetus to biblical theology. From ancient times, and particularly after the Reformation, there had been a general consensus that theology should be biblical. It was only as a result of the historical studies of the last two centuries, however, that scholars had become acutely aware of the distance between them and the biblical sources. Therefore, those who sought to develop a "biblical theology" were now faced with an unprecedented situation:

No period of Christian theology has been as radically exposed to a consistent attempt to relive the theology of its first adherents. The ideal of an empathetic understanding of the first century without borrowing categories from later times has never been an ideal before, nor have the comparative sources for such an adventure been as close at hand and as well analyzed. There have always been bits and pieces of an appeal to the original meaning over against different later dogmas and practices of the church. . . . But never before was there a frontal nonpragmatic, nonapologetic attempt to describe OT or NT faith and practice from within its original presuppositions.[44]

How do we bridge the acknowledged gap between the times and cultures of the Bible and ours? Barth himself argued that the subject of the text itself, God, bridges that gap. Barth's epochal *Commentary on Romans* made the "otherness" of God the connecting point between Paul and his contemporary readers. Others, notably Rudolf Bultmann, followed the lead of existentialism, claiming that the bridge that allows us to appropriate the message of the NT is self-authenticity and self-understanding— a position that tended to dehistorize the NT. Still others sought other points of contact and continuity, such as a particular understanding of time (O. Cullmann) or a theological motif (the Lundensians). Quite naturally, the debate among all these positions brought the hermeneutical question once more to the fore.

Meanwhile, particularly during the second half of the twentieth century, other concerns have af-

fected the hermeneutical question. These have been basically two: the literary and the sociopolitical.

The literary concern has given rise to what Carl Holladay calls "the literary paradigm." Suffice it to say that in recent decades there has been a lively discussion in the field of literary criticism regarding the meaning and interpretation of texts, and that this discussion is being applied to the question of biblical interpretation. Thus one finds attempts to approach the biblical text on the basis of rhetorical criticism, narrative criticism, reader-response criticism, deconstructionism, etc.

Finally, a word must be said about the sociopolitical concern in biblical interpretation. In recent decades, partly as the result of the growing dialogue with Christians in different social and political settings, we have learned that the social and cultural location of the reader and of the reading community have much to do with what one finds in a text. No one who approaches a text does so as a *tabula rasa*. We all bring our perspectives and presuppositions. Today, as we look back at the most recent centuries of biblical scholarship and interpretation, we realize the degree to which that tradition has been dominated by a particular sector of the human race and of the Christian church. As OT scholar Norman K. Gottwald has put it: "The massive datum is that biblical scholars of the last two centuries have been firmly located in the middle class and have synthesized their scholarly humanistic ideals with bourgeois capitalism and, furthermore, have done so with surprisingly little sense of the inherent tensions and contradictions in such a synthesis."[45]

What is true of class, as Gottwald so clearly states, is also true of gender, race, and culture. By and large, women have been excluded from the hermeneutic task, and biblical scholarship has been the preserve of white Western men. For this reason, many of the most significant discoveries being made today in the biblical text are the result, not so much of historical-critical inquiry, as of new perspectives from which the text is being read.[46]

Equipped with the tools and the results of historical and critical research, the believing community

43. "The Rise of Modern Biblical Scholarship," in *The Cambridge History of the Bible*, 3:322.
44. Stendahl, "Biblical Theology," 425.

45. Norman K. Gottwald, *The Tribes of Yahweh: A Sociology of the Religion of Liberated Israel, 1250–1050 B.C.E.* (Maryknoll, N.Y.: Orbis, 1979) 11.
46. See in this volume the articles by Chan-Hie Kim, James Earl Massey, Carolyn Osiek, Fernando F. Segovia, and George E. Tinker. See also the chapter "Visions of the Word," in J. L. González, *Out of Every Tribe and Nation: Christian Theology at the Ethnic Roundtable* (Nashville: Abingdon, 1992) 38-60.

is now ready to undertake the task of a new reading of Scripture—and, therefore, a new reading of itself. This reading will take into account the contributions of many whose voices have scarcely been heard in the past, but whose insights are already proving to be both valuable and disturbing. The result could well be a theological upheaval and reformation rivaling those of the sixteenth century.

BIBLIOGRAPHY

Abrams, M. H. *The Mirror and the Lamp: Romantic Theory and the Critical Tradition* (Oxford: Oxford University Press, 1953).

Ackroyd, P. R., and C. E. Evans, eds., *The Cambridge History of the Bible*. 3 vols. (Cambridge: Cambridge University Press, 1963–70).

Bainton, R. H., "The Bible in the Reformation." In *The Cambridge History of the Bible*. 3:1-37.

Barton, J., and R. Morgan. *Biblical Interpretation* (Oxford: Oxford University Press, 1988).

Burrows, Mark S., and Paul Rorem, eds. *Biblical Hermeneutics in Historical Perspective: Studies in Honor of Karlfried Froelich on His Sixtieth Birthday* (Grand Rapids: Eerdmans, 1991).

Crehan, F. J. "The Bible in the Roman Catholic Church from Trent to the Present Day." In *The Cambridge History of the Bible*. 3:199-237.

González, Justo L. *Christian Thought Revisited: Three Types of Theology* (Nashville: Abingdon, 1989).

Grant, Robert M., and David Tracy. *A Short History of the Interpretation of the Bible* (Philadelphia: Westminster, 1984).

Greer, Rowan A. *Theodore of Mopsuestia: Exegete and Theologian* (Westminster: Faith Press, 1961).

Hanson, R. P. C. *Allegory and Event: A Study of the Sources and Significance of Origen's Interpretation of Scripture* (London: SCM, 1959).

Kugel, James L., and Rowan A. Greer. *Early Biblical Interpretation* (Philadelphia: Westminster, 1986).

Pelikan, Jaroslav. *Luther the Expositor*. Companion volume to *Luther's Works* (St. Louis: Concordia, 1959).

Neil, W. "The Criticism and Theological Use of the Bible, 1700–1950." In *The Cambridge History of the Bible*, 3:238-93.

Richardson, Alan. "The Rise of Modern Biblical Scholarship and Recent Discussion of the Authority of the Bible." In *The Cambridge History of the Bible*. 3:294-338.

Rogers, J. B., and D. K. McKim. *The Authority and Interpretation of the Bible: An Historical Approach* (New York: Harper & Row, 1979).

Smalley, Beryl. "The Bible in the Medieval Schools." In *The Cambridge History of the Bible*. 2:197-220.

CONTEMPORARY THEORIES OF BIBLICAL INTERPRETATION

MOISÉS SILVA

OUTLINE

INTRODUCTION AND OVERVIEW

The Jewish and the Christian traditions have always been characterized by a fervent interest in the proper ways to interpret the Bible. From the debates between Alexandrians and Antiochenes in the ancient period of the church to the heated discussion of the use of the Bible at the time of the Reformation, the meaning of Scripture has been a major—often the overriding—focus of concern. To scholars in the late nineteenth and early twentieth centuries, when biblical criticism seemed to have fully matured, their own age must have seemed the triumphant culmination of that history. Had not the

new historical approach to the Bible, informed by the principles of the Enlightenment, brought in a definitive, scientific method of interpretation?

In fact, however, modern historical criticism was far from successful in putting an end to the debate. If anything, the second half of the twentieth century has been witness to a bewildering variety of interpretive theories, most of them developed in reaction to the standard critical approach. Even a cursory look at lists of recent publications makes clear not merely that the debate has continued but that it has reached a level of complexity and intensity unparalleled in the history of biblical study. The contemporary landscape is not easily described, but a brief introductory overview of the major approaches will help to orient the reader to the issues discussed in this article. It should be noted, however, that the various theories listed here are not necessarily exclusive of one another; in some cases they are in fact so closely related that treating them separately is artificial.

1. In the first place, we may use the term *traditional* to describe the general approach to biblical interpretation that characterized the Christian church prior to the development of modern scientific thought in the seventeenth century; with some qualifications, such an approach continues to be used by many readers of the Bible. This viewpoint affirms that the Bible is primarily a divine book, that, therefore, it is characterized by perfect unity and infallible teaching, and that recognizing this unique character is essential for proper interpretation. Thus, for example, any reading of Scripture that entails contradiction or error would seem to be precluded.

Within this traditional approach, however, a variety of theories has been used. According to the allegorical method, which was especially prevalent during the ancient and medieval periods, the Bible as a divine book is characterized by multiple meanings. A competing viewpoint has emphasized the importance of the "literal sense" intended by the author (*sensus literalis*), but many—especially Roman Catholic scholars—who are not satisfied with the allegorical approach have nevertheless argued for the validity of a "fuller sense" (*sensus plenior*—that is, a meaning intended by God but not necessarily understood by the biblical author). Another important issue in dispute pertains to the role of the church and its tradition in the process of interpretation; the Protestant Reformation of the sixteenth century argued, in distinction from the teaching of the Roman Catholic and Eastern Orthodox churches, that ultimate authority resides in Scripture alone (*sola scriptura*) and that, therefore, tradition must play a subservient role.[1]

2. A second major approach is the *historical* method, which arose in the context of the Age of Enlightenment and has dominated biblical scholarship even to this day.[2] Of course, interest in the historical meaning of the Bible had characterized important groups of biblical interpreters for centuries, and much of what developed in the modern scientific period was clearly compatible with earlier approaches. Nevertheless, the new emphasis on human reason and on the task of "criticism" entailed treating the Bible as one would treat any other book. This principle meant different things to different thinkers; for some, though certainly not for all, it meant abandoning the traditional notion of biblical authority.

In any case, belief in the divine character of the Bible, even when not rejected, became irrelevant to historical criticism, which insisted on using an approach that is not prejudiced by dogmatic assumptions. And since the Bible, like all other books, was subjected to the judgment of human reason, the historical-critical method normally assumed the existence of biblical errors and contradictions. As this approach matured in the nineteenth century, it made dramatic progress in textual and philological analysis, but at the same time the theological significance of the Bible receded more and more into the background.

In addition, the desire to develop a method that was consistently historical led many biblical students to embrace the "history-of-religions" school.[3] Because this method viewed Christianity as simply one among many religious phenomena of antiquity, a belief in the uniqueness and divine authority of the Bible seemed to be excluded. Consequently, biblical interpretation became dominated by the attempt to explain the text on strictly naturalistic grounds.

3. In reaction to these developments, many influential thinkers began, soon after World War I, to argue for the importance of *theological* interpretation. Associated primarily with the name of Karl Barth (1886–1968), this approach denounces the sterility of the historical method (but not the method itself), seeks to restore confidence in the unity and authority of the Bible without abandoning the advances of historical-critical scholarship (hence the label neo-orthodox), and stresses the relevance of the Bible for today. The implications of this movement, which were considerable, will be examined below.

---

1. I stand within this "Protestant evangelical" tradition, particularly as that has come to expression in classical Reformed theology. Such a perspective, however, does not necessarily exclude important and valid insights provided by the other approaches discussed in this essay.

2. For important treatments of this period, see H. G. Reventlow, *The Authority of the Bible and the Rise of the Modern World,* trans. John Bowden (Philadelphia: Fortress, 1985) esp. Part 2; W. G. Kümmel, *The New Testament: The History of the Investigation of Its Problems* (Nashville: Abingdon, 1972) esp. Parts 2 and 3.

3. This movement, which is akin to the discipline known as "comparative religions," flourished at the beginning of the twentieth century. The attempt to explain the origins of Christianity by taking into account its religio-historical environment usually focused either on Jewish apocalypticism or on the Hellenistic religions, especially gnosticism.

4. A fourth major approach takes us back to the beginnings of the nineteenth century. Mainly through the work of Friedrich Schleiermacher (1768–1834), the concept of *general* or *philosophical hermeneutics* was introduced into the theological discussion but did not play a prominent role until the twentieth century. The term *hermeneutics,* at least in its earlier context, meant simply "the science [or art] of interpretation." The term *general* emphasizes the need to develop a broad theory of understanding that is applicable to any text, but to accomplish such a task we cannot dispense with *philosophical* tools and concepts. Almost by definition, this approach involves a strongly interdisciplinary perspective. Indeed, one of the most influential figures in the development of general hermeneutics, Wilhelm Dilthey (1833–1911), was primarily concerned with the process of understanding in all of the humanities and the social sciences. More recently, as we shall see, this approach has been developed vigorously within the framework of existentialist philosophy.

5. Quite a different perspective is that provided by *modern linguistics.* The scientific study of language made some extraordinary advances in the nineteenth century, and these were appropriated by biblical scholarship. At that time, however, the focus of linguistics was on the historical and comparative method: How have languages developed and how are they related to one another? A fundamental change in approach is usually credited to the Swiss scholar Ferdinand de Saussure (1857–1913), who argued that linguistic study should be primarily *synchronic* in character, focusing not on the evolution of a language (*diachronic* perspective) but on its system or structure at a particular time. These and related ideas had a crucial impact on the development of so-called structural linguistics, but it was not until the 1960s that biblical scholarship began to appropriate those insights.[4] (Saussure's work also served as a springboard for a broader and quite distinct movement known as *structuralism,* which in turn has influenced some aspects of biblical interpretation.)

6. Interestingly, a parallel development known as *linguistic analysis* took place about the same time in the English-speaking world. Also known as analytic philosophy, it may be viewed as a reaction to

certain speculative and abstract currents of thought that were popular at the turn of the century. According to the proponents of the new approach, the real task of philosophy should be the clarification of concepts, which requires a careful analysis of language. Later developments in this philosophical tradition—such as "speech act theory"—have strongly influenced the contemporary theological debates.

7. Another discipline that has obvious contacts with biblical interpretation is *literary criticism.* Several approaches that emerged in the twentieth century will need to be taken into account below. The dominant tendency, however, has been one of minimizing the significance of the author so as to emphasize either the independent value of the text or the active role played by the reader.

These seven major approaches do not constitute an exhaustive list, and readers of the Bible are often discouraged by the very complexity of the subject. Nevertheless, some overarching ideas can be identified that may help to isolate the most fundamental questions.

KEY DEVELOPMENTS IN THE TWENTIETH CENTURY

Barth and Bultmann. It is no exaggeration to say that the contemporary interest in hermeneutics signals a new epoch in the scientific study of the Bible. Observers commonly see the beginning of that epoch in the work of Karl Barth, one of the most influential theologians of modern times. Barth had been trained by highly respected scholars in the classical liberal tradition. Nevertheless, as he left the academic world and took up a pastorate, he found that training of little value for the life of the church.

Then in 1914 came the tragedy of World War I, which affected theological developments quite directly in Europe. Liberalism, believing that the proclamation of a "social gospel" would bring God's kingdom of peace to the earth, had relied heavily on an optimistic view of human nature. Those hopes were crushed by the war. Barth would, of course, have been personally affected by these events. But there was an additional element. He saw his revered teachers adopt political positions that, he felt, contradicted the very principles they had taught. The only course left open to him was to break with his theological past.

Soon after the war, Barth published a commen-

---

4. Primarily as a result of James Barr, *The Semantics of Biblical Language* (Oxford: Oxford University Press, 1961).

tary on Paul's Epistle to the Romans that sent shock waves through academia. As someone said, it was as though a bomb had been dropped in the garden where the theologians were playing. Even today his book seems more than a little strange. It bears little resemblance to a typical exegetical commentary. Instead of focusing on the historical meaning of the text, Barth seemed to ignore that meaning because of his preoccupation with the *relevance* of the text for today's reader. Predictably, the commentary made no advance on Romans scholarship. His bold approach, however, set in motion a dramatic change in the way theologians view biblical interpretation.

Enter Rudolf Bultmann (1884–1976), whose relationship with Barth was rather friendly at the beginning. Primarily a New Testament (NT) scholar with special interest in the history-of-religions school, Bultmann shared with Barth a deep concern about the relevance of Christianity. For a variety of reasons, however, they soon parted company. One important factor was Bultmann's adoption of existentialism, particularly as set forth by the philosopher Martin Heidegger.

Among Bultmann's articles, few are more interesting than one entitled "Is Exegesis Without Presuppositions Possible?"[5] The answer to his own question was no. To be sure, Bultmann was not suggesting that readers of the Bible may decide ahead of time the specific meaning of a text: he always believed that objectivity (properly understood) is the aim of the exegete. His point, however, was that all of us bring a world view to the text and that suppressing that world view is out of the question. Boldly, Bultmann went on to argue as follows:

The historical method includes the presupposition that history is a unity in the sense of a closed continuum of effects in which individual events are connected by the succession of cause and effect. . . .

This closedness means that the continuum of historical happenings cannot be rent by the interference of supernatural, transcendent powers and that therefore there is no "miracle" in this sense of the word.[6]

Bultmann was quite right to argue that it is impossible to interpret the Bible (or any other text,

for that matter) without presuppositions.[7] The kind of neutral objectivity that earlier scholars had aimed for does not exist. It is another issue, however, whether Bultmann's own presuppositions were in line with those of the biblical writers. A genuine Christian commitment, one could argue, must be compatible with the faith of those through whom the Christian revelation came. The inevitable question is thus raised: Just what sense does it make to hold on to our Christian identity if our most basic assumptions (the question of God's so-called "interference" in this world) conflict with those of the Christian Scriptures?

Bultmann's theological aims, like Barth's, were greatly affected by a concern for relevance. If we moderns cannot believe in miracles, he argued, then we must reclothe the primitive Christian message in terms that are understandable to us. This principle led Bultmann to develop a hermeneutical method known as *demythologization* (but perhaps more accurately described as *remythologization*). He believed that the early Christians used mythical categories to give expression to their Easter faith. One must not think of myths as fabrications intended to deceive. Bultmann's approach did not precisely involve rejecting the myths but translating them into modern myths. By the latter Bultmann meant primarily the categories of existentialist philosophy.

Some of Bultmann's disciples, though dissatisfied by various elements in their teacher's ideas, sought to build on those ideas during the 1950s and 60s. For example, a movement that came to be known as "the new quest for the historical Jesus" attempted to bring the Jesus of history and later Christian faith closer together than Bultmann had allowed. More significant for our purposes was the development of the "New Hermeneutic." This movement had very little to do with the traditional concerns of hermeneutics,[8] except in the rather general sense that it

5. Rudolf Bultmann, "Is Exegesis Without Presuppositions Possible?" in *Existence and Faith: Shorter Writings of Rudolf Bultmann,* ed. Schubert M. Ogden (New York: World Publishing, 1960) 289-96.

6. Ibid., 291-92.

7. This emphasis was hardly unique to Bultmann. Many challenges to the supposed objectivity and impartiality of the scientific enterprise have been thrown by scholars in a variety of fields. In theology, note in particular the work of Cornelius Van Til; building on the philosophy of Abraham Kuyper, he developed a system of apologetics in which the role of presuppositions was fundamental. See especially his book *The Defense of the Faith,* 3rd ed. (Phillipsburg, N.J.: Presbyterian and Reformed, 1967; repr. 1985).

8. The very use of the singular form *hermeneutic* reflects the changed perspective. The term "can become coterminous with Christian theology as the statement of the meaning of Scripture for our day" (James R. Robinson, "Hermeneutic Since Barth," in *The New Hermeneutic,* New Frontiers in Theology, eds. J. R. Robinson and John B. Cobb, Jr. [New York: Harper & Row, 1964] 1-77, esp. 6). The term *hermeneutics* had been used in a much narrower sense: a discipline that deals with the principles and methods of interpretation.

focused on the concept of *understanding*. Indeed, the scholars representative of the New Hermeneutic seldom discussed the methods by which we determine the historical meaning of the biblical text. Rather, they were interested in developing a theology that built on certain Continental views about language and thought, mainly the teachings of the existentialist philosopher Martin Heidegger. Because these ideas have broad implications, however, the movement has made a significant impact on subsequent discussions about biblical interpretation.

Literary Theory and Philosophy. Even as these developments were taking place in biblical and theological scholarship, a parallel set of ideas was coming to expression in the field of literary criticism. As early as the 1930s, important literary scholars were arguing that the traditional approach to criticism was unsatisfactory—that the usual concern with the author was misguided. What a poet may have intended in writing a poem, for example, may be of some historical interest, but that has little relevance to our understanding of that poem. Known as the "New Criticism," this approach treated the text as an artifact independent of its author and thus reopened the question of textual meaning.

The interrelationship among the disciplines of literary criticism, philosophy, and theology has deeply affected the debate during the past several decades. Perhaps the most prominent figure has been the German philosopher Hans-George Gadamer, whose name is usually (though not always fairly) associated with a *relativistic* approach to interpretation. Indeed, Gadamer went so far as to give the impression that truth in interpretation is a matter of personal taste.[9]

It is important to keep in mind, however, the context of his argument. What Gadamer was most concerned to refute was the claim that the scientific method alone is able to arrive at the truth. At the root of this method is doubt—that is, doubt about anything that has not been repeated and verified. Accordingly, tradition is "prejudice" and must be eliminated. But the humanities, and history in particular, are not subject to this kind of repetition and

verification, so the inference might be drawn that the humanities cannot arrive at the truth.

Over against that viewpoint, Gadamer argued that "prejudice" cannot be eliminated. Indeed, "prejudice" is essential for consciousness and understanding. His intent was to rehabilitate tradition (particularly the classics), which provides the presuppositions that can be tested as they are applied to the texts. Gadamer also placed much emphasis on the view that the past is not fixed, that prior events and texts change inasmuch as they are continually being understood. If so, it is not possible to identify the meaning of the text simply with the author's intention.

Ironically, soon after the publication of Gadamer's work, modern science underwent some radical changes, largely as a result of the work of Thomas Kuhn.[10] It is now generally recognized that the sciences are not so fundamentally different from the humanities; the former no less than the latter are deeply involved in hermeneutics, so that no field of study can escape some measure of relativity. Be that as it may, Gadamer's thought had a deep impact not only on philosophical discussion but also on the study of literature and, therefore, on theological and biblical scholarship.

Particularly well-known in this connection is the work of Paul Ricoeur. Among his numerous suggestive ideas, we should take note of his emphasis on the distinction between the speaking-hearing and the writing-reading relation. In spoken discourse, the meaning overlaps the intention of the speaker. "With written discourse, however, the author's intention and the meaning of the text cease to coincide. . . . The text's career escapes the finite horizon lived by its author. What the text means now matters more than what the author meant when he wrote it."[11] In written texts, there is a "surplus of meaning" not intended by the author. While Ricoeur himself is not a biblical scholar, he is

9. Joel C. Weinsheimer, *Gadamer's Hermeneutics: A Reading of Truth and Method* (New Haven: Yale University Press, 1985), puts it this way: "Whether an interpretation is true is a matter of taste. If this seems to denigrate truth, that is only because we have denigrated taste as a cognitive capacity able to arrive at the truth. It is only because we have thought truth is exclusively something that has been or can be proven" (111).

10. Thomas S. Kuhn, *The Structure of Scientific Revolutions*, 2nd ed., International Encyclopedia of Unified Science 2/2 (Chicago: University of Chicago Press, 1967). For the relevance of Kuhn's work to hermeneutics, see Vern S. Poythress, *Science and Hermeneutics: Implications of Scientific Method for Biblical Interpretation*, Foundations of Contemporary Interpretation 6 (Grand Rapids: Zondervan, 1988) chaps. 3–4.

11. Paul Ricoeur, *Interpretation Theory: Discourse and the Surplus of Meaning* (Fort Worth: Texas Christian University, 1976) 29-30; see also *Essays on Biblical Interpretation*, intro. by Lewis S. Mudge (Philadelphia: Fortress, 1980). Among various important assessments of Ricoeur, see especially Kevin J. Vanhoozer, *Biblical Narrative in the Philosophy of Paul Ricoeur: A Study in Hermeneutics and Theology* (Cambridge: Cambridge University Press, 1990).

deeply interested in religious thought, and so many theologians and biblical students have been affected by his work.

J. S. Croatto is an especially interesting example, since his writings, which arose in the context of Latin American liberation theology, have become popular in the English-speaking world.[12] According to Croatto, the Bible must not be viewed as a fixed deposit that has already said everything; it is not so much that the Bible "said" but that it "says." In committing their message to writing, the biblical authors themselves disappeared, but their absence means semantic richness. The "closure" of authorial meaning results in the "opening" of new meaning. Croatto even tells us that the reader's responsibility is not *exegesis*—bringing out a pure meaning the way one might take an object out of a treasure chest—but properly *eisegesis*, that is, we must "enter" the text with new questions so as to produce new meaning.

One can hardly overemphasize the radical character of these developments. To a practitioner of the historical method, it is simply shocking to hear that eisegesis may be a permissible—let alone the preferable!—way to approach the text. For nineteen centuries the study of the Bible had been moving away from just such an approach (especially in the form of allegorical interpretation), so that with the maturing of the historical method a great victory for responsible exegesis had been won. But now we are told that historical interpretation is passé. And although no one is arguing that we should return to the uncontrolled allegorizing of some ancient and medieval interpreters, the search for a meaning other than that intended by the original author does seem, at first blush, as though one is giving up centuries of hermeneutical progress.

But the situation is even more complicated. During the past several decades we have witnessed the arrival of a variety of more specialized, even esoteric, approaches, such as structuralism, post-structuralism, deconstruction, and so on (see below, "The Role of the Reader"). At their most extreme, some schools question the very foundations of Western thought and thus suggest the impossibility of interpreting texts.

To be sure, there have been some eminent defenders of "authorial intention" in the contemporary scene, best known among them E. D. Hirsch. Arguing for a distinction between *meaning* (the invariable sense intended by the writer) and *significance* (the changeable application of a writing to different contexts), Hirsch believed he could preserve the crucial role of the original author against the attacks of thinkers like Gadamer.[13] Moreover, the vast majority of books and articles dealing with the biblical text continue to place priority on its historical meaning. Especially puzzling is the fact that, from time to time, one may hear a scholar at a professional meeting who seems to adopt the newer approach theoretically but whose actual interpretive work does not appear substantially different from standard historical exegesis. The abandonment of authorial and historical interpretation would be difficult to document from the usual articles published in the recognized journals of biblical scholarship.

Nevertheless, it would be a mistake to infer that the contemporary debates in hermeneutics are mere games. The challenges to traditional approaches are serious and need to be weighed carefully. In particular, these challenges have a direct bearing on the relevance of the Bible for the communities of faith. After all, whatever the scholars may be doing in their specialized publications, one must still ask what is the responsibility of preachers as they address their congregations and of individual believers as they approach their reading and study of Scripture.

THE HISTORICAL-CRITICAL METHOD

Before looking in greater detail at the various aspects of the current debate, we must be clear as to what contemporary thinkers are reacting *against*. Unfortunately, the terminology is not always as precise as one might hope. Up to this point I have used phrases such as "historical interpretation" and

12. J. Severino Croatto, *Biblical Hermeneutics: Toward a Theory of Reading as the Production of Meaning,* trans. R. R. Barr (Maryknoll, N.Y.: Orbis, 1987) ix, 17, 66.

13. E. D. Hirsch, Jr., *Validity in Interpretation* (New Haven: Yale University Press, 1967). This work has been embraced by many evangelical writers, such as W. C. Kaiser, Jr., *The Uses of the Old Testament in the New* (Chicago: Moody, 1985), and some other biblical scholars concerned with the objectivity of historical meaning, but Hirsch has not been well received by the mainstream of philosophical and literary thinkers. For a brief criticism see Anthony C. Thiselton, *New Horizons in Hermeneutics: The Theory and Practice of Transforming Biblical Reading* (Grand Rapids: Zondervan, 1992) 13. Ben Meyer, *Critical Realism and the New Testament,* Princeton Theological Monograph Series 17 (Allison Park, Pa.: Pickwick, 1989) chap. 2, defends the intended sense of texts while recognizing weaknesses in Hirsch's argument.

"biblical criticism" to represent the work done by the mainstream of biblical scholarship. Understood in a general way, this approach fairly characterizes the vast majority of scholars, even though their theological views about the character of the Bible may differ from each other in fundamental ways.

At this general level, perhaps the best descriptor is "grammatical-historical exegesis." This is an old phrase that focuses attention on the detailed analysis of the text in conformity with the original language and the original historical situation. The approach was developed in self-conscious opposition both to allegorical interpretation and to the natural tendency we all have to interpret the text on the basis of English (or some other modern language) and in the light of our own customs and experiences. An important corollary of this approach was that before we could use, say, Romans 8 for our needs, we must first set aside our prejudices and ask what the original author meant. According to this viewpoint, only after we have figured out what Paul wished to communicate to the Roman Christians could we claim the right to *apply* that passage to our situation.

Is this viewpoint, however, to be equated with the "historical-critical method"? Many students of the Bible have rejected this method on the grounds that it is incompatible with the divine character of Scripture. Here is where the confusion begins, since the label "historical-critical" is not used in precisely the same sense by everyone. Scholars who reject the method—usually referred to as "conservative" or "evangelical" scholars—certainly do not object to reading the Bible historically. Quite the contrary, they have been among the most vocal supporters of historical, authorial meaning in opposition to current trends. Moreover, there are many aspects of "critical" study in which they have participated without misgivings.[14]

Unfortunately, there is a deep ambiguity in the term *criticism*. Even apart from the negative associations the word has in popular usage, several meanings must be distinguished. In the fields of art and literature, it refers to the skill of evaluating the artistic quality of specific works. When used with reference to biblical scholarship, the primary idea is that of investigating in scientific fashion the historical origins, text, composition, and transmission of literary documents. For anyone who acknowledges that the Bible has human as well as divine characteristics, there can be no objection to such a study.

The problem arises, however, because of the close ties between the critical method and the principles of the Enlightenment. The priority given to human reason during that period dictated that the Bible must be treated "like any other book," a phrase that need not be offensive to evangelicals as long as it is also recognized that the Bible is uniquely divine in origin and so, with respect to this factor, it must be treated *unlike* any other book. As far as the Age of Reason was concerned, however, such a qualification was unacceptable; obviously, it would have been destructive of the principle of human autonomy. Accordingly, "biblical criticism" came to mean not simply the scientific investigation of biblical documents, but a method that assumed from the start the critic's right to pass judgment on the truth claims of the Bible. Thus, for example, to interpret the Bible historically meant almost by definition to acknowledge that it contains contradictions; indeed, one of the standard textbooks on the subject simply assumes that any approach is unhistorical that does not accept those contradictions.[15] In short, assent to the view that the Bible was not totally reliable became one of the operating principles of the "historical-critical method."

It goes without saying that anyone who was theologically committed to the traditional view of inspiration could not do "criticism" in this sense. Subsequent developments, however, created further complications. The formulations of so-called "higher criticism"[16] regarding the historical origins of biblical documents tended more and more to denigrate the religious value of the Bible. By the beginning of the twentieth century, conservative and liberal approaches had become almost totally polarized, though the former continued to make extensive use of critical studies insofar as these could be integrated into the framework of theological orthodoxy.

The significance of these developments for the

---

14. Among the most prominent conservative scholars of the last two centuries are such NT specialists as J. B. Lightfoot, Theodore Zahn, Bernhard Weiss, J. Gresham Machen, Herman Ridderbos, and F. F. Bruce. In the field of the Old Testament (OT), note such names as E. Hengstenberg, Franz Delitzsch, Robert Dick Wilson, Edward J. Young, and the Jewish scholar Umberto Cassuto.

15. W. G. Kümmel, *The New Testament: The History of the Investigation of Its Problems* (Nashville: Abingdon, 1972) 29-31 and passim.
16. This label served to distinguish the more controversial approaches from investigations focusing on language and textual transmission, which were referred to as "lower criticism."

present article is fairly obvious, but two points need emphasis. In the first place, the fundamental antitheses between the conservative and critical schools must not obscure their common goal of discovering the historical meaning of the text. Committed to the priority of authorial intent, both sides assumed the need for an objective, unbiased, scientific approach, which was to be distinguished from the task of application.

In the second place, ironically, this history also reminds us that theological commitments can hardly be separated from decisions about hermeneutical principles. Given the claims of the Bible and the religious expectations it places on its readers, theological neutrality is a mirage. This is not to deny that people with widely differing theological assumptions can come to the same conclusions on numerous points of detail and even on significant issues. But we fool ourselves if we think we can approach the text of Scripture with unprejudiced minds. Current emphasis on the role of the reader's "pre-understanding" is, therefore, a salutary development.

THE AUTONOMY OF THE TEXT

The Interpretive Triangle. Determining the meaning of a text is not a simple task. For interpretation to take place, there must be an author, a text, and an interpreter (reader or hearer), and it is precisely this three-pronged relationship that can create confusion. Even when we come across a statement whose meaning is "obvious," the truth is that an enormous amount of previous knowledge and experience has prepared our minds to handle the new information. However, there is no guarantee that our minds are quite ready to process the message.

For example, in the process of determining the meaning of a specific word or sentence in the letters of Paul, interpreters often ask themselves: Would the original readers of the letter have grasped such-and-such a meaning? Not infrequently, a particular interpretation will be rejected precisely on the grounds that those readers could not have been expected to come up with it. On the other hand, however, probably all scholars acknowledge that some of the apostle's richer or subtler nuances would have been beyond the reach of his original audience.

In the introduction to his famous dictionary of NT Greek, Walter Bauer raised:

the possibility that what . . . Paul said, conditioned as he was by his Jewish past, was not always understood in the same terms by his gentile Christian hearers, who were also unable to dissociate themselves entirely from their previous ways of thought . . . .

. . . With this in mind we might conclude that sometimes there are two meanings for the same passage, one from the standpoint of the writer and another which becomes evident when one puts one's self in the place of the recipient intellectually and spiritually; the lexicographer naturally feels an obligation to draw the proper conclusions. The way a passage is understood by its first readers has an immediate effect upon its later interpretation.[17]

While this quotation raises several interesting questions, we need only note at this point the recognition that an appeal to the original readers does not always work—that in itself such an appeal is not a satisfactory solution to problems of interpretation. In other words, we have to cope with the possibility of a "disturbance" between two points of the interpretive triangle, the author and the reader.

The moment we acknowledge this problem, however, we have also conceded that writing a text (and, in somewhat different ways, speaking an utterance) involves a risk. That text, as it were, has a life of its own. It is subject to being understood in ways different from those intended by the author. This complication increases the further that text moves (geographically, temporally, culturally) away from its author, particularly as one loses the possibility of asking the author for an explanation.

Of course, biblical scholars interested in the original author's historical meaning have not been unaware of this problem, though one may wonder whether they fully realized its implications. For them, however, the problem was simply a challenge to be overcome. At times the definitive solution may be beyond the interpreter's reach, but one makes every effort to discover what the author meant.

With the rise of the New Criticism, on the other hand, American students of literature began to see this phenomenon not as a problem to be solved, but as an opportunity for interpretive creativity.

Instead of asking "Does the text mean this or that?" with a "Tea or coffee?" intonation, implying that only one answer can be chosen, critics began to ask "Can the text mean this or that?" with a "Cigarettes or liquor?" intonation, seeing a text as a bag of mysteries not advertised on the surface. (There is some debate whether the author

17. BAGD, xxiv.

knows what he has packed.) To take an example, in Marvell's lines:

Meanwhile the mind, from pleasure less,
Withdraws into its happiness

should we understand that the mind is less because of pleasure or that because of pleasure the mind withdraws? The answer now was to be "Both—and what else can you find?"[18]

Freed from the constraints of authorial intent, critics could now proclaim the autonomy of the text. This perspective became dominant in American literary criticism through the 1940s and 50s, although its impact on biblical scholarship was slow in coming. When finally it did come, other currents of thought were entering the picture as well.

Structuralism. One of these was French structuralism, a movement that derived its name—but little more than the name and some terminology—from modern linguistics. Even in linguistics, the term *structuralism* is not free of ambiguity. If all we mean is the recognition that language is a structured system (so that individual sounds and forms have value not simply in themselves but in relationship to the whole), then virtually all modern linguists are "structuralists." The term, however, is more often applied narrowly to several schools that dominated the linguistic landscape in the first half of this century.[19]

The anthropologist Claude Lévi-Strauss, finding some of the structuralist concepts helpful, borrowed them, possibly in an attempt to give scientific credibility to his cultural analyses. In the process, however, terms were stretched well beyond their use in linguistics. It was this watered-down terminology that became the source for key intellectual developments in France in the late 1960s. One historian has commented: "But the linguistics of French structuralism and poststructuralism was a mirage. Those who used its notions understood neither the technical aspects of linguistics nor the theoretical stakes involved."[20]

18. G. W. Turner, *Stylistics* (Baltimore: Penguin, 1973) 100-101. It is important to note that this approach focuses primarily on poetry, a medium that frequently uses deliberate ambiguity and thus invites imaginative response.

19. Perhaps the best-known representative is Leonard Bloomfield's classic work *Language* (New York: Holt, 1933).

20. Thomas G. Pavel, *The Feud of Language: A History of Structuralist Thought* (Oxford: Blackwell, 1992), vii; see also 76 and 130-32. Even if Pavel's criticisms are exaggerated, it is clear that the links between French structuralism and linguistics were superficial and tenuous. From a different, but also critical, perspective, see the important comments by Martin Krampen, "Ferdinand de Saussure and the Development of Semiology," in *Classics of Semiotics,* eds. M. Krampen et al. (New York and London: Plenum, 1987) 59-88, esp. 78-83.

In any case, these new ideas began to be applied to biblical literature in the 1970s, often under the rubric of "structural exegesis." Much use was also made of *semiotics* (the theory of signs), since the approach puts great emphasis on language as a network of symbols. The structuralist jargon was daunting, and many biblical scholars who expended the effort to learn the method were greatly disappointed with the results (though at the hands of some moderate practitioners the questions asked can shed new light on the text). Part of the reason was that structuralists focused their attention not on what a text means but on *how* it produces meaning; indeed, their concerns fall more easily under the category of epistemology (or even the study of culture) than that of traditional hermeneutics.

The significance of this movement for the purposes of the present article lies in the fact that it embodies, sometimes in a radical way, the principle of the semantic autonomy of texts. In the view of structuralists, biblical criticism had been much too preoccupied with both the original author and the historical referent of the text. Instead, they proposed to examine the text independently of those considerations and to determine the self-contained value of narratives.

At its most extreme, structuralism gives way to *deconstruction,* a point of view normally associated with the name of Jacques Derrida. Deconstruction is nothing less than an attack on some fundamental concepts of Western culture, since it appears to call into question the very possibility of literary communication by insisting on the absence of a fixed language. As applied to the parables of Jesus, for example, this approach emphasizes the polyvalence (multiple meanings) of metaphor. The reason a parable can mean numerous things, we are told, is not precisely that it has a "surplus of meaning" (Ricoeur's phrase) but that it has a *"void of meaning* at its core." Having made that point, and a few others, one will be drawn to accept

the permanence of paradox at the heart of the human. And the fundamental one which generates all the others is presumably *the paradox that, if perception creates reality, then perception (mine, yours, ours together) must also be creating the perceiver (me, yours, us together). . . . The core paradox of the per-*

ceived perceiver, is, once again, a destiny to be accepted, not a difficulty to be solved.[21]

Many readers find this kind of language confusing and have little patience with it, but at the very least it serves to underline the almost incalculable distance that separates historical exegesis from some forms of the structuralist approach.

Text versus History. One of the more controversial elements in this modern emphasis on the autonomy of the text has been the tendency to play down the extraliterary, particularly the historical, reference of literary works. In other words, an emphasis on the text's autonomy means that the text is cut off not only from the author but also from the extralinguistic reality to which the text apparently refers. Earlier biblical scholarship (both liberal and conservative) is often criticized for paying too much attention to the question of historicity. If conservative scholars wonder what may have motivated a biblical character to act in a particular way, they are chastised for focusing on the historical event rather than on the literary skills of the biblical author. If liberal scholars take to task a conservative reading of some historical portion, they too are criticized for missing the point. In short, the very asking of historical questions is seen as basically irrelevant. One proponent of this point of view suggests that "the new literary criticism may be described as inherently ahistorical." He further comments: "Consideration of the Bible as literature is itself the beginning and end of scholarly endeavor. The Bible is taken first and finally as a literary object."[22]

As is usually the case when a provocative new idea makes its appearance and is taken hold of by enthusiastic thinkers, the notion of the autonomy of the text has proven to be a mixed blessing. Both positive and negative results are clearly discernible. Predictably, formulations that appear extreme tend to prejudice our acceptance of the positive elements. Even the most objectionable views, however, are likely to reflect some important truth, and the effort must be made to do justice to it.

Undoubtedly, historical exegesis—in spite of some notable exceptions—has tended to ignore the intrinsic literary quality of the biblical documents. The New Criticism and later developments related

to it have taught us to pay attention to the "texture" of biblical literature. One need not view this quality as the beginning and end of our interest. To do so would be to undermine what traditionally has been recognized as a foundational element of biblical religion—namely, its essentially historical character.

Nevertheless, biblical narrative, as well as other biblical genres that include historical reference, must not be treated as neutral in character, free of interpretive and theological "bias." (Belief in biblical inspiration and infallibility does not preclude—in fact, it intensifies—the importance of this interpretive element.) Now the theological perspective of the biblical authors is seldom expressed in explicit terms; rather, it is reflected in their composition of the text. Accordingly, close attention to the literary quality of narrative, even if considered in relative independence from its historical reference, can be of immense value in understanding the *significance* of the history that narrative presents.

THE ROLE OF THE READER

Scientific Method and Hermeneutics. Throughout the centuries people have assumed without a second thought that our perception of data corresponds exactly with objective reality: If we see a black horse, it *must* be black—and it certainly must be a horse! After all, how could the work of science proceed without such assurance? Now what is true of the scientific observer is presumably true as well of someone interpreting literature, though it might be recognized that in this case there is more room for ambiguity and misunderstanding. Biblical interpreters prior to this century have, of course, been conscious of the role played by personal bias, but they have simply taken for granted that such a bias can be overcome.

This is no longer true. If there is anything distinctive about contemporary hermeneutics it is precisely the emphasis on the *subjectivity* and *relativity* of interpretation. The roots of this perspective may be found in the philosophy of Immanuel Kant (1724–1804), whose work was undoubtedly a major turning point between modern thought and everything that preceded it. The effect of Kant's contribution was so broad and so fundamental in character that no intellectual discipline could escape its impact—not even biblical interpretation, though it took a while for exegetes to figure out what was happening.

21. John Dominic Crossan, *Cliffs of Falls: Paradox and Polyvalence in the Parables of Jesus* (New York: Seabury, 1980) 9-10, 71.
22. D. Robertson, "Literature, the Bible as," in *IDBSup*, 547-51, esp. 548.

In very simple terms, we may remind ourselves that Kant was deeply preoccupied with the unbearable tension that the Enlightenment had created between science and religion (this is, of course, the old philosophical problem of reason vs. faith in new dress). His own solution to the problem was to divorce the two by circumscribing their roles. Religion, for example, must recognize its limitations: The basic tenets of faith cannot be proved by theoretical reason. But science is also restricted: Observers never see things as they are in themselves, since the mind is no mere receptacle molded by physical sensations, but rather an active organ that brings order to the chaotic stream of data it confronts. One might as well admit that the world *as we know it* is one created by our own ordering of sensations.

To be sure, most scientists went about their work in blissful ignorance, but the seed had been sown for fundamental changes in scientific outlook. Indeed, some of the most significant questions debated in twentieth-century philosophy of science have to do with the relativity of scientific thought. As already mentioned, the controversial writings of Thomas Kuhn have served to sensitize the scientific community to this issue. Kuhn's primary interest was to understand the human process by which major changes in our interpretation of the natural world have taken place. If we look carefully, for example, at the "scientific revolution" associated with the work of Galileo and Copernicus, we do not find a simple change of opinion based on the impartial investigation of objective data. Respectable scientists, in the face of newly discovered evidence, continued to hold on to traditional views of physics and astronomy. Whenever possible, they managed to integrate the new evidence into their general interpretation; otherwise, they temporarily set it aside as yet-to-be-explained-data ("anomalies").

As part of his argument, Kuhn called attention to a fascinating psychological experiment. In it, the experimenters used a deck of playing cards that contained a few "anomalies," such as a *red* six of spades or a *black* four of hearts. The cards were quickly displayed one by one, and the subjects were asked to identify them. As a rule, the subjects did not even seem aware of the anomalies; *they readily integrated the new facts into a system that was incompatible with those facts*. With somewhat lengthier exposures, most of the subjects became aware of a problem but were unable to figure out the anomaly; it took even lengthier exposures for them to be able to identify the cards correctly. A few subjects, however, even after exposures many times longer than the others required, continued to experience difficulties and became very anxious; it was as though an interpretive inflexibility prevented them from accepting the new evidence.[23]

Relativity in Interpretation. The old retort "I've made up my mind—don't bother me with the facts" is usually spoken tongue-in-cheek, but there is more truth to it than we realize or are willing to admit. And this is not necessarily a matter of willful obstinance or dishonesty. When someone misinterprets what we say, we may find solace in the fact that "people hear what they want to hear." Perhaps more accurately, we could say that people hear only what their minds are already prepared to hear. It is impossible for us to understand and assimilate new information except by relating it to what we already know—that is, by filtering it in a way that fits our "pre-understanding." A few wise individuals, however, seem able to identify an anomaly quickly, to recognize that they are unable to assimilate it, and to adjust their interpretive framework in a way that takes account of the new fact.

Be that as it may, the point is that contemporary thinkers have learned to accept the role played by the subjectivity of the observer in scientific research.[24] But now, if these things are true in the "hard sciences," where objective measurement lies at the core of research, what shall we say with regard to the humanities, and particularly the interpretation of literature, where the subjective factor seems so much more prominent? For one thing, these developments tell us that we probably have overestimated the differences between the sciences and the humanities. In both of these broad disciplines, the researcher is faced with a set of data that can be interpreted *only in the light of previous commitments*; in both cases, therefore, an interpreter comes—consciously or unconsciously—with a "theory" that seeks to account for as many facts as possible. Given the finite nature of every human interpreter, no explanation accounts for the data exhaustively. And in many, many cases, it is a set of

23. Kuhn, *Scientific Revolutions*, 62-64.
24. I must leave out of account here many other relevant developments, such as the implications of the "uncertainty principle" in the field of quantum physics.

prior commitments, rather than the weight of the evidence, that determines the final conclusion.

That much is widely agreed upon in our day. Some thinkers, however, will argue that, at least in the case of literary interpretation, we need to go further. It is even suggested that the role of the reader is and should be virtually the only thing that matters. For practitioners of both the historical method (which emphasized the original author's meaning) and the New Criticism (which disregarded any such authorial intention), the one thing that could be relied on was the objectivity of the text. For proponents of "reader-response theory," however—at least in its more extreme forms—there is no such thing as an objective text. Insofar as every reader brings an interpretive framework to the text, to that extent every reader generates a new meaning and thus creates a new text.

This approach, moreover, does not stop at describing what happens when a text is read; after all, traditional interpreters might recognize that there is a sense in which that description may be accurate—just as long as an effort is made to control the tendency! The message of reader-response theorists, rather, is that this way of reading is legitimate and should be encouraged in all its many-splendored varieties. Accordingly, specific points of view become self-conscious hermeneutical strategies. Prominent in the last decade or two have been Marxist readings of the Bible, feminist approaches, and studies in African American hermeneutics; but in principle there should be no objection to taking any ideology as a point of departure (say, an explicitly capitalist approach to the prophecy of Amos, or a self-consciously racist reading of the Gospel of John).

Edgar V. McKnight, a respected proponent of reader-response theory, suggests that, since we cannot completely break out of our self-validating systems, ultimate meaning is unreachable: All we can hope for is to discover and express truth "in terms that make sense within a particular universe of meaning." We may, therefore, continue to discover or create meaning, "which is satisfying for the present location of the reader."[25]

A specific exegetical example helps to understand what all of this means for the actual interpretation of Scripture. In 2 Samuel 11 we are told that, after committing adultery with Bathsheba, David tried to get her husband, the soldier Uriah, to go home. Uriah, however, refused to do so. Since the rest of the army was in the open fields, he protested, "How could I go to my house to eat and drink and lie with my wife?" (see v. 11). Most readers, of course, will wonder whether Uriah had found out about the affair, but the Hebrew narrative, so often characterized by gaps of information, does not tell us. "The gap may be filled legitimately by both affirmative and negative answers. . . . The text demands that both hypotheses be utilized to shed their different light on details in the text; different plots must be organized on the basis of the hypotheses. Moreover, the text requires the reader to maintain both hypotheses simultaneously."[26]

Stated in that fashion, it is difficult to object to the approach, for it simply attempts to do justice to the literary power of the narrative. Behind this example, however, lies a commitment to the relativity of truth in human experience and, therefore, to the validity of multiple, perhaps even contradictory, meanings. While McKnight himself is careful to deny that *"anything goes,"*[27] it is not always easy to see how an extreme application can be logically avoided. In a famous essay that argues against the determinacy of meaning, Stanley Fish concludes by assuring us that we need not worry that such an approach leads to relativism; after all, in spite of indeterminacy of meaning, people continue to participate in communication with confidence because their beliefs are communal.[28] Yet, it remains unclear whether Fish's reassurance works out in practice.

The Theological Factor. The application of this principle to biblical studies inevitably becomes embroiled in fundamental theological disputes. For most of their historical existence, both Jewish and Christian communities held—and substantial groups within them still hold—that the Bible does communicate and make accessible to us ultimate

---

25. Edgar V. McKnight, *Postmodern Use of the Bible: The Emergence of Reader-Oriented Criticism* (Nashville: Abingdon, 1988) 28, 59, 60.

26. Ibid., 240, with reference to Meir Sternberg, *The Poetics of Biblical Narrative: Ideological Literature and the Drama of Reading* (Bloomington: Indiana University Press, 1985) 201-2.

27. Ibid., 61.

28. Stanley Fish, "Is There a Text in This Class?" in *Is There a Text in This Class? The Authority of Interpretative Communities* (Cambridge, Mass.: Harvard University Press, 1980) 303-21, esp. 21. On the same page he affirms that his views do not give rise to solipsism or idiosyncrasy, and the reason for this confidence is reflected in the subtitle of his book. As he puts it in the preface: it *is* possible to identify "a structure of meanings that is obvious and inescapable from the perspective of whatever interpretive assumptions happen to be in force" in a community (p. viii). For his more recent formulations, see *Doing What Comes Naturally: Change, Rhetoric, and the Practice of Theory in Literary and Legal Studies* (Oxford: Clarendon, 1989).

truth. How is that commitment to be reconciled with the notion that conflicting interpretations of the Bible, since they have behind them the authority of their respective communities, are all valid?

Is a Roman Catholic believer, for example, supposed to acknowledge the truthfulness of a Protestant doctrine even if that doctrine contradicts and thus undermines an important Roman Catholic tenet? And if an interpretive community decides that the reader-response approach is invalid, is that community's interpretation valid too? The term *valid* is seldom if ever defined in these contexts.[29] According to what may be described as a "soft" approach, the point is that no community has a monopoly on the whole truth; therefore, diverse communities, recognizing that their respective traditions have emphasized different aspects of biblical truth, may prove mutually enriching. Given human finiteness, such an emphasis is unobjectionable. What remains unaddressed and troubling is whether any two views may be mutually exclusive and, if so, whether it is helpful to regard them both as valid.

Unquestionably, current emphases on the role of the reader cover a wide variety of approaches. Included under the general category are profound insights into the process of interpretation as well as faddish ideas. The danger is that, troubled by what appear to be extreme formulations, we may close our eyes to the invaluable contributions made by this movement. Such an overreaction would be particularly unfortunate in view of the character of Scripture as a book that speaks to all generations. If there is anything demonstrable in the history of biblical study it is the vigor and consistency with which believers have "actualized" its teachings in their lives.

This relevance is not the result of the Bible's "timelessness," if we mean by that a transcendent meaning totally unconditioned by historical factors. The very fact that the biblical message has proven relevant to remarkably diverse people living in different ages and different lands is itself evidence of its essentially historical character; it was given to people in the context of their life situation, and it has been readily contextualized by subsequent readers. (To me, the theological explanation is that the same Holy Spirit who authored the Scriptures—thus biblical inspiration—is the one who brings understanding to the reader.) It is worth pointing out, incidentally, that Stanley Fish, whatever other controversial things he may say, places a premium on the contextual aspect of communication.[30]

Some thinkers view the concept of contextualization as a relativizing of the Bible that deprives it of its authority. It may well be that the concept has been abused in specific instances, but biblical authority can just as easily be undermined by minimizing the reality of historical variation. The divine authority of Scripture comes to human beings in their concrete situations, which of course are susceptible to change. The absoluteness of God's commands thus would not be preserved but rather compromised if those commands were so general and vague that they were *equally* applicable to all situations.

The Legitimacy of Reader Involvement. Our discussion so far may be viewed as an acknowledgment of the intense involvement of the reader in the process of interpreting Scripture. We should not be misled by the apparent novelty, or even avant-garde quality, of reader-response theory. While it is true that the current preoccupation with the reader is very much a modern phenomenon, the newness in question has to do mainly with the self-conscious and explicit character of the descriptions. But there is unquestionably a reality to which those descriptions point, and that reality has always been there.

Whether we like it or not, readers can—and routinely do—create meanings out of the texts they read. That being so, several options are available to us. At one extreme, we could legitimize all reader responses, or at least the ones that have the authority of some community behind them; it is doubtful, however, whether the integrity of Christianity can be preserved within such a framework. At the other extreme, we could attempt to suppress the reader's prejudice. In effect, this is what historical exegesis has had as its goal: total objectivity on the part of the interpreter. But such objectivity does not exist. And if it did exist, it would be of little use, because then we would simply be involved in a bare repeti-

---

29. For some, perhaps, it simply means that all views deserve to be tolerated.

30. Arguing that his viewpoint does not imply an "infinite plurality of meanings," he points out that "sentences emerge only in situations, and within those situations, the normative meaning of an utterance will always be obvious or at least accessible, although within another situation that same utterance, no longer the same, will have another normative meaning that will be no less obvious and accessible" (ibid., 307-8). Again: "It is impossible even to think of a sentence independently of a context, and when we are asked to consider a sentence for which no context has been specified, we will automatically hear it in the context in which it has been most often encountered" (310).

tion of the text that takes no account of its abiding value. Paradoxically, the success of modern biblical criticism was obtained at the great cost of losing biblical relevance.

The historical method was not necessarily wrong in *distinguishing* what the Bible originally meant from what it means today. In practice, however, it also *separated* the two. The new approach teaches us, or rather reminds us, that if we do not know what the Bible means today, it is doubtful that we know what it meant then. At all stages of interpretation some human need is being met. None of those activities presents us with a "purely objective" truth that is removed from all human questions and concerns. Every request for "meaning" is a request for an application because whenever we ask for the "meaning" of a passage we are expressing a lack in ourselves, an ignorance, an inability to use the passage. Asking for "meaning" is asking for an application of Scripture to a need; we are asking Scripture to remedy that lack, that ignorance, that inability. Similarly, every request for an "application" is a request for meaning; the one who asks doesn't understand the passage well enough to use it.[31]

In short, it is not necessary to suppress our present context to understand the text. On the contrary, at times we need to approach Scripture with our problems and questions if we would truly appreciate what it says. And that is to recognize that in order to value the text, the reader must have a commitment to it. Commitment, however, entails pre-understanding, and such a "prejudice" is not only permissible—it is required.

Users of *The New Interpreter's Bible* will note, in the very format for the commentaries, a deliberate attempt to avoid a false dichotomy between "what it meant" and "what it means." Although individual contributors reflect a variety of viewpoints with regard to reader-response theory, the project as a whole acknowledges, in contrast to the older method, the legitimacy of the interpreter's self-involvement.

IS THE AUTHOR REALLY DEAD?

Authorial Intent. It should be clear by now that modern hermeneutics has moved further and fur-

ther away from an interest in the meaning of the original author. Other than for antiquarian purposes, authorial intent is regarded, at least by a number of prominent thinkers, as more or less irrelevant. This approach clashes with the "common sense" of the average reader. Moreover, as already noted, it is vigorously rejected by not a few scholars. We need to consider, therefore, whether reports of the death of the author have been greatly exaggerated.[32]

There is undoubtedly a certain legitimacy to the claim that the meaning of a text should not be identified with the author's intention *in an exclusive and absolute fashion.* Every teacher, for example, has probably experienced the delight of having a student ask a question that rephrases, interprets, and expands points mentioned in a lecture. Although it would not be quite right to say that all of what the student says was part of the teacher's conscious intention, the instructor is happy to take credit for the "new" meaning insofar as it is a legitimate inference from the lecture.

May we say that the student's interpretation was part of the meaning of the lecture? In some sense, yes, and we can confirm that by the very fact that the instructor accepts the interpretation. Now, if the same interpretation had arisen in a conversation among the students, with the instructor being absent and thus unable to confirm it, it would still have been part of the meaning. This potential for semantic expansion increases in the case of a written document, for now the text becomes widely available to a large and diverse number of people who are more and more removed from the original setting of the author. The apostle Paul, let us say, could not have possibly anticipated certain specific problems in twentieth-century Christian churches. Whether we admit it or not, the "application" of a Pauline statement to those problems entails a decision about the "meaning" of the text that certainly was not part of the original author's conscious intent.

The matter becomes even more pressing for believers who regard God as the ultimate author of Scripture. This conviction of a dual authorship— both human and divine—has, of course, been the motivating factor behind many controversial uses of the Bible throughout the centuries. Whether we think of that strand of Jewish exegesis associated

---

31. John M. Frame, *The Doctrine of the Knowledge of God* (Phillipsburg, N.J.: Presbyterian and Reformed, 1987) 83.

32. See Roland Barthes, *The Pleasure of the Text* (London: Cape, 1975) 27: "As an institution, the author is dead: his civil status, his biographical person have disappeared."

with Rabbi Akiba that saw a significant meaning in every detail, or the allegorical program of Origen of Alexandria, or the so-called typological approach of the Antiochenes, or the appeal to *sensus plenior* ("fuller meaning"; see above p. 108), or simply the common devotional reading of thousands of believers—all of these assume that there is "more" to the biblical message than is apparent on the surface. Indeed, anyone who believes that the primary origin of the Bible lies in an omniscient and foreseeing God can hardly doubt that there is considerable "meaning" in the biblical text that the human authors were not fully aware of.[33]

In short, we may concede, on both literary and theological grounds, that the meaning of a biblical passage need not be identified *completely* with the author's intention. It is quite a different question, however, to suggest that authorial meaning is dispensable or even secondary. The position I take (and presumably shared in a general way by most of the *NIB* contributors, who are expected to present a historical exegesis of the text) is that, while in certain cases the task of identifying what the biblical author meant is not the *only* legitimate way of proceeding; such a task is *always* legitimate and indeed must continue to function as an essential goal.

Respect for the Author. One could argue that this is the only honest way of proceeding before further considerations are brought to bear on the text. Our social interaction with one another is anchored on this principle. We all recognize that it is utterly unjust to take a conversation we have just heard and interpret the words of one of the speakers in a sense different from—let alone contradictory to—the sense meant by that speaker. Indeed, we routinely denounce that sort of thing as morally unacceptable behavior. The notion that such a principle can simply be suspended in the case of written documents cannot be justified.

Consider, for example, liberation theologian Croatto's claims (summarized early in this article) that interpreters should read into the text their own

meaning. One suspects that Croatto would be deeply offended (and rightly so) if we were to interpret his book to mean that the best kind of hermeneutics is the fundamentalist approach, or that his book sets forth a capitalist ethics on the basis of which the United States is justified in exerting imperialist pressures on Latin America. Such an interpretation of Croatto's work would be deplorable.

In response, some may suggest that he was only referring to works that have become classics, whether religious or otherwise. There is no doubt a measure of truth in this argument: A classic work becomes part of a given community, whose members, by their very use of the work, put their own imprint on it. But to admit that much is a far cry from what some moderns are suggesting. Can it reasonably be argued that the more important a work is the greater liberties we may take with it? That the more we respect a text, the more justified we are to disregard its author? Whatever *other* functions a classic may have, it continues to be a historical document, requiring historical interpretation. It should be kept in mind, incidentally, that Bultmann's own emphasis on preunderstanding, far from removing the need for historical interpretation, was intended to do real justice to serious texts.[34]

Part of the difficulty arises from the role played by poetry in most societies. It is, of course, true that if someone composes a poem or produces a painting—that is, a purely artistic product—the creator is inviting us to "interpret" that work in a variety of ways. But the biblical texts are not art in this sense. Even the Hebrew poetry of the OT cannot be reduced to pure art. Whatever literary and artistic features we may find in Scripture, its primary purpose is to communicate an intelligible message that requires a response.

The Character of Scripture. Here, however, once again we come across a theological issue that has a history of vigorous controversy. Is God's revelation really *propositional* in character (that is, conveying information) or is it *personal* (establishing a relationship)? The so-called dialectical approach associated

---

33. Walter Kaiser, to be sure, has argued that the divine meaning must be the same as the human meaning, because otherwise the real meaning of Scripture would be inaccessible to us; after all, grammatical-historical exegesis is our only way to determine what the actual text says (see above, n. 12). This approach appears to restrict unnecessarily the meaning of the word *meaning*. Kaiser's legitimate concerns can be preserved by insisting that the historical sense constitutes the semantic center, to which any other meaning ("application"?) must be demonstrably related. For a nuanced discussion, see Vern S. Poythress, "Divine Meaning of Scripture," *WTJ* 48 (1986): 241-79.

34. See Robinson, "Hermeneutic Since Barth," 23: "One's subjectivity does not simply introduce distortions; it ensures that the phenomena with which the text was grappling—if it is a serious text—are not overlooked or distorted into curiosities. It is this relevance of 'Bultmannian' hermeneutic *for the understanding of the past in its own right* (in distinction from any modern appropriation of the message of the past) that is often overlooked" (italics added).

with the theology of Karl Barth, concerned that orthodox Christianity downgraded the Bible to the level of a static document, emphasized the relational quality of the Word of God (this view, with some modifications, became the dominant position and continues to be widely held). Evangelical theology, on the other hand, concerned about the subjectivity implied in Barth's approach, has insisted that the biblical revelation is propositional.

While I am committed to the latter perspective, one must be careful not to fall into indefensible disjunctions. The whole of the biblical text can hardly be reduced to a sourcebook of information—there is much more to Scripture than that.[35] But neither can we suggest that God's revelation consists of a personal encounter void of content. Indeed, nothing is more basic to Scripture than the fact that it *communicates* to us God's good *news*. The question is, then, whether, by an appeal to the autonomy of the text or the role of the reader, we have the liberty to subvert that message.

LANGUAGE AND MEANING

Historical Background. At various points in this article, the significance and function of language have proven to be a central issue. Certainly, meaning is inextricably tied to language, and so it is only a mild exaggeration to say that the whole contemporary debate about interpretation is a discussion about language. A brief background on the history of this issue may help to place that debate in perspective.

During the nineteenth century, which saw the flowering of linguistic *science* as a primarily historical discipline (comparative philology), language philosophy was largely dominated by so-called idealism. On the European continent, this general approach was tied to phenomenology and existentialism, which placed great emphasis on the fundamental significance of language. Not averse to the use of paradox, Continental philosophy has tended to express its ideas in less than perfectly clear terms. The New Hermeneutic, for example, builds on Heidegger's ontology (language as the "house of being") and views speech not so much as human expression but as the self-speaking of language.

The basic thing about a text is not what the author intended to express in words by following up a given point of view. Rather, basic is *what wills fundamentally to show itself and have its say prior to or apart from any subjective intent.* The question to the text would then not be the question as to the [author's] perspective, but rather: "What shines forth in this text? What shows itself in this text?"[36]

Concerns of this sort are what lies behind the subsequent development of structuralism and related approaches.

Quite a different point of view, however, has dominated Anglo-American language philosophy in recent times. Indeed, at the beginning of the twentieth century British thought experienced something of a revolution that came to be known as "the linguistic turn."[37] Tired of the abstract quality of the idealist tradition, such brilliant British thinkers as G. E. Moore and Bertrand Russell decided that the real task of philosophy was to clarify our concepts and, therefore, our language. The Austrian Ludwig Wittgenstein and other prominent philosophers took up this theme and generated a new subdiscipline known as analytic philosophy. (The question of "God-talk," incidentally, often emerged in this context and so ties in quite directly to the issue of meaning in biblical revelation.) Although working independently of twentieth-century linguistic science, these philosophers developed principles and methods that were very similar indeed to what linguists were doing. The isolation between linguists and philosophers has gradually given way to cooperation, and it is no longer unusual to find philosophers fully abreast of developments in linguistics or linguists who capably try their hand at philosophical investigation.[38]

One important consequence, out of many, is the

---

35. Traditionally, evangelical thought has been inclined to the view that such concepts as biblical inerrancy, propositional revelation, and authorial intent entail one another. While the connections among them are indeed close, some distinctions are necessary. For a nuanced discussion of the variety of biblical genres and how that variety relates to biblical authority, see Kevin J. Vanhoozer, "The Semantics of Biblical Literature: Truth and Scripture's Diverse Literary Forms," in *Hermeneutics, Authority, and Canon,* eds. D. A. Carson and J. W. Woodbridge (Grand Rapids: Zondervan, 1986) 53-104.

36. Helmut Franz, "Das Wesen des Textes," *ZTK* 3, 69 (1962) 190, italics added. Quoted in Robinson, "Hermeneutics Since Barth," 46.
37. See Richard Rorty, ed., *The Linguistic Turn: Recent Essays in Philosophical Method* (Chicago: University of Chicago Press, 1967). It is important to distinguish "philosophy of language," which indicates one of the subject matters of philosophy, from "linguistic (or analytic) philosophy," which refers to a particular method of doing philosophy.
38. See Colin Lyas, ed., *Philosophy and Linguistics* (New York: Macmillan, 1971). For more recent developments, see Alice ter Meulen, "Linguistics and the Philosophy of Language," in *Linguistics: The Cambridge Survey,* 4 vols., ed. F. J. Newmeyer (Cambridge: Cambridge University Press, 1988) 1:430-46.

value attached to *semantics* in contemporary linguistics, a subject broached somewhat gingerly by earlier (structural) linguists. Already in 1951, Stephen Ullmann, a Hungarian-born scholar who eventually became professor of Romance languages and literature at Oxford, had published a foundational work on the question of meaning that was fully informed by developments in the scientific study of language.[39] Within two decades, it was no longer unusual for linguists to deal extensively with problems of meaning; indeed, one of the major linguistic contributions of the 1970s, by John Lyons, was entitled *Semantics*.[40] Drawing on advances in several disciplines, including philosophy (but not of the Continental variety) and psychology, Lyons produced an admirable synthesis that continues to serve as a base for further debate. Lyons appears to be innocent of the controversy regarding authorial intent in literary studies. He asserts without any hesitation that the speaker's intention is a necessary element in communication.[41]

Semantic Theories. In any case, the careful empirical work of modern linguistics should provide a solid foundation for discussions about meaning (and, therefore, about the interpretation of texts). A variety of theories have been propounded; we need not identify them all, but several emphases deserve mention. One long-standing explanation—more or less discredited among professionals but unconsciously assumed by most speakers even today—is the reference or denotation theory of meaning. According to this view, words function like names—that is, labels attached to extralinguistic objects. As a comprehensive explanation, this theory is most inadequate. Even when applied to "names," the concept of reference is only part of the picture; both "New York City" and "The Big Apple" refer to, or stand for, the same extralinguistic entity, but it would be misleading to say that their meaning is identical. The problem is even more serious when we take into account words for which it is difficult to identify a referent (e.g., *beautiful*).

A competing approach is the functional view of meaning, which stresses the contextual use of language. This explanation has been proposed in various forms by such philosophers as Gilbert Ryle, Ludwig Wittgenstein, and J. L. Austin.[42] The emphasis on context is congenial to scholars in the field of general linguistics. This approach can be easily integrated, for example, into a view of language as a structured system, in which value arises from the relationship that holds among the diverse linguistic elements. Thus the potential meaning of the word *good* depends on its relationship to words of similar meaning that could occupy the same context, such as *nice* and *excellent*; the actual meaning of the word in an utterance is determined by its relationship with the other words in that specific sentence.[43]

Although much more satisfying than the reference theory of meaning—at least when discussing the meaning of vocabulary items—the contextual approach cannot account for every semantic problem in language. Other perspectives and emphases can and should be used to shed greater light on the question of linguistic meaning. In particular, it is worth pointing out that to recognize the strong connection between meaning and usage does not do away with the concept of reference, especially in the case of whole utterances or propositions. Take the sentence *Abraham Lincoln delivered a powerful speech at Gettysburg.* The two proper names in that sentence certainly denote (that is, have a one-to-one correspondence with) extralinguistic realities. The terms *delivered* and *speech* are not totally devoid of reference, but their meaning is to a large extent determined by linguistic relationships. This is even more true of the adjective *powerful,* for its semantic value depends almost entirely on both the presence of other adjectives that could occupy that spot in the sentence and the specific combination of the adjective with the noun *speech.*

Note, however, that the recognition of these facts does not in any way undermine the denotative character of *the sentence as a whole.* As a historical proposition, the meaning of that statement is inextricably tied to the referent to which it points. (Moreover, the referential character in view is independent of its truthfulness. If we replace *Abraham*

39. Stephen Ullmann, *The Principles of Semantics* (Oxford: Blackwell, 1951). In the second edition, published in 1957, Ullmann noted the "remarkable" affinity between L. Wittgenstein's functional theory of meaning and modern linguistic thought (303; Wittgenstein had a great impact on Anglo-American language philosophy). See also James Barr, *Biblical Words for Time,* 2nd ed., SBT 1/33 (London: SCM, 1969) 197.

40. John Lyons, *Semantics,* 2 vols. (Cambridge: Cambridge University Press, 1977).

41. Ibid., 1:4, 33; 2:733. It would not be fair to say that Lyons's remarks apply only to oral communication. Much of his own early research, in fact, focused on ancient Greek literature, especially Plato's writings.

42. On the basis of Austin's work, more detailed "speech-act" theories have appeared, with subsequent application by some biblical scholars. See Thiselton, *New Horizons,* esp. chap. 8.

43. The adjectives *paradigmatic* and *syntagmatic,* respectively, are used to describe these two kinds of relationships.

Lincoln with *Plato,* the sentence, though false, would still denote something outside of language itself.) In sum, it is important to keep in mind that competing theories of meaning need not be mutually exclusive of each other. More important, one must not conclude that an emphasis on inner-linguistic semantics results in the destruction of objective meaning.

CONCLUSION

Exposure to contemporary theories of meaning and interpretation can not only prove dizzying but they can also create personal angst about the uncertainty of human experience. We need to keep in mind, however, that the same scholars who challenge the determinacy and objectivity of meaning go on in their daily lives assuming that interpretation is both possible and essential. They engage in conversations with the clerk at the bank and believe that the money they were told had been deposited is really there. They read the newspaper account of a fire in another city and do not experience an emotional crisis, wondering whether the fire actually took place in the very house where they are reading the newspaper. They even write books about the death of the author and expect the reader to believe that they themselves are alive.

The view that it is the reader who creates meaning calls to mind the old paradox of whether a tree falling in the forest produces a noise if no one is there to hear it. Suppose that I receive a letter, but afraid of what it might tell me, I decide to burn it without reading it. It could be argued that, since the very reader for whom the letter was intended never read it, there was no meaning at all. Yet the objective reality of the communication is not undone by my reaction—and it certainly would be folly to think that I am personally unaffected as a result of the decision not to read the letter (which happened to say, "You must come in for an operation this Friday or you will die").

For those who believe what the Scriptures claim to be—God's very message to us—an additional consideration must be brought to bear. The Bible presents God as the Creator of all things, including human speech. In fact, the ability of men and women to speak appears to be closely related to their being created in the image of God, who made

the world by speaking the word of command, "Let there be. . . . " The reality and effectiveness of human communication is a reflection of God's own speaking. To be sure, human speech is finite and, more important, is deeply affected by the presence of sin. Not surprisingly, therefore, legitimate questions arise concerning the interpreter's subjectivity, the relative features of culture, and ambiguity in meaning. These problems must not be ignored or set aside by an appeal to theological considerations.

Nevertheless, the purposes of the Creator, who is also the Savior, cannot be thwarted by human weakness. Indeed, just as the snow and the rain do not return to the sky without producing fruit on the earth, "so is my word that goes out from my mouth:/ It will not return to me empty,/ but will accomplish what I desire/ and achieve the purpose for which I sent it" (Isa 55:11 NIV). For the Christian, the meaning of that revelation is inextricably bound to Christ, who came to "explain" or "interpret" the Father (John 1:18, ἐξηγέομαι *exēgeomai*), and whose words, we are assured, will never pass away (Mark 13:31).[44]

44. A few of the ideas and descriptions in this article are treated in greater detail in Moisés Silva, *Has the Church Misread the Bible? The History of Interpretation in the Light of Current Issues,* Foundations of Contemporary Interpretation (Grand Rapids: Zondervan, 1987).

BIBLIOGRAPHY

Fish, Stanley. *Is There a Text in This Class? The Authority of Interpretative Communities.* Cambridge, Mass.: Harvard University Press, 1980.

Gadamer, Hans-Georg. *Truth and Method.* 2nd rev. ed. Translated and revised by Joel C. Weinsheimer and Donald G. Marshall. New York: Continuum, 1993.

Hirsch, E. D., Jr. *Validity in Interpretation.* New Haven: Yale University Press, 1967.

McKnight, Edgar V. *Postmodern Use of the Bible: The Emergence of Reader-Oriented Criticism.* Nashville: Abingdon, 1988.

Osborne, Grant R. *The Hermeneutical Spiral: A Comprehensive Introduction to Biblical Interpretation.* Downers Grove, Ill.: InterVarsity, 1991.

Palmer, Richard E. *Hermeneutics: Interpretation Theory in Schleiermacher, Dilthey, Heidegger, and Gadamer.* Northwestern University Studies in Phenomenology and Existential Philosophy. Evanston: Northwestern University Press, 1969.

Ricoeur, Paul. *Essays on Biblical Interpretation.* Introduction by Lewis S. Mudge. Philadelphia: Fortress, 1980.

Robinson, James R., and John B. Cobb, Jr., eds. *The New Hermeneutic.* New Frontiers in Theology: Discussions Among Continental and American Theologians. New York: Harper & Row, 1964.

Stuhlmacher, Peter. *Historical Criticism and Theological Interpretation of Scripture: Towards a Hermeneutics of Consent.* Translated by Roy A. Harrisville. Philadelphia: Fortress, 1977.

Wilson, Barrie A. *About Interpretation: From Plato to Dilthey—A Hermeneutic Anthology.* American University Studies 5, 30. New York: Peter Lang, 1989.

CONTEMPORARY METHODS OF READING THE BIBLE

CARL R. HOLLADAY

OUTLINE

Recent biblical study has been characterized by dissatisfaction with established methods based on inherited assumptions and a corresponding willingness to explore new methods of interpretation. This survey will look at some of the reasons for the dissatisfaction and describe some of the newer approaches. But rather than inventorying the various forms of biblical criticism that have developed over the last two centuries, here we sketch three "paradigms," or "theories of biblical literature," that have emerged historically and still provide fundamental options for modern readers of the Bible.[1]

There are no neutral methods of biblical interpretation. Readers of the Bible rarely operate with an explicitly formulated theory of the text. Yet theoretical assumptions are undeniably present, and they undergo change. Identifying these assumptions, their distinctive configurations, and established pat-

---

1. See N. Petersen, *Literary Criticism for New Testament Critics* (Philadelphia: Fortress, 1978) 9-12.

terns of use enables us to speak of *paradigms,* by which is meant distinctive ways of conceiving the biblical text that are identifiable across a broad range of use and that constitute the pre-understanding that leads to the development of certain methods of interpretation. Seen in this way, different interpretive approaches (e.g., literal versus allegorical interpretation) or different forms of biblical criticism (e.g., source criticism, form criticism, etc.) may be understood, not as different paradigms, but as debates or methodological developments operating within a single paradigm. Contemporary methods of biblical interpretation can be classified according to whether they relate essentially to one of three different paradigms: divine oracle, historical, or literary.

THE DIVINE ORACLE PARADIGM

Several basic principles informing the divine oracle paradigm can be identified.[2] One fundamental assumption is the conviction that *the Bible constitutes a single genre.* Even though it is recognized that the Bible is composed of diverse literary materials (e.g., law, prophets, writings), nevertheless, when properly arranged as a completed collection, it is seen as unfolding a single, continuous, coherent story of salvation history. For Jewish readers, the Tanakh (i.e., the Hebrew Scriptures) unfolds the continuous story of Israel, which Christian readers believe is continued in the NT. In both cases, some continuity is presupposed in their respective canons.

A second critical assumption is the *direct (extraordinary) divine origin of Scripture,* usually expressed in terms of divine authorship of all the writings. To speak of God as the author of Scripture in an unqualified sense makes it possible to say that the Bible *is* the Word of God in an equally unqualified sense. The metaphor of divine authorship is, of course, an extended metaphor, based on the simple observation that the Scriptures were written by numerous authors speaking, in some direct sense, on behalf of God. By extension, God is the real author.

An important corollary of this second principle is the view that the various biblical authors were inspired by God. This can be asserted in a strict or loose sense. The strict form implies direct rather than indirect divine authorship: God is the "Active Cause," primarily responsible for the origin and production of Scripture. The stricter the form this takes, the less individuality or creativity is attributed to the human authors. When prophets or apostles speak, they are giving God's message, not their own. As passive instruments, they may be characterized with such metaphors as "pens of the Holy Spirit."[3] An especially strict understanding of divine dictation is reflected in a rabbinic tradition describing God's dictating the Torah to Moses. It is reported that when Moses began to write Gen 1:26 ("God said, 'Let us make humankind' " [NRSV]), Moses said, "Lord of the world, why do You give a good argument for the heretics?" To which God responded, "Write, and whoever wants to err may err!" God, not Moses, decides what is written in Scripture.[4]

A third principle, which results from the first two, is *uniformity of revelation.* If one's canon is assumed to be a unified, coherent collection of writings that directly derive from God, it naturally follows that God is speaking in all its parts. Every passage of Scripture is one word in a larger "speech" made by God. In any given verse we can hear God's voice, and we can expect it to resonate with all the other parts. God does not sing on key in one part and off key somewhere else. We expect it all to harmonize.

One of the classic statements of this principle occurs in the rabbinic tractate *Sanhedrin* 99a: "He who says, 'The Torah is not from God,' or even if he says 'The whole Torah is from God with the exception of this or that verse which not God but Moses spoke from his own mouth'—that soul shall be rooted up."

This third principle also has a corollary: Scripture as a repository of divine revelation. Regardless of the canon one uses, whether it is Jewish, Roman Catholic, or Protestant, Scripture is regarded as a collection of divine utterances. Because God is speaking with equal force anywhere, and everywhere, in Scripture, the Bible represents the sum total of what God has spoken "on the record." To gain a comprehensive understanding of God's will requires systematic examination of all these statements and relating them to each other in some plausible scheme. This view naturally lends itself to proof-texting, which means that any passage, located anywhere throughout the

2. What is here called the divine oracle paradigm roughly corresponds to what Farley and Hodgson call the "scripture principle" (E. Farley and P. C. Hodgson, "Scripture and Tradition," in P. C. Hodgson and R. H. King, *Christian Theology: An Introduction to Its Traditions and Tasks,* 2nd ed. [Philadelphia: Fortress, 1985] 61-87, esp. 62).

3. Augustine *Confessions* 7.21.27.
4. *Gen. Rab.* 8.8.

Bible, can be adduced to support a claim made about God's will. They all are of equal weight theoretically.

With this view of Scripture, theology—the task of articulating how God is known and experienced in the world—essentially becomes biblical theology. When the Bible is read as the exclusive, or even primary, sourcebook of divine revelation, the basic task of theology is biblical interpretation, and one of the main forms of theological reflection is the biblical commentary.

A fourth principle is the assumption that *Scripture is directly expressive of the divine will.* This presupposes a direct correspondence between Scripture and divine intent and assumes that the will of God is somehow embodied within and expressed by the text. The text becomes the primary focus of the reader's attention, and the primary locus of revelation. The place the reader looks for, or listens to, the Word of God is within the sacred pages of the Bible. One imagines that God is somehow standing behind the curtain of the text, speaking to the reader, and that the attentive reader/listener will hear God speaking directly *through the text.* It is also assumed that God's will can be discerned and followed, and that doing so on the part of the believing individual or community can serve to implement God's will in the world. Thus the message of the text can be appropriated and used to create within the reader's world identifiable profiles of behavior or certain social structures and religious institutions (cult, priesthood, church, etc.) that express God's intentions. As such, the biblical text may be read as an architectural plan or blueprint that, when executed, results in forms of human society that represent the fulfillment of God's will.

In this paradigm, since the biblical text and the divine voice are so closely identified, one may be said to read the Bible as a divine oracle. A divine oracle is a form of direct revelation, in which a divine being speaks to an individual without using an intermediary. The words of the oracle are the very words of the deity. Thus the Scriptures, taken as a whole, are "living oracles," words of God that are perennially current, timeless in their significance.

The origins of this paradigm can be traced to the exilic and post-exilic periods of Israelite history, even though the stages of its development remain obscure. At what point the Jewish Scriptures achieved definable limits and came to be regarded as uniformly authoritative is not easy to define, but it was likely as late as the first century CE. Once the paradigm was firmly established in both post-70 Judaism and early Christianity, it essentially remained in effect through the ancient and medieval periods and was not seriously challenged until the late fifteenth and early sixteenth centuries.

Throughout these earlier periods there were intense debates about how Scripture should be interpreted. Jews and Christians disagreed sharply about whether certain Old Testament (OT) passages should be interpreted typologically (i.e., whether certain OT persons, events, or institutions pre-figured Christian persons, events, or institutions), or whether certain OT prophecies were actually fulfilled in Christ. Closely related was the debate about levels of meaning or the different senses in Scripture, whether a text should be understood in a straightforward, literal sense or whether it also had a higher or deeper spiritual sense.

Alexandria and Antioch came to symbolize two fundamentally different interpretive approaches; yet the debate between them over the relative value of the literal versus the spiritual meaning was not so much about two different paradigms as it was over the most appropriate method for making sense of the divine oracle paradigm they shared. The issue was not whether there was a literal meaning in the biblical text, but whether one quickly bypassed it to get to the deeper, spiritual or allegorical meaning (Alexandria), or whether one stayed focused on the literal meaning while also looking for the deeper meaning (Antioch).

Even though the precise formula for giving weight to the literal and spiritual senses could vary, the conviction remained through the ancient and medieval periods that Scripture yielded multiple levels of meaning. Yet, in spite of differences concerning the relative weight to attach to the literal meaning of Scripture, the divine oracle paradigm during this time is *presupposed* rather than *challenged.*

The hegemony of this paradigm was seriously challenged in the seventeenth and eighteenth centuries; yet, it continues to be used by many biblical interpreters today. This is largely the case in Eastern Orthodox Christian traditions; in conservative Roman Catholic and Protestant traditions, especially fundamentalist Protestant traditions; and also in Orthodox and more conservative Jewish traditions.

This is not to say that the methods by which modern readers of the Bible appropriate the divine oracle paradigm are the same as those used in earlier centuries, although there are often close resemblances. Modern interpreters no longer read Scripture using the scheme of the fourfold meaning in the way Origen or Augustine did. Nor does one find elaborate schemes of allegorical interpretation comparable to those found in Philo of Alexandria or medieval Christian interpreters.

Yet the divine oracle paradigm continues to operate in certain settings, most notably in liturgical settings. Because lectionaries were developed during periods when this paradigm was used, the assumptions for selecting lectionary texts for certain liturgical days or seasons derive from this paradigm. Thus on certain days the OT and New Testament (NT) readings are selected and read because they are understood to belong to the one continuous story of God's revelation and traditionally have been related to each other in a typological or prophecy-fulfillment interpretive scheme. Moreover, when lectionary texts are designated in worship as "the Word of God," the relationship between the reading of Scripture and the audience is essentially the one presupposed by this paradigm. Scripture is being read and heard as divine oracle.

This is also often the case in private devotional settings, where one reads Scripture expecting to hear the Word of God coming directly from the sacred page. In such settings, the relationship between the reader and the text is one of immediacy where God speaks to the reader directly through the words of Scripture.

Today, in Jewish and Christian traditions that firmly adhere to the principles of the divine oracle paradigm, Scripture tends to be regarded as a sourcebook of divine revelation. Through various schemes of interpretation attempts are made to make sense of the story the text tells, and while such interpretive schemes may vary widely, they tend to operate with the common assumption that the biblical text is directly expressive of the divine will. Consequently, in these traditions consistent efforts are made to correlate Scripture with the contemporary reader's own situation.

THE HISTORICAL PARADIGM

The historical paradigm refers to a set of assumptions and overall approach to Scripture that came to prominence during the seventeenth and eighteenth centuries and eventually gave rise to a set of interpretive methods that have come to be called the historical-critical method.[5] Even though this paradigm was anticipated in important respects in earlier periods of Jewish and Christian biblical interpretation, it received special impetus during the Renaissance and Reformation. It served as the major interpretive paradigm during the nineteenth and early twentieth centuries. Although never without opposition, it has come under special criticism in the latter half of the twentieth century.

Features of the Historical Paradigm. In the historical paradigm, Scripture is understood as historical in several senses. First, as *historical narrative,* it relates, or unfolds, a story of Israel and the church, generally designated as salvation history, that is essentially continuous. The historical paradigm shares this element with the divine oracle paradigm, although historical critics more readily acknowledge that the Bible contains multiple versions of this story. Second, the text is seen as *historical artifact,* serving as historical evidence used to construct a critical history that stands alongside the official history presented by the biblical text. Third, the text is seen as a *historical product* that has grown and developed through time. Since the text is conceived as having its own history, it becomes possible to speak of the history *of* the text—its formation, stages of development, and evolution.

So understood, the biblical text (a) relates history, (b) conceals and (through critical historical work) reveals another history, and (c) has its own history. The interpreter is now able to think of the history *in* the text—the story it tells, the official, canonical version; the history *behind* the text—the story to which it bears witness; the history *of* the text—the story of its origin, formation, and development.

Whereas the locus of revelation in the divine oracle paradigm is within the text itself, in the historical paradigm it tends to shift outside the text. Rather than reading the words of Scripture, and expecting to hear the Word of God coming directly through the sacred page or through the sacred story unfolded in the sacred page, the reader now looks behind, or beyond, the biblical text to another story that is independent of the biblical text.

With this shift in the locus of divine revelation from biblical text to critical history, certain theologi-

5. See E. Krentz, *The Historical-Critical Method* (Philadelphia: Fortress, 1975).

cal problems in the official canonical version(s) may be more easily explained. Since the text is no longer viewed as the (exclusive) carrier of divine revelation, but relinquishes this function to a much more complex historical process (of which it is a part), discrepancies and conflicting points of view within the text no longer impugn God, for God is no longer seen as directly responsible for having put them there. Rather, they represent the best, most earnest efforts of inspired, but nevertheless flawed, human beings, bearing witness to God's presence and work.

Moreover, the canonical ordering is seen to be the result of a historical process. In order to construct a critical history, the biblical canon is dismantled and rearranged. Individual books or sections (e.g., the Pentateuch) are seen to be compilations of smaller, shorter units. The canonical order and arrangement no longer have any official status. Biblical writings can be analyzed into sources, divided and sub-divided, arranged in new chronological sequences. Nor do attributions of authorship carry the same weight. In many instances, the names attached to writings come to be seen as anachronisms, attempts to ensure them an earlier and, therefore, more authoritative place in the developmental time line. Scripture is no longer seen as a single fiber but as a rope with many strands of different sizes woven together.

With this shift in the understanding of the text, the interpreter becomes a historian and is required to think historically. What does this entail? First, recognition that each writing, or group of writings, has its own history, and consequently the theoretical possibility of determining its historical circumstances: date and place of writing, identity of author(s) and addressees, and the religious, theological, social, historical, and political circumstances that occasioned the writing. The reader of any biblical text thus becomes obligated, at least minimally, to become acquainted with the history surrounding the text. Inevitably, this means becoming a student of the ancient world, the ancient Near East in the case of the OT, and the Hellenistic-Roman world in the case of the NT. It also involves familiarity with the ancient languages in which the books were written: Hebrew, Aramaic, and Greek.

Second (and this is an extension of the notion that a text has its own history), is the recognition that the history of the text can be conceived in stages: those stages leading up to its canonical form (its pre-history) and what happened after it reached its final, or near-final, form (its post-history). In the historical paradigm, special attention is given to the pre-history of the text: what happened before the text reached its canonical form. This requires that the biblical texts be analyzed and arranged in ways that make it possible to identify previous stages of development. Larger units (e.g., the Gospels) are arranged in some plausible chronological, or genetic, sequence, so that Matthew and Luke are read as revised, expanded versions of Mark, or Chronicles is read as an expanded version of Kings. The Pastorals are read as appendices to the genuine Pauline letters, reflecting subsequent stages of development within Pauline Christianity. With smaller units, especially those that are similar and seem to have some genetic relationship, either to each other or to an earlier common tradition, the reader tries to determine which came first and how the texts are related to each other. Thus the various accounts of the Decalogue in the Pentateuch, or the two versions of the Beatitudes in Matthew and Luke, are placed in a developmental scheme. The assumption here is that understanding the final form of the text is illuminated by learning about its pre-history.

Methodologically, this means that the reader constantly seeks to correlate a specific biblical text with other biblical texts by arranging them, or understanding them, in some chronological or developmental sequence, or at least comparing them with other texts within this reconstructed historical framework. Thus the book of Deuteronomy is seen to come not from the time of Moses, but from a much later period, because of features within the text that can be correlated with a critically reconstructed history of Israel. Even though 1 Thessalonians comes late in the canonical ordering of Paul's letters, it is read as his earliest writing chronologically. Similarly, although Mark comes after Matthew in the canon, it is read as (probably) older; thus Matthew represents a later stage of development historically, and thus a different historical situation.

If a strict chronological sequence is not followed, the writings may be arranged according to common traditions: Jahwistic (J), Elohistic (E), Deuteronomistic (D), Priestly (P); the Deuteronomic history; the Synoptic tradition; the Johannine tradition, where the Johannine letters are grouped with the Fourth Gospel; or the Pauline tradition. Here, too, the historical principle is at work, because it is assumed that writings, or groups of writings, are best understood as belonging to some identifiable historical tradition, perhaps related to a historical figure (e.g., Paul or John); and that the texts belonging to that tradition can be arranged chronologically: the earlier Pauline letters followed by the later ones, or the disputed letters. Once these traditions are identified and isolated, it is then possible to relate them to each other. One envisions the Johannine tradition as separate from the Synoptic tradition, and then decides how they are related historically—whether, for example, the Johannine tradition is historically derived from the Synoptic tradition, or whether they are independent of each other.

In effect, the reader works with a rearranged canon. The writings are arranged according to some historical principle, rather than some other ordering principle, such as length, relative theological importance, or topical similarity.

Past and present serve as the two primary foci for interpretation: The biblical text is set within the past, and the contemporary reader resides within the present. One becomes especially aware of the chronological, linguistic, and cultural distance between the reader and the text. A major interpretive task is to bridge this gap, and this is done by the reader's becoming acquainted with the earlier historical period, its languages, customs, and political and social history.

Since the original historical circumstances that produced the text are given such a high premium, determining "what the text meant" becomes a major aim for the interpreter. What did the author, or community, that produced the text *intend* to convey? How was the text heard and understood by its original audience? Recognizing the distance between past and present, the contemporary reader's ultimate concern, however, is not with "what the text meant" then (or even in subsequent generations) but "what it means" now.[6] How should it be read and understood in the reader's present situation? Does it have basically the same meaning and significance? Or must it, for some reason, have a fundamentally different meaning and significance?

Thus the interpreter's chief task is to negotiate this distance between past and present, to adjudicate between "what it meant" and "what it means." Or, using the imagery of an interpretive journey, the

reader must leave the modern world and enter the past, live in the world of the text until it becomes familiar, and, having broken through the barrier of the text's unfamiliarity, return again to the modern world. The reader thus constantly oscillates between the two worlds of past and present—leaving one's own world, entering the text's past, returning to one's own world. Every interpretive act is a journey there and back again.

But this does not mean that one is a student of the past only. It is equally important to become a student of the present, a modern cultural historian who understands the language(s), customs, world views, and various histories of one's own setting. This is done for the purposes of correlating the message of the past with the needs of the present. But the aim remains the same: to bring a word spoken in the past to bear on the present, or to hear a spoken word speak again.

The historical paradigm represents a direct challenge, although in different ways, to the main principles of the divine oracle paradigm. The single-genre view of Scripture gives way to the perception that it contains not only multiple literary genres, but also multiple outlooks. As the divisions and subdivisions of Scripture are closely examined, it becomes clear that many different theological perspectives are found in Scripture and that the Bible unfolds not one story but several. This directly challenges the notion that Scripture as a whole represents a single theological perspective. Scripture becomes highly differentiated and is seen as a collection of writings with many different perspectives.

The claim for direct divine authorship becomes modified as the role of individual authors and communities is more clearly recognized. As human authors are given greater responsibility for composing, collecting, and transmitting Scripture, God's direct responsibility for the origin and production of Scripture diminishes proportionately.

If the various parts of Scripture reflect many theological outlooks, revelation cannot be uniform in the sense that it has been understood. The image of Scripture as a repository of divine revelation becomes more difficult to hold. If statements from various parts of Scripture are in conflict, and they are traceable to an immutable God, Scripture cannot be directly expressive of God. The changes can more easily be explained as the result of historical contin-

6. For the classic statement of this formulation, see K. Stendahl, "Biblical Theology," *IDB* 1:418-32.

gencies or as representing different historical stages in the process of revelation.

With these changes it becomes increasingly difficult to claim that Scripture *is* the Word of God in an unqualified sense. This also complicates the hermeneutical task. The interpreter must compare what the text meant then with what it might mean now. The text also must be interpreted in the light of an independently reconstructed history, understood at various levels: history in, behind, and of the text. To locate God and discern the will of God in these various histories is inevitably more complicated, and it becomes more difficult for the reader, operating within the historical paradigm, to regard the text as directly expressive of the will of God, and to know how God's intention as revealed in Scripture might be translated into some definable reality, either in the reader's life or within society.

Methods of the Historical Paradigm. Just as certain methods of interpreting the Bible developed in connection with the divine oracle paradigm, so also has this occurred with the historical paradigm. Many of these interpretive methods were pioneered by German biblical scholars, and their designations are noteworthy in that they usually include the term *history* (*Geschichte*): the *religionsgeschichtliche Schule,* the "history-of-religions school"; *Traditionsgeschichte,* "history of traditions"; *Formsgeschichte,* "history of forms"; *Redaktionsgeschichte,* "history of redactions," or "editorial history." Although they are sometimes translated using the term *criticism*— "tradition criticism," "form criticism," and "redaction criticism"—they function within the historical paradigm. These types of criticism now represent accepted methods of interpreting the Bible and are widely used across a broad range of contemporary scholarship.

Generally speaking, historical criticism, or the historical-critical method,[7] describes the interpretive approach associated with the historical paradigm. The term *historical* underscores the pivotal role history plays in this approach, and it reflects the conviction that the Bible is understood primarily within a historical framework. The term *critical* signals the interpreter's recognition that the history of Israel and early Christianity reconstructed from the biblical text may differ fundamentally from the biblical history that is presented in the narrative

itself. At every turn the interpreter must be prepared to weigh carefully the claims made by a text and decide whether they may be taken at face value, or whether they must be reinterpreted and represented because of other overriding concerns that might be brought to bear on the text. Thus, even though a text might claim to be attributed to a particular author, a critical reading of the text might recognize the impossibility of such a claim and posit a more convincing origin for the text. The interpretive methods and approaches described below are treated as specific methods that have been developed as part of the larger historical-critical enterprise.

Lower and Higher Criticism. Earlier scholarship distinguished between these two types of criticism.[8] "Lower" meant that it was more basic. It refers to the reader's first step: trying to establish what the text originally said, what is now commonly designated text (or textual) criticism. Once this basic question is decided, one can move to a "higher" range of questions, such as identifying the author and the addressees, and inquiring about other aspects of the text.

Textual Criticism. No original copy (autograph) of any biblical writing has been preserved, only copies of copies. As long as there have been written biblical texts, scribes and other biblical specialists have compared the various versions and manuscripts in order to determine which text is likely to be the most reliable. Notable in this regard was the work of Origen and Jerome, but they had predecessors and many successors. Now a highly developed, technical field of study, textual criticism draws on numerous disciplines, ranging from paleography to lexicography, all of which are employed to determine the origin and transmission of the biblical text.[9] The rise of modern textual criticism may be traced to the fifteenth century, when the discovery of numerous classical texts from antiquity made it possible to develop more precise comparative methods. This, in turn, enabled the production of printed editions of the Bible, based on better textual witnesses. Among the more notable of these was Erasmus's edition of the Greek NT.

Some of the questions textual critics try to answer

---

7. See Petersen, *Literary Criticism,* 9-23, and literature cited there.

8. See J. Barton, *Reading the Old Testament: Method in Biblical Study* (Philadelphia: Westminster, 1984) 20-21, 213n. 2; Petersen, *Literary Criticism,* 29.

9. See P. K. McCarter, Jr., *Textual Criticism: Recovering the Text of the Hebrew Bible* (Philadelphia: Fortress, 1986); B. M. Metzger, *The Text of the New Testament,* 3rd ed. (Oxford: Oxford University Press, 1992).

are these: When different wordings of a verse have been preserved in the manuscript tradition, which one is likely the more original? How does one account for different readings? Did they result from scribal errors, or were they intentional corrections? What is the most plausible way of explaining how the surviving manuscripts relate to each other? Can they best be grouped in families? Do they point to a common origin, such as a single manuscript from which all the others within a given family derive?

Source Criticism. This method seeks to determine the sources on which a biblical writing is based, or from which it has been compiled.[10] The sources may be either oral or written. Early theories of both Pentateuchal and Gospel composition envisioned periods of oral tradition prior to the composition of a writing, when traditions circulated at first in unwritten form before eventually being written down. While the oral period is often regarded as a time when the traditions remained quite fluid, the possibility that traditions could become relatively fixed, and grouped together based on various organizing schemes, is usually admitted.

In the earliest stages of the historical paradigm, source criticism primarily involved analyzing stylistic features of the biblical text, such as the recurrence of the names of God and the patterns of usage this reflected. It is treated here as a method of the historical paradigm because these observations about language and style were put to work in the service of the historical paradigm, providing clues that helped scholars identify and unravel the several strands comprising the canonical text, arrange them in a likely chronological sequence, and finally suggest some developmental explanation that described the *history of the formation of the text*. Since identifying and evaluating sources is a prerequisite for doing historical work, source criticism becomes an indispensable task when the interpreter reads the biblical text with a historical agenda.

Traditio-Historical Criticism. This hyphenated expression designates the interpretive method that sees the Bible primarily in terms of the "history of traditions" (*Traditionsgeschichte*), an approach that has dominated OT studies until very recently.[11] As noted earlier, this method has several critical ingre-

dients: the community as the generative matrix where biblical traditions are formed; the ability to classify traditions according to distinguishable, formal (literary) features and correlate them with specific settings within the community's life; and the resulting ability to identify stages in the development of the tradition, which can be correlated with the biblical text itself, and thereby describe their "history"—that is, their movement and development through successive periods of time.

One of the most influential works embodying this approach is G. von Rad's two-volume *Old Testament Theology,* which presents a comprehensive treatment of the development of Israel's history and faith as seen through the OT, which is seen as the final stages in this long process. By focusing attention on Israel's traditions that are discernible through the text, von Rad essentially attempts to unfold the *history of Israel's faith.* The locus of revelation thereby shifts away from the text itself to the historical process to which the text bears witness, but it is still a theologically motivated enterprise. Even though canon is dissolved in the sense that the canonical order of writings is massively rearranged and the biblical text is used as a source for reconstructing the history of theological tradition, it nevertheless does serve to establish the limits of the sources that are utilized for his reconstruction. The canonical paradigm remains operative to the extent that it is Israel's faith that is being presented, rather than that of other ancient Near Eastern religions.

Similarly, R. Bultmann's seminal study of the Synoptic Gospels, *History of the Synoptic Tradition,* whose title preserves the critical terms *history* and *tradition,* provides a monumental example of this approach applied to the study of the formative decades of the Jesus movement, out of which the canonical Gospels eventually arose. Like von Rad, Bultmann's primary interest is to investigate the sources for what they reveal about the church's faith. This results from his insistence that the Gospels serve as *secondary* sources for reconstructing a history of Jesus, but as *primary* sources for reconstructing the church's faith about Jesus. Even though the time span through which the history of the Synoptic tradition can be traced is much shorter than that presupposed by the history of Israel's traditions, the aforementioned assumptions are basically the same.

This model could be extended to other parts of the NT. Thus it has become commonplace to speak

10. See J. Barton and D-A Koch, "Source Criticism," *ABD* (1992) 6.162-71.
11. See D. A. Knight, "Tradition History," *ABD* (1992) 6.633-38; W. Rast, *Tradition History and the Old Testament* (Philadelphia: Fortress, 1972).

of the history of the Pauline tradition or the Johannine tradition. In these latter two instances, the seminal role of a single individual is recognized, yet the traditions that come to be associated with that person are seen to be transmitted primarily through communities related in some way to that figure.

Form Criticism. Being able to distinguish among various literary forms found in the biblical text is an essential element of the "traditio-historical" method, yet form criticism can be treated usefully as a separate interpretive method.[12] It first involves a type of literary analysis that seeks to identify formal features of a text, analyze recurrent structural literary patterns, and then classify these into different groups. The OT is seen to contain a wide range of literary genres and sub-genres: narrative, legal material, wisdom sayings, prophetic oracles, liturgical texts (various types of psalms, prayers, and confessions), to name just a few. Within the narrative portions of the NT, one finds miracle stories, stories in which a significant pronouncement is made by Jesus, and stories that essentially relate controversies between Jesus and his opponents, among others. The various letters not only reflect different genres—letters of thanksgiving, friendship, exhortation, instruction, etc.—but also contain smaller identifiable units: sermon summaries, confessions, prayers, and hortatory material. Both the OT and the NT contain writings that are themselves apocalypses, but also works that include apocalyptic sections.

Identifying and classifying literary genres or forms is done for several reasons. First, it assists in tracing the history of particular traditions. By correlating certain recurrent literary forms with certain sociological contexts (e.g., enthronement psalms with coronation events in Israel's history, or controversy stories in the Gospels with controversies in the life of Jesus and the early church), form critics propose concrete historical, sociological settings in which to understand these texts. And if several written versions of a biblical text occur (e.g., the different accounts of the feeding of the five thousand in the four Gospels), it then becomes possible to propose some developmental sequence to explain them. One thus does *Formsgeschichte* ("history of forms") by constructing a history of the (literary) forms that explains the stages through which the story has passed and why they finally occur in their present location in the Gospels. Form criticism thus serves as a way of doing historical criticism.

But attention to literary forms can have a second function not directly related to reconstructing the history of biblical traditions. It may serve an essentially interpretive function. Positing some direct connection between what a text says (content), how it says it (form), and in what setting it is said (context) provides some interpretive advantage to the reader of the text. The meaning or significance of the text may be unclear, until one realizes, through careful attention to literary form, that it is, for example, a particular type of psalm, such as a communal lament that likely stemmed from a crisis within the community and reflects an antiphonal structure. By identifying its literary form and correlating this with its likely social and religious context, the reader recognizes it as a set of antiphonal responses within a liturgical setting and can make better sense of its meaning. A NT example is provided by 1 Corinthians where, for a long time, Paul's line of thought seemed to be inconsistent. But when form critical analysis of the letter suggested that in certain parts of the text Paul is quoting Corinthian slogans and in other parts correcting those slogans, and that this way of reading the text made sense of the historical context of the letter, a more plausible interpretation was possible. Thus identifying the literary form (dialogue) and relating this to its probable "life setting" (Paul's responding to libertine tendencies within the Corinthian church) makes it possible to render a more coherent interpretation of the message of the text (content).

Redaction Criticism. Drawing on the insights and results of form criticism, redaction criticism, presupposes the "history of traditions" model, thinks of texts as having pre-histories, and relates texts to each other as sources and revisions of sources.[13] Yet it may be seen as a refinement of form criticism, and as an important corrective.

Whereas form criticism focuses on smaller literary units, and especially seeks to reconstruct their pre-history, redaction criticism shifts the focus to a later stage in the history of the tradition. While redaction critics remain interested in the text's preceding history, they are more interested in identifying the points at which the tradition has been edited, or

---

12. See J. Barton and V. Robbins, "Form Criticism," *ABD* (1992) 2.837-44; G. M. Tucker, *Form Criticism and the Old Testament* (Philadelphia: Fortress, 1971); "Form Criticism, OT," *IDBSup* 2:342-45.

13. See N. Perrin, *What Is Redaction Criticism?* (Philadelphia: Fortress, 1969).

redacted, but especially in determining how these changes reflect certain theological points of view. To be sure, redaction critics are interested in tracing the history of these redactional changes through the tradition, hence the term *Redaktionsgeschichte* ("history of redactions"); yet they are typically more interested in seeing how these changes have affected the final form of the canonical text as a whole.

Redaction criticism is most fruitful when it is fairly certain that one text, either a single passage or an entire work, has depended directly on an earlier text. Thus source criticism is indispensable to redaction criticism. Assuming the widely held view that Matthew has used Mark, it then becomes possible to assess the significance of the ways Matthew has altered Mark. By thinking of the editorial process as it has affected the entire writing, redaction critics have sought to determine the overall theological viewpoint of the work. As a consequence, redaction critics think of the final editor not so much as a collector of traditions but as a creative theologian.

By focusing on the distinctive theological elements of entire biblical writings, redaction critics have called attention to the diverse theological viewpoints found in the biblical canon, thereby enabling useful comparisons between the theologies of biblical writings.

Composition Criticism. Coined by E. Haenchen in connection with his work on Mark, composition criticism can be seen as a further refinement of redaction criticism.[14] Whereas redaction criticism focuses especially on specific redactional changes made by an author or editor, and how these reflect an identifiable theological outlook, composition criticism is more interested in the cumulative effect of all such changes when the finished work is viewed as a whole. It thus goes a step beyond redaction criticism. In shifting emphasis from editorial redaction to the combined effect of such redaction for the work as a whole, compositional criticism represents a move toward canonical criticism, and in certain important respects, more recent versions of literary criticism.

The composition critic tries to determine the overall effect of redactional changes, but to look at these, along with all other relevant aspects of a text,

with a view to assessing the work in its literary entirety. Once a comprehensive view of the writing as a whole is obtained, the composition critic then tries to relate each part to the whole, as well as interpret each part in the light of the whole. In effect, the composition critic acknowledges the importance of the text's pre-history, but is more concerned with the finished composition.

In certain senses the work of Cadbury, Dibelius, Conzelmann, and Haenchen illustrates composition criticism's interest in the finished narrative as a whole. The method is consciously applied to Luke–Acts by R. F. O'Toole.[15]

Audience Criticism. As already noted, historical-critical analysis has typically been interested in determining the original audience to which a text is addressed, whether it is relatively specific historically (e.g., the addressees of certain Pauline letters), or whether it is largely hypothetical and indirect, as in the case of the Gospels. By drawing special attention to this part of historical investigation, J. A. Baird seeks to give more formal definition to this approach.[16] In important respects, this emphasis anticipates the more rigorous attention given to the reader in reader-response criticism (see below).

Canonical Criticism. Like redaction criticism, canonical criticism works with the "history of tradition" model and focuses attention on the final, written form of the text rather than on its earlier stages of development.[17] But whereas redaction criticism tends to focus on single writings, and the overall theological message of each writing, canonical criticism affirms this and emphasizes an even later stage—the final canonical collection.

Since canonical criticism operates with the basic assumptions of the historical paradigm, it is treated here as one of the methodological approaches of that paradigm. Even though its proponents have often been critical of certain features of the historical paradigm, these criticisms should be seen as arising from within the paradigm and not external to it.

By accenting what is actually an even later moment in the history of the tradition, canonical critics take seriously the significance, not simply of the

---

14. See S. D. Moore, *Literary Criticism and the Gospels: The Theoretical Challenge* (New Haven: Yale University Press, 1989) 4-7; E. Haenchen, *Der Weg Jesu: Eine Erklärung des Markus-Evangeliums und der kanonischen Parallellen,* 2nd ed. (Berlin: Walter de Gruyter, 1968).

15. See R. F. O'Toole, *The Unity of Luke's Theology: An Analysis of Luke–Acts* (Wilmington: Michael Glazier, 1984).

16. See J. A. Baird, *Audience Criticism and the Historical Jesus* (Philadelphia: Westminster, 1967).

17. See J. A. Sanders, *Canon and Community: A Guide to Canonical Criticism* (Philadelphia: Fortress, 1984); also Barton, *Reading the Old Testament,* 77-103.

historical development of Israel and the church's traditions and institutions, but also the historical process by which their biblical canons developed. Their specific focus of interest is to trace and assess the process through which traditions became normative for believing communities. There is an explicit interest in history, with some canonical critics especially emphasizing the history of the canonizing process. By refocusing attention away from the *history behind the text* or the *history prior to the text* toward the *history of the text* as it acquired canonical status, proponents of canonical criticism have sought to relocate the locus of revelation more directly within the biblical texts themselves. Primary attention is given to the final form of the biblical text—the received text—since it represents the final stage in the community's theological reflection. In this sense, canonical criticism represents a corrective move within the historical paradigm.

Canonical criticism as an interpretive method has several distinctive elements besides its focused attention on the final form of the texts and their canonical arrangement. The first element might be termed *explicit concern for the canonical context of a biblical writing.* Canonical critics try to take seriously not only the inclusion of a writing in the canon but its placement as well—where it has been included and the difference this makes for its interpretation. The placement of a writing makes a difference in how it is read. It would make a decisive difference, for example, if the order of the biblical books were reversed: if the OT began with the prophets and ended with the Torah, or if the NT began with Revelation, and the Gospels were placed between the Pauline epistles and the general epistles. This is not to imply that the canonical order is itself authoritative, but to underscore that the cumulative message of the entire collection and how the writings are arranged do affect the way we construe the message of a single writing. If the book of Ecclesiastes is read as an isolated work apart from the canon, it is thoroughly pessimistic, but if read as part of the larger canon, its pessimism is modulated by the sheer fact that it is juxtaposed with other writings that are more hopeful in their outlook. By the same token, the sheer presence of Ecclesiastes within the canon affects the way the rest of the canon is read.

If canonical criticism's emphasis on the final form of the text is taken seriously, the reader's first question is not to ask about the pre-history of the text. Rather, the reader's initial move is to see the text within the broader spectrum of the complete collection. It is less important to think of the biblical writings in their chronological relation to each other than it is to see their canonical interrelationships. Canonical critics see the biblical writings as a dealt hand of cards that is arranged in suits, looked at, primarily, in relation to each other.

The more traditional historical-critical approach and a canonical-critical approach might be contrasted as follows: Whereas a historical critic might enter a room full of paintings and begin to arrange them in chronological order and ask questions about the historical circumstances that led to their being painted, a canonical critic would tend to ignore these questions. Instead, the canonical critic would tend to accept the painting for what it is—a finished work—and look at it in its own right. The aim would be to make sense of each painting from what one sees on its canvas. Having looked at all the paintings, one would try to assess each painting in the light of all the others and then try to interpret the significance of the overall collection.

Another distinctive feature of canonical criticism is that *it operates with an explicitly theological agenda.* For canonical critics, it is important that religious communities have accepted these writings as normative for their faith and practice. So regarded, they may be read and interpreted as writings that make explicit theological claims and ethical demands. The reader can be expected to take seriously such claims and demands because, as part of a canonical collection, they express the collective judgment of the believing communities that preserved and transmitted them. As such, the canonical critic places the locus of revelation more squarely within the communities of faith, not in a reconstructed historical process that can be seen through the text. In this sense, canonical criticism seeks to recapture the emphasis of the canonical paradigm that sees Scripture as a single genre, and as a much more direct medium of divine revelation.

Social History and Sociological Analysis. Although this does not constitute an interpretive method in the same sense as those just mentioned, it does represent an approach to Scripture directly related to the historical paradigm.[18] A recent trend

18. See R. Morgan and J. Barton, *Biblical Interpretation* (Oxford: Oxford University Press, 1988) 133-66; the entire issue of *Interpretation* 36 (1982) is devoted to sociological approaches to biblical study. See also N. Gottwald and S. R. Garrett, "Sociology," *ABD* (1992) 6.79-99.

in biblical interpretation has sought to refine our understanding of the history of Israel and early Christianity by emphasizing their social aspects. In one sense, this interest was anticipated by form criticism's interest in the life setting in which texts arose. Quite often, this meant the social context surrounding the text—those aspects of social life and institutions that recur. The implicit assumption of form criticism was that certain social settings (e.g., worship) remain relatively constant from age to age.

But the interest in social history extends beyond that of form criticism. Biblical scholars engaged in doing social history have attempted a much more comprehensive understanding of the social worlds of Israel and early Christianity. To do so, they have consciously appropriated analytical methods and perspectives developed by modern sociologists and have sought to use these in interpreting biblical texts. One difference this has made for interpreting biblical texts is a much richer understanding of the social dynamics of the early religious communities out of which these texts arose, and consequently fresh perspectives on the texts themselves.

One portion of the biblical writings that has directly benefited from this approach is the study of Jewish and Christian apocalyptic. These texts in both the OT and the NT, as well as in the so-called intertestamental writings, have been subjected to extensive sociological analysis. A greater understanding of the sociological origins of apocalpytic movements has led to a fuller appreciation of its distinctive world view and language imagery. It has also been possible to see clearer correlations between the communities that produced these texts and the outlook of the texts themselves.

This approach to biblical literature is included here as part of the historical paradigm because it essentially reads and uses biblical texts as sources for doing social-historical reconstruction or sociological analysis. But recent use of social-scientific approaches for radically revisioning the way Israelite history should be studied by modern interpreters, represented most vividly in the work of N. Gottwald, has not only posed a serious challenge to the historical paradigm but also has moved beyond it by proposing an explicitly ideological reconstruction of Israel's history from a Marxist perspective.[19]

THE LITERARY PARADIGM

It is probably too early to tell whether we can speak meaningfully of literary paradigm, and thus of a theory of biblical literature or a theory of the text that derives from such a paradigm.[20] Yet we do so here because there does appear to be a set of theoretical assumptions and methodological approaches that represent a fundamental shift in the way Scripture is construed as text and that have enough in common to be grouped together in this manner.

To speak of this paradigm as literary is perhaps confusing because of the different ways the term has been used, especially in connection with the historical paradigm. As already noted, literary criticism has meant many things.[21] In the present context, "literary" describes a set of assumptions and approaches commonly associated with critical literary theory, especially New Criticism, but also a range of other approaches that either directly challenge the historical paradigm or provide plausible alternatives for modern biblical readers.

What makes this paradigm literary is the distinctive way in which the biblical text is conceived. Rather than being read primarily as a sacred text through which we can hear God speaking to us quite directly, or as a (historical) source that assists us indirectly in doing something else, whether it is reconstructing history or some other constructive enterprise independent of the text itself, in the literary paradigm the text itself is the reader's sole focus. What is said in the text is understood as the voice of the text, and the reader does not read the text listening for some other voice, such as God's voice or the author's voice, behind the text; nor does the reader assume that the voice of the text is primarily testifying to something outside the text, whether it is the author's intention or historical,

19. See especially N. Gottwald, *The Tribes of Yahweh* (Maryknoll, N.Y.: Orbis, 1979).
20. Barton and Morgan, in their treatment of the "literary study of the Bible," speak of the literary paradigm (*Biblical Interpretation*, 203-68, esp. 213). Similarly, E. V. McKnight, *Postmodern Use of the Bible: The Emergence of Reader-Oriented Criticism* (Nashville: Abingdon, 1990) 104-6. For helpful treatments of literary approaches to the Bible, see especially Moore, *Literary Criticism*; Morgan and Barton, *Biblical Interpretation*, 203-68; Barton, *Reading the Old Testament*, 8-29, 140-79.
21. See K. R. Gros Louis, "Some Methodological Considerations," in K. R. Gros Louis, J. S. Ackerman, and T. S. Warshaw, *Literary Interpretations of Biblical Narratives* (Nashville: Abingdon, 1982) 2.7-34, esp. 14.

social realities referred to, or presupposed, by the text. Rather, the text is understood as having its own voice, and as the words of a text are read, this textual voice speaks. What the term *literary* is intended to capture is this focal emphasis on the words of the text and the conviction that the message and meaning of a text somehow inhere within the literary texture. By closely identifying the words and message of a text, and thereby ascribing such generative power to the words of the text, it might be appropriate to speak instead of the *textual paradigm.*

M. H. Abrams's theoretical model of the interpretive process has been used to clarify the distinctive features of the literary paradigm and distinguish it from the divine oracle and historical paradigms.[22] In Abrams's scheme, the "work" (text) is located at the center of a triangle whose points represent "universe" (world), "artist" (author), and "audience" (reader), and the act of interpretation can be understood in terms of how the text is related to each of the points of the triangle.

In the historical paradigm, the interpreter obviously focuses on the text but does so *primarily* for what it says about the world and the author. In relating text to world, the reader correlates what is said in the text about certain historical, social, or conceptual realities with these realities as they are known or understood from sources independent of the text. Thus the world that is depicted or referred to in the text is related to the reader's own understanding of that world. In relating text to author, the reader conceives of the text as having been authored by someone, either an individual or a community, and thus reading the text with primary reference to this author. This may mean trying to discern the author's intention, relating the text to other writings by the same author, or interpreting the text in the light of biographical information about the author.

The interpreter makes similar moves in the divine oracle paradigm, for there too the reader relates text to author, but the author is primarily God. If the reader is trying to discern authorial intent, it is more likely to be God's will as it comes to expression in the text. Similarly, the reader may try to relate the text to God's "biography" by correlating what is said in the text with what the reader understands as God's character or typical form of behavior. In the

divine oracle paradigm, efforts to relate text to world are quite similar to those in the historical paradigm. They usually take the form of correlating what the text says or implies about the world with the reader's own understanding of the world. The main difference is that in the historical paradigm "world" is ordinarily construed in historical terms, whereas in the divine oracle paradigm it is ordinarily, although not exclusively, construed in either metaphysical or doctrinal terms.

In the literary paradigm, by contrast, there is very little, if any, interest in relating text either to world or to author, for in a very real sense the text is construed as both its own author and world. If anything, reader, the third point of the triangle, replaces world and author as the primary element to which text is related. The primary relationship that is presupposed in the act of interpretation is that between the reader and the text. In certain appropriations of the literary paradigm, most notably reader-response criticism, the focus of attention shifts away from text toward reader.

Features of the Literary Paradigm. Although the literary paradigm takes many different forms, it represents, in a fundamental sense, a reaction against the historical paradigm. Several of its distinguishing features may be mentioned.

Ahistorical View of Texts. In the historical paradigm, interpreters tend to think in chronologically linear terms. Since texts and traditions are understood as originating at specific points in time and then developing over time, establishing reliable dates for them and constructing chronological frameworks in which to trace their development are critically important. One reason for this is that interpreters tend to think in terms of historical cause and effect, and consequently read texts, analyze issues, and propose explanations that are framed in terms of historical causality. This often takes the form of identifying previous influences on a text and determining whether and how previous texts, traditions, or events have formatively shaped the text. The interpreter thus tries to establish genetic relationships between these various elements, but also between them and the text being interpreted.

In the literary paradigm, by contrast, interpreters do not employ history as the defining category for construing the process of interpretation, and for thinking about the text as it relates to its world, author, and reader. There is less interest in how

22. M. H. Abrams, *The Mirror and the Lamp: Romantic Theory and the Critical Tradition* (New York: Oxford University Press, 1953), esp. 6-7; used by Barton, *Reading the Old Testament,* 200-204.

previous texts, traditions, or events have influenced a text, in ascertaining the historical process through which a text might have developed over time, or in what historical causes led to the writing of a text. Rather than seeing a text as the product of historical causes, those who work within the literary paradigm tend to view a text as a finished product. The reader is not so much concerned with what preceded the writing of the text as with the finished writing itself. Consequently, there is less interest in assigning texts to specific times and relating them to each other within some historical, developmental scheme.

This does not mean that the reader is uninterested in comparing one text with other texts, even from different periods. It simply means that the interpreter's comparisons are essentially spatial rather than temporal, or literary rather than historical. One tends to make comparisons between texts without asking whether one text preceded another chronologically or whether there is some genetic relationship of literary dependence or historical influence.[23] Instead, texts are compared because of their formal similarities regardless of their chronological, historical relationship.

This way of reading texts and relating them to each other is possible because in the literary paradigm texts tend to be thought of in *ahistorical,* or *atemporal,* terms.[24] Time and history are not the primary reference points for reading texts in the literary paradigm.

Since the literary paradigm works with an understanding of the text that is, in a real sense, timeless, a different form of analysis is required for interpretation. Thus it is now common to distinguish between *diachronic* and *synchronic* analysis.

To analyze a text diachronically (literally, "through time") means that one examines the language of the text or other aspects of the text as they have developed over time. Thus one might trace how the meaning and use of a term have evolved or changed over time, or how its use in the text being studied relates to one or another of these usages. The term *synchronic,* which literally means "with time" and by extension "at the same time," designates a different form of analysis where the inter-

preter looks at a text at a particular moment in time, usually its time of composition, and makes comparisons from other texts as they relate to that single moment. Thus in diachronic analysis, the interpreter thinks in terms of a linear time line along which the development of language and texts can be plotted. Synchronic analysis, by contrast, focuses on a single point in the time line and draws comparisons from other texts that are either roughly contemporary or otherwise relevant. In the literary paradigm, synchronic analysis may also involve comparing texts, or aspects of language, from different chronological periods, but doing so as if they occupied the same moment in time.

The fact that the relationship between the text being interpreted and all other texts is not viewed historically nor related to each other chronologically does not mean that the interpreter makes no use of the categories of time and history. If a text relates a story or develops a plot that moves through time or unfolds history, then certainly the interpreter is required to think both temporally and historically, and to use these basic categories in trying to make sense of the text. But such historical analysis is required because of what is being said in the text. Thus the interpreter must think in these terms to the extent that the voice of the text requires it. But this is quite different from relating a given text *historically* to texts, traditions, and events outside the text, which is the main emphasis in the historical paradigm.

Autonomy of the Text. A second defining characteristic of the literary paradigm is the *autonomy of the text.* Ordinarily, this is a way of saying that the text serves as the reader's primary, if not exclusive, focus. It stands by itself, speaks for itself, and provides clues within it that serve as the basis for interpretation. The text is understood to have its own voice, and the interpreter's task is to recognize its independence, take seriously what the voice says and how it says it, and give it full authority to define the limits of the interpretive agenda.

This axiom could be said to derive from the tenet of ahistoricity. The text is seen as autonomous, since it is not essentially connected to its historical setting, its author, indeed, to anything outside the text that constitutes its (historical) environment. Once completed, the text is seen as a finished work, with a life of its own. As such, it can be thought of as possessing meaning or as a message-bearing voice in its own

---

23. As Petersen puts it, cause/effect explanations give way to parts/whole explanations, whether the reader is trying to relate one part of a single text to the text as a whole, or parts of one text to parts of other texts, or one text to a body of defined literature as a whole (*Literary Criticism,* 26).

24. See Gros Louis, "Methodological Considerations," 14.

right, but neither its meaning nor its message has a life apart from the text itself.

From this principle of autonomy emerge some important corollaries. First, attention is focused on *the final form of the text.* Proponents of the literary paradigm may acknowledge that texts have pre-histories, or recognize the importance of establishing a reliable text using textual criticism. But for the most part these concerns are relegated to secondary or tertiary importance, since they deal with the text's past. Generally, these interpreters concentrate primarily on the final stage of composition, the finished form of the text. In biblical interpretation, this usually means the form of the text that was included in the canon—the received text.

A second corollary is that *the text is viewed as a whole.* In the literary paradigm, a text is ordinarily conceived of as a self-contained writing that can be regarded as a single, complete work. Thus even if a writing is clearly composed of many smaller units that have been edited to form a more coherent whole, the emphasis is on the whole rather than the composite parts. It is usually assumed that a text should be read and interpreted holistically, which means read as a whole from start to finish. Even when one is examining parts, this is done with a constant sense of the whole. As Cleanth Brooks remarks, "The primary concern of criticism is with the problem of unity . . . the kind of whole which the literary work forms or fails to form, and the relation of the various parts to each other in building up this whole."[25]

This insistence on the importance of the unified work may also be seen as a form of protest against the historical paradigm, where texts tend to be dealt with by dividing them into literary strands or fragments, or by analyzing them atomistically, which is especially the case with source and form criticism, and to some extent with redaction criticism.

A third corollary is the conviction that *texts are intrinsically meaningful.* According to this principle, all necessary clues for meaningful interpretation are to be found within the text itself. A common distinction is made between intrinsic and extrinsic dimensions of the text. While these terms have been used to connote different things, they essentially serve to distinguish what belongs to the interior of the text and a wide range of concerns that are seen as exterior

to the text. Of the two, the former is more heavily emphasized in the act of interpretation.

This principle may be expressed in other ways. It is sometimes referred to as the principle of text-immanence, which means that somehow the meaning of the text inheres within the text itself. Or it may be stated as the principle of formalism, the conviction that form and meaning are inseparable. A text's meaning cannot be construed apart from its form. *What is said* in a text is inextricably intertwined with *how it is said.*

Meaning as Aesthetics. A third defining feature of the literary paradigm relates to its theory of meaning, the way a text is understood to express meaning, as well as the way the interpreter gets at or construes the text's meaning. Because of the special emphasis on the final form of the text and its literary contours, in the literary paradigm *meaning is understood as aesthetics.*

Several things are implied by this. First, because meaning is thought to inhere in a text, as something intrinsic to the text, it is not seen as derived from anything outside the text. Thus meaning is not a concept or intention originally residing in the author's mind that the text helps the interpreter to recover. Nor is it something that is ascertained by relating the text to its historical setting or context. Meaning is not a function of correlating a text with its setting. It is, rather, part and parcel of the text itself. In a sense, the text *is* the meaning. A text is like an art object: The interpreter looks at it in order to experience its meaning. Or, in the case of the text, one reads it. Meaning is an experience one has with the text by reading it, reciting it, or hearing it.

Second, since the text in its relationship to other texts, traditions, and events, is viewed ahistorically or atemporally, the locus of meaning shifts from the past to the present. Because meaning inheres in the text, to the extent that a text exists in the reader's present, its meaning always occurs in the present. The interpreter comes to the text with one question: What does it mean? or What is its meaning? not, What did it mean? or What has it meant to previous readers? The interpreter's task is to read the text *meaningfully.* If this involves relating it to another body of texts, this is done as if they all occupy a timeless present.

Third, the act of interpretation is bifocal: text and reader. In terms of Abrams's model, the text is no longer related primarily either to its world or author,

25. Cleanth Brooks, "The Formalist Critics," *Kenyon Review* 13 (1951) 72-81, esp. 72; cf. Moore, *Literary Criticism,* 1.

but to the reader. Meaning occurs when the received text is read and interpreted by a (fresh) reader.

Fourth, interpretation is essentially an aesthetic act that calls for the ability to read and grasp the text as a whole, see its parts in relation to each other and to the whole, establish meaningful correlations, and render an appropriate judgment about them. One experiences the text as one experiences a work of art.

Methods and Approaches. Some may wonder whether the various methods and approaches treated below should be included under the literary paradigm. In some instances, they are closely, if not genetically, related, while in other cases, the relationships may be less direct, or even nonexistent. Boundaries between the various approaches are sometimes unclear, often because they are highly interdisciplinary. The blurred distinctions and confused pictures themselves indicate recent biblical interpretation. Some critics have abandoned older methods in pursuit of newer, innovative approaches, while others, adopting a more eclectic approach, have tried to combine new and old.

Literary Criticism. For a long time biblical critics have used the term *literary criticism* to include a broad range of interpretive questions that pertain to intrinsic (e.g., language and style of writing) as well as extrinsic (e.g., historical setting of the writing) aspects of the text.[26] But when recent biblical critics describe their work as a literary approach to the Bible or biblical literary criticism, they tend to use the expression in its more limited sense to refer to interpretive approaches that focus on intrinsic aspects of the text. Used in this way, it refers to an approach to the text that embodies the principles of the literary paradigm mentioned above.

Rhetorical Criticism. To the extent that rhetoric is thought of as "the art of expressive speech or of discourse, especially of literary composition,"[27] efforts to identify those aspects of a text that constitute its distinctive literary form and determine how they serve to express its message may be characterized as rhetorical criticism.[28] Since the term

rhetoric is especially used to designate the formal study of oratory in the Greco-Roman world, and the application of these principles to various forms of writing, rhetorical criticism has often taken the form of identifying points of correspondence between the biblical text and the Greco-Roman rhetorical tradition.[29] This was the case early in the Christian tradition, owing to the strong influence of the classical tradition on Christian exegetes. Augustine, for example, in *On Christian Doctrine* identifies numerous examples of classical rhetorical literary devices within the biblical text.

The exegetical tradition of establishing significant points of contact between the Greco-Roman rhetorical tradition and the Bible and trying to ascertain the difference this makes in the way one reads the biblical text has been continuous. It not only informed the divine oracle paradigm but figured centrally in the historical paradigm because of the importance it attached to the original historical and literary context of the biblical writings. Consequently, adducing parallel texts from classical authors became a well-established feature of biblical commentaries that employed the historical paradigm, and this remains the case.

Yet rhetorical criticism is included under the literary paradigm because the rhetoric of a text is essentially part of its literary texture. And if the literary paradigm conceives of what is said in the text as the voice of the text, rhetorical criticism seeks to identify the distinctive elements of that voice, its patterns of vocal expression, and how they are arranged in order to convey the message of the text.

The rhetoric of the gospel to which Wilder draws attention is the symbolic and aesthetic dimension of biblical language. In OT studies, most notably J. Muilenburg's work on the prophetic books, rhetorical criticism has been used to analyze literary features of the Hebrew Bible, especially as compared with the formal principles of literary composition used in other ancient Near Eastern traditions.

Structuralism. Structuralism is more than an interpretive method or set of methods.[30] Since its

---

26. For example, D. Aune's definition: "Literary criticism deals with the interpretation and evaluation of a literary work through the careful examination and analysis of the work itself on the basis of both internal factors (e.g., genre, structure, content, style, sources) and external factors (e.g., historical setting, social setting, biographical data, psychological information)." (*The New Testament in Its Literary Environment* [Philadelphia: Westminster, 1987] 19.)

27. *Webster's New International Dictionary,* 2nd ed. (Springfield, Mass.: G. & C. Merriam, 1958) 2138.

28. J. Muilenburg, "Form Criticism and Beyond," *JBL* 88 (1969) 1-18; R. Majercik, T. B. Dozeman, and B. Fiore, "Rhetoric and Rhetorical Criticism," *ABD* (1992) 5.710-19.

29. See especially G. Kennedy, *New Testament Interpretation Through Rhetorical Criticism* (Chapel Hill, N.C.: University of North Carolina Press, 1984); also B. Mack, *Rhetoric and the New Testament* (Minneapolis: Fortress, 1990).

30. See especially Barton, *Reading the Old Testament,* 104-39; also his article "Structuralism," in *ABD* (1992) 6.214-17. For specific examples, see D. Patte, *What Is Structural Exegesis?* (Philadelphia: Fortress, 1979); *Paul's Faith and the Power of the Gospel: A Structural Introduction to the Pauline Letters* (Philadelphia: Fortress, 1983); or H. Boers, *Neither on This Mountain Nor in Jerusalem: A Study of John 4,* SBLMS, 35 (Atlanta: Scholars Press, 1988).

theory of meaning and its consequent understanding of the interpretive process are closely related to a comprehensive theory of culture, it is more a philosophical system whose interpretive theory has been appropriated by specific disciplines, including anthropology, linguistics, and literary criticism. Several assumptions inform its theory of meaning and interpretive approach.

First, it operates with a complex theory of language that takes into account both the personal and the social dimensions of language. It sees language as an individual human activity that presupposes and reflects a complex network of social activities and relationships that are tied to particular cultures. As a system of signs and symbols, language is the expressed manifestation of this complex system of social relationships and cultural norms, and thus provides clues for detecting the organizing principles, or structures, on which the culture is based. As a function of culture, language is both culturally derivative and culturally expressive.

Second, the function of language is to differentiate. Because language serves to detect and express differences within a culture, or social system, meaning occurs when language is at work. It is not something inherent in language. Words and sentences do not "have [some inherent] meaning"; instead they "relate meaning." Rather than having content, words and sentences serve to establish intelligible, meaningful connections between a speaker/listener and the social, cultural context within which the language expression occurs. Language "meaning" has more to do with *social function* than *word content*. Thus in the structuralist theory of language, the relationship between meaning and language is functional rather than ontological.

Third, the principle of binary opposition is seen as a basic category for analyzing social relationships and cultural patterns, and as such becomes a basic interpretive category. The principle is based on the conviction that cultural patterns tend to emerge as sets of opposites. Meaning is seen as a process of differentiation because "contrast" is such a central category within structuralist thought. To define what something is requires one to know what something is not. One can build a house, and know it is a house, only if one has some way of knowing when something is not a house. These basic oppositions may be abstract concepts (e.g., love and hate, good

and evil, justice and injustice); natural, biological categories (e.g., female and male, plants and animals, animate and inanimate objects, night and day); or social, cultural categories (e.g., weeds and flowers, tragedy and comedy, north and south, married and unmarried). Since the function of language is to differentiate, it becomes an important pointer to these binary oppositions.

Even with this cursory summary of some of the basic tenets of structuralism, it can be seen why structuralist interpretation fits within the literary paradigm. The interpreter's attention is focused on a given text, which is seen as a complex system of interconnecting language symbols. The approach is ahistorical, since the structuralist critic typically has little interest in relating the text to historically conceived traditions or historically arranged bodies of texts. Rather, the interpreter listens to the voice of the text as it is heard through the literary texture. This is done through aesthetic analysis, by looking for literary patterns within the text, or other literary structures intrinsic to the text that might provide clues to how the language of the text functions. Throughout the analysis, the structuralist critic assumes that the language of the text, properly understood, will provide clues to underlying social or cultural structures, especially binary opposites that are inherent within the particular culture.

In one sense, the search for these deeper structures of meaning that exist as something approaching philosophical principles beyond the text takes the interpreter outside the text. And to this extent, the structuralist critic becomes concerned with extrinsic dimensions of the text. Yet the principle of the text's autonomy is preserved, since these deep structures are seen to be inherent qualities resident within the text itself.

Structuralist interpretation may also seek to relate a given text to other written texts. Such comparison is possible because of the structuralist theory of literature, which may be seen as a direct extension of its theory of language. If language is seen as culturally derivative and culturally expressive, all writings (literature) within a particular culture have these characteristics. The interpreter is thereby able to compare texts within this body of literature in hopes of correlating particular language expressions with more universal social structures and cultural norms. But in doing so, one works within a cultural system that is conceived spatially rather than temporally. Thus a given religious text can profitably be interpreted as one piece of the larger set of all religious texts in that culture because it is assumed that the ways religious ideas, values, and claims are expressed in one religious text are (possibly) structurally analogous to the ways they are expressed in all other religious texts.

In structuralist criticism, the interpretive aim shifts away from trying to find the meaning resident within the words and sentences of a text as though they are the medium through which an author's or community's *intentions* come to be expressed. Since language is understood more functionally, the aim is to see *how language works* in a text—not what meaning it contains but how it makes meaning. The task is to determine how it relates to various social, cultural conventions, not simply from the historical period from which it derives but from any period, and how the uses of language and the patterns it reflects within a particular text work or make meaning within that text, but also within that text as it relates to other texts from the literature of the culture. Thus meaning is construed not in terms of authorial intent. It is not something that can be gotten at through the language the author uses, but rather as reflective of language significations that are in one sense imposed on the author.[31]

Narrative Criticism. Interpretive approaches deriving from the literary paradigm have been fruitfully applied to biblical narratives. Auerbach's seminal work focused on narrative material in Genesis,[32] and R. Alter first analyzed the "art of biblical narrative" before turning to the "art of biblical poetry."[33] The narratives of Luke–Acts served as the basis for the innovative literary analysis of H. Cadbury and M. Dibelius, and recent NT literary critics have focused especially on the Gospels and Acts.[34]

D. Rhoads, who collaborated with the literary critic D. Michie in producing *Mark as Story: An Introduction to the Narrative of the Gospel* (1982), characterizes narrative criticism as focusing principally on "plot, conflict, character, setting, narrator,

point of view, standards of judgment, the implied author, ideal reader, style, and rhetorical techniques."[35] Rather than serving as a formal definition, this characterization usefully identifies the focal interests of narrative critics.

When narrative critics approach a biblical text with the principles and assumptions mentioned earlier, they tend to focus on the final form of the text, not what preceded it or what stands outside it, but the text and what is in it: what it reports and how it reports it. The text is assumed to have a message that is neither external to the text nor extractable from the text, but inherent within the text as something that can be discerned only by actually reading the narrative itself. Only as the text is read and experienced as an unfolding story can its message be transmitted to the reader. To read the text is to receive its message.[36]

As early as Aristotle, it has been recognized that a narrative has certain well-defined features, such as movement and plot. Characters are introduced, developed, and portrayed by employing well-established techniques, such as the use of dialogue. Various dramatic devices may be employed to develop the narrative: flashback techniques, visions and dreams, and a host of others. All of these are employed and deployed in order to move the story from its beginning to its end. Narrative critics assume that these literary techniques and compositional devices, which are both built into the narrative and identifiable from reading the narrative, provide the reader with the clues for meaningful interpretation.

In analyzing narratives, some critics have distinguished between *the story that is told in the narrative* and *the way the narrative tells the story,* or between the story's content and its rhetorical form. But this distinction between form and content as complementary elements of a narrative is not meant to suggest that the narrative is the literary "shell" that contains the "nut" of the story, for this fails to do justice to the linear dimension of narrative. To use a dramatic metaphor, we might think of a play as having a story that unfolds as the play unfolds, but what enables it to unfold is the structure of the

31. See Moore, *Literary Criticism,* 3-68; D. N. Fewell and D. M. Gunn, "Narrative, Hebrew," in *ABD* (1992) 4.1023-27.

32. E. Auerbach, "Odysseus' Scar," in *Mimesis* (Princeton: Princeton University Press, 1965).

33. R. Alter, *The Art of Biblical Narrative* (New York: Basic Books, 1981); *The Art of Biblical Poetry* (New York: Basic Books, 1985).

34. H. J. Cadbury, *The Style and Literary Method of Luke,* Harvard Theological Studies 6 (Cambridge, Mass.: Harvard University Press, 1920; reprint New York: Kraus Reprint, 1969); M. Dibelius, *Studies in the Acts of the Apostles,* ed. H. Greeven (London: SCM, 1956).

35. Gros Louis lists the kinds of questions literary critics use in approaching texts ("Some Methodological Considerations," 17-20).

36. Gros Louis aptly summarizes the approach: "Our approach is essentially ahistorical; the text is taken as received, and the truth of an action or an idea or a motive, for literary criticism, depends on its rightness or appropriateness in context. Is it true, we ask, not in the real world but within the fictive world that has been created by the narrative?" ("Some Methodological Considerations," 14.)

play (acts and scenes), the speech and movements of the actors and actresses (the lines), and the staging. All of these elements that serve to move the story along constitute its rhetoric or discourse.

Since there is such a close correlation between what story is told and how it is told, the literary texture of the narrative itself is of crucial interest to the narrative critic. By analyzing the how, the reader is given access to the what. For this reason, the eyes of the narrative critic are focused on the narrative text, its literary components (speeches, dialogues, movements of characters through space and time, transitions, etc.), their arrangement, their repetition or other patterns of relationship with each other. As a result, the narrative critic primarily makes interpretive moves that are internal to the story itself. The main concern is to trace how the story unfolds, see how this is achieved through various literary devices and strategies, and assess the way this is done. Thus the narrative critic may ask whether the overall plot is coherent, whether the story reaches successful resolution in terms of the way it begins and unfolds, and in terms of the expectations that are created early in the story.

But narrative critics are not interested merely in identifying and assessing literary strategies or other rhetorical features of the narrative. Such analysis is done to see how the story functions to portray a particular point of view—for example, how reality is being envisioned in the story, whether the outlook is optimistic or pessimistic, comic or tragic. Narrative critics may ask about the moral vision of the main characters and thus try to discern whether the narrative as a whole presents a definable perspective, such as a way of viewing death, mortality, or evil. In asking such questions, narrative critics are not trying to reduce the story to a single point, nor are they trying to abstract a message, or set of messages, from the story. They are, rather, trying to determine and assess what the story, understood comprehensively and as an intrinsic part of the narrative, can be said to mean in the sense that it presents an intelligible, definable point of view. The interpreter's task, then, is to determine how the story, as expressed in the narrative—the narrative world—is construing reality, or the particular angle of vision it takes on some aspect of reality.

When narrative critics approach the biblical text this way, they are essentially trying to ascertain what is intrinsic to the text itself. Comparison with similar literary texts may be made, but usually not to determine redactional changes or to establish historical connections with a literary tradition or other historical setting. Instead, they are trying to read the text in its own terms, think of it as a closed literary system with numerous cross-referential clues that assist in determining how the various parts relate to each other and to the whole. But unlike redaction critics, narrative critics do not try to determine the author's theology. Instead, they try to ascertain the overall narrative point of view: how reality is being construed through the narrative world, not how the author was trying to construe reality.

Reader-Response Criticism. Rather than being seen as a single method, reader-response criticism should be understood as a general interpretive approach that encompasses a broad range of viewpoints and methodologies where attention is primarily focused on the role of the reader in the communication process.[37] This emphasis on the reader, and how the reader responds to a text, is part of a broader pragmatic concern with how language actually functions as it is used in texts. This allows for a much more fluid understanding of what a text is, and the recognition that a text is not a fixed entity. Of particular interest are the effects of a text on the reader(s). In this approach more attention is paid to how a text is received than to how it originated or how it is arranged.

In terms of Abrams's model, rather than being primarily concerned with how the text relates to some external world, or to its author, reader-response critics are more centrally interested in that part of the communication process that involves the text and its reader(s). Of special interest is the reader, and the reader's role in construing meaning. If rhetorical criticism, structuralism, and narrative criticism focus more exclusively on the text and its literary aspects, reader-response criticism, while retaining this interest, focuses special attention on the dynamic interplay between the text and the reader.

Like other methodological approaches related to the literary paradigm, this one has been accompanied or influenced by theoretical innovation. An especially influential role has been exercised by the

37. B. C. Lategan, "Reader Response Theory," *ABD* (1992) 5.625-28; McKnight, *Postmodern Use of the Bible* (see n. 20 above); J. P. Tompkins, ed., *Reader-Response Criticism: From Formalism to Post-Structuralism* (Baltimore: Johns Hopkins University Press, 1980). See also J. Darr, *On Character Building: The Reader and the Rhetoric of Characterization in Luke–Acts* (Louisville: Westminster/John Knox, 1992).

seminal work on "reception theory" by R. Jauss and W. Iser in the 1960s and 1970s.[38]

In its emphasis on the text and its effects on the reader, reader-response criticism expresses its reformative agenda. By focusing on how a text is received, it critiques preoccupation with how a text originated. In shifting the accent from the text to the reader, it represents a critique of the tenet of text autonomy that tends to see meaning as immanent within the text. By contrast, reader-response criticism sees meaning more as a function of the reader than as a property of the text.

One of the benefits of reader-response criticism is an expanded understanding of "reader," construed in various ways. It may recognize the legitimacy of the historical paradigm's interest in the actual, historical reader(s), whether among the original circle of addressees or among subsequent addressees in later generations. Yet, also recognizing that these original addressees may be impossible to identify, it nevertheless recognizes that every thoughtfully composed text presupposes a reader, designated by Iser as the implied reader, who can be regarded as an intrinsic element in the text itself. It is a theoretical rather than an actual reader, although it is conceivable that any given actual reader might correspond to what the author envisioned as the ideal reader. This theoretical, or literary, reader may then be envisioned in other ways, for example, as the first-time reader or the experienced reader or the reader envisioned in some other relationship to the text. It has been an especially fruitful concept because of the fresh angles of vision it provides on the text itself. For example, in narrative texts characters in the story might themselves be construed, at some level, as readers, with whom the implied readers are expected to identify. Thus it is possible to distinguish between internal readers, who can be construed in some sense as standing within the text and its story, and external readers, who are on the outside looking in. Whether the reader is viewed as a historical figure or an imagined, literary figure envisioned by the text itself, the reader's role in the interpretive process is of focal concern.

One task of the interpreter is to determine how the text envisions the relationship between the text and its readers, and what literary techniques or other narrative strategies are employed to enable the text to have an effect on the reader. The effect may be construed as cognitive or emotive. One might ask how the reader was (or is) expected to *understand* the text, or how the reader was (or is) *to be affected* by the text. In either case, as one reads a narrative, one tries to project how a reader—an actual reader, an implied reader, or the critic as reader—actually engages and experiences the narrative as it unfolds. Here the emphasis is on the reader's engagement with the text and what this entails: how the reader might identify, or fail to identify, with characters in the text; how the reader is affected by the mood of the text, or the dramatic effect of various rhetorical techniques that occur in the text; how the reader's point of view is being challenged by the text's (or author's) point of view.

In narrative criticism, it may be assumed that certain literary features intrinsic to the text have a kind of objective quality. They are there in the text, and the interpreter's responsibility is to detect literary features and patterns that are in the text, determine how they relate to each other, and assess their significance for understanding the narrative point of view. In reader-response criticism, where the accent tends to shift away from the text toward the reader, the interpretive process tends to be seen in more subjective terms. In its more radical form, represented, for example, by Stanley Fish, reader-response criticism would insist that there is no text per se.[39] Rather, the text is essentially something created in the reader's mind as the reader interacts with the words on a printed page of text. To the extent that meaning is a function of the reader's intellectual engagement with a text, meaning is imposed on, or brought to, a text; at least, it is something that takes place in the interpretive dynamic that lies between the text and a reader. Seen this way, meaning lies in the foreground of the text and occurs as the dynamic interplay between a text and its symbols, on the one hand, and a reader and the reader's thought-world on the other.

When the reader's role is given such prominence, the autonomy of the text can shift to the reader, who is seen more as a maker than a receiver of meaning. As Fish states, "Once the locus of signification is firmly fixed in the reading consciousness rather than

38. See W. Iser, *The Implied Reader* (Baltimore: Johns Hopkins University Press, 1974); *The Act of Reading: A Theory of Aesthetic Response* (Baltimore: Johns Hopkins University Press, 1978).

39. S. E. Fish, *Is There a Text in This Class? The Authority of Interpretive Communities* (Cambridge, Mass.: Harvard University Press, 1980).

in the printed page or between the covers of a book, literature yields up its traditional image of stable artifact and becomes an activity that readers perform, a 'kinetic art.' "[40]

Deconstruction. As an interpretive approach pioneered by the French philosopher J. Derrida, deconstruction stands within the structuralist tradition because it shares some of the same basic theoretical assumptions.[41] Like other approaches treated under the literary paradigm, deconstruction is concerned with the "received text," the final form of a particular text, not its earlier stages of development or the editorial process. Moreover, it works with a holistic understanding of the text; once the limits of a given text are set, the interpreter tries to understand it comprehensively rather than focusing only on some part of it. To an extent, it shares the formalist conviction that understanding a text can occur only in relation to its overall formal structure. Like structuralism, it views language as a system of signs that must be interpreted in relation to each other; discerning meaning is more a matter of discovering how language works within a particular system than of trying to correlate what is being said with some other world outside the text. Yet, for all these similarities and lines of continuity, deconstruction moves beyond structuralism, challenging some of its most fundamental assumptions, and for this reason is said to be post-structuralist.

Deconstruction is strongly anti-metaphysical in outlook. It denies "logocentrism," the view that certain foundational principles or ideas (e.g., truth, reason, God) have an existence independent of language, and thus the corresponding notion that language should be seen as a vehicle used to give expression to such metaphysical realities that exist beyond language. This is especially the case with pairs of opposites (e.g., beginning/end, form/content, presence/absence), which structuralists regard as foundational realities, or deep structures, that underlie all human thought and language. If there is one philosophical given in deconstructionism, it is language itself, or more specifically, writing understood as a theoretical construct. For only in so far as basic concepts or foundational principles are expressed in language do they have a life of their own. For this reason, deconstruction has been called linguistic idealism or linguistic monism.[42]

Joined with this philosophical outlook is a theory of the human personality that denies that the individual is an autonomous, thinking subject—an "I" who discovers some external truth through thought and uses language self-consciously to express those thoughts. Instead, the individual is seen primarily as a language user: What defines us as humans is our unique capacity to use language. But because the language we use, and the way we use it, is determined by many factors beyond our control, there is a sense in which language uses us. Thus when we speak (or write), we reveal much about ourselves of which we are unaware; our use of language is as much *subconscious* as it is *self-conscious.*

This means that any given "text," whether a speech, story, essay, or some other oral or written composition, is always a partial success. A gap always exists between what we want our words to say and what they actually say. Since our words have connotations we do not even realize, especially when they are heard or read by someone else, when we speak (or write) we always say both more and less than we wish. This is especially the case if our language reveals how we subconsciously reflect the myths and beliefs, the fears and anxieties shared by all other human beings. Thus a text both reveals and conceals. At one level, it expresses what we think we are saying, or what we would like to think we are saying; at another level, it expresses what we may not even know we are saying.

The deconstructionist operates with the assumption that the spoken or written truth is never the whole truth. Looked at closely, any text will yield slip-ups that somehow challenge, if not subvert, its

40. Quoted in Moore, *Literary Criticism,* 114. "Kinetic art" is Fish's term (*Is There a Text?* 43).

41. See J. Derrida, *Of Grammatology* (Baltimore: Johns Hopkins University Press, 1976); *Writing and Difference* (Chicago: University of Chicago Press, 1978). Especially useful treatments introducing deconstructionism include the unusually clear ninety-page preface to *Grammatology* by the translator, G. C. Spivak; Iris Murdoch's chapter, "Derrida and Structuralism," in *Metaphysics as a Guide to Morals* (Harmondsworth, Middlesex: Penguin Books/Allen Lane, 1992) 185-216; W. A. Beardslee, "Poststructuralist Criticism," in S. L. McKenzie and S. R. Haynes, eds., *To Each Its Own Meaning: An Introduction to Biblical Criticisms and Their Application* (Louisville: Westminster/John Knox, 1993) 221-35; M. Sarup, *An Introductory Guide to Post-Structuralism and Postmodernism* (Athens: Univeristy of Georgia Press, 1989), esp. 34-62.

For discussions of post-structuralist approaches, most notably deconstructionism, as related to biblical studies, see E. L. Greenstein, "Deconstruction and Biblical Narrative," *Prooftexts* 9 (1989) 43-71; S. D. Moore, *Literary Criticism and the Gospels: The Theoretical Challenge* (New Haven: Yale University Press, 1989), esp. 131-70; *Mark and Luke in Poststructuralist Perspectives: Jesus Begins to Write* (New Haven: Yale University Press, 1992); "Deconstructive Criticism: The Gospel of Mark," in J. C. Anderson and S. D. Moore, eds., *Mark and Method: New Approaches in Biblical Studies* (Minneapolis: Fortress, 1992) 84-102.

42. Murdoch, "Derrida and Structuralism," 185.

overall point of view. From the outset, the deconstructionist distrusts the text and proceeds by trying to locate those points in the text that betray it. These may be single words, incidental phrases, or isolated parts of the overall argument; or they may be larger, more significant elements of the text. In either case, they are the interpreter's points of entry into the text that are used to open it up for exposure.

For the deconstructionist, a text can be seen as a "fabric of signs" that the reader seeks to decipher. Operating with the commonly accepted distinction between "signified" (something being described—e.g., an idea, event, person, or object) and "signifier" (the language used to describe it), the reader is able to comprehend a text primarily because the language signs are distinguishable—that is, because of their conspicuous "differences." For one thing, it is clear to the reader that there is a difference between the expression itself (signifier) and what is being expressed (signified). At each interpretive point, the signifier bears a "trace" of what it signifies, enough of a trace to establish a connection between the two, but not enough to render them exact equivalents. As the reader deciphers these signs in the text, a meaningful reading begins to be produced, and this is made possible because of observable "differences." Yet because the process of deciphering can go on endlessly, meaning is "deferred." It both occurs and is postponed. The technical term *differance* (intentionally spelled with an *a*) expresses this two-pronged sense of "differing" and "deferring." What enables the reader to move through the text meaningfully is the capacity to detect "differences" between various language signs; yet, the very act of differentiating is also an act of deferral.

The interpreter's task is to follow the scent of meaning, moving from signifier to signifier, and he or she is able to do so because the language markers are distinguishable—they do not look entirely alike. Their differences, and the gaps separating them, become the roads the reader travels. In this way, the reader produces a criticial reading of a text by a rigorous process of differentiating.

With the interpretive agenda defined this way, the reader's task is to find those elements in the text that disturb the equilibrium of the text and call its coherence into question, and then use these to frame a set of interpretive questions. The overall effect is to dismantle the text, but not in the way earlier critics did. No effort is made to identify the various literary strands of a text, disentangle and identify them, as earlier source critics did. Nor is the aim to identify underlying sources and trace the way editorial changes have produced these points of dissonance within the text, as form and redaction critics did. Instead, the text is dismantled in the sense that its overall point of view—its story, its argument, its case—is undermined or subverted, so that what the text ostensibly says is negated or redefined.

To further clarify the interpretive process: It is not simply that we read a text, understand it, grasp its meaning or general thrust, only to disagree with it, then stand over against it, and perhaps finally reject it. Rather, the text itself is understood to supply clues that suggest countervailing points of view that lead to its own dismantling, or that perhaps suggest alternative interpretations that run against the grain of the text, or even undermine it. In deconstructionist reading, a text is understood as a "house divided against itself," and the reader's task is to promote civil war.

Using problematic parts of the text that appear "superclumsy" or "supersmooth," the reader tries to produce a comprehensive interpretation of the text. Rather than trying to understand the meaning of the text, the interpreter is expected to produce a reading that exposes structures of meaning—viewpoints, assumptions, arguments—that the text itself somehow conceals, or that otherwise lie hidden within the text. This is done by deconstructing the text, locating "the moment that is undecidable in terms of the text's apparent system of meaning, the moment in the text that seems to transgress its own system of values."[43]

It is in this sense that the reader is said to deconstruct in order to reconstruct, to undo the text in order to redo it. The text that appears is dismantled in order to construct another, better reading. The written text remains intact, yet the reconstructed reading constitutes another text, superimposed, as it were, on the original text. Through such a series of deconstructions and reconstructions, with each reading there is a fresh appraisal of the significations in the text; each reading is another turn of the kaleidoscope. The same set of signs is being read, but never the same way.

Deconstructionist interpretation proceeds with the confident optimism that "the *real* work of litera-

---

43. Spivak, "Translator's Preface," in Derrida, *Grammatology,* xlix.

ture is what the *critic* produces. The deconstructed work is the real work."[44]

SUMMARY AND CONCLUSIONS

We have attempted to review contemporary methods of interpreting the Bible by setting them within the framework of three different paradigms. Broadly speaking, the three paradigms might be said to correspond respectively to a pre-modernist, modernist, and postmodernist outlook. In some cases, they may represent the stages through which individual biblical interpreters have moved. Perhaps as much as anything else, this review has shown the difficulties inherent in working with a single paradigm. Each of them centers on critically important aspects of Scripture that interpreters have prized as being of paramount concern.

From this review of interpretive methods, several things have become clear. First, the inherent difficulty of viewing Scripture as a single genre. The notion of a single genre can only be retained in a very restricted sense. On the one hand, we must recognize the existence of "canon" as both a historical and a social reality. Certain well-defined collections of biblical writings are regarded as authoritative by different believing communities. Even though the precise limits of these canons differ, the "scripture principle" remains intact for a variety of contemporary religious traditions, including Jewish, Christian, and Muslim. At some level, each of these traditions speaks of and thinks of a "Bible" in some definable, theologically realistic sense.

Yet, in the modern period there is much greater awareness of the complexity of Scripture and its multiplicity of genres and sub-genres. Many new interpretive methods are especially appropriate for narrative, but not equally appropriate for nonnarrative texts (e.g., OT wisdom literature or NT epistles). It has now become necessary to use interpretive methods appropriate for interpreting different types of biblical writing. In order to frame appropriate questions, it will be necessary to develop different "literary competencies" for reading different types of material.

Second is the need for devising interpretive methods that are appropriate to a theological use of the Bible. At issue here is developing a theory of Scrip-

ture, or a theory of revelation that takes seriously Scripture's own claims, yet at the same time meaningfully relates those claims to theories of knowledge within the interpreter's contemporary setting. The relation between explicit theological claims and biblical interpretation is clearly addressed by the divine oracle paradigm. In the early stages of the historical paradigm, it was also a concern. Some of the criticisms of the historical paradigm are protests against the undue narrowing of the interpretive focus to historical, or historicistic, questions. Moreover, corrective movements within the historical paradigm (e.g., canonical criticism) are attempts to recapture this explicitly theological dimension of Scripture. This question has been approached in different ways in the literary paradigm, but this explicit correlation has been largely unexplored.[45] It still remains to be seen how the various methods related to the literary paradigm will develop "theories of revelation" that attend to the specifically theological claims of Scripture. To put it another way, it is still not clear how literary critical methods, more narrowly understood, will be adopted and incorporated by believing communities who regard the biblical texts as normative for life and faith.

Third is the challenge posed by disenfranchised Bible readers. Because of the experience of oppression and marginalization of many biblical readers, and the related conviction that the Bible has played a central role in creating or authorizing oppressive structures, the various theological approaches that have been developed can be seen as types of "liberation theology." Regardless of their diversity, both in perspective and approach to the Bible, there is a sense among these various Bible readers that they are interpreting the Bible from a marginalized position, one in which their particular point of view has been either silenced or muted. They are seeking liberation from the constraining elements of the biblical tradition.

These approaches challenge those parts of the biblical tradition that have helped contribute to situations of oppression, most notably its patriarchialism, androcentrism ("man-centeredness"), and hierarchicalism. This has resulted not only in fresh appraisals of certain biblical texts (e.g., Genesis 1–3) and reinvestigation of how the ancient evidence has been collected and evaluated, but also reconceptions

---

44. Murdoch, "Derrida and Structuralism," 190.

45. See, however, G. O'Day, *Revelation in the Fourth Gospel: Narrative Mode and Theological Claim* (Philadelphia: Fortress, 1986).

of how the biblical tradition should be read and appropriated by modern readers.[46]

Feeling the burden of oppression, "readers from below" or "readers on the margin" are less content to read the Bible with an "objectivist-realist" aim in order to determine what the ancient text said or meant, or how it helps us to understand "what really happened" then. Instead, many prefer a "constructionist" approach that allows them to reconstrue the biblical text and tradition.[47] By reading it critically and identifying those parts of the texts that negate their experience, this approach seeks to develop alternative historical reconstructions or theological approaches that respect the autonomy and freedom of the interpreter and her or his communities of faith, regardless of their ethnicity, social location, or gender; include them as full, meaningful participants in the debate; and acknowledge the vested interest of all methods of interpretation.

Fourth is the different ways of appropriating these three paradigms. Even though the three paradigms have developed over time, they are employed in different ways in the contemporary setting. As we have seen, certain trends within the historical paradigm, such as canonical criticism, may be seen as corrective attempts that seek to recover some emphases of the divine oracle paradigm. Similarly, the literary paradigm developed as a way of responding to what were perceived as deficiencies of the historical paradigm (e.g., the notion of authorial intent).

Within theological traditions that have come into prominence over the last several decades, the Bible is being read and appropriated in many different ways. It has continued to play a central role not only in traditional forms of theology, but also in more recently developed theological traditions, such as liberation theology, feminist theology, black theology, and womanist theology. Rather than each of these having its own method of biblical interpretation, or even developing an interpretive method that is distinctive to its approach, it is more correct to say that each uses the three paradigms in different ways. Thus it is important to distinguish among the three paradigms, the methods of interpretation that have

been derived from them, and the specific application of those methods by various readers of the Bible.

Liberation theology, for all its variety, generally seeks to recapture the divine oracle paradigm's insistence that the Bible can be seen as addressing the present needs and situation of the reader. It operates with the fundamental conviction that through the Bible God is speaking now. And yet many liberation theologians, having been trained in the historical-critical method, also recognize the value of seeing the Bible as historical source.

Reading the Bible from this perspective has enabled them to see, for example, that much of the Bible consists of traditions that have been received in one form, appropriated and applied in a new setting, and then transmitted in another form. This perspective has been helpful in providing liberation theologians a way of appropriating the biblical text to their own situation. Thus they have seen that the interpreter's task is not simply one of determining "the meaning" of a particular text, either what it meant then or even what it means to the reader now, and then "applying" it to the present situation. Instead, the interpretive task is seen as one of contextual appropriation: finding ways of taking a received text and reconceiving it by adapting it and shaping it to the new situation of the reader.

Or, in other instances, liberation theologians have made more explicit appeal to the historical Jesus as a model for prophetic reform, and historical-critical reading of the Gospels has given sharpness to their understanding of how Jesus related to the historical and social situation of first-century Palestine.

By the same token, certain perspectives and emphases of the literary paradigm have also been usefully appropriated by liberation theologians—for example, the recognition that the reader's own perspective and social location are an important ingredient in the interpretive process. Also important to some liberation theologians is the structuralist understanding of language as culturally derivative and culturally expressive, which has meant that biblical texts have been read not only to discern their "content" but also for what they reveal about the social matrix of the communities that produced them.[48]

46. See, for example, P. Trible, *God and the Rhetoric of Sexuality* (Philadelphia: Fortress, 1978).

47. On this distinction, see E. Schüssler Fiorenza, "Remembering the Past in Creating the Future: Historical-Critical Scholarship and Feminist Biblical Interpretation," in A. Y. Collins, ed., *Feminist Perspectives on Biblical Scholarship* (Chico, Calif.: Scholars Press, 1985) 43-63.

48. For an especially helpful treatment of the use of the Bible in liberation theology, see C. Rowland and M. Corner, *Liberating Exegesis: The Challenge of Liberation Theology to Biblical Studies* (Louisville: Westminster/John Knox, 1989).

The case is similar with feminist criticism, where the three paradigms have been used in quite different ways, depending on the particular approach of a given feminist theologian.[49] Feminist criticism has found historical criticism useful in reframing the question of biblical authority.[50] Rather than seeing biblical passages that depict women negatively, or that promote a patriarchal point of view, as authoritative statements that are to be taken as timeless truths by every age, feminist interpreters have been able to account for them as part of an ancient world view that does not necessarily need to be retained by later interpreters. As in other cases, historical criticism has helped to relativize the biblical perspective in ways that make it more understandable as well as more available to modern critical readers. In proposing that biblical "texts must be evaluated *historically* in terms of their own time and culture and assessed *theologically* in terms of a feminist scale of values," E. Schüssler Fiorenza argues that historical-critical study of the Bible, properly conceived and executed, benefits feminist theology.[51]

Various types of structuralist and post-structuralist approaches have also been appropriated by feminist critics. By recognizing the interconnectedness of language and social reality, some feminist interpreters have employed deconstructive analysis of the biblical text as an alternative way of relativizing the "surface meaning" of the text.[52]

Fifth is the danger of methodological imperialism. In this survey, we have reviewed the variety of methods that have been employed to interpret Scripture. We have attempted to identify the main assumptions underlying the various methods in order to show that, given these assumptions as well as the explicit purpose for which they were devised, these methods have value. But when one method extends its reach far beyond its grasp and becomes imperialistic, its practitioners tend to assume that it is *the* method to use in interpreting all material, or is the method by which all other methods are judged. When method becomes dogma, revisionism is inevitable, for it provides a way of addressing aspects of the text that have been left unattended, either because they would not be addressed or could not be addressed by the previous reigning method.

The way forward is to be more modest and recognize both the possibilities and the limitations of different approaches, and to recognize that informed reading will require knowledge and experience in many methods and approaches. Actual interpretation will involve a combination of approaches.

BIBLIOGRAPHY

Barton, J. *Reading the Old Testament: Method in Biblical Study.* Philadelphia: Westminster, 1984.

Farley, E., and P. C. Hodgson. "Scripture and Tradition." In *Christian Theology: An Introduction to Its Traditions and Tasks.* Edited by P. C. Hodgson and R. H. King, 61-87. 2nd ed. Philadelphia: Fortress, 1985.

Grant, R. M., with D. Tracy. *A Short History of the Interpretation of the Bible.* 2nd ed. Philadelphia: Fortress, 1985.

McKenzie, S. L., and S. R. Haynes, eds. *To Each Its Own Meaning: An Introduction to Biblical Criticisms and Their Application.* Louisville: Westminster/John Knox, 1993.

Moore, S. D. *Literary Criticism and the Gospels: The Theoretical Challenge.* New Haven: Yale University Press, 1989.

Morgan, R., with J. Barton. *Biblical Interpretation.* Oxford: Oxford University Press, 1988.

Petersen, N. R. *Literary Criticism for New Testament Critics.* Philadelphia: Fortress, 1978.

Wilder, A. *Early Christian Rhetoric: The Language of the Gospel.* Cambridge, Mass.: Harvard University Press, 1964; reissued 1971.

49. See Collins, ed., *Feminist Perspectives* (n. 47 above); also, D. Fewell, "Reading the Bible Ideologically: Feminist Criticism," in McKenzie and Haynes, *To Each Its Own Meaning,* 237-51.

50. See C. De Swarte Gifford, "American Women and the Bible: The Nature of Woman as a Hermeneutical Issue," in Collins, ed., *Feminist Perspectives,* 11-33, esp. 22-23.

51. Schüssler Fiorenza, "Remembering the Past," 56-57.

52. See Fewell, "Reading the Bible Ideologically," 246-47; also, T. Docherty, *Postmodernism: A Reader* (New York: Columbia University Press, 1993) esp. the essays on feminist criticism, 363-442.

READING THE BIBLE FROM PARTICULAR SOCIAL LOCATIONS: AN INTRODUCTION

JAMES EARL MASSEY

Interpretation of the Bible depends largely on the social perspectives of the interpreter. This statement should not surprise, because whether one is dealing with Holy Writ or any other written materials, there is usually some influence on our thinking from the sociocultural setting that has affected our lives. To a more than considerable extent, our thinking has been influenced by elements of rationalism, or by some brand of nationalism, or perhaps by a narrow individualism, but always by some communal identity. In various combinations, these factors have affected us; they have shaped the way we view the world, and that world view influences the way we read the Word of God and use that Word in teaching and preaching.

The quest to be able interpreters and effective sharers of biblical meanings needs to be allied with an understanding of how our thinking and world view have been shaped. We need to recognize and appreciate how the differing social communities within the larger society have given us not only our identities but also our different perspectives on Scripture. Those perspectives become evident when we speak from within the experiences shaped by our social locations. That is, particular approaches to Bible reading have been influenced by differing

social locations. African Americans, Native Americans, Asian Americans, Hispanic Americans, and women of various ethnic backgrounds read and interpret the Bible from a set of understandings influenced by a history of experience as members of a particular social community.

Those who are familiar with developments in biblical studies since the 1970s know that the social-scientific method has gained increasing prominence as an exegetical tool. Applied to the Bible with accented seriousness, the social-scientific method enabled biblical scholars to gain a fuller and more accurate understanding of the social environment and cultural dimensions of the biblical world. Using sociology and anthropology as additional tools, several scholars have identified and described in detail data regarding the social location of the communities whose life stands reflected in the Bible. The published works of Norman K. Gottwald, Howard Clark Kee, Abraham J. Malherbe, and Bruce J. Malina, among others, have made accessible more strategic information about the social, economic, political, and religious influences that conditioned and shaped the spiritual communities whose experiences and institutions are reported in the biblical record.[1] Thus, benefited by an increased understanding of how biblical texts have been socially and religiously conditioned, those who preach and teach from the Bible can more meaningfully relate to its frame of reference, its world view, and its intended witness to the world.

Bible reading in our time has been transformed. That transformation is due not only to the use of new methods to interrogate, analyze, and relate texts, but also, among other approaches, to a *community-situation approach* used by persons in communities with a history of experienced oppression and social deprivation. Identifying the social location and concerns of the ancient communities reflected in the biblical record is one thing; learning something about the Bible from contemporaries whose social location has granted them different perspectives for Bible reading is a different, but not unrelated, possibility.

The community-situation approach in reading the Bible involves a hermeneutic that takes the community's life experiences into account. The relation of Scripture to the contemporary community's needs is one of the critical principles by which those who use this method discern the import and application of biblical texts. For example, the historical memory of African Americans about the slavery period, the victimizing system that the churches in the American South endorsed and sought to buttress with texts misused to justify human oppression for commercial gain, found hope and meaning through a different point of reference in reading the same Bible. Given their situation, which paralleled ancient Israel's plight in Egypt, African Americans have valued the biblical witness about freedom, justice, divine deliverance, and the means by which these were enacted and sustained.[2]

Native Americans have been increasingly vocal about their historical memory, their concept of sacred space, and the principle of creation that are basic to their world view. However deeply entrenched other North Americans are in highly romanticized notions and ideologies about Western culture, the historical memory of their own meaning, background, concepts, and values continues to influence the way Native Americans read the Bible.[3]

Hispanic Americans and Asian Americans also have their own respective approaches as Bible readers (as the associated articles show), and so do women, whose history has been compounded by the problem of social placement, even in many of the biblical accounts.[4]

Despite a common confession as Christians, members of communities that have experienced oppression or marginalization read the Bible from a different perspective, always wary of so-called objective approaches and interpretations that are insensitive to human need and problems resulting from exploitation of others. Communities that have a remembered history of injustices perpetrated against them by the dominant society do not find meaning, identity, or affirmation in "mainstream biblical interpretations" that overlook or disregard their social location.

Life in the hierarchically organized West has usually been socially problematic and painful for minorities, certain immigrants, and women. Native Americans, Hispanic Americans, Asian Americans, African Americans, and women all have social histories that explain why they read the Bible with an interest in their human concerns and needs. As those who have been disinherited (Native Americans), as those who have been marginalized (Asian Americans and Hispanic Americans), as those who have been oppressed (African Americans), and as those who have known subjugation (women), these groups have found in the biblical accounts much that parallels their own communal experience. All of them have known the social pain of life in America, while some of them have experienced the added misfortune of having had Scripture used as a weapon against them, as a tool *for* the "strong" *against* the "weak." But in their own reading of the Bible, they all located a point of reference by which to define and affirm themselves in the midst of a problematic social environment whose skewed perspectives and sub-Christian values steadily

1. Among a growing body of literature in the field, see Norman K. Gottwald, *The Tribes of Yahweh: A Sociology of the Religion of Liberated Israel, 1250–1050 B.C.E.* (Maryknoll, N.Y.: Orbis, 1979); Howard Clark Kee, *Christian Origins in Sociological Perspective* (Philadelphia: Westminster, 1980); Abraham J. Malherbe, *Social Aspects of Early Christianity*, 2nd ed., enlarged (Philadelphia: Fortress, 1983); Bruce J. Malina, *The New Testament World: Insights from Social Anthropology* (Atlanta: John Knox, 1981); John E. Stambaugh and David L. Balch, *The New Testament in Its Social Environment* (Philadelphia: Westminster, 1986).

2. See the article "Reading the Bible as African Americans" in this volume.

3. See the article "Reading the Bible as Native Americans" in this volume.

4. See the articles "Reading the Bible as Asian Americans," "Reading the Bible as Hispanic Americans," and "Reading the Bible as Women," in this volume.

and systematically worked against them. The writers of the five articles that follow all report, with clarifying detail, on the meaningful point of reference their social communities identified in the Bible and the impact of that perspective on their communal way of interpreting and applying its message.

In recent years, those whose histories of experience have much in common have begun to make common cause. The reference here is not to the many published complaints and public protests evidenced on the wider social scene; it is, rather, to the collaborative work among Christians who have sought to confer in shaping a theology appropriate to their heritage of suffering, their spiritual vision, and their perspectives on the Bible.[5] Some of the results of that collaboration are instructive, and impressive, as one may readily discover in examining the plethora of works that treat Christian theology from the respective experiences of each group of people. Many texts once used to promote Western ideologies, or previously interpreted so as to legitimate oppression and social control, have been reassessed, recontextualized, and explained anew in ways that liberate and affirm the readers. In all such instances, the Bible is being read from the standpoint of the respective community's own experience and needs. This way of reading the Bible is guided by questions raised within the readers' communal experience.

It is natural, expected, and perhaps inevitable that life in a particular social location helps to shape a group's hermeneutic and apologetic. But beyond the questions and history that stand behind that hermeneutic and its rationale, there is always the broader context and larger message of the entire Bible that continually brings every reading approach under scrutiny. In addition, there is the active presence and reading perspective of all others who look to the Bible as authoritative text. It is important, then, that the "community-situation approach," and every other, be critiqued under the light of the entire Bible, on the one hand, and used in a spirit of open dialogue with the entire church, on the other. The various reading perspectives discern and identify sometimes overlooked aspects and accents within the Bible; they call attention to how these are

strategic in the life and faith of a particular people. Viewed with openness, each perspective can inform us, raise our consciousness, advise us, and increase awareness of our mutual responsibilities as believers. This is as it should be, because the Bible is the property of the entire church, and each reading community within the church has insights to share with an interest to enlarge the church's vision of God and God's work among and through us in the world. The quest to understand and rightly utilize the Bible makes that sharing necessary. The plurality of reading perspectives makes that sharing possible. Meanwhile, we must understand that although readings of the Bible can be influenced by life within a particular social location, no reading should lead to an isolating hermeneutic, nor should it end as a reading that is location-controlled.

Across the changing centuries of its life and witness, the church has believed, taught, and treasured the texts of the canonized Christian Scriptures, which are viewed as the authoritative written source of witness about God, Christ, salvation history, Christian experience, hope in the midst of life, and life beyond death. Christianity moves forward in connection with the witness recorded in its Bible, and the Christian missionary enterprise rightly uses that record of witness in its quest to reach and "make disciples of all nations" (Matt 28:19). One of the special challenges to that unfinished enterprise is how effectively to contextualize the gospel, retaining its true distinctiveness while honoring indigenous theologies shaped from communal perspectives on Scripture that mutually correct and enrich believers as they learn to appreciate their God-given differences. Justo L. González has aptly reminded us that

The church calls all the "nations" to the gospel, not only because the "nations" need the gospel, but also because the church needs the "nations" in order to be fully "catholic." If "catholic" means "according to the whole," as long as a part of the whole remains outside, or is brought in without being allowed *to speak from its own perspective,* catholicity itself is truncated.[6]

Aspects of that catholicity are represented in the five following articles, in which five scholars "speak" from the perspective of their own social commu-

5. For a report on how one denomination (The United Methodist Church) has sought to facilitate such dialogue by means of an "ethnic roundtable," see Justo L. González, *Out of Every Tribe and Nation: Christian Theology at the Ethnic Roundtable* (Nashville: Abingdon, 1992).

6. González, *Out of Every Tribe and Nation,* 29, emphasis added.

nity's way of "reading" the Bible. Each reading is singular, but all of the approaches represented agree about what is the basic concern in reading the Bible: to gain faith, affirmation, hope, courage and wisdom for living, and a glimpse of the means by which the horizons of personal and social reality can be altered in the direction of human good.

BIBLIOGRAPHY

Atkins, Robert A., Jr. *Egalitarian Community: Ethnography and Exegesis.* Tuscaloosa: University of Alabama Press, 1991.

Clements, R. E., ed. *The World of Ancient Israel: Sociologial, Anthropological and Political Perspectives.* Cambridge: Cambridge University Press, 1989.

Cormie, Lee. "Revolution in Reading the Bible." In *The Bible and the Politics of Exegesis: Essays in Honor of Norman K. Gottwald on His Sixty-fifth Birthday.* Edited by David Jobling, Peggy L. Day, and Gerald T. Sheppard. Cleveland: Pilgrim, 1991.

Elliot, John H. *What Is Social-Scientific Criticism?* Minneapolis: Fortress, 1993.

Gill, Robin. *The Social Context of Theology: A Methodological Enquiry.* London: Alden & Mowbray, 1975.

González, Justo L. *Out of Every Tribe and Nation: Christian Theology at the Ethnic Roundtable.* Nashville: Abingdon, 1992.

Holmberg, Bengt. *Sociology and the New Testament: An Appraisal.* Minneapolis: Fortress, 1990.

Osiek, Carolyn. "The New Handmaid: The Bible and the Social Sciences," *Theological Studies 50 (1989) 260-78.*

Paris, Peter J. "The Bible and the Black Churches." In *The Bible and Social Reform.* Edited by Ernest R. Sandeen. Philadelphia: Fortress/Scholars Press, 1982.

Perkins, Richard, and Brian Sayers. "Between Alienation and Anomie: The Integration of Sociology and Christianity." In *Christian Scholar's Review* 17, 2 (December 1987) 122-42.

Ronda, James P. "The Bible and Early American Indian Missions." In *The Bible and Social Reform.* Edited by Ernest R. Sandeen. Philadelphia: Fortress/Scholars Press, 1982.

Said, Edward W. *The World, the Text, and the Critic.* Cambridge, Mass.: Harvard University Press, 1983.

Schreiter, Robert J. *Constructing Local Theologies.* Maryknoll, N.Y.: Orbis, 1985.

Thiselton, Anthony C. *New Horizons in Hermeneutics.* Grand Rapids: Zondervan, 1992.

Tracy, David. "A Plurality of Readers and a Possibility of a Shared Vision." In *The Bible and Its Readers.* Edited by Wim Beuken, Sean Freyne, and Anton Weiler. Philadelphia: Trinity Press International, 1991.

Zikmund, Barbara Brown. "Biblical Arguments and Women's Place in the Church." In *The Bible and Social Reform.* Edited by Ernest R. Sandeen. Philadelphia: Fortress/Scholars Press, 1982.

READING THE BIBLE AS AFRICAN AMERICANS

JAMES EARL MASSEY

The bearing of social location and experience upon the reading and interpretation of the Bible is revealed in graphic, detailed fashion in the history, religious heritage, music, folklore, and literature of African Americans. Innumerable songs, speeches, sermons, and writings give evidence of African American approaches to, attitudes toward, and interpretation of biblical materials.[1] In addition to these, the very mention of "the Bible" in relation to African Americans recalls, on the one hand, the unswerving drive for literacy and schooling among black slaves in the antebellum South—and the part their contact with the Bible played in fueling that desire and shaping their religious life—and, on the other hand, how questions about basic human capacities and the risk of literacy and religious instruction with respect to slaves became both a sectional and a national issue that resulted in costly divisions in several national church bodies and in the nation itself.[2]

Earl E. Thorpe writes that "the master-slave relationship was not an ideal posture for white Americans to introduce transplanted Africans to the Christian religion. Despite this very serious difficulty," he adds, "an effective transmission was made, and this religion became not only the dominant thought stream in the mind of the Negro, but a major vehicle for transmitting Occidental culture to this alien race."[3] The Bible was a major instrument

---

1. On early African American music and songs, one of the most comprehensive studies is John Lovell, Jr., *Black Song: The Forge and the Flame—The Story of How the Afro-American Spiritual Was Hammered Out* (New York: Paragon, 1972). See also Miles Mark Fisher, *Negro Slave Songs in the United States* (New York: Cornell University Press, 1953). On some early speeches and writings, see Carter G. Woodson, *Negro Orators and Their Orations* (Washington, D.C.: Associated Publishers, 1925), and Carter G. Woodson, ed., *The Mind of the Negro as Reflected in Letters Written During the Crisis: 1800–1860* (Washington, D.C.: The Association for the Study of Negro Life and History, Inc., 1926); for some orators and sermonizers of a later period, see Marcus Hanna Boulware, *The Oratory of Negro Leaders: 1900-1968* (Westport, Conn.: Negro Universities Press, 1969). An additional helpful study that provides some insight into reflections of biblical motifs in black narratives is Bernard W. Bell, *The Afro-American Novel and Its Tradition* (Amherst: University of Massachusetts Press, 1987), esp. the sections that treat the writings of James Baldwin and Zora Neale Hurston, among others. Earlier, Benjamin E. Mays sought to distinguish between what he termed "mass" and "classical" black literature (from within the period 1760–1937); he arbitrarily placed spirituals, sermons, and Sunday school materials in the "mass" category and poetry, fiction, and various essays in the "classical" category. See Benjamin E. Mays, *The Negro's God as Reflected in His Literature* (New York: Chapman & Grimes, 1938; reprinted by Atheneum, 1969).

2. The literature treating these matters is vast, but for an overview see Sydney E. Ahlstrom, *A Religious History of the American People* (New Haven: Yale University Press, 1972), esp. Part 6, which discusses "Slavery and Expiation," 635-729, and the extensive bibliography Ahlstrom has listed for the section on 1117-18. See also Winthorp D. Jordan, *White Over Black: American Attitudes Toward the Negro, 1550–1812* (Chapel Hill, N.C.: University of North Carolina Press, 1968); Louis Ruchames, ed., *Racial Thought in America*, vol. 1: *From the Puritans to Abraham Lincoln, A Documentary History* (Amherst: University of Massachusetts Press, 1969); John R. McKivigan, *The War Against Proslavery Religion: Abolitionism and the Northern Churches, 1830–1865* (Ithaca: Cornell University Press, 1984); and Janet Duitsman Cornelius, *When I Can Read My Title Clear: Literacy, Slavery and Religion in the Antebellum South* (Columbia, S.C.: University of South Carolina Press, 1991).

3. Earl E. Thorpe, *The Mind of the Negro: An Intellectual History of Afro-Americans* (Westport, Conn.: Greenwood, 1961) 104.

in that transmission process, although the possibility must be considered that some Africans transplanted to North America as slaves might have brought with them some knowledge of the Christian faith and/or some acquaintance with the Christian Scriptures, since Christianity had been active in North Africa and Ethiopia as early as the first century (see Acts 2:10; 8:26-40). John S. Mbiti, African scholar, states that long before the start of Islam in the seventh century "Christianity was well established all over north Africa, Egypt, parts of the Sudan and Ethiopia," and that because of this early entrance upon the African continent, Christianity "can rightly be described as an indigenous, traditional and African religion."[4] Notwithstanding this, other scholars have disputed any prior Christian influence on the enslaved Africans, since most of them were brought from the coastal states of West Africa, where traditional African religions and Islam were observed.[5]

THE BIBLE AND THE SLAVES: PROBLEMS AND PROSPECTS

Every slave master who sought to give religious instruction to his slaves was placed in a situation that was immediately and steadily ironic: (1) The very act of *teaching* slaves argued the case for their capacity for learning and nurture; (2) every conversion among the slaves argued for a relationship between master and slave as fellow Christians, begging the question of the rightness of holding a fellow believer in slavery; and (3) the use of the Bible, the master's sacred book, as the prime instrument of authority in religious instruction continually fed the slaves' interest in becoming literate in order to read on their own. Legal restrictions were instituted and maintained in slave-holding states to help slave masters handle some of the complexities and risks inherent in such an ironic situation, but despite legal barriers, brutal sanctions, and grim threats designed

to intimidate and control slaves, many learned to read and secretly shared their skills with other slaves.

The arguments were many for providing religious instruction to slaves.[6] The first was that of duty, if the master was a professing Christian, for some viewed their plantation as a mission field and sought to show concern for the eternal salvation of their slaves. The second was that of profit, since religious instruction, if successful, was expected to influence the character, morale, behavior, and work output of the slave. The third argument was that of decreased risk of possible slave rebellions, since converted slaves would be expected to obey the Pauline injunction to be obedient to their master (Eph 6:5). As for this third concern, many slave narratives document the persistent way the masters kept the Pauline injunction about slave obedience before them. J. W. Lindsay, a former slave, reported in an 1863 interview what has been paralleled in many of the documented interviews with former slaves. Speaking about the chief Bible passages quoted to slaves during religious services conducted by the master's minister, Lindsay stated: "Their biggest text is, 'Servants, obey your masters'; and 'he that knoweth his master's will & doeth it not, shall be beaten with many stripes,' is a favorite text with them."[7]

Howard Thurman (1900–81), grandson of slaves, described the attitude his grandmother held toward such texts after being freed. Born in slavery, she lived until the Civil War on a plantation near Madison, Florida, and she never learned to read or write. "Two or three times a week I read the Bible aloud to her," Thurman reported:

I was deeply impressed by the fact that she was most particular about the choice of Scripture. For instance, I might read many of the more devotional Psalms, some of Isaiah, the Gospels again and again. But the Pauline epistles, never—except, at long intervals, the thirteenth

4. John S. Mbiti, *African Religions and Philosophy* (Garden City, N.Y.: Anchor/Doubleday, 1970) 300. In Ethiopia, Christianity became the state religion, boasting of a tradition of beginnings traceable back to the Acts 8:26-40 account of the conversion of the Ethiopian treasurer who served Candace, queen of Ethiopia (Nubia).

5. See C. Eric Lincoln, "The Development of Black Religion in America," in *African American Religious Studies: An Interdisciplinary Anthology*, ed. Gayraud Wilmore (Durham: Duke University Press, 1989) esp. 7-9. See also Gayraud S. Wilmore, *Black Religion and Black Nationalism: An Examination of the Black Experience in Religion*, C. Eric Lincoln Series on Black Religion (Garden City, N.Y.: Anchor/Doubleday, 1973) esp. 1-39.

6. See Thomas L. Webber, *Deep Like the Rivers: Education in the Slave Quarter Community, 1831–1865* (New York: W. W. Norton, 1978) esp. 43-58; Albert J. Raboteau, *Slave Religion: The "Invisible Institution" in the Antebellum South* (New York: Oxford University Press, 1978) esp. 96-150; Carter G. Woodson, *The Education of the Negro Prior to 1861* (Washington, D.C.: The Association for the Study of Negro Life and History, 1919; reprint, New York: Arno and The New York Times, 1968) esp. chaps. 2, "Religion with Letters," 18-50, and 8, "Religion Without Letters," 179-204; Eugene E. Genovese, *Roll, Jordan, Roll: The World the Slaves Made* (New York: Vintage Books, 1976) esp. 561-66.

7. See John W. Blassingame, ed., *Slave Testimonies: Two Centuries of Letters, Speeches, Interviews, and Autobiographies* (Baton Rouge: Louisiana State University Press, 1977) 402; for additional similar testimonies, see also 130-31, 411, 420, 465-66, and 642.

chapter of First Corinthians. My curiosity knew no bounds, but we did not question her about anything.[8]

When he was older and half through Morehouse College, Thurman mustered enough courage to ask his grandmother why it was that she had not allowed him to read any of the Pauline letters to her. "What she told me I shall never forget," he said:

"During the days of slavery," she said, "the master's minister would occasionally hold services for the slaves. Old man McGhee was so mean that he would not let a Negro minister preach to his slaves. Always the white minister used as his text something from Paul. At least three or four times a year he used as a text: 'Slaves, be obedient to them that are your masters . . . as unto Christ.' Then he would go on to show how it was God's will that we were slaves and how, if we were good and happy slaves, God would bless us. I promised my Maker that if I ever learned to read and if freedom ever came, I would not read that part of the Bible."[9]

The sense of selectivity and value expressed by Howard Thurman's grandmother—a sense rooted solidly in rejection of every selfish manipulation of Scripture to control others, a deep faith in self-worth, an intuitive understanding that God is just, and a hermeneutical alertness about how the Bible is to be rightly "read"—was widespread among religiously sensitive slaves. That valuing and acute selectivity with respect to portions and central teachings within the Bible was later institutionalized in the churches and theology African Americans shaped.

Stirring reflections of the basic theology shaped by the slaves from their experiential reading of the Bible are found in the spirituals, an extensive repository of religious folk music, each creation a testament of both individual and communal religious experience and aspirations. Variously termed "spirituals," "folk religious songs," "folk hymns," and "plantation melodies," the clue to the meaning of these slave creations is religious experience and aspirations both spiritual and social. With the social location and experience of African American slaves in his view, and with an awareness of the religious significance and spiritual discernment reflected in the songs the slaves created to inform and sustain them during their troubles, Howard Thurman wrote:

There were three major sources from which the raw materials of Negro spirituals were derived: the Old and New Testaments, the world of nature, and the personal experiences of religion that were the common lot of the people, emerging from their inner life. Echoes from each source are presently in practically all the songs.[10]

John Lovell, Jr., whose work *Black Song: The Forge and the Flame* is regarded one of the most comprehensive studies of the spirituals, includes in his treatment not only the religious and spiritual concerns expressed in these songs but also the ways the songs became agents and models of transformation. The spirituals, whether sung privately or communally, fostered a sense of well-being; an increased determination and fortitude to struggle, resist, and hold fast; a deepened awareness of a just God and a meaningful world; and a renewed commitment to gain freedom.[11] Crucial to these ends were understandings based on "readings" about major Bible characters, decisive events, suggestive expressions, and faith-inspiring promises. As Lovell says: "To say that the slave poet borrowed from or utilized the Bible is to say little about his literary propensities or values. His special attitude towards the Bible, his selectivity with respect to its contents, and his special way of turning Biblical materials to imaginative purposes make him quite distinctive."[12]

Eileen Southern has more recently traced the way improvisations made by later African Americans upon their spiritual songs contributed to the development of a black hymnody, spiritual ballads, and the well-known gospel music tradition so widely honored in the churches of African Americans.[13] John Michael Spencer's *Protest and Praise* chronicles, among other things, the way many traditional

8. Howard Thurman, *Jesus and the Disinherited* (Nashville: Abingdon-Cokesbury, 1949) 30.

9. Ibid., 30-31.

10. Howard Thurman, *Deep River: Reflections on the Religious Insight of Certain of the Negro Spirituals* (New York: Harper and Bros., 1955) 12. For additional theological interpretations of the spirituals, see Thurman's *The Negro Spiritual Interprets Life and Death* (New York: Harper and Bros., 1947); Mays, *The Negro's God as Reflected in His Literature,* esp. 19-30; James H. Cone, *The Spirituals and the Blues: An Interpretation* (New York: Seabury, 1972).

11. John Lovell, Jr., *Black Song: The Forge and the Flame* (New York: Paragon House, 1972) esp. chaps. 17-20.

12. Ibid., 255. See also Lovell's chart on the use of biblical items in the spirituals, 258-62; and see Charles B. Copher, "Biblical Characters, Events, Places and Images Remembered and Celebrated in Black Worship," *Journal of the Interdenominational Theological Center* 14 (Fall 1986/Spring 1987) 75-86.

13. See E. Southern, *The Music of Black Americans: A History,* 2nd ed. (New York: W. W. Norton, 1983) esp. 127ff, 259-61, 444-56, 461-74. See also Eileen Southern, "Hymns of the Black Church," *The Journal of the Interdenominational Theological Center* XIV, 1/2 (Fall 1986/Spring 1987) 127-40; Wendell Philips Whalum, "Black Hymnody," *Review and Expositor: A Baptist Theological Journal* 70 (Summer 1973) 341-55. For ballads and gospel music, see Bernice Johnson Reagon, ed., *We'll Understand It Better By and By: Pioneering African American Gospel Composers* (Washington, D.C.: Smithsonian Institution, 1992).

spirituals were creatively adapted for use as freedom songs during the civil rights movement era, while his *Black Hymnody* has treated the history of how the spirituals have been incorporated with other music forms, including formal hymns, in contemporary hymnals of ten prominent mainline African American denominations.[14]

THE BIBLE AND AFRICAN AMERICAN CHURCHES

The history and theology reflected in the spirituals, the rise of the African American churches—independent from white control,—and a particularized way of "reading" the Bible are not separate but integrally related stories. Victimized by a slavery system "Christianized" by a skewed reading of Scripture by the Southern church, and dominated, even after emancipation, by a racist majority culture, African Americans were faced with the necessity of constructing a world view and world of their own, a world in which their selfhood, meaning, pride, solidarity, and advancement could be nurtured. One result of that world-shaping effort was the development of an independent religious movement rooted in a unique *black* Christian tradition. Peter J. Paris writes about this development and its relation to a biblical rationale: "In the Bible, blacks found a perspective on humanity that was wholly different from that which they experienced in the teachings and practices of white Americans. The universal parenthood of God implied a universal kinship of humankind. This is the basic proposition of the hermeneutic designated as the black Christian tradition."[15]

Paris also observes: "Accordingly, the black churches have never hesitated to disavow any interpretation of Scripture that would attempt to legiti-mate racism, slavery, or any other form of human bondage. One can conclude that there have been no sacred scriptures for blacks apart from the hermeneutical principle immortalized in the black Christian tradition."[16]

Writing to address the need for a working outline of the history of the role of the Bible in the religious traditions of African Americans, from the slavery era to the twentieth century, Vincent L. Wimbush offers a schema divided into five "reading periods."[17]

According to Wimbush, Reading Period One involved the first decades of the enslaved Africans in the New World, and their response of suspicion and rejection as a "Book Religion" was forced upon them. But although well-established in sometimes elaborate oral traditions, their final response was one of awe and a willingness to deal with their sense of disorientation and social death by entering into the language world of the Bible. This accommodation proved successful because it gave the slaves a common ground upon which to "meet" and engage their captors.

Reading Period Two marks the time when the slaves transformed the "Book Religion" of their captors into a religion informed by their own experience. This occurred, Wimbish suggested, during the time of the mass conversions associated with evangelical activities and agencies during the eighteenth century. "By the end of the century 'the Book' had come to represent a virtual language-world that they, too, could enter and manipulate in light of their social experience."[18] The results of their engagement with Scripture stand documented in spirituals, sermons, and testimonies from the period. "The spirituals reflect the process of the transformation of the Book Religion of the dominant peoples into the religion reflective of the socio-political and economic status of African slaves," Wimbush asserts.[19] He further explains that the hermeneutic discerned in these creative interpretations and uses of Scriptures by the slaves is "a hermeneutic characterized by a looseness, even playfulness, vis-à-vis the biblical texts themselves." He adds, "The interpretation was not controlled by the literal words of the texts, but

14. Jon Michael Spencer, *Protest and Praise: Sacred Music of Black Religion* (Minneapolis: Fortress, 1990) esp. 83-105; John Michael Spencer, *Black Hymnody: A Hymnological History of the African-American Church* (Knoxville: The University of Tennessee Press, 1992). In their massive study *The Black Church in the African American Experience* (Durham: Duke University Press, 1990) 346-81, C. Eric Lincoln and Lawrence H. Mamiya devote a chapter to sociological analysis regarding the musical forms and styles favored by contemporary African Americans for their worship, distinguishing traditional spirituals from standard hymnody, jazz forms, and the gospel music tradition. See also Portia K. Maultsby, "The Use and Performance of Hymnody, Spirituals and Gospels in the Black Church," *Journal of the Interdenominational Theological Center* XIV, 1/2 (Fall 1986/Spring 1987) 141-59.

15. Peter J. Paris, "The Bible and the Black Churches," in *The Bible and Social Reform,* ed. Ernest R. Sandeen (Philadelphia and Chico, Calif.: Fortress/Scholars Press, 1982) 135.

16. Ibid.

17. See Vincent L. Wimbush, "The Bible and African Americans: An Outline of an Interpretative History," in *Stony the Road We Trod: African American Biblical Interpretation,* ed. Cain Hope Felder (Minneapolis: Fortress, 1991) 81-97.

18. Ibid., 86.

19. Ibid., 87.

by social experience. The texts were heard more than read; they were engaged as stories that seized and freed the imagination," making the songs and sermons of the enslaved "reflect a type of indirect or veiled commentary on the social situation that the African slaves faced."[20]

All other readings to come would in some sense be built upon and judged against it. This reading is in fact the classical reading of the biblical text for African Americans; it reflects the classical period in the history of African Americans (the eighteenth century).[21]

Thus African Americans accepted the Bible, "but not in the way white Americans accepted it or in the way the whites preferred that others accept it."[22]

The third reading period Wimbush isolates in his schema included the beginnings of the independent church movements in the nineteenth century, the time when independent black churches and local and regional denominational bodies developed among African Americans. The reading of the Bible during this period strongly informed the churches for oppositional action in the face of societal racism. Claims were made and pressed from a black consciousness and self-assertiveness, based on a reading of the Bible that had made African Americans view their experience and position as a true antitype of the ancient Hebrews.

According to Wimbush, the fourth and fifth reading periods are embraced within the twentieth century, with blacks influenced, like many others with religious interests, to emphasize religious differences in esoteric and elitist religious sects and cults, or in many ways showing the marks of a fundamentalism that emphasized an inductive reading of Scripture and an insistence upon a "Bible-believing" stance that sometimes clashed with the traditionally social and experiential reading.

Scholars on the subject will differ about what is the most useful schematic to trace the history of how African Americans have read, appropriated, and used the Bible, but there is unanimous agreement among them that their reading, appropriation, and use has been complex rather than simple, and while definite, quite diverse. The Black Church movement has never been homogeneous, and it remains as diverse and complex in form and activities as are

those members who comprise it. While all the African American churches agree with the basic hermeneutical principle of the parenthood of God and the kinship of humankind, the ways that hermeneutic informs church activities and emphases are quite diverse.

In his essay "The Bible and the Black Churches," referred to above, Paris explains how the basic hermeneutic of "the black Christian tradition" has influenced at least four different forms of religious life and action in the African American church setting. Sifting the history of the churches in general and the sermons of five representative and highly influential African American preachers in particular, Paris isolates four major strands of emphasis in the way the black Christian tradition has been taught and applied. There is the "pastoral" emphasis, in which the Bible is used mainly to comfort, console, and nurture in the faith. There is the "prophetic" emphasis, in which Scripture is used to provide a base of understanding for redemptive action toward social change. There is the "reformist" emphasis, which uses Scripture to strengthen resolve and assure one of victory because of divine support for efforts to seek peace and effect justice. Paris categorized the fourth emphasis as "nationalist," a use of the Bible to liberate blacks and build the race into a distinct, independent, central, and productive nation. Each emphasis had its beginning in a particular historical period, and although modified some by time and changing circumstances, each one continues to influence the present.[23]

FOOTPRINTS OF A BROADENED AFRICAN AMERICAN HERMENEUTIC

Some have criticized what Paris has isolated as the basic hemeneutic within "the black Christian tradition," discussed above, as too narrow to allow for an adequate reading of the Bible. In actual fact, a much broader hemeneutic for reading the Bible has evolved within the African American church setting of late.

Because of a growing interest among contemporary African Americans in religion in general and in the Bible in particular, an increased number of black biblical scholars have been at work assessing and

20. Ibid., 88.
21. Ibid., 89.
22. Ibid., 90.

23. See Paris, "The Bible and the Black Churches," 133-54.

reporting what the Bible is really about, and how its contents are best understood and appropriated. Some among that number have addressed themselves to the problem of the way many European and American exegetes and commentary writers have overlooked or, at worst, distorted the factual details about an active African presence within the biblical record itself. As an example, in a descriptive essay, "Three Thousand Years of Biblical Interpretation with Reference to Black Peoples," Charles B. Copher offers a critical assessment of some skewed interpretations of selected biblical accounts.[24] Copher's published studies reflect extensive historical and exegetical work not only within the biblical texts themselves but within correlative ancient periods, documents, places, and languages as well.[25] Influenced by both the "assured benefits" of the historical-critical method and an appreciation for the African American heritage of biblical understandings, several contemporary black biblical scholars have been busy broadening and writing about the African American hermeneutic. Among those who emerged as leaders in the field, mention must be made of Charles B. Copher, David T. Shannon, Cain Hope Felder, Thomas Hoyt, Jr., John R. Waters, Robert A. Bennett, Vincent L. Wimbush, Renita J. Weems, Clarice J. Martin, William H. Myers, Lloyd A. Lewis, and Randall C. Bailey.

A seminal and trailblazing volume on the subject was published in 1991, *Stony the Road We Trod: African American Biblical Interpretation,* with Cain Hope Felder as editor.[26] The book was the culmination of a five-year collaboration of African American biblical scholars in the United States, all of them professors in theological seminaries. Some of these black scholars served in predominantly white schools, and others within predominantly black institutions. In his preface to the volume, Felder explains that the presupposition for the book was to "engage the new challenge to recapture the ancient biblical vision of racial and ethnic pluralism as shaped by the Bible's own universalism" and to "gain a new appreciation for the varied uses of Scripture within the Bible itself as a means of devel-

oping more sensitivity for the positive elements in such phenomena as modes of African American biblical interpretation, which at times are closer to scriptural usage within the Bible and with first-century churches."[27] Felder adds:

Thus, we arrive at the burning question that makes this volume distinctive: How can the Bible break down the "dividing walls of hostility" (Eph 2:14) that recent centuries of Eurocentric biblical translations and interpretations have, however unwittingly in some cases, erected between us? To this question, the present volume attempts to provide some answers; in this regard, such answers take the form of both descriptive and prescriptive narratives and studies.[28]

Stony the Road We Trod reflects a combination of historical inquiry, sophisticated exegesis, and a special sensitivity for the African American heritage of experience. The volume redefined, reshaped, and restated the questions, basic concerns, and scholarly methods that should determine how the Bible is to be read, not only by African Americans but also by the church at large, by the academy, and by the larger society.

Programmatic works directed toward applying a broader hermeneutic in pulpit ministry have also appeared. This was to be expected, given the leading role African American clergy continue to play in their churches and the black community. Such prominence for black clergy within church and community has a long and treasured history behind it, dating back to the antebellum era. As Howard Thurman once explained it:

The ante-bellum Negro preacher was the greatest single factor in determining the spiritual destiny of the slave community. He it was who gave to the masses of his fellows a point of view that became for them a veritable Door of Hope. His ministry was greatly restricted as to movement, function, and opportunities of leadership, but he himself was blessed with one important insight: he was convinced that every human being was a child of God. This belief included the slave as well as the master.[29]

African American preachers are still entrusted with and expected to model and convey that biblical "point of view, providing vision, wisdom, and spiritual guidance to bless the lives and paths of those

24. See Charles B. Copher, "Three Thousand Years of Biblical Interpretation with Reference to Black Peoples," in *African American Religious Studies: An Interdisciplinary Anthology,* ed. Gayraud Wilmore (Durham: Duke University Press, 1989) 105-28.

25. See esp. Copher's essay on "The Black Presence in the Old Testament," in Felder, ed., *Stony the Road We Trod,* 146-64.

26. See footnote 17.

27. Felder, ed., *Stony the Road We Trod,* ix-x.

28. Ibid., x.

29. Howard Thurman, *Deep River,* 11.

who look to them. Crucial to such necessary ends is the *preacher's* reading and handling of the Bible."[30]

African Americans accept the Bible as an adequate, practical, and immediate statement of the divine intention for humankind. Although like all others they must interrogate the manifold forms and genres in the Bible for their "life-meanings," blacks seldom, if ever, read the Bible to gain some analytical absoluteness about the nature and scope of Scripture. The concern is forever practical—to discern the voice of God addressing oneself and one's people in the context of life's immediacies. The cultural rootage of this approach to the Bible honors the folk appeal reflected throughout its pages, and it explains why most African American pulpits have remained free of divisive controversies and why the sermons preached from them have escaped becoming deadening abstractions. In the African American reading of the Bible, and the preaching that flows from it, the ruling principle has been to read Scripture in the light of the deliverance theme. This approach places even Paul's more creative contribution in clearer perspective, especially since his shared understanding about what God has accomplished in the human interest through Jesus Christ is best summed up in the word *freedom*. To sense the many dimensions within the word as the apostle used it, one need only consider how he applied it: freedom from sin (Romans); release from subjection to the powers of an evil age (Ephesians); escape from bondage to the elemental spirits of the universe (Colossians); freedom from confinement in legalisms (Galatians); and even ultimate release from a limiting morality by means of a promised resurrection of the body-self from death (Corinthians).[31]

African Americans readily acknowledge that approaching the Bible to understand its contents in the light of its theme of freedom does not answer all of the questions that inevitably arise when confronting its pages. But neither does the covenant theme answer all of such questions, nor does the promise and fulfillment approach, nor the revelation-as-history framework, nor the sacrifice motif. African American interpreters and preachers know that more than one conceptual framework must be utilized in order to view and appropriate the meanings within the Bible with fruitful understanding, that not everything in the Bible can be made to fit neatly into any one interpretive scheme. Meanwhile, however, the one perspective that rules every reading of Scripture is to test all that is read by the human need for freedom, since God as Deliverer is one of the obvious thematic continuities by which the two testaments cohere. That theme has surely had the strongest and most fruitful appeal as African Americans have read the Bible, and as it has been used to address them in their history of oppression and social trauma.

BIBLIOGRAPHY

Felder, Cain Hope. *Troubling Biblical Waters: Race, Class, and Family.* Maryknoll, N.Y.: Orbis, 1989.

———, ed. *Stony the Road We Trod: African American Biblical Interpretation.* Minneapolis: Fortress, 1991.

Jones, Amos, Jr., *Paul's Message of Freedom: What Does It Mean to the Black Church?* Valley Forge: Judson, 1984.

Lincoln, C. Eric, and Lawrence H. Mamiya. *The Black Church in the African American Experience.* Durham: Duke University Press, 1990.

Massey, James Earl. "An African-American Model." In *Hermeneutics for Preaching: Approaches to Contemporary Interpretation of Scripture.* Edited by Raymond Bailey. Nashville: Broadman, 1992.

Paris, Peter J. "The Bible and the Black Churches." In *The Bible and Social Reform.* Edited by Ernest R. Sandeen. Philadelphia and Chico, Calif.: Fortress/Scholars Press, 1982.

Spencer, Jon Michael. *Protest and Praise: Sacred Music of Black Religion.* Minneapolis: Fortress, 1990.

---

30. For an interpretative overview of the hemeneutical perspectives that inform the contemporary African American pulpit, see James Earl Massey, "An African-American Model," in *Hermeneutics for Preaching: Approaches to Contemporary Interpretations of Scripture,* ed. Raymond Bailey (Nashville: Broadman, 1992) 135-59.

31. See also Amos Jones, Jr., *Paul's Message of Freedom: What Does It Mean to the Black Church?* (Valley Forge: Judson, 1984).

READING THE BIBLE AS ASIAN AMERICANS

CHAN-HIE KIM

Asian American Christians read the Bible as "Holy Scripture." The Bible is the canon of the Asian American Christian community, just as it is the canon of other Christian communities. Asian Americans approach the Bible not as an ordinary book but as the revealed "Word of God," gaining from it an understanding of who they are in the light of their faith in God. Thus they find their identity and the meaning of their presence in a land where people from all over the world and their descendants live together as a nation called the United States of America.

But who are those called Asian Americans? It is necessary to clarify this identity before treating the way Asian Americans read the Bible.

THE DIVERSITY OF ASIAN AMERICANS

Asian Americans are a people whose forebears emigrated from many different countries in Asia. They include first-generation immigrants, a majority of whom came to this side of the Pacific Ocean beginning in 1965, but who share very little in common among themselves. First-generation Asian Americans do not have a common language. Their cultural heritage is multifarious, although they belong to either the Chinese or the Indian cultural realm—the two dominant cultures in Asia. Each

group also has a distinct and divergent history of immigration, and their patterns of settlement are different and diverse, depending on the social, political, and economic climate of the United States at the time of their entry. Strictly speaking, there is no monolithic group of "Asian Americans." There are, rather, specific subgroups, like Chinese Americans, Japanese Americans, Filipino Americans, and Korean Americans, among others.

Despite all these differences, however, Asian Americans yet share something in common that does justify the use of the designation "Asian American." Asian Americans have a similar history in America in that the dominant group neither recognizes nor regards the many differences among people of Asian ancestry. They are simply grouped together and labeled "Asian Americans," and their history and cultural particularities are disregarded. In addition, those who emigrated from Asia and those born in the United States to Asian parents share in common experiences of oppression. In this kind of situation, the cultural and historical differences of their own ancestral lands became less meaningful in their struggle for justice and survival. Once they joined the people called "Americans," they came to understand themselves not as a particular ethnic or racial group of their ancestry but as "Asian Americans."

One needs to take into account the diversity of

Asian Americans in order to understand the total picture of their social location in the United States. No particular segment of Asian Americans can represent the whole. The numbers, social status, political orientation, household income, and preference of cultural values among Asian Americans are quite diverse.

There are four major Asian American groups in the United States: Chinese, Filipinos, Japanese, and Koreans. The rest of Asian Americans are from other groups, such as Indians, Vietnamese, Indonesians, Thai, Cambodians, and others. The rapid growth of Asians in the United States began in 1965 when the discriminatory quota system that favored European immigrants was abolished by the Immigration and Naturalization Act (PL 89-236).

Economic conditions among Asian Americans also vary. Whereas some Chinese and Korean immigrants arrived here with sufficient capital to start their businesses, Cambodians and Vietnamese often came as penniless refugees.

With respect to religious affiliation among Asian Americans, here again a wide variance can be observed. The absolute majority of Filipino Americans is Catholic, while Korean Americans are heavily Protestant. The percentage of Chinese Americans and Japanese Americans who are Christians is very small. However, compared to religious preference in their ancestral countries, the percentage of Christian population among Asian Americans is extremely high.

It is not necessary to document the unpleasant historical experiences that each Asian American group underwent in the United States, but it must be remembered that all the Asian American groups had to win their place in American life, fighting against racism and oppression. Although federal and state laws and restrictive municipal codes against Asian Americans have been rescinded as a result of the civil rights movement of the 1960s, the struggle against racism and stereotypical thinking still continues.

Asian Americans are not completely acculturated, despite tremendous pressure to conform from the basically European environment in America. The Asian world views, value systems, ethos, and behavioral patterns are still very much part of the Asian American mentality. The way of thinking and viewing the world is still basically Asian, even though many have become acculturated to a certain degree.

Family, for instance, is still viewed as the most important social unit, and interpersonal relationships among family members is regarded as more valuable than any other social contact. Respecting the elderly and giving more significance to the family union rather than to individuals in marriage are additional examples.[1]

HERMENEUTICAL PRINCIPLES

How, then, do Asian Americans read the Scriptures? What are the hermeneutical principles that inform their reading? The answer to these questions may be stated simply: Asian American Christians read the Bible from their own historical and cultural context in the United States. They read and understand the Bible from their present social location, which has a long history of struggle for survival in the midst of discrimination and inequity. Such a reading is not intentional, but a natural response to circumstance.

Regrettably, for too long Asians and Asian Americans have been deprived of their right and privilege to read the Bible from their own historical and cultural perspectives. When Christianity was introduced to the Asian countries, a Eurocentric hermeneutic was taught as the only viable way of understanding the Bible. Contextual reading was suppressed and ridiculed as unlearned. Although Asian cultures are well prepared to be able to narrow the cultural and temporal gap between the biblical texts and ourselves, Western Christian scholarship has until recently denied the legitimacy of reading the Bible from a non-European perspective. Because of a life-setting similar to the ancient Mediterranean culture, Asians and Asian Americans feel very close to the biblical world. They often understand the core meaning of the biblical passages without the help of elaborate hermeneutical tools and theories developed by European scholarship.

This does not mean that Asian Americans deny the importance of historical-critical study of the Bible, a great contribution that Western biblical scholarship has made, based on insights from the

1. For more information about the history of Asian Americans and their social location, read Bok-Lim C. Kim, *The Asian Americans: Changing Patterns, Changing Needs* (Montclair, N.J.: AKCS, 1978); and Roy Sano, ed., *The Theologies of Asian Americans and Pacific Peoples: A Reader* (Berkeley: Asian Center for Theology and Strategies, Pacific School of Religion, 1976). For more up-to-date information about written and other media resources, consult the Asian American study centers and institutes at UCLA, UC Berkeley, and other higher educational institutions.

Enlightenment. We recognize its usefulness without question, and we neither underestimate nor devalue its contribution to biblical scholarship. We appreciate and appropriate it. In fact, the very ability to recognize the importance of contextual interpretation itself is a result of the historical-critical study of the Bible. Such study has taught us that the Bible is a historical document with a long history of formation, extending almost a thousand years. The Bible is also a historical document in the sense that it contains the story of God's dealing with a chosen people in various stages of their history. It is a record from the people who struggled for their national identity and survival, and who, like us, had great joys as well as sufferings. In other words, we find in the Bible a historical people, a faith community of people who understood themselves as created and constantly encountered by God throughout their history. They were a people who honored their own history and, yet, whose retelling of that history was decisively influenced by their own changing historical contexts. This fact legitimates our approach to the Scriptures from our own historical context.

Asian Americans recognize an inalienable link between themselves and the people of God in the Bible. They identify themselves with the people who have not only produced the Bible, but who have encountered God in it. The narratives, poems, hymns, laws, lamentations, proverbs, and all the other forms of biblical literature reflect the story of not only the biblical people but of us as well. Thus the most important presupposition of the biblical hermeneutic for Asian Americans is that the Bible is not an irrelevant ancient document but our own story and history and, therefore, the very source from which we understand our existential place before God.

Such an understanding of the Bible makes it the absolute authority on every level of Christian life for the Asian American Christian community. Particularly for Protestants, there exists no greater authority than the Scriptures to regulate community life and give guidance to spiritual disciplines. *Sola scriptura* (Scripture alone) is very much alive in the Asian American Christian churches, where the Bible is valued and revered as the Word of God, in which the message of truth transcends the historical limitations of its original settings.

Consequently, it is inevitable that we sometimes have to *read into* the Scriptures—a practice commonly called *eisegesis*—to do justice to our pre- and self-understanding. If the truthfulness of the Bible transcends its historicity, the division of the "original meaning" (meaning then) and the "meaning for us" (meaning now) loses its significance and validity in understanding the Scriptures. As long as a genuine dialogue exists between the reader and the text that illumines the reader's self-understanding, even eisegesis is an acceptable method for us. Strictly speaking, unbiased, objective reading of the scriptural text is an impossible task. Readers come to the Scriptures with questions, expecting answers from it. In this process of dialogue, eisegesis is not only inevitable but a valid and acceptable method as well.

Asian Americans do recognize the importance of historical-critical exegesis on given texts, as mentioned above. But we are aware, at the same time, of the danger of biblical historicism, which denies the capacity of the Bible to be the Word of God. One way to avoid the pitfall of biblical historicism is to utilize various methods of interpretation, and Asian Americans seek to employ those other methods when they read the Bible and preach from it. Often we take certain portions of the biblical texts as a paradigm, parable, analogy, metaphor, allegory, or illustrative story—just as the early Christian readers did with the text of the Hebrew Bible. We practice such a reading because we take our own historical context seriously into account, just as the New Testament writers did when viewing and using the Hebrew Scriptures. Our self-understanding is a primary goal of reading the Bible as the "Scriptures."

IMMIGRATION AND SETTLEMENT SEEN IN BIBLICAL TERMS

Let us consider an example of how Asian Americans read the Scriptures with a specific question in mind—namely, understanding of the immigration and settlement of Asian Americans in the United States. Some of the fundamental questions Asian Americans raise in this historical circumstance are How do we understand our existence on this continent in the light of our faith in God? What does the Bible tell us about ourselves, a group of latecomers? What does the Bible say about our own particular situation? Can we use any paradigms, images, metaphors, or analogies from the Scriptures to help us understand our own life situations and to show us future directions we should take? Do we have any right to demand to be a part of this established "kingdom" and to be treated justly and equally with those who settled here earlier than we? Our answer to all of these questions is positive: The Bible does help us to answer these questions.

First of all, we need to deal with the misleading notions many Asian Americans hold about the United States as "a good and broad land, a land flowing with milk and honey" (Exod 3:8 NRSV). Early Asian immigrants and recent newcomers alike have looked upon America as a "land flowing with milk and honey." The first Asian immigrants, the Chinese, came to California seeking fortunes in gold mines in the 1850s. They were followed by the Japanese in the late nineteenth and early twentieth centuries, who were looking for better wages in the sugar plantations of the Hawaiian Islands. The Filipinos and Koreans were no exceptions. Their early immigrants migrated to Hawaii on the promise of good wages, even though the harsh reality they experienced there was far from what they expected. But the analogy is still heard, particularly among recent Asian immigrants. This analogy used to be one of the most frequently used catch phrases in Korean American pulpits in the late 1960s and early 1970s. Even if we do not hear the phrase explicitly these days, the basic imagery projected by this analogy is still popular among Asian American Christians.

The appeal to the "golden age" of Israelite history is understandable. After all, Asians came to this land at that juncture of American history when the wealth of the country was at its maximum—like the glorious era of Solomon's reign. However, it must not be overlooked that there was once a period of Joshua and Judges in the history of America. Even in this period of the "kingdom of Solomon" there are still unpleasant realities.

The Solomonic kingdom in America was possible only because there was a period of conquest under Joshua and struggles under the Judges before the Israelite monarchy was firmly established. The monarchy is a result of the bloody battles for expansion of territories. In the process of territorial expansion, "the Canaanites, the Hittites, the Amorites, the Perizzites, the Hivites, and the Jebusites"—the nations of the Native Indians—were pushed to what the early migrating conquerors called reservations. Solomon's glory and wealth are the result of the westward movement of the conquering tribes. We do not want to hide the fact that Asian Americans are certainly a beneficiary of American expansionism.

Modern Old Testament scholarship generally accepts the theory that not all twelve tribes experienced the exodus but only a few of them, including perhaps the Benjaminites. Later, after the tribes had formed a tribal federation (or amphyctyony), the tradition of the exodus became the tradition of all of the tribes, although some of them had never taken part in it. Although recent Asian American immigrants have nothing to do with the history of America's Joshua and Judges, that history has become and still is *our* history, since we now participate in the shaping of America today. What happened in America's past is relevant to Asian Americans because we are unavoidably affected by that history today.

Since we have become one of the tribal groups that have joined the existing tribal league of the United States, the event of exodus and the subsequent history of Joshua and Judges have become *our own* history. In this respect, we need to repent and be grateful to all the nations of Native Americans who are sharing their land with us. Likewise, we too have to repent for what the early settlers did to African Americans, even though we, particularly Japanese Americans, became victims of racism during World War II.

We discovered that the land to which our parents and grandparents came is not a land dominated by various independent tribes. They had already lost control over most of their previous territories, and in their place monarchy under the leadership of Saul was established. When we came to this "promised land," Saul was no longer the ruling monarch, but Solomon was reigning over the kingdom. The campaign for territorial expansion initiated by David continued, and, by the time of Solomon, the kingdom was enjoying glory and power in the region. The kingdom subdued many tribes and nations. Some tribes completely lost their identities after being conquered by the Israelites. Enjoying here the glory of Solomonic wealth, we are in a country that, like no other nation in the world, offers abundant material wealth and luxuriant life-styles. Surely this land is the promised land "flowing with milk and honey."

On the other hand, this land is not the sweet paradise Asian Americans expected. Our participation in the mainstream of American life is limited not by our language handicaps but by our very ethnicity. Some sociologists say that structural assimilation in American society is an impossible dream as long as our physical appearance is different from that of the dominant race. Even second- and third-generation Asian Americans find it very difficult to move freely in the mainstream of American life, because, despite its wealth and commendable features, this country does not wholly reflect the good biblical image depicted in the words "a land flowing with milk and honey."

Contrary to the standard ideals of the founders of this nation, the descendants of "the Canaanites, the Hittites, the Amorites, the Perizzites, the Hivites, and the Jebusites" in America do not enjoy the same freedom the Israelites enjoyed. The dreams Asians had at the time of their entry into this "promised land" were shattered by the harsh reality of arduous American life as they got a better understanding of the country they had made home.

OLD TESTAMENT CONCEPTS OF JUSTICE

Unfortunately, the Bible does not always present God as the liberator, as liberation theologians claim. Sometimes it depicts God as the oppressor of the Canaanites on behalf of the invading Israelites.

It is regrettable that liberation theology of all types generally does not take note of the suffering and humiliation of the people conquered by the invading Israelites; it does not notice the fact that the liberated Israelites become, in turn, the conqueror and oppressor of people already settled in the promised land. The Pilgrims who risked their lives crossing the Atlantic Ocean on the Mayflower in quest of religious freedom were no longer the persecuted Puritans once they landed on this shore. Their freedom led to oppression for other races on this continent. If the God of Israel is also the God of all nations, why does God fulfill justice by annihilating other nations?

The individual Bible texts some liberation theologians quote reveal only a limited view of God's justice. Numerous other biblical texts can be cited to claim quite the opposite—that is, oppression of the innocent as God's just action.[2] When one takes

a close look at the concept of "justice" in the Old Testament, one recognizes immediately that there are diverse theological dimensions in this concept. Individual OT texts understand "justice" differently, depending on different historical circumstances and conditions.

There can be no doubt that justice means liberation from oppression. But there is another and even more important aspect of justice in the OT. Not only the liberation of people from oppression, but also Yahweh's fulfillment of the promise to give Israel "a land flowing with milk and honey" is viewed as justice.[3] This theology is common in the books of Exodus–Joshua and in some other related OT texts. The presence of two seemingly mutually exclusive concepts of justice in the OT is a problem, especially its claim that Israel's oppression of the Canaanite nations as well as Israel's liberation from Egyptian oppression are both *just* actions. Such a claim involves the reader in an apparent contradiction or inconsistency, which demands an answer.

The recognition of the election of the Israelites as Yahweh's people might lead us to a solution. The Deuteronomistic historian contends that not only liberating the Israelites from the pharaoh but fulfilling God's promise to give the promised land to the children of Abraham is itself justice, even though it takes thousands of innocent lives in Canaan. The people of Canaan must be eradicated because the land was promised to the children of Israel. Once we understand the killing and oppression of the people of Canaan in this context, the action of the Israelites in Canaan can easily be understood.

Of course, the OT also gives another rationale for dispossessing the Canaanites of their lands— namely, their idolatry, sins, abominations, and wickedness. But a closer look at the applicable texts reveals that these reasons are all related to Israel's very existence in the newly occupied land; the Israelites are simply threatened by the polytheistic environment of the land. Thus the sins of the Canaanites themselves are not the reason for their elimination, as a superficial reading of the texts purports them to be. The annihilation of the Canaanites has something to do with the preservation of Israel's own religious identity in the new environ-

2. For example, "Let my people go" (Exod 5:1 and *passim*) against "Now go and attack Amalek, and utterly destroy all that they have . . . kill both man and woman, child and infant" (1 Sam 15:3 NRSV).

3. I am indebted to Prof. Rolf Knierim for this observation. His 1989 lecture series entitled "The Interpretation of the Old Testament," delivered at the United Methodist Seminary in Sao Paulo, Brazil, was published in Portuguese in 1990, and the English version will be forthcoming by Eerdmans.

ment. Here, Asian Americans find a biblical message relevant to our own immigration to this country.

If one does not take note of the theology of the Deuteronomistic historian and its ramification within OT theology, one might find justification for oppression in biblical texts that are really talking about the righteousness of God. The concept of Israel's election as Yahweh's people is sufficient ground to justify the oppression of the Canaanite nations. In this sense, the concept of justice inherent in the Deuteronomistic history—namely, fulfilling justice at the expense of oppressing other nations—might be considered unique.

The preservation of Asian American cultural heritages and ethnic identities is desirable and not to be overlooked. The contamination of Yahwism through contact with the native Canaanites was the Israelites' greatest fear. Asian Americans did not and are not bringing with them their own religion as the Israelites had, but they do have their own precious cultural heritage from their forebears. Like the Israelites, who cherished their heritage and identity as integral to the fulfillment of God's promise, Asian American churches honor and treasure the values inherent in our traditions. Without these, we would not be able to keep our identity in this multicultural society.

A NEW AGE OF PACIFIC AMERICA

We are very much aware of the changing reality of the world today, particularly in the Pacific region. Western civilization, rooted in the Nile valley and Mesopotamia, is today interacting with another group of civilizations emerging from the rivers Yangtze and Huang in the arena of the Pacific Ocean. For many centuries, the center of the world was concentrated in the fertile crescent and the Mediterranean basin before it moved to the European continent. With the presence of the Roman Empire in the Mediterranean region at the beginning of the first century BCE, world activity moved to the European continent. However, the "discovery" of America in 1492 induced another change in the world scene. For the past five hundred years, especially since the birth of the United States, the Atlantic Ocean has been the center of world activity. Now the central arena of world history is moving once again. The dawn of a new era of political and economic order since the end of World War II in the Pacific Ocean is clearly noticeable. Interaction of the Pacific Rim countries will play a major role in shaping the new political and economic order in the future.

The shaping of the future America depends on how the people from the Pacific Rim countries interact with the people of North America. As the descendants of Pacific Rim nationalities, Asian Americans can and should play a leading role in a country dominated by the descendants of European immigrants and their cultures. The United States in the next millennium will not be "Euro-America" but "Pacific America." This is not a naive belief but a reality, the signs of which are already appearing on the horizon. There is no need to seek its sign as Jesus' disciples did: "Tell us, when will this be, and what will be the sign of your coming and of the end of the age?" (Matt 24:3 NRSV). The new generation of Asian Americans has tremendous opportunities in the new age, despite all the obstacles and shackles imposed on us. The apocalyptic vision of "a new heaven and a new earth" (Rev 21:1) is not a wild dream but a present reality already dawning on us.

Once the nation called Israel, formed out of the various ethnic tribes, became an established kingdom in the land of Canaan, there were no longer the Josephites, the Benjamites, the Reubenites, and others. They were all called the "children of Israel." We also look forward to the day when all the "tribes" of America become known simply as the "people of America" and not as hyphenated Americans. Like the first-generation Israelites, the first-generation Asian Americans may not be able to see the real Land of Promise. But they believe firmly that their descendants will see it someday and have an abundant life in the new Canaan.

READING THE BIBLE AS HISPANIC AMERICANS

FERNANDO F. SEGOVIA

The title of this article reflects the fundamental change that has taken place in biblical studies in the last quarter century and signals a clear and exciting path for the future direction of the discipline. This change forms part of a much broader transformation at work in the theological and ecclesiastical worlds at large, characterized by the emergence of the issue of perspective, or standpoint, with its explicit and critical focus on the theologian or interpreter and his or her social location, and thus ultimately on the relationship between theology or interpretation and the social context of the theologian or interpreter.

In large part, this ongoing transformation has been occasioned by the irruption of the voice of the voiceless, of those who had remained silent, of the colonized and the marginalized—an irruption that has begun to give way to a profound, multifaceted, and indigenous process of decolonization and globalization with regard to interpretation, theology, and the church.

First, the presence of the comparative clause "as Hispanic Americans" presupposes that all readings of the Bible are contextual—readings from a particular historical and cultural situation—and that no reading can claim or pretend to be ahistorical or acultural. The clause lets it be known that, at the very least, ethnic background and sociopolitical status do have an effect on the reading and interpretation of the Bible. This article moves, therefore, far beyond the implicit theoretical orientation

of historical criticism, the dominant criticism in biblical studies through the 1970s. Instead of an ideal reader as posited by historical criticism (informed, objective, universal), this article argues for a full contextuality in the reading of the Bible, an open and explicit acknowledgment and analysis of flesh-and-blood readers in biblical criticism and interpretation. A theoretical orientation for this approach lies in both reader-response criticism and cultural studies. The meaning of a text lies not in the text itself, properly secured and retrieved by an ideal reader via the use of scientific methods, but is rather the result of a complex interaction between a historically and culturally conditioned text and a historically and culturally conditioned reader, with the reader as an ever-present and inescapable filter in the reading of a text.[1]

---

1. For the shift in the discipline, the theoretical orientation of historical criticism, and the theoretical orientation of this particular type of reader-response criticism, see F. Segovia "The Text as Other: Towards a Hispanic American Hermeneutics," in *Reading from This Place. Social Location and Biblical Interpretation: The American Scene,* eds. Fernando F. Segovia and Mary Ann Tolbert (Minneapolis: Fortress, 1993). For reader-response criticism and its interpretive spectrum, see Vincent B. Leitch, *American Literary Criticism from the Thirties to the Eighties* (New York: Columbia University Press, 1988) 211-37; Susan R. Suleiman, "Introduction: Varieties of Audience-Oriented Criticism," in *The Reader in the Text: Essays on Audience and Interpretation,* eds. Susan R. Suleiman and Inge Crossman (Princeton: Princeton University Press, 1980) 3-45; Jane P. Tompkins, "An Introduction to Reader-Response Criticism," in *Reader-Response Criticism: From Formalism to Post-Structuralism,* ed. Jane P. Tompkins (Baltimore: Johns Hopkins University Press, 1980) ix-xxvi. For cultural studies, see Renato Rosaldo, *Culture and Truth: The Remaking of Social Analysis* (Boston: Beacon Press, 1989).

Second, given its emphasis on contextuality and flesh-and-blood readers, the comparative clause demands more than a simple description of the reader's social location; it also requires a critical analysis of the reader's context in terms of an informed theoretical framework. Just as historical criticism called for a radical contextualization of the text (a focus that must by no means be abandoned but rather properly expanded and grounded), so does this type of reader-response criticism call for a radical contextualization of the reader of the text. The present article focuses on biblical interpretation as influenced by the social location of Hispanic Americans, a contextualization involving both ethnic background and sociopolitical status.[2] A wide variety of other identity factors is also important for this type of analysis, such as gender, racial background, socioeconomic class, educational level, ideological stance, socioreligious tradition and affiliation, and sociocultural conventions. The content of the comparative clause thus varies as the different factors are isolated for critical analysis.

Finally, given the enormous scope of these factors as well as their interdependence, the reach of the comparative clause must be carefully and explicitly circumscribed, if it is not to be misleading. Hispanic Americans, for example, exhibit many and profound similarities that allow them to be seen as a distinct and readily identifiable social group. At the same time, however, many and profound differences also distinguish members of the group from each other—we come from many different areas and countries, each with its own distinctive history and culture. It would be utterly presumptuous of me to pretend to know how Hispanic Americans actually read the Bible as a group or even in terms of subgroups; the aim here is much more circumscribed. In effect, it is to investigate how Hispanic American theologians, as representatives of the group at large, read and use the Bible in their own constructive work.

This article, then, treats the question of how Hispanic Americans read and interpret the Bible in terms of the reading strategies adopted, consciously or unconsciously, by a number of theologians from the group. After delineating a variety of such strategies, I argue for another and very different strategy, which can be called the strategy of intercultural criticism.

FOUR HISPANIC AMERICAN READING STRATEGIES

Hispanic American theology has quite understandably followed the methodology of liberation theology.[3] I say "quite understandably" given the precarious social conditions of the group as a whole, a situation characterized by (1) sustained and pervasive discrimination, regardless of origin or status, fueled by a dominant view of the group as inferior, undeveloped, and uncivilized; and (2) widespread and entrenched social marginalization—political powerlessness, economic disadvantage, and educational fragility. Not at all surprisingly, therefore, the goal of liberation from such oppressive and dehumanizing conditions has emerged as a common thread in the rapidly expanding corpus of this movement. Given this fundamental theological option, Hispanic American theology has also opted for a hermeneutic of liberation with regard to the Bible, a hermeneutic that encompasses a wide variety of reading strategies. Four such strategies, taken from the work of four prominent Hispanic American theological voices, can serve as representative.[4]

A Canon Within the Canon from the Inside. A first reading strategy, adopted by Virgilio Elizondo in his elaboration of *mestizaje* theology from the point of view of the borderland experience and reality of Mexican Americans in the Southwest, represents a variation of the canon within the canon approach and employs the principle of correspondence.[5] Elizondo defines the normative experience of the faith community in terms of the tradition of the church, especially the founding tradition of the New Testament (NT) and the writings of the Church Fathers; however, it is clear that for him pride of place belongs to the Synoptic Gospels—the Fourth Gospel is hardly mentioned—and, more specifically, the figure of the historical Jesus, faithfully preserved and conveyed by these Gospels. Thus the canon

---

2. For a definition of Hispanic Americans, its reach and rationale, see F. Segovia "Two Places and No Place on Which to Stand: Mixture and Otherness in Hispanic American Theology," *Listening: A Journal of Religion and Culture* 27 (1992) 26-40.

3. On this point see F. Segovia "A New Manifest Destiny: The Emerging Theological Voice of Hispanic Americans," *Religious Studies Review* 17 (1991) 101-9.

4. For an extended critical exposition of these strategies, see Segovia, "Hispanic American Theology and the Bible: Effective Weapon and Faithful Ally," in *We Are a People! Initiative in Hispanic American Theology*, ed. Roberto S. Goizueta (Minneapolis: Fortress, 1992) 21-50.

5. V. Elizondo, *Galilean Journey: The Mexican American Promise* (Maryknoll: Orbis, 1983) II:47-88.

within the canon is provided from inside the Bible by Jesus of Nazareth, whose life and message as recounted in the Gospels establish the basic parameters for all Christian theology across time and cultures.

For Elizondo, a retrieval of the historical Jesus is imperative; this retrieval yields two main features. First, Jesus' identity as a Galilean takes on paramount importance. On the one hand, he is said to come from a region that represented a crossroads of cultures and peoples with an openness to each other, a place of *mestizaje,* of racial and cultural mixture. On the other hand, this place of *mestizaje* is rejected by Gentiles and Jews alike as impure and inferior, with the Galileans as a clear example of a marginalized and oppressed people. As a Galilean, Jesus was a *mestizo,* and, as *mestizo,* Jesus embodies the option of God for the poor of the world—in Jesus, the Son of God becomes one of the lowly and despised of the world.

Second, the overall pattern of Jesus' life becomes very important as well, with the Galilee-Jerusalem-resurrection cycle as the way of transformation and liberation. The ministry in Galilee confirms the primary option for the oppressed, with a message of inclusion for all Jews in the kingdom of God, based on a new relationship with God as Father and a radical new association with each other and society as brothers and sisters in God. The journey to Jerusalem reveals a necessary turn to, confrontation with, and exposé of the powers of oppression, with a message of nonviolence and unconditional love. And the resurrection appearances in Galilee demonstrate both his triumph over violence and the path of new life, with a message of inclusion, of fellowship, and of celebration for all nations in the kingdom of God.

This portrayal of the historical Jesus sets the boundaries for all proper Christian theology via the principle of correspondence: As Jesus functioned in his time and culture, so must the church function in its time and culture. Thus the region of Galilee takes on a symbolic character—it exists wherever the marginalized and the oppressed live. Similarly, Jesus' life acquires a typological dimension—the church must opt for the Galilees of the world, confront its Jerusalems, and preach the message of new life, of universal inclusion and fellowship in God. Any theology that fails to take into account the life and message of Jesus represents a misreading of the gospel, ultimately substituting its own version of the gospel for *the* gospel and its own version of the faith for *the* faith.

Elizondo sees his own theology of *mestizaje* as being in full accord with this normative criterion of the church for all ages and thus grounded in a correct reading of the Bible. As a *mestizo* people, Mexican Americans represent a Galilee of the contemporary world, a modern example of a marginalized and oppressed people. As such, they can see the Galilean Jesus as the way of transformation and liberation, not only anticipating but also giving meaning and purpose to their own struggle for identity, integration, and celebration. Thus Mexican Americans can see Jesus as present and active among them (the Galilean principle of inclusion), calling them to witness out of their own exclusion and rejection (the Jerusalem principle of confrontation), to the message of global *mestizaje,* of universal inclusion and fellowship in God (the resurrection principle of universal inclusion).

A Canon Within the Canon from the Outside. A second reading strategy, followed by Ada María Isasi-Díaz in her formulation of *mujerista* theology from the perspective of Hispanic American women, provides a different variation of the canon within the canon approach, with recourse to the principle of liberative praxis.[6] For Isasi-Díaz the Bible must cease to be the peripheral force that it has been for Hispanic women and must begin to play a central role in their everyday religious lives. In effect, not only is the Bible—more accurately, parts of the Bible, such as the core of the gospel message—in fundamental accord with the values of justice and love in their popular religiosity, but also the Bible can serve as an effective weapon in their daily struggle for survival, given its importance in and for the dominant culture.

However, such a recovery of the Bible must be accompanied by correct use, defined according to the principles and vision of *mujerista* theology. On the one hand, the point of departure for this theology lies in the experience of oppression, in terms of both sexism and racism, which Hispanic women face in their daily lives, with survival itself, physical and/or cultural, always at risk. On the other hand, its *modus*

---

6. Ada María Isasi-Díaz, "The Bible and *Mujerista* Theology," in *Lift Every Voice: Constructing Theologies from the Underside,* eds. Susan Brooks Thistlethwaite and Mary Potter Engel (San Francisco: Harper & Row, 1990) 1-15.

operandi is defined as a praxis: critical, reflective action based on the lived experience of Hispanic women with liberation in mind. Consequently, the principle of liberative praxis guides and informs a proper use of the Bible. Thus neither the Bible nor any part thereof passes judgment on the praxis of Hispanic women, but rather such praxis passes judgment on the Bible. In other words, the Bible can be both liberating and oppressive for Hispanic women, and only Hispanic women can make a decision in this regard in the light of their experiential norm. The canon within the canon is determined, therefore, from outside the Bible by a superior, external canon—a Hispanic, feminist, liberative canon. The consequences are clear: Whatever traditions contribute to and advance the liberation of Hispanic women are accepted as revelatory and salvific; whatever traditions detract from and impede such liberation are to be considered neither normative nor authoritative. In the end, therefore, the Bible remains subordinate to the praxis of Hispanic women.

The Bible as Straightforward Liberation. The third reading strategy, proposed by Harold Recinos in his development of *barrio* theology from the experience and reality of Puerto Ricans in the inner cities of the Northeast, looks upon the whole of the Bible as liberating and makes use, once again, of the principle of correspondence.[7] For Recinos, the message of the Bible throughout, in both the Old Testament (OT) and the NT, is one of straightforward liberation: The God of the Bible, the God of the cross, sides with the poor and the oppressed and actively works their liberation. This option for the marginalized—which is called "prophetic" theology—is traced from the early traditions of the Pentateuch, with the exodus story at its very center; through the prophetic tradition; to its climax in Jesus' proclamation of the kingdom; and on to the message of the early church through the first century. However, with the gradual accommodation of the church to imperial society in the second through the fourth centuries, this "prophetic" theology—this option for the poor—is replaced by a "royal" theology, with an option for the status quo and a corresponding loss of the radical message of the Bible.

For Recinos, therefore, a correct reading of the Bible must begin with the prophetic perspective rather than the royal stance, with the principle of correspondence at its very core: Only from the perspective of the poor, the perspective of the people of God in the Bible, can the God of the Bible, the God of the poor, be discerned. As the people of the *barrio,* Puerto Ricans—and Hispanic Americans in general—represent a marginalized and oppressed people, overwhelmed, both as a group and as individuals, by their sociocultural situation. As such, they can identify with the people of God in the Bible, who share a parallel sociocultural story of oppression. They discover a God who sides with the oppressed and works for their liberation, and they see the kingdom of God as pointing to a world of justice and equality. For Recinos, such a reading of the Bible allows the people of the *barrio* to make sense of their reality of oppression and regain a fundamental sense of human dignity, to struggle against all dehumanizing structures, and to work for a world based on justice and equality.

The Bible as Non-innocent Liberation. A fourth reading strategy, proposed by Justo González in his elaboration of *mañana* theology from the perspective of Hispanic Americans as a people in exile, also takes the whole of the Bible as liberating but in a non-innocent way, again with recourse to the principle of correspondence.[8] González sees the whole message of the Bible, in both the OT and the NT, as one of liberation, but with a twist, insofar as it is a liberation repeatedly snatched by God out of the clutches of human failings and failures.

Thus, on the one hand, the message of liberation is described as highly political. The Bible argues for a salvation that is deeply social and historical, not just otherworldly. It affirms a reign of God that is already at work in the world, not just in the future, and it identifies a God who demands peace and justice in human affairs, not just interested in souls and life after death. On the other hand, however, the message of liberation is also said to be highly ironic. Since the biblical protagonists of the OT and the NT all carry (including Jesus himself) closets full of skeletons and by no means represent embodiments of high ideals, purity, and perfection, the real heroes of the Bible are rather history itself, which keeps moving despite such unlikely channels and repeated, even radical, failures, and the God of history, who chooses such people for the divine plan.

7. Harold J. Recinos, *Hear the Cry! A Latino Pastor Challenges the Church* (Louisville: Westminster/John Knox, 1989) esp. 65-81.

8. Justo L. González, *Mañana: Christian Theology from a Hispanic Perspective* (Nashville: Abingdon, 1990) esp. 75-87.

Thus, in effect, the liberation of the people of God in the Bible is carried out by the God of liberation and life in spite of the people of God. In other words, God remains fully at work in and through such a non-innocent and concrete history.

For González, such a reading of the Bible is possible only from the perspective of a people "in exile," such as that of Hispanic Americans, thereby calling into play the principle of correspondence: The situation and liberation of Hispanic Americans are anticipated in the life and call of the people of God in the Bible. First, Hispanic Americans do represent a people in exile, not only as alien and powerless, living in a land that does not recognize them as its own and facing sustained discrimination and marginalization at every level of life, but also as painfully aware of their own non-innocent history and identity, of their beginnings in violence and injustice. Second, as a people in exile, Hispanic Americans can come to a correct reading of the Bible, what González calls a reading "in Spanish": *beyond innocence,* from a people aware of its own painful beginnings and history; *from exile,* from an alien and disadvantaged people called to liberation and new life by God; and *naive,* from a people not afraid to lay claim to its own reading of the Bible, fully inserting itself into biblical history. As a result, Hispanic Americans can see the Bible as addressed to them as the people of God; seeing in the people of God their own non-innocent history and identity, their many failures and skeletons; and seeing the God of the Bible as one who calls them nonetheless to liberation and new life, to social change and a transformation of the world in terms of peace and justice.

This reading "in Spanish" involves a very specific "grammar," with four main principles at work: (1) It must focus throughout on the question of power and powerlessness in the Bible. (2) It must see the Bible as addressing the community of faith. (3) It must be particularly attuned to what the poor and the simple find in the Bible. (4) It must let itself be interpreted by the Bible in terms of its own historical pilgrimage.

Concluding Comments. These four reading strategies represent, once again, variations of a hermeneutic of liberation, which involves the use of the Bible as an effective weapon and faithful ally in the struggle for liberation. All four strategies presuppose, to one degree or another, rather direct access to the biblical texts on the part of present-day readers; the identification of a locus of liberation within the Bible; an entrée to the text in an experience of marginalization; a call for a specific and correct way of reading the Bible; and a utopian reading of the Bible.

I propose, not at all by way of displacement but rather by way of addition, another reading strategy grounded in the reality and experience of Hispanic Americans as a bicultural people.

THE READING STRATEGY OF INTERCULTURAL CRITICISM

The fundamental purpose of this strategy is to read the biblical text as an "other"—not to be overwhelmed or overridden, but acknowledged, respected, and engaged in its very otherness. This strategy emerges from a hermeneutic of otherness and engagement and is ultimately grounded in a social location of radical otherness as a bicultural people.[9]

The Otherness of Hispanic Americans. For many Hispanic Americans, biculturalism represents a fundamental and inescapable way of life, involving two essential dimensions. On the one hand, we live in two worlds at the same time, operating relatively at ease within each world and able to go in and out of each in an endless exercise of human and social translation. On the other hand, we live in neither one of these worlds, regarded askance by their respective populations and unable to call either world home. Thus our biculturalism results in a very paradoxical and alienating situation involving a continuous twofold existence as permanent strangers or aliens, as the permanent others. It is a situation that can be accurately described as having two places and yet no place on which to stand.

Insofar as we have no place on which to stand, we find ourselves always defined by somebody else. In our present, permanent, and everyday world of the United States, we *begin* as strangers and *remain* strangers throughout—the undesirable others, the ones who do not fit. In our former, traditional, and distant world of Latin America, we gradually and inevitably become and remain aliens as well—the distant others, the ones who left. As such, we find ourselves with neither a voice nor a home of our

9. For a beginning and fuller exposition of this reading strategy, see Segovia, "The Text as Other: Towards a Hispanic American Hermeneutics."

own. Such otherness overwhelms and overrides us, depriving us not only of a present or self-definition, but also of a past and a future, self-appropriation and self-direction.

However, insofar as we do have two places on which to stand, such otherness can also be turned into a point of departure for the formulation of our own voice, using it constructively and creatively in the interest of liberation, not only on our own behalf but on behalf of others as well. In so doing, we turn the very source of our alienation into the very source of our identity. While regarded as "others" in both worlds of our existence, we do live in both worlds and we know how to proceed, at a moment's notice, from one world to the other. We know both worlds from the inside and outside, and this privileged knowledge gives us a rather unique perspective. We know that both worlds, that all worlds, are constructions, solid and firm, to be sure, but constructions nonetheless. Such knowledge allows us in the end to see our own reality as "others" in terms of construction; to use it to our own advantage, giving it a voice of its own; and to do so critically, in terms of our own power to construct ourselves and "others."

Giving a voice to our "otherness" entails a process of self-affirmation. On the one hand, it requires an active refusal to be bound by our imposed definitions, with a corresponding commitment to understand, expose, and critique such definitions. On the other hand, it involves an active determination to offer our own self-definitions, with a corresponding commitment not only to the self-affirmation of others but also to a critical exchange with such others and their own corresponding self-affirmations. This process confers dignity, liberation, and openness not only on the group itself but on all other groups as well. From such a voice emerges a profound commitment not to overwhelm or override the other but rather to acknowledge it, value it, and engage it—a hermeneutic of otherness and engagement.

Intercultural Criticism. Out of such a hermeneutic emerges in turn the reading strategy of intercultural criticism, with three basic dimensions at work. First, the text is to be regarded, like any contemporary social group, as a historically and culturally conditioned "other." The question of access is crucial. Rather than positing any type of direct or immediate entrance into the text, the hermeneutic of otherness and engagement argues for distance

from the text as a working principle, emphasizing thereby the historical and cultural remoteness of the text. For intercultural criticism, therefore, the contextuality and otherness of the text must be acknowledged, valued, and analyzed. This process of setting at a distance is helped immensely by a view of the text as a literary, rhetorical, and ideological product in its own right. It is an artistic construction with underlying strategic concerns and goals in the light of its own point of view, its own vision of the world and reality, within a given historical and cultural matrix. The ultimate aim of such a view is an understanding of the text as a whole, as a world of its own, as a construct within a more comprehensive historical-cultural framework, no matter how strange or remote.

Second, the reader is also to be regarded as historically and culturally conditioned, as an "other" to both the text and other readers. The question of critical honesty is crucial. Rather than seeking after objectivity or universality, intercultural criticism argues for a self-conscious exposition and analysis of the reader's strategy for reading, the theoretical foundations behind this strategy, and the social location underlying such a strategy. For intercultural criticism, therefore, the contextuality and otherness of readers must also be acknowledged, valued, and analyzed. This process of self-conscious reflection is helped immensely by a view of the reader as a product, a "text" as it were, in his or her own right—a historical and cultural construction involving a view of the past, the present, and the future. The ultimate aim of such an analysis would be an understanding of the reader as a whole, as a world of his or her own, as a construct within a more comprehensive historical and cultural matrix—again, no matter how strange or remote.

Finally, the interaction between the text and the reader is to be regarded not as a neutral encounter between two independent, historically and culturally conditioned entities or worlds, but rather as an unavoidable filtering of the one world or entity by and through the other, of the text by and through the reader. In this regard the question of access and the question of critical honesty are crucial. Despite the attitude of distance from the text, intercultural criticism argues that the historical and cultural remoteness of the text as an "other" is in itself not a reconstruction but a construction of the past on the part of the reader. Despite the attitude of conscious self-reflection, this strategy further argues that such a construction of the past is dependent as well on the reader's own social location.

For intercultural criticism, therefore, the interchange between the reader and the text must be seen in terms of both construction and engagement. On the one hand, the process of setting at a distance is helped immensely by a view of all reconstruction as construction. In other words, even when attempting to understand the text as an "other" to us, historically and culturally removed, we ultimately play a major role in the construction of such otherness; thus even when considering the text as a literary, rhetorical, and ideological product, we ultimately have a major hand in the very identification and articulation of its literary structure and development, its rhetorical concerns and aims, its ideological thrust, and its relationship to its historical and cultural matrix.

On the other hand, the process of self-reflection is helped immensely by a comprehensive and critical engagement with both the text as "other" and with "others" regarding their constructions of the text. First, an understanding of the text as an "other" demands critical engagement with it—a thorough evaluation of its world, strategy, and applicability in terms of the reader's own historical and cultural context; the goal of such an engagement is none other than that of liberation itself. Second, in attempting to understand the text as an "other" to us, it is necessary to understand as well how the text has been interpreted by "others," by readers in a variety of different historical situations and cultural frameworks. Such an understanding also demands critical engagement with these "others"—a thorough evaluation of reading strategies, theoretical orientations, social locations, as well as interpretive results, reception, and aftereffects; again, the goal of such an engagement is none other than liberation itself.

Such then are the essential characteristics of the envisioned hermeneutic of otherness and engagement and the basic principles for its proposed reading strategy of intercultural criticism. In conclusion, this Hispanic American hermeneutic is one with a manifest destiny of liberation: It begins with and aims for contextualization, and it seeks not to overwhelm or override the other but rather to acknowledge it, respect it, and engage it. Furthermore, intercultural criticism is not advanced as the sole and definitive Hispanic American strategy for reading but rather as one strategy among many, with a similar dream and task of liberation in mind.

BIBLIOGRAPHY

Elizondo, Virgilo. *Galilean Journey: The Mexican-American Promise.* Maryknoll: Orbis, 1983.

González, Justo L. *Mañana: Christian Theology from a Hispanic Perspective.* Nashville: Abingdon, 1990.

_____. *Out of Every Tribe and Nation: Christian Theology at the Ethnic Roundtable.* Nashville: Abingdon, 1992.

Isasi-Díaz, Ada María. "The Bible and *Mujerista* Theology." In *Lift Every Voice: Constructing Theologies from the Underside.* Edited by Susan Brooks Thistlethwaite and Mary Potter Engel. San Francisco: Harper & Row, 1990.

Leitch, Vincent B. *American Literary Criticism from the Thirties to the Eighties.* New York: Columbia University Press, 1988.

Recinos, Harold J. *Hear the Cry! A Latino Pastor Challenges the Church.* Louisville: Westminster/John Knox, 1989.

_____. *Jesus Weeps: Global Encounters on Our Doorstep.* Nashville: Abingdon, 1992.

Romero, C. Gilbert. "Tradition and Symbols as Biblical Keys for a U.S. Hispanic Theology." In *Frontiers of Hispanic Theology in the United States.* Edited by Allan Figueroa Deck. Maryknoll, N.Y.: Orbis, 1992.

Rosaldo, Renato. *Culture and Truth: The Remaking of Social Analysis.* Boston: Beacon, 1989.

Segovia, Fernando F. "Hispanic American Theology and the Bible: Effective Weapon and Faithful Ally." In *We Are A People! Initiatives in Hispanic American Theology.* Edited by Roberto S. Goizueta. Minneapolis: Fortress, 1992.

_____. "A New Manifest Destiny: The Emerging Theological Voice of Hispanic Americans." *Religious Studies Review* 17 (1991) 101-9.

_____. "The Text as Other: Towards a Hispanic American Hermeneutics." In *Reading from This Place. Social Location and Biblical Interpretation: The American Scene.* Edited by Fernando F. Segovia and Mary Ann Tolbert. Minneapolis: Fortress, forthcoming.

_____. "Two Places and No Place on Which to Stand: Mixture and Otherness in Hispanic American Theology." *Listening: A Journal of Religion and Culture* 27 (1992) 26-40.

Suleiman, Susan R. "Introduction." In *The Reader in the Text: Essays on Audience and Interpretation.* Edited by Susan R. Suleiman. Princeton: Princeton University Press, 1980.

Tompkins, Jane P. "An Introduction to Reader-Response Criticism." In *Reader-Response Criticism: From Formalism to Post-Structuralism.* Edited by Jane P. Tompkins. Baltimore: Johns Hopkins University Press, 1990.

READING THE BIBLE AS NATIVE AMERICANS

GEORGE E. TINKER

A Native American reading of the Bible presents an interesting challenge to the predominant, Eurocentric tradition of biblical scholarship. Western biblical scholarship has long struggled with the task of accurately and adequately translating a text from one language to another. Since languages are never simply codes for one another, there are always things one can say clearly in one language that may not be able to be said at all in another language. More recently, scholars have begun to understand that their task also includes the greater difficulty of translating from one culture into another culture. The lack of this understanding necessarily caused Christian missionaries, with the best of intentions, to function so genocidally with respect to Native American cultures.[1] Today we are beginning to gain some clarity about the cultural otherness of the biblical text and, more important, the cultural otherness of exegesis and interpretation for modern readers.

A Native American reading of the Bible will differ from usual Euro-American interpretations on at least three counts. First, the theological function of the Old Testament (OT) in a Native American context will differ. Second, the sociopolitical context of Native American peoples will characteristically generate interpretations that are particularly Native American. Moreover, the discrete cultural particu-

larities of cognitive structures among Native Americans will necessarily generate "normatively divergent" readings of Scripture.

THE IMPOSITION OF A FOREIGN HISTORY

There is, of course, an initial theological issue with respect to the role of the OT in a Native American context. Many Native American Christian congregations will give considerable prominence to the OT. The nature of OT narrative is far more compatible with Native American narrative traditions than, for instance, the discursive style of New Testament (NT) epistolary literature. At the same time, because of the surviving narrative traditions of many Native American communities, a theological problem is inherent in any attempt to accord the same status to the OT that it receives in Euro-American church communities.

Each Native American tribal community in North America had a relationship with God as Creator that was healthy and responsible long before they knew of or confessed the gospel of Jesus Christ. That relationship with Creator was solidified in the stories they told around the camp fires, in their prayers, and especially in their ceremonies. Many Native American Christians today would claim their own histories, cultural traditions, narratives, and traditional

1. See G. E. Tinker, *Missionary Conquest: The Gospel and Native American Genocide* (Minneapolis: Fortress, 1993).

174

ceremonies as the appropriate traditional covenant (old testament) for their communities.

The imposition of the Hebrew Bible on Native American Christians as an old testament functions in two dysfunctional ways in Native American communities. First, it functions to proscribe (explicitly or implicitly) the validity of Native American traditions. Second, it inherently prescribes replacing one's own history with someone else's history as a prerequisite for conversion.

SOCIOPOLITICAL CONTEXT AND A NATIVE AMERICAN HERMENEUTIC

The sociopolitical context of imperial Europe generated a colonial conquest interpretation of the Exodus account. This interpretation provided inspiration to John Winthrop and the seventeenth-century Puritan conquerors of New England, who consistently saw themselves as a New Israel settling in a new promised land. Nineteenth-century German imperialism, along with the prominence of German exegetical research continuing into the twentieth century, gave rise to conquest exegesis that has influenced most if not all Euro-American scholarship. More recently, Gottwald and others, under the influence of Marxist socialism, have argued for a "peasant revolt" paradigm for interpreting the same event.[2] Both interpretations are problematic for Native American readers.

As Warrior has demonstrated, the Israelite conquest has little historical affinity with the Native American experience. To the contrary, the closest analogy to Native American history in the OT seems to be the experience of the Canaanites, dispossessed of their land and annihilated by a foreign invader. In Native American eyes, the liberation of Israel is inexorably linked to the conquest and destruction of the Canaanites. For the same reason, the peasant revolt model has no affinity with Native American experience.[3] Moreover, Native American cultures traditionally knew nothing of such class distinctions that resulted historically in Europe in a classification of peoples as peasants. While the revolt paradigm

has some superficial appeal because of the more egalitarian nature of Native American communities, the Marxist inclination to overlook or deny cultural distinctions in favor of an imposed, classless social homogenization is antithetical to Native American social thought.[4]

NATIVE AMERICAN CULTURE AND COGNITIVE STRUCTURES

The third difference in a Native American reading of the Bible has to do with more fundamental differences in the structures of cognition in a culturally discrete community. Even when scholars more fully understand the task of translating languages and cultures, they must knowingly take the risk of mistranslating. The risk is not that they may have failed to understand the other culture or language, but that they are not fully aware of their own foundational cultural presuppositions. Those presuppositions are the foundational metaphors of existence, which become formative for thought processes and out of which evolve the discursive category system of every discrete cultural community.

The distinction between temporal and spatial as foundational cognitive categories provides us with an example that distinguishes Native American from Euro-American thought. Further, the application of the spatial as a Native American hermeneutical principle can clarify a particularly creational interpretation of the βασιλεια του θεου (*basileia tou theou,* Kingdom of God).

Spatiality and Creation as Hermeneutical Principles. The spatial orientation of Native American peoples, and their spiritual and political attachment to place and land, is well noted in the literature.[5] As a corollary to this spatial orientation, Native American religious thought begins with some sense of creation. Likewise, the most

2. See Norman K. Gottwald, *Tribes of Yahweh: A Sociology of the Religion of Liberated Israel* (Maryknoll, N.Y.: Orbis, 1979).

3. Robert Warrior, "Canaanites, Cowboys and Indians: Deliverance, Conquest, and Liberation Theology Today," *Christianity and Crisis* 4, 9 (1989) 261-65.

4. G. Tinker, "Spirituality, Native American Personhood, Sovereignty and Solidarity," *Ecumenical Review* 44 (1992) 312-24; Glenn T. Morris and Ward Churchill, "Between a Rock and a Hard Place: Left-Wing Revolution, Right-Wing Reaction and the Destruction of Indigenous People," *Cultural Survival Quarterly* 11 (1987) 17-24.

5. Vine Deloria, Jr., *God Is Red* (New York: Dell, 1973); and *The Metaphysics of Modern Existence* (New York: Harper & Row, 1979); Ward Churchill, "The Earth Is Our Mother: Struggles for American Indian Land and Liberation in the Contemporary United States," in *The State of Native America,* Annette Jaimes, ed. (Boston: South End, 1992) 139-88; G. Tinker, "Native Americans and the Land: The End of Living and the Beginning of Survival," *Word and World* 6 (1986) 66-74; and "American Indians and the Arts of the Land: Spatial Metaphors and Contemporary Existence," *Voices from the Third World: 1990* (Sri Lanka: EATWOT, 1991) 170-93.

THE NEW INTERPRETER'S BIBLE

successful appropriations of Christianity and the Bible by Native Americans interpret both from a referential perspective on creation.

Creation, in a Native American context, is an ongoing eschatological act and not just God's initiatory act. A Native American Christian hermeneutic will press toward seeing Creation as the eschatological basis even for the Christ-event. If this is difficult, it may be so because the Western cultures in which the gospel has traditionally come to find a home are so fundamentally oriented toward temporality and so disoriented toward spatiality. As a result, all of the categories of analytical discourse in the Western intellectual tradition function out of a temporal base and pervade our understanding of all reality.[6] This, then, characterizes both Euro-American theologies and especially how key biblical themes and texts are interpreted.

The fact that all Native American spiritual insights, and hence theology, must begin with Creation is reflected already in the basic liturgical posture of members of many North American tribes. Prayers are most often said with the community assembled into some form of circle—the circle being a key symbol for self-understanding in these tribes, representing as it does the whole of the universe and our part in it. All see themselves as co-equal participants in the circle, standing neither above nor below anything else in God's Creation. There is little sense of hierarchy in this cultural context, even of species, because the circle has no beginning or end. Hence all the "createds" (two-leggeds, four-leggeds, wingeds, and living, moving ones) participate together, each in its own way, to preserve the wholeness of the circle. It is important to note that the formation of the circle is itself prayer, a prayer for the harmony and balance of creation, and in some ceremonies no words need be spoken.

The Lakota and Dakota peoples have a phrase used in all their prayers that aptly illustrates the Native American sense of the centrality of creation. *Mitakuye oyasin* functions somewhat like the word *amen* in European and American Christianity. As such, it is used to end every prayer, and often it is in itself a whole prayer, being the only phrase spoken. The usual translation offered is: "For all my relations." Yet, like most Native American symbols, *mitakuye oyasin* is polyvalent in its meaning. Certainly, one is praying for one's close kin, aunts, cousins, children, grandparents, etc. "Relations" can be understood as fellow tribal members or even all Indian people. At the same time, the phrase includes all human beings, all two-leggeds as relatives of one another, and the ever-expanding circle does not stop there. Every Native American who prays this prayer knows that his or her relatives necessarily include the four-leggeds, the wingeds, and all the living, moving ones, including trees, rocks, and mountains.

Perhaps one can begin to understand the extensive image of interrelatedness and interdependence symbolized by the circle and the importance of reciprocity and respect for one another for maintaining the wholeness of the circle. The Native American concern for starting theology with Creation is a need to acknowledge the goodness and inherent worth of all of God's creatures. We experience evil or sin as a disruption in that delicate balance, which negates the intrinsic worth of any of our relatives.

A Native American Interpretation of basileia. A comparison of a Native American interpretation of the *basileia* with those generally proposed by Western biblical scholars provides us with an example of how the Native American hermeneutical principles of creation and spatiality might function.[7] The Euro-American scholarly discussion for the last century has been predicated on an intuitive assumption of a fundamental cross-cultural sameness when otherness may have been the case. In particular, a Native American reading begins with a primarily spatial understanding of the *basileia* as opposed to a predominantly temporal understanding argued by Western biblical scholarship. In the Native American world of spatiality, then, it is natural to read *basileia tou theou* as a creation metaphor.

As it stands in the Greek, or even in literal English translation, the "kingdom" metaphor is radically disjunctive for any Native American hearer quite beyond the inherent sexism of the usual "kingdom" translation. Of course, few North American hearers have any experiential analogues for understanding

---

6. So argues Robert A. Nisbet, *Social Change and History: Aspects of the Western Theory of Development* (London: Oxford University Press, 1969). While Nisbet rightly sees temporality as important for understanding all Western culture, he finds this aspect to be wholly positive. I, of course, find it problematic.

7. For a fuller treatment of this example, see Marie-Therese Archambault and G. Tinker, "A Native American Interpretation of Basileia tou Theou," paper delivered at the Cassassa Conference on Cultural Exegesis, at Loyola Marymount University, Los Angeles, California, April 1992. Publication of proceedings forthcoming from Sheffield University Press, Daniel L. Smith-Christopher, ed.

the political referent for this phrase, and it must be disjunctive for all except as religious language that has taken on symbolic value quite apart from the original meaning of the word in first-century Palestine. For Native American peoples, who come out of communities that are more egalitarian, genuinely democratic, and participatory, the metaphor must be completely recast. The only possible analogue for the notion of *basileia* might be the Bureau of Indian Affairs or the U.S. War Department.

Since the emergence of eschatology as a central aspect of the interpretation of the NT, especially the critical interpretation of the Gospels in the work of Johannes Weis and Albert Schweitzer,[8] until very recently the *basileia tou theou* has been given over completely to temporal interpretations.[9] That is, the only appropriate question to ask about the *basileia* has been When? It is not that scholars did not consider other possibilities, but in fact, the question Where? has been consistently disallowed. Norman Perrin spoke for some seventy years of scholarly dialogue in Europe and North America when he wrote in 1967 that the *basileia* "is not a place or community ruled by God."[10] From Weis and Schweitzer to Perrin and beyond, the question had been When will the *basileia tou theou* happen? When will it appear? In the course of the dialogue, a wide variety of answers has been argued, each generating a new technical term to label the theory. So we have argued between "realized eschatology," "actualized eschatology," "immanent eschatology," and "future eschatology."

In the mid 1970s, Norman Perrin and his student Werner Kelber announced a major shift in the interpretation of *basileia*. Kelber first put forth arguments for a consistent spatial understanding of the *basileia* in the Gospel of Mark, linking its meaning to expanding territorial or geographical developments in that Gospel.[11] Perrin decisively articulated the metaphoric nature of *basileia* language, distinguishing between "steno" and "tensive" symbols and identi-

fying *basileia* as the latter. So we now can begin to understand the *basileia tou theou* as a "symbol," which Perrin defines with Wheelwright as "a relatively stable and repeatable element of perceptual experience, standing for some larger meaning or set of meanings which cannot be given, or not fully given in perceptual experience itself."[12]

It seems obvious enough that spatial categories do not necessarily exclude the temporal, nor vice versa. Yet the orientation assumed by the interpreter becomes crucial. As Boring argued, temporality cannot be excised from Mark's proclamation of the *basileia*, yet to assume that the *basileia* sayings in Mark must be read in terms of an "overwhelming temporal orientation" is surely an overstatement of the case.[13] On the contrary, there exists the possibility of spatial priority in language of the *basileia*, perhaps in Mark particularly. That possibility becomes pronounced in any Native American reading of the text, because the American Indian world is as decidedly spatial in its orientation as the modern Western world is temporal in its orientation. In fact, any Indian reader of Mark or the Synoptics is bound to think first of all in terms of the question Where? with regard to *basileia*.[14]

A Native American spatial interpretation raises the possibility that Western biblical scholarship has worked for a century with a transcultural blind spot. Why, after all, would the kingdom of God not be a realm or a place where God rules or a community that God rules? What we have here are two very different ways of thinking, of seeing the world, of sorting out reality. Western biblical scholarship has developed a system of discourse that has become dominant and highly differentiated, and many affected by that system may have no immediate way of acknowledging those who think differently.

The argument here is that those two different ways of thinking have to do with time and space, the when and the where of the *basileia* in Mark.

8. J. Weis, *Die Predigt Jesu von Reich Gottes* (1892); A. Schweitzer, *Das Abendmahl in Zusammenhang mit dem Leben Jesu und der Geschichte des Urchristentums* (1901) and *Von Reimarus zu Wrede: Eine Geschichte der Leben-Jesu-Forschung* (1906).

9. See Bruce Chilton, ed., *The Kingdom of God in the Teaching of Jesus* (Minneapolis: Fortress, 1984); and Wendell Willis, ed., *The Kingdom of God in 20th Century Interpretation* (Peabody, Mass.: Hendrickson, 1987).

10. Norman Perrin, *Rediscovering the Teaching of Jesus* (New York: Harper & Row, 1967) 55.

11. W. Kelber, *The Kingdom in Mark: A New Place and a New Time* (Minneapolis: Fortress, 1974).

12. N. Perrin, *Jesus and the Language of the Kingdom: Symbol and Metaphor in New Testament Interpretation* (Minneapolis: Fortress, 1976) 30. See also Philip Wheelwright, *Metaphor and Reality* (Bloomington: Indiana University Press: 1962) 92.

13. M. Eugene Boring, "The Kingdom of God in Mark," in Willis, *The Kingdom of God in 20th Century Interpretation,* 140.

14. Realizing that the metaphor presents problems to modern readers, many scholars have attempted to offer new translations, emphasizing the resulting relationship between believer and God or emphasizing, as Perrin did originally, the activity of God as King. The most common translation offered is "Reign of God," which Bultmann uses throughout his *Theology of the New Testament*. On the other hand, the translation "Realm of God" is consistently disallowed as an unthinkable translation, because it would introduce spatiality unto the discussion.

Space and time are not necessarily two equal coordinates in human thinking. On the contrary, one is usually primary and the other secondary for any given culture. Native Americans tend to think out of a spatial viewpoint. Space is primary for them, and their most fundamental and powerful images, metaphors, and myths have to do primarily with space and places. For the Western intellectual tradition, the opposite is demonstrably the case; time is primary and space is a subordinate category.[15] From notions of progress to the casual revelation that "time is money," from the sacred hour on Sunday morning to the seven-day cycle of work, play, and spiritual obligation, according to the philosophical and scientific inquiry of the West, time always reigns supreme. Think what the world might be like if Heidegger had written *Being and Space* instead of *Being and Time,* or if Hegel had not had at his disposal the temporal categories that generated his philosophy of history in terms of thesis, antithesis, synthesis. Charles Darwin built on temporal modalities in thinking through his *On the Origin of the Species,* and Western theoretical physicists developed the same temporal modalities in ways that enabled Albert Einstein to reduce the whole of the physical world to temporal categories. From this perspective in Western thought, all of space becomes a mere function of time. It is no wonder that the *basileia tou theou* is also discussed consistently as a function of time.

Mark and Spatiality. This Native American hermeneutic of spatiality might be seen as normatively divergent—i.e., an aberrant cultural reading of the *basileia.* Yet, the Gospel of Mark has other clear indications of attention to issues of spatiality. In Mark 10:46-52, Jesus is coming out of Jericho where a blind beggar, Bartimaeus, cries out to him for help. The important words here have to do with where Bartimaeus is sitting and where he is to go afterward. He is sitting παρὰ τὴν ὁδόν (*para tēn hodon*), "beside the roadside" or "by the highway" or "by the way." After the healing, Bartimaeus is told by Jesus to leave ὕπαγε (*hypage,* "to return home"). Instead, Bartimaeus "follows" Jesus—a discipleship word—ἐν τῇ ὁδῷ (*en tē hodō,* "on the way"). The word ὁδός (*hodos*) is used in both places, yet in all English translations there is a consistent tendency to translate the Greek word differently in

each case, losing what might be Mark's intentional play on that word. To wit, the healing of Bartimaeus comes at the end of the section beginning with the healing of a blind person in chapter 8. In between these two literary parentheses of two healings of blind people, we have just been told that the disciples who followed Jesus, even though their eyes appear to be open, are really blind. Bartimaeus, it turns out, has a greater claim to sight than do the Twelve. Bartimaeus, who had been sitting "by the way," who had not been following Jesus, now has a better claim to follow Jesus "on the way." Is it possible that "the way" here is a techincal term spelling out or pointing to the spatial bases of Mark's thinking?

The word *hodos* occurs also at the beginning of the Gospel in the quote from Malachi, and may already be a coded word in that context: "See, I am sending my messenger ahead of you, who will prepare your way" (Mark 1:2 NRSV). Is this notion of spatiality consistently there all the way through Mark? What would this possibility mean for our interpretation of the kingdom of God in Mark?

Any Native American reader would naturally think of *hodos* in these verses as the Red Road, the Good Way, the Way of Life. In much of Plains Indian culture, two lines inscribed in a circle to form a balanced cross are used to symbolize not only the four directions but also Plains Indian ethics. They symbolize the choice each person must make between the Good Road and the Road of Difficulties, the road of community wholeness versus the road of individual achievement, the Red Road and the Blue Road. Native people functioning within their own cultural frame of reference have little choice but to understand the Way in Mark as an ethical, spatial designation.[16]

Basileia as a Spatial Metaphor for Creation. A Native American spatial reading of the Gospels, then, must combine spatiality and creation, resulting in a reading that interprets *basileia tou theou* as a creation metaphor, imaging ideal harmony and balance. It represents a symbolic value whose parameters might be filled in as follows: (a) The Gospels seem to view the divine hegemony as something

---

15. For the priority of temporality in Western thought, see again Robert Nisbet, *Social Change and History.*

16. Lohmeyer and Lightfoot, although they were firmly committed to an eschatological interpretation, which was the fashion of the time, already saw geography as an important interpretive issue in the Gospels. See Ernst Lohmeyer, *Galiläa und Jerusalem* (Göttingen: Vandenhoeck and Ruprecht, 1936); and Robert H. Lightfoot, *Locality and Doctrine in the Gospels* (New York: Harper, 1938). The use of geography in the enigmatic ending of the Gospel becomes another indication of spatiality that might argue for a spatial interpretation of *basileia.*

that is in process. It is drawing near; it is emerging (Mark 1:15). Yet it is also "among us," in our midst (Luke 17). It is something that can be experienced by the faithful here and now, even if only proleptically, with its full emergence still in the future. (b) The symbolic value captured by the imagery in no small part includes a view of an ideal world. Finally, (c) the structural definition of that ideal world is, above all else, relational and spatial.

The imagery of divine rule in the OT is essentially Creation imagery. That is, the ideal world symbolically represented in the OT image builds on the divine origin of the cosmos as an ideal past and points to an ideal future. To this extent, the ideal world is the real world of creation in an ideal relationship of harmony and balance with the Creator. It is relational, first of all, because it implies a relationship between the created order of things and its Creator, and, second, because it implies a relationship between all of the things created. As Creator, God is perforce the rightful ruler of all. Hence, the ideal world to which Jesus points in the Gospels is precisely the realization of that proper relationship between the Creator and the created in the real, spatial world of creation.

For a Native American reader, whether human beings were created first (Genesis 2) or last (Genesis 1) of all the created is not nearly as important as affirming the harmony and balance of the created order. While the balance of that order has been shaken by the human createds, it is still the ideal state toward which all look forward in Christ Jesus. While the ideal state of balance and harmony can never be achieved for all time, all (including all of creation) are part of the ongoing process of restoring balance. As Paul says, all of Creation groans in travail, in childbirth (Rom 8:22).

In this Native American interpretation, the *basileia* must be understood as all-inclusive. If it symbolizes the harmony and balance of all creation, then it must include all things created. In a Native American anthropology, consistent with the prayer of *mitakuye oyasin,* the *basileia* must include two-leggeds, four-leggeds, wingeds, and the living, moving ones, since all are created by the same creative force. Perforce, then, it is inclusive of all human beings, whether all recognize the divine hegemony or not. Those who are seen as standing outside the kingdom are outside because they have somehow excluded themselves in their lack of recognition,

perhaps attempting to establish their own hegemony instead.

Removing the Euro-American emphasis of temporality, of course, lessens the emphasis on eschatology. In a Native American reading, the *basileia* has less to do with what happens in the future than how one images oneself in the present in relationship to the Creator and the rest of creation.

Repentance as a Spatial Notion of Return. In Mark 1:15 the *basileia* is linked with the imperative, μετανοεῖτε (*metanoeite,* "repent!"). It is helpful to acknowledge the cyclical, seasonal nature of the word καιρός (*kairos*) as used in the verse, as over against the more linear concept of χρόνος (*chronos*),[17] so that Mark's mention of a time element does not distract us from a spatial understanding to which attention has been directed. Nor at this point is it necessary to elaborate on the verb ἤγγικεν (*ēggiken,* "has drawn near"), which has both spatial and temporal connotations.

More important to a Native American reading of that text is a spatial understanding of *metanoiete.* Here, the underlying Aramaic (spatial) sense of שׁוּב (*šûb*) as "return" rather than the Greek notion of "change of mind" is at stake. Repentance is key to the establishment of divine hegemony because it involves a "return"—namely, a return to God. Feeling sorry for one's sins is not a part of repentance at all, though it may be the initial act of confession. Even in the most "Greek" of the Gospel writers, in Luke's Acts of the Apostles, repentance is not a penitential emotion but instead carries the Hebrew sense of return. In Acts 2:37-38, people feel penitential emotion as a result of Peter's sermon and come to him to ask what they must do. His response is to say: "Repent and be baptized." Since they already feel sorry for their sins, that is not what Peter requires of them. The Hebrew notion of repentance really is calling on God's people to recognize the divine hegemony, to return to God, to return to the ideal relationship between Creator and the created, to live in the spatiality of creation fully cognizant of God's hegemony, of human createdness, and of the

---

17. If Mark is, indeed, talking about cyclical time, we ought to consider the notion that he does not have in mind some linear progression of history such as what Western scholars have called in the past forty or fifty years the history of salvation, with its mid-point being the birth, the life, and the death of Jesus. That has been most explicitly spelled out by Hans Conzelmann in a book about the Gospel of Luke, titled *Die Mitte der Zeit,* loosely translated into English as *The Theology of St. Luke* (New York: Harper, 1960). For a more general treatment, see Oscar Conzelmann, *Salvation in History* (New York: Harper, 1967).

interrelatedness of all the createds. In the Native American world, we recognize that interrelatedness as a peer relationship between the two-leggeds and all the others: four leggeds, wingeds, and living, moving things. That is the real world within which we hope to actualize the ideal world of balance and harmony.

The Native American understanding of Creation as sacred, of Grandmother Earth as the source of all life, goes far beyond the concerns articulated by various environmental groups. It embraces far more than concern for harp seals or a couple of ice-bound whales. It embraces all of life from trees and rocks to international relations. And this knowledge informs all of the community's activity, from hunting to dancing and even to writing grant proposals or administering government agencies. It especially concerns itself with the way we all live together. It has to do with issues of justice and fairness in the community, and ultimately with peace. If one takes seriously the spatiality of *basileia* as a metaphor for Creation and the interrelationship of all the createds under Creator's hegemony, then it becomes very difficult to pursue acts of exploitation or oppression of others. The reciprocity of male and female in both Creator and creation necessitates a repentance (return) to relationships of balance. It mandates a model of *basileia* that obviates male-female oppression and the resulting power imbalances. Competition between human communities is replaced by cooperation or at least mutual respect. Even environmental devastation is necessarily impeded under the paradigm of *mitakuye oyasin,* because mutual respect and cooperation are then seen as extended beyond the foolish nation of two-leggeds to include all the four-legged, winged, and living, moving relatives, even the trees and hills and the earth itself.

These examples begin to articulate something of a Native American reading of the Bible. The fact that this reading of the *basileia* may be quite disparate from standard Euro-American interpretations should also signal that in a multicultural, pluralistic world of diversity there will necessarily be many readings of the Bible. Normative interpretation, a valid hermeneutic, demands something more than the limited system of Western biblical scholarship.

BIBLIOGRAPHY

Chilton, Bruce, ed. *The Kingdom of God in the Teaching of Jesus.* Minneapolis: Fortress, 1984.

Churchill, Ward. "The Earth Is Our Mother: Struggles for American Indian Land and Liberation in the Contemporary United States." In *The State of Native America,* Annette Jaimes, ed. (Boston: South End Press, 1992) 139-88.

Deloria, Vine, Jr. *God Is Red.* New York: Dell, 1973.

————. *The Metaphysics of Modern Existence.* New York: Harper & Row, 1979.

Morris, Glenn T., and Ward Churchill. "Between a Rock and a Hard Place: Left-Wing Revolution, Right-Wing Reaction and the Destruction of Indigenous People," *Cultural Survival Quarterly* 11 (1987) 17-24.

Tinker, G. E. "American Indians and the Arts of the Land: Spatial Metaphors and Contemporary Existence." In *Voices from the Third World: 1990.* Sri Lanka: EATWOT, 1991.

————. *Missionary Conquest: The Gospel and Native American Genocide.* Minneapolis: Fortress, 1993.

————. "Native Americans and the Land: The End of Living and the Beginning of Survival," *Word and World* 6 (1986) 66-74.

————. "Spirituality, Native American Personhood, Sovereignty and Solidarity," *Ecumenical Review* 44 (1992) 312-24.

Warrior, Robert. "Canaanites, Cowboys and Indians: Deliverance, Conquest, and Liberation Theology Today," *Christianity and Crisis* 4, 9 (1989) 261-65.

Willis, Wendell, ed. *The Kingdom of God in 20th Century Interpretation.* Peabody, Mass.: Hendrickson, 1987.

READING THE BIBLE AS WOMEN

CAROLYN OSIEK

Do women read the Bible differently from men? To judge from recent studies on gender differences, the answer must be yes, since such studies indicate that, based on the differences of socialization and experience due to gender, women generally interpret their world differently than do men.[1]

Since the middle of the nineteenth century there has been a growing awareness on the part of some women that our very devotion to the Bible has put us in a conflictive situation and that the Bible itself is partly responsible for the ambiguity and even outright oppression we suffer in societies that claim the Bible as their moral and creedal foundation. The origins of modern religious feminism in America have often been traced in recent years, so they need not be repeated here, except to acknowledge that women like Elizabeth Cady Stanton, Sarah Grimké, Angelina Grimké, and Frances Willard were consciously engaged with the problems of biblical interpretation and discrimination. They read their Bible as women, took it seriously enough to struggle with it, and even, assuming the received text and its interpretation to be that of men, published a new version from their reading, *The Woman's Bible.*[2]

RECENT HISTORY OF WOMEN'S BIBLICAL INTERPRETATION

With the rediscovery and growing popularity of religious feminism in the middle of the twentieth century, there was a surge of new interest in how women relate to the Bible and in how women are represented in it. Some of the leading early efforts were done by men, an indication that women as biblical theologians were not at first granted the credibility they deserved. Work done in the late 1960s and early 1970s concentrated on text-based studies and was less methodologically self-conscious than would be the case today. The approach tended to be "the role of women in. . . . " Thus, for example, Krister Stendahl's *The Bible and the Role of Women* was a landmark. Written originally in Swedish in 1958 as a contribution to the question of the

---

1. See, for example, Elaine Showalter, "Feminist Criticism in the Wilderness," in *The New Feminist Criticism: Essays on Women, Literature, and Theory* (New York: Pantheon, 1985) 243-70; Elizabeth A. Flynn and Patrocinio P. Schweickart, eds., *Gender and Reading: Essays on Readers, Texts, and Contexts* (Baltimore: Johns Hopkins, 1986); Judith Spector, ed., *Gender Studies: New Directions in Feminist Criticism* (Bowling Green: Bowling Green State University Press, 1986).

2. For an excellent summary of their story, see Carolyn De Swarte Gifford, "American Women and the Bible: The Nature of Woman as a Hermeneutical Issue," in Adela Yarbro Collins, ed., *Feminist Perspectives on Biblical Scholarship* (Chico, Calif.: Scholars Press, 1985) 11-33 and works suggested there; see also C. Newsom and S. Ringe, eds., *The Women's Bible Commentary* (Louisville: Westminster/John Knox, 1992) xiii-xix.

ordination of women in the Church of Sweden, it was published in English eight years later.[3]

But a more explicitly feminist critique was already entering into the dialogue and developed more fully in the mid-1970s. Questions like "Was Jesus a feminist?" and "Was Paul a chauvinist?" were being discussed. For example, Leonard Swidler's "Jesus Was a Feminist" (1971) was followed in 1972–1974 by the published dialogue between Robin Scroggs and Elaine Pagels on "Paul and the Eschatological Woman," an ongoing discussion of the intentions behind some of the difficult Pauline passages about women.[4] Even earlier, women biblical scholars were beginning to analyze the difficult biblical texts about women with the tools of historical criticism.[5]

In the late 1970s to mid-1980s, feminist scholars began using more than the traditional historical-critical methods of interpretation, adding the newer hermeneutical tools of literary criticism and liberation theology. Phyllis Trible's *God and the Rhetoric of Sexuality* and *Texts of Terror: Literary-Feminist Readings of Biblical Narrative*[6] indicated that a new wave of women's biblical interpretation was on the way. From that point on, traditional ways of reading biblical narratives, like the Genesis creation account, in such a way as to use them for exclusion or oppression of women would no longer be tenable. At the same time came feminist critical reconstructions with a consciously liberationist methodology adapted to the special situation of women, as exemplified in Elisabeth Schüssler Fiorenza's groundbreaking *In Memory of Her: A Feminist Theological Reconstruction of Christian Origins.*[7] It was no longer enough to look at the roles of women in the Bible or the early church, or to employ only the traditional tools of historical criticism, though they remained necessary foundations. Now feminist biblical theologians were using new hermeneutical methods in an explicitly feminist way. Words like *androcentrism* (the social normativity of the male) and *patriarchy* (the rule of male elders) began to be accepted terminology to describe the situation in which women found themselves in the biblical world—as well as in Western society ever since.

The period of the late 1980s has seen a blossoming of new insights and approaches. The question was more consciously asked: How did ancient women themselves hear and respond to the biblical message in their own context? The very different tools of archaeology and rhetorical criticism are currently being better used to this end. For instance, Carol Meyers employed archaeology and social history to reconstruct the lives of Israelite women in *Discovering Eve: Ancient Israelite Women in Context.*[8] Lillian Portefaix's *Sisters Rejoice: Paul's Letter to the Philippians and Luke-Acts as Read by First-Century Philippian Women* used both archaeology and rhetorical criticism to understand the religious experience of the first-century Philippian women whom Paul would have encountered in his missionary efforts.[9] In addition, Antoinette Wire's *The Corinthian Women Prophets: A Reconstruction Through Paul's Rhetoric* was a rhetorical study of 1 Corinthians with a view to reconstructing the other side of the argument, especially that of the Corinthian women whom Paul was trying to control.[10] An extensive study of biblical women's experience from the social-science perspective has yet to be written.

Still another important aspect of women's relationship to the Bible was being raised to general consciousness through these years. Earlier feminist theologians, mostly white middle-class, were made aware by the emerging voice of minority-group feminists that their claims to speak for "women's experience" were in fact a female version of the same white male dominance that had always been present. African American and Hispanic American female voices began to articulate their different experiences of patriarchy. African American writers like Renita Weems and Clarice Martin have probed the double experience of oppression of being a black

3. K. Stendahl, *The Bible and the Role of Women* (Philadelphia: Fortress, 1966).

4. L. Swidler, "Jesus Was a Feminist," *Catholic World* (Jan. 1971) 177-83; R. Scroggs, "Paul and the Eschatological Woman," *JAAR* 40 (1972) 283-303; "Paul and the Eschatological Woman: Revisited," *JAAR* 42 (1974) 532-37; E. Pagels, "Paul and Women: A Response to Recent Discussion," *JAAR* 42 (1974) 538-49.

5. See articles by M. Kathleen Lane, Winsome Munro, and Martha M. Wilson in *Women and Religion: Proceedings; Working Group on Women and Religion,* ed. Judith Plaskow Goldenberg (Waterloo, Ont.: AAR, 1973).

6. P. Trible, *God and the Rhetoric of Sexuality,* Overtures to Biblical Theology (Philadelphia: Fortress, 1978); *Texts of Terror: Literary-Feminist Readings of Biblical Narrative,* Overtures to Biblical Theology (Philadelphia: Fortress, 1984).

7. E. Schüssler Fiorenza, *In Memory of Her: A Feminist Theological Reconstruction of Christian Origins* (New York: Crossroad, 1983).

8. C. Meyers, *Discovering Eve: Ancient Israelite Women in Context* (New York: Oxford University Press, 1988).

9. L. Portefaix, *Sisters Rejoice: Paul's Letter to the Philippians and Luke-Acts as Read by First-Century Philippian Women* (Uppsala: Almqvist & Wiksell, 1988).

10. A. Wire, *The Corinthian Women Prophets: A Reconstruction Through Paul's Rhetoric* (Minneapolis: Fortress, 1990).

woman seeking to live a biblical faith. Hispanic writers like Ada María Isasi-Díaz and Yolanda Tarango have reminded us that the view is different from a macho culture burdened with the effects of centuries of colonialism.[11]

The year 1992 marked the appearance of the first complete one-volume biblical commentary written expressly *by* women *for* women from a feminist perspective.[12] Studies about biblical women continue to abound, such that a full bibliographic survey cannot be attempted here. However, it has become clear that the feminist perspective in biblical interpretation is no longer optional, nor is it a passing fad.

Perhaps the full integration of women into biblical interpretation will occur only when it is no longer necessary to publish special studies about women, no longer necessary to include paragraphs and sections about women in major studies and commentaries, because the consideration of women will have been so well included that it is no longer meaningful to single us out for attention. But such a time remains in the future. At present, the deeply rooted androcentrism of our interpretation is still revealed in the way that general statements about aspects of culture and history are assumed to be generic, when in fact they often refer only to men. Women are meant to identify with assertions about the male world, which is presented as the norm, and have been doing it for so long that it takes a critical consciousness to break the habit. On the other hand, men are not expected to identify with assertions about the female world, which is a subset of "reality." Biblical theologians from developing countries and ethnic minorities have made us aware that African American exegesis, liberation exegesis, etc., are considered specialized branches of a generic tree, "exegesis," which is supposedly bias-free. In reality, this "exegesis" is white, middle-class, North American, and Northern European. It is also male.

11. See Renita J. Weems, "Reading *Her Way* Through the Struggle: African American Women and the Bible," in *Stony the Road We Trod: African American Biblical Interpretation,* ed. Cain Hope Felder (Minneapolis: Fortress, 1991) 57-97; Clarice Martin, "The *Haustafeln* (Household Codes) in African American Biblical Interpretation: 'Free Slaves' and 'Subordinate Women,' " in ibid., 206-31; Ada María Isasi-Díaz and Yolanda Tarango, *Hispanic Women: Prophetic Voice in the Church.* San Francisco: Harper & Row, 1988.

12. Newsom and Ringe, *The Women's Bible Commentary.*

CRUCIAL QUESTIONS AND SOME RESPONSES

Beyond the flourishing scholarship by women for women about biblical women that continues today, however, the fundamental questions remain, the questions that must be asked by every woman of biblical faith whose consciousness has been raised this far: Is the Bible redemptive for women? Taking the question a step further, is the Bible redeemable for women? There is an unavoidable problem with the foundational document of Jewish and Christian faith, in that it sometimes ignores women or treats us only as threats to men (androcentrism), sometimes expresses contempt and fear of us (misogynism), and sometimes treats us as dangerously ignorant beings that must be controlled (patriarchalism).

The Bible has been used throughout the centuries as authorization for the abuse, exploitation, and derision of women by men in the name of God. Does the problem lie only with the fallible and sinful biblical interpreters, including the many women who have acquiesced voluntarily to such treatment in the name of religion, or is the problem in the biblical text itself, to such an extent that it is unredeemable for a faith that proclaims the full equality of all persons? The dilemma was already clearly caught in the 1890s by Elizabeth Cady Stanton, who refused to attend a suffragist meeting that began with the hymn "Guide Us, O Thou Great Jehovah," because Jehovah had "never taken any active part in the suffrage movement."[13] Yet she went on to edit the ground-breaking *Woman's Bible,* demonstrating that even she could not reject the entire tradition, but still took the Bible seriously enough to work with it in whatever way possible to salvage its importance for women.

There is no clear answer to these questions, with which every biblical faith community and every female reader and interpreter must struggle. Women who do engage these questions answer them in varying ways. For some, the evidence of exploitation is so overwhelming that their own integrity leads them to painful separation from biblical communities into other forms of faith expression rooted in nonbiblical religious traditions. For them, the answer to the double question is a resounding, though

13. Quoted in Schüssler Fiorenza, *In Memory of Her,* 7.

often regretful, *no;* the Bible is neither redemptive nor capable of being redeemed for women.

For other women, the oppressive texts and historical and social realities about women in the Bible are not as significant as the feminine symbolism that appears in some key passages and seems to exalt femininity as an important aspect of theology: God's compassionate love of children, Israel and Jerusalem as the bride of God, wisdom as a feminine figure, the church as the bride of Christ, Jesus depicted as mother hen, the transcendent role of Mary. Both the relational quality of "the feminine" and its otherness in the patriarchal realm are important contributions to religion, without which it would be abandoned to rigidity and calcification. Here complementarity, not equality, is the issue.

For still other women, the problem lies not with the Bible but with its interpreters. In this case, the task of careful study and reinterpretation has only just begun. According to this way of thinking, biblical interpretation in church contexts must be purified of its biases about women that have allowed difficult biblical passages to be used in ways not intended by the authors to oppress or control women, but rather to affirm the unique differences between men and women; indeed, such differences are now being confirmed by modern scientific gender studies. Moreover, these unique differences suggest diverse gifts and functions based on gender, while the basic equality of women and men before God is vigorously affirmed. In other words, difference of roles and functions does not mean inequality; the Bible is not only redeemable but redemptive.

For other women, the task is a historical and methodological one that sidesteps the question of the Bible's redemptivity and leaves open that of its redeemability. As an ancient document, the Bible bears part of our past, and for that reason it is inherently important. The historical and literary reconstruction of the life of biblical women will lead to a better assessment of the interpretive issues involved for contemporary women. Thus reexamination of archaeological remains, literary texts, and comparative anthropology leads to new insights and shatters old conclusions when we approach the material with new questions about the mostly silent half of the population of ancient cultures. Even biblical narratives that include the action and speech of women can be illumined by analysis of the patterns of relationship between women and men in the culture. Thus the role of historical research is essential, and cannot be bypassed in favor of contemporary hermeneutical issues.

Finally, for some, these same contemporary hermeneutical issues are indeed the focus. The question of the Bible's redeemability, let alone its redemptivity, for many contemporary women depends entirely on whether the Bible can be seen as a proclamation of redemption and liberation for the oppressed of whatever kind. The prophetic challenge to social justice and the gospel exigency to live the reign of God are the clarion calls around which all biblical interpretation must rally. With historical and literary studies as a firm foundation, a contemporary biblical hermeneutic must be focused on the imperative to create a just and egalitarian society for all. It cannot proclaim the liberation of some and not others; it cannot, for instance, declare slavery an outmoded historical remnant and continue to subordinate women. Without full acceptance of this imperative for justice as being integral to the biblical message itself, and without its consistent application to all, there is no redemptive power at the heart of the biblical witness.

Within these various responses, minority women often have somewhat different views because of their cultural experience. Thus, for instance, because African American women's relationship to the Bible has traditionally been largely oral rather than literary, many have been able to be freer and more selective in screening out the difficulties and welcoming the comfort brought by the Bible than are those women more closely bound to the written text. The social and political context of Hispanic women often brings them most easily to be fundamentally committed to a liberation hermeneutic in reaction to centuries of colonial exploitation, and to insist on the grounding of any biblical interpretation in the concrete reality of social life and the people's faith.

Women's responses to the critical questions about the Bible are quite varied, depending on differences of experience and interpretive community. What is undeniable, however, is that consciousness of how these differences affect their reading of the Bible continues to grow.

ONGOING CHALLENGES

Three major issues could be singled out as the most difficult to resolve in any satisfactory, long-term way: androcentrism, actively oppressive texts, and the inclusion of the voices of all women of faith.

Androcentrism. One of the basic tenets of feminist critique is that in the biblical world, as well as our own, androcentrism—the assumption that the male is the norm of humanity—is pervasive. Speeches that address only "men and brothers" (Acts 2:37) or refer to the "sons of Israel" (Acts 7:23) do not intend such expressions as generic, contrary to what opponents of gender-inclusive language argue today. Rather, in a male-dominated and male-oriented culture, women are simply discounted as part of the active audience. Narratives that count only men (Mark 6:44), leave women nameless when men are named (Judg 12:29-40), or treat women as expendable (Judg 19:24-25) reveal the problem most clearly. Moral exhortation that addresses women only to criticize their behavior or prescribe their submission to men (Eph 5:22-24; 1 Pet 3:1-6), but most often gives even these directives in the third person (1 Cor 11:2-16; 14:34-35), shows that these passages are addressed primarily to men.

Language mirrors life and in turn creates images of life. The problem of gender-inclusive language has been tackled at many levels. On the "horizontal" plane (language about persons), the first step is to eliminate unnecessary gender-exclusive terminology in translation when not present in the original language (the first guiding principle of the NRSV). A second step is to alter it even when present in the original, on the basis that when biblical texts are proclaimed today, the proclaimer intends to address the message to both men and women, even if the ancient author did not. Horizontal gender-inclusive language is becoming standard in many lectionaries and worship books, and its use will undoubtedly continue to expand wherever people become fully aware of the issues involved. Altering nouns and pronouns, however, cannot supply the presence and activity of women in narratives where it is absent. That is a different and more difficult challenge.

On the "vertical" plane (language about God), sensitivity is stronger and the stakes are higher. For some, the overriding masculinity of the biblical and traditional portrayal of God is a terrible impoverishment of religious representation for women, and of religious imagination for all. For others, the biblical language about God is embedded in the message of revelation in such a way that to tamper with the language is to tamper with the revelation itself. For this reason, vertical gender-inclusive language still has a long way to go toward general acceptance. The portrayal of God in almost exclusively masculine terms aggravates the problem of male social normativity by projecting it beyond the human into the divine realm. Regardless of how many disclaimers are made that the ascription of gender to God is only metaphorical, the connection between images of God and masculinity is deeply rooted in the spirituality of both women and men, as demonstrated by the nervous reactions of many when female language is used of God. Those nervous reactions are well worth examining carefully, for they reveal the depth of our mistrust of femaleness as redeemed and redemptive. As long as exclusive masculine language is retained for God, the phantom of supposedly God-given male centeredness, male authority over women, and male identification with God in a way that excludes women will remain. On the other hand, the use of gender-inclusive language conceals the androcentrism of the text and can gradually make us oblivious of the problem.

Overtly Oppressive Texts. Another serious obstacle is the presence in the Bible of overtly oppressive texts—i.e., passages that seem directly to teach a theory of male superiority and female inferiority and subordination. The most problematic texts are the Pauline and Petrine ones in the New Testament (NT): women's head covering (culturally, a symbol of female modesty and male control), justified by women's theological derivation from men (1 Cor 11:2-16); the injunctions to women's public silence and submission to male authority (1 Cor 14:34-35; 1 Tim 2:11-16); and the submission of wives to husbands for christological and theological reasons (Eph 5:22-24; Col 3:18; 1 Pet 3:1-6).

There is no room here for a detailed study of these passages, all of which have been closely studied and carefully exegeted elsewhere. Together they symbolize the blockage experienced by many women for whom reading the Bible is problematic. Can a woman simply read selectively and ignore such passages? Can she believe that subordination does not mean inequality, but simply diversity of roles? Or must she accept the Bible itself as an instrument for the oppression of women through the faith community's claim to its authority? Few women who belong to worshiping communities cannot recall incidents in which these texts or others like them have been used to justify abuse, exploitation, or exclusion of women from full and equal participation in church or family.

This problem is, of course, part of the larger issue of the role of biblical authority in theology and church praxis. It is a point at which that authority intersects with the life of persons in a particularly direct way. It is, in fact, a laboratory in which the questions of biblical authority and normativity are tested in the crucible of everyday church and family life. It is insufficient to dismiss such texts as culturally backward, for then careful criteria must be formulated to distinguish a culturally backward prescription from one that is not time-bound. On the other hand, it is equally unacceptable to take such passages at face value, as similar texts condoning slavery demonstrate (e.g., 1 Cor 7:21-24; Eph 6:5-9; Col 3:22–4:1; 1 Pet 2:18-25). A headache for biblical conservatives and an embarrassment for biblical liberals, the problem of oppressive texts will not soon go away.

Inclusion of the Voices of All Women. The third ongoing issue is the full incorporation of minority women's voices and experience into what has been until very recently a dominant-culture account of "women's experience." While every bit as trenchant in their critique of patriarchal structures as dominant-culture white women, minority women who have had to build racial and ethnic solidarity with men of their own culture in defense against a dominant alien culture are not so quick to take a stand over against men as are women from the dominant culture, secure in their economic and political position. Women who are part of highly corporate family and social structures are not enthusiastic about the individualist values of liberal feminism that white middle-class women can import into their religious ethic almost without thinking.

Minority women have learned from their collective experience that "all women" do not necessarily stand in solidarity against the oppression of women, but that racism and classism have determined the relationships of rich and poor, slave and free women. Some identify with Sarah, the legitimate wife who benefits from the patriarchal system, and others with Hagar, the slave woman used for procreation and then rejected by her mistress (Genesis 16; 21). Some

by reason of economic and, therefore, educational privilege identify with Mary, who had the leisure to be a student of Jesus, others with Martha, who did not feel authorized to assume that privilege (Luke 10:38-42).

We are learning slowly and painfully that women's reading of the Bible and of their lives is affected by race and class as much as by sex. The myth of "value-free exegesis" must be abandoned not only by white males, but by white females as well.

It has sometimes been argued that Christianity improved the condition of women as contrasted to the Greco-Roman society in which it took shape, but especially in respect to the Judaism of its time, from which it mutated. Such arguments are now recognized by most historians of ancient Mediterranean cultures as erroneous and ethnocentric. Moreover, in the case of Judaism, they have the potential for being anti-Jewish; the subtle, or sometimes not so subtle, implication is that Christianity is an improvement on Judaism. In fact, Christianity absorbed many of the mores of its world and sifted them according to its own internal principles, as did every other philosophical and religious system of the day, including Judaism. The fact that the full personhood of women was affirmed by Christianity in most cases is well grounded, but the same was true elsewhere. The fact that the actual dignity and well-being of women improved in Christian cultures is highly debatable.

ON THE POSITIVE SIDE

In spite of the obstacles, women continue in great numbers to find in the Bible our source of inspiration and strength. More recently, many have been helped by the focus on great biblical women, always known but often forgotten. Heroines like Sarah, Hagar, Rebecca, Leah, Rachel, Miriam, Deborah, Jael, Hannah, Ruth, Judith, Esther, Elizabeth, Mary of Nazareth, Mary and Martha of Bethany, the Samaritan woman at the well, and Mary of Magdala—whether held to be historical or not—may function as inspiration or models of courage and devotion for contemporary women and men. They are disciples, prophets, apostles, mothers, daughters, sisters, friends, political leaders, unwed mothers, mother and friends of an executed political prisoner. The joys and sorrows of women's lives are present in the testimony of biblical women. They are models for all of us every bit as much as are the biblical heroes with whose exploits we are more familiar.

Elisabeth Schüssler Fiorenza's triple hermeneutic of *suspicion, remembrance,* and *celebration* is a helpful framework from which to approach the problematic and yet rewarding challenge of reading the Bible as women. The hermeneutic of suspicion assumes androcentric and patriarchal bias in the texts themselves, in the ways stories are narrated and teaching is given. This gender bias must be critically searched out, addressed, and modified or eliminated where possible. The hermeneutic of remembrance leads to the reconstruction of the story from the women's point of view by raising up with interpretive imagination their concerns and their experience. It is especially here that the interpreter must be sensitive to race and class bias; the remembrance must be inclusive of the lives of women from many corners of the social spectrum. Finally, the hermeneutic of celebration prompts the joyful lifting up of biblical women as our foremothers in the faith who have gone before and marked the way.

To read the Bible as women is to participate in a long and rich tradition, to be ready to critique the parts of that tradition that no longer serve, and to celebrate our belonging in a way that will make our contribution to generations to come.

BIBLIOGRAPHY

Bowe, Barbara, Kathleen Hughes, Sharon Karam, Carolyn Osiek, eds. *Silent Voices, Sacred Lives: Women's Readings for the Liturgical Year.* Mahwah, N.J.: Paulist, 1992.

Isasi-Díaz, Ada María, and Yolanda Tarango. *Hispanic Women: Prophetic Voice in the Church.* San Francisco: Harper & Row, 1988.

Martin, Clarice J. "The *Haustafeln* (Household Codes) in African American Biblical Interpretation: 'Free Slaves' and 'Subordinate Women.' " In *Stony the Road We Trod: African American Biblical Interpretation.* Edited by Cain Hope Felder. Minneapolis: Fortress, 1991.

Newsom, Carol A., and Sharon H. Ringe, eds. *The Women's Bible Commentary.* Louisville: Westminster/John Knox, 1992.

Osiek, Carolyn. "The Feminist and the Bible: Hermeneutical Alternatives." In *Feminist Perspectives on Biblical Scholarship.* Edited by Adela Yarbro Collins. SBL Centennial Publications; Biblical Scholarship in North America 10. Chico, Calif.: Scholars Press, 1985.

Schüssler Fiorenza, Elisabeth. *In Memory of Her: A Feminist Theological Reconstruction of Christian Origins.* New York: Crossroad, 1983.

Tolbert, Mary Ann, ed. *The Bible and Feminist Hermeneutics.* Semeia 28. Chico, Calif.: Scholars Press, 1983.

———. "Protestant Feminists and the Bible." In *The Pleasure of Her Text: Feminist Readings of Biblical and Historical Texts.* Edited by Alice Bach. Philadelphia: Trinity, 1990.

Trible, Phyllis. *God and the Rhetoric of Sexuality.* Overtures to Biblical Theology. Philadelphia: Fortress, 1978.

———. *Texts of Terror: Literary-Feminist Readings of Biblical Narratives.* Overtures to Biblical Theology. Philadelphia: Fortress, 1984.

Weems, Renita J. "Reading *Her Way* Through the Struggle: African American Women and the Bible." In *Stony the Road We Trod: African American Biblical Interpretation.* Edited by Cain Hope Felder. Minneapolis: Fortress, 1991.

THE USE OF THE BIBLE IN PREACHING

DAVID G. BUTTRICK

For centuries preachers have preached from Scripture. Sometimes they have launched from a single verse; at other times they have interpreted longer passages. Sometimes they have worked their way through whole books of the Bible, page after page and verse after verse. Of course, we must be quick to admit that preaching from the Bible does *not* make a sermon more or less godly. There are "biblical" sermons that are tedious, trivial, or even baldly heretical. Preaching from Scripture does not guarantee a better or more Christian enterprise. Likewise, there are sermons that never mention Scripture but are truly "biblical" in spirit and in content. Yet, down through the ages, more often than not, preachers have had recourse to the Bible when preaching within Jewish and Christian communities.

Why do preachers reach for biblical texts? Is the lectionary tradition an impetus? Lectionaries have been around for centuries. Synagogue preaching followed a schedule of readings from the Law and the Prophets, which may have coordinated with a slate of one hundred and fifty psalms. But lectionaries derive from the practice of speaking from Scripture; they do not cause the custom. What of the idea of an authoritative canon? Doesn't an official canon require biblical preaching? The earliest attempt to designate a fixed collection of Hebrew writings was late in the first century (90 CE), but it did not have substantial impact. Likewise, although Christian writings were circulating during the first two centuries, Christians did not decide on a compendium of writings until sometime in the fourth century, and debate over some books (e.g., Revelation) continued until the time of the Reformation and beyond. Do we not still publish some Bibles without the so-called Apocryphal books, even though our Christian Scriptures quote them often and with obvious approval? What of the supposed "inspiration" of Scripture? While Christians believe that the scriptures have been provided under the guidance of God, we must be wary. Certainly we must not give credence to the notion that the Bible is a magic "Word of God" book. Without the interpretation of the Spirit, the Bible is nothing more than an interesting collection of religious literature that stands alongside the Koran or the Upanishads and that, for some reason, seems to show up in most hotel rooms! We must probe the matter more deeply.

What does the Bible offer preaching? Obviously the gospel can be preached without recourse to Scripture and, possibly, with greater freedom and social relevance. What's more, even if we do turn to the Scripture in preaching, we soon discover that much of the Bible may not be "preachable" and, indeed, may not seem to *want* to be preached! There has always been a "homiletic canon" within the canon of Holy Scripture. So why do we begin sermons with a biblical text? Traditionally, preachers have defended the use of Scripture by pointing to the sheer scope and profound depth of the Bible's presentation of the human condition. Further, they have insisted that the Bible contains records of "revelation"—that is, disclosures that have opened to us the mystery of God. Sometimes preachers have appealed to an intrinsic biblical "authority," suggesting that the Bible both commands our religious activity and provides a court of final appeal in church disputes. But claims of authority are not always convincing. John Fry has satirized notions of biblical authority: "The New Testament says the Apostles say that God says the Gospel is the Word of God."[1] No, the question deserves a more probing answer.

The Bible, written over thousands of years, presents a kind of narrative structure—a story of God-with-us. The narrative structure of Scripture begins with creation, rolls out of early primal myth, and tells the story of a people, Israel, interacting with God. Finally, the Bible comes to a grand conclusion in the eschatological poetry of the last chapters of Revelation, a descending Holy City filled with the presence of God and a throned Lamb. The only way in which our lives have meaning is within some broadly structured story of God and humanity, a story that embraces all our stories and assumes the continuing interactive reality of God-with-us. Note that the biblical story has a beginning and an end, without which stories are senseless. In addition, in the early portion of Genesis (1–11) the Bible offers huge meaningful myths that undergird "the whole story" and interpret human life. Preaching, which need not embrace a narrative form, nonetheless draws on the narrativity of Scripture's story for meaning. The Bible, however, is not *our* story, a *church* story that provides us with a separate religious identity to preserve, so much as it is *humanity's* story within God's great purpose for the universe. Above all, preaching works from creation, from myths of theological meaning, and looks toward a consummation of all things—a pattern provided by the Hebrew Bible.

Before the early Christians had a completed collection of writings, a Bible, they had a structure of remembrance and anticipation; they lived in time between memory and hope. Inevitably, they recalled the life, death, and resurrection of Jesus Christ,

events that created the early Christian movement. As a community, had they not died with Christ's dying and revived again with his rising? They "had passed from death to life." No wonder that in the years that followed immediately after Jesus, they remembered him liturgically. They remembered many of his teachings and, impelled by the Spirit, apparently added more. They remembered the crowded, cruel happenings of what we now call Holy Week. Could they forget the terror of Good Friday or the lost emptiness of the Sabbath after? And were they not bound to celebrate Easter Day? Their Lord was risen, indeed enthroned "at the right hand of God." Why were the Christian Scriptures written and why were early letters preserved? They have been collected to preserve memory; they document the constitutive event of Christianity, the "Christ event" remembered and grasped within the primitive community of faith. We must still remember. The basic structure of the church year recurs to aid our recollection, and, in turn, the Scriptures assist our celebration of the Christian calendar. But, please note, the Scriptures do not cause the church year; theologically they serve the preaching of the church year.

Christian worship and piety have always been "through Jesus Christ." Inescapably, Christians believe that they know God through God's humanity—namely, the event of Jesus Christ. We know God, then, through the figure of Christ, whom we study in faith. In a way, we relate to God by interacting with the figure of Christ; Christ can be described as a "disclosure symbol" for faith. How does Christ come to us? Christ comes and joins us through preaching. In turn, preachers study Christ through Scripture. To know Christ—who did not spring from history *de novo*—we must search the Hebrew Scriptures, which surely shaped his mind and determined his piety. We must become what we are—namely, true Jewish descendants. But we will also attend to the Pauline correspondence, the earliest documents we possess, for they offer a key to the reading of Christ's story. Christian writings function "in between." We draw on them as we seek to understand symbols, including the symbol of the risen Lord Jesus Christ, in the midst of our contemporary being-saved communities.

Although we can sense the role of Scripture in the life of the church, what about the custom of a sermon text—a verse, a pericope, or more? Can we believe that some limited piece of Scripture, written

---

1. John R. Fry, *The Great Apostolic Blunder Machine: A Contemporary Attack upon Christendom* (San Francisco: Harper & Row, 1978) 17.

centuries ago, often taken out of context by a lectionary and proscribed for preaching, contains some sort of divine truth? Do we believe that every single verse of Scripture can be emptied out like a Christmas stocking to give us some sweet nougat of God's truth hidden there for us? No, we cannot. Nor can reasonable preachers affirm that many lections, some of which are snipped from a larger narrative or broken out of a Pauline epistle, contain some sort of God-meaning that cannot be found elsewhere. The Bible is not a magic book. Obviously, there are classics of faith that may well be far more helpful and Christian than some rather dubious sections of the canon. If we are slavishly bound to Scripture by a prescribed lectionary or our own often unexamined theological convictions, we may be prevented from addressing God's Word to specific sociopolitical moments or to present-day Christian churches in our nation. Is it possible that some pulpits excuse their silence with regard to bitter prejudice or unjust warfare because "we follow the lectionary"?

Let us affirm our central calling. As preachers we are called by God through the voice of the church to preach the gospel message. Please note: We are preachers of the gospel, *not* necessarily of the Bible. The gospel is good news of a new state of affairs brought about by God through Jesus Christ. We are forgiven and can be set free, not only from ourselves but from dominating forms of social bondage as well. We can live toward God's promised new order in which God will be one with reconciled humanity, where there will be no more war, no more injustice, no more disfiguring prejudice, no more oppressive poverty, no more religious intolerance, and, ironically, no more church! The gospel is a message of social and personal liberation addressed not only to the in-group of believers but especially to those who may appear to be "on the outs" with God. So we are not called to preach *about* the Bible. Nor are we called to a chain reaction understanding of preaching from the Bible: God is revealed in Christ, Christ is written down in the Bible, and we in turn transfer biblical revelation to present-day faith through preaching. In such a model, preaching derives secondhand authority from the Bible. No, Luther insisted that the word of preaching is God-in-Christ's own liberating word: "It is a wonderful thing that the mouth of every pastor is the mouth of Christ."[2]

And, again: "You ought to listen to the pastor not as a man but as God."[3] For Luther, preaching was God's word because it announced news of justifying grace to sinners and not because it was drawn from Scripture. For Luther, the Bible existed for preaching, and not preaching for the Bible:

The gospel should really not be something written, but a spoken word. . . . This is why Christ himself did not write anything but only spoke. He called his teaching not scripture but gospel, meaning good news or a proclamation that is spread not by pen but by word of mouth.[4]

Luther said another quite scandalous thing about the Bible. He implied that if we did not have Christian writings we could write our own "Gospels" by drawing on the Hebrew Scriptures with the aid of the Holy Spirit.[5] His remark has made Christians uneasy for centuries. But what he meant was obvious. We have heard the gospel of "Jesus Christ and him crucified." We stand in a community of faith that, no matter how blasé, is at least dimly aware of the transforming activity of God in common life. We break bread together and, in so doing, enact the promises of God in the presence of Christ. Out of the reality of God-with-us, surely we too could write our own unique witness. The purpose of our preaching is not a book, the Bible, particularly in an age when linear literacy is crumbling under the onslaught of other media. (How can we be a "people of the Book" when books may become passé?) No, the purpose of our preaching is to announce the saving good news of Jesus Christ and to glorify God!

What about notions of biblical authority? The early Christian communities broke bread and preached good news without any developed notion of authority. Their authority was Christ crucified and risen, understood in the midst of their lively, astonished, being-saved communities. They read the Bible, along with first-century rabbis, as a good gift of God for their faith. Gifts are eagerly unwrapped. Gifts are full of thankfulness and delight. Beyond the fights over authority that will no doubt continue to disfigure American Christianity, we can still receive Scripture gladly and gratefully as a gift of God for the people of God.

---

2. WA 37.381.

3. Ibid., 49.140.
4. *Luther's Works,* vol. 35: *Word and Sacrament, 1* (Philadelphia: Muhlenberg Press, 1960) 123.
5. WA 21, 235-36.

PREACHING IN AND OUT OF CHURCH

Ever since the resurrection, preachers have preached the gospel. Preaching has taken two forms: out-church evangelical preaching to the world and in-church preaching, which seeks to "form" the community of faith. Out-church preaching has always had an apologetic character; it takes shrewdness to be "fishers of people." In-church preaching, on the other hand, seems to be designed for faith seeking understanding. As Karl Barth suggested, it answers the question, Who are we who break bread together?[6]

Obviously, out-church preaching is culturally alert. It attempts to relate the gospel to contemporary thought and, therefore, is seldom overtly biblical. The idea of speaking from a limp Bible in evangelistic rallies is a relatively recent and somewhat peculiar practice. According to Acts, Christian preaching took place in many settings and did *not* necessarily begin with Bible verses. Early disciples announced the good news in synagogues, streets, marketplaces, public buildings, courtrooms and, of necessity, prisons. Evidently, homiletic strategies varied according to the audience. In early days, following the resurrection of Jesus Christ, the message was probably an invitation to join in the world's new beginning; like Jesus' own preaching, it declared the Kingdom of God, a new social order for a new humanity. In other words, the earliest preaching may have been influenced by patterns of apocalyptic thought: The aeon of Adam and the new aeon of Christ, the present age and an age to come that, with the resurrection of Christ, had already arrived. Our earliest Christian writings, the letters of Paul and the Gospel of Mark, feature such apocalyptic thought.

Subsequently, Luke/Acts provides quite different summaries of the gospel message in a series of "sermons." The sermons in Acts, though influenced by rhetorical conventions, are no doubt Lukan compositions in which he attempts to rehearse an official *kerygma.* But even Luke's sermons seem to invite people to enter a new state of affairs by repentance and faith. Out-church preaching called people to be baptized into God's new humanity.

Within the church, preaching seemed to be dedicated to making sense of the great Christ event.

Obviously, early Christians were aware that some new mode of living together seemed to be forming in their common life; redemptive new life was happening among them. They knew they were being-saved. Somehow the reality of a salvific newness had to be connected with the dreadful death of Christ, the rejected, crucified one whom God had raised up. Early Christians searched the Hebrew Scriptures trying to make sense out of all that had happened and, in fact, was continuing to happen among them. So, in-church preaching turned to Scripture. Early preachers interpreted Scripture within an inherited understanding of Israel's faith and religious practices.

Obviously, primitive Christianity was Jewish in character. Did the early Christians preach from lections as was usual in synagogue practice? We cannot say. From the Pauline correspondence, we know that they read from the scriptures when they gathered together, no doubt from the Septuagint Greek. But was preaching from the outset an exposition of Scripture? They read from Hebrew Scriptures, and, if we can trust the record in Acts, they also read from apostolic memoirs, such as Paul's epistles. But we cannot claim that there were assigned lections during the earliest years. Recently scholars have argued that there were also "prophets" who spoke to the community on behalf of the risen Christ, apparently without benefit of any specific biblical materials.[7] What we can say with certainty is that early in-church preaching sought to interpret the event of Jesus Christ to a being-saved community and, what is more, to transmit practical directions for their common ministry in the world. In-church preaching spoke to the baptized.

EARLY CHRISTIAN COMMUNITIES

While it is obvious that early Christians preached both to the wider world and within their own assemblies, their preaching was scarcely lodged in a pulpit, written out in manuscripts, or always an exposition of Scripture. We must not read our own peculiar proclivities back into earlier ages. Apparently, within the first Christian communities, members saw themselves and their leaders as continuing

6. Karl Barth, *Homiletics,* trans. G. W. Bromily and D. E. Daniels (Louisville: Westminster/John Knox, 1991) 58.

7. M. Eugene Boring, *The Continuing Voice of Jesus: Christian Prophecy and the Gospel Tradition* (Louisville: Westminster/John Knox, 1991).

the ministry of Jesus Christ. Not only were they extending Christ's ministry—speaking and healing and helping and teaching—but, in doing so, they were directed by the risen Christ and enabled by his bold Spirit. Apparently there were many kinds of "preaching." The apostles preached as witnesses to Jesus Christ, but so also did "prophets," who evidently believed they were giving voice to the risen Christ. Surely "teachers" taught within the community as well, not to mention "charismatic" speakers such as those who troubled Paul in Corinth. Scriptures were read, but there is no sure evidence that Synagogue traditions were recapitulated at table in Christian assemblies. Suffice it to say that the good news of God's new order was declared out-church and in; the mystery of Christ, his death and resurrection, was explored in relation to the Hebrew Scriptures; and instruction was offered, interpreting current situations and advocating moral behavior. But we cannot read back expository preaching into the earliest years of Christian community. The first sermons we possess, a sermon by Clement and a somewhat forced sermon by Melito of Sardis, come from mid-second century. They are primarily moral exhortations and may have been connected loosely to some Hebrew scripture reading.

During the first few hundred years, the only scriptures on hand were the writings of the Hebrew Bible. No doubt the letters of Paul were circulated among Christian groups, and, here and there, some Gospels or pre-Gospels may have been known, but neither the Gospels nor the epistles had achieved anything like canonical status. The second century displayed many different views with regard to the Hebrew Scriptures. Marcion of Pontus, filled with enthusiasm for Paul, rejected the writings of the Hebrew Scriptures on the basis of a still popular theological position—namely, that there are two Gods, the Hebrew God of Law and the loving God and Father of our Lord Jesus Christ. In his *Antithesis,* Marcion reread Paul and Luke, amending them so they would support his own somewhat singular theological contentions. One of Marcion's opponents, Justin Martyr, argued that all of the Hebrew Scriptures were, in fact, Christian as was all great Greek philosophy as well. The Gnostic Ptolemaeus argued that Christ is God's ultimate truth and in Christ, therefore, we can approve or discard selectively the laws of the Hebrew Bible. Irenaeus responded by insisting that there is but *one* God, who

is disclosed in both Hebrew and Christian writings. Irenaeus set forth some basic ways of biblical study, including a preference for the plain meaning of Scripture, typological interpretation, and the insistence that Scripture must be understood in the light of the church's confessional tradition. The issue of the interrelation of the Hebrew and Christian scriptures is with us still and is often still skewed by both the triumphalism and unacknowledged anti-Semitism of Christian tradition.

ANTIOCH AND ALEXANDRIA

Early Christian interpretation of Scripture took what is often described as two different directions, usually labeled Antiochian and Alexandrian. It should be said that preaching during the third, fourth, and fifth centuries was strongly influenced by both Greek and Asiatic rhetorical traditions. In turn, these traditions may have influenced biblical interpretation. Asiatic rhetoric is more florid and metaphorical, while Greek rhetoric encourages a degree of plain spoken terseness. Perhaps the whole history of biblical preaching can be understood as an alternating current between Antioch and Alexandria, between an expressive and a serviceable rhetoric.

Alexandrian interpretation emerged as Christian faith, originating as a Jewish sect, moved into the Greco-Roman world. In order to explain aspects of Christian faith, early preachers ventured analogies, "Christian faith is *like . . . * " and sometimes even elaborate allegories, directly equating Christian ideas with Greek notions. Earlier, the Jewish apologist Philo had adopted much the same method in explaining Hebrew faith: to oversimplify, Torah = Logos; Messiah = Divine Emanation; God = Being; etc. So Clement of Alexandria, influenced by Philo, understood the words of Scripture to be a mysterious symbolic language that could be interpreted on many levels, not only historically or morally but also doctrinally, typologically, philosophically, and mystically. The most famous of the Alexandrians, Origen (c. 230 CE), a noted preacher and theologian, recognized that Scripture is historical, indeed that most Scripture has a direct historical referent; but he also proposed "spiritual" meanings as well. The literal, historical meaning of Scripture is for the simple believer, the beginner, who may not readily cope with metaphor or symbol, whereas the deeper spiritual meanings are lures for mature faith. Origen's sermons apparently proceeded from Scripture verse by verse, with each verse often receiving an allegorical reading. For example, Origen interprets a metaphor in Numbers 23:24, "like a lion!/ It does not lie down until it has eaten the prey/ and drunk the blood of the slain" (NRSV), as a reference to consuming body and blood in the Eucharist.

By contrast, Antiochian interpretation was grounded in Jewish Christianity, and flatly rejected the speculative Alexandrian allegorizations. The Antiochian interpreters set what they called "theory"—namely, a true, literal reading of a text, over against allegory. The leading exponents of the Antiochian school were Theodore of Mopsuestia, the preacher John Chrysostom, and, subsequently, the Scripture scholar Jerome, who, though originally committed to allegorization, became a champion of the Antiochian position. Basically, Antiochian interpretation preferred the plain, obvious, historical meaning of Scripture. With regard to prophecy, Antiochian interpreters did not view messianic passages as mysterious prescient symbols of Christ, but as historical prophecy subsequently fulfilled in Christ. Both approaches are drawn together in Augustine. In 397 CE, he wrote his *De doctrina christiana,* laying down rules for understanding Scripture. Obviously, Augustine understood preaching to be an act of biblical interpretation. Generally, he accepts the plain meaning of the Bible, but he is willing to allegorize so as to bring out deeper meaning. While he asserts that Scripture interprets Scripture, he flatly rejects what is sometimes called the "private interpretation of Scripture" and insists, as did Irenaeus, that ultimately the confession of the church must rule interpretation.

CATHOLIC AND PROTESTANT

During the medieval period, trajectories of Antioch and Alexandria maintained their influence. Preaching was important and was usually expected to be an exposition of Scripture. There were handbooks for biblical interpretation, which often built on the work of Augustine. In the eighth century Carolingian reforms, preaching was usually from the Gospel lection, or sometimes the epistle. The lesson was explained and exhortations followed. During medieval years, collections of homilies were produced for clergy use. Later illustration books appeared as well as some homiletic "how-to" manuals provided for the Dominican and Franciscan preaching orders. For the most part, medieval preachers accepted a fourfold sense of scriptural meaning that offered homiletic latitude:

The letter shows us what God and our fathers did;
The allegory shows us where our faith is hid;
The moral meaning gives us rules of daily life;
The anagogy shows us where we end our strife.[8]

Protestant preachers are apt to groan with disapproval and, yet, employ much the same method of interpretation today. While they may look for a historical referent, if stumped, they will draw out psychological meaning or hidden narrative meaning or some sort of existential meaning.

The greatest interpreter of the medieval period was Thomas Aquinas, who affirmed the authority of Scripture, urged its literal meaning, and insisted that the Bible's use of metaphor was natural rather than esoteric. He also argued that if texts have other meaning, such other "senses" rest on the literal historical sense. But, wisely, Aquinas also believed that Scripture must be interpreted in accord with the confessions of the church.

Protestants like to suppose that the Reformation once more restored the Antiochian literal meaning of Scripture after centuries of Alexandrian excessive misinterpretation; however, as we have seen, such is not the case. Reformation interpretive principles were not far from those of Thomas Aquinas. What was different was the locus of authority, transferred from church tradition to the Bible. According to the Reformers, *sola scriptura* was now the rule, since the gospel message to be found in Scripture was proclaimed by prophets and apostles before there was a self-aware church. Luther renounced allegorical interpretation in favor of "one simple solid sense." And both Luther and Calvin insisted that the Bible is essentially self-interpreting and that the key to biblical meaning is the good news in Christ Jesus for believers. For Luther, the message of Christ was justification by grace through faith, a principle by which he judged all biblical writings, boldly discarding some materials (e.g., James) as sub-Christian. Calvin's understanding of Scripture was somewhat broader. While he clung to the entire collection of

---

8. A sixteenth-century jingle cited in Robert Grant and David Tracy, *A Short History of the Interpretation of the Bible,* 2nd ed. (Philadelphia: Fortress, 1984) 85.

biblical books, he found christological meaning throughout. The real difference in the Reformation period was preaching. The Reformers preached from Scripture, often working their way systematically through whole books passage by passage. They attempted to create a biblically educated laity and a biblically ordered piety. Later, as the invention of movable type took hold and spread, printed Bibles were provided for even the most modest home.

"I THINK; THEREFORE I QUESTION"

Of course, the supremacy of Scripture did not go unchallenged, not in an age that could announce: *"cogito ergo sum"* ("I think; therefore I am"). The rise of scientific method was bound to challenge biblical preaching. As early as the mid-seventeenth century, philosophers Hobbes and Spinoza questioned biblical "truth" in the name of an autonomous human reason. Hobbes, a cautious Anglican, looked to Scripture, interpreted by reason, as a moral foundation for responsible human society. His interests were political rather than theological. The point of attack for Spinoza was the miracle tradition as reported in Scripture. Miracles in both Hebrew and Christian writings stretched the credulity of objective reason, not to mention the subsequent *Common Sense* of a Thomas Paine. But, strangely enough, the same autonomous reason that questioned Scripture came to its defense in the writings of Bishop Berkeley. In spite of conflict, the rationalism of the eighteenth century finally led to the emergence of a supposedly "scientific" historical-critical method. Preaching began to be marked by rational explanation of troubling passages ("storms rise and fall almost instantly on the Sea of Galilee") on the one hand, and a method of preaching whereby propositional "truths" were distilled from often embarrassing biblical narratives, on the other. Single verse texts could be reduced to rational "truths" with ease.

In the nineteenth century, biblical interpretation took a philosophical turn. The rationalism of the previous era persisted and indeed flourished in objective "higher criticism" of the Bible. But the century also saw the rise of a kind of romanticism as well. Friedrich Schleiermacher's hermeneutic lectures had major impact. Although he employed philological and historical methods, he pushed further, insisting on entering "the inner form or animating idea of [a text], then to the mind of the author," by a kind of intuition.[9] Texts found meaning as they were grasped by an inner Christian piety. As a result, Schleiermacher tended to regard the Hebrew Scriptures as subordinate to the Christian writings. But the Christian Scriptures themselves were scarcely ultimate. In his *On Religion,* Schleiermacher was outspoken: "The holy books have become the Bible in virtue of their own power, but they do not forbid any other from being or becoming a Bible in its turn."[10] For Schleiermacher, the person of Christ and the redeemed life flowing from him are authority alone.

The most important biblical scholar of the century was probably F. C. Bauer. Following Hegel, he supposed that ideas evolved gradually by a process involving opposition and synthesis. Thus conflict between Judaizers and Paul led to the synthesis of the Gospels. D. F. Strauss, one of Bauer's students, is usually regarded as the most radical scholar of the era. He argued that orthodoxy regarded the Gospels as both history and supernatural history. Rationalism rejected the supernatural, but clung to history. He argued that scientific scholarship had to complete the task and question the history of biblical records. Strauss's *Life of Jesus* stripped away what he considered to be mythological elaborations in search of a factual Jesus. The century produced a procession of lives of Christ, which in turn fed popular preaching. The idea of evolving religious ideas led to the work of Julius Wellhausen, a professor of Hebrew Scripture, whose approach to the Bible influenced subsequent twentieth-century scholarship.

One of the most influential figures in the century was the poet Samuel Taylor Coleridge. Although he acknowledged that Scripture spoke profoundly to his piety, Coleridge opposed any claim of biblical infallibility. The Bible must be read as a "believed book," and each literary part should be interpreted in the light of the whole. Coleridge urged the right of private interpretation in conversation with the church's judgment.

The nineteenth century was split between two notions of truth: objective truth, rationally determined, and subjective inner truth, mediated by

---

9. James D. Wood, *The Interpretation of the Bible: A Historical Introduction* (London: Gerald Duckworth, 1958) 129.
10. Quoted in Grant and Tracy, *A Short History of the Interpretation of the Bible,* 111.

imagination or intuition. Biblical interpretation moved in both directions. So, in large part, did preaching. Clearly the pulpit was influenced by the rise of rationalism; either it preached an apologetic gospel based on Jesus' teaching or it addressed the inner world of religious experience.

THE TWENTIETH CENTURY

How can we assess the twentieth century? Two words may get at patterns: *history* and *psychology*. In a way, they continue nineteenth-century preoccupation with both piety and historical fact. In our century, we have seen the flourishing of historical-critical research; multivolume encyclopedias of religion; Bible dictionaries, commentaries, atlases; Kittel's theological word books; plus more dissertations than can be counted. As a result, sermons have frequently begun with historical description as if context is somehow a form of truth.

But psychology has been on the rise as well. In 1928, Harry Emerson Fosdick asked, "What is the matter with preaching?" in a now famous article. He rejected both topical and expository preaching in favor of addressing human problems, most of which were analyzed with Fosdick's early-day psychology. Following Fosdick, white Protestant pulpits interpreted both sin and salvation personally and, often, psychologically. The Bible became a religious resource for problem solving.

The same year that Fosdick's article appeared, Karl Barth's *The Word of God and the Word of Man* appeared in an English translation. Barth wrote more about preaching than any theologian. He called the pulpit back to biblical fidelity by setting historical revelation over against impotent human wisdom. The First World War, followed by the Great Depression, shook optimistic turn-of-the-century theological liberalism. So Barth and other neo-orthodox theologians found an eager audience. And, when a mid-century liturgical revival handed out reworked lectionaries, in general preaching became compulsively biblical.

Of course, even within neo-orthodoxy there were tensions. Rudolf Bultmann, writing from a Lutheran heritage and influenced by the philosopher Heidegger, raised sharp questions with regard to a necessary "demythologizing" of biblical concepts. His followers, departing from the rationalist tradition, viewed preaching as a "word-event" in which the saving power of Christ encounters contemporary people.

The African American preaching tradition had its own ways of opening the Scriptures. In the twentieth century, African American congregations which, since the Civil War, had been concerned primarily with survival, emerged as a public influence. All things considered, the African American pulpit has provided America with remarkably fine preaching. Why didn't African American preaching succumb to therapeutic preaching? A common "black consciousness," aware of oppression, united African American congregations; personal psychological problems were secondary. And why didn't African American preaching turn Barthian? Perhaps because the Scriptures were read as eschatological promise rather than past-tense historical revelation. African American pulpits have preached a gospel of liberation. Surely the words of Martin Luther King, Jr., addressed the world.

THE BIBLE, CULTURE, AND PREACHING

Now let us frame still another set of distinctions. Can we admit that Christian faith is never pure but always an admixture? Have theologians ever successfully distilled an "essence of Christianity"? Never. Instead we talk about Byzantine Christianity, medieval Christianity, Christianity of the Reformation, or Enlightenment Christianity. Christianity never seems to travel alone. It cannot be separated into "fundamentals" without courting heresy. Christianity is always embodied within a "cultural formulation"—namely, the world view, the tacit assumptions, and the shared beliefs of any given social order.[11] For example, can we not distinguish recent American Christianity—a pragmatic, capitalist, "habit of the heart"—from an earlier Puritan Calvinism? Although Christian faith is always embodied, perhaps we can distinguish phases in the always ambiguous, often scandalous relationship between Christian faith and cultural formulations. If we review the Christian centuries, we can begin to sense patterns.

In certain periods, the church is engaged in an evangelical ministry. These are eras in which the

---

11. The term "cultural formulation" is used by Crane Brinton, *A History of Western Morals* (New York: Harcourt, Brace and Co., 1959).

church is moving into some new culture, seeking to interpret the gospel in a new language, amid new social symbols. The Christian faith soon moved out of Palestine and into the Greco-Roman world. When the ancient world was overrun and the Roman Empire toppled, Christian faith was again translated into many different tongues and was related to different cultural groups. After the collapse of the medieval synthesis, during the Renaissance and the Reformation, once more Christianity spread evangelically, interpreting itself in relationship to an emerging Enlightenment mind. In reaching-out eras such as these, biblical faith is interpreted broadly as it seeks to relate to new cultural "minds," to seed itself into a new social language. Evangelical preaching employs translation, metaphor, and analogy to explain itself in every new setting. Moreover, such missionary preaching usually stresses an incarnational theology, reveling in "God-with-us."

Of course, the terrible risk of evangelism is accommodation. Can Christian faith lose itself in dalliance with a cultural formulation? It may seem so in "high" periods when a cultural world view is in ascendancy. Did not the early nineteenth century translate theological categories into common ideas? Thus the biblical idea of Torah became rational "laws of Nature"; the conflict between Law and Grace, as understood by D. H. Lawrence and Paul Gauguin, was a battle between natural instincts and social constraints; original sin became either transmitted social custom or an evolutionary lag; providence gave way to a Hegelian historical dialectic; and the idea of the "Kingdom" turned into Utopia. Although we can spot the same tendency to accommodation in the Greco-Roman era and again at the height of the medieval synthesis, somehow the relationship between Christian faith and a cultural formulation can never be reduced to an equal sign. The same stumbling blocks seem to occur: the biblical understanding of God as "person," the biblical doctrine of creation, and the biblical notion of resurrection. Cultures tend to denigrate the physical world, while the God of Gen 1:31 shouts, with obvious approval, "Very good!" Cultures view God as an impersonal force, as Being, whereas the Bible speaks of God in personal terms as our Mother or Father. Cultural high periods are marked by notions of correspondence—something "out there" (or "up there") is like us—and, therefore, embraces dreams of immortality. Christian faith announces "All flesh is grass," but then celebrates resurrection as an act of sheer graciousness by God. In the high periods of cultural synthesis, there is a tendency for Christian faith to lose itself in the patterns of a cultural philosophy. But there always seems to be an alien, perhaps scandalous, quality to the preached Christian message; Christianity and cultural formulations live together in a peculiar tension.

Now, by contrast, are there not other eras when somehow Christian faith attempts to distinguish itself dialectically from the world view to which it has been embodied? Immediately we think of the time of Augustine or the early sixteenth century or perhaps the twentieth century. In such eras, the church seems to return to biblical categories and toward Antiochian literalism in biblical interpretation. Once more, scholars turn to original sources and to the languages in which sources have been written. Theologians begin to deny analogy, particularly *analogia entis*; God is *not* like us! God is utterly transcendent and, in fact, unknowable apart from God's own self-revelation. Moreover, because Christianity is based on God's chosen moments of self-revelation, it is quite unlike the "religions." They grope in the dark because there is no such thing as general revelation. What is the biblical theology of our century (epitomized by Karl Barth) if not a strategy for cultural disengagement? In periods of disengagement, we announce the transcendent holy "otherness" of God.

Notice that we have inadvertently described changing patterns of preaching. Missionary preaching reaches out and interprets itself within strands of cultural thought; by translation it seeks embodiment, by analogy it embraces ideas. In periods of high culture, preaching tends to become an ally of social stability. It dispenses a somewhat static "vertical" gospel without much apocalyptic edginess. In times of disengagement, when a cultural formulation may be breaking up, Christian preaching is apt to become fiercely biblical but unable or unwilling to converse apologetically with culture. Essentially it becomes a dialectical enterprise. In times of cultural breakdown, such as our own "in between" era, preaching may tend to split between evangelical impulses and a desire for biblical disengagement. In the new pluralism of a broken-down cultural formulation, Christian preaching struggles to relate and, at the same time, to hold on to the primal faith of the biblical witness.

YESTERDAY AND TODAY

When the first volume of *The Interpreter's Bible (IB)* was published in 1951, the biblical theology movement was riding high. Turn-of-the-century theological liberalism had been vanquished, and the religious scene was dominated by neo-orthodox giants: Brunner, Barth, the Niebuhrs, Tillich. As a result, certain theological assumptions were taken for granted: Revelation was historical; revelation history was scribbled in the Bible; and the Bible could be cracked open by the historical-critical method to yield a "Word of God." A decade later, James Barr surveyed the era: "Historians of theology in a future age will look back on mid-twentieth century and call it the revelation-in-history pe-riod."[12]

The biblical theology movement eschewed fun-damentalism. The *IB* was published nearly fifty years after the height of the fundamentalist/mod-ernist controversies. Although the editors of the *IB* were scarcely fundamentalist (most were on the faculty of New York's Union Theological Semi-nary and, therefore, in the tradition of the "Auburn Declaration"), they did affirm the Bible as the Word of God; and they firmly believed that the Bible handed out crucial theological mean-ings. The world of the 1950s was a chastened world, a post-war, post-Depression world that had witnessed the dead stacked like cord wood in the German concentration camps. Earlier notions of inevitable progress and missionary conquest—"The Kingdom of God in our generation!"—seemed no longer tenable. Once more people turned to Scrip-ture, some moved by Barth's astonishing *Der Romer-brief* (1918), others swayed by Reinhold Niebuhr's dour Gifford Lectures, *The Nature and Destiny of Man* (1941 and 1943), still others influenced by the biblical homiletics of P. T. Forsyth's *Positive Preach-ing and the Modern Mind* (1909). In general, neo-orthodoxy wrote the *IB,* and its tacit assumptions were those of the biblical theology movement.

What were the assumptions of the biblical theo-logians?[13] For the most part, they embraced dialec-tical theology, thus rejecting notions of general revelation in nature or in religious experience. In-stead, they affirmed revelation in "the mighty acts of God" and, singularly, in the historic event of Jesus Christ. They asserted the notion of a unique, biblical (Hebrew) "mind" over against pagan religions of the ancient world as well as against the speculations of Greek philosophy. They believed in the unity of Scripture. Scripture portrayed a biblical point of view and embodied a common underlying kerygmatic meaning. They enthroned notions of biblical author-ity; the Bible was the "Word of God." Since the mid-1960s, almost all of these positions have been challenged. In addition, the supremacy of the his-torical-critical method itself has been shaken. In 1973, the first sentence in a book on biblical inter-pretation baldly announced, "Historical biblical criti-cism is bankrupt."[14]

So *The New Interpreter's Bible (NIB)* is written in a quite different social world. Since the *IB,* we have witnessed a huge revolution in hermeneutics that began in a Barth-Bultmann controversy over "demythologizing" but since has moved in many directions. We have listened to sharp critiques by feminist, African American, and other liberationist interpreters, not to mention the profound suspicion of the Frankfort School's so-called Critical Theory, pointing to white European, male, capitalist com-mitments that may lie hidden in the supposed ob-jectivity of biblical research. We have learned from literary critics, structuralists, deconstructionists, reader-response analysts, as well as critics operating out of various theories of "social world." Biblical criticism has taken a literary turn, which some theorists suggest is both more appropriate to the material itself (biblical writings are *not* objective history but are writings from and for faith) and, thus, more theologically perceptive. So *The New Inter-preter's Bible* reflects new, or at least transitional, biblical scholarship. And newer methods of biblical research may reflect very different theological com-mitments. If the past fifty years could be labeled a "revelation-in-history period," perhaps in the future we will speak of revelation through symbol to social consciousness and, therefore, regard the Bible in a quite different light.

In the fifties, an article on "The Bible in Preach-ing" would have rung with confident assurance, paying tribute to a sure "Word of God" in the Bible. Even though most homiletic textbooks at the time

12. James Barr, "Revelation in History in the Old Testament and in Modern Theology," *New Theology No. 1,* eds. Martin E. Marty and Dean G. Peerman (New York: Macmillan, 1964) 62.
13. See Brevard S. Childs, *Biblical Theology in Crisis* (Philadelphia: Westminster, 1970) Part I.

14. Walter Wink, *The Bible in Human Transformation: Toward a New Paradigm for Biblical Study* (Philadelphia: Fortress, 1973) 1.

of the *IB* bowed in the direction of Scripture, many suggested the use of one-verse texts for preaching that, in practice, were often pretexts for topical orations. Yes, there were churches that still embraced a tradition of lectionary preaching—such as Catholic, Lutheran, and Anglican confessions, to name a few. But for many Protestant groups, choice of a scriptural text was still prompted by a kind of ministerial "eeny, meeny, miney, mo"; many pastors picked a topic and then leafed through the pages of a concordance for some sort of text.

Then, in the sixties, a second wave of liturgical renewal produced a batch of new worship books. The Presbyterian *Worshipbook* printed a modified version of the Vatican II Catholic lectionary revision, which, in turn, was picked up by several other Protestant bodies. Suddenly, local clergy discovered that they could study Scripture together in lectionary-based groups, doing mutual sermon preparation. Of course, the idea of lectionary preaching was reinforced by a rise in Barthian "Word of God" theology. Barth himself insisted that preachers must preach the Bible *and nothing more.*[15] He even went so far as to suggest that a sermon should be like the lip movements of a person reading the Bible.[16] All of a sudden, the notion caught on, and religious publishers hustled lectionary commentaries off presses. For pastors, books that chased down specific Bible passages without having to grope through intimidating commentaries seemed a godsend. Besides, many pastors had begun to regard their task as maintenance; they would maintain people through counseling and churches through management. So in the sixties and seventies, preaching became a secondary concern supported by the lectionary handbooks.

At the same time, homiletic theory was up for grabs. In the 1950s, preaching methods split into three options: (1) Sermons could distill topics from brief snatches of Scripture, making points in order to "apply" biblical ideas to daily life; (2) in the style of Harry Emerson Fosdick, sermons could begin with diagnosed human problems and bring Scripture in as an available resource; or (3) they could proceed verse by verse through scriptural passages, drawing out a series of often disconnected meanings for late-night radio listeners. After the mid-fifties, signifi-

cant homiletic texts seemed almost to disappear. Around 1970, however, we began to see ventures in homiletic theory, some prompted by the so-called "new hermeneutic" or by a renewed interest in ecclesiology, others reflecting a cultural "triumph of the therapeutic." So in the 1990s, we have homiletic theory moving in very different directions. In a variety of narrative approaches, Scripture is regarded as a story to tell that provides insight or identity to God's people. Inductive homiletic approaches seem to begin in human self-understanding, with which Scripture converses powerfully. In addition, there have been other proposals: structuralist, phenomenological, psychological, etc. What these homiletic positions share is a rejection of an older, rationalist preaching that distilled objective "truths" and made points about them. Instead, most of the recent ventures in homiletic theory argue that sermon design must relate appropriately to subject matter or to biblical form. Biblical language is regarded as "performative," as a language that not only instructs but *does.* How could God's Word be anything less? Newer homiletics regards sermon design as a *doing* in common consciousness; meaning and form are always to be interrelated. No wonder that contemporary homiletics has greeted recent literary-critical approaches to Scripture with considerable enthusiasm.

ON LOOKING INTO THE FUTURE

One of the peculiar notions of the biblical theology movement was the idea that preachers could move directly from the biblical text to a sermon without recourse to homiletics or theology; biblical research was regarded as sufficient. Under the indirect influence of Barthian thought, guidebooks on biblical preaching that appeared in the sixties were deeply suspicious of rhetoric as well as speculative philosophical-theology. Therefore, they seemed to suppose that the Bible, informed by historical-critical scholarship, would automatically form the preacher's sermon. Preachers would translate a text, do appropriate word study, look up other related biblical texts, determine something called an "original meaning," and—presto!—the preacher's mind would readily produce a "biblical sermon." As a result, many sermons related considerable historical reconstruction, plus information about the Bible gleaned from study, before adding some sort of

---

15. Karl Barth, *The Preaching of the Gospel,* trans. B. E. Hooke (Philadelphia: Westminster, 1963) 43.
16. Barth, *Homiletics,* 76.

contemporary "application." A self-sufficient "biblical preaching" skipped theology. But theology interprets Scripture and, arm in arm with rhetoric, does homiletics. For the foreseeable future, preaching may have to dedicate itself to remedial theology!

What is important about the Bible? Ultimately, it is a message, a saving message. In a way, we already know that saving message. Almost all of us can articulate some version of what we call "gospel," the good news. We have argued that the Bible offers a narrative that sets our lives into a larger story of God and humanity, between creation and eschaton; an account of God's interactive relating to humanity as a paradigm for our common lives; the memory of Jesus Christ's life and death and resurrection, the church's constitutive event. Above all, the Bible offers us a source for the study of Jesus Christ, his own Jewish faith, and a revelation of God-with-us. Thus we will draw on Scripture as we faithfully do in-church preaching. As for lectionaries, they are useful guides to the seasons of faith, unless they turn into law. We can seek to live in freedom with lectionaries. Some of the passages of Scripture listed in a lectionary are not useful for preaching; they lack literary unity and, as fragments of Scripture, may have little to say to our more modern age.

But we live "between the ages." On the one hand, we seem to be concerned with the self-preservation of our separate denominational identities; on the other hand, we sense an evangelical task of immense proportions. How can we seed the gospel into a forming new age? So we cling to a kind of biblical concern and, yet, sense an apologetic task that may demand a very different kind of preaching.

Have we made a model error? We have labeled the Bible "Word of God" and handed it over to preachers to preach in a secondary or reiterative way. In so doing we have reversed a traditional model. According to the Reformers as well as to ancient church tradition, preaching itself is a "Word of God." So let us begin with the words of the Second Helvetic Confession: "The preaching of the word of God is the word of God." Because God speaks through the risen Christ to the church via preaching, preachers have an awesome burden: They must get the message straight. In so doing, they will avail

themselves of Christian tradition: theology, liturgy, and, of necessity, Scripture. How does preaching use Scripture? Out-church preaching in a missionary age preaches the gospel message with great savvy to secular people. Thus out-church preaching will risk "translating" the message of Scripture for a new age. While out-church evangelism may not mention the Bible, it will draw on the biblical sense of narrative and also on the gestalt image of Christ that the Bible happens to provide as it calls people into a new humanity. In-church preaching may still begin with passages from Scripture as they relate to the patterns of memory in the Christian calendar. But all preaching will have recourse to Scripture as it performs its primary tasks: joining the baptized to the living symbol of Jesus Christ and interpreting the world in which we share our common ministry.

Above all, preaching at the edge of the twenty-first century must once more turn to a traditional task; it must dare to stand before the huge mystery in which we live and invoke the presence of God for those in and out of the church. We will speak "without authority," yet with utter commitment to the calling of God. Of course, we will feed on the Scriptures and be glad that they have been given to us. But we will also be culturally alert and theologically perceptive. We will speak God's "Word," news of the new order, which even now is breaking into our world, and we will tell of Christ crucified and risen with all the homiletical skill we can muster. Above all, we will speak, where for centuries every preacher has preached, knee-deep in grace.

BIBLIOGRAPHY

Barr, James. *The Bible in the Modern World.* New York: Harper & Row, 1973.

Brilioth, Yngve. *A Brief History of Preaching.* Translated by Karl E. Mattson. Philadelphia: Fortress, 1965.

Cooke, Bernard. *Ministry to Word and Sacraments.* Philadelphia: Fortress, 1976.

Grant, Robert M., and David Tracy. *A Short History of the Interpretation of the Bible.* Philadelphia: Fortress, 1984.

McKim, Donald K. *The Bible in Theology and Preaching.* Nashville: Abingdon, 1994.

Van Olst, E. H. *The Bible and Liturgy.* Translated by John Vriend. Grand Rapids: Eerdmans, 1991.

Wilson, Paul Scott. *A Concise History of Preaching.* Nashville: Abingdon, 1992.

THE USE OF THE BIBLE IN HYMNS, LITURGY, AND EDUCATION

CATHERINE GUNSALUS GONZÁLEZ

How does a congregation of the Christian church come to know the Scripture? The public reading of a text in the Scripture lessons and the preaching of a sermon on that text is one way. However, in our culture this is not the only—or even the most effective—way. In an oral culture, where few could read the Scriptures, there was a facility for learning the text through its public reading. In the early church, where not many had access to copies of Scripture, the congregation gathered before the worship service to hear the Bible read, in addition to any reading that was part of the service. This was probably a very effective means in that situation. In a letter St. Augustine of Hippo wrote to Jerome, there is an account of the reading of a text from Jonah during a service in a church in Roman North Africa.[1] Because the reading was from Jerome's new Latin version and not from the familiar old Latin version, the people shouted out the traditional words and refused to listen to the new translation. Augustine wrote that the bishop would have lost his church, rejected by his congregation, had he not agreed to go back to the traditional reading. Augustine stated that the congregation had memorized the passage through hearing, having sung it for generations.

In the Roman Empire, even during its decline in

the West, there were educational systems, considerable literacy, and the possibility of private copies of at least portions of Scripture for the reasonably well-to-do. The Germanic invasions that began in the fourth century put an end to the Western Empire and also to the limited availability of the Bible outside of corporate worship. Educational systems were destroyed, not to be rebuilt for centuries. Multitudes of new people who were not literate were added to what became Europe and added to the church. The society became increasingly oral.

Today, most of us in Western society no longer live in an oral culture. We do not readily learn by hearing; especially we do not memorize easily in that fashion. If we really want to learn what we have heard, we generally ask to see the text and read it for ourselves. In comparison to earlier cultures, we are a literate, not an oral, people. With the advent of new media forms that stress the visual, we may be moving beyond literacy, but we are not moving back to an oral society.

What means do we have in the church to learn and appropriate Scripture in our day? We can make use of the written text and adapt our methods to a literate culture. We can also find ways in which oral learning can be assisted, ways also used in the history of the church. We can also develop forms that use the newer media with which rising generations are more familiar.

1. Augustine, Letter 71.

It is significant that the Protestant movement of the sixteenth century began shortly after the development of the movable type printing press. With the rise of a commercial class, vernacular culture, and educational centers, literacy had been increasing for several generations. Luther soon came to understand the power of the new press. Relatively inexpensive editions of Scripture in the vernacular languages could be published. Catechisms filled with scriptural allusions could be widely and cheaply distributed. Hymns could be written based on the biblical texts and could be made readily available. Although the sixteenth-century Reformers still were in a somewhat oral culture, they set the stage for a Protestantism highly dependent upon literacy. To be a Protestant implied having a Bible and being able to read it. Scripture was to be read in the home, as part of family worship. It was to be studied. Its language was to permeate the whole life of the believer. This literate heritage is the legacy of most Protestants in the West.

That is not the situation today. Some in our churches do read Scripture privately every day, but family worship that includes such reading is not as common as it once was. As the whole society becomes increasingly secular, the basic knowledge of Scripture is no longer a part of the cultural norm. Without basic knowledge of biblical history, themes, names, and places, many in the church consider the Bible a formidable and inaccessible book. Perhaps because of this, as well as the fragmented character of much of contemporary family life and the dwindling tradition of family worship with the reading of Scripture, adults who grew up in this new situation may find it difficult to begin a serious study of Scripture on their own. Furthermore, when they hear Scripture read in congregational worship, they may lack the background to comprehend what has been read.

Why does a congregation need to know Scripture? Several answers could be given, and the way in which a church goes about intentionally teaching Scripture might depend on the purposes that are uppermost in that congregation's life. Let us consider two possible reasons for teaching Scripture. First, the purpose might be to ensure orthodoxy by having a basis upon which to judge, individually and corporately, the preaching and actions of the church. In that case, doctrine and law would be the chief portions stressed. A second purpose might be to give the believers resources for their individual and corporate lives of faith, to give reassurance, hope, comfort, strength in times of trial; to provide means of thanksgiving and praise in times of joy; to assist in the life of prayer by inculcating a vocabulary and a set of images that help them to understand and put into words their relationship with God through Christ. The Psalms, Isaiah, and the book of Revelation would be more helpful for these purposes. Distinctions of purpose cannot be drawn too sharply, but they do point to the variety of ways Scripture is used, or can be used, with great benefit in the life of the church. They also point out that the style and content of teaching may vary with a particular congregation's understanding of the function of the Bible.

SCRIPTURE IN CHRISTIAN EDUCATION

It is somewhat arbitrary to separate worship and Christian education, since for centuries worship was the major means of education in the church. Worship lasted much longer than an hour on Sunday, and Christian congregations often worshiped more than once a week. Children were part of the service, so their education also took place within the liturgy. During the first three centuries of the church's life, it was clear that most members were coming into the church from outside and needed to attend catechetical classes. Such classes could extend over two or three years. They included the study of the content of Scripture, particularly as the time approached for baptism. In a sermon given in the late fourth century to those who had just been baptized at Easter, Bishop Ambrose of Milan rehearsed what they had been taught and experienced in the baptismal service, pointing out the meaning of the various actions. The amount of Scripture that they learned is obvious.[2]

In subsequent centuries, this educational system broke down, overwhelmed by the sheer numbers who wished to be baptized. These numbers were caused by two different factors. First, in the early fourth century, Emperor Constantine's support of the church meant that great numbers of Roman citizens came into the church. Second, beginning later in that century, various Germanic tribes were

2. See Ambrose "On the Mysteries."

converted in large groups. The number of teachers was insufficient for this changed situation, so people were baptized without the previously required preparation. Also, children born into church families were baptized. As these became the vast majority of the population of Europe, there was no place for the traditional catechetical training.

The Protestant Reformation brought change, including a determined effort to educate the congregation about the biblical message, particularly as churches developed written catechisms. The congregation provided catechetical classes for children already baptized. Thanks to the development of the printing press, catechisms could be studied in the home as well as taught at church. Parents were expected to review and support the assigned study during the week. Special catechetical sessions were often held at the church for parents and children. The work on the catechism as well as the expected family worship, which included Bible study, were the major forms of Christian education.

Other forms of education developed later. The Sunday school movement began in the nineteenth century as a form of evangelism for unchurched children. Also, new forms of adult education emerged: Missionary study groups for women were part of the Evangelical Revival of the late eighteenth and early nineteenth centuries; small groups were part of the German Pietist and Methodist movements of the same period. Eventually, many of these forms merged into adult church school classes that became a normal part of the life of Protestant congregations. Where there was such a strong emphasis on Bible study, one could anticipate at least a basic familiarity with the major events and themes of the Bible. For those with little or no church connection, the public schools provided at least some acquaintance with the Bible.

Today, with the increased religious pluralism and secularism of Western society in general and American culture in particular, such basic knowledge can no longer be assumed, even on the part of those who are asked to teach in the church schools. Adults often are embarrassed about their lack of knowledge, and assume that they are the only ones to be so lacking. Congregations have increasingly recognized this situation and have addressed the problem through innovative Christian education programs. Instead of a rather casual study to which people give about half an hour a week with little preparation, congrega-

tions may be involved in intensive series on biblical knowledge, demanding a serious time commitment from members, perhaps outside of the traditional church school time, and over a period of months or years. These more intensive programs have helped to improve the general level of biblical knowledge.

Aside from providing basic biblical literacy, educational programs in the church have sought to deal more intensively and personally with particular portions of Scripture. This is done in a variety of ways. Different forms of the International Lesson Series are a part of denominational and nondenominational literature. These lessons are based on a selected and organized set of Scripture portions that help church school classes study a significant amount and variety of Scripture throughout the years. Material has been prepared for all levels of the church school, from children to adults, which gives some unity to what all the members of the family are studying. In congregations that use the ecumenical three-year lectionary cycle in Sunday worship, there may be church school classes that also deal with this material, perhaps in advance of the time it is scheduled to be used in the worship service. These classes may also help the preacher to prepare and reflect. Specific Bible studies are often a part of the programs for women's groups in the life of the church. Even beyond the local congregation, retreats and conferences provide opportunities for the study of Scripture with a clear intent to deal with its effect on our lives.

New materials for Christian nurture have also been developed for individual, family, or group devotional use. These help church members in personal and family devotions. Some are very simple suggestions of a passage to be read, with a brief comment and prayer added. Others are more complex, including liturgical elements based on the ancient monastic offices, as well as providing a context for the reading of Scripture.

Our era presents a very strange contrast to earlier centuries. In the past, Protestants were expected to know and study Scripture. But now, Protestant churches in our culture are having to learn how to cope with biblical illiteracy within their own membership. Roman Catholics, on the other hand, were not encouraged to study Scripture in the past; now, with the reforms of the Second Vatican Council, they have been encouraged to read and study the Bible both privately and in groups. The ecumenical horizon for the development of materials for the basic study of Scripture among Christians is exciting.

SCRIPTURE SET TO MUSIC

To the degree that great musical compositions that use biblical texts become part of the wider cultural horizon, Scripture is also taught. Many Christians know the words of Handel's *Messiah* and from that source have learned a great number of passages of Scripture, though they might find it difficult to locate them in the Bible. Even those well outside of the church also know the words. Anthems within the worship service also provide a way of hearing and learning Scripture. Many churches print the words in the bulletin so that the congregation will understand them clearly, a recognition of the non-oral character of our culture.

Hymns, however, are the great source of musical settings of Scripture for church members. In some, the words are directly taken from Scripture, as in the pattern of the metrical psalms of the Scottish tradition. Others are more indirectly paraphrased, as in Luther's "A Mighty Fortress." In an earlier time, hymn singing in the home was more common than it is now. Families had a variety of hymn books, and family or wider groups often gathered as a social event for the singing of hymns. In the African American tradition, spirituals were a significant means for developing a knowledge of the events and themes of biblical history, as well as a means for expressing the believers' faith, both in the worship of the congregation and in other settings.

It is not surprising that hymns are often the main source of learning biblical imagery. Many Christians, when seeking spiritual strength or guidance, are more likely to turn to hymns than to the Bible itself. Words and phrases that are sung may more readily slip into the mind than those that are only heard or read silently. Perhaps it is the versification or the music itself that helps us to remember the words and phrases. For whatever reason, most church members are far more likely to know the words " 'When through the deep waters I call thee to go,/ the rivers of woe shall not thee overflow' "[3] than the words of Isa 43:2: "When you pass through the waters, I will be with you;/ and through the rivers, they shall not overwhelm you" (NRSV). In fact, they

might not know that the words were really a paraphrase or where exactly they could be found in Scripture. Even Christians who would think of themselves as relatively unacquainted with some portions of Scripture, the book of Revelation for example, would be surprised at the allusions to it they do know because of the hymns they have learned.

Nor should we be surprised by the enormous number of biblical references in our hymnody. The Scriptures have been the major source of our imagery of the gospel and the Christian life. In addition, for centuries in some traditions, metrical versions of the psalms were considered the only legitimate form of hymnody in worship. The Puritan strand of the church was particularly noted for this. The result is an abundance of metrical psalms and psalm tunes that continue to play a vital part in worship, even though a wider variety of hymnody is now accepted.

The Protestant Reformation was known almost as much for its singing as for its stress on Scripture. In fact, revivals in the life of the Protestant churches have usually begun, or been accompanied by, great hymn writing and singing. The Wesleyan Revival in England, the Great Awakenings, and the development of African American Christianity in this country were accompanied by new hymnody. Many know the great narratives of the Bible through spirituals like "Go Down, Moses" and eschatological hopes through "My Lord! What a Morning." The strong vocabulary and imagery of Scripture are found throughout John Newton's "Amazing Grace" and Charles Wesley's "O For a Thousand Tongues." Almost direct scriptural quotations are in Fanny Crosby's "To God Be the Glory" (from the Gospel of John) and Thomas Chisholm's "Great Is Thy Faithfulness" (from Lamentations). In many of the newer ecclesiastical traditions, notably the Pentecostal, congregational singing is a major means for the learning of Scripture. This is particularly true in areas of the world where literacy or access to printed material is not high. Much of the new music used ecumenically comes out of Roman Catholic congregations in Latin America, where musical settings of biblical texts play a vital role in the renewal of that church.

The great hymn writers of the past knew Scripture well. Those of the present also do. Their music is able to bring the world of the Bible into our lives. We live in a time when a large body of great new

---

3. The third stanza of "How Firm a Foundation."

hymnody, closely tied to Scripture, is being written. These new hymns often build upon biblical themes that are more significant to the church now than they would have been a century or two ago. Some of these are emphasized because of the liturgical renewal movement. For instance, there are now many more hymns that stress the sacraments. Whereas many of the earlier hymns that were often used on occasions of the Lord's Supper were based on a substitutionary or satisfaction view of the atonement, such as "When I Survey the Wondrous Cross" or "Beneath the Cross of Jesus," the newer hymns tend to stress more the joy of the victory of Christ over the powers of evil, shown in the Resurrection, as in "This Is the Feast of Victory for Our God" and "Let Us Talents and Tongues Employ." There are also many more hymns that directly speak of baptism. More of the hymns are oriented to the faith of the community rather than to the faith of the individual. Many come from situations of oppression and speak to the presence and victory of Christ, even in those circumstances. Ecological concerns find a place in the new hymns as well, as do prayers for peace.

We have new hymns, and we have inherited a wealth of hymnody. Both the old and the new are a marvelous means for the learning and appropriation of Scripture. Yet many in the traditions that stem from the sixteenth century no longer sing with the enthusiasm of their forbearers. Older members seem reluctant to learn new hymns, and younger members do not find that older hymns reflect the issues primary in their Christian lives. What is needed are more congregations nurtured by both old and new hymns. If congregations realized the significant role hymns play in the learning and loving of Scripture, the obstacles that inhibit their vital use could be lessened. In fact, a solid study of how hymns convey biblical awareness, in which the old or new hymns could be judged on the basis of the degree to which they are biblically oriented, might well alleviate prejudices on both sides. Musical value obviously does need to be considered, but often prejudice arises out of the assumption that particular hymns represent or come out of theological movements with which we disagree. Looking at the words of hymns and judging them on a scriptural basis may help to overcome some of the passion that opposes them.

In past generations, when church members knew the Bible much better, singing a biblically based hymn might well have brought to mind the specific passage to which it alluded. In our own day, there may not be such recognition. If we wish to increase the knowledge of Scripture on the part of the congregation, we may have to help the church members see how much they already do know and make the link from the hymns and liturgical elements back to the Bible. In an earlier generation worship grew out of an immersion in the biblical texts. Today, however, we may need to reverse the process, and use the hymns to take the congregation back into the biblical material. In this endeavor, the hymn books or liturgical materials that contain an index or notation of biblical references or allusions are a great help. Intentional collaboration on the part of worship leaders and church musicians can promote significant learning within the context of worship.

In addition to anthems and hymns, biblical texts and music are often combined in what is generally termed "Service Music." The liturgical renewal of recent years has increased the number of congregations using such musical settings.

SCRIPTURE IN THE LITURGY

The role of Scripture in the liturgy of the Christian church is obviously a complex issue, since there is such a variety of liturgies historically, including those of churches that consider themselves nonliturgical, and we are presently in the midst of a major liturgical revolution.

There are basically three historical roots of the uses of Scripture in the liturgy of the Western church: the monastic office, the medieval eucharistic service, and the particular requirements of the Protestant churches. It is almost impossible to deal with these sources separately; they all need to be considered. In the following discussion of various elements of Christian worship, all three will be discussed where they apply in regard to each aspect of the worship service. Because the monastic office is not generally understood as a source for contemporary worship, or at least not understood as readily as the other two sources, it would perhaps be helpful to begin with some discussion of the use of Scripture in those services.

The Daily Office. The monastic order of prayer is variously referred to as the Daily Office, the Divine Office, or the Breviary. It may stem originally from forms of daily prayer that were used in the early church, perhaps based on synagogue use. As a monastic liturgy, it was developed over centuries, and in the West was made fairly uniform under the Benedictine Order in the early Middle Ages. However, there have been a number of reforms and changes, most recently after the Second Vatican Council. From the basic form used in monastic houses, there are adaptations for the use of individuals or families, or for religious groups that need a more abbreviated version. Although this order of prayer has been a major part of monastic life, it originated among ordinary Christians, who have continued to use it throughout history.

The basic content of the whole Office is the book of Psalms, divided into about eight different times of prayer for each day. The entire Psalter is read over a period of one or two weeks, divided into psalms appropriate for the different days of the week or the different times of the day. Morning and evening prayer, brief times of prayer during the day, and prayer at bedtime is the basic structure. More elaborate liturgical forms developed within the monastic setting, where the services were more formal and there could be training and preparation. Eventually the whole service was sung to Gregorian chant.

Antiphons play an important role in the Office. These are brief responses that are said or sung before and after, and sometimes during, each of the psalms. They are frequently taken from that psalm or from another part of Scripture, and they help to focus the particular emphasis of the day or the season. In addition, in the longer times of prayer there are fairly long passages of Scripture to be read. In the brief times of prayer, a short verse or two of Scripture is recited. These brief verses are repeated with sufficient frequency during the day and the season that it would be difficult not to memorize them. Also, other brief responsive forms, directly related to the particular time of day or season, are composed largely of portions of Scripture. There are also brief prayers, as well as the Lord's Prayer. Several of the New Testament (NT) psalms or canticles are used in these Offices, such as Mary's song in Luke 1:47-55 (the Magnificat) and Simeon's song in Luke 2:29-32 (*Nunc Dimittis*). The traditional liturgical names for these hymns come from the words that begin the Latin versions.

Anyone who seriously used the Divine Office would be thoroughly immersed in Scripture. Since it was required for monastics and priests, the vast majority of the Protestant reformers of the sixteenth century were trained in this form. Through the Divine Office, the Roman Catholic Church preserved a knowledge of Scripture. The objection of the Reformers, aside from particular biblical interpretations they opposed, was that persons who were not able to understand Latin were deprived of the knowledge of Scripture. The Reformers themselves, however, had been strongly influenced by the Psalms that they had learned in this fashion.

Precisely because the Office developed for the use of lay Christians rather than ordained ones, it requires no ordained leadership. It is appropriate for use in a variety of settings. No sacrament or sermon is expected. At the time of the Protestant Reformation, serious issues concerning the meaning of the mass led several Reformers to develop forms for Sunday worship that did not include the Eucharist. The services of morning and evening prayer in the monastic Office were one of the models they used. They were adapted for the new circumstances so that they would now be led by clergy, include sermons, be in the language of the people, and use congregational hymns rather than Gregorian chant. In the Anglican tradition, the *Book of Common Prayer* still has strong elements of the monastic forms in its services of morning and evening prayer.

More recently, many Protestant churches, seeking to find ways of increasing the devotional use of the Bible, have developed forms of daily prayer that are clearly based on the ancient monastic form. The specific Roman Catholic elements have been removed, the number of psalms limited, and hymns are suggested; but the form is still there, and is very useful.

The basic understanding underlying the Office is quite different from that of most contemporary Protestants who are seeking a deeper devotional life. The Office assumes that the great prayer life of the church is going on, regardless of the individual. Others throughout the world are praying this Office. Those who decide to use this method of prayer are joining something that is already going on. In other words, the Office is part of a corporate prayer life, even if a solitary person is praying it alone in a room. The sense is that they all are joined in an already existing corporate prayer life. If at some point they do not join this prayer, their voice may be missed, but the prayer goes on, waiting for them to rejoin. This is in great contrast to the individualism that usually marks our modern life. For many, it is precisely this corporate sense that is the great strength of the Divine Office. It is the church that is praying. In addition, because the Office is related to the church year, its use can reinforce the rest of liturgical life. It can tie the devotions of the home into the celebrations of the congregation.

The monastic Office is also an excellent source for liturgical elements that can be used as calls to worship, or in a variety of ways within a more traditional Sunday service. Its method of using Scripture in a liturgical fashion is often extremely creative, and can be very helpful as a model for worship leaders who are seeking to incorporate more Scripture into worship. Within a liturgical setting, there is a freedom to combine brief lines from one passage with those from another. The grammatical forms are readily changed from the singular to the plural, or from first to third person, so that they are authentic expressions of worship for those who are using them. In other words, there is a freedom in the liturgical use of Scripture that would not be appropriate in the Scripture lesson or in the exegetical work for a sermon.

A few examples may help to show what is meant. The Office at bedtime is brief and has few variations through the year, since the major theme that is considered is the time of sleep rather than the season of the year. The medieval form of the Night Office for Sunday night began with a blessing: "May the all-powerful Lord grant us a peaceful night and a perfect end." Then followed a brief verse from Scripture (1 Pet 5:8-9) that speaks of the need to be watchful in the face of temptation. The response was "Our help is in the name of the Lord, who made heaven and earth" (Ps 124:8). Then the Lord's Prayer was said. The Psalms followed. The new form begins with a hymn and then goes directly to the Psalms. The Psalms in both forms are Psalms 4, 91, and 134, all of which are appropriate preparation for sleep. Some of the antiphons before these psalms are: "Have mercy on me, Lord, and hear my prayer" (an adaptation of Ps 51:1); and "Night holds no terrors for me sleeping under God's wings." There is a brief biblical verse, this time Jer 14:9, which speaks of God's presence in our midst. Then comes a responsive form combining biblical phrases from a variety of places. The words are "Into your hands, O Lord, I commend my spirit. You have redeemed

us, O Lord, God of truth. Into your hands, O Lord, I commend my spirit." The medieval form added these words: "Keep us, O Lord, as the pupil of your eye. Shelter us under the shadow of your wings." The Song of Simeon (*Nunc Dimittis*) is said, which begins, "Master, now you are dismissing your servant in peace. . . . " (Luke 2:29ff). The antiphon for this canticle is a very ancient one: "Protect us, Lord, while we are awake and safeguard us while we sleep, that we may keep watch with Christ and rest in peace." Some brief prayers and responses follow, and the Office concludes with the blessing "May the all-powerful Lord grant us a restful night and a peaceful death."

Anyone who prays the Divine Office for several years would be very well acquainted with a wide variety of Scripture, particularly the Psalms.

The Call to Worship or Introit. The medieval mass proper began with an introit, or entrance antiphon, which was usually a responsive form based on a psalm or other biblical material. It was a statement of the particular emphasis or theme of the day's worship. It differs from what is usually referred to as a call to worship, which is an invitation to worship. The difference is not that one is sung and the other spoken, which is often the way the terms are distinguished in Protestant churches. Both forms are traditionally based on Scripture, but the understanding of their function differs. The function of a call to worship is to invite the congregation to enter into worship. The function of an introit is to set the theme for the whole service. On major days of the Christian year, the difference may be negligible, since the call to worship may reflect the specific season, but the rest of the year, there is often a clear distinction.

Introits are closely related to the church year and to the particular themes that emerge from a stress on the year. They are proper for the day, and specific ones are listed for each mass of the year. For instance, the medieval introit for the second Sunday in Advent included Psalm 80:1: "Give ear, O Shepherd of Israel,/ you who lead Joseph like a flock!" (NRSV). For the third Sunday in Lent, it was various verses from Psalm 25:

To you, O LORD, I lift up my soul.
O my God, in you I trust;
    do not let me be put to shame;
. . . .

My eyes are ever toward the LORD,
    for he will pluck my feet out of the net.
Turn to me and be gracious to me,
    for I am lonely and afflicted.
(vv. 1-2, 15-16 NRSV)

For the seventeenth Sunday after Pentecost, it was from Psalm 119, vv. 1, 124, and 137:

Happy are those whose way is blameless,
    who walk in the law of the LORD.
. . . .
Deal with your servant according to your steadfast love,
    and teach me your statutes.
. . . .
You are righteous, O LORD,
    and your judgments are right. (NRSV)

These tended to be responsive and to conclude with the Gloria Patri. In each case, they related quite closely to the themes articulated by the passages assigned by the traditional lectionary for these particular Sundays.

When the introit form is used, there is exposure of a congregation to a wider variety of passages. If they are sung or said responsively by the congregation, and if the source of the text is listed, the people are being educated about Scripture as a part of worship. In Protestant services where the call to worship is not normally specifically set by the denomination, a verse or two from the psalm assigned for the day or from another of the lectionary passages may be used in the fashion of an introit.

The Daily Office had an influence on the development of Protestant worship, and may well be the source of the call to worship form. The monastic Daily Office begins with Psalm 95:

O come, let us sing to the LORD;
    let us make a joyful noise to the
        rock of our salvation!
Let us come into his presence with thanksgiving;
    let us make a joyful noise to
        him with songs of praise! (NRSV)

This is more like a call to worship than the introit forms of the mass.

In recent years, some of the educational opportunity of the call to worship has been lost. Perhaps out of a concern to make worship more personal or directly relevant to the congregation, calls to worship have been created that are not based on biblical sources, but are more a reflection of the assumed frame of mind of the congregation. They often begin with a statement such as, "We are not sure why we are here" or "We are here hoping something will happen." It may be helpful to lift up such issues, but what this has meant is that an opportunity has been lost for increasing the knowledge and appropriation of Scripture by the congregation. It also points to a concentration on the congregation's own feelings rather than on the actions of the God who has called them together.

Confession and Pardon. One of the points of controversy in the Reformation was the role of the clergy in the forgiveness of sins. For this reason, many Protestant churches avoided any form of absolution after the prayer of confession, preferring to read words directly from Scripture, assuring those who are penitent that their sins are forgiven. Where this is done, the congregation often learns the passages from these assurances of pardon. Typical of the passages used are 1 John 2:1-2; John 3:16; 1 Tim 1:15. Passages may focus on the need for repentance, on the mercy and love of God, on the promise of forgiveness, or on some combination of these. This is an excellent point for the use of Scripture, and it may well provide the congregation with the words they will be able to draw on in their own Christian lives.

As part of the sequence of confession and forgiveness, churches have used a variety of other materials, including the Ten Commandments or the two Great Commandments, often read with a musical or spoken response. Historically these have been used either before the prayer of confession, as a guide to what needs to be confessed, or as a response to forgiveness, indicating the kind of life we are now free to live.

Other possible responses to the prayer of confession are some ancient forms, one that begins "Lord have mercy upon us" (the Kyrie), a second that begins "Glory to God in the highest" (the Gloria) and one that begins "Lamb of God, you take away the sins of the world" (the Agnus Dei), all of which draw on biblical themes or phrases, though without extensive quotation.

The Responsive Psalm. The form that has already been described in the monastic Office, the psalm read responsively, often with an antiphon, was also a part of the traditional eucharistic service. In many Protestant services, stemming either from the mass or from the monastic morning or evening prayer, there remains a responsive reading, which has usually been a psalm. Some Protestant traditions had metrical settings of psalms. Recently, many new psalm settings for cantor and congregational response have been written by both Catholics and Protestants, and their use has enjoyed a renaissance. The response functions as an antiphon, and may not be taken from the psalm itself. The response may be from a very different portion of Scripture and serve to tie the psalm very directly to the liturgical season being celebrated. For instance, the Roman Catholic Christmas midnight mass has Psalm 96 as the responsive reading, with the simple antiphon, "Today is born our Savior, Christ the Lord." The second Sunday after Christmas mass uses Ps 147:12ff, with an antiphon from the first chapter of the Gospel of John: "The Word of God became man, and lived among us." The first Sunday in Lent uses Psalm 51, and the antiphon is a simple restatement of one of the verses, put into the plural for the congregation: "Be merciful, O LORD, for we have sinned."

The Peace. In liturgies that include the passing of the peace, various words from Scripture serve to introduce it. These vary from the simple greeting of "Peace be with you," the words of Jesus to the disciples after the resurrection (John 20:19), to the more extensive passage from Matt 5:23-24, concerning the need to be reconciled with others before bringing gifts to the altar. The particular placement of the passing of the peace in the service will probably determine which passages are most helpful. Its traditional place was based on the Matthew passage, before the elements were brought to the table. Some congregations have placed it following Communion, or at some other point. If there is no bringing of the elements to the table, the Matthew passage is not as useful.

The Offertory. This term is very confusing, especially for Protestants in the United States, for whom the tradition of receiving an offering of money for the support of the church and its mission is an essential part of worship. Obviously, in state churches of the Old World such support came in a very different manner. Yet the traditional services included an offertory. In the early church, it was the presentation by members of the congregation of the bread and wine to be used in the eucharistic service. Later, it often became the transfer of the elements by the priest from a table at the side of the chancel to the altar. As part of the liturgical renewal of our own day, the practice of having the elements brought forward by members of the congregation at the point of the eucharistic prayer has been revived. In some traditions, the two meanings have been combined, so that the money offering is brought forward as part of the same procession as the elements.

In either case, biblical passages have been used at this point. In the case of money, the verses have usually had to do with being a cheerful giver (2 Cor 9:7) or the self-giving of Christ that we are called to imitate (2 Cor 8:9). The medieval mass included offertory verses, generally from the Psalms, which dealt more with the theme of the day. When the elements for Communion are brought forward at this time, words about God's graciousness in feeding the people are appropriate, such as Ps 145:15-16: "The eyes of all look to you,/ and you give them their food in due season./ You open your hand,/ satisfying the desire of every living thing" (NRSV).

The Creed. The texts of the traditional creeds, either Apostles' or Nicene, are clearly not from Scripture. And yet something needs to be said about their relationship to Scripture. Biblical phrases are included, especially in the Apostles' Creed, but the purpose of the creeds is to give a basic guide to the interpretation of Scripture. That is, they give a brief description of the whole of Scripture on basic issues so that no single passage can be taken out of context and misinterpreted. Both creeds were developed in order to avoid the heresies that were prevalent in the early centuries of the church's life. They were the touchstone to determine which congregations and bishops were part of the one great church, and which should not be so considered. The Apostles' Creed developed as the confessional statement required for baptism. The ancient heresies have not gone forever, but can reappear in any generation, whenever a single part of Scripture is looked at apart from the whole, as did the ancient heresies that denied the humanity or the divinity of the Redeemer, or the goodness of the material creation, or the identity of the God of Israel as the God of the Christians. Creeds are not in themselves biblical, but they need to be seen as functioning in relation to Scripture. Some congregations use more recent confessional statements of their own traditions for this function. These would perform some of the same tasks as the early creeds, though less ecumenically, and probably would be used because they deal with theological issues that the early creeds did not consider. On these grounds they may be useful on occasion, but congregations need to confess the faith of the wider church and on the basic issues of the faith with great frequency. The other documents need to find a place in the life of the church, and even in worship, but not at the expense of the ancient and ecumenical creeds.

Many congregations use biblical passages for creedal statements in the service. Particularly useful are some from the Pauline epistles, such as sections of Romans 8 or Philippians 2. One needs to be aware that such passages, since they are from Scripture itself, cannot perform the task of providing a general framework for the interpretation of Scripture.

Prayers. Most Christian worship includes the Lord's Prayer, which is clearly a passage from Scripture. Only in the period of the strong Puritan reaction to the *Book of Common Prayer* with its set prayers did some propose using the Lord's Prayer as a model for the pastoral prayer, rather than as something to be memorized and said by all. However, today that prayer is so familiar to most Christians that even when worshiping in a language totally foreign one can pick up the cadences and the relative lengths of phrases and know what is being said.

Litanies may have biblical responses to the various petitions, either sung or said. Other prayers in the life of the church generally draw on biblical imagery and occasional phrases, but are not quotations.

The Sacraments. Many Protestant traditions have wished to make very clear that the particular sacraments or ordinances they use have scriptural warrant. For this reason, the words of institution of the Lord's Supper have often not been part of the prayer of consecration, but were said before that prayer as the clear indication that the sacrament was commanded by Christ. In baptismal services, the concluding verses of Matthew are often read for the same reason. Even in nonsacramental services, such as marriage or the setting apart of church officers, various passages have been used as warrant for the church's action. To the degree that such use of Scripture is a part of Scholastic Protestantism it has lost its dominance, and the placement of the words of institution within the eucharistic prayer is becoming more common.

The Eucharist prayer often includes other portions of Scripture, particularly the Sanctus ("Holy, holy, holy Lord," based on Isa 6:3) with or without the Benedictus ("Blessed is he who comes in the name of the Lord," Luke 19:38), both with biblical roots. The prayer usually includes the words of institution, based on 1 Cor 11:23-26.

Protestant traditions often include some form of invitation to the Table, clarifying who is invited. This clarification in the early generations of Protestantism had the purpose of warning those who were not prepared to stay away, what was termed "fencing the Table." More recently it has been stated in more positive terms as an invitation. The most common traditional form of invitation in English-speaking churches is taken from the *Book of Common Prayer,* and begins, "Ye who do truly and earnestly repent of your sins. . . . " In many of the newer liturgies, passages of Scripture have been used at this point, and may therefore be fairly similar to an offertory— words of Jesus, "I am the bread of life . . . " (John 6:35), or words of the psalmist, "O taste and see that the LORD is good!" (Ps 34:8), or from the Gospel narratives, "When our risen Lord was at table with his disciples . . . " (adapted from Luke 24:30). These passages have less the character of "fencing the table" against sinners and more that of a positive invitation to a feast.

Since the Bible is composed of words, one could expect that only words would be examples of its use in worship, but that is not totally the case. The most dominant themes in Scripture are narratives of events in which God has acted for the redemption of the people. In the life of Israel, the supreme event was the exodus from Egypt, with the return from the exile in Babylon a later parallel. In the Gospels, the event above all is the cross and resurrection of Jesus. Scripture does not see these as totally separate and disparate events. Even as the return from exile seems to be a new exodus, so also the cross and resurrection are seen as an exodus from sin and death. Paul paralleled the Passover with the Christian celebration of Easter; and the crossing of the Red Sea with baptism. The Gospel of John points to Jesus as the Bread of Heaven that is like manna, but far superior. These repeated parallel events or typologies also find a major place in liturgy. What this implies is that in the worship setting, particularly in its sacramental forms, but also in the liturgical year, the events of which Scripture speaks can come to life and be participated in, not simply spoken of. The sermon is a central piece of this event-character of worship, but the rest of the liturgy, the various elements that have been mentioned here, from hymns to offertories and benedictions, also have an essential role to play.

Without an understanding of such biblical typology, the early liturgies seem very strange indeed. Think of the "Apostolic Tradition," also known as the "Rite of Hippolytus," which stems from the third century, though purports to represent an earlier, second century form. There, baptism is paralleled with the exodus. The whole baptismal service, because it is held on Easter Eve, links the baptism of the new candidate with the death and resurrection of Jesus, which is in turn linked to Israel's crossing of the Red Sea and the Jordan. In other words, the release from bondage that God had effected for Israel, followed by the entrance into the Promised Land across the Jordan, was reenacted, relived, redone in an even greater fashion by Jesus, who freed humanity from the greater bondage to sin and death and all the powers of evil, and delivered us to a greater land, the Kingdom, the Reign of God.

When baptism was performed on Easter Eve, the candidate was not simply reminded of those past events, but the parallel was relived at that very moment. If the cross and resurrection form the archetype to which the exodus points as a type, then baptism is also a type pointing back to the cross and resurrection of Jesus and to the exodus. To say that the cross and the resurrection are the archetype is to say that the types that occur earlier in history lead to this center, and types occurring later stem from it.

It can be stated more clearly: Baptism and the Eucharist are types. The liturgical event in our own midst is the latest in the series of such types. It depends for its power on the archetype, on the cross and the resurrection of Jesus. It has no independent source or power. But in the same way that the exodus and the death and resurrection of Jesus were actual events in history, so too is this baptism a specific moment in history, in a chain of events linked by their typological pointing to the cross and resurrection.

The "Rite of Hippolytus" sheds more light on the parallels. After the candidates were baptized and anointed with oil—that is, made Christs, "anointed ones," with royal and priestly powers—they are joined to the whole congregation as the Easter Eucharist is celebrated. For these candidates, their first Communion included not only the traditional chalice of wine, but also a chalice of milk and honey, to indicate that through baptism, they have been brought into the Promised Land, that the water in which they were baptized was a type not only of the Red Sea but also of the Jordan.

Other types abound in the ancient liturgies: the manna in the wilderness and the bread of Communion, which the Gospel of John links with the words of Jesus: "I am the Bread of Heaven." Those who are baptized may truly have entered the Promised Land, but there is also a sense in which they still are pilgrims through the wilderness, preparing to enter that land. The image of new birth is also clearly present, along with death and resurrection. Again, the words of the Gospel of John are helpful: Even as Jesus was born, not of the will of the flesh but of God, so too in baptism those who once were born of the flesh are now born of God. And these words from the Prologue of John's Gospel come just before the account of the baptism of Jesus: "To all who received him, who believed in his name, he gave power to become children of God, who were born, not of blood or of the will of the flesh or of the will of man, but of God" (vv. 12-13 NRSV).

Types are not simple representations of past history, but complex, evocative, symbolic, poetic forms that can be combined in myriad ways within liturgy. Yet they retain the character of a new historical moment in which these types come to life, with the power they possess because of those earlier moments. If in the Scripture itself we find frequent use of typology, much of it pointing to the liturgy, then it would appear that the liturgy of the church may be the best setting in which to understand fully the significance of much of Scripture. It is in the liturgy, most specifically in baptism and the Eucharist as well as in aspects of the liturgical year, that the types with which Scripture has to do reach us and become events in our time. Baptisms were situated on Easter Eve because in our baptism we died with Christ and rose with him. The Eucharist was on Sunday because it was the day of the resurrection. The calendar and the sacraments became events, typologically, not simply rituals that were performed for reasons of tradition. To know and participate in the liturgy is to become more and more familiar with Scripture. To know Scripture is to be better prepared to participate in liturgy. Worship is not only for the sake of the adoration of God, but it is also for the sake of forming in character and values, in life and attitudes, those who are the church, the Body of Christ in the world, the worshipers. Those who know that baptism has indeed called them to live as a priestly people are able to have a greater appreciation for the prayers of intercession in the liturgy, since priests stand before God to pray for others. Luther understood this in stressing "the priesthood of all believers."

In the sixteenth century and beyond one of the debates among the churches was whether something "happened" in baptism and the Lord's Supper. Roman Catholics had understood that what "happened" in the Eucharist was a change in the elements, not a repetition of a type. Protestants were asking whether these were purely symbolic acts or whether something really changed. To view the sacraments typologically is to see that question differently. Yes, something happens: At a specific moment in history in a liturgical setting a type recurs. What Scripture records as happening in the past now occurs in our presence. It is an event. How we respond to that event may be as ambiguous as is our response to all of history. The possibilities may only be known to faith. But an event is an event. It is not the symbol of an event. An event is a moment in which something happens. It is a specific moment in history. It is a moment in which Scripture is not only spoken and explained, but also happens.

The Blessing. In the medieval mass, the blessing was simple and invariable: "May almighty God bless you, the Father, and the Son, and the Holy Spirit." In Protestant services, a wider variety of benedictions has been used, many of which were taken from the conclusions to Pauline epistles.

As with the call to worship, many congregations now use benedictions that are not taken from Scripture but are specifically written to deal with current concerns of Christians, or to carry out the message of the sermon. Where this is done, an opportunity has been lost for a word of blessing from Scripture to be learned and appropriated.

CONCLUSION

A knowledge of Scripture and an ability to use it and to reflect on it are a necessity for the Christian life. This was recognized from the earliest days of the church. The church in the West has experienced centuries when many of its members had only minimal knowledge of Scripture. Renewal in the life

of the church has been tied to the expansion of the love of Scripture and its appropriation in the daily lives of Christians. Sometimes this was limited to those who entered monastic life, but always renewal and Scripture were tied together.

In our own day and culture, we face the problem of a serious lack of biblical knowledge. It is more than that, however. As was mentioned in the sections on the call to worship and the benediction, in many contemporary congregations nonbiblical writings considered to be more relevant to the situation of the worshipers are substituted for biblical forms. Church school classes also often avoid serious study of Scripture, preferring topics that appear more related to their lives. What is reflected here is not only an ignorance of Scripture, but the sense that it has little relevance to daily lives. Merely scheduling classes to fill in knowledge will not suffice, if there is the underlying presupposition that such knowledge will be irrelevant.

In this regard, we have much to learn from the early church. Education was a major preparation for worship, which was a major bearer of the educational task. There was a strong tradition of devotional use of Scripture in the corporate life of the church which was related to the devotional life of the individual and family. Music played a great part in the worship and education of Christians.

We can learn three lessons from this that would be helpful in our own day. First, knowledge about the Bible is not enough. What is needed is a corporate setting in which such knowledge is directly applied to the lives of the congregation. This is obviously a major task of the sermon, but it cannot be left to that alone. The whole worship and educational life of the church needs to include such application. Perhaps as a result of the Enlightenment and the scientific and technological society in which we live, we tend to view knowledge as a collection of objective facts to be learned. In this sense, a knowledge of the Bible is not particularly helpful. The early church viewed biblical knowledge as a form of wisdom, a path to holy and blessed life. It was not a matter of the mind only, but of the heart and the will as well.

Second, we have also tended to separate worship and devotion, thinking that worship is objective and appropriate for corporate gatherings, and devotion is subjective, and, therefore, a private matter for the individual. This may be the result of the Pietist reaction to Orthodoxy in the seventeenth and eighteenth centuries. The early church was able to have subjective formation of the Christian life in the midst of what was strongly objective worship of the transcendent God. It was also able to have a corporate form of devotional use of Scripture in the monastic Office, which could also be adapted for family worship. It could also give a corporate sense to individual devotion.

Third, there cannot be a separation of worship and Christian education. These are not two independent tracks in the life of the church. Education needs to be related to joyful and intelligent participation in worship and devotion, and worship and devotion need to be educational. All should be geared to the involvement in and appropriation of Scripture. If this is done, then there is excellent reason for having classes related to a variety of contemporary issues, based on a corporate Christian life growing out of the Bible.

Our church life often divides worship, education, and personal devotion. It takes great coordination in the church, both denominationally and locally, to relate worship and education, and a program for devotional use in the home. Such coordination may have to begin slowly, but it is most helpful. In addition, the music program of the church can be coordinated with worship, devotion, and education. All need to be geared to a variety of ages. Scripture can provide the basic focus, perhaps with the church year as the overarching structure based on the lectionary. The resulting program may involve thinking through what being baptized means or what being part of the Body of Christ in the world means, based on particular passages. It may involve understanding the creeds more deeply, or Communion in relation to a particular passage. It may also provide simple suggestions for home use, especially for ways of involving children. One of the major seasons of the year, either Advent and Christmas or Lent and Easter, might provide the best time to try such an experiment. It has been interesting to note the degree to which the Advent wreath has become readily accepted recently in both the church and the home. This has been true even for Christians who have little or no liturgical tradition. One reason may be that it does provide the kind of simple link between the worship of the church and the renewal of family devotions. It provides something in which children can participate and begin to understand. There is a hunger for such links as a means to develop and nurture Christian lives.

In our own time there is a lack of appreciation for the power of Scripture, partly because of a lack of acquaintance with it. This has affected the worship and the educational life of the church, since these aspects of the church's life depend on such knowledge. The challenge of the church today is to find ways to so immerse congregations in the Scripture that they begin again to view all of life through its lens. Worship in all of its fullness, as well as the educational program of the church, are needed in this effort. Both will be enriched by it.

BIBLIOGRAPHY

Brueggemann, Walter. *The Creative Word: Canon as a Model for Biblical Education.* Philadelphia: Fortress, 1982.

Carson, D. A. *Teach Us to Pray: Prayer in the Bible and the World.* Grand Rapids: Baker, 1990.

Consultation on Common Texts. *The Revised Common Lectionary.* Nashville: Abingdon, 1992.

Holbert, John C., S T Kimbrough, and Carlton R. Young. *Psalms for Praise and Worship: A Complete Liturgical Psalter.* Nashville: Abingdon, 1992.

Lengeling, E. J. "Pericopes." In *New Catholic Encyclopedia* 11. New York: McGraw-Hill, 1967.

Reumann, John. "A History of Lectionaries." *Int* 31 (1977) 116-30.

Reynolds, William Jensen, and Milburn Price. *A Survey of Christian Hymnody.* Carol Stream, Ill.: Hope, 1987.

Rogal, Samuel J. *A General Introduction to Hymnody and Congregational Song.* Metuchen, N.J.: Scarecrow, 1991.

Spencer, Jon Michael. *Black Hymnody: A Hymnological History of the African-American Church.* Knoxville: The University of Tennessee Press, 1992.

White, James F. *Sacraments as God's Self-giving: Sacramental Practice of Faith.* Nashville: Abingdon, 1983.

LIFE IN ANCIENT PALESTINE

DAVID C. HOPKINS

Life in ancient Palestine was a complex constellation of political forces, social and religious forms, economic patterns, and cultural traditions. This complexity is easy to overlook when observed from the standpoint of the biblical literature. Yet new windows that have opened up on ancient Palestine in recent decades increasingly expose a heterogeneous tableau. Israelite and Judean society was composed of contrasting, though interlaced, fragments of urban and rural life. Conditions of life varied to such an extent that the term *society* itself only has meaning in the most general sense. Geography alone created a fragmented landscape: Regionalism was the basic fact of life. Moreover, the Palestinian social scene was radically splintered by class divisions and degrees of wealth and political power. Both human life and the biblical literature that emerged from it were stamped by the conflict inherent in these divisions. In addition, the larger political and military powers that influenced the western rim of the Mediterranean Sea encouraged regional and social strife in their struggle to control Palestine's strategic landscape. Pressed by external forces and tossed by internal struggle, the people of ancient Palestine developed a distinct life and culture of which the Bible is the most enduring legacy.

SOURCES OF DATA

The Bible. While life in ancient Palestine was complex, a general picture does emerge. The Bible naturally provides an essential source for this picture. Yet it is more helpful in some areas than others and particularly unhelpful in reconstructing crucial aspects of daily life. The biblical records focus first and foremost on the political and religious history of Israel and Judah, the history of events dominated by strong personalities. The everyday life of the region comes into play only tangentially and is not itself an area of interest for biblical poets, chroniclers, and storytellers. Moreover, the texts offer a distinct perspective on daily life, one governed by the social location of the Bible as the product of a literary elite. However "rural" the world of the Bible may appear at first glance or in comparison to the modern world, an urban outlook controls most portraits of life presented in the Bible. Inasmuch as the urban world—the world of politics and government—was ruled by men, the Bible's orientation also regularly excludes female perspectives and subjects. The private and domestic sphere where women held sway is by and large neglected. Thus the urban, male authorship of most biblical literature circumscribes its testimony about life lived outside the public arena. The formal character of the biblical texts themselves, many of them originating as "official documents" of major social institutions (e.g., Deuteronomy) magnifies the normative or idealist nature of their presentation. Reality seldom matches such portraits. In fact, it may be consciously obscured as these ancient authors attempt to influence rather than to describe the life of their times. With these caveats in mind, one may claim that the Bible offers a cardinal witness to the basic structure and many facets of life in its place of origin, from the agrarian nature of the society to the basic social, economic, and political institutions along with the ideas that animated them.

Archaeology. The biblical data on life in ancient Palestine is complemented by the data emerging from ongoing archaeological investigation. Archaeology, the study of the material record of the past, contributes to the portrait of life in Palestine. Calls to reform and royal pronouncements do not leave traces in the dirt unless they are acted on by human hands. The material remains unearthed by archaeologists are the frozen deeds of the ancient communities. Archaeological research into the nature of the ancient environment illuminates the real conditions under which communities of biblical times made their homes, an area passed over by our biblical sources. Whereas the Bible contains the ideas of an elite segment of the Israelite and Judean communities, archaeology displays the broad spectrum of the material culture. Its contribution includes the recovery of how ordinary people actually lived, especially when excavation leaves the city precinct and ventures into the countryside. While we cannot often be certain which actors created which remains, taken as a whole, archaeology exposes the unfiltered, unauthorized products of the rich and poor, urban and rural, female and male residents of ancient Palestine.

Anthropology and Comparative Sociology. Both the data of archaeology and the critical study of the biblical literature require a systemic model—some means of integrating the disparate pieces of information—in order to be understood. Anthropological research, in particular ethnography, and the work of comparative sociology provide this coherence in numerous recent studies. Models of social structure and function drawn from these disciplines affirm the interrelationship between various elements of ancient life. Such work helps to guard against abstract claims and unrealistic reconstructions. Ethnographic analogies guide the interpretation of particular artifacts (e.g., stone-cut oil presses) and social institutions (e.g., kinship structures). Moreover, study of pre-industrial societies, when situated in demographically, technologically, and environmentally parallel locations, can augment the portrait of life in ancient Palestine. Where the Bible does not inform us and archaeology cannot reveal much (e.g., regarding gender roles), ethnographic analogy can at least whet our imagination. No such model is able to allow for the unique solutions to the problems of life conceived and carried out by ancient Israelites and Judeans. Yet models describing, for example, the nature of monarchical government, the role of the temple in pre-industrial states, or the influence of population growth on agricultural production, remain indispensable and unavoidable guides to interpreting archaeological and biblical data.

GEOGRAPHY

Strategic Location. The shape and sense of life in ancient Palestine responds substantially to three key aspects of its geography, both local and geopolitical. First, Palestine is a strategically crucial commercial and military crossroad. Located at the eastern end of the Mediterranean Sea and at the western end of the fertile crescent, which stretches from the top of the Persian Gulf toward the valley of the Nile, Palestine constituted a land bridge connecting Egypt and Mesopotamia, the two major centers of ancient Near Eastern civilization. Moreover, this narrow strip of land offered a port of entry for contact between the Near East and Greek and Roman civilizations of Europe. Major trade routes funneled through Palestine from all four compass points: from Europe through the Phoenician ports, from Egypt along the Mediterranean coast, from Arabia and East Africa through the Gulf of Aqaba, and from Syria and Mesopotamia skirting the Arabian desert. Because of its commercial importance, Palestine was rarely exempt from larger struggles that it could do little to control. Campaigning armies of the empires often crossed its soil. The prosperity of Palestine depended in large measure upon the political and economic situation in these distant lands.

Limited Natural Resources. The interest directed by the ruling political powers of the ancient world toward Palestine rarely went beyond control of its strategic location. There was little else to be exploited. Hence, limited natural resources constitute a second determining characteristic of Palestine. The land does not possess any great mineral wealth, only some pockets of iron ore east of the Jordan and copper in the south. Forests of small trees and dense undergrowth satisfied limited local building needs, but were cut down for fuel rather than harvested for lumber. Lebanon, not Palestine, is famous for timber. The region's predominantly limestone rocks and clay soils provided most of the material for construction. The amount of level land for agriculture was generally restricted, and the Mediterranean climate, while well suited for farming, was highly erratic and caused significant hardships three or four years out of ten. The possibilities for irrigation were minimal, and not all of the region received sufficient rainfall for dry farming. A variable border of aridity (at 200 mm of rainfall) ran through the land, marking the oscillating frontier between the desert and the sown. Under these limitations of natural resources, the success of settlement in the area was often marked by the ability to cope with economic failure. The relative poverty of the land stands out in the material record: There are few finds of precious objects comparable with those of Egypt, Mesopotamia, or Syria. This paucity of resources explains why imperial rulers of Palestine rarely saw the need to displace the local leaders and incorporate Palestine more fully into their realm. Outside investment attracted to Palestine merely concentrated on developing its transit networks and a few key agricultural industries, such as olive oil and wine production.

Geographical Diversity. Although resource poor and small in total area, Palestine boasted remarkable diversity. The geological history of the area has shaped a third geographic attribute: a complex landscape that can aptly be described as fragmented. Palestine's diversity extended to land forms, natural vegetation, soils, climate, subsistence potential, and accessibility or seclusion. The patchwork introduced a high degree of regionalism into the life of its inhabitants. While some sections of the country could never escape involvement in their larger political and cultural environment, other regions were inaccessible or inhospitable; they supported insulated communities and afforded refuge for drifters and outlaws or impermanent occupation by pastoral nomads. Unlike Egypt's Nile or Mesopotamia's Tigris and Euphrates, Palestine's major river, the serpentine, saline, and deeply incised Jordan, did not unify its complex map. This variegated landscape rendered political and economic unification of the region fraught with difficulties. When achieved, unification was never long-lived.

RURAL LANDSCAPE

The dominant locus of human life and settlement across this fragmented landscape of the Iron Age monarchies of Israel and Judah was rural. Although the Bible's preoccupation with urban life and archaeology's one-time fixation on famous tells (sites of successive ancient settlement) suggest otherwise, most ancient Israelites and Judeans did not live in cities or even towns, but in the countryside. This asymmetry of settlement has always been true of the pre-industrial world, and until very recently characterized our own world as well. According to the famous Domesday book (an economic inventory), to take one medieval example, the English countryside at the time of William the Conqueror (eleventh century CE) contained about 90 percent of the total population. Cities and towns held much the smaller fraction. This relative demographic weight cannot be far from the case for ancient Palestine, especially for Israel's earliest era at which time the collapse of the urban culture of the Late Bronze Age was nearly complete. The reurbanization that commenced with the formation of the monarchy in the tenth century certainly brought more of the population back behind city walls; yet most royal subjects still lived in the hinterlands.

Village Life. Village life represents the primary mode of settlement on the rural landscape.[1] Iron Age villages consisted of a tiny or small cluster of dwellings housing a consolidated community engaged in economic activities in its immediate environment. The best preserved and most thoroughly excavated sites matching this definition date to the Early Iron Age and make possible a portrait of village life. None of these villages amounted to very much. The tiny sites would fit on a half acre, what would be a fairly nice sized suburban lot. A small village covered about two and one-half acres, about the area of two adjacent soccer fields, hardly home to a sizable populace. None of these villages showed any interest

1. This description of rural life (as well as that of urban life below) does not treat the religious life of Palestine's inhabitants. This omission should not be taken as a sign of the unimportance of religious belief. To the contrary, religious belief was integral to all aspects of the life of ancient Palestine, though it also provided another source of division: Urban belief systems had little in common with those of the villages.

in defensive fortification. While the sites were not designed to exclude anybody, they were constructed to offer some sort of containment. One set of sites forms a group of "enclosed villages," constituted by a ring of houses, not adjoining, but arranged in an oval line. Apparently the internal area of these sites was free of dense building, perhaps serving as a pen for the residents' livestock. A second set of sites suggests the classic agglomerative village, with a busy site layout containing irregular house clusters. The clusters provided only a tenuous site perimeter, and no system of streets made its presence felt. The village was not planned, but grew and wore a disorganized street tangle as an emblem of its origins. Village houses frequently shared walls and may also have shared courtyards, but they existed in a great variety of spatial configurations. The layouts of these villages were marked by the absence of public building of any kind, whether religious or administrative. Instead, these villages were constituted by domestic buildings, predominantly the well-known pillared courtyard or four-room house.

The prominence of this four-room house in the villages permits a number of important generalizations regarding their inhabitants and the nature of the "consolidated community" that they comprised. In keeping with the small size of the villages themselves, their constituent courtyard house was a small structure encompassing between 30 and 70 square meters of roofed floor space. Based on a cross-culturally derived estimate of per person space allotment, these houses provided room for three to seven occupants. This strikingly small range could only have been filled by a nuclear family. Under pre-industrial demographic constraints, such a group would have been fragile indeed. Infant mortality seized at least twice as many children as survived into adulthood. Male life expectancy was set at about forty years. The dangers of childbirth stole an additional decade from the women who might anticipate seeing their thirtieth birthday. Poor diet and disease susceptibility due to chronic malnutrition were the chief agents of this dismal demography. To characterize family life in the village as an inexorable struggle against death would not be far wide of the mark. Composed of such small and inherently unstable units, it is understandable why the population of the small Iron Age villages never mounted very high. A densely packed average sized village, such as Ai, could have

boasted no more than 200–300 persons. Thinly built enclosed villages would have claimed less than a third of that total.

The family of the courtyard house probably called on an extended family grouping as a more stable context in which to maintain itself. The apparent clusters of dwellings in Early Iron Age villages have been regarded as hard evidence for the existence of the extended family that provided an anchor in Israelite society. That extended family was known in the Bible as the בית אב *(bêt 'āb,* "father's house"). A three-house cluster at the site of Khirbet Raddana offers the most lucid example. A large, 55-square meter house provided the focal point for two smaller dwellings that circled around a courtyard. Thus constituted, the extended family of grandparents, parents, aunts, uncles, and children might have comprised a total of ten to twelve persons. At such a size even the extended family faced the challenge of reproduction. Few would be the extended families that were not repeatedly nipped in the bud and reduced, de facto, to nuclear families. Although hard pressed to achieve stability through increased household size, it was this unit that provided the context for family survival.

The small villages of the Iron Age presumably constituted social units in and of themselves, though archaeological data neither confirms nor questions this judgment. The biblical term for this community would be משפחה *(mišpaḥâ),* often translated "clan." However the resident village community is envisaged—one scholar defines it as a "protective association of families"—there is no place for the imagination of a happy "main-street" town. The extended families themselves were hardly simple harmonious households. They struggled to subsist and to produce children. They simmered with strife created by contention for patrimony and progeny similar to that which drives so many Israelite folk stories (e.g., Jacob and Esau [Genesis 25–33] and Hannah and Peninnah [1 Samuel 1–2]). Although villages as a whole were rife with such conflict, all levels of the village community functioned in an interdependent way, which provided their only real chance for survival.

Economic activities also shaped village community. Villagers devoted their lives to work in the fields, forests, pastures, and marshes of their environment. Every indication suggests that subsistence farming and herding absorbed the lion's share of village energy. Tools—grindstones, sickleblades, and spindle whorls—highlight archaeological finds. Goat and sheep bones rule the refuse pit. Wheat, barley, and lentils turn up in storage jars, grain pits, and soil samples from kitchen floors. In addition to food-producing activities, villagers saw to their own clothing and utensil needs as well. Crafts such as clothes making were carried out within each household. Barter secured other essentials, such as pottery from the village workshop and metals from itinerant peddlers or more-or-less distant market towns.

The structure and dynamics of this subsistence activity were shaped by the village environment, which involved a range of agricultural and pastoral conditions. Most highland village locations were not as well endowed as Tell Qiri, nestled on low hills overlooking the western margin of the Jezreel Valley and boasting an extremely well-watered site surrounded by a broad combination of rich land types. Ai was more typical, offering thin soils and little level land. Such villages had to contend with three key environmental constraints: Palestine's sharp wet-dry seasonality; its erratic pattern of rainfall and unreliable annual precipitation totals and a hilly terrain covered by a thin mantle of fertile, but easily eroded, red clay soil.

Water availability was the decisive environmental constraint under which village economics operated. Intense rainfall was concentrated in a few winter months. When it rained, it poured. The same amount of rainfall that today London sees spread over three hundred rain days fell onto Jerusalem in only fifty. This intense rainfall meant high rates of runoff such that precious water was lost to agriculture. When it was not raining, the climate was subject to a vigorous sun. During the summer months, this extreme insolation browned every natural pasture; flocks and herds had to be led to water every two or three days. The summer sun drained the soil of whatever small quantity of moisture remained from the wet season. Unlike the middle latitudes, where the dead season (winter) is wet, the crops of the region's planting season depended completely on the rains of planting season for their germination and growth. Thus the winter plantings were highly vulnerable to any hiatus of precipitation after they germinated. Sowing of the fields could not even begin until sufficient moisture had accumulated in the soil, left hard-baked by the summer heat. Delay of the rains constricted the most

propitious plowing and planting season, putting pressure on limited cultivation resources (e.g., plow oxen).

Alongside the frustrating seasonality of rainfall, farmers faced precipitation that varied with potentially devastating consequences (both with respect to the distribution of rainfall throughout the year and to the achievement of the average annual accumulation). Three years out of ten experienced problem patterns of rainfall, for example, very wet in the beginning of the season, very dry toward the end. There could be agricultural drought even though total rainfall reached the average measure. Additionally, the rainfall totals of one or two years out of ten dropped more than 25 percent. Drought years also bunched up, thus compounding subsistence difficulties.

Around most villages soil profiles offered a fairly productive environment, one not yet stripped of its mantle of soil by radical deforestation. Nevertheless, the relative scarcity of bottom land meant that hillside slopes would come into cultivation, whereupon their soils were easily eroded. Furthermore, soil nutrients were depleted with each season's crop. This was particularly true in Palestine, where the climate limits the rate of soil formation and the vegetational cover was not generous in its contribution of organic matter. Once opened for agriculture, fields easily succumbed to erosion and over-cropping. All told, there is no mistaking a very high risk environment: thin, hilly, erodible soils; erratic—all or nothing—rainfall; circumscribed planting and harvest seasons. In this environment the strategies adopted by subsistence cultivators were of two basic types. On the one hand, farmers endeavored to reduce the chance of a meager harvest of poorly developed grains and vegetables or even total crop failure due to drought and soil depletion by capturing more water for agriculture, planting more crops in diverse locations, and stabilizing the soil base.

Unfortunately, ancient villagers were hard pressed to achieve any of these objectives. It is worth recalling how truly small and demographically unstable these villages were. Most potential strategies for reducing the risks of subsistence were labor intensive and in most periods demanded more hands than could generally be supplied. Hill slopes could have been terraced. By building stone walls running across the hillsides and hauling soil up from the valleys to fill behind the walls, farmers could create a series of steps shelving thin strips of level land. Such terraces trapped water flowing downhill and retained precious soil. But terracing to conserve soil and water was a costly, long-term investment that villagers were customarily unable or unwilling to make. During the early centuries of Israel's life in Palestine, evidence for terrace construction is meager at best; it does not mount until the monarchical period. Similarly, no technological development, such as iron metallurgy, abetted the opening of fields or advanced the progress of the plow during the pre-monarchical period. Even later, the traditional plow (the ard) continued to be fitted to bronze, iron, and, haphazardly, steel plowpoints, making no gain in efficiency or efficacy. Villagers certainly fallowed their fields and applied manure by grazing their herds on harvested plots. But the outcome of such husbandry did not boost but only halted the decline of the all-important grain yields. Village communities had to be satisfied with fairly low crop yields, which they could do little to enhance on a broad scale. Precisely what these yields were is not easy to determine, since evidence for them comes only indirectly. There are no economic records to illuminate the yielding characteristics of Early Iron Age crops and cultivation techniques. A meager ten- to fifteenfold harvest would probably have been welcome by any farming family. Household gardens may have offered an exception to this bleak canvas; special attention, the application of composted manure, and hand watering would have been repaid by significant produce.

On the other hand, villagers pursued the option of spreading out their risks. This second type of challenge prompted villagers to distribute their efforts across the broadest possible spectrum of agricultural pursuits. The greatest contribution to risk spreading was provided by a substantial commitment to herding. The presence of animal stalls in many courtyard houses signals its place in the village economy. At the village level, livestock rearing was both indispensable to and complementary with farming. The grazing of livestock—predominantly sheep and goats—added greatly to the resiliency of communities struck by crop failure. Animals were a mobile resource subject to a different set of environmental constraints than were fixed fields of crops. The dietary contribution of herd animals was significant as well, offering milk and milk foods. Animals were also used directly for food (though never

incautiously, for they constituted a major capital investment). Otherwise, sheep and goats contributed wool and hair to home industry. Livestock husbandry also made use of land marginal for cultivation, provided needed fertilizer, and did not compete for agricultural labor, since shepherding could be carried out by youths (e.g., David, the youngest of Jesse's sons, who nearly missed Samuel's visit because he was out pasturing the flock).

Risk spreading was further accomplished through diversification of farming activities. Farming communities planted a variety of crops in locations as diverse as possible. The natural diversity of the Palestinian environment—e.g., highland and coastal plain—often aided this effort. The crop mix included not just the staple cereals—barley and wheat—and vegetables, but tree and vine crops as well. These perennials spread risk by diversifying the subsistence base. The calendar of attention required by grapes, olives, and figs made them complementary pursuits, again permitting optimal use of a limited labor pool. The repertoire of highlands crops also included fruit and nut trees (e.g., pomegranate and almond) as well as many important vegetables, such as broad beans, lentils, chick-peas, onions, leeks, gourds, and condiments, all of which have been attested archaeologically. The list of agricultural seasons on a tenth-century limestone tablet, recovered from the Shephelah site of Gezer, strikingly manifests the diversity of endeavors characteristic of village agriculture; it alludes to activities involving olives, wheat, barley, grapes, and summer fruit. It reads:

line 1: two months of [olive] harvest;
lines 1-2: two months of sowing;
line 2: two months of late sowing;
line 3: a month of hoeing weeds;
line 4: a month of harvesting barley;
line 5: a month of harvesting and [measur]ing;
line 6: two months of cutting [grapes];
line 7: a month of [collecting] summer fruit.

In another way to spread risk, villagers developed ways to preserve produce from a year of plenty for a year of want. Many of the tree and vine crops were stored as fruits or processed juice and oil. Large storage jars—in the pre-monarchical period, the collared rim pithoi—and household grain pits unearthed at the village sites are nearly ubiquitous manifestations of this strategy. Perhaps the crucial attribute of flocks and herds was their ability to act as a kind of storage—"a disaster bank on the hoof"—capable of receiving deposits in good years, withstanding withdrawals in years when crops did not suffice.

The labor required for the conduct of agriculture consumed the daylight hours for most parts of the year. Farming families—women, men, children—carried this unrelenting burden. Emphasis was placed on economic activities whose schedules melded rather than those that conflicted. Food had to be produced, processed, and prepared for consumption. These latter two endeavors probably fell disproportionately on women, who controlled the domestic sphere in which wool was carded and spun, raisins dried, chick-peas sorted, cheese curdled, and grain ground into flour. No less than childbirth and rearing, household survival hinged upon the woman's management of its multifarious economic footing.

The constellation of strategies adopted to spread risk stands out as the primary means by which villages secured their sustenance. The village life underwritten by these labors was tenuous and arduous. The dominating tenor of the village was hardship. Small and unfortified, demographically unstable, focused on short-term survival, pushed to combine diverse farming and herding pursuits and pressed to the limits of its labor resources, village life flickered between life and death. There are a few examples of village sites where life succeeded itself generation after generation. But such sites as Tell Qiri and Tell es-Seba (Beer Sheba), which survived over much of the course of the Iron Age, are far outnumbered by villages like Ai, which failed after a brief boom.

Nomadic Pastoralists. Villages were not alone on the rural landscape of ancient Palestine. Villagers were joined by a floating medley of refugees and renegades and, under certain conditions, by the occupants of isolated farmsteads and seasonal installations who also populated the hinterlands. Among these other rural inhabitants, nomadic pastoralists contributed the most potent presence, and archaeologists are beginning to discern their traces. Pastoralists do construct permanent fixtures such as stone corrals near places of preferred encampments. Surveys have documented numerous sites composed of a few scattered structures that represent the permanent but seasonal camps of nomadic herders. An excellent example of a herding station has been excavated on a barren outpost in the Judean hills (Giloh). Isolated cultic structures existing apart from permanent sites and cemeteries located in peripheral areas could have attended to the religious and mortuary needs of nonsedentary pastoralists. The herders of ancient Palestine concentrated on sheep and goats. Other beasts were present—horses, asses, camels, cattle, and pigs—but none approached the prominence of sheep and goats. Horses and asses could not be bred for subsistence. Camels became a focal animal upon which deep-desert nomadic communities relied during the second half of the Iron Age. Cattle and pigs were extremely important in the pastoral economy of the village and town, but both required daily water and were generally not herded from one pasture to the next in Palestine. The ubiquity of sheep and goats is attested by manifold references in biblical literature as well as by archaeological evidence in the bone refuse of ancient sites.

Ancient pastoral families probably herded between fifty and one hundred animals, to judge by contemporary pastoralists. Such a herd was approximately five times larger than that of settled villagers. Sheep and goats were characteristically herded together because of their complementary herding and dietary traits. The sight of a mob of dirty-white, fat-tailed sheep ranging a hillside along with a smattering of brown goats remains familiar throughout the region. Nomadic movement with such herds was dictated by the conflict between the unrelenting dietary needs of livestock and the seasonal variation in the availability of pasture.

Milk, wool and hair, hides, bone and horn, meat, manure, and young animals for trade or sale were the familiar products of sheep and goats. The catalog of secondary products derived from these animals was enormous and encompassed a wide variety of bone tools and implements, wool clothing, blankets, and rugs; a huge assortment of milk products (yogurt, butter, and storable cheese), as well as the black, goat-hair tent itself.

Yet the herd did not run autonomously; it was managed to enhance its productivity in specific ways. Goats were immensely more valuable than sheep as milk providers. Shorter life cycles and higher reproductive rates made goats a more productive meat source as well, mostly in the form of slaughtered male offspring. Sheep provided less meat and milk, but, unlike goats, produced wool, a fiber of much greater value than goat hair. Lower reproduction and longer maturation rates increased the value of the sheep itself. Thus, because of both its wool and its innate value, the sheep was a more market- or trade-oriented animal. The goat was the animal of choice for household subsistence. With an eye to economic conditions, such as the rise or decline of markets and the needs of subsistence, the pastoralists adjusted the balance of animals across the rural landscape.

The most telling characteristic of the herd of sheep and goats was its potential for explosive growth. Early sexual maturation (one year of age) and short gestation periods (approx. five months) made these small animals fecund. These rates stood out markedly in contrast to larger beasts such as camels (five year maturity, twelve- to thirteen-month gestation) and cattle (three-year maturity, nine-month gestation). A large herd of cattle represented the work of decades, while a sizable herd of sheep could have taken shape in a matter of years. A set of conservative flock demographics—birthrates, cull rates, and mortality rates—yields a yearly growth rate of a hypothetical flock of sheep and goats of 11.2 percent. This rate of increase doubles flock size within six years.[2]

Such a rate of increase was ideal. Rapid flock growth was matched by the herd's susceptibility to precipitous decline. Pastoral disasters were frequent in the Near East: Drought and epidemic joined animal predators and human thieves to give an Asian proverb the ring of truth; "the herd belongs to the first adverse season or powerful enemy."[3] Disaster came with unpredictable frequency. Thus the economic basis of nomadic pastoralism was given to extreme fluctuations, shaping a boom or bust venture of high gain and high risk.

Integration of Farming and Herding. The oscillation of the herding community's economic base brings into focus an important contrast between pastoral and agricultural life in Palestine. Productivity in cultivation tended to be inelastic compared to the productivity of pastoralism. Land and labor needs did not rise and fall in tandem with the success or failure of the crops, but remained relatively constant. In the herding sector, tremendous increases

during pastoral boom cycles were matched by tremendous declines during bad years. Labor and pasturage needs rose and fell correspondingly. These diverse productive tendencies of herding and crop production were fundamental to the dynamics of rural life. They provided incentives to the integration of the two sectors in Palestine's erratic and uncertain environment, especially at the household and village level. The ability of settled cultivators to turn to pastoral pursuits added buoyancy to their subsistence. In addition, pastoral nomadic households sought stability when making investments in arable land.

This picture of pastoral-agricultural integration stands at a significant remove from the more traditional view of nomads as fierce, land-hungry desert dwellers who emerge from one or another wasteland to challenge settled society. Within the past two decades, the study of pastoral nomadic life in the ancient Near East has veered sharply from this and other such imaginations. Modern ethnographic studies have dissolved the cultural dichotomization of wandering herder and settled cultivator. In place of the desert *versus* the sown, there stands a portrait of the desert *and* the sown as an economically and politically charged continuum. This notion of the integration of pastoralists and agriculturalists, of nomadic and sedentary life-styles within the same society, has become fundamental to our understanding of the ancient Near East. At any given moment the pattern of relationships on this nomadic-sedentary continuum may appear more or less continuous, more or less fragmented. Yet none of the farmers and herders who inhabit this spectrum can be understood in isolation. Indeed, the fluidity of their location is such that people of the same ancestry, even the same household, may be found at a variety of locations along the continuum. This cultural integration finds expression in the portrait of two brothers: agriculturalist Cain and pastoralist Abel (Genesis 4).

The nature of the relationship between the two primary occupants of the rural landscape, villagers and nomadic pastoralists, depended on the extent to which their productive characteristics were advanced, channeled, or blocked by larger regional and inter-regional forces. Periods of well-oiled, forceful central authority based in cities and demands for territorial stability often encouraged more village labor intensive cultivation of the land. At the same

2. R. Cribb, *Nomads in Archaeology* (Cambridge: Cambridge University Press, 1991) 28-34, provides an especially clear and helpful analysis of flock demographics.
3. Cited in ibid., 31.

time, such central forces checked the territorial expansionism inherent in pastoralism's potential for explosive growth. Under these circumstances, pastoral pursuits became more specialized as market outlets for herd output, and excess labor appeared in the urban-dominated sector. The energetic growth during the monarchic period, especially during the eighth century, presented such conditions. Conversely, weak rule and disordered social and economic institutions undercut conditions for optimal cultivation and expanded incentives that swelled the numbers of nomadic pastoralists, spurred herd management for subsistence production, and offered opportunities for territorial aggrandizement. Both the Late Bronze Age and the Early Second Temple Period were characterized by such conditions. Thus variations in the forms of village agriculture of ancient Palestine were innately connected with the political and economic power of the urban world.

URBAN LIFE

The Bible prominently displays the role played by urban life in Israelite and Judean history and society. Within the past few decades, perspectives on the role of cities in the Bible have changed markedly. It was once thought that a "nomadic bias," a wholesale rejection of the sedentary life, shaped the biblical view of the city. But this view of ancient Israel as fundamentally antagonistic to "city life" has been abandoned. The "city" does come under criticism, notably from prophets who vilify specific cities (e.g., Babylon, Nineveh, and Tyre) that symbolize Israel's imperial foes as well as the "royal" cities (Jerusalem and Samaria) of Israel's monarchs. Nevertheless, the biblical tradition as a whole has a decidedly urban orientation. Its literature originates in the city, was preserved and transmitted by Jerusalem-based groups, and its chief eschatological vision projects future life in a new city (Mic 4:1-5; Isa 65:17-25).

City Size. Perceptions of the life in Israelite and Judean cities have been enlivened through a tremendous investment of archaeological energy in excavating the prominent mounds of ancient Palestine. These urban sites developed at places usually rich in natural resources, accessible to economic networks, offering good defensive position, and often preserving ancient religious traditions. Yet the most favorable conditions never generated cities of mod-

ern proportions. Palestine's small-sized cities had correspondingly small populations, though estimates of the sizes of ancient cities are very rough, based on an average density figure of 160 to 200 tightly packed persons per urban acre. Jerusalem, the largest by far (approx. 150 acres), reached a population no greater than 30,000 by the late eighth century. Judah's next largest city, the provincial capital Lachish, achieved only about one-eighth of Jerusalem's measure. The capital of Israel, Samaria, possessed a rectangular royal acropolis that covered four acres, but the extent of the surrounding city remains unknown.

City Types and Structures. Jerusalem was a capital city, like Samaria, and housed an array of administrative functions. Other urban sites served secondary roles or more specialized functions: major administrative centers, such as Megiddo and Lachish; secondary administrative centers, such as Beer Sheba; and fortified towns, such as Tell en-Nasbeh. All of these sites distinguish themselves from villages by the presence of monumental architecture that demands a large organized and directed labor force for its construction.

The typical city's most important monumental feature was its fortification system. The gate was the centerpiece of the system and the hub of civic and commercial activity. Most often, traffic climbed an incline parallel to the city wall and then turned sharply to enter through the gate. The path through the gate was dominated by two, three, or four sets of piers that jutted out into it and created a series of chambers on either side. The chambers were lined with benches for guards, officials, or elders who were said to administer justice "in the gate" (Deut 21:19; Josh 20:4; Ruth 4). A wooden door secured the outside entrance (Judg 16:3), whose width stretched to about four meters. Towers rose above the doorway on either side, providing added firepower around this weak point in the defense system. A variety of wall types led away from the gates to encompass the city; "casemate walls," consisting of solid outside and inside walls connected at intervals by perpendicular walls to create a series of "cases"; and solid walls of stone designed with salients and recesses. Both were usually mounted with mud brick superstructures. City walls were often strengthened by a *glacis,* a sloping earth and stone structure that protected their foundations. Although only their foundations are generally preserved, the

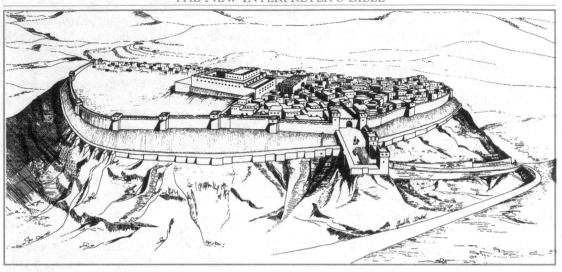

Figure 1: A reconstruction of the Iron Age city of Lachish, showing its fortification system and huge acropolis.

walls probably reached an average height of eight to ten meters.

Inside these circular perimeter defenses, most cities show evidence of planning. In the major administrative centers, a rectangular acropolis or citadel was specially demarcated behind its own wall and elevated above the remainder of the city. This focal area was the site of the temple, palace, and other buildings associated with governance. Samaria and Lachish offered notable examples of this basic plan; the acropolis of Lachish commandeered considerably more than half the entire site (*see Fig. 1*). Besides organizing essential administrative functions, the acropolis served as a place of last resort in battle (Judg 9:50-52). Dominating the visual appearance of the city, these inner cities were potent symbols of the political power that the city wielded.

The area adjoining the gate on the inside of the city was also directed toward special purposes. At Beer Sheba, the gate empties out into a complex of administrative buildings on the west and a series of storehouses on the east (*see Fig. 2*). The proximity of gate and storehouse was presumably consistent with the cities' functions as armories or centers for tax collection. Beyond the gate area, the fortified towns manifested a ring design with a casemate wall integrated into an outer belt of buildings that were separated from the middle of the city by a circular road. Inside this outer belt, the system of streets was not so recognizably organized.

The strong and often indomitable fortification systems that protected cities elicited the siege as a military strategy. To enable the city to withstand a protracted siege, considerable energy and engineering skill were marshaled to guarantee access to water. Waterworks were a conspicuous feature of the most important cities of Palestine. In Jerusalem, Hezekiah's tunnel (2 Kgs 20:20), built in anticipation of the Assyrian siege, stands as the most well-known example. It cut through over 500 meters of hard limestone to direct the waters of the spring at the foot of the city to a secure outlet within the walls. The outside entrance to the spring was sealed off. At many cities, shaft systems aimed to tap a water-bearing layer of rock by tunneling a vertical shaft down to its level from within the city. The cities of Gezer, Gibeon, Hazor, Jerusalem, and Megiddo all boasted such massive "wells." The vast scale and ingenuity of these projects speak eloquently about both the resources and the fears of the ancient Israelite urbanites.

City Populace. Cities appear to have been governed by a body of "elders," composed of the heads of the leading family or families of the city. This "city council" was related to the central authorities through the royal service of some of its members (Jer 26:16; Job 29:7-10). The capital cities, Samaria and Jerusalem, were administered by the "prince of the city" (1 Kgs 22:26; 2 Kgs 23:8), while other cities may have come under the command of the district officials (1 Kgs 4:7-19; 20:14).

The leaders of the capital cities and major admin-

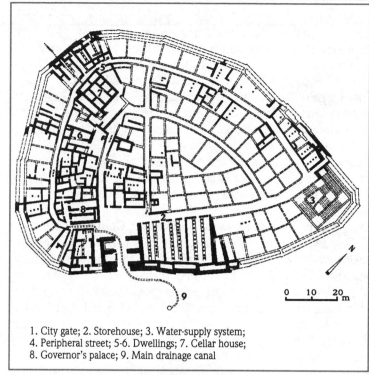

1. City gate; 2. Storehouse; 3. Water-supply system;
4. Peripheral street; 5-6. Dwellings; 7. Cellar house;
8. Governor's palace; 9. Main drainage canal

Figure 2: Site Plan of Beer Sheba

City Life. The city's concentration of resources produced a diverse urban scene. To facilitate this urban life, ancient Israelite and Judean cities provided few of what modern city dwellers expect in the way of public services. The great energy directed toward the water supply was exceptional in this respect, though the water systems owed their existence to military rather than domestic motives. Sanitation was not wholly lacking—channels beneath main streets carried the rainfall out the city gate—but no provisions were made for solid waste, domestic or industrial. Garbage and garbage eaters—dogs and rats—were omnipresent in the ancient city. Fire protection and health care were, of course, nowhere to be found. Security was afforded by the fortifications. Although these walls kept undesirable elements out of the city, there was no "policing" within the urban domain, apart from the palace guard such as Rehoboam is said to have equipped with bronze shields (1 Kgs 14:27). Individuals were responsible for their own protection and apparently for apprehending and bringing before the court any putative law breakers. Yet, the city's judicial services constituted one of its key social contributions, especially when commercial arrangements came into play. The availability of judicial arbitration and conflict resolution, backed by armed might and divine sanction, lowered the costs of business transactions by reducing the risk of default and fraud.

Although the city marketplace *(agora)* provided the primary emblem of urban life in Hellenistic times, Israelite and Judean city plans do not appear to have offered such a commercial area. Artisans sold out of their workshops, which served at the same time as their homes, perhaps in distinct "quarters" or "streets" specializing in particular merchandise. Jerusalem contained a locale known as the "bakers' street" during Jeremiah's day (Jer 37:21). Produce sellers may have erected temporary stalls, either inside or outside the city gate. While members of the tiny elite class had access

istrative centers constituted the elite stratum of Israelite and Judean society and probably amounted to no more than 2 percent of the total population. This leadership was predominantly, if not totally, male. Thus, compared to the village scene, the role of women was significantly attenuated in the urban setting. The ruling class was composed of members of the royal house, royal retainers and administrators, cultic officials, judicial officers, and military commanders. Such urbanites were at the same time the principal landowners and manufacturers, though by no means the cultivators and laborers. The population of their cities was filled out by "townspeople" who served the elite rulers and the administrative apparatus. Some were direct personal servants. Artisans and fabricators produced clothes, furniture, metal items, and other desired articles. Manufacturers processed agricultural products—olives into olive oil and grapes into wine—using small-scale installations. Merchants procured goods unavailable locally. Unskilled laborers worked in maintenance and building construction. Assorted governmental workers (scribes, priests, soldiers) also made their homes behind these city walls. The less prominent fortified towns contained more significant numbers of families who owned and worked their own fields and orchards in the area surrounding the town.

to the products of their own estates, townspeople depended on these markets for their daily fare. Though spared the preoccupation with farming, the women of the city would still have invested enormous amounts of time at the market, at the well, and with the preparation of meals. They may also have kept small kitchen gardens wherever the jumble of housing permitted. City homes belonged to the pillared courtyard house type that was also common in the villages. Sometimes these homes appeared in their more elaborate "four-room" variety (e.g., at Tirzah in the north), sometimes in a smaller rendition, such as those whose rear rooms constituted part of the casemate wall at Beer Sheba. Two stories were doubtless the rule for these dwellings, which were furnished with baking ovens, storage bins, and a variety of other installations.

The dependence of the city upon grain imported from the countryside for market, whether destined for sowing or baking, encouraged state intervention to ensure supplies as well as to generate profits. The anti-merchant tirade of Amos 8:4-6 leaves the impression that the grain market of eighth-century Samaria was not an open market, but solidly in the hands of a coterie of dealers, probably sponsored by the royal court. The workings of the state were also perceptible in the standardization of weights, such as the dome-shaped stone weights that came into use in seventh-century Judah for transactions in silver. Markets equipped with such weights provided for the needs of urbanites as well as for episodic needs of villagers who would commute to the cities to purchase specialized goods, though barter no doubt continued to dominate most economic exchange.

The urban environment included industry components. Best known are the olive pressing installations from the seventh-century Philistine and Judean lowlands. Olive oil manufacture employed crushing basins and beam (lever) presses to extract the oil into vats at such sites as Tell Beit Mirsim, Timnah (Tel Batash), and Ekron. The olive oil industry also made profuse demands for water, storage, and shipping facilities. The scores of presses at Ekron amply justify the label "industrial city" and render it an exceptional site whose economy was geared to the international export trade in olive oil. The mass production of necessary commodities like oil, cloth, pottery, and tools for local consumption may also have taken place within the urban sphere. The fact that workshops for ceramics, textiles, and the products of metallurgy have not yet come to light signals the inherent economic limitations—low consumer demand and high transportation costs—on the development of these industries. Like the olive presses, any such shops would have been small-scale operations, by no means "factories" of the industrial revolution. City industry in ancient Palestine focused nearly exclusively on transforming the products of farming and herding. Thus the city never severed its bond with its agricultural hinterlands by developing an economically sustainable "industrial base."

City as Administrative Center. A fair number of city residents served as regional administrators and tax collectors. Several cities—Kinneret, Hazor, Megiddo, and Beer Sheba—contained warehouses, often located near the gate complex. These mirrored the city's function as collector and distributor of commodities. Ostraca, discovered in the Late Iron Age citadel of Arad, exemplify this function. These inked potsherds record the receipt of flour, oil, and wine from the region of southern Judah. Other letters authorize the citadel's military commander to distribute the foodstuffs from the citadel's store. The famous jars—stamped with the phrase *lmlk*, "belonging to the king"—bespeak the same pattern of royal management, and perhaps even production, of agricultural commodities. The discovery of numerous such jars, with their inscribed handles, in the storerooms of Lachish and Timnah attests to the involvement of urbanites in the royal administration of the economy. Seals employed to make such impressions on wet clay jars or *bullae* (clay seals placed on documents) occur frequently in excavations of city precincts and add further testimony to the urban administration of economic and judicial affairs. The seals carried personal names as well as titles such as "steward," "city governor," "king's minister," "in charge of the house," and "in charge of the tax." The ostraca found in an eighth-century storehouse in Samaria provide evidence for the flow of oil and wine from the agriculturally productive environs of the capital. These delivery records or tax receipts suggest the kind of complex bureaucracy that would have employed significant numbers of city residents.

Elite Life-style. The spiced wine and fine oil delivered to Samaria may have found their way onto the tables of the ruling elite. Biblical texts and archaeological finds document one element of an elite, urban and luxurious life-style known as the מרזח (marzēaḥ, "feast"). This banquet, forbidden to Jeremiah (Jer 16:5-9) and castigated by Amos (Amos 6:4-7), involved communal feasting and possibly sexual activities. It served a funereal or memorializing function emphasizing continuity between human generations. Amos's denunciation of the marzēaḥ censures feasting on wine and meat, anointing with oil, and reclining on ivory inlaid furniture, all to a musical accompaniment. Archaeologically recovered ivory carvings from Ahab's palace at Samaria—cow and calf, infant on a lotus, woman at the window—may have adorned the "ivory" furniture used at the marzēaḥ. The artistic motifs focus on life transformations (birth and death) and were particularly appropriate on memorial occasions or contexts involving royal succession. The marzēaḥ served symbolically to express the legitimacy of the elite rule while displaying the privileges of the powerful. The marzēaḥ thus exemplified the concerns and preoccupations of the urban enclave: lavish consumption of foodstuffs produced by others and maintenance of the political power that made an elevated life-style possible.

URBAN-RURAL RELATIONS

The tenth-century formation of the Israelite and Judean monarchical states brought an end to a brief era of relatively autonomous nomadic pastoral and sedentary village life in Palestine. The monarchy built upon and intensified a process of urbanization that not only renewed the city life of Palestine but altered the character of rural landscape as well. Based in its urban centers, the state organization imposed itself upon the rural productive base, moving in the direction of a "command" or "mobilization" economy. At least five factors influenced this economic development. Population growth was perhaps the most basic, pushing the economy to produce more from a limited amount of land in order to feed the growing population. Second, incorporation of the lowland regions into Israelite control during the process of state formation under David added broad grain fields to the monarchical endowment, permitting the highland zone to develop more efficiently the production of olive oil and wine. The upswing in trade throughout the Mediterranean region, and the ancient Near East generally, consti-

tuted a third stimulus and whetted royal interest in trade both as transit agent and trading partner. Involvement in trade further encouraged the process of intensification and the development of industries that produced desirable trade commodities. The presence of the monarchy itself was a fourth major factor in economic development. The royal house offered a new, nonagricultural locus of employment and spawned a new social class of royal retainers and administrators, denizens of the swelling urban environment. The monarchy's own agenda was dictated in large measure by a final factor: the emergence of competitor states, e.g., Syria and Moab, and especially the growth of the powerful Assyrian Empire, which began to exert its influence within the first century of Israel and Judah's national lives. Military provisions (e.g., expenditures for armaments and fortifications) and diplomatic matters (e.g., gifts and tribute) played a dominant role in economic decision making.

The rural world felt the burden of these developments most acutely through the taxation by which the royal house siphoned the productive wealth of the hinterlands into the urban centers. The royal state expropriated no less than half of the total village productive output. The riches thus garnered financed the lavish life-style of the marzēaḥ, palatial construction of fine ashlar masonry, as well as military enterprises. Prophetic diatribe (e.g., Mic 2:1-2, 8-9) charged that monarchical taxation and conscription plundered the countryside. Furthermore, state policies of taxation and procurement, judicial regulation, and land development set the economic agenda for the hinterlands. In particular, the monarchical demand for the most readily transportable and exchangeable commodities—olive oil and wine—pushed village agriculture toward specialization. Villagers who had previously invested in risk-spreading and self-sufficiency found themselves spending energy on costly long-term improvements (terracing), engaging in commodity production, and depending on regional networks of exchange. Nomadic pastoralists moved toward the periphery and oriented themselves to the urban market for their wool and meat products.

The effects of these developments were spread unevenly through Palestine, depending especially upon each region's distance from trading networks. Yet overall they produced a boom, marked especially in the eighth century, in population size and settlement, monumental architecture, luxury imports, and other measures of economic florescence. The primary beneficiaries of this boom were not the subsistence-oriented villagers caught up in the process of intensification, those who built the terraces, spent extra hours in the fields, and hauled and processed the harvest. Rather, those who governed the use of village lands reaped the benefits. Even in the pre-state period, village land was not "owned" outright by the villagers who worked it. Ownership was multi-stranded, not single-stranded as we know it. Rights were held not only by those who worked the land, but also by village leaders and by the tribal groups that had sponsored the Early Iron Age rural rejuvenation. Under the monarchy's land grant and patronage systems, these land rights passed to the members of the urban ruling class and certain well-placed village headmen who represented the village to the monarchy. Further, it was just these persons associated with monarchical governance who were in a position to perceive the opportunities offered by agricultural intensification and investments in commodity production. The attractiveness of costly intensification is often invisible to capital-poor, security-conscious, risk-spreading village farmers.

Farming families doubtless resisted intensifying their field work—i.e., specializing in specific crops and entering into the market system, since these processes stood in conflict with the perceived best interests of rural life. Although biblical literature scarcely mentions such resistance or the friction it generated, ethnographic study suggests that peasant resistance took the form of passivity in the face of urban demands. Although no peasant himself, Naboth's refusal to sell his vineyard to the king (1 Kings 21) may have exemplified such defiance. To this open response, villagers added subterfuge and deceit in dealings with tax agents, as well as engaging in various forms of village solidarity, such as periodic land distribution (Mic 2:5), which provided insurance for individual households and screened them from bureaucratic inspection. The minimal capabilities of urban-based management—note the problems associated with conducting a census, 2 Samuel 24—abetted village reluctance to surrender both its decision-making capabilities and its produce. The urban-directed constellation of armed might and judicial right produced a centralized economy dominated by the objectives of the state. During the eighth century, prophetic denunciations lashed out at landlord exploitation (Amos 5:11), farmers' debt (Amos 2:8; 8:6), land forfeiture (Mic 2:2), and slavery (Amos 2:6), which epitomized the new economic system. Prophetic activity may have contributed to moments of amelioration for village cultivators, notably debt-easements promulgated by the royal house (e.g., Josiah [Deut 15:1-18]), but such relief would have been short-lived. Tied to a historical course of increasing militarization, monarchical command of the economy inducted the life of Palestine into a world of incessant discord. Insecure in the best of times, villagers faced homelessness and starvation in the grip of the monarchically "managed" economy (Mic 2:9; 3:2-3; Job 24:9-12). Regularly, crises erupted into devastation. At the end of the eighth century, for example, the market economy collapsed in the wake of Sennacherib's army. Jerusalem may have escaped as Isaiah predicted, but the Judean countryside was traumatized. As with the ultimate international fate of ancient Israel and Judah themselves, so the preponderance of life in Palestine was violently tossed and turned in a world of economics and politics that was beyond its means of control or escape.

LIFE AND LITERATURE

While most rural life of Palestine falls outside the gaze of the biblical authors, the prevalence in the Bible of metaphors drawn from the hinterland—images of shepherding, vines, cisterns, and fertile fields—justifies every effort spent in reconstructing its portrait. The same holds true for urban life, all the more so in the light of our increasing understanding of the role of the urban world in producing and transmitting the Scriptures. Besides offering an aid to understanding the rhetorical intention of the ancient biblical literature and the potency of its metaphor, the recovery of the life of ancient Palestine plays a crucial role in recovering aspects of real life in biblical times. Biblical literature omits much of ancient life and, particularly, the role of women in giving shape and meaning to that life. Study of the social and material world of the ancient Levant renders the lives of the overlooked individuals visible in a way that buffers the imbalances of the biblical presentation. Examination of the lives of men and women in the distant past, with its attendant discovery of a world strange to modern readers, renders what might be perceived as offensive cultural practices, such as primogeniture, debt slavery, and surrogate motherhood, understandable in their own contexts.

Gains made by the study of the social and material world of ancient Israel and Judah help to ransom ancient texts from the generality that historical distance often enforces. The necessity of recovering the "situation in life" of biblical discourse is a century-old theme of exegetical method that has been given new life in the sociologically conscious reconstruction of Palestinian life. Placed in the context of ancient Israel's and Judah's politically charged eighth- and seventh-century economic transformation, for example, both prophetic pronouncement and royal legislation take on new meanings. Both can be understood in the light of the debt and disenfranchisement of village agriculturalists and the struggles of elite urbanites to maintain power within agrarian societies, which were influenced significantly by potent international forces. Some of the most "idealistic" and "revolutionary" ethics, such as the Deuteronomic call for the periodic release of debts (Deuteronomy 15), emerge out of these economic and political struggles. Such ethics were the product of neither religious idealizations nor brute economics, but emerged from a history in which the material and spiritual were inseparably intertwined. The reconstruction of the life of ancient Palestine offers the challenge and holds the promise of grasping the full embodiment of the Bible—that complex and fractious world.

BIBLIOGRAPHY

Coote, Robert B. *Early Israel: A New Horizon.* Minneapolis: Fortress, 1990.
Cribb, Roger. *Nomads in Archaeology: New Studies in Archaeology.* Cambridge: Cambridge University Press, 1991.
Finkelstein, Israel. *The Archaeology of the Israelite Settlement.* Jerusalem: Israel Exploration Society, 1988.
Frick, Frank S. *The City in Ancient Israel.* SBLDS 36. Missoula, MT: Scholars, 1977.
Hopkins, David C. *The Highlands of Canaan: Agricultural Life in the Early Iron Age.* Social World of Biblical Antiquity, 3. Decatur: Almond, 1985.
Jobling, David, Peggy L. Day, and Gerald T. Sheppard, eds. *The Bible and the Politics of Exegesis.* Cleveland: Pilgrim, 1991.
Kautsky, John H. *The Politics of Aristocratic Empires.* Chapel Hill: University of North Carolina Press, 1982.
Mazar, Amihai. *Archaeology of the Land of the Bible: 10,000-586 BCE.* The Anchor Bible Reference Library. New York: Doubleday, 1990.
Meyers, Carol. *Discovering Eve: Ancient Israelite Women in Context.* New York: Oxford University Press, 1988.
Stager, Lawrence E. "The Archaeology of the Family in Ancient Israel." *BASOR* 260 (1985) 1-35.

THE ANCIENT NEAR EASTERN LITERARY BACKGROUND OF THE OLD TESTAMENT

SIMON B. PARKER

OUTLINE

INTRODUCTION

Since the fixing of the contents of the Jewish and Christian Bibles in the first centuries of our era, the defining literary context in which most Christians have interpreted the OT has been the Christian Bible. More particularly, the New Testament (NT) has usually been seen as the key to the Old Testament (OT).[1]

As the NT makes clear, early Christians were interested in the meaning of OT literature for their own times, not in its earlier meaning for ancient Israelites. The latter did receive some attention in subsequent centuries, but remained a minority interest during most of the church's history. The dominant theologies, both before and after the Reformation, tended to depreciate an interest in or need for establishing the literary context of the authors of the OT. In any case, because no other literature from the ancient Near East was known, no literary con-

---

1. For Jews, the defining literary context for interpreting the Hebrew Bible became the Talmud.

text was available other than that preserved in the Bible itself. Thus for theoretical and practical reasons there was no interest in the original literary context or background of biblical literature.

In the last two centuries a considerable amount of ancient Near Eastern literature has gradually been recovered, some by accidental discovery, most as a result of the systematic excavation of ancient sites in the Middle East. Previously unknown ancient scripts and languages have been deciphered and ancient literary genres and conventions have been discovered. Our understanding of these texts improves with each passing decade, and more reliable and readable translations of long-known texts, as well as initial translations of recently recovered texts, are appearing (see Bibliography). Today, it is possible to interpret the OT in the context of ancient Near Eastern literature in general.

Despite its availability, however, many interpreters of the Bible continue to ignore this material. There are both religious and secular reasons why this is so. On the one hand, many believe that the Bible is a direct communication from God to us. We know the author—God. We are the audience. The Bible is the message the Author has given to the audience. The Bible must be comprehensible on its own, without having to read the literature of cultures that Israel—indeed God—condemned. In addition, some feel an anxiety about discovering the Bible's human dimension or historical rootedness, which, in their view, might lessen the divine character of the message.

On the other hand, many modern readers take the Bible as an object in our world and at our disposal. More deliberately, many secular literary critics are increasingly emphasizing the creative role of the reader in interpretation. Whether aware of this academic trend or not, many readers feel free to interpret the Bible within their own context and against the background of their own culture.

Religious or secular, the crucial transaction is between the Bible and the reader. What determines the meaning or significance of a passage tends to be what meets the reader's needs or interests. Other dimensions of the interpretive process are devalued or ignored.

It is certainly possible to interpret texts in these ways. Readers simply make a prior judgment that what the Spirit says to them through the Bible is more important than what the biblical authors were saying or intending; or that what they can create out of the biblical text is more important than what the biblical authors created.

But if we consider the original purposes of the biblical writings important, and give priority to discovering the historical sense of the texts before they are assigned significance by later interpreting communities, then we must seek to recover the traditions and understandings of the communities in which they were produced. That means attending to any literary or social context that we can recover. In this article we are concerned with the literary context—although we cannot ignore the social context, since literature does not exist or have meaning in a social vacuum.

THE IMPORTANCE OF LITERARY BACKGROUND

All literature, including religious literature, and specifically the Bible, uses conventions and traditions—even when it is adapting or resisting them. An awareness of the conventions and traditions that are being used, resisted, or adapted assists the reader in discerning the intentions and meanings of the author. If we interpret a work of literature in the light of earlier or contemporary works of the same kind or treatment of the same subject, we are constrained to recognize the commonalities among the works and so to appreciate more sharply what is unique in the work before us. Interpreting a work of literature without any knowledge of its literary background allows for a high degree of arbitrariness.

The biblical writings do not normally refer to the literary background or antecedents with which (or against which) their authors were working, any more than modern novels refer explicitly to those novels that have most influenced their authors. But there are exceptions.

Current readers interpreting Ezekiel's vision of the valley of dry bones (Ezek 37:1-14), for example, may reflect on the rather bizarre choice of image and perhaps speculate about Ezekiel's mentality. Alternately, they may see in it an expression of the doctrine of resurrection. But in this case the author gives us the literary background of the vision when he quotes a current saying among his compatriots: "Our bones are dried up, our hope is gone; we are doomed" (v. 11*b* TNK). This saying, in which the Jews picture themselves as dried-up skeletons, expresses their feeling, following the fall of Jerusalem, that they have no future. Against this background we can see what Ezekiel has done and what his purpose is in this passage. He has taken the people's image (accepting their account of their present state—as hopeless as dried-up bones—and has used it to make the opposite case. Through the image of God's clothing the bones with flesh and putting breath into them, he shows his audience that God will give them new life and hope.

Because Ezekiel quotes the literary saying that provides the basic image for his message, we can see that he is not using bizarre language, expressing the fantasies of a disturbed mind, or depicting a literal resurrection. Rather, he is playing off a popular saying, using a popular image of hopelessness to construct an image of hope in a hopeless situation. Without the miniature literary background that the author himself provides we might well have come up with one of the two alternative interpretations suggested, depending on our presuppositions (a belief in psychic disturbance as the cause of religious visions, or a belief in the resurrection as something already known to God's intimates during OT times). Knowledge of the literary background, here supplied by the text itself, allows readers of different presuppositions to recognize how that background has shaped the author's message, to perceive more precisely what that message is, and so to make more fitting use of it today.

If such references to current literary expressions are rare, overt references to literary traditions known to us from outside Israel are even rarer. Ezekiel 14:12-20 refers to Noah, Daniel, and Job as people who, if now living in a land that God decided to punish, would save none but themselves by their righteousness—not even their children. (This implies that people in Ezekiel's audience believed that the presence of people of great righteousness would guarantee the salvation of others in the community.) It is immediately understandable to readers of the OT why Noah and Job should be mentioned here—Noah by his righteousness saved his family from God's judgment by the flood (Genesis 6–8); and Job, while losing his children initially, by his righteousness got a new family (Job 1; 42; in the oral version familiar to Ezekiel he may possibly have saved his original family). But no story of the biblical Daniel (in the book of that name) refers to his saving his family, nor indeed is there any reference to his

having a family. (In addition, the stories of the book of Daniel are all dated to well after Ezekiel's time.) To whom does Ezekiel refer? A fourteenth-century text from the northwest Syrian city state of Ugarit recounts the story of a pious and righteous patriarch called Danel, who has a son who is killed.[2] We do not have the end of the text, but it seems most likely that this figure of antiquity (resembling Noah and Job) is referred to in Ezekiel, and that in the version of the story familiar to the Jews of the early sixth century Danel got his son back—or a new son (cf. Job). Hence an Ugaritic text suggests a fitting background to a biblical reference that is quite obscure on biblical evidence alone.

Even biblical texts which seem quite comprehensible on their own presuppose traditions. Certainly the traditions of Israel itself are the primary literary context in which to read biblical literature. But we have only a small selection of those traditions, so any examples of related traditions from the larger Near East have the potential to shed light on the background and purposes of a given text.

THE NATURE AND RANGE OF ANCIENT NEAR EASTERN LITERATURE

Orality, Writing, and the Alphabet. Prior to the invention of writing all literature throughout the world was entirely oral. Literature was known through performance, and every performance was given by a live performer before a live audience. The degree of consistency or innovation in repeated performances depended on cultural values and audience expectation and began to appear in both regions, the beginning of two literary traditions that continued down to the beginning of the Common Era. While some oral literature found its way into written form, the invention of writing probably did not significantly affect the transmission of oral literature.

Mastery of the complex cuneiform and hieroglyphic writing systems required an extensive, highly specialized education. Literacy was, therefore, necessarily limited to the scribal guilds. These guilds developed their own traditions and canons. Many literary texts survived because they became

2. All dates in this article are BCE.

part of the scribal schools' traditional curriculum and were repeatedly copied by student scribes.

The gap between the literati and the rest of the population is most clearly exposed by the language in which the literature was written. Babylonian and Assyrian literary texts of the first millennium were written in a literary dialect distinct from the contemporary language used for, e.g., correspondence. Egyptian literature of the second and first millennia was largely written in Middle Egyptian, the language of the early second millennium. This functioned as a kind of classical language and was rather different from the evolving spoken language, which attained written form in the later first millennium.

The alphabet (the Canaanite alphabet) was invented in Palestine around the middle of the second millennium. Soon afterward a second (cuneiform) alphabet was also devised and used for writing the native language of Ugarit. (The Ugaritic alphabet was abandoned in the widespread social upheavals around 1200.) The alphabet reduced the hundreds of signs of the cuneiform and hieroglyphic scripts to the number of consonants in the language. It was much easier to master than previous writing systems, and its use probably spread through a much wider spectrum of officialdom. But it is unlikely that officials in Syria-Palestine promoted literacy beyond their own circles.

With the exception of the texts from Ugarit virtually all of the alphabetic inscriptions that have been recovered are monumental or immediately functional. Outside the Bible, literary texts—in our sense of that term—are almost nonexistent in the Canaanite alphabet, as compared with the extensive literary traditions now attested in cuneiform and hieroglyphic. Thus we should envisage in Syria-Palestine a lively and extensive oral literature of which we have only very occasional written deposits outside the OT.

Transmission and Innovation. We are accustomed to thinking of the OT as a fixed text, which indeed it has been since the early centuries CE (although it was considerably less stable and more varied in the preceding centuries). In those cases in which we have more than one copy of an ancient Near Eastern literary work, it is clear that many minor and even major changes might be introduced over a period of a few centuries. Fresh influence from the ever-changing oral tradition, developments internal to the scribal tradition, and shifts in the

political and cultural context produced changes in style, in ideology, and in artistic and social goals. The textual evidence for the *Epic of Gilgamesh* (see below), ranging over almost two thousand years, provides the fullest evidence for how ancient literature might change over time.[3] Other situations in which creativity was called for are suggested in the introduction to the so-called "Memphite Theology": "His majesty found [this writing] to be a work of the ancestors which was worm-eaten, so that it could not be understood from beginning to end. His majesty copied it anew so that it became better than it had been before."[4] Major changes in the tradition— innovative literary works—can often be assigned safely to a particular period. To this extent we can speak of the date of composition of a particular work. But unless it can be demonstrated that a work is strictly a scribal composition (like those Egyptian texts that extol the virtues of the scribal profession[5]), or a direct response to particular historical events, the ultimate roots of a work may reach back into the fertile soils of oral tradition.

At times during the long writing traditions of Mesopotamia and Egypt, some writers strove to imitate older models, producing an archaizing style that mixed the old and the new. Some works are pseudepigrapha—compositions composed as if written by some ancient scribe, king, or other authority.

Poetry and Prose. Basic to ancient Near Eastern (including biblical) poetry is a rather consistent use of parallelism, in which a line of poetry is paired with another line that repeats, recalls, or in other ways plays on the syntax and/or meaning of the first line. (Sometimes three lines are so correlated—or indeed larger groupings.) This convention tends to produce lines of comparable length and rhythm. It also tends to give the modern reader the sense that the poetry is repetitious and verbose. But parallelism invites the reader to read not rapidly and silently, as we are accustomed to do, but slowly and aloud, as in ancient performance, contemplating the relations between parallel lines and enjoying the poetry as if it were a series of pictures—each drawn from two

3. See J. H. Tigay, *The Evolution of the Gilgamesh Epic* (Philadelphia: University of Pennsylvania Press, 1982); and, for a similar approach to biblical literature, J. H. Tigay, ed., *Empirical Models for Biblical Criticism* (Philadelphia: University of Pennsylvania Press, 1985).
4. M. Lichtheim, *Ancient Egyptian Literature: A Book of Readings,* 3 vols. (Berkeley: University of California Press, 1973–1980) I:52.
5. See ibid., I:184-92, II:167-78; W. K. Simpson, ed., *The Literature of Ancient Egypt: An Anthology of Stories, Instructions, and Poetry,* 2nd ed. (New Haven: Yale University Press, 1973) 329-36, 343-47.

(or more) different views, rather than from a single perspective or, to emphasize the aural element, as if it were a musical theme immediately followed by its transposition or variation, rather than by new thematic material.

Formal prose also may exhibit a high degree of parallelism of phrases or clauses, but without the density of imagery, compactness of language, richness of vocabulary, or other marks of poetry. For Egyptian literature, Lichtheim has tentatively proposed a mediating category (between prose and poetry), which she calls "orational style."[6]

Individual Literatures of the Ancient Near East.

Sumerian, Babylonian, and Assyrian. Only small samples of Mesopotamian literature have survived from the third millennium.[7] But from early in the second millennium, we have numerous literary texts. Some are in Sumerian, a language perhaps related to the Turkic languages. This was the dominant language in the third millennium but was no longer spoken in the second. Other texts are in Akkadian, from this time on the reigning spoken language of Mesopotamia. In the later second millennium, Akkadian became the international language of trade and diplomacy. From this period Akkadian literary texts, used in the training of scribes, have been found in Canaan and as far away as central Egypt (el-Amarna).

Most Sumerian literature is known from copies made in the early second millennium. Among these are several short myths and epics, including some independent stories about Gilgamesh (see below). Sumerian literature also comprises hymns and prayers, collections of laws, lamentations over fallen cities, wisdom literature, etc.[8]

Best known among Akkadian literary works is the *Epic of Gilgamesh*.[9] Enkidu, made by the gods as a match for the boisterous Gilgamesh, king of Uruk (biblical Erech), becomes Gilgamesh's comrade-in-arms. Their joint adventures end with Enkidu's death. Gilgamesh then sets out in search of immortality. The epic concludes with a recognition of the limits of human striving. First composed in the early second millennium out of several separate Sumerian stories, the epic further developed down into the first millennium. Fragments have been found as far afield as Megiddo. The more recently recovered *Atrahasis* myth dates from the same period (early second millennium).[10] The majority of the gods strike and rebel because of the work imposed on them by the high gods. Their leader is killed so that the high gods can create humanity out of his remains to take over the work and provide for the gods. In time the newly created humans also become noisy and troublesome, and the gods decide to dispose of them, finally doing so by a massive flood that Atrahasis, duly warned by one of the gods, survives in a boat. The so-called *Epic of Creation* or *Enuma elish*, probably composed around the eleventh century, recounts the defeat of the primeval sea monster by the Babylonian god Marduk, his creation of the world out of her corpse, and his elevation to supreme status in his sanctuary in Babylon—the real point of the whole.[11]

Besides other myths, there are several works treating in varying ways the plight of an innocent sufferer,[12] several collections of laws,[13] hymns and prayers (including a great hymn to the sun god, Shamash[14]), proverb collections,[15] and historiographic narratives especially in the form of royal annals and chronicles.[16]

Hurrian and Hittite. The cuneiform system of writing spread to the northwest, where it was used already in third-millennium Ebla and adopted in the second millennium by the peoples of Syria and Asia Minor. These include the Hurrians and the Hittites (who also developed their own hieroglyphic writing system). Although the Hurrian language is still not completely understood, some Hurrian literature has been preserved in the Indo-European language of the Hittites, a group that dominated the area of Turkey c.1600–1200. A major Hurrian myth has been partially recovered, notably the Kumarbi cycle, which recounts the origins and progress of the conflict between the storm god and the underworld

---

6. Lichtheim, *Ancient Egyptian Literature*, I:11.

7. There are a few samples of Sumerian literature in third millennium Elba, in Syria.

8. For a sampler of Sumerian literature, see T. Jacobsen, *The Harps That Once . . . Sumerian Poetry in Translation* (New Haven: Yale University Press, 1987).

9. D. Dalley, *Myths from Mesopotamia* (Oxford: Oxford University Press, 1989) 39-153.

10. Ibid., 1-38.

11. Ibid., 228-77.

12. *ANET*, 596-604.

13. Ibid., 161-68, 197-98.

14. For a translation and literary appreciation of this hymn, see E. Reiner, *Your Thwarts in Pieces, Your Mooring Rope Cut: Poetry from Babylonia and Assyria* (Ann Arbor: Horace H. Rackham School of Graduate Studies at the University of Michigan, 1985) 68-84.

15. *ANET*, 593-96.

16. See ibid., 265-317, 558-64. For a literary appreciation of examples of several genres of Akkadian literature, mostly translated, see Reiner, *Your Thwarts in Pieces.*

deity, Kumarbi.[17] Excavations at the Hittite capital have also produced a number of indigenous myths and folktales, especially two versions of an account of how the storm god defeated a dragon with the aid of a mortal,[18] and several versions of a myth in which a god disappears and has to be found and won back.[19] There is also a fragmentary version of a Canaanite myth about the gods El and Baal, and the goddesses Asherah and Anat.[20]

Hittite literature also includes prayers,[21] rituals,[22] a law collection,[23] a number of carefully drafted treaties with neighboring powers,[24] and a variety of official court documents that are historiographic and literary in conception and form.[25]

Egyptian. The Egyptians spoke and wrote their own literature in the African-Asiatic language we now call ancient Egyptian. Egyptian literature includes a body of often powerful, imaginative religious texts designed to ensure that the deceased passes safely from this life to a blessed new life in the hereafter. These are enshrined in the third millennium royal Pyramid Texts,[26] the slightly later Coffin Texts, which extended this privilege to other people of wealth and influence, and finally The Book of the Dead of the later second millennium, which made the afterlife more generally accessible.[27] A tradition extending from the earliest period to the Hellenistic period is the "Instruction"—a collection of wisdom sayings and advice first designed for success at court but later developing into general reflections on living well in this world.[28] The Egyptians also produced several literary works on the breakdown of social order and on whether life is worth living.[29]

No continuous mythical narratives or properly epic literature has been recovered from Egypt, though there are extracts from and allusions to myths in the mortuary and hymnic literature, and

some royal inscriptions have epic characteristics. There are, however, several tales—some fantastic, others more realistic. The latter include *The Story of Sinuhe,* who flees Egypt during a palace coup and spends several years in Canaan before being invited back to the palace by the new king,[30] and *The Report of Wenamun,* who sails to various Phoenician ports to get wood for the god Amun-Re.[31] The Egyptians also had a tradition of hymns and prayers. *The Great Hymn to the Aten* (the divine sun disk)[32] has many topics in common with Psalm 104. Compare with Ps 104:25-6 the following: "Ships fare north, fare south as well,/Roads lie open when you rise; The fish in the river dart before you, Your rays are in the midst of the sea."[33] Many monumental inscriptions are literary creations, and from the later second millennium come several collections of love poems.[34]

Ugaritic, Phoenician, and Aramaic. The earliest literature recovered from Syria-Palestine, dating from the fourteenth to thirteenth centuries, appears at Ugarit. It includes a series of myths about the storm god Baal, including his defeat of the god Sea/River and his struggle with the god Death; the story of King Kirtu (or Keret), who is saved from various plights by the patriarchal god El, and the already-mentioned story about the patriarch Danel and his son, Aqhat. These are all poetic in form.[35] Among other texts from second-millennium Syria, the (pseudo-) autobiographical inscription of Idrimi of Alalakh (near Aleppo),[36] though written in (rough) Akkadian, is of Western literary inspiration.

In the first millennium the two dominant Semitic dialects of Syria-Palestine were Phoenician and Aramaic. Of the numerous Phoenician and Aramaic monumental inscriptions, a few exhibit marked literary features that hint at a developed literary tradition now largely lost except in the Bible.[37] A rare find from that tradition is the tale and proverbs

17. H. A. Hoffner, *Hittite Myths,* Society of Biblical Literature: Writings from the Ancient World, vol. 2 (Atlanta: Scholars Press, 1990) 38-61.
18. Ibid., 10-14.
19. Ibid., 14-31, 35-37.
20. Ibid., 69-70.
21. *ANET,* 393-401.
22. Ibid., 346-61.
23. Ibid., 188-87.
24. Ibid., 201-6, 529-30.
25. Ibid., 318-19.
26. Lichtheim, *Ancient Egyptian Literature,* I:29-50; Simpson, *The Literature of Ancient Egypt,* 269-78.
27. Lichtheim, *Ancient Egyptian Literature,* II:119-32.
28. Ibid., I:58-80, 97-109, 135-39; II:135-63; III:159-217; Simpson, *The Literature of Ancient Egypt,* 159-200, 241-65.
29. Lichtheim, *Ancient Egyptian Literature,* I:139-69; Simpson, *The Literature of Ancient Egypt,* 102-240.

30. Lichtheim, *Ancient Egyptian Literature,* I:222-35; Simpson, *The Literature of Ancient Egypt,* 57-74.
31. Lichtheim, *Ancient Egyptian Literature,* II:224-30; Simpson, *The Literature of Ancient Egypt,* 142-55.
32. Lichtheim, *Ancient Egyptian Literature,* II:96-100; Simpson, *The Literature of Ancient Egypt,* 289-95.
33. Lichtheim, *Ancient Egyptian Literature,* II:97.
34. Ibid., II:181-93; Simpson, *The Literature of Ancient Egypt,* 296-325.
35. See M. C. Coogan, *Stories from Ancient Canaan* (Philadelphia: Westminster, 1978).
36. *ANET,* 557-58.
37. Ibid., 653-62.

of Ahiqar, written in Aramaic on papyrus and preserved in the fifth-century Jewish colony at Elephantine on the first cataract of the Nile.[38] This is the first known version of a work that became very popular in the Middle East in subsequent centuries, being translated into some dozen languages. A more recent find, a badly damaged inscription from Tell Deir Alla in Jordan, tells of the visions of Balaam son of Beor (see Numbers 22–24).

RELATIONS BETWEEN THE LITERATURE OF THE ANCIENT NEAR EAST AND THE OT

The Objects of Comparison. As the preceding brief overview shows, ancient Near Eastern literature allows us to see a larger, longer tradition of virtually all the major categories of biblical literature—tales, historiography, laws, hymns and prayers, love songs, lamentations over fallen cities, proverbs, and so on.

On the other hand there is nothing from the ancient Near East quite like most biblical "books" (to use our modern term). These "books," in which biblical literature finally reached more or less its present form, are the product of the codifying efforts of Jewish scribes during the Persian and Hellenistic periods (fifth to second centuries) and already reflect the preoccupations of a new era. This might indicate that we too should be more engaged with the form, structure, and cultural context of the books than with the literary traditions they enshrine. However, attention to the traditions from which the books have been compiled is warranted by several facts.

First, a focus on smaller component parts of the literature corresponds to an essential characteristic of most OT books, which are not made from whole cloth but rather of various traditional materials. The degree to which the various source materials are assimilated varies from book to book. In most cases, even when we appreciate the larger patterns and themes of the whole, a book's richness of meaning derives to a considerable extent from the diversity and individual character of the parts.

Second, many biblical books consist of literature of diverse types—thus Deuteronomy consists of homilies, laws, and poems. And the basic genres of Israelite literature cut across later divisions into

38. Ibid., 427-30.

books—thus cultic songs, characteristic of the book of Psalms, also appear in books of law (Deuteronomy 32), of historiography (1 Sam 2:1-10), and of prophecy (Isa 63:7–64:12). To appreciate these component types of literature, it is necessary to focus on traditional genres and their ancient Near Eastern background. This emphasis on genre does not, however, imply inattention to other aspects of the literature, such as themes or topics, imagery, social settings, or literary settings.

Finally, attention to the component literary units of the books gives more direct access to the expressions, beliefs, and experiences of the ancient Israelites before they had anything approaching a Bible. In other words, it gives us access to aspects of the history of Israel's experience. That history is of considerable theological significance.

The Validity of Comparison. Within the last century and a half, considerable use has been made of the emerging ancient Near Eastern literary background of the OT. Many older comparative studies have been invalidated by additional sources, more careful and comprehensive analysis, and greater knowledge. But presuppositions often shape comparisons too. Some interpreters emphasize the OT's similarity to and continuity with ancient Near Eastern literature—perhaps to show that the OT is authentic or, on the other hand, that it is merely a product of its environment. Others emphasize its divergence from and contrast with its background—perhaps to show that it is absolutely different or that each of the ancient Near Eastern literatures should be appreciated on its merits, not just in comparison with the others.

A just comparison gives due weight to both commonalities and differences and seeks to explain both—as respectively part of the common culture Israel shared with its neighbors and antecedents, or as part of the particular culture or sub-culture of the individual work—or indeed of the creativity of its author(s).

Specific Comparisons. It is impossible within the compass of this article to give a useful survey of all the fruitful comparisons that have been made or can be made between biblical and extra-biblical literature. In the following pages, a few smaller literary phenomena from diverse parts of the OT are set against their ancient Near Eastern literary background. The intention is to cover various types of material, to illustrate diverse kinds of relationships, and to suggest different contributions to interpretation. Where possible, I have concentrated on materials from Syria-Palestine, on the assumption that these may best represent the literary culture that most substantially and continuously influenced Israel. These materials are generally less familiar, and unfortunately still less accessible, to the general reader than are the great works of Egypt and Mesopotamia.

None of the following cases represents an exhaustive comparison; indeed, in most cases only a few salient features are noted. They are designed to alert the reader to three things: the rich literary resources from the ancient Near East now available to the student of the OT; the striking continuities that can be observed between the literature of the OT and its antecedents; and, ultimately, the assumptions that must replace our modern presuppositions if we are to appreciate the literature of the OT on its own terms.

Rhetoric. Many of the turns of phrase, images,

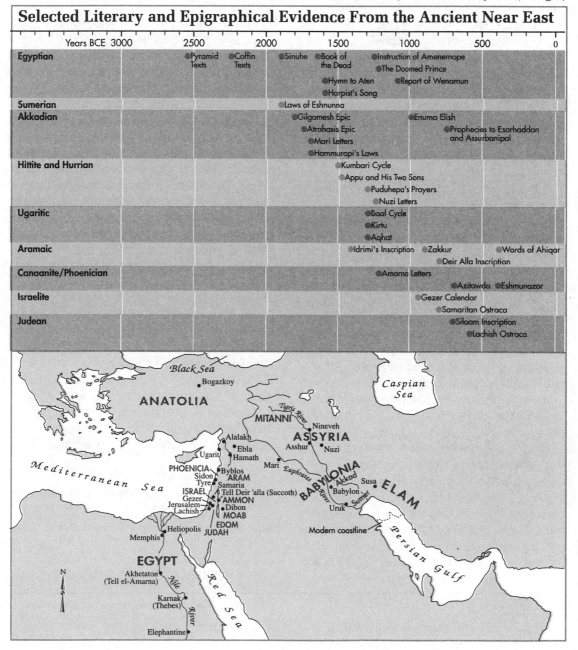

Selected Literary and Epigraphical Evidence From the Ancient Near East

	3000	2500	2000	1500	1000	500	0
Egyptian		Pyramid Texts • Coffin Texts		Sinuhe • Book of the Dead • Hymn to Aten • Harpist's Song	Instruction of Amenemope • The Doomed Prince • Report of Wenamun		
Sumerian				Laws of Eshnunna			
Akkadian				Gilgamesh Epic • Atrahasis Epic • Mari Letters • Hammurapi's Laws	Enuma Elish • Prophecies to Esarhaddon and Assurbanipal		
Hittite and Hurrian				Kumbari Cycle • Appu and His Two Sons • Puduhepa's Prayers • Nuzi Letters			
Ugaritic				Baal Cycle • Kirtu • Aqhat			
Aramaic				Idrimi's Inscription • Zakkur • Deir Alla Inscription	Words of Ahiqar		
Canaanite/Phoenician				Amarna Letters	Azitawda • Eshmunazor		
Israelite					Gezer Calendar • Samaritan Ostraca		
Judean					Siloam Inscription • Lachish Ostraca		

235

and general sentiments that we think of as biblical turn out to be attested elsewhere in the rhetoric of the ancient Near East. In other words, they were part of the Israelite authors' inherited stock of traditional expressions. This does not mean that they always expressed their authors' views, however, or that the Israelite authors always used them in precisely the same way as their predecessors or neighbors.

In the divine oracle in Psalm 89, God pronounces that the dynasty of David will perdure as long as the sun and moon (vv. 37-38). Psalm 72 expresses the wish that the king might live as long as the sun and moon (v. 5), and that his "name" (which may include reputation and descendants) endure as long as the sun (v. 17a). In the ancient Near East the sun and moon are cited as stereotypical models of longevity. This use is especially common in statements supporting a monarch. Thus the eighth-century Phoenician inscription of king Azatiwada concludes with the wish that his " 'name' might be forever like the 'name' of the sun and moon."[39]

The fifth-century Phoenician inscription of King Eshmunazor of Sidon includes a curse on anyone disturbing his sarcophagus: "May they have no root below, nor fruit above."[40] Amos 2:9 uses the same imagery for God's destruction of the Amorites, and Bildad speaks of the fate of the wicked in similar language in Job 18:16. It is used affirmatively of the recovery of the remnant of Judah in 2 Kgs 19:30/Isa 37:31.

Ugaritic literature has revealed many poetic conventions and expressions to which Israelite poets were heirs. It has also exposed some of the mythological antecedents of Hebrew expressions of faith. Both may be illustrated with the following example: When Baal is first felled in his conflict with the god Yamm ("Sea"), the craftsman god rallies him with the words: "Now your enemy, O Baal,/now your enemy you will smite,/now you will destroy your opponent." Psalm 92:9 exhibits an almost identical poetic structure, but transfers the address to Yahweh, generalizing the deity's victory and using it in a song of thanksgiving: "For your enemies, O LORD,/for your enemies shall perish;/all evildoers shall be scattered."[41]

Mythical phenomena sometimes underlie what to us may seem merely poetic language in the OT. For example, Mot, the god of death, appears at Ugarit as a ravening, insatiable monster. This is echoed in Isa 5:14 ("Sheol has enlarged its appetite/ and opened its mouth beyond measure") and in Hab 2:5b, where the arrogant "open their throats wide as Sheol;/ like Death they never have enough." The Ugaritic literature suggests that such expressions are not "merely" poetic, but are vestiges of powerful religious symbols.

The assertion of universal human mortality found in the Old Babylonian *Gilgamesh Epic* (III.iv.6-8; X.iii.3-5) and an Egyptian harpist's song[42] was clearly a commonplace long before it was taken up in Israelite literature (Josh 23:14a; Job 30:23; Eccl 2:14-16; 3:19-20; 9:1-3).

The belief that "God does what he wishes" is expressed at the end of an Egyptian autobiographical inscription.[43] In Jonah 1:14b the sailors, desperate to survive a storm without offending God, express the same sentiment (in the second person). In both cases this expression of the deity's freedom and power is a gesture of submissiveness behind which lies a hope for divine favor.[44] On the other hand, the identical sentiment in Pss 115:3 and 135:6 glories in God's freedom and sovereignty over all other gods.

These expressions and many others indicate that the literature in question drew on a common stock of poetic and mythical formulae, metaphors, similes, and sentiments.[45] Imagery in the OT and ancient Near East generally functions very differently from the imagery prized in modern literary criticism; rather than being novel, particular, and suggestive, it is traditional, general, and fixed in reference.[46] This is not to deny that Israel had its own traditional images, nor that individual poets might use such

---

39. Ibid., 654b.

40. Ibid., 622b.

41. Unless otherwise noted, Scripture quotations in this article are from the New Revised Standard Version.

42. Lichtheim, *Ancient Egyptian Literature,* II:116.

43. Ibid., III:17.

44. The annals of the ninth-century Assyrian king Assurnasirpal II claim that the leaders of a city threatened by his army threw themselves on the king's mercy by ascribing to him the same absolute freedom to do whatever he pleases. They came out to him crying: "If it pleases you, kill! If it pleases you, spare! If it pleases you, do what you will!" (A. K. Grayson, *Assyrian Royal Inscriptions,* vol. 2, Records of the Ancient Near East [Wiesbaden: Harrassowitz, 1976] 547).

45. While some may not be essentially literary, but rather part of ordinary speech, others imply a more formal, artistic, literary tradition.

46. See D. R. Hillers, "Dust: Some Aspects of Old Testament Imagery," in *Love and Death in the Ancient Near East: Essays in Honor of Marvin H. Pope,* eds. J. H. Marks and R. M. Good (Guilford, Conn.: Four Quarters, 1987), 105-9.

images in fresh ways. Indeed, the biblical evidence shows that they were used both in conventional and in fresh and distinctive ways. But the meaning of a simile or metaphor is always to be understood in the light of its traditional use.

Genres: Prophecies, Laws, Vows and Psalms, Proverbs, and Narratives. Most of the smaller literary genres found in the Bible—e.g., prophecies, laws, vows, psalms, proverbs, narrative motifs, episodes, and tales—are well attested in ancient Near Eastern literature.

Prophecies. Officials in and around eighteenth-century Mari (on the middle Euphrates) sometimes quoted prophetic oracles in letters informing the king about the prophecy—often on the day the oracle was delivered. Some of these letters have been recovered from the palace archives.[47] We can get no closer to hearing an oracle directly from a prophet's mouth!

Prophecies are also enshrined in more literary form. A prophecy by a group of prophets (see 1 Kings 22) is quoted by Zakkur, king of Hamath, in a monumental Aramaic inscription that he installed in a temple to commemorate the main events of his reign (c.800).[48] Brief collections of oracles addressed to the last two great kings of Assyria, Esarhaddon and Assurbanipal (c.680–627), were compiled and preserved in Nineveh.[49]

The Deuteronomistic history (dating ultimately from the exilic period and covering Joshua to 2 Kings), and especially Samuel and Kings, often quotes individual oracles delivered by prophets in earlier centuries. If we set aside the typically Deuteronomistic themes that the historians incorporate into these older oracles, we discover that many of the original prophecies had topics and purposes similar to those of the Mari prophecies, in which international relations, warfare, cultic matters, and the king's welfare are addressed with promises and assurances, demands or requests, warnings, and threats against other kings or states.

Letters from Mari show that the officials who report prophecies have already at that earliest stage of transmission begun the process of interpretation. It is not surprising, therefore, that the much longer process of transmission of the biblical prophetic books has produced multiple layers of interpretation.

The language of the prophecy quoted by King Zakkur demonstrates that Israel's contemporary prophets used expressions almost identical to those of their neighbors. Besieged by a confederacy of other kings, Zakkur reports that he prayed to Baal-shamayn ("Lord of the Heavens"), who answered him through seers and prophets: "Do not be afraid, for I made you king, and I will stand with you, and I will deliver you from all these kings." Individually, each of these clauses is found in divine speech in the Bible. Most of them appear together in an oracle attributed to the prophet Jeremiah: "Do not be afraid of the king of Babylon . . . for I am with you, to save you and to rescue you from his hand" (Jer 42:11).

While all the extra-biblical oracles (like those of Samuel and Kings) are addressed to individuals (usually the monarch), Jeremiah, like most of the classical prophets, is here addressing not just the king, but all the leaders of the nation and indeed "all the people." When there is no longer a monarch, the exilic Isaiah reiterates the same themes in an address to Israel: "Do not fear, for I am with you . . . I will uphold you with my victorious right hand . . . those who strive against you shall be as nothing and shall perish" (Isa 41:10-11). Oracles addressed to the nation, especially those critical of the nation and its religious practice, such as are preserved in the books of the classical prophets, are without antecedent or analogue in the ancient Near East. However, the variety and sophistication of the classical prophetic literature invites comparison with a variety of other literary genres from the ancient Near East.

The literary records of oracles from Mesopotamia and Syria are exceptional. Mesopotamian scribes had a greater interest in preserving the more "scientific" literature of the diviners, especially the omens read off animals' entrails.[50] Divination literature exceeds in volume all other literary categories in Akkadian. But in Israel discerning the deity's will is not handed over to the specialized custodians of an impersonal science. This suggests a greater appreciation for the freedom of the deity and also of the people.

Laws. Biblical laws take several different forms. The most common form is termed casuistic: If a person does such and such, then such and such shall happen. The casuistic formulation had long been the standard way in the ancient Near East of describing the just resolution

---

47. *ANET,* 623-25, 629-32.
48. Ibid., 655, there spelled Zakir.
49. Ibid., 605.

50. On Mesopotamian divination and its literature, see A. L. Oppenheim, *Ancient Mesopotamia,* 2nd ed. (Chicago: University of Chicago Press, 1977) 206-27.

of a hypothetical case. It is the almost universal form of laws in the various cuneiform law collections. The fact that Israel not only shared this conventional form but also was familiar with the larger Near Eastern legal tradition is obvious from certain specific cases. For example, Exod 21:28-32 consists of a group of laws concerned with an ox that gores someone to death. This problem is addressed also in the laws of Eshnunna (pars. 53-55)[51] and the laws of Hammurapi (pars. 250-2).[52] Both of these collections distinguish three cases: (1) an ox simply gores another ox (Eshnunna) or person (Hammurapi) to death; (2) an ox is publicly known to be prone to such behavior; its owner has been warned, but it still gores someone to death; and (3) the victim is a slave. The Exodus laws treat of precisely the same three cases as the Hammurapi laws. This is neither coincidence nor a necessary feature of all Near Eastern cultures. It can only be a case of inherited tradition. Even when the biblical version introduces certain additions, spelling out that the victim may be a man or a woman or, in the second case, a dependent son or daughter, it is simply drawing on a common feature of the cuneiform tradition.

The disposition of the three cases appears to differ more sharply. In the first case, Hammurapi states that the case is not actionable. Exodus similarly declares the owner of the offending ox innocent, but also prescribes that the ox is to be stoned to death and its meat not eaten. The Israelite laws about the goring ox are consistently distinguished from the cuneiform tradition by their insistence that the ox be killed. But this is a matter of spelling out what was doubtless taken for granted in the earlier tradition. An ox that had not been disposed of posed an ongoing threat.

In the case of the owner who has already been warned, Hammurapi and Eshnunna prescribe that he shall pay a stated sum of silver. Exodus has both ox and owner put to death (v. 29), although it allows the substitution of a ransom for the owner's life. The alternative penalties may reflect the fact that the case does not quite correspond with either murder or manslaughter (see vv. 12-13). According to the Exodus law, the penalty is the same, even if the victim is only a dependent. The cuneiform laws in other contexts lessen penalties in accordance with the victim's family status. Thus Exodus asserts, against the tradition, that the value of the life of a

dependent family member is equal to that of a head of household.[53]

This example, while pointing up a small but significant distinction in the valuation of dependent family members, demonstrates the clear continuity of the literary tradition in the cuneiform records and in Exodus with respect to both literary form and judicial measures. Admittedly each collection deals with a different selection of cases, so that the same ones do not appear in all collections. But it has been plausibly argued that each law collection presupposes the same general system of law, and that the selection of individual laws on a given topic in one collection can be best understood on the basis of knowledge of all the collections.[54]

Comparison of all the biblical law collections, however, shows that in Israel an increasingly wide range of material was included, varying in form and topic from what is found in the cuneiform collections. Moreover, while the latter are based in the civil establishment and concerned entirely with secular law, the Israelite law collections increasingly distance themselves from the monarchy (see Deut 17:14-20) and assume the character of religious law. A still wider focus, including the present literary settings of the biblical laws (in which they are received from God and declared to the people by Moses as part of God's covenant), would require a comparison of these settings with the prologues and epilogues of the cuneiform collections (in which the monarch proclaims his fulfillment of his divine calling to establish justice in the land), and with the Hittite and Assyrian treaties with vassal states.

Vows and Psalms. Vows are, in effect, prayers to the deity that seek to motivate a response by promising something in return. More specifically, a vow is a promise made to the deity conditional upon the deity's delivering the vower from a need or threat. The vow is to be fulfilled when the need or threat has been removed. This is made clear in Ps 66:13-14: "I will pay you my vows, those that . . . my mouth promised when I was in trouble." Several biblical narratives quote specific vows. These reveal both

51. *ANET,* 163.
52. Ibid., 176.

53. In all three law collections—Eshnunna, Hammurapi, and Exodus—the fine imposed on the owner of the ox when the gored victim is a slave is less than that when the victim is a free person, indicating that the slave was of less social value throughout the ancient Near East.
54. On this point, as well as the treatment of the laws of the goring ox, see R. Westbrook, *Studies in Biblical and Cuneiform Law,* Cahiers de la Revue Biblique 26 (Paris: Gabalda, 1988).

the general form in which vows were expressed ("O God, if only you will do X, then I will give you Y"), and, in the first conditional part of this expression, the specific circumstances in which the vow is made (barrenness, 1 Sam 1:11; a military crisis, Num 21:2; Judg 11:30-31; exile, Gen 28:20-22; 2 Sam 15:8).

The use and form of the vow are traditional. A cultic text from Ugarit envisages the city under siege and commends prayer to Baal under such circumstances in the form of a vow: "O Baal, if you will drive the mighty from our gates, the warrior from our walls. . . . " The vow continues with a promise of sacrifices and of a procession to the temple of Baal. In this case the vow is communal, rather than individual. In the tale of King Kirtu, the wifeless and childless hero, on his way to win another king's daughter as his wife, makes a vow to the goddess Asherah, promising her a silver and gold image of the woman if he succeeds in marrying her.

In both these cases the literary form is essentially that of the Hebrew. The same is true among the Hittites, from whom we have a whole series of vows by a queen, Puduhepa, who prays to various deities for the life and health of her evidently sick husband and promises in return a variety of material gifts to the deity.

From this background it is clear that the vow was a common institution in all these societies and was expressed in the same way in each. Knowledge of the vows in extra-biblical literatures, all of which express or imply the conditions from which the vower is appealing for deliverance, expand our appreciation of the range of circumstances in which vows might be made. This in turn helps us to imagine the various plights in which those reciting complaints found themselves and from which those reciting songs of thanksgiving had been delivered. (The Psalms themselves do not specify such plights, since they are designed for use on multiple occasions.)[55] Although the complaints in the psalter—which appeal to God to do something for an individual in a desperate plight—do not contain vows so explicit as the one in Queen Puduhepa's prayer to the goddess Lelwani on behalf of her sick husband, some do include a promise of thanksgiving (e.g., Pss 7:17; 56:12; 109:30). This conjunction of expression of need and promise of thanksgiving constitutes an implied vow, which explains the

number of songs of thanksgiving in which the delivered individual speaks of fulfilling the vows made during the crisis or in the complaint.

According to the Psalms, the promise and fulfillment of a vow in Israel generally concerned songs and sacrifices of thanksgiving (Pss 50:14; 66:13, 15; 116:17-18). The Psalms also make clear that the fulfillment of a vow was not just a matter of paying a debt to God, but also an occasion for testifying within the community to God's responsiveness (see esp. Pss 22:23-26; 66:16-19; 116:18-9). Aramaic, Phoenician, and Punic votive inscriptions are a similar public testimony.[56] They report that they are what the donor had vowed (promised) and that they have now been made because the deity has heard (and acted upon) the donor's prayer (the conditional part of the vow). As the votive inscription makes public written acknowledgment of the deity's aid in response to a vow, so more broadly the thanksgiving song makes public oral acknowledgment of God's aid in response to a complaint.[57]

In sum, ancient Near Eastern literature shows that the vow is identical in general form and function among Israelites and their neighbors, and that the biblical laments and thanksgiving songs, so familiar from the book of Psalms and elsewhere in the Bible, have functional counterparts in rather different form in the immediately surrounding cultures. All of these phenomena express in a public way an appeal to the deity when one fears the worst and gratitude to the deity for being spared. A broader perspective would take into account the longer, more literary prayers of the Egyptians, Hittites, and Mesopotamians.

Proverbs. Proverbs are a universal genre, so it is not surprising to find them throughout the ancient Near East. In the Bible we think first of the book of Proverbs, but proverbs are scattered through other books of the Bible as well. Both the prophetic books of Jeremiah and Ezekiel quote the proverb "The parents have eaten sour grapes, and the children's teeth are set on edge" (Jer 31:29; Ezek 18:2). Similarly, in ancient Near Eastern literature proverbs are quoted in a variety of contexts. Puduhepa, in the prayer just mentioned, quotes the proverb, "To a woman in travail the god yields her wish."[58] In such cases the authors are generally quoting popular

---

55. *ANET,* 393-94.

56. See, for example, ibid., 655 (Ben-hadad), 658*a* [c].
57. J. M. O'Brien, "Because God Heard My Voice: The Individual Thanksgiving Psalm and Vow-Fulfilment," *The Listening Heart,* JSOTSup 58 (Sheffield: Almond, 1987), 281-98.
58. *ANET,* 393.

sayings. What marks the proverbs in the book of Proverbs, and in the Near Eastern proverb collections, as part of a common literary tradition is the recurrence of similar artistic forms and themes.

The one West Semitic proverb collection outside the Bible is that of Ahiqar, which shares both forms and themes with material in the book of Proverbs.[59] Numerical sayings are found there (e.g., no. 12: "Two things are good, a third is pleasing to Shamash [the sun-god]"—these then being listed), as in the book of Proverbs (30:15-31). Ahiqar No. 21 ("How can sticks contend with fire, meat with a knife, a man with a king?") illustrates two formal features found in Israelite proverbs: the rhetorical question (e.g., Prov. 17:16) and the prefixing of parallel phrases or clauses that prove to be metaphors sharpening the point of the final phrase or clause (e.g., Prov. 26:3).

Certain themes are common to the two collections: Wisdom is "from the gods . . . precious to the gods" (no. 12; cf. Prov 8:22-31); a monarch is not like the rest of humanity, but godlike ("A king is like the Compassionate One" [no. 25]; "A king is as glorious to see as Shamash" [no. 26; cf. Prov 25:2-3; 16:15]); a monarch's anger is to be avoided ("Do not oppose the king; his anger is more fleet than lightning" [no. 19; cf. Prov 16:14]). The wise keep their own counsel ("Guard your mouth more than anything . . . for a word is a bird—anyone who releases it is a fool" [no. 15; cf. Prov 12:23]); children benefit from physical punishment ("Do not withhold your son from the rod; otherwise will you be able to save him?" [no. 3; cf. Prov 23:13-14]); parents are to be respected ("Whoever takes no pride in the name of his father or mother, may Shamash not shine on him" [no. 49; cf. Prov 20:20]); the wicked will be destroyed ("[The city] of the wicked will be overwhelmed . . . " [no. 75; cf. Prov 14:11]). Clearly many of the proverbs in the biblical book of Proverbs are part of a larger wisdom tradition.

A more extensive and direct influence can be seen in the Egyptian *Instruction of Amenemope*,[60] dating from toward the end of the second millennium. This has long been seen as a source or model for the collection of proverbs in Prov 22:17–24:22 (esp. 22:22–23:11). The latter speaks of "thirty sayings" (22:20), a precise reflection of the thirty chapters into which Amenemope is divided.[61]

Within the Egyptian tradition, each "Instruction" has its own character. Similarly there are discernible differences among the various collections within the book of Proverbs (chaps. 1–9 being most sharply distinguished from all the others)—even though they are now juxtaposed in one "book." The historically distinct, and sometimes distant, settings of the various Egyptian "Instructions" suggest the importance of discovering the different settings in which the various biblical proverb collections flourished before being gathered into one context.

Narratives. The narrative literature from the ancient Near East exhibits a wide range of genres, from folk tale to epic, from autobiographical account of royal achievements to national myth. Again, in this context, we shall concentrate on some smaller narrative elements.

Of religious significance is the motif in which a capital crime causes a reaction in nature (see Hos 4:2-3 and Jer 12:4) and the punishment of the offender is the only remedy (expressed as a legal principle in Num 35:33). After the murder of Aqhat in the Ugaritic story of that name, vegetation withers. Daniel and his daughter seek in vain to bring back the rain and revive the plant life. Pughat's mission of vengeance, with which the preserved part of the story ends, suggests that nature will revive only after the murderer's punishment. This is what happens in 2 Sam 21:1-14. There is a persistent famine in the land. David seeks an oracle that would explain why. He is told that it is because of Saul's killing of some Gibeonites (vv. 1-2). Only when this act has been expiated by the killing (and burial) of some of Saul's surviving family can the land be restored. In v. 14*b* the restoration is then depicted not as an automatic, impersonal revival, but as a divine act in response to the "land's" supplication.

A common narrative episode is set in the divine council where the high god appeals for a volunteer to undertake a mission, saying: "Who will do X?" Some member of the council volunteers: "I will do X." The high god then commissions him: "Do X." In 1 Kgs 22:19*b*-22 the prophet Micaiah recounts a vision that consists of just such an episode (in which the members

---

59. Reference to the proverbs of Ahiqar is according to their enumeration in the translation of J. M. Lindenberger in J. H. Charlesworth, ed., *The Old Testament Pseudepigrapha*, vol. 2 (Garden City, N.Y.: Doubleday, 1987) 498-507. Lindenberger also translates the narrative (494-98) and provides a useful introduction to the whole work (479-93).

60. Lichtheim, *Ancient Egyptian Literature*, II:146-63; Simpson, *The Literature of Ancient Egypt*, 241-65.

61. A list of comparable passages in the two texts appears in *ANET*, 42n. 46.

of the council are called "spirits"). Commonly, as there, the assembly is shown to be at a loss until the volunteer finally steps forward. Thus in the Ugaritic tale of Kirtu, all the gods remain utterly speechless as the high god, El, repeatedly calls for someone to heal the sick king. In this case, El himself finally volunteers to undertake the task. The episode is used to display El as the king's sole hope.

Another creative adaptation of this episode is found in Isa 6:8-9, where, as in 1 Kings 22, the narrator is recounting a vision (v. 1). In this case, the narrator reports that he himself, present at the scene he sees, speaks up as the volunteer. Thus the prophet claims to have received his commission in the same way as a member of the divine court (or "angel").

Folktales incorporated into literary works reflect a common concern with making a good marriage and having children. One tale type introduces the protagonist as being devoid of spouse or children, then recounts an expedition to get a spouse and lengthy negotiations leading to a marriage agreement, the ceremony, and the birth of children. The first third of the preserved part of *Kirtu* is precisely such a story, highlighting the divine directions under which Kirtu operates. Genesis 24 is another example, in which Abraham's steward represents the bridegroom's family. Again, divine guidance (of the envoy) is emphasized. (The birth of children is postponed to chap. 25.) A special mutation of the same story appears in the book of Ruth, with some reversals of the traditional form: The protagonist is a woman looking for a husband; the expedition is, for Naomi, a homecoming. Finally, the story of Jacob reflects a similar structure and theme (Genesis 28–29). While the same tale type clearly underlies, and the same familial concerns inform, all these examples, the treatment in each is quite different.

Marriage does not guarantee children, however, and childlessness is a shameful condition in many of our sources. Hence the type of tale in which a childless individual appeals to the deity for a child, and the deity grants his or her request. The story of the birth of Samuel is a good example (1 Samuel 1; see also Gen 25:21; 30:1*a*, 22-23*a*). Neighboring literatures exhibit other uses of the same: the Ugaritic tale of Aqhat and the Hurrian tale of *Appu and His Two Sons*.[62] The Egyptian tale of *The Doomed Prince* opens with another version of the same story, which is brief enough to be quoted:

It is said, there once was a king to whom no son had been born. [After a time his majesty] begged a son for himself from the gods of his domain, and they decreed that one should be born to him. That night he slept with his wife and she [became] pregnant. When she had completed the months of childbearing, a son was born.[63]

While all of these stories share the same general structure, each has distinctive local features and functions differently in the larger story that it initiates. The account of the birth of Samuel is alone in having this result achieved by a woman's prayer. In the context of the book of Samuel, the peculiar significance of Hannah's prayer (which is actually a vow; 1 Sam 1:11) is that it explains how Samuel comes to be living in the sanctuary where he receives his first message from God (1 Samuel 3).

In all of these cases, the common underlying structure is best explained as a popular oral tradition taken up and adapted for each of the literary works we now have. There are probably no grounds for suspecting any direct influence among the latter.

The last examples were stories focusing on family concerns. The Aramaic *Ahiqar* is a court story. The wise Ahiqar, adviser to the Assyrian king, is accused of treachery by his nephew and heir, Nadin. The king dispatches an officer to put Ahiqar to death, but the man saves him, because once, when he himself had been condemned to death, Ahiqar hid him, told the king he was dead, and then produced him again when the king seemed favorable. The story of Mordecai in the book of Esther follows the same bipartite structure. In both, because X had previously saved Y, who was threatened by A, Y now saves X, who is threatened by B.

More generally, the story of Ahiqar, like those of Esther, Joseph, and the early chapters of Daniel, illustrates and promotes a morality for court life in the great Near Eastern empires with its rivalries, intrigues, and risk of treachery. But while Ahiqar saves himself, Esther, Joseph, and (by implication) Daniel save their communities; and while specifically religious acts, miracles, and divine intervention are completely absent from *Ahiqar,* they are variously used in the biblical stories (least in Esther, which is closest in this respect to *Ahiqar*).

62. Hoffner, *Hittite Myths,* 63-65.

63. Lichtheim, *Ancient Egyptian Literature,* II:200.

Numbers 22–24 relates how Balaam was hired by the Moabite king to curse the people of Israel, but was in fact constrained to bless them. It is now clear that Balaam the seer, like Daniel the patriarch, was a popular subject of story—specifically in Transjordan—for he reappears in another narrative, unfortunately in very fragmentary condition, found at Tell Deir Alla, just east of the Jordan. In this he is identified as "Balaam son of Beor, seer of gods," to whom gods come at night with a message. The next day, when his people ask him why he is mourning, he recounts his vision. This begins with a divine assembly and proceeds with language reminiscent of the more poetic and symbolic oracles and visions of the late classical prophets.

Balaam was already portrayed as a seer of legendary reputation; this is clearly implied by Balak's message to him in Num 22:5-6. It is now confirmed that the authors of Numbers 22–24 were neither inventing a character nor reporting a historical event, but taking this legendary figure, a "pagan" seer known for his visions from the gods, as an object lesson. They depict him almost as God's plaything in chap. 22. More specifically, by showing that he had less spiritual perception than an ass (22:22-35), and that God turned his intended curse of Israel into a blessing (chaps. 23–24), the authors are assuring Israelites that they have little to fear from prestigious foreign prophets.

There are also connections between larger ancient Near Eastern and biblical narrative works. The two Ugaritic narratives most closely related to biblical narratives are *Aqhat* and *Kirtu,* stories of a patriarch and a king respectively. In these, as in *Gilgamesh* and often in epic, divine beings affect the plot by appearing as actors in the human realm (as in Genesis 18–19; 32:24-34; Judg 6:11-22; 13:3-23), or by taking action in the divine realm (as in Job 1–2 and, according to Micaiah, in 1 Kgs 22:19-22). Doubtless early Israelite storytellers used these devices much more freely, but the dominant theology of the later transmitters has severely limited their appearance in our Bible—as it both blurs Yahweh's appearances and limits the divine status of his representatives and members of the divine court in the cited passages. Modern readers unable to interpret such unrealistic scenes may find it helpful to recognize that these are conventional narrative means of representing the divine impact on human lives.

More fantastic elements of divine activity found in *Aqhat* and *Kirtu* are absent from the Bible. While the Ugaritic narratives make much more use of epic repetition than is found in Israelite narrative, they are devoid of the authorial explanations, summaries, or judgments commonly interjected into biblical narrative.

Kirtu treats of three situations to which kings were vulnerable: lack of progeny, sickness, and threat of deposition. Kirtu (and his community) are helpless to do anything about these problems, and he is saved only by the power, wisdom, and benevolence of the high god, El, on whom he is totally dependent. Thematic connections with OT narratives will be obvious. *Aqhat* focuses on the boy of that name, received by Danel in answer to an appeal to the gods, but later killed by the goddess Anat for his refusal to give her his bow, a gift of the gods. When Danel (accompanied by his daughter) learns of the murder, he proceeds to look for and bury the remains, curse the places closest to the site of the murder (see the law in Deut 21:1-9), observe a period of mourning, and offer a sacrifice. Pughat, the daughter, then seeks his blessing on her errand of vengeance. The story emphasizes not only traditional familial roles, especially duties and rituals, but also a reversal of gender roles sought by Anat and assumed by Pughat. Many biblical narratives portray families in which members do not play ideal roles (e.g., the patriarchal narratives, the story of David's court), and some depict women who are not seen in family roles at all (e.g., Deborah and Jael in Judges 4–5; Miriam in Exodus 15 and Numbers 12 [but cf. the anonymous sister of Moses in Exodus 2]; the wise woman of Tekoa in 2 Samuel 14 [though she gives a convincing dramatic performance of the part of a mother]; Huldah in 2 Kgs 22:14-20).

Again, a broader perspective would include especially the Akkadian epics, but also the more literary and historiographic of the royal inscriptions from throughout the Near East, all of which have exercised some influence on the larger narrative works of the OT.

CONCLUSION

Reading OT literature against its background in the literature of the ancient Near East allows us to appreciate common conventions and presuppositions, but also to identify more precisely the particular developments and interests that distinguished the Israelite authors and their communities. Similar or even identical forms do not necessarily imply identical meaning. It is always necessary to ask how, and for what purpose, a literary form or expression is being used in a particular text. Answers to such questions require careful attention to the larger literary, cultural, and social contexts.

This article has sought to stimulate and encourage readers to explore some ancient Near Eastern literature for themselves (see Bibliography), to discover relations between this literature and the OT, and so to deepen their understanding and appreciation of the literature of the OT.

Some knowledge of ancient Near Eastern literature helps us to see how the OT literature grew out of a larger tradition and how its authors adapted that tradition to serve new needs, values, and goals. The church is involved in another set of relations—between the messages and purposes of biblical texts and the situation of the world today. Our own awareness of the tradition to which we are heirs—including different interpretations of the Bible—gives us a similar opportunity and obligation to seek the wisdom to adapt that tradition to serve the needs, values, and goals of God's work in the world today.

BIBLIOGRAPHY

Pritchard, J. B., ed. *Ancient Near Eastern Texts Relating to the Old Testament.* 3rd ed. Princeton: Princeton University Press, 1969. Abbreviated *ANET,* this is a standard collection of most significant genres, but many texts are translated only in part, and many translations are now out of date.

The following are more recent translations of complete (so far as preserved) literary texts:

Coogan, M. D. *Stories from Ancient Canaan.* Philadelphia: Westminster, 1978.

Dalley, D. *Myths from Mesopotamia.* Oxford: Oxford University Press, 1989.

Foster, B. R. *Before the Muses: An Anthology of Akkadian Literature.* 2 vols. Bethesda: CDL, 1993.

Hoffner, H. A. *Hittite Myths.* Society of Biblical Literature: Writings from the Ancient World, vol. 2. Atlanta: Scholars Press, 1990. (New volumes are appearing from year to year.)

Jacobsen T. *The Harps That Once . . . Sumerian Poetry in Translation.* New Haven: Yale University Press, 1987.

Lichtheim, M. *Ancient Egyptian Literature: A Book of Readings.* 3 vols. Berkeley: University of California Press, 1973–1980.

Simpson, W. K., ed. *The Literature of Ancient Egypt: An Anthology of Stories, Instructions, and Poetry.* 2nd ed. New Haven: Yale University Press, 1973.

INTRODUCTION TO THE HISTORY OF ANCIENT ISRAEL

J. MAXWELL MILLER

OUTLINE

ANCIENT ISRAEL IN GEOGRAPHICAL CONTEXT

One naturally associates ancient Israel with Palestine, the term used here in its traditional geographical sense. This is essentially correct, but three important qualifications need to be made. First, Palestine is not a geographically discrete region, but continuous with the eastern Mediterranean seaboard. Second, the history of ancient Israel must be understood as having unfolded in a broader geographical context than either Palestine or the Mediterranean seaboard. Third, while the history of ancient Israel must be understood as having un-

244

folded in a broader geographical context than Palestine, center stage was actually smaller. The ancient Israelites are to be associated primarily with the central and southern hill country of western Palestine.

Palestine is the southern end of the eastern Mediterranean seaboard (often called Syria-Palestine or the Levant), which itself is a strip of cultivable land sandwiched between the Mediterranean Sea and the Arabian Desert. This strip averages between seventy and one hundred miles east-west, extends from Mt. Taurus in the north to the Sinai Desert in the south, and exhibits four features of physical geography that also extend north-south throughout the length of the seaboard. These features are most obvious in the north, where they are represented by the Phoenician coast, the Lebanon Mountains, the Bekaa Valley, and the Anti-Lebanon Mountains. Continuing southward into Palestine, they are represented by the coastal plain (the Sharon and Philistia), the hill country of western Palestine (Galilee, the central or "Ephraimite" hill country, and the southern "Judean" hill country), the Jordan Valley (with the Sea of Galilee and the Dead Sea) and the Transjordanian highlands (the regions of ancient Gilead, Ammon, Moab, and Edom). With the topography of the seaboard broken by mountain ranges and valleys, agricultural possibilities are modest and tend toward small-plot farming augmented with sheep and goat herding. There are no major river valleys suitable for extensive irrigation or to encourage political unity. Thus the physical circumstances of Syria-Palestine predisposed the area to regionalism during ancient times, characterized by small urban centers and localized political structures rather than large empires.

However, this Mediterranean seaboard was strategic territory in ancient times because it served as a land bridge between Africa, Asia, and Europe. Consequently its population tended to be somewhat heterogeneous and, especially along the main trade routes, cosmopolitan. While benefiting from the commercial traffic that passed through, the inhabitants of the region were constantly vulnerable to the aggressive commercial and military policies of imperial powers at opposite ends of the seaboard, especially those of Egypt and Mesopotamia, and were caught up in virtually every major conflict between these powers. It cannot be overemphasized, therefore, that the small cities and kingdoms of Syria-Palestine did not exist in isolation. Their history must be understood in the broader context of ancient Near Eastern politics and international commerce.

The book of Joshua envisions a unified Israel to whom Yahweh had granted all of Palestine except for limited Ammonite, Moabite, and Edomite holdings in the Transjordan. It is explained that a significant amount of this divine land grant "remained to be conquered" (Josh 13:2-7), however; in fact, most of the narratives of the book have as their setting the hill country north and south of Jerusalem. The narratives of the book of Judges focus primarily on the hill country north of Jerusalem. Saul's kingdom was centered in that area as well, even though occasional military excursions into the northern Transjordan and the Negeb are reported for him (1 Sam 11:1-11; 15:1-9). Whatever the extent of David's and Solomon's kingdom, they ruled from Jerusalem, nestled deep in the hill country, and their expanded realm did not survive Solomon's death. The two kingdoms that emerged after Solomon—Israel and Judah—were centered in the central and southern hill country respectively, and only a few of the stronger Israelite and Judean kings were able to exert political authority beyond their hill-country base. In short, ancient Israel is to be associated primarily with the hill country of western Palestine. Palestine as a whole was shared by a diversity of people. The fact that this southern end of the Mediterranean seaboard came to be called "Palestine" serves as a reminder of that; *Palestine* is the anglicized form of *Philistia,* the land of the Philistines.

One further clarification is in order regarding the geographical setting of ancient Israel. Although the Hebrew Bible (HB) tends to use the name *Israel* in a broadly inclusive fashion, it is more appropriate from a historical perspective to distinguish between Israel and Judah. The fact that Israel and Judah were separate kingdoms with separate histories following Solomon's death is taken for granted even by the biblical writers. But there is much to suggest that the Israelites and Judeans were essentially separate peoples even in pre-monarchical times. More specifically, as will be explained in further detail below, (a) the name *Israel* probably referred originally to a group of loosely associated clans and tribes whose settlement was concentrated in the central hill country north of Jerusalem; (b) Judah was a separate group that settled in the southern hill country south of Jerusalem; and (c) the affairs of Israel and Judah did not become significantly entangled until the time of David.

ANCIENT ISRAEL IN HISTORICAL CONTEXT

The earliest known written materials date some 5,000 years ago, appearing first in Mesopotamia and soon after in Egypt. Although the very earliest of these texts remain undeciphered, they signal humankind's entering a new phase of existence. Appearing about the same time were the earliest cities and various other developments generally associated with advanced civilization—e.g., differentiated societal structures, occupational diversity, the accumulation of wealth and building projects on a monumental scale. There would be still other developments and endless local variations over the next 3,000 years, but likewise significant continuity of cultural patterns throughout the Near East. Locally based agricultural economies were the norm, typically involving a fortified urban center surrounded by smaller villages and hamlets. These city-states often were at war with each other, and occasionally a city would be able to extend its authority far afield. Egypt and Mesopotamia, able to draw upon the rich agricultural resources and dense population of their river valleys, were especially successful in this regard. Prominent cities that became the seat of small empires at different times during these three millennia were Memphis and Thebes in Egypt, Ebla and Aleppo in Syria, Hattusha in Anatolia, Ashur on the bank of the Tigris River, and Isin, Larsa, and Babylon further south in Mesopotamia, where the Tigris and Euphrates flow alongside each other before reaching the Persian Gulf.

Archaeologists working in Palestine, where relatively few written materials have been recovered from ancient times, divide these three millennia into four major ages: Early Bronze, Middle Bronze, Late Bronze, and Iron. These archaeological divisions are based on changes that occurred over time in the material culture, usually very gradual changes that included, but were by no means limited to, developments in metal technology. Thus the names of the archaeological divisions should not be taken too literally. The following are some correlations between these archaeological divisions and historical developments outside of Palestine.

Early Bronze Age (c. 3200–2000 BCE). Among the urban centers that emerged at the beginning of the Early Bronze Age were Sumerian cities that flourished in southern Mesopotamia (Ur, Warka, Shuruppak, Nippur, and others). Later on in that same region, although he was of Semitic rather than Sumerian heritage, Sargon of Akkad made a name for himself as a great conqueror. The "Old Kingdom" and "First Intermediate" periods of Egyptian history correspond roughly to the Early Bronze Age; it was during the Old Kingdom that the famous pyramids of Giza were built. Also, the recently discovered city of Ebla in Syria flourished during the Early Bronze Age. In Palestine there occurred at the end of this age a general decline of urban life. For unknown reasons, much of the population seems to have abandoned the cities for small villages and pastoral nomadism.

Middle Bronze Age (c. 2000–1550 BCE). Fortified cities began to reappear in Palestine early in this period, while Amorite dynasties gained control of many of the Mesopotamian cities (Isin, Larsa, Mari, Babylon, and others). Perhaps the most famous of the Amorite rulers was Hammurabi (c. 1792–1750 BCE) under whose rule Babylon enjoyed an early phase of grandeur. Although drawing upon motifs from earlier Sumerian literature, three major literary works were composed during this age: the so-called Babylonian Creation Account, the Atrahasis Epic, and the *Gilgamesh Epic*. Egypt's "Middle Kingdom" and "Second Intermediate" periods correspond roughly to the Middle Bronze Age. The latter part of the age witnessed an influx of Kassites in Mesopotamia and Hyksos rule in Egypt.

Late Bronze Age (c. 1550–1200 BCE). While Egypt enjoyed its heyday, Mesopotamia experienced a period of "dark ages," apparently initiated by the Kassites, and Palestine entered another phase of urban decline. Specifically, the Late Bronze Age corresponds to the "New Kingdom" period of Egypt's history, when the powerful pharaohs of dynasties XVIII and XIX ruled from Thebes. Under Thutmose III (c. 1479–1425 BCE), Egyptian armies reached northern Syria, where they met with resistance from the Middle Euphrates (Hurrian) state of Mitanni. Later pharaohs clashed in that region with armies of the Hittite Empire, centered in Anatolia. Egyptian texts from the Late Bronze Age provide our earliest written information of consequence regarding circumstances in Palestine. Especially important in this regard are the Amarna Letters (correspondence between the Egyptian court and subject rulers in Syria-Palestine) and inscriptions that report Egyptian military campaigns into Syria-Palestine.

Iron Age (c. 1200–300 BCE). Both the Egyptian and the Hittite empires experienced rapid decline after c. 1200 BCE, a turn of events that was exacerbated if not brought about by disruptive movements of the so-called "Sea Peoples." A brief revival of Egyptian influence in Palestine lasted until the mid-twelfth century. This was followed by a power vacuum that allowed for the rise of several minor city-states and small territorial kingdoms along the eastern Mediterranean seaboard. Included among these were the two Hebrew kingdoms, Israel and Judah. Assyria began a new phase of imperial expansion during the ninth century BCE, and under Tiglath-pileser III (744–727 BCE) gained a firm grip on the whole seaboard. From that time on, except for occasional brief moments, the city-states and local kingdoms of Syria-Palestine remained under foreign rule. When the Assyrian Empire collapsed in 612 BCE, the region fell quickly into the hands of Babylon, and when Babylon capitulated to Cyrus in 539 BCE, the region passed into Persian hands. The Persian Empire included more territory than ever before had been under single rule. Darius's invasion of Greece was halted with the battle of Marathon in 490 BCE, however, and a subsequent Persian attempt to conquer Greece ended with the defeat of Xerxes' fleet at Salamas in 480 BCE. Following Salamas, about the same time that Nehemiah was attempting to restore Jerusalem, Athens enjoyed its golden age of Pericles (d. 429 BCE). Alexander's conquest of the Persian Empire approximately a century later (334–331 BCE) marked the end of the Iron Age and the beginning of a new era to which we will return our attention below.

General Observations. The preceding brief outline of Near Eastern history from the earliest cities to Alexander the Great invites some general observations regarding ancient Israel. First, while the Israelites were indeed an ancient people, they did not live at the dawn of history. On the contrary, in the context of the long sweep of Near Eastern history, they were relative latecomers. The actual circumstances of Israel's origins is a vigorously debated topic among contemporary scholars and will require attention below. Regardless of how individual scholars understand the circumstances, however, virtually all agree that Israel's appearance on the scene as a self-conscious people is to be associated with the Late Bronze Age at the earliest, and more specifically with the opening centuries of the Iron Age. Thus the Israelites were preceded by some two thousand years of recorded history and impressive cultural achievements. Most of the spectacular achievements are to be associated with Egypt, Mesopotamia, and Syria. But excavations at ancient sites in Palestine reveal that there also the Israelites were heirs to a long and sophisticated civilization.

A second observation is that the transition from the Late Bronze Age to the Iron Age in Palestine was a time of political turbulence and socioeconomic change. Many of the old Bronze Age cities, which were located primarily in the Palestinian lowlands and had been experiencing decline throughout the Late Bronze Age, were destroyed at the end of Late Bronze (Hazor, Beth-Shean, Megiddo, Aphek, Gezer, and Lachish, to name a few). Those that survived into the Iron Age continued as much less impressive cities in size and architecture. Simultaneously, there began to emerge in the Palestinian hinterland numerous small villages and hamlets. Archaeological remains of these early Iron Age hinterland settlements are best represented in Galilee, the central hill country north of Jerusalem, the northern Negeb, and the Transjordanian highlands—regions that had relatively sparse sedentary population during the Middle and Late Bronze Ages. These new Iron Age settlements were of various sorts, from simple groupings of huts to respectable villages; but all were small and unfortified.

These two developments, the disturbances and further decline among the urban centers in the Palestinian lowlands and simultaneous small village settlement of the hinterland, were related to Egypt's dominant role in Palestinian affairs during the Late Bronze Age and radically reduced role thereafter. Egyptian inscriptions and letters reveal that Late Bronze Age Palestine had a heterogeneous population, which the pharaohs (after Thutmose III) were able to dominate through vassal rulers positioned in the main urban centers. As an example of urban change and decline already under way during the Late Bronze Age while Palestine was under Egyptian domination, archaeologists note that city fortifications tended to be neglected in deference to fortified palaces or citadels. These fortified citadels presumably were intended for the protection of the local nobility who would have been overshadowed in turn by the Egyptian pharaohs. Near the end of the Late Bronze Age, moreover, there appear at several Palestinian sites buildings with clear Egyptian influence identified tentatively as "governor's residences." Some of the old Bronze Age cities continued occupation into the Iron Age, and in fact there seems to have been a brief revival of Egyptian influence in Palestine during the reigns of Rameses III to Rameses VI. The era of Egyptian domination clearly had come to an end by the mid-twelfth century, however, and it is against this background—while the already declining cities were dealing first with a tightening of the Egyptian grip and then a relaxing altogether of Egyptian control and security—that the numerous small settlements began to appear in the Palestinian hinterland (including the central hill country that is the setting of so many of the narratives pertaining to Israel's early tribal period). Whatever the connection between these settlements and early Israel (see below), one can easily imagine the sort of circumstances reflected in the book of Judges. This was a time of political change and realignment, a time when "there was no king in Israel" and "all the people did what was right in their own eyes" (Judg 17:6 NRSV).

Gradually a new political configuration emerged consisting of the local city-states and kingdoms that one encounters further on in the HB. In addition to Israel and Judah, there were the Philistine pentapolis (Gath, Gaza, Ekron, Ashdod, and Ashkelon), several Phoenician cities (Tyre, Sidon, Byblos, etc.) with their faces to the Mediterranean Sea, which they dotted with trading colonies (such as Carthage in North Africa), several relatively strong Aramean cities (the nearest one being Damascus), and the three Transjordanian kingdoms (Ammon, Moab, and Edom). These city-states (all with their surrounding villages and hamlets) and petty kingdoms existed alongside each other, sometimes peacefully but often at war, until they were engulfed by the Assyrian Empire. Some were annexed by Assyria fairly early, such as Israel in 722 BCE. Others, as in the case of Judah, survived for a while longer as vassal kingdoms subject first to Assyria and then to Babylon.

A third point to be made, therefore, is that the early movements toward monarchy in Israel that occurred approximately 1000 BCE (under Saul, David, and Solomon), the internal and external affairs of the two kingdoms that emerged after Solomon, and the final demise of both these kingdoms under Assyrian and Babylonian might were entirely consistent with the unfolding pattern of political developments witnessed by the various peoples of Syria-Palestine during the Iron Age. The Phoenicians, Philistines, Ammonites, Moabites, and Edomites also fell under the domination of the Assyrians, Babylonians, and eventually the Persians.

SOURCES OF INFORMATION

The available information pertaining specifically to the history of ancient Israel falls essentially into three categories: epigraphical texts (monumental inscriptions, royal records, correspondence, seal impressions, and other such recovered written materials), archaeological evidence (material remains, occasionally bearing epigraphical texts but typically nonverbal), and the HB. Certain nonbiblical documents (especially Josephus's *Antiquities of the Jews*) are not to be ignored, but are useful primarily as sources of information for Hellenistic and Roman times (see below). Theoretically it makes sense to give priority to epigraphical and archaeological evidence, since both are "firsthand" in contrast to the HB and other later sources. However, these firsthand sources also present difficulties in interpretation. Moreover, the epigraphical and archaeological evidence alone, in and of itself, really tells us surprisingly little about ancient Israel.

Epigraphical Evidence. Interpretation problems characteristic of epigraphic texts involve difficulties of decipherment and translation, biased and selective reporting on the part of the ancient scribes (often associated with a royal court and writing for propagandistic purposes), and uneven coverage. The epigraphical evidence pertaining to ancient Israel is especially disappointing in the latter regard. Abraham, Isaac, Jacob, Joseph, Moses, the Exodus from Egypt, Joshua, the conquest of Canaan, Saul, David, Solomon—none of these are mentioned in any ancient sources outside of the HB. With a single exception, in fact, the epigraphical record for Israel does not begin until the mid-ninth century BCE, the time of Omri and Ahab.

The exception is a passing reference to "Israel" in a hieroglyphic inscription from the reign of Merneptah, an Egyptian pharaoh of dynasty XIX. Thus it dates from the late thirteenth century BCE, the end of the Late Bronze Age. Carved on a stone stela that was discovered in the ruins of Merneptah's mortuary temple at Thebes, the inscription commemorates the pharaoh's military victories primarily in the area of present-day Libya. However, it concludes with a hymnic section that alludes to a campaign conducted by Merneptah into Syria-Palestine, and Israel is mentioned in the hymnic section along with three Palestinian cities: Ashkelon, Gezer, and Yanoam:

The princes are prostrate, saying, "Mercy!"
　　Not one raises his head among the Nine Bows.
Desolation is for Tehenu; Hatti is pacified;
　　Plundered is the Canaan with every evil;
Carried off is Ashkelon; seized upon is Gezer;
　　Yanoam is made as that which does not exist;
Israel is laid waste, his seed is not;
　　Hurru is become a widow for Egypt!
All lands together, they are pacified;
　　Everyone who was restless, he has been bound.[1]

The hieroglyphic presentation of the name suggests that Israel was understood by the Egyptian scribe to be a people—i.e., a loosely defined population group of some sort—rather than a city or an organized kingdom. Otherwise, one learns from the inscription only that Israel was located somewhere in Palestine. It is not even necessary, some Egyptologists contend, to conclude that Merneptah's army actually clashed with Israel. Israel may have been included in the list so as to render it representative of all the inhabitants of Palestine.

Another Egyptian inscription from the tenth century reports Pharaoh Shoshenq's military campaign into Palestine, an event that is mentioned also in 1 Kgs 14:25-28 (where he is called Shishak). But while Shoshenq claims to have conquered many cities in Palestine, some of which presumably would have belonged at that time to the separate kingdoms of Israel and Judah, his inscription conspicuously fails to mention either of these kingdoms. The prophet Balaam is featured in some very poorly preserved Aramaic texts dis-covered at Tell Deir 'Alla in the Jordan Valley and dating to the end of the eighth century BCE. But these texts are fragmentary, difficult to interpret, and belong to a much later time than the Bible presupposes for Balaam.

For all practical purposes, therefore, the epigraphical record for ancient Israel begins in the mid-ninth century BCE, and it is not abundant even then. Especially noteworthy from Palestine are the Mesha Inscription, the Siloam Inscription, and several groups of ostraca (an ostracan [singular] is a fragment of pottery containing a written inscription).[2] The Mesha Inscription, discovered in 1868 at the site of the ancient Moabite city of Dibon, reports the royal accomplishments of King Mesha, who ruled Moab from Dibon in the ninth century. Clearly Mesha regarded as his major accomplishment a successful struggle to rid Moab of Israelite domination, and the inscription identifies Omri as the Israelite king who had subjected Moab in the first place. This same King Mesha figures in the narrative of 2 Kgs 3:4-28, which reports that Jehoram, Omri's grandson, attempted unsuccessfully to restore Israelite control over Moab. The Siloam Inscription was discovered at Jerusalem in 1880 in the tunnel hewed out of solid rock for the purpose of transferring water from the Gihon Spring to the Siloam Pool. Intended to commemorate the completion of the tunneling project, the inscription was vandalized soon after its discovery, and the remaining legible portion does not name the king who commissioned the project. Almost certainly, however, it should be attributed to Hezekiah (see 2 Chr 32:30). Discovered among the ruins at Sebastiyeh (ancient Samaria) were approximately sixty ostraca bearing administrative records concerning dispatches of wine and oil. While the ostraca include no references to known persons or events that enable scholars to date them, the archaeological context of their discovery, the script, and certain clues from their content suggest that they derive from the time of Jehu's dynasty (late ninth to early eighth centuries BCE). Two other important ostraca groups have been uncovered at Tell Arad (ancient Arad) and Tell ed-Duweir. Both groups contain letters apparently sent to military commanders at these two places in the seventh and sixth centuries BCE.

---

1. J. B. Pritchard, *ANET,* 378.

2. See *ANET* 320-21.

Royal records of the Assyrian and Babylonian rulers provide valuable information regarding international circumstances throughout the Near East, especially from the mid-ninth to the mid-sixth centuries BCE. Moreover, since these rulers often can be dated fairly securely, the occasional points of contact between their records and the biblical account serve as valuable benchmarks for working out the chronology of Israel's history. Usually these are only passing references, typically in reports of military campaigns that these rulers conducted into Syria-Palestine or records of tribute they collected from the various peoples encountered there.[3] Assyria was just beginning its imperial expansion westward under Shalmaneser III, who claims to have defeated a coalition of Syro-Palestinian kings that included "Ahab of Israel." The battle, fought at Qarqar on the Orontes River in Syria, is reported for Shalmaneser's sixth year, which would have been 853 BCE. Other inscriptions from later in Shalmaneser's reign report that he conducted several more western campaigns and, in 841 BCE, collected tribute from "Jehu the son of Omri." Adad-nirari III (810–783 BCE) claims in one inscription to have received tribute from "the land of Omri" and in another to have received tribute from "Joash of Samaria." Tiglath-pileser III (744–727 BCE) reports tribute from Menahem of the land of Omri and claims to have confirmed Hoshea on the throne in Samaria after the people of the city overthrew Pekah (cf. 2 Kgs 15:19-20; 29-31). Sargon II (722–705 BCE) claims to have conquered Samaria, exiled much of its population, and resettled the city with exiles from other places (cf. 2 Kgs 17:5-6).

Jehoahaz, also listed among the local Palestinian rulers who paid tribute to Tiglath-pileser III, is the first Judean king to turn up in the ancient epigraphical sources (cf. 2 Kgs 16:7-9). But surely the most notable Assyrian inscriptions relevant to the history of Judah are two annalistic prisms from the reign of Sennacherib (704–681 BCE) that provide almost duplicate accounts of his invasion of Palestine and siege of Jerusalem in 701 BCE (cf. 2 Kgs 18:9–19:37). Assyria held a firm grip on all of Syria-Palestine during the reigns of Esarhaddon (680–669 BCE) and Ashurbanipal (668–627 BCE), and both of these rulers report tribute from Judah, Edom, and Moab. With the collapse of Assyria and the

rise of Babylon, the local Palestinian kingdoms that had survived Assyrian domination fell into Babylonian hands. One of the Babylonian Chronicles reports Nebuchadnezzar's conquest of Jerusalem in March of 597 BCE. According to the biblical account of this event, Jehoiachin was on the throne in Jerusalem when the city fell (2 Kgs 24:1-17) and was taken captive to Babylon. Babylonian lists of food rations mention Jehoiachin along with other exiles resident in Babylon during Nebuchadnezzar's reign (604–561 BCE).

Under the Persians, Palestine belonged to the fifth satrapy known as "the land beyond the river" (i.e., beyond the Euphrates). Coins were struck in the province of *Yehud* (Judah), but there are no specific references to either the province of Samaria or of Judah in the surviving Persian records, and no mention of Zerubbabel, Ezra, Nehemiah, or of any of the official letters mentioned in the books of Ezra and Nehemiah. A group of papyri from Elephantine Island (in the upper Nile) witnesses to the existence of a Jewish military colony living there during the fifth century BCE.

Archaeological Evidence. It would be difficult to overestimate the importance of archaeology for historical research. With systematic analysis of the artifactual evidence surviving in a given area (ancient settlement ruins; architectural remains; remnants of weapons, tools, potsherds, and other material remains), archaeologists can reconstruct to a surprising degree the settlement patterns and life-styles of the people who lived there in times past. A major disadvantage of archaeological evidence from a historian's point of view, however, is that the artifacts are typically nonverbal. This means that they are not ethnic specific in and of themselves, and only rarely are they very useful for clarifying matters of historical detail. In other words, if the people who lived in the settlements, used the tools, and produced the pottery are to be identified in terms of their ethnic identity, or if any details are to be known about specific individuals and events of their history, the artifactual record must be coordinated with and interpreted in the light of written evidence. The artifacts themselves occasionally bear inscriptions, so that the distinction made here between epigraphical and archaeological evidence cannot be maintained absolutely. Nevertheless, whatever the source, any extensive use of artifactual evidence toward understanding the specifics of the history of

3. See *ANET* 227-86, 288-301, 308, 564.

a particular people must rest ultimately on verbal information. Consider the following examples of how artifactual evidence from Palestine has been brought to bear on ancient Israelite history.

As indicated above, the archaeological record shows the end of the Late Bronze Age and opening centuries of the Iron Age to have been a time of socioeconomic change and population shift in Palestine. On one hand, many of the cities that had dominated the lowlands during the Middle and Late Bronze Ages were in decline. The Palestinian hinterland, on the other hand, where there is little archaeological evidence of Bronze Age occupation, became strewn with small settlements during the Early Iron Age. Nothing has been found in any of these Early Iron Age ruins of the hinterland that reveals the identity of the new settlers, much less identifies them as Israelites. Nevertheless, on the basis of the Merneptah inscription and the HB, it seems reasonable to associate the early Israelites with these Early Iron Age settlements in some way; for instance, the Merneptah inscription places Israel on the scene in Palestine by the beginning of the Iron Age when the hinterland settlements were emerging, while the biblical materials place the core of early Israelite tribal settlement in the Palestinian hinterland, specifically the central hill country. It would be an oversimplification, however, to suppose that all of the early Iron Age settlements in the central hill country were Israelite villages. The settlement phenomenon was not limited to the central hill country where the biblical narratives place the early Israelite tribes; the same biblical narratives that place the early Israelite tribes in the central hill country speak also of other peoples living there (e.g., Hivites, Jebusites); and, as explained above, archaeological evidence typically is not ethnic specific. In other words, archaeologists have no way of determining which of the Early Iron Age settlements were Israelite and which were not.

It is often possible, especially when the modern Arabic place name corresponds linguistically to the ancient biblical place name, to identify an archaeological ruin as the remains of a specific city, town, or village mentioned in the Bible. Sometimes, moreover, although not always (see below), the results of excavations at a site thus identified can be reasonably correlated with the biblical record. Strong cases can be made, for example, for identifying Tell Qedah as the ruin of biblical Hazor, Tell Mutesellim

as the ruin of ancient Megiddo, and Tell Jezer as ancient Gezer. Excavations at all three of these sites reveal remains of relatively impressive fortifications with similar architectural design that can be dated to roughly 1000 BCE. This evidence seems to connect with 1 Kgs 9:15, which reports that Solomon levied forced labor "to build the house of the LORD and his own house, the Millo and the wall of Jerusalem, Hazor, Megiddo, Gezer" (NRSV). Again, nothing in the archaeological evidence itself from any of the three sites, no inscriptions and nothing about the architectural design, identifies the builder as Solomon. Nevertheless, in view of the biblical record, which suggests a date of c. 1000 BCE for Solomon and credits him with rebuilding these three cities, it seems reasonable to many scholars to identify the fortifications at the three corresponding sites as Solomonic.

Sebastiyeh (ancient Samaria) serves as an example of how archaeologists and historians go about correlating written evidence and the stratigraphy of ancient ruins. First Kings 16 introduces Omri with chronological data that would place him during the first half of the ninth century BCE and reports in verse 24 that he "bought the hill of Samaria from Shemer for two talents of silver; he fortified the hill, and called the city that he built, Samaria, after the name of Shemer, the owner of the hill" (NRSV). Centuries later, Herod the Great rebuilt Samaria, renamed it Sebastos, and this Herodian name is preserved in that of the present-day Arabic village, Sebastiyeh, which covers only a portion of an ancient ruin. Thus it was anticipated even before excavations were begun at the ruin that it would include the Iron Age remains of ancient Samaria, that the earliest occupational phase would be Omri's city, and that later phases would represent later stages of Samaria's history. Very little of the earliest phase was actually uncovered, but the pottery and building remains do in fact seem to date from roughly the ninth or tenth century BCE, and so this phase generally is dated to Omri's reign. The next phase, which seems to have followed soon after the first and presents more impressive architecture, usually is associated with Omri's son Ahab, who is credited in 1 Kgs 22:39 with building activities. The third phrase of occupation at Sebastiyeh is characterized by less impressive buildings that departed from the basic plan of phase two. This departure was interpreted by the excavators to suggest that the phase-two city had been largely destroyed before the phase-three rebuild, and this hypothesized destruction was attributed in turn to disturbances associated with the political coup reported in 2 Kgs 8:28–10:31 which brought Jehu to the throne. Accordingly, the third phase of occupation at Sebastiyeh is generally associated with Jehu and the early rulers of his dynasty. Later phases of the ruins correlate in similar fashion with later phases of Samaria's history as known from the Bible and Assyrian texts.

To summarize, archaeology is primarily useful in helping us understand the material culture and settlement patterns of the inhabitants of Palestine during biblical times. It is less useful for dealing with the specifics of Israelite history. Indeed, were we to depend on the nonverbal artifactual evidence alone, we would not even know that ancient Israel existed. The artifactual record takes on an added dimension, however, when correlated with and interpreted in the light of written evidence. Given the fact that the epigraphical references to ancient Israel are relatively few in number, this means that the HB usually plays a dominant role when archaeological data is interpreted as relating to Israelite history.

The Hebrew Bible. A large portion of the HB presents itself as Israelite history—i.e., narrative accounts of the people and events of Israel's past. To be sure, this is not history written for the sake of history. Indeed, the biblical narrators and compilers are more akin to theologians than to historians. Nevertheless, it is not insignificant that they chose to cast their theological messages in the form of historical narrative. Moreover, it is not just the so-called historical books that come into consideration in this regard. Other parts of the HB, especially prophetic books, also reveal a strong consciousness of Israel's historical past and make numerous references to contemporary national and international circumstances.

First attention goes to the two extensive and composite "theological histories," one represented by the books of Genesis through 2 Kings (read in sequence and excluding the book of Ruth) and the other represented by 1–2 Chronicles, Ezra, and Nehemiah. The Genesis–Kings account begins with Adam (although it provides little more than genealogies for the time prior to David) and concludes with Nehemiah's activities in Jerusalem under Persian rule. These two works, especially the Genesis–Kings account, provide the overall historical

framework against which information relevant to the history of Israel gleaned from other sources usually is interpreted. The preceding discussion of epigraphical and archaeological evidence provides several illustrations of how this works. Without the Genesis–Kings account, for example, specifically the narratives in Judges and 1 Samuel, there would be no basis for connecting Merneptah's enigmatic Late Bronze Age reference to Israel with the anonymous early Iron Age settlements in the Palestinian highlands and relating both the inscriptional reference and the settlements to Israel's early tribal period. Without the narratives concerning Saul, David, and Solomon in these two "theological histories," it would be difficult to determine from the other biblical references to these three figures even approximately when they lived or how their careers were related. Assyrian records mention some of the later Israelite and Judean kings and provide occasional chronological benchmarks, but only in the Genesis–Kings account do we have a complete list of Israelite and Judean kings and an overall chronological framework against which to relate the Assyrian data.

Unfortunately, both the Genesis–Kings account and the Chronicles–Nehemiah account present major problems of interpretation for historians. First, elementary historical-critical logic forces the conclusion that both works are composite and reached their final form long after most of the events they report. Specifically, the Genesis–Kings account was compiled (or reached essentially the form in which we have received it) no earlier than the exilic period, while the Chronicles–Nehemiah account reached essentially its present form no earlier than the Persian period. Second, both works, largely because of their composite character, present distracting internal inconsistencies. Compare Josh 10:36-37 with 14:6-12, for example, on the matter of when and under what circumstances Hebron and its vicinity were conquered. Third, both works exhibit very noticeable theological agendas that determined what was reported and how it was reported. The editors of Genesis–Kings, for example, evaluated all of the kings after Solomon on the basis of whether they were loyal to the Jerusalem cult. The Israelite kings naturally received low marks in this regard, and very little is said about any of their accomplishments. Yet, these editors tended to make rather much of the relatively mediocre accomplishments of certain Judean kings, such as Josiah. The Israelite kings are ignored altogether by the editors of Chronicles–Nehemiah, except when they serve as foils for the presentation of the reigns of the Judean kings. Fourth, especially for the distant past, both works presuppose schematic and ideal notions of history. The Genesis–Kings account presupposes a primeval golden age when people lived fantastically long lives, for example, as well as the notion that the various peoples of the world are descended in unilinear fashion from individual male ancestors. Also the Genesis–Kings account presents the time of the patriarchs, Moses, Joshua, and Solomon as normative for virtually every aspect of later Israelite history and, accordingly, project practices and circumstances (actual and ideal) of the editors' own time back into these supposedly normative ages of the distant past. Fifth, close comparison of the Genesis–Kings account with the Chronicles–Nehemiah account reveals that the former (or possibly a very similar version of the Samuel–Kings section of that work) served as one of the main sources for 1–2 Chronicles; and the editors of Chronicles, in addition to offering a rather distinctive interpretation of Israel's past, often revised the material derived from Genesis–Kings so that it would fit this interpretation (e.g., cf. 1 Kgs 22:48 with 2 Chr 20:35-37). Thus one must consider the possibility that the editors of Chronicles–Nehemiah handled all of their sources in that fashion, and not only they, but the editors of Genesis–Kings and Chronicles–Nehemiah transmitted early materials reasonably accurately; it does not necessarily follow that these early materials provide historically useful information. Most of the individual narratives that comprise these two works appear to be legends, folktales, artfully constructed stories, and the like.

APPROACHES TO THE STUDY OF ANCIENT ISRAELITE HISTORY

When scholars disagree on matters pertaining to the history of ancient Israel, and there is both widespread and radical disagreement at the moment, it is not because they have different "facts" at their disposal, but because they interpret the available information differently. Also they may place more or less confidence in some of the kinds of information discussed above and take different methodological approaches in their interpretations. The variety of methodological approaches is especially evident when one considers the range of views regarding the origins of ancient Israel.

The Traditional Approach. The Genesis–Kings account (specifically the books of Genesis–Joshua) is the only ancient written source that speaks directly to the matter of Israel's origins. Merneptah's inscription mentions Israel only in passing, as we have seen, and for all practical purposes the Chronicles–Nehemiah account begins its coverage with David. According to the Genesis–Kings account, Israel descended from a single ancestor, Jacob, later named Israel. Jacob's family multiplied into a nation of 600,000 men plus women and children while in Egypt; they escaped from Egypt and wandered for forty years in the wilderness under the leadership of Moses. Then, under Joshua's leadership, they conquered the land of Canaan, distributed the land, and settled down. Subsequent treatments of Israel's history have tended until modern times to paraphrase this Genesis–Kings account with elaborations here and there (e.g., Josephus's *Antiquities of the Jews*). Some contemporary scholars continue to follow this traditional approach—i.e., assuming that the Genesis–Kings account is historically accurate, thus attempting to correlate it "as is" with ancient Near Eastern history as known from other written sources and archaeological finds.

These scholars encounter serious difficulties, however, if for no other reason than that the chronological specifics of the biblical account simply do not "square" with evidence from other sources. For example, biblical chronology seems to require a late–fifteenth-century (or Late Bronze Age) date for the Israelite conquest of Canaan. Accordingly, it is reasonable to expect archaeological evidence of Late Bronze Age occupation at the ruins of the cities that figure in the biblical account of the conquest and evidence of destruction at the cities reported to have been destroyed by the Israelites. Archaeologists have found little or no evidence of Late Bronze Age occupation at the ruins of the key conquest cities, however, much less evidence of destruction. This is the case specifically with Tell Arad (biblical Arad), Tell Hesban (Heshbon), Tell es-Sultan (Jericho), and et-Tell (Ai). Since there is archaeological evidence of numerous city destructions in Palestine at the end of the Middle Bronze Age, several of the scholars who take this traditional approach incline to accept a proposal advanced by John Bimson.[4] Specifically,

4. John Bimson, *Redating the Exodus and Conquest* (Sheffield: University of Sheffield Press, 1978).

Bimson lowers the date of the end of the Middle Bronze Age from the mid sixteenth to the late fifteenth century BCE and attributes the city destructions that marked the end of that age to the conquering Israelites, rather than to the Hyksos (see below), as generally supposed. Few archaeologists find this redating of the Middle Bronze Age acceptable, however, while scholars who take a historical-critical approach to the Bible find the whole exercise misguided. Bimson's redating of the Middle Bronze Age provides only a partial solution to the problem, moreover, since the ruins of three of the crucial conquest cities (Arad, Heshbon, and Ai) show no archaeological evidence of Middle Bronze Age occupation or destruction either. Thus he must argue further that the ruins of these three remaining problematic cities have been either misidentified or misinterpreted.

W. F. Albright and John Bright. Other scholars favor a methodologically similar, but less rigid, approach. They regard the Genesis–Kings account of Israel's origins to be historically trustworthy in general, in overall outline for example, but not necessarily so in the details. Thus they do not hesitate to depart from the specifics of the biblical account where this seems necessary in order to correlate it with the archaeological record. This approach was championed by W. F. Albright and is represented by John Bright's *A History of Israel,* which remains very popular, although it was first published in 1959.[5] Bright's history begins with the patriarchs (Abraham, Isaac, and Jacob), who are presented as historical figures associated with Amorite movements thought to have been underway in Syria-Palestine approximately 2000 BCE (during the period of urban decline at the end of the Early Bronze and the beginning of the Middle Bronze Ages), but understood as representative of a much longer "Patriarchal Age," which would have continued through the Middle Bronze and into Late Bronze Ages. The exodus group was of mixed Semitic-Egyptian heritage; their ancestors would have entered Egypt at various times and under various circumstances during the Bronze Age, some of them no doubt during the Hyksos period. The exodus itself would have occurred during the reign of Rameses II (c. 1279–1213 BCE), thus allowing the Israelites time to arrive in Palestine by the reign of Merneptah (Rameses'

successor). This means that the Israelite conquest of Canaan would have occurred in the closing century of the Late Bronze Age, which is known from the archaeological record to have been a time of disturbances and city destructions.

It is difficult to argue with scenarios for Israel's origins produced in accordance with this second approach because the correlations made between the biblical account and ancient Near Eastern history are so loose. The patriarchs are individuals in Bright's history, for example, but their dates are negotiable within a time frame of up to 800 years. The Israelite conquest of Canaan is associated with the city destructions that marked the end of the Late Bronze Age, even though the cities that show archaeological evidence of having been destroyed at that time are not identical with the cities the Bible claims to have been destroyed; indeed, some of the crucial cities mentioned in the biblical account were not even occupied during the Late Bronze Age. None of this is regarded as fatal to the scenario because the proponents of this approach do not read the biblical account in a rigidly literalistic fashion. All details are negotiable. Regarding the absence of Late Bronze Age remains at Ai, for example, Bright followed Albright's suggestion that the Israelites really destroyed Bethel and that the event came to be associated incorrectly with Ai in Israel's folk memory. Yet, the very looseness of this approach, which renders it resistant to counterarguments, is also its major weakness. As it usually turns out, rather than coordinating the biblical account of Israel's origins with ancient Near Eastern history, this approach results in compromise scenarios for Israel's origins, which, in addition to being exceedingly vague on details, are not firmly anchored in either the biblical account or extra-biblical evidence.

Albrecht Alt and Martin Noth. Still other scholars, in view of the composite, schematic, and theologically ideal character of the Genesis–Kings account of Israel's origins, are doubtful of its historicity even in overall outline. Indeed, it is especially the overall outline that they find unconvincing—the notion that a whole people might have descended from a single male ancestor, escaped from Egypt, wandered for a generation in the wilderness, and then conquered a region as large as Palestine, whose indigenous population seems conveniently to have disappeared from the scene. All of this is "revisionist" history, they con-

5. John Bright, *A History of Israel,* 2nd ed. (Philadelphia: Westminster, 1972).

tend, a fanciful scenario of how Israel came to be, produced by the editors of Genesis–Kings. Accordingly, those who take this third approach begin with a thorough historical-critical analysis of the biblical materials in an effort to identify older literary units and traditions that have survived in the later canonical versions of the biblical books and that presumably provide more authentic glimpses of early Israel. The bits of information thus derived are interpreted, along with whatever epigraphic and archaeological evidence seems relevant, in the light of models and theories informed by ancient historical parallels, ethnography, and sociology. The earliest critical treatments of Israel take basically this approach.[6] Perhaps the most outstanding champions of this approach during the present century were A. Alt and his student M. Noth. Noth's *Geschichte Israels* (1959),[7] for example, does not treat the patriarchs as historical figures and presupposes neither an exodus from Egypt nor a military conquest of Canaan. Instead, drawing upon Alt's studies, his own extensive traditio-critical analysis of Genesis–Kings, what he thought to be close parallels between early Israelite society and that of ancient Greek and Italian tribal leagues (known as *amphictyonies*), and upon the sociological theories of Max Weber, Noth argued that the ancestors of Israel probably were semi-nomads (or transhumance nomads) who ranged between the desert fringe and Canaan in search of pasture until they gradually settled down and took up agriculture. In the process of settlement, and in stages suggested by early traditions that Noth thought he could isolate in the Pentateuch, these tribes formed an amphictyonic cultic league. Thus earliest Israel came into existence, not as a genetically homogeneous ethnic people but as a tribal league organized around a central cult. The conquest of Canaan occurred not at the beginning of the Israelite presence in the land, according to Noth, but much later under Saul and David. The weakness of this approach, also well illustrated by Noth's history, is that it builds elaborate theory on top of theory. All of the main underpinnings of Noth's scenario are regarded as problematic by contemporary scholars: his analysis and interpretation of the early traditions preserved in Genesis–Kings, the

relevance of the amphictyonic model for understanding early Israel, and Weber's theories regarding transhumance nomads.

Norman Gottwald. Another approach, similar in basic methodology to the above, but with radically different emphases and conclusions, initiated by G. E. Mendenhall in 1962, has been championed most aggressively by Gottwald, especially in his *The Tribes of Yahweh*[8] and still has some following, especially among liberation theologians. Specifically, this approach places less confidence in historical-critical analysis of biblical texts as an appropriate starting point for understanding earliest Israel and focuses, rather, on ethnographic parallels and sociological models. Moreover, the proponents of this new perspective challenged one of the basic assumptions of Weber, Alt, and Noth—namely, that transhumance nomadism in ancient Palestine would have represented an essentially different social structure with a different origin than that of peasant farmers and city dwellers. On the contrary, the proponents of this fourth approach refer to ethnographic studies that seem to suggest that semi-nomadic herding more likely would have been a derivative of sedentary agriculture in ancient Palestine than an intrusive element from the desert fringe. Gottwald, therefore, contends that the Israelite tribes did not enter Palestine from elsewhere, either as conquerors or as nomads, but emerged from the indigenous Canaanite population. Late Bronze Age society, dominated by the declining city-states of the lowlands, whose rulers were themselves overshadowed by Egypt, would have been oppressive for Palestinian peasants. During the turbulent time at the close of the Late Bronze Age, therefore, many of the peasants supposedly revolted against the oppressive system and retreated to the highlands, where they formed an egalitarian, tribal society under the banner of Yahweh. The objection raised above to building theory on top of theory applies also to this scenario for the origins of Israel. In this case, moreover, the scenario rests almost entirely on social theory. The HB, whether taken at face value or dissected in search of early traditions, knows nothing of a peasant revolt.

While the peasants' revolt scenario seems to have

---

6. See H. G. A. Ewald's *Geschichte des Volkes Israel bis Christus* (1843–55) and J. Wellhausen's *Prolegomena zur Geschichte Israels* (1878).

7. Published in English as Martin Noth, *The History of Israel* (New York: Harper & Row, 1960).

8. Norman Gottwald, *The Tribes of Yahweh: A Sociology of the Religion of Liberated Israel* (Maryknoll, N.Y.: Orbis, 1979).

lost most of its following except among liberation theologians, two aspects of the approach remain very influential in the current discussion: the notion that early Israel emerged from the indigenous Canaanite population, and the recognition that any satisfactory explanation as to how this came about must be grounded in ethnographic and sociological research. At the same time, the point is being made with increasing insistence that any satisfactory explanation of Israel's origins must also have some tangible grounding in epigraphy, archaeology, or the HB—i.e., it cannot be constructed entirely, or even nearly so, from ethnographic parallels and sociological theory.

Other Recent Approaches. All of the approaches and scenarios discussed above presuppose an early "pan-Israelite" tribal confederation of some sort from which emerged a united Israelite monarchy under Saul, David, and Solomon. Correspondingly, even the scholars mentioned above who question the very basics of the Genesis–Kings story of Israel's origins generally are more trusting of its account of the emergence of the monarchy and of the divided kingdoms. However, an increasing number of scholars have come to regard this also as highly contrived, especially the notion of an early unified Israel that reached a golden age under Solomon. J. A. Soggin, for example, expressed strong reservations about the existence of a twelve-tribe Israelite league preceding the monarchy.[9] J. M. Miller and J. H. Hayes dispensed with the notion altogether and treated the Israelites and Judeans as essentially separate peoples who were joined together only temporarily under the rules of David, Solomon, and possibly some of the later Israelite kings.[10] David and especially Solomon are seen as largely legendary figures, moreover, who were "re-imaged" first by the editors of Genesis–Kings in accordance with their idealistic notions about Israel's past and then again by the editors of Chronicles–Nehemiah to suit their theological purposes. Beginning with a close literary-critical analysis of the biblical materials, it is contended that the Davidic-Solomonic kingdom was neither as unified nor as extensive as the late Judean compilers of Genesis–Kings and Chronicles–Nehemiah wished

to believe. Especially Solomon's golden age may have been largely fiction.

This tendency to question the basic accuracy of the biblical account of the early monarchical period becomes programmatic in Thomas L. Thompson's *Early History of the Israelite People.*[11] Thompson contends that the whole story of the rise and fall of the ancient Israelite monarchy was artificially constructed during the Persian period in response to Persian administrative policies. The Persians wished to present themselves as benevolent rulers who, in contrast to the Assyrians and Babylonians, supported the local ethnic groups of their realm, honored national traditions, and restored national gods. But the Judean community living in and around Jerusalem had neither a glorious past nor unifying religious traditions to be restored. Thus the editors of Genesis–Kings created a past. Using the name "Israel" (although this name historically had nothing to do with Judah), they constructed a nationalistic history that claimed ethnic and religious unity from earliest times and projected, as an appropriate setting for the founding of the Jerusalem cult and Temple, a glorious golden age under the legendary David and Solomon. Thompson concedes that the editors of Genesis–Kings drew upon older traditions in constructing their account. But the older traditions were so thoroughly reworked and the resulting account so thoroughly contrived, in his opinion, that modern critical historians had best lay it aside and say nothing more about ancient Israel than can be determined from epigraphical sources and archaeology. And that, as explained above, is very little. Actually, according to Thompson, we have no trustworthy evidence of either an Israelite or a Judean monarchy before the ninth century BCE. The Israelite kingdom probably was founded at that time by Omri and lasted only about two and a half centuries, until the Assyrians destroyed Samaria in 722 BCE. Judah was a separate (and very minor) kingdom that probably emerged slightly later than Israel but survived into the Babylonian period.

It does seem likely to the present writer that the late Judean editors of Genesis–Kings and Chronicles–Nehemiah overplayed the matter of early Israelite tribal unity, the continuity between Saul's Israelite kingdom and David's Jerusalem city-state, and certainly the glory of Solomon's reign. Yet

9. J. A. Soggin, *A History of Israel: From the Beginnings to the Bar Kochba Revolt* (London: SCM, 1985).

10. J. Maxwell Miller and John H. Hayes, *A History of Ancient Israel and Judah* (Philadelphia: Westminster, 1986).

11. Thomas L. Thompson, *Early History of the Israelite People* (Leiden and New York: Brill, 1992).

Thompson's skepticism goes too far. It is one thing to question the historicity of the stories about Saul, David, and Solomon, for example, but Thompson calls into question even the general setting of these stories, which the narrator assumes the audience will take for granted. Also, if there was no Israelite monarchy before Omri, what do we do with the earlier Israelite and Judean kings reported in 1 Kings (Rehoboam, Jeroboam, Asa, Ahijah, etc.) and the chronological data provided for them? Again, it is one thing to suggest that this chronological data has been skewed and some of it perhaps fabricated to fit the overall schematic chronology of the Genesis–Kings account. If the pre-Omride chronology of Genesis–Kings is total fabrication, however, how were the editors of this account able to calculate a date of Shishak's invasion, which corresponds so closely to Egyptian chronology? In short, any thought of laying aside altogether the biblical accounts of the monarchical period and working solely with extra-biblical sources only raises new questions that by their very nature call for reconsideration of the biblical materials.

Obviously, in view of the wide range of approaches and views described above, it is impossible to present a reconstruction of the history of ancient Israel that represents scholarly consensus. There simply is no such consensus at the moment. It will be useful to make some further observations regarding contemporary trends, however, and in the process to suggest the broad outlines of a very tentative reconstruction that avoids some of the problems and extreme positions discussed above. The following suggestions depend heavily on the two "theological histories" of the HB, especially the Genesis–Kings account, examined in accordance with the standard procedures of historical criticism. This is done with full awareness of the problems involved. Historical criticism is not an exact science in the first place, and attempts to extract historical information from these biblical sources, regardless of how carefully examined, take one deep into the realm of speculation.

ISRAEL'S ORIGINS

As observed above, scholars who regard the Genesis–Joshua account of Israel's origins as historically trustworthy even in overall outline have had little success in correlating it with ancient Near Eastern history in general and Palestinian archaeology in particular. The often highly publicized expeditions launched in search of Noah's ark have yet to produce a shred of evidence regarded as credible by the scientific community, and are unlikely to do so in the future, since these ark searchers operate with "creationist" assumptions that are in conflict with scientific methodology. Those who regard the characters featured in Genesis–Joshua as historical individuals have no place to turn for biographical information other than to the biblical stories themselves. Some of the names of these characters are authentic enough, and numerous parallels have been pointed out between the practices and customs presupposed by the biblical stories and those presupposed in epigraphical sources from the Bronze and Iron Ages. However, authentic names and customs do not of themselves imply historicity, since one would expect a folktale or even fiction to exhibit authentic features of that sort. Neither are these features very useful for dating the characters or the stories, since the names and customs involved tend to be of a general sort rather than specific to a particular period.

Although traffic between the peoples of Syria-Palestine and Egypt apparently was common in ancient times, the search in Egyptian records for evidence of Israelites in Egypt has been equally unsuccessful. There is no hard evidence for identifying Rameses II as the pharaoh of the exodus, for example, and contemporary scholars generally have given up on finding any direct connection between the Israelites and the Hyksos. Egyptologists date the Hyksos period in Egypt approximately 1700–1550 BCE, which does not fit well with any of the scenarios described above. According to Bimson's late–fifteenth-century BCE dating of the exodus (which involves lowering the date of the end of the Middle Bronze Age), the Israelites would have entered Egypt earlier and left later than the Hyksos. According to Bright's scenario, the expulsion of the Hyksos rulers from Egypt would have occurred approximately three centuries before the Israelite exodus.

Thus contemporary treatments of Israelite history typically begin with Israel already settled in the central Palestinian hill country (i.e., at the time of the Judges) and leave it for the reader to decide whether Abraham, Isaac, Jacob, Moses, or Joshua (a) were historical individuals whose time and place in history can no longer be ascertained, (b) legendary and folk characters, (c) literary creations on the part of the editors of the Genesis–Kings account, or (d) combinations of the above. For example, some of these early biblical characters may have been historical individuals whose memory survived in Israel's legends and folk traditions, which were embellished and edited in turn by the editors of Genesis–Kings.

THE EARLY TRIBAL PERIOD

It seems reasonable on the grounds explained above to associate the early Israelite tribes with the increase in sedentary population that occurred in the central Palestinian hill country at the close of the Late Bronze Age and the opening centuries of the Iron Age. Specifically, the Merneptah Inscription witnesses to the existence of a population group or political entity of some sort known as Israel on the scene in Palestine at the end of the Late Bronze Age, while the narratives of the book of Judges presuppose Israelite tribes settled in the central Palestinian hill country during the opening centuries of the Iron Age—i.e., prior to the emergence of the Israelite monarchy, a development that itself is probably to be dated approximately 1000 BCE (see below). This is not to suggest, however, a direct correspondence between the early Israelites and the Early Iron Age towns and villages reported by archaeologists in the hill country. The surge of small town and village settlements that characterized this period was not confined to the hill country region where the biblical narratives place the early Israelite tribes. The same biblical narratives that place the early Israelite tribes in the central hill country also speak of other peoples settled there, and archaeologists are unable to distinguish Israelite settlements from non-Israelite ones. Perhaps archaeology will be able to shed some light on the conditions and circumstances that resulted in the Early Iron Age settlement of the Palestinian hinterland. Thus far, however, the evidence is ambiguous. It is not clear from the archaeological record, in other words, whether most of the new hill country settlers were immigrants from the Palestinian lowlands, transhumance nomads from the desert fringe, or indigenous hill country population that had been there all along but following a nomadic life-style.

Some of the Genesis stories about Abraham, Isaac, and Jacob may relate to this early tribal period, with intertribal relationships expressed in terms of patriarchal figures, family traditions, and genealogies. The Judges narratives must serve as our main written source of information about this period, however, in spite of the fact that these narratives are largely legendary and that all of them have been edited to fit the format and theological message of the Genesis–Kings account. Namely, these narratives are presented in an editorial framework that implies that the various figures whose exploits are described (Othniel, Ehud, Jabin, Deborah, etc.) were all national heroes who delivered and judged "all Israel" in chronological sequence. Examined apart from the editorial framework, however, most of these stories clearly have to do with very localized affairs and concern the exploits of a mixed bag of characters, some of whom may have lived contemporarily. Certainly, the individual narratives do not presuppose a unified Israel composed of twelve tribes. The Judges narratives must be read very critically, therefore, and perhaps the most a cautious historian can hope to derive from them are glimpses of the general structures and conditions of pre-monarchical times. Occasionally, these glimpses can be amplified or sharpened with comparative data from archaeology, epigraphy, and ethnography.

Studies of the kinship pattern reflected in the biblical materials with attention to ethnographic parallels suggest, for example, that the extended family and the clan (or village, which in many cases may have corresponded roughly to the claim) probably were more basic to the social structure of pre-monarchical Israel than the tribe. Tribal connections seem to have been somewhat fluid, in fact, and tended to be more territorial than genealogical in nature. Families, clans, and villages living in the same area over several generations, struggling for survival under the same physical conditions, exchanging sons and daughters in marriage, and often having to defend against common enemies, would come to think of themselves as related and to express this in terms of tribes, tribal groupings, and tribal genealogies.

Yet, while the notion of an early Israel composed of twelve discrete tribes is artificial, obviously some distinction was made between Israelite and non-Israelite clans and villages (see Judg 19:12). Probably the name *Israel* in its earliest usage was roughly synonymous with the tribe of Ephraim, but extended to include certain other tribes (principally

Manasseh, Benjamin, and Gilead) that were closely associated with (or satellite to) Ephraim and also settled in the central hill country north of Jerusalem with some spill over into the adjacent lowlands and the Transjordan. This is suggested in the first place by the genealogical assumptions underlying the stories about the patriarchs in Genesis and the tribal divisions in Joshua. Note that the stories about Jacob (also named "Israel") have their primary setting in the hill country north of Jerusalem (Gen 32:27-28; 35:10). Joseph and Benjamin are depicted as the favorite sons of Jacob/Israel. Manasseh and Ephraim are identified as Joseph's sons, in turn, with Manasseh the older and Ephraim destined to dominate (Genesis 48). The occasional references to "the house of Joseph" in the book of Joshua clearly pertain to these three related tribes: Ephraim, Benjamin, and Manasseh (Josh 17:14-18). Most of the Judges narratives find their setting among the Ephraim/Israel tribes; most of the so-called "minor judges" listed in Judg 10:1-5 and 12:8-15 are identified as being from one of these tribes or from villages of the central hill country. This same region was to become the core of the kingdom of Saul, himself a Benjaminite. Finally, this region accounted for a large portion of the territory of the post-Solomonic kingdom of Israel that was called "Ephraim" on occasion.

Political organization would have been rather loose among the early "Israelite" tribes and clans, centered in the clans and villages with authority vested in the clan and village elders. Naturally elders of large and wealthy families with extensive marriage connections would have been able to assert more than usual influence. This seems to have been the case with Tola, Jair, Ibzan, Elon, and Abdon, for example, all of them wealthy men with numerous offspring (Judg 10:1-5; 12:8-15). Also, especially in times of conflict and enemy threat, leadership would have shifted to persons with military daring and ability. One thinks here of Ehud (Judg 3:15-30), Gideon (Judges 6–8), Abimelech (Judges 9), and Jephthah (Judg 11:1–12:7). The stories of Abimelech and Jephthah suggest that from time to time semi-professional military chieftains arose and maintained small private armies.

Finally, close examination of the Judges narratives reveals that the religious beliefs and practices of the early Israelites were neither as uniform nor as different from those of their neighbors as the compilers of the Genesis–Kings account would have it. This is especially obvious from the narratives about Gideon and Abimelech in Judges 6–9 and Micah the Ephraimite in Judges 17–18. Apparently, numerous shrines, high places, and altars were scattered among the clans. Some of these, such as Bethel, would have had broader influence than others. Yet, one does not get the impression that a single cultic center or a single priestly line had any sort of monopoly. Neither did Yahweh have the allegiance of the early Israelite tribes to the exclusion of other gods. It was indeed a time when "all the people did what was right in their own eyes" (Judg 17:6 NRSV).

SAMUEL, SAUL, DAVID, AND SOLOMON

Gradually, as reflected in the archaeological record, the situation seems to have stabilized in Palestine. Villages expanded into towns and towns into small cities with fortifications and public buildings, which suggests that centralized political structures were gaining importance. By approximately 1000 BCE, Syria-Palestine was relatively free of external political influences and the area was dominated by local monarchies, including an array of autonomous city-states (e.g., Phoenician and Aramean cities), coalitions of prominent cities (such as the Philistine pentapolis), and small localized kingdoms (Ammon, Moab, Edom, and Israel). However, one should be careful not to read medieval and modern conceptions of monarchy back into Early Iron Age Palestine, such as the conception of an autocratic king ruling over an expansive territorial realm with clearly defined boundaries. The numerous "kings" who present themselves in the biblical materials seem to fall essentially into two categories—city kings (everything from small-time mayors to rulers over powerful city-states) and tribal chieftains (including some who maintained private armies). The city kings represented a long Bronze Age tradition that would have survived in Palestine in spite of the misfortunes that the urban centers experienced at the end of that age. The stories about Abimelech (Judges 9) and Jephthah (Judg 11:1–12:7) illustrate the second type, powerful tribal chieftains and local warlords whose range of authority may have included cities but apparently was not city based. Both Jephthah and Abimelech had private armies, which they maintained with spoils from raids and "contributions" from those whom they protected and ruled. The story about Abimelech is especially instructive, since he is depicted as a king (Judg 9:16) whose constituency included the populations of both a city (Shechem) and surrounding Israelite clans.

Although constructed from earlier traditions (see below), the Genesis–Kings account of the origins of monarchy in Israel clearly represents in its present form the idealized thinking of its editors, who themselves lived a half millennium later than Samuel, Saul, David, and Solomon. Specifically, they depict the beginnings of monarchy in Israel as a matter of negotiations between the Israelites and the prophet Samuel. Samuel had grown old, we are told, and his sons took bribes and perverted justice, so the people appealed to him to appoint a king (1 Samuel 8). Samuel resisted, but consulted Yahweh, who instructed him to comply with the people's request. Still guided by Yahweh, therefore, Samuel anointed Saul as Israel's first king. This turned out to be a mistake, because Saul failed to follow some of Samuel's instructions after becoming king and on two occasions took inappropriate liberties in matters of cultic ritual (1 Sam 13:8-15; 15:1-35). Thereupon Samuel announced that Yahweh had rejected Saul and secretly anointed David to rule in Saul's place (1 Samuel 16). With divine support, David displaced Saul and established a secure kingdom centered in Jerusalem (1 Samuel 17–2 Samuel 24). David was a man of war, however, so it remained for his son Solomon to build a temple to Yahweh (2 Samuel 7). Israel prospered under Solomon's wise rule; he amassed fabulous wealth, and Yahweh expanded his realm so that it extended from the Egyptian frontier to the Euphrates (2 Kings 3–10). Also Solomon was a great builder, we are told, his greatest achievement being the construction of Yahweh's Temple in Jerusalem.

As indicated above, the editors of Genesis–Kings constructed this clearly idealized account of the beginnings of monarchy in Israel from earlier narratives and narrative clusters. Often they incorporated these earlier materials into the larger Genesis–Kings account with little revision or editing, so that items occasionally are preserved that conflict with the editor's idealized views. These narratives suggest that Saul was much loved by his countrymen to the very end of his reign, while others reveal that David was forced to put down at least two rebellions among his people, one of which was led by his own son. Unfortunately, the only other written source that treats this period of Israel's history, the Chronicles–Nehemiah account, relies heavily on the Genesis–Kings account and presents David and Solomon in even more idealistic fashion. For example, the editors of Chronicles–Nehemiah screened virtually everything in the Genesis–Kings account that might have distracted in any way from their presentation of David as the man after Yahweh's own heart. The same is true of their treatment of Solomon. There is no hint of the conflict surrounding Solomon's accession to the throne; of his oppressive policies, which led to resistance even among his high officials; or of his inability to deal with Aramaean and Edomite forces well within his supposed territorial realm (see 1 Kings 1; 9:15-23; 11:14–12:21).

Our best hope of getting a realistic picture of Israel's earliest kings, therefore, is to examine the older narratives from which the editors of Genesis–Kings constructed their account. Separating these older narrative traditions from the later editorial overlay is not easy. Moreover, even these older traditions, to the extent that they can be isolated, are largely legendary and show evidence of political bias. The stories in 1 Samuel about Saul's and David's dealings with each other, for example, clearly are concerned to justify David's displacement of Saul's heirs by showing that it was all God's doing, that David always was morally upright in his dealings with Saul, and that even Saul's son Jonathan supported David. This perspective would have been popular in Judah, where David's descendants continued to rule until the fall of Jerusalem. But one must suspect that the people of the Northern Kingdom, whose ancestors had rebelled against Solomon's oppression and chosen their own kings, would have remembered things differently. In the final analysis, therefore, it must be conceded that we know nothing for certain about the historical Samuel, Saul, David, and Solomon. Even their dates are uncertain, as will be explained below. The following scenario is very much an "educated guess."

Saul. Saul's "kingdom" probably should be understood as being similar to those of Jephthah and Abimelech. Although he was from a prominent and relatively wealthy Benjaminite family, he apparently had made a name for himself by expelling the Philistines from the central hill country. A small army collected around him, and soon we hear of military adventures as far afield as the northern Transjordan (Jabesh Gilead) and the Negev (against the Amalekites). Saul's kingdom seems to have consisted essentially of Ephraim and the closely associated tribes (i.e., Ephraim/Israel as identified above). He made his residency at Gibeah, one of the small towns in the central hill country, and his Benjaminite kinsmen served as his administrative staff. Rather than a territorial kingdom with precise boundaries, therefore, one should think in terms of a core area (Ephraim/Israel) with somewhat vaguely defined frontiers over which Saul provided protection and collected "gifts" from those he protected. In peripheral areas, such as the Judean hill country, recognition of his authority would have varied from time to time depending on the proximity of his army and whether the local population needed his protection against other threats.

David. David also came to the fore as a soldier of fortune, getting his start as a Philistine fighter among Saul's troops. Soon we find him operating in the southern hill country with his own private army, however, posing as the protector of that region in competition with Saul and extracting material support from those whom he supposedly was protecting (1 Sam 25:7-8, 21-22). Apparently his services were not entirely welcomed because the local people kept informing him of David's whereabouts and the movements of his army. After several narrow escapes from Saul, therefore, David placed himself and his army in the service of the Philistines, which was his status when the Philistines met and defeated Saul's army on Mount Gilboa. With Saul and Jonathan dead and Israel's army in disarray, Saul's "kingdom" was reduced to nothing more than his family and a remnant of loyal soldiers who retreated into Gilead east of the Jordan. David moved with his troops back into the Judean hill country, therefore, and chose Hebron, the central city in that region, as his "kingdom."

David's rule over Hebron, reported to have lasted seven years, must have been similar to Abimelech's rule over Shechem. David's army was his power base—there is nothing to suggest that the Hebronites invited him into their city—and his rule extended beyond the city to the surrounding region.

The major difference, of course, is that David was more successful than Abimelech and was able to expand his realm of political influence beyond the Judean hill country. The taking of Jerusalem and transferral of his residency there was the next major step, and one that had significant consequences not only for David but also for the future of his dynasty. On the one hand, Jerusalem's central location made it an ideal base from which to control the whole Palestinian hill country and to expand east of the Jordan. On the other hand, Jerusalem was an old city with its own cultural heritage, including cultic and political traditions, which did not disappear with the arrival of David and his troops. In the final analysis, David's "kingdom" can perhaps best be described as a city-state with Jerusalem as the center of a political realm that eventually included most of Palestine. The core of this realm would have consisted of Jerusalem's own immediate vicinity, the Judean hill country to the south and the region of Ephraim/Israel to the north. Beyond that, David's authority seems to have been recognized to some degree in the northern Transjordan, Jezreel, and Galilee. He is reported to have conquered the Ammonites, Moabites, and Edomites, but this does not necessarily mean that he subdued and ruled all of the territory associated with these Transjordanian peoples. His encroachment on Moabite territory, for example, probably was limited to the region north of the Arnon (present-day Wadi el-Mujib). Also, while he completed the task undertaken by Saul of expelling the Philistines from the hill country, he probably did not encroach on Philistine territory itself.

Solomon. The nature and extent of Solomon's "kingdom" is a controversial issue among biblical scholars and historians. The biblical writers present his reign as Israel's golden age and describe him as an exceedingly wise, wealthy, and powerful ruler whose realm extended from the Egyptian frontier to the Euphrates. This complemented their emphasis on his role as builder of the Jerusalem Temple. If all of this is true, it is amazing that Solomon's glorious kingdom left no epigraphical traces and made such an insignificant archaeological impact. As indicated above, relatively impressive city gates and fortifications were constructed at Gezer, Megiddo, and Hazor about the time of Solomon's reign and usually are attributed to him (see 1 Kgs 9:15-19). Yet one would have expected something more from a ruler who supposedly received an annual income of 666 talents of gold (about 25 tons) in addition to income received from commerce, the kings of Arabia and the governors of the land (1 Kgs 10:14-15). Also, in view of the international gifts and trade goods that supposedly were flowing into the land during Solomon's reign, surprisingly little evidence of foreign goods has turned up among the archaeological remains of the period. Finally, there are the occasional details one encounters in the Genesis–Kings account of Solomon's reign that seem to undercut the biblical claims regarding the splendor of his reign—e.g., the report that he gave Hiram of Tyre twenty cities in payment of a debt for timber and gold used in his building program (1 Kgs 9:11-14).

Scholars generally agree that the biblical writers have exaggerated the splendor of Solomon's reign, but are of different minds regarding the extent of the exaggeration. Some contend that, allowing for normal royal hyperbole, the biblical presentation of Solomon is reasonably accurate; he really was a wise potentate who ruled over a fabulous mini-empire that extended from the Egyptian frontier to the Euphrates. Others contend that Solomon's glory is largely literary fiction, an idealistically constructed golden age considered appropriate for the building of the Temple, that the real Solomon probably was unable to hold on to much of the territory he inherited from David, and that his show of wealth involved squandering the assets of the kingdom and supplementing this with heavy taxes and forced labor extracted from his people. Otherwise, it is argued, how does one explain the circumstances Rehoboam encountered following Solomon's death?

SEPARATE KINGDOMS: ISRAEL AND JUDAH

Whatever the character and extent of Solomon's kingdom, only a remnant survived his death. The inhabitants of the central hill country north of Jerusalem, the region of the Ephraim/Israel tribes who had constituted the core of Saul's kingdom, rejected Solomon's successor, Rehoboam, and established their own monarchy. This northern kingdom took the name Israel, although the biblical writers occasionally refer to it as Ephraim or Samaria (after the city that became its capital). The earliest rulers of Israel resided at Shechem and at Tirzah, but Omri,

under whom this northern kingdom began to play a relatively significant role in international affairs, transferred the royal residency and center of government to Samaria. The inhabitants of Jerusalem remained loyal to the Davidic dynasty, and Rehoboam was able to secure control of the southern hill country, where David's own tribe of Judah was prominent. This southern loyalist kingdom took the name Judah, therefore, although occasionally it is referred to in the biblical narratives simply as Jerusalem.

The Genesis–Kings account (specifically 1–2 Kings) continues as our main source of information for the separate kingdoms. Chronicles–Nehemiah (specifically 2 Chronicles) covers the period also, but is interested only in Judean affairs and offers little new information beyond what it derives from 1–2 Kings (the list of Rehoboam's "Cities of Defense" in 2 Chr 11:5-12 is a notable exception). Beginning with the reign of Omri and his son Ahab in the mid-ninth century, epigraphical sources provide additional information. For the eighth century and following, the prophetic books of the HB also come into consideration. Especially in the pronouncements of the books of Amos, Hosea, Micah, Isaiah, and Jeremiah, one catches glimpses of the social, economic, political, and religious conditions of the day. Some of the prophets, such as Isaiah and Jeremiah, were directly involved in Judean politics.

Among the epigraphical sources, the royal Assyrian and Babylonian texts are especially useful in that they provide benchmark dates for working out the chronology of the Israelite and Judean kings. Even with this epigraphical data, however, precise dates rarely can be established with confidence. The dates given below (see Fig. 1) for the Judean kings following Hezekiah probably are accurate within one or two years. However, some of those given for the earlier kings of both Judah and Israel may be as much as ten years off. Modern calculations for the date of Rehoboam's accession to the throne at Solomon's death have ranged from as early as 932 BCE to as late as 922 BCE. Dates attributed to Solomon, David, and Saul by modern historians are even less certain. These are calculated by beginning with whatever date is determined for Rehoboam's accession and working backward, allowing forty years for Solomon's reign, forty for David's, and two for Saul's (1 Sam 13:1; 2 Kgs 2:11; 11:42).

Figure 1: KINGS OF ISRAEL AND JUDAH

Kings of Judah	Kings of Israel	
Rehoboam (924–907) Abijah (907–906) Asa (905–874)	Jeroboam I (924–903) Nadab (903–902) Baasha (902–886) Elah, Zimri (886–885)	**Four decades of hostilities** (c. 924–885) From Solomon's death to Omri's rise to power, the two kingdoms were weak and often at war with each other.
Jehoshaphat (874–850) Jehoram (850–843) Ahaziah (843)	Omri (885–873) Ahab (873–851) Ahaziah (851–849) Jehoram (849–843)	**Era of the Omride dynasty** (c. 885–843) Israel emerged in strength and played a significant role in international affairs. Judah, allied with Israel, also shared in the resulting prosperity.
Athaliah (843–837) Joash (837–?) Amaziah (?–?) Uzziah (?–?) Jotham (?–742)	Jehu (843–816) Johoahaz (816–800) Joash (800–785) Jeroboam II (785–745) Zechariah, Shallum (745)	**Era of the Jehu dynasty** (c. 843–745) Israel and Judah were overshadowed by Damascus, then recovered and, under Jeroboam II and Uzziah, experienced a brief period of prosperity and expansion.
Jehoahaz I (742–727) Hezekiah (727–698) Manasseh (697–642) Amon (642–640) Josiah (639–609) Jehoahaz II (609)	Menahem (745–736) Pekahiah (736–735) Pekah (735–732) Hoshea (732–723) **Fall of Samaria (722)**	**Assyrian domination** (c. 745–605) Israel's monarchy ended with the fall of Samaria, and the former Israelite territory was annexed into the Assyrian province system.
Jehoiakim (608–598) Jehoiachin (598–597) Zedekiah (597–586) **Destruction of Jerusalem (586)**		**Babylonian domination** (605–539) Judah's monarchy survived the long years of Assyrian domination but fell then into Babylonian hands, which it did not survive.

But surely the forty-year reigns attributed to David and Solomon in 2 Kgs 2:11 and 11:42 are more theologically symbolic than historically accurate, while 1 Sam 13:1, which suggests a two-year reign for Saul, is a corrupt text. The most we can say with confidence, therefore, is that Saul, David, and Solomon probably lived approximately 1000 BCE. The single date given below that has been established with precision and certainty is the date of the surrender of Jerusalem to Nebuchadnezzar's army, an event reported in both 2 Kgs 24:10-17 and one of the Babylonian Chronicles. Specifically, the Babylonian Chronicle places this event in the second day of the month of Addaru of the seventh year of Nebuchadnezzar's reign. This would have been March 15/16, 597 BCE.

The biblical sources for the period of the separate kingdoms are decidedly pro-Judean and give a somewhat skewed picture of the relationship between Israel and Judah. The editors of Genesis–Kings wish to convey the impression that Israel was an apostate kingdom with a turbulent history that God brought to an early end because the evil kings refused to recognize the primacy of Jerusalem. No doubt the inhabitants of Israel regarded Judah as the apostate kingdom, a non-Israelite dynasty that succeeded in dominating Ephraim/Israel for a time, but whose oppressive policies were justifiably rejected at Solomon's death. In any case, Israel clearly was the most cosmopolitan of the two kingdoms, played a more significant role in international affairs, and left the most impressive archaeological remains. Beginning with Omride kings, moreover, Israel seems to have dominated Judah much of the time, to the extent that Judah may have been looked upon as a satellite of Israel. Note in this regard that neither Judah nor any of its kings get any mention in the epigraphical sources until the reign of Tiglath-pileser III, who brought Israel under Assyrian control during the 730s BCE.

The kingdoms of Israel and Judah existed alongside each other for approximately two centuries—from c. 924 BCE to the fall of Samaria in 722 BCE, approximately a decade after Tiglath-pileser's conquests, at which time the former Israelite territories were annexed into the Assyrian province system and resettled with political refugees from other parts of the Assyrian Empire. Judah would survive under the domination of first Assyria and then Babylon for approximately 135 years longer, until the fall of Jerusalem in 586 BCE. For purposes of overview, it is useful to divide these three and a half centuries into five sub-periods.

Four Decades of Hostilities (c. 924–885 BCE). The two fledgling kingdoms that emerged following Solomon's death were small, weak, and hostile toward each other. Much of their energy seems to have been expended in skirmishes along their mutual frontier, which was precariously close to Jerusalem. For Jeroboam I, the first ruler of Israel, the first order of business was to establish (or revive) a sense of national identity for his people and to introduce (or revive) cultic practices that did not depend on Jerusalem. Rehoboam, Solomon's successor in Jerusalem, may have faced the potential of further rebellion among the towns and villages of the hill country south of Jerusalem. This is suggested by the locations of the "cities of defence" that he fortified and provisioned throughout the southern hill country (2 Chr 11:5-12); their locations suggested that these cities were intended as much to secure and maintain control over the interior of Judah as to defend against encroachment from the outside. Thus the Davidic dynasty (supported by royal Zion theology) held secure in Jerusalem, and when Rehoboam died he was followed successively by Abijah, Asa, and Jehoshaphat, apparently with no serious resistance from any quarter. The Northern Kingdom, by contrast, having rejected the Davidic dynasty, was rarely successful at transferring the crown from one ruler to the next without bloodshed. Jeroboam I was succeeded in turn by Nadab, Baasha, Elah, Zimri, and Omri, of whom only Baasha and Omri were able to hold the throne until they died a natural death. Both kingdoms will have suffered, if only temporarily, from Shishak's *blitzkreig* campaign into Palestine, which 1 Kgs 14:25-28 places in the fifth year of Rehoboam's reign. The fact that Shishak failed even to mention these two kingdoms in his own report of the campaign confirms their fledgling character.

The Era of the Omride Dynasty (c. 885–843 BCE). Omri's accession to the throne in approximately 885 BCE marked the beginning of an era of prosperity for both Israel (under Omri, Ahab, Ahaziah, and Jehoram) and Judah (under Jehoshaphat, Jehoram, and Ahaziah). This prosperity seems to have resulted from policies initiated by Omri that combined military strength with international alliances. Omri was a successful military leader; the Mesha Inscription, for example, credits him with conquering northern Moab. But Omri also played a major role in negotiating a two-way alliance that joined Israel with Phoenicia on one side (sealed with the marriage of Omri's son Ahab to Jezebel, daughter of Ethbaal of Sidon) and Israel with Judah on the other (sealed with the marriage of Athaliah, Omri's daughter or granddaughter, to Jehoram, son of Jehoshaphat). The benefits of Omri's military successes and international policies reached fruition during the reigns of Ahab and Jehoshaphat. Indeed, Ahab's reign, rather than Solomon's, probably has the best claim to be Israel's golden age. The prosperity of the period is reflected in the archaeological remains at Samaria, Hazor, and Megiddo. As indicated above, excavations at Samaria have revealed what probably are the remains of the Omride palace. Expanded fortifications and impressive water systems were built at Hazor and Megiddo about the same time and probably also are to be attributed to the Omride rulers. Omri and Ahab are the first Israelites to receive notice in the epigraphical sources (Omri in the Mesha Inscription and Ahab in Shalmaneser III's reports of his western campaigns), and for years to come Israel would be referred to as "the land of Omri" in the Assyrian records. The stories about Elijah in 1 Kings 17–19, 21 and 2 Kgs 1:2-16 offer another view of the Omride period, suggesting that it was a time of royal arrogance and religious conflict. The political and economic situation deteriorated rapidly after Ahab's death, and the era of military strength, international alliances, and resulting prosperity came to an abrupt end with Jehu's coup during or soon before 841 BCE (843, according to the chronology presented in Fig. 1).

The Era of the Jehu Dynasty (c. 843–745 BCE). Jehu's coup resulted in simultaneous throne changes for both kingdoms. The Jehu dynasty would remain in place for roughly a century (from approximately 843 to 745 BCE), but during the first half of the century both Israel (under Jehu and Jehoahaz) and Judah (under Athaliah, Joash, and Amaziah) were overshadowed by the kings of Damascus (Hazael and Benhadad). Elisha's career may have overlapped the Omride period, but most of the stories pertaining to him (2 Kings 2; 4:1–8:15), as well as the three battle accounts in 1 Kings 20 and 22:1-38, actually pertain to the early years of the Jehu dynasty and reflect the difficult conditions at that time. Judah may have felt the Syrian oppression less directly than did Israel, but had the additional problem of an unstable government. All three of the Judean rulers mentioned above were executed or assassinated.

During the second half of the century of Jehu dynasty rule in Israel (during the reigns of Joash, Jeroboam II, and Zechariah in Israel, and Uzziah and Jotham in Judah) both kingdoms seem to have enjoyed a brief period of national recovery and modest territorial expansion. This brief revival is to be associated especially with the reigns of Jeroboam II and Uzziah, who were roughly contemporary. Uzziah's Judah probably was overshadowed by Jeroboam's Israel, however, and may not have been entirely independent from it. The oracles of Amos and Hosea reflect conditions of this period. Both books witness to a wide range of social and cultic ills attributed to Israel's leaders—wealthy people who took advantage of the poor, priests who led their followers astray, and so on. Zechariah's assassination (ca. 745 BCE) brought the Jehu dynasty to an end after a century of rule; of the five kings who ruled during the remaining two decades of Israel's national existence (Shallum, Menahem, Pekahiah, Pekah, and Hoshea), only Menahem avoided assassination or removal from office.

Assyrian Domination and the End of Israel (c. 745–605 BCE). Israel's internal politics during these last two turbulent decades must be understood in the context of international developments, specifically the rise and western expansion of the Assyrian Empire. Shalmaneser III's western campaigns during the reigns of Ahab and Jehu and the western campaigns of Adad-nirari III during the reign of Jehu's grandson Joash were only the early rumblings of storm clouds. The storm broke when Tiglath-pileser III (744–727 BCE) ascended the Assyrian throne and initiated a highly successful program of expansion and consolidation of Assyrian control over the surrounding peoples. In 754 BCE he invaded northern Syria, and by 732 he had subdued the whole of Syria-Palestine. For approximately the next hundred years, through the reign of Ashurbanipal (688–627 BCE), the peoples of Syria-Palestine were firmly in Assyria's grip. Attempted revolts were ruthlessly crushed. Hoshea, for example, whom Tiglath-pileser III had confirmed on the throne of Israel, was disloyal to Tiglath-pileser's successor, Shalmaneser V (727–722 BCE), possibly as part of a widespread anti-Assyrian movement. The Assyrians managed to capture Hoshea and conquered Samaria after a three-year siege (2 Kgs 17:1-6). Shalmaneser died soon thereafter, but Sargon II (722–705 BCE) returned in 720 to settle affairs throughout the southern Levant. This was the end of Israel. Sargon organized the region as an Assyrian province, rebuilt Samaria as the administrative center with an appointed governor, and resettled both the region and the city with peoples exiled from other conquered places.

Hezekiah was on the throne of Judah at the time

and thus witnessed the demise of Israel. Nevertheless, some two decades later, he involved Judah in an anti-Assyrian movement. This occasioned Sennacherib's march on Philistia and Judah in 701 BCE (2 Kgs 18:7–19:37; 2 Chr 32:1-21; Isaiah 36–37). Although Sennacherib did not actually take Jerusalem (a development regarded locally as a miracle), Hezekiah seems to have learned his lesson and remained a loyal tribute-paying vassal thereafter, as were Manasseh and Amon after him. Isaiah, whose career spanned the end of Uzziah's reign (Isaiah 6) through the reign of Hezekiah, witnessed all of these events as well and was directly involved in some of them. Also, the oracles of the prophet Micah pertain to this period.

Assyria began to encounter difficulties already during the last years of the reign of Ashurbanipal (668–627 BCE). Scythians had pressed in upon and occupied an extensive area from approximately the Halys river in Asia Minor to the northwestern reaches of the Iranian plateau. The Medes, another nomadic group centered in northwestern Iran, had united and thus posed another threat. Also the ancient city of Babylon was positioning itself to challenge Assyria. Nabopolassar gained the throne of Babylon in 626, the year after Ashurbanipal's death, and fourteen years later (612 BCE) joined forces with the Medes (ruled now by Cyaxares) to capture the Assyrian capital Nineveh. A remnant of the Assyrian army retreated westward and, supported by an Egyptian army, attempted to make a stand at Haran. But Nabopolassar and his allies (possibly the Scythians this time, or a combination of Scythians and Medes) took Haran in 610 BCE. A counterattack on the part of the Assyrians and the Egyptians (led now by Pharaoh Neco II) in 609 recovered Haran temporarily but eventually failed. This was the end of the Assyrian Empire. Thereafter the competition was between Egypt and Babylon for control of the Mediterranean seaboard, until Nebuchadnezzar's defeat of the Egyptians at Carchemish in 605 BCE.

During this turbulent period, while Assyria was struggling for survival, Josiah initiated cultic reform in Judah, sought to expand his realm, and then was killed by Neco at Megiddo (probably during Neco's march north to join the Assyrians at Harran in 609 (see 2 Kgs 22:1–23:30; 2 Chronicles 34–35). Jeremiah's early career overlapped this period also, while the book of Nahum celebrates the fall of Nineveh. Usually it is assumed that Assyria's struggle for survival left a power vacuum in Palestine, and that this circumstance allowed Josiah to regain Judah's independence temporarily, initiate his reform, and begin to expand his realm. A case can be made, however, that the Egyptians (specifically the twenty-sixth Saite dynasty, which Neco II represented) was closely allied with Assyria already before Assyria's difficulties set in, and that as the Assyrians withdrew from Palestine the Egyptians followed immediately behind. Thus Josiah would have been an Egyptian vassal throughout his reign and it was his Egyptian overlord who executed him at Megiddo.

Babylonian Domination and the End of Judah (c. 605–539 BCE). The story of the last years of the kingdom of Judah (2 Kgs 23:28–25:29) is to be understood against the backdrop of the collapse of Assyria, the rush of the Medes, Scythians, Egyptians, and Babylonians to "pick the pieces," and the rise of Babylon for a brief period of empire. Babylon had been the seat of empire under Hammurabi (1792–1750 BCE) during the Middle Bronze Age, thus this brief revival of international strength is sometimes referred to as the Neo-Babylonian Empire. However, Nebuchadnezzar and his successors were never able to dominate Near Eastern affairs to the extent that the Assyrians had earlier or that the Persians would later. The Medes, for example, who had participated in the defeat of Assyria, continued to control the highlands north and east of Mesopotamia and expanded from there into Urartu and Asia Minor. Thus Babylon was forced to exert its military and economic interests more to the west where, in spite of the victory at Carchemish, which secured Babylonian control of the interior of Syria-Palestine, Egypt competed for a share of the maritime commerce in the eastern Mediterranean. Moreover, Nebuchadnezzar was followed by a succession of weak rulers, concluding with Nabonidus, who was on the throne when Babylon capitulated to Cyrus in 539 BCE.

The last five Judean kings (Josiah, Jehoahaz, Jehoiakim, Jehoiachin, and Zedekiah) all met their deaths or were exiled in connection with the international struggle during Nebuchadnezzar's reign. Jerusalem was conquered twice (597 and 586 BCE) and was destroyed the second time. Its walls were broken down, the Temple burned, and other prominent buildings dismantled. The leaders of Judean society were deported to Mesopotamia for resettlement, and many more fled to Egypt. Although the Assyrians also practiced deportation in order to break the nationalistic spirit of the peoples whom they conquered (their treatment of Samaria being an example) this Babylon deportation of the people of Judah has come to be known as "the exile." With Jerusalem in ruins and both Jehoiachin and Zedekiah imprisoned in Babylon, Nebuchadnezzar appointed Gedaliah, from a prominent Judaean family, to administer Judah (2 Kgs 25:22; Jer 40:7). Gedaliah chose Mizpah, just north of Jerusalem, as the new seat of government, and Mizpah probably continued to play that role until Nehemiah refortified Jerusalem almost a century and a half later. It is unclear whether Gedaliah was appointed as governor or designated as king to follow Zedekiah. He was soon assassinated in any case, which prompted a second wave of Judean refugees to Egypt in anticipation of further Babylonian reprisals. Jeremiah was active during these last years of the Kingdom of Judah, was among those who fled to Egypt following Gedaliah's assassination (apparently against his will; see Jeremiah 42–44), and the book that bears his name is an important source of historical information for the period. The Genesis–Kings account ends its coverage with the exile and may have been compiled at this time. Also, the books of Habakkuk and Lamentations and many of the psalms (e.g., 74 and 137) pertain to this period.

THE PERSIAN PROVINCE OF JUDAH

Cyrus II of the Achaemenid dynasty of Anshan in Persia defeated his grandfather, Astyages, king of the Medes, approximately 550 BCE. Victory was added to victory during the following decade as Cyrus conquered lands as far west as Lydia in Asia Minor and as far east as Bactria in present-day Afghanistan. The climax of this amazing decade of conquests was his defeat of a Babylonian army at Opis (near present-day Baghdad) in 539 BCE and the surrender of the city Babylon itself (apparently without a struggle) later that same year. Thus Samaritans, Jews, and many other peoples who had been subject first to the Assyrians and then to the Babylonians found themselves in the hands of a new master: Cyrus the Great, king of the Medes and the Persians.

However, Cyrus and at least his early successors seem to have taken a rather different approach to the governance of their subjects, many of whom had been uprooted from their ancestral lands by the Assyrians and Babylonians and resettled in other places. Cyrus and his successors chose instead to present themselves as liberators of the various peoples who now fell under their rule and as patrons of local gods and local temples. This clearly is the intended message of the so-called Cyrus Cylinder, an inscribed barrel dating from the reign of Cyrus that makes his claim to have restored the proper worship of Marc in Babylon. Near the end of the inscription, Cyrus claims to have restored sanctuaries in many other places as well, to have returned the images that had been looted from these various local sanctuaries, and to have allowed also for the return of peoples associated with the local cults.[12] In short, the decree attributed to Cyrus in 2 Chr 36:23 and Ezra 1:2-4 does seem in keeping with official Persian policy. The fact that Cyrus is looked upon with such favor in Isa 44:24–45:7 is not surprising.

The Persian Empire would dominate the Near East for the next two centuries, until Alexander the Great brought it to an end early in the fourth century BCE. The overall contours of the history of these two centuries of Persian domination are fairly well known from official Persian sources—mostly inscriptions in various languages (Babylonian, Old Persian, and Elamite) but typically in cuneiform script—and from the works of several Greek historians who treat portions of the period in considerable detail. Especially important in this latter regard are Herodotus, Thucydides, and Xenophon. Herodotus, for example, reports that Darius I (522–486 BCE) organized the Persian Empire into twenty administrative and military satrapies and identifies each geographically. Palestine would have belonged to the satrapy of Babylon and Ebir-Nari ("Beyond the River"—i.e., west of the Euphrates).

A group of papyri discovered in Egypt witness to the existence of a Jewish military colony living on Elephantine Island (in the upper Nile) during the fifth century BCE.[13] Among the various legal and business documents in this group of papyri are letters to Jerusalem and Samaria, including one addressed

12. *ANET,* 316.
13. *ANET,* 491-92.

to Bagoas, governor of Judah, regarding the rebuilding of a temple to Yaho by the Elephantine Jews. In closing, the writer mentions that a similar letter regarding the matter had been sent to "Delaiah and Shelemiah, the sons of Sanballat the governor of Samaria." Otherwise, for information pertaining specifically to the Samaritan and Jewish inhabitants of Palestine during the Persian period, we are limited essentially to archaeology and the biblical materials. Archaeological evidence suggests that the Palestinian hill country was somewhat off the beaten track of international affairs, which helps to explain why neither Samaria nor Judah turns up in any Persian records—namely, the material remains from the Palestinian hill country and the Transjordan are rather unimpressive for the Persian period and (in contrast to those of Galilee and the Mediterranean coastal plain) show little influence of Phoenician and Greek culture. Persian influence is most obvious in coins, seals, and seal impressions, many of which bear the name *Yehud* ("Judah," apparently with reference to the province of Judah).

The main biblical source for the Persian period is the Chronicles–Nehemiah account (specifically Ezra–Nehemiah). In addition to the highly composite and tendentious character of this work, its record of events for the Persian period is very uneven in coverage and raises many puzzling questions. Basically, it reports two clusters of events, the first having to do with early returnees from Babylonian exile under the leadership of Sheshbazzar, Zerubbabel, and Jeshua and their rebuilding of the Jerusalem Temple (Ezra 1–6; see also Haggai and Zechariah); the second involving the careers of Ezra and Nehemiah (Ezra 7–Nehemiah 13). Ezra 6:15 reports that the temple was completed in the sixth year of Darius (516 BCE), which means that the first cluster of events would have occurred between 539 and 516. Ezra and Nehemiah are said to have arrived in Jerusalem in the seventh and twentieth years respectively of Artaxerxes, almost certainly Artaxerxes I (464–424 BCE), which means that they came in 458 and 445 respectively. Nehemiah apparently left Jerusalem and returned sometime after 433 BCE (Neh 13:6-7). The Chronicles–Nehemiah account stops there. Nothing is reported for the last half of the Persian period, during which time the Peloponnesian Wars were fought and Persian armies crossed Palestine numerous times in attempts to maintain

control of Egypt. Even for the first century of the Persian period for which there is some coverage, the focus is almost entirely on the Jews who returned to Jerusalem from Mesopotamia. There are only passing references to the Samaritans, for example, or even to the Jews who had remained in the land and not gone into exile. To what extent were the latter involved in the restoration efforts? Did Jewish exiles return also from other places, such as Egypt? Among the puzzling questions is the shadowy role of Sheshbazzar. Ezra 1:8-11 and 5:14-16 identify him as a "prince of Judah" to whom Cyrus entrusted the Temple vessels, who led the first group of returnees, and who laid the foundation of the Temple. Otherwise, he disappears from the scene, eclipsed by Zerubbabel and Jeshua. Zerubbabel also seems to drop out of sight unexpectedly between the completion of the Temple and its dedication ceremony. The connection between Ezra and Nehemiah is another puzzling question. Supposedly they were active in Jerusalem at the same time, with Ezra arriving slightly earlier. Yet the accounts of their activities indicate surprisingly little interaction between the two, and several bits of information reported seem to require that Ezra's career be placed later than Nehemiah's.

Thus treatments of biblical history during the Persian period differ almost as radically as do treatments of Israel's origins, and for basically the same reasons: very little tangible information to work with and significant differences of opinion regarding the historical trustworthiness of the biblical materials. At one end of the spectrum are conservative scholars who place much confidence in the Chronicles–Nehemiah account and attempt to correlate it "as is" with the overall framework of Persian history known from other sources. E. M. Yamouchi illustrates this approach with Daniel on the scene in Babylon when Cyrus took the city, explaining that "Sheshbazzar, who was older, was probably viewed as the official governor, while Zerubbabel served as the popular leader,"[14] maintaining the traditional order of Ezra and Nehemiah, and so on. Representing a more critical and cautious approach to the biblical account is L. L. Grabbe, who sees the book of Daniel as an apocalyptic work from the reign of Antiochus IV (as do most critical scholars) and is unwilling to make any firm statements regarding Sheshbazzar and Zerubbabel except

14. E. M. Yamouchi, *Persia and the Bible* (Grand Rapids: Baker, 1990).

that Zerubbabel was governor and may have succeeded Sheshbazzar in that office.[15] He is confident that Neh 1:1–7:23*a* represents an authentic Nehemiah "memoir" of some sort. Regarding Ezra, on the other hand, he contends that more basic questions need to be asked than whether he came before or after Nehemiah, the first one being: Did Ezra exist?

PTOLEMIES, SELEUCIDS, AND HASMONEANS

Alexander of Macedon crossed the Hellespont and defeated a Persian army at the Granicus River (present-day Koca Çayi in northwestern Turkey) in 334 BCE. Two further victories, at Issus (southeastern Turkey) in 333 and Gaugamela (upper Tigris River) in 331, finished off the Persian Empire. Between Issus and Gaugamela, Alexander secured control of Syria-Palestine and entered Egypt, where he founded Alexandria. By the time of his sudden death in Babylon in 323, Alexander's conquests extended as far as present-day Afghanistan. Alexander's brief but amazing career signaled a major change in the history of the ancient Near East. Heretofore, Mesopotamia and Egypt had been the main centers of political and cultural influence. For approximately the next thousand years, until the expansion of Islam in the seventh century CE, the Near East would be dominated by Greek- and Latin-speaking peoples. Note that this cultural and political watershed occurred between the last events reported in the HB (the time of Ezra and Nehemiah) and those presupposed by the books of the Apocrypha and the New Testament. The history of Old Testament times is to be understood as unfolding primarily in the context of the fertile crescent, in other words, with the strongest influences on Israel, cultural as well as political, coming from the directions of Egypt, Syria, and Mesopotamia. After Alexander, the history of Syria-Palestine is to be understood in the context of the Mediterranean world with the strongest cultural and political influences coming from the west.

Following his death, Alexander's vast empire was fragmented between his warring generals (the *Diadochi):* Antigonus, Seleucus, Lysimachus, and Ptolemy. Antigonus held Macedonia but sought to control Asia Minor and Syria also. Thus Palestine changed hands several times between him and Ptolemy (who held Egypt) until the battle of Ipsus, in which Antigonus was killed and the international situation stabilized. Specifically, there emerged four major Hellenistic powers who would dominate the Near East for the next two and half centuries, until the coming of the Romans during the first century BCE. These powers were Macedonia, with its capital at Pella; the Pergamum city-state in Asia Minor (much smaller than the other four); the extensive Seleucid realm, with its capital at Antioch on the Orontes and included Mesopotamia, northern Syria, and much of Asia Minor; and the Ptolemaic kingdom centered in Egypt, with its capital at Alexandria. The dynasty founded by Seleucus ruled until Pompey brought it to an end in 64 BCE. Ptolemy's descendants ruled in Egypt until Cleopatra, the last member of the dynasty, committed suicide after Mark Antony's defeat at Actium in 31 BCE.

The Ptolemies and Seleucids were strong antagonists and fought five major wars during the third century (while the Romans and Carthagenians were fighting the Punic Wars). Control of Coele-Syria (southern Syria, including Palestine) was one of the main points of contention. The Ptolemies managed to hold this region throughout the century, but the Seleucids claimed it and eventually, as a result of the fifth "Syrian war" (201–198 BCE), were able to take it. Thus Judah, having been under Ptolemaic rule for almost exactly a century, became a part of the Seleucid Empire. The Seleucid kingdom was in an expansion mode at the time, ruled by the vigorous Antiochus III (223–187 BCE). Later Seleucid rulers would have increasing difficulty holding the empire together, however, as illustrated by the situation that developed in Judah during the reign of Antiochus IV (175–164 BCE). A Jewish rebellion broke out at that time and led eventually (late in the second century BCE) to an essentially independent Judean state ruled by a local Judean dynasty. This was the so-called Maccabean Rebellion, which is featured in the books of 1–2 Maccabees and gave rise to the Hasmonean dynasty.

Various Greek and Roman writers provide useful information regarding circumstances in Palestine during the Hellenistic period. Some of these works have survived independently (such as the writings of Polybius and portions of Diadorus Siculus). Por-

15. L. L. Grabbe, *Judaism from Cyrus to Hadrian* (Minneapolis: Fortress, 1992).

269

tions of others (such as Eupolemus, Hecataeus of Abdera, and Alexander Polyhistor) survive only as long quotes in the works of other authors, such as Josephus and Eusebius. Also extremely useful for understanding the history of Palestine during the Hellenistic period are two papyrus groups. The Wadi ed-Daliyeh papyri, discovered in a cave near Jericho, are fragmentary remains of legal documents of various sorts, apparently brought to the cave by refugees from Samaria when the city was destroyed by Alexander. The Zenon papyri provided a glimpse of local circumstances under Ptolemaic rule. Zenon was a minor official in the Egyptian court of Ptolemy II who visited Palestine in 260–58 BCE. Perhaps the most important sources of information about developments in Judah during the Hellenistic period, however, are the books of 1–2 Maccabees and the writings of Josephus, who was a Jewish historian in the latter half of the first century CE and wrote two major narrative accounts: *The Antiquities of the Jews,* which is his version of the history of the Jews from creation to Nero, and *The Jewish War,* which recounts events from the time of Antiochus IV and the Maccabean Rebellion through the First Jewish Revolt in 66–70 CE. For the early part of *The Antiquities of the Jews,* Josephus's narrative is largely a paraphrase of the biblical materials. As he approached his own time, however, and especially for the centuries following Alexander, Josephus drew upon other classical sources, many of which are no longer available. One must read the books of Maccabees and Josephus with critical caution, of course, since they were written to convey particular perspectives on the events reported. Josephus is an especially valuable source of information about the First Jewish Revolt, for example, since he was personally involved in it. But one of his purposes in writing was to respond to the charge that he had turned traitor and joined the Romans during the revolt.

The Ptolemies and Seleucids were proud of their cultural heritage. Thus it was only natural that both dynasties, although ruling from Egypt and Syria respectively, would use Greek as their official administrative language and seek to improve, develop, and beautify their realms in accordance with Hellenistic tastes and ideals. Both conflict and synthesis between Hellenism and the cultural traditions of the East were inevitable. Moreover, it was not just a matter of conflict between the Hellenistic intruders and the indigenous peoples such as the Jews. Much of the conflict reflected in Jewish writings of the period (e.g., the books of the Apocrypha) was between Jews who were receptive to Hellenism and those who were not. For example, although the Maccabean Rebellion is depicted in the books of Maccabees as a struggle for the restoration of traditional Jewish faith and practices, the Hasmonean dynasty, which emerged from the rebellion, was itself essentially Hellenistic in outlook and faced constant opposition from Jews of more traditional persuasion.

The Maccabean Rebellion was led by the three brothers each in turn (Judas "the Maccabee," Jonathan, and Simeon). It remained for Simeon's son, John Hyrcanus (135/4–104), to free Jerusalem completely of the Seleucids, who were having serious troubles with the Romans by that time. Hyrcanus assumed the office of high priest, but ruled as a monarch and expanded his realm to include virtually all of the territory west of the Jordan and parts of the Transjordan. Employing a policy of conversion by force, moreover, he incurred the hatred of the Samaritans when he destroyed their temple on Mount Gerizim. Hyrcanus's son, Alexander Jannaeus (103–76), expanded the Hasmonean realm still further into the Transjordan with victories at Gadara, Pella, and Gerasa. Alexander was succeeded by his wife, Salome Alexandra (76–67 BCE); after her death, a power struggle ensued between their two sons, Aristobulus II and Hyrcanus II. Aristobulus seized the throne, but the dispute remained unsettled when Pompey invaded Syria in 64 BCE and ended the Seleucid kingdom. Pompey marched on Jerusalem the following year and placed Hyrcanus on the throne. From that time on the rulers of Judah were answerable to Rome.

PREVIEW OF THE ROMAN PERIOD

Rome had become increasingly involved in eastern Mediterranean affairs during the half century preceding Pompey's invasion and for almost four centuries thereafter would dominate Syria-Palestine. Having defeated the Seleucids, Pompey annexed Syria as a Roman province with Antioch on the Orontes as its administrative capital. The Judean kingdom that he left in the hands of Hyrcanus II was, in addition to being subject to Rome, much reduced in territory. For example, Pompey separated from

Jerusalem a number of Palestinian cities whose inhabitants were largely Hellenistic in cultural orientation, after which they came to be known as "the Decapolis." Judah became a Roman province for all practical purposes after the death of Herod the Great in 4 BCE, even though Herod's sons (Archelaus, Herod Antipas, and Philip), a grandson (Agrippa I), and a great-grandson (Agrippa II) were allowed periods of rule (not always with the title "king") over various parts of Palestine. Agrippa II, for example, remained loyal to Rome during the First Jewish Revolt (66–70 CE), which involved his domain only indirectly. Egypt, in the meantime, had become a Roman province in 30 BCE following the Cleopatra-Mark Antony episode; and Domitian combined the Decapolis cities with Perea in 90 CE to form the province of Arabia. Finally, in 106 CE, Trajan annexed Nabataea to the province of Arabia, after which it was known as Arabia Petraea, and began construction of a major road system (the *via nova Traiana*) along the age-old trade route that extended north-south through the Transjordan. By the early second century, therefore, during which the Roman Empire reached the height of its power and broadest expanse, Syria-Palestine was firmly embedded in it and began to enjoy the benefits of the *Pax Romana*. Hadrian's visit to the eastern provinces in 129 CE was received with great fanfare and prompted his decision to rebuild Jerusalem as a proper Roman city with a proper name, Aelia Capitolina. This occasioned the Second Jewish Revolt (the Bar Kochba Revolt, 132–135 CE) which Rome crushed easily.

BIBLIOGRAPHY

Aharoni, Y., *The Land of the Bible: A Historical Geography.* Translated by A. F. Rainey. Philadelphia: Westminster, 1962.

Avi-Yonah, M. *The Holy Land: From the Persian to the Arab Conquests (536 B.C. to A.D. 640): A Historical Geography.* Rev. ed. Grand Rapids: Baker, 1977.

Hayes J. H., and J. M. Miller, eds. *Israelite and Judean History.* Philadelphia: Westminster, 1977.

Mazar, A. *Archaeology of the Land of the Bible, 10,000–586 BCE.* New York: Doubleday, 1990.

Miller, J. M., and J. H. Hayes. *A History of Ancient Israel and Judah.* Philadelphia: Westminster, 1986.

Pritchard, J. B. *Ancient Near Eastern Texts Relating to the Old Testament.* Princeton: Princeton University Press, 1955.

Shanks, H., ed. *Ancient Israel: A Short History from Abraham to the Roman Destruction of the Temple.* Washington, D.C.: Biblical Archaeology Society, 1988.

Soggin, J. A. *A History of Israel: From the Beginnings to the Bar Kochba Revolt.* London: SCM, 1985.

INTRODUCTION TO ISRAELITE RELIGION

GARY A. ANDERSON

The study of Israelite religion should be distinguished from biblical theology. The latter aims at a systematic presentation of ancient Israel's religious legacy. Its intention is to make the Bible serviceable to the faithful. The study of Israelite religion, on the other hand, is a purely descriptive enterprise. Its goal is a historical presentation of the religious life and thought of ancient Israel in all of its variety. Often the results of such a historical presentation will not easily fit into a theological system. Among most religious thinkers, it is still a debated issue as to how these two modes of approaching the Bible are to be reconciled.

In this article we will not attempt to solve this problem. Rather, we will present some of the more salient examples of what the historian of Israel's religion has learned. The legacy of the Bible is a complex one. Although in the final analysis it presents us with a theological framework that is unique in the ancient world—that is, the monotheistic principle that there is only one God—this principle did not come into complete existence at the beginning of the biblical period. Historical research has shown that this monotheistic principle emerged only after centuries of struggle, both political and spiritual. It is the task of the historian of Israel's religion to show what the roots of this struggle were.

This article will examine the historical origins of Israel's monotheistic heritage. We will then turn to the manner by which the Israelites heard and responded to the divine word both directly through the agency of the prophetic oracle and in their liturgical life, through the mediation of the Temple, sacrifice, and personal holiness.

CANAANITE AND ISRAELITE BELIEFS ABOUT THE GODS

At first glance it would seem that one area of strong discontinuity between Canaanite and Israelite religion would be their attitudes toward the gods. For many, the most distinctive aspect of Israelite religion is the belief in *one* God. Yet there are texts in the Bible that seem to presume some sort of polytheistic belief. For example, in Exod 15:11, the song that Moses and the Israelites sing when they are redeemed at the Sea of Reeds, having just left Egypt, reads: "Who is like you, O LORD, *among the gods?*" (NRSV, italics added). This curious expression presumes a company of divine beings among whom the Israelite Deity stands preeminent. Later Jewish and Christian tradition would come to understand lines like this as either poetic metaphor (*"if there were other gods,* who among them would be like you, O LORD?") or evidence for the angelic host who surround the divine throne in heaven ("Who is like thee, O LORD, among the [*semi-*] divine beings?").[1] But the historian of Israel's religion will attempt to understand this verse against the Canaanite background out of which Israelite culture arose, for the historian has found evidence in the Bible that would suggest a more complicated origin. Israel's distinctive monotheistic beliefs evolved over a long period of time and so, not surprisingly, showed a strong degree of continuity with the polytheism of ancient Canaan in its earlier periods.

Among the deities of ancient Canaan, the most important was El, the chief god of the tribal clan, who directed the wars of his patrons and intervened on behalf of childless couples. He also presided over the "council of the gods," which convened on his holy mountain. El was both the father of these gods and their leader. This ancient Canaanite deity was well known to the early Israelites. Indeed, the Bible claims that during the pre-Mosaic period the patriarchs themselves identified their God by the name *El* (אל).[2] This is plainly stated in Exod 6:3: "I appeared to Abraham, Isaac, and Jacob as God Almighty [*El Shaddai*], but by my name, 'The LORD' [YHWH], I did not make myself known to them" (NRSV).[3]

After the revelation of God's personal name to Moses, the name *El* functions primarily as a common noun meaning "[a/the] god," instead of a title for the deity. The revelation to Moses of the new name constitutes a turning point in Israel's religion, and the Bible is conscious of this dramatic change. But what of this deity El, whom we meet in the stories of Genesis?

Most scholars would say that this El who figures so prominently in the early patriarchal narratives is none other than the El of Canaanite religion. In other words, during the patriarchal era, the supreme deity of the proto-Israelites was the chief god of the Canaanite pantheon. What evidence could support such a claim? First of all is the titles used to describe the god of the patriarchs. In Genesis 12–50, El is identified or described by a distinct set of adjectives. These include *El Elyôn* (אל עליון) "El, the highest

one") *El Shaddai* (אל שדי) "El, the mountain-dwelling one"), *El Olam* (לא עלם) "El, the eternal one"), *El Elôhê Yisrael* (אל אלהי ישראל) "El, the [patron] god of Israel"), *Abbir Ya'aqob* (אביר יעקוב) "the Bull of Jacob"). A number of these are associated with particular regional shrines in ancient Canaan, which suggests that they may have been local manifestations of El that the patriarchs encountered upon entering those respective places. But what is most striking about these names is their close conformity to well-known images and descriptions of El from extra-biblical sources. Some are identical word for word. This close agreement between the Israelite and Canaanite titles for El cannot be mere coincidence. The biblical descriptions had a pre-history in the religion of ancient Canaan.

Not only the titles of El but also the very *mode* of religious life presupposed in the patriarchal material shows close parallels with the Canaanite world. The God of the patriarchs appear to his clients in visions and takes a special interest in their progeny. Both of these aspects are very prominent in the epic lore from the ancient Canaanite city of Ugarit. Two famous epics from this collection, *Danel* and *Kirta,* concern the securing of offspring for the purpose of inheritance, the same concern of the patriarchal legends. In addition, the mode of El's appearance to these figures is similar to that of Genesis: He appears in dreams, which often occurred while the individual in question is sleeping on holy ground (see Genesis 28).

There is, perhaps, no better expression of Canaanite thinking about the role of El in Israelite thought than the surprising text found in Deut 32:8 (NRSV):

When the Most High *[Elyôn]*
     apportioned the nations,
when he divided humankind,
he fixed the boundaries of the peoples,
     according to the number of the gods *[sons of El]*.

When we realize that *Elyôn* is simply a standard title for El, the verse appears to express a standard mythic world view of the Canaanites; El, the head of the divine assembly, has apportioned the kingdoms of the earth to the various national deities (sons of El). Perhaps in certain Israelite circles, YHWH was merely one of these local deities who had received the fiefdom of Israel. Nothing in this text would contradict such a notion, though one must be fair here and note that other circles in Israel identified

---

1. This is certainly how all the archaic "polytheistic" verses in the Bible were read by later Jewish interpreters. This type of interpretation is already in evidence by the time the Bible was being translated into Greek just prior to the birth of Christ. In the Greek Bible, the Hebrew term for "gods" is often rendered "angels." Later Christian interpreters used these plural references to the divine realm as evidence of the Trinity.

2. Actually the Hebrew most often renders the name in the plural, אלהים *Elohim,* but with a singular meaning.

3. The term שדי *Shaddai* is just an adjectival qualifier of the noun *El,* or "god." Shaddai probably means the "one of the mountains," or "El, the mountain-dwelling god."

Elyon and El as alternate titles of YHWH and so understood this text as depicting the apportionment of the kingdoms of the earth as a witness to the supreme authority of the Israelite God. But even in this more "orthodox" perspective there are problems; belief in other national deities is presumed!

Before abandoning the alternative that for some early Israelite thinkers YHWH was just a "local" figurehead, it is worth citing the unusual tale found in Judg 11:12-28. In this story the leader of the Israelite militia, Jephthah, engages the kings of the Ammonites in a political/theological dispute. In pressing for peace, Jephthah tries to dissuade an Ammonite invasion of Israel by appealing to a common theological principle. He asserts that just as their national god (here incorrectly identified as Chemosh) has apportioned to them a particular patrimony, so the god of Israel has provided in a similar fashion for his own people. If either nation oversteps the bounds of these "divine estates" it will incur the wrath of a higher order. Now one might argue that Jephthah has employed this language for rhetorical purposes alone and never would equate the two deities in other circumstances; nonetheless, when this tale is compared to Deut 32:8 we can see that the imprint of Canaanite thought had a vital reflex in the earliest layers of Israelite literature.

Next to El, the most important figure is Baal, the god of the storm. In his gracious mode, Baal is the provider of rain, the source of fertility, but in his ferocious aspect he is the god of war, whose roaring thunderbolts and shafts of lightning wreak havoc among denizens of Canaan. In the mythic literature, Baal's most notable feature is his struggle against the forces of death; he defeats the watery monster of chaos, emerges as king among the gods, and is, accordingly, fitted with a temple. Neglect of temple duty would result in the displeasure of the resident deity and the infertility of the land. This theme of the life-giving nature of the temple (and the king who oversees it) is quite evident in the rhetoric of temple-building found in the prophet Haggai, who argues that YHWH's restoration of Judea cannot begin until the Temple and its royal patron are fully established (Hag 1:7-11; 2:20-23).

The influence of Baal worship on Israelite religion is evident from a comparison of how Baal and YHWH are said to manifest their power in nature. For example, in the Baal myth we read:

Baal opened a slit in the clouds,
  Baal sounded his holy voice,
  Baal thundered from his lip . . .
the earth's high places shook.[4]

This description is extremely close to that found in Judg 5:4-5 (NRSV):

The earth trembled,
  and the heavens poured,
  the clouds indeed poured water.
The mountains quaked before the
    LORD, the One of Sinai,
  before the LORD, the God of Israel.

The use of poetic descriptions of Baal and YHWH are so close that some have suggested that Psalm 29 was originally a hymn to Baal that was later adapted by an Israelite by merely changing the god named within!

The most important reflex of Baal imagery in the Bible concerns that of the storm god's doing battle with the watery forces of chaos. In Canaanite mythology, Baal destroys the agent of Chaos, Prince Sea/Judge River (an unnamed being identified by these two titles). After Baal destroys him, Baal becomes king. Strong resonances of this mythic motif are found in various retellings of the exodus story in the Bible. Compare the hymn found in Ps 77:16-17 (NRSV):

When the waters saw you, O God,
  when the waters saw you, they were afraid,
  the very deep trembled.
The clouds poured out water;
  the skies thundered;
  your arrows flashed on every side.

In this poem, the enemy is not the Egyptians, as it is in Exodus 14–15, but the turbulent, chaotic forces of evil, personified in watery terms. Similar imagery can be found in Ps 114:3, where the watery enemy is given a double name, Sea and (Jordan) River, a description that cannot help suggesting the enemy of Baal. This mythic complex also appears in later portions of the Bible, such as Isaiah 40–66. In one passage of this work, the victory at the Red Sea is described as YHWH's victory over the sea dragon Rahab (Isa 51:9). If a reader had only the biblical account of the exodus, it would be difficult to know

4. This comparison was first drawn by M. Coogan, *Stories from Ancient Canaan* (Philadelphia: Westminster, 1978) 21.

how the prophet could have understood such an event as a battle with chaos. But the Canaanite material, in conjunction with evidence of poetic accounts like Psalm 77, helps us to understand how this foundational event in Israelite history could be subject to mythological development at the hand of an accomplished bard.

Another way in which the god Baal may have influenced Israelite religion can be seen in how both Baal and YHWH are depicted as the source of fertility. As an agricultural society, the ancient Israelites celebrated three religious festivals in conjunction with the major harvest seasons—unleavened bread (Matzoth) at the beginning of the barley harvests, "weeks" (Pentecost) at the end of the wheat harvest, and "ingathering" (Succoth) following the date, grape, and olive harvests. Ingathering was the principal festival, which "closed out" the year. These three festivals, each of which required a pilgrimage to a local place of worship to present an offering (Exod 23:14), are seen by some scholars as reflecting a common Canaanite heritage and are, in some cases, dated by the Canaanite calendar. Passover, a rite originally marked by the moving of flocks from winter to summer pasturage, was observed at the spring equinox and was celebrated in the home. As time passed, the Israelites gave these festivals fixed dates and associated them with YHWH's historical saving events. Passover was celebrated on the eve of Matzoth (the two being viewed as one festival), both associated with the Exodus event and celebrated from the first to the eighth days of the first month (Abib). "Weeks" came seven weeks (fifty days) later and was

associated with the covenant at Sinai (Exod 19:1). Rosh ha-Shanah (New Year's Day) was the first day of Tishri; Yom Kippur (the Day of Atonement) the tenth; and Booths the fifteenth through the twenty-second—all three commemorating Israel's time in the wilderness (in particular, New Year's Day was associated with the first time the tabernacle was set up [Exod 40:17], as well as with the dedication of Solomon's Temple in Jerusalem [1 Kings 8]).

In the Bible itself, the most common references to Baal are derisive. This is well illustrated by the figure of Elijah, who constantly chastises his fellow Israelites for confusing the power of Baal for that of YHWH. Because this confusing of YHWH and Baal was so widespread in ancient Israel, it is important to understand why such an identification would have suggested itself in the first place. The most obvious explanation is the similar natures of YHWH and Baal, which we have just seen. These similarities would have led many Israelites to presume that YHWH (the more "recent" figure in the history of ancient Canaan) was not a unique god but rather just an alternative local title for an older pan-Canaanite deity. From the perspective of the common Israelite, it was not so much a matter of rejecting YHWH in preference for Baal, but of seeing the two as equitable or interchangeable in certain fundamental ways. For the prophets, however, this merging of deities was nothing other than a rejection of the absolute uniqueness of the biblical God and the requirement to revere God alone. Not only does this comparison of the biblical story to Canaanite religion

AGRICULTURAL AND CIVIL CALENDAR

The Gezer Calendar	Season	Labor	Babylonian (Canaanite) Numbering	Months	Israelite Numbering	Religious Festivals	
Two months of [olive] harvest;	Former (autumn) rains	*Olive, grape, fig harvests	1st	Tishri (*Ethanim)	Sept/Oct	7th	**High Holy Days**
		*Plowing	2nd	Marchesvan (*Bul)	Oct/Nov	8th	Trumpets — 1 Tishri; Day of Atonement — 10 Tishri; Booths-Ingathering — 15-22 Tishri
Two months of sowing;		*Sowing of wheat, barley, and spelt	3rd	*Chislev	Nov/Dec	9th	
	Winter rains 70% of yearly precipitation	(Second plowing) Late planting	4th	*Tebeth	Dec/Jan	10th	Hanukkah — 25 Chislev (eight days)
Two months of late sowing;		(Sheep shearing) Flax harvest	5th	*Shebat	Jan/Feb	11th	
A month of hoeing weeds;	Latter (spring) rains	*Barley harvest	6th	*Adar	Feb/Mar	12th	Purim — 14 Adar
A month of harvesting barley;		*Wheat harvest	7th	*Nisan (*Abib)	Mar/Apr	1st	Passover — 14 Nisan; Unleavened Bread — 15-21 Nisan; First Fruits
A month of harvesting and [measur]ing;		Early figs ripen Grapes ripen	8th	Iyyar (*Ziv)	Apr/May	2nd	
Two months of cutting [grapes];	Summer Dry Season	*Date, fig, grape, and pomegranate harvests	9th	*Sivan	May/June	3rd	Weeks (Pentecost) — 7 weeks after Passover
			10th	Tammuz	June/July	4th	
A month of [collecting] summer fruit.			11th	Ab	July/Aug	5th	
		*Times of intense labor demand.	12th	*Elul	Aug/Sept	6th	[Vintage Festival at Shiloh]
				* Used in the Bible			

allow us to understand the Israelites' tendency toward syncretism, but it also puts in far greater relief the innovative and radical theological program of the prophets. How easy it would have been for these religious leaders to acquiesce to the convention of the times and correlate the activity of Israel's God to that of its neighbors.

Monotheism and Covenant. Our discussion so far has shown how the figure of YHWH was similar to the figures of El and Baal and how early Israelite belief did not rule out the possibility of other gods. In this respect, the early religion of Israel looks similar to that of ancient Canaan. Yet the similarity stops short of absolute convergence. Although certain streams within Israel attempted to correlate their god to those of the surrounding cultures and to achieve a more radical form of convergence, prophetic opposition assured that this never became standard. On two points, the normative thinking of early Israel was quite distinctive: the prohibition against venerating other gods and the command to construct no graven images. The first point is best summed up in the famous declaration of Deut 6:4: "Hear, O Israel: The LORD is our God, the LORD alone" (NRSV). Here the adverbial qualifier *alone* neatly summarizes the distinctiveness of Israelite thought. Although it does not rule out the *theoretical possibility* that other gods might exist, it asserts as a *practical orientation* the fact that only one god can be worshiped.

It is no accident that this text occurs in a book that is thoroughly tied to the theme of the covenant. The terminology comes from ancient Near Eastern vassal treaties in which a vassal was bound by an oath to serve one sovereign (human) lord among the many potential lords who reigned among the surrounding nations. This legal rubric was then transferred from the human realm to the divine in early Israelite thought, an act that has no parallel in the ancient world. Thus the monotheistic principle in Israel began from a quite practical framework. This contrasts quite sharply with the development of monotheism in the Greek world, in which the concept of a single God developed in philosophical circles, largely as a result of deductive logic and the search for an original primary cause. In the biblical period, this practical feature of obeying only one lord and refusing to adorn the deity with images led to the idea that this lord was the only God and that other deities in surrounding lands were little more

than sticks and stones (e.g., Isa 44:9-20). But even in this more reflective (albeit polemical) literature, the concern for monotheism is never a purely ideational construct; it is always rooted in the notion of allegiance and service.

Although the importance of the idea of covenant has always been recognized by scholars, the historical origin of the idea has been the subject of some controversy. Julius Wellhausen, writing at the end of the nineteenth century, argued that the idea of the covenant arose very late in Israel's history. His chief piece of evidence was the fact that the covenant form appears in full dress only in Deuteronomy, and in that book it is wedded to the concept of centralization of all liturgical life to the city of Jerusalem. Since this concept of centralization is a relatively late one—indeed, prophets like Elijah and Hosea have no familiarity with it—it would appear that so was the concept of covenant, which undergirded it. The lateness of covenant form led Wellhausen to the startling conclusion that the religion of the prophets preceded the religion of the covenant or law.

Wellhausen's reconstruction of the role of covenant held sway for quite some time. Not until 1954, when George Mendenhall published his famous article on covenant, did the pendulum begin to shift. Mendenhall argued that the covenant formula found in the Bible was closely parallel to the covenant form found in Hittite texts from the Late Bronze Age (1500–1200 BCE). Mendenhall argued that biblical writers from the Mosaic period were conversant with this ancient Near Eastern legal form and employed it for their own religious purposes. The covenant, then, in Mendenhall's view, not only preceded the prophets, but also provided the very foundation upon which Israel's most distinctive religious ideas were built. Recently, Mendenhall's thesis has come under attack, and counterproposals have been suggested that argue for a return to a position more or less like that of Wellhausen. It is probably safe to say that certain features of Mendenhall's argument need to be amended, but certainly the extreme lateness for the covenant form that was argued by Wellhausen cannot stand.

For most biblical writers, the notion of the covenant was the most significant principle of Israelite religion. Although the covenant form has a number of features, most of which closely parallel other ancient Near Eastern documents,[5] two in particular are worth highlighting: the *historical prologue* and the *commandments*. The historical prologue includes a narrative that accounts for the special relationship between the (divine) sovereign and his subjects. In the Bible, this usually means a detailed account of the specific acts of deliverance God has effected for the people (see Josh 24:2-13). This recital of a saving history, though, is not merely an account of the ancient past. Rather, its function is to instill within its hearers the proper attitude of reverence, obedience, and love (see Deut 11:1; Josh 24:14-15). This aspect is brought out quite well in a post-biblical Jewish tradition that tries to explain why the covenant was not brought into full realization until the period after the Exodus:

Why were the Ten Commandments not said at the beginning of the Torah? They give a parable. To what may this be compared? To the following: A king who entered a province said to the people: May I be your king? But the people said to him: Have you done anything good for us that you should rule over us? What did he do then? He built the city wall for them, he brought in the water supply for them and he fought their battles. Then when he said to them: May I be your king? They said to him: Yes, Yes. Likewise God . . . [6]

The reverence and obedience demanded by the covenant cannot be formalized by mere verbal assent; it must be concretized through the keeping of commandments. A favorite metaphor in the Old Testament (OT) for the type of relationship represented by this covenantal bond is that of marriage (Hos 2:14-23). Just as the love of a husband for his wife will be defined by specific obligations and not simply a feeling of mutual attraction, so also the love Israel feels for God will be manifested by the observance of the divine commandments. In the past, biblical scholars have stressed the value of God's gracious historical acts on behalf of Israel over the notion of Israel's subsequent legal obligation to God, no doubt in conformity with the Christian principle

that sees the era of the Law coming to its closure with the advent of the Messiah. Yet a true understanding of the function of the covenant in Israelite religion cannot make any separation between these two ideas. Because God has redeemed Israel, Israel must keep God's commandments. The commandments are not the means by which entry into the covenant is secured, but rather are the fitting vehicle by which Israel showed gratitude for the existence of this covenantal relationship.

THE MANIFESTATION OF GOD IN RITUAL

The Temple. The cultic or liturgical life of ancient Israel centered on the institution of the Temple. As in other cultures of the ancient world, the Temple in Israelite religion was a spot where God's presence was available in an extraordinary way. In the Bible the notion of God's residing in the Temple often stood in uneasy tension with the idea that God was free to reside anywhere. Thus at the moment the Ark of the Covenant was moved into the holiest room of the Temple—inaugurating God's visible entry into the shrine—Solomon asks, "But will God indeed dwell on the earth? Even heaven and the highest heaven cannot contain you, much less this house that I have built!" (1 Kgs 8:27 NRSV). Yet, significantly, Solomon built the Temple regardless of these reservations and presumed that in some fashion God's presence would dwell within its confines. For Solomon, and indeed much of biblical thought, the Temple was a supra-mundane location in which God quite freely chose to become visible.

This special locus of the divine presence in the Temple is best expressed in the story of the founding of Bethel in Gen 28:10-22. In this story, Jacob was on his way to Aramea to find a wife when he happened upon the city of Luz. There, during a dream, Jacob saw a ladder erected between heaven and earth with members of the divine council ("angels") moving up and down on it. When Jacob awoke, realizing the special nature of the place, he set up a pillar, consecrated it, and renamed the site Bethel. Later, an Israelite temple was built there, obviously as a result of the founding vision. Jacob's explanation of the sanctity of the site is significant: "This is none other than the house [*Beth*] of God [*El*], and this is the gate of heaven" (Gen. 28:17 NRSV). The sacred site, then, provides an aperture

---

5. The common features to the covenant include (a) a preamble in which the king identifies himself, (b) the historical prologue in which the king recites the many kind deeds he has performed on behalf of the vassal, (c) the stipulations or the terms of the treaty itself, (d) the provision for depositing the text of the treaty in the temple. In conjunction with this, reference was often made to the need for public recitation of the treaty during periodic intervals; (e) a list of witnesses, this usually included the gods of the two parties involved; and (f) a series of curses and blessings. This guaranteed the vassal's loyalty, for it stipulated certain rewards for obedience (blessings) and punishments for disobedience (curses).

6. The translation is from *Mekhilta de Rabbi Ishmael,* ed. and trans. J. Z. Lauterbach (Philadelphia: JPS, 1933) 2:229-30.

to the world of the gods. Whereas Jacob by chance stumbled upon this holy soil, later generations, because of the erection of a temple on this site, would be able to have continual access.

The name Jacob gave to this place is significant for understanding the Temple. The name *Bethel* means "the house of God." The presumption here is not that God entirely resides in this earthen structure, but that this earthen building stands in a parallel relation to God's heavenly abode. The earthly Temple mirrors the heavenly. The Temple is the *axis mundi,* or point of linkage, between heaven and earth. In order to concretize this point, ancient Near Eastern writers described their temples as high mountains. Sometimes actual, physical mountains become the special locus of the divine presence (so Mt. Sinai), but more often than not, the imagery and symbolism of the mountain was transferred to temple buildings, regardless of their physical nature. In Sidon, a Canaanite city sitting astride the coastal plain of Phoenicia, the temple precinct was called "the high heavens," a mythic image that stood in strong contrast to earthly reality. So also the Temple in Jerusalem could be called God's "holy mountain, beautiful in elevation" (Ps 48:2), in spite of the fact that the Temple mount was a rather inconspicuous hill, overshadowed by the immediately adjacent Mount of Olives.

Canaanite myths associated the sacred mountain upon which the Temple is situated with the source of the world's fresh water. This image proved to be quite significant for biblical writers as well. It certainly is present in the Eden traditions that describe this location as the source of the world's four great rivers (Gen 2:10-13). It is also evident in certain psalmic descriptions of Zion (Pss 36:8; 46:4). Perhaps nowhere is this tradition more evident than in Ezekiel's vision of how the rebuilt Jerusalem will appear (Ezekiel 47). In this text, Jerusalem's water source becomes so magnificent that it is capable of transforming much of the Judean desert and the stagnant waters of the Dead Sea into a region teeming with life. The picture these poetic images provide stands in strong contrast to the actual water source that served the city of Jerusalem, the Gihon Spring, a tiny tributary. Here again we see that the hymnic praises of this city utilize the world of myth over that of history. The descriptions of Jerusalem in the Bible conform to a spiritual norm of truth and so must hold in suspension cartographic or geologic criteria.

The notion that the Temple could serve as an *axis mundi* and that the architecture of this earthly building was constructed so as to correlate with its heavenly archetype helps to clarify the famous commission of the prophet Isaiah (Isaiah 6). In this scene, Isaiah seems to have miraculously ascended into heaven wherein he sees the Lord upon the throne, with seraphim in attendance; an incense altar is used to purify his lips. In brief, what Isaiah glimpses is a session of the divine council. What is often not noted, however, is that all of the physical items Isaiah sees in this vision actually exist in artistic form within the Temple in Jerusalem. The Ark, which resides in the holiest room, was the throne upon which God was thought to sit, and on this Ark were carved two representative members of the divine assembly, the cherubim. Just outside this throne room stood the incense altar and its assorted cultic utensils. Isaiah's experience, then, could be understood as a transformation of the artistic iconography of the Temple into the spiritual realities it represented. The symbolic forms took life, and the mythos of the Temple as an aperture to the heavenly realm was realized in the everyday experience of this eighth-century BCE Judean prophet. Such was the possibility of divine encounter within this sacred shrine.

Because the earthly Temple had such a crucial role in mediating the divine presence, the imagery used to describe it was often trans-historical or mythic in scope. Although all Israelites were certainly aware that the actual Temple building in Jerusalem was constructed at the behest of David and Solomon, the description of its construction in hymnic poetry ignores this mundane information. For the psalmist, the building of the Temple compares to the founding of the earth itself: "He built his sanctuary like the high heavens,/ like the earth, which he has founded forever" (Ps 78:69 NRSV).

Even less poetic accounts of the founding of the Temple emphasize creation themes. Just as the world was created in seven days, so also the Temple was created over seven years. These cycles of seven obviously serve to correlate Temple building with the construction of the world. In addition, just as the creation of the world culminated in the sabbath, the moment at which God rested, so also the building of the Temple afforded for the deity a place of rest.

Much of the Temple's architecture reflects creation imagery as well. The huge, molten basin that sat just outside the Temple is said to contain the "sea." The term for "sea," ים *yām* is used to identify the enemy of the storm god in Canaanite mythology and represents the powers of chaos, which the biblical God subdued at the time of creation. The presence of this "sea" residing within a huge basin in front of the Temple was striking testimony to the domestication of this potential source of chaos by the Israelite God. So, too, the pillars that flanked the entrance to the Temple proper had a cosmic role. These two poles, named Jachin and Boaz, did not support any part of the Temple itself but seemed to stretch effortlessly toward the heavens. Like other such pillars from the ancient Near East, they were probably understood to support the surface of the firmament (understood as a beaten, physical surface in the Bible), which divided the earthly and heavenly realms. Indeed the names of the pillars themselves were probably part of an archaic liturgical formula: "by [his] strength, [the world] was established."

The powerful mythic dimensions of the Temple—present in both the psalmic hymns and the architecture—helps us to appreciate the pride of place shown for the very physicality of the Temple. Most readers are not at all surprised that the Bible would require Temple worshipers to be moral, to offer sacrifices and prayers, and to consider the great deeds God has wrought for the people. But occasionally the psalmist exhorts hearers simply to gaze upon the Temple:

Walk about Zion, go all around it,
    count its towers,
consider well its ramparts;
    go through its citadels,
that you may tell the next generation
    that this is God. (Ps 48:12 NRSV)

This rather surprising text associates the very description of God's being with buildings in Zion. There is no better testimony to the fact that the iconography of the Temple was a veritable witness to the power of God. Perhaps this iconographic interest accounts for the double narrative concerning the erection of the tent shrine in Exodus 25–30, 35–40. For many modern readers, repetition of detail seems needless if not tedious, but considered against the background of a culture that put a high premium on iconographic reality, such interest in repeated visual detail surely had its value. Such

extended descriptions of Temple appurtenances had a profound influence on later Jewish mystical texts that took delight in describing, in infinite detail, the various chambers (היכלות *hēkālôt)* of the supernal temple.

Sacrifice. The phenomenon of sacrifice cannot be appreciated apart from the mythic notion that the Temple serves as the very house of God. In order to concretize the fact of this *physical* or sacramental encounter, biblical law took special care to outline the responsibilities that went along with it. Chief among these were the requirements to attend to the daily needs of this resident deity and to dispose of material the deity found offensive. The former concern resulted in the sacrificial system; the latter led to the concern for purity. Although both should be understood as an essential unity—for each in its own way serves to highlight in a ritual fashion the material consequences of housing a deity—we will begin our discussion with the concept of sacrifice.

The laws of sacrifice presume a *sacramental* mentality that believes that God's presence is made manifest within the confines of the material world (Exod 20:24). Neither the Israelites nor the Canaanites were wont to conceive of a god's existence apart from a concrete referent to that deity's mode of manifestation. This is most obvious in the gods of nature who were thought to reside within the phenomena they represented, whether rivers and seas or various agricultural items. But even the higher gods, those not explicitly identified with an aspect of nature, are constrained by this sacramental principle to physically manifest themselves within liturgical practice. Rituals such as sacrifices evolved to help concretize the manner in which the deity was truly present in the human community. Although God is beyond nature and history, through the medium of the Temple God's presence is manifested. But this presence cannot be merely stated; it must be lived and experienced. Thus, following through with this logic, the deity who assumes residence in the Temple must be revered and honored with the proper trappings of such a setting—an elaborate throne room, finely crafted paneling, handsome vestments for servants, and, most important, sumptuous food. *What holds together all of these images is the notion of God's assuming and maintaining residence within a particular place.* Sacrifice, considered here as the provisioning of the deity's banquet table, is simply one among a number of ritual acts that symbolize the miraculous availability of the deity within the Temple and allow this reality to be lived and experienced by the human community.

Within the biblical narratives, the act of sacrifice is the single most important feature of the liturgical life of the Temple. The tremendous importance of the sacrificial system is certainly related to the fact that it—unlike most other dimensions of temple life—requires daily maintenance and upkeep by the community of worshipers. In other words, this mode of affording honor and reverence toward the deity is unique in so far as it requires constant human attention. And it should cause no surprise that the same word for "service" [עבדה ʿǎbōdâ] in the Bible is also the term for divine worship. In the act of providing a sacrifice, Israelites were not only providing a service to the deity, but also setting themselves in a position of subservience to that very God.

The performative role of sacrifice has long been a topic of reflection among anthropologists. This role has sometimes been caricatured as nothing more than the secondary application of the fundamental principle of secular mercantile exchange: *do ut des,* "I have given [a gift to the god] so grant me [a blessing in return]." Although no one would doubt that an aspect of "exchange" is present in the sacrificial act—people do present sacrifices in the hope of gaining a blessing in return—recent thinking on the topic of sacrifice has suggested a more subtle aspect to the type of exchange envisioned. Gift exchange among unequal partners is never a purely mercantile affair—i.e., one party gives with the single intention of securing a future benefit. Rather, the very act of exchange serves to embody and communicate the relative status of the partners in question. Thus, for example, when a person offers a mere animal in the hope that God will in turn grant that person a child, the unequal nature of the items exchanged cannot help creating within the person a feeling of dependency and gratitude. Understood in this manner, we would do well to translate *do ut des* as "I give [so precious little] but [nevertheless, please] grant [so very much]." This may appear to be an overly subtle and perhaps quibbling type of distinction, but in reality the results of such a distinction are quite profound. When the sacrificial act of giving is viewed this way, the exchange can hardly be considered a crude bargain oriented at "twisting the arm" of the deity. Instead, the act of sacrifice becomes a liturgical

"realization" of the absolute dependence of the human giver upon the graces of God. Sacrifice is an essential vehicle for establishing and *expressing* this relationship of God to humanity; it could hardly be considered optional.

Understood this way, sacrifice provides an occasion for the Israelite to "dramatize" subservient status before God. The word *drama* has been chosen with some care, for the Israelite hymns of thanksgiving, which often were accompanied by sacrifices, always require that the Israelite perform this event before the assembled community (see Ps 66:13-20). Sacrifice was a *public* event. Yet the drama of this presentation before the deity could have meaning only if one accepted the fundamental principle upon which it was based: God resided within this building, and God's residence required the honor of a well-provisioned table. Here resided the great danger of Israelite temple theology—indeed it is a danger inherent in any sacramental form of revelation and a danger to which the prophets paid particular attention—the notion that God's cultic availability could be subject to ritual manipulation. It is against this background that one can understand the evolution of the laws of purity and holiness, for lurking behind these apparently irrational collections of rules and regulations is the idea that God's presence is a "potent" one, possessing both potential benefits and dangers. Thus we can understand the Israelites' fear of being too close to that presence while at Sinai and their insistence that Moses be their intercessor (Exod 20:19). It is not that God is a tempestuous being whose unstable nature casts fear into the hearts of the Israelites. Rather, God is a holy being, whose requirements for human perfection caused the Israelite community to reflect on their inadequateness. The benefits of God's presence could accrue only to those who respect these rules for holiness and purity; for those who are less than circumspect in this regard, the dangers that lurk within the divine teem with mortal ill.

Purity and Holiness. The divine holiness was fundamental to the concept of God's presence. God's presence could not be made manifest before those who had no respect for proper decorum. God's own holiness required that only those who were holy could approach. Within the Israelite system, personal holiness was of two kinds: ascribed and earned. In the former, holiness was graded according to rank, the high priest being the most holy, followed in turn by the other priests, the Levites, and finally the laity. Earned holiness is readily apparent in the fulfillment of special vows (e.g., the Nazirite vow in Numbers 6) and in the keeping of certain rituals. Thus when the Israelites approached the sacred mountain at Sinai they were instructed to wash their clothes and abstain from sexual relations (Exod 19:10-15). Holiness could also accrue to those who were faithful to the commandments. Hence the act of keeping the commandments is summed up with the rubric "You shall be holy, for I the LORD your God am holy" (Lev 19:2 NRSV).

Any encroachment on the holiness of God was dangerous. Thus those who usurped the prerogatives of priesthood were either cut off from the Temple (Uzziah in 2 Chronicles 16) or put to death (the Korahites in Numbers 16). Similarly neglect of the laws for holiness and purity by the population at large could result in the eviction of those people from their land (Lev 19:22).

Closely related to, if not at times almost inseparable from, the issue of holiness is the concern for maintaining the laws of purity. Purity in the Bible has two dimensions: physical and moral. The moral requirements hardly need any elaboration; it is altogether expected that those who reside beside the Temple would maintain a certain level of personal righteousness. The best evidence for this idea comes from Temple entrance litanies. Thus the liturgical question of Ps 15:1 ("Who may dwell on your holy hill?" [NRSV]) is answered, "Those who walk blamelessly, and do what is right,/ and speak the truth from their heart" (Ps 15:2 NRSV).

The rules that regulate physical purity are often difficult for the modern person to appreciate. No one has yet provided a compelling explanation for why a sexual emission or contact with a menstruating woman or the carcass of an animal renders one impure. However different moral and physical impurity may appear to us, for the ancient Israelite they were inseparable. For the ancient Israelite, requirements to avoid physical impurities when possible, and when not, to undergo the proper rites of purgation, seemed as indelibly written into the order of the cosmos as were the Ten Commandments. Indeed, we could argue that for the Israelite religion they were just as important, for by attending to these physical requirements for purity one was forced to reflect on the high demands the Temple placed on human sanctity.

Although no explanation has been offered that makes sense of every purity law, the one common thread that does seem to follow through most of them is the notion of human mortality. Or to put it in just a slightly altered form, because the Temple is perceived to be a spot of perfection, "a place in which reality is perceived as whole, fresh and untarnished, where costs exacted by harshness of normal life are not paid,"[7] then it would follow that anything that pointed to mortal frailty would be forbidden within the inner sanctum of the Temple. As a result of such an understanding, it is only natural that those items alone that approximated such a status could gain access to its courts. Hence the concern that the bodies of the priests remain unblemished, that the animals offered on the altar be whole, and that those who have recently handled dead flesh undergo purificatory rites before entering the Temple courts. The purity laws, in effect, establish an important and essential split between the human and the divine realms that must be respected. Although God had provided access to the divine presence within the Temple, this presence was not to be presumed upon. By the act of maintaining these physical rules and boundaries, Israel was made to reflect on the high demands of access to God.

An essential by-product of any system of purity is the formation of a set of rituals designed to remove offending impurities. For the intrusion of impurity into the community need not be merely the result of human sin but could result from activities that God had commanded the Israelites to perform (e.g., preparation of a corpse for burial). For the mildest forms of impurity, all that was required was the passage of a set time; others could be removed by ablutions. The most serious forms required animal sacrifice. This sacrifice was called the חטאת (ḥaṭṭāʾt), or "sin-offering" (perhaps better rendered "purification offering" in the light of its function), and its most essential purpose was the removal of impurity from unintentional human sin (Leviticus 4–5). In Israelite thinking, the resulting impurity from unintentional human sin produced a miasmic substance that embedded itself within the sacred confines of the Temple itself. The resulting pollution was offensive to the holy and august God whose presence graced that building, and it had to be removed to assure God's continued availability. The sin offering furnished the means by which the offending impurity could be

7. J. Levenson, *Sinai and Zion* (San Francisco: Harper & Row, 1987) 127-28.

removed. This process may seem crudely mechanistic, but it is really nothing but a corollary to the theological idea that God resides in the Temple. If God can be *physically* present there—even if in a limited way, as through the mediation of the divine name—then it would follow that this holy-yet-real presence can be contaminated by the effects of human sin. To think otherwise would be to mock God's sanctity and the concomitant moral responsibility toward that sanctity.

Human sin poses a true physical danger to the presence of God. The impurity that results threatens this continued presence, hence a sacrificial system is put in place to allow for the containment and disposal of such impurities. The general laws that set forth how this sacrifice is to be applied take great care to emphasize that these sacrifices can only undo the effects of inadvertent sin (Lev 4:2; Num 15:30-31). How was the impurity of intentional sins dealt with? The priestly legislation of the Pentateuch seems to be of two minds. On the one hand, the annual scapegoating procedure of the Day of Atonement mentions conscious infractions פשע (*pĕšaʿ*, "conscious violations"; Lev 16:21) and, therefore, must have taken care of at least some of them. On the other hand, Num 15:30 asserts that any person who commits a sin in such a high-handed fashion will be "cut off" from the community. This irregularity in the priestly system is quite significant, for it subtly discloses the nonmechanical nature of the atoning practice in its complete application. Although the priestly system has made arrangements for all inadvertent sins, and probably many conscious ones as well, one must be wary of presuming that God will forgive *all* human sin. For the individual or community who sins in a truly brazen fashion, the stakes are high. Such high-handed acts of arrogance are very dangerous and *could* place the person or community (temporarily) outside the realm of forgiveness. It is not an accident that the priestly writer of Num 15:30-31 dispenses with cultic idiom and slips into the rhetoric of prophetic speech: "The person who intentionally sins . . . he is a blasphemer . . . he has despised the word of the Lord and broken his commandment." The force of such language suggests that willful, conscious violation of God's covenant, though having a place in the rites of the Day of Atonement, could just as easily result in placing the individual outside the power of the sacrificial system of atonement. In so doing, the priestly code protects the freedom of God to reject the Temple and so abandon the people.

Prophetic Attitude to the Cult. Most often in the Bible such acts of abandonment or, in biblical terms, "hiding the face," were short lived and rectified by public displays of penance. Thus the unlawful appropriation of sacred property in a moment of battle resulted in the absence of the deity in the next military exchange (see Joshua 7) and served as the occasion for the community to come together in penance before their God. Repentance, more often than not, mollified the anger of the offended, righteous God. But much more serious was the cumulative effect of flagrant violations of these laws. Because the priestly system viewed the impurity as a miasmic substance that defiled not only the person in question but also the sacred shrine, over time the Temple could become sufficiently unclean so that the ability of the deity to reside there was called into question. Like clothes that were soiled for too long, no amount of cleansing could remove the indelible signs of pollution. The first case of such abandonment was the fall of the Northern Kingdom of Israel, recounted in 2 Kings 17 as the result of a persistent flagrant violation of the Lord's commands. But certainly the most catastrophic example was the fall of Jerusalem itself in 587. According to the prophet Ezekiel, the fall of Jerusalem was the result of God's choosing to abandon his city. For this prophet, the profanation of the sanctuary through the impious activities of the Judean elite (Ezekiel 8) necessitated the deity's departure (Ezekiel 10–11). The resulting impurity had grown so massive that normal procedures used to eliminate it lost their effectiveness. As a result, God is depicted as mounting the throne within the holy of holies and traveling upon it as though it were a chariot to a region outside the city. Once the deity has left the city, the inhabitants are left defenseless and the overthrow of the nation and destruction of the land are inevitable.

This tale of God's departure from the city would seem to call into question certain theological voices in the Bible that strongly proclaim the promise that God will *always* abide in Zion and that the city's safety is secure from any possible encroachment. Exactly this mode of thinking is found in Isaiah 7–8 when the prophet exhorts the Judean king Ahaz to rely on the security of Jerusalem as opposed to seeking its military safety through various international alignments of power (Isa 8:6-7). Isaiah's message (see also 29:1-8) would seem to be in absolute contradiction to the voice of Jeremiah (or Ezekiel, see above), who denounced those whose sole trust was in the Temple. Although there is some truth to this view, and one would commit a fundamental error in trying to achieve a complete harmonization of these variant perspectives, there is room for some clarification. Jeremiah's harsh words against the Temple were not a condemnation of the Zion theology *in toto,* but rather a pointed critique of those who would cling to only a part of it. As we noted above, the promise of God's presence in (and so his protection of) the city of Jerusalem is inextricably linked to the demands for purity and holiness. Jeremiah's generation was more interested in deriving benefits from the former than attending to the responsibilities of the latter; thus Jeremiah was forced to call into question God's fundamental obligation to stand by the city. Isaiah, on the other hand, faced a different problem. In his day, king Ahaz made an effort to gain political security by aligning himself militarily with the kings of Aramea and Assyria. This, to Isaiah's thinking, represented nothing less than an inability to trust in the power of God to protect his chosen city. Isaiah, trying to lead the Judean leadership toward such faith, embellishes his prophecy with the promises God has made to protect and cherish Zion. In other words, Isaiah and Jeremiah find themselves addressing a population that has neglected different aspects of the Zion myth; the generation of Isaiah ignored the promise of protection, whereas that of Jeremiah ignored the claims this protection made on personal holiness.

In many instances, the prophets are portrayed as critical voices in regard to the Temple. This has led certain scholars to presume that a fundamental rift existed between priestly and prophetic religion. No doubt there is some truth here. The fact that prophets were called to their profession and priests were chosen by virtue of genealogy would have instilled within them vastly different feelings of responsibility toward the fixed institutions of their culture. The tenuous claim to authority and permanence allowed for a far more critical spirit to emerge among certain prophets. But we must note that in actual practice the many prophets' means of sustenance depended on the favors of the royal house, hence their message was much more compliant with national self-interest than is often witnessed in the biblical prophets. The narrative about the opponents of Jeremiah (chap.

28) is a good example of this. The shapers of the canon, on the other hand, did not see these numerous compliant figures as true prophets. They saw fit to define the prophetic office as one that often had a quite critical message to deliver (see Deut 18:15-22).

We must also admit that in its final form, the priestly material has much prophetic spirit in it. The concepts of holiness and purity act as firm boundaries against any attempt to manipulate the presence of God for personal ends. God's presence was potentially dangerous, and the moral and physical demands for purity necessitated a strict moral vigilance on the part of the priests and people. What, then, was the prophetic role *vis-à-vis* the cult? The prophets' role was to oversee its covenantal foundation. The cultic availability of God was rooted in God's covenantal promise to abide with the people and the attendant responsibility to keep the commandments. If the covenantal rootage was compromised in a serious fashion, the prophet called the people and their leaders to account. In most instances this was in the form of an oracle of woe whose purpose was to foster repentance (see Hos 5:15–6:16). But in extreme cases, such as the fall of Jerusalem in 587 BCE, the very foundation on which the covenant rested appeared to crack. Prophets addressed this problem through the notion of divine abandonment. For Jeremiah, this meant that neither the repentance of the people nor prophetic intervention could be of any assistance. Ezekiel was more mythic in scope; in his writings, God physically mounts a storm chariot and departs the city, leaving it vulnerable to outside attack and devastation. Much of Second Temple religion is devoted to the void created by these prophetic judgments. These later writings attempt to provide assurance that the covenant has been refashioned and that God again has assumed residence within the chosen city.

BIBLIOGRAPHY

Coogan, M. *Stories from Ancient Canaan.* Philadelphia: Westminster/John Knox, 1978.

Cross, F. *Canaanite Myth and Hebrew Epic.* Cambridge: Harvard University Press, 1973.

Levenson, J. *Sinai and Zion.* San Francisco: Harper & Row, 1987.

Mendenhall, G. "Ancient Oriental and Biblical Law," *Biblical Archaeologist* 17 (1954) 26-46.

———. "Covenant Forms in Israelite Traditions," *Biblical Archaeologist* 17 (1954) 50-76.

Pope, M. *El in the Ugaritic Texts.* Leiden: Brill, 1955.

Smith, M. *The Early History of God.* San Francisco: Harper & Row, 1990.

Wellhausen, J. *Prolegomena to the History of Ancient Israel.* Gloucester: Peter Smith, 1973. First published in 1883.

INTRODUCTION TO EARLY JEWISH RELIGION

JOHN J. COLLINS

The transition from ancient Israel to early Judaism was brought about by the Babylonian exile. Except for an interlude of a century or so under the Hasmoneans (from the Maccabean revolt to the Roman intervention in 63 BCE), Israel would not enjoy political independence again until modern times. An increasing proportion of the Jewish people now lived outside the land of Israel. Judaism, named for the Persian province of Judah, would henceforth be defined by ethnic and religious considerations rather than national, political allegiance. While the land would always play a prominent part in Jewish aspirations, Judaism flourished in exile and came to be regarded as a distinctive form of worship and way of life rather than as a national religion.

Older handbooks often gave a uniform picture of what they called "normative Judaism," which relied heavily on the great rabbinic compendia of the Mishnah, Talmud, and midrashim.[1] Recent scholarship has recognized the importance of chronology. The earliest rabbinic collection, the Mishnah, dates from the end of the second century CE, and while all the rabbinic works contain older traditions, they cannot safely be used as independent witnesses for the period before 70 CE. Recent scholars also emphasize the diversity of Judaism in this period, to the point where Jacob Neusner insists on using the plural "Judaisms."[2] The truth lies somewhere between these extremes. Judaism had definite parameters, and we are seldom in doubt as to who was a Jew. Nonetheless, the diversity was undeniably greater than was envisaged in the older handbooks.

SYMBOLS OF UNITY

Unlike other religions, such as Christianity, Judaism has always acquired cohesion from its ethnic bond. The importance of this bond is dramatized in the book of Esther, a book notable in its Hebrew form for its lack of reference to God. When he becomes enraged against Mordecai, Haman seeks the destruction of all Jews. Esther is moved to intercede for her compatriots by Mordecai's warning: "Do not think that in the king's palace you will escape any more than all the other Jews" (4:13 NRSV). Ethnic solidarity is a pervasive factor in Jewish identity, but it is normally accompanied by religious considerations. The Greek translators of Esther took care to introduce prayers and explicit acknowledgment of God.

---

1. The classic example is George Foot Moore's *Judaism,* 3 vols. (Cambridge, Mass.: Harvard University Press, 1927).

2. See Neusner's preface to *Judaisms and Their Messiahs,* eds. J. Neusner, W. S. Green, and E. Frerichs (Cambridge: Cambridge University Press, 1987).

The most basic religious element in Judaism is, of course, the worship of the one God. The Jewish military colony at Elephantine in southern Egypt in the fifth century appears to have worshiped several deities, presumably through ignorance. Some wealthy Jews in the Hellenistic period acknowledged other gods through indifference or social assimilation. But these were exceptions. Judaism was distinguished throughout the Second Temple period by its rejection of idolatry. The problems to which this position gave rise in a Gentile setting are dramatized in the stories of the fiery furnace and the lions' den in the book of Daniel. In Egypt, Jews were accused of "atheism" because they did not worship the same gods as everyone else.[3] This was an issue for which Jews were willing to die. Those who succumbed to the worship of other gods were renegades.

Closely related to the worship of the one God was the distinctiveness of Jewish laws. Even in the book of Esther, Haman's charge against the Jews is that "their laws are different from those of every other people, and they do not keep the king's laws" (3:8 NRSV). To be sure, the laws admitted of different explanations and different levels of observance. Especially in the Hellenistic Diaspora, Jews were embarrassed by some of the purity laws and resorted to allegorical explanations. On the whole, however, Jews were distinguished by stricter attitudes than their neighbors on such matters as abortion and homosexuality. Adherence to the law, in some form, would seem to be essential to Jewish identity in antiquity.

Finally, the Jerusalem Temple served as a unifying symbol and spiritual center of Judaism. All Jews were expected to contribute to its upkeep by the temple tax, at least in the Roman period, and to visit it on pilgrimage if they could afford to do so. Its significance can be seen most clearly at those moments when it was endangered. The profanation of the Temple by the Syrian king Antiochus Epiphanes sparked the Maccabean revolt. In the first century, Jewish multitudes showed themselves willing to face death rather than permit profanation of the Temple by a statue of Caligula.[4] Philo of Alexandria, who was best known for his allegorical interpretation of Jewish law, referred to the Temple as "that most notable and illustrious shrine whose beams like the sun's reach everywhere, beheld with awe both by east and west."[5] The destruction of the Temple by the Romans marked the end of an era and was the cause of long-standing grief. Some groups, such as the Dead Sea sect, were at variance with the current temple cult. The Damascus Document admonishes the members of the new covenant "not to enter the Temple to light His altar in vain" (CD 6:12), but even here the Temple remains an important point of reference, and the issue is proper temple practice, not the importance of the Temple as such. The high priesthood, of course, was closely linked to the Temple, and for much of the Second Temple period (down to the time of the Maccabees) the high priest was the undisputed leader of Judaism. Thereafter, however, the high priesthood had a checkered history, and no longer commanded the near universal respect accorded to the Temple.[6]

THE LAW

Perhaps the most abiding stereotype of ancient Judaism is that it was a religion of the Law. Christian perceptions on this subject have been shaped to a great degree by the portrayal of the Pharisees in the Gospels as rigid observers of the letter of the Law. It is now recognized that this portrayal is polemical in nature and cannot be taken as an objective description.

There can be no doubt that the Law, as contained in the Pentateuch or Torah, occupied a central place in the religion of Judaism. The centrality of the Law was promoted already before the exile by the Deuteronomic reform in 621 BCE. The Deuteronomic law code, promulgated by King Josiah, forbade sacrificial worship outside of Jerusalem. Some Jews flouted this law in the post-exilic period. The Jewish military colony at Elephantine in southern Egypt had its own temple in the fifth century, and the fugitive High Priest Onias IV founded a temple at Leontopolis in Egypt in the second century BCE. These were unusual cases, however. The sacrificial cult outside of Jerusalem was replaced by the synagogue, where the emphasis was on the reading of the Law. This was the first part of the canon to attain authoritative status, and it provided a common point of reference across the various strands of Judaism.

The name of Ezra is often taken to be synonymous

---

3. Josephus *Against Apion* 65.
4. Josephus *Jewish War* 2.195-98; *Antiquities of the Jews* 18.269-72.

5. Philo of Alexandria *Embassy to Gaius,* 191.
6. There are a few exceptions in the Hellenistic Diaspora. The fourth Sibylline Oracle, written in the late first century CE, declares that God does not have a temple made of stone (*Sib. Or.* 4:8). Compare Isa 66:1-2 and Acts 7:48-49.

with the attitude to the Law in Second Temple Judaism. Ezra was "a scribe skilled in the Law of Moses" (Ezra 7:6 NRSV) who was authorized by King Artaxerxes of Persia "to make inquiries about Judah and Jerusalem according to the law of your God, which is in your hand" (7:14 NRSV). When he came to Jerusalem, he was outraged to find that many Jews had intermarried with the people of the land. He insisted that they divorce their non-Jewish wives, and send them away with their children (10:44). The impact of Ezra on the Judaism of his time is open to question, however. Nehemiah's sojourn in Jerusalem is most plausibly dated a mere thirteen years after Ezra's mission.[7] Yet he found Jerusalem still in ruins and beset by various social problems. Ben Sirach's Praise of the Fathers (Sir 44–50), written in the early second century BCE, mentions Nehemiah, but not Ezra. Although Ezra later came to be regarded as the father of Judaism, he apparently had not attained this status in Ben Sirach's time.

Ben Sirach himself gives us another perspective on the attitude to the Law. Ben Sirach was a scribe and teacher of wisdom. The wisdom tradition prior to his time was conspicuous for its lack of attention to specifically Israelite traditions. It was Sirach who first integrated Israelite history and law in a sapiential book. Moreover, he identifies wisdom with the law. A long passage in praise of wisdom concludes: "All this is the book of the covenant of the Most High God,/the law that Moses commanded us" (Sir 24:23 NRSV). Yet his use of the law is indirect. His book is made up of traditional wisdom sayings and admonitions. These are generally compatible with the Torah and often informed by it, but they base their authority on empirical observation and tradition, not on Mosaic revelation.

Ben Sirach was relatively conservative. Some of his contemporaries attempted to set aside the law of Moses and accommodate Judaism to the ways of the Gentiles. The so-called Hellenistic reform, which involved the introduction of a gymnasium into Jerusalem, is described in colorful detail in the books of Maccabees. This "reform" culminated in a struggle for control of the Jerusalem Temple, and eventually led to the violent intervention of the Syrian king, Antiochus Epiphanes. The Maccabees, who led the Jewish resistance, had as their rallying cry "zeal" for the law and the covenant. Yet the Maccabees were

no purists. When some Jews refused to defend themselves on the Sabbath, in strict observance of the law, and consequently were slaughtered, the Maccabees decided that survival took precedence over the sabbath rest (1 Macc 2:40-41). There was, then, a spectrum of ways in which the law might be observed. The variety of attitudes is also represented in the fictional literature of the period. The book of Esther depicts a heroine who risks her life for her people. While the book makes much of ethnic solidarity, it does not even ask whether a consort of the King of Persia could observe Jewish purity laws. In contrast, the book of Judith describes another heroine who risks her life for her people, but in this case she pointedly refuses Gentile food, and her custom of going out at night to bathe becomes the cover for her escape from the enemy camp.

SECTARIANISM

The interpretation of the law figures prominently in sectarian disputes of the Hellenistic and Roman periods. Our clearest examples of sectarianism come from the Dead Sea Scrolls. The so-called halakhic letter (4QMMT) is apparently written by a sectarian leader and addressed to an authoritative religious figure, probably the high priest in Jerusalem. It gives the reasons why the author and his group had "separated ourselves from the majority of the people." The issues are halakhic in character (that is, they are concerned with issues of legal observance). They concern the true calendar and various purity laws. The author challenges the addressee "that you should examine the book of Moses [and the words of the Pr]ophets and in Davi[d]" to see whether these things are so. The Damascus Document claimed that all Israel had gone astray with respect to "the hidden things," which were revealed to the sect. These involved the calendar ("His holy Sabbaths and His glorious feasts") and other halakhic matters ("the desires of his will which a man must do in order to live," CD 3:14-15). The Temple Scroll, a remarkable document in which God speaks to Moses in the first person, has similar concerns. The fact that these sectarians followed a different calendar from that followed in the Jerusalem Temple would obviously put them at variance with most Jews in their observance of the festivals.

The classic account of Jewish sectarianism is provided by Josephus, who gives a lengthy account in the *Jewish War* and a much shorter one in the

---

7. Nehemiah came to Jerusalem in 445 BCE. Ezra is usually dated to the seventh year of Artaxerxes I (458 BCE), but some scholars argue for a date under Artaxerxes II (398 BCE).

Antiquities.[8] Josephus distinguishes three "schools of philosophy": the Pharisees, the Sadducees, and the Essenes. The bulk of his account, however, is devoted to the Essenes, a fact that is all the more surprising since they are not even mentioned in the New Testament or the rabbinic sources. It is likely that Josephus drew on an account of the Essenes by Nicholas of Damascus. He portrays them as ascetics who shun marriage, despise wealth, and practice community of goods. He describes their common meals and their complex process of admission to the group, and notes their hierarchical structure. He attributes to them a belief in the immortality of the soul and a strong sense of determinism. He claims that they live in no one city, but settle in every town, and he acknowledges that one order of Essenes practices marriage. His account of the Pharisees is much more brief. They are considered the most accurate interpreters of the laws and are considered the leading sect. Like the Essenes, they believe in the immortality of the soul and have a sense of fate, but combine it with an affirmation of free will. The Sadducees, in contrast, deny any form of afterlife and insist on free will. They also hold no observance apart from the laws (apparently in contrast to the Pharisaic acceptance of the oral law).

The reliability and accuracy of Josephus's account is open to question. At least the characterization of the sects as philosophical schools is misleading. On Josephus's own account, the Pharisees first appear on the scene in the late second century BCE, in the time of John Hyrcanus, when they appear to be a political force.[9] By the first century CE, however, they no longer enjoy political prominence. In the New Testament they are primarily concerned with purity laws and ritual observance. These concerns are also typical of the *ḥabûrôt,* or associations, mentioned in a number of places in the rabbinic literature,[10] and which are often assumed to be Pharisaic. These ritualistic concerns need not necessarily indicate a withdrawal from the political sphere, but the Pharisees do not appear to have enjoyed political power in the last century of the Second Temple. Little can be said of the Sadducees except that they were a prominent and well-established group who often differed from the Pharisees on halakhic matters.

The Essenes, long considered the most obscure of the Jewish sects, have come into considerable prominence since the discovery of the Dead Sea Scrolls. The consensus of scholarship has favored the identification of the Dead Sea sect with the Essenes. This identification is based on a number of considerations. The Roman author Pliny the Elder mentions an Essene settlement on the west bank of the Dead Sea between Jericho and Engedi. The procedures of admission to the Essenes, as described by Josephus, are similar to those specified in the Qumran Community Rule. Other features of the Essenes that are paralleled in the Scrolls include some form of community property, common meals, estrangement (not necessarily total) from the Jerusalem Temple, and preoccupation with purity. Josephus's claim that they believed in the immortality of the soul is compatible with the scrolls.

The correspondences are certainly not complete. The Scrolls reveal a dualistic world, divided between light and darkness; the archangel Michael; and the satanic Belial. The elect were thought to enjoy fellowship with the heavenly host and anticipated the resolution of history in an eschatological battle. None of this appears in the Greek sources. Moreover Philo, Josephus, and Pliny all emphasize that the Essenes were celibate. Celibacy is never required in the Scrolls, and some documents legislate for marriage and families. This discrepancy is mitigated by two considerations: (1) The Community Rule makes no mention of marriage, and (2) Josephus allows that one order of Essenes did marry.[11] Most scholars have assumed that the dualism and eschatology of the sect were omitted in the Greek accounts because Hellenized readers would find them obscure or repellent. The sect described in the Scrolls is closer to the Essenes than to any of the other sects described by Josephus, but the identification should be held with some reservation.

Josephus also refers to a "fourth philosophy" that agreed with the Pharisees in everything except that it rejected Roman rule and insisted that God alone should be master.[12] In some scholarly literature there has been a tendency to group all resistance to Rome under the single heading of the "Zealots," which was the name of one faction at the time of the revolt against Rome in 66–70 CE. In fact, however, there were several different groups at various times in the first century. The rejection of Gentile sovereignty

8. Josephus, *War* 2.119-166; *Antiquities* 18.11-22.
9. Ibid., 13.288-98.
10. *m. Dem.* 2:2-3; *t. Dem.* 2:2–3:9.
11. Josephus *War* 2.160-61.
12. Josephus *Antiquities* 18.23.

was a principle that might be held by people who were of various persuasions in matters of halakha and doctrinal belief. It did not constitute a "philosophy" or a sect in itself, although it gave rise to various factions, especially at the time of the war.

The main impulse to sectarianism in Second Temple Judaism arose from the interpretation of the Law in matters of practical observance of purity and ritual. Judaism has always been concerned with orthopraxy (right practice) rather than orthodoxy (right belief). Beliefs, however, were also important. The literature of Judaism in the late Second Temple period suggests greater variety than is implied by Josephus's account of the sects. There were probably many more groupings, even though we lack direct evidence of their social formation.

APOCALYPTICISM

Perhaps the most striking new development in Judaism of the late Second Temple period was the rise of apocalypticism. The apocalyptic world view was marked by a strong interest in a heavenly world, peopled by angels and demons, and the expectation of a final judgment. It differed from earlier biblical religion most decisively in its affirmation that individuals are judged after death. Traditional biblical religion was this-worldly in focus. Salvation was long life in the land and was essentially communal. The apocalyptic belief in life beyond death opened the way to a new kind of spirituality, which inclined to asceticism and placed greater emphasis on the salvation of the individual. Jewish apocalypticism still had a strong communal character and was far from individualistic, but it marked a shift in a direction that would be taken much farther in Christianity.

Belief in life, and judgment, after death entered Judaism in the context of apocalypticism, but spread rapidly. It was shared by the Essenes and the Pharisees, but not by the Sadducees. In the Hellenistic Diaspora, it was influenced by the Platonic idea of the immortality of the soul. Biblical scholars have often contrasted this Greek notion of immortality with the Jewish belief in the resurrection of the body. In fact, however, Jewish belief had many forms. The early apocalypses of Daniel and Enoch expected that the righteous dead would shine like the stars, or become companions to the angelic host. The Dead Sea Scrolls also seem to envisage some kind of spiritual afterlife. In the first century CE, Paul of Tarsus envisaged resurrection in terms of a spiritual body (1 Cor 15:44), a notion that corresponds neither to the immortality of the soul nor to corporeal resurrection. Expectation of physical resurrection became more common in the first century CE, but it is not possible to speak of a normative Jewish view on the subject in this era.

The earliest apocalypses appear in the Hellenistic period and are attributed to Enoch and Daniel. Pseudepigraphy, the attribution of works to fictitious authors, is a standard feature of this kind of writing, and was also popular in other genres in that era. Presumably it enhanced the authority of the works in question, but we can only guess as to how the real authors understood the validity of the practice. The books of Enoch and Daniel represent two strands in Jewish apocalypticism. Enoch was allegedly taken up to heaven on a cloud, and there he was shown the mysteries of the universe. These included the preparations for the final judgment. The primary emphasis in the Enoch tradition is on mysticism, exemplified by Enoch's tour of the heavens and the ends of the earth, and his vision of the divine throne. At the time of the Maccabean revolt, some apocalypses with a more historical focus were also attributed to Enoch. These described the course of history and its culmination in a great crisis and judgment.

This "historical" kind of apocalypse, however, found its classic expression in the book of Daniel. The visions of Daniel (chaps. 7–12) were written at the time of the Maccabean revolt.[13] Like those of Enoch, they are pseudepigraphic, and their author is supposed to have lived at a much earlier time. Daniel's visions take the form of historical allegories. Four beasts from the sea symbolize four kingdoms, which are judged and condemned by God, while "the kingdom," or universal sovereignty, is given to "one like a son of man" and the people of the holy ones (chap. 7). Antiochus Epiphanes, the persecutor of the Jews, is represented as "the little horn" on the fourth beast. In another revelation, Daniel is told that at the time of the end the archangel Michael will arise in victory and that those who sleep in the dust will awaken, some for glory and some for

13. The majority of biblical scholars agree that the book of Daniel was written, or at least reached its final form, in the second century BCE. But in any case, see Peter Craigie's caution against elevating disagreements about the book's dating to a major theological issue. *The Old Testament: Its Background, Growth, and Content* (Nashville: Abingdon, 1986) 245-47.

shame. This is the only clear reference to the resurrection of individuals in the Hebrew Bible.[14]

The book of Daniel is much closer than the book of Enoch to the language and imagery of the prophets. Perhaps for this reason it was also more widely accepted and cited as authoritative Scripture. Both Daniel and Enoch were treasured by the Dead Sea sect. The beliefs attested in the Scrolls differ somewhat from those of the early apocalypses, but the sect can also be described as an apocalyptic movement. The Community Rule contains a treatise on the Two Spirits of Light and Darkness, and describes how they struggle for dominion over humanity until the final age. Another document, the War Scroll, describes the final battle between the Sons of Light, led by Michael, and the Sons of Darkness, led by Belial. The sectarians evidently believed that they were living in the final era. The Scrolls contain commentaries on the prophetic books, which were written on the assumption that the meaning of the prophecies had been hidden but was now revealed to them through their Teacher. They also contain hymns that express the belief that the sectarians were already rescued from death and were mingling with the angelic host.

Yet another strand of apocalypticism emerges at the end of the first century, after the destruction of the Jerusalem Temple by the Romans. This strand is represented by 4 Ezra and 2 Baruch, and is often associated with the Pharisees because of its interest in the Law. These books lament the catastrophe that had befallen Judaism and look for a glorious restoration in a world to come.

MESSIANISM

One of the distinguishing features of apocalyptic literature is the role of intermediate figures. God seldom speaks directly to the visionaries. The revelations are usually mediated by angels. Also in the eschatological drama, there are savior figures who act for God in the deliverance of the people. In the book of Daniel, the archangel Michael plays this role (12:1), and he is probably the enigmatic "one like a son of man" who appears in Daniel's vision in chapter 7. Michael also plays a key role in the Qumran War Scroll, and his prominence in Judaism

is reflected in the book of Revelation, where it is he who casts Satan from heaven (Rev 12:7).

The early apocalypses (Daniel, Enoch) make no mention of human messianic figures. (In Daniel 9, the word *messiah,* "anointed one," is used with reference to high priests.) In the Dead Sea Scrolls, however, we find an expectation of two messianic figures. One is the "messiah of Israel," who is also called "the shoot of David" and the "Prince of the Community." The other is the "messiah of Aaron," or the eschatological high priest. (The Community Rule also speaks of an eschatological prophet, who is expected in conjunction with them.) In the sectarian rule books, the Community Rule and the Damascus Document, these messianic figures are only mentioned, with no indication of the roles they will play. The emphasis here seems to be on the restoration of the Jewish community to an ideal state, under the leadership of a Davidic king and Aaronic high priest. Some of the fragmentary scrolls are more eloquent in their descriptions of the messianic figures. Especially noteworthy for the New Testament (NT) is a scroll that anticipates a figure who will be called Son of God and Son of the Most High.[15] While the word *messiah* is not used, the most probable referent is the Davidic messiah.

The "Son of God" text from Qumran has many allusions to the book of Daniel, and the "Son of God" may represent an interpretation of Daniel's "one like a son of man." This figure played an important part in Jewish expectations around the turn of the era. In one apocalypse, the *Similitudes of Enoch,* Enoch sees "one who had the appearance of a man," in the company of an aged divine figure. This "son of man," as he is subsequently called, is enthroned as the eschatological judge. He is also called messiah, but he is not of human origin as he was "named" before the creation of the world. Another apocalypse at the end of the first century CE, 4 Ezra, explicitly reinterprets Daniel's fourth kingdom as Rome. It goes on to describe a vision of a human figure rising from the sea on clouds. This figure is clearly inspired by Daniel's vision. Here he is called messiah and God's son, and he destroys the wicked with a fiery breath, in the manner of the Davidic messiah (Isa 11:4).

Interpretation of older Scriptures played an important part in the formation of messianic ideas, and of eschatological ideas in general. The prophet Jere-

14. Some scholars find an earlier reference in Isa 26:19, but that passage probably refers to the metaphorical resurrection of the Jewish people, in a manner similar to Ezekiel's famous vision of the valley full of dry bones.

15. 4Q246.

miah had predicted that Jerusalem would be desolate for 70 years (Jer 25:11; 29:10). Daniel (chap. 9) reinterpreted this to mean 70 weeks of years, or 490 years. Attempts to calculate this period figured prominently in both Jewish and Christian eschatology down to the Middle Ages.

Messianism was not an academic exercise, however. It arose directly from a sense of frustration with the present. One of the earliest witnesses to messianic expectation in the Hellenistic-Roman period is found in the *Psalms of Solomon.* These were written in reaction to the violation of the Temple in 63 BCE by the Roman general Pompey, who insisted on entering the Holy of Holies. The *Psalm of Solomon* 17 asks God to "raise up unto them their king, the son of David . . . that he may reign over Israel thy servant," and predicts that he will rebuke sinners.

Throughout the first century a series of messianic pretenders attracted some following, but ended in failure.[16] Each of the Jewish revolts against Rome, in the late first and early second centuries CE, was accompanied by a messianic movement. The revolt of 66–70 CE involved two royal claimants, first Menahem,[17] and later Simon bar Giora, who was paraded through Rome and executed as the Jewish leader at the end of the war.[18] The great Diaspora revolt of 115–119 CE was led by a messianic pretender named Andreas or Lukuas. The leader of the last great revolt in 132 CE, Simon bar Kochba, was, according to legend, hailed as messiah even by Rabbi Akiba. The response of another rabbi on that occasion captures the disillusionment with messianic expectations that set in after the failure of the revolts: "Rabbi Yohanan b. Torta answered him: 'Akiba, grass will grow out of your cheek-bones and the Son of David will still not have come.' "[19]

It is not clear what relation there was between these popular messianic movements and the more learned speculations of the apocalypses, but it is reasonable to suppose that there was some relationship. Josephus claims that one of the factors responsible for the Jewish revolt against Rome in 66 CE was "an ambiguous oracle, likewise found in their sacred scriptures, to the effect that at that time one from their country would become ruler of the world."[20]

16. These are reported by Josephus *Antiquities* 17.271-85. He places the first instances shortly after the death of Herod, about the turn of the era.
17. Josephus *War* 2.422.42.
18. Ibid., 7.153-55.
19. *j. Ta'an* 4.8 (68d, 48-51).
20. Josephus *War* 6.312.

In this area, distinctions between religious and social history, or between biblical interpretation and political action, can be difficult to maintain.

DIASPORA JUDAISM

Jewish life in the Diaspora was somewhat different from the situation in Israel. We are especially well informed about the Jewish community in Alexandria, which was unusually large and prosperous. At an early point (third century BCE) the Torah was translated into Greek to meet the needs of this community. The books of the Prophets and Writings were translated in the third and second centuries. The translation (known as the Septuagint, or seventy, because of a legend that it was translated by seventy scribes) was rather literal. It differs sharply from the Hebrew in some books, such as Job and Jeremiah. In some cases, however, a Hebrew text corresponding to the Greek has now been found in the Dead Sea Scrolls. Jeremiah is a notable example. The Greek translators tried to render the Hebrew that was before them as accurately as possible.

Nonetheless, translation inevitably involved some transformation of meaning. The most famous example is found in Exod 3:14, where God responds to Moses' question about God's name with the enigmatic sentence "I AM WHO I AM" (NRSV). In the Greek, this was rendered as "I am the one who is," a formulation that suggested that the God of Israel was equivalent to the Greek notion of Being. This misleading translation became a proof text for philosophical theology in the Church Fathers.

The Hellenistic Diaspora was distinguished by its attempt to express the Jewish faith in Greek cultural forms. This attempt was expressed in various ways. Jews wrote oracles in the name of the pagan Sibyl, who supposedly extolled the virtues of Judaism and its God. (Use of the Sibylline form was later continued by Christianity.) A writer named Ezekiel recast the story of the Exodus in the form of a Greek tragedy. The most influential aspect of this enterprise, however, was the Jewish appropriation of Greek philosophy. This is attested already in the second-century work of Aristobulus and is reflected to some degree in the Wisdom of Solomon. It reached its climax in the work of Philo of Alexandria in the time of Christ. Philo's voluminous writings were mainly taken up with an allegorical interpretation of the Jewish law, in terms of Greek philosophy. One of the noteworthy aspects of his philosophy was the role he assigned to the Logos, or Word. The Logos was a concept of Stoic philosophy, for the rational spirit that pervades the universe. Philo combines this concept with the Jewish concept of Wisdom, and also speaks of the Logos as an angel and as the firstborn son of God. The assumption that undergirds his work is that the truth is one and that Plato and Moses must ultimately be saying the same thing.

Some scholars have assumed that the attempt to express Judaism in Greek cultural forms was an attempt to win Gentile converts. It is more likely that it was an attempt to satisfy the Jews themselves, who were profoundly Hellenized by their surroundings and education. We do not know whether Jewish writings had any impact on the Greeks. They leave very few traces in Greek literature. We know from various sources, however, that many Gentiles were attracted to Judaism. Josephus says that the Jews of Antioch "were constantly attracting to their religious ceremonies multitudes of Greeks, and these they had in some measure incorporated with themselves."[21] He also claims that Jewish customs, such as Sabbath observance, had also spread to the Gentiles; this is confirmed, reluctantly, by Roman authors, notably Juvenal in his 14th Satire. Some scholars have inferred from this evidence that there was a whole class of righteous Gentiles (called "God-fearers" in the Acts of the Apostles) who observed much of the Jewish law but stopped short of circumcision. In fact, however, Gentiles related to Judaism on various levels. Several inscriptions recognize Gentiles as *theosebēs,* or pious, but they seldom specify what their piety involved. In some cases it may have involved observance of Jewish laws; in others it may merely connote benefactors of the synagogue.

Needless to say, the Gentile reaction to Judaism was not uniformly positive. In the Roman era the community in Alexandria became embroiled in a dispute over its legal standing. It is unclear whether the Jews aspired to Roman citizenship, which would normally have involved recognition of Roman gods. At the least they demanded a status equal to that of citizens, distinct from the despised Egyptian natives. After a lengthy dispute, the Emperor Claudius issued a decree that reaffirmed certain rights and privileges, but firmly excluded the Jews from citizenship and denied them any special status. Alexandrian Greeks, who themselves were subject to the Romans, vented some of their frustrations on the Jews, who were perceived as an alien body. There were pogroms in Alexandria in 38 CE and again in 66. Relations deteriorated further in the wake of the Jewish War of 66–70 CE. The Jewish community in Alexandria was almost wiped out in the crushing of the Diaspora revolt of 115–118 CE.

CONCLUSION

The Jewish community in the land of Israel also suffered widespread destruction in the late first and early second centuries CE in the catastrophic revolts against Rome. Judaism survived, in large part because of the work of the Rabbis who codified the laws and collected the midrashic traditions. (There were also many Jewish communities, from Babylon to Rome, that suffered no destruction.) Rabbinic Judaism developed its own forms of expression and its own spirituality, but there is no doubt that much of the rich variety of Second Temple Judaism was lost or obscured after the revolts. There was no Jewish successor to Philo until the Middle Ages. Many of the apocalyptic writings were lost. Some were transmitted in translation in Christian churches, and some have only recently come to light in the Dead Sea Scrolls. Rabbinic Judaism, however, was not the only heir to Second Temple Judaism. Christianity grew from the same root, although it too neglected some aspects of the tradition (especially the halakhic ones) and developed its own new forms in the Hellenistic world.

BIBLIOGRAPHY

Detailed surveys of ancient Judaism can be found in:

Safrai, S., M. Stern, et al. *The Jewish People in the First Century.* 2 vols. Compendia Rerum Iudaicarum ad Novum Testamentum. Philadelphia: Fortress, 1974–76.

Schuerer, E. *The History of the Jewish People in the Age of Jesus Christ.* 3 vols. Revised and edited by G. Vermes, M. Black, et al. Edinburgh: T & T Clark, 1973–87.

Stone, M. E., ed. *Jewish Writings of the Second Temple Period.* Compendia Rerum Iudaicarum ad Novum Testamentum. Philadelphia: Fortress, 1984.

A more popular treatment can be found in:

Murphy, F. J. *The Religious World of Jesus: An Introduction to Second Temple Palestinian Judaism.* Nashville: Abingdon, 1991.

On the topics treated in this article, see further:

Collins, J. J. *The Apocalyptic Imagination.* New York: Crossroad, 1984.

———. *Between Athens and Jerusalem: Jewish Identity in the Hellenistic Diaspora.* New York: Crossroad, 1983.

Horsley, R. A., and J. S. Hanson. *Bandits, Prophets, and Messiahs.* Minneapolis: Winston, 1985.

Saldarini, A. J. *Pharisees, Scribes and Sadducees in Palestinian Society.* Wilmington: Glazier, 1988.

Sanders, E. P. *Judaism, Practice and Belief 63 BCE–66 CE.* Philadelphia: Trinity, 1992.

21. Ibid., 7.45.

ANCIENT TEXTS AND VERSIONS OF THE OLD TESTAMENT

JUDITH E. SANDERSON

THE IMPORTANCE OF ANCIENT TEXTS AND VERSIONS

The Old Testament (OT) was written primarily in the Hebrew language, with several chapters of Ezra and Daniel in Aramaic,[1] and the deuterocanonical books either composed or at least chiefly transmitted in Greek.[2] Although the Aramaic sections of Ezra and Daniel are in a different (but very closely related) language, they share a common history with the rest of the Hebrew Bible (HB) and henceforth will not be mentioned specifically. For a discussion of the history behind and reasons for the inclusion or exclusion of individual works in the Bibles of various faith communities, see the article "Introduction to the Canon." The present article concerns the contents and wording of a biblical book, apart from the issue of its canonical status.

The basic text from which English versions of the HB are translated is called the Masoretic Text (MT), with the deuterocanonical books being translated chiefly from the Greek Septuagint (LXX). Yet there are many other—and more ancient—sources that

provide evidence for the contents and wording of biblical books, both in Hebrew ("texts") and in languages into which ancient Jews and Christians translated their Bibles ("versions"): Aramaic, Syriac, Greek, Latin, Coptic, Ethiopic, and others.

Perhaps the chief contribution of these ancient sources is in teaching us more about the history of the biblical text after it had reached substantially the form in which we now know it and until the invention of printing revolutionized methods of preserving the Bible. On the one hand, these ancient documents attest to the remarkable stability of the biblical text. Due to the careful work of numerous scribes over two millennia, the words of our Bibles are translated from texts very much like the scrolls that Jesus and his followers found in their synagogues. On the other hand, the documents give evidence of a remarkable degree of variation. Precisely as Christianity was emerging, biblical manuscripts (MSS) exhibited a diversity—in relatively minor features—that has surprised many in the twentieth century. Finally, a comparison of all witnesses reveals much about the new period of standardization that had already begun during the earliest days of Christianity. In the light of that earlier diversity, why does the OT exist today in only three main forms: MT, LXX, and Samaritan Pentateuch? How much like the ancient texts are the forms we have today? Who is responsible for their transmis-

---

1. Ezra 4:8; 6:18; 7:12-26; Dan 2:4; 7:28; see also Gen 31:47 and Jer 10:11.

2. The deuterocanonical writings are those accepted in the Roman Catholic and Orthodox canons but not in the Jewish and Protestant canons. They include both complete works, such as Sirach, and additions to books, such as the Additions to Daniel. Protestants customarily refer to these writings as apocryphal texts.

sion and their development? As will become clear, each biblical book developed and was transmitted separately, and each must be studied on its own.

Also of great significance is the contribution these witnesses make to the translation and exegesis of each individual passage within the Bible. They offer a variety of readings to those searching for the text that is to be translated and interpreted. Comparing all the ancient witnesses to a given passage can help in determining which differences are due to mistakes in copying, which to a greater degree of freedom among scribes (many of whom considered themselves more than merely copyists), and which to a lesser degree of concern to prevent variations. In a typical brief paragraph of biblical text, one can detect the following illustrative sorts of alterations: A tired scribe misread a ד *(dalet)* as an ר *(rēš)* because these two Hebrew characters are so similar and transposed two other letters; a preoccupied scribe accidentally omitted a sentence, a scribe who liked precision added a proper name to make the subject of a sentence explicit and also added a clarifying prepositional phrase, while a scribe who preferred simplicity took the liberty of substituting a more common expression for a less familiar one. Furthermore, sources exist for many passages—and for several entire books—that present much greater differences; a few examples will be mentioned below.

Sometimes this variety among witnesses can be bewildering, even to the extent of raising questions about the definition of "the biblical text." Was there ever one original copy (*Urtext*) of the finished biblical book from which all other copies derived, or does the fluidity of content and wording exhibited in the first century BCE reflect fluidity that goes back to the origins of the biblical writings? Should the MT continue to serve as the basic text to be translated, supplemented by other texts and versions only when it is problematic? Or should all witnesses be appreciated on their own, not as supplements but as valuable witnesses to the biblical text even when the MT makes good sense?

ANCIENT HEBREW TEXTS

The ancient texts are of special value because they are written in the same language in which the Bible was written and, therefore, provide direct evidence of the state of the biblical text in the early centuries, as opposed to the indirect evidence provided by the

ancient translations into other languages. This fact can be misleading, however; while they are in the original language, they do not necessarily preserve the original wording. The fact that a MS is written in Hebrew does not guarantee that it preserves a better or more original reading than does a MS in Greek translation.

In any discussion of texts and versions it is important to distinguish the age of the oldest MSS of each developed witness and the age of the emergence of the tradition behind those MSS. So many truly ancient documents have been entirely or partially lost that in the case of each tradition only relatively late representatives are extant in complete form. Thus the most ancient texts are forerunners, and usually fragmentary ones at that. They represent an earlier stage of the long process of development behind the final forms of the Bible known today, and they represent that earlier stage only in a partial way. The Dead Sea Scrolls (DSS)—the oldest biblical witnesses known today—include the first such fragmentary forerunners.[3]

Dead Sea Scrolls. Fragments from more than two hundred biblical MSS have been found since 1947 in the Judean desert close to the Dead Sea, chiefly in caves near Wadi Qumran, as well as in caves in two other river valleys, Wadi Murabba'at and Nahal Hever, and in the fortress of Masada.[4] Eleven caves at Qumran have yielded more than 190 MSS of biblical books, with by far the largest number coming from Cave 4. Since the DSS were copied between 250 BCE and 135 CE, with the majority coming from the first century BCE and the first century CE, they show us what the various biblical books looked like toward the end of the Second Temple period and

3. The oldest portion of the Bible found so far is the priestly benediction in Num 6:24-26, inscribed on two tiny silver rolls in the seventh or sixth century BCE. They were discovered in 1979 in a grave just outside the walls of Jerusalem. A text containing the Ten Commandments and the *Shema* (Deut 6:4-5), copied in the second or first century BCE presumably for liturgical purposes, was discovered in Egypt in 1902 and was named the Nash papyrus. These are not biblical texts in the strict sense, however.

4. The term "Dead Sea Scrolls" is often used in a narrow sense to refer only to the MSS found at Qumran. Here it is used more broadly to refer to MSS found in several different sites in the Judean desert and dated between 250 BCE and 135 CE. On the other hand, the discussion focuses here on biblical MSS in the strict sense. Fragments from roughly six hundred other scrolls have also been found in the Judean Desert. Many of these MSS contain portions from the Bible (e.g., phylacteries and mezuzas), quote the Bible (e.g., biblical commentaries), or are composed of biblical paraphrases, all of which shed some light on the state of the biblical text but are, nonetheless, to be distinguished from biblical MSS in the strict sense. None of these nonbiblical MSS are described or included in the statistics here. Further, since a full assessment of the extant DSS is not possible until all have been published, this entire section must be understood as preliminary.

immediately thereafter—in the case of some books, only a century or two after they were written. Most of the MSS are in the Hebrew language, with a few in Aramaic and Greek. Every book of the Hebrew Bible except Esther and Nehemiah[5] is represented among the fragments, as well as the deuterocanonical books of Tobit (in Aramaic and Hebrew), Sirach (in Hebrew), and the Letter of Jeremiah (in Greek). Copies of the Psalms, Deuteronomy, Isaiah, Genesis, and Exodus far outnumber the other books. The majority of the Hebrew MSS were written in the so-called square or Aramaic script, much like the script in which Bibles are printed today, but at least twelve from the Torah and one of Job were in the so-called Paleo-Hebrew script, a successor of the ancient Canaanite alphabet used during the Israelite period. Some scribes used the square script for all but the names and titles of God, which appear in Paleo-Hebrew characters. The MSS have been named according to where they were found, the book(s) of the Bible they contain, the number of the copy of that book found in that location, as well as by unusual features, such as material (papyrus) or language (Greek). Thus 4QpaleoDeut[r], a scroll of the book of Deuteronomy was found in the fourth cave at Qumran, was written in the Palaeo-Hebrew script, and is preceded by 4QDeut[a-q]. 8HevXIIgr is a Greek translation of the twelve Minor Prophets found in cave 8 at Nahal Hever.

What did the Bible look like in the Judean desert?[6] There was not yet a sense of "the Bible" as one work such as is common today. There were no books in the modern sense of pages bound together in a single volume, but only individual scrolls, most of which seem to have contained only one book of the Bible. The twelve Minor Prophets, however, were treated as one book, and at least in the Torah some scrolls contained two consecutive books. Most of the scrolls are of leather, with a few made of papyrus. The leather skins were sewn together side by side to form scrolls of varying lengths (papyrus sheets were glued). Only one side was inscribed. Vertical lines were drawn by a sharp dry point to delineate the columns, with horizontal ruling for the lines of text. There was as yet no division by chapters and verses. Many scribes, however, were already showing divisions into paragraphs by leaving blank spaces. A few scribes wrote poetic passages stichometrically (i.e., arranged by poetic lines). All of the MSS have spaces between words, and a few have a dot between each word to ensure recognition of word divisions. Scribes relying on spaces sometimes squeezed their words so that some divisions are unclear.

Ancient Hebrew was written in consonants only (of which there are twenty-two), which meant that readers had to supply the vowel sounds. To demonstrate using English, *ths prctc ws lss dffclt thn t snds.* But it left room for multiple interpretations of some words and phrases. Hebrew vocabulary is built on the interplay of two factors: a fixed combination of consonants that gives the general field of meaning and a variety of patterns of pronunciation that narrow the sense. Thus the consonant combination *lmd* provides the general meaning "learn," while *lāmad* means "he learned"; *limdû,* the imperative "learn"; *limmad,* "he taught"; *limmud,* "accustomed to"; *talmîd,* "disciple"; and *talmûd,* "study"—to give only a few possibilities. Even in English, *sng* could be pronounced *sang, sing, song,* or *sung,* and *lvs* could mean *leaves, lives,* or *loves* (each as a verb or a noun), or *loaves* or *laves.*

By the time of the DSS, however, scribes were inserting so-called weak consonants, such as ה *h,* ו *w,* and י *y,* to show how some syllables should be pronounced. These "vowel letters" (*matres lectionis*) represent one of the first methods of biblical exegesis, since they narrowed the possibilities of pronunciation and meaning. Some DSS have very few such vowel letters and thus retain the earlier ambiguities, while others have a very large number of them, reflecting a great deal of interpretation on the part of a scribe.

The DSS are of paramount importance in biblical study first of all, because they are the oldest extant witnesses to the text of the Bible. All other Hebrew texts have reached us only by being copied and recopied throughout twelve or more centuries. The DSS, on the other hand, were produced after a much shorter period of copying—less than one century in the case of two MSS of Daniel, up to several centuries for the older books. After that they were frozen—or more aptly for the Dead Sea, baked—apart from human contact in hot, dry, forgotten, and almost inaccessible caves. We still lack entirely any textual evidence from those first centuries prior to the DSS, so that the early history of the finished biblical

---

5. Since all of the finds are so fragmentary and random, no conclusions can be drawn from the absence of Esther and Nehemiah. Nehemiah was probably included with Ezra as one book. Only one fragment was found of the 65 chapters of Chronicles.

6. The following discussion is limited to the Hebrew biblical scrolls.

text—let alone the history of its composition—remains without contemporary documentation and must be inferred from other evidence. But we now have a much clearer idea of what the biblical text looked like as Christianity was emerging, including a greater appreciation for the antiquity of many variations. Variant readings that before 1947 were known only from the Greek translation, for instance, have now been found in Hebrew texts, which has forced a reevaluation of the techniques used by ancient translators. It is now clear that in many cases what used to be considered paraphrastic and sometimes even tendentious for the sake of a theological point was simply a legitimate, careful translation of a different Hebrew text from that preserved in the MT. Second, the scrolls give us more insight into how scribes understood their task and how they carried it out. Some scribes, for example, brought a conservative attitude to their work, while others exhibited a much freer approach that allowed for additions and changes. The scrolls reveal the details of their work, including the physical data of the scrolls and the scribal writing habits such as those described above. Furthermore, they show how omissions, expansions, and changes occurred in the text, and how corrections were made. Third, simply by providing so many more examples of the text of a given book, each agreeing sometimes with one later witness against another and each with its own unique variations, they have broadened our understanding of how fluid—within narrow confines—the text was during that period. With the new evidence of the DSS we can now revise our understanding of the development of the biblical text and recognize the much greater diversity that existed in the last centuries of the Second Temple period. The significance of the DSS will become clearer below as a few examples of readings are mentioned in relation to the later texts and versions.

As significant as the DSS are, however, it is nonetheless true that almost all of them are fragmentary. While 4QIsa[a] is a major tourist attraction in Jerusalem because it is still a beautiful scroll containing all sixty-six chapters of Isaiah, the vast majority of the "scrolls" exist in tiny scraps that look like the remains of a jigsaw puzzle that has been mostly lost; even the surviving pieces are damaged and hard to read. While significant portions of forty-three columns (out of a presumed original fifty-seven) of 4QpaleoExod[m] are extant, only one piece remains of 4QExod[h], with five complete words and parts of eight more. These words come from a passage in which the other known Hebrew witnesses happen to agree with each other, and 4QExod[h] agrees precisely with them. If the fragment had come from just three verses later, where the other witnesses show significant disagreement, it would have told us whether it agreed with one of them or presented a unique reading hitherto unknown. Unfortunately, the testimony of 4QExod[h] is forever lost on that point. And it should always be remembered that a similar randomness characterizes the discovery of the DSS as a whole. We have access to ancient MSS found only from these centuries and only in the Judean desert, not from earlier or later periods and from nowhere else in Palestine, let alone in other major centers of ancient Judaism, such as Egypt and Babylon. Because it seems clear, however, that many of the scrolls were not copied at Qumran, there is good reason to take the Qumran evidence of textual diversity as typical at least of Palestine, if not of other Jewish communities, during the late Second Temple period. Also, in all specific instances where the DSS are silent, we are thrown back on the general lessons we have learned from them: The history of the text is much more complicated than was guessed before 1947. Moreover, in many passages there was a greater variety of possible readings than was handed down to us, such that witnesses other than the MT should be appreciated more as possibly offering preferable readings.

Moving on from the DSS entails leaving the ancient world behind and entering the Middle Ages, moving on to Hebrew MSS that are almost one thousand years younger. It also means leaving behind the age of diversity among biblical MSS, moving on to a new age of history when textual fluidity was no longer tolerated and only two basic forms of the entire Bible (three of the Torah) were preserved: the MT (preserved in Hebrew and in translations from the MT by Jews wherever their communities were located), the Septuagint (preserved in Greek and in translations from Greek by a variety of Christian communities scattered around the world), and the Samaritan Pentateuch (preserved in Hebrew by the very small but remarkably long-lived Samaritan community still today centered on Mount Gerizim near ancient Shechem in Palestine). Part of the success with which each community has preserved its own distinctive identity since ancient times is attributable to the fact that each has preserved its own distinctive canon and its own distinctive form of the text of that canon.

Masoretic Text. The Masoretic Text (MT) owes its name to the Masoretes, a group of scribes who transmitted and improved it between the sixth and eleventh centuries CE. Texts that reflect this tradition in the centuries before the Masoretes did their work are labeled proto-Masoretic. We possess evidence of that earlier tradition from four periods. The oldest evidence is provided by predecessors of the MT from the last three centuries BCE and the first two centuries CE: many of the scrolls found at Qumran and most of those from Masada, Wadi Murabba'at, and Naḥal Ḥever are proto-Masoretic. The very high degree of agreement among these MSS demonstrates that the consonantal text behind the MT (i.e., the consonants and vowel letters) was being treasured in a particular way, guarded, and copied with meticulous care since the first century CE or even before, presumably under the auspices of influential Jewish circles in Palestine. Witnesses from the second, still proto-Masoretic, period are biblical quotations in rabbinic literature and those translations into other languages which were based on proto-Masoretic texts. The third period is that of the almost fully developed MT, attested by MSS from the ninth century onward found in the 1890s in the *genizah* (a storage place for old MSS) of the Ben-Ezra synagogue in Old Cairo. The fourth period is that of the fully developed MT. The earliest extant MS, now called the Cairo Prophets, was copied in 895 CE, and contains twenty-one books. Two of the oldest MSS of the entire Hebrew Bible, now called the Aleppo Codex (severely damaged by fire in 1947, it is now in Jerusalem) and the Leningrad Codex (still intact), date from approximately 930 and from 1009, respectively, and represent the pinnacle of Masoretic achievement. All three are codices, or books in the modern sense, with pages inscribed on both sides and bound together. For liturgical use, Jewish communities have always used scrolls, and still do so today. More than 6,000 MSS of the MT still exist, and when proto-Masoretic MSS and MSS of versions translated from them are added, together they constitute the largest group of witnesses to the HB. The large quantity is naturally given the authoritative status of the MT for rabbinic Judaism.

The beauty of the MT is that it has been exceedingly carefully preserved, transmitted, and improved through the centuries by the Jewish community; it is the only (more or less) complete Bible written in Hebrew; it is easily accessible to non-Jews, printed in modern type, bound as one volume, and endowed with a complete guide to pronunciation, with punctuation, paragraph divisions, chapter and verse numbers, and even a partial list of variant readings. Some of the problems with the MT arise from those same characteristics. Its very existence in Hebrew; its completeness, accessibility, and legibility; and its traditional name, the "received text," can be a stumbling block, causing a reader to think that—or at least proceed as if—it is *the* HB rather than a witness to the HB, and further that the books it contains are uniform in the nature of their text. Its guide to pronunciation, punctuation, and sense divisions, while making it much easier to read and understand, can cause a reader to forget that those aids were created at a relatively late date and reflect the exegetical work of interpreters, rather than authors and editors, of the Bible.

Scholars do not yet know exactly how this particular collection of texts came to be especially treasured by the official Jewish community and ultimately to be considered their Bible. The inconsistent textual quality of the various books within the MT has given rise to a variety of explanations. It has been suggested that these were either prestigious texts stored in the Temple and meticulously analyzed, corrected, and transmitted by highly trained Temple scribes, or that they are simply the only texts that could be salvaged when Palestine was overrun and Jerusalem was destroyed in 70 CE. In either case, the textual quality of the collection is uneven. While the text of the Torah is very good, the text of Samuel is rather poor, having suffered many accidental omissions, large and small. One of the larger examples is the text that is now, belatedly, enumerated as 1 Sam 10:27*b*, which does not appear in the NIV or the RSV because it is not in the MT and formerly was known only from Josephus's account of Israelite history.[7] Fortunately, the text is included in the NRSV because it appears in 4QSam[a], which has been dated to the first century BCE.

Once the text for each book had been chosen—perhaps by default after the catastrophe of 70 CE—by the group that was to become the mainstream within Judaism, the work of preserving, transmitting, and

---

7. Josephus *Antiquities of the Jews* 6.68-71.

improving that text began in earnest. The task of preservation and transmission meant that scribes (the *Sopherim* of the early centuries CE) began taking great pains to ensure that no more changes—omissions or additions, however slight—would occur deliberately, and that amazingly few would occur accidentally. For instance, not even one more vowel was to be added for the sake of pronunciation. Counting the number of letters and words of each book, marking the middle letter of each book, and recording and marking a variety of linguistic features were some of the methods used to prevent further changes that, by then, would have been considered corruption of the text. The verb from which the name *Sopherim* comes means, appropriately, both to write and to count!

The other task—that of improving the text—was taken up especially by the Masoretes (scribes who owe their name to the Masorah, "tradition," they created) of the sixth through eleventh centuries. Leaving the consonantal text exactly as they received it from the *Sopherim,* the Masoretes in Babylon and Palestine developed various systems of adding "points"—various configurations of tiny lines and dots—above, below, and in the middle of the consonants to show exactly how each word should be pronounced.[8] One such vocalization system in Palestine, the Tiberian, which reached its most highly developed form in the eighth through the tenth centuries, eventually won out; it can be seen in any printed Hebrew Bible today. The Masoretes also added a complex system of accent signs that indicate the proper way to chant the text in the liturgy and, in effect, provide punctuation for each sentence. While specific punctuation that English readers might expect, such as quotation marks and question marks, do not appear, the entire Bible received the equivalent of paragraph and verse divisions, periods, and commas. (For the numbering of the verses [sixteenth century] and for chapter divisions [thirteenth century], we have Christian sources to thank; these were introduced first into the Vulgate [see below] and subsequently were transferred to copies of the MT.) All of these additions, while they constituted improvements for the reader, should be recognized for what they are: the result of interpretation that narrowed the possibilities of what the consonantal text could mean.

---

8. These vowel points and the other additions mentioned below were added only to codices for study, not to scrolls used in liturgy.

The Masorah is an apparatus, a collection of notes written—in Aramaic—in the margins of the biblical MSS and in companion volumes to preserve meticulous records regarding details of the text, especially peculiarities of spelling. Only one feature of the Masorah is described here, that most likely to be mentioned in Christian commentaries: the notation of קרא (*Qěrē'*) and כתיב (*Kětîb*). The Masoretes were very aware that, although their text was the authoritative one, there were other ways of pronouncing and, therefore, understanding the consonants of some words and phrases as well as other ways of writing the consonantal text. Other forms of the text apparently still existed, some in writing (whether in biblical MSS or in citations) and some in the oral tradition. While the tradition of how the MT was to be written (*Kětîb* or כ) could no longer be altered, the Masoretes wrote many of these variants in the margins, where they now appear with the instruction to read the word thus (*Qěrē'* or ק). The original purpose of these marginal notations is disputed today. Did the early Masoretes consider all of the Qere forms to be superior, or were they merely collecting interesting variants, the value of which could be debated? Regardless of their original intent, however, these variants became a part of the Masoretic tradition and are thus, unfortunately, often more acceptable to commentators today than other variants that did not find their way into the margins of the MT. In the most frequent case, the purpose is clear: to avoid what had come to be considered blasphemy. The "perpetual Qere" directs the scribe to write the divine name with the ancient consonants יהוה (*YHWH*) but directs the reader to read a euphemism, usually אדני (*'ǎdōnay,* "Lord"). Most English translations still obey this instruction, rendering *YHWH* as LORD to distinguish occurrences of the divine name from those where the word *Lord* was originally meant.

An example of a reading that has not been preserved in either the text or the margins of the MT and that, therefore, has not found its way into English Bibles or their marginal notes, though it is sometimes discussed in commentaries, occurs in Exod 1:15, where the MT refers to "the Hebrew midwives" but the LXX to "the midwives of the Hebrews." Did the ancient Israelite story honor Shiphrah and Puah as Hebrew women, like Moses' mother and sister in Exod 2:1-10, who saved their own people's babies, or as women of unspecified ethnic/national identity who saved Hebrew babies, perhaps Egyptian like Pharaoh's daughter in Exod 2:5-10? The consonants of the MT allow either interpretation, but its pointing has removed the ambiguity and made the women Hebrew. The LXX has preserved the ambiguity. English Bibles, following the MT, present the midwives as unambiguously Hebrew.

In summary, we have Jewish communities throughout the centuries, especially the *Sopherim* and Masoretes, to thank for what has become a major contribution to Christianity: a complete HB that can be easily read and, for the most part, easily understood, and that is very much like some biblical texts in existence in the first century BCE. It must be recognized, however, that this Bible is the end result of more than a thousand years of copying and exegetical work, that the *Sopherim* and Masoretes arrived on the scene rather late in the day, after many corruptions and changes had already entered the text, and that it represents one—often but not always the best—witness to the Bible.

Samaritan Pentateuch. The Samaritan Pentateuch (SP) owes its name to the community that has preserved it for at least two millennia, maintaining a distinctive identity. Insisting on the uniqueness of the old sacred site, Gerizim (near Shechem), the Samaritans reject both the sanctity of Jerusalem, sacred to Israelites only since David, and the Prophets and Writings of the Jewish canon, which focus so largely on Jerusalem. The oldest complete MSS of the SP date from the twelfth century.[9] While the Samaritans copy their Bibles in their own developed form of the Paleo-Hebrew script, printed editions in the square script have been produced by and for outsiders. This form of the SP shares with the MT the advantages of having been very carefully preserved, transmitted, and improved through the centuries by a religious community, of presenting a complete Hebrew text of the Torah bound as one volume with (Christian) chapter and verse numbers, and of being accessible.

The differences between the SP and the MT fall into several categories. Minor differences include

grammatical features of interest to historians of the Hebrew language as well as changes in the SP for the sake of clarification. More significant are several types of additions to the text ranging in length from a sentence to a lengthy paragraph. For example, additions created by repeating what was already in the immediate context include the eight cases in the plague narratives in Exodus, where YHWH's threats (see Exod 7:16-18) appear twice: (1) when YHWH tells Moses what to say, and (2) when Moses relays the message to the pharaoh. Additions from a remote parallel passage include frequent importations from Deuteronomy into the earlier books (e.g., the insertion of Deut 1:6-8 before Num 10:11).

Since the early seventeenth century, when Westerners discovered the SP, its history and its value for determining the preferable text have been much debated. The discovery of six DSS, especially the relatively well-preserved 4QpaleoExod[m] and 4QNum[b], which contain many of these significant additions and grammatical variations, as well as other variants previously known only from the SP, has shed light on both questions. It is now clear that the Samaritans adopted for their community a type of text that was current in Judaea in the first century BCE, and then slightly adapted it to their own unique tradition. Hence these six DSS are best labeled *pre*-Samaritan. The prefix is meant to show that they do not share with the SP the continuity that the *proto*-Masoretic MSS have with the MT. While these DSS share most of the distinguishing features of the SP, they betray absolutely no connection with the Samaritan community. Before distinguishing the pre-Samaritan and the Samaritan stages in the development of the SP, it may be helpful to look more broadly at an important aspect of scribal activity during the Second Temple period.

During the Second Temple period, scribes made a variety of additions to the text—creating an expansionist version—with various intents: to clarify, to explain, to harmonize parallel texts; to heighten the dramatic effect; and to emphasize a theological point. Virtually all of the oldest texts and versions exhibit the results of these activities, although the MT Torah has fewer such expansions. An example of a harmonizing addition that is preserved in only two extant biblical MSS occurs in the Ten Commandments, which are stated in almost identical terms in Exodus and Deuteronomy, except that two different motives are given for the Sabbath commandment. The motive from creation in

---

9. A total of about 150 MSS survive, beginning with a fragment apparently from the ninth century and coming up to the twentieth century. Indirect witnesses to the text of the SP are its translations into Greek (the *Samareitikon*), Aramaic (the paraphrastic Samaritan Targums), and Arabic, as well as quotations in early Samaritan inscriptions, liturgies, and commentaries.

Exod 20:11 has been brought in to supplement the motive from Israel's slavery in Egypt in Deut 5:14-15 (4QDeutⁿ), a first-century BCE Hebrew MS, and in Codex Vaticanus, a fourth-century CE Greek MS (see below). This particular harmonizing addition does not appear in the SP, where it might have been expected. An example of a harmonizing addition that found its way into the MT and SP, as well as more ancient witnesses, is Exod 32:9, the entire verse having been imported, with appropriate modification, from the parallel narrative in Deut 9:13.

Two expansions in the Sinai narrative (Exodus 20) will illustrate how the pre-Samaritan DSS and the SP are alike and how they are different, thus indicating which expansions are attributable to the spirit of the times and which to the socioreligious needs of the Samaritan community. Both 4QpaleoExodᵐ and the SP share a two-part expansion in Exod 20:19, 21, where an unknown scribe combined Deut 5:24-31 and 18:18-22 and imported the resulting passage to supplement the Exodus form of the Sinai narrative so that the second narration in Deuteronomy 5 and 18 (see Deut 18:16-17) would correspond to the first. The SP alone, on the other hand, has an expansion two verses earlier, following Exod 20:17, where a Samaritan scribe combined Deut 11:29-30 and 27:2-7 and imported the resulting passage to create a new Tenth Commandment, thereby giving greater prominence to already-existing commands to build an altar at Gerizim. When these two importations are compared, it is clear that the Samaritans took an already existing expansionist text (similar to the pre-Samaritan DSS) and created their own ideologically distinct Bible by following the same methods already being used elsewhere among Jews.

A comparison of the pre-Samaritan DSS and the SP shows several things. First, the number of significant features attributable to Samaritan scribes is small. Besides the importation of the Gerizim commandment, the main Samaritan activity was the deletion of one Hebrew letter in 21 verses in Deuteronomy (e.g., 12:5, 11, 14; also Exod 20:24) to alter "the place that YHWH will choose" to "the place that YHWH has chosen"—thus preserving the uniqueness of Gerizim. Second, these ideological changes may well have occurred about 100 BCE. Third, there is a high degree of agreement between scrolls that froze at least by 70 CE and a tradition that has continued to be copied until today. This new understanding of the SP as a remarkably faithful

rendering of texts from the Second Temple period calls for a new appreciation of Samaritan scribes and a new appraisal of the usefulness of the SP for determining preferable readings.

By comparing several ancient witnesses, it is easy to recognize the relatively few harmonizing and clarifying expansions in the pre-Samaritan DSS and the SP. When those are discounted, the SP agrees substantially with the text behind the MT and, at times, offers a reading that is preferable to that of the MT. Moreover, since it is unpointed—i.e., since it presents consonants only—it is a constant reminder on a large scale of how the Bible used to look before the Masoretes added vowel signs. The ambiguity of the identities of the above-mentioned midwives in Exod 1:15, for instance, is preserved. The SP has experienced some clearly recognizable and classifiable expansions that affect only certain parts of its text, but it has not undergone the interpretation that has been a necessary component of the other two most ancient complete witnesses: the pointing and punctuating of the MT and the translation activities that produced the LXX. The SP thus serves as a salutary reminder—on a large scale—of how the Bible appeared during the Second Temple period.

ANCIENT VERSIONS

Early translations that were made from a variety of Hebrew and Greek MSS challenge today's scholars to reconstruct those diverse sources as part of the twofold search for the history of the biblical text and for the best reading to be translated into modern languages. Some translations are important because they exist in complete MSS (in contrast to the fragmentary DSS, which are centuries older than extant complete MSS of the MT and the SP), and because they often represent an earlier form of the text than does either the MT or the SP. Yet, the antiquity of the versions must be balanced against the limitations inherent in any translation, since the Hebrew and Greek sources can be reconstructed only with probability. Hence the versions provide only indirect evidence to the text of the HB, though they are of great value in illuminating the history of biblical exegesis as well as of their various languages.

Septuagint. The Septuagint (LXX) owes its name to the delightful ancient tale of seventy-two Jewish elders (not seventy, but six from each of the twelve tribes) who translated the Torah into Greek at the behest of Ptolemy II Philadelphus of Alexandria. According to the most highly embellished form of the story, each pair of elders worked independently for seventy-two days, and upon bringing their translations together found all thirty-six to be identical! While the tale must sadly be relegated to the realm of legend, the time and place are generally considered to be historical; there was a complete Greek translation of the Torah by the third century BCE in Alexandria, a major center of Greek-speaking Jews. Over the next century or so, the rest of the HB was translated and the deuterocanonical works were variously composed in or translated into Greek. As a result, the name Septuagint soon expanded to include the entire Greek Bible.[10] Unfortunately, the name Septuagint kept on expanding to include a number of revisions and fresh translations over the centuries, with the result that it has become a quite slippery term that frequently requires clarification.

The LXX bears the distinction of deriving from Jewish origins but then becoming the Bible of the Christians. It thus reveals how the HB was understood by both Jews and Christians, and illuminates the thought of writers such as Philo, Josephus, Paul, and Luke, to mention only four. It is the oldest complete witness to the entire OT of the Roman Catholic and Orthodox communities, it remains today the liturgical Bible of many Orthodox Christians, it is easily accessible and beautifully printed, and it preserves a very good and faithful early translation of the Bible. One currently popular edition is bound in two volumes and is convenient to use. Other editions, however, give a better indication of the complexity of the Greek Bible; each book of the Bible fills an entire volume, and more of each page is devoted to notes offering variants than to the text itself. The history of the LXX is complicated, involving as it does Jewish and Christian activities, and a number of revisions (recensions) by persons with very different goals and methods.

Although the oldest complete MSS are no older than the fourth century CE, the preceding seven centuries saw an extremely complex set of developments, of which some are only recently

becoming clear, and many are still being investigated and debated. Further, what was the case for Hebrew texts is, if anything, more true for the books in their Greek manifestations: The nature of both the translation and the transmission of each biblical book (or section of a book) must be studied separately. A widely held view on these matters is reported here in simplified form. Not only does it represent a scholarly reconstruction of what can no longer be known certainly, but also almost every detail mentioned is subject to complicated qualification, if not outright dispute.

The oldest primary witnesses to the LXX are a few leather and papyrus fragments found at Qumran and papyrus fragments found in Egypt. These attest to the presence of texts presumably very much like the original translation, often called the Old Greek (OG), in Palestine as well as Egypt during the last two centuries BCE. The OG is of enormous value for biblical study because two facts taken together distinguish it from all other versions: It was translated (1) directly from Hebrew and (2) in the days before the proto-Masoretic tradition had become authoritative. Unfortunately, the OG was not allowed to remain in its original state for very long, as we shall see.

According to one theory, already in the last two centuries BCE, the OG was systematically revised to bring it into conformity with Hebrew MSS (not proto-Masoretic) that were by that time being preferred in certain Jewish circles to those from which the OG had been translated. Some scholars claim, on the basis of Hebrew MSS found at Qumran as well as various sorts of further evidence, that some or all of the revisional activity that has traditionally been attributed to Lucian, a Christian in Antioch around 300 CE, actually occurred centuries earlier. They have labeled this early revision "proto-" or "Ur-Lucianic" and have questioned the nature and extent of the contribution of the actual Lucian to the history of the Greek Bible.

Perhaps a greater number of scholars have accepted the first-century BCE Greek MS of the Minor Prophets found at Naḥal Ḥever (8ḤevXIIgr) as undeniable evidence of (further?) revisional work in Palestine that brought the Greek of all or most of the OT into conformity with Hebrew texts that were very similar to proto-Masoretic ones. This revision is variously designated *kaige* in honor of one of the Greek words used consistently and in a deliberately

---

10. The role of the LXX shifts when moving from the HB to the larger OT. While it constitutes a *version*—a translation—of the HB, it constitutes the *text* of those deuterocanonical books that were originally written in Greek (e.g., Wisdom). Further, it is the primary form in which others have been transmitted, since the Semitic originals were lost (e.g., Tobit and the Additions to Daniel).

non-idiomatic fashion to render a particular Hebrew expression; "proto-" or "Ur-Theodotion" because much of it was traditionally attributed to Theodotion, a Jewish proselyte who lived in Ephesus in the second century CE; and, perhaps most helpfully, "*kaige*-Theodotion." As was the case with "Lucian," the new understanding that much or all of the traditional "Theodotion's" work actually occurred centuries before his lifetime has called into question the nature and extent of the role of the historical Theodotion. In any case, the literal "Semitic Greek" ensures that readers today can, with a relatively high degree of accuracy, reconstruct the Hebrew wording of the MSS on which these revisions were based.

Early in the second century CE a Jewish proselyte named Aquila made a further revision of *kaige*-Theodotion. His aim was to bring it into line with the newly authoritative proto-Masoretic texts and to perfect the techniques of literal translating. His Greek even more consistently and unnaturally represents those features of Hebrew—such as word choice, word order, and grammatical phenomena—that cannot be reflected in idiomatic Greek. Based on MSS that had by now become the standard for the Jewish community, Aquila's revision became their accepted Greek Bible, while henceforth the LXX belonged solely to the Christians. Aquila's version has been preserved chiefly in fragmentary quotations and notes, except in Ecclesiastes, for which it appears as "the LXX." Later in the second or third century, Symmachus, whose identity and dates are disputed, produced a new translation using *kaige*-Theodotion and OG as well as Hebrew sources. The idiomatic Greek he produced is more valuable for the history of exegesis and was more appreciated by Jerome, but is less valuable for textual criticism than is Aquila's literal version. Like Aquila's, however, it survives today only in fragments.

Origen, a Christian scholar who lived in Caesarea in Palestine in the mid-third century CE, attempted to bring order out of the chaos of all these translations and revisions. His apparent aim was to provide Christians with an accurate understanding of the differences between the Jewish and Christian Bibles of that day, so that they could more effectively debate with Jews on their own terms. To accomplish this, Origen wrote in six parallel columns (hence the name *Hexapla*) the Hebrew consonantal text with which he was familiar, a transliteration of the Hebrew in Greek characters, Aquila, Symmachus, the traditional LXX, and what he called Theodotion. For those books where he had other witnesses at his disposal, he wrote up to seven or eight columns. He then proceeded to refine his fifth column, the LXX, in two ways: by enclosing in an obelus (÷) and metobelus (✕) those words present in the LXX but not in his Hebrew sources, and by inserting within an asterisk (※) and a metobelus a Greek translation (usually from his "Theodotion") for whatever he found in his Hebrew text that was lacking in his LXX. Unfortunately, Origen is thought to have revised the LXX much more than his three critical symbols would indicate. For instance, when the discrepancy between his Hebrew and Greek sources involved not length but choice of expression, he seems to have preferred the equivalent of the Hebrew. In other words, he seems to have fallen prey to the common notion that a text preserving the original *language* necessarily preserves the original *wording*. Thus in many places his fifth column was no longer the LXX but a Greek translation of proto-Masoretic Hebrew, amounting to a new revision of the LXX. To make matters worse, a work of such mammoth proportions was unlikely ever to be recopied as a whole, and thus it was preserved very poorly, with two deleterious results. For one thing, citations of his various columns were sometimes misnamed. Perhaps even more seriously, when his most popular column, the fifth, was copied or quoted the three symbols frequently were misplaced or omitted altogether, with the result that unsuspecting scribes began producing what are now called hexaplaric MSS, full of the supplements and changes that corresponded to proto-Masoretic texts of the third century CE rather than to the OG of the Second Temple period. Thus Origen's massive effort to bring order only complicated the situation further.

Even when textual critics have satisfied themselves that, on the basis of a careful comparison of all the variant readings in Greek, Hebrew, Latin, and other languages, they have arrived at the original translation, use of that OG nonetheless remains complicated. Each book must be studied and evaluated on its own, since numerous translators brought a variety of methods to the original translation of Hebrew MSS, which themselves reflected several stages of development and corruption. The OG of both Samuel and Jeremiah, for example, were translated from Hebrew MSS that predated the text preserved in the MT, but varied significantly from each other. The OG of Samuel is longer in many places than the MT, but frequently superior, since it preserves so many readings that were accidentally omitted in the MT. The OG of Jeremiah, on the other hand, is roughly one-seventh shorter than the MT, and the sequence of material differs in several places, since it was translated before many expansions were introduced. The fact that these differences derive from Hebrew MSS and are not attributable to the translator is now clear from two Hebrew scrolls, 4QJer[b,d]. Though only fragments still remain, they include enough text from characteristic passages to show that the scrolls agreed with the LXX in matters of both order and length. Also, each book must be studied individually to determine the techniques and aims of its translator. Those who have done so have found a wide range from literal and non-idiomatic (e.g., in Joshua and the Psalms) to relatively literal but idiomatic (e.g., in the Torah) to a freer, more paraphrastic style (e.g., in Isaiah and Job). These findings are of paramount importance in assessing the value of individual readings within each book.

The OG suffered long from the assumption that its translators contributed many exegetical and theological expansions and alterations. Whenever the OG differed from the MT the first guess was that the MT (thought of as "the Hebrew") was more likely to preserve the original and the OG to exhibit the results of the translator's tinkering (an attitude going back at least as far as Origen). The tinkering was assumed to reflect a desire to make the text clearer or more dramatic, perhaps, or even to bring it in line with the theological ideas of the translator. But the discovery of the DSS has demonstrated the existence in Hebrew texts of so many of the variant readings previously known only from translations that we now must be more cautious in attributing such activities to the translators. Frequently, it turns out, they were carefully and even literally translating a Hebrew text that was different from—and often earlier than—the MT. Because the DSS confirm the reliability of the OG, we now have more faith in it even where there is no confirmatory reading from the DSS. In general, the OG is the witness that presents the greatest degree of variation from the MT, and since many parts of it clearly reflect very early Hebrew sources that are forever lost, these OG readings are highly significant for the textual critic.

About 1,800 Greek MSS have been preserved in a variety of forms. The format may be either a scroll or a codex, and the material may be papyrus, leather, or parchment. Further, the script may be uncials (large, formal, separate block characters similar to capital letters) or minuscules (a smaller, cursive script used only since the ninth century CE). The oldest and best complete (or almost complete) MSS are parchment uncial codices. Codex Vaticanus from c. 350 is, in many books, the best single witness to the OG (though it should never be used alone!), and Codex Sinaiticus from the same century reflects for the most part a similar text. There are about 1,500 minuscule MSS, but since they date from the ninth century onward, they only occasionally offer a text superior to that of earlier witnesses. Secondary witnesses to the LXX occur as quotations found in ancient Christian commentaries and sermons as well as the ancient translations of the LXX, e.g., Old Latin (OL).

Other Versions. The other versions are much less significant than the OG for establishing the text that should be translated and interpreted today, since they were, by and large, translated or revised either from strictly proto-Masoretic texts or from texts that were already the result of translation, chiefly into Greek. In the first case they reflect only the proto-Masoretic tradition, for which we possess many witnesses in Hebrew. They very often agree with the MT against other more ancient witnesses, yet without actually adding any weight to the evidence in favor of the MT reading. In the second case, they can be called second-generation witnesses, since they often provide evidence of Greek MSS based on Hebrew sources written earlier than or at least different from the proto-Masoretic. However, that evidence is only indirect, requiring textual reconstruction. Since their contribution to the study of the history of exegesis and to the history of Jewish and Christian communities and their languages can be quite significant, it is important to know of their existence. But since their contribution to the text-critical enterprise is of much lesser value, only those most important for reconstructing the LXX will be described briefly.

Targums. During the course of the Second Temple period, as Jews in Palestine and to the east began speaking Hebrew less, they needed the Bible in Aramaic, first orally for synagogue liturgy then in writing for private study and for educating children. Although *targum* is simply the Hebrew word for "explanation" or "translation," it is used specifically for translations of the Bible into Aramaic. At least one Jewish targum exists for every book of the HB except Ezra, Nehemiah, and Daniel. Each targum—and each revision thereof—for a biblical book must be analyzed individually. The targums (or *targumim,* Hebrew plural) have not been treated like other ancient versions; no one book or even one comprehensive collection presents a targum for each part of the Bible. Some targums carefully and strictly follow their Hebrew sources, whereas others include extensive midrashic expansions (while often strictly following the Hebrew text in the unexpanded passages). When the targums provide literal translations, they can provide evidence on minor points of a passage discernible only in a Semitic language, since Aramaic is so similar to Hebrew (as Italian is to Spanish). However, a major disadvantage is that almost all of the targums were translated or revised from proto-Masoretic MSS. Thus many targums, especially those with expansions, reveal more of the history of Jewish biblical exegesis than of the history of the biblical text.

A few fragmentary targums have been found among the DSS (e.g., 11QtgJob, one of the few targums that reflect a source other than proto-Masoretic) and more in the Cairo Genizah, including some as early as the seventh century CE. Complete targums are known only from late MSS, which reflect a very long, and now much disputed, process of evolution. The two most authoritative targums for the rabbis were Targum Onqelos for the Torah and Targum Jonathan for the Former and Latter Prophets, which have been preserved in a number of MSS. They appear to have originated in Palestine in the first two centuries CE but then to have been revised thoroughly in talmudic Babylon to conform to the tradition behind the MT. Thus they lost many of their distinctive features, especially readings other than those reflecting the MT. For the Torah there are a variety of witnesses to the more paraphrastic Palestinian targum(s), each of which had its own complicated history: Pseudo-Jonathan, *Neofiti 1,* the Fragmentary Targum(s), the Toseftot, and the much older fragments from the Cairo Genizah. Similar complexity is present for the other biblical books.

Syriac Versions. Syriac, an eastern dialect of Aramaic, has been the language of many Christians since the emergence of that new religion. While Syriac long ago gave way to other languages as the vernacular, it is still the liturgical language of many Orthodox and Roman Catholic communities from Lebanon east to India, as well as of their emigrants to the Americas.

Scholars differ as to whether there was an early translation of the HB, called Old Syriac. If it ever existed, it has survived only in ancient quotations. In any case, since at least the fifth century the Peshitta has been the OT of the Syriac churches. While the oldest dated MSS were copied in 460 and 464, the oldest complete MS comes from the sixth or seventh century. Translators worked primarily from Hebrew MSS that were very close to what was to become the MT, but were also influenced by targums as well as the LXX. The quality of the Peshitta varies from book to book. Its name means "simple," and may refer to its being written in the vernacular or to its offering only one text, an idiomatic one, as opposed to the more complicated Syro-Hexapla. The latter is an early-seventh-century translation of the fifth column of Origen's Greek Hexapla, the LXX (see above). Since it was produced from very good sources and is one of the few witnesses preserving the critical symbols indicating discrepancies between Origen's LXX and his Hebrew sources, and since it renders the Greek so literally, the Syro-Hexapla is of great value to textual critics in reconstructing Origen's otherwise poorly preserved LXX.

Latin Versions. Prior to 400 CE, Latin translations were made from Greek rather than Hebrew, which means that they provide evidence of the history of the OG and its various revisions—i.e., second-generation evidence of early, non-Masoretic Hebrew sources. Much of this indirect evidence is significant, because many witnesses to OL (*Vetus Latina)* are older than extant Greek MSS, and because many OG readings have survived only in OL. A number of such OL translations and revisions were made. The first seven books of the Bible, all produced by the same translator, have been preserved in OL. Also, an OL form of several deuterocanonical books (e.g., Sirach) survived intact in the Vulgate, since Jerome refused to translate those books. Other sections have been retrieved piecemeal from a variety of quotations in early Christian commentaries and other works, from marginal glosses (e.g., in Vulgate MSS), as well as from MSS in widely varying conditions of preservation.

Jerome, in his earliest work, continued the Western Christian tradition of producing Latin translations from Greek, but finally, between 389 and 406 in Bethlehem, began working directly from Hebrew MSS preserved among Jews. In this effort, he was aided by Jewish scholars and exegetical writings, as well as by the LXX, Symmachus, and Aquila. Although his Hebrew MSS were proto-Masoretic, since he was translating into a non-Semitic language and receiving guidance from Jewish sources and from a variety of Greek MSS, his work suggests the state not only of the proto-Masoretic tradition but also of Jewish and Christian exegetical traditions in Palestine at that time. Jerome's translations formed the basis of what eventually came to be called the Vulgate, because it had become the "common" or standard Latin Bible, gradually replacing the many OL texts and serving as the preeminent Bible of Western Christians during the later Middle Ages. *Vulgate* remains an ambiguous term, used retroactively to refer to ten thousand MSS that reflect a very complex history. The Vulgate version was not stabilized until the end of the sixteenth century.

Coptic Versions. Since the second century CE, *Coptic,* deriving from the Greek word for "Egyptian," has been the Christian form of the Egyptian language. It is written in the Greek alphabet with a few added characters. Since Egyptian is an Afroasiatic language, translation from Greek into Coptic necessitated a great deal of paraphrasing, which makes the use of these versions exceedingly complicated. The Coptic language and biblical translations exist in a number of dialects, two of which are especially important: Sahidic (in southern Egypt), which gave way in the eleventh century to Bohairic (in northern Egypt), still today the Coptic Christians' liturgical language. Manuscripts of Coptic translations of individual books are extant from the fourth century.

Ethiopic Version. Although Ethiopic is a Semitic language, the Ethiopic translation was made for Christians from the Greek OT (possibly with an eye on Syriac and Hebrew), sometime after 350. The Ethiopic Bible is written in the classical Ge'ez dialect, distinct from modern spoken Ethiopic. The earliest translation was rather literal. Taken in conjunction with Codex Vaticanus (see above) the Ethiopic version often provides evidence of the OG. Only a very few MSS predate the fourteenth century.

BIBLIOGRAPHY

Ackroyd, P. R., and C. F. Evans, eds. *The Cambridge History of the Bible.* Vol. I: *From the Beginnings to Jerome.* Cambridge: Cambridge University Press, 1970.

Albrektson, B. "Reflections on the Emergence of a Standard Text of the Hebrew Bible." *VT Sup* 29 (1978) 49-65.

Birdsall, J. Neville, et al. "Versions, Ancient." *The Anchor Bible Dictionary* 6:787-803.

Cross, Frank Moore, and Shemaryahu Talmon, eds. *Qumran and the History of the Biblical Text.* Cambridge, Mass.: Harvard University Press, 1975.

Deist, F. E. *Towards the Text of the Old Testament.* Pretoria: D. R. Church, 1978.

Jellicoe, Sidney. *The Septuagint and Modern Study.* Oxford: Clarendon, 1968.

———, ed. *Studies in the Septuagint: Origins, Revisions, and Interpretations. Selected Essays with a Prolegomenon.* New York: KTAV, 1974.

Klein, Ralph W. *Textual Criticism of the Old Testament: The Septuagint after Qumran.* Philadelphia: Fortress, 1974.

O'Connell, Kevin G. "Texts and Versions." In *The New Jerome Biblical Commentary.* Edited by Raymond E. Brown, Joseph A. Fitzmyer, and Roland E. Murphy. Englewood Cliffs, N.J.: Prentice Hall, 1990.

Tov, Emanuel. *Textual Criticism of the Hebrew Bible.* Minneapolis: Fortress, 1992.

Ulrich, Eugene. "Horizons of Old Testament Textual Research at the Thirtieth Anniversary of Qumran Cave 4." *CBQ* 46 (1984) 613-36.

Würthwein, Ernst. *The Text of the Old Testament: An Introduction to the Biblia Hebraica.* Translated by Erroll F. Rhodes. Grand Rapids: Eerdmans, 1979.

INTRODUCTION TO THE PENTATEUCH

JOSEPH BLENKINSOPP

THE PENTATEUCH IN THE BIBLICAL CANON

The designation Pentateuch, deriving from the Greek ἡ πεντάτευχος βίβλος (*hē pentateuchos biblos,* "the fivefold book"), is not attested before the second century CE, though the fivefold division was in place much earlier. Josephus gives pride of place to the five books of Moses among authoritative Jewish records, which he compares favorably with those of the Greeks, but does not name the individual books.[1] The titles were, however, known to his older contemporary Philo, who refers to Deuteronomy as "The Protreptics," a not inappropriate title.[2] Occasional allusions in the New Testament (NT) to "the law and the prophets" (e.g., Matt 5:17; Luke 16:16; Rom 3:21) reflect contemporary Jewish usage, but the NT nowhere refers to the fivefold division or names any of the individual books. This division was, nevertheless, in place no later than the time of Ben Sira, who wrote his treatise in the early decades of the second century BCE; the fact that this author is familiar with the division of Latter Prophets into three and twelve (Sir 48:20–49:10) creates a strong presumption that he also knew the fivefold division of Torah. Frequent allusions to "the law," "the law of Moses," and "the book of the law" in

earlier Second Temple compositions (e.g., 2 Chr 30:16; Ezra 10:3; Neh 8:3) refer to the legal content of the corpus, most frequently the Deuteronomic law, rather than to the entire Pentateuch.

Designations current in Judaism—חמישה חומשי התורה (*hămîšâ hûmšê hattôrâ,* "the five fifths of the Law") or, more briefly, חומש (*hûmāš,* "the fivefold book") and, of course, תורה (*tôrâ,* "instruction, law")—imply the preeminence of the legal material that takes up more than one fifth of the Pentateuch. And since all the laws were believed to have been delivered to Israel through Moses, it was practically inevitable that the entire corpus came to be attributed to him as sole author.

In due course, the Pentateuch, or Torah, became the first and most important segment of the tripartite canon for Jews, and it alone enjoyed canonical status in the Samaritan community. We should add, however, that the term *canon,* meaning an authoritative corpus of sacred writings, originated in a Christian milieu no earlier than the fourth century (in Athanasius's *Decrees of the Council of Nicaea,* c. 350), though lists of biblical books were in circulation from the early second century. In Judaism there is nothing comparable prior to the well-known passage in *b. B. Bat.* 14b-15a listing the biblical books and their reputed authors. The process by which the canon in its different forms (Jewish, Protestant, Catholic, Eastern Orthodox) reached its final formulation is

---

1. *Against Apion* 1:37-41.
2. *De Fuga et Inventione* 170.

now acknowledged to have been much more complex and less clearly defined than was once thought, and the role of "the men of the Great Assembly" at the time of Ezra and "the Council of Jamnia [Yavneh]" after the fall of Jerusalem to the Romans in 70 CE is now known to be anachronistic and unhistorical. In any case, the Pentateuch had in all essentials reached its final form much earlier in the Second Temple period.

THE PENTATEUCHAL NARRATIVE

In spite of the designation Torah current in Judaism, the Pentateuch is basically a narrative. The sequence of events begins with creation and the early history of humanity in which the structurally decisive event is the deluge, after which the descendants of Noah are dispersed around the earth. In the tenth generation after the deluge, Abram (later Abraham) is called by God to leave Mesopotamia for a new land, with the promise of divine blessing and numerous progeny contingent on his answering this call. The history of Israel's ancestors is traced through four generations, particular attention being devoted to the twenty-year exile of Jacob (later called Israel) in Mesopotamia, his eventual return to the promised land, and the emigration of his family, now seventy in number, to Egypt. The story of the ancestors, therefore, begins and ends outside the land, hence the promise made initially to Abraham and often repeated awaits fulfillment in the future. In Egypt the original settlers grow into a numerous and powerful people until a new pharaoh ascends the throne and, for reasons that are not entirely clear, launches a genocidal campaign against them.

One of Jacob's descendants called Moses, son of Levitical parents, survived the massacre of Hebrew male infants decreed by Pharaoh and, after killing an Egyptian overseer, was forced to take refuge in Midian. There he had the extraordinary experience of a deity's self-revelation to him as Yahweh, God of the ancestors, who sent him on a mission to persuade Pharaoh to let the oppressed Hebrews leave Egypt. A first attempt proved unsuccessful, but with the assistance from his brother, Aaron, and after a series of ecological disasters visited on the Egyptians culminated in the death of their firstborn, a second mission succeeded. The Israelites headed out into the wilderness and the pursuing Egyptians were

destroyed as they attempted to cross a body of water. After further vicissitudes, the Israelites, now 600,000 strong, not counting women and children, reached the wilderness of Sinai. There Moses received laws from Yahweh: First, ten commandments promulgated to the people at once; then a collection of laws communicated to Moses alone. There followed a covenant ritual and the revelation of the plan for the construction of the sanctuary and detailed instructions for the cult to be carried on in it. During Moses' absence on the mountain, an act of apostasy by the people, aided and abetted by Aaron, led to the breaking and remaking of the Law tablets and the giving of further statutes, mostly of a ritual sort. The cult was then set up as prescribed, the priesthood under Aaron was inaugurated, and after a lapse of about a year the Israelites continued on their way.

After an abortive attempt to invade Canaan, the Israelite throng under Moses arrived in Moab east of the Jordan. The attempt of the Moabite king to block their passage by hiring a seer to curse them was thwarted, and those Israelites who succumbed to the temptation to engage in sexual rites were executed. Preparations were made for occupying land both east and west of the Jordan, and on the last day of his life Moses addressed the people, reminding them of past favors bestowed on them by their God and the obligations they had thereby incurred. This last address included a new set of laws and was followed by a new covenant. Moses commissioned Joshua as his successor before his death and burial in an unmarked grave at the age of 120.

NARRATIVE ANOMALIES

The uneven narrative tempo of the Pentateuch story will be obvious even on a cursory reading. According to the chronology provided by the narrative itself, the events unfold over a period of 2,706 years, yet the sojourn at Sinai, the account of which occupies about one fifth of the total length, lasts less than one year (Exod 19:1; Num 10:11), while another fifth is dedicated to the last day in the life of Moses (Deut 1:3; 32:48). The most obvious explanation of this anomalous feature is that all laws, whenever promulgated, came in the course of time to be backdated to the lifetime of Moses. But the narrative also contains numerous repetitions and digressions and is punctuated at frequent intervals by genealogies and lists. These features suggest that the Pentateuchal story has been formed as the result of an incremental process over a considerable period of time.

Another structural problem is that the ending, with Moses and his people camped in Moab, east of the Jordan, appears to leave the promise of land, prominent in the history of the ancestors, up in the air. According to the Deuteronomic author-editor of Joshua, the conquest of Canaan was viewed as the fulfillment of that promise (see esp. Josh 21:43-45), so that it might seem more appropriate to speak of a Hexateuch (Pentateuch plus Joshua) as the basic literary unit and explain the omission of the conquest from the Pentateuch as a later move dictated by the needs of the post-exilic community. But in the context of the dominant documentary hypothesis (see below), we then have the problem that the principal continuous early sources—namely, J and E—are not clearly attested in Joshua, which reflects, rather, the language and ideology of Deuteronomy. This has led several scholars, conspicuously Martin Noth, to read Deuteronomy as the preface to the Deuteronomic History (Joshua–2 Kings) and the first four books as a more or less self-contained Tetrateuch. But a glance at the conclusion of Numbers will suffice to show that the Tetrateuch is no more a well-rounded and self-contained narrative than the Pentateuch; indeed, less so, since it not only leaves Israel outside the land but also omits the death of Moses. Noth's Tetrateuchal hypothesis would be further weakened if, as several scholars have since argued, the Deuteronomic hand is much more in evidence in Genesis–Numbers than he and others at that time were prepared to allow.

It is at least clear that the present divisions in the narrative continuum from creation to the Babylonian exile resulted from successive editorial adjustments. The most important of these was the inclusion of the Deuteronomic law and its homiletic framework in the narrative of Israelite origins, a move that necessitated the displacement of the commissioning of Joshua and the death of Moses from their original position in the Priestly narrative (Num 27:12-23) to the end of Deuteronomy (32:48-52 and 34:1, 7-9, also of P origin). Once this was done, Moses' death marked the closing of the normative epoch in which everything necessary for the sustenance of the Israelite commonwealth had been revealed and promulgated. In its final form, there-fore, the Pentateuch is centered on the law and the unique mediatorial role of Moses.

STRUCTURE, DIVISIONS, THEME

The chapter divisions of the Pentateuch begin to appear in Hebrew MSS in the later Middle Ages, but had already been introduced into the Vulgate by Stephen Langton, Archbishop of Canterbury (1150–1228). By the Talmudic period, individual sentences or brief pericopes were being identified by words or phrases (סימנים sîmānîm, "signs"), but verse numbering is first attested in Christian Bibles at the time of the Reformation. The division of the Hebrew Bible (HB) into longer pericopes for liturgical reading is also attested from an early date. These sections (סדרים sĕdārîm) were subdivided into short paragraphs (פסקות pisqôt) separated by a space of at least three letters, a practice already attested in the Qumran biblical texts. According to an early tradition, this had the purpose of giving Moses time to reflect on the meaning of the text between each subsection.[3]

While the division of the Pentateuch into five books clearly owed something to the need for convenient scroll handling, it is equally clear that the material could have been divided in a different way. Genesis and Deuteronomy have their own distinctive character as self-contained narratives, though the former could as well have concluded with the recapitulating genealogy of the Israelite family in Egypt in Gen 46:8-27. This is not the case with Exodus and Numbers, which are almost exactly equal in length. The break between Exodus and Leviticus is quite artificial, for the latter falls within the Sinai pericope that ends only in Numbers 10. Moreover, the ordination ceremony in Leviticus 8 is the sequel to the prescriptions for carrying out that ceremony in Exodus 29. It is possible that the fivefold arrangement had the purpose of highlighting Leviticus, by far the shortest of the five books, as the central panel defining Israel as a holy community distinct from other nations. The structure itself could then be read as encoding an important aspect of the self-understanding of the emergent Jewish commonwealth after the return from exile.

Another significant structural feature is the division of Genesis into sections entitled אלה תולדות

3. *Sipra* 1:1.

('ēlleh tôlĕdôt, "these are the generations . . . "). They are arranged in two pentads (groups of five) covering, respectively, the early history of humanity (Gen 2:4a; 5:1; 6:9; 10:1; 11:10) and the ancestral history (Gen 11:27; 25:12, 19; 36:1; 37:2). As with the fivefold division of the Pentateuch itself, this arrangement draws attention to the central panel of each pentad—namely, the deluge in the first and the vicissitudes of Jacob/Israel in the second. While the title tôlĕdôt is particularly apt for genealogical material, most of these sections contain far more narrative than genealogy.

A structuring and periodizing feature of a different kind is the series of precise chronological markers punctuating the narrative, especially in Genesis (e.g., Gen 7:6, 11; Exod 12:40-41; Num 10:11). Attempts to decode this chronological schema are complicated by the different numbers in the MT, LXX, and Samaritan Pentateuch, and no one solution has won universal acceptance. What can be said is that the schema is undoubtedly fictive and that it extends beyond the Pentateuch, taking in the building of Solomon's Temple (1 Kgs 6:1) and the 430 years between the construction and the destruction of the Temple, identical with the length of the sojourn in Egypt, according to Exod 12:40. It has also been observed that the interval of 2,666 years between creation and the exodus is two-thirds of a total of 4,000 years, which may have been thought of as a world epoch or "Great Year." Whatever the solution, this chronological grid expresses the conviction that the course of events has a direction and a goal predetermined and willed by God.

Since the Pentateuch contains materials from successive periods in the history of Israel and early Judaism that have been combined and reshaped in response to different situations, it is difficult to identify a single theme or organizing principle. The fact that it concludes with the death of Moses prior to the occupation of and residence in the land suggests that what is centrally important is the complex of institutions and laws that serve as a kind of blueprint for the commonwealth and polity to be established. But the story of the ancestors begins with the command to Abraham to go to a land in which his descendants would become a great nation replete with blessing and a source of blessing for other peoples (Gen 12:1-3). For those who postulate a Hexateuch from which the Pentateuch was formed by detaching Joshua, the fulfillment of these prom-ises would be seen in the conquest and settlement of Canaan (see Josh 21:43-45 which reads like a finale to the story); and for those who postulate a Yahwist (J) source from the early monarchy, the terminus would be the "Greater Israel" of David and Solomon. If, however, the Pentateuch *in its final form* is read in the context of the emergent Judaism that produced it, the ancestral promises would reflect the aspirations of those who elected to return to the homeland under Persian rule. The addition of the early history of humanity in Genesis 1–11, in keeping with well-established historiographical tradition in the Near East and the Levant (the countries bordering the eastern edge of the Mediterranean Sea), placed the history of the nation in the context of world history and allowed for a realistic and profound diagnosis of the human condition.

THE FORMATION OF THE PENTATEUCH

From Ibn Ezra to Wellhausen. The view long traditional in both Judaism and Christianity, and still maintained in the more conservative denominations of both religions, is that Moses authored the entire Pentateuch with the possible exception of the last verses recounting his death and burial. The beginnings of this belief can be traced to the close association between Moses and the law. From a fairly early time, it became standard procedure to attribute all laws to Moses in the same way that sapiential compositions came to be attributed to Solomon and Psalms to David. And since the laws are embedded in narrative, it was a short step to assigning the entire corpus to Moses in spite of the fact that this is nowhere affirmed in the Pentateuch itself.

One of the earliest to raise questions about the attribution was the twelfth-century Jewish scholar Abraham Ibn Ezra, who alluded cryptically, in his commentary on Deuteronomy, to certain passages that presuppose situations and events long after the time of Moses; e.g., the remark that at that time the Canaanites were in the land (Gen 12:6) and the allusion to the iron bed of King Og of Bashan, which was a tourist attraction at the time of his writing (Deut 3:11). Further difficulties were raised by other commentators in the following centuries, with the result that by the seventeenth century writers as diverse as Spinoza and Hobbes simply rejected Mosaic authorship altogether. Even scholars within the ecclesiastical mainstream, while not denying the traditional view outright, were beginning to acknowledge the composite nature of the Pentateuch. One of the earliest of these was the French Oratorian priest Richard Simon. In his *Histoire Critique du Vieux Testament* (1678) he acknowledged the role of Moses in the production of the Pentateuch but went on to suggest that it owed its final form to scribes at the time of Ezra. The outcome was that his work was placed on the Roman Catholic Index of Prohibited Books and most of the copies printed were destroyed. One of the surviving copies was, however, translated into German by Johann Salomo Semler about a century later and, in that form, contributed significantly to research on the Pentateuch, then well underway in German universities.

By the early eighteenth century, evidence for the use of sources was becoming more and more apparent. Repetitions, parallel versions of the same event, and notable differences in language and point of view seemed to render this conclusion inevitable. The first to exploit the occurrence of divine names—Elohim and Yahweh—as a means of distinguishing between sources was Henning Bernhard Witter, Lutheran pastor of Hildesheim, who wrote a monograph on the subject in 1711 that remained practically unnoticed until rediscovered by the French biblical scholar Adolphe Lods in 1925. Somewhat along the same lines, the French physician and amateur Old Testament (OT) scholar Jean Astruc published a book forty-two years later in which he distinguished three sources in the Pentateuch, the first two of which were characterized by use of the names Elohim and Yahweh respectively. By assuming that these sources were used by Moses in compiling the Pentateuch, Astruc sought to preserve the traditional dogma. By the end of that century, nevertheless, the existence of parallel sources was widely acknowledged, at least for Genesis and the first part of Exodus up to the point where the divine name YHWH (Yahweh) was revealed to Moses (Exod 3:13-15).

A minority opinion, first proposed by the Scottish Roman Catholic priest Alexander Geddes in the late eighteenth century and developed by J. S. Vater, professor at Halle in the early years of the following century, rejected the hypothesis of two continuous parallel sources in favor of a much greater number of quite disparate blocks of material that were combined long after the time of Moses to form the Pentateuch (the Fragmentary Hypothesis). Another alternative assumed that a single base narrative, or *Grundschrift,* was subsequently filled out with additional material (the Supplementary Hypothesis). But in whatever form it was proposed, the view that the Pentateuch is the result of a long process of literary formation was firmly established by the early nineteenth century, in academic if not in ecclesiastical circles.

During that period of political and cultural upheaval, the most important contribution to understanding the formation of the Pentateuch was that of Wilhelm Martin Leberecht de Wette (1780–1849), colleague of Schleiermacher at the newly founded University of Berlin. De Wette's study of Chronicles persuaded him that the legal and cultic system that the author of Chronicles presumes to have been in place since Mosaic times or, with respect to the Jerusalem cult, from the time of David, is unattested in the early records and must, therefore, be a projection into the past of the situation obtaining at the time of writing in the post-exilic period. The greater part of the legal and cultic material in the Pentateuch, therefore, belongs to the early history of Judaism rather than to that of Israel. In keeping with this conclusion, de Wette divided his *Biblical Dogmatics* (1813) into two sections entitled "Hebraism" and "Judaism." True to the dominant Romanticism of the time, de Wette contrasted the spontaneity and vigor of early Israelite religion with the formalism and empty ritualism that he believed characterized early Judaism and Judaism as a whole, a contrast that would be set out in much starker terms by Wellhausen toward the end of the same century. In another important monograph, de Wette identified the lawbook that the priest Hilkiah claimed to have found in the Temple during the reign of Josiah (640–609 BCE) with an early draft of Deuteronomy (see 2 Kgs 22:8-10). According to de Wette, this composition claimed for itself Mosaic authorship but was actually a recent pseudepigraphal work "planted" by the priests to serve as a basis for the religious reforms that followed its "discovery." By thus placing the Deuteronomic Law (Deuteronomy 12–26) in the seventh century BCE, de Wette believed it possible to distinguish between earlier legislation unfamiliar with this compilation and later laws that presupposed it.

Throughout the nineteenth century OT scholars concentrated on the identification and dating of sources, rather less so on the editorial processes by which they were assembled into a coherent whole. Briefly, the most important advances following de Wette were, first, the discovery that the Elohist source (E), by most considered the earliest, contained an earlier and a later strand. First suggested by Karl David Ilgen in 1798, the distinction was worked out in detail about a half century later by Hermann Hupfeld, resulting in the emergence of a priestly and theocratic source (later to be known under the siglum P). The second and decisive proposal, already implicit in the results obtained by de Wette at the beginning of the century, was that this newly discovered Priestly source was to be located at the end, not the beginning, of the process of formation. First advanced by Edouard Reuss in lectures delivered at the University of Strasbourg, the hypothesis of the late P source appeared in print in a book published by Karl Heinrich Graf, student of Reuss, in 1866. The way was thus cleared for the definitive formulation of what came to be known as "the newer documentary hypothesis," with the sources in the chronological order JEDP, in the *Prolegomena to the History of Israel* of Julius Wellhausen (1883).

With benefit of hindsight, it is not too difficult to detect the philosophical and cultural determinants of this lengthy and persistent attempt to identify and date sources. It is important to bear in mind that the goal of this massive effort to identify and date sources was not so much a theological or aesthetic appreciation of the texts in themselves but rather the reconstruction of the history, and especially the religious history, of Israel. Throughout the nineteenth century, scholars emphasized development, specifically of ideas. Although sometimes exaggerated, the impact of Hegel's dialectical philosophy of history was felt in both OT and NT studies. It can be detected, for example, in the tendency for a tripartite periodization of the history—typically, Mosaism, propheticism, early Judaism. As noted above, influences were also felt from the Romantic movement, especially in the positive evaluation of the early and naive stage of religious development, the high estimation of the prophet as the religious individualist *par excellence,* and the marked lack of enthusiasm for post-exilic Judaism, generally characterized as a decline into religious formalism and ritualism. While, perhaps, few OT scholars professed to be anti-Jewish, academic study of the Pentateuch, and

the OT in general, was carried on in an atmosphere decidedly unfavorable to Judaism. It is, therefore, not surprising that Jewish scholars, with few exceptions, turned their attention elsewhere.

From Wellhausen to the Mid-Twentieth Century.

The four-source or newer documentary hypothesis as set out by Wellhausen soon became the critical orthodoxy, though opposed by scholars of more conservative ecclesiastical affiliation. It was not clearly perceived at the time, but the Graf-Wellhausenian construct was threatened less from conservative reaction than it was from the ongoing analysis of the sources themselves. The requirement of a fairly high level of consistency in terminology, style, and theme had already led to the division of an originally unitary E source into P and E, and it was not long before the E source itself suffered the same fate,[4] resulting in E^1 and E^2. However, J proved to be especially friable, resulting either in J^1 and J^2 as constituent sources[5] or in the postulation of a more primitive strand within J, variously described as of lay origin,[6] or of Kenite,[7] Edomite,[8] or nomadic provenance.[9] Wellhausen himself had argued for two strands in Deuteronomy, and the existence of a Josian and exilic redaction, from the seventh and sixth centuries BCE respectively, is now widely accepted. At the beginning of the century, Bruno Baentsch identified as many as seven strands in P, each with its own redactional history, and while few were prepared to press source division to that extreme, many agreed that additions were made at different times to the P narrative and laws,[10] though there is still no agreement as to whether P is a distinct source or an editorial reworking of earlier material.

The problem inherent in this kind of detailed analysis of sources is not difficult to detect. To the

4. See Abraham Kuenen, *Historisch-Kritische Einleitung in die Bücher des Alten Testaments ihrer Entstehung und Sammlung* (Leipzig: J. C. Hinrichs, 1887); Otto Procksch, *Das nordhebräische Sagenbuch. Die Elohimquelle* (Leipzig: J. C. Hinrichs, 1906).

5. See Karl Budde, *Die Biblische Urgeschichte (Gen. 1–12, 5)* (Giessen: A. Töpelmann, 1883); Rudolph Smend, *Die Erzählung des Hexateuch. Aufe ihre Quellen untersucht* (Berlin: Walter de Gruyter, 1912); Cuthbert Simpson, *The Early Traditions of Israel: A Critical Analysis of the Pre-Deuteronomistic Narrative of the Hexateuch* (Oxford: Blackwell, 1948).

6. *Laienquelle* is a source of the Pentateuch, according to Otto Eissfeldt. See his *The Old Testament: An Introduction* (Oxford: Blackwell, 1965).

7. Julius Morgenstern, "The Oldest Document of the Hexateuch," *Hebrew Union College Annual* 4 (1927) 1-138.

8. Robert Pfeiffer, "A Non-Israelite Source of the Book of Genesis," *Zeitschrift für die alttestamentliche Wissenschaft* 48 (1930) 66-73.

9. Georg Fohrer, *Introduction to the Old Testament* (Nashville: Abingdon, 1968).

10. See Gerhard von Rad, *Die Priesterschrift im Hexateuch literarisch untersucht und theologisch gewertet* (Stuttgart: W. Kohlhammer, 1934).

degree that the requirement of inner consistency is pressed, the sources tend to disintegrate into a bewildering variety of smaller units or strands, and the entire hypothesis is undermined. A challenge of a different nature emerged from the work of Hermann Gunkel (1852–1932), the first edition of whose commentary on Genesis appeared in 1901. Gunkel accepted the Graf-Wellhausen construct, but the innovative study of literary forms, in his work and that of his students Gressmann and Baumgartner, was to create serious problems for the documentary hypothesis. The influence of the History of Religions school on Gunkel can be seen in his first significant publication, entitled *Creation and Chaos* (*Schöpfung und Chaos,* 1895); following the lead of this school, Gunkel brought a comparative study of genres to bear on the narrative material in Genesis, concentrating on the smallest literary units, their oral prehistory, and the social situations that generated them. His description of these narratives as saga has occasioned difficulties, since in English the term applies to medieval Icelandic prose narratives, not necessarily composed and transmitted orally. In German, however, the corresponding term *Sage* can have a more general meaning, including legend and folktale, and it is in this sense that Gunkel used it, depending on the work of the Danish folklorist Axel Olrik. Gunkel's application of this kind of literary analysis, which he called *Literaturgeschichte* (literary history) or *Gattungsforschung* (the investigation of genres), but which has since been known as *Formgeschichte* (the history of forms, form criticism), shifted the emphasis away from extensive written documents to individual pericopes and the oral tradition underlying them. Although it was not clearly perceived at the time, Gunkel's investigations were to lead in a quite different direction from that of Graf and Wellhausen.

The concept of oral tradition also played an important role in the work of von Rad, whose study entitled "The Form-Critical Problem of the Hexateuch," published in 1938, proved very influential, and whose ideas were further developed in his commentaries on Genesis and Deuteronomy as well as in the first volume of his *Old Testament Theology.*[11] According to von Rad, the Hexateuchal

narrative was elaborated on the basis of the kind of liturgical and confessional statement found in Deut 26:5-9, the form of words pronounced by the Israelite farmer at the offering of the firstfruits. He observed that this "Hexateuch in a nutshell," as he called it, memorialized the descent into Egypt, the exodus, and settlement in the land but omitted any mention of the giving of the Law. To explain this omission, he postulated two separate streams of tradition that came together only in the work of the Yahwist author (J): the exodus-occupation tradition rooted in the Festival of Weeks at Gilgal; and the Sinai tradition, originating in the Festival of Tabernacles at the ancient tribal sanctuary of Shechem. The Yahwist prefaced the literary elaboration of these conflated traditions with the early history of humanity in Genesis 1–11 and the ancestral history in Genesis 12–50, thus laying the groundwork for the Hexateuch as we have it. Cultic recital rooted in the tribal federation of the prestate period was thus transformed into religious literature, the catalyst for the transformation being what von Rad called "the Solomonic enlightenment."

Von Rad's high evaluation of the Yahwist as a literary and religious genius was very influential, especially during the heyday of the "biblical theology movement" in the two decades following World War II and residually down to the present. Books and articles began to appear on the kerygma, or the theology, of the Yahwist.[12] There were even attempts to penetrate the veil of anonymity by identifying him as a member of Solomon's entourage, the favored candidates being Nathan, Abiathar, and Ahimaaz. In recent years serious questions have been raised about the date, extent, and even existence of J as a continuous and integral narrative source.

Other proponents of a cultic origin for the narrative and legal traditions of ancient Israel were the Norwegian scholar Sigmund Mowinckel, who located the Decalogue in a pre-monarchic New Year festival; Johannes Pedersen, who read Exodus 1–15 as the deposit of cultic recital for Passover; and Albrecht Alt, whose influential essay "The Origins of Israelite Law"[13] grounded the apodictic laws in

11. Published in English in *The Problem of the Hexateuch and Other Essays* (New York: McGraw-Hill, 1966) 1-78. See *Genesis: A Commentary,* rev. ed. (Philadelphia: Westminster, 1973), first published in 1953; *Deuteronomy: A Commentary* (Philadelphia: Westminster, 1966), first published in 1964; *Old Testament Theology,* vol. 1: *The Theology of Israel's Historical Traditions,* trans. D. M. G. Stalker (New York: Harper and Row, 1962), first published in 1957.

12. See Hans-Walter Wolff, "Das Kerygma des Yahwisten," *Evangliche Theologie* 24 (1964) 73-98; Peter Ellis, *The Yahwist: The Bible's First Theologian* (Collegeville: Liturgical Press, 1968).

13. Albrecht Alt, "Die Ursprünge des israelitischen Rechts," *Bericht über die Verhandlungen der Sächischen Akademie der Wissenschaften zu Leipzig. Philologisch-historische Klasse,* vol. 86, 1 (Leipzig: S. Hirzel, 1934).

the cult of the Israelite amphictyony. Following the same form-critical and traditio-historical procedures, Martin Noth[14] identified five major themes (guidance out of Egypt, progress through the wilderness, entry into the arable land, promise to the ancestors, and the revelation at Sinai) whose origin and early development were in the tribal amphictyony and its cult. These traditions were combined and molded into a consecutive narrative to form the Tetrateuch. Noth's acceptance of the documentary hypothesis was fairly laconic, since he maintained that the essential lines of the narrative tradition had been present from the beginning, whether in oral or written form is unclear (his reference to a base narrative or *Grundschrift* remained undeveloped).

Noth's studies provided the basis for his account of the origins and early development of Israel in his *A History of Israel.*[15] His main point was that the combination of the five themes, originating in different segments of what later became Israel, went hand in hand with the consolidation of these diverse groups into the Israelite tribal federation, or amphictyony, of the pre-monarchic period. Here, too, more recent studies have called into question Noth's amphictyonic thesis, first advanced in 1930, and his understanding of Israelite origins in general. His hypothesis of a Deuteronomistic historical work (Dtr) covering Joshua through 2 Kings, first advanced in 1943, has on the other hand stood the test of time and is still almost universally accepted.

We can see now how von Rad and Noth, neither of whom questioned the regnant documentary hypothesis, followed Gunkel in shifting the emphasis back into the preliterary origin of the Pentateuchal traditions. While this displacement has had important consequences, many of the specific conclusions of both scholars have since been called into question. The creedal statements von Rad took as the starting point of the literary development eventuating in the Hexateuch, especially Deut 26:1-15, are now seen to be Deuteronomic and, therefore, no earlier than the seventh century BCE. The separate origin of the exodus-occupation and Sinai traditions has been generally abandoned, and the high antiquity of the covenant formulation can no longer be taken for granted. More recent comparative studies of oral tradition have given us a better understanding of the relation between oral and written transmission and have made it more difficult to determine the oral origin of written narrative.[16] Moreover, one might ask how the cult, which can certainly serve to transmit a narrative tradition, can also originate it.

During the same period, more radical theories of oral tradition were popular with Scandinavian scholars, especially with respect to the Pentateuch and the prophetic books. Drawing on the work of the Uppsala scholars H. S. Nyberg and Harris Birkeland, Ivan Engnell argued strongly for a traditio-historical approach rather than the Wellhausenian emphasis on literary sources. Engnell maintained that the narrative material in the Tetrateuch was transmitted orally throughout the pre-exilic period and was committed to writing only after the Babylonian exile in what he called "the P circle." This final redaction was quite distinct from the roughly contemporary "D work" comprising Deuteronomy and Dtr. At some point Deuteronomy was detached from the history and built into the Priestly Tetrateuch, resulting in the Pentateuch more or less as we have it. Some aspects of Engnell's critique of the documentary hypothesis are reproduced in recent revisionist writings, but his extreme advocacy of oral tradition has since been abandoned.

Recent Developments. While there have always been those who rejected the documentary hypothesis outright[17] and others who were critical of some aspect of it,[18] it is only in the last two decades or so that the Graf-Wellhausen construct can be said to be in serious and possibly terminal crisis. The main line of attack has focused on the existence of *continuous* sources from the early period of the monarchy. It has become apparent that Otto Eissfeldt's description of J as expressing "enthusiastic acceptance of agricultural life and national-political power and cultus"[19] may apply to some parts of the narrative but not at all to the substantial J component of Genesis 1–11, which speaks of the curse on the soil and emphasizes the vanity of human pretensions in general and in the political sphere in particular. Considerations such as this have led several scholars—

14. Martin Noth, *A History of Pentateuchal Traditions* (Englewood Cliffs, N.J.: Prentice-Hall, 1972). First published in 1948.

15. Martin Noth, *A History of Israel,* 2nd ed. (New York: Harper and Row, 1960), first published in 1950.

16. Robert Culley, *Studies in the Structure of Hebrew Narrative* (Philadelphia: Fortress, 1976).

17. E.g., the Jewish scholar Umberto Cassuto, *Torat hatte'udot vesiddurim shel sifre hattorah* (Jerusalem: Magnes, 1941).

18. E.g., Wilhem Rudolph and Paul Volz, *der Elohist also Erzähler. Ein Irrweg der Penteteuchkritik? An der Genesis erlautert* (Berlin: Walter de Gruyter, 1933).

19. Eissfeldt, *The Old Testament,* 200.

Norman Wagner, Rolf Rendtorff, Erhard Blum, among others[20]—to argue that the several narrative blocks in the Pentateuch had their own distinctive processes of formation until they were redacted together at a late date. Doubts about the early dating of J (in the tenth or ninth century BCE) have coalesced to the point where such an early date can no longer be taken for granted. The Canadian scholar F. V. Winnett[21] argued for a post-exilic J in Genesis, while John Van Seters, one of his students, postulated an exilic J whose work reflects the exigencies and aspirations of the Jewish community at that time. In later studies, Van Seters went on to argue that the Yahwist, an individual author and not a school or circle, produced a historiographical work that can be profitably compared with, and was influenced by, early Greek mythography and historiography, including Herodotus and the Hesiodic *Catalogue of Women*.[22] It is still too early to evaluate adequately this new direction, but at least one scholar of note has taken a similar line.[23]

Another development threatening to undermine the existing paradigm involves the contribution of Deuteronomic authors to the narrative in the first four books of the Bible. We have seen that Martin Noth made a sharp distinction between the Tetrateuch and Dtr prefaced by Deuteronomy; until recently, this position was widely accepted. In recent years, however, several scholars have argued for a substantial D contribution to the narrative continuum in Genesis–Numbers, especially in key passages such as "the covenant of the pieces" in Genesis 15 and the Sinai/Horeb pericope in Exodus 19–34.[24] Others have noted prophetic and Deuteronomic features in passages routinely attributed to J—e.g., the call of Moses in Exodus 3–4, reminiscent of prophetic commissionings—and have concluded that the first consecutive account of the founding events was put together by members of the Deuteronomic school who linked existing units of tradition by means of the promise of land, nationhood, and divine blessing.[25] These conclusions—the displacement of J to a much later period, a significant D component in Genesis–Numbers, the absorption of J into the D school—are still open to debate, but if they are sustained it is difficult to see how the documentary hypothesis can survive in anything like its classical form. And it goes without saying that they would lead to a very different way of reconstructing the history and religion of Israel.

A more radical attack on the documentary hypothesis, and the historical-critical methods employed by its advocates, has come in recent years from a quite different direction, that of literary-critical theory. The emergence of the New Criticism in the twenties and thirties of this century marked a decisive turning away from the historical, philological, and referential approach to literature with an emphasis on the circumstances of the production and first reception of texts, the psychology and intention of the author, and the like. The proponents of this theory, including such major figures as I. A. Richards and William Empson, favored a text-immanent approach that concentrated on the internal organization and aesthetics of the literary composition without regard to its social and psychological coordinates. A similar concentration on "the text in itself," the text as a closed system, characterizes more recent trends in formalist, structuralist, and post-structuralist interpretation, and it was inevitable that sooner or later such approaches would be applied to biblical texts. This is not the place to evaluate the many essays in interpretation of Pentateuchal narratives of these kinds that have appeared over the last two decades or so. Several (e.g., Roland Barthes's analysis of the Jabbok ford narrative in Genesis 32) have been stimulating, but the results have been uneven, and the best readings have come from professional literary critics familiar with and sensitive to the original language.[26] Synchronic analysis, which takes the text as it is can open up valuable new perspectives, but without disposing of the need for diachronic—i.e., historical-critical—

20. Norman E. Wagner, "Pentateuchal Criticism: No Clear Future," *Canadian Journal of Theology* 13 (1967) 225-32; Rolf Rendtorff, "Pentateuchal Studies on the Move," *JSOT* 3 (1977) 2-10, 43-45; Erhard Blum, *Die Komposition der Vätergeschichte* (Neukirchen-Vluyn: Neukirchener Verlag, 1984), and *Studien zur Komposition des Pentateuch* (Berlin: Walter de Gruyter, 1990).

21. F. V. Winnett, "Re-examining the Foundations," *JBL* 84 (1965) 1-19.

22. John Van Seters, "Recent Studies on the Pentateuch: A Crisis in Method," *JAOS* 99 (1979) 663-67; and *In Search of History: Historiography in the Ancient World and the Origins of Biblical History* (New Haven: Yale University Press, 1983).

23. R. N. Whybray, *The Making of the Pentateuch: A Methodological Study* (Sheffield: JSOT Press, 1987).

24. See Lothar Perlitt, *Bundestheologie im Alten Testament* (Neukirchen-Vluyn: Neukirchener Verlag, 1969); and Ernst Kutsch, *Verheissung und Gesetz* (Berlin: Walter de Gruyter, 1973).

25. See esp. Hans Heinrich Schmid, *Der sogenannte Jahwist: Beobachtungen und Fragen zur Pentateuchforschung* (Zurich: Theologischer Verlag, 1976).

26. E.g., Robert Alter, *The Art of Biblical Narrative* (New York: Basic Books, 1981).

reconstructions, the principal aim of which has never been aesthetic appreciation of the text.

Similar in some respects is the approach that, since the 1970s, has come to be known as "canonical criticism."[27] Both the new critical and the canonical approaches concentrate on the final form of the text, but with the difference that the latter has an explicitly theological agenda. The contribution of Brevard S. Childs in particular seems to aim at reaffirming the nature of the Bible as a confessional document originating in a faith community. Attention is, therefore, focused on the final form, rather than on the hypothetical origins or sources, of the biblical texts as the proper object of theological inquiry. With respect to the Pentateuch, therefore, Childs seeks to show how the five books are related thematically and how the final editorial stage was based on a reading of the Pentateuch as a whole.[28]

The Final Stage of Formation. It is generally agreed that the Pentateuch achieved its final form during the two centuries (538–334 BCE) when Jews in the province of Judah, and most Jews elsewhere, were subject to Iranian rule. Some, including Wellhausen himself, have been prepared to go further and identify the Pentateuch, or at least its legal content, with the law, which Ezra was commissioned to teach and enforce in the Transeuphrates satrapy of the Achaemenid Empire (Ezra 7:1-26). This hypothesis has ancient precedent in the Ezra Apocalypse (late first century CE), which depicts Ezra's reproducing under divine inspiration the sacred books after they had perished in the fall of Jerusalem (2 Esdras 14). The law administered by Ezra was certainly no innovation, since it was presumed to be familiar to Jews in the area under Ezra's jurisdiction (Ezra 7:25). It would be reasonable to assume that, at least in the mind of the author of the Ezra narrative, it was identical with the law referred to on numerous occasions elsewhere in Chronicles–Ezra–Nehemiah, and therefore included legal material from both Deuteronomy and the Priestly writers. But there is no evidence that Ezra "canonized" the law in such a way that no further additions or modifications could be introduced into it. Thus the Temple tax, which is a third of a shekel in Neh 10:33-34, has increased to half a shekel in Exod

30:11-16 (see also 38:25), and the solemn day of fasting and repentance occurs on the twenty-fourth of Tishri, according to Neh 9:1, and on the tenth of the same month in the Priestly law (Lev 16:29; 23:27-32; Num 29:7-11). Admittedly, these divergences could be explained otherwise, but they are consistent with the conclusion that the Pentateuchal law had not attained its final form by the mid-fifth century BCE but was well on its way to doing so.

Our knowledge of Achaemenid imperial administration also suggests that the Pentateuchal law came to serve as the civic constitution of the Jewish ethnos at that time. It was the Persian custom to insist on the codification of local and traditional laws and entrust their implementation to the provincial authorities, including priesthoods, with the backing of the central government. A document example comes from Egypt, since we know from the Demotic chronicle[29] that Darius I appointed a commission composed of representatives of the different orders charged with the task of codifying the traditional laws. After a labor of several years, these laws were redacted in Aramaic and demotic Egyptian. While there is no direct evidence of such activity in Judah, the proximity of Judah to Egypt and its location in the same satrapy, as well as the consistency of Persian policy in this respect, suggest that something similar may have happened in Judah.

The circumstances under which the narrative achieved its final form are even more obscure. The great importance of the laws as the civic constitution of the nascent Jewish commonwealth would help to explain why the story ends with the death of the lawgiver, and the exclusion of the conquest narrative would be understandable in view of the delicate situation of a small subject province in the vast Achaemenid Empire. The need for a comprehensive corpus of laws resulted in the incorporation of the Deuteronomic law with its historical and homiletic framework into the structure of the Priestly work, which also features law and narrative. This was accomplished by the simple expedient of adding a date of the P type at the beginning of Deuteronomy (1:3), which aligned the book with the overall P chronology. It appears that in the original form of the P narrative Moses' death, preceded by the commissioning of Joshua as his successor, occurred at an earlier point in the wilderness itinerary (Num

---

27. Brevard S. Childs, *Introduction to the Old Testament as Scripture* (Philadelphia: Fortress, 1979); and *Old Testament Theology in a Canonical Context* (London: S.C.M., 1985).

28. Childs, *Introduction to the Old Testament as Scripture,* 112-35.

29. Papyrus 215 of the Bibliothèque Nationale in Paris.

314

27:12-23) following on the deaths of Miriam and Aaron (Num 20:1, 22-29). God commands Moses to ascend Mount Abarim, view the land, and die; the natural implication is that this is to happen at once, delayed only by the need to appoint a successor. But Moses' death is not recorded at this point, because he must first promulgate the second law and covenant in Moab. Only toward the end of Deuteronomy, therefore, do we find a revised version of the appointment of Joshua as successor (32:48-52) and an account of Moses' death (34:1, 7-9), both passages from the hand of a later P writer. The work is then rounded off with a statement denying parity between the Mosaic revelation and prophetic revelations subsequent to Moses' death; a statement that, in effect, establishes the Mosaic age as normative and confers authoritative status on the record of Moses' life and work (Deut 34:10). By this means the post-exilic commonwealth laid a firm foundation in the past for its own self-understanding as a community based on covenant and law.

If, then, we view the process of formation beginning with this final stage and working backward we must assign a decisive role to the Priestly and Deuteronomic writers. The former, whose contribution is relatively easy to detect, were responsible for the basic structuring of the work. The narrative framework within which the massive corpus of Priestly law is presented begins with creation and ends with the establishment of the sanctuary in the promised land (Joshua 18–19). The Deuteronomic contribution is not confined to the book of Deuteronomy but is in evidence elsewhere in the Pentateuch (e.g., Genesis 15; Exodus 32–34), though to what extent still remains to be clarified. If, for the sake of continuity, we continue to speak of J and E, we must now acknowledge that there is no longer any certainty about the origin, date, and extent of these sources. Some of the material assigned to them is either Deuteronomic or of unknown provenance. The J material in Genesis 1–11 may even be later than P, serving as a reflective supplement and commentary in the manner of the later stages. Both D and P have certainly incorporated early traditions and written sources in prose and verse, but the entire issue of pre-exilic source material in the Pentateuch—its extent, its origins written and oral, and its editorial history—remains to be clarified.

READING THE PENTATEUCH THEOLOGICALLY

A theological reading of the Pentateuch must take account not only of the final form but also of the successive restructurings, re-editings and expansions that, according to a historical-critical reading, eventuated in the final form. This process implies that any theologically significant theme will have undergone a process of development. In addition, different traditions, notably those of the Priestly and Deuteronomic writers, have been allowed to coexist even where they differ in significant respects. Reducing these perspectives to a common theological denominator would risk missing the richness and variety of religious thinking in the Pentateuch.

Theological understanding is also conditioned by the point of view, the perspective, of the reader and the convictions of the community within which the text is read. Neither Judaism nor Christianity has assigned absolute and exclusive authority to the Pentateuch. In Judaism functional canonicity includes Mishnah, Gemarah, and Toseftah, understood as the deposit of the oral law. Early Christianity continued to regard the Law and the Prophets as authoritative but read them in the light of the new reality in Christ. Persons and events in the Pentateuch were interpreted as prefiguring this new reality and the prophets as predicting it. The laws in the Pentateuch were evaluated in widely different ways from the apostolic period on. From an early date, the Decalogue served as a compendium of moral teaching (e.g., in the *Didache*), a circumstance that, when taken with the neglect of the ritual laws, explains why it played a very minor role in Jewish teaching. (It is mentioned only twice in the Mishnah.) This issue came to the fore with particular clarity at the Reformation. The Lutheran distinction between law and gospel, reinforced by Luther's own often-expressed aversion to Judaism, resulted in a distinct undervaluation of the legal content of the Pentateuch. Calvinism, on the other hand, tended rather to overestimate the place of law in Christian theology and church polity. The result is that only in recent years have Christian biblical scholars begun to give serious and unprejudiced attention to the legal material, including the ritual law.

While this is clearly not the place to attempt a comprehensive survey or synthesis of religious ideas in the Pentateuch, which would be tantamount to writing a history of Israelite religion, some account should be given of the leading theological symbols and ideas in the major literary strands.

The Priestly Writers (P). While several Jewish scholars have followed Yehezkel Kaufmann[30] in dating P to the pre-exilic period, the majority opinion has placed this school in the sixth or fifth century BCE while allowing that much of the legal and cultic material may have originated earlier. There is no consensus on the issue of P's relation to earlier narrative material, some viewing it as basically commentary and editorial expansion and others as an independent narrative source. In favor of the latter alternative, at least with regard to the narrative core of the P material, are the thematic and linguistic correspondences between the creation account in Gen 1:1–2:3, the construction of the wilderness sanctuary in Exodus 35–40 (see especially 39:32; 40:33), and its establishment at Shiloh in the land of Canaan (Josh 18:1; 19:51).[31] One implication of this structural feature is that the created order exists for the worship and praise of God. The seven days of creation represent the liturgical week. Sabbath is rooted in the created order, and the fact that its celebration concludes the construction of the wilderness sanctuary signals a close association between world building and sanctuary building (Exod 31:12-17). The heavenly bodies are created on the fourth day as a means of establishing the religious calendar. If we confine ourselves to the P strand, the Sinai event consists exclusively in the reception by Moses in a vision of the specifications for the sanctuary and its cult (Exod 19:1; 24:15-18; 25–31), which can be inaugurated only after the ordination of priests, a ceremony that also lasts seven days (Leviticus 8–9).

Even if it is argued that the P version was intended to be read together with other, and presumably earlier, accounts of the Sinai/Horeb event, it is still remarkable that this source omits any reference to a covenant. The P source in fact represents a rather radical rethinking of the covenant idea, no doubt in response to the situation of exile. The first covenant is made with the new humanity after the flood, long before Israel appears on the historical scene (Gen 9:8-17). All of humanity had received a religious qualification at creation (Gen 1:26-28), and now is

offered a new dispensation, including the so-called Noachide laws, and an unconditional commitment on the part of God to preserve the new creation. The only covenant with Israel recorded in P is with Abraham, to whom is promised nationhood, land, and the divine presence (Gen 17:1-21). Both of these covenants, with humanity and with Israel, are unilateral and unconditional, since circumcision is the sign of Israel's covenant and not a stipulation on the observance of which God's promise is contingent. Both are also "everlasting covenants" (Gen 9:16; 17:7-8, 13) that, therefore, do not require periodic renewal as do most covenants. All that is called for is that God *remember* the covenant commitment, which God does when the people are languishing in exile (Exod 2:24; 6:5; Lev 26:42, 45).

According to P the covenant promise of divine presence is fulfilled through the erection of the sanctuary and the inauguration of the cult, a conclusion implicit in the structure of the core narrative. Throughout the wilderness journey, presence is signified by the mysterious glory or effulgence (כבוד *kābôd*) that comes to rest in the sanctuary (Exod 40:34-35), appears when important decisions have to be taken (e.g., Num 14:10; 16:19), and guides Israel in its progress to the land. In P, all aspects of the liturgical life of the people are revealed in orderly fashion. Only rituals not requiring presence in the sanctuary and the participation of the priesthood are revealed before the cult is inaugurated; namely, sabbath (Exod 31:12-17; cf. 16:22-30), circumcision (Gen 17:9-14), and Passover (Exod 12:1-28). The P version of the flood story, therefore, omits mention of the distinction between clean and unclean animals and Noah's sacrifice on leaving the ark. The basic rationale for the sacrificial cult, as of the laws governing clean and unclean and sexual relations, is to preserve and, where necessary, restore the cosmic order established at creation. That order is disturbed by sin, even involuntary sin (e.g., bodily discharges), and can be restored only by the mandatory purgation and reparation sacrifices (Lev 4:1–6:7). The tenfold occurrence in the creation recital of the phrase "according to its/their kind" suggests that the distinction between clean and unclean fauna (Leviticus 11–15) was intended to preserve the norms established in creation and to inculcate a reverent regard for the created order. Although often dismissed as archaic and irrational, these and similar regulations reflect an ecological

---

30. Y. Kaufmann, *The Religion of Israel from Its Beginnings to the Babylonian Exile* (New York: Schocken, 1972).

31. J. Blenkinsopp, "The Structure of P," *CBQ* 38 (1976) 275-92.

concern in the broadest sense, a discriminating ethical attitude to the taking of life for human nourishment, and a concern for the body as that part of the world for which each one is more directly responsible.

The Deuteronomists (D). A significantly different perspective is apparent in the Deuteronomic corpus, consisting in Deuteronomy, the Deuteronomistic History (Joshua–2 Kings), additions to the narrative in the Tetrateuch, and editorial accretions in several prophetic books, especially Jeremiah. Deuteronomy presents not so much a law as a program or polity for the future Israelite commonwealth. Endowed with the authority of Moses as lawgiver and founder of the nation, it grounds the social existence of the people on the new covenant made on the eve of entry into the land. Unlike the P covenant, that of the Deuteronomists is genuinely bilateral and conditional in that its maintenance is contingent on a faithful and trustful commitment on the part of Israel to the observance of the Law. In this respect, it is comparable to, and was probably influenced in its formulation by, more or less contemporary Assyrian vassal treaties. The emphasis, therefore, is on Israel as a moral community. The connection between the fulfillment of the promises and faith that finds expression in fidelity to the law is already clearly articulated in the Deuteronomic profile of Abraham (Gen 18:17-19; 22:16-18; 26:4-5), the starting point for the presentation of Abraham in both Judaism and Christianity as the model and paradigm of faith (e.g., Heb 11:8-12). On numerous occasions, the Mosaic homilies in Deuteronomy emphasize that the gift of land is contingent on fidelity to the Law, and it is made abundantly clear that without faith Israel cannot fulfill its destiny (see Deut 1:32; 9:23).

The covenant is also the basis for Israel's election and its consequent special status vis-à-vis the nations of the world. While the dangerous ambiguities inherent in this idea of election are abundantly clear, the Deuteronomists emphasize repeatedly both its origin in a divine initiative (see Deut 4:32-40; 7:7-11) and the obligations it entails (7:7-11). The uniqueness of Israel, thus defined and circumscribed, is emphasized at every turn. Thus the law is seen as the counterpart of the intellectual tradition or wisdom of other peoples (Deut 4:5-8), and prophecy is contrasted with divination and similar forms of mediation practiced elsewhere (13:1-5; 18:9-22). Most important, Deuteronomy insists on an exclusive relationship with one God: Yahweh, God of Israel. This conviction, of immense significance for the future, is enshrined in the שמע *šĕmaʿ* (Deut 6:4-9), a confessional formula that has sustained the faith of the Jewish people down to the present.

The incorporation of Deuteronomy into the framework of the P narrative resulted in the juxtaposition within the same corpus of different theological perspectives, those of the two major schools and those of their sources. Thus the covenant of obligation of D is balanced against the promissory and indefectible covenant of the P writers, and the more limited and nationalistic perspective of Deuteronomy is offset by the more universalistic range of the P work. The extension of the narrative back to creation and the early history of humanity also permitted the grounding of institutions—sabbath and covenant—in antecedents of unimpeachable antiquity. This combination also provides an illustration of the tension between tradition and situation. Like Israel, both synagogue and church draw their self-understanding, their ability to survive and flourish, from the myth of their origins, constantly repeated and reactualized in recital and ritual. Appeal to a shared memory, so prominent in Deuteronomy, is a central feature of the Pentateuch. It appears with particular clarity in the festivals that memorialize the founding events of the community. It is also a prominent feature of the legal tradition. It is noteworthy, for example, how care for the rights of the resident alien is enjoined on the grounds of collective memory: "You shall not oppress a resident alien; you know the heart of an alien, for you were aliens in the land of Egypt" (Exod 23:9 NRSV). But allegiance to the past must also allow for openness to the demands imposed by life in a changing world, requiring an ongoing testing and reinterpreting of what has been received. A careful and critical reading of the Pentateuch shows that this process of incorporating and reinterpreting the past continued throughout the history of Israel.

Other Sources. While the existence of *continuous* early, pre-exilic sources can no longer be taken for granted, the Pentateuch in its final, post-exilic form has clearly incorporated much pre-exilic narrative and legal source material. With the possible exception of Abraham, of whom we first begin to hear in exilic texts (Ezek 33:24), traditions about the ancestors were in circulation from an early time (e.g., Hos 12:4-5, 13), as also about the exodus (e.g., Amos

3:1; 9:7; Hos 2:15; 11:1) and wilderness period (e.g., Hos 2:14-15; 9:10). In whatever form these traditions circulated, they served to sustain a sense of corporate identity strong enough to survive the destruction of the state and the experience of exile, and they have continued down to the present to exercise this function for the different "interpretive communities" that have accepted them.

The J version of the early history of humanity in Genesis 1–11 has generally been assigned a date in the early monarchy period, perhaps as early as Solomon's reign, though we have seen reason to suspect that a much later date would be more appropriate. Using ancient Mesopotamian mythic traditions as a model, the author projects on to human origins a psychologically profound and disturbing diagnosis of human existence. In a manner reminiscent of some of the later prophets (e.g., Jer 17:9-10) and sages (e.g., Job 14:1-6), the author emphasizes both the ineradicable human tendency to evil (see especially Gen 6:5 and 8:21) and the reality of divine mercy and forgiveness. In their own quite different way, the stories about the ancestors (however they originated and in whatever form they were known to the post-exilic redactors) also succeed in rendering the richness and complexity of human existence in the presence of God. These stories are unified by the promise of land, progeny, and divine blessing, announced at the outset (Gen 12:1-3) and repeated at regular intervals throughout (e.g., 13:14-17; 15:7-21; 26:2-4; 46:2-3). Yet at the crucial points of the narrative—at the beginning, in the middle, and at the end—the protagonists are outside the land, and the story ends with exile in Egypt. In this situation of deferred fulfillment, Abraham is presented as the model of trust and fidelity, especially in the climactic scene of the near-sacrifice of Isaac (Genesis 22). The Jacob narrative, less schematic and psychologically more realistic than that of Abraham, is organized around the twenty-year exile of the protagonist and the transformation he must undergo in order to bear the name Israel (Gen 32:22-32; cf. 35:9-15 P).

The "Song at the Sea" (Exod 15:1-18), one of the oldest poems in the HB, celebrates deliverance from slavery in Egypt by miraculous, divine intervention. The accompanying prose account narrating the sequence of events leading up to this point is also based on ancient tradition, though we are no longer able to identify its earliest formulation or trace its development in detail. These events were decisive for Israel's self-identity and its relationship with its God ("I am Yahweh your God from the land of Egypt" [Hos 12:9; 13:4]). Commemorated in the Passover ceremony, they achieved paradigmatic status for both community and individual: "In every generation one must look upon oneself as if one had in one's own person come out of Egypt." Something similar can be said of the wilderness narratives (Exod 15:22–18:27; Num 10:29–36:13), also based on ancient tradition, as exemplifying divine guidance and providence and legitimating the institutional life of the community. This context, then, confers on the law given at Sinai/Horeb its character as gift and grace.

BIBLIOGRAPHY

Alter, Robert. *The Art of Biblical Narrative.* New York: Basic Books, 1981.

Blenkinsopp, Joseph. *The Pentateuch: An Introduction to the First Five Books of the Bible.* Anchor Bible Reference Library. New York: Doubleday, 1992.

———. *Prophecy and Canon.* Notre Dame: University of Notre Dame Press, 1977.

Knight, Douglas A. "The Pentateuch." In Douglas A. Knight and Gene M. Tucker, eds. *The Hebrew Bible and Its Modern Interpreters.* Chico, Calif.: Scholars Press, 1985.

Noth, Martin. *A History of Pentateuchal Traditions.* Englewood Cliffs, N.J.: Prentice-Hall, 1972.

Rendtorff, Rolf. "Pentateuchal Studies on the Move," *JSOT* 3 (1977) 2-10, 43-45.

Van Seters, John. *In Search of History: Historiography in the Ancient World and the Origins of Biblical History.* New Haven: Yale University Press, 1983.

———. "Recent Studies on the Pentateuch: A Crisis in Method," *JAOS* 99 (1979) 663-67.

von Rad, Gerhard. "The Form-Critical Problem of the Hexateuch." In *The Problem of the Hexateuch and Other Essays.* New York: McGraw-Hill, 1966, 1-78.

———. *Old Testament Theology.* Vol. 1: *The Theology of Israel's Historical Traditions.* Translated by D. M. G. Stalker. New York: Harper & Row, 1962.

Whybray, R. Norman. *The Making of the Pentateuch: A Methodological Study.* Sheffield: JSOT, 1987.

Winnett, F. V. "Re-examining the Foundations," *JBL* 84 (1965) 1-19.

THE BOOK OF GENESIS

INTRODUCTION, COMMENTARY, AND REFLECTIONS
BY
TERENCE E. FRETHEIM

THE BOOK OF
GENESIS

INTRODUCTION

The book of Genesis stands at the head of the canon. Its range is breathtaking, moving from cosmos to family, from ordered world to reconciled brothers, from the seven days of the creation of the universe to the seventy descendants of Jacob entering the land of their sojourn. Hence, it stands as a monumental challenge to the interpreter.

The canonical placement of Genesis is important for various reasons. Genesis is a book about beginnings, from the beginnings of the universe and various orderings of humankind to the beginnings of the people of Israel. It also witnesses to the beginnings of God's activity in the life of the world. But creation is more than chronology. Genesis stands at the beginning because creation is such a fundamental theological category for the rest of the canon. God's continuing blessing and ordering work at every level is creational. Moreover, only in relationship to the creation can God's subsequent actions in and through Israel be properly understood. The placement of creation demonstrates that God's purposes with Israel are universal in scope. God's work in redemption serves creation, the *entire* creation, since it reclaims a creation that labors under the deep and pervasive effects of sin. Even more, the canonical placement makes clear that God's redemptive work does not occur in a vacuum; it occurs in a context that has been shaped in decisive ways by the life-giving, creative work of God. Redemption can never be understood as *ex nihilo* without denigrating God's gifts given in creation.

THE CRITICAL STUDY OF GENESIS

For more than two hundred years, *source criticism* has provided the predominant literary approach to the study of Genesis and the Pentateuch. In fact, Genesis has often been studied only as part of this larger literary whole. Hence, Genesis is usually seen as a composite work, consisting primarily of three interwoven sources (Yahwist [J], Elohist [E], Priestly [P]), with some texts attributed to other traditions (e.g., chaps. 14 and 49). Genesis thus grew over time, with these sources gradually brought together by redactors over five hundred years or more, from the United Monarchy to the post-exilic era.

This long-prevailing scholarly consensus has come under sharp challenge from a number of perspectives in the last generation. From within the source-critical perspective, the nature, scope, and dating of the sources have been regular subjects of debate. Few doubt that Genesis consists of traditions from various historical periods, but there is little consensus regarding the way in which they have been brought together into their present form.[1]

I view Genesis as a patchwork quilt of traditions from various periods in Israel's life. The earliest stories date from before the monarchy; over time certain traditions began to coalesce around key figures, such as Abraham and Jacob, and more extensive blocks were gradually built up. The fact that the major sections of Genesis (generally, chaps. 1–11; 12–25; 26–36; 37–50) remain identifiable clusters within a relatively thin, overarching framework sustains this theory. A redactor (probably J) wove these clusters of tradition together into a coherent whole, provided a basic framework (perhaps focused on the ancestral promises), and integrated them with the larger story of the Pentateuch. While J probably worked early in the monarchical period, arguments for a later date for the Yahwist are attractive (not least because of the sophisticated form of its anthropomorphisms). Over the centuries reworkings of this collection took place, drawing on other, as yet unintegrated, traditions (the Elohist may be one such supplementary reworking). One major redaction is to be identified with P (probably during the exile); this redactor drew on materials from a wide variety of sources, older and more recent, and placed a decisive stamp on the entire corpus. It is possible that deuteronomistic redactors worked over this material at a later time, integrating it into a still larger collection with only minor touch-ups.

The purpose of these retellings of the material is not entirely clear and may vary, involving sociopolitical and religious issues. Each reworking made it ever more difficult to discern where the inherited traditions and the retellings begin and end. It is likely, however, that theological and kerygmatic interests come more and more into play, so that finally one must speak of the essential testimonial character of the material, a witness to the complex interrelationships of divine action and human response.[2]

Newer literary approaches have also called into question many of the assumptions and

---

1. For a recent survey, see R. N. Whybray, *The Making of the Pentateuch* (Sheffield: *JSOT*, 1987); and J. Blenkinsopp, *The Pentateuch: An Introduction to the First Five Books of the Bible* (New York: Doubleday, 1992) 1-30.
2. See W. Brueggemann and H. W. Wolff, *The Vitality of Old Testament Traditions* (Atlanta: John Knox, 1982).

conclusions of the source-critical consensus. These strategies focus on issues of literary criticism rather than literary history, on the texts as they are rather than any history prior to their present shape. Such readers attempt to hear the texts as we now have them and to discern their various rhetorical features as they work together to form a coherent whole. At times, this analysis has been undertaken with an eye to literary parallels in other ancient Near Eastern literature (e.g., the *Gilgamesh Epic*).[3]

The book of Genesis has been one of the most popular workshops for these approaches. Over the last two decades hundreds of articles and sections of books have mined the literary riches of these chapters and unearthed many insights into the ways in which they can be read with greater profit. Yet, it is not so clear how these gains are to be integrated with the more historical approaches. While historical issues continue to be important, this commentary will emphasize literary approaches in order to perceive what makes these texts work.

Literary studies and analyses of the theological movement within these texts have not kept pace with one another. For example, many literary (and other) studies simply work with the assumptions and conclusions of classical theism in the analysis of the theological material the texts present. On the other hand, some studies take pains to treat the theological elements at the same level as any other (e.g., God becomes a character like every other). I will attend to the theological dynamic of the text and recognize its special stature in view of the community of faith that produced it and the canonical place eventually given to it.[4]

Another lively concern in Genesis studies has to do with ancient Near Eastern parallels (and beyond, possibly even Greece). Since the unearthing of the Mesopotamian accounts of creation and the flood over a century ago, augmented since by numerous discoveries, scholars have devoted considerable attention to discerning possible links with Genesis. While this is true of Genesis as a whole, parallels to chaps. 1–11 have constituted a special focus. Although direct points of dependence do not seem common, it is clear that Israel participated in a comprehensive ancient Near Eastern culture that had considerable impact on its ways of thinking and writing, both in details and with larger themes. Apart from more formal links, such as language, some have tended to view these parallels largely in negative terms. At the same time, Israel's deep dependence upon its cultural context extends even to theological matters (e.g., the understanding of moral order or creation by word) and to the very creation-disruption-flood structure of chaps. 1–11. Interpreters must maintain a fine balance between recognizing such dependence (finally, a witness to the work of the Creator) and Israel's genuinely new and imaginative ideas and formulations.

Feminist scholarship has produced important studies that have influenced this commentary at numerous points. This work has attended particularly to the place of the woman in chaps. 1–3 and the prominent role of women in the ancestral narratives. Phyllis Trible's

3. On new literary approaches, see R. Alter, *The Art of Biblical Narrative* (New York: Basic Books, 1981). On extra-biblical parallels, see D. Damrosch, *The Narrative Covenant* (San Francisco: Harper & Row, 1987).
4. On theology and narrative, see Terence Fretheim, *Exodus* (Louisville: Westminster/John Knox, 1991) 10-12.

work, in particular, has had an immense and salutary influence. In addition, anthropological and sociological studies have expanded our knowledge of the issues of kinship and culture.[5] Generally, a proliferation of approaches is elucidating ever new dimensions of these important biblical materials.

LITERARY FORM

There are basically two types of literature in Genesis, narrative and numerative, to use Westermann's language.[6] Poetic pieces are integrated into the narratives as well (e.g., 2:23; 3:14-19; 16:11-12; 25:23; 27:27-29, 39-40; 49:1-27).

1. Narratives. Little consensus has emerged regarding the proper label for these narratives, though *saga* has been used often. The issues in chaps. 1–11 are particularly complex (see below). "Family narrative (story)" emphasizes the family unit as central to these texts, and in a way that has no real parallel elsewhere in the OT. While not historiographical in character and with much imagination used in the telling, the narratives do possess certain features associated with history writing, e.g., a chronological framework and some cumulative and developmental character.[7]

The language of story may be most helpful in determining how these materials functioned for Israel.[8] They are told in such a way that they could become the story of each ensuing generation. The readers could participate in a great, yet often quite hidden, drama of divine action and human response. At this juncture of past story and present reality Israel came to know what it meant to be the people of God. The faith was not fundamentally an idea, but an embodiment, a way of life. The language and experience of faith thus remained concrete and personal. Thus it has the capacity to keep the reader anchored in this world. It does not dissolve into myth, into some mystical world of the gods that suppresses the human or the natural, or some religious world far removed from the secular sphere. By and large, the world reflected in these stories is ordinary, everyday, and familiar, filled with the surprises and joys, the sufferings and the troubles, the complexities and ambiguities known to every community.

At the same time, the story form allows (in a way that history proper does not) an admixture of Israel's story and God's story. But even the latter is seen to be this-worldly, as God works toward the divine purposes in and through less than perfect individuals and world. And God's story has the ultimate purpose, not of bringing people into some heavenly sphere, but of enabling a transformation of this life.

The capacity of the story to draw one into it in such a way as to encompass the full life

5. Phyllis Trible, *God and the Rhetoric of Sexuality* (Philadelphia: Fortress, 1978) 72-143; see also the work of R. Hendel and C. Meyers, listed in the bibliography.

6. C. Westermann, *Genesis 1–11: A Commentary* (Minneapolis: Augsburg, 1984) 6.

7. On the Pentateuch as a historiographical work in comparison with early Greek histories, see the assessment of John van Seters in Blenkinsopp, *Pentateuch,* 37-42.

8. See T. Fretheim, *Deuteronomic History* (Nashville: Abingdon, 1983) 39-40; R. W. L. Moberly, *The Old Testament of the Old Testament: Patriarchal Narratives and Mosaic Yahwism* (Minneapolis: Fortress, 1992) 130-46; D. Steinmetz, *From Father to Son: Kinship, Conflict and Continuity in Genesis* (Louisville: Westminster/John Knox, 1991) 134-55.

of the reader has the effect of overcoming the distance between past story and present reader; the horizons merge. At the same time, readers will encounter that which is often different from their own stories; there are surprises and discontinuities as past and present life stories come into contact with one another. Some hearers may reject the story, but for those who respond positively the story may provide a means of shaping identity (a constitutive function), a mirror for self-identity (a descriptive function), or a model for the life of faith (a paradigmatic function). One may thereby not only become a member of the people of God, but also come to know who one is, and what shape the life of faith ought to take in the world.

The narratives offer an exercise in self-understanding. They become a vehicle through which a new generation can learn its identity once again as the people of Abraham, a people who have trod in his footsteps, who have taken his journey. It is one more retelling of the past, not to find patterns for moral behavior, but to understand who we are as the people of God who have inherited these commands and promises, who have ventured down similar paths. We can thereby see where we have been, who we now are, and the shape of our paths into the future.

2. Genealogies. "Genesis is a book whose plot is genealogy."[9] Israel formulated family trees, often with social and political overtones. As with us, they were concerned about kinship interrelationships and tracking family origins and "pedigrees," especially for important figures. Also similar is the way in which genealogies are woven into family stories. Major portions of seven chapters in Genesis consist of genealogies, an interest evident in other OT texts (e.g., Chronicles) as well as in the NT (see Matthew 1; Luke 1).

The ten תולדות (tôlēdôt translated either "genealogy"/"generations" or "account"/"story")—2:4 (heaven and earth); 5:1 (Adam); 6:9 (Noah); 10:1 (Noah's sons); 11:10 (Shem); 11:27 (Terah); 25:12 (Ishmael); 25:19 (Isaac); 36:1, 9 (Esau); 37:2 (Jacob)—constitute a prominent structuring device in Genesis. These Priestly genealogies are supplemented by a few others (e.g., that of Cain, 4:17-26). Genealogies have an enumerative style, but at times they are "broken" by narrative pieces (e.g., 10:8-12). They usually introduce a section, but at times they look both backward and forward (2:4; 37:2). One type of genealogy is linear (one person in each generation, 5:1-32); the other is segmented (multiple lines of descent), characteristic of branches of the family outside the chosen line (table of nations; Ishmael; Esau). Because genealogies cut across the break between chaps. 11 and 12, they witness to the fundamental creational unity of Genesis.

The historical value of the genealogies is much debated, but their function of providing continuity over these chapters probably means that they were understood as some kind of historical anchor for the larger story. Their original setting was the family or tribe, those most interested in such matters, and within which they were often transmitted orally over many generations. They show that every character is kin to every other, a key to Israelite

9. N. Steinberg, "The Genealogical Framework of the Family Stories in Genesis," *Semeia* 46 (1989) 41. Generally, see R. Wilson, *Genealogy and History in the Biblical World* (New Haven: Yale University Press, 1977).

self-identity, especially in times of conflict or dispersion. Hence, Genesis is fundamentally about one big extended family. The genealogies also demonstrate that Israel is truly kin to all the surrounding peoples, a fact that helps to develop the meaning of the people's special role. The genealogies thus are integrally related to the essential concerns of the narratives.

Because genealogies order people into families, and witness to the continued existence of families in spite of much difficulty and dysfunctionality, they fit most fundamentally within a theology of creation (so explicitly in 5:1-2). They present "the steady, ongoing rhythm of events which stamp the course of human existence—birth, length of life, begetting, death" in which both God and human beings participate.[10] Moreover, because the first of the *tôlēdôt* includes the nonhuman, genealogies link human and nonhuman into a larger *creational family,* in which every creature is, in effect, kin to every other. Even more, because genealogies also encompass larger human groupings (10:1-32; 25:12-18), they witness to the range of the divine creative activity in the ordering of the world.

The narratives, on the other hand, "are inherently messy . . . take account of much that is problematic and contingent, all the vagaries of human life . . . pursuing a far less predictable course of surprise and unanticipated events."[11] Naomi Steinberg speaks of genealogies reintroducing equilibrium into such messy family lives, restabilizing them for the next journey into a volatile future. Yet, she shows that this perspective is too simple. Some genealogies also contain elements of disequilibrium, contingency, and open-endedness (see 11:30; 25:19-26; 37:2); hence, the genealogies do not witness so univocally to order and stability as one might initially think.[12] Indeed, most genealogies contain such an unusual element (e.g., 5:24 on Enoch; 5:29; 6:9 on Noah; 10:8-12 on Nimrod). Such features integrate narrative messiness into the very heart of the genealogical order. They show thereby that the genealogies do not witness to a *determined* order of reality. Cain's genealogy (4:17-26) testifies further to this integration; it *intensifies* the contingencies of the prior narratives. Genealogies are finally *insufficient* for ordering purposes; another type of divine activity will be needed in order to reclaim the creation—namely, redemption.

FAITH AND HISTORY IN GENESIS

The book of Genesis does not present the reader with historical narrative, at least in any modern sense. Its primary concerns are theological and kerygmatic. Those responsible for the material as we now have it (and no doubt at other stages in its transmission) were persons of faith concerned to speak or reflect on a word of God to other persons of faith. The voice of a living community of faith resounds through these texts. Rooted in history

---

10. Westermann, *Genesis 1-11,* 7.
11. R. Robinson, "Literary Functions of the Genealogies of Genesis," *CBQ* 48 (1986) 597.
12. Steinberg, "The Genealogical Framework," 43.

In this way, Genesis is not socially or historically disinterested; it was written—at each stage of transmission—with the problems and possibilities of a particular audience in view.

Although scholars have a difficult time discerning those audiences, the text is linked to specific times and places. While the latest redactors may well have made the witness of the text more generally available to ongoing communities of faith, the material has not been flattened out into generalities. The most basic shaping of Genesis probably occurred in exile. Traditions in Genesis are consistent with other examples of creation language during this era, as evidenced by Isaiah 40–55, which relates Israel's future to the universal purposes of God. Affirmations of divine faithfulness to ancient promises—a veritable litany in these texts—speak volumes in a time when the future appears to stand in jeopardy. In attending to Israel's ancestral heritage, both in narrative and in genealogy, the authors address sharp issues of communal identity. The various stories of the ancestors often seem to mirror the history of Israel, assisting the exiles in coming to terms with their own past (this will often be noted in the commentary; e.g., the parallels between 12:10-20 and the exodus). These texts spoke a clear word of God to exiled people.

The literary vehicle in and through which this word of God is addressed narrates a story of the past. Although the ancient writers were not concerned with reconstructing a history of this early era, modern scholars have had a great interest in determining the extent to which these texts reflect "what actually happened" (on chaps. 1–11, see below). This task has been made difficult by the nature of the texts themselves as well as by the difficulties of assessing extra-biblical parallels.

Scholarly efforts at historical reconstruction of the ancestral period have had mixed results.[13] A period of some confidence in the basic historicity of these texts within the second millennium BCE has faded in recent years in view of the character of the texts and challenges to the interpretation of putative archaeological evidence. Since the biblical texts underwent a long period of transmission, they reflect aspects of Israel's history all along the way. For example, relationships between these texts and other tribal and genealogical OT materials suggest that various historical realities from both before and after the United Monarchy are reflected in them. Various ancient Near Eastern parallels to patriarchal names, customs, and modes of life have at times been overdrawn; yet they are not finally without historical value, even for a second-millennium dating at some points. While it is not possible to determine whether the women and men of Genesis were actual historical persons, it seems reasonable to claim that the narratives carry some authentic memories of Israel's pre-exodus heritage. At the same time, Israel's valuing of these materials for its own faith and life appears not to have centered on issues of historicity; however, it is likely that Israel thought these traditions derived from pre-exodus times.

The religion of the ancestors reflected in the texts also figures in this discussion about historical background. The religious (and other) practices of these chapters are often

13. See a survey in G. Ramsey, *The Quest for the Historical Israel* (Atlanta: John Knox, 1981) 28-43. See also K. McCarter, "The Historical Abraham," *Int* 42 (1988) 341-52.

distinctive when compared to later Israelite convention.[14] Hence, later Israelites did not simply read their own religious lives back into these texts (though nothing seems to be incompatible with later Yahwism). They preserved some memories of earlier practices, including worship of God under various forms of the name El (see 16:13; 21:33; 33:20; El is the high god in the Canaanite pantheon), referred to as the God of my/our/your father(s), the God of Abraham, the God of Isaac, and the God of Jacob. The ancestral God was understood to be a personal deity who accompanied this family on its journeys, providing care and protection. Some traditions understand that Yahweh was a name revealed only at the time of Moses (Exod 3:14-16; 6:2-3) and that El was an earlier name for God (although the OT generally understands El to be an alternate name for Yahweh). The frequent use of Yahweh in Genesis is anachronistic in some ways, but it conveys an important theological conviction—namely, that the God whom the ancestors worshiped under the name El had characteristics common to Yahweh and, in fact, is to be identified with Yahweh.

UNITY, STRUCTURE, AND THEME

It has long been the practice in Genesis study to drive a sharp wedge between chaps. 1–11, the so-called Primeval History (Story), and chaps. 12–50, the Patriarchal (Ancestral) History. More recently, under the impact of literary-critical readings, there has been renewed interest in the integrity of Genesis as a whole.[15]

In some ways this division is appropriate, with chap. 12 marking a new stage in God's relationship with the world. Even those who sharpen this division often note that 12:1-3 is a fulcrum text, linking Abraham with "all the families of the earth." Hence, it has been common to claim that God's choice of Abraham had a universal purpose: to extend God's salvific goals through this family to the entire world. Even more, this theme has been tracked through chaps. 12–50, with particular attention not only to its verbal repetition (e.g., 18:18; 22:18; 26:4; 28:14), but also to the numerous contacts made between Israel's ancestors and the "nonchosen" peoples. Remarkably little polemic is directed against outsiders in the Genesis text. The promises of God to Abraham are intended for the world. The way in which Israel's ancestors did or did not respond to this intention served as a negative or positive model for every generation.

The focus of such discussion has been so sharply placed on "salvation history" that creation themes have been neglected. Even more, it is striking the extent to which the more emphatic themes of chaps. 12–50 are grounded in chaps. 1–11, wherein God promises and blesses, elects and saves. God first establishes a covenant and makes promises, not to Abraham, but to Noah (6:18 and 9:8-17); God's promissory activity

14. For a review, see Moberly, *The Old Testament.*

15. See D. Clines, *The Theme of the Pentateuch* (Sheffield: *JSOT*, 1978); B. Childs, *Introduction to the Old Testament as Scripture* (Philadelphia: Fortress, 1979) 136-60; B. Dahlberg, "On Recognizing the Unity of Genesis," *TD* 24 (1977) 360-67; T. Mann, "All the Families of the Earth: The Theological Unity of Genesis," *Int* 45 (1991) 341-53; and Overview sections in this commentary.

in Israel participates in God's promissory relation to the larger world (see the manifold promises to Ishmael and Esau). God's work of blessing in the world does not begin with Abraham; it is integral to chaps. 1–11 (see 9:1, 26) and so God's blessing work through Abraham must involve intensification and pervasiveness, not a new reality. Since God saves Noah, his family, and the animals (Ps 36:6), God does not become a savior with Abraham or Israel. Issues of creation and redemption are integrated throughout Genesis (see p. 321). God's promises and salvific acts must finally be seen as serving all of creation. God acts to free people, indeed the entire world, to be what they were created to be.[16]

Scholars have noted various forms of evidence for structured unity in Genesis, especially in the genealogies (extending from 2:4 to 37:2; see p. 325) and the divine promises (from 8:21 to 50:24). More refined efforts to discern structures throughout the book have been less successful, with the focus of attention on the four major, distinct sections.[17] Links within Genesis have been discerned in chaps. 1–11 and 37–50, from family discord/harmony, to fertility (1:28 and 47:27), to the extension of life to a flood/famine-filled world (41:57), to the "good" that God is about in the creation and through this family (50:20); in some sense Joseph functions as a new Adam (41:38).

At the same time, the Joseph story does not occasion a return to Eden. Sin and its ill effects remain very much in place. Human life, more generally, becomes ever more complex as one moves from Adam to Joseph. These developments are matched by shifts in the imaging of God, whose words and deeds become less direct and obtrusive. God's actions are never all-controlling in Genesis, but a more prominent role is given to the human in the Joseph story, from the transmission of promises to the exercise of leadership. These developments correlate with narratives that become less and less episodic.[18]

The following themes in Genesis as a whole may be gathered; creation themes remain prominent throughout. (1) The presence and activity of God in every sphere of life, among nonchosen and chosen, for purposes of judgment and salvation. These two themes tie chaps. 1–11 closely to chaps. 12–50: God responds to ongoing human sinfulness through sentence and judgment (often involving creational realities, from flood to plague to fire and brimstone); God also responds in a gracious way to humankind, even though their lives have been deeply affected by sin and its consequences. (2) Blessing is a creational category in which both God and humankind, nonchosen and chosen, are engaged. This theme includes the continuity of the family through the struggles of barrenness and birth, and the fertility of fields and animals, often juxtaposed with famine. Blessing also relates to land, raising ecological considerations that are not far from the surface (from the flood to Sodom and Gomorrah). (3) The pervasive concern for kinship and family, an order of creation. One contemporary way of looking at chaps. 12–50 is through the lens of family systems theory and the manifestations of a dysfunctional family one sees throughout. The various dimensions of family life belong within the sphere of God's concern. God

16. See T. Fretheim, "The Reclamation of Creation," *Int* 45 (1991) 354-65.
17. See Overview sections; G. Rendsburg, *The Redaction of Genesis* (Winona Lake: Eisenbrauns, 1986).
18. See R. Cohn, "Narrative Structure and Canonical Perspective in Genesis," *JSOT* 25 (1983) 3-16.

is at work in and through family problems and possibilities for purposes of reconciliation (50:20). (4) Concern for the life of the nation also entails one of the most basic orders of creation. In the Joseph story especially, the writers devote attention to issues of economics, agriculture, and the dynamics of political and governmental life more generally, in and through which God is at work for blessing (41:53-57; 47:13-26). (5) The role of the human in the divine economy. It is not uncommon to denigrate the importance of human activity in these chapters. For example, von Rad states: "The story of Hagar shows us a fainthearted faith that cannot leave things to God and believes it necessary to help things along. . . . [A child] conceived . . . in little faith cannot be the heir of promise."[19] But divine promise, appropriated by faith, does not entail human passivity in working toward God's goals for the creation. The high place given to the human role, from creation to Joseph, testifies to the depth of God's engagement with human beings as the instruments of God's purpose.

19. Von Rad, *Genesis* (Philadelphia: Westminster, 1972) 196.

BIBLIOGRAPHY

1. The following are standard commentaries that deal with the full range of issues faced by the interpreter. Those by Westermann contain the most extensive discussions of issues the text presents, from textual matters to the history of interpretation.

Hamilton, Victor. *The Book of Genesis, Chapters 1–17.* NICOT. Grand Rapids: Eerdmans, 1990.

Sarna, Nahum. *Genesis.* JPS Torah Commentary. Philadelphia: Jewish Publication Society, 1989.

Von Rad, Gerhard. *Genesis.* OTL. Philadephia: Westminster, 1972.

Wenham, Gordon. *Genesis 1–15.* Word Biblical Commentary. Waco: Word, 1987.

Westermann, Claus. *Genesis 1–11: A Commentary; Genesis 12–36: A Commentary;* and *Genesis 37–50: A Commentary.* Minneapolis: Augsburg, 1984–86.

2. The following are commentaries or studies on Genesis geared for use in preaching, teaching, and personal study. The commentary of Brueggemann should be cited for its thoughtful discussions of the text in view of the issues presented by contemporary American culture.

Brueggemann, Walter. *Genesis.* Interpretation. Atlanta: John Knox, 1982.

Fretheim, Terence. *Creation, Fall and Flood: Studies in Genesis 1–11.* Minneapolis: Augsburg, 1969.

Gowan, Donald E. *From Eden to Babel: A Commentary on the Book of Genesis 1–11.* Grand Rapids: Eerdmans, 1988.

Jeansonne, Sharon. *The Women of Genesis.* Minneapolis: Fortress, 1990.

Mann, Thomas. *The Book of the Torah: The Narrative Integrity of the Pentateuch.* Atlanta: John Knox, 1988.

Rogerson, John. *Genesis 1–11.* Old Testament Guides. Sheffield, England: *JSOT,* 1991.

Roop, Eugene F. *Genesis.* Scottdale, Pa.: Herald, 1987.

3. The following are studies of special issues in Genesis from a particular angle of vision. Various articles of interest are cited in appropriate sections of the commentary.

Alter, Robert. *The Art of Biblical Narrative.* New York: Basic Books, 1981.

Anderson, B. W., ed. *Creation in the Old Testament.* IRT 6. Philadelphia: Fortress, 1984.

Blenkinsopp, Joseph. *The Pentateuch: An Introduction to the First Five Books of the Bible.* ABRL. New York: Doubleday, 1992.

Bonhoeffer, Dietrich. *Creation and Fall: Temptation.* New York: Macmillan, 1966.

Brueggemann, Walter, and H. W. Wolff. *The Vitality of Old Testament Traditions.* Atlanta: John Knox, 1982.

Clines, David. *The Theme of the Pentateuch.* JSOTSup 10. Sheffield, England: *JSOT,* 1978.

Coats, George W. *From Canaan to Egypt: Structural and Theological Context for the Joseph Story.* CBQMS 4. Washington: Catholic Biblical Association of America, 1976.

———. *Genesis: With an Introduction to Narrative Literature.* The Forms of the Old Testament Literature 1. Grand Rapids: Eerdmans, 1983.

Damrosch, David. *The Narrative Covenant.* San Francisco: Harper & Row, 1987.

Fishbane, Michael. *Text and Texture: Close Readings of Selected Biblical Texts.* New York: Schocken, 1979.

Fokkelman, J. P. *Narrative Art in Genesis.* Assen: Van Gorcum, 1975.

Fretheim, Terence. *Deuteronomic History.* Nashville: Abingdon, 1983.

Gunkel, Hermann. *The Legends of Genesis: The Biblical Saga and History.* New York: Schocken, 1964. This is a translation of the introduction to his 1901 commentary.

Hendel, Ronald. *The Epic of the Patriarch: The Jacob Cycle and the Narrative Traditions of Canaan and Israel.* HSM 42. Atlanta: Scholars Press, 1987.

Humphreys, W. L. *Joseph and His Family: A Literary Study.* Studies in Personalities of the Old Testament. Columbia: University of South Carolina Press, 1988.

Levenson, Jon. *Creation and the Persistence of Evil.* San Francisco: Harper & Row, 1988.

Meyers, Carol. *Discovering Eve: Ancient Israelite Women in Context.* New York: Oxford University Press, 1988.

Miller, Patrick D., Jr. *Genesis 1–11: Studies in Structure and Theme.* JSOTSup 8. Sheffield, England: *JSOT,* 1978.

Moberly, R. W. L. *The Old Testament of the Old Testament: Patriarchal Narratives and Mosaic Yahwism.* Minneapolis: Fortress, 1992.

Niditch, Susan. *Chaos to Cosmos: Studies in Biblical Patterns of Creation.* Chico: Scholars Press, 1985.

———. *Underdogs and Tricksters: A Prelude to Biblical Folklore.* San Francisco: Harper & Row, 1987.

Rendsburg, Gary. *The Redaction of Genesis.* Winona Lake, Ind.: Eisenbrauns, 1986.

Rendtorff, Rolf. *The Problem of the Process of Transmission in the Pentateuch.* JSOTSup 89. Sheffield, England: *JSOT,* 1990.

Steinmetz, Devorah. *From Father to Son: Kinship, Conflict and Continuity in Genesis.* Louisville: Westminster/John Knox, 1991.

Sternberg, Meir. *The Poetics of Biblical Narrative.* Bloomington: Indiana University Press, 1985.

Thompson, Thomas. *The Historicity of the Patriarchal Narratives.* BZAW 133. Berlin: de Gruyter, 1974.

Trible, Phyllis. *God and the Rhetoric of Sexuality.* Overtures to Biblical Theology. Philadelphia: Fortress, 1978.

Turner, Lawrence. *Announcements of Plot in Genesis.* JSOTSup 96. Sheffield, England: *JSOT,* 1990.

Van Seters, John. *Abraham in History and Tradition.* New Haven: Yale University Press, 1975.

Wallace, Howard. *The Eden Narrative.* HSM 32. Atlanta: Scholars Press, 1985.

White, Hugh C. *Narration and Discourse in the Book of Genesis.* Cambridge: Cambridge University Press, 1991.

Whybray, R. N. *The Making of the Pentateuch.* JSOTSup 53. Sheffield, England: *JSOT,* 1987.

Wilson, R. R. *Genealogy and History in the Biblical World.* New Haven: Yale University Press, 1977.

OUTLINE OF GENESIS

I. Genesis 1:1–11:26, The Primeval Story

A. 1:1–6:4, The Creation and Disruption of the Universe
1:1–2:3, The Creation
2:4-25, Another Look at Creation
3:1-24, The Intrusion of Sin
4:1-26, Cain and Abel
5:1-32, Adam's Family Tree
6:1-4, Sin Becomes Cosmic

B. 6:5–8:22, The Flood: The Great Divide

C. 9:1–11:26, A New World Order
9:1-17, God's Covenant with Noah
9:18-29, Curse and Blessing in Noah's Family
10:1-32, The Table of Nations
11:1-9, The City of Babel
11:10-26, From Shem to Abraham

II. Genesis 11:27–25:18, The Story of Abraham

A. 11:27–12:9, The Call of Abram

B. 12:10-20, Abram and Sarai in Egypt

C. 13:1-18, Abram and Lot

D. 14:1-24, Abram and Melchizedek

E. 15:1-21, The Covenant with Abram

F. 16:1-16, Hagar and Sarai

G. 17:1-27, Covenant and Circumcision

H. 18:1-15, God Visits Abraham and Sarah

I. 18:16–19:38, Abraham, Lot, and Sodom

GENESIS 1:1–11:26

THE PRIMEVAL STORY

OVERVIEW

The last century has seen a proliferation of new directions in the study of these chapters, including comparative studies based on the discovery of ancient Near Eastern creation and flood accounts, new literary approaches and historiographical methods, innovative theological developments, and issues generated by scientific research, environmentalism, feminism, and other liberation movements. These realities have sharply complicated the interpretation of these chapters: Did Israel inherit theological perspectives from the larger ancient Near Eastern culture? How old is the earth? What about evolution? Does the dominion passage commend the exploitation of the earth? Are these texts inimical to the proper role of women in church and society?

It will not do to suggest that such questions violate the integrity of the text, which knew of no such modern problems. Every question asked of the text is contemporary; every reader will study the text through modern eyes. Indeed, personal questions can often make a text come alive. Nonetheless, the public canons of accountability, which historical-critical approaches provide, can introduce some objectivity into the interpretive process.

Even though the rest of the OT makes few specific references to these chapters (see Isa 54:9), rather too much can be made of this fact. The same may be said for other narratives in the Pentateuch. There is, for example, no mention of the Akedah (Genesis 22) and only passing reference to Jacob's wrestling with God (see Hos 12:3-4). This situation stands in some contrast to the prominent use made of these texts in intertestamental literature, which may explain NT interest in them, at least in part (e.g., Mark 10:6-8; Rom 5:12-21).[20] The NT use of these passages will, no doubt, shape one's angle of vision in some way.

Yet, the fact that these NT citations cannot be allowed to have a privileged position in interpreting the OT seems clear from the use of Genesis 2–3 in 1 Tim 2:8-15. Each NT interpretation must be integrated with other evidence and methods as one attends to the meaning of these chapters.

TYPE OF LITERATURE

Determining the type(s) of literature present in these chapters has proven difficult. One confronts terms as diverse as a report of actual events or myth. Scholars generally agree that there is an admixture of narrative and numerative materials, but a more precise understanding of the former has been difficult to achieve, whether it be in terms of saga, legend, myth, fairy tale, etiology, story, or theological narrative. This discussion has not been very fruitful in helping readers understand the texts themselves, not least because there is no agreed-upon definition of words like *myth*. The word *story*, though imprecise, will probably serve us best.

One may identify these materials in two distinct, but not unrelated, ways:

1. They are *typical* or archetypical stories; that is, they explain aspects of human life in every age, including interhuman, human-nonhuman, and creature-Creator relationships. The various uses of the word אדם (*'ādām*) point the reader in this direction (generic—1:26-27; 2:5; 3:22-24; 5:1-2; 6:1-7; the first man—2:7–4:1; Adam–4:25–5:5). This movement back and forth between humankind and first man suggests an effort to portray the human in both typical and atypical ways. The admixture of symbolic (e.g., the tree of knowledge) and literal language also pushes in this direction, as do the parallels with ancient Near Eastern myth.[21]

---

20. For a survey of texts, see D. Gowan, *From Eden to Babel: A Commentary on the Book of Genesis 1–11* (Grand Rapids: Eerdmans, 1988) 3-6.

21. See J. Rogerson, *Genesis 1–11* (Sheffield: *JSOT*, 1991) 41-55.

Clines emphasizes this typicality. "Genesis 1-11 is not for [Israel], as it is for us, universal history; it is their own history."[22] For example, the flood symbolizes the destruction of Jerusalem for its sinful ways, and the dispersion in chap. 11 alludes to Israel's own Diaspora. Yet, while these texts may indeed mirror Israel's own reality, the claims of the text are more extensive. The past and the present are not simply collapsed into each other.

2. These texts tell *a story of the past,* more particularly a story of beginnings. They speak, not simply of the general human condition, but also of the beginnings of life.[23] This is not to say that the material is historical in any modern sense, nor does it necessarily make any historical judgments. Rather, these narratives offer Israel's own understandings.

(a) There are *atypical* aspects to some texts, showing that Israel did not simply collapse their own (or any later) time into the time of the text. The long-lived patriarchs would be one clear example; Israel knew that it would never live through such a time again. Such a reality belonged to the irretrievable past; indeed, to live such a long life was *totally* beyond Israel's experience. Other texts showing that the time of the text was understood to be different from Israel's own include 2:25 (nakedness and shame); 3:23-24 (driven from Eden, never to return); 6:1; and 11:1 (explicitly unique world situations). On the other hand, 6:4 speaks of continuity between the primeval era and a later time.

(b) There is an etiological concern, wherein the origins of later practices or phenomena are rooted in the distant past. We could cite 4:20-22 and the origins of certain cultural activities, or marriage practices (2:24), or national origins (10:2-31), even certain divine decisions that God will "remember" (8:21; 9:14-16). More generally, we could cite the creation itself; e.g., the actions of God in 2:7 and 2:22 will never be repeated. Creation is not an annual event, but a once-for-all moment that stands at the beginning of time. Somewhat different are the sentences in 3:14-19, which are etiological. They too are typical, but such typicality will not happen *whenever* people sin; rather, these distorted relationships reflect a *common* human reality.

(c) The concern for chronology is evident in the various genealogies (see p. 325), which allow us to track the years from Adam (5:5) through every generation to Israel. We can discern this same motif in the flood story (7:11; 8:13-14). The presence of such chronology in chaps. 1–11 and chaps. 12–50 means that these two sections of Genesis share a fundamental understanding regarding typicality and atypicality.

In sum, these texts present an interweaving of the typical and what belongs to the past. The interpreter must regularly walk a fine line between these two possibilities.

STRUCTURE AND THEME

Numerous efforts have been made to discern the structure in Genesis 1—11.[24] Most basic is the interweaving of genealogies and narratives.

Narrative pattern provides one type of structure. What transpires in 3:1-24 recurs in subsequent stories (4:1-16; 6:1-4; 6:5–8:22; 9:20-27; 11:1-9): Sinful Act (3:6); Speech (Decision) of Judgment (3:14-19); Act of Mercy/Blessing (3:21); Act of Punishment (3:22-24). While this pattern highlights a certain rhythm in the texts, it is not exact and leaves chaps. 1–2 dangling.

Another type of structure consists of parallel panels: A/A'—Creation from watery chaos (1:1–3:24) stands parallel to the flood (6:9–9:17); B/B'—discordant sons of Adam (4:1-16) to the sons of Noah, a second Adam (9:18-29); C/C'—technological development of humankind (4:17-26) to ethnic development (10:1-32); D/D'—ten generations, Adam to Noah/three sons (5:1-32) to ten generations, Noah to Terah/three sons (11:10-26); E/E'—downfall, Nephilim (6:1-8) to the Tower of Babel (11:1-9). The Shem genealogy and Babel story are reversed in order to connect Abram in 11:26 with 12:1-3. However, this theory presents difficulties, as may be seen in the prominent role given to 6:1-8 as over against 3:1-24, which is collapsed into the creation accounts.

These structures may be linked to a more general one wherein chaps. 1–11 depict an ever-increasing growth of sin and severity of punishment. Yet, the Babel story seems anti-climactic after the flood; this episode suggests a modification, with a distinct break after the flood, and then a recapitulation. The first

22. Clines, *Theme*, 98.
23. Von Rad, *Genesis*, 65.

24. See Clines, *Theme*, 61-79; T. Fretheim, *Creation, Fall and Flood: Studies in Genesis 1–11* (Minneapolis: Augsburg, 1969) 18-22; Rendsburg, *Redaction.*

movement is the primeval era, moving from sinful individuals (3:1-24) through family (4:1-26) out into the larger world (6:1–8:22), ending in catastrophe. Then there is another beginning (9:1-17, parallel to 1:1–2:25), moving also through sinful family and individuals (9:18-27) out into the world (10:1–11:9), only this time into a world that Israel clearly knows. The genealogy of Shem (11:10-26), once again, provides an individual point of reference that reaches out into the world (12:3*b*).

The larger structure is particularly helpful because it accounts for both stories and genealogies. It also attends to a variety of themes within these chapters: the growth and spread of sin, to which God's acts of judgment are explicitly related (and hence not arbitrary), accompanied by continuing acts of divine grace, as well as the themes of creation-uncreation-new creation (see 6:5–8:22).

Fundamental to Genesis is the divine creative activity, which involves not only the beginnings of the cosmos and all of its creatures but also God's continuing ordering and blessing activity within and without Israel (see p. 329). This anchor gives a horizon, scope, and purpose to God's particular act of election and words of promise to Israel's ancestors (see Reflections on 1:1). Indeed, even God's promises to Israel are grounded in God's promissory relationship to the world more generally (8:21–9:17), as is the activity of God as Savior (6:5–8:20).

Throughout these chapters issues of relationship are addressed from every conceivable perspective. Most basic are the relationships between God and the creatures, especially humans. The recurrent litany that all is created "good" stands as a beacon regarding the nature of God's creative work and the divine intentions for the creation. The *subsequent* entrance of human sin, while not finally effacing the God-human relationship or the important role human beings play in the divine economy, has occasioned deep and pervasive ill effects upon all relationships (human-God; human-human at individual, familial, and national levels; human-nonhuman) and dramatically portrays the need for a reclamation of creation. Through the experience of the flood story, God rejects annihilation as the means to accomplish this reformation and graciously opts instead for a more vulnerable, long-term engagement, working from within the very life of the world itself. The world continues to live and breathe because God makes a gracious, unconditional commitment to stay with the world, come what may in the wake of human sinfulness.

GENESIS 1–11 AND MODERN SCIENCE

To claim that God created the world and all that exists is a matter of faith, grounded fundamentally in God's self-revelation (see Heb 11:3). At this level the opening chapters of Genesis are a confession of faith. At the same time, in witnessing to God's creative activity the biblical writers made use of the available knowledge of the natural world. Israel had no little interest in what we today would call "scientific" issues (see 1 Kgs 4:33). These chapters are prescientific in the sense that they predate modern science, but not in the sense of having no interest in those types of questions. "Pre-scientific" knowledge is evident in God's use of the earth and the waters in mediating creation (1:11, 20, 24), the classification of plants into certain kinds and a comparable interest in animals, as well as the ordering of each day's creation. Despite claims to the contrary (often in the interest of combating fundamentalism), such texts indicate that Israel's thinkers were very interested in questions of the "how" of creation, and not just questions of "who" and "why."

Israel's theologians used this kind of "scientific" knowledge to speak of creation. They recognized that the truth about creation is not generated simply by theological reflection; we must finally draw from various fields of inquiry in order to speak the full truth about the world. The key task, finally, becomes that of integrating materials from various fields into one coherent statement about the created order. In effect, Genesis invites every generation to engage in this same process.

Difficulties arise when it becomes evident that not everything in these chapters can be made congruent with modern knowledge about the world (recognizing that no field of endeavor has arrived at the point of full understanding). If our view of the Bible insists that all information in it, of whatever sort, must correspond to scientific reality, then we will have to engage in all sorts of exegetical antics to make it work. But if we recognize that those authors did not know everything about the world (e.g., a source for light independent of the luminaries; the age of the world), then we just recognize that and move on. We have to take all the additional knowledge we have gained or will gain about the world (e.g., some form of evolution) and integrate it with our confession about God the Creator.

We are not called to separate the theological material from the "scientific" material and rewrite the chapter from our own scientific perspectives (however much that task must be accomplished for other purposes). The Genesis text remains both an indispensable theological resource and an important paradigm on the way in which to integrate theological and scientific realities in a common search for the truth about the world.

GENESIS 1:1–6:4, THE CREATION AND DISRUPTION OF THE UNIVERSE

Genesis 1:1–2:3, The Creation

NIV

1 In the beginning God created the heavens and the earth. ²Now the earth was*ᵃ* formless and empty, darkness was over the surface of the deep, and the Spirit of God was hovering over the waters.

³And God said, "Let there be light," and there was light. ⁴God saw that the light was good, and he separated the light from the darkness. ⁵God called the light "day," and the darkness he called "night." And there was evening, and there was morning—the first day.
⁶And God said, "Let there be an expanse between the waters to separate water from water." ⁷So God made the expanse and separated the water under the expanse from the water above it. And it was so. ⁸God called the expanse "sky." And there was evening, and there was morning—the second day.
⁹And God said, "Let the water under the sky be gathered to one place, and let dry ground appear." And it was so. ¹⁰God called the dry ground "land," and the gathered waters he called "seas." And God saw that it was good.
¹¹Then God said, "Let the land produce vegetation: seed-bearing plants and trees on the land that bear fruit with seed in it,

NRSV

1 In the beginning when God created*ᵃ* the heavens and the earth, ²the earth was a formless void and darkness covered the face of the deep, while a wind from God*ᵇ* swept over the face of the waters. ³Then God said, "Let there be light"; and there was light. ⁴And God saw that the light was good; and God separated the light from the darkness. ⁵God called the light Day, and the darkness he called Night. And there was evening and there was morning, the first day.
6And God said, "Let there be a dome in the midst of the waters, and let it separate the waters from the waters." ⁷So God made the dome and separated the waters that were under the dome from the waters that were above the dome. And it was so. ⁸God called the dome Sky. And there was evening and there was morning, the second day.
9And God said, "Let the waters under the sky be gathered together into one place, and let the dry land appear." And it was so. ¹⁰God called the dry land Earth, and the waters that were gathered together he called Seas. And God saw that it was good. ¹¹Then God said, "Let the earth put forth vegetation: plants yielding seed, and fruit trees of every kind on earth that bear fruit with the seed in it." And it was so. ¹²The earth brought forth vegetation: plants yielding seed of every kind, and trees of every kind bearing fruit with the seed

ᵃ2 Or possibly became

ᵃ Or when God began to create *or* In the beginning God created
ᵇ Or while the spirit of God *or* while a mighty wind

NIV

according to their various kinds." And it was so. ¹²The land produced vegetation: plants bearing seed according to their kinds and trees bearing fruit with seed in it according to their kinds. And God saw that it was good. ¹³And there was evening, and there was morning—the third day.

¹⁴And God said, "Let there be lights in the expanse of the sky to separate the day from the night, and let them serve as signs to mark seasons and days and years, ¹⁵and let them be lights in the expanse of the sky to give light on the earth." And it was so. ¹⁶God made two great lights—the greater light to govern the day and the lesser light to govern the night. He also made the stars. ¹⁷God set them in the expanse of the sky to give light on the earth, ¹⁸to govern the day and the night, and to separate light from darkness. And God saw that it was good. ¹⁹And there was evening, and there was morning—the fourth day.

²⁰And God said, "Let the water teem with living creatures, and let birds fly above the earth across the expanse of the sky." ²¹So God created the great creatures of the sea and every living and moving thing with which the water teems, according to their kinds, and every winged bird according to its kind. And God saw that it was good. ²²God blessed them and said, "Be fruitful and increase in number and fill the water in the seas, and let the birds increase on the earth." ²³And there was evening, and there was morning—the fifth day.

²⁴And God said, "Let the land produce living creatures according to their kinds: livestock, creatures that move along the ground, and wild animals, each according to its kind." And it was so. ²⁵God made the wild animals according to their kinds, the livestock according to their kinds, and all the creatures that move along the ground according to their kinds. And God saw that it was good.

²⁶Then God said, "Let us make man in our image, in our likeness, and let them rule over the fish of the sea and the birds of the air, over the livestock, over all the

NRSV

in it. And God saw that it was good. ¹³And there was evening and there was morning, the third day.

14And God said, "Let there be lights in the dome of the sky to separate the day from the night; and let them be for signs and for seasons and for days and years, ¹⁵and let them be lights in the dome of the sky to give light upon the earth." And it was so. ¹⁶God made the two great lights—the greater light to rule the day and the lesser light to rule the night—and the stars. ¹⁷God set them in the dome of the sky to give light upon the earth, ¹⁸to rule over the day and over the night, and to separate the light from the darkness. And God saw that it was good. ¹⁹And there was evening and there was morning, the fourth day.

20And God said, "Let the waters bring forth swarms of living creatures, and let birds fly above the earth across the dome of the sky." ²¹So God created the great sea monsters and every living creature that moves, of every kind, with which the waters swarm, and every winged bird of every kind. And God saw that it was good. ²²God blessed them, saying, "Be fruitful and multiply and fill the waters in the seas, and let birds multiply on the earth." ²³And there was evening and there was morning, the fifth day.

24And God said, "Let the earth bring forth living creatures of every kind: cattle and creeping things and wild animals of the earth of every kind." And it was so. ²⁵God made the wild animals of the earth of every kind, and the cattle of every kind, and everything that creeps upon the ground of every kind. And God saw that it was good.

26Then God said, "Let us make humankind[a] in our image, according to our likeness; and let them have dominion over the fish of the sea, and over the birds of the air, and over the cattle, and over all the wild animals of the earth,[b] and over every creeping thing that creeps upon the earth."
27 So God created humankind[a] in his image,
    in the image of God he created them;[c]
    male and female he created them.
²⁸God blessed them, and God said to them, "Be fruitful and multiply, and fill the earth and subdue it; and have dominion over the fish of the sea

a Heb *adam*   b Syr: Heb *and over all the earth*   c Heb *him*

NIV

earth,[a] and over all the creatures that move along the ground."

27So God created man in his own image,
  in the image of God he created him;
  male and female he created them.

28God blessed them and said to them, "Be fruitful and increase in number; fill the earth and subdue it. Rule over the fish of the sea and the birds of the air and over every living creature that moves on the ground."

29Then God said, "I give you every seed-bearing plant on the face of the whole earth and every tree that has fruit with seed in it. They will be yours for food. 30And to all the beasts of the earth and all the birds of the air and all the creatures that move on the ground—everything that has the breath of life in it—I give every green plant for food." And it was so.

31God saw all that he had made, and it was very good. And there was evening, and there was morning—the sixth day.

2 Thus the heavens and the earth were completed in all their vast array.

2By the seventh day God had finished the work he had been doing; so on the seventh day he rested[b] from all his work. 3And God blessed the seventh day and made it holy, because on it he rested from all the work of creating that he had done.

a26 Hebrew; Syriac *all the wild animals*   b2 Or *ceased*; also in verse 3

NRSV

and over the birds of the air and over every living thing that moves upon the earth." 29God said, "See, I have given you every plant yielding seed that is upon the face of all the earth, and every tree with seed in its fruit; you shall have them for food. 30And to every beast of the earth, and to every bird of the air, and to everything that creeps on the earth, everything that has the breath of life, I have given every green plant for food." And it was so. 31God saw everything that he had made, and indeed, it was very good. And there was evening and there was morning, the sixth day.

2 Thus the heavens and the earth were finished, and all their multitude. 2And on the seventh day God finished the work that he had done, and he rested on the seventh day from all the work that he had done. 3So God blessed the seventh day and hallowed it, because on it God rested from all the work that he had done in creation.

COMMENTARY

Many scholars consider the opening two chapters of Genesis as two creation stories, assigning 1:1–2:4a to the Priestly writer and 2:4b-25 to the Yahwist. Moreover, considerable effort has been expended in comparing and contrasting them (see commentary on 2:4-25). Newer approaches to biblical texts, however, have raised anew the question of the shape of the present form of the text. While the two accounts certainly have different origins and transmission histories, they have also been brought together in a coherent way by a redactor. As such, they function together to provide the canonical picture of creation. We cannot be certain that either account ever appeared in their present form, so theological perspectives based on these accounts in isolation are speculative and problematic.

Israel was not the only people in the ancient Near East to compose stories of creation. Sumerian, Mesopotamian, and Egyptian accounts have been unearthed in the nineteenth and twentieth centuries. As a result of comparing these extra-biblical texts with the biblical accounts, it is apparent that Israel participated in a culture with a lively interest in these questions. While in the past some claimed that Israel depended directly on one or more of these accounts, it is now more common to speak of a widespread fund of images and ideas upon which Israel drew and shaped into its own creation account(s). Early scholarly efforts focused on the Babylonian *Enuma Elish* in the century following its appearance in 1876; more recent efforts have concentrated on the Babylonian *Epic of Atrahasis* (about 1600 BCE), primarily because its sequence of creation-disruption-flood corresponds to the biblical account. Special attention has also been given to Egyptian parallels (e.g., creation by means of the word).

It is important to examine all such accounts and seek to determine their relationship, if any, to the biblical texts. The delineation of similarities and dissimilarities has long belonged to such work. Such dissimilarities as the basic purpose (e.g., the absence of explicit Israelite political interests), the lack of a theogony and a conflict among the gods, the absence of interest in primeval chaos, the prevailing monotheism, and the high value given human beings have often been noted. At the same time, to conceive of the biblical account's relationship to these other stories fundamentally in disjunctive or polemical terms can miss their genuine contribution to a perception of Israel's own reflection about creation.

Israel itself conceptualized the beginnings of things and told creation stories in several ways. Creation by word (followed by deed) is majestically presented in chap. 1; God as potter and builder working with already existing materials occurs as a prominent image in chap. 2. We may also discern traces of a creation account in which God fought with and achieved victory over chaotic forces (see Ps 74:12-15). It is notable, however, that these references are allusive in character, may refer to the exodus, and are present only in poetic literature. To assume that Israel understood such imagery in a literal way is as profound a mistake as to think of these Genesis chapters as journalistic prose.

Despite this important comparative and historical-critical work, we must not forget that these texts are most fundamentally the product of a community of faith engaged in theological reflection on creation. God is the primary subject of this chapter, which relates God in various ways to every creature. Even more, the chapter, with its rhythmic cadences, has a certain doxological character. Hence, the material may have grown out of liturgical use and the regular round of the community's praise of God the Creator (see Job 38:7). Worship interests also clearly appear in the links among creation, tabernacle, and temple as well as in sabbath and religious festivals.[25] Although these roots seem clear, we should not identify this chapter as an actual liturgy. While it may be identified as a didactic account, it has been shaped by liturgical use and worship interests.

At the same time, we should not collapse every concern in chapters 1 and 2 into a theological mold. This material provides considerable evidence of what we today would call scientific reflection on the natural world. Israel takes the available knowledge of that world and integrates it with theological perspectives, recognizing thereby that both spheres of knowledge must be used to speak the truth about the world (see Overview).

Structure. The first account possesses an obvious seven-day structure, signifying unity and comprehensiveness (the number 7 also serves this purpose). But other structures have been observed. Eight creative acts on six days (two acts occur on days three and six) may reflect originally diverse accounts, though such a scheme is more likely a deliberate structure in view of certain natural correspondences:

Day 1: Light	Day 4: Luminaries
Day 2: Waters/	Day 5: Fish/Birds
Firmament	Day 6: Land animals/
Day 3: Dry land/	People
Vegetation	Vegetation for food

In addition, the repetition of phrases provides a discernible rhythm: "God said . . . let there be . . . and it was so . . . and God made . . . and God saw that it was good . . . and it was evening and morning." It is important to note that this rhythm is not absolutely regular (additions in the LXX

---

25. See J. Levenson, *Creation and the Persistence of Evil* (San Francisco: Harper & Row, 1988) 66-99.

sought to make it so). In sum, various structures overlap and, together, betray a less than perfect symmetry.

1:1-2, The Beginning. The difficulties in translating vv. 1-3 are evident in the NIV and the NRSV, each of which is grammatically defensible. We may note three possible translations. (1) Verse 1 is a temporal clause, subordinate to the main clause in v. 3, with v. 2 a parenthesis regarding prior conditions (see JPS). When God began to create heaven and earth, God said, "Let there be light" (v. 2). Although this translation may be compared to 2:4-7 (cf. 5:1*b*-2) and ancient Near Eastern texts, each of these parallels is inexact (e.g., using the phrase "in the day"). Moreover, such a long opening sentence is uncharacteristic of the style of this chapter and other genealogies. (2) Verse 1 is a temporal clause, subordinate to the main clause in v. 2 (NRSV; also NAB; NEB; GNB). This rendering is less problematic, especially with the emphasis provided by the phrase "in the beginning." (3) Verse 1 is an independent sentence (NIV; also KJV; RSV; JB; NJB; REB). We could interpret v. 1 as depicting the first act of creation followed by further phases, though such a view breaks up the seven-day pattern.[26] Or, preferably, v. 1 may be seen as a summary of the chapter (v. 2 describes the prior conditions and v. 3 narrates the first act of creation). The most convincing evidence for this position derives from the genealogies in 5:1; 6:9; 10:1; and 11:10, all of which begin with an independent clause that provides a summary of what follows.

The word *beginning* probably does not refer to the absolute beginning of all things, but to the beginning of the ordered creation, including the temporal order. Time began with God's ordering, and the seven-day time of God's creating establishes a temporal pattern throughout all generations (see 2:1-3). The author does not deny that God created all things, but God's creative work in this chapter begins with something already there, the origins of which are of no apparent interest. Also, the writer presupposes the existence and basic character of God.

The first of two primary words for God's creative activity is introduced in Gen 1:1 (ברא *bārā'*). Only God serves as the subject of this verb in the

OT, and the verb has no object of material or means (though some uses refer to re-creation or a transformation of existing realities; see Pss 51:10; 102:18; Isa 41:20; 65:18). The word *bārā'* may be a technical term used to speak about the fundamental newness and uniqueness of what God brings into being. This view has sometimes led to the formulation of a *creatio ex nihilo* view of creation (see p. 356). While the word *bārā'* may speak of what only God can do, it remains metaphorical language. That God's creating is analogous to the human sphere is shown by the common use of the everyday word *make* (עשה *'āśâ*; integrated in 1:26-27; 2:1-3; Isaiah 41–45) and the images of creating present in chap. 2 (e.g., God as potter or builder). Yet, no analogy from the human sphere can exhaust the meaning of God's creative activity.

"Heaven and earth" specifies the ordered universe (see Ps 89:11), the totality of the world in which everything has its proper place and function. This phrase also testifies to a bipartite structure, wherein "the heavens are the LORD's heavens,/ but the earth he has given to human beings" (Ps 115:16). The heavens are an integral aspect of the world *as created.* Other texts show that heaven as God's abode is built into the very structure of the created order (Ps 104:1-3; Isa 40:22; Amos 9:6), a shorthand reference to the abode of God *within* the world.

Verse 2 describes the conditions before God began to order the cosmos. The language used to describe this pre-creation state of affairs is difficult to comprehend (on chaos, see p. 356). There are three parallel descriptions: (1) The "formless void" (תהו ובהו *tōhû wābōhû*) is neither "nothing" nor an undifferentiated mass; the earth, the waters (deep), the darkness, and the wind are discrete realities (see Jer 4:23-26). As a parallel to 2:4-7, but with a watery image, it refers to the earth as "void/empty" in the sense of something desolate and unproductive. The earth, present here, only "appears" in v. 9. (2) The "deep" (תהום *tĕhôm*) has often been compared with Tiamat of the Babylonian creation story, but a specific link seems unlikely in view of both language and content. Yet, the motif of water as the primal element in other ancient accounts no doubt influenced this writer. In Genesis 1, the "deep" may be equated with the waters that cover the earth

26. See G. Wenham, *Genesis 1–15* (Waco: Word, 1987) 11-13.

(see v. 9; cf. 49:25; Deut 33:13; Prov 8:24). Darkness may not be an absolute absence of light, given the act of separation in v. 4. As with the other realities in this verse (except wind), darkness becomes an integral part of God's ordered world; darkness is not called "good" in v. 4, but neither are the creations of the second day; "everything" is included in the "very good" evaluation of 1:31.[27]

(3) A "wind/spirit from/of God" are common translations of the רוח אלהים *rûaḥ 'ĕlōhîm* (NIV's capitalized "Spirit" implies a Trinitarian view; the superlative "mighty wind" would be unique for this phrase in the OT). The verb (used in Deut 32:11 and Jer 23:9 for a hovering eagle and a drunken walk) may be translated in various ways—"move," "sweep," "hover over"—suggesting the ever-changing velocity and direction of the wind. But to what end? Since the wind is related to God, it involves purposeful movement. God was present, hence the activity was in some sense creative (which tips the translation toward "spirit"). A comparable use of this language occurs in the flood story (8:1) and at the Red Sea (Exod 14:21; see the creative use of spirit in Job 33:4; Ps 104:30).

The writer placed the three clauses in v. 2 in grammatical parallelism; yet the third clause works differently because the wind is the sole entity not picked up in the rest of the chapter. The reference to God moves toward the rest of the chapter; it brings God and raw material together, in motion rather than static, preparing for the ordering process to follow (see p. 355).

1:3-13, Days One–Three. God as speaker is another key metaphor for God's creative activity (see Pss 33:6, 9; 148:5; 2 Esdr 6:38; 2 Cor 4:6). The centrality of the Word means that the creation is not an accident, but a deliberate act of the divine will; it expresses what God intends. The Word personalizes the activity; God enters into the creative deed. The Word bespeaks transcendence, expressing the separateness of God from the created order, which is not a divine emanation or birth. At the same time, God's speech reveals divine vulnerability, for God's speaking does not occur in isolation or function as command. The use of the jussive "let there be" leaves room for

creaturely response (vv. 11, 24); the cohortative "let us make" leaves room for consultation (v. 26); the "let them have dominion" (v. 26) entails a sharing of power. God's way of speaking creation communicates with others, makes room for others, with the attendant risks. God no longer chooses to be alone.

God's speaking does not stand isolated from God's making (e.g., 1:6-7, 14-16; see also Ps 33:6; Isa 48:3). This speaking-doing rhythm may reflect earlier forms of the text that have now been decisively integrated. Hence, the word itself does not explain sufficiently what comes to be; the word is accompanied by the deed. God does not create by "word events" but by "word-deed events." Hence, existing in the image of God means having a vocation that consists of both word and deed.

The divine speaking often involves a speaking *with* whatever is *already* created (vv. 11, 20, 22, 24, 28) in such a way that the receptor of the word helps to shape the result. The earth itself assists importantly in creative activity (vv. 11, 24). While God's work creates the potential for this creaturely response, it is creation from within the creation, not from without. Both human and nonhuman creatures are called to participate in the creative activity made possible by God.

Light. On "day" and "evening and morning," see the commentary on 2:1-3. Inasmuch as the sun had not yet been created, this verse probably refers to a divine manipulation of light as a creative act. Light was thought to have another source (Job 38:19; Isa 30:26; e.g., light on cloudy days and before and after sunset). The sun, when created, augmented the already existing light. Israelites believed light, often a symbol of life and salvation (Pss 27:1; 56:13) and characteristic of the presence of God (Ps 104:2), was fundamental to the creation, pushing back the darkness and making life possible. Every morning was a kind of new creation.

"And God saw that it was good." God acts as an evaluator. In this remarkable and recurring phrase, God responds to the work, making evaluations of it (2:18 implies that the evaluation is part of an ongoing process, within which improvement is possible). The "subdue" language (1:28) implies that "good" does not mean perfect or static or in no need of development. This state-

---

27. See D. Tsumara, *The Earth and the Waters in Genesis 1 and 2: A Linguistic Investigation* (Sheffield: *JSOT,* 1989).

ment carries the sense of achieving the divine intention, which includes elements of beauty, purpose, and praise. This evaluative move (as with naming or blessing) means that God remains involved with the creation once it has been brought into being. God sees the creature, experiences what has been created, and is affected by what is seen. God's response leads to the further development of the creation and of intra-creaturely relationships. God's creative activity may thus in part be determined by that which is not God.

"And God separated . . . " (vv. 4, 7). In this activity, too, God works with what has already been created to develop the creation still further, suggesting a continued unfolding of the creation. This divine cosmic activity may be intended to ground certain ritual distinctions (e.g., clean and unclean).

God acts as name-giver in vv. 5-10; God names the day, the night, the sky, the earth, and the seas. God's naming stands parallel to, but does not overlap, the human naming in 2:19-20. The naming (either divine or human) does not thereby create these realities. In naming, the deity *responds* to the creation. In effect, God looks at what has come into being, evaluates it, and discerns its place in the creation. The Creator thus not only speaks and acts, but also reacts to what has been brought into being and continues further. The act of creation constitutes, thus, no simple punctiliar act, but also involves a process of action and interaction with what has been created. In this process, naming entails knowledge of and relationship with the thing named.

Dome, Expanse, Firmament. Having no idea of infinite space, the writer thought the sky was something solid (Job 37:18), either metal or ice, held up by pillars (Job 26:11). This "dome" provided living space between the waters above (the source of rain and snow, flowing through windows, 7:11) and the waters on and below the earth.

The irregular placement of the recurrent phrase "and it was so" makes it likely that the divine speech announces the divine *intention* to create. Yet, the creative act is not complete until this phrase has so informed the reader.[28] Sometimes

28. Rogerson, *Genesis 1–11,* 58-60.

this phrase occurs as a summary; sometimes it occurs between God's speaking and acting (vv. 11, 14, 24). Even the creation of light is not complete until it is separated from the darkness (v. 4).

The creative word functions as an ordering word, especially in v. 9, where the dry land *appears* after the waters have been gathered into seas (the earth is already present in v. 2).

Verses 11-13 witness to a shift in God's way of creating; the earth itself participates in the creative process (see above). The description of the plants and trees with their capacity to reproduce by themselves gives evidence for a probing interest in what we would call "natural science" (see 1 Kgs 4:33). Israel had not yet related plant growth to the sun, ascribing it entirely to the powers of the earth.

1:14-23, Days Four–Five. In vv. 14-19—arranged in a chiasm—the heavenly lights are created to divide day and night, to give (additional) light, and to serve as signs (i.e., time markers) for days, years, and fixed seasons (the word for "season" is also the word for religious festival). The tasks of separating and ruling (מָשַׁל *māšal*) are, notably, also divine roles, here delegated to certain creatures. Once again, the involvement of the nonhuman in the continuing ordering of the world achieves prominence. The fact that the sun and moon are not specifically named, and the stars are just mentioned, may reflect a polemic against religious practice in Mesopotamia, where heavenly bodies were considered divine and astrology played an important role in daily life. All are here acclaimed as the creations of the one God.

In vv. 20-23 two new elements are introduced: life and blessing. Animals and human beings alike (not plants, whose reproductive powers are inherent) share a blessing—the power of sexual reproduction. The NRSV and the NIV offer different understandings of the verbal form used in v. 20. In the NRSV, the waters would be parallel to the earth in vv. 11 and 24 in mediating the creative work of God. The NIV's "teem" specifies a more direct creative act. In either case, ultimate responsibility lies with God. The fact that the sea monsters (תַּנִּינִם *tannînîm*) are specifically mentioned may polemicize theories of a divine chaos monster in other creation stories, ascribing their creation to God; imagery associated with this myth occurs in some poetic texts (e.g., Isa 27:1; 51:9; Ps 74:13). In language similar to 1:28, God's blessing extends to birds and fish, focusing on the life-giving powers. That no land animals receive a specific blessing is something of a puzzle.

1:24-31, The Sixth Day. God's creations on the sixth day all share the habitat of dry land. It may be something of a disappointment to human beings that they have to share this day! As with the vegetation in v. 11, the earth mediates the creation of the land animals (2:19 will speak of God's forming the animals). The NIV interprets "creeping things" accurately with its "creatures that move along the ground."

On the last half of the sixth day, God creates human beings. God's way of speaking and acting signals the importance of this development—namely, inner divine reflection, the cohortative "let us make" (followed by "our"), and the speaking/doing rhythm continues. The plural may refer to the divine council or heavenly court (see Job 38:7; 1 Kgs 22:19; Jer 23:18-23).[29] Other interpretations of the plural are not convincing (the plural of *majesty* is without parallel, and the plural of *deliberation* does not account for 3:22; see 11:7; Isa 6:8).

The "let us" language refers to an image of God as a consultant of other divine beings; the creation of humankind results from a dialogical act—an inner-divine communication—rather than a monological one. Those who are not God are called to participate in this central act of creation. Far from either slighting divine transcendence or concealing God within the divine assembly, it reveals and enhances the richness and complexity of the divine realm. God is not in heaven alone, but is engaged in a relationship of mutuality within the divine realm, and chooses to share the creative process with others. Human beings are the product of such a consultation (אדם ' *ādām* is used generically here). The "let us make" thus implicitly extends to human beings, for they are created in the image of one who chooses to create in a way that shares power with others.

The phrase "image of God" has been the subject of much discussion over the centuries.[30] This language occurs only in Genesis 1–11 (though implied elsewhere, e.g., Psalm 8). In describing the relationship between Adam and Seth (5:3; cf. 5:1; 9:6), the words *image* and *likeness* are reversed, suggesting that the second word dominates. In 1:26, *likeness* may specify the meaning more closely, so that *image* should not be construed in the sense of identity. Fundamentally, it means that "the pattern on which [human beings are] fashioned is to be sought outside the sphere of the created."[31] The inner-divine communication, which makes interhuman and God-human communication possible, constitutes one basic element of the pattern. Generally, human beings are given such gifts that they can take up the God-given responsibilities specified in these verses. The "image" refers to the entire human being, not to some part, such as the reason or the will. As for likeness in body, one may suggest that this notion appears in the later physical appearances of the "messenger of God" (see 16:7).

The image functions to mirror God to the world, to be God as God would be to the nonhuman, to be an extension of God's own dominion. In the ancient Near East the king as image of God was a designated representative of the gods, ruling on their behalf. Genesis 1 democratizes this royal image so that all humanity belongs to this sphere and inter-human hierarchical understandings of the image are set aside. That both male and female are so created (see also 5:2) means that the female images the divine as much as the male; both are addressed in the command of v. 28. The reference to both implies that their roles in life are not identical, and that likeness to God pertains not only to what they have in common but also to what remains distinctive about them (the emergence of both male and female images for God could be grounded in this text). The fact that the words *male* and *female* are not used for animals indicates that both sexuality and procreation are involved.

The involvement in the creative process of those created in the divine image takes the form of a command (1:28). These first divine words to human beings are about their relationship, not to God, but to the earth. They constitute a sharing of the exercise of power (dominion). From the

---

29. P. Miller, *Genesis 1–11: Studies in Structure and Theme* (Sheffield: *JSOT,* 1978).

30. For a survey, see G. Jonsson, *The Image of God: Genesis 1:26-28 in a Century of Old Testament Research* (Lund: Gleerup, 1988).

31. G. von Rad, *Old Testament Theology* (New York: Harper, 1962) I:145.

---

beginning God chooses not to be the only one who has or exercises creative power. The initiative has been solely God's, but once the invitation has been issued, God establishes a power-sharing relationship with humans. This initiative remains in the post-sin world as demonstrated in the use of God language in 5:1-3 and 9:6 as well as the use of these themes in Psalm 8. Hence, God appears less meticulously present in the life of the world; God serves as the supreme delegator of responsibility (for becoming like God in chap. 3, which bears negative connotations, see commentary on 3:22).

The command to be fruitful, to multiply, and to fill the earth immediately follows the word of blessing and involves a sharing of the divine creative capacities. God has brought the first human beings into existence, and the powers of propagating their own kind are now given over to the creatures (see 1:22; continued after the flood, 9:1, 7). The writer was obviously concerned about populating the earth. There was plenty of room for the human race to expand and grow. But should the point arrive at which the earth appears to be filled (the definition of which would need discussion), then the human responsibility in this area would need adjustment. New situations will teach new duties regarding the created order.

A study of the verb *have dominion* (רדה *rādâ*) reveals that it must be understood in terms of care-giving, even nurturing, not exploitation. As the image of God, human beings should relate to the nonhuman as God relates to them. This idea belongs to the world of the ideal conceptions of royal responsibility (Ezek 34:1-4; Ps 72:8-14) and centers on the animals. The command to "subdue the earth" (כבשׁ *kābaš*) focuses on the earth, particularly cultivation (see 2:5, 15), a difficult task in those days. While the verb may involve coercive aspects in interhuman relationships (see Num 32:22, 29), no enemies are in view here. More generally, "subduing" involves development in the created order. This process offers to the human being the task of intra-creational development, of bringing the world along to its fullest possible creational potential. Here paradise is not a state of perfection, not a static state of affairs. Humans live in a highly dynamic situation. The future remains open to a number of possibilities

in which creaturely activity will prove crucial for the development of the world.

When God conveys blessing (see 1:22; 2:3) God gives power, strength, and potentiality to the creatures. Such action, therefore, constitutes an integral part of the power-sharing image, a giving over of what is God's to others to use as they will. God will not pull back from this act of commitment, which God renews after the flood (9:1).

God as a giver (נתן *nātan,* 1:29-30) provides vegetation to human beings and animals to sustain their lives. When combined with 9:2-3, we discover that human beings were intended to be vegetarians (Isa 11:7; 65:25 imply that animals would be herbivorous in the new creation).

2:1-3, Creation and Sabbath. The repetitive character of this segment stresses the importance of the seventh day. The divine *act* of finishing the creation occurs on the *seventh* day (the NIV's pluperfect, "God had finished," is possible but not likely). The divine resting concludes creation—namely, sabbath belongs to the created order; it cannot be legislated or abrogated by human beings. "Finishing" does not mean that God will not engage in further creative acts (the absence of the typical concluding formula cannot be appealed to, for the structure of the creation account is not exact). These days did not exhaust the divine creativity! The seventh day refers to a specific day and not to an open future. Continuing creative work will be needed, but there is a "rounding off" of the created order at this point.

The meaning of the word *day* (יום *yôm*) has occasioned much debate. The days, with evening and morning rhythm, are "to be understood as actual days and as a unique, unrepeatable lapse of time in this world."[32] Other possibilities (symbolic; sequential but not consecutive; liturgical) are less likely. While seven-day patterns of various sorts are present in ancient Near Eastern texts, no sabbath day or seven-day week or seven-day creation account has been discovered. Yet, the writer highlights not individual days, but the seven-day pattern. This very temporal framework, a work/rest rhythm, inheres as a part of the created order of things. Creation thus has to do, not simply with spatial order, but with temporal order as well.

32. Von Rad, *Genesis,* 65.

Exodus 20:11 and 31:17 (which make sense only if the days are actual days) appeal to Genesis in order to claim that sabbath observance belongs to the creation as God intended it to be; hence its importance for all peoples, not just Israel. As with God, so with human beings; their six days of work are brought to fulfillment when integrated with keeping sabbath. On the far side of sin, resting on the sabbath becomes a *sign* that God's creative order continues to exist in the present. When all the world rests on the sabbath (a sign that all are in right relationship with the Creator—Exod 31:12-17), God's created order will once again be complete, will be realized as at the beginning. Yet, the noun for "sabbath" does not occur; this does not constitute its *earthly* institution (God does not command human beings about the sabbath here).

The divine act of blessing the sabbath is an unspoken report of God's act of giving power and potentiality to a particular temporal order, in the sense that human honoring of the work/rest rhythm has the capacity of deeply affecting life itself (as does its neglect). The setting aside of one day when human beings attend, not to their own responsibilities and freedoms, but to God's ordering of life honors the larger creative purposes of God and integrating oneself into them. It acknowledges that God is indeed the Creator and provider of all things.

In the act of sanctifying, God sets aside one day as different from other days, the full significance of which becomes apparent only later in the Pentateuch (e.g., Exod 20:11; 31:17). This work stands parallel to other divine acts of separation in the account.

Genesis 2:4-25, Another Look at Creation

NIV

⁴This is the account of the heavens and the earth when they were created.

When the LORD God made the earth and the heavens— ⁵and no shrub of the field had yet appeared on the earth*ᵃ* and no plant of the field had yet sprung up, for the LORD God had not sent rain on the earth*ᵃ* and there was no man to work the ground, ⁶but streams*ᵇ* came up from the earth and watered the whole surface of the ground— ⁷the LORD God formed the man*ᶜ* from the dust of the ground and breathed into his nostrils the breath of life, and the man became a living being.

⁸Now the LORD God had planted a garden in the east, in Eden; and there he put the man he had formed. ⁹And the LORD God made all kinds of trees grow out of the ground—trees that were pleasing to the eye and good for food. In the middle of the garden were the tree of life and the tree of the knowledge of good and evil.

¹⁰A river watering the garden flowed from Eden; from there it was separated into four headwaters. ¹¹The name of the first is the Pishon; it winds through the entire land of Havilah, where there

ᵃ5 Or land; also in verse 6   ᵇ6 Or mist   ᶜ7 The Hebrew for man (adam) sounds like and may be related to the Hebrew for ground (adamah); it is also the name Adam (see Gen. 2:20).

NRSV

4These are the generations of the heavens and the earth when they were created.

In the day that the LORD God made the earth and the heavens, ⁵when no plant of the field was yet in the earth and no herb of the field had yet sprung up—for the LORD God had not caused it to rain upon the earth, and there was no one to till the ground; ⁶but a stream would rise from the earth, and water the whole face of the ground— ⁷then the LORD God formed man from the dust of the ground,*ᵃ* and breathed into his nostrils the breath of life; and the man became a living being. ⁸And the LORD God planted a garden in Eden, in the east; and there he put the man whom he had formed. ⁹Out of the ground the LORD God made to grow every tree that is pleasant to the sight and good for food, the tree of life also in the midst of the garden, and the tree of the knowledge of good and evil.

10A river flows out of Eden to water the garden, and from there it divides and becomes four branches. ¹¹The name of the first is Pishon; it is the one that flows around the whole land of Havilah, where there is gold; ¹²and the gold of

ᵃ Or formed a man (Heb adam) of dust from the ground (Heb adamah)

NIV

is gold. [12](The gold of that land is good; aromatic resin[a] and onyx are also there.) [13]The name of the second river is the Gihon; it winds through the entire land of Cush.[b] [14]The name of the third river is the Tigris; it runs along the east side of Asshur. And the fourth river is the Euphrates.

[15]The LORD God took the man and put him in the Garden of Eden to work it and take care of it. [16]And the LORD God commanded the man, "You are free to eat from any tree in the garden; [17]but you must not eat from the tree of the knowledge of good and evil, for when you eat of it you will surely die."

[18]The LORD God said, "It is not good for the man to be alone. I will make a helper suitable for him."

[19]Now the LORD God had formed out of the ground all the beasts of the field and all the birds of the air. He brought them to the man to see what he would name them; and whatever the man called each living creature, that was its name. [20]So the man gave names to all the livestock, the birds of the air and all the beasts of the field.

But for Adam[c] no suitable helper was found. [21]So the LORD God caused the man to fall into a deep sleep; and while he was sleeping, he took one of the man's ribs[d] and closed up the place with flesh. [22]Then the LORD God made a woman from the rib[e] he had taken out of the man, and he brought her to the man.

[23]The man said,

"This is now bone of my bones
    and flesh of my flesh;
she shall be called 'woman,[f]'
    for she was taken out of man."

[24]For this reason a man will leave his father and mother and be united to his wife, and they will become one flesh. [25]The man and his wife were both naked, and they felt no shame.

---

[a]12 Or *good; pearls*   [b]13 Possibly southeast Mesopotamia
[c]20 Or *the man*   [d]21 Or *took part of the man's side*   [e]22 Or *part*
[f]23 The Hebrew for *woman* sounds like the Hebrew for *man*.

NRSV

that land is good; bdellium and onyx stone are there. [13]The name of the second river is Gihon; it is the one that flows around the whole land of Cush. [14]The name of the third river is Tigris, which flows east of Assyria. And the fourth river is the Euphrates.

[15]The LORD God took the man and put him in the garden of Eden to till it and keep it. [16]And the LORD God commanded the man, "You may freely eat of every tree of the garden; [17]but of the tree of the knowledge of good and evil you shall not eat, for in the day that you eat of it you shall die."

[18]Then the LORD God said, "It is not good that the man should be alone; I will make him a helper as his partner." [19]So out of the ground the LORD God formed every animal of the field and every bird of the air, and brought them to the man to see what he would call them; and whatever the man called every living creature, that was its name. [20]The man gave names to all cattle, and to the birds of the air, and to every animal of the field; but for the man[a] there was not found a helper as his partner. [21]So the LORD God caused a deep sleep to fall upon the man, and he slept; then he took one of his ribs and closed up its place with flesh. [22]And the rib that the LORD God had taken from the man he made into a woman and brought her to the man. [23]Then the man said,

"This at last is bone of my bones
    and flesh of my flesh;
this one shall be called Woman,[b]
    for out of Man[c] this one was taken."

[24]Therefore a man leaves his father and his mother and clings to his wife, and they become one flesh. [25]And the man and his wife were both naked, and were not ashamed.

---

[a] Or *for Adam*   [b] Heb *ishshah*   [c] Heb *ish*

COMMENTARY

In the present form of the text, this section is probably intended to describe in detail several days of chap. 1, particularly the sixth one. Genesis 2 was likely not understood as a parallel creation account; it probably was once part of a larger story, evident particularly in vv. 5-6, which could describe a state of affairs after 1:9-10 (with dry land in place, but the separated waters not yet providing fertility).

Differences from chap. 1 have often been observed (e.g., literary type; structure, style, and vocabulary; center of concern). But there are also key similarities: God as sole Creator of a good and purposeful world, the key place of the human among the creatures, the co-creative role of the human and the nonhuman, the social character of the human as male-female. The chapter focuses on humankind and the particularities of their life, signaled by the shift from "heaven and earth" to "earth and heaven" (v. 4). Elohim, the generic term for the deity, occurs throughout 1:1–2:3. In linking the names Yahweh and Elohim in 2:4-25, the writer may have intended to identify Israel's special name for God with the creator of the world (allowing Elohim to stand alone in 1:1–2:3 makes clear that we are dealing with pre-Israel realities).

While no parallel to this story exists elsewhere in the ancient Near East, certain paradise motifs, e.g. the tree of life, may be found elsewhere. Other OT passages suggest that this was once part of a more comprehensive story (see 13:10; Isa 51:3; Ezek 28:13-19; 31:8-9).

2:4-9, The Role of the Human. Verse 4 has long been considered the point of division between the two creation stories, with v. 4*a* usually associated with what precedes—with "genealogy" and "create"—and v. 4*b* with what follows. Some scholars view v. 4 as an introduction to the following story. I construe it as a hinge verse that looks both backward and forward (2:25 may play a similar role), signaled by the reversal of heaven/earth, the creation of which is *assumed* in chap. 2. The phrase "in the day that" (NIV, "when") in v. 4*b* reaches back into the account of the creation of earth and heavens at a point before everything had been sorted out. Verse 5

functions similarly to v. 18, providing a perspective on the creation process before "not good" became "good."

The word used for "generations"/"account" (תולדות *tôlēdôt*) is the first of ten such occurrences in Genesis (see Introduction), each of which introduces what is to follow. The phrase, though, remains linked with someone/something that has already been introduced in the narrative. The usage in Gen 2:4 functions most like 25:19 and 37:2, which also introduce new developments in story form.

Verse 5 startles the reader due to the parallel it draws between the rain and human labor (עבד *'ābad*), both of which are considered indispensable to produce edible plants/herbs ("stream[s]" is of uncertain meaning, but insufficient for vegetation). The earth remains in a pre-creation state, not only because God has not yet done something, but also because no human beings are active. The divine purpose for the man in 2:15 is expressed with the same word (שמר *šāmar*, "keep," "protect"). This change gives responsibility to the human being, not simply for maintenance and preservation, but for intra-creational development, bringing the world along toward its fullest possible potential. God intends from the beginning that things not stay just as they were initially created. God creates a paradise, not a static state of affairs, but a highly dynamic situation in which the future lies open to various possibilities.

Various images of God as Creator are presented in this section. (a) God as a potter (יצר *yāṣar;* see Isa 41:25; 45:9; 64:8; Jer 18:1-6) shapes the man according to the divine design (2:7) and forms *every* animal and *every* bird (2:19) from the dust or clay (see Job 10:9) of the ground. The writer uses the same verb to narrate both human and nonhuman creation. The image of the deity as a potter creating humankind from clay occurs elsewhere in the ancient Near East. This image reveals a God who focuses closely on the object to be created and takes painstaking care to shape each one into something useful and beautiful. At the same time, the product of the potter's work remains very much bound to the earth and bears essential marks of the environment from which it derives (see 3:19). This combination of being made from clay and the image of God, being made of the same substance as the earth but made for dominion over it, constitutes a profound statement about human identity (links to royal themes have been noted). (b) God as a bellows breathes life into what has been formed. This "breath of life" is not the air in general, but God's own living breath. God shares this divine "breath of life" with the human and with the animals (see 7:22, which adds רוח *rûaḥ*). The result for both human beings and animals is "a living being" (נפש חיה *nepeš ḥayyâ*; 2:7, 19; 1:20-30; 9:12-16). The divine act of breathing into the human (though it may be implied in 7:22) provides the only distinction between humans and animals. (c) God as farmer/gardener (נטע *nāṭaʿ*, 2:8-9) plants a garden and makes the trees grow out of the ground (אדמה *ʾădāmâ*, the source of trees, animals, and human beings). Here the garden lies *in* Eden (probably meaning "luxuriant"), a wider geographical area (in 3:22-24 the garden and Eden seem to be equated). These verses refer to the trees of the garden and not to vegetation generally (see 1:11-12, 29, where the earth itself acts). Verse 5 refers to edible plants/herbs of the field, which God planted, but they do not grow apart from rain and human toil. The writer devotes special attention to the beauty of the trees and to their provision of food (two characteristics of the tree of knowledge noted by Eve in 3:6), and hence placed there for the good of the human inhabitants. God provides for bodily nourishment and also for other pleasures of life—more than food and clothing! People will find that they depend on that which is outside themselves in order to live fully. The theme of a primeval paradise occurs only rarely elsewhere in the ancient Near East.

The tree of life (2:9; 3:22, 24). The awkward syntax of these texts, which occur at the beginning and end of the story, suggests that stories with different trees have been combined. Some think that only one tree is intended ("the tree of life, namely, the tree of knowledge"), but most interpreters discern two trees in the middle of the garden. The first tree mentioned symbolizes the fullest possible life, the eating of which would grant continuing life (such a tree or plant occurs in the *Gilgamesh Epic* and elsewhere). The reference in 3:22 indicates that one would need to

eat from that tree only once, as was also the case with the tree of knowledge.

The narrator gives no indication that the man and woman know of this tree's existence until 3:22. Readers encounter the tree of life in 2:9 and then again only in 3:22-24. Genesis 3:22 implies that the man and woman, having eaten of the other tree and knowing that death has become a near possibility, would with their new knowledge become aware of the tree of life and its import and, by eating of it, live forever.

The relationship between the tree of life and the breath of life (2:7-9; חיים *ḥayyîm*) remains uncertain. When humans are excluded from the tree of life (3:22), they obviously retain God's breath of life. Hence, the tree must represent possibilities for life not entailed in the breath of life. The fact that more is at stake than issues of quality of life seems clear since the deity expresses concern in 3:22 regarding the possibility of humans living forever. Having the breath of life does not entail immortality. Human beings are created mortal, but eating of the tree of life was a means by which human beings might receive a special blessing—namely, ongoing life; no ontological change seems in view, hence *immortality* would not be the right word to describe the result of their eating the fruit. Some this-worldly form of "eternal life" (not an afterlife) may be in mind.

The tree of the knowledge of good and evil (2:9, 17). (The woman refers to it in 3:3 as implied by 3:6; the changes she makes in the command mean that her description of the trees may be less than exact.) The name of this tree gives it a symbolic value, but that value has proved to be difficult to discern. In view of 3:22 (which the serpent affirms, 3:5), God knows good and evil, and human beings attain that godlike knowledge upon eating of the tree, though it is a knowledge with which they cannot live very well. Any meaning assigned to the tree must recognize that it has to do with a "knowledge" that God has. This makes it unlikely that it has to do either with sexual knowledge/experience, which 2:24-25 and 1:27-28 already imply, or knowledge of/experience with sin or wickedness.

The phrase "good and evil" functions as an idiomatic expression in which the individual words do not have their normal meanings (hence the phrase does not speak to the question of the existence of evil; a knowledge of the "good" is assumed from 2:9; 3:5). For example, the NIV translates the phrase in 24:50 with "one way or the other," referring to a divine decision, not the servant's (see 31:24, 29). The phrase with the verb *know* (ידע *yāda'*) occurs twice elsewhere (Deut 1:39; 2 Sam 19:35; cf. Isa 7:15-16), specifying those too young or too old to decide for themselves what serves their own best interests. Comparable phrases in 1 Kgs 3:9 and 2 Sam 14:17 speak of kings discerning the best interests of those who come within their jurisdiction.

For the writer, the key issue involves the discernment of what is in one's own best interests, not the fruit of the tree as fruit or any specific content of the knowledge or knowledge generally.[33] The text defines who finally decides what is in the best interests of the human. The tree and the command *together* define the limits of creatureliness; to transgress these limits entails deciding about one's own best interests, to become autonomous, independent of the will of God for one's life. To refrain from eating recognizes creaturely limitations and the decisiveness of the will of God for true human life. This creational command presents a positive use of law, wherein certain limits are recognized as being in the best interests of human life and well-being.

2:10-14, The Rivers. This material both retards the action of the narrative and prepares for the end of chap. 3. The narrator creates a specific link between the beginning of things and the later world (see 2:24); vv. 10-14 belong to an identifiable place on the map (though its location is disputed). The Garden of Eden does not equate with the world. We have a glimpse of the world outside the garden. The river that waters the garden flows out of Eden and through the major sections of the then known world, making the latter dependent on the former. Even more, things in the garden are "good" *in their own right* (v. 12), hence in continuity with the good and diverse creation of chap. 1. Moreover, the worlds out beyond Eden already have names, suggesting that they were believed to be inhabited (which would coincide with the fuller population in chap. 4). Rivers and places no longer known to us

(Pishon, Gihon, Havilah, and Cush[34]) combine with the known—Assyria and the Tigris-Euphrates valley. Even life outside the garden (eventually to be home to Adam and Eve) has significant continuities with life inside the garden. The two humans will not move from a world of blessing to one devoid of blessing.

2:15-17, Permission and Prohibition. God places the man in the garden—resuming v. 8—to work/serve ('*ābad*) the ground and care for it (*šāmar*) in fulfillment of the command to subdue the earth (ארץ '*ereṣ* and '*ădāmâ* are often interchangeable). Given the use of '*ābad* in v. 5, this role involves not only simple maintenance or preservation, but a part of the creative process itself. The role given the human in v. 15 may be compared to the dominion/servant role in 1:28.

God addresses the man in vv. 16-17 (given the anthropomorphisms, God is probably embodied), giving permission to eat from every tree (which would include the tree of life) except the tree of knowledge, and a prohibition; in effect, this constitutes a version of the first commandment (see commentary on 2:9), a concern not evident in chap. 1. God's first speech to humans does not center on God's place in the world, but focuses instead on the creatures, on their place and role, and the gifts they are given. The deity expresses no concern that the creature might exalt itself at God's expense.

The permission establishes an incredible range of freedom for the creatures; hence, the command that follows certainly does not seem repressive. The command may appear surprising, but it indicates the important role law has to play as a creational, pre-sin reality; command inheres as an integral part of the created order. To be truly a creature entails limits; to honor limits becomes necessary if the creation will develop as God intends. Yet, while the language takes the form of command, the issue involves trust in the word of God. Decisions faced by the humans will concern not only themselves, but also choices that have implications for their relationship with *God*. The command involves the visible and tangible (see the testing of Abraham, 22:1). Trust in God will often manifest itself in concrete matters.

Over against the tree of life, the tree of knowl-

33. See W. M. Clark, "A Legal Background to the Yahwist's Use of 'Good and Evil' in Genesis 2–3," *JBL* 88 (1969) 266-78; Fretheim, *Creation,* 73-77.

34. See Sarna, *Genesis* (Philadelphia: JPS, 1989) 19-20.

edge raises the possibility of human death. The two trees represent two possible futures: life and death. To be separated from the tree of life (3:22-24) represents the broken nature of the relationship, with death being inevitable. "The fruit of the righteous is a tree of life,/ but lawlessness takes away lives" (Prov 11:30 RSV; see Prov 3:18; 13:12; 15:4; Dan 4:10-12). The metaphor of eating, so prominent in this text, signifies the taking of something into one's very self with effects on one's total being ("you are what you eat").

"You shall surely die" stipulates a negative consequence, a specific penalty for eating, but the meaning remains difficult to discern. It does not mean "you shall become mortal"; they already are mortal beings. Death as such belongs to God's created order. It seems to imply capital punishment without delay (though "in the day" could mean "when" more generally, so the NIV); yet, they do not die and God nowhere takes back the threat. It may be that death (and life) has a comprehensive meaning in this story (as in the OT generally; see Hos 13:1), associated with a breakdown in relationships to God, to each other, and to the created order.[35] This larger view of death comes to a climax when humans are excluded from the tree of life and lose the opportunity to overcome their natural mortality. So death does become pervasive within their lives even in the garden. At the same time, physical death would not have occurred had they managed to eat from the tree of life. If God had not acted, the serpent would have been right regarding physical death.

If humans obey the command, they recognize that they do have limitations in the exercise of their God-given responsibilities and that a right relationship to God provides an indispensable matrix for the proper exercise of that power.

2:18-25, The Creation of Woman. God evaluates the situation and declares that something is not (yet?) good; the man remains alone (God's presence does not suffice).[36] God, probably, speaks within the divine council; so the reader, again, overhears the inner divine reflective process (see 1:26). The man's not being alone correlates with God's not being alone. God identifies a problem with the state of creation at this point and moves to make changes that would improve it.

For the woman to be called "helper" ('ēzer)—a word used by both God and the narrator—carries no implications regarding the *status* of the one who helps; indeed, God is often called the helper of human beings (Ps 121:1-2). The NRSV's "partner" may capture the note of correspondence more than "suitable" or "fitting." The notion of Eve as "helper" cannot be collapsed into procreation, not least because the immediate outcome specified in vv. 24-25 does not focus on this concern; the term does not offer evidence of a hierarchy.[37]

Initially, God "forms" *every* animal and bird. Indeed, God does not simply create them, but "brings" them to the human in a kind of parade (the same verb is used in 6:19). This is a remarkable image of God. Twice, God "brings" a creature—first the animals, then the woman—before the man. God thereby is placed at the service of the "good" of the human being, presenting creative possibilities before him. Twice, God lets the human being determine whether the animals or the woman are adequate to move the evaluation from "not good" to "good." And *whatever*—without qualification—the man called every living creature, that was its name (v. 19). Phyllis Trible observes that God, who dominates the narrative up to this point, now recedes into the background, "not as the authoritarian controller of events but as the generous delegator of power who even forfeits the right to reverse human decisions."[38] In the first case, the man does not accept what God presents; God accepts the human decision and goes back to the drawing board.

The man recognizes that the woman will address the stated need. God recognizes the creational import of this human decision, for no additional divine word or act follows. God lets the man's exultation over the woman fill the scene; the *human* word (the first one uttered) serves as an evaluation that this situation may be termed "good." The narrator (vv. 24-25) then draws the reader into the closeness of the male-female bond, citing the implication of the human

---

35. See R. Moberly, "Did the Serpent Get It Right?" *JTS* 39 (1988) 1-27.

36. See W. Brueggemann, *Genesis* (Atlanta: John Knox) 47.

37. For an opposing view, see D. Clines, *What Does Eve Do to Help?* (Sheffield: *JSOT,* 1990).

38. Trible, *Rhetoric,* 93.

decision for the future. These verses show that the bond involves more than issues of procreation; the relationship includes companionship, intimate and otherwise.

The naming by the human parallels God's naming (1:5-10); it belongs as a part of the creative process, discerning the nature of intra-creaturely relationships. For the woman to be named by the man does not subordinate the named to the namer, any more than does Hagar's naming of God subordinate the deity to her (16:13).[39] Naming involves *discernment* regarding the nature of relationships (the male "rule" over the female derives from sin, 3:16).

God designs and builds (בנה *bānâ*) woman out of already existing material. This image may be compared to that of the potter who both designs and fashions an object. The "rib" is only one step removed from the dust, and hence stresses common ultimate origins, but the different image may reflect differences in design (no known ancient parallel exists for the separate creation of woman). The relationship of the woman to the "rib" entails no subordination, any more than man's being created from the ground implies his subordination to it. (Some suggest "side," Exod 25:12-14, but "rib" best links with the bone/flesh reference. See "boards" in 1 Kgs 6:15-16; the word usually occurs in architectural descriptions.) Unlike the dust, the rib is living material. The theological force of this creation is implied in 1:26-27—namely, the explicit equality of man and woman in the image of God (being created first or last remains immaterial). This description of the human creation emphasizes the personal attention implicit in the image of God as builder.

Contrary to some recent opinions,[40] the אדם (*'ādām*) ought not to be considered an "earth creature" without sexual identity until after the creation of woman. Without an explicit linguistic marker that the meaning of *'ādām* changes from "earth creature" to "the man," this word should be read with the same meaning throughout. Indeed, the word *'ādām* would have to be read with two different meanings *within* v. 22 if this distinction were licit. Moreover, v. 22, which speaks explicitly of God's creation of the woman, would lack a comparable creation account for the man. Verse 23 also refers to the man by the word איש (*'îš*; unambiguously male) as the one from whom the woman was taken.

The point at which *'ādām* becomes the proper name Adam remains uncertain. Genesis 4:25 provides the first unequivocal instance of *'ādām* without the definite article (so NRSV), though the NRSV provides footnotes for 2:20 (NIV begins Adam here); 3:17 (so RSV); and 3:21 (so NEB). These three texts are ambiguous (the NIV also uses the proper name in 3:20 and 4:1, but footnotes "the man"). The movement of the meaning of *'ādām* back and forth between generic humankind (1:26-27; 5:1-2), the first man, and Adam probably reflects an effort both to tell a story of a past and to provide a mirroring story for every age.

The language of "one flesh" (v. 24) functions as a literal reference at one level. The man is less than what he was before this surgery, and yet humankind has become more than it was—i.e., now male and female. The writer has not depicted a "birth" of the woman from the man, as if the man's creative powers were now in focus. The man was in a deep sleep; not to guard the mystery, but to stress that *God* was working creatively! The deity's initiative remains as central in the creation of woman as it was with the man.

In the wake of this divine act, the man's first words are recorded (note the assumption of a full-blown vocabulary), unlike the "silent" naming of the animals. The naming entails a difference from but no authority over the woman. The use of איש (*'îš*, "man") and אשה (*'iššâ*, "woman") in the naming discerns and formally *recognizes* the sameness and difference within humanity; the similarity in sound may emphasize equality. The narrator had already so named the woman in v. 22, contrasting the *'iššâ* with the *'ādām* from whom she was made *and* to whom she was brought.

The man's words recognize that the "not good" situation of v. 18 has now become good. "Bone of my bones and flesh of my flesh," a phrase that specifies kinship (29:14; 2 Sam 19:12-13; a broader reference than in English idiom), literally highlights mutuality and equality. The immediately recognizable bodily differences between them occasions the difference in the name. The

39. See G. Ramsey, "Is Name-Giving an Act of Domination in Genesis 2:23 and Elsewhere?" *CBQ* 50 (1988) 24-35.

40. Trible, *Rhetoric*, 79-81.

man thereby has a new level of knowledge of his identity as a sexual being in relationship to the woman.

One Flesh. Verse 24 stands out from its context by the way in which it makes explicit reference to a later time—namely, when children are born and one can speak of fathers and mothers (the NRSV is more explicit than the NIV). The narrator thereby links God's original intention for creation and later practice in providing an etiology of marriage. The previous verses provide the reason for this practice—namely, a man leaves his parents and clings to his wife. Inasmuch as it was usually the woman who left the parental home, such departure probably does not have a spatial reference, but alludes to leaving one family identity and establishing another with his wife. These verses make no mention of children; rather, the writer focuses on the man-woman relationship, not on the woman as the bearer of children. God's creation values sexual intimacy as being good. Although the text does not speak explicitly about single human existence, it does not imply that, in order to be truly human, one must be married.

"One flesh" does not refer to sexual intimacy in a narrow way, but recognizes that man and woman constitute an indissoluble unit of humankind from *every* perspective. Hence the author refers to but does not focus on the sexual relationship. Leaving one's parents certainly implies marriage in that culture, and marriage certainly entails sexual intimacy. Being naked in the presence of the other was natural, with no embarrassment attached to total bodily exposure. Inasmuch as this is still generally true for married persons, nakedness must be understood in both literal and metaphorical senses (3:7, 10, 21); spouses also have no fear of exposure in the broader sense, no need to cover up.

REFLECTIONS

1. Is Genesis 1–2 an adequate statement about creation for the modern or postmodern context in which we live? In many ways this question must be answered in the negative. We have learned truths about the origins, development, and nature of the world from modern science of which the biblical authors never dreamed. We are confronted with issues never faced by these authors, from the environment to the role of women. In some ways the text, at least as it has been commonly interpreted, creates problems for any adequate consideration of these issues. While the commentary suggests that these problems have been created more by interpreters than by the text itself, the reader must not discount the history of the *negative effects* of such interpretations, from the exploitation of the environment to a second-class place for women. It will take generations for newer readings to overcome these effects.

In seeking finally to address these issues in a responsible manner, we must go beyond the text and draw on insights from other parts of the Scriptures and from our own experience in and through which God continues to speak. At the same time, these chapters will continue to provide the modern reader with an indispensable foundation for these reflections, including the images of God and the human, the relationship between God and the world, and human and nonhuman interrelationships. Perhaps, above all, these chapters provide a paradigm that we can use to integrate truths about the world gathered from all spheres of life.

2. The fact that the creation account rather than the birth of Israel stands at the head of the canon remains of considerable importance. The theological factors reflected in this ordering include the following: (a) The Bible begins with a testimony to the universal activity of God. God's creative activity not only brought the world into being but also was effectively engaged in the lives of individuals and peoples long before Israel came into being. The canonical ordering reflects the actual sequence of God's activity in the world. God was at work on behalf of the divine creational purposes before Israel understood what this activity was all about. (b) *God's* actions in the world achieve priority of place over human knowledge of what God has done. When Israel does begin to articulate the place of creation in the divine economy, this amounts to Israel's "catching up" with what God has long been about. The development of a creation theology in Israel occurs secondary to God's actual engagement with the world. At the same time, such a creation theology probably emerged much earlier in Israel than has commonly been supposed. Creation theology seems to be a given for those who first formulated a theology of Israel's redemption (see Exodus 15). (c) This canonical ordering corresponds to human experience of God's activity. Human beings in all times and places have experienced (even if they have not known) God's creative acts prior to and alongside of God's redemptive acts. Human beings receive their life and all their native gifts from the Creator quite apart from their knowledge of its source. The redemptive work of God takes place within a world and individual lives that have been brought into being and sustained by God's care. God's redemptive activity does not occur in a vacuum, but within a context decisively shaped by the life-giving work of God within and without Israel. (d) The position of Genesis 1–2 demonstrates that God's purpose in redemption does not, finally, center on Israel. God as Creator has a purpose that spans the world, and since divine deeds are rooted in the divine will, God's redemptive activity must be understood to serve this universal intention. Israel's place in the purposes of God are clear only from within this creation-wide perspective. Israel's election furthers God's mission on behalf of the entire universe.[41]

3. Traditional interpretations of Genesis have tended to favor the lofty formulations and familiar cadences of chap. 1 at the expense of the more "naive" story in chap. 2. Critical decisions, which tend to see the latter as older and more primitive (J) while considering the former (P) to be the product of more sophisticated theological reflection on creation, tend to fortify this tendency. Such views reinforce the traditional image of God as a radically transcendent Creator, operating in total independence, speaking the world into being.

Whatever the history of the transmission of these accounts, they now stand together as a single witness to the creation of the world. In this canonical perspective on creation each chapter stands in interaction with the other. Praiseworthy language about a transcendent Creator has been placed in a theological context in which other images for God and the God-creature relationship come more clearly into view, providing for a more relational model of creation than has been traditionally presented.

Both God and the creatures have an important role in the creative enterprise, and their spheres of activity are interrelated. God has shaped the created order in such a way that the Creator and the creatures share overlapping spheres of interdependence and creative responsibility.[42] Moreover, the creatures are interdependent among themselves. Both human beings and animals depend on vegetation for their food (1:29-30); humans are to preserve the independent role of the animals (1:22). In addition, the nonhumans depend on varying forms of dominion exercised by the humans.

God is God and freely brings into being that which is not God. The creatures depend on the Creator for their existence and continuing life. Chapter 1 stresses divine initiative, imagination, transcendence, and power in a way that chap. 2 does not. The position of chap. 1 implies that these divine characteristics should stand at the beginning and in the foreground in any discussion. Yet, no simple or static hierarchy emerges, since some features of chap. 1 already lean toward chap. 2.

On the other hand, the realm of the divine and the realm of the creature are not two radically unrelated spheres; there are overlapping powers, roles, and responsibilities, to which image language testifies. God is not powerful and creatures powerless, as if the Godness of God could be bought at the expense of creaturely diminishment. In the very act of creating, God gives to others a certain independence and freedom. God moves over, as it were, and

---

41. Fretheim, "Reclamation," 355-57.
42. See M. Welker, "What Is Creation? Rereading Genesis 1 and 2," *TToday* 45 (1991) 56-71.

makes room for others. Creation involves an ordered freedom, a degree of openness and unpredictability wherein God leaves room for genuine decisions on the part of human beings as they exercise their God-given power. Even more, God gives them powers and responsibilities in a way that *commits* God to a certain kind of relationship with them. Divine constraint and restraint operate in the exercise of power within the creation (e.g., God will not singlehandedly be involved in procreation), still further restrained by the promise at the end of the flood story.

Human beings have been given freedom enough to destroy themselves, though God does not will such destruction. God does not have a final and solitary will in place from the beginning regarding every aspect of the created order. Things may develop, divine and human creativity may continue (see Ps 104:30), in view of which God will make adjustments in the divine will for the world. Yet, these divine acts will always be in tune with God's absolute will regarding the life and salvation of all.

These chapters imply that the divine sovereignty in creation is understood, not in terms of absolute divine control, but as a sovereignty that gives power over to the created for the sake of a relationship of integrity. Such a view involves risk, since it entails the possibility that the creatures will misuse the power they have been given, which does occur. A reclamation of creation will be needed.

4. Some observations on "chaos": The "deep" is probably not related to Tiamat in the Babylonian story in terms of either language or content (see commentary). Yet, some claim that "chaos" is a reality that persists beyond God's ordering activity, providing a negative backdrop and/or a potential threat to God's creation. Such language of "chaos" seems problematic, since *God* decides when to destroy (and promises not to). No reality independent of God is a threat to the creation. Such allusions do, later, provide deeply negative *images* for the world (e.g., Jer 4:23-26), but these are subsumed under the wrath of God in response to creaturely wickedness. Moreover, once Noah finds favor with God (6:8), the deity no longer threatens to destroy all creation, and specific temporal limits are placed on the flood (7:4, 12, 17). In 7:11 the fountains and windows function in an intensive way; they do not break down. When the flood waters abate, the created order of chap. 1 emerges into the light of day.

A different perspective on v. 2 seems appropriate. God's creative activity in the rest of Genesis 1 makes use of the "raw material" in v. 2 for new purposes. The author may not have had the philosophical perspective to call it "matter," but this verse testifies to a pre-temporal reality. As such, it describes a state of affairs prior to God's ordering that is *not yet* consonant with the divine purposes in creation (see the "not good" of 2:18).

God relates to this pre-ordering situation in and through the wind/spirit. The writer thus confesses that God constitutes a reality prior to the "beginning," and in the form of an active reality (wind or spirit). Even at this point, God acts creatively. Genesis 1:2 thus leans toward the rest of the chapter when God makes use of raw materials. Hence, the situation does not run out of control or in opposition to God. God does not reject it or say no to it; God simply uses it as part of a more comprehensive creative activity. Once God has ordered creation, the realities of v. 2 become part of a new world order. No independent threat to the cosmos (or to God) occurs at any stage.

Although the doctrine of "creation out of nothing" has often been grounded in this verse (see 2 Macc 7:28; Rom 4:17; Heb 11:3), it speaks almost exclusively of the ordering of already existing reality. We may justify a very limited use of this notion, only if we think of certain creative acts (sky and its luminaries). God brings everything else into being out of the not-yet-ordered reality, in the ultimate origins of which the author has no apparent interest. Any comprehensive doctrine of *creatio ex nihilo* must be found in other texts or theological perspectives.

(On relationships between these chapters and contemporary science, see the Overview.)

5. In 2:18-23, God takes the human decision into account when shaping new directions for the creation. Divine decisions interact with human decisions in the creation of the world. Creation involves process as well as moment; it is creaturely as well as divine.

The future stands genuinely open here. All depends on what the humans does with what God presents. The question of not only *how,* but indeed whether humanity *will* continue beyond this first generation remains open-ended, suspended in this creative moment. What the humans decide will determine whether there will be a next human generation. Human judgment will shape the nature of the next divine decision, indeed the future of the world.

This situation is similar to our own, where ecological sensitivity or the use of nuclear weapons may have a comparable import for the world's future. Such decisions could put an end to the human race as decisively as the man's choice of the animals would have. Human beings do not have the capacity to stymie God in some absolute way. But God has established a relationship with human beings such that their decisions about the creation truly count.

Genesis 3:1-24, The Intrusion of Sin

NIV

3 Now the serpent was more crafty than any of the wild animals the LORD God had made. He said to the woman, "Did God really say, 'You must not eat from any tree in the garden'?"

²The woman said to the serpent, "We may eat fruit from the trees in the garden, ³but God did say, 'You must not eat fruit from the tree that is in the middle of the garden, and you must not touch it, or you will die.'"

⁴"You will not surely die," the serpent said to the woman. ⁵"For God knows that when you eat of it your eyes will be opened, and you will be like God, knowing good and evil."

⁶When the woman saw that the fruit of the tree was good for food and pleasing to the eye, and also desirable for gaining wisdom, she took some and ate it. She also gave some to her husband, who was with her, and he ate it. ⁷Then the eyes of both of them were opened, and they realized they were naked; so they sewed fig leaves together and made coverings for themselves.

⁸Then the man and his wife heard the sound of the LORD God as he was walking in the garden in the cool of the day, and they hid from the LORD God among the trees of the garden. ⁹But the LORD God called to the man, "Where are you?"

¹⁰He answered, "I heard you in the garden, and I was afraid because I was naked; so I hid."

¹¹And he said, "Who told you that you were

NRSV

3 Now the serpent was more crafty than any other wild animal that the LORD God had made. He said to the woman, "Did God say, 'You shall not eat from any tree in the garden'?" ²The woman said to the serpent, "We may eat of the fruit of the trees in the garden; ³but God said, 'You shall not eat of the fruit of the tree that is in the middle of the garden, nor shall you touch it, or you shall die.'" ⁴But the serpent said to the woman, " 'You will not die; ⁵for God knows that when you eat of it your eyes will be opened, and you will be like God,ᵃ knowing good and evil." ⁶So when the woman saw that the tree was good for food, and that it was a delight to the eyes, and that the tree was to be desired to make one wise, she took of its fruit and ate; and she also gave some to her husband, who was with her, and he ate. ⁷Then the eyes of both were opened, and they knew that they were naked; and they sewed fig leaves together and made loincloths for themselves.

8They heard the sound of the LORD God walking in the garden at the time of the evening breeze, and the man and his wife hid themselves from the presence of the LORD God among the trees of the garden. ⁹But the LORD God called to the man, and said to him, "Where are you?" ¹⁰He said, "I heard the sound of you in the garden, and I was afraid, because I was naked; and I hid

ᵃ Or *gods*

NIV

naked? Have you eaten from the tree that I commanded you not to eat from?"

¹²The man said, "The woman you put here with me—she gave me some fruit from the tree, and I ate it."

¹³Then the LORD God said to the woman, "What is this you have done?"

The woman said, "The serpent deceived me, and I ate."

¹⁴So the LORD God said to the serpent, "Because you have done this,

"Cursed are you above all the livestock
 and all the wild animals!
You will crawl on your belly
 and you will eat dust
 all the days of your life.
¹⁵And I will put enmity
 between you and the woman,
 and between your offspringᵃ and hers;
he will crushᵇ your head,
 and you will strike his heel."

¹⁶To the woman he said,

"I will greatly increase your pains in
 childbearing;
 with pain you will give birth to children.
Your desire will be for your husband,
 and he will rule over you."

¹⁷To Adam he said, "Because you listened to your wife and ate from the tree about which I commanded you, 'You must not eat of it,'

"Cursed is the ground because of you;
 through painful toil you will eat of it
 all the days of your life.
¹⁸It will produce thorns and thistles for you,
 and you will eat the plants of the field.
¹⁹By the sweat of your brow
 you will eat your food
until you return to the ground,
 since from it you were taken;
for dust you are
 and to dust you will return."

²⁰Adamᶜ named his wife Eve,ᵈ because she would become the mother of all the living.

a15 Or seed   b15 Or strike   c20 Or The man
d20 Eve probably means living.

NRSV

myself." ¹¹He said, "Who told you that you were naked? Have you eaten from the tree of which I commanded you not to eat?" ¹²The man said, "The woman whom you gave to be with me, she gave me fruit from the tree, and I ate." ¹³Then the LORD God said to the woman, "What is this that you have done?" The woman said, "The serpent tricked me, and I ate." ¹⁴The LORD God said to the serpent,

"Because you have done this,
 cursed are you among all animals
 and among all wild creatures;
upon your belly you shall go,
 and dust you shall eat
 all the days of your life.
¹⁵ I will put enmity between you and the
  woman,
 and between your offspring and hers;
he will strike your head,
 and you will strike his heel."

¹⁶To the woman he said,

"I will greatly increase your pangs in
  childbearing;
 in pain you shall bring forth children,
yet your desire shall be for your husband,
 and he shall rule over you."

¹⁷And to the manᵃ he said,

"Because you have listened to the voice of
  your wife,
 and have eaten of the tree
about which I commanded you,
 'You shall not eat of it,'
cursed is the ground because of you;
 in toil you shall eat of it all the days of
  your life;
¹⁸ thorns and thistles it shall bring forth for
  you;
 and you shall eat the plants of the field.
¹⁹ By the sweat of your face
 you shall eat bread
until you return to the ground,
 for out of it you were taken;
you are dust,
 and to dust you shall return."

²⁰The man named his wife Eve,ᵇ because she was the mother of all living. ²¹And the LORD God

a Or to Adam   b In Heb Eve resembles the word for living

NIV

²¹The Lord God made garments of skin for Adam and his wife and clothed them. ²²And the Lord God said, "The man has now become like one of us, knowing good and evil. He must not be allowed to reach out his hand and take also from the tree of life and eat, and live forever." ²³So the Lord God banished him from the Garden of Eden to work the ground from which he had been taken. ²⁴After he drove the man out, he placed on the east side*a* of the Garden of Eden cherubim and a flaming sword flashing back and forth to guard the way to the tree of life.

a24 Or placed in front

NRSV

made garments of skins for the man*a* and for his wife, and clothed them.

22Then the Lord God said, "See, the man has become like one of us, knowing good and evil; and now, he might reach out his hand and take also from the tree of life, and eat, and live forever"— 23therefore the Lord God sent him forth from the garden of Eden, to till the ground from which he was taken. 24He drove out the man; and at the east of the garden of Eden he placed the cherubim, and a sword flaming and turning to guard the way to the tree of life.

a Or for Adam

COMMENTARY

This chapter does not stand isolated. It has long been recognized as an integral part of the story, stretching from 2:4 to 4:16 (24). Some scholars have suggested that the story had an earlier form, particularly in view of the role of the trees (see p. 350), but no consensus has emerged. Given the high value this text has had through the centuries, the reader may be surprised to learn that the OT itself never refers to it (Eden is mentioned in 13:10; Isa 51:3; Ezek 31:9, 16, 18; 36:35; Joel 2:3). The closest parallel to the story is Ezek 28:11-19, a lamentation over the king of Tyre: "You were in Eden, the garden of God . . . were blameless in your ways from the day that you were created, until iniquity was found in you . . . and the guardian cherub drove you out" (vv. 12, 15-16). Ezekiel 28, however, includes no mention of prohibited trees, the serpent, eating, or cursing of the ground. Genesis 3 offers no mention of riches, precious stones, or holy mountains. Some version of Ezekiel 28 was probably a source for the writer of Genesis 3. Unlike the Mesopotamian parallels, this story develops a sharp sense of human responsibility for the disruption of God's good creation.

One may discern a similar structure in Genesis 3 and 4:7-16. There is an unusual ordering in the appearance of the principals: vv. 1-7: Transgression—serpent, woman, man; vv. 8-13: Inquest—man, woman, (serpent); vv. 14-19: Sentence—serpent, woman, man.[43] That the woman plays the lead role in the transgression and the man in the inquest may suggest an interest in balance.

No word for "sin" occurs in the chapter (though in some ways that would defeat the art of storytelling; to have to name the game means one has not told the story very well). This situation parallels, in some ways, the absence of language about feeling; the chapter focuses instead on what the humans see and know and hear and do.

3:1-7, The Temptation. Verse 1 reaches back into the previous chapter in several ways. The writer identifies the serpent ("snake" would probably present fewer connotations) as a "beast"/"animal of the field" that God had formed and the man had named (the NRSV and the NIV introduce the word *wild* in 3:1 but not in 2:19-20, probably reflecting the history of the interpretation of the serpent). The serpent is characterized as "more crafty" (ערום *ʿārûm*) than any of the others God formed; this is a play on the word for "naked" (ערומים *ʿărûmmîm*) in 2:25. The link suggests that human beings may be *exposed* at times to shrewd or crafty elements in the world, language often associated with temptation.

Much debate has centered on the identity of the serpent. While the OT has no interest in this question, the situation changes in the intertes-

43. Fretheim, *Creation*, 82.

tamental period. The association of the serpent with the "devil" in Wisd 2:24 (see Rev 12:9; 20:2) has enjoyed a long history. While this interpretation may be a legitimate extension of the relationship between the serpent and temptation (see below), the text does not assume such metaphysical considerations.

The text does not focus on the serpent per se, but on the human response to the possibilities the serpent presents. As such, the serpent presents a metaphor, representing anything in God's good creation that could present options to human beings, the choice of which can seduce them away from God. The tree itself becomes the temptation, while the serpent facilitates the options the tree presents.

The author introduces the serpent abruptly, in a rather matter-of-fact way. The woman shows no fear or surprise or concern; conversations with snakes about God are presented as nothing unusual. Indeed, the reader receives an initial impression that the serpent is not a villain, but a neutral observer of the God-human relationship and a conversation partner, positively disposed toward the woman. The serpent only *becomes* a facilitator of temptation as the conversation progresses.

The reader appears to be overhearing the middle of a theological dialogue, leaving questions about the source of the serpent's knowledge unsettled, but suggesting that these words have grown out of a broader conversation. The reader first hears a question from the serpent to the woman (why the woman was chosen to play this role remains unknown, perhaps because she did not receive the prohibition firsthand; see 1 Tim 2:13-15; Sir 25:21-24). The question focuses on the prohibition, explicitly referring to God. The serpent raises a question about the amount of freedom God has given humans (always a sensitive topic). This tactic sets the agenda, which centers on God, and provokes a response by suggesting that the woman knows more about the prohibition than the serpent does: "Have I got this straight? Did God really say that you were not to eat of *any* tree?" The question is clever, to which a simple yes or no response is impossible, *if* one decides to continue the conversation (a key move in such situations). The "you" is plural in Hebrew, so that both the man and the woman are implied

(the man stands "with her," v. 6, and so acts as a silent partner to the entire conversation).

Eve's response (vv. 2-3) seems motivated by an effort to explain the situation to the serpent. We may deem her response noteworthy in a number of ways. She evidences familiarity with the prohibition (not established to this point in the narrative); she both paraphrases the permission/prohibition in her own words and quotes God directly. In quoting God, she uses the plural "you," understanding that the prohibition applies to her (as in the "we"), though God's original prohibition was in the singular (2:16-17). One puzzles over the reference to touching (the serpent interprets her indefinite reference to the tree in the middle of the garden—see commentary on 2:9—as the tree of knowledge). She may have heard it this way from the man; yet, because the text does not settle the issue, we do not know that *either* the man or the woman misstated it. The text does not offer a judgment or a defense of God, as the word order shows ("God" is delayed until after the second "garden"; the NRSV and the NIV advance the reference; see TNK, NAB). That she (or the man) makes the prohibition more severe than God made it has been explained in various ways (from anxiety to confusion to innocent defensiveness to hyperbole to a contribution in the search for truth). Most likely, the woman's reasons are revealed in the serpent's reply, which immediately focuses on death. The reference to touching thus reveals a key vulnerability—namely, anxiety about death. She exaggerates because she wants to avoid death at all costs (anxiety does not necessarily involve sin). The exaggeration offers evidence of reflection that the woman (and/or the man) has had about the prohibition.

The serpent responds (vv. 4-5) precisely at the point of exaggeration and vulnerability, and with a promise at that: The humans will not die. This response could be a contradiction of what God has said (but not all that the woman has said). But it may be more subtle than that. In 3:22, God recognizes that they could eat and not die, *if* they eat of the tree of life. Expulsion from the garden becomes necessary for death to occur. So the serpent speaks a word that has the potential of being true (at least at the physical level). The reason: They will be like God/divine beings (1:26

and 3:22 include both), knowing good and evil (the phrase could refer either to God or to minor deities, and may be purposely ambiguous). Inasmuch as God said nothing about being like God(s) a new element has been drawn into the picture (3:22 confirms that the serpent was right); yet, because this issue plays no role in the woman's reflection (v. 6) we have difficulty assessing its importance. Hence, we should temper efforts to see the primal sin as a desire to become like God. The serpent was subtle in holding out the possibility of avoiding death, while not conveying all the possible futures, not least a broader definition of death and another option that God had available (expulsion).

The serpent, then, is correct in saying the humans would become like God(s), knowing good and evil, and that eating in itself would not necessarily mean death in at least some sense. The serpent speaks a key phrase: "God knows." It claims that God has not told them the full truth about the matter, that God keeps something back. In this, the serpent acts not as a deceiver but as *a truth-teller*. But what was God's motivation for not telling them the whole story? The serpent makes it sound as if God's motivation is self-serving; the humans will become like God. Has God, in keeping the full truth from them, divine interests more at heart than interest in humans? The issue of knowledge thus becomes at its deepest level an issue of *trust*. Is the giver of the prohibition one who can be trusted with their best interests? Can the man and the woman trust God even if God has not told them everything, indeed not given them every possible "benefit"?

The writer leaves the woman to draw her own conclusions. The serpent has only presented some possibilities. The serpent engages in no coercion here, no arm-twisting, no enticement through presentation of fruit from the tree; everything happens through words. The word of the serpent ends up putting the word of God in question. At the same time, the issue focuses on the visible and tangible, which belong to God's creation.[44]

The woman does not speak (the lack of communication reinforces the element of mistrust); she only looks, contemplates, and eats. She considers explicitly neither God nor the prohibition,

in terms of either complaint or rejection; she focuses only on the potential the tree offers. The observation that the tree was good for food and pleasant to the sight means, in view of 2:9 (see 1:29), that this tree becomes like other trees to her; it also happens to be "desirable for gaining wisdom." While one may "desire" (נחמד *neḥmād,* 2:9) the trees for their beauty, the humans shall not "desire" wisdom (i.e., knowledge of good and evil). The command seems to forbid an immediate acquisition of knowledge, though without suggesting that humans should not have wisdom. The issue involves *the way in which wisdom is gained.* The fear of the Lord is the beginning of wisdom (see Rom 1:20-21). By using their freedom to acquire wisdom in this way, they have determined that the creational command no longer applies to them. That command refers primarily, not to the intellect, but to success in making decisions in life—true wisdom involves knowing good and evil, the discernment of what is one's own best interests (see at 2:9). What it means can be seen from the result. Only God has a perspective that can view the created order as a whole; human beings (even with their new knowledge) will never gain that kind of breadth, for they make their decisions from within the creation.

The woman takes some of the fruit and gives it to her husband. As a silent partner "with her" throughout this exchange, the man puts up no resistance, raises no questions, and considers no theological issues; he simply and silently takes his turn. The woman does not act as a temptress in this scene; they both have succumbed to the same source of temptation. They stand together as "one flesh" at this point as well.

The result is fourfold: Their eyes are opened (as the serpent had promised, v. 5); they know that they are naked; they make loincloths for themselves (an interhuman act); and they hide from God's presence. With eyes opened, they see the world differently, *from a theological perspective.* They realize that, now having to decide for themselves what is in their own best interests, everything looks somewhat different. Having decided to be on their own, they see the world entirely through their own eyes. They now operate totally out of their own resources.

The humans first see each other's nakedness.

44. See H. White, *Narration and Discourse* (Cambridge: Cambridge University Press, 1991) 133-37.

It becomes clear (v. 10) that nakedness has more than a bodily reference. It reverses the lack of shame between them in 2:25 (see 9:21-23; Isa 20:4; Lam 1:8; Ezek 16:37). They respond initially by providing garments for themselves, which involves more than a physical act; they attempt to cover up their shame. This response addresses only the symptoms of the problem. Their human resources prove inadequate, as they recognize in seeking to hide their nakedness from God (3:10)—their clothing reveals more than it conceals—as God's action in clothing the already clothed indicates (3:21).

3:8-13, The Inquest. In this section God conducts a judicial inquiry. Whereas the woman functioned as the dialogue partner in vv. 1-5, the man serves that function in vv. 9-12. Hence, the author creates a certain balance between them in the story as a whole.

The Creator of the universe and all creatures chooses not to relate to the world at a distance, but takes on human form, goes for a walk among the creatures, and personally engages them regarding recent events. The writer presents no naive theology, but a deeply profound understanding of how God chooses to enter into the life of the world and relate to the creatures. Even more, this God comes to the man and the woman subsequent to their sin; God does not leave them or walk elsewhere.

Hearing God walking about in the garden, the man and woman try to hide from the divine presence. Not encountering the couple (as usual?), God calls for the man (the "you" is singular). The man interprets the question correctly as a probing inquiry and attempts to deflect the conversation away from what has happened. But his response reveals that something disastrous has occurred. He is afraid—the fear is explicit—because he was naked and, feeling shame at what has happened, hides himself, even though he is now clothed (v. 7). While the nakedness in v. 7 focuses on their relationship to each other, in v. 10 it shifts to their relationship with God. Although the feelings about nakedness are new, their clothing prompts the response; "clothedness" must be hidden from God. (It is ironic that the words for "hearing" and "fearing" can also be used for "obedience" and "awe.")

God's response centers on their nakedness, not on their fear. How would the man have known that he was naked? Something must have happened so that nakedness had become a problem *to the someone who told him* so (namely, the woman). God immediately puts the right question (again, to elicit a confession), asking whether he has eaten of the prohibited tree.

The responses could be viewed as a consequence of achieving autonomy; the man could not handle the new "knowledge." He appears fearful, insecure, and ashamed, seeking to justify himself and deflecting blame, both to God for giving him the woman and to the woman for giving him the fruit to eat, which had been guaranteed to alienate them from each other. Yet he does admit having eaten (though without mentioning motives). This situation attests to a breakdown in interhuman relationships as well as in the relationship with God, whom he does not engage in a straightforward manner.

God then turns to the woman, again asking a leading question. The woman deflects the responsibility as well (though she does not blame God as the man does), this time laying the blame on the trickery of the serpent (blaming it on the source of temptation), yet admitting that she too has eaten. That there is no inquiry of the serpent may show that the purpose in the interrogation of the humans was to elicit confession.

3:14-19, The Sentence. God proceeds with the sentencing, accepting full human responsibility and bringing all parties within the scope of the announcement. God acts as judge (see p. 369), calling each of the participants before the bench (in the order of vv. 1-6) and pronouncing sentence on each in typical courtroom speech (which immediately takes effect). Yet, even in the sentencing, God remains in relationship with the creatures involved, connected and concerned enough to identify further what has just happened.

What are the effects of the sentencing? Most basically, the sentences pertain to their primary roles in life (in that culture), roles of stature among the animals, roles of wife and mother, roles of tiller of soil and provider of food. Every conceivable relationship has been disrupted: among the animals; between an animal and humans; between the ground and humans; between human beings and God; between an animal and God; within the individual self (e.g., shame). More abstractly, one could speak of humiliation, domination and subordination, conflict, suffering, and struggle. The sentences touch every aspect of human life: marriage and sexuality; birth and death; work and food; human and nonhuman. In all of these areas, one could speak of death encroaching on life. Disharmony reigns supreme.

We may deem the judgment announced to the serpent unusual in a number of ways. First, God does not interrogate the serpent, although the judgment recognizes some responsibility on the part of the serpent for what happened. Second, the serpent receives a curse, becoming isolated from the community of animals (a word play with the initial description: "more crafty [ערום *ʿārûm*]" becomes "more cursed" [ארור *ʾārûr*]), a moral order correspondence—what goes around comes around. Third, in the future the serpent will move on its belly and "eat" dust (given the role that eating plays in the temptation, this is moral order talk). While this sentence may present an explanation of why the snake crawls on its belly, it signifies humiliation; eating dust symbolizes degradation (see Mic 7:17; cf. Ps 72:9; Isa 49:23). In some sense, vv. 14-15 create a symbol out of the serpent, which will remind all who encounter it of the subtleties of temptation as well as of the humiliating and conflicting consequences.

God places enmity between the serpent and the woman, and between the offspring of both. On the surface, the writer may be offering an origin of the legendary revulsion human beings have for snakes, which may relate back to 1:28 and show how the human task of dominion has been much complicated (see 9:2-3). Interpreters through the centuries (who have often linked the serpent and the devil) have seen in this text an ongoing struggle at a deeper level, even considering the text messianic, foretelling the struggle between the seed of the woman (i.e., the Messiah) and Satan. Yet, the word for "seed" functions as a collective noun (9:9; 12:7) or refers to the immediate offspring (4:25), not a distant one. It probably refers more generally to ongoing centuries of conflict between people and various sources of temptation. The "head" and "heel" are the natural targets against each other and point to no resolution of the conflict (the NRSV correctly reflects the fact that the same verb is used in both). Yet, striking the head of the serpent would more likely prove decisive and would give at least potential superiority to the human over the animal (perhaps reflecting 4:7).

The sentence on the woman—with whom no curse language is associated—has also been much discussed. Carol Meyers has placed this material in a sociohistorical setting just before the monarchy, a time when the place of women was related to the harsh realities of agricultural life in the central highlands.[45] She translates (with help from different versions) the first line of v. 16 to reflect the arduous field work in which women had to participate ("I will greatly increase your toil and your pregnancies"), and thinks it has an etiological force originally not present in Gen 3:16. While this view has not been fully tested, most scholars continue to translate along the lines of the NRSV and the NIV, so that the first clause in the poetry refers only to the pain of childbirth (hence paralleling the second clause). In any case, whatever the sociohistorical background of the text, the final literary context presents these verses as a consequence of the man's and the woman's sin. The fulfillment of the command to multiply in 1:28 has become more difficult.

The "desire" of the woman for the man remains unclear. It could involve a desire for mastery (as with this verb in 4:7), which will be thwarted by the husband. More likely, it means that, despite the pains of childbirth, she will still long for sexual intimacy. The "rule" of the husband could be a more general reference to patriarchy, which would be a departure from what God intended in creation (see 2:18-23). Trible states that the rule of the male "is neither a divine right nor a male prerogative. Her subordination is neither a divine decree nor the female destiny. Both their positions result from shared disobedience."[46] The "rule" of the man over the woman is part and parcel of the judgment on the *man* as much as the woman. This writer understood that patriarchy and related ills came as a consequence of sin rather than being the divine intention. How easy it would have been to build patriarchy into the created order!

God allocates the most extensive sentence to the man, whose attempt to pass off the blame to his wife the deity has rejected out of hand. One

45. C. Meyers, *Discovering Eve: Ancient Israelite Women in Context* (New York: Oxford University Press, 1988) 117-19.
46. Trible, *Rhetoric*, 128.

may discern moral order talk, since eating plays a role in both sin and sentence. Although the man does not receive the curse, the ground from which he was formed does. The ground brings forth thorns and thistles as well as the plants of the field, which human beings will continue to need for food, but the thistles will make it more difficult to obtain. This also means that God's command to subdue the earth will be more difficult to fulfill. A concern for relief from the curse on the ground appears in 5:29 and 8:21. The same word that was used for "toil" in v. 16 for woman's pain in childbirth occurs in this sentence as well (both striking at a primary role in life). The man's work does not receive a curse (he still does in 3:23 what he was called to do in 2:15), but it has become more difficult and more energy has to be expended to gain a living from the soil.

"All the days of your life . . . You are dust and to dust you shall return" expands upon "until you return to the ground." This part of the sentence stipulates that the toil shall not let up until death. Death seems to be assumed rather than introduced as a part of the sentence. While the word *death* does not occur here, certain features of death within life are evident, beginning even before the sentencing. It remains to be seen whether the still remaining possibility of eating from the tree of life and gaining immortality will be realized.

3:20-24, The Expulsion. The note about Eve in v. 20 seems intrusive, but it probably functions as a positive development in the midst of the judgment, anticipating that life will still go on (a negative assessment of this verse incorrectly associates naming with subordination). The NIV future tense seems correct (since the perfect verb expresses certainty). Adam gives his wife the more personal name Eve ("Eve" resembles the word for "living"), as a way of expressing confidence that children will be born; indeed, the unity of the human race ("all") appears implied, which would fulfill the command in 1:28.

Verse 21 has both positive and negative dimensions. The use of clothing is a common thread throughout Genesis as a sign of many things (see Tamar in 38:14, 19; Joseph in 37:3). Here God is imaged as a tailor, using animal skins (not necessarily killing to procure them). This same image for God is used in Ezek 16:8-14, where it

is a profoundly gracious act, assuring continuing divine presence in the midst of the judgment; that is likely one theme here. If nakedness has to do with shame, exposure, and vulnerability, and they already had made clothes for themselves, God's act of clothing them may relate to issues of salvation (Job 29:14; Ps 132:16). God acts to cover their shame and defenselessness. At the same time, this act recognizes continuity in their estranged relationship; this is something with which they must now live (the more substantial skins may also stress this).

Verse 22 introduces inner-divine communication once again (see 1:26 for the "us"; see also 11:6-7). The sentence could break off abruptly (see NRSV), matching the effect of the action—namely, expulsion from the garden. Or it could be concluded with an exclamation point (see TNK). We should note that 'ādām functions generically here. The expulsion becomes necessary because God envisions radical possibilities regarding the tree of life and human immortality. Expulsion does not mean that an innate immortality has been lost; rather, the possibility of ever attaining it has been eliminated. Preventing humans from living forever might seem to be a defensive move by the deity, yet if death (in the comprehensive sense) has already become a significant part of life, then never-ending life offers no blessing. God continues to protect human beings. In apocalyptic literature, this motif recurs in an eternal frame, and when eternal life becomes a reality, it is not accompanied by sin and its consequences.

The author provides no specific description of the apparently coercive means used to drive the humans out of the garden. Yet, the divine vocation for the human remains the same: tilling the ground (see 2:15) from which he was taken (2:7-8). Hence, the humans leave the garden with a certain integrity, remaining an integral part of the divine purpose for the world (2:5). While being "like God" carries tremendous burdens and ambiguities, it also bears some potential for good and advancement. The cherubim—a human and animal/bird composite (a common phenomenon in the ancient Near East)—are usually associated with sanctuaries in Israel, associated with the divine presence in the ark, the tabernacle, and the temple. They assumed various functions, including guarding the sanctuary from unauthorized intrusion. The turning sword (unique in the OT) may or may not be in the hands of the cherubim, but its purpose is clear: to prevent human beings from returning to Eden; paradise on earth no longer remains a possibility.

The ending of this chapter bears some remarkable similarities both to Israel's being sent/driven out of Egypt (Exod 6:1) and to Israel's exile to Babylon, a banishment from the land (see Leviticus 26). The latter, in particular, may have been viewed as a parallel experience to this primeval moment in Israel's eyes.

REFLECTIONS

1. Inasmuch as God made the serpent, the text raises the issue of God's responsibility for what happens. God holds ultimate responsibility in the sense that God did not create puppets, but made human beings in such a way that they could resist the will of God (human beings would not be commanded not to eat if they were unable to do so). The temptation to reach beyond the limits of creatureliness belongs to created existence for the sake of human integrity and freedom (and God does not have absolute knowledge of future human behaviors, 22:12). At the same time, the text does not bring God's responsibility closer to hand and speak of God as the tempter or the instigator of the serpent's wiles or the source of sin and evil. The author does not use the language of evil to describe the serpent; indeed, the word about the serpent as God's creature recalls the litany of the goodness of all that God has created. Sin and evil have emerged only subsequent to the creation of the world. The first human beings are presented as individuals who are not sinful, but with clear choices available to them, with no response coerced or inevitable; they live in a world where choices count and God has not programmed the divine-human relationship.

We may see the serpent from a number of angles. The word *crafty* seems purposely ambiguous, as words like *clever, cunning,* and *shrewd* commonly are; it depends on the use to which these characteristics are put. Although used to describe human beings in both a good and a bad sense (e.g. Job 5:12; esp. Prov 12:16), no other biblical writer used this word for an animal; yet people often associate animals with characteristics usually reserved for humans (a sly fox; a wise owl). The serpent stands as an ambivalent symbol, associated with both life and death (see Num 21:4-9), often used figuratively for evil people (Pss 58:4; 140:3). Serpents were considered dangerous and probably always poisonous, a threat to life (Ps 91:13); they were "naked" in appearance, silent and "innocent" in their approach, suddenly there with little or no warning. As occasional symbols of deity, they could have been associated with that which was religiously seductive and hence dangerous to Israel's religious health.

The writer views the serpent as an animal of the field, and when God sentences the serpent (v. 14) it is included again among these fauna. Yet, this animal's knowledge and abilities seem not to outmatch those of any other animal. It may have been thought, however, that animals had unusual capabilities in paradise, or even beyond (see Balaam's ass [Num 22:22-30] and animals that have a knowledge of God, Job 12:7-9). When it comes to actions, however, the serpent seems to stand in a class by itself. Yet, a question remains: Is the serpent out to seduce human beings and challenge God or is it more of a neutral figure, serving to mediate possibilities within God's good creation? We should note that the woman occasions no surprise or fear or wonderment about the serpent. From every sign in the text, the woman understands it to be a natural part of her world.

The serpent, neither divine nor human, stands over against both as a "third party." In some sense, Genesis 3 reverses or makes less certain the dominion of humans over animals (1:28). God's sentence makes enmity a part of life. The serpent elicits certain characteristics in the human. "The serpent's 'subtlety' is the ability to provoke reflection on the true meaning of freedom, to reveal by means of conversation that the woman had the ability to think for herself, to suggest to her that she had the power to decide for herself. So it is the course of the conversation that is truly important, and not the existence of a talking serpent. . . . The serpent is a tempter in a sense, but only as a catalyst, assisting the woman's own mental processes to discover the freedom she had the power to grasp."[47]

The identification of the serpent as a "beast of the field" means that the reality embodied in the serpent should not be viewed as either primordial or transhistorical. It is not an evil being or supernatural/metaphysical force opposed to the divine purposes. The serpent exists within this world and is encountered by humans there. Nevertheless, the reality embodied in the serpent is transpersonal, not simply a product of the individual will. Language about the seed of the serpent, as well as God's judgment upon it, prevents us from seeing here *simply* an externalization of an inward struggle. In one sense, the serpent becomes transgenerational. The serpent may be a metaphor, yet no "mere metaphor"; it bears some correspondence with reality beyond the individuals involved.

2. Descriptions of paradise have, at times, been drawn in overly romantic terms. The text, however, shows remarkable restraint. It emphasizes basics: life, freedom, food, a place to call home, a family, harmonious relationships, and a stable natural environment. The contrast with the situation portrayed in 3:7-19 stands sharp and clear; yet, care must be used not to overdraw the differences. For example, suffering is often considered to be only part of the broken world. But it would be truer to the text to speak of the effects of sin as an intensification of suffering, so that it becomes a burden, tragic, no longer serving of life. Eden, though, does include suffering. D. J. Hall speaks of four Edenic dimensions of "the suffering of becoming" (and draws parallels with the life of Jesus): loneliness (2:18); limits (not only the command in 2:17, but the very nature of creaturely existence); temptation; and anxiety (of ignorance, dependency, uncertainty). "Life without suffering would be no life at all; it would be a form of death. Life depends in some mysterious way on the struggle to be."[48] Genesis 1 may recognize this reality in the language of "subdue" (1:28).

3. What is the sin? Although the word *sin* or other such words do not appear in the chapter (4:7 is the first occurrence), we should not overvalue its absence. Stories are similar to games in that certain things do not need to be named. Nonetheless, interpreters have had difficulty identifying the nature of the primal sin. The story remains complex and devoid of abstract reflection. Even God's responses focus on the act of eating itself and its effects (vv. 11, 13, 17). God deems what they have done to be clearly wrong. But no single word appears to be satisfactory to describe it.

Disobedience may be the most common suggestion. Yet, though humans transgress God's prohibition (2:17), that action symptomizes a more fundamental problem. The vocabulary of pride (or hubris) also appears frequently, centered particularly in the "becoming like God(s)" theme. The serpent does mention this issue (3:5), but as part of a larger point being made regarding the divine motivation for the prohibition (for "God knows"). Moreover, the woman does not mention it in her own reflection; she uses language that normally would not be associated with pride (3:6). Even God mentions their having become like God(s) in a matter-of-fact way (3:22). Finally, language of rebellion also presents problems. No storming of the heavens language occurs here, no expressed effort to take over the divine realm. We might speak of their desire for autonomy, but not to run the universe. Even then, the reader finds no declaration of independence and no celebration of a newfound freedom.

The primal sin may be best defined as mistrust of God and the word of God, which then manifests itself in disobedience and other behaviors (e.g., blaming others). The serpent, in

47. Gowan, *Genesis 1–11*, 52.
48. D. J. Hall, *God and Human Suffering* (Minneapolis: Augsburg, 1986) 53-62.

telling the truth about God (v. 4, "God knows"), informs the humans of something that God had not conveyed to them. This information centers on certain benefits that would accrue to them upon eating from the tree, benefits that appear to be in their best interest. This raises the question of God's motivation; even more, it suggests that God's motivation might be more focused on God than on their welfare. Can the humans trust that God has their best interests at heart even if they do not know everything? Even more, can the humans trust that God will be able to discern that not all such "benefits" are in their best interests, that true creaturely freedom entails acknowledging limits?

4. Commentators often use the language of "fall" with reference to this chapter. Such language begins to emerge only in post-OT interpretation, both in Judaism (Sir 25:24; Wis 2:24; see 2 Esdr 3:7-22; 7:118) and in Christianity (Rom 5:12-21; 1 Cor 15:21-22, 45-49), and has been a staple of Christian theological reflection through the centuries.[49]

Readers, thereby, have given this text a level of significance found nowhere else within the OT (some themes are picked up here and there). But care must be used not to overdraw this statistical observation (this would be particularly the case if the Yahwist wrote in the exilic period!). Canonical placement has given to this text a certain theological stature (as with chaps. 1–2). Moreover, frequency of reference does not provide an absolute criterion for determining theological importance (one thinks of the suffering servant songs in Isaiah). We can only decry the elevation of this story into a dogma, though that often develops on the basis of many other considerations. Further questions need to be raised: To what extent does the "Fall" constitute a metaphor grounded in this text? This question relates to issues raised by the postbiblical language of "original sin." We take up the latter first.

This chapter in itself cannot support a notion of original sin. "Original" refers to the universality or inescapability of human sinfulness, not to its point of origin or to a particular mode of transmission—say, genetic (though the claim has often been made). At most one could speak of an "originating" sin (see below). Chapters 3–6 together, however, support a view approximating this, especially as seen in the snowballing effects of sin, climaxing in the statement of 6:5, "Every inclination of the thoughts of their hearts was only evil continually" (reaffirmed in 8:21). This suggests a process by which sin became "original."

The text includes the image inside/outside the garden to probe this issue, with progressively greater distances from the near presence of God (3:22-24; 4:16; see also the decreasing ages of human beings).[50] Humans live outside the garden (3:14-19 describes such conditions). Cain makes his decision to kill outside the garden, in a state of alienation from the relationship with God that presence together in the garden implies; 4:7 even gives "sin" an enticing, possessive character. At the same time, 4:7 implies that being "outside the garden" does not exhaust the analysis of a sinful act. Hence, something approximating a distinction between "sin" and "sins" is made; at the least, sin cannot be reduced to individual acts in these chapters.

What, then, of the "Fall" as a metaphor for what happens in this text? At least two issues present themselves: (1) the congruence of this metaphor with the metaphors in the text, and (2) the idea of the sin of Adam and Eve as a decisive rupture in the history of the relationship between God and humans. I believe that we may speak of a fundamental disruption, though this specific metaphor finds no textual basis. The most basic theological issue at stake involves whether sin is collapsed back into God's creational work and intention.

"Fall" theorists commonly assume that the text presents straightforward chronological terms: creation, paradise, fall. I have sought to show that these chapters, for all their typological character, tell a story of the past. They are placed within a *temporal framework*, particularly

---

49. See S. Towner, "Interpretations and Reinterpretations of the Fall," *Modern Biblical Scholarship*, ed. F. Eigo (Villanova: Villanova University Press, 1984) 53-85; G. Tucker, "The Creation and the Fall: A Reconsideration," *LTQ* 13 (1978) 113-24.

50. Fretheim, *Creation*, 97-99.

in the distinctions drawn between past and present and in the common chronological references.

Other readers assume that human beings were not created as sinful or evil creatures. If they were "perfect," how could they have failed? Rather, they were "good," which entails considerable room for growth and the development of potentialities. By the way human responsibility for what happens is lifted up, the writer does not assign the problem of human sinfulness to God or consider it integral to God's creational purposes. Certainly God creates the potential for such developments for the sake of human freedom. Especially important are the effects of this human decision, which range in an amazingly wide arch; it disrupts not only their own lives, but (given the symbiotic character of creaturely relationships) that of the entire cosmos as well, issuing in disharmonious relationships at every level. The narrative signals some kind of fundamental break by the journey of the nakedness theme from 2:25 through chap. 3, to which 9:3-5 also testifies. At the same time, the attention given to "process" noted above means that such human developments are not simply collapsed into a single moment.

The metaphor of "fall" does not do justice to these texts. Traditionally, this metaphor has been used to refer to a fall "down." Others typically emphasize the "becoming like God" theme, where human beings strive for and, indeed, assume godlike powers for themselves. This kind of a fall "up" (see above) violates the basic thrust of the metaphor (perhaps one could speak of a reaching up only to fall down, for the humans are not able to handle what they have become).

Such an upward move in the texts has been interpreted positively (at least since Irenaeus) in the sense that human beings move out from under the parental hand of God; they are pioneers on the road to moral autonomy and maturity, a necessary move if they are to become truly human. "The position reflects the mounting consciousness of the last few decades that rebellion against the yoke of authority is both an inevitable and a necessary element in human maturation."[51] However, one has difficulty in sustaining a totally positive view of God's response to the human violation of the prohibition. We would have to assign the problem to God, who acts arbitrarily in the setting of limits, and who opposes maturity and overreacts to what has happened. There are, in fact, few signs that the human lot improves, from either the divine or the human perspective. All the signs are that death (in the comprehensive sense) has become a pervasive reality with which humanity must deal, and that far from being marked by a new maturity or freedom, human life now entails broken relationships with God and every other creature (see 9:3-5 as well).

Perhaps these themes allow a variation on the "Fall" metaphor—namely, a fall "out." The primary images in the text are those of separation, estrangement, alienation, and displacement.[52] In these respects, the story is written not only to reflect a story of the past, but also to claim that in fundamental ways it reflects the character of human life in every age, which is filled with disharmonious relationships at all levels of life. Human beings always "reject their God-given vocation, scorn their permission modestly to enjoy the good gifts of the Garden, and break across into the area of prohibition outside the sphere of human competence."[53]

In view of these suggestions, does the text wish to claim that these events have *universal* effects on *all* subsequent generations? This combination of considerations, particularly the cosmic motifs present in chaps. 3 and 6, suggests that it does (reaffirmed in 8:21). The possible negative consequences for one's view of God need to be considered in the light of the moral order rather than a forensic divine decision. To this end, a consideration of 3:14-19 is helpful.

51. S. Towner, "Interpretations," 80.
52. See A. Hauser, "Genesis 2–3: The Theme of Intimacy and Alienation," *Art and Meaning,* ed. D. Clines et al. (Sheffield: *JSOT,* 1982) 20-36.
53. S. Towner, "Interpretations," 78.

5. Finding the right language to describe vv. 14-19 has been difficult. Some would say that the language functions descriptively, but not prescriptively. The language does describe what has been commonly true about the human situation; it serves more as a statement about *condition* than a typical effect of specific human sins. Hence, this dimension of the story has a more than typological force; it works as a story of the past, presenting consequences of human sin that have taken hold in human life.

Some interpreters have hesitated to use the language of judgment (or punishment), often narrowly conceived. Yet, God's judgment facilitates the moral order, the working out of the effects of sinful acts. The man and woman reap the consequences of their own deeds. They wanted control over their own lives; they now have control in grievously distorted and unevenly distributed forms. They wanted to transcend creaturely limits, but they have found newly intensified forms of limitation. They now have the autonomy they so desired, but neither the perspective nor the wherewithal to handle it very well.

The language of prescription does not help if it means that God puts this particular state of affairs into place for all time to come. These judgments are not a divine effort to put a new order of creation into place. And these effects are not cast in stone, determining human fate forever. The judgment of Jerusalem in 587 BCE did not mean that it should remain forever in ruins, for it was soon rebuilt. Correspondingly, the toil of the man and the pain of the woman are not such that no effort should be made to relieve them. In fact, the intense efforts, particularly in recent years, to overcome these effects of sin harmonize with the creational intentions of God. At the same time, continuing human sinfulness impedes these efforts, and other forms of the distorting effects of sin break out among us with extraordinary regularity. We have a smoldering forest fire on our hands.

6. What about death in particular? In some sense this story includes an etiology of death (at least for human beings). Human beings were created mortal; nothing inherent in human beings would have enabled them to live forever. Death per se belongs as a natural part of God's created world. At the same time, the tree of life presents the possibility of continuing life as a special blessing. Since humans violate the prohibition, God cuts off that possibility by excluding them from access to the tree of life (3:22). In effect, sin leads to a death that would have been possible to avoid. It would be a mistake to think of death in these chapters as defined solely in terms of the cessation of heartbeat; death becomes a pervasive reality within life before the exclusion. Yet, these intrusions of death into life would not have led to physical death if the human beings had discovered the tree of life. Only God's act of exclusion in 3:22-24 forecloses that option.

The interpretation of Rom 5:12-21 ought not to be set up in such a way that it presents Paul as either all wrong or all right in his interpretation of the Genesis story. He certainly develops these themes beyond the scope of the story. Paul is, after all, basically interested in soteriological issues and develops an Adam-Christ typology as a way of interpreting the significance of what God has done in Jesus.[54] But, in some sense, he was right to read the story in terms of an etiology of *the reality of* death, if not death as such.

7. In vv. 17-18 the moral order bears a close relationship to the cosmic order, since human sin has ill effects upon the ground. While human behaviors today may affect the nonhuman order in ways different from then, or the cause-and-effect relationship may have been conceived differently, the link remains important.

The concern for the relationship between the human and nonhuman, often neglected, pervades these texts. This connection ranges from the deep concern evident in the detail regarding God's creating of the various creatures, to the assignment of the human to the further

---

54. See Ernst Käsemann, *Commentary on Romans,* trans. and ed. Georffrey W. Bromiley (Grand Rapids: Eerdmans, 1980) 139-58 for a balanced view.

development of and care for the nonhuman world. The naming of the animals, while not finally solving human loneliness, establishes a "by name" relationship between the human and the nonhuman. God's continuing concern for the animals in the story of Noah's ark shows that God's delegation of responsibility does not issue in a deistic perspective regarding the divine care for the world. The symbiotic relationship among the creatures, in which humans participate, remains a prominent theme throughout the OT (see Lev 18:24-28; 26:14, 20; Hos 4:1-3; Rom 8:19-23).

Genesis 4:1-26, Cain and Abel

NIV

4 Adam[a] lay with his wife Eve, and she became pregnant and gave birth to Cain.[b] She said, "With the help of the LORD I have brought forth[c] a man." [2]Later she gave birth to his brother Abel.

Now Abel kept flocks, and Cain worked the soil. [3]In the course of time Cain brought some of the fruits of the soil as an offering to the LORD. [4]But Abel brought fat portions from some of the firstborn of his flock. The LORD looked with favor on Abel and his offering, [5]but on Cain and his offering he did not look with favor. So Cain was very angry, and his face was downcast.

[6]Then the LORD said to Cain, "Why are you angry? Why is your face downcast? [7]If you do what is right, will you not be accepted? But if you do not do what is right, sin is crouching at your door; it desires to have you, but you must master it."

[8]Now Cain said to his brother Abel, "Let's go out to the field."[d] And while they were in the field, Cain attacked his brother Abel and killed him.

[9]Then the LORD said to Cain, "Where is your brother Abel?"

"I don't know," he replied. "Am I my brother's keeper?"

[10]The LORD said, "What have you done? Listen! Your brother's blood cries out to me from the ground. [11]Now you are under a curse and driven from the ground, which opened its mouth to receive your brother's blood from your hand. [12]When you work the ground, it will no longer

NRSV

4 Now the man knew his wife Eve, and she conceived and bore Cain, saying, "I have produced[a] a man with the help of the LORD." [2]Next she bore his brother Abel. Now Abel was a keeper of sheep, and Cain a tiller of the ground. [3]In the course of time Cain brought to the LORD an offering of the fruit of the ground, [4]and Abel for his part brought of the firstlings of his flock, their fat portions. And the LORD had regard for Abel and his offering, [5]but for Cain and his offering he had no regard. So Cain was very angry, and his countenance fell. [6]The LORD said to Cain, "Why are you angry, and why has your countenance fallen? [7]If you do well, will you not be accepted? And if you do not do well, sin is lurking at the door; its desire is for you, but you must master it."

[8]Cain said to his brother Abel, "Let us go out to the field."[b] And when they were in the field, Cain rose up against his brother Abel, and killed him. [9]Then the LORD said to Cain, "Where is your brother Abel?" He said, "I do not know; am I my brother's keeper?" [10]And the LORD said, "What have you done? Listen; your brother's blood is crying out to me from the ground! [11]And now you are cursed from the ground, which has opened its mouth to receive your brother's blood from your hand. [12]When you till the ground, it will no longer yield to you its strength; you will be a fugitive and a wanderer on the earth." [13]Cain said to the LORD, "My punishment is greater than I can bear! [14]Today you have driven me away from the soil, and I shall be hidden from your face; I shall be a fugitive and a wanderer on the earth, and anyone who meets me may kill me."

---

a1 Or *The man*   b1 *Cain* sounds like the Hebrew for *brought forth* or *acquired*.   c1 Or *have acquired*   d8 Samaritan Pentateuch, Septuagint, Vulgate and Syriac; Masoretic Text does not have *"Let's go out to the field."*

---

a The verb in Heb resembles the word for *Cain*   b Sam Gk Syr Compare Vg: MT lacks *Let us go out to the field*

NIV

yield its crops for you. You will be a restless wanderer on the earth."

[13]Cain said to the LORD, "My punishment is more than I can bear. [14]Today you are driving me from the land, and I will be hidden from your presence; I will be a restless wanderer on the earth, and whoever finds me will kill me."

[15]But the LORD said to him, "Not so[a]; if anyone kills Cain, he will suffer vengeance seven times over." Then the LORD put a mark on Cain so that no one who found him would kill him. [16]So Cain went out from the LORD's presence and lived in the land of Nod,[b] east of Eden.

[17]Cain lay with his wife, and she became pregnant and gave birth to Enoch. Cain was then building a city, and he named it after his son Enoch. [18]To Enoch was born Irad, and Irad was the father of Mehujael, and Mehujael was the father of Methushael, and Methushael was the father of Lamech.

[19]Lamech married two women, one named Adah and the other Zillah. [20]Adah gave birth to Jabal; he was the father of those who live in tents and raise livestock. [21]His brother's name was Jubal; he was the father of all who play the harp and flute. [22]Zillah also had a son, Tubal-Cain, who forged all kinds of tools out of[c] bronze and iron. Tubal-Cain's sister was Naamah.

[23]Lamech said to his wives,

"Adah and Zillah, listen to me;
    wives of Lamech, hear my words.
I have killed[d] a man for wounding me,
    a young man for injuring me.
[24]If Cain is avenged seven times,
    then Lamech seventy-seven times."

[25]Adam lay with his wife again, and she gave birth to a son and named him Seth,[e] saying, "God has granted me another child in place of Abel, since Cain killed him." [26]Seth also had a son, and he named him Enosh.

At that time men began to call on[f] the name of the LORD.

[a]15 Septuagint, Vulgate and Syriac; Hebrew *Very well*   [b]16 Nod means *wandering* (see verses 12 and 14).   [c]22 Or *who instructed all who work in*   [d]23 Or *I will kill*   [e]25 *Seth* probably means *granted.*   [f]26 Or *to proclaim*

NRSV

[15]Then the LORD said to him, "Not so![a] Whoever kills Cain will suffer a sevenfold vengeance." And the LORD put a mark on Cain, so that no one who came upon him would kill him. [16]Then Cain went away from the presence of the LORD, and settled in the land of Nod,[b] east of Eden.

[17]Cain knew his wife, and she conceived and bore Enoch; and he built a city, and named it Enoch after his son Enoch. [18]To Enoch was born Irad; and Irad was the father of Mehujael, and Mehujael the father of Methushael, and Methushael the father of Lamech. [19]Lamech took two wives; the name of the one was Adah, and the name of the other Zillah. [20]Adah bore Jabal; he was the ancestor of those who live in tents and have livestock. [21]His brother's name was Jubal; he was the ancestor of all those who play the lyre and pipe. [22]Zillah bore Tubal-cain, who made all kinds of bronze and iron tools. The sister of Tubal-cain was Naamah.

[23]Lamech said to his wives:

"Adah and Zillah, hear my voice;
    you wives of Lamech, listen to what I say:
I have killed a man for wounding me,
    a young man for striking me.
[24] If Cain is avenged sevenfold,
    truly Lamech seventy-sevenfold."

[25]Adam knew his wife again, and she bore a son and named him Seth, for she said, "God has appointed[c] for me another child instead of Abel, because Cain killed him." [26]To Seth also a son was born, and he named him Enosh. At that time people began to invoke the name of the LORD.

[a] Gk Syr Vg: Heb *Therefore*   [b] That is *Wandering*
[c] The verb in Heb resembles the word for *Seth*

COMMENTARY

This story of conflict between brothers (assigned to J) has long captivated interpreters. Many factors no doubt contribute to this popularity, from the way in which it mirrors the reality of family life in every age to the many puzzles the text itself presents.

The story has long been recognized as having origins independent of its present context. The verses presuppose a much more densely populated world than the immediate context would allow (e.g., the potential killer of Cain, vv. 14-15; Cain's wife and building of a city, v. 17). Moreover, Adam and Eve are active in the opening and closing verses, but do not appear in vv. 2*b*-24. Many have suggested that the conflict between a shepherd (Abel) and a farmer (Cain) betrays its origin, but God's regard for Abel's offering has nothing to do with Cain's occupation; after all, tilling the soil (עבד *ābad*) was Adam's vocation (2:15) and what the creation needed (2:5).

The story clearly sets themes such as primogeniture and sibling rivalry in place, providing continuity across the whole of Genesis. Yet the narrator seems especially concerned not in the brief notice of the murder itself, but in God's interaction with the words and deeds of Cain.

The chapter combines various types of literature: a tale of two brothers (vv. 2*b*-16), enclosed by genealogical materials and expanded by etiological elements regarding various cultural realities (vv. 17-22), concluded by a song (vv. 23-24) and the introduction of the line of Seth (vv. 25-26), which links this genealogy to that in chap. 5. It seems likely that a more compact genealogy has been expanded along the way to include the story of Cain and Abel and the song of Lamech.

Structurally, vv. 7-15 are similar to chap. 3, moving from temptation to sinful deed to divine interrogation and response to divine sentence and its mitigation to expulsion to the east.[55] This and other thematic links (e.g., 3:16 and 4:7; the pervasive concern for the ground, אדמה *ădāmâ*) imply that the two chapters, though having different origins, are to be interpreted in the light of each other.

Chapter 3 establishes a pattern that will be

55. See Fretheim, *Creation*, 93-94.

followed down through the generations. What happens in the garden in chap. 3 and begins to manifest itself in disharmonious relationships of all sorts accompanies the history of humankind outside the garden in chap. 4. The reality of sin continues and intensifies Cain's problematic relationship to God, to other people (especially to family), to his own feelings and actions, and to the ground. On the structural similarities with other stories in chaps. 1–11, see the Introduction.

4:1-16. The rather abrupt transition to life outside the garden appears initially positive, with the intimacy between wife and husband and the birth of a child; these themes recur in the chapter (vv. 1, 17, 25). Eve lives up to her name (3:20), and the divine blessing of creation (1:28) develops appropriately. In addition, Cain and Abel, in their professions, take up the creational commands to have dominion over the animals and to subdue the earth (1:28).

Readers may find the relation between God and Eve in v. 1 ambiguous. The verb קנה (*qānâ*, "produced, acquired") plays on Cain's name, but its meaning as well as the preposition *with* remain uncertain. The context suggests a creational theme, "I have created a man with the LORD" (see Exod 18:22; Num 11:17). The verb can refer to God's creative activity (14:19, 22); the preposition can have the sense of "together with" (see BDB, 86; Exod 18:22; Num 11:17). Eve's word implies human-divine cooperation in fulfillment of 1:28 (see 16:2; 17:16). Her words also refer to Adam's cry that woman was taken out of man (איש *'îš*; 2:23); now the woman cries out that she has produced an *'îš* (the link explains the unusual use of this word for a child). Her cry expresses no more a prideful boast than does that of the man. Eve's response appears similar to that of Leah and Rachel (29:32–30:24), expressing gratitude to Yahweh (a woman first speaks this name) for the child and acknowledging divine participation, which probably refers generally to God's blessing of fertility and child-bearing capability.

The writer handles the birth of Abel more perfunctorily as the narrator quickly moves toward the heart of the story. Abel's status as the younger brother sets the stage for the issue of primogeniture in the rest of Genesis. The brothers grow up to become shepherd and farmer (see 1:28). Although these occupations were often at odds with each other, the text presents no specific signs of such conflict.

The text initially focuses on their worship, thereby placing the reality of worship within a *creational* context, distinct from God's revelation to Israel. They bring offerings without any command to do so; the writer assumes that human beings worship and conduct sacrifices. No altars or cult personnel are evident, and it seems unlikely that later Israelite regulations would apply. The narrator stipulates no motive, but gratitude seems likely. Since the offerings derive from the yield of their labors, they are an extension of the two brothers. All seems to be in order. Cain even brings his offering "to Yahweh" (which entails invoking the name, see v. 26). God clearly could accept both kinds of offerings (as in Israel's worship); neither appears inherently right or wrong.

It thus comes as something of a surprise that God accepts Abel's offering but not Cain's. Two puzzles emerge: (1) We are not told how Cain discovered that neither he nor his offering was accepted. Given God's way of responding in the story, Cain may have been told directly. (2) No rationale is given, hence God's action appears arbitrary (to readers and probably to Cain).[56] Most commonly, scholars have appealed to differences in their offerings. Abel offers the firstlings (Exod 22:19) and choice fat portions (Lev 3:3-17); Cain's offering is not described in such detail. Yet it seems unlikely that later Israelite practice would apply. Their motivation or attitudes may have differed; God looks at both the offerer and the offering (so Heb 11:4; cf. 1 Sam 16:7). God's response suggests that Cain did not "do well." In any case, God makes a decision for the younger brother. Cain's response to that decision sets the rest of the story in motion.

Cain's response (NAB, "resentful"; TNK, "distressed")—the downcast face (the external manifestation of the inner feeling [see 3:7])—reveals more the idea of dejection, feelings associated with rejection, than anger. Cain must care about

what God thinks of him and his sacrifice. But the basic issue becomes *not* that Cain acts in a dejected fashion, but how he responds to God's interaction with him about his dejection. That God responds at all reveals a divine concern for Cain, and God's questions (v. 6)—repeating the description of v. 5*b*—disclose an insightful empathy for his situation. They imply that God's decision should not be the occasion for dejection, that a further response from Cain can put the situation right.

Although clearly a key to the entire story, v. 7 presents difficulties. In view of Cain's rejection and dejection, God graciously lays out Cain's options and their consequences. If he acts properly in response to his brother's acceptance and his own rejection (see Jer 7:5), then he will be accepted (namely, God will have regard for him and he can lift up his head again). On the other hand, if he does not do what is right, sin—occurring here for the first time in Genesis—lurks/crouches at the door (of his life), desiring to gain entrance. The image of sin lurking (the "enmity" of the serpent in 3:15 may be in mind; see Deut 19:11) symbolizes temptation. The reality of temptation is portrayed as something active, close at hand, predatory, eager to make inroads into Cain's life; it can consume his life, take over his thinking, feeling, and acting. Cain must not let it rule his life; he (the "you" is emphatic) can or must master it (see Ps 19:13). The text reflects the implications of 3:16 in the use of the words *desire* and *rule/master,* specifying continuity in such post-sin realities. Cain responds to a particular situation—namely, the working out of his feelings toward his brother (see p. 377).

Cain does not attend well to God's warning. When the brothers are in open country, Cain overpowers Abel and kills him (note the lack of emotion or drama). Cain may have invited Abel, but the explicit invitation was not preserved in the Hebrew text. Although God warns that the violation of the command will lead to death (2:17), the fact that a human being and not God sounds death into the world introduces an ironic note.

Once again, God immediately interrogates the offender in order to elicit Cain's response (cf. 3:9-13). Cain takes the road of denial rather than hiding from God; even more, he turns the ques-

---

56. For a survey of opinion, see Wenham, *Genesis 1–15,* 104.

tion back to God ("Am I my brother's keeper?"), implying impropriety in God's question. "Keeping" is not something human beings do to one another in the OT; only God keeps human beings (see Num 6:24; Ps 121:3-8); hence *God* should know the answer to the question. In effect, if God does not know Abel's whereabouts, God has not been "keeping" him and should be blamed for his present situation. Cain seeks to relieve himself of any responsibility for Abel by focusing on God's task of "keeping."

God ignores the counterquestion and offers a sharp reply that keeps the conversation on course. Human actions are evaluated by the deity. Once again, God asks Cain a question (actually more an accusation), prompted by Abel's blood crying out *to God* from the ground (see Job 16:18; the verb often describes those experiencing injustice, see commentary on 18:20-21; 19:13; see also blood as polluting the land in 6:11-13; Num 35:33). This idea assumes that blood as the conveyor of life belongs to God and spilled blood cannot be covered up, leaving the issue of exacting justice in divine hands. God knows Abel has been killed by Cain and seeks to elicit from him a confession to that end. God does not wait for a response, but proceeds to sentence Cain for his crime (vv. 11-12)—though technically he has violated no law against murder (9:6). Nonetheless, Cain's acts certainly violated God's creational intentions. The penalty in 9:6 does not apply to Cain.

God does not curse Cain directly ("from the ground"; unlike 3:17), but the ground, which has opened its mouth and received Abel's blood, mediates the curse to him by rejecting his labors and no longer yielding its fruit (vv. 11-12 belong together). In effect, the earlier curse of the ground (3:17) applies to Cain in an intensified way so that it does not yield produce at all (the banishment, the hiddenness from God, and the journey east are also intensifications of earlier judgments on humanity). God condemns Cain to be a "restless wanderer" (the NIV captures the hendiadys), rootless, living from hand to mouth, away from the supportive relationships of family. As Cain recognizes, he has received the equivalent of a death penalty. The breakdown of the human relationship to the ground, begun in 3:17, contin-

ues here and reaches a climax in the flood story (6:11-13).

Cain does not passively accept the divine sentence. He complains that his punishment—i.e., the consequences of his sin (the word עון *'āwōn*, a common word for "sin," refers to a continuum from sinful act to its effects; see 1 Sam 28:10) is greater than he can bear. (When faced with his own murder, the murderer laments!) In his use of sin language, he accepts the relationship between his sin and God's sentence; he admits guilt. He picks up on language God has just used: If the ground will not yield its produce and he must wander, he will be the target of Abel's avengers (perhaps God or siblings, 5:4, but see p. 377). Even more, being driven away from the soil will break his basic relationship to the land itself. Speaking theologically, he will be hidden from the face (i.e., presence) of God (note the implied relationship with God, v. 16), i.e., driven from the near presence of the garden. God will no longer be available to him for care and protection, or even prayers relating thereto.

God disagrees emphatically, though without taking back the basic sentence. Cain's plea occasions a divine amelioration of the sentence, reflecting a divine responsiveness to a human cry, an openness to taking a different way into the future in view of what human beings have to say (see 18:22-33; Exod 32:9-14). God promises ("Not so" could be translated, "I promise," so TNK) that should anyone kill Cain, he will be avenged sevenfold (an idiom expressing intensity or severity). The story depicts not vengeance in the sense of revenge, but an effort to stop the violence from spiraling out of control by intensifying the workings of the moral order. The legal formulation gives it the force of law, hence applicability to all people. God will be Abel's brother's keeper. God's mercy embraces the murderer.

God then puts a mark on Cain as a *protective* device (the "mark of Cain" mistakenly carries a sense of public stigma). Only he would know why he received it; probably this mark (tattoo?; see Exod 12:13; Ezek 9:4-6) would be understood by any who encountered him. The mark does not protect him absolutely, as the word about vengeance shows.

The narrator leaves him as one who has been placed under the very special care of God. Hence, the story ought not to be interpreted in basically negative terms, but rather as the activity of one who lives under divine protection and care.

Cain leaves the presence of the Lord—i.e., the region of the garden, where God's presence was especially evident (see v. 14). This move does not refer to an absolute separation from God; indeed, God remains present in the conception and birth described in v. 17 (see Jonah [1:3], who does not leave God's presence absolutely either). The divine blessing follows Cain through all his wandering. He settles still further to the east of Eden (see 3:24), in a place called Nod (location unknown; it means "wandering" and plays on the word נד [nād, "wander"] in vv. 12, 14). To "settle" in "Wandering," an ironic comment (see also the city he builds), may refer to a division within the self, wherein spatial settledness accompanies a troubled spirit (see Isa 7:2). That Cain founded a city (nothing is said about the nature of this city) suggests that rootlessness means more than simple physical wandering. Those who live in cities can also be restless wanderers.

4:17-26. This section begins as did 4:1 (see v. 25). The genealogy of Cain, seven generations in all, occurs in linear form, with only the firstborn mentioned until Lamech, whose wives and three sons are named (5:32; 11:26). We hear nothing of Cain or any of his descendants beyond this chapter (an association with the Kenite peoples is problematic and of no evident concern here; on the relationship to similar names in chap. 5, see commentary on 5:1-32).

What are we to make of the origins of certain cultural advances—namely, urban life, animal husbandry (a more general reference than Abel's work), music (both stringed and wind instruments) and metallurgy? Inasmuch as such developments were ascribed to divine beings in the Mesopotamian world, this genealogy may provide a demythologized form of that tradition.

Many scholars have suggested that, inasmuch as these developments belong to the genealogy of Cain, these cultural achievements should be interpreted negatively. However, a positive assessment seems more likely. The seven generations of Cain may mirror the seven days of creation, thus placing human creativity parallel to the divine. Just as one may marvel at the great diversity of God's creation, so also human creativity mirrors

God's in producing numerous gifts and interests (and to which the Creator God seems related). This relation may be evident even in the names of Lamech's four children; the similar names of the three sons are related to a semantic root having to do with capability and productivity, while the name of the daughter, Naamah, means "pleasant" or "beautiful."

The writer does not condemn Lamech for having two wives (cf. Abraham; Jacob). Lamech's song, probably of ancient origin, occurs in poetic form; in its parallelism, the second line uses different words to repeat the essential point of the first (e.g., listen to me/hear my words; wounding me/injuring me). He probably makes reference to only one incident (though "man" and "young man" are not strictly identical). The piece may be identified as a taunt song by one about to do battle (hence translated future, NIV footnote) or a boasting song upon completion of a mission (revenge), a macho song performed before women. Commentators usually interpret it negatively.[57] Whereas God avenged the death of Abel, Lamech takes vengeance into his own hands; he exacts death only for an injury; he appropriates God's own measures and intensifies the level of retribution, so much so that only a blood feud could ensue (see Matt 18:21-22 for Jesus' reversal of Lamech's boast). The song shows how Cain's violence had been intensified through the generations. Progress in sin and its effects matches the progress in civilization.

The birth of Seth constitutes an important moment; through him the human line will move into the future. Yet, his line involves no less evil than Cain's, as the introduction to the flood story soon reminds the reader. Eve's response at his birth, recalling the names of all her children, plays on Seth's name (שׁית šît, "put," "set") as God's replacement for Abel. The word translated "child" (זרע zera') may also be translated "seed" or "offspring" (see 3:15). Genesis 4:25 offers the first certain instance of אדם ('ādām) as a proper name (without article or preposition; so NRSV, with footnotes to possible prior instances in 2:20; 3:17, 21). The name of Seth's son, Enosh, has the same meaning as 'ādām; there is no good reason for giving it a sense of weakness or frailty.

---

57. See J. Sailhamer, *The Pentateuch as Narrative* (Grand Rapids: Zondervan, 1992) 115.

"To invoke" the name of Yahweh (v. 26*b*) refers in general to worship. Such activity should not be linked to Seth in any special way. The phrase refers to this primeval period and parallels other notes about the beginnings of culture. Cain's offerings to Yahweh (4:3; see also 4:1) already imply the invocation of the deity's name. Yahweh's name was probably first associated with Israel at the time of Moses (see Exod 3:14-16; 6:2-3); using the name here attests that Israel's God should be identified with the God active from the morning of the world. Even more, pre-Israelite worship should not be written off as illegitimate. It was genuine and stands in continuity with Israel's later worship (see also the phrase in 12:8; 13:4; 26:25). This language testifies to a relationship with God that people had before there ever was an Israel and must, in some ways, have continued alongside Israel at a later time (see Mal 1:11).

REFLECTIONS

1. The first story of human life outside the garden includes elements regarding human potential for the best and the worst: from creating life to destroying life, from intimacy to jealousy and resentment, from invoking the name of the Lord to lying to God, from the development of the arts and culture to the use of human ingenuity for violent purposes, from living in the presence of God to alienation from God, from being at home to being displaced.

2. Gowan proposes that the story provides an illustration of the often savage inequalities that life inexplicably visits upon equally gifted or qualified people and the issue of how people should appropriately respond.[58] Yet, the narrator understands that *God* created the problem, and one ought not risk the inference that divine action lies behind each inequality of life. Hence, the text may address more narrowly ways of approaching seemingly unjust and arbitrary *divine* preferences (e.g., God's choice of the younger son in the stories that follow).

3. Verse 7 presents difficulties, but to claim that it is secondary or that God's response is "feeble" is not helpful. God's word evidences a deep concern about Cain's future and the two courses he can take with his life. God gives a gift to Cain by naming his feelings (v. 6) and pointing out the character of his inner struggle. Cain now knows that God understands him. Cain knows how God relates to people in the midst of such struggles; God will not intervene and force Cain to decide one way or another. Cain must decide how to respond, with the help of the knowledge God has given him. More generally, Cain ought not to view even such a divinely generated moment in life as devastating; God wills people to move on from such moments and be on with life.

The text implies that human beings are able to make decisions about *specific* matters of temptation (the issue is not whether to be sinless or not); we do *not* have to do with compulsion here, as if God holds out illusory possibilities to Cain. God clearly speaks an "if" and an "if not"; what human beings decide to do makes a difference regarding the shape of the future.[59]

4. Cain's feelings or actions are not directed toward God, the one who made the decision, but misdirected toward Abel. In effect, Abel becomes a scapegoat, the one who takes the blame for something God did. In some sense, *God's* action leads to Abel's death. Does this fact explain why God mitigates the penalty for Cain? We should note the importance of the lament psalms and remonstrating responses on the part of persons like Abraham and Moses when confronted with difficult circumstances. In these expressions, God takes the "guff"; the deity helps prevent the blame from being misdirected toward other human beings. The suffering and death of Jesus, who takes on himself the violence and blame for something human beings have done, can be helpfully related to this text (see Heb 12:24 for the Abel-Jesus link).

58. See Gowan, *Genesis 1–11*, 67.
59. For a discussion of Steinbeck's use of the statement "you can master it" in *East of Eden*, see Brueggemann, *Genesis*, 58.

5. The fact that the first murder arises over a conflict regarding religious practices, between two worshipers of God, presents another ironic twist in the story. Sin lurks within the community of faith, too, and no little conflict has developed over the centuries within that community over disagreements regarding worship and who is being true to God's will in such matters. In the wake of such experiences, the "losers" should be especially watchful, for the temptation to retaliate may be especially powerful.

6. Cain, guilty of murder and standing outside the line of promise, becomes the recipient of a promise from God (see also Ishmael, Esau). Even more, rather than exacting an eye-for-an-eye retribution on Cain, God protects him from an avenger. This incident raises questions about the appropriateness of later eye-for-eye legislation (see Exod 21:23-24) and capital punishment (see 9:6).

7. The sevenfold use of "brother" in the story intensifies concern for that relationship. These two persons are not strangers; they grew up in the same household, had the same family environment, were exposed to the same family values over many years. Yet, even such deep commonalities do not prevent hatred and violence. If sin can have this kind of effect on those who are so close and who share so many values, it presents a deep and pervasive problem for all human beings (see 1 John 3:11-15; Matt 5:21-25 links worship and conflict between brothers and sisters). Cain's act violates the family, an integral part of God's created order. Even more, by taking a life, Cain arrogates to himself a godlike power over Abel's life.

This story sets a key theme for the rest of the book of Genesis, with intrafamilial conflict moving from an exception to the norm. The stories of Abraham, Isaac, Jacob, and Joseph are filled with the legacy of the relationship between Cain and Abel, often involving primogeniture.

8. Once again, the story reflects the close relationship between humans and the land, an intimate link between moral order and cosmic order. Humans and the nonhuman world live in a symbiotic relationship. Although Cain's behaviors are not specifically directed against the land, the shedding of human blood adversely affects the productivity of the soil (see Hos 4:1-3). Even human behaviors that do not come to the attention of other persons have such an effect; they will in any case come to the attention of God.

9. Advances in civilization are not made ambiguous by being incorporated into a narrative so centered on violence. These references, as well as continuing testimony to intimacy and new life (vv. 1, 17, 25), suggest a powerful rhythm within life that works for good. Although material progress "frequently outruns moral progress and that human ingenuity, so potentially beneficial, is often directed toward evil ends,"[60] such a point moves beyond these verses. We must keep the positive accomplishments of Cain and his descendants *alongside* the negative word about Lamech. While the latter can have a negative impact on the former, it does not so contaminate the other that the products of human creativity become innately evil. The positive point needs to be made clearly: "The story of civilization . . . is ennobled by the fact that it is a human being, God's creature, who leads the way along the path of progress, invention and discovery."[61] The redactor probably did not think that the pre-flood origin of the arts of civilization was a problem; knowledge was passed down through the family of Noah, finally to be inherited by Israel. In this, Israel acknowledges its debt to earlier creative efforts (Deut 6:10-11).

10. Those long-asked questions about who endangered Cain, where Cain got his wife, and who would have purchased all the houses he built are difficult. We may explain these disjunctions by appealing to the original setting of the story; it originated at a time when the

60. Sarna, *Genesis*, 36.
61. Westermann, *Genesis 1–11*, 326.

world was populated, and the disjunctions were not smoothed over when it was incorporated into its present context. Yet, it seems unlikely that the redactor would have overlooked these elements. The redactor may have thought of Cain's siblings (see 5:4), but more likely these texts belong with those (e.g., 2:24) that collapse the distance between the "then" of the story and the "now" of the redactor. They are evidence that the story functioned, not as a straightforward account of ancient events, but as a mirror for human reality in every age. Cain may not have been threatened by anyone, but he reflects a concern that would have been voiced by later generations. Cain may not actually have built a city, but urban existence was a reality with which all subsequent generations lived.

Genesis 5:1-32, Adam's Family Tree

NIV

5 This is the written account of Adam's line.

When God created man, he made him in the likeness of God. [2]He created them male and female and blessed them. And when they were created, he called them "man.[a]"

[3]When Adam had lived 130 years, he had a son in his own likeness, in his own image; and he named him Seth. [4]After Seth was born, Adam lived 800 years and had other sons and daughters. [5]Altogether, Adam lived 930 years, and then he died.

[6]When Seth had lived 105 years, he became the father[b] of Enosh. [7]And after he became the father of Enosh, Seth lived 807 years and had other sons and daughters. [8]Altogether, Seth lived 912 years, and then he died.

[9]When Enosh had lived 90 years, he became the father of Kenan. [10]And after he became the father of Kenan, Enosh lived 815 years and had other sons and daughters. [11]Altogether, Enosh lived 905 years, and then he died.

[12]When Kenan had lived 70 years, he became the father of Mahalael. [13]And after he became the father of Mahalael, Kenan lived 840 years and had other sons and daughters. [14]Altogether, Kenan lived 910 years, and then he died.

[15]When Mahalael had lived 65 years, he became the father of Jared. [16]And after he became the father of Jared, Mahalael lived 830 years and had other sons and daughters. [17]Altogether, Mahalael lived 895 years, and then he died.

[18]When Jared had lived 162 years, he became the father of Enoch. [19]And after he became the

NRSV

5 This is the list of the descendants of Adam. When God created humankind,[a] he made them[b] in the likeness of God. [2]Male and female he created them, and he blessed them and named them "Humankind"[c] when they were created.

[3]When Adam had lived one hundred thirty years, he became the father of a son in his likeness, according to his image, and named him Seth. [4]The days of Adam after he became the father of Seth were eight hundred years; and he had other sons and daughters. [5]Thus all the days that Adam lived were nine hundred thirty years; and he died.

[6]When Seth had lived one hundred five years, he became the father of Enosh. [7]Seth lived after the birth of Enosh eight hundred seven years, and had other sons and daughters. [8]Thus all the days of Seth were nine hundred twelve years; and he died.

[9]When Enosh had lived ninety years, he became the father of Kenan. [10]Enosh lived after the birth of Kenan eight hundred fifteen years, and had other sons and daughters. [11]Thus all the days of Enosh were nine hundred five years; and he died.

[12]When Kenan had lived seventy years, he became the father of Mahalael. [13]Kenan lived after the birth of Mahalael eight hundred and forty years, and had other sons and daughters. [14]Thus all the days of Kenan were nine hundred and ten years; and he died.

[15]When Mahalael had lived sixty-five years, he became the father of Jared. [16]Mahalael lived after the birth of Jared eight hundred thirty years,

[a]2 Hebrew *adam*   [b]6 *Father* may mean *ancestor;* also in verses 7-26.

[a] Heb *adam*   [b] Heb *him*   [c] Heb *adam*

NIV

father of Enoch, Jared lived 800 years and had other sons and daughters. ²⁰Altogether, Jared lived 962 years, and then he died.

²¹When Enoch had lived 65 years, he became the father of Methuselah. ²²And after he became the father of Methuselah, Enoch walked with God 300 years and had other sons and daughters. ²³Altogether, Enoch lived 365 years. ²⁴Enoch walked with God; then he was no more, because God took him away.

²⁵When Methuselah had lived 187 years, he became the father of Lamech. ²⁶And after he became the father of Lamech, Methuselah lived 782 years and had other sons and daughters. ²⁷Altogether, Methuselah lived 969 years, and then he died.

²⁸When Lamech had lived 182 years, he had a son. ²⁹He named him Noah*a* and said, "He will comfort us in the labor and painful toil of our hands caused by the ground the LORD has cursed." ³⁰After Noah was born, Lamech lived 595 years and had other sons and daughters. ³¹Altogether, Lamech lived 777 years, and then he died.

³²After Noah was 500 years old, he became the father of Shem, Ham and Japheth.

a29 Noah sounds like the Hebrew for comfort.

NRSV

and had other sons and daughters. ¹⁷Thus all the days of Mahalalel were eight hundred ninety-five years; and he died.

18When Jared had lived one hundred sixty-two years he became the father of Enoch. ¹⁹Jared lived after the birth of Enoch eight hundred years, and had other sons and daughters. ²⁰Thus all the days of Jared were nine hundred sixty-two years; and he died.

21When Enoch had lived sixty-five years, he became the father of Methuselah. ²²Enoch walked with God after the birth of Methuselah three hundred years, and had other sons and daughters. ²³Thus all the days of Enoch were three hundred sixty-five years. ²⁴Enoch walked with God; then he was no more, because God took him.

25When Methuselah had lived one hundred eighty-seven years, he became the father of Lamech. ²⁶Methuselah lived after the birth of Lamech seven hundred eighty-two years, and had other sons and daughters. ²⁷Thus all the days of Methuselah were nine hundred sixty-nine years; and he died.

28When Lamech had lived one hundred eighty-two years, he became the father of a son; ²⁹he named him Noah, saying, "Out of the ground that the LORD has cursed this one shall bring us relief from our work and from the toil of our hands." ³⁰Lamech lived after the birth of Noah five hundred ninety-five years, and had other sons and daughters. ³¹Thus all the days of Lamech were seven hundred seventy-seven years; and he died.

32After Noah was five hundred years old, Noah became the father of Shem, Ham, and Japheth.

COMMENTARY

This, the second of ten genealogies in Genesis, presents ten generations from Adam to Noah, the hero of the flood (see 11:10-26). The genealogy is linear/vertical in form (see Introduction). The author created a generally consistent pattern, except for the first and last, with Enoch, the seventh entry, a special case. This list, commonly identified with the Priestly (v. 29 is a J fragment) source, bridges creation and the flood. In the present narrative it provides a link between major

stories and accounts for every generation from the creation. The immediately preceding verses (4:25-26, J) clarify that the Seth of chap. 5 is actually Adam's third child.

Mesopotamian traditions also feature ten (or so) generations before the flood. In a similar list, eight to ten kings live a total of 432,000 years in one version, 241,200 in another (the kings in postflood lists have much shorter reigns). Major differences from the biblical lists include the names;

semi-divine kings vs. human beings (a motif of democratization comparable to the image of God); shorter lifespans (777-969 years; approx. a ratio of five years to one week). The biblical list participates in a common folklore about the ages of early humans. The ages were probably understood literally (see below). The ancient texts do not agree about the years involved; the years in the Hebrew text total 1,656; the Samaritan text, 1,307; the Septuagint, 2,242.

Some of the names in the Cain genealogy in 4:17-24 are similar to those in Genesis 5. Certain parallels are based on sound, others in form: Cain-Kenan; Irad-Jered; Mehujael-Mahalalel; Methushael-Methuselah; Lamech-Lamech; Enoch-Enoch-Enosh. Moreover, the last person in each list (Lamech, Noah) has three sons. Many scholars consider these lists as doublets (J and P), having a common origin but with different developments, or one being a reworking of the other or having differing forms because of differing functions (variations in the length of genealogies are common). Whatever the history, the present redaction regards them as two separate family lines.

After the murder perpetrated by Cain and the vengeful response of Lamech, Genesis 5 may represent a fresh start, building upon the reference to the worship of Yahweh at the end of chap. 4. The two narrative elements in the chapter are positive (vv. 22-24, 29), though the language regarding Enoch suggests he is something of an exception (so also Noah).

5:1-3. The opening sentence may refer to a larger book that included the other genealogies in Genesis. The "written account" of NIV may more accurately reflect the Hebrew ספר (*sēper*).

Verses 1-2 essentially repeat 1:26-28. The variations may only be stylistic, but the divine naming of male and female parallels the naming in 1:3-9, and gives male and female a decisive place within the created order (*'ādām* functions both generically and as a proper name). This delayed report may affirm humanity in the wake of the preceding stories. The absence of a specific blessing (see 1:28; cf. 9:1, 7) may also show that the creational command remains intact, as does image and likeness of God language. The words *image* and *likeness* in v. 3 are reversed from their order in 1:26. If the second word helps us to understand the phrase, the relationship between son and father embodies the notion of image (only "likeness" appears in v. 1 with reference to God).

5:4-32. Two elements stand out in an otherwise rhythmic genealogy, the notes about Enoch and Noah.

Enoch. Twice he is said to have walked with God (the phrase is used elsewhere only of Noah [6:9; see 17:1; 48:15]), which testifies to a close relationship with God in the midst of a "fallen" world. That God "took" this one who "walked with God" anticipates God's saving of Noah (see "take" in 7:2), a special act of divine deliverance. "He was not" may refer to death (Job 7:8; Pss 39:13; 104:35; Ezek 28:19) or an uncertain disappearance (42:13, 32, 36). It could mean that he died prematurely or disappeared unexpectedly. "God took him" (no place is noted) could be a way of speaking of death (Jonah 4:3), but it has been linked with God's "taking" of Elijah in 2 Kgs 2:1 (see Pss 49:15; 73:24), which may be how the postbiblical traditions of Enoch's escaping death and receiving divine secrets arose (see Sir 44:16; 1–2 Enoch; Jubilees; Heb 11:5; Jude 14-15). His living 365 years (see the year-long flood, 8:13-14) depends on the solar year, but explanations are only speculative. It may refer to a complete or fulfilled life as well.

Noah. The name is a word play on נחם (*niḥam*, "relief, comfort"), though it probably means "rest." His father, Lamech, who anticipates Noah's role in the following chapters, expresses confidence—or a wish—rather than prophecy (it may stand in contrast to the word of the other Lamech in 4:23-24). The nature of the relief remains ambiguous, but may include a dual reference to 8:21 and 9:20. The former refers to a promise that provides for a constant natural order within which life can develop; the latter offers a specific instance—namely, Noah's development of viticulture and less onerous methods of farming (not the pleasure that wine-drinking brings). The "relief" would ameliorate the curse on the ground (3:17), but not remove it. From another angle, the author uses the Hebrew root for "toil"/"pain" that refers to Yahweh's grief in 6:6; both human beings and God suffer the painful effects of human sin. Moreover, the root for "comfort"/"relief" repeats the vocabulary of God's sorrow/repentance in 6:6-7. God's grieving/repenting actions concerning the human situation are more decisive than anything

Noah might do. At the same time, Noah, the one who "walks with" this God, becomes the vehicle in and through which God enables a new beginning for humankind.[62]

62. See H. Wallace, "The Toledot of Adam," *Studies in the Pentateuch,* ed. J. Emerton (Leiden: Brill, 1990) 28.

Noah, who is unusually old at the time he begins a family, is the first person to be born after the death of Adam. Noah's genealogy brackets the flood story with its resumption in 9:18. Due to the location of his story, Noah is also the ancestor of all human beings.

REFLECTIONS

1. We may compare the structure of this genealogy with that of Shem in 11:10-26, which also climaxes in a key juncture within the larger story. These two genealogies balance each other, each bringing an era to a close, and with a key figure (Noah, Terah) having three sons. They serve both a literary and a chronological purpose in uniting key elements in the story (see Introduction). Scholars dispute the theological significance of this structure. Three developments may be noted: (1) The fulfillment of the divine blessing (1:28), which entails both human and divine elements. Divine in origin and empowering the creature to fulfill the command, it cannot be effected without human participation (the importance of which is clear in a negative way in 38:8-10). (2) The continuing creation. The order and stability that God the Creator initially brought to the world continues in the shaping of the human community. Even more than in chaps. 1–2, this creational activity involves human participation. Although not absent in this move from one generation to the next, the lack of God language gives the human a special place. (3) Some concern to express the unity of humankind may be present. Yet, because all but Noah's family are lost in the flood, it would not be a point well made. The table of nations (10:1-32) seems more clearly to be concerned about this matter.

2. Readers often puzzle over the long lives of these patriarchs. While they might be idealizations of the world's early history, the overall concern for chronology suggests that they are meant to be taken literally. The decrease in lifespan as time goes along constitutes a notable feature of the ages of these and other ancestral figures: Adam to Noah (969-777); Noah to Abraham (600-200); Israel (100-200); Ps 10:10 (70 years). The author may use these statistics to chart the effects of sin upon human life (see the above discussion on "Fall"), though diminishing life spans are also characteristic of Mesopotamian lists. Most basically, these ages are consonant with other features of chaps. 1–11 that indicate that this age differs from later ages; indeed, it belongs to an irretrievable past. In fact, the ages of these individuals lies *completely* beyond our experience (if not our desires).

The repetitive references to the image/likeness of God are important in several ways (see 1:26). First, it indicates that the identification of the human in the image of God has not been effaced by the events of chaps. 3–4. Not only Adam and Eve, but all subsequent generations (also affirmed at 9:6) are to be so described. Second, the use of likeness/image language to speak of the relationship between Adam and Seth establishes a link between the creativity of God and that of humans. The dialogical character of the divine creation of the human in 1:26 here explicitly draws the human up into that creative enterprise.

Genesis 6:1-4, Sin Becomes Cosmic

NIV

6 When men began to increase in number on the earth and daughters were born to them, ²the sons of God saw that the daughters of men were beautiful, and they married any of them they chose. ³Then the LORD said, "My Spirit will not contend with^a man forever, for he is mortal^b; his days will be a hundred and twenty years."

⁴The Nephilim were on the earth in those days—and also afterward—when the sons of God went to the daughters of men and had children by them. They were the heroes of old, men of renown.

^a3 Or *My spirit will not remain in*　^b3 Or *corrupt*

NRSV

6 When people began to multiply on the face of the ground, and daughters were born to them, ²the sons of God saw that they were fair; and they took wives for themselves of all that they chose. ³Then the LORD said, "My spirit shall not abide^a in mortals forever, for they are flesh; their days shall be one hundred twenty years."

⁴The Nephilim were on the earth in those days—and also afterward—when the sons of God went in to the daughters of humans, who bore children to them. These were the heroes that were of old, warriors of renown.

^a Meaning of Heb uncertain

COMMENTARY

This brief segment is one of the most difficult in Genesis both to translate and interpret. Certain words are rare or unknown ("abide"/"contend with" and "for" in v. 3; Nephilim in v. 4); issues of coherence arise at many points. These verses may be a fragment of what was once a longer story, or scribes may have added to or subtracted from the text. The fact that the text presents ambiguity may be precisely the point, however: The mode of telling matches the nature of the message.

This fragment may reflect mythical roots, yet parallels in West Semitic cultures (unlike Greek) have been hard to come by, and very little help has been gained from such comparative work. The text has been traditionally assigned to J, yet links with Priestly material can be discerned.

Consistent with other sections in chaps. 1–11, this material reflects an era no longer accessible to Israel. The text does not mirror a typical human situation (though parallels to specific items may be noted; see "also afterwards" for the Nephilim), but speaks of a time long past when God decreed a specific length to human life.

6:1. The narrative follows naturally what has preceded it. The divine blessing of 1:28 on humanity (האדם *hāʾādām*) to be fruitful and multiply moves ahead. The language of birth and the reference to daughters pervaded chap. 5. The link of human beings to "the face of the ground אדמה [*ʾădāmâ*]" continues the creational theme of chaps. 2–4. Yet, these themes become distorted in what follows. The blessing to be fruitful and multiply catches up those who are not part of the human realm. Moreover, the earthly character of creaturely existence is compromised with an apparent breakdown of the earth-heaven distinction.

6:2. The author introduces the "sons of God" (or "sons of the gods") as a matter of course, as if the reader needs no explanation. But the modern reader does; indeed, much depends on their proper identification. There are three basic options: (1) The sons of Seth in chap. 5—the daughters are descendants of Cain; the godly sons are Sethites who sin by mixing with unbelievers. Or the daughters are referred to in chap. 5, while the "godly sons" are descendants of Cain (Eve's son "with the help of the LORD," 4:1). Or the "sons of God" are those who have "become like God" (3:22), assuming divine prerogatives. (2) They may be royal or semi-divine figures who accumulated women in their harems. Texts such as Psalms 2 and 82 have been related to this discussion; the links between semi-divine kings in the lists comparable to chap. 5 are also noted. (3) They are divine beings of the heavenly court (see

1:26). This widely held view, which seems most likely, may be grounded in the use of the phrase elsewhere in the OT (Job 1:6; 2:1; 38:7; Ps 29:1; as old as the LXX) and at Ugarit. These divine beings take the initiative and breach the boundary between heaven and earth by taking human wives. The strangeness of such events in and of themselves (e.g., actual marriages are in view) should not count against this interpretation.

The reader may observe other links with the preceding narrative. The sons of God "see" the daughters who are "fair, beautiful" (טוב *ṭôb*, "good") and "take" them. These three words occur together in 3:6, describing Eve's eating of the fruit from the tree of knowledge. This parallel must mean that the actions described are inappropriate. The "seeing" narrows the appreciation of women to their beauty or, simply, physical desire. Their "taking" of multiple wives seems arbitrary ("take" is ambiguous; it can mean proper or forced behavior; the parallel with 3:6 suggests the latter); it implies the misuse of women (the "seeing" and "taking" of Sarai by Pharaoh in 12:15 and of Bathsheba by David in 2 Sam 11:2-4 have been cited). At the same time, more is at issue here than the acts of the sons of God. Why should human beings, who did not initiate this matter, bear a divine judgment?

6:3. The placement and interpretation of this verse provide a major crux. Regarding placement, some have thought that God's judgment should be a conclusion to the entire segment and that vv. 3 and 4 should be interchanged. The present placement, however, signals that the judgment relates most fundamentally to the problem, not the product.

The expression "my spirit shall not abide in mortals forever" presents another problem. The NRSV translation "abide," following the LXX and Vulgate, fits the context best. The mortals are humans generally (including any offspring of these unions). Spirit (רוח *rûaḥ*) signifies the breath of life as in 6:17; 7:15, 22 (a variant of 2:7), that divine life that enables life for both humans and animals.

"Forever" refers to 3:22 and the concern that God expresses regarding access to the tree of life. The divine-human link in this text has become another way in which immortality (or very long lives?) might be realized by human beings. Whether they have taken initiative in this matter may be finally irrelevant, for immortality would become a reality in any case (hence, the question of the assignation of fault does not pertain to the basic issue). God issues a decree that such a union will not result in human beings who live forever; indeed a specific limit is set. Without the animation of divine spirit, the flesh will perish.

If we translate *"for* they are flesh" (as in the LXX), we understand why God thought it necessary to set this more limited lifespan. Immortality raises the issue of humans being able to live such a length of time with their fleshly nature (bodies wear out; see Isa 31:3 for flesh as weakness, not sinful nature). The divine decree becomes necessary, and has in mind what it would mean for a body of flesh to be animated by a spirit that lives forever. God, again, acts graciously.

6:4. Scholars dispute the identification and place of the Nephilim (literally it could be "fallen ones"; Num 13:33 suggests persons of gigantic stature). The first line may be an aside to the reader, giving a contemporary reference ("also afterward") concerning the offspring of these unions. This interpretation seems more likely than that they were actually the offspring of this union; the latter are identified as warriors of renown. Hence this verse does not present an etiology of any persons known to Israel. But if the ancient reader wanted to know what these warriors were like, the Nephilim would be a good analogy.

REFLECTIONS

1. Readers have usually thought these verses illustrate the increasingly ungodly state of affairs before the flood. Although words for "sin," "evil," or "judgment" are not present, they are implied, as was the case in chap. 3.

This downward development occurs at three levels: (1) Human sin has drawn the entire cosmic order into its orbit. Chapter 3 showed that human sin has an effect on the natural order; here those effects move even into heavenly places and entrap divine beings. In effect, the separation between divine and human worlds has broken down; the orders of creation have become confused. Evil has become cosmic in its scope. The flood must have a comparable scope. (2) The text illustrates the "becoming like God" theme only indirectly, for the initiative in the text comes from the divine realm. Likeness to God entails the possibilities for immortality (though still limited, for they are flesh). In this regard, the text relates to 3:22. Whereas that divine action had cut off humankind from the tree of life as a means to immortality, this divine decree cuts off another way in which that end might have been accomplished. The number 120 may also relate to the long life spans of chap. 5. (3) The resulting violence constitutes another level. The reference to heroes and warriors in v. 4 may relate to vv. 11-13. The mix of divine and human resulted in new forms of human life with intensified capacities for violence. The actions of these Nephilim-like figures thus signify another distorting effect of sin on the life of the world.

2. This text became the source of much speculation in postbiblical reflection (and it may have informed such texts as Job 4:18-19 and Isa 14:12-20). Indeed, it became the focus of interpreters more than did Genesis 3 (see 1–2 Enoch; Jubilees 5; 2 Pet 2:4; Jude 6). This text pushed speculation in the direction of dualism, wherein sin and evil are realities for both divine and human realms. Stories associated with a revolt in heaven followed by the casting out of these beings from the heavenly realm led to conclusions regarding the demonic sphere (which did not solve the problem of the origin of evil; it was only pushed back one step). Regarding the fate of the divine beings involved in this episode, however, the text remains remarkably silent. We may assume that they, too, were destroyed in the cosmic flood; indeed they may have precipitated its cosmic character. However, Gen 11:7 suggests that the heavenly council was again in proper working order after the flood.

GENESIS 6:5–8:22, THE FLOOD: THE GREAT DIVIDE

NIV

⁵The Lord saw how great man's wickedness on the earth had become, and that every inclination of the thoughts of his heart was only evil all the time. ⁶The Lord was grieved that he had made man on the earth, and his heart was filled with pain. ⁷So the Lord said, "I will wipe mankind, whom I have created, from the face of the earth—men and animals, and creatures that move along the ground, and birds of the air—for I am grieved that I have made them." ⁸But Noah found favor in the eyes of the Lord.

⁹This is the account of Noah.

Noah was a righteous man, blameless among the people of his time, and he walked with God. ¹⁰Noah had three sons: Shem, Ham and Japheth.

¹¹Now the earth was corrupt in God's sight and was full of violence. ¹²God saw how corrupt the earth had become, for all the people on earth had

NRSV

5The Lord saw that the wickedness of humankind was great in the earth, and that every inclination of the thoughts of their hearts was only evil continually. ⁶And the Lord was sorry that he had made humankind on the earth, and it grieved him to his heart. ⁷So the Lord said, "I will blot out from the earth the human beings I have created—people together with animals and creeping things and birds of the air, for I am sorry that I have made them." ⁸But Noah found favor in the sight of the Lord.

9These are the descendants of Noah. Noah was a righteous man, blameless in his generation; Noah walked with God. ¹⁰And Noah had three sons, Shem, Ham, and Japheth.

11Now the earth was corrupt in God's sight, and the earth was filled with violence. ¹²And God saw that the earth was corrupt; for all flesh had corrupted its ways upon the earth. ¹³And God said

NIV

corrupted their ways. [13]So God said to Noah, "I am going to put an end to all people, for the earth is filled with violence because of them. I am surely going to destroy both them and the earth. [14]So make yourself an ark of cypress[a] wood; make rooms in it and coat it with pitch inside and out. [15]This is how you are to build it: The ark is to be 450 feet long, 75 feet wide and 45 feet high.[b] [16]Make a roof for it and finish[c] the ark to within 18 inches[d] of the top. Put a door in the side of the ark and make lower, middle and upper decks. [17]I am going to bring floodwaters on the earth to destroy all life under the heavens, every creature that has the breath of life in it. Everything on earth will perish. [18]But I will establish my covenant with you, and you will enter the ark—you and your sons and your wife and your sons' wives with you. [19]You are to bring into the ark two of all living creatures, male and female, to keep them alive with you. [20]Two of every kind of bird, of every kind of animal and of every kind of creature that moves along the ground will come to you to be kept alive. [21]You are to take every kind of food that is to be eaten and store it away as food for you and for them."

[22]Noah did everything just as God commanded him.

7 The LORD then said to Noah, "Go into the ark, you and your whole family, because I have found you righteous in this generation. [2]Take with you seven[e] of every kind of clean animal, a male and its mate, and two of every kind of unclean animal, a male and its mate, [3]and also seven of every kind of bird, male and female, to keep their various kinds alive throughout the earth. [4]Seven days from now I will send rain on the earth for forty days and forty nights, and I will wipe from the face of the earth every living creature I have made."

[5]And Noah did all that the LORD commanded him.

[6]Noah was six hundred years old when the floodwaters came on the earth. [7]And Noah and his sons and his wife and his sons' wives entered

a14 The meaning of the Hebrew for this word is uncertain.
b15 Hebrew 300 cubits long, 50 cubits wide and 30 cubits high (about 140 meters long, 23 meters wide and 13.5 meters high)
c16 Or Make an opening for light by finishing   d16 Hebrew a cubit (about 0.5 meter)   e2 Or seven pairs; also in verse 3

NRSV

to Noah, "I have determined to make an end of all flesh, for the earth is filled with violence because of them; now I am going to destroy them along with the earth. [14]Make yourself an ark of cypress[a] wood; make rooms in the ark, and cover it inside and out with pitch. [15]This is how you are to make it: the length of the ark three hundred cubits, its width fifty cubits, and its height thirty cubits. [16]Make a roof[b] for the ark, and finish it to a cubit above; and put the door of the ark in its side; make it with lower, second, and third decks. [17]For my part, I am going to bring a flood of waters on the earth, to destroy from under heaven all flesh in which is the breath of life; everything that is on the earth shall die. [18]But I will establish my covenant with you; and you shall come into the ark, you, your sons, your wife, and your sons' wives with you. [19]And of every living thing, of all flesh, you shall bring two of every kind into the ark, to keep them alive with you; they shall be male and female. [20]Of the birds according to their kinds, and of the animals according to their kinds, of every creeping thing of the ground according to its kind, two of every kind shall come in to you, to keep them alive. [21]Also take with you every kind of food that is eaten, and store it up; and it shall serve as food for you and for them." [22]Noah did this; he did all that God commanded him.

7 Then the LORD said to Noah, "Go into the ark, you and all your household, for I have seen that you alone are righteous before me in this generation. [2]Take with you seven pairs of all clean animals, the male and its mate; and a pair of the animals that are not clean, the male and its mate; [3]and seven pairs of the birds of the air also, male and female, to keep their kind alive on the face of all the earth. [4]For in seven days I will send rain on the earth for forty days and forty nights; and every living thing that I have made I will blot out from the face of the ground." [5]And Noah did all that the LORD had commanded him.

6Noah was six hundred years old when the flood of waters came on the earth. [7]And Noah with his sons and his wife and his sons' wives went into the ark to escape the waters of the flood. [8]Of clean animals, and of animals that are

a Meaning of Heb uncertain   b Or window

NIV

the ark to escape the waters of the flood. [8]Pairs of clean and unclean animals, of birds and of all creatures that move along the ground, [9]male and female, came to Noah and entered the ark, as God had commanded Noah. [10]And after the seven days the floodwaters came on the earth.

[11]In the six hundredth year of Noah's life, on the seventeenth day of the second month—on that day all the springs of the great deep burst forth, and the floodgates of the heavens were opened. [12]And rain fell on the earth forty days and forty nights.

[13]On that very day Noah and his sons, Shem, Ham and Japheth, together with his wife and the wives of his three sons, entered the ark. [14]They had with them every wild animal according to its kind, all livestock according to their kinds, every creature that moves along the ground according to its kind and every bird according to its kind, everything with wings. [15]Pairs of all creatures that have the breath of life in them came to Noah and entered the ark. [16]The animals going in were male and female of every living thing, as God had commanded Noah. Then the LORD shut him in.

[17]For forty days the flood kept coming on the earth, and as the waters increased they lifted the ark high above the earth. [18]The waters rose and increased greatly on the earth, and the ark floated on the surface of the water. [19]They rose greatly on the earth, and all the high mountains under the entire heavens were covered. [20]The waters rose and covered the mountains to a depth of more than twenty feet.[a,b] [21]Every living thing that moved on the earth perished—birds, livestock, wild animals, all the creatures that swarm over the earth, and all mankind. [22]Everything on dry land that had the breath of life in its nostrils died. [23]Every living thing on the face of the earth was wiped out; men and animals and the creatures that move along the ground and the birds of the air were wiped from the earth. Only Noah was left, and those with him in the ark.

[24]The waters flooded the earth for a hundred and fifty days.

8 But God remembered Noah and all the wild animals and the livestock that were

[a]20 Hebrew *fifteen cubits* (about 6.9 meters)   [b]20 Or *rose more than twenty feet, and the mountains were covered*

NRSV

not clean, and of birds, and of everything that creeps on the ground, [9]two and two, male and female, went into the ark with Noah, as God had commanded Noah. [10]And after seven days the waters of the flood came on the earth.

[11]In the six hundredth year of Noah's life, in the second month, on the seventeenth day of the month, on that day all the fountains of the great deep burst forth, and the windows of the heavens were opened. [12]The rain fell on the earth forty days and forty nights. [13]On the very same day Noah with his sons, Shem and Ham and Japheth, and Noah's wife and the three wives of his sons entered the ark, [14]they and every wild animal of every kind, and all domestic animals of every kind, and every creeping thing that creeps on the earth, and every bird of every kind—every bird, every winged creature. [15]They went into the ark with Noah, two and two of all flesh in which there was the breath of life. [16]And those that entered, male and female of all flesh, went in as God had commanded him; and the LORD shut him in.

[17]The flood continued forty days on the earth; and the waters increased, and bore up the ark, and it rose high above the earth. [18]The waters swelled and increased greatly on the earth; and the ark floated on the face of the waters. [19]The waters swelled so mightily on the earth that all the high mountains under the whole heaven were covered; [20]the waters swelled above the mountains, covering them fifteen cubits deep. [21]And all flesh died that moved on the earth, birds, domestic animals, wild animals, all swarming creatures that swarm on the earth, and all human beings; [22]everything on dry land in whose nostrils was the breath of life died. [23]He blotted out every living thing that was on the face of the ground, human beings and animals and creeping things and birds of the air; they were blotted out from the earth. Only Noah was left, and those that were with him in the ark. [24]And the waters swelled on the earth for one hundred fifty days.

8 But God remembered Noah and all the wild animals and all the domestic animals that were with him in the ark. And God made a wind blow over the earth, and the waters subsided; [2]the fountains of the deep and the windows

NIV

with him in the ark, and he sent a wind over the earth, and the waters receded. [2]Now the springs of the deep and the floodgates of the heavens had been closed, and the rain had stopped falling from the sky. [3]The water receded steadily from the earth. At the end of the hundred and fifty days the water had gone down, [4]and on the seventeenth day of the seventh month the ark came to rest on the mountains of Ararat. [5]The waters continued to recede until the tenth month, and on the first day of the tenth month the tops of the mountains became visible.

[6]After forty days Noah opened the window he had made in the ark [7]and sent out a raven, and it kept flying back and forth until the water had dried up from the earth. [8]Then he sent out a dove to see if the water had receded from the surface of the ground. [9]But the dove could find no place to set its feet because there was water over all the surface of the earth; so it returned to Noah in the ark. He reached out his hand and took the dove and brought it back to himself in the ark. [10]He waited seven more days and again sent out the dove from the ark. [11]When the dove returned to him in the evening, there in its beak was a freshly plucked olive leaf! Then Noah knew that the water had receded from the earth. [12]He waited seven more days and sent the dove out again, but this time it did not return to him.

[13]By the first day of the first month of Noah's six hundred and first year, the water had dried up from the earth. Noah then removed the covering from the ark and saw that the surface of the ground was dry. [14]By the twenty-seventh day of the second month the earth was completely dry.

[15]Then God said to Noah, [16]"Come out of the ark, you and your wife and your sons and their wives. [17]Bring out every kind of living creature that is with you—the birds, the animals, and all the creatures that move along the ground—so they can multiply on the earth and be fruitful and increase in number upon it."

[18]So Noah came out, together with his sons and his wife and his sons' wives. [19]All the animals and all the creatures that move along the ground and all the birds—everything that moves on the earth—came out of the ark, one kind after another.

NRSV

of the heavens were closed, the rain from the heavens was restrained, [3]and the waters gradually receded from the earth. At the end of one hundred fifty days the waters had abated; [4]and in the seventh month, on the seventeenth day of the month, the ark came to rest on the mountains of Ararat. [5]The waters continued to abate until the tenth month; in the tenth month, on the first day of the month, the tops of the mountains appeared.

6At the end of forty days Noah opened the window of the ark that he had made [7]and sent out the raven; and it went to and fro until the waters were dried up from the earth. [8]Then he sent out the dove from him, to see if the waters had subsided from the face of the ground; [9]but the dove found no place to set its foot, and it returned to him to the ark, for the waters were still on the face of the whole earth. So he put out his hand and took it and brought it into the ark with him. [10]He waited another seven days, and again he sent out the dove from the ark; [11]and the dove came back to him in the evening, and there in its beak was a freshly plucked olive leaf; so Noah knew that the waters had subsided from the earth. [12]Then he waited another seven days, and sent out the dove; and it did not return to him any more.

13In the six hundred first year, in the first month, the first day of the month, the waters were dried up from the earth; and Noah removed the covering of the ark, and looked, and saw that the face of the ground was drying. [14]In the second month, on the twenty-seventh day of the month, the earth was dry. [15]Then God said to Noah, [16]"Go out of the ark, you and your wife, and your sons and your sons' wives with you. [17]Bring out with you every living thing that is with you of all flesh—birds and animals and every creeping thing that creeps on the earth—so that they may abound on the earth, and be fruitful and multiply on the earth." [18]So Noah went out with his sons and his wife and his sons' wives. [19]And every animal, every creeping thing, and every bird, everything that moves on the earth, went out of the ark by families.

20Then Noah built an altar to the LORD, and took of every clean animal and of every clean bird, and offered burnt offerings on the altar. [21]And

NIV

[20]Then Noah built an altar to the LORD and, taking some of all the clean animals and clean birds, he sacrificed burnt offerings on it. [21]The LORD smelled the pleasing aroma and said in his heart: "Never again will I curse the ground because of man, even though[a] every inclination of his heart is evil from childhood. And never again will I destroy all living creatures, as I have done. [22]"As long as the earth endures,
 seedtime and harvest,
 cold and heat,
 summer and winter,
 day and night
 will never cease."

[a]21 Or man, for

NRSV

when the LORD smelled the pleasing odor, the LORD said in his heart, "I will never again curse the ground because of humankind, for the inclination of the human heart is evil from youth; nor will I ever again destroy every living creature as I have done.
[22] As long as the earth endures,
 seedtime and harvest, cold and heat,
 summer and winter, day and night,
 shall not cease."

COMMENTARY

Literary analysts consider this narrative an admixture of differing versions of a single story (J and P). Other literary readings have discerned unity in the story, including elaborate chiastic structures.[63] While such schemas are often forced, unified readings of this composite text remain an important task.

That Israel would have preserved several versions of the flood story is not surprising since numerous versions circulated in the ancient Near East. The most widely known today occurs as part of the *Gilgamesh Epic.* An older, but less complete, version may be found in the *Atrahasis Epic.* The 3rd-century BCE history of Babylon by Berossus contains a retelling of the story. A Sumerian version of the flood also exists. Similarities in the basic creation-flood structure between *Atrahasis* and the biblical story are particularly striking (creation; early proliferation and disruption of humankind, including long-lived antediluvians; the gods sending a flood to stop human disruption; the saving of a hero). This structure, as well as commonalities in theme and vocabulary, indicate that these stories are in some way interdependent, though questions of direct dependence remain unresolved.[64]

The existence of numerous flood stories has stimulated efforts to discern the basis of the story. The above-noted stories are set in the Tigris-Euphrates River valley; alluvial deposits show that it was periodically flooded in ancient times. No such deposits have been found in the land of Canaan, and archaeological and geological remains provide no evidence of a worldwide flood. These factors suggest that the Genesis account should be related to a major flood in the Mesopotamian valley, which in time was interpreted as a flood that covered the then known world (one severe flood has been dated around 3000 BCE). Stories from other cultures should be tracked back to their own local flood traditions. No credence should be given to the occasional rumors regarding the discovery of Noah's ark.[65]

Some interpreters think the flood story is enclosed by the genealogical references in 6:9 and 10:1. Other interpreters, however, argue that the story begins at 6:5. Certainly the repetitions of 6:5 in 8:21 are linked formally and thematically, centering in God's relationship to a sin-filled world. Many readers view God's remembrance of Noah and the animals in 8:1 as the pivotal center of the story. The rising of the waters leads up to

63. See Wenham, *Genesis 1–15,* 155-58.
64. For a summary, see Westermann, *Genesis 1–11,* 399-406.

65. For more details, see L. Bailey, *Noah: The Person and the Story in History and Tradition* (Columbia: University of South Carolina Press, 1989).

8:1, and their subsidence leads to a newly ordered world.

The story's characteristics include a repetition of key scenes, words, and phrases that focus attention on important aspects of the story; little direct speech (no speaking between 7:4 and 8:15) and no dialogue; no words from Noah, and he assumes little initiative, simply doing what he is told—so his portrayal is rather flat; no description of Noah's family members; a minimum of description of the disaster itself, with little attention given to the plight of the victims or the scene of death or Noah's family's reaction to what must have been a fearful and heart-rending time (how different from the way in which the media would have handled it today!); no communication with or reaction from those most affected negatively by these events—only the one to be saved is told what is coming; the images of God focus less on judgment (no anger language) than on sorrow, pain, disappointment, regret, and mercy.

On the other hand, the author devotes repeated (four times in 6:18–7:15!) attention to the boarding of the ark, to lists of people and animals and birds that are saved, and to the chronology of the event (though not for the construction of the ark). Attention centers on salvation rather than on judgment, on what God does to preserve the creation.

6:5-8, Prologue to the Flood. These verses (assigned to J) are central to an interpretation of the flood story.[66] Together with 6:11-13, they provide the deity's rationale for the flood. God's seeing (v. 5; see 6:12) reflects an inquiry into the human situation (see 11:5; 18:21), which issues in a general indictment of humankind (not a specific sinful act). In contrast to "all" the "good" that God "saw" in 1:31, here God sees that "every inclination of the thoughts of their hearts was only evil continually" (v. 5; see 8:21 for a comparable assessment at the end of the flood). "Wickedness" refers to both sinful acts and their consequences. The indictment encompasses not simply actions, but the inner recesses of the human heart. "Inclination" (יצר *yēṣer*) denotes the conceiving of possibilities for thought, word, and deed. The words *only, every,* and *continually* specify the breadth and depth of the sinful human condition

(see Jer 17:9-10 for a similar appraisal). These assessments signify that God does not act from sudden and arbitrary impulses.

Having made this evaluation, the narrator describes the inner-divine reaction stunningly. The basic character of the human heart is set alongside the response of the divine heart. God appears, not as an angry and vengeful judge, but as a grieving and pained parent, distressed at what has happened. God "regrets" having proceeded with the creation in the first place, given these tragic developments (repeated in vv. 6-7; the NIV's "grieved" seems too weak a translation of נחם [*niḥam*]; the force of the verb has to do with genuine change; see 1 Sam 15:11, 35). We may discern divine consternation and disappointment, since God's vision for what the world might have been has been dashed by a narrow and self-centered human vision.[67]

Even more, and the NIV says it best, God's "heart was filled with pain" (used of human grief and pain, 45:5, as well as divine, Ps 78:40; Isa 63:10; Eph 4:30). God experiences the pain characteristic of man and woman in 3:16-17. These developments strike deeply into the divine heart and create tensions regarding the shape the future should take. How can God's deep suffering be reconciled to the forthcoming judgment (see Hos 11:8-9)? God does not stand in an indifferent or remote relationship to what has happened, but personally enters into its brokenness and works on it from within. The future of the creation that becomes a possibility in and through Noah and the ark is rooted in this divine pain and sorrow, leading first to the divine choice of Noah (6:8) and finally to the promises in 8:21–9:17.

God, whose heart has been broken, announces a judgment (v. 7), which is nonetheless thoroughgoing and uncompromising. The verb ("blot out, wipe away") may carry the sense of erasing away, as written letters (Num 5:23); it is used positively for washing away sins (Ps 51:2, 9). Hence the image of the flood would involve cleansing. This action seems to leave no room for qualification or exception (as in 7:4, 23, also followed by a note on Noah). God's showing favor to Noah (v. 8), however, moderates the judgmental decision (see Moses' argument on the relationship between

---

66. See von Rad, *Genesis,* 116-17.

67. See T. Fretheim, "The Repentance of God," *HBT* 10 (1988) 47-70; *The Suffering of God* (Philadelphia: Fortress, 1984) 107-26.

finding favor in God's sight and judgment in Exod 33:12-17; חן [ḥēn] is a play on Noah). God's action does not depend on Noah's character (though Noah's potential in God's eyes cannot be discounted). God's gracious choice of Noah results from the divine agony over what to do about the creation. Yet, having been chosen, Noah's *subsequent* faithfulness (v. 9) is not just a blip on the cosmic screen, somehow irrelevant to God (see 7:1). Verse 9 is not presented as Noah's response to the divine choice, but as a consequence of God's prior action.

The relationship between vv. 5-8 and vv. 11-13 is comparable to that between 8:21-22 and 9:8-17, with a divine soliloquy followed by direct divine speech (cf. Exod 2:23-25 with 3:7-10).

6:9-10, Genealogy of Noah. These verses begin in a way typical of the P genealogies in the book of Genesis; they pick up on 5:32, but with the new information (anticipated in 5:29) that Noah's faithful relationship with God provides a channel through which God can start afresh. The negative evaluations of creation (vv. 5, 11-12) enclose the positive reference to Noah. Even in the midst of such a tragedy, one individual faithfully walks with God. But, most fundamentally, God's choice of Noah enables a glimmer of hope in the midst of all that makes for decay and deterioration.

The descriptions of Noah say essentially the same thing from different points of view. He is a righteous man (צדיק ṣaddîq). God matches this judgment by the narrator (7:1). The point is not that Noah measures up to certain moral standards. Rather, he stands in a right relationship with God and has done it justice in various dimensions of his life (see 38:26). He acts blamelessly (תמים tāmîm) as compared to his contemporaries (see 1 Kgs 9:4; Ezek 14:14-20). This term, typical in ritual contexts for an unblemished animal, does not mean that Noah is sinless; rather, he is a person of high integrity (see Ps 15:2-5). He walks with God, suggesting an unusually close relationship (Enoch, 5:24; see 17:1; 48:15; Mic 6:8). These characteristics are exemplified by Noah's response to God's commands in the narrative that follows (6:22; 7:5, 9, 16; 8:18).

6:11-22, Preparations. Scholars often view vv. 11-13 to be a P version of the divine rationale for sending the flood, a vision of the world from God's viewpoint (see 6:5 for God's seeing). These verses belong with 6:5-7; the latter more clearly specify the depths of human sin, the former the cosmic implications. The indictment followed by the announcement of judgment appears prophetic in form, but only Noah hears the word.

The author focuses on what has happened to the *earth,* a word repeated six times. God deems the earth to be corrupt (vv. 11*a*, 12*a*) because it is filled with violence. Corruption (שחת šāḥat) involves ruin, decadence, or decay, the effect of violence; it stands over against the "good" God saw in chap. 1. The earth (not just the creatures) has not continued as it was created to be (on defiling or polluting of the earth, see 4:10-12; Num 35:33-34; Isa 24:5-7; Jer 3:1-3). Violence (חמס ḥāmās) includes lawlessness or injustice, a willful flaunting of the moral order, manifested in deeds that violate the lives of others, perhaps especially murder (in view of 9:5-6; see 49:5; Ezek 12:19-20).

Some interpreters understand the phrase "all flesh" to refer to both humans and animals, as in 6:17, 19; 9:11, 15-17 (9:2, 5 is at times appealed to). The NIV, however, translates "flesh" as "people" in vv. 12-13 ("life" or "[living] creatures" elsewhere). Here, the place of animals is not explicit; yet it means that v. 13 (unlike v. 17) would not refer directly to animals. Hence, the inclusion of the animals in the promise (9:8-17) does not appear symmetrical with the pre-flood scene. In either case, at least some animals suffer innocently in the corruption of the earth and in the destruction. Because the moral order does not have a tight causal weave, and given the interconnectedness of life, the innocent often suffer with the guilty (see 18:25).

According to the NIV and the NRSV, the earth along with the creatures will be destroyed (v. 13*b*). However, this seems problematic (cf. NAB, "destroy them and all life on earth"), because v. 13*a* refers only to "all flesh"; people and animals are destroyed "*from* the earth" (7:23), the waters swell and recede from the earth (7:24; 8:3), and the earth is not re-created. The violence does corrupt the earth, and so judgment must be comparably comprehensive, but the effect on the earth functions more as a cleansing than a destruction (see p. 394).

God informs Noah of the "end of all flesh" (i.e., doom, see Amos 8:2; Lam 4:18). The verb *destroy* derives from the same root as "corrupt" (*šḥt*, "ruin/ruined," would capture the point well), which signals the functioning of the moral order (what goes around comes around). God does not need to introduce judgment into the situation (God does not act to trigger the destructive elements). The seeds of destruction are contained within the very nature of the situation. Unlike some biblical figures (e.g., Moses), Noah does not interact with God's announcement. But he must decide whether to obey God's command, trusting God enough to build the ark when nary a cloud is in the sky. God the architect tersely lays before Noah the plans for the ark. The dimensions (450 x 75 x 45 feet, a cubit is about 18 inches; the boat in the *Gilgamesh Epic* was a perfect cube) and other features suggest the image of a floating house rather than a boat, with no rudder, sail, or crew. The word for "ark" (תבה *tēbâ*) occurs elsewhere only for Moses' basket of rushes (Exod 2:3-5), where Moses becomes a new Noah.[68] Noah faced a daunting task in constructing this enormous boat (five times longer than the *Mayflower!*) and getting all the animals and necessary food on board in a short time—and the narrator tells the story in a matter-of-fact way, unlike many extra-biblical versions of the story. The significant issue for the narrator is that Noah obeyed the divine directive (v. 22).

In v. 17 God specifies the means for the destruction of all living creatures (those with the "breath of life" are human beings and animals) by means of a "flood of waters" (מבול *mabbûl*, probably the waters above the firmament [1:7], used elsewhere only in Ps 29:10). Death will overwhelm everyone everywhere, except the occupants of the ark. The covenant (v. 18) assumes a right relationship, as do all of God's covenants in the OT. The covenant probably refers to God's commitment to Noah and his family at this moment of danger and anticipates 9:8-17 in a general way. Noah can move into this horrendous experience surrounded by a promise from God that ensures a future relationship with him and, by implication, the entire creation.

God commands Noah to bring onto the ark his family of eight persons, a pair (or pairs) of "every living thing, of all flesh," and food for all (see

68. On this and parallels between the ark and the tabernacle, see Fretheim, *Exodus*, 38, 268-69.

1:29-30). Noah does all that God has commanded him; in view of 7:5, this compliance refers to vv. 14-16 and the completion of the ark, regarding which the author provides no details; vv. 17-21 provide some information about what God intends to do and what will be expected of Noah when the ark is completed.

7:1-10, The Embarkation. These verses stem mostly from J (except vv. 6, 9). God's recognition of Noah's unique righteousness (v. 1) derives from Noah's trust in God and obedience in building the ark (see Heb 11:7). The righteous Noah of 6:9 has done justice to the relationship with God in which he stands. If he had not responded positively to the command, presumably he would have perished like the rest (see the assessment of Abraham in 22:12; cf. 38:26). God's confidence in Noah is seen to be well placed.

Verses 2-4, wherein God actually gives the command to board the ark, introduce problems of coherence with 6:17-20. While 6:19-20 spoke of pairs of animals and birds, here God directs Noah to take seven pairs of clean animals and birds (on clean birds, see 8:20) and a pair of unclean animals (in view of 9:3, clean and unclean refer to sacrifice rather than diet). Also, whereas 6:17 spoke of a "flood of waters" (see 7:11, 24) as the cause of the flood, 7:4 (see v. 12) speaks of forty days and nights of rain. Noah, once again, does all that God commands him (7:5).

Source criticism has explained this variety in terms of a shift from P to J materials; a redactor retained both versions. Yet, the redactor may not have thought this to be a problem; 6:19-20 speaks of pairs of animals generally, while 7:2-3 specifies the number and kind of pairs (needed for the sacrifice, 8:20). Verse 5 may be paired with v. 9*b*, which encloses the act of obedience to God's command. Verse 10 indicates that God does what God promised (v. 4).

The author provides a precise chronology, but contemporary readers have had difficulty in sorting it out, probably due to our lack of information about ancient calendars. Some details suggest a symbolic level of meaning. According to v. 4 the rain would come in seven days and last forty days; God *applies a temporal limit* to the flood from the beginning. Hence, the "flood" (vv. 6-7) does in fact come in seven days (v. 10) and lasts forty days (vv. 12, 17). The forty-day mark of v. 17 concludes the entry of water, the mountain-covering results of which are described in vv. 17-20. The 150-day mark of v. 24 marks the end of the time the flood had such an effect; in 8:3, these 150 days also mark the time the waters had subsided enough for the ark to rest on the mountains. These periods equal the five thirty-day months from the second month of 7:11 to the seventh month of 8:4. This sequence suggests that the forty days are included within the 150 days. The earth was dried up in the 601st year, the twenty-seventh day of the second month (8:14), totaling some 365-370 days (perhaps a solar year). The New Year's day of 8:13 marks the key point in the abatement of the flood (see Exod 40:2). Several scholars have noted the chiasm of seven waiting days (twice, 7:4, 10), forty days of rain (7:12, 17), 150 days of flood prevailing (7:24; 8:3), forty days of waiting (8:6) to seven days (twice, 8:10, 12).[69]

7:11-24, The Flood. The editor created, in this section, an admixture of J (vv. 12, 16*b*-17, 22-23) and P, with the renewed reference to the entry into the ark and Noah's obedience somewhat intrusive (vv. 13-15). Verses 6-9 are recapitulated in vv. 10-16 in more precise detail. The writer makes clear that all those specified had indeed gotten on board and were delivered from the flood. Yahweh shut the door of the ark (unparalleled in the Mesopotamian versions), signifying divine care (v. 16).

Right on God's announced schedule the flood begins, with water pouring in from below and above. The bursting forth (or splitting open) of the deep (תהום *tĕhôm*, v. 11; cf. Ps 78:15; Isa 51:10) suggests a breakdown of the division between waters above and below (1:6-7). The windows of the heavens, however, seem simply to be the source of rain (Mal 3:10; but see Isa 24:18). The presence of this event within a time frame remains important, for it keeps the destruction within created temporal limits.

The swelling of the waters (vv. 17, 24) encloses reference to death for all living creatures; the earth itself receives no mention, but there is repeated mention of the animals in the destruction (drowning language does not appear). The water rose

above the highest mountains, and all living creatures died (language from 2:7 and 6:17 is used in v. 22). The writer describes the flood in quite natural terms; only with the subsiding of the waters does God's explicit activity now become apparent.

8:1-12, God Remembers Noah and the Animals. In 8:1-5 (essentially P), v. 1 constitutes the turning point in the story: God remembers (see 9:15: Exod 2:24; Lev 26:42-45) Noah and the animals, both wild and domestic. (God's remembering may be compared to that in Ps 25:7). While this divine act is of no little import, the promise of God's covenant with Noah (6:18) and the placing of a temporal limit on the waters (7:4, 12, 17) means that God's remembering would occur.

Verses 1-2 describe divine activity prior to the end of the 150 days (reference to which brackets these verses; the NIV partially recognizes this action of the deity by putting v. 2 in the pluperfect). God made a wind (רוח *rûaḥ*) to blow over the earth, and it began to dry things up; indeed v. 2 reverses the deeds of 7:11. This divine activity recalls 1:2; it suggests that the creation had begun to fail, and that God now begins the task of restoration. The *rûaḥ* has a re-creative effect, bringing the cosmic "plumbing" back into proper repair. Unlike the frightened gods of the Mesopotamian stories, Israel's God remains in charge of the situation.

Five months after the flood began, the ark came to rest on a mountain in an area called Ararat (2 Kgs 19:37; Jer 51:37), most likely in extreme northeastern Turkey, near the sources of the Tigris and Euphrates rivers. The waters continue to abate for some months thereafter (v. 5 speaks of seventy-three more days until the tops of the mountains were seen; this chronology implies that the ark was grounded seventy-three days before the mountain on which it was grounded actually could be seen, though the two sources do not seem coherent here).

In vv. 6-12 (J), after forty more days, Noah sends out a succession of four birds (one raven, and a dove three times) to discern the condition of the earth (a comparable scene appears in an extra-biblical account and corresponds to a practice of ancient mariners). Note the use of practical wisdom rather than divine direction to discern the nature of the situation, as well as the salvific use

69. Wenham, *Genesis 1–15*, 157, 179-81.

of animals. The raven's going to and fro suggests it made various trips out from the ark, finally stopping when the waters dried up. Noah could probably determine whether the dove had found land by examining its feet when it returned. The olive branch brought back by the dove has long been deemed a symbol of peace (see Pss 52:8; 128:3 for its symbolic value of strength, beauty, and new life).

8:13-22, Disembarkation and Promise. In vv. 13-19 (essentially P), the author provides notice about varying stages of drying, from the appearance of the dry land (on New Year's Day, v. 13, an important moment for the beginning of the new creation) to a completely dry earth (v. 14); the verb stems from the same root as "dry land" in 1:9, hence it parallels the first creation.

God personally gives the directive for everyone to leave the ark (see 7:1, 16). The birds and animals are released for the purpose of multiplying on the earth (see 1:22, where birds but not land animals are blessed). Upon their release they find an earth accommodating to the purposes God intended for them.

In vv. 20-22 (J) Noah responds by building an altar and offering burnt offerings of every clean animal and bird (given the number of animals, this is an offering of consequence!). In the Babylonian epic the gods "gather like flies around the sacrifice," having been without food for many days. Here, God's smelling the odor of the sacrifice provides a lively metaphor for God's positive reception of the sacrifice (cf. Lev 26:31 with Amos 5:21-22) Noah remained unaware of this response. The offering in gratitude serves as a means for God to act on behalf of the worshiper, and hence has atoning value for Noah and his family. To claim, however, that it has perduring, universal significance, shifting God's future relation to *all* humankind and the world, isolates the sacrifice from other features of God's relationship to Noah.[70]

God initially responds with an internal commitment to the future of the creation (vv. 21-22), conveyed as an unconditional promise to Noah in 9:8-17 (formally comparable to 6:7 and 6:13). God's response expresses faithfulness not only to Noah but also to the larger creation. According

70. Wenham, *Genesis 1–15*, 190.

to 6:18, God's commitment to Noah remains firm and involves more than his personal future. God's recognition of Noah's righteousness (7:1) and God's remembering of Noah *and* the animals (8:1) also reveal a committed relationship. Noah's sacrifice is thus not simply an occasion for or the cause of God's response; it symbolizes a vital relationship. The totality of Noah's relationship with God (not just the sacrifice) mediates God's new relationship with the creation.

Verse 21 has occasioned much discussion. The phrase "never again curse the ground [or hold it in contempt]" (קלל *qālal*) could refer to no more floods, to no additional curses on the ground (ארר *'ārar*, 3:17), to the abandonment of the existing curse, or, more generally, to the end of the reign of the curse. The last seems likely; curse will no longer be the decisive divine relationship to the earth. God enters into the unfolding effects of the curse (of which the flood was a climactic instance), not allowing it to control the future of humankind or the creation. In effect, God places an eternal limit on the functioning of the moral order. Positively, the divine blessing and promise enter anew upon the scene and begin to break down the effects of the curse.

God's internal reason for giving the promise of no more floods appears highly unusual: "For the inclination of the human heart is evil from youth" (v. 21). A comparable statement occurs in 6:5, which serves as the reason for the flood; it now becomes the reason for *not* sending a flood. The differences between 6:5 and 8:21 are minimal (omission of "every"; replacement of "continually" with "from his youth"). The flood has not changed the basic human character. No new people are in view in 8:21, just fewer of them!

God chooses to take another course of action. The deity does not resign to the presence of sin (God sets only a certain type of judgment off limits), but offers a new way of relating to a wicked world. In view of this, God changes the ways and means of working toward divine goals for the creation (see p. 395).

God promises that the rhythm of the natural order—disrupted by the flood—will continue "as long as the earth endures" (v. 22)—literally, "as long as all the days of the earth." At first glance, one wonders what kind of promise this is, if another flood could simply be one way in which the earth no longer endures! But this phrase does not qualify the promise. It does not have an "end of the world" in view (though 2 Pet 3:6-7 suggests one could think of "the fire next time"); it speaks only of the life of the earth in an indefinite future. The phrase alludes to the "permanence" of the earth.[71] The promises focus on matters ecological, involving agricultural life, climate, seasons, and the daily rhythm. The first implies the continuing existence of human work in seeding and harvesting. All elements are necessary for continued life in the world, providing a basic rhythm as life reaches forward to the future. Come what may, the cosmic order will remain steady and regular.

71. See Westermann, *Genesis 1–11*, 457.

REFLECTIONS

1. The situation that led to the flood is described clearly enough. The wickedness of God's creatures had become so deep and broad (by the tenth generation) that the creation was reeling in negative response. God had to do something. Scholars have suggested overlapping interpretations for the purpose of the flood.

(a) God intended to *purge* the world of its corruption. Water may thus be understood in both a literal and a metaphorical way, as flood and as a cleansing agent, i.e., the language of blotting out or wiping away, wiping the slate of the world clean of its wickedness and beginning anew. This interpretation has some merit, but 8:21 reminds the reader that the flood did not cleanse human beings of sin. If God's purpose was to cleanse, it was in some sense a failure.

(b) God wanted to *undo* creation ("uncreation") and to begin again ("recreation"). Water functions literally and metaphorically, as flood and as instrument of destruction. Wenham's language conveys this interpretation: The flood was "the day when the old creation died"; it "destroyed the old world, God's original creation, and out of it was born a new world."[72] This could be seen in the return of a watery chaos (תהום *tĕhôm*) and the collapse of the division of the waters (7:11). Then, in a recreative act, God reverses the movement toward chaos, evident in the use of the רוח (*rûaḥ*) and the return of the waters (8:1-2), the emergence of dry land (8:13-14), and the blessings of 8:17 and 9:1, 7. (See p. 356, Reflections on chaos.)

This interpretation also presents some problems. The journey back from chaos works differently from the journey depicted in chap. 1. The old world was not destroyed; major continuities with the original creation remain (vegetation [the olive leaf]; light; firmament; luminaries; the ark occupants). *God sets limits to the flood from the start,* from the saving of a remnant of human beings and animals, to the covenant with Noah (6:18), to placing a temporal limit to the onrush of the waters (7:4). Hence, from a point early in the account, God did not intend to undo the creation, or for that matter to re-create an undone world according to some design. There is a beginning again, but the pre-flood creation remains.

(c) Another approach appeals to mythological or typological elements. Water often occurs as an archetypal symbol of chaos: "The potency of water as a symbol for the threat to all ordered life . . . lurks at the edges of controlled, meaningful existence."[73] Water appears in various texts (e.g., lament psalms) as an image for difficulty and suffering. The story reflects this-worldly reality of every age. For Westermann the story is the product of "a series of identical or similar events which have been fashioned into a type. The flood is the archetype of human catastrophe."[74] The flood story illustrates how God relates to the world in judgment and grace, from the prophetic indictments and announcements of judgment and salvation to the apocalyptic images of the end of the world.

72. Wenham, *Genesis 1–15*, 177, 206; see also Clines, *Theme*, 73-76, who notes this theme in chaps. 3–6 as well.
73. Gowan, *Genesis 1–11*, 92.
74. Westermann, *Genesis 1–11*, 398-99.

While flood language can indeed be appropriated to depict such moments (see Isaiah 24–27; Matt 24:37-44), this approach to the story is deeply inadequate. The promises that chart God's new relationship to the world indicate that the flood was a not-to-be-repeated event. As such, the flood should *never* be used as a type or illustration of divine judgment. The flood has a unique character, frozen in place by the divine promise never to do this again. Hence, the flood functions for Israel as an illustration of the certainty of God's promises (Isa 54:9-10). The flood typifies the inviolability of God's promises.

The biblical authors did not consider the flood as simply one event among others. It was an epoch-making event that deeply affected the future relationship between God and the world (see below). Such a perspective may explain why the flood story is so long, when compared with other narratives in Genesis 1–11.

(d) Another approach to the story involves its relationship to other flood stories in that world. However, we must do more than probe similarities and dissimilarities, and speculate regarding issues of dependence and interdependence. One often finds a tendency to show the "obvious" superiority of the biblical account to the other stories, or to reduce everything to Israelite polemic against other religions. While the task of comparison remains important, the hegemonic agenda does not prove helpful.

A more useful approach recognizes that the Israelites drew on understandings generated by other peoples and cultures. This angle of vision acknowledges that God the Creator was at work among other peoples before Israel appeared, and appreciates that significant insights, even theological insights, have been borrowed and developed by Israel. Israel inherits a way of thinking about beginnings—including the very structure of the account—that enables the community of faith to think about the creation in innovative ways.

From another perspective, we must recognize that God's saving act occurs in the world outside Israel. God *as Creator* acts in *saving* ways on behalf of creational goals. Such actions are not confined to Israel and need not be mediated by the community of faith.

(e) The flood story focuses on God as well as God's decisions and commitments regarding the creation. "The beginning and goal of the event lie with God."[75] The images of God developed in the story are striking: a God who expresses sorrow and regret; a God who judges, but doesn't want to, and then not in arbitrary or annihilative ways; a God who goes beyond justice and determines to save some creatures, including *every* animal and bird; a God who commits to the future of a less than perfect world; a God open to change and doing things in new ways; a God who promises never to do this again. The story reveals and resolves a fundamental tension within God, emphasizing finally, not a God who decides to destroy, but a God who wills to save, who is committed to change based on experience with the world, and who promises to stand by the creation.

The ascription of human feelings to God (see 6:5-7 in particular) reveals something about God. The grieving divine response at *Israel's* sin (Ps 78:40; Isa 63:10) harks back to the morning of the world and relates to all creatures. God, from creation on, continues to be open to and affected by the world. "God's judgment is not a detached decision . . . like flicking a switch or sending an impersonal command through a subordinate. God is caught up in the matter . . . the judgment is a very personal decision, with all the mixed sorrow and anger that go into the making of decisions that affect the people whom one loves. Grief is always what the Godward side of judgment looks like."[76] God experiences such sorrow *as God*, but real continuities with human sorrow exist.

Even more fundamental to the story is "the change wrought in God which makes possible a new beginning for creation. . . . The flood has effected no change in humankind. But it has effected an irreversible change in God. . . . It is now clear that such a commitment [to the

75. Ibid., 394.
76. Fretheim, *The Suffering of God,* 112.

creation] on God's part is costly. The God-world relation is not simply that of strong God and needy world. Now it is a tortured relation between a grieved God and a resistant world. And of the two, the real changes are in God."[77] What God does "recharacterizes" the divine relationship to the world. "God decides to put up with this state of evil."[78] This divine commitment signals the end of any simple sin-consequence schemas; this story does not exactly fit that way of construing other narratives in chaps. 1–11.

But the issue involves something other than a patient tolerance of human sin. For God to promise never to do something again, and to be faithful to that promise, entails self-limitation regarding the exercise of divine freedom and power. God thereby accepts limited options, in this case, the way in which God relates to evil in the world—no more flood-like responses. But God does not simply resign to evil (see below). Therefore, God *must* find a new way of engaging evil. Genesis 6:5-7 suggests that God takes the route of suffering. Deciding to endure a wicked world, while continuing to open up the divine heart to that world, means that God will continue to grieve. God thus decides to take suffering into God's own self and bear it there for the sake of the future of the world.[79]

God's regretful response assumes that humans have successfully resisted God's will for the creation. To continue to interact with this creation involves God's decision to continue to live with such resisting creatures (not your typical CEO!). In addition, God's regret assumes that God did not know for sure that all this would happen. As is evident throughout Genesis and the OT, God does not know the future in some absolute way (see commentary on 22:12). The text provides no support for a position that claims that God knew, let alone planned, that the creation would take this course.

God decides to go with the world, come what may in the way of human wickedness. God makes this promise, not simply in spite of human failure, but *because* human beings are sinful (8:21). The way into the future cannot depend on human loyalty; sinfulness so defines humanity that, if human beings are to live, they must be undergirded by the divine promise. Hence, *because* of human sinfulness, God promises to stay with the creation (see Exod 34:9 for an identical understanding of God's future with Israel in the wake of the golden calf debacle).[80]

We find an admixture of realism and promise here. On the one hand, human beings remain sinful creatures through and through. The flood cuts them off from any Edenic paradise; access to that world cannot be bridged or developed by gradual improvement. For the sake of creation, God must formulate laws to restrain negative human tendencies and behavior. On the other hand, human beings remain in the image of God (9:6); they are so highly valued that commands must be put in place to conserve their life, and they retain fundamental responsibility for the larger created order. But humans do not possess sufficient resources for the task; only God can assure creation's future. To this end, God ameliorates the workings of divine judgment and promises an orderly cosmos for the continuation of human and nonhuman life. Humans may, by virtue of their own behaviors, put themselves out of business, but not because God has so determined it or because the created order has failed.

2. There are significant ecological dimensions in the text. Human behavior has had a deeply adverse impact on the created order. The growth of thorns and thistles in the wake of human sin (3:18) has here grown to cosmic proportions. A close relationship exists between moral order and cosmic order, a point needing little argument in the modern world. Positively, it is striking that God puts such stock in the saving of the animals; indeed, God's remembrance of the animals belongs to the same initiative as God's remembering Noah. The lives of animals and humans are so interconnected that our future on this planet is linked to one another's

---

77. Brueggemann, *Genesis*, 73, 81.
78. Westermann, *Genesis 1–11*, 456; see von Rad, *Genesis*, 133-34, who speaks of "forbearance" and cites Rom 3:25.
79. Fretheim, *Suffering of God*, 72, 112.
80. Fretheim, *Exodus*, 303-5.

well-being. Although human sin has had significant negative consequences for the earth, if humans assume appropriate responsibility we may anticipate significant potential for good.

3. The theme of God delivering through dangerous water is in a number of biblical texts: e.g., Exodus 14–15 (and the other texts dependent on this tradition, e.g., Isa 43:2); Jonah; various lament psalms; Jesus stilling the storm and walking on the water (Mark 4:35-41); baptism (1 Pet 3:18-22). Flood water imagery also appears in later divine judgments (Isa 8:7-8). Nonetheless, God's promise remains sure: never again will there be the like of Noah's flood.

GENESIS 9:1–11:26, A NEW WORLD ORDER

Genesis 9:1-17, God's Covenant with Noah

NIV

9 Then God blessed Noah and his sons, saying to them, "Be fruitful and increase in number and fill the earth. ²The fear and dread of you will fall upon all the beasts of the earth and all the birds of the air, upon every creature that moves along the ground, and upon all the fish of the sea; they are given into your hands. ³Everything that lives and moves will be food for you. Just as I gave you the green plants, I now give you everything.

⁴"But you must not eat meat that has its lifeblood still in it. ⁵And for your lifeblood I will surely demand an accounting. I will demand an accounting from every animal. And from each man, too, I will demand an accounting for the life of his fellow man.

⁶"Whoever sheds the blood of man,
   by man shall his blood be shed;
 for in the image of God
   has God made man.

⁷As for you, be fruitful and increase in number; multiply on the earth and increase upon it."

⁸Then God said to Noah and to his sons with him: ⁹"I now establish my covenant with you and with your descendants after you ¹⁰and with every living creature that was with you—the birds, the livestock and all the wild animals, all those that came out of the ark with you—every living creature on earth. ¹¹I establish my covenant with you: Never again will all life be cut off by the waters of a flood; never again will there be a flood to destroy the earth."

NRSV

9 God blessed Noah and his sons, and said to them, "Be fruitful and multiply, and fill the earth. ²The fear and dread of you shall rest on every animal of the earth, and on every bird of the air, on everything that creeps on the ground, and on all the fish of the sea; into your hand they are delivered. ³Every moving thing that lives shall be food for you; and just as I gave you the green plants, I give you everything. ⁴Only, you shall not eat flesh with its life, that is, its blood. ⁵For your own lifeblood I will surely require a reckoning: from every animal I will require it and from human beings, each one for the blood of another, I will require a reckoning for human life.

⁶ Whoever sheds the blood of a human,
   by a human shall that person's blood be
      shed;
   for in his own image
   God made humankind.

⁷And you, be fruitful and multiply, abound on the earth and multiply in it."

⁸Then God said to Noah and to his sons with him, ⁹"As for me, I am establishing my covenant with you and your descendants after you, ¹⁰and with every living creature that is with you, the birds, the domestic animals, and every animal of the earth with you, as many as came out of the ark.ᵃ ¹¹I establish my covenant with you, that never again shall all flesh be cut off by the waters of a flood, and never again shall there be a flood to destroy the earth." ¹²God said, "This is the sign

ᵃ Gk: Heb adds *every animal of the earth*

NIV

¹²And God said, "This is the sign of the covenant I am making between me and you and every living creature with you, a covenant for all generations to come: ¹³I have set my rainbow in the clouds, and it will be the sign of the covenant between me and the earth. ¹⁴Whenever I bring clouds over the earth and the rainbow appears in the clouds, ¹⁵I will remember my covenant between me and you and all living creatures of every kind. Never again will the waters become a flood to destroy all life. ¹⁶Whenever the rainbow appears in the clouds, I will see it and remember the everlasting covenant between God and all living creatures of every kind on the earth."

¹⁷So God said to Noah, "This is the sign of the covenant I have established between me and all life on the earth."

NRSV

of the covenant that I make between me and you and every living creature that is with you, for all future generations: ¹³I have set my bow in the clouds, and it shall be a sign of the covenant between me and the earth. ¹⁴When I bring clouds over the earth and the bow is seen in the clouds, ¹⁵I will remember my covenant that is between me and you and every living creature of all flesh; and the waters shall never again become a flood to destroy all flesh. ¹⁶When the bow is in the clouds, I will see it and remember the everlasting covenant between God and every living creature of all flesh that is on the earth." ¹⁷God said to Noah, "This is the sign of the covenant that I have established between me and all flesh that is on the earth."

COMMENTARY

These speeches of God to Noah are conventionally assigned to the Priestly writer, but must now be read in view of 8:21-22 and other non-Priestly texts. Recalling key elements from chap. 1 in the light of the experience with a devastated creation, God lays out the dynamics of a renewed relationship to the post-flood world. Although Noah is in some sense a new Adam, God must take into account that the inclination of his heart is evil (8:21). The world is no new Eden. Generally, these texts seek to assure Noah and his family (and readers) that God has not withdrawn from the creation; God still rules and the basic shape of the divine relationship to the world still holds, with its blessings, commands, and promises.

God chooses to safeguard the creation, making provisions from the human (vv. 1-7) and the divine sides (vv. 8-17). Verses 1-7, with their recognition of murder and human-nonhuman conflict, assume that the pre-flood, but post-Eden, state of affairs will continue in post-flood times. God's continuing valuing of and care for the creation, regarding both animals and humans (vv. 1-7) and then more universally with respect to the future of the entire created order (vv. 8-17), provides the primary link between these two sections. The God who blesses (v. 1) and the God

who promises (v. 11) come together in this text, and lay the foundations for the future of the post-flood world.

9:1-7. This segment is enclosed by formulations from chap. 1: to be fruitful, to multiply, and to fill the earth; v. 7 even speaks of "swarming" (used for sea creatures, 1:20; cf. 8:17 with 1:22). As in 1:28, God blesses Noah and his sons before offering commands. This blessing language stresses that, in the midst of death and destruction, God wills life; that will remains firmly in place even with the "inclination of the human heart" (8:21) and the negative effects of continuing violence, injustice, and disorder.

Verse 2 assumes the charge to have dominion, though now complicated by the "fear and dread" of the violence of which human beings are capable (military language, Deut 11:25), and developed in the wake of sin's effect on human domination (v. 5 also knows about violence against humans by animals). Human dominion over that world has often been more a matter of tyranny than benevolence. That all animals are "given/delivered" into human hands (also military language, Deut 20:13) entails power over their life, though not a license for exploitation nor a diminution in the task of dominion. This verse recognizes that the realities of fear make relationships to the animal world much more difficult and complex, with new levels of responsibility. The prophets envision a return to the deity's earlier plan, according to which humans would relate to the animals (see Hos 2:17-18; Isa 11:6-9).

Human diet constitutes another issue carried over from chap. 1. Earlier, God grants green plants to humans for food (v. 29); here God expands that to include *"every* moving thing that lives."￼ A vegetarian diet is supplemented with meat, probably a concession to the need for food in a famine-ridden world. Yet restrictions remain (the formulation of vv. 3-4 is similar to 2:16-17). No distinction between clean and unclean occurs (see 8:20), but the flesh of a living animal or the meat of a slaughtered animal may not be eaten if the blood remains in it, since blood equals life (see Lev 17:11; external evidence for the ancients would be the pulse). Humans must drain animal blood before eating meat. This directive, without parallel in the ancient Near East, recurs in the OT (see Lev 17:10-14; Deut 12:15-27) and has authority in the NT (Acts 15:20; 21:25). It was not uncommon for ancients to drink blood for the renewal of vitality it was thought to bring. Israel, however, believes that life belongs to God and should be returned to its source. This proscription regarding blood—and the attention needed to fulfill it—stands as a sharp reminder that killing animals ought not to be taken lightly, for God is the source of their life. As such, it guards against brutality, carelessness, and needless killing. Concern for the life of animals immediately leads into the concern for human life.

The lifeblood of human beings should not be shed, much less eaten (v. 5). Using personal language, God declares that murderers will be directly accountable to God; indeed, the writer states three times that *God* will require a reckoning. This includes even the animals (for a case, see Exod 21:28-29). Although the text does not specify an executor in v. 5, yet "by a human" in v. 6 assumes, in a matter-of-fact way, that human beings will administer the sanctions. The chiastic formulation of v. 6 provides a shorthand expression, probably proverbial, of the repercussions that fall upon a murderer (v. 6): If a human life is taken, the life of the one taking it shall be required (see Matt 26:52). The chiasm formally expresses

the point; in such cases, justice will involve the principle of measure for measure. No persons shall be allowed to pay their way out of such a situation (see Num 35:31). Capital punishment, though referred to here, remains limited compared to many other cultures (e.g., never in property cases). This text does not advocate or authorize or justify capital punishment; rather, it recognizes the way in which human beings would participate in the moral order as executors of the divine judgment (later laws institute a legal system; see Rom 13:4). This saying expresses God's point of view regarding the high value of human life.

The writer links the rationale given for this command to the fact that human beings have been made in the image of God (see 1:26), an understanding that still pertains in a post-flood world. In the killing of a human, the created order is threatened; the status and role of humans within God's creation is violated. At the same time, humans are not absolutely inviolable; they can forfeit their right to life if they take a life. The divine image rationale may relate to both halves of v. 6a—"for" may refer both to the victim and to the human executor on God's behalf, providing a deeper link with 1:26.

9:8-17. God moves to promises, a personal witness to humans regarding what they can expect from God. The covenant God establishes fulfills the promise God made in 6:18. Originally a doublet of 8:21-22, the latter verses now serve as divine reflection that leads to this public statement of promise (cf. 6:7 with 6:13).

Similar to vv. 1-7, these verses are enclosed by reference to the covenant being established (v. 8) and, in a final peroration, to having been established (v. 17) with all flesh. The many repetitions of key words and phrases emphasize the promissory character of the covenant and the inclusiveness of the recipients throughout all generations, assuring the listeners (and readers) of a hopeful future. The promises may be compared to those given Israel after the fall of Jerusalem (see esp. Isa 54:9-10, which describes this covenant in terms of a divine oath). God stands as the subject of the verbs throughout; God establishes/makes the covenant, sets the bow in the clouds, and remembers the covenant.

We may observe a basic structure: vv. 8-10, the recipients of the covenant; v. 11, the content of the covenant; vv. 12-17, the sign of the covenant, in chiastic form; vv. 12-13, 17, the sign; vv. 14-15a, 16, God's remembering when the bow is in the clouds; v. 15b is the essence of the promise.

God establishes this covenant, not only with Noah, his sons, and all their descendants, but with "every living creature"—that is, "all flesh"—and with the earth as well (v. 13). The involvement of the nonhuman in the promise parallels their presence in the expectations of vv. 1-7 (see also 6:11-13). We hear a word of comfort and reassurance in the wake of the horrendous experience of the flood (and readers can plug in their own disasters).

Covenant functions as an equivalent to promise; God is obligated, unilaterally and unconditionally. God initiates and establishes the covenant, and remembering it becomes exclusively a divine responsibility. The covenant will be as good as God is. God establishes it in goodness and love and upholds it in eternal faithfulness. It will never need to be renewed; it stands forever, regardless of what people do. Humans can just rest in the arms of this promise. And the promise offers this (comparable to 8:21-22): Never again will God send a flood to destroy the earth. There may well be judgments yet to come, but not one that will annihilate everything (see Isa 54:6-10).

God did not create the rainbow for this moment; it had existed but was now filled with new significance for the future. Although elements of the natural order could function as virtual signs (see Jer 31:35-36; 33:19-26), the bow is different since it reminds God (see Exod 12:13), not human beings (see 17:9-14). When God sees the rainbow, God remembers the covenant. This does not mean that God forgets in between rainbows. Yet, at times Israel believed that God had in fact forgotten them (see Ps 13:1; Lam 5:20). To attest God's remembering assures those who think that

God appears to have forgotten. God's remembering entails more than mental activity; it involves action with specific reference to a prior commitment (see 8:1; Exod 2:24; 6:5; Lev 26:42). As a sign for God it becomes a secondary sign for people, one in which they can take comfort and hope.

In the ancient Near East and Israel (in poetic texts; see Pss 7:12-13; 18:14; 144:6; Lam 2:4; 3:12; Hab 3:9-11) the (rain)bow was a divine weapon, and lightning bolts were arrows that exacted judgment. Hence, possible interpretations of the bow in this text arise: (a) Associating the rainbow with *promise* rather than judgment changes the meaning of the symbol, becoming a sign of peace rather than war; God will not use the bow for this judgmental purpose again. This view seems difficult since the *broken* bow becomes a symbol of peace (Ps 46:9); (b) Associating the rainbow with *both* promise and judgment keeps the normal meaning of the symbol intact, but focuses it on the means by which God keeps the promise— namely, God uses the bow to *protect* creation from such disasters.[81] This interpretation also presents problems because the buildup of clouds in vv. 14 and 16 implies that the divine judgment gathers momentum (see Jer 4:13; Ezek 38:16; Joel 2:2) and the appearance of the bow occasions a shift in God's direction. No bow appears unless there are clouds; the bow thus suggests restraint in the midst of deserved judgment. It thus seems best to retain it as a symbol of peace and divine good will toward the creation. In either case, the bow serves as an important sign of God's ongoing, deep commitment to the life of the creation, and in such a way that God is limited regarding its possible futures (see below).

81. E. Zenger, *Gottes Bogen in den Wolken* (Stuttgart: Katholisches Bibelwerk, 1983).

REFLECTIONS

1. Since the commands in vv. 1-7 are formulated for a pre-Israel world, they present a universal dimension. In fact, God must only be formalizing an already existing "natural law," for such allowed the author to speak of responsibility and accountability in the earlier chapters. For example, Cain was held accountable for his murder of Abel, as were the pre-flood generations for their violence. Numerous other instances occur in Genesis (e.g., 20:1-10; 26:5, 10) and in the rest of the OT (e.g., the oracles against the nations, Amos 1–2). The NT seems cognizant of the status of these laws in such texts as Acts 15:20; 21:25 (see p. 396).[82]

2. In the wake of the troubles caused by human beings, God continues to place confidence in them by giving them hope (vv. 1-7). They are neither reduced to automatons nor considered untrustworthy in any respect, but are directly addressed in light of responsibilities they have within the created order. Whatever else one might say about the effect of the fall on human beings, it does not mean that God has ceased to trust them or refuses to work in and through them.

3. Since God calls the murderer to account, the deity serves as the final arbiter concerning the taking of human life. Although humans have been made the executors of this divine reckoning, they should examine the situation in these terms: Do we understand that such a penalty in this case is the will of God? Are we willing to carry it out in the name of God?

4. Although God promises never again to punish the earth with a flood, that affirmation does not invalidate what human beings might do with nuclear power at their disposal, or by despoiling the environment. This promise also does not speak to issues regarding the "wearing out" of the physical universe over billions of years, or the "Big Crunch." It has been suggested that the text speaks only to a destruction of the earth by water. A recent song has the line, "God gave Noah the rainbow sign—no more water—the fire next time" (see 2 Pet 3:17). But such a perspective would violate the text, which speaks clearly not simply of the means of destruction, but of the end: Earth's destruction (v. 11) or the destruction of all flesh (v. 15).

5. The covenant with Noah involves all people. God, active in this way with all creation quite apart from Israel's life and mission, upholds this covenant *independent* of the community of faith. All people experience its effects, even though they may not have heard Genesis 9. Israel occupies a privileged position because it knows the promise, but is not to keep that knowledge to itself.

This universal covenant provides the context within which other covenants become possible. Since God has covered the earth with promises, other and more particular promises can be made. The creational promise to Noah makes possible, provides grounding for, the promise to Abraham. God's promissory relationship with the world *generates* more particular promises in order to enable these universal promises. Nonetheless, all covenants are directed to the same end—namely, the good creation intended by God. There are correspondences between this covenant and the one with Abraham (chap. 17). There, too, God "establishes" an "everlasting" covenant. However, the sign of Abraham's covenant—circumcision—becomes a sign for Abraham to keep, whereas the sign of the rainbow serves to remind God.

6. The covenant has significant ecological implications because God has established it with "all flesh," with birds and animals and the earth itself, even though they are now alienated from human beings. What does it mean for our ecological considerations that God has made promises to nonhumans? God cares for their life and seeks to enhance it in various ways.[83] Human beings should follow the divine lead. For another, humans, with our knowledge of the promise, have a responsibility to the nonhuman recipients of the promise to tend to the earth and all of its inhabitants. Hosea 2:18 envisions a future in which all the recipients of this covenant will no longer be estranged and can experience God's salvation together.

---

82. For a discussion of the so-called Noachic commandments (often idolatry, blasphemy, bloodshed, incest/adultery, robbery, injustice, eating flesh with blood), see Sarna, *Genesis*, 377.
83. See T. Fretheim, "Nature's Praise of God," *Ex Auditu* 3 (1987) 16-30.

7. Von Rad speaks correctly here of divine forbearance, calling attention to Rom 3:25.[84] God's power in response to evil in the world restrains itself in a permanent fashion (see 8:21-22). God's use of power in dealing with evil is eternally self-limited. No simple retributive system applies. God will not respond with total destruction, no matter the human response. God's internal musings (8:21) make clear that God makes this move with eyes wide open, regarding human possibilities for evil; God remains a realist. But God cares so much for creation and its potential that God determines to take a new direction. As noted above, God changes over the course of the flood, not human beings, and this for the sake of the creation.

84. Von Rad, *Genesis,* 133-34.

Genesis 9:18-29, Curse and Blessing in Noah's Family

NIV

[18]The sons of Noah who came out of the ark were Shem, Ham and Japheth. (Ham was the father of Canaan.) [19]These were the three sons of Noah, and from them came the people who were scattered over the earth.

[20]Noah, a man of the soil, proceeded[a] to plant a vineyard. [21]When he drank some of its wine, he became drunk and lay uncovered inside his tent. [22]Ham, the father of Canaan, saw his father's nakedness and told his two brothers outside. [23]But Shem and Japheth took a garment and laid it across their shoulders; then they walked in backward and covered their father's nakedness. Their faces were turned the other way so that they would not see their father's nakedness.

[24]When Noah awoke from his wine and found out what his youngest son had done to him, [25]he said,

"Cursed be Canaan!
The lowest of slaves
will he be to his brothers."

[26]He also said,

"Blessed be the LORD, the God of Shem!
May Canaan be the slave of Shem.[b]
[27]May God extend the territory of Japheth[c];
may Japheth live in the tents of Shem,
and may Canaan be his[d] slave."

[28]After the flood Noah lived 350 years. [29]Altogether, Noah lived 950 years, and then he died.

a20 Or *soil, was the first*   b26 Or *be his slave*
c27 *Japheth* sounds like the Hebrew for *extend.*   d27 Or *their*

NRSV

18The sons of Noah who went out of the ark were Shem, Ham, and Japheth. Ham was the father of Canaan. [19]These three were the sons of Noah; and from these the whole earth was peopled.

20Noah, a man of the soil, was the first to plant a vineyard. [21]He drank some of the wine and became drunk, and he lay uncovered in his tent. [22]And Ham, the father of Canaan, saw the nakedness of his father, and told his two brothers outside. [23]Then Shem and Japheth took a garment, laid it on both their shoulders, and walked backward and covered the nakedness of their father; their faces were turned away, and they did not see their father's nakedness. [24]When Noah awoke from his wine and knew what his youngest son had done to him, [25]he said,

"Cursed be Canaan;
lowest of slaves shall he be to his
brothers."
[26]He also said,
"Blessed by the LORD my God be Shem;
and let Canaan be his slave.
[27] May God make space for[a] Japheth,
and let him live in the tents of Shem;
and let Canaan be his slave."
28After the flood Noah lived three hundred fifty years. [29]All the days of Noah were nine hundred fifty years; and he died.

a Heb *yapht,* a play on *Japheth*

COMMENTARY

On the far side of the flood story, the texts begin to reflect known historical realities. Even more, stories of individuals within a family begin to extend into relationships among larger communities. Although especially evident in chap. 10, such a move occurs *within* this text (assigned to J): intrafamilial conflicts within Noah's family (vv. 20-24) lead to communal difficulties among his descendants (vv. 25-27). Noah's sons may be understood in both individual and eponymous terms, thus preparing the way for the table of nations. Both Noah and Adam remain "typical" characters. Moreover, both their families produce sharp repercussions for their descendants. Even more, the relationships anticipated among the descendants of Noah's sons apply to various historical situations. The narrative thus serves complex purposes, including typological, ethnological, and etiological issues.

This brief text consists of an unusual admixture of literary types, from genealogy to story to curse and blessing. This multiform text reflects a complex tradition history, which no redactor has smoothed over. Whether a fuller form of this story ever existed remains uncertain. The text presents numerous difficulties, often so intractable that little scholarly consensus has been achieved. What is the nature of Ham's indecent act? Why is his son Canaan cursed? Why is Canaan to become a slave to his brothers? Why does Noah refer to what his "youngest son" has done, when Ham seems to be the second son (see 7:13; 9:18)? Why are Shem and Japheth aligned?

The redactor may have worked with two different traditions regarding the identity of Noah's sons: (1) Shem, Japheth, and Canaan; (2) Shem, Ham, and Japheth. Two ways of conceiving the resulting amalgamation are thus: The first has been overlaid by the insertion of "Ham, the father of" (vv. 18, 22); or the second has been overlaid with material about Canaan, based on Israel's later experience in the land. The latter seems more likely, but uncertainty abounds. No known parallels to this story exist in other ancient Near Eastern literature.

The story is enclosed by brief genealogical notices. Verses 18-19 resume earlier references to the sons of Noah and announce the spreading out of their families (detailed in chaps. 10–11). Verses 28-29 give chronological notes about Noah's life and death, completing the genealogy of chap. 5. The references to grape-bearing vines and Canaan as a mature grandson make clear that the story takes place many years after the flood. Also, these verses present the first Genesis story in which God does not appear directly.

The story involves the themes of blessing and curse.

1. Blessing pertains to both nonhumans and humans in this text. God's post-flood blessing begins to take effect amid the world of the curse in all its aspects, hence ameliorating the effects of the curse.

Noah is the first to plant a vineyard and practice winemaking, discoveries ascribed to the *gods* elsewhere in the ancient Near East. Noah's skill at farming and crop development provides some relief from being totally at the mercy of what the ground brings forth on its own, so intimated in the words of his father, Lamech (5:29). As such, he stands in the tradition of the family of Cain (4:21-22), founders of other cultural blessings. He also functions as a new Adam, whose original calling was to till the ground and keep it (2:15).

This focus on vineyards and wine may seem a small matter for modern people, but these were important economic realities for Israel, celebrated in the feast of Booths (Deut 16:13-16). Vines, the grape harvest, and wine symbolize God's blessings of life and fertility (see Pss 80:8-16; 104:15; Isa 5:1-7; 27:2-6; Hos 2:15; 9:10). Blessings can be abused, however; that which makes the heart glad can also promote drunkenness (see the warnings in Prov 20:1; 23:31-35; 31:6-7; Isa 5:11). What is good within God's creation can be made perverse by inappropriate human behavior.

At another level, the blessing on Shem (v. 26) first hints at God's blessing of Israel. Shem begins the line that will lead to Abraham, in and through whom this blessing will reach out to all the earth (see 12:1-3).

2. Sin and the Curse. The flood did not rid the world of sin (so 8:21). In this text, sin manifests itself in the effects of drunkenness, disrespect of parents, and familial conflict.

The narrator offers no explicit judgment about Noah's drunkenness; yet, it opens Noah to victimization and provides the occasion for all the suffering and conflict that follow. He has drunk himself into an unconscious state and lies naked in his tent (see Lam 4:21; Hab 2:15). The theme of nakedness (chaps. 2–3) involves issues of shame and exposure, an issue of no little consequence in Israel, in both religious (Exod 20:26) and social (2 Sam 6:20; 10:4-5) life. The prophets use this same theme to portray Israel's apostasy (Ezek 16:36) and the resulting divine judgment, in which Israel's shameful behavior will be exposed for all to see (Isa 47:3; Ezek 16:37-39).

What Noah's youngest son "had done" has prompted numerous conjectures. Some readers hypothesize about an inappropriate sexual act, from sodomy to incest. Some even appeal to Lev 18:7-8, which condemns "uncovering the nakedness of one's father," a reference to sexual activity with one's *mother*. Yet, the OT does not normally shrink from "telling it like it is" (see chaps. 18–19). Here the text makes clear that Noah uncovers himself. Moreover, Ham's *seeing* his father naked constitutes the problem, as confirmed by the detailed report of how his two brothers make sure they do not (v. 23; a chiasm of v. 22). Yet, the problem involves more than seeing (which may have been inadvertent); Ham errs in what he does with what he has seen. Rather than keep quiet or seek to remedy the situation, Ham tells tales to a wider public. The matter entails not simply a breach of filial piety, but the *public* disgrace of his father. Parent-child relationships were considered to be of the highest importance in Israel (see Deut 21:18-21, which prescribes capital punishment for sons who rebel).

When Noah awakens from his stupor, he learns what has been done, probably because it is now public knowledge, and speaks his first and only words. The reference to his "youngest son" may mean that earlier references to Shem, Ham, and Japheth (5:32; 6:10; 7:13) do not occur in chronological order. Noah's blessing and cursing words stand in the tradition of Isaac (27:27-29, 39-40) and Jacob (49:1-27), though one cannot help wondering whether he is overreacting. The curse

on Canaan appears most prominent; indeed, his enslavement also becomes part of the blessing of Shem and Japheth. Yet, for Canaan to become a slave of his brothers in an individual sense seems difficult. It almost certainly bears an eponymous force at this point, condemning the wickedness of the Canaanites in advance (see 15:16; Deut 9:4-5). In the blessings of Shem and Japheth (the NIV more literally translates that *God* is being blessed/praised, as in 24:27, but for unstated reasons), Noah calls for God to act (unlike the curse). The blessings *request* a future divine action and are not understood to be inevitably effective (see 25:23; chap. 27).

Noah's cursing of Canaan is most puzzling: He does not curse Ham, but Ham's son, Noah's grandson. Perhaps both father and son were responsible in an originally longer text; this telescoping would be a way of involving both. Perhaps the author alludes to the effects of the sins of the parents on the children (see Exod 20:5). More probably, those reading the text in terms of ethnic units as much as individuals would not have made a clear distinction between Canaanites and Hamites (see 10:6). An original reference to Ham was narrowed to one Hamite group, the Canaanites, when they came into conflict with Israel. Not changing the details keeps the Hamite link intact.

Although chap. 10 identifies many peoples in the lineage of Noah's sons, the author focuses on a narrower range, which is most prominent here: Shem represents the Israelites (but this is unique in the OT); Canaan the Canaanites; Japheth the sea-faring peoples, such as the Philistines; Ham the Egyptians, probably. The first three are the most prominent groups occupying Palestine in the early years of Israel's life in the land; their relationships may be foreshadowed in these verses. The Israelites and the Philistines entered Canaan from east and west, respectively, in this period, resulting in the subjugation (i.e., enslavement?) of the Canaanites. The blessing regarding Japheth may represent a qualification of the fulfillment of the promise. Japheth's dwelling in the tents of Shem may mean that Israel does not have the land to itself, but shares it with others, a situation prevailing at various times (as with the Philistines). Ham was the progenitor of nations in the Egyptian orbit (10:6; see Pss 78:51; 105:23-27);

Canaan was controlled by (was the son of) Egypt from 1550 to 1200 BCE. The various nations in chap. 14 may represent another level of the fulfillment of vv. 25-27, since all three branches of Noah's genealogy are represented in that conflict.

REFLECTIONS

1. The often-cited parallels between this narrative and the Eden story, especially as interpreted through 5:29, make it typical. Noah, a new Adam, takes up the creational task once again in "planting" and tilling the "ground"; his skill leads to a taming of what the ground produces and hence ameliorates the curse (3:17; 5:29). Yet, Noah as the new Adam (and one child) also fails as miserably as the old Adam. Similar themes appear in both stories: nakedness after eating fruit, and intrafamilial conflict, including human subservience and its affect. The curse on the serpent and the ground parallels the curse on Canaan, both of which affect life negatively. Yet, the act of Shem and Japheth in covering the naked one mirrors earlier action of the deity (3:21).

These parallels strongly suggest that, in the post-flood movement to the world of nations, "good and evil" patterns in life persist. God's work of blessing influences the worlds of human and nonhuman, family and nation; but there are also deep human failures due to the "evil inclination of the human heart" (8:21). This mix of goodness and evil will accompany every human endeavor, whether familial or sociopolitical, and every relationship, whether personal or communal, down through the ages to our own time.

2. It seems incredible that this story could have been used to justify the enslavement of Africans. Suffice it to say that, inasmuch as Canaan among all the sons of Ham, is not the father of a Negroid people (see 10:15-19, where all the peoples listed are Semitic or Indo-European), any attempt to justify the slavery of African peoples is a gross misuse of this text. Regarding slavery in general, however, neither the OT nor the NT condemns this inhumane institution. Various OT laws seek to regulate (never commend) this practice (Exod 21:1-11). And an increasing concern for issues of humaneness may be discerned in later laws (see Deut 15:12-18; Lev 25:39-46). The "enslavement" of Canaanites envisaged in this text probably reflects their later subjugation rather than any practice of slavery.

This text mentions enslavement in the wake of sinful behavior; such a human practice is thus clearly set at odds with God's creational intentions. As with the sentence in 3:14-19, humans should, appropriately, work to overcome this effect of sin.

3. Noah's word (no word from God occurs here) about the future of his sons should not be interpreted in fatalistic terms. What happens over the course of history affects what in fact will happen in the aftermath of such a word (see 25:23).

4. The chief point of this text may involve relationships between children and their parents,[85] a negative illustration of the commandment, "Honor your father and your mother." Israelites considered the family of extreme importance in the created order; any deterioration in the quality of family life could only disrupt the creational intentions of God. Such a perspective would be in line with chaps. 3–4, which speak of other familial relationships that have been distorted in the wake of human sin. At the same time, the author has in view broader relationships among peoples and nations, which are profoundly affected by what happens within families. Dysfunctional families affect our communal life together.

85. Westermann, *Genesis 1–11,* 494.

Genesis 10:1-32, The Table of Nations

10 This is the account of Shem, Ham and Japheth, Noah's sons, who themselves had sons after the flood.

[2] The sons[a] of Japheth:

Gomer, Magog, Madai, Javan, Tubal, Meshech and Tiras.

[3] The sons of Gomer:

Ashkenaz, Riphath and Togarmah.

[4] The sons of Javan:

Elishah, Tarshish, the Kittim and the Rodanim.[b] [5] (From these the maritime peoples spread out into their territories by their clans within their nations, each with its own language.)

[6] The sons of Ham:

Cush, Mizraim,[c] Put and Canaan.

[7] The sons of Cush:

Seba, Havilah, Sabtah, Raamah and Sabteca.

The sons of Raamah:

Sheba and Dedan.

[8] Cush was the father[d] of Nimrod, who grew to be a mighty warrior on the earth. [9] He was a mighty hunter before the LORD; that is why it is said, "Like Nimrod, a mighty hunter before the LORD." [10] The first centers of his kingdom were Babylon, Erech, Akkad and Calneh, in[e] Shinar.[f] [11] From that land he went to Assyria, where he built Nineveh, Rehoboth Ir,[g] Calah [12] and Resen, which is between Nineveh and Calah; that is the great city.

[13] Mizraim was the father of

the Ludites, Anamites, Lehabites, Naphtuhites, [14] Pathrusites, Casluhites (from whom the Philistines came) and Caphtorites.

[15] Canaan was the father of

Sidon his firstborn,[h] and of the Hittites,

a2 *Sons* may mean *descendants* or *successors* or *nations*; also in verses 3, 4, 6, 7, 20-23, 29 and 31.   b4 Some manuscripts of the Masoretic Text and Samaritan Pentateuch (see also Septuagint and 1 Chron. 1:7); most manuscripts of the Masoretic Text *Dodanim*   c6 That is, Egypt; also in verse 13   d8 *Father* may mean *ancestor* or *predecessor* or *founder*; also in verses 13, 15, 24 and 26.   e10 Or *Erech and Akkad—all of them in*   f10 That is, Babylonia   g11 Or *Nineveh with its city squares*   h15 Or *of the Sidonians, the foremost*

10 These are the descendants of Noah's sons, Shem, Ham, and Japheth; children were born to them after the flood.

2 The descendants of Japheth: Gomer, Magog, Madai, Javan, Tubal, Meshech, and Tiras. 3 The descendants of Gomer: Ashkenaz, Riphath, and Togarmah. 4 The descendants of Javan: Elishah, Tarshish, Kittim, and Rodanim.[a] 5 From these the coastland peoples spread. These are the descendants of Japheth[b] in their lands, with their own language, by their families, in their nations.

6 The descendants of Ham: Cush, Egypt, Put, and Canaan. 7 The descendants of Cush: Seba, Havilah, Sabtah, Raamah, and Sabteca. The descendants of Raamah: Sheba and Dedan. 8 Cush became the father of Nimrod; he was the first on earth to become a mighty warrior. 9 He was a mighty hunter before the LORD; therefore it is said, "Like Nimrod a mighty hunter before the LORD." 10 The beginning of his kingdom was Babel, Erech, and Accad, all of them in the land of Shinar. 11 From that land he went into Assyria, and built Nineveh, Rehoboth-ir, Calah, and 12 Resen between Nineveh and Calah; that is the great city. 13 Egypt became the father of Ludim, Anamim, Lehabim, Naphtuhim, 14 Pathrusim, Casluhim, and Caphtorim, from which the Philistines come.[c]

15 Canaan became the father of Sidon his firstborn, and Heth, 16 and the Jebusites, the Amorites, the Girgashites, 17 the Hivites, the Arkites, the Sinites, 18 the Arvadites, the Zemarites, and the Hamathites. Afterward the families of the Canaanites spread abroad. 19 And the territory of the Canaanites extended from Sidon, in the direction of Gerar, as far as Gaza, and in the direction of Sodom, Gomorrah, Admah, and Zeboiim, as far as Lasha. 20 These are the descendants of Ham, by their families, their languages, their lands, and their nations.

21 To Shem also, the father of all the children of Eber, the elder brother of Japheth, children were born. 22 The descendants of Shem: Elam,

a Heb Mss Sam Gk See 1 Chr 1.7: MT *Dodanim*   b Compare verses 20, 31. Heb lacks *These are the descendants of Japheth*   c Cn: Heb *Casluhim, from which the Philistines come, and Caphtorim*

NIV

¹⁶Jebusites, Amorites, Girgashites, ¹⁷Hivites, Arkites, Sinites, ¹⁸Arvadites, Zemarites and Hamathites.

Later the Canaanite clans scattered ¹⁹and the borders of Canaan reached from Sidon toward Gerar as far as Gaza, and then toward Sodom, Gomorrah, Admah and Zeboiim, as far as Lasha.

²⁰These are the sons of Ham by their clans and languages, in their territories and nations.

²¹Sons were also born to Shem, whose older brother was[a] Japheth; Shem was the ancestor of all the sons of Eber.

²²The sons of Shem:

Elam, Asshur, Arphaxad, Lud and Aram.
²³The sons of Aram:

Uz, Hul, Gether and Meshech.[b]
²⁴Arphaxad was the father of[c] Shelah,

and Shelah the father of Eber.
²⁵Two sons were born to Eber:

One was named Peleg,[d] because in his time the earth was divided; his brother was named Joktan.
²⁶Joktan was the father of

Almodad, Sheleph, Hazarmaveth, Jerah, ²⁷Hadoram, Uzal, Diklah, ²⁸Obal, Abimael, Sheba, ²⁹Ophir, Havilah and Jobab. All these were sons of Joktan.

³⁰The region where they lived stretched from Mesha toward Sephar, in the eastern hill country.

³¹These are the sons of Shem by their clans and languages, in their territories and nations.

³²These are the clans of Noah's sons, according to their lines of descent, within their nations. From these the nations spread out over the earth after the flood.

a21 Or Shem, the older brother of   b23 See Septuagint and 1 Chron. 1:17; Hebrew Mash   c24 Hebrew; Septuagint father of Cainan, and Cainan was the father of   d25 Peleg means division.

NRSV

Asshur, Arpachshad, Lud, and Aram. ²³The descendants of Aram: Uz, Hul, Gether, and Mash. ²⁴Arpachshad became the father of Shelah; and Shelah became the father of Eber. ²⁵To Eber were born two sons: the name of the one was Peleg,[a] for in his days the earth was divided, and his brother's name was Joktan. ²⁶Joktan became the father of Almodad, Sheleph, Hazarmaveth, Jerah, ²⁷Hadoram, Uzal, Diklah, ²⁸Obal, Abimael, Sheba, ²⁹Ophir, Havilah, and Jobab; all these were the descendants of Joktan. ³⁰The territory in which they lived extended from Mesha in the direction of Sephar, the hill country of the east. ³¹These are the descendants of Shem, by their families, their languages, their lands, and their nations.

³²These are the families of Noah's sons, according to their genealogies, in their nations; and from these the nations spread abroad on the earth after the flood.

a That is Division

COMMENTARY

This, the fourth *tôlēdôt,* introduces the reader to the world of nations, the history of the world "after the flood." Noah's three sons provide the outline, each point of which closes with statements about land, language, family, and nation (vv. 5, 20, 21). Opening and closing summary verses bracket the chapter (vv. 1, 32). The author provides Shem with a double introduction because of his importance for the Hebrews (Eber), significance also attested by the extension of his genealogy to six generations, while those of his brothers continue for only three. Other elements are embedded in the genealogy (cf., v. 19), usually associated with later Israelite history (i.e., Babylonians/Assyrians; Philistines; Canaanites). Scholars think the chapter consists of interwoven strands of P and J. The beginning verse establishes a connection with the end of the Adam genealogy in 5:32.

Many names in this list function eponymously, whereby the origin of a city/people/nation is explained by derivation from an individual progenitor. The names stand for peoples or nations, represented as "sons" of the group ancestor; smaller groups are represented as "grandsons" (cf., fatherland, mother country). The reader may discern this strategy most clearly in the use of the plural ending (-îm; vv. 13-14) and the use of a definite article and a suffix that specifies ethnic identification (vv. 16-18). This same feature also occurs in the genealogies of Abraham (25:1-4), Ishmael (25:12-16), and Esau (chap. 36).

The horizon of the list extends from Crete and Libya in the west to Iran in the east, from Arabia and Ethiopia in the south to Asia Minor and Armenia in the north. However, there are many problems in identifying peoples and places. The peoples seem to be listed on the basis of various factors: geographical, sociocultural, political, and commercial relationships (literary factors may also be at work; i.e., the similar names of v. 7). Issues of language, color, and race do not appear significant; e.g., the Canaanites are not listed with Shem, but the Elamites (whose language was non-Semitic) are. We do not know whether the narrator thought these peoples were actually genealogically related. Scholars dispute the historical situation that this list reflects. The most likely candidates are the end of the second millennium or a time after 600 BCE.[86] On the significance of this chapter's location, see commentary on 11:1-9.

10:2-5. Japheth represents the peoples in Asia Minor (and even farther north) and Greece, to the north and west of Palestine; it includes seven

---

86. Some names occur in Ezekiel 27; for details about the various names, see Sarna, *Genesis,* 70-80.

"sons" and "grandsons." Many are maritime peoples. The movement of the "coastland peoples" may reflect population shifts in the Aegean and Mediterranean islands around 1200 BCE.

10:6-20. Ham serves as progenitor of the peoples (thirty in all) within the Egyptian political and commercial orbit, including sections of Africa, Arabia, and Mesopotamia. The inclusion of the latter (who are Semitic) may be attributed to similar-sounding names, Cush in Africa and the Kassites, who ruled in the Mesopotamian region during 1600 to1200 BCE. Canaan may be included here because it came under Egyptian control in 1500–1200 BCE.

Verses 8-12, associated with Mesopotamia, include prose fragments about a warrior named Nimrod, who established a kingdom in Shinar (Babylonia) and Assyria (see Mic 5:5). The results of scholarly efforts to identify him with a god or a king are uncertain; legends of the heroic exploits of various figures may have resulted in a composite figure. The specific and repeated reference to Yahweh (v. 9) is unusual, but probably indicates that Nimrod's activity should be interpreted in a positive light, as are references to the deity in chap. 5 (a negative construal would see v. 9 as anticipating 11:1-9, with links to Cain as builder and to the warriors of 6:4).

The peoples mentioned in vv. 15-19 include a number who occupied Canaan, whose boundaries may be specified because of later history (though they correspond to no other boundary list); some are mentioned in the promises to the ancestors (see 15:19-21; Heth = Hittites; Jebusites; Amorites; Girgashites; Hivites).

10:21-31. The double introduction to Shem's genealogy, with the premature introduction of Eber (v. 21), signals its importance for what follows. Shem stands as the ancestor of peoples in Syria/Assyria/Iran and environs as well as part of the Arabian peninsula (twenty-six are listed in two groups of thirteen). His genealogy encloses the story of the city of Babel. This is a branched or segmentary genealogy, with all the descendants of Shem listed; 11:10-26 presents his genealogy in linear form only through his third son, Arpachshad.

The author places Eber, who is the progenitor of the Hebrews (see 11:16) as well as other tribal groups, among the descendants of Shem. The genealogy of Eber's son Peleg continues in

11:18-26 (the division of the earth in v. 25 remains unexplained, though it has been linked to the scattering in 11:1-9). Eber's other son, Joktan, had thirteen sons, also related to the Hebrews; they may be linked with various Arabian groups near Yemen and had important commercial links to Israel (e.g., Seba, v. 10).

REFLECTIONS

1. These figures are understood in political, rather than mythological, terms; they come into being by virtue of human activity, not divine initiative. Such political structures are part of the ordering work of God the Creator, which promotes good and checks evil in the life of the world. Yet, they are not structured into the created order itself, but participate in all the foibles and flaws of human leadership, hence "they can be changed and are subject to criticism."[87]

2. For the first time in these chapters Israel comes into view, though with no special virtues assigned to its ancestors; indeed, the author provides no reference to God's relationship with them. The repeated reference to "families" (vv. 5, 20, 31-32) links up with 12:3b: through the family of Abraham all the families of the earth shall be blessed. At the same time, the chapter testifies to God's work of blessing already active in the lives of these peoples (v. 9); hence, the blessing brought through Abraham continues an earlier reality.

The isolation of the family of Shem places no negative judgment on the families of Ham and Japheth (on Canaan, see commentary on 9:20-27). The writer focuses on the commonalities of the family of Shem (hence of Israel) with all other persons, not on their differences. Shem shares his humanity "before the LORD" with all others, who are given a place in the life of God's creation independent of any relationship to Israel.

3. The fact that seventy peoples are mentioned (excluding Nimrod) is probably important, but its explanation remains uncertain (see 46:27; Exod 1:5; 24:9). The number may signify that the entirety of the known world has been included (even if some were omitted, v. 5) and that all peoples share ultimate unity in spite of the differences of language, race, and color. That the geographical areas appear to overlap and interlock to some degree may testify to a genuinely international community, an integration of peoples across traditional boundaries. In spite of significant differences, we belong to one world. The table thus becomes a natural extension of the creation account. This chapter constitutes a theological witness to a common humanity shared by all.

4. The repeated phrase "before the LORD" (v. 9) probably connotes the help of Yahweh (see TNK, "by the grace of the LORD"). The narrator believed that God the Creator was involved in the lives and activities of such kings and peoples. This would not mean that Nimrod had explicit knowledge of Yahweh, but that the deity associated with his life would later be identified with Israel's God (Isa 10:5; 45:1; Acts 17:26-27 may be dependent on this chap.).

5. The multiplication of peoples across the face of the earth constitutes a fulfillment of the divine blessing and the divine command to "fill the earth" (1:28; renewed in 9:1, 7).

87. Brueggemann, *Genesis,* 93.

Genesis 11:1-9, The City of Babel

NIV

11 Now the whole world had one language and a common speech. [2]As men moved eastward,[a] they found a plain in Shinar[b] and settled there.

[3]They said to each other, "Come, let's make bricks and bake them thoroughly." They used brick instead of stone, and tar for mortar. [4]Then they said, "Come, let us build ourselves a city, with a tower that reaches to the heavens, so that we may make a name for ourselves and not be scattered over the face of the whole earth."

[5]But the LORD came down to see the city and the tower that the men were building. [6]The LORD said, "If as one people speaking the same language they have begun to do this, then nothing they plan to do will be impossible for them. [7]Come, let us go down and confuse their language so they will not understand each other."

[8]So the LORD scattered them from there over all the earth, and they stopped building the city. [9]That is why it was called Babel[c]—because there the LORD confused the language of the whole world. From there the LORD scattered them over the face of the whole earth.

[a]2 Or *from the east*; or *in the east*   [b]2 That is, Babylonia
[c]9 That is, Babylon; *Babel* sounds like the Hebrew for *confused*.

NRSV

11 Now the whole earth had one language and the same words. [2]And as they migrated from the east,[a] they came upon a plain in the land of Shinar and settled there. [3]And they said to one another, "Come, let us make bricks, and burn them thoroughly." And they had brick for stone, and bitumen for mortar. [4]Then they said, "Come, let us build ourselves a city, and a tower with its top in the heavens, and let us make a name for ourselves; otherwise we shall be scattered abroad upon the face of the whole earth." [5]The LORD came down to see the city and the tower, which mortals had built. [6]And the LORD said, "Look, they are one people, and they have all one language; and this is only the beginning of what they will do; nothing that they propose to do will now be impossible for them. [7]Come, let us go down, and confuse their language there, so that they will not understand one another's speech." [8]So the LORD scattered them abroad from there over the face of all the earth, and they left off building the city. [9]Therefore it was called Babel, because there the LORD confused[b] the language of all the earth; and from there the LORD scattered them abroad over the face of all the earth.

[a] Or *migrated eastward*   [b] Heb *balal*, meaning *to confuse*

COMMENTARY

The reader may find difficulty in fathoming the import of this final narrative of chaps 1–11. The first problem involves its relationship with chap. 10. The linguistic division of peoples has already appeared in 10:5, 20, 31, as has the spreading abroad (פרד *pārad*, 10:5, 32) or scattering (פוץ *pûṣ;* נפץ *nāpaṣ*, 9:19; 10:18; cf. 11:4, 8-9) of the nations; moreover, Babel has already been named (10:10). Source critics provide a "solution" by assigning the sections to P and J. In the text's present form, however, interpreters often view 11:1-9 as a supplement to 10:1-32 (and 9:18-19), perhaps especially the segment concerning Nimrod and Babel (10:8-12).

The two sections do not stand in chronological order; rather, the second reaches back and complements the first from another perspective. In 10:1-32 the author has associated the realities of pluralism with the natural growth of the human community after the flood. This positive word may have seemed important to state first (structural considerations may also have dictated placement). Genesis 11:1-9, however, gives these developments a negative cast in terms of human failure and divine judgment. The writer depicts the same reality from different points of view (11:1-9 does not cover all that happens in 10:1-32) by juxtaposing texts rather than interweaving them.

This same literary tactic also occurs elsewhere in chaps. 1–11 (see Overview). Genesis 2:4–4:16

relates to chap. 1 in this way (cf. also 6:1-8 with 4:17–5:32; 9:20-29 with 9:18-19; 12:1-9 with 11:10-32 breaks the pattern). In the admixture of story and genealogy, the editor places continued creational blessing in the ongoing generations alongside continuing evidence of breakdown in various relationships. These images do not occur simply as pictures in white and black; genealogies contain elements of disequilibrium (see 10:8-12) and stories exhibit acts of human goodness and divine graciousness. As we will see, Gen 11:1-9 returns to the concerns of creation in chaps. 1–2, providing an inclusio for chaps. 1–11.

No other story like this has been found in the ancient Near East, but some parallels in detail exist, such as the origin of languages, matters of building construction, and the function of towers in Mesopotamian culture. Traditional links between creation and temple building in Mesopotamia may be reflected in the structure of chaps. 1–11, though Gen 11:1-9 does not refer explicitly to a temple. In the flood story preserved by Berossus, the survivors migrate to Babylon, as in the biblical account. The journey of Abraham's family from Ur (11:31) could be understood as a part of the migration from Babel (11:9).

The author clearly intends the text to be a typical story of humankind ("whole earth"), not a reflection on a specific event. Hence, we may read the text from a variety of contexts. From an exilic perspective, the city could represent Jerusalem and the exile, a theme prominent in prophetic materials from that era (Ezek 11:16-17; 12:15; 20:34, 41; 34:5-6, 12). Less probably, the text might be viewed as a critique of royal building programs in Israel or as a negative comment on the history of the Babylonians, a judgment on the prideful stance of such nations in the world. Yet, the text offers no sign of this building project as an imperial enterprise; in fact, the discourse and motivation are remarkably democratic, reinforcing the view that the problem here is generally human, not that of any particular institution or nation.

The writer has structured this narrative symmetrically, wherein the situation of vv. 1-4 is reversed in vv. 6-9.[88] The direct speech of the people's plans in vv. 3-4 parallels that of God's plans in vv. 6-7 (note esp. the consultative "come, let us"). The divine decision to conduct a judicial

inquiry (v. 5) sits between these speeches; its central position constitutes the turning point. The bracketing verses (vv. 1-2, 8-9; note the reversal "language" and "whole [all the] earth") describe the human situation before and after the discourses of vv. 3-7, from the human (vv. 1-2) and the divine perspective (vv. 8-9). The fact that the divine and the humans do not stand in dialogue with one another constitutes one of the most ominous elements in this text (in contrast to the divine-human conversation that begins once again with Abraham). The careful structure suggests that this story should not be read as an amalgam of originally distinct narratives.

11:1-4. The story describes the "whole earth" from a communal perspective (no individuals are mentioned), which is consistent with the emphasis on families, soon to be noted (12:3). All members of this community, relatively few in number, speak the same language and have a common vocabulary. They migrate to (13:11; or in, 2:8; or from, 4:16) the east and settle in the land of Shinar (Babylonia; see 10:10). Verses 8-9 specify that this "whole earth" community moves from this one place (now called Babel), and various peoples who speak different languages (see 10:5, 20, 31) emerge across the "whole earth." Hence, the narrative describes how peoples of common origin had come to speak various languages (despite the historical unlikelihood).

The building of a city with a tower (vv. 3-5, in v. 8 only the city is mentioned, an instance of synecdoche, though the import of the tower is thereby diminished) reflects knowledge of Mesopotamian construction methods. In the absence of natural stone, people made bricks of kiln-baked clay; burning gave them greater durability. The text offers no reason to suppose that the building efforts as such are pernicious; we might in fact think of human creativity and imagination in developing such materials and projects. The author focuses on their motivations, not that they build or what they build. The precise nature of their failure remains elusive, however, resulting in various scholarly formulations.

The effort to secure a place to call home seems natural enough, not even new (see 4:17), and the builders raise no explicit theological issues. Even the tower may not be an issue, as either a fortified city tower (see Deut 1:28; 9:1; Judg 9:46-47) or

88. On literary features, see Wenham, *Genesis 1–15,* 234-35.

a temple tower (ziggurat), a stepped, mountain-shaped structure. In Babylonian culture, the latter provided for communication between earthly and heavenly realms through priestly intermediaries. The base of the tower was on earth and "its top in the heavens"— a popular description of ziggurats.[89] The ziggurat represents an *indirect* relationship between heaven and earth; in 28:10-22, a writer implicitly faults the ziggurat for the *distance* it creates between God and the world. As such, it seems insufficient to carry theories about a storming of heaven or transgressing the limits of creatureliness or usurping the place of God. There may be some gibes at Babylonian religious practice, but this seems too specific to constitute a "whole earth" problem. Besides, Babylon appears at the *end* of the story; thus it does not stand at the center of attention.

The objective of "making a name (שׁם *šēm*) for ourselves" is more problematic. This phrase may recall the renown that accrued to kings associated with major building projects in Mesopotamia and Israel or other heroic efforts (see 6:4). It may signal an autonomous attempt to secure the future by their own efforts, particularly in view of the use of *šēm* in 12:2, where God is the subject of any accrued renown (note also that the genealogy of Shem encloses the account). The name they actually receive—though not a divine judgment—becomes Babel ("confusion"), ironically testifying to the futility of their efforts. The project may also intimate a search for the kind of immortality implicit in a famous name (but not in the sense of 3:22, which implies a literal immortality). Yet, David does not come under judgment for such efforts in 2 Sam 8:13 (see 18:18); the desire for fame, even self-generated, does not seem reprehensible enough *in and of itself* to occasion the magnitude of God's response.

The key is in the motivation, "otherwise we shall be scattered abroad upon the face of the whole earth." This central human failure inheres in the straightforward moral-order talk (the punishment fits the crime); it corresponds precisely to God's judgment (vv. 8-9). Most basically, humans fear what the future might bring, evincing deep anxiety and insecurity about what lies ahead. We do not discover fear of other human beings, but

fear of not being able to keep their community intact in the face of a perceived peril of dispersion into a threatening world. Only because of this motivation do their objectives of building a city/tower and making a name for themselves become problematic. The building projects constitute a bid to secure their own future as a unified community, isolated from the rest of the world.

Hence, their action constitutes a challenge to the divine command to fill the earth (1:28, renewed in 9:1; already seen by Josephus. *Antiquities* I.iv.1), but *not* simply in a spatial sense. Their resistance to being scattered (this word occurs positively in 10:18; cf. 9:19; 10:5, 32) occasions a divine concern for the very created order of things, for only by spreading abroad can human beings fulfill their charge to be caretakers of the earth. According to 1:28 and 2:5 (cf. 2:15), the proper development of the creation depends on human activity. For the builders to concentrate their efforts narrowly on the future of the (only) human community places the future of the rest of creation in jeopardy. An isolationist view of their place in the world, centered on self-preservation, puts the rest of the creation at risk. The building project thus understeps rather than oversteps human limits, for it prevents scattering and taking up the creational command that put the creation at risk.

11:5-9. In v. 5 God "comes down" to conduct a judicial inquiry (see 18:21; their project was *not* so meager that God, ironically, had to descend to see it). God's descent (see Exod 3:8) demonstrates God's deep engagement on behalf of the creation. Heaven is that place *within* the created world where God's presence remains uncontested.[90] The relation between this descent and that of v. 7 represents the difference between inquiry and action. As in 18:21, the inquiry appears genuine, preliminary to a final decision (the NIV's "were building" recognizes that the project was incomplete, v. 8).

Verse 6 constitutes a summary of the results of the inquiry; v. 7 calls on the council to assist in taking the necessary actions. Verse 7 indicates that in v. 6 God speaks to the divine council (see 1:26; 2:18; 3:22), with whom God consults about the matter (Abraham assumes the role of the divine

89. See Sarna, *Genesis*, 82-83.

90. See Fretheim, *Suffering of God,* 37-39.

dialogically between God and the council. While Yahweh carries out the sentence (vv. 8-9; the text does not report the actual act of confusing, suggesting that the scattering is central), v. 7 indicates that this punishment stems from the divine council.

God's response focuses, not on their present project, but on other possibilities of united human endeavor (v. 6). The *unity* of peoples with isolationist concerns for self-preservation could promote any number of projects that would place the creation in jeopardy. Their sin concentrates their energies on a creation-threatening task; even the finest creative efforts can subvert God's creational intentions. Although the text does not impugn cities, it does recognize that sin and its potential for disaster accompanies human progress of whatever sort.

In response, God judges, but in the interests of the future of the creation, "the face of all the earth" (vv. 8-9). God's judgment, though creating difficulties, has a fundamentally gracious purpose. The garbling of languages and consequent scattering prevents any comparable projects that could be carried out by a self-serving, self-preserving united front; humans might engage in feats that could be even more destructive of themselves and God's creation (Job 42:2 uses similar language of God). God's gracious action places limits on human possibilities for the sake of creation (see 3:22; 6:3).

God thus counters their efforts to remain an isolated community by acting in such a way that they have no choice but to obey the command. God does this by making their languages so diffuse that they can no longer communicate, having to leave off what they are doing, move apart from one another, and establish separate linguistic communities. The confusing that leads to their scattering (confusion is the only means cited by which God does this) thus becomes a means to another end: the filling of and caring for the earth in fulfillment of the creational command. God thereby promotes diversity at the expense of any form of unity that seeks to preserve itself in isolation from the rest of the creation.

The divine action of scattering corresponds exactly to what the people sought to prevent (v. 4). The verb *bālal* ("confuse"; vv. 7, 9, see footnotes) plays on the word *Babel* (in English it would approximate "babble"). The very name they sought to make for themselves becomes a name for confusion, making them famous for their failure. (The literal meaning of *Babel*, "gate of god" [see 28:17] is given an ironic, if imaginative, etymological link.) Verse 9 functions similarly to 2:24 ("therefore") by the way the narrator steps outside of the story and summarizes what has happened.

REFLECTIONS

1. The story has a universal ("whole earth") perspective, speaking of what is true of humankind generally; yet the function of that universalism in a context where historically identifiable peoples are very much in view, and itself speaks of Babel, makes it somewhat different from the other primeval narratives. This universalistic/specific combination probably shows that 11:1-9 serves as an *illustration* of the typical developments in 10:1-32; this darker side of developments among the peoples of the world could be multiplied indefinitely. In other words, what is described here characterizes the peoples mentioned in the previous chapter.

2. One tension in the text involves an ambivalent view of unity and diversity. On the one hand, the spreading abroad correlates with God's creational intentions of filling the earth. On the other hand, such scattering constitutes God's judgment. One should distinguish between divine judgment and punishment in any conventional sense. God evaluates the situation negatively and moves to correct it.

Brueggemann notes that human unity is a complex reality in this text.[91] Ordinarily, we regard unity in the human community as desirable and in tune with God's purposes for the creation. But here, because the unity desired and promoted stands over against the divine will

---

91. Brueggemann, *Genesis*, 99.

to spread abroad throughout the world, a unity that seeks self-preservation at all costs, God must resist it and act to advance the divine will for scattering. Those who seek to save their life will lose it. The right kind of unity occurs only when the community encompasses the concerns of the entire world and encourages difference and diversity to that end. Proper unity manifests itself in an ability to live together without conflict, oppression, and having common objectives in tune with God's purposes for the world. At the same time, scattering should not result in fragmentation or divided loyalty to God. The story of the chosen one, Jacob, also conceives of a false unity that focuses on self-preservation; he also receives the call to "spread abroad" (*pāraṣ*, 28:14) throughout the world so that all the families of the earth can be blessed.

Diversity inheres in God's intention for the world, as is evident from the marvelously pluriform character of God's creation in the first place or the blessing evident in the table of nations. In tune with those creational intentions, God makes a decisive move here on behalf of diversity and difference.[92]

3. We find a contemporary parallel in the often-isolated way in which the church relates to the world. In the interests of unity and preserving its own future, the members often stay close to home and don't risk venturing forth (see Jonah). The command of Matt 28:18-20 calls for the church to scatter across the face of the earth. If the church refuses this call, God may well enter into judgment against the church and find some way of getting us beyond our own church cliques out into the world on behalf of the creation. The unity of the church is not to be found by focusing on unity, building churches and programs that present a unified front before the temptations of the world. We receive true unity finally as a gift, found in those things that are not tangible or centered on one's own self-interests. Unity will be forged most successfully in getting beyond one's own kind on behalf of the word in the world.

4. At Pentecost (Acts 2), each of the peoples present heard the gospel in their native tongue. The gift of the Spirit results in a linguistic cacophony, but all receive the gospel. This gift of a new hearing transcends language barriers, but at the same time maintains the differences that languages reflect. The testimony of Acts 2 does not then overturn the multiplicity of languages, but enables people who speak various languages to hear and understand the one gospel for all the earth. The people are then scattered over the face of the earth (Acts 8:1-4) to proclaim the gospel rather than their own concerns (Acts 2:11).

Speaking different languages probably presents more blessing than bane, more gift than problem. Linguistic diversity enriches people's understanding of the world around them and is expressed in the world's literature. Speaking and hearing, broadly conceived, become a more complex reality in everyday life, and include not simply hearing other languages, but truly hearing others in their various life situations. Difficulties in communication can often lead to difficulties in relationships, but this usually involves the failings of people who seek to communicate than the reality of differences in language as such.

92. See B. Anderson, "Unity and Diversity in God's Creation: A Study of the Babel Story," *CTM* (1978) 69-81.

Genesis 11:10-26, From Shem to Abraham

NIV	NRSV
[10]This is the account of Shem. Two years after the flood, when Shem was 100 years old, he became the father[a] of Arphaxad. *a10 Father* may mean *ancestor,* also in verses 11-25.	10These are the descendants of Shem. When Shem was one hundred years old, he became the father of Arpachshad two years after the flood; [11]and Shem lived after the birth of Arpachshad five hundred years, and had other sons and daughters.

NIV

¹¹And after he became the father of Arphaxad, Shem lived 500 years and had other sons and daughters.

¹²When Arphaxad had lived 35 years, he became the father of Shelah. ¹³And after he became the father of Shelah, Arphaxad lived 403 years and had other sons and daughters.^a

¹⁴When Shelah had lived 30 years, he became the father of Eber. ¹⁵And after he became the father of Eber, Shelah lived 403 years and had other sons and daughters.

¹⁶When Eber had lived 34 years, he became the father of Peleg. ¹⁷And after he became the father of Peleg, Eber lived 430 years and had other sons and daughters.

¹⁸When Peleg had lived 30 years, he became the father of Reu. ¹⁹And after he became the father of Reu, Peleg lived 209 years and had other sons and daughters.

²⁰When Reu had lived 32 years, he became the father of Serug. ²¹And after he became the father of Serug, Reu lived 207 years and had other sons and daughters.

²²When Serug had lived 30 years, he became the father of Nahor. ²³And after he became the father of Nahor, Serug lived 200 years and had other sons and daughters.

²⁴When Nahor had lived 29 years, he became the father of Terah. ²⁵And after he became the father of Terah, Nahor lived 119 years and had other sons and daughters.

²⁶After Terah had lived 70 years, he became the father of Abram, Nahor and Haran.

^a*12,13 Hebrew; Septuagint (see also Luke 3:35, 36 and note at Gen. 10:24) 35 years, he became the father of Cainan. ¹³And after he became the father of Cainan, Arphaxad lived 430 years and had other sons and daughters, and then he died. When Cainan had lived 130 years, he became the father of Shelah. And after he became the father of Shelah, Cainan lived 330 years and had other sons and daughters*

NRSV

12When Arpachshad had lived thirty-five years, he became the father of Shelah; ¹³and Arpachshad lived after the birth of Shelah four hundred three years, and had other sons and daughters.

14When Shelah had lived thirty years, he became the father of Eber; ¹⁵and Shelah lived after the birth of Eber four hundred three years, and had other sons and daughters.

16When Eber had lived thirty-four years, he became the father of Peleg; ¹⁷and Eber lived after the birth of Peleg four hundred thirty years, and had other sons and daughters.

18When Peleg had lived thirty years, he became the father of Reu; ¹⁹and Peleg lived after the birth of Reu two hundred nine years, and had other sons and daughters.

20When Reu had lived thirty-two years, he became the father of Serug; ²¹and Reu lived after the birth of Serug two hundred seven years, and had other sons and daughters.

22When Serug had lived thirty years, he became the father of Nahor; ²³and Serug lived after the birth of Nahor two hundred years, and had other sons and daughters.

24When Nahor had lived twenty-nine years, he became the father of Terah; ²⁵and Nahor lived after the birth of Terah one hundred nineteen years, and had other sons and daughters.

26When Terah had lived seventy years, he became the father of Abram, Nahor, and Haran.

COMMENTARY

This is the fifth of the ten genealogies in Genesis. We find a line of nine (or ten) generations, matching the line before the flood (5:1-32), except in one basic respect: The ages of the figures have been scaled down considerably, with a consequent younger child-begetting age (after Seth's 600 years, the next three live 433-464 years, the

last six 148-239 years; as with chap. 5 the versions differ regarding ages).

In linear form, the genealogy moves from Shem, one of three sons of Noah, to Terah, who also has three sons, one of whom is Abraham. A branched genealogy of Shem precedes the story of the city of Babel (10:21-31), the basic elements of which are now included in vv. 10-17 (note that Arpachshad is not Shem's oldest son, a pattern in Genesis). Some names in the genealogy are associated with names in the upper reaches of the Euphrates River valley, from which Abraham migrates and with which Isaac and Jacob continue to associate (e.g., Haran, Serug, Nahor).

REFLECTIONS

1. In a fashion similar to other genealogies, this one brings an orderly, stabilizing rhythm into the scattering images of 11:8-9. The fact that the name *Shem* has a form identical to the word for "name" (in 11:4 and 12:2) may suggest even more—namely, that this family line will be a vehicle in and through which God will magnify the human name.

2. The author does not present Abraham's family line in isolation but sets it in the midst of all the family units of the known world and, in so doing, keeps the chosen line embedded in the life of the world. These are deep roots, which Israel ought not to forget or set aside. God as Creator has been active all the way with this line leading to Abraham (note that Abraham's family is already on the way to Canaan when God's call comes in 12:1-3). God chooses Abraham, not to escape the world out of which he was hewn, but to return to it. All the contacts that Israel's ancestors have with this world in chaps. 12–50 are certainly intended to say something about the nature and scope of this task.

GENESIS 11:27–25:18

THE STORY OF ABRAHAM

OVERVIEW

Postulating a sharp division between chaps. 1–11 and 12–50, between "primeval 'history'" and "patriarchal history," has long been a staple of Genesis study. While the exact dividing point has been disputed (from 11:10 to 11:27 to 12:1), there certainly are good reasons for such a division as the narrator's eye now focuses on the progenitors of Israel. The text, which has had the world as a stage, narrows down to a small town in Mesopotamia, to a single family, to the mind and heart of a single individual—Abraham. At the same time, the world stage remains very much in view. Abraham is both deeply rooted in that earlier history and continues to be in contact with the peoples of that larger world. The narrator ties these two parts of Genesis together in ways that are rich and deep. Too sharp a distinction between these two "histories" will not serve the interpreter well (see Introduction).

We might claim that God chooses to begin with chap. 1 all over again, except that this time around Abraham steps onto a world stage out of tune with God's creational intentions. The downward spiral that began in Eden plunged the world into a cosmic catastrophe, and the post-flood world seems once again on the way into a negative future. Not much of a future seems to be in store for the family of Terah, with early death, infertility, and interrupted journeys (11:27-32).

Yet, the continuities are positive as well. God did not abandon the creation to the consequences of its own sins within that "primeval" time. The genealogies testify that life, however troubled, continues. Even more, God's covenant with Noah has given the post-flood world a sign, in the shape of a rainbow, wherein God's promise ensures its future. This shift to Abraham does not mean a new world or a new divine objective for the world. God's goal of reclaiming the world so that it reflects its original divine intention remains in place. However, we now have a clearer view about the *divine strategy* for moving toward this objective. God devises a means by which the creation will be reclaimed through Abraham's family.

We do not know why God chose Abraham rather than another person or family. But we do know that God chose him so that the human and nonhuman creation might be reclaimed and live harmoniously with the original divine intention. God's choice of Abraham constitutes an initially exclusive move for the sake of a maximally inclusive end. Election serves mission.

The Abraham cycle appears episodic in character, often with little discernible coherence. While it is less episodic than chaps. 1–11, the reader does not encounter as sustained a narrative as that of Jacob and especially Joseph. This development coincides with the characterization of the chief personalities, with Abraham least well developed (but more than Noah); Jacob and especially Joseph are more fully portrayed. Moreover, the God who directly engages the life of Abraham is depicted in more unobtrusive ways in the remainder of Genesis, especially in the story of Joseph.

Classical source criticism has identified J, E, and P materials scattered throughout the Abraham cycle (with some texts undesignated, chap. 14). With the recent demise of the Elohist, scholars have discerned J (or JE) and P as the primary sources. Whatever the identity and perspective of these sources at one level or another,[93] they have now been decisively reshaped by theological viewpoints that encompass the entire cycle. We may identify three basic perspectives:

1. A Theology of Creation. We have already identified some of the links between chaps. 1–11 and 12–50 (see Introduction). The call of Abraham does not narrow God's channel of activity

93. See Brueggemann and Wolff, *Vitality.*

417

down to a history of salvation. These texts speak to creational issues such as life and death, birth and marriage and burial, family and community, economic and political realities, human conflicts and ambiguities and joys, and divine blessings that reach into every sphere of life. These are matters characteristic of the human community as a whole, matters in and through which God works to carry forth the larger divine designs for the world, and often in ways independent of the chosen community.

More specific modes of God's activity in the world are handled well theologically only in the context of this all-pervading presence and activity of God in the created order. Without this perspective as a given, the idea of a God who works in more focused ways can be perceived only as an interruption of the created order of things, or as radically discontinuous from life in creation generally. These broader creational understandings provide the necessary context for understanding more specific and concrete ways of divine presence in the community of faith.

2. Promise. While God's promises to Abraham are decisive for the future of this community (and through it, the world), they continue the promising and saving activity in which God has been active earlier, i.e., especially in the unconditional word of *promise* to Noah and all flesh and the *salvation* of a family from the ravages of the flood. These divine actions signal a new divine commitment concerning the future of the world. This divine *promissory* relationship with the entire world grounds and generates the more particular promises to Abraham. In order for God to oversee the promise to the world, God must make particular promises. These promises now specify *how* God will relate to the larger world, which now rests secure from destruction, enfolded within the divine promise. Indeed, the God who acts with Abraham is so familiar to the narrator (and implicitly, to Abraham) that God does not even have to be (re)introduced (12:1).

Promises stand at the beginning of the narrative (12:1-3), at the climax (22:16-18), and are repeated at key junctures throughout (12:7; 13:14-17; 15:1-7, 18-21; 17:1-21; 18:10-14, 18; 24:7). They even give decisive shape to the Hagar-Ishmael texts (16:10-12; 21:13, 18). In their present form and arrangement—the rationale for which

is not always discernible—these theologically charged texts reflect the perspective of the final redactor, who thereby gives one internal hermeneutic for the interpretation of the whole (the other is faithfulness).

Interpreters regularly consider the promise of a son to be the oldest; the promises of nation, name, many descendants, and land are extensions that depend on new times and places. In other words, the traditio-historical process *enhances* the promissory element. This process of development extends the promises beyond Abraham's own lifetime (within which only the promise of a son was fulfilled) to an open future. For every new generation the promises continue to function *as promises* independently of specific fulfillments, though with sufficient experience of fulfillment to ground the community's hopes (e.g., land).

David Clines speaks about the *partial* fulfillment of the promises to Israel's ancestors.[94] This insight helps, but such an analysis places too much emphasis on fulfillment and gives insufficient attention to the way in which the promise *functions as promise*. A passage such as 12:1-3, for example, does not really announce a plot for the story of Abraham. These verses attest to the generative event, a profoundly creative moment in his life in which God speaks command and promise, and it propels a faithful Abraham and his family into a future, which takes shape most fundamentally by living with promises. What shape the future takes will depend on many things, but Abraham can be assured that, amid all that makes for trouble in his life and the world, it holds promise for goodness and well-being. And that makes a profound difference for all life.

Son. This promise, though presupposed in the promise of descendants, comes specifically only in chap. 15 and provides the focus for chaps. 16–21. Even then we do not immediately know which son it will be (Ishmael, then Isaac), and the resolution does not appear until near the end of Abraham's journey (chap. 22). Initially it appears that Ishmael will be *the* son, then Isaac comes into focus; but even Isaac does not appear as a fulfillment until God tests Abraham's fidelity.

Land. We may discern this theme in the opening chapters (12:7; 13:14-17; 15:7, 18-21; 17:8).

94. Clines, *Theme.*

God does not make this promise to a landless individual, at least initially. Abraham starts from a homeland (see chaps. 24, 29–31), becomes a sojourner and resident alien, and looks toward a new land for the future. Yet, though he knows the identity and size of the land and procures a down payment (chap. 23), he lives and dies only with the promise. But, again, living with the promise *as promise* profoundly shapes his life and thought; the promise constantly generates new possibilities for living short of fulfillment. Moreover, although God promised to give the land "forever," faithfulness is not an option for participation in the fulfillment. The promise of land functions much like this in Hebrews; those who, like Abraham, journey in faith do not finally need an enduring city (11:8-16; 13:14).

Nation, Name, Kings, Descendants. The promises of nation, name, and kings probably find an initial fulfillment in the Davidic empire. At the same time, Christians claim this language, recognizing that "Jesus the Messiah" may be linked through David to Abraham (Matt 1:1). Moreover, the language of descendants is much broader than the descendants of the "son"; it includes the descendants of Ishmael and Abraham's children by Keturah.

Even more, "descendants" has taken on a much broader spiritual meaning than the text probably knows. The legacy of Abraham includes not only both testaments, but also the Koran. Abraham became the father of the religious heritages embodied in Judaism, Islam, and Christianity. The various religious appropriations of the story of Abraham must be cognizant of not only their similarities and differences in interpreting this story, but also the possibilities that this commonality may hold for continuing conversation with one another. Christians also should recognize among themselves that the NT does not draw on the story of Abraham in a univocal way, as comparisons of Paul, James, and Hebrews show.

Blessing. The specific language of blessing appears nearly one hundred times in chaps. 12–50 and undergirds a key theme in the fulcrum text of 12:1-3 (see Reflections there). *Blessing* becomes a catchall word, encompassing all the promises noted heretofore, as well as a host of creational blessings (e.g., life and fertility). At the same time, simply to collapse the promises into blessing would fail to recognize the prior role of promise. The specific divine promises enable blessing to be brought into the sphere of redemption. Blessing is basically a creational category; all of God's creatures, to one degree or another, experience blessing apart from their knowledge of God (it rains on the just and the unjust alike). The promises bring a particular focus to God's activity in and through a chosen people, ultimately for the purpose of redemption.

The mediation of the blessing to those outside of the chosen family becomes a centerpiece in the chapters that follow.[95] To that end, these texts relate Abraham with virtually every people in Israel's sociohistorical context, from Egypt (12:10-20) to numerous Near Eastern nations, including the king of Jerusalem (chap. 14); Hagar and Ishmael (16; 21); Sodom and Gomorrah (18–19); Lot, and sons Moab and Ammon (19:30-38); Abimelech and the Philistines (20:1-18; 21:22-34). The biblical authors are interested in the way Abraham relates to these peoples and how he does or does not function as a mediator of God's special blessing to them. The relationship between Abraham and Lot may have the special purpose of relating Abraham to land issues and to the larger world scene.

3. Faithfulness. Abraham's faithfulness also functions centrally in these stories, a centrality made especially evident in the story of Isaac (26:3-5, 24). Key texts provide the center for this concern: 15:1-6; 12:1-9; 22:1-19; they appear at the beginning and end of the cycle, and in the key covenant section. The shape of the future is determined, not simply by the one who speaks the promise, but by the way the recipient responds to it. Abraham does not act as the passive recipient of a drama shaped solely by the divine will and word. What Abraham does and says has an effect on what happens in the future beyond the promise. Nonetheless, Abraham can neither preserve nor annul the promise, since God will be faithful to promises made.

None of the ancestral figures (Abraham, Sarah, Rebekah) is perfect, but familial strife proves more inimical to God's intentions than isolated actions of individuals. The text presents the story of a family, with all the flaws and foibles characteristic

95. See Brueggemann and Wolff, *Vitality,* 41-66.

of such institutions. The fact that this conflicted family still mediates God's promise and blessing to the world constitutes one of the marvels in God's way of relating to the world.

The general way God states promises (e.g., nation, blessing, descendants) highlights the human role. God leaves room for human freedom in response, so that the track from promise to fulfillment cannot be precisely determined in advance. Hence, when God promises descendants, but is not specific regarding Sarah, especially in view of her barrenness, the reader must struggle with the other possibilities. To suggest, for example, that if Abraham and Sarah had simply settled back in their married life, God would have seen that a son was born in due time remains (a) pure speculation; (b) insufficient regard for the narrative where Ishmael appears as a fulfillment; (c) a denial of a *genuine* and active role God has given to the human (e.g., God takes Abraham's counsel into account regarding Sodom and Gomorrah). What human beings do makes a difference to God, and hindsight may not reveal the value their actions actually had. In considering matters of this sort, the God portrayed in these texts does not have absolute foreknowledge of the future (see 22:12). Once again (1:26-28), God uses human beings as instruments in and through whom to carry out the divine creational intentions. God gives them responsibilities within this intention, choosing to trust humans with a significant role, while continuing to see to the promises in an attentively personal way.

The NT picks up on the Abrahamic narrative at the points of promise and faithfulness, from Romans 4 to Galatians 3–4 to Hebrews 11 (see 11:27–12:9; 15:6 esp.). Paul grounds some of his basic understandings of faith on narratives that are pre-Mosaic and pre-Sinaitic, giving Abraham a profound relationship with the faith of which he speaks.

Structure. Scholars have made numerous efforts to discover the structure of the Abrahamic narratives.[96] While a certain chiastic ordering may be discerned, we must use care not to overdraw the parallels or neglect overlapping structures. Most efforts have had difficulty incorporating 22:20–25:18 into any finely tuned chiasm. Generally, we may observe a doubling of key stories over the course of the narrative:

1. As with other major sections, genealogies enclose the story of Abraham, those of his ancestors (11:10-32) and of his descendants (25:1-18), although 22:20-24 is a complicating factor.

2. The story of the endangering of Sarah (12:10-20; 20:1-18).

3. Stories pertaining to Lot (13–14; 18:16–19:38).

4. Chapters focusing on covenant (15; 17). Most analyses find the center of the text in these covenants.

5. Stories focusing on Hagar and Ishmael (16; 21:8-21).

6. Segments focusing on the birth of Isaac (18:1-15; 21:1-7).

7. Stories relating to Abimelech (20; 21:22-34).

8. Stories providing a "test" and a journey for Abraham (11:27–12:9; 22:1-19).

9. Stories pertaining to land (13; 23).

These doublings give to the narrative an ongoing mirroring effect, inviting another look at Abraham and the development of God's purposes in and through him from different perspectives along the course of his journey.

More generally, the Abrahamic story may be structured by the parallels regularly drawn with the history of Israel. That is to say, the overall structure of Israel's history provides a grid into which the various Abrahamic stories are fit (see Introduction and each episode).

96. See Rendsburg, *Redaction,* 27-52.

GENESIS 11:27–12:9, THE CALL OF ABRAM

NIV	NRSV
27This is the account of Terah.	27Now these are the descendants of Terah. Terah was the father of Abram, Nahor, and Haran;

NIV

Terah became the father of Abram, Nahor and Haran. And Haran became the father of Lot. [28]While his father Terah was still alive, Haran died in Ur of the Chaldeans, in the land of his birth. [29]Abram and Nahor both married. The name of Abram's wife was Sarai, and the name of Nahor's wife was Milcah; she was the daughter of Haran, the father of both Milcah and Iscah. [30]Now Sarai was barren; she had no children.

[31]Terah took his son Abram, his grandson Lot son of Haran, and his daughter-in-law Sarai, the wife of his son Abram, and together they set out from Ur of the Chaldeans to go to Canaan. But when they came to Haran, they settled there.

[32]Terah lived 205 years, and he died in Haran.

12 The LORD had said to Abram, "Leave your country, your people and your father's household and go to the land I will show you.

[2]"I will make you into a great nation
  and I will bless you;
I will make your name great,
  and you will be a blessing.
[3]I will bless those who bless you,
  and whoever curses you I will curse;
and all peoples on earth
  will be blessed through you."

[4]So Abram left, as the LORD had told him; and Lot went with him. Abram was seventy-five years old when he set out from Haran. [5]He took his wife Sarai, his nephew Lot, all the possessions they had accumulated and the people they had acquired in Haran, and they set out for the land of Canaan, and they arrived there.

[6]Abram traveled through the land as far as the site of the great tree of Moreh at Shechem. At that time the Canaanites were in the land. [7]The LORD appeared to Abram and said, "To your offspring[a] I will give this land." So he built an altar there to the LORD, who had appeared to him.

[8]From there he went on toward the hills east of Bethel and pitched his tent, with Bethel on the west and Ai on the east. There he built an altar to the LORD and called on the name of the LORD. Then Abram set out and continued toward the Negev. [9]Then Abram set out and continued toward the Negev.

[a]7 Or seed

NRSV

and Haran was the father of Lot. [28]Haran died before his father Terah in the land of his birth, in Ur of the Chaldeans. [29]Abram and Nahor took wives; the name of Abram's wife was Sarai, and the name of Nahor's wife was Milcah. She was the daughter of Haran the father of Milcah and Iscah. [30]Now Sarai was barren; she had no child.

[31]Terah took his son Abram and his grandson Lot son of Haran, and his daughter-in-law Sarai, his son Abram's wife, and they went out together from Ur of the Chaldeans to go into the land of Canaan; but when they came to Haran, they settled there. [32]The days of Terah were two hundred five years; and Terah died in Haran.

12 Now the LORD said to Abram, "Go from your country and your kindred and your father's house to the land that I will show you. [2]I will make of you a great nation, and I will bless you, and make your name great, so that you will be a blessing. [3]I will bless those who bless you, and the one who curses you I will curse; and in you all the families of the earth shall be blessed."[a]

[4]So Abram went, as the LORD had told him; and Lot went with him. Abram was seventy-five years old when he departed from Haran. [5]Abram took his wife Sarai and his brother's son Lot, and all the possessions that they had gathered, and the persons whom they had acquired in Haran; and they set forth to go to the land of Canaan. When they had come to the land of Canaan, [6]Abram passed through the land to the place at Shechem, to the oak[b] of Moreh. At that time the Canaanites were in the land. [7]Then the LORD appeared to Abram, and said, "To your offspring[c] I will give this land." So he built there an altar to the LORD, who had appeared to him. [8]From there he moved on to the hill country on the east of Bethel, and pitched his tent, with Bethel on the west and Ai on the east; and there he built an altar to the LORD and invoked the name of the LORD. [9]And Abram journeyed on by stages toward the Negeb.

[a] Or by you all the families of the earth shall bless themselves
[b] Or terebinth   [c] Heb seed

COMMENTARY

Genesis 11:27, beginning with the genealogy of Abraham's father and enclosing the story with genealogies (cf. 25:1-18), provides the likely starting point for the story of Abraham. The story of Jacob (25:19) and the story of Joseph and his brothers (37:2) also begin this way. This segment is an admixture of P and J materials.

11:27-32. These genealogical, geographical, and travel notes introduce 12:1-9 and anchor Abram in the story of the nations (Genesis 1–11). Starting the story at 12:1 would give the impression that the call of Abram marks a highly disjunctive event in his life, a bolt out of the blue. But 11:27-32 makes it clear that his family had already begun a journey to Canaan from their home in "Ur of the Chaldeans" (probably the ancient center about 70 miles south of modern Baghdad; Chaldea was a less ancient name of Babylonia from neo-Babylonian times [see Jer 50:1, 8]). Such movement links the call of Abram to the Tower of Babel story and may also relate to the exiles in Babylon. Terah and his family had gotten stalled along the way, settling in Haran (in southeastern Turkey, on a tributary of the Euphrates). God's call thus spurs Abram to complete the journey once begun (in which God had been involved, 15:7), only now leaving all but his immediate family (which included Lot, who was under Abram's care because his father had died) behind in Haran. These details indicate that efforts to portray Abram's move as especially agonizing may be overdrawn; moving on was a way of life with this family (though verbal links with 22:1 suggest it was not altogether easy).

Other important elements that specifically link up with chaps. 12–50 include the infertility of Sarai (see commentary on 29:31–30:24), which becomes a central theme for the story, and Lot, whose enigmatic place in this family the author explores at key points (chaps. 13–14; 18–19). More generally, links with the family in Haran continue through the story of Abraham (22:20-24; 24) and Jacob (27:43–28:7; 29–31), as both Isaac and Jacob return to marry members of their family (Rebekah; Rachel).

Interpreters dispute whether Abram's call at age seventy-five (12:4) occurred before or after Terah's death (11:32). The NIV pluperfect in 12:1 ("had said") apparently derives from the interpretation of Acts 7:2-4 that Abram received his call in Ur rather than Haran (perhaps based on the general observations of divine leading in 15:7; Neh 9:7). But Terah takes the initiative in 11:31, and Abram leaves from Haran in 12:4-5 (*if* Abram is Terah's firstborn, 11:26, then Terah lived for sixty more years, which may not be the case).[97]

At the end of this short passage, the author reports Terah's death, his uncompleted journey to Canaan, the death of one of his sons, the barrenness of the wife of another, and an orphaned grandson (Lot). The word of God (vv. 1-3) enters into a point of great uncertainty for the future of this family.

12:1-4a. Interpreters universally consider vv. 1-3 to provide the key for the rest of Genesis, indeed the Pentateuch. They constitute a fulcrum text, thoroughly theological in focus, especially written to link chaps. 1–11 ("all the families of the earth") with the ancestral narratives, and to project forward to the later history of Israel ("a great nation"). Although Abram will never see this future, his response will shape it (see 26:4-5, 24). The promises focus on nationhood, renown, and blessing for Abram's family and others through them. The promises are somewhat general, yet the emphasis on greatness entails a level of particularity that can be discerned by others. The promises are brought into play in the following narrative again and again in various formulations, with the implied themes of descendants and land made more specific; further imperatives also play a role (17:1; see 22:1).

The command/promise structure of these verses seems most like 26:2-6*a;* it is similar to others (e.g., 46:1-5*a*) but surprisingly lacks a divine self-identification. The narrator assumes that Abram knows the one who speaks these words. Verses 1-3 serve as the narrator's summary of the "call" (cf. Isa 51:2), laying out a theological agenda in general terms, rather than an actual report thereof. The passage may be outlined as follows:

---

97. See Victor Hamilton, *The Book of Genesis 1–17,* NICOT (Grand Rapids: Eerdmans, 1990) 366-68.

(1) An imperative. God appears suddenly and without introduction, calling Abram to leave (in order of increasing level of intimacy) his country, his clan, and his home (as in 24:4), and journey to a land God will reveal to him (22:1-2), which must happen quickly given their travel plans (v. 5, as in 22:3-4). Verse 4a reports Abram's positive response to the divine directive.

(2) A series of four cohortative verbs that express emphatically the intention of the speaker, each of which provides gracious divine promises to Abraham, but whose full realization lies beyond his own lifetime (see Overview). *God* will (note the recurrent "I") make Abraham a great nation; bless him; make his name great; and bless those who bless him (and curse anyone who abuses him). God, in essence, promises a new community with a new name (unlike 11:4, given by God). The author, here, recognizes that Abram embodies later Israel (in the subsequent narratives, Abraham's life will mirror that of later Israel). How these promises are related to Sarai's infertility (11:30) sets up a key issue, though the promises at this point

do not necessarily involve Sarai in the fulfillment. Lot possibly came to mind for Abram (this is pure speculation), but so much is open-ended in what God says that the point seems to be the *absence* of calculation on Abram's part and a simple trust that God will find a way (Abram's first concern is expressed in 15:2).

The reader might conceive all the promises to encompass the promise of blessing, so that the promises of nation and name are more precise forms of that blessing. Yet, placing the "I will bless you" in second position implies that the promise of "a great nation" (גוי *gôy;* as a political entity it has later Israel in view) creates a key to what follows ; fulfillment of the other promises will follow on the heels of that fulfillment. It is *as a nation* that Israel will be blessed and given a great name or renown. One may discern royal connotations in these materials (2 Sam 7:9; Ps 72:17). This promise of future blessing, however, does not involve moving from night to day at some future date; the divine promise will already begin its work

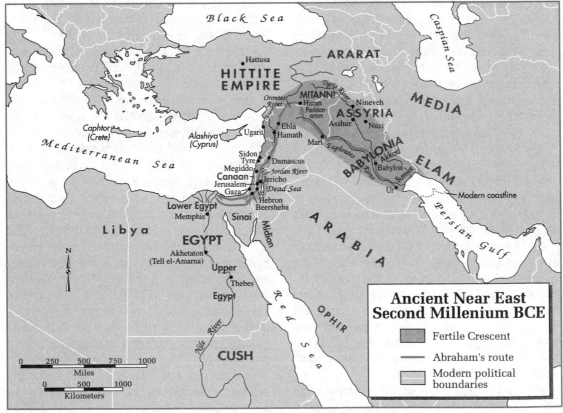

Ancient Near East Second Millenium BCE

- Fertile Crescent
- Abraham's route
- Modern political boundaries

within Abram's own life and continue on in the lives of his descendants (see Overview).

The promise of "blessing those who bless you" brings Abraham into relationship with those outside the chosen community. Those who treat Israel in life-sustaining ways will receive a response of blessing from God.

The intervening imperative could express either result or intention "so that [and] you will be a blessing," or retain its imperative sense ([you are to] be a blessing). In either case, it (a) indicates that God's fulfillment of the three previous promises will enable Israel's life to take the shape of blessing in the world; and (b) stands as preliminary to v. 3, which specifies that other peoples will experience blessing through their relationship with this family, who are to play an active role on behalf of this divine intention.

(3) The statement "the one who curses you I will curse" makes two shifts, to the singular (the one who, NRSV) and to an imperfect verb. This phrase does not offer another free-standing promise, but a note on the previous promise—namely, should any persons treat Israel with contempt they will reap the consequences of their deed (see Deut 5:9-10; 7:9-10); to put it positively, part of Israel's blessing means that they will be protected from those who mistreat them. The first word for "curse" (קלל *qālal*) has reference to any form of mistreatment; the second (ארר *'ārar*) is the opposite of blessing, reaping the consequences of such behaviors.

(4) Verse 3*b*, which presents translation difficulties, shifts to the perfect tense, and "families" serves as the subject of the verb. The NRSV has changed to the passive voice (so the NIV throughout) from the reflexive RSV (see footnote), as in the other texts where the Niphal form of the verb occurs (18:18; 28:14). With the Hithpael form, the NRSV shifts to the middle voice (the response of the other is more in play), "gain blessing for themselves" through Abram's offspring (22:18; 26:4). The RSV (NRSV footnote) translation makes Israel's role more passive; Abraham's blessing will become so commonplace that people will bless themselves by invoking his name (see 48:20). Yet, even here the blessing received by Abram extends to all the families of the earth.

This final phrase presents the objective of all the previous clauses—God's choice of Abraham will lead to blessings for *all* the families of the earth (see 10:32; note the corporate focus). God's choice of Abram serves as an initially exclusive move for the sake of a maximally inclusive end. Election serves mission (in the broadest sense of the term).

12:4b-9. These verses report Abram's silent, but actively positive, response to God's call and review his travels to and through the land he has been shown, during which he is accompanied by God, builds altars, and worships God. Thereby God's promise does not float above the life experience of the recipient; the author emphasizes Abram's faithful and worshipful response at the onset of the story. Indeed, Abraham's fidelity shapes God's promised future (see 22:16-18; 26:4-5, 24).

Sarai and Lot accompany Abram, along with slaves and possessions (all his wealth does not come from Egypt; v. 16). When Abram reaches Canaan, God appears to him to inform him that this is the land promised to his descendants. Abraham then moves through the land, from north to south, anticipating God's request in 13:17 and perhaps the eventual Israelite settlement—from Shechem to near Bethel, toward the Negeb in the south (eventually Hebron, 13:18). The reference to Canaanites (i.e., all pre-Israelite inhabitants; see 15:19-21) reflects the perspective of a later period, long after Moses. The basically positive view of Canaanites in Genesis probably reflects v. 3*b* more than later problems. At this point the future seems open-ended.

Abram's journey functions paradigmatically for the one made by Jacob/Israel in chap. 35, including attention to trees and altars. Worship is obviously an integral part of his life and gives a shape to what will come. This journey seems not to be associated with the founding of sanctuaries, but with building altars at known sacred sites (without personnel or buildings), marked by trees (commonly associated with oracles; Moreh is probably a well-known site, 35:4; Josh 24:26) or stones. The later association of these natural markers with idolatry (Deut 12:2; 16:21) does not characterize this early period. Abraham's altar building belongs to a personal and familial act of worship, probably with sacrificial acts (see 8:20; 22:13), here a vehicle for expressing gratitude to God for the promise (each is built "to the LORD," 13:18).

"Invoking the name of Yahweh" (4:26; 13:4; 26:25) refers to worship generally. These forms of early worship allow for movement, and are not tied down to priests or sanctuaries. The altar also functions as a continuing marker, perhaps a kind of public sign of God's promise of land.

Verse 7 speaks of a divine appearance to Abraham (in human form, see 16:7; cf. 17:1; 18:1; 26:2, 24; 35:9) in which the deity promises *this* land to Abraham's descendants (the corporate view of later Israel, evident in vv. 1-3, remains). God continues to give promises; as life moves along, new times and places elicit new promises. Although land is implied in the promise of nationhood (and descendants!) and in God's directive, this promise now refers to the land of Canaan. What God would *show* Abram is now *given*.

REFLECTIONS

1. Verses 1-3 link chaps. 1–11 with Israel's ancestral story. This is most evident in the relationship Abram is to have to "all the families of the earth" (cf. 10:32). This family does not come onto the world scene out of the blue; it has deep familial connections to *all* the nations of the world. This family thereby enables God's cosmic purposes and activity. The author does not even introduce the God who speaks to Abram in 12:1; we assume that this is the God who created the world and who has been engaged in the life of all peoples in the previous chapters. The call of Abram may be understood as God's response to the dilemma created by the sin and evil that had become so pervasive among all the families of the earth.

2. Blessing becomes a key theme in the narratives that follow, used eighty-eight times in Genesis, with many indirect references (see Overview). It shapes the life of this family in varying ways as well as the lives of the many outsiders they encounter. Blessing stands as a gift of God (mediated through a human or nonhuman agent) that issues in goodness and well-being in life. It involves *every* sphere of existence, from spiritual to more tangible expressions. Blessing manifests itself most evidently in fertility and the multiplication of life, from herds and flocks, to field and forest, to new human life; it embraces material well-being, peace, and general success in life's ventures (see the list in Deut 28:3-15).

Blessing belongs fundamentally to the sphere of creation. The creation narratives make clear that blessing inheres as an integral part of God's purposes for the world, human and nonhuman, both before (1:22, 28; 2:3) and after (5:2; 9:1) the entrance of sin. The emphasis on blessing in the ancestral narratives (signaled by the fivefold reference in these verses) shows that God's original intentions for the world are being mediated in and through this family. Yet, the "families of the earth" are *not* totally dependent on their relationship to the chosen for blessing; the blessings of God the creator (e.g., sun and rain) continue to flow to all independently of their relationship to Abraham's family. The genealogies of chaps. 1–11 testify amply to the presence and power of blessing within even a fallen creation. The difference remains this: Blessings will be intensified or made more abundant (30:27-30) by this contact, made even more correspondent to God's intentions for the creation.

3. While blessing appears central in Genesis, it is inadequate and incomplete without *promise.* Promise is the most basic category with which this and the following narratives work.[98] The blessing that God promises to Abram has deep levels of continuity with the blessing he has experienced in his life to this point. But his new promise is something more, something beyond what the creation in and of itself can provide. Within creation, blessing is powerful, life-enabling, and life-sustaining, but finally insufficient for the fullest possible life. *The promises bring blessing into the sphere of redemption.*

98. See White, *Narration,* 107-12, 169-73.

God speaks to Abram, but very little has been said about him; he has spoken no words and has barely acted. By calling him, God brings Abram into the new day provided by promise. The divine word of command and promise newly constitutes Abram (though, as we have seen, not a *creatio ex nihilo*). God's new commitment to the relationship with Abram that promising entails makes for a new identity for the one who now responds in trust and obedience. Abram now takes into his life the character of the promises made; *he is now one whose future looks like this.* The future is not yet, but because God has been faithful to earlier promises, Abram's very being takes on the character of that future, though not apart from his own faithful response to the word of God, which created his faith in the first place. More generally, the promise stands at the beginning of Israel's ancestral story. We may understand not only the stories that follow, but also the entire history of Israel, as constituted and shaped by God's promises.

Even more, promise as promise serves as a key here. What counts about God's promises finally is their *continuing status as promise,* which can then be appropriated by the community of faith in later generations as still applicable to them and their future (see Overview).

4. Abram's trust in the promise and his move from Haran to Canaan will certainly mean a new level of meaning and life for him. But the God who commands and promises will also change forever as well. Having made promises, and being faithful to those promises, means that God is now committed to a future with the one who has faithfully responded. The text describes not only human faithfulness, but also divine faithfulness to promises made to a specific family. God will never be the same again. By his word, God has created a new family, indeed a new world for both Abraham and God, which gives to *each* a revised job description, though the goal of a reclaimed creation remains the same.

5. This text has many children in both the OT and the NT. It works itself out in the kingship of David and the associated promises (2 Sam 7:9; Pss 47:9; 72:17). The prophets address the theme of blessing on the nations (see Isa 19:24-25; Jer 4:2), which in turn arises in the NT and grounds the inclusion of Gentiles in the community of faith (see Acts 3:25; Gal 3:8).

On another point, Heb 11:8-16 celebrates Abraham and Sarah's journey of faith, but also recognizes its unfinished character. Their pilgrimage becomes one of faith and hope in the promises, but they do not live to see their fulfillment (a theme also present in Acts 7:2-5). As such, the pilgrimage of Abram and Sarai becomes a metaphor for the Christian life, a journey that reaches out toward a promised future, but comes up short of final fulfillment within one's own lifetime. Not that there are no signs of that future along the way; indeed, God provides blessings for the journey in an amazing range of sizes and colors. But persons of faith will realize that hope never becomes obsolete, for "here we have no lasting city" (Heb 13:14); the "better country" (Heb 11:16) will remain stretched out before us until our dying day.

GENESIS 12:10-20, ABRAM AND SARAI IN EGYPT

NIV	NRSV
¹⁰Now there was a famine in the land, and Abram went down to Egypt to live there for a while because the famine was severe. ¹¹As he was about to enter Egypt, he said to his wife Sarai, "I know what a beautiful woman you are. ¹²When the Egyptians see you, they will say, 'This is his	10Now there was a famine in the land. So Abram went down to Egypt to reside there as an alien, for the famine was severe in the land. ¹¹When he was about to enter Egypt, he said to his wife Sarai, "I know well that you are a woman beautiful in appearance; ¹²and when the Egyptians

NIV

wife.' Then they will kill me but will let you live. [13]Say you are my sister, so that I will be treated well for your sake and my life will be spared because of you."

[14]When Abram came to Egypt, the Egyptians saw that she was a very beautiful woman. [15]And when Pharaoh's officials saw her, they praised her to Pharaoh, and she was taken into his palace. [16]He treated Abram well for her sake, and Abram acquired sheep and cattle, male and female donkeys, menservants and maidservants, and camels.

[17]But the LORD inflicted serious diseases on Pharaoh and his household because of Abram's wife Sarai. [18]So Pharaoh summoned Abram. "What have you done to me?" he said. "Why didn't you tell me she was your wife? [19]Why did you say, 'She is my sister,' so that I took her to be my wife? Now then, here is your wife. Take her and go!" [20]Then Pharaoh gave orders about Abram to his men, and they sent him on his way, with his wife and everything he had.

NRSV

see you, they will say, 'This is his wife'; then they will kill me, but they will let you live. [13]Say you are my sister, so that it may go well with me because of you, and that my life may be spared on your account." [14]When Abram entered Egypt the Egyptians saw that the woman was very beautiful. [15]When the officials of Pharaoh saw her, they praised her to Pharaoh. And the woman was taken into Pharaoh's house. [16]And for her sake he dealt well with Abram; and he had sheep, oxen, male donkeys, male and female slaves, female donkeys, and camels.

17But the LORD afflicted Pharaoh and his house with great plagues because of Sarai, Abram's wife. [18]So Pharaoh called Abram, and said, "What is this you have done to me? Why did you not tell me that she was your wife? [19]Why did you say, 'She is my sister,' so that I took her for my wife? Now then, here is your wife, take her, and be gone." [20]And Pharaoh gave his men orders concerning him; and they set him on the way, with his wife and all that he had.

COMMENTARY

This is a thrice-told tale. In 20:1-18 Abraham will again seek to pass Sarah off as his sister; Isaac does the same with respect to Rebekah (26:1-11). Many interpreters view this as a single story retold in somewhat disparate ways and set into the narrative at different points by later redactors (chaps. 12 and 26 are J; chap. 20 is E). Genesis 12 may be the more original, with chaps. 20 and 26 being reworkings in view of issues in different locales. Stories of this sort were common in the ancient world, however, and these may reflect such a convention.[99] These stories now serve three distinctive, but not unrelated, functions within the narrative.

In addition, the Exodus story provides a structure for the narrative (see p. 429). The text is bracketed by Abram's descent to and return from Egypt (12:10; 13:1) and by the only speaking in the narrative, between Abram and Sarai (vv. 11-13) and between Abram and Pharaoh (vv. 18-19). Historically, journeys from Canaan to Egypt at a

time of famine (usually occasioned by drought) are known from Egyptian sources.

The next two chapters follow naturally this narrative by showing an interest in problems with the land that Abram has been promised.

12:10-16. The promise of the land has just been made to Abram (12:7), and he has been moving about its various territories (cf. the journeys of Jacob in chap. 35). His worship has expressed his gratitude to God (12:8). But now this land of promise cannot support him; the repetition (chiastic) of famine language in 12:10 stresses its severity. He must move out of the land in order to survive.

The narrator has yet to put a word in Abram's mouth. His first words, spoken to Sarai, are difficult to understand (vv. 11-13). The issue is not that Abram lies; in 20:12, we are informed—probably correctly—that Sarai was his half-sister (forms of sister marriage in the Near East are not applicable). Abram does, however, ask (not demand) that Sarai speak less than the full truth, to conceal

99. On type scenes, see Alter, *Art*, 47-62.

the nature of their relationship, because the Egyptians might kill him to procure such a beautiful woman (the redaction puts her age at sixty-five!). This presupposes a situation where adultery is forbidden, but a murder might be arranged (cf. David and Bathsheba).

Abram's premonitions about Egypt are on target in some respects. Both the populace and the officials of the unnamed pharaoh do make the anticipated judgment about Sarai's beauty. They praise Sarai so much that she is taken into Pharaoh's house to become his "wife" (v. 19; cf. 16:3; 2 Sam 11:27, with possible parallels with David); the lack of any marker to distinguish the uses of "wife" in v. 19 means they have the same force. These references, as well as the time that passes (v. 16), make it likely that the marriage is consummated (to deny this seems a case of special pleading). Because of Sarai ("for her sake"), Pharaoh treats Abram well (anticipated in v. 13, but with a different scenario). Prosperity comes to Abram at the expense of Sarai; indeed, Pharaoh makes Abram a wealthy man (cf. 24:35; 16:1 implies that one slave was Hagar). His life is preserved from famine and Pharaoh, but it has cost him the loss of Sarai, and it has cost Sarai her honor and dignity.

Abram fails to anticipate the Egyptian situation in other respects: (a) Pharaoh himself enters the picture. There is no hint in this scenario that any other than Egyptians generally are in view (confirmed by the broad reference in v. 14). The problem appears cultural, certainly out in the open, and not a peculiarly royal issue. To suggest that Abram intends to entrap Pharaoh goes beyond the text. (b) An Egyptian takes her for a wife. Abram does not even suggest this as a possibility. If it had been any Egyptian but Pharaoh, he may have thought he could negotiate as Sarai's "brother" (cf. 24:55) and been able to forestall her marriage. (c) Abram expects the worst from the outsider. From the way Pharaoh responds when the ruse becomes known, it seems unlikely he would have mistreated or killed Abram, if he had told the truth from the beginning. Pharaoh's response (vv. 18-20) seems genuine, even if offered under some duress. (d) Abram underestimates the consequences of his actions. Note the disastrous effects of Sarai's presence on Pharaoh and his household. If Sarai should be

taken, one must doubt that Abram thought the moral order would function in some mechanical way and would deliver Sarai back quickly (v. 16 assumes no little time) or would gain him considerable wealth.

12:17-20. Pharaoh's action is relationally inappropriate, even though he participates unknowingly, so that it brings divine judgment in its wake (objective guilt). While we do not know the identity of the "serious" plague, diseases are probably in mind (see 2 Chr 26:20; Ps 73:5, 14). The phrase "because of Sarai" (v. 17) points in two directions, God's working within the moral order and the saving of Sarai. God's action constitutes the turning point in the story, in spite of Abram's duplicity. A comparison with the plague stories (Exod 11:1) brings out a notable contrast. While plagues are visited upon the Egyptians in both cases, the reasons differ. In Exodus, the conduct of the Egyptians elicits them. Here the behavior of God's own chosen one leads to Pharaoh's action, which engenders the plagues. Abram brings a curse rather than a blessing upon the nations (12:3). In his very first contact with outsiders, Abram fails in his response to the call of God. Even more, Pharaoh cuts the Egyptians off from this source of blessing.

Nonetheless, Abram does not reap the full negative effects of his behavior; this happens because of Sarai (v. 16) and Pharaoh (v. 20). No mechanically conceived moral order at work here! Human activity can cut into the act-consequence spiral and ameliorate its effects. We do not know how Pharaoh establishes the link between his actions toward Sarai and the plagues; yet, the immediate juxtaposition of the plagues and his interrogation shows that it involves *his own insight* (note the stress on "wife").

Pharaoh asks Abram exactly the same question that God asked Eve in the garden (3:13; similarly of Cain, 4:10). His "sending away" (שׁלח šālaḥ) Abram and his family is similar to God's banishing Adam and Eve from the garden (3:23). Not unlike them, Abram (in this only recorded meeting with Pharaoh) may have experienced shame and dread at being peppered by the (nonjudicial) questions of an angry emperor, but the narrator makes a different point. Just as Sarai had no response in vv. 11-13, so also Abram offers no response in this, the only other dialogue. Abram is reduced to silence, too! They are sent away abruptly and ignominiously, escorted to the border; yet, Pharaoh exhibits a remarkably generous spirit. While the plagues no doubt prompt this treatment of Abram, Pharaoh also acts in a way more liberally than he has to. Pharaoh not only lets Abram off the hook, but also lets him keep all the possessions he had accumulated because of the ruse (v. 20). Ironically, Pharaoh proves to be more of a behavioral model in this instance than Abram, alleviating the negative consequences that might well have befallen Abram. God's purposes are also served by Pharaoh.

REFLECTIONS

1. Many readers sympathize with Abram's equivocation; after all, he not only comes to Egypt with hat in hand, but he understands his life to be in danger as well. Faced with such a dilemma and preparing for the worst, he puts life ahead of honor, life for himself at the potential expense of Sarai's honor. That this entails the potential loss of the promised future seems unlikely, given her barrenness and her not yet being associated with the promise. At this point the promise need not be fulfilled through Sarai; his death, on the other hand, would be decisive.

Other readers have pronounced his actions cowardly and lacking in integrity (see chap. 20). At what price does he seek to assure his personal safety? A repeated focus on self fills his speech. He puts Sarai at the disposal of his personal concerns. In fact, as his sister, she seems even more likely to be taken; he may lose her altogether (see below).

The truth probably rides the cusp between these two views. Abram had few options, none of them perfect. He chooses to enter into a situation fraught with danger and ambiguity and devises a careful strategy, albeit imperfect, self-serving, and dishonoring of Sarai.

2. The parallels with Exodus are striking: (a) Abram goes down to Egypt because of famine (see 42:1-5; 43:1, 15; 47:4, 13). To "sojourn" (גור *gûr*) is also used in 20:10 and 47:4. In 26:1-3 God tells Isaac *not* to go down to Egypt and sojourn there. Is it not yet the appropriate time? (b) Egypt is both life-threatening and life-enhancing. (c) Use of a ruse (Exod 5:1-3). (d) Sarai like Moses is taken into Pharaoh's house. (e) Conflict with Pharaoh. (f) Plagues on Egypt (נגע *nāga'*; cf. Exod 11:1). (g) Enrichment/despoiling in Egypt. (h) "Take and go" (לקח *lāqaḥ;* הלך *hālak;* 12:19 and Exod 12:32). (i) Let Abram/Israel go (*šālaḥ*).

Abram's story prefigures the experience of Israel. Abram functions as the father of Israel in more than a genealogical way; Israel's story plays out Abram's story. Yet, the author portrays the Egyptians more positively here; indeed, throughout Genesis, the Egyptians appear in a positive light (see chaps. 39–50), which seems remarkable, given what is to come in Exodus. The Egyptians are not the embodiment of evil; they are not destined to a certain way of being. Other futures are available to them. Given the number of links with the Exodus story, the chosen family itself may in some respects be responsible for what the Egyptians become. In some sense Abram (and others) is to blame for the Egyptian oppression.

The chosen ones are not inevitably the bringers of blessing to others. They can so comport themselves in daily life that others will suffer, rather than be blessed. How the people of God respond to others has great potential for both good and ill. In addition, just because a given people are not believers ought not occasion suspicion or a lack of basic human trust. Benevolent behavior by those who are unchosen testifies to the continuing work of God the Creator in the lives of all people. Those who are instruments of God's redemptive activity ought to recognize these wide-ranging positive effects of God's creative work, and seek to join hands with such persons in working toward God's goals of a reclaimed creation. The most basic root of these problematic ways of relating to others, according to this text, lies in a deeply rooted centering on self.

3. We do not know why the narrator gives Sarai no voice. It could reflect the patriarchy of the time. Yet, the powerful voice given women in Genesis (e.g., Rebekah) intimates that Sarai's silence may be intentional (see 20:5). Either it is a characteristic of her relationship to Abram or she chooses to suffer silently, tacitly agreeing to risk her honor and her life for Abram's sake. In view of later initiatives she takes (16:2), the latter is more likely. It is striking that Abram has no response when Sarai is "taken" (cf. his reaction to Lot in 14:14).

Even though she remains silenced, the story unfolds around Sarai; as such, the author gives her a position of no little power and influence. It is because of her that Abram feels threatened, that things may go well with him and that his life may be spared (v. 13), that Pharaoh is "good" to him (v. 16), and that God afflicts Pharaoh (v. 17). The story refers to her thirteen times, moving from being Abram's wife to his sister to "the woman" to Pharaoh's wife and back to Abram's wife. This focus on the silent, but nonetheless powerful, role of Sarai should be allowed to have its full interpretive import. She is no minor figure and should be given a prominent role in any retelling of the story.

4. While Abram can depend on the *promise* of land (12:7), he cannot depend on the land itself. God offers a creational gift that almost immediately fails the recipient—no land of milk and honey for Abram. Does God promise Abram a fractured gift? The very gift has a certain precarious character. In this case, the land does not sustain—at least consistently—the human population so dependent on its riches. The fruitfulness of the land seems precarious; the gifts of God can become something other than what they were created to be.

5. The author intends such talk of famine to recall aspects of the creation story (1:11-12, 29-30; 3:17-18). The land (אֶרֶץ *eres*) was created to bring forth every green thing; it did so, and God saw that it was good. The land was to supply all living creatures with food. Genesis 1 claims that God does not intend famine for the creation. Genesis 3, however, claims that the creation has become at odds with that intention. More specifically, Gen 3:17-18 speaks of an inescapable link between sin and the fruitfulness of the land; human sin has negative creational effects. Ever since, the land has not produced as God originally intended; human beings may indeed suffer famine. Such was the creational situation within which God's promise to Abram occurs. God promises a land, but it falls short of paradise.

Abram committed no sin that led to this famine; this is the way things are in the land when God makes the promise. While the land is full of creational potential, presently it falls short of its promise and contributes to human suffering. So God's gift to Abram can fail, having been spoiled through what human beings have done (see Lev 26:18-20; Deut 11:13-17). The land needs healing, as it often does during Israel's history. In eschatological vision, when God's promises are fulfilled on a cosmic scale, famine will be no more (Isa 65:21; Amos 9:13-14).

6. Abram no sooner receives the promise than he has to leave it behind. Promises often work this way. The promises are real and reliable, because God has made them. But one cannot settle into what has been promised, forever secure in its reality. Promises do not result in certainty; certainty exists only in myth. Promises can only be trusted, believed in; the journey toward the fulfillment of the promise involves faith, not sight (Hebrews 11). This text describes the first of a number of such journeys into alien and dangerous territory for Israel, away from the land of promise. Israel's way of being in the land often appears this way; it will not be otherwise for many another sojourning community of faith.

7. Some have suggested that the absence of reference to God by Abram should be important in evaluating his actions; he should have appealed to or shown confidence in divine help as he faced this dilemma. This direction of thought does not prove helpful. Characters in Genesis often make decisions and pursue actions without specific reference to God, and without being judged for it. In fact, Abram's actions here meet with no little success and wealth (v. 16).

Humanly devised strategies are not in and of themselves out of order; in fact, "the narrator presents his character in a world where natural crises arise with no relation to the divine, and where the person of faith makes independent decisions in response to them."[100] It ought not to be thought that Abram's actions entail taking the divine promises into his own hands; that would be a docetic way of viewing God's way of working in the world. Moreover, the alternative could be viewed as tempting God to provide miracles (Exod 17:1-7) or an unreal divine protection plan of some sort. The narrative speaks not one word of Abram's faith in God or lack thereof; it centers on the way he handles a problem in daily life, with all of its complexities and ambiguities.

8. Given the correspondence between act and consequence, one might expect the plagues as an appropriate response (see Exod 11:1; 1 Kgs 15:5; Isa 53:4). Both act and consequence occur within the sphere of creation; an unnatural relationship leads to disease. The consequence inherently follows the deed. Yet the text does not present a deistic process; God midwifes the consequences. A contemporary restatement of such divine action should call on the fuller language of the nature of the divine involvement evident in other biblical texts: "[You] have delivered us into the hand of our iniquity" (Isa 64:7; cf. Rom 1:24-32); "I am going to bring disaster on this people,/ the fruit of their schemes" (Jer 6:19; cf. 21:14). God delivers Pharaoh into the hands of his own iniquity, the fruit of which is disease.

One might well wonder about the fairness of this effect, given both Abram's success and Pharaoh's unwitting activity. Abram has occasioned this problem, as Pharaoh discerns (v. 18). He blames Abram, not Abram's God! He puts the blame right where it belongs (and only Pharaoh does so). But the workings of the moral order do not discriminate between those who commit sins knowingly or unknowingly. This has been true generally throughout human history. People do experience great disasters in life "through no fault of their own." They also experience great benefits.

100. White, *Narration,* 179.

GENESIS 13:1-18, ABRAM AND LOT

NIV

13 So Abram went up from Egypt to the Negev, with his wife and everything he had, and Lot went with him. [2]Abram had become very wealthy in livestock and in silver and gold.

[3]From the Negev he went from place to place until he came to Bethel, to the place between Bethel and Ai where his tent had been earlier [4]and where he had first built an altar. There Abram called on the name of the LORD.

[5]Now Lot, who was moving about with Abram, also had flocks and herds and tents. [6]But the land could not support them while they stayed together, for their possessions were so great that they were not able to stay together. [7]And quarreling arose between Abram's herdsmen and the

NRSV

13 So Abram went up from Egypt, he and his wife, and all that he had, and Lot with him, into the Negeb.

[2]Now Abram was very rich in livestock, in silver, and in gold. [3]He journeyed on by stages from the Negeb as far as Bethel, to the place where his tent had been at the beginning, between Bethel and Ai, [4]to the place where he had made an altar at the first; and there Abram called on the name of the LORD. [5]Now Lot, who went with Abram, also had flocks and herds and tents, [6]so that the land could not support both of them living together; for their possessions were so great that they could not live together, [7]and there was strife between the herders of Abram's livestock

NIV

herdsmen of Lot. The Canaanites and Perizzites were also living in the land at that time.

[8]So Abram said to Lot, "Let's not have any quarreling between you and me, or between your herdsmen and mine, for we are brothers. [9]Is not the whole land before you? Let's part company. If you go to the left, I'll go to the right; if you go to the right, I'll go to the left."

[10]Lot looked up and saw that the whole plain of the Jordan was well watered, like the garden of the LORD, like the land of Egypt, toward Zoar. (This was before the LORD destroyed Sodom and Gomorrah.) [11]So Lot chose for himself the whole plain of the Jordan and set out toward the east. The two men parted company: [12]Abram lived in the land of Canaan, while Lot lived among the cities of the plain and pitched his tents near Sodom. [13]Now the men of Sodom were wicked and were sinning greatly against the LORD.

[14]The LORD said to Abram after Lot had parted from him, "Lift up your eyes from where you are and look north and south, east and west. [15]All the land that you see I will give to you and your offspring[a] forever. [16]I will make your offspring like the dust of the earth, so that if anyone could count the dust, then your offspring could be counted. [17]Go, walk through the length and breadth of the land, for I am giving it to you."

[18]So Abram moved his tents and went to live near the great trees of Mamre at Hebron, where he built an altar to the LORD.

[a]15 Or *seed*; also in verse 16

NRSV

and the herders of Lot's livestock. At that time the Canaanites and the Perizzites lived in the land.

[8]Then Abram said to Lot, "Let there be no strife between you and me, and between your herders and my herders; for we are kindred. [9]Is not the whole land before you? Separate yourself from me. If you take the left hand, then I will go to the right; or if you take the right hand, then I will go to the left." [10]Lot looked about him, and saw that the plain of the Jordan was well watered everywhere like the garden of the LORD, like the land of Egypt, in the direction of Zoar; this was before the LORD had destroyed Sodom and Gomorrah. [11]So Lot chose for himself all the plain of the Jordan, and Lot journeyed eastward; thus they separated from each other. [12]Abram settled in the land of Canaan, while Lot settled among the cities of the Plain and moved his tent as far as Sodom. [13]Now the people of Sodom were wicked, great sinners against the LORD.

[14]The LORD said to Abram, after Lot had separated from him, "Raise your eyes now, and look from the place where you are, northward and southward and eastward and westward; [15]for all the land that you see I will give to you and to your offspring[a] forever. [16]I will make your offspring like the dust of the earth; so that if one can count the dust of the earth, your offspring also can be counted. [17]Rise up, walk through the length and the breadth of the land, for I will give it to you." [18]So Abram moved his tent, and came and settled by the oaks[b] of Mamre, which are at Hebron; and there he built an altar to the LORD.

[a] Heb *seed*   [b] Or *terebinths*

COMMENTARY

Bracketed by an itinerary (vv. 1-4, 18), this text (mostly J) includes a quarrel narrative (vv. 5-13) and an oracle of promise (vv. 14-17). Verse 1 serves as a hinge verse. This report of Abram and his family leaving Egypt and settling in the land again mirrors later events. What Abram does, his descendants will do; he anticipates Israel's history in his own life. This takes its most concrete form in the promises of land and posterity in vv. 14-17.

Jacob's journey from Bethel to Hebron in chap. 35 replicates Abram's and links both patriarchs to these important centers in later Israel and Judah.

The author has included some ethnological features in the story inasmuch as Lot is the progenitor of the Moabites and the Ammonites (19:37-38), peoples often at odds with Israel (Deut 2:9-19; 23:3-4). Lot's "separation" anticipates that of Ishmael and other sons of Abraham (25:1-18) and Esau (36:6-8), and continues that evident more generally in the table of nations (10:32). This story works as an integral part of the larger story of Lot continued in chaps. 14 and 18–19, though it probably never existed apart from an Abramic context.

13:1-4. Verses 1-4 are ordered in terms of Israel's early history.[101] Abram's going up (עלה 'ālâ) from Egypt presents language used of Israel (Exod 13:18); note also the belongings, in detail (12:35-38). In both cases, *Egypt* has willingly enabled this prosperity (12:36). Abram's journeying in "stages" toward the promised land (and the tents) mirrors the exodus and wanderings (17:1; Num 10:12). Lot's being "with him" with "flocks and herds" recalls Exod 12:38. When Lot compares the Jordan valley to "the land of Egypt," the wilderness murmurings come to mind (Exod 16:3; see below), as does the strife (מריבה *mĕrîbâ*, used only for the murmurings; Exod 17:7). Israel encounters the descendants of Lot along the way (Deut 2:9-19). The references to Bethel and Ai (v. 3) and to Canaanites (v. 7; cf. 12:6), as well as the theme of strife, call to mind the early narratives in Joshua, albeit initially without violence (cf. chap. 14; cf. also vv. 14-15 and the language for the land in Deut 3:27). The repeated language concerning Abram's "beginnings" (vv. 3-4) in the land links this family to this land from the start. Neither Lot nor Sarai should be evaluated negatively in view of their absence in v. 4 (or in 12:7-8).

13:5-13. Strife arises between the families of Abram and Lot (vv. 7-8 speak of strife between groups, only potentially between the individuals) because "their possessions were so great that they could not live together" (v. 6; note the repetition). Other groups no doubt intensified such tension (v. 7; cf. 26:12-22), reference to which helps explain why the land is already too small for Abram's family.

Abram takes the initiative to settle the intrafamilial squabble. The explicit motivations are twofold: (1) They are brothers (kinsmen) and hence should not be quarreling (see Ps 133:1); (2) an interest in peace: "Let there be no strife between you and me" (v. 8). The herdsmen extend the family unit. Abram's enlightened self-interest may

101. See Wenham, *Genesis 1–15,* 300.

be a third reason. This separation would probably lead to greater prosperity, as all would have recognized. Abram makes the first move, given his seniority; it entails no evaluation of Lot (in view of 12:7, the story does not imply that Lot was Abram's heir).

Abram's resolution creates family separation (the verb occurs in vv. 9, 11, 14), with each group occupying different territories. Historically, quarreling among nomads over pastures and wells for their cattle was commonplace in that era (see chaps. 21; 26), and it was common for families to separate (see 10:5, 32). Hence, one ought not think of either Lot or Abram as especially quarrelsome, as if different temperaments would have enabled them to live together. The text does not blame either person, or even regard separation as unfortunate; it works as a responsible way of responding to crowded conditions. The criterion for evaluation should be whether the act helps to achieve peace and well-being.

Abram allows Lot to choose between two lands (given Abram's settlement in Hebron and v. 11, the axis seems to be east-west, though some think it to be north-south). This ploy appears magnanimous, but is it? Too many unresolved questions remain. Did Abram have a sense for the choice Lot might make? He may not have wanted the land that Lot was apt to choose. Or was he tired of strife and willing to take anything for the sake of peace? Did Abram know what the implications of Lot's choice might be? Does he know about Sodom, and if so, does he set up Lot to fail (v. 13)? That Lot thinks through his reasons rather than talking them through relieves Abram of some responsibility for the choice, but his motivations remain ambiguous.

Some think that Abram puts the promise in jeopardy: If Lot had chosen the other portion of land, the promise would have failed. This seems problematic for at least three reasons: (1) Given what became of Lot, his decision could hardly be "right." (2) On the basis of 12:7, Abram does not know what "this land" includes. (3) The promised land does not become co-extensive with either of these options. Verse 9 ("the whole land") and vv. 14-15 (what Abram sees includes what Lot saw, more than the "Canaan" of v. 12) show that the choices of *both* Lot and Abram were included within the land promised at this point, though Lot journeys to the eastern edge.

Lot's silence appears striking. Yet, v. 10 reports his thoughts regarding the choice Abram has put before him. What are the crucial factors in his decision? Some say that Lot was drawn by the beauty of the land and his own greed. But this explanation works too simplistically. What Lot sees occasions his choice, but so also does other knowledge he has regarding the garden of the Lord (see 2:8; Isa 51:3) and the land of Egypt.

If it were like the Garden of Eden, why would that be a bad choice? There can be no going back to Eden; but even more, v. 13 makes clear that Sodom is no Eden. Lot does not perceive accurately the reality of things. His "seeing" provides too limited a perspective (see 3:5). Regarding Egypt, the links to Exodus point the way. The issue focuses on Egypt as a garden, from which Lot has recently returned (13:1; cf. Deut 11:10). In view of Israel's wandering in the wilderness begging to return to Egyptian flesh pots, Egypt represents a desire for a pre-redemption state of affairs. Likeness to Egypt connects with the later language of "outcry" about Sodom (18:21; 19:13; cf. Exod 3:7-9); note also Abram's identification of a problem in Egypt (12:11-13), of which Lot would have been aware. The narrator's comments about Sodom (vv. 10, 13) say something about Lot's choice, rather than simply anticipating a later aspect of the story. Lot's ethical-theological perspective creates the problem. While this perspective does not determine how Lot will respond within his new locale, his behavior in chap. 19 suggests he begins to take on the character of his new environment. The reference to "eastward" may link up with Abraham's sons by Keturah (25:6) rather than with Adam, Eve, and Cain (3:24; 4:16).

13:14-18. Verses 14-15, 17 consist of a repeated promise of land, enclosing a promise of posterity (v. 16). The dust image relates to the land in which Abraham lives; it provides a traditional image for an unimaginably large number (a new emphasis from 12:1-3; see 15:5; 28:14). The promise to Abram comes as a direct, unconditional proclamation. It extends the promise that appears in 12:7, with a new word about perpetuity. Three factors contribute to its reiteration: (1) It signals another key transition in Abram's journey. The promise stands just as clearly after Abram's Egyptian

sojourn as before. This anticipates what the situation will be after the next Egyptian sojourn. Generally, the promises are repeated so often and in such variety over the course of chaps. 12–50 in order to assure readers from later generations, perhaps especially exiles, that God's promises still stand, no matter the experience.

(2) Lot's decision makes necessary greater precision regarding the extent of the promised land. The promise includes Lot's land (hence his departure?)! The decision by Lot may be a division *within* the promised land; in some sense the family of Abram remains intact within this land. The promise does not express a divine approval of Abram's treatment of Lot; his conduct toward Lot remains much too ambiguous.

(3) The author uses legal language for the transfer of property.[102] Abram lifts up his eyes, looks around, and walks through the land. These actions are probably a legal way of concretely laying claim to something (cf. Lot in vv. 10-12; Josh 1:3; 24:3). They also highlight the fact that heavenly visions are related to earthly realities— i.e., an actual piece of real estate. God thereby transfers the land to Abram; it is *actually given* to him. The text does not describe simply a promise of what will belong to Abram's descendants, but a gift now in place (the NRSV has future tense in v. 17; the NIV is closer to the mark with its "I am giving"). This may explain Abram's inclusion in the promise at this point; only his descendants were in view in 12:7.

Abram follows through on God's instructions in a somewhat oblique way as the narrator reports his journey to Hebron (cf. Jacob in chap. 35; Deut 11:24). Abram "moves his tent" (as did Lot, vv. 12, 18) and settles near a stand of trees, where he (unlike Lot) builds an altar—his third!—in the open air, not at a sanctuary. Mamre, near Hebron, is not mentioned outside of Genesis. The text attests to the importance of this area with Abraham's later purchase of land for a burial place (chap. 23).

Lot begins life in the land from essentially the same point as Abram, recipient of the blessings of God in great bounty. What will the two individuals now make of the blessings they have received?

---

102. For Near Eastern parallels, see Sarna, *Genesis,* 99-100.

REFLECTIONS

1. This text harks back to Genesis 1–11. The language of "beginning" and the declaration "Abram called on the name of the LORD" (v. 4; cf. 12:8; 4:26) recall creational texts. Note also the strife between "brothers" (cf. vv. 8, 11 with 4:8-11) and the explicit reference to the "well watered . . . garden of the LORD" (v. 10; cf. 2:6). Abram's well-being and wealth and his settlement in the promised land constitute a claim that basic *creational* intentions are being realized (see Exod 3:8).

The author uses the word *evil* (רע *ra'*, cf. 2:9) for the first time since the flood (v. 13; cf. 6:5; 8:21), and the root חטא (*ḥaṭṭā'*, "sin[ner]") for the first time since 4:7. The Sodomites are the first historical people described in this negative way and to experience the destruction (שחת *šḥt*) of the divine judgment as a result (v. 10; cf. 6:12-17; 9:11, 15). The author points to continuity with the primeval period. The language of sin/evil/destruction occurs only in these texts in the Abraham cycle. Whatever lack of trust in God that Abram or his family exhibit in these chapters, the writer never uses the language of sin and evil to describe it (see 20:9).

This positive/negative reference back to chaps. 1–11 indicates that the ancestral stories have been placed within a creational matrix and are to be interpreted through the lens provided by the opening chapters of Genesis. This means not only that God's creational activity manifests itself in the life of this family, but also that the forces that make for evil and sin hover near and threaten its future (see 4:7). Israel lives in a world in which the forces of evil are very much a reality; Lot's being drawn into that orbit of life serves as a reminder of negative possibilities for the people of God and the importance of the choices they make. At the same time, these texts look forward to a reclamation of what God has created through Abram's family.

2. The reference to Sodom and Gomorrah (v. 10) also emphasizes the drastic change in the ecology of the area within Abram's lifetime (see chap. 19). Zoar also anticipates this change (see 19:22-23, 30). In some sense the Sodom story, begun here, continues the history of the interweaving of human choices and cosmic effects sketched in Genesis 3–8. Lot's beautiful land will become an ecological disaster, which the author relates implicitly to the wickedness of Sodom (v. 13). Verse 10 (which assumes readers know the Sodom story) does not imply that Lot moves into a situation already doomed before his arrival, but suggests a link between his decision and the future of the area. What characterized humankind as a whole has intruded into the very heart of the family chosen by God to reclaim that creation. It should remind the community of faith that the choices its members make with respect to the land and economic issues have a potential ecological impact on God's blessings of the land.

3. The blessings God showers on people create problems as well as possibilities. The families of Lot and Abram have been blessed with many possessions, but the blessing provides the occasion for strife and separation. A situation of material well-being does not necessarily mean that life will go well; it raises its own set of problems. What people do with their blessings will determine whether they remain blessings or become curses. The text gives a strong premonition of what will happen to Lot's choice. At the same time, the promise to Abram includes Lot's land (vv. 14-15); thus he does not stand outside the reach of God's special blessing (see 14:14). Even more, Abram's land is also potentially within reach of a Sodom and Gomorrah experience. Israel will later be visited with judgments that are described in such terms (see chap. 19).

4. Westermann suggests that this text stands over against later Israelite ways of using war as a way of settling disputes; Abram shows a different way, achieving peace without violence. "The narrative of Abraham, who brought a dispute to peaceful solution by personal renunciation, still spoke across the era of Israel's wars; it was a pointer to another way of solving a conflict. The promise of a king of peace had a predecessor."[103] If this theological background can be assumed, then one might extend it to include an implicit critique of the Joshua parallels noted above. In any case, chap. 14 makes clear that Abraham was not a pacifist.

5. "Forever" language occurs for the first time with the land (see 17:8; 48:4), linked to a countless posterity. This language does not carry the sense of eternity, however, but indefiniteness into the future. This motif should be tied to such issues as who are the heirs of the Abrahamic promises, especially in view of Romans 4. While the gift of land remains always in place, disloyal recipients can remove themselves from the sphere of fulfillment (see 22:15-19; 26:5).

103. Westermann, *Genesis 12–36: A Commentary* (Minneapolis: Augsburg, 1985) 181.

GENESIS 14:1-24, ABRAM AND MELCHIZEDEK

NIV

14 At this time Amraphel king of Shinar,[a] Arioch king of Ellasar, Kedorlaomer king of Elam and Tidal king of Goiim [2]went to war against Bera king of Sodom, Birsha king of Gomorrah, Shinab king of Admah, Shemeber king of Zeboiim, and the king of Bela (that is, Zoar). [3]All these latter kings joined forces in the Valley of Siddim (the Salt Sea[b]). [4]For twelve years they had been subject to Kedorlaomer, but in the thirteenth year they rebelled.

[5]In the fourteenth year, Kedorlaomer and the kings allied with him went out and defeated the Rephaites in Ashteroth Karnaim, the Zuzites in Ham, the Emites in Shaveh Kiriathaim [6]and the Horites in the hill country of Seir, as far as El Paran near the desert. [7]Then they turned back and went to En Mishpat (that is, Kadesh), and they conquered the whole territory of the Amalekites, as well as the Amorites who were living in Hazazon Tamar.

[8]Then the king of Sodom, the king of Gomorrah, the king of Admah, the king of Zeboiim and the king of Bela (that is, Zoar) marched out and drew up their battle lines in the Valley of Siddim [9]against Kedorlaomer king of Elam, Tidal king of Goiim, Amraphel king of Shinar and Arioch king of Ellasar—four kings against five. [10]Now the Valley of Siddim was full of tar pits, and when the kings of Sodom and Gomorrah fled, some of

a1 That is, Babylonia; also in verse 9   b3 That is, the Dead Sea

NRSV

14 In the days of King Amraphel of Shinar, King Arioch of Ellasar, King Chedorlaomer of Elam, and King Tidal of Goiim, [2]these kings made war with King Bera of Sodom, King Birsha of Gomorrah, King Shinab of Admah, King Shemeber of Zeboiim, and the king of Bela (that is, Zoar). [3]All these joined forces in the Valley of Siddim (that is, the Dead Sea).[a] [4]Twelve years they had served Chedorlaomer, but in the thirteenth year they rebelled. [5]In the fourteenth year Chedorlaomer and the kings who were with him came and subdued the Rephaim in Ashteroth-karnaim, the Zuzim in Ham, the Emim in Shaveh-kiriathaim, [6]and the Horites in the hill country of Seir as far as El-paran on the edge of the wilderness; [7]then they turned back and came to En-mishpat (that is, Kadesh), and subdued all the country of the Amalekites, and also the Amorites who lived in Hazazon-tamar. [8]Then the king of Sodom, the king of Gomorrah, the king of Admah, the king of Zeboiim, and the king of Bela (that is, Zoar) went out, and they joined battle in the Valley of Siddim [9]with King Chedorlaomer of Elam, King Tidal of Goiim, King Amraphel of Shinar, and King Arioch of Ellasar, four kings against five. [10]Now the Valley of Siddim was full of bitumen pits; and as the kings of Sodom and Gomorrah fled, some fell into them, and the rest fled to the hill country. [11]So the enemy took all

a Heb Salt Sea

NIV

the men fell into them and the rest fled to the hills. [11]The four kings seized all the goods of Sodom and Gomorrah and all their food; then they went away. [12]They also carried off Abram's nephew Lot and his possessions, since he was living in Sodom.

[13]One who had escaped came and reported this to Abram the Hebrew. Now Abram was living near the great trees of Mamre the Amorite, a brother[a] of Eshcol and Aner, all of whom were allied with Abram. [14]When Abram heard that his relative had been taken captive, he called out the 318 trained men born in his household and went in pursuit as far as Dan. [15]During the night Abram divided his men to attack them and he routed them, pursuing them as far as Hobah, north of Damascus. [16]He recovered all the goods and brought back his relative Lot and his possessions, together with the women and the other people.

[17]After Abram returned from defeating Kedorlaomer and the kings allied with him, the king of Sodom came out to meet him in the Valley of Shaveh (that is, the King's Valley).

[18]Then Melchizedek king of Salem[b] brought out bread and wine. He was priest of God Most High, [19]and he blessed Abram, saying,

"Blessed be Abram by God Most High,
    Creator[c] of heaven and earth.
[20]And blessed be[d] God Most High,
    who delivered your enemies into your
    hand."

Then Abram gave him a tenth of everything.

[21]The king of Sodom said to Abram, "Give me the people and keep the goods for yourself."

[22]But Abram said to the king of Sodom, "I have raised my hand to the LORD, God Most High, Creator of heaven and earth, and have taken an oath [23]that I will accept nothing belonging to you, not even a thread or the thong of a sandal, so that you will never be able to say, 'I made Abram rich.' [24]I will accept nothing but what my men have eaten and the share that belongs to the men who went with me—to Aner, Eshcol and Mamre. Let them have their share."

a13 Or a relative; or an ally   b18 That is, Jerusalem
c19 Or Possessor, also in verse 22   d20 Or And praise be to

NRSV

the goods of Sodom and Gomorrah, and all their provisions, and went their way; [12]they also took Lot, the son of Abram's brother, who lived in Sodom, and his goods, and departed.

[13]Then one who had escaped came and told Abram the Hebrew, who was living by the oaks[a] of Mamre the Amorite, brother of Eshcol and of Aner; these were allies of Abram. [14]When Abram heard that his nephew had been taken captive, he led forth his trained men, born in his house, three hundred eighteen of them, and went in pursuit as far as Dan. [15]He divided his forces against them by night, he and his servants, and routed them and pursued them to Hobah, north of Damascus. [16]Then he brought back all the goods, and also brought back his nephew Lot with his goods, and the women and the people.

[17]After his return from the defeat of Chedorlaomer and the kings who were with him, the king of Sodom went out to meet him at the Valley of Shaveh (that is, the King's Valley). [18]And King Melchizedek of Salem brought out bread and wine; he was priest of God Most High.[b] [19]He blessed him and said,

"Blessed be Abram by God Most High,[b]
    maker of heaven and earth;
[20] and blessed be God Most High,[b]
    who has delivered your enemies into
        your hand!"

And Abram gave him one tenth of everything. [21]Then the king of Sodom said to Abram, "Give me the persons, but take the goods for yourself." [22]But Abram said to the king of Sodom, "I have sworn to the LORD, God Most High,[b] maker of heaven and earth, [23]that I would not take a thread or a sandal-thong or anything that is yours, so that you might not say, 'I have made Abram rich.' [24]I will take nothing but what the young men have eaten, and the share of the men who went with me—Aner, Eshcol, and Mamre. Let them take their share."

a Or terebinths   b Heb El Elyon

COMMENTARY

This chapter stands among the most difficult in the book of Genesis, evident not least in the unusual number of its unique or rare words and phrases. Scholars have not been able to identify all of these persons and places. To the extent that they are known, and may be set in the second millennium BCE, they are not simply to be taken at face value, but have some typological significance. Moreover, the portrayal of Abram as a military leader stands in some tension with the rest of the cycle (see 23:6). The historical basis of the story remains difficult to discern.[104] The chapter derives from several traditions, but the component parts are usually not associated with the pentateuchal sources (occasionally J, as part of a Lot-Abram tradition). The silence regarding Abram in vv. 1-11 has often led to their separation from vv. 12-24, set entirely within the land of Canaan. Within the latter, vv. 18-20 interrupt reference to the king of Sodom and are associated commonly with Davidic/Zion traditions. While probably originally unrelated, the three segments in the chapter have been verbally and thematically integrated into a broader story by an editor.[105]

Regarding form, vv. 12-24 may stem from an old hero story about Abram, similar to liberation stories from the period of the judges. Verses 18-20 may have been added as a midrash to link David and Jerusalem with Abram. Verses 1-11 are a report of a military campaign, though with few details; it may have been non-Israelite in origin, perhaps Babylonian. The dating (vv. 4-5) and other stylistic features accord with royal inscriptions from the ancient Near East. Dialogue comes into play only in the aftermath of the entire affair (vv. 21-24).

An editor has integrated this chapter into Abram's story for several reasons: (1) It belongs to a larger pattern wherein Abram mirrors the early history of Israel in his own life, especially the conquest of the land (see below). (2) It serves as an integral part of the larger story of Lot and Abram. (3) The kings' responses prepare us for the response of God in chap. 15. (4) It gives Israel a role in the world of nations, which attests to God as creator. While the chapter may well exalt Abram "as a great and powerful prince who encounters victoriously the united kings of the great kingdoms of the east,"[106] it also says something about Israel. God's call to Abram (12:1-3) has a purpose that spans the globe. This chapter and the table of nations (10:1-32) have many links; together they enclose chaps. 11–13, placing Israel's beginnings through Abraham within a universal context.

This redaction involves Israel's self-understanding, not least within a probable exilic provenance, when the Abrahamic tradition receives renewed attention (Isa 41:8; 51:2). While one concern may be to "awaken a glorious past which opened broader horizons to those currently humiliated,"[107] the focus should be placed on mission rather than on national self-aggrandizement.

14:1-16. Verse 1 presents names and places that are otherwise unattested (Shinar is Babylon, see 10:10; 11:2). Also, we know of no such international coalition, apparently from the Mesopotamian region. Whatever the historical basis, this coalition could be viewed as a gathering of forces that endangers Israel's future in the land.

The names of the five kings of the Pentapolis in the region of the Dead Sea (v. 2) remain unidentified. The five cities occur together only here (four appear in 10:19 and Deut 29:23); in the report of events (vv. 10-11) only Sodom and Gomorrah appear (as in chap. 19). Scholars have been unable to locate the valley of Siddim, but it must be near the Dead Sea. The author depicts Abram as a Hebrew (v. 13), probably to distinguish his people from the others mentioned.

The eastern kings (v. 1) go to war against the Pentapolis (vv. 2-3), which had rebelled after twelve years of subjugation (v. 4). On their way to putting down that rebellion (described in vv. 8-12), they conquer six peoples in the area (vv. 5-7), who may also be participating in a general rebellion against the eastern kings. The first three are original inhabitants of the land, described in legendary terms as giants (Deut 2:10-12, 20); the

104. For detail, see Sarna, *Genesis,* 101-11; Wenham, *Genesis 1–15,* 318-20.
105. See Wenham, *Genesis 1–15,* 305-7.
106. Westermann, *Genesis 12–36,* 192.
107. Ibid., 207.

next three are well-known. The land of two of these six peoples had been promised to Abram (15:18-20). The reference to Kadesh recalls a stopping place of the Israelites in the Negeb (Num 20:1), in which area the Amalekites were also subdued by the Israelites (Exod 17:8-16; Num 13:29). The reference to the Amorites seems unusual in that it refers to a city near the Dead Sea (see 2 Chr 20:2) rather than a region (Num 21:13; Deut 1:27, 44). Abram is allied with some Amorites (14:13)!

The reference to the "four kings against five" (v. 9) suggests something of the power of the four; this reference highlights Abram's later victory against those four kings (vv. 14-16). The plight of the kings of Sodom and Gomorrah, mentioned in vv. 10-11, may anticipate chaps. 18–19, as does the reference to the geology of the valley of Siddim. Also, the fleeing to the hills anticipates what happens to Lot (19:17-20, 30).

In conquering the Pentapolis, the eastern kings capture people and possessions, including Lot, and leave the area. When Abram hears this report, he takes his trained men, joins forces with other "allies," pursues the kings to the vicinity of Damascus, and brings back all that had been captured, including Lot. In effect, Abram thereby assumes control over the promised land.

Verse 14 provides the reason for Abram's entrance into this perilous situation: He acts on behalf of Lot, who remains very much a part of the family in spite of chap. 13. The story here moves from the world of nations to a single individual. Lot's fate moves Abram to act against the armies of four major nations!

The reference to the wickedness of Sodom (13:13) hangs over this story. Just as Abram would later intercede for these cities for the sake of the righteous in them (18:22-33), so also here he risks his life in ways that will benefit them. Abram centers his efforts on Lot's freedom, but in the process he liberates "great sinners." The move from Sodom and Gomorrah to just Sodom in 14:10-17 (as in 13:10, 13) shows that Lot's domicile is clearly in view.

In this military exploit Abram forms a coalition with non-Hebrews (vv. 13, 24). Living in community means cooperating with other families. These allies join Abram's trained group of 318, "born in his house" (14:14). The latter are dedicated and trained persons who serve the family of Abram. In view of this text (see also 15:2; 17:12-13, 23, 27; 24:2), Abram's household appears large, perhaps several thousand with women and children, although historically Abram's retinue was probably somewhat smaller.

14:17-24. When Abram returns from battle, the king of Sodom meets him (vv. 17, 21-24), soon joined by the king of Salem (vv. 18-20) in the King's Valley, of uncertain location but probably near Jerusalem. They respond in different ways to the liberation. Their appearance together, although probably not original, invites comparison. Yet, the king of Sodom has reaped too much negative comment from commentators; inasmuch as he appears with Melchizedek, the reader ought not adjudge his response in an isolated way.

The king of Salem, Melchizedek (vv. 18-20), also serves as a priest of God Most High (*El Elyon*). He brings Abram food and drink, blesses him in the name of God Most High, the Creator, and blesses Abram's God for delivering Abram. These verses give a theological interpretation of the previous events.

Melchizedek is a mysterious figure, mentioned elsewhere only in Ps 110:4 (a royal psalm) and Hebrews 5–7, where the author interprets him in messianic terms. His name, similar to the Canaanite king Adonizedek (Josh 10:1), probably means "my king is salvation [righteousness]." His priest/king status may mean that the Canaanite kingship was understood as a sacral/political office, an understanding not foreign among Israel's kings (see Ps 110:4).

These verses may be traced to Davidic-Solomonic apologists, when relationships with the pre-Israelite leaders of Jerusalem (i.e., Salem; see Ps 76:2) were important. They sought to anchor new forms of royal/temple practice in Abrahamic times in order to legitimize them, perhaps in view of questions raised about "new" practices associated with the Davidic regime.

The priestly name Zadok (2 Sam 8:17; 15:24-35) also derives from this root; he was a pre-Israelite Jerusalem priest associated with David. His descendants, the Zadokite priestly line, were linked with the Davidic dynasty through the centuries. Abram's encounter with Melchizedek may have been understood as legitimizing the Zadokite priesthood.

In view of these links, ancient readers may have viewed Melchizedek as a precursor of both the royal and the priestly lines in the Davidic empire. Melchizedek is a priest of El Elyon, God Most High. Elyon is probably an epithet rather than a name (it is usually translated "Most High," see the NRSV footnote). *El* occurs as the general word for "deity" throughout the ancient Near East (*Elyon* was also used outside of Israel). The two words occur together elsewhere only in Ps 78:35, but *Elyon* appears in parallel with *El* (Num 24:16; Ps 73:11), with other divine names (Pss 18:13; 46:4), and independently (Deut 32:8; Ps 82:6).

Melchizedek's bringing of bread and wine, intended to refresh Abram after his battles, also had a religious import because Melchizedek was a priest. The meal cannot be separated from the blessing by Melchizedek that follows. It is (a) a blessing on Abram by God the Creator. Melchizedek thus exercises a truly mediatorial function. An outsider blesses Abram (cf. Balaam, Num 24:1); he does not do the blessing. (b) It blesses God in direct address; this is an act of praise and thanksgiving for their deliverance from a common enemy. In both cases, the blessing increases power and renown; it bestows strength on Abram from God and fosters an increase of God's renown in the world. Praise is always a word to God and a word about God; it witnesses to God and thereby increases the divine renown in the world (see Exod 18:10, also spoken by a nonchosen one in the wake of an experience of salvation). The text sets both dimensions of blessing in Israel's later worship during the time of Abram.

The tithe Abram gives to Melchizedek refers to the spoils; Abram leaves the other 90 percent with the king of Sodom, except for what the young men take (v. 24). Abram thereby gratefully acknowledges what Melchizedek has proclaimed to him on behalf of God and implicitly recognizes the legitimacy of Melchizedek's priesthood of the same God whom Abram worships. The OT mentions the tithe elsewhere only in connection with regular worship practices; hence we may infer that it functions here as part of the larger ritual of meal and blessings.[108] In this typical exchange, the priest gives the blessing and the worshiper responds. Tithing serves as an act of worship, not a military-political settlement. This account may legitimize later worship practices by rooting them in the story of Abram (cf. Jacob's vow of a tithe in 28:22).

Verse 17 introduces the king of Sodom, but then he drops into the background after Melchizedek's arrival. The two kings have different agendas. The king of Sodom represents the cities liberated by Abram. With worship completed, he generously indicates that Abram should keep the recaptured goods, but the persons (such as Lot) are to be returned. The king focuses on the disposition of the booty (v. 21), a major portion of which was Lot's (vv. 11-12, 16). The problem of who should keep the spoils of war troubled Israel at various times (see Joshua 7), though here it is a matter of getting their own goods back.

The issue here is not simply whether Abram will take the spoils, but whether he will take Lot's goods and use them (and that of others) for gaining hegemony in Lot's land, a matter that had just been settled (13:6-12). In some sense, this discussion recapitulates chap. 13: Abram refuses an explicit opportunity to invest himself in Lot's land. Abram would thereby have become rich at Lot's expense and complicated his relation to Lot's land (e.g., he would have been obligated to the king of Sodom; cf. Gideon, who refuses to accept the offer of kingship for himself, Judg 8:22-23). Abram's refusal also gives his later intercession on behalf of Sodom a higher level of credibility. Abram refuses to go back on his agreement with Lot. His refusal depends on an oath, sworn to God Most High, the Creator, that he would not take anything, not even a thread or a shoestring (the smallest items). Abram did let his allies take their share, however.

This text, then, does not simply focus on Abram's choosing not to enrich himself, but centers on an issue of justice—his own agreement with Lot. The author presented Abram's behavior as a model for later Israelite leaders (see 1 Kings 21).

108. Ibid., 203.

REFLECTIONS

1. As with chaps. 12–13, this chapter also mirrors a subsequent period of Israel's history: the land settlement, the judges, and the Davidic empire.

The six peoples listed in 14:5-7 (from the region around the Pentapolis of 14:2, 8) are among those encountered by Israel on its journey to Canaan. For the four kings (14:1, 9)—representing the world powers known from that era—to have conquered these peoples means gaining control of routes and lands that are integral to Israel's later movement into the promised land. Abram, in conquering the kings, not only frees the peoples there, but clears that region of powerful outside forces. More basically, Abram, as military leader, embodies later Israel. In effect, Abram takes over the promised land by conquest!

We have noted the formal similarity of this story with those of the judges. In this way Abram becomes *a savior figure* for Israel. Continuities with the Gideon story are especially strong. The 300 men of Gideon (Judg 7:7) face a situation not unlike that encountered by Abram's 318 men, and they effect comparable liberation. Moreover, the link between Abram and Melchizedek anticipates later relationships between David and the Jebusites of Jerusalem (Psalm 110; 2 Sam 5:6-10); compare also David's campaign against the Amalekites (1 Samuel 30). The covenant in chap. 15 occurs now with good reason. Abram's own history also parallels that of David.

2. In Abram's military action against the four kings, a solitary individual comes into view: Lot. For Abram, the individual does not get lost amid all the movements of kings and armies. His actions could be ascribed to human foolishness, but Abram's concern for his nephew reaches beyond simple common sense or a careful calculation of possible gains and losses. Moreover, when it comes to the disposition of the booty, Abram remains true to his agreement with Lot and returns his goods.

Moreover, Abram does not pursue a strategy of rescuing only Lot from among those captured. He acts in such a way as to liberate all captives from Sodom and Gomorrah, apart from an assessment of whether they deserved it, or whether their behaviors up to this point would justify the risk. This action links up with Abram's intercession on behalf of these cities in chap. 18.

3. The author describes Abram's group almost entirely in the language of the family. The story pits family against nation. When combined with the focus on Lot, family interests take priority over those of nations and kings. For the sake of the family, it may be necessary to challenge efforts made by national forces. Peace and war are matters that affect nations because they deeply affect families. It is for the sake of the family that Abram finally makes his decisions regarding war and peace.

This text presents issues of war and peace not as matters for chosen people only; all who oppose the subjugation of others (e.g., v. 24) become involved, whether they are people of God or not. God the Creator has an impact on the lives of "outsiders" so that they work toward the peace and well-being of communities not their own. The "goodness" of the creation as stated by God in Genesis 1 manifests itself in the lives of communities outside those who have been specifically called and chosen.

4. Although v. 20 attests that God is effectively engaged in this conflict, the text offers no reference to divine intervention (or speaking). The report of the battle recalls only Abram's abilities as a military strategist and leader. Hence, the battle involves multiple (divine and human) agencies. Nonetheless, Melchizedek ascribes the victory to God. In fact, the battle is not simply a victory, but a rout. The reader receives the image of kings and armies tumbling all over themselves to get away (the same language describes the victories of these kings in vv. 5, 7!)—no doubt designed to impress the reader with the boldness and cleverness of Abram in defeating a much larger force and rescuing the kidnapped persons and their possessions. Abram, as a Gideon-like figure, comes through in larger-than-life proportions. Although Abram's talents and skills are not to be played down, God makes the victory possible.

5. El Elyon probably carries the sense of "God of gods." While Melchizedek's God language is not new to Abram—indeed he claims it as his own in the oath he swore prior to his encounter with Melchizedek (v. 22)—he also claims that *Yahweh* is the name of El Elyon. Each worships the same God; even more, Melchizedek confesses their God as both creator (v. 19) and redeemer (v. 20). But Abram *knows* that the name of this God of gods is Yahweh.

This narrative confesses God the Creator, maker of heaven and earth (קנה *qānâ;* see Exod 15:16; Deut 32:6; Ps 139:13), as the *liberator.* Earlier confessional language for the Creator, evident in both Abram's earlier oath (v. 22) and Melchizedek's blessing (v. 19), appears in doxological service for this moment of salvation. The God confessed as creator of heaven and earth (not simply of human beings) becomes central to the faith of principals from this early period, including both Abram and Melchizedek; the narrator does not introduce a later theological development. The fact that both men worship God with this language also indicates that ancient Israelites presumed some commonality in faith to exist between the progenitors of the later Israelites and Canaanites. This shared belief, too, witnesses to the work of God the Creator in both communities; even more, it is witness to the *knowledge* of God the Creator, indeed a Creator who liberates, outside of the chosen family.

6. The theme of blessing relates to its use elsewhere in Genesis. In 12:1-3, God promises blessing to Abram; Melchizedek helps to fulfill that promise, mediating the divine blessing to him. Although Abram earlier experienced God's blessing in his life, Melchizedek explicitly does what God has promised to do. Moreover, he thus recognizes Abram as the blessed one of God, even though Melchizedek stands outside that family. Consistent with 12:1-3, Abram has been a blessing to Melchizedek (and others) in and through what he has done in ridding the country of its predators. The text presents a triangular repetition of blessing, from God to Abram to Melchizedek (representing the nonchosen), and then back again from Melchizedek to Abram to God. Significant religious links are thus made between Israel and at least some elements of the Canaanite populace.

7. Why would Abram make the disposition of the booty a matter of oath to God (v. 22)? We have suggested that Lot's presence explains much here, though in the context of other factors. Some look to Abram's generosity of spirit, or a recognition that Sodom's goods were not his to do with as he would, for Sodom was not the defeated one; it would be improper for the liberator to enrich himself at the expense of the liberated. Is there a concern here for the enrichment of the "church" at the expense of its liberated members? The Sodomites had just experienced deliverance; to take away from that experience by keeping all their goods would be to intrude on the salvific experience itself. It might even appear to make the liberation conditional upon receiving the gift! How religious leaders handle the issue of "giving" may obscure the graciousness of the saving experience.

8. Hebrews 5–7 depends more heavily on Ps 110:4 than on Genesis 14. Basically the argument runs like this: Abram (hence his descendant Aaron, father of the Levitical priesthood) acknowledged the primacy of Melchizedek and his priesthood through the giving of a tithe. Hence, Jesus Christ, who belongs to the priestly order of Melchizedek, reaches back beyond Aaron's priesthood in typological (not historical) fashion. This establishes ancient, pre-Abrahamic, pre-Israelite priesthood roots for the Christly priesthood, thereby declaring its preeminence, and so Hebrews uses Melchizedek not unlike David and Solomon did.

GENESIS 15:1-21, THE COVENANT WITH ABRAM

NIV

15 After this, the word of the LORD came to Abram in a vision:

"Do not be afraid, Abram.
I am your shield,[a]
your very great reward.[b]"

[2]But Abram said, "O Sovereign LORD, what can you give me since I remain childless and the one who will inherit[c] my estate is Eliezer of Damascus?" [3]And Abram said, "You have given me no children; so a servant in my household will be my heir."

[4]Then the word of the LORD came to him: "This man will not be your heir, but a son coming from your own body will be your heir." [5]He took him outside and said, "Look up at the heavens and count the stars—if indeed you can count them." Then he said to him, "So shall your offspring be."

[6]Abram believed the LORD, and he credited it to him as righteousness.

[7]He also said to him, "I am the LORD, who brought you out of Ur of the Chaldeans to give you this land to take possession of it."

[8]But Abram said, "O Sovereign LORD, how can I know that I will gain possession of it?"

[9]So the LORD said to him, "Bring me a heifer, a goat and a ram, each three years old, along with a dove and a young pigeon."

[10]Abram brought all these to him, cut them in two and arranged the halves opposite each other; the birds, however, he did not cut in half. [11]Then birds of prey came down on the carcasses, but Abram drove them away.

[12]As the sun was setting, Abram fell into a deep sleep, and a thick and dreadful darkness came over him. [13]Then the LORD said to him, "Know for certain that your descendants will be strangers in a country not their own, and they will be enslaved and mistreated four hundred years. [14]But I will punish the nation they serve as slaves, and afterward they will come out with great possessions. [15]You, however, will go to your fathers in peace and be buried at a good old age. [16]In the

NRSV

15 After these things the word of the LORD came to Abram in a vision, "Do not be afraid, Abram, I am your shield; your reward shall be very great." [2]But Abram said, "O Lord GOD, what will you give me, for I continue childless, and the heir of my house is Eliezer of Damascus?"[a] [3]And Abram said, "You have given me no offspring, and so a slave born in my house is to be my heir." [4]But the word of the LORD came to him, "This man shall not be your heir; no one but your very own issue shall be your heir." [5]He brought him outside and said, "Look toward heaven and count the stars, if you are able to count them." Then he said to him, "So shall your descendants be." [6]And he believed the LORD; and the LORD[b] reckoned it to him as righteousness.

[7]Then he said to him, "I am the LORD who brought you from Ur of the Chaldeans, to give you this land to possess." [8]But he said, "O Lord GOD, how am I to know that I shall possess it?" [9]He said to him, "Bring me a heifer three years old, a female goat three years old, a ram three years old, a turtledove, and a young pigeon." [10]He brought him all these and cut them in two, laying each half over against the other; but he did not cut the birds in two. [11]And when birds of prey came down on the carcasses, Abram drove them away.

[12]As the sun was going down, a deep sleep fell upon Abram, and a deep and terrifying darkness descended upon him. [13]Then the LORD[b] said to Abram, "Know this for certain, that your offspring shall be aliens in a land that is not theirs, and shall be slaves there, and they shall be oppressed for four hundred years; [14]but I will bring judgment on the nation that they serve, and afterward they shall come out with great possessions. [15]As for yourself, you shall go to your ancestors in peace; you shall be buried in a good old age. [16]And they shall come back here in the fourth generation; for the iniquity of the Amorites is not yet complete."

[17]When the sun had gone down and it was dark, a smoking fire pot and a flaming torch

[a]1 Or *sovereign* [b]1 Or *shield; / your reward will be very great*
[c]2 The meaning of the Hebrew for this phrase is uncertain.

[a] Meaning of Heb uncertain [b] Heb *he*

NIV

fourth generation your descendants will come back here, for the sin of the Amorites has not yet reached its full measure."

[17]When the sun had set and darkness had fallen, a smoking firepot with a blazing torch appeared and passed between the pieces. [18]On that day the LORD made a covenant with Abram and said, "To your descendants I give this land, from the river[a] of Egypt to the great river, the Euphrates— [19]the land of the Kenites, Kenizzites, Kadmonites, [20]Hittites, Perizzites, Rephaites, [21]Amorites, Canaanites, Girgashites and Jebusites."

[a]18 Or *Wadi*

NRSV

passed between these pieces. [18]On that day the LORD made a covenant with Abram, saying, "To your descendants I give this land, from the river of Egypt to the great river, the river Euphrates, [19]the land of the Kenites, the Kenizzites, the Kadmonites, [20]the Hittites, the Perizzites, the Rephaim, [21]the Amorites, the Canaanites, the Girgashites, and the Jebusites."

COMMENTARY

From a source-critical perspective, vv. 1-6 have at times been considered the beginning of the E source, with much of vv. 7-21 assigned to J. In recent years, scholars have advanced many differing proposals regarding the history of this material, but no consensus has emerged. An ancient author may have woven a narrative around three originally independent God speeches. Links with the Davidic tradition seem particularly prominent, and suggest one stage for the material. The final redaction presents perceptible unity, centering on promise, possibly with an exilic provenance (cf. Lev 26:44-45).

This chapter differs from the usual ancestral story, being more like 18:16-33 or chaps. 1–3; therefore, it could be called a theological narrative. The reader may discern movement within the chapter in the dialogue between God and Abram (the first recorded in the Abraham story), centering on key questions Abram raises regarding offspring and land. The two narrative segments (vv. 1-6, 7-21) have similar structures: divine promise (vv. 1, 7), Abram's questioning (vv. 2-3, 8), and God's response with reassuring words and deeds (vv. 4-5, 9-21). At another level, the chapter moves from Abram's vision (vv. 1-11) to his sleep (vv. 12-21).

Some scholars identify this structure as the lament-salvation oracle pattern;[109] however, each section *begins* with a divine promise. They are

more like narratives in which a question or objection follows the promise (e.g., Judg 6:12-13). Hence, this text should be viewed more in terms of theological disputation (see 18:23-33). The text's mood may reflect exilic discussions regarding divine promises.

15:1-5. The expression "the word of the LORD came" (vv. 1, 4), so common in the prophets, occurs only here in the Pentateuch (cf. Abraham as prophet in 20:7 and the link to Davidic promises in 2 Sam 7:4). This link to prophetic texts gives to the promises a special status; this is not "just another" divine word. That the word comes in a "vision" (see 46:2) reinforces this prophetic quality. Theophanies share similar formal features: the divine self-identification, the reassuring word not to fear, and the promise (see 26:24; 46:3). The vision may continue through v. 11.

The phrase "after these things" attests a close relation to the preceding narrative (see 22:1). This word provides God's response to Abram's actions in chap. 14, confirming the judgment of Melchizedek.[110] The link between the identification of Yahweh as "shield" (מגן *māgēn*) in 15:1 and 14:20, where God Most High has "delivered" (*miggēn*) Abraham, is especially important (for God as shield in Davidic contexts, see 2 Sam 22:3, 31, 36; Ps 144:2). Abram had refused any spoils, but God now sees to Abram's "reward." God promises that Abram will receive his "spoils" from

109. Ibid., 216-17.

110. For ties between the chapters, see Sarna, *Genesis*, 112.

God (cf. v. 14; Psalm 132 for David; Isa 40:10). (The NIV has God as the reward, but no such image for God occurs elsewhere.)

The "reward" in v. 1 thus involves neither deliverance nor a promise of land or posterity (those have already been promised). In the context provided by chap. 14, God's "reward" introduces a promise of spoils—the content of which is not made clear—in recognition of Abram's faithful action on behalf of others, including the king and people of Jerusalem. The promises of offspring and land come later, not in view of what Abram has done, but in response to his questions.

God's promise prompts Abram's question in vv. 2-3 ("Lord GOD" is rarely used, and its import uncertain). In royal terms, Abram raises the question of dynasty: What good will spoils be, if I cannot pass them on to my children? (Cf. Davidic texts: 2 Sam 7:11-16; Ps 132:11-12, 17-18.) The question turns the issue from "reward" generally to an unfulfilled promise, God's promise of off-spring (12:7; 13:15-16). This impatience is repeated in v. 3, but now centered on "seed," suggesting the depth of his concern; the focus of the verb—now in a statement rather than a question—has moved to what God has *not* given rather than to what God will give. The repetition about his servant may be designed to motivate God, as if to make sure God understands the implication of nonfulfillment: Eliezer will be Abram's heir. Is the promise of offspring still in place? The text focuses not on whether there will be an heir (Eliezer of Damascus—a difficult Hebrew phrase—could be adopted), but whether the heir will be from Abram's own line, a matter of great importance in that culture. What God had promised was "seed," not simply an "heir."

God speaks to Abram's concerns, with "heir" repeated and word order designed to emphasize the point: No, Eliezer will not be your heir. Yes, one whom you will father will be your heir (see 2 Sam 7:12). Indeed, his "seed" will be as numerous as the stars in the sky. The stars are not a sign to Abram, but a rhetorical move to make a point about the promise in the face of his questions: God keeps promises (cf. Deut 1:10; 10:22 for fulfillment). The image does not center on power, but on stability and sheer numbers (note the repetition). This rhetorical shift from dust (13:16) to stars suggests stability and security

in a way that dust does not (see Jer 33:20-26 for its reference to Davidic offspring; 31:35-37).

15:6. This verse is commonly cited, not least because of its prominent use in the NT (Rom 4:3, 20-24; Gal 3:6; James 2:23).

Unlike his response to the promise of v. 1, Abram *believes* God; i.e., he trusts in the one to whom his faith clings. Abram fixes his heart on God, rests back in the arms of the promise-giver. The narrator, and not Abram, states this, perhaps to move more naturally (from within the vision) into theological reflection. Here the narrator interprets Abram's faith. This does not speak to the (need for such) faith in the narrator's own time; Abram's faith is not restricted to this later generation.

Abram's faith was "reckoned to him as right-eousness." The verb for "reckon" likely has a cultic background wherein the priest formally declares that a gift has been properly offered (Lev 7:18; 17:4).[111] In response to Abram's faith, God in effect functions as a priest, although outside of a worship setting, and *formally* declares that Abram is righteous (cf. Ps 106:31). Righteousness (צדקה *ṣĕdāqâ*) often involves doing justice to a relationship in which one stands (cf. 38:26; 18:23-26; 7:1); here it refers to what Abram *becomes* by virtue of God's declaration *in view of his faith*. (Credit language [see NIV] is less than adequate because it suggests a divine keeping of account books.)

15:7-21. The author structures this section in a way similar to vv. 1-6. It begins with a divine self-identification: "I am the LORD who brought you [יצא *yāṣāʾ*] from Ur of the Chaldeans" (v. 7; see 11:28). This language may also refer to the exodus, so that Abram's journey anticipates Israel's (see v. 14; Exod 3:7-10; 6:6-7; 20:2). God's promise here focuses on the gift of a land, a creational goal—life in a land he can call his own.

Abram requests a sign, some concrete indication that this will be so (v. 8), to which God responds positively. While the question in v. 2 focuses on *God's giving,* this question focuses on *Abram's knowing.* God clearly responds to this new issue (v. 13): *Know* for certain (with infinite absolute verb, cf. 24:14). A key point: Abram's

111. Von Rad, *Genesis,* 184-85.

knowing will come not only from what God says, but also from what God *does*.

God's response to Abram's question involves a rite, for which Abram must prepare. *God,* rather than the human being, goes through the rite and submits to its terms. While there are extra-biblical parallels to some of the details,[112] Jer 34:18-20 provides the only biblical analogy, where participants walked between divided animals and thereby invoked death upon themselves should they be unfaithful to the terms of the covenant. Not a regular sacrificial act (animals used for sacrifice are specified, but too many elements of the sacrificial ritual are missing), it is a special rite for the formalization of a solemn oath or promise, which is what "making a covenant" entails in this context (v. 18). The promise works itself out as a ritual event, involving both word and deed.

God asks Abram to become involved in the preparation of the rite. The narrative focuses not simply on what God will *say*; the *entire rite* will constitute an answer to Abram. He goes beyond the divine directive (v. 10), suggesting that he is familiar with the rite. Note that Abram brings the animals directly *to God* (v. 10), so that we should think of the messenger of God in human form. We do not know why the birds were the only animals not divided, why the animals had to be three years old, or the meaning of v. 11. It does evoke some basic themes of the rite, involving a life-and-death matter. At the least, it stresses Abram's vigilance and care in the preparation. An allegorical interpretation, where, for example, the birds of prey are foreign nations, perhaps Egypt, whom Abram drives away, seems strained in view of Jer 34:18-20.[113]

The rite (vv. 12-19) begins at sunset (v. 12) and concludes in total darkness (v. 17). The darkness in v. 5 seems at odds with v. 12, but vv. 1-11 are visionary (so v.1).

Abram falls into a deep sleep, with all dark and foreboding (see Job 4:12-16). Darkness appears integral to the rite, perhaps to shroud what God does. Such darkness symbolizes dreamlike seeing and knowing (cf. 28:10-22), which penetrates to the deepest recesses in Abram's being.

God, symbolized by the smoke and fire, actually passes through the divided animals (v. 17). God

here acts alone; this specifies the unilateral character of the promise. The deity takes on the only obligation in this covenant (royal grants in the ancient Near East are a possible parallel). God's personal involvement constitutes the unusual character of the rite. In an act of self-imprecation, God in effect puts the divine life on the line, "writing" the promise in blood! "God's swearing by his own self" refers to this promise (and 22:16; 24:7; 26:3; 50:24). The author uses this phrase because God cannot invoke a higher power regarding the penalty. In some sense Abram functions as a witness, because he is involved in the preparations. God's "swearing" also alludes to promises to David (2 Sam 3:9; Pss 89; 100:4; 132:11) and to Noah (Isa 54:9).

Verses 13-16 are a divinely spoken word about the future, for Abram personally (v. 15) and his descendants (vv. 13-14, 16). Then, in conjunction with God's passing through the divided animals (v. 17), the deity proclaims an unconditional promise of the land (vv. 18-21).

We may discern that vv. 13-16 (and not just vv. 18-21) are integral to Abram's request expressed in the language of knowing (v. 13). The upshot of this prophetic word resides in v. 16*b* (the only proper name occurs here), because it explains the long delay before the fulfillment of the promise of v. 7. The sins of the Amorites (i.e., Canaanites) will not have "yet reached [their] full measure"; it takes time for sins to have their full effects (see Exod 20:5, note the reference to the fourth generation; Lev 18:24-25). Verses 13-16 involve the nations, as does chap. 14; God judges them, whether they oppress Israel (v. 14) or are iniquitous more generally (v. 16), and thereby delivers Abram's descendants (this time with spoils) and enables them to have a home of their own.

The relationship between the 400 years of v. 13 (Acts 7:6; 430 years in Exod 12:40; cf. Gal 3:17) and the fourth generation of v. 16 remains uncertain and may reflect different traditions. The "generation" probably refers to a lifetime (more or less than 100 years, see 6:3; Ps 90:10; Isa 65:20). It could, however, refer literally to the fourth generation— namely, Jacob's sons; they come back from a kind of exile (in Haran) and begin to settle in the land (cf. the "Amorites" in 48:22), a process not completed for centuries. Since "Egypt" does not appear in v. 13, the author does not appear concerned to

---

112. See Sarna, *Genesis,* 114-15.
113. See Wenham, *Genesis 1–15,* 332.

speak about the future with precision. Hence, readers might apply the word to more than one life situation (fourth-generation language would work well for the exiles).

Abram himself will not see the land, and his descendants will do so only after considerable delay. Abram's relationship to the land remains tied to a much larger divine purpose than his own personal life. Because Abram knows that God will continue to be at work on behalf of the promise, he can die in peace after a full life and will "go to" his ancestors (see 25:8, "gathered to his people"; on Sheol, see 37:35). This personal note about a good life and death also responds to Abram's question about knowing, for in some sense it prefigures that of his descendants (and that may be why v. 15 comes before v. 16). His descent into death will be the experience of his descendants as well. Unlike him they will return to the land, but Abram will receive a kind of immortality.

The ancestral promise, yet delayed in its fulfillment, will come to pass. Verses 18-21, which recollect an earlier moment in the rite ("on that day"), return to the basic promise in greater detail and in specific association with God's commitment (v. 17). The narrative here returns to the beginning (v. 7) in its reiteration of the promise. This involves more than an inclusio; the situation at the end of this text has changed from the beginning. The promise depends decisively on the very nature of God; God has staked God's very own life on the promise.

These boundaries are important to the people of God at various times in their history (cf. Deut 11:24; Josh 1:4; Isa 27:12). They extend from the Euphrates to the "Brook of Egypt" (not the Nile, but of uncertain location). That God has promised such a land, however, does not necessarily mean that they *must* possess every territory noted or at all times. Only with Solomon does the land even approach this size, and then not totally (1 Kgs 5:1, 4; 8:65). This list of ten peoples stands unique and in contrast with most OT lists, which have five to seven names enumerated; they all lived within a territory smaller than that envisaged in v. 18.

We do not hear Abram's response to God's unilateral promise. This may be because of the way God enables Abram's knowing. The event functions at levels of consciousness deeper than in vv. 1-6. Yet, the point of this rite lies elsewhere. God's response to Abram more than matches Abram's faith in God (v. 6). God, in swearing by the divine self, does justice to the relationship with Abram and thereby shows forth the divine righteousness. Abram trusts, and God can be trusted. Abram's faith is matched by God's faithfulness.

REFLECTIONS

1. If our analysis of Genesis 12–14 is correct, wherein the later history of Israel from the descent into Egypt to the kingship of David is prefigured in Abram's own life, then Genesis 15 caps that story off in its talk about covenant. The covenant with Abram prefigures the covenant with David. The latter exists in fundamental continuity with God's commitments to Abraham; in the Davidic kingship, God's promises to Abram find a renewed realization.

The covenant in these chapters parallels that of David. God chooses Abram (12:1-3); God chooses David (1 Samuel 16). God saves Abram from Egypt (12:10-20); God saves David from his enemies (2 Sam 5:24-25; 7:1). Abram worships God (12:7-8; 13:18); David worships as well (2 Sam 6:15-17). God establishes the covenant with both (15:18; 2 Samuel 7). We may discern a consistent order: election, deliverance, faith/worship, covenant. God's choosing and saving actions constitute the foundation of the covenant; God establishes the covenant with those who have faith, evidenced not least in worship. The covenant does not establish the relationship; it becomes a moment where God's promises spoken to faithful ones carries an obligation for God.

Moreover, God's "bringing out" Abram from one land to another (v. 7) prefigures more than exodus and land settlement. The prophets use similar language to speak of a new bringing out of Israel by God (Jer 16:14-15; 23:7-8; Ezek 34:13). Abram prefigures the return of the exiles from that same far country to the land promised them. The specification of boundaries in vv. 18-21 proclaims that God's promises concerning this expanse of land are still in place (cf. Lev 26:44-45).

2. Regarding Abram's "reward," God expresses concern about the faithfulness of human beings, since they affect the future of God's intentions for the world. What people do counts for God as well as for the world. Hence, reward ought not to be thought of in simplistic terms, a "stars in my crown" mentality. The matter remains interrelational, not unlike the role that recognitions play among human beings. God, too, recognizes the contributions people make toward realizing God's plans for the world.

3. Abram believes in God without having any concrete evidence that God's promise will come to pass (Heb 11:1, 8-12). Abram's faith (v. 6) has been enabled by what God has done in the previous verses. God's word makes Abram's faith possible, indeed creates faith; faith arises not from within him or by his own resources. Rather, God particularizes the promise for Abram by *addressing the specific situation* opened up by Abram's question. Abram has expressed some very particular needs concerning the future of his family, and God responds directly to those questions. Not just any word from God will do; the promise of v. 1 did not issue in v. 6. God put the promise in relation to the need, and in a particular rhetorical fashion.

This way of speaking of Abram's faith may be related to the context in which the passage was written. It could be the exile or any time of great difficulty for the Israelites' faith. How can anyone believe the promises of God in such a time? Nothing in the present situation provides a reason to believe. The task for the proclaimer of promises is to link the promise to actual life situations using the most penetrating rhetorical images possible. One may so speak the promises that the hearer will come to believe that nothing is so difficult in the present circumstance as to prevent God from seeing them through to completion.

4. Upon reading v. 8, one may well ask, What has happened to Abram's faith, so amply evident in 15:6? Should such faith be seeking signs? Evidently, believing and seeking signs do not necessarily stand over against each other (see Exod 3:11-12). It is not unnatural to faith, or unbecoming to the believer, that questions persist in the midst of belief. Indeed, if the just-declared statement of righteousness indicates that the God-Abram relationship exists in good order, then his question is appropriate.

5. In this context, covenant means a promise under oath, solemnly sworn, not an agreement or contract, and the making ("cutting") has reference to the rite with cut animals. God unilaterally declares and swears to it at his own initiative. The promise grants the land with specific boundaries to Abram's descendants. Not a future gift, it is now theirs (they are in a land that is "not theirs," v. 13). God makes the covenant with one who has faith.

God will never nullify this promise. It is *by* Yahweh, as God assumes obligation (and hence not strictly "legal"). Yet, the covenant has been made *with* Abram, a person whose faith has just been acclaimed, though not in a contractual sense. The relational element cannot be divorced from the content of covenant. Making and keeping promises to Abram entails a relationship of consequence, an ongoing attending to the promise as it relates to the lives of Abram and his descendants. Yet, while the promise is everlasting, God does not guarantee that every person or generation will participate in its fulfillment. The promise always remains available for believers to cling to, knowing that God remains available to fulfill it, but a rebellious generation may not live to see it. Faith does not function as a condition for the giving of the promise, but one can, by unbelief, leave the sphere of the promise. "Unconditional" promises do not make faithfulness irrelevant (see chaps. 17; 22; 26:5).

6. When compared to 12:7 and 13:14-17, the divine oath constitutes the new reality in this reiteration of the promise. God enters into that promise at a depth not heretofore evident, at least from Abram's perspective. This kind of divine involvement responds to Abram's question! Abram thereby moves God to take steps to assure Abram of the irrevocable nature of the promises. Abram should now "know" how deeply God has entered into this commitment.

7. Some commentators have had difficulty conceiving of God as a participant in an oath of self-imprecation; one's view of God does affect one's reading. However, that God would swear that the animal's fate would apply to God should the promises be broken is the most natural, and the more difficult, reading of the rite. This should give the reader pause before backing away from it. God commits to the promise at such a depth that God considers an experience of suffering and even death. This reveals the depth of the divine faithfulness to Abram and the divine willingness to become vulnerable for the sake of the promise. This text should be associated with other passages about divine suffering (e.g., Hos 11:8).[114] These levels of divine vulnerability resonate in the minds of Christians because of a comparable move that God makes in the incarnation and at the cross. In that event, God actually does enter into suffering and death on behalf of the promises. In Jesus Christ, those possibilities are not only a potential divine move, but they become actual as well, and all for the sake of the promises.

8. In v. 16, the descendants of Abram will receive the land, not because of their own qualities of being or life, but because the sins of its present inhabitants will reach such proportions that they will be engulfed in their effects (see Deut 9:4-5; Lev 18:24-28; 1 Kgs 21:26). The relationship between sin and judgment means that sins do not necessarily have immediate deleterious effects. The judgment of God may work in an accumulative way, as a buildup of forces, and not as the result of a forensic divine act. Particularly in thinking about communities, it may take time for the effects to build up and overwhelm its perpetrators. The story of Sodom and Gomorrah may be considered the beginning of the fulfillment of this word, and the prophets did not hesitate to apply the very same principle to Israel itself. It invites reflection by the reader on the various communal contexts to which one belongs; how close might we be to experiencing the "completion" of our iniquities?

The text remains open regarding some details of these matters, given the virtual absence of proper names and the ambiguity regarding timing. If so, the "plan of God" language for this text can be used only in a general way as well.[115] There is no effort to lay out the future with precision. As such, it opens up the text to generations of the people of God other than those of Abram. The text allows us to speak of comparable ways in which the people of God will experience life in the world, often as exiles and sojourners, oppressed and under just judgment. It also speaks to the way in which God will be involved in their lives, judging oppression and iniquity, delivering the people of God, and giving them a home in which to dwell.

9. God makes clear to Abram that there will be a delay in the fulfillment of the promise; 400 years is a long time. The story of God's people during those centuries attests that God's promises will move through dark and complex times. The people of God often want immediate fixes, instant gratification; this text might help teach the faithful to live with delay.

10. This chapter, particularly v. 6, is central to the apostle Paul (Romans 4; Galatians 3). For Paul, faith does not earn or merit righteousness. God's gracious action preceded anything that Abram is or does, and the word announcing that gracious action creates Abram's faith; at the same time, God's word can be resisted. Abraham becomes the father of all who have faith (see Eph 2:8-9). God observes Abraham's faith and declares Abraham to be righteous.

The Epistle of James uses this material for somewhat different reasons (2:18-24); he focuses not on faith but on response in life on the part of one who has faith. Faith should issue in a shape for life that corresponds to what God wills for the world. James draws on a common

114. See Fretheim, *Suffering of God.*
115. See Westermann, *Genesis 12–36,* 227.

understanding of righteousness: to do justice to the relationship in which one stands. Abraham's works do justice to the relationship and thereby witness to his righteousness.

GENESIS 16:1-16, HAGAR AND SARAI

NIV

16 Now Sarai, Abram's wife, had borne him no children. But she had an Egyptian maidservant named Hagar; ²so she said to Abram, "The LORD has kept me from having children. Go, sleep with my maidservant; perhaps I can build a family through her."

Abram agreed to what Sarai said. ³So after Abram had been living in Canaan ten years, Sarai his wife took her Egyptian maidservant Hagar and gave her to her husband to be his wife. ⁴He slept with Hagar, and she conceived.

When she knew she was pregnant, she began to despise her mistress. ⁵Then Sarai said to Abram, "You are responsible for the wrong I am suffering. I put my servant in your arms, and now that she knows she is pregnant, she despises me. May the LORD judge between you and me."

⁶"Your servant is in your hands," Abram said. "Do with her whatever you think best." Then Sarai mistreated Hagar; so she fled from her.

⁷The angel of the LORD found Hagar near a spring in the desert; it was the spring that is beside the road to Shur. ⁸And he said, "Hagar, servant of Sarai, where have you come from, and where are you going?"

"I'm running away from my mistress Sarai," she answered.

⁹Then the angel of the LORD told her, "Go back to your mistress and submit to her." ¹⁰The angel added, "I will so increase your descendants that they will be too numerous to count."

¹¹The angel of the LORD also said to her:

"You are now with child
  and you will have a son.
You shall name him Ishmael,ᵃ
  for the LORD has heard of your misery.
¹²He will be a wild donkey of a man;
  his hand will be against everyone
  and everyone's hand against him,

ᵃ11 Ishmael means God hears.

NRSV

16 Now Sarai, Abram's wife, bore him no children. She had an Egyptian slave-girl whose name was Hagar, ²and Sarai said to Abram, "You see that the LORD has prevented me from bearing children; go in to my slave-girl; it may be that I shall obtain children by her." And Abram listened to the voice of Sarai. ³So, after Abram had lived ten years in the land of Canaan, Sarai, Abram's wife, took Hagar the Egyptian, her slave-girl, and gave her to her husband Abram as a wife. ⁴He went in to Hagar, and she conceived; and when she saw that she had conceived, she looked with contempt on her mistress. ⁵Then Sarai said to Abram, "May the wrong done to me be on you! I gave my slave-girl to your embrace, and when she saw that she had conceived, she looked on me with contempt. May the LORD judge between you and me!" ⁶But Abram said to Sarai, "Your slave-girl is in your power; do to her as you please." Then Sarai dealt harshly with her, and she ran away from her.

⁷The angel of the LORD found her by a spring of water in the wilderness, the spring on the way to Shur. ⁸And he said, "Hagar, slave-girl of Sarai, where have you come from and where are you going?" She said, "I am running away from my mistress Sarai." ⁹The angel of the LORD said to her, "Return to your mistress, and submit to her." ¹⁰The angel of the LORD also said to her, "I will so greatly multiply your offspring that they cannot be counted for multitude." ¹¹And the angel of the LORD said to her,

"Now you have conceived and shall bear a
    son;
  you shall call him Ishmael,ᵃ
  for the LORD has given heed to your
    affliction.
¹² He shall be a wild ass of a man,
  with his hand against everyone,

ᵃ That is God hears

NIV

and he will live in hostility
toward[a] all his brothers."

[13]She gave this name to the LORD who spoke to her: "You are the God who sees me," for she said, "I have now seen[b] the One who sees me." [14]That is why the well was called Beer Lahai Roi[c]; it is still there, between Kadesh and Bered.

[15]So Hagar bore Abram a son, and Abram gave the name Ishmael to the son she had borne. [16]Abram was eighty-six years old when Hagar bore him Ishmael.

[a]12 Or *live to the east / of* [b]13 Or *seen the back of*
[c]14 *Beer Lahai Roi* means *well of the Living One who sees me.*

NRSV

and everyone's hand against him;
and he shall live at odds with all his kin."
[13]So she named the LORD who spoke to her, "You are El-roi";[a] for she said, "Have I really seen God and remained alive after seeing him?"[b] [14]Therefore the well was called Beer-lahai-roi;[c] it lies between Kadesh and Bered.

[15]Hagar bore Abram a son; and Abram named his son, whom Hagar bore, Ishmael. [16]Abram was eighty-six years old when Hagar bore him[d] Ishmael.

[a]Perhaps *God of seeing* or *God who sees* [b]Meaning of Heb uncertain [c]That is *the Well of the Living One who sees me* [d]Heb *Abram*

COMMENTARY

Interest in this story has at times focused on the history of the Ishmaelites, bedouin tribes to the south and east of Canaan (see 25:12-18). More recent interest in Islam, which traces its religious heritage to Abraham through Ishmael, has renewed study in Ishmael's heritage in this and related texts (17:15-25; 21:8-21). Whatever its history, the present narrative has been decisively shaped by theological interests and integrated within the story of Abraham. The story has often been identified with the J source (with Priestly framing elements).

In terms of form, scholars have described the story as a "conflict narrative," centering on a conflict between two women, Sarai and Hagar.[116] The nature of this conflict has been much debated in recent years, not least by feminist scholars, who have provided much insight into the text.[117] At the same time, the conflict should be more broadly conceived in terms of the family of Abraham. This text must be placed within the whole of Genesis, which reveals, in contemporary terms, a highly dysfunctional family system in which individuals—both male and female—are caught up in swirls of dissension beyond their own making or ability to control. This text narrates, fundamentally, a family problem. Yet, because the

116. See Westermann, *Genesis 12–36,* 235.
117. For a survey see K. P. Darr, *Far More Precious Than Jewels: Perspectives on Biblical Women* (Louisville: Westminster/John Knox, 1991).

story occurs in a patriarchal system, the males involved deserve special blame, and this does not go entirely unrecognized by the narrator.

In terms of structure and plot, the story begins with a statement of the problem, and in a highly compact way moves through various difficulties toward an ambiguous resolution. While a division might be made between vv. 1-6 and vv. 7-14 from the perspective of the history of traditions, the inclusio provided by the repeated word *bear* (ילד *yālad*) in vv. 1-2 and 15-16 ties the chapter together into a unified whole. The chapter relates to what precedes by references to Egypt (12:10-20; 13:1, 10; 15:18) and the promise of a son—linking son with the blessing on nations. The text now shifts from a focus on land in chaps. 13–15 to a focus on a son in chaps. 16–21.

16:1-6. Sarai remains barren (see 11:30), and Abram has no children. The story moves quickly to Sarai's strategy, as she (not Abram) takes the initiative to resolve the matter. The author does not mention previous discussions or the shame associated with childlessness in that culture; nor does Sarai raise a moral issue, as if she were being judged for something she did. She raises only a theological issue; she *interprets* her situation to mean that God has kept her from having children, whether such were actually the case (see 20:18; 25:21; 29:31; 30:2, 22). At the same time, she recognizes that God does not act alone, that human agency is important ("by her"; cf. 4:1;

17:16; 19:32; 30:3-4). Humans can thwart the will of God concerning progeny by their sexual practices (38:9-10).

Sarai certainly knows that God has promised *Abram* offspring (15:4), but not necessarily by her. At the same time, she wants to have children she can call her own. To accomplish this, she makes a self-sacrificing move. She not only shares her husband sexually, but allows Hagar to be a *wife* to Abram; 16:3 portrays a formal act on Sarai's part. Ancient Near Eastern parallels show that this was common practice.[118] Rachel and Leah take a similar initiative in 30:3-13, with God's apparent approval (30:6, 18). Since Sarai's strategy appears customary, she should not be condemned. Her decision stems not only from an interpretation of God's action, so that "she must do as she does,"[119] but from a recognition that God works through human agents.

Abram accedes to the plan, though without speaking. A problem arises when, after becoming pregnant with Abram's child, Hagar's attitude toward Sarai changes. The verb קלל (*qālal*) describes her action (also used in 12:3 for contempt shown to Abram's family), which would bring Hagar under the divine curse. Hagar somehow diminishes Sarai's status in view of her new place as mother-to-be of Abram's child (cf. Prov 30:23).

Hagar's *qālal* action certainly justifies Sarai's sharp raising of the issue with Abram (v. 5). Rather than voice her objections to Hagar, she speaks to Abram, the husband of both of them, presumably with the authority in such matters (and 12:3 was spoken to him). In language from the legal sphere, she accuses Abram and gives a rationale; he bears responsibility for this distressful situation (see the NIV). It was within his power to stop this kind of treatment of Sarai and his to settle now, and God will be the judge of how he handles the issue. By so appealing to God, Sarai gives evidence of her own relationship with God.

Abram's only speech in the chapter comes at this point (v. 6). Admitting no responsibility, he puts Hagar into Sarai's hand (i.e., power), giving Sarai authority to do as she wills. Abram thus tips the balance in favor of Sarai, giving no apparent regard for the effect it might have on Hagar. Abram has not handled this conflict very well, to

say the least. Sarai seeks no reconciliation with Hagar, but treats her harshly. Sarai acts strongly (ענה *ʿānâ*, vv. 6, 9, 11) against the Egyptian and invites comparison with Exodus texts, for the author uses this verb to describe Israel's oppression *by Egypt* (15:13; Exod 1:11-12; Deut 26:6-7). Hagar, taking her future and that of Sarai and Abram's child into her own hands, flees (see Exod 14:5) toward her home in Egypt (Shur is near the border). She prefers the dangers of the wilderness to continuing life in Abram's household. Ironically, she thinks she can find more freedom in Egypt than among God's chosen people! With this problem seemingly resolved, the issue of v. 1 seems to be front and center again, but not in this narrative. God remains focused on Hagar. Sarai and Abram have sent Hagar away, not God. God appears on the scene on behalf of this oppressed one, as one day God would for oppressed Israel.

16:7-16. Out in the same wilderness where Israel would later wander, Hagar encounters the "angel of the LORD" (repeatedly introduced, vv. 7, 9-11; cf. Moses in Exod 3:2). This figure, better called a messenger, should not be confused with later angelic beings. The narrator's report in v. 13 shows that Yahweh speaks to Hagar, and Hagar recognizes that she has seen God. This messenger is God in human form (cf. 21:17-19; 22:11-12, 15-16; 31:11, 13).[120]

Hagar's partial reply to God's inquiries (v. 8)—God does not predict her reply—suggests that she envisions no future; she can speak only of the past. God responds by focusing on the future. First, God directs Hagar to return to Sarai and to submit to her (Hagar's return is not noted). Given her treatment of Sarai in view of 12:3, she needs to get this matter resolved. She will not find salvation in being freed from Sarai and Abram as yet (though in her faith she stands on her own).

Instead of following through on the curse, as a mechanical view of the moral order might suggest, God responds to her affliction and makes promises to her (vv. 10-12). In fact, God names Hagar's affliction in exodus-like terms (*ʿānâ*, v. 11). Unlike Abram and Sarai, God addresses her by name, and for the first time she speaks. God is present to

118. See Sarna, *Genesis,* 119.
119. See Westermann, *Genesis 12–36,* 238.

120. For detail, see Fretheim, *Suffering of God,* 79-107.

her and draws her into conversation rather than reducing her to silence (vv. 8, 13).

The salvation Hagar receives focuses on the promise of a son. We can recognize the Abrahamic promises regarding offspring in v. 10 (13:16; 15:5), while in v. 11 we hear the familiar cadences of the annunciation in Isa 7:14. Although the oracle in v. 12 is more difficult, Hagar's response remains positive (the narrator has a comparable view).[121] Ishmael will be free, roving the wilderness (the "wild ass" is celebrated by God in Job 39:5-8), and he will not be submissive to oppressive people like Sarai and Abram. He will be frequently at odds with others, but such tension often occurs between sedentary and nomadic groups in that world (OT texts project similar difficulties for the other side of Abram's family, too; cf. 25:23; 27:28-29, 39-40). He will live at odds with his kin (some translations [TNK] have him living "alongside"), but no OT text speaks of a fulfillment in these terms; such oracles are not interpreted as a precise shaping of the future (see 25:23).

Hagar will follow through on bearing the child for Abram; the possibilities for a future of nonoppression will thereby be opened up for her own family (see 21:13-21). While the reader might wish for a freer future for Hagar at this point, she moves with what has become possible in that situation, trusting in the word of God that the future will contain a new form of freedom. Salvation for Hagar must take the form of waiting, but she knows that God sees and hears the afflicted, and so she can rest in the knowledge that God keeps promises.[122]

Hagar's response in v. 13 shows her not only as a trusting spirit but a person of faith. She recognizes the messenger as the voice of God, though he offers no word of self-identification (cf. 31:11-13). Moreover, she publicly confesses that God has come to her rescue ("You are El-roi"— that is, a God of seeing or a God who sees me). The last phrase in v. 13 presents difficulties, but at the least it speaks of a mutual seeing on the part of God and Hagar (so the NIV), and may include the idea of still living after having seen God (so the NRSV; cf. Exod 33:20).

Hagar's new name for God presents a metaphor born of her experience of having been given a future and a hope, rather than an already existing name/epithet. This is not a "new" God who needs a name; the word to her from the messenger uses the name Yahweh (v. 11), as does the narrator (v. 13). Her confession focuses on a God who sees rather than a God who speaks. Her experience mirrors that of Leah and Jacob (29:32; 31:42) and Israel in Egypt, whom God also "sees" and delivers (Exod 2:25; 3:7; 4:31). The name she gives to the well also centers on the God who sees "me" (see the NRSV footnote to v. 14). By these namings the event is pressed into the memory of succeeding generations in terms of a seeing God. A parallel theme is sounded about a God who hears (v. 11). The name Ishmael, meaning "God hears," witnesses to God's hearing one in distress (see 17:20; 21:17; 29:33; 30:6, 17, 22). In this naming of God, Hagar (like Sarai) shows that she has an independent relationship with God.

The text presents God's promises of a son and descendants as *a genuine fulfillment* of God's promise to Abram (cf. v. 10 with 13:16; 15:5; cf. also 17:20; 21:13). Abram has a son in Ishmael and numerous descendants through him (25:12-18). In addition, v. 10 picks up on the promise in 1:28; God's designs for the creation are being fulfilled in and through him. One may assume that the promise of nationhood includes land (17:20), although language about covenant does not occur. Hence, we ought not to minimize or set aside the vigorous promises given to Hagar and Ishmael.

Verses 15-16 confirm this understanding; they form an inclusio with vv. 1-2, with the verb *bear* (ילד *yālad*) occurring five times. Hagar bears "Abram a son," and Abram gives "his *son*" the name that *God* had given him (v. 11). This assumes that Abram was told of the encounter between Hagar and God and that Abram knows the significance of the name. Sarai does not appear; her intention (v. 2) seems not to be realized.

Genesis 17:15-27 allows such questions at this stage of the narrative (and to some extent in 21:10-13), where the decision as to Ishmael's status remains up in the air; only a new word from God resolves the issue. The reader of chap.

121. See von Rad, *Genesis*, 195.
122. See J. G. Janzen, "Hagar in Paul's Eyes and the Eyes of Yahweh (Genesis 16)," *HBT*, 13 (1991) 1-22.

16 must not underinterpret these developments, as if Ishmael were a dead-end issue. Chapter 17 must be interpreted with the understanding that God's promise to Abraham has apparently been fulfilled. The passing of thirteen years between 16:16 and 17:1 reinforces this judgment.

REFLECTIONS

1. Hagar is Sarai's trusted servant; she no doubt came out of Egypt with Abram and his family (see 12:16). With this status, she possesses no choice and has no voice in becoming a surrogate mother; she is simply taken and given to Abram (v. 3). However much she may have accepted the customs of the time, her vulnerability ought not to be played down. She has no powers or rights should she be mistreated by those in authority over her. Since neither Abram nor Sarai ever names her (only God does, v. 8), and even though the narrator never calls her a slave, we are to be mindful of her precarious situation. Even more, the text stresses that Hagar is an *Egyptian* (vv. 1, 3; 21:9)! She is thus an outsider and an African.[123]

Hagar is the first person in Genesis to be encountered by the angel of God, and the first woman to be given promises (see 25:23). In response, Hagar becomes the *only* person in the OT to name God. She engages in theological formulation, using her own experience with God and the knowledge of God gained thereby to shape new language for God. She thereby shapes contemporary language for God in view of ever-changing human experience and new experiences of God in the midst of that change. Being open to naming God in new ways based on personal experience was not a luxury, but a necessity if God would accompany people in their changing lives.

2. At the same time, Sarai comes onto the scene for the first time as a character in her own right. She takes the initiative with her husband, taking charge on the issue of offspring and not backing away from issues that need to be addressed. Although she treats Hagar harshly, Abram tacitly participates as well. Many commentators are hard on Sarai, claiming that she seeks to fulfill the promise by her own efforts. Von Rad is typical: Sarai's is "a fainthearted faith that cannot leave things with God and believes it necessary to help things along . . . a child so conceived in defiance or in little faith cannot be the heir of promise."[124] Such a judgment reflects a docetic view of God's ways of working in the world. God often works in and through humans to carry out the divine purposes in Genesis (and the rest of the OT). Theologically, it should be stated as strongly as possible: Sarai should not in any way be faulted for taking the initiative, and the means she uses are typical for that culture.

3. Language about Sarai's (and tacitly Abram's) mistreatment of Hagar (ענה '*ānâ*, v. 6) also describes Israel's oppression by the Egyptians (15:13; Exod 1:11-12) and commandments that forbid oppression binding on Israel (Exod 22:21-22). The story of the outcast contains themes and experiences parallel to that of the insider. Given the prefiguring concerns played out in chaps. 12–15, this chapter may also reflect how Israel, or any who have been delivered, can quickly deny their own history. It is a sad dimension of Israel's story and that of the people of God in every age that the liberated so often become the oppressor.[125] While this kind of behavior can occur at the level of community or society, this text would have us examine the family sphere more closely, not least the relationship between husband and wife or parents and children.

4. The author gives this tale, so attentive to persons outside the chosen family, considerable space in the story of Abraham; it will not be the last time. In terms of the usual recounting of the salvation history, this story doesn't belong; it's a dead end. At best, the story seems to

123. For a portrayal of Hagar, see P. Trible, *Texts of Terror: Literary-Feminist Readings of Biblical Narratives* (Philadelphia: Fortress, 1984) 9-35.
124. Von Rad, *Genesis*, 196.
125. See Westermann, *Genesis 12–36*, 241.

have only a negative purpose. The fact that women play a key role in this story has probably meant for a certain neglect as well.

Such narrow perspectives will not do. Israel's God plays an important role in the lives of these "unchosen" ones. Indeed, God appears to Hagar, converses with her, and makes promises to her that approximate those given to Abram (vv. 10-11). This divine concern will continue in chap. 21. The author portrays God as a *Creator* who makes *promises* to those who do not belong to the "people of God" (which should include their descendants, both physical and spiritual, in Islam). God acts in *both word and deed* outside the boundaries of what we normally call the community of faith. God's attentiveness to Hagar and Ishmael comes more in spite of what Abram's family has done than because of their concern for outsiders and their welfare. Indeed, God enters the picture most decisively at precisely that point when *exclusion* from the chosen family has taken place (the move from v. 6 to v. 7). The chosen people cannot confine God's works and ways—even words of gospel and promise (vv. 10-11)—within their often oppressive and narrowly conceived structures. One ought to recognize that "God has not exclusively committed himself to Abram-Sarai."[126]

What does it mean that Hagar and Ishmael receive the *continuing* promises of God? What might the fulfillment of such promises mean for the people of God, not least for their continuing relationships to the descendants of Ishmael in Islam? What might it mean to continue to confess in and through the retelling of this story that the Ishmaelites are who they are because God has kept promises? A key question for the modern interpreter thus becomes, Has God been faithful to these promises made to Hagar and Ishmael? In search of the answer, we should remember that Ishmael does not receive negative treatment in the rest of the OT, and the Ishmaelites never seem to be in conflict with Israel. When Isaac and Ishmael bury their father, no sign of conflict appears (25:9). One of David's sisters married an Ishmaelite (1 Chr 2:17), and an Ishmaelite and a Hagrite were administrators for David (1 Chr 27:30-31).

5. At times the community of faith can so center on the speaking God that the theme of the seeing God is left aside. Not so with Hagar, and not so with Israel either. Israel's confession includes the claim that its God sees the human situation and responds to it (see 29:31-32; 31:12, 42; Exod 2:25; 3:7; 4:31). God's seeing (and hearing) remains crucial, because it means that God's speaking will address the human need in a precise way. God's word can bring a future and a hope because God has seen the situation and, hence, has been able to address actual needs in a specific way. God's saving acts respond directly to creaturely need.

On Paul's use of this story in Galatians 4 and other aspects of its significance, see commentary on chap. 21.

126. Brueggemann, *Genesis*, 153.

GENESIS 17:1-27, COVENANT AND CIRCUMCISION

NIV

17 When Abram was ninety-nine years old, the LORD appeared to him and said, "I am God Almighty[a]; walk before me and be blameless.

a1 Hebrew *El-Shaddai*

NRSV

17 When Abram was ninety-nine years old, the LORD appeared to Abram, and said to him, "I am God Almighty;[a] walk before me, and

a Traditional rendering of Heb *El Shaddai*

NIV

²I will confirm my covenant between me and you and will greatly increase your numbers."

³Abram fell facedown, and God said to him, ⁴"As for me, this is my covenant with you: You will be the father of many nations. ⁵No longer will you be called Abram*a*; your name will be Abraham,*b* for I have made you a father of many nations. ⁶I will make you very fruitful; I will make nations of you, and kings will come from you. ⁷I will establish my covenant as an everlasting covenant between me and you and your descendants after you for the generations to come, to be your God and the God of your descendants after you. ⁸The whole land of Canaan, where you are now an alien, I will give as an everlasting possession to you and your descendants after you; and I will be their God."

⁹Then God said to Abraham, "As for you, you must keep my covenant, you and your descendants after you for the generations to come. ¹⁰This is my covenant with you and your descendants after you, the covenant you are to keep: Every male among you shall be circumcised. ¹¹You are to undergo circumcision, and it will be the sign of the covenant between me and you. ¹²For the generations to come every male among you who is eight days old must be circumcised, including those born in your household or bought with money from a foreigner—those who are not your offspring. ¹³Whether born in your household or bought with your money, they must be circumcised. My covenant in your flesh is to be an everlasting covenant. ¹⁴Any uncircumcised male, who has not been circumcised in the flesh, will be cut off from his people; he has broken my covenant."

¹⁵God also said to Abraham, "As for Sarai your wife, you are no longer to call her Sarai; her name will be Sarah. ¹⁶I will bless her and will surely give you a son by her. I will bless her so that she will be the mother of nations; kings of peoples will come from her."

¹⁷Abraham fell facedown; he laughed and said to himself, "Will a son be born to a man a hundred years old? Will Sarah bear a child at the age of ninety?" ¹⁸And Abraham said to God, "If only Ishmael might live under your blessing!"

a5 Abram means *exalted father.*   *b5 Abraham* means *father of many.*

NRSV

be blameless. ²And I will make my covenant between me and you, and will make you exceedingly numerous." ³Then Abram fell on his face; and God said to him, ⁴"As for me, this is my covenant with you: You shall be the ancestor of a multitude of nations. ⁵No longer shall your name be Abram,*a* but your name shall be Abraham;*b* for I have made you the ancestor of a multitude of nations. ⁶I will make you exceedingly fruitful; and I will make nations of you, and kings shall come from you. ⁷I will establish my covenant between me and you, and your offspring after you throughout their generations, for an everlasting covenant, to be God to you and to your offspring*c* after you. ⁸And I will give to you, and to your offspring after you, the land where you are now an alien, all the land of Canaan, for a perpetual holding; and I will be their God."

9God said to Abraham, "As for you, you shall keep my covenant, you and your offspring after you throughout their generations. ¹⁰This is my covenant, which you shall keep, between me and you and your offspring after you: Every male among you shall be circumcised. ¹¹You shall circumcise the flesh of your foreskins, and it shall be a sign of the covenant between me and you. ¹²Throughout your generations every male among you shall be circumcised when he is eight days old, including the slave born in your house and the one bought with your money from any foreigner who is not of your offspring. ¹³Both the slave born in your house and the one bought with your money must be circumcised. So shall my covenant be in your flesh an everlasting covenant. ¹⁴Any uncircumcised male who is not circumcised in the flesh of his foreskin shall be cut off from his people; he has broken my covenant."

15God said to Abraham, "As for Sarai your wife, you shall not call her Sarai, but Sarah shall be her name. ¹⁶I will bless her, and moreover I will give you a son by her. I will bless her, and she shall give rise to nations; kings of peoples shall come from her." ¹⁷Then Abraham fell on his face and laughed, and said to himself, "Can a child be born to a man who is a hundred years old? Can Sarah, who is ninety years old, bear a child?"

a That is *exalted ancestor*   *b* Here taken to mean *ancestor of a multitude*   *c* Heb *seed*

NIV

¹⁹Then God said, "Yes, but your wife Sarah will bear you a son, and you will call him Isaac.ᵃ I will establish my covenant with him as an everlasting covenant for his descendants after him. ²⁰And as for Ishmael, I have heard you: I will surely bless him; I will make him fruitful and will greatly increase his numbers. He will be the father of twelve rulers, and I will make him into a great nation. ²¹But my covenant I will establish with Isaac, whom Sarah will bear to you by this time next year." ²²When he had finished speaking with Abraham, God went up from him.

²³On that very day Abraham took his son Ishmael and all those born in his household or bought with his money, every male in his household, and circumcised them, as God told him. ²⁴Abraham was ninety-nine years old when he was circumcised, ²⁵and his son Ishmael was thirteen; ²⁶Abraham and his son Ishmael were both circumcised on that same day. ²⁷And every male in Abraham's household, including those born in his household or bought from a foreigner, was circumcised with him.

ᵃ19 Isaac means he laughs.

NRSV

¹⁸And Abraham said to God, "O that Ishmael might live in your sight!" ¹⁹God said, "No, but your wife Sarah shall bear you a son, and you shall name him Isaac.ᵃ I will establish my covenant with him as an everlasting covenant for his offspring after him. ²⁰As for Ishmael, I have heard you; I will bless him and make him fruitful and exceedingly numerous; he shall be the father of twelve princes, and I will make him a great nation. ²¹But my covenant I will establish with Isaac, whom Sarah shall bear to you at this season next year." ²²And when he had finished talking with him, God went up from Abraham.

23Then Abraham took his son Ishmael and all the slaves born in his house or bought with his money, every male among the men of Abraham's house, and he circumcised the flesh of their foreskins that very day, as God had said to him. ²⁴Abraham was ninety-nine years old when he was circumcised in the flesh of his foreskin. ²⁵And his son Ishmael was thirteen years old when he was circumcised in the flesh of his foreskin. ²⁶That very day Abraham and his son Ishmael were circumcised; ²⁷and all the men of his house, slaves born in the house and those bought with money from a foreigner, were circumcised with him.

ᵃ That is he laughs

COMMENTARY

Interpreters usually understand this chapter (assigned to P) as an alternate version of the covenant in chap. 15. Although the two texts do have distinct origins, the redactor of the present text probably does not so view the matter. Most likely we should view this covenant as a *revision* (not simply a renewal) of the earlier covenant in view of events that seem to take the future of the promise in directions not fully satisfactory (cf. the relationship between the covenants in Exodus 24 and 34, with the intervening sin in Exodus 32). The promise of a son (15:4) has been fulfilled, and thirteen years pass between 16:16 and 17:1 (vv. 24-25), during which time Abram lives with what 16:15-16 and 17:18 suggest to be a settled matter. It may be that, during these years, everyone—including God—lives with Ishmael to see

what opens up regarding the future. Experience shows (for reasons unknown) that Ishmael will not do. The story begins again, this time with Sarai as mother (v. 19), not simply Abram as father. In a new moment for God, he reveals a new name and shapes a somewhat different future. This new divine identity, correlating with newly shaped promises, associates with *both* Abraham and Sarah, who are also given new names.

God particularizes the promises in other new ways. For example, the promise focuses less on land and more on Abraham as a progenitor of a *multitude* of nations and kings (vv. 4-6), which also involves a promise to Sarah (v. 16). The covenant as *everlasting* is new, though the land was so viewed in 13:15. The links with creation (cf. 1:28) are also new; in some sense the command within creation is focused in this family (cf. Exod 1:7). God being God to Abraham and his descendants (mentioned thirteen times) provides a new element, or at least a new formulation (v. 7). Finally, the text highlights Abraham's response within this covenant.

17:1-22. The author structures this segment as a typical theophanic narrative. (a) God's appearance: Given the appearances in human form elsewhere in the cycle (e.g., 16:7; 18:1) the reader should think of the divine messenger (note that God "went up" in v. 22). (b) Self-identification (El Shaddai): the meaning of this name remains uncertain, perhaps "God of the Mountains" (Breasts?; recalled in Exod 6:3), commonly translated "God Almighty" (based on Greek and Latin renderings). (c) A word to the recipient, including commands as well as promises: The three introductions focus on God (v. 4, "as for me"), Abraham (v. 9, "as for you"), and Sarah (v. 15, "as for Sarah"). (d) Abraham responds to the word (vv. 17-18), occasioning a more emphatic and particular divine word (vv. 19-21), after which God departs. The narrative concludes with a report of Abraham's obedience to God's command (vv. 23-27).

The word of God dominates the narrative. (1) God begins with imperatives (v. 1; cf. 12:1-2). As Noah did (6:9; cf. Pss 15:2; 101:2; Prov 20:7), Abraham is to walk before God (i.e., be loyal; 24:40 and 48:15; cf. 5:22-24) and be blameless (i.e., unreserved faithfulness in every aspect of the relationship, but not sinless; so also Jacob, 25:27, and David, 2 Sam 22:24; cf. 1 Kgs 3:6). The second imperative presents the consequence of obeying the first (and you *will be* blameless). Walking before God does not constitute a condition for giving the covenant, but Abraham intends to do so; walking before God becomes obligatory for relationship *within* the covenant. As in chap. 15, God establishes the covenant with one who has faith (15:6; the same pattern occurs in covenants with Noah, Israel, and David). For Abraham to fall on his face (v. 3; cf. v. 17) involves a response of faith, agreeing to what God expects for one in a covenant relationship. Hence, v. 2 provides an announcement of what God will do if Abram acknowledges in faith that he intends to walk before God.

(2) God, having taken the initiative, makes

(literally, gives) a covenant (i.e., speaks promises) with Abraham and with his descendants (note the ABBA structure in vv. 4b-5). The content of the covenant consists of vv. 4b-8 (note the colon at the end of v. 4a). One should understand covenant here as a royal grant, attested elsewhere in the ancient Near East. It bears close similarities to the covenants with Noah (9:10-17; see 6:9) and David (2 Sam 23:5; 7:8-17) involving stability, eternity, and unconditionality (though not apart from faithfulness). These are the components of this word of God:

(a) Abraham will be exceedingly fruitful (vv. 2, 6). These words recall the creation account (1:28; 9:1, 7). But that creational command here becomes a promise (and in 22:17). Looking forward, it will be conveyed to Isaac in 26:4, 24, from Isaac to Jacob in 28:3, but restated as a command by God in 35:11, and again as promise in 48:4. It also involves a promise made to Ishmael in 16:10 and 17:20. This command/promise is fulfilled in Exod 1:7 (anticipated in Gen 47:27). In other words, in Abraham's family the commands of creation are being fulfilled because of God's promise. The command reaches fulfillment because promise accompanies it. "Abraham is the first fruit of the new creation."[127]

(b) Abraham and Sarah will be ancestors of a multitude of nations and kings, those whose physical ancestry can be traced to Abraham (see 28:3; 35:11; 48:4), for example, Edomites and Ishmaelites. Yet, as Sarna notes, the phrase "has a more universal application in that a larger segment of humanity looks upon Abraham as its spiritual father," including Christians and Muslims (see John 1:13).[128] "Kings" has Davidic links (see 49:8-12) and later takes on messianic overtones (see Matt 1:1).

(c) God will be God to Abraham and his descendants (vv. 7-8), a statement of divine commitment (see Exod 6:7). The repeated emphasis on descendants (vv. 7-10, 20) understands this promise to stand for all generations.

(d) Abraham will receive the land in which he now resides as an alien for an everlasting possession (v. 8; NRSV "perpetual holding"; cf. 13:15; 48:4). And so he lived in the land, but could not yet consider it his. The promise was for the future; it would not be fully realized in his lifetime (see

127. Ibid., 153.
128. Sarna, *Genesis,* 124.

chap. 23). This would have been an especially important word for landless exiles.

(3) God changes Abram's name to Abraham, a dialectal variation of the name Abram ("exalted father"), but here understood to carry a different meaning: "father of a multitude." A name change does not refer to a change in personality or character, but marks a new stage in his identification with the divine purpose. He must now live up to his new name, which focuses not on his personal relationship with God but on his relationship to the nations. The name looks outward, centered on the lives of others. Abraham's election involves mission.

(4) Abraham and his descendants (including Ishmael) are commanded to keep (שמר *šāmar*) the covenant. Genesis 18:19 and 26:5 articulate more precisely Abraham's "keeping," which involves more than circumcision (cf. Exod 19:5, referring to this covenant).[129] Generally, "keeping" means doing justice to, being faithful to, the relationship with the promising God. Verse 10 does not identify covenant with circumcision (cf. v. 4); v. 13*b* signifies that the covenant is marked in the flesh, an instance of synecdoche, a physical sign referring to the whole (covenant).

Circumcision serves as a *sign* of faithfulness to the covenant from the *human* side (different from the rainbow in 9:12-17, which is a sign for God); it resembles the sabbath of Exod 31:16-17. Although we read about Isaac's (21:4) and Jacob's sons' circumcisions (34:15), the OT seldom mentions the practice elsewhere.

The last clause in v. 14 does not derive causally from the first clause. Neglecting circumcision does not constitute the essence of breaking the covenant; such neglect signifies unfaithfulness, a mark of an already broken relationship. An act of omission symbolizes an act of commission. Those who are unfaithful can remove themselves from the sphere of the covenant; the promises of God, however, will always remain in place for the faithful to cling to.

God will never be unfaithful, yet human unfaithfulness can lead to severe consequences (v. 14). What being "cut off" from the people entails is not certain (note the play on "cut"). The text does not refer explicitly to any action by court or cult—execution or excommunication; the matter is left up to God (see Lev 20:1-6). One has difficulty imagining that noncircumcised children would have "broken" the covenant. Rather, the text refers to the community in which circumcision functions as a sign (see the admixture of singular and plural "you"). The author may have in mind a situation where Israel had become lax, perhaps the exile. The repeated reference to slaves (vv. 12-13, 23, 27; is their status in question?) indicates that presence in the community is what matters, not racial stock or social standing.

(5) Sarai receives a new name and promises of blessing (twice!), nations, and kings (v. 16). The name Sarah (princess?) presents a less archaic form of Sarai; it may be related to the name Israel, and hence recognizes Sarah as the forebear of Israel and other nations. These promises are repeated for Sarah (even if spoken to Abraham); the text does not subsume her under Abraham, finding her importance for the future only through him. She participates genuinely in the covenant.

Abraham first responds by *internal* musing and laughter based on their ages as potential parents (v. 17; cf. 18:12; יצחק [*yiṣḥāq*], a play on the name for Isaac ["he laughs"], becomes a narrative theme, 18:12-15; 19:14; 21:6, 9). Then, he asks God (or claims?) that Ishmael be the one who bears the promise (v. 18). While Abraham responds by falling on his face in obeisance in v. 3, here he falls on his face in laughter. His questions suggest that this laughter expresses incredulity (contrast 15:6), or possibly bewilderment. Abraham's laughter appears similar to Sarah's (18:12), demonstrating that Sarah was not told what he here learns. He accepts the goal but not the means of gaining descendants.

Remarkably God does not chide Abraham; he simply says no, and speaks of a new son, to be named Isaac (God also names Ishmael, 16:11), with whom God will establish the covenant. God responds to Abraham's concerns, however. He speaks promises regarding Ishmael similar to those given Isaac; these amount to a covenant (though that word does not appear), which includes nationhood and royalty (see 21:13, 18; 25:12-16 lists the twelve princes). The heart of the difference would seem to be 12:3*b*, the role of mediating blessing to the nations.

God answers Abraham's questions of v. 17 by

---

129. See Fretheim, *Exodus*, 209-11.

asserting again that Sarah will be the mother of his son (21:1-7), and Isaac the one with whom the covenant will be continued (26:3-5). God's own decision results in the selection of Isaac. The reference to a male son (cf. 18:14) does not testify to absolute foreknowledge, but to God's knowing what God will do.

After the conversation, God leaves the scene, and the narrator repetitively reports that Abraham follows through on the divine command, himself wielding the knife for all male members of his household. The author refers to the circumcision of Ishmael, "his son," *three* times, and to that of the others twice (vv. 23-26). Abraham responds to the covenant on behalf of his own generation.

REFLECTIONS

1. The common translation "God Almighty" (from Greek and Latin renderings) presents an unfortunate abstraction; it unpacks (and hence limits) the concrete image of mountains in a single direction; the image should be retained in translation or (typical for names) transliterated. The image of mountains for God occasions a variety of reflections (cf. Ps 36:7). As Hagar gave a new name to God in 16:13, so here God reveals a new name. God's new name matches the new names for Abraham and Sarah, signaling a new beginning in their relationship. The community of faith must be open to new names for God, names that may be more congruent with the life experiences of people in new times and places.

2. Circumcision was common among Israel's neighbors (and beyond), often as a rite of passage (see Jer 9:25-26; God assumes that Abraham knows the rite). God does not institute a new rite that would set Israel apart from its neighbors. God takes an existing practice—a sign from the world of creation—and "baptizes" it for use within the community of faith.

Circumcision provides a mark on the body, which symbolizes the command to walk before God, involving all aspects of the person's life. Relationship with God does not express itself simply as a spiritual journey; it draws in the bodily dimensions of life to which God lays claim. Women are included only by virtue of being members of a household where the males are circumcised (clitoridectomy, female circumcision, was and is practiced in other cultures). Yet, the later metaphoric use of circumcision (see below) becomes a way of including women.

The physical act of circumcision does not provide the primary sign of faithfulness to the covenant (v. 11). Although external and ineradicable, it was not a visible sign of belonging. Hence, it was, essentially, a sign of belonging for the individual, though also a sign for the community, who are thereby true to God's command. The eighth day may refer to the completion of creation in seven days, here applied to the individual, so that covenant becomes the realization of creation.

Having fulfilled this obligation, the way one's life is shaped remains consequential. Circumcision never guarantees; other traditions will speak of judgment on circumcised ones with an "uncircumcised heart" (Jer 4:4; 9:25; Ezek 44:7-9; cf. Deut 10:16; 30:6). One senses the danger in isolating religious forms from faith, as if the sign in and of itself will suffice. Circumcision will not be a sign if it points to nothing; it becomes an empty sign. The NT picks up on this spiritual circumcision (Phil 3:3; Col 2:11-13 links it to baptism). The NT neither condemns nor makes the sign decisive for membership in the Christian community (1 Cor 7:18-19; Gal 5:6; 6:12-15), a principle framed against those who thought it essential. Paul argues (Rom 4:9-12) that Abraham's faith was decisive for inclusion in the community before he was circumcised.

3. The use of the word *everlasting* with respect to the covenant (vv. 7, 13, 19) and the land (v. 8; cf. 13:15) may occasion questions about continuing applicability. These "terms" involve the promises *from God's side.* If those to whom such promises are made do not walk before God (namely, remain faithful) they can remove themselves from the sphere of promise and *everlasting* no longer applies to them in terms of either covenant or land. This possibility does not take away from the unconditionality of the covenant. Nonetheless, humans must remain faithful (22:16-19; 26:5, 24).

4. Ishmael, the one who stands outside the chosen line, remains integrally related to it due to his circumcision. Generally, the rite provides democratization: slaves as well as sons, foreigners as well as family, chosen as well as unchosen—are all included within its scope. Circumcision allows for a genuine openness to the outsider.

GENESIS 18:1-15, GOD VISITS ABRAHAM AND SARAH

NIV

18 The LORD appeared to Abraham near the great trees of Mamre while he was sitting at the entrance to his tent in the heat of the day. ²Abraham looked up and saw three men standing nearby. When he saw them, he hurried from the entrance of his tent to meet them and bowed low to the ground.

³He said, "If I have found favor in your eyes, my lord,*a* do not pass your servant by. ⁴Let a little water be brought, and then you may all wash your feet and rest under this tree. ⁵Let me get you something to eat, so you can be refreshed and then go on your way—now that you have come to your servant."

"Very well," they answered, "do as you say."

⁶So Abraham hurried into the tent to Sarah. "Quick," he said, "get three seahs*b* of fine flour and knead it and bake some bread."

⁷Then he ran to the herd and selected a choice, tender calf and gave it to a servant, who hurried to prepare it. ⁸He then brought some curds and milk and the calf that had been prepared, and set these before them. While they ate, he stood near them under a tree.

⁹"Where is your wife Sarah?" they asked him.

"There, in the tent," he said.

¹⁰Then the LORD*c* said, "I will surely return to you about this time next year, and Sarah your wife will have a son."

Now Sarah was listening at the entrance to the tent, which was behind him. ¹¹Abraham and

a3 Or *O Lord* *b6* That is, probably about 20 quarts (about 22 liters)
c10 Hebrew *Then he*

NRSV

18 The LORD appeared to Abraham*a* by the oaks*b* of Mamre, as he sat at the entrance of his tent in the heat of the day. ²He looked up and saw three men standing near him. When he saw them, he ran from the tent entrance to meet them, and bowed down to the ground. ³He said, "My lord, if I find favor with you, do not pass by your servant. ⁴Let a little water be brought, and wash your feet, and rest yourselves under the tree. ⁵Let me bring a little bread, that you may refresh yourselves, and after that you may pass on—since you have come to your servant." So they said, "Do as you have said." ⁶And Abraham hastened into the tent to Sarah, and said, "Make ready quickly three measures*c* of choice flour, knead it, and make cakes." ⁷Abraham ran to the herd, and took a calf, tender and good, and gave it to the servant, who hastened to prepare it. ⁸Then he took curds and milk and the calf that he had prepared, and set it before them; and he stood by them under the tree while they ate.

9They said to him, "Where is your wife Sarah?" And he said, "There, in the tent." ¹⁰Then one said, "I will surely return to you in due season, and your wife Sarah shall have a son." And Sarah was listening at the tent entrance behind him. ¹¹Now Abraham and Sarah were old, advanced in age; it had ceased to be with Sarah after the manner of women. ¹²So Sarah laughed to herself, saying, "After I have grown old, and my husband is old, shall I have pleasure?" ¹³The LORD said to Abraham, "Why did Sarah laugh, and say, 'Shall

a Heb *him*   *b* Or *terebinths*   *c* Heb *seahs*

NIV

Sarah were already old and well advanced in years, and Sarah was past the age of childbearing. ¹²So Sarah laughed to herself as she thought, "After I am worn out and my master[a] is old, will I now have this pleasure?"

¹³Then the LORD said to Abraham, "Why did Sarah laugh and say, 'Will I really have a child, now that I am old?' ¹⁴Is anything too hard for the LORD? I will return to you at the appointed time next year and Sarah will have a son."

¹⁵Sarah was afraid, so she lied and said, "I did not laugh."

But he said, "Yes, you did laugh."

[a]12 Or husband

NRSV

I indeed bear a child, now that I am old?' ¹⁴Is anything too wonderful for the LORD? At the set time I will return to you, in due season, and Sarah shall have a son." ¹⁵But Sarah denied, saying, "I did not laugh"; for she was afraid. He said, "Oh yes, you did laugh."

COMMENTARY

Since Abraham's name does not occur until v. 6 (on v. 1, see the textual notes), we may judge that the editor has fully integrated this narrative into the larger story. While the story may not have originally centered on an appearance of God, it now does (18:1). While it differs in some ways from typical theophanic narratives (e.g., no self-identification of the deity), we may view the story as a variant of the form (cf. 16:7-14; 26:24). The divine appearance reaches completion when the deity leaves (18:33). We are not certain at what point Abraham recognizes that God has appeared to him.

Scholars often think this narrative (usually J) centers in the announcement of the birth of a son. Yet, inasmuch as the promise of a son through Sarah has just been emphasized (17:16), a somewhat broader function for the story seems likely. Both biblical and nonbiblical parallels combine the themes of hospitality and birth announcement; 2 Kgs 4:8-17, a story of a "man of God" and a Shunammite woman, provides a good example. Parallels in Greek literature—perhaps late developments of Near Eastern prototypes—include a story in which three gods in human form are received hospitably and give the childless host a son.[130] Stories about visits from strangers are found in many cultures.

The relationship between vv. 1-8 and vv. 9-15

130. See Westermann, *Genesis 12–36*, 275-76.

remains difficult to discern. Chapter 17 makes it unlikely that the promised son constitutes a "reward" for Abraham's hospitality or a "gift" from the guests. Verses 1-8 set the issue as one of hospitality extended to strangers; Abraham may pass a "test" of some sort in this. Verses 9-15 retain some interest in hospitality, with their focus on Sarah's *reception* of the announcement: How hospitable will Sarah be to this word? Will her response be similar to Abraham's (17:17)? Issues of hospitality relate to both receiving others and the words they may speak.

This theme (with men/angels) plays a key role in 19:1-3 (Lot) and 24:18-20 (Rebekah). Moreover, in 18:16-33, issues of *divine* hospitality are raised, especially regarding God's reception of the human. God receives the "outcry" from those affected by the conduct of the people of Sodom and Gomorrah and moves to deal with it. God tends to Abraham's words and takes them into account when moving into the future. Another link with vv. 16-33 involves the prominence of questions, from Abraham and God. In all cases, the questions are serious, posed for the purpose of continuing the conversation. God's conveyance to Abraham of matters concerning the future also tie vv. 10-13 with vv. 17-19.

18:1-8. From the narrator's point of view, Yahweh appears to Abraham at his home (v. 1). From Abraham's point of view, however, three men stand near him (v. 2). Yahweh has assumed human form (see 16:7), appearing among the three men;[131] the other two are angelic attendants (so 19:1; perhaps presented in abstract form in Pss 23:6; 43:3). The separation between Yahweh and two of the messengers in 18:22 and 19:1, 13 supports this, as does the singular "you, your" in v. 3 and the shift from plural (v. 9) to a single spokesman (vv. 10-15; a comparable move occurs in 19:17-19, cf. NIV footnotes). All are involved in destroying the city, as the angels mediate God's action (cf. 19:13 with 19:14, 24). But Abraham does not yet know these identities, so the reader understands more at this point than he does. Abraham does not act hospitably due to a desire to please a divine visitor. Sarah's response (vv. 9-15) also must be interpreted with this same intentionality in mind.

Abraham's hospitality has several characteristics: It extends to strangers, toward those who appear unexpectedly; it follows a certain protocol: seeing, running to meet, honoring, inviting, refreshing, preparing, serving. Bowing, an everyday gesture, was appropriate for all visitors, not only for important people. "Haste" language appears five times (vv. 2, 6-7; cf. 24:18-20). Abraham gives of the best he has (a calf!), makes and serves food, remains available to them and concerned about their welfare, and accompanies them on their way (v. 16). The phrase "find favor in your eyes" (v. 3; see 19:19; 32:5; 33:8-15) includes courtesy; it gives the visitors a higher status and so the freedom to respond without embarrassment. Abraham depicts what the visitors may expect (vv. 4-5), in view of which they accept the invitation, and he goes beyond what he promised in providing meat—these heavenly beings eat! As the visitors stand near Abraham (v. 2), so he stands near them (v. 8); he reciprocates in being attentive. He understands himself to be their servant (vv. 3, 5).

18:9-15. The home setting integrates Sarah into the conversation. Yet (unlike 17:16), neither Sarah nor Abraham seems to be clear that God speaks. Initially, all three persons are involved (v. 9), then one takes the lead (the NIV's "Lord" in v. 10 is an inference drawn from the words that follow). In v. 13 only the narrator identifies the

speaker as Yahweh; v. 14 speaks about Yahweh, but the identity of the "I" remains unclear. The fear shown by Sarah (v. 15) comes from knowing what this person has said about her (including her laughing to herself where she could not be seen). This introduces an element of mystery, amazement that this one could speak for God.

The reader will remember that God had spoken such a promise to Abraham and that he had also laughed to himself, asking essentially the same questions (17:16-17). Abraham's falling on his face implies a more explicit negative response, however. The narrator inserts a word about their age (cf. 17:17) and that Sarah no longer menstruates (v. 11), as if to provide an objective view on Sarah's own comments (v. 12). These comments soften Sarah's response, making it more understandable, as does her observation about the end of sexual pleasure (note that Abraham fathers other children, 25:1-4). For Sarah, the issue has become more than barrenness (cf. 11:30).

All of the questions directed to Abraham in this section seem genuine. The question in v. 9 ensures Sarah is within earshot of what will be said; the narrator states (v. 10) that she listens "off camera." God inquires about Sarah's laughter in v. 13. If an accusatory question, then it could claim that Sarah should know better than to laugh, for nothing is too wonderful for God. Yet, it seems unlikely that God would be critical of Sarah if not of Abraham in 17:19. More likely, the "why" introduces a genuine question designed to continue the conversation, especially if one or both of them do not know God speaks in v. 10. God's question in v. 14, also a genuine question, moves Abraham and Sarah beyond their limited view of the future to a consideration of God's possibilities. Then the author repeats v. 10, as if to start over again in the light of the intervening conversation.

That the deity directs the questions of vv. 13-14 to Abraham means that God seeks a response from *him* regarding Sarah's laughter. God holds him accountable for her response. This may be due to Abraham's not informing her of the events of chap. 17, which means that he shares blame for Sarah's response. Abraham remains silent, as questionable a response as Sarah's. At the same time, if the author intended Sarah to hear the promise expressed in v. 10, the same must be true for vv.

---

131. For the idea that "Yahweh appeared in all three," see von Rad, *Genesis,* 204.

13-14 as well, as her response suggests (v. 15). She does not step forward to speak, so hers may be a voice from "off stage." Her denial of laughter (v. 15) could be a lie, or an attempt to withdraw her laughter,[132] now being more aware of the nature of the moment and the probable identity of the one who has spoken. But the messenger says it remains a fact. This affirmation keeps both Sarah and Abraham on the same level regarding the reception of the promise and also links her response to the naming of Isaac ("he laughs").

Sarah's incredulous response belongs to a literary convention for such announcements, (e.g., the Shunammite woman to a "man of God" [2 Kgs 4:16] and Mary to an angel [Luke 1:34!]); so also the "due time" reference (2 Kgs 4:16), which is the one innovation beyond chap. 17. The relation between the twice-stated temporal—but general—reference "due time" (vv. 10, 14) and Sarah having a son finds its explanation in 21:1, which

132. See Westermann, *Genesis 12–36*, 282.

speaks of God visiting Sarah "as he had said." Although God enables Sarah to become pregnant, the normal time for the child to develop in the womb is not set aside.

The precise meaning of the verb פלא (*pālē'*), translated "to be wonderful" or "to be hard/difficult" (v. 14), remains obscure. Does the word push in the direction of competence (Deut 17:8) or ability to accomplish something (Jer 32:17, 27) or something extraordinary or marvelous (Pss 118:23; 139:14)? The related plural noun commonly refers to God's wonderful deeds of redemption and judgment (Exod 3:20; 34:10), not a claim that only God possesses power, or that the divine power is irresistible. The term claims God's promises will not fail, that God will always find a way into the future.

The end of this segment seems incomplete, but the intent may well be to leave the reader (and Sarah and Abraham) in a state of some uncertainty concerning what the future will bring.

REFLECTIONS

1. The motif of hospitality extends into the NT. Jesus specifies that the lack of hospitality serves as grounds for judgment (Matt 25:43). Hebrews 13:2 stresses its importance, for "some have entertained angels without knowing it" (see Acts 14:11; 28:1-6; those visited by Paul say, "The gods have come down to us in human form!"). Hospitality is commended to all Christians (see 1 Pet 4:9; 3 John 5-8), especially leaders (1 Tim 3:2; Titus 1:8). See Luke 24:29 on welcoming the risen Christ.

This text involves not only human hospitality, but also hospitality toward God. One could speak in terms of Matthew 25; acting on behalf of one of "the least of these" constitutes an act on behalf of God. Hospitality toward God is not simply a spiritual matter, but a response of the whole self in the midst of the quite mundane affairs of everyday life. Although we are not always able to identify the presence of God in the midst of life, God assumes flesh and blood in the neighbor (1 John 4:20).

Modern culture presents numerous challenges to the practice of hospitality toward others. Hospitality may be defined as acts of benevolence toward those outside of one's usual circle of family and friends. In North American culture, people live increasingly isolated lives, seldom reaching out beyond a very close circle. We live in a self-protective age where parents must warn their children about strangers; who knows what might be lurking beneath a kind and gentle facade? Hence, we seldom move out toward strangers. Hospitality in the modern world entails some risk of moving toward the stranger with less than full certainty as to how one might be received. Such hospitality should be especially important in the life of worship; worship ought to be a setting in which the stranger is welcomed in premier ways.

2. A text such as this calls for sentences in which God appears as the subject. God makes the promised future possible. God serves as the source of hope in situations where the way into the future seems entirely blocked off. God gives shape to possibilities when all around us seems impossible. The active engagement of God in the midst of the problems of daily life opens up the future rather than closing it down.

3. The question "Is anything too wonderful [hard] for the LORD?" (v. 14), is difficult to understand. The text probably presents a genuine question designed to continue the conversation, not a rhetorical question, which would declare that nothing is too hard. Brueggemann recognizes that the question has no simple yes or no answer.[133] If the answer is yes, then we could delimit in a specific way what is possible for God. No human construct can finally define God's possibilities in a given situation. If the answer is no, "that is an answer which so accepts God's freedom that the self and the world are fully entrusted to God and to no other." It would fail to recognize that God has given *genuine* power into the hands of the creation (so 1:28) and that what is possible for God must be consistent with who God is.[134] One must deal with the issues of divine self-limitation raised by many OT texts. But, in this text, God finds a way into the future of a promised son. And this, in spite of the seemingly insurmountable hurdles of human bodily limits (postmenopausal births have been documented in modern times) and the uncertain responses of both Abraham and Sarah. No situation can *finally* stymie the divine purposes.

New Testament texts use such language, e.g., Mark 10:27 and Luke 1:37. We also need to consider texts such as Matt 17:20 (nothing is impossible for faithful *human beings*); Matt 26:39 (where Jesus' "if it is possible" raises questions of divine self-limitation), and Mark 6:5 (where Jesus' healing powers are limited by the dynamics of a situation).

4. Male commentators discussing this passage have often been unfair to Sarah, excusing Abraham's laughter (17:17) but judging Sarah severely.[135] Neither Abraham nor Sarah responds in exemplary ways to the word of God; at the same time, we should not call it unbelief, especially given the conventional form present here (see Mary in Luke 1:34). Many OT texts depict humans questioning God as a natural part of a genuine God-human conversation, and Abraham will shortly do just that (vv. 23-25; cf. Moses; Gideon in Judg 6:13). In this case, God's response continues the conversation, and God makes no judgment, even when Sarah denies that she laughed.

133. Brueggemann, *Genesis*, 159.
134. For the larger OT context, see Fretheim, *Suffering of God*, 72.
135. See examples in S. Jeansonne, *Women in Genesis* (Minneapolis: Fortress, 1990) 121n 28.

GENESIS 18:16–19:38, ABRAHAM, LOT, AND SODOM

Genesis 18:16-33, Abraham's Intercession

NIV

[16]When the men got up to leave, they looked down toward Sodom, and Abraham walked along with them to see them on their way. [17]Then the LORD said, "Shall I hide from Abraham what I am about to do? [18]Abraham will surely become a great and powerful nation, and all nations on earth will be blessed through him. [19]For I have chosen him, so that he will direct his children and his house-

NRSV

16Then the men set out from there, and they looked toward Sodom; and Abraham went with them to set them on their way. [17]The LORD said, "Shall I hide from Abraham what I am about to do, [18]seeing that Abraham shall become a great and mighty nation, and all the nations of the earth shall be blessed in him?[a] [19]No, for I have chosen[b]

a Or and all the nations of the earth shall bless themselves by him
b Heb known

NIV

hold after him to keep the way of the LORD by doing what is right and just, so that the LORD will bring about for Abraham what he has promised him."

[20]Then the LORD said, "The outcry against Sodom and Gomorrah is so great and their sin so grievous [21]that I will go down and see if what they have done is as bad as the outcry that has reached me. If not, I will know."

[22]The men turned away and went toward Sodom, but Abraham remained standing before the LORD.[a] [23]Then Abraham approached him and said: "Will you sweep away the righteous with the wicked? [24]What if there are fifty righteous people in the city? Will you really sweep it away and not spare[b] the place for the sake of the fifty righteous people in it? [25]Far be it from you to do such a thing—to kill the righteous with the wicked, treating the righteous and the wicked alike. Far be it from you! Will not the Judge[c] of all the earth do right?"

[26]The LORD said, "If I find fifty righteous people in the city of Sodom, I will spare the whole place for their sake."

[27]Then Abraham spoke up again: "Now that I have been so bold as to speak to the Lord, though I am nothing but dust and ashes, [28]what if the number of the righteous is five less than fifty? Will you destroy the whole city because of five people?"

"If I find forty-five there," he said, "I will not destroy it."

[29]Once again he spoke to him, "What if only forty are found there?"

He said, "For the sake of forty, I will not do it."

[30]Then he said, "May the Lord not be angry, but let me speak. What if only thirty can be found there?"

He answered, "I will not do it if I find thirty there."

[31]Abraham said, "Now that I have been so bold as to speak to the Lord, what if only twenty can be found there?"

He said, "For the sake of twenty, I will not destroy it."

[32]Then he said, "May the Lord not be angry,

[a]22 Masoretic Text; an ancient Hebrew scribal tradition *but the LORD remained standing before Abraham* [b]24 Or *forgive;* also in verse 26 [c]25 Or *Ruler*

NRSV

him, that he may charge his children and his household after him to keep the way of the LORD by doing righteousness and justice; so that the LORD may bring about for Abraham what he has promised him." [20]Then the LORD said, "How great is the outcry against Sodom and Gomorrah and how very grave their sin! [21]I must go down and see whether they have done altogether according to the outcry that has come to me; and if not, I will know."

22So the men turned from there, and went toward Sodom, while Abraham remained standing before the LORD.[a] [23]Then Abraham came near and said, "Will you indeed sweep away the righteous with the wicked? [24]Suppose there are fifty righteous within the city; will you then sweep away the place and not forgive it for the fifty righteous who are in it? [25]Far be it from you to do such a thing, to slay the righteous with the wicked, so that the righteous fare as the wicked! Far be that from you! Shall not the Judge of all the earth do what is just?" [26]And the LORD said, "If I find at Sodom fifty righteous in the city, I will forgive the whole place for their sake." [27]Abraham answered, "Let me take it upon myself to speak to the Lord, I who am but dust and ashes. [28]Suppose five of the fifty righteous are lacking? Will you destroy the whole city for lack of five?" And he said, "I will not destroy it if I find forty-five there." [29]Again he spoke to him, "Suppose forty are found there." He answered, "For the sake of forty I will not do it." [30]Then he said, "Oh do not let the Lord be angry if I speak. Suppose thirty are found there." He answered, "I will not do it, if I find thirty there." [31]He said, "Let me take it upon myself to speak to the Lord. Suppose twenty are found there." He answered, "For the sake of twenty I will not destroy it." [32]Then he said, "Oh do not let the Lord be angry if I speak just once more. Suppose ten are found there." He answered, "For the sake of ten I will not destroy it." [33]And the LORD went his way, when he had finished speaking to Abraham; and Abraham returned to his place.

[a]Another ancient tradition reads *while the LORD remained standing before Abraham*

but let me speak just once more. What if only ten can be found there?"

He answered, "For the sake of ten, I will not destroy it."

³³When the LORD had finished speaking with Abraham, he left, and Abraham returned home.

COMMENTARY

This passage picks up a narrative thread from chaps. 13–14. The author introduces an intercessory dialogue between God and Abraham concerning the fate of Sodom and Gomorrah (vv. 23-33) by means of divine reflections on the role of Abraham as God's chosen one (vv. 17-21). The entire text constitutes a *judicial inquiry*. Abraham's intercession functions as a judicial rather than a worshipful act (prayer formulae are absent). More broadly, in this theological narrative, the author does not report an event in Abraham's life, but reflects on theological issues by juxtaposing an ancient tradition about a natural disaster and a religious crisis in the community of the redactor. This tactic grounds theological reflection deeply within Israel's ancestral heritage.

The crisis prompts the question Will the righteous fare as the wicked? (v. 25; cf. Job 9:22-24). Such issues were prominent at those points in Israel's history when its future seemed to be at stake, from the fall of Samaria (Amos 7:1-9, also an intercessory dialogue regarding a "shower of fire") to the fall of Jerusalem (Jer 5:1; Ezek 14:12-20; 18:1-32). Why would God sweep away the faithful with the wicked, not save all of Israel for the sake of the righteous few? So, while commonly assigned to J, the narrative in its present form is also a relatively late composition.

The shift from Sarah's laughing to the long episode on Sodom and Gomorrah seems abrupt. The fulfillment of God's promise remains up in the air. Perhaps Sarah's laughing and the jesting of Lot's son-in-law (19:14) are linked to highlight the potentially devastating effects of taking God's words lightly (note the prophetic parallels). The road to fulfillment is precarious, through many a dark valley, and faith and hospitality will not be irrelevant. Perhaps, too, the reader catches a glimpse of the kind of world within which this new son of Abraham is to be a blessing.

18:16-19. The men of v. 16 are the three who had appeared to Abraham (v. 2). Three transitional phrases mark developments regarding the fate of Sodom: The three men/angels (then two) "looked toward Sodom" (18:16; cf. 19:28); "went toward Sodom" (18:22); and "came to Sodom" (19:1). This progression correlates with developments in the judicial inquiry. While both Sodom and Gomorrah are in view in the larger narrative, the author focuses on Sodom, the home of Lot.

Verses 17-21 are spoken by Yahweh to the other two men and are overheard by Abraham (v. 23 presupposes their content). In effect, these verses work as inner divine reflection about the situation in Sodom and Abraham's relationship to it (cf. 1:26; 2:18; 11:6-7). We receive insight into God's thoughts as background for the dialogue.

Abraham should not be kept in the dark regarding what God is "about to do," for God has chosen him (ידע [*yādaʿ*, "known"]; cf. Amos 3:2) and made promises to him. God does not intend human ignorance of God's work (cf. Amos 3:7). Even more, God consults with Abraham because he *and his descendants* are chosen to have a role among the "nations" ("families" in 12:3; cf. 22:18; 26:4). Abraham responds by interceding on behalf of the righteous, none of whom would be among the chosen, not even Lot (as in 20:17).

God calls Abraham to charge his family "to keep the way of the LORD by doing righteousness [צדקה *sĕdāqâ*] and justice [משפט *mišpāṭ*]" (v. 19; cf. Ps 33:5; Prov 21:3). These key words—uncommon in Genesis—are picked up in the dialogue, *mišpāṭ* in v. 25 and the root *ṣdq* seven times in vv. 23-28 (cf. 6:9; 7:1; 15:6; 20:4; 30:33; 38:26). The two words are closely related, characterizing individuals and communities that exemplify and promote life and well-being for all in every relational sphere, human and nonhuman. As such, their lives would correspond to God's creational intentions for the world order, including blessing on all nations. After so charging Abraham, God brings to his attention a case where these divine purposes are being subverted. To be a blessing to all nations, Abraham must become involved in situations of injustice. Just as God enters into the life of the chosen regarding these issues, so also God identifies the divine way with the world more generally.

The author deems the transmission of the faith to subsequent generations an appropriate topic in view of the imminent birth of Isaac. This brings *Israel's* life into view and its practice of "justice and righteousness" and the implications thereof (including judgment). Hence, the question of Sodom's fate could become a question of the fate of Israel (Isa 1:10; Jer 23:14; Ezek 16:49) or any people.

The fact that God raises the issue of justice (in vv. 17-19) before Abraham does is important. If God chooses Abraham to address issues of justice within his household, then God's ways of relating to these issues must be clear (raised by a non-Israelite in 20:4). God's people are to walk in all of God's ways (v. 19; cf. Deut 8:6; 10:12; Jer 5:4-5) and so they should know what justice means for God.

Verse 19 may seem to make God's promises conditional. Yet, the text focuses on Abraham's *transmitting the faith to the next generation,* without which there would be no community to whom the promises apply. The promises are not genetically transmitted. The community of faith can continue only if children receive instruction. If the generations to come are not faithful, they remove themselves from the sphere of the promise. Nonetheless, the faith of Abraham and his descendants will survive (see commentary on 22:16-18 and 26:5, 24).

18:20-22. God reports the cries of unidentified persons about the gravity of the sins of Sodom and Gomorrah (against their own?). Outcry language (also 19:13) describes the oppressed (4:10; 27:34), including Israel in Egypt (Exod 2:23; 3:7, 9). The sins of Sodom involve social injustice (to which Jer 23:14 and Ezek 16:49 also testify).

Verse 20, with a new introduction, reports the decision of God as Judge (v. 25) formally to investigate the situation; Abraham will be involved in this judicial inquiry (11:5; Num 12:5; on "seeing" as judicial activity, see 6:5, 12; Exod 3:7-9; 32:9). God will consult with him to discover whether the situation is in fact so grave that it warrants the judgment that God has *preliminarily* drawn.[136] The dialogue thus follows naturally from this divine intent. Abraham understands that he has been invited into such a conversation.

This inquiry is not just rhetorical, so God's words, "and if not, I will know [acknowledge, recognize]" (v. 21). This divine knowing for judicial purposes depends on the inquiry. God admits the possibility of an "if not." For God to use "if" language means the future remains open (Exod 4:8-9; Jer 7:5; 22:4-5; Ezek 12:3). God holds out the prospect that the inquiry will issue in a verdict other than that preliminarily drawn. Abraham presumes the integrity of this consultation; what he has to say will be taken seriously (cf. Exod 32:9-14; Num 14:11-20).

The departure of two of the men marks the transition to dialogue (cf. 19:1, v. 16). Abraham now stands before God, though originally the text read that God stood before Abraham (NRSV footnote). The subjects were reversed by scribes who thought it indecorous for God to stand before a human being. "Remained" refers more appropriately to God, who remains behind while the two men depart. God seeks to communicate with Abraham, not the other way around.

18:23-33. Abraham proceeds to raise very specific questions regarding God's preliminary decision. He is blunt, persistent, and nontraditional. His questions (vv. 23-25) pull no punches; he gets right to the point without preliminary niceties. The author stresses this confrontative approach by the "indeed?" (vv. 23-24; cf. 18:13; Job 34:17), as well as the repeated "far be it from you" (cf. 44:7, 17). Abraham understands his relationship with God to be such that direct questions are not only in order but welcome (cf. Exod 32:11-14). Indeed, God exhibits no disapproval. Abraham does become more deferential as the dialogue

---

136. Not finally drawn, see Fretheim, *Suffering of God,* 49-53.

proceeds. His motives for this shift are not stated, but God's positive response to his candor may have humbled him. We may not know enough about ancient methods of argumentation to assess this shift properly.

One could suggest that God plays with Abraham, for God knows the number of righteous persons in Sodom. But this would deny the integrity of the inquiry. Something may emerge out of this consultative interaction that calls for a different divine direction. Given the divine "if," God does not appear certain just how far and in what direction Abraham might push the discussion.

Abraham's argument moves in stages to its climactic question at the end of v. 25. Abraham first expresses concern that God not "sweep away" (19:15, 17) the righteous (not sinless—righteousness is measured in terms of creational relationships, cf. 38:26) with the wicked; they must not be treated in the same way. He raises a more specific question: How many righteous must there be in order for God to save the city (see below)?

While Lot may have prompted Abraham's action (as in 14:14, see 19:29), he places the matter on a much broader canvas of concern, i.e., the number of righteous he mentions (fifty!) and the absence of Lot. The "righteous" are any who had not participated in the behaviors that led to the "outcry." While Abraham focuses on them, he knows their deliverance would mean the saving of many wicked. In not suggesting that the few righteous simply be removed (which is what happens) he shows his concern for the many. God's fourfold "for the sake of" carries a double meaning: God will not destroy for the sake of saving the few; for the sake of the few, the many will not be destroyed (in 12:13, 16, Pharaoh dealt well with Abraham *for the sake of* Sarah; see 26:24; 1 Sam 12:22; 2 Sam 5:12; 9:1, 7). The verb נשא (*nāśā'*, "spare") means to annul the decision to destroy. The righteous do not exercise an *atoning* function for the others, yet the effect is comparable. Certainly God's mercy toward those who deserve another future grounds this divine response.

Abraham's most direct question is Will not the Judge of all the earth do right (*mišpāṭ*)? (cf. 1 Sam 2:10; 1 Kgs 8:32; Ps 9:7-8). If God expects Abraham and his family to do *mišpāṭ* (v. 19),

justice must be God's own way. Only then would "doing justice" be keeping "the way of the LORD." Abraham's question does not accuse; it provides a debating point, warranted by what God has said (v. 19).

This question suggests an implicit theology. Abraham considers God to be subject to an existing moral order. God has freely created that order but is bound to attend to it faithfully. That is, God cannot ignore doing justice to established relationships (i.e., righteousness) and still be faithful, not least because God expects this of Abraham and his family. God thus is held to certain standards in dealing with issues of justice. Hence in Abraham's eyes, God cannot ignore differences between the righteous and the wicked in acts of judgment. God accepts Abraham's argument.

As Abraham continues to raise the numbers question, God responds in a consistently positive way. Abraham's concerns are matched by God's. The author reveals here the ends to which God will go to save the righteous and the divine patience in matters of judgment. God's will to save over the will to judge so predominates that no reward-punishment schema can explain what happens. The text is making one basic point: No retributionary schema will explain why disastrous events do *not* occur. The wicked may not suffer the consequences of their own sins because of the presence of the righteous.

We should not move too quickly past this point, not least because it answers most clearly why Abraham cut the questioning off at ten, a number not to be taken literally. It may be that "the number ten represents the smallest group"[137] and that a smaller number would be dealt with as individuals, who could be (and were) led out of the city. It may be that it represents the point at which Abraham saw that God's justice had been established beyond the shadow of a doubt; he could now leave the fate of the few righteous up to God. It may be that Abraham realizes that this "numbers game" cannot be pressed exactly, for that would mean a precise number "out there," which would trigger a divine decision, as if all that counts is "counting noses." God has no quota system in these matters.

Most basically, however, the numbers speak to

137. Westermann, *Genesis 12–36*, 292.

the issue of a critical mass in relation to the moral order. The wickedness of a few can have a contaminating effect on the larger group of which they are a part (cf. Deut 21:1-9). Here the issue is reversed; the righteousness of a few can so permeate a wicked society that they can save it from the destructive effects of its own evil ways. However, a buildup of wickedness can become so deep and broad that nothing can turn the potential for judgment around. The "critical mass" effect of the presence of the righteous can be so diminished as not to be able to affect positively the shape of the future. There may come a point where even God cannot turn the situation around and still be just; judgment must fall. Abraham recognizes this by not taking the numbers lower than ten. He tacitly admits that a few righteous may indeed "fare as the wicked" (v. 25). Eschatological thinking will speak finally of a distinction in the world to come rather than in this world.

God does not reappear as an agent until 19:24. Abraham, too, reappears only in 19:27, looking down on the destroyed cities. Chapter 19 now brings readers into the city of Sodom. They will be given an example of behaviors that occasioned the "outcry" and be asked to judge for themselves whether God's judgment appears just. (See Reflections at the end of the next section.)

Genesis 19:1-38, Sodom and Gomorrah

NIV

19The two angels arrived at Sodom in the evening, and Lot was sitting in the gateway of the city. When he saw them, he got up to meet them and bowed down with his face to the ground. ²"My lords," he said, "please turn aside to your servant's house. You can wash your feet and spend the night and then go on your way early in the morning."

"No," they answered, "we will spend the night in the square."

³But he insisted so strongly that they did go with him and entered his house. He prepared a meal for them, baking bread without yeast, and they ate. ⁴Before they had gone to bed, all the men from every part of the city of Sodom—both young and old—surrounded the house. ⁵They called to Lot, "Where are the men who came to you tonight? Bring them out to us so that we can have sex with them."

⁶Lot went outside to meet them and shut the door behind him ⁷and said, "No, my friends. Don't do this wicked thing. ⁸Look, I have two daughters who have never slept with a man. Let me bring them out to you, and you can do what you like with them. But don't do anything to these men, for they have come under the protection of my roof."

⁹"Get out of our way," they replied. And they said, "This fellow came here as an alien, and now he wants to play the judge! We'll treat you worse

NRSV

19¹The two angels came to Sodom in the evening, and Lot was sitting in the gateway of Sodom. When Lot saw them, he rose to meet them, and bowed down with his face to the ground. ²He said, "Please, my lords, turn aside to your servant's house and spend the night, and wash your feet; then you can rise early and go on your way." They said, "No; we will spend the night in the square." ³But he urged them strongly; so they turned aside to him and entered his house; and he made them a feast, and baked unleavened bread, and they ate. ⁴But before they lay down, the men of the city, the men of Sodom, both young and old, all the people to the last man, surrounded the house; ⁵and they called to Lot, "Where are the men who came to you tonight? Bring them out to us, so that we may know them." ⁶Lot went out of the door to the men, shut the door after him, ⁷and said, "I beg you, my brothers, do not act so wickedly. ⁸Look, I have two daughters who have not known a man; let me bring them out to you, and do to them as you please; only do nothing to these men, for they have come under the shelter of my roof." ⁹But they replied, "Stand back!" And they said, "This fellow came here as an alien, and he would play the judge! Now we will deal worse with you than with them." Then they pressed hard against the man Lot, and came near the door to break it down. ¹⁰But the men inside reached out their

NIV

than them." They kept bringing pressure on Lot and moved forward to break down the door.

¹⁰But the men inside reached out and pulled Lot back into the house and shut the door. ¹¹Then they struck the men who were at the door of the house, young and old, with blindness so that they could not find the door.

¹²The two men said to Lot, "Do you have anyone else here—sons-in-law, sons or daughters, or anyone else in the city who belongs to you? Get them out of here, ¹³because we are going to destroy this place. The outcry to the LORD against its people is so great that he has sent us to destroy it."

¹⁴So Lot went out and spoke to his sons-in-law, who were pledged to marry[a] his daughters. He said, "Hurry and get out of this place, because the LORD is about to destroy the city!" But his sons-in-law thought he was joking.

¹⁵With the coming of dawn, the angels urged Lot, saying, "Hurry! Take your wife and your two daughters who are here, or you will be swept away when the city is punished."

¹⁶When he hesitated, the men grasped his hand and the hands of his wife and of his two daughters and led them safely out of the city, for the LORD was merciful to them. ¹⁷As soon as they had brought them out, one of them said, "Flee for your lives! Don't look back, and don't stop anywhere in the plain! Flee to the mountains or you will be swept away!"

¹⁸But Lot said to them, "No, my lords,[b] please! ¹⁹Your[c] servant has found favor in your[c] eyes, and you[c] have shown great kindness to me in sparing my life. But I can't flee to the mountains; this disaster will overtake me, and I'll die. ²⁰Look, here is a town near enough to run to, and it is small. Let me flee to it—it is very small, isn't it? Then my life will be spared."

²¹He said to him, "Very well, I will grant this request too; I will not overthrow the town you speak of. ²²But flee there quickly, because I cannot do anything until you reach it." (That is why the town was called Zoar.[d])

²³By the time Lot reached Zoar, the sun had risen over the land. ²⁴Then the LORD rained down

NRSV

hands and brought Lot into the house with them, and shut the door. ¹¹And they struck with blindness the men who were at the door of the house, both small and great, so that they were unable to find the door.

12Then the men said to Lot, "Have you anyone else here? Sons-in-law, sons, daughters, or anyone you have in the city—bring them out of the place. ¹³For we are about to destroy this place, because the outcry against its people has become great before the LORD, and the LORD has sent us to destroy it." ¹⁴So Lot went out and said to his sons-in-law, who were to marry his daughters, "Up, get out of this place; for the LORD is about to destroy the city." But he seemed to his sons-in-law to be jesting.

15When morning dawned, the angels urged Lot, saying, "Get up, take your wife and your two daughters who are here, or else you will be consumed in the punishment of the city." ¹⁶But he lingered; so the men seized him and his wife and his two daughters by the hand, the LORD being merciful to him, and they brought him out and left him outside the city. ¹⁷When they had brought them outside, they[a] said, "Flee for your life; do not look back or stop anywhere in the Plain; flee to the hills, or else you will be consumed." ¹⁸And Lot said to them, "Oh, no, my lords; ¹⁹your servant has found favor with you, and you have shown me great kindness in saving my life; but I cannot flee to the hills, for fear the disaster will overtake me and I die. ²⁰Look, that city is near enough to flee to, and it is a little one. Let me escape there—is it not a little one?—and my life will be saved!" ²¹He said to him, "Very well, I grant you this favor too, and will not overthrow the city of which you have spoken. ²²Hurry, escape there, for I can do nothing until you arrive there." Therefore the city was called Zoar.[b] ²³The sun had risen on the earth when Lot came to Zoar.

24Then the LORD rained on Sodom and Gomorrah sulfur and fire from the LORD out of heaven; ²⁵and he overthrew those cities, and all the Plain, and all the inhabitants of the cities, and what grew on the ground. ²⁶But Lot's wife, behind him,

a14 Or were married to b18 Or No, Lord; or No, my lord
c19 The Hebrew is singular. d22 Zoar means small.

a Gk Syr Vg: Heb he b That is Little

471

NIV

burning sulfur on Sodom and Gomorrah—from the LORD out of the heavens. ²⁵Thus he overthrew those cities and the entire plain, including all those living in the cities—and also the vegetation in the land. ²⁶But Lot's wife looked back, and she became a pillar of salt.

²⁷Early the next morning Abraham got up and returned to the place where he had stood before the LORD. ²⁸He looked down toward Sodom and Gomorrah, toward all the land of the plain, and he saw dense smoke rising from the land, like smoke from a furnace.

²⁹So when God destroyed the cities of the plain, he remembered Abraham, and he brought Lot out of the catastrophe that overthrew the cities where Lot had lived.

³⁰Lot and his two daughters left Zoar and settled in the mountains, for he was afraid to stay in Zoar. He and his two daughters lived in a cave. ³¹One day the older daughter said to the younger, "Our father is old, and there is no man around here to lie with us, as is the custom all over the earth. ³²Let's get our father to drink wine and then lie with him and preserve our family line through our father."

³³That night they got their father to drink wine, and the older daughter went in and lay with him. He was not aware of it when she lay down or when she got up.

³⁴The next day the older daughter said to the younger, "Last night I lay with my father. Let's get him to drink wine again tonight, and you go in and lie with him so we can preserve our family line through our father." ³⁵So they got their father to drink wine that night also, and the younger daughter went and lay with him. Again he was not aware of it when she lay down or when she got up.

³⁶So both of Lot's daughters became pregnant by their father. ³⁷The older daughter had a son, and she named him Moabᵉ; he is the father of the Moabites of today. ³⁸The younger daughter also had a son, and she named him Ben-Ammiᶠ; he is the father of the Ammonites of today.

e37 *Moab* sounds like the Hebrew for *from father.*   f38 *Ben-Ammi* means *son of my people.*

NRSV

looked back, and she became a pillar of salt.

27Abraham went early in the morning to the place where he had stood before the LORD; 28and he looked down toward Sodom and Gomorrah and toward all the land of the Plain and saw the smoke of the land going up like the smoke of a furnace.

29So it was that, when God destroyed the cities of the Plain, God remembered Abraham, and sent Lot out of the midst of the overthrow, when he overthrew the cities in which Lot had settled.

30Now Lot went up out of Zoar and settled in the hills with his two daughters, for he was afraid to stay in Zoar; so he lived in a cave with his two daughters. 31And the firstborn said to the younger, "Our father is old, and there is not a man on earth to come in to us after the manner of all the world. 32Come, let us make our father drink wine, and we will lie with him, so that we may preserve offspring through our father." 33So they made their father drink wine that night; and the firstborn went in, and lay with her father; he did not know when she lay down or when she rose. 34On the next day, the firstborn said to the younger, "Look, I lay last night with my father; let us make him drink wine tonight also; then you go in and lie with him, so that we may preserve offspring through our father." 35So they made their father drink wine that night also; and the younger rose, and lay with him; and he did not know when she lay down or when she rose. 36Thus both the daughters of Lot became pregnant by their father. 37The firstborn bore a son, and named him Moab; he is the ancestor of the Moabites to this day. 38The younger also bore a son and named him Ben-ammi; he is the ancestor of the Ammonites to this day.

COMMENTARY

This chapter brings the story of Lot to an end, concluding with the faintest of hopes for the future. Lot was part of Abraham's journey of faith (12:5). A conflict over land rights concludes when Lot picks the region around Sodom. The author makes three telling comments (13:10-13): a fertile area like the garden of the LORD; like "the land of Egypt," where *Israel's* "outcry" will be heard by God; its people are "wicked, great sinners against the LORD" (see 18:20). From this chapter, it appears that Lot has taken on some qualities of his environment.

This text (assigned to J) is the most frequently cited Genesis passage in the rest of the Bible. Sodom and Gomorrah become a conventional image for heinous sins and severe disaster. Apparently these cities symbolize the worst that can be imagined. The nature of Sodom's sins may vary, but the mistreatment of other human beings tops the list; inhospitality lends itself to diverse development (Jer 23:14). Later texts recall Sodom's judgment, even its specific form (see Ps 11:6; Ezek 38:22; Rev 21:8).

We do not know where these cities were located, but some now place them southeast of the Dead Sea (rather than under the southern part of the sea). The area lies in a geological rift, extending from Turkey to East Africa, the Dead Sea being its lowest point (1,305 feet below sea level). The area has extensive sulphur and bitumen deposits and petrochemical springs, which the text points out (14:10; 19:24; cf. Deut 29:23; Zeph 2:9). An earthquake with associated fires (19:28; brimstone is sulfurous fire) may have ignited these deposits, producing an explosion that "overthrew" these cities.

The tradition has taken up tales of some such ecological disaster and woven them into the story of Abraham and his family. The area around the Dead Sea had not always been desolate, and its present state was due to *human* wickedness. Such an interrelationship of human and cosmic orders stands in continuity with 3:16 and the flood story (see 13:10). Scholars have noted parallels with the latter, from the lack of sexual restraint (6:1-4), to natural disaster (note v. 24, "rained" on Sodom), to the saving of a remnant (and God's

remembering, 8:1; 19:29), to the drunken aftermath (cf. 9:20-27 with vv. 30-38). The NT also appropriates these texts (see Luke 17:26-32; 2 Pet 2:5-8, which identifies Lot as righteous). We may also discern continuities with the exodus events, such as the outcry of the oppressed, the ecological disasters (plagues), the fate of the Egyptians, and Lot's being brought out of the city (יָצָא *yāsāʾ*, vv. 12, 16, 17).

We may also view this chapter from the vantage of its close parallel in Judg 19:22-30, a text that depends heavily on this passage.[138] Sexual abuse comes from Israelites, however, not from foreigners. While the inhospitable mistreatment of others in the two stories contains similar components, the focus in Genesis on divine judgment through a natural disaster and the preservation of a remnant push the story in somewhat different directions.

19:1-11. Readers are not explicitly informed about the upshot of the conversation in 18:23-33. For all they know, God has found ten righteous people in Sodom and the city will be saved. The narrator now gives readers an inside view, enabling them to judge for themselves what ought to be done to Sodom. So 19:1-11 develops an *illustration* of Sodom's character; in view of this, readers should have little difficulty agreeing with the verdict—even Lot comes off as one whose righteous behavior we might question.

The author develops this illustration in relationship to 18:1-15. Both chapters share the basic thematic link of *hospitality,* which should not be narrowly conceived, as if it were a matter of putting out a welcome mat. Hospitality involves a wide-ranging image, revealing fundamental relationships of well-being for individuals and society. Abraham shows hospitality in exemplary fashion. Lot follows suit to some extent, but he fails at a key juncture. The people of Sodom show no sign of what hospitality entails at all.

It seems wise not to overdraw the differences between Abraham's hospitality in 18:1-8 and Lot's in 19:1-3. Initially, Lot's hospitality parallels Abraham's; thus, when the differences appear, they

---

138. See S. Lasine, "Guest and Host in Judges 19," *JSOT* 29 (1984) 37-59.

have a greater shock value. Lot does engage the crowd on behalf of his guests, and he names directly the sin of the Sodomites (v. 7; רע ra'). At the same time, his language to them as "brothers" raises problems, and his treatment of his daughters reveals deep levels of inhospitality.

Abraham had welcomed his visitors wholeheartedly and treated them in an exemplary way. Lot behaves in a basically similar way: He rises (but does not run), bows before them, speaks of them as "lords," provides for their rest and refreshment (the preparations are less thorough and the provisions less sumptuous). He also invites them to stay the night to protect them from the street, which also makes for problems. The visitors accept only upon his strong urging. The word brought to Abraham was one of hope (18:9-10); the word to Lot is one of destruction (19:13-14). Both words are introduced with a question regarding the whereabouts of others (18:9; 19:12). Both households respond to the word in similar fashion; they consider it laughable (צחק ṣāḥaq), both Sarah (and Abraham) and Lot's sons-in-law (v. 14). While the response to Sarah was left up in the air (18:15), the narrative pursues the issue of Sodom to its disastrous conclusion. Is the reader invited to draw parallels?

The author makes the depth of Sodom's inhospitality immediately evident. Verse 4 (cf. v. 11) shows that *every* man (!) in the city was caught up in this threat of violence through homosexual activity (they even threaten Lot himself, v. 9). If the assault had succeeded, the result could only be described as gang rape, not a private act. The text presents the sins of Sodom more as social than individual, something that characterizes the entire city. This deed would be but one example of Sodom's sins, as other texts show (see below). Inasmuch as Sodom serves as the evil counterpart to Abraham's hospitality, we trivialize the narrative if we focus on this one sin.

Lot's reply (v. 8) borders on the incredible. Interestingly, he thinks that the men of Sodom would be satisfied with *heterosexual* abuse (as in Judges 19–20, where it is condemned). The offer of his daughters to be abused "as you please" provides but another example of the depravity of Sodom (ironically, Lot will become the abuser of his own daughters, see below). His daughters were betrothed (v. 14); Israel condemned to death those who rape betrothed women (Deut 22:23-24). Threatened sexual abuse and violence, both homosexual and heterosexual, constitutes sufficient evidence to move forward with judgment.

The men of Sodom now raise the issue of justice, which God and Abraham had broached

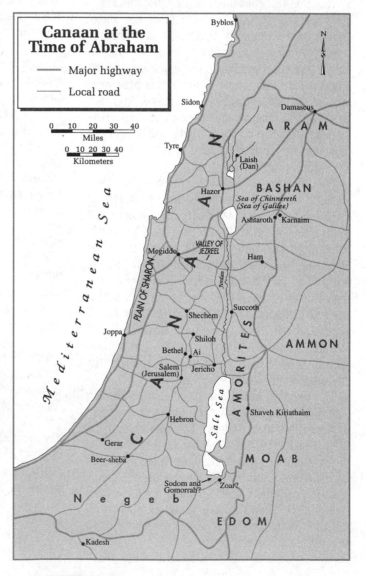

474

earlier (v. 9); the men of Sodom alone can judge the rightness of their own action—no external standard obtains here. The strangers save Lot—who sought to save them—from their violence and strike them with temporary blindness, perhaps a sudden flash of light (see 2 Kgs 6:18; Acts 9:3-9). We hear no more from the men of Sodom; they are left still blindly groping for the door to complete their objective! But God (and the reader) who came to "see" them has seen enough for the judgment to fall.

19:12-23. The angels mediate *God's* destruction (v. 13; so also Lot and narrator, vv. 14, 24); they save Lot and his family. In spite of Lot's warning, the sons-in-law treat it as a laughable matter (cf. 18:12-15). The word for "punishment" in v. 15 is עָוֹן (ʿāwōn,) a common word for "sin" (cf. 4:7). The effects of sin flow out of the sin itself; they are not introduced by God from outside the situation.

These are tension-filled moments, emphasized by the use of imperatives alongside Lot's lingering. Lot's dallying ends only when he is forced to leave the city, an effort due to the undeserved mercy, graciousness, and kindness (חֶסֶד ḥesed) of God (vv. 16, 19). Commanded not to look back lest his family be delayed and engulfed by the fallout, Lot still hesitates out of fear of the open hills (to which he later retreats, v. 30); the angels agree to exclude the city of Zoar. They are "not able" to do anything until Lot is safe (v. 22). In view of v. 29, God's delay for Lot's sake testifies to the efficacy of Abraham's intercession.

Verses 18-23 explain the meaning of the name Zoar ("little"), but more remains at stake. Because of Lot, one of the smaller cities to be destroyed is saved from destruction, *as are the wicked living there.* Hence, God honors one of the principles for which Abraham argued in 18:22-33. The emphasis on its smallness suggests that the presence of Lot and his family were sufficient to provide the "critical mass" of righteous among the wicked.

19:24-26. The author describes the destruction only briefly. The repetition in v. 24 suggests that the brimstone and fire—a traditional expression—come from the very presence of God. Verse 25 describes its calamitous effects, from the cities and environs to the people and the vegetation. The verb *overthrow* may not fit the nature of the event precisely (but cf. *catastrophe,* which has the same meaning; see Jon 3:4).

The fate of Lot's wife echoes a common motif in folklore. Lot's wife mirrors his irresoluteness, only she lingers to the point of death. The nature of the cataclysm could explain the salt pillar; she was engulfed in the fallout of fire and chemicals. Human-shaped pillars of salt still found in the area may have prompted this element in the story (see Wis 10:4).

19:27-29. Abraham retraces his steps (18:33) and "freezes in the awe-inspiring horror of the sight."[139] He says nothing. He simply witnesses the judgment of God, and his silence speaks volumes. The nations of the earth are to find blessing through him, but not inevitably so. In spite of his efforts, intercession could not turn the situation around (cf. Jer 11:14; 14:11).

God rescues Lot *both* because God is merciful toward him (19:16, 19) and because God remembers Abraham (19:29). God does attend to his prayers; without him Lot would have been lost. The repetition in v. 29 stresses the destruction from which he escaped. Both judgment and rescue witness to the universal work of God the Creator, here powerfully at work outside of the chosen community.

19:30-38. The author/editor has integrally related this text to the preceding story (cf. Zoar). Interpreters have tended in two directions. Most commonly, they understand this passage as the conclusion to the story of Lot, the final stage of a downward spiral, showing the depths to which this man of faith had fallen. It presents one possible journey for any person of faith, and in view of 18:19, even for Abraham. Lot meets an end as destructive as the cities from which he is taken, having taken on their character in his own life. Yet, his fear of dwelling in Zoar may mean he was not accepted among these people either. He is a person without a home. The man who had chosen paradise (13:10) ends up in a barren cave, far removed from others, utterly destitute.

Lot, who earlier had offered his daughters for sexual abuse, ironically becomes the one who engages in such acts, but passively so. He becomes the passive sexual object he had determined his daughters should become. The narrator thereby passes sharp judgment on Lot for offering his daughters; his fate corresponds precisely to his earlier deed. What goes around comes around.

139. Westermann, *Genesis 12–36,* 307.

The only "positive" note involves his lack of knowledge; his daughters get him drunk to engage in incest.

Other interpreters see the story as a new beginning; Lot's daughters take the initiative to continue the family line, a larger narrative theme (vv. 32, 34). Parallels with 9:18-27 have been noted, including drunkenness, sexual impropriety, ethnological concerns, and the issue of continuing progeny (the emphasis on Zoar in v. 30 shows that the daughters are concerned about their family line, not a repeopling of the earth). Such a "desperate deed" resonates, especially, with that of Tamar (chap. 38; cf. also the midwives in Exodus 1). Westermann speaks of "acts of revolt against prevailing standards of morality and customs" for the laudable goals of life and family well-being.[140] Given the precarious situation into which their father had led them, their options had narrowed to a single one. Hence, no negative judgment on them seems to be in order, except the judgment of Judah regarding Tamar, "She is more righteous than I" (38:26 NIV).

The reader should also note the genealogical interest in the text. The reference to the Moabites and Ammonites (vv. 37-38) may attest that these peoples were rarely on friendly terms with later Israel (see Deut 23:3). Yet, Ruth was a Moabite, making this son of Lot's daughter an ancestor of both David and Jesus (Ruth 4:18-22; Matt 1:5). The messianic line has one of its roots in this initiative by Lot's daughter. Even out of the worst of family situations, God can bring goodness, life, and blessing to the world.

140. Ibid., 315.

REFLECTIONS

1. Abraham concerns himself with the future of the nonchosen, both righteous and unrighteous, those who are outside the community of faith, almost all of them strangers. He does so by focusing, not on narrowly religious matters (e.g., idolatry), but on issues of justice. This testifies to an interpretation of 12:1-3 that involves the chosen in their relationship to the nations. The fact that God also enters into the lives of others *on the issue of justice* sets a pattern for those who are "to keep the way of the LORD" (18:19).

Sodom is condemned, not because they have no faith in God, but because of the way in which they treat their brothers and sisters. God holds the nonchosen accountable for such behaviors. This assumes an understanding of natural law, wherein God's intentions for all people are clear in the creational order (cf. the oracles of the prophets against the nations, e.g., Amos 1–2).

2. One wonders whether those who think God's decision about Sodom is final from the beginning do so because of a view of God that does not allow for consultation. But God takes Abraham's thinking into account in deciding what the divine action will finally be. God takes seriously what human beings think and say, which can contribute in a genuine way to the shaping of the future. While God would have thought of all the options, to have them articulated by Abraham gives them a new level of significance that God will take into account. Abraham brings new ingredients into the situation—energies, words, insights—that give God new possibilities with which to work. This interaction has the potential of changing the divine decision (see Exod 32:9-14).

Abraham participates with God in matters of divine judgment. Hence, Abraham's role may be compared to that of the pre-exilic prophets (cf. 18:17 with Amos 3:7). We are accustomed to thinking about God working through human beings on behalf of what is positive and good. The nature of the continuing role of the people of God in matters of judgment needs closer scrutiny (see Rom 13:4).

3. This text centers on the future of a corporate entity, not individuals in isolation. It does not deny that individuals are to be held accountable, but it focuses on communal responsibility, on what happens when sin and its effects become so pervasive that the entire community is caught up in it.

The text links corporate responsibility and ecology, a strikingly contemporary concern. Human behavior affects, not simply the human community, but the entire cosmos (though the link may be difficult to discern). Although we often consider individual sins in an analysis of environmental problems, the ecological issue may involve a social dimension in which the innocent (from children to the ozone layer) are caught up in the disastrous consequences. Historical evil can cause creational havoc, as moderns know all too well.

But does not *God* cause all the damage? The text links God to this catastrophe (19:24) as an ecological disaster of divine judgment. God sees to a *creational* form for this disaster; it corresponds to the *anticreational* form of human wickedness, focused especially in the language of outcry and the deprivation of life and well-being (18:20-21; 19:13). God midwifes or sees to the moral order, through already existing human or nonhuman agents.[141] Many such events are just part of the normal workings of the natural order (the rain falls, or does not fall, on the just and the unjust, Matt 5:45). Yet, both Israelites and moderns know that human behaviors have led and will lead to cosmic disaster (flood story; plagues). The devastation of Sodom and Gomorrah and their environs offers a major instance; the depletion of the ozone layer may be another.

The destruction of Sodom and Gomorrah serves as a warning of what could (and did) become of Israel's own land; the text may allude to the fall of Jerusalem (Deut 29:22-23; Jer 4:23-26). The link between the practice of justice and righteousness and the future of the land remains very close, as the prophets often point out (see Hos 4:1-3). They focus their message of judgment in a sharply corporate manner, rooted in God's concern for the oppressed, deeply embedded in the law (Exod 22:21-23). The prophets do voice a hope regarding the regardening of the land (Isa 51:3; Ezek 36:35), but only on the far side of ecological and historical disaster.

While judgment language may be difficult to accept, for God not to be concerned about the oppression of people would mean that God does not finally care about evil and its effects. What are misdemeanors to us may be disasters to God, not least because God sees the evil effects they have on the creation in a way that we do not. At the same time, this story shows that God is not eager that judgment fall. God consults with Abraham about the possibility of another future short of judgment; God appears open to alternatives. The speech of God in Ezek 18:32 (NRSV), "I have no pleasure in the death of anyone," also characterizes the God of this text. This cuts against the grain of any notion that Israel's God acts as a punitive God focused on the punishment of the wicked. Israel's God is "slow to anger," even with the nonchosen.

4. This text *illustrates* the situation in Sodom as homosexual activity (condemned for males in Israel [Lev 18:22; 20:13]), but refers specifically to the abusive violence and savage inhospitality. The text does not talk about homosexual activity or orientation generally, or nonviolent sexual behavior. Other biblical references to Sodom lift up a wide range of behavior, from neglect of the poor and needy to lies, greed, luxury, heterosexual abuse, and inhospitality to strangers (Isa 1:9-10; Jer 23:14; Lam 4:6; Ezek 16:48-55; Zeph 2:9). Jesus remains true to the text in condemning a town to a fate like Sodom's because of its refusal to receive strangers who bear the word of God (Matt 10:14-15; 11:23-24; Luke 10:12; 17:29; 2 Pet 2:8; only in Jude 7 does the reference to homosexual behavior possibly become explicit).

5. Abraham forthrightly raises the issue of theodicy. He brings questions about the justice of God directly to God, who fields them in a way that does not close off conversation. These issues are raised so sharply because of crisis contexts in which this material functioned. The fate of the righteous, not least the children (Lam 2:20; 4:10), in the judgment of Samaria

---

141. See discussion of plagues in Fretheim, *Exodus,* 105-12.

(Amos 7:1-6) or Jerusalem (Ezek 14:12-20) was a lively issue, as was the saving role of the few for the many (see Isa 53:1-12; Jer 5:1). In such events the innocent (many more than ten!) often have perished with the guilty. Would it be Abraham's view that the Judge of all the earth has *often* not acted correctly?

We usually conceive of the relationship between act and consequence in individual terms, letting the judicial system "take care of" the penalty. We think less often about corporate sin and judgment, but actions against a corporate aggressor (e.g., war) are rooted in such understandings. In God's concern for the moral order at this level, the righteous are caught up in the judgment of the wicked and suffer with them, e.g., children in the fall of Jerusalem (or the World Wars). In such cases, we are seldom able precisely to sort the innocent and the righteous from the wicked. More generally, the interconnectedness of life means that evil actions will have dire consequences for those who are not guilty. The innocent often suffer the consequences of acts committed by the wicked.

Abraham's question focuses on the fairness of the moral order. Should the innocent perish when the wicked are judged? But Abraham argues for the saving of not only the righteous, but also the entire city because of the presence of the righteous, more precisely in order to save the righteous. The priority ought to be given to the righteous. In effect, the presence of the righteous would lead to the extension of the divine mercy upon all. This, of course, would mean that the wicked would not receive their just deserts. So Abraham seeks to abandon any exact retribution system, but discovers in the process that no such system exists.

Abraham, however, introduces a qualification. He raises the precise *number* of righteous people that ought to be present. The numbers ought not to be taken literally; that would establish a kind of quota to which divine judgment would be bound. Yet, the numbers are important (the dialogue focuses there) and indicate the kind of issue Abraham raises. Two questions will help to address this issue:

Why does Abraham not *begin* with one righteous person or take it all the way down to one? If he wanted to reverse this approach completely, the presence of one would be sufficient to make his case. He must want to make another point. Moreover, he stops at ten. God takes leave at that juncture, with Abraham and God in apparent agreement. Why are fifty or ten righteous persons enough to spare the city, but one or so not? Sarna pushes in the right direction.[142] Ten represents the limit of the number of righteous who could outweigh the cumulative evil of the community. Ten constitutes the "minimum effective social entity," a critical mass, *for this situation* (for other situations, the number would vary considerably). The buildup of wickedness and its effects in Sodom are such that ten righteous would not be able to turn around the potential for judgment. So few righteous could not affect the shape of the future in a positive way.

Through this conversation, Abraham recognizes that God will indeed act justly concerning Sodom, and indeed any corporate entity. But, with respect to corporate justice, there comes a point when justice must be done, even radical surgery undertaken, even if some righteous people get caught up in the judgment. Other options are not finally tolerable, especially an option where the Sodomites would not be brought to account in any way for the terrible injustice they are visiting upon people. To avoid judgment would allow evil to go unchecked in the world.

God agrees that the righteous few can often save a city. But Abraham recognizes that there comes a point when even the righteous are too few to turn a situation around (fewer than ten). Even then, what the righteous do in such situations will make a difference, but not a predictable one. Perhaps even ten (or whatever) will not finally be enough. Abraham persuades

142. Sarna, *Genesis,* 134.

God to think of a lower number of righteous that might make a difference in Sodom's situation, but finally he chooses not to seek to overturn the moral order, recognizing the justice in it.

Genesis 19:29 presents one other point of persuasion when God remembers Abraham and saves Lot. Abraham is concerned about *all* righteous persons who may have been in the city (he begins with fifty!). Although Abraham does not specifically mention Lot, neither does the author identify Lot as righteous; one has difficulty in linking God's remembering in 19:29 with anything other than Abraham's expressed advocacy. Does God then make an extraordinary exception to the judgment that will catch up the righteous in Sodom? Does God save Lot (and the people of Zoar!) arbitrarily?

For one thing, the fact that the righteous will suffer judgment with the wicked does not belong, necessarily, to the order of things. The moral order does not involve a tight causal weave, with no room for chance or randomness, for the serendipitous or the extraordinary event.

For another, intercession counts for something; Abraham's intercessory advocacy makes a difference. The community of faith tends to intercede for those of whom it approves or causes it endorses. We do not often intercede for the Lots and Sodoms of this world, persons who have disappointed us by the direction they have taken with their lives. Jesus identifies our obligation: "Love your enemies and pray for those who persecute you" (Matt 5:44-47 NRSV; see Jer 29:7).

At the same time, such activity cannot be separated from the kind of response to the warnings one sees in Lot and his family in chap. 19. If such alarms are deemed to be in jest, the potential effect of intercession will be cut off. Lot illustrates how the journey of faith may end on a very tragic note. Choices people make can adversely affect the power of intercession and the divine engagement in their lives.

This text witnesses to the significance of the presence of the righteous in any situation; they can subvert the effects of sin and evil *from within the city* so that the consequences are less severe, perhaps even sparing the wicked and reclaiming the city. This author argues against fatalism among the righteous, the belief that nothing can be done about society's problems, that plays down the potential impact of human activity and resigns itself to sin's consequences. The righteous can indeed make a difference, to the world and to God.

The positive note in vv. 30-38 entails an understanding of a God who works for good in the midst of great evil (50:20). The decision of Lot's daughters correlates to their father's earlier abuse of them. A father who would offer them to the entire male population of the town for the purpose of sexual services could hardly have had an appropriate relationship with them, no matter how patriarchal the family structures may have been. Their father showed them the way, as have abusive fathers over the centuries; it takes little imagination to recall abusive situations just as devastating in our own society. In such moments, hope in a God who keeps promises through the worst of times can sustain one through to another day. Even then, the journey of a family may continue to be filled with troubles, as the Genesis narrative unfolds. Yet, that one grandson of Lot (Moab), an ancestor of David and Jesus, witnesses to what God can bring out of the worst of situations. Someday God will raise up a single innocent one who does have the power to save the many unrighteous, not by resigning himself to that wickedness or ignoring it, but taking it into himself and exploding the powers of death from within (Isa 53:5, 10: Hos 11:8-9).

GENESIS 20:1-18, ABRAHAM, SARAH, AND ABIMELECH

NIV

20 Now Abraham moved on from there into the region of the Negev and lived between Kadesh and Shur. For a while he stayed in Gerar, [2]and there Abraham said of his wife Sarah, "She is my sister." Then Abimelech king of Gerar sent for Sarah and took her.

[3]But God came to Abimelech in a dream one night and said to him, "You are as good as dead because of the woman you have taken; she is a married woman."

[4]Now Abimelech had not gone near her, so he said, "Lord, will you destroy an innocent nation? [5]Did he not say to me, 'She is my sister,' and didn't she also say, 'He is my brother'? I have done this with a clear conscience and clean hands."

[6]Then God said to him in the dream, "Yes, I know you did this with a clear conscience, and so I have kept you from sinning against me. That is why I did not let you touch her. [7]Now return the man's wife, for he is a prophet, and he will pray for you and you will live. But if you do not return her, you may be sure that you and all yours will die."

[8]Early the next morning Abimelech summoned all his officials, and when he told them all that had happened, they were very much afraid. [9]Then Abimelech called Abraham in and said, "What have you done to us? How have I wronged you that you have brought such great guilt upon me and my kingdom? You have done things to me that should not be done." [10]And Abimelech asked Abraham, "What was your reason for doing this?"

[11]Abraham replied, "I said to myself, 'There is surely no fear of God in this place, and they will kill me because of my wife.' [12]Besides, she really is my sister, the daughter of my father though not of my mother; and she became my wife. [13]And when God had me wander from my father's household, I said to her, 'This is how you can show your love to me: Everywhere we go, say of me, "He is my brother." ' "

[14]Then Abimelech brought sheep and cattle and male and female slaves and gave them to Abra-

NRSV

20 From there Abraham journeyed toward the region of the Negeb, and settled between Kadesh and Shur. While residing in Gerar as an alien, [2]Abraham said of his wife Sarah, "She is my sister." And King Abimelech of Gerar sent and took Sarah. [3]But God came to Abimelech in a dream by night, and said to him, "You are about to die because of the woman whom you have taken; for she is a married woman." [4]Now Abimelech had not approached her; so he said, "Lord, will you destroy an innocent people? [5]Did he not himself say to me, 'She is my sister'? And she herself said, 'He is my brother.' I did this in the integrity of my heart and the innocence of my hands." [6]Then God said to him in the dream, "Yes, I know that you did this in the integrity of your heart; furthermore it was I who kept you from sinning against me. Therefore I did not let you touch her. [7]Now then, return the man's wife; for he is a prophet, and he will pray for you and you shall live. But if you do not restore her, know that you shall surely die, you and all that are yours."

8So Abimelech rose early in the morning, and called all his servants and told them all these things; and the men were very much afraid. [9]Then Abimelech called Abraham, and said to him, "What have you done to us? How have I sinned against you, that you have brought such great guilt on me and my kingdom? You have done things to me that ought not to be done." [10]And Abimelech said to Abraham, "What were you thinking of, that you did this thing?" [11]Abraham said, "I did it because I thought, There is no fear of God at all in this place, and they will kill me because of my wife. [12]Besides, she is indeed my sister, the daughter of my father but not the daughter of my mother; and she became my wife. [13]And when God caused me to wander from my father's house, I said to her, 'This is the kindness you must do me: at every place to which we come, say of me, He is my brother.' "[14]Then Abimelech took sheep and oxen, and male and female slaves, and gave them to Abraham, and restored his wife Sarah to

NIV

ham, and he returned Sarah his wife to him. ¹⁵And Abimelech said, "My land is before you; live wherever you like."

¹⁶To Sarah he said, "I am giving your brother a thousand shekels^a of silver. This is to cover the offense against you before all who are with you; you are completely vindicated."

¹⁷Then Abraham prayed to God, and God healed Abimelech, his wife and his slave girls so they could have children again, ¹⁸for the LORD had closed up every womb in Abimelech's household because of Abraham's wife Sarah.

a16 That is, about 25 pounds (about 11.5 kilograms)

NRSV

him. ¹⁵Abimelech said, "My land is before you; settle where it pleases you." ¹⁶To Sarah he said, "Look, I have given your brother a thousand pieces of silver; it is your exoneration before all who are with you; you are completely vindicated." ¹⁷Then Abraham prayed to God; and God healed Abimelech, and also healed his wife and female slaves so that they bore children. ¹⁸For the LORD had closed fast all the wombs of the house of Abimelech because of Sarah, Abraham's wife.

COMMENTARY

This text (often assigned to E) closely parallels 12:10-20 and 26:1-11 but includes more dialogue and theological reflection. These ties invite a comparison, but such analyses ought to center on the text's role within its present literary context. The narrative provides a return look at Abraham after all that has happened in chaps. 12–19. Given these events, especially Abraham's developing relationship with God, how might he fare in a situation like the one he faced in 12:10-20?

Links with chaps. 18–19 are especially strong: issues of justice, human and divine (Abraham proves to be closer to the Sodomites than Abimelech!), sin and consequence, Abraham as intercessor. Chapter 21 will return to contact between Abraham and Abimelech (vv. 22-34), but sandwiched in between is a narrative of birth and separation. Focus on the closing of wombs in 20:18 leads into the story of the conception and birth of Isaac (21:1-7), where God's action and Abraham's paternity reinforce 20:4-6.

The author builds this story around three dialogues: Abimelech with God (vv. 3-7), Abimelech with Abraham (vv. 9-13), and Abraham and Sarah (vv. 15-16).

20:1-7. Abraham journeys (נסע *nāsa'*) and sojourns (גור *gûr*) for the first time since 12:9-10, which introduced the previous story of threat to Sarah. Now Abraham sojourns in the city-state of Gerar (in the southwestern corner of Canaan in what became Philistine territory, see 21:34).

In 12:10-20, the narrator presented early the reasoning behind Abraham's calling Sarah his sister; here the rationale is delayed until vv. 11-13. Abraham, already in Gerar, initially claims that Sarah is his sister. Only in v. 5 are we told that Abraham spoke these words to Abimelech, the king of Gerar, and that Sarah had concurred. Placing Abraham's claim at the onset of the story suggests that he has not learned from the previous experience. Once again, he deliberately betrays Sarah. Her acquiescence notwithstanding, Abraham knowingly places her life and well-being in jeopardy. Even more, he apparently still does not believe that God's promise of a son includes Sarah (see 17:16-17). In spite of all the divine words and deeds in his life, Abraham does not address the issue in theological terms. Even more, he fails to consider the effects of his actions on outsiders. These actions may well provide some of the backdrop for the testing in chap. 22.

In view of what Abraham does, and Abimelech's taking Sarah, God abruptly enters the situation to protect Sarah. God speaks to Abimelech in a dream (see 28:10-22; 37; 40–41; dreams were considered a medium of divine revelation and no less real or personal than a direct divine encounter). Abimelech and God carry out a conversation within the dream; Abimelech claims innocence since he did not know that Sarah was married to Abraham. This interchange (vv. 3-7) appears unusual in a number of respects.

(a) God speaks to one who stands outside the community of faith (cf. 31:24; Num 22:20), indeed engages in dialogue with him. Abimelech's response (vv. 4-5) occasions a positive response in God (vv. 6-7), which opens up the possibilities for life rather than death.

(b) Similar to Abraham in 18:22-33, Abimelech acts in a situation of perceived injustice. He not only pleads with God, but sharply questions God and flatly states his innocence ("pure heart and clean hands" may be a legal formula; cf. 17:1; Pss 24:4; 78:72); he places his action in the context of his general loyalty to interhuman relationships. He refuses to acquiesce in the face of a divine decision or resign himself to the announced fate of death. He expects his innocence to be acknowledged if justice is to be served. His question in v. 4 appears like Abraham's in 18:25: "Lord, will you destroy an innocent people [גּוֹי *gôy*]?" Verses 7, 9, 17-18 indicate the events have affected more than Abimelech as an individual. God acknowledges Abimelech's innocence.

(c) Verse 6 states that God has been so active in his life that Abimelech was prevented from touching Sarah (we learn from v. 17). Because God states this reason, the claim is incontestable.

(d) God announces that Abimelech is a dead man because of what he has done (v. 3), even though v. 6 makes clear that God knew he was innocent. Hence, the announcement of v. 3 serves not as a forensic judgment, but as a matter-of-fact divine statement regarding the moral order and its effects on Abimelech. We learn from vv. 17-18 that Abimelech's death would have been caused by a malady that was capable of being healed and that the women of his household were unable to conceive. The moral order means that certain deeds have an effect just by virtue of their having happened, and people reap the consequences quite apart from their intentions or their knowledge of what they have done (a reality just as true today as then).

(e) God devotes attention to the *effects* of the deeds apart from questions of guilt or innocence. In preventing Abimelech from touching Sarah through an illness, God has prevented a worse deed from occurring and even more serious effects. So the situation is not as bad as it might have been! Possibilities for the future are more hopeful as a result.

God specifies that two things must happen for Abimelech's life to be preserved (v. 7): He should restore Sarah to Abraham, and then Abraham, a prophet, should pray for him. Indeed, if he does not so proceed, his entire family will be claimed by death. Abimelech must do more than restore the situation to the point where it started. He also must consider all the effects that his action has let loose. God deems prayer necessary in order to deal with such realities (see v. 17).

God's word about Abraham's being a prophet serves a double purpose. It protects Abraham from any precipitous judgment that Abimelech may wish to pass, for it makes his life dependent on Abraham's intercession. It also shows God's concern for Abimelech, providing a means by which he can be brought through this difficulty alive. To use the word *prophet* for Abraham is anachronistic, and may be used because prophets were commonly associated with intercessory activity (cf. 1 Sam 12:23; Jer 11:14).

20:8-18. Abimelech reacts in two basic ways. (1) He calls *all* his servants together and reports the event to them (cf. 41:8). Their response is fear; the fallout from this act will adversely affect their lives (see v. 17). (2) Having been assured by God that he has acted innocently, Abimelech confronts Abraham and in effect conducts a judicial inquiry. He does this with knowledge regarding Abraham's complicity that Abraham does not know he has. He does not reveal where he got the information, however, and seeks to get Abraham to tell the story from his own point of view. His charges, expressed as assertions and as rhetorical questions, are on target. Given what Abimelech knows and has suffered, he shows notable restraint and magnanimity toward the guilty one.

Two striking things occur in this: (1) the outsider pronounces Abraham guilty: "You have done things to me that ought not to be done" (v. 9). Abimelech's sin language reveals the essence of the problem. He has not sinned (חטא *ḥāṭā*ʾ) against Abraham, but Abraham has brought a "great guilt" (חטאה *ḥăṭāʾâ*) on him. *Abraham's* sin lies at the root of the problem, and its effects have reached out through Abimelech's innocent deed and engulfed his entire kingdom. Gerar faces a situation not unlike Sodom and Gomorrah, but this time due to *Abraham's* unrighteousness. (2) God uses the outsider as a confessor, eliciting a confession from Abraham himself.

In responding (vv. 10-13), Abraham does not deny his guilt, but becomes very defensive and seeks to justify his actions. He gives three reasons: (a) He had determined with certainty (רק *raq*) that there was no fear of God in this place and so had to protect himself (as in 12:10-20, killing an alien was considered less an offense than adultery). In view of what *Abraham* has done, and what the reader has learned about Abimelech, this reason appears highly ironic (and may explain its delay). The "fear of God" may indeed be found in this place. Not all cities are like Sodom! It is *Abraham* who has not exhibited the fear of God; this lays the groundwork for the testing of Abraham's fear of God (22:12; to distinguish between Abimelech's and Abraham's fear of God misses this point).

(b) Sarah, his half-sister, became his wife (a permissible practice, later forbidden, Deut 27:22). This rationale does not speak to the point being made. Abraham had not given Abimelech sufficient knowledge to make a proper decision regarding Sarah.

(c) Genesis 20 does not offer a special case; Abraham has done this at every place where they have sojourned! His focus on kindness (חסד *ḥesed*) to himself, and laying the blame back on God for making him wander (not the full truth of the matter), have a self-serving ring. This suggests a less than trusting relation to God, let alone an inability to develop strategies for life that are in the best interests of all those who might be affected.

Given the defensiveness of Abraham's reply, Abimelech's response seems magnanimous indeed. He not only restores Sarah (the use of "brother" means he either accepts Abraham's explanation or keeps his deed front and center in the midst of the generosity), he gives Abraham a significant sum of money for the purpose of vindicating her within her family (literally, a "covering of eyes")—a public demonstration that she has not been wronged and hence can be held in honor within her community. He also gives them animals and servants and offers them a place to live in his land (unlike 12:19-20).

Abraham responds by interceding on Abimelech's behalf (see 18:22-33; Num 12:13; 21:7). God responds to his prayer and heals Abimelech (of an uncertain malady) and his wife and female slaves so that they can once again bear children (illness? Was Sarah included?). Instead of being an agent of blessing, Abraham had been an agent of curse; but by praying he can begin to turn around what he has done. Note that the narrator uses the name Yahweh for the first time in this narrative (v. 18), perhaps to make clear that this activity functions consistently with the work of God, whom Abimelech's community confesses. This community of outsiders receives, thereby, order (salvation).

REFLECTIONS

1. God attends to what Abimelech has to say in vv. 4-5; it affects the shape of the future. God takes seriously religious questioning by the "unchosen" ones. Moreover, God engages them directly, albeit through less than "orthodox" channels (such as dreams). The fact that Abimelech is a Canaanite ruler makes this point even more notable.

The reader finds goodness and a keen sense of justice among the outsiders. "The Canaanite king hears the voice that speaks as God's voice because it says what he recognizes to be just and valid."[143] The narrator, of course, understands this voice as that of the God of Abraham. Throughout the ages, nonchosen people often have had a profound sense of justice and truth, and they have often been teachers of the community of faith regarding such matters. The text functions with a sense of natural law as a part of the created order of things that can be discerned and observed apart from faith. (See Jesus' evaluation of the centurion in Matt 8:10: "In no one in Israel have I found such faith" [NRSV].)

143. Westermann, *Genesis 12–36*, 322.

Once again, God uses an outsider to convict the chosen ones of their sinful deeds (see 12:18-19). Persons of faith have not listened to outsiders as often as they should, perhaps thinking that they cannot be called to account by such persons on moral issues. Many people who are not a part of the community of faith have consciences more sensitive than the people of God, who do not have a corner on discerning right and wrong. One might claim that Abimelech is motivated by self-interest, for he needs Abraham's intercession to be healed. Yet, the overall portrayal of Abimelech suggests a person of character. Although not the root cause of this problem, he seeks to bring healing to the situation far beyond the level of his own involvement.

2. For God to hold an individual back from sinning (v. 6) raises a theological issue. If God can enter into people's lives and, at will, prevent them from sinning (in this case, through Abimelech's illness), then human sin reflects a divine choice, occurring only when God chooses *not* to hold individuals back from doing so. A more likely interpretation would be that Abimelech does not sin because he responds to the work of God in his life.

Texts such as this should prompt reflection concerning God's relationship with those outside the chosen community. It should prevent easy assumptions about God's presence and activity in their lives. Whether such persons recognize the transcendent reality at work is another matter, of course. They often may be unable to name the experience for what it is. The community of faith faces a challenge to speak about the faith with these persons in such a way that connections can be made with the God experiences they have already had, enabling them to move toward naming that experience for what it in fact has been. God speaks with Abimelech fundamentally to preserve Sarah, but also because of a concern for Abimelech.

3. References to the effect of Abimelech's deed upon his people highlight the communal impact of an individual's sin, insufficiently recognized in modern individualistic understandings of sin and guilt. Words for "sin" can refer to any point on a continuum from the sinful act (the first reference in v. 9) to its far-reaching effects (the second). An innocent person, indeed an entire nation, has been caught up in the effects of another's sin. Because of the seamless web of life, the interconnectedness of all things, those who are innocent are often caught up in the consequences of the sinful deeds of others (from personal abuse to wars).

In a related matter, this narrative clarifies the importance of distinguishing between forgiveness and salvation. One may be forgiven for a sin committed and thereby be restored within the broken relationship; but forgiveness, however many positive results it may have, does not wipe out with one stroke the *effects* of the sin. Those effects have to be dealt with in other ways, the result of which may be called salvation. Isaiah 40:1-11 is an illustration: God announces forgiveness in vv. 1-2, but salvation still lies in the future. A contemporary illustration: A parent may be forgiven for the abuse of a child, but the effects of that abuse in the child's life will need considerable attention over the months and years to come before the child is healed.

4. Abraham, once again, has brought trouble rather than blessing to outsiders (v. 9). He has not attended very well to the call to be a blessing to all families. This no doubt mirrors the people of God in later generations, who have often mistreated strangers and aliens in their midst (a concern deeply rooted in Israel's law, cf. Exod 22:21-27). Deeds of the chosen have all too often led to the suffering of others.

5. God does not heal directly, but works through Abraham's prayers. The prayer of a righteous person may avail much (James 5:16), but here the prayer of an *unrighteous* Abraham proves effective. The righteous one needs the prayers of the unrighteous chosen one. God has chosen to work through even such persons to carry out the divine purposes. Other texts will speak of additional means (e.g., 2 Kgs 20:7), but prayer appears here as a powerful vehicle through which God works to heal.

6. God works for life and goodness, both within and without the community of faith, and often in spite of the words and deeds of the chosen ones. Although they may complicate and frustrate the divine activity, they cannot finally stymie it; God will find a way to work toward the divine purposes. The next narrative speaks about other ways in which God continues this task.

Genesis 21:1-34, ISAAC, ISHMAEL, AND ABIMELECH

OVERVIEW

The three episodes in this chapter are sewn together by word plays and other verbal and thematic links. The stories of the birth of Isaac and the expulsion of Hagar and Ishmael are internally linked, and together they are enclosed by stories about Abimelech. The first (20:1-17) is tied to 21:1-7 by the references to God's involvement in the lives of women having difficulty bearing

children; the second (21:22-34) follows a story in which water and wells, and relationships between insiders and outsiders, also play a role. The birth of Isaac is surrounded by many texts associated with nonchosen people, suggesting that issues of Israel's relationship to such people (see 12:3) are central. The story of Hagar and Ishmael also has many links with chap. 22 (see below).

Genesis 21:1-7, The Birth of Isaac

NIV

21 Now the LORD was gracious to Sarah as he had said, and the LORD did for Sarah what he had promised. ²Sarah became pregnant and bore a son to Abraham in his old age, at the very time God had promised him. ³Abraham gave the name Isaac*a* to the son Sarah bore him. ⁴When his son Isaac was eight days old, Abraham circumcised him, as God commanded him. ⁵Abraham was a hundred years old when his son Isaac was born to him.

⁶Sarah said, "God has brought me laughter, and everyone who hears about this will laugh with me." ⁷And she added, "Who would have said to Abraham that Sarah would nurse children? Yet I have borne him a son in his old age."

a3 Isaac means he laughs.

NRSV

21 The LORD dealt with Sarah as he had said, and the LORD did for Sarah as he had promised. ²Sarah conceived and bore Abraham a son in his old age, at the time of which God had spoken to him. ³Abraham gave the name Isaac to his son whom Sarah bore him. ⁴And Abraham circumcised his son Isaac when he was eight days old, as God had commanded him. ⁵Abraham was a hundred years old when his son Isaac was born to him. ⁶Now Sarah said, "God has brought laughter for me; everyone who hears will laugh with me." ⁷And she said, "Who would ever have said to Abraham that Sarah would nurse children? Yet I have borne him a son in his old age."

COMMENTARY

Isaac's birth brings a key aspect of the story of Abraham to a climax. The writer depicts it in quite straightforward fashion, considering all the problems and possibilities that have led up to this moment (some twenty-five years have passed since 12:4).

The work of the redactor (the narratives are a mix of JEP) includes cross-references, with four citations back to earlier narratives (vv. 1, 2, 4). They stress that God has made good on the promises (17:15-21) and that Abraham has been obedient in naming and circumcising Isaac (17:12,

19; cf. 17:23). Readers will recall the ages of Sarah and Abraham; that constitutes the wonder of the occasion (see 24:36; barrenness is no longer in view). The theme of laughter associated with Isaac's name continues. Only Sarah speaks in response to Isaac's birth (vv. 6-7). Abraham remains silent here and throughout much of the chapter, for reasons that are not entirely clear.

The distinct divine acts in v. 1 (cf. Luke 1:68) stress that God has made Isaac's birth possible. The first verb (פקד *pāqad,* various translations are possible) links this act of God with Exodus events (50:24-25; Exod 3:16; 4:31), showing the import of Isaac for the larger divine purpose. The promise language in 17:16 focuses on blessing, so one should think of a divine *creative* activity that makes Sarah's pregnancy possible (see 11:30).

God's naming of Isaac leads to his naming by both Abraham (v. 3) and Sarah (implicitly in v. 6). Whether vv. 6-7 contain one or two explanations of the name *Isaac* is debated, but the element of shame is unlikely. Verse 6 refers to Sarah's joy at the *birth* of Isaac; others who hear about the birth will rejoice *with* her. Verse 7 gives the reason: No one would have dreamed of announcing to Abraham that two such old people would become parents. They themselves did not believe it could be so!

Isaac's name thus expresses the joy at his birth, with only an indirect reference to the earlier laughter at God's promise of a son. Indeed, the author construes the former disbelief as something anyone would do. We best understand the final line in v. 7 (an inclusio with v. 2) as a cry of joy: "I have borne him a son in his old age" (see Reflections).

REFLECTIONS

1. Isaac, though the son of promise, will also cause problems, tearing this family apart. But at this moment he is the source of deep joy. The cynical laughter of these parents has not been held against them; it has been turned into genuine joy at this new life made possible by God. God has brought an end to cynicism and despair of the future; joyful hope fills the scene.

2. God does not act independently when dealing with Sarah (v. 1). The author uses the verb *bear/beget* (ילד *yālad,* used five times, twice in v. 3, but obscured in NRSV/NIV; cf. 17:17) to describe the roles of both Abraham and Sarah. At the same time, this event occurs only because God has become involved in some way, when all the roads into the future seem blocked (the text stresses their age). God works in and through human beings to carry out his purposes in the world, with all the complications and potential difficulties related thereto. The unusual cross-references stress not only the fulfillment of God's word, but also that this was not the only future possible for God. The faith of Abraham and Sarah remains relevant to all of this (as Rom 4:16-21 and Heb 11:11-12 make clear).

A modern question arises, however: In what sense can we (do we!) still speak of God's involvement in bringing a new life into being? The question is especially poignant for those parents who have had difficulty having children. The OT speaks graphically of this in some texts (e.g., Job 10:8-12; Ps 139:13). One might speak of multiple agency; both God and parents are involved in the shaping of new life. We do not normally understand God's power as all-determinative; the parental situation can profoundly affect matters, e.g., cocaine babies. Genetics or unknown factors appear more complicated. One should think of God's creative involvement in and through the medical community seeking to overcome these realities, resulting in breakthroughs for many parents.

This text might suggest that God can set aside natural processes (in this case, age) for his own special purposes. At the same time, the NT texts noted above indicate that this divine action relates to human response (in this case, faith in a specific promise). A likely reason for the long delay in the fulfillment of the promise relates to the developing response of Abraham and Sarah (including their lack of trust in 17:17; 18:12). Generally, God's perseverance within a human situation may find openings into the future that seem impossible to us, but God's will may also be frustrated in view of human response.

Genesis 21:8-21, Hagar and Ishmael

NIV

[8]The child grew and was weaned, and on the day Isaac was weaned Abraham held a great feast. [9]But Sarah saw that the son whom Hagar the Egyptian had borne to Abraham was mocking, [10]and she said to Abraham, "Get rid of that slave woman and her son, for that slave woman's son will never share in the inheritance with my son Isaac."

[11]The matter distressed Abraham greatly because it concerned his son. [12]But God said to him, "Do not be so distressed about the boy and your maidservant. Listen to whatever Sarah tells you, because it is through Isaac that your offspring*a* will be reckoned. [13]I will make the son of the maidservant into a nation also, because he is your offspring."

[14]Early the next morning Abraham took some food and a skin of water and gave them to Hagar. He set them on her shoulders and then sent her off with the boy. She went on her way and wandered in the desert of Beersheba.

[15]When the water in the skin was gone, she put the boy under one of the bushes. [16]Then she went off and sat down nearby, about a bowshot away, for she thought, "I cannot watch the boy die." And as she sat there nearby, she*b* began to sob.

[17]God heard the boy crying, and the angel of God called to Hagar from heaven and said to her, "What is the matter, Hagar? Do not be afraid; God has heard the boy crying as he lies there. [18]Lift the boy up and take him by the hand, for I will make him into a great nation."

[19]Then God opened her eyes and she saw a well of water. So she went and filled the skin with water and gave the boy a drink.

[20]God was with the boy as he grew up. He lived in the desert and became an archer. [21]While he was living in the Desert of Paran, his mother got a wife for him from Egypt.

a12 Or seed   b16 Hebrew; Septuagint the child

NRSV

8The child grew, and was weaned; and Abraham made a great feast on the day that Isaac was weaned. [9]But Sarah saw the son of Hagar the Egyptian, whom she had borne to Abraham, playing with her son Isaac.*a* [10]So she said to Abraham, "Cast out this slave woman with her son; for the son of this slave woman shall not inherit along with my son Isaac." [11]The matter was very distressing to Abraham on account of his son. [12]But God said to Abraham, "Do not be distressed because of the boy and because of your slave woman; whatever Sarah says to you, do as she tells you, for it is through Isaac that offspring shall be named for you. [13]As for the son of the slave woman, I will make a nation of him also, because he is your offspring." [14]So Abraham rose early in the morning, and took bread and a skin of water, and gave it to Hagar, putting it on her shoulder, along with the child, and sent her away. And she departed, and wandered about in the wilderness of Beer-sheba.

15When the water in the skin was gone, she cast the child under one of the bushes. [16]Then she went and sat down opposite him a good way off, about the distance of a bowshot; for she said, "Do not let me look on the death of the child." And as she sat opposite him, she lifted up her voice and wept. [17]And God heard the voice of the boy; and the angel of God called to Hagar from heaven, and said to her, "What troubles you, Hagar? Do not be afraid; for God has heard the voice of the boy where he is. [18]Come, lift up the boy and hold him fast with your hand, for I will make a great nation of him." [19]Then God opened her eyes and she saw a well of water. She went, and filled the skin with water, and gave the boy a drink.

20God was with the boy, and he grew up; he lived in the wilderness, and became an expert with the bow. [21]He lived in the wilderness of Paran; and his mother got a wife for him from the land of Egypt.

a GkVg: Heb lacks with her son Isaac

COMMENTARY

This story has often been considered a doublet with chap. 16 (J and E versions; see the distinctive use of Yahweh and Elohim). Through this "doubling," Hagar and Ishmael become more prominent figures in the story of Abraham, receiving almost as much attention as Isaac. They cannot be set aside as minor diversions in the larger story.

The fulfillment of the divine promise in Isaac's birth occasions problems as well as possibilities. The immediate problem has to do with the relationship between Abraham's two sons. Ishmael and Isaac are both children of promise (see their parallel genealogies in 25:12, 19). In 17:19-20, however, God has made clear to Abraham the difference between the sons. God would make a covenant with Sarah's son, the yet-to-be-born Isaac. But God would not overlook Ishmael; indeed, God makes promises to him as well (16:10; 17:20; 21:13, 18). God's redemptive purposes on behalf of the world (including Ishmael!) will manifest themselves through Isaac. Some of the dynamics associated with this divinely determined distinction are worked out in these verses.

21:8-14. The author begins by noting that Isaac is growing up; hence, the relationship with Ishmael will need attention. At the same time, the relationship between Sarah and Hagar (16:3-9) was either not resolved amicably or has deteriorated in the three years since Isaac's birth. The references to Hagar as an Egyptian and bearer of Abraham's child are linked to the conflict in chap. 16, as is Sarah's repeated reference to Hagar as the "slave woman" (cf. 16:2, 5) and her concern about inheritance rights (legally, both sons would inherit). Sarah expresses concern about her maturing son's future.

These factors are sufficient explanation for Sarah's action. Yet, the difficulty in translating v. 9 (see Gal 4:29, where Ishmael "persecutes" Isaac) prompts a closer look. The verb צחק (*sāḥaq,* "mocking" [NIV]; "playing" [NRSV, adding "with her son Isaac," see footnote]) can have positive or negative senses (cf. 19:14). The verb has appeared in earlier narratives—the name *Isaac* and Sarah's and Abraham's laughter (17:17-19; 18:12-13). The word play associated with Ishmael's activity may have reminded her of the divine decision (17:19-20). Not unlike Rebekah (cf. 25:23), she decides it is time to act; Abraham must choose between his sons. Inasmuch as God will support her objective, at least in this regard the author views Sarah's action in positive terms.

Sarah's *strategy* is also difficult to understand, however. She demands that Abraham send Hagar and Ishmael away, using language that recalls Pharaoh's action in Exod 12:39 (and led to Israel's freedom!). She also chooses the festival associated with the weaning of Isaac, a time of rejoicing because he has survived the difficult first years. Her timing and means seem unnecessarily harsh, and (unlike chap. 16) she does not speak to Hagar. Yet God, agreeing with Sarah's objective, chooses not to interfere with her strategy.

Abraham appears distressed at Sarah's request (v. 11). His concern centers on Ishmael rather than Hagar (cf. 17:18), because Sarah insists that he choose between his two sons; God's reply (v. 12) expresses concern about Hagar as well. The narrator's use of "his son" (i.e., Ishmael) intensifies his anguish. Abraham is genuinely torn. This characteristic of Abraham has recurred in the narrative (cf. 16:6; 17:18). He has difficulty taking decisive action or following through on what God has said; yet, he shows deep levels of concern for the plight of the persons involved, and he does not finally stand in the way of God's directive.

In responding to Abraham (perhaps in a dream, v. 14), God sides with Sarah, adopts some of her language, and tells him to do as she says! God supports her objective and lets her set the strategy; Abraham must set his own feelings aside. God's rationale basically repeats what had been told to Abraham earlier (17:19-21), making it doubly clear that Abraham must make a choice. Both sons are recognized as Abraham's offspring (vv. 12-13; literally, "seed"), but God's particular future will be worked out through Isaac, however difficult or unpleasant that may be. God announces that it is through Isaac that descendants will be "named" for Abraham (NRSV), which probably refers to the covenantal line. At the same time, Abraham can be assured that God will care for the future of Ishmael. God will make of him a great nation also (vv. 13, 18).

This divine concern appears immediately (vv. 15-21). Abraham does as God tells him (שלח [*šālaḥ*, "send away"] again—see chap. 16—is language for Israel's *freedom* in Exodus, e.g., 5:1-2). The author creates a poignant picture in v. 14—not a single word is spoken (the text remains ambiguous as to whether Ishmael—now about sixteen years old—is placed on Hagar's shoulder). This verse stands parallel to 22:3, as do other elements in this text (see below).

21:15-21. The parallels with Exodus continue in

Hagar and Ishmael's "wandering in the wilderness," again mirroring Israel's later experience (as does the provision of water). With water supplies depleted, Hagar puts Ishmael under a bush and moves away in deep sorrow; she cannot bear to watch him die. God hears "the voice of the boy" (her lament and Ishmael's are telescoped) and responds to "her" (by name; no "slave-girl") with a salvation oracle: God quells her fear and assures her of Ishmael's future in words used with Abraham (v. 13). God opens Hagar's eyes and she sees (cf. the seeing in 16:13) the source of water needed to save Ishmael's life. The now-familiar God/messenger of God rhythm appears (see 16:7).

The story closes with three themes that bode well for the future of both mother and child: "God was with the lad" (as with Abraham in v. 22); Hagar exhibits no little strength in continuing to care for his needs (finding a wife for him among her own people, the only time a mother does this in the OT); and he becomes an expert hunter. All these are important for shaping Ishmael's life well, but God's presence with him and God's promise to be creatively at work in his life stand out. His twelve sons parallel Jacob's progeny (25:12-18). Ishmael and Isaac, both as "sons," will return for the burial of their father (25:9).

REFLECTIONS

1. The modern reader may tend to side with Abraham rather than Sarah on the issue of sending Hagar and Ishmael away. Yet, some such move must occur if the sons are to shape their separate futures consistent with God's choice (17:19-20), a historical and theological reality for the narrator. Her objective seems to be on target, even if the means are unnecessarily harsh. It may be more troubling that God lets Sarah set the strategy for the separation. Here, again, God chooses to work through complex situations and imperfect human beings on behalf of the divine purposes. God works with individuals on the scene; God does not perfect people before deciding to work through them. God may see Sarah's strategy, however inadequate, as the best possible way into the future for this particular moment in the life of this family.

2. Although Genesis 22 has received most of the attention, this story of Ishmael is certainly just as difficult and heart-rending. The father-son relationship between Abraham and Ishmael is close and strong. Note some of the parallels between the episodes: In 21:14 and 22:3 Abraham rises "early in the morning" and wordlessly proceeds to put his son's future in jeopardy; both seem to move relentlessly toward death. In both cases, Abraham obeys God's command and trusts in the divine promise, leaving the future of his sons in the hands of God. Hagar voices her lament, while Abraham voices his confidence that God will provide; the sons voice laments, though only Isaac speaks. The angel of the Lord calls from heaven and speaks of a role for their hands, assuring each parent that the son will live. The eyes of both see a source of life that saves their sons.

These are parallel events in Abraham's life. What he endures as a parent of what is now an "only son" (22:2, 12, 16) appears all the more extraordinary. The character of God's "test" of Abraham in chap. 22 is intensified; God's promises are placed in jeopardy in both cases. This should occasion reflection about why the threat to the life of the "outsider" (see chap. 16) is so widely neglected compared to the threatened life of the chosen one of God. The narrator thinks otherwise. The narrative holds us to "the tension between the one *elected* and the not-elected one who is *treasured*" by God.[144]

3. Hagar's lament ensues in the assurance of salvation. This typical rhythm characterizes *Israel's* communal and individual life, so evident in the Psalms. In this story the people of God should recognize and rejoice that God's saving acts are not confined to their own community. God's acts of deliverance occur out and about in the seemingly godforsaken corners of the world, even among those who may be explicitly excluded from the "people of God." Here we see God at work

144. Brueggemann, *Genesis*, 183.

among the outcasts, the refugees of the world—who fill our world as much as they did then. Persons of faith are to participate in their lives, to lift them up and hold them fast until the wells become available. They are also to discern where God's delivering activity may have occurred, to name these events for what they are, and publicly to confess them as such to the participants and to all the world. Once again, we see how Genesis witnesses to the workings of the *Creator* God. Telling and retelling stories like this one keeps that testimony alive and serves to remind the chosen that their God is the God of all the world, including the outcasts.

Phyllis Trible speaks eloquently about Hagar's becoming many things to many people (see chap. 16): "Most especially, all sorts of rejected women find their stories in her. She is the faithful maid exploited, the black woman used by the male and abused by the female of the ruling class, the surrogate mother, the resident alien without legal recourse, the other woman, the runaway youth, the religious fleeing from affliction, the pregnant young woman alone, the expelled wife, the divorced mother with child, the shopping bag lady carrying bread and water, the homeless woman, the indigent relying upon handouts from the power structures, the welfare mother, and the self-effacing female whose own identity shrinks in service to others."[145] How does the community of faith respond to these Hagars of our world?

The text does affirm that God chooses the line of Isaac, not that of Ishmael. This is a strong claim, and it occasions a sharper question for Isaac's descendants than if the treatment had been more "even-handed." What one does with the Ishmaels of this world in the face of the claims for Isaac comes front and center. Abraham was chosen so that all families might be blessed through him. This means that the children of Abraham who are also the children of *Isaac* are so to comport themselves that blessing rather than curse comes upon the nations.

4. This text reminds us that the world is filled with both physical *and spiritual* (as Christians relate to Abraham) descendants of Ishmael. Nearly one billion Muslims, 85 percent of whom live outside the Middle East, call Abraham father, too. Even more, they are the descendants of God's promise to Ishmael, which remains a contemporary theological reality. How is the other half of Abraham's family going to relate to these brothers and sisters in ways that acknowledge this ongoing work of God? Our words and actions may run so counter to God's activity that the divine will for this people, embodied in the promises, is thereby frustrated and hence less effective than it might otherwise be.

Paul's use of this text in Gal 4:21-31 picks up on the story in a somewhat narrow way, but does not finally stand over against this point. Using an allegorical approach, Hagar and Sarah symbolize two different ways of conceiving of life in God's world: Hagar, the way of slavery and law (Sinai); and Sarah, the way of promise and the freedom of the Spirit. Ishmael was produced in natural, humanly planned ways; Isaac came only as a gift of God's promise. Paul uses this contrast to address differences between Christianity and Judaism, with Christians belonging to the line of promise. From another angle, Hagar could be the embodiment of Paul's argument, with her combination of necessity (her return to Sarah) and freedom.[146] Paul's word in Gal 3:28-29, that there are neither slave nor free, but that all are one in Christ Jesus, could provide another perspective on Hagar, who bears public witness to the God of Abraham and Sarah.

145. Trible, *Terror*, 28.
146. See Janzen, "Hagar in Paul's Eyes."

Genesis 21:22-34, Abraham and Abimelech

NIV	NRSV
[22]At that time Abimelech and Phicol the commander of his forces said to Abraham, "God is	22At that time Abimelech, with Phicol the commander of his army, said to Abraham, "God

NIV

with you in everything you do. ²³Now swear to me here before God that you will not deal falsely with me or my children or my descendants. Show to me and the country where you are living as an alien the same kindness I have shown to you."

²⁴Abraham said, "I swear it."

²⁵Then Abraham complained to Abimelech about a well of water that Abimelech's servants had seized. ²⁶But Abimelech said, "I don't know who has done this. You did not tell me, and I heard about it only today."

²⁷So Abraham brought sheep and cattle and gave them to Abimelech, and the two men made a treaty. ²⁸Abraham set apart seven ewe lambs from the flock, ²⁹and Abimelech asked Abraham, "What is the meaning of these seven ewe lambs you have set apart by themselves?"

³⁰He replied, "Accept these seven lambs from my hand as a witness that I dug this well."

³¹So that place was called Beersheba,ᵃ because the two men swore an oath there.

³²After the treaty had been made at Beersheba, Abimelech and Phicol the commander of his forces returned to the land of the Philistines. ³³Abraham planted a tamarisk tree in Beersheba, and there he called upon the name of the LORD, the Eternal God. ³⁴And Abraham stayed in the land of the Philistines for a long time.

ᵃ31 Beersheba can mean well of seven or well of the oath.

NRSV

is with you in all that you do; ²³now therefore swear to me here by God that you will not deal falsely with me or with my offspring or with my posterity, but as I have dealt loyally with you, you will deal with me and with the land where you have resided as an alien." ²⁴And Abraham said, "I swear it."

25When Abraham complained to Abimelech about a well of water that Abimelech's servants had seized, ²⁶Abimelech said, "I do not know who has done this; you did not tell me, and I have not heard of it until today." ²⁷So Abraham took sheep and oxen and gave them to Abimelech, and the two men made a covenant. ²⁸Abraham set apart seven ewe lambs of the flock. ²⁹And Abimelech said to Abraham, "What is the meaning of these seven ewe lambs that you have set apart?" ³⁰He said, "These seven ewe lambs you shall accept from my hand, in order that you may be a witness for me that I dug this well." ³¹Therefore that place was called Beer-sheba;ᵃ because there both of them swore an oath. ³²When they had made a covenant at Beer-sheba, Abimelech, with Phicol the commander of his army, left and returned to the land of the Philistines. ³³Abrahamᵇ planted a tamarisk tree in Beer-sheba, and called there on the name of the LORD, the Everlasting God.ᶜ ³⁴And Abraham resided as an alien many days in the land of the Philistines.

ᵃ That is Well of seven or Well of the oath   ᵇ Heb He
ᶜ Or the LORD, El Olam

COMMENTARY

This episode explores the relationship between Abraham and Abimelech, which began in chap. 20 (cf. Isaac in 26:1-33). It may be an interweaving of two covenant stories (from J and E?) that explain the name Beersheba (cf. 26:33) as the "well of the oath" and the "well of seven [ewe lambs]."

Abimelech appears as a character in two separate episodes, a common feature in the Abraham cycle (witness the wife-sister theme, covenant, Lot, Hagar, and Ishmael). This "doubling" brings greater coherence to the larger story. Here it suggests that the relationship between Abraham and other peoples (especially those in Canaan) matters. Isaac's birth

occurs in the midst of a world filled with various problems. The story also highlights Abraham's initial acquisition of land in Canaan (cf. chap. 23). Beersheba, at the southernmost boundary of Judah, did not become a city until later times.

The transition between vv. 21 and 22 is abrupt but presupposes the problems created for Abimelech by Abraham in chap. 20. There are few links to the story of Hagar and Ishmael, but both relate Abraham to non-Israelite peoples, and in ways that exhibit the importance of positive relationships about which God expresses concern.

We may compare the content of vv. 22-24 to

the report about Isaac and Abimelech/Phicol in 26:26-33. Abimelech's testimony regards God's presence with Abraham and Abimelech's concern that the basic human loyalty (חסד ḥesed) he has shown Abraham be returned to his family (and to the land!). Abraham swears that he will do so. The reference to posterity brings the problematic relationships between Israelites and Canaanites over the years into view. Abraham serves as a mirror in which those generations can reflect about such relationships.

Within the relationship just established, Abraham complains to Abimelech about his servants' actions in seizing a well (v. 25), an important resource in that world (see 26:27). Abimelech pleads ignorance, but also notes that he had not been informed until this moment (in view of chap. 20, this response is not evasive). This exchange concludes with a nonaggression pact, according to which the two agree to maintain a relationship of integrity. Abraham contributes sheep and oxen for his part, but from among them sets seven ewe lambs apart and gives them a special significance. Abraham's reply to Abimelech's natural query about the lambs indicates that, by accepting them as an addendum to the oath, Abimelech makes a public witness that the well is not his but Abraham's.

This shrewd move settles the conflict over the well. Beersheba receives its name based on this sworn oath and the gift/acceptance of the seven lambs. In this way, the story provides grounding for *both* meanings—well of seven or well of the oath (NRSV)—of the name Beersheba.

Abimelech and Phicol return to their own territories. The "land of the Philistines" could be an anachronism (the Philistines settled in that land around 1200 BCE), yet it probably represents the knowledge of the Abrahamic era available to the narrator. Philistines may represent all pre-Israelite inhabitants of the land. Abraham plants a tree at Beersheba as a permanent sign of the treaty and worships God. The epithet used for God (only here)—El Olam, the Everlasting God—may testify to the appropriation of an epithet/name of the god El for Yahweh (cf. Ps 102:24-29). When related to the nature of this specific event, it expresses a confidence in God's tending to this relationship long after the death of the present participants. The final note that Abraham sojourned for an extensive period of time in Abimelech's land testifies not only to the effectiveness of the treaty, but also to Abraham's continuing alien status in a land included in the promise (15:18-21).

REFLECTIONS

Abimelech again discerns the character of Abraham's situation theologically. He *interprets* Abraham's relationship with God: "God is with you in all that you do" (v. 22), in language identical to the narrator's interpretation of Ishmael in v. 20. In other words, God has blessed Abraham in all observable circumstances of life. In spite of the way Abimelech was treated in chap. 20, he discerns that God's presence functions decisively in Abraham's life. Given God's promise (12:3), Abimelech participates in God's blessings to Abraham and Abraham gains some rights in the land. That an outsider like Abimelech makes such a confession and treats Abraham well in spite of what happened earlier testifies notably to God's work as Creator in his life.

Abraham enters into a mutually agreed-upon covenant with outsiders. God's purposes in the world are for the good order of the creation, which includes relationships with all, regardless of their faith commitments. The story implies that Abraham is not somehow inevitably trustworthy; specific agreements will be needed by the outsider, because loyalty on the part of chosen ones all too often fails.

In response to the *secular* event of reconciliation, Abraham worships Yahweh. This connection made by Abraham between peacemaking events of everyday life and the worship of God is significant. Linking such events of peace and justice explicitly to God recognizes that God has been involved behind the scenes, enabling such salutary effects. The OT regularly refuses to separate sacred and secular, though God-talk is often reserved for explicitly religious matters in the modern world. The confession of the community of faith should be clear: "All things work together for good for those who love God" (Rom 8:28 NRSV). This should issue in worshipful gratitude to God whenever *any* good thing happens.

GENESIS 22:1-19, THE TESTING OF ABRAHAM

NIV

22 Some time later God tested Abraham. He said to him, "Abraham!"

"Here I am," he replied.

²Then God said, "Take your son, your only son, Isaac, whom you love, and go to the region of Moriah. Sacrifice him there as a burnt offering on one of the mountains I will tell you about."

³Early the next morning Abraham got up and saddled his donkey. He took with him two of his servants and his son Isaac. When he had cut enough wood for the burnt offering, he set out for the place God had told him about. ⁴On the third day Abraham looked up and saw the place in the distance. ⁵He said to his servants, "Stay here with the donkey while I and the boy go over there. We will worship and then we will come back to you."

⁶Abraham took the wood for the burnt offering and placed it on his son Isaac, and he himself carried the fire and the knife. As the two of them went on together, ⁷Isaac spoke up and said to his father Abraham, "Father?"

"Yes, my son?" Abraham replied.

"The fire and wood are here," Isaac said, "but where is the lamb for the burnt offering?"

⁸Abraham answered, "God himself will provide the lamb for the burnt offering, my son." And the two of them went on together.

⁹When they reached the place God had told him about, Abraham built an altar there and arranged the wood on it. He bound his son Isaac and laid him on the altar, on top of the wood. ¹⁰Then he reached out his hand and took the knife to slay his son. ¹¹But the angel of the LORD called out to him from heaven, "Abraham! Abraham!"

"Here I am," he replied.

¹²"Do not lay a hand on the boy," he said. "Do not do anything to him. Now I know that you fear God, because you have not withheld from me your son, your only son."

¹³Abraham looked up and there in a thicket he saw a ram*ᵃ* caught by its horns. He went over and took the ram and sacrificed it as a burnt

ᵃ13 Many manuscripts of the Masoretic Text, Samaritan Pentateuch, Septuagint and Syriac; most manuscripts of the Masoretic Text a ram behind ˌhimˌ

NRSV

22 After these things God tested Abraham. He said to him, "Abraham!" And he said, "Here I am." ²He said, "Take your son, your only son Isaac, whom you love, and go to the land of Moriah, and offer him there as a burnt offering on one of the mountains that I shall show you." ³So Abraham rose early in the morning, saddled his donkey, and took two of his young men with him, and his son Isaac; he cut the wood for the burnt offering, and set out and went to the place in the distance that God had shown him. ⁴On the third day Abraham looked up and saw the place far away. ⁵Then Abraham said to his young men, "Stay here with the donkey; the boy and I will go over there; we will worship, and then we will come back to you." ⁶Abraham took the wood of the burnt offering and laid it on his son Isaac, and he himself carried the fire and the knife. So the two of them walked on together. ⁷Isaac said to his father Abraham, "Father!" And he said, "Here I am, my son." He said, "The fire and the wood are here, but where is the lamb for a burnt offering?" ⁸Abraham said, "God himself will provide the lamb for a burnt offering, my son." So the two of them walked on together.

9When they came to the place that God had shown him, Abraham built an altar there and laid the wood in order. He bound his son Isaac, and laid him on the altar, on top of the wood. ¹⁰Then Abraham reached out his hand and took the knife to kill*ᵃ* his son. ¹¹But the angel of the LORD called to him from heaven, and said, "Abraham, Abraham!" And he said, "Here I am." ¹²He said, "Do not lay your hand on the boy or do anything to him; for now I know that you fear God, since you have not withheld your son, your only son, from me." ¹³And Abraham looked up and saw a ram, caught in a thicket by its horns. Abraham went and took the ram and offered it up as a burnt offering instead of his son. ¹⁴So Abraham called that place "The LORD will provide";*ᵇ* as it is said to this day, "On the mount of the LORD it shall be provided."*ᶜ*

ᵃ Or to slaughter   ᵇ Or will see; Heb traditionally transliterated Jehovah Jireh   ᶜ Or he shall be seen

NIV

offering instead of his son. [14]So Abraham called that place The LORD Will Provide. And to this day it is said, "On the mountain of the LORD it will be provided."

[15]The angel of the LORD called to Abraham from heaven a second time [16]and said, "I swear by myself, declares the LORD, that because you have done this and have not withheld your son, your only son, [17]I will surely bless you and make your descendants as numerous as the stars in the sky and as the sand on the seashore. Your descendants will take possession of the cities of their enemies, [18]and through your offspring[a] all nations on earth will be blessed, because you have obeyed me."

[19]Then Abraham returned to his servants, and they set off together for Beersheba. And Abraham stayed in Beersheba.

[a]18 Or seed

NRSV

[15]The angel of the LORD called to Abraham a second time from heaven, [16]and said, "By myself I have sworn, says the LORD: Because you have done this, and have not withheld your son, your only son, [17]I will indeed bless you, and I will make your offspring as numerous as the stars of heaven and as the sand that is on the seashore. And your offspring shall possess the gate of their enemies, [18]and by your offspring shall all the nations of the earth gain blessing for themselves, because you have obeyed my voice." [19]So Abraham returned to his young men, and they arose and went together to Beer-sheba; and Abraham lived at Beer-sheba.

COMMENTARY

Recent readers of this famous story have been particularly interested in delineating its literary artistry.[147] Significant gains have resulted, but one wonders whether this approach has overplayed its hand by overdramatizing the story and reading too much between the lines. Likewise, religious interpretations, especially in the wake of Kierkegaard's *Fear and Trembling,* seem often to intensify the contradictoriness of the story, perhaps in the interests of heightening the mystery of the divine ways. While the frightening, even bizarre, character of the divine command ought not to be discounted, it should not be exaggerated either.

This story (commonly assigned to E, with supplements) remains firmly within the circle of the family, which suggests an original pre-Israelite setting. At the same time, the theological force of the story takes on new contours as it is passed through many generations (especially vv. 15-19).[148] Exilic Israel may have seen itself in both Abraham and Isaac: God has put Israel to a test in which many children died, has called forth its

continuing faith, has delivered it through the fires of judgment and renewed the promises.

Israelite ritual regarding the firstborn informs this text. Israel knew that God could require the firstborn (Exod 22:29), but that God had provided for their redemption (Exod 13:13; 34:20). Here, God does just this: God asks that Isaac be sacrificed and provides an animal "instead of" Isaac. This issue belongs indisputably to the story, but with a metaphorical understanding of *Israel* as God's firstborn (see below). The text bears no mark of an etiology of sacrifice (see 4:3-4; 8:20) or a polemic against child sacrifice, clearly abhorrent to Israel, though it was sometimes a problem (cf. Lev 20:2-5; 2 Kgs 3:27; Jer 7:31; 32:35).

This text fits into the larger sweep of Abraham's life. The relationship between God and Abraham is in progress; it has had its ups and downs, in which each has affected the other. Abraham has exhibited a deep faith and engaged God in significant theological conversation, while God has consulted with Abraham regarding the fate of Sodom and Gomorrah. At the same time, Abraham's response has been less than exemplary, even distrusting the promise (17:17) and not showing the "fear of God" in relationship to outsiders (see

147. Most influential is E. Auerbach, "Odysseus' Scar," in *Mimesis* (Princeton: Princeton University Press, 1965) 1-22.

148. See R. Moberly, "The Earliest Commentary on the Akedah," *VT* 38 (1988) 302-23.

20:11). His response has raised an issue for God, indeed what God truly knows (v. 12).

Generally, though, this text presupposes "familiar mutual trust" built over no little experience together.[149] From Abraham's perspective, the God who commands has filled his life with promises; he understands that God has Abraham's best interests at heart. He has already learned to trust this God. He has no reason to distrust the God from whom this word comes, however harsh and frightening it may be.

The test appears especially poignant in view of the parallels with the story of Ishmael (see 21:8-21). Abraham has just lost his son Ishmael, hence the repeated reference to Isaac as "only son." Now he is asked to sacrifice his remaining son. We may view these stories as mirrors of each other, focusing on the potential loss of both sons, as well as on God's providing for both children.

Parallels between Gen 12:1-4 and Genesis 22 provide an overarching structure. Although this divine command does not appear as abrupt as in 12:1, they are similar in other ways, in vocabulary ("take, go" to a "place that I shall show you"), along with Abraham's silent, but faithful, response. Both are ventures in faith and enclose the story of Abraham; Abraham begins and ends his journey with God by venturing out into the deep at the command of God. The former cuts Abraham off from his past; the latter threatens to cut him off from his future.

We may observe the structure of the entire text in the threefold reference to "your son, your only son" (vv. 2, 12, 16). Also, the repetition of Abraham's "Here I am," spoken to God (v. 1), then Isaac (v. 7), and finally God (v. 11) highlights basic moments in the story.

22:1-14. God commands Abraham not to kill or murder his son, but to present him "on the altar" as a burnt offering to God (עלה *'ōlâ;* cf. Exod 29:38-46; Lev 1:3-17). The offering language places this entire episode within the context of the sacrificial system. The deed will be a specifically religious act, an act of faith, a giving to God of what Abraham loves (only then would it be a true sacrifice). Inasmuch as sacrifice involves a vehicle in and through which God gives back the life that has been given, the hope against hope for Abraham would be that

God would somehow find a way of giving Isaac—or another life—back (hence the link made to the resurrection by Heb 11:17-19). We should note that Abraham does, finally, offer a sacrifice.

Abraham's silent response to God's command (on test, see below) may be designed to raise questions in the mind of the reader. Why is Abraham being "blindly" obedient, not raising any questions or objections (especially in view of 18:23-25)? Abraham's trust in God seems evident in his open stance ("Here I am") and unhesitating response. At the same time, the text gives us no clue as to his emotional state (e.g., whether he was deeply troubled).

God's command is accompanied by נא (*na'*), a particle of entreaty or urgency. Rarely used by God (cf. Judg 13:4; Isa 1:18; 7:3), God thereby may signal the unusual character of the moment and the relationship of mutual trust. It may help Abraham to see that God has as much stake in this matter as he does; God needs to know about Abraham's faith. This may account for Abraham's silence. However, God does not engage in a ploy, but offers a genuine command. Yet, the command pertains to a particular moment; it is not universally valid. Moreover, God does not intend that the commandment be fully obeyed. Hence, God revokes the command when the results of the test become clear and speaks a second command that *overrides* the first (v. 12).

We should note the emphasis on "seeing." Twice, Abraham lifts up his eyes (vv. 4, 13), and five times the verb "to see" (ראה *rāʾâ*) is used of Abraham (vv. 4, 13) and God (vv. 8, twice in 14). From a distance, Abraham sees the place where God told him to sacrifice Isaac and then, close up, he sees the ram provided at that very place. This process testifies to a *progressively clearer seeing.* Abraham places his trust in *God's seeing* (v. 8) and that trust finally enables him to see the lamb that God has seen to. Seeing saves the son (cf. Hagar's seeing in 16:13; 21:19, which saves Ishmael).

The writer offers another important feature: "the mountains that I shall show you" (v. 2; cf. 12:1). The narrative stresses it early on (vv. 3-5, 9) and returns to it in v. 14, when a name appears: God will provide. *God* shows Abraham that place (by v. 3 NRSV). It is as if God has

149. Westermann, *Genesis 12–36,* 356.

prepared the scene ahead of time, ram and all, and hence Abraham must be precisely directed to it. Moriah, three days' journey away (a general reference), a place unknown to us, but not to him, may refer to Jerusalem (2 Chr 3:1; cf. "the mount of Yahweh" [v. 14] in Ps 24:3; Isa 2:3). The place name *Moriah* gives the command a special quality: Abraham will not sacrifice at any altar, but in a specific God-chosen place a great distance away. Might this arrangement have given Abraham a clue to what God intended?

Verses 7-8 are central. The statement "the two of them walked on together" encloses this interchange between Abraham and Isaac. Abraham's statement of faith that God will provide (v. 8) is the only time Abraham responds more fully than "Here I am." This is also the only time that Isaac speaks. Note also the movement from the more distancing language of "boy" in v. 5 to the repeated "my son" in vv. 7-8, perhaps testifying to a shift in perspective.

By this point Abraham stays on course because he trusts that God will act to save Isaac. He conveys to Isaac what he believes to be the truth about his future: God will provide. He testifies to this form of divine action in v. 14, as does Israel's witness to the event "to this day" (v. 14). God tests precisely the nature of Abraham's response as unhesitating trust in the deity. As God puts it (v. 12), it involves Abraham's fear of God, a faithfulness that accords with God's purposes and works itself out in daily life as truth and justice (see 20:11). Abraham obeys because he trusts God; trust out of which obedience flows remains basic. Disobedience would reveal a lack of trust. At least by v. 8 Abraham's obedience is informed and undergirded by a trust that God will find a way through this dark moment.

Anticipations of this trust occur earlier. In v. 5 Abraham tells his servants that both of them will worship and both will return; the servants *witness* to this conviction. The author relates the trustful reference to worship with the worship in v. 8. To suggest that Abraham is equivocating or being ironic or deceptive or whistling in the dark finds no basis in the text; such ideas betray too much interest in dramatization. It would be strange for a narrative designed to demonstrate Abraham's trusting obedience to be punctuated with acts of deception.

Verses 7-8 also focus on Isaac. The author initially devotes attention to Isaac as a child (without recalling the promise). Abraham loves this child (in *God's* judgment, v. 2); we should not assume an abusive relationship. Although ignorant of the journey's purpose, Isaac does not remain entirely passive. He breaks the silence with a question of his father (v. 7)—the only recorded exchange between them. He senses that something is not right (his lack of reference to the knife no more suggests this than does the absence of fire in vv. 9-10). Yet, Isaac does not focus on himself. (Isaac's emotions are often overplayed.) Isaac addresses Abraham as a loving father, mirroring Abraham's trusting relationship to God. Abraham responds in like manner.

Abraham centers on what his son has to say, attending to him as he has attended to God ("Here I am"). He does not dismiss Isaac's question, as if inappropriate. It even elicits Abraham's trust in God in a *public* form. Isaac enables his father's trusting action to be joined with trusting words. While not telling him everything, Abraham does answer Isaac's question directly and conveys to him what he believes will happen. What had been implicit (v. 5) here becomes explicit. Their walking on together conveys indirectly Isaac's response. He exhibits no resistance, even later when his father prepares him for the sacrificial moment (some descriptions of the knife go beyond the text). Isaac believes his father's trust to be well placed. Abraham's trust in God has become Isaac's trust: God will provide a lamb, which is God's intention from the beginning, of course, and Abraham and Isaac are now both attuned to that intention and trust it.

The text also focuses on Abraham's *continuing* trust in God. The trusting departure does not settle the issue, or God could have cut off the journey much earlier. The question becomes: Will Abraham stay with the journey? The author stresses the journey as such, which provides opportunity for second thoughts (vv. 6, 8) following each expression of trust (vv. 5, 8). Abraham exhibits his trust in God by staying the course. Only at the end of the journey can God say, "Now I know."

Tensions in the text also center on God. *What is at stake in this for God?*

1. God's testing. God and the reader know

this is a test; Abraham does not. God intends not to kill Isaac but to test Abraham's faithfulness, which is essential if God is to move into the future with him. In responding, Abraham no doubt observes (as do all commentators) the apparent contradictory character of the command: God, having fulfilled the promise of a son, asks Abraham to sacrifice that son and the future that goes with him. The fact that Abraham obeys shows that he trusts God will find a way into the future. God had found a way to fulfill the promise of a son when nothing seemed possible (see 18:14); given that experience, Abraham trusts that this comparably impossible situation will not be beyond God's ability. Abraham trusts that God's promise and command are not finally contradictory; whatever conflict there may be, it is up to God to resolve it, and God is up to it.

If Abraham had known in advance that it was a test, it would have been no real test; for he (or anyone) would respond differently to a test from a more indirect method of discernment. Moreover, the test would not work simply at the verbal level; words might not lead to action. Abraham may recognize this fact by his silence, responding in deed rather than word. In the OT, God tests Israel to discern whether they will do justice to a relationship in which they stand (Deut 8:2-3). God can test by discerning the human response to a command: Is Abraham's loyalty undivided? God initiates the test to gain certainty.

2. God's knowledge. Brueggemann notes correctly that this test "is not a game with God; God genuinely does not know. . . . The flow of the narrative accomplishes something in the awareness of God. He did not know. Now he knows."[150] The test is as real for God as it is for Abraham.

The test is *not* designed to teach *Abraham* something—that he is too attached to Isaac, or that Isaac is "pure gift," or that he must learn to cling to God rather than to the content of the promise. Experience always teaches, of course, and Abraham certainly learns. But nowhere does the text say that he now trusts more in God or has learned a lesson of some sort. Rather, the test *confirms a fact:* Abraham trusts deeply that God has his best interests at heart so that he will follow

where God's command leads (a point repeated in vv. 12 and 16). The only one said to learn anything from the test is *God:* "Now I know" (v. 12; on the angel, see commentary on 16:7). God does not teach; rather, God learns. For the sake of the future, God needs to know about Abraham's trust.

While God knew what was likely to happen, God does not have absolute certainty as to how Abraham would respond. God has in view the larger divine purpose, not just divine curiosity or an internal divine need. The story addresses a future that encompasses all the families of the earth: Is Abraham the faithful one who can carry that purpose along? Or does God need to take some other course of action, perhaps even look for another?

Is the promise of God thereby made conditional? In some sense, yes (see vv. 16-18). Fidelity was not optional. God could not have used a disloyal Abraham for the purposes God intends.

3. God's vulnerability. Some people read this story as if God were a detached observer, a heavenly homeroom teacher watching from afar to see if Abraham passes the test. But God puts much at risk in this ordeal. *God* had chosen Isaac as the one to continue the line of promise (at one point Abraham would have chosen Ishmael, 17:18; 21:11). Although God does not intend that Isaac be killed, the test places *God's own* promise at risk, at least in the form of the person of Isaac. The command has the potential of taking back what God has taken so many pains to put in place.

This story presents a test not only of Abraham's faith in God, but of God's faith in Abraham as well, in the sense that Abraham's response will affect the moves God makes next. God places the shape of God's own future in Abraham's hands. Given his somewhat mixed responses to God up to this point, God took something of a risk to put so much on the line with this man. As E. Roop puts it: "God took the risk that Abraham would respond. Abraham took the risk that God would provide."[151] One cannot project what God would have done had Abraham failed, or if Abraham had actually killed Isaac, but God would have had to find another way into the future, perhaps another way with Abraham.

Why would God place the promise at risk in

150. Brueggemann, *Genesis,* 187; on the less than absolute character of divine foreknowledge, see Fretheim, *Suffering of God,* 45-59.

151. Eugene F. Roop, *Genesis* (Scottdale, Pa.: Herald, 1987) 151.

order to see whether *Abraham* fears God? Why not just get on with it, or wait to put Isaac to the test? But, according to vv. 16-18 (and 26:3-5, 24), it is not enough for the sake of the history of the promise that Isaac be born. There are also other promises to be fulfilled. Abraham's continuing faithful response to God remains a central issue. God waits upon him before getting on with the promised future.

The interpreter may find difficulty in relating Genesis 22 to the divine promises of chap. 15, where God participates in an act of self-imprecation; God's potential sacrifice there (reinforced here by God's own oath) correlates with Abraham's potential sacrifice of Isaac. While the promises are not given a new shape in Genesis 22, they receive a new emphasis in view of Abraham's response.

4. God's trustworthiness. The test raises the question of whether God can be trusted. This God promises, proceeds to fulfill that promise, and then seems to take it back. Can readers trust this God only because they know this is a test, and that God does not intend to kill Isaac? For Abraham, trust was there without this knowledge. What will God's response be?

Abraham departs for the place of sacrifice because he believes that God can require Isaac of him (and of God!); yet he trusts that God will somehow find a way to fulfill the promises. By v. 8 in his long journey, his trust has taken the form that God will provide a lamb. His public confession constitutes *a new situation* with which God must work. This ups the ante for *God.* The test no longer involves simply Abraham's trust but becomes a matter of God's providing as well. Will Abraham's trust in God be in vain? Is God free to ignore Abraham's trust? If God did not provide, then that would constitute *another kind of test,* at a much deeper level than the one initiating this journey.

If God tests within relationship to determine loyalty, then God cannot disdain the expression of such loyalty. Given God's previous commitments (especially in chap. 15), God is bound to stay with a trusting Abraham. So God does speak,

forbidding the sacrifice of Isaac and providing an animal; even more, God provides it as a substitute for Isaac, "instead of his son."

5. God's providing. Why should God be praised as a provider for following through on God's own test? God appears praiseworthy for being faithful to the commitment to Abraham. But why was the ram even necessary? After discerning that Abraham did fear God, God stopped him *before* he saw the ram (vv. 12-13). Yet, God provided the ram, and Abraham offered it "instead of his son." A sacrifice seems necessary, even if not expressly commanded. If not Isaac, then it must be another.

The redemption of the firstborn remains as a concern in this text (Exod 13:13; 22:29; 34:20). But the interest is not etiological or historical. This motif underscores *Israel* as the firstborn of God (Exod 4:22), an issue faced by the exiles (Jer 31:9, 20; cf. 2:3). This story presents a *metaphor* for Israel's life with God, in which Israel becomes both Abraham and Isaac (see below).

22:15-19. These verses report God's response in straightforward language (reinforced by 26:3-5, 24, but often obscured by efforts to wiggle out of the implications), twice spoken as if to ensure the point: *Because* Abraham has done this, previously spoken divine promises can be reiterated. The promises were originally made (12:1-3) independently of Abraham's response. God's promises create his faith (15:6), though Abraham could still be unfaithful. That is not reversed here so that his faith creates the promises. The covenant in chap. 15 was made with Abraham as a person of faith (as all covenants in the OT are). Here the promises are reiterated (in an emphatic way) to a trusting Abraham. If he had been unfaithful to God, we do not know what would have happened (God may have given Abraham another opportunity), but we do know that the promises would always be there for Abraham to cling to. Having seen Abraham's faithfulness, God swears *an oath* for the first time in the narrative, in effect laying the divine life on the line, putting the very divine self behind the promise.

REFLECTIONS

1. This is a classic text. It has captivated the imaginations of numerous interpreters, drawn by both its literary artistry and its religious depths. It has played a special role in both Jewish and Christian traditions. Before its depth and breadth one stands on holy ground. But this text also presents problems. It has occasioned deep concern, especially in a time when the abuse of children has screamed its way into the modern consciousness.

Psychoanalyst Alice Miller claims this text may have contributed to an atmosphere that makes it possible to justify the abuse of children. She grounds her reflections on some thirty artistic representations of this story over the centuries. In two of Rembrandt's paintings, Abraham faces the heavens rather than Isaac, as if in blind obedience to God and oblivious to what he is about to do. Abraham's hands cover Isaac's face, preventing him from seeing or raising a cry. Not only is Isaac silenced, but only his torso shows—his personal features are obscured. Isaac "has been turned into an *object*. He has been dehumanized by being made a sacrifice; he no longer has a right to ask questions and will scarcely even be able to articulate them to himself, for there is no room in him for anything besides fear."[152]

We may not simply dismiss the possible negative impact of this text; it would not be the first time the Bible has been used knowingly or unknowingly for such purposes. The text contributes to such an understanding, as God asks and then twice commends Abraham for not withholding his son, his only son (vv. 2, 12, 16). Abraham asks no questions, and God offers no qualifications. The child seems to be a pawn in the hands of two "adults" who need to work out an issue between them.

Yet, while moderns might wonder about the psychological abuse Isaac endures in all of this, the narrator gives him a questioning voice, and his father attentively responds to his query. This dialogue leads Isaac to place himself trustingly in the arms of his father and his God. The text offers no evidence that trust in God ever wavers for either father or son. We must be careful to stress these elements for the sake of a proper hearing of the text. Children must be allowed to ask their questions about this text, to which adults should be highly alert.

2. Once again, an Abrahamic text mirrors a later period in Israel's life. Israel, God's firstborn, had been sentenced to death *by God* in the fires of judgment. But exilic Israel remains God's firstborn (so Jeremiah affirms, 31:9), the carrier of God's purposes into the future. As Isaac was saved from death, so was Israel delivered from the brink of annihilation. But what of the future? Out of this matrix the Israelites developed an understanding that a sacrifice was necessary to assure Israel's future, shaped most profoundly in Isaiah 53 (see the use of שֶׂה (*śeh*), lamb, in 53:7 and vv. 7-8; cf. Jer 11:19). Israel's redemption would not occur without cost. At the same time, Israel's faithfulness was not an optional matter as it moved into a future shaped by God's promises. The emphasis on descendants in v. 17 also connects well with these exilic concerns (see Isa 51:2, and the renewed interest in Abraham in exile). The NT use of this story to understand the sacrifice of God's only Son constitutes an appropriate extension of the text (see John 1:14).

3. To trust God does not mean always to respond in an unquestioning way; this text does not commend passivity before God. Chapters 18 and 22 must be kept together, showing that Abraham's faithfulness to God works itself out in various ways. Perhaps Abraham responds as he does in chap. 22 because he learned from the encounter in chap. 18 that God is indeed just, and that he need only trust on this occasion. The confession that God will provide pertains as much to times of questioning and challenging as to moments of 'blind' trust. It may well be the *reader* who, having learned from Abraham in chap. 18, responds with questions to God's command to sacrifice Isaac.

Abraham does not simply obey; he obeys because he trusts. He could have obeyed because he was ordered to do so; if God commands, he had better respond. But v. 8 makes clear that he obeys because he trusts God, that God will be faithful and will act in his best interests.

152. Alice Miller, *The Untouched Key: Tracing Childhood Trauma in Creativity and Destructiveness* (New York: Doubleday, 1990) 139.

Hebrews 11:17-19 posits the Resurrection at this point; if necessary, the promises will remain in and through death. Moreover, Abraham does not claim ownership of the promise, as if it were his possession, as if his faithful response counts for little or nothing (see Jas 2:18-26).

4. This story presents the last dialogue between Abraham and God and between Abraham and Isaac. It follows closely on the heels of the birth of Isaac and precedes Sarah's death (23:2). The narrative's literary setting intimates a concern for the (unprecedented) turning of the generations; Isaac now moves out into the world on his own. The absence of an explicit reference to Isaac at the end (v. 19) may witness to a future open to the next generation, with uncertainty as to what will happen to the promises as Abraham moves off the scene.[153]

One promise has been fulfilled. Yet, promises of land, numerous descendants, and being a blessing to the nations remain. What status do these other divine promises have now? Are they a matter of course, to be fulfilled irrespective of Abraham's (or anyone else's) faith in God? Are God's promises now to be carried by genetics, by a natural biological succession? What happens if Abraham ceases to trust God? At times scholars speak of the unconditionality of God's promise to Abraham in such a way that faith becomes irrelevant. Verses 16-18 together with 26:3-5, 24 make clear, however, that God reiterates the promise to Isaac because of the way in which Abraham responded in faithfulness. Hence, the promise does not automatically or naturally carry on into the family's next generation.

Although God will never invalidate the promise, people do not participate in the sphere of the promise independently of a faithful response. Abraham could have said no to God, and complicated God's moves into the future, though not finally stymied them. While the divine word of promise inspires Abraham's trust (15:6), he could resist the word of God; if that were not the case, then the command would have been no test at all, for the outcome would have been settled in advance. God, however, does not coerce or program Abraham's fidelity.

The apostle Paul incorporates this point when making the claim that the promises of God cannot be reduced to genetics (Rom 4:16-25; Gal 3:6-9). Those who have faith in the God of Abraham have received the promises irrespective of biological succession.

At the same time, the text does not imply a spiritual succession across the centuries, for the promise takes shape in the actual lives of people, whose *own words and deeds* are centrally involved in its transmission. This means that the word of God, in some general way, does not provide for the continuity across the generations. God places the promise in the hands of those who are faithful, and their witness ought not to be discounted.

Another way of putting the issue: What happens to faith when the promise reaches fulfillment? Granted, other promises reach out to the future. But receiving the promised son could have tempted Abraham to push other promises to the side: I now have what I want. How do promises already fulfilled affect the relationship with God? Will Abraham's trust in God still be the core of his life? Will Abraham still ground his life in the divine promises rather than bask in the sunshine of fulfillment? In order to explore these questions, the test focused precisely on the point of fulfillment: Isaac.

5. Testing must be considered relationally, not legalistically. Life in relationship will inevitably bring tests; individuals will often find themselves in situations where their loyalty is tested. What constitutes testing will be determined by the nature of the relationship and the expectations the parties have for it. As a relationship matures and trust levels are built up, faithful responses to the testing of the relational bond will tend to become second nature. Yet, even in a mature relationship, sharp moments of testing may present themselves. Abraham may have faced this kind of moment.

Is the relationship with the deity one in which the people of God can expect to be put to

153. See White, *Narration,* 187-203.

the test again and again? Are there absurd, senseless experiences in life that can become the occasion to turn away from God? There may well be a deep, dark, and seemingly hopeless valley through which we travel. Maybe we think God protects us from such moments, especially those who have been given promises; if God does not protect us, then we will turn away from God. We should learn from this story that receiving promises does not entail being protected from moments where those promises seem to be called into question.

To move to the NT, God does not expect of Abraham something that God would be unwilling to do. God puts Jesus through a time of testing to see if he will be faithful, and hence could be a vehicle for God's redemptive purposes in the world. God risked that Jesus would not be found faithful. Even more, God put Jesus through a time of testing in the Garden of Gethsemane. How was it possible for Jesus to believe that God would be faithful to promises in such a time? Jesus trusts himself to the will of God, trusting that God will find a way to be faithful to the promises even in the face of death. And God does prove faithful in raising Jesus from the dead.

Some NT words on testing may be helpful: "Because he himself was tested by what he suffered, he is able to help those who are being tested" (Heb 2:18 NRSV; cf. 4:15). We are promised by 1 Cor 10:13, "God is faithful, and he will not let you be tested beyond your strength, but with the testing he will also provide the way out so that you may be able to endure it" (NRSV). These affirmations do not make trust an option, but we can count on the faithfulness of God, who in the midst of the worst possible testings will provide a way through the fire.

GENESIS 22:20-24, REBEKAH'S FAMILY

NIV

[20]Some time later Abraham was told, "Milcah is also a mother; she has borne sons to your brother Nahor: [21]Uz the firstborn, Buz his brother, Kemuel (the father of Aram), [22]Kesed, Hazo, Pildash, Jidlaph and Bethuel." [23]Bethuel became the father of Rebekah. Milcah bore these eight sons to Abraham's brother Nahor. [24]His concubine, whose name was Reumah, also had sons: Tebah, Gaham, Tahash and Maacah.

NRSV

[20]Now after these things it was told Abraham, "Milcah also has borne children, to your brother Nahor: [21]Uz the firstborn, Buz his brother, Kemuel the father of Aram, [22]Chesed, Hazo, Pildash, Jidlaph, and Bethuel." [23]Bethuel became the father of Rebekah. These eight Milcah bore to Nahor, Abraham's brother. [24]Moreover, his concubine, whose name was Reumah, bore Tebah, Gaham, Tahash, and Maacah.

COMMENTARY

The author encloses this section (22:20–25:18), having to do with concluding events in Abraham's journey, with genealogies (22:20-24; 25:1-18; cf. 33:18–36:43 and 47:27–50:26 for other closing accounts). The stories share a common focus: the preparation for the future of the family, as that involves both land and posterity.

This brief genealogy chronicles the family of Abraham's brother Nahor, including children of his wife Milcah and his concubine Reumah (see 11:27-29; 31:53). As with Jacob, Nahor has twelve sons; their names later become associated with tribes and places (see Job 1:1; 32:2).

The insertion of the genealogy at this point anticipates the role of Rebekah (granddaughter of Nahor), shortly to be introduced (see 24:15, 24). The writer thus makes clear that Isaac's wife comes from the same family (cf. Ishmael, 21:21). The genealogy lists the children of both the wife and the concubine; the list identifies Rebekah as a granddaughter of the wife.

GENESIS 23:1-20, ABRAHAM BUYS LAND IN CANAAN

NIV

23 Sarah lived to be a hundred and twenty-seven years old. [2]She died at Kiriath Arba (that is, Hebron) in the land of Canaan, and Abraham went to mourn for Sarah and to weep over her.

[3]Then Abraham rose from beside his dead wife and spoke to the Hittites.[a] He said, [4]"I am an alien and a stranger among you. Sell me some property for a burial site here so I can bury my dead."

[5]The Hittites replied to Abraham, [6]"Sir, listen to us. You are a mighty prince among us. Bury your dead in the choicest of our tombs. None of us will refuse you his tomb for burying your dead."

[7]Then Abraham rose and bowed down before the people of the land, the Hittites. [8]He said to them, "If you are willing to let me bury my dead, then listen to me and intercede with Ephron son of Zohar on my behalf [9]so he will sell me the cave of Machpelah, which belongs to him and is at the end of his field. Ask him to sell it to me for the full price as a burial site among you."

[10]Ephron the Hittite was sitting among his people and he replied to Abraham in the hearing of all the Hittites who had come to the gate of his city. [11]"No, my lord," he said. "Listen to me; I give[b] you the field, and I give[b] you the cave that is in it. I give[b] it to you in the presence of my people. Bury your dead."

[12]Again Abraham bowed down before the people of the land [13]and he said to Ephron in their hearing, "Listen to me, if you will. I will pay the price of the field. Accept it from me so I can bury my dead there."

[14]Ephron answered Abraham, [15]"Listen to me, my lord; the land is worth four hundred shekels[c] of silver, but what is that between me and you? Bury your dead."

[16]Abraham agreed to Ephron's terms and weighed out for him the price he had named in the hearing of the Hittites: four hundred shekels

NRSV

23 Sarah lived one hundred twenty-seven years; this was the length of Sarah's life. [2]And Sarah died at Kiriath-arba (that is, Hebron) in the land of Canaan; and Abraham went in to mourn for Sarah and to weep for her. [3]Abraham rose up from beside his dead, and said to the Hittites, [4]"I am a stranger and an alien residing among you; give me property among you for a burying place, so that I may bury my dead out of my sight." [5]The Hittites answered Abraham, [6]"Hear us, my lord; you are a mighty prince among us. Bury your dead in the choicest of our burial places; none of us will withhold from you any burial ground for burying your dead." [7]Abraham rose and bowed to the Hittites, the people of the land. [8]He said to them, "If you are willing that I should bury my dead out of my sight, hear me, and entreat for me Ephron son of Zohar, [9]so that he may give me the cave of Machpelah, which he owns; it is at the end of his field. For the full price let him give it to me in your presence as a possession for a burying place." [10]Now Ephron was sitting among the Hittites; and Ephron the Hittite answered Abraham in the hearing of the Hittites, of all who went in at the gate of his city, [11]"No, my lord, hear me; I give you the field, and I give you the cave that is in it; in the presence of my people I give it to you; bury your dead." [12]Then Abraham bowed down before the people of the land. [13]He said to Ephron in the hearing of the people of the land, "If you only will listen to me! I will give the price of the field; accept it from me, so that I may bury my dead there." [14]Ephron answered Abraham, [15]"My lord, listen to me; a piece of land worth four hundred shekels of silver—what is that between you and me? Bury your dead." [16]Abraham agreed with Ephron; and Abraham weighed out for Ephron the silver that he had named in the hearing of the Hittites, four hundred shekels of silver, according to the weights current among the merchants.

17So the field of Ephron in Machpelah, which was to the east of Mamre, the field with the cave that was in it and all the trees that were in the

---

[a]3 Or *the sons of Heth*; also in verses 5, 7, 10, 16, 18 and 20
[b]11 Or *sell*   [c]15 That is, about 10 pounds (about 4.5 kilograms)

NIV

of silver, according to the weight current among the merchants.

¹⁷So Ephron's field in Machpelah near Mamre—both the field and the cave in it, and all the trees within the borders of the field—was deeded ¹⁸to Abraham as his property in the presence of all the Hittites who had come to the gate of the city. ¹⁹Afterward Abraham buried his wife Sarah in the cave in the field of Machpelah near Mamre (which is at Hebron) in the land of Canaan. ²⁰So the field and the cave in it were deeded to Abraham by the Hittites as a burial site.

NRSV

field, throughout its whole area, passed ¹⁸to Abraham as a possession in the presence of the Hittites, in the presence of all who went in at the gate of his city. ¹⁹After this, Abraham buried Sarah his wife in the cave of the field of Machpelah facing Mamre (that is, Hebron) in the land of Canaan. ²⁰The field and the cave that is in it passed from the Hittites into Abraham's possession as a burying place.

COMMENTARY

Within the inclusio provided by the death and burial of Sarah, the chapter (usually assigned to P) provides a report about negotiations between Abraham and the Hittites for purchase of a family burial place. Since Sarah is the first member of the core family of promise to die, the textual moment is appropriate. The prominent use of burial language (thirteen times), especially the expression "bury your [my] dead," demonstrates the centrality of this concern. The matter concludes (23:20) with this particular space within the promised land transferred legally to Abraham. No explicit theological language occurs in the chapter; any such understandings must be developed out of the larger context.

Ancient Near Eastern documents provide parallels to aspects of this transaction.[154] Abraham negotiates with the Hittites, a people infrequently encountered in the OT. Their eponymous ancestor Heth, the second son of Canaan, appears in 10:15, while 28:1 seems to equate Hittites and Canaanites (see Judg 1:10). Esau marries two Hittite women (26:34), and Rebekah expresses concern that Jacob might do the same (27:46). Although the Hittite kingdom was centered in Anatolia, and their empire did not extend into Canaan, there may have been enclaves of such non-Semitic peoples in Canaan. To the ancient reader of Genesis, the Hittites would have been one of the pre-Israelite peoples living in the promised land; here the author calls

them "the people of the land" (vv. 7, 12-13; see 15:20).

Abraham's chosen burying place, Machpelah, was located in the southern part of Canaan near Mamre. This became the burial place not only of Sarah and Abraham (25:9), but also of Isaac, Rebekah, Jacob, and Leah. It was an important site during the biblical period and has remained so during subsequent centuries. Jacob's request to be buried there underscores the importance of a person's burial site (49:29-33; 50:13). And although Joseph is buried at Shechem (Josh 24:32), the importance of burial in the promised land is similarly evident (50:24).

The Story. Sarah has died, and the report of the purchase of land for her burial place begins with Abraham acting much as he did in chap. 14. While he identifies himself as a lowly outsider without property rights, the Hittites immediately recognize and acknowledge his reputation ("mighty prince," v. 6; cf. 24:35). Perhaps in view of his status, the Hittites openly receive his initially quite general request for a burial place (v. 4; "give" probably means "sell"). Abraham negotiates with them as an apparent equal, but with proper deference, at the place for such legal transactions, the city gate (v. 10).

The Hittites grant Abraham's request in a general way; in fact, they offer him the pick of available tombs (v. 6). But Abraham has his sight on a particular cave. One of the elders, Ephron, owns the burial cave he wants to buy, and Abra-

154. See Sarna, *Genesis,* 156-60.

ham requests that he be allowed to proceed with negotiations for it. Ephron twice publicly offers to "give" him not only the cave for burying, but the surrounding field as well (v. 11). This may be an opening gambit for a sale, not generosity. In any case, Abraham, who will not be obligated to strangers (cf. 14:22-24) and wants use of the land, insists on paying for it. Ephron, seemingly not concerned about payment, claims that it is worth 400 shekels; we do not know whether this was a fair price (cf. Jer 32:7). Abraham agrees and, without speaking a word, gives him the money on the spot, carefully measuring it according to local standards.

Verses 17-18 summarize the transaction, with the narrator specifying that the entire plot of land—field, cave, trees—is deeded to Abraham "in the presence of the Hittites," who have been witnesses to all that has transpired. After Sarah's burial, which confirms the agreed-upon use of the land and makes the transaction firm, v. 20 seems concerned to attest Abraham's legal claim to this land one more time.

REFLECTIONS

1. This account has generated a number of interpretations. The text provides no evidence that Machpelah was a hallowed spot or sanctuary. A more theological explanation relates the text to the land promise.[155] In death, these Israelite ancestors are no longer strangers and aliens in the land (Abraham's self-identification in v. 4), but heirs; they come to rest in the land promised them by their God. The repeated language of "possession" (אחזה, 'ăḥuzzâ, vv. 4, 9, 20; cf. 49:29-30; 50:13) relates to its immediately prior use in 17:8, where God promised the land to Abraham as an "everlasting possession" (repeated in 48:4; cf. 36:43; Lev 14:34; 27:24; Num 32:32; Josh 22:4, 19). Hence, one can make an explicitly theological interpretation on intertextual grounds (cf. also Jacob's purchase in 33:19 and Jeremiah's in Jer 32:1-15, a text of similar antiquity that bears an explicitly theological meaning).

2. When one places the repetitive burial language within an exilic context, other meanings may emerge.[156] The text may address the issue of exiles' having to bury their dead outside of the land and their interest in having a special burial place in both exile and Canaan (cf. the interest in transporting bodies from Egypt back to Canaan in 50:12-14, 24-25). These exiles were, like Abraham, sojourners and aliens; Israelites may have understood burial places in Canaan in terms of the land as an everlasting possession. This text shows that Abraham comes by the land on terms that were both legal and fair, and hence should be honored by future generations.

The chapter may also involve issues of family life, as do 17:9-14 (circumcision) and 27:46–28:9 (marriage). Burial practices were an important matter in ancient societies, and texts such as these grounded customs in ancient times.

While these factors may seem to be nontheological, they relate in direct ways to creation, particularly the proper ordering of individual, family, and communal life. A comprehensive theology of creation includes concerns for social order, which in the ancient (and modern!) world is intimately connected with cosmic order. If the social fabric is in disrepair, deleterious effects on the cosmic order may ensue. So the good order of the entire cosmos may be at stake. Hence, this chapter relates to chap. 1 and creational concerns. There are also connections between creation and the promise of the land as an everlasting possession. For the promise to be fulfilled, land must be available. The promise of a specific land for one's own possession presupposes the creational activity of God.

3. Abraham's purchase of a plot in the land does not stand over against God's promise to

155. Von Rad, *Genesis,* 250.
156. See Westermann, *Genesis 12–36,* 376.

give the land to his descendants. Again and again, God works through humans on behalf of divine purposes. The purchase of land provides a symbol of hope, a concrete anticipation of what God has in store for those who trust in the promises.

GENESIS 24:1-67, THE WOOING OF REBEKAH

NIV

24 Abraham was now old and well advanced in years, and the LORD had blessed him in every way. [2]He said to the chief[a] servant in his household, the one in charge of all that he had, "Put your hand under my thigh. [3]I want you to swear by the LORD, the God of heaven and the God of earth, that you will not get a wife for my son from the daughters of the Canaanites, among whom I am living, [4]but will go to my country and my own relatives and get a wife for my son Isaac."

[5]The servant asked him, "What if the woman is unwilling to come back with me to this land? Shall I then take your son back to the country you came from?"

[6]"Make sure that you do not take my son back there," Abraham said. [7]"The LORD, the God of heaven, who brought me out of my father's household and my native land and who spoke to me and promised me on oath, saying, 'To your offspring[b] I will give this land'—he will send his angel before you so that you can get a wife for my son from there. [8]If the woman is unwilling to come back with you, then you will be released from this oath of mine. Only do not take my son back there." [9]So the servant put his hand under the thigh of his master Abraham and swore an oath to him concerning this matter.

[10]Then the servant took ten of his master's camels and left, taking with him all kinds of good things from his master. He set out for Aram Naharaim[c] and made his way to the town of Nahor. [11]He had the camels kneel down near the well outside the town; it was toward evening, the time the women go out to draw water.

[12]Then he prayed, "O LORD, God of my master Abraham, give me success today, and show kindness to my master Abraham. [13]See, I am standing beside this spring, and the daughters of the towns-

NRSV

24 Now Abraham was old, well advanced in years; and the LORD had blessed Abraham in all things. [2]Abraham said to his servant, the oldest of his house, who had charge of all that he had, "Put your hand under my thigh [3]and I will make you swear by the LORD, the God of heaven and earth, that you will not get a wife for my son from the daughters of the Canaanites, among whom I live, [4]but will go to my country and to my kindred and get a wife for my son Isaac." [5]The servant said to him, "Perhaps the woman may not be willing to follow me to this land; must I then take your son back to the land from which you came?" [6]Abraham said to him, "See to it that you do not take my son back there. [7]The LORD, the God of heaven, who took me from my father's house and from the land of my birth, and who spoke to me and swore to me, 'To your offspring I will give this land,' he will send his angel before you, and you shall take a wife for my son from there. [8]But if the woman is not willing to follow you, then you will be free from this oath of mine; only you must not take my son back there." [9]So the servant put his hand under the thigh of Abraham his master and swore to him concerning this matter.

10Then the servant took ten of his master's camels and departed, taking all kinds of choice gifts from his master; and he set out and went to Aram-naharaim, to the city of Nahor. [11]He made the camels kneel down outside the city by the well of water; it was toward evening, the time when women go out to draw water. [12]And he said, "O LORD, God of my master Abraham, please grant me success today and show steadfast love to my master Abraham. [13]I am standing here by the spring of water, and the daughters of the townspeople are coming out to draw water. [14]Let the girl to whom I shall say, 'Please offer your jar that I may drink,' and who shall say, 'Drink,

a2 Or oldest   b7 Or seed   c10 That is, Northwest Mesopotamia

NIV

people are coming out to draw water. ¹⁴May it be that when I say to a girl, 'Please let down your jar that I may have a drink,' and she says, 'Drink, and I'll water your camels too'—let her be the one you have chosen for your servant Isaac. By this I will know that you have shown kindness to my master."

¹⁵Before he had finished praying, Rebekah came out with her jar on her shoulder. She was the daughter of Bethuel son of Milcah, who was the wife of Abraham's brother Nahor. ¹⁶The girl was very beautiful, a virgin; no man had ever lain with her. She went down to the spring, filled her jar and came up again.

¹⁷The servant hurried to meet her and said, "Please give me a little water from your jar."

¹⁸"Drink, my lord," she said, and quickly lowered the jar to her hands and gave him a drink.

¹⁹After she had given him a drink, she said, "I'll draw water for your camels too, until they have finished drinking." ²⁰So she quickly emptied her jar into the trough, ran back to the well to draw more water, and drew enough for all his camels. ²¹Without saying a word, the man watched her closely to learn whether or not the LORD had made his journey successful.

²²When the camels had finished drinking, the man took out a gold nose ring weighing a beka^a and two gold bracelets weighing ten shekels.^b ²³Then he asked, "Whose daughter are you? Please tell me, is there room in your father's house for us to spend the night?"

²⁴She answered him, "I am the daughter of Bethuel, the son that Milcah bore to Nahor." ²⁵And she added, "We have plenty of straw and fodder, as well as room for you to spend the night."

²⁶Then the man bowed down and worshiped the LORD, ²⁷saying, "Praise be to the LORD, the God of my master Abraham, who has not abandoned his kindness and faithfulness to my master. As for me, the LORD has led me on the journey to the house of my master's relatives."

²⁸The girl ran and told her mother's household about these things. ²⁹Now Rebekah had a brother named Laban, and he hurried out to the man at

_{a22 That is, about 1/5 ounce (about 5.5 grams)   b22 That is, about 4 ounces (about 110 grams)}

NRSV

and I will water your camels'—let her be the one whom you have appointed for your servant Isaac. By this I shall know that you have shown steadfast love to my master."

¹⁵Before he had finished speaking, there was Rebekah, who was born to Bethuel son of Milcah, the wife of Nahor, Abraham's brother, coming out with her water jar on her shoulder. ¹⁶The girl was very fair to look upon, a virgin, whom no man had known. She went down to the spring, filled her jar, and came up. ¹⁷Then the servant ran to meet her and said, "Please let me sip a little water from your jar." ¹⁸"Drink, my lord," she said, and quickly lowered her jar upon her hand and gave him a drink. ¹⁹When she had finished giving him a drink, she said, "I will draw for your camels also, until they have finished drinking." ²⁰So she quickly emptied her jar into the trough and ran again to the well to draw, and she drew for all his camels. ²¹The man gazed at her in silence to learn whether or not the LORD had made his journey successful.

²²When the camels had finished drinking, the man took a gold nose-ring weighing a half shekel, and two bracelets for her arms weighing ten gold shekels, ²³and said, "Tell me whose daughter you are. Is there room in your father's house for us to spend the night?" ²⁴She said to him, "I am the daughter of Bethuel son of Milcah, whom she bore to Nahor." ²⁵She added, "We have plenty of straw and fodder and a place to spend the night." ²⁶The man bowed his head and worshiped the LORD ²⁷and said, "Blessed be the LORD, the God of my master Abraham, who has not forsaken his steadfast love and his faithfulness toward my master. As for me, the LORD has led me on the way to the house of my master's kin."

²⁸Then the girl ran and told her mother's household about these things. ²⁹Rebekah had a brother whose name was Laban; and Laban ran out to the man, to the spring. ³⁰As soon as he had seen the nose-ring, and the bracelets on his sister's arms, and when he heard the words of his sister Rebekah, "Thus the man spoke to me," he went to the man; and there he was, standing by the camels at the spring. ³¹He said, "Come in, O blessed of the LORD. Why do you stand outside when I have prepared the house and a place for

NIV

the spring. ³⁰As soon as he had seen the nose ring, and the bracelets on his sister's arms, and had heard Rebekah tell what the man said to her, he went out to the man and found him standing by the camels near the spring. ³¹"Come, you who are blessed by the LORD," he said. "Why are you standing out here? I have prepared the house and a place for the camels."

³²So the man went to the house, and the camels were unloaded. Straw and fodder were brought for the camels, and water for him and his men to wash their feet. ³³Then food was set before him, but he said, "I will not eat until I have told you what I have to say."

"Then tell us," ₗLabanₗ said.

³⁴So he said, "I am Abraham's servant. ³⁵The LORD has blessed my master abundantly, and he has become wealthy. He has given him sheep and cattle, silver and gold, menservants and maidservants, and camels and donkeys. ³⁶My master's wife Sarah has borne him a son in herᵃ old age, and he has given him everything he owns. ³⁷And my master made me swear an oath, and said, 'You must not get a wife for my son from the daughters of the Canaanites, in whose land I live, ³⁸but go to my father's family and to my own clan, and get a wife for my son.'

³⁹"Then I asked my master, 'What if the woman will not come back with me?'

⁴⁰"He replied, 'The LORD, before whom I have walked, will send his angel with you and make your journey a success, so that you can get a wife for my son from my own clan and from my father's family. ⁴¹Then, when you go to my clan, you will be released from my oath even if they refuse to give her to you—you will be released from my oath.'

⁴²"When I came to the spring today, I said, 'O LORD, God of my master Abraham, if you will, please grant success to the journey on which I have come. ⁴³See, I am standing beside this spring; if a maiden comes out to draw water and I say to her, "Please let me drink a little water from your jar," ⁴⁴and if she says to me, "Drink, and I'll draw water for your camels too," let her be the one the LORD has chosen for my master's son.'

⁴⁵"Before I finished praying in my heart, Re-

ᵃ36 Or his

NRSV

the camels?" ³²So the man came into the house; and Laban unloaded the camels, and gave him straw and fodder for the camels, and water to wash his feet and the feet of the men who were with him. ³³Then food was set before him to eat; but he said, "I will not eat until I have told my errand." He said, "Speak on."

³⁴So he said, "I am Abraham's servant. ³⁵The LORD has greatly blessed my master, and he has become wealthy; he has given him flocks and herds, silver and gold, male and female slaves, camels and donkeys. ³⁶And Sarah my master's wife bore a son to my master when she was old; and he has given him all that he has. ³⁷My master made me swear, saying, 'You shall not take a wife for my son from the daughters of the Canaanites, in whose land I live; ³⁸but you shall go to my father's house, to my kindred, and get a wife for my son.' ³⁹I said to my master, 'Perhaps the woman will not follow me.' ⁴⁰But he said to me, 'The LORD, before whom I walk, will send his angel with you and make your way successful. You shall get a wife for my son from my kindred, from my father's house. ⁴¹Then you will be free from my oath, when you come to my kindred; even if they will not give her to you, you will be free from my oath.'

⁴²"I came today to the spring, and said, 'O LORD, the God of my master Abraham, if now you will only make successful the way I am going! ⁴³I am standing here by the spring of water; let the young woman who comes out to draw, to whom I shall say, "Please give me a little water from your jar to drink," ⁴⁴and who will say to me, "Drink, and I will draw for your camels also"—let her be the woman whom the LORD has appointed for my master's son.'

⁴⁵"Before I had finished speaking in my heart, there was Rebekah coming out with her water jar on her shoulder; and she went down to the spring, and drew. I said to her, 'Please let me drink.' ⁴⁶She quickly let down her jar from her shoulder, and said, 'Drink, and I will also water your camels.' So I drank, and she also watered the camels. ⁴⁷Then I asked her, 'Whose daughter are you?' She said, 'The daughter of Bethuel, Nahor's son, whom Milcah bore to him.' So I put the ring on her nose, and the bracelets on her

NIV

bekah came out, with her jar on her shoulder. She went down to the spring and drew water, and I said to her, 'Please give me a drink.'

⁴⁶"She quickly lowered her jar from her shoulder and said, 'Drink, and I'll water your camels too.' So I drank, and she watered the camels also.

⁴⁷"I asked her, 'Whose daughter are you?'

"She said, 'The daughter of Bethuel son of Nahor, whom Milcah bore to him.'

"Then I put the ring in her nose and the bracelets on her arms, ⁴⁸and I bowed down and worshiped the LORD. I praised the LORD, the God of my master Abraham, who had led me on the right road to get the granddaughter of my master's brother for his son. ⁴⁹Now if you will show kindness and faithfulness to my master, tell me; and if not, tell me, so I may know which way to turn."

⁵⁰Laban and Bethuel answered, "This is from the LORD; we can say nothing to you one way or the other. ⁵¹Here is Rebekah; take her and go, and let her become the wife of your master's son, as the LORD has directed."

⁵²When Abraham's servant heard what they said, he bowed down to the ground before the LORD. ⁵³Then the servant brought out gold and silver jewelry and articles of clothing and gave them to Rebekah; he also gave costly gifts to her brother and to her mother. ⁵⁴Then he and the men who were with him ate and drank and spent the night there.

When they got up the next morning, he said, "Send me on my way to my master."

⁵⁵But her brother and her mother replied, "Let the girl remain with us ten days or so; then you*ᵃ* may go."

⁵⁶But he said to them, "Do not detain me, now that the LORD has granted success to my journey. Send me on my way so I may go to my master."

⁵⁷Then they said, "Let's call the girl and ask her about it." ⁵⁸So they called Rebekah and asked her, "Will you go with this man?"

"I will go," she said.

⁵⁹So they sent their sister Rebekah on her way, along with her nurse and Abraham's servant and his men. ⁶⁰And they blessed Rebekah and said to her,

ᵃ55 Or she

NRSV

arms. ⁴⁸Then I bowed my head and worshiped the LORD, and blessed the LORD, the God of my master Abraham, who had led me by the right way to obtain the daughter of my master's kinsman for his son. ⁴⁹Now then, if you will deal loyally and truly with my master, tell me; and if not, tell me, so that I may turn either to the right hand or to the left."

50Then Laban and Bethuel answered, "The thing comes from the LORD; we cannot speak to you anything bad or good. ⁵¹Look, Rebekah is before you, take her and go, and let her be the wife of your master's son, as the LORD has spoken."

52When Abraham's servant heard their words, he bowed himself to the ground before the LORD. ⁵³And the servant brought out jewelry of silver and of gold, and garments, and gave them to Rebekah; he also gave to her brother and to her mother costly ornaments. ⁵⁴Then he and the men who were with him ate and drank, and they spent the night there. When they rose in the morning, he said, "Send me back to my master." ⁵⁵Her brother and her mother said, "Let the girl remain with us a while, at least ten days; after that she may go." ⁵⁶But he said to them, "Do not delay me, since the LORD has made my journey successful; let me go that I may go to my master." ⁵⁷They said, "We will call the girl, and ask her." ⁵⁸And they called Rebekah, and said to her, "Will you go with this man?" She said, "I will." ⁵⁹So they sent away their sister Rebekah and her nurse along with Abraham's servant and his men. ⁶⁰And they blessed Rebekah and said to her,

"May you, our sister, become
    thousands of myriads;
may your offspring gain possession
    of the gates of their foes."

⁶¹Then Rebekah and her maids rose up, mounted the camels, and followed the man; thus the servant took Rebekah, and went his way.

62Now Isaac had come from*ᵃ* Beer-lahai-roi, and was settled in the Negeb. ⁶³Isaac went out in the evening to walk*ᵇ* in the field; and looking up, he saw camels coming. ⁶⁴And Rebekah looked up, and when she saw Isaac, she slipped quickly from the camel, ⁶⁵and said to the servant, "Who is the

ᵃ Syr Tg: Heb from coming to   ᵇ Meaning of Heb word is uncertain

"Our sister, may you increase
to thousands upon thousands;
may your offspring possess
the gates of their enemies."

[61]Then Rebekah and her maids got ready and mounted their camels and went back with the man. So the servant took Rebekah and left.

[62]Now Isaac had come from Beer Lahai Roi, for he was living in the Negev. [63]He went out to the field one evening to meditate,[a] and as he looked up, he saw camels approaching. [64]Rebekah also looked up and saw Isaac. She got down from her camel [65]and asked the servant, "Who is that man in the field coming to meet us?"

"He is my master," the servant answered. So she took her veil and covered herself.

[66]Then the servant told Isaac all he had done. [67]Isaac brought her into the tent of his mother Sarah, and he married Rebekah. So she became his wife, and he loved her; and Isaac was comforted after his mother's death.

[a]63 The meaning of the Hebrew for this word is uncertain.

man over there, walking in the field to meet us?" The servant said, "It is my master." So she took her veil and covered herself. [66]And the servant told Isaac all the things that he had done. [67]Then Isaac brought her into his mother Sarah's tent. He took Rebekah, and she became his wife; and he loved her. So Isaac was comforted after his mother's death.

COMMENTARY

In this lengthy family story, Joseph-like in character (assigned to J), the author focuses on the search for a wife for Isaac among family members back in the old country (the Nahor of v. 10 is near Haran). In the course of this last story in which Abraham plays a role, interest passes to "master" Isaac (v. 65). Abraham's good and faithful servant (possibly Eliezer, 15:2) serves as the mediator of this transition. The story follows a pattern ("type-scene") similar to that of Jacob/Rachel in 29:1-14 and Moses/Zipporah in Exod 2:15-22—a meeting between a man and a woman at a well that results in a marriage (cf. John 4; Ugaritic parallels have also been noted). We may also discern a literary form used to depict the commission of a messenger, a pattern similar to the calls of the prophets (cf. Exodus 3; Isaiah 6), evident not least in the objection that the servant raises (vv. 5, 39).

Within the larger story of Abraham, this chapter (esp. vv. 1-7, 35-41) provides an inclusio with

12:1-7, with specific references to the call and initial journey, as well as the promises of land and blessing. Genesis 24 provides a similar introduction to the beginning of the second generation. In some sense, however, *Rebekah* rather than Isaac parallels Abraham; she continues the faithful response of leaving home and family that furthers God's purposes. The story also includes recapitulations of scenes that have already occurred (cf. vv. 17-19 with 13-14; vv. 34-49 with 1-27), a technique that retards the action and helps to interpret the event, especially God's important role.

Abraham initiates the journey by commissioning his servant to find a wife for Isaac (vv. 1-9). The servant carries out the commission (vv. 10-27), and Rebekah and her family respond (vv. 28-61), resulting in the marriage of Rebekah and Isaac (vv. 62-67).

24:1-9. Abraham's final days provide an occasion to note how God has filled his life with blessings. God has indeed kept the promise to him, a promise worked out largely through God's work as Creator.

Abraham now focuses on finding a proper wife for Isaac. Functioning without divine directive, he commissions the most senior of his servants for the task. (In what follows, God's leading actually responds to Abraham's initiative!) He binds the servant with an oath (placing his hand under the genitals, a vehicle of life, vv. 2, 9; cf. 47:29) to find a woman only among family members, not from among the resident Canaanites (see 28:1, but not applicable to Jacob's sons; cf. Deut 7:3-4 for Israel's later history). After an objection by the servant and Abraham's response (note his emphasis on the woman's own decision, v. 8; cf. v. 58), the servant takes the oath. The author explains in v. 7 the twice-expressed concern that Isaac not be brought back to Haran (vv. 6, 8; not recalled in vv. 34-41): for Isaac to settle in the place from which Abraham migrated would be untrue to God's call and the promise for the land. Abraham follows through faithfully on the implications of his own call and subjects Isaac to the same call. At the same time, *Rebekah* will follow exactly in Abraham's footsteps (cf. v. 38 with 12:1) and will receive the same blessing (cf. v. 60 with 22:17). In all things, the servant will prove to be loyal to his commission, while unafraid to take appropriate initiatives.

Abraham, in his last words, does not know what will come of this venture. He makes his servant swear (not) to do certain things (vv. 3-4, 6, 8), but his conduct and that of others are not predetermined. In fact, Abraham considers it possible that this venture might fail because "the woman" might refuse to cooperate (v. 8; in v. 41, the woman's family can decide). Failure might result, even though God would "send his angel before you" (see 32:1; Exod 23:20; 32:34). The servant takes human behaviors into account when carrying out the task—what people customarily do counts (v. 11), and the numerous gifts (v. 10) are certainly an effort to persuade. These factors suggest that one should not say that "the success or failure of the commission depends on whether God grants success or not."[157] Although success may well depend on God, the activity of human

beings may occasion failure even though God intends success.

24:10-27. The author encloses this episode with prayer and doxology. Having arrived at his destination, the servant prays that he will be successful in this venture, which would mean that God show kindness or steadfast love (חסד *ḥesed*) to Abraham—namely, manifest love in this particular way. Without God's steadfast love there would be no success (cf. v. 21). The author presents no claim that lack of success would mean that God had withheld kindness; it could simply result from human decision making (vv. 8, 41). Divine providence does not mean that the future is somehow predetermined or that human decision making can never frustrate the divine designs. The servant refers to Yahweh as "God of my master Abraham," an explicit reference to the language used in vv. 3, 7; only a God of heaven and earth, active throughout those spheres, could grant success in Aram-naharaim (v. 10).

Verse 13 does not constitute a naive effort to inform God; it states the servant's present situation, in which he hopes success will be forthcoming. He then prays in a way that is less precise than it sounds (and may still be too precise for a good prayer) that the woman to whom he will speak *in a certain way* and who will respond *in a certain way* (the words of vv. 17-19 are not identical; cf. vv. 42-46) will be the one whom God has chosen to be Isaac's wife. Note that this interchange will not necessarily signal the presence of the right woman (v. 21). He also hopes and prays that *God will let her be* the chosen one, which implies additional divine action. "By this" (v. 14) refers to the entire complex of events. The servant's prayer to God correlates well with his own sense of what might take place at the well.

The narrator's description of Rebekah (vv. 15-16) enables the reader to know she will be Isaac's wife before the servant does; the focus thus falls on the servant's faithful handling of the situation. When the anticipated conversation does occur (vv. 17-19; it is not represented as an answer to prayer), the servant does *not* immediately know that this is the woman. Rather, he gazes "at her in silence to learn whether or not the LORD had made his journey successful" (v. 21; not reported in vv. 46-47). In other words, he deems a period

157. Ibid., 382.

of reflection and observation necessary. We do not know how he gained this knowledge, but an inner certainty through God-given insight regarding the divine decision seems likely (and leads to the giving of gifts before he is absolutely certain, vv. 22-24).

When it becomes clear to the servant that Rebekah is the woman (and he had all the time it would take to water *all* those camels with a pitcher!), he immediately gives public thanks to the Lord, praising (i.e., blessing; see v. 48; Exod 18:10) God for his kindness (*ḥesed*), faithfulness (אמה *ʾĕmet*), and guiding presence. Rebekah's hospitality mirrors that of Abraham in 18:2-8 (vv. 18-20; cf. also vv. 23, 25).

Relationships in Rebekah's family are not easy to discern, but the following seems likely: Rebekah is the granddaughter of Nahor, Abraham's brother; her father, Bethuel, and Isaac are cousins; her "mother's household" (v. 28) refers naturally to a girl's family (Cant 3:4). The leading role of her brother Laban and minor role of Bethuel (only v. 50) may reflect that culture (in 29:5 Laban is called the son [NIV "grandson"] of Nahor; in 24:48, the NIV has granddaughter-brother; the NRSV has daughter-kinsman).

24:28-61. Rebekah, having informed her family, leaves the official welcoming to her brother, Laban. His theological language, coming after he has observed the expensive gifts, may be more calculated than sincere (v. 31). Yet, his welcome testifies that such symbols of prosperity result from God's work of blessing in the servant's life, a perspective again voiced in v. 50.

The servant insists on telling his story to Rebekah's family, the better to persuade them that Rebekah should marry Isaac (enclosing it with words of blessing, vv. 35, 48). In giving God such a prominent role, he testifies publicly to all the blessings God has wrought on Abraham's behalf (cf. psalms of thanksgiving, e.g., Ps 66:16). He also lifts up Abraham, his "master" (ten times; twenty-four times in the chapter; "servant" fifteen times) rather than himself. He repeats in somewhat different language the conversation he had with Abraham prior to leaving (cf. vv. 37-41 with vv. 3-8); one difference occurs in v. 41, which places the onus of responsibility on the family, whereas v. 8 had spoken of Rebekah (the decisions of both prove to be important, vv. 51, 58).

He also does not repeat Abraham's charge (vv. 6, 8) to avoid taking Isaac back to the home country. Both of these shifts are politic deployments of Abraham's directives.

The servant then recalls his prayer upon arriving at the well in basically the same words (vv. 42-44) and rehearses the events that followed (vv. 45-48), including his acts of worship. This fifteen-verse rehearsal of the story comes to a climax in v. 49: The servant asks Laban and Bethuel to give their daughter to become Isaac's wife. The servant's request includes language he had used of God—to show kindness and faithfulness to Abraham (cf. vv. 12, 27; the NIV retains this verbal link). In other words, Laban and Bethuel will be acting toward Abraham as God does if they allow Rebekah to go. Turning either "to the right hand or to the left" expresses an idiom captured well in the NIV's paraphrase, "so I may know which way to turn." What he does next depends on their response.

Laban and Bethuel respond directly; they believe the witness of the servant constitutes a word from Yahweh (vv. 50-51). As a consequence, "nothing one way or the other" (NIV; the NRSV's "bad or good" is more literal, which the NIV retains in 31:24, 29) can contribute to the discussion, except to formalize the matter (v. 51). These statements testify to a rich and deep faith in Yahweh present in this family, about which we have not heard since Abraham left the home country (cf. 31:53).

Having heard their response, Abraham's servant again worships God (v. 52). He does not respond verbally, but distributes gifts (a dowry?; cf. 34:12) and takes part in a meal. Note the reference to her mother in vv. 53, 55, whereas v. 50 speaks of Bethuel, her father. In vv. 59-60 they refer to Rebekah only as a sister.

In v. 55, Rebekah's family seeks to delay her departure for a few days, as was the custom (cf. Tob 7:15). When the servant insists on leaving so the good news can be brought to Abraham, they call on Rebekah to make her own decision. When she agrees, they send her and her attendants (her nurse Deborah [35:8] anticipates later children) away with their blessing. This blessing takes a traditional form, focusing on victory over enemies and fertility (as in God's word to Abraham in 22:17-18). It lacks explicitly religious language, as befits a narrative addressing everyday family concerns.

24:62-67. The author concludes the story in a brief and direct way. The servant identifies Isaac as the "master," an indication of the transition from Abraham to Isaac. The servant's retelling the story one more time (v. 66) becomes an occasion for the next stage of the story. Isaac and Rebekah are married, and what might have been just an arranged marriage grows into a loving relationship. The veil may be a signal from Rebekah that she accepts Isaac as her husband; her presence in Sarah's tent signifies her new role as matriarch of this family.

REFLECTIONS

1. This novella highlights in an unusually expansive way the motif of divine guidance, especially in the servant's prayers and in his rehearsal of earlier events (vv. 1-27) in vv. 34-48. This retelling constitutes a public testimony to the presence and activity of God, to which Laban and Bethuel respond with their own witness (v. 50). The repetition of vv. 12-14 in vv. 17-19 links prayer for divine guidance with daily life and highlights the place given to worship and prayer, both petition and thanksgiving, throughout the narrative (vv. 12-14, 26-27, 42-44, 48, 52). While these witnessing and worshiping actions of the servant in the story provide a model for the life of God's servants in every age, the servant remains anonymous, subservient to the divine action in the life of this family. The servant illustrates what life is like for many servants of God. They enter into the service of their master and proceed faithfully in quite ordinary situations, remaining anonymous in the overall scheme of things, but they are crucial vehicles for the leading and blessing work of God in daily affairs.

2. The narrator initially portrays God as one who has a history of blessing Abraham. Because blessing involves creation, this history testifies to God's work as creator, which is consonant with the characterization of Yahweh as "the God of heaven and [the God of] earth" (v. 3) and more briefly as "the God of heaven" (v. 7 NRSV). Such universal claims for the God of Abraham match those of 14:19, 22. While these divine epithets are often considered late because of their use in post-exilic literature (e.g., Ezra 1:2; 5:12), the narrator thought that such universal understandings of God were necessary in order to speak adequately about God's activity in this ancestral period.

The material content of these verses may further explain this usage. Abraham's servant is to swear regarding matters that reach out into the wider world of Mesopotamia (vv. 4, 7). Such a universal understanding of God becomes necessary if matters relating to the larger world of this family are to make theological sense. In other words, the theological affirmations of Genesis 24 correlate with the opening chapter of Genesis and its claim about God as creator of heaven and earth.

In addition, we may discuss God's work as creator in and through the ordinary, everyday workings of this family rather than in miraculous or extraordinary events. We do not have here a divine "management of events";[158] to the contrary, our exposition has shown that human activity can shape the future, though not finally stymie God's purposes. We can speak of God's highly effective work behind the scenes without resorting to such deterministic descriptions.

3. The story understands Abraham's wealth to result from the blessing of God (vv. 1, 31, 35-36, 60). Moreover, the author emphasizes that God gives success (vv. 12, 21, 40, 56). Blessing and success involve tangible realities, from wealth and property to posterity. "The blessings of heaven come packaged for earth."[159] The author does not claim that wealth and success are always due to the blessing work of God. People can come by possessions and prosperity through evil means. Humans *interpret* whether or not one can ascribe such material

---

158. Von Rad, *Genesis,* 260.
159. Brueggemann, *Genesis,* 198.

well-being to the blessing work of God. The servant attempts to convince the family in Haran that the wealth they see is indeed due to God's work in Abraham's life, but finally they themselves must make an interpretive judgment in faith.

4. The variations in the servant's retelling (vv. 34-49) say something important about the continuing use of this story in our own time. We use biblical texts properly not simply by quoting a biblical passage or providing an exact rendering of this or that biblical story. The biblical materials themselves provide the reteller sanction to play with the details of the story in view of the context in which the teller stands.

5. The God language of Laban and Bethuel (vv. 31, 50-51) invites speculation; certainly the narrator understands that the Yahwistic faith was established within Abraham's family before Abraham left for Canaan (see 31:53). Such faith apparently continues outside of Abraham's family and the specific promises that undergirded his relationship with God. Once again, this situation testifies to the work of God the Creator.

6. Many commentators have observed the importance of prayer in the life of the servant; it is spontaneous, personal, and focused on the individual's relationship to God. Westermann puts its well: These prayers indicate that "spontaneous address to God in petition and thanks arising therefrom is the natural expression of life with God. . . . Just as the personal relationship of trust in God and his guidance remains the same throughout the Bible, so too does prayer as a response to this guidance when experienced in one's personal life."[160]

7. Regarding v. 67, we must say more than that a new generation is appearing, or even that God's promises of posterity through Isaac can now be realized. Isaac loves Rebekah! Life in God's good creation involves more than divine promises and religious practice; it includes such creational gifts as the love between husband and wife. We should relate this theme to that of faithfulness and steadfast love. While these words depict God's relation to this family (vv. 12, 14, 27), they also characterize human relationships (v. 49) and are integral to God's purposes for all creation.

160. Westermann, *Genesis 12–36*, 392.

GENESIS 25:1-18, THE DEATH OF ABRAHAM AND THE FAMILY OF ISHMAEL

NIV

25 Abraham took[a] another wife, whose name was Keturah. ²She bore him Zimran, Jokshan, Medan, Midian, Ishbak and Shuah. ³Jokshan was the father of Sheba and Dedan; the descendants of Dedan were the Asshurites, the Letushites and the Leummites. ⁴The sons of Midian were Ephah, Epher, Hanoch, Abida and Eldaah. All these were descendants of Keturah.

⁵Abraham left everything he owned to Isaac. ⁶But while he was still living, he gave gifts to the sons of his concubines and sent them away from his son Isaac to the land of the east.

a1 Or had taken

NRSV

25 Abraham took another wife, whose name was Keturah. ²She bore him Zimran, Jokshan, Medan, Midian, Ishbak, and Shuah. ³Jokshan was the father of Sheba and Dedan. The sons of Dedan were Asshurim, Letushim, and Leummim. ⁴The sons of Midian were Ephah, Epher, Hanoch, Abida, and Eldaah. All these were the children of Keturah. ⁵Abraham gave all he had to Isaac. ⁶But to the sons of his concubines Abraham gave gifts, while he was still living, and he sent them away from his son Isaac, eastward to the east country.

7This is the length of Abraham's life, one hundred seventy-five years. ⁸Abraham breathed

NIV

⁷Altogether, Abraham lived a hundred and seventy-five years. ⁸Then Abraham breathed his last and died at a good old age, an old man and full of years; and he was gathered to his people. ⁹His sons Isaac and Ishmael buried him in the cave of Machpelah near Mamre, in the field of Ephron son of Zohar the Hittite, ¹⁰the field Abraham had bought from the Hittites.ᵃ There Abraham was buried with his wife Sarah. ¹¹After Abraham's death, God blessed his son Isaac, who then lived near Beer Lahai Roi.

¹²This is the account of Abraham's son Ishmael, whom Sarah's maidservant, Hagar the Egyptian, bore to Abraham.

¹³These are the names of the sons of Ishmael, listed in the order of their birth: Nebaioth the firstborn of Ishmael, Kedar, Adbeel, Mibsam, ¹⁴Mishma, Dumah, Massa, ¹⁵Hadad, Tema, Jetur, Naphish and Kedemah. ¹⁶These were the sons of Ishmael, and these are the names of the twelve tribal rulers according to their settlements and camps. ¹⁷Altogether, Ishmael lived a hundred and thirty-seven years. He breathed his last and died, and he was gathered to his people. ¹⁸His descendants settled in the area from Havilah to Shur, near the border of Egypt, as you go toward Asshur. And they lived in hostility towardᵇ all their brothers.

ᵃ10 Or *the sons of Heth*   ᵇ18 Or *lived to the east of*

NRSV

his last and died in a good old age, an old man and full of years, and was gathered to his people. ⁹His sons Isaac and Ishmael buried him in the cave of Machpelah, in the field of Ephron son of Zohar the Hittite, east of Mamre, ¹⁰the field that Abraham purchased from the Hittites. There Abraham was buried, with his wife Sarah. ¹¹After the death of Abraham God blessed his son Isaac. And Isaac settled at Beer-lahai-roi.

12These are the descendants of Ishmael, Abraham's son, whom Hagar the Egyptian, Sarah's slave-girl, bore to Abraham. ¹³These are the names of the sons of Ishmael, named in the order of their birth: Nebaioth, the firstborn of Ishmael; and Kedar, Adbeel, Mibsam, ¹⁴Mishma, Dumah, Massa, ¹⁵Hadad, Tema, Jetur, Naphish, and Kedemah. ¹⁶These are the sons of Ishmael and these are their names, by their villages and by their encampments, twelve princes according to their tribes. ¹⁷(This is the length of the life of Ishmael, one hundred thirty-seven years; he breathed his last and died, and was gathered to his people.) ¹⁸They settled from Havilah to Shur, which is opposite Egypt in the direction of Assyria; he settled downᵃ alongside ofᵇ all his people.

ᵃ Heb *he fell*   ᵇ Or *down in opposition to*

COMMENTARY

The story of Abraham ends as it began, with genealogies (a mix of J and P). They link up with 22:20-24 and enclose the final segment of the Abraham story. Although commentators often view v. 18 as the break point, a better ending may come at 25:11, with its reference to the divine blessing of Isaac (cf. 24:1). Verses 12-18 would then be an interlude (vv. 12 and 19 are parallel). This pattern occurs also with Isaac; after his death and burial by his sons (35:29) comes an interlude with the genealogy of Esau (36:1-42), a secondary line parallel to Ishmael (25:19 could be considered parallel to 37:2 as well; cf. also 25:11 and 37:1). One may view Ishmael's genealogy as a new beginning, much briefer than that of Isaac, naturally, but exactly parallel (the same might be said of Esau and Jacob). Generally, the narrator has so closely linked these genealogies and stories that no separation seems finally satisfactory.

An editor has placed the death and burial of Abraham (vv. 7-10) between genealogies, as if to suggest that Abraham's life continues on in many children (cf. 17:5). These names may refer primarily to peoples with whom Israel as a nation was engaged over the years.[161] Most involve various Arabian groups, but the historical setting remains unclear; they do not seem to be sharply distinguished geographically, as might be expected of groups that are partly sedentary, partly nomadic.

161. For details, see Sarna, *Genesis,* 170-77.

The various peoples by whom Israel was surrounded were, ultimately, a part of their family.

25:1-6. In vv. 1-6, the narrator introduces us to a side of Abraham's life hitherto completely unknown. Given all the divine and human activity necessary for Abraham to have a son, the reader may be surprised to read about Keturah, who bore him six more children. These names (developed in part to the third generation) are generally associated with the Syro-Arabian desert; we know most about the Midianites (see 37:28, 36). *Keturah* is closely related to the Hebrew word for "spice"; this and other biblical and extra-biblical evidence links these peoples to the lively commerce in these commodities.

We do not know when this marriage of Abraham's occurred, though its place after the death of Sarah suggests that the narrator understood it to postdate that event; Abraham did live seventy-five years after the birth of Isaac and thirty-eight after Sarah died (17:17; 23:1). But, if so, the previous comments about having a son in his old age (cf. also 24:1) seem trivial. Perhaps the segment (vv. 1-6) provides nothing more than an addendum, a tradition that the narrator chose not to integrate into the major story itself. The apparent reference in v. 6 to the sons of both Hagar and Keturah ("concubines"; perhaps correlated with "wife" [v. 1; 16:3] to set them off from Sarah) draws Ishmael and the sons of Keturah together as those whom Abraham "sent away" (cf. 21:14). They are sent away to "the east" (as are Cain and Lot). This action settles the place of Isaac and issues of inheritance (cf. 21:10 with 25:5). Yet, they receive largess from Abraham, which attests to a relationship of concern and generosity.

25:7-11. Abraham died at the ripe old age of 175, a nice round 100 years after he had responded to the divine call (12:4). The writer describes his death in quite matter-of-fact ways. Death appears not as the enemy, but simply as the end of a good and full life (see 15:15; cf. 47:9). Being "gathered to his people" (vv. 8, 17; 35:29; 49:33; a phrase unique to the Pentateuch) does not refer to death or burial, but probably alludes to Sheol or some other form of afterlife. Isaac and Ishmael, with no sign of disharmony between them, see to his burial beside Sarah in the cave he had purchased (chap. 23). The return of Ishmael but not the sons by Keturah is striking, testifying to the special place of Ishmael as a child of promise (see 17:18; 21:11).

25:12-18. The author depicts Ishmael (v. 12) in terms identical to Isaac (v. 19); both are "sons of Abraham." The reference to his life span is unique outside of the chosen line (v. 17). Moreover, the twelve princes (v. 16) mirror the twelve tribes of Israel. The many descendants of Ishmael testify to the fulfillment of God's promises (17:20; 21:18). Ishmael has a future, too. Some of the names are unknown, but other identifications have been made with Arabian tribal groups to the east and south of Canaan. The translation of v. 18 remains uncertain (see the footnotes), but may be linked to an earlier pronouncement about Ishmael's future, anticipating intrafamilial difficulties (16:12).

REFLECTIONS

The story of Abraham ends by specifying his role as the father of a multitude of nations; his descendants are numerous, indeed. While the author does not recall the language of promise, it goes without saying that these descendants are a fulfillment of key divine promises to Abraham. At the same time, vv. 12-18 witness to the fulfillment of God's promises to Ishmael (17:20; 21:13, 18). God has been faithful to those both within and without the chosen family.

The story of Abraham does not culminate with reference only to Isaac, an important theological affirmation. Given the variety of negative and positive relationships Israel will have with these peoples over the years, it is striking that, at the beginning of Israel's history, stands this word about their place in the family of Abraham. The relationships among people in that part of the world ought to be conceived most fundamentally in familial rather than national or political or religious terms. Differences have emerged over the years that cannot be lightly set aside. But there are significant commonalities as well, to which very deep roots in Abraham's family testify. These links should provide some continuing basis for working with differences among these peoples in a creative and peaceful way.

THE STORY OF JACOB

OVERVIEW

Jacob is Israel; that overriding consideration informs and propels these chapters. The biblical authors present a story about an individual, one whose character and personality emerge in ways both subtle and direct over the course of the story. Jacob remains very much a person in his own right, but in time he *becomes* Israel. Finally, Jacob is more than an individual.

In another sense, Jacob also becomes Israel during the development of these traditions. The experiences of later, corporate Israel have shaped the telling of this story. The narrative portrays the story of Jacob-Israel as *both* a story of the past—whatever the degree of historicity modern historians say the story may have—and a story of every contemporary Israelite. Israel understands itself as possessing characteristics that are often mirrored in the story of Jacob-Israel (one could make similar, but less fully developed, statements about Esau-Edom and Laban-Aram).

This portrayal presents self-critical realism. The traditions do not whitewash Jacob-Israel, as if to suggest an Eden-like origin for itself. The story possesses remarkably little pretense. Here Jacob stands with qualities negative and positive, clear and ambiguous, simple and complex. Take him or leave him. The most astounding claim of the story is that God takes him.

A writer introduces this section of Genesis with a summary reference to the story of Isaac (see the NIV), yet the reader quickly discovers that his sons, especially Jacob, overshadow him. The story of Isaac himself exists only in an abbreviated form (chap. 26), almost as an interlude in the larger family chronicle. It may be that few Isaac traditions actually existed or that one or more storytellers, for unknown reasons, chose to leave them aside; the obscure references to Isaac in 31:42 and Amos 7:9, 16 suggest that more was available at one time.

The stories of Jacob in chaps. 25–36 are presented in a somewhat episodic fashion, tied together by itineraries (primarily) or genealogical references, yet less so than with the Abraham stories. Chapters 29–31 provide a sustained narrative that bears similarities to the Joseph story. Moreover, a plot pervades most of the chapters and provides internal cohesion. Any attempt to depict the complex history of the story must come to terms with evidence for both compositeness and unity.

Scholars commonly agree that the story betrays diverse origins, pieced together from a variety of sources, though each part retains its character as a family narrative. These scholars think of J, E, P, and redactors, who used various Jacob traditions that had already been brought together from oral and written materials composed over an extensive period of time. More specific theories of origin remain quite uncertain, though special associations with the northern kingdom seem likely (e.g., the special interest in the northern cities Bethel and Shechem).

During the past two decades there has been increasing interest in reading the Jacob story as a unity. As a literary entity, the text has a life of its own, and we have to come to terms with its final form. This approach does not deny the need to consider issues of source and redaction, but the basic concern involves hearing the text as we now have it. That will be the perspective of this commentary.

We have already noted that the overriding theme is Jacob as Israel. Interpreters often suggest that family conflict provides the basic focus of the story. This may be so, but we must resist the temptation of reducing the text to a sociological phenomenon, to claim that the story fundamentally addresses dysfunctional family systems. Or we may reduce the discussion to moral issues, regarding the ethical behavior of the characters. As important as these matters are, the story makes certain theological claims regarding this family's relationship to God and to God's purposes in the world through them. Most basically, *God's choosing and speaking* generates and propels the story of this family, yet without discounting the important role humans play.

1. The Divine Promise. As with the Abraham stories, promises function at two levels. (a) The basic ancestral promises continue—promises of land, descendants, and blessing on them and through them to the families of the earth (28:3-4, 13-14; 35:11-12). (b) Promises directed to Jacob's particular situation also occur—promises of divine presence and care in his journeyings (28:15; 31:3). Without these promises, and God's tending to them, there would be no story of Jacob. The promises for this family exist for the sake of God's mission in the world. Election and promise involve, finally, the other "families" (12:3; 28:14) of the world, so that they too might receive the life that God intends for creation.

2. The Divine Blessing. The narratives treat blessing basically in creational terms, whether of fertility in the field (26:12; 27:27-28), among the animals (30:30), in the birth of children (29:31–30:24; 33:5), or more generally (26:13, 29; 30:27, 43; 33:11). The blessing extends through Isaac to Jacob (27:28-29; 28:1-4) and Esau (27:39-40), from God to Jacob (32:29; 35:9), and even from Laban to his family (31:55). It constitutes the central issue between Jacob and Esau (27:1-45). God's promises as continuing blessings remain basic for this family and to others through them (26:3-4, 24; 28:4, 14). Blessings are conveyed through both the spoken word and God's working in creational processes, both human and nonhuman. The divine purpose behind the blessings functions identically to that of the promises: to enable the fullest possible life for all the families in God's good creation.

3. God. God speaks promises, brings blessing, and accompanies this family along its various journeys. Even more, God engages this conflicted family directly in the service of these promises. God not only puts these promises in verbal form, but also enters into the fray on their behalf, even if it means engaging Jacob himself in "hand-to-hand combat."

As with Abraham, God appears in order to speak; this speaking defines the story. God speaks two times to Isaac, to command and to promise (26:3-4, 24), and six times to Jacob to promise (28:13-15; 31:3; 35:11-12), to command (31:3, 13; 35:1), to bless (32:29), to name (32:28; 35:10) and to advise (31:12). God also speaks to Rebekah (25:23) and to Laban (31:24). The response of the various principals to this divine speaking helps give shape to the development of the story.

Attention to God language helps us to understand the story. It appears most pervasively with the birth of the children (29:31–30:24), where Leah and Rachel witness powerfully to the gracious activity of God in responding to their laments. These women also interpret the Jacob-Laban conflict theologically (31:16). Other individuals offer theological interpretations of events: Isaac (26:22), Abimelech (26:28-29), Laban (30:27), and Jacob (30:30; 31:5-9, 42; 32:2, 30; 33:5, 11). These persons testify to a pervading divine presence working in and through people and events within and without the community of faith on behalf of the divine purposes. God language also appears in connection with prayers and rituals by Isaac (27:28; 28:3-4), Jacob (32:9-12), and Laban (31:49-50, 53); though twice Jacob uses God language in less than appropriate ways (27:20; 30:2). We find God language when God speaks to Jacob (28:16-22; 31:11; 35:3) and Laban (31:29). Nonetheless, the narrator uses God talk relatively infrequently, aside from divine appearances (the birth of the children [29:31; 30:17, 22; 31:53; 33:20] and events in chap. 35 [vv. 5, 7, 15]). The narrator obviously prefers that the characters themselves give voice to the place of God in their lives.

4. Conflict. The conflict theme arises from within these theological matters. In the Abraham/Sarah stories, barrenness and childbearing, and their implications for the promise, constitute the prevailing motif; parents rather than sons stand at the center of the conflict. In the Isaac and Jacob stories, while issues of barrenness and birth continue, the narratives focus more on conflict between sons. At the same time, the intrafamilial conflict often extends beyond the brothers, and catches up parents, wives, children, more extended family members (e.g., Laban), the neighbors (from Abimelech to Shechem), and even

God. The vital and positive role that women—especially Rebekah, Leah, Rachel, and Dinah—play in these conflicts has only recently received significant attention.

The Jacob story begins with conflict (25:19-34), which sets the stage for much of what follows, issuing finally in a less than full reconciliation. Conflict begins with issues of kinship and inheritance, especially primogeniture, which in turn catches up the characters in acts of deception and all of their spiraling consequences. We might, today, call this a dysfunctional family, with all of its relational difficulties, complexities, and ambiguities. One of the difficulties in interpreting this conflict has to do with character depiction.

Commentators have tended to portray virtually every individual in extreme and unfortunate directions: Jacob is a cheat and rascal, Esau an idiot, Isaac a dottering old man, Rebekah a manipulator. To be sure, there are no gods or demons among these people, but the interpreter will be truer to the text by striving for as much balance as possible in sketching out the ways these characters work in and through the conflict.

At the same time, these texts witness to a God who engages this family in the very midst of its conflicted life from the start. In fact, God's oracle to Rebekah (25:23) stands at the beginning. While the oracle presents a divine interpretation of already existing conditions, and the characters do inherit a way of being a family from their Abrahamic forebears, in some sense it becomes God's own word that generates and intensifies the conflict. The entire story involves a divine decision to elect one person rather than another to carry on the Abrahamic line of promise. At its most profound level, the problems and possibilities created by the divine election constitute the essence of the conflict in the story of Jacob and Esau. We should understand the conflicted relationships in the story as a result of God's decision to choose one family.

The way in which the principals involved respond to this divine election can, of course, intensify the conflict even further. They can complicate and frustrate the divine purpose, even place it in jeopardy. The story should not be seen as "the actualization of a predetermined fate."[162]

God is, indeed, bound to this family, but they are to respond faithfully (see 26:5), and the way they work through the divine choices and promises shapes the future, including God's future, in significant ways. Not least, the chosen ones themselves must come to see that election should not be understood in isolated terms. Such a perception could only lead to exclusivistic understandings, to an isolation from the world while basking in the glory of having been divinely chosen (an understanding not foreign to later Israel, cf. Amos 3:2; 9:7). Election always serves mission, the choice of one family for the sake of all other families (12:3; 28:14). This orientation outward helps to explain why these chapters "reveal an astounding degree of empathy with Israel's antagonists."[163]

Structure. One may outline the Jacob story broadly as a journey: flight from Canaan to Haran and back to Canaan. To this we should add the journey through the land of promise in 33:18–35:27, after the return. This itinerary gives to the story a strong sense of movement, presenting a person and a family on the go, never staying in one spot for too long. The journeys both within and without the promised land mirror the life of later Israel, especially the experiences of exodus and exile. The most basic movement in the Jacob story is linear, climaxing in the settlement of Jacob and his family in the land of promise.

Others have observed a chiastic structure within the story (especially as refined by Fishbane and others). However, though certain patterns can indeed be observed, we must be highly cautious about forcing the material into complex and detailed chiasms. A number of structures overlap and help to prevent any easy reading of the story according to a single model.

In discerning structure (and content) one should note the prominent parallels between this story and that of Moses in Exod 2:1–4:31.[164] The following brief observations may be helpful.

Genealogies, those of Ishmael (25:12-18) and Esau (36:1-43), bracket the Jacob story. The former provides a link with the Abraham story, as does the latter for the Joseph story. This bracketing of the chosen by the nonchosen may be a way

---

162. Michael Fishbane, *Text and Texture: Close Readings of Selected Biblical Texts* (New York: Schocken, 1964) 62.

163. John Gammie, "Theological Interpretation by Way of Literary and Tradition Analysis: Genesis 25–36," *Encounter with the Text*, ed. M. Buss (Philadelphia: Fortress, 1979) 130.

164. Ronald Hendel, *The Epic of the Patriarch: The Jacob Cycle and the Narrative Traditions of Canaan and Israel* (Atlanta: Scholars Press, 1987) 140.

in which these groups of people are held together, not least in the service of God's mission of blessing *all* "families" (28:14).

One may discern a similar interest in the two chapters that occur at comparable points early and late in the story. They relate the Canaanite peoples to Isaac and Jacob (26; 34), drawing out ways in which Israel's relationship to outsiders takes both positive and negative (mostly) directions.

The centerpiece of the story may well be the birth of Jacob's children (29:31–30:24). This judgment is supported by the sudden and pervasive use of God language, by the lament-deliverance-thanksgiving rhythm revealed in the responses of Leah and Rachel, and by the overriding concern for the birth of Israel. Different elements of the Jacob-Laban conflict enclose this birth narrative (29:1-30; 30:25–31:54).

Some scholars have suggested that two texts focusing on Jacob and Esau are also parallel (27:1-45; 33:1-17), moving from conflict to some sort of resolution. This judgment, however, tends to reduce the important conflict story in 25:23-34 to the status of an introduction.

The appearances of God constitute the "pillars" of the story. Here the structure becomes more complex than typical chiasms allow. Some interpreters view the dream at Bethel (28:10-22) and the struggle at the Jabbok (32:22-32; or encounters with angels of God, 32:1-2, 22-32) as parallel, enclosing the Jacob-Laban story. However, one may discern more significant levels of correspondence between the texts related to Bethel (28:10-22; 35:1-15). Moreover, the divine oracle to Rebekah (25:23) regarding "struggling" is linked to the struggle at the Jabbok, especially the text's mirroring of the Jacob-Esau and the Jacob-God struggle (see 33:10). One should view these four instances of divine speaking as informing each other in complex ways and propelling the story along.

GENESIS 25:19-34, JACOB AND ESAU

NIV

19This is the account of Abraham's son Isaac.

Abraham became the father of Isaac, 20and Isaac was forty years old when he married Rebekah daughter of Bethuel the Aramean from Paddan Aram[a] and sister of Laban the Aramean.
21Isaac prayed to the LORD on behalf of his wife, because she was barren. The LORD answered his prayer, and his wife Rebekah became pregnant. 22The babies jostled each other within her, and she said, "Why is this happening to me?" So she went to inquire of the LORD.
23The LORD said to her,

"Two nations are in your womb,
  and two peoples from within you will be
    separated;
one people will be stronger than the other,
  and the older will serve the younger."

24When the time came for her to give birth, there were twin boys in her womb. 25The first

[a]20 That is, Northwest Mesopotamia

NRSV

19These are the descendants of Isaac, Abraham's son: Abraham was the father of Isaac, 20and Isaac was forty years old when he married Rebekah, daughter of Bethuel the Aramean of Paddan-aram, sister of Laban the Aramean. 21Isaac prayed to the LORD for his wife, because she was barren; and the LORD granted his prayer, and his wife Rebekah conceived. 22The children struggled together within her; and she said, "If it is to be this way, why do I live?"[a] So she went to inquire of the LORD. 23And the LORD said to her,

"Two nations are in your womb,
  and two peoples born of you shall be
    divided;
the one shall be stronger than the other,
  the elder shall serve the younger."

24When her time to give birth was at hand, there were twins in her womb. 25The first came out red, all his body like a hairy mantle; so they named named him Esau. 26Afterward his brother came

[a] Syr: Meaning of Heb uncertain

NIV

to come out was red, and his whole body was like a hairy garment; so they named him Esau.[a] ²⁶After this, his brother came out, with his hand grasping Esau's heel; so he was named Jacob.[b] Isaac was sixty years old when Rebekah gave birth to them.

²⁷The boys grew up, and Esau became a skillful hunter, a man of the open country, while Jacob was a quiet man, staying among the tents. ²⁸Isaac, who had a taste for wild game, loved Esau, but Rebekah loved Jacob.

²⁹Once when Jacob was cooking some stew, Esau came in from the open country, famished. ³⁰He said to Jacob, "Quick, let me have some of that red stew! I'm famished!" (That is why he was also called Edom.[c])

³¹Jacob replied, "First sell me your birthright."

³²"Look, I am about to die," Esau said. "What good is the birthright to me?"

³³But Jacob said, "Swear to me first." So he swore an oath to him, selling his birthright to Jacob.

³⁴Then Jacob gave Esau some bread and some lentil stew. He ate and drank, and then got up and left.

So Esau despised his birthright.

ᵃ25 Esau may mean hairy; he was also called Edom, which means red.
ᵇ26 Jacob means he grasps the heel (figuratively, he deceives).
ᶜ30 Edom means red

NRSV

out, with his hand gripping Esau's heel; so he was named Jacob.[a] Isaac was sixty years old when she bore them.

27When the boys grew up, Esau was a skillful hunter, a man of the field, while Jacob was a quiet man, living in tents. ²⁸Isaac loved Esau, because he was fond of game; but Rebekah loved Jacob.

29Once when Jacob was cooking a stew, Esau came in from the field, and he was famished. ³⁰Esau said to Jacob, "Let me eat some of that red stuff, for I am famished!" (Therefore he was called Edom.[b]) ³¹Jacob said, "First sell me your birthright." ³²Esau said, "I am about to die; of what use is a birthright to me?" ³³Jacob said, "Swear to me first."[c] So he swore to him, and sold his birthright to Jacob. ³⁴Then Jacob gave Esau bread and lentil stew, and he ate and drank, and rose and went his way. Thus Esau despised his birthright.

ᵃ That is He takes by the heel or He supplants   ᵇ That is Red
ᶜ Heb today

COMMENTARY

These verses introduce in almost snapshot fashion the leading figures of the chapters to follow: Isaac, Rebekah, Jacob, and Esau. Events associated with the birth of Jacob and Esau (vv. 21-26) and their early life (vv. 27-34), while presented in brief and episodic fashion, set the stage well for the conflicted family relationships that ensue. The oracle in v. 23 specifies that national issues are at stake (Edomite and Israelite relationships), but the text grounds those realities in the experiences of individuals. The two principals shape history both before and after birth, with not a little help from their parents.

25:19-26. The story begins with genealogical notes, wherein Abraham's relationship to Isaac is

stated twice (the NIV is probably correct in seeing v. 1a as a summary statement of the chapters that follow, cf. 37:2a). Verses 19b-20 recapitulate earlier material (cf. 24:67), though Isaac's age is new information and Rebekah's family roots are described in greater detail.

The story of Rebekah/Isaac parallels that of Sarah/Abraham. Isaac and Rebekah are identified with some precision (cf. 11:27-32). Like Sarah, Rebekah is barren (cf. also 30:1-2), though that does not become a major motif in this story. Isaac, like Abraham, is old when he becomes a father (sixty years). Unlike Abraham, Isaac prays concerning the barrenness of Rebekah, and God, the narrator testifies, responds to (more precisely, is moved to answer) his prayer so that she conceives.

Rebekah's prayer soon follows Isaac's prayer. God responds differently to the two prayers, however. In the first, God enables conception; hence, one might speak of an "answer." The second involves a more complicated issue. The pregnancy is difficult for Rebekah; the story dictates that the (fraternal) twins' subsequent relationship has its *roots* in genetic rather than environmental factors. To suggest, however, that genetics equals destiny goes beyond the text, especially given the parental favoritism. She brings her lament to God in prayer (the language suggests a trip to a sanctuary), wondering whether life is worth all this suffering (the NRSV and the NIV differ on whether this has become a life-and-death matter for her; cf. 27:46).

God responds directly (an inner voice?) to her with an oracle. The oracle responds to an already existing situation; it does not start from "scratch." God explains to her the reason for the painful pregnancy (twins) and *interprets* this as a sign of the future relationship between them and their descendants (v. 23); the struggle itself does not result from divine action. More specifically, the narrative moves beyond laws of primogeniture; either the older (Esau) will be the weaker of the two and will serve the younger (Jacob), or, more likely, the older will be the stronger but will serve the weaker and younger. If the latter, there would be a play on the word for "strength." Either Esau is stronger physically—he wins the battle in the womb—and Jacob is stronger in other ways, or the one shall be stronger initially (Esau) but not finally (2 Sam 8:13-14). God is not described as an agent in these developments, which underscores the importance of human activity.

This oracle (consonant with Isaac's later blessings on the sons, 27:29, 40; cf. also 49:8), as well as the plays on words, reflects later conflict between the two "nations" (i.e., peoples) of Israel and Edom and the hegemony of the former over the latter (see 2 Sam 8:13-14). They help to ground (perhaps even justify) that later reality in these ancient family events. At the same time, the move from present oracle to future reality was not necessary or inevitable. This oracle will inform Rebekah's subsequent relationships to her sons in significant ways (see 25:28; 27:5-15, 42-46; 28:7).

When the twin boys are born, the narrator portrays them with features of their subsequent relationship: Esau, physical features; Jacob, action (this is reversed to some degree in v. 29). The Hebrew word for "red" (אדמוני *'admônî* [or "ruddy"]; see 1 Sam 16:12) is a play on *Edom*, linked to the "red stuff" at v. 30 (see 36:1). The word for "hairy" (שער *śē'ār*) is a play on *Seir*, the region where the Edomites lived, and is linked to the deception in 27:23. Why he is named Esau is uncertain. The meaning of *Jacob* (יעקב *ya'ăqōb*), also uncertain, plays on the word for "heel," עקב (*'āqēb*), "grasp the heel," or, less likely, the verb *'āqab* ("he supplants, deceives"; see Esau's interpretation in 27:36; Hos. 12:4). The name *Jacob* is associated with a feature of his birth and implies a uterine struggle to be born first, a struggle that Esau wins.

25:27-34. The following two vignettes not only illustrate this birth relationship between the two brothers, but establish specific grounds for later conflict. The first (vv. 27-28) speaks to issues of life-style and intrafamilial relationships, the second (vv. 29-34) to economics and personal values.

The author describes the young men by referring to ways of life that often stood in tension: Esau with those who are at home in the wild, on the move with animals, and Jacob with those who live a more settled, pastoral way of life. The writer characterizes Jacob with the word תם (*tām*), which both the NRSV and the NIV translate as "quiet" or mild-mannered; it normally means "innocent, upright" (see Job 1–2), which seems appropriate, at least at this point in his life. The writer juxtaposes the twins' different interests and temperaments with the love of the parents (cf. 37:4), a realistic note, common among parents. Isaac's love of Esau involves his ability to provide food (see Rebekah's use of this knowledge in 27:7, 14), but also remains independent of the oracle, of which Isaac was unaware. The author offers no specific reason to explain Rebekah's love for Jacob, but we may suppose it relates to what she knows about Jacob from the oracle.

How the second vignette is related to the oracle presents somewhat of a problem: Neither man was aware of the oracle or of the promise. Jacob does not act directly on the basis of the oracle, but Rebekah's favoritism may have helped to shape the way he acts toward his brother. His "cooking" (an ambiguous word) scene may even be contrived on the basis of his knowledge of Esau's habits.

The birthright—namely, the conferral of rights and privileges on the eldest son (normally)—entails a leadership position in the family and establishes claims regarding inheritance, indeed a double share of it—no small matter in view of 25:5 (see Deut 21:15-17). This story (and ancient Near Eastern parallels) indicates that such rights could be forfeited by the one born into such a privileged position. Esau and Jacob relate to the birthright in different ways. Esau comes across as callous and uncaring, easily outwitted regarding what might "naturally" be his, desiring more a satisfied present than a secure future (though his reference to death may not be as hyperbolic as is usually thought). He sells or barters his birthright for Jacob's lentil stew (i.e., "red stuff," another play on his identity); that Esau initially identifies the "red stuff" as blood stew seems possible, but too uncertain to guide interpretation. Five verbs depict the moment: *ate, drank, rose, departed*, and *despised*. The last verb specifies the narrator's judgment that more is at stake than a lapse in judgment. Although not justifying Jacob's actions, that final verb demonstrates that Esau bears responsibility for what happens here. At the same time, Esau continues to live, in the light of the oracle that he, like Jacob, will become a people or nation (v. 23).

The author, on the other hand, presents Jacob as a clever and opportunistic individual, who knows what he wants. He takes advantage of a brother in need (of which Esau is later rightfully critical, 27:36) and his hospitality to his brother contrasts with both Abraham and Lot (chaps. 18–19). He carefully covers the legal bases when the opening for advancement presents itself, having Esau swear an inviolable oath in the urgency of the moment regarding the transfer of the birthright.

REFLECTIONS

1. The story and Jacob and Esau begins with a struggle, which sets the stage for a complex and difficult journey for everyone within this conflicted family. At the same time, the texts witness to a God at work in and through this situation. The problems and possibilities created by the interaction between God and this family constitute the essence of the story of Jacob and Esau.

We should not cast struggle and conflict in totally negative terms. Hence, for God to subvert the law of primogeniture for the sake of the divine purposes opens the situation up to conflict; those who hold on for dear life to the way things are will not give up easily, not least because they have law and custom on their side. At the same time, we may have difficulty in discerning when and how change (and hence often conflict) stands in service of God's purposes. The furtherance of God's mission in the world would be one basic criterion.

2. We are not told what sort of divine action Rebekah's conception was thought to entail. "Barrenness" means childlessness, but not necessarily infertility. We do not know the degree to which physiological or psychological factors, or some combination, faced these parents. They had been childless for twenty years. Rebekah's conception witnesses to God's work as Creator, enabling new life to emerge.

3. The role of prayer on the part of *both* Isaac and Rebekah continues an emphasis of chap. 24, and demonstrates its importance in the lives of these figures; they obviously believe God would be concerned about such matters and had resources to do something about them (see 18:22-33). Prayer occurs prominently in Genesis as an unself-conscious practice of nearly every major figure, attesting to the personal nature of their relationship with God.[165]

4. God's oracle to Rebekah achieves a profound effect; it sets into motion a certain *direction*

---

165. On prayer, see S. Balentine, *Prayer in the Hebrew Bible: The Drama of Divine-Human Dialogue* (Minneapolis: Fortress, 1993).

for the future. This oracle recognizes that what happens in one generation (especially a word from God) may have a profound influence on those that follow, particularly with respect to certain formative periods in Israel's (or any people's) life. Later Israel understood the ancestral period to be such a time.

One might claim that the future of the two boys has been predetermined by this divine word. Yet, it shortly becomes clear that Rebekah does not understand that the oracle absolutely determines her sons' futures. What she does or says assumes that she thinks she can shape that future. She enters into their lives in decisive, at times manipulative, fashion, acting in ways that she thinks will contribute toward the future of which God has spoken (the narrator passes no judgment on her activity). The oft-suggested idea that just by pursuing such activities one seeks to take the divine promises into one's own hands constitutes a docetic view of the way in which God works in the world. God chooses to work in and through human activity in pursuing the divine purposes.

The future about which God speaks is not set in concrete. This is true of divine announcements about the future generally, particularly in prophetic material (see 2 Kgs 20:1-7; Jonah 3).[166] These utterances express the future as God sees it (or would like to see it). God's knowledge of future human behaviors is not absolute (evident in other texts; see 22:12). Moreover, the divine will can be frustrated by human behaviors (e.g., sin); though God's way into the future cannot, finally, be stymied.

Why would God speak directly to Rebekah about such matters? God takes sharp risks in being misunderstood. Giving Rebekah (or any human being) such information will tend to predispose her to act in certain ways toward her sons. Although she could have ignored God's word or actively worked against it, she chooses to tilt toward Jacob. God knows such behavior is likely, of course. The narrator has already reported Rebekah's preference (25:28), where she is said to love Jacob, and she doubtless knows that this runs counter to Isaac's "love." So God apparently gives Rebekah this information because God wants her to speak and act in such a way that this oracle will have a greater likelihood of coming to pass! The oracle expresses the future that God desires, and he hereby enlists Rebekah to work with God toward that end. That God chooses Rebekah rather than Isaac seems remarkable, given this patriarchal society; it suggests that God has more confidence in Rebekah than in Isaac. The reader might ask: Is this fair? Not according to any known human standard. At this point we are smack up against the mysteries of the divine election of Jacob (or Abraham or Israel . . .).

5. The narrator depicts the situation in such a way as to demonstrate that the inversion of priorities in the oracle does not derive from the boys' behaviors. The decision occurred pre-birth. Both act in ignorance of the oracle. The writer portrays both Jacob and Esau in such a way that disinterested readers would probably disagree on who acted the most reprehensibly. Both are guilty of violating basic family relationships, and any effort to excuse either one cuts against the grain of the text. Jacob takes egregious advantage of another person in need and sets the stage for major family conflict. Esau comes off as the dullard, careless with family interests and despising of the birthright. We do not know why God would choose either one to carry out his purposes. From another angle, inasmuch as God typically chooses weak instruments, then both Esau and Jacob would qualify! It would be precarious to talk about God's choosing the weak to shame the strong on the basis of this passage (unless *strength* is defined in a very narrow way).

The narrator probably "sets up" the reader with this text. The temptation for later Israel (and all who consider themselves to be God's elect) would certainly be to side with Jacob against Esau, to somehow justify his behaviors or even to suggest that whatever he did to obtain the birthright was appropriate to or congruent with God's choice. At one level, such

---

166. Contrary to White, *Narration*, 207, it can be a question of what as well as how.

thinking is ethically dangerous, for it suggests that the elect are free to act as they please, without regard for the consequences. At another level, such thinking is theologically wrong-headed, for personal behaviors did not ground God's choice to have the elder serve the younger.

Moreover, to note with Brueggemann, the pottage and the birthright ought not to be interpreted "as a contrast of spiritual and material . . . the birthright is fully as historical and material as is the pottage. It concerns security, prosperity, fertility and land."[167]

6. The reader must also use care in discussing primogeniture and the reversal of the rights of the firstborn. To be sure, the oracle overturns traditional customs and understandings and opens the future to possibilities not inherent in existing structures and institutions. But it is just as true that one can idolize the reversal of the traditional for its own sake. Even more, one can be tempted to understand election in terms comparable to primogeniture! Election, too, can be used as a vehicle to exclude others and exalt one's rights and privileges. Against such an understanding the prophets will speak very sharply (Amos 3:2; 9:7).

7. Family conflicts have far-reaching consequences, extending into personal, political, economic, and religious spheres. The conflict within this family will become more and more sharply evident as the narrative moves on. What will this mean for the future of God's people? Are seeds being sown in these dim recesses of history that will one day reap bitter fruit for the descendants of this family? What the people of God do with the conflicts with which they are inevitably presented will make a difference. And, amid all of this intrafamilial difficulty, what will become of the promises of God? Will they transpire as God intends? Neither the oracles nor the promises of God give a precise shape to the future. God will be faithful, that will never be in doubt; but what the recipients of the promise do and say along the way will make a difference regarding the shape of fulfillment.

167. Brueggemann, *Genesis*, 219.

GENESIS 26:1-33, STORIES ABOUT ISAAC

NIV

26 Now there was a famine in the land—besides the earlier famine of Abraham's time—and Isaac went to Abimelech king of the Philistines in Gerar. [2]The LORD appeared to Isaac and said, "Do not go down to Egypt; live in the land where I tell you to live. [3]Stay in this land for a while, and I will be with you and will bless you. For to you and your descendants I will give all these lands and will confirm the oath I swore to your father Abraham. [4]I will make your descendants as numerous as the stars in the sky and will give them all these lands, and through your offspring[a] all nations on earth will be blessed, [5]because Abraham obeyed me and kept my requirements, my commands, my decrees and my laws." [6]So Isaac stayed in Gerar.

[7]When the men of that place asked him about

a4 Or *seed*

NRSV

26 Now there was a famine in the land, besides the former famine that had occurred in the days of Abraham. And Isaac went to Gerar, to King Abimelech of the Philistines. [2]The LORD appeared to Isaac[a] and said, "Do not go down to Egypt; settle in the land that I shall show you. [3]Reside in this land as an alien, and I will be with you, and will bless you; for to you and to your descendants I will give all these lands, and I will fulfill the oath that I swore to your father Abraham. [4]I will make your offspring as numerous as the stars of heaven, and will give to your offspring all these lands; and all the nations of the earth shall gain blessing for themselves through your offspring, [5]because Abraham obeyed my voice and kept my charge, my commandments, my statutes, and my laws."

a Heb *him*

NIV

his wife, he said, "She is my sister," because he was afraid to say, "She is my wife." He thought, "The men of this place might kill me on account of Rebekah, because she is beautiful."

[8]When Isaac had been there a long time, Abimelech king of the Philistines looked down from a window and saw Isaac caressing his wife Rebekah. [9]So Abimelech summoned Isaac and said, "She is really your wife! Why did you say, 'She is my sister'?"

Isaac answered him, "Because I thought I might lose my life on account of her."

[10]Then Abimelech said, "What is this you have done to us? One of the men might well have slept with your wife, and you would have brought guilt upon us."

[11]So Abimelech gave orders to all the people: "Anyone who molests this man or his wife shall surely be put to death."

[12]Isaac planted crops in that land and the same year reaped a hundredfold, because the LORD blessed him. [13]The man became rich, and his wealth continued to grow until he became very wealthy. [14]He had so many flocks and herds and servants that the Philistines envied him. [15]So all the wells that his father's servants had dug in the time of his father Abraham, the Philistines stopped up, filling them with earth.

[16]Then Abimelech said to Isaac, "Move away from us; you have become too powerful for us."

[17]So Isaac moved away from there and encamped in the Valley of Gerar and settled there. [18]Isaac reopened the wells that had been dug in the time of his father Abraham, which the Philistines had stopped up after Abraham died, and he gave them the same names his father had given them.

[19]Isaac's servants dug in the valley and discovered a well of fresh water there. [20]But the herdsmen of Gerar quarreled with Isaac's herdsmen and said, "The water is ours!" So he named the well Esek,[a] because they disputed with him. [21]Then they dug another well, but they quarreled over that one also; so he named it Sitnah.[b] [22]He moved on from there and dug another well, and no one quarreled over it. He named it Rehoboth,[c] saying,

a20 Esek means *dispute*.   b21 Sitnah means *opposition*.
c22 Rehoboth means *room*.

NRSV

[6]So Isaac settled in Gerar. [7]When the men of the place asked him about his wife, he said, "She is my sister"; for he was afraid to say, "My wife," thinking, "or else the men of the place might kill me for the sake of Rebekah, because she is attractive in appearance." [8]When Isaac had been there a long time, King Abimelech of the Philistines looked out of a window and saw him fondling his wife Rebekah. [9]So Abimelech called for Isaac, and said, "So she is your wife! Why then did you say, 'She is my sister'?" Isaac said to him, "Because I thought I might die because of her." [10]Abimelech said, "What is this you have done to us? One of the people might easily have lain with your wife, and you would have brought guilt upon us." [11]So Abimelech warned all the people, saying, "Whoever touches this man or his wife shall be put to death."

[12]Isaac sowed seed in that land, and in the same year reaped a hundredfold. The LORD blessed him, [13]and the man became rich; he prospered more and more until he became very wealthy. [14]He had possessions of flocks and herds, and a great household, so that the Philistines envied him. [15](Now the Philistines had stopped up and filled with earth all the wells that his father's servants had dug in the days of his father Abraham.) [16]And Abimelech said to Isaac, "Go away from us; you have become too powerful for us."

[17]So Isaac departed from there and camped in the valley of Gerar and settled there. [18]Isaac dug again the wells of water that had been dug in the days of his father Abraham; for the Philistines had stopped them up after the death of Abraham; and he gave them the names that his father had given them. [19]But when Isaac's servants dug in the valley and found there a well of spring water, [20]the herders of Gerar quarreled with Isaac's herders, saying, "The water is ours." So he called the well Esek,[a] because they contended with him. [21]Then they dug another well, and they quarreled over that one also; so he called it Sitnah.[b] [22]He moved from there and dug another well, and they did not quarrel over it; so he called it Rehoboth,[c] saying, "Now the LORD has made room for us, and we shall be fruitful in the land."

a That is Contention   b That is Enmity   c That is Broad places or Room

"Now the LORD has given us room and we will flourish in the land."

²³From there he went up to Beersheba. ²⁴That night the LORD appeared to him and said, "I am the God of your father Abraham. Do not be afraid, for I am with you; I will bless you and will increase the number of your descendants for the sake of my servant Abraham."

²⁵Isaac built an altar there and called on the name of the LORD. There he pitched his tent, and there his servants dug a well.

²⁶Meanwhile, Abimelech had come to him from Gerar, with Ahuzzath his personal adviser and Phicol the commander of his forces. ²⁷Isaac asked them, "Why have you come to me, since you were hostile to me and sent me away?"

²⁸They answered, "We saw clearly that the LORD was with you; so we said, 'There ought to be a sworn agreement between us'—between us and you. Let us make a treaty with you ²⁹that you will do us no harm, just as we did not molest you but always treated you well and sent you away in peace. And now you are blessed by the LORD."

³⁰Isaac then made a feast for them, and they ate and drank. ³¹Early the next morning the men swore an oath to each other. Then Isaac sent them on their way, and they left him in peace.

³²That day Isaac's servants came and told him about the well they had dug. They said, "We've found water!" ³³He called it Shibah,ᵃ and to this day the name of the town has been Beersheba.ᵇ

a.33 *Shibah* can mean *oath* or *seven*.   b.33 *Beersheba* can mean *well of the oath* or *well of seven*.

²³From there he went up to Beer-sheba. ²⁴And that very night the LORD appeared to him and said, "I am the God of your father Abraham; do not be afraid, for I am with you and will bless you and make your offspring numerous for my servant Abraham's sake." ²⁵So he built an altar there, called on the name of the LORD, and pitched his tent there. And there Isaac's servants dug a well.

26Then Abimelech went to him from Gerar, with Ahuzzath his adviser and Phicol the commander of his army. ²⁷Isaac said to them, "Why have you come to me, seeing that you hate me and have sent me away from you?" ²⁸They said, "We see plainly that the LORD has been with you; so we say, let there be an oath between you and us, and let us make a covenant with you ²⁹so that you will do us no harm, just as we have not touched you and have done to you nothing but good and have sent you away in peace. You are now the blessed of the LORD." ³⁰So he made them a feast, and they ate and drank. ³¹In the morning they rose early and exchanged oaths; and Isaac set them on their way, and they departed from him in peace. ³²That same day Isaac's servants came and told him about the well that they had dug, and said to him, "We have found water!" ³³He called it Shibah;ᵃ therefore the name of the city is Beer-shebaᵇ to this day.

ᵃ A word resembling the word for *oath*   ᵇ That is *Well of the oath* or *Well of seven*

COMMENTARY

Isaac is the least well known of the ancestral figures. We are most familiar with Isaac as the boy portrayed in the stories of Abraham. Chapter 26 presents the only block of material devoted solely to Isaac. Even then, it occurs after the introduction of Jacob and Esau and their emerging conflict, so it has the feel of an interlude within that more comprehensive story. The fact that the two boys are not yet born seems evident from 26:7, so an editor has positioned this chapter in a nonlinear fashion.

Whatever the origins and history of these materials (scholars typically point to J), many interpreters now consider the chapter a unity. Isaac's contacts with Abimelech provide episodes that highlight the promises to Isaac and the formation of peaceful relationships with "nonchosen" people of the land. There are numerous links between this chapter and the story of Abraham. In some basic sense, Isaac is a mirror of Abraham.

26:1-5. The chapter begins with the first of several links to the story of Abraham and the initial famine (12:10). Isaac also leaves his home in time of famine and heads for Egypt, but he gets only as far as Gerar, in Philistine country, when God appears to him. We have previously encountered Gerar, Abimelech, and the Philistines. (See chaps. 20–21. Some have questioned whether this can be the same king, given the expanse of some seventy-five years; yet, the ages of people in Genesis [Abraham died at 175] and the absence of any report to the contrary means the author thinks this Abimelech is probably the same person.)

God appears to Isaac twice (vv. 2, 24), probably in the form of a messenger (see 16:7). In both cases, the deity extends to Isaac the promises previously given to Abraham.

The first instance (vv. 2-5) contains both a command regarding a journey (which Isaac obeys) and a promise, mirroring Abraham's word from God in 12:1-4a; both are also followed by famines and journeys during which the patriarchs place their wives in danger. God intends to *stop* Isaac from doing what Abraham did, going down to Egypt for relief from the famine (see 12:10). He should "sojourn" (be a resident alien) among the Philistines. Enduring the famine here would seem to entail more hardship for the family, but such does not happen. While the command may be intended to deter Isaac from repeating Abraham's experience (that would be ironic in view of what happens), it also highlights God's blessings even in the midst of famine. In another such time God approves Jacob's journey to Egypt (46:3). Looking to Egypt for relief may be a difficult political question for later Israelites.

This divine word fulfills the promise to Abraham regarding the covenant with Isaac (17:19). God's promises are confirmed to Isaac: (a) I will be with you. God offers this word for the first time to Isaac, and then, later, to Jacob (28:15; 31:3); (b) I will bless you (see 12:2); this promise pertains to the goodness that comes to Isaac as well as to his descendants; (c) I will give "all these lands," a collocation peculiar to this context and stated twice; it includes the lands of the various peoples noted earlier (15:18-19), but focuses on the land in which Isaac lives now as an alien; (d) the multiplication of descendants as the stars (see 15:5), i.e., too numerous to count; (e) the blessing upon the nations in and through Isaac and his descendants (see 12:3). This promise takes con-

crete form in this context in Isaac's relationship to the Philistines.

On the difficult v. 5, see Reflections.

26:6-11. We have already encountered two similar episodes involving the endangering of a wife of a patriarch (12:10-20; 20:1-18). This story begins with language that links it to Abraham's sojourn in the same city, Gerar (20:1-18). The juxtaposition of command/promise and the endangerment episode also occur in chap. 12 (vv. 1-9, 10-20). Moreover, all three versions are followed by texts concerned with land (13:1-18; 21:22-34; 26:12-33). This version of the story presents minimal complexity: little tension, no divine involvement, no actual contact with Rebekah by the king, and less disparagement of the patriarch, who responds only when confronted with interest in Rebekah (and apparently for good reason, v. 10).

Once again, an ancestor of Israel tries to pass off his beautiful wife as his sister in the presence of foreigners. Once again, fear for his own life (twice stated) leads him to do this. This guise had been successful for "a long time" when Abimelech (unlike chap. 20, he was not personally involved) quite by chance observes intimate behaviors between them that suggest a husband/wife relationship. He immediately challenges Isaac, insists on an explanation but ignores it, and berates him for endangering that community. If someone had thought Rebekah was unmarried and had had sexual relations with her, that would have brought "guilt" on his people. In the face of this threat, Abimelech warns all citizens to keep their hands off both Rebekah and Isaac. This edict assures a safe setting in which God's blessings now flow to Isaac. Here, as in chaps. 12 and (especially) 20, the author portrays a foreign king in congenial terms, both personally and religiously.

26:12-22. As with Abraham in Egypt (12:16) and in Gerar (20:14-16), Isaac emerges from this potentially disastrous situation not only unscathed, but also immeasurably enriched. His material prosperity occurs quickly in the very midst of the famine and enfolds every aspect of his life. Unlike chaps. 12 and 20, Isaac's wealth derives only indirectly from the king (the edict protected him, v. 11), whereas the author highlights God's blessing activity. This prosperity attests to the promise in v. 3; the blessing comes in spite of the patriarch's actions. This result qualifies Abimelech's concern about guilt, at least if he thought the moral order functioned mechanically. If people *always* reaped the effects of their deeds, then Isaac (and Abraham) would have reaped disaster rather than blessing.

This picture of great wealth (mentioned three times in v. 13) has become important to these stories. God's promise of blessing works itself out in every sphere of their life. The sojourning life experienced by Israel's ancestors on that land gives a foretaste of what it will be like when Israel lives in the land of milk and honey.

However, not everyone receives well God's work of blessing. Isaac's wealth becomes the object of envy by the Philistines, who stop up some wells Abraham's servants had dug (see 21:22-34; the NIV translation of v. 15 is clearer than the NRSV). Given this tension, Abimelech thinks that Isaac's power endangers (again, cf. v. 10) the Philistine hegemony, and asks him to leave the area. This he does without hesitation, but he remains close by, in territory adjacent to Gerar (v. 17), where Abraham had spent some time (21:34) and had also dug wells.

Conflict over wells and water rights continues in this new territory (vv. 17-22). Isaac and his servants reopen other wells (opposed to those in v. 15) that Abraham had dug and that the Philistines had stopped up; he gave them their old names as a sign of renewed ownership (v. 18). Verses 19-22 speak of Isaac's digging three new wells (finding fresh water in one); the Philistines in the area quarrel over the first two, but not the third (reasons are not given, but v. 16 suggests Isaac's power). Isaac gives names to the wells that correspond to this life experience (see NRSV and NIV footnotes). The author explains the third name (Rehoboth) as a divine gift of land, in which they will be able to spread out and be fruitful. These incidents may reflect Israel's later experience with the people of the land, but we should observe that Isaac does not use his stronger position to claim every well. Verse 22, with its reference to room and fruitfulness in the land of promise, leads into a fuller statement of the promise in v. 24.

26:23-33. The second divine appearance to Isaac (vv. 24-25) occurs after his return to Beersheba (22:19). The author presents a typical theo-

phanic narrative, with self-identification, quelling of fear, and word of God. For the first time, God is identified as "the God of your father." Abraham is the first such "father," and the epithet now becomes common in referring to the continuity of God's promise. The epithet (used as well for other gods in the ancient Near East) specifies the singularity of this deity from one generation to the next and the faithful response of each "father" to God. The link with persons rather than places emphasizes the personal character of the faith between God and these persons.

The God of Isaac's own father reiterates the basic promises spoken in vv. 2-4 (except the land promise, just treated in v. 22). The promises may recur at this point because the conflicts seem to jeopardize Isaac's relationship to the promises and because land that Abraham held has been reclaimed. The phrase "for the sake of [on account of] Abraham" refers to v. 5. Because of Abraham's faithfulness, the promises are transmitted to Isaac. The designation of Abraham as a servant, an image with a focus on loyalty, stresses exactly this point. This does not involve a "fund of spiritual credit" upon which subsequent generations may draw.[168] For the first time, Isaac responds with worship (v. 25), calling on God as Yahweh (see 4:25). This appearance also establishes Beersheba as a cultic center (Jacob stops here in 46:1). The digging of a well by Isaac's servants (v. 25*b*) may have prompted the visit from Abimelech. The well brackets his visit (vv. 25*b*, 32-33).

Verses 26-33 closely parallel 21:22-34. Abimelech and his top advisers leave their own area to initiate better relationships with the more powerful Isaac; Isaac exhibits caution in view of their history with each other. For all Abimelech's concern about future relations with Isaac, however, he emphasizes another motivation. He observes that *Yahweh* has been with Isaac and has blessed him (vv. 28-29); these affirmations enclose his words and signal their import—they are more than flattery. Because of what God has done—and the reiteration of the promises in v. 24 reinforces this—Isaac draws Abimelech into a peaceful relationship.

The two men express some difference of opinion regarding their common past. Isaac speaks of

168. Sarna, *Genesis*, 187.

hostility and expulsion (cf. v. 16); Abimelech claims that no harm, indeed nothing but good, has been done—Isaac was sent away in peace (cf. v. 11). Isaac ignores the differences (no further words between them are reported) and takes a peaceful initiative by preparing a meal for all concerned (common in treaty making; cf. 31:46). The next day they formally enter into a covenant, a bilateral, nonaggression pact. It results in peace (שלום *šālôm*) between Isaac and Abimelech (cf. 31:44-54), less than idyllic but still peace.

The references to well digging and finding water (vv. 32-33), begun in v. 25, symbolize the newly won peace. Isaac's servants dig a well and discover water, thereby supporting life, and no conflict ensues. Isaac gives essentially the same name to the place—Beersheba—reported in 21:31 (as was his practice, 26:18), testifying to the sworn oath that enables peace rather than conflict to prevail.

REFLECTIONS

1. This chapter as a whole testifies to the way Isaac, exhibiting both weakness and strength, yet repeatedly surrounded by the promises and blessings of God, works through relationships with outsiders and enables peace to prevail amid numerous possibilities for conflict.

2. Verse 5 provides two sorts of difficulties. (1) It seems to indicate that the continuance of the promise depended on Abraham's obedience. (2) The various words for the law seem to presuppose the giving of the law at Sinai.

The initial "because" has been used before in 22:18 (cf. Deut 7:12; 8:20), though there associated only with obeying the "voice" of God. Westermann states that Abraham is "the exemplar of obedience to the law in return for which God bestowed the promises on him." Similarly, Coats states that obedience "offers the basis for the promise."[169] This should be stated differently. God gave the promise to Abraham independently of his obedience (12:1-3). Similarly, God repeats the promise twice to *Isaac* because of the obedience of *Abraham* (vv. 5, 24). Isaac's obedience does not enable him to be the *recipient* of the promise. God announces the promise to him because of someone else's faithfulness. The community of faith throughout the centuries has also received the promise because of someone else's faithfulness.

The issue involves the transmission of the promise to the next generation. Genes, independent of the faithfulness of the one to whom the promise has been given, do not transmit the promise (see commentary on chap. 22). Isaac's faithfulness will be as important for generational transmission as was Abraham's. The reference to the "God of Isaac" in 28:13-15 covers the same point, as does 48:15, where Jacob confesses that Isaac walked before God. This chapter, in its various parallels to Abraham's story, illustrates Isaac's faithful response. Isaac responds to the initial command/promise of God as does Abraham (12:1-4a); he moves through comparable times of failure, but nevertheless remains blessed by God and receives anew the divine promises; and he responds in worship and peacemaking.

The language about the law certainly means that the author knows about the law given at Sinai. But this is no simple anachronism; it carries significance for understanding the place of law in the pre-Sinai period. God introduces law initially at creation (1:26-28; 2:16-17) and other divine commands emerge along the way (e.g., 9:1-7). The law given at Sinai does not emerge as a new reality; it stands in basic continuity with earlier articulations of God's will for the creation.[170] Abraham's conforming to the will of God shows that his life is in tune with God's creational purposes and models for later Israel the right response to law, which cannot

169. Westermann, *Genesis 12–36*, 424; George W. Coats, *Genesis: With an Introduction to Narrative Literature* (Grand Rapids: Eerdmans, 1983) 189.
170. See Fretheim, "Reclamation," 362-65.

be collapsed into that given at Sinai. The fivefold "my" shows that obedience to law is seen in terms of interpersonal response.

3. The author presents Abimelech as the only named outsider who extends across more than one generation. He must have grown weary encountering this family, who had a habit of passing off wives as sisters and with whom he had to negotiate about water and wells one more time. One more pre-Israelite, nonchosen inhabitant of the promised land receives remarkably good press, and acts with integrity that often matches the patriarch.

4. The story in vv. 6-11, as others in Genesis, assumes the idea of objective guilt. Even if a sinful act is unknowingly committed (in this case, sexual relations with a married woman), one incurs guilt. Whether the text also presumes corporate guilt ("us") remains unclear. The word translated "guilt" (אשם 'āšām) may only refer more generally to negative communal consequences. Isaac, in protecting himself from danger, places an entire city under threat from the fallout of sins committed because he has not considered fully the possible effects of his action. Yet, this was only a risk, for the moral order does not function in a mechanical fashion.

5. Verse 22 foreshadows settlement in the land, but it also describes a preliminary *fulfillment* of the promise of a "broad" land (cf. Exod 3:8) and their growth as a people (see 17:6; 47:27), which in turn fulfills God's word in creation (1:28; 9:1, 7). Isaac's utterance also provides a good word for people in exile, whose lives often parallel the ancestors. To have a home, a place one can call one's own, means to "make room" (give space). The OT construes the experience of salvation in similar ways (see Pss. 4:1; 18:19, 36; 31:8 ["You have set my feet in a broad place," NRSV]); the blessing that comes in the midst of famine attests to an experience of salvation.

6. Abimelech confirms that the divine promises (v. 3) have been fulfilled (vv. 28-29)! Even more, we see Isaac/Israel as one with whom the kings and nations of the world must come to terms. But this claim does not function simply at the political level; whatever greatness comes to Israel (see v. 13; 12:2) comes because of God's blessing and not its own powers. Even more, if and when power or greatness comes, it does not necessarily involve establishing hegemony over others or undermining their reconciling efforts, perhaps in retaliation for past actions. Israel should be an instrument of peace among the nations (vv. 29, 31).

GENESIS 26:34–28:9, JACOB, ESAU, AND THE BLESSING

NIV

34When Esau was forty years old, he married Judith daughter of Beeri the Hittite, and also Basemath daughter of Elon the Hittite. 35They were a source of grief to Isaac and Rebekah.

27 When Isaac was old and his eyes were so weak that he could no longer see, he called for Esau his older son and said to him, "My son."

"Here I am," he answered.

2Isaac said, "I am now an old man and don't know the day of my death. 3Now then, get your weapons—your quiver and bow—and go out to the open country to hunt some wild game for me.

NRSV

34When Esau was forty years old, he married Judith daughter of Beeri the Hittite, and Basemath daughter of Elon the Hittite; 35and they made life bitter for Isaac and Rebekah.

27 When Isaac was old and his eyes were dim so that he could not see, he called his elder son Esau and said to him, "My son"; and he answered, "Here I am." 2He said, "See, I am old; I do not know the day of my death. 3Now then, take your weapons, your quiver and your bow, and go out to the field, and hunt game for me. 4Then prepare for me savory food, such as I like,

NIV

⁴Prepare me the kind of tasty food I like and bring it to me to eat, so that I may give you my blessing before I die."

⁵Now Rebekah was listening as Isaac spoke to his son Esau. When Esau left for the open country to hunt game and bring it back, ⁶Rebekah said to her son Jacob, "Look, I overheard your father say to your brother Esau, ⁷'Bring me some game and prepare me some tasty food to eat, so that I may give you my blessing in the presence of the LORD before I die.' ⁸Now, my son, listen carefully and do what I tell you: ⁹Go out to the flock and bring me two choice young goats, so I can prepare some tasty food for your father, just the way he likes it. ¹⁰Then take it to your father to eat, so that he may give you his blessing before he dies."

¹¹Jacob said to Rebekah his mother, "But my brother Esau is a hairy man, and I'm a man with smooth skin. ¹²What if my father touches me? I would appear to be tricking him and would bring down a curse on myself rather than a blessing."

¹³His mother said to him, "My son, let the curse fall on me. Just do what I say; go and get them for me."

¹⁴So he went and got them and brought them to his mother, and she prepared some tasty food, just the way his father liked it. ¹⁵Then Rebekah took the best clothes of Esau her older son, which she had in the house, and put them on her younger son Jacob. ¹⁶She also covered his hands and the smooth part of his neck with the goatskins. ¹⁷Then she handed to her son Jacob the tasty food and the bread she had made.

¹⁸He went to his father and said, "My father."

"Yes, my son," he answered. "Who is it?"

¹⁹Jacob said to his father, "I am Esau your firstborn. I have done as you told me. Please sit up and eat some of my game so that you may give me your blessing."

²⁰Isaac asked his son, "How did you find it so quickly, my son?"

"The LORD your God gave me success," he replied.

²¹Then Isaac said to Jacob, "Come near so I can touch you, my son, to know whether you really are my son Esau or not."

²²Jacob went close to his father Isaac, who touched him and said, "The voice is the voice of

NRSV

and bring it to me to eat, so that I may bless you before I die."

5Now Rebekah was listening when Isaac spoke to his son Esau. So when Esau went to the field to hunt for game and bring it, ⁶Rebekah said to her son Jacob, "I heard your father say to your brother Esau, ⁷'Bring me game, and prepare for me savory food to eat, that I may bless you before the LORD before I die.' ⁸Now therefore, my son, obey my word as I command you. ⁹Go to the flock, and get me two choice kids, so that I may prepare from them savory food for your father, such as he likes; ¹⁰and you shall take it to your father to eat, so that he may bless you before he dies." ¹¹But Jacob said to his mother Rebekah, "Look, my brother Esau is a hairy man, and I am a man of smooth skin. ¹²Perhaps my father will feel me, and I shall seem to be mocking him, and bring a curse on myself and not a blessing." ¹³His mother said to him, "Let your curse be on me, my son; only obey my word, and go, get them for me." ¹⁴So he went and got them and brought them to his mother; and his mother prepared savory food, such as his father loved. ¹⁵Then Rebekah took the best garments of her elder son Esau, which were with her in the house, and put them on her younger son Jacob; ¹⁶and she put the skins of the kids on his hands and on the smooth part of his neck. ¹⁷Then she handed the savory food, and the bread that she had prepared, to her son Jacob.

18So he went in to his father, and said, "My father"; and he said, "Here I am; who are you, my son?" ¹⁹Jacob said to his father, "I am Esau your firstborn. I have done as you told me; now sit up and eat of my game, so that you may bless me." ²⁰But Isaac said to his son, "How is it that you have found it so quickly, my son?" He answered, "Because the LORD your God granted me success." ²¹Then Isaac said to Jacob, "Come near, that I may feel you, my son, to know whether you are really my son Esau or not." ²²So Jacob went up to his father Isaac, who felt him and said, "The voice is Jacob's voice, but the hands are the hands of Esau." ²³He did not recognize him, because his hands were hairy like his brother Esau's hands; so he blessed him. ²⁴He said, "Are you really my son Esau?" He answered, "I am."

Jacob, but the hands are the hands of Esau." [23]He did not recognize him, for his hands were hairy like those of his brother Esau; so he blessed him. [24]"Are you really my son Esau?" he asked.

"I am," he replied.

[25]Then he said, "My son, bring me some of your game to eat, so that I may give you my blessing."

Jacob brought it to him and he ate; and he brought some wine and he drank. [26]Then his father Isaac said to him, "Come here, my son, and kiss me."

[27]So he went to him and kissed him. When Isaac caught the smell of his clothes, he blessed him and said,

"Ah, the smell of my son
     is like the smell of a field
     that the LORD has blessed.
[28]May God give you of heaven's dew
     and of earth's richness—
     an abundance of grain and new wine.
[29]May nations serve you
     and peoples bow down to you.
Be lord over your brothers,
     and may the sons of your mother
          bow down to you.
May those who curse you be cursed
     and those who bless you be blessed."

[30]After Isaac finished blessing him and Jacob had scarcely left his father's presence, his brother Esau came in from hunting. [31]He too prepared some tasty food and brought it to his father. Then he said to him, "My father, sit up and eat some of my game, so that you may give me your blessing."

[32]His father Isaac asked him, "Who are you?"

"I am your son," he answered, "your firstborn, Esau."

[33]Isaac trembled violently and said, "Who was it, then, that hunted game and brought it to me? I ate it just before you came and I blessed him— and indeed he will be blessed!"

[34]When Esau heard his father's words, he burst out with a loud and bitter cry and said to his father, "Bless me—me too, my father!"

[35]But he said, "Your brother came deceitfully and took your blessing."

[25]Then he said, "Bring it to me, that I may eat of my son's game and bless you." So he brought it to him, and he ate; and he brought him wine, and he drank. [26]Then his father Isaac said to him, "Come near and kiss me, my son." [27]So he came near and kissed him; and he smelled the smell of his garments, and blessed him, and said,

"Ah, the smell of my son
     is like the smell of a field that the LORD
          has blessed.
[28] May God give you of the dew of heaven,
     and of the fatness of the earth,
     and plenty of grain and wine.
[29] Let peoples serve you,
     and nations bow down to you.
Be lord over your brothers,
     and may your mother's sons bow down
          to you.
Cursed be everyone who curses you,
     and blessed be everyone who blesses
          you!"

30As soon as Isaac had finished blessing Jacob, when Jacob had scarcely gone out from the presence of his father Isaac, his brother Esau came in from his hunting. [31]He also prepared savory food, and brought it to his father. And he said to his father, "Let my father sit up and eat of his son's game, so that you may bless me." [32]His father Isaac said to him, "Who are you?" He answered, "I am your firstborn son, Esau." [33]Then Isaac trembled violently, and said, "Who was it then that hunted game and brought it to me, and I ate it all[a] before you came, and I have blessed him?— yes, and blessed he shall be!" [34]When Esau heard his father's words, he cried out with an exceedingly great and bitter cry, and said to his father, "Bless me, me also, father!" [35]But he said, "Your brother came deceitfully, and he has taken away your blessing." [36]Esau said, "Is he not rightly named Jacob?[b] For he has supplanted me these two times. He took away my birthright; and look, now he has taken away my blessing." Then he said, "Have you not reserved a blessing for me?" [37]Isaac answered Esau, "I have already made him your lord, and I have given him all his brothers as servants, and with grain and wine I have sustained him. What then can I do for you, my

NIV

³⁶Esau said, "Isn't he rightly named Jacob*a*? He has deceived me these two times: He took my birthright, and now he's taken my blessing!" Then he asked, "Haven't you reserved any blessing for me?"

³⁷Isaac answered Esau, "I have made him lord over you and have made all his relatives his servants, and I have sustained him with grain and new wine. So what can I possibly do for you, my son?"

³⁸Esau said to his father, "Do you have only one blessing, my father? Bless me too, my father!" Then Esau wept aloud.

³⁹His father Isaac answered him,

"Your dwelling will be
away from the earth's richness,
away from the dew of heaven above.
⁴⁰You will live by the sword
and you will serve your brother.
But when you grow restless,
you will throw his yoke
from off your neck."

⁴¹Esau held a grudge against Jacob because of the blessing his father had given him. He said to himself, "The days of mourning for my father are near; then I will kill my brother Jacob."

⁴²When Rebekah was told what her older son Esau had said, she sent for her younger son Jacob and said to him, "Your brother Esau is consoling himself with the thought of killing you. ⁴³Now then, my son, do what I say: Flee at once to my brother Laban in Haran. ⁴⁴Stay with him for a while until your brother's fury subsides. ⁴⁵When your brother is no longer angry with you and forgets what you did to him, I'll send word for you to come back from there. Why should I lose both of you in one day?"

⁴⁶Then Rebekah said to Isaac, "I'm disgusted with living because of these Hittite women. If Jacob takes a wife from among the women of this land, from Hittite women like these, my life will not be worth living."

28 So Isaac called for Jacob and blessed*b* him and commanded him: "Do not marry a Canaanite woman. ²Go at once to Paddan Aram,*c*

a36 Jacob means *he grasps the heel* (figuratively, *he deceives*).
b1 Or *greeted*   *c2* That is, Northwest Mesopotamia; also in verses 5, 6 and 7

NRSV

son?" ³⁸Esau said to his father, "Have you only one blessing, father? Bless me, me also, father!" And Esau lifted up his voice and wept.

39Then his father Isaac answered him:

"See, away from*a* the fatness of the earth
shall your home be,
and away from*b* the dew of heaven on
high.
⁴⁰ By your sword you shall live,
and you shall serve your brother;
but when you break loose,*c*
you shall break his yoke from your neck."

41Now Esau hated Jacob because of the blessing with which his father had blessed him, and Esau said to himself, "The days of mourning for my father are approaching; then I will kill my brother Jacob." ⁴²But the words of her elder son Esau were told to Rebekah; so she sent and called her younger son Jacob and said to him, "Your brother Esau is consoling himself by planning to kill you. ⁴³Now therefore, my son, obey my voice; flee at once to my brother Laban in Haran, ⁴⁴and stay with him a while, until your brother's fury turns away— ⁴⁵until your brother's anger against you turns away, and he forgets what you have done to him; then I will send, and bring you back from there. Why should I lose both of you in one day?"

46Then Rebekah said to Isaac, "I am weary of my life because of the Hittite women. If Jacob marries one of the Hittite women such as these, one of the women of the land, what good will my life be to me?"

28 Then Isaac called Jacob and blessed him, and charged him, "You shall not marry one of the Canaanite women. ²Go at once to Paddan-aram to the house of Bethuel, your mother's father; and take as wife from there one of the daughters of Laban, your mother's brother. ³May God Almighty*d* bless you and make you fruitful and numerous, that you may become a company of peoples. ⁴May he give to you the blessing of Abraham, to you and to your offspring with you, so that you may take possession of the land where you now live as an alien—land that God gave to Abraham." ⁵Thus Isaac sent Jacob away; and he

*a*Or *See, of*   *b*Or *and of*   *c*Meaning of Heb uncertain
d Traditional rendering of Heb *El Shaddai*

NIV

to the house of your mother's father Bethuel. Take a wife for yourself there, from among the daughters of Laban, your mother's brother. ³May God Almighty[a] bless you and make you fruitful and increase your numbers until you become a community of peoples. ⁴May he give you and your descendants the blessing given to Abraham, so that you may take possession of the land where you now live as an alien, the land God gave to Abraham." ⁵Then Isaac sent Jacob on his way, and he went to Paddan Aram, to Laban son of Bethuel the Aramean, the brother of Rebekah, who was the mother of Jacob and Esau.

⁶Now Esau learned that Isaac had blessed Jacob and had sent him to Paddan Aram to take a wife from there, and that when he blessed him he commanded him, "Do not marry a Canaanite woman," ⁷and that Jacob had obeyed his father and mother and had gone to Paddan Aram. ⁸Esau then realized how displeasing the Canaanite women were to his father Isaac; ⁹so he went to Ishmael and married Mahalath, the sister of Nebaioth and daughter of Ishmael son of Abraham, in addition to the wives he already had.

a3 Hebrew *El-Shaddai*

NRSV

went to Paddan-aram, to Laban son of Bethuel the Aramean, the brother of Rebekah, Jacob's and Esau's mother.

6Now Esau saw that Isaac had blessed Jacob and sent him away to Paddan-aram to take a wife from there, and that as he blessed him he charged him, "You shall not marry one of the Canaanite women," ⁷and that Jacob had obeyed his father and his mother and gone to Paddan-aram. ⁸So when Esau saw that the Canaanite women did not please his father Isaac, ⁹Esau went to Ishmael and took Mahalath daughter of Abraham's son Ishmael, and sister of Nebaioth, to be his wife in addition to the wives he had.

COMMENTARY

The author has enclosed this major story of Isaac's deception (27:1-45, assigned to J or JE) by reports associated with the wives of the two sons (26:34-35; 27:46–28:9; assigned to P). These reports intensify the conflicted character of the family. At the same time, Isaac's freely given blessing of Jacob (28:3-4) softens the impact of Jacob's deception in gaining the blessing. The origin of these texts remains obscure, but they may reflect later Israel/Edom alignments. Two old poetic pieces provide the focus for the chapter (vv. 27-29, 39-40).

26:34-35. Chapter 26 concludes on a negative note. Family relationships remain conflicted in spite of peace in the larger community. Esau's act of marrying, without parental consent, two Hittite (Canaanite) women (cf. 24:3; 28:1, 6) first provides evidence of difficulties. Esau's wives' making

life bitter for both parents involves more than their family lineage. Yet, placement of these verses before chap. 27 reinforces a negative sense about Esau and disposes the reader to be less critical of the moves made by Jacob and Rebekah. Moreover, Esau's actions create sympathy for the dilemma Isaac faces as a parent. However, one must be careful not to fall into the trap of placing Esau and Jacob on some kind of "fitness" scale, as if God's choices were determined by measuring morality. Jacob is no plaster saint either.

27:1-40. Jacob and Esau never appear together in the four major scenes of this story, nor do Rebekah and Esau, which symbolizes a lack of communication within the family. The author uses vocabulary to create a sensuous story: seeing, hearing, tasting, touching and smelling make it a story one can almost feel. Also, repeated language of blessing (twenty-eight times) demonstrates its centrality in the story.

The relationship between the story of the birthright (בכרה *bĕkōrâ*; 25:29-34) and this story of the blessing (ברכה *bĕrākâ*) appears problematic. They may be two different ways of thinking about the same reality, but that may be too simple. Esau distinguishes them but thinks they bear comparable importance (27:36); to lose both produces a double loss. The former relates basically to issues of inheritance; the latter to deathbed blessing (cf. 48:22 with 49:22-26). Both deal with issues raised by the oracle in 25:23, the overturning of primogeniture; both involve Jacob in an active role; his actions are duplicitous in both cases. The former reflects, initially, a private arrangement (of which Isaac is not aware until 27:36), the latter a more public matter.

Verses 1-4. Isaac, advanced in years, takes steps to prepare his family for the future (cf. 24:1; he does not die until 35:29). Isaac directs Esau to hunt for game and prepare his favorite food (cf. 25:28); then Isaac would give him a personal (נפשי *napšî*) blessing. The provision of a meal constitutes an essential part of the blessing ritual (see below).

Verses 5-17. Overhearing Isaac's request, Rebekah reports its essentials to Jacob, including Esau's absence, but she adds "before Yahweh" (v. 7). This interpretation sets Isaac over against God's speech (25:23) and establishes Rebekah's theological motivation; she responds to the word of God, which Esau's behaviors have reinforced (26:34-35). Blessing is not a justice issue for her. Taking the initiative, she devises a ruse by which Jacob can receive the blessing, and "commands" him to help out (v. 8; "obey" in v. 13). He should act in just the way Isaac commanded Esau, but before Esau returns.

Jacob does not immediately agree, not because he thinks it wrong, but because he doubts its feasibility. His participation becomes explicit when he raises a complicating issue; Esau is hairy and Jacob is not, and their nearly blind father can still feel (an ironic touch since "smooth" can also mean deceptive, Ps 55:21). Jacob worries that Isaac may pronounce a curse on him. Their mother's willingness to bear the brunt of any response (note that the curse could be transferred!) reassures him, and he quickly (conveyed

by three verbs in rapid sequence, v. 14) "obeys" her directives. Only then does Rebekah address her son's concern by "clothing" him so that he feels and smells like Esau (cf. Jacob's being deceived by clothing in 37:31-33; 38:14). Jacob proceeds without hesitation. We cannot help wondering whether such crude disguises will do the trick.

Verses 18-29. Carrying out the ruse is now up to Jacob, and he executes it without hesitation. His verbal deception takes two forms: He lies about his identity (vv. 19, 24), and he sanctimoniously draws God into the deceit by claiming, with supreme irony, that *Isaac's* God, Yahweh, has granted him success (v. 20). But from v. 20 on, Jacob utters only one word (v. 24); otherwise he only acts in response to Isaac's queries and commands.

These verses are informed by a blessing ritual (though without magical allusions):[171] the command of the father, here recalled by the son (vv. 18-19); identification of the son (vv. 19, 24); a shared meal—for communion, not strength (v. 25); approach and kiss—to seal the blessing, not to transfer life (vv. 26-27*a*); pronouncement of blessing (vv. 27*b*-29). The various elements of the ritual are essential for the transmission of blessing. At the same time, Isaac utilizes this ritual in remarkable ways to pursue his questions. Isaac may be an unknowing vehicle for Rebekah's wishes, but he has not thereby turned into an automaton!

Interpreters often adjudge Isaac's behavior to be naive, even bumbling, yet the repeated questions and ritual delays reveal that he pursues his deep suspicions carefully. He uses all the senses available to him (in this order: sound, touch, taste, smell) to discern the truth. He trusts hearing less than touching (vv. 22-23); his blindness and age create varying sensitivities. We should note especially his manipulation of the ritual. Rather than wait for full clarity before proceeding, he uses its various elements to test his suspicions. Twice he questions Jacob's identity; in the meal and kiss rituals he probes with taste and smell. The smell (mentioned four times in v. 27!) *seems* finally to be sufficient, if not conclusive evidence. The smell

---

171. Westermann, *Genesis 12–36*, 439.

recalls a fertile field and then moves to the blessing of fertility!

In view of what follows, v. 23 proves startling. If it means what it says, then Isaac utters the blessing, but quickly has further doubts, the import of which would be that a blessing once spoken may not be final. But these words could also refer to Isaac's decision to proceed with the blessing ritual even in the face of uncertainty. In either case, Isaac begins the ritual once again, still concerned with the issue of identity (v. 24).

Isaac never calls Jacob by the name *Esau* (contrast chap. 49) or concludes that he now knows this is Esau. The (sevenfold) "my son" remains constant from beginning (v. 18) to end (v. 27); in fact, its use in v. 25 seems unusual, since "your game" would have been more natural. The narrator claims nonrecognition only at the story's mid-point (v. 23). Isaac probably gives the blessing with less than full certainty, and probably suspects he is dealing with Jacob (note his musings in v. 22).

Although Isaac reacts strongly when he finds he has been tricked (v. 33); and calls it deceit (v. 35), he never chides Jacob. In fact, the next time he speaks to him (28:1-4), Isaac proceeds as if all is well. He then reinforces the blessing, explicitly linking it with Abraham. Isaac's acceptance seems to lie, not in a magical notion of blessing, but in a conviction that he acted properly (vv. 33, 37). After all, he has just learned about the birthright incident for the first time (v. 36); another factor may have been the parental pain Esau's marriages caused (26:35).

The blessing centers on fertility (v. 28) and dominion (v. 29; cf. 24:60). The parallels between this blessing and those Jacob extends to both Judah and Joseph in 49:8-12, 22-26 are noteworthy. Verse 28 (cf. 49:25; Deut 33:13-16, 28) speaks of divine blessing as rain and mist (i.e., the dew of heaven), rich produce (i.e., fatness of the earth), and a plentiful harvest of grain and grapes. Progeny and land are assumed, but are not mentioned as part of the ancestral promises. Isaac calls upon God the Creator, who blesses in the agricultural sphere, to be active in the life of Jacob. Verse 29 (cf. 49:8)—with only an implicit reference to God—speaks of blessing as dominion over other nations/peoples, including his "brothers/mother's sons" (cf. v. 37; the plural may refer to family members, so NIV). At this point, Isaac

unknowingly echoes God's word to Rebekah (25:23) and anticipates the blessing of Judah (49:8). Then, in the only explicit reference to 12:3a in Genesis (see Num 24:9), Isaac links his blessing with God's promise: Whether people are cursed or blessed depends on their treatment of Jacob/Israel.

Verses 30-40. These verses begin as did vv. 18-19. Having obeyed his father's directive, Esau approaches him with the prepared food and requests a blessing, to which Isaac responds with questions about his identity. His inquiry about the perpetrator is only rhetorical (v. 33), for he identifies him as "your brother" immediately (v. 35). Yet, Jacob remains blessed; Isaac refers not simply to the word of blessing but to the accompanying ritual meal as reasons why Jacob remains blessed (v. 33).

Crying out in exasperation and deep disappointment, Esau pleads that his father bless him also. Isaac replies that, even though his brother was deceitful, he has taken his blessing. Esau bitterly retorts that Jacob is rightly named (see 25:26), for he deceived him of both blessing and birthright—news for Isaac. Esau begs for his own blessing, believing it possible that Isaac might have "reserved" a blessing for him (see 49:1-28 on open and multiple blessings). Since Isaac's blessing does, in principle, extend to him, Esau correctly pursues the matter.

Isaac summarizes the blessing given Jacob (v. 37); Isaac acts as the agent, not mentioning God. He has said "I do" to Jacob; in view of the prevailing convention regarding blessings, what can he do for Esau now that Jacob is his lord? Yet, when Esau insistently cries out, Isaac responds to his lament with a secondary blessing (vv. 39-40). Esau will dwell in an area without (or with, NRSV footnote; the Hebrew may be purposely ambiguous) rich land and adequate rainfall, and his life will be filled with violence. Although he will be subject to his brother, at times he will break free from that yoke (see 33:3-7; 2 Kgs 8:20-22). This statement *qualifies* Jacob's blessing (v. 29) in response to Esau's plea; it becomes somewhat less comprehensive than it was. Esau's deep lament proves to be potent, and Isaac responds. "Here is a clear theology of liberation—for Esau/Edom!."[172] For all the negative

172. Gammie, "Genesis 25–36," 130.

correspondence to Jacob's blessing, Esau will have a (fruitful?) land in which to dwell, life, progeny, and periods of freedom from his brother. Esau receives blessing—attenuated, compared to Jacob's—but not a curse or even nonblessing.

27:41-45. We can understand why Esau hates Jacob, but Esau's vow to kill him once Isaac has died (cf. 50:15) threatens the future of the promise. Once again Rebekah hears Esau's plans (speaking "to himself" expresses his resolve), and her actions shape the next scene. She informs Jacob and directs him to flee to her home in Haran until Esau's fury has passed (repeated for emphasis). When time has healed the wounds, she will send for him again. She remains hopeful; Esau will drop his threat, but Rebekah will not see Isaac again. Her lament shows a concern for Esau too (though she never speaks to him); if Esau were to kill Jacob, he would be executed. Once again she believes she must act, for the divine oracle of 25:23 will not inevitably protect Jacob. Nor will Isaac's blessing.

27:46–28:9. This section relates to 26:34-35 with its concern about wives, and to the immediately preceding 27:41-45. Her differing motivations are true to the story; she remains anxious about both Jacob's life and wife. Rebekah does not speak to Isaac about the threat to Jacob, perhaps to conceal her own involvement. She raises the issue of Esau's marriages, which had "made life bitter" for *both* Isaac and Rebekah (26:35). If Jacob follows suit, her life will not be worth living; she may be thinking about the way she became Isaac's

wife (24:2-4). Her concern about wives gives Jacob's departure a sense of legitimacy.

Isaac responds positively. Speaking with Jacob for the first time *as Jacob* in Genesis, Isaac enjoins him from marrying a Canaanite and directs him to go to Haran and marry a cousin, a daughter of Rebekah's brother, Laban. Using language that derives from God's covenant with Abraham in chap. 17, he blesses Jacob for the journey based on the promises he had received from God (26:3-4, 24). This blessing elaborates the blessing in 27:27-29, only Isaac knowingly and freely blesses Jacob this time and without reproach for his deceit; this softens Jacob's deception in obtaining Esau's blessing. Although similar in form ("May God . . . "), the language this time appears more specifically Abrahamic (the link is with v. 29c). Isaac conveys promise in the form of a blessing. Isaac does not transmit the promises formally, but anticipates God's own speaking "the blessing of Abraham" to him, which occurs in 28:13-15. Jacob obeys without a word.

Meanwhile, Esau catches wind of what has happened to Jacob. Suppressing the hatred expressed in 27:41, Esau focuses on his father's concern about wives for his sons and Jacob's obedient response to *both* parents. In an effort to please his *father* (v. 8), he takes a (third) wife from within the family, the family of Ishmael, his father's brother (25:12-18). This favorable portrayal of Esau appears similar to that given to Ishmael (21:8-21). Yet, like Ishmael, he remains on the fringes of the family.

REFLECTIONS

1. This story has long been a favorite of Bible readers. It is well told and filled with intrigue. Some readers think it tells of a cheat and a rascal who, nonetheless, remains the chosen of God. That has occasioned both wonderment and hope on the part of the elect in every age: Why would God choose such a character? If God includes Jacob, who can be excluded? This may be an appropriate direction to take with this text, yet one cannot help wondering if such a negative picture of Jacob is justified.

2. How should one assess Jacob's and Rebekah's actions? They are motivated by an oracle from God (25:23), by Esau's treatment of his parents (26:35; 28:8), and by the birthright (25:33). Jacob's experience and self-understanding link up with Rebekah's theological convictions and familial sensitivities; this is a formidable duo. But, while the end they achieve may be fitting in view of the oracle, do not the means lack integrity, even basic decency (cf. Deut 27:18)? While their actions can be explained, can they be justified? White claims that they may be justified in opening a closed system: "Deception and desire may now have positive roles to play so long as they are subservient to the contingency of the promissory Word and faith, rather than serving the interest of symbiotic personal behavior and structures of power."[173] One thinks of Tamar and the midwives, whose deception was not only tolerated but commended (38:26; Exod 1:20).

One often hears this attractive approach, but it is sometimes bought at the expense of "demonizing" Esau and even Isaac or "whitewashing" Jacob and Rebekah. Neither demons nor plaster saints are here, and the way the story pursues blessing for Jacob retains no little ambiguity. The way in which "what goes around comes around" for Jacob in 29:25-26 and 37:31-33 suggests that Jacob reaps the consequences of his deceptions of Esau and Isaac. At the same time, pursuance of the "right" often carries negative consequences, and with respect to Rebekah one must reckon with issues of patriarchy (see below). One must be careful not to become too defensive regarding Jacob's actions, lest God's choices be grounded in "righteousness" or "uprightness of heart" (cf. Deut 9:4-5). God chooses to work in and through what human beings make available. This reveals a deep divine vulnerability, for it links God with people whose reputations are not stellar and opens God's ways in the world to sharp criticism.

3. Readers should note some additional features of Rebekah's actions.[174] Rebekah could have conceivably pursued other, less deceptive options, such as informing Isaac about God's oracle. But, while we are not privy to her reflections, she doubtless thought this matter through carefully. She had to consider, above all, Isaac's special relationship to Esau (25:28), even though 28:8 (cf. 26:35) indicates Isaac's displeasure with him. Another likely factor involves the prevailing patriarchy, which rendered her opinions on such matters of little import. She must rely on secondary means to discover what goes on in the family (vv. 5, 42), and must be careful in approaching Isaac about Jacob's predicament (27:46; cf. also Isaac's reaction in 27:33—because his authority has been undercut?). In the face of the powerlessness patriarchy engenders, manipulation often remains the only route open to the future. On another matter, her response to Jacob's hesitance in 27:13 indicates a resolve to take upon herself any curse that Isaac might pronounce. She expresses an openness to suffering, even death, on behalf of both her son and the divine purposes she serves.

4. Blessing. This motif probably has its origins in the leave-taking of everyday life (24:60) or in the departure from life itself (see chap. 49). It is important to stress, however, that the word of blessing does not have a magical sense—either in terms of (a) the transmission of vitality from blesser to blessed, so that Isaac has no life left to give Esau; or (b) the speaking of a word that becomes an autonomous force, independent of Isaac or God.

Yet, the latter view especially has been popular. The blessing of the father "inexorably determined destiny: the father's horror [v. 33] stands powerless before the unalterable."[175] So also the Oxford Annotated NRSV notes: "The blessing, like the curse, released a power that effectively determined the character and destiny of the recipient . . . the spoken blessing, like an arrow shot toward its goal, was believed to release a power which could not be retracted."[176]

However, this understanding of the word is incorrect, both generally and in this text. Acts of blessing in the OT rest on accepted *conventions.* Such words produce effects because of certain social understandings about the function of these speech-acts. These words must be spoken in a particular situation by the appropriate person in the proper form to be effective.[177] If the blessing *could* not be revoked by Isaac, it was because no convention was available for its revocation. If there were such a convention, Isaac chooses not to make use of it. Esau, in

173. White, *Narration,* 225.
174. See Jeansonne, *Women in Genesis,* 53-69.
175. So Westermann, *Genesis 12–36,* 442.
176. *The New Oxford Annotated Bible,* eds. B. Metzger and R. Murphy (New York: Oxford University Press, 1991) 34-35.
177. See T. Fretheim, "Word of God," in *The Anchor Bible Dictionary,* vol. 6, ed. D. Freedman (New York: Doubleday, 1992) 961-68, and literature cited therein.

asking for *another* blessing, appears to believe that no such convention exists. Even then, Isaac's response to Esau (vv. 39-40) demonstrates that actions can be taken to qualify the impact of a blessing already spoken.

One basic reason cited by Isaac for not retracting the blessing involves the consumption of a meal (v. 33; cf. vv. 4, 7, 10, 19, 25, 31). The meal was an integral part of a conventional blessing ritual (see above), without which it would not have been valid. In this understanding of ritual, we are not far from certain realistic views of, say, the Christian sacraments, or liturgy more generally.

5. It would be too simple to suggest that the known histories of Israel and Edom are here retrojected into early times and thought to have been determined by these early oracles (see 25:23). Certainly the text recognizes that words and deeds do shape history, but not in some detailed, inevitable way. For example, Israel over the course of its history did not always have "plenty of grain and wine" (v. 28; see Deut 11:13-17), nor were the nations of the world, including Edom, always subservient. Esau has Jacob over the barrel not infrequently (see Psalm 137)! Moreover, Esau is not alone in living by the sword (see 34:25; 48:22).

6. It may be that the issue of marrying within one's own community, so evident in this segment, arose at a time when this issue was a lively concern for readers during the exile and later. However, Genesis does not present a consistent picture regarding the matter. Judah and Joseph marry outside the family, with no censure or criticism. The same openness could be claimed for the relationship between Dinah and Shechem in chap. 34, where two of her brothers are rebuked for their actions against Shechem and his family. The issue involves, not a general principle regarding such marriages, but certain moments in the life of a community when a distinctive identity is deemed to be crucial to ensure the future. Such may be the case for the first two generations of Abraham's family, but before the end of Genesis, the issue no longer seems so important.

7. The blessing extended to Esau by his father testifies to blessing as a reality outside the community of chosen ones. Esau's blessing, though attenuated, should be linked with other Genesis narratives, where the "outsider" becomes the recipient of divine blessing (e.g., Ishmael; see chaps. 16; 21). God the Creator works among these peoples with blessings that take various forms, the most basic of which is life itself, often apart from contact with the community of faith (though such contact may produce special blessings, v. 29). The interests of the people of promise are not served well by finding ways of speaking negatively about those outside that community, or seeking to limit the blessing activity of God among them.

8. Jacob's receiving the birthright and the blessing does not issue in a trouble-free life. In fact, they expose his life to more conflict than would probably otherwise have been the case, not least because of what he does with it. God's choices are not always well received, by both the chosen and the not chosen. Certainly, God designs blessing for all the peoples of the world. But, because of the recalcitrance and deception of the chosen themselves, blessing sometimes has the effect of dividing as often as uniting. One should reflect deeply on this story from the perspective of those who believe themselves to be chosen and how they relate to those who are the "unchosen." The degree to which religious convictions have provoked strife in the modern world should occasion deep shame on the part of members of the community of faith and a renewed sense of what it means to be a responsible recipient of divine blessing.

GENESIS 28:10-22, JACOB'S DREAM AT BETHEL

NIV

¹⁰Jacob left Beersheba and set out for Haran. ¹¹When he reached a certain place, he stopped for the night because the sun had set. Taking one of the stones there, he put it under his head and lay down to sleep. ¹²He had a dream in which he saw a stairway[a] resting on the earth, with its top reaching to heaven, and the angels of God were ascending and descending on it. ¹³There above it[b] stood the LORD, and he said: "I am the LORD, the God of your father Abraham and the God of Isaac. I will give you and your descendants the land on which you are lying. ¹⁴Your descendants will be like the dust of the earth, and you will spread out to the west and to the east, to the north and to the south. All peoples on earth will be blessed through you and your offspring. ¹⁵I am with you and will watch over you wherever you go, and I will bring you back to this land. I will not leave you until I have done what I have promised you."

¹⁶When Jacob awoke from his sleep, he thought, "Surely the LORD is in this place, and I was not aware of it." ¹⁷He was afraid and said, "How awesome is this place! This is none other than the house of God; this is the gate of heaven."

¹⁸Early the next morning Jacob took the stone he had placed under his head and set it up as a pillar and poured oil on top of it. ¹⁹He called that place Bethel,[c] though the city used to be called Luz.

²⁰Then Jacob made a vow, saying, "If God will be with me and will watch over me on this journey I am taking and will give me food to eat and clothes to wear ²¹so that I return safely to my father's house, then the LORD[d] will be my God ²²and[e] this stone that I have set up as a pillar will be God's house, and of all that you give me I will give you a tenth."

a12 Or ladder   b13 Or There beside him   c19 Bethel means house of God.   d20,21 Or Since God . . . father's house, the LORD   e21,22 Or house, and the LORD will be my God, 22then

NRSV

10Jacob left Beer-sheba and went toward Haran. ¹¹He came to a certain place and stayed there for the night, because the sun had set. Taking one of the stones of the place, he put it under his head and lay down in that place. ¹²And he dreamed that there was a ladder[a] set up on the earth, the top of it reaching to heaven; and the angels of God were ascending and descending on it. ¹³And the LORD stood beside him[b] and said, "I am the LORD, the God of Abraham your father and the God of Isaac; the land on which you lie I will give to you and to your offspring; ¹⁴and your offspring shall be like the dust of the earth, and you shall spread abroad to the west and to the east and to the north and to the south; and all the families of the earth shall be blessed[c] in you and in your offspring. ¹⁵Know that I am with you and will keep you wherever you go, and will bring you back to this land; for I will not leave you until I have done what I have promised you." ¹⁶Then Jacob woke from his sleep and said, "Surely the LORD is in this place—and I did not know it!" ¹⁷And he was afraid, and said, "How awesome is this place! This is none other than the house of God, and this is the gate of heaven."

18So Jacob rose early in the morning, and he took the stone that he had put under his head and set it up for a pillar and poured oil on the top of it. ¹⁹He called that place Bethel;[d] but the name of the city was Luz at the first. ²⁰Then Jacob made a vow, saying, "If God will be with me, and will keep me in this way that I go, and will give me bread to eat and clothing to wear, ²¹so that I come again to my father's house in peace, then the LORD shall be my God, ²²and this stone, which I have set up for a pillar, shall be God's house; and of all that you give me I will surely give one tenth to you."

a Or stairway or ramp   b Or stood above it   c Or shall bless themselves   d That is House of God

COMMENTARY

This text stands as one of the pillars of the Jacob story. God transmits to him the ancestral promises, fulfilling the expressed wish of his father (28:3-4). This is the first time Jacob appears by himself; hence it represents a new beginning for the larger story. Jacob flees from the hatred and threats of his brother, seeming to reap the consequences of his own duplicity, and the future does not seem bright. At precisely this deeply vulnerable moment in his life, God appears, not in judgment, but to confirm him as the one chosen to carry on the promise.

Some readers think this story has its roots in a concern to ground the later Bethel sanctuary and worship life in the ancestral period (see 1 Kgs 12:26-33). Although possible, the episode has now been drawn into the larger orbit of stories about Jacob (often assigned to JE) and serves a more comprehensive purpose. It shares a basic structure with the fragment in 32:1-2 (cf. 32:22-33), an encounter with angels on his way back home. Together with another appearance of God to Jacob at Bethel on his return journey (35:1-15), this episode brackets the narrative. A note about setting (vv. 10-11) is followed by the dream (vv. 12-15) and Joseph's response to it (vv. 16-22).

The author introduces Jacob en route. He is traveling from Beersheba to Haran, from which the Abrahamic family migrated and where he will find a temporary home and two wives. While still within Canaan, he spends the night out in the open, using an ordinary, if large, stone to support and protect his head. The text does not depict it as a holy site, but "place" anticipates vv. 11, 16, 17, and 19 and "stone" anticipates vv. 18 and 22; God transforms an ordinary stone and an ordinary place. It probably was a religious center for people in earlier times (cf. the name change in v. 19), but the text stakes a claim for Bethel's religious importance on the basis of this event (and perhaps Abraham's visit in 12:8; 13:3-4).

A remarkable dream fills Jacob's night. He dreams that a ladder (better, a stairway or ramp) extends from earth to heaven. We may compare this stairway to those attached to temple towers (ziggurats) elsewhere in the ancient Near East; these were microcosms of the world, with the top of the tower representing heaven, the dwelling place of the gods. Such structures provided an avenue of approach from the human sphere to the divine realm. Priests or divine beings traversed up and down the stairway, providing communication between the two realms. This text polemicizes such an understanding.

Ascending and descending divine beings are a part of Jacob's dream, but they have no specific function. In fact, their presence makes a negative point. While such beings may serve as messengers, here they do *not* serve as intermediaries for divine revelation. Rather, Yahweh stands beside Jacob and speaks directly to him (so NRSV; the NIV's "above it" is possible but unlikely in view of the immediacy in the deity's communication to Jacob). The angels do not speak; God does. Jacob hears the divine promises directly from God, who in turn promises God's very own presence rather than that of a surrogate. "Earth is not left to its own resources and heaven is not a remote self-contained realm for the gods. Heaven has to do with earth. And earth finally may count on the resources of heaven."[178]

God is identified in terms of Jacob's family, referring to Abraham as father rather than Isaac. Jacob thus has the same relationship to Abraham and Abraham's God as his father, Isaac, has had (see 26:3-4, 24). The use of the name *Yahweh* provides clearer continuity with Abraham (cf. 15:7) than the generic word for God.

God's word to Jacob moves directly from self-identification to promise, which fulfills Isaac's benedictory wish of 28:3-4 and constitutes *God's* confirmation of Jacob's gaining of birthright and blessing. God's promises are unusually extensive (eight different elements), to which Jacob adds another (v. 20, food and clothing). The promises are: land; many descendants; dispersion of posterity throughout the land (not the world, cf. 13:14-17); the extension of blessing to others through him; presence; keeping; homecoming, and not leaving. All the promises spoken in the narrative to this point are gathered up and focused on Jacob. The last four (v. 15) relate directly to Jacob's status as a traveler, extending the promise given to his father in comparable circumstances (26:3, 24).

Upon awakening, Jacob realizes the import of his dream, and he proceeds to *interpret* its significance. He recognizes that he has some new knowledge; he has moved from not knowing to knowing that God has been present with him. (Except for the ruse in 27:20, this is the first time he mentions God.) He also expresses awe that in

178. Brueggemann, *Genesis*, 243.

this ordinary place he has been confronted by the God of whom his father spoke (28:3-4), indeed granted direct access to God's promise-speaking (see Reflections). His "naming" of the place occurs in two stages. The first (v. 17) attests to his encounter with the divine presence: the "house of God" (i.e., *Beth-el*) and the "gate of heaven." These building metaphors represent concretely his experience of direct divine access. The stairway and the angels have been reduced to props, metaphors now inadequate for depicting the dynamics of immediate divine-human communication. The second (v. 19), more formal, naming emphasizes the continuity between the immediate experience and the ongoing significance of this particular place.

Jacob's response the next day takes more concrete forms. He sets up as a pillar the stone that had supported him as a "pillow." What was quite ordinary now becomes a sacred symbol for his experience. (Such standing stones are often set up at Israelite sanctuaries and at other places of historical import; cf. 35:14, 20.) The stone has now become recognizable for use by others who may pass by this way. The anointing with oil consecrates or sets the stone apart from others (cf. 31:13; Exod 40:9-11). The oil also stains the stone so that it can be properly identified by those who follow. Although not itself a sanctuary, the stone can become an integral part of a worship center; Jacob vows he will establish such a site (v. 22;

35:1-15). At the same time, the stone becomes a public witness to his own experience (on stones as witness, see Josh 24:27).

Finally, Jacob makes a vow (recalled by God in 31:13). Although vows are common in the OT (cf. Num 21:2; Judg 11:30-31; 1 Sam 1:11; 2 Sam 15:8, all spoken at sanctuaries), this vow seems unique since God has already unconditionally promised what Jacob states as a condition. By repeating God's promises in the vow, Jacob *claims* them as his own. Hence, to see this as bargain language does not do justice to the vow; rather, Jacob wants to hold God to his promises (those associated with his journey, v. 15). If God does *not* do these things, of course, then *God* will not have been faithful, and Jacob's relationship to such a God would be problematic, to say the least. If God keeps the promises, then Jacob will do certain things: Yahweh will be his God (namely, Jacob will remain loyal); he will construct a sanctuary (fulfilled in 35:7, 14-15) and offer a tithe (see 14:20; Deut 26:12-15), apparently a one-time gift, perhaps for the care of the sanctuary. In essence, if God acts faithfully, Jacob will be faithful.

From this point on, Jacob's journeys are filled with a new sense of vocation, for he now bears the promise. At the same time, he remains Jacob and does not know immediately what this experience entails for his life.

REFLECTIONS

1. God's relation to Jacob, through both his father and his grandfather, stresses not only a familial link, but *divine* continuity across the generations as well. The story involves *God* as well as Jacob's ancestors. God's own self is identified in the context of a divine journey, which God now promises to continue with Jacob. And this journey exists outside of the land of promise, "wherever you go" (see Josh 1:9; Psalm 23; Isa 43:1-2; 46:3-4).

2. The dream (see 31:11-3; chaps. 37; 40–41). Dreams do not witness to the dreamer's psychological state, working out stress or anxiety or subconscious fears; they are external forms of divine communication, in which actual encounters with God take place. They are one means by which God's own self is revealed. When Jacob refers to this event, he speaks of divine appearance but never of dream (35:1-9; 48:3; cf. also 1 Kgs 11:9), apparently understanding God's appearance in the dream to be comparable to other such appearances (cf. 35:9). When Jacob awakens, he does not speak of God's presence in his dream; he speaks of God's presence in this *place!* The dream reflects not simply a mental world, but an actual world that can be slept on, touched, and built on.

Jacob's dream contains both symbolism and divine verbal communication. Jacob interprets the significance of *both* dimensions in his response in vv. 16-22. In turn, he mirrors the dream in responding both verbally and in more concrete terms. The visual and auditory aspects of the dream belong together, not least because human beings are not simply minds or "big ears," and God chooses to address the whole person (e.g. Incarnation; sacraments). The visual "speaks" in its own way, and the word gives "concreteness" to the visual.

The dream comes entirely at the divine initiative; Jacob was asleep, not in control of what happened *within* him (in contrast to the nocturnal wrestling of chap. 32). At the same time, Jacob's responses to God's word of promise shape the future. It may be tempting to explain away such dream experiences, though dreams are much less difficult for the modern consciousness to accept than are direct divine appearances. The text helps us to recognize that "the world is a place of such meetings," and God can use such moments as a vehicle for getting through to us, even today.[179]

3. The word of promise involves more than simply a word about a communal future; God also particularizes the promise for Jacob as an individual, for the specific situation in which he finds himself. God's promises of being with and keeping/protecting Jacob (v. 15) are distinct, for God can also be present to judge, which Jacob may have expected. Yet they are not separate, for God's presence never means passivity. God's "not leaving" gathers up the three previous promises to Jacob, yet it constitutes a further promise centering on the temporal unbrokenness of the divine presence.

4. In Jacob's response to the dream, awesomeness and the themes of presence and access come together. The transcendence of God is not compromised by closeness to humans. The awe that Jacob expresses depends on the fact that *God has come near.* The confession of God as transcendent and awesome correlates this text to God's coming to be present rather than God's remaining afar off. Far from being a place forbidden to human beings, this site becomes a place where humans can be assured of the divine presence.

5. The importance of places of worship. Setting aside a place for a sanctuary does not stand at odds with the God who is with Jacob wherever he goes. Both are significant dimensions of God's being present in the world. Specific places for worship are needed because human beings are shaped by place as well as time. A sanctuary provides (a) order, discipline, and focus to the worship of God; (b) a tangible aspect to worship; (c) assurance that God is indeed present in this place because God has so promised. At the same time, such understandings must guard against a "house of God" syndrome, as if the divine presence could be fixed or localized, as if this were the only place where God could be found. God's being present at the sanctuary is not coextensive with God's presence in the world. Jacob can count on God's being present at this place (hence he returns in 35:1-15) *and* with him during his journey. The rhythms of the ancestors include the rhythm of journeying and worship; their journeys are punctuated by moments of worship at specific places. Yet the place never becomes a final objective, where one settles in; it provides sustenance for the ongoing journey.

6. This text also says something about God. God can bind God's own self with unconditional promises to tricksters and deceivers. Although Jacob leaves this moment with divine promises ringing in his ears, God leaves this moment with the divine options for the future more limited than before, because God will be faithful to these promises Jacob has just spoken. God's promises may have come to Jacob as a surprise, but Jacob will not know them again as such. God can be counted on to be faithful. Jacob need no longer wonder about God; God is a promise-keeper, as Jacob must be also. There is a "must" for God in this text, and a "must" for Jacob as well.

179. Brueggemann, *Genesis,* 242.

7. To understand this vow, we would remember it as a word spoken by a person in dire straits, concerned about his safety and his future. Such vows are common in the lament psalms (e.g., 7:17; 13:6) and have been used by people in distress in every age!). Because of the context in which they are uttered, we should not press them for theological niceties. But we, as Jacob, should expect God to keep the promises unconditionally.

GENESIS 29:1–31:55, THE BIRTH OF JACOB'S CHILDREN

NIV

29 Then Jacob continued on his journey and came to the land of the eastern peoples. ²There he saw a well in the field, with three flocks of sheep lying near it because the flocks were watered from that well. The stone over the mouth of the well was large. ³When all the flocks were gathered there, the shepherds would roll the stone away from the well's mouth and water the sheep. Then they would return the stone to its place over the mouth of the well.

⁴Jacob asked the shepherds, "My brothers, where are you from?"

"We're from Haran," they replied.

⁵He said to them, "Do you know Laban, Nahor's grandson?"

"Yes, we know him," they answered.

⁶Then Jacob asked them, "Is he well?"

"Yes, he is," they said, "and here comes his daughter Rachel with the sheep."

⁷"Look," he said, "the sun is still high; it is not time for the flocks to be gathered. Water the sheep and take them back to pasture."

⁸"We can't," they replied, "until all the flocks are gathered and the stone has been rolled away from the mouth of the well. Then we will water the sheep."

⁹While he was still talking with them, Rachel came with her father's sheep, for she was a shepherdess. ¹⁰When Jacob saw Rachel daughter of Laban, his mother's brother, and Laban's sheep, he went over and rolled the stone away from the mouth of the well and watered his uncle's sheep. ¹¹Then Jacob kissed Rachel and began to weep aloud. ¹²He had told Rachel that he was a relative of her father and a son of Rebekah. So she ran and told her father.

NRSV

29 Then Jacob went on his journey, and came to the land of the people of the east. ²As he looked, he saw a well in the field and three flocks of sheep lying there beside it; for out of that well the flocks were watered. The stone on the well's mouth was large, ³and when all the flocks were gathered there, the shepherds would roll the stone from the mouth of the well, and water the sheep, and put the stone back in its place on the mouth of the well.

4Jacob said to them, "My brothers, where do you come from?" They said, "We are from Haran." ⁵He said to them, "Do you know Laban son of Nahor?" They said, "We do." ⁶He said to them, "Is it well with him?" "Yes," they replied, "and here is his daughter Rachel, coming with the sheep." ⁷He said, "Look, it is still broad daylight; it is not time for the animals to be gathered together. Water the sheep, and go, pasture them." ⁸But they said, "We cannot until all the flocks are gathered together, and the stone is rolled from the mouth of the well; then we water the sheep."

9While he was still speaking with them, Rachel came with her father's sheep; for she kept them. ¹⁰Now when Jacob saw Rachel, the daughter of his mother's brother Laban, and the sheep of his mother's brother Laban, Jacob went up and rolled the stone from the well's mouth, and watered the flock of his mother's brother Laban. ¹¹Then Jacob kissed Rachel, and wept aloud. ¹²And Jacob told Rachel that he was her father's kinsman, and that he was Rebekah's son; and she ran and told her father.

13When Laban heard the news about his sister's son Jacob, he ran to meet him; he embraced him and kissed him, and brought him to his

NIV

¹³As soon as Laban heard the news about Jacob, his sister's son, he hurried to meet him. He embraced him and kissed him and brought him to his home, and there Jacob told him all these things. ¹⁴Then Laban said to him, "You are my own flesh and blood."

After Jacob had stayed with him for a whole month, ¹⁵Laban said to him, "Just because you are a relative of mine, should you work for me for nothing? Tell me what your wages should be."

¹⁶Now Laban had two daughters; the name of the older was Leah, and the name of the younger was Rachel. ¹⁷Leah had weak*a* eyes, but Rachel was lovely in form, and beautiful. ¹⁸Jacob was in love with Rachel and said, "I'll work for you seven years in return for your younger daughter Rachel."

¹⁹Laban said, "It's better that I give her to you than to some other man. Stay here with me." ²⁰So Jacob served seven years to get Rachel, but they seemed like only a few days to him because of his love for her.

²¹Then Jacob said to Laban, "Give me my wife. My time is completed, and I want to lie with her."

²²So Laban brought together all the people of the place and gave a feast. ²³But when evening came, he took his daughter Leah and gave her to Jacob, and Jacob lay with her. ²⁴And Laban gave his servant girl Zilpah to his daughter as her maidservant.

²⁵When morning came, there was Leah! So Jacob said to Laban, "What is this you have done to me? I served you for Rachel, didn't I? Why have you deceived me?"

²⁶Laban replied, "It is not our custom here to give the younger daughter in marriage before the older one. ²⁷Finish this daughter's bridal week; then we will give you the younger one also, in return for another seven years of work."

²⁸And Jacob did so. He finished the week with Leah, and then Laban gave him his daughter Rachel to be his wife. ²⁹Laban gave his servant girl Bilhah to his daughter Rachel as her maidservant. ³⁰Jacob lay with Rachel also, and he loved Rachel more than Leah. And he worked for Laban another seven years.

³¹When the LORD saw that Leah was not loved,

a17 Or delicate

NRSV

house. Jacob*a* told Laban all these things, ¹⁴and Laban said to him, "Surely you are my bone and my flesh!" And he stayed with him a month.

15Then Laban said to Jacob, "Because you are my kinsman, should you therefore serve me for nothing? Tell me, what shall your wages be?" ¹⁶Now Laban had two daughters; the name of the elder was Leah, and the name of the younger was Rachel. ¹⁷Leah's eyes were lovely,*b* and Rachel was graceful and beautiful. ¹⁸Jacob loved Rachel; so he said, "I will serve you seven years for your younger daughter Rachel." ¹⁹Laban said, "It is better that I give her to you than that I should give her to any other man; stay with me." ²⁰So Jacob served seven years for Rachel, and they seemed to him but a few days because of the love he had for her.

21Then Jacob said to Laban, "Give me my wife that I may go in to her, for my time is completed." ²²So Laban gathered together all the people of the place, and made a feast. ²³But in the evening he took his daughter Leah and brought her to Jacob; and he went in to her. ²⁴(Laban gave his maid Zilpah to his daughter Leah to be her maid.) ²⁵When morning came, it was Leah! And Jacob said to Laban, "What is this you have done to me? Did I not serve with you for Rachel? Why then have you deceived me?" ²⁶Laban said, "This is not done in our country—giving the younger before the firstborn. ²⁷Complete the week of this one, and we will give you the other also in return for serving me another seven years." ²⁸Jacob did so, and completed her week; then Laban gave him his daughter Rachel as a wife. ²⁹(Laban gave his maid Bilhah to his daughter Rachel to be her maid.) ³⁰So Jacob went in to Rachel also, and he loved Rachel more than Leah. He served Laban*c* for another seven years.

31When the LORD saw that Leah was unloved, he opened her womb; but Rachel was barren. ³²Leah conceived and bore a son, and she named him Reuben;*d* for she said, "Because the LORD has looked on my affliction; surely now my husband will love me." ³³She conceived again and bore a son, and said, "Because the LORD has heard*e* that I am hated, he has given me this son also"; and

a Heb *He*   *b* Meaning of Heb uncertain   *c* Heb *him*
d That is *See, a son*   *e* Heb *shama*

NIV

he opened her womb, but Rachel was barren. ³²Leah became pregnant and gave birth to a son. She named him Reuben,ᵃ for she said, "It is because the LORD has seen my misery. Surely my husband will love me now."

³³She conceived again, and when she gave birth to a son she said, "Because the LORD heard that I am not loved, he gave me this one too." So she named him Simeon.ᵇ

³⁴Again she conceived, and when she gave birth to a son she said, "Now at last my husband will become attached to me, because I have borne him three sons." So he was named Levi.ᶜ

³⁵She conceived again, and when she gave birth to a son she said, "This time I will praise the LORD." So she named him Judahᵈ Then she stopped having children.

30 When Rachel saw that she was not bearing Jacob any children, she became jealous of her sister. So she said to Jacob, "Give me children, or I'll die!"

²Jacob became angry with her and said, "Am I in the place of God, who has kept you from having children?"

³Then she said, "Here is Bilhah, my maidservant. Sleep with her so that she can bear children for me and that through her I too can build a family."

⁴So she gave him her servant Bilhah as a wife. Jacob slept with her, ⁵and she became pregnant and bore him a son. ⁶Then Rachel said, "God has vindicated me; he has listened to my plea and given me a son." Because of this she named him Dan.ᵉ

⁷Rachel's servant Bilhah conceived again and bore Jacob a second son. ⁸Then Rachel said, "I have had a great struggle with my sister, and I have won." So she named him Naphtali.ᶠ

⁹When Leah saw that she had stopped having children, she took her maidservant Zilpah and gave her to Jacob as a wife. ¹⁰Leah's servant Zilpah bore Jacob a son. ¹¹Then Leah said, "What good fortune!"ᵍ So she named him Gad.ʰ

ᵃ32 *Reuben* sounds like the Hebrew for *he has seen my misery;* the name means *see, a son.* ᵇ33 *Simeon* probably means *one who hears.* ᶜ34 *Levi* sounds like and may be derived from the Hebrew for *attached.* ᵈ35 *Judah* sounds like and may be derived from the Hebrew for *praise.* ᵉ6 *Dan* here means *he has vindicated.* ᶠ8 *Naphtali* means *my struggle.* ᵍ11 Or *"A troop is coming!"* ʰ11 *Gad* can mean *good fortune* or *a troop.*

NRSV

she named him Simeon. ³⁴Again she conceived and bore a son, and said, "Now this time my husband will be joinedᵃ to me, because I have borne him three sons"; therefore he was named Levi. ³⁵She conceived again and bore a son, and said, "This time I will praiseᵇ the LORD"; therefore she named him Judah; then she ceased bearing.

30 When Rachel saw that she bore Jacob no children, she envied her sister; and she said to Jacob, "Give me children, or I shall die!" ²Jacob became very angry with Rachel and said, "Am I in the place of God, who has withheld from you the fruit of the womb?" ³Then she said, "Here is my maid Bilhah; go in to her, that she may bear upon my knees and that I too may have children through her." ⁴So she gave him her maid Bilhah as a wife; and Jacob went in to her. ⁵And Bilhah conceived and bore Jacob a son. ⁶Then Rachel said, "God has judged me, and has also heard my voice and given me a son"; therefore she named him Dan.ᶜ ⁷Rachel's maid Bilhah conceived again and bore Jacob a second son. ⁸Then Rachel said, "With mighty wrestlings I have wrestledᵈ with my sister, and have prevailed"; so she named him Naphtali.

9When Leah saw that she had ceased bearing children, she took her maid Zilpah and gave her to Jacob as a wife. ¹⁰Then Leah's maid Zilpah bore Jacob a son. ¹¹And Leah said, "Good fortune!" so she named him Gad.ᵉ ¹²Leah's maid Zilpah bore Jacob a second son. ¹³And Leah said, "Happy am I! For the women will call me happy"; so she named him Asher.ᶠ

14In the days of wheat harvest Reuben went and found mandrakes in the field, and brought them to his mother Leah. Then Rachel said to Leah, "Please give me some of your son's mandrakes." ¹⁵But she said to her, "Is it a small matter that you have taken away my husband? Would you take away my son's mandrakes also?" Rachel said, "Then he may lie with you tonight for your son's mandrakes." ¹⁶When Jacob came from the field in the evening, Leah went out to meet him, and said, "You must come in to me; for I have hired you with my son's mandrakes." So he lay with her that night. ¹⁷And God heeded Leah, and

---

ᵃ Heb *lawah* ᵇ Heb *hodah* ᶜ That is *He judged* ᵈ Heb *niphtal* ᵉ That is *Fortune* ᶠ That is *Happy*

NIV

¹²Leah's servant Zilpah bore Jacob a second son. ¹³Then Leah said, "How happy I am! The women will call me happy." So she named him Asher.ᵃ

¹⁴During wheat harvest, Reuben went out into the fields and found some mandrake plants, which he brought to his mother Leah. Rachel said to Leah, "Please give me some of your son's mandrakes."

¹⁵But she said to her, "Wasn't it enough that you took away my husband? Will you take my son's mandrakes too?"

"Very well," Rachel said, "he can sleep with you tonight in return for your son's mandrakes."

¹⁶So when Jacob came in from the fields that evening, Leah went out to meet him. "You must sleep with me," she said. "I have hired you with my son's mandrakes." So he slept with her that night.

¹⁷God listened to Leah, and she became pregnant and bore Jacob a fifth son. ¹⁸Then Leah said, "God has rewarded me for giving my maidservant to my husband." So she named him Issachar.ᵇ

¹⁹Leah conceived again and bore Jacob a sixth son. ²⁰Then Leah said, "God has presented me with a precious gift. This time my husband will treat me with honor, because I have borne him six sons." So she named him Zebulun.ᶜ

²¹Some time later she gave birth to a daughter and named her Dinah.

²²Then God remembered Rachel; he listened to her and opened her womb. ²³She became pregnant and gave birth to a son and said, "God has taken away my disgrace." ²⁴She named him Joseph,ᵈ and said, "May the LORD add to me another son."

²⁵After Rachel gave birth to Joseph, Jacob said to Laban, "Send me on my way so I can go back to my own homeland. ²⁶Give me my wives and children, for whom I have served you, and I will be on my way. You know how much work I've done for you."

²⁷But Laban said to him, "If I have found favor in your eyes, please stay. I have learned by divination thatᵉ the LORD has blessed me because of

---

ᵃ13 Asher means happy.   ᵇ18 Issachar sounds like the Hebrew for reward.   ᶜ20 Zebulun probably means honor.   ᵈ24 Joseph means may he add.   ᵉ27 Or possibly have become rich and

NRSV

she conceived and bore Jacob a fifth son. ¹⁸Leah said, "God has given me my hireᵃ because I gave my maid to my husband"; so she named him Issachar. ¹⁹And Leah conceived again, and she bore Jacob a sixth son. ²⁰Then Leah said, "God has endowed me with a good dowry; now my husband will honorᵇ me, because I have borne him six sons"; so she named him Zebulun. ²¹Afterwards she bore a daughter, and named her Dinah.

22Then God remembered Rachel, and God heeded her and opened her womb. ²³She conceived and bore a son, and said, "God has taken away my reproach"; ²⁴and she named him Joseph,ᶜ saying, "May the LORD add to me another son!"

25When Rachel had borne Joseph, Jacob said to Laban, "Send me away, that I may go to my own home and country. ²⁶Give me my wives and my children for whom I have served you, and let me go; for you know very well the service I have given you." ²⁷But Laban said to him, "If you will allow me to say so, I have learned by divination that the LORD has blessed me because of you; ²⁸name your wages, and I will give it." ²⁹Jacob said to him, "You yourself know how I have served you, and how your cattle have fared with me. ³⁰For you had little before I came, and it has increased abundantly; and the LORD has blessed you wherever I turned. But now when shall I provide for my own household also?" ³¹He said, "What shall I give you?" Jacob said, "You shall not give me anything; if you will do this for me, I will again feed your flock and keep it: ³²let me pass through all your flock today, removing from it every speckled and spotted sheep and every black lamb, and the spotted and speckled among the goats; and such shall be my wages. ³³So my honesty will answer for me later, when you come to look into my wages with you. Every one that is not speckled and spotted among the goats and black among the lambs, if found with me, shall be counted stolen." ³⁴Laban said, "Good! Let it be as you have said." ³⁵But that day Laban removed the male goats that were striped and spotted, and all the female goats that were speckled and spotted, every one that had white on it, and every lamb that was black, and put them in

---

ᵃ Heb sakar   ᵇ Heb zabal   ᶜ That is He adds

you." ²⁸He added, "Name your wages, and I will pay them."

²⁹Jacob said to him, "You know how I have worked for you and how your livestock has fared under my care. ³⁰The little you had before I came has increased greatly, and the LORD has blessed you wherever I have been. But now, when may I do something for my own household?"

³¹"What shall I give you?" he asked.

"Don't give me anything," Jacob replied. "But if you will do this one thing for me, I will go on tending your flocks and watching over them: ³²Let me go through all your flocks today and remove from them every speckled or spotted sheep, every dark-colored lamb and every spotted or speckled goat. They will be my wages. ³³And my honesty will testify for me in the future, whenever you check on the wages you have paid me. Any goat in my possession that is not speckled or spotted, or any lamb that is not dark-colored, will be considered stolen."

³⁴"Agreed," said Laban. "Let it be as you have said." ³⁵That same day he removed all the male goats that were streaked or spotted, and all the speckled or spotted female goats (all that had white on them) and all the dark-colored lambs, and he placed them in the care of his sons. ³⁶Then he put a three-day journey between himself and Jacob, while Jacob continued to tend the rest of Laban's flocks.

³⁷Jacob, however, took fresh-cut branches from poplar, almond and plane trees and made white stripes on them by peeling the bark and exposing the white inner wood of the branches. ³⁸Then he placed the peeled branches in all the watering troughs, so that they would be directly in front of the flocks when they came to drink. When the flocks were in heat and came to drink, ³⁹they mated in front of the branches. And they bore young that were streaked or speckled or spotted. ⁴⁰Jacob set apart the young of the flock by themselves, but made the rest face the streaked and dark-colored animals that belonged to Laban. Thus he made separate flocks for himself and did not put them with Laban's animals. ⁴¹Whenever the stronger females were in heat, Jacob would place the branches in the troughs in front of the animals so they would mate near the branches, ⁴²but if

charge of his sons; ³⁶and he set a distance of three days' journey between himself and Jacob, while Jacob was pasturing the rest of Laban's flock.

³⁷Then Jacob took fresh rods of poplar and almond and plane, and peeled white streaks in them, exposing the white of the rods. ³⁸He set the rods that he had peeled in front of the flocks in the troughs, that is, the watering places, where the flocks came to drink. And since they bred when they came to drink, ³⁹the flocks bred in front of the rods, and so the flocks produced young that were striped, speckled, and spotted. ⁴⁰Jacob separated the lambs, and set the faces of the flocks toward the striped and the completely black animals in the flock of Laban; and he put his own droves apart, and did not put them with Laban's flock. ⁴¹Whenever the stronger of the flock were breeding, Jacob laid the rods in the troughs before the eyes of the flock, that they might breed among the rods, ⁴²but for the feebler of the flock he did not lay them there; so the feebler were Laban's, and the stronger Jacob's. ⁴³Thus the man grew exceedingly rich, and had large flocks, and male and female slaves, and camels and donkeys.

31 Now Jacob heard that the sons of Laban were saying, "Jacob has taken all that was our father's; he has gained all this wealth from what belonged to our father." ²And Jacob saw that Laban did not regard him as favorably as he did before. ³Then the LORD said to Jacob, "Return to the land of your ancestors and to your kindred, and I will be with you." ⁴So Jacob sent and called Rachel and Leah into the field where his flock was, ⁵and said to them, "I see that your father does not regard me as favorably as he did before. But the God of my father has been with me. ⁶You know that I have served your father with all my strength; ⁷yet your father has cheated me and changed my wages ten times, but God did not permit him to harm me. ⁸If he said, 'The speckled shall be your wages,' then all the flock bore speckled; and if he said, 'The striped shall be your wages,' then all the flock bore striped. ⁹Thus God has taken away the livestock of your father, and given them to me.

10During the mating of the flock I once had a dream in which I looked up and saw that the

NIV

the animals were weak, he would not place them there. So the weak animals went to Laban and the strong ones to Jacob. 43In this way the man grew exceedingly prosperous and came to own large flocks, and maidservants and menservants, and camels and donkeys.

31 Jacob heard that Laban's sons were saying, "Jacob has taken everything our father owned and has gained all this wealth from what belonged to our father." 2And Jacob noticed that Laban's attitude toward him was not what it had been.

3Then the LORD said to Jacob, "Go back to the land of your fathers and to your relatives, and I will be with you."

4So Jacob sent word to Rachel and Leah to come out to the fields where his flocks were. 5He said to them, "I see that your father's attitude toward me is not what it was before, but the God of my father has been with me. 6You know that I've worked for your father with all my strength, 7yet your father has cheated me by changing my wages ten times. However, God has not allowed him to harm me. 8If he said, 'The speckled ones will be your wages,' then all the flocks gave birth to speckled young; and if he said, 'The streaked ones will be your wages,' then all the flocks bore streaked young. 9So God has taken away your father's livestock and has given them to me.

10"In breeding season I once had a dream in which I looked up and saw that the male goats mating with the flock were streaked, speckled or spotted. 11The angel of God said to me in the dream, 'Jacob.' I answered, 'Here I am.' 12And he said, 'Look up and see that all the male goats mating with the flock are streaked, speckled or spotted, for I have seen all that Laban has been doing to you. 13I am the God of Bethel, where you anointed a pillar and where you made a vow to me. Now leave this land at once and go back to your native land.'"

14Then Rachel and Leah replied, "Do we still have any share in the inheritance of our father's estate? 15Does he not regard us as foreigners? Not only has he sold us, but he has used up what was paid for us. 16Surely all the wealth that God took away from our father belongs to us and our children. So do whatever God has told you."

NRSV

male goats that leaped upon the flock were striped, speckled, and mottled. 11Then the angel of God said to me in the dream, 'Jacob,' and I said, 'Here I am!' 12And he said, "Look up and see that all the goats that leap on the flock are striped, speckled, and mottled; for I have seen all that Laban is doing to you. 13I am the God of Bethel,[a] where you anointed a pillar and made a vow to me. Now leave this land at once and return to the land of your birth.'" 14Then Rachel and Leah answered him, "Is there any portion or inheritance left to us in our father's house? 15Are we not regarded by him as foreigners? For he has sold us, and he has been using up the money given for us. 16All the property that God has taken away from our father belongs to us and to our children; now then, do whatever God has said to you."

17So Jacob arose, and set his children and his wives on camels; 18and he drove away all his livestock, all the property that he had gained, the livestock in his possession that he had acquired in Paddan-aram, to go to his father Isaac in the land of Canaan.

19Now Laban had gone to shear his sheep, and Rachel stole her father's household gods. 20And Jacob deceived Laban the Aramean, in that he did not tell him that he intended to flee. 21So he fled with all that he had; starting out he crossed the Euphrates,[b] and set his face toward the hill country of Gilead.

22On the third day Laban was told that Jacob had fled. 23So he took his kinsfolk with him and pursued him for seven days until he caught up with him in the hill country of Gilead. 24But God came to Laban the Aramean in a dream by night, and said to him, "Take heed that you say not a word to Jacob, either good or bad."

25Laban overtook Jacob. Now Jacob had pitched his tent in the hill country, and Laban with his kinsfolk camped in the hill country of Gilead. 26Laban said to Jacob, "What have you done? You have deceived me, and carried away my daughters like captives of the sword. 27Why did you flee secretly and deceive me and not tell me? I would have sent you away with mirth and songs, with tambourine and lyre. 28And why did

[a] Cn: Meaning of Heb uncertain   [b] Heb the river

¹⁷Then Jacob put his children and his wives on camels, ¹⁸and he drove all his livestock ahead of him, along with all the goods he had accumulated in Paddan Aram,^a to go to his father Isaac in the land of Canaan.

¹⁹When Laban had gone to shear his sheep, Rachel stole her father's household gods. ²⁰Moreover, Jacob deceived Laban the Aramean by not telling him he was running away. ²¹So he fled with all he had, and crossing the River,^b he headed for the hill country of Gilead.

²²On the third day Laban was told that Jacob had fled. ²³Taking his relatives with him, he pursued Jacob for seven days and caught up with him in the hill country of Gilead. ²⁴Then God came to Laban the Aramean in a dream at night and said to him, "Be careful not to say anything to Jacob, either good or bad."

²⁵Jacob had pitched his tent in the hill country of Gilead when Laban overtook him, and Laban and his relatives camped there too. ²⁶Then Laban said to Jacob, "What have you done? You've deceived me, and you've carried off my daughters like captives in war. ²⁷Why did you run off secretly and deceive me? Why didn't you tell me, so I could send you away with joy and singing to the music of tambourines and harps? ²⁸You didn't even let me kiss my grandchildren and my daughters good-by. You have done a foolish thing. ²⁹I have the power to harm you; but last night the God of your father said to me, 'Be careful not to say anything to Jacob, either good or bad.' ³⁰Now you have gone off because you longed to return to your father's house. But why did you steal my gods?"

³¹Jacob answered Laban, "I was afraid, because I thought you would take your daughters away from me by force. ³²But if you find anyone who has your gods, he shall not live. In the presence of our relatives, see for yourself whether there is anything of yours here with me; and if so, take it." Now Jacob did not know that Rachel had stolen the gods.

³³So Laban went into Jacob's tent and into Leah's tent and into the tent of the two maidservants, but he found nothing. After he came out of Leah's tent, he entered Rachel's tent. ³⁴Now

you not permit me to kiss my sons and my daughters farewell? What you have done is foolish. ²⁹It is in my power to do you harm; but the God of your father spoke to me last night, saying, 'Take heed that you speak to Jacob neither good nor bad.' ³⁰Even though you had to go because you longed greatly for your father's house, why did you steal my gods?" ³¹Jacob answered Laban, "Because I was afraid, for I thought that you would take your daughters from me by force. ³²But anyone with whom you find your gods shall not live. In the presence of our kinsfolk, point out what I have that is yours, and take it." Now Jacob did not know that Rachel had stolen the gods.^a

³³So Laban went into Jacob's tent, and into Leah's tent, and into the tent of the two maids, but he did not find them. And he went out of Leah's tent, and entered Rachel's. ³⁴Now Rachel had taken the household gods and put them in the camel's saddle, and sat on them. Laban felt all about in the tent, but did not find them. ³⁵And she said to her father, "Let not my lord be angry that I cannot rise before you, for the way of women is upon me." So he searched, but did not find the household gods.

³⁶Then Jacob became angry, and upbraided Laban. Jacob said to Laban, "What is my offense? What is my sin, that you have hotly pursued me? ³⁷Although you have felt about through all my goods, what have you found of all your household goods? Set it here before my kinsfolk and your kinsfolk, so that they may decide between us two. ³⁸These twenty years I have been with you; your ewes and your female goats have not miscarried, and I have not eaten the rams of your flocks. ³⁹That which was torn by wild beasts I did not bring to you; I bore the loss of it myself; of my hand you required it, whether stolen by day or stolen by night. ⁴⁰It was like this with me: by day the heat consumed me, and the cold by night, and my sleep fled from my eyes. ⁴¹These twenty years I have been in your house; I served you fourteen years for your two daughters, and six years for your flock, and you have changed my wages ten times. ⁴²If the God of my father, the God of Abraham and the Fear^b of Isaac, had not been on my side, surely now you would have sent

a18 That is, Northwest Mesopotamia   b21 That is, the Euphrates

a Heb them   b Meaning of Heb uncertain

Rachel had taken the household gods and put them inside her camel's saddle and was sitting on them. Laban searched through everything in the tent but found nothing.

[35]Rachel said to her father, "Don't be angry, my lord, that I cannot stand up in your presence; I'm having my period." So he searched but could not find the household gods.

[36]Jacob was angry and took Laban to task. "What is my crime?" he asked Laban. "What sin have I committed that you hunt me down? [37]Now that you have searched through all my goods, what have you found that belongs to your household? Put it here in front of your relatives and mine, and let them judge between the two of us.

[38]"I have been with you for twenty years now. Your sheep and goats have not miscarried, nor have I eaten rams from your flocks. [39]I did not bring you animals torn by wild beasts; I bore the loss myself. And you demanded payment from me for whatever was stolen by day or night. [40]This was my situation: The heat consumed me in the daytime and the cold at night, and sleep fled from my eyes. [41]It was like this for the twenty years I was in your household. I worked for you fourteen years for your two daughters and six years for your flocks, and you changed my wages ten times. [42]If the God of my father, the God of Abraham and the Fear of Isaac, had not been with me, you would surely have sent me away empty-handed. But God has seen my hardship and the toil of my hands, and last night he rebuked you."

[43]Laban answered Jacob, "The women are my daughters, the children are my children, and the flocks are my flocks. All you see is mine. Yet what can I do today about these daughters of mine, or about the children they have borne? [44]Come now, let's make a covenant, you and I, and let it serve as a witness between us."

[45]So Jacob took a stone and set it up as a pillar. [46]He said to his relatives, "Gather some stones." So they took stones and piled them in a heap, and they ate there by the heap. [47]Laban called it Jegar Sahadutha,[a] and Jacob called it Galeed.[b]

[48]Laban said, "This heap is a witness between you and me today." That is why it was called

a47 The Aramaic *Jegar Sahadutha* means *witness heap.*
b47 The Hebrew *Galeed* means *witness heap.*

me away empty-handed. God saw my affliction and the labor of my hands, and rebuked you last night."

[43]Then Laban answered and said to Jacob, "The daughters are my daughters, the children are my children, the flocks are my flocks, and all that you see is mine. But what can I do today about these daughters of mine, or about their children whom they have borne? [44]Come now, let us make a covenant, you and I; and let it be a witness between you and me." [45]So Jacob took a stone, and set it up as a pillar. [46]And Jacob said to his kinsfolk, "Gather stones," and they took stones, and made a heap; and they ate there by the heap. [47]Laban called it Jegar-sahadutha:[a] but Jacob called it Galeed.[b] [48]Laban said, "This heap is a witness between you and me today." Therefore he called it Galeed, [49]and the pillar[c] Mizpah,[d] for he said, "The LORD watch between you and me, when we are absent one from the other. [50]If you ill-treat my daughters, or if you take wives in addition to my daughters, though no one else is with us, remember that God is witness between you and me."

[51]Then Laban said to Jacob, "See this heap and see the pillar, which I have set between you and me. [52]This heap is a witness, and the pillar is a witness, that I will not pass beyond this heap to you, and you will not pass beyond this heap and this pillar to me, for harm. [53]May the God of Abraham and the God of Nahor"—the God of their father—"judge between us." So Jacob swore by the Fear[e] of his father Isaac, [54]and Jacob offered a sacrifice on the height and called his kinsfolk to eat bread; and they ate bread and tarried all night in the hill country.

[55][f]Early in the morning Laban rose up, and kissed his grandchildren and his daughters and blessed them; then he departed and returned home.

a In Aramaic *The heap of witness*   b In Hebrew *The heap of witness*
  c Compare Sam: MT lacks *the pillar*
d That is *Watchpost*   e Meaning of Heb uncertain
f Ch 32.1 in Heb

NIV

Galeed. ⁴⁹It was also called Mizpah,^a because he said, "May the LORD keep watch between you and me when we are away from each other. ⁵⁰If you mistreat my daughters or if you take any wives besides my daughters, even though no one is with us, remember that God is a witness between you and me."

⁵¹Laban also said to Jacob, "Here is this heap, and here is this pillar I have set up between you and me. ⁵²This heap is a witness, and this pillar is a witness, that I will not go past this heap to your side to harm you and that you will not go past this heap and pillar to my side to harm me. ⁵³May the God of Abraham and the God of Nahor, the God of their father, judge between us."

So Jacob took an oath in the name of the Fear of his father Isaac. ⁵⁴He offered a sacrifice there in the hill country and invited his relatives to a meal. After they had eaten, they spent the night there.

⁵⁵Early the next morning Laban kissed his grandchildren and his daughters and blessed them. Then he left and returned home.

^a49 Mizpah means watchtower.

COMMENTARY

These three chapters constitute a unified "novella" or short story (assigned to J or JE). They follow Jacob's flight from Esau and lead the reader quickly through Jacob's twenty years in Haran to the point of his return to Canaan. Family ties to "the old country" continue (chap. 24), but with Jacob there will now be a permanent break from this part of the family. The text maintains strong ties with Mesopotamian customs and culture; it may reflect Israelite/Aramaean relationships of a later era.

The narrator's primary interest lies in the birth of eleven sons (all but Benjamin), progenitors of the tribes of Israel. The sudden and pervasive God talk (29:31–30:24), as well as structural considerations, underline the importance of these chapters. The story may be outlined as follows: Jacob's arrival in Haran (29:1-14); Jacob's struggles with Laban over Leah and Rachel (29:15-30); the birth of the sons (29:31–30:24); Jacob's struggle with

Laban over the departure (30:25-43); preparations for the return to Canaan (31:1-54). The birth of the children stands as the central text, surrounded by parallel narratives arranged chiastically. The text begins and ends with Jacob's arrival in and departure from Haran.

29:1-14. In a type-scene reminiscent of other well stories issuing in marriage (24:15-33; Exod 2:15-22), Jacob meets Rachel, who keeps sheep for her father, Laban. An emerging problem involves watering rights for shepherds. A stone covering the well is so large that only when all shepherds using the well are present can they remove it; this protects fair community access to the water (note the repetition in vv. 2-3, 8, 10; cf. the interest in stones in 28:10-22; 31:45-50). Jacob becomes impatient with waiting for all the shepherds and rolls the stone away so Rachel can water her flock. This becomes a feat of some consequence; it also violates community customs

(v. 8). This act establishes Jacob as a person of both strength and authority within this unfamiliar community. Jacob, the father of Israel, is a man to be reckoned with.

Jacob's inquiry about welfare (שלום šālôm, v. 6; cf. 28:21), the wordless and emotional recognition scene of kissing and weeping with Rachel (v. 11-12), and the warm welcome and acknowledgment of kinship by Laban (vv. 13-14) depict familial harmony. It contrasts sharply with the story of deception and conflict that follows. This sense of a developing relationship seems preferable to the idea that Laban was duplicitous and self-serving already in his welcome.

29:15-30. This scene begins on a harmonious note, with Laban expressing concern about Jacob's welfare in view of what would certainly be a lengthy stay (v. 15). His use of "serve" language (and the aside introducing Leah and Rachel) signals the conflict to come; that Jacob "serves" anyone in view of prior oracles seems ironic (25:23; 27:29, 37, 40). Yet, Laban invites Jacob to name his own "salary," and Jacob himself suggests that he "serve" Laban as a free man under contract for seven years for Rachel's hand. This length of time, unreal to readers in a less family-oriented world, reveals both the depth of Jacob's love for Rachel (v. 18) and what he deems to be the equivalent of a dowry for her (see 31:15; 24:53). Jacob considers it no burden at all (v. 20).

Laban's warm welcome and open offer may have created an ironic, unsuspecting trust in Jacob; on the other hand, if Jacob told Laban *everything* ("all") that had happened in Canaan (v. 13; cf. v. 26), Laban would have had good reason to be wary of Jacob. This combination of factors may bring out the worst in Laban. He thinks he can take advantage of Jacob, perhaps even that Jacob should "pay" for his deception of Isaac. The relationship quickly deteriorates as Laban, through deceit (concealing a local custom, v. 26), gets Rachel and Leah married off. The deceiver has been deceived (v. 25; 27:35).

At the end of seven years, Jacob not only must request payment of "my wife" (v. 21; betrothed women have the status of wives, Deut 20:7), but receives Leah rather than Rachel (the NRSV and the NIV in v. 17 reflect the uncertainty as to whether Leah's eyes were "weak" or "lovely"). The brief report of the surprise on the "morning

after" is stunning (v. 25a); it seems ironic that Leah knows what Jacob does not know. One can sympathize with Jacob's accusatory questioning, while realizing that what goes around comes around.

Laban's appeal to tradition after the fact (v. 26) appears duplicitous, but by directly raising firstborn issues he establishes an explicit link with Jacob's own deception on the same matter. His reference to "our country" functions similarly. In matching deception for deception, the narrator must have understood Jacob's activity in chap. 27 as reprehensible. Jacob must now know something of how Esau felt. At the same time, he has met in Laban someone not unlike himself.

Jacob's desire for Rachel and his reflection about deception result in his agreement—without a word!—to Laban's terms: He can wed Rachel at the end of seven days, if he completes the bridal week with Leah and serves Laban for seven more years. Jacob thus gains two wives in a week (cf. Lev 18:18 on marrying sisters). Yet, the narrator makes clear that Jacob loves Rachel more than Leah (v. 30; the "unloved" of v. 31 may also refer to preference), which Leah interprets as no love at all (vv. 32-33). Laban's devious orchestration could not force Jacob to love both women; love cannot be so manipulated. Once again, an appeal to custom (v. 26) fails to satisfy. The narrator gives love between a man and a woman a high role here, but it remains complicated by other issues that make for conflict and rivalry: between Laban and Jacob, Leah and Rachel, and Jacob with each wife.

Laban's ruse, made possible through the use of veils (see 24:65) and heavy festival drinking, violates Rachel and Jacob and their love for each other. It violates Leah as well, whose feelings about the matter are not considered, but whose suffering in all of this will shortly be voiced (29:32-35). God responds to her laments first of all (29:31), while Rachel remains childless initially (29:31; 30:1). Neither woman speaks directly in vv. 1-30 (cf. v. 12); their lives are arranged for them. The same also obtains for Zilpah and Bilhah (vv. 24, 29), maids customarily given to a bride by her father. The fact that God responds in so many ways to Leah's suffering in the next episode reveals the divine perspective on her mistreatment and an implicit judgment on her oppressors. She bears seven children, more than all the others. But in so doing, the Leah-Rachel conflict intensifies.

29:31–30:24. This section reads rather like a genealogy, but the conflict between Leah and Rachel and the divine *response* to the oppression of the women provide a basic story line. While these elements may have had separate origins, the interweaving of a gracious divine action in and through a complex fabric of human love and conflict mirrors the story of Israel's life.

The author has made this segment the centerpiece for chaps. 29–31. It narrates the birth of eleven sons and one daughter to Jacob and his wives, Leah and Rachel, and their maids, Bilhah and Zilpah (on Benjamin, see 35:16-18). Leah and Rachel name the children, including the children of their maids, usual Israelite practice. The word plays on the children's names (see the NIV and NRSV footnotes) are not really etymologies, but reflections on the familial conflicts and God's actions related thereto. While their tribal descendants may be in view, the text remains remarkably familial in its orientation, with the mothers playing the major role throughout. Jacob, in fact, appears remarkably passive (speaking only in 30:2).

The conflicting elements both recapitulate and anticipate other intrafamilial struggles. The friction between Leah and Rachel bears resemblances to both the Sarah/Hagar (16:1-6) and the Jacob/Esau conflicts (27:1-45); it anticipates the conflict between Joseph (a child of Rachel) and his brothers. Issues of succession bubble beneath the surface: Will just one of Jacob's sons be the inheritor of the blessing (as has been the case up to this point)? If so, which one? At the same time, the conflict remains personal in its focus, as Leah struggles with her esteem in the eyes of Jacob (29:32, 33, 34; 30:15, 20; the issue for her moves from love to honor), and Rachel with the reproach of childlessness in the eyes of Jacob (30:1-2, 6, 23). While

Laban's deception set up the conflict in the first place, Jacob perpetuates it.

God is now mentioned for the first time in this story, and the interweaving of divine and human roles will shape the rest of our discussion of this section. God is invoked thirteen times by Leah (29:32, 33, 35; 30:18, 20), Rachel (30:6, 23, 24), Jacob (30:2), and the narrator (29:31; 30:17, 22)—the maids never speak—in connection with the birth of seven of the twelve children. These references to God underline the importance of this section for the larger story.

God serves as the subject of the following activities: God sees the affliction of the women, hears their cry, remembers them, takes away their disgrace, and vindicates/rewards them. God both opens the womb and withholds (cf. 16:2) and

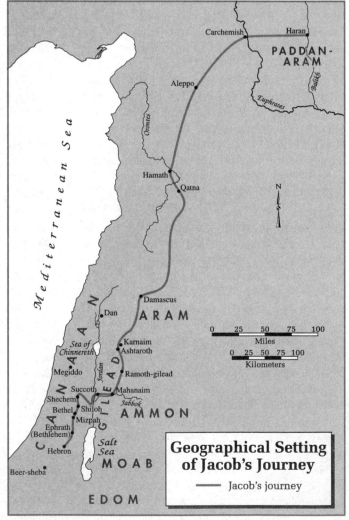

Geographical Setting of Jacob's Journey

—— Jacob's journey

gives/adds a son. The God language occurs as a gracious response to the women's laments (a common OT rhythm, cf. Exod 2:24-25; 3:7). The eight references to God by the women are always in the spirit of praise and gratitude for the gift of a child; the only reference by Jacob—surely an important statistic—is negative and in the form of an angry question.

The narrator does not mention God at the births of Levi, Naphtali, Gad, Asher, or Dinah. Combined with other factors, this suggests that the author did not think God to be the sole, or even the initiating, agent in conception. For the narrator (29:31; 30:17, 22), God *responds* to concrete human situations, but does not initiate a process. For example, God acts with a specific view to the women's cries. Even when God is not mentioned, the mother's response normally assumes the human need (the author offers no explanation of Dinah in 30:21). From another angle, when *both* the narrator and the women do mention God, it occurs only in connection with the births of Reuben, Joseph, and Issachar (the firstborn of Leah and Rachel and the first child born to Leah after she had "ceased bearing"). The narrator apparently thinks God's agency to be decisive, even if not initiatory, in connection with the firstborn or in problematic cases (see 16:2).

We should note other important factors regarding divine and human involvement:

In 30:1-2, Rachel blames Jacob for her childlessness (see 11:30). Her reference to death may reflect concerns about security and inheritance. Jacob's response could be a theological corrective (but can he speak for God?), yet the deep anger suggests otherwise. It probably constitutes a blatant attempt to lay the blame elsewhere (the narrator makes no such claim for God).

First-person references (e.g., "I have borne"; 29:34; 30:20) highlight the importance of human activity. God and the women are brought together in the blessing of Ruth 4:11: "May the LORD make . . . like Rachel and Leah, who together built up the house of Israel" (NRSV). The author specifically mentions Jacob in connection with only six sons (the four sons by the maids and Leah's last two).

Leah and Rachel—in the tradition of Sarah (16:2)—give their maids to Jacob to bear children for them; even God approves (30:18). Why Leah did this after bearing four children stems from issues of equality in her conflict with Rachel (v. 8). She may have "ceased bearing" (29:35; 30:9) because Jacob avoided her (see 30:15). The reference to bearing on "my knees" (v. 3) legitimates the maids' children (cf. 48:12; 50:23). The reference to good fortune (30:11; text uncertain) may suggest an element of chance in issues of birthing.

Conflict between the two women emerges explicitly in 30:1. It consists of envy (30:1) and "wrestling" (30:8; cf. 32:28), climaxing in the discussion over the use of mandrakes (a wild fruit used as an aphrodisiac, v. 14) provided by Reuben, Leah's oldest. This exchange indicates that the women—for all their theological conversation—thought that nondivine factors might be effective in enhancing potency. The narrator makes clear (vv. 17-19, 22) that God enables Leah and Rachel to conceive, and probably, though not necessarily, independently of the mandrakes (but certainly not Jacob!). Rachel—who had access to Jacob in a way that Leah did not—makes a deal with Leah—who still desired Jacob's love—so as to improve her chances of having children: Leah's mandrakes for one night with Jacob ("lie" has negative associations, v. 15)! This hiring/bartering results in a fifth child for Leah. Verses 19-21 show that it turned into more than one night, but we see no sign of Jacob's love for Leah—ever. The conflict between Leah and Rachel may be resolved, given their concerted action in 31:14. It finally works itself out at the familial level, however, only when *all* of their children become the children of promise (50:24).

30:25-43. This story of the rivalry between Jacob and Laban no doubt has complex origins, not least because the progression of thought remains unclear. The unit may have been glossed by an editor with agricultural or other interests.

With the birth of Joseph, Jacob decides that the time has come to return home (this now becomes a key theme for the remainder of the story). He asks that, in view of his service, Laban give him his wives and children and "let him go" (echoing Moses' word to Pharaoh). This constitutes a request for a separation of families. Laban is reluctant to do so, for God has prospered him because of Jacob's labor, and Laban would like that to continue (v. 27; the NIV captures the sense with its "please stay"; cf. 39:2-5, 21-23). Laban even offers to renegotiate Jacob's wages if he will stay (v. 28; cf. 29:15). Laban's reference to divination (v. 27), however, is theological hocus-pocus. Jacob tells it straight: Laban knows that God has blessed him through Jacob from his own experience (without divine revelation); he can see for himself what has happened. As for wages, Jacob needs to make provisions for his family, and he wonders when he can be about that responsibility (v. 30). Once again, Laban asks Jacob to set his own "salary" (v. 31*a*).

Jacob realizes that Laban will not let him go easily, and so he devises a cunning plan that will get him out of the country and provide for his family's future (vv. 31*b*-33). In all of this, the deceiver who has been deceived turns the tables one more time. Jacob refuses any wages, but agrees to work for Laban if, at the end of the work period, he can take his "wages" in multicolored animals and black sheep from the flock he tends. He suggests an onsite inspection plan to demonstrate his honesty (צדקה *ṣĕdāqâ*)—that is, his loyalty to the relationship.

Since animals with such markings are uncommon, Laban thinks he has a deal, but to be on the safe side he deceitfully puts all such colored animals he presently has under his sons' care (three days journey away!) so they would not breed stock for Jacob (vv. 34-36). Jacob responds by devising a plan that produces such animals (vv. 37-43). While difficult to understand, it may assume an ancient belief that what animals look toward when breeding (either striped rods for multicolored animals, vv. 37-39, or the flock tended by Laban's sons for the black or partly black animals, v. 40) determines the coloration of their offspring. In this process, Jacob separates the weaker animals from the others and breeds only the strong animals for his purposes (vv. 41-42; cf. modern efforts at genetic manipulation). Hence, over time, Laban ends up with feebler animals and Jacob has the strong ones (ironically mirroring Laban's manipulation of "weak" Leah).

At the same time, it becomes clear (31:7*b*-12) that God has been involved in and through this process (see below). Jacob's means—through which God works—are effective; he manipulates the flocks to outwit Laban, free himself from dependence on him, and become a wealthy man (over a six-year period, 31:41).

31:1-55. An editor or author has united various traditions here in order to maintain the narrative tension of 30:25-43. The text centers on the continuing dispute both Jacob and God have with the oppressive behaviors of Laban and the difficulties associated with Jacob's flight. The narrative reaches its climax in Jacob's speech (vv. 36-42), especially his witness to a God who sides with him in his affliction. It concludes with a covenant of peace between Jacob and Laban (vv. 43-54).

Jacob's successful breeding practices raise suspicions in the minds of Laban's sons, and conflict with Laban intensifies. In the face of these developments, God tells Jacob to return home (in effect, reinforcing Jacob's own decision, v. 25); God will make good on his promise of presence (v. 3). Jacob consults with Leah and Rachel—a high tribute to them and to the importance of their opinion—about leaving (vv. 4-13) and fills in the details of the story, to which they respond positively (vv. 14-16). The differing agendas of Laban's sons and daughters brackets the central episode. The daughters prove to be stronger and more independent than their brothers.

Jacob testifies that their father has cheated him and changed his wages many times (given Laban's invitations to Jacob, this seems hyperbolic). God, on the other hand, has been working behind the scenes against Laban's arbitrary decisions regarding wages so that whatever changes Laban made actually worked to Jacob's advantage (v. 8); God's activity in vv. 7*b* and 9 encloses Laban's deceit. God has transferred the animals from their father to him. Jacob then recalls a dream in which God revealed how it was that the multicolored animals were the active ones in the breeding process. (Verses 11-12 report the actual dream introduced in v. 10—"once had"; the author telescopes the command to leave the land with the directions about breeding the animals.) God has been so involved because Jacob has been oppressed (v. 12).

Verses 7*b*-12 provide a theological interpretation of the events reported in 30:35-43. God as Creator has been involved in the natural order, in the actual breeding behaviors of animals, resulting in the increase of Jacob's multicolored flock. But God did not give full instructions; Jacob took this divine word and used it to develop effective procedures with the animals. Although

Jacob's techniques were important, Jacob gives all the credit to God in this report to his wives.

God's involvement in Jacob's life correlates to promises made at Bethel (28:10-22): "I am the God of Bethel" (v. 13; the angel in v. 11 is identified as God). God has been faithful to the promises made to Jacob (28:13-15), witnessed to in 31:3b, 5b, 7b, 9, 12b, and 13. The divine command to return can be trusted in view of Jacob's own experience. These verses also reveal a faithful Jacob, whose witness to God's faithfulness in the presence of his wives remains pervasive and without equivocation.

Jacob's wives—acting in concert!—respond with comparable trust: "Do whatever God has told you" (see vv. 14-16). But they base their case on their father's abuse of them rather than on Jacob's experience. In a rhetorical question they use legal language to renounce their father (v. 14; see 1 Kgs. 12:16). He has engaged in false dealings, misappropriating their dowry (money Laban did not have available to give to Jacob; 29:15) and regarding them as aliens; Laban has treated them as property. Such a strong, public stand on the part of these women against the abuse of their father seems remarkable. When Jacob gained wealth, God acted on their behalf as well! In the face of such oppression, God and Jacob have acted justly and properly. The implication: They will accompany Jacob back to Canaan. Their comments put the lie to Laban's later claims (vv. 26, 43).

Upon hearing Rachel and Leah, but without telling Laban, Jacob gathers his family and possessions and begins to flee (vv. 17-21). Unbeknownst to Jacob (v. 32), and after Laban had left the area, Rachel steals Laban's household gods—human-shaped images of gods that were symbols of Laban's authority over his household, perhaps tokens of inheritance. This mirrors Jacob's action of "stealing" Laban's heart (vv. 20, 26)—namely, deceiving him. Because Laban never discovers what Rachel did, her act functions symbolically (see v. 35).

When Laban hears of the flight, he and his men pursue the family for seven days, to the hills of Gilead where Jacob was encamped (east of the Jordan). At this point, God speaks to Laban in a dream in order to protect the fleeing family (cf. 20:3), commanding him not to speak good or bad

to Jacob (vv. 22-24)—namely, to do Jacob no harm (v. 29). The question now is whether Laban will obey the word of God. When Laban overtakes Jacob, he adheres to God's word, but his emotional language appears designed to turn Rachel and Leah against Jacob.

Laban has a list of complaints against Jacob (vv. 25-30). He begins by accusing Jacob of deception and handling his daughters like prisoners. He also berates Jacob by appealing—once again—to custom: Jacob fled in secret; hence, Laban could not give his own flesh and blood a proper send-off. His charge of foolishness (v. 28) seeks to shame Jacob in the presence of his daughters. Self-righteously he appeals to the word from God as a reason for his kindness, but he still could ignore it. He continues in this vein; by suggesting that they have fled out of a desire to see Jacob's family (v. 30), he dissociates himself as a factor in the flight. Then, he concludes with a question designed to turn the entire situation to his own advantage: Why did you steal my gods? Why would he even need them if he was returning to Canaan?

Again, Jacob does not equivocate (vv. 31-32); he fled out of fear of what Laban might do. But he heightens the tension when he unwittingly condemns to death anyone caught stealing Laban's gods (cf. 44:9). Laban pokes around for the gods in the tents (vv. 33-35). But the gods are nowhere to be found, primarily because of Rachel's cleverness; Rachel had put the gods in the camel's saddle, sat on them, and then used menstruation (see NIV) as an excuse for remaining seated. This interchange symbolizes Rachel's defeat of her abusive father and, should the occasion ever arise, provides evidence that he has no claim to their possessions (see vv. 14-16).

Jacob now takes the initiative and angrily makes countercharges. He presents a legal defense of his rights (vv. 36-42), calls on witnesses, and challenges Laban to find cause to prevent him from proceeding to Canaan with his possessions and wives. There is no evidence that anything has been stolen, and he has worked very hard and long (twenty years is stressed, vv. 38, 41) for what he has, going beyond what he was obligated to do. He brings his defense to its high point by claiming that the God of his father has been with him in all of this. (The Fear [or Refuge] of Isaac is an epithet for the God of Israel's ancestors, appropriated for Yahweh.) This God has sided with him, the oppressed one, rather than with Laban; God has sent him away rich rather than empty-handed (see Deut 24:14-15; 1 Sam 2:1-10; Psalm 124). In fact, God spoke to Laban in order to rebuke him, not simply to protect Jacob.

Laban, refusing to admit defeat publicly, claims that everyone and everything really belongs to him (he views all in terms of property), but that he will be magnanimous and conclude a nonaggression pact with Jacob (vv. 43-44). Laban no doubt realizes that he has been had and seeks to protect his own future from further maneuvers by Jacob. Although Jacob appears as an equal partner in what follows, the author gives Laban alone direct speech, specifying the terms of what appear to be two forms of the treaty: (1) interfamilial relationships (vv. 49-50); in effect, they ask God to keep watch over them when they are unable personally to keep track of one another (this "Mizpah Benediction" is not all that positive!); (2) land boundaries (vv. 51-52), which both are to recognize as inviolate.

In connection with each are (a) two sets of stones (vv. 45-46, 51), only the first of which is named (vv. 47-49, cf. NRSV and NIV for different attempts to resolve a textual difficulty), which function as continuing witnesses to the treaty; (b) two communal meals (vv. 46, 54), in which only Jacob's kin appear to participate; (c) two invocations of God (vv. 50, 53; Nahor is Abraham's brother). Isaac adds the Fear of Isaac to replace Laban's second name, not to designate a different God, but to replace Laban's epithet in view of his own experience. This act effectively cuts off Jacob and his family from this particular strand of religious tradition. Jacob's relationship to the family in Haran now ends.

The fact that these two individuals, after deception upon deception, could part in peace, however strained the relationship (note that Laban does not speak to Jacob in v. 55), testifies to the work of God. They go their separate ways; Laban is not heard from again.

REFLECTIONS

1. The story reports a watershed period in the life of this family. We find a thoroughgoing break between the family in Haran and the family in Canaan. Although 27:46–28:9 lifted up the importance of Jacob's marrying within the family, resulting in his journey to Haran, that concern now ends. Marital relationships outside the family now become a part of their reality (34:1-24; 38:1-11; 41:45; 46:10). Indeed, a number of texts suggest that Jacob's family are aliens in Haran (31:15; 32:4); the families are distinct from one another (30:30; 31:37, although Laban claims otherwise, 31:43), and even their deities are distinct (31:53). God stresses the importance of Jacob's returning to his own homeland (30:25; 31:3, 13, 18).

This text witnesses to profound changes, even with respect to family structures and human relationships, to which God often calls the community of faith. As those changes develop, however, they may well entail considerable anxiety and conflict. Discerning God's call into a different future may prove difficult and take considerable time and effort.

2. These chapters continue the theme of sharp and deep levels of intrafamilial conflict and deception, with focus now on the family in the "old country." The family in Haran more than matches the family in Canaan. They are chips off the same block; such familial tendencies run deep. At the same time, this picture derives in many ways from Jacob's own duplicity in chap. 27; Jacob is the only link between chaps. 25–28 and chaps. 29–31. Jacob reaps the fruits of his own deception of Esau and in the process intensifies the problems in another community.

The author creates this central text, highlighting the birth of the tribes of Israel, permeated with negative realities. How easy it would have been to paint a rosy, idyllic picture of Israel's origins, a Garden of Eden sort of beginning. But the narrator, with a realistic understanding of the human condition, knew that this would not be realistic. The more deeply the probe into Israel's own past, the more the present looks like more of the same. Yet, precisely because of this continuity, at the level of both human and divine action, readers can see themselves as if in a mirror, gaining new levels of self-understanding and being assured of God's continuing involvement in their troubled lives.

3. At the same time, human love (stressed in 29:18, 20; cf. 24:67) and human service (forms of עבד ʿābad occur thirteen times) can counter human deception. And we ought not to overlook the humor sprinkled throughout (e.g., 31:33-35). Moreover, as we shall see, God makes use of human wisdom and ingenuity in effecting the divine purposes in and through this family. Both human beings and God act with favorable consequences, from the women (29:31–30:24) to Jacob (30:27, 30). Even people like Laban listen to God's voice and participate in the divine purposes (31:24, 29). Jacob may not be entirely free of arrogance (30:30; 31:42), but God extends abundant blessings through Jacob's service. God's blessings are always mediated, whether through created orders (e.g., the fertility of animals) or human activity or a combination thereof.

4. The author emphasizes the role of the women as mediators of the divine blessing in and through their bearing of children. Jacob, though indispensable, remains deeply in the background, as the voices and actions of the women fill these verses (remembered in Ruth 4:11). In the midst of a patriarchal culture, the tradition gives these women a central place in the story of the birth of the people of Israel. " 'Israel' has emerged out of the intense struggle between Rachel and Leah, just as 'Israel' will emerge from the struggle between Jacob and God."[180] These mothers order the Jacob genealogy (46:8-26).

At the same time, the important role that Leah and Rachel play in the story is not limited to their role as mothers. The text recognizes their abuse at their father's hand and that they give this abuse public voice (31:14-16); such action is of no little importance for a community of faith that has all too often engaged in a cover-up regarding such abusive familial situations. Their sharp critique of their father and renunciation of his authority in their lives witnesses to a possible avenue of approach to abusive situations. Their renunciation takes not only verbal form but also courageous, concrete action in Rachel's theft of the gods and her defiance of him when he comes looking for them. When Leah also voices her abuse at the hands of her husband, Jacob (29:31-34; 30:20), she adds an additional positive dimension to the way in which these women confront tragic situations in their lives.

In addition, the use of God language by the women, both in connection with the birth of their children and with Jacob (31:16), testifies not only to their personal faith, but also to their ability to engage in theological formulation and discussion. The women make confessions, not on the basis of some special revelation, but by the deep-down links they see between their experience and what they know their God to be about in the world.

5. The community of faith is fortunate in having a God who does not insist on perfection before choosing to work in and through it. Israel has a God who blesses this family in the very midst of its conflicts (29:31–30:24; 30:27, 30; 31:3, 5, 7, 9, 42), making life possible even within a dysfunctional system. God does not work in isolation, but within a complex context to bring about the birth of Israel's children and enable goodness to emerge.

In the births of these children we may see God at work on behalf of new life and families. This *creative* work of God remains indispensable for the history of the promise, for it enables the coming into being of persons to whom promises can be given and for whom they can be realized. God's promises are given on behalf of "families" (12:3*b*; 28:14). God's most fundamental objective in giving the promises to Abraham, Isaac, and Jacob—and Leah and Rachel—is the blessing of families. In all of this, of course, God is at work in quite

---

180. Thomas W. Mann, *The Book of the Torah: The Narrative Integrity of the Pentateuch* (Atlanta: John Knox, 1988) 57.

unobtrusive ways, hidden from public view (in this respect, these chapters are similar to the Joseph story).

The author places the birth of Israel as a community of faith within an admixture of familial conflict, human love and service, and ongoing divine blessing in the midst of failure. As such, the story is not simply about origins; it reveals the fundamental character of Israel's continuing life with God through the generations. And it shapes the very heart of Israel's understanding of God as one who works on behalf of families like this one. Indeed, it speaks about and to the community of faith in every age.

6. This mirroring function of the text occurs at another level. Jacob's journey to a foreign land and his return reflect Israel's later journey to Egypt and back. For example, Israel's founding family, though virtually in place in 30:25-43, resides in a foreign land. The situation appears similar to that faced by the adult "children of Israel" in Egypt (Exod 1:1-8). They are not free to leave. Jacob's request of Laban to let his family go echoes Moses' request of Pharaoh (30:25-26; the verbs שלח [šālaḥ, "send"] and הלך [hālak, "go"] are used by Moses with Pharaoh, e.g., Exod 5:1-3; cf. also [ʿābad, "serve"] used twice here and often in Exodus). We may compare Moses and Jacob in the ways they gain freedom from Pharaoh and Laban. They begin with relationships in good order, but end with angry exchanges, threats, involvement of women and children, pursuit and interrupted flight, and carrying the wealth of the land with them as they go (cf., 31:18 with Exod 12:35-38). We have seen this mirroring before in Genesis, e.g., Abraham's journey to Egypt (12:10-20). These parallels suggest that the great rhythms of life are usually not unique to any historical period. Human life has a way of returning ever again to face problems and possibilites that are comparable to those of their predecessors in the faith. When we study carefully these texts, we receive a potential source for a word from God to address our own problems and possibilities.

7. The identity of the oppressor and oppressed varies. Jacob, for example, can be both. Initially Laban and Jacob oppress Leah. Her own father uses her for his deceptive purposes (29:23; 31:15), forcing her into a marital situation that he knows will bring trouble. Jacob, in turn, accepts the marriage and relates to her sexually (four children in quick succession), but treats her as nothing compared to Rachel. Leah's cries of affliction (עני ʿānî) are heard (שמע šāmaʿ) by God (29:32-33; 30:17). Rachel's cries concerning the distress of her childlessness are also heard (30:6, 22) and remembered (זכר zākar; v. 22) by God. This pattern is later matched by Jacob's affliction (31:42), which is seen (ראה rāʾâ) by God (31:12). Such language reflects the Exodus events (Exod 2:24-25; 3:7, 17; 4:31), as well as psalms of lament and thanksgiving (see 29:35; 30:23).

This divine commitment to the oppressed is already central to the biblical narrative. This is *not* a theme that surfaces for the first time in Egypt; God's remembrance of Abraham, Isaac, and Jacob grounds the divine response in the exodus (Exod 2:24; 3:6, 16; 6:2-8). And the OT includes Leah and Rachel in this remembrance; they "built up the house of Israel" (Ruth 4:11) and Rachel becomes a metaphor for those who lament the death and dying of the children of Israel; indeed, she even becomes a metaphor for the suffering of God (Jer 31:15-20; cf. Matt 2:18).

GENESIS 32:1-21, JACOB PREPARES TO MEET ESAU

NIV

32 Jacob also went on his way, and the angels of God met him. ²When Jacob saw them, he said, "This is the camp of God!" So he named that place Mahanaim.ᵃ

³Jacob sent messengers ahead of him to his brother Esau in the land of Seir, the country of Edom. ⁴He instructed them: "This is what you are to say to my master Esau: 'Your servant Jacob says, I have been staying with Laban and have remained there till now. ⁵I have cattle and donkeys, sheep and goats, menservants and maidservants. Now I am sending this message to my lord, that I may find favor in your eyes.'"

⁶When the messengers returned to Jacob, they said, "We went to your brother Esau, and now he is coming to meet you, and four hundred men are with him."

⁷In great fear and distress Jacob divided the people who were with him into two groups,ᵇ and the flocks and herds and camels as well. ⁸He thought, "If Esau comes and attacks one group,ᶜ the groupᶜ that is left may escape."

⁹Then Jacob prayed, "O God of my father Abraham, God of my father Isaac, O LORD, who said to me, 'Go back to your country and your relatives, and I will make you prosper,' ¹⁰I am unworthy of all the kindness and faithfulness you have shown your servant. I had only my staff when I crossed this Jordan, but now I have become two groups. ¹¹Save me, I pray, from the hand of my brother Esau, for I am afraid he will come and attack me, and also the mothers with their children. ¹²But you have said, 'I will surely make you prosper and will make your descendants like the sand of the sea, which cannot be counted.'"

¹³He spent the night there, and from what he had with him he selected a gift for his brother Esau: ¹⁴two hundred female goats and twenty male goats, two hundred ewes and twenty rams, ¹⁵thirty female camels with their young, forty cows and ten bulls, and twenty female donkeys and ten male donkeys. ¹⁶He put them in the care

NRSV

32 Jacob went on his way and the angels of God met him; ²and when Jacob saw them he said, "This is God's camp!" So he called that place Mahanaim.ᵃ

3Jacob sent messengers before him to his brother Esau in the land of Seir, the country of Edom, ⁴instructing them, "Thus you shall say to my lord Esau: Thus says your servant Jacob, 'I have lived with Laban as an alien, and stayed until now; ⁵and I have oxen, donkeys, flocks, male and female slaves; and I have sent to tell my lord, in order that I may find favor in your sight.'"

6The messengers returned to Jacob, saying, "We came to your brother Esau, and he is coming to meet you, and four hundred men are with him." ⁷Then Jacob was greatly afraid and distressed; and he divided the people that were with him, and the flocks and herds and camels, into two companies, ⁸thinking, "If Esau comes to the one company and destroys it, then the company that is left will escape."

9And Jacob said, "O God of my father Abraham and God of my father Isaac, O LORD who said to me, 'Return to your country and to your kindred, and I will do you good,' ¹⁰I am not worthy of the least of all the steadfast love and all the faithfulness that you have shown to your servant, for with only my staff I crossed this Jordan; and now I have become two companies. ¹¹Deliver me, please, from the hand of my brother, from the hand of Esau, for I am afraid of him; he may come and kill us all, the mothers with the children. ¹²Yet you have said, 'I will surely do you good, and make your offspring as the sand of the sea, which cannot be counted because of their number.'"

13So he spent that night there, and from what he had with him he took a present for his brother Esau, ¹⁴two hundred female goats and twenty male goats, two hundred ewes and twenty rams, ¹⁵thirty milch camels and their colts, forty cows and ten bulls, twenty female donkeys and ten male donkeys. ¹⁶These he delivered into the hand

NIV

of his servants, each herd by itself, and said to his servants, "Go ahead of me, and keep some space between the herds."

¹⁷He instructed the one in the lead: "When my brother Esau meets you and asks, 'To whom do you belong, and where are you going, and who owns all these animals in front of you?' ¹⁸then you are to say, "They belong to your servant Jacob. They are a gift sent to my lord Esau, and he is coming behind us.' "

¹⁹He also instructed the second, the third and all the others who followed the herds: "You are to say the same thing to Esau when you meet him. ²⁰And be sure to say, "Your servant Jacob is coming behind us.' " For he thought, 'I will pacify him with these gifts I am sending on ahead; later, when I see him, perhaps he will receive me." ²¹So Jacob's gifts went on ahead of him, but he himself spent the night in the camp.

NRSV

of his servants, every drove by itself, and said to his servants, "Pass on ahead of me, and put a space between drove and drove." ¹⁷He instructed the foremost, "When Esau my brother meets you, and asks you, 'To whom do you belong? Where are you going? And whose are these ahead of you?' ¹⁸then you shall say, 'They belong to your servant Jacob; they are a present sent to my lord Esau; and moreover he is behind us.' " ¹⁹He likewise instructed the second and the third and all who followed the droves, "You shall say the same thing to Esau when you meet him, ²⁰and you shall say, 'Moreover your servant Jacob is behind us.' " For he thought, "I may appease him with the present that goes ahead of me, and afterwards I shall see his face; perhaps he will accept me." ²¹So the present passed on ahead of him; and he himself spent that night in the camp.

COMMENTARY

This text, a unified composition (mostly J), prepares the reader for Jacob's encounters with God (32:22-32) and with Esau (33:1-20). These verses center on the prayer of Jacob (vv. 9-12), the interpretation of which shapes the approach to the narratives that follow. The prayer is framed by encounters with God (vv. 1-2, 22-32) and, within that, by the dispatch of messengers to Esau (vv. 3-8, 13-21). At the same time, the tension in the narrative sharply increases after the prayer, to such an extent that the encounter with God in vv. 22-32 becomes, in turn, the centerpiece of chaps. 32–33. These verses thus combine with 33:1-20 to enclose the encounter with God in 32:22-32. Jacob's "facing" both Esau and God are important to keep together.

Chapters 29–31 have demonstrated that Haran cannot be home for Jacob. Hence, he must return to Canaan, where a hornet's nest may well await him. Nonetheless, he returns under God's command.

32:1-2. The author structures this section similarly to 28:10-22. Jacob experienced angels when he left Canaan (28:12), when he was in Haran

(31:11), and now when he returns (32:1). The angels may be God in human form (on the plural, see 18:2). The angels are associated with revelation in the two prior texts, but in this text no word from God is heard. The angels may be linked to the promise of divine presence (28:15) and, less directly, to 31:42, 49. They also point forward to the dangers of the meeting with Esau and his militia-sized group of 400 men, hence the reference to angels in terms of an entire company or encampment, probably with military connotations (see Josh 5:13-15; 1 Chr 12:22), is fitting. The coalescence of some of these themes in Ps 34:7 ("The angel of the LORD encamps/ around those who fear him, and delivers them" [NRSV]) supports their role as protectors.

The name Jacob gives to the place, Mahanaim (its location is uncertain; it must have had some link with Jacob), "two camps [or companies]," refers to God's company and his own or to the two divisions of his own people (vv. 7-8). The exclamation appears similar to 28:16-17 and conveys Jacob's clear sense of ongoing divine presence and protection. It may embolden Jacob for the dangerous journey ahead; his response suggests that it does.

32:3-8. In conventional language, Jacob sends messengers (the same word as "angels") on ahead to discern from Esau himself the nature of the situation. His actions reflect the memory of Esau's intentions to kill him (v. 11; 27:41-42). Esau is already settled in Seir (i.e., Edom; though see 36:6-8), to the southeast of Canaan. Jacob tells the messengers what to say: where he has been, about his wealth, and his interest in reconciliation. Indeed, Jacob's use of lord/servant language (vv. 4, 6, 18, 20) in the message itself suggests his willingness to reverse the blessing gained by deceiving Esau. The return to this language in chap. 33 shows that Jacob is serious about such reconciliation. The author does not describe the encounter of the messengers with Esau (though note the "brother" language), only that Esau comes to meet Jacob, accompanied by 400 men (v. 6). Jacob appears distressed and uncertain about the meaning of the report, but he prepares for the worst. He divides his company into two parts so that, should Esau attack, at least one group might be saved.

32:9-12. In the midst of this fearful moment, Jacob prays. Scholars are divided about the sincerity of this prayer. A judgment that Jacob is attempting to deceive God depends not on the prayer itself, but on a negative assessment of Jacob in the larger narrative. Such an interpretation seems unlikely.[181]

The structure of the prayer is similar to the individual lament for deliverance from an enemy (cf. Pss 31:15-16; 40:11-13; 69:13-14; 86:13-15): (1) An invocation, with a threefold naming of God, linking him with the God of his fathers; (2) A recollection of God's command to return to Canaan and what God has done for him. The language recalls God's command to Abraham (12:1) and suggests again a break from the family in Haran. Jacob's use of the terms חסד (ḥesed,

"steadfast love") and אמת (ʾĕmet, "faithfulness") recalls the use of these terms in 24:27 and links Jacob with basic creedal language for God in the OT (cf. the psalms noted above). (3) A confession of his unworthiness for even a modicum ("least") of God's love. The request does not depend on what he brings to this moment. (4) A request for deliverance; Jacob fears not only for his own life, but for his wives and children; (5) A claiming of the divine promises. This grounds Jacob's plea in God's loyalty to promises made. He appropriately claims God's promises (eight in number; cf. 28:13-15) for this moment.

Jacob quotes God two times in his prayer, referring to the command to return to Canaan (31:3) and the promises regarding divine presence and numerous progeny (28:13-15). The word "do you good" (repeated in vv. 9 and 12, stressed in the latter) summarizes the divine promises and frames the prayer. The reference to posterity derives from this specific situation.

32:13-21. After the prayer, Jacob begins to move his retinue toward confrontation with Esau. In an effort to cover his guilt for past behaviors (כפר *kāpar*) and to effect acceptance (נשׂא *nāśāʾ*) by Esau (v. 20), Jacob sends his servants on ahead in stages with a major gift: over 550 animals! He cleverly designs the threefold staging of the gift in droves to break down any initial resistance that Esau might exhibit. Jacob instructs his servants carefully concerning their response to Esau's questions. He stresses that the animals are a gift to "my lord [Esau]" from "your servant Jacob" (vv. 18, 20, cf. vv. 4, 6), who is coming along behind. The fourfold mention of gift (מנחה *minḥâ*, vv. 14, 19, 21-22, a play on Mahanaim) may suggest tribute from a vassal to his lord (cf. 2 Sam 8:2, 6; 1 Kgs 4:21 for this combination).

Prior to the encounter between Jacob and Esau, the narrative pauses for a description of an encounter between Jacob and God. How they are to be related will not be easy to resolve (see 33:1-20).

---

181. For a negative view, see S. Balentine, *Hebrew Prayer*, 64-71.

REFLECTIONS

1. The presence of divine messengers (v. 1) does not obviate the need for human messengers (v. 3). This juxtaposition suggests that, in situations of danger and interpersonal difficulty, the coalition of divine presence and human initiative and planning is important. God's presence does not control so much that what human beings think, do, and say in such moments is irrelevant. At the same time, the struggle with the "messenger" (God) in vv. 22-32 makes clear that God may enter anew into human plans.

2. Jacob does not blame God for the problem he now faces (v. 9); he simply states the truth and claims a coherent relationship between the God who commands and the God who promises. The one who promises can be trusted not to subvert the promises in issuing commands; the one who commands will see somehow to the promises (cf. 22:1). Jacob has been faithful to God and in this dangerous moment claims God's promises; hence the appeal to divine steadfastness and faithfulness. The text does not report that Jacob is delivered from Esau until after the struggle with God (32:30). Given that experience, the confrontation with Esau seems anticlimactic. God answers the prayer for deliverance in a way somewhat different from what Jacob imagined.

3. The language the messengers are to speak to Esau implies Jacob's willingness to reverse his earlier deception and return the blessing to Esau (not the blessing in 28:3-4, and nothing is said of the birthright). The reversal in the use of lord/servant language from 25:23 and 29:29, 37, 40, where Esau became Jacob's servant, demonstrates this interest. Also, the word used for Jacob's "gift" in 33:11 is ברכה (bĕrākâ, "blessing"; see 27:36-41). The word פנים (pānîm, "face") occurs seven times (vv. 16, 17, 20-21); this anticipates its prominence in the next sections (32:30; 33:3, 10). Seeing the face of God before seeing the face of Esau turns the meeting with Esau into a less dangerous moment, though seeing the face of God presents its own dangers.

GENESIS 32:22-32, JACOB WRESTLING WITH GOD

NIV

[22]That night Jacob got up and took his two wives, his two maidservants and his eleven sons and crossed the ford of the Jabbok. [23]After he had sent them across the stream, he sent over all his possessions. [24]So Jacob was left alone, and a man wrestled with him till daybreak. [25]When the man saw that he could not overpower him, he touched the socket of Jacob's hip so that his hip was wrenched as he wrestled with the man. [26]Then the man said, "Let me go, for it is daybreak."

But Jacob replied, "I will not let you go unless you bless me."

[27]The man asked him, "What is your name?"

"Jacob," he answered.

[28]Then the man said, "Your name will no longer be Jacob, but Israel,[a] because you have struggled with God and with men and have overcome."

[a]28 *Israel* means *he struggles with God.*

NRSV

[22]The same night he got up and took his two wives, his two maids, and his eleven children, and crossed the ford of the Jabbok. [23]He took them and sent them across the stream, and likewise everything that he had. [24]Jacob was left alone; and a man wrestled with him until daybreak. [25]When the man saw that he did not prevail against Jacob, he struck him on the hip socket; and Jacob's hip was put out of joint as he wrestled with him. [26]Then he said, "Let me go, for the day is breaking." But Jacob said, "I will not let you go, unless you bless me." [27]So he said to him, "What is your name?" And he said, "Jacob." [28]Then the man[a] said, "You shall no longer be called Jacob, but Israel,[b] for you have striven with God and with humans,[c] and have prevailed." [29]Then Jacob asked him, "Please tell me your name." But he said, "Why is it that you

[a] Heb *he*   [b] That is *The one who strives with God* or *God strives*
[c] Or *with divine and human beings*

NIV

²⁹Jacob said, "Please tell me your name."

But he replied, "Why do you ask my name?" Then he blessed him there.

³⁰So Jacob called the place Peniel,^a saying, "It is because I saw God face to face, and yet my life was spared."

³¹The sun rose above him as he passed Peniel,^b and he was limping because of his hip. ³²Therefore to this day the Israelites do not eat the tendon attached to the socket of the hip, because the socket of Jacob's hip was touched near the tendon.

^a30 Peniel means *face of God.*   ^b31 Hebrew *Penuel,* a variant of *Peniel*

NRSV

ask my name?" And there he blessed him. ³⁰So Jacob called the place Peniel,^a saying, "For I have seen God face to face, and yet my life is preserved." ³¹The sun rose upon him as he passed Penuel, limping because of his hip. ³²Therefore to this day the Israelites do not eat the thigh muscle that is on the hip socket, because he struck Jacob on the hip socket at the thigh muscle.

^aThat is *The face of God*

COMMENTARY

This text has long fascinated commentators. Its meaning is so elusive that a variety of interpretations is credible. The "breaks and joints . . . and the looseness in the inner connection of the statements to one another [make] room for many ideas" and give it an "essential spaciousness."[182]

Although the story has been edited in the course of its transmission (e.g., v. 32), most scholars assign the present passage to J. An early pre-Yahwistic story of a supernatural encounter at a river crossing may have informed the narrative; yet, the relatively sophisticated image of God and the centrality of the name *Israel* make any such links remote. Hosea 12:3-4 may attest to a somewhat different form of the passage. The text also differs from typical stories of attacks to prevent the completion of a mission; in this case, the one who commanded the return (31:3, 13) becomes the assailant.

This text stands between God's two appearances at Bethel (28:10-22; 35:9-13), one of the primary pillars in the story of Jacob. It presents special parallels to the first story. Just as God encountered Jacob when he fled the promised land because of his brother's anger, so also God now encounters him at the point of reentry, with his brother's anger once again focusing his energies. In both cases, Jacob appears deeply vulner-

able and alone, in need of divine care. This time, however, God approaches him in a much more ambiguous manner. God's second appearance at Bethel brings Jacob's return home full circle and clarifies the shape of his future. In another sense, this text has its closest relationship to 33:1-17, Jacob's meeting with Esau, which constitutes a mirror image of this episode (see chap. 33). This confrontation with God shapes Jacob's final encounter with Esau.

Among its literary features, the story plays on various words, especially the names *Jacob* (יבק [yabbōq, Jabbok]; אבק [ʾābaq, "wrestle"]) and *Israel* (שרה [śārâ, "struggle"]), and the word *face* (פנים pānîm), especially in 32:21, 30 and 33:10. Also, the author delays identifying the assailant. Initially, he appears only as a "man" (איש ʾîš, v. 24); the reader gradually comes to realize that this is no ordinary assailant; it is God in human form (the מלאך malʾāk, cf. 16:7). Ancient and modern readers familiar with the story would hear it with this identification in mind from the beginning, as I will in the exposition.

Having sent his gift to Esau on ahead, later that same night Jacob sends his entire caravan across the Jabbok (an eastern tributary of the Jordan about twenty miles north of the Dead Sea), a frontier point for the promised land (Deut 3:16). Jacob stays behind at the border for reasons un-

182. Von Rad, *Genesis*, 324.

known. He remains filled with fear and distress (32:7, 11); for all he knows, Esau still plans to kill him (27:41-42). The narrative stresses that Jacob is alone. He will not be able to call for help should trouble come.

And come it does. During the night and in a surprise attack, God wrestles him to the ground. Jacob may well have thought it was Esau. God and Jacob struggle for a considerable period of time. When God sees that daybreak is near and that he has not been able to prevail in straightforward wrestling, God strikes Jacob in the hollow of the thigh (the exact spot is uncertain). The NRSV's "struck" is truer to the context than the NIV's "touched," though both translations are possible.

This blow has a crippling effect and brings the struggle to its climactic moment, but it does not dictate the terms of the outcome. Jacob retains such a hold that God cannot escape from it; Jacob alone has the power to grant God's request for release. At the same time, God alone has the power to grant a blessing. Jacob's insistence that release be contingent upon blessing results in God's giving the name *Israel* to Jacob (though both names are retained in the narratives that follow) and the gift of blessing. Jacob is forever marked by the struggle, as he limps away toward the promised land. His mark attests to success and not to defeat.

Rather than move through the text verse by verse, we approach it through some questions it raises. God takes Jacob seriously enough to engage him in a struggle, but God seems also concerned not to be revealed fully to Jacob. Why is this the case?

First, it was a commonplace that God's face would not be seen: "no one shall see me and live" (Exod 33:20 NRSV). This reflects a concern not for God, but for the life of the one seeing. In this story, God is not the one endangered by the daylight, it is Jacob! To see God in the full light of day would have meant death for Jacob. If Jacob holds on until daybreak, he is a dead man! At the same time, the continued grasping of God on Jacob's part in the near-dawn light also says something about Jacob. He is willing to risk death for the sake of the divine blessing. Jacob's action suggests that he will risk seeing the face of Esau, too.

Second, Jacob's request to know the name of God is respectful: "Please." Not unlike Moses (Exod 3:13), Jacob knows that he is dealing with God, seen in the request for blessing (v. 26) and from God (v. 28). He wants neither the generic name *God* (אל '*ēl*) nor the names God has already given him (28:13). As with Moses, Jacob requests a divine name commensurate with this new development in his relationship with God, a new name for God to go with the new name for Jacob (cf. 16:13; 21:33; 31:13).

God replies to the question with a question (as in Judg 13:18): Why do (למה זה *lāmmâ zeh*) you ask my name? The Jacob-Esau meeting will also end abruptly with such a question (33:15). God does not seek information from Jacob. At the least, God thereby signals the intent to close off the conversation and move on, while leaving Jacob with a question rather than a refusal. The fact that the question is followed by a blessing suggests the latter as an indirect answer; God is a God of blessing, a deity positively disposed toward Jacob.

In what sense does God not prevail (v. 25) and Jacob prevail (v. 28)? Neither emerges as the unqualified winner; God's blow moves the struggle to a new level, yet Jacob is able to prevent God from leaving (v. 26). One could say that Jacob's struggling and holding his own has helped turn a potentially negative situation into a positive, blessing-filled one.

Who is changed because of this struggle? God? Jacob? Both? Certainly their relationship has changed. They hold fast to each other; neither will turn away. Certainly Jacob is not so changed that he loses his identity. We find no evidence of a purging of his sin or his negative character traits. Yet, we can discern important changes.

Jacob has a new name. Although *Israel* may actually mean something like "God rules," the narrator claims otherwise. The NRSV footnotes suggest a purposeful ambiguity in the name: "God strives" (God initiates and engages in the wrestling) *and* "the one who strives with God" (Jacob responds in kind). Jacob cannot struggle with God if God refuses to be so engaged. God's giving this name, then, has implications for God as well as for Jacob. It affirms a divine commitment to stay with Jacob in the struggle. God will be caught up in this relationship. God's promise (28:15) involves not a passive presence, but an active, engaged relationship.

From Jacob's side, the new name attests to and affirms the strength he has exhibited in this encounter with God *and* throughout his lifetime. It is important to note that name changes do not, necessarily, signal a change in character (cf. 17:5); here God gives the name to Jacob in recognition of *who he has been and presently is*, not what he becomes in this moment. The name change immediately follows Jacob's refusal to let God go and his demand for a blessing from God; these responses prompt God's response. God explains the name *only* in positive terms: It represents Jacob's *strength* and *capacity for struggling well*. If Jacob had not struggled and prevailed, there would have been no new name, at least not the name *Israel*.

This change significantly assures Jacob. If he can hold his own even with God, certainly he should be able to live up to his name with Esau. Although the name *Israel* describes part of Jacob, yet he also exhibits Jacob-like characteristics in this encounter by grasping God. Unlike Abram/Abraham, both names continue to be used in the subsequent narrative, suggesting that both aptly describe this individual. (The repetition of the name change in 35:10 reflects a different origin for the name *Israel*.)

Jacob is blessed. Jacob will not let God go until he receives a blessing (v. 26). God responds positively (v. 29), but not until the exchange over names. What is the content of the blessing? Blessings are normally not gained through struggle. However, Jacob here holds God to the freely given promises (see 28:13-15); Jacob claims what God has promised. Intercession occurs here in physical terms, not unlike Exod 32:10-14. Through such blessings (cf. 35:9) God continues the blessing put in place by Isaac, and the strength for life and well-being it implies (27:27-29). In other words, the blessing spoken here by God enables the promises to be realized in Jacob's life.

Just as Jacob enters the promised land, God seals the promise with him (28:15)—at just the point where Jacob's life appears most in danger. At the moment of deepest vulnerability for Jacob, God enters into the very depths of the struggle, *binding God's own self to Jacob at that level*. In fulfillment of the promise, God will go with Jacob into future dangerous moments. God helps to make Jacob ready for the encounter ahead, arming him with continuing blessings for the journey. Jacob can now face any foe, no matter how hostile (cf. Moses). Jacob is about to embark on a life-and-death struggle, and he now knows that God the wrestler will be at his side.

Jacob sees God face to face. Jacob names the place Peniel ("the face of God"; usually spelled *Penuel*, v. 31). Unlike at Bethel, no altar is built nor are issues of holiness raised. He gives it this name not because of any later historical significance (cf. 1 Kgs 12:25), but because he has had a particular experience—namely, seeing God face to face and living to tell the tale (as Moses does in Num 12:8; cf. Judg 13:22). The references to dawn (vv. 24, 26, 31) make clear that God and Jacob parted company before the full light of day. Hence, seeing God's face was for Jacob at best a twilight experience.

Jacob sustains an injury. The author presents a poignant portrayal of Jacob limping down the road toward the promised land as the sun's first rays peek over the horizon. Jacob may now move on toward his goal. At the same time, Jacob has been sharply, and perhaps permanently, marked by this struggle with God (the exact nature of the injury remains unclear). What is the significance of the mark? On the one hand, it signifies Jacob's *success*, not his failure or defeat; he has struggled and prevailed. As such, Jacob does not become a victim of God, reduced to groveling or to nothing before the power of the Almighty. On the other hand, it attests to God's graciousness; Jacob has wrestled with God to the break of day, yet his life is preserved. So the mark symbolizes *both* who Jacob is and who God is.

By means of a dietary regulation (not mentioned elsewhere in the OT) Israel's memory will be continually jogged regarding this struggle between Jacob and God. This regulation institutionalizes the memory. It provides an ongoing mark of self-identification for Jacob's descendants. This memory, associated with bodily ritual, draws attention to Jacob/Israel's self-identity, involving not simply a spiritual reality, but all of Israel's life as well. An animal—part of God's creation—focuses this human memory.

The author does not report that Jacob let go of God or even that God has left him. The story moves immediately into the confrontation with Esau. In some sense this means that God and Jacob remain bound to each other, facing this future.

REFLECTIONS

1. Both God and Jacob identify the "man" as God (אלהים *'ĕlōhîm;* vv. 28, 30). His assailant speaks of Jacob as having striven with *God.* Jacob understands this to mean that he confronted God: "I have seen God face to face" (v. 30). Other texts connect "man" and "God" in a comparable way (see 18:1-8; Judg 13:6, 21-22). The OT links the human figure with the divine messenger (מלאך *mal'āk*), understanding that God is present and active in human form (see 16:7; Hos 12:3-4 identifies the *'ĕlōhîm* figure with the *mal'āk*, messenger).

Some interpreters view this story as involving *only* an inner struggle between God and Jacob. But the stress on the blow to the body and the resultant limp (vv. 25, 31) indicate that Jacob's physical self is affected. The fact that the struggle involves a figure in human form, rather than a disembodied God, also shows that the author describes more than a dark night of the soul, as does the lack of reference to dreaming or sleeping (cf. 28:10-22). This is no nightmare; Jacob remains fully awake. Jacob struggles with more than his own conscience or fears; his entire person is engaged. The dietary etiology also keeps the story grounded in a physical encounter, as does the parallel drawn with Esau's face (33:10).

2. Why does God wrestle with Jacob? Many suggest that God responds to Jacob's history of deception; the story constitutes a disciplinary move on God's part to teach Jacob that he cannot proceed into the future relying on his own devices. Hence, some claim the story presents Jacob's conversion to a life more attuned to the ways of God. Yet, we find no evidence of that in the narrative—no negative judgment of Jacob's behaviors, no repentance on Jacob's part, and no fundamental change in Jacob's subsequent life pattern. Indeed, in giving Jacob a new name, God commends Jacob for struggling and names him in view of who he has been in the past and, given his response to the divine challenge, still is.

God will act in ways that are in the best interests of the life of the chosen one, however undeserving. At the same time, God sharply challenges Jacob in a "let's-see-what-this-guy's-made-of-when-the-going-really-gets-rough" sense. We may compare how Jacob will respond when faced with such a challenge to God's test of Abraham in chap. 22. The way in which Jacob responds to the divine challenge is as relevant as that of Abraham for the future of this family. Just as God's tests of Abraham and Jacob are attuned to their particular way of being and doing (Abraham is no wrestler!), so also is Jacob's response (like Abraham's) true to who he is. And God's commendation responds directly to the strengths they exhibit in this challenge (cf. 22:16 with 32:28).

Others have compared this text with Exod 4:24-26, a divine attack on Moses.[183] The goal there is more explicit ("seek to kill"); here it is, at least, an act of bodily coercion, a challenging of Jacob at the deepest levels of his being. We do not know the motivation of the assailant in either text, but both texts are associated with a dangerous moment of transition in their lives.

Such struggles might be viewed as divinely initiated exercises in human becoming, of shaping and sharpening the faithfulness of the human beings involved for the deep challenges to be faced. God's engagement in such moments in people's lives is always a gracious move, informed most basically by faithfulness to promises made, and in the interests of health, peace, and well-being.

3. How could Jacob even stay in the ring with God? First, this text does not speak of God

183. See discussion in Fretheim, *Exodus*, 75-81.

in all of God's glory; God has taken on human form and stooped to encounter Jacob at his own level. Second, contrary to most commentators, we find no hint that God could have overwhelmed Jacob at any moment God chose. God does not play games with Jacob; God actually struggles with him. With human beings such as Jacob (cf. Abraham; Moses), God commits to a genuine encounter, entering deeply into the struggle with Jacob with a kind of power that doesn't simply overpower him. The power God has available appears commensurate with the nondivine power present in the situation. The divine power differs from the human by the way in which it is exercised. We see a divine restlessness and relentlessness in this moment of encounter, and an indomitable divine will at work on behalf of Jacob. God watches for openings, for opportunities to enhance the divine purpose in Jacob's life. Further, God retains certain kinds of power; God is able to do with Jacob's name what Jacob is not able to do with God's. The blessing comes from God; Jacob does not generate blessings for himself. For all of Jacob's powers, he recognizes the need of a blessing that he can finally only receive from God.

4. The confrontation with Esau mirrors the encounter with God. In some sense, God functions as a substitute for Esau, yet the "man" does not equal Esau. Jacob moves from seeing the face of God to seeing the face of Esau, and he testifies that seeing Esau's face is *like* seeing God's face (33:10). The obverse also seems true in retrospect: Seeing God's face is like seeing Esau's face. What Jacob had expected from Esau was hostility; he got graciousness. What Jacob might have expected from God was graciousness (in view of the prayer in vv. 9-12); he did get that, but only on the far side of an attack. The actual encounter between Jacob and Esau proves to be different from the experience Jacob has with God, but there are still a number of similarities (see commentary on chap. 33).

At the same time, the victory appears ambiguous, for Jacob recognizes that, if he had truly seen God, he would have died. Hence Jacob confesses that God has been his deliverer, and he experiences graciousness at God's (and Esau's) hand. God puts him through the encounter in advance.

The prayer for deliverance (נצל *nāṣal*) from Esau (32:11) is realized initially in being preserved (*nāṣal*, 32:30) in the struggle with God. Jacob prays for deliverance from Esau; God delivers Jacob from *God*. This prior deliverance does not resolve the conflict with Esau, however. Jacob still must face that. But the deliverance from God symbolizes Jacob's future deliverance from Esau. Jacob does not say he has prevailed; only God says that. Jacob understands the event, rather, in terms of his own deliverance.

5. God may encounter people in conflictual times by taking the very form of the anticipated difficulty. "In the night, the divine antagonist tends to take on the features of others with whom we struggle in the day."[184] Having been through such a time with God provides a gracious rehearsal for the actual life circumstance. To refuse to engage with God in that struggling moment denies oneself a God-given resource. To go through it with God before we go through it with others provides resources of strength and blessing for whatever lies in the wings of life.

Israel knows that wrestling with God can have both internal and external effects, even though God has not been seen and no blows to the body have been felt. Other texts about a *verbal* wrestling between God and key figures function similarly to this one (one thinks of Abraham in chap. 18 or Moses).

6. While we might conclude that the members of the community of faith ought to learn from Jacob to struggle with God, we should remember that God takes the initiative here. The issue is how Israel will *respond* to God's initiative. At the least, this means that Israel's response

184. Brueggemann, *Genesis*, 267.

to God ought not to be passive or submissive, acquiescent in the face of God's engagement with us. Moses appears as a new Jacob in this regard. An individual may hang on to God, claiming the promises, persisting in the relationship.

When it comes to struggles in daily life, we can count on God's mixing it up with us, challenging us, convicting us, evaluating us, judging us. We may have to place our life at risk, knowing that the one who loses life will find it. God honors the relationship both by engaging in the struggle in the first place and by persisting in that struggle through thick and thin. The most meticulous of preparations cannot guarantee a certain shape for the future. God may break into life and force a new direction for thought and action.

7. This text belongs to a larger story about the experience of two communities (Israel and Edom). Jacob's descendants know that this wrestler with God symbolizes their own experience with their neighbors as well as with God and that, somehow, these relationships are interrelated. Conflicts at the interhuman level have an effect on the God-human relationship, and vice versa. Hence we should understand this text not only in terms of the dynamics of the relationship between individuals or between an individual and God, but in communal terms. "This event did not simply occur at a definite biographical point in Jacob's life, but as it is now related it is clearly transparent as a type of that which Israel experienced from time to time with God. Israel has here presented its entire history with God almost prophetically as such a struggle until the breaking of the day."[185]

185. Von Rad, *Genesis*, 325.

GENESIS 33:1-17, JACOB'S MEETING WITH ESAU

33 Jacob looked up and there was Esau, coming with his four hundred men; so he divided the children among Leah, Rachel and the two maidservants. ²He put the maidservants and their children in front, Leah and her children next, and Rachel and Joseph in the rear. ³He himself went on ahead and bowed down to the ground seven times as he approached his brother.

⁴But Esau ran to meet Jacob and embraced him; he threw his arms around his neck and kissed him. And they wept. ⁵Then Esau looked up and saw the women and children. "Who are these with you?" he asked.

Jacob answered, "They are the children God has graciously given your servant."

⁶Then the maidservants and their children approached and bowed down. ⁷Next, Leah and her children came and bowed down. Last of all came Joseph and Rachel, and they too bowed down.

⁸Esau asked, "What do you mean by all these droves I met?"

33 Now Jacob looked up and saw Esau coming, and four hundred men with him. So he divided the children among Leah and Rachel and the two maids. ²He put the maids with their children in front, then Leah with her children, and Rachel and Joseph last of all. ³He himself went on ahead of them, bowing himself to the ground seven times, until he came near his brother.

4But Esau ran to meet him, and embraced him, and fell on his neck and kissed him, and they wept. ⁵When Esau looked up and saw the women and children, he said, "Who are these with you?" Jacob said, "The children whom God has graciously given your servant." ⁶Then the maids drew near, they and their children, and bowed down; ⁷Leah likewise and her children drew near and bowed down; and finally Joseph and Rachel drew near, and they bowed down. ⁸Esau said, "What do you mean by all this company that I met?" Jacob answered, "To find favor with my lord."

NIV

"To find favor in your eyes, my lord," he said.

9But Esau said, "I already have plenty, my brother. Keep what you have for yourself."

10"No, please!" said Jacob. "If I have found favor in your eyes, accept this gift from me. For to see your face is like seeing the face of God, now that you have received me favorably. 11Please accept the present that was brought to you, for God has been gracious to me and I have all I need." And because Jacob insisted, Esau accepted it.

12Then Esau said, "Let us be on our way; I'll accompany you."

13But Jacob said to him, "My lord knows that the children are tender and that I must care for the ewes and cows that are nursing their young. If they are driven hard just one day, all the animals will die. 14So let my lord go on ahead of his servant, while I move along slowly at the pace of the droves before me and that of the children, until I come to my lord in Seir."

15Esau said, "Then let me leave some of my men with you."

"But why do that?" Jacob asked. "Just let me find favor in the eyes of my lord."

16So that day Esau started on his way back to Seir. 17Jacob, however, went to Succoth, where he built a place for himself and made shelters for his livestock. That is why the place is called Succoth.a

a17 Succoth means shelters.

NRSV

9But Esau said, "I have enough, my brother; keep what you have for yourself." 10Jacob said, "No, please; if I find favor with you, then accept my present from my hand; for truly to see your face is like seeing the face of God—since you have received me with such favor. 11Please accept my gift that is brought to you, because God has dealt graciously with me, and because I have everything I want." So he urged him, and he took it.

12Then Esau said, "Let us journey on our way, and I will go alongside you." 13But Jacob said to him, "My lord knows that the children are frail and that the flocks and herds, which are nursing, are a care to me; and if they are overdriven for one day, all the flocks will die. 14Let my lord pass on ahead of his servant, and I will lead on slowly, according to the pace of the cattle that are before me and according to the pace of the children, until I come to my lord in Seir."

15So Esau said, "Let me leave with you some of the people who are with me." But he said, "Why should my lord be so kind to me?" 16So Esau returned that day on his way to Seir. 17But Jacob journeyed to Succoth,a and built himself a house, and made booths for his cattle; therefore the place is called Succoth.

a That is Booths

COMMENTARY

This chapter (mostly J) concludes the Jacob-Esau segment of the story of Jacob (except for the burial of their father, 35:29). While a reconciliation of integrity does take place between Jacob and Esau, they will not share a future together. They address past offenses (vv. 1-11), but they spar over the shape the future should take, and, finally, part ways (vv. 12-17). Such is the relationship between Jacob and Esau, Israel and Edom.

33:1-11. The opening verse is filled with tension. The gifts of 32:13-21 have arrived (v. 8), but we have not yet heard Esau's response. Jacob sees Esau coming with four hundred men and the

reader expects to hear about a fearful Jacob (as in 32:7, 11). But such will not be the case; moreover, the two companies' strategy has disappeared. Rather, Jacob arranges the women and children (only) in such a way that the most esteemed (Rachel and Joseph) come last, and hence will be introduced last (v. 7). Jacob himself goes ahead of them, bowing seven times like a vassal before his lord (perhaps an acceptance of wrongdoing). The author repeatedly notes that the women and children behave in comparable ways toward Esau (vv. 5-7).

This behavior suggests that Jacob's basic stance

toward Esau involves submission and stands as a fulfillment of the oracle in 27:40, a (temporary?) reversal of the oracle of 25:23 and the blessing of 27:29, 37. Key repetitions support this assessment: "lord" for Esau five times (33:8, 13-15; cf. 32:4-5, 18), his self-reference as "servant" of Esau (33:5, 14; cf. 32:4, 18, 20), and his concern to find favor in Esau's eyes (33:8, 10, 15; cf. 32:5). This language continues with that used by Jacob before Jabbok; the struggle at Jabbok introduces no changes in this language.

Yet, there are also points of discontinuity in Jacob from before Jabbok: (1) The encounter with God appears to have stayed his fear of Esau and eliminated fear-based strategies; Jacob makes himself vulnerable by moving toward Esau alone, unaccompanied by any of his company. (2) The gift remains intact, but the reason for it changes from appeasement (32:20) to gratitude (33:10). Although this development takes place after the encounter (see below), the encounter with God makes it possible. (3) The submissive language appears genuine. (4) Yet, Jacob does not grovel; he seeks to demonstrate through word and deed the change, indeed the reversal in the relationship between the brothers. (5) Jacob now functions more clearly as the progenitor of a people rather than as just an individual.

Jacob's solitary limping toward Esau and bowing to the ground constitutes clearly the vulnerable move that makes possible what happens next. But Esau, too, takes an important initiative: He runs to meet Jacob, embraces him, throws his arms around him, kisses him, and weeps with him. This impressive list of welcoming activities is unparalleled elsewhere in Genesis (the closest is 45:14-15, where Joseph makes himself known to his brothers; see also 29:11-13; 46:29; 48:10; 50:1; Luke 15:20). Hence, one should interpret Esau's moves positively; in fact, in that culture they may well have entailed forgiveness. Then, at Esau's initiative, Jacob's wives and children are introduced (vv. 5-7). Jacob witnesses publicly to God's graciousness (חן *ḥēn*, "undeserved favor") concerning his family's growth (cf. with v. 11 below), language most closely related to his prayer (32:10; cf. 31:5, 7, 42). Previously, Jacob had never done this. Here he attests to the theological role played previously by his wives, Leah and

Rachel (29:31–30:24). They have shown him the way.

Esau also asks about the "company" (מחנה *maḥăneh*) he has encountered (v. 8). This query plays on the word מנחה *minḥâ* (32:13, 18, 20-21), meaning the gift or tribute that Jacob sent on before him. Esau wants to know the *meaning* of this gift. Jacob's response repeats the earlier message to Esau (32:5): "to find favor [חן *ḥēn*] in his eyes" (v. 8). Jacob thereby links God's favor (v. 5) with Esau's, but in a wrong-headed manner. God's graciousness had come to him in a quite undeserved way, but now he would seek, in essence, to buy Esau's favor with all this property.

Esau's refusal of the gift on these grounds (v.9) brings Jacob's response to a new level. Jacob realizes from Esau's reply (e.g., "my brother") that he has *already* found favor with Esau (v. 10): "If I *have found* favor in your eyes . . . now that you *have received* me favorably" (italics added). Verse 10 proceeds from this new ground: Jacob now gives a *new* reason for extending the gift— namely, *gratitude;* because you have received me as God received me, accept my gift. The gift that was originally offered for purposes of appeasement (32:20) is, in fact, not necessary for reconciliation. Esau has forgiven Jacob quite apart from such an "offering." The "sacrifice" can now function as a "gift."

Jacob, once again, experiences the graciousness of God, this time extended through the face of his brother. Verse 11 testifies to this experience: Jacob now offers the gift not simply in gratitude to Esau, but in gratitude to *God.*

Verse 11 extends this discussion along other lines. The "gift" becomes "my blessing" (ברכה *běrākâ*), a clear reference to 27:35-37 (note the lord/servant language), but not to 28:3-4. It may be that Esau also accepts the gift because of the language of blessing that Jacob now uses for the first time. God's blessing has been at work in Jacob's life, and he now has all he needs. He now wants to give that blessing to Esau. He does not give the blessing "back" to Esau,[186] but the blessing that he has received has been so bountiful that it can flow through him to Esau as well (he does not give everything he has to Esau, vv. 13-14, 17). Hence, God's word to Jacob (28:14)

186. Compare Westermann, *Genesis 12–36*, 526.

is specifically fulfilled with Esau: "All the families of the earth shall be blessed through you."

33:12-17. Esau accepts Jacob's offer. Even more, he offers to accompany Jacob on his journey. Surprisingly, Jacob deflects Esau's offer, asking him to pass on ahead to Seir; Jacob will follow with his company, but at a slower pace. Two observations are in order: (1) Jacob uses language that continues to defer to Esau—though not deceptive, it betrays that theirs has not become a truly brotherly relationship; (2) the reason Jacob gives (vv. 13-14) remains somewhat obscure, but it may mean that Jacob's family needs some independence to develop properly. Now separated from the family in Haran, Jacob's family must establish its own identity (see 30:30). Jacob's response may have been prompted by a perception that Esau's offer (v. 12) suggested a merger of their families. Yet, Jacob does offer to come along to Seir in due time. The fact that he doesn't (v. 17) must have something to do with the next exchange between them.

Esau takes Jacob's hesitation at face value and offers some of his people to help with the journey, thereby insisting on a close, ongoing relationship (v. 15). In response, Jacob puts an end to the conversation rather abruptly, but what he says is puzzling (compare NIV and NRSV). In view of the parallel expression in 32:29 (למה זה *lāmmâ zeh*), the NIV seems best[187]: "But why do that? . . . Just let me find favor in the eyes of my lord" (v. 15)—i.e., "This is all the further our relationship should go; it ought not to result in the merging of our families. I trust that we are reconciled, but our families and our futures should remain separate." Jacob's decision not to go to Seir comes in the wake of Esau's continuing to press against this matter (unwittingly?). We should also note that going back to Seir would have delayed fulfilling God's command to return to Canaan (31:3, 13).

Jacob and Esau separate, coming together again only at their father's funeral (35:29). But this shared responsibility, as well as the economic factors cited for Esau's return to Seir (see 36:6-8) make it clear that theirs is a separate relationship, but not without conversation and cooperation. Jacob goes to Succoth, on the east side of the Jordan, and settles his company there for an unknown period of time (v. 17).

187. Also ibid., 523.

REFLECTIONS

1. The narrative concludes in *reconciliation with separation and an open-ended future*. In view of what happens over time between their descendants (Edom and Israel; see Obadiah), this text seems remarkably evenhanded in its treatment of the relationship, even drawing an analogy between the graciousness of Esau and the graciousness of God (v. 10)! Overall, the narrator claims that continued conflict between the two is not a *necessary* future, set for all eternity by some word of the distant past. Even more, it claims that no matter how severe the conflict, or how deeply rooted in past history, reconciliation among brothers remains a possibility, even if that does not finally eventuate in a close relationship. The oracles in 25:23 and 27:27-29 stand in continuing tension with 27:40 (see 33:11), and that tension, in fact, describes their history with each other.

2. Seeing Esau's face so graciously turned toward him works not only parallel to, but as *an extension of* God's face, which Jacob finally saw (32:30). In metaphorical terms, Esau's face *is* the face of God for Jacob one more time: (a) their confrontation begins on a note of danger, with the potential of death; (b) they confront each other face to face, not simply at the psychological level, and engage in bodily struggle, involving the whole person; (c) they are both struggles or wrestlings; in fact, for Esau and Jacob it goes back into their mother's womb (25:22, 26). Struggle so characterizes Jacob that it will shape his relationship with everyone; (d) they both end on a gracious note, though only on the far side of the struggle; Jacob does not die—"my life is preserved." (e) Jacob does not deserve the kindness shown by both God and Esau. (f) They both end up on a "crippling" note: Jacob comes up lame in the encounter with God, and Jacob's encounter with Esau ends short of full reconciliation. (g) They both issue in new corporate realities. Jacob becomes Israel, and the families of Jacob and Esau proceed on to their lives in separate lands. "It is hard to identify the players. In the *holy God*, there is something of the *estranged brother*. And in the *forgiving brother*, there is something of the *blessing God*."[188]

The life one lives with God and the life one lives with other human beings are two sides of the same coin. They affect each other in deep and profound ways; what happens in one relationship has effects for good or evil on the other. Life with God cannot somehow be lived in isolation from one's sisters and brothers without harming both relationships (see Matt 5:22-24; 1 John 3:17; 4:20-21). Life with other humans cannot truly be lived out in isolation from God if we are to be what the Creator intended us to be. In either case, God will find a way to engage in such lives on behalf of the gracious divine purposes.

3. In and through Esau, God works to fulfill the promises of life and goodness on behalf of Jacob, not simply through salvation-historical ("churchly") events, but through the way in which individuals—even former enemies, whether within the family or without—respond to one another. This involves God's *creational* activity, at work beyond the borders of churchly properties and promised lands. But such creational activity remains fundamentally related to God's promissory work, not simply with Jacob but with nonchosen ones like Esau. God fulfills the promises through creative activity as well as through redemptive acts. The result for these related types of divine activity is the same: salvation, in this case, reconciliation between former enemies and the extension of blessings that have the potential of shaping families for the good.

188. Brueggemann, *Genesis*, 272.

GENESIS 33:18–34:31, THE RAPE OF DINAH

NIV

18After Jacob came from Paddan Aram,^a he arrived safely at the^b city of Shechem in Canaan and camped within sight of the city. 19For a hundred pieces of silver,^c he bought from the sons of Hamor, the father of Shechem, the plot of ground where he pitched his tent. 20There he set up an altar and called it El Elohe Israel.^d

34 Now Dinah, the daughter Leah had borne to Jacob, went out to visit the women of the land. 2When Shechem son of Hamor the Hivite, the ruler of that area, saw her, he took her and violated her. 3His heart was drawn to Dinah daughter of Jacob, and he loved the girl

a18 That is, Northwest Mesopotamia   b18 Or *arrived at Shalem, a*
c19 Hebrew *hundred kesitahs;* a kesitah was a unit of money of unknown weight and value.   d20 El Elohe Israel can mean *God, the God of Israel* or *mighty is the God of Israel.*

NRSV

18Jacob came safely to the city of Shechem, which is in the land of Canaan, on his way from Paddan-aram; and he camped before the city. 19And from the sons of Hamor, Shechem's father, he bought for one hundred pieces of money^a the plot of land on which he had pitched his tent. 20There he erected an altar and called it El-Elohe-Israel.^b

34 Now Dinah the daughter of Leah, whom she had borne to Jacob, went out to visit the women of the region. 2When Shechem son of Hamor the Hivite, prince of the region, saw her, he seized her and lay with her by force. 3And his soul was drawn to Dinah daughter of Jacob; he loved the girl, and spoke tenderly to her. 4So

a Heb *one hundred qesitah*   b That is *God, the God of Israel*

NIV

and spoke tenderly to her. ⁴And Shechem said to his father Hamor, "Get me this girl as my wife."

⁵When Jacob heard that his daughter Dinah had been defiled, his sons were in the fields with his livestock; so he kept quiet about it until they came home.

⁶Then Shechem's father Hamor went out to talk with Jacob. ⁷Now Jacob's sons had come in from the fields as soon as they heard what had happened. They were filled with grief and fury, because Shechem had done a disgraceful thing in*ᵃ* Israel by lying with Jacob's daughter—a thing that should not be done.

⁸But Hamor said to them, "My son Shechem has his heart set on your daughter. Please give her to him as his wife. ⁹Intermarry with us; give us your daughters and take our daughters for yourselves. ¹⁰You can settle among us; the land is open to you. Live in it, trade*ᵇ* in it, and acquire property in it."

¹¹Then Shechem said to Dinah's father and brothers, "Let me find favor in your eyes, and I will give you whatever you ask. ¹²Make the price for the bride and the gift I am to bring as great as you like, and I'll pay whatever you ask me. Only give me the girl as my wife."

¹³Because their sister Dinah had been defiled, Jacob's sons replied deceitfully as they spoke to Shechem and his father Hamor. ¹⁴They said to them, "We can't do such a thing; we can't give our sister to a man who is not circumcised. That would be a disgrace to us. ¹⁵We will give our consent to you on one condition only: that you become like us by circumcising all your males. ¹⁶Then we will give you our daughters and take your daughters for ourselves. We'll settle among you and become one people with you. ¹⁷But if you will not agree to be circumcised, we'll take our sister*ᶜ* and go."

¹⁸Their proposal seemed good to Hamor and his son Shechem. ¹⁹The young man, who was the most honored of all his father's household, lost no time in doing what they said, because he was delighted with Jacob's daughter. ²⁰So Hamor and his son Shechem went to the gate of their city to speak to their fellow townsmen. ²¹"These men are

ᵃ7 Or against   ᵇ10 Or move about freely; also in verse 21
ᶜ17 Hebrew daughter

NRSV

Shechem spoke to his father Hamor, saying, "Get me this girl to be my wife."

5Now Jacob heard that Shechem*ᵃ* had defiled his daughter Dinah; but his sons were with his cattle in the field, so Jacob held his peace until they came. ⁶And Hamor the father of Shechem went out to Jacob to speak with him, ⁷just as the sons of Jacob came in from the field. When they heard of it, the men were indignant and very angry, because he had committed an outrage in Israel by lying with Jacob's daughter, for such a thing ought not to be done.

8But Hamor spoke with them, saying, "The heart of my son Shechem longs for your daughter; please give her to him in marriage. ⁹Make marriages with us; give your daughters to us, and take our daughters for yourselves. ¹⁰You shall live with us; and the land shall be open to you; live and trade in it, and get property in it." ¹¹Shechem also said to her father and to her brothers, "Let me find favor with you, and whatever you say to me I will give. ¹²Put the marriage present and gift as high as you like, and I will give whatever you ask me; only give me the girl to be my wife."

13The sons of Jacob answered Shechem and his father Hamor deceitfully, because he had defiled their sister Dinah. ¹⁴They said to them, "We cannot do this thing, to give our sister to one who is uncircumcised, for that would be a disgrace to us. ¹⁵Only on this condition will we consent to you: that you will become as we are and every male among you be circumcised. ¹⁶Then we will give our daughters to you, and we will take your daughters for ourselves, and we will live among you and become one people. ¹⁷But if you will not listen to us and be circumcised, then we will take our daughter and be gone."

18Their words pleased Hamor and Hamor's son Shechem. ¹⁹And the young man did not delay to do the thing, because he was delighted with Jacob's daughter. Now he was the most honored of all his family. ²⁰So Hamor and his son Shechem came to the gate of their city and spoke to the men of their city, saying, ²¹"These people are friendly with us; let them live in the land and trade in it, for the land is large enough for them; let us take their daughters in marriage, and let us

ᵃ Heb he

NIV

friendly toward us," they said. "Let them live in our land and trade in it; the land has plenty of room for them. We can marry their daughters and they can marry ours. 22But the men will consent to live with us as one people only on the condition that our males be circumcised, as they themselves are. 23Won't their livestock, their property and all their other animals become ours? So let us give our consent to them, and they will settle among us."

24All the men who went out of the city gate agreed with Hamor and his son Shechem, and every male in the city was circumcised.

25Three days later, while all of them were still in pain, two of Jacob's sons, Simeon and Levi, Dinah's brothers, took their swords and attacked the unsuspecting city, killing every male. 26They put Hamor and his son Shechem to the sword and took Dinah from Shechem's house and left. 27The sons of Jacob came upon the dead bodies and looted the city where*a* their sister had been defiled. 28They seized their flocks and herds and donkeys and everything else of theirs in the city and out in the fields. 29They carried off all their wealth and all their women and children, taking as plunder everything in the houses.

30Then Jacob said to Simeon and Levi, "You have brought trouble on me by making me a stench to the Canaanites and Perizzites, the people living in this land. We are few in number, and if they join forces against me and attack me, I and my household will be destroyed."

31But they replied, "Should he have treated our sister like a prostitute?"

a27 Or because

NRSV

give them our daughters. 22Only on this condition will they agree to live among us, to become one people: that every male among us be circumcised as they are circumcised. 23Will not their livestock, their property, and all their animals be ours? Only let us agree with them, and they will live among us." 24And all who went out of the city gate heeded Hamor and his son Shechem; and every male was circumcised, all who went out of the gate of his city.

25On the third day, when they were still in pain, two of the sons of Jacob, Simeon and Levi, Dinah's brothers, took their swords and came against the city unawares, and killed all the males. 26They killed Hamor and his son Shechem with the sword, and took Dinah out of Shechem's house, and went away. 27And the other sons of Jacob came upon the slain, and plundered the city, because their sister had been defiled. 28They took their flocks and their herds, their donkeys, and whatever was in the city and in the field. 29All their wealth, all their little ones and their wives, all that was in the houses, they captured and made their prey. 30Then Jacob said to Simeon and Levi, "You have brought trouble on me by making me odious to the inhabitants of the land, the Canaanites and the Perizzites; my numbers are few, and if they gather themselves against me and attack me, I shall be destroyed, both I and my household." 31But they said, "Should our sister be treated like a whore?"

COMMENTARY

Many scholars have thought this chapter to be an isolated narrative, inserted haphazardly into the story of Jacob. Newer literary-critical work, on the other hand, tends to view the chapter as an integral part of Jacob's story.[189] Moreover, one may

189. For different readings, see M. Sternberg, *The Poetics of Biblical Narrative* (Bloomington: Indiana University Press, 1985) 445-75; D. Fewell and D. Gunn, "Tipping the Balance: Sternberg's Reader and the Rape of Dinah," *JBL* 110 (1991) 193-211.

discern continuities with other Genesis narratives—e.g., the interrelationship of this family with outsiders, or the way the narrative helps to fill in the story of the children of Jacob (especially Dinah, Simeon, and Levi). In addition, there are continuities regarding issues of marriage with those outside the family, circumcision, deception, and family conflict and violence. Perhaps most important, the sharp and unambiguous judgment (indeed, a curse!) by Jacob on the violence of Simeon and Levi must stand as the primary clue about how we should interpret this chapter (49:5-7).

Although the narrative may reflect early tribal history, including issues of land settlement in the Shechem area (see Joshua 24), ethnological considerations should play a minimal role in interpreting the chapter in its present context. Simeon, Levi, and the other sons of Jacob do attack a city (vv. 25-29), but they are not presented as tribes in this text. Moreover, given the basically positive assessment of the Canaanites here and elsewhere in Genesis, later Canaanite issues are probably not mirrored in this chapter, except to suggest that the roots of those later troubles may stem from this ancestral time.

The story consists of six scenes: Jacob's settlement in the Shechem area (33:18-20); Shechem's rape of Dinah and his request to make Dinah his wife (34:1-4); the negotiations between the two families regarding this request (34:5-18); the fulfillment of the agreement by Hamor's family (34:19-24); the rape of the city of Shechem by Simeon and Levi (34:25-29); the exchange between Jacob and his sons (34:30-31). Moreover, since 35:1 appears as God's response to the question broached in 34:31, chaps. 34 and 35 are drawn more closely together.

33:18-20. The transition to vv. 18-20 seems abrupt, introducing a new stage in Jacob's life. No longer associated with the land of Laban, he enters the land of promise, safely or "whole" (שלם *šālēm*), fulfilling the divine command (31:3, 13). His purchase of a plot near Shechem parallels the action of Abraham in chap. 23 and signals another claim to the promised land (as a burial ground, see Josh 24:32). Shechem is both the name of the city in which Jacob settles (33:18)—later, a significant Israelite center (Joshua 24)—and the name of the son of Hamor, from whom Jacob buys the land (33:19).

At this auspicious moment of entering the land of promise, Jacob erects an altar and calls it El Elohe Israel ("God, the God of Israel"; cf. 35:7). Inasmuch as *El* was the name of the Creator God worshiped at pre-Israelite Shechem, this act signals yet another claim: The God of this land is the God of Israel. The "Israel" in God's name has a dual reference: to Jacob, whose name is *Israel*

(32:29), and to his "household" (34:30), for whom this moment is an important point in their historical journey.

34:1-4. Dinah is the first child of Jacob to whom the narrator devotes attention (30:21). She pays a visit to other (Canaanite) women in the Shechem area; such openness to outsiders is not unusual for Genesis. The author depicts this visit as entirely natural. The reference to Leah alludes to Dinah's full brothers, Simeon and Levi (vv. 25, 31; Judah is also a full brother), and ought not to be viewed negatively. The journey proves to be unsafe. Suddenly, a Hivite (i.e., Canaanite) named Shechem, the "most honored" (v. 19) member of the ruling family of the city-state, rapes her (see below). The narrator may assume that they know each other (see 33:19); he immediately moves to Shechem's next action.

In the *narrator's* words, Shechem proceeds to act in a way atypical of rapists: He clings to Dinah (as in 2:24), loves her (as Isaac and Jacob love Rebekah and Rachel—24:67; 29:18, 30), and speaks to her heart (as Joseph does to his brothers, 50:21). The latter phrase may cause Dinah's positive response.[190] As revolting as the rape of Dinah is, this turn of events shifts the reader's response to Shechem in more positive directions. Moreover, the presence of love language for Dinah on the part of both Hamor and the narrator (vv. 8, 19, words also used of God's love and delight) reinforces Shechem's sincerity. Sympathy for Shechem continues to develop based on his generous statement in vv. 11-12. At the same time, this language predisposes the reader to be alert to the sons of Jacob.

In asking his father to make arrangements for Dinah to become his wife ("get" is typical language for this; cf. 24:3-7, 37-40), Shechem conforms to Israel's own legal tradition (Exod 22:16-17; Deut 22:28-29). If a man rapes an unbetrothed virgin, he has to pay the father, marry the woman, and is "not permitted to divorce her as long as he lives." This law sought to preserve as much honor in the situation as possible, including the honor of the raped woman, who would live in disgrace if she remained unmarried in her father's house. In that world, Shechem's offer was in Dinah's best interests (cf. 2 Sam 13:16). All

190. See Fewell and Gunn, "Balance," 196.

indications are that Dinah had been drawn into the house of Shechem and the two had fallen in love. Hence, when the brothers murder Shechem and "take" Dinah (לקח *lāqaḥ,* v. 26, the word also used for the rape, v. 2) without consulting her, they ignore this legal tradition.

34:5-18. When Jacob first hears of the rape of Dinah (by means unknown), he holds his peace (used in 24:21 to buy time for learning); he waits to consult with his sons before taking action. The author understands this reticence positively (cf. v. 30). In the verses enclosing chap. 34 (33:20; 35:1-4), Jacob focuses properly on the God who has made promises to him. One can best assess Jacob's attitude in chap. 34 as one of prudence and care, informed by the worship of God and in view of a future in the land of promise that is in some jeopardy.

Hamor consults with Jacob (vv. 6-8); the sons' entry in v. 7 interrupts the fathers. When they heard what had happened, but without benefit of consultation with Jacob (as he had hoped, v. 5), the sons were upset and angry, expressed in the phrase "an outrage in [or, against] Israel" (v. 7), which clearly has later Israel in view (cf. Deut 22:21; Judg 20:6, 10; 1 Sam 13:12). At this point, they seem to have the interests of the larger community at heart. Yet, the "outrage" focuses, not on Dinah's rape, but on her having been "lain with," something that "ought not to be done." Their response focuses on the past; without apparent concern for the future (vv. 13, 27).

Both Shechem and his father enter into negotiations with Jacob and (now) his sons for Dinah's hand. The rapist and lover of Dinah, as well as the head of his family, seek to make things right; indeed, they go beyond Israel's own law in doing so. Hamor speaks first (vv. 8-10). His proposal is expansive, piling up verbs denoting generosity (cf. Abimelech's offer in 20:15; cf. 13:9). He moves beyond Shechem's marriage to Dinah to include openness to other marriages and an invitation for Jacob's family to live freely among them and to own property. Verses 20-23 make clear that this is sincere, with mutual benefits—theirs will be ours, and ours theirs. Whereupon Shechem enters the negotiations; he is even more generous and open to the future, offering to give any gift (cf. Exod 22:16-17) and to pay any price, perhaps to Dinah, for her hand in marriage. The language of

"taking" has turned into the language of "giving." In fact, he opens himself to being cheated by Jacob's sons. Such generosity was certainly not necessary on his part, given the numerical advantage (v. 30).

The sons of Jacob (all of them!), without their father, resume the negotiations (vv. 13-17), even though Jacob had been addressed earlier (vv. 6, 8, and 11). A possible explanation for his absence is the word *deceitfully* in v. 13 (cf. 27:35); that word does not describe Jacob, though apparently he is not opposed to the form of the negotiations. Hamor would not have made the move he does in vv. 20-24 if Jacob had not been included. The fact that the phrase "because he had defiled their sister Dinah" immediately follows the word *deceitfully*—such evaluations are rare for the narrator in Genesis—is instructive. They believe that what Shechem has done justifies a deceitful response. Thus the reader finds no ambiguity regarding their motivation; this is a trick, pure and simple; they intend to exact vengeance. And they use religion as a vehicle for their deception!

What Shechem did to Dinah, "the outrage in Israel," has dropped from view altogether; the uncircumcised status has become the "disgrace"—a disgrace *to the brothers.* Somehow their honor, rather than Dinah's, has become the issue. In effect, Jacob's sons are promising that Shechem and his family will be incorporated into the family of Abraham: "You will become as we are"; "we will . . . become one people" (repeated in vv. 21-22). If they do not agree, the parties will go their separate ways (the NRSV's "daughter" and the NIV's "sister" are both possible, but see NIV in v. 8). We find no sign of the violence that is to come.

34:19-24. Hamor and Shechem consider the proposal "good," though the reader knows (v. 13) what they consider good will destroy them. But the author presents them as trusting, even naive, persons who deeply want to bring Dinah and Shechem together. Shechem apparently immediately moves to be circumcised (v. 19). The writer places the phrase "most honored of all his family" strategically; it accents the integrity with which he responds. His honor will bring honor to Dinah, precisely what Israel's law called for in such a situation. The fifth (!) reference to his love for

Dinah reinforces the sincerity of his desire for this marriage.

In vv. 20-24, Hamor and Shechem take the negotiated terms to their "city council" for ratification (cf. chap. 23). Their speech is marked by hortatory language designed to persuade an understandably reluctant group, hence the emphasis on economic advantage; no deceit appears, for they could simply have confiscated Jacob's goods if they had wanted. They do not mention the rape, but given the extent to which the word had spread (vv. 5, 7), we may presume the council knew about it. Hamor's and Shechem's words about friendship (šālēm is translated "safely" in 33:18) stand in ironic contrast with the "deceit" of v. 13. By disclosing what Hamor says in the privacy of his own council, the narrator emphasizes that Hamor negotiates in good faith. This integrity intensifies when the entire council agrees to submit to this painful and *identity-establishing* ritual. In other words, they recognize Israel's peculiar chosenness and make the necessary overtures to join them; hence Israel has made no compromise at this point.

Circumcision as an identity-establishing rite makes it an even greater gesture on the part of the Shechemite community. (Does not their circumcision in fact incorporate them?) Certainly, for the reader, this would in effect mean—in view of chap. 17 and the repetition of 17:10 in 34:15—the Shechemites have agreed to be integrated into the Abrahamic family. The repetition in v. 24 (the threefold use of כל [kol, "all," "every"]) stresses the unanimity of the city council.

34:25-29. Simeon and Levi (two of Dinah's full brothers) take the initiative in following through on the deceit they and their brothers have schemed; they break faith with their new blood brothers, weakened by the circumcision. (Note that the noun for "pain" is also used for Israel in Egypt, Exod 3:7!) Entering the city by stealth (necessary for two people to kill so many), they murder Hamor, Shechem, and all the males of the city in cold blood. The "sons of Jacob" (v. 27; the NRSV inserts "other," but 49:5-7 assumes that Simeon and Levi are also involved) take advantage of the situation and pillage the city, taking all of the women (lāqaḥ must include rape, v. 2), children, animals, indeed, everything they could lay their hands on. The text specifically identifies this wholesale action against the city as revenge for what had been done to Dinah (v. 27; the NIV expresses not cause but place, "where"). Yet, the extensive detail (the accusative particle is used nine times!) yields an "overkill," a blood feud mentality. Even more, the fact that the brothers kept their "spoil" for themselves is highly problematic.[191] In addition, they "take" (lāqaḥ, cf. v. 2!) Dinah out of Shechem's house without consulting her. The narrative implies that Dinah was not being detained against her will, so this was probably not a happy occasion for her.

34:30-31. In this concluding exchange, Jacob opposes the violent actions of Simeon and Levi because of what it may mean for the future of the family (i.e., Israel); this verse must be read in the canonical context provided by 49:5-7, with its reference to the sons' violence, murder, anger, and cruelty against people and animals. Israel's reputation has been besmirched and the trust gained has been violated, with developing good relationships between the families, once so promising, now deeply compromised. If the Canaanites should decide to seek revenge, Jacob's family in its minority status would certainly be destroyed. The future may well have been put at risk.

Ignoring Jacob's perspective on the matter, Simeon and Levi voice an opinion: "Should our sister be treated like a whore?" Note that the brothers introduce a new thought—harlotry. What actually happened to Dinah is thereby blurred; what happens to harlots is not usually called rape. The focus thereby shifts from the violent abuse of Dinah and her rights (appropriate legal restitution) to the brothers' own reputation or honor. The brothers may be accusing their father of mistreating Dinah by his comment, "selling" her for "peace at all costs." If so, that would be ironic, for they have just *used* Dinah and her situation and *taken* her without her consent in order to gain for themselves honor and great wealth (cf. God's response to Achan's comparable actions in Josh 7:11, where the language of "trouble" also appears, 6:18; 7:25). By leaving the reader with the sons' question, standing over against the word of the head of the family oriented toward life and promise, the narrator shows how narrow and self-serving their perspective and actions have

---

191. See Brueggemann, *Genesis*, 278.

been. The question also leaves the reader with an agenda to consider: How would they respond?

God responds to the question with a word about settling elsewhere and worshiping God (35:1). Jacob's response exhibits faithfulness, commanding his household (cf. 34:30), including his sons, to put away foreign gods and to purify themselves. The earlier distress Jacob recalls (35:3) may be parallel to this moment; he is in special need of divine protection (forthcoming in 35:5).

REFLECTIONS

1. The literary brackets provided by vv. 1-2 and v. 31 raise the issue of Dinah's abusive treatment. Two types of references to Dinah stand in counterpoint: (1) the many-faceted love that Shechem has for her (vv. 3, 8, 19); it is no small tribute to Dinah that her rapist goes to the lengths he does (finally giving his life!) to obey the law and arrange for marriage with her; (2) the violence against her: seized and raped (v. 2); defiled (vv. 5, 13, 27); suffered an outrage (v. 7); "taken" by her own brothers (v. 26); treated like a whore (v. 31). The same verb (ענה 'ānâ) for what Dinah suffered (v. 2) describes Israel's oppression in Egypt (15:13; Exod 3:7); it was also used for Sarah's treatment of Hagar (16:6). Dinah, an oppressed one, prefigures Israel's own violation at the hands of other outsiders (cf. Isa 53:4).

Why is Dinah, the only daughter of Israel, made the victim of rape and then silenced? One could simply decry the patriarchy involved, but this text gives Bible readers permission to talk openly about rape and the sorry history of society's response, including the silencing of victims. Has this text contributed to that silence?

2. The text raises another issue: the role of the family of Hamor and their interaction with Jacob's family. The larger Genesis context helps in assessing the role of this Canaanite family. While outsiders are almost always viewed in a positive light, the relationship of Abraham's family to them has often stood in sharp contrast to the divine intention (12:3*b*). This chapter offers another instance in which the community of faith fails to serve as a channel for the blessing of God to outsiders. Rather than treat the rape of Dinah according to the law, as Hamor's family was openly willing to do, Israel takes the way of anarchy and violence. Rather than honor a genuine change on the part of Dinah's victimizers, the brothers ignore it and take a sharply overdrawn retributive form of behavior that serves to alienate the outsider. Dinah certainly suffered injustice at the hands of outsiders, but her brothers respond in kind. The deep suffering that Dinah had to undergo could have served as a vehicle for a greater good, but the violent response deepens her suffering. Israel loses the opportunity to bring good out of suffering, and Dinah becomes even more of a victim.

The temptation for the oppressed to become oppressors themselves offers an all too prevalent possibility, a turning-the-tables kind of mentality that places them precisely in the position of those who perpetrated the violence in the first place. The frequently used motif that Israelites should treat the stranger as God would treat them reminds them of this temptation (Exod 23:9).

3. The claim that the text expresses concern about intermarriage with Canaanites, or exogamy generally, appears unlikely (Deut 7:2-3 reflects a later concern shaped by particular contextual realities). The generations following Jacob, now cut off from the family in Haran, must necessarily take wives outside the family; witness Judah (and his sons; chap. 38) and Joseph (41:45; cf. Moses). Some may have deemed intermarriage with the Shechemites a positive development, but Dinah's brothers subvert it by their violent behaviors. Issues of the "politics of sex," sexual hospitality for purposes of political advantage, may have informed an earlier version of this story, but not in its present form.

4. Jacob's concern (v. 30) sharply raises the issue of the future of the chosen family. In fact, Jacob envisions the possibility that his family will be "destroyed." Jacob obviously desired a positive relationship with the inhabitants of the land. But how will the promises of God to this family be fulfilled in view of this changed relationship to the people of the land? The relationship between Israel and these peoples, two of whom are mentioned (Canaanites and Perizzites), reaches back to 13:7 and 15:18-21. In the latter text God promises Abraham the land of these peoples. But the fulfillment of the promise does not necessarily entail violence. The divine intention may have included a less violent relationship with the present inhabitants (15:16 lifts up a note of judgment). This chapter may seek to explain one reason for the violent shape of the later conflict between Israel and these peoples. The behaviors of Jacob's family subverted divine intentions and promoted violence in relationship to the Canaanites (again, see 49:5-7). Is it possible that these actions set up the situation in the land in such a way that only violence could bring about the fulfillment of the promise? This would lead to formulations such as those found in Exod 23:23; 33:2; 34:11; and Deut 7:1-5.

5. Jacob's response (v. 30) focuses on the effects of the violence for the larger issues of life and well-being for the *community* ("I and my household"); this implies a judgment on the violence (made explicit in 49:5-7). Communal well-being remains a key issue. How the family relates to its neighbors becomes relevant for the shape that its life takes, both internally (for Israel) and externally (for the fulfillment of 12:3*b*). The brothers have sacrificed long-range objectives for the sake of short-term advantage, using their sister's predicament as an excuse to perpetrate violence. Such settling of accounts sounds suspiciously like modern governments or individuals that use a wrong done at one level to justify a long-contemplated action that seeks to defend "honor."

The author presents issues of violence at multiple levels. The violence against Dinah and the violence against the Canaanites both come in for criticism. The story illustrates how violence begets violence; a response of violence sets in motion even deeper levels of violence and in the end places the future of the chosen family in jeopardy. This makes it necessary for God to enter into a much more compromised situation in order to answer the divine promises. This way of violence on the part of Jacob's sons continues in the story of Joseph. Violence against the outsider leads to violence within the family (cf. Matt 26:52 [NRSV]: "All who take the sword will perish by the sword").

This development would be congruent with Jacob's evaluation in 49:5-7; their violence results in the families of Simeon and Levi being divided and scattered. Simeon does not survive as a tribe, being absorbed into other groups; members of the tribe of Levi do become a priestly class, but with no tribal land.

6. The brothers' use of circumcision in their deception doubtless constituted an effort to make the Shechemites "pay" in the bodily organ that was the instrument of Dinah's rape. Yet, the inclusion of "every male" goes way beyond any measure-for-measure understanding; adding the rape of all the women of Shechem extends the irresponsible character of the brothers' response. Moreover, the use of circumcision for such a purpose appears highly questionable. They use circumcision as a vehicle for death rather than life, for separating people rather than uniting them in a single community. This will not be the first time that the people of God have used religious practice as a vehicle for deception and violence!

7. We find no explicit God language in this chapter. The persons involved are entrusted with decision making that matters, and they will reap the effects of their own behaviors. At the same time, the chapter is bracketed by God language (33:20; 35:1); God is engaged behind the scenes, working in and through even these levels of violence on behalf of the divine purposes. Yet, the actions of Jacob's sons have drawn their God into a highly compromised situation; God now must work in and through the violence in order to move toward the fulfillment of the divine purposes. Explicitly religious concerns are evident in references to defilement and circumcision, implying that theological issues are close to the surface.

GENESIS 35:1-29, THE JOURNEYS OF JACOB

NIV

35 Then God said to Jacob, "Go up to Bethel and settle there, and build an altar there to God, who appeared to you when you were fleeing from your brother Esau."

²So Jacob said to his household and to all who were with him, "Get rid of the foreign gods you have with you, and purify yourselves and change your clothes. ³Then come, let us go up to Bethel, where I will build an altar to God, who answered me in the day of my distress and who has been with me wherever I have gone." ⁴So they gave Jacob all the foreign gods they had and the rings in their ears, and Jacob buried them under the oak at Shechem. ⁵Then they set out, and the terror of God fell upon the towns all around them so that no one pursued them.

⁶Jacob and all the people with him came to Luz (that is, Bethel) in the land of Canaan. ⁷There he built an altar, and he called the place El Bethel,ᵃ because it was there that God revealed himself to him when he was fleeing from his brother.

⁸Now Deborah, Rebekah's nurse, died and was buried under the oak below Bethel. So it was named Allon Bacuth.ᵇ

⁹After Jacob returned from Paddan Aram,ᶜ God appeared to him again and blessed him. ¹⁰God said to him, "Your name is Jacob,ᵈ but you will no longer be called Jacob; your name will be Israel.ᵉ" So he named him Israel.

¹¹And God said to him, "I am God Almightyᶠ; be fruitful and increase in number. A nation and a community of nations will come from you, and kings will come from your body. ¹²The land I gave to Abraham and Isaac I also give to you, and I will give this land to your descendants after you." ¹³Then God went up from him at the place where he had talked with him.

¹⁴Jacob set up a stone pillar at the place where God had talked with him, and he poured out a drink offering on it; he also poured oil on it. ¹⁵Jacob called the place where God had talked with him Bethel.ᵍ

ᵃ7 *El Bethel* means *God of Bethel.*   ᵇ8 *Allon Bacuth* means *oak of weeping.*   ᶜ9 That is, Northwest Mesopotamia; also in verse 26
ᵈ10 *Jacob* means *he grasps the heel* (figuratively, *he deceives*).
ᵉ10 *Israel* means *he struggles with God.*   ᶠ11 Hebrew *El-Shaddai*
ᵍ15 *Bethel* means *house of God.*

NRSV

35 God said to Jacob, "Arise, go up to Bethel, and settle there. Make an altar there to the God who appeared to you when you fled from your brother Esau." ²So Jacob said to his household and to all who were with him, "Put away the foreign gods that are among you, and purify yourselves, and change your clothes; ³then come, let us go up to Bethel, that I may make an altar there to the God who answered me in the day of my distress and has been with me wherever I have gone." ⁴So they gave to Jacob all the foreign gods that they had, and the rings that were in their ears; and Jacob hid them under the oak that was near Shechem.

5As they journeyed, a terror from God fell upon the cities all around them, so that no one pursued them. ⁶Jacob came to Luz (that is, Bethel), which is in the land of Canaan, he and all the people who were with him, ⁷and there he built an altar and called the place El-bethel,ᵃ because it was there that God had revealed himself to him when he fled from his brother. ⁸And Deborah, Rebekah's nurse, died, and she was buried under an oak below Bethel. So it was called Allon-bacuth.ᵇ

9God appeared to Jacob again when he came from Paddan-aram, and he blessed him. ¹⁰God said to him, "Your name is Jacob; no longer shall you be called Jacob, but Israel shall be your name." So he was called Israel. ¹¹God said to him, "I am God Almighty:ᶜ be fruitful and multiply; a nation and a company of nations shall come from you, and kings shall spring from you. ¹²The land that I gave to Abraham and Isaac I will give to you, and I will give the land to your offspring after you." ¹³Then God went up from him at the place where he had spoken with him. ¹⁴Jacob set up a pillar in the place where he had spoken with him, a pillar of stone; and he poured out a drink offering on it, and poured oil on it. ¹⁵So Jacob called the place where God had spoken with him Bethel.

16Then they journeyed from Bethel; and when they were still some distance from Ephrath, Ra-

ᵃ That is *God of Bethel*   ᵇ That is *Oak of weeping*
ᶜ Traditional rendering of Heb *El Shaddai*

NIV

¹⁶Then they moved on from Bethel. While they were still some distance from Ephrath, Rachel began to give birth and had great difficulty. ¹⁷And as she was having great difficulty in childbirth, the midwife said to her, "Don't be afraid, for you have another son." ¹⁸As she breathed her last—for she was dying—she named her son Ben-Oni.ᵃ But his father named him Benjamin.ᵇ

¹⁹So Rachel died and was buried on the way to Ephrath (that is, Bethlehem). ²⁰Over her tomb Jacob set up a pillar, and to this day that pillar marks Rachel's tomb.

²¹Israel moved on again and pitched his tent beyond Migdal Eder. ²²While Israel was living in that region, Reuben went in and slept with his father's concubine Bilhah, and Israel heard of it.

Jacob had twelve sons:
²³The sons of Leah:
    Reuben the firstborn of Jacob,
    Simeon, Levi, Judah, Issachar and Zebulun.
²⁴The sons of Rachel:
    Joseph and Benjamin.
²⁵The sons of Rachel's maidservant Bilhah:
    Dan and Naphtali.
²⁶The sons of Leah's maidservant Zilpah:
    Gad and Asher.
These were the sons of Jacob, who were born to him in Paddan Aram.

²⁷Jacob came home to his father Isaac in Mamre, near Kiriath Arba (that is, Hebron), where Abraham and Isaac had stayed. ²⁸Isaac lived a hundred and eighty years. ²⁹Then he breathed his last and died and was gathered to his people, old and full of years. And his sons Esau and Jacob buried him.

ᵃ18 Ben-Oni means *son of my trouble.*   ᵇ18 Benjamin means *son of my right hand.*

NRSV

chel was in childbirth, and she had hard labor. ¹⁷When she was in her hard labor, the midwife said to her, "Do not be afraid; for now you will have another son." ¹⁸As her soul was departing (for she died), she named him Ben-oni;ᵃ but his father called him Benjamin.ᵇ ¹⁹So Rachel died, and she was buried on the way to Ephrath (that is, Bethlehem), ²⁰and Jacob set up a pillar at her grave; it is the pillar of Rachel's tomb, which is there to this day. ²¹Israel journeyed on, and pitched his tent beyond the tower of Eder.

22While Israel lived in that land, Reuben went and lay with Bilhah his father's concubine; and Israel heard of it.

Now the sons of Jacob were twelve. ²³The sons of Leah: Reuben (Jacob's firstborn), Simeon, Levi, Judah, Issachar, and Zebulun. ²⁴The sons of Rachel: Joseph and Benjamin. ²⁵The sons of Bilhah, Rachel's maid: Dan and Naphtali. ²⁶The sons of Zilpah, Leah's maid: Gad and Asher. These were the sons of Jacob who were born to him in Paddan-aram.

27Jacob came to his father Isaac at Mamre, or Kiriath-arba (that is, Hebron), where Abraham and Isaac had resided as aliens. ²⁸Now the days of Isaac were one hundred eighty years. ²⁹And Isaac breathed his last; he died and was gathered to his people, old and full of days; and his sons Esau and Jacob buried him.

ᵃ That is *Son of my sorrow*   ᵇ That is *Son of the right hand* or *Son of the South*

COMMENTARY

Few biblical chapters give such clear evidence of their composite character as this one (all major sources are probably represented). Apparently, bits and pieces of tradition regarding Jacob's journeys and family have been placed at the end of his story, not unlike the way texts have been woven into the seams of the stories of Abraham (chap. 25) and Joseph (chap. 50). Some linkages occur within the chapter. We should note especially the portrayal of Jacob journeying through the promised land from north to south. Jacob's journey basically recapitulates the journey of Abraham. It begins with a similar command of God (12:1). They both journey from Haran to Shechem to Bethel toward the Negeb (12:6-9), include a promise of land (12:7), and travel in stages to Mamre (13:18), with references to oaks and altars all along the way. In addition, the separation of the families of Jacob and Esau because "their possessions were too great for them to live together" (36:7) parallels exactly the land division between Abraham and Lot (13:6). Verses 9-13 parallel significantly the covenant with Abraham in chap. 17 (see below), including a name change, with a focus on circumcision (as in chap. 34). All of these parallels may mean that Jacob has now arrived at that point in his life where he is a true successor in the line of Abraham.

The links with chap. 34 are somewhat indirect, but important. (a) The purification rites may be tied to the defilement of Dinah (34:5, 13, 27) and more generally to what was done to Shechem. (b) The inclusion of people beyond Jacob's own family (v. 2) may refer to the captives of Shechem (34:29), which may in turn explain the presence of "foreign gods." (c) The "terror" (v. 5) may be a divine response to Jacob's fear of revenge at the hands of the Canaanites in 34:30. (d) Reuben's sexual/political act (v. 22) has parallels with the actions of Simeon and Levi in chap. 34. Both are criticized by Jacob in chap. 49 and lose their place in the family. (e) The focus on Jacob's family as a community occurs in both.

Bethel receives some attention in this chapter, which, with 28:10-22, encloses the story of the adult Jacob.

35:1-15. These verses combine segments revolving around events at Bethel (see 28:10-22). God commands Jacob to go from Shechem to Bethel and build an altar; later God appears there, and Jacob again responds with worship. Worship issues frame the section.

The fact that *God* tells Jacob to make an altar is unusual (cf. Exod 27:1); elsewhere in Genesis this occurs as a human response. God appeared to Jacob (v. 1) and made promises to him there (v. 7). God has fulfilled those promises, answering him in distress and accompanying him (v. 3). These references suggest that God, who has been faithful, now holds Jacob to his own vow at Bethel (28:10-22; 31:13).

In response to God, Jacob commands his household and "all who were with him" (see 34:29) to put away foreign gods, purify themselves (see Exod 19:10; Deut 27:15), and accompany him to Bethel. The presence of persons in his retinue who are not members of Jacob's family explains the reference to "foreign" gods; Rachel's household gods (31:19) may also still be in view. Such a double reference to the "gods" corresponds to the similar command in Josh 24:14-15, 23. This action of Joshua also occurred at Shechem and was associated with entry into the land (cf. Judg 10:16; 1 Sam 7:3-4). This element of the text may also be related to the issues of defilement raised in chap. 34:5, 13, 27 (cf. Lev 11:47; 16:19). These texts support the idea that this ritual involved an internal renunciation, the shaping of thought and life toward what pleases God. The ritual implies an in-depth reading of the divine command relevant to the new family situation in the land. Jacob's action may be understood as a *paradigm* for worship practices in later Israel.

Everybody responds positively to Jacob's request (not all of Jacob's directives are reported in v. 4, and earrings are added). They give Jacob their idols and their golden earrings, a potential resource for making idols (cf. Exod 32:3-4; Judg 8:24-27). Jacob buries them under the oak at Shechem, another link with Abraham (see 12:6). The immediate reference to God's protection implies that God's action responds to these worship activities.

Jacob and his family undertake the journey from Shechem to Bethel (about thirty miles). God's protection on the way may refer to 34:30 and Jacob's fear of the local inhabitants; the "terror" probably refers to a God-inspired fear instilled in those who may have threatened Jacob (see Exod 23:27; Josh 10:10). They arrive at Bethel unharmed and fulfill the command of God, which, in turn, fulfills Jacob's vow (28:22). The name *El-Bethel* is given to the altar site and not to the city. On Deborah, see Reflections.

God appears to Jacob "again" (v. 9; see 28:10-22). The word God speaks alludes to a number of previous promises, especially 17:2-8, which also includes Abraham's name change. It provides a second realization of Isaac's benediction in 28:3-4 (the first, 28:13-15), but this time it has a community-oriented focus (as in Jacob's recollection of this appearance in 48:3-4). The presence of his entire family and others (see vv. 2, 5-6, 16) makes this more of a corporate experience than the others. God gives a promise (vv. 10-12) to a community that has just renounced other gods. This new, corporate setting in the land of promise may have led to the repetition of Jacob's name change.

One senses that all previous appearances of God in Genesis are caught up in this one, especially the promises to Abraham, and are applied directly to one who gives his name to the people as a whole. God gives these promises to Jacob—that is, Israel. (1) The language and form of appearance are similar to those used with Abraham (17:1); God's "going up" (v. 13; see 17:22) no doubt means the appearance of the messenger in human form (see 16:7). (2) The repetition of the promises of the land (17:8; 26:3; 28:13), a nation, indeed a community of nations and kings (cf. 17:4-6), maintains the continuity between Jacob and Abraham/Isaac. (3) It bridges God's earlier appearance to Jacob at Bethel (28:10-22), including parallels to appearance, promise, and Jacob's response. (4) It parallels the Peniel story: being blessed by God (32:29); the change of his name to Israel (32:28). (5) The command to be fruitful and multiply occurs as a command for the first time since chaps. 1–11 (1:28; 9:1, 6); it took the form of a promise to Abraham (17:6) and is recalled *as promise* in 48:4 (cf. 28:3).

Jacob's response (vv. 14-15) also repeats earlier actions; he names Bethel again (28:19), and he erects another pillar and anoints it (28:18-19). Verses 14-15 have as much to do with the fulfillment of the vow as does 35:7 (e.g., the pillar and the name *Bethel*, the house of God, cf. 28:22). These texts establish the authority of the sanctuary at Bethel for a later generation. Jacob pours the drink (wine) offering, unique to Genesis, on the pillar rather than the altar. These cross-references testify to continuities in Jacob's relationship with God and bracket his life from the point of leaving home until his return. They also establish continuities with Israel's later, more elaborate ritual activities.

35:16-20. These verses portray the birth of Benjamin and the death of Rachel on the way from Bethel near Ephrath/Bethlehem (see 48:5-7); Rachel's grave lies near Ramah in Benjaminite territory in 1 Sam 10:2 and Jer 31:15, however. There were two Ephraths in Israel, Bethlehem and near Ramah, hence the confusion. The immediate family of Jacob is now complete. The comforting words of the midwife about a son inform Rachel that her desires for a second son (30:24) have been fulfilled. Rachel's naming of her son (*Ben-oni*, "son of my sorrow") is partially changed by Jacob (*Benjamin*, "son of the right hand"—i.e., power—or "son of the south" or "son of days," see 44:20), to link the child less closely to the sorrowful past.

35:21-26. Only here, in chaps. 25–36, does the author refer to Jacob by his new name, Israel, but it may well have a corporate reference. Eder is near Jerusalem; it constitutes one more point in Israel's journey through the promised land ("Israel journeyed on"). The shocking note about Reuben's cohabiting with Rachel's maid (and mother of Dan and Naphtali) probably explains why Reuben lost his status as the firstborn son (cf. 48:5; 49:3-4; 1 Chr 5:1). His act appears more a political move than a sexual one. The death of Rachel occasions an effort on Reuben's part to assume the role of the family leader (see Absalom's efforts with his father's concubines in 2 Sam 16:20-22; cf. 2 Sam 3:7; 12:8) and illustrates again the conflict in this family.[192]

Since a list of Jacob's sons follows this note about Reuben, the author may be addressing the transition in leadership from Jacob to his sons; Reuben makes the first move. He also remains on the list in spite of his deed. The point finally would be that, unlike the previous generations, the blessing and the promise will be shared by the sons as a group, rather than be assumed by any one of them (see 49:1-28; 50:24). The fact that Benjamin is included among those born in Paddan-aram may refer to the home of the mother. Dinah's omission from the list indicates that tribal considerations are at stake here. The list is followed closely by a list of Esau's descendants (chap. 36).

35:27-29. Jacob finally returns to the place from which he left in 28:1-5 (see 31:18), another piece of evidence for the bracketing function of this chapter. The writer reports Isaac's death in terms almost exactly the same as those used for Abraham (25:7-9), being buried by his two sons (from 49:31) in the grave at Machpelah.

---

192. For details, see Sarna, *Genesis*, 244-45.

REFLECTIONS

1. One best interprets this chapter as a series of snapshots from a Jacob scrapbook that provided an episodic look at his later life. The references to 28:10-22 and the notices of various journeys that take him the length of the promised land in a manner parallel to Abraham (see above) provide linear coherence. The journeys are punctuated by one birth (Benjamin), three deaths (Deborah, Rachel, Isaac), and continuing family trouble (v. 22). God continues to be with Jacob, with appearances to command (v. 1), to panic (v. 5), to name (v. 10), and to promise (vv. 11-12). Jacob always responds in positive ways, by putting away gods (vv. 2-4), building altars (vv. 3, 7), and worshiping God (vv. 14-15). Amid this amazing variety, the author lists the twelve sons of Jacob according to their mothers (vv. 22c-26).

The author seems to say: "Your lives as Israel will be as complex and varied as was that of your father, Israel, but you will be undergirded by the presence of God catching you up in creation-wide purposes." Such a picture is typical of communities of faith; the surface image resembles more a scrapbook than a harmonious, logical presentation. There are the ongoing rhythms of life and death, joy and sorrow, family conflict and unity. Yet, beneath the surface of these apparently incoherent details, the journey moves toward a divinely established goal.

2. The author appends a curious note about the death of Rebekah's nurse, Deborah (see 24:59), to this story; the narrative does not report the death of Rebekah (cf. 49:31). That a name ("oak of tears") is attached to the place where Deborah is buried may be associated with the oak of v. 4. This text provides striking testimony to the memory of a faithful servant that lives on in the community of faith. Amid all the great movements of these major ancestral figures, the author includes a note about "little" people, who are more important in the larger story than one typically appreciates.

3. The renunciation of other gods embeds the first commandment in the heart of the ancestral story. More broadly, it sets the community of faith apart from certain values and commitments of the surrounding cultures. It lifts up the importance of ritual activity for life in the land, as a way of responding to the problems faced by the community of faith, and as a vehicle in and through which God acts on behalf of the community.

The task of "putting away" whatever is harmful to the community moves beyond just "gods" in other texts, incorporating more specific directives for the shape of a faithful life—putting away crooked speech (Prov 4:24), violence and oppression (Ezek 45:9), and sin (2 Sam. 12:13). Israel should move beyond specific ritual activities and speak of daily commitments and responsibilities. The NT picks up this same language, speaking of putting away "your former way of life, your old self" (Eph 4:22-32 NRSV) and, more specifically, putting off anger, wrath, malice, slander, and abusive language (Col 3:8; cf. 1 Pet 2:1). Putting away foreign gods has been translated into the Christian tradition by referring to the renunciation of sinfulness or "devil and all his works and all his ways."

Changing clothes also works as a symbol of moving from the old to the new. Clothing plays an important role in Genesis, symbolizing significant changes in the narrative (from 3:21 to 41:14). The washing of clothes is a symbol of removing defilement (cf. Lev 15:5-27); all of our own deeds are like a polluted garment (Isa 64:6). Yet, because of what God has done, we are clothed "with the garments of salvation," covered with "the robe of righteousness" (Isa 61:10 NRSV; 52:1). The NT also uses the image of clothing to symbolize this change (cf. Mark 2:21), and persons of faith are called upon to clothe themselves in the characteristics of the new life in Christ (Eph 4:24; 6:13-17; 1 Pet 5:5). "The new community is found by *renunciation, renaming, reclothing,* and finally, *receiving a promise.*"[193]

---

193. Brueggemann, *Genesis,* 283.

---

4. Rachel's weeping lives on in Israel's memory, noted not least in the reference to Jacob's pillar, "which is there to this day" (v. 20). This image works powerfully in Jer 31:15-17 to express the deep effects of suffering on Israel and in Matt 2:17-18, in reference to the slaughter of the innocents in and around Bethlehem at Jesus' birth. In Jeremiah, Rachel is used to express feminine and suffering images for God (31:15-20). This devastating moment for both Rachel and Jacob does not slip into the past or remain only a negative memory; it continues to generate fresh theological reflections. It (along with much else in this chapter) witnesses to the generative power of even "scraps" of the tradition for the ongoing life of the people of God.

GENESIS 36:1-43, THE FUTURE OF ESAU

NIV

36 This is the account of Esau (that is, Edom).

²Esau took his wives from the women of Canaan: Adah daughter of Elon the Hittite, and Oholibamah daughter of Anah and granddaughter of Zibeon the Hivite— ³also Basemath daughter of Ishmael and sister of Nebaioth.

⁴Adah bore Eliphaz to Esau, Basemath bore Reuel, ⁵and Oholibamah bore Jeush, Jalam and Korah. These were the sons of Esau, who were born to him in Canaan.

⁶Esau took his wives and sons and daughters and all the members of his household, as well as his livestock and all his other animals and all the goods he had acquired in Canaan, and moved to a land some distance from his brother Jacob. ⁷Their possessions were too great for them to remain together; the land where they were staying could not support them both because of their livestock. ⁸So Esau (that is, Edom) settled in the hill country of Seir. .

⁹This is the account of Esau the father of the Edomites in the hill country of Seir.

¹⁰These are the names of Esau's sons:
   Eliphaz, the son of Esau's wife Adah, and
   Reuel, the son of Esau's wife Basemath.
¹¹The sons of Eliphaz:
   Teman, Omar, Zepho, Gatam and Kenaz.
¹²Esau's son Eliphaz also had a concubine named Timna, who bore him Amalek. These were grandsons of Esau's wife Adah.
¹³The sons of Reuel:
   Nahath, Zerah, Shammah and Mizzah.

NRSV

36 These are the descendants of Esau (that is, Edom). ²Esau took his wives from the Canaanites: Adah daughter of Elon the Hittite, Oholibamah daughter of Anah son[a] of Zibeon the Hivite, ³and Basemath, Ishmael's daughter, sister of Nebaioth. ⁴Adah bore Eliphaz to Esau; Basemath bore Reuel; ⁵and Oholibamah bore Jeush, Jalam, and Korah. These are the sons of Esau who were born to him in the land of Canaan.

6Then Esau took his wives, his sons, his daughters, and all the members of his household, his cattle, all his livestock, and all the property he had acquired in the land of Canaan; and he moved to a land some distance from his brother Jacob. ⁷For their possessions were too great for them to live together; the land where they were staying could not support them because of their livestock. ⁸So Esau settled in the hill country of Seir; Esau is Edom.

9These are the descendants of Esau, ancestor of the Edomites, in the hill country of Seir. ¹⁰These are the names of Esau's sons: Eliphaz son of Adah the wife of Esau; Reuel, the son of Esau's wife Basemath. ¹¹The sons of Eliphaz were Teman, Omar, Zepho, Gatam, and Kenaz. ¹²(Timna was a concubine of Eliphaz, Esau's son; she bore Amalek to Eliphaz.) These were the sons of Adah, Esau's wife. ¹³These were the sons of Reuel: Nahath, Zerah, Shammah, and Mizzah. These were the sons of Esau's wife, Basemath. ¹⁴These were the sons of Esau's wife Oholibamah, daughter of Anah son[b] of Zibeon: she bore to Esau Jeush, Jalam, and Korah.

a Sam Gk Syr: Heb *daughter*   *b* Gk Syr: Heb *daughter*

NIV

These were grandsons of Esau's wife Basemath. [14]The sons of Esau's wife Oholibamah daughter of Anah and granddaughter of Zibeon, whom she bore to Esau:

Jeush, Jalam and Korah.

[15]These were the chiefs among Esau's descendants:

The sons of Eliphaz the firstborn of Esau:
Chiefs Teman, Omar, Zepho, Kenaz, [16]Korah,[a] Gatam and Amalek. These were the chiefs descended from Eliphaz in Edom; they were grandsons of Adah. [17]The sons of Esau's son Reuel:
Chiefs Nahath, Zerah, Shammah and Mizzah. These were the chiefs descended from Reuel in Edom; they were grandsons of Esau's wife Basemath. [18]The sons of Esau's wife Oholibamah:
Chiefs Jeush, Jalam and Korah. These were the chiefs descended from Esau's wife Oholibamah daughter of Anah.

[19]These were the sons of Esau (that is, Edom), and these were their chiefs.

[20]These were the sons of Seir the Horite, who were living in the region:
Lotan, Shobal, Zibeon, Anah, [21]Dishon, Ezer and Dishan. These sons of Seir in Edom were Horite chiefs. [22]The sons of Lotan:
Hori and Homam.[b] Timna was Lotan's sister. [23]The sons of Shobal:
Alvan, Manahath, Ebal, Shepho and Onam. [24]The sons of Zibeon:
Aiah and Anah. This is the Anah who discovered the hot springs[c] in the desert while he was grazing the donkeys of his father Zibeon. [25]The children of Anah:
Dishon and Oholibamah daughter of Anah.

a16 Masoretic Text; Samaritan Pentateuch (see also Gen. 36:11 and 1 Chron. 1:36) does not have *Korah*.   b22 Hebrew *Hemam*, a variant of *Homam* (see 1 Chron. 1:39)   c24 Vulgate; Syriac *discovered water*; the meaning of the Hebrew for this word is uncertain.

NRSV

[15]These are the clans[a] of the sons of Esau. The sons of Eliphaz the firstborn of Esau: the clans[a] Teman, Omar, Zepho, Kenaz, [16]Korah, Gatam, and Amalek; these are the clans[a] of Eliphaz in the land of Edom; they are the sons of Adah. [17]These are the sons of Esau's son Reuel: the clans[a] Nahath, Zerah, Shammah, and Mizzah; these are the clans[a] of Reuel in the land of Edom; they are the sons of Esau's wife Basemath. [18]These are the sons of Esau's wife Oholibamah: the clans[a] Jeush, Jalam, and Korah; these are the clans[a] born of Esau's wife Oholibamah, the daughter of Anah. [19]These are the sons of Esau (that is, Edom), and these are their clans.[a]

[20]These are the sons of Seir the Horite, the inhabitants of the land: Lotan, Shobal, Zibeon, Anah, [21]Dishon, Ezer, and Dishan; these are the clans[a] of the Horites, the sons of Seir in the land of Edom. [22]The sons of Lotan were Hori and Heman; and Lotan's sister was Timna. [23]These are the sons of Shobal: Alvan, Manahath, Ebal, Shepho, and Onam. [24]These are the sons of Zibeon: Aiah and Anah; he is the Anah who found the springs[b] in the wilderness, as he pastured the donkeys of his father Zibeon. [25]These are the children of Anah: Dishon and Oholibamah daughter of Anah. [26]These are the sons of Dishon: Hemdan, Eshban, Ithran, and Cheran. [27]These are the sons of Ezer: Bilhan, Zaavan, and Akan. [28]These are the sons of Dishan: Uz and Aran. [29]These are the clans[a] of the Horites: the clans[a] Lotan, Shobal, Zibeon, Anah, [30]Dishon, Ezer, and Dishan; these are the clans[a] of the Horites, clan by clan[a] in the land of Seir.

[31]These are the kings who reigned in the land of Edom, before any king reigned over the Israelites. [32]Bela son of Beor reigned in Edom, the name of his city being Dinhabah. [33]Bela died, and Jobab son of Zerah of Bozrah succeeded him as king. [34]Jobab died, and Husham of the land of the Temanites succeeded him as king. [35]Husham died, and Hadad son of Bedad, who defeated Midian in the country of Moab, succeeded him as king, the name of his city being Avith. [36]Hadad died, and Samlah of Masrekah succeeded him as king. [37]Samlah died, and Shaul of Rehoboth on the Euphrates succeeded him as king. [38]Shaul died,

a Or *chiefs*   b Meaning of Heb uncertain

26The sons of Dishon*a*:

Hemdan, Eshban, Ithran and Keran.

27The sons of Ezer:

Bilhan, Zaavan and Akan.

28The sons of Dishan:

Uz and Aran.

29These were the Horite chiefs:

Lotan, Shobal, Zibeon, Anah, 30Dishon, Ezer and Dishan. These were the Horite chiefs, according to their divisions, in the land of Seir.

31These were the kings who reigned in Edom before any Israelite king reigned*b*:

32Bela son of Beor became king of Edom. His city was named Dinhabah.

33When Bela died, Jobab son of Zerah from Bozrah succeeded him as king.

34When Jobab died, Husham from the land of the Temanites succeeded him as king.

35When Husham died, Hadad son of Bedad, who defeated Midian in the country of Moab, succeeded him as king. His city was named Avith.

36When Hadad died, Samlah from Masrekah succeeded him as king.

37When Samlah died, Shaul from Rehoboth on the river*c* succeeded him as king.

38When Shaul died, Baal-Hanan son of Acbor succeeded him as king.

39When Baal-Hanan son of Acbor died, Hadad*d* succeeded him as king. His city was named Pau, and his wife's name was Mehetabel daughter of Matred, the daughter of Me-Zahab.

40These were the chiefs descended from Esau, by name, according to their clans and regions:

Timna, Alvah, Jetheth, 41Oholibamah, Elah, Pinon, 42Kenaz, Teman, Mibzar, 43Magdiel and Iram. These were the chiefs of Edom, according to their settlements in the land they occupied.

This was Esau the father of the Edomites.

a26 Hebrew *Dishan*, a variant of *Dishon*   *b31* Or *before an Israelite king reigned over them*   *c37* Possibly the Euphrates   *d39* Many manuscripts of the Masoretic Text, Samaritan Pentateuch and Syriac (see also 1 Chron. 1:50); most manuscripts of the Masoretic Text *Hadar*

and Baal-hanan son of Achbor succeeded him as king. 39Baal-hanan son of Achbor died, and Hadar succeeded him as king, the name of his city being Pau; his wife's name was Mehetabel, the daughter of Matred, daughter of Me-zahab.

40These are the names of the clans*a* of Esau, according to their families and their localities by their names: the clans*a* Timna, Alvah, Jetheth, 41Oholibamah, Elah, Pinon, 42Kenaz, Teman, Mibzar, 43Magdiel, and Iram; these are the clans*a* of Edom (that is, Esau, the father of Edom), according to their settlements in the land that they held.

a Or *chiefs*

COMMENTARY

These highly composite lists (cf. 1 Chr 1:35-54) include Esau's descendants (vv. 1-19); those of Seir the Horite, whose name is given to the region (vv. 20-30); the Edomite king list (vv. 31-39); and an appendix (vv. 40-43). The king list carries the story of Esau and Edom well beyond the narrative in which it is embedded, down to the time of David and Solomon (2 Sam 8:13-14; 1 Kgs 11:14), probably the time of the narrator. This chapter thus constitutes a *projection* of Edomite peoples and leaders into the future.

These lists were probably gathered by the Davidic monarchy after its subjugation of Edom. Over half of these names are not otherwise identifiable, having no connection with an existing narrative; many of the known names have a close relationship with Judah; some are both personal and place names; some have been taken over from other lists; others are used in more than one way in this text; and still others are not in full agreement with the surrounding story (e.g., Esau's wives in 26:34; cf. 28:9 to 36:1-3, 10, 14).

The lists document stages in the history of the people involved, from family (vv. 1-14) to tribal units (vv. 15-30) to more national entities (vv. 31-39). They probably reveal comparable developments in the life of Israel. Generally, the relationships in the list reflect historical developments among tribal groups (e.g., the intermarriage of Canaanites and Edomites, 36:2).

This list parallels that of Ishmael (25:12-18) in both structure and concern for the nonchosen brother. As with Ishmael, Esau's genealogy relates to previous oracles of blessing (25:23; 27:39-40); God attends to their realization in the development of this people. The move from Esau to Edom in this chapter (vv. 8-9, 43) also leads into chaps. 37–50, where the most basic subject is the movement from Jacob to Israel (36:31; see Josh 24:4).

36:1-19. The lists begin with a genealogy of the five sons of Esau and his three wives. Verses 1-5 focus on Esau's family, vv. 9-14 on that of his sons. The parenthetical reference to Amalek (v. 12) reflects antipathetic relationships between the Amalekites and the Israelites (Exod 17:8-16; Deut 25:17-19). In vv. 15-19 the sons are listed in their political role as chiefs (NIV, or as clans, NRSV) over Edomite territories.

Verses 6-8 constitute the major narrative piece within the chapter (cf. vv. 24, 35); they relate back to relationships between Jacob and Esau, established earlier (33:1-17; 35:29); both have been highly successful. The division between the families of Jacob and Esau are here grounded in socioeconomic reality (cf. Abraham and Lot, 13:5-7), with no sign of previous personal conflict evident. Earlier links in the text between Esau and Seir (32:4; 33:14-16; cf. 14:6) are difficult to justify with these verses; some have suggested this text speaks of a permanent settlement of a nomadic people having a sometime relationship to Seir.

The author presents Esau's family positively, highlighting stability, growth, and continuity. The fact that Esau moves, rather than Jacob, says something about their historical relationships as well as the divine promise regarding Canaan; at the same time, the tradition speaks of the land of Seir as a divine gift for Esau (Deut 2:5; Josh 24:4), and the oracle in 27:39-40 assumes a land.

36:20-30. These verses present a genealogy of the seven sons of Seir the Horite (vv. 20-28), also listed as chiefs (NIV) or clans (NRSV), vv. 29-30. The Horites are also known as Hurrians, a non-Semitic people in origin (but here having Semitic names). These people occupied Seir before the sons of Esau subjugated them (described in Deut 2:12, 22; cf. Gen 14:6). We do not know whether individuals or tribes are primarily in view here, but probably the latter.

36:31-39. This list (not a genealogy) of eight nondynastic kings of Edom (vv. 31-39) may be best understood as chiefs similar to Israelite judges; they probably do not always reign successively or over the same territory. They pre-date Israel's entry into Canaan (see Num 20:14; Judg 11:17) and continue down to the time of the United Monarchy, at which time David conquered the Edomites (2 Sam 8:13-14; 1 Kgs 11:14-17). The last of the kings (Hadar [Hadad]) may be a contemporary of Saul, whose son or grandson may be the Hadad mentioned in 1 Kgs 11:14. Reference to the kings of Israel (v. 31) reflects the oracle (25:23) that Esau was the older son who came to serve the younger. One of these groups, the Midianites, descend from Abraham (25:2).[194]

36:40-43. This appendix probably specifies

194. For details, see Sarna, *Genesis*, 408-10.

eleven Edomite chiefs (or clans) in terms of their localities at the time of the last-named king. Redactionally, they balance the twelve sons of Jacob in 35:22-26.

REFLECTIONS

To the average reader of Genesis, these lists (with over 200 names!) are to be read quickly while getting on with the story of Joseph. Moreover, it may be thought that because this chapter focuses on those who are "not chosen," whose history seemingly goes nowhere, it need not delay the reader. Yet, the inclusion of the stories of these peoples (known only from Israelite sources) is significant, for it makes the reader pause over the place of nonchosen ones and ponder their relationship to the chosen. Their story is not expunged or reduced to something of no account by the narrators of the story of the chosen people.

The testimony of this chapter, with its references to Esau's land, material blessings, and the succession of generations is that God the Creator is indeed at work outside Israel, giving life and blessing to the nonchosen. The blessings given to Esau (27:39-40) continue to be realized down through the centuries. In fact, the promises to Abraham and Sarah include a promise of kings and nations (17:5, 16), so that the very existence of Edom depends on divine promises. In these respects we may compare Esau's story to the story and genealogy of Ishmael (see chaps. 16–17; 21; 25).

While Esau is not the "chosen," these texts do not forget that the story is about brothers. This is made clear in other texts, where Esau is a "brother" of Israel (Num 20:14), who is not to be "abhorred" by Israel, "because [the Edomites] are your kin" and are even to be welcomed into the "assembly" of Israel (Deut 23:7-8). It is thereby recognized that, though the division between chosen and nonchosen may slice down the middle of a family, that does not nullify the continuing familial relationship and the obligations the chosen ones have for the welfare of the other. Their responsibility to be a blessing to all the "families" of earth (12:3*b;* 28:14) includes those within the family as well as those who stand without. Election is for the purposes of mission.

It is clear from the historical record that severe conflicts between Edom and Israel took place from time to time, from David to the post-exilic period, issuing in some harsh judgments on Edom (2 Sam 8:13-14; Psalm 137; Obadiah; Mal 1:2-5; cf. Rom 9:12-13). Since these basically positive stories of Esau in Genesis continued to be transmitted through difficult times, they demonstrate that family ties cannot finally be subverted by the behaviors of one or more generations of brothers and sisters. This perspective may attest to a countercultural origin and transmission for these texts, not uncommon for Israel's literature. These texts witness to bonds of family that reach across the centuries. They should inform the continuing relationships among all peoples, no matter how difficult they may be at any given moment.

We may observe links between the two excluded sons, Ishmael and Esau, not only in the promises spoken to them, but also in their roles as progenitors of the Arab peoples, many of whom claim adherence to Islam (see chaps. 16–17; 21; 25). These texts may be especially important as the chosen in the modern world seek to relate to these "others" in as positive a way as possible; they demonstrate that we have common roots in the faith of Abraham and Sarah and that heritage may enhance our conversations with each other.

591

JOSEPH, JUDAH AND JACOB'S FAMILY

OVERVIEW

We know this last major section of the book of Genesis as the story of Joseph; and for good reason, since it involves, primarily, the fortunes and misfortunes of Joseph, Jacob's son. At the same time, the text announces that "this is the story of the family of Jacob" (37:2), and concludes with reference to the promises God "swore to Abraham, to Isaac, and to Jacob" (50:24). At the least this means that, despite all the focus on Joseph, the reader must think fundamentally in corporate terms; this story narrates the emergence of Israel's family as Israel, the people of God.

The reader must also seek to come to terms with chaps. 37–50 as a unified whole. Modern scholarship has usually regarded the story as a composite work (J, E, P, and redactors), a view prompted in particular by so-called doublets. There has been a decisive move away from this approach over the past generation, however, with renewed efforts to understand the story as a unity. Hence, for example, we now may read the repetitions as a deliberate literary device, perhaps reflecting an oral culture. This usually does not entail a denial of the composite character of these chapters in some respects (or the need to probe redactional issues).

Yet, for all the talk about unity, many still regard certain sections as intrusive, especially chaps. 38 and 49 (and often portions of chaps. 46–48; 50). Such an approach seems guided especially by a concern to isolate those segments that focus on Joseph or reflect a particular literary style. However, such claims diminish the corporate perspective of the present redaction. For example, chaps. 48–49 have the emergent tribal groups of Israel in view. Chapter 38 highlights Judah, who has a key role in the larger story (43:3-10; 44:18-34) and whose descendants are of central importance in later Israel. These chapters coordinate the pervasive role that the "brothers" play in the story, but because they are so often mentioned as a collective body, they tend to be less visible. Whatever place the story may have had as an independent piece of literature (of whatever length), it now focuses on the move from Israel as an individual to Israel as a family, to Israel as a people.

Chapters 12–36 are basically individual stories, presented in episodic fashion and tied together by genealogies and itineraries. This story, though episodic at some points (38; 46–50), is more a single narrative. As such, we may designate it a short story or novella, with a plot moving from crisis to resolution (similar to books like Ruth and Esther). At the same time, its self-designation as the "story of a family" (37:2) accents continuities with the previous family narratives. Yet, the differences from chaps. 12–36 suggest that the story emanates from different circles than the earlier stories.

What, then, can be said about its origins? Scholars have often pointed to the influence of the wisdom movement on the book.[195] Wisdom influence may be evident at some points, as in the portrayal of Joseph as an ideal young man or a model administrator. Yet, such ideas were widespread in Israel's world and should not be used to support a specific intellectual matrix for its origins. A royal setting is likely, given leading themes; and the Solomonic era (with its positive relationship with Egypt; see 1 Kgs 9:16) affords a probable background. We must remain agnostic about the story's history, except to say that the Priestly writer probably integrated it into its present ancestral context (Priestly influence can be discerned at a few points [e.g., 37:1-2; 47:27-28; 48:3-6]).

195. See von Rad, Genesis, 433-40.

Function. The Joseph story functions in several ways within Genesis and the Pentateuch.

1. The story follows the genealogy of Esau, Jacob's brother. The reason for this juxtaposition seems clear: Both present the movement from individual to people. Chapter 36 announces that "Esau is Edom" (vv. 1, 8-9, 43) and assumes a comparable movement for Jacob (36:31; cf. Josh 24:4). Chapters 37–50 trace this movement, depicting the journey from individual Israel to people Israel (from 37:1 to 47:27 to 50:25), which is recapitulated in Exod 1:1-7.

2. The story leads into the book of Exodus. At one level, the story has a narrow geographical purpose, moving the family from Canaan to Egypt, the setting for Exodus events. References to "settling" (יָשַׁב *yāšab*) signals this motif. The story begins with Jacob's settling in the land of Canaan (37:1), moves to his settling in Egypt (47:27; cf. vv. 4, 6, 11), and finally shifts to Joseph's "settling" there *with his father's household* (50:22), with a not unimportant aside about the Canaanites as "settlers" in Canaan (50:11). The journeys of this family back and forth between Canaan and Egypt anticipate Exodus journeys.

At another level, the story "sets up" issues for the book of Exodus—for example, the Egyptian context. The story acquaints the reader with a remarkable range of life in Egypt, particularly the court of Pharaoh. Generally, a highly positive portrayal of Pharaoh and the Egyptians emerges, from the pharaonic treatment of Joseph, to the welcome of Jacob's family, to the significant participation in Jacob's funeral (including prolonged and "grievous mourning," 50:3, 11). One should also note the Egyptians' openness to Israel's God (e.g., 39:3; 41:38-39; 43:23). This material provides essential background for events in Exodus 1–15, so 1:8, "A new king arose over Egypt, who did not know Joseph." Genesis prevents us from "demonizing" the Egyptians of Exodus, suggests potentially positive relationships, and may well prepare for such prophetic words as Isa 19:18-25: "Blessed be Egypt my people" (Isa 19:25 NRSV)!

"Servant/slave" (עֶבֶד *'ebed*) appears as an important theme. The nearly 100 uses of this root in Exodus should make one attentive to its use in Genesis 37–50. Just as Exodus insists that Israel is the servant of God, not Pharaoh, so also Genesis claims that Israel is not the servant of *Joseph* (read

any Israelite leader). Life, growth, and blessing are another significant theme. Lifted up in a prominent way in chaps. 37–50 (esp. 45:5-8), it becomes a creational issue around which Exodus revolves (beginning in 1:7), which also relates to the theme of promise. While this theme appears more muted in chaps. 37–50 (except for blessing), it occurs at key junctures (46:3-4; 48:3-4, 21-22), ends on this note (50:24), and grounds God's activity in the Exodus events (2:24; 3:16-17; 6:2-8).

3. The story continues *and develops* the story of Jacob and his forebears in chaps. 12–36. The story of the family of Abraham/Isaac/Jacob moves on, rampant with conflicting relationships, yet chosen by God to be the recipient of promises and responsibilities. Significant developments occur:

Family and promise. Family issues continue to play a primary role, particularly tensions created by intrafamilial conflict. They create a major movement in the story, resulting in brotherly reconciliation, not an end in itself, however; it happens for the sake of the future, particularly as seen in the promises. The families of Abraham and Isaac had been divided over the issue of the promises (Isaac/Ishmael; Jacob/Esau). Will this "tradition" continue in Jacob's family? The story begins that way; Joseph seems to be eliminated (chap. 37), then Judah (chap. 38). But in time, when Jacob first speaks God's promise to Joseph, he refers to *all* of his offspring (48:3-4; cf. 35:12); Joseph follows through on this by speaking the promise to all his brothers (50:24). Family conflicts are resolved for the sake of *a unified family* moving toward those promises.

Individual, family, and nation. The story integrates family history with national and political history.[196] At times the author focuses on the family (chaps. 37; 42–45), at times on the broader political arena (chaps. 39–41; 47). Yet, because there is no interest in foreign affairs (e.g., wars), the focus throughout remains on issues that affect interhuman relationships.

This integration may speak to a conflictual reality in Israel's history. Put generally, the evolution of Israel's history from a family/clan orientation to monarchy occasioned numerous conflicts.

196. Westermann highlights this throughout his *Genesis 37–50*.

This story conveys the importance of a symbiotic relationship between government and family, embodied in the figure of Joseph, who remains both brother and national leader. Government, in its effect on citizens, should function like a good family system. Yet, if the family is conflicted or natural disaster strikes—as with Jacob—it takes wise governmental leaders—as with Joseph—to bring the good order needed for life and well-being. Because his leadership in social and economic spheres and his rise to power are ascribed to the work of God, the story views national structures in a positive light. They, in effect, mirror God in valuing and preserving life in families. Yet, the potential for the misuse of authority appears evident as well (see Exod 1:8). The story could be interpreted as an essay on the use and abuse of power (from Jacob as a father, to the brothers' treatment of Joseph, to the role of the pharaoh and Potiphar's wife, to Joseph in various roles).

In Joseph, especially, the story highlights the importance of the individual; what he says and does has considerable positive impact. Once placed in a leadership position, Joseph is no passive member of the community, but rather becomes deeply engaged on behalf of the public good. He rejects violence and revenge, and hence brings some closure to the snowballing effects of dysfunctionality. Although no angel—himself the product of such a family—Joseph chooses an approach that, however justifiable, causes no little discomfort among the brothers; finally he does not return in kind, though it is within his power to do so. The one who has ample reason to retaliate chooses reconciliation instead of retribution.

God. The action of God and the relationship to God are seen as central, enabling life and well-being for individual, family, and nation. God, not human heroes, provides the unity in the story; the deity works toward the divine purposes in and through these spheres of society and their deep and pervasive levels of sin and evil. Thereby the family is preserved alive and unified, and enabled to move on as the bearer of God's promises to the world. The story highlights God's presence with Joseph (chap. 39), blessing him at every turn; but God has a larger canvas in view. Joseph's relationship with God, accented at key junctures, affects his personal life, but moves beyond him to affect wide ranges of public life. The move from

his encounter with Potiphar's wife to his wise leadership in community affairs suggests that personal and public life are to be linked for maximum effectiveness as a leader.

This story depicts God in ways quite different from chaps. 12–36. Although not mentioned less often (some fifty times), God is portrayed differently. Never obvious, God acts unobtrusively, behind the scenes. God does not overpower or offer oracles and miracles; God's presence weaves the threads of goodness, mercy, *and judgment* into the texture of ordinary life, working toward the best possible end.

Moreover, God never appears to Joseph; unlike his forebears in the faith, he receives no word from God. God appears only in 46:1-4 (48:3-4 recalls an appearance), but to Jacob, not to Joseph. The promises seem hidden to ordinary view. Joseph builds no altars and associates with no centers of worship. Yet God is with him, and he is imbued with God's spirit (41:38). Joseph hears the promises for the first time from Jacob in 48:3-4, 21-22. Such differences may help to explain why the text never includes Joseph in the common formula: the God of Abraham, Isaac, and Jacob. Yet, another important dynamic operates in this way of conveying the knowledge of God. Jacob, not God, passes the promise on to Joseph, who in turn passes it on to his brothers (50:24); also, the word of Joseph to the brothers in 45:3-8 is formally similar to a typical theophany. The human community now becomes responsible for the transmission of the word of God. The former mode of revelation will return almost immediately (Exod 3:1-10), but a new method for transmitting the word of God across the generations has developed.

Why does the author present God differently in this story? This story may have been produced in a more secular time, when human thought and action seemed to carry the day, and God was experienced in less direct ways. Or God's actions correlate with the new reality of a people; God relates to the entire people of Israel, not just to individuals. Or it may be an introduction to the opening chapters of Exodus, where God acts in much the same way (cf. 2:23-25). Whatever the case, Genesis does portray the different ways in which God conveys the divine word to the community of faith.

4. The story picks up on key themes from Genesis 1–11 and, together, they enclose the unity of that book. God appears as one who works on behalf of not only the chosen family, but also the Egyptians; indeed the entire world serves as the divine horizon. The primary issues throughout the story are creational, from issues of family order to natural disaster, from socioeconomic crisis to national structures. God's purposes throughout are to preserve life and well-being, which in 45:5-8 includes the world community. The author focuses on divine blessing, blessings of the land, of wise leadership, of family growth, fulfilling the creational words of 1:28 (47:27), which are in turn extended to Pharaoh (47:7-10), the Egyptians (47:13-26), and the world (41:53-57) through this blessed family (cf. 12:3). God's choosing to work through this weak, conflicted family constitutes a divine irony, using the weak to bless the strong, which leads into important themes in Exodus.

Structure. The story begins with a conflicted family situation; two brothers, Joseph (37:1-36) and Judah (38:1-30), seem to be eliminated from the line of promise. It ends with the inclusion of all of Jacob's offspring within the orbit of the promise (47:29–50:26), grounded in God's word (48:4). Their futures are marked out in chaps. 48–49; chap. 50 depicts the reconciliation that enables their reception of the promise as a corporate entity (50:24).

Chapters 45:1-9 and 46:1-4 stand parallel and establish the divinely ordered creational setting of life and well-being in Egypt that enables the events of chaps. 48–50. The author describes the family's growth in Egypt, summarized in 47:27 and detailed in the genealogy (46:8-27). The setting makes this possible—filled with the blessings associated with Pharaoh (45:16-20; 47:7-10) and the Egyptians (47:13-26), interwoven with reports about their settlement and provision in that land (45:9-15, 21-28; 46:28–47:6, 11-12).

Chapters 39–44 develop *both* the Egyptian context and the family relationships in such a way that the events of chaps. 46–50 become possible; chaps. 39–41 focus on the public, Egyptian setting, with Joseph's rise to power; chaps. 42–44 develop the family issues.

GENESIS 37:1-36, JOSEPH AND HIS BROTHERS

NIV

37 Jacob lived in the land where his father had stayed, the land of Canaan.

²This is the account of Jacob.

Joseph, a young man of seventeen, was tending the flocks with his brothers, the sons of Bilhah and the sons of Zilpah, his father's wives, and he brought their father a bad report about them.

³Now Israel loved Joseph more than any of his other sons, because he had been born to him in his old age; and he made a richly ornamented[a] robe for him. ⁴When his brothers saw that their father loved him more than any of them, they hated him and could not speak a kind word to him.

⁵Joseph had a dream, and when he told it to his brothers, they hated him all the more. ⁶He

a3 The meaning of the Hebrew for *richly ornamented* is uncertain; also in verses 23 and 32.

NRSV

37 Jacob settled in the land where his father had lived as an alien, the land of Canaan. ²This is the story of the family of Jacob.

Joseph, being seventeen years old, was shepherding the flock with his brothers; he was a helper to the sons of Bilhah and Zilpah, his father's wives; and Joseph brought a bad report of them to their father. ³Now Israel loved Joseph more than any other of his children, because he was the son of his old age; and he had made him a long robe with sleeves.[a] ⁴But when his brothers saw that their father loved him more than all his brothers, they hated him, and could not speak peaceably to him.

5Once Joseph had a dream, and when he told it to his brothers, they hated him even more. ⁶He said to them, "Listen to this dream that I dreamed.

a Traditional rendering (compare Gk): *a coat of many colors*; Meaning of Heb uncertain

said to them, "Listen to this dream I had: [7]We were binding sheaves of grain out in the field when suddenly my sheaf rose and stood upright, while your sheaves gathered around mine and bowed down to it."

[8]His brothers said to him, "Do you intend to reign over us? Will you actually rule us?" And they hated him all the more because of his dream and what he had said.

[9]Then he had another dream, and he told it to his brothers. "Listen," he said, "I had another dream, and this time the sun and moon and eleven stars were bowing down to me."

[10]When he told his father as well as his brothers, his father rebuked him and said, "What is this dream you had? Will your mother and I and your brothers actually come and bow down to the ground before you?" [11]His brothers were jealous of him, but his father kept the matter in mind.

[12]Now his brothers had gone to graze their father's flocks near Shechem, [13]and Israel said to Joseph, "As you know, your brothers are grazing the flocks near Shechem. Come, I am going to send you to them."

"Very well," he replied.

[14]So he said to him, "Go and see if all is well with your brothers and with the flocks, and bring word back to me." Then he sent him off from the Valley of Hebron.

When Joseph arrived at Shechem, [15]a man found him wandering around in the fields and asked him, "What are you looking for?"

[16]He replied, "I'm looking for my brothers. Can you tell me where they are grazing their flocks?"

[17]"They have moved on from here," the man answered. "I heard them say, 'Let's go to Dothan.' "

So Joseph went after his brothers and found them near Dothan. [18]But they saw him in the distance, and before he reached them, they plotted to kill him.

[19]"Here comes that dreamer!" they said to each other. [20]"Come now, let's kill him and throw him into one of these cisterns and say that a ferocious animal devoured him. Then we'll see what comes of his dreams."

[21]When Reuben heard this, he tried to rescue him from their hands. "Let's not take his life," he

[7]There we were, binding sheaves in the field. Suddenly my sheaf rose and stood upright; then your sheaves gathered around it, and bowed down to my sheaf." [8]His brothers said to him, "Are you indeed to reign over us? Are you indeed to have dominion over us?" So they hated him even more because of his dreams and his words.

9He had another dream, and told it to his brothers, saying, "Look, I have had another dream: the sun, the moon, and eleven stars were bowing down to me." [10]But when he told it to his father and to his brothers, his father rebuked him, and said to him, "What kind of dream is this that you have had? Shall we indeed come, I and your mother and your brothers, and bow to the ground before you?" [11]So his brothers were jealous of him, but his father kept the matter in mind.

12Now his brothers went to pasture their father's flock near Shechem. [13]And Israel said to Joseph, "Are not your brothers pasturing the flock at Shechem? Come, I will send you to them." He answered, "Here I am." [14]So he said to him, "Go now, see if it is well with your brothers and with the flock; and bring word back to me." So he sent him from the valley of Hebron.

He came to Shechem, [15]and a man found him wandering in the fields; the man asked him, "What are you seeking?" [16]"I am seeking my brothers," he said; "tell me, please, where they are pasturing the flock." [17]The man said, "They have gone away, for I heard them say, 'Let us go to Dothan.' " So Joseph went after his brothers, and found them at Dothan. [18]They saw him from a distance, and before he came near to them, they conspired to kill him. [19]They said to one another, "Here comes this dreamer. [20]Come now, let us kill him and throw him into one of the pits; then we shall say that a wild animal has devoured him, and we shall see what will become of his dreams." [21]But when Reuben heard it, he delivered him out of their hands, saying, "Let us not take his life." [22]Reuben said to them, "Shed no blood; throw him into this pit here in the wilderness, but lay no hand on him"—that he might rescue him out of their hand and restore him to his father. [23]So when Joseph came to his brothers, they stripped him

NIV

said. ²²"Don't shed any blood. Throw him into this cistern here in the desert, but don't lay a hand on him." Reuben said this to rescue him from them and take him back to his father.

²³So when Joseph came to his brothers, they stripped him of his robe—the richly ornamented robe he was wearing— ²⁴and they took him and threw him into the cistern. Now the cistern was empty; there was no water in it.

²⁵As they sat down to eat their meal, they looked up and saw a caravan of Ishmaelites coming from Gilead. Their camels were loaded with spices, balm and myrrh, and they were on their way to take them down to Egypt.

²⁶Judah said to his brothers, "What will we gain if we kill our brother and cover up his blood? ²⁷Come, let's sell him to the Ishmaelites and not lay our hands on him; after all, he is our brother, our own flesh and blood." His brothers agreed.

²⁸So when the Midianite merchants came by, his brothers pulled Joseph up out of the cistern and sold him for twenty shekels*ᵃ* of silver to the Ishmaelites, who took him to Egypt.

²⁹When Reuben returned to the cistern and saw that Joseph was not there, he tore his clothes. ³⁰He went back to his brothers and said, "The boy isn't there! Where can I turn now?"

³¹Then they got Joseph's robe, slaughtered a goat and dipped the robe in the blood. ³²They took the ornamented robe back to their father and said, "We found this. Examine it to see whether it is your son's robe."

³³He recognized it and said, "It is my son's robe! Some ferocious animal has devoured him. Joseph has surely been torn to pieces."

³⁴Then Jacob tore his clothes, put on sackcloth and mourned for his son many days. ³⁵All his sons and daughters came to comfort him, but he refused to be comforted. "No," he said, "in mourning will I go down to the grave*ᵇ* to my son." So his father wept for him.

³⁶Meanwhile, the Midianites*ᶜ* sold Joseph in Egypt to Potiphar, one of Pharaoh's officials, the captain of the guard.

ᵃᵇ28 That is, about 8 ounces (about 0.2 kilogram)   *ᵇ35* Hebrew *Sheol*   *ᶜ36* Samaritan Pentateuch, Septuagint, Vulgate and Syriac (see also verse 28); Masoretic Text *Medanites*

NRSV

of his robe, the long robe with sleeves*ᵃ* that he wore; ²⁴and they took him and threw him into a pit. The pit was empty; there was no water in it.

25Then they sat down to eat; and looking up they saw a caravan of Ishmaelites coming from Gilead, with their camels carrying gum, balm, and resin, on their way to carry it down to Egypt. ²⁶Then Judah said to his brothers, "What profit is it if we kill our brother and conceal his blood? ²⁷Come, let us sell him to the Ishmaelites, and not lay our hands on him, for he is our brother, our own flesh." And his brothers agreed. ²⁸When some Midianite traders passed by, they drew Joseph up, lifting him out of the pit, and sold him to the Ishmaelites for twenty pieces of silver. And they took Joseph to Egypt.

29When Reuben returned to the pit and saw that Joseph was not in the pit, he tore his clothes. ³⁰He returned to his brothers, and said, "The boy is gone; and I, where can I turn?" ³¹Then they took Joseph's robe, slaughtered a goat, and dipped the robe in the blood. ³²They had the long robe with sleeves*ᵃ* taken to their father, and they said, "This we have found; see now whether it is your son's robe or not." ³³He recognized it, and said, "It is my son's robe! A wild animal has devoured him; Joseph is without doubt torn to pieces." ³⁴Then Jacob tore his garments, and put sackcloth on his loins, and mourned for his son many days. ³⁵All his sons and all his daughters sought to comfort him; but he refused to be comforted, and said, "No, I shall go down to Sheol to my son, mourning." Thus his father bewailed him. ³⁶Meanwhile the Midianites had sold him in Egypt to Potiphar, one of Pharaoh's officials, the captain of the guard.

ᵃ See note on 37.3

COMMENTARY

The author/editor juxtaposes chaps. 36 and 37–50 because they involve the movement from individual to people. The announcement that "Esau is Edom" (36:1, 8-9, 43) assumes a comparable movement for Jacob (36:31; cf. Josh 24:4). Chapters 37–50 trace this journey from individual Israel to people Israel (cf. 37:1; 47:27; 50:25). Jacob will also migrate from Canaan, as does Esau (36:6-8); unlike Esau, Jacob claims God's promise of an eventual return.

This story begins in a familiar way: Jacob as an inept father; the deception of the father by sons; the conflict among brothers. Will only one brother receive the promise this time, too? Much of chaps. 37–50 addresses this question. Joseph begins the chapter as the leading candidate to succeed Isaac and Jacob, but he seems to be out of the picture at the end.

Scholars have commonly thought that two sources are interwoven in this chapter, suggested by the roles of Reuben/Judah and the Midianites/Ishmaelites, as well as various geographical and familial details. Yet, other explanations are possible. The use of the names *Jacob* and *Israel* also suggests such a theory. However, the emergence of the name *Israel* for a people (e.g., 47:27; 48:20) may mean that later Israel sees itself mirrored in the story. The fact that Rachel remains alive (v. 10; see 35:19) may also create some confusion; yet, Genesis does not always present events in a precisely linear orientation.

Verses 1-4 set the stage for this episode, indeed for the story as a whole. The remainder of the chapter quickly moves through three scenes to a preliminary climax, the exclusion of Joseph; Joseph's dreams intensify intrafamilial conflict (vv. 5-11); the isolation of Joseph and the violence he experiences at the hands of his brothers (vv. 12-28); Jacob's grieving reaction (vv. 29-36).

37:1-4. Jacob settles in the land of promise (v. 1), which is linked with 47:27 and 50:22, where "Israel" and Joseph settle in Egypt. This sets up two themes for the story: the movement from Canaan to Egypt and the development from individual to people.

The reference to *Jacob's* genealogy (37:2) indicates that the story of Joseph unfolds *from within*

the story of Jacob's family. Indeed, Jacob himself remains a central character in this story until his death and burial at the end (49:33).

The author introduces Joseph as a teenager and as a shepherd, helping four older brothers (Dan, Naphtali, Gad, and Asher). He first acts as an interpreter, a key role he will play in the story; he brings a criticism of his brothers back to Jacob (which they may or may not have deserved).

Joseph evidently now has a relationship with his father that the others do not have. It suggests that Joseph becomes the chosen son of the promise; the eleven are "Esau." This perception has been fostered by Jacob himself, who "loves" Joseph more than his other children (see 33:2, 7); Joseph was a child of Jacob's old age (see 30:22-24). Although not a problem in itself, it takes public form, specifically the gift of a costly robe, long and sleeved, perhaps with royal connotations (see 2 Sam 13:18; the traditional translation "a coat of many colors" is based on the Greek and Latin). Once again, an article of clothing plays an important role in a Genesis story.

As it became obvious that Joseph was his father's pet, the brothers grew to hate him (rather than Jacob!) and could not speak to him peaceably (בשלם *běšālôm;* see 45:15; 50:21). Communication breaks down. The stage is set for deep intrafamilial conflict. "In a few short sentences the narrator has sketched out an unusually complex world of fateful familial stratification, relations, and emotions: youth versus old age, intra-familial social hierarchy, concealed realms of discourse, rivalry, betrayal, obsessive love, ill-considered gifts of passion, hatred, shunning. The balance with which this system is presented leaves no heroes and no villains."[197]

37:5-11. Joseph, like his father, is a dreamer, and also an interpreter of dreams. The narrator heightens the importance of interpretation by offering no words (cf. 28:12-15; 31:10-13), only symbols. Dreams play a key role in the story, with three scenes of two dreams each (see chaps. 40–41). Yet, too much can be made of them as well.[198] They do introduce an important external

---

197. White, *Narration,* 242.
198. See Brueggemann, *Genesis,* 298-307.

reality into the family situation, but basically they serve a provisional function. They intensify the conflict through Joseph's telling of them and enable Joseph's testing of his brothers (42:9); but Joseph will finally deny the dreams' continuing applicability for shaping the future.

The meaning of Joseph's two dreams may be transparent, but *interpretations,* implied in their questions, are made only by the brothers and the father (cf. 40:8!): Joseph stands in a position of authority over them. That Joseph chooses to share uninterpreted dreams with those most affected makes for deeper misunderstanding; his silence regarding their interpretations intensifies the difficulties. He could have talked about what "rule" might mean (a key issue in the larger narrative); he could have responded to Jacob's comment about "bowing to the ground" before him (which never happens!). Joseph may be seeking to gain an advantage in the intrafamilial conflict, but he acts insensitively, even arrogantly, and only exacerbates the problems.

In the dream about the sheaves—anticipating the food/famine theme—the brothers bow down to Joseph. The brothers understand this as a threat to their place in the family. This provides a variant on the younger/older brother theme so common in Genesis (see 25:23), but finally *no one*—Joseph or brothers—will be excluded (50:24). The brothers respond with repeated, sarcastic, rhetorical questions about Joseph's becoming their ruler.

The second dream expands upon the first: The luminaries (sun and moon are parents; eleven stars are brothers) add Joseph's parents to those doing obeisance (Rachel seems still to be alive). No astrological links are evident, but the use of luminaries suggests that Joseph's role has taken on "astronomical" proportions! Only Jacob responds with rebuking, nonrhetorical questions this time, but finally he ponders what this might mean (v. 11). The dreams are the final step in a buildup of hatred. They are the catalyst for the first voicing of the brothers' attitude toward Joseph. The dreams finally tip the balance toward violence.

37:12-17. The scene changes abruptly; this enables the brothers to act outside their father's purview. The brothers journey some fifty miles from Hebron (35:27) to pasture the flock where there is good grassland, in this case near Shechem (a place with family links, 33:18-20). Joseph stays home, a change from established practice (37:2), about which Jacob wonders. Jacob (certainly not innocent regarding brotherly relationships) sends him to look into the well-being (šālôm) of the brothers and of their flocks and to report back (cf. David in 1 Samuel 17). This seems ironic given previous "reports" (v. 2) and the absence of šālôm between the brothers (v. 4). Even more, it leads the reader to wonder about Jacob's motivation. Is this the naive, loving father (the giver of the coat) who hopes that the brothers can work things out? Is he completely innocent of possible violence? *Shalom* will be hard to come by before this book, let alone this chapter, is over.

Because the brothers had moved to Dothan (fifteen miles north of Shechem), even farther away from their father, Joseph has difficulty locating them, and only then through the hospitality of a stranger. This delay heightens the drama, leaving Joseph vulnerably "suspended between father and brothers, between love and hatred."[199] It may also show how acts of hospitality are often "neutralized" by the context of trouble in which they occur.

37:18-28. This scene describes the brothers' plotting against Joseph and its convoluted effects. When the brothers see him approaching, they conspire to kill him. Their motivation centers on Joseph's dream (they sarcastically call him a "master of dreams"); by killing him, they will make certain that the dream does not become a reality. Ironically, by selling him to Egypt they enable it to become so! They think that human action can affect the outcome of what has been depicted in a dream.

Interpreters debate the meaning of this section. The brothers agree to sell him to passing Ishmaelites (vv. 27-28); yet, Midianite traders are also mentioned (vv. 28, 36). The text reports that both groups sell him in Egypt (v. 36; 39:1). Also, both Reuben (vv. 21-22) and Judah (vv. 26-27) intervene in comparable ways on his behalf. Some would resolve the issue by identifying the Midianites with the Ishmaelites (see Judg 8:24), or claim that the redactor does. Others posit two interwoven traditions: (1) Reuben and the Midianites, who kidnap Joseph; (2) Judah and the Ishmaelites, to whom Joseph is sold.

199. W. Lee Humphreys, *Joseph and His Family: A Literary Study* (Columbia: University of South Carolina Press, 1988) 35.

Since the antecedent of "they" in v. 28*a* is ambiguous (so NRSV; the NIV interprets "they" as the brothers) we do not know who sold Joseph. The author may have intended ambiguity, the effect being to destabilize the brothers' planning and leave the details of Joseph's transition to Egypt clouded in mystery (as 40:15 and 45:4-5 do). The fact that both groups are descended from half-brothers of Isaac (hence Joseph's kin, see 25:2) suggests an interest in having the descendants of Abraham through each of his three wives involved in the deed.

The brothers prove not to be of one mind in the matter and two voice their misgivings. Reuben, the oldest son (hence responsible to his father), intervenes on behalf of Joseph and begs the brothers not to take his life, but to throw him into a cistern (holes dug out to store rain water). The narrator informs us that his intention is heroic; he will return to the pit at a later time and restore Joseph to their father (if this happened, Joseph's reports to his father would, of course, intensify familial conflict). The brothers agree, and without a word from them or Joseph (though 42:21 refers to his pleas), they strip him of his robe (namely, his status), throw him into a waterless cistern (to a position *below* them), and sit down to eat (cf. 43:31-34 for the next meal).

Judah intervenes, sensing problems. When Ishmaelite traders bound for Egypt (with goods for use in medicine, cosmetics, and embalming; 43:11) enter the scene, he suggests a compromise, designed to appeal to self-interest: a "profit" motive (there is nothing to gain from killing him, though there would be if they sold him); they cannot conceal his blood (cf. 4:10) and will bear guilt; he is a brother, their own flesh and blood. The brothers agree and sell him for twenty shekels (see Lev 27:5) to the Ishmaelites (or the Midianites kidnap him), and he is sold on the Egyptian slave market. (Historically, a lively slave trade existed between Canaan and Egypt.)

37:29-36. This scene describes the effect of the brothers' convoluted conspiracies. Reuben (who was not with his brothers when they sold Joseph; see 42:22) returns to the pit to release Joseph (v. 22). He discovers to his grief (tearing his clothes) that he is gone. What can be done? His brothers are silent, displaying no knowledge or emotion; all of them simply get on with a ruse to convince Jacob of Joseph's death. Together, they dip Joseph's coat—so despised by them—in goat's blood and take it to their father (NRSV—they had it sent on ahead of them) for identification, following a legal process of substantiating a death. Jacob recognizes it and imagines a story of Joseph's death uncannily similar to the one the brothers had planned (v. 20). He has been tricked just as he had tricked his father (27:9), though 42:36 suggests he may suspect them. Expecting a report from Joseph, Jacob receives a report about him. Hoping for a word of *shalom,* Jacob hears a word that destabilizes his life. The coat, given to confirm love, becomes a confirmation of death.

Jacob cries out for his son with deep intensity. With traditional signs of mourning, Jacob laments for many days; his children (daughters, i.e., Dinah and his daughters-in-law) are unable to comfort him. He will lament until the day of his death, when he will go down to Sheol—where Joseph already is (cf. 42:38). Sheol is the realm of the dead, a shadowy, silent existence (more than the NIV's "grave"). Perhaps Jacob thought his mourning would continue even beyond death. The brothers sought to displace Joseph in their father's affections, but ironically Joseph will retain a preeminent place in his father's love even in death. Will the promise go down to Sheol with him? As if to confirm Jacob's wishes, Jacob disappears from the narrative until 42:1.

The author concludes by noting that the Midianites sell Joseph to Potiphar, one of Pharaoh's officials (anticipating chap. 39). At least Joseph is alive. But his journey to become ruler has taken a detour through slavery; his status at this point mirrors Israel's later life in Egypt. The story will resume again in 39:1, where the Ishmaelites sell him to Potiphar, perhaps another reference to the ambiguity regarding Joseph's fate, noted above.

REFLECTIONS

1. The dual movement from Canaan to Egypt and from individual Israel to people Israel shapes the Joseph story. This episode sets into motion a concatenation of events that will come to a climax in the formation of a people and the exodus from Egypt, and finally conclude in the promised land, with the deposition of Joseph's bones (Josh 24:32). The narrative as a whole witnesses to a God who uses even the evil designs of people to bring about good, indeed leads to events constitutive of the very character of Jacob's sons. Sinful behaviors do indeed frustrate the divine purposes in the world, but they do not, finally, stymie them.

2. Dreams in that world were usually understood to be externally and divinely generated (cf. Jer 23:25-26), not the result of an interior psychological process. Yet the brothers interpret Joseph's dreams as if they are the product of Joseph's own arrogance rather than a divine word about destiny. This ambiguity provides some of the tension in the narrative. Dreams also create tension by their "prophetic" character, as they move from announcement to realization (see 42:6; 43:26, 28; 44:16-17), yet without the brothers' realizing it! And not inevitably so, for example, since nowhere does *Jacob* "bow down" to Joseph (37:10). Moreover, the brothers *believe* that they can cut off the fulfillment by killing the dreamer, not least because (unlike a prophecy) Joseph himself remains integral to the plot depicted in the dream.

Eventually, Joseph denies the dreams' continuing applicability (see 50:19); the brothers are *not* to be his slaves, for he is not in the place of God. That role will be assumed by Pharaoh in the book of Exodus. Slavery cannot shape the relationship of Joseph to his brothers if they are to move toward reconciliation. Joseph takes the place of honor at the end of the story not least because he gives up on the dream. In so doing, Joseph demonstrates what it means truly to be a ruler.

The dreams do point to a future, but their import depends on the one who hears them and—always a second step—interprets them. One is reminded of the various responses to the visions of the prophets. For the brothers, Joseph's dreams are understood negatively; for Joseph, they are interpreted in a narrowly personal way; for Jacob, they become a matter for reflection. Jacob's response seems particularly admirable. He does not appear gullible, nor does he reject the dreams' potential import. He initially asks questions concerning the nature and implications of the dreams. But he takes these things and ponders them in his heart (see Luke 2:19), revealing an openness to future possibilities.

3. The narratives in Genesis have depicted the exclusion of various family members from the inner circle: Lot, Ishmael, the sons of Keturah, and Esau. On the basis of this chapter, the reader could think Joseph has joined the list. It is not to be so. The fact that the brothers are progenitors of the twelve tribes of Israel does cast their conflicted story in a different light. Eventually no one will be excluded; all twelve carry the promises into the future (50:24). These intrafamilial conflicts mirror exclusivistic efforts among the people of God in every age. This story finally witnesses to reconciliation among the brothers and the end of exclusion.

4. No individual in this story emerges innocent. Even Joseph, though certainly the primary victim, furnishes fuel for his own troubles. Everyone in his own way contributes to the mess in which the family finds itself; at the same time, to level out the sins of the characters and to make everyone equally irresponsible is to fail to consider issues of communal consequence. Or to turn God into an all-determining power undermines human responsibility for sin and encourages human passivity in the face of the power of evil.

5. Once again, the author tells this story without a single reference to God. The reader will learn (45:5) that God has not been absent from these activities. God works in and through even the worst that this family can perpetrate; in everything—even evil—God works for good. This relationship between human action and divine providence characterizes the entire narrative. The reader will be tempted to fall into one ditch or another in interpreting this dialectic: either divine determinism, where God fully controls events, or deism, where God must simply make do with whatever human action turns up and acts with no independent initiative. Neither of these options grasps the theological perspective that governs the story.

The absence of God language in this chapter commonly results in an emphasis on moral lessons, for example, related to parent/child relationships or intrafamilial disputes and deceptions. One must be careful not to draw easy moralisms, say, about parental favoritism—at most it is a lack of commonsense parenting! Favoritism per se does not constitute the problem; rather, the problem involves the way in which favoritism manifested itself publicly, on the part of both chooser and chosen. In some sense, the same problems arise for the electing God and Israel! Does the text mean to speak about problems in the way Israel dealt with its chosenness?

GENESIS 38:1-30, TAMAR AND JUDAH

NIV

38 At that time, Judah left his brothers and went down to stay with a man of Adullam named Hirah. [2]There Judah met the daughter of a Canaanite man named Shua. He married her and lay with her; [3]she became pregnant and gave birth to a son, who was named Er. [4]She conceived again and gave birth to a son and named him Onan. [5]She gave birth to still another son and named him Shelah. It was at Kezib that she gave birth to him.

[6]Judah got a wife for Er, his firstborn, and her name was Tamar. [7]But Er, Judah's firstborn, was wicked in the LORD's sight; so the LORD put him to death.

[8]Then Judah said to Onan, "Lie with your brother's wife and fulfill your duty to her as a brother-in-law to produce offspring for your brother." [9]But Onan knew that the offspring would not be his; so whenever he lay with his brother's wife, he spilled his semen on the ground to keep from producing offspring for his brother. [10]What he did was wicked in the LORD's sight; so he put him to death also.

[11]Judah then said to his daughter-in-law Tamar, "Live as a widow in your father's house until my son Shelah grows up." For he thought, "He may die too, just like his brothers." So Tamar went to live in her father's house.

[12]After a long time Judah's wife, the daughter of Shua, died. When Judah had recovered from his grief, he went up to Timnah, to the men who were shearing his sheep, and his friend Hirah the Adullamite went with him.

[13]When Tamar was told, "Your father-in-law is on his way to Timnah to shear his sheep," [14]she took off her widow's clothes, covered herself with a veil to disguise herself, and then sat down at

NRSV

38 It happened at that time that Judah went down from his brothers and settled near a certain Adullamite whose name was Hirah. [2]There Judah saw the daughter of a certain Canaanite whose name was Shua; he married her and went in to her. [3]She conceived and bore a son; and he named him Er. [4]Again she conceived and bore a son whom she named Onan. [5]Yet again she bore a son, and she named him Shelah. She[a] was in Chezib when she bore him. [6]Judah took a wife for Er his firstborn; her name was Tamar. [7]But Er, Judah's firstborn, was wicked in the sight of the LORD, and the LORD put him to death. [8]Then Judah said to Onan, "Go in to your brother's wife and perform the duty of a brother-in-law to her; raise up offspring for your brother." [9]But since Onan knew that the offspring would not be his, he spilled his semen on the ground whenever he went in to his brother's wife, so that he would not give offspring to his brother. [10]What he did was displeasing in the sight of the LORD, and he put him to death also. [11]Then Judah said to his daughter-in-law Tamar, "Remain a widow in your father's house until my son Shelah grows up"—for he feared that he too would die, like his brothers. So Tamar went to live in her father's house.

12In course of time the wife of Judah, Shua's daughter, died; when Judah's time of mourning was over,[b] he went up to Timnah to his sheepshearers, he and his friend Hirah the Adullamite. [13]When Tamar was told, "Your father-in-law is going up to Timnah to shear his sheep," [14]she put off her widow's garments, put on a veil, wrapped herself up, and sat down at the entrance to Enaim, which is on the road to Timnah. She saw that

[a] Gk: Heb *He*   [b] Heb *when Judah was comforted*

NIV

the entrance to Enaim, which is on the road to Timnah. For she saw that, though Shelah had now grown up, she had not been given to him as his wife.

¹⁵When Judah saw her, he thought she was a prostitute, for she had covered her face. ¹⁶Not realizing that she was his daughter-in-law, he went over to her by the roadside and said, "Come now, let me sleep with you."

"And what will you give me to sleep with you?" she asked.

¹⁷"I'll send you a young goat from my flock," he said.

"Will you give me something as a pledge until you send it?" she asked.

¹⁸He said, "What pledge should I give you?"

"Your seal and its cord, and the staff in your hand," she answered. So he gave them to her and slept with her, and she became pregnant by him. ¹⁹After she left, she took off her veil and put on her widow's clothes again.

²⁰Meanwhile Judah sent the young goat by his friend the Adullamite in order to get his pledge back from the woman, but he did not find her. ²¹He asked the men who lived there, "Where is the shrine prostitute who was beside the road at Enaim?"

"There hasn't been any shrine prostitute here," they said.

²²So he went back to Judah and said, "I didn't find her. Besides, the men who lived there said, 'There hasn't been any shrine prostitute here.'"

²³Then Judah said, "Let her keep what she has, or we will become a laughingstock. After all, I did send her this young goat, but you didn't find her."

²⁴About three months later Judah was told, "Your daughter-in-law Tamar is guilty of prostitution, and as a result she is now pregnant."

Judah said, "Bring her out and have her burned to death!"

²⁵As she was being brought out, she sent a message to her father-in-law. "I am pregnant by the man who owns these," she said. And she added, "See if you recognize whose seal and cord and staff these are."

²⁶Judah recognized them and said, "She is more righteous than I, since I wouldn't give her to my son Shelah." And he did not sleep with her again.

²⁷When the time came for her to give birth,

NRSV

Shelah was grown up, yet she had not been given to him in marriage. ¹⁵When Judah saw her, he thought her to be a prostitute, for she had covered her face. ¹⁶He went over to her at the road side, and said, "Come, let me come in to you," for he did not know that she was his daughter-in-law. She said, "What will you give me, that you may come in to me?" ¹⁷He answered, "I will send you a kid from the flock." And she said, "Only if you give me a pledge, until you send it." ¹⁸He said, "What pledge shall I give you?" She replied, "Your signet and your cord, and the staff that is in your hand." So he gave them to her, and went in to her, and she conceived by him. ¹⁹Then she got up and went away, and taking off her veil she put on the garments of her widowhood.

²⁰When Judah sent the kid by his friend the Adullamite, to recover the pledge from the woman, he could not find her. ²¹He asked the townspeople, "Where is the temple prostitute who was at Enaim by the wayside?" But they said, "No prostitute has been here." ²²So he returned to Judah, and said, "I have not found her; moreover the townspeople said, 'No prostitute has been here.'" ²³Judah replied, "Let her keep the things as her own, otherwise we will be laughed at; you see, I sent this kid, and you could not find her."

²⁴About three months later Judah was told, "Your daughter-in-law Tamar has played the whore; moreover she is pregnant as a result of whoredom." And Judah said, "Bring her out, and let her be burned." ²⁵As she was being brought out, she sent word to her father-in-law, "It was the owner of these who made me pregnant." And she said, "Take note, please, whose these are, the signet and the cord and the staff." ²⁶Then Judah acknowledged them and said, "She is more in the right than I, since I did not give her to my son Shelah." And he did not lie with her again.

²⁷When the time of her delivery came, there were twins in her womb. ²⁸While she was in labor, one put out a hand; and the midwife took and bound on his hand a crimson thread, saying, "This one came out first." ²⁹But just then he drew back his hand, and out came his brother; and she said, "What a breach you have made for yourself!"

NIV

there were twin boys in her womb. [28]As she was giving birth, one of them put out his hand; so the midwife took a scarlet thread and tied it on his wrist and said, "This one came out first." [29]But when he drew back his hand, his brother came out, and she said, "So this is how you have broken out!" And he was named Perez.[a] [30]Then his brother, who had the scarlet thread on his wrist, came out and he was given the name Zerah.[b]

[a]29 *Perez* means *breaking out.*   [b]30 *Zerah* can mean *scarlet* or *brightness.*

NRSV

Therefore he was named Perez.[a] [30]Afterward his brother came out with the crimson thread on his hand; and he was named Zerah.[b]

[a]That is *A breach*   [b]That is *Brightness*; perhaps alluding to the crimson thread

COMMENTARY

Interpreters have devoted considerable attention in recent years to the human passions and literary tensions presented in this text. A source-critical approach (usually J) no longer seems sufficient. Despite its independent origins, this narrative plays an important role within its present literary context.[200] This is a family story, not tribal history, that has a "wonderful openness to what is human—passions, guilt, paternal anxiety, love, honor, chivalry, all churning up the narrow circle of one family in labyrinthine entanglement."[201]

The preceding narrative centers on the conflict between Joseph and his brothers, concluding with Joseph's being sold to Egypt (37:36). Chapter 38 proceeds as if that were the end of the story for Joseph, taking us into the continuing life of one of the other brothers, in this case Judah (cf. 37:26), who separates himself from the family. It covers some twenty years in his life, and then, in 39:1, the story of Joseph abruptly picks up at the point where it left off in 37:36.

What is accomplished by this break in the story? From a literary perspective, it slows the action of the story and creates suspense concerning Joseph's fate. Moreover, it shows that the story of Jacob's family continues alongside that of Joseph, especially important in view of Judah's later role. It also anticipates and helps to interpret certain features of the story to follow: (a) issues of sexuality (39:9-11); Judah's serving as a foil for Joseph; (b) the theme of recognition, where

Joseph "hides" from his brothers for the sake of their future, not unlike what Tamar does with Judah; (c) the theme of reversal, in view of which Joseph's return from a seemingly impossible situation parallels that of Tamar; and (d) the theme of deception, through the use of tangible evidence (37:32-33; 38:25-26).

At the same time, chap. 38 picks up many themes from the ancestral story: (1) Judah stands over against the tradition of marriage to Canaanites (24:3; 28:1; Joseph also marries outside the family). Although the Canaanites occupy an ambiguous place in Genesis, the line of promise carries on through Tamar, a Canaanite. The repeated reference to Judah's Canaanite "friend" (vv. 12, 20) may also provide a positive rather than a negative note. (2) As with Abraham and Isaac, the firstborn sons of neither Jacob nor Judah continue the line of promise leading to David. (3) Onan's refusal of responsibility toward Er mirrors the conflict between brothers. (4) The symbolic use of Tamar's clothing has parallels throughout Genesis, from Adam and Eve to various incidents in Joseph's life. (6) Other women, like Tamar, confront the problem of childlessness. (7) Other women—e.g., Rebekah, like Tamar—act over against established order, thereby furthering God's purposes. (8) The web of deception, not least those cases where the deceiver is himself deceived, continues.

This story also relates to the development of Jacob's older sons. Judah's older brothers have been sharply criticized up to this point (Reuben in 35:22; Simeon and Levi in 34:30). Judah, the

200. See Alter, *Art,* 3-12.
201. Von Rad, *Genesis,* 361.

fourth son, played a slave-dealer (37:26), and he here leaves the rest of the family. This raises a question comparable to chap. 37: Is Judah, too, being excluded from the line of promise? But he returns to become a risk-taker for the sake of the family (see 43:3-10; 44:18-34) and receives high praise in Jacob's blessing (49:8-12). The story of Joseph becomes, also, the story of Judah, both of whom receive equal prominence in Jacob's blessing (49:8-12, 22-26).

38:1-5. Judah settles near Bethlehem (the place names in the chapter are all in this vicinity) and marries an unnamed Canaanite woman; they have three children: Er, Onan, and Shelah. Early normality quickly devolves into dysfunctionality.

38:6-11. Tamar (probably a Canaanite) appears on the scene as the wife of Er. Because Er is a wicked man, God puts him to death (through unspecified means; see below). Judah then directs his second son, Onan, to "perform the duty of a brother-in-law to her" (though marriage is not mentioned, consummation probably entails it; cf. v. 14)—namely, to raise up an heir to carry on the name and inheritance of the deceased brother (cf. Deut 25:5-10; Ruth 4).

Onan sabotages the intent of the relationship in order to gain Er's inheritance for himself upon Judah's death—the firstborn would receive a double share. He regularly uses Tamar for sex, but makes sure she does not become pregnant by not letting his semen enter her (*coitus interruptus*, not masturbation). He thereby formally fulfills his duty, lest the role be passed on to his other brother and he lose Er's inheritance in this way. This willful deception would be observable to Tamar, but God's observation leads to Onan's death (again, by unspecified means).

Judah, having lost two sons and perhaps wondering whether Tamar were the problem, seeks to protect his own future by keeping his last son from her. He does so at Tamar's expense, directing her to return to her own father's house, where she would not have inheritance rights or be free to remarry. This act cuts her off from her husband's family and places her future welfare in jeopardy (cf. 30:1). Verse 26 shows v. 11 to be central; Judah deceives Tamar rather than risk his third son.

38:12-23. Tamar does as Judah says, but she does not settle for such an arrangement. When she realizes that Judah has withheld Shelah from her (v. 14b delays this notice), she takes the matter into her own hands and assumes the duty of providing an heir for Er. Having no recourse to the courts, she will move beyond the law to fulfill the law, even at the cost of her honor and her life. As Judah will say (v. 26), Tamar's risk-taking on behalf of her husband exceeds his and proves her to be the righteous one in this situation.

The death of Judah's wife provides the opportunity for Tamar; he will be open to sexual diversion. Hearing of his trip to Timnah, Tamar makes plans to confront him. She dresses in such a way as to attract Judah's attention and situates herself on the way she knows he will take (see Jer 3:2). The narrator does not speak of her intentions. Although her dress and action could imply prostitution (the veil both invites and conceals), the narrator does not mention it. Judah so interprets the veil and propositions her (vv. 15-16). In v. 21, his friend speaks of her as a "temple prostitute," probably only more discreet language for a prostitute (with no official cultic reference). The townspeople deny having seen a prostitute, a matter stressed in the friend's report to Judah (v. 22). When it becomes evident that Tamar is pregnant, "friends and neighbors" of Judah (not the narrator) draw the inference regarding harlotry (v. 24).

Was Tamar playing the harlot? It depends on one's point of view. Judah and his friend understood her to be a prostitute, and Judah's not recognizing her seems startling (did she remain veiled? cf. 29:23-25). But she was not publicly so identified by the people of Enaim. While Judah's friends assume such upon hearing of her pregnancy, the narrator's perspective does not interpret her action as harlotry. Whatever her intentions and actions, she must not be *identified* as a prostitute. Tamar's putting her widow's garments off and on (vv. 14, 19) symbolizes continuity in identification as the widow of Er. Judah's failure to regain the signs of his identity signifies discontinuity. His identity becomes ambiguous; will he gain it back?

Before Tamar allows Judah to have his way with her, she exacts a price; Judah (apparently unprepared for such an eventuality) agrees on a young goat from the flock, but she wisely insists on a pledge. Judah naively agrees to what she suggests: his staff (specially marked) and his signet and cord (a seal, suspended on a neck cord, used to stamp one's "signature" in wet clay), signs of personal identification. Having completed the sexual act, each goes his or her way, with Tamar's identity intact and Judah's identity in the hands of Tamar. The immediate reference to conception establishes her intent in all of this. The narrative draws no moral conclusions about the behavior of either Judah or Tamar (cf. Lev 18:15).

When Judah seeks to fulfill the pledge, he discreetly sends his friend; but he can find no prostitute. Judah contents himself with the fact that he kept his pledge, and he does not risk having his male ego publicly bruised for being taken by a prostitute. He remains a man without identity.

38:24-26. When Tamar's pregnancy becomes evident, she is charged with harlotry. Upon hearing the news, Judah assumes the role of judge (she was under his authority, though with her family) and exacts the death penalty (cf. Lev 20:10; Deut 22:22). The irony is sharp: When Judah saw her as a prostitute (זונה zônâ, v. 15), he used her; when he sees her in this capacity as his daughter-in-law (זנה zānâ, v. 24), he condemns her. Clearly Judah applies a double standard.

Tamar, however, produces the pledge given her by Judah and sends the items on ahead (less embarrassing?). Judah responds magnanimously; his words and actions go beyond what would have been necessary. His guilt-admitting recognition that Tamar has been more righteous (צדקה ṣadĕqâ!) than he means that Tamar has done justice to *this* relationship in a way that he has not in failing to give her to his third son. Tamar and Judah do not speak face to face, and he does not touch her again, though he may have been entitled to (perhaps a reference to the reestablishment of her proper place in Judah's family). We are not informed whether she ever marries again.

38:27-30. The narrative concludes quickly, with the concern for which Tamar fought brought to fruition. Twins are born to Judah and Tamar in an abnormal birth, reminding the reader of the birth of Jacob and Esau (25:22-26). Again we encounter confusion about the firstborn; although Perez is actually born first, Zerah's arm had already come out, and so he is designated firstborn. Once again, the second born carries on the line of promise, for David (Ruth 4:18) and Jesus (Matt 1:3) descend from Perez.

REFLECTIONS

1. The direct statements that God put Er and Onan to death are unusual for the OT. Such divine actions at the individual level seem reserved for moments when the future of the people of God is at stake (see 1 Sam 2:25). The narrator may understand that here, particularly since the line leading to David is at risk. The narrator does not specify the means by which the brothers meet their death (e.g., sickness; cf. God's role in the death of Saul according to 1 Chr 10:14). These texts provide no basis upon which to draw general conclusions about death as God's will. Generally, God wills life, not death (see 45:5-7; Ezek 18:23, 32). Yet, the fact that God may work toward the death of certain persons ought not be ruled out. One thinks of the theological rationale given by some who plotted Hitler's death.

2. This text involves the continuation of the line of promise, which leads to David (see Ruth 4:18). We have noted links with the story of David (e.g., name similarity, such as Tamar in 2 Samuel 13) and with the Abrahamic promises regarding kings (17:6; 35:11). This line continues through the younger son of Tamar and Judah, Perez (Er drops from the genealogy, perhaps because he had never actually received the inheritance). Tamar is specifically mentioned in the genealogy of Jesus (Matt 1:3), along with three other women who engage in sexual activity of a questionable sort: Rahab, Ruth, and Bathsheba. These women contribute in a direct way to the birth of the Messiah. Such an explicit connection with the birth of Jesus affirms that this royal lineage does not somehow float above the maelstrom of life. This fact presents divine irony: God works in and through what appears weak and despised according to worldly standards in order to accomplish

God's purposes (see 1 Cor 1:18-31). Tamar distinguishes herself more than does Jacob's own son toward this end.

3. This text lifts up issues of social responsibility and justice in an especially forceful way, with a focus on the plight of women. The text offers two primary perspectives. On the one hand, the ancient author recognized Tamar as one misused by a key authority figure in her life. In spite of her oppression, she possesses resources to find a way into a more hopeful future (see below). She subverts Judah's intentions and accomplishes a stunning reversal of authority. Tamar's resourcefulness occurs within the order of creation; God does not directly act.

On the other hand, the author presents Judah as one who misuses his authority and fails in both his familial and communal responsibilities. He chooses a self-serving route that places in jeopardy the future of both Tamar and the community to which they belong. The text thus speaks sharply about the use and abuse of power within the family and in the community of faith. But the text is not finally pessimistic regarding changes that can take place within individuals to transform such situations into good. Judah does change and acknowledges that the person he had abused is indeed the one who has been righteous. His experience with Tamar, leading to his public confession, may be decisive; when he risks his life for the sake of the family's future (43:9; 44:32), he follows Tamar's example.

4. Tamar's actions constitute a rebellion against established authority and custom and would normally be considered offensive; most religious people would condemn this act out of hand. But the word used for Tamar's act is *ṣādĕqâ* (v. 26). Her action cannot be universalized so as to be declared righteous wherever it is committed; at the same time, such action may be righteous in another time and place if it becomes the way of doing justice to a relationship. It may be necessary to go beyond the law in order to fulfill the law, which should enable life and well-being to a community (see Deut 6:24; Jesus' sabbath-breaking, Mark 2:27). Here the OT narrative gives especially high value to the future of the community, in view of which individual acts, which might be normally condemned, are viewed positively. Relationships are more important than rules; faithfulness may mean going beyond the law. We cannot help wondering whether this story has informed Jesus' saying that "the prostitutes are going into the kingdom of God ahead of you" (Matt 21:31 NRSV) as well as his open response to the woman who was a "sinner" (Luke 7:36-50).

We should not "secularize" this note about righteousness; in v. 10, God is explicitly involved in judgment regarding this matter. Hence, Tamar has been truer to her relationship with *God* than Judah has. Once again in the ancestral narrative, a person who stands outside of the community of promise proves to be faithful to what God intends for human community, indeed for the community of promise. In fact, she is a Canaanite! At least in part because of his evaluation of Tamar, Judah receives a praiseworthy place in the ancestral narrative (49:8), and his staff becomes a scepter that "shall not depart from Judah" (49:10).

GENESIS 39:1-23, JOSEPH, GOD, AND SUCCESS

NIV

39 Now Joseph had been taken down to Egypt. Potiphar, an Egyptian who was one of Pharaoh's officials, the captain of the guard, bought him from the Ishmaelites who had taken him there.

NRSV

39 Now Joseph was taken down to Egypt, and Potiphar, an officer of Pharaoh, the captain of the guard, an Egyptian, bought him from the Ishmaelites who had brought him down there. [2]The LORD was with Joseph, and he became a

NIV

²The LORD was with Joseph and he prospered, and he lived in the house of his Egyptian master. ³When his master saw that the LORD was with him and that the LORD gave him success in everything he did, ⁴Joseph found favor in his eyes and became his attendant. Potiphar put him in charge of his household, and he entrusted to his care everything he owned. ⁵From the time he put him in charge of his household and of all that he owned, the LORD blessed the household of the Egyptian because of Joseph. The blessing of the LORD was on everything Potiphar had, both in the house and in the field. ⁶So he left in Joseph's care everything he had; with Joseph in charge, he did not concern himself with anything except the food he ate.

Now Joseph was well-built and handsome, ⁷and after a while his master's wife took notice of Joseph and said, "Come to bed with me!"

⁸But he refused. "With me in charge," he told her, "my master does not concern himself with anything in the house; everything he owns he has entrusted to my care. ⁹No one is greater in this house than I am. My master has withheld nothing from me except you, because you are his wife. How then could I do such a wicked thing and sin against God?" ¹⁰And though she spoke to Joseph day after day, he refused to go to bed with her or even be with her.

¹¹One day he went into the house to attend to his duties, and none of the household servants was inside. ¹²She caught him by his cloak and said, "Come to bed with me!" But he left his cloak in her hand and ran out of the house.

¹³When she saw that he had left his cloak in her hand and had run out of the house, ¹⁴she called her household servants. "Look," she said to them, "this Hebrew has been brought to us to make sport of us! He came in here to sleep with me, but I screamed. ¹⁵When he heard me scream for help, he left his cloak beside me and ran out of the house."

¹⁶She kept his cloak beside her until his master came home. ¹⁷Then she told him this story: "That Hebrew slave you brought us came to me to make sport of me. ¹⁸But as soon as I screamed for help, he left his cloak beside me and ran out of the house."

NRSV

successful man; he was in the house of his Egyptian master. ³His master saw that the LORD was with him, and that the LORD caused all that he did to prosper in his hands. ⁴So Joseph found favor in his sight and attended him; he made him overseer of his house and put him in charge of all that he had. ⁵From the time that he made him overseer in his house and over all that he had, the LORD blessed the Egyptian's house for Joseph's sake; the blessing of the LORD was on all that he had, in house and field. ⁶So he left all that he had in Joseph's charge; and, with him there, he had no concern for anything but the food that he ate.

Now Joseph was handsome and good-looking. ⁷And after a time his master's wife cast her eyes on Joseph and said, "Lie with me." ⁸But he refused and said to his master's wife, "Look, with me here, my master has no concern about anything in the house, and he has put everything that he has in my hand. ⁹He is not greater in this house than I am, nor has he kept back anything from me except yourself, because you are his wife. How then could I do this great wickedness, and sin against God?" ¹⁰And although she spoke to Joseph day after day, he would not consent to lie beside her or to be with her. ¹¹One day, however, when he went into the house to do his work, and while no one else was in the house, ¹²she caught hold of his garment, saying, "Lie with me!" But he left his garment in her hand, and fled and ran outside. ¹³When she saw that he had left his garment in her hand and had fled outside, ¹⁴she called out to the members of her household and said to them, "See, my husband[a] has brought among us a Hebrew to insult us! He came in to me to lie with me, and I cried out with a loud voice; ¹⁵and when he heard me raise my voice and cry out, he left his garment beside me, and fled outside." ¹⁶Then she kept his garment by her until his master came home, ¹⁷and she told him the same story, saying, "The Hebrew servant, whom you have brought among us, came in to me to insult me; ¹⁸but as soon as I raised my voice and cried out, he left his garment beside me, and fled outside."

19When his master heard the words that his wife spoke to him, saying, "This is the way your

ᵃ Heb *he*

NIV

[19]When his master heard the story his wife told him, saying, "This is how your slave treated me," he burned with anger. [20]Joseph's master took him and put him in prison, the place where the king's prisoners were confined.

But while Joseph was there in the prison, [21]the LORD was with him; he showed him kindness and granted him favor in the eyes of the prison warden. [22]So the warden put Joseph in charge of all those held in the prison, and he was made responsible for all that was done there. [23]The warden paid no attention to anything under Joseph's care, because the LORD was with Joseph and gave him success in whatever he did.

NRSV

servant treated me," he became enraged. [20]And Joseph's master took him and put him into the prison, the place where the king's prisoners were confined; he remained there in prison. [21]But the LORD was with Joseph and showed him steadfast love; he gave him favor in the sight of the chief jailer. [22]The chief jailer committed to Joseph's care all the prisoners who were in the prison, and whatever was done there, he was the one who did it. [23]The chief jailer paid no heed to anything that was in Joseph's care, because the LORD was with him; and whatever he did, the LORD made it prosper.

COMMENTARY

Chapters 39–41 constitute a unified narrative, telling the story of the problems and successes associated with Joseph's rise to a high official in Pharaoh's court. Within this narrative, the author has divided chap. 39 into three scenes, the first two set in Potiphar's home. Verses 1-6 portray Joseph's initial advancement to a position of power, vv. 7-20, his fall associated with encounters with Potiphar's wife, and vv. 21-23, a new rise to prominence in prison.

This story bears some resemblance to the Egyptian *Tale of Two Brothers.* The course of each story is similar; similar phraseology occurs in both, including theological language (e.g., "the strength of a god was in him"; adultery as the "great sin"). Such stories and motifs were probably common in the ancient Near East.

39:1-6. Chapter 37 ended with the reader's being left in some suspense regarding Joseph's fate. Chapter 39 picks up the story at that point. Joseph has been sold by the Ishmaelites to an otherwise unknown Egyptian named Potiphar, an official of Pharaoh, in whose home Joseph takes up residence. Now, through chap. 41, we find no reference to Joseph's home and family. This absence intensifies Joseph's isolation and may explain the emphasis placed on God's presence with him.

When Potiphar observes how he prospers under Joseph's care, he appoints Joseph to a position of authority, entrusting him with the care of his

entire household. The narrator interweaves what God has done (vv. 3, 5) with Joseph's rise to power (vv. 4, 6). By this repetition, the narrator stresses that this success has been made possible because of God's involvement. The only concern Potiphar has is eating; this reference hints subtly to a lack of interest in anything else, including his own wife. This could explain her sexual interest in Joseph, who was well built and handsome (v. 6*a* should not be split off from v. 6*b*).

39:7-20. This famous episode of Joseph and Potiphar's wife has often been interpreted as a morality tale, designed to specify limits regarding sexuality for persons of faith. A closer look reveals a more complex purpose. The text has also received attention because of the role of Potiphar's wife, the only woman given a role of consequence in the Joseph story. Although she remains unnamed throughout (Potiphar is named only in 37:36; 39:1 and, unlike his wife, never utters a word), she has much independence and freedom and exercises no little power in the confrontation with Joseph and her own husband. Both Potiphar and his wife are almost always defined in terms of their place in life (e.g., master's wife; captain of the guard; master).

The description of Joseph (words used for his mother in 29:17) leads immediately to a scene in which his master's wife—whose appearance the author does not describe—commands Joseph to go to bed with her: "Lie with me." Forgoing all preliminaries, she presents the matter in terms of power rather than love, of command rather than seduction; she is "his master's wife." But she misunderstands the power issues involved. Joseph resists her demands and responds to her in terms of authority (both human and divine; he begins with master and ends with God) rather than sexuality. He emphasizes that her husband has entrusted him with their household. This element of trust appears central, for his relationship with Potiphar—and perhaps his own life—depends on it (as his later reaction shows). But the text also presents an issue of the responsible exercise of his office; he and Potiphar are in effect equals with respect to authority in the household, hence he need not obey her command. At the same time, he has no rights to her. In fact, it appears that Potiphar has explicitly held his wife back from Joseph (v. 9).

Joseph's reply also specifies a "great wickedness" (or evil) against God, almost certainly a phrase designating adultery (cf. 20:9). The author has identified at least an implicit moral standard on this matter (cf. Deut 22:22), though not addressed in the abstract (nor in chap. 38). The focus: If he should commit this act with his master's wife, he would thereby sin against God. He remains true to God by remaining true to his master. He sees adultery as an irresponsible use of power and a violation of the trusting relationship he has both with Potiphar and with God.

The concern for Joseph's relationship with God appears striking, since the author has not mentioned it. Sin (or wrong, blame) elsewhere in the Joseph story refers to sins or offenses against others (40:1; 42:22; 43:9; cf. also 20:6, 9). From the perspective of Potiphar's wife, Joseph was guilty of an outrage or insult (NRSV; NIV, "making sport") not only against her but against "us," presumably the entire household (vv. 14, 17).

Potiphar's wife does not accept Joseph's reply—she continues to request sexual favors from him (v. 12). He persists in refusing her overtures; indeed, he stays away from her. But one day while he is going about his work alone, she encounters him, grabs his cloak, repeats her command, and retains the garment as he flees her grasp. She now finds herself in a position not unlike Tamar (38:25), except Joseph is the innocent one. She holds Joseph's garment as did his brothers (37:23, 31-32), using it in a deceitful way against him. She accuses him falsely, and she gets away with it (note the absence of retribution, a recognition of the loose causal weave in the moral order).

With Joseph's garment in her hand, and Joseph in her power, she immediately calls her servants together and fabricates a story involving an insult to all of them ("us") wherein Joseph is accused of doing what, in fact, she did. The reference to "a Hebrew" may play on their natural suspicion of foreigners (43:32). She also implicitly blames her husband for hiring him in the first place (vv. 14, 17), thereby raising the stakes. She, in turn, repeats the story in more subtle terms to her husband ("his master"), focusing on the insult to her ("me") and calling him *"your* servant" (vv. 17, 19). She cleverly makes it as much Potiphar's problem as Joseph's. If he hadn't hired Joseph, this would not have happened! This assures that Potiphar's response will be driven as much by guilt as by anger.

39:21-23. Potiphar becomes enraged by what he hears (probably for many reasons) and puts Joseph into prison—another pit (37:20)—without either facing him with the evidence or giving him an opportunity to reply to the accusation. Prison (especially the king's prison) was probably a lesser penalty than what was typical in such situations (Israelite law called for death, Lev 20:10; Deut 22:22). Joseph is an innocent victim, reduced to silence. Yet, in time he responds to the prison warden in a way similar to his response to Potiphar (vv. 4-6), with much the same effect (v. 22): The warden entrusts Joseph with responsibility for the warden's prison work (so the NIV; he did not do everything, so the NRSV). The narrator interprets what happens in theological terms; reports of God's enabling activity enclose the chapter (cf. vv. 2-6).

REFLECTIONS

1. These developments in the story are explicitly linked to the activity of God. Many references to God occur at the deepest point of Joseph's journey. Not since 35:1-15 have God's presence and action been so directly reported. Generally, reference to God occurs more often in the story than interpreters commonly recognize (some fifty times). Yet, the type of reference to God pushes in somewhat different directions, as will become evident.

The narrator provides eight of the nine references to God in this chapter, and they enclose the story (vv. 2-5, 21-23). They include the only occurrences of "Yahweh" (eight times) in the Joseph story, none spoken by a character. Unlike the immediately preceding chapters, the narrator thereby gives an explicitly theological interpretation to what occurs and links the story with key "God" texts later in the narrative (45:5-9; 50:20). Moreover, the use of *Yahweh* connects with usage in previous chapters, assuring continuity. More generally, it links up with Israel's subsequent history.

God works at multiple levels in these events—with both Joseph and Potiphar, and in such a way that the relationship between the two of them develops favorably. Moreover, God's work in and through Joseph leads to life and well-being for everything to which Joseph puts his hand, both human and nonhuman.

2. We focus on the nine references to God in this chapter (see vv. 2, 3, 5, 9, 21, 23). Four of these references specify that Yahweh was with Joseph. Even more, God remains present (1) outside the promised land, (2) in the life of one not of the line of promise, and (3) in everyday spheres of life, especially the political. Two passages occur at those points where Joseph's future appears uncertain. Although Joseph was without the support of his family (v. 2) and in prison (v. 21), the narrator assures the reader that Joseph has not been abandoned. Although all human supports have failed, and Joseph is far removed from the community of faith and the land of promise, God stays with him. God's presence, neither localized geographically nor dramatic or spectacular, is an unobtrusive, working-behind-the-scenes kind of presence.

In addition, God's presence with Joseph encompasses human abandonment and prison. Moreover, the text offers no evidence that such sin-generated events are the will of God for Joseph; sin is "against God" (v. 9); hence it is contrary to the divine will. God does not always get God's way in the world. Divine presence does not mean "preventive medicine" or a "quick fix" of whatever may befall a person of faith. There are implications here for how God works in the world: not in overwhelming power, but in and through the ambiguities and complexities of the relationships of integrity God has established.

The narrator thereby speaks not simply of divine presence but of the kind of God who acts in these events. Presence is one thing; the nature and effect of that presence are another. Verse 21 speaks of this God as one who shows steadfast love (חסד *hesed*); this word occurs elsewhere in the Joseph story only for human kindness and loyalty (40:14; 47:29). The author emphasizes here divine loyalty to the promise (see 32:10). God also works with Potiphar, so that Joseph finds favor in his eyes. Thus God appears active, not only within the lives of the family of promise, but also within those who do not confess the name of God.

Other references to God's presence are unusual: The Egyptian Potiphar recognizes that Yahweh is with Joseph and that Yahweh has prospered Joseph (vv. 3, 23). How should we explain an Egyptian's making this theological interpretation? It probably presupposes that Joseph's presence "in the house of his Egyptian master" entails theological conversation, or at least sufficient knowledge of Joseph to make the connection between his God and his words and deeds. This may also stand behind v. 21, which witnesses to a divine action within Potiphar—mediated through Joseph's presence at least—that enables him to view Joseph favorably. We should compare this response to those events in Exodus where God acts with Pharaoh and the Egyptians toward a comparable end (7:17; 8:10; 14:4); the Israelites gain favor at least in the eyes of the Egyptians, if not with the pharaoh (11:3; 12:36).

Two further references to Yahweh focus on the divine blessing brought on Potiphar's household and all that he has (v. 5). The author notes that God gives this blessing "because of Joseph" (as with Jacob, 30:27-30). This divine blessing goes beyond the blessings that come to all in and through the created order. Not simply God's presence but Joseph's presence as well makes a difference to the Egyptian situation. We hear this stated explicitly: *From the time that* Potiphar made Joseph an overseer, such blessings were forthcoming. Joseph's activity thus becomes a vehicle in and through which God works to bless in ways *that would not otherwise be effective in the same way.* In other words, Joseph's presence intensifies and enhances the general blessing work of God. We may relate this understanding to 12:2-3 (and parallels): In and through the members of Abraham's family, blessing extends to those who are not the elect. What God's people say and do makes a difference regarding the welfare of others; God has chosen to depend on them in carrying out the divine work in the world. While God is not explicitly the subject of verbs conveying blessing to the Egyptians, the entire narrative presupposes that God works among them in and through the person and work of Joseph. Indeed, 41:53-57 makes it clear that this blessing extends to include the entire world!

Three references to Yahweh in this chapter involve God's making Joseph's way prosperous, successful (vv. 2-3, 23; cf. 1 Sam 18:14; 2 Kgs 18:7). Once again, this activity of God relates explicitly to what *Joseph does.* Who Joseph is and the way in which Joseph speaks and acts have a positive effect.

The narrative portrays the impact of Joseph's behavior in a number of ways. For example, the narrator does not neglect the effective methods Joseph uses to bring about well-being (e.g., 41:46-49). Joseph works as an efficient, diligent, and competent administrator, which enables God to work more effectively through him. Moreover, the narrator delves into Joseph's character; he is loyal, patient under stress, and filled with wisdom (his loyalty mirrors God's, v. 21). The trust that Potiphar places in him (v. 6), as well as the incident with Potiphar's wife, are probably intended to speak directly to this point. The author provides the reader a clue to this end with the reference to God in v. 9, the only time a human character utters the word *God.* Joseph does justice to relationships, both with human beings and with God—and both are important in their own right. Joseph does not succumb to the very real temptations of power and sex. His actions have considerable effect on how God works in and through him. Who Joseph is and what Joseph does make a difference to God's work in the world. In turn, God's work in Joseph enables him to mature and develop in ways that would not otherwise be possible.

3. Success and prosperity are not a necessary or inevitable result of either God's presence or Joseph's faith or action. Joseph appears genuinely vulnerable and could have failed even with God's presence and the divine intention for success. Joseph's success depends not simply on his own devices, but on God's engagement in the situation.

4. Interpreters have often pointed to thematic parallels with the story of the rise of David (1 Sam 16:18; 18:12, 14, 28). This comparison suggests a particular interest in associating the presence of God with the political sphere. God accompanies this family as it moves out of the domain of the domestic into the broader sphere of national and political life. God works in every aspect of life.

5. Once again a story in Genesis mirrors a later experience of the people of God or an individual Israelite: Israel from Egypt to the kingship of David and Solomon; David from shepherd boy to king. Also parallel are the theological themes of divine presence and blessing. Different, however, is the basically positive assessment of those who stand outside the community of faith, something typical of Genesis. The incident with Potiphar's wife indicates the potential for the misuse of power by those in high positions. Yet, in Genesis, the author views political power, both when Joseph is in power and when he is not, much more positively. Rather than mirroring later Israel, this aspect of the story provides rulers with an ideal toward which to strive. The Joseph figure—particularly as mediated through David—provides images for the development of messianic themes.

GENESIS 40:1-23, JOSEPH, INTERPRETER OF DREAMS

40Some time later, the cupbearer and the baker of the king of Egypt offended their master, the king of Egypt. ²Pharaoh was angry with his two officials, the chief cupbearer and the chief baker, ³and put them in custody in the house of the captain of the guard, in the same prison where Joseph was confined. ⁴The captain of the guard assigned them to Joseph, and he attended them.

After they had been in custody for some time, ⁵each of the two men—the cupbearer and the baker of the king of Egypt, who were being held in prison—had a dream the same night, and each dream had a meaning of its own.

⁶When Joseph came to them the next morning, he saw that they were dejected. ⁷So he asked Pharaoh's officials who were in custody with him in his master's house, "Why are your faces so sad today?"

⁸"We both had dreams," they answered, "but there is no one to interpret them."

Then Joseph said to them, "Do not interpretations belong to God? Tell me your dreams."

⁹So the chief cupbearer told Joseph his dream. He said to him, "In my dream I saw a vine in front of me, ¹⁰and on the vine were three branches. As soon as it budded, it blossomed, and its clusters ripened into grapes. ¹¹Pharaoh's cup was in my hand, and I took the grapes, squeezed them into Pharaoh's cup and put the cup in his hand."

¹²"This is what it means," Joseph said to him. "The three branches are three days. ¹³Within three days Pharaoh will lift up your head and restore you to your position, and you will put Pharaoh's cup in his hand, just as you used to do when you were his cupbearer. ¹⁴But when all goes well with you, remember me and show me kindness; mention me to Pharaoh and get me out of this prison. ¹⁵For I was forcibly carried off from the land of the Hebrews, and even here I have done nothing to deserve being put in a dungeon."

¹⁶When the chief baker saw that Joseph had given a favorable interpretation, he said to Joseph,

40Some time after this, the cupbearer of the king of Egypt and his baker offended their lord the king of Egypt. ²Pharaoh was angry with his two officers, the chief cupbearer and the chief baker, ³and he put them in custody in the house of the captain of the guard, in the prison where Joseph was confined. ⁴The captain of the guard charged Joseph with them, and he waited on them; and they continued for some time in custody. ⁵One night they both dreamed—the cupbearer and the baker of the king of Egypt, who were confined in the prison—each his own dream, and each dream with its own meaning. ⁶When Joseph came to them in the morning, he saw that they were troubled. ⁷So he asked Pharaoh's officers, who were with him in custody in his master's house, "Why are your faces downcast today?" ⁸They said to him, "We have had dreams, and there is no one to interpret them." And Joseph said to them, "Do not interpretations belong to God? Please tell them to me."

9So the chief cupbearer told his dream to Joseph, and said to him, "In my dream there was a vine before me, ¹⁰and on the vine there were three branches. As soon as it budded, its blossoms came out and the clusters ripened into grapes. ¹¹Pharaoh's cup was in my hand; and I took the grapes and pressed them into Pharaoh's cup, and placed the cup in Pharaoh's hand." ¹²Then Joseph said to him, "This is its interpretation: the three branches are three days; ¹³within three days Pharaoh will lift up your head and restore you to your office; and you shall place Pharaoh's cup in his hand, just as you used to do when you were his cupbearer. ¹⁴But remember me when it is well with you; please do me the kindness to make mention of me to Pharaoh, and so get me out of this place. ¹⁵For in fact I was stolen out of the land of the Hebrews; and here also I have done nothing that they should have put me into the dungeon."

16When the chief baker saw that the interpretation was favorable, he said to Joseph, "I also had a dream: there were three cake baskets on

"I too had a dream: On my head were three baskets of bread.[a] [17]In the top basket were all kinds of baked goods for Pharaoh, but the birds were eating them out of the basket on my head."

[18]"This is what it means," Joseph said. "The three baskets are three days. [19]Within three days Pharaoh will lift off your head and hang you on a tree.[b] And the birds will eat away your flesh."

[20]Now the third day was Pharaoh's birthday, and he gave a feast for all his officials. He lifted up the heads of the chief cupbearer and the chief baker in the presence of his officials: [21]He restored the chief cupbearer to his position, so that he once again put the cup into Pharaoh's hand, [22]but he hanged[c] the chief baker, just as Joseph had said to them in his interpretation.

[23]The chief cupbearer, however, did not remember Joseph; he forgot him.

a16 Or three wicker baskets   b19 Or and impale you on a pole
c22 Or impaled

my head, [17]and in the uppermost basket there were all sorts of baked food for Pharaoh, but the birds were eating it out of the basket on my head." [18]And Joseph answered, "This is its interpretation: the three baskets are three days; [19]within three days Pharaoh will lift up your head—from you!—and hang you on a pole; and the birds will eat the flesh from you."

[20]On the third day, which was Pharaoh's birthday, he made a feast for all his servants, and lifted up the head of the chief cupbearer and the head of the chief baker among his servants. [21]He restored the chief cupbearer to his cupbearing, and he placed the cup in Pharaoh's hand; [22]but the chief baker he hanged, just as Joseph had interpreted to them. [23]Yet the chief cupbearer did not remember Joseph, but forgot him.

COMMENTARY

This unified episode fits as an integral part of chaps. 39–41. Set in an Egyptian prison, its very inhospitableness provides the context for an important advance in Joseph's return to a position of power in Egypt. Joseph's ability to interpret the dreams of two court officials focuses this development. While Joseph's own dreams have resulted in his slavery, the dreams of others now become the means for his release from slavery.

40:1-8. The occasion commences with an encounter between Joseph and two recently disemployed, unnamed members of Pharaoh's "kitchen" staff: the chief cupbearer and the chief baker. These were important positions in Egypt; the former personally served wine to the pharaoh. Having committed unnamed offenses against Pharaoh (if poisoning, both could be under suspicion), they are detained in the captain of the guard's house where Joseph has been placed in charge of prisoners. Since they are in detention, their futures have not yet been determined (because they still have their status, Joseph serves them as he did Potiphar, 39:4). Joseph is obviously aware of their situation, which shapes his interpretation of their dreams.

After some time, these servants of Pharaoh have dreams on the same night; they are troubled, probably because they relate the dreams to their uncertain fate. Joseph, here the alert caregiver, asks about their dejection. They report having had dreams, but in prison no interpreters are available (v. 8, פתר *pōtēr*, used only in the Joseph story). Joseph replies that interpretations belong to God (interestingly, he does not say the dreams themselves do)—i.e., God gives the gift of dream interpretation (note TNK translation, "Surely God can interpret!"). Without skipping a beat, Joseph urges them to tell him the dreams. In effect he says: I have the gift of divine interpretation (cf. 41:16). Joseph thereby brings a public witness to God to bear on the situation. God works in and through the dreams of the nonchosen (so also in chap. 41) to develop the future of the chosen.

40:9-19. Joseph proceeds to interpret the dreams (vv. 12, 18). Once again, as in chap. 37, there are two dreams. They are integrally related to the profession of each dreamer. Elements common to both dreams include the number three, food/drink for Pharaoh in a container, and the hand/head body reference. One key difference is that the cupbearer acts in his dream, while the baker does not (though birds do). Another difference is that Pharaoh is served in the first dream, but not in the second. Commonalities in Joseph's interpretations are the use of "three days" to represent a short time and the expression "lift up your head," though in different senses. "Lift up [not off] the head" in v. 13 is a metaphor for freedom from blame; in v. 19 it is literal, to be hanged; in v. 20 it does double duty. This play on words may relate to audiences before Pharaoh, wherein he lifted the bowed head of one seeking royal amnesty.

These dreams provide mixtures of allegorical elements and literal descriptions of what will happen. Allegorical elements in the interpretations include the three branches/baskets (i.e., three days), the instant blossoming and ripening (i.e., soon, the compression of time), and the baked goods (i.e., flesh of the baker). These dreams require an interpreter more so than those of chap. 37; this will be even more the case in chap. 41.

The chief cupbearer tells his dream to Joseph first (vv. 9-15). In it, a vine with three branches, upon budding, immediately puts forth blossoms, and its clusters ripen into grapes. He presses the grapes into Pharaoh's cup and gives it to Pharaoh. Joseph's interpretation is that in three days the cupbearer will be restored to his office and will give Pharaoh his cup as usual.

Joseph uses the interpretive moment to ask the cupbearer to show kindness (חסד *ḥesed*)—hence

to act as God does in 39:21—and to intercede for Joseph's release before Pharaoh. He has been deprived of his rights wrongfully (kidnapping probably refers to the Midianites in 37:28, but may be a general description) and has done nothing to deserve his imprisonment. He thereby anticipates the laments of his people in Egypt.

The chief baker then takes his turn (vv. 16-19), ironically, as it turns out, after the initial favorable interpretation. In his dream, three baskets of baked goods are on his head, and birds are eating from the topmost one. Joseph's interpretation is that in three days Pharaoh will have him hanged (the NRSV's "from you!" captures the point) and will leave him hanging on the tree for the birds to pick clean. Joseph does not ask the baker to remember him to the pharaoh, for obvious reasons!

40:20-23. These verses report what happens after three days. The dreams are realized as Joseph had interpreted them, on a public occasion, Pharaoh's own birthday, when such decisions were regularly announced. Each man has his head lifted, but in quite different ways; for one it means death, for the other life (these are important themes for the story as a whole).

The cupbearer does not remember Joseph, so he remains forgotten in prison; it will take two more years (41:1) for human memory to be jogged. For now, Joseph's future remains uncertain. Joseph's journey from slavery to freedom is filled with frustration and disappointment (it will take thirteen years in all, 41:46).

REFLECTIONS

1. Verse 8 contains the only reference to God in the chapter. Joseph seems to claim that only God can interpret dreams, and then proceeds to have the dreams told to him in order to interpret them. One should read this verse within the context of other references to God in 41:16, 25, 28, and 38-39.

The text suggests that dream specialists are not needed; God does such business: "It is not I [I cannot do it]; God will give Pharaoh a favorable answer" (41:16). Yet, Joseph repeatedly interprets dreams—without explicit reference to any divine inspiration: "This is its interpretation" (40:12, 18). Moreover, others publicly recognize him as an interpreter (41:12-13).

Another perspective draws on Joseph's knowledge of royal protocol. Such statements as Joseph's are polite disclaimers, devices "for detaching the interpretation from the interpreter; the interpreter bears no responsibility but merely announces what is to come. Joseph in each episode shows himself a sure master of the complexities of court protocol."[202] Such political

---

202. Humphreys, *Joseph,* 143.

---

realities would mean that we must be extraordinarily careful so as not to overdraw the theological import of v. 8.

It would seem best to see Pharaoh's statement in 41:38-39 as ironically putting this data together in an appropriate way: "God has shown you all this, there is no one so discerning and wise as you." Both human and divine agents are recognized. The initiative and the "showing" come from God, but human wisdom and discernment remain necessary. Joseph's gifts are not irrelevant (as if any person would do). His abilities come into play and are *used* by God in the interpretive process. Note Joseph's knowledge regarding the royal context, his discernment of the officials' situation, and his skill at word play.

Joseph is thus engaged at two levels: He receives divine inspiration, and his own gifts of discernment come into play in the interpretation. Yet, Joseph does not boast in his own abilities; he diminishes himself and gives the glory to the God who works in and through him, without whom the appropriate interpretation would not be possible. Comparable language in our own time would be the naming of a sermon as the proclamation of the word of God.

In addition, we find no evidence of polemic in this chapter, as if dream specialists are being put down, or that only God's people can interpret dreams. Moreover, not all dreams come from God (see Deut 13:1-5; Jer 23:16-17; cf. Eccles 5:7), though in such cases God may choose to enter into the interpretive process. These dreams are so straightforward that special inspiration for their interpretation seems unnecessary for astute persons such as Joseph.

2. The "prophetic" dreams come to pass as Joseph had interpreted them. Unlike modern interpretations, in the OT (and the ancient Near East generally) dreams relate more to the future than the past or present. But would the dreams have been realized apart from Joseph's interpretation? As for the future of the two officials, is what Joseph says finally irrelevant (except in a "pastoral" function, to reduce or intensify anxiety)? Does not the interpretation in some sense activate the dream (cf. the prophetic word)? Might it have some effect on the shape of the realization? Even more, might not subsequent events also shape the nature of the realization? One thinks of the interpretations of the brothers and the father in chap. 37, where Joseph's second dream remains unfulfilled. The narrator finally appears to be interested, however, not in the dreams as such, but in Joseph's interpretive abilities because of the reputation that accrues to him as a consequence (see also chap. 37:5-11).

3. We hear, for the first time, Joseph speaking openly about his own life—for the first time in the narrative (42:21 recalls an earlier moment) he becomes aggressive regarding his situation. Although Joseph has the God-given ability to interpret dreams, he still needs *human* help. The one inspired by God pleads with a fellow prisoner for help. He asks to be remembered by another—as God remembers Noah (8:1), Abraham (19:29), Rachel (30:22), and the people of Israel (also in bondage in Egypt [Exod 2:24; 6:5]). But to be in need of human help also involves being open to human frailties. The one upon whom Joseph depends will forget Joseph (cf. Exod 1:8), but not forever (see 41:9). Human help will finally be a key to Joseph's future, as it will be for virtually everybody.

Joseph's lament anticipates those of his descendants in Egypt, who also are "brought out of the house" of bondage (see Exod 13:14; 20:2). With Joseph, as with the people of Israel, the lament plays an important role in the development of the deliverance (note the integral relationship between lament and divine remembrance in Exod 2:23-25; 6:5). Such language would also recall psalms of lament (and thanksgiving), which often use the word *pit* to refer to the depths of despair (Pss 28:1; 30:3, 9; 35:7; 40:2; 88:4, 6).

GENESIS 41:1-57, JOSEPH'S ELEVATION TO POWER

NIV

41 When two full years had passed, Pharaoh had a dream: He was standing by the Nile, ²when out of the river there came up seven cows, sleek and fat, and they grazed among the reeds. ³After them, seven other cows, ugly and gaunt, came up out of the Nile and stood beside those on the riverbank. ⁴And the cows that were ugly and gaunt ate up the seven sleek, fat cows. Then Pharaoh woke up.

⁵He fell asleep again and had a second dream: Seven heads of grain, healthy and good, were growing on a single stalk. ⁶After them, seven other heads of grain sprouted—thin and scorched by the east wind. ⁷The thin heads of grain swallowed up the seven healthy, full heads. Then Pharaoh woke up; it had been a dream.

⁸In the morning his mind was troubled, so he sent for all the magicians and wise men of Egypt. Pharaoh told them his dreams, but no one could interpret them for him.

⁹Then the chief cupbearer said to Pharaoh, "Today I am reminded of my shortcomings. ¹⁰Pharaoh was once angry with his servants, and he imprisoned me and the chief baker in the house of the captain of the guard. ¹¹Each of us had a dream the same night, and each dream had a meaning of its own. ¹²Now a young Hebrew was there with us, a servant of the captain of the guard. We told him our dreams, and he interpreted them for us, giving each man the interpretation of his dream. ¹³And things turned out exactly as he interpreted them to us: I was restored to my position, and the other man was hanged.^a"

¹⁴So Pharaoh sent for Joseph, and he was quickly brought from the dungeon. When he had shaved and changed his clothes, he came before Pharaoh.

¹⁵Pharaoh said to Joseph, "I had a dream, and no one can interpret it. But I have heard it said of you that when you hear a dream you can interpret it."

¹⁶"I cannot do it," Joseph replied to Pharaoh,

^a13 Or *impaled*

NRSV

41 After two whole years, Pharaoh dreamed that he was standing by the Nile, ²and there came up out of the Nile seven sleek and fat cows, and they grazed in the reed grass. ³Then seven other cows, ugly and thin, came up out of the Nile after them, and stood by the other cows on the bank of the Nile. ⁴The ugly and thin cows ate up the seven sleek and fat cows. And Pharaoh awoke. ⁵Then he fell asleep and dreamed a second time; seven ears of grain, plump and good, were growing on one stalk. ⁶Then seven ears, thin and blighted by the east wind, sprouted after them. ⁷The thin ears swallowed up the seven plump and full ears. Pharaoh awoke, and it was a dream. ⁸In the morning his spirit was troubled; so he sent and called for all the magicians of Egypt and all its wise men. Pharaoh told them his dreams, but there was no one who could interpret them to Pharaoh.

⁹Then the chief cupbearer said to Pharaoh, "I remember my faults today. ¹⁰Once Pharaoh was angry with his servants, and put me and the chief baker in custody in the house of the captain of the guard. ¹¹We dreamed on the same night, he and I, each having a dream with its own meaning. ¹²A young Hebrew was there with us, a servant of the captain of the guard. When we told him, he interpreted our dreams to us, giving an interpretation to each according to his dream. ¹³As he interpreted to us, so it turned out; I was restored to my office, and the baker was hanged."

¹⁴Then Pharaoh sent for Joseph, and he was hurriedly brought out of the dungeon. When he had shaved himself and changed his clothes, he came in before Pharaoh. ¹⁵And Pharaoh said to Joseph, "I have had a dream, and there is no one who can interpret it. I have heard it said of you that when you hear a dream you can interpret it." ¹⁶Joseph answered Pharaoh, "It is not I; God will give Pharaoh a favorable answer." ¹⁷Then Pharaoh said to Joseph, "In my dream I was standing on the banks of the Nile; ¹⁸and seven cows, fat and sleek, came up out of the Nile and fed in the reed grass. ¹⁹Then seven other cows came up after them, poor, very ugly, and thin.

NIV

"but God will give Pharaoh the answer he desires."

[17]Then Pharaoh said to Joseph, "In my dream I was standing on the bank of the Nile, [18]when out of the river there came up seven cows, fat and sleek, and they grazed among the reeds. [19]After them, seven other cows came up—scrawny and very ugly and lean. I had never seen such ugly cows in all the land of Egypt. [20]The lean, ugly cows ate up the seven fat cows that came up first. [21]But even after they ate them, no one could tell that they had done so; they looked just as ugly as before. Then I woke up.

[22]"In my dreams I also saw seven heads of grain, full and good, growing on a single stalk. [23]After them, seven other heads sprouted—withered and thin and scorched by the east wind. [24]The thin heads of grain swallowed up the seven good heads. I told this to the magicians, but none could explain it to me."

[25]Then Joseph said to Pharaoh, "The dreams of Pharaoh are one and the same. God has revealed to Pharaoh what he is about to do. [26]The seven good cows are seven years, and the seven good heads of grain are seven years; it is one and the same dream. [27]The seven lean, ugly cows that came up afterward are seven years, and so are the seven worthless heads of grain scorched by the east wind: They are seven years of famine.

[28]"It is just as I said to Pharaoh: God has shown Pharaoh what he is about to do. [29]Seven years of great abundance are coming throughout the land of Egypt, [30]but seven years of famine will follow them. Then all the abundance in Egypt will be forgotten, and the famine will ravage the land. [31]The abundance in the land will not be remembered, because the famine that follows it will be so severe. [32]The reason the dream was given to Pharaoh in two forms is that the matter has been firmly decided by God, and God will do it soon.

[33]"And now let Pharaoh look for a discerning and wise man and put him in charge of the land of Egypt. [34]Let Pharaoh appoint commissioners over the land to take a fifth of the harvest of Egypt during the seven years of abundance. [35]They should collect all the food of these good years that are coming and store up the grain under the authority of Pharaoh, to be kept in the cities for

NRSV

Never had I seen such ugly ones in all the land of Egypt. [20]The thin and ugly cows ate up the first seven fat cows, [21]but when they had eaten them no one would have known that they had done so, for they were still as ugly as before. Then I awoke. [22]I fell asleep a second time[a] and I saw in my dream seven ears of grain, full and good, growing on one stalk, [23]and seven ears, withered, thin, and blighted by the east wind, sprouting after them; [24]and the thin ears swallowed up the seven good ears. But when I told it to the magicians, there was no one who could explain it to me."

25Then Joseph said to Pharaoh, "Pharaoh's dreams are one and the same; God has revealed to Pharaoh what he is about to do. [26]The seven good cows are seven years, and the seven good ears are seven years; the dreams are one. [27]The seven lean and ugly cows that came up after them are seven years, as are the seven empty ears blighted by the east wind. They are seven years of famine. [28]It is as I told Pharaoh; God has shown to Pharaoh what he is about to do. [29]There will come seven years of great plenty throughout all the land of Egypt. [30]After them there will arise seven years of famine, and all the plenty will be forgotten in the land of Egypt; the famine will consume the land. [31]The plenty will no longer be known in the land because of the famine that will follow, for it will be very grievous. [32]And the doubling of Pharaoh's dream means that the thing is fixed by God, and God will shortly bring it about. [33]Now therefore let Pharaoh select a man who is discerning and wise, and set him over the land of Egypt. [34]Let Pharaoh proceed to appoint overseers over the land, and take one-fifth of the produce of the land of Egypt during the seven plenteous years. [35]Let them gather all the food of these good years that are coming, and lay up grain under the authority of Pharaoh for food in the cities, and let them keep it. [36]That food shall be a reserve for the land against the seven years of famine that are to befall the land of Egypt, so that the land may not perish through the famine."

37The proposal pleased Pharaoh and all his servants. [38]Pharaoh said to his servants, "Can we find anyone else like this—one in whom is the spirit of God?" [39]So Pharaoh said to Joseph, "Since

[a] Gk Syr Vg: Heb lacks *I fell asleep a second time*

NIV

food. ³⁶This food should be held in reserve for the country, to be used during the seven years of famine that will come upon Egypt, so that the country may not be ruined by the famine."

³⁷The plan seemed good to Pharaoh and to all his officials. ³⁸So Pharaoh asked them, "Can we find anyone like this man, one in whom is the spirit of God*?"

³⁹Then Pharaoh said to Joseph, "Since God has made all this known to you, there is no one so discerning and wise as you. ⁴⁰You shall be in charge of my palace, and all my people are to submit to your orders. Only with respect to the throne will I be greater than you."

⁴¹So Pharaoh said to Joseph, "I hereby put you in charge of the whole land of Egypt." ⁴²Then Pharaoh took his signet ring from his finger and put it on Joseph's finger. He dressed him in robes of fine linen and put a gold chain around his neck. ⁴³He had him ride in a chariot as his second-in-command,^b and men shouted before him, "Make way^c!" Thus he put him in charge of the whole land of Egypt.

⁴⁴Then Pharaoh said to Joseph, "I am Pharaoh, but without your word no one will lift hand or foot in all Egypt." ⁴⁵Pharaoh gave Joseph the name Zaphenath-Paneah and gave him Asenath daughter of Potiphera, priest of On,^d to be his wife. And Joseph went throughout the land of Egypt.

⁴⁶Joseph was thirty years old when he entered the service of Pharaoh king of Egypt. And Joseph went out from Pharaoh's presence and traveled throughout Egypt. ⁴⁷During the seven years of abundance the land produced plentifully. ⁴⁸Joseph collected all the food produced in those seven years of abundance in Egypt and stored it in the cities. In each city he put the food grown in the fields surrounding it. ⁴⁹Joseph stored up huge quantities of grain, like the sand of the sea; it was so much that he stopped keeping records because it was beyond measure.

⁵⁰Before the years of famine came, two sons were born to Joseph by Asenath daughter of Potiphera, priest of On. ⁵¹Joseph named his first-born Manasseh^e and said, "It is because God has

---

a38 Or *of the gods*   *b43* Or *in the chariot of his second-in-command;* or *in his second chariot*   *c43* Or *Bow down*   *d45* That is, Heliopolis; also in verse 50   *e51* Manasseh sounds like and may be derived from the Hebrew for *forget.*

NRSV

God has shown you all this, there is no one so discerning and wise as you. ⁴⁰You shall be over my house, and all my people shall order themselves as you command; only with regard to the throne will I be greater than you." ⁴¹And Pharaoh said to Joseph, "See, I have set you over all the land of Egypt." ⁴²Removing his signet ring from his hand, Pharaoh put it on Joseph's hand; he arrayed him in garments of fine linen, and put a gold chain around his neck. ⁴³He had him ride in the chariot of his second-in-command; and they cried out in front of him, "Bow the knee!"^a Thus he set him over all the land of Egypt. ⁴⁴Moreover Pharaoh said to Joseph, "I am Pharaoh, and without your consent no one shall lift up hand or foot in all the land of Egypt." ⁴⁵Pharaoh gave Joseph the name Zaphenath-paneah; and he gave him Asenath daughter of Potiphera, priest of On, as his wife. Thus Joseph gained authority over the land of Egypt.

⁴⁶Joseph was thirty years old when he entered the service of Pharaoh king of Egypt. And Joseph went out from the presence of Pharaoh, and went through all the land of Egypt. ⁴⁷During the seven plenteous years the earth produced abundantly. ⁴⁸He gathered up all the food of the seven years when there was plenty^b in the land of Egypt, and stored up food in the cities; he stored up in every city the food from the fields around it. ⁴⁹So Joseph stored up grain in such abundance—like the sand of the sea—that he stopped measuring it; it was beyond measure.

⁵⁰Before the years of famine came, Joseph had two sons, whom Asenath daughter of Potiphera, priest of On, bore to him. ⁵¹Joseph named the firstborn Manasseh,^c "For," he said, "God has made me forget all my hardship and all my father's house." ⁵²The second he named Ephraim,^d "For God has made me fruitful in the land of my misfortunes."

⁵³The seven years of plenty that prevailed in the land of Egypt came to an end; ⁵⁴and the seven years of famine began to come, just as Joseph had said. There was famine in every country, but throughout the land of Egypt there was bread.

---

^a *Abrek,* apparently an Egyptian word similar in sound to the Hebrew word meaning *to kneel*   ^b Sam Gk: MT *the seven years that were*   ^c That is *Making to forget*   ^d From a Hebrew word meaning *to be fruitful*

NIV

made me forget all my trouble and all my father's household." ⁵²The second son he named Ephraimᵃ and said, "It is because God has made me fruitful in the land of my suffering."

⁵³The seven years of abundance in Egypt came to an end, ⁵⁴and the seven years of famine began, just as Joseph had said. There was famine in all the other lands, but in the whole land of Egypt there was food. ⁵⁵When all Egypt began to feel the famine, the people cried to Pharaoh for food. Then Pharaoh told all the Egyptians, "Go to Joseph and do what he tells you."

⁵⁶When the famine had spread over the whole country, Joseph opened the storehouses and sold grain to the Egyptians, for the famine was severe throughout Egypt. ⁵⁷And all the countries came to Egypt to buy grain from Joseph, because the famine was severe in all the world.

ᵃ52 Ephraim sounds like the Hebrew for twice fruitful.

NRSV

55When all the land of Egypt was famished, the people cried to Pharaoh for bread. Pharaoh said to all the Egyptians, "Go to Joseph; what he says to you, do." ⁵⁶And since the famine had spread over all the land, Joseph opened all the store-houses,ᵃ and sold to the Egyptians, for the famine was severe in the land of Egypt. ⁵⁷Moreover, all the world came to Joseph in Egypt to buy grain, because the famine became severe throughout the world.

ᵃGk Vg Compare Syr: Heb opened all that was in (or, among) them

COMMENTARY

The scene changes from Pharaoh's prison to Pharaoh's palace, mirroring Joseph's rise from weakness to strength. The dreams continue; this time Pharaoh himself has two dreams (vv. 1-7), which enable Joseph's dream to come full circle. After the cupbearer remembers him (vv. 8-13), Joseph is called forth from prison to interpret the dreams and to give advice based on them (vv. 14-36). As a result, Pharaoh elevates Joseph to prime minister (vv. 37-46), in which capacity he proves to be an effective administrator of Egypt's economy (vv. 47-57).

This episode contains a storyline common to many cultures: elevation of a person from low to high status because he or she solves a problem. This chapter has long been considered a composite, but the occasional roughness of expression may be ascribed to its history of transmission. The chapter is a literary unity, thoroughly integrated into the larger segment of chaps. 39–41 (cf. vv. 9-13).

41:1-7. After a note indicating that Joseph has languished in prison for two more years, these verses describe Pharaoh's two dreams. In the first, the setting is the Nile, Egypt's lifeline. Seven sleek and fat cows come out of the Nile and begin to

graze; then seven ugly and gaunt cows appear and eat the fat ones. In the second, seven plump and good ears of grain grow on one stalk; then seven ears of grain, thin and scorched by the hot desert wind, sprout on that stalk and devour the healthy ones. Although the second is somewhat shorter, the dreams mirror each other; this becomes an important point in Joseph's interpretation (vv. 25-26, 32). Pharaoh retells the dreams to Joseph in vv. 17-24, with some variations. This same theme, the weak prevailing over the strong, characterized Joseph's own dreams.

41:8-13. Pharaoh is deeply disturbed by his dreams because their bizarre nature may portend a troubled future, an intrusion that he can neither interpret nor control. Such a God-generated intrusion provides the opening that Joseph needs. Pharaoh calls in specialists to sort out their meaning, but none can interpret them to his satisfaction. They are now in over their heads. Although they are decisively bested by Joseph, the story makes little of their failure (unlike Exodus 7–8 or Daniel 1–2).

These events trigger the cupbearer's memory, and he recalls his experience with Joseph (cf. 40:14), both his interpretation and its accuracy.

Quite remarkably, he even uses the language of sin (as in 39:9; 40:1) to describe his forgetfulness. This human act changes the future for all concerned.

41:14-36. Pharaoh hurriedly brings Joseph from the "pit" (signaling the end of his journey from the pit in 37:20-29). His shaving and fresh clothing symbolize the change in his circumstance. Pharaoh reports to Joseph what has been said about him; Pharaoh's expectations are high.

Joseph's reply in v. 16 has a number of dimensions: Pharaoh's dreams come from God (cf. vv. 25, 28); he will receive an answer about their meaning, which will effect שלום (šālôm) for him (NIV "desired"; NRSV "favorable"). Joseph has not yet heard the dream! *Shalom* thus relates to Pharaoh's troubled spirit, that Pharaoh would be satisfied with Joseph's interpretation because it comes from God. Joseph, not having heard the dream, acts in a straightforward manner here; in effect he puts God on notice that an interpretation will be needed. At stake are the reputations of both Joseph and God.

Pharaoh tells the dream to Joseph (vv. 17-24). The retelling basically matches the first report. Yet, the differences are important; they are in the first person, they anticipate that the meaning is negative, and they reveal Pharaoh's deep concern: exaggeration (the scrawny cows are unprecedented in their ugliness, and the thin ears of grain are even more withered) and additional bizarre information (the eating did not change the ugly cows' appearance). The dreams contain both literal and allegorical elements, though the latter predominate here. The number seven (four times) refers to years, with the healthy cows/grain referring to years of plenty and the sickly ones years of grievous famine. The famine will so consume the land that the years of plenty will be forgotten (vv. 30-31).

The heart of Joseph's interpretation takes the form of announcements about the future (vv. 29-32), though he does not construe them as divine judgment. He gives a fuller theological explanation than that given in chap. 40, followed by a clear recommendation as to what Pharaoh ought to do about the situation the dreams portend (vv. 33-36).

The theological explanations that punctuate this section (vv. 25, 28, 32) accomplish three things: (1) They emphasize that God reveals this meaning; in other words, this is serious business; (2)

they indicate that God speaks through Joseph; and (3) they provide a structure for the section.

The enclosing verses (25, 32) stress the dreams' identical meaning and significance. Verses 26-27 focus on the number seven, vv. 29-31 on the sequence of the events; the author introduces each by a statement that God has revealed to Pharaoh what will happen. The interpretation centers on the years of famine, the better to impress upon Pharaoh the need to take action.

Joseph offers more than just an interpretation. Without waiting for Pharaoh's response and using bold speech, yet cognizant of his status (note the repeated "let," stressing Pharaoh's decision), Joseph puts forward a plan whereby these events can effectively be addressed, preventing much damage to the country (vv. 33-36). Pharaoh should not resign himself to the disaster, as if all the famine's effects were a matter of fate. Pharaoh has the freedom to make decisions, though within a context provided by God's decision. Joseph believes that he can persuade Pharaoh to develop a plan of action so that Egypt will be able to endure the famine in a way that brings the greatest possible well-being to all.

Joseph proposes that a wise and discerning person be appointed (used for an obedient Israel in Deut 4:6 and for Solomon in 1 Kgs 3:12). He carefully articulates the plan in the hopes that he himself will be chosen, not some local expert. Other astute overseers should also be appointed to manage the economic policy. He proposes that enough food—20 percent of the crop each year (i.e., the "all" of v. 35)—be stored during the years of plenty to provide a reserve for the years of famine. Everything will be under "the authority of Pharaoh." (A historical note: Egypt was renowned in that part of the world for its granaries.)

41:37-46. Joseph emphasizes throughout that God has revealed the meaning of the dream to *Pharaoh* (vv. 16, 25, 28). Joseph thereby identifies a direct relationship between Pharaoh and God. This emphasis, along with Joseph's candor and bold speech, as well as his concern for *national* well-being (rather than himself), convinces Pharaoh. While he gives all the "credits" to God, Joseph obviously mediates the divine revelation.

Pharaoh astutely puts these matters together; we ought not discount his theological insightfulness. He recognizes that God has revealed these things to *Joseph* (v. 39); hence he must be the one in whom the Spirit of God rests (v. 38). Pharaoh addresses his question to the court (v. 38), thus drawing them into accepting his conclusion.

Hence, Pharaoh chooses Joseph as the "discerning and wise" person Joseph himself had suggested and had modeled through his speech. Pharaoh makes Joseph the prime minister, in charge of both the palace (v. 40) and the country (vv. 41, 43), second in command only to Pharaoh, with wide-ranging authority. Verse 44 specifies the unlimited character of his command, against which no one shall lift up hand or foot—namely, rebel. Once again, the author portrays Pharaoh as a wise and discerning person in his own right due to his elevation and empowerment of Joseph.

Verses 41-44 describe an act of installation. Pharaoh opens and closes with a formal statement of Joseph's authority (v. 41, 44; cf. Jer 1:10) and gives him the symbols of his new office: his signet ring (with Pharaoh's own "signature," cf. 38:18), a royal garment, and a gold chain. His clothing may mirror the cloak given him by his father. He rides in a royal chariot throughout the city, before which Egyptian heralds call to the crowds to acclaim him: "Bend the knee" (or "Attention"). At some point later, he travels through the entire land so that people can recognize him in his new position (v. 46*b;* cf. 13:17). Through all this, Joseph remains silent; only in the naming of his sons will he reveal his reaction.

Pharaoh gives Joseph an Egyptian name to signal his new status, Zaphenath-paneah (i.e., God speaks and lives), and provides him a wife from the nobility, Asenath (i.e., she who belongs to the goddess Neith). She is the daughter of Potiphera (i.e., the one whom Re gave; probably identical in meaning to Potiphar), priest of On (i.e., Heliopolis), a prominent center for worship of the sun god Re.

A historical note: There is some evidence that slaves from the ancient Near East achieved positions of high standing in Egyptian royal circles.

The rite of installation also has parallels in that world, and rings, chains, and chariots that were used on such occasions have been found. Finally, famines were not uncommon; a seven-year famine occurs as a literary convention in Israel (2 Sam 24:13), in Egypt, and in Mesopotamia.[203]

41:47-57. Joseph is thirty years old when these events occur, thirteen years after his enslavement (37:2-3). As prime minister, he carries out the economic program needed to prevent the disaster that Pharaoh's dreams portend. During the seven years of plenty—more than could actually be measured—he stores up food in all the cities. The image of the sand of the sea continues the blessing of the family of Abraham (22:17).

Verses 50-52 are not intrusive; the fruitfulness of Joseph and Asenath mirrors the fruitfulness of the land. They have two sons, Ephraim and Manasseh. Joseph names them in recognition of God's involvement in this massive change in his life: Manasseh, because God has enabled Joseph's slavery in Canaan and Egypt to be forgotten; Ephraim, because God has prospered Joseph in the very land in which he has experienced so much misfortune. These names reveal Joseph's life experience: God's preserving and prospering activity in the very midst of great personal hardship. External appearances provide no clear barometer of the depth and breadth of God's blessings. This family reference also anticipates chapters to come.

When the years of famine come, it affects every country, not just Egypt. But only Egypt has grain. The success of Joseph redounds to his reputation. When Egyptians cry out for bread due to the famine's severity, they can get relief from Joseph (note that they buy grain; it is not given away). In fact, Joseph's wisdom enables Egypt to become the bread basket for "all the world" (vv. 54, 56, 57).

203. See Sarna, *Genesis,* 290.

REFLECTIONS

1. The Spirit of God rests on Joseph (v. 36). Some have suggested that Joseph was a charismatic personality and should be understood from within the prophetic tradition. One may also appeal to the relationship between God and wise kings like Solomon (see 1 Kings 3–4). Generally, Joseph's empowerment should be understood in terms of Exod 31:3; 35:31 (cf. Dan 5:14), which connect particular *gifts suitable for the task at hand* with the presence of the divine spirit. These texts recognize God-given talents rather than a pouring out of the Spirit for the occasion, a way in which the people of God might well speak of the work of the Spirit of God in every age. Joseph's portrayal has no single antecedent tradition.

2. The realities of dreams and their interpretation issue in a complex configuration of divine, human, and nonhuman agency (see chap. 40). God sets the context, but does not override human discernment, care, and planning. Humans channel the divine blessings to their most effective ends. Dreams and their God-given interpretation do not necessarily shape the future in detail. Creaturely response also shapes the future. Natural disasters (the famine) do not have predetermined effects; wise human planning can ameliorate their negative impact.

3. Policies are to be developed "so that the land may not perish through the famine" (v. 36). The dreams do not determine the future *in every respect.* God has firmly established the future to which the dreams point, and God will act soon (v. 32). At the same time, the full future that the dreams open up depends on more than God's becoming involved. The economic policies adopted during the years of plenty mean that the land will not be consumed, the dreams will not have their fullest possible negative effects.

Inasmuch as famine results from the failure of the Nile's waters to overflow, and the Nile is a pharaonic symbol of fertility, the story calls into question the very future of the pharaoh. The future does not lie within his control; he appears subject to a future that comes from God. Since Pharaoh listens to Joseph, however, and takes appropriate action, he helps to shape his future. Although his choices are limited, he exercises power, and his elevation of Joseph reveals considerable insight.

4. The story reflects the various ways in which God can work in and through people. God works outside the religious sphere, in economics and government. Moreover, Joseph was not the obvious choice, but was raised up from the lowest rungs to lead a people from the highest levels of authority. Joseph becomes part of a hierarchical structure of power (see chap. 47). With the proper leadership, such structures of authority need not be oppressive.

The problems presented by this chapter have been faced by virtually every generation in every country. The issues have to do with agriculture and related industries, with the difficulties of feeding people when crops are not produced in sufficient amounts. It also presents issues of the management of an economy. God's work in the world through wise leaders affects every sphere of life.

5. God's work of blessing in this chapter includes the entire human race, not just the chosen ones. God works in Pharaoh's life in ways Pharaoh does not know, even communicating in and through a dream. This experience testifies to significant levels of divine activity in human lives outside the community of faith. At the same time, the chosen have the God-given mandate and capacity to enhance God's blessings in such a way that enables them to become more than they would be without human participation.

Moreover, Joseph's *work of interpretation,* his wisdom and discernment, provides an entry point into the life of Pharaoh. Deuteronomy 4:6 uses this same language to speak about Israel; other people will see their obedience and say: Surely this great nation is a wise and discerning people. This work of interpretation—not simply of dreams—has the potential to draw outsiders into conversation regarding God and God's ways in the world, and can, as with Pharaoh, actually lead to their public witness regarding God's involvement in their lives. Indeed, Pharaoh becomes a theologian of no little consequence when he interprets these events (vv. 38-39).

6. Joseph does not boast about what he has done or will do: "It is not I, but God." He speaks of God as the one without whom interpretation would be impossible; God has given him the ability to interpret dreams (cf. 40:8). God enables Joseph to play the critical role (v. 16). Joseph links the chosen people with the unchosen people to bring blessing on the latter.

Precisely because of his disclaimers, Joseph appears as an ideal figure: patient through numerous setbacks and deep suffering; loyal to God, honoring of human relationships in the midst of severe trials and temptations. His bold speech, especially in the presence of persons and systems of power, reveals courage and integrity. He acts wisely and in a discerning manner in all of his dealings with people and their problems. Joseph stands as a model for the godly life, but moving far beyond the religious sphere; it is a life lived in the midst of the full range of human problems and the complexities of human existence.

7. In Joseph's naming of his children, the themes of forgetfulness and fruitfulness are highlighted; God has enabled both. What an incredible gift: God enables one to forget, to put the past behind, to move beyond dwelling on misfortunes and get on with the ever-new gifts that God brings. Joseph's confession should guide the reader's interpretation of the way in which he works with his brothers in the following chapters.

As for fruitfulness, *Egypt* becomes the context for this blessing, anticipating Exod 1:7 and the growth of Israel in that same land. Joseph's life anticipates Israel's. Blessing comes in the midst of affliction (ענה *ʿānâ*, used for Israel's oppression in Egypt, Gen 15:13; Exod 3:7). These acts of naming could be profitably compared with the naming of Joseph and his brothers in 29:31–30:24, where the mothers do the naming, in view of their life experience and to praise God. Joseph's naming of his sons testifies to the continuing link between tradition and personal life experience and the importance of their interaction.

8. Both Joseph and his brother Judah (see chap. 38) marry women outside the family and its religious heritage. Later legends speak of Asenath's conversion, but Genesis has no interest in this. The text attests to a remarkable capacity for the integration of Yahwistic faith and other religious communities and expressions (similarly 2 Kgs 5:15-19). Many OT texts do not tolerate such practices, but the reasons are contextual rather than normative (e.g., dangers of syncretism). Joseph functions as an ideal for Israel at this point, demonstrating that the later intolerance is *not characteristic of the Yahwistic faith in and of itself.* Joseph illustrates that such integration can be a positive experience and need not carry negative effects.

GENESIS 42:1-38, JOSEPH MEETS HIS BROTHERS

NIV

42 When Jacob learned that there was grain in Egypt, he said to his sons, "Why do you just keep looking at each other?" ²He continued, "I have heard that there is grain in Egypt. Go down there and buy some for us, so that we may live and not die."

³Then ten of Joseph's brothers went down to buy grain from Egypt. ⁴But Jacob did not send Benjamin, Joseph's brother, with the others, because he was afraid that harm might come to him. ⁵So Israel's sons were among those who went to buy grain, for the famine was in the land of Canaan also.

⁶Now Joseph was the governor of the land, the one who sold grain to all its people. So when

NRSV

42 When Jacob learned that there was grain in Egypt, he said to his sons, "Why do you keep looking at one another? ²I have heard," he said, "that there is grain in Egypt; go down and buy grain for us there, that we may live and not die." ³So ten of Joseph's brothers went down to buy grain in Egypt. ⁴But Jacob did not send Joseph's brother Benjamin with his brothers, for he feared that harm might come to him. ⁵Thus the sons of Israel were among the other people who came to buy grain, for the famine had reached the land of Canaan.

6Now Joseph was governor over the land; it was he who sold to all the people of the land. And Joseph's brothers came and bowed them-

Joseph's brothers arrived, they bowed down to him with their faces to the ground. [7]As soon as Joseph saw his brothers, he recognized them, but he pretended to be a stranger and spoke harshly to them. "Where do you come from?" he asked.

"From the land of Canaan," they replied, "to buy food."

[8]Although Joseph recognized his brothers, they did not recognize him. [9]Then he remembered his dreams about them and said to them, "You are spies! You have come to see where our land is unprotected."

[10]"No, my lord," they answered. "Your servants have come to buy food. [11]We are all the sons of one man. Your servants are honest men, not spies."

[12]"No!" he said to them. "You have come to see where our land is unprotected."

[13]But they replied, "Your servants were twelve brothers, the sons of one man, who lives in the land of Canaan. The youngest is now with our father, and one is no more."

[14]Joseph said to them, "It is just as I told you: You are spies! [15]And this is how you will be tested: As surely as Pharaoh lives, you will not leave this place unless your youngest brother comes here. [16]Send one of your number to get your brother; the rest of you will be kept in prison, so that your words may be tested to see if you are telling the truth. If you are not, then as surely as Pharaoh lives, you are spies!" [17]And he put them all in custody for three days.

[18]On the third day, Joseph said to them, "Do this and you will live, for I fear God: [19]If you are honest men, let one of your brothers stay here in prison, while the rest of you go and take grain back for your starving households. [20]But you must bring your youngest brother to me, so that your words may be verified and that you may not die." This they proceeded to do.

[21]They said to one another, "Surely we are being punished because of our brother. We saw how distressed he was when he pleaded with us for his life, but we would not listen; that's why this distress has come upon us."

[22]Reuben replied, "Didn't I tell you not to sin against the boy? But you wouldn't listen! Now we must give an accounting for his blood." [23]They

selves before him with their faces to the ground. [7]When Joseph saw his brothers, he recognized them, but he treated them like strangers and spoke harshly to them. "Where do you come from?" he said. They said, "From the land of Canaan, to buy food." [8]Although Joseph had recognized his brothers, they did not recognize him. [9]Joseph also remembered the dreams that he had dreamed about them. He said to them, "You are spies; you have come to see the nakedness of the land!" [10]They said to him, "No, my lord; your servants have come to buy food. [11]We are all sons of one man; we are honest men; your servants have never been spies." [12]But he said to them, "No, you have come to see the nakedness of the land!" [13]They said, "We, your servants, are twelve brothers, the sons of a certain man in the land of Canaan; the youngest, however, is now with our father, and one is no more." [14]But Joseph said to them, "It is just as I have said to you; you are spies! [15]Here is how you shall be tested: as Pharaoh lives, you shall not leave this place unless your youngest brother comes here! [16]Let one of you go and bring your brother, while the rest of you remain in prison, in order that your words may be tested, whether there is truth in you; or else, as Pharaoh lives, surely you are spies." [17]And he put them all together in prison for three days.

[18]On the third day Joseph said to them, "Do this and you will live, for I fear God: [19]if you are honest men, let one of your brothers stay here where you are imprisoned. The rest of you shall go and carry grain for the famine of your households, [20]and bring your youngest brother to me. Thus your words will be verified, and you shall not die." And they agreed to do so. [21]They said to one another, "Alas, we are paying the penalty for what we did to our brother; we saw his anguish when he pleaded with us, but we would not listen. That is why this anguish has come upon us." [22]Then Reuben answered them, "Did I not tell you not to wrong the boy? But you would not listen. So now there comes a reckoning for his blood." [23]They did not know that Joseph understood them, since he spoke with them through an interpreter. [24]He turned away from them and wept; then he returned and spoke to them. And he picked out Simeon and had him

NIV

did not realize that Joseph could understand them, since he was using an interpreter.

24He turned away from them and began to weep, but then turned back and spoke to them again. He had Simeon taken from them and bound before their eyes.

25Joseph gave orders to fill their bags with grain, to put each man's silver back in his sack, and to give them provisions for their journey. After this was done for them, 26they loaded their grain on their donkeys and left.

27At the place where they stopped for the night one of them opened his sack to get feed for his donkey, and he saw his silver in the mouth of his sack. 28"My silver has been returned," he said to his brothers. "Here it is in my sack."

Their hearts sank and they turned to each other trembling and said, "What is this that God has done to us?"

29When they came to their father Jacob in the land of Canaan, they told him all that had happened to them. They said, 30"The man who is lord over the land spoke harshly to us and treated us as though we were spying on the land. 31But we said to him, 'We are honest men; we are not spies. 32We were twelve brothers, sons of one father. One is no more, and the youngest is now with our father in Canaan.'

33"Then the man who is lord over the land said to us, 'This is how I will know whether you are honest men: Leave one of your brothers here with me, and take food for your starving households and go. 34But bring your youngest brother to me so I will know that you are not spies but honest men. Then I will give your brother back to you, and you can trade^a in the land.'"

35As they were emptying their sacks, there in each man's sack was his pouch of silver! When they and their father saw the money pouches, they were frightened. 36Their father Jacob said to them, "You have deprived me of my children. Joseph is no more and Simeon is no more, and now you want to take Benjamin. Everything is against me!"

37Then Reuben said to his father, "You may put both of my sons to death if I do not bring him

a34 Or move about freely

NRSV

bound before their eyes. 25Joseph then gave orders to fill their bags with grain, to return every man's money to his sack, and to give them provisions for their journey. This was done for them.

26They loaded their donkeys with their grain, and departed. 27When one of them opened his sack to give his donkey fodder at the lodging place, he saw his money at the top of the sack. 28He said to his brothers, "My money has been put back; here it is in my sack!" At this they lost heart and turned trembling to one another, saying, "What is this that God has done to us?"

29When they came to their father Jacob in the land of Canaan, they told him all that had happened to them, saying, 30"The man, the lord of the land, spoke harshly to us, and charged us with spying on the land. 31But we said to him, 'We are honest men, we are not spies. 32We are twelve brothers, sons of our father; one is no more, and the youngest is now with our father in the land of Canaan.' 33Then the man, the lord of the land, said to us, 'By this I shall know that you are honest men: leave one of your brothers with me, take grain for the famine of your households, and go your way. 34Bring your youngest brother to me, and I shall know that you are not spies but honest men. Then I will release your brother to you, and you may trade in the land.'"

35As they were emptying their sacks, there in each one's sack was his bag of money. When they and their father saw their bundles of money, they were dismayed. 36And their father Jacob said to them, "I am the one you have bereaved of children: Joseph is no more, and Simeon is no more, and now you would take Benjamin. All this has happened to me!" 37Then Reuben said to his father, "You may kill my two sons if I do not bring him back to you. Put him in my hands, and I will bring him back to you." 38But he said, "My son shall not go down with you, for his brother is dead, and he alone is left. If harm should come to him on the journey that you are to make, you would bring down my gray hairs with sorrow to Sheol."

NIV

back to you. Entrust him to my care, and I will bring him back."

³⁸But Jacob said, "My son will not go down there with you; his brother is dead and he is the only one left. If harm comes to him on the journey you are taking, you will bring my gray head down to the grave^a in sorrow."

_a38 Hebrew *Sheol*

COMMENTARY

Chapters 39–41, focused on Joseph in Egypt, are now balanced by chaps. 42–44, which center on a new relationship for Joseph and his family. The former developments make the latter possible. The two journeys of the brothers to Egypt mirror the doubling of the dreams in the previous chapters.

This chapter may be a composite of J and E, but works now as a unified whole. Linked with chaps. 37 and 39–41, bringing those different scenes and people together, it also reverses the situation of chap. 37; Joseph now has the power, and the brothers are at the mercy of his decisions. The text now addresses Joseph's use of that power. While some scholars have a basically negative view of Joseph's use of authority, we side with those who take a more positive view.

The scene in this chapter shifts back and forth between Egypt and Canaan, between palace and local village. The reader encounters Jacob and Joseph's brothers (except for Judah) for the first time since chap. 37. Famine has affected Canaan, too. Egypt has grain, however, and this means a trip to procure it (vv. 1-5; cf. 12:10-20). The stage is now set for Joseph and his brothers to encounter one another again, described in vv. 6-24. Verses 25-38 portray the brothers' return to Canaan and the associated difficulties occasioned by Joseph's testing of their integrity.

42:1-5. Verse 1 brings the reader into the middle of a conversation—something of a to-do in the family of Jacob. It is the same old story, but unbeknownst to them, a massive change is in

the offing. The famine in Canaan has created a problem, and the brothers are reduced to "looking at one another," waiting for a solution. Jacob, a stabilizing influence in this scene, reports that Egypt has grain, telling his sons to journey there and purchase some. Unknowingly and ironically, he tells them to go to Joseph just as he once sent Joseph to them (37:13-14). Only ten of Joseph's brothers go to Egypt; Jacob holds Benjamin back for fear of his life. As the one remaining son of his beloved Rachel, Benjamin is now the favorite; Jacob will not repeat the mistake he made with Joseph. This decision sets up a key development in the story. The end of the chapter will return to his concern about Benjamin.

The life-and-death matter presented here is a theme struck by Jacob himself in v. 2, and it reappears at important points in the subsequent narrative (vv. 18, 20; 43:8; 45:5-7). Jacob articulates thereby a key objective for the entire story, one that will be picked up by Joseph and even by the brothers.

Verse 5 seems to be set already in Egypt. It blends the brothers into a crowd of peoples who have made the journey for the same purpose, picking up on the theme of 41:57. The phrase "sons of Israel" (cf. 46:5, 8) appears purposely ambiguous; it refers to Jacob, but also anticipates the Israel of the exodus. The journeys in and out of Egypt mirror later developments.

42:6-24. These verses describe the first of four dialogues between Joseph and his brothers (cf. 43:27-31; 44:15–45:13; 50:15-21), a scenario not unlike the encounter between Jacob and Esau, only here the recognition is not mutual. In vv. 8-9*a* the narrator provides a key comment to make sure the reader understands who recognizes whom and that Joseph recalls his earlier dream just before the interrogation begins.

Verse 6 immediately brings the brothers into the presence of the highest official in Egypt, upon whom they now depend. The fact that they bow down before Joseph fulfills the dream in 37:7, reinforced by the brothers' repeated use of lord/servant language (vv. 10, 11, 13, 30, 33). Verse 9*a* shows that Joseph recognizes this; his dream has now come full circle. This recognition now propels the story over the next chapters. The brothers' lack of recognition enables Joseph to manipulate the situation toward the objective he chooses.

What will Joseph do in view of his recollection of the dream? *Now that the dream has been realized,* and in view of 41:51, he begins to move toward healing the breach. But this becomes a complex task. He cannot simply speak to them, for he may not discern equivocation (cf. God's test of Abraham). He must set up situations that will enable him to observe them without their realizing it and to bring their common story to the surface so that it can be dealt with properly. Again and again, these situations will mirror their treatment of him, forcing the issue into the front of their consciousness.

Joseph decides to treat them as if they were strangers, thus creating an artificial relationship. He speaks in an abrupt, officious manner, refusing to take them at their word. He questions them sharply, repeatedly accusing them of spying (historically, an Egyptian concern; the "nakedness of the land" refers to exposed borders), ironically exposing *their* defenselessness. The tables have been turned on the brothers; they experience what Joseph did in chap. 37, including the possibility of being assigned to a comparable fate. The accusation achieves its purpose; it draws out information about the family, including Benjamin, and, when combined with Joseph's shifting strategies regarding their future, it leads the brothers into confessional/theological reflection.

The brothers refuse to accept the evaluation and proceed with a defense born of surprise and fear, revealing more than they need to. They repeatedly insist on two things: (1) They are a family ("sons of one man"). This makes sense as a defense; it would be unusual for an espionage group to place in jeopardy so many from the same family. Ironically, the brothers appeal to family solidarity, so sharply violated in their treatment of Joseph. In this concern they unwittingly join forces with Joseph. (2) They are "honest people," men of integrity. This note recurs (vv. 11, 19, 31, 33, 34)—are the brothers honest or not? This claim recalls that their dealings with Joseph and their father were marked by a lack of integrity. Joseph needs to test this point: "whether there is truth in you" (vv. 16, 20). Joseph sharply continues his accusation and sets up a test. No doubt noting their equivocation regarding his fate ("one is no more"), he picks up on their unnecessary reference to Benjamin. This may have given him a clue that not all was right with his family. If Benjamin had simply displaced him in Jacob's affection, then the problem between father and brothers (see v. 36) had only been papered over. Benjamin thus becomes a passive vehicle for getting this issue out in the open.[204] One brother is to return for him, while the rest remain in prison. Joseph's repeated use of the oath "as Pharaoh lives" mirrors Israel's use of God or kings in their oaths (cf. 1 Sam 17:55; 2 Sam 15:21), and to rhetorical effect. Together with talk about life and death, it emphasizes the seriousness of the conversation. Joseph then has all of them peremptorily taken into custody (v. 17; cf. 40:4). This arbitrary act gives them a taste of the "pit" experience they put Joseph through and helps to prompt their memory (vv. 21-22).

After three days, Joseph approaches them with a less onerous plan, allowing all but one of them to leave. This extends the test: Will the brothers sacrifice one more brother? This plan mirrors still another dimension of his own experience. Yet, in this plan Joseph gives them an experience of graciousness. This combination of

204. See White, *Narration,* 260-61.

judgment and graciousness elicits their confession (vv. 21-22). Joseph's comments this time are positive in tone; he expresses interest in life for them and their family (vv. 18-19), though death still lingers in the air (v. 20). His rationale for these positive directions touches base with their own tradition: "for I fear God" (see 20:11), and stands in ironic contrast to their lack of concern for life.

The brothers agree to the plan (are they sincere?) and begin to lament their plight, not realizing that Joseph, having spoken through an interpreter (unique in Genesis), could understand them. They are "paying the penalty" (or are certainly guilty). The word אשם ('āšēm; v. 21) means both guilt and its ill effects. Their speech becomes a *public* confession of guilt for what they did to Joseph, whose anguished cries went unheeded. The detailed recollection after so many years is striking; it reveals a stricken conscience. Even more, ironically, their cry now mirrors his. They engage in moral order talk (what goes around comes around). They see that their present experience corresponds to Joseph's (the punishment fits the crime). More specifically, one brother will suffer the same fate as did Joseph. But the brothers do not perceive that Joseph himself executes the moral order.

Reuben enters an "I told you so" speech (cf. 37:21-22) into the conversation, which could only intensify their sense of guilt; he had told them not to harm (i.e., sin against) the boy, for such crimes cannot finally be concealed. He knew there would be a "reckoning" someday (cf. 9:5). His speech is met with silence, suggesting some level of acceptance.

When Joseph hears their guilt-ridden response, he almost gives himself away, turning from them to weep. Having calmed himself, Joseph turns back to the brothers and proceeds with the test. He binds Simeon (the second oldest; because of Reuben's defense?) as the one to stay behind to guarantee their return with Benjamin, which would confirm the brothers as honest men.

42:25-28. Joseph, however, has another gambit. He orders not only that they be given grain and food, but also that the money paid for the grain be placed in their sacks. This ploy explores the theme of integrity rather than being a sign of love or harshness. Even more, it ironically relates to their selling him for silver (כסף *kesep*,

37:28). This elicits further reflections regarding what they have done, including God's activity in their lives (v. 28).

The brothers depart for Canaan without Simeon; en route one brother discovers the money. Their "hearts sink"—they could be accused of being thieves as well as spies. Perhaps catching the irony of the silver, they feel themselves at the mercy of powers beyond their own. But this now takes explicit theological form, not some general dis-ease. Joseph, of course, had done this; yet, his discernment and wisdom are God-given. Hence, the brothers do get it right in one sense: God indeed remains active in these exchanges among the brothers, not least in seeing to the moral order at work in their lives. Their first reference to God represents another advance in their development (cf. 44:16; 50:17, their only other explicit God statements). In 50:20, Joseph will answer this question: God has been at work in their lives for good—a response anticipated by Joseph's steward (43:23!).

42:29-38. The brothers' return to Jacob follows a pattern similar to 37:32-36; they report their encounter with "the man" (vv. 29-34), but with subtle differences, perhaps to protect "their father" (a rare designation). They stress the positive (even exaggerate, v. 34b), with no mention of this as a life-and-death matter, and fewer references to Benjamin (two times vs. four times). But the author heightens the issue of honesty (three times vs. two times) in the formula: "By this I shall know" that you are honest men (v. 33). The brothers also do not speak of being jailed or the discovery of the money. The narrator also reports the new discovery of money by the other brothers. These verses (sometimes seen as a doublet) double the effect of Joseph's action; the returned money affects the brothers on their journey and at home, not only themselves but Jacob as well. It also intensifies the memory of the brothers' selling Joseph for silver (Judah's comment in 43:21 that *all* the brothers had discovered money at the lodging place telescopes vv. 27-28 and 35).

Jacob responds by lamenting the tragedies of his family: you are making me childless (does he suspect them?)! Two sons are gone, and now Benjamin is threatened. This sort of thing is always happening to me! He may be concerned about preserving the family, but tones of self-pity are evident. Reuben asks that Benjamin be put in his care and, in a sign of desperation, offers the life of his two sons should Benjamin not return (how could a loss from the *next* generation help?). Jacob refuses the offer, for if harm should come to Benjamin (cf. v. 4), he would die in great sorrow (cf. his comments about Rachel's other son in 37:35). Better that Simeon be lost than risk losing Benjamin, too.

REFLECTIONS

1. Various suggestions have been made regarding Joseph's motive for giving the test: (1) To exact revenge or punish his brothers. This seems unlikely, given the "test" language—and he is up front about this—and given the diminished test, with one brother detained. While his response may be somewhat harsh, the author's emphasis on Joseph's wisdom and discernment (as well as 41:51 and 42:9) suggests that he has everyone's best interests at heart. (2) To learn whether they are spies, but he knows they are not spies. This issue provides a facade, necessary only to serve another purpose. (3) To bring Benjamin to Joseph.[205] He wants to see his brother (vv. 15-16, 20) and weeps when he does (43:30). Yet, in the larger narrative (cf. 50:15-24) Benjamin becomes a means of achieving family unity, presupposed by the events of Exodus. (4) To determine whether the brothers have changed and are acting more like brothers. Although certainly true in part (v. 16), they may act so only to satisfy the needs of the moment—hence the need for more than one test. (5) To achieve a larger objective: the best possible future for this family *as a unit,* whose very future is at stake. The brothers need to pass through an ordeal in order to bring their memories and guilt to the surface, where it can be dealt with adequately, before reconciliation can truly take place, and hence safeguard the future of the family. This process transpires (see vv. 21-22, 28; 44:16; 50:16-17).

2. The recurring theme of Joseph's weeping (43:30; 45:1-2, 14-15; 46:29; 50:1, 17) has two basic purposes: (1) It breaks "the tension with progressing signs of hope for a full reconciliation."[206] The brothers' remorse prompts the first such sign. (2) Even more, it reveals "Joseph's growing feelings of compassion for his brothers behind his harsh facade, so that the reader can be aware that the meaning of Joseph's actions is not to be found in their surface appearance."[207] The author conveys Joseph's thoughts and feelings through this device.

3. The issue of guilt and punishment surfaces in a number of ways. It involves, however, not forensic acts of divine judgment, but the functioning of the moral order. The moral order does not function in some exact temporal way; the brothers' actions against Joseph come home to roost only after some thirteen or more years. Moreover, it does not function mechanically. The brothers certainly reap the consequences of their sins and relive many dimensions of Joseph's own experience of suffering; yet both human and divine actions are capable of breaking into that spiral, and reconciliation among the brothers finally comes. Nor does the moral order function in some deistic way. God works within it to bring about good (see 45:5-9; 50:15-21). Yet, God does not have full control over human behaviors, else one could not speak of sin as in any sense a human responsibility. But human sin cannot finally stymie God, who can draw everything that has happened into the orbit of larger purposes for good.

205. See von Rad, *Genesis,* 382.
206. Coats, *Genesis,* 286.
207. White, *Narration,* 259-60.

GENESIS 43:1-34, THE SECOND JOURNEY TO EGYPT

NIV

43 Now the famine was still severe in the land. ²So when they had eaten all the grain they had brought from Egypt, their father said to them, "Go back and buy us a little more food."

³But Judah said to him, "The man warned us solemnly, 'You will not see my face again unless your brother is with you.' ⁴If you will send our brother along with us, we will go down and buy food for you. ⁵But if you will not send him, we will not go down, because the man said to us, "You will not see my face again unless your brother is with you.'"

⁶Israel asked, "Why did you bring this trouble on me by telling the man you had another brother?"

⁷They replied, "The man questioned us closely about ourselves and our family. 'Is your father still living?' he asked us. 'Do you have another brother?' We simply answered his questions. How were we to know he would say, 'Bring your brother down here'?"

⁸Then Judah said to Israel his father, "Send the boy along with me and we will go at once, so that we and you and our children may live and not die. ⁹I myself will guarantee his safety; you can hold me personally responsible for him. If I do not bring him back to you and set him here before you, I will bear the blame before you all my life. ¹⁰As it is, if we had not delayed, we could have gone and returned twice."

¹¹Then their father Israel said to them, "If it must be, then do this: Put some of the best products of the land in your bags and take them down to the man as a gift—a little balm and a little honey, some spices and myrrh, some pistachio nuts and almonds. ¹²Take double the amount of silver with you, for you must return the silver that was put back into the mouths of your sacks. Perhaps it was a mistake. ¹³Take your brother also

NRSV

43 Now the famine was severe in the land. ²And when they had eaten up the grain that they had brought from Egypt, their father said to them, "Go again, buy us a little more food." ³But Judah said to him, "The man solemnly warned us, saying, 'You shall not see my face unless your brother is with you.' ⁴If you will send our brother with us, we will go down and buy you food; ⁵but if you will not send him, we will not go down, for the man said to us, 'You shall not see my face, unless your brother is with you.' " ⁶Israel said, "Why did you treat me so badly as to tell the man that you had another brother?" ⁷They replied, "The man questioned us carefully about ourselves and our kindred, saying, 'Is your father still alive? Have you another brother?' What we told him was in answer to these questions. Could we in any way know that he would say, 'Bring your brother down'?" ⁸Then Judah said to his father Israel, "Send the boy with me, and let us be on our way, so that we may live and not die—you and we and also our little ones. ⁹I myself will be surety for him; you can hold me accountable for him. If I do not bring him back to you and set him before you, then let me bear the blame forever. ¹⁰If we had not delayed, we would now have returned twice."

11Then their father Israel said to them, "If it must be so, then do this: take some of the choice fruits of the land in your bags, and carry them down as a present to the man—a little balm and a little honey, gum, resin, pistachio nuts, and almonds. ¹²Take double the money with you. Carry back with you the money that was returned in the top of your sacks; perhaps it was an oversight. ¹³Take your brother also, and be on your way again to the man; ¹⁴may God Almighty*

ᵃTraditional rendering of Heb El Shaddai

NIV

and go back to the man at once. [14]And may God Almighty[a] grant you mercy before the man so that he will let your other brother and Benjamin come back with you. As for me, if I am bereaved, I am bereaved."

[15]So the men took the gifts and double the amount of silver, and Benjamin also. They hurried down to Egypt and presented themselves to Joseph. [16]When Joseph saw Benjamin with them, he said to the steward of his house, "Take these men to my house, slaughter an animal and prepare dinner; they are to eat with me at noon."

[17]The man did as Joseph told him and took the men to Joseph's house. [18]Now the men were frightened when they were taken to his house. They thought, "We were brought here because of the silver that was put back into our sacks the first time. He wants to attack us and overpower us and seize us as slaves and take our donkeys."

[19]So they went up to Joseph's steward and spoke to him at the entrance to the house. [20]"Please, sir," they said, "we came down here the first time to buy food. [21]But at the place where we stopped for the night we opened our sacks and each of us found his silver—the exact weight—in the mouth of his sack. So we have brought it back with us. [22]We have also brought additional silver with us to buy food. We don't know who put our silver in our sacks."

[23]"It's all right," he said. "Don't be afraid. Your God, the God of your father, has given you treasure in your sacks; I received your silver." Then he brought Simeon out to them.

[24]The steward took the men into Joseph's house, gave them water to wash their feet and provided fodder for their donkeys. [25]They prepared their gifts for Joseph's arrival at noon, because they had heard that they were to eat there.

[26]When Joseph came home, they presented to him the gifts they had brought into the house, and they bowed down before him to the ground. [27]He asked them how they were, and then he said, "How is your aged father you told me about? Is he still living?"

[28]They replied, "Your servant our father is still alive and well." And they bowed low to pay him honor.

a14 Hebrew *El Shaddai*

NRSV

grant you mercy before the man, so that he may send back your other brother and Benjamin. As for me, if I am bereaved of my children, I am bereaved." [15]So the men took the present, and they took double the money with them, as well as Benjamin. Then they went on their way down to Egypt, and stood before Joseph.

16When Joseph saw Benjamin with them, he said to the steward of his house, "Bring the men into the house, and slaughter an animal and make ready, for the men are to dine with me at noon." [17]The man did as Joseph said, and brought the men to Joseph's house. [18]Now the men were afraid because they were brought to Joseph's house, and they said, "It is because of the money, replaced in our sacks the first time, that we have been brought in, so that he may have an opportunity to fall upon us, to make slaves of us and take our donkeys." [19]So they went up to the steward of Joseph's house and spoke with him at the entrance to the house. [20]They said, "Oh, my lord, we came down the first time to buy food; [21]and when we came to the lodging place we opened our sacks, and there was each one's money in the top of his sack, our money in full weight. So we have brought it back with us. [22]Moreover we have brought down with us additional money to buy food. We do not know who put our money in our sacks." [23]He replied, "Rest assured, do not be afraid; your God and the God of your father must have put treasure in your sacks for you; I received your money." Then he brought Simeon out to them. [24]When the steward[a] had brought the men into Joseph's house, and given them water, and they had washed their feet, and when he had given their donkeys fodder, [25]they made the present ready for Joseph's coming at noon, for they had heard that they would dine there.

26When Joseph came home, they brought him the present that they had carried into the house, and bowed to the ground before him. [27]He inquired about their welfare, and said, "Is your father well, the old man of whom you spoke? Is he still alive?" [28]They said, "Your servant our father is well; he is still alive." And they bowed their heads and did obeisance. [29]Then he looked

a Heb *the man*

NIV

²⁹As he looked about and saw his brother Benjamin, his own mother's son, he asked, "Is this your youngest brother, the one you told me about?" And he said, "God be gracious to you, my son." ³⁰Deeply moved at the sight of his brother, Joseph hurried out and looked for a place to weep. He went into his private room and wept there.

³¹After he had washed his face, he came out and, controlling himself, said, "Serve the food."

³²They served him by himself, the brothers by themselves, and the Egyptians who ate with him by themselves, because Egyptians could not eat with Hebrews, for that is detestable to Egyptians. ³³The men had been seated before him in the order of their ages, from the firstborn to the youngest; and they looked at each other in astonishment. ³⁴When portions were served to them from Joseph's table, Benjamin's portion was five times as much as anyone else's. So they feasted and drank freely with him.

NRSV

up and saw his brother Benjamin, his mother's son, and said, "Is this your youngest brother, of whom you spoke to me? God be gracious to you, my son!" ³⁰With that, Joseph hurried out, because he was overcome with affection for his brother, and he was about to weep. So he went into a private room and wept there. ³¹Then he washed his face and came out; and controlling himself he said, "Serve the meal." ³²They served him by himself, and them by themselves, and the Egyptians who ate with him by themselves, because the Egyptians could not eat with the Hebrews, for that is an abomination to the Egyptians. ³³When they were seated before him, the firstborn according to his birthright and the youngest according to his youth, the men looked at one another in amazement. ³⁴Portions were taken to them from Joseph's table, but Benjamin's portion was five times as much as any of theirs. So they drank and were merry with him.

COMMENTARY

This chapter continues the segment begun in chap. 42 and follows a similar outline, though with contrasting content (e.g., the brothers' reception).[208] The chapter begins with a conversation between the brothers and Jacob (43:1-15) and moves to a description of the brothers' journey to Egypt and their encounter with the steward (vv. 16-25), followed by another audience with Joseph (vv. 26-34).

This doubling of the journey to Egypt has raised the question of sources, suggesting to some that there is really only one journey, twice-told. Others insist on two different journeys, which is the shape of the final redaction in any case. Thus, although Simeon is neglected, he is not forgotten (v. 14). Also, the details of the second journey often presuppose the first (e.g., vv. 2-9). One may recognize a delay in returning (v. 10; see Joseph's concern in 45:9), though perhaps no more than a month or so, given the two weeks needed to make a round trip to Egypt.

43:1-15. Because of the severity of the famine (as in 41:57), the need to return to Egypt for food arises once again (as Joseph anticipated). Israel

(Jacob's only name in chap. 43) again tells his sons to go to Egypt, but they will not go without Benjamin (whose age is difficult to discern; cf. "boy" in v. 8).

Judah becomes a resolute spokesman for the brothers (cf. Reuben in 42:37) and remains so for the balance of the story. He plays a key role in helping to overcome the impasse centered on Benjamin. This conversation ought not to be considered a doublet of the report to Jacob in 42:29-34, not least because it focuses solely on the condition regarding Benjamin.

Judah forcefully reminds his father of the conversation with "the man" about Benjamin. Joseph had "solemnly" warned them. To reinforce this, Judah repeats Joseph's words: "You shall not see my face [i.e., me] unless your brother is with you" (vv. 3, 5). Israel wonders why his sons had even mentioned another brother, knowing how he would feel. They (i.e., all the brothers, v. 7) say it was in response to Joseph's questioning. This appears to skirt the truth, for in 42:13 they volunteer the information; yet, Joseph does not object when Judah reports the conversation to him (44:19-20). So we have difficulty discerning whether the brothers are "honest

208. See Humphreys, *Joseph,* 97.

men." This may be exactly the question the narrator intends the reader to raise.

Judah proceeds with what proves to be a highly persuasive speech (vv. 8-10). He pleads with Israel to let Benjamin return with them, claiming this to be a life-and-death matter for the family—even the children (he echoes the words of both Jacob and Joseph, 42:2, 20). Jacob had not heard the matter put in such terms by the brothers before (42:29-34). Then Judah, in a way more laudable and magnanimous than Reuben (42:37), places himself on the line as the personal guarantor of Benjamin's safety (see 44:32). Finally, Judah notes the delay in returning, indirectly pointing to Jacob's own refusal to send Benjamin (42:38). Joseph's concern about the delay (cf. 45:9) could have raised the issue of the *brothers'* integrity (in view of their agreement, 42:20) and prompted further testing.

Israel realizes that he must allow Benjamin to go, but he seeks to assure his return by sending gifts to "the man." They are to bring the best produce available in Canaan (cf. 24:10), ironically acting like Joseph's traders (37:25). They are also to take double the money (including the money found in the sack), a matter not raised by the brothers (unusual in view of their fears in v. 18). Jacob thus rescues his sons' integrity on this matter. They are to do this posthaste. Then Israel pronounces a benediction upon the success of their journey. Having done as much as he can, Jacob resigns himself to whatever may come; if deprived of children, his will be a deep loss indeed. The author does not name Simeon ("your other brother"), leaving room in the readers' mind for Joseph. The importance of Benjamin to Jacob sharply informs the brothers' subsequent behaviors (see esp. 44:18-34).

43:16-25. The brothers follow Israel's directives and proceed to Egypt, immediately presenting themselves to Joseph. But they do not get an audience with Joseph right away. Joseph, having observed Benjamin's presence without being seen, chooses to have his steward—an alter ego—deal with the brothers first (v. 16). The narrative purpose for the role of the steward allows Joseph to observe his brothers' behavior at some distance. They have fulfilled his demand regarding Benjamin, but the issue of the money and their honesty (so stressed in 42:11-34) remains open.

The brothers are received cordially this time

(cf. 42:7). A dinner is to be prepared, and the brothers are to dine with Joseph. Yet, when they are brought in (probably to the courtyard), they become frightened, a fear born of their last experience with Joseph. They suspect a trap, that they will be overpowered and enslaved because of the money, with the means for their return to Canaan (donkeys) taken away. They take the initiative, telling the steward about the money that mysteriously appeared in their sacks; they are returning it and have additional money for grain. They conclude their defense by pleading ignorance of how this happened. They would appear to have passed the honesty test, but Joseph continues to pursue the issue in the next episode. Does Joseph suspect what the reader knows—namely, that Jacob had to see to the return of the money?

The steward responds graciously, even though he keeps them off balance by the way he talks about the money and God. He assures them that everything is in order (literally, *"shalom* [שלום] be with you"); they need not be afraid. He tells them that God must have put the "treasure" in their sacks. His statement about receiving their money renounces any claim to it; he does not offer a half-truth.[209] He thus does not feign ignorance about the money; rather, he puts the truth in theological terms.

The scene concludes without dialogue. The steward brings Simeon out to fulfill Joseph's pledge to release him if Benjamin was brought along. The steward sees that the brothers' needs are met, as well as those of their animals, and they ready themselves and their gift for Joseph. They are Joseph's guests. The story invites us to think that everything will now be fine between Joseph and his brothers. But not yet.

43:26-34. When Joseph makes his appearance, the brothers present their gift and again bow before him to pay him honor (two times!). The realization of Joseph's dream continues (37:7). At the same time, the theme of peace (*shalom*), introduced by the steward (v. 23), is repeated by Joseph (v. 27)—recall 37:14—and is picked up by the brothers (v. 28). This marks an important transition in the narrative. At least from Joseph's perspective, the relationship between the brothers has shifted toward the positive. This exchange of

209. Sarna, *Genesis,* 301.

peace, which occurs in an everyday context of greeting, outside of the land of promise and apart from a liturgical setting, provides evidence of its importance for interpersonal relationships.

At the same time, the brothers' obeisance (vv. 26, 28), even if now marked by honor rather than simply submission, makes clear that their relationship with Joseph remains difficult. One verb used in v. 28, קדד (qādad, "bow down") occurs only with God as the object elsewhere in the Pentateuch (cf. 24:26, 48). Joseph will claim in 50:19 that he does not stand in the place of God, and thereby recognizes that such obeisance is not appropriate to a proper relationship between himself and his brothers.

Joseph begins by asking about their welfare and that of their aged father (see 44:20). Joseph then shifts his attention to Benjamin. Although Joseph recognizes him, he continues the ruse by asking into Benjamin's identity. Without waiting for a reply, he pronounces a blessing on Benjamin in language that echoes Jacob's blessing (v. 14), as well as Joseph's own gracious treatment by Potiphar (39:4, 21).

The encounter with Benjamin, for whom Joseph shows much affection, so moves Joseph that he excuses himself and weeps privately. The second time that Joseph weeps will not be the last (see Reflections on chap. 42). Having composed himself (see 45:1), he returns and directs the meal to begin. The brothers are now guests rather than enemies. Yet, the one with whom they are eating still appears as a stranger, signaled by the absence of conversation between them (until 45:3). The relationship has progressed, but Joseph still holds back his identity. For reasons not stated, Joseph believes the time is not yet right to reveal himself to his brothers. Given the events of the next chapter, a further test seems necessary. The brothers have not reached the end of their journey.

The author reports no further dialogue, but notes certain unusual incidents. Separate servings are given to Joseph, to the brothers, and to the Egyptians, because of religious scruples (Joseph sits between communities!). This information shows that reconciliation has not yet truly taken place. The brothers are seated at Joseph's direction (i.e., "before him")[210] according to their age, a strange procedure at which the brothers are astonished: How would he know how to seat them without being asked? Benjamin's portion is five times greater than that of his brothers, demonstrating pleasure at Benjamin's presence, though Joseph also wants to see the brothers' reaction to this favoritism. Benjamin may be the guest of honor, but the absence of any speech on his part (in the entire story!) diminishes his role. The comment about this being a happy occasion sets up the not-so-happy turn of events that follows.

210. Ibid., 302.

REFLECTIONS

1. The tensions created for the reader of this chapter revolve around difficult decisions that deeply affect family life. The author addresses feeding one's family in the midst of famine, but also the danger presented by the strange request that getting more food from Egypt is contingent on the presence of Benjamin. In weighing options, Jacob finally decides that seeing to the future of the community overrides the fate of a beloved individual family member and his own personal well-being (cf. 34:30).

2. In v. 14, Jacob first mentions God (*El Shaddai*, see 17:1) in this story; he uses the language of mercy (רחמים *raḥămîm*), undeserved divine favor, a frequent element in Israel's confession about God (cf. Exod 34:6). The success of his sons' journey depends on the mercy of God. The stress on mercy lifts up the reality of this dysfunctional family. Although hopeful, Jacob knows—and wisely so—that things may not work out as well as he anticipates. His hopes have been dashed before, for anti-God forces are powerful, often frustrating divine purposes. Yet, his trust in God enables him to continue to express hope for the future, for he believes that God's work does have good effects in ways beyond his knowing and beyond external observation.

Joseph's use of the verb meaning "be gracious" (חנן *ḥānan*) in v. 29 recalls an important theological claim made by Israel for the nature of its God (see Ps 86:15-17). As elsewhere in benedictions (see Num 6:25; Ps 67:1), it functions here as a welcoming word. And as in laments (see Pss 4:1; 86:15-17), it suggests here a response to Jacob's lament about Benjamin—God has been gracious. This word relates back to creedal language used by Jacob at the sending of the brothers (v. 14; see above). Israel's creedal statement about its God (Exod 34:6) attests to this kind of experience with God. Jacob also used this language at the reconciliation with Esau and in the wake of God's graciousness at Jabbok (33:5, 11). God, indeed a gracious one, extends blessings to all, freely and undeservingly (see Exod 33:19).

3. The steward's theological observations in v. 23 are noteworthy. The brothers are extended a word of peace (*shalom*) and told that they need not be afraid, for God, the God of their father (namely, their family) has taken care of them by putting the money in their sacks. This announcement of peace and the removal of fear recurs as a motif in other biblical texts, especially in theophanies (see 26:24) and in Second Isaiah (e.g., 43:1-5). One who stands outside the community announces this word of comfort to the people of God (even if he learned it from Joseph). This may be disconcerting to insiders, but they must be open to God's capability of working on their behalf in and through such persons. Outsiders, too, can be the vehicle for a word of God's peace.

We do not know the extent to which the steward's theology reflects that of Joseph or the narrator. It could be a generic reference to God that the brothers can interpret as they please. Most likely (as in 41:38-39), he offers a way of speaking about God, indeed a gracious, rather than a retributive, God (cf. 42:28), that helps us to understand other aspects of the story, particularly 45:8, "It was not you who sent me here, but God." In 43:23, God did not personally insert the money in their sacks (cf. 42:25), but because this human action was in tune with the divine purposes, one could claim God as the subject of the action. Such a claim does not mean that Joseph's decision to fill the sacks was necessary; he could have taken other actions. The author's direct use of God language seems purposely ambiguous, for the divine activity is not obvious, but remains confessional, as no empirical claims can be made. It becomes a statement of faith.

GENESIS 44:1-34, JOSEPH'S FINAL TEST

NIV

44 Now Joseph gave these instructions to the steward of his house: "Fill the men's sacks with as much food as they can carry, and put each man's silver in the mouth of his sack. ²Then put my cup, the silver one, in the mouth of the youngest one's sack, along with the silver for his grain." And he did as Joseph said.

³As morning dawned, the men were sent on their way with their donkeys. ⁴They had not gone far from the city when Joseph said to his steward, "Go after those men at once, and when you catch up with them, say to them, 'Why have you repaid good with evil? ⁵Isn't this the cup my master drinks from and also uses for divination? This is a wicked thing you have done.'"

NRSV

44 Then he commanded the steward of his house, "Fill the men's sacks with food, as much as they can carry, and put each man's money in the top of his sack. ²Put my cup, the silver cup, in the top of the sack of the youngest, with his money for the grain." And he did as Joseph told him. ³As soon as the morning was light, the men were sent away with their donkeys. ⁴When they had gone only a short distance from the city, Joseph said to his steward, "Go, follow after the men; and when you overtake them, say to them, 'Why have you returned evil for good? Why have you stolen my silver cup?ᵃ ⁵Is it not from this that my lord

a Gk Compare Vg: Heb lacks *Why have you stolen my silver cup?*

NIV

⁶When he caught up with them, he repeated these words to them. ⁷But they said to him, "Why does my lord say such things? Far be it from your servants to do anything like that! ⁸We even brought back to you from the land of Canaan the silver we found inside the mouths of our sacks. So why would we steal silver or gold from your master's house? ⁹If any of your servants is found to have it, he will die; and the rest of us will become my lord's slaves."

¹⁰"Very well, then," he said, "let it be as you say. Whoever is found to have it will become my slave; the rest of you will be free from blame."

¹¹Each of them quickly lowered his sack to the ground and opened it. ¹²Then the steward proceeded to search, beginning with the oldest and ending with the youngest. And the cup was found in Benjamin's sack. ¹³At this, they tore their clothes. Then they all loaded their donkeys and returned to the city.

¹⁴Joseph was still in the house when Judah and his brothers came in, and they threw themselves to the ground before him. ¹⁵Joseph said to them, "What is this you have done? Don't you know that a man like me can find things out by divination?"

¹⁶"What can we say to my lord?" Judah replied. "What can we say? How can we prove our innocence? God has uncovered your servants' guilt. We are now my lord's slaves—we ourselves and the one who was found to have the cup."

¹⁷But Joseph said, "Far be it from me to do such a thing! Only the man who was found to have the cup will become my slave. The rest of you, go back to your father in peace."

¹⁸Then Judah went up to him and said: "Please, my lord, let your servant speak a word to my lord. Do not be angry with your servant, though you are equal to Pharaoh himself. ¹⁹My lord asked his servants, 'Do you have a father or a brother?' ²⁰And we answered, 'We have an aged father, and there is a young son born to him in his old age. His brother is dead, and he is the only one of his mother's sons left, and his father loves him.'

²¹"Then you said to your servants, 'Bring him down to me so I can see him for myself.' ²²And we said to my lord, 'The boy cannot leave his father; if he leaves him, his father will die.' ²³But you told

NRSV

drinks? Does he not indeed use it for divination? You have done wrong in doing this.' "

6When he overtook them, he repeated these words to them. ⁷They said to him, "Why does my lord speak such words as these? Far be it from your servants that they should do such a thing! ⁸Look, the money that we found at the top of our sacks, we brought back to you from the land of Canaan; why then would we steal silver or gold from your lord's house? ⁹Should it be found with any one of your servants, let him die; moreover the rest of us will become my lord's slaves." ¹⁰He said, "Even so; in accordance with your words, let it be: he with whom it is found shall become my slave, but the rest of you shall go free." ¹¹Then each one quickly lowered his sack to the ground, and each opened his sack. ¹²He searched, beginning with the eldest and ending with the youngest; and the cup was found in Benjamin's sack. ¹³At this they tore their clothes. Then each one loaded his donkey, and they returned to the city.

14Judah and his brothers came to Joseph's house while he was still there; and they fell to the ground before him. ¹⁵Joseph said to them, "What deed is this that you have done? Do you not know that one such as I can practice divination?" ¹⁶And Judah said, "What can we say to my lord? What can we speak? How can we clear ourselves? God has found out the guilt of your servants; here we are then, my lord's slaves, both we and also the one in whose possession the cup has been found." ¹⁷But he said, "Far be it from me that I should do so! Only the one in whose possession the cup was found shall be my slave; but as for you, go up in peace to your father."

18Then Judah stepped up to him and said, "O my lord, let your servant please speak a word in my lord's ears, and do not be angry with your servant; for you are like Pharaoh himself. ¹⁹My lord asked his servants, saying, 'Have you a father or a brother?' ²⁰And we said to my lord, 'We have a father, an old man, and a young brother, the child of his old age. His brother is dead; he alone is left of his mother's children, and his father loves him.' ²¹Then you said to your servants, 'Bring him down to me, so that I may set my eyes on him.' ²²We said to my lord, 'The boy cannot leave his father, for if he should leave his father, his father

NIV

your servants, 'Unless your youngest brother comes down with you, you will not see my face again.' [24]When we went back to your servant my father, we told him what my lord had said.

[25]"Then our father said, 'Go back and buy a little more food.' [26]But we said, 'We cannot go down. Only if our youngest brother is with us will we go. We cannot see the man's face unless our youngest brother is with us.'

[27]"Your servant my father said to us, 'You know that my wife bore me two sons. [28]One of them went away from me, and I said, "He has surely been torn to pieces." And I have not seen him since. [29]If you take this one from me too and harm comes to him, you will bring my gray head down to the grave[a] in misery.'

[30]"So now, if the boy is not with us when I go back to your servant my father and if my father, whose life is closely bound up with the boy's life, [31]sees that the boy isn't there, he will die. Your servants will bring the gray head of our father down to the grave in sorrow. [32]Your servant guaranteed the boy's safety to my father. I said, 'If I do not bring him back to you, I will bear the blame before you, my father, all my life!'

[33]"Now then, please let your servant remain here as my lord's slave in place of the boy, and let the boy return with his brothers. [34]How can I go back to my father if the boy is not with me? No! Do not let me see the misery that would come upon my father."

[a]29 Hebrew *Sheol*; also in verse 31

NRSV

would die.' [23]Then you said to your servants, 'Unless your youngest brother comes down with you, you shall see my face no more.' [24]When we went back to your servant my father we told him the words of my lord. [25]And when our father said, 'Go again, buy us a little food,' [26]we said, 'We cannot go down. Only if our youngest brother goes with us, will we go down; for we cannot see the man's face unless our youngest brother is with us.' [27]Then your servant my father said to us, 'You know that my wife bore me two sons; [28]one left me, and I said, Surely he has been torn to pieces; and I have never seen him since. [29]If you take this one also from me, and harm comes to him, you will bring down my gray hairs in sorrow to Sheol.' [30]Now therefore, when I come to your servant my father and the boy is not with us, then, as his life is bound up in the boy's life, [31]when he sees that the boy is not with us, he will die; and your servants will bring down the gray hairs of your servant our father with sorrow to Sheol. [32]For your servant became surety for the boy to my father, saying, "If I do not bring him back to you, then I will bear the blame in the sight of my father all my life.' [33]Now therefore, please let your servant remain as a slave to my lord in place of the boy; and let the boy go back with his brothers. [34]For how can I go back to my father if the boy is not with me? I fear to see the suffering that would come upon my father."

COMMENTARY

This segment continues the episode of chaps. 42–43. It begins in Egypt (vv. 1-5), moves to a point along the way between Egypt and Canaan (vv. 6-13), and concludes once again in Egypt at Joseph's house (vv. 14-34). Joseph controls the situation from beginning to end. At the same time, Judah, now the leader of the brothers, makes a passionate and persuasive speech before Joseph, in the wake of which Joseph finally reveals himself (chap. 45).

44:1-5. Joseph commands his steward to put food and money (i.e., silver) in the brothers' sacks for their return to Canaan. This repeats the directive

of 42:25, except that Joseph's silver cup is also to be placed in Benjamin's sack. An important personal possession allows one more test of his brothers. The return of the money once again has troubled commentators. Yet, while it plays no further role in this chapter, it reinforces the focus on silver and makes clear that Joseph will not keep any money his family has paid for food (see chaps. 42–43).

Shortly after the brothers depart, Joseph sends his steward after them. He takes a hard-line approach, firing questions that assume they stole the silver cup (NRSV/NIV footnotes). The steward's (Joseph's) questions focus on the personal character of the deed; the silver cup is Joseph's own. In some sense it stands in for him, so that he is more personally violated when they "take" *this* silver; it more sharply mirrors his own violation at their hands when they sold him for silver.

Joseph uses the cup to divine, to seek the meaning of, events through observing patterns in the liquid (cf. the modern use of tea leaves or coffee grounds). God could work through such means, which is linked with Joseph's ability as a dream interpreter (cf. 40:8). It may be that Joseph does not actually practice divination (cf. v. 15), but he certainly wants the brothers to think he does. They must have had an increasing sense of being hemmed in, at the mercy of powers beyond their control (v. 16*a*).

44:6-13. When the steward repeats Joseph's words to the brothers, they strongly deny their guilt; they are "honest" men (using עבד ['*ebeb*, "servant"] three times; this word occurs nineteen times in vv. 7-33!). As evidence, they cite their return of the money (cf. 43:12). If they hadn't kept that money, why would they steal again? They naively offer to become Joseph's servants/slaves should the cup be found; indeed, they pronounce a death sentence on the thief (harsher than Israelite law required). By these words they play right into Joseph's hand (see below). Their innocence, which mirrors Joseph's innocence, seems ironic. Moreover, they prescribe *for themselves* a double fate that mirrors his—death for one and slavery to the Egyptians for the rest. Their cries of innocence also parallel Joseph's (42:21).

While v. 10 remains ambiguous, the steward does not fully accept their self-sentencing. He speaks graciously before the evidence sees the light of day. He agrees only to the enslavement of the culpable one; the rest are to go free. The steward thereby sets Joseph up for a response (v. 17) that will provide the breakthrough in this prolonged process of testing.

The brothers confidently subject themselves to a search. When the cup is found in Benjamin's sack, the brothers do not respond verbally; they express their distress by tearing their clothes (cf. 37:34). Rather than proceeding to Canaan, all of them return to Egypt for a confrontation with Joseph himself. Their actions are informed by knowing how their father would respond if they returned without Benjamin (see 42:38).

44:14-17. When the brothers prostrate themselves before Joseph (cf. 37:7), he picks up the steward's accusations. Expressing amazement at what they have done, he claims that he could have (has?) discovered their deed through divination (v. 15). Judah interprets this exposure of guilt as a divine act (v. 16).

Judah, the spokesman for the brothers, acknowledges that they are entirely at Joseph's disposal; they can do nothing to clear themselves. Although he never confesses that a crime has been committed, Judah makes a public confession of guilt for *all* the brothers and throws them on the mercy of this "lord." For him to include all the brothers suggests that he has more than this event in mind, including their actions against Joseph (see 42:21), though Joseph does not recognize this dynamic.

Joseph sharply refuses to make them all his slaves, asking only that the possessor of the cup (Benjamin is not named) be made a slave. The other brothers will return to their father in peace (*shalom*), an irony, given what their father has said about Benjamin (see 42:38; 43:14). On the surface, this proposal appears magnanimous, but Joseph knows that they cannot return to their father without Benjamin. Joseph has tightened the screws; how will the brothers respond?

By this action, Joseph has placed Benjamin in a relationship to his brothers not unlike the way his own had once been (see other such parallels in chap. 42). In this test, Joseph will certainly gain knowledge about his brothers. Will they act toward Benjamin as they once had toward him? Will they allow Benjamin to become a slave, while they save their own skins?

44:18-34. Judah responds with a passionate speech, the longest in Genesis and a literary masterpiece, not least in the way it gathers up the story to this point. In a way similar in its rhetorical power to his speech to Jacob in 43:3-10, Judah seeks to persuade Joseph to keep him rather than Benjamin. To this end, Judah makes selective and expansive use of previous conversations, with Joseph himself (cf. vv. 20-23 with 42:12-20) and Jacob (cf. vv. 24-29, 32 with 37:33-35; 42:36-38; 43:2-14). Joseph hears for the first time his father's reaction to his own abduction, and that Jacob still mourns for him (cf. v. 28 with 37:33).

Judah speaks straightforwardly and sincerely, conveying what is at stake for this family in quite direct ways. At the same time, he speaks in a highly deferential manner, in initial approach ("you are like Pharaoh himself"), in general language (lord/servant is used twenty times!), and in omitting any harshness from prior conversations (e.g., Joseph's charge of spying and threat of death). The speech also has strong emotional content, especially regarding the negative effect on their aged father (mentioned fourteen times!), whose life has been so filled with hardship and loss (vv. 19-20, 22, 27-29, 30-31, 34). Judah stresses that this is a matter of life and death for him (vv. 22, 29-31). He also recalls the violence done to Joseph (vv. 20, 27-29) and refers to Jacob's special love for Benjamin, with whom "his life is bound up" (v. 30; cf. vv. 20, 22, 27-29, 31, 34). Judah speaks of this in nonjudgmental ways, recognizing and accepting

such preferential treatment by his father. The climax of the speech refers to the suffering their father will endure (v. 34), a contrast to the brothers' concern in 37:31-35.

Judah also underscores the extent to which the brothers have acceded to Joseph's requests, even more, how he has placed his own future on the line (v. 32). This makes clear that he is following through on his promise to his father (cf. 43:9). Judah's speech accents his integrity and gives further evidence of a change in the brothers. Judah's willingness also appears ironic, for he would then become the slave of the very one he had made a slave (cf. 37:26-27).

As with Jacob (43:11-14), Judah's speech persuades Joseph, whose response is detailed in chap. 45. Judah's references to their father seem to have been particularly effective (45:3, 9, 13, 23).

REFLECTIONS

1. Some commentators believe that Joseph turns the test into "an insolent, almost wanton game."[211] This seems unlikely. As noted, testing must involve action and not just words. Whether there has been a change in fact can more readily be discerned by the way people act. Moreover, the testing gives the brothers an experience not unlike Joseph's own (as in chap. 42). This mirroring process enables the brothers to recognize their guilt and makes reconciliation possible.

2. Note the important language in vv 5-6. The brothers have done wrong (רעע *rāʿaʿ*); they have returned evil (רע *raʿ*) for the good (טוב *ṭôb*) they had received from Joseph. This anticipates the use of good and evil in 50:20. Here the brothers are accused of doing evil (without so intending), and Joseph does good; there they are said to do evil (with intention), and God does good. Regarding the evil, their "innocence" actually mirrors their guilt in selling Joseph for silver, so that this verse and 50:20 are finally parallel. Regarding the good, we see, once again, an elision of divine and human activity; both are engaged in doing good.

3. The author mentions God only once in this chapter (v. 16), but it is significant. Although the brothers had previously acknowledged their guilt to one another (42:21), they now confess before Joseph. Moreover, although the brothers now use God language for the second time (cf. 42:28), previously it took the form of a question. Judah here brings guilt and God together, thereby confessing that God has been engaged in these events, working to expose their guilt in and through what has happened. When we combine this with other changes, we understand that Joseph's testing (though rigorous) has finally served a positive purpose.

It seems somewhat strange to say that *God* has "found out," as if God did not know what had transpired. The author links God and Joseph again (see 43:23). This use of God language also reflects Joseph's speech in 45:8, where human and divine agency are combined. Moreover, in 45:5-9 Joseph will speak of God as one who has been engaged in preserving life; the reference in 44:16 to God as one before whom guilt stands exposed is directed toward the

211. Von Rad, *Genesis,* 391.

same end. The exposure of guilt serves life and well-being, not to perpetuate self-loathing. God's activity in convicting the brothers, therefore, brings about reconciliation in this family.

4. Judah's speeches (to Jacob, 43:3-10; and to Joseph, 44:18-34) relate directly to the events of chap. 38 and play a critical role in the Joseph story. Genesis 37–50 also involves a story about Judah. In and through what he says, not least his confession of guilt and the changes he exemplifies in his interpretation of what has happened, he enables the story of this family to move to a new level, setting the stage for the reconciliation that follows. Without Judah, Joseph's ensuing speech would not have been possible. Joseph's theological interpretation of events builds upon Judah's confession.

Even more, unlike his earlier attitude (37:26-27), Judah—like Tamar—chooses to risk himself rather than risk the life of another brother. First, he makes this promise to his father. Second, he follows through on it, in spite of his innocence. This self-effacing act—certainly not his only option—serves the future of both father and brother. Self-sacrifice in conflicted situations may lead to reconciliation.[212]

At the same time, Joseph refuses to accept this sacrifice in his response in chap. 45. Joseph recognizes that self-sacrifice is not necessarily a good thing, not least because it can be used in abusive ways to promote the elevation of one person over another. And so finally, in 50:19-21, Joseph will reject any hierarchical relationship among the brothers. Nevertheless, this does not discount the integrity of Judah's offer, and it stands in the narrative as a sign of the great change that has come over the brothers.

212. Westermann speaks of "vicarious suffering," *Genesis 37–50*, 137-38.

GENESIS 45:1-28, JOSEPH MAKES HIMSELF KNOWN

NIV

45 Then Joseph could no longer control himself before all his attendants, and he cried out, "Have everyone leave my presence!" So there was no one with Joseph when he made himself known to his brothers. [2]And he wept so loudly that the Egyptians heard him, and Pharaoh's household heard about it.

[3]Joseph said to his brothers, "I am Joseph! Is my father still living?" But his brothers were not able to answer him, because they were terrified at his presence.

[4]Then Joseph said to his brothers, "Come close to me." When they had done so, he said, "I am your brother Joseph, the one you sold into Egypt! [5]And now, do not be distressed and do not be angry with yourselves for selling me here, because it was to save lives that God sent me ahead of you. [6]For two years now there has been famine in the land, and for the next five years there will not be plowing and reaping. [7]But God sent me ahead of you to preserve for you a remnant on

NRSV

45 Then Joseph could no longer control himself before all those who stood by him, and he cried out, "Send everyone away from me." So no one stayed with him when Joseph made himself known to his brothers. [2]And he wept so loudly that the Egyptians heard it, and the household of Pharaoh heard it. [3]Joseph said to his brothers, "I am Joseph. Is my father still alive?" But his brothers could not answer him, so dismayed were they at his presence.

4Then Joseph said to his brothers, "Come closer to me." And they came closer. He said, "I am your brother, Joseph, whom you sold into Egypt. [5]And now do not be distressed, or angry with yourselves, because you sold me here; for God sent me before you to preserve life. [6]For the famine has been in the land these two years; and there are five more years in which there will be neither plowing nor harvest. [7]God sent me before you to preserve for you a remnant on earth, and to keep alive for you many survivors. [8]So it was not you who sent me here, but God; he has made

NIV

earth and to save your lives by a great deliverance.[a]

⁸"So then, it was not you who sent me here, but God. He made me father to Pharaoh, lord of his entire household and ruler of all Egypt. ⁹Now hurry back to my father and say to him, 'This is what your son Joseph says: God has made me lord of all Egypt. Come down to me; don't delay. ¹⁰You shall live in the region of Goshen and be near me—you, your children and grandchildren, your flocks and herds, and all you have. ¹¹I will provide for you there, because five years of famine are still to come. Otherwise you and your household and all who belong to you will become destitute.'

¹²"You can see for yourselves, and so can my brother Benjamin, that it is really I who am speaking to you. ¹³Tell my father about all the honor accorded me in Egypt and about everything you have seen. And bring my father down here quickly."

¹⁴Then he threw his arms around his brother Benjamin and wept, and Benjamin embraced him, weeping. ¹⁵And he kissed all his brothers and wept over them. Afterward his brothers talked with him.

¹⁶When the news reached Pharaoh's palace that Joseph's brothers had come, Pharaoh and all his officials were pleased. ¹⁷Pharaoh said to Joseph, "Tell your brothers, 'Do this: Load your animals and return to the land of Canaan, ¹⁸and bring your father and your families back to me. I will give you the best of the land of Egypt and you can enjoy the fat of the land.'

¹⁹"You are also directed to tell them, 'Do this: Take some carts from Egypt for your children and your wives, and get your father and come. ²⁰Never mind about your belongings, because the best of all Egypt will be yours.'"

²¹So the sons of Israel did this. Joseph gave them carts, as Pharaoh had commanded, and he also gave them provisions for their journey. ²²To each of them he gave new clothing, but to Benjamin he gave three hundred shekels[b] of silver and five sets of clothes. ²³And this is what he sent to his father: ten donkeys loaded with the best things of Egypt, and ten female donkeys loaded with

a7 Or save you as a great band of survivors   a22 That is, about 7 1/2 pounds (about 3.5 kilograms)

NRSV

me a father to Pharaoh, and lord of all his house and ruler over all the land of Egypt. ⁹Hurry and go up to my father and say to him, "Thus says your son Joseph, God has made me lord of all Egypt; come down to me, do not delay. ¹⁰You shall settle in the land of Goshen, and you shall be near me, you and your children and your children's children, as well as your flocks, your herds, and all that you have. ¹¹I will provide for you there—since there are five more years of famine to come—so that you and your household, and all that you have, will not come to poverty.' ¹²And now your eyes and the eyes of my brother Benjamin see that it is my own mouth that speaks to you. ¹³You must tell my father how greatly I am honored in Egypt, and all that you have seen. Hurry and bring my father down here." ¹⁴Then he fell upon his brother Benjamin's neck and wept, while Benjamin wept upon his neck. ¹⁵And he kissed all his brothers and wept upon them; and after that his brothers talked with him.

16When the report was heard in Pharaoh's house, "Joseph's brothers have come," Pharaoh and his servants were pleased. ¹⁷Pharaoh said to Joseph, "Say to your brothers, 'Do this: load your animals and go back to the land of Canaan. ¹⁸Take your father and your households and come to me, so that I may give you the best of the land of Egypt, and you may enjoy the fat of the land.' ¹⁹You are further charged to say, "Do this: take wagons from the land of Egypt for your little ones and for your wives, and bring your father, and come. ²⁰Give no thought to your possessions, for the best of all the land of Egypt is yours.'"

21The sons of Israel did so. Joseph gave them wagons according to the instruction of Pharaoh, and he gave them provisions for the journey. ²²To each one of them he gave a set of garments; but to Benjamin he gave three hundred pieces of silver and five sets of garments. ²³To his father he sent the following: ten donkeys loaded with the good things of Egypt, and ten female donkeys loaded with grain, bread, and provision for his father on the journey. ²⁴Then he sent his brothers on their way, and as they were leaving he said to them, "Do not quarrel[a] along the way."

25So they went up out of Egypt and came to

a Or be agitated

grain and bread and other provisions for his journey. ²⁴Then he sent his brothers away, and as they were leaving he said to them, "Don't quarrel on the way!"

²⁵So they went up out of Egypt and came to their father Jacob in the land of Canaan. ²⁶They told him, "Joseph is still alive! In fact, he is ruler of all Egypt." Jacob was stunned; he did not believe them. ²⁷But when they told him everything Joseph had said to them, and when he saw the carts Joseph had sent to carry him back, the spirit of their father Jacob revived. ²⁸And Israel said, "I'm convinced! My son Joseph is still alive. I will go and see him before I die."

their father Jacob in the land of Canaan. ²⁶And they told him, "Joseph is still alive! He is even ruler over all the land of Egypt." He was stunned; he could not believe them. ²⁷But when they told him all the words of Joseph that he had said to them, and when he saw the wagons that Joseph had sent to carry him, the spirit of their father Jacob revived. ²⁸Israel said, "Enough! My son Joseph is still alive. I must go and see him before I die."

COMMENTARY

Chapter 45 provides the climax to the story, but must be seen as closely coordinate with chap. 46 (especially 45:5-8 and 46:1-4). The actual descent belongs together with the preparations for it. After Joseph reveals himself to his brothers (vv. 1-8), Joseph (vv. 9-15, 21-24), Pharaoh (vv. 16-20), the brothers, and Jacob (vv. 25-28) prepare for the descent to Egypt in their own ways.

One of the puzzles regarding this section involves its relationship to 50:15-21. Those verses seem to replicate the events of this chapter, but that is not the case. The key difference lies in Joseph's relationship with his brothers. Three observations make clear that a full reconciliation does not occur here.

First, in this chapter the brothers do not respond specifically to what Joseph says; v. 15 testifies only to general conversation. In 50:15-18, the brothers still fear Joseph; they still stand in a lord/servant relationship with him, in fact, they seek to perpetuate it. This means that Joseph's goal of ameliorating their anxieties was not finally successful.

Second, Joseph, in chap. 45, does not specifically deal with the lord/servant reality. His first question relates to his father, not to his brothers (v. 3). He leaves questions of accountability and penalty aside (cf. 42:21-22). These issues burst forth at the point of their father's death (between 45:26 and 50:15, the brothers speak only at 47:4).

Third, Joseph is the direct object of every verb, with God as subject (vv. 5, 7, 8, 9): God has sent

me; God has made *me;* indeed, he repeats that God has made him "lord." The author encloses the report that Joseph asks be brought to his father by language that could be described as self-congratulatory (vv. 9, 13). Initially, Joseph calls himself a brother (v. 4), but father/lord/ruler language finally predominates (vv. 8-9, 13; cf. v. 26). Moreover, directives to the brothers abound, and Joseph even appears paternalistic (v. 24; 46:31-33).

The new question addressed in 50:15-21 addresses the nature of the relationship between Joseph and his brothers. There Joseph will reject the ruler/slave image. The dream of 37:7 was earlier realized, without the brothers' knowledge (do they now realize it?), but the images of that dream must not be allowed to shape their ongoing life together.

45:1-3. Judah's speech proves to be highly effective. Joseph can no longer control his emotions, but rather than leave (see 42:24; 43:30), he dismisses all attendants so that family members can deal with these issues privately. Yet, he weeps so loudly that it proves not to be a private affair after all (Joseph's weeping encloses the section, vv. 1-2, 14-15). Standing alone with his brothers, he reveals his identity. All the brothers are alive.

In view of Judah's speech, Joseph asks whether their father is really still alive ("life" could refer simply to good health). His brothers, however, are reduced to an agitated, fearful silence. This silence provides a break in the reunion; how Joseph will move past this awkwardness and deal with his brothers' fear becomes the question. The task of reconciliation is no simple matter.

45:4-15. Joseph asks his brothers to come closer, not to see him more clearly, but thereby to cross the official barrier. He identifies himself further by recalling their common history, going directly to the heart of the issue: You sold me into Egypt (v. 4).

Joseph's next comment (v. 5*a*) proves decisive. He discerns that his brothers are dismayed or terrified (NIV), distressed (cf. 42:21), and angry at each other (42:22), no doubt for many reasons, not least what this means for their own future. Joseph does not scold or blame them; he does not try to make them feel either guilty or shameful. He asks for no confession of sin and issues no absolution.[213] Rather, he wants to allay their fears (see the "for/because"). His formulations are thus designed for pastoral purposes, and they take on a confessional or doxological character; they must be interpreted not unlike other such language (e.g., the hymns of the psalter; oracles of salvation in response to laments). Even so, Joseph does not fully accomplish his objective.

Joseph's speaking takes a form similar to that of a theophany narrative (see 26:24), with self-identification, the quelling of fear, and the announcement of what God has done (not *will* do). The formal parallels between 45:3-8 and 46:2-4 should be especially noted, because they bring creational and promissory themes together.

Joseph says, fundamentally, that in spite of their past history, all will be well because what has happened corresponds to God's purposes. He invites them to view the past from the perspective of the present: Everybody is alive. Hence, their particular past can be interpreted as having a fundamentally (not totally, 50:20) positive dimension. God has "taken over" what they have done and used it to bring about this end. Their actions have *become* God's by being woven into his life-giving purposes. Even more, *Pharaoh's* actions—elevating Joseph as ruler—have *become* God's! The author leaves aside the role of the human for a specific purpose (not unlike referring to a sermon as the word of God)—the role of the human returns in 50:20. Human actions could have resulted in different ends; these ends have

213. Contra Westermann, *Genesis 37–50,* 144.

come to pass, however, and the result means that the decisive actor has been God.

Some scholars think that the narrator's perspective appears most transparently at this point; yet, it certainly needs 50:15-21 for proper interpretation. The important new developments in 50:15-21 move theologically beyond this text, so that Joseph's perspective becomes more mature (see above). Moreover, we are not fully clear about how God's activity should be interpreted. Certainly, God acts unobtrusively, hidden beneath the ordinary course of events. God is the subject of two verbs, שלח (*šālaḥ,* "send"; vv. 5, 7, 8), and שׂים (*śîm,* "make"; vv. 8, 9), in every case with Joseph as the object. God acts to preserve life, particularly the life of Jacob's family (vv. 5, 7).

Famine provides the sociohistorical context for the divine activity. Famine, a life-and-death issue, no doubt cost many lives, which explains references to "remnant" and "survivors" (prophetic use of these words links Israel's hardships with the experience of their ancestors; cf. Isa 10:20; 37:32). The author interprets Joseph's being sent to Egypt and his elevation to leadership in Egypt ("father to Pharaoh" is a title for a king's counselor) as God's means of preserving life. What God did provides the *decisive* reality *within* this larger concatenation of events that has led to life and well-being. God's concern for life also embraces Egypt, indeed the entire world, as already evident in Joseph's wise administration (see 41:56-57). The divine objective encompasses every sphere of life within both family and nation.

In vv. 9-13, Joseph now seeks to preserve his family's life in ways that correspond directly to God's activity. Joseph acts as father, lord, and ruler (all used as images for God in the OT) in tune with God's purposes. Joseph tells the brothers to hurry home, report these events to their father, return with family and possessions, and settle in the land of Goshen near him (of uncertain location on the eastern edge of the delta region, near the border facing Canaan). Joseph assures them that he will provide for all their needs—adults, children, animals—during the continuing famine.

Joseph concludes by repeating his identity, with special notice of Benjamin (v. 12). Joseph's word to hurry to "my father" with the news (so different from the news in 37:32!) encloses his directives to the brothers (vv. 9, 13), revealing deep concern for Jacob.

The episode concludes as it began, with a description of the tearful reunion. The author singles out Joseph's reunion with Benjamin, Joseph's only full brother, the only time in the story that we hear about Benjamin's own feelings. The episode also concludes with a reference to the brothers' conversation with one another, harking back to 37:4, where the brothers could not talk peaceably with one another.

45:16-24. Joseph's instructions to the brothers become those of Pharaoh himself. They are to return to Canaan and bring their father and their families back to Egypt, with the assurance that they will have no worries about possessions. The royal household not only rejoices in the good fortune of Israel's family, but also provides the best land and choicest products (i.e., fat) that Egypt has to offer. Both Pharaoh and Joseph will take care of them. Pharaoh's pleased response, filled with generosity and good will, proves startling. In view of events in Exodus, this positive portrayal of the Egyptians commands attention, alluding to possible reconciliation for nations—even Egypt and Israel—as well as families. Historically, pharaohs were generous to Semitic peoples in time of famine.

Joseph carries out Pharaoh's wishes with respect to his family, perhaps interpreting Pharaoh's directive somewhat generously. He provides for his full brother, Benjamin, in a special way, and seems emphatically lavish in the provisions for his father (which later serve as evidence, v. 27). Reference to the gift of clothing recalls for the reader that Joseph's coat precipitated this family conflict in the first place; clothing now becomes a sign of reconciliation. Finally, Joseph realistically but paternalistically admonishes his brothers not to quarrel among themselves on the journey (cf. 42:21-22).

45:25-28. When the brothers report the news, Jacob is skeptical. But, when they repeat Joseph's words and display the evidence, he believes and resolves to go to Egypt to see his son before he dies. "Enough" is shorthand for Jacob's willingness to put the past behind him and get on with the new possibilities presented by this surprising good news. The parental trauma that Jacob experienced in 37:31-35 now comes full circle; life and joy once more fill the family scene. God enables the past to be forgotten (see 41:51) and makes new beginnings possible. Yet, more will come.

REFLECTIONS

1. For the reader following Joseph's development closely over these eight chapters, his theological presentation may come as something of a surprise. Joseph's God talk has been comparatively rare (see 39:9; 40:8; 41:16, 25, 28, 32, 51-52; 42:18; 43:29), but a sufficient basis on which to build. In addition, God talk by other individuals may reveal the narrator's perspective, particularly those texts that mention God as the seemingly exclusive subject (see esp. 41:38-39; 43:23; 44:16). Such a way of speaking is not new to this text.

Joseph's theology involves life, not promise. The latter awaits later developments, for Joseph has not yet been the recipient of the promises given to his ancestors (see 46:1-4; 48:3-4). But life remains necessary for the continuation of the promises.

2. At this climactic point in their relationship, Joseph sits in a position to do with his brothers as he pleases. Yet, he makes no effort to hold their feet to the fire; his language and demeanor (loud weeping) evidence no anger or irritation. He manifests more weakness than strength; he sets aside the trappings of royalty and enters into the pathos of the situation, all for the sake of reconciliation. Whereas Joseph's testings were indispensable in bringing the family to this moment, a display of power and control was insufficient finally to heal them. Joseph must step outside his role as Egyptian ruler (hence the dismissal of others), and join the family at an intimate and vulnerable level. Yet, as we have noted, Joseph's language does not always match these behaviors. The brothers remain uncertain. A full reconciliation must await later events (50:15-21).

Joseph does not require sorrow or regret from the brothers (cf. 50:17-19). Rather, he confesses that God has been at work in all these events to preserve life, and that is the decisive reality in this moment. What God has done stands *independent of the brothers' repentance.* The word, for the brothers, thus serves as a straightforward gospel word, spoken by one who has experienced it deep within his own life: God has acted so that life, rather than death, now abounds. So the activity of the brothers, however reprehensible in itself, has been used by God as a vehicle for sustaining the life of this family.

3. The relationship between divine and human agency in vv. 5-9 is much debated. One view understands v. 8*a* in a literal fashion: God sends Joseph to Egypt, not the brothers. God is the *only* effective agent in this event ("this all-sufficiency of divine sovereignty makes human action almost irrelevant").[214] A number of difficulties attend such a view, however. (1) The text explicitly ascribes effective agency to the brothers: They "sold" (מכר *mākar*) Joseph into Egypt (vv. 4, 5; 37:28; cf. 42:21). The brothers are not considered puppets in the hands of God (see also the agency of Joseph in vv. 9-13). (2) The larger story uses the language of sin (חטא *ḥāṭā*', 42:22; 50:17) and evil (רעה *rā'â,* 50:15, 17, 20) to refer to the brothers' action, for which they are guilty (אשם *'āšēm,* 42:21; עון *'āwōn,* 44:16). To consider God as the actual subject of these words would be problematic and would rule human responsibility for such activity out of order. (3) The notion of testing is integral to understanding the story (cf. 42:15-16). If God serves as absolute subject of events, there would be no real test of the brothers, for God would bend their wills to respond as God saw fit. All of Joseph's activities would be only a facade for a divine game. (4) Later, 50:20 speaks of both human and divine intentions effectively at work in these events, though in the service of different purposes. Joseph's perspective at this point, however, does not seem as mature as it later becomes.

Another view speaks of effective agency on the part of both God and the brothers, but considers God's intentions as inevitably overriding the brothers' intentions. This view could be correct if understood in the sense that no human activity can *finally* stymie God's purposes for life. On the other hand, such a view seems problematic if it means that God's will can never be rejected or frustrated, so that human sin becomes in effect God's will for the moment. The OT as a whole often testifies to the resistibility of God's word and will.[215]

Either of these perspectives would profoundly affect how one portrays the development of the story. Talk about the drama of the story should then be cast so that everything happens consonantly with the divine will, and any analysis of human words and deeds, *even thoughts,* should be peppered with talk about the controlling divine subject. And, of course, no negative judgment should be placed on the activities of any human subjects, for they are only doing the will of God.

A more acceptable view would speak of the effectiveness of both divine and human agency in the drama, in which both can influence and be influenced, resist and be resisted. As with doxological language more generally, however, God acts decisively, and should thus be celebrated.

We should not evaluate the brothers' life-diminishing activity against Joseph as good (see 50:20) or deem irrelevant how they conduct themselves within God's economy. Rather, God's activity *from within the context set in part by the brothers' sinful behaviors* has proved, finally, to be decisive. Hence, what *God* has done *now* counts in charting a way into the future. God has preserved life; God has kept this family intact in the threat of death. To use a different image, the brothers' sinful objectives have been thwarted by being drawn into the larger orbit of God's purposes and used by God in such a way as to bring life rather than death. To repeat, God has "taken over" what they have done and used it to bring about this end. Their actions have *become* God's by being woven into God's life-giving purposes. Even more, *Pharaoh's* actions—elevating Joseph as ruler—have *become* God's!

4. The extent to which one can draw inferences from this text concerning God's more

---

214. Von Rad, *Genesis,* 438.
215. See T. Fretheim, "Will of God in the OT" and "Word of God" in *The Anchor Bible Dictionary,* 6:914-20, 961-69.

general activity in the world (providence) remains difficult to discern. Westermann denies this possibility, claiming that the text focuses on specific salvific actions of God in this situation.[216] Yet, such actions are stretched out over a considerable period of time; they are also "salvific" in creational rather than redemptive terms. The narrator would certainly claim that the way in which God acts in the world more generally bears basic continuities with God's actions at any moment. While the text testifies to God as an actor in human affairs, these acts are understood in ways quite different from, say, the Exodus events (or 46:1-4, for that matter); they are more hidden to ordinary sight, much less disruptive of ordinary life.

Such an understanding of God's involvement in the life of the cosmos seems especially pertinent in our own world, wherein the tracks of God seem so often ambiguous at best. We might confess that God's activity counts as a factor to be reckoned with in all events, but these same events *could* be interpreted without reference to God at all. But those who make this confession would also go on to say that, wherever there are signs of life rather than death, signs of reconciliation rather than estrangement, God has been at work in, with, and under human affairs. Depending on the context, it may be that God should be the only subject of such verbs so that we know whose life-giving purposes and activity have been decisive.

216. Westermann, *Genesis 37–50,* 143.

GENESIS 46:1–47:26, THE DESCENT INTO EGYPT

NIV

46 So Israel set out with all that was his, and when he reached Beersheba, he offered sacrifices to the God of his father Isaac.

²And God spoke to Israel in a vision at night and said, "Jacob! Jacob!"

"Here I am," he replied.

³"I am God, the God of your father," he said. "Do not be afraid to go down to Egypt, for I will make you into a great nation there. ⁴I will go down to Egypt with you, and I will surely bring you back again. And Joseph's own hand will close your eyes."

⁵Then Jacob left Beersheba, and Israel's sons took their father Jacob and their children and their wives in the carts that Pharaoh had sent to transport him. ⁶They also took with them their livestock and the possessions they had acquired in Canaan, and Jacob and all his offspring went to Egypt. ⁷He took with him to Egypt his sons and grandsons and his daughters and granddaughters—all his offspring.

⁸These are the names of the sons of Israel (Jacob and his descendants) who went to Egypt:

Reuben the firstborn of Jacob.
⁹The sons of Reuben:

NRSV

46 When Israel set out on his journey with all that he had and came to Beer-sheba, he offered sacrifices to the God of his father Isaac. ²God spoke to Israel in visions of the night, and said, "Jacob, Jacob." And he said, "Here I am." ³Then he said, "I am God,[a] the God of your father; do not be afraid to go down to Egypt, for I will make of you a great nation there. ⁴I myself will go down with you to Egypt, and I will also bring you up again; and Joseph's own hand shall close your eyes."

5Then Jacob set out from Beer-sheba; and the sons of Israel carried their father Jacob, their little ones, and their wives, in the wagons that Pharaoh had sent to carry him. ⁶They also took their livestock and the goods that they had acquired in the land of Canaan, and they came into Egypt, Jacob and all his offspring with him, ⁷his sons, and his sons' sons with him, his daughters, and his sons' daughters; all his offspring he brought with him into Egypt.

8Now these are the names of the Israelites, Jacob and his offspring, who came to Egypt. Reuben, Jacob's firstborn, ⁹and the children of

a Heb *the God*

NIV

Hanoch, Pallu, Hezron and Carmi.

[10]The sons of Simeon:

Jemuel, Jamin, Ohad, Jakin, Zohar and Shaul the son of a Canaanite woman.

[11]The sons of Levi:

Gershon, Kohath and Merari.

[12]The sons of Judah:

Er, Onan, Shelah, Perez and Zerah (but Er and Onan had died in the land of Canaan). The sons of Perez:

Hezron and Hamul.

[13]The sons of Issachar:

Tola, Puah,[a] Jashub[b] and Shimron.

[14]The sons of Zebulun:

Sered, Elon and Jahleel.

[15]These were the sons Leah bore to Jacob in Paddan Aram,[c] besides his daughter Dinah. These sons and daughters of his were thirty-three in all.

[16]The sons of Gad:

Zephon,[d] Haggi, Shuni, Ezbon, Eri, Arodi and Areli.

[17]The sons of Asher:

Imnah, Ishvah, Ishvi and Beriah.

Their sister was Serah.

The sons of Beriah:

Heber and Malkiel.

[18]These were the children born to Jacob by Zilpah, whom Laban had given to his daughter Leah—sixteen in all.

[19]The sons of Jacob's wife Rachel:

Joseph and Benjamin. [20]In Egypt, Manasseh and Ephraim were born to Joseph by Asenath daughter of Potiphera, priest of On.[e]

[21]The sons of Benjamin:

Bela, Beker, Ashbel, Gera, Naaman, Ehi, Rosh, Muppim, Huppim and Ard.

[22]These were the sons of Rachel who were born to Jacob—fourteen in all.

[23]The son of Dan:

Hushim.

[24]The sons of Naphtali:

a13 Samaritan Pentateuch and Syriac (see also 1 Chron. 7:1); Masoretic Text Puvah   b13 Samaritan Pentateuch and some Septuagint manuscripts (see also Num. 26:24 and 1 Chron. 7:1); Masoretic Text Iob   c15 That is, Northwest Mesopotamia   d16 Samaritan Pentateuch and Septuagint (see also Num. 26:15); Masoretic Text Ziphion   e20 That is, Heliopolis

NRSV

Reuben: Hanoch, Pallu, Hezron, and Carmi. [10]The children of Simeon: Jemuel, Jamin, Ohad, Jachin, Zohar, and Shaul,[a] the son of a Canaanite woman. [11]The children of Levi: Gershon, Kohath, and Merari. [12]The children of Judah: Er, Onan, Shelah, Perez, and Zerah (but Er and Onan died in the land of Canaan); and the children of Perez were Hezron and Hamul. [13]The children of Issachar: Tola, Puvah, Jashub,[b] and Shimron. [14]The children of Zebulun: Sered, Elon, and Jahleel [15](these are the sons of Leah, whom she bore to Jacob in Paddan-aram, together with his daughter Dinah; in all his sons and his daughters numbered thirty-three). [16]The children of Gad: Ziphion, Haggi, Shuni, Ezbon, Eri, Arodi, and Areli. [17]The children of Asher: Imnah, Ishvah, Ishvi, Beriah, and their sister Serah. The children of Beriah: Heber and Malchiel [18](these are the children of Zilpah, whom Laban gave to his daughter Leah; and these she bore to Jacob—sixteen persons). [19]The children of Jacob's wife Rachel: Joseph and Benjamin. [20]To Joseph in the land of Egypt were born Manasseh and Ephraim, whom Asenath daughter of Potiphera, priest of On, bore to him. [21]The children of Benjamin: Bela, Becher, Ashbel, Gera, Naaman, Ehi, Rosh, Muppim, Huppim, and Ard [22](these are the children of Rachel, who were born to Jacob—fourteen persons in all). [23]The children of Dan: Hashum.[c] [24]The children of Naphtali: Jahzeel, Guni, Jezer, and Shillem [25](these are the children of Bilhah, whom Laban gave to his daughter Rachel, and these she bore to Jacob—seven persons in all). [26]All the persons belonging to Jacob who came into Egypt, who were his own offspring, not including the wives of his sons, were sixty-six persons in all. [27]The children of Joseph, who were born to him in Egypt, were two; all the persons of the house of Jacob who came into Egypt were seventy.

[28]Israel[d] sent Judah ahead to Joseph to lead the way before him into Goshen. When they came to the land of Goshen, [29]Joseph made ready his chariot and went up to meet his father Israel in Goshen. He presented himself to him, fell on his neck, and wept on his neck a good while. [30]Israel said to Joseph, "I can die now, having seen for

a Or Saul   b Compare Sam Gk Num 26.24; 1 Chr 7.1: MT Iob
b Gk: Heb Hushim   c Heb He

NIV

Jahziel, Guni, Jezer and Shillem. ²⁵These were the sons born to Jacob by Bilhah, whom Laban had given to his daughter Rachel— seven in all.

²⁶All those who went to Egypt with Jacob— those who were his direct descendants, not counting his sons' wives—numbered sixty-six persons. ²⁷With the two sons*ᵃ*who had been born to Joseph in Egypt, the members of Jacob's family, which went to Egypt, were seventy*ᵇ* in all.

²⁸Now Jacob sent Judah ahead of him to Joseph to get directions to Goshen. When they arrived in the region of Goshen, ²⁹Joseph had his chariot made ready and went to Goshen to meet his father Israel. As soon as Joseph appeared before him, he threw his arms around his father*ᶜ* and wept for a long time.

³⁰Israel said to Joseph, "Now I am ready to die, since I have seen for myself that you are still alive."

³¹Then Joseph said to his brothers and to his father's household, "I will go up and speak to Pharaoh and will say to him, 'My brothers and my father's household, who were living in the land of Canaan, have come to me. ³²The men are shepherds; they tend livestock, and they have brought along their flocks and herds and everything they own.' ³³When Pharaoh calls you in and asks, 'What is your occupation?' ³⁴you should answer, 'Your servants have tended livestock from our boyhood on, just as our fathers did.' Then you will be allowed to settle in the region of Goshen, for all shepherds are detestable to the Egyptians."

47 Joseph went and told Pharaoh, "My father and brothers, with their flocks and herds and everything they own, have come from the land of Canaan and are now in Goshen." ²He chose five of his brothers and presented them before Pharaoh.

³Pharaoh asked the brothers, "What is your occupation?"

"Your servants are shepherds," they replied to Pharaoh, "just as our fathers were." ⁴They also said to him, "We have come to live here awhile,

ᵃ27 Hebrew; Septuagint the nine children   ᵇ27 Hebrew (see also Exodus 1:5 and footnote); Septuagint (see also Acts 7:14) seventy-five   ᶜ29 Hebrew around him

NRSV

myself that you are still alive." ³¹Joseph said to his brothers and to his father's household, "I will go up and tell Pharaoh, and will say to him, 'My brothers and my father's household, who were in the land of Canaan, have come to me. ³²The men are shepherds, for they have been keepers of livestock; and they have brought their flocks, and their herds, and all that they have.' ³³When Pharaoh calls you, and says, "What is your occupation?' ³⁴you shall say, 'Your servants have been keepers of livestock from our youth even until now, both we and our ancestors'—in order that you may settle in the land of Goshen, because all shepherds are abhorrent to the Egyptians."

47 So Joseph went and told Pharaoh, "My father and my brothers, with their flocks and herds and all that they possess, have come from the land of Canaan; they are now in the land of Goshen." ²From among his brothers he took five men and presented them to Pharaoh. ³Pharaoh said to his brothers, "What is your occupation?" And they said to Pharaoh, "Your servants are shepherds, as our ancestors were." ⁴They said to Pharaoh, "We have come to reside as aliens in the land; for there is no pasture for your servants' flocks because the famine is severe in the land of Canaan. Now, we ask you, let your servants settle in the land of Goshen." ⁵Then Pharaoh said to Joseph, "Your father and your brothers have come to you. ⁶The land of Egypt is before you; settle your father and your brothers in the best part of the land; let them live in the land of Goshen; and if you know that there are capable men among them, put them in charge of my livestock."

7Then Joseph brought in his father Jacob, and presented him before Pharaoh, and Jacob blessed Pharaoh. ⁸Pharaoh said to Jacob, "How many are the years of your life?" ⁹Jacob said to Pharaoh, "The years of my earthly sojourn are one hundred thirty; few and hard have been the years of my life. They do not compare with the years of the life of my ancestors during their long sojourn." ¹⁰Then Jacob blessed Pharaoh, and went out from the presence of Pharaoh. ¹¹Joseph settled his father and his brothers, and granted them a holding in the land of Egypt, in the best part of the land, in the land of Rameses, as Pharaoh had instructed.

NIV

because the famine is severe in Canaan and your servants' flocks have no pasture. So now, please let your servants settle in Goshen."

⁵Pharaoh said to Joseph, "Your father and your brothers have come to you, ⁶and the land of Egypt is before you; settle your father and your brothers in the best part of the land. Let them live in Goshen. And if you know of any among them with special ability, put them in charge of my own livestock."

⁷Then Joseph brought his father Jacob in and presented him before Pharaoh. After Jacob blessed*a* Pharaoh, ⁸Pharaoh asked him, "How old are you?"

⁹And Jacob said to Pharaoh, "The years of my pilgrimage are a hundred and thirty. My years have been few and difficult, and they do not equal the years of the pilgrimage of my fathers." ¹⁰Then Jacob blessed*b* Pharaoh and went out from his presence.

¹¹So Joseph settled his father and his brothers in Egypt and gave them property in the best part of the land, the district of Rameses, as Pharaoh directed. ¹²Joseph also provided his father and his brothers and all his father's household with food, according to the number of their children.

¹³There was no food, however, in the whole region because the famine was severe; both Egypt and Canaan wasted away because of the famine. ¹⁴Joseph collected all the money that was to be found in Egypt and Canaan in payment for the grain they were buying, and he brought it to Pharaoh's palace. ¹⁵When the money of the people of Egypt and Canaan was gone, all Egypt came to Joseph and said, "Give us food. Why should we die before your eyes? Our money is used up."

¹⁶"Then bring your livestock," said Joseph. "I will sell you food in exchange for your livestock, since your money is gone." ¹⁷So they brought their livestock to Joseph, and he gave them food in exchange for their horses, their sheep and goats, their cattle and donkeys. And he brought them through that year with food in exchange for all their livestock.

¹⁸When that year was over, they came to him the following year and said, "We cannot hide from our lord the fact that since our money is gone

NRSV

¹²And Joseph provided his father, his brothers, and all his father's household with food, according to the number of their dependents.

13Now there was no food in all the land, for the famine was very severe. The land of Egypt and the land of Canaan languished because of the famine. ¹⁴Joseph collected all the money to be found in the land of Egypt and in the land of Canaan, in exchange for the grain that they bought; and Joseph brought the money into Pharaoh's house. ¹⁵When the money from the land of Egypt and from the land of Canaan was spent, all the Egyptians came to Joseph, and said, "Give us food! Why should we die before your eyes? For our money is gone." ¹⁶And Joseph answered, "Give me your livestock, and I will give you food in exchange for your livestock, if your money is gone." ¹⁷So they brought their livestock to Joseph; and Joseph gave them food in exchange for the horses, the flocks, the herds, and the donkeys. That year he supplied them with food in exchange for all their livestock. ¹⁸When that year was ended, they came to him the following year, and said to him, "We can not hide from my lord that our money is all spent; and the herds of cattle are my lord's. There is nothing left in the sight of my lord but our bodies and our lands. ¹⁹Shall we die before your eyes, both we and our land? Buy us and our land in exchange for food. We with our land will become slaves to Pharaoh; just give us seed, so that we may live and not die, and that the land may not become desolate."

20So Joseph bought all the land of Egypt for Pharaoh. All the Egyptians sold their fields, because the famine was severe upon them; and the land became Pharaoh's. ²¹As for the people, he made slaves of them*a* from one end of Egypt to the other. ²²Only the land of the priests he did not buy; for the priests had a fixed allowance from Pharaoh, and lived on the allowance that Pharaoh gave them; therefore they did not sell their land. ²³Then Joseph said to the people, "Now that I have this day bought you and your land for Pharaoh, here is seed for you; sow the land. ²⁴And at the harvests you shall give one-fifth to Pharaoh, and four-fifths shall be your own, as seed for the field and as food for yourselves and your house-

and our livestock belongs to you, there is nothing left for our lord except our bodies and our land. [19]Why should we perish before your eyes—we and our land as well? Buy us and our land in exchange for food, and we with our land will be in bondage to Pharaoh. Give us seed so that we may live and not die, and that the land may not become desolate."

[20]So Joseph bought all the land in Egypt for Pharaoh. The Egyptians, one and all, sold their fields, because the famine was too severe for them. The land became Pharaoh's, [21]and Joseph reduced the people to servitude,[a] from one end of Egypt to the other. [22]However, he did not buy the land of the priests, because they received a regular allotment from Pharaoh and had food enough from the allotment Pharaoh gave them. That is why they did not sell their land.

[23]Joseph said to the people, "Now that I have bought you and your land today for Pharaoh, here is seed for you so you can plant the ground. [24]But when the crop comes in, give a fifth of it to Pharaoh. The other four-fifths you may keep as seed for the fields and as food for yourselves and your households and your children."

[25]"You have saved our lives," they said. "May we find favor in the eyes of our lord; we will be in bondage to Pharaoh."

[26]So Joseph established it as a law concerning land in Egypt—still in force today—that a fifth of the produce belongs to Pharaoh. It was only the land of the priests that did not become Pharaoh's.

[a]21 Samaritan Pentateuch and Septuagint (see also Vulgate); Masoretic Text *and he moved the people into the cities*

holds, and as food for your little ones." [25]They said, "You have saved our lives; may it please my lord, we will be slaves to Pharaoh." [26]So Joseph made it a statute concerning the land of Egypt, and it stands to this day, that Pharaoh should have the fifth. The land of the priests alone did not become Pharaoh's.

COMMENTARY

This chapter begins a new episode, but the parallels between 45:5-8 and 46:1-4 (see below) suggest that chap. 45, as preparation for the descent, must be drawn more closely to this section, which describes the actual trip of Jacob's family to Egypt. Joseph's reconciliation with his brothers has been a leading objective of the narrative, but the reunion of father and son has yet to occur. That, too, constitutes an important dimension of the story.

The segment 46:28–47:12 describes issues of settlement in Egypt. After the reunion of Jacob and Joseph (vv. 28-30), Joseph prepares his brothers for conversations with Pharaoh (vv. 31-33); 47:1-12 reports that audience, leading to the settlement in Goshen; 47:13-26 describes Joseph's agrarian reforms to cope with the effects of the famine; 47:27 concludes this episode with a summary of these events and their effect on Jacob's family.

The remaining chapters in Genesis are more

episodic than 39–45, with a disparate range of genres, which reveal a composite character. Verses 1-4 link this story with divine appearances and related promises in Genesis 12–35 (cf. 26:23-25), as do the itineraries and the genealogy-like list in 46:5-27. At the same time, these texts point forward to Exodus, toward which these chapters begin to lean more and more. Together, these sections help both to unify Genesis and to integrate it with Exodus.

46:1-7. Jacob initially journeys from Hebron (cf. 37:14) and comes to Beersheba, where God once appeared to his father (26:23-25). Jacob worships at the altar built by Isaac *before* he has his vision (note the sacrifices, rare in Genesis, cf. 31:54). At this juncture in life—once again on leaving the land (cf. chap. 28)—Jacob builds upon the faith of his family heritage, "the God of his father."

God acknowledges this tradition by appearing to Jacob in visions of the night as the "God of your father" (cf. 15:1; 28:11) and affirms the decision to go to Egypt (cf. 26:2). The plural "visions" seems difficult; it may refer to the intensity of the experience, and could be either oral or oral with a visual component. God's double call and Jacob's obedient response are identical to Abraham's experience in 22:11.

These verses appear formally similar to 45:3-8. Both move from self-identification to the quelling of fear to an announcement, only this time regarding the future. While parallel in form, Joseph's word to his brothers and God's word to Jacob are complementary in content. Together they link creation and promise. God's life-enabling work makes possible the continued articulation of the promises. Without life, there would be no promise. The creative work of God stands in service of the promise.

God allays Jacob's fears regarding the move by making promises, drawing on past promises, but adjusting them in view of the changed circumstances that Egypt presents. Hence, "I will make of you a great nation *there*" (v. 3; cf. 12:2; 18:18), indicates that their development into a people will occur in Egypt (see Exod 1:7). Moreover, God will go down with him to Egypt. This statement constitutes a new version of God's promise of presence to Jacob in 28:15; it not only specifies presence, but emphasizes that this will be *a journey for God.* This represents a deep commitment

of God to enter into all the dynamics of the Egyptian experience. With the promise that God will bring him back to Canaan, the exodus and related events come into view. Inasmuch as Jacob himself does not return to Canaan alive (cf. 47:30; 50:4-14), we may interpret the promise of return in corporate terms as well. Finally, Joseph will close his eyes, implying that Joseph will be with him when he dies (cf. 50:1).

Jacob journeys from Beersheba, accompanied by his family and all their belongings (contrary to Pharaoh's expectations? 45:20). While the following roll focuses on the brothers and their children, this introductory list identifies the women accompanying Jacob. The daughters of Jacob include daughters-in-law (clearer in v. 15; cf. 37:35).

46:8-27. The author provides a list of Jacob's descendants—individuals, not clans—who made the migration to Egypt (cf. Exod 1:1). Its relationship to other lists appears to be highly complex (cf. Numbers 26; 1 Chronicles 1–9).[217] It is based on the number seventy (v. 27; cf. Exod 1:5) and ordered according to Jacob's wives (vv. 15, 18, [19], 22, 25; note the double reference to Rachel), who are called the mothers of both children and grandchildren (e.g., v. 22). The list includes Dinah (v. 15), one granddaughter (v. 17), and four great-grandsons (vv. 12, 17). The author names only Joseph's wife (v. 20; cf. v. 26) and mentions that a Canaanite woman bore one of Simeon's children (v. 10). The list assumes knowledge of the previous narratives (e.g., vv. 12, 15, 18, 20, 25), suggesting that an independent list has been adapted to fit this context, breaking the natural continuity between vv. 7 and 28.

Verses 26 and 27 are difficult, perhaps due to several editorial hands; not everything can be sorted out. The numbers in vv. 15, 18, 22, and 25 total seventy (adding Jacob, Joseph's sons, and one other person, possibly Dinah); the number sixty-six (v. 26), however, takes into account that Er and Onan (v. 12) and Joseph's two sons (v. 20) never made a trip to Egypt.

46:28-30. These verses begin an episode that continues through 47:12, describing the settlement of Joseph's family in Egypt.

Jacob recognizes Judah's leadership in having

217. For details, see Westermann, *Genesis 37–50,* 158-61.

him prepare the way for their entry into Egypt. When Joseph hears of their arrival in the land of Goshen, he takes the initiative to greet his father. Tears—not words—once again flow for this sensitive man as father and son embrace at length, joyfully reunited after so many years apart. Joseph appears before his father as a son, not as a public official, with appropriate levels of emotional intensity (no fulfillment of his second dream seems in view).

Verse 30 brings one dimension of the Joseph story full circle. The violence of chap. 37 has been turned into life. Jacob, who had lamented that he would go into death mourning (37:33-35) and whose life has been so pervaded by this loss (42:38; 43:14; 44:28-29), now announces that he can die with the joy of knowing that his son who was lost has been found (cf. 45:28).

46:31–47:12. Joseph takes charge of the situation. Having prepared his father and brothers, he mediates with Pharaoh the settlement in Goshen. Pharaoh might be concerned about a settlement in Goshen, which Joseph wanted because his family would be nearby, but which Pharaoh could find difficult for some reason (a border region?). Because Goshen is somewhat removed from the settled areas of Egypt, Joseph devises a plan that would allow his family to move there (a convenient placement for escape?). He directs his brothers to stress that they are shepherds (i.e., keepers of livestock), because shepherding was an unappealing occupation to Egyptians (v. 34). Thus Pharaoh would be glad to have them at a distance, and Joseph would not compromise his own position among the Egyptians.

Joseph announces to Pharaoh that the family has arrived and are in Goshen (also called Rameses, v. 11, elsewhere referred to as a city, Exod 1:11). The brothers respond to Pharaoh's questions as directed, describing themselves as shepherds (see 46:32, 34) and, going beyond the question, as aliens (גרים *gērîm*, cf. 15:13) in the land, temporary residents seeking pasture for their flocks ("holding" in v. 11 suggests permanence; does Joseph disagree with his brothers here?). The brothers request settlement in Goshen; both Pharaoh and the narrator describe this as "the best part of the land" (vv. 6, 11), which Pharaoh had promised them (45:18).

Pharaoh, speaking officially to Joseph (vv. 5-6), supportively acknowledges his statement of v. 1 and agrees to this arrangement. Moreover, going beyond previous conversations, he offers to allow the capable ones among them to oversee his own livestock, guaranteeing the security of the family under pharaonic authority. (Historically, pharaohs possessed herds and used such persons.) The Egyptians are the ones who violate the agreement (Exod 1:8-11); hence they have only themselves to blame for the destruction that comes.

Joseph presents his father to Pharaoh, and Jacob proceeds to bless Pharaoh (rather than do obeisance). He also blesses Pharaoh when he departs (v. 10). We should understand this greeting and farewell more broadly in terms of the blessing motif in chaps. 12–50. This prompts Pharaoh's question about his age; Jacob's blessing might speak to issues of longevity. Jacob states that his 130 years have been "few and hard" compared with his ancestors (see 25:7; 35:28), referring to difficulties endured over the years, not least with Joseph. Yet, characteristic of each patriarch has been the sojourning shape of life, its unsettled character, moving toward a goal set by the promises of God. To be a recipient of God's blessing does not in and of itself mean a trouble-free life. Jacob provides a word of realism for Pharaoh.

Joseph settles his family "in the best part of the land" and provides them with food in this time of famine. We do not know whether Joseph's family suffers the effects of the famine that afflicted the rest of Egypt. Inasmuch as the author never mentions the Israelites in vv. 13-26, they probably had enough food.

These conversations attest to the fact that Egypt will not, finally, be the home of these people. They cannot be integrated with the Egyptians. They remain transients, forced by famine to live here and not able to call it home. Yet, Egypt will prove to be hospitable for the growth of many generations (cf. Exod 1:7).

47:13-26. This segment seems unrelated to its present context. It is most closely connected with Joseph's skilled economic leadership in 41:46-57, which it may continue—though links with the seven-year famine are not made (see the inexact reference to years in v. 18; cf. v. 14 with 41:56). These verses illustrate Joseph's administrative wisdom (and show that it continues beyond the climax in chap. 45). At the same time, such harsh measures made necessary by emergency can be abused if successive leaders are not comparably wise (as in Exod 1:8). Joseph could be faulted for having insufficient vision, especially in making his emergency measures permanent "to this day" (v. 26).

An editor may have placed these verses in their present position because of two themes. First is the report about food in v. 11, where Joseph provides food not only for his family but also for all the Egyptians. Second is the blessings on Pharaoh (vv. 7, 10). Through these economic measures, Joseph serves as the channel for blessing on Pharaoh and his people (stated seven times!).

The reader has some difficulties following the text, which may reflect the redactional process and our lack of knowledge regarding ancient Egyptian economics.[218] The interpreter should thus be cautious in drawing conclusions about Joseph's role. His policy results in a concentration of property and power in the crown, but the language of "slavery" appears insufficiently nuanced (note the textual difficulties in v. 21). One should think about "tenant farmers of the state" as well as the draconian measures of nationalization.[219]

218. For details, see Westermann, *Genesis 37–50*, 173.
219. Sarna, *Genesis*, 321-23.

The severity of the famine in Egypt and Canaan (Canaan drops out after v. 15) prompts Joseph to develop new food distribution systems. He responds to the cries of the Egyptian people for bread, and even takes their opinions into account (v. 19). Whatever effects the measures have on the people, the idea has come from them; they affirm it after the actions have been taken (v. 25).

The progressively more severe measures include the money supply's no longer sufficing to buy food; livestock depletion in exchange for food; Joseph's buying their land in exchange for food (actually, for seed to grow food). They make this request even though it will mean that they and their lands will come under Pharaoh's control (v. 19).

Joseph proceeds as they request. All Egyptian lands (the priests had an agreement with Pharaoh) become royal property, and the people become tenant farmers, even though it deprives them of some freedom. Joseph gives them seed for sowing, and they agree that Pharaoh will receive 20 percent of the harvests (making the emergency policy of 41:34 permanent)—not excessive in that world. They are grateful to Joseph for having saved their lives, and ask for his continuing favor, even as they affirm their status as tenant farmers.

REFLECTIONS

1. These chapters begin to move from the story of the person called Israel to the story of the people called Israel. Literarily, the author interweaves Joseph's reunion with Jacob and the list of the seventy members of Jacob's family who migrate to Egypt. Rather than simply juxtaposing these developments, the list occurs before the reunion. Beginning with "the Israelites" (46:8) and concluding with "the house of Jacob" (v. 27; cf. v. 31; 50:8), the list signals the shift to a new era as the family becomes a people, anticipating the book of Exodus (cf. Exod 1:1 with 1:7).

The author provides a preface, grounded in a promise with corporate dimensions. These promises, long absent from the narrative (see 35:9-13), still operate in spite of all that has occurred. The promise of a "great nation" in 46:3 gives divine direction to this development. The elision of the individual and the corporate in v. 4 ("I will bring you up again") anticipates Exodus events. The move from family to people is presented as divinely sanctioned. The reader thereby begins to shift attention to the new reality of Israel as the people of God.

2. The purpose of the story, especially as articulated in 45:5-9, now comes more clearly into view. God's concern in this entire story has been to "preserve life," to make sure that there would be a "remnant," enough "survivors" from this family to move out into God's larger purposes for the world. This divine purpose for life does not relate narrowly to Jacob's family, but to the larger world. All the attention given to Joseph must be related to these overarching purposes. At the same time, the particular promise to Israel now becomes integrated with this purpose.

3. The author integrates Jacob's twofold blessing of Pharaoh (47:7, 10) with the aforementioned dynamic. As announced in 12:2-3, the chosen family will be a blessing to all, not least to those who extend blessing upon them (as Egypt and Pharaoh certainly have). This entails—even if not actually stated—a blessing for life and well-being for Pharaoh and his family and fertility for his lands and animals. One notes no little irony here, as a lowly foreign shepherd pronounces a blessing upon this paragon of wisdom and power who was understood to participate in the very life of the divine. The text does not state explicitly that Pharaoh, potentate though he is, needs blessing (as his question in 47:8 suggests). Moreover, Jacob represents one who is Lord even of Pharaoh, and from whom all blessings flow.

By this action Jacob adheres to the calling of this chosen family, whose words and deeds on behalf of their God should reach out beyond themselves and include within the circle of blessing even *those who seem least in need of it.* The need for God's blessing cuts across socioeconomic strata and political boundaries; Jacob and Pharaoh stand together as recipients of blessing. Even more, the blessing ought to extend to those whose relationship to the chosen may become problematic and difficult. Jacob's blessing of this pharaoh stands in the background of the later conflict with the pharaohs in Exodus; it remains a sign of the desirable relationship with the Egyptians.

4. In 47:13-26, we see comparable, if more concrete, blessing activity on Joseph's part. This Israelite, whose authority extends over a nonchosen people, responds to their cries for bread. The links between this text and 45:7 show that the preservation of life remains important for all people. The issues of life and death for Jacob's family over the course of the narrative have become issues for the Egyptians (note the repeated concern in vv. 19, 25). The place to which Israel has gone to seek relief is now itself caught up in the famine's effects; Joseph, in effect, returns the favor. The people of God are here engaged in seeking to alleviate the devastating effects of the famine on people who stand outside of their own community, by working in and through a variety of governmental structures. Their methods may not be a model of perfection, but taking the opinions of the hurting people themselves into account, they enter into the fray on behalf of life rather than death.

5. The Egyptians view the famine as a life-and-death issue not only for themselves but also for their land (vv. 18-19). Their cry to Joseph involves the future of the land ("that the land may not become desolate") as much as their own. They thereby recognize that such events have important ecological consequences and that the human future is inextricably linked with the future of the land. This testifies to the wisdom of the nonchosen regarding the care of creation—a wisdom often evident through the centuries, including our own, and to which the community of faith should be as responsive as Joseph.

6. We now understand better the statement that a later pharaoh did not "know Joseph" (Exod 1:8). Later generations of pharaohs will not remember that frequently Joseph served as the mediator of blessings for Egyptian royalty. There may be some irony in that, as Joseph makes "slaves" of the Egyptians (though not to himself), so the later pharaohs—who do not have the wisdom and commitments of Joseph—will make "slaves" of his family. While we cannot be certain, this reversal raises the question of whether later pharaohs extend Joseph's economic policy to include the Israelites. Any governmental policy can be twisted in such a way as to become demonic. Yet, that must not be allowed to immobilize people in their efforts to work for life in and through imperfect structures.

GENESIS 47:27–50:26, THE EMERGENCE OF UNIFIED ISRAEL

OVERVIEW

These chapters, evidently a composite, have been pieced together from various sources and given their present unity by the Priestly redactor. We may conclude that they are concerned primarily with the story of Jacob, his final days, his testamentary activities, his death and burial. Certainly they show that Jacob dies in peace (46:30), after numerous indications that it might not be so (cf. 37:35; 42:38; 44:29-31). Yet, Joseph's role remains important as well. One might suggest that 47:27-28 and 50:22-23 lift up both persons by the way they bracket the section (both "settle" in Egypt, are fruitful, and die at a certain age).

But these chapters possess a more fundamental purpose together with chaps. 46–47: They speak of the transition from the individual sons of Jacob to corporate Israel and the tribal dynamics and interrelationships characteristic of a people. This story comes to a climax in 50:24, with the recnciled brothers receiving the promise from Joseph (who had received it from Jacob in 48:3-4, 21-22). As such, chaps. 48–50 provide a bracket with chaps. 37–38 for the entire story, moving from the apparent exclusion of Joseph and Judah to their special role associated with promises in a unified family.

Subsequent *tribal* history has shaped these chapters. Hence, the relationship between Joseph's sons, Ephraim and Manasseh, in chap. 48 plays off the development and history of Israelite tribes with these names, collectively called the house of Joseph (e.g., Amos 5:6). The blessing of Jacob in chap. 49 does so in a comparable way for all of Jacob's sons, though recognizing the ascendancy of the Joseph and Judah tribes in the north and south.

Genesis 47:27–48:22, Joseph and His Sons

NIV	NRSV
²⁷Now the Israelites settled in Egypt in the region of Goshen. They acquired property there and were fruitful and increased greatly in number. ²⁸Jacob lived in Egypt seventeen years, and the years of his life were a hundred and forty-seven. ²⁹When the time drew near for Israel to die, he called for his son Joseph and said to him, "If I have found favor in your eyes, put your hand under my thigh and promise that you will show me kindness and faithfulness. Do not bury me in Egypt, ³⁰but when I rest with my fathers, carry me out of Egypt and bury me where they are buried." "I will do as you say," he said. ³¹"Swear to me," he said. Then Joseph swore to him, and Israel worshiped as he leaned on the top of his staff.^a **48** Some time later Joseph was told, "Your father is ill." So he took his two sons	27Thus Israel settled in the land of Egypt, in the region of Goshen; and they gained possessions in it, and were fruitful and multiplied exceedingly. ²⁸Jacob lived in the land of Egypt seventeen years; so the days of Jacob, the years of his life, were one hundred forty-seven years. 29When the time of Israel's death drew near, he called his son Joseph and said to him, "If I have found favor with you, put your hand under my thigh and promise to deal loyally and truly with me. Do not bury me in Egypt. ³⁰When I lie down with my ancestors, carry me out of Egypt and bury me in their burial place." He answered, "I will do as you have said." ³¹And he said, "Swear to me"; and he swore to him. Then Israel bowed himself on the head of his bed. **48** After this Joseph was told, "Your father is ill." So he took with him his two sons, Manasseh and Ephraim. ²When Jacob was told,

NIV

Manasseh and Ephraim along with him. [2]When Jacob was told, "Your son Joseph has come to you," Israel rallied his strength and sat up on the bed.

[3]Jacob said to Joseph, "God Almighty[b] appeared to me at Luz in the land of Canaan, and there he blessed me [4]and said to me, 'I am going to make you fruitful and will increase your numbers. I will make you a community of peoples, and I will give this land as an everlasting possession to your descendants after you.'

[5]"Now then, your two sons born to you in Egypt before I came to you here will be reckoned as mine; Ephraim and Manasseh will be mine, just as Reuben and Simeon are mine. [6]Any children born to you after them will be yours; in the territory they inherit they will be reckoned under the names of their brothers. [7]As I was returning from Paddan,[c] to my sorrow Rachel died in the land of Canaan while we were still on the way, a little distance from Ephrath. So I buried her there beside the road to Ephrath" (that is, Bethlehem).

[8]When Israel saw the sons of Joseph, he asked, "Who are these?"

[9]"They are the sons God has given me here," Joseph said to his father.

Then Israel said, "Bring them to me so I may bless them."

[10]Now Israel's eyes were failing because of old age, and he could hardly see. So Joseph brought his sons close to him, and his father kissed them and embraced them.

[11]Israel said to Joseph, "I never expected to see your face again, and now God has allowed me to see your children too."

[12]Then Joseph removed them from Israel's knees and bowed down with his face to the ground. [13]And Joseph took both of them, Ephraim on his right toward Israel's left hand and Manasseh on his left toward Israel's right hand, and brought them close to him. [14]But Israel reached out his right hand and put it on Ephraim's head, though he was the younger, and crossing his arms, he put his left hand on Manasseh's head, even though Manasseh was the firstborn.

[15]Then he blessed Joseph and said,

a31 Or Israel bowed down at the head of his bed
b3 Hebrew El-Shaddai   c7 That is, Northwest Mesopotamia

NRSV

"Your son Joseph has come to you," he[a] summoned his strength and sat up in bed. [3]And Jacob said to Joseph, "God Almighty[b] appeared to me at Luz in the land of Canaan, and he blessed me, [4]and said to me, "I am going to make you fruitful and increase your numbers; I will make of you a company of peoples, and will give this land to your offspring after you for a perpetual holding.' [5]Therefore your two sons, who were born to you in the land of Egypt before I came to you in Egypt, are now mine; Ephraim and Manasseh shall be mine, just as Reuben and Simeon are. [6]As for the offspring born to you after them, they shall be yours. They shall be recorded under the names of their brothers with regard to their inheritance. [7]For when I came from Paddan, Rachel, alas, died in the land of Canaan on the way, while there was still some distance to go to Ephrath; and I buried her there on the way to Ephrath" (that is, Bethlehem).

8When Israel saw Joseph's sons, he said, "Who are these?" [9]Joseph said to his father, "They are my sons, whom God has given me here." And he said, "Bring them to me, please, that I may bless them." [10]Now the eyes of Israel were dim with age, and he could not see well. So Joseph brought them near him; and he kissed them and embraced them. [11]Israel said to Joseph, "I did not expect to see your face; and here God has let me see your children also." [12]Then Joseph removed them from his father's knees,[c] and he bowed himself with his face to the earth. [13]Joseph took them both, Ephraim in his right hand toward Israel's left, and Manasseh in his left hand toward Israel's right, and brought them near him. [14]But Israel stretched out his right hand and laid it on the head of Ephraim, who was the younger, and his left hand on the head of Manasseh, crossing his hands, for Manasseh was the firstborn. [15]He blessed Joseph, and said,

"The God before whom my ancestors
    Abraham and Isaac walked,
the God who has been my shepherd all my
    life to this day,
[16] the angel who has redeemed me from all
    harm, bless the boys;

a Heb Israel   b Traditional rendering of Heb El Shaddai
c Heb from his knees

NIV

"May the God before whom my fathers
   Abraham and Isaac walked,
the God who has been my shepherd
   all my life to this day,
[16]the Angel who has delivered me from all harm
   —may he bless these boys.
May they be called by my name
   and the names of my fathers Abraham and Isaac,
and may they increase greatly
   upon the earth."

[17]When Joseph saw his father placing his right hand on Ephraim's head he was displeased; so he took hold of his father's hand to move it from Ephraim's head to Manasseh's head. [18]Joseph said to him, "No, my father, this one is the firstborn; put your right hand on his head."

[19]But his father refused and said, "I know, my son, I know. He too will become a people, and he too will become great. Nevertheless, his younger brother will be greater than he, and his descendants will become a group of nations." [20]He blessed them that day and said,

"In your[a] name will Israel pronounce this
      blessing:
   'May God make you like Ephraim and
      Manasseh.'"

So he put Ephraim ahead of Manasseh.
[21]Then Israel said to Joseph, "I am about to die, but God will be with you[b] and take you[b] back to the land of your[b] fathers. [22]And to you, as one who is over your brothers, I give the ridge of land[c] I took from the Amorites with my sword and my bow."

a20 The Hebrew is singular.   b21 The Hebrew is plural.
c22 Or And to you I give one portion more than to your brothers—the portion

NRSV

and in them let my name be perpetuated,
   and the name of my ancestors
      Abraham and Isaac;
and let them grow into a multitude on the
      earth."

17When Joseph saw that his father laid his right hand on the head of Ephraim, it displeased him; so he took his father's hand, to remove it from Ephraim's head to Manasseh's head. 18Joseph said to his father, "Not so, my father! Since this one is the firstborn, put your right hand on his head." 19But his father refused, and said, "I know, my son, I know; he also shall become a people, and he also shall be great. Nevertheless his younger brother shall be greater than he, and his offspring shall become a multitude of nations." 20So he blessed them that day, saying,

"By you[a] Israel will invoke blessings, saying,
   "God make you[b] like Ephraim and like
         Manasseh.'"

So he put Ephraim ahead of Manasseh. 21Then Israel said to Joseph, "I am about to die, but God will be with you and will bring you again to the land of your ancestors. 22I now give to you one portion[c] more than to your brothers, the portion[d] that I took from the hand of the Amorites with my sword and with my bow."

a you here is singular in Heb   b you here is singular in Heb
c Or mountain slope (Heb shekem, a play on the name of the town and district of Shechem)   d Or mountain slope (Heb shekem, a play on the name of the town and district of Shechem)

COMMENTARY

This segment begins with a summary statement (47:27-28; v. 27 does double duty) then moves to Joseph's oath regarding Jacob's burial (47:29-31), to Jacob's adoption and blessing of Joseph's two sons (48:1-22), to Jacob's "blessing" on all his sons (49:1-28), and his death and burial (49:29–50:14). It closes with the brothers' reconciliation (50:15-21) and the promise to the unified family (50:24) during Joseph's final days (50:22-26).

47:27. This verse serves as a preliminary conclusion to the story (see the parallel with 37:1). The people of Israel—note the corporate reference—not only survive in Goshen, but they thrive, gaining many possessions and, in fulfillment of the divine promise (35:11; 1:28; cf. 48:4), growing considerably (cf. Exod 1:7). The connections with both Genesis 1 and 35 provide a link between God's creative work and God's promissory activity.

47:28-31. This episode begins with a summary statement about Jacob's life and death. He lives his last seventeen years in Egypt (cf. 37:2).

Prior to his death, Jacob requests that Joseph swear an oath regarding his burial in Canaan (cf. 24:2 for the phrase "hand under thigh"). In 49:29-32, Jacob will charge all the brothers with this task, specifying the cave at Machpelah, near Hebron (23:1-20; 50:5, 12-13). Jacob asks Joseph to "show kindness and faithfulness" (חסד ואמת *ḥesed we'ĕmet*), two significant theological terms (v. 29). This oath presents strong commitment language for what seems an insignificant issue to moderns, but burial in Canaan is no minor matter to Jacob (and Joseph, 50:25), not least because of God's own promise (46:4). It may be a not so subtle effort to assure the continuance of his family in Canaan rather than Egypt.

The phrase "lie down with my ancestors [fathers]" is an idiom for death (cf. 15:15; 25:8); the phrase "bow at the head of the bed" (the NIV adopts another text) probably refers to a worshipful gesture in the bed to which Jacob is confined (48:2; cf. Heb. 11:21). It has nothing to do with bowing down to Joseph, as if the dream in 37:9 were partially fulfilled in this gesture; in the immediately following text, Jacob exercises authority over Joseph.

48:1-7. Upon hearing that his father is ill, Joseph takes his two sons to their grandfather for a proper farewell. Because Joseph has not been told of God's promises (or himself received a revelation), at least in the storyline, Jacob recalls God's (*El Shaddai,* 17:1) appearance to him at Luz (Bethel) in Canaan (35:9-13). The major elements of the promise were that his family would experience considerable growth (see 47:27), become a "community/company of peoples" (see 28:3), and receive Canaan as

a perpetual holding (see 17:8; perpetuity does not appear in chap. 35).

This report moves immediately to Jacob's adoption of Ephraim and Manasseh as his own sons, "just as Reuben and Simeon are" (Jacob's oldest sons), a legal act with parallels in the ancient Near East (see Ruth 4:16-17).[220] The "therefore" (NRSV) of v. 5 shows that Jacob makes this decision on the basis of the previous promise: As its recipient, he assumes power to designate its inheritors. This act places Joseph's sons on a par with Jacob's own sons. Should Joseph have other offspring, they are to be his own, though for purposes of inheritance they will participate with the families of Ephraim and Manasseh.

Then (v. 7), for reasons not entirely clear, Jacob recalls Rachel's death at the time of his own death (quoting from 35:16, 19, perhaps because it follows the just-cited 35:9-13). The link between Rachel and this adoption of her grandchildren could be rooted in Jacob's special love for the wife who died in childbirth. The fact that the mother of the two sons is Asenath, the daughter of an Egyptian priest (46:20), may also be a factor.

48:8-20. A ritual of blessing now follows (cf. chap. 27) as a concluding part of the adoption ceremony. It begins with a verification of the boys' identity (cf. 27:18), as Joseph confesses them to be God's gift to him (so 41:51). The nearly blind Jacob (cf. 27:1) asks that they be brought near so that he can bless them. After kissing and embracing the sons and having them placed near (on?) his knees (v. 12, a symbolic act legitimating their status as sons; cf. 30:3; 50:23), he confesses that God has let him live long enough to see both Joseph and his sons. Jacob certainly had had other opportunities to see his grandsons—here understood to be boys. Hence, these chapters should not be conceived in a linear way.

After bowing his face to the earth (a gesture of honor), Joseph stands them next to his father, Ephraim on the left and Manasseh on the right, the place of honor, assuming that the oldest (Manasseh) would be the recipient of Jacob's right hand. Jacob, however, crosses his hands so that his right hand rests on Ephraim (v. 14; cf. Num 27:18, 23). When Joseph sees this (v. 17), he interrupts the ritual, thinking of Jacob's failing

220. Ibid., 325.

sight (ironic, considering his own story; 27:1), and begins to switch his father's hands. But Jacob calmly insists, knowing full well what he has done. He explains: Both sons will become a great people, but Ephraim shall be greater, the father of a multitude of nations. Ephraim will truly be preeminent, so prominent that Ephraim becomes a name for the northern kingdom (cf. Jer 31:9; Hosea). "So he put Ephraim ahead of Manasseh" (v. 20). In terms of tribal history, Ephraim and Manasseh replace the nonterritorial tribe of Levi, thus retaining the number twelve.

The two "blessings" of the sons by Jacob are distributed over the course of the action (vv. 15-16, 20). Jacob *verbally* treats Ephraim and Manasseh equally, building on the act of adoption. Only in the ritual and the explanation given to Joseph (v. 19) does a distinction become evident.

In the first, Jacob "blessed *Joseph,*" though it seems that only the sons are blessed (as in v. 20), but, as in vv. 21-22, reference to the father includes the sons (see Deut 33:13-17; cf. Gen 49:22-26). Jacob begins a threefold invocation, in liturgical language, with a structure similar to the Aaronic benediction in Num 6:24-26. The specific content of the blessing (v. 16) consists of (1) their families' being included within the ongoing traditions that include the names of Abraham, Isaac, and Jacob; and (2) their considerable growth as families, blessed by God with the power of life (already by Num 26:28-37 their numbers exceed those of Reuben and Simeon; cf. also Deut 33:17).

The second blessing (v. 20) is complicated by the use of the singular "you" (see the NRSV footnote); the first instance probably refers to the sons individually (cf. the use of plural and singular in Num 6:23-26), the second to the one being blessed. The sons' names can be invoked when Israel (the people, cf. 47:27) pronounces blessings on others: God bless you as he has blessed Ephraim and Manasseh, with all that means in terms of life, fertility, and well-being (cf. 12:3; 18:18; 22:18; 26:4; 28:14). What God has done to them will be an exemplary instance of divine blessing.

48:21-22. These verses show that the adoption of Joseph's sons does not entail a displacement of Joseph. This elevation of his sons, in effect, represents an elevation of Joseph to the status of firstborn, who *in his sons* receives a double share (cf. 49:26; Deut. 33:13-17; 1 Chr 5:1-2). Double shares go to the firstborn. The placement of this chapter before the blessings of chap. 49, within which the Joseph sayings (vv. 22-26) are really the only ones that directly relate to the blessings promised his ancestors, attest to this elevation.

Jacob here speaks more directly to Joseph. Jacob has included him in the blessing of his sons up to this point (v. 15), made especially clear in the transmission of the promise of presence and land to Joseph and his family (the "you" is plural). God will be with them; this promise, usually associated with a journey (28:15), anticipates the exodus. God will also bring them back to the land of promise. These are promises heretofore not extended to Joseph; he in turn will transmit them to his brothers in 50:24. In Canaan he will be given one more portion than that received by his brothers (namely, the portions assigned to his two sons; see Josh 17:14-18).

The word translated "portion" (NRSV) or "ridge of land" (NIV) is שְׁכֶם (*šĕkem*), usually meaning "shoulder," but here probably a play on the city of Shechem. Jacob purchased land there (33:18-19), and Joseph will be buried there (Josh 24:32); it became a central city in the northern kingdom (i.e., Ephraim). The defeat of the Amorites (the pre-Israelite population of Canaan; cf. 15:16) may refer to the violent acts of Simeon and Levi in 34:25-29. Yet, it speaks of Jacob's own sword and bow. Jacob judged those actions harshly (34:30; and in the blessing to be pronounced [49:5-7]). It may be a fragment, recognized also in Israel's never having to conquer the Shechem area. If it alludes to Genesis 34, Jacob would now be simply dealing with reality; it is past history and can now be assigned to the family of Joseph (*not* to Simeon and Levi).

REFLECTIONS

1. The close reader of Genesis might have predicted the turn of events in chap. 48. As throughout the ancestral stories, Jacob's included, primogeniture is set aside; the younger has been given priority over the older. The reader will also recall the deathbed blessing of Jacob's father, Isaac (chap. 27). Such a deathbed blessing was believed to have a special efficacy.

Israelites believed that Jacob's act of putting Ephraim ahead of Manasseh accounted, in part, for the later history of these tribes. While both tribes were powerful during the early years, Ephraim became the more powerful by the time of the monarchy. As Westermann says, the account provides a " 'prehistorical' conception of history," wherein "events were explained by the family structures underlying them."[221] Jacob's decision shapes the future, yet not in such a way that his decision floats above the realities of history until it comes to pass. Jacob's decision continues to be remembered and has effects on the subsequent history of the family, which involves the relative status of each of these tribes.

2. Jacob's threefold invocation of God (48:15-16) provides a gathering of themes from the Genesis narrative.

God is the one before whom Abraham and Isaac walked (recalling 17:1; 24:40; cf. 5:22; 6:9). The author focuses here *not* on God's action, but on human "walking." Their faithfulness becomes important for what Jacob now has to say. God's action preceded their response; the deity has been engaged in every aspect of the lives of Jacob's grandfather and father. Jacob can now testify twice to God's involvement in his own life (but not his own "walking").

God is the one who has been his shepherd all the days of Jacob's life, thereby placing a concrete image on the promise of 28:15 (cf. 35:3). The image of God as shepherd includes the ideas of guidance, protection, and the provision of sustenance for the journey (cf. 49:24; Pss 23:1; 80:2). Jacob certainly draws this image of God out of his own experience as shepherd. This integration of life experience and divine revelation illustrates how new images for God develop within the community of faith. It prompts reflection on how new images for God might be developed out of the interplay of modern experience and inherited traditions.

God is the one who has redeemed (גאל *gōʾēl*) him from all harm (רע *raʿ*). The text actually reads "the angel [מלאך *malʾāk*]," i.e., God who appears in human form (see 31:11-13; cf. 16:7-13; 21:17-19; 22:11-12, 15-16). Jacob's use of "angel" could be informed by his struggle with the "man" at the Jabbok (32:22-33). The language of redemption (*gōʾēl*) rarely refers to God's action on behalf of individuals (cf. Pss 19:14; 103:4). The OT uses it chiefly for God's salvific acts at the Red Sea (Exod 6:6; 15:13), which this anticipates, as well as in the exile (Isaiah 40–55; Jer 31:9-11). Divine activity on behalf of Jacob thus moves beyond the providential, ongoing activity of the second predicate and more specifically speaks of God's activity as one of salvation. The author thus integrates creation and redemption themes in these wide-ranging statements about God.

221. Westermann, *Genesis 37–50,* 191.

Genesis 49:1-33, The Last Words of Jacob

NIV	NRSV
49 Then Jacob called for his sons and said: "Gather around so I can tell you what will happen to you in days to come.	**49** Then Jacob called his sons, and said: "Gather around, that I may tell you what will happen to you in days to come.
2 "Assemble and listen, sons of Jacob; listen to your father Israel.	2 Assemble and hear, O sons of Jacob; listen to Israel your father.
3 "Reuben, you are my firstborn, my might, the first sign of my strength,	3 Reuben, you are my firstborn, my might and the first fruits of my vigor,

NIV

excelling in honor, excelling in power.
⁴Turbulent as the waters, you will no longer excel,
  for you went up onto your father's bed,
  onto my couch and defiled it.

⁵"Simeon and Levi are brothers—
  their swords*a* are weapons of violence.
⁶Let me not enter their council,
  let me not join their assembly,
 for they have killed men in their anger
  and hamstrung oxen as they pleased.
⁷Cursed be their anger, so fierce,
  and their fury, so cruel!
 I will scatter them in Jacob
  and disperse them in Israel.
8"Judah,*b* your brothers will praise you;
  your hand will be on the neck of your
    enemies;
  your father's sons will bow down to you.
⁹You are a lion's cub, O Judah;
  you return from the prey, my son.
 Like a lion he crouches and lies down,
  like a lioness—who dares to rouse him?
¹⁰The scepter will not depart from Judah,
  nor the ruler's staff from between his feet,
 until he comes to whom it belongs*c*
  and the obedience of the nations is his.
¹¹He will tether his donkey to a vine,
  his colt to the choicest branch;
 he will wash his garments in wine,
  his robes in the blood of grapes.
¹²His eyes will be darker than wine,
  his teeth whiter than milk.*d*

¹³"Zebulun will live by the seashore
  and become a haven for ships;
  his border will extend toward Sidon.

¹⁴"Issachar is a rawboned*e* donkey
  lying down between two saddlebags.*f*
¹⁵When he sees how good is his resting place
  and how pleasant is his land,
 he will bend his shoulder to the burden
  and submit to forced labor.

¹⁶"Dan*g* will provide justice for his people

a5 The meaning of the Hebrew for this word is uncertain.   *b8 Judah*
sounds like and may be derived from the Hebrew for *praise.*
c10 Or *until Shiloh comes;* or *until he comes to whom tribute belongs*
d12 Or *will be dull from wine, / his teeth white from milk*
e14 Or *strong*   *f14* Or *campfires*   *g16 Dan* here means *he*
provides justice.

NRSV

excelling in rank and excelling in power.
⁴ Unstable as water, you shall no longer excel
  because you went up onto your father's
    bed;
  then you defiled it—you*a* went up onto
    my couch!

⁵ Simeon and Levi are brothers;
  weapons of violence are their swords.
⁶ May I never come into their council;
  may I not be joined to their company—
  for in their anger they killed men,
  and at their whim they hamstrung oxen.
⁷ Cursed be their anger, for it is fierce,
  and their wrath, for it is cruel!
 I will divide them in Jacob,
  and scatter them in Israel.

⁸ Judah, your brothers shall praise you;
  your hand shall be on the neck of your
    enemies;
  your father's sons shall bow down before
    you.
⁹ Judah is a lion's whelp;
  from the prey, my son, you have gone up.
 He crouches down, he stretches out like a
    lion,
  like a lioness—who dares rouse him up?
¹⁰ The scepter shall not depart from Judah,
  nor the ruler's staff from between his feet,
 until tribute comes to him;*b*
  and the obedience of the peoples is his.
¹¹ Binding his foal to the vine
  and his donkey's colt to the choice vine,
 he washes his garments in wine
  and his robe in the blood of grapes;
¹² his eyes are darker than wine,
  and his teeth whiter than milk.

¹³ Zebulun shall settle at the shore of the sea;
  he shall be a haven for ships,
  and his border shall be at Sidon.

¹⁴ Issachar is a strong donkey,
  lying down between the sheepfolds;
¹⁵ he saw that a resting place was good,
  and that the land was pleasant;

a Gk Syr Tg: Heb *he*   *b* Or *until Shiloh comes* or *until he comes to*
Shiloh or *(with Syr) until he comes to whom it belongs*

NIV

as one of the tribes of Israel.
¹⁷Dan will be a serpent by the roadside,
a viper along the path,
that bites the horse's heels
so that its rider tumbles backward.

¹⁸"I look for your deliverance, O LORD.

¹⁹"Gadᵃ will be attacked by a band of raiders,
but he will attack them at their heels.
²⁰"Asher's food will be rich;
he will provide delicacies fit for a king.

²¹"Naphtali is a doe set free
that bears beautiful fawns.ᵇ
²²"Joseph is a fruitful vine,
a fruitful vine near a spring,
whose branches climb over a wall.ᶜ
²³With bitterness archers attacked him;
they shot at him with hostility.
²⁴But his bow remained steady,
his strong arms stayedᵈ limber,
because of the hand of the Mighty One of Jacob,
because of the Shepherd, the Rock of Israel,
²⁵because of your father's God, who helps you,
because of the Almighty,ᵉ who blesses you
with blessings of the heavens above,
blessings of the deep that lies below,
blessings of the breast and womb.
²⁶Your father's blessings are greater
than the blessings of the ancient mountains,
thanᶠ the bounty of the age-old hills.
Let all these rest on the head of Joseph,
on the brow of the prince amongᵍ his brothers.

²⁷"Benjamin is a ravenous wolf;
in the morning he devours the prey,
in the evening he divides the plunder."

²⁸All these are the twelve tribes of Israel, and this is what their father said to them when he blessed them, giving each the blessing appropriate to him.
²⁹Then he gave them these instructions: "I am about to be gathered to my people. Bury me with my fathers in the cave in the field of Ephron the

NRSV

so he bowed his shoulder to the burden,
and became a slave at forced labor.

¹⁶ Dan shall judge his people
as one of the tribes of Israel.
¹⁷ Dan shall be a snake by the roadside,
a viper along the path,
that bites the horse's heels
so that its rider falls backward.

¹⁸ I wait for your salvation, O LORD.
¹⁹ Gad shall be raided by raiders,
but he shall raid at their heels.

²⁰ Asher'sᵃ food shall be rich,
and he shall provide royal delicacies.

²¹ Naphtali is a doe let loose
that bears lovely fawns.ᵇ

²² Joseph is a fruitful bough,
a fruitful bough by a spring;
his branches run over the wall.ᶜ
²³ The archers fiercely attacked him;
they shot at him and pressed him hard.
²⁴ Yet his bow remained taut,
and his armsᵈ were made agile
by the hands of the Mighty One of Jacob,
by the name of the Shepherd, the Rock
of Israel,
²⁵ by the God of your father, who will help
you,
by the Almightyᵉ who will bless you
with blessings of heaven above,
blessings of the deep that lies beneath,
blessings of the breasts and of the womb.
²⁶ The blessings of your father
are stronger than the blessings of the
eternal mountains,
the bountiesᶠ of the everlasting hills;
may they be on the head of Joseph,
on the brow of him who was set apart
from his brothers.

²⁷ Benjamin is a ravenous wolf,
in the morning devouring the prey,

NIV

Hittite, ³⁰the cave in the field of Machpelah, near Mamre in Canaan, which Abraham bought as a burial place from Ephron the Hittite, along with the field. ³¹There Abraham and his wife Sarah were buried, there Isaac and his wife Rebekah were buried, and there I buried Leah. ³²The field and the cave in it were bought from the Hittites.^a"

³³When Jacob had finished giving instructions to his sons, he drew his feet up into the bed, breathed his last and was gathered to his people.

^a32 Or *the sons of Heth*

NRSV

and at evening dividing the spoil."

28All these are the twelve tribes of Israel, and this is what their father said to them when he blessed them, blessing each one of them with a suitable blessing.

29Then he charged them, saying to them, "I am about to be gathered to my people. Bury me with my ancestors—in the cave in the field of Ephron the Hittite, ³⁰in the cave in the field at Machpelah, near Mamre, in the land of Canaan, in the field that Abraham bought from Ephron the Hittite as a burial site. ³¹There Abraham and his wife Sarah were buried; there Isaac and his wife Rebekah were buried; and there I buried Leah—³²the field and the cave that is in it were purchased from the Hittites." ³³When Jacob ended his charge to his sons, he drew up his feet into the bed, breathed his last, and was gathered to his people.

COMMENTARY

Many scholars deem this poem—Jacob's final words to his sons—to be one of the oldest pieces of literature in the OT. Its language, aphorisms, metaphors, word plays, and other poetic features make for many difficulties in text, translation, and interpretation. The poem has no doubt had a complex compositional history, evident, for example, in the differing length and character of each saying. One confronts difficulties in assessing the literary and historical relationships with a similar list of tribal sayings in Deuteronomy 33 (cf. Judg 5:14-18).

Only the sayings of Reuben and Judah occur in the second person, directly addressed to them; only in those of Reuben, Simeon/Levi, and Judah does Jacob refer to himself in the first person (also in the interlude, v. 18). The order of the sons corresponds to no other text; Leah's six sons come first and Rachel's last, with Bilhah's sons (Dan, Naphtali) enclosing those of Zilpah. The form of the sayings regarding Reuben, Simeon/Levi, Judah, and Joseph is more oracular, that of the others more aphoristic.

The prose context in which the poem is set occasions further difficulties. Verse 28 names this word of Jacob a blessing; yet curse and censure

occur. The "blessings" of Reuben, Simeon, and Levi are sharply negative (cf. vv. 4-7). Jacob's telling his sons "what will happen to you in days to come" presents a similar difficulty. While most of the sayings bear on the future, not all do. Moreover, they also often focus on past events or present circumstance.

The differences among the sayings provide evidence for their independent origins in widely disparate settings. They have been brought together into a larger poem over an extensive period of time, the present composite form emerging sometime late in the period of the judges or in the early monarchy. The sayings were then inserted into a narrative that originally moved directly from 49:1*a* ("Jacob summoned his sons") to 49:28*b*, a reference to blessing but with no specific content. The structural element that most informs the present shape is Jacob's repeated charge regarding his burial that encloses the two blessings of chaps. 48–49, first to Joseph (47:29-31) and then to all the sons (49:29-32). Enclosing each of these in turn are the references to Jacob's death (47:28; 49:33).

These sayings have to do less with the persons in the previous narrative than with tribal entities, reflecting the history of the tribes during the early centuries in Canaan. Only those of Reuben and Simeon/Levi are explicitly related to earlier incidents; otherwise, only Judah and Joseph mention intrafamilial relationships. The negative words about Reuben and Simeon reflect both their ill-begotten behaviors and their later disappearance as tribal entities; they are the only sayings with a crime/punishment schema. The two lengthiest blessings, those of Judah and Joseph (vv. 8-12, 22-26), reflect both their dominance in the ancestral story and their predominance in tribal history. Only the Joseph sayings mention God explicitly (v. 18 is an interlude); they provide the most direct link to the ancestral promises of blessing. Many of the sayings include lively metaphors from the nonhuman world.

49:1-2. Jacob asks his sons to gather around his deathbed to hear a word about their future. Not all the sayings allude to the future, but in all cases they move beyond the lifetime of the sons. Hence, there is overall movement from individual to tribal entity, which parallels other elements in these final chapters that move from Jacob to Israel (see 46:8; 47:27). This future, already beginning to emerge out of the present, is conceived in historical, not eschatological, terms.

49:3-4. Jacob addresses Reuben directly. Reuben, Jacob's firstborn and the product of his youthful vigor, excels in rank and power. But like sea waters, he seems unreliable, inconsistent in behavior. He will not excel, because he disgracefully lay with Bilhah, his father's wife (35:22). Jacob, in effect, deposes Reuben from his status as firstborn (see chap. 48). That future of instability (see Deut 33:6) works itself out historically: The tribe, whose territory lay east of the Dead Sea, was absorbed by the Moabites.

49:5-7. Simeon and Levi are the only sons considered together, no doubt because of the slaughter at Shechem (34:25-30). The poem includes strong language about them; they were murderous, violent, fiercely angry, arbitrary, cruel, and harsh in their treatment of animals. Consequently, Jacob will not participate in their counsels (cf. 34:30). He curses their anger (i.e., "them," an instance of metonymy) and announces the dispersion of their families throughout the nation. Historically, their "dispersion" appears quite different. Simeon (omitted in Deuteronomy 33) was absorbed into the tribe of

Judah. Levi later becomes a nonterritorial priestly group, elect by God (Num 8:14-19; 18:24), a development not in view here (cf. Deut 33:8-11). Jacob's repeated use of the first person reflects a prophetic mode of discourse; strikingly, Jacob himself (namely, his word) serves as the agent of judgment in v. 7.

49:8-12. Jacob praises Judah highly in recognition of his increasingly prominent role in the preceding narrative. The heart of the saying contains a promise: All his brothers will recognize him as preeminent because he will defeat his enemies in battle (i.e., seize them by the neck). The poet employs the image of a lion/lioness/lion's cub for Judah because he is cleverly successful in his ventures (i.e., he always returns to the lair with his prey) and no one dares to provoke him (cf. Num 24:9; "lion of Judah" becomes a messianic image, Rev 5:5).

Verse 10 appears especially difficult, particularly the word שׁילה (*šîlōh*), variously translated as a place (Shiloh) or a person ("ruler," the one to whom rule belongs; so the NIV) or tribute (NRSV). It most likely refers to a person. The basic image is clear: The poet depicts Judah as a royal figure, whose rule (i.e., scepter, staff standing between feet; cf. Ps 45:6) will continue for a lengthy period until a climactic event occurs that assures a glorious future, when he will reign over obedient nations and a fertile earth.

But what will happen to enable this future? Judah experiences some growth over the years, but achieves prominence only during the time of Saul and David. Hence, many scholars suggest that this verse refers to the Davidic monarchy, at which point Judah's preeminence as a tribe will assume a broader sovereignty over the nations. The imagery has also been interpreted in messianic terms—e.g., the Balaam oracles (see Num 24:17). In such contexts, Judah will rule until the Messiah comes, and all the peoples of the world will serve him in a time of great abundance. Historically, an original Davidic reference was probably given a messianic interpretation during the course of Israel's history (cf. Psalm 2; Isa 11:1-9).

Although the images are somewhat obscure, vv. 11-12 speak of the new prosperity brought about by Judah's hegemony. There will be so many vineyards that he can use the tender stalks to tether his donkey (a royal animal, Zech 9:9) and a grape harvest so abundant that he can even wash his clothes in blood-colored wine. He will be a person of surpassing beauty, with dark eyes and white teeth (see Ps 45:2; the images in Num 24:5-7).

49:13. This verse focuses on geographical location (cf. Josh 19:10-16, where Zebulun is not on the coast). Zebulun shall have an advantageous position, with access to the sea, at or near the port of Sidon (=Phoenicia).

49:14-15. The poet describes Issachar as a strong donkey that has been domesticated and rests at ease rather than roaming free (i.e., lives among the sheep, or saddlebags); this may allude to the fertile plain of Esdraelon in northern Canaan. The image suggests one content with his lot, in exchange for which it will (NIV) or has (NRSV) become a servant to others (e.g., the Canaanites or Solomon's forced levy, 1 Kgs 9:21?). These verses seem to present a negative future (contrast Judg 5:15).

49:16-17. In this positive saying, Dan (a name similar to the word for "judge") will become active in seeking justice for the tribes of Israel (note the tribal reference; cf. Judges 18). The image of a poisonous snake suggests Dan as a small tribe struggling for survival, but which will successfully strike at more powerful groups ("horse and rider") and so advocate the causes it has assumed. The history of this tribe, which had difficulty settling within its original borders and migrated to the north, is very complex.[222]

49:18. This confession of trust in God provides an interlude reflected in the Psalms (25:5; 38:15; 119:166). Jacob waits for God. He interrupts the blessings on his sons with a word of anticipation for the salvation (ישועה *yĕšûâ*) that Yahweh (the only occurrence in chap. 49) will bring to him. This is probably not a word about Jacob personally, but a corporate reference, expressing trust in God's eventual salvation on behalf of Jacob's sons.

49:19. Gad settled east of the Jordan and was especially vulnerable to desert marauders. Gad will continue to be victimized by bands of raiders (גדוד יגודנו *gĕdûd yĕgûdennû*, a word play on גד *Gad*), but will be able to respond effectively by seemingly minor acts of bravery.

49:20. Asher's coastal land was agriculturally fertile, hence he would provide rich food for

royalty, including the export of delicacies. The reference appears positive.

49:21. The positive, but puzzling, image of Naphtali as a doe that has been set free and bears beautiful fawns suggests that he will enjoy freedom, vitality, and increase of numbers in the mountain areas of his home (north of the Sea of Galilee).

49:22-26. The relationship between Joseph and his sons in the previous chapter (see 48:15, 21-22) shows that the mention of either could count for both (cf. Deut 27:12; 33:13-17).

The image of a fruitful, well-watered bough whose branches extend ever outward suggests a growing community that moves into surrounding territories. Joseph's enemies attacked him (his brothers?), but he held his own with strength, courage, and agility. This response was made possible because of divine aid, specified by an unusually concentrated series of images, drawn from liturgical practice (cf. 48:15-16): (a) Mighty One of Jacob (see Ps 132:2, 5; Isa 49:26; 60:16); God has seen Jacob through thick and thin during his numerous lengthy and troubled journeys. (b) Shepherd (see 48:15). (c) The epithet "Rock of Israel" (cf. Deut 32:15, 31; 1 Sam 7:12) stresses the strength and constancy of God on behalf of the weak and helpless. God's faithfulness remains steadfast even when being buffeted about by people and events. (d) The title "God of your father" (see Exod 3:6) represents continuity from one generation to the next, informed most fundamentally by God's faithfulness to promises made. (e) The Almighty (*Shaddai*, see 17:1).

This God will continue to help and bless Joseph (note the creation and redemption themes). These themes tie Joseph most closely to the promises given to his ancestors (12:2-3) and are expanded (cf. the parallels in Deut 28:3-6; 33:13-16): the blessing of water for crops—so important in an arid land—from both the heavens above (rain) and the earth beneath (springs) as well as the blessing of the fertility of the females (breasts and womb). The word *blessing* occurs six times!

Verse 26 has a benedictory form. The blessings extended by Jacob (received from Isaac, 27:28) are richer than any others (if they exceed the mountains, they exceed all). They are now given to Joseph, who has been set apart from his brothers (a reference to chap. 48). The reference to

---

222. See ibid., 340.

head and brow may be synecdoche or refer to the laying on of hands (cf. 48:13-18).

49:27. The image of a ravenous wolf for Benjamin, though basically positive, does not correspond to anything in the narrative (cf. Judg 5:13-14; 20:15-25). The poem portrays him as relentless and successful in battle with other peoples, which could be related to his territory's central geographical location between Judah and Ephraim.

49:28. This concluding comment stresses that each of Jacob's blessings was appropriate to the son—i.e., each was suitable to its person, history, and life situation. The narrator here, for the first time, mentions the twelve tribes.

49:29-33. In this final charge to his sons, Jacob reinforces the oath taken by Joseph (47:29-31); he knows that oaths no more control the future than do blessings. Jacob requests that he be buried in the place purchased by Abraham at Machpelah (chap. 23), where three generations are already buried (the only reference to the burial of Rebekah and Leah). The detail in the text makes the charge unmistakably clear; the repeated clause regarding purchase from the Hittites (vv. 29b, 32a) encloses the place reference, emphasizing its legal standing and authenticating the claim that this is the land promised to Jacob's descendants. Having completed this charge, Jacob dies (cf. 27:30).

REFLECTIONS

1. Tribal considerations appear in chap 49. While most scholars think these words were written soon after the history they reflect, the text presents these materials as Jacob's own word. *Prophecy* would not be fully adequate to describe these materials. We understand them better as Jacob's judgment regarding the future of his sons' lives on the basis of his thoroughgoing knowledge and evaluation of them. The past and present life of the son signals the way in which each future will be shaped. While this becomes explicit only with Reuben and Simeon/Levi, these cases function paradigmatically for the others. Hence, the future sketched out does not appear arbitrary, unrelated to experience. The wisdom exhibited by Jacob—an important link with the Joseph story as a whole—involves discerning how the future for each son grows out of past and present experience.

2. The last words of Jacob in chap 49 unify the book of Genesis in significant ways. Links with the divine promises to each ancestor are drawn up into this poem. The promises regarding a nation/people (cf. 12:2; 46:3), numerous posterity (cf. 26:24; 48:4), and blessings in abundance (22:17) become a reality in the twelve tribes. Within chaps. 37–50, special attention was initially given to both Joseph (chap. 37) and Judah (chap. 38); now in these last words, Joseph and Judah dominate the scene (in terms of quantity of material [some 40 percent]), the extent to which the divine blessing affects their lives, and their role and influence in shaping Israel's future.

Moreover, the efficacy of the word links the beginning and the end of Genesis, from the creative word of God to the effective word of the patriarch. At the same time, just as one finds a certain vulnerability of the divine word as its waits upon creaturely response, so also the patriarch's word waits upon the contingencies of historical process as it moves into the future. This appears particularly evident concerning the role of the tribe of Levi, whose "dispersion" can hardly be considered negative due to its special election by God to priestly status (Num 8:14-19; 18:24; Deut 10:8-9). Thus Jacob's words do not determine fully the future of the tribes.

3. A poet used striking metaphors to depict Jacob's sons, including lion, donkey, snake, deer, fruit, tree, and wolf. We need to ask how such metaphors function. They have been created on the basis of observations made of commonalities between human beings and the animal and plant worlds. In congruence with the use of metaphor, the enemies of the various tribes are never named (the same phenomenon can be observed in Psalms); this gives the poem a more timeless quality, enabling the reader to relate it to a multitude of situations. We must thus be careful not to seek to pin down each saying to a particular historical moment. The movement back and forth between individual personalities and corporate identities also contributes to this fluidity. Hence, the sayings could link the ancestral period with virtually every succeeding period of the tribal history.

4. We should devote special consideration to 49:10-12 and should not consider this text a straightforward parallel to the messianic oracles of the prophets. First, the text is insufficiently clear to establish this claim. Second, it suggests, wrongly, that a full-blown messianism is present wherever these themes occur. It seems better to think that these verses provide early reflections concerning the future, particularly in view of the failure of the monarchy. These traditions of promise are associated with words of indictment and judgment on Reuben and Simon/Levi.

5. While one rightly should attend to the details associated with each of Jacob's sons, one should also consider the overall picture of this family that emerges. The sayings suggest both unity and diversity. One could use the image of a body, moving back and forth between corporate identity and individual expression, with the various members of the body contributing in their own unique way to the functioning of the whole. At the same time, not all the members make equally important contributions; Judah and Joseph are evidently the head and the heart of the people. Moreover, not all play a positive role; among the tribal groups there is excellence and mediocrity, vigor and weakness, goodness and evil. Overall, the author presents a realistic, warts-and-all portrayal of the people of Israel. Yet, the word for the future is positive, most fundamentally because God is at work among them, saving and blessing.

Genesis 50:1-14, The Burial of Jacob

NIV

50 Joseph threw himself upon his father and wept over him and kissed him. ²Then Joseph directed the physicians in his service to embalm his father Israel. So the physicians embalmed him, ³taking a full forty days, for that was the time required for embalming. And the Egyptians mourned for him seventy days.

⁴When the days of mourning had passed, Joseph said to Pharaoh's court, "If I have found favor in your eyes, speak to Pharaoh for me. Tell him, ⁵'My father made me swear an oath and said, "I am about to die; bury me in the tomb I dug for myself in the land of Canaan." Now let me go up and bury my father; then I will return.' "

⁶Pharaoh said, "Go up and bury your father, as he made you swear to do."

⁷So Joseph went up to bury his father. All Pharaoh's officials accompanied him—the dignitaries of his court and all the dignitaries of Egypt— ⁸besides all the members of Joseph's household and his brothers and those belonging to his father's household. Only their children and

NRSV

50 Then Joseph threw himself on his father's face and wept over him and kissed him. ²Joseph commanded the physicians in his service to embalm his father. So the physicians embalmed Israel; ³they spent forty days in doing this, for that is the time required for embalming. And the Egyptians wept for him seventy days.

4When the days of weeping for him were past, Joseph addressed the household of Pharaoh, "If now I have found favor with you, please speak to Pharaoh as follows: ⁵My father made me swear an oath; he said, 'I am about to die. In the tomb that I hewed out for myself in the land of Canaan, there you shall bury me.' Now therefore let me go up, so that I may bury my father; then I will return." ⁶Pharaoh answered, "Go up, and bury your father, as he made you swear to do."

7So Joseph went up to bury his father. With him went up all the servants of Pharaoh, the elders of his household, and all the elders of the land of Egypt, ⁸as well as all the household of Joseph, his brothers, and his father's household.

NIV

their flocks and herds were left in Goshen. [9]Chariots and horsemen[a] also went up with him. It was a very large company.

[10]When they reached the threshing floor of Atad, near the Jordan, they lamented loudly and bitterly; and there Joseph observed a seven-day period of mourning for his father. [11]When the Canaanites who lived there saw the mourning at the threshing floor of Atad, they said, "The Egyptians are holding a solemn ceremony of mourning." That is why that place near the Jordan is called Abel Mizraim.[b]

[12]So Jacob's sons did as he had commanded them: [13]They carried him to the land of Canaan and buried him in the cave in the field of Machpelah, near Mamre, which Abraham had bought as a burial place from Ephron the Hittite, along with the field. [14]After burying his father, Joseph returned to Egypt, together with his brothers and all the others who had gone with him to bury his father.

[a]9 Or charioteers   [a]11 Abel Mizraim means mourning of the Egyptians.

NRSV

Only their children, their flocks, and their herds were left in the land of Goshen. [9]Both chariots and charioteers went up with him. It was a very great company. [10]When they came to the threshing floor of Atad, which is beyond the Jordan, they held there a very great and sorrowful lamentation; and he observed a time of mourning for his father seven days. [11]When the Canaanite inhabitants of the land saw the mourning on the threshing floor of Atad, they said, "This is a grievous mourning on the part of the Egyptians." Therefore the place was named Abel-mizraim;[a] it is beyond the Jordan. [12]Thus his sons did for him as he had instructed them. [13]They carried him to the land of Canaan and buried him in the cave of the field at Machpelah, the field near Mamre, which Abraham bought as a burial site from Ephron the Hittite. [14]After he had buried his father, Joseph returned to Egypt with his brothers and all who had gone up with him to bury his father.

[a]That is mourning (or meadow) of Egypt

COMMENTARY

The author reports on the events associated with the death and burial of Jacob. Weeping and mourning, on the part of both Joseph and the Egyptians, move in and out of this scene (vv. 1, 3-4, 10-11).

Once again Joseph weeps, marking another major stage in the development of the story (see 42:24). He directs the physicians to embalm Jacob, a forty-day task, included within the seventy days of mourning. The OT reports mummification only for Jacob and Joseph (hence it genuinely reflects the Egyptian setting). Since this practice was customary for Egyptian monarchs, the writer depicts Jacob's receiving a royal funeral. In contrast, it seems ironic that the burial of Joseph, the royal official, is described in the simplest of terms (v. 26). The Egyptians mourn for Jacob in a grand way (the brothers are never so singled out).

Joseph attends to the oath he had sworn to his father about burial in Canaan (see 47:29-31). Contrary to usual practice (see 47:1), perhaps because of the mourning, Joseph indirectly asks permission of Pharaoh to go to Canaan to bury

his father. Pharaoh grants it, and Joseph proceeds exactly according to his request.

Joseph and a "very great company" (v. 9) make the journey to Canaan with Jacob's body. This return anticipates the exodus and subsequent events, only this time the Egyptians accompany them! The group includes not only all the members of the "household" of both Joseph and Jacob (except children—probably with mothers—and livestock), but also "all" of Pharaoh's servants and "all" the elders of the land of Egypt, with full chariot (i.e., military) accompaniment. Once again, in purposeful hyperbole, the full participation of the Egyptians appears stunning. The Egyptians seem to agree with the claims of Jacob's family to the land of Canaan. The author reinforces this claim (ironically?) by the "objective" observation of the Canaanites that the Egyptians engaged in such "a very great and sorrowful mourning" (vv. 10-11).

Jacob's burial place remains unclear. In v. 5, Joseph quotes his father's request to be buried "in the tomb that I hewed out for myself in the land of Canaan." We do not find this description in either of Jacob's charges (47:29-31; 49:29-32). The language probably reflects Pharaoh's understanding rather than a different burial tradition. For reasons unknown, they hold a wake at the threshing floor at Atad (renamed Abel-mizraim, "mourning of Egypt," by the Canaanites), a place otherwise unknown. While "beyond the Jordan" could mean the Transjordan, if the writer were east of the Jordan it could be Canaan (as the reference to Canaanites suggests). If the latter, the journey would not be a major detour from a direct Egypt-Mamre (Hebron) route. Hence, we would not need to think of another tradition regarding Jacob's place of burial. Only Joseph observes a seven-day time of mourning (the usual Israelite practice, 1 Sam 31:13), and only the sons continue on to the burial place.

The text stipulates that Jacob's sons did exactly what their father had instructed them to do (v. 12). This claim must refer to the following verse, hence v. 12 should conclude with a colon (so NIV). This episode concludes with the return of the entire party to Egypt (as Joseph had promised to Pharaoh, at least regarding himself, v. 5).

REFLECTIONS

It would appear that the positive references to Egyptian participation (indeed, Egyptian burial practices) in Jacob's funeral are intended to stand in sharp contrast to the changed relationship between Israel and the Egyptians in the following Exodus narrative. Genesis speaks of the kind of relationship that can be possible with other, nonchosen peoples. Exodus records an aberration. Genesis, not Exodus, should inform Israel's post-Exodus relations with the Egyptians.

Genesis 50:15-21, The Full Reconciliation of Israel's Sons

NIV

[15]When Joseph's brothers saw that their father was dead, they said, "What if Joseph holds a grudge against us and pays us back for all the wrongs we did to him?" [16]So they sent word to Joseph, saying, "Your father left these instructions before he died: [17]'This is what you are to say to Joseph: I ask you to forgive your brothers the sins and the wrongs they committed in treating you so badly.' Now please forgive the sins of the servants of the God of your father." When their message came to him, Joseph wept.

[18]His brothers then came and threw themselves down before him. "We are your slaves," they said.

[19]But Joseph said to them, "Don't be afraid. Am I in the place of God? [20]You intended to harm me, but God intended it for good to accomplish what is now being done, the saving of many lives. [21]So then, don't be afraid. I will provide for you and your children." And he reassured them and spoke kindly to them.

NRSV

15Realizing that their father was dead, Joseph's brothers said, "What if Joseph still bears a grudge against us and pays us back in full for all the wrong that we did to him?" [16]So they approached[a] Joseph, saying, "Your father gave this instruction before he died, [17]'Say to Joseph: I beg you, forgive the crime of your brothers and the wrong they did in harming you.' Now therefore please forgive the crime of the servants of the God of your father." Joseph wept when they spoke to him. [18]Then his brothers also wept,[b] fell down before him, and said, "We are here as your slaves." [19]But Joseph said to them, "Do not be afraid! Am I in the place of God? [20]Even though you intended to do harm to me, God intended it for good, in order to preserve a numerous people, as he is doing today. [21]So have no fear; I myself will provide for you and your little ones." In this way he reassured them, speaking kindly to them.

[a] Gk Syr: Heb *they commanded*   [b] Cn: Heb *also came*

COMMENTARY

The author sets this story of reconciliation between two deaths, though it is difficult to relate it to the story in chap. 45. It may be simply a recapitulation, but its purpose seems more complex (see discussion on chap. 45).

In v. 15, the brothers express apprehension about how Joseph will treat them now that their father has died; he may decide to exact retribution (see 27:41). Given the lack of resolution in chap. 45, this is understandable. Moreover, in the face of the death of a common parent, particularly a parent of such influence and renown, typical patterns of behavior may no longer continue. Life among the siblings has to be renegotiated.

In vv. 16-17, the brothers send a messenger (cf. 37:32) to present their concerns to Joseph, suggesting their high anxiety (the NRSV adopts the LXX reading, omitting the messenger). They couch their concerns in terms of their father's deathbed wish, rather than a direct personal request. The upshot of Jacob's request was that the brothers be reconciled, more specifically that Joseph forgive them the crime they committed. No evidence exists that Jacob actually said this, but Joseph remains as much in the dark on this as the reader! This is the only text in which Jacob gives a clear indication that he knows what the brothers did to Joseph (cf. 42:36). Nothing suggests it is a fabrication, spun out of the brothers' anxiety. In fact, the last reference to a report from the brothers about what Jacob said (44:24-29) appears truthful. The progress of the story toward the unified family of chap. 50 reinforces their speech as an honest report.

Building on their father's request, the brothers call themselves "servants" (anticipating a key theme in Exodus) of "the God of your father." The author grounds their appeal in their common faith in the God of Jacob; this binds them to one another in the heritage of their father. The theme of forgiveness occurs twice in v. 17, in Jacob's request and voiced by the brothers. Words for "sin" and "evil" are used four times, in both their father's speech and in their own words. This high consciousness of their crime suggests that the encounter in chap. 45 did not resolve the matter for the brothers. Even with the assurances given them by Joseph, they still live with the guilt of what they have done.

Joseph weeps, though not in the presence of his brothers (cf. NRSV). Once again, this marks a move toward the resolution of the conflict. He had wept with his brothers in 45:1-2, 14-15 at the occasion of a reconciliation. Here he weeps over their message, words revealing an ongoing mistrust. The weeping may also signal to the reader that he will not seek revenge, marking another stage in the development of the story (see 42:24).

The reference to Joseph's weeping leads into the brothers' coming before him (the NRSV's "wept" is based on an emendation of the Hebrew), without waiting for any response from the messenger. The brothers do obeisance before Joseph and declare themselves his servants/slaves (once again, the Exodus theme). They intensify the messenger's words with these personal actions. The brothers' bowing before Joseph does *not* fulfill his dream in 37:7 (as it does in 42:6; 43:26; 44:14). Joseph will now reject such status as an inappropriate relationship between himself and his brothers.

The words to have no fear enclose Joseph's response (vv. 19-21). This signals an oracle of salvation, a word of comfort and assurance. Such language commonly appears as God's first word in theophany (see 21:17; 26:24; 46:3); Second Isaiah uses it to speak to the exiles (41:10-14). We also find this language in an oracle of salvation at the birth of Jesus and at his resurrection (Matt 28:10; Luke 2:10).

Joseph gives three reasons to ease their fears. First, he responds in tones that are both rebuke and reassurance: "Am I in the place of God?" The question portrays a profound human judgment in this matter, not a "humble declaration of noncompetence."[223] It probably has a double reference—to their request for forgiveness and to their offer to become slaves. (a) The latter occurs immediately before his response. Joseph is not God, thus they can be assured that he will not behave as a pharaoh to them. He remains subject to God as the brothers are; they stand together under the

223. Von Rad, *Genesis,* 432.

authority of a divine other who works purposefully on behalf of them all. This theme anticipates the acts of the pharaoh who did not know Joseph (Exod 1:8) and the fivefold use of servant language in Exod 1:13-14, with the authoritarianism and potential for oppression. The implication here functions as it does in Exodus; the people of Israel will be the servants of God alone. (b) Regarding forgiveness, Joseph seems to reject a guilt/forgiveness approach (as in 45:3-8), leaving that up to God. At the same time, his words and deeds reveal a conciliatory spirit, showing that no revenge on his part is in view.

Second, regardless of their intentions, and Joseph names them evil (רע *ra'*; see 44:4-5), they can be assured their actions have been drawn into God's larger purposes for goodness, and these have come to prevail. The God who created the world and called it good has been about life and its preservation in and through all of these events, despite their intentions for death. Joseph, by clearly naming the brothers' actions as "evil"— something not done in 45:3-9—makes this matter public. His positive action has their evil behaviors in clear view, and the brothers now know that the evil they have done no longer counts against them.

Third, they will be cared for. In v. 21, Joseph comforts them and speaks tenderly/kindly to them (both words are used in Isa 40:1-2 in a context of forgiveness), assuring them that he will provide for them, with special attention to the children, and hence their future (as in 45:10-11; 47:12). This involves not just words, but concrete practical realities. The brothers do not respond, and though vv. 24-25 assume a positive response, the brothers' final silence in the narrative may indicate a sense of foreboding, or at least openness, about future relationships.

REFLECTIONS

1. The theme of goodness in Genesis comes full circle here.[224] In Genesis 1, God created everything "very good." This "good" did not entail perfection or deny the need of development. Throughout Genesis, God has been pursuing these good intentions for the created order. Even more, God recruited human beings to participate in that pursuit of goodness; God's creative work leads to specific vocations. Joseph's work in Egypt, for example, served creation (41:33-37, recognized by Pharaoh as "good"), providing for the daily needs of *all* persons (cf. 45:11; 47:12; 50:21). God's *creational* purposes for goodness, life, and well-being in and through people do not cease even in the face of their weakness or failure.

2. The narrator gathers up a key theme of these chapters (50:20) concerning what both the brothers and God have done (see also 45:5-9). The verb חשב (*ḥāšab*) is translated in various ways; either "plan" or "intend" will do, though "plan" lifts up the concrete side of intention more directly. This term also more clearly alludes to the plots of the brothers against Joseph. In their very plans, God, too, has been working on a plan for goodness (see Jer 18:11-12, 18; 29:11).

God does not have a highly detailed plan all worked out that will come to fruition regardless of what humans do. The people involved are not automatons, whose good or evil actions count for nothing. Positively, they can act for good in the face of those who plan for evil. Negatively, they can frustrate God's intentions, so that the future may look different from what would have been the case had only the divine plan been realized. Yet, however much these planners may complicate the divine planning, God's way into the future will never *finally* be stymied. God will persevere, will stay with plans for life, though it may entail changes in the ways and means to that goal in view of human intractability and failure. We should remember this perspective, voiced at the end of Genesis, as we move into the "evil" evident in the book of Exodus.

This divine action has been behind the scenes, unobtrusive. Dissimilar to the rest of Genesis, it has been more subtle, interweaving the threads of goodness and mercy among the various

224. See Brueggemann, *Genesis,* 373-76.

strands of evil in their lives, working toward the best possible end. God can take what such persons do and draw it into God's larger purposes. We do not find a situation in which "even the evil design is included in God's plan." God does not intend human evil. Rather, God's plan "is to bring the evil devised by the brothers to good effect."[225] Paul echoes this text in Rom 8:28: In everything, in even the worst that evildoers may throw God's way, God will draw it into the divine plans for good. For Joseph, finally, one must trust in these persistent divine purposes on behalf of life.

3. God's purposes are not confined to the reconciliation of the brothers. Joseph's word of comfort and assurance does address the context of their fear and guilt. But these words effect salvation in their lives, in the broadest sense of the term, which moves beyond forgiveness to include life and well-being.

This story demonstrates that the moral order does work, but not in any exact or inevitable way. It can be ameliorated by God's reconciling work as well as human comfort and compassion. The brothers do, indeed, reap many consequences for their deeds (cf. 42:14; 44:16); even forgiveness would not bring those to a sudden end. The issue becomes whether the evil consequences (hence the sin that triggered them) will be allowed to claim the day. God's move, in and through Joseph, means that sin and its consequences are not allowed to have the last word. The people of God can trust that, in the midst of sin and evil, God pursues his purposes for good.

Joseph does not deal directly with his brothers' guilt. In spite of their efforts to discern a word of forgiveness, we hear no such word from Joseph's mouth. "The speech transcends their preoccupation with guilt and turns them to a fresh way of understanding what has happened."[226] The narrative seeks to "restore their personal dignity and parity with Joseph"; a confession of sin "would make their status dependent upon his grace and would thus establish them in a position spiritually inferior to him."[227] What the brothers have done, God has been able to transmute into good, so their guilt no longer remains; therefore, no word from Joseph appears necessary. Although a word of forgiveness certainly could be appropriate in a general way, yet such a word may be used (consciously or unconsciously) to initiate or maintain a hierarchical relationship between the forgiver and the forgiven. The author seems concerned to make sure that, in the end, all parties to the dispute maintain their self-respect as moral equals.

4. God finally brings unity to this story. God is the only one who has been active in the story with a constant good purpose from beginning to end—that there might be life for all.

God is the only one who has been active at every level of the story, from the highest tier of governmental authority to the lowest sphere of everyday family life, suffusing them with the divine purposes for good. God holds life together in all of its personal and social complexity and ambiguity.

God has been active among both the chosen and the unchosen, including the Egyptians, with exactly the same purpose in mind: life. Genesis attests to God's universal purpose in this story of Israel.

225. Westermann, *Genesis 37–50,* 205.
226. Brueggemann, *Genesis,* 373.
227. White, *Narration,* 267.

Genesis 50:22-26, The Promise Transmitted

NIV

²²Joseph stayed in Egypt, along with all his father's family. He lived a hundred and ten years ²³and saw the third generation of Ephraim's children. Also the children of Makir son of Manasseh were placed at birth on Joseph's knees.ª

²⁴Then Joseph said to his brothers, "I am about to die. But God will surely come to your aid and take you up out of this land to the land he promised on oath to Abraham, Isaac and Jacob." ²⁵And Joseph made the sons of Israel swear an oath and said, "God will surely come to your aid, and then you must carry my bones up from this place."

²⁶So Joseph died at the age of a hundred and ten. And after they embalmed him, he was placed in a coffin in Egypt.

ª23 That is, were counted as his

NRSV

22So Joseph remained in Egypt, he and his father's household; and Joseph lived one hundred ten years. ²³Joseph saw Ephraim's children of the third generation; the children of Machir son of Manasseh were also born on Joseph's knees.

24Then Joseph said to his brothers, "I am about to die; but God will surely come to you, and bring you up out of this land to the land that he swore to Abraham, to Isaac, and to Jacob." ²⁵So Joseph made the Israelites swear, saying, "When God comes to you, you shall carry up my bones from here." ²⁶And Joseph died, being one hundred ten years old; he was embalmed and placed in a coffin in Egypt.

COMMENTARY

This epilogue portrays Joseph's final years, pulls together a key theme, and serves as a bridge to the next stage of Israel's story. Indeed, the reference to Joseph's bones pushes on to the land settlement (Josh 24:32; cf. Exod 13:19). The first reference to "Abraham, Isaac, and Jacob" presupposes the unity of the previous narrative. Joseph's death at 110 years provides an inclusio for this section (and with 48:28), while Joseph's "staying" (שׁב *yāšab*) in Egypt in v. 22 ties back to Jacob's "settling" in 37:1, completing the movement from Canaan to Egypt (cf. 47:27).

Joseph remains in Egypt along with the rest of Jacob's family, living long enough to see his great-grandchildren. They were born on his knees—i.e., claimed as his descendants. The future of his family, and hence the promises regarding posterity, relates to the rest of the family. At the same time, the length of time indicates that the family has stayed in Egypt generations beyond the famine, anticipating the hardships of Exodus.

When Joseph is at the point of death, he extends to his brothers (all are assumed to be alive) both a promise and a charge. Jacob had

never spoken the promise to his sons, except to Joseph in 48:21, though there are links in chap. 49. He assures them that God will *surely* visit them in Egypt (see Exod 3:16; 4:31; 13:19) and bring them out of the land of Egypt (see Exod 3:8, 17; 13:19) and into the land of Canaan, the land promised to their ancestors in the previous chapters. Egypt was not to be their permanent home. Joseph's words create the bridge to the next stage in Israel's story, just as it has been his actions in this story that have enabled the brothers to go into Exodus as a unified family.

Joseph also charges them that, after these events, they are to take his bones to Canaan (see Exod 13:19). He trusts his brothers to see to his proper burial, as together they had seen to their father's. He does not insist on a replication of his father's burial, but he links his future with that of his father and the rest of the family. According to Josh 24:32, Joseph was buried in Shechem. Joseph's death marks the end of Genesis, but the stage has been set for a series of events that will constitute Israel's family as the people of God.

THE BOOK OF EXODUS

INTRODUCTION, COMMENTARY, AND REFLECTIONS
BY
WALTER BRUEGGEMANN

THE BOOK OF
EXODUS

INTRODUCTION

T he book of Exodus is, according to tradition, the "Second Book of Moses"—i.e., the second book of the Pentateuch. This traditional formula refers not to Mosaic authorship but to the foundational character of the literature in relation to the unrivaled authority of Moses. The book of Exodus stands at the center of Israel's normative faith tradition.

RELATIONSHIPS WITHIN THE PENTATEUCH

We may identify three relationships within the Pentateuch that are pertinent to the book of Exodus.

1. The relation between the books of Genesis and Exodus is important but uneasy.[1] On critical grounds, it is clear that the community of the Exodus has no direct (historical) connection to the "ancestors" of Genesis. Nonetheless, the text itself gives considerable attention to that connection, which is theologically crucial. On the one hand, the God known in Genesis is only in Exodus made fully known by name (see 3:14; 6:2). On the other hand, the text is insistent that the old promises of Genesis are still operative in Exodus—promises made at creation (Gen 1:28; Exod 1:7), and promises of land to the ancestors (Gen 12:1). Indeed, those promises are the driving force that causes God to be engaged on behalf of the slaves (see Exod 2:24; 3:16-17; 6:8). Thus the connection between the two pieces of literature is promissory (i.e., theological rather than historical) but for that no less decisive.

---

1. R. W. L. Moberly, *The Old Testament of the Old Testament: Patriarchal Narratives and Mosaic Yahwism,* OBT (Minneapolis: Fortress, 1992).

2. The relation of the book of Exodus to the books of Leviticus and Numbers is very different. Insofar as these later books are the extended proclamation of the Torah, they simply continue the work of Moses at Sinai. They belong completely within the orbit of Moses' authorizing work and in fact constitute no new theme.

3. The relation of Exodus to Deuteronomy is again very different. Deuteronomy consists of a restatement of the Ten Commandments (5:6-21), which then receive a full and belated exposition that is placed in the mouth of Moses. There is enormous interpretive freedom in Deuteronomy, so that what we are given is what Moses could have said in a later, very different circumstance.

Thus the book of Exodus reaches in three quite different directions to gather together the main threads and themes of Israel's faith. As the focal point of all this literature, it is the force of the book of Exodus that makes the Torah (Pentateuch) a profoundly Mosaic book, relying primarily upon his authority.

THE DOCUMENTARY HYPOTHESIS

It is not necessary to review here the complex account of recent critical scholarship, which for the past two centuries has been preoccupied with the complex history of the literature that now bears the authority of Moses. Specifically, this complexity is articulated by scholars in "the Documentary Hypothesis," which identifies four major recastings (sources) of the material around four demanding theological crises. This hypothesis is a way of speaking in critical fashion (largely in nineteenth-century modes) about dynamic vitality in the ongoing development of the tradition. Current scholarship finds the hypothesis in its classical form less and less useful. This commentary makes very little use of the Documentary Hypothesis, though it is fully aware of the textual realities that have evoked the hypothesis.

Specifically, it has been necessary to recognize that the "Priestly texts" are of a peculiar kind, easy to recognize, with very specific ideological interests. I have not found any way to avoid the odd juxtaposition of the liberation narrative and the "sacerdotal" accent.[2] Acknowledging the juxtaposition, what has interested me is the way in which the final form of the text has been able to bring these very different accents into serious, sustained interaction.

MAJOR THEOLOGICAL THEMES

We may identify four major theological themes that order the book of Exodus and that provide focal points for interpretation.

1. Liberation. The "narrative of liberation" (chaps. 1–15) is primarily concerned with the transformation of a social situation from oppression to freedom. This liberation is indeed

---

2. George V. Pixley, *On Exodus: A Liberation Perspective* (Maryknoll, N.Y.: Orbis, 1987) 35 and *passim,* has used the term *sacerdotal* rather than the more conventional *Priestly,* escaping a bit the pejorative usage attached to *Priestly* and suggesting that this layer of tradition is a continuing angle of interpretation, rather than a late, "degenerate" form of faith.

a sociopolitical-economic operation that delegitimates and overthrows the throne of Egypt. The odd claim of this literature is that social transformation of revolutionary proportion is wrought through the holy intentionality of a "new God" (see Judg 5:8), whose name is known only in and through this wondrous happening.

2. Law. The meeting at Sinai (which continues through Num 10:10) is the announcement of God's will for all aspects of Israel's personal and public life. The God who liberates refuses to be limited with reference only to "religion." Three aspects of this proclamation of law may be noted. First, the giving of the Law is situated in a frightening theophany, whereby the holy God intimidates and threatens Israel (19:16-25). The purpose of the theophany, so far as the canonical form of the literature is concerned, is to ground law in holy authority beyond any human agent or construct. This Law is God's law! Second, the Ten Commandments, and only they, come directly from God's own mouth. This is an extraordinary phenomenon, an act of sovereignty that orders the world, and an act of graciousness whereby Israel need not guess about God's intention for it or for the world. Third, the rest of the laws in Exodus (20:22-26; 21:1–23:19; 34:11-26) are given by Moses, who is the designated and accepted mediator (20:18-21). That is, Israel has devised a stable human arrangement whereby God's will and purpose continue to be available.

3. Covenant. The proclamation of Law has as its purpose the making of a covenant, a binding relation whereby Yahweh and Israel are intimately, profoundly, and non-negotiably committed to each other. In this act, a social novelty is introduced into the world, a community founded on nothing other than an act of faith and loyalty.

Moreover, the present form of Exodus 32–34 is now positioned as a new or renewed covenant, after the nullification of the covenant of 19–24. The relation between 19–24 and 32–34 suggests that covenant is a once-for-all commitment. It is endlessly impinged upon by the contingencies of history, so that the covenant rooted in fidelity must struggle with the reality of infidelity. This dynamic, on the one hand, permits the savage warning of the pre-exilic prophets that the relation will end because Israel persists in disobedience. On the other hand, this same dynamic of fidelity in the face of infidelity permits the daring assertion in the Exile that the God who "plucks up and tears down" will also "plant and build" a new covenant people (Jer 1:10; 31:27-28). Thus the theme of covenant permits the terrible tension of judgment and hope already anticipated in 34:6-7 and asserted in pre-exilic prophets (e.g., Hosea), but worked out in the great prophets of the Exile—Jeremiah, Isaiah 40–55, and Ezekiel.[3]

4. Presence. The book of Exodus is concerned not only with an *event* of liberation, but with a *structure* that will ensure in some concrete institutional form the continued presence of God in the midst of Israel. This God, however, is not casually or easily available to Israel, and the emerging problem is to find a viable way in which to host

3. See W. Brueggemann, *Hopeful Imagination: Prophetic Voices in Exile* (Philadelphia: Fortress, 1986); Gerhard von Rad, *Old Testament Theology II* (London: Oliver and Boyd, 1965) 188-278.

the Holy. The second half of the book of Exodus is preoccupied with this problem and this possibility (25:1–40:38). Israel devises, through daring theological imagination, structure (tabernacle) that makes possible "glory" both as abiding presence and as traveling assurance (40:34-38).

These four themes converge to make the poignant claim that Israel is a profound *novum* in human history. It is a community like none that had yet been—the recipient of God's liberating power, practitioner of God's sovereign Law, partner in God's ongoing covenant, and host of God's awesome presence. This astonishingly odd community is, of course, made possible only by this incomparable God who dares to impinge upon the human process in extravagant and unprecedented ways (see 33:16).

LOCUS

The current view of scholarship is that the book of Exodus reached its present, final form during the sixth-century exile or soon thereafter, with the final shaping of the Priestly tradition. This judgment provides a chronological reference point for the literature. More important, however, this critical judgment also suggests a context in which to understand the pastoral intention and interpretive issues at work in the literature as it comes to us.

The exilic (or post-exilic) community had to practice its faith in a context where the primary guarantees of the Jerusalem establishment (both political and religious) had been terminated, and where foreign powers (Babylon, Persia) governed. The book of Exodus thus is to be understood as a literary, pastoral, liturgical, and theological response to an acute crisis. Texts that ostensibly concern thirteenth-century matters in fact are heard in a sixth- to fourth-century crisis.

This judgment that Exodus is an exilic document does two things. On the one hand, it requires a rereading of the main themes of the book. Thus *liberation* now concerns the freedom given in faith in an imperial context of a Babylonian or Persian "pharaoh." *Law* concerns a counter-ethic in an empire that wants to preempt and commandeer all of life. *Covenant* is a membership alternative to accommodation to the empire. And *presence* is a sense of energy, courage, and divine accompaniment in an empire that wants to "empty" life of such resources. In that imperial context, the book of Exodus becomes a counter-document that voices and legitimates the odd identity of this community in the face of an empire that wants to crush such oddity.

On the other hand, the identity of the book of Exodus as an exilic document suggests the interpretive vitality that belongs inherently to this text. Our own interpretive work, then, is not to reflect on an ancient history lesson about Egypt or about cult, but to see how this text, in new, demanding, and dangerous circumstances, continues to offer subversive possibilities for our future.

METHOD

The older critical commentaries (of which Noth's is a primary example) largely reflect and build upon nineteenth-century questions and methods.[4] They are especially concerned with the history behind the present text, both concerning what happened as "event," and how the text itself was developed and formed. This commentary is written in a context of great methodological ferment. It is increasingly clear that the older "critical perspective" is a product and example of the prevailing epistemological situation in the service of modernism. Any probe of these commentaries suggests how greatly our epistemological situation is changed by the receding of modernity. We are, however, only beginning to articulate new methods, none of which yet claims any consensus of scholarly support. This commentary seeks to make use of three emerging methods that are more congenial to the intellectual, epistemological context at the turn of the century, and to the context of Jewish and Christian faith communities in a postmodern context.

1. Literary Criticism. The newer "literary criticism" is no longer preoccupied with the history of hypothetical sources and documents, but seeks to focus on the internal, rhetorical workings of the text, assuming that the text itself "enacts a world" in which the reader may participate. Focus is not on external references, but on what is happening in the transactions of the text itself. This approach devotes great attention to the details, dramatic tensions, and rhetorical claims of the text itself. Such an approach requires great discipline to stay inside the world of text, and great patience in noticing the subtle nuances of the text. From a theological perspective, it operates with a "high view" of the text, suggesting that the world inside the text may be more real, more compelling, and more authoritative than other worlds construed behind or beyond the text.

While this method is everywhere important, Exodus 32–34 provides a marvelous example of its fruitfulness. In these chapters the demanding, insistent role of Moses over against God is noteworthy. Such a role requires that God should also be considered a character who can be impinged upon by action in the text, and who is placed at risk by the rhetoric and transactions of the text. Thus the decision of 34:10 that God will grant a new covenant to Israel results from Moses' insistent petition in v. 9, which in turn results from God's statement of available options in vv. 6-7. Moreover, in 32:10, Yahweh seems almost to be seeking Moses' consent or permission to "burn hot" and consume Israel. Such a dramatic treatment of God in the text does not serve well the interests of either conventional historicism or conventional orthodoxy. It does, however, let the text become a field of imagination in which the listening community catches a glimpse of an alternative world that lives in and through the text.

2. Social Criticism. "Social criticism" sees the text itself as a practice of discourse that is loaded with ideological power and interest. Texts are never innocent or disinterested, but are always acts of advocacy. Most especially, textual material about

4. Martin Noth, *Exodus: A Commentary,* OTL (Philadelphia: Westminster, 1962).

God is never "mere religion," but is discourse in which God is a party to social conflict and social interest.

In Exodus are many such voices of interest and advocacy; we will comment on two. First, in the narrative of liberation (chaps. 1-15), the dominant voice of the text is that of revolutionary criticism, which mounts a vigorous assault on every (Pharaonic) establishment of abusive power. The work of such revolutionary discourse is to expose the power of Pharaoh as null and void, and to assert that other social possibilities are available, if enacted with freedom, courage, and faith.

Conversely, in chaps. 25–37, 35–40, and more specifically in 28–29 and 39, the centrality of the Aaronide priesthood is established.[5] There can be no doubt that these texts are ideologically interested and that they work hard to establish the preeminence and monopoly of the Aaronide priesthood.[6] Thus even a text about presence is a form of political discourse about power. Theological terms and social forces are always and everywhere intimately connected and cannot be rent asunder. Indeed, to imagine that they can be separated is a maneuver that keeps real power masked in benign God-talk.

In the book of Exodus, the ideological force of the liberation narrative (1–15) and the monopolizing program of the Aaronides (25–40) are in profound tension with each other, one being revolutionary and the other consolidating if not reactionary.[7] It may be that Exodus leaves us with that tension. However, it is also possible that in its final form, the book intends to show the victory of the "liberation narrative" over the "pattern of presence." This may be subtly suggested in the fact that in 25–31 and 35–40, Aaron does nothing, but passively depends on Moses, who takes all the initiatives. Thus the priest of presence is derivative from the authority of the great liberator. More directly, Exodus 32–34 constitutes a massive critique of the Aaronides and establishes Moses' Levites as the faithful priests.

3. Canonical Criticism. "Canonical criticism" is based on the insistence that one gains very little by probing the complexity of the pre-history of the text. One must seek to read the text in its final, canonical form, taking the joints and seams in the text as clues to the intention of the text.

The final form of the book of Exodus follows a definite sequence from liberation to covenantal law to abiding presence. That is, the purpose of liberation is to live in covenantal obedience, in communion with God's glory. As Yahweh "gets glory" over Pharaoh (14:4, 17), the book of Exodus intends to wean Israel away from the glory of Pharaoh to an alternative glory encountered on the mountain of covenantal law. For Christians, that "alternative glory," a "greater glory," is found in Jesus (see 2 Cor 3:10-11). For the book of Exodus, the culmination

5. Ellis Rivkin, "The Revolution of the Aaronides," in *The Shapers of Jewish History* (New York: Charles Scribner's Sons, 1971) 21-41.

6. See Frank M. Cross, *Canaanite Myth and Hebrew Epic: Essays in the History of the Religion of Israel* (Cambridge, Mass.: Harvard University Press, 1973) 195-215; Paul D. Hanson, *The Dawn of Apocalyptic* (Philadelphia: Fortress, 1975); O. Plöger, *Theocracy and Eschatology* (Richmond: John Knox, 1968); and Morton Smith, *Palestinian Parties and Politics That Shaped the Old Testament* (New York: Columbia University Press, 1971).

7. See the statement on this ongoing tension between "the constitutive" and the "prophetic" by James A. Sanders, "Hermeneutics," *IDBSup,* ed. Keith Crim (Nashville: Abingdon, 1976) 402-7.

of glory in 40:34-38 is already in view in Exodus 1. In bondage, as the story begins, Israel has no glory and has no access to glory. By this sequence from liberation through covenantal encounter to assured presence, it is clear that the distinct political and religious themes of liberation, covenant, and presence cannot be kept separated.

In reading from liberation to glory, one may attend to the deep ideological tension present in Exodus. Thus the Mosaic accent on emancipation wrought through the destabilization and overthrow of Pharaoh is uneasy with the stable "presence" linked to Aaron. I suggest that 29:43-46 shows that traditionists are aware of the tension and deliberately establish the juxtaposition of the two. A canonical reading must take seriously a sociocritical reading.[8] The canonical reading does not nullify the sociocritical dimension of the text, but makes a second-level, intentional use of them. Only in this way is the final form genuinely "post-critical."

INTERPRETIVE ISSUES

The fact that the old memory can serve a later (exilic) community in a pastoral, liturgical way suggests that questions of the recurring contemporaneity of the text are not inappropriate, even concerning our own context as "contemporary." From the very beginning, Israel's authorizing text must always be reread and reinterpreted.

1. This text is understood as dynamic and under way, open to a fresh hearing. The mode of such a text is liturgical—i.e., it is used regularly in public worship, where texts are always and inevitably heard with enormously liberated imagination. In worship one does not ask historical-critical questions of when and where, nor does one ask scientific questions of rational possibility. For the moment, one agrees to a willing suspension of disbelief, giving oneself over to the voice of the text.

The Exodus text itself shows Israel practicing exactly that kind of imaginative freedom. Thus the "report" of the Exodus eventuates in the festival of remembrance, whereby new generations enter into the memory and possibility of liberations (12–13). In parallel fashion, I imagine many generations of girls and boys, upon hearing the "pattern of the tabernacle," imagine it, construct it, and at least for a moment "see" the glory that is there.

2. There is no doubt that the core claim of the book of Exodus is covenantal liberation. The text, and a long Jewish history of Passover celebration, has been a voice of alternative possibilities in the world. The structures, policies, and agents of oppression that have seemed ordained to perpetuity are here delegitimated and overthrown. The text permits the entertainment of a world that is different, which in turn permits different kinds of behavior. What happens in the text thus serves to make abused, oppressed persons subjects of their own history, able and authorized to take responsibility for their future. In liturgical celebration, one is not given strategies, policies, or procedures for freedom. Rather, what is given are imaginative possibilities in which the God who hears the cries of the abused Hebrews

---

8. Norman K. Gottwald, "Social Matrix and Canonical Shape," *TToday* 42 (1985) 307-21.

hears the cries of other abused persons as well and enacts promises that authorize and embolden.

There are, to be sure, current objections to the notion that the Exodus text is related to "liberation theology"; Fretheim offers three objections to such a construal of the material.[9] However, his objections are largely based on a caricature, infused by a kind of dualism that splits religious affirmation and social reality. Thus when Fretheim insists that the exodus is God's doing, and not "violent revolutionary activity," he fails to see that Moses is indeed engaged in such activity in the center of the narrative, and that it is precisely Moses' words and actions that delegitimate the Egyptian power structure. No one imagines that it is Moses alone who liberates. But if the text is taken seriously, it also is not "Yahweh alone" who liberates, for Moses, not Yahweh, must "go to Pharaoh." Fretheim's separation of religious idea from social practice ends with a kind of "idealism," an approach that Gottwald has decisively critiqued.[10]

Gottwald has rightly argued that Yahweh is a "function" of the revolution, even as the revolution is a "function" of Yahweh. The text precludes and denies a separation between the powerful intentionality of Yahweh and the determined action of disobedience that brings freedom to the slaves. The same ill-advised split is evident in Fretheim's second objection that separates "anti-God" activity from "political" activity. Such a split fails to see that God-talk is intrinsically and inevitably political talk. I propose, thus, that one can resist the agenda of liberation in the text only by a seriously distorted reading of the text.

3. Conversely, Fretheim is enormously helpful in suggesting that Exodus champions the theme of creation. The book of Exodus is indeed concerned with God's will for creation and with the destructive capacity of Pharaoh to undo creation.[11] In a context where one might think about "sustainable creation," this text is urgent. Just as Pharaoh defeats creation, so also the laws of Yahweh are intended as ways to honor and enhance creation.

4. Because this text refuses to remain "history," but insists on contemporary liturgical engagement, the contemporary interpreter is permitted considerable imaginative maneuverability, disciplined, of course, by the detailed specificity of the text. As hearers of this text, we are like youths entering into the Passover liturgy and hearing with our own ears the wonder of God's power over Pharaoh. Or we are like children in a ritual of covenant renewal, watching again the frightful theophany, frightened to death, hearing the law proclaimed afresh, claimed in innocent obedience. Or we are like children dazzled by the "pattern of presence," free to imagine how the glory comes and where it dwells, in our midst. Then, upon hearing the wonder of liberation and the poignancy of the law

9. See Terence E. Fretheim, *Exodus,* Interpretation (Louisville: Westminster/John Knox, 1991) 18-20. See also Lyle Eslinger, "Freedom or Knowledge? Perspective and Purpose in the Exodus Narrative (Exodus 1–15)," *JSOT* 52 (1991) 43-60; Jon D. Levenson, "Exodus and Liberation," *HBT* 13 (1991) 134-74; and in response, Walter Brueggemann, "Pharaoh as Vassal: A Study of a Political Metaphor," forthcoming in *CBQ.*

10. Norman K. Gottwald, *The Tribes of Yahweh: A Sociology of the Religion of Liberated Israel 1250–1050 B.C.E.* (Maryknoll, N.Y.: Orbis, 1979) 592-607.

11. Terence E. Fretheim, "The Plagues as Ecological Signs of Historical Disaster," *JBL* 110 (1991) 385-96. Fretheim has elaborated this suggestive theme in his commentary, *Exodus.*

proclaimed, and being dazzled by the presence, we break out in an innocent *Te Deum,* when it is all "finished" (39:32; 40:33)!

Scholarly niceties are not unimportant, but must, in the end, be mobilized for our own work of contemporary interpretation. The book of Exodus is now, for us in our reading, set down in a context of profane, self-indulgent consumer culture, in which technological capacity is matched and mobilized by self-serving ideology. In such a culture (either in market-driven licentiousness or in state-practiced brutality), human beings, human community, and human possibility are increasingly neglected and muted, if not nullified. In such a culture, the voice of Exodus sounds where it has courageous interpreters, who simply and uncompromisingly voice the alternative intention the Holy One has for creation.

The dramatic rendition of *liberation* takes place in a society where the question of liberation is little honored. Ours is increasingly a shut-down culture in which "freedom" is reduced to a range of "product choices," but in which the soaring of the human spirit, the dignity of the human body, and the health of the body politic are little cared for, honored, or financed. The question posed by the Exodus tradition is whether liberation is possible in such a shut-down world. The answer given by this Jewish voice of God is that God's own will to end the bondage status of the marginated is relentless and cannot finally be resisted.

The revolutionary possibility of *covenant* is resisted when power is closed, settled, and monopolized. Covenant, the text claims, is a revolutionary possibility. Against both authoritarianism and individual autonomy, the Sinai text enacts a covenant rooted in a holy authority that deabsolutizes every other authority. Moreover, in law and command the God of Sinai grounds human dignity and mobilizes the strong for the sake of the weak. Since those awesome days at Sinai, Jews and Christians have believed that a community of mutuality, rooted in the command of God, is indeed a social possibility and a social mandate.

The pattern for *presence* imagines God's awesome magisterial, life-giving glory being present concretely in the world. That "pattern" given us in the text makes its statement now in an utterly profane cultural context in which sacrament is reduced to technique and magisterial "signs" are driven out by mindless slogans and manipulative ideology. The text continues to ask whether sacramental power and presence are possible in an "emptied" culture.[12] This text asserts that God is willing and yearning to be present, but that presence requires a community of generous faith, which gives its best skills, disciplines, and goods for the housing of the holy.

When we depart the text of Exodus, our world is not miraculously transformed by our reading and interpretation. What is effected by our reading and interpretation is only the slow, unnoticed work of transformed imagination. The book of Exodus invites the reader to Passover imagination (i.e., counterimagination), rooted in the sufferings of our ancestors who cried out. It is powered by our ancestors of the Exile who treasured the alternative.

---

12. See George Steiner, *Real Presences* (Chicago: University of Chicago Press, 1989). Concerning an "emptied, shut-down" culture, see Herbert Marcuse, *One-Dimensional Man* (Boston: Beacon, 1964).

Now our reading, amid the suffering of the world, in the presence of exiles and of exile-producing institutions and policies, invites us to leave off the paralyzing fantasy of Pharaoh for the One who will be gracious.

THREE NEW TESTAMENT EXTRAPOLATIONS

Richard Hays has shown with reference to Paul that the Christian use of the Old Testament (OT) is done in rich and varied modes, but always with respect for and a careful reading of the OT.[13] This is clearly true of the New Testament (NT) use of the book of Exodus. The interrelations between the book of Exodus and the NT take many forms, and one cannot reduce that usage to any single interpretive principle of method. Each such usage attends carefully to the claim of Exodus, and each usage focuses on the decisiveness and finality of Jesus. Here I will mention characteristic interactions that refer to each of the three great themes of the book of Exodus.

1. Exodus Deliverance and Liberation. The entire Moses recital of deliverance becomes the center piece and primary material of Stephen's great sermon (Acts 7:17-44). One is especially impressed with the detailed way in which the Moses narrative is followed all the way from the birth of Moses in the midst of a death-dealing Egyptian regime (v. 19) to the "tent of testimony" (v. 44). The story of Moses is for Stephen the primary model for the work of the Holy Spirit and for the persecution of the prophets. (See a different casting of the same recital in Heb 11:23-29.)

2. The Covenant at Sinai. The Covenant at Sinai is clearly definitional for Christians. Paul, however, in relating "Moses and Sinai" to his own generation of Jews and the continuing community of Judaism, which did not accept Jesus as Messiah, speaks of a "new covenant" (1 Cor 11:25; 2 Cor 3:6; and the subtle argument of Romans 9–11). Yet for all his brave language of "new covenant," Paul can never cleanly and unambiguously declare that the old covenant is null and void.[14]

3. The Presence. The argument of Hebrews 7–10 depends completely on the Levitical-Aaronide theory of priesthood and presence in Exod 25–40. Again, a complete contrast is made between the once-for-all priestly work of Jesus and the priesthood of Aaron, which is said to be unreliable and insufficient.

In these several uses the New Testament writers are passionately focused on the distinctiveness and finality of Jesus. In our ecumenical and reconciling context, this supersessionism is awkward, but nonetheless evident in the text. It is equally clear, however, that for all such bold claims, the New Testament can never freely and fully escape the claims and categories of the Old Testament and the faith of Moses. Even when the claim of Christian displacement is most powerful, the truth of the Mosaic witness

13. Richard B. Hays, *Echoes of Scripture in the Letters of Paul* (New Haven: Yale University Press, 1989).

14. See the carefully nuanced discussion by Paul M. van Buren, *A Theology of the Jewish-Christian Reality. Part 3; Christ in Context* (San Francisco: Harper & Row, 1988); and Norbert Lohfink, *The Covenant Never Revoked: Biblical Reflections on Christian-Jewish Dialogue* (New York: Paulist, 1991).

persists in the New Testament. Thus, for example, the thematic use of Exodus in the Gospel of Mark argues for a sense of continuity between the narrative of the God of Exodus and the story of Jesus.

BIBLIOGRAPHY

The following books will be helpful reading:

Commentaries:

Calvin, John. *Commentaries on the Last Four Books of Moses (Arranged in the Form of a Harmony)*. Vols. II, III. Grand Rapids: Baker, 1979. A magisterial evangelical commentary, informed by the best criticism of his time, but undistracted from a theological focus.

Childs, Brevard. *The Book of Exodus*. OTL. Philadelphia: Westminster, 1974. An erudite, comprehensive commentary, the most important of this generation, which summarizes the critical tradition of scholarship and moves boldly to theological (canonical) issues.

Fretheim, Terence. *Exodus*. Interpretation. Louisville: Westminster/John Knox, 1991. An excellent commentary, reflecting newer methods of reading, offering rich suggestion for pastoral interpretation, committed to an accent on creation theology.

Greenberg, Moshe. *Understanding Exodus*. New York: Behrman House, 1969. A discerning statement that makes full use of Jewish interpretive voices, sensitive to the powerful theological voice of the text.

Noth, Martin. *Exodus*. OTL. Philadelphia: Westminster, 1962. The standard critical German commentary, the most influential of the last generation, largely concerned with the prehistory of the text.

Pixley, George V. *On Exodus, a Liberation Perspective*. Maryknoll, N.Y.: Orbis, 1987. A brief, but important, reading with a liberation hermeneutic alive to the sociocritical issues in the text.

Sarna, Nahum. *The JPS Torah Commentary: Exodus*. Philadelphia: JPS, 1991. A discerning, balanced interpretation, critically informed, but paying primary attention to the religious claims of the text.

Other suggestive studies:

Bloom, Harold, ed. *Exodus: Modern Critical Interpretations*. New York: Chelsea House, 1987. Offers a rich collection of classic articles, with special emphasis on Jewish contributions, valuable for theological sensitivity and artistic discernment.

van Iersel, Bas, and Anton Weiler, eds. *Exodus: A Lasting Paradigm*. Concilium. Edinburgh: T. & T. Clark, 1987. A collection of studies, suggesting the varied modes and contexts of a contemporary Exodus hermeneutic.

Walzer, Michael. *Exodus and Revolution*. New York: Basic Books, 1985. A judicious study by a political theorist of the ways in which Exodus has provided impetus for revolution in many parts of the modern world.

OUTLINE OF EXODUS

I. 1:1–15:21, The Narrative of Liberation

A. 1:1–4:31, Preparation for Deliverance
1:1-22, A New King Comes to Power
2:1-10, The Birth of Moses

EXODUS 1:1–15:21

THE NARRATIVE OF LIBERATION
OVERVIEW

This great narrative of liberation voices themes central to the faith of the Bible, the core of Jewish identity, and the categories in which Christians will subsequently articulate their faith. It concerns a process of social transformation wrought by the revolutionary intervention of God.

At the center of this narrative, as its key actor, is Yahweh, a God known provisionally in the book of Genesis, and now known fully by God's proper name (3:14; 6:2). This God initiates a social transformation and effects the power of a new social possibility in the world. The God of the Bible is in fact and in principle deeply embedded in this narrative, and cannot be fully known apart from this narrative.

The beneficiaries of Yahweh's powerful action are "Hebrews," a collection of marginated people who have no communal identity of their own and are powerless to change their social circumstance. In the telling of the narrative, however, these Hebrews are, or become, "Israel," a community for whom God cares and acts in unprecedented ways. Derivatively, it is clear that this story of liberation has a rich variety of social futures, for many other abused peoples, ancient and contemporary, have found this narrative to be their story as well.[15]

While the work of Exodus is clearly God's work, the human Moses is indispensable as an agent in social transformation. As becomes characteristic in the Bible, God's action in the world is undertaken by human agents who are summoned into Yahweh's dangerous service. The book of Exodus is a statement that establishes and celebrates the authority of Moses as the founder and generator of all things Israelite, including Israel's faith and freedom.

The dramatic power of the narrative is found in its presentation of Yahweh in deep conflict and combat with the gods (the legitimating powers) of Egypt (see 12:12). Thus this is the story of a *theological* triumph, whereby the God of Israel defeats all the powers of death that continue to stalk the earth with threatening authority.

That theological triumph, however, has socio-economic and political dimensions. The exodus can never be kept safely as a "religious event." Yahweh's conflict is not simply with Egyptian gods, but is with the Egyptian "social system," which is delegitimated and finally nullified through the process of this narrative. This critical dimension of the narrative has fed subsequent prophetic faith. As Michael Walzer has shown, this text has become the *fount* of revolutionary faith and practice right into the contemporary world.[16]

The structure of the narrative of liberation has dramatic force and power. It starts at a certain place (oppression) and ends at a very different place (liberation and celebration). It invites the listener to participate in that dramatic sequence from hurt to joy. The dramatic form of the narrative suggests that it has its function and use in liturgical recital.[17] This means that the text is not primarily interested in the historical facticity of the story, nor can the dramatic claim of the text be reduced to theological proposition. There is no secondary or alternative language by which this tale of God and Israel can be told. It must be kept, transmitted, and received precisely in its dramatic form.

In the modern world, with its singular preoccupation with the cerebral and the programmatic, we have failed to notice that the concrete, dramatic voicing of social truth and social possibility has enormous transformative power. The liturgical

---

15. See Bas van Iersel and Anton Weiler, *Exodus: A Lasting Paradigm,* Concilium (Edinburgh: T. & T. Clark, 1987). Jon Levenson, "Exodus and Liberation" *HBT* 13 (1991) 169, has agreed that when rightly construed, the exodus is "the paradigmatic instance" of liberation.

16. Michael Walzer, *Exodus and Revelation* (New York: Basic Books, 1985).
17. See J. Pedersen, *Israel, Its Life and Culture III-IV* (London: Oxford University Press, 1940) 728-37.

force of the text is now evident in many social revolutions in our time that begin in imagining an alternative. Moreover, as Freud understood, personal transformation happens in the same way, by acts of criticism and possibility that take the form of subverting narrative.

The exodus story is a narrative construal of reality in which the substance of transformative possibility and the form of narrative discourse effectively converge. This means, first, that one cannot communicate or "practice" Yahweh apart from this narrative in which Yahweh speaks and acts in characteristic ways. Second, it means that the text requires listeners (participants in the liturgy) to imagine and construe themselves through the actions of this drama, so that we know ourselves as offspring and children of this narrative. Third, this narrative is in profound conflict with other narratives by which we can imagine and construe ourselves. In our own Western context, one rival story this narrative defeats is that of individual consumerism. It is the intent of this narrative to evoke repentance, whereby one switches stories and so exchanges worlds.

This text is the release into the practicing community of a daring, subversive, alternative imagination. This narrative is a powerful and primary example of what is meant by the "dangerous" stories of the Bible. In its Passover celebration, Israel regularly practices that dangerous imagination that entertains new possibilities, and that delegitimates all that goes against the freedom and justice Yahweh intends.

EXODUS 1:1– 4:31, PREPARATION FOR DELIVERANCE

OVERVIEW

These chapters function as an introduction to the liberation narrative of 1–15 and prepare the way for the initial confrontation between Moses (with Aaron) and Pharaoh. This section of text is made up of a collection of quite different materials, expressed in a variety of different genres, but intricately woven together. Michael Fishbane has shown how these chapters introduce the themes that will recur in and dominate chapters 5–19.[18] We may identify four elements of text and assert four primary themes.

1. Chapter 1 characterizes the slave community for the story that follows. On the one hand, the narrator deliberately connects this community of slaves to the Genesis story, indicating that the promise made to the ancestors is still operative and decisive for this community of slaves. On the other hand, in a candid characterization of the present, the community is shown to be in the throes of brutal oppression at the hands of a death-dealing pharaoh. The narrator has deftly

juxtaposed the continuing power of an enduring promise and an exposé of current social helplessness. That juxtaposition creates a tension between past promise and present struggle, a tension that the ensuing narrative will adjudicate.

2. In 2:1-22, Moses is introduced. The narrator's interest in Moses is quite limited, treating only two matters. First, is the wondrous birth and survival of the baby who is in severe jeopardy (vv. 1-10). Cheryl Exum and James Ackermann have noticed the way in which the baby Moses survives, due to the courage and imagination of women who preserve his life from the death decreed by the mad king.[19] Moses is kept safe through the inscrutable protection of God, which in the narrative is credited only to the women. Second, the adult career of Moses is quickly traced through three social conflicts (vv. 11-22). In these brief episodes, it is evident that Moses has an

---

18. Michael Fishbane, "Exodus 1–4: The Prologue to the Exodus Cycle," *Text and Texture: Close Readings of Selected Biblical Texts* (New York: Schocken, 1979) 63-76.

19. J. Cheryl Exum, "'You Shall Let Every Daughter Live': A Study of Exodus 1:8–2:10," *Semeia* 28 (1983) 63-82; James S. Ackerman, "The Literary Context of the Moses Birth Story (Exodus 1–2)," *Literary Interpretations of Biblical Narratives,* eds. Kenneth R. R. Gros Louis et al. (Nashville: Abingdon, 1974) 74-119; and Ana Flora Anderson and Gilberto da Silva Gorgulho, "Miriam and Her Companions," *The Future of Liberation Theology: Essays in Honor of Gustavo Gutiérrez,* eds. Marc H. Ellis and Otto Maduro (Maryknoll, N.Y.: Orbis, 1989) 205-19.

acute concern for justice and a keen awareness of his own exploited people.

3. Only in 2:23–3:10 does Yahweh, the God of the promise, enter actively and decisively into the narrative. In 2:23, attention is turned from the life of Moses to the crisis of the people. This section is focused on the appearance and speech (theophany) of Yahweh, who now decisively intervenes to connect the life of Moses to the plight of Israel. The element of the narrative that has attracted the most attention is the appearance in the burning bush (3:1-6). But more important are the words spoken from the bush (3:6-10).

That speech includes the following elements: (a) a reiteration of the promise to the ancestors, (b) an acknowledgemnt of the Israelites' present suffering, and (c) a self-disclosure including the utterance of God's enigmatic name (3:14). These three elements all lead to the fourth climactic accent in 3:10: (d) Moses is abruptly summoned to a decisive and dangerous role in the life of Israel.

4. In 3:11–4:26, the call of Moses into the purpose of God for Israel is further developed.

This "call narrative" is reminiscent of the standard genre of call narratives, also utilized in the prophetic materials. The dominant feature of this section is Moses' fivefold resistance to the call. It is in response to Moses' resistance that God's self-disclosure is given (3:13-15), and the question of Moses' authority is posed, a question that will frequently recur in the book. In the end, Moses' resistance is overcome, and he is prepared to address Pharaoh (4:21-23).

This section of text thus lays out the large drama of God versus Pharaoh, which concerns the future of Israel. That large, almost cosmic, drama, however, focuses on the fearful human agent Moses—i.e., the great clash between Yahweh and the gods of Egypt depends on this human agent. Through these chapters we watch and wait while Moses prepares for the confrontation upon which everything depends. The driving energy of the narrative is from Yahweh. When the drama begins, however, it will be Moses (all alone except for Aaron) before the great power of Egypt. We are prepared for an unequal contest, the outcome of which is unclear, especially to Moses.

Exodus 1:1-22, A New King Comes to Power

NIV

1 These are the names of the sons of Israel who went to Egypt with Jacob, each with his family: [2]Reuben, Simeon, Levi and Judah; [3]Issachar, Zebulun and Benjamin; [4]Dan and Naphtali; Gad and Asher. [5]The descendants of Jacob numbered seventy[a] in all; Joseph was already in Egypt.

[6]Now Joseph and all his brothers and all that generation died, [7]but the Israelites were fruitful and multiplied greatly and became exceedingly numerous, so that the land was filled with them.

[8]Then a new king, who did not know about Joseph, came to power in Egypt. [9]"Look," he said to his people, "the Israelites have become much too numerous for us. [10]Come, we must deal shrewdly with them or they will become even more numerous and, if war breaks out, will join our enemies, fight against us and leave the country."

[a]5 Masoretic Text (see also Gen. 46:27); Dead Sea Scrolls and Septuagint (see also Acts 7:14 and note at Gen. 46:27) *seventy-five*

NRSV

1 These are the names of the sons of Israel who came to Egypt with Jacob, each with his household: [2]Reuben, Simeon, Levi, and Judah, [3]Issachar, Zebulun, and Benjamin, [4]Dan and Naphtali, Gad and Asher. [5]The total number of people born to Jacob was seventy. Joseph was already in Egypt. [6]Then Joseph died, and all his brothers, and that whole generation. [7]But the Israelites were fruitful and prolific; they multiplied and grew exceedingly strong, so that the land was filled with them.

8Now a new king arose over Egypt, who did not know Joseph. [9]He said to his people, "Look, the Israelite people are more numerous and more powerful than we. [10]Come, let us deal shrewdly with them, or they will increase and, in the event of war, join our enemies and fight against us and escape from the land." [11]Therefore they set taskmasters over them to oppress them with forced labor. They built supply cities, Pithom and Rameses, for Pharaoh. [12]But the more they were op-

NIV

¹¹So they put slave masters over them to oppress them with forced labor, and they built Pithom and Rameses as store cities for Pharaoh. ¹²But the more they were oppressed, the more they multiplied and spread; so the Egyptians came to dread the Israelites ¹³and worked them ruthlessly. ¹⁴They made their lives bitter with hard labor in brick and mortar and with all kinds of work in the fields; in all their hard labor the Egyptians used them ruthlessly.

¹⁵The king of Egypt said to the Hebrew midwives, whose names were Shiphrah and Puah, ¹⁶"When you help the Hebrew women in childbirth and observe them on the delivery stool, if it is a boy, kill him; but if it is a girl, let her live." ¹⁷The midwives, however, feared God and did not do what the king of Egypt had told them to do; they let the boys live. ¹⁸Then the king of Egypt summoned the midwives and asked them, "Why have you done this? Why have you let the boys live?"

¹⁹The midwives answered Pharaoh, "Hebrew women are not like Egyptian women; they are vigorous and give birth before the midwives arrive."

²⁰So God was kind to the midwives and the people increased and became even more numerous. ²¹And because the midwives feared God, he gave them families of their own.

²²Then Pharaoh gave this order to all his people: "Every boy that is born[a] you must throw into the Nile, but let every girl live."

a22 Masoretic Text; Samaritan Pentateuch, Septuagint and Targums *born to the Hebrews*

NRSV

pressed, the more they multiplied and spread, so that the Egyptians came to dread the Israelites. ¹³The Egyptians became ruthless in imposing tasks on the Israelites, ¹⁴and made their lives bitter with hard service in mortar and brick and in every kind of field labor. They were ruthless in all the tasks that they imposed on them.

15The king of Egypt said to the Hebrew midwives, one of whom was named Shiphrah and the other Puah, ¹⁶"When you act as midwives to the Hebrew women, and see them on the birthstool, if it is a boy, kill him; but if it is a girl, she shall live." ¹⁷But the midwives feared God; they did not do as the king of Egypt commanded them, but they let the boys live. ¹⁸So the king of Egypt summoned the midwives and said to them, "Why have you done this, and allowed the boys to live?" ¹⁹The midwives said to Pharaoh, "Because the Hebrew women are not like the Egyptian women; for they are vigorous and give birth before the midwife comes to them." ²⁰So God dealt well with the midwives; and the people multiplied and became very strong. ²¹And because the midwives feared God, he gave them families. ²²Then Pharaoh commanded all his people, "Every boy that is born to the Hebrews[a] you shall throw into the Nile, but you shall let every girl live."

a Sam Gk Tg: Heb lacks *to the Hebrews*

COMMENTARY

The exodus narrative, as constantly reiterated in the Passover liturgy, portrays an abrupt newness, a liberation wrought by God for this particular body of slaves. That abruptness, however, has important antecedents in Israel's memory. The story of the exodus begins with a brief, dense retrospective on the memory of Genesis.

1:1-7. This people about to be liberated have a memory and a genealogy. More than that, they have a remembered promise from the "God of

the ancestors." Thus the abrupt newness about to be narrated in the book of Exodus is framed in vv. 1-7 by the antecedents of genealogy, blessing, and promise. These people, regarded by the empire as nameless slaves, in fact have a powerful shaping pedigree. This treasured past carries power and potential that the empire does not recognize and cannot in the end contain.

The Exodus narrative begins with remembering. The last of the great fathers, Jacob, had come to Egypt with a great entourage, affluent, dignified, and honored by Pharaoh (Gen 47:7-12). He is indeed somebody of importance! Our narrative quickly lists his sons, born to two wives and two slave-maidens (see Gen 29:31–30:24). This is the family, blessed by God, that carries the promises of God.

In the listing of the sons, Joseph is not mentioned (vv. 2-4). His name is deliberately withheld. There were seventy persons (see Gen 46:8-27). The number bespeaks vulnerability and fragility. At the threshold of liberation, this family is small in number (see Deut 10:22), but then, this family in Genesis was in every generation small in number, vulnerable, and fragile. Such precariousness, however, is matched (or perhaps overridden) by the mention of Joseph (v. 5). His name was absent from the list in vv. 2-4, because it deserves to be mentioned separately.

Unlike his fragile brothers, Joseph's name bespeaks power, authority, and substance to the Israelites. Joseph, as his name indicates, is one who "adds" (יסף *yāsap*), who expands and accumulates. The name *Joseph* conjures Egyptian royal power, the power of surplus through coercive accumulation, the power of property and military might, the power of severe policy and ruthless enforcement (see Gen 41:37-57; 47:13-26). With Joseph established, Israel (Jacob) need have no fear. Genesis brings Israel to the horizon of Egypt, with all its gifts and, in the end, with its enormous threat.

The threat of the empire is hinted at in v. 6 and voiced in v. 8. Joseph could not last forever; he had died, as even powerful people do. With his death, the favored status of Israel, so deliberately fabricated, collapsed. The move from Genesis to Exodus reflects the flow of the generations, the drastic shift in the fortunes of this special people, and the fickleness of great power.

Verse 7 provides a summary to the book of Genesis. Because of the promise of God, the fidelity of Jacob, and the strategies of Joseph, who took care of his own, the Israelites were filled with vitality. Four verbs describe Israel's powerful position. Two of these verbs, *fruitful* and *multiply* are also used both for God's will for creation (Gen 1:28), and for God's promise to father Jacob concerning Israel (Gen 35:11). Like creation, Israel is to "be fruitful and multiply"; and now, says this narrative, it has happened! The third verb, *prolific,* characterizes teeming life, evidencing the

power of blessing in creation (see Gen 1:21; 8:17; 9:7). Israel, like creation, teems with abundant life. The fourth verb, *be strong,* suggests might and staying power. Moreover, the four verbs are reinforced by a double adverb, *exceedingly much*—i.e., "very, very." Israel is the arena in which God's verbs for creation become embodied and enacted.

1:8-14. We are scarcely prepared for v. 8 after the celebrative affirmation of vv. 1-7. Indeed, the narrative does not intend us to be prepared. Verse 7 left us with a sense of Israel's well-being, its preparedness for a good future. But now, abruptly and decisively, there is a new king with a short memory! He is not committed to any policies of his predecessors. His forgetting Joseph means that state commitments are abandoned; the privileges previously granted to Jacob's family are, in an instant, forfeited.

Now the new king speaks (vv. 9-10). He is the first one to speak in the book of Exodus. The first word is a royal decree addressed to the royal entourage, "his people," concerning the "sons of Israel." The king reiterates the sense of v. 7, "numerous and more powerful." The words that had been signs of blessing in v. 7, however, now come with the force of threat. The fact that Israel is fruitful and powerful makes it a threat to the empire. Thus in the reuse of the terms, the stakes are upped. The new king proposes to counteract the power of blessing under which Israel prospers.

The king worries that, because of its fruitfulness, Israel will be strong and escape. It is odd that the king's worry is escape, for he might have feared being defeated by them, especially since the term *strong* is used to describe them in v. 7. Defeat, however, is not the agenda. It is escape; they might "go up" (v. 10). The king's speech sounds the crucial Exodus word עלה (*ʿālâ*). The new king anticipates the exodus, the departure of cheap labor that the imperial government is no longer able to control.

Out of his anxiety, the new king generates a fresh policy of forced labor toward his feared workers. Two words are used twice to characterize imperial practice. Twice the Israelites are "oppressed" (ענון *ʿanôn;* vv. 11-12); twice the Egyptians are "ruthless" (עבד *ʿābad;* vv. 13-14). The forced labor practice whereby some are coerced to serve the ends of others is not mere abusiveness. Rather, it is an essential part of the great state building program. Great governments must build great buildings in order to produce permanent monuments to their power and greatness. Thus the slaves must enhance precisely the power they most fear, resent, and hate.

The program of the new king, however, is more pragmatic than abuse or self-aggrandizement. The forced labor is to build royal storehouses in the royal cities of Pithom and Rameses. Archaeological remains show evidence that the nineteenth dynasty in Egypt did indeed undertake such ambitious building projects, and the name of one city, Rameses, is also the name much used as a royal name of prowess, as in Rameses II or Rameses III. While a great deal of scholarly energy has been given to the specific dating and geography of these cities, such specificity should not mislead us.

The "storehouses" constitute not only grain policies, but are also metaphors for state policy, an elitist control of economic surplus and the means of production. Such storehouses are not an outcome of economic "good luck." They are, rather, evidence of a policy of coercion and accumulation. Already in Gen 12:10, the hungry Israelites know that Egypt controls a monopoly on food, while everyone else suffers from famine.

We are told in v. 12, however, that this aggressive state policy did not work. The more the empire abuses and oppresses, the more this slave community "multiplied and spread." This phrase repeats one of the verbs of vv. 3 and 8, *multiply,* and introduces a new term: *spread*—i.e., to expand over the land. Thus the narrative unobtrusively suggests that the power for blessing is at work in this community, and the empire is helpless either to slow it or to preempt it for its own ends.

The episode functions primarily to establish the fierce adversarial relationship of Israel and Egypt, and to show that disadvantaged Israel has a decisive advantage in the narrative. This rhetorical shaping of the memory, utilized repeatedly in the larger Exodus liturgy, serves to nurture a deep resentment of state power, a deep yearning for an alternative, and a treasured sense of distinctiveness. Moreover, the lack of historical, factual specificity about the king permits the account to become a paradigmatic presentation that, in every new generation of Israelites, can be reapplied and

reasserted against whomever is the current agent of abusive power.

1:15-22. Now the narrative becomes more concrete. The king of Egypt (still not named or even called Pharaoh) undertakes a policy of genocide against the slave population, clearly a self-defeating policy. This paragraph thus escalates the harshness of policies, commensurate with an escalation of anxiety.

In this narrative unit, the king speaks three times. The first time, he issues a command to the two midwives who assist in birthing among the slaves (v. 16). His command is that all boy babies should be eliminated. It is of peculiar importance that in this entire unit, "the Israelites" are not at all mentioned (unlike 1:9, 13). Now it is all "Hebrews." This term, with its cognates known all over the ancient Near East, refers to any group of marginal people who have no social standing, own no land, and who endlessly disrupt ordered society. They may function variously as mercenaries, as state slaves, or as terrorists, depending on governmental policies and the state of the economy. They are "low-class folks" who are feared, excluded, and despised. It is the common assumption of scholars that the biblical "Hebrews" are a part of this lower social class of *hapiru* who are known in nonbiblical texts.

The king's second speech is again addressed to the midwives (v. 18). The instruction of v. 16 has been ignored. Now the king, accustomed to obedience, conducts an investigation into this defiance of imperial command. Finally, he speaks a third time and issues a massive and programmatic command (v. 22). In v. 16, the instruction is only to the midwives, but in the third speech it is "to all his people" (as in v. 9). The deep fear of the outcasts has evoked a policy of systematic murder of precisely the babies who might be the most productive workers in the state system. The new policy is indeed irrational, suggesting that fear and rage have produced a deep insanity in imperial policy.

Over against the two royal decrees of vv. 16 and 22, the narrative juxtaposes a seemingly weak counterforce. The midwives, instructed in v. 16 to kill, are said to disobey the king (v. 17). The reason given for such disobedience is that they "feared God" more than they feared the new king, and for that reason they refused to participate in the state-authorized killing. When questioned about their insubordination, they do not explicitly bear witness to their faith in God. Rather, they attest to the surging power for life that is present in the Hebrew mothers, a power for life that is not known among the women of the empire. Hebrew babies, they say, are born with such vigor and at such a rate that the midwives simply cannot be present in time for each birth. In asserting their innocence, however, the midwives do not accuse the Hebrew mothers. The miracle of such births is beyond the fault of any human agent, for the fault is that of the God who will not be deterred by the new king. What counts is that Hebrew mothers are invested with dangerous, liberated power for life, which no one can deter.

The narrative sweep of chapter 1 leads us to the specifics of the exodus in three large concentric circles. In the most comprehensive circle (vv. 1-7), the horizon of the reader is fixed in the large promissory past preceding the book of Exodus. The lines refer to the ancestral memory—i.e., the stories of the fathers and mothers in Genesis 12–50. The verbs, however, look back even to the promises of creation. In this large look backward to treasured roots, the life-force of God's blessing is brought powerfully into the present of this narrative.

In the second, closer concentric circle (vv. 8-14), we are introduced to a concrete, albeit paradigmatic, unnamed character, "a new king." In uttering that phrase, the narrator brings the large memory of Israel immediately into the purview of their ominous oppression by Egypt. What has been a large, unspecified blessing is now transformed into the specificity of Israel versus Egypt. This narrative features the power of a state policy of abusive labor vis-à-vis the power of blessing operative peculiarly in the life of Israel.

In the third, closest circle of textuality (vv. 15-22), the narrative brings us into a quite specific conversation. The exchange is between a desperately fearful king and nervy midwives who are unafraid. The oddest reality in this raw conflict is that the people of Israel are never mentioned. The subject here is not an identifiable political community. It is "Hebrews," that floating mass of unacknowledged, unnamed humanity who are socioeconomic nobodies with not yet enough nerve or wherewithal to claim peoplehood. This is the unformed chaos of social reality that seethes against the ordered empire. Such images suggest that behind the political-ethical conflict is the reality of a class conflict, the center resisting the margin, the "haves" alarmed by the insistent presence of the "have-nots."

The exchange between the king and the midwives is ominous, touching the bottom of social reality. The midwives (whose names we know, Shiphrah and Puah) and the king (who is given no name) voice life and death respectively. Their encounter is a revisit of the drama of chaos versus order (Gen 1:2). Ironically, the champion of imperial order is, in fact, the agent of chaos, for he will terrorize the very possibility of life. The outcome of the confrontation is not certain. The threat of death now stalks this people of promise. Against such a force, there is only an old promise, and the mothering that persists among the outcasts, a mothering force that refuses to halt or capitulate.

REFLECTIONS

This narrative plunges the listening congregation into a world of danger, brutality, and desperation. It is a world into which a settled congregation does not easily go, a world largely screened out for a church that has romanticized the Bible. This text invites the congregation to reenter a world peopled by extreme characters—a frightened king, abused laborers, and defiant midwives. Or the congregation is invited to stand in the company of Jewish boys and girls at Passover as they are permitted to imagine and envisage a world of ominous, high-stakes conflict. Exodus 1 sets the context and shape for a Passover-imagined world.

1. The world in this text is one in which the power of blessing from God is assured and can be trusted. Throughout this narrative, which counts on the newness of Genesis, the verbs of multiplication, fruitfulness, and life are everywhere. Life is understood and affirmed as blessed, hallowed, and authorized by God to be a productive, fruitful place. That power of blessing, which is assured and affirmed, however, is received in deep jeopardy, for there is always some regime that wants to nullify it.

2. This is a world in which irrational destructive power is unloosed in the person and policies of the new king. There is here no romanticism about a world that is "user friendly" or that is "getting better." Moreover, that irrational, destructive power is not the work of a disturbed individual. It is, rather, brutalizing public policy that is legitimated by imperial ideology and exercises the appearance and force of rationality. Pharaoh's program is a corporate, systemic operation that has at its disposal enormous technical capacity and that relies on immense ideological authority, thus generating actions that are mere policy. The practitioners themselves do not perceive it as brutal, for it is all for reasons of state. The narrative is, in fact, an intense critical judgment against such brutalizing policy, exposing it for what it is. Thus the narrative invites the listening congregation to acute social criticism of such "policy."

3. This word of blessing and of destructive power focuses on the little community of promise, which is profoundly vulnerable in this deep dispute. The narrative is not interested in generalized or objective social criticism. Rather, it speaks from and for the powerless, who are victims of state power and who depend on the elusive power of blessing for survival. The narrative makes this little, unnoticed community the focus of our attention, as though the whole world depends on the possible survival of this community in formation.

4. This imagined world of the text shows us the destiny of Israel. It also pushes behind Israel to the inchoate reality of "Hebrews." That is, the text does not let the listeners stay with competing political identities, but goes underneath to the least-formed, vulnerable, and despised. It invites notice that the world is still ordered in terms of threat and violence, and still includes amorphous, ill-formed communities under threat.

5. In this dangerous mix of power and powerlessness, the narrative places Shiphrah and Puah. Amazing! They are nowhere else named or known, and certainly not celebrated. Yet we remember them by name. We remember these two discreet, defiant, cunning, mothering agents. At great risk, they counter genocide; in so doing, they bear witness to the mothering power of God, whose will for life overrides the killing, and whose power for life is undeterred by the death dispensed by the powerful.

6. The purpose of hearing such a text is not to identify the contemporary counterparts of "the new king," though that could be done. It is, rather, to see that the dynamic of this story is a reassuring and pervasive model for social relations. There is no doubt that the text reflects the endlessly jeopardized situation of Jews in a world bent on their destruction. The fact that the state often acts against Jews is a tale that runs all the way from the book of Esther to the modern Holocaust.

The New Testament parallel to this text is "the Slaughter of the Innocents," wherein Herod sets out to eliminate all the young boys who are potential rivals for power (Matt 2:16-18). Thus the story in Exodus has an opening to christological reality, for the baby Jesus is born exactly in such jeopardy, which persists until implemented on Good Friday in a state execution.

The sphere of Passover imagination, however, is not limited to the risk of the Jews or the destiny of Jesus. There are, in our own day, "little peoples" who, as a threat or an inconvenience for established power, are eliminated in wars and invasions, or are simply denied the right to live. In different parts of the world, different peoples play the role of "Hebrew." They are nonethnic, pre-formed, devalued folk who suffer at the hands of violent, legitimated policy.

Genocide can be blatant, as we have often witnessed. We need not neglect, however, the more "respectable" genocide wrought by our admired technology in which the destroyers never contact the victims. So-called "smart bombs" can take out an enormous civilian population without any need for hand-to-hand combat. The listening congregation may wonder about contemporary policies and practices that nullify the innocent.

The power of God is almost hidden in this text and is scarcely made visible. Nevertheless an undeniable "preferential option for the poor" is at work in this narrative. The power for life surges among the hopeless slave community through blessed women. Thus the issue of liberation surfaces inescapably through these "carriers of liberation." The birthing turns the hopeless into powerful, dangerous hopers.

A sermon on this text need not be confrontational. It would, rather, suggest that our common, uncritical reading of social reality ignores powerful class distinctions. That pervasive misreading screens out not only the hidden surprise of God's power for life, but also the faithful women strong enough to withstand genocide. This interpretation invites what may be an unnoticing, unacknowledging community (perhaps unwittingly allied with the policies of Pharaoh) to enter a season of Passover imagination, wherein one baby born overrides the brutalizing fear of Pharaoh.

On that mismatch between brutal power and the defiant miracle of birth that refuses genocide, Zora Neale Hurston comments: "The birthing beds of Hebrews were matters of state. The Hebrew womb had fallen under the heel of Pharaoh. . . . Hebrew women shuddered with terror at the indifference of their wombs to the Egyptian law."[20]

The capacity of the Hebrews to be indifferent to Egyptian law permits the exodus narrative to proceed. If they had submitted, there would have been no narrative of liberation, no Passover imagination, no gospel.

20. Zora Neale Hurston, *Moses, Man of the Mountain* (Chicago: University of Chicago Press, 1984) 11.

Exodus 2:1-10, The Birth of Moses

NIV	NRSV
2 Now a man of the house of Levi married a Levite woman, ²and she became pregnant and gave birth to a son. When she saw that he was a fine child, she hid him for three months. ³But when she could hide him no longer, she got a papyrus basket for him and coated it with tar and pitch. Then she placed the child in it and put it among the reeds along the bank of the Nile. ⁴His sister stood at a distance to see what would happen to him.

⁵Then Pharaoh's daughter went down to the Nile to bathe, and her attendants were walking along the river bank. She saw the basket among the reeds and sent her slave girl to get it. ⁶She opened it and saw the baby. He was crying, and she felt sorry for him. "This is one of the Hebrew babies," she said.

⁷Then his sister asked Pharaoh's daughter, "Shall I go and get one of the Hebrew women to nurse the baby for you?"

⁸"Yes, go," she answered. And the girl went and got the baby's mother. ⁹Pharaoh's daughter | **2** Now a man from the house of Levi went and married a Levite woman. ²The woman conceived and bore a son; and when she saw that he was a fine baby, she hid him three months. ³When she could hide him no longer she got a papyrus basket for him, and plastered it with bitumen and pitch; she put the child in it and placed it among the reeds on the bank of the river. ⁴His sister stood at a distance, to see what would happen to him.

5The daughter of Pharaoh came down to bathe at the river, while her attendants walked beside the river. She saw the basket among the reeds and sent her maid to bring it. ⁶When she opened it, she saw the child. He was crying, and she took pity on him, "This must be one of the Hebrews' children," she said. ⁷Then his sister said to Pharaoh's daughter, "Shall I go and get you a nurse from the Hebrew women to nurse the child for you?" ⁸Pharaoh's daughter said to her, "Yes." So the girl went and called the child's mother. ⁹Pharaoh's daughter said to her, "Take this child and |

NIV

said to her, "Take this baby and nurse him for me, and I will pay you." So the woman took the baby and nursed him. [10]When the child grew older, she took him to Pharaoh's daughter and he became her son. She named him Moses,[a] saying, "I drew him out of the water."

[a]10 *Moses* sounds like the Hebrew for *draw out.*

NRSV

nurse it for me, and I will give you your wages." So the woman took the child and nursed it. [10]When the child grew up, she brought him to Pharaoh's daughter, and she took him as her son. She named him Moses,[a] "because," she said, "I drew him out[b] of the water."

[a] Heb *Mosheh*   [b] Heb *mashah*

COMMENTARY

The Exodus story is not fundamentally interested in the person of Moses. It is not a "hero story." The story cannot, however, manage without Moses. In these verses, the quick sketch we are given of Moses' life moves quickly from the startling miracle of childhood survival (vv. 1-10) to the restless, violent urgency of adulthood (vv. 11-22). The story shrewdly conceals God in the life of Moses where that presence is not explicit or visible. Speaking of God's providential care, Calvin concludes, "All things which led to the preservation of Moses, were disposed by his guidance, and under his auspices, and by the secret inspiration of his spirit."[21]

We have just heard the harsh, massive decree of "the new king" (1:22). All male babies, the very ones who could do the slave labor of the empire, are to be drowned in the Nile River. Pharaoh misuses and distorts the Nile, which is characteristically a power for life, just as he misuses and distorts the lives of those around him.

In spite of this royal decree for death, which violates the "natural processes" of life, those processes continue; Pharaoh cannot stop them. There is a marriage (v. 1), and there is a birth (v. 2). These are two quick acts for life that intrinsically defy Pharaoh, even as the midwives had defied him in chapter 1. The marriage does not occupy the narrative for long (v. 1), and the birth receives only slightly more attention than the marriage (v. 2). An incongruity is immediately established. Death is decreed; birth nevertheless happens. The birth, an act of defiance of Pharaoh much like the births of

1:17-19, is also an act of raw danger. Commentaries observe that this narrative recapitulates something of the earlier narratives of Genesis. The nameless mother looked at the baby and saw "that he is a fine [טוב *ṭôb*] baby," the formula closely echoing the familiar verdict of creation, when God found creation "good" *(ṭôb)* (Gen 1:31). This birth is a new act of creation, an act of new creation. The world begins here again, precisely out of the chaos that "the new king" had decreed.

There are limits to hiding this baby, perhaps because the baby has become too big, too active, too noisy. The still unnamed mother, however, is up to this crisis. She makes a waterproof basket of bitumen and pitch. The narrative uses the term *basket* (תבה *tēbâ*), frequently used in the flood narrative. This new "ark" floats on the river, which was intended for his death. This unnamed baby reenacts the flood narrative; thus the basket, in the imagination of Israel, looks back to Genesis. The basket-ark is placed in the reeds (סוף *sûp*) at the edge of the Nile. The term used here for "reeds" is used subsequently in the exodus narrative to name the waters through which Israel came to liberation (13:18). The baby is at the edge of the waters of freedom, there before his people.

The narrative moves to the third crisis of the baby. Abruptly, the daughter of Pharaoh, also unnamed, comes to the river to bathe and finds the baby (v. 5). Was this discovery planned by the mother? Did Pharaoh's daughter bathe in that place regularly? Did she willfully bathe in the very river now burdened by her father with death? What will she do when she sees the baby? Will she replicate her raging father and kill the baby?

No, she sees the baby as the mother before her

21. John Calvin, *Commentaries on the Four Last Books of Moses Arranged in the Form of a Harmony Volume First* (Grand Rapids: Baker, 1979) 44.

had seen him. Her reaction to the baby is surprise and immediate recognition: "A Hebrew!" She "had pity" (חמל *ḥāmal*), or as the NIV renders, she "felt sorry." But the word is stronger than these renderings. She spared the baby, entering into an alliance with him, and prepared to be his protector. Moreover, the princess knows exactly what she is doing. She recognizes that the baby is a "Hebrew baby," a child from the slave community, a child under royal ban, a child under death sentence from her father—and she spares his life!

Princesses, even well-intentioned ones, however, do not tend to babies. They may knowingly save a baby in defiance of a royal decree, but a nursemaid must be found. All this time, watching at a distance, silent but palpably present, the unnamed sister of the unnamed baby takes initiative (vv. 4, 7). She volunteers to get help, and the help she offers is "from the Hebrew women," the same Hebrew women in 1:19 who are so vigorous and productive.

The response of the Egyptian princess is to issue two commands. To the unnamed sister, she says, "Go" (לכי *lēkî*). To the unidentified mother, she says, "Go [הילִיכִי *hêlîkî*] . . . nurse [הינקהו *hêniqihû*]" (v. 9) and she promises to pay. The narrative reports that "the woman" obeyed the princess. The woman is unnamed, but we know her identity; this is the mother. We have come full circle from "the woman" in v. 2 who conceived and bore to "the woman" in v. 9 who took and nursed. She is at the beginning and the end of this rhetorical unit, the key player. The jeopardized baby who had to be taken from the mother because of the royal threat is now safe again with the mother, because of royal sparing.

The narrative permits a considerable time to elapse between vv. 9 and 10. We do not know how much time, but it is the timespan for growth and maturation. The unnamed child is now old enough to leave his unnamed mother. She yields up her child to the care of the princess who had spared him. The future of the baby is now all in the hands of the princess, for the mother has finished her risky work and now disappears from the narrative. In this single climactic verse, Pharaoh's daughter now adopts him as her own son, and by implication makes him an Egyptian prince. Moreover, in the act of adoption, she names him Moses (v. 10), indicating that he is now fully in her orbit.

In this narrative, Moses is the first person named. The name is Egyptian, used as a part of many royal names in Egypt. The etymology given for the name, placed in the mouth of the princess, however, is of another sort. The term *draw* (משה *māšâ*) is not related to *Moses* (משה *mōšeh*), but is in fact a homonym. The term *māšâ* is used only in 2 Sam 22:17 (cf. Ps 18:16) wherein David says of Yahweh, "He drew me out of mighty waters." The strophe of the poem that includes this verse also includes other active verbs with God as subject, e.g., *delivered* (נצל *nāṣal* and חלץ *ḥālaṣ*) and *brought out* (יצא *yāṣā'*). Thus the term is used with reference to God's mighty acts of rescue. What may be a royal Egyptian name is transposed by the proposed etymology into Israelite praise for deliverance. Thus the rescue of little Moses from the waters anticipates a larger rescue to be wrought through the power of Moses.

REFLECTIONS

This narrative is framed by two notations that might mislead. At the outset, we are given a priestly genealogy (v. 1). At the conclusion, we are given an Egyptian name (v. 10). Neither of these plays an important part in the narrative, for the crucial action takes place between these notations.

1. God is not mentioned as a character or agent in the plot (before this, God is evident only in 1:20, in a rather understated way). There is no doubt that God is present but quite below the surface of the rhetoric. Although God will be visibly active in the exodus narrative to follow, here the mode of discourse is not unlike the Joseph narrative wherein the outcome of the story is governed by a God who never makes an appearance (see Gen 45:5-8; 50:20).

2. The main action is wrought through a series of three unnamed women, who are to be linked to the two midwives of 1:15-22. The key characters are "the daughter of Pharaoh," who spares; "the woman," who is the mother; and "the sister." Pixley observes that even in the Egyptian "den of death," "allies of life" are found.[22] The narrator has wrought a powerful interface between the hiddenness of God and the daring visibility of the women. One might conclude that the women act out of the hidden providence of God. Or, closer to the voice of the text itself, the women have displaced the providence of God and are the ones who assure the baby's future. They permit Israel's liberated future.

3. The narrative has unobtrusively injected class consciousness into the narrative. The tension in the narrative is not all focused on the baby. Rather, the action takes place between the daughter of Pharaoh—the powerful Egyptian—and the marginal Hebrews, mother and daughter. These latter women have been designated as enemies by the royal decree of the powerful new king. The three women, however, refuse to live out their assigned hostility to one another. In fact, they become unwitting allies, each playing an unexpected role in the life of the baby. It is a story beyond their ken, for the princess hardly wanted liberated slaves, and the Hebrew women scarcely believed liberation to be possible.

4. This is in fact a rescue narrative. While scholars often cite parallels to other birth legends, this story is not much interested in the birth, which receives only half a verse (v. 2*a*). What counts is the jeopardy of the child (because of the decree of 1:22) and the series of small, emergency maneuvers that move the baby from caring hand to caring hand, until he arrives at safety and is named and valued. The listener is left in astonishment at the rescue.

5. The story of Moses' survival is deeply embedded in the larger, communal memory of Israel. We have mentioned the verdict "good," the basket as an ark, and the reference to the watery reeds. Israel is able to hear in this story of a baby the story of its entire life. The last phrase of v. 10 sounds and anticipates the desperate petitions and the glad thanks of Israel for the many rescues made in its life.

6. This is a people who always live under the threat of chaos, always about to be inundated by the chaotic waters, helpless lest the Lord of chaos act and intervene. Thus the story of Moses is paradigmatic for Israel's life and faith. It not only anticipates the exodus narrative, but it also resonates with the deepest spirituality of Israel, a practice of plea and praise, of need and hope.

22. George V. Pixley, *On Exodus: A Liberation Perspective* (Maryknoll, N.Y.: Orbis, 1987) 7.

Exodus 2:11-22, Moses Flees from Pharaoh

NIV

[11]One day, after Moses had grown up, he went out to where his own people were and watched them at their hard labor. He saw an Egyptian beating a Hebrew, one of his own people. [12]Glancing this way and that and seeing no one, he killed the Egyptian and hid him in the sand. [13]The next day he went out and saw two Hebrews fighting. He asked the one in the wrong, "Why are you hitting your fellow Hebrew?"

[14]The man said, "Who made you ruler and judge over us? Are you thinking of killing me as you killed the Egyptian?" Then Moses was afraid

NRSV

11One day, after Moses had grown up, he went out to his people and saw their forced labor. He saw an Egyptian beating a Hebrew, one of his kinsfolk. [12]He looked this way and that, and seeing no one he killed the Egyptian and hid him in the sand. [13]When he went out the next day, he saw two Hebrews fighting; and he said to the one who was in the wrong, "Why do you strike your fellow Hebrew?" [14]He answered, "Who made you a ruler and judge over us? Do you mean to kill me as you killed the Egyptian?" Then Moses was afraid and thought, "Surely the thing

NIV

and thought, "What I did must have become known."

¹⁵When Pharaoh heard of this, he tried to kill Moses, but Moses fled from Pharaoh and went to live in Midian, where he sat down by a well. ¹⁶Now a priest of Midian had seven daughters, and they came to draw water and fill the troughs to water their father's flock. ¹⁷Some shepherds came along and drove them away, but Moses got up and came to their rescue and watered their flock.

¹⁸When the girls returned to Reuel their father, he asked them, "Why have you returned so early today?"

¹⁹They answered, "An Egyptian rescued us from the shepherds. He even drew water for us and watered the flock."

²⁰"And where is he?" he asked his daughters. "Why did you leave him? Invite him to have something to eat."

²¹Moses agreed to stay with the man, who gave his daughter Zipporah to Moses in marriage. ²²Zipporah gave birth to a son, and Moses named him Gershom,ᵃ saying, "I have become an alien in a foreign land."

ᵃ22 *Gershom* sounds like the Hebrew for *an alien there.*

NRSV

is known." ¹⁵When Pharaoh heard of it, he sought to kill Moses.

But Moses fled from Pharaoh. He settled in the land of Midian, and sat down by a well. ¹⁶The priest of Midian had seven daughters. They came to draw water, and filled the troughs to water their father's flock. ¹⁷But some shepherds came and drove them away. Moses got up and came to their defense and watered their flock. ¹⁸When they returned to their father Reuel, he said, "How is it that you have come back so soon today?" ¹⁹They said, "An Egyptian helped us against the shepherds; he even drew water for us and watered the flock." ²⁰He said to his daughters, "Where is he? Why did you leave the man? Invite him to break bread." ²¹Moses agreed to stay with the man, and he gave Moses his daughter Zipporah in marriage. ²²She bore a son, and he named him Gershom; for he said, "I have been an alienᵃ residing in a foreign land."

ᵃ Heb *ger*

COMMENTARY

The narrative makes an important leap in time from v. 10 to v. 11. In v. 10, Moses is a child who grows up (גדל *gādal*). In v. 11, he is "grown up" (*gādal*), now fully an adult. The narrative is divided into two locations, Egypt (vv. 11-15*a*) and Midian (vv. 15*b*-22).

2:11-15a. In the Egyptian scene, the narrator loses no time coming to the subject, "forced labor" (v. 11; cf. 1:11; 5:4-5; 6:6-7). When Moses went out, forced labor is what he saw, humans forcibly engaged in oppressive labor for the sake of the imperial government. Others might have seen other matters: royal splendor, extravagant living, well ordered society. But Moses saw only forced labor.

Verse 11 twice uses the term *brother* ("people," "kinsman"). In the first use, we cannot tell if "his people" are the slaves or the imperial overlords. Verses 1-10 make it possible for Moses to claim and

enact either identity. The second use resolves our uncertainty. It is a "Hebrew" who is "one of his kinsfolk." We now know whose side Moses is on.

Moses' intervention in the beating of the Hebrew produces three sub-scenes in quick succession. First, Moses intervenes to kill the abusive Egyptian (v. 12). Coote and Ord opine that this act of violence in the face of an oppressive, unequal social relation is the core event for Israel's founding memory.[23] The narrative uses the same word, for "kill" (נכה *nākâ*) that was used for the actions of the Egyptian against the Hebrew, "beat." The Egyptian is killing the Hebrew slave, and Moses inverts the power relation and does to the Egyptian what he is doing to the slave.

23. Robert B. Coote and David Robert Ord, *The Bible's First History* (Philadelphia: Fortress, 1989) 220-30.

The second sub-scene is "the next day" (v. 13). Two "Hebrews" (two of Moses' now embraced kinsmen) are fighting. Of course, the marginated dare not strike out at the master, but work out their unresolved violence on each other, an arrangement that reassures and maintains the position of the unthreatened, unassaulted overseers. A second time, Moses intervenes. Unlike the struggle of Egyptian versus Hebrew, slave versus overseer, this dispute is only between Hebrew slaves. In this intervention, Moses already asserts a judicial function in the community (see 18:13-27), for he identifies and addresses the "guilty one" (רשע rāšā').

Note well that Moses does not scold or judge or reprimand; he only stops the violence. He understands very well that any alternative future for the marginated Hebrews depends on solidarity, which is precluded by internal conflict. The "guilty one" predictably is not happy about the intervention, and promptly and daringly rebukes Moses (v. 14). He chides Moses for his presumptuousness, acting as ruler and judge when no one has authorized him to serve such a function.

Then, as an escalation of the rebuke, the one in the wrong lets Moses know that the killing of the Egyptian is no secret in the slave community. While the slaves might be grateful for Moses' intervention, their awareness of his killing the Egyptian is now used against Moses as a threat.

This challenge to Moses has its immediate and desired effect. The speech of the one "in the wrong" questions the authority of Moses, and at the same time threatens him by communicating that his attack on the Egyptian is well known. If his deed is known among the Hebrews, no doubt it is known (or soon will be) in the royal entourage. This threat (which also serves as a warning) abruptly changes the focus of the narrative. The real danger is not from the knowing Hebrews, but from the Egyptians who will also know.

The narrative thus turns to the third sub-scene (vv. 14b-15a). Moses' own pondering in v. 14 is reinforced by the verdict of the narrator in v. 15: Pharaoh knows. Again, Pharaoh is unnamed, but he is in any case the same new king who had issued the desperate decree of 1:22. Pharaoh now seeks Moses. Pharaoh intends to "kill" (הרג hārag). The verbs of this Egyptian episode are relentlessly violent and brutal. At the outset, the Egyptian "strikes" (v. 11), and at the end, Pharaoh seeks to "kill" (v. 15). In between, Moses "strikes" (v. 12), and is accused of murder (v. 14). The Egyptians kill, and the Hebrews are driven into responding brutality.

2:15b-22. In order to escape the killing reach of Pharaoh, Moses flees (v. 15b). His flight changes the venue of the story. We now begin the second scene of Moses' adult life, this time in Midian. We are not told anything about Midian, except that it is not Egypt. It is evidently a pastoral society, and it is free of the dangers, threats, and abusiveness of the Egyptian kingdom.

The narrator immediately situates Moses at a well. In a pastoral economy, a well is a place of well-being and sustenance. The pastoral opening of this narrative account in v. 15b is heightened in v. 16, with a notice that is almost predictable. In a pastoral economy, women invariably come to the well for water. The narrative introduces us to an appropriate "type-scene," and our imagination recalls the servant of Abraham meeting Rebekah (Gen 24:10-21), and Jacob meeting Rachel at the well (Gen 29:9-12). Almost incidentally, we are introduced to "the priest of Midian," but we are told nothing about him. At this point, his only function is to be the father of seven daughters.

The narrative permits the idyllic scene of Moses, daughter, and water to last for only one verse. That type scene, which holds a potential for romance, is immediately and violently interrupted in v. 17 with the arrival of the shepherds. The work of shepherds is to lead their sheep "beside still waters," but the only available water is at the well where Moses is. The shepherds are stronger than the daughters, so they prevail. The NRSV says that Moses "came to their defense," but that rendering of the Hebrew is weak. The Hebrew term is ישע (yāšaʿ); he "saved" them, he rescued them, and so their flocks had water. Moses intervenes powerfully, so that the weak are not deprived of what is needed for their life. Moses is clearly cast as a rescuer.

Now the action moves from the well to the habitat of the priest, the father of the seven daughters. His name is given only here as Reuel (cf. Num 10:29). He notices that his daughters' schedule has varied, and he inquires why. Their response is telling in two regards. First, Moses is identified in their answer as an Egyptian. This is not at all what we expected. In the preceding episode, Moses has clearly identified himself with the Hebrews and has visibly set himself against Egypt. Now, however, he has enough remaining marks of his royal station that this is how he appears to the daughters. This identification is telling, because it suggests that Moses is at a liminal moment in his life, moving to a new identity.

Second, Moses' action is described by the daughters with the verb נצל (*nāṣal*). He "snatches" the daughters from danger at the hands of the shepherds. Again the NRSV's "help" is much too weak. The use of *nāṣal* here echoes *yāšā* in v. 17. Moses is a powerful intervenor who has yet again entered into a dangerous situation on the side of the weak against the strong.

Reuel, the father, immediately recognizes that this "Egyptian" is a remarkable man and that his debt to Moses is very great. Now the story moves quickly. Reuel offers hospitality to Moses, inviting him to "eat bread"—i.e., to enjoy his household and to enter into solidarity with him (v. 20). Moses accepts the proffered hospitality. The narrative promptly escalates hospitality into marriage, and the marriage immediately eventuates in a son.

We can now see, as we arrive at v. 22, that this story has been moving quite intentionally to the name of the son, "alien." The term גרשם (*gēršōm*) appears to be a combination of the word גר (*gēr*, "alien") with the adverb שם (*šām*, "there"). The narrative, which culminates in the term *alien*, is reinforced by the final word of the narrative, *foreigner* (נכרי *nākĕrî*). Moses' powerful intervention has transformed him from a well-situated member of Pharaoh's household to a fugitive. His passion for the well-being of the Hebrews has made him a fugitive from Egyptian order and power. He is a hunted, unwelcome man. He has indeed become an alien in his own land.

REFLECTIONS

This narrative concerning Moses' formation as an adult is not much known or read in the church. We tend to skip directly from the idyllic birth story (2:1-10) to the account of the burning bush (3:1-6). Skipping over this material permits the narrative to be a rather romantic tale of religious experience under the hidden protection of God. This material in vv. 11-22, however, forces the narrative of Moses into the arena of deep social conflict, and of violence and brutality that are inescapable in an unjust society.

1. The narrative lets us see that the social reality in which Moses is formed and out of which he emerges is one of conflict in which he is deeply and riskily enmeshed. Moreover, that social conflict is not just because people are mean-spirited. Rather, the conflict concerns real issues of social, economic, and political power. Thus there is conflict between Egyptian and Hebrew over forced labor practices, between two Hebrew men over a "wrong" (רשע *rāšā*), and between daughters and shepherds over water, which is no doubt scarce. In each of these three cases, Moses intervenes on the side of the victim.

2. While this story focuses on the person of Moses, we should not miss the fact that the narrator operates with a larger, acute social analysis. It is, perhaps, too much to say that the narrative does a "class reading" of social power, but it makes unmistakably clear the enormous contrast between the powerful and the powerless, and shows that this contrast assures that social relations are marked by relentless and recurring violence. The narrative does not comment on the violence, but only voices it and lets us see it for what it is. Moreover, Moses' own activities are themselves acts of compensatory violence, effectively countering the violence of the powerful. This overriding ethos of violence does not permit us to romanticize rescue or salvation in the Bible, which regularly consist of an intrusion into cycles of violence taken at great risk, in order to permit a new pattern of social relations.

3. The story is structured as an interplay between Egypt and Midian. Egypt is a place of power, order, and affluence. It is also Moses' "home" in which he is homeless, and from which he must flee because of his passion for justice. By contrast, Midian is a pastoral society. The main point about Midian is that it is non-Egypt, non-imperial, non-stratified. There is no forced labor policy there. It is in this "other place" that Moses finds hospitality and, in the end, his true family and home. Midian is his chance for a new identity, but his vocation drives him always back to Egypt.

4. Like the geography of his narrative, Moses himself is portrayed as a man with something of a fluid and unsettled identity. In this account, no one calls him by name, except the narrator. On the one hand, the rebuke of the Hebrew man seems to identify him as another Hebrew who is reprimanded for acting presumptuously as an Egyptian (v. 14). On the other hand, late in the narrative, the daughters still perceive him to be an Egyptian. Presumably, Moses still had options and choices. Moses did not have to make the choice he did; had he not so chosen, he would not have had to flee to Midian. Thus his choices made from his passion for justice in fact bestow upon him the role of fugitive (*gēr*, "alien").

5. The series of choices through which this liminal character emerges culminates in his final characterization, "an alien am I" (v. 22). Moses never sets out to be an alien, but finds himself so, one choice at a time. While God is nowhere present in the narrative (as also in 2:1-10), it is clear that attention to the freedom and justice intended by God predictably culminates in being excluded as an outsider.

This characterization of Moses' adult life as an outsider has important christological overtones. One becomes an outsider by making choices to continue as savior on the side of the marginated, in order to break the cycles of brutality. It is no wonder that in the story of Jesus, the one who had "nowhere to lay his head" is finally executed "outside the city," almost completely abandoned. Jesus' story is one of choices that make him a feared outsider.

This role of the continuing outsider has important ecclesiastical overtones as well. Whenever the faithful community accepts a role as an intervener for the marginal in order to break cycles of violence, it invariably becomes a community of "resident aliens." The church does not need to give up its "imperial status" in the company of the Egyptians. But whenever it acts in its passion for "the Hebrew," it accepts its own fugitive vocation.

Exodus 2:23-25, God Hears Their Groaning

NIV

²³During that long period, the king of Egypt died. The Israelites groaned in their slavery and cried out, and their cry for help because of their slavery went up to God. ²⁴God heard their groaning and he remembered his covenant with Abraham, with Isaac and with Jacob. ²⁵So God looked on the Israelites and was concerned about them.

NRSV

23After a long time the king of Egypt died. The Israelites groaned under their slavery, and cried out. Out of the slavery their cry for help rose up to God. ²⁴God heard their groaning, and God remembered his covenant with Abraham, Isaac, and Jacob. ²⁵God looked upon the Israelites, and God took notice of them.

COMMENTARY

These three verses function as something of a pivotal marker, a transition point between the preliminary narrative of chapters 1–2 and the narrative of liberation that follows. The action of these verses occurs when the oppressive king dies.

Such an occurrence is not uncommon. When an oppressive ruler dies, everything comes unglued and there is an opportunity to reconfigure patterns of social power.

This readily observable political pattern, however, is matched by an even more powerful theological reality. The nullification of this pseudo-king makes room for the real king. The historical sequence and theological dynamic of these verses is not unlike the more familiar statement of Isa 6:1, which we may paraphrase: "In the year that King Uzziah died, I saw the real king." In times of social discontinuity, the kingship of Yahweh becomes powerfully active and visible.

After the framing phrase of v. 23, these verses are cast in two parts: the voicing of Israel and the response of God. The first speaker is Israel (v. 23). It is at the moment of the death of the king that Israel finds its voice. Of course, the voice of rage, resentment, and insistence may have been present in Israel, but stifled. A totalitarian regime can keep such voices silent for a long time. When, however, there is a hint of transition or a show of weakness, that stifled voice can sound with enormous force and energy.

We have not had mention of "Israel" since 1:13. Since that verse, the subject of the narrative has been "the Hebrews." Now, however, the narrative becomes theologically self-conscious and speaks of "Israel." Israel finds its voice and sounds its pain. It dares to engage in a public process of letting its pain have voice. When such pain is voiced, it takes on energy and becomes an active agent in the process of public power. Four terms, two verbs (אנח *'ānaḥ*, "groaned"; זעק *zā'aq*, "cried out") and two nouns (שועה *šaw'â*, "cry;" נאקה *nĕ'āqâ*, "groaning"), are used for Israel's speech, and twice the statement is reinforced by the phrase "from their slavery." The terms themselves are not exceptional. Together they constitute a characteristic vocabulary of those who cry out in rage, protest, insistence, and expectation concerning an intolerable situation. The two terms *groan* and *groaning* serve as an unfocused expression of distress. The other terms serve to summon help. None of the terms, however, is addressed to anyone in particular.

The focus of our reading need not be on the nuance of any particular term. It is much more important that Israel cried out at all. In the moment of crying out, of letting pain become public and audible, the slaves broke with the definitions of reality imposed by the policies and values of the empire. The empire characteristically preferred silent slaves, who present no social embarrassment or administrative inconvenience. Silence among the oppressed means that they have conceded to the oppressors the right to define reality.

The startling moment of this narrative is when the silence is broken. Israel cries out. We are not told why. No theological reason is given; the cry is neither God-induced nor God-directed. The beginning point of the exodus is rooted not in any explicitly theological claim, but in this elemental fact that human bodies can absorb so much, and then will rebel and assert and initiate. The crying, groaning bodies of the slaves found enough voice to say that their circumstance is not right, acceptable, or sustainable. In a quite distinct rhetorical maneuver, the narrator reports that God heard their cry (v. 24). The one who hears was not explicitly addressed. Perhaps there is something about this God that makes hearing possible. Perhaps this God is especially attentive to cries of oppression. In any case, now and only now, God takes a critical role in the narrative. Until now God has been mentioned only briefly in chapter 1 and not at all in chapter 2.

Only now, after the cries, is there a sustained statement about God. God is now the subject of four crucial verbs: God *heard* (שמע *šāma'*), God *remembered* (זכר *zākar*), God *saw* (ראה *rā'â*), and God *knew* (ידע *yāda'*). God heard their groaning. These were not groans addressed to God, but the hearing caused the remembering. The voicing of pain drives God back into the book of Genesis, to the ones to whom God is already committed. The memory is powered by those unambiguous carriers of the promise who are now named: Abraham, Isaac, Jacob. God connects present slaves and old promises. God has one eye on the old covenant oaths in Genesis. The other eye, however, is on the present circumstance of Israel in bondage. The text does not say, as the NRSV has it, "God took notice *of them*" (emphasis added). It is only, "God knew," without an object. We are left to imagine what God knew. God knew that these slaves were connected to the people of Genesis. God knew that promises were yet to be kept, requiring powerful intervention. God knew, because of old memories, abiding promises, present pain, and audible groans. God knew and so had to act. All of chapters 1–2 have built toward these powerful verbs that witness to God's powerful, sovereign purpose.

REFLECTIONS

The two points I mention are to be taken in reverse order. First, God is moved to care in decisive and powerful ways for this slave community. The good news is that God is motivated to act in a situation of terrible hurt. Priority should be given, however, to the second point: Israel's voice of hurt and rage. That is the catalyst for the entire Exodus story; it is the cry that evokes God's care.

It is difficult to imagine a more radical theological statement than this; it is voiced grief that mobilizes God to act in saving ways. This affirmation, when fully comprehended, challenges us on two fronts. On the one hand, this sequence of events challenges all talk about divine priority and sovereign initiative. The Exodus is not initiated by either the power or the mercy of God. God is the second actor in the drama of liberation. It is Israel's self-assertion that begins the process. That self-assertion is a remarkable matter, for the first task of every marginated community is to find its voice when it has had its voice, wind, and identity knocked out of it. God is a crucial agent in the story of liberation, but is second and not first.

On the other hand, this sequence of events goes against all of our refined notions of propriety and decorum. There is here no respectful distance from God, no waiting in silence, no trustful awe. The Exodus process begins with a raging cry of self-assertion. The action of Israel in slavery is not unlike blind Bartimaeus (Mark 10:46-52). His well-meaning contemporaries tried to silence him in his need, but he refused. He knew that silence could only mean continued disability. Thus, against a theology that leaves too much to God, and against an etiquette that prefers peaceable waiting, Israel is vigorous and bold, insistent and importunate. Israel shatters the docile silence, asserts its hurt and its hope. In doing so, it not only terrifies the empire, but it mobilizes holiness on its behalf as well. As a result of Israel's cry, God knows now that God must act.

This text is not perceived as overly urgent in most of our bourgeois congregations. If, however, this story is not only a concrete memory of a past time, but also a present paradigm, it might help us to hear differently the disruptive noise of those who cry out of their hurt and voice their insistent hope. The world of Exodus is where the holiness of God lives in staggering response to the hurt of the slaves. For both parties, Israel and God, there must be a voicing!

Exodus 3:1– 4:31, Moses Is Sent to Pharaoh

NIV

3 Now Moses was tending the flock of Jethro his father-in-law, the priest of Midian, and he led the flock to the far side of the desert and came to Horeb, the mountain of God. [2]There the angel of the LORD appeared to him in flames of fire from within a bush. Moses saw that though the bush was on fire it did not burn up. [3]So Moses thought, "I will go over and see this strange sight—why the bush does not burn up."

[4]When the LORD saw that he had gone over to

NRSV

3 Moses was keeping the flock of his father-in-law Jethro, the priest of Midian; he led his flock beyond the wilderness, and came to Horeb, the mountain of God. [2]There the angel of the LORD appeared to him in a flame of fire out of a bush; he looked, and the bush was blazing, yet it was not consumed. [3]Then Moses said, "I must turn aside and look at this great sight, and see why the bush is not burned up." [4]When the LORD saw that he had turned aside to see, God

NIV

look, God called to him from within the bush, "Moses! Moses!"

And Moses said, "Here I am."

[5]"Do not come any closer," God said. "Take off your sandals, for the place where you are standing is holy ground." [6]Then he said, "I am the God of your father, the God of Abraham, the God of Isaac and the God of Jacob." At this, Moses hid his face, because he was afraid to look at God.

[7]The LORD said, "I have indeed seen the misery of my people in Egypt. I have heard them crying out because of their slave drivers, and I am concerned about their suffering. [8]So I have come down to rescue them from the hand of the Egyptians and to bring them up out of that land into a good and spacious land, a land flowing with milk and honey—the home of the Canaanites, Hittites, Amorites, Perizzites, Hivites and Jebusites. [9]And now the cry of the Israelites has reached me, and I have seen the way the Egyptians are oppressing them. [10]So now, go. I am sending you to Pharaoh to bring my people the Israelites out of Egypt."

[11]But Moses said to God, "Who am I, that I should go to Pharaoh and bring the Israelites out of Egypt?"

[12]And God said, "I will be with you. And this will be the sign to you that it is I who have sent you: When you have brought the people out of Egypt, you[a] will worship God on this mountain."

[13]Moses said to God, "Suppose I go to the Israelites and say to them, 'The God of your fathers has sent me to you,' and they ask me, "What is his name?' Then what shall I tell them?"

[14]God said to Moses, "I AM WHO I AM.[b] This is what you are to say to the Israelites: 'I AM has sent me to you.'"

[15]God also said to Moses, "Say to the Israelites, 'The LORD,[c] the God of your fathers—the God of Abraham, the God of Isaac and the God of Jacob—has sent me to you.' This is my name forever, the name by which I am to be remembered from generation to generation.

[16]"Go, assemble the elders of Israel and say to them, 'The LORD, the God of your fathers—the

a12 The Hebrew is plural.   b14 Or I WILL BE WHAT I WILL BE
c15 The Hebrew for LORD sounds like and may be derived from the Hebrew for I AM in verse 14

NRSV

called to him out of the bush, "Moses, Moses!" And he said, "Here I am." [5]Then he said, "Come no closer! Remove the sandals from your feet, for the place on which you are standing is holy ground." [6]He said further, "I am the God of your father, the God of Abraham, the God of Isaac, and the God of Jacob." And Moses hid his face, for he was afraid to look at God.

7Then the LORD said, "I have observed the misery of my people who are in Egypt; I have heard their cry on account of their taskmasters. Indeed, I know their sufferings, [8]and I have come down to deliver them from the Egyptians, and to bring them up out of that land to a good and broad land, a land flowing with milk and honey, to the country of the Canaanites, the Hittites, the Amorites, the Perizzites, the Hivites, and the Jebusites. [9]The cry of the Israelites has now come to me; I have also seen how the Egyptians oppress them. [10]So come, I will send you to Pharaoh to bring my people, the Israelites, out of Egypt." [11]But Moses said to God, "Who am I that I should go to Pharaoh, and bring the Israelites out of Egypt?" [12]He said, "I will be with you; and this shall be the sign for you that it is I who sent you: when you have brought the people out of Egypt, you shall worship God on this mountain."

13But Moses said to God, "If I come to the Israelites and say to them, 'The God of your ancestors has sent me to you,' and they ask me, 'What is his name?' what shall I say to them?" [14]God said to Moses, "I AM WHO I AM."[a] He said further, "Thus you shall say to the Israelites, 'I AM has sent me to you.'" [15]God also said to Moses, "Thus you shall say to the Israelites, 'The LORD,[b] the God of your ancestors, the God of Abraham, the God of Isaac, and the God of Jacob, has sent me to you':

This is my name forever,
and this my title for all generations.

[16]Go and assemble the elders of Israel, and say to them, "The LORD, the God of your ancestors, the God of Abraham, of Isaac, and of Jacob, has appeared to me, saying: I have given heed to you and to what has been done to you in Egypt. [17]I declare that I will bring you up out of the misery

a Or I AM WHAT I AM or I WILL BE WHAT I WILL BE   b The word "LORD" when spelled with capital letters stands for the divine name, YHWH, which is here connected with the verb hayah, "to be"

God of Abraham, Isaac and Jacob—appeared to me and said: I have watched over you and have seen what has been done to you in Egypt. [17]And I have promised to bring you up out of your misery in Egypt into the land of the Canaanites, Hittites, Amorites, Perizzites, Hivites and Jebusites—a land flowing with milk and honey.'

[18]"The elders of Israel will listen to you. Then you and the elders are to go to the king of Egypt and say to him, 'The LORD, the God of the Hebrews, has met with us. Let us take a three-day journey into the desert to offer sacrifices to the LORD our God.' [19]But I know that the king of Egypt will not let you go unless a mighty hand compels him. [20]So I will stretch out my hand and strike the Egyptians with all the wonders that I will perform among them. After that, he will let you go.

[21]"And I will make the Egyptians favorably disposed toward this people, so that when you leave you will not go empty-handed. [22]Every woman is to ask her neighbor and any woman living in her house for articles of silver and gold and for clothing, which you will put on your sons and daughters. And so you will plunder the Egyptians."

4 Moses answered, "What if they do not believe me or listen to me and say, 'The LORD did not appear to you'?"

[2]Then the LORD said to him, "What is that in your hand?"

"A staff," he replied.

[3]The LORD said, "Throw it on the ground."

Moses threw it on the ground and it became a snake, and he ran from it. [4]Then the LORD said to him, "Reach out your hand and take it by the tail." So Moses reached out and took hold of the snake and it turned back into a staff in his hand. [5]"This," said the LORD, "is so that they may believe that the LORD, the God of their fathers—the God of Abraham, the God of Isaac and the God of Jacob—has appeared to you."

[6]Then the LORD said, "Put your hand inside your cloak." So Moses put his hand into his cloak, and when he took it out, it was leprous,[a] like snow.

[a]6 The Hebrew word was used for various diseases affecting the skin—not necessarily leprosy.

of Egypt, to the land of the Canaanites, the Hittites, the Amorites, the Perizzites, the Hivites, and the Jebusites, a land flowing with milk and honey.' [18]They will listen to your voice; and you and the elders of Israel shall go to the king of Egypt and say to him, "The LORD, the God of the Hebrews, has met with us; let us now go a three days' journey into the wilderness, so that we may sacrifice to the LORD our God.' [19]I know, however, that the king of Egypt will not let you go unless compelled by a mighty hand.[a] [20]So I will stretch out my hand and strike Egypt with all my wonders that I will perform in it; after that he will let you go. [21]I will bring this people into such favor with the Egyptians that, when you go, you will not go empty-handed; [22]each woman shall ask her neighbor and any woman living in the neighbor's house for jewelry of silver and of gold, and clothing, and you shall put them on your sons and on your daughters; and so you shall plunder the Egyptians."

4 Then Moses answered, "But suppose they do not believe me or listen to me, but say, 'The LORD did not appear to you.'" [2]The LORD said to him, "What is that in your hand?" He said, "A staff." [3]And he said, "Throw it on the ground." So he threw the staff on the ground, and it became a snake; and Moses drew back from it. [4]Then the LORD said to Moses, "Reach out your hand, and seize it by the tail"—so he reached out his hand and grasped it, and it became a staff in his hand— [5]"so that they may believe that the LORD, the God of their ancestors, the God of Abraham, the God of Isaac, and the God of Jacob, has appeared to you."

6Again, the LORD said to him, "Put your hand inside your cloak." He put his hand into his cloak; and when he took it out, his hand was leprous,[b] as white as snow. [7]Then God said, "Put your hand back into your cloak"—so he put his hand back into his cloak, and when he took it out, it was restored like the rest of his body— [8]"If they will not believe you or heed the first sign, they may believe the second sign. [9]If they will not believe even these two signs or heed you, you shall take some water from the Nile and pour it on the dry

[a] Gk Vg: Heb no, not by a mighty hand   [b] A term for several skin diseases; precise meaning uncertain

NIV

[7]"Now put it back into your cloak," he said. So Moses put his hand back into his cloak, and when he took it out, it was restored, like the rest of his flesh.

[8]Then the LORD said, "If they do not believe you or pay attention to the first miraculous sign, they may believe the second. [9]But if they do not believe these two signs or listen to you, take some water from the Nile and pour it on the dry ground. The water you take from the river will become blood on the ground."

[10]Moses said to the LORD, "O Lord, I have never been eloquent, neither in the past nor since you have spoken to your servant. I am slow of speech and tongue."

[11]The LORD said to him, "Who gave man his mouth? Who makes him deaf or mute? Who gives him sight or makes him blind? Is it not I, the LORD? [12]Now go; I will help you speak and will teach you what to say."

[13]But Moses said, "O Lord, please send someone else to do it."

[14]Then the LORD's anger burned against Moses and he said, "What about your brother, Aaron the Levite? I know he can speak well. He is already on his way to meet you, and his heart will be glad when he sees you. [15]You shall speak to him and put words in his mouth; I will help both of you speak and will teach you what to do. [16]He will speak to the people for you, and it will be as if he were your mouth and as if you were God to him. [17]But take this staff in your hand so you can perform miraculous signs with it."

[18]Then Moses went back to Jethro his father-in-law and said to him, "Let me go back to my own people in Egypt to see if any of them are still alive."

Jethro said, "Go, and I wish you well."

[19]Now the LORD had said to Moses in Midian, "Go back to Egypt, for all the men who wanted to kill you are dead." [20]So Moses took his wife and sons, put them on a donkey and started back to Egypt. And he took the staff of God in his hand.

[21]The LORD said to Moses, "When you return to Egypt, see that you perform before Pharaoh all the wonders I have given you the power to do. But I will harden his heart so that he will not let

NRSV

ground; and the water that you shall take from the Nile will become blood on the dry ground."

[10]But Moses said to the LORD, "O my Lord, I have never been eloquent, neither in the past nor even now that you have spoken to your servant; but I am slow of speech and slow of tongue." [11]Then the LORD said to him, "Who gives speech to mortals? Who makes them mute or deaf, seeing or blind? Is it not I, the LORD? [12]Now go, and I will be with your mouth and teach you what you are to speak." [13]But he said, "O my Lord, please send someone else." [14]Then the anger of the LORD was kindled against Moses and he said, "What of your brother Aaron, the Levite? I know that he can speak fluently; even now he is coming out to meet you, and when he sees you his heart will be glad. [15]You shall speak to him and put the words in his mouth; and I will be with your mouth and with his mouth, and will teach you what you shall do. [16]He indeed shall speak for you to the people; he shall serve as a mouth for you, and you shall serve as God for him. [17]Take in your hand this staff, with which you shall perform the signs."

[18]Moses went back to his father-in-law Jethro and said to him, "Please let me go back to my kindred in Egypt and see whether they are still living." And Jethro said to Moses, "Go in peace." [19]The LORD said to Moses in Midian, "Go back to Egypt; for all those who were seeking your life are dead." [20]So Moses took his wife and his sons, put them on a donkey and went back to the land of Egypt; and Moses carried the staff of God in his hand.

[21]And the LORD said to Moses, "When you go back to Egypt, see that you perform before Pharaoh all the wonders that I have put in your power; but I will harden his heart, so that he will not let the people go. [22]Then you shall say to Pharaoh, "Thus says the LORD: Israel is my firstborn son. [23]I said to you, "Let my son go that he may worship me." But you refused to let him go; now I will kill your firstborn son.'"

[24]On the way, at a place where they spent the night, the LORD met him and tried to kill him. [25]But Zipporah took a flint and cut off her son's foreskin, and touched Moses'[a] feet with it, and said, "Truly you are a bridegroom of blood to

[a] Heb *his*

the people go. ²²Then say to Pharaoh, 'This is what the LORD says: Israel is my firstborn son, ²³and I told you, "Let my son go, so he may worship me." But you refused to let him go; so I will kill your firstborn son.'"

²⁴At a lodging place on the way, the LORD met ₍Moses,₎ᵃ and was about to kill him. ²⁵But Zipporah took a flint knife, cut off her son's foreskin and touched ₍Moses'₎ feet with it.ᵇ "Surely you are a bridegroom of blood to me," she said. ²⁶So the LORD let him alone. (At that time she said "bridegroom of blood," referring to circumcision.)

²⁷The LORD said to Aaron, "Go into the desert to meet Moses." So he met Moses at the mountain of God and kissed him. ²⁸Then Moses told Aaron everything the LORD had sent him to say, and also about all the miraculous signs he had commanded him to perform.

²⁹Moses and Aaron brought together all the elders of the Israelites, ³⁰and Aaron told them everything the LORD had said to Moses. He also performed the signs before the people, ³¹and they believed. And when they heard that the LORD was concerned about them and had seen their misery, they bowed down and worshiped.

ᵃ24 Or ₍Moses' son₎; Hebrew him   ᵇ25 Or and drew near ₍Moses'₎ feet

me!" ²⁶So he let him alone. It was then she said, "A bridegroom of blood by circumcision."

27The LORD said to Aaron, "Go into the wilderness to meet Moses." So he went; and he met him at the mountain of God and kissed him. ²⁸Moses told Aaron all the words of the LORD with which he had sent him, and all the signs with which he had charged him. ²⁹Then Moses and Aaron went and assembled all the elders of the Israelites. ³⁰Aaron spoke all the words that the LORD had spoken to Moses, and performed the signs in the sight of the people. ³¹The people believed; and when they heard that the LORD had given heed to the Israelites and that he had seen their misery, they bowed down and worshiped.

COMMENTARY

3:1-10. After the formal, public notice of 2:23-25, we are taken back into the narrative of Moses. He has made for himself a new life in the service of his father-in-law, Jethro, presumably another name for Reuel in 2:18. Moses herds sheep and comes to new grazing land. The place to which Moses comes is Horeb, here called "the mountain of God." Elsewhere in the tradition, the same mountain is called Sinai, and even here the term for "bush" is סנה (sĕneh), likely an allusion to Sinai.

We are quickly put on notice that this narrative concerns no ordinary happening, and we must not expect to understand it through our usual categories. The narrative features an angel (messenger), a bush that burns but is not burned, and God's own voice. At the outset, we do well to recognize that this narrative is of a peculiar genre, a vehicle for the appearance of God's presence, God's first

presence in the exodus narrative. We need not and must not seek explanations for what happens according to the norms of other genre.

The theophany (i.e., "appearance of God") happens in two parts. First, there is the visible element (vv. 2-3). The better-known part of the appearance is the burning bush. But along with the bush a messenger appears. It is odd that the angel appears, but says nothing and carries no message. It is as though the visible presence in the narrative is designed only to get Moses' attention, which it does.

The second part of the encounter is the speech of God (vv. 4-6). This speech is quite extended, but our immediate concern is only vv. 4-6. The narrator is no longer interested in or troubled by the bush. What counts is the speech of God, which contains three elements. First, there is the sovereign summons. God calls Moses in a double summons, not unlike Gen 22:11 and 1 Sam 3:10 (v. 4). Moses' response, following convention, is "Here am I," indicating readiness to submit and obey.[24] This exchange establishes the right relation of sovereign and servant. This is the first hint we have that the life of Moses has a theological dimension, for the categories of his existence until now have been political.

Second, the commanding voice in the bush asserts an awesome limit, caused by the reality of God's holiness (v. 5). The key term is *holy.* The voice in the fire asserts that God's own preemptive presence is here. That presence transforms everything at hand, including the place and the conversation. The crushing, awesome reality of God's holiness requires respectful distance (cf. 19:23). The removal of sandals is an act of willing submission. The place has been transformed by the speech and presence of God. Moses is now taken up into the sphere of that awful holiness.

God now speaks a third time, offering God's own self-identity (v. 6). The formula of v. 6 connects the experience of Moses to the book of Genesis, and to the promises operative there (see 2:24).

Moses' response is abrupt and appropriate; he "hides his face." He would not look at God. Note well, this narrative does not suggest that God is invisible. Quite the contrary. God is visible, but must not be seen, for to see God is to impinge upon God's holiness and freedom. Thus Moses' act of submissive deference is undertaken so that God's sovereignty is not crowded. Later on, Moses will become daring and emboldened (33:17-23). But this is after a long, troubled history together.

The unit concerning the bush has much occupied commentators.[25] We must not, however, be overly inquisitive about these strange events. In fact, the theophany has no life of its own, but is only the launching pad in the text for what must come next. The voice in the bush, taken by itself, might be evidence of all sorts of religious manifestation, and has been interpreted in many, varied ways. We are told promptly, however, that this is not a generic religious presence. This is the nameable, identifiable voice of the God of Gene-

sis, the one who has made faithful promises, who "goes with," who guards fugitives like Jacob, who keeps outsiders like Joseph, and who births babies to barren mothers.

The God who summons (v. 4) and warns (v. 5) and discloses an enduring commitment (v. 6) now speaks more fully and characteristically concerning the slaves (vv. 7-9). Fretheim observes that this is Yahweh's first direct speech in Exodus, and is indeed prognostic for what follows.[26] In these verses, the tradition has placed in the mouth of God at the bush the standard credo that Israel in its Passover imagination regularly recites. Here it is God's own speech of self-disclosure that makes available to Moses (and Israel) all that needs to be known of God.

God's first self-announcement echoes the great responding verbs of 2:24-25. In v. 7, three of the verbs of 2:24-25 are reiterated, "I have seen . . . I have heard . . . I have known." (The fourth verb of v. 24, "God remembered," is absent here, but is implied in the formula of v. 6.) These are the three actions that God characteristically takes toward Israel, for Israel is the object of God's intense attentiveness. The verbal sentences here differ in important ways from those of 2:24-25. The first verb, "I have seen," acknowledges affliction, and instead of "sons of Israel" claims the slaves as "my people." The second verb, "I have heard," is roughly the same. The third verb, "I have known," ends cryptically in 2:25, but here has the object, "sufferings." That is, with all three verbs God acknowledges and engages the troubles of Israel: afflictions, cries, sufferings.

The fourth verb here is not paralleled in 2:24-25 and decisively advances the action: "I have come down." God not only knows, but God is now physically(!) mobilized to be present in the midst of the trouble. The verb articulates decisively what is crucial for Israel's understanding of God, which for Christians culminates in the incarnation—God has "come down" into human history in bodily form.

The verb *come down* is followed by two other verbs of enormous power: *deliver, bring up.* The first of these (נצל *nāṣal*) is the same verb used of Moses in 2:19 when he "snatches" the daughters from the destructive power of the shepherds. So

---

24. Calvin, *Commentaries,* 63.

25. See the overview of the passage by Samuel Terrien, *The Elusive Presence,* Religious Perspectives (San Francisco: Harper & Row, 1978) 109-12, together with full documentation.

26. Fretheim, *Exodus,* 53.

God now snatches Israel from the destructive power of Egypt. The second verb, *bring up* (עלה *'ālâ*) is regularly used for the exodus. This verb is followed by a double use of the term *land*, used both negatively and positively, "from the land" of Egypt "to the land" of promise. In this sequence of verbs, God's speech introduces the major elements in Israel's normative memory, succinctly anticipating the entire story from exodus to the promised land. In v. 8, God's speech fully anticipates the new land, which in every way contrasts the present land of oppression and bondage. The new land that God now promises is "good." It is filled with the power of blessing rather than curse, broad and nonrestrictive rather than confining like the place of the slaves, and filled with plenty, rather than the close rations that must have been the lot of the slaves. This characteristic expression of Israel's faith readily, and without effort or embarrassment, joins what is everywhere else divided: God/slaves, God's promise/land. The rhetoric of Israel easily holds together the power of religious claim and the needed resources for public life. This linkage redefines both God and human history, a connection that is the driving impetus for the exodus narrative.

The last part of v. 8 moves to the present occupants of the land of promise. The list of peoples is stylized and is not to be taken as an actual description of the land. The list is a foil for God's promise, in order to affirm that God's powerful intentionality will override all present power arrangements. (While this warrant for taking the land occupied by others subsequently has dangerous and destructive implications, those implications are not now on the horizon of the land-hungry who desperately believe they are destined by God for land.)

Verse 9 reiterates God's awareness from vv. 7-8, employing the verb *hear* and repeating the verb *see* and introducing yet another word for "oppression" (לחץ *lāḥaṣ*). God knows Israel's present circumstance and is prepared to counter it decisively. Thus 2:24-25 and 3:7-9 portray God as the only and crucial character in creating for Israel an alternative to the situation of oppression in Egypt.

Verse 10 makes a radical and decisive break, which must have stunned Moses when he heard it, and must have stunned Israel each time it was reiterated. What had been all pious promise now becomes rigorous demand: "Come." In one brief utterance, the grand intention of God has become a specific human responsibility, human obligation, and human vocation. It is Moses who will do what Yahweh said, and Moses who will run the risks that Yahweh seemed ready to take. The connection of God and Moses, of heaven and earth, of great power and dangerous strategy is all carried in the statement "I will send you." After the massive intrusion of God, the exodus has suddenly become a human enterprise. It is Moses (not God) who will meet with Pharaoh. It is Moses (not God) who will "bring out" (יצא *yāṣā'*) "my people." It is Moses who acts in God's place to save God's people. Again, this is the odd joining of God and human history. The joining is done, however, through the vulnerable, risk-taking body of Moses, on whom everything now depends.

It is no wonder that the narrative that follows shows Moses voicing a series of serious doubts and resistances to the summons, for he has been summoned to do a remarkably dangerous deed. There is, moreover, substantive reason for such resistance, especially in the case of Moses. The call and the imposition of the verb *yāṣā'* are a summons for him to return to the dangerous, conflictual arena of Egypt where his own identity is at risk and where he must frontally challenge the enormous imperial power of the status quo. Clearly, Moses' chances of success in Egypt are modest indeed, and his chances for survival are no better.

3:11–4:17. Moses offers five points of resistance concerning his awesome new vocation. Childs observes that each objection looks to a past reality, and each response of God moves Moses to a new future.[27] The first resistance is that he is a genuine nobody: "Who am I?" Moses' words anticipate the later resistance by Gideon (cf. Judg 6:15). Moses, like Gideon, is nobody important and lacks authority. In his resistant question, Moses juxtaposes his own insignificance to the great task of Exodus, reiterating the awesome verb *yāṣā'* and invoking the dreadful name of Egypt. God's response to Moses is equally massive and characteristic: "I will be with you" (3:12). Moses must go, but not Moses alone. This is the same answer later to be given to Gideon (Judg 6:16). Neither text says how God is

---

27. Brevard S. Childs, *The Book of Exodus: A Critical, Theological Commentary,* OTL (Philadelphia: Westminster, 1974) 72.

present. It is enough that Moses' person is fully invested with God's accompanying presence.

Moses' second point of resistance is more substantive and requires a more substantive response (vv. 13-22). Moses must know the name of the one who authorizes such a dangerous mission. The mission is dangerous not only for Moses, but also for the Israelites, who are asked to engage in massive civil disobedience against Pharaoh. Such a risk will require unambiguous warrant. Moses already accepts that he is dealing with "the God of your ancestors"—the promise-making God of Genesis (cf. 2:24; 3:6). But he wants something more explicit. He wants, as Israel will require, a personal name.

God's answer is extensive and complicated (vv. 14-16). The best known and most enigmatic part of the answer to Moses is the formula of v. 14: "I AM WHO I AM." Without pursuing the endless critical opinions about the origin of the formula, it is enough to see that the formula bespeaks power, fidelity, and presence.[28] This God is named as the power to create, the one who causes to be. This God is the one who will be present in faithful ways to make possible what is not otherwise possible. This God is the very power of newness that will make available new life for Israel outside the deathliness of Egypt. This reading of the formula is, of course, a theological interpretation, not a philological analysis. Whether by design or by accident, the name in fact tells Moses almost nothing. Moses still depends on more traditional formulations to flesh out what is suggested in this formula.

That fleshing out, as though recognized as needed by the tradition builders, is given in v. 15. The God with the enigmatic name is in fact the one already known in the Genesis narratives concerning the ancestors (see v. 13). Thus we come full circle to what Moses already knows in v. 13. Moses' knowledge of God has advanced little, but the old memory contains everything Israel needs to know. Everything is already present there, and now is freshly enacted in this encounter with Moses. In the formulation of v. 15, the name *Yahweh* is uttered as a summary of the longer ancestral formulation. The name *Yahweh* (יהוה) ostensibly derives from some form of the verb *to be* (היה *hāyâ*) so that God is the power for life,

the power of being, the power of newness. This strange formula leaves the door open toward "being"—toward "ontology."[29]

Childs vigorously holds to a "historical" understanding, seeing that in the *present* crisis, the formulation looks to the *past* in order to envision an utterly new *future*.[30] Israel, however, does not pursue the point, because even its flirtation with ontology is narratively framed. It is a God with a narratively framed name who will be present and decisive for Israel. This reading of the exchange with Moses insists upon the narrative quality of Israel's faith, which refuses to go behind the narrative or to bring the narrative to a question of abstract "being." What Israel receives of God can be appropriated only by the retelling of the stories in which Yahweh is embedded. Thus Yahweh is "told" and "retold" and is about to be retold again in the face of Pharaoh.

The response to Moses' question in v. 13 extends only through v. 15. In vv. 16-22, the narrative departs from the actual exchange with Moses in order to suggest a three-step strategy for the actual departure from Egypt.

In the first step, Moses is to recruit and mobilize the elders of Israel—i.e., the heads of the families and clans (vv. 16-18*a*). While Moses is the initiator of action, he does not act alone. Notice that unlike the Hebrews, who appear to be amorphous and without visible social structure, this narrative imagines Israel's already having in place a coherent, visible structure of leadership.

Moses' word to the elders reiterates the fundamental promise of God, already voiced in vv. 7-9. Moses' appeal is to the God of Genesis. (Notice that reliance is placed upon the formula of v. 15, to the neglect of the enigmatic statement of v. 14.) The God of the Genesis ancestors has taken note of the Egyptian situation. The acknowledgment of the situation of oppression is expressed with an infinitive absolute: "I have *really* visited you" (v. 16); NRSV, "given heed"; NIV, "watched over." (See the important reuse of this formula in 13:20, with reference to Gen 50:24-25.) This assurance is followed by a recognition of what has been "done to you" by the Egyptians and by the use of the term *affliction* ("misery").

---

28. See Dennis J. McCarthy, "Exodus 3:14: History, Philosophy and Theology," *CBQ* 40 (1978) 311-22.

29. See Childs, *Exodus*, 83, 88, on the issue of ontology in this formulation.
30. Ibid., 87-88.

This verse uses forceful language to sound again the assurance of 2:25 and 3:7: "I know." This is followed by the verb *bring up,* which was assigned to Moses in v. 10. Now it is God who will "bring up." Again, the Exodus verbs are stretched to include deliverance into the new land of well-being and abundance. That is, Moses is to announce that the God of Genesis is about to act to transform the situation of the present slave community. In v. 18, God adds a powerful assurance, "They will listen to your voice." They (the elders) will be persuaded to act in solidarity with Moses and to place themselves at risk even as Moses is at risk.

The second element in the strategy is that Moses with the elders will directly confront the king of Egypt (vv. 18*b*-19). The elders and Moses are to assert to the king that Yahweh is the "God of the Hebrews." This is the God who is allied with the amorphous, low-class work force. The slave community is to propose a work strategy to worship this counter-God three days' journey into the wilderness. This demand might be read in very different ways. Such a proposed three-day journey may be a ruse for escape, or it may be that such a proposed act of worship is a dramatic act that delegitimates the religious claims of the empire through the sacramental acknowledgment of a counter-God. This latter reading lacks the intent of a planned escape, but in the end holds a greater threat.

Whatever the intent of the demand, it will, of course, not be granted by the king (v. 19). If it is a ruse for escape, the king will not permit such an escape. If it is an intended assault on royal ideology, the king cannot risk such an assault. Neither the narrator nor God is naive about the stakes of the confrontation or about the possibilities for success. The narrator understands that power is not willingly or easily surrendered. It requires counterpower, "a mighty hand," to force the hand of Pharaoh (v. 19).

The third element in this strategy is that God's own powerful hand will be at work against the empire. This resolve on God's part anticipates the extensive plague narrative that follows. Two elements of God's resolve are worth noting. First, the verb for "strike" (נכה *nākâ*) is the same verb in 2:12 whereby Moses "struck" the Egyptian. Thus Moses' act anticipates the same action of

Yahweh against Egypt. Moses' enormous anger against abusive Egypt has penetrated even into the heart of Yahweh, who now also has enormous anger against abusive Egypt. Second, Yahweh resolves to do "all my wonders." The term *wonders* (נפלאה *niplā'ōt*) bespeaks the extraordinary acts of power that violate all present constructions of reality and make possible what the world thinks is impossible. Such acts are staggering ways of shattering the status quo, inexplicable except that they are credited to God's own inscrutable resolve.

As a result of these "wonders," the slave community in Egypt is to be placed in quite a new relation vis-à-vis the resentful Egyptians (v. 21). Likely, this affirmation is laden with heavy irony. The assertion made to Moses is that Israel will have "favor" (חן *ḥēn*) with the Egyptians, believing the threat of the "mighty hand" and "wonders" that intimidate and coerce Egypt.

The provision thus is cast as a grand euphemism. Each slave woman will "ask" for jewelry of silver and gold from her masters, but in fact the asking is taking, and receiving is seizing. The last phrase exposes the euphemism. Thus you shall "plunder" (*nāṣal* in the *pi'el*) the Egyptians." The text anticipates a forcible redistribution of wealth.

This extended digression in the mouth of Yahweh (vv. 16-22) is only loosely related to vv. 14-15, which respond to Moses' question in v. 13. Although vv. 16-22 are a quite distinct piece, they are placed here to function as an exposition of vv. 14-15. It is implicit in the ancestral and enigmatic name of Yahweh that promises are operative now, as in Genesis. The force of the promise will cause the elders to listen, will cause the king of Egypt to resist, and will cause the slave women to take plunder as they depart from slavery. In a less than direct way, all of these rhetorical elements testify to the dynamism and energy of this God, whose name is permeated with promise and with the capacity to work a new thing. Moses asked for a name; in response, he received a scenario of all that comes along with Yahweh's promissory activity.

Moses' third objection is that he fears rejection by his own people (4:1). The NRSV casts the protest conditionally: "Suppose they do not believe me." The Hebrew text, however, does not require such a construction. It may be a straight indicative statement: "They will not trust me."

The second negative, "They will not listen to my voice," is a direct refutation of the assurance given by God in 3:18. Thus in raising this objection, Moses refuses the very assurance God has given. Read psychologically, this exchange from 3:18 to 4:1 suggests that because the stakes are very high, Moses' anxiety is equally high. Read as a piece of strategic rhetoric, the protest serves to heighten suspense and to permit (or require) an even more extreme response from God.

Moses is no longer satisfied with verbal assurances from God, so God's response to this third objection is an act that makes its own irrefutable statement. The action is designed to show what Yahweh is capable of. The purpose of the wonders is to evoke belief (v. 5). The first wonder wrought in response to Moses' anxiety is to turn a staff into a snake, and then in the twinkling of an eye, to turn the snake back into a staff. This feat belongs to the genre of "wonder story" to make its own witness. We are offered no hint of the effect or persuasiveness of the wonder. Given Moses' own misgivings about his mission, we may speculate that the miracle is in fact aimed at Moses and not his doubting comrades, but the narrative provides no clue for such a notion.

It is immediately recognized that the first wonder might not be compelling (cf. v. 8). A second miracle is promptly worked, presumably because it will be more compelling. The structure of this miracle report parallels the first. Whereas the first required a stick-made-snake, now the sequence is leprous hand-restored hand. This is the God who can create weal and create woe (cf. Isa 45:7), who can accomplish life and death.

Yahweh, however, is mindful that even two such remarkable wonders may not be convincing. For that eventuality, a third possibility is left open: Moses will turn the water of the Nile into blood. This third wonder, held in abeyance, is remarkable because Moses is said to be the agent, whereas in the first two Moses is the benefactor and recipient of the wonder. The narrative assumes that such wonders will establish Moses' credibility in the eyes of Israel.

Moses' fourth objection concerns his own speech (4:10-12). Moses protests that he cannot speak effectively. This objection sounds more like the making of excuses. The response of Yahweh suggests irritation, if not indignation, as though Yahweh is losing patience with this endless sequence of objections (vv. 4:11-12).

Yahweh's response is in two parts. In the first part, Moses is asked two questions: Who? Who? The subject is not in specifically Israelite categories. Here speaks the creator God, the one who makes, orders, and dispatches all of creation. The topic concerns creation and endowment of all humanity (אדם 'ādām). The answer to the rhetorical question is brief and sweeping: "Is it not I, Yahweh?" Yahweh is the maker of heaven and earth, birds, fish, creeping things, and human persons with speech and sight and hearing (cf. Ps 94:9). Moses' pitiful excuse disregarded his own status as creature, and the fact that all of his life must be referred to the creator God who endows and invests human persons as is expedient for God. Moses is not autonomous or abandoned in his difficult calling. He need, therefore, have no anxiety about his speech.

On the basis of this sweeping assurance, God issues a command to Moses (4:12). The imperative is the same as the one issued in 3:10, "Go." The God who promised to "be with" him in 3:12 now reiterates that promise and accepts responsibility for Moses' speech. When Moses speaks, it will be God speaking.

Finally, a fifth objection is lodged by Moses (4:13-17). This statement may, perhaps, be a continuation of the same point raised in 4:10. While God has powerfully assured Moses of adequate speech, Moses is unpersuaded. This time in the response, Yahweh is angry (4:14), perhaps impatient and exhausted, but he concedes much of Moses' point. Moses wants another sent, and God agrees to send Aaron along with him. Fretheim terms this God's "Plan B," after Moses has refused "Plan A."[31] That is, Moses' resistance is taken seriously by God, who must adapt.

The actual role of Aaron in the Exodus tradition is more than a little problematic. As a champion and emblem of the priesthood, his entry into the narrative mostly appears to be an intrusion. Indeed, it might be that all of 4:13-16 is an intrusion to accommodate Aaron's entry into the tradition. In v. 11, Yahweh seems to have put to rest any problem with the speech of Moses, but now the concern has resurfaced.

31. Fretheim, *Exodus*, 53, 73.

When we take the text as it stands, without reference to any external priestly agenda, we may conclude simply that Yahweh has devised a procedure that honors Moses' anxiety about speech, a problem apparently not finally resolved in v. 11. Moses and Aaron are to share responsibility for speech, but their roles are by no means symmetrical. Aaron is to Moses as a mouth; Moses is to Aaron as a god (see 6:28–7:2). Moses retains unshared and unchallenged authority.

4:18-31. The remainder of chapter 4 is four brief rhetorical elements, all of which serve as a transition, moving Moses back from Midian to Egypt.

In vv. 18-20, Moses seeks permission from his father-in-law, Jethro, to return to Egypt. It is telling that Moses resolves to go back (v. 18) before he is commanded by God to do so (v. 19). We are not told here why he will go back. In the light of the preceding, especially 3:10, the reason given to Jethro in v. 18 is clearly less than candid. He receives an assurance from Yahweh (cf. Matt 2:20) and is authorized by "the staff of God," now an emblem of special power and authority.

Moses is now given instructions by God (vv. 21-23). First, he is told what to do (v. 21). He is to do "wonders" (מפתים *mōpĕtîm*). This is the first use of this term in our narrative, a term different from the one used in 3:12 and 4:9. This term also refers to extraordinary deeds that intrude upon settled, controlled life and generate new possibilities. Nowhere has Moses been instructed about the wonders that are in his power to perform. To be sure, in 4:1-9, we were offered three representative examples, but that is less than "all the wonders."

The mention of "wonders," oddly enough, evokes the first mention of God's resolve to "harden the heart" of Pharaoh. The juxtaposition is striking. The *wonders* are on behalf of Israel against Egypt; the *hardening* is against Egypt, but only indirectly, on behalf of Israel. God works both sides of the street. God does wonders that shatter all present reality, but God also sponsors resistance to the newness on behalf of the status quo. The juxtaposition makes perfectly good sense, even if we judge only by what is visible and conventional. Gestures and acts that violate the present and anticipate newness do indeed evoke resistance in defense of the status quo. Moreover, the response of resistance tends to be proportionate to the threat of the "wonder." As the pitch of wonder intensifies, so the intensity of resistance is sure to increase as well. The text shows that Yahweh intends to escalate both the wonder and the resistance.

The statement of the text, however, is more than a comment upon what is politically visible and conventional in the trouble evoked by revolutionary activity. The additional factor below the surface, and which changes everything, is the fact that the "hardening" does not just happen, is not merely chosen by Pharaoh, but is caused by Yahweh, who is the subject of the active verb *harden.* The narrator is willing to entertain the awareness that Yahweh operates negatively to heighten the drama, to make the clash between oppressor and victim as pointed as is bearable in the narrative. God's speech serves to give the conflict enormous dramatic scope, so that all experienced reality of the characters is gathered into this single momentous abrasion.

Second, Moses is instructed in what to say (vv. 22-23). The words to be uttered by Moses are not his own words, but Yahweh's. The words of Yahweh include three staggering affirmations. First, there is a dramatic embrace of Israel, who is given a stunning identity as firstborn. Previously, Israel has been called by the epithet "my people," but never by this distinctive phrase. In something like a formula of adoption, Israel is marked as the one best loved and most treasured. Pharaoh is put on notice that this oppression is serious business. There are no limits to how far this watchful father will go on behalf of this son. God's second statement is a retrospect. Referring to 3:18, God has asked leave for the "son" to worship the father—i.e., to enact in a liturgical way an alternative loyalty and alternative identity. There God suggests that Pharaoh would, of course, refuse, because he could not bear such a delegitimating gesture. This second statement suggests that Pharaoh would have one last chance, and he would refuse it.

The third statement of God looks back to the first statement, playing again on "firstborn." In the face of Pharaoh's refusal, Yahweh establishes a *quid pro quo:* Your firstborn for my firstborn. It might be contended that Pharaoh's firstborn is to be understood literally, whereas Yahweh's firstborn is a metaphorical reference and, therefore, not as unequivocal. Childs makes this unhelpful contrast between "metaphorical" and "literal," which dissolves the power of the rhetorical point.[32] The narrative, however, will allow no such contrast. The usage of "firstborn" for Israel is no less serious and concrete. This is a son valued like a son, and so Yahweh's statement is severe and uncompromising. That community that appears to be state property is in fact Yahweh's beloved heir. To misidentify them as Pharaoh has done inevitably leads to mistreatment. Pharaoh abuses because he misconstrues who this people is. The cost of such a misconstrual is very high.

Genesis 4:24-26 is among the most enigmatic verses in the entire book of Exodus. The episode is not framed in time or space, nor does it seem to be related to its context. Moses is "on the way," but to where we do not know. The narrative concerns a meeting that seems to happen at night. This is no ordinary meeting but sounds not unlike the meetings of Jacob at Bethel (Gen 28:10-22) and Penuel (Gen 32:22-32). The premise of the meeting is indeed odd: Yahweh seeks to kill Moses. The statement is barren and unqualified, and especially odd in the light of the preceding designation of Israel as firstborn. God seems to take action against those most treasured. The best we can do is to let the narrative witness to the deep, untamed holiness of God. In vv. 22-23, that wildness is aimed at the well-being of Israel, but here it is unleashed in all its destructiveness. There is no hint that God is testing or measuring Moses, but only that Yahweh operates in inexplicable, undisciplined freedom. To be present at all in Yahweh's history is a high risk venture, for Moses as well as for Pharaoh.

The response that rescues Moses from the terror of God is as odd as the terror itself. Zipporah, daughter of Jethro and wife of Moses, intervenes to rescue. Perhaps she enacts a very old, primitive rite that requires blood and is connected with sexual organs. She apparently circumcises her son in a crude way. Perhaps this is the son of 2:22, the one signifying displacement (גֵּר *gēr*). It may be that "feet" here is a euphemism for Moses' genitals, which are touched with the blood.

After her act, Zipporah issues a verdict, giving Moses yet another identity, very different from

the one suggested in 4:16. She asserts that he is a "bridegroom of blood," variously with the addition "to me" (v. 25) and "by circumcision." Moses' status is thereby changed, and by this curious act, Moses is made safe from the inscrutable threat of Yahweh.

It is conventional to take this narrative as an etiology for circumcision, to explain why (and how) the practice of circumcision came about in Israel. At one level, this may be so, but taken in context this seems an inadequate comment on the text. We should not forget the nature of this text and of the larger narrative. We are dealing with a story built around the resolve of this holy one, who will not be tamed or explained. Yahweh is set loose for the sake of Israel, but Yahweh is also set loose by the narrator in savage ways against Pharaoh and (here at least) in savage ways against Moses. The larger narrative is not solely about liberation. It concerns, rather, the claim that all parties, Israelite as well as Egyptian, must live in the presence of unleashed, unlimited holiness. There are provisional strategies for safety in the face of holiness, but none that will finally tame this dangerous God. One is struck at the end of this brief encounter with the peculiar juxtaposition of threat and safety, a resolve to kill and safety found only in a primitive act of blood and genitalia. But then, holiness is perplexing beyond all explanation.

Now Aaron makes his first active appearance in the narrative (vv. 27-31). He has been previously authorized as Moses' mouthpiece (4:13-17), but now he is directly recruited by God. It is important that he goes to meet Moses and not the other way round. The primary authority of Moses vis-à-vis Aaron is made clear. The meeting between the two is at "the mountain of God," at the place of ultimate encounter (cf. 3:1). The two are about no ordinary business together.

The mandate to Aaron in vv. 14-16 is for him only to speak for Moses. Here, however, Aaron has taken over authority not only to speak the words of Moses, but also to enact the "signs" (wonders) of Moses. The narrative itself, however, pays no attention to such a development or discrepancy. What counts is that the elders and the people believe. The entire discussion of vv. 1-9 had been preoccupied with bringing Israel to faith. Now this people is converted.

Coming to this faith is no small matter for

32. Childs, *Exodus*, 102.

Israel. What is believed is not simply that Moses had been the receiver of an appearance from Yahweh. What is believed is not simply that Yahweh intends to emancipate Israel. What is believed is that Yahweh has attended to (פקד *pāqad*) and has seen (ראה *rā'â*, "taken note of") Israel's oppression. No wonder they "bowed down and worshiped." No wonder they cast their lot with this new God whose name was not even known a chapter ago.

This act of worship is not a frivolous act of religiosity or piety. It is, rather, an extraordinary decision to define authority in a certain way and to embrace a specific view about public reality. The act of worship, already rejected and refused by Pharaoh (cf. 3:19; 4:23), was an act of enormous political courage as well as social credulity. The Yahweh now embraced by Israel is in every way contrasted with Pharaoh. Yahweh is the God who has seen, known, heard, remembered, and come down. This God is so unlike the king of Egypt, who has noticed nothing of the suffering, who has heard nothing of the protest, who has known nothing of their anguish, who has remembered nothing of old promises, and who has never come down to relieve.

This narrative witnesses to possibilities outside imperial totalism. The "signs" are hopes and affirmations that there is life beyond the empire. The narrative invites the people around Moses and Aaron to a high-risk venture, to trust in the God who gives signs, reveals a name, threatens Pharaoh, and even assaults Moses. This trust is no casual undertaking, but it is a formidable act of letting life start from a different point toward a different possibility.

REFLECTIONS

1. This extended narrative invites reflection upon the nature of vocation, and the power of "call" in the life of faith. An uncalled life is an autonomous existence in which there is no intrusion, disruption, or redefinition, no appearance or utterance of the Holy. We may imagine in our autonomous existence, moreover, that no one knows our name until we announce it, and no one requires anything of us except that for which we volunteer. The life of Moses in this narrative, as the lives of all people who live in this narrative of faith, is not autonomous. There is this One who knows and calls by name, even while we imagine we are unknown and unsummoned.

2. The resolve of Yahweh to transform, to let the oppressed go free, is met by Moses' determined resistance. Moses offers reasons, alibis, and excuses against the call of Yahweh, but he never goes behind these excuses to state the reason for his reluctance and refusal. We are left to conclude that Moses understands immediately and intuitively that this summons from the God of promise and liberation is a threat to his very life. So it is with God's call. In our time, the notion of call has often been trivialized, institutionalized, and rendered innocuous as bland calls to "obedience" and to "ministry." Moses, however, knows better than this. A right sense of call (and its danger) derives from a right sense of Yahweh's intention. And when the call of Yahweh is made safe through trivialization (which Moses refuses to do), it is because Yahweh's intention has already been distorted and domesticated.

Moses' excuses are altogether reasonable, the kind anyone might make who understands the risks at hand. In the end, however, the narrative is not much interested in his resistance. Yahweh does not find his excuses compelling, nor does the narrator. The narrative does not answer or refute the reasons of Moses, but simply overrides them with a more vigorous assertion of Yahweh's intentionality, which in fact dismisses Moses' reluctance as unacceptable. Thus Moses' sense of his own inadequacy (3:11) is not met with an assurance of his adequacy, but with an assertion of Yahweh as the God who will be present (3:12). Moses wants to know the name (3:13), but all he receives is a formula already known (3:15; cf. v. 6), and an enigma (3:14) that yields no name at all.

Moses' worry about disbelief on the part of Israel (4:1) is countered by an assertion that Moses will, as he acts in courage, have resources he does not yet know he has (4:2-7). But his possession of these resources will not be evident until he is at risk in his ominous vocation. And even these stunning acts of power are his only by the assurance of God, so that God's sign overpowers the unfaith of Israel.

Moses' protest about poor speech (4:10) is not answered by an assurance of good speech, but by an assurance that Yahweh presides over speech and gives tongues as they are needed (4:11-14). And even the granting of Aaron as spokesperson in response (4:14-17) to the fifth objection (4:13) gives Moses no slack, for he is still the "point man" in the confrontation to come.

This exchange over five objections and five responses produces a powerful drama of vocation and resistance (3:11–4:17). In the end, Moses exercises no freedom of choice, but is compelled by the power and resolve of Yahweh, which is relentless and unaccommodating. The work and character of this human life are settled in God's own intention, and Moses has no vote or voice in the shape of his future.

3. Yahweh's resolve is not just that of a political sovereign (though it is that), but is also the passion of a parent who will see about the honor and well-being of the beloved heir and firstborn. Thus the great political issue of Exodus is given familial intensity. The danger invited by Pharaoh's politics of oppression concerns not simply politics, but Pharaoh's own most intimate treasure, his crown prince. No one and nothing is safe that stands against Yahweh's resolve to act on behalf of this enslaved, oppressed people. It should not surprise us that the God who has been relentless with Moses (3:11–4:17) should be uncompromising in the world of Pharaoh (4:22-23). Yahweh is now playing for keeps, the way only a treasuring, concerned parent can care.

We might reflect on how odd and unlikely this move to familial images is. The anticipated confrontation between lordly Pharaoh and frightened Moses is so unfair and one-sided. Except, of course, that Moses is not on his own, but is simply the voice and agent of this sovereign whom Pharaoh will not acknowledge (5:2), but before whom he must eventually yield (12:31-32). The terrible challenge to Pharaoh and the public outcome of the narrative anticipate the way in which this Easter God will subsequently challenge and defeat the powers of chaos and death in the world. Moses, it turns out, is a tool of Yahweh in that deep, dangerous conflict between fathers over firstborn sons, with its assured outcome in emancipation for Israel and dread death for Egypt (cf. 14:30-31).

4. In the enigmatic account of 4:24-26, we are given a glimpse of Yahweh in raw and devastating power. In these verses, there is nothing of blessing or promise, nothing of liberation, not even an effort to give assurance to Moses. We are at the end of the narrative, and Moses is now on his way in obedience (4:18-20), the very obedience he had so long resisted (3:11–4:17). Yahweh has prevailed, and Moses has yielded.

Nonetheless, in this odd account, Yahweh seeks to kill the very one who has just been recruited for this singular work of emancipation. Whatever may have been the earlier function of this text in terms of the institution of circumcision, now in this locus, we are given to see Yahweh in dread, inexplicable holiness, enemy and threat even to this called one. Yahweh will not finally be thematized even in a narrative of liberation, much less in a single account of creation and redemption. There is indeed something visceral, untamed, and hostile about this God. Those who are called by this God to service find on occasion that more dangerous than the task is the danger of Yahweh's own person, who in inexplicable ways is partly threatened. That threat pertains even to God's closest associate, and Israel must take care not to count unguardedly on God's intimate friendliness.

5. In the concluding notice of this unit (4:27-31), the call process is given a reassuring closure. Sometimes the call process does work! Moses had needed his brother Aaron, and now he has him as an aide (4:27-28). Much more crucially, the people believed (4:31)! Such faith is always a gift and always a mystery. We do not know why the presence of Moses, called by the God of liberation, was credible to these slaves, when he himself feared disbelief (4:1). But the summons is credible, and there arises in the historical process of oppression the conviction that an alternative is offered, rooted in the very holiness of God. Certainly there was nothing on the surface of Moses' words or acts to give credibility. Trust in the prospect of liberation is indeed a theological reality.

6. In this text converge the large themes of divine purpose and human vocation, and the human drama that arises from that purpose and vocation. Thus, this text enunciates some of the largest, most problematic themes of biblical faith.

Israel knows that the one who speaks here is the Lord of creation and the governor of all of Israel's life. The two credo recitals of 3:7-8 and 3:17 announce that this holy one takes as an overriding purpose the transformation of Israel's life from bondage in an alien land to "at-homeness" in its own land. The plot of the text, and therefore the imagination of the listener, is dominated by this resolve for public transformation.

Pursuant to this large purpose of God, the purpose and intent of Moses' life are reshaped and redefined. It may be that Moses in 2:11-22 was already, unbeknownst to him, embracing the holy purpose of his life. Without any divine disclosure, he already acted as the liberator that he subsequently was called to be. God's call to him does not make him something other than he himself truly was. Moses' vocation is not imposed, but is intrinsic to the context of his life.

The two themes of *divine resolve for transformation* and *a human vocation of liberation* converge to assert something decisive about the public, human process. This text announces that the affairs of nations and of human persons (Egypt, Pharaoh, Moses, Israel, Midian) are in fact elements of the large drama where *divine resolve* and *human vocation* conspire for transformation. Both elements matter decisively; when they are both recognized, the public process is inevitably discerned as laden with alternatives yet to be wrought.

7. This narrative is more fully saturated with "signs" than is often noted (see 3:12; 4:1-9, 17, 27-30). The signs assert that there is more at work in the human process than what is defined by conventional power. They are regarded neither as acts of magic nor as violations of "natural law," but as evidences that a surplus of intention is present in human life at the behest of God. They are not acts of overt force or coercion; they do not directly impinge upon human decision making or policy or rationality, but are hints that the historical process is more open than might be imagined. Thus such "gestures of the holy" outdistance any scientific positivism, any hard orthodoxy, or any critical toning down that imagines it already knows the limits of the possible. We may conclude that attentiveness to such gestures of the holy (wrought by God through human persons) is a precondition of liberation and transformation.

The intention of this foundational narrative may be echoed in John 20:30-31. In something of a signature to the Fourth Gospel, the writer describes the move from "sign" to "faith" through text: "Now Jesus did many other *signs* in the presence of his disciples, which are not written in this book. But these are written so that you may come to *believe* . . . and that through believing you may have life in his name" (emphasis added).

Our text in Exodus is closely parallel in its intention and claim. There will be "many signs," which are *written* in order to evoke faith. Note well that they are written, not in this wording, "acted." The telling of signs in Exodus 3–4 (and in 5–12) is to bring listeners into this alternative future. The text grows out of the powerful signs, but the signs themselves continue to have power because they are embedded in and mediated by the text. The text and its interpretation are to bring the people (see 4:31) to believe and to have life.

EXODUS 5:1–11:10, "LET MY PEOPLE GO"

OVERVIEW

The plague narrative is a great dramatic contest between Yahweh, the Lord of liberation, and Pharaoh, the entrenched power of exploitation. The "plagues" are a series of "wonders" (miracles) whereby the stunning power of Yahweh is exhibited in the world, designed to intimidate Pharaoh until the Egyptian empire sees that it cannot withstand God's will for freedom and justice.

As early as 1940, Johannes Pedersen argued that this textual material closely reflects a liturgic drama.[33] That is, the episodes in the plague narrative are highly stylized, repetitive, and cumulative in their dramatic force. This liturgic exercise (which has as its intention the incorporation of the young into the memory) need not have been slavishly disciplined about "what happened" in any specific detail. Liturgical freedom permits the community to engage in grand, sweeping, hyperbolic rhetoric, the subject of which is the inversions that occur in the historical process, inversions of power that are inexplicable by any commonsense reading.

On the one hand, such a regularly reenacted drama serves to establish these events as paradigmatic for the faith and imagination of Israel. These events become the authoritative reference point and clue by which the community continues to discern its true situation in the world. Israel's shaping of historical reality is characteristically done in the categories of oppressed and oppressor, with Yahweh as the third actor who regularly intervenes to break open and transform a situation in which the oppressor seems endlessly in charge and the oppressed seems endlessly hopeless. (Note well that Israel utilized the categories long before any modern—e.g., Marxist—analysis.) That this paradigmatic event became enduring script thus provides an ongoing counterreading of social reality that generates revolutionary restlessness, unintimidated social criticism, and buoyant hope to be rediscerned in many circumstances and settings. It is this paradigmatic event that has made Jews characteristically attentive to the "underdog."[34] Because this liturgy is most plausibly situated in Passover (so Pedersen), I have termed the use of this material a practice of "Passover imagination," the continual rereading of social reality according to this cast of characters and this recital of inexplicable miracles. (Observe Amos 9:7, where Yahweh is said to be a God who causes exoduses for many other peoples and not exclusively for Israel.)

It goes without saying then, that the prospect for asking critical questions about what happened in the plagues is irrelevant. Greta Hort has provided the classic modern attempt to make the plagues scientifically credible.[35] While her analysis is careful, disciplined, and discerning, in the end it does not touch the dramatic issues that are at the center of the narrative. Thus the text does not stress that a number of odd events occurred. Rather, it accents the fact that Yahweh the creator mobilized all of creation to work this liberation. Thus the text insists that the narrative serves a theological point: It witnesses to the power of Yahweh on behalf of the Hebrew slaves, even in the face of Pharaoh and his power to resist.

We may suggest two productive tensions in the long drama that warrant attention. First, while the plagues feature the resolve, activity, and power of Yahweh (and are, therefore, accounts of miracles), the human work of Moses is decisive. The narrative is to be read as a long, studied process of bargaining, negotiation, intimidation, and deception. A careful reading of the text will not sustain the view that the wonder of liberation concerns no human initiative, for Moses has a crucial role to play. Indeed, the juxtaposition of God's initiative and Moses' cruciality is a characteristic way in which the Bible refuses to cut apart the roles of Yahweh and humanity.

The second tension concerns earnestness and

---

33. Pedersen, *Israel,* 728-37.

34. On the Jewish passion for the underdog, see Cynthia Ozick, *Metaphor and Memory: Essays* (New York: Knopf, 1989) 265-83; Herbert N. Schneidau, "Let the Reader Understand," *Semeia* 39 (1987) 140-42.

35. Greta Hort, "The Plagues of Egypt," *ZAW* 69 (1957) 84-103. See critical responses to Hort by Childs, *Exodus,* 168, and J. Philip Hyatt, *Commentary on Exodus,* New Century Bible (London: Oliphants, 1971) 336-45.

humor. This confrontation is enormously serious, as the stakes are very high. The very future of Israel rests on the outcome of these transactions; as it turns out, Pharaoh's future is also at stake. At the same time, however, the narrator has a good time and wants the listener to have a good time, largely at the expense of Pharaoh, who in the end turns out to be a pitiful character—indecisive, foolish, and self-destructive. The capacity of the oppressed to laugh at their oppressor is a way for the weak to delegitimate the strong.[36]

The plague cycle makes the point that the processes of human power are not as cut, dried, and foreclosed as the powerful imagine. Another power is loose in the world that finally precludes any system of power that overrides the fragility of human persons and human community. This inscrutable power will not finally tolerate such abuse. At the center of public history is "wonder," which no ruthless pharaoh can resist or squelch. It is that wonder wrought by God that in the end creates human possibilities for freedom and justice, for well-being and covenant.

Alongside the stylized series of confrontations and plagues, the text includes three elements that function to introduce the plagues themselves. First, chapter 5 is a series of conversations within the Egyptian labor structure designed to characterize the foolish and brutal Egyptian policy of oppressive labor. That chapter has the effect of heightening the suspense and creating rage toward the empire. Second, 6:2-9 presents a self-disclosing decree of God. This is a formal self-declaration that connects to the Genesis promise, discloses God's name (cf. 3:14), and pronounces a formal covenant formula. As Walther Zimmerli has shown, the passage is dominated by the expression "I am Yahweh," which places God's sovereignty in the center of the narrative.[37] Third, 6:14-25 presents the only genealogy in Exodus, this one to present the priestly pedigree of the Levitic-Aaronide priests. They will play a larger role later in the book, and are perhaps the community that brought Exodus to its final form.

The drama of the plagues themselves revolves around several recurring formulas. On the one hand, the imperative "Let my people go" states the overriding agenda of emancipation. (While one may eschew "liberation theology," one cannot avoid the fact that liberation stands as the core agenda of this text.) On the other hand, the indicative "You shall know that I am Yahweh" focuses on the power struggle between Yahweh and Pharaoh, without any particular reference to Israel. In this second formula, the liberation of Israel is only instrumental in exhibiting the rule of Yahweh to which Pharaoh inescapably must submit. Moreover, this latter theme of Yahweh's coming sovereignty is served by the odd formula, "Yahweh hardened Pharaoh's heart." This formula indicates that Yahweh's sovereign will is worked, even through Pharaoh's resistance.

The two governing formulas "Let my people go" and "You shall know I am Yahweh" together join the social and theological issues. The imperative of freedom and the indicative of sovereignty cannot be separated in the rhetoric or in the faith of Israel.

While these fixed formulas do recur and provide the rhetorical structure of the passages, one should not imagine that the several episodes are simply reiterations. In fact, each plague episode is distinct and merits careful attention to rhetorical detail. The narrator is able to handle the stable and recurring formulas with great imagination and playfulness. The outcome is not only imaginative rhetoric and bold theological affirmation, but also a cunning articulation of the ways the social crisis develops through deception and negotiation. In the end, it is clear that the forms of power held by and presided over by Pharaoh do not at all match the reality of power, which has now passed to Moses and the Israelites.

The storyline of the plague cycle does indeed subvert all established power by its witness to Yahweh's irresistible will for social transformation. The community that shares in this dramatic recital continues to affirm that public miracles of transformation will still be wrought by God, no matter what the odds.

---

36. This is a major element in Minjung theology, on which see Kim Yong Bock, ed., *Minjung Theology: People as the Subjects of History* (Singapore: The Commission on Theology Concerns, The Christian Conference of Asia, 1981); and Cyris H. S. Moon, *A Korean Minjung Theology: An Old Testament Perspective* (Maryknoll, N.Y.: Orbis, 1985). See also James C. Scott, *Weapons of the Weak* (New Haven: Yale University Press, 1987).

37. Walther Zimmerli, *I Am Yahweh* (Atlanta: John Knox, 1982) 7-13 and *passim*. See also Zimmerli's study of the formula in his Ezekiel commentary.

Exodus 5:1–6:1, Bricks Without Straw

NIV

5 Afterward Moses and Aaron went to Pharaoh and said, "This is what the LORD, the God of Israel, says: 'Let my people go, so that they may hold a festival to me in the desert.'"

[2]Pharaoh said, "Who is the LORD, that I should obey him and let Israel go? I do not know the LORD and I will not let Israel go."

[3]Then they said, "The God of the Hebrews has met with us. Now let us take a three-day journey into the desert to offer sacrifices to the LORD our God, or he may strike us with plagues or with the sword."

[4]But the king of Egypt said, "Moses and Aaron, why are you taking the people away from their labor? Get back to your work!" [5]Then Pharaoh said, "Look, the people of the land are now numerous, and you are stopping them from working."

[6]That same day Pharaoh gave this order to the slave drivers and foremen in charge of the people: [7]"You are no longer to supply the people with straw for making bricks; let them go and gather their own straw. [8]But require them to make the same number of bricks as before; don't reduce the quota. They are lazy; that is why they are crying out, 'Let us go and sacrifice to our God.' [9]Make the work harder for the men so that they keep working and pay no attention to lies."

[10]Then the slave drivers and the foremen went out and said to the people, "This is what Pharaoh says: 'I will not give you any more straw. [11]Go and get your own straw wherever you can find it, but your work will not be reduced at all.'" [12]So the people scattered all over Egypt to gather stubble to use for straw. [13]The slave drivers kept pressing them, saying, "Complete the work required of you for each day, just as when you had straw." [14]The Israelite foremen appointed by Pharaoh's slave drivers were beaten and were asked, "Why didn't you meet your quota of bricks yesterday or today, as before?"

[15]Then the Israelite foremen went and appealed to Pharaoh: "Why have you treated your servants this way? [16]Your servants are given no straw, yet we are told, 'Make bricks!' Your servants are

NRSV

5 Afterward Moses and Aaron went to Pharaoh and said, "Thus says the LORD, the God of Israel, 'Let my people go, so that they may celebrate a festival to me in the wilderness.'" [2]But Pharaoh said, "Who is the LORD, that I should heed him and let Israel go? I do not know the LORD, and I will not let Israel go." [3]Then they said, "The God of the Hebrews has revealed himself to us; let us go a three days' journey into the wilderness to sacrifice to the LORD our God, or he will fall upon us with pestilence or sword." [4]But the king of Egypt said to them, "Moses and Aaron, why are you taking the people away from their work? Get to your labors!" [5]Pharaoh continued, "Now they are more numerous than the people of the land[a] and yet you want them to stop working!" [6]That same day Pharaoh commanded the taskmasters of the people, as well as their supervisors, [7]"You shall no longer give the people straw to make bricks, as before; let them go and gather straw for themselves. [8]But you shall require of them the same quantity of bricks as they have made previously; do not diminish it, for they are lazy; that is why they cry, 'Let us go and offer sacrifice to our God.' [9]Let heavier work be laid on them; then they will labor at it and pay no attention to deceptive words."

10So the taskmasters and the supervisors of the people went out and said to the people, "Thus says Pharaoh, 'I will not give you straw. [11]Go and get straw yourselves, wherever you can find it; but your work will not be lessened in the least.'" [12]So the people scattered throughout the land of Egypt, to gather stubble for straw. [13]The taskmasters were urgent, saying, "Complete your work, the same daily assignment as when you were given straw." [14]And the supervisors of the Israelites, whom Pharaoh's taskmasters had set over them, were beaten, and were asked, "Why did you not finish the required quantity of bricks yesterday and today, as you did before?"

15Then the Israelite supervisors came to Pharaoh and cried, "Why do you treat your servants

[a] Sam: Heb *The people of the land are now many*

being beaten, but the fault is with your own people."

[17]Pharaoh said, "Lazy, that's what you are—lazy! That is why you keep saying, 'Let us go and sacrifice to the LORD.' [18]Now get to work. You will not be given any straw, yet you must produce your full quota of bricks."

[19]The Israelite foremen realized they were in trouble when they were told, "You are not to reduce the number of bricks required of you for each day." [20]When they left Pharaoh, they found Moses and Aaron waiting to meet them, [21]and they said, "May the LORD look upon you and judge you! You have made us a stench to Pharaoh and his officials and have put a sword in their hand to kill us."

[22]Moses returned to the LORD and said, "O Lord, why have you brought trouble upon this people? Is this why you sent me? [23]Ever since I went to Pharaoh to speak in your name, he has brought trouble upon this people, and you have not rescued your people at all."

6 Then the LORD said to Moses, "Now you will see what I will do to Pharaoh: Because of my mighty hand he will let them go; because of my mighty hand he will drive them out of his country."

like this? [16]No straw is given to your servants, yet they say to us, 'Make bricks!' Look how your servants are beaten! You are unjust to your own people."[a] [17]He said, "You are lazy, lazy; that is why you say, 'Let us go and sacrifice to the LORD.' [18]Go now, and work; for no straw shall be given you, but you shall still deliver the same number of bricks." [19]The Israelite supervisors saw that they were in trouble when they were told, "You shall not lessen your daily number of bricks." [20]As they left Pharaoh, they came upon Moses and Aaron who were waiting to meet them. [21]They said to them, "The LORD look upon you and judge! You have brought us into bad odor with Pharaoh and his officials, and have put a sword in their hand to kill us."

[22]Then Moses turned again to the LORD and said, "O LORD, why have you mistreated this people? Why did you ever send me? [23]Since I first came to Pharaoh to speak in your name, he has mistreated this people, and you have done nothing at all to deliver your people."

6 Then the LORD said to Moses, "Now you shall see what I will do to Pharaoh: Indeed, by a mighty hand he will let them go; by a mighty hand he will drive them out of his land."

[a] Gk Compare Syr Vg: Heb *beaten, and the sin of your people*

COMMENTARY

After Moses' extended narrative in Midian, at "the mountain of God" (3:1–4:31), the narrative moves the action back to Egypt and to the court of Pharaoh. This narrative on the surface simply portrays a struggle for political power and influence, and the action in this chapter takes place completely on Pharaoh's terms. This is the last episode in which Pharaoh will be the unchallenged master of his own house and his own policy. The narrative lets us see unambiguously that where Pharaoh works his will, there is sure to be abuse, brutality, and violence. It is striking that Yahweh, the God of the Hebrews, appears nowhere as an actor in this narrative. To be sure, Yahweh is spoken about by the other characters, but in the end, all that is said of the "God of the Hebrews"

is that this God is noticeably absent and ineffective. Moses and Aaron, for the extent of this narrative, are left on their own with Pharaoh, and it is not a hopeful picture for those in bondage.

Along with Pharaoh and Moses-Aaron, there are three other "characters" in the narrative: the taskmasters (נגשׁים *nōgĕśîm*), the supervisors (שׁטרים *šōṭĕrîm*), and the slaves. While the taskmasters and supervisors participate in the action and voice important lines in the plot, they occupy no independent place in the narrative. They function to pass along the brutality downward from above, or the indignation upward from below. At the bottom of the vertical arrangement of the narrative are the peasants-slaves-Hebrews. They are a real presence and a "character" in the plot, even though they are not permitted to speak.

The chapter consists of two related, but asymmetrical, conversations. The one conversation is a confrontation between would-be equals, Pharaoh and Moses-Aaron (vv. 1-5). It is a struggle for control and a conflict between competing visions of social reality. The other conversation is a vertical one between Pharaoh and the Hebrews, in which the taskmasters and supervisors are intermediaries who pass information back and forth (vv. 6-19). In this conversation, the Hebrews do not speak, except to sigh and groan under severe abuse; this in itself, however, is an important voicing, as we have seen in 2:23.

It is important that Moses and Aaron do not participate in this vertical, hierarchial conversation, for they do not share the view that Pharaoh is at the top of power. They stand outside that conversation as the voice of Yahweh, who challenges Pharaoh's claim to priority. Nonetheless, the voice of Moses-Aaron (i.e., the voice of Yahweh) impinges upon the vertical conversation, because it brings to speech the silenced agenda of the muted Hebrews. Yahweh functions to speak with power for the muted slaves, who have no voice of their own. Pharaoh can ignore the slaves' silence, but he cannot ignore the abrasive, demanding, sovereign speech of Yahweh on the lips of Moses and Aaron.

5:1-9. The chapter consists of a series of sharp, brief exchanges, with only occasional narrative elements to connect the speeches. Moses and Aaron speak first (v. 1), voicing Yahweh's decree and the yearning of the Hebrews. They reiterate the most elemental decree of Yahweh: "Send my people." The conventional reading, "Let my people go," sounds like a request or a plea. In fact, it is an imperative on the lips of Yahweh, as though Yahweh addresses a political subordinate (Pharaoh) who is expected to obey. The reason for the "sending" is a festival in the wilderness, with no hint that the festival is a ploy in order to escape, though later an escape is implied (10:10).

What is intended, rather, is a religious observance that will assert loyalty to Yahweh, thereby delegitimating the claims of Pharaoh to loyalty. Thus the proposed worship "in the wilderness"— i.e., outside Pharaoh's controlled arena—constitutes a threat to Egypt, but that threat is not as blatant as an escape. (On subversive energy that comes from the wilderness, outside the governed territory, see Luke 3:1-6).

Pharaoh's defiant response to the imperative is not an inquiry (v. 2). It is, rather, a hostile, high-handed dismissal of Yahweh. The tone is not unlike that of Yahweh's speech in 4:11, wherein Yahweh dismisses a challenge from Moses. Pharaoh insists that Yahweh is a nobody, has no right to issue a decree, and certainly will not be obeyed. Pharaoh imagines that he is autonomous and refuses his role as an underling to Yahweh. Pharaoh makes two interdependent assertions in response. First, "I do not know Yahweh" (i.e., "I do not acknowledge the status of Yahweh as overlord"). *Know* here means not only "to be familiar with," but also "to recognize authority." Second, and consequently, Pharaoh will not release the slaves. The double point of resistance, as is characteristic of the exodus narrative, joins the *theological* ("I do not know") and the *sociopolitical* ("I will not send").

Political transformation derives from theological commitment. Negatively, Pharaoh's brutalizing political policies derive from his sense of autonomy from Yahweh. Pharaoh cannot practice liberation without acceding to the rule of Yahweh, which he cannot do without giving up his claim to power and authority. Thus the first couplet of speeches (vv. 1-2) sets the conflict in its sharpest, most comprehensive and uncompromising form.

In the second couplet of speeches (vv. 3-5), the two positions are stated with greater intensity and both parties receive more elaborate titles. Yahweh is named "God of the Hebrews," and Pharaoh is called "King in Egypt." The speech of Moses-Aaron indirectly answers Pharaoh's haughty question of v. 2, "Who?" Calvin observes that Pharaoh's defiant question is paralleled by Pilate's question, "What is truth?" (John 18:37-38).[38] Yahweh is "God of the Hebrews," the patron, guarantor, and advocate of the silenced slaves. Thus the title both gives information and intensifies the conflict, for Pharaoh cannot countenance such a God in his realm.

Pharaoh's response does not touch the theological issue raised by Moses and Aaron. His answer concerns work, the only thing he has on his

---

38. Calvin, *Commentaries,* 114.

horizon. That is, in his answer, Pharaoh refuses to think beyond the technical requirements of the economy of the state. The counter to Yahwistic worship is a greater commitment to the abusive status quo. The ideology of Pharaoh could be affirmed under either totalitarian socialism or abusive capitalism: "Work makes free." Such work-produced well-being is clearly not the intent of the wilderness festival. Pharaoh's response indicates that the confrontation is now between two systems of reality. It touches everything from religious claim to economic policy. There can be no compromise.

This double exchange in vv. 1-2 and 3-5 leads to a narrative interlude in which Pharaoh intensifies his policy of abusive labor practice (vv. 6-9). Here for the first time the bureaucratic structure of the empire is mentioned, including taskmasters and supervisors. Their presence reminds us that the problem for the slaves is not simply the fierceness of a single leader, but the systemic force and abuse that supports him.

The new policy intensifies the work schedule. Straw is required for the production of bricks. Presumably the production schedule was so organized that straw was supplied for the brickmakers. The necessary supplies were on a regular work schedule, suggesting high efficiency. Now that a continuous supply of straw is curtailed, the brickmakers must add to their own work time in order to gather straw, but nonetheless meet the same schedule of brick production.

This policy is clear enough; the reasons for the policy are more interesting (vv. 8-9). In v. 8, the brick-producing slaves themselves are said to cry, "Let us go and offer sacrifice to our God." Verse 9 takes a different position. It recognizes that it was not the slaves who issued such a cry. The slaves themselves are not the speakers of this yearning, but are only the hearers and receivers of such an option. The verse does not specify, but it is clear that in v. 9 (unlike v. 8) it is Moses-Aaron who have spoken the troublesome words that threaten the empire.

Thus by inference, Moses-Aaron are outsiders in the slave community, troublemakers who come to agitate, and the brick-producing slaves are only exposed to the seduction of their words. Pharaoh concludes his policy statement with the concern that the slaves should be "saved" (יָשַׁע *yāša'*) by

false words—i.e., should be misled. Moses and Aaron are labeled "false" (שֶׁקֶר *šeqer*) in their appeal to Yahweh (cf. Isa 36:5-7). This conclusion not only dismisses Moses-Aaron, but in fact dismisses Yahweh as well, as a god who has no power to enact what is decreed. Pharaoh's strategy is not to silence them, but to keep the slaves too busy to heed, to listen, to respond, or to organize. This approach is ideologically self-deceiving, for it assumes that keeping workers on board with intense work keeps the purposes and warrants of the work from scrutiny. It mistakenly assumes that if they are busy, suffering people will not notice what is going on.

5:10-21. After Pharaoh's decree (vv. 6-9), the narrative pauses to expose the working out of the new, aggressive policy. The action is in two parts: the general implementation (vv. 10-14) and the peculiar problem of the supervisors (vv. 15-21). Pharaoh's underlings (taskmasters and supervisors) are loyal to him in implementing the new policy, the purpose of which is to screen out the counter-vision of Moses and Aaron. The taskmasters, the more senior officers, insist on the punctual and complete fulfillment of the work schedule (v. 13).

In v. 14, it is clear that the supervisors have a different role to play from that of the taskmasters. Indeed, the breaking point between management and labor seems to fall between taskmasters and supervisors and not, as one might expect, between supervisors and slaves.[39] As a result, the supervisors are directly held accountable for production, and are punished for a failure to meet quotas.

Moreover, the supervisors are closer to the exploited work force and sensitive to their lot under the new policy. The supervisors are said to be "supervisors of the Israelites." The language suggests that they are in fact members of the Hebrew community who have been given modest leadership roles. If so, they are most vulnerable. On the one hand, they must answer for the work and are subject to discipline if the work does not go well. On the other hand, they must have been viewed by their own work force with suspicion, as compromisers with and accommodators to the exploitative work schedule and its benefactors.

The double bind of the supervisors is evident in vv. 15-21, where they undertake two quite

39. See Pixley's shrewd analysis, *Exodus*, 33.

heroic confrontations. The first confrontation is with Pharaoh. They "cry out" (צעק *ṣāʿaq*; cf. v. 8; 2:23). They issue a protest on behalf of the slaves who are beaten for their inability to meet production schedules. Finally, their speech makes a direct accusation against Pharaoh: "You are unjust" (following the Greek text). The Hebrew text asserts, "You have violated ["sinned against," חטא *ḥāṭāʾ*] your people." Thus royal policy is identified (with either rendering) as inhumane and unacceptable. Such an assertion in such a high place is indeed a high-risk venture. It is clear that Moses and Aaron were not the only daring and courageous voices in the slave community.

Pharaoh is unresponsive and intransigent. He refuses the protest, reiterates the policy, and accuses the protesting supervisors of being lazy and trying to get out of work (vv. 17-18). Pharaoh reiterates the critical proposal of v. 1 (cf. v. 18). The narrator adds that the supervisors were "in trouble" (רע *rāʿ*, "get evil for themselves"), for they had issued a protest and were left severely exposed when their request was not heeded.

The second confrontation the supervisors undertake is with Moses and Aaron (vv. 20-21). This meeting happens immediately after the first one, perhaps in reaction to it. It is as though Moses and Aaron are waiting to see what comes out of the supervisors' meeting with Pharaoh. Nothing came out of it but trouble and yet one more insidious resolve on the part of Pharaoh. The supervisors are now exposed and in jeopardy. It is for that reason, not surprisingly, that their attack is now turned promptly upon Moses and Aaron.

Speaking out of their own jeopardy, the supervisors issue a charge against Moses and Aaron not unlike the one they made against Pharaoh. Whereas Pharaoh is "unjust," Moses and Aaron need to be "judged"—i.e., shown to be irresponsible. The charge against them is not, as against Pharaoh, abusiveness. Rather, it is that the protesting supervisors (and the slaves they represent) have become a "bad smell" to Pharaoh, loathsome, repellent, and likely needing to be eliminated (cf. 1 Sam 27:12). That is, acting on the word of Moses-Aaron, the supervisors have now called attention to themselves in a terribly dangerous way. The term "bad smell" (באש *bĕʾōš*) regularly is used for those who become unaccept-

able to other, stronger people (cf. Gen 34:30; 1 Sam 13:4; 2 Sam 10:6; 16:21).

5:22–6:1. This narrative ends on an odd and unexpected note (vv. 22-23). Moses has just been accused by the supervisors. Indeed, the supervisors leave the impression that Pharaoh was correct in v. 9; their words are "false," without substance. It is odd and telling that Moses makes no response to them, either to defend himself or to refute the charge. Rather, he turns abruptly to a different conversation in which the supervisors have no part. Moses turns to Yahweh, who thus far has been completely absent in this narrative.

Moses issues a severe rebuke to Yahweh, one to which Yahweh makes only a belated response. The accusation turns on the double use of the term *mistreat* (*rāʿ*). We have already seen the term in v. 19, where the protesting supervisors are said to be "in trouble." Now Moses accuses Yahweh: "You are the one who has caused trouble ["evil," *rāʿ*] for this people." In making this accusation against Yahweh, Moses is deftly declaring his own innocence in response to the charge in v. 21.

Moses' accusation is exceedingly harsh. You have not "really snatched" this people. The word used for "snatch" or "deliver" (נצל *nāṣal*) means to drag out of danger at the last minute (cf. 1 Sam 17:37; Amos 4:11). Two items interest us in this statement. First, already in 3:9, Yahweh had used the term *nāṣal* in the initial promise to rescue Israel from the power of Egypt. Thus Moses here accuses Yahweh of not doing what has been promised. Second, the verb here is in the infinitive absolute; it is an intense, strong verb. Moses is very clear about what needs to be done and what Yahweh has not done. This acute address to Yahweh is the first in what will become a series of attacks Moses makes upon Yahweh.

The accusation is that Yahweh has been absent from this dangerous confrontation, in which Yahweh promised to be the decisive player. A quick reading of the chapter indicates that Yahweh has indeed been absent; the risk-taking parties, Moses-Aaron and the supervisors, have been left on their own. As a result, they are dangerously exposed, with no visible gain or assurance. Moses' protest accuses Yahweh of having offered false words, with no follow-through in action; as a result, Pharaoh does indeed seem to prevail.

However, we must read more closely. I suggest

that this "interim narrative," between promise and deliverance, is governed by Yahweh's preceding speech in 4:21. In that verse, Yahweh gives Moses his lines to speak to Pharaoh. Yahweh resolves, "I will harden his heart"; "he will not let the people go." That is precisely what has happened in chapter 5. Pharaoh has not, as Yahweh anticipated he would not, let this people go.

But Pharaoh's heart has indeed been made harder and more resistant. This is evident in the dismissal of Yahweh (v. 2), in the policy of "no straw" (vv. 6-9) and in the reiteration of the harsh policy, the maintenance of the production schedule, and the accusation of laziness (vv. 17-18). As in any exploitative regime, Pharaoh has begun a policy of escalation, believing that more repression, applied a little at a time, is a workable policy. Pharaoh apparently does not know that he is facing a revolution, an exodus. All he knows is that there is more protest, shrill outside agitation; and the way to deal with agitation is to tighten control and be repressive. That is all that is visible in the narrative, all that was visible to the slaves, to the supervisors, to the taskmasters, or even to Moses.

The narrator, however, has let us see a bit more than the participants have been able to notice. This seemingly inhumane strategy whereby Pharaoh becomes more demanding is only the visible element of Yahweh's hidden work of hardening. The hardening and escalation of repression are a necessary step in creating a social situation so laden with pressure that it will blow open with rage and liberation. After all, the exodus is not a transcendental occurrence, but a social revolution accomplished by real people through public protests. Yahweh may be invisible in the narrative, but Yahweh is not absent. Liberation is slow, hard work. It entails making the oppressed odious. It requires making the oppressor stupid and abusive and blind to his own real interest. Liberation takes time, but the time is full of the resolve of Yahweh. No party in the narrative can see the painful requirement of time, not even Moses.

The narrator does not, however, leave the narrative with the rebuke of Yahweh by Moses as the last word. Yahweh is permitted to speak one time (6:1), asserting, against this rebuke, that the present situation of the Israelite community is not the last state. There is more to come from Yahweh. On the basis of what Yahweh will do, Pharaoh will act differently. This enigmatic statement seems, in retrospect, to be an allusion to the last plague of chapters 11–12. The other interesting point about Yahweh's response is that Pharaoh will act "by a mighty hand." The first intent of the statement is that the "mighty hand" is that of Pharaoh. Yet the term hand is twice without a pronominal suffix, where we might expect "his hand." Thus the way is open to suggest that the "mighty hand" by which Pharaoh will act is in the end the mighty hand of Yahweh, who is at work through Pharaoh. It is finally Yahweh who mobilizes Pharaoh to become engaged recalcitrantly in the mighty work of liberation. Yahweh acts with high resolve, but in the public process mostly by indirection.

REFLECTIONS

This is an "interim narrative"; it stands between the announcement of God's intention (chaps. 3–4) and the enactment of that intention (chaps. 6–11). In terms of God's own speech, it stands between the resolve to "harden Pharaoh's heart" (4:21) and the time when "You shall see what I will do" (6:1). In this text, Israel must wait in its dangerous, exposed position where Pharaoh is unjust, Moses causes a "bad smell," and Yahweh has "done nothing." Such waiting provides an opportunity for a more reflective perspective on the text, when there is nothing direct to proclaim.

1. This text invites reflection on the integral relation of theological claim and political possibility, or, if one will, the relation between faith and politics. In much of the church that connection is not understood, and is often resisted. The first exchange between Moses-Aaron and Pharaoh makes the linkage in a subtle and knowing way (vv. 1-2). The decree of Yahweh in the mouth of Moses-Aaron understands that "a sacrifice in the wilderness to Yahweh" is not merely a religious act, but in fact is a threatening political act that implicitly delegitimates

the deep claims of Pharaoh to command the loyalty of the Hebrews. Pharaoh understands this connection as well, for in his defiant response, he refuses to acknowledge Yahweh and (consequently) he refuses to let the slaves go.

Given the identification of Yahweh with the slaves, it follows that biblical faith is inevitably concerned with political questions, with an inescapable tilt not only toward justice, but also toward liberation. Thus Pharaoh, with his oppressive policies, is accused of being unjust (v. 16) (following the Greek text). This text relates justice to the character of God, and will not let faith stray far from justice questions that focus on oppression and labor policy. This text invites the listening church to rethink the categories through which it practices the future.

2. The strategy of Pharaoh is worth study. His notion is that the pressure of productivity is the way to keep social relations from changing. That is, the lazy and unproductive have time to listen to voices that authorize dangerous change. Productivity numbs attention to the voice of new possibility. This mode of enslavement is worth considering in a society that is aimed at the acquisition of goods in the pursuit of greed and affluence.

Two dimensions of numbing through productivity might be identified. On the one hand, consumerism, the driving ideology of Western society, is based in the capacity to produce and acquire wealth as a sign of personal worth. While production quotas may not be as abusive and demeaning as in this narrative, the pressure to produce and achieve is enormous in our society, so enormous that it robs energy from every chance for justice and freedom. On the other hand (and more subtly), in a moral posture that is focused on "doing," even the doing of "goodness" leads to a passion for busyness that leaves little time for "being." One can imagine that the exodus narrative is an exercise in weaning the imagination of the listening community away from an ideology of productivity, in order to have room and energy to "be."

3. The supervisors in this narrative are of special interest to us. The large drama of Moses versus Pharaoh makes them decidedly subordinate in the plot. Nonetheless, in this narrative, they occupy considerable attention. They are the "persons in the middle," in the uneasy place of having sympathy for those below, but also appearing to be excessively compromised with those above. Many people who look to this text for help are cast in our society precisely as those "in the middle" of such abusive arrangements. Few among us are as powerful or as brutal as Pharaoh, who has the power to change matters by decree. Many more of us are positioned where we notice and care, where we can protest injustice, but only at risk.

The supervisors are bold characters on two counts. On the one hand, they present a strong critique of Pharaoh on behalf of the slaves. On the other hand, they are accountable for productivity and are beaten when schedules are not met. They rely on the word of Moses-Aaron and seem to be left holding the bag when Moses does not triumph. This narrative provides no solution for those cast in this dangerous role. The narrative, however, is illuminating in letting us see precisely where we may be located. The supervisors do not turn their backs on the abused. Nor do they flinch from protest against abusive power. They are the very ones who keep the justice question visible in the narrative, after the extreme "pronouncement" of Moses-Aaron. They live an exceedingly exposed life.

4. Only near the end is this narrative explicitly theological. The story encourages reflection upon some difficult questions: What is God doing in the story? What is God doing in the world? How is God delivering on God's promises? This story holds no brief for an easy kind of supernaturalism that imagines that God will swoop in and cause freedom. Rather, the exodus is wrought slowly, painfully through hurt and risk, through sociopolitical processes that are not unlike our own experience. The notion of "hardening the heart" suggests that God unleashes increasing injustice, stubbornness, and resistance to change, so that the old order must give way to God's new intention. If a benign status quo can be maintained, nothing will ever change. Only when brutality escalates to an unbearable level can genuine public newness surface. The community that trusts this text is invited to think and notice again God's "strange work" in the public process that makes newness possible.

This muted text makes rigorous demands on our theological categories. It is not that the affirmations are so esoteric or subtle. Rather, they are so strange to us in our conventional, status quo perception of the gospel, or in our expectation that healing, liberating change should be visible and developmental. This narrative invites us to enter into that story of the absence of God in a radical and daring way, in order to perceive the very places that seem closed and hopeless as laden with potential newness. The whole of this narrative stands under a relentless promise and a sovereign decree. Along the way to that promise's fulfillment, there is abuse, trouble, and a "bad smell." This is narrative candor on the way to a new possibility. The community watches to see "what I will do" (6:1). The one who will do is the one whom Pharaoh disdainfully refuses to acknowledge.

Exodus 6:2-30, "I Am Yahweh"

NIV

²God also said to Moses, "I am the Lord. ³I appeared to Abraham, to Isaac and to Jacob as God Almighty,ᵃ but by my name the Lordᵇ I did not make myself known to them.ᶜ ⁴I also established my covenant with them to give them the land of Canaan, where they lived as aliens. ⁵Moreover, I have heard the groaning of the Israelites, whom the Egyptians are enslaving, and I have remembered my covenant.

⁶"Therefore, say to the Israelites: 'I am the Lord, and I will bring you out from under the yoke of the Egyptians. I will free you from being slaves to them, and I will redeem you with an outstretched arm and with mighty acts of judgment. ⁷I will take you as my own people, and I will be your God. Then you will know that I am the Lord your God, who brought you out from under the yoke of the Egyptians. ⁸And I will bring you to the land I swore with uplifted hand to give to Abraham, to Isaac and to Jacob. I will give it to you as a possession. I am the Lord.' "

⁹Moses reported this to the Israelites, but they did not listen to him because of their discouragement and cruel bondage.

¹⁰Then the Lord said to Moses, ¹¹"Go, tell Pharaoh king of Egypt to let the Israelites go out of his country."

¹²But Moses said to the Lord, "If the Israelites will not listen to me, why would Pharaoh listen to me, since I speak with faltering lipsᵈ?"

ᵃ3 Hebrew *El-Shaddai* ᵇ3 See note at Exodus 3:15. ᶜ3 Or *Almighty, and by my name the Lord did I not let myself be known to them?* ᵈ12 Hebrew *I am uncircumcised of lips*; also in verse 30

NRSV

2God also spoke to Moses and said to him: "I am the Lord. ³I appeared to Abraham, Isaac, and Jacob as God Almighty,ᵃ but by my name 'The Lord'ᵇ I did not make myself known to them. ⁴I also established my covenant with them, to give them the land of Canaan, the land in which they resided as aliens. ⁵I have also heard the groaning of the Israelites whom the Egyptians are holding as slaves, and I have remembered my covenant. ⁶Say therefore to the Israelites, 'I am the Lord, and I will free you from the burdens of the Egyptians and deliver you from slavery to them. I will redeem you with an outstretched arm and with mighty acts of judgment. ⁷I will take you as my people, and I will be your God. You shall know that I am the Lord your God, who has freed you from the burdens of the Egyptians. ⁸I will bring you into the land that I swore to give to Abraham, Isaac, and Jacob; I will give it to you for a possession. I am the Lord.' " ⁹Moses told this to the Israelites; but they would not listen to Moses, because of their broken spirit and their cruel slavery.

10Then the Lord spoke to Moses, ¹¹"Go and tell Pharaoh king of Egypt to let the Israelites go out of his land." ¹²But Moses spoke to the Lord, "The Israelites have not listened to me; how then shall Pharaoh listen to me, poor speaker that I am?"ᶜ ¹³Thus the Lord spoke to Moses and Aaron, and gave them orders regarding the Israelites and

ᵃ Traditional rendering of Heb *El Shaddai* ᵇ Heb *YHWH*; see note at 3.15 ᶜ Heb *me? I am uncircumcised of lips*

NIV

¹³Now the LORD spoke to Moses and Aaron about the Israelites and Pharaoh king of Egypt, and he commanded them to bring the Israelites out of Egypt.

¹⁴These were the heads of their families^a:

The sons of Reuben the firstborn son of Israel were Hanoch and Pallu, Hezron and Carmi. These were the clans of Reuben.

¹⁵The sons of Simeon were Jemuel, Jamin, Ohad, Jakin, Zohar and Shaul the son of a Canaanite woman. These were the clans of Simeon.

¹⁶These were the names of the sons of Levi according to their records: Gershon, Kohath and Merari. Levi lived 137 years.

¹⁷The sons of Gershon, by clans, were Libni and Shimei.

¹⁸The sons of Kohath were Amram, Izhar, Hebron and Uzziel. Kohath lived 133 years.

¹⁹The sons of Merari were Mahli and Mushi.

These were the clans of Levi according to their records.

²⁰Amram married his father's sister Jochebed, who bore him Aaron and Moses. Amram lived 137 years.

²¹The sons of Izhar were Korah, Nepheg and Zicri.

²²The sons of Uzziel were Mishael, Elzaphan and Sithri.

²³Aaron married Elisheba, daughter of Amminadab and sister of Nahshon, and she bore him Nadab and Abihu, Eleazar and Ithamar.

²⁴The sons of Korah were Assir, Elkanah and Abiasaph. These were the Korahite clans.

²⁵Eleazar son of Aaron married one of the daughters of Putiel, and she bore him Phinehas.

These were the heads of the Levite families, clan by clan.

²⁶It was this same Aaron and Moses to whom the LORD said, "Bring the Israelites out of Egypt by their divisions." ²⁷They were the ones who spoke to Pharaoh king of Egypt about bringing the Israelites out of Egypt. It was the same Moses and Aaron.

^a14 The Hebrew for *families* here and in verse 25 refers to units larger than clans.

NRSV

Pharaoh king of Egypt, charging them to free the Israelites from the land of Egypt.

14The following are the heads of their ancestral houses: the sons of Reuben, the firstborn of Israel: Hanoch, Pallu, Hezron, and Carmi; these are the families of Reuben. ¹⁵The sons of Simeon: Jemuel, Jamin, Ohad, Jachin, Zohar, and Shaul,^a the son of a Canaanite woman; these are the families of Simeon. ¹⁶The following are the names of the sons of Levi according to their genealogies: Gershon,^b Kohath, and Merari, and the length of Levi's life was one hundred thirty-seven years. ¹⁷The sons of Gershon:^c Libni and Shimei, by their families. ¹⁸The sons of Kohath: Amram, Izhar, Hebron, and Uzziel, and the length of Kohath's life was one hundred thirty-three years. ¹⁹The sons of Merari: Mahli and Mushi. These are the families of the Levites according to their genealogies. ²⁰Amram married Jochebed his father's sister and she bore him Aaron and Moses, and the length of Amram's life was one hundred thirty-seven years. ²¹The sons of Izhar: Korah, Nepheg, and Zichri. ²²The sons of Uzziel: Mishael, Elzaphan, and Sithri. ²³Aaron married Elisheba, daughter of Amminadab and sister of Nahshon, and she bore him Nadab, Abihu, Eleazar, and Ithamar. ²⁴The sons of Korah: Assir, Elkanah, and Abiasaph; these are the families of the Korahites. ²⁵Aaron's son Eleazar married one of the daughters of Putiel, and she bore him Phinehas. These are the heads of the ancestral houses of the Levites by their families.

26It was this same Aaron and Moses to whom the LORD said, "Bring the Israelites out of the land of Egypt, company by company." ²⁷It was they who spoke to Pharaoh king of Egypt to bring the Israelites out of Egypt, the same Moses and Aaron.

28On the day when the LORD spoke to Moses in the land of Egypt, ²⁹he said to him, "I am the LORD; tell Pharaoh king of Egypt all that I am speaking to you." ³⁰But Moses said in the LORD's presence, "Since I am a poor speaker,^d why would Pharaoh listen to me?"

^aOr *Saul*   ^bAlso spelled *Gershom*; see 2.22   ^cAlso spelled *Gershom*; see 2.22   ^dHeb *am uncircumcised of lips*; see 6.12

NIV

²⁸Now when the LORD spoke to Moses in Egypt, ²⁹he said to him, "I am the LORD. Tell Pharaoh king of Egypt everything I tell you."

³⁰But Moses said to the LORD, "Since I speak with faltering lips, why would Pharaoh listen to me?"

COMMENTARY

This chapter, on any reading, constitutes something of a disruptive oddity in the exodus narrative. According to the older source analysis (which in this particular case seems not only cogent but important), this text is by consensus taken as a part of the Priestly source. The evidence for assignment to this source includes the peculiar language for covenant making whereby the covenant is unilaterally imposed by God (v. 4), the name of El Shaddai for God (v. 2), the preoccupation with priestly genealogy (vv. 14-25), and the peculiar prominence of Aaron in that genealogy (vv. 20-25). It is clear that the texture and intent of this chapter is very different from what precedes and what follows.

Priestly texts are commonly dated either to the exile or soon thereafter.[40] They are addressed to a community in exile (or just out of exile) that is rootless and displaced. By appealing to the very old tradition, the P source seeks to construct for the exiles a sense of structured, stable reality, in order to give coherence, order, and legitimacy to communal life. The ordering that is offered is cultic in character, so that it is around liturgic claims that life is said to be properly arranged. Consequently, the antidote offered in the narrative is no longer political emancipation or economic restitution, but a stabilizing sacral order.

This Priestly block of material includes God's speech of self-disclosure (vv. 2-8), an account of resistance to that speech (vv. 9-13), a priestly genealogy (vv. 14-27), and a reprise of assertion and resistance (vv. 28-30).

6:2-8. In this extended speech of God, we have the fullest self-disclosure of God that is offered in the exodus narrative, (a very different speech of God's self-disclosure is given in 34:6-7). W. Zimmerli has shown that this lean utterance, "I am Yahweh," is the complete self-giving God, the full revelation of God's intentionality, and the way in which God makes God's own self available to Moses and to Israel.[41] The meaning of the name *Yahweh* is endlessly problematic (as we have seen concerning 3:14). Nonetheless, it is clear that as construed in the Exodus tradition, even in the later P casting of the Exodus tradition, the name bespeaks presence, fidelity, and emancipatory power released in the world. Moreover, in his study of the book of Ezekiel, Zimmerli has shown that this theological formula is peculiarly prized by Israel in exile.[42] When all other modes of theological stability and forms of theological identity were in jeopardy, Israel clung to the name of Yahweh as the summary and foundation of its entire structure of faith and identity.

The remainder of this speech (vv. 3-8) is an exposition of the intent and substance of the brief formula of v. 2. Verse 3 makes clear the proposal of this (Priestly) tradition of the self-disclosure of Yahweh, somewhat differently paralleled in 3:14. The tradition wants to affirm the full continuity of God in the exodus narrative with God in the ancestral tales of Genesis. It is God's memory of promises to the ancestors in Genesis that operates in Exodus for liberation. But with equal resolve, the tradition wants to assert a discontinuity between these two sets of narratives. The God now fully known by name was indeed known by the

40. But see the important alternative proposal by Jacob Milgrom, *Leviticus 1–16: A New Translation with Introduction and Commentary,* AB 3 (New York: Doubleday, 1991) 3-13.

41. Zimmerli, *I Am Yahweh,* esp. 1-28.

42. Walther Zimmerli, *Ezekiel 1: A Commentary on the Book of the Prophet Ezekiel, Chapters 1–24,* Hermeneia (Philadelphia: Fortress, 1979) 406-14. See also Moshe Greenberg, *Ezekiel 1–20: A New Translation with Introduction and Commentary,* AB 22 (Garden City, N.Y.: Doubleday, 1983) 376-88.

Genesis ancestors, but not *fully* known and not by name.

This hypothesis of continuity/discontinuity in v. 3 is wondrously exposited in vv. 4-5. In v. 4, it is unambiguous that God fully and unilaterally declared and imposed a covenant upon the ancestors of Genesis. They had no choice or option. The covenant results from God's providential, generous sovereignty (cf. Gen 17:7-8). Moreover, the gift of covenant contained, as its key factor, the gift of the land of the Canaanites. That is, the covenant by definition anticipated receiving of land already held by others.

The ancestors to whom the promise of the land is made (cf. Gen 17:8) are in fact only aliens ("sojourners," גרים *gērîm*) there. The usage also recalls Exod 2:22; like the ancestors, Moses is required to live where he does not belong, without a home. While v. 3 recalls the laden past, v. 5 focuses on the painful present tense. God has heard the groaning of the people in oppression (cf. 2:7-8, 16, 24); God is fully attentive to the present. The present pain, however, serves primarily to drive God back to the memory of the covenant made in Genesis. Thus there is a dynamic movement back and forth between old covenant commitment and immediate pain, between an authorizing past and a demanding, insistent present.

Out of this meditation on the dynamic of past and present, God issues a powerful promise to Israel through Moses (vv. 6-8). This promise is one more classic formulation of Israel's core faith, not unlike 3:7-8, 17. The promise is dominated by first-person verbs, with Yahweh as subject. God's own action will dominate Israel's future. Before the active verbs, however, there is a second solemn sounding of the basic affirmation: "I am Yahweh." The verbs of hope and liberation arise from this self-disclosure and belong intrinsically to Yahweh's own self:

"I will free you" (יצא *yāṣaʿ*): This is the verb assigned to Moses in 3:10, but characteristically has God as its subject.

"I will deliver you" (נצל *nāṣal*). The verb is the same used by Moses in 5:23 in the infinitive absolute to accuse God of doing nothing.[43]

"I will redeem you" (גאל *gāʾal*). The verb has the force of a kinsman who acts for the honor and well-being of a wounded or abused member of the family, thus bespeaking God's intimate solidarity as a member of the slave community.

This recital of active verbs of rescue takes a curious turn in v. 7, which departs from the standard form of the recital. There is another powerful first-person verb: "I will take you" (לקח *lāqaḥ*). This verb, however, is not a "historical deed," but the establishment of a relation, as though elevating liberated Israel to a new status. This verb affirms a covenant relation. The symmetrical formula "You shall be my people and I shall be your God" is unusual in the Exodus tradition and is known primarily in the exilic formulations of Jeremiah (11:4; 24:7; 30:22; 31:33; 32:38) and Ezekiel (11:20; 14:11; 36:28; 37:23, 27).[44] Israel, who has been a nobody, now is publicly and irreversibly marked and honored as Yahweh's people. Or in the horizon of P, exiles without identity, in this liturgical context, are given a peculiar and treasured identity.

The formulation of relationship and status at the end of v. 7, however, is still derived from a deed. Again, the statement "I am Yahweh" is linked to the exodus. Moreover, it is introduced by a second stylized expression, "You shall know." Zimmerli has shown that this second formulation is a device whereby theological certitude is rooted in and derived from concrete acts of rescue, well-being, and judgment.[45] Thus the exodus is converted into a datum of theological certitude. The exodus event is not only a covenant about Israel's future, but about Yahweh's character as well.

In v. 8, the standard recital is continued from v. 6, which was disrupted by the different sort of speech in v. 7. In v. 8, the promise of the land, already guaranteed in the old promise of Genesis, is now reiterated. The promise of v. 8 is characteristically the counterpart to the deliverance of v. 6. These three verses, then, have an intentional structure:

---

43. See above, 704, 712, 728.

44. See Rudolf Smend, *Die Bundesformel,* Theologische Studien 68 (Zürich: EVZ-Verlag, 1963).

45. Zimmerli, *I Am Yahweh,* 35-36.

v. 6 Exodus as   v. 8 land as
    emancipation   possession
    ("bring out,"   ("bring in,"
    יָצָא *yāṣā'*)   בוא *bô'*)
                v. 7 covenant formula

The whole of the disclosure from God concludes with a climactic reassertion, "I am Yahweh" (v. 8), which balances the statement at the beginning of this assertion in v. 6.

Thus the completed affirmation is bracketed by this self-disclosure. Between "I am Yahweh" (v. 6) and "I am Yahweh" (v. 8) is both the usual *recital of Exodus-land* (vv. 6, 8) and the *covenantal formula* of v. 7. The primary intent of the whole is that this hopeless people should have a firm offer of the character and resolve of Yahweh, whose very self-disclosure completely reshapes and reconstrues Israel's circumstance in bondage (or in exile). The self-disclosure of God to the slaves (vv. 6-8) grows out of the dynamic between past and present, and promise and suffering (vv. 3-5). The entire text pivots on the single root claim "I am Yahweh." This elemental reality of Yahweh makes a whole alternative history available to the hopeless ones.

6:9-13. This powerful, authoritative redefinition of reality might be expected to evoke delight, exuberance, and energy (vv. 9-13). It does not, however. We are in turn given two responses that in sequence fail to resonate with this remarkable self-offer of God.

The first response is that of the people to whom Moses delivered the self-disclosure of God (v. 9). The people "do not listen." Their response, however, is not because of stubbornness or resistance. It is, rather, because of "a broken spirit." The narrative is subtle and sensitive. The slaves, addressed by hope, have become saturated with hopelessness. The adjective *broken* bespeaks "exhausted," "spent," "short-lived." They cannot muster the vitality needed to accept the imagined alternative future just voiced. Why? Because of "their cruel slavery." They have become so deeply enmeshed in their bondage, so burdened by their brick quotas, so overwhelmed by the coercive legitimacy of Pharaoh's system, and so exhausted with survival issues that they are incapable of entertaining the alternative. The response is not one of recalcitrance, but of exhaustion. The text

accepts the fact that the depth of despair can (at least in the short term) defeat the hope of God. In this utterance, despair prevails.

Following the negative response of Israel comes a second mandate of God, and a second response of resistance, this time from Moses (vv. 10-12). God, who had sent Moses to the spent Israelites (v. 6), now sends Moses to Pharaoh (v. 11). The verb addressed to Pharaoh is the same used in 4:23, again an imperative addressed to Yahweh's presumed subordinate, Pharaoh.

The message to Pharaoh, however, never gets delivered. This time Pharaoh does not have the opportunity to refuse Yahweh's decree, for the refusal is made by Moses, the messenger (v. 12). Moses has been permeated by Israel's despair. When the ones for whom the word is good news will not heed, surely Pharaoh, for whom the word is bad news, will not heed either. Besides, adds Moses, "I have uncircumcised lips." This self-disqualification is not quite, as the NRSV has it, an appeal concerning poor speech, as in 4:10. Rather, to plead "uncircumcised lips" may mean that his lips are not adequate. Or it may mean that he is an outsider to Pharaoh, who will never take him seriously. In either case, Moses successfully resists the command of God.

The narrative adds a concluding statement (v. 13). This statement is interesting because it introduces Aaron into the chapter, thus preparing the way for the priestly genealogy to follow. Moreover, the move toward Aaron in the narrative means that the refusals of Israel (v. 9) and of Moses (v. 12) are completely ignored. Rather, these lines sound the good news one more time. Yahweh, via Moses and Aaron, has given command to Israel and to Pharaoh to work on Exodus. The construction of this sentence is odd and unclear. What is clear is that both parties to the Exodus, Israel and Egypt, are under the same command. Both are to work the liberation. Neither welcomes the new intrusion into their life, for Yahweh will cause both parties a staggering inconvenience. Freedom is a terribly disruptive gift from God, unwelcome in the midst of bondage, unwelcome for both perpetrators and victims.

6:14-27. Now that Aaron has been introduced into the narrative, we turn abruptly to a list of the "heads of ancestral houses." The genealogy begins with a roll call of the sons of Jacob:

Reuben, Simeon, Levi . . . but the list goes no farther than Levi (v. 16), for this is the point of interest and concern for the narrative. In turn, Levi's sons are three (vv. 16-19). The first of these sons, Gershon, is said to have two sons (v. 17), and Merari two sons (v. 19). The remainder of the genealogy is concerned with the lineage of Kohath, who has four sons and who eventually produces Moses and Aaron, the real subject of this piece. (Moses and Aaron are here fully legitimated, deeply rooted in the oldest and most respected priestly lines, which can be traced to the house of Levi.)

We may usefully reflect on why Moses and Aaron are given this emphasis. When we understand that, we shall likely understand the function of the genealogy in its setting. We have seen in v. 9, taken in its canonical context, that despair precludes Israel from hearing Moses' message of Moses. Despair, in fact, dismisses the message. The pedigree of Moses and Aaron argues against such dismissal. The slaves may despair, but this is not adequate ground for disregarding the message of Yahweh's emancipating self-disclosure. Moses and Aaron warrant a hearing, in spite of despair.

Conversely, taken in a critical context—i.e., in the context of exile (according to the P source)—the exiles may be reluctant to hear a message concerning emancipation from the power of Babylon, or from their role of powerless victim. They may prefer to conclude that the old exodus memory is not germane 600 years late in exile, because it seems so remote and liberation is, then as always, a costly inconvenience. If that be so, then the genealogy is a device for bringing the old story inescapably into the present. For Moses and Aaron, as presented in this list, are not simply ancient leaders, but are the focal references for present priestly authority. The genealogy thus provides an interpretive connection between ancient text and present legitimation of the message, making it contemporarily unavoidable.

6:28-30. The concluding verses are stunning, if this suggested battle for authority is cogent. One last time in this unit, the text sounds the root claim "I am Yahweh." Thus the unit ends as it began. There derives from this disclosure the second piece of news: "Tell Pharaoh." The claim of Yahweh is that Yahweh is able to command Pharaoh.

It would be a different matter if this episode ended with the triumphal assertion of v. 29. Verse 30, however, completely reverses field. One more time, Moses voices his resistant doubt, already surfaced in v. 12. Moses and Yahweh seem to have reached a stalemate. In 5:22-23, Moses cannot get Yahweh to save ($n\bar{a}ṣal$). Now in 6:28-30, Yahweh cannot get Moses to speak. We have seen in 3:7-10 that the Exodus is the doing of God, but that doing is through this human agent. At the end of chapter 6, we do not know whether God's resolve can move beyond Moses' resistance.

REFLECTIONS

1. As much as any text in the Exodus tradition, this one invites reflection upon the character of the God of Israel. Childs observes the "tremendous theocentric emphasis" of this text.[46] God's self-disclosure requires Israel to break with every generic understanding of God, with any notion that life with this God is a standard, conventional religious tale. The angular particularity of this God is an abrasion not only in our culture, but in the church as well.

This is God's self-disclosure freely given. God is subject and not object. God is the speaker and the initiator who gives what will be given. Israel's fresh chance derives from Yahweh's initiative.

God discloses a full, complete personal name: Yahweh. This is the surprising risk of particularity in ancient Israel. God has become fully available to Israel. Israel decided subsequently that this name must not be uttered. This refusal is out of awe and fear, not because Israel does not know or because Yahweh has withheld God's own self. The disclosure of the name completely changes the calculus between God and people, for this community now has leverage with God, which God has willingly given.

46. Childs, *Exodus,* 119.

God's very character is to make relationships, bring emancipation, and establish covenants. The covenantal formulation of v. 7 suggests not only that Israel is now always Yahweh connected, but also that Yahweh is always Israel connected, and will not again be peopleless. Moreover, the fact that this symmetrical formula has most currency precisely in the exile means that at the time of the deepest rupture of faith, this relatedness persists. The God of Israel is defined by that relatedness.

The utterance of the name of Yahweh contains within it the urge of the exodus. As Käsemann asserted, "Jesus means freedom."[47] So here, "Yahweh means exodus." Liberation is integral and intrinsic in Yahweh's very character. This is what has made the utterance of the name of Israel's God so endlessly disruptive and dangerous. Any talk of narrative theology must come finally to the shape and claim of this narrative. The story that most faithfully characterizes Israel (and Yahweh) is categorically and nonnegotiably a resolve for emancipation.

2. The move in the narrative between vv. 8 and 9 is devastating. It acknowledges that Yahweh's marvelous self-disclosure toward emancipation does not always and everywhere prevail. The reasons for resistance are not to be found in some dark theological category of "original sin" or in a psychological analysis. Rather, resistant despair is understood in terms of a political-economic analysis. It is "cruel slavery," which creates a "broken heart" and makes trust in Yahweh's emancipation impossible.

We may ponder the power of despair in two quite different directions. On the one hand, it seems clear enough that people who live under brutal repression might be reluctant to run the risk of theological talk of freedom, which invites wholesale civil disobedience. On the other hand, the same paralysis of despair may be more common in the Western church, not among the oppressed, but among the seduced who live in the consumptive end of Pharaoh's productive apparatus. Consumer ideology (not experienced quite as "cruel bondage") may also lead to a "broken spirit"—i.e., to the inability to think, believe, hope, or imagine outside the present tense. Despair is no more powerful among the brutalized than it is among those who are psychologically numbed by consumer satiation. Thus the realism of v. 10 concerning "broken spirit" may apply to more than one kind of bondage.

3. In this text, focused on God's self-disclosure, the cruciality of the human agent, Moses, is accented. After God's grand self-disclosure, Moses is dispatched (v. 6). It is again Moses who is sent to Pharaoh (v. 11). It is this "same Moses and Aaron" (vv. 26, 27); it is Moses who is to tell Pharaoh (v. 29). The entire operation intended by Yahweh, that brings the future to political reality, depends on this human agent. And this human agent can doubt and refuse (vv. 12, 30).

The intended emancipation is clearly rooted in God's own character and fully depends on the capability and willingness of Moses. It is, therefore, an intention that is fragile and vulnerable, because Moses is not easily commandeered. This dramatic interplay of divine resolve and human decisiveness, which is left unresolved in this chapter, gives us pause. God's resolve awaits human readiness. The Christian tradition affirms that in Jesus of Nazareth the gospel of God found a ready human agent, but this text leaves the issue where God's emancipatory impetus seems often left, unresolved and still waiting on a willing human agent.

47. Ernst Käsemann, *Jesus Means Freedom: A Polemical Survey of the New Testament* (London: SCM, 1969).

Exodus 7:1-13, Aaron's Staff

NIV	NRSV
7 Then the LORD said to Moses, "See, I have made you like God to Pharaoh, and your	**7** The LORD said to Moses, "See, I have made you like God to Pharaoh, and your brother

brother Aaron will be your prophet. ²You are to say everything I command you, and your brother Aaron is to tell Pharaoh to let the Israelites go out of his country. ³But I will harden Pharaoh's heart, and though I multiply my miraculous signs and wonders in Egypt, ⁴he will not listen to you. Then I will lay my hand on Egypt and with mighty acts of judgment I will bring out my divisions, my people the Israelites. ⁵And the Egyptians will know that I am the LORD when I stretch out my hand against Egypt and bring the Israelites out of it."

⁶Moses and Aaron did just as the LORD commanded them. ⁷Moses was eighty years old and Aaron eighty-three when they spoke to Pharaoh.

⁸The LORD said to Moses and Aaron, ⁹"When Pharaoh says to you, 'Perform a miracle,' then say to Aaron, 'Take your staff and throw it down before Pharaoh,' and it will become a snake."

¹⁰So Moses and Aaron went to Pharaoh and did just as the LORD commanded. Aaron threw his staff down in front of Pharaoh and his officials, and it became a snake. ¹¹Pharaoh then summoned wise men and sorcerers, and the Egyptian magicians also did the same things by their secret arts: ¹²Each one threw down his staff and it became a snake. But Aaron's staff swallowed up their staffs. ¹³Yet Pharaoh's heart became hard and he would not listen to them, just as the LORD had said.

Aaron shall be your prophet. ²You shall speak all that I command you, and your brother Aaron shall tell Pharaoh to let the Israelites go out of his land. ³But I will harden Pharaoh's heart, and I will multiply my signs and wonders in the land of Egypt. ⁴When Pharaoh does not listen to you, I will lay my hand upon Egypt and bring my people the Israelites, company by company, out of the land of Egypt by great acts of judgment. ⁵The Egyptians shall know that I am the LORD, when I stretch out my hand against Egypt and bring the Israelites out from among them." ⁶Moses and Aaron did so; they did just as the LORD commanded them. ⁷Moses was eighty years old and Aaron eighty-three when they spoke to Pharaoh.

⁸The LORD said to Moses and Aaron, ⁹"When Pharaoh says to you, 'Perform a wonder,' then you shall say to Aaron, 'Take your staff and throw it down before Pharaoh, and it will become a snake.'" ¹⁰So Moses and Aaron went to Pharaoh and did as the LORD had commanded; Aaron threw down his staff before Pharaoh and his officials, and it became a snake. ¹¹Then Pharaoh summoned the wise men and the sorcerers; and they also, the magicians of Egypt, did the same by their secret arts. ¹²Each one threw down his staff, and they became snakes; but Aaron's staff swallowed up theirs. ¹³Still Pharaoh's heart was hardened, and he would not listen to them, as the LORD had said.

COMMENTARY

Now begins the stylized account of the drama between Yahweh and Pharaoh, a struggle for power, control, and sovereignty (Exod 7–11). The entire corpus of the plague narrative is cast as a response to the exchange between Yahweh and Moses in 6:28-30. Yahweh has uttered a magisterial "I am Yahweh," and Moses has resisted in his paralyzing doubt. The dynamic of resistance (from Moses) and resolve (from Yahweh) is characteristic of calls to obedience, as in the cases of Gideon (Judg 6:11-24) and Jeremiah (Jer 1:4-10).

7:1-7. In vv. 1-2 of our chapter, Yahweh issues to Moses both an assurance (v. 1) and a command (v. 2). The assurance defines Moses' relation to

Pharaoh, and it structures Moses' relation to Aaron. Vis-à-vis Pharaoh, Moses is "a god," with enormous magisterial authority and sure to be obeyed. The Hebrew text, unlike the NRSV, does not say "like a god," but only "a god." Moses relates to Aaron as a god to a prophet; there is no doubt to who is superior and who is subordinate in their relationship.

The command, to be transmitted through Aaron to Pharaoh, is dominated by the verb *"let us go"*—i.e., *send* (שלח *šālaḥ*). Moses' "office" is instrumental to God's intention for the exodus.

Verse 3 promptly undermines and threatens both the assurance and the command of vv. 1-2.

In the very same breath, Yahweh now escalates the power struggle with Pharaoh. On the one hand, Yahweh will "harden" Pharaoh. On the other hand, Yahweh will do "signs and wonders," gestures of dazzling, inscrutable power. The fact that Yahweh both hardens and does signs appears to be simply a literary device for intensification, but there is a quality of political realism in the escalation. That is, action for liberation leads to greater repression, and greater repression produces more intense resolve for liberation. In that process, it is never known who will be first to lose nerve. Moreover, the very sign itself becomes the means whereby the hardening is accomplished, as the very gesture toward liberation is what evokes more repression—i.e., hardening.

Yahweh is undeterred by Pharaoh's refusal to listen (v. 4). Yahweh will (no matter what) bring Israel out from Egypt. Yahweh's "hand" (massive power) will rest on Egypt, and in the end it cannot be resisted. Yahweh's power will be evident in great "acts of judgment." The phrase suggests that the coming plagues are to be understood as acts that enforce Yahweh's sovereign governance, as the punishment of a recalcitrant vassal. (Cf. Ezekiel 28 for a critique of Egypt's imagined autonomy.) In his abuse of Israel, Pharaoh has sought to secede from Yahweh's magisterium. The sure indication of a "break-away state" is that it refuses to practice justice toward the powerless, a practice to which Yahweh is fully committed in all areas of Yahweh's realm.

The beginning paragraph of 7:1-7 is presented as a general introduction to the extended plague narrative, announcing most of the important theological themes that follow. Verse 6 suggests an important literary device that we shall see repeatedly in the structure of the book of Exodus. The whole of the paragraph is put together as *command and obedience*. Here the command is that Moses and Aaron shall speak to Pharaoh. In v. 6, we are told, they obeyed and confronted Pharaoh. In spite of his doubts and misgivings (cf. 6:12, 30), Moses is fully obedient to Yahweh. The information of v. 7 no doubt reflects the interest of the tradition (P) in such statistical data. More than that, however, the data voices the "scandal of particularity." Speech, to Pharaoh, is not simply generic and paradigmatic; Israel knows exactly when the speech occurred, who did it, and how old they were.

7:8-13. The narrative now becomes specific with the first of the "plagues" (vv. 8-13). Yahweh anticipates Pharaoh's testing of Moses and Aaron and their capacity to perform (v. 9). The anticipated challenge of Pharaoh is almost flippant: "Do a miracle!" Do something extraordinary to show that you are more than an ordinary protesting political figure. Verse 9 constitutes a command of Yahweh ("Take, throw"), and v. 10 is a report of immediate obedience. Moses and Aaron do promptly and exactly as Yahweh intends. Thus the "first wonder" is the amazing feat of transforming a staff, a symbol of authority into a "snake" (תַּנִּין *tannîn*).

The translation "snake" is far too innocuous and bland. What Moses and Aaron conjure is not a garden-variety snake. Rather, the term in most of its uses (and surely here) is a great sea "monster," bespeaking God's unleashing of chaos in the midst of Pharaoh's well-ordered realm. The production of the "monster" thus may announce in the empire that God is unleashing powerful disorder and elemental destabilization, which are the outcome of brutal oppression. In Gen 1:21 and Ps 148:7, the same "monster" is in fact an obedient creature of Yahweh. Thus what is a devastating threat against Egypt is a useful tool of Yahweh in the exercise of rightful sovereignty (cf. 104:26).

It is clear even to Pharaoh that Moses had worked "a wonder." He has demonstrated that he operates with a "surplus" of power given by Yahweh. What Moses has not yet established is whether that "surplus" is great enough to be a serious challenge to entrenched Pharaoh. Repressive regimes always think of the assertion of freedom as an inconvenience to be silenced. Pharaoh counters the wonder of Moses and Aaron by having his own technicians and "intelligence community" (wise men, sorcerers, and magicians who also possess extraordinary "secrets") match the feat of Moses and Aaron (vv. 11-12a).

In fact, the contest that is staged between these functionaries is really between Yahweh and Pharaoh, between the God of emancipation and the awesome power of evil and brutality. That power of brutal oppression also has "tricks" of its own to perform. It is not difficult to imagine that the court of Egypt possessed special skills and techniques, since it no doubt controlled the most advanced "research and development" available.

The surprise is that the disadvantaged slaves, dispatched by Yahweh, could do the same as the powers of the empire.

The contest ends in a stalemate; both sides produce "monsters." The narrative, however, will not leave the matter quite at a stalemate. It adds, "The staff of Aaron swallowed the Egyptian one" (v. 12*b*). That is, the chaos produced by Israel overpowers the chaos sanctioned by Pharaoh. The "swallowing" is an ominous threat to the order of the empire. Yahweh (and Israel) will unleash disorder beyond the control of the empire.

REFLECTIONS

This first episode only introduces an extended drama of the plagues. Nothing yet is resolved here; therefore, too much should not be claimed at this beginning point in the drama.

1. At the most obvious level, we witness here a show of power that concerns authority outside of the ordinary. We may, if we choose, call this show of power "magic," but we may also see that the "holy" enters the political with inscrutable force. The casting of the narrative already suggests that public power is more than arms and brute force. There is another kind of power that will not be denied or explained away; it is this other power that is endlessly troublesome for established tyrannical power. If there were no such "holy power," then might alone would make right, established power with superior weapons would govern to perpetuity, and tyrants would never be overthrown. Indeed, every established power that moves toward tyranny, public or more personally, dreams of such perpetuity. This narrative, however, tells us that there is more to the public process of power than surface control through brute force. There are ominous signs and wonders that are in fact the "hardening" way in which Yahweh does great "acts of judgment." This narrative is a reflection on that other sort of power that is only belatedly acknowledged.

2. The reference to "know" in v. 5 suggests that this episode is about not only the freedom of the slaves, but also the legitimate governance of Yahweh. The power struggle concerns bringing recalcitrant Pharaoh to acknowledge the rule of Yahweh. In recent times, with unlimited weapons capable of untold destruction, we have witnessed powerful political regimes imagine that they can operate autonomously and unchecked, only to be brought to heel by the force and assertion of the brutalized. Moreover, this text gives pause to any supposed super-power that imagines it is free to do what it wants with its seemingly unchecked power and with the lives of those entrusted to its governance.

3. The strategy of the drama depends on the complete obedience and daring of Moses and Aaron, an obedience that requires enormous nerve against ostensibly uneven odds. One need not turn this narrative into a tract for "revolutionary politics," but must observe that the critics of liberation theology are not correct in their insistence that the exodus is done by God and not by human initiative. In this and in the following narratives, all that is visible in the ongoing confrontation is human courage and human claims of authority. Behind that human action are certainly the references, claims, and allusions to the power and purpose of Yahweh, but they function primarily to give authorization and legitimacy to the human actors.

Exodus 7:14-25, The Plague of Blood

NIV	NRSV
[14]Then the LORD said to Moses, "Pharaoh's heart is unyielding; he refuses to let the people	14Then the LORD said to Moses, "Pharaoh's heart is hardened; he refuses to let the people go.

NIV

go. ¹⁵Go to Pharaoh in the morning as he goes out to the water. Wait on the bank of the Nile to meet him, and take in your hand the staff that was changed into a snake. ¹⁶Then say to him, 'The LORD, the God of the Hebrews, has sent me to say to you: Let my people go, so that they may worship me in the desert. But until now you have not listened. ¹⁷This is what the LORD says: By this you will know that I am the LORD: With the staff that is in my hand I will strike the water of the Nile, and it will be changed into blood. ¹⁸The fish in the Nile will die, and the river will stink; the Egyptians will not be able to drink its water.' "

¹⁹The LORD said to Moses, "Tell Aaron, 'Take your staff and stretch out your hand over the waters of Egypt—over the streams and canals, over the ponds and all the reservoirs'—and they will turn to blood. Blood will be everywhere in Egypt, even in the wooden buckets and stone jars."

²⁰Moses and Aaron did just as the LORD had commanded. He raised his staff in the presence of Pharaoh and his officials and struck the water of the Nile, and all the water was changed into blood. ²¹The fish in the Nile died, and the river smelled so bad that the Egyptians could not drink its water. Blood was everywhere in Egypt.

²²But the Egyptian magicians did the same things by their secret arts, and Pharaoh's heart became hard; he would not listen to Moses and Aaron, just as the LORD had said. ²³Instead, he turned and went into his palace, and did not take even this to heart. ²⁴And all the Egyptians dug along the Nile to get drinking water, because they could not drink the water of the river.

²⁵Seven days passed after the LORD struck the Nile.

NRSV

¹⁵Go to Pharaoh in the morning, as he is going out to the water; stand by at the river bank to meet him, and take in your hand the staff that was turned into a snake. ¹⁶Say to him, 'The LORD, the God of the Hebrews, sent me to you to say, "Let my people go, so that they may worship me in the wilderness." But until now you have not listened.' ¹⁷Thus says the LORD, "By this you shall know that I am the LORD." See, with the staff that is in my hand I will strike the water that is in the Nile, and it shall be turned to blood. ¹⁸The fish in the river shall die, the river itself shall stink, and the Egyptians shall be unable to drink water from the Nile.' " ¹⁹The LORD said to Moses, "Say to Aaron, 'Take your staff and stretch out your hand over the waters of Egypt—over its rivers, its canals, and its ponds, and all its pools of water—so that they may become blood; and there shall be blood throughout the whole land of Egypt, even in vessels of wood and in vessels of stone.' "

20Moses and Aaron did just as the LORD commanded. In the sight of Pharaoh and of his officials he lifted up the staff and struck the water in the river, and all the water in the river was turned into blood, ²¹and the fish in the river died. The river stank so that the Egyptians could not drink its water, and there was blood throughout the whole land of Egypt. ²²But the magicians of Egypt did the same by their secret arts; so Pharaoh's heart remained hardened, and he would not listen to them; as the LORD had said. ²³Pharaoh turned and went into his house, and he did not take even this to heart. ²⁴And all the Egyptians had to dig along the Nile for water to drink, for they could not drink the water of the river.

25Seven days passed after the LORD had struck the Nile.

COMMENTARY

In this second plague, the ante is upped in the terrible contest of repression and freedom. The episode is arranged as command (vv. 14-19), obedience (vv. 20-21), Egyptian response (vv. 22-23), and verdict (vv. 24-25).

The plague is the out-working of the sovereign command of Yahweh, which will not be retracted (vv. 14-19). Yahweh's speech takes note of the resistance of Pharaoh (v. 14), and Yahweh sends Moses to meet Pharaoh (v. 15). The place of confrontation is "the water." In an arid climate, society depends on the water; therefore, the maintenance of the water is the regime's first order of business. The water is the power for life in Egypt, and so it is the place of most dangerous challenge.

Moses is directed by Yahweh to issue one more time the most elemental demand, so that Pharaoh will not doubt the subject of the confrontation. The conflict concerns the power and will of "the God of the Hebrews," the God who has taken for a people this amorphous band of the marginal whom Pharaoh in his scorn and contempt keeps helpless and powerless. It is the will of this outsider God that this outsider people be permitted to worship Yahweh and so enact their primal and defining loyalty. Yahweh's instruction adds this chiding notice to Pharaoh: "Until now, you have not listened."

This statement suggests two matters. First, Pharaoh is expected to listen. The king of Egypt is assumed to be subordinate to the command of the "king of the slaves." Such listening would signify a complete transfiguration of politics, whereby the strong one becomes an obedient suppliant.[48] Second, the statement is one of ominous teasing: "Until now" implies "Not yet . . . but you will!" The speech of Yahweh is boldly confident, completely without doubt about the ultimate outcome of the power struggle.

In v. 17, Yahweh moves the speech toward the new "wonder." The next wonder will let Pharaoh "know," or acknowledge as sovereign, this outsider. Pharaoh will come to face Yahweh's awesome majesty when he sees that the Nile, the single source of life, is turned to blood and becomes a sign and channel for death. The Egyptians will not be able to drink from the Nile; life will shrivel, death will come, power will evaporate, and Pharaoh will be no more. Yahweh proposes to strike at the jugular of Pharaoh, for no king can survive in Egypt who does not control the Nile. On behalf of the brutalized, Yahweh will sabotage the life-support system of the empire.

Moses and Aaron obey the decree of Yahweh, and the river of life becomes a source of death (vv. 20-21). The description of their act is graphic and realistic. The fish all die and there is a terrible smell—the smell of death. There is, perhaps, some irony in the notion of the "stench," if this text is related to 5:21. In that verse, the supervisors of the

labor force dispute with Moses and Aaron, urging that their actions have made the Hebrews a "bad odor" to Pharaoh (i.e., an unwelcome presence in the regime). Now it is clear, however, that the smell of death from the Nile makes the "inconvenient odor" of the slaves benign and innocent.

Like every entrenched authority under assault, Pharaoh learns very slowly and very little (vv. 22-23). The technical community already knows how to turn the Nile of life into a channel of death. Perhaps that cynical, uncritical technical capacity is anticipated in 1:22. It is astonishing that the agents of Pharaoh have developed the capacity to undo the Nile of life. It is even more astonishing that they do not hesitate to unleash that power and knowledge against their own people in the context of exhibiting and maintaining royal power. But such are the costs of technology when driven by uncritical ideology. It is now clear that Pharaoh will stop at nothing, not even the death of his own people, to refuse and refute this new power threatening his order.

The decisive turn in the narrative that brings the episode to a conclusion is not the responding "wonder" of Egypt. It is, rather, Pharaoh's refusal to listen. He learns nothing, acknowledges nothing, and grants nothing. He just goes home (v. 23).

This confrontation, once again, ends in a stalemate, with both parties having enacted the same wonder. But once again it is an uneven stalemate. The battle has been fought on Pharaoh's home turf. It is *his Nile* that has been polluted. It is *his people* who must scramble for survival. It is *his land* now in the grip of death and its smell. It is *his power* in deep jeopardy. The slaves lose very little in this crisis, for they long ago learned to survive on almost nothing. Chaos threatens most those who have come to prize their own contrived order. As the slaves are not threatened, so Yahweh is not threatened. Yahweh can wait. Yahweh has set in motion a powerful process whereby Yahweh will repossess the Nile and reclaim sovereignty that Pharaoh has usurped.

Yahweh can wait. The narrator adds enigmatically "seven days" (v. 25). The drama is paced. The third episode can wait, to let death sink in, to let the dramatic turn take its full effect on the imagination of Egypt (and those who listen). Imagine, the king shut up for seven anxious days— Egyptians scrambling for water for seven days.

48. See Paul Lehmann, *The Transfiguration of Politics* (New York: Harper & Row, 1975), esp. his exposition of the Johannine Passion narrative, 48-70.

Seven days of chaos! It took seven days to enact the old story of creation, seven days to establish a new order of livelihood, seven days to cancel out the terrible deathliness of chaos (Gen 1:1–2:4a). Pharaoh loves chaos too much, relies upon it, embodies it. The slaves await a newness from God, who will finally claim the Nile. The slaves will wait for seven days. It is like waiting for sabbath, when even slaves shall not work and shall come to blessed rest.

REFLECTIONS

Our interpretation should focus on what is distinctive in this text—namely, the importance of the Nile. The Nile, taken in its historical specificity, is indeed the source of life for Egypt. Taken metaphorically, the Nile is not only Egypt's source of life, but it is also a symbol of authority. Whoever controls the Nile has power over life.

According to this account, the Nile in fact belongs to Yahweh, and Yahweh can dispose of it according to Yahweh's larger purposes. Conversely, Pharaoh has misunderstood both his own status as a creature who is dependent upon the Nile and his relation to Yahweh as a vassal who must obey Yahweh. The sorry outcome of this narrative makes clear that when the relation of creator and creature is distorted, life is put profoundly at risk (cf. Rom 1:20-25).

The large horizon of this narrative poses the question of arrogant power that tries to dispose of life on its own terms. In a scientific-technological society, it is seductive and easy to mistake the richness of creation entrusted to us, and imagine that it is a possession to be used at will. Conversely, given enormous technical and political power, it is easy to disregard one's status as a creature and to imagine there are no enduring lines of accountability in the use of power.

The result of distorted creaturehood and disturbed creation is the pitiful picture of the empire brought to its knees, humbled by the inescapable smell of death. One wonders whether the smell could penetrate even the sealed-off royal apartments with their up-to-date ventilation systems. There is also the ludicrous picture of formidable members of society digging desperately with their fingernails to find water enough to live. The empire is reduced to a caricature of itself. And, of course, they thought it couldn't happen here!

In the meantime, the creator waits a full seven days, the time of creation. Israel waits the same seven days, to see if God's newness will bring life for them.

Exodus 8:1-15, The Plague of Frogs

NIV

8 [1]Then the LORD said to Moses, "Go to Pharaoh and say to him, 'This is what the LORD says: Let my people go, so that they may worship me. [2]If you refuse to let them go, I will plague your whole country with frogs. [3]The Nile will teem with frogs. They will come up into your palace and your bedroom and onto your bed, into the houses of your officials and on your people, and into your ovens and kneading troughs. [4]The frogs will go up on you and your people and all your officials.'"

[5]Then the LORD said to Moses, "Tell Aaron, 'Stretch out your hand with your staff over the

NRSV

8 [a]Then the LORD said to Moses, "Go to Pharaoh and say to him, 'Thus says the LORD: Let my people go, so that they may worship me. [2]If you refuse to let them go, I will plague your whole country with frogs. [3]The river shall swarm with frogs; they shall come up into your palace, into your bedchamber and your bed, and into the houses of your officials and of your people,[b] and into your ovens and your kneading bowls. [4]The frogs shall come up on you and on your people and on all your officials.'" [5c]And the

[a] Ch 7.26 in Heb   [b] Gk: Heb upon your people   [c] Ch 8.1 in Heb

NIV

streams and canals and ponds, and make frogs come up on the land of Egypt.'"

⁶So Aaron stretched out his hand over the waters of Egypt, and the frogs came up and covered the land. ⁷But the magicians did the same things by their secret arts; they also made frogs come up on the land of Egypt.

⁸Pharaoh summoned Moses and Aaron and said, "Pray to the LORD to take the frogs away from me and my people, and I will let your people go to offer sacrifices to the LORD."

⁹Moses said to Pharaoh, "I leave to you the honor of setting the time for me to pray for you and your officials and your people that you and your houses may be rid of the frogs, except for those that remain in the Nile."

¹⁰"Tomorrow," Pharaoh said.

Moses replied, "It will be as you say, so that you may know there is no one like the LORD our God. ¹¹The frogs will leave you and your houses, your officials and your people; they will remain only in the Nile."

¹²After Moses and Aaron left Pharaoh, Moses cried out to the LORD about the frogs he had brought on Pharaoh. ¹³And the LORD did what Moses asked. The frogs died in the houses, in the courtyards and in the fields. ¹⁴They were piled into heaps, and the land reeked of them. ¹⁵But when Pharaoh saw that there was relief, he hardened his heart and would not listen to Moses and Aaron, just as the LORD had said.

NRSV

LORD said to Moses, "Say to Aaron, 'Stretch out your hand with your staff over the rivers, the canals, and the pools, and make frogs come up on the land of Egypt.'" ⁶So Aaron stretched out his hand over the waters of Egypt; and the frogs came up and covered the land of Egypt. ⁷But the magicians did the same by their secret arts, and brought frogs up on the land of Egypt.

8Then Pharaoh called Moses and Aaron, and said, "Pray to the LORD to take away the frogs from me and my people, and I will let the people go to sacrifice to the LORD." ⁹Moses said to Pharaoh, "Kindly tell me when I am to pray for you and for your officials and for your people, that the frogs may be removed from you and your houses and be left only in the Nile." ¹⁰And he said, "Tomorrow." Moses said, "As you say! So that you may know that there is no one like the LORD our God, ¹¹the frogs shall leave you and your houses and your officials and your people; they shall be left only in the Nile." ¹²Then Moses and Aaron went out from Pharaoh; and Moses cried out to the LORD concerning the frogs that he had brought upon Pharaoh.ᵃ ¹³And the LORD did as Moses requested: the frogs died in the houses, the courtyards, and the fields. ¹⁴And they gathered them together in heaps, and the land stank. ¹⁵But when Pharaoh saw that there was a respite, he hardened his heart, and would not listen to them, just as the LORD had said.

ᵃ Or frogs, as he had agreed with Pharaoh

COMMENTARY

The structure of the third plague narrative is by now in a general way familiar to us. Verses 1-7 are the full enactment of the plague. The narrative consists of a charge and warning to Pharaoh, an instruction to Moses, an enactment by Aaron, and a matching "wonder" by the Egyptians. The second part of the narrative, however, exhibits a negotiation about the threat that was not present in the first two cases (vv. 8-15). The narrative has become more complex than in the first two plagues, and the center of interest is no longer in the wonder itself, but in the derivative transaction.

8:1-7. At the outset, Yahweh gives a word to Moses that is to be relayed to Pharaoh (vv. 1-4). The primary insistence of Yahweh is unchanged: Pharaoh is to send the people of Yahweh to worship Yahweh (cf. 6:26-27; 7:2, 16). This command is followed, however, as it was not in the preceding scenes, with a quite specific and extensive threat.

The cost of refusing the command of Yahweh is to be a plague of frogs. The commandment concerning the frogs is brief (v. 2), but the portrayal of their coming is designed to produce dismay in the listener. The frogs with their filth, repulsiveness, disease, and smell will permeate everything: palace, bedchamber, bed, houses of the officials and of people, ovens, and kneading bowls. The frogs will be there "when you are at home, and when you are away, when you lie down and when you rise up" (cf. Deut 6:7). The rhetorical power of this catalogue is parallel to that of 7:19; in both cases the intent is to announce, "No escape." It costs a great deal to continue practices of exploitative labor that contradict the intentions of Yahweh. At least Pharaoh now knows the other side of the bargain and can make an informed decision about the costs he will undertake.

Yahweh's instruction to Moses quickly follows (v. 5). We all know the choice of one whose heart has been hardened, and there is no need to wait. Yahweh's command is to conjure frogs everywhere, all over the land. Aaron's performance follows immediately upon the command of Yahweh (v. 6), and the land is covered. This is saturation bombing with frogs! Almost as an aside, we are told that the Egyptian technicians match the "wonder" (v. 7). Powerful gestures of freedom are matched, so that the regime does not yet perceive itself as being under serious threat, certainly not anything that requires a review or adjustment of oppressive policy.

8:8-15. In the encounter that follows, the tone and mood are profoundly changed. Whereas the frogs had seemed rather routine in v. 7, by v. 8 it is acknowledged that there is indeed a crisis in the realm. It is as though Pharaoh urges, "Remove the frogs, and then we can talk." This first admission of such trouble on the part of the seemingly impervious Pharaoh suggests that Moses has won a first tactical victory. Speakers for the oppressed regularly have a problem receiving even recognition as a presence worthy of conversation. Moses has now made that case.

Pharaoh requests that Moses and Aaron "make supplication to Yahweh" (cf. Isa 19:22). In this appeal, Pharaoh concedes three matters: that the frogs are genuinely a problem beyond his capacity; that Moses and Aaron can do for him what he cannot do for himself; and, most important, that Yahweh can do what he cannot do—namely, revoke the threat and remove the frogs. This is the same Pharaoh who had haughtily dismissed Yahweh (5:2). But now something is happening in Pharaoh's alleged realm over which he has no

competence. Indeed, Pharaoh is urgent about the frogs, so urgent that he will bargain. He offers the most crucial trade-off, the one that Yahweh, Moses, and Aaron all want. Pharaoh will send the people to worship Yahweh, which act will affirm a withdrawal of any alleged loyalty to Pharaoh.

The enactment of Pharaoh's urgent petition is playful and leisurely, and Moses' response to Pharaoh seems mocking (v. 9). The initial term of his response is not *kindly,* as in the NRSV. Rather, it is a term of honor and praise. Either it is a sarcastic comment by Moses to this king who has now come as a suppliant (which seems likely), or it is a no-nonsense address, acknowledging the office of the king, but conceding nothing excessive by the way of honor or authority. Moses' question sounds like he is toying with Pharaoh. "When shall I pray?" invites an indication of how urgent the crisis is in the purview of Pharaoh. Moreover, Moses seems to add a qualification: The frogs will be withdrawn, but they will not be nullified. They will be kept in the Nile, ready at hand to be recalled.

Pharaoh's answer to the question (accepting the condition "only in the Nile" without comment) is "tomorrow"—i.e., "quickly" (מחר *māḥār*), without delay (v. 10). Moses in turn responds quickly and sharply: "As you say!" Moses and Yahweh, the frog removers, will act promptly. The purpose of the removal, however, is not primarily to accommodate the desperate king, or even to liberate the slaves. Rather, the frog removal is so that Pharaoh (and all his ilk) may come to know that "there is none like Yahweh." From the beginning, the plagues have been designed to bring Pharaoh to "knowledge," to acknowledge Yahweh's sovereignty (cf. 7:5). Here, however, the rhetoric is intensified.

The formula of v. 10 voices the incomparability of Yahweh. There is no other like Yahweh, none who proposes what Yahweh does, none who does what Yahweh does. This verse exhibits Israel's characteristic way of doing theology. The doxology moves from a quite specific act, in this case frog removal, to a sweeping theological affirmation. Pharaoh, the outsider and rival claimant to power, is expected to make the same doxological move as does Israel. Again, Moses adds his uncontested proviso, "left only in the Nile" (v. 11). The addition is to assert that Yahweh has not been duped, nor has Yahweh conceded anything to the power of Pharaoh.

The frog-removal operation is, of course, effective (vv. 12-14). Pharaoh gets what he wants, the lifting of the emergency; Yahweh is shown to be the full and final arbiter of frog deployment. Moses "cried out" to move Yahweh to act, even as the slaves had initially cried out (2:23); Moses' petition depends on this crucial verb. As Yahweh hears the cries of the slaves (3:7, 16), so now Yahweh hears the cries made for Egypt in its vexation. The voicing of effective petition and its positive reception dramatically assert that Egypt and Pharaoh belong to the regime of Yahweh, and that Yahweh is attentive even to their need. This is a God who answers those in trouble, even if it is the voice of the great nemesis, Pharaoh. The frogs are removed, but the land stinks (cf. 7:21)! Yahweh has left a calling card, one to remind Pharaoh, each time he breathes, that he has been bested.

The conclusion of this episode evidences that Moses is not in a fair fight (v. 15). Yahweh had warned Pharaoh in good faith (v. 2). Pharaoh has seemed to bargain in good faith (v. 8). Whether the bargain in v. 8 was a trick, or whether Pharaoh meant what he said at the time and then reneged,

we are not told, and we cannot know. In either case, Pharaoh did not do as he said in v. 8. When he saw that the threat of the frogs was withdrawn, he saw no need to keep his part of the bargain.

It may be easy to conclude (because it is most demeaning of Pharaoh) that Pharaoh had indeed tricked Moses and Yahweh. Such a reading, however, is not necessary. The crisis of frogs may have been acute enough to permit a serious promise by Pharaoh concerning the release of the slaves, but when the crisis is relaxed, making an actual concession seems both foolish and unnecessary. Making a promise and then reneging is a perfectly credible sequence for a major power under duress. The episode has, nonetheless, genuinely changed the tilt of the playing field. By his desperate petition and by his willingness to bargain at all, Pharaoh has in fact given recognition of the power, authority, and reality of Yahweh. By the end of this episode, Pharaoh is strategically and psychologically weakened, though not enough so that he knows it, not enough to warrant substantive concessions. Conversely, Yahweh, Moses, and Aaron are in a measurably strengthened position for the continued struggle for authority.

REFLECTIONS

Along with the standard rhetorical elements of the plague episodes, we may identify the following interpretive points:

1. Covering the earth with frogs that swarm is an appeal to Yahweh's sovereign governance as creator. The verb for "swarm" (שׁרץ *šāraṣ*) is used in 1:7 concerning the fruitfulness of Israel. Here the creator has reversed the process of creation in the face of Pharaoh, the great disturber and distorter of creation. Instead of a creation that teems with life, the teeming now is an invasion of the power of death, sent at the behest of God. God mobilizes the deathly capacity present in creation against this disobedient power.

2. Pharaoh's petition evidences the willingness of Yahweh to be seriously engaged with non-Israelites, even those who have resisted Yahweh's purpose. Pharaoh's petition is heard, honored, and positively answered. Yahweh intends the well-being even of Pharaoh and of Egypt. Note that Yahweh's readiness to hear prayer for Pharaoh is based on the hint in the narrative that Pharaoh has at least in part acknowledged the rule of Yahweh. Prayer is heard from those who accept the rule of Yahweh, to whom prayer is addressed.

3. The willingness of Yahweh to deal with Pharaoh and with Egypt, however, is uncompromising. Graciousness on the part of Yahweh is not to be construed as accommodation to any rival sovereignty. This lesson is so urgent for a "super power," or for any of us who imagine a piece of our lives where we have final say. Pharaoh here imagines he can enlist the goodness of Yahweh and yet retain his imperial turf. The subsequent narrative makes clear that Pharaoh cannot have it both ways.

4. The God who is disclosed here, whom Pharaoh must come to "know," is without rival, partner, competitor, or ally. This God is unlike any other. This affirmation hints at the abrasiveness of biblical faith in a culture that craves "user-friendly," benign religion. The narrative anticipates the poet of the exile in the assertion, "I am the LORD, and there is no other" (Isa 45:6 NRSV). Pharaoh has not yet come to that realization.

5. Perhaps the most interesting dramatic element in this narrative is the wavering of Pharaoh. After making a promise to Moses (v. 8), he promptly reneges on that promise (v. 15). The narrative is on sound psychological ground in this portrayal of Pharaoh. The narrator understands that in a place of acute crisis, we do resolve to make important changes that are responsible, healing, and large-hearted. However, when the pressure lifts, such costly changes are frequently seen to be neither necessary nor practical. (Cf. the same vacillating resolve in Judah [Jeremiah 34].) Pharaoh here exemplifies the way of a powerful agent (person or community) whose life is strewn with unkept promises and unpaid pledges. Without sustained pressure, it is not easy to listen, and less easy to change. The ongoing narrative shows Yahweh's capacity to keep the pressure on.

Exodus 8:16-19, The Plague of Gnats

NIV

[16]Then the LORD said to Moses, "Tell Aaron, 'Stretch out your staff and strike the dust of the ground,' and throughout the land of Egypt the dust will become gnats." [17]They did this, and when Aaron stretched out his hand with the staff and struck the dust of the ground, gnats came upon men and animals. All the dust throughout the land of Egypt became gnats. [18]But when the magicians tried to produce gnats by their secret arts, they could not. And the gnats were on men and animals.

[19]The magicians said to Pharaoh, "This is the finger of God." But Pharaoh's heart was hard and he would not listen, just as the LORD had said.

NRSV

16Then the LORD said to Moses, "Say to Aaron, 'Stretch out your staff and strike the dust of the earth, so that it may become gnats throughout the whole land of Egypt.'" [17]And they did so; Aaron stretched out his hand with his staff and struck the dust of the earth, and gnats came on humans and animals alike; all the dust of the earth turned into gnats throughout the whole land of Egypt. [18]The magicians tried to produce gnats by their secret arts, but they could not. There were gnats on both humans and animals. [19]And the magicians said to Pharaoh, "This is the finger of God!" But Pharaoh's heart was hardened, and he would not listen to them, just as the LORD had said.

COMMENTARY

This brief narrative of the fourth plague is introduced abruptly, presumably as a response to the bad faith of Pharaoh in v. 15. Again the narrative is divided as performance of the plague (vv. 16-17) and Egyptian response to it (vv. 18-19).

The affliction of gnats is brief and conventional. Yahweh issues a command to Aaron through Moses; Aaron obeys, and gnats invade the whole land. Of the damage caused by these pesky insects, Calvin comments: "But let us learn from this history, that all creatures are ready at God's lightest command, whenever He chooses to make use of them to chastise His enemies, and again that no animal is so vile and contemptible as not to have the power of doing injury when God employs it."[49]

As Fretheim has noticed, the sweeping rhetoric used to describe the "saturation bombing" of gnats is the language of creation. Fretheim suggests that

49. Calvin, *Commentaries,* 165.

"dust" refers to death—i.e., the end of the Egyptians (cf. Gen 3:19; Ps 104:29).[50] The gnats cover all the earth, humankind, and beasts. That is, God has sent a crippling vexation upon the whole earth as a response to the distortion of social relations on the part of Pharaoh. The well-being of the earth depends on the well-being of the human community.

The Egyptians' response to this plague is by now predictable. They will match the miracle of Aaron. In what may be a modest irony, the verb rendered "to produce" in the NRSV is יצא (yāṣā'), the term regularly used for "bringing out"—i.e., the exodus. The Egyptian technicians attempt to cause an exodus of the gnats.

The narrator, however, has set up the listener for a stunning surprise: "They could not!"(18a). The Egyptians were unable to match the Israelite miracle. From the outset, the first three plagues have been aimed at this dramatic moment in the sequence when the confrontation between Yahweh and Pharaoh reaches to the limit of Egyptian scientific-religious capability.

The verb for "could not" (יכל yākōl) elsewhere is rendered without the negative as "be able, prevail," assert one's way. It is used on occasion for a struggle with God. Thus in Gen 32:22-32, Jacob wrestles with a night-stranger (ostensibly God). In that struggle, the night-stranger does not "prevail" against Jacob (v. 25), but in the end salutes Jacob: "You have striven with God and with humans, and have prevailed [yākōl]" (v. 28 NRSV).

Conversely, in Jer 20:7-13, as Fishbane has shown, the same verb is used to very different effect.[51] In this complaint, Jeremiah is "not able" (v. 9). His opponents hope to "prevail" (v. 10), but in the end cannot prevail against God (v. 11). In this poem, unlike the Jacob narrative, God indeed prevails, against both Jeremiah and his opponents. From the outset, Jeremiah has lived

with the assurance from God that his enemies would not prevail—i.e., be able to destroy him—because of God's promise (cf. 1:19; 15:20). The poem in 20:7-13 seeks to claim this promise for the prophet one more time.

In these two examples, Gen 32:22-33 and Jer 20:7-13, it is evident that a struggle with the power of God can lead to different outcomes. Thus Jacob prevails, but Jeremiah and his opponents do not. The result of such a struggle is not known ahead of time. In our text, it was not known until v. 18 that Egypt "could not." This moment marks a dramatic turn in the power struggle between Yahweh and Pharaoh. The remainder of v. 18 adds laconically, "There were gnats on both humans and animals." This innocent statement, however, asserts that such a blanketing of the earth accents the power of Yahweh in contrast to the pitiful impotence of Egypt.

As a result of this dramatic and massive defeat, the technicians of the Egyptian empire are required to report their findings to Pharaoh (v. 19). Their report is astonishing, doxologically impressive on behalf of Yahweh, and ominous for the Egyptians. To be sure, the Egyptians do not name the name of Yahweh. Their language is more generic, but their statement is an acknowledgment that a power other than their own has been loosed in the empire.

Characteristically and sadly, Pharaoh will not listen, even to his own advisers. Pharaoh now has sufficient evidence, plus the council of his best scientists, to conclude that he cannot win the battle he is engaged in with Yahweh. The reason he cannot prevail is that he labors not simply against "flesh and blood" (i.e., Moses and Aaron), but against the power that drives all of creation. Increasingly, members of the narrative cast know this. Indeed, everyone knows it now except Pharaoh. The isolation of failed, decadent power encourages enormous self-deception.

---

50. Fretheim, *Exodus*, 118.
51. Michael Fishbane, *Text and Texture: Close Readings of Selected Biblical Texts,* 91-102.

REFLECTIONS

This brief narrative concerns the sovereignty of God, which overrides the power of the empire. Even the Egyptian scientists discover the limits of their power. It is clear to them that the empire cannot deliver the goods, cannot keep its promises, and cannot guarantee life. The empire, by its religious ideology and its technological posturing, wants to present itself as an ultimate source of life. One of the pastoral tasks invited by this text is the exploration of the limits of every "empire," every concentrated hosting of an illusion of life-power, in order to discern that such empires, public and personal, cannot keep their promises and cannot give life.

Surprisingly, by the very mouth of the Egyptians, the power of Yahweh to give life is confessed. Yahweh, an outsider to the empire, allied only with the marginal in Egypt, is here shown to be the one capable of creative power. The "power of Yahweh" is a strange and difficult theme in our modernist environment. The language of power concerning Yahweh is sure to be misunderstood, given our dominant models of power. In any case, the text suggests that power for life is not reliably situated where there are the usual forms and appearances of power. We are invited to look to the margins of life, among "the Hebrews," for God's power toward life. Publicly this suggests that those excluded from formal power may finally have the capacity to generate newness. More personally, it suggests that we look to the censored, less honorable, and denied parts of self in order to have life.

Exodus 8:20-32, The Plague of Flies

NIV

20Then the LORD said to Moses, "Get up early in the morning and confront Pharaoh as he goes to the water and say to him, 'This is what the LORD says: Let my people go, so that they may worship me. 21If you do not let my people go, I will send swarms of flies on you and your officials, on your people and into your houses. The houses of the Egyptians will be full of flies, and even the ground where they are.

22" 'But on that day I will deal differently with the land of Goshen, where my people live; no swarms of flies will be there, so that you will know that I, the LORD, am in this land. 23I will make a distinction[a] between my people and your people. This miraculous sign will occur tomorrow.' "

24And the LORD did this. Dense swarms of flies poured into Pharaoh's palace and into the houses of his officials, and throughout Egypt the land was ruined by the flies.

25Then Pharaoh summoned Moses and Aaron and said, "Go, sacrifice to your God here in the land."

26But Moses said, "That would not be right. The sacrifices we offer the LORD our God would be detestable to the Egyptians. And if we offer sacrifices that are detestable in their eyes, will they not stone us? 27We must take a three-day journey into the desert to offer sacrifices to the LORD our God, as he commands us."

28Pharaoh said, "I will let you go to offer

NRSV

20Then the LORD said to Moses, "Rise early in the morning and present yourself before Pharaoh, as he goes out to the water, and say to him, 'Thus says the LORD: Let my people go, so that they may worship me. 21For if you will not let my people go, I will send swarms of flies on you, your officials, and your people, and into your houses; and the houses of the Egyptians shall be filled with swarms of flies; so also the land where they live. 22But on that day I will set apart the land of Goshen, where my people live, so that no swarms of flies shall be there, that you may know that I the LORD am in this land. 23Thus I will make a distinction[a] between my people and your people. This sign shall appear tomorrow.' " 24The LORD did so, and great swarms of flies came into the house of Pharaoh and into his officials' houses; in all of Egypt the land was ruined because of the flies.

25Then Pharaoh summoned Moses and Aaron, and said, "Go, sacrifice to your God within the land." 26But Moses said, "It would not be right to do so; for the sacrifices that we offer to the LORD our God are offensive to the Egyptians. If we offer in the sight of the Egyptians sacrifices that are offensive to them, will they not stone us? 27We must go a three days' journey into the wilderness and sacrifice to the LORD our God as he commands us." 28So Pharaoh said, "I will let you go to sacrifice to the LORD your God in the wilderness, provided you do not go very far away. Pray for me." 29Then Moses said, "As soon as I

a23 Septuagint and Vulgate; Hebrew *will put a deliverance*

a Gk Vg: Heb *will set redemption*

NIV

sacrifices to the LORD your God in the desert, but you must not go very far. Now pray for me."

²⁹Moses answered, "As soon as I leave you, I will pray to the LORD, and tomorrow the flies will leave Pharaoh and his officials and his people. Only be sure that Pharaoh does not act deceitfully again by not letting the people go to offer sacrifices to the LORD."

³⁰Then Moses left Pharaoh and prayed to the LORD, ³¹and the LORD did what Moses asked: The flies left Pharaoh and his officials and his people; not a fly remained. ³²But this time also Pharaoh hardened his heart and would not let the people go.

NRSV

leave you, I will pray to the LORD that the swarms of flies may depart tomorrow from Pharaoh, from his officials, and from his people; only do not let Pharaoh again deal falsely by not letting the people go to sacrifice to the LORD."

30So Moses went out from Pharaoh and prayed to the LORD. ³¹And the LORD did as Moses asked: he removed the swarms of flies from Pharaoh, from his officials, and from his people; not one remained. ³²But Pharaoh hardened his heart this time also, and would not let the people go.

COMMENTARY

The narrative moves on quickly to the fifth plague. Again the narrative may be divided as performance (vv. 20-24) and Egyptian response (vv. 25-32). Note that the response is more extensive than the enactment of the plague itself.

8:20-24. The performance of the plague of flies is peculiar, because here Yahweh speaks (vv. 20-23) and acts (v. 24) without either Moses or Aaron. It is as though the confrontation has now become so urgent that Yahweh must act swiftly and decisively. To be sure, there is an initial command to Moses (v. 20*a*). Moses is to address Pharaoh at "the water." The king, in his anxiety, is presumably checking the condition of the Nile. Moses, however, is absent from the action and takes no part in the narrative.

In Yahweh's own mouth is a theological statement in three parts. First, Yahweh issues one more time the basic intention of the entire narrative: "Let my people go" (v. 20). All that is required is that Pharaoh act toward Yahweh in obedience as the vassal he is. Second, as in 8:2, Yahweh states the cost of disobedience and warns of flies that will penetrate everywhere (as did the frogs in 8:2-6). The flies will "fill the earth" (and subdue it?). Yahweh is prepared to place all of creation in jeopardy, because of Pharaoh's distortion of the human community. Third, Yahweh now exposits the notion of "my people," named

in v. 20 and often in this programmatic command (vv. 22-23*a*). The creator God who has just exhibited cosmic power now distinguishes and specifies that a particular people (group) in the empire is the object of Yahweh's special attention and concern. The one who speaks is "the God of the Hebrews" (cf. 7:16; 9:1). Thus "my people" who are to be let go are the Hebrews, that amorphous group of marginated outsiders who have not yet become a real community. The distinctions made by Yahweh are exactly the kinds of distinctions refused by the empire.

After the long speech of Yahweh's resolve, the actual implementation of the threat of flies is quick and devastating (v. 24). The flies come everywhere, and the land is "ruined," left like a land invaded and abandoned in the devastation of war. (In Gen 6:11-12, the term for "ruined" describes the land before the flood—"ruined" by corruption.)

8:25-32. The devastation is enough to evoke a desperate concession from Pharaoh (v. 25-28). He cleverly appears to give in and to grant the primal request so frequently stated (cf. v. 20). He will, indeed, let the people offer a sacrifice to their God. That is an enormous admission in itself, one echoing the admission of the scientists in v. 19. As in all such duplicitous bargaining positions, however, a qualification undermines the entire offer. The permit is for sacrifice "within the land," still under the aegis and scrutiny of Pharaoh. This qualification domesticates the act of worship and robs it of its dramatic, ideological power and subverts the entire offer.

Moses, of course, is quick to notice the cunning footnote to the offer, and so he also bargains (vv. 26-27). Moses' words suggest cool-headed negotiations, but in fact Moses abruptly rejects Pharaoh's modest concession. Worship of Yahweh "in the land" would put the slaves at risk, for they would be worshiping Yahweh where the rule of Pharaoh is still evident and assumed. Such an act would be odious and unacceptable (cf. 5:21). If Israel is to worship Yahweh, that worship must be unfettered and unconditional.

Pharaoh counters with a second offer, giving only slightly more ground (v. 28). Now Pharaoh agrees to let the worship of Yahweh take place in the wilderness, outside his domain. Pharaoh's statement indicates that he understands very well what is at stake in the debate about a worship permit. He understands *to whom* the worship is addressed: to Yahweh, his great adversary. He understands *where* the worship is to happen: in the wilderness, outside his domain and beyond his control.

Like every good negotiator, Pharaoh will not grant that much to Moses without getting something in return. Pharaoh seeks to impose two conditions. First, they cannot go far away. He wants to compromise on where, not far removed from his governance. He does not yet understand that a hair's breadth from his rule into the rule of Yahweh is a leap of light years from one governance to another. To this condition, Moses makes no response, and in fact ignores the proposal.

The second condition is "Pray for me." The LXX adds, as in 8:8, "Pray for me *to Yahweh.*"

The added condition of the Greek text is astonishing. It is a reluctant, but necessary, admission on the part of Pharaoh that Yahweh holds the power for life and that Pharaoh must finally submit to Yahweh's requirements. Moses is not excessively eager to accept this last proposal, which concedes a great deal.

Moses is very clear about what comes before what (v. 29). First comes the exodus, the departure. Then, only then, comes prayer to Yahweh on behalf of Pharaoh. Prayers to Yahweh are among Moses' few bargaining chips, and he will not use them lightly. Neither Moses nor Pharaoh doubts that Moses' prayer will effect a removal of the flies, but departure of the slaves is a condition of the removal of the flies. The flies come because of social abuses, and the flies can depart only when those abuses are rectified.

With the added warning of v. 29*b*, Moses proceeds to act out the condition set by Pharaoh: He prays to Yahweh (v. 30), and the prayer is promptly effected. Yahweh answers by removing all the flies from Pharaoh, from the officials, from the people. So far, so good—except that the narrative ends the account with a twist that violates everything negotiated. Moses had been right to be suspicious, but he had not been fearful enough. Moses had shrewdly sequenced matters in this agreement with Pharaoh: first exodus, then prayers (v. 29). But Moses had promptly disregarded his own condition and had made prayers for Pharaoh before there was an exodus. One more time, Pharaoh has triumphed and bested Moses. One more time, Pharaoh refuses to listen. One more time, Pharaoh acts with a hard heart. One more time, Yahweh is refused, and the slaves stay in bondage.

REFLECTIONS

Three new factors appear in this episode:

1. In the mouth of Yahweh is affirmed a distinction between peoples, between Hebrews and Egyptians. This is an exceedingly important and problematic affirmation. It is important because the entire narrative depends on this scandal of particularity. It is problematic because the notion of distinction flies in the face of our pervasive penchant for even-handed treatments.

Two very different readings are possible of this special people. On the one hand, it is conventional to take this people as "the Israelites," which leads directly to the affirmation that the Jews are the treasured people of God. This is the beginning point of the "mystery of Israel," which continues to be important for Christian theology.

A second, less obvious but more expansive, interpretative possibility suggests that this chosen people is not any ethnic community (or about-to-become ethnic community), but is in fact a sociological allusion to the Hebrews, the socially marginated, wherever and whomever they may be.[52] Inside the narrative itself, this later reading of a sociological distinction has peculiar cogency. Such an affirmation leads to a "class reading" of social relations, to the relationships between haves and have-nots, between the center and the margin. Given Yahweh's special care for the marginated, all social relations are now to be transformed, so that the ones conventionally dismissed as unimportant become peculiarly important.

2. The negotiations between Pharaoh and Moses reach new delicacy and subtlety here. Two facets are worth exploring. First, negotiation belongs to the reality of emancipation. Thus Moses' story will eventually culminate in a massive power play by Yahweh that overrides all possible negotiations. But along the way, Moses is prepared to do business with "the evil empire." Second, the negotiations in the end are not conducted in good faith. Pharaoh is endlessly resourceful, imaginative, devious, and deceptive in his zeal to preserve the status quo. At one level, this procedure simply squares with Niebuhrian realism. Power is not readily relinquished. At another level, if Pharaoh can be seen as an embodiment of demonic power, it is evident that historical-political embodiments of evil are massively resistant and do not easily give up privilege. One is left to adjudicate the extent to which Pharaoh is "normal" in the retention of power, and the extent to which he is an embodiment of larger-than-life evil.

We know already from 8:18 that Egypt cannot prevail. From the perspective of the narrator, that crucial point is settled. Pharaoh, however, has not yet conceded the point, and along the way, he still prevails in many immediate skirmishes. Moses and his folk keep their faith in this ultimate verdict of 8:18 to sustain them in the face of more immediate defeats. Thus the story is a model for enduring resolve in the face of hostile, even demonic, resistance.

3. Given this mismatch between *a special marginated people* and the *resilient bad faith of Egypt,* we may note a third element already evident in 8:28. Moses prays efficaciously, and his prayer matters in the public arena. Indeed, prayer appears to be Moses' major mode of power and point of bargaining. Prayer is a powerful activity in the narrative, deriving from the power of Yahweh, which is inadvertently acknowledged by Pharaoh. This narrative affirms that the public process of power is not reduced to visible imperial might. If it were, the story would have ended before now, and Pharaoh would have been secure and unbothered. There is, however, another sort of power at work in the public arena, according to this narrative. Prayer is where that other power becomes visible and effective.

While the narrative does not permit any easy, pious claim for the "power of prayer," it is nonetheless clear that prayer is a mode of political power that operates as an equalizer between the marginated, seemingly powerless, and the resilient power of Pharaoh's evil. Moses is utterly convinced of Yahweh's will for transformed social relations, and even Pharaoh must from time to time acknowledge the point. The narrative is not yet to the place where Pharaoh will, like Moses, "know that I am Yahweh." But then, the narrator has not yet finished with Pharaoh!

---

52. In a carefully nuanced way, Paul M. van Buren, *A Theology of the Jewish-Christian Reality Part II: A Christian Theology of the People Israel* (San Francisco: Harper & Row, 1983) 179-83, suggests that the suffering of the Jews may indeed be an important learning for marginated African Americans. And even Jon Levenson, "Exodus and Liberation," 169, concludes his polemical study: "The liberation of which the exodus is the paradigmatic instance is a liberation from degrading bondage for the endless service of the God who remembers his covenant, redeems from exile and oppression, and gives commandments through which the chosen community is sanctified." The "paradigmatic" character of the text-event opens its claims beyond its first "Hebrew" participants.

Exodus 9:1-12, The Plague on Livestock and the Plague of Boils

9 Then the LORD said to Moses, "Go to Pharaoh and say to him, 'This is what the LORD, the God of the Hebrews, says: "Let my people go, so that they may worship me." ²If you refuse to let them go and continue to hold them back, ³the hand of the LORD will bring a terrible plague on your livestock in the field—on your horses and donkeys and camels and on your cattle and sheep and goats. ⁴But the LORD will make a distinction between the livestock of Israel and that of Egypt, so that no animal belonging to the Israelites will die.' "

⁵The LORD set a time and said, "Tomorrow the LORD will do this in the land." ⁶And the next day the LORD did it: All the livestock of the Egyptians died, but not one animal belonging to the Israelites died. ⁷Pharaoh sent men to investigate and found that not even one of the animals of the Israelites had died. Yet his heart was unyielding and he would not let the people go.

⁸Then the LORD said to Moses and Aaron, "Take handfuls of soot from a furnace and have Moses toss it into the air in the presence of Pharaoh. ⁹It will become fine dust over the whole land of Egypt, and festering boils will break out on men and animals throughout the land."

¹⁰So they took soot from a furnace and stood before Pharaoh. Moses tossed it into the air, and festering boils broke out on men and animals. ¹¹The magicians could not stand before Moses because of the boils that were on them and on all the Egyptians. ¹²But the LORD hardened Pharaoh's heart and he would not listen to Moses and Aaron, just as the LORD had said to Moses.

9 Then the LORD said to Moses, "Go to Pharaoh, and say to him, 'Thus says the LORD, the God of the Hebrews: Let my people go, so that they may worship me. ²For if you refuse to let them go and still hold them, ³the hand of the LORD will strike with a deadly pestilence your livestock in the field: the horses, the donkeys, the camels, the herds, and the flocks. ⁴But the LORD will make a distinction between the livestock of Israel and that of Egypt, so that nothing shall die of all that belongs to the Israelites.'" ⁵The LORD set a time, saying, "Tomorrow the LORD will do this thing in the land." ⁶And on the next day the LORD did so; all the livestock of the Egyptians died, but of the livestock of the Israelites not one died. ⁷Pharaoh inquired and found that not one of the livestock of the Israelites was dead. But the heart of Pharaoh was hardened, and he would not let the people go.

8Then the LORD said to Moses and Aaron, "Take handfuls of soot from the kiln, and let Moses throw it in the air in the sight of Pharaoh. ⁹It shall become fine dust all over the land of Egypt, and shall cause festering boils on humans and animals throughout the whole land of Egypt." ¹⁰So they took soot from the kiln, and stood before Pharaoh, and Moses threw it in the air, and it caused festering boils on humans and animals. ¹¹The magicians could not stand before Moses because of the boils, for the boils afflicted the magicians as well as all the Egyptians. ¹²But the LORD hardened the heart of Pharaoh, and he would not listen to them, just as the LORD had spoken to Moses.

COMMENTARY

This unit consists in two brief plague episodes in which themes familiar to us are reiterated.

9:1-7. The first of these two plagues concerns "a very heavy pestilence," a contagious disease that will be out of control and will kill livestock. Fretheim suggests a play on *pestilence* (רבד *deber*) and *word* (רבד *dābār*), both attesting to the power of Yahweh.[53] This narrative account includes the

53. Fretheim, *Exodus*, 121.

usual elements of performance (vv. 1-6) and response (v. 7).

Yahweh again announces the primal intention of liberation, as a command of "the God of the Hebrews." The God of the Hebrews wants for them exactly what they have never had: freedom and the end of abusive dependence. Again the cost of disobedience to Yahweh's decree is stated (vv. 2-3). As usual, the promised vexation will penetrate all of Egyptian society—horses, donkeys, camels, herds, flocks—nothing is immune. Pha-raoh is given a clear choice.

This plague episode includes a variation. Yahweh sets a deadline—i.e., issues an ultimatum (v. 5). Pharaoh is very much treated like a recalcitrant vassal who needs to come back into obedience to the real authority. Oddly enough, no space or time is allowed between vv. 5 and 6. Pharaoh is given no slack time in the narrative to reflect upon or to ponder Yahweh's ultimatum. The threat of the deadline is followed promptly by execution of the threat. Yahweh does exactly what has been threatened. The contrast is as complete as promised: "all died/not one died."

Only now, and that briefly, is Pharaoh permitted to respond to the disaster. He conducts an investigation concerning the extent of the damage inflicted by Yahweh. One can imagine the imperial statisticians carefully reviewing the numbers, reporting a census of dead cattle. All the numbers are consistent, except for one fluke. One oddity defies normal explanation: In the land of Goshen, among the slave camps, there are no dead cattle. Scientists that they are, they can only give the data, drawing no large conclusions, either political or theological.

Pharaoh, however, receives the reports and draws conclusions as he must (v. 7). It is true! Yahweh really does make distinctions. The Hebrews really are an exempt people. The evidence makes unmistakably clear that what is happening in his realm no longer has any relation to the policies or interests of Pharaoh. The revolution has happened, and Pharaoh is increasingly ineffective and irrelevant. It is as though power is being wielded from somewhere else.

Pharaoh makes no comment about the odd statistic. But he knows! He nonetheless draws a conclusion, as though he has taken leave of his senses. He will refuse to acknowledge the new, emerging reality. He will persist in what must surely be, clear even to him, a lost cause. A hard heart leads him to maintain his own interest, even if he must refuse overwhelming reality.

9:8-12. The second of these two plague accounts concerns boils caused by soot. This sixth plague report is highly stylized and contains almost no narrative variation from the conventional form. In this account, there is no voicing of a command from Yahweh to Pharaoh, as is usual, nor is any negative condition stated that leaves Pharaoh an option to avoid the threat. In this account, the threat is not undertaken in order to urge an action by Pharaoh. It is simply announced as punishment. The initial speech of Yahweh to Moses moves immediately to "soot," which will cause boils (vv. 8-9).

The language of Yahweh's speech again reflects a comprehensive governance over humans and animals throughout the whole land. The implementation of the threat by Moses and Aaron is as expected (v. 10). The comment about the Egyptian experts utilizes the language of 8:18, though to somewhat different effect (v. 11). As in 8:18, the magicians "are not able" (יכל *yākōl*), but here the sentence does not refer to a counterattempt at a wonder. It suggests only that Pharaoh's experts are routed, cannot compete, and are finally disabled themselves by the boils. Pharaoh's response, even in the light of the failure of his own experts, is as defiant as usual (v. 12).

REFLECTIONS

These two truncated episodes advance no new themes and are among the most stylized and predictable of any of the narrative units concerning the plagues, but this may let us see more clearly the primary theological claims operative here, as elsewhere, in the plague cycle. The principle claim is that Yahweh, little by little, is establishing sovereignty over Egypt as part of Yahweh's rightful realm. Conversely, Pharaoh is being effectively delegitimated and is, little by little, abandoning his claims and his rule. It is for that reason that Pharaoh responds in desperate resistance. The real issue is not even the loss of the slaves but the loss of legitimacy, as Egypt is seen to be a territory over which Yahweh exercises control. The narrative portrays the way in which Yahweh "must increase," growing "stronger and stronger," and Pharaoh "must decrease," growing "weaker and weaker" (cf. 2 Sam 3:1; John 3:30).

Derivative from that main point about conflicting sovereignties are two interrelated subpoints. On the one hand, the Israelites, subjects of Yahweh's exodus intention, are treated distinctively under social protection (v. 4). Nothing bad can happen to Israel (vv. 6-7). On the other hand, Egypt is subject to Yahweh's special assault. Egypt, at the command of Yahweh, is saturated with the power of death (vv. 3-4, 6) and is unable to resist (v. 11).

The interpretive task is to see how the exodus narrative (or the classic Christian proclamation, for there are obvious connections here), touches in pastoral ways the lived reality of contemporary people. In truth, contemporary people, like ancient people, have in endless ways sworn allegiance or found themselves in bondage to false authorities who intend no good, but who only exploit and abuse. The pastoral office has as its work the emancipation of persons from all seductive bondages. This may entail the dramatic disclosure that the old loyalties are discredited. It also invites people to the hard, slow work of boldly withdrawing allegiance and refusing to obey or submit to these loyalties.

In this pastoral work, Pharaoh's role may take many forms. In public life, it may be the demanding, massive ideologies of sexism, racism, ageism, or nationalism or the seductive sloganeering of greed, anxiety, despair, or amnesia. Taken more personally, this false loyalty, which robs one of life may involve a false sense of self that leads to an abusive underliving or a destructive overliving that, in either case, is death-dealing. A popular phrasing of such false loyalties is "addiction" (or "co-dependency"), but the language of these narrative texts has long ago voiced the crisis more poignantly and more powerfully. Our more analytical language is not an advance on the narrative sketching of the conflict between freedom and bondage, life and death.

Exodus 9:13-35, The Plague of Hail

NIV

13Then the LORD said to Moses, "Get up early in the morning, confront Pharaoh and say to him, 'This is what the LORD, the God of the Hebrews, says: Let my people go, so that they may worship me, 14or this time I will send the full force of my plagues against you and against your officials and your people, so you may know that there is no one like me in all the earth. 15For by now I could have stretched out my hand and struck you and your people with a plague that would have wiped you off the earth. 16But I have raised you up[a] for this very purpose, that I might show you my power and that my name might be proclaimed in all the earth. 17You still set yourself against my people and will not let them go. 18Therefore, at this time tomorrow I will send the worst hailstorm that has ever fallen on Egypt, from the day it was founded till now. 19Give an order now to bring your livestock and everything you have in the field

[a]16 Or have spared you

NRSV

13Then the LORD said to Moses, "Rise up early in the morning and present yourself before Pharaoh, and say to him, 'Thus says the LORD, the God of the Hebrews: Let my people go, so that they may worship me. 14For this time I will send all my plagues upon you yourself, and upon your officials, and upon your people, so that you may know that there is no one like me in all the earth. 15For by now I could have stretched out my hand and struck you and your people with pestilence, and you would have been cut off from the earth. 16But this is why I have let you live: to show you my power, and to make my name resound through all the earth. 17You are still exalting yourself against my people, and will not let them go. 18Tomorrow at this time I will cause the heaviest hail to fall that has ever fallen in Egypt from the day it was founded until now. 19Send, therefore, and have your livestock and everything that you have in the open field brought to a secure

NIV

to a place of shelter, because the hail will fall on every man and animal that has not been brought in and is still out in the field, and they will die.'"

²⁰Those officials of Pharaoh who feared the word of the LORD hurried to bring their slaves and their livestock inside. ²¹But those who ignored the word of the LORD left their slaves and livestock in the field.

²²Then the LORD said to Moses, "Stretch out your hand toward the sky so that hail will fall all over Egypt—on men and animals and on everything growing in the fields of Egypt." ²³When Moses stretched out his staff toward the sky, the LORD sent thunder and hail, and lightning flashed down to the ground. So the LORD rained hail on the land of Egypt; ²⁴hail fell and lightning flashed back and forth. It was the worst storm in all the land of Egypt since it had become a nation. ²⁵Throughout Egypt hail struck everything in the fields—both men and animals; it beat down everything growing in the fields and stripped every tree. ²⁶The only place it did not hail was the land of Goshen, where the Israelites were.

²⁷Then Pharaoh summoned Moses and Aaron. "This time I have sinned," he said to them. "The LORD is in the right, and I and my people are in the wrong. ²⁸Pray to the LORD, for we have had enough thunder and hail. I will let you go; you don't have to stay any longer."

²⁹Moses replied, "When I have gone out of the city, I will spread out my hands in prayer to the LORD. The thunder will stop and there will be no more hail, so you may know that the earth is the LORD's. ³⁰But I know that you and your officials still do not fear the LORD God."

³¹(The flax and barley were destroyed, since the barley had headed and the flax was in bloom. ³²The wheat and spelt, however, were not destroyed, because they ripen later.)

³³Then Moses left Pharaoh and went out of the city. He spread out his hands toward the LORD; the thunder and hail stopped, and the rain no longer poured down on the land. ³⁴When Pharaoh saw that the rain and hail and thunder had stopped, he sinned again: He and his officials hardened their hearts. ³⁵So Pharaoh's heart was hard and he would not let the Israelites go, just as the LORD had said through Moses.

NRSV

place; every human or animal that is in the open field and is not brought under shelter will die when the hail comes down upon them.'" ²⁰Those officials of Pharaoh who feared the word of the LORD hurried their slaves and livestock off to a secure place. ²¹Those who did not regard the word of the LORD left their slaves and livestock in the open field.

²²The LORD said to Moses, "Stretch out your hand toward heaven so that hail may fall on the whole land of Egypt, on humans and animals and all the plants of the field in the land of Egypt." ²³Then Moses stretched out his staff toward heaven, and the LORD sent thunder and hail, and fire came down on the earth. And the LORD rained hail on the land of Egypt; ²⁴there was hail with fire flashing continually in the midst of it, such heavy hail as had never fallen in all the land of Egypt since it became a nation. ²⁵The hail struck down everything that was in the open field throughout all the land of Egypt, both human and animal; the hail also struck down all the plants of the field, and shattered every tree in the field. ²⁶Only in the land of Goshen, where the Israelites were, there was no hail.

²⁷Then Pharaoh summoned Moses and Aaron, and said to them, "This time I have sinned; the LORD is in the right, and I and my people are in the wrong. ²⁸Pray to the LORD! Enough of God's thunder and hail! I will let you go; you need stay no longer." ²⁹Moses said to him, "As soon as I have gone out of the city, I will stretch out my hands to the LORD; the thunder will cease, and there will be no more hail, so that you may know that the earth is the LORD's. ³⁰But as for you and your officials, I know that you do not yet fear the LORD God." ³¹(Now the flax and the barley were ruined, for the barley was in the ear and the flax was in bud. ³²But the wheat and the spelt were not ruined, for they are late in coming up.) ³³So Moses left Pharaoh, went out of the city, and stretched out his hands to the LORD; then the thunder and the hail ceased, and the rain no longer poured down on the earth. ³⁴But when Pharaoh saw that the rain and the hail and the thunder had ceased, he sinned once more and hardened his heart, he and his officials. ³⁵So the heart of Pharaoh was hardened, and he would not let the Israelites go, just as the LORD had spoken through Moses.

COMMENTARY

This seventh plague narrative is not only more extended than what has gone before, but it is also much more complex. The narrative divides into three parts: (1) decree and announcement (vv. 13-21), (2) implementation (vv. 22-26), and (3) response (vv. 27-35). In large sweep, this account is like all the others. Wholesale destruction of Egypt is wrought by Yahweh, and in the end, Pharaoh refuses to change. What is interesting and important in the narrative is not a changed outcome (which does not occur), but the process of the story itself.

9:13-21. Yahweh's decree (vv. 13-19) receives an initial mixed response from the Egyptians (v. 20-21). In the decree, Yahweh once more dispatches Moses to Pharaoh to issue again the unchanging resolve of the God of the Hebrews to have this people worship Yahweh in freedom (v. 13). What follows functions as a negative threat that is not unlike 8:2 or 9:2, though the actual "if" clause is lacking. That is, Yahweh declares in a straight, unqualified indicative that all the plagues will be sent. But, in fact, a condition is implied. This time, in the event of Pharaoh's resistance, Yahweh will empty the arsenal of plagues and exhaust the entire repertoire of threats. The reason for this wholesale resolve is not God's exhaustion or impatience. It is, rather, that Yahweh now knows that nothing less than this will affect Pharaoh.

The intention of this massive assault on Pharaoh, so far as this decree goes, is not primarily the liberation of the Hebrews, though that is implied as well. Rather, it is that Pharaoh might know (come to knowledge) that there is none like Yahweh in all the earth (v. 14). The plague thus is a means of theological instruction and persuasion. Pharaoh may have mistaken Yahweh to be like other gods, as do the Assyrian theologians later on (cf. Isa 36:18-20). If Yahweh is like the others, then this threat from Yahweh is neither dangerous nor serious, and the power of Yahweh is not much of a threat. The other gods will either fail in their weakness or be bought off in their greed. Yahweh's willingness to engage Pharaoh on behalf of the Hebrews, however, is an incontrovertible message to Pharaoh (if only Pharaoh will

pay attention), that Yahweh is not weak, not fickle, not vain, not for sale.

Then the inescapable question arises: If this is Yahweh's intent, why have there been two and one half chapters of only partial action? Why not do the whole job in the beginning? The narrative seems to recognize this wonderment and seeks to respond to it. There is no doubt, according to the narrative, that Yahweh could have obliterated Pharaoh by now. Yahweh's capacity to do this is not in doubt for the narrator. Yahweh, however, has not done so, but has chosen this slower strategy in order to evidence power, to let Yahweh's reputation (name) be noticed by the other nations. It is as though Yahweh always has one eye on public relation gains and knows that the other nations are watching (cf. Num 14:13-16). Moreover, the narrator seems to recognize that the "events" of the plagues are essentially a literary phenomenon and the delay is appropriate in order to generate more texts that provide more material for liturgic reenactment.

After that odd reflection on strategy, the speech of Yahweh returns to criticize Pharaoh and to justify the coming assault (v. 17). The telling indictment against Pharaoh is that he continues to "lift himself up" (סלל *sālal*) at the expense of the slaves, "my people." The verb used here is a quite distinctive one, used nowhere else in the Hebrew text in this way. It refers to the distortion of social relations whereby the high one towers over the low one. The verb suggests actual physical distance, and it is this distance between power and powerlessness that Yahweh will not tolerate in the earth.

The statement in vv. 14-17 is an odd departure from the conventional sequence of these episodes. Very often these narratives move directly from command (v. 13) to attack (vv. 18-19). The intervening verses provide a rich theological reflection, which joins together the incomparability of Yahweh and the indictment of Pharaoh for self-exaltation. That Yahweh is so preoccupied with Pharaoh's self-exaltation provides substance to the claim of incomparability and, in fact, means that Yahweh will tolerate no competitor.

The plague now to be enacted (cf. v. 14 on

"all my plagues") is very heavy hail, like no hail that had ever been in Egypt (v. 18). While v. 18 sounds a note of uncompromising severity, v. 19 provides a way out of the threat, suggesting that Yahweh wants not so much to destroy as to send a decisive signal to Pharaoh. The instruction gives the Egyptians a choice. The response to the instruction is mixed (vv. 20-21); some heed it, and some do not. It is interesting that the ones who heed the urging are not said to act simply in prudence or in terror. They are characterized as "fearing the word of Yahweh." It is likely that this fear intends nothing like faith, but means simply that they took wise precautions in the face of a real danger. That they took the threat to be a real danger, however, means they credit the word. They are, the story suggests, in an elemental way converted to the rule of Yahweh.

9:22-26. The implementation of the promised hail happens through word and act (vv. 22-26). The word to Moses is expansive in scope, reflecting the rule of the creator over all the land, over humans, animals, and plants (v. 22). Moses' act yields very heavy hail. True to the warning of v. 19, everything left exposed in the field is completely devastated (v. 25). The negatives of vv. 19 and 25 correlate precisely. The positives of vv. 19 and 26 do not correlate so completely. The positive warning indicates that anyone, any Egyptian could have had protection from the hail. The outcome introduced by "only" (רק *raq*) in v. 26, however, reports respite and protection only in Goshen where the Israelites dwell. Evidently there is some instability in these statements.

Our propensity, however, should be to let the text have its own clear say. Thus the warning in v. 19, now fully implemented in v. 26, suggests that Yahweh has a modest inclination to want to exempt even Egyptians from the assault, if only they "feared the word of the LORD." Calvin suggests that the Egyptians who feared the word of the Lord did so for "immediate and monetary terror," and did not seriously repent.[54] Using a class reading of the text to which I am sympathetic, Pixley suggests that as some of the Egyptians feared the word of the Lord, "we discern a crack in the solidarity of the state bureaucratic class . . . certain sectors of the state bureaucracies

were allied with the peasant uprising."[55] Accepting Yahweh as a force for the uprising, Pixley (unlike Calvin) regards their repentance as serious, including its profound political implications. The text itself passes over this odd relation of warning and outcome without comment.

9:27-35. The response of Pharaoh is poignant and urgent (vv. 27-28). The tone of his response is no longer that of a political ploy. Pharaoh moves to first-level theological talk: "I have sinned this time" (חטא *ḥāṭā'*). The statement is direct, unqualified, and unadorned. This initial term is supported by the double statement of Pharaoh: "Yahweh is righteous [צדיק *ṣaddîq*]; I [and my people] are wicked" [רשע *rāšaʿ*]." Taken at face value, the words show Pharaoh fully capitulating to Yahweh. The great power of Egypt is in this moment assessed by the covenantal notions of righteousness and wickedness.

Our suspicion about Pharaoh's statement is immediately evoked, however, when we read on into v. 28. The urgency of Pharaoh's full statement is indicated by the fact that no qualifications, conditions, or bargaining points are added. Nonetheless, it is clear that the purpose of Pharaoh's entire theological exercise is to curtail the threat of devastating hail. Pharaoh is being eminently practical. This confession of guilt is not a statement made for its own sake. It functions only to support the imperative petition which comes next: "Pray to Yahweh" (v. 28).

Moses' response and Pharaoh's ultimate resistance enact a sad tale, one we have heard before (vv. 29-35). Again Moses responds, as in 8:29, with the sequence, "First exodus, then intercession." This time Moses adds a phrase, reiterating the claim of v. 29. The purpose of stopping the hail, like the purpose of sending the hail (v. 14), is in order that Pharaoh may acknowledge what he does not want to acknowledge. In v. 14, the purpose is to know the incomparability of Yahweh; here the purpose is to know that all the earth belongs to Yahweh (and none of it to Pharaoh, v. 29). Thus the sending and withholding of hail are here not directly related to the emancipation of the Hebrews. They are, rather, to exhibit the authority of Yahweh in administer-

54. Calvin, *Commentaries*, 187.

55. Pixley, *On Exodus*, 52.

ing the power both to enhance and to diminish creation.

The wondrous doxological statement on the part of Moses (v. 29) is followed by an amazing strategic comment (v. 30). Moses had been conned by Pharaoh in 8:29-29, and he now recalls that occasion. He lets Pharaoh (and the reader) know that he is not unaware that he is being conned. He is under no illusions. He knows that the words of Pharaoh are only a ploy and he does not believe them.

The parenthetical comment of v. 31 is odd; it provides Pharaoh with a rationale for his capitulation to Moses at this time. The hail had already destroyed the flax and barley crops, and this is a land that must worry about famine. It was not too late to save the wheat and spelt. Thus Pharaoh has a most pragmatic reason for his seeming capitulation: He is buying time for the crops. If Moses knows about v. 31, if he is privy to the narrator's parenthetical comment, and if he knows about the crops, he may also know about Pharaoh's pragmatic reason. It happens, however, that Pharaoh's pragmatic effort to save the crops converges with Moses' witness to the power of the creator. How better to save the crop than to honor the God who gives both wheat and spelt!

Moses implements his plan as he said he would (v. 33). He prays, the hail stops, and the wheat and spelt are presumably saved. Moses, however, has not been duped. His theological witness does not depend on the reliability of Pharaoh. Moses wants to exhibit the power of the creator God, and that can happen regardless of what Pharaoh intends. The concluding response of Pharaoh does not surprise us (v. 34-35). Indeed, Moses in v. 30 has led us to expect this response. Pharaoh, who has acknowledged his sin (v. 27), sins more and increases his resistance. He resists Yahweh and he the exodus. He maintains distance between himself and the slaves, exalting himself at their expense (cf. v. 17).

Nothing in the empire has changed by the process of this narrative. Yahweh has delivered his heaviest blow in the hail, to no visible effect. Yahweh has, however, by sending and ending hail, been glorified as creator. Yahweh is about the business of "getting glory." That work of Yahweh, without regard to the exodus, does not depend on Pharaoh's cooperation. Indeed, Pharaoh's stubborn resistance makes the glory of Yahweh all the more spectacular.

REFLECTIONS

The sending of hail is the most extreme and severe plague yet wrought in this larger narrative. The severe hail, however, does not liberate Israel, for at the end of the narrative Pharaoh is as unresponsive as at the beginning (v. 35).

Yet, the episode is not futile. The peculiar accent of this encounter between the God of the Hebrews and the power of Egypt is on the twofold "know" that Moses announces in vv. 14-16 and 29.

1. The first of these affirmations is that Yahweh is incomparable, "There is no one like me in all the earth" (v. 14). The phrase "all the earth" is reiterated in v. 16. The plague is not aimed at the emancipation of the Hebrews, but at the manifestation of Yahweh in Yahweh's complete incomparability, for all of creation to see.

Such an affirmation invites reflection on Yahweh's incomparability. Of what does it consist? On the one hand, Yahweh is *incomparable in power.* The sending of hail of such destructive intensity is a show of force that, according to this narrative, no other hand (and certainly not any god of the Egyptian variety) could match. Yahweh is known not only to be "in all the earth" but, as will be asserted in v. 27, the earth belongs to Yahweh (see 19:5).

On the other hand, Yahweh's incomparability is known in Yahweh's *solidarity with the needy and the marginal.* In this text, this element of Yahweh's character is signaled in the nomenclature "God of the Hebrews." Unlike every other god in Egypt, or anywhere else for that matter, Yahweh's natural habitat is not in the royal palace or royal temple as patron and guarantor of the central establishment. Unlike all such gods, Yahweh's primary habitat is in the slave huts, and Yahweh's primary inclination is to attend to the cries and groans of the abused.

This aspect of Yahweh's incomparability is exceedingly difficult in a theological context of popular religion informed by a "theology of Zeus" and supported by a scholastic notion of God's omnipotence, omniscience, and omnipresence, in which "godness" is flatly equated with power. Clearly there is more to Yahweh's incomparability than raw power, the "more" being the solidarity that subverts and jeopardizes all established power in an advocacy of the powerless.

Israel's witness to the incomparability of Yahweh is delicate and subtle, holding together *power* and *solidarity,* majesty and mercy, so that each impinges upon and modifies the other without either being nullified. In much mistaken and careless trinitarian theology, this awesome dialectic is transposed so that "the Father" is an agent of power and "the Son" enacts solidarity with the weak. That, of course, will not do, for both elements belong everywhere to the wholeness and oneness of God. Both elements together give the Exodus story (and biblical faith more generally) their force and attractiveness. Thus the narrative of devastating hail shows forth not only *the enormous power of Yahweh which impresses Pharaoh,* but *power in the service of emancipation* for the Hebrews, those who have no power to emancipate themselves; and that angers and jeopardizes Pharaoh.

2. The second statement of "know" in this narrative asserts that Yahweh is the creator God who by right owns and administers all of creation: "The earth is the LORD's" (v. 29). This formula, which Pharaoh is supposed to learn and accept from the giving and removing of hail, is an exact parallel to the familiar doxology of Ps 24:1: "The earth is the LORD's and all that is in it,/ the world, and those who live in it."

The phrasing of Psalm 24 is commonly heard as a benign doxological statement to which we all assent in a kind of romantic gesture. The quote of the same claim in our text shows, however, that the formula is not at all benign and should not be heard simply as a vacuous celebration of the doxological loveliness of "nature." Rather, the statement, even in Psalm 24, is essentially confrontational and polemical. To assert that the earth belongs to Yahweh clearly implies as well that it does not belong to Pharaoh; and Pharaoh should not imagine that any part of the land is his to own or control.

In our own context, when oil spills, "smart bombs," and nuclear contamination are on the loose and at our door, the same phrasing is a polemical statement against the abuse of the earth by super powers who have the technical capacity to govern and to ruin the earth. Or closer, the formula draws a line of warning and relief against our compulsive consumerism. The fact that the earth belongs to Yahweh draws a line against our *greed,* for we are not able to possess the earth to satiation. The fact that the earth belongs to Yahweh draws a line against our *anxiety,* for we do not need to worry about our inability to possess (cf. Matt 6:25, 31). Thus the claim about the governance and control of the creator God is not simply a reassurance about the "character of the cosmos." That claim, in this narrative, is a direct warning against idolatrous political-economic aims.

Exodus 10:1-20, The Plague of Locusts

NIV

10 Then the LORD said to Moses, "Go to Pharaoh, for I have hardened his heart and the hearts of his officials so that I may perform these miraculous signs of mine among them ²that

NRSV

10 Then the LORD said to Moses, "Go to Pharaoh; for I have hardened his heart and the heart of his officials, in order that I may show these signs of mine among them, ²and that you

you may tell your children and grandchildren how I dealt harshly with the Egyptians and how I performed my signs among them, and that you may know that I am the LORD."

³So Moses and Aaron went to Pharaoh and said to him, "This is what the LORD, the God of the Hebrews, says: 'How long will you refuse to humble yourself before me? Let my people go, so that they may worship me. ⁴If you refuse to let them go, I will bring locusts into your country tomorrow. ⁵They will cover the face of the ground so that it cannot be seen. They will devour what little you have left after the hail, including every tree that is growing in your fields. ⁶They will fill your houses and those of all your officials and all the Egyptians—something neither your fathers nor your forefathers have ever seen from the day they settled in this land till now.' " Then Moses turned and left Pharaoh.

⁷Pharaoh's officials said to him, "How long will this man be a snare to us? Let the people go, so that they may worship the LORD their God. Do you not yet realize that Egypt is ruined?"

⁸Then Moses and Aaron were brought back to Pharaoh. "Go, worship the LORD your God," he said. "But just who will be going?"

⁹Moses answered, "We will go with our young and old, with our sons and daughters, and with our flocks and herds, because we are to celebrate a festival to the LORD."

¹⁰Pharaoh said, "The LORD be with you—if I let you go, along with your women and children! Clearly you are bent on evil.ᵃ ¹¹No! Have only the men go; and worship the LORD, since that's what you have been asking for." Then Moses and Aaron were driven out of Pharaoh's presence.

¹²And the LORD said to Moses, "Stretch out your hand over Egypt so that locusts will swarm over the land and devour everything growing in the fields, everything left by the hail."

¹³So Moses stretched out his staff over Egypt, and the LORD made an east wind blow across the land all that day and all that night. By morning the wind had brought the locusts; ¹⁴they invaded all Egypt and settled down in every area of the country in great numbers. Never before had there been such a plague of locusts, nor will there ever

ᵃ10 Or Be careful, trouble is in store for you!

may tell your children and grandchildren how I have made fools of the Egyptians and what signs I have done among them—so that you may know that I am the LORD."

3So Moses and Aaron went to Pharaoh, and said to him, "Thus says the LORD, the God of the Hebrews, 'How long will you refuse to humble yourself before me? Let my people go, so that they may worship me. ⁴For if you refuse to let my people go, tomorrow I will bring locusts into your country. ⁵They shall cover the surface of the land, so that no one will be able to see the land. They shall devour the last remnant left you after the hail, and they shall devour every tree of yours that grows in the field. ⁶They shall fill your houses, and the houses of all your officials and of all the Egyptians—something that neither your parents nor your grandparents have seen, from the day they came on earth to this day.' " Then he turned and went out from Pharaoh.

7Pharaoh's officials said to him, "How long shall this fellow be a snare to us? Let the people go, so that they may worship the LORD their God; do you not yet understand that Egypt is ruined?" 8So Moses and Aaron were brought back to Pharaoh, and he said to them, "Go, worship the LORD your God! But which ones are to go?" 9Moses said, "We will go with our young and our old; we will go with our sons and daughters and with our flocks and herds, because we have the LORD's festival to celebrate." ¹⁰He said to them, "The LORD indeed will be with you, if ever I let your little ones go with you! Plainly, you have some evil purpose in mind. ¹¹No, never! Your men may go and worship the LORD, for that is what you are asking." And they were driven out from Pharaoh's presence.

12Then the LORD said to Moses, "Stretch out your hand over the land of Egypt, so that the locusts may come upon it and eat every plant in the land, all that the hail has left." ¹³So Moses stretched out his staff over the land of Egypt, and the LORD brought an east wind upon the land all that day and all that night; when morning came, the east wind had brought the locusts. ¹⁴The locusts came upon all the land of Egypt and settled on the whole country of Egypt, such a dense swarm of locusts as had never been before,

NIV

be again. [15]They covered all the ground until it was black. They devoured all that was left after the hail—everything growing in the fields and the fruit on the trees. Nothing green remained on tree or plant in all the land of Egypt.

[16]Pharaoh quickly summoned Moses and Aaron and said, "I have sinned against the LORD your God and against you. [17]Now forgive my sin once more and pray to the LORD your God to take this deadly plague away from me."

[18]Moses then left Pharaoh and prayed to the LORD. [19]And the LORD changed the wind to a very strong west wind, which caught up the locusts and carried them into the Red Sea.[a] Not a locust was left anywhere in Egypt. [20]But the LORD hardened Pharaoh's heart, and he would not let the Israelites go.

[a]19 Hebrew *Yam Suph*; that is, Sea of Reeds

NRSV

nor ever shall be again. [15]They covered the surface of the whole land, so that the land was black; and they ate all the plants in the land and all the fruit of the trees that the hail had left; nothing green was left, no tree, no plant in the field, in all the land of Egypt. [16]Pharaoh hurriedly summoned Moses and Aaron and said, "I have sinned against the LORD your God, and against you. [17]Do forgive my sin just this once, and pray to the LORD your God that at the least he remove this deadly thing from me." [18]So he went out from Pharaoh and prayed to the LORD. [19]The LORD changed the wind into a very strong west wind, which lifted the locusts and drove them into the Red Sea;[a] not a single locust was left in all the country of Egypt. [20]But the LORD hardened Pharaoh's heart, and he would not let the Israelites go.

[a]Or *Sea of Reeds*

COMMENTARY

This eighth plague narrative contains many rhetorical elements that are by now familiar to us. Indeed, they are so familiar and predictable that we are likely to lose patience in listening and skip over the story too lightly. Liturgy (for which this material was designed) has reiterative, cumulative force. Just when we want to quit with the excessive familiarity of the material, we are addressed yet again. If, as listeners, we place ourselves in the position of the first subjects of the story—the Hebrew slaves—then, of course, the story is not old or boring or repetitious. This community of the marginated is ready to tell and hear the "old, old story" because it has become "the new, new song" of hope and possibility.

The intent of Yahweh, so Moses is to tell Pharaoh, is to keep the confrontation underway (v. 1). It is for that reason that Yahweh continues to harden Pharaoh's heart. The lines seem to suggest that Yahweh could stop this ongoing confrontation at any time. If Yahweh were to quit hardening the heart of Pharaoh (stop propping him up as an agent of resistance), Pharaoh would immediately collapse and the story would end

with an uncontested triumph for Yahweh. The reason for continuing to keep this fragile, dependent character afloat is to give Yahweh more opportunities to enact signs and to commit powerful gestures of solidarity with the Hebrews.

Verse 2 moves outside the confrontation, however, to the production of a text. The story of "hardening" and "signs" is kept going so that the confrontation may be "retold" (ספר *sipēr*). It is clear that the purpose of the text that is being generated is not simply to report or to remember, but to instruct coming generations of "Hebrews," "children and grandchildren," and induct them into the world of wonder, where God's signs override established, oppressive power.

Verse 2 clearly wants subsequent listening generations to participate in this "class reading" of political reality, for this is a story designed for the use and encouragement of the marginated against the establishment. The story tells us that the powerful can be duped, outflanked, overpowered, and made fools of. The playful quality of this statement means that the confrontation is not one of sheer power, but of a strategic mocking and trivialization of Pharaoh's power. Moreover, if Pharaoh stands as a paradigm for all established, oppressive power, then all subsequent generations of text-listeners are inducted into a mocking resentment toward such power. The ongoing story of hardening and sign is to generate a reading of one's own reality that enacts hope and possibility, precisely for those who seem defeated and hopeless.[56]

The process of downgrading Pharaoh, however, is only the penultimate intent of the narrative. Behind that is the hope that the children and grandchildren should come to know (as Pharaoh may come to know in 9:16, 29) that "I am Yahweh." It is, finally, acknowledgment of Yahweh that is the purpose of the narrative cycle. The purpose, astonishingly enough, is not to convert Pharaoh or to liberate the slaves, but to recruit the next generation of Israelites into this daring scenario of courage and confidence, passion and faith. In this case, the narrative is not aimed at Egypt at all, but is an in-house tale, for faith and against despair, resignation, and capitulation.

After this singularly reflective and candid statement, the narrative resumes with more familiar elements. Again, there are the elements of announcement (vv. 3-6), implementation (vv. 12-15), and Egyptian response (vv. 16-20), with an interlude for bargaining (vv. 7-11).

Yahweh's announcement to Pharaoh, through Moses and Aaron (vv. 3-6), again begins with a demand from the God of the Hebrews that the Hebrews be released (v. 3). Yahweh is uncompromising and unchanging in this resolve. The only new element in this statement is that Pharaoh's acceptance of the ultimatum from Yahweh would be to "humble" himself (ענה ʿānâ)—i.e., give up his haughty, exploitative distance from the Hebrews. The term for "humble" here is the counterpart to that translated "exalt" (סלל sālal) in 9:17. Pharaoh is thus urged to give up his pretensions, which fly in the face of Yahweh's governance.

The cost of Pharaoh's refusal to liberate the Hebrews this time is a locust swarm, which will come with massiveness, to devastate the land and to make the land genuinely uninhabitable. Like the anticipated hail in 9:18, the locust swarm will be unprecedented in severity. The reference to parents and grandparents in v. 6 is especially interesting in the light of "children and grandchildren" in v. 2. It may be that the reference to the generations in Egypt looks back because there is no Egyptian future, whereas the Israelite generations look forward to a people with a liberated future. Whereas the Egyptians have no future, the Hebrews have not been permitted by Egypt to have any past that is "recorded glory." Their whole life lies in front of them.

Moses' departure from Pharaoh is defiant and haughty (v. 6). As the plagues escalate, those closest to Pharaoh begin to catch on: Yahweh (and Moses) will not stop until Egypt is destroyed beyond recovery. Pharaoh's advisers counsel him to cut his losses (v. 7). After all, this pack of Hebrews is not a life-and-death matter to a great empire. The advisers now can see realistically and ask for an end to Pharaoh's obsession. Pixley observes that Pharaoh's political base is cracking, a base without which he cannot long endure.[57]

Pharaoh gives his advisers no sign of his reaction to their counsel. He does, however, resume his conversation with Moses and Aaron. Such a resumption of talks leads one to expect concessions, as has just been urged. Indeed, Pharaoh's opening statement to Moses and Aaron sounds like acceptance of the advice of his colleagues: "Go, worship the LORD your God!" (v. 8). It is as though Pharaoh just cannot bring himself to follow such a prudent policy, for immediately after his initial permission, he counters it with a question. The question appears to be a negotiating gesture, but it is in fact a nullification of the permit just granted (v. 8). Pharaoh certainly knows, as his advisers know, that Moses will not go unless all go.

There must have been a groan and a sigh and a sinking feeling in the room among both the royal advisers and the Israelite negotiators, when Pharaoh spoke. It is as though Pharaoh is "fated" ("hardened") to resist the simple act that is, among other things, in his own best interest. Pharaoh is portrayed not only as a fool, but as a man destined to self-destruction in his incredible "march of folly." Barbara Tuchman, in her book

---

56. Walzer, *Exodus and Revolution,* 149, concludes his stunning exposition with a threefold extrapolation from the text:
"—wherever you live, it is probably Egypt";
"—there is a better place,"
"—the way to the land is through the wilderness."

57. Pixley, *On Exodus,* 57.

The March of Folly, has used the phrase to describe the pursuit of self-destructive public policy, even when the policy is manifestly self-destructive and when there is visible counsel to the contrary.[58] Our narrator would say that what happens in such cases is the hardening that is inscrutably done by God. So it is with Pharaoh. He is made a fool of (v. 2) in quite a public, pitiful way.

Moses' answer to Pharaoh's bad faith question is hardly unexpected (v. 9). Everybody goes, or nobody goes! It is as though Moses now had assumed initiative in the talks. When a situation of abuse is too far deteriorated, it happens that the party of the victims comes to hold great moral power before which the establishment is largely delegitimated and, therefore, feeble. The narrator, in this case, knows that at a certain point the moral authority of the abused is so unavoidable that the shift of power and influence cannot be stopped. At this point, Moses seems to gain a profound edge in the debate with Pharaoh.

Moses' simple, non-negotiable statement evokes in Pharaoh an impossible condition, one he knows will be rejected: "Leave the children," presumably as hostages, to assure the slaves' return. Pharaoh concludes that Moses has "evil" in mind—that he intends to escape (v. 10). Pharaoh asserts that the initial request was for "man" to worship, and he will grant that, but he will not agree to a change in the terms (v. 11). Pharaoh manages a pious rescinding, as though he is the one who has been deceived. He holds to the letter of the request, but flagrantly violates its intention.

The mention of children (טַף *tap*) here is especially poignant in the light of v. 2. Pharaoh wants to bargain precisely the children, so as to deny to the slave community its future into the next generation, just as they are at the threshold of receiving such a future. The children and grandchildren in time to come are to be told that Moses insisted that "our sons and daughters" are to go with us, and we will not go without them. Chil-

dren in coming generations are to know that this beleaguered community, even in the face of this insane overlord, valued its children and refused to negotiate about them.

With negotiations failed, Moses does what Yahweh had promised (vv. 12-16). The invasion of locusts is as Yahweh had indicated. The narrator takes time and energy to give a full description of the invasion. Fretheim calls attention to the deliberate, frequent use of "all" in these verses, voicing a panoramic view of all creation.[59] (For a positive view of creation, see the frequent use of "all" in Ps 145:13-20.) Distorted social relations by the king who would not humble himself evokes the unleashing of chaos.

Pharaoh's response to the devastation of locusts is by now predictable (vv. 16-20). As in 9:27, Pharaoh confesses his sin, this time not only against Yahweh, but also against the Hebrews. The language of his request is intensified from 8:28 and 9:28. Now Pharaoh asks not only that Moses pray "for me to Yahweh," but that Moses should forgive him. This time Moses makes no interpretive comment; he promptly prays, and the locusts vanish.

It is perfectly credible, given what we have seen of recalcitrant tyrants in modern times, that Pha-raoh should choose to be destroyed rather than to yield (v. 20). Even such choices, however, do not (according to the narrator) fall outside Yahweh's sovereign intention. The juxtaposition of *fate and choice* in Pharaoh's behavior is not unlike that of Saul in the narratives of 1 Samuel. He is, indeed, fated by Yahweh to fail, but he also chooses his own destruction in a series of choices. Paul Ricoeur has observed about the power of sin in the narrative of Genesis 3 that the human couple are both *victims* and *perpetrators* of their destruction.[60] So it is with Saul, and so it is with Pharaoh. And so it is with all of our hard-heartedness in which we choose what has been given us.

---

58. Barbara W. Tuchman, *The March of Folly: From Troy to Vietnam* (New York: Ballantine, 1984).

59. Fretheim, *Exodus,* 127.
60. Paul Ricoeur, *The Symbolism of Evil* (Boston: Beacon, 1967) 252-60. On 258, Ricoeur notices that humanity in the primal story of sin is both "author and servant" of ethical demands, but there is more to disobedience than willfulness.

REFLECTIONS

This by now familiar storyline offers three distinct elements, along with the enduring struggle for sovereignty and emancipation.

1. The narrative about the plagues should be understood to have an educational purpose and potential (vv. 1-2). The narrative is enacted and retold as text in order that coming generations of young people can be inducted into this very tendentious reading of historical reality. The purpose of this education is to teach a most controversial angle of vision that plunges the young into radical social awareness that is resentful of cynical power, and militantly hopeful for the marginated. Such education, rooted in the partisan character of God, is a dangerous education in revolutionary evangelicalism. It makes the insistent affirmation that God intrudes against every abusive power for the sake of a reordered world. It is this nurture in a kind of evangelical restlessness that generates missional courage and energy.

2. The notion of using children as potential bargaining chips in power politics, and Moses' refusal of such bargaining, is a telling innovation in this episode.

The affirmation of the value of children is so obvious as not to require comment. Yet, if one probes more deeply into economic and military matters, it is clear that agents of aggressive, ambitious power regularly treat children as bargaining chips in large games of leverage. Such "useful" purposes for children are evident economically, when children become pawns of the market and are devalued in terms of health care, housing, and education because they do not serve the market. Or, more blatantly, children are easy pawns of power militarily, both in sacrificing young boys (and lately young girls) to military escapades, or in the ruthless abuse of "civilians" in wars that serve only the dominant economy. Against such cynical abuse, the community of Moses stands as an enduring witness. No amount of raw, abusive power is worth holding one child as a pawn or a hostage.

Out of the tradition of Moses, Jesus continued to value the "little ones" who had no political significance or market value (see Matt 10:42; 18:6, 10, 14). In his hands, children become an example of how the world will be organized when God's intention is actualized.

3. As Fretheim has so well observed, the plagues concern the undoing of creation. As a case in point, the locusts are indeed the unleashing of chaos. The reduction of biblical faith to pastoral-psychological categories (so widespread among us) leads to the domestication of some of its great themes. The imagination of the church will be well served by a recovery of the large theme of creation and chaos. God's power to undo creation because human power has gone mad in its abuse permits two affirmations. On the one hand, the maintenance of created order is a fragile task. On the other hand, "He's got the whole world in his hand," little-bitty children and massive Egyptian power. Even the terror of chaos, in God's hand, is in the service of a new world of emancipation.

Exodus 10:21-29, The Plague of Darkness

NIV

²¹Then the LORD said to Moses, "Stretch out your hand toward the sky so that darkness will spread over Egypt—darkness that can be felt." ²²So Moses stretched out his hand toward the sky,

NRSV

21Then the LORD said to Moses, "Stretch out your hand toward heaven so that there may be darkness over the land of Egypt, a darkness that can be felt." ²²So Moses stretched out his hand

NIV

and total darkness covered all Egypt for three days. ²³No one could see anyone else or leave his place for three days. Yet all the Israelites had light in the places where they lived.

²⁴Then Pharaoh summoned Moses and said, "Go, worship the LORD. Even your women and children may go with you; only leave your flocks and herds behind."

²⁵But Moses said, "You must allow us to have sacrifices and burnt offerings to present to the LORD our God. ²⁶Our livestock too must go with us; not a hoof is to be left behind. We have to use some of them in worshiping the LORD our God, and until we get there we will not know what we are to use to worship the LORD."

²⁷But the LORD hardened Pharaoh's heart, and he was not willing to let them go. ²⁸Pharaoh said to Moses, "Get out of my sight! Make sure you do not appear before me again! The day you see my face you will die."

²⁹"Just as you say," Moses replied, "I will never appear before you again."

NRSV

toward heaven, and there was dense darkness in all the land of Egypt for three days. ²³People could not see one another, and for three days they could not move from where they were; but all the Israelites had light where they lived. ²⁴Then Pharaoh summoned Moses, and said, "Go, worship the LORD. Only your flocks and your herds shall remain behind. Even your children may go with you." ²⁵But Moses said, "You must also let us have sacrifices and burnt offerings to sacrifice to the LORD our God. ²⁶Our livestock also must go with us; not a hoof shall be left behind, for we must choose some of them for the worship of the LORD our God, and we will not know what to use to worship the LORD until we arrive there." ²⁷But the LORD hardened Pharaoh's heart, and he was unwilling to let them go. ²⁸Then Pharaoh said to him, "Get away from me! Take care that you do not see my face again, for on the day you see my face you shall die." ²⁹Moses said, "Just as you say! I will never see your face again."

COMMENTARY

In this episode of the ninth plague, no command for emancipation is voiced. The narrative moves immediately to the performance of the plague itself (vv. 21-23), as though God is eager to get on with the escalation. After the plague, there is a twofold confrontation in response (vv. 24-26, 27-29).

10:21-23. In the performance of the plague itself, no message is sent to Pharaoh, no demand, no condition, no threat (vv. 21-23). Moses is commanded by Yahweh to create a darkness; Yahweh's intention is that the darkness should be "felt," palpable, intense, ominous, and impinging (v. 21). In the conjuring of the darkness, what Moses causes is described by a second word, *dense* (אפלה 'ăpēlâ) *darkness*, which is filled with the dread of God. The same word is used in Amos 5:21, Zeph 1:15, and Joel 2:2 to characterize the coming of God's terrible wrath and judgment.

It is exceedingly difficult in our positivistic, technically controlled, "Enlightenment" environment to grasp the threat of such darkness. In that

ancient "peopled" world (a world untamed, not unlike the dark) this darkness is one of unqualified terror. In that world, one is vulnerable, unprotected, and in severe danger in the dark. With the coming of the darkness, the modest, flimsy ordering of reality by Pharaoh is easily dismissed and set aside. Pharaoh and all his company are exposed to the raw, unnoticing, silent power of chaos, from which there is no refuge or escape. The rhetoric wants to bring the listener to a sense of profound threat, where all safeguards of an ordered world are withdrawn and dysfunctional. The empire is completely at risk.

However, "all the Israelites had light where they lived" (v. 23)! The contrast of darkness in Egypt and light in Israel is indeed peculiar. The Egyptians, the ones who bask in blessing and well-being (of the Sun-God?) are destined for the dread of chaos. The Israelites, the ones exposed and unprotected by present power arrangements, are in fact the ones who are given a cosmic safe conduct. This people, who walked in utter darkness, are now given light.

10:24-29. The first exchange between Pharaoh and Moses again gives the impression that Pha-raoh is prepared to negotiate (vv. 24-26). Again, as in v. 8, Pharaoh seemingly authorizes the departure of the slaves and then, in the next breath, qualifies his permission in an unacceptable way (v. 24). Pharaoh is determined to have hostages, though this time he proposes keeping only herds and cattle, and not children. Here as in v. 10, the purpose of retaining children or herds and flocks as hostages is never stated. The most likely "evil" that Pharaoh fears (cf. v. 10) is a complete escape with no return. In proposing to keep cattle as hostages, the narrator has Pharaoh acknowledge that this demand is less intense than the previous one concerning children. That is, Pha-raoh admits that this time he is not even considering the retention of the children. He lowers his asking price.

Moses' response is quick, unambiguous, and decisive (vv. 25-26). He identifies herds and flocks as material needed for an adequate sacrifice to Yahweh, so that to leave them behind would preclude a proper festival for Yahweh. Moses' language is uncompromising: "Not a hoof [פרסה *parsâ*] shall be left behind," not one small element of Israel can be left in the hands of Pharaoh. The exodus must be total, comprehensive, uncompromised.

The confrontation between Pharaoh and Moses has moved from the possibility of negotiations (vv. 24-26) to hard hostility and stiff resistance (vv. 27-29). As the negotiations collapse, Pharaoh is once more smitten by Yahweh to refuse any accommodation to Israel at all. Pharaoh promptly retracts even the qualified permission of v. 24. Indeed, Moses' refusal to make a deal has enraged Pharaoh. Instead of sending the slaves away to freedom, Pharaoh sends Moses away from court. Negotiations are over, and Moses is banished from any further negotiations. The narrator has now escalated the issue to its full, most extreme form. Moses will not beg or grovel. In fact, he assents to Pharaoh's hard verdict. Moses agrees that any time for negotiation is past. Both parties now will go for broke, with no accommodation, no bargaining of cattle or children, no concession, and no compromise. In retrospect, perhaps, there never was any chance for a compromise. The narrator, however, has continued to seduce us into thinking a compromise might happen. Now it becomes clear that there was nothing over which Moses could reach an accommodation with Pharaoh. From the outset, given Yahweh's character, the drama concerns a rigorous "either/or," with no middle ground.

This escalation makes perfectly good literary, liturgical, and theological sense. The narrator creates a situation in which Yahweh's victory is spectacular. This escalation also makes perfectly good political sense. Aligned against each other is a liberation movement now confident of victory and a tired, decadent regime unable to see the depth or power of the resistance that still imagines that Moses voices a fringe threat. Resolving this conflict cannot be put off much longer. As Yahweh's patience is exhausted, so the imagination of the narrator must also be near exhaustion, as more ways are needed to sustain the drama.

REFLECTIONS

The struggle for sovereignty takes shape in this episode around the struggle of light and darkness. There is little doubt that the darkness here refers to the portentous threat of chaos, which is what the terrorizing presence of Israel evokes in the empire.

1. Israel is clear that Yahweh governs darkness as well as light, that God can make use of either to effect Yahweh's purpose. This central conviction in Israel works against our "Enlightened," bourgeois theology, which imagines that God is singularly and everywhere light and love. Not so the God of Moses, the God of the Bible. This God works "the darkness" as well as the light (see Isa 45:7).

At the core of this latter affirmation is the assertion "I am Yahweh." The incomparability of Yahweh is as one who presides over heaven and earth, over life and death, over chaos and creation. This same God dispatches both darkness and light, decrees "weal" (שלום *šālôm*) and "evil" (רע *rāʿ*). Or the same affirmation is put by Hannah in more directly sociopolitical category: "The LORD makes poor and makes rich; he brings low, he also exalts" (1 Sam. 2:7 NRSV).

Our narrative is simply one concrete evidence of the two-sided capacity of Yahweh.

This view of God, to be sure, is a scandal to a religious culture that wants to associate only the "good things" with God. But such a cleaned-up version of God is faithful neither to our experience nor to the witness of Scripture itself. In biblical modes, God has a rich interior life and is endlessly processing and adjudicating the available options.

2. While the text itself focuses on the threat to Egypt, the assurance of light to Israel is a positive counterpart in the text. The children and grandchildren who are to be told this narrative are to learn of God's protection from the witness of God's own people. We have no better affirmation of this protective side of God than the statement of trust in Psalm 91.

The psalm, like Israel's faith in general, is content with doxological assurance. No explanation is given. No effort is used on those who are stricken with the darkness. This affirmation grows out of the experience-based confidence of the faithful. Thus the "sign" of darkness and light, in our narrative, is no isolated wonder. This narrative is well situated in the Psalmic tradition of Israel, which knows that God's darkness is ominous, but that light is given to protect the faithful.

This connection between light and trust in God, and darkness and abuse of God's intention is incontrovertible for Israel. Pharaoh, of course, cannot understand this faith. In his arrogant power, Pharaoh seeks to break the connection between obedience and light, but he cannot have his way. Interpreters of this narrative are wise to ponder both the savage release of chaos upon God's abusers and the odd, protective exception made for those who belong to God. Those who have learned to rely on God find the darkness dispelled.

3. Quite incidentally, without anything being made of it, v. 33 asserts that in the darkness, the Egyptians were immobilized "for three days." They could not see enough to move. It is likely that "three days" is a quite incidental time reference and is not intended as a precise measure. It may be worth noting that the same measure of time is used in the story of Jesus' death. Indeed, the whole earth is then like Egypt, for three days in the grip of death that prevented any freedom of action (cf. Matt 27:45-54). In that narrative, Easter is the dawn of God's light, which gives again the possibility of liberated life. The phrase "three days" is not used here with any special intentionality, nor does this text explicitly relate to the Easter narrative. Rather, in this context, it is evident that the Easter drama is not an isolated story. In Israel's narrative imagination, there were other times when chaos was unleashed, when the power of God's light broke in, making new life possible.

Exodus 11:1-10, Warning of the Final Plague

<table>
<tr><td>NIV</td><td>NRSV</td></tr>
<tr><td>

11 Now the LORD had said to Moses, "I will bring one more plague on Pharaoh and on Egypt. After that, he will let you go from here, and when he does, he will drive you out completely. ²Tell the people that men and women alike are to ask their neighbors for articles of silver and gold." ³(The LORD made the Egyptians favorably disposed toward the people, and Moses himself was highly regarded in Egypt by Pharaoh's officials and by the people.)

</td><td>

11 The LORD said to Moses, "I will bring one more plague upon Pharaoh and upon Egypt; afterwards he will let you go from here; indeed, when he lets you go, he will drive you away. ²Tell the people that every man is to ask his neighbor and every woman is to ask her neighbor for objects of silver and gold." ³The LORD gave the people favor in the sight of the Egyptians. Moreover, Moses himself was a man of great

</td></tr>
</table>

NIV

⁴So Moses said, "This is what the Lord says: 'About midnight I will go throughout Egypt. ⁵Every firstborn son in Egypt will die, from the firstborn son of Pharaoh, who sits on the throne, to the firstborn son of the slave girl, who is at her hand mill, and all the firstborn of the cattle as well. ⁶There will be loud wailing throughout Egypt—worse than there has ever been or ever will be again. ⁷But among the Israelites not a dog will bark at any man or animal.' Then you will know that the Lord makes a distinction between Egypt and Israel. ⁸All these officials of yours will come to me, bowing down before me and saying, 'Go, you and all the people who follow you!' After that I will leave." Then Moses, hot with anger, left Pharaoh.

⁹The Lord had said to Moses, "Pharaoh will refuse to listen to you—so that my wonders may be multiplied in Egypt." ¹⁰Moses and Aaron performed all these wonders before Pharaoh, but the Lord hardened Pharaoh's heart, and he would not let the Israelites go out of his country.

NRSV

importance in the land of Egypt, in the sight of Pharaoh's officials and in the sight of the people.

4Moses said, "Thus says the Lord: About midnight I will go out through Egypt. ⁵Every firstborn in the land of Egypt shall die, from the firstborn of Pharaoh who sits on his throne to the firstborn of the female slave who is behind the handmill, and all the firstborn of the livestock. ⁶Then there will be a loud cry throughout the whole land of Egypt, such as has never been or will ever be again. ⁷But not a dog shall growl at any of the Israelites—not at people, not at animals—so that you may know that the Lord makes a distinction between Egypt and Israel. ⁸Then all these officials of yours shall come down to me, and bow low to me, saying, 'Leave us, you and all the people who follow you.' After that I will leave." And in hot anger he left Pharaoh.

9The Lord said to Moses, "Pharaoh will not listen to you, in order that my wonders may be multiplied in the land of Egypt." ¹⁰Moses and Aaron performed all these wonders before Pharaoh; but the Lord hardened Pharaoh's heart, and he did not let the people of Israel go out of his land.

COMMENTARY

This final plague narrative, the most intensive and extreme action by Yahweh against Pharaoh, is brief. The narrative in chapter 11 is not in fact a narrative about the plague itself, but only a statement of Yahweh's intention and resolve. Thus, unlike any of the other plague episodes, here the announcement is separated from the actual implementation, which does not take place until 12:29-36.

This brief narrative is divided into three parts, a conversation between Yahweh and Moses (vv. 1-3), a statement of Moses to Pharaoh, including a comment by the narrator (vv. 4-8), and a second address of Yahweh to Moses (v. 9). The chapter concludes with a brief narrative statement (v. 10).

11:1-3. Yahweh's address to Moses lets Moses see the larger picture of Yahweh's strategy and intent (vv. 1-2). In 10:1-2, Yahweh had told Moses why this dramatic confrontation with Pha-

raoh continued for so long, scene after scene, crisis after crisis. Now Moses learns that Yahweh intends to conclude the drama. Presumably the encounter has gone on long enough to establish Israel's knowledge of Yahweh (cf. 10:2). Since the drama has continued only because Yahweh has persistently kept Pharaoh in the game by "hardening" him, Yahweh need only stop that action, and Pharaoh will cease to play his defiant role.

The narrative concedes that Pharaoh's position cannot be defended or justified rationally, because it is sustained only irrationally. Thus Yahweh informs Moses that this is the last plague, the most severe, and the one to bring sure results. Indeed, this plague will be so severe that not only will Pharaoh "send" (שלח *šālaḥ*) Israel away, but Pharaoh will "forcibly drive" them out. The verb נרש (*gāraš*) is stated with an infinitive absolute, indicating that Pharaoh will not only lose his reluctance about the exodus, but will be an adamant advocate of the departure. Pharaoh will finally come around to the view his advisers expressed in 10:7. The departure of Israel from bondage is the price of saving the throne of Egypt.

The exodus turns out to be a high price for Pharaoh. In vv. 2-3a, Yahweh instructs Moses that the Israelites are to "ask" from the Egyptians silver and gold. That is, they are not merely to escape, but are to leave with economic support granted by the Egyptians. This anticipation echoes Exod 3:21-22, where the escaping Israelites are authorized by Yahweh to take Egyptian jewelry and clothing when they leave.

David Daube has supplied the most suggestive interpretation of this authorization from Yahweh.[61] Daube observes that the language of 3:31, and the entire idea of 3:21-22 and 11:2-3a, is informed by the Mosaic "year of release" in Deut 15:1-11. In that most radical of all Mosaic laws, the Hebrew slave who is being freed from bondage is not only set free, but is "furnished liberally" with economic wherewithal to rejoin the economy in a fully functioning manner. This law is of interest to us because it voices a remarkably humane notion of debt bondage. On the one hand, it affirms that liberated slaves are to be treated with dignity and respect, they are to be measured in the terms that count most: economic terms. On the other hand, the law of Moses assumes that a responsible slaveholder will act fairly, honestly, and generously in respecting those rights. The slave, upon release, is to compensate from the master's goods, sufficient to resume a full and viable life.

Daube has seen that this law lies behind and informs the narratives of 3:20-21 and 11:2-3a. Bringing the exodus transaction into the horizon of this law, the tradition has decisively redefined the drama of the exodus. No longer is this a desperate, frantic, forced escape. For an instant, the instant of this interpretive moment, the exodus is pictured as an ordered, proper, regulated "letting go." The two main points of the law are implied: Israel has certain entitlements that will not be denied, and Pharaoh will act like a proper and responsible slave master and will give of his wealth for the sake of the renewed, liberated life of the slave community.

This presentation, in its own context, is palpa-

---

61. David Daube, *The Exodus Pattern in the Bible* (London: Faber and Faber, 1963) 55-61.

bly a fiction. At best, we may imagine that the slaves seized what they wanted on the run and the Egyptians conceded their right to nothing. But such "realism" contradicts the intentional, magisterial construal of these verses. Thus, according to these verses (which contradict the flow of the main narrative), there is no need to seize goods or to hurry, because the slaves are entitled to their well-equipped departure, guaranteed by torah provision. (The same construal is suggested for the exilic indenture in Babylon; cf. Isa 40:2.)

Moreover, the narrative adds that the slave community was granted (by Yahweh) "favor" in Egyptian eyes—i.e., it was well regarded according to legal requirements. Pharaoh's government also participated (for this one instant) in the redefinition of the Exodus crisis as an ordered economic transaction. The comment in v. 3b concerning Moses appears to be something of an afterthought to v. 3a. As Israel is granted favor, so Moses is respected. Perhaps it is better to reverse the matter: Moses is greatly feared by the Egyptians; *therefore,* the Israelites gain favor. Either way, the narrative makes clear that the authority of Moses (and of Yahweh) is now visible and powerful enough that Pharaoh's government is willing to play the role required by the law of the "year of release"—that of benign, benevolent creditor who respects and rehabilitates the debtor, in spite of Pharaoh's recalcitrance. By the power of Yahweh, Moses has wrought this redefinition of the relationship.

11:4-8. The second part of the narrative, Moses' speech to Pharaoh, fully rejects the benign portrayal of vv. 2-3. In this speech, Israel is not easily granted any rights or "favor." Pharaoh is not credited with any gracious behavior, and Moses does not sound like a greatly respected leader. Thus vv. 4-8, in contradiction to vv. 2-3, rejects any redefinition of the departure according to the law of the year of release and portrays the Exodus as a raw contest of power, with no quarter asked and none given. The fact that vv. 2-3 and 4-8 stand side by side suggests that the Israelite tradition had a variety of narrative-liturgical options in construing and constructing its past, as does every remembering community. Israel took no great pains to harmonize all of these options, but simply included them. The main tendency is to portray an intensely adversarial relation (as in

vv. 4-8), but it is not the only option (as evidenced in vv. 2-3a).

Moses' speech to Pharaoh is filled with ominous threat: "At midnight," in the middle of the darkness shaped and governed by Yahweh; "at midnight," when the rule of chaos is most formidable and Pharaoh is most vulnerable; "at midnight," when the covering deception of royal ideology in the daylight ceases to function in a protective way—then will come God's intrusion. God's most ominous, awesome assault against the empire will be hidden; it will be beyond both description and resistance. Pharaoh will be unable to counter the onslaught of Yahweh.

It will also be hidden from Israel and from Israel's storytellers. They will not know what happened or how it happened. They will be given no clues about how to describe the terrible onslaught, for who dares describe how the "rulers of this age" are made weak and finally destroyed! Yahweh's action, nonetheless, is as sure and powerful as it is hidden. Israel is reduced to elusive language.

In Yahweh's speech in the mouth of Moses, Yahweh uses the strong first-person pronoun "I" (אני 'ănî). But the "I" of Yahweh with the predicate "go out" is followed only by a stative verb, "shall die." It is not said, "I will kill." Thus the narrative itself is cautious and restrained in telling anything specific. Moreover, for this long and comprehensive threat, the verb is used only once. It is enough for the one verb to govern all of the sentence. The construction of the sentence is enormously elusive, and the relation between the parts of the sentence is enigmatic: "I go out/first-born die." That is all; we (and Pharaoh) are told nothing more.

Why is such brutal power arrayed against the firstborn? Why is there such a savage departure from the ordered image of vv. 2-3? The answer is suggested already in 4:22. Israel is Yahweh's firstborn. Israel is Yahweh's treasured son and precious heir and the chance for Yahweh's own future in the world. Pharaoh has brought Yahweh's own treasured heir under threat. If vv. 2-3 are informed by the law of Deut 15:1-11, perhaps this image is informed by the law of Deut 21:15-17. The firstborn has certain rights that may not be denied or compromised. The passion of Yahweh in these verses, however, is more than the enforcement of a legal requirement. It is more like the passion of a mother bear in defense of a cub (see Hos 13:8). The mother bear is ferocious and unreasoned in its attack on anything or anyone that threatens the cub. So Yahweh reacts irrationally and beyond measure for Israel. The empire must pay at every level for its refusal to honor this vulnerable heir.

The response to the slaughter of the firstborn in Egypt (slaughter of the innocents? [cf. 1:16-22]) is as might be expected (v. 6). There will be "a cry" (צעקה sĕ'āqâ) like there has never been nor ever will be. The tradition has preferred superlatives as it moves toward this dénouement of the struggle of Yahweh and Pharaoh. Thus both the hail (9:18) and the locusts (10:6) are said to be unparalleled in any part of the empire. The superlative used to describe the cry, however, is more extreme than that for hail or locust, because it reaches into the future: "will ever be again."

This unprecedented cry is a complete and intentional counterpart to the cry of Israel, reported in 2:23-24 and 3:7. Egypt's cry, however, is more intense, more severe, and more pain-filled than even the cry of Israel. Thus the liturgic tradition works an inversion, so that the people who impose the cry upon Israel are now the ones who cry. The one who continues to exalt himself (9:17) and refuses to humble himself (10:3) now has ended in a terrible humiliation. God will not be mocked; therefore, the empire has arrived at its terrible undoing.

The narrative does not go the full extent to complete the syllogism to say that the humiliated are now exalted (cf. Phil 2:9). It is, however, on its way to such an affirmation in v. 7. The terrible invasion by Yahweh at midnight is everywhere, except—! Yahweh does make a distinction! Yahweh does sort out and treat people differently. Even in the pitch dark of midnight, Yahweh can identify Yahweh's own firstborn, perhaps like a mother finding her child in the dark of the night, by smell, by touch, by instinct too deep to identify. Yahweh makes a distinction in the night, as Yahweh has been doing in the most recent plagues (cf. 8:23; 9:7, 26; 10:24). Israel sleeps through the deathwatch, sleeps so peacefully that not even its dogs are disturbed. Its livestock are valued and protected as well (see 9:7), and now its dogs are as well off as its cows. The contrast with Egypt could not be more complete or dramatic.

Moses goes on to assert that when this stark contrast of death and life is worked against Egypt, Egyptian officials will finally order Israel to leave (v. 8). The Egyptians will bow down to Moses, at long last recognizing his vast authority (cf. v. 3). They will use an imperative form of the Exodus word for "leave" (אֵצֵ *ṣēʾ*). The officials will finally enact the wisdom they had already reached in 10:7. Perhaps our verse suggests that they will finally overrule or persuade Pharaoh. In any case, they will gladly send Israel away, because the cost of keeping them has become too great. Then, says Moses, "I will go out" (אֵצֵא *ʾēṣēʾ*)! Moses' tone is not one of defeat. He has not been chased out. Rather, he envisions a triumphal, dignified exit, with the awareness of having prevailed over Egypt.

Moses' speech concludes. And then he goes out (יָצָא *yāṣāʾ*) "in hot anger"; he enacts his own exodus from Pharaoh. The narrator shrewdly uses the same verb for his exit. It is now clear that initiative in this conversation has passed from Pharaoh to Moses. In this account, Pharaoh and his officials listen in complete silence. They no longer have a voice in the terms of separation. It is no longer the case that Moses is "driven" from

their presence, as in 10:12. Now Moses decides when to come and go. Moses "goes out" whenever he will, and Pharaoh is helpless and mute before him.

11:9-10. After this remarkable and defiant announcement by Moses to the court of Egypt, Yahweh is permitted one more reprise. The verses once again juxtapose "signs" and "hardening." Gestures of sovereignty are matched by intensified hardening. Yahweh had announced in v. 1 that this was to be the final plague, the one to resolve everything. But we do not yet know. In v. 9, Yahweh pauses, almost against the promise of v. 1. Yahweh (or the narrator) is not yet ready to have the drama collapse into triumph and liberation. Moses is adamant, but Pharaoh will not yield. There are new threats, but no new yielding. Moses may go out from the presence of the court in defiance, but the larger "going out" of the Hebrews remains still in prospect. Could it be that Yahweh has miscalculated or has second thoughts? Yahweh allows that Pharaoh, even now, will not listen. But if this action against the firstborn will not persuade Pharaoh, it is difficult to imagine anything that will affect the Egyptian king. We are left to wait with oppressed Israel—at least until midnight.

REFLECTIONS

1. The ordered release of slaves (vv. 2-3), informed by the legal provision of Deut 15:1-11, suggests that power relations between slave and master, between power and powerlessness, between center and margin, are here radically revisioned. In the midst of a conventional relation of slave and master, Israel's narrative tradition introduces the very different notion of covenantal mutuality. In this relation, the slave has *rights* in relation to the material substance of the master, and the master has corresponding *obligations* to the slave. The conventional relation of indifference and disconnectedness is undermined and redefined.

This reconstrual of social relations is taken up in the NT in the Pauline formulation of freedom in Gal 3:28 and in the reflections on power relations in the epistle to Philemon. Further, this undermining of conventional power relations and redefinition in terms of mutuality in rights and obligations is suggestive for power relations in our contemporary world. The notion of creditor and debtor nations, the empowerment of emerging states that move beyond patterns of dependency, and the notion of mutuality in interpersonal relations are all touched by a rearticulation of rights and obligations. If even Pharaoh can, for a moment, be regarded as a responsible slave owner who liberates with dignity, then any contemporary relation based on power is subject to a very different construal.

2. The inversion of Israel and Egypt, in terms of who cries now and those who cried earlier, suggests something like an eschatological proviso on any set pattern of power relations. At the beginning of the Exodus story, one might have thought Egypt would abuse forever, and Israel could cry in agony to perpetuity, but now in this narrative, Egypt becomes the voice of the most extreme cry. The narrative affirms that drastic revision does indeed take place in power relations where no revision seemed possible. They change because in the end, the God of the Hebrews will not stay unengaged where the Hebrews are oppressed.

In an inchoate form, this belated new voice of cry anticipates the ominous words of Jesus: " 'Blessed are you who weep now,/ for you will laugh . . . / Woe to you who are laughing now,/ for you will mourn and weep' " (Luke 6:21, 25 NRSV).

Those who weep now will not weep forever, but will eventually laugh. And those who laugh now in their well-being will not be so joyous forever, for a time for crying will come (cf. Eccl 3:4). There is more to one's social situation than is visible in the daylight. There are nights and midnights, filled with both heavy loses and astonishing gifts.

3. Yahweh's brutal passion for the firstborn may astonish or even offend us. Yahweh is the partisan advocate who is prepared to go to any extreme in defense of this vulnerable child. That commitment is stated in 4:22 and is now to be enacted in a grossly irrational way against Pharaoh, who has sought to damage the firstborn.

This theme does not need to be turned in a christological direction, but it can be. Thus the role of Israel as firstborn in the NT lives in tension with Jesus as "the beloved Son." In christological usage, the irrational passion for the beloved Son who is heir greatly intensifies the risky offer of the Son for the sake of the world. Thus God's passion for the firstborn son in the exodus narrative plays against the offer of the Son in christological images. In Matt 21:33-41, the son who is heir (and therefore presumably the firstborn) is killed by the tenants. That much sounds like a generous risk on the part of the landlord. The hard saying at the end of the parable (vv. 41, 43-44, the part usually skipped in the reading of the church), suggests that the passion for the firstborn in our text persists in the NT metaphor. Contrary to much sweet, romantic Christian faith, this lord and father does not look lightly upon the killing of the son and heir. Just as Yahweh wars against Pharaoh, who has violated the beloved son and heir, so also the landlord in the Gospel story will kill and destroy those who hurt the Son. The metaphor leads to a hard saying for Pharaoh and the Egyptian system, and it becomes no less hard and ruthless in NT use.

EXODUS 12:1–15:21, THE LORD WILL REIGN

OVERVIEW

This material completes the liberation narrative of 1:1–15:21. The section is made up of quite diverse elements. In chapters 12–13, the predominant materials concern specific regulations for cultic remembrance and reenactment of the exodus from bondage, situated in the festivals of Passover and Unleavened Bread. In the midst of the cultic regulations, there are brief notices that form a conclusion to the events left unfinished in chapter 11—the implementation of the final "plague." The position of chapters 12–13 in the larger narrative suggests that the historical event fades off into or has been cast primarily in, through, and for liturgical reenactment. It is, therefore, impossible to sort out what in the narrative is reportage (in a modern fashion) and what is cultic rubric. This means that remembering and celebrating in Israel are acts that have no great interest in the kind of question of historical origin that readily occupies us. Rather, the central concern is that the ancient victory and liberation should be present now and for the coming generations as a way of redefining and reshaping present social reality.

In chapter 14, we have the only specific narrative of the actual crossing of the "sea." The force of reiterated phrases and the different conversations provided in the text suggest that this most dramatic narrative also is designed to serve cultic reiteration and replication. George Coats has argued persuasively that the crossing of the sea is a late entry into the narrative that had no necessary connection to the deliverance from Egypt.[62] Thus the sea motif tilts the narrative of liberation toward cosmic-mythic themes that are concerned with the struggle for created order against the surging threat of chaos, which is here embodied in Pharaoh.[63] By this interpretive development, the "historical liberation" is shown to be part of the larger enterprise of Yahweh in governing the unruly waters of chaos.[64] Such a theme in this prose narrative prepares the way for the magisterial poetry of 15:1-21.

Exodus 15:1-21 provides a great lyrical conclusion to the recital of liberation. It consists in two poems, connected by the prose remarks of v. 19. These poems are commonly thought to be among the most ancient and most radical in the OT.[65] The earlier poem is most likely the brief lyric of Miriam and the other women (vv. 20-21), providing a poignant counterpart to the role of the women in chaps. 1–2 in initiating the story of liberation through the nurture and protection of the baby Moses. Its doxological intent is to celebrate Yahweh's victory over the forces of injustice and chaos.

The second poem (15:1-18) lays down the primary themes that govern the entire Moses tradition. Indeed, the poem may lie behind and generate the longer narrative that now constitutes chaps. 1–15. The poem has as its theme the struggle with Pharaoh, leading to the triumph and glorious enthronement of Yahweh (v. 18). Whereas chaps. 5–11 narrate the *struggle* with Pharaoh, 12–15 narrate the complete *triumph* of Yahweh and the massive defeat of Pharaoh. Whereas the outcome is far from clear in the plague cycle, in these chapters the outcome is sure and unambiguous. It is a triumph and a defeat that this community continued to reenact and reiterate, both as a practice of hope and as an act of powerful, subversive social criticism. Israel is relentless in its conviction of the outcome and restless in the meantime about the pretensions of the chaotic powers.

---

62. George W. Coats, "The Traditio-Historical Character of the Red Sea Motif," *VT* 17 (1967) 253-65.

63. See Frank Moore Cross, *Canaanite Myth and Hebrew Epic* (Cambridge: Harvard University Press, 1973) 112-44; and Patrick D. Miller, Jr., *The Divine Warrior in Early Israel* (Cambridge: Harvard University Press, 1973).

64. For cautious or even negative judgments about the liberation motif in the exodus narrative, see Fretheim, *Exodus,* 18-20; Levenson, "Exodus and Liberation," 134-74; and Lyle Eslinger, "Freedom or Knowledge? Perspective and Purpose in the Exodus Narrative (Exodus 1–15)," *JSOT* 52 (1991) 43-60; and in response, Walter Brueggemann, "Pharaoh as Vassal: A Study of a Political Metaphor," forthcoming in *CBQ.*

65. See David Noel Freedman, "Divine Names and Titles in Early Hebrew Poetry," *Magnalia Dei: The Mighty Acts of God; Essays on the Bible and Archaeology in Memory of G. Ernest Wright,* eds. Frank Moore Cross et al. (Garden City, N.Y.: Doubleday, 1976) 55-107; and Bernhard W. Anderson, "The Song of Miriam Poetically and Theologically Considered," in *Directions in Biblical Hebrew Poetry,* ed. by Elaine R. Follis, JSOTSup 40 (Sheffield: Sheffield Academic, 1987) 285-96.

Exodus 12:1-28, The Passover Instituted

NIV

12 The LORD said to Moses and Aaron in Egypt, [2]"This month is to be for you the first month, the first month of your year. [3]Tell the whole community of Israel that on the tenth day of this month each man is to take a lamb[a] for his family, one for each household. [4]If any household is too small for a whole lamb, they must share one with their nearest neighbor, having taken into account the number of people there are. You are

a3 The Hebrew word can mean *lamb* or *kid*; also in verse 4.

NRSV

12 The LORD said to Moses and Aaron in the land of Egypt: [2]This month shall mark for you the beginning of months; it shall be the first month of the year for you. [3]Tell the whole congregation of Israel that on the tenth of this month they are to take a lamb for each family, a lamb for each household. [4]If a household is too small for a whole lamb, it shall join its closest neighbor in obtaining one; the lamb shall be divided in proportion to the number of people who eat of

to determine the amount of lamb needed in accordance with what each person will eat. [5]The animals you choose must be year-old males without defect, and you may take them from the sheep or the goats. [6]Take care of them until the fourteenth day of the month, when all the people of the community of Israel must slaughter them at twilight. [7]Then they are to take some of the blood and put it on the sides and tops of the doorframes of the houses where they eat the lambs. [8]That same night they are to eat the meat roasted over the fire, along with bitter herbs, and bread made without yeast. [9]Do not eat the meat raw or cooked in water, but roast it over the fire—head, legs and inner parts. [10]Do not leave any of it till morning; if some is left till morning, you must burn it. [11]This is how you are to eat it: with your cloak tucked into your belt, your sandals on your feet and your staff in your hand. Eat it in haste; it is the LORD's Passover.

[12]"On that same night I will pass through Egypt and strike down every firstborn—both men and animals—and I will bring judgment on all the gods of Egypt. I am the LORD. [13]The blood will be a sign for you on the houses where you are; and when I see the blood, I will pass over you. No destructive plague will touch you when I strike Egypt.

[14]"This is a day you are to commemorate; for the generations to come you shall celebrate it as a festival to the LORD—a lasting ordinance. [15]For seven days you are to eat bread made without yeast. On the first day remove the yeast from your houses, for whoever eats anything with yeast in it from the first day through the seventh must be cut off from Israel. [16]On the first day hold a sacred assembly, and another one on the seventh day. Do no work at all on these days, except to prepare food for everyone to eat—that is all you may do.

[17]"Celebrate the Feast of Unleavened Bread, because it was on this very day that I brought your divisions out of Egypt. Celebrate this day as a lasting ordinance for the generations to come. [18]In the first month you are to eat bread made without yeast, from the evening of the fourteenth day until the evening of the twenty-first day. [19]For seven days no yeast is to be found in your houses. And whoever eats anything with yeast in it must

it. [5]Your lamb shall be without blemish, a year-old male; you may take it from the sheep or from the goats. [6]You shall keep it until the fourteenth day of this month; then the whole assembled congregation of Israel shall slaughter it at twilight. [7]They shall take some of the blood and put it on the two doorposts and the lintel of the houses in which they eat it. [8]They shall eat the lamb that same night; they shall eat it roasted over the fire with unleavened bread and bitter herbs. [9]Do not eat any of it raw or boiled in water, but roasted over the fire, with its head, legs, and inner organs. [10]You shall let none of it remain until the morning; anything that remains until the morning you shall burn. [11]This is how you shall eat it: your loins girded, your sandals on your feet, and your staff in your hand; and you shall eat it hurriedly. It is the passover of the LORD. [12]For I will pass through the land of Egypt that night, and I will strike down every firstborn in the land of Egypt, both human beings and animals; on all the gods of Egypt I will execute judgments: I am the LORD. [13]The blood shall be a sign for you on the houses where you live: when I see the blood, I will pass over you, and no plague shall destroy you when I strike the land of Egypt.

14This day shall be a day of remembrance for you. You shall celebrate it as a festival to the LORD; throughout your generations you shall observe it as a perpetual ordinance. [15]Seven days you shall eat unleavened bread; on the first day you shall remove leaven from your houses, for whoever eats leavened bread from the first day until the seventh day shall be cut off from Israel. [16]On the first day you shall hold a solemn assembly, and on the seventh day a solemn assembly; no work shall be done on those days; only what everyone must eat, that alone may be prepared by you. [17]You shall observe the festival of unleavened bread, for on this very day I brought your companies out of the land of Egypt: you shall observe this day throughout your generations as a perpetual ordinance. [18]In the first month, from the evening of the fourteenth day until the evening of the twenty-first day, you shall eat unleavened bread. [19]For seven days no leaven shall be found in your houses; for whoever eats what is leavened shall be cut off from the congregation of Israel, whether an alien

NIV

be cut off from the community of Israel, whether he is an alien or native-born. ²⁰Eat nothing made with yeast. Wherever you live, you must eat unleavened bread."

²¹Then Moses summoned all the elders of Israel and said to them, "Go at once and select the animals for your families and slaughter the Passover lamb. ²²Take a bunch of hyssop, dip it into the blood in the basin and put some of the blood on the top and on both sides of the doorframe. Not one of you shall go out the door of his house until morning. ²³When the Lᴏʀᴅ goes through the land to strike down the Egyptians, he will see the blood on the top and sides of the doorframe and will pass over that doorway, and he will not permit the destroyer to enter your houses and strike you down.

²⁴"Obey these instructions as a lasting ordinance for you and your descendants. ²⁵When you enter the land that the Lᴏʀᴅ will give you as he promised, observe this ceremony. ²⁶And when your children ask you, 'What does this ceremony mean to you?' ²⁷then tell them, 'It is the Passover sacrifice to the Lᴏʀᴅ, who passed over the houses of the Israelites in Egypt and spared our homes when he struck down the Egyptians.'" Then the people bowed down and worshiped. ²⁸The Israelites did just what the Lᴏʀᴅ commanded Moses and Aaron.

NRSV

or a native of the land. ²⁰You shall eat nothing leavened; in all your settlements you shall eat unleavened bread.

²¹Then Moses called all the elders of Israel and said to them, "Go, select lambs for your families, and slaughter the passover lamb. ²²Take a bunch of hyssop, dip it in the blood that is in the basin, and touch the lintel and the two doorposts with the blood in the basin. None of you shall go outside the door of your house until morning. ²³For the Lᴏʀᴅ will pass through to strike down the Egyptians; when he sees the blood on the lintel and on the two doorposts, the Lᴏʀᴅ will pass over that door and will not allow the destroyer to enter your houses to strike you down. ²⁴You shall observe this rite as a perpetual ordinance for you and your children. ²⁵When you come to the land that the Lᴏʀᴅ will give you, as he has promised, you shall keep this observance. ²⁶And when your children ask you, 'What do you mean by this observance?' ²⁷you shall say, 'It is the passover sacrifice to the Lᴏʀᴅ, for he passed over the houses of the Israelites in Egypt, when he struck down the Egyptians but spared our houses.'" And the people bowed down and worshiped.

²⁸The Israelites went and did just as the Lᴏʀᴅ had commanded Moses and Aaron.

COMMENTARY

These verses interrupt the flow of the plague narrative, continued in vv. 29-39, in order to introduce a regularized liturgical practice that commemorates and reenacts the saving events of the exodus. In these verses we witness the transformation of a specific, concrete, remembered event into a liturgical convention that is available for replication. Indeed, as the text stands, the *liturgical festival* precedes the *saving event.* Thus the saving event itself is, in its very first casting, a liturgical event. The particularity of biblical memory is regularly converted into routine practice. That conversion is never easy or straightforward, as it is by no means obvious how that shift takes place. It is nonetheless a required shift in a community of faith that stakes its identity on

once-for-all events that must be kept present-tense in each new generation and in each new circumstance. In the Christian tradition, the obvious parallel is the way in which the "Last Supper" has been converted into the "Eucharist," with a host of interpretive problems and possibilities attached to it.

The text is divided into command (vv. 1-27) and obedience (v. 28). It is immediately clear that the relation between the two is disproportionate. It is assumed in the voicing of the command that there will be obedience, so that the second part of the equation does not need much attention.

The first extended command of Yahweh divides into two parts: a description of concrete procedures for the festival (vv. 1-10) and an interpretive comment on the meaning of the procedures (vv. 11-13). Two practices converge: putting of blood on the doorposts and the eating of unleavened bread. Those two practices together are treated now as part of a single event.

12:1-10. It is thought by many scholars that the provision for the protection by the blood of the lamb may reflect a more ancient rite, taken over by the Israelites, that in its origin had nothing to do with the exodus. While that may be so, the text itself exhibits no interest in such pre-Exodus antecedents, nor in offering explanations for what is required in the observance. This text is simply a manual for what must have been a consensus of right practice. The instructions are concerned for a certain kind of *blood* and a certain kind of *food.* For both food and blood, the festival revolves around the importance of the lamb, its supply, its distribution, and its use. For the celebration, each family unit must have a lamb. But since sheep are a treasured commodity in this pastoral economy, the requirement may be financially excessive for a family, so that a lamb might be more generally shared. The important matter is that each family unit, therefore each member of the community, must have access to a lamb.

12:11-13. In the interpretive comment of vv. 11-13, the twofold accent on food and blood is again maintained. Verse 11 suggests the dramatic intention of the eating. Those who share in this festal meal must be ready to go, ready to travel, ready to depart from the empire. Being ready to go requires that traveling clothes be worn, that shoes be on, and that staff be in hand. The entire drama must be done in a hurry in order to reenact the memory that leaving Egypt is a dangerous, anxiety-ridden business.

Verses 12-13 connect the blood, for the first time, with the exodus. The festival of Passover (פסח *pesaḥ*) marks the time when Yahweh "passes over" (עבר *ʿābar*) the community of Israel. The two Hebrew terms for "Passover" (*pesaḥ*) and "pass over" (*ʿābar*) are not the same, and it is only in our English translation that the terms appear to be equivalent. Nonetheless, the interpretive comment in vv. 11-13 refers to 11:4-7 when Yahweh shall "go out" (יצא *yāṣāʾ*) through the land as a "destroyer." In all the previous places where Yahweh makes a distinction (8:23;

9:6, 26; 10:23), Yahweh has known where the special people are and has needed no marking signal. Thus in the primal narrative, the sign of blood that is pivotal for the festival is for Yahweh superfluous. Nonetheless, the blood of the lamb has now become a sign, which quite concretely, publicly, and explicitly marks those who are to be exempt from destruction. Moreover, it is a sign that makes visible the promise of God and assures the protection of Israel.

Verse 12 adds a new element to the familiar formula of destruction. The assault of Yahweh against Egypt for the first time now includes "Egyptian gods." Now the narrative is understood as theologically defined. What finally needs to be overcome is not only the rulers and officials, but also the gods of the empire who sanction oppression and legitimate abusive policy. It may be that this inclusion of the gods only refocuses the festival to make it more "religious." Or it may be that the interpreters are now more discerning about the power of ideology and have come to see that political abuse depends on theological warrants.

12:14-20. The second element of command from Yahweh concerns the festival of unleavened bread (as distinct from Passover). The term for "festival" (חג *ḥag*) is now used; the same word was used for "worship" in 5:1 and 10:9. Three items are reiterated for this festival. First, it is important to have unleavened bread. Second, this special diet shall be followed in all generations. Third, anybody who violates this practice and uses leavened bread shall be "cut off" (i.e., excommunicated).

We are not told in the command why this practice is so important and demanding, but in the reflective comment of v. 11 we find out why. The reason for "unleaven" is that the slaves left in a hurry and could not wait around until the yeast worked and the bread rose. Anybody who has leavened bread is not "hurrying"—i.e., is not participating in the urgency and anxiety of the memory. Such a casualness may suggest being at ease in Egypt, where faithful Israel must never be at ease.

12:21-27. The third element of the celebration focuses on the blood and the Passover (vv. 21-27). The blood functions as a sign for the fundamental distinction God makes between Israel and Egypt, thus marking out Israel's special identity. This festival provides for the special status of Israel under the rule of God.

12:28. The narrative ends with the terse, cru-cial note "Israel obeyed" (v. 28). Israel is prepared to sustain its special identity, and to accept its odd role in the governance of Yahweh.

REFLECTIONS

These verses provide opportunity to reflect on the cruciality of worship for the maintenance of the identity of a historical community and on the importance of doing worship rightly. The text also suggests the wisdom of avoiding excessive explanation for what is done in worship. Much Christian worship is either excessively doctrinal and rational or excessively moralistic and didactic. In either case, it is excessively self-conscious. Worship entails a willing suspension of disbelief, a reentering of a definitional memory, and a readiness to submit to the memory as identity-bestowing for both parents and children. This community, in every time and place, is prepared to reengage this primitive, unreflective act.

1. Such worship requires pre-rational activity that is simply done without explanation or even understanding. Such worship violates our sophisticated rationality whereby we keep control of what we do and screen out less sophisticated gestures. Childs observes that the rites are "uninterpreted."[66] Serious worship requires violating our sophisticated rationality in order to participate alongside our more credulous ancestors.

In these particular provisions, such activity includes eating in a hurry (perhaps standing up), anxious, at risk, ready to leave. Such activity includes blood on a door post to mark specialness, a sense of being wondrously protected, valued, and safe. Both eating in a hurry and being marked for safety are acts in which children can engage. It is no wonder that it is a child who asks, "What do you mean by this observance?" (v. 26).

2. Such pre-rational activity, however, must be accompanied by a storied account that persists through all seasons of fads and criticism. If there is not a storied account that is understood, cherished, and verbalized, then the pre-rational activity may take on magical meanings, as though in and of itself the act has some intrinsic merit. This activity is not generalized religious practice, but belongs to a known time, place, and people.

The storied meaning is twofold. First, the blood marking enacts a large sense of protectedness from the midnight violence that is loosed in the empire. This is an act that lets us confess to each other that we are abidingly cared for in a world that is under profound threat. Second, eating the food asserts that we are able to depart Egypt. If Egypt and Pharaoh are to be understood as references to any and every agent of oppression and abuse (including one's own socioeconomic system), then this festival evokes an important restlessness. Indeed, when the community of faith no longer has this "festival of urgent departure," it runs the risk of being excessively and in unseemly ways at home in the empire. In such a posture, there will never be a departure; therefore, every celebration is an act of bad faith.

Such interpretive commentary is important to prevent these festival acts from degenerating into superstition. Conversely, it will not do simply to have the interpretation without the acts themselves, for then the memory becomes excessively cognitive and cerebral, and we forget that it is in our bellies that we practice the hurried departure and on our door posts that we mark our safety. There must be no cerebral shortcuts away from actual practice, for we hold the precious memories in our bodies, not in our heads. It was our bodies that were oppressed, and it was our bodies that cried out and were liberated.

66. Childs, *Exodus,* 204.

3. This festival is clearly Jewish. No doubt Christians need Jews to help us concretely engage these practices, but the Christian community needs to move beyond curiosity about Jewish practices in order to claim these festivals as our own. This, of course, does not mean to usurp or preempt them from Jews, but to see that as the OT is Christian Scripture even while it is thoroughly Jewish, so this festival is a part of our Christian memory and identity. Christians, like Jews, are *children of these marked door posts,* marked for safety in the midnight of chaos and crying. Christians, like Jews, are *children of this hurried bread,* postured to depart the empire, destined for freedom outside the norms and requirements of the empire. Such an embrace will not only draw us into closer solidarity with practicing Judaism, but also let us see the peculiar shapes of humanness given us in our narrative theological tradition.

4. The aim of celebrating these marked door posts and hurried bread is that the children may be recruited into this odd angle of vision. Thus the festival is intended to evoke a probing question from the children. The children will not know, unless they wonder and unless they are told, that this community holds an odd identity in the world—odd over against established power, odd because of the inscrutable protective attentiveness of Yahweh. The practitioners of these festivals and the tellers of these tales are indeed sojourners dreaming of a better land, filled with God's abundance. The engaged memory of pain evokes hope for a transformed world. The children of this community cannot afford to be protected from either the pain or the hope.

Exodus 12:29-39, Death of the Firstborn

NIV

29At midnight the LORD struck down all the firstborn in Egypt, from the firstborn of Pharaoh, who sat on the throne, to the firstborn of the prisoner, who was in the dungeon, and the firstborn of all the livestock as well. 30Pharaoh and all his officials and all the Egyptians got up during the night, and there was loud wailing in Egypt, for there was not a house without someone dead.

31During the night Pharaoh summoned Moses and Aaron and said, "Up! Leave my people, you and the Israelites! Go, worship the LORD as you have requested. 32Take your flocks and herds, as you have said, and go. And also bless me."

33The Egyptians urged the people to hurry and leave the country. "For otherwise," they said, "we will all die!" 34So the people took their dough before the yeast was added, and carried it on their shoulders in kneading troughs wrapped in clothing. 35The Israelites did as Moses instructed and asked the Egyptians for articles of silver and gold and for clothing. 36The LORD had made the Egyptians favorably disposed toward the people, and they gave them what they asked for; so they plundered the Egyptians.

37The Israelites journeyed from Rameses to Suc-

NRSV

29At midnight the LORD struck down all the firstborn in the land of Egypt, from the firstborn of Pharaoh who sat on his throne to the firstborn of the prisoner who was in the dungeon, and all the firstborn of the livestock. 30Pharaoh arose in the night, he and all his officials and all the Egyptians; and there was a loud cry in Egypt, for there was not a house without someone dead. 31Then he summoned Moses and Aaron in the night, and said, "Rise up, go away from my people, both you and the Israelites! Go, worship the LORD, as you said. 32Take your flocks and your herds, as you said, and be gone. And bring a blessing on me too!"

33The Egyptians urged the people to hasten their departure from the land, for they said, "We shall all be dead." 34So the people took their dough before it was leavened, with their kneading bowls wrapped up in their cloaks on their shoulders. 35The Israelites had done as Moses told them; they had asked the Egyptians for jewelry of silver and gold, and for clothing, 36and the LORD had given the people favor in the sight of the Egyptians, so that they let them have what they asked. And so they plundered the Egyptians.

coth. There were about six hundred thousand men on foot, besides women and children. [38]Many other people went up with them, as well as large droves of livestock, both flocks and herds. [39]With the dough they had brought from Egypt, they baked cakes of unleavened bread. The dough was without yeast because they had been driven out of Egypt and did not have time to prepare food for themselves.

37The Israelites journeyed from Rameses to Succoth, about six hundred thousand men on foot, besides children. [38]A mixed crowd also went up with them, and livestock in great numbers, both flocks and herds. [39]They baked unleavened cakes of the dough that they had brought out of Egypt; it was not leavened, because they were driven out of Egypt and could not wait, nor had they prepared any provisions for themselves.

COMMENTARY

These verses resume the narrative of 11:8. The passage includes the conventional plague materials of the assault itself (vv. 29) and the Egyptian response (vv. 30-36), plus an initial glimpse into the beginning of the journey from Egypt (vv. 37-39).

12:29. The description of the assault itself is brief (v. 29). It is exactly as Moses had announced in 11:5. At midnight, in the darkness, which Pharaoh cannot control, Yahweh strikes. The term *firstborn* occurs four times and pounds at the listener. The first use is generic and comprehensive. The other three uses are sub-sets of the first: firstborn of Pharaoh (i.e., the heir apparent), firstborn of the cattle, firstborn of all things Egyptian. Nothing in Egypt is protected from the harsh midnight incursion of Yahweh. Of course, the narrative does not tell what happened in the darkness or how it happened. Nobody saw anything!

12:30-36. The response of Egypt is exactly as was anticipated in 11:6, and is what might be expected in such a crisis. There was a great cry from every part of Egypt. The desperate cry of loss and protest began on the lips of Israel (2:23-24; 3:7), and it has now been transferred to the pathos-filled mouths of Egypt. The empire is now saturated with the reality of death; as had been anticipated in 11:5, Pharaoh cannot maintain the life of the empire against the God who gives both life and death. The extreme, brutal loss brings Pharaoh to his first wise decision. He finally gives to Yahweh and Moses all they have been asking. Yahweh had promised in 11:1 that this would be the end of the struggle, and so it is. Pharaoh completely capitulates to the God of Israel.

Pharaoh summons Moses and Aaron "at night,"

at the time when he is in least control and most subject to the powers of chaos (v. 31). He summons Moses and Aaron with an urgent imperative, so urgent that it cannot wait until morning. The four imperatives he speaks are the ones Pharaoh has most resisted, which he now desperately wants to utter: "arise" (קוּמוּ *qûmû*), "go out" (צְאוּ *ṣĕ'û*), "go" (לְכוּ *lĕkû*), "serve" (עִבְדוּ *'ibdû*). The words are finally on Pharaoh's lips, but the command has been instigated by Yahweh. They are words of release, departure, permission, and complete capitulation. Here the word *serve* is not "worship" (חַג *ḥag*), but means to accept one as master, to enter a new servitude. Pharaoh is conceding that the Hebrew slaves are no longer in his servitude, but now owe allegiance to a different master. (See the point expressed in Lev 25:42, with a double use of *serve* [עבד *'ābad*].) In v. 32, two more imperatives are sounded by Pharaoh, "take" (קְחוּ *qĕḥû*) and "go" (*lĕkû*).

Finally, Pharaoh utters a seventh imperative, this one most astonishing: "Bless me also!" In this utterance, the role reversal of Israel and Egypt is complete. According to all appearances, it was Pharaoh who carried the power of blessing, the capacity to bestow life and well-being. The blessing, however, is not where it appears to be, but is carried by this band of slaves who seem to possess nothing. This theme of reassigned blessing has been anticipated in the initial encounter between Jacob and another Pharaoh (Gen 47:7-12). The old man was ushered into the presence of the great king, who ostensibly possessed everything. Then, however, we are told, "Jacob blessed Pharaoh" (Gen 47:7, 10). Pharaoh needs what Israel has: the gift of life.

The departure scene shows the Egyptians acting desperately and frantically, with the Israelites hurriedly but pointedly taking whatever they are able to carry. The Egyptians' desperation is due to their recognition that the retention of Israel in its midst will only guarantee death (cf. 10:7). The verb for "urged" (חזק *ḥāzaq*) is regularly used against the Egyptians as "harden." Now the Egyptians are subject to the same verb, but to very different effect. Whereas "harden" was to prevent the departure of Israel, here "urge" is to encourage and insist on that same departure. This use of the term bespeaks not power, but a needy supplication to be rid of Israel. The notation in vv. 35-36 has been anticipated in 3:21-22 and 11:2. The statement of 36, echoing 11:3, is likely ironic; it is because of favor from Yahweh that they successfully "asked." The language of "favor from Yahweh" and "asking" in fact disguises marauding and plundering, which the erstwhile slaves work against their deeply resented masters. This seizure of goods is driven partly by a desire to have for the first time, and partly by a mocking scorn of triumph that now lets the hated symbols of arrogant indifference pass through their fingers. They "plundered" (נצל *nāṣal*) the Egyptians. The same term *nāṣal* is used to mean "save" or "rescue" elsewhere, connoting "to snatch from." Here, as in 3:22 and 2 Chr 20:25, the term is used negatively, presumably to seize or snatch, to take violently for oneself. The term makes clear that power has now fully shifted to Israel, and Israel may take whatever it wants.

12:37-39. In an almost understated way, the narrative finally has Israel on its way: "Israel journeyed" (v. 37). The actual moment of departure is always a non-moment in the narrative after the enormous conflict to bring it about. This freedom to journey (journey to freedom), however, is what the entire drama has been about. Slaves have no mobility; they are fixed to a place and are kept there. Now the limit has been broken, and the erstwhile slaves can go as they

have not been able to do. Verse 37 gives specific detail about place and numbers. Israel departs Rameses, the hated storehouse city on which it had worked; a city that symbolized Egyptian power, accumulation, and monopoly (cf. Gen 47:13-21; Exod 1:11).

A much more interesting and suggestive statement is offered in vv. 38-39. The narrator describes the scene of initial travel, the "long march," noting four aspects of this company of relaxed bond servants. First, it is a "mixed multitude" of great number. The phrase suggests that this is no kinship group, no ethnic community, but a great conglomeration of lower-class folk who have no time or energy for bloodlines or pedigrees. (On the term *mixed* [ערב *'ēreb*], see Neh 13:3; Jer 25:20, 24; 50:37. This term is important for the view that earliest Israel was not an ethnic community, but a sociological grouping of the marginated who had been liberated from their oppressed socioeconomic status.)

Second, they are not only great in number but also have great numbers of herds and cattle. That is, Pharaoh is able to keep back nothing the Hebrews want to take (cf. 10:24; 12:32). They are completely free and without any supervisory restraint. Third, they carry their dough not yet risen. The narrative continues to refer to the unleavened bread as a reference point for their hurried departure. That is, these first actors in the drama of departure are already characters in the liturgy. They do what they do, not only to get out of slavery, but also to authorize and "institute" the ritual meal.

Fourth, they had made no promises, but leave quickly, because they cannot wait. We are not told why, but, clearly, their waiting might have given Pharaoh a chance to change his mind or to regroup or to continue their servitude. They leave with only what they can hurriedly pick up, nothing more than they can carry in their hands and wear on their backs. But it is enough, because they are on their way!

REFLECTIONS

1. The interpreter's core theme in these narratives is this incredible inversion whereby the last and the first change places. The text does not linger over the collapse of Egypt. It is much more preoccupied with the astonishing appearance of Israel as a new reality in the world. The narrative shows that God has relentlessly valued this firstborn son, so devalued by the world of brutalizing power.

2. In this story, the Israelites are the powerless multitude, abruptly transformed into a community of power and significance, "on their way rejoicing." Pharaoh finally recognizes that Moses and Aaron (Israel) now have the power and authority to bestow blessing. We listen and watch power come to this powerless people. This is indeed the people regarded as "having nothing, and yet possessing everything" (2 Cor 6:10 NRSV). The early church was also a feeble community filled with power. Thus in Acts 3:6, Peter is able to say to the lame man, "I have no silver or gold, but what I have I give you" (NRSV). This encounter faithfully reflects how it is that this completely powerless people is filled with power to transform.

3. Conversely, this narrative is a study of how worldly power, the dazzling grandeur of Egypt, turns out to be an empty shell of powerlessness. Who would have thought that this "bread basket" of the ancient world would at midnight suffer an inexplicable, humiliating reversal of fortunes? Who could have known that its silver and gold would be plundered and seized by its oppressed workforce? Indeed, oppressive regimes vanish in the twinkling of an eye and leave only stories told by those newly endowed with power.

Exodus 12:40-51, Directions for the Passover

NIV

40Now the length of time the Israelite people lived in Egypt[a] was 430 years. 41At the end of the 430 years, to the very day, all the Lord's divisions left Egypt. 42Because the Lord kept vigil that night to bring them out of Egypt, on this night all the Israelites are to keep vigil to honor the Lord for the generations to come.

43The Lord said to Moses and Aaron, "These are the regulations for the Passover:

"No foreigner is to eat of it. 44Any slave you have bought may eat of it after you have circumcised him, 45but a temporary resident and a hired worker may not eat of it.

46"It must be eaten inside one house; take none of the meat outside the house. Do not break any of the bones. 47The whole community of Israel must celebrate it.

48"An alien living among you who wants to celebrate the Lord's Passover must have all the males in his household circumcised; then he may take part like one born in the land. No uncircumcised male may eat of it. 49The same law applies to the native-born and to the alien living among you."

a40 Masoretic Text; Samaritan Pentateuch and Septuagint *Egypt and Canaan*

NRSV

40The time that the Israelites had lived in Egypt was four hundred thirty years. 41At the end of four hundred thirty years, on that very day, all the companies of the Lord went out from the land of Egypt. 42That was for the Lord a night of vigil, to bring them out of the land of Egypt. That same night is a vigil to be kept for the Lord by all the Israelites throughout their generations.

43The Lord said to Moses and Aaron: This is the ordinance for the passover: no foreigner shall eat of it, 44but any slave who has been purchased may eat of it after he has been circumcised; 45no bound or hired servant may eat of it. 46It shall be eaten in one house; you shall not take any of the animal outside the house, and you shall not break any of its bones. 47The whole congregation of Israel shall celebrate it. 48If an alien who resides with you wants to celebrate the passover to the Lord, all his males shall be circumcised; then he may draw near to celebrate it; he shall be regarded as a native of the land. But no uncircumcised person shall eat of it; 49there shall be one law for the native and for the alien who resides among you.

50All the Israelites did just as the Lord had commanded Moses and Aaron. 51That very day

⁵⁰All the Israelites did just what the Lord had commanded Moses and Aaron. ⁵¹And on that very day the Lord brought the Israelites out of Egypt by their divisions.

the Lord brought the Israelites out of the land of Egypt, company by company.

COMMENTARY

These verses include a ritual provision inside a narrative frame. The narrative frame of vv. 40-42*a* and 51 envisions the exodus as an ordered departure of all of Yahweh's "companies." The term צבאות (*sĕbā'ôt,* "companies") is a military usage, referring to regiments and battalions. The most interesting phrase in this narrative is that the night of departure (cf. vv. 29, 31) is for Yahweh "a night of vigil." The phrase suggests that the departure is a time in which Yahweh is especially alert and attentive, supervising to see that all are on the move, acting as a reviewing officer and as a guard to keep all the companies ordered, on the move, and safe from any last-minute Egyptian harassment. Alternatively, the image is one of Yahweh waiting at headquarters, anxiously awaiting the call that slaves have safely crossed the border into freedom. Yahweh is deeply invested in this revolutionary operation.

Inside that narrative is a provision for a ritual practice, designed to remember and to reenact that "night of all nights" (vv. 42*b*-50). The night was a "vigil for Yahweh"—i.e., done *by Yahweh*—but now it is to become a watch in honor of and reference *to Yahweh.* That is, the same phrase, "vigil for Yahweh," is used in two different senses, the first *by* Yahweh, the second in devotion *to* Yahweh. With the use of the same preposition, the original event has been made into

a routine liturgic practice. Fretheim nicely says, "Israel's keeping remembers God's keeping."[67]

The night of vigil—the night of watching, waiting, and glad remembrance—is the night of Passover. These verses, then, institute the festival sacrament of Passover. Emerging in this text are the most elemental remembrances of Israel and the most precise procedural rules to protect that memory. The text suggests that over time, Passover had many interpretations and many practices, many disputes that require careful and authoritative adjudication. The procedures specify who may participate, and the distinctions are drawn quite firmly. Excluded are foreigners (נכרי *nokrî*), bonded or hired servants, and uncircumcised persons. Conversely, those permitted to celebrate include circumcised slaves and circumcised aliens (גר *gēr*). These distinctions are very close, and we do not know why a line is drawn so closely between slave and hired servant, or between foreigner and sojourner. Apparently what matters is a readiness and willingness to be counted an Israelite, and that is signified by a readiness to be circumcised. Thus the regulation is inclusive (though obviously gender specific), but it is not careless or casual. Finally, we are told that Israel obeys and practices Passover as commanded (v. 50).

67. Fretheim, *Exodus,* 145.

REFLECTIONS

1. The primary accent in this text is that the hidden night of liberation, the miracle of transferring public power, must be remembered by a replication of the event. That night was a concrete, specific, unrepeatable event. It becomes, however, a paradigmatic event, continually mediating in the community a passion for freedom and a critical posture toward any practice of oppression.

2. The community must reflect with discipline upon how to maintain the integrity and power of that festival-sacrament. The text clearly struggles with a desire for inclusiveness and a need for some intentional exclusivity. There is no "moral qualification" for participation, and no "doctrinal test," but a readiness to let this festival define one's life in the world. Those who do not want their lives redescribed in this way are not free to participate.

3. The "spill over" of these "words of institution" is evident in rethinking the Christian Eucharist. The Eucharist does not replace Passover, but may carry many more of the accents of Passover than is commonly recognized. The Passover connection can keep the Eucharist focused on this-world reality of emancipation, feeding, and healing, rather than floating off into liturgical escapism.

4. This festival invites a "night of vigil," a watchful, grateful remembering into the darkness, which we cannot control. On the one hand, that it is at night means paying attention to the inscrutable quality of ominous holiness. On the other hand, that it is for watching means an active, glad waiting for an initiative other than our own. The Passover recalls not an act taken by Israel, but a gift received from Yahweh, precisely at midnight when nothing seems possible.

Exodus 13:1-16, Special Observances

NIV

13 The LORD said to Moses, 2"Consecrate to me every firstborn male. The first offspring of every womb among the Israelites belongs to me, whether man or animal."

3Then Moses said to the people, "Commemorate this day, the day you came out of Egypt, out of the land of slavery, because the LORD brought you out of it with a mighty hand. Eat nothing containing yeast. 4Today, in the month of Abib, you are leaving. 5When the LORD brings you into the land of the Canaanites, Hittites, Amorites, Hivites and Jebusites—the land he swore to your forefathers to give you, a land flowing with milk and honey—you are to observe this ceremony in this month: 6For seven days eat bread made without yeast and on the seventh day hold a festival to the LORD. 7Eat unleavened bread during those seven days; nothing with yeast in it is to be seen among you, nor shall any yeast be seen anywhere within your borders. 8On that day tell your son, 'I do this because of what the LORD did for me when I came out of Egypt.' 9This observance will be for you like a sign on your hand and a reminder on your forehead that the law of the LORD is to be on your lips. For the LORD brought you out of Egypt with his mighty hand. 10You must keep this ordinance at the appointed time year after year.

11"After the LORD brings you into the land of the Canaanites and gives it to you, as he promised

NRSV

13 The LORD said to Moses: 2"Consecrate to me all the firstborn; whatever is the first to open the womb among the Israelites, of human beings and animals, is mine.

3Moses said to the people, "Remember this day on which you came out of Egypt, out of the house of slavery, because the LORD brought you out from there by strength of hand; no leavened bread shall be eaten. 4Today, in the month of Abib, you are going out. 5When the LORD brings you into the land of the Canaanites, the Hittites, the Amorites, the Hivites, and the Jebusites, which he swore to your ancestors to give you, a land flowing with milk and honey, you shall keep this observance in this month. 6Seven days you shall eat unleavened bread, and on the seventh day there shall be a festival to the LORD. 7Unleavened bread shall be eaten for seven days; no leavened bread shall be seen in your possession, and no leaven shall be seen among you in all your territory. 8You shall tell your child on that day, 'It is because of what the LORD did for me when I came out of Egypt.' 9It shall serve for you as a sign on your hand and as a reminder on your forehead, so that the teaching of the LORD may be on your lips; for with a strong hand the LORD brought you out of Egypt. 10You shall keep this ordinance at its proper time from year to year.

11"When the LORD has brought you into the

NIV

on oath to you and your forefathers, [12]you are to give over to the LORD the first offspring of every womb. All the firstborn males of your livestock belong to the LORD. [13]Redeem with a lamb every firstborn donkey, but if you do not redeem it, break its neck. Redeem every firstborn among your sons.

[14]"In days to come, when your son asks you, 'What does this mean?' say to him, 'With a mighty hand the LORD brought us out of Egypt, out of the land of slavery. [15]When Pharaoh stubbornly refused to let us go, the LORD killed every firstborn in Egypt, both man and animal. This is why I sacrifice to the LORD the first male offspring of every womb and redeem each of my firstborn sons.' [16]And it will be like a sign on your hand and a symbol on your forehead that the LORD brought us out of Egypt with his mighty hand."

NRSV

land of the Canaanites, as he swore to you and your ancestors, and has given it to you, [12]you shall set apart to the LORD all that first opens the womb. All the firstborn of your livestock that are males shall be the LORD's. [13]But every firstborn donkey you shall redeem with a sheep; if you do not redeem it, you must break its neck. Every firstborn male among your children you shall redeem. [14]When in the future your child asks you, 'What does this mean?' you shall answer, 'By strength of hand the LORD brought us out of Egypt, from the house of slavery. [15]When Pharaoh stubbornly refused to let us go, the LORD killed all the firstborn in the land of Egypt, from human firstborn to the firstborn of animals. Therefore I sacrifice to the LORD every male that first opens the womb, but every firstborn of my sons I redeem.' [16]It shall serve as a sign on your hand and as an emblem[a] on your forehead that by strength of hand the LORD brought us out of Egypt."

[a] Or as a frontlet; Meaning of Heb uncertain

COMMENTARY

This passage includes two provisions for ritual, reflecting themes already introduced in the exodus narrative.

13:1-2. The first theme, that of the firstborn, is introduced in v. 1, but is not explicated until vv. 11-16 (see below). The initial decree is flat, comprehensive, and unconditional. The notion that the firstborn, human and animal, belong to Yahweh likely reflects land-ownership practices and rent arrangements. It is instructive that in v. 11 the regulation is linked to the land. In an agricultural economy, the way of rental payment by a tenant farmer is that the owner of land receives the first share of the produce for the use of the land. The payment of the firstborn animal or first fruits of the crop is an acknowledgment of ownership and, by extrapolation, an acknowledgment of sovereignty.

In extending this provision to the human firstborn in the context of the exodus narrative, the provision may signify that members of the human family—i.e., the community of Israel—belong to and owe allegiance to Yahweh and not to Pha-

raoh. Thus a land practice seems to be extended in the rhetoric of this provision to underscore the radical claim of loyalty, implicit in the event of the exodus. Whether this language of consecration refers at any time to an actual sacrifice of a human life, or rather is metaphorical is open to question. But there is no doubt that in Israel's purview consecration to Yahweh meant loyalty and allegiance, and not the taking of a life. To make the notion more than a metaphor for loyalty and allegiance would be to contradict the core affirmations of Yahwism, and to think in the categories of Pharaoh's abusive practices.

13:3-10. The second theme of ritual is that of the Feast of Unleavened Bread. We have already seen that unleavened bread is a reminder (and reenactment) that the slave community left Egypt in a hurry and did not wait around for the yeast to rise (cf. 12:11). Thus this festival is a reminder and participation in the drama of a hurried departure from bondage. Two sub-points are important in this provision.

First, the festival is especially designed for the

time when Israel is settled in the luxurious land already promised in the book of Genesis (cf. Exod 3:8, 17). The dramatic contrast between present-tense settlement in the good land and past-tense memory of hurried departure from oppression is crucial for understanding this text and the intention of the festival. The tradition knows, perhaps from very specific experience, that present-tense well-being causes disregard of past-tense tribulation. Moreover, such forgetting causes a disregard of dependence on Yahweh and a sense of one's independence, autonomy, and self-sufficiency. Thus the festival intends to keep Israel in touch with a more difficult past, so that it will know that its present situation properly evokes wonder and gratitude, and not self-congratulations.

The second element in this provision is that the practice of eating unleavened bread is to evoke in the watching children questions about the festival and its intent. When the child's question is asked, the community of adults has ready and waiting a normative, canonical answer (vv. 8-9). The answer, which the child could never guess ahead of time, is that the festival is practiced because of what Yahweh did in the exodus. Notice that the recital is first-person singular. The answer is, no doubt, communal. But the text envisions that the questions will be asked by a particular child and answered by a particular parent. Moreover, the conversation may be many generations removed from the exodus, but the answer is nonetheless "When I came out of Egypt." The purpose of the festival is to keep the past present, authoritative, and powerfully identity-giving.

In v. 9, it is not clear what the antecedent of "it" is. The "it" no doubt refers to some aspect of the festival that shall be a visible sign and remembrance. The text does not specify. What is important is that the visible reminder on head and hand is to keep *torah* on the lips, which presumably means the recital of the exodus event and its intrinsic obligations.

13:11-16. The text now refers to the theme of the firstborn, introduced in v. 1. This practice,

like the feast of unleavened bread, is explicitly related to, and geared for, the land. The primary command of v. 12 reiterates v. 1 with the same flat, non-negotiable tone. In vv. 13-15*b*, the uncompromising quality of the initial command is toned down. These verses introduce the term *redeem* (פדה *pādâ*), which here refers to a transaction whereby a substitute can be made for the firstborn, so that a less valuable object can be offered to Yahweh in place of the more valuable—e.g., a sheep instead of a donkey. In vv. 13*a* and 15*b*, provision is made for the redemption of a male child, but the approved substitute is not named. On this reading, it seems likely that the primary command of v. 1 is taken literally and that these later verses seek an alternative to the costly demand. The relation between vv. 1 and 12 (which give a flat command) and vv. 13 and 15 (which provide alternatives) is of interest, because they place in juxtaposition an unqualified demand and a qualification of the demand made by "trading downward." The qualifying provisions clearly affirm that the substitute is an adequate equivalent and, in fact, reflects no compromise of value, devotion, or commitment.

The practice of committing the firstborn and/or a substitute to Yahweh may be a highly sacramental gesture. Its main use here, however, is its instructional value. Either the offer of the firstborn or the presentation of a substitute serves to evoke in a watching child wonderment about its meaning. Again the adult community has ready its canonical answer to the anticipated question (vv. 14*b*-15*a*). The practice is related in this answer (as it may not have been in origin) to the exodus and to the liberation wrought by Yahweh. The particular work of liberation could be wrought in Egypt only by killing all the Egyptian firstborn. That is, this payment of "rent" is a way to recall the savage act of Yahweh's power in the service of liberation.

Again in v. 16, it is not at all clear what "it" is, except that the text makes a connection between a ritual gesture and an identifying memory.

REFLECTIONS

1. The biblical community of faith is a community of memory, working at its precious identity in a culture devoted to amnesia. The market forces that encourage a consumer consciousness are largely controlled by ideology that wants to abandon the past and forsake the future in order to live in an absolute "now." Those who neither remember nor hope are profoundly vulnerable to consumerism, busy filling the void left by eradication of that extra dimension of historical awareness that belongs to healthy humanness. Thus when the community says, "This do in remembrance," it is not engaged in a mere history lesson or a simple act of piety. It is, rather, engaged in an act of resistance against an ideology that will destroy any Passover-driven humanness. While such a critique of the ideology of amnesia is not explicit in this text, there is no doubt that as the community struggles for its memory, it seeks to resist the forgetful abandonment of peculiar identity to which it is always vulnerable.

2. The festival of unleavened bread is a dramatic affirmation that freedom is given only at the last moment, only at great risk, only by the skin of our teeth, and only by the midnight urgency of Yahweh. An alternative future is never given or received casually. The festival invites reflection upon the urgency of faith, and how late freedom is characteristically given in a world set against liberation.

3. The lesson taught the children in vv. 14-15 requires enormous interpretive agility. The child is told that God must kill all the firstborn in order to bring about their freedom. Such a voicing of violence, especially by the hand of God, may be unsettling to a child. Implicit in the answer, however, is a drastic (albeit subtle) maneuver. The child learns in this telling that the God who killed the firstborn is also the God who has risked everything for the beloved firstborn. This text does not shield the child from the brutal reality of God's work of liberation, which always requires a tough struggle. In the caring process of the telling, however, this text does not fear that children will understand themselves as the ones exposed to such violence. The case is just the opposite. The surrounding action of the community in the festival permits children to experience the inordinate valuing of the firstborn in this community, without deceiving them about the high price and high risk of freedom as the gift of God.

The text is not (as the interpreter also should not be) insensitive to the hazards of this story. Nonetheless, the root story of faith is a story of deep conflict. Unless the community of faith falsely nurtures a kind of romanticism about the real world in which God brings newness, then the children of the community must come to know this story as their own, of being bought at a terrible price. The terrible price bespeaks the inordinate passion of God and the deep expectation of new obedience that belongs to the liberation.

4. The reference to "redeem" obviously introduces important theological vocabulary. The term *redeem* (פדה *pādâ*) refers to a trade-off whereby a substitute is offered to meet God's demand. Peter Stuhlmacher has shown that this metaphorical use of exchange or substitution (ransom) lies behind the christological formulation of Mark 10:45: "For the Son of Man came not to be served, but to serve and to give his life a *ransom* (λύτρον *lytron*) for many" (NRSV, emphasis added).[68]

In this formulation, the Son of Man is accepted as a substitute for others who are in deep need. That same notion of substitution is already evident in our text. Note well, however, that the substitution is not related to any "satisfaction" of God's requirement. It is, rather, an economic transaction, whereby something especially treasured is bought out of hock.

68. Peter Stuhlmacher, *Reconciliation, Law, & Righteousness: Essays in Biblical Theology* (Philadelphia: Fortress, 1986) 16-29.

Exodus 13:17-22, Pillars of Cloud and Fire

NIV

¹⁷When Pharaoh let the people go, God did not lead them on the road through the Philistine country, though that was shorter. For God said, "If they face war, they might change their minds and return to Egypt." ¹⁸So God led the people around by the desert road toward the Red Sea.ᵃ The Israelites went up out of Egypt armed for battle.

¹⁹Moses took the bones of Joseph with him because Joseph had made the sons of Israel swear an oath. He had said, "God will surely come to your aid, and then you must carry my bones up with you from this place."ᵇ

²⁰After leaving Succoth they camped at Etham on the edge of the desert. ²¹By day the LORD went ahead of them in a pillar of cloud to guide them on their way and by night in a pillar of fire to give them light, so that they could travel by day or night. ²²Neither the pillar of cloud by day nor the pillar of fire by night left its place in front of the people.

ᵃ18 Hebrew *Yam Suph*; that is, Sea of Reeds   ᵇ19 See Gen. 50:25.

NRSV

17When Pharaoh let the people go, God did not lead them by way of the land of the Philistines, although that was nearer; for God thought, "If the people face war, they may change their minds and return to Egypt." ¹⁸So God led the people by the roundabout way of the wilderness toward the Red Sea.ᵃ The Israelites went up out of the land of Egypt prepared for battle. ¹⁹And Moses took with him the bones of Joseph who had required a solemn oath of the Israelites, saying, "God will surely take notice of you, and then you must carry my bones with you from here." ²⁰They set out from Succoth, and camped at Etham, on the edge of the wilderness. ²¹The LORD went in front of them in a pillar of cloud by day, to lead them along the way, and in a pillar of fire by night, to give them light, so that they might travel by day and by night. ²²Neither the pillar of cloud by day nor the pillar of fire by night left its place in front of the people.

ᵃ Or *Sea of Reeds*

COMMENTARY

This "journey report" resumes the account of the journey from 12:37-39. That account has been interrupted by a set of procedural regulations for celebration and remembering in 12:40–13:16. Thus the present text intermingles *guidelines for present celebration* with *narrative accounts of the past*. The narrative in its present form is shaped to create a lively interface between past and present, so that even the narratives that remember are given to us with attentiveness to their present "voice."

This unit briefly reports on the route taken in the departure from Egypt. Scholars have spent great energy on the route, and especially on the Sea of Reeds (יַם-סוּף *yam-sûp*). It is clear, however, that the paragraph that incidentally mentions geography is principally concerned to make a theological statement, pivoting on the word *lead* (נחה *nāḥâ*). Two statements at the beginning and at the end of this unit focus on the leadership of God.

At the beginning, God "leads" by a circuitous route in order to avoid conflict with the Philistines (vv. 17-18*a*). That decision about an alternative route, however, is not made because of the threat of the Philistines. The reason for this decision is given us by the rhetoric of a divine soliloquy. The expression "God thought" is, in Hebrew, "God said." God said out loud, perhaps only to God's own self. God is mindful that the Israelites, in the face of danger, may have a "change of mind." The verb *"change* their mind" is נחם (*nāḥam*), which in many other places means "repent" (Gen 6:6-7; Exod 32:14; Amos 7:2, 5). Israel may repent of its resolve for freedom, may abandon its liberated destiny, and may accept the bondaged fate of Egypt.

At the end of the unit, *lead* is related to a very different set of images (vv. 21-22). Now God is much more transcendent and impersonal, being present neither personally nor through reflective speech, but only through the cultic devices of "cloud" and "fire." This part of the tradition has devised a sign of God's full presence that is stable and visible. God is not directly available, but only through mediation. (Clearly this is a very different leadership from that in vv. 17-18a.) Two facets of this leadership are important. First, it is for "day and night," all of the time. Both the day and the night are filled with enormous danger, and this people is completely vulnerable (cf. Ps 91:5-6). The cloud shields from the sun; the fire protects from darkness.

Thus the verb *lead* in vv. 17-18a and vv. 21-22 means that Israel in its journey, like the shape of this text, is surrounded behind and before by reliable, attentive leadership. Within these references to "leading," two items are mentioned. First, the journey is one into conflict (v. 18b). The departure of Pharaoh was only the beginning of battle, for the journey of freedom includes the struggle to stake out a zone of well-being in a busy, crowded world that is already organized without any reference to Israel's existence or freedom. The term rendered "prepared for battle" (חמשים *ḥămušîm*) specifically means organized into military units of fifty, thus conjuring a well-organized, highly disciplined company. Such language is no doubt an overstatement for this "mixed crowd" (12:38), but the term does signal the coming struggle.

The second, rather odd motif is the report that Moses carries the bones of Joseph on the journey. The book of Genesis ends with Joseph's insistence, finalized in a solemn oath, that his bones must be taken up with the departing Israelites and carried to the land of promise (Gen 50:24-26). It is as though at the last moment Joseph, who as an Israelite was an incredible compromiser with Egyptian definitions of reality, finally asserts unequivocally his Israelite identity. He is clearer about this in his death than he was in his successful political career. Most important, Joseph twice uses the same infinitive absolute, "will surely come" (פקד יפקד *pāqōd yipqōd*), to state his firm conviction that God will not leave this people in bondage but will notice them and liberate them. The inclusion of Joseph's bones on the journey once again binds the exodus community to the old promises of Genesis, as in Exod 2:24; 3:16; and 6:3. Moreover, the paragraph appeals to the firm faith of the dying father Joseph, not usually cited as a carrier of faith. The people who make the journey carry with them, in the tangible form of these bones, very old promises and very sure faith.

REFLECTIONS

The departure from Egypt is not the end, but only the beginning of the long struggle for freedom and well-being, a struggle for the identity and destiny of God's beloved community apart from the life-robbing, life-denying definitions of Egypt. The central interpretive point here is that the community that attends to this text is an inheritor and practitioner of this still unfinished struggle for a distinctive identity and destiny.

1. The primary affirmation of this passage is that God's leadership is thoughtful, prudent, and utterly reliable. The form of that leadership in vv. 17-18a is not described, but in vv. 21-22 it is given a more concrete, substantive identity. Compare Ps 23:2-3, perhaps the best-known use of the image of God's leadership. The metaphor in the psalm is of a shepherd who leads sheep safely to good pastures and well-supplied water, even though the terrain to be traveled is dangerous and threatening. The notion of God's leadership is a primary datum in Israel's creedal recital, in Deut 8:2-4. Both texts affirm that God supplies every needed thing.

2. Following the dangerous, demanding lead of Yahweh requires continual fresh resolve and reinforcement. Israel is addicted to the order, oppression, and regular food supply of the empire, and Yahweh's leadership is aimed exactly against that death-dealing addiction. Thus the interpretive point of contact concerns those powerful loyalties currently termed "addictions." Every breaking of an addiction is like departing the reassuring structures of Egypt. This text affirms that the departure is difficult, that the temptation to return is great, and that Yahweh takes steps to make the departure as palatable as possible.

3. The "bones of Joseph" invite reflection on the intergenerational character of biblical faith. The exodus is initiated only because "God remembered" (2:24-25; 6:5). The book of Exodus cannot do without the book of Genesis, even if the relation is awkward and disjointed. The generation of emancipation is not the first generation in the story, but depends on the generations of hopeful ones who believe before them and on whose hope we trade as recipients.

There are two dangers to which this motif may be referred. First, there is the danger that the "now generation" in the church (particularly in a mobile, displacing society) may scuttle all the old ancestors (their names and their bones) and seek to live in a vacuum, excessively focused on the present. Second, there is the danger that a preoccupation with ancestors may treat the past like a relic—i.e., an act of nostalgia that resists present-tense requirements. Against both temptations, the bones of Joseph are understood as an urgent, fervent bet on Israel's future with God: "By faith Joseph, when his end was near, spoke about the exodus of the Israelites from Egypt and gave instructions about his bones" (Heb 11:22 NIV).

Joseph trusted in God's coming liberation. He made that bet on God's future by faith. It is in the same way, by faith, that the journey can be undertaken in the present, dangerous as it is.

Exodus 14:1-31, Crossing the Sea

NIV

14 Then the LORD said to Moses, [2]"Tell the Israelites to turn back and encamp near Pi Hahiroth, between Migdol and the sea. They are to encamp by the sea, directly opposite Baal Zephon. [3]Pharaoh will think, 'The Israelites are wandering around the land in confusion, hemmed in by the desert.' [4]And I will harden Pharaoh's heart, and he will pursue them. But I will gain glory for myself through Pharaoh and all his army, and the Egyptians will know that I am the LORD." So the Israelites did this.

[5]When the king of Egypt was told that the people had fled, Pharaoh and his officials changed their minds about them and said, "What have we done? We have let the Israelites go and have lost their services!" [6]So he had his chariot made ready and took his army with him. [7]He took six hundred of the best chariots, along with all the other chariots of Egypt, with officers over all of them. [8]The LORD hardened the heart of Pharaoh king of Egypt, so that he pursued the Israelites, who were marching out boldly. [9]The Egyptians—all Pharaoh's horses and chariots, horsemen[a] and troops—pursued the Israelites and overtook them as they camped by the sea near Pi Hahiroth, opposite Baal Zephon.

[10]As Pharaoh approached, the Israelites looked

[a]9 Or *charioteers*; also in verses 17, 18, 23, 26 and 28

NRSV

14 Then the LORD said to Moses: [2]Tell the Israelites to turn back and camp in front of Pi-hahiroth, between Migdol and the sea, in front of Baal-zephon; you shall camp opposite it, by the sea. [3]Pharaoh will say of the Israelites, "They are wandering aimlessly in the land; the wilderness has closed in on them." [4]I will harden Pharaoh's heart, and he will pursue them, so that I will gain glory for myself over Pharaoh and all his army; and the Egyptians shall know that I am the LORD. And they did so.

[5]When the king of Egypt was told that the people had fled, the minds of Pharaoh and his officials were changed toward the people, and they said, "What have we done, letting Israel leave our service?" [6]So he had his chariot made ready, and took his army with him; [7]he took six hundred picked chariots and all the other chariots of Egypt with officers over all of them. [8]The LORD hardened the heart of Pharaoh king of Egypt and he pursued the Israelites, who were going out boldly. [9]The Egyptians pursued them, all Pharaoh's horses and chariots, his chariot drivers and his army; they overtook them camped by the sea, by Pi-hahiroth, in front of Baal-zephon.

[10]As Pharaoh drew near, the Israelites looked back, and there were the Egyptians advancing on them. In great fear the Israelites cried out to the LORD. [11]They said to Moses, "Was it because there

NIV

up, and there were the Egyptians, marching after them. They were terrified and cried out to the LORD. [11]They said to Moses, "Was it because there were no graves in Egypt that you brought us to the desert to die? What have you done to us by bringing us out of Egypt? [12]Didn't we say to you in Egypt, 'Leave us alone; let us serve the Egyptians'? It would have been better for us to serve the Egyptians than to die in the desert!"

[13]Moses answered the people, "Do not be afraid. Stand firm and you will see the deliverance the LORD will bring you today. The Egyptians you see today you will never see again. [14]The LORD will fight for you; you need only to be still."

[15]Then the LORD said to Moses, "Why are you crying out to me? Tell the Israelites to move on. [16]Raise your staff and stretch out your hand over the sea to divide the water so that the Israelites can go through the sea on dry ground. [17]I will harden the hearts of the Egyptians so that they will go in after them. And I will gain glory through Pharaoh and all his army, through his chariots and his horsemen. [18]The Egyptians will know that I am the LORD when I gain glory through Pharaoh, his chariots and his horsemen."

[19]Then the angel of God, who had been traveling in front of Israel's army, withdrew and went behind them. The pillar of cloud also moved from in front and stood behind them, [20]coming between the armies of Egypt and Israel. Throughout the night the cloud brought darkness to the one side and light to the other side; so neither went near the other all night long.

[21]Then Moses stretched out his hand over the sea, and all that night the LORD drove the sea back with a strong east wind and turned it into dry land. The waters were divided, [22]and the Israelites went through the sea on dry ground, with a wall of water on their right and on their left.

[23]The Egyptians pursued them, and all Pharaoh's horses and chariots and horsemen followed them into the sea. [24]During the last watch of the night the LORD looked down from the pillar of fire and cloud at the Egyptian army and threw it into confusion. [25]He made the wheels of their chariots come off[a] so that they had difficulty driving. And

[a]25 Or He jammed the wheels of their chariots (see Samaritan Pentateuch, Septuagint and Syriac)

NRSV

were no graves in Egypt that you have taken us away to die in the wilderness? What have you done to us, bringing us out of Egypt? [12]Is this not the very thing we told you in Egypt, 'Let us alone and let us serve the Egyptians'? For it would have been better for us to serve the Egyptians than to die in the wilderness." [13]But Moses said to the people, "Do not be afraid, stand firm, and see the deliverance that the LORD will accomplish for you today; for the Egyptians whom you see today you shall never see again. [14]The LORD will fight for you, and you have only to keep still."

[15]Then the LORD said to Moses, "Why do you cry out to me? Tell the Israelites to go forward. [16]But you lift up your staff, and stretch out your hand over the sea and divide it, that the Israelites may go into the sea on dry ground. [17]Then I will harden the hearts of the Egyptians so that they will go in after them; and so I will gain glory for myself over Pharaoh and all his army, his chariots, and his chariot drivers. [18]And the Egyptians shall know that I am the LORD, when I have gained glory for myself over Pharaoh, his chariots, and his chariot drivers."

[19]The angel of God who was going before the Israelite army moved and went behind them; and the pillar of cloud moved from in front of them and took its place behind them. [20]It came between the army of Egypt and the army of Israel. And so the cloud was there with the darkness, and it lit up the night; one did not come near the other all night.

[21]Then Moses stretched out his hand over the sea. The LORD drove the sea back by a strong east wind all night, and turned the sea into dry land; and the waters were divided. [22]The Israelites went into the sea on dry ground, the waters forming a wall for them on their right and on their left. [23]The Egyptians pursued, and went into the sea after them, all of Pharaoh's horses, chariots, and chariot drivers. [24]At the morning watch the LORD in the pillar of fire and cloud looked down upon the Egyptian army, and threw the Egyptian army into panic. [25]He clogged[a] their chariot wheels so that they turned with difficulty. The Egyptians said, "Let us flee from the Israelites, for the LORD is fighting for them against Egypt."

[a] Sam Gk Syr: MT removed

the Egyptians said, "Let's get away from the Israelites! The LORD is fighting for them against Egypt."

26Then the LORD said to Moses, "Stretch out your hand over the sea so that the waters may flow back over the Egyptians and their chariots and horsemen." 27Moses stretched out his hand over the sea, and at daybreak the sea went back to its place. The Egyptians were fleeing toward[a] it, and the LORD swept them into the sea. 28The water flowed back and covered the chariots and horsemen—the entire army of Pharaoh that had followed the Israelites into the sea. Not one of them survived.

29But the Israelites went through the sea on dry ground, with a wall of water on their right and on their left. 30That day the LORD saved Israel from the hands of the Egyptians, and Israel saw the Egyptians lying dead on the shore. 31And when the Israelites saw the great power the LORD displayed against the Egyptians, the people feared the LORD and put their trust in him and in Moses his servant.

a27 Or *from*

26Then the LORD said to Moses, "Stretch out your hand over the sea, so that the water may come back upon the Egyptians, upon their chariots and chariot drivers." 27So Moses stretched out his hand over the sea, and at dawn the sea returned to its normal depth. As the Egyptians fled before it, the LORD tossed the Egyptians into the sea. 28The waters returned and covered the chariots and the chariot drivers, the entire army of Pharaoh that had followed them into the sea; not one of them remained. 29But the Israelites walked on dry ground through the sea, the waters forming a wall for them on their right and on their left.

30Thus the LORD saved Israel that day from the Egyptians; and Israel saw the Egyptians dead on the seashore. 31Israel saw the great work that the LORD did against the Egyptians. So the people feared the LORD and believed in the LORD and in his servant Moses.

COMMENTARY

The journey to freedom has begun in 12:37-39. Israel, however, is not yet free. Pharaoh will make one last effort to block the departure. This most dramatic narrative of the departure is arranged in a sequence of quite distinct scenes. While the action turns on the two wonders of the waters divided (vv. 21-25) and the waters returned (vv. 26-28), the actual confrontation is concerned with far more than the miracles of the waters.

14:1-4. The narrative begins, characteristically, with Yahweh's command to Moses. Yahweh knows well before the events themselves that one more crisis with Pharaoh is still to be faced. The reason for this last, desperate effort of the king, so far as the narrative asserts, is not in fact Pharaoh's willfulness, but is yet again Yahweh's act of "hardening."

The reason for Yahweh's action is crucial for our interpretation. The last confrontation will be staged so that "I will get glory over Pharaoh!" (v. 4). Yahweh arranges the confrontation as an exhibition of enormous power, not for the sake of Israel. The final, decisive intention is not Israelite freedom, but Yahweh's glory, which is decisive. The outcome of the power struggle (which Yahweh will win!) is that Pharaoh in all his recalcitrance shall come at last to know "I am Yahweh."

14:5-9. With this disclosure to Moses and to the listener, we are given the same scene a second time, this time from Pharaoh's perspective. In this scene, the action gives the surface appearance that Pharaoh has freely chosen this new initiative against Israel. We are told simply that Pharaoh changes his mind (יהפך לבב *yēhāpēk lēbab*) and acts with new resolve. The Egyptians now focus not on relief that the "troublemakers" are gone, but on the lost slave labor. What a short memory! Pharaoh cannot remember back to 12:31-32, when he was desperate for their departure. So, with a radical change of policy and strategy, Pharaoh seeks to block the departure of Israel with a display of enormous power and resolve.

The narrative, however, insists that Egyptian power, resolve, and strategy are not what they seem. Everything has been preempted by Yahweh, who manages all sides of the drama. This is an enormously heavy dose of sovereignty. But then, the entire meeting concerns competing sovereignties. In this scene, the double use of "heart" (change of heart, hardened heart) nicely calls attention to the conflict of sovereignties. Fretheim observes that Yahweh's impact on Pharaoh strengthens Pharaoh's own proclivity.[69] The hardening by Yahweh does not violate Pharaoh's own intention.

14:10-14. In the third scene, neither Pharaoh nor Yahweh is present. Now the exchange is between Moses and Israel, who appears as a character in the plot for the first time. The speeches are arranged as a petition (vv. 10-12) and a responding salvation oracle (vv. 13-14).

The renewed attack of Pharaoh is an enormous threat to escaping Israel. The erstwhile slave community is completely vulnerable and without resources. Indeed, in this moment the entire departure is once more in profound jeopardy. As a result, the Israelites do the only thing they can do, the thing they always do in fear, and the thing they did in 2:23-24 at the beginning of the emergency: They cry out to Yahweh. Their cry is characteristic of Israel's faith, modeling the way in which the troubled turn to God. The slaves have now found their insistent voice. They cry out to Yahweh in protest, complaint, demand, and hope.

In fact, their speech is not a petition for help; in fact, it is not addressed to Yahweh, as is stated in v. 10. Rather, it is an accusation against Moses (vv. 10-12). The new threat of Egypt is not viewed as a theological emergency, does not even concern Yahweh, who figures more for Moses than for the community. The threat of Pharaoh evokes a crisis of political leadership. The accusation is in three rhetorical questions that are attacks on Moses for his unwise, dangerous, miscalculated, stupid initiative: Was it because . . . ? What have you done . . . ? Is this not . . . ?

69. Fretheim, *Exodus*, 155.

Moses had provided a revolutionary alternative for the slaves, an alternative to the demands of Egypt. In prospect, such emancipation had been attractive. In hand, however, it is only a profound hardship. It is difficult to sustain a revolution, because one loses all the benefits of the old system, well before there are any tangible benefits from what is promised.

In their three angry questions, Moses' opponents utter the name *Egypt* five times. It is the only name they know, the name upon which they rely, the name they love to sound. In the speech of the protesting, distrusting people, the name of Yahweh, however, is completely absent. They do not perceive Yahweh as being in any way a pertinent, active member of the plot. On their own terms, of course, without Yahweh, their reasoning is sound and their complaint is legitimate. Without Yahweh, they have no resources against Egypt and no hope of success. Moses by himself—without Yahweh—is no adequate resource against Egypt.

Moses' response to the challenge, introduced by "fear not," is a characteristic salvation oracle in which the voice of the gospel, rooted in God's own power and fidelity, is offered as a resolution to the voice of protest and trouble (vv. 13-14).

Moses' speech begins with three reassuring imperatives that serve to seize the initiative from the protesters: "Do not fear, stand, see." Moses refuses to accept the despairing picture of reality offered by the protesters. Their picture includes only themselves and the Egyptians, and there is no hope in such a scenario. Moses asserts that such a construal is a severe distortion of reality, for it eliminates Yahweh as an active player. Thus, in his response, Moses twice mentions Yahweh, the very name the protesters were either unable or unwilling to utter. Moreover, Moses' entire self-defense is staked on the claim that Yahweh is indeed a live, active, decisive character in this crisis. Thus the dispute turns on the relevance or irrelevance of Yahweh to the crisis.

Moses' imperatives refuse to respond to the three accusatory sentences just uttered. The first imperative, "fear not," is an enormously preemptive statement, used to override fear by the giving of assurance that lies outside and beyond fear. His other two imperatives invite Israel to stop and pay attention, to notice a presence in their crisis that they had neither noticed nor acknowledged. Thus Moses reframes the crisis of Israel around the presence, power, and fidelity of Yahweh, whom the Israelites have not permitted on their horizon.

Before the very eyes of fearful Israel, Moses asserts, Yahweh will work a deliverance (ישועה *yĕšûʿâ*) today. Indeed, in this statement, it is Yahweh alone who acts to deliver. Israel need only "be still and watch." Yahweh's singular action here precludes any other agent in the liberation. The deliverance will be the evaporation of Egypt as a threat, for Egypt will be removed and never seen again. Moses not only introduces into the picture Yahweh, whom the complainers deny, but he in turn denies the Egyptian reality, the one with whom his adversaries are preoccupied. A second time, Moses names Yahweh as the one who will fight for Israel. Israel can desist from its feverish activity and only witness the battle. The Israelites who protest are given no chance to answer Moses, to reject his affirmations, or to quarrel with his leadership. The narrator gives Moses the last word.

14:15-18. Now Yahweh reemerges in the narrative. Yahweh's initial rebuke of Moses is odd (v. 15), because Moses has not cried out and no one, not even complaining Israel, has addressed Yahweh (cf. vv. 11-12). The rebuke is clearly aimed over the head of Moses against the people, whose cry constitutes lack of faith and readiness to credit the reality of Pharaoh over the reality of Yahweh. As an alternative to the cry of fear and the lack of faith, Yahweh issues an imperative that calls for daring action: "Journey!" (נסע *nāsaʿ*; NRSV "go forward"; NIV "move on").

After that word addressed to the community, Yahweh issues a long statement to Moses (vv. 16-18). It includes the imperative "extend your hand" (i.e., power). It is followed by a reiteration of Yahweh's resolve, stated in v. 4, in which the departure of the people from Egypt is seen to be a way of exalting Yahweh. The outcome again will be an acknowledgment, "I am Yahweh." Thus the imperative of v. 15 is an instrument of the glorification of Yahweh, who effectively changes the subject on Moses and on Israel. The real crisis is not the emancipation or survival of Israel, but the triumph of Yahweh over Pharaoh.

14:19-20. The next paragraph is peculiar and without parallel anywhere in the preceding narrative. It concerns two modes of Yahweh's protective presence. On the one hand, "the angel of God" is a rearguard. We have not had an angel in the narrative since the meeting at the burning bush (3:2). The angel here is an escort to assure safe passage (cf. Ps 91:11-13). One might think of a public person walking through a crowd that pushes and shoves to touch, with the angels as those who push the crowd back to make a safe way; no one can lay a hand on Israel with such protection!

On the other hand, the protective cloud is both before and behind Israel as a protective screen. The narrator seems to play on the motif of cloud and fire in 13:21-22, but here there is only a cloud. In addition to being protective covering, the cloud takes over the function of the fire, providing light as well as covering. By appealing to both "angel" and "cloud," these verses are an extravagant way of characterizing the vigilant protection God gives Israel, which Moses promised in vv. 13-14.

14:21-25. Following the command of v. 16, Moses enacts a double "wonder" that both rescues Israel and glorifies Yahweh. First, as commanded, Moses (and Yahweh!) drives back the waters and creates a dry path for escaping Israel (vv. 21-22). Critics have long noted that in v. 21, the "east wind" blew back the waters in something like a natural event, but in v. 22, there is a "wall of water" so that Moses' action is heightened as a miracle. Such an analysis, based on source criticism, is of little help to the interpreter; in fact, it detracts from the narrator's intention. Indeed, making such distinctions is an attempt to read the event through the eyes of explanatory suspicion, whereas the narrative insists on being taken through the eyes of helpless Israel without resources.

Moses' capacity to divide the waters or drive them back suggests that he is replicating the coming of dry land in creation, when the sea is divided for the sake of inhabitable land. In this moment of liberation, God does a deed as powerful, original, and life-giving as the very newness of creation. Conversely, the Egyptians are caught in the power of the waters and the disorder—the powers of chaos, which are mobilized by Yahweh to foil the enemies of liberation. The narrative shrewdly juxtaposes the waters of the Nile in chaps. 1–2 with the large, ominous waters of chaos and the specificity of liberation with the majesty of new creation. It is no wonder (but a "wonder") that the Egyptians are forced to a confession of Yahweh (v. 25), an Egyptian affirmation of Moses' assurance in v. 14. Indeed, in this utterance over what they have seen, the Egyptians are at long last forced to "know" (as Yahweh intended in vv. 4, 18) that this is Yahweh, that Yahweh is at work on behalf of the Israelites, and that Egypt is helpless in the face of Yahweh's enduring, passionate resolve.

Thus the Egyptians are made to confess what the Israelites themselves had doubted (vv. 11-12), and what Moses himself had affirmed (v. 14). When one hears the Egyptian confession, one may conclude that we have not seen such faith in all of Israel (cf. Matt 8:10). The Egyptians become, against their will, confessors of Yahweh. Thus the miracle of the water is instrumental to the miracle of faith, to which Egypt is resistantly brought. When Egypt comes to this confession, Yahweh is indeed acknowledged, exalted, and glorified as the real sovereign.

14:26-29. The work of faith (for Israel) and glorification (of Yahweh) accomplished, Moses performs his second "wonder": the return of the waters to their proper course, which is, in fact, the unleashing of the power of chaos, the "mighty waters," before which Pharaoh and the Egyptian army are completely helpless. By the conclusion of the narrative, the contrast between these two antagonists, so long locked in an unequal struggle, is complete. Israel is safe on dry land, untouched by the surging waters of chaos. Egypt is completely nullified, so that "not one of them remained" (v. 28).

14:30-31. The narrator adds a reprise that serves as a conclusion to this chapter, and possibly to the entire exodus narrative: "Yahweh saves" (יָשַׁע yāša') (v. 30)! Yahweh commits an act of inscrutable power that breaks the power of Egypt. Then the camera does a slow, sweeping survey of the shore, at the edge of the deathly waters. The Israelites are not visible in the deathly scene. They are behind the camera looking in astonishment. All that is visible are dead Egyptians: Egyptian soldiers, Egyptian horses, Egyptian chariots, Egyptian power, and Egyptian arrogance. The term *dead* looms over the picture and over the text. The word is not new, even on Egyptian lips. Already in 12:33, the Egyptians understand that having Israel among them will bring death.

The watching Israelites are driven to two unavoidable conclusions. First, they fear Yahweh. This is the counterpoint to the imperative of Moses in v. 13, "Do not fear." Israel is to fear Yahweh and, therefore, to fear none other. They finally know beyond any doubt that Yahweh, with power and fidelity, will do for them what they cannot do for themselves.

Second, the Israelites "believe in" (אָמַן 'mn) Yahweh and Moses. While both Yahweh and Moses are named, and Israel comes to rely on both of them, Moses is clearly in a subordinate, derivative position. Nevertheless, the ones who were fearful and doubting in vv. 11-12 have come to faith and confidence in the leadership of Moses. It is most important that fear of Yahweh is linked to the concrete, specific, political leadership of Moses. As early as 4:1-9, Moses had doubted that he would be trusted or believed in. Now that question has been resolved by the massive, decisive action of Yahweh.

REFLECTIONS

The narrative invites silence before this stunning reversal of the processes of power. This outcome is no ordinary turn of affairs, to be explained by any human stratagem or by any natural phenomenon. Any attempt to have the story on such terms is a violation of what we are intended to hear in the narrative. In the purview of this narrative, there is only one possible explanation, and the name of that "explanation" is Yahweh, who brings both life and death.

Interpreting this passage, then, requires that we clear our minds (as much as possible) of any of the haunting misgivings of modernity. One cannot ask merely how this rescue could happen or whether it is possible. One cannot proceed by seeking to explain the miracle of the water, for any convincing explanation would only lead away from the intent of the text itself. This text is not argument, but witness and summons; it is *a witness to the power of Yahweh* and *a consequent summons to faith.*

1. The key actor in this narrative is Yahweh. It is Yahweh who issues the decisive decree to Moses and who is the target of doubt, the goal of defiance, and the focus of faith. It is Yahweh who is the subject of the crucial verbs, even the "hands-on" verbs, like *clogged* (v. 25) and *tossed* (v. 27), as well as the more magisterial *saved* (v. 30).

The explicit purpose of the narrative is to "get glory" over Egypt, so that Egypt will "know" (acknowledge) that Yahweh warrants allegiance. That is, the large purpose of the narrative is not to comfort the Israelites, but to look beyond Israel to the doubting, cynical reality of worldly power. This focus on Yahweh and Yahweh's exaltation is brought to fruition in the Egyptian confession, stated in desperation in v. 25. The confession, a grudging admission of defeat, anticipates the parallel statement in Mark 15:39, whereby the power of Rome at long last concedes the power of Jesus. The story thus culminates in a loud, grand "Gloria!"

2. The story of the stunning triumph of Yahweh over the great power of Egypt is told in order to summon Israel to faith. Gerhard von Rad has shrewdly seen that the assurance of Moses given in vv. 13-14 (and echoed in Isa 7:9) is a formula now removed from the primary context of battle and has become an invitation to faith.[70] The context and metaphor of battle may at first glance be offensive—faith is to trust the power of God in the face of one's enemies. Yet that same battle metaphor is used by faith in this wondrous and familiar Pauline affirmation of trust in God: "No, in all these things we are more than *conquerors* through him who loved us" (Rom 8:37 NRSV; emphasis added). Paul would likely not have had this triumphant metaphor available to him if not for the exodus narrative.

3. Both the exaltation of Yahweh and the summons to faith are situated in and dependent upon a concrete, public struggle about power. That is, the glorification of Yahweh and the trust of Israel are not religious ideas or affirmations made in a vacuum unscathed by the reality of life. This narrative insists that the celebration of God and the faith of Israel are inescapably mediated through the transformation of public life. Characteristically, the Bible points to specific, concrete places where the triumph of Yahweh is evident. Faith points to transformation, and liturgy recites and replicates these transformations.

The matter is made both more problematic and more compelling because this is a public event in the face of the empire. Even those of us who are inclined to faith are also inclined to reiterate the cynical question of Stalin about the danger of war: "How many divisions does the Pope have?" Pharaoh might have asked the same cynical question: "How many troops does Yahweh have?" The military metaphors and martial rhetoric of the text make the claim that Yahweh has sufficient troops for the battle.

Such a claim sounds like nonsense, except for two matters. First, the text celebrates the outcome. It did happen! Second, over time, it is the marginal, with no other troops, who in all kinds of emergencies have trusted in the strong arm of Yahweh and have not been disappointed. The faith to which Israel is here summoned is not a faith the world easily believes and is arrived at by common sense. It is trust against the evidence, risk in the face of the odds, that life can come even in the public domain, where Yahweh governs.

70. Gerhard von Rad, *Holy War in Ancient Israel* (Grand Rapids: Eerdmans, 1991) 88-90.

Exodus 15:1-21, Songs of Moses and Miriam

NIV

15 Then Moses and the Israelites sang this song to the LORD:

"I will sing to the LORD,
  for he is highly exalted.
The horse and its rider
  he has hurled into the sea.
²The LORD is my strength and my song;
  he has become my salvation.
He is my God, and I will praise him,
  my father's God, and I will exalt him.
³The LORD is a warrior;
  the LORD is his name.
⁴Pharaoh's chariots and his army
  he has hurled into the sea.
The best of Pharaoh's officers
  are drowned in the Red Sea.*a*
⁵The deep waters have covered them;
  they sank to the depths like a stone.

⁶"Your right hand, O LORD,
  was majestic in power.
Your right hand, O LORD,
  shattered the enemy.
⁷In the greatness of your majesty
  you threw down those who opposed you.
You unleashed your burning anger;
  it consumed them like stubble.
⁸By the blast of your nostrils
  the waters piled up.
The surging waters stood firm like a wall;
  the deep waters congealed in the heart of the
    sea.

⁹"The enemy boasted,
  'I will pursue, I will overtake them.
I will divide the spoils;
  I will gorge myself on them.
I will draw my sword
  and my hand will destroy them.'
¹⁰But you blew with your breath,
  and the sea covered them.
They sank like lead
  in the mighty waters.

¹¹"Who among the gods is like you, O LORD?

NRSV

15 Then Moses and the Israelites sang this song to the LORD:
  "I will sing to the LORD, for he has
    triumphed gloriously;
  horse and rider he has thrown into the
    sea.
² The LORD is my strength and my might,*a*
  and he has become my salvation;
this is my God, and I will praise him,
  my father's God, and I will exalt him.
³ The LORD is a warrior;
  the LORD is his name.

⁴ "Pharaoh's chariots and his army he cast
    into the sea;
  his picked officers were sunk in the Red
    Sea.*b*
⁵ The floods covered them;
  they went down into the depths like a
    stone.
⁶ Your right hand, O LORD, glorious in
    power—
  your right hand, O LORD, shattered the
    enemy.
⁷ In the greatness of your majesty you
    overthrew your adversaries;
  you sent out your fury, it consumed
    them like stubble.
⁸ At the blast of your nostrils the waters piled
    up,
  the floods stood up in a heap;
  the deeps congealed in the heart of the
    sea.
⁹ The enemy said, 'I will pursue, I will
    overtake,
  I will divide the spoil, my desire shall
    have its fill of them.
I will draw my sword, my hand shall
    destroy them.'
¹⁰ You blew with your wind, the sea covered
    them;
  they sank like lead in the mighty waters.

¹¹ "Who is like you, O LORD, among the gods?
  Who is like you, majestic in holiness,

---

*a4 Hebrew *Yam Suph*; that is, Sea of Reeds; also in verse 22

a Or *song*   *b* Or *Sea of Reeds*

NIV

Who is like you—
majestic in holiness,
awesome in glory,
working wonders?
[12]You stretched out your right hand
and the earth swallowed them.

[13]"In your unfailing love you will lead
the people you have redeemed.
In your strength you will guide them
to your holy dwelling.
[14]The nations will hear and tremble;
anguish will grip the people of Philistia.
[15]The chiefs of Edom will be terrified,
the leaders of Moab will be seized with
trembling,
the people[a] of Canaan will melt away;
[16] terror and dread will fall upon them.
By the power of your arm
they will be as still as a stone—
until your people pass by, O LORD,
until the people you bought[b] pass by.
[17]You will bring them in and plant them
on the mountain of your inheritance—
the place, O LORD, you made for your dwelling,
the sanctuary, O Lord, your hands
established.
[18]The LORD will reign
for ever and ever."

[19]When Pharaoh's horses, chariots and horse-men[c] went into the sea, the LORD brought the waters of the sea back over them, but the Israelites walked through the sea on dry ground. [20]Then Miriam the prophetess, Aaron's sister, took a tambourine in her hand, and all the women followed her, with tambourines and dancing. [21]Miriam sang to them:

"Sing to the LORD,
for he is highly exalted.
The horse and its rider
he has hurled into the sea."

[a]15 Or rulers   [b]16 Or created   [c]19 Or charioteers

NRSV

awesome in splendor, doing wonders?
[12] You stretched out your right hand,
the earth swallowed them.

[13] "In your steadfast love you led the people
whom you redeemed;
you guided them by your strength to
your holy abode.
[14] The peoples heard, they trembled;
pangs seized the inhabitants of Philistia.
[15] Then the chiefs of Edom were dismayed;
trembling seized the leaders of Moab;
all the inhabitants of Canaan melted away.
[16] Terror and dread fell upon them;
by the might of your arm, they became
still as a stone
until your people, O LORD, passed by,
until the people whom you acquired
passed by.
[17] You brought them in and planted them on
the mountain of your own
possession,
the place, O LORD, that you made your
abode,
the sanctuary, O LORD, that your hands
have established.
[18] The LORD will reign forever and ever."

[19]When the horses of Pharaoh with his chariots and his chariot drivers went into the sea, the LORD brought back the waters of the sea upon them; but the Israelites walked through the sea on dry ground.

[20]Then the prophet Miriam, Aaron's sister, took a tambourine in her hand; and all the women went out after her with tambourines and with dancing. [21]And Miriam sang to them:
"Sing to the LORD, for he has triumphed
gloriously;
horse and rider he has thrown into the sea."

COMMENTARY

This unit includes a long poem, usually called "The Song of Moses" (vv. 1-18); a short poem, commonly termed "The Song of Miriam" (vv. 20-21); and a brief narrative interlude between the two poems (v. 19).

15:1-18. The Song of Moses is commonly recognized as one of the oldest, most radical, and most important poems in the OT. It not only sounds the crucial themes of Israel's most elemental faith, but it also provides a shape and sequencing of that faith, which we may take as "canonical." The most important recent development in interpretation is to see that the poem holds together a distinctive articulation of *the story of liberation,* with Israel moving from the world of Pharaoh's oppression to the safe land of promise and the undercurrent thematic of *a creation liturgy,* which portrays and enacts God's victory over the powers of chaos and the forming of the earth as a safe, ordered place for life.

The poem begins with an introduction whereby Moses and the Israelites prepare to sing to Yahweh (vv. 1-2). Such an introduction is a standard element in Israel's hymnody. This declaration is itself an exuberant act of self-abandonment, wherein one yields oneself to the subject of praise. That is, the introduction effectively changes the subject of the song from the intention of the singers to the reality of the one praised. There is no doubt that the "I" of the song is the whole community of Israel, now publicly declaring that its life is rooted in and derived from this other one.

The subject of this act of exuberant self-abandonment is Yahweh, named three times in these introductory verses. This Yahweh has been the subject of the entire exodus narrative, in whom Israel has come to believe (14:31), and whom Pharaoh finally comes to know (14:25). This naming of Yahweh is not only an act of praise, but it is also a polemical act, whereby Israel dismisses and nullifies any rival to Yahweh, for no other has undertaken the liberation now being celebrated.

The first verse of the hymn apparently is a quotation from the older independent song of v. 21. The older song is by "Miriam and all the women." Thus Moses, the official leader, has taken over and preempted the singing first done by the women. This act of preemption is not unlike the early witness to the resurrection of Jesus in Luke 24:10-12. The women were the first witnesses, but it took the verification of the male leaders to authenticate their report. The reference to "sea" here no doubt refers to the Egyptian waters of death, but more largely refers to the waters of chaos, which Yahweh has utilized for the purposes of liberation. That single core act of the defeat of "the horse and rider" becomes the elemental claim from which all else in Israel's doxological tradition derives.

From this single event, now celebrated in all its inscrutable wonder, the poem uses a series of first-person pronouns to draw close to Yahweh in adoration and allegiance: Yahweh—my strength, my song, my deliverance, my God, God of my father. The singer knows that all of life is owed to this one who will be lifted up and enthroned in this act of praise. Reference to "my father's God" may be a modest connection to the Genesis tradition, a connection that was decisive in Exod 2:24-25; 3:17; and 6:2-3.

The rhetoric in v. 3 moves into a somewhat more formal statement. Israel's faith depends in important ways on a military metaphor. While such a metaphor may offend our modern sensibilities, the whole claim of rescue, deliverance, and salvation depends on the reality that God can do for us what we cannot do for ourselves. It is as though the utterance of Yahweh's name is a defiant challenge to any power that might try to undo the liberation and force the singer back into bondage. The singer anticipates the Pauline assertion: "I am not ashamed of the gospel" (Rom 1:16 NRSV). This singer is not embarrassed to take a strong stand for the future in this affirmation. The singer is buoyant and delighted at the new possibilities the reality of this God makes possible. The remainder of the poem explicates this passionate faith and sure confidence.

The body of the song in its first half focuses on the rescue, understood as a victory for Yahweh (vv. 4-10). The victory song, characteristic of Israel, celebrates by retelling the dangerous, hard-fought conflict and its happy resolve. Thus the whole drama of Exodus is summarized briefly in v. 4, looking back to v. 1, reiterating the event whereby the waters governed by Yahweh were used to protect Israel and to defeat the formidable troops of Egypt. In v. 5, we have a dramatic picture of the soldiers and horses of the empire slowly sinking into the waters (cf. v. 10*b*). One can hear in the poem the blub, blub, blub of water as the bodies disappear into the depths, defeated and helpless. That graphic picture is voiced in the boldest terms possible, for "floods" (תהמת *těhōmōt*) and "depths" (מצולה *měṣôlōt*) are allusions to cosmic waters. By the surging of these waters, the residue of defeated Egypt disappears from creation and succumbs to the resilient, indifferent power of chaos, a power operating here at the behest of Yahweh.

After the description of the pivotal act of defeat, the poem breaks into a fresh doxology, voicing Yahweh's incomparable power (vv. 6-8). These verses, dominated by the pronoun *your,* acknowl-edge the unrivaled power of Yahweh. The wonder of this rescue is effected by Yahweh's "right hand"—i.e., Yahweh's most potent capacity for action (cf. 14:31 on Yahweh's "great hand"). Accent on Yahweh's power only underscores the pitiful impotence of Pharaoh, who now has no power at all. The rhetoric includes to "your majesty, your adversaries, your fury, your nostrils." All is "yours"! Israel withholds nothing in its glad acknowledgment of Yahweh as the only one capable of working such an inversion. Yahweh's power, moreover, is aimed exactly against "enemy" (אויב *'ôyēb*), a word that occurs without any definite article; against your "adversary" (קמיך *qāmêkā*), the one who "rises up" in opposition (vv. 6-7). Yahweh is at work against rivals for power, or against recalcitrant subjects of Yahweh's rightful governance.

In vv. 7b-8, we are given two contrasting images for Yahweh's power. On the one hand, Yahweh's "fury" (חרון *ḥārôn*) is like a consuming fire, for which "stubble" (straw) is most flammable. On the other hand, Yahweh is like a great sea monster. The "wind" (רוח *rûaḥ*) out of Yahweh's nostril blows the waters of the sea; the primordial waters stand aside in a wall. The poetry here moves well beyond the specific enactment of the Exodus and appeals to the language of the creator's victory over and administration of chaos. The images of warrior, fire, and monster are attempts to voice the extravagant power of Yahweh.

The struggle with "enemy" (*'ôyēb*) escalates. Yahweh does not prevail easily. The enemy, the surging, recalcitrant power of chaos, issues a resolve against Yahweh in a speech dominated by defiant first-person pronouns, with more than a little arrogance (v. 9):

I will pursue [רדף *rādap*], I will overtake [נשׂג *nśg*],
I will divide [חלק *ḥālaq*] the spoil, my desire
 shall have its fill [מלא *mālē'*] of them.
I will draw [ריק *rîq*] my sword, my hand
 shall destroy [ירשׁ *yāraš*] them.

The enemy has not yet been defeated or become convinced of Yahweh's power.

The shift from v. 9 to v. 10 is abrupt and complete. There is no conjunction or preposition, but the rhetoric breaks off as it moves from the "I" of the enemy to the "You" of the doxology. "You blew your wind" (*rûaḥ*). That is all, but that is enough. The wind of God moves over the mighty waters, and the enemy is inundated, destroyed, and nullified. The voice of this poem is positioned as a witness who sees and attests to the contest between Yahweh and Egypt, between creation and chaos, and between life and death. It is no contest. In two lines of poetry, the battle is over, and the enemy is not heard from again.

At the center of the poem is a reflective, doxological reprise that looks back on the victory of vv. 4-10 and articulates an exultant affirmation (vv. 11-12). These two verses stand at the center of the poem, poised between the two main elements of vv. 4-10 and 13-17. The conclusion drawn from the struggle just described concerns the incomparability of Yahweh: "Who is like you?" That issue, here voiced as a rhetorical question, has been voiced in an indicative conclusion in 8:10 and 9:14. The hymn is situated in an openly polytheistic context. It does not say there are no other gods, just that there are no parallels to Yahweh. On the other hand, however, Yahweh is named (the only one named) and in truth has no rivals among the other gods. No other people has a doxology about a god who has won a victory for the oppressed against the oppressor in the real world of power politics.[71]

In the drama of the poem, the world is made utterly safe for the adherents of Yahweh. Slavery is banished, and chaos is eliminated. The doxology of v. 11 is sanctioned and legitimated by the specificity of v. 12, which looks back to vv. 4-10. Again there is reference to Yahweh's right hand. Look out for Yahweh's right hand, for it is lethal! The last line of v. 12 reverts to very different language. The verb *swallow* suggests something like a monster that gulps down the enemy. (See the verb poignantly used in 7:12.) In this case,

---

71. See Herbert Schneidau, "Let the Reader Understand," 140-42.

the earth (dry land) swallows up the sea, the surging power of chaos. In the narrative of chapter 14, that is what Israel saw: Dry land swallowed up the water, creation swallowed up chaos, and order swallowed up disorder (14:21-22). Yahweh has won! Earth is ordered! Israel is safe!

In the second half of the main body of the poem (vv. 13-17), the setting and tone have changed. We are not now at the waters as in vv. 4-10, but are moving through occupied territory. In the literary-liturgical antecedents to Israel's song, the genre amounts to *a victory parade, a triumphal procession,* in which the winning God moves in processional splendor to take up his throne. Along the parade route, those who watch the victory parade stand in silent awe, witnesses filled both with respect and dread. These verses portray Yahweh and Israel moving triumphantly on to the land of promise, moving without resistance, because all the potential resisters have seen Yahweh's great victory and are duly intimidated.

The dominant image here is not power, as in vv. 4-10, but the "steadfast love" (חסד *ḥesed*) of the God who journeys now in protective leadership (v. 13). This part of the poem characterizes Israel's journey after the exodus on its way to the land of promise, a journey already anticipated in 3:7-9. This brief outline of the journey sketches the itinerary that is later followed in more detail in the book of Numbers. Here, however, the intention is not to recall all of those encounters, but to witness to the power and fidelity of Yahweh. Already in 13:21-22, we have been introduced to the protective leadership of Yahweh for this people that is "between places." The journey is dangerous, because it is through territory already occupied, in the face of peoples who are hostile, threatened, and suspicious. This hostility and suspicion are countered, so says the poem, by the fidelity of Yahweh, which is committed to this people whom Yahweh has "redeemed" (גאל *gāʾal,* v. 13) and "acquired" (קנה *qānâ,* v. 16). Both of these verbs connote an economic transaction. Yahweh has purchased the slaves and then has set them free. Yahweh now "possesses" these erstwhile slaves and can dispose of them as Yahweh chooses. What Yahweh chooses is to give them a safe place that is, in fact, God's own "holy abode" (v. 13).

Israel is protected by Yahweh, who embodies cosmic law. The watching peoples hear about this "invasion" and tremble, enormously agitated (v. 14). That is, they are seized by a powerful urge to do something to resist their loss of territory. "The peoples," here treated generically, include Israel's standard list of adversaries whose land they occupy: Philistines, Edomites, Moabites, and Canaanites. The poem assigns to each of these resentful witnesses a verb of anxiety and hostility: *seized, dismayed, trembling, melted.* Then in v. 16, is a summary statement of their common condition: "terror and dread."

The source of their immobilizing fear, however, is not Israel: It is Yahweh! Each of these peoples has its own god who protects its own territory. Each of these peoples, however, now knows that Yahweh is more powerful than their gods. It is the might of Yahweh's arm (which saves, which drowns) that reduces these peoples to sullen submission. They know the sorry tale of the resistant pharaoh. If the great king of Egypt could not compete with Yahweh, then much smaller peoples and much weaker gods have no chance.

How long must this grim spectacle persist? How long must these watching witnesses remain immobilized by fear? For as long as Yahweh wants; for as long as it takes to get every Israelite—every man, woman, child, cow, and sheep of Israel—safely pastured. The poem uses a double "until" (v. 16). Now, for the first time in the second half, Yahweh is named, and only with reference to Israel: "Until your people, O Yahweh, have passed by." Normal life in all these places is suspended, until this community, which is possessed and treasured by Yahweh, is brought to safety.

It is not completely clear what this poem intends as a destination. While we expect the goal to be the land, the language of the poem suggests, rather, a sanctuary, perhaps the Temple to be established in Jerusalem (cf. the "mountain" in v. 17). Scholars are uncertain whether the reference is to land or sanctuary; perhaps the elusive rhetoric of the poem does not require a decision. The conventional accent on the "credo" (cf. 3:7-9, 17) would tilt our reading toward the land. In the book of Exodus itself, however, the text culminates with the establishment of a right sanctuary (see Exodus 35–40). Taken either way, the goal is a safe place that is marked by the majestic and protective presence of God.

Verse 18 provides a conclusion to the poem that is structurally the counterpart to vv. 1-3. At the outset, the poem celebrates the military prowess of Yahweh. Now in v. 18, Israel sounds a great doxological affirmation of Yahweh's enthronement. That enthronement, however, does not leave Yahweh in splendid isolation. Rather, the enthronement has required both the safe establishment of Israel and the proper deference of the nations. Yahweh's enthronement entails a reordering of human power for the enhancement of those who have been despised by the nations.

The poem is exceedingly difficult and complicated, and many interpretive problems persist. We may, however, see that in one possible reading the poem is organized in a chiastic fashion:

A *The introduction* announces the core theme: that Yahweh is to be praised for throwing the horse and rider into the sea (vv. 1-3).

  B The *first core element* is *a victory song* (vv. 4-10). In a struggle for divine authority, which in the experience of Israel is constituted by exodus; Yahweh has "gotten glory" over all adversaries.

    C At the center is *the doxological reprise* affirming the distinctiveness and incomparability of Yahweh (vv. 11-12).

  B′ The *second core element* is the triumphal entry of the victor in majestic procession on the way to the throne (vv. 13-17). In Israel's experience, this procession is constituted by the journey toward the land of promise; Yahweh's triumphal entry is at the same time the entry of Israel into well-being.

A′ *The conclusion* is an enthronement formula that anticipates Yahweh's very long-term governance (v. 18).

This extraordinary poem dramatizes and reenacts the story of Yahweh. In Israel's imagination, however, the story of Yahweh can never be told without its being at the same time the story of Israel. As the latter, this poem is the account whereby a helpless company of vulnerable slaves traverses the dangerous territory to a safe land of their own. To be sure, Israel's story could not happen unless this was first of all Yahweh's story.

But it is equally clear that Yahweh's story can never be told unless it is at the same time the story of Israel. Humanly speaking, one can conclude that Israel is unwilling or unable to tell Yahweh's story unless it is also a story about "us." Theologically, the poem asserts that Yahweh will not undertake this story unless Israel can be its subject. In the end, the two stories—*the story of victory and enthronement* and *the story of liberation and homecoming*—are deeply intertwined and cannot be told apart from each other.

15:19. After Moses' poem, the narrator has added a prose comment that gives closure to the entire unit of the Exodus narrative. This prose comment only reiterates in summary fashion the second wondrous act of Yahweh (there wrought through Moses) in 14:26-29, whereby the waters return. After the rescue, Yahweh puts things back where they belong. Now life goes on with the "normal" arrangement of land and sea, creation and chaos.

15:20-21. Finally, as the great rhetorical climax to this long tale of inversion, we are given a brief poem, commonly called "The Song of Miriam." This poem is regarded by scholars as being very old, perhaps the oldest Israelite poem we have and perhaps composed very close to the time of these remembered events. The poem itself in v. 21 has already been encountered in v. 1, where it is quoted.

This brief hymn follows the convention of Israel's hymns in its two parts. First, there is an imperative summons, in this case, "Sing to Yahweh." The summons to praise is itself an act of praise, an exuberant acknowledgment of Yahweh and a glad ceding over of energy and loyalty to Yahweh. Second, reasons for praise are given, introduced by the particle *for* (כִּי *kî*, "because"). The reason for praise of Yahweh, the incomparable one, is quite specific. Yahweh has overcome the seemingly invincible power of armed might that enforced aggression. The "power" in this poem is not specifically Pharaoh and Egypt. The lack of specificity permits the poem to be readily available as a paradigm for every doxology that celebrates death to tyrants.

The poem (song) is placed on the lips and in the dancing feet of Miriam and the Israelite women. We know elsewhere that there were women especially skilled in the singing required by the community for grief and death (Jer 9:17; 2 Chr 35:25). In the same way, no doubt there were women, perhaps the same ones, skilled in singing and dancing with joy and exultation for liberation, victory, and well-being (cf. 1 Sam 18:7). The OT lets us see a community that is easily and readily evoked into the "surplus" activity of liturgy for the emotional, political extremities of joy and grief, well-being and loss.

It may be that at the exodus itself there was such singing and dancing, such glad release of stifled yearning, such freedom for which bodies in Israel had long ached. How could it be otherwise! There is also no doubt that as the exodus liberation became a stylized liturgical event, this song and its unfettered dancing must have become standard practice. It is the liturgic remembering and hoping of every community of the oppressed that catches a glimpse of freedom and authorizes liturgical (and eschatological) exaggeration to say, "Free at last!" When the song is sung, clearly this is not yet "at last." The community at worship, however, can dare such exaggeration,

because its hope is more powerful and more compelling than any present circumstance.

Finally, no doubt, this song, rooted in exodus experience and preserved in exodus liturgy, is taken up for the canonical telling of the biblical story. Now the story of Miriam and the women is placed as the ultimate verdict of Israel's faith. As such, it stands as a massive, lyrical resolution to the grief and cry of 2:23-25. Israel's *initial cry* (which began the liberating work of Yahweh) and *concluding shout* stand in an arc of faith. The larger narrative of Israel—the old, old story that Israel loves to tell (and act out)—is the Passover tale of grief and joy, trouble and resolution, oppression and liberation. Passover imagination, centered in the one who hears the cry and dances in delight, dares to see all of Israel's existence, all of human existence (indeed, the tale of all creation) as a drama from hurt to well-being. Israel claims, moreover, to know the name of the elusive character who makes the story relentlessly and recurrently true, visible, and actualized in the very bodies of the Israelites.

REFLECTIONS

1. God is portrayed here in embarrassingly anthropomorphic categories (i.e., God has qualities of emotion and body that may offend our "metaphysical propensities"). Our Western inclination to portray God as removed from the human drama of our experience, however, is a highly dubious gain. Such anthropomorphic portrayals as we have in this text belong to the core of biblical faith, and are not incidental footnotes. Moreover, such earthiness brings the questions and resources of faith very close to how we experience and live reality. Such speech in this poem opens up the most elemental struggles and hopes that are part of the human enterprise. No other mode of theological speech so well touches the human concreteness of faith.

2. More specifically, the military metaphors for God raise problems. Yahweh is "a man of war," a description that seems to evoke and authorize violence in the world. Our primary way of dealing with this problem is to transpose the political-historical violence into ontological violence—i.e., God's struggle with death. No doubt there is something positive in such an interpretive move (made even in the Bible itself). Such a maneuver, however, may on occasion be a bourgeois device. It is evident that theological rhetoric about God's use of force against the power of oppression is not experienced as violent by those who are, in fact, oppressed. In a situation of victimization, one is not so worried about violence in the power of one's rescuer. Metaphors of violence are problematic, but we must take care not to escape them by ideological dismissal. There is in the gospel a model of conflict and a deep struggle for power and authority. To miss this element is to distort biblical faith into a benign, innocent affair. We are (as the Bible recognizes) caught in a deep battle for humanness, a battle larger than we ourselves can manage. This, finally, is what faith asserts in its claim that "God is for us."

3. The power of God for well-being, in the sub-currents of this text, concerns the power of cosmic ordering in the face of the surging threat of chaos. Thus the imagery of water and the sea are allusions to the elemental disordering that lives all around our safety and well-being. The news of God's management of the waters and the capacity of the dry land to swallow up the threat is good news: The world is not, in the end, chaotic.

4. This affirmation about holy power clearly has a public, political dimension. It is precisely Pharaoh and his tools of domination (horses and chariots) that are destroyed. The good news of the poem is that God's power for life is arrayed against, and victorious over, every enemy of human well-being in every present power arrangement.

5. Derivatively, this poem is good news in our personal dramas as well. The poem asserts paradigmatically that God is for us, that we as listeners are invited into the world of God's fidelity to be a member of this people whom God has now acquired and treasures.

6. The peculiar image for the show of God's rescuing power is God's רוח (*rûaḥ*.). The "wind" here refers concretely to the force that blows the waters back. We may see this usage in v. 8 ("blast") and in v. 10 ("wind") as references to God's force, which moves the world toward life. This "spirit" (as the Hebrew may also be rendered) is not to be read as "the third person of the Trinity," but is the active force of God's irresistible intention unleashed into the world. This force is unadministered, unintimidated, undomesticated, insatiable, and able to move the world toward life.

The wind of God is, in the Christian confession, no doubt profoundly focused in the power of Easter, where God's inscrutable capacity to work life in the face of the determined power of death is demonstrated. Indeed, in the categories of Christian faith, this great poem has its counterpart in the Easter narratives of the Gospels and in the great Pauline lyric of 1 Corinthians 15. Paul can scarcely find words with which to utter the inscrutable power of life in the world that refuses the governance of death. Ezekiel 37:1-14 already provides the language whereby the work of the Spirit and the power of the resurrection are deeply linked to each other.

7. This poem, framed around the crisis of exodus liberation (vv. 4-10) and sojourn-conquest (vv. 13-17), shapes the credo tradition of Israel.[72] These verses assert, in what may be Israel's most crucial articulation of its creed, that Israel's life consists in *liberation from* and *entry into*. These are the two points already promised in 3:7-8. That is, life is shaped as departure from bondage and access to liberated well-being. This same modeling of reality is mediated in Christian liturgy and characterizes the Christian pilgrimage of life in Christ. That life consists in dying with Christ and being raised to new life, in taking the form of a servant and being exalted, in denying oneself and having life given abundantly.

72. See Miller, *The Divine Warrior in Early Israel,* 166-75.

"IS THE LORD AMONG US OR NOT?"

OVERVIEW

These chapters articulate a subordinate theme in the book of Exodus: the wilderness sojourn. With the book of Numbers, the wilderness sojourn will come to occupy a much larger place in the completed narrative.

Here the wilderness sojourn functions primarily as a geographical device for the larger narrative. It provides a way to move action from one place to another, or to indicate the passage of time. Specifically, these materials and this theme help move the action from the "Sea of Reeds" to Mt. Sinai. Careful attention has been given by scholars to the historical, geographical, and archaeological elements of the narrative.[73] It is, however, completely impossible to assess the "historical" reliability of any of these narratives.

What may have been a transitional literary convenience, however, has become a freighted theme that makes its own contribution to the larger theological claims of the completed tradition. The wilderness through which Israel traverses comes to be a metaphor for a zone of life not properly ordered and without the usual, reliable life-support systems. The several narrative episodes characteristically revolve around the need of Israel, the distrust of Israel (which becomes an attack on Moses' leadership), and the generous, life-sustaining gifts of Yahweh (cf. Ps 78:19-20). Thus the theological issues regularly come to the fore, and the narrative exhibits little interest in geographical, historical details. Moreover, the wilderness metaphor serves as an effective cipher for exile, thus being crucial for the exilic and post-exilic community that brought the text to its final form.

The paradigmatic narrative in this small grouping of texts is, of course, chapter 16. In that story about manna, the need of Israel is more than met by the powerful generosity of Yahweh. The derivative themes of the sabbath and the fearful hoarding of bread suggest the broad range of issues present in the theme of the wilderness sojourn. The brief episodes concerning Marah, Elim, and Rephadim witness to the same suppleness of the tradition.

Two narratives do not fit this general pattern of need and gift. First, the encounter with the Amalekites is odd in this context and serves a quite distinct ideological interest (17:8-16). Second, chapter 18, with its reference to Jethro, stands all alone and does not seem to relate to anything in its context. Both 17:8-16, concerning perpetual war, and 18:13-27, concerning judicial procedures, portray Moses as devising new institutional practices (war and justice) in the process of nation building.[74]

Primary interpretive attention, however, will most likely be given to the other narratives concerning need and gift. Yahweh is indeed able to give life, especially in circumstances where resources for life are not evident and where Pharaoh could not give life. Yahweh's capacity to give life where there is none, to give bread from heaven and water from rock, are examples of *creatio ex nihilo,* God's capacity to form a people out of "no people" (cf. 1 Pet 2:9-10).

---

73. See George W. Coats, *Rebellion in the Wilderness: The Murmuring Motif in the Wilderness Traditions of the Old Testament* (Nashville: Abingdon, 1968); and Graham I. Davies, *The Way of the Wilderness: A Geographical Study of the Wilderness Itineraries in the Old Testament* (Cambridge: Cambridge University Press, 1979).

74. On Moses as a political leader, see Aaron Wildavsky, *The Nursing Father: Moses as a Political Leader* (Tuscaloosa: The University of Alabama Press, 1984).

EXODUS 15:22-27, BITTER WATER MADE SWEET

NIV

²²Then Moses led Israel from the Red Sea and they went into the Desert of Shur. For three days they traveled in the desert without finding water. ²³When they came to Marah, they could not drink its water because it was bitter. (That is why the place is called Marah.ª) ²⁴So the people grumbled against Moses, saying, "What are we to drink?"

²⁵Then Moses cried out to the LORD, and the LORD showed him a piece of wood. He threw it into the water, and the water became sweet.

There the LORD made a decree and a law for them, and there he tested them. ²⁶He said, "If you listen carefully to the voice of the LORD your God and do what is right in his eyes, if you pay attention to his commands and keep all his decrees, I will not bring on you any of the diseases I brought on the Egyptians, for I am the LORD, who heals you."

²⁷Then they came to Elim, where there were twelve springs and seventy palm trees, and they camped there near the water.

ª23 Marah means bitter.

NRSV

²²Then Moses ordered Israel to set out from the Red Sea,ª and they went into the wilderness of Shur. They went three days in the wilderness and found no water. ²³When they came to Marah, they could not drink the water of Marah because it was bitter. That is why it was called Marah.ᵇ ²⁴And the people complained against Moses, saying, "What shall we drink?" ²⁵He cried out to the LORD; and the LORD showed him a piece of wood;ᶜ he threw it into the water, and the water became sweet.

There the LORD ᵈ made for them a statute and an ordinance and there he put them to the test. ²⁶He said, "If you will listen carefully to the voice of the LORD your God, and do what is right in his sight, and give heed to his commandments and keep all his statutes, I will not bring upon you any of the diseases that I brought upon the Egyptians; for I am the LORD who heals you."

²⁷Then they came to Elim, where there were twelve springs of water and seventy palm trees; and they camped there by the water.

ª Or Sea of Reeds   ᵇ That is Bitterness   ᶜ Or a tree   ᵈ Heb he

COMMENTARY

The journey away from bondage to well-being and from Egypt to the new land, begun in 12:37-39, continues. The setting is "the wilderness," the territory not under the control of Pharaoh. It is also, however, the territory where there is no ordered, reliable life-support system. Wilderness habitation is life at risk. This brief unit features Israel at two "watering holes" (oases): Marah (vv. 23-25a) and Elim (v. 27). The two oases reports sandwich a divine oracle voiced by the God who commands and who heals (vv. 25b-26). Another way to see the construction of this passage is that it moves from "no water" (v. 22) to "water" (v. 27), by way of God's speech (v. 26).

The first encounter at Marah concerns a water shortage, which is promptly transposed into a crisis of leadership (vv. 23-25a). The name of the place

is Marah ("bitter"). It is commonly thought by scholars that the tale is told to explain how the oasis got its name, "bitter." What may have been such a name-tale (etymological saga) is, however, transposed by the tradition into a serious theological crisis. There is no water, exactly what one might expect in the wilderness where life is at risk. Without water, the people will soon die.

The people "complain" against Moses. They are restless and discontented with his leadership. The trust they have placed in him (v. 14:31) is soon dissipated, perhaps with the general wonderment, "What has Moses done for us lately?" Moses, however, does not respond to the complaint. Rather, he himself turns into a complainer against Yahweh: "He cried out to Yahweh." There is a two-tiered leadership in which the people deal with Moses, and

Moses deals with Yahweh. Thus Moses promptly turns the water crisis over to Yahweh.

We have already seen the rhetorical construct of "complaint-assurance" in 14:11-14, wherein Israel's complaint receives from Moses a salvation oracle that overcomes the cause of complaint. This narrative is structured in the same way, except that Yahweh's response is not a speech, but an act: Yahweh provides a means whereby bitter water becomes sweet. The crisis is averted, and Moses'

leadership is again accepted. The life-threatening situation of the wilderness is overcome by a "wonder."

The second element of the unit is a decree of Yahweh (v. 25b-26). This decree has no visible connection to the preceding "wonder," except that the God who presides over life-processes is now entitled to assert sovereignty. This verse makes unmistakeably clear that the liberation from Egypt does not lead to autonomy for Israel, but rather to an alternative sovereignty that imposes

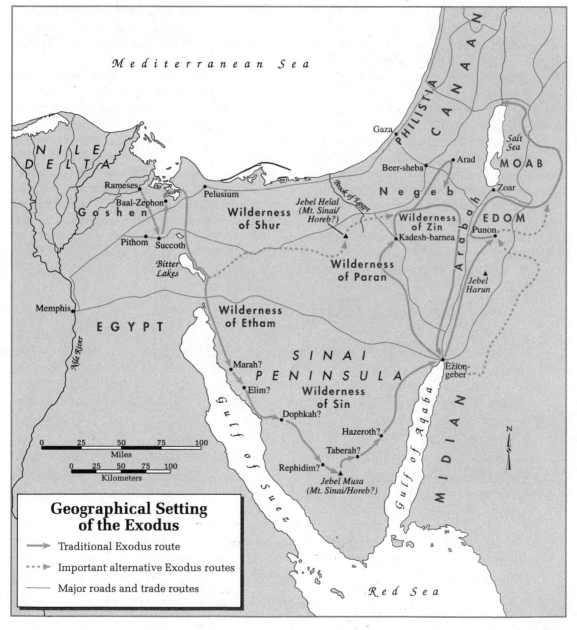

Geographical Setting of the Exodus

→ Traditional Exodus route

┈→ Important alternative Exodus routes

— Major roads and trade routes

an alternative regimen on the liberated slaves. This single verse presents Yahweh as the God who commands, and it anticipates the larger tradition of command in the Sinai meeting to come.

The decree of Yahweh issues a comprehensive command and makes an extraordinary promise. The command is introduced with a conditional "if," followed by an infinitive absolute, "if you will *really* hear," exactly the same instruction as in 19:5 and Deut 15:5. This statement of urgency is followed by three additional verbs of command—*do, give heed,* and *keep*—which are all roughly synonymous. These verbs govern the terms *right, commandments,* and *statutes,* which are synonymous references to the intention and purpose of Yahweh, the new possessor of the liberated slaves. In this triad following the conditional infinitive absolute, Israel is bound, securely and finally, to the will and purpose of Yahweh. So far, this mention of Yahweh's commands is given no substance, and the statement remains completely formal. In this utterance, nonetheless, Israel is radically redefined as a community whose single purpose is the doing of Yahweh's command.

The second half of Yahweh's decree is an assurance. It is odd that the second half of the statement is not in any effective way related to the preceding. We expect an "if . . . then" construction, but there is no "then" in the text. Perhaps it is understood; however, it is not certain whether freedom from Egyptian "diseases" depends on the preceding command, though that is likely implied.

As a seal and guarantee of both the command and the promise, Yahweh issues a magisterial statement of self-identity and self-disclosure: "I am Yahweh." This is not Pharaoh, not a god of burdensome obedience, not a power that generates disease, but a genuine alternative power. Moreover, that magisterial formula is now exposited in a new and remarkable way: "who heals you." The participle might also be translated as a noun, "your healer," or "your doctor." Thus there is introduced into Israel's rhetoric God's concern for the therapeutic, which stands in complete contrast to the Egyptian powers who generate disease.

The final verse of this unit (v. 27), perhaps, has no integral relation to the preceding. It seems to stand alone. In its context, however, Elim, a luxurious oasis, stands in complete contrast to Marah. There is nothing bitter here; therefore, there is no contentiousness among the people. Instead of "no water," there is water. The wilderness contains adequate resources for life! The text itself makes no explicit connection between v. 27 and what precedes. In its present sequence, however, it is fair to think that v. 27 is offered as a case in point of what the new life looks like when the commands and assurances of Yahweh are taken seriously.

REFLECTIONS

1. This is a concrete case of utter dependence. Water is required for life and is urgent in the wilderness. Water cannot be invented, devised, or manufactured. It can only be given and received. These two tales of water assert both Israel's vulnerability and utter dependence, and Yahweh's fidelity in giving what is needed for life. God's people are shown here in their deep precariousness; God is shown in utter, sovereign fidelity. There is no doubt that biblical faith takes "water" as a metaphor for the gift of life in the gospel, most clearly in John 4:7-15.

2. The exodus is construed as a healing, as restoration to healthy existence. The situation of bondage in which Israel finds itself is one of disorder and pathology, not a true state of human existence. This God as "healer" is the one who liberates, redeems, ransoms, restores to the true intention of creation.

So much that is silly and trivial has been said in recent time about therapy.[75] It is indeed a deep misfortune that therapy and healing have in popular parlance become so trivialized. The cost of such a mistaken, truncated notion of "healing" is chronicled in Robert Bellah et al., *Habits of the Heart.*[76] Such caricatures of therapy, however, have nothing to do with the

75. See the critical analysis of Philip Rieff, *The Triumph of the Therapeutic: Uses of Faith After Freud* (New York: Harper and Row, 1966).
76. Robert N. Bellah et al., *Habits of the Heart: Individualism and Commitment in American Life* (Berkeley: University of California Press, 1985).

healing intention of God, which is to restore persons, communities, and ultimately the whole of creation to their rightful status of health, as creatures loved by and responsive to the purposes of the creator. This "therapy" is not some act of self-indulgence that touches nothing serious. True therapy, the kind worked by the living God, is a radical reconstrual of reality, a radical recharacterization of self before God, a deep revision of power arrangements in the world, and a demanding embrace of God's good purposes for self and world.[77] This same work of healing, moreover, is entrusted by Jesus to his disciples, who are to do the work of God (Luke 10:9). The claim of the gospel is not only that God is about the work of restoring creation to health, but that God's resolve to effect wholeness is entrusted to human agents.

3. The structure of Yahweh's decree appears to be completely an "if . . . then" statement of conditionality. There is no free offer of healing. One cannot be healed of a pathology if one insists on continuing the practices that initially produced the condition. In this case, the healing of the diseases of Egypt requires coming under the command of Yahweh and renouncing the commands of Egypt.

This statement of conditionality is not a petty supernaturalism that says God will not heal if one does not act right. Rather, it is better understood through serious social criticism. The systemic pathologies of an exploitative system can be escaped only if one stops colluding with the system. The way to stop such collusion, says the decree of Yahweh, is to commit to a different pattern of obedience that is rooted in a different vision.

Specifically, if consumerism is destroying the human spirit among us and crushing the values of family and community, and if consumerism produces a pathology of abused persons in inadequate relations, then there is no remedy within that system. Remedy requires breaking with that system for the sake of a different set of relations that are authorized by the commands of torah. Like the Israelites who lust for Egyptian "fleshpots," so we can be endlessly seduced precisely by the system that generates the disability. The decree of Yahweh invites, authorizes, and requires a deep and intentional break with Egypt in order to be healed. There is no cheap, easy healing, but there is healing. Those who trust the decree of Yahweh and make the break will find themselves at the oasis with an abundance of sweet water.

77. For a classic, public notion of "therapy," see Robert E. Cushman, *Therapeia: Plato's Conception of Philosophy* (Westport, Conn.: Greenwood, 1958).

EXODUS 16:1-36, MANNA AND QUAIL

NIV

16 The whole Israelite community set out from Elim and came to the Desert of Sin, which is between Elim and Sinai, on the fifteenth day of the second month after they had come out of Egypt. [2]In the desert the whole community grumbled against Moses and Aaron. [3]The Israelites said to them, "If only we had died by the LORD's hand in Egypt! There we sat around pots of meat and ate all the food we wanted, but you have brought us out into this desert to starve this entire assembly to death."

[4]Then the LORD said to Moses, "I will rain down

NRSV

16 The whole congregation of the Israelites set out from Elim; and Israel came to the wilderness of Sin, which is between Elim and Sinai, on the fifteenth day of the second month after they had departed from the land of Egypt. [2]The whole congregation of the Israelites complained against Moses and Aaron in the wilderness. [3]The Israelites said to them, "If only we had died by the hand of the LORD in the land of Egypt, when we sat by the fleshpots and ate our fill of bread; for you have brought us out into this

NIV

bread from heaven for you. The people are to go out each day and gather enough for that day. In this way I will test them and see whether they will follow my instructions. [5]On the sixth day they are to prepare what they bring in, and that is to be twice as much as they gather on the other days."

[6]So Moses and Aaron said to all the Israelites, "In the evening you will know that it was the LORD who brought you out of Egypt, [7]and in the morning you will see the glory of the LORD, because he has heard your grumbling against him. Who are we, that you should grumble against us?" [8]Moses also said, "You will know that it was the LORD when he gives you meat to eat in the evening and all the bread you want in the morning, because he has heard your grumbling against him. Who are we? You are not grumbling against us, but against the LORD."

[9]Then Moses told Aaron, "Say to the entire Israelite community, 'Come before the LORD, for he has heard your grumbling.'"

[10]While Aaron was speaking to the whole Israelite community, they looked toward the desert, and there was the glory of the LORD appearing in the cloud.

[11]The LORD said to Moses, [12]"I have heard the grumbling of the Israelites. Tell them, 'At twilight you will eat meat, and in the morning you will be filled with bread. Then you will know that I am the LORD your God.'"

[13]That evening quail came and covered the camp, and in the morning there was a layer of dew around the camp. [14]When the dew was gone, thin flakes like frost on the ground appeared on the desert floor. [15]When the Israelites saw it, they said to each other, "What is it?" For they did not know what it was.

Moses said to them, "It is the bread the LORD has given you to eat. [16]This is what the LORD has commanded: 'Each one is to gather as much as he needs. Take an omer[a] for each person you have in your tent.'"

[17]The Israelites did as they were told; some gathered much, some little. [18]And when they measured it by the omer, he who gathered much

[a]16 That is, probably about 2 quarts (about 2 liters); also in verses 18, 32, 33 and 36

NRSV

wilderness to kill this whole assembly with hunger."

[4]Then the LORD said to Moses, "I am going to rain bread from heaven for you, and each day the people shall go out and gather enough for that day. In that way I will test them, whether they will follow my instruction or not. [5]On the sixth day, when they prepare what they bring in, it will be twice as much as they gather on other days." [6]So Moses and Aaron said to all the Israelites, "In the evening you shall know that it was the LORD who brought you out of the land of Egypt, [7]and in the morning you shall see the glory of the LORD, because he has heard your complaining against the LORD. For what are we, that you complain against us?" [8]And Moses said, "When the LORD gives you meat to eat in the evening and your fill of bread in the morning, because the LORD has heard the complaining that you utter against him—what are we? Your complaining is not against us but against the LORD."

[9]Then Moses said to Aaron, "Say to the whole congregation of the Israelites, 'Draw near to the LORD, for he has heard your complaining.'" [10]And as Aaron spoke to the whole congregation of the Israelites, they looked toward the wilderness, and the glory of the LORD appeared in the cloud. [11]The LORD spoke to Moses and said, [12]"I have heard the complaining of the Israelites; say to them, 'At twilight you shall eat meat, and in the morning you shall have your fill of bread; then you shall know that I am the LORD your God.'"

[13]In the evening quails came up and covered the camp; and in the morning there was a layer of dew around the camp. [14]When the layer of dew lifted, there on the surface of the wilderness was a fine flaky substance, as fine as frost on the ground. [15]When the Israelites saw it, they said to one another, "What is it?"[a] For they did not know what it was. Moses said to them, "It is the bread that the LORD has given you to eat. [16]This is what the LORD has commanded: 'Gather as much of it as each of you needs, an omer to a person according to the number of persons, all providing for those in their own tents.'" [17]The Israelites did so, some gathering more, some less. [18]But when they measured it with an omer, those who gath-

[a]Or "It is manna" (Heb man hu, see verse 31)

NIV

did not have too much, and he who gathered little did not have too little. Each one gathered as much as he needed.

¹⁹Then Moses said to them, "No one is to keep any of it until morning."

²⁰However, some of them paid no attention to Moses; they kept part of it until morning, but it was full of maggots and began to smell. So Moses was angry with them.

²¹Each morning everyone gathered as much as he needed, and when the sun grew hot, it melted away. ²²On the sixth day, they gathered twice as much—two omers* for each person—and the leaders of the community came and reported this to Moses. ²³He said to them, "This is what the Lord commanded: 'Tomorrow is to be a day of rest, a holy Sabbath to the Lord. So bake what you want to bake and boil what you want to boil. Save whatever is left and keep it until morning.'"

²⁴So they saved it until morning, as Moses commanded, and it did not stink or get maggots in it. ²⁵"Eat it today," Moses said, "because today is a Sabbath to the Lord. You will not find any of it on the ground today. ²⁶Six days you are to gather it, but on the seventh day, the Sabbath, there will not be any."

²⁷Nevertheless, some of the people went out on the seventh day to gather it, but they found none. ²⁸Then the Lord said to Moses, "How long will you^b refuse to keep my commands and my instructions? ²⁹Bear in mind that the Lord has given you the Sabbath; that is why on the sixth day he gives you bread for two days. Everyone is to stay where he is on the seventh day; no one is to go out." ³⁰So the people rested on the seventh day.

³¹The people of Israel called the bread manna.^c It was white like coriander seed and tasted like wafers made with honey. ³²Moses said, "This is what the Lord has commanded: 'Take an omer of manna and keep it for the generations to come, so they can see the bread I gave you to eat in the desert when I brought you out of Egypt.'"

³³So Moses said to Aaron, "Take a jar and put an omer of manna in it. Then place it before the Lord to be kept for the generations to come."

³⁴As the Lord commanded Moses, Aaron put

*a22 That is, probably about 4 quarts (about 4.5 liters)
b28 The Hebrew is plural.   c31 Manna means What is it? (see verse 15).

NRSV

ered much had nothing over, and those who gathered little had no shortage; they gathered as much as each of them needed. ¹⁹And Moses said to them, "Let no one leave any of it over until morning." ²⁰But they did not listen to Moses; some left part of it until morning, and it bred worms and became foul. And Moses was angry with them. ²¹Morning by morning they gathered it, as much as each needed; but when the sun grew hot, it melted.

²²On the sixth day they gathered twice as much food, two omers apiece. When all the leaders of the congregation came and told Moses, ²³he said to them, "This is what the Lord has commanded: 'Tomorrow is a day of solemn rest, a holy sabbath to the Lord; bake what you want to bake and boil what you want to boil, and all that is left over put aside to be kept until morning.'" ²⁴So they put it aside until morning, as Moses commanded them; and it did not become foul, and there were no worms in it. ²⁵Moses said, "Eat it today, for today is a sabbath to the Lord; today you will not find it in the field. ²⁶Six days you shall gather it; but on the seventh day, which is a sabbath, there will be none."

²⁷On the seventh day some of the people went out to gather, and they found none. ²⁸The Lord said to Moses, "How long will you refuse to keep my commandments and instructions? ²⁹See! The Lord has given you the sabbath, therefore on the sixth day he gives you food for two days; each of you stay where you are; do not leave your place on the seventh day." ³⁰So the people rested on the seventh day.

³¹The house of Israel called it manna; it was like coriander seed, white, and the taste of it was like wafers made with honey. ³²Moses said, "This is what the Lord has commanded: 'Let an omer of it be kept throughout your generations, in order that they may see the food with which I fed you in the wilderness, when I brought you out of the land of Egypt.'" ³³And Moses said to Aaron, "Take a jar, and put an omer of manna in it, and place it before the Lord, to be kept throughout your generations." ³⁴As the Lord commanded Moses, so Aaron placed it before the covenant,^a for safekeeping. ³⁵The Israelites ate manna forty years,

a Or treaty or testimony; Heb eduth

the manna in front of the Testimony, that it might be kept. ³⁵The Israelites ate manna forty years, until they came to a land that was settled; they ate manna until they reached the border of Canaan.

³⁶(An omer is one tenth of an ephah.)

until they came to a habitable land; they ate manna, until they came to the border of the land of Canaan. ³⁶An omer is a tenth of an ephah.

COMMENTARY

The wilderness continues to be a profoundly troubling place for Israel, where the necessities for survival are not immediately supplied. This long narrative is paradigmatic for the crisis of faith that occurs between bondage and well-being. Israel has no other story that lays out the theme so clearly. We may take this text as representative for the faith issues with which Israel must deal in its times of displacement (e.g., exile). After an introduction, establishing the nature of the crisis (vv. 1-3), there is the giving of the gift of bread (vv. 4-15), the reception of bread (vv. 16-30), and the "sacramentalization" of the bread (vv. 31-36).

16:1-3. The departure from Elim portends the lack of adequate food, water, and life-support. The crisis of the wilderness is a material crisis with great anxiety over what to eat and what to drink. It predictably becomes a crisis over leadership. The beginning point of the narrative is an assault upon the leadership of Moses and Aaron, who have chosen for Israel trouble (liberation) instead of bondage.

The complaint of Israel (which does not mention Yahweh at all) makes a sharp and unfavorable contrast between the wilderness and Egypt. The wilderness is a place of hunger and will inevitably lead to death. By contrast, Egypt is remembered as a place of "pots of flesh" (i.e., meat) and bread, so that even in bondage there may be material satiation. The contrast, so far as it goes, is no doubt correct; there is no hint that the bondaged Hebrews in Egypt lacked bread.

What is striking in this assaulting contrast is how present anxiety distorts the memory of the recent past. Egypt is known to be a place of deep abuse and heavy-handed oppression. Here, however, none of the oppression or abuse is men-

tioned, only meat and bread. The seductive distortion of Israel is that, given anxiety about survival, the immediacy of food overrides any long-term hope for freedom and well-being. The desperate, fearful choice that Israel voices in this contrast is reminiscent of Esau, who was willing to forego his birthright for immediate satisfaction in food (Gen 25:29-34).

In its anxiety, Israel is willing to make a very poor trade. Israel is not reprimanded in this narrative for its anxious concern, but receives an immediate, positive response. Israel is not required to repent its yearning for food; rather, they can expect to receive food from another source, one that requires dependence but does not lead to a fresh bondage.

16:4-15. The response to the complaint is the enactment of a "wonder" that redescribes the wilderness as a place of life. It is striking, however, that the response is not made by Moses, to whom the complaint is addressed. Nor does Moses transmit the complaint to Yahweh. Rather, Yahweh takes over the complaint addressed to Moses and answers the complaint directly (vv. 4-5).

Yahweh's promise has two parts. First, there will be bread "from heaven"—i.e., bread given out of God's rich storehouse, so that it need not come from Pharaoh's storehouses (v. 4; cf. 1:11; Gen 47:13-19). Quail is also given in answer to a yearning for meat. (Notice that in Ps 78:26 "the wind of heaven" brings bread and meat. On that wind, see Job 38:24 as well as Exod 14:21.)

Second, there is a special provision for sabbath, so that the bread given on the sixth day is enough for the seventh (v. 5). As we shall see, the theme of sabbath is woven throughout this narrative concerning free bread. Between these two provisions concerning "bread from heaven" and sabbath, God resolves to "test" Israel in order to determine whether Israel is prepared to receive bread and life under wholly new terms and completely changed conditions. The ways of receiving bread in Egypt are completely inappropriate here. Israel will be under scrutiny to see if old ways of receiving bread in Egypt (in anxiety, oppression, hoarding) can be resisted.

On the basis of this promise from Yahweh to Moses, there now follows a speech of Moses-Aaron to the people (vv. 6-8), a statement of Moses to Aaron (v. 9), a statement of Yahweh to Moses (vv. 11-12), and narrative reports on the implementation of God's promise (vv. 10, 13-15). This sequence of exchange reiterates three themes: First, it is affirmed four times that God has *heard* Israel's complaint (vv. 7-9, 12). This is, in fact, the crucial theme in the drama. The narrative insists on this point, because the hearing by Yahweh overrides the complaint. Second, it is twice asserted on the basis of being heard that "you shall know" (vv. 6, 12). You shall *know* that it was Yahweh who rescued. You shall know that the key character in this new, precarious life is precisely Yahweh and none other. Third, the wilderness, which appears bereft of any life-giving presence, will be the host context of God's glory. The glory is promised (v. 7); then the glory is *seen* (v. 10). Israel knows that wilderness is not empty but is inhabited by the powerful presence of God. In these three rhetorical moves of hearing, knowing, and seeing, Israel's complaint is dealt with by a massive disclosure that God is powerfully and decisively present.

Moses (through Aaron) invites Israel, the congregation (עדה 'ēdâ) to "draw near," or to gather in worship (v. 9). When they do, they see "the glory" (v. 10). This verse is cast in the language of worship, not only with the verb "draw near," but also with an emphasis on "glory" as a real, visible presence in the midst of worship. Although cast in the language of worship, the coming of God's glory is at the same time a remarkable and dramatic turn in the larger narrative. "Glory" bespeaks magisterial and wondrous presence, embodying God's sovereignty. The complaint of v. 3 indicates that Israel still associates "glory" (and the power to give life) with the splendor, wealth, prestige, and extravagance of Egypt. Compared to the glory of Egypt, the wilderness holds little attraction.

In drawing near, however, Israel dramatically turns its face away from Egypt and looks again toward the wilderness. It sees there what it always thought to see in Egypt, and what it never expected to see in the wilderness. It is not an empty, deathly place, but the locus of God's sovereign splendor. The wilderness is more brilliant than Egypt, because Yahweh has "gotten glory over Pharaoh" (14:4, 17). By God's rule, the wilderness is completely redefined.

After these several speeches, there still remains the concrete problem of delivering bread to a hungry, protesting people (vv. 13-15). Everything finally depends not on theological talk or religious manifestation, but on the availability of food for life. And then it happens—enough quail to blanket the camp, meat all over the place! Next morning, there is a kind of bread under the dew that the Israelites have never seen before. Moses must tell them that it is "bread that the LORD has given you to eat" (v. 15). Thus their complaints are answered precisely. In place of Egyptian flesh, they are given quail; in place of Egyptian bread, they have bread from God. The wilderness, which seemed a threat, has become a nurturing place.

The brief exchange of v. 15 about the name of the bread is interesting, though perhaps not very significant. This is bread Israel has never seen; it is not the bread of coercion and affliction. So they say מן הוא (*mān hû'*, "What is it?"), and this question provides the popular name for the bread: *Manna.* That name, however, has no positive content. It is only a question, one that indicates that this is strange, unfamiliar bread without any antecedents or parallels. The positive identification of the bread is in Moses' explanation: It is bread given by Yahweh to eat.

16:16-30. There are, however, two conditions for the right reception of bread. The people shall harvest just enough bread for the day and gather no surplus, so that everyone has enough and nobody has too little. The provision for the bread becomes a model for the right distribution of food and a paradigm for a covenant community that is trustfully organized around God's unfailing generosity. The wondrous reality about the distribution of this bread is that their uncompetitive, non-hoarding practice really does work, and it works for all! The ones who gather a lot do not have too much; the ones who gather a little have no lack (vv. 17-18). The bread has a way of being where it is needed, with everyone having a sufficiency. Thus the bread becomes a means whereby (a) God's reliability is to be trusted, and (b) neighbors are to live together in trustful equity.

Israel, however, refuses to trust the God who promised and supplies the bread. They refuse to live in vulnerable equity with neighbors. Some seek to store up bread in violation of Moses' warning. They want to establish a surplus, to develop a zone of self-sufficiency. The people in the wilderness immediately try to replicate the ways of Egypt by storing up and hoarding out of anxiety and greed. However, this bread (bread of another kind given by God) cannot be stored up. The narrator takes pains to underscore that stored-up, surplus bread is useless. Bread that reflects self-sufficient anxiety and greed will have no food value for Israel, so that the bread of disobedience breeds worms, turns sour, and melts (vv. 20-21).

A special practice is permitted, however, on the sixth day in order to provide food for the sabbath day, which follows (vv. 22-26). What is permitted for the sake of the sabbath directly contradicts what is prohibited for all the other days. What cannot be carried over from one day to the next is now carried over to the day of sabbath. The sabbath authorizes storing up bread, because when designed for sabbath, the extra bread does not reflect either anxiety or greed.

Once again, however, Israel disobeys. In v. 27, some of the people go out to gather on the sabbath, in direct violation of the command just given. Yet, when they go out to gather they find no bread. Not only must the people refrain from working on the sabbath, but also God's own bakeries are closed for the day. Creation is shut down, and the heavens rest. Moses' rebuke of them is sharp: "How long?" The answer is not given, but we may anticipate that the refusal of the commands will last a very long time in Israel.

Verse 30, which concludes this unit, is somewhat surprising. It is as though the community has been converted, as though it has belatedly become convicted to the sabbath command and honors it. This verse is remarkable because it puts a good end to what has been essentially a narrative account of stubborn resistance. (This interpretive maneuver is the antithesis of 17:7, which puts a negative interpretation on a "wonder.")

16:31-36. After the gift of bread and its hard-hearted reception, the chapter ends as the bread is solidified into a sacramental memorial. Now the dispute about the bread has disappeared. A measure of this bread is placed in a jar to be preserved and witnessed to in perpetuity. It is to be kept visible and seen by Israel through the generations as a witness and reminder. Happily, the memory that inhabits the jar is a selective, corrected memory. According to the text, the jar of manna does not allude to the hoarding that violates the provision for dailiness. Nor does the jar refer to the sabbath violation against the provision for rest. Rather, the jar is a positive testimony. It attests only to the generous fidelity of Yahweh in the wilderness after the exodus. It asserts that bread is given, that God is faithful, that life in wilderness is possible, that Israel is safe.

REFLECTIONS

1. The good news of this text is that God gives bread and nourishment for life as the sovereign ruler and governor of all creation. Fretheim wants to insist on the "naturalness" of manna, that it is produced in ways that can be understood according to natural phenomena.[78] By contrast, Calvin takes enormous pains to argue that the bread of heaven is "contrary to the order of nature."[79] Clearly, Calvin and Fretheim have very different agendas. I suggest that the bread is given according to God's providential ordering of creation. That, however, is an ordering not impinged upon by the mechanisms of technology or bureaucracy. To imagine providence unencumbered by these is well nigh miraculous. God does not depend on the

78. Fretheim, *Exodus,* 181-82.
79. Calvin, *Commentaries,* 276.

technical apparatus or the bureaucratic arrangements of Egypt for the delivery of bread, but gives bread out of the richness of God's own treasure house.

2. This affirmation of God's good bread pertains precisely to the wilderness, those regions of life wherein Israel is peculiarly dependent and without resources of its own. Verse 35 identifies the zone of free bread as extending "until they came to a habitable land." And Josh 5:12 affirms that on the day they ate the produce of the land, "the manna ceased" for the Israelites. In the wilderness, the primary concern is anxiety about survival; in the land, the temptation is complacency about self-sufficiency. This story of manna is not for all of life. It is for life in those zones of bereftness when the problem is not self-sufficiency but despair, need, and anxiety. From first to last, wilderness is subject to God's ongoing providential generosity.

3. Because the gospel stays so close to concrete, material reality, it is not surprising that this narrative is taken up in powerful ways in the story of Jesus.

On the one hand, the story of manna is replicated in the actions of Jesus. Thus in his feeding of the crowds of 5,000 persons (Mark 6:30-41; John 6:1-4) and of 4,000 persons (Mark 8:1-10), Jesus acts messianically to give bread where there is none. These narratives are cast in eucharistic language, suggesting that the church fully understood the paradigmatic quality of the manna narrative.

On the other hand, in Jesus' discourse about his own person and his mission (John 6:25-59), reference to our text is crucial. The connection to this narrative is direct and explicit: "It is my Father who gives you the true bread from heaven" (John 6:32 NRSV). The narrative is turned in a very different direction with the claim, "I am the bread that came down from heaven" (John 6:41 NRSV). The peculiar mode of discourse in the Fourth Gospel permits the manna story to be taken up and refocused as a christological affirmation. While the listening community in John 6 is bewildered by Jesus' statement, there is no doubt that Jesus is presented as the sign, assurance, and reality of God's generous fidelity, which supplies the need of all those who are faithful (who accept his messianic person).

4. Just as the text provides a model for christology, so also it functions as a model for ecclesiology. In his discussion of the collection for the Jerusalem church, Paul directly quotes this narrative (2 Cor 8:8-15). He suggests that equity in the Christian community results when the ones with abundance and the ones with need live in generosity to each other. The way the bread is distributed in the manna story is a model for the way the church shares and distributes goods with equity and liberality.

5. Woven all through the manna narrative is an argument about the character and cruciality of the sabbath.

I suggest that sabbath is a way of contrasting wilderness with Egypt positively. Egypt is a place where bread is gotten only for labor, where bread is given only as a reward for productivity, and where bread is always received in and with fearful anxiety. The gift of bread, then, is a decisive break with the exploitative conditions of Egyptian bread. "Bread from heaven" is an invitation to break with the destructive politics of bread production and the pressures upon which the empire depends for productivity—namely, fear, abuse, anxiety, and exploitation. Sabbath is yet another opportunity to depart economically and psychologically from Egyptian modes of social reality. The alternative in this narrative is a world of glad dependence and utter fidelity, devoid of all anxiety and threat. The conclusion of the narrative, "So the people rested on the seventh day" (v. 30), is an affirmation that at least for this narrative Egyptian patterns of existence have been nullified.

6. It is striking that in the Sermon on the Mount, Jesus' instructions for prayer (Matt 6:7-15) and against anxiety (Matt 6:25-33) are closely related. In the prayer, the community of disciples is summoned to pray daily for bread. That is, they are to rely on God for each day's supply, without anxious hoarding. The instruction about anxiety thus plays upon the theme from the prayer.

There is a temptation to serve two masters, Yahweh and Pharaoh, and to trust in two bread supplies, the bread of heaven and the bread of the sweat of our brow (cf. Matt 6:24). This teaching of Jesus urges that seeking to have it both ways generates endless anxiety. The only way out of the anxiety is to make a clean, unambiguous decision. The gospel is the affirmation, made earlier in the wilderness, that God knows what is needed and that God faithfully supplies everything required for life.

7. In the life of the church, this narrative that culminates in a jar has been preserved in the form of the "jarring" narrative of the Eucharist. The Eucharist reenacts and keeps visioning what the world will be like when the bread from heaven is not hoarded, but is trusted in by the human community on a daily basis. Thus the Eucharist is not some otherworldly act of spirituality, but a glad affirmation that this counterstory of bread continues to be haunting and, therefore, powerful. This community continues to believe that bread that is broken and shared has power for life that bread does not have when it is unbroken and unshared—when it is guarded and hoarded.

It is not accidental that at the end of the miracle of the bread, Mark reports that they "did not understand about the loaves" (6:52 NRSV). They did not understand because "their hearts were hardened." It is a high irony that in an allusion to the manna story, it is now the disciples, not the people of Pharaoh, who have "hard hearts." Hard hearts make us rely on our own capacity and our own bread. In the end, they render all of these stories of alternative bread too dangerous and too outrageous for consideration. As a result, the bread practices of Pharaoh continue to prevail among us. In the presence of those practices, this community continues to watch the jar, tell the story, and imagine another bread that is taken and given, blessed and broken.

EXODUS 17:1-7, WATER FROM THE ROCK

NIV

17 The whole Israelite community set out from the Desert of Sin, traveling from place to place as the LORD commanded. They camped at Rephidim, but there was no water for the people to drink. ²So they quarreled with Moses and said, "Give us water to drink."

Moses replied, "Why do you quarrel with me? Why do you put the LORD to the test?"

³But the people were thirsty for water there, and they grumbled against Moses. They said, "Why did you bring us up out of Egypt to make us and our children and livestock die of thirst?"

⁴Then Moses cried out to the LORD, "What am I to do with these people? They are almost ready to stone me."

⁵The LORD answered Moses, "Walk on ahead of the people. Take with you some of the elders of Israel and take in your hand the staff with

NRSV

17 From the wilderness of Sin the whole congregation of the Israelites journeyed by stages, as the LORD commanded. They camped at Rephidim, but there was no water for the people to drink. ²The people quarreled with Moses, and said, "Give us water to drink." Moses said to them, "Why do you quarrel with me? Why do you test the LORD?" ³But the people thirsted there for water; and the people complained against Moses and said, "Why did you bring us out of Egypt, to kill us and our children and livestock with thirst?" ⁴So Moses cried out to the LORD, "What shall I do with this people? They are almost ready to stone me." ⁵The LORD said to Moses, "Go on ahead of the people, and take some of the elders of Israel with you; take in your hand the staff with which you struck the Nile, and go. ⁶I will be standing there in front of you on the rock

which you struck the Nile, and go. ⁶I will stand there before you by the rock at Horeb. Strike the rock, and water will come out of it for the people to drink." So Moses did this in the sight of the elders of Israel. ⁷And he called the place Massah*ᵃ* and Meribah*ᵇ* because the Israelites quarreled and because they tested the LORD saying, "Is the LORD among us or not?"

ᵃ7 Massah means *testing.*   *ᵇ7 Meribah* means *quarreling.*

at Horeb. Strike the rock, and water will come out of it, so that the people may drink." Moses did so, in the sight of the elders of Israel. ⁷He called the place Massah*ᵃ* and Meribah,*ᵇ* because the Israelites quarreled and tested the LORD, saying, "Is the LORD among us or not?"

ᵃ That is *Test*   *ᵇ* That is *Quarrel*

COMMENTARY

Israel's life in the wilderness, in the aftermath of liberation and in pursuit of Yahweh's promise of the land, is precarious indeed. Israel proceeds "as the LORD commanded" (v. 1), but there is no water to drink. In the wilderness, Israel lacks the most elemental resource for life. This problem leads to two exchanges with Moses (vv. 2-3), which result in a "wonder" (vv. 5-6) and a reflective comment (v. 7).

The first exchange is brief and serves to question the leadership of Moses (v. 2). The people file a complaint (רִיב *rîb*) against Moses for his ineffectiveness and his incompetence. Moses has not and cannot produce drinking water. Moses' response consists in two rhetorical questions that repudiate the charge. The first question asks, in effect, "Why blame me?" We expect Moses to say, as he did in 16:7-8, that he is innocent and that the grievance should be addressed against Yahweh instead of him.

The second question in this case, however, surprises us. Moses reprimands Israel not only for criticizing him, but also for testing Yahweh. What Moses has done is to equate his leadership with that of Yahweh, for the two parts of the question are exactly parallel and equivalent. As it is unthinkable to "test" Yahweh (i.e., to make demands of Yahweh), so it is now unthinkable to challenge Moses.

Because the problem of water is neither acknowledged nor alleviated, it is predictable that there must be a second exchange with Moses (vv. 3-6). Again, the people accuse Moses (as in 16:3) of having caused death by instigating the exodus. Because the escalation of rhetoric is severe, Moses

this time turns to Yahweh. His petition, however, is not for the well-being of the people, but for his own safety. Moses petitions Yahweh so that he himself will not be assaulted.

Unlike the first, the second exchange includes Yahweh as a speaker and actor. The second exchange, because of Yahweh's involvement, can have a life-giving outcome as the first exchange, without Yahweh, could not. Yahweh's response to Moses does not address the problem of Moses' leadership or safety, but directly addresses the people's problem of thirst. Moses is to use again his staff, which embodies his authority from Yahweh. Now Moses is to use his staff for a life-giving wonder for Israel.

The center of Yahweh's response, however, is in Yahweh's own commitment to the process: "Behold, I will be standing before you." Yahweh is involved with all the sovereignty that can be mustered to preside over this "wonder." The staff, the rock, the courage of Moses, the witness of the elders, and the guarantee of Yahweh all converge. After Yahweh's careful, detailed instruction, the narrator adds laconically, "He did so." The narrator does not even tell us whether there is water, the people drink, or that the problem is solved. All of that is already certain in the speech of Yahweh, which is much more interesting and crucial than is the implementation. The narrator is clear on the main point: Only Yahweh can give the resources for life, but Yahweh will do so through the work of Moses.

This small, rhetorical unit has the standard structure of *problem* and *resolution,* the movement from the one to the other wrought through a wonder.[80] The presence and power of Yahweh are perfectly capable of transforming rock to water and death to life. It is likely important that the rock is "in Horeb," located in the peculiar precincts where Yahweh's presence is palpable and immediate. In the sphere of Yahweh's sovereignty, life is wrought in situations of death.

The narrator adds a comment that gives to the narrative an unexpected interpretive direction (v. 7). We might expect the conclusion of the narrative will celebrate in amazement the life-giving wonder wrought by Yahweh. Instead the narrator focuses on the two verbs that concern the plaintiff action of the people: *test* (נסה *nissâ*, thus "Massah") and *quarrel* (ריב *rîb*, thus "Meribah"). The story is slanted as a story of unfaith. It may be that the narrator is preoccupied with a limitation the two verbs impose, which serves to ground a "name tale." In larger context, however, the narrator is not interested in the explanation of place names but with issues of faith and unfaith. It is not that Yahweh must demonstrate a capacity for giving life; that is assumed. What is to be exhib-

ited is not the power of God, but Israel's inappropriate and remarkable lack of faith. In the context of the narrative account of wonders in Egypt, Israel should have known and trusted.

Here, however, Israel is remarkably stubborn and arrogant. Israel dares to ask a demanding question that presumes upon Yahweh (v. 7). The only evidence of Yahweh's presence that Israel will accept is concrete action that saves. Thus Israel collapses God's promise into its own well-being and refuses to allow Yahweh any life apart from Israel's well-being. The question makes the religious issue completely pragmatic, resulting in an affirmation about Yahweh that in fact is a demand that Yahweh must now (right now!) give an account of Yahweh's faithful sovereignty. Thus the focus on *quarrel* and *test* accuses Israel of having inverted the relation with Yahweh, so that Yahweh must now *perform* at Israel's behest. As it turns out, Yahweh does so by producing water. According to the narrator, however, Israel badly misconstrues this act if it imagines that Yahweh's sovereignty can be reduced to meeting Israel's questions and demands.

80. On the narrative structure, see Robert C. Culley, *Studies in the Structure of Hebrew Narrative* (Philadelphia: Fortress, 1976).

REFLECTIONS

1. The story itself provides nearly a model for the structure of evangelical narrative, a structure that is replicated many times in the actions of God and in the saving miracles of Jesus. It is worth considering that the same structure is used as the standard form for television commercials in the United States. The problem is presented, and a need is boldly voiced, in this case thirst. There is a powerful *intervention by God,* here through Moses. There is *a happy resolution* of the problem through a gift of God, in this case water.

At the center of the narrative is the faithful, powerful intervention of God. The story is told as a witness of faith in order to place God's powerful fidelity and attentiveness as the middle term of the whole human drama, as life is moved from hunger to fullness, from thirst to water, from blindness to sight, from leprosy to cleanness, from poverty to well-being, and in the end, from death to life.

The derivative TV use of this structure falsely substitutes for God "the product." The problem may be loneliness, stress, or bad odor. When the "product" is used, life is powerfully transformed to one of companionship, calmness, popularity, peace, joy, and well-being. An evangelical critique of such advertisements is that they are in principle false. Whereas the product may deal with the presenting problem, it cannot in fact generate the joy and well-being that are characteristically promised. Thus the biblical claim in this structure is not only formal, but it is also a substantive claim that only the intervention of Yahweh can work a miracle. There are no other miracle workers.

2. Verse 7 constitutes something of an interpretive problem and offers a fresh interpretive possibility. This "clue" to interpretation suggests that the story is to be understood as a critique of utilitarian religion in which God is judged by the desired outcomes for the asking community. Thus the community in this story would conclude that if the Israelites lack well-being, then God is not present for them. This temptation to reduce religion to utilitarian effect is the problem with which the book of Job struggles. In the end, the whirlwind speeches of Job 38–41 assert (and Job accepts in 42:1-6) that the reality of God is not commensurate with human prosperity. This text provides the ground for criticism of communities of faith that seek to "program" the capacity of God to do the wonders required by the community.

EXODUS 17:8-16, AMALEK IS DEFEATED

NIV

[8]The Amalekites came and attacked the Israelites at Rephidim. [9]Moses said to Joshua, "Choose some of our men and go out to fight the Amalekites. Tomorrow I will stand on top of the hill with the staff of God in my hands."

[10]So Joshua fought the Amalekites as Moses had ordered, and Moses, Aaron and Hur went to the top of the hill. [11]As long as Moses held up his hands, the Israelites were winning, but whenever he lowered his hands, the Amalekites were winning. [12]When Moses' hands grew tired, they took a stone and put it under him and he sat on it. Aaron and Hur held his hands up—one on one side, one on the other—so that his hands remained steady till sunset. [13]So Joshua overcame the Amalekite army with the sword.

[14]Then the LORD said to Moses, "Write this on a scroll as something to be remembered and make sure that Joshua hears it, because I will completely blot out the memory of Amalek from under heaven."

[15]Moses built an altar and called it The LORD is my Banner. [16]He said, "For hands were lifted up to the throne of the LORD. The[a] LORD will be at war against the Amalekites from generation to generation."

[a]16 Or "Because a hand was against the throne of the LORD, the

NRSV

[8]Then Amalek came and fought with Israel at Rephidim. [9]Moses said to Joshua, "Choose some men for us and go out, fight with Amalek. Tomorrow I will stand on the top of the hill with the staff of God in my hand." [10]So Joshua did as Moses told him, and fought with Amalek, while Moses, Aaron, and Hur went up to the top of the hill. [11]Whenever Moses held up his hand, Israel prevailed; and whenever he lowered his hand, Amalek prevailed. [12]But Moses' hands grew weary; so they took a stone and put it under him, and he sat on it. Aaron and Hur held up his hands, one on one side, and the other on the other side; so his hands were steady until the sun set. [13]And Joshua defeated Amalek and his people with the sword.

[14]Then the LORD said to Moses, "Write this as a reminder in a book and recite it in the hearing of Joshua: I will utterly blot out the remembrance of Amalek from under heaven." [15]And Moses built an altar and called it, The LORD is my banner. [16]He said, "A hand upon the banner of the LORD![a] The LORD will have war with Amalek from generation to generation."

[a] Cn: Meaning of Heb uncertain

COMMENTARY

As we have seen in 15:13-17, Israel's way to the land of promise was not without trouble and conflict. The way is fraught with adversaries, because Israel constitutes a political-military threat to the peoples who already occupy the land. This particular narrative, offensive as it is, identifies the Amalekites as the quintessential enemy of Israel. The narrative consists of two parts: the account of the victory itself (vv. 8-13) and the literary, interpretive process whereby this specific enemy is demonized and turned into a permanent, paradigmatic enemy (vv. 14-16).

17:8-13. The victory account itself makes nothing special or noteworthy out of the defeated Amalekites. It is a report of a confrontation, a battle, and a victory. Even here, however, the narrator presents two very different themes.

First, Joshua is introduced as the warrior who recruits the army, fights with the Amalekites, and defeats them (vv. 9-10a, 13). This is the first mention of Joshua in the Bible. He is introduced almost incidentally, as if the reader already knows who he is. His presence at this point in the narrative suggests the overlap of the traditions of Moses and Joshua—i.e., the traditions of exodus and "conquest."

Joshua will subsequently emerge as the pivotal figure in Israel's faith after Moses (and before Samuel). It will be the work of Joshua to lead Israel, to fight its battles as it seizes the land of promise, and to consolidate the victory by dividing the land among the tribes. His name in Hebrew is from יָשַׁע (yāšaʿ, "save"). It is unmistakable in the OT that "save" (i.e., salvation, savior) is first of all military imagery, so that the use of this term bespeaks a struggle with those too strong for Israel. That military metaphor comes in Paul to be a battle against Satan, sin, and death. Even in our contemporary parlance, the same imagery survives, so that we speak not only of the "war" against communism but also of the "war" on cancer and the "war" on poverty. Israel's life does indeed emerge out of struggle and conflict, when Israel wins victories of well-being in situations where one might soberly expect defeat.

Second, in this narrative are the intervening vv. 10b-12, which are sandwiched by Joshua's actions. In these verses, Moses, who does not go into battle, is nonetheless the key figure in assuring Israel's victory. Theologically, these verses not only assert that the power and authority of Moses matter decisively, but also that the battle and the victory are no ordinary military action. What is decisive for the outcome of the conflict is the staff held in the powerful hand of Moses, which bespeaks the power of Yahweh. Childs (with special reference to Barth) sees these two themes, Joshua's leadership and Moses' hands, as "a delicate balance which neither impaired God's will nor destroyed man's genuine activity."[81]

81. Childs, *Exodus*, 317.

Taken more practically, we may wonder how the raised hands of a leader at a distance from the battle could matter for the outcome of the battle. I have no desire to "explain" the narrative, but to indicate how such a statement might be credible in a self-conscious community in conflict. After all the military strategy, material, and technology is assembled, battles require passion, energy, and sheer adrenalin, which are usually generated not by technicians but by public leaders who can mobilize imagination and play on the passions of the military community.

17:14-16. The tradition has taken up this particular report of victory and, by a literary, interpretive maneuver, has converted it into an enduring theological passion in Israel. The victory tale itself might have been routine. Moses is instructed by God to reduce the tale of victory to writing, which is to be read to Joshua (to the generation that struggles with the Canaanites), so that it will have enduring authority for all time to come. We are given no reason why this command is issued to Moses. We are told only that from the very mouth of God comes the resolve that God has declared unending hostility toward the Amalekites. God's decree includes an intense infinitive absolute: "I will utterly blot out." The patron and guarantor of Israel has sworn to obliterate an enemy of Israel.

Moreover, as Yahweh has solemnly sworn, so Moses is instructed to create a sign and symbol, rooted in theology, crediting this deep and perpetual hostility, not to any human imagination but to the very God of Israel. Thus the altar and the banner are to make it clear for all time to come that hostility toward Amalek is deep, for perpetuity, and authorized by Yahweh.

When we try to understand this statement, we are reduced to bewildered, awkward silence. We are given no hint of why the report in vv. 8-13, in itself not unusual, leads to the ideological intensification of vv. 14-16. We know of nothing from any other text (except possibly Deut 25:17-19, on which see below) why Amalek is singled out in this way. We have no evidence of more than conventional conflict, and nothing is noticeably barbaric in the relationship between the two peoples. It is as though in an unguarded, undisciplined moment the tradition (or the God of the tradition) has given vent to a deep, irrational hunger to have a permanent enemy.

We may briefly review the sequence of Amalek texts to discern the function of this interpretive maneuver (though we will not find a rationale for this brutal pronouncement).

Verse 14 enjoins Moses to write "in a book" the abiding enmity of God toward Amalek. That written piece is ostensibly found in Deut 25:17-19, which would seem to fulfill the requirement of v. 14. Here we are given one piece of "information" that we have nowhere else: The Amalekites attack Israel in its weakness and are especially vicious toward stragglers.

But this notice is suspect on at least three grounds. First, such attacks on the vulnerable are not uncommon in war, and it cannot have been the only enemy of Israel who engaged in such a practice. Second, there is no hint of such a criticism of Amalek in the narrative of the battle itself in Exod 17:8-13. Third, and consequently, the reason given comes late in the development of the ideology, thus creating wonderment whether this is rationale after the fact. One gains the impression that this "reason" in itself is not a compelling basis for the enshrinement of hostility in such a remarkable way.

In the curses of Balaam against the enemies of Israel, Amalek is singled out, both as the "first of many nations" and as destined for perpetual destruction (see Num 24:20). The same ideology is clearly at work here.

We can see this powerful ideology most concretely in 1 Sam 15:1-33. As Israel moves toward monarchy (and more ordered, "rational" governance) with Saul, the old tribal ideologies become less compelling. Saul is portrayed as one who, for pragmatic reasons, compromises this piece of old ideology. He "spares" Amalek and takes Amalekite spoils. Saul's explanation of his act to Samuel evidences one who squirms under the power of

ideology, because it is difficult to provide rationale for action that contradicts an all-consuming ideology.

By contrast, Samuel is portrayed as the upholder and guarantor of the Amalekite curse. He uses that ideological claim as a ground from which to depose Saul. Moreover, without flinching, Samuel proceeds to execute the curse against Amalek (1 Sam 15:32-33). In v. 33, Samuel suggests that Amalek has in the past murdered pregnant women, perhaps a notion linked to Deut 25:18. There is no way to determine whether this claim is historical. What strikes one about the narrative, rather, is that Samuel is presented as an unconditional adherent to the old ideology, which he fully and gladly implements.

Finally, we may mention David's action in 1 Sam 30:18-31. While it is not the case that David actually "spares" an Amalekite, he does take spoils (herds and flocks) in a quite pragmatic way, to give to "his friends, the elders of Judah." This is a remarkable report, because Saul has been rebuked and finally deposed for daring to keep even Amalekite cattle.

We do not know how to adjudicate David's action. It may be simply that the power of the ideology was weakened and, with the death of Samuel, lost its most passionate, dangerous adherent. Or it may be that David was both pragmatic and strong enough to risk offending old political-theological opinion, and he got away with his pragmatic action. In any case, it is clear that David was able to break the vicious cycle of hate that seems to have persisted long after Amalek constituted any concrete political threat. Eventually, ideological hatred that is no longer connected to political reality may be broken. It can, however, persist for a long time, producing enormous political damage when ideology holds sway without reference to reality.

REFLECTIONS

This is a most problematic text. We may identify four points of interpretive exploration that move from theological affirmation to interpretive suspicion.

1. As we have seen in 15:3 where "Yahweh is a man of war," the military metaphor is crucial in the Bible for making an affirmation that God saves. To the extent that biblical faith is a religion of salvation, the military metaphor is crucial, because it identifies the agonistic context in which God, in power and in fidelity, saves from enemies. Moreover, this way of rhetoric is not an abstract intellectual invention, but arose from quite concrete conflicts. Such concrete conflict is not "nice" but is inevitably brutal and violent. Our capacity to confess the God of the Bible as sovereign depends on the stories of the specific places in which the community has known rescue from those powers that bring death.

2. There is no doubt that the rhetoric of the "victories of Yahweh" has been handled in Jewish faith and certainly in Christian theology by converting such language into metaphor. That is, the concreteness of battle has been transposed into battles against evil and against all the manifestations of evil (personal and public) that take place in human experience. There is no doubt that the process of metaphor is both necessary and legitimate.

Care must be taken, however, when turning these concrete narratives into metaphor, that one does not lose specificity and the connections to socioeconomic reality. When metaphor serves to remove the specific bite of a narrative so that it now becomes "spiritual," remote, or otherworldly, then the metaphor serves to enhance the status quo, and to neutralize the threat inherent in the story. In the end, oppressed communities do not move too quickly away from the conviction that their enemies are God's enemies as well (cf. Ps 139:21-22). That conviction lives close to this sort of text, even as it offends those of us who are less oppressed.

3. The most interesting interpretive point is how the move is made from vv. 8-13 to vv. 14-16. The victory itself is the sort of outcome that happens in the processes of public conflict. The institutionalization of hostility, however, is another matter. This move in the text is the process of *theological demonization,* whereby an enemy in a particular war (perhaps an adversary because of a legitimate conflict of interest) is now absolutized as an embodiment of evil, without regard to any historical circumstance or visible vested interest.

Examples of this in our public life might include the demonizing of Germans ("Remember Munich") or the Japanese ("Remember Pearl Harbor") or the Russians ("Never Trust a Commie"). Perhaps the most blatant example of such demonization has been our fixation on communism, which was uncritically assumed to be monolithic. Such an uncritical act of demonization led us into the morass of the Vietnam war without taking into account the geopolitical realities of China and Southeast Asia. It was far easier to hate "the enemy" than to sort out the nuances of political reality.

In the Persian Gulf War, we watched the ideological demonization of Saddam Hussein of Iraq, an aggressive tribal chieftain, without any acknowledgment of the sorry, shameful imperial history of the West in controlling oil in the Middle East. Saddam was treated as an ontological principle of evil. This demonization justified the defense of other tribal chieftains who practiced an equal brutality. Demonization is easier, quicker, and more immediately satisfying than dealing with political reality.

On a more personal level, our propensity to refuse forgiveness to our enemies causes us to freeze and absolutize relationships, attitudes, and perceptions at one point of hurt and rage. This happens in families, in churches, and in communities of all kinds. Such a freezing and absolutizing precludes any further development in relations and justifies continued irrational negativities that are no longer appropriate. The resolve to remember forever hurt, hate, rage, and fear ensures the shut-down of the political processes of newness.

Forgiveness, by contrast, is the political, creative process of negotiating old wounds in ways that lead to newness. Such negotiations are impossible in a world where hurts are absolutized and institutionalized. David's action toward the Amalekites may be a daring example of de-demonizing, an inclination that may in the end lead even to forgiveness.[82]

---

82. On the larger public issues of forgiveness, see Carter Heyward et al., *Revolutionary Forgiveness: Feminist Reflections on Nicaragua* (Maryknoll, N.Y.: Orbis, 1987).

---

4. Finally, we are left with the awareness that the interpretive move of v. 14 is on the lips of Yahweh. It is, according to the tradition, none other than Yahweh who has authorized the writing of Deut 25:17-19 and the canonization of this ideology in the imagination of Israel. Of course, it is legitimate to say that some powerful human agent created this text, and no one doubts that the tradition of Deuteronomy was a powerful ideological force in Israel. If, however, we are to think theologically (and beyond critical explanations) about the text, then we must deal with a God who speaks this way and authorizes such a text. I must confess I find responsibility for comment overwhelming. I suggest two lines of thought.

First, the God of the Bible is the source and product of a martial propensity, placing conflict, violence, and brutality in the center of the tradition. The Bible and the God of the Bible are, to a large extent, cast in conflictual categories. This perspective has been most visible in the Christian Crusades (perhaps including twentieth-century examples) and in Islamic rhetoric about "holy war." It may also be that this reality about God is evident in church practice whereby established authority silences those with whom it disagrees, or in the tendency of conservatives and liberals to demonize each other because of passionately held ethical views. As Christians come increasingly into contact with persons of other faiths and become aware that there are other categories through which faith is practiced, we are destined for a dangerous, demanding rethinking of the oppositional mapping of our faith.

Second, it is clear that this propensity of the God of the Bible is not the only way God has been disclosed in the text. Critically, it is easy enough to insist that our understanding of God evolved. But if we are to think theologically (post-critically), we do better to take these texts in tension, as *unresolved issues in God's own heart.* Thus the God who will always remember is also the God who will "remember . . . no more" (Jer 31:34). To be sure, the disparate texts disclosing God differently have arisen in very different contexts and horizons. They are all there, nonetheless, purporting to be disclosures of this God.

EXODUS 18:1-12, JETHRO COMES TO MOSES

NIV

18 Now Jethro, the priest of Midian and father-in-law of Moses, heard of everything God had done for Moses and for his people Israel, and how the Lord had brought Israel out of Egypt.

²After Moses had sent away his wife Zipporah, his father-in-law Jethro received her ³and her two sons. One son was named Gershom,ª for Moses said, "I have become an alien in a foreign land"; ⁴and the other was named Eliezer,ᵇ for he said, "My father's God was my helper; he saved me from the sword of Pharaoh."

⁵Jethro, Moses' father-in-law, together with Moses' sons and wife, came to him in the desert, where he was camped near the mountain of God. ⁶Jethro had sent word to him, "I, your father-in-

NRSV

18 Jethro, the priest of Midian, Moses' father-in-law, heard of all that God had done for Moses and for his people Israel, how the Lord had brought Israel out of Egypt. ²After Moses had sent away his wife Zipporah, his father-in-law Jethro took her back, ³along with her two sons. The name of the one was Gershom (for he said, "I have been an alienª in a foreign land"), ⁴and the name of the other, Eliezerᵇ (for he said, "The God of my father was my help, and delivered me from the sword of Pharaoh"). ⁵Jethro, Moses' father-in-law, came into the wilderness where Moses was encamped at the mountain of God, bringing Moses' sons and wife to him. ⁶He sent word to Moses, "I, your father-in-law Jethro, am coming to you, with your wife and her two sons."

ª3 *Gershom* sounds like the Hebrew for *an alien there.*   ᵇ4 *Eliezer* means *my God is helper.*

ª Heb *ger*   ᵇ Heb *Eli,* my God; *ezer,* help

NIV

law Jethro, am coming to you with your wife and her two sons."

⁷So Moses went out to meet his father-in-law and bowed down and kissed him. They greeted each other and then went into the tent. ⁸Moses told his father-in-law about everything the LORD had done to Pharaoh and the Egyptians for Israel's sake and about all the hardships they had met along the way and how the LORD had saved them.

⁹Jethro was delighted to hear about all the good things the LORD had done for Israel in rescuing them from the hand of the Egyptians. ¹⁰He said, "Praise be to the LORD, who rescued you from the hand of the Egyptians and of Pharaoh, and who rescued the people from the hand of the Egyptians. ¹¹Now I know that the LORD is greater than all other gods, for he did this to those who had treated Israel arrogantly." ¹²Then Jethro, Moses' father-in-law, brought a burnt offering and other sacrifices to God, and Aaron came with all the elders of Israel to eat bread with Moses' father-in-law in the presence of God.

NRSV

⁷Moses went out to meet his father-in-law; he bowed down and kissed him; each asked after the other's welfare, and they went into the tent. ⁸Then Moses told his father-in-law all that the LORD had done to Pharaoh and to the Egyptians for Israel's sake, all the hardship that had beset them on the way, and how the LORD had delivered them. ⁹Jethro rejoiced for all the good that the LORD had done to Israel, in delivering them from the Egyptians.

10Jethro said, "Blessed be the LORD, who has delivered you from the Egyptians and from Pharaoh. ¹¹Now I know that the LORD is greater than all gods, because he delivered the people from the Egyptians,ᵃ when they dealt arrogantly with them." ¹²And Jethro, Moses' father-in-law, brought a burnt offering and sacrifices to God; and Aaron came with all the elders of Israel to eat bread with Moses' father-in-law in the presence of God.

ᵃ The clause *because . . . Egyptians* has been transposed from verse 10

COMMENTARY

This entire chapter, which concerns Moses' relation to his father-in-law, Jethro, is most peculiar and seems to disrupt the storyline of the journey from Egypt to "the mountain." The narrative of 17:8-15 has Israel at the oasis of Rephidim, and Israel is still at that oasis in 19:2. Likely chapter 18 is an independent tradition that insisted upon inclusion in the larger narrative.

An older scholarly hypothesis, advocated by Karl Budde, has proposed that it was through Jethro the Midianite that Yahweh was first known and mediated to Israel.[83] We shall not linger over the hypothesis, for two reasons. First, the text as it now stands is not interested in such a pre-history of Yahweh and will not entertain an alternative to the canonical story of an original revelation to Moses through the burning bush (3:1-6). Second, as the text stands, in v. 11 Jethro makes an

exclamation that he now knows about the greatness of Yahweh. Thus, contrary to Budde's hypothesis, the text insists that knowledge of Yahweh has gone from Moses to Jethro.

The text as it stands has as its surface plot the return of Moses to the wilderness after the exodus. However, the weight of the narrative falls on *the witness of Moses* (v. 8) and the *doxological response of Jethro* in word (vv. 10-11) and in liturgic act (v. 12). Whatever pre-history may be reflected here, the function of the present text is to plant in the midst of the larger narrative a pause to permit a model of *testimony and response,* whereby faith in Yahweh is transmitted from Moses to Jethro and the Midianites.

18:1-7. Moses returns to his family. In these verses there is no direct speech but only the narrator's report concerning news of the deliverance shared by Moses and Jethro.

The geographical movements assumed by the text are ambiguous. In 4:18-20 Moses takes his wife and sons with him back to Egypt. In that

---

83. H. H. Rowley, *From Joseph to Joshua: Biblical Traditions in the Light of Archaeology,* The Schweich Lectures (London: Oxford University Press, 1950) 153-56 and *passim.* Rowley thoroughly reviews the data pertinent to the hypothesis. Note his reference to Budde, 156 n.3.

text, his wife and sons seem to be with him in Egypt, but in our text they are in Midian with Jethro. Several commentaries suggest that in v. 2 Moses sent his wife and sons to Jethro with news and Jethro then returned with them. This would be supported by the name of the second son (v. 4), which reflects Egyptian deliverance and suggests he was born after the deliverance. This, however, runs beyond the explicit statement of the text.

In vv. 3-4, the narrative pauses to elucidate the names of the two sons of Moses. The first, Gershom, is already known in 2:22. The second, Eliezer, is not previously known. The names of the two sons together witness to the shape and destiny of Moses' life. On the one hand, Moses is an "alien there" (גרשׁם *gēr-šōm*), vulnerable and at risk. On the other hand, God has indeed been Moses' "help" (אליעזר *'ĕlî-ezer*), whereby Moses has survived and wrought the deliverance from Egypt. The name of each son is essential to the characterizations of both Moses and Israel, a people that is both "alien" (גר *gēr*) and "helped" (עזר *'āzar*).

Moses' return home is one of joyous hospitality, as well as mutual interest and concern (vv. 5-7). The narrative seems uninterested in such matters, but reports them to create a context for the exchange that happens next. (Cf. the structure in Gen 18:1-15, in which vv. 1-8 function as a narrative preface for the exchange of vv. 9-15.)

18:8-12. The exchange between Moses and Jethro is a model of theological testimony. Moses' brief speech is an abbreviated form of the narrative credo recital of Israel (v. 8). The phrase "all that Yahweh had done to Pharaoh and to the Egyptians" echoes v. 1, though this is now a direct speech. Moreover, it focuses on Yahweh's action, whereas v. 1 focuses on Moses and "his people

Israel." Moses quickly tells of the exodus and the hardship of the wilderness sojourn, and culminates with the verb *deliver* (נצל *nāṣal*), which Moses uses in 5:23 to accuse God of indifference.

Jethro's response to Moses' testimony is more extended (vv. 9-12). He "rejoices in the good"; that is, he is completely taken with the news and delights as in a victory (Ps 21:1-7) or the birth of a child (Jer 20:15). Jethro delivers a conventional doxological blessing that acknowledges and celebrates Yahweh as the giver of new life. Jethro confesses that Yahweh is more powerful, more reliable, and more worthy of allegiance than any other god, even the gods of Egypt. Jethro fully discerns the power struggle that went on between Moses and Pharaoh and between the gods of Egypt and Yahweh. He understands that in the end, Yahweh will not be mocked, dismissed, or belittled. In his exuberant confession, Jethro uses the word *nāṣal* three times (vv. 9, 10, 11), echoing the term Moses used in v. 8. Thus Jethro's speech is a litany of *nāṣal*, whereby he joins in celebration of the God who can override the power of the empire, giving new life and new possibility to the slave community that has no power of its own. Jethro thus becomes a voice for the celebrative faith of Israel.

Verse 12 reports an action that gives liturgical shape to Jethro's doxology. The offerings and sacrifices are not only an act of celebration but of allegiance as well. It is curious that Aaron and the elders, until now absent in the narrative, appear for the official sacrifice. Thus v. 12 serves to give institutional form and stability to the new faith of Jethro. The narrator has recalled the full cast of characters necessary to perform this cultic act of consolidation.

REFLECTIONS

1. The names of Moses' two sons provide an inchoate theological confession that characterizes not only Moses and early Israel, but also the community of faith whenever it is intentional about its dangerous call and destiny. This community is by definition "alien" to every culture, living only by the "help" of God.[84] These names are important reminders against two primary temptations of every established church. On the one hand, "alien" reminds us that the community of faith is not "at home" in any cultural context, any more than Moses dared to be at home in Egypt. On the other hand, "help" reminds us that the community of faith is neither self-sufficient nor abandoned.

---

84. The notion of the community of faith as "alien" to its cultural context, and in some way in an antagonistic relation to it, has been articulated in a contemporary mode by Stanley Hauerwas and William H. Willimon, *Resident Aliens* (Nashville: Abingdon, 1989).

2. Moses voices the testimony that comes most readily to Israel's lips: "God delivered," and "God led" on the way. These two verbs are the foundation of Israel's faith, which is astonished by deliverance that is public, concrete, and political. Israel never forgets that its life consists in being saved and that salvation is not any private or otherworldly business. This is a community utterly amazed that it is given life in a context where no real life is on the horizon. Israel's mode of faith is simply to "tell" (ספר *sāpar*) (as Moses did) without justification, proof, or rationalization. There are no larger criteria or categories that make this odd turn of affairs any more credible or palatable.

3. Jethro receives the news and is immediately convicted by it. He is a model for the way in which biblical faith is heard and embraced by those once removed from the events (cf. John 20:29). This second version of the news is the basis of all biblical evangelism. The same verb for "tell" (*sāpar*) is used in 10:2 for communicating to the children and the grandchildren (cf. 9:16). The same dynamic (with the verb בשׂר *biśśar* rather than *sāpar*) is assumed in Isa 52:7 where the "messenger" from exile brings "news" of events to Jerusalem. This is the text by which Paul makes his case for retelling the news of the gospel (Rom 10:14-15).

Moreover, this telling and hearing become the core activity of the early church in Acts, whereby those who have not witnessed the saving events come to share in their reality and their power. Thus in his hearing and in his response in doxology and sacrifice, Jethro becomes a model for evangelism.

EXODUS 18:13-27, JETHRO'S ADVICE

NIV

13The next day Moses took his seat to serve as judge for the people, and they stood around him from morning till evening. 14When his father-in-law saw all that Moses was doing for the people, he said, "What is this you are doing for the people? Why do you alone sit as judge, while all these people stand around you from morning till evening?"

15Moses answered him, "Because the people come to me to seek God's will. 16Whenever they have a dispute, it is brought to me, and I decide between the parties and inform them of God's decrees and laws."

17Moses' father-in-law replied, "What you are doing is not good. 18You and these people who come to you will only wear yourselves out. The work is too heavy for you; you cannot handle it alone. 19Listen now to me and I will give you some advice, and may God be with you. You must be the people's representative before God and bring their disputes to him. 20Teach them the decrees and laws, and show them the way to live and the duties they are to perform. 21But select capable men from all the people—men who fear

NRSV

13The next day Moses sat as judge for the people, while the people stood around him from morning until evening. 14When Moses' father-in-law saw all that he was doing for the people, he said, "What is this that you are doing for the people? Why do you sit alone, while all the people stand around you from morning until evening?" 15Moses said to his father-in-law, "Because the people come to me to inquire of God. 16When they have a dispute, they come to me and I decide between one person and another, and I make known to them the statutes and instructions of God." 17Moses' father-in-law said to him, "What you are doing is not good. 18You will surely wear yourself out, both you and these people with you. For the task is too heavy for you; you cannot do it alone. 19Now listen to me. I will give you counsel, and God be with you! You should represent the people before God, and you should bring their cases before God; 20teach them the statutes and instructions and make known to them the way they are to go and the things they are to do. 21You should also look for able men among all the people, men who fear God, are

God, trustworthy men who hate dishonest gain— and appoint them as officials over thousands, hundreds, fifties and tens. ²²Have them serve as judges for the people at all times, but have them bring every difficult case to you; the simple cases they can decide themselves. That will make your load lighter, because they will share it with you. ²³If you do this and God so commands, you will be able to stand the strain, and all these people will go home satisfied."

²⁴Moses listened to his father-in-law and did everything he said. ²⁵He chose capable men from all Israel and made them leaders of the people, officials over thousands, hundreds, fifties and tens. ²⁶They served as judges for the people at all times. The difficult cases they brought to Moses, but the simple ones they decided themselves.

²⁷Then Moses sent his father-in-law on his way, and Jethro returned to his own country.

trustworthy, and hate dishonest gain; set such men over them as officers over thousands, hundreds, fifties, and tens. ²²Let them sit as judges for the people at all times; let them bring every important case to you, but decide every minor case themselves. So it will be easier for you, and they will bear the burden with you. ²³If you do this, and God so commands you, then you will be able to endure, and all these people will go to their home in peace."

²⁴So Moses listened to his father-in-law and did all that he had said. ²⁵Moses chose able men from all Israel and appointed them as heads over the people, as officers over thousands, hundreds, fifties, and tens. ²⁶And they judged the people at all times; hard cases they brought to Moses, but any minor case they decided themselves. ²⁷Then Moses let his father-in-law depart, and he went off to his own country.

COMMENTARY

The shift from vv. 1-12 to this rhetorical unit is abrupt. The units have in common the key role of Jethro, but the subject is completely different. This text, in contrast to the preceding, has little explicit reference to the exodus or the God of liberation. Yahweh is nowhere explicitly mentioned. Now the text is concerned with the quite practical matter of judicial procedure. This text shows that Israel has a crucial concern for institution building, for the establishment of stable procedures and due process, which will make justice everywhere available and reliable.

The narrative that Jethro dominates may be divided into three characteristic parts: the statement of a problem (vv. 13-16), Jethro's intervention with a proposed solution to the problem (vv. 17-23), and the resolution by Moses (vv. 24-27).

18:13-16. The problem is that Moses is overworked. The text begins abruptly: "Moses sat as judge." The text affirms and assumes that the practice of justice is a primary concern for his leadership and for Israel from day one. It is worth noting, by contrast, that the matter of justice nowhere comes up as an Egyptian concern.

Moreover, Moses is quite clear that the concern for justice is not simply political pragmatism, but

derives from and belongs to the very character of God. Jethro asks Moses why he shoulders such an impossible burden. In his answer, Moses asserts that he is preoccupied with "inquiries of God" (i.e., pronouncing oracles from God) and "instruction [תורה *tôrâ*] of God" (vv. 15-16). Moses is not dispensing mere practical advice or positive law, but the very torah of God. The God of Israel cares about the concrete, day-to-day matters of justice.

18:17-23. Jethro sees immediately that Moses is committed to an unworkable practice. Moses cannot handle the heavy docket. We do not know whether Moses is so concerned with control that he wants to handle all the cases himself, or if he is unreflective and has never thought about a more workable, practical system. Moses seems not to have much common sense about administrative matters. But then, such dominating figures often do not. Jethro fears for Moses that he will "burn out"; Jethro's solution is that Moses must learn to delegate.

Jethro thus proposes a judicial system, distinct from the primitive practice of one-man adjudication. The proposal includes (a) the recruitment of good people (v. 21); (b) their training and preparation (v. 20); (c) a system of courts for different social units (v. 21); (d) a "high court" over which Moses would preside (v. 22); and (e) continued affirmation that the entire system would be referred to the will of God (vv. 19, 23).

Perhaps the most important matter in Jethro's plan concerns the qualifications of the judges (v. 21). They are to be able, God-fearing, haters of dishonest (violent) gain. This list of qualifications is both theologically referenced and aware that corruption is not likely to be about large, theological matters, but about the modest temptations of bribery and economic manipulation.

Such a system will save Moses from burnout, but more important, it will let the community go home in שלום (šālôm)—i.e., in harmony and wholeness, free of conflict, enjoying a stable, shared welfare (v. 23).

18:24-27. Moses accepts the proposals of Jethro and implements them. Moses was able to delegate. He does not need to control all details of judicial administration. The text ends with a notice of Jethro's departure, leaving Moses at the mountain of God, ready for the great encounter that comes next.

Two texts are commonly educed to illuminate this encounter with Jethro. First, Deut 17:8-13 shows in more exacting fashion the establishment of a judiciary system with a central high court. In contrast to our passage, which moves from Moses down to "able men," Deuteronomy 17 moves up to levitical priests. The principle espoused is the same, however: a system of courts that permit appeal. It is worth observing that in this text, the occupants of the high court positions are to be levitical priests—i.e., those who claim to survive from the lineage of Moses and Aaron (cf. 6:14-25). Thus we observe that the person of Moses has been converted into an "office" that claims the continuing authority of Moses.

There is here no strict constructionism. The book of Deuteronomy itself is abundant evidence that even the most treasured of all "law" requires continued interpretation and extrapolation in order to be pertinent to new situations. Indeed, if there were no need for continued, authoritative construal, there would be no need for such a high, authorized, trusted court. The text knows very well that the ultimate administration of justice is not the handing out of programmed, fortune-

cookie decisions but the articulation of wise, faithful, reasoned, imaginative new judgments. It is ironic that advocates of strict constructionism who want to resist contextual reinterpretation of the law appeal characteristically to the "absolutes" of the Bible. Such a notion itself is not strict constructionism of the text but a bold, self-serving construal of the biblical text. The tradition of Moses knows from the outset that serious justice requires imaginative, unending interpretation.[85]

Norbert Lohfink has suggested that Deut 17:8-13 belongs to the wider text of Deuteronomy 16–19, which serves as something like a constitution in ancient Israel, providing for a constitutional separation of powers.[86] Lohfink sees this as a crucial principle of government in ancient Israel whereby absolutizing authority is resisted and precluded. In Exod 18:13-27, we may see a safeguard against the absolutizing of the Mosaic office, though enormous authority continues to be assigned to it.

A second text usefully related to ours is 2 Chr 19:4-11, where king Jehoshaphat in the ninth century institutes an important judicial reform in Jerusalem. Historical-critical judgment may suggest that the Jethro narrative is in fact a retrospect from the narrative of Jehoshaphat. We do not need to accept that judgment in order to let this text illuminate our text. It is enough to cite this text concerning Jehoshaphat to see that this is how Israel at its best characteristically thought and spoke about the matter of social justice.

In this narrative the king establishes a judicial system for his entire realm "from Beer-sheba to the hill country of Ephraim." The most important matter for those newly appointed judges is their moral, personal qualification (vv. 6-7). The new judges are to be clear that justice concerns not human wishes, but Yahweh's agenda. This agenda provides that if Yahweh be "dreaded" (פחד pāḥad), taken with ominous seriousness, then it follows that there will be no partiality in judgment or the taking of bribes.

This same provision is fully explicated in Deut

85. On the interpretive trajectory of the Mosaic tradition, see Gerhard von Rad, *Studies in Deuteronomy,* SBT 9 (Chicago: Henry Regnery, 1953) 16, and his notion of "preached law." Derivatively, see Walter Brueggemann, *Interpretation and Obedience: From Faithful Reading to Faithful Living* (Minneapolis: Fortress, 1991) 100-18.

86. Norbert Lohfink, *Great Themes from the Old Testament* (Edinburgh: T. & T. Clark, 1982) 55-75.

16:19-20, a passage closely connected to Exod 17:8-13: "You must not distort justice; you must not show partiality; and you must not accept bribes, for a bribe blinds the eyes of the wise and subverts the cause of those who are in the right. Justice, and only justice, you shall pursue, so that you may live and occupy the land that the LORD your God is giving you" (Deut 16:19-20 NRSV; cf. Deut. 1:9-18).

Israel (and Jehoshaphat) knows that the judicial system must remain free of the leverage of economic power. Put positively, the courts must be a place where the economically disadvantaged receive an equitable hearing.

These two texts, Deut 17:8-13 and 2 Chr 19:4-11 (see also Deut 16:18-20) provide categories and terms for the ways Israel thinks about justice and its cruciality for maintaining an equitable community. It is astonishing that this issue of fair justice arises so early in the tradition and is dealt with so precisely. Moreover, this concern for justice pays peculiar attention from the very beginning to economic matters. But this is what we might expect in a community that poignantly remembers economic exploitation.

REFLECTIONS

1. We may reflect on the odd juxtaposition of vv. 1-12 and vv. 13-27. As we have seen, the first of these units is a *celebration of the exodus* and the second is about *the institutionalization of justice.* No explicit connection is made between the two texts beyond the fact that both feature the work of Jethro. Their juxtaposition, however, is more than incidental. The exodus celebration of vv. 8-12 clearly looks back to the exodus and the beginning of the sojourn with its "hardships." It exults in God's stunning, sovereign act of liberation. The judicial initiative of vv. 17-23, by contrast, looks forward to the Sinai covenant and its legal provisions for a covenantal ordering of society in the books of Exodus and Deuteronomy.

The juxtaposition affirms that this liberated community must develop institutions that will sustain and stabilize the exodus vision in daily social practice. Moses acts on the assumption that the power and passion that made the exodus possible are the same power and passion that can make possible a society free of exploitation. Biblical faith is not simply a recital of odd, isolated events of rescue. It is also about the hard, sustained work of nurturing and practicing the daily passion of healing and restoring, and the daily rejection of dishonest gain.

2. Israel intends here to institutionalize "exodus-justice." This is a very special kind of justice almost everywhere assumed in the Bible, but not much understood.

Our common understandings of justice are Aristotelian in character, assuming that justice is a system of close retribution in which people receive their "just desserts." Such a system is especially prized by the well-off and the "deserving," who prefer to see that the "undeserving" get exactly what they "deserve," and nothing else.

Exodus-justice is very different from such retributive justice.[87] The slaves in bondage had no rights and were entitled to no serious consideration. The wonder of the exodus is that Yahweh did not give to the Hebrews what they "deserved," according to settled Egyptian values. Rather, God made a distinction (8:23) and gave the Hebrews what they *needed* in order to have a viable life. Exodus-justice is compensatory, giving to the needy and disadvantaged well beyond what is deserved. For that reason, in Deuteronomy and in the prophets, when justice is urged for widows and orphans, they are not to be given what they "deserve," but what they need for a viable human existence.

---

87. The best discussion of exodus-justice known to me is José Miranda, *Marx and the Bible: A Critique of the Philosophy of Oppression* (Maryknoll, N.Y.: Orbis, 1974).

EXODUS 19:1–24:18

THE CHARTER OF A
HOLY NATION

OVERVIEW

The "Sinai pericope" stands at the very center of the book of Exodus and as the pivotal point for Mosaic faith. The theological claims of this unit are intimately tied to *the liberation of the exodus* (cf. 19:4; 20:1). The God who here commands (20:1-17; 21:1–23:19) is the God who has liberated (chaps. 1–15). The voice of command that is most decisive here anticipates the *pattern of presence* that is soon to follow (chaps. 25–40). In this text, it is the holy God of command who is known in full, fearful majesty and who speaks a sovereign word. This text, then, is a disclosure of that God, offered in Israel's most characteristic categories. The upshot of Yahweh's command is twofold. First, and most important, a new community is created. In this event, a collection of erstwhile slaves, not identified by common blood, language, or territory, is formed into a community based solely on allegiance to the command of Yahweh. Second, at the center of this unit (20:18-21) stands the authorization of Moses, who is to be the sole legitimator and go-between for Yahweh and Israel. Moses' role, however, is subordinated to the existence of Israel. Through the self-disclosure of Yahweh, the formation of a new community of radical obedience occurs.

There is no doubt that this unit has a complex literary history, comprised of distinct strands of tradition.[88] These difficult matters have been considered by a number of scholars.[89] Given that

complexity, however, it is nevertheless possible to trace out something of a coherent, orderly pattern that reflects some theological intentionality. This was done most boldly by Klaus Baltzer and George Mendenhall, who found in this pericope an orderly form of covenant making.[90] Mendenhall proposed that this form is a reflection of international treaties. It is now commonly agreed that Mendenhall's claim is an overstatement.[91] Nonetheless it is possible to see in these texts a sequence and procedure that aims, in a liturgically stylized way, to form a people newly sworn to obey the radical commands of Yahweh.

The completed form of the text consists in six elements. Chapter 19, after a thematic announcement of covenant obedience rooted in the exodus (vv. 3-6), presents a theophany of the coming of God to the mountain in fearful and devastating sovereignty to meet Israel. This meeting requires ritual preparation and evokes from Israel a preliminary oath of allegiance (v. 8).

The theophany provides the context for God's utterance of the Ten Commandments, the most crucial and authoritative command in the faith of Israel (20:1-17). The text is so familiar to us that we may fail to notice that it is a speech from the very mouth of God. This speech gives to Israel God's full intention for the life of creation. All

---

88. Childs, *Exodus,* OTL (Philadelphia: Westminster, 1974) 749-51.
89. See, for example, Murray Newman, *The People of the Covenant* (Nashville: Abingdon, 1962); Walter Beyerlin, *Origins and History of the Oldest Sinaitic Traditions* (New York: Oxford University Press, 1965); and Thomas B. Dozeman, *God on the Mountain: A Study of Redaction, Theology and Canon in Exodus 19–24,* SBLMS 37 (Atlanta: Scholars Press, 1989).

90. Klaus Baltzer, *The Covenant Formulary in Old Testament, Jewish, and Early Christian Writings* (Philadelphia: Fortress, 1971); George E. Mendenhall, *Law and Covenant in Israel and the Ancient Near East* (Pittsburgh: The Biblical Colloquium, 1955).
91. See the judicious mediating position of McCarthy and the summary of Nicholson: Dennis J. McCarthy, *Treaty and Covenant: A Study in Form in the Ancient Oriental Documents and in the Old Testament,* Analecta Biblica 21 (Rome: Biblical Institute Press, 1978); Ernest W. Nicholson, *God and His People: Covenant and Theology in the Old Testament* (Oxford: Clarendon, 1986).

other law in Israel is reflective commentary upon this decree.[92]

The address of God to Israel in 20:1-17 so frightens Israel that Moses is designated mediator (20:18-21). From now on, Yahweh will address Israel only indirectly, but Moses will be accepted by Israel as the single, true voice of Yahweh. It is entirely plausible that this text reflects the creation of a Mosaic "office."

The "Covenant Code" of 20:22–23:19 stands in this larger unit as a counterpart to the Decalogue of 20:1-17. However, it is not on a par with the Decalogue in terms of significance or authority; whereas the Decalogue comes out of God's own mouth (before Moses is made mediator), the Covenant Code is Moses' word and comes after the authorization of a mediator. Thus the juxtaposition of the two groups of laws serves to accent both the peculiar authority of the Decalogue and the authority of Moses.

The brief section of 23:20-33 concludes the proclamation of law with a promise and a warning. This speech relates the Sinai pericope to the larger Israelite tradition of promise and land. It indicates how demanding the law of Yahweh is, and how vulnerable Israel is as it seeks to live out its peculiar vocation.

Chapter 24 corresponds to chapter 19 in two aspects. First, it provides contact with God in a theophany. Second, it voices Israel's oath of allegiance to Yahweh (vv. 3, 7). The final verses (vv. 15-18), which situate Moses in the cloud of glory, prepare the way for Exodus 25–31 and anticipate the conclusion of 40:34-38.

In large design this passage is chiastically arranged:

A theophany (19)
  B law (20:1-17)
    C mediator (20:18-21)
    C' (vv. 22-26)
  B' law (21:1–23:19, 20-33)
A' theophany (24)

The juxtaposition of *theophany* and *law* roots Israel's definitional commands in nothing less than the sovereign voice and will of Yahweh. The law that constitutes Israel's existence originates outside Israel's historical horizon and beyond the reach of Moses or of any king. Israelite life is mandated from the awesome region of heaven, and Moses must enter glory to receive all that is given. The effect of this textual arrangement is to assert that Israel is neither a historical accident nor an ordinary political entity, but a peculiar community willed and destined by God. Its earthly vocation, to be a priestly kingdom mediating God's intention for the world, is grounded in a holy, heavenly purpose. That holy purpose must be practiced in the dailyness of human history.[93]

92. The most helpful interpretive comment on the Decalogue is Walter Harrelson, *The Ten Commandments and Human Rights,* OBT (Philadelphia: Fortress, 1980). See also Childs, *Exodus,* 383-439; Johann Jakob Stamm and Maurice Edward Andrew, *The Ten Commandments in Recent Research,* SBT 2 (Naperville: Alec R. Allenson, 1967); and Anthony Phillips, *Ancient Israel's Criminal Law: A New Approach to the Decalogue* (Oxford: Blackwell, 1970).

93. See Martin Buber and his notion of theopolitics, *Kingship of God* (New York: Harper & Row, 1967) 99-107, 121-62, and portions of *Moses: The Revelation and the Covenant* (Atlantic Highlands, N.J.: Humanities Press International, 1988). Echoes of Buber may be sounded in Nicholson, *God an His People,* chap. 10.

EXODUS 19:1-25, AT MOUNT SINAI

NIV

19 In the third month after the Israelites left Egypt—on the very day—they came to the Desert of Sinai. [2]After they set out from Rephidim, they entered the Desert of Sinai, and Israel camped there in the desert in front of the mountain.

[3]Then Moses went up to God, and the LORD

NRSV

19 On the third new moon after the Israelites had gone out of the land of Egypt, on that very day, they came into the wilderness of Sinai. [2]They had journeyed from Rephidim, entered the wilderness of Sinai, and camped in the wilderness; Israel camped there in front of the mountain. [3]Then Moses went up to God; the LORD called to

NIV

called to him from the mountain and said, "This is what you are to say to the house of Jacob and what you are to tell the people of Israel: ⁴'You yourselves have seen what I did to Egypt, and how I carried you on eagles' wings and brought you to myself. ⁵Now if you obey me fully and keep my covenant, then out of all nations you will be my treasured possession. Although the whole earth is mine, ⁶youᵃ will be for me a kingdom of priests and a holy nation.' These are the words you are to speak to the Israelites."

⁷So Moses went back and summoned the elders of the people and set before them all the words the LORD had commanded him to speak. ⁸The people all responded together, "We will do everything the LORD has said." So Moses brought their answer back to the LORD.

⁹The LORD said to Moses, "I am going to come to you in a dense cloud, so that the people will hear me speaking with you and will always put their trust in you." Then Moses told the LORD what the people had said.

¹⁰And the LORD said to Moses, "Go to the people and consecrate them today and tomorrow. Have them wash their clothes ¹¹and be ready by the third day, because on that day the LORD will come down on Mount Sinai in the sight of all the people. ¹²Put limits for the people around the mountain and tell them, 'Be careful that you do not go up the mountain or touch the foot of it. Whoever touches the mountain shall surely be put to death. ¹³He shall surely be stoned or shot with arrows; not a hand is to be laid on him. Whether man or animal, he shall not be permitted to live.' Only when the ram's horn sounds a long blast may they go up to the mountain."

¹⁴After Moses had gone down the mountain to the people, he consecrated them, and they washed their clothes. ¹⁵Then he said to the people, "Prepare yourselves for the third day. Abstain from sexual relations."

¹⁶On the morning of the third day there was thunder and lightning, with a thick cloud over the mountain, and a very loud trumpet blast. Everyone in the camp trembled. ¹⁷Then Moses led the people out of the camp to meet with God, and they stood at the foot of the mountain.

ᵃ5,6 Or possession, for the whole earth is mine. ⁶You

NRSV

him from the mountain, saying, "Thus you shall say to the house of Jacob, and tell the Israelites: ⁴You have seen what I did to the Egyptians, and how I bore you on eagles' wings and brought you to myself. ⁵Now therefore, if you obey my voice and keep my covenant, you shall be my treasured possession out of all the peoples. Indeed, the whole earth is mine, ⁶but you shall be for me a priestly kingdom and a holy nation. These are the words that you shall speak to the Israelites."

⁷So Moses came, summoned the elders of the people, and set before them all these words that the LORD had commanded him. ⁸The people all answered as one: "Everything that the LORD has spoken we will do." Moses reported the words of the people to the LORD. ⁹Then the LORD said to Moses, "I am going to come to you in a dense cloud, in order that the people may hear when I speak with you and so trust you ever after."

When Moses had told the words of the people to the LORD, ¹⁰the LORD said to Moses: "Go to the people and consecrate them today and tomorrow. Have them wash their clothes ¹¹and prepare for the third day, because on the third day the LORD will come down upon Mount Sinai in the sight of all the people. ¹²You shall set limits for the people all around, saying, 'Be careful not to go up the mountain or to touch the edge of it. Any who touch the mountain shall be put to death. ¹³No hand shall touch them, but they shall be stoned or shot with arrows;ᵃ whether animal or human being, they shall not live.' When the trumpet sounds a long blast, they may go up on the mountain." ¹⁴So Moses went down from the mountain to the people. He consecrated the people, and they washed their clothes. ¹⁵And he said to the people, "Prepare for the third day; do not go near a woman."

16On the morning of the third day there was thunder and lightning, as well as a thick cloud on the mountain, and a blast of a trumpet so loud that all the people who were in the camp trembled. ¹⁷Moses brought the people out of the camp to meet God. They took their stand at the foot of the mountain. ¹⁸Now Mount Sinai was wrapped in smoke, because the LORD had descended upon it in fire; the smoke went up like the smoke of a

ᵃ Heb lacks with arrows

NIV

[18]Mount Sinai was covered with smoke, because the LORD descended on it in fire. The smoke billowed up from it like smoke from a furnace, the whole mountain[a] trembled violently, [19]and the sound of the trumpet grew louder and louder. Then Moses spoke and the voice of God answered him.[b]

[20]The LORD descended to the top of Mount Sinai and called Moses to the top of the mountain. So Moses went up [21]and the LORD said to him, "Go down and warn the people so they do not force their way through to see the LORD and many of them perish. [22]Even the priests, who approach the LORD, must consecrate themselves, or the LORD will break out against them."

[23]Moses said to the LORD, "The people cannot come up Mount Sinai, because you yourself warned us, 'Put limits around the mountain and set it apart as holy.'"

[24]The LORD replied, "Go down and bring Aaron up with you. But the priests and the people must not force their way through to come up to the LORD, or he will break out against them."

[25]So Moses went down to the people and told them.

[a]18 Most Hebrew manuscripts; a few Hebrew manuscripts and Septuagint *all the people*   [b]19 Or *and God answered him with thunder*

NRSV

kiln, while the whole mountain shook violently. [19]As the blast of the trumpet grew louder and louder, Moses would speak and God would answer him in thunder. [20]When the LORD descended upon Mount Sinai, to the top of the mountain, the LORD summoned Moses to the top of the mountain, and Moses went up. [21]Then the LORD said to Moses, "Go down and warn the people not to break through to the LORD to look; otherwise many of them will perish. [22]Even the priests who approach the LORD must consecrate themselves or the LORD will break out against them." [23]Moses said to the LORD, "The people are not permitted to come up to Mount Sinai; for you yourself warned us, saying, 'Set limits around the mountain and keep it holy.'" [24]The LORD said to him, "Go down, and come up bringing Aaron with you; but do not let either the priests or the people break through to come up to the LORD; otherwise he will break out against them." [25]So Moses went down to the people and told them.

COMMENTARY

This extensive, complicated chapter serves as an introduction to the meeting between Yahweh and Israel at "the mountain." Cast in liturgical form, its work is the preparation by Israel to be properly qualified for worship of Yahweh. Rhetorically, the central portion of the text reports a theophany—a disciplined account of the powerful, disruptive, cataclysmic coming of God into the midst of the community. The chapter begins with a geographical note (vv. 1-2), followed by a speech of God to Moses (vv. 3-6). The remainder of the chapter is constituted by a series of transactions that make the meeting possible (vv. 7-25). We may note three factors operating in this long and not well-ordered narrative of preparation.

First, the meeting is an entry into "the holiness" for the purpose of worship. Such an entry and meeting is a high-risk venture for which careful preparation must be made. This focus on worship makes this chapter pivotal for the entire book of Exodus. On the one hand, this act of worship implements the long-standing, oft-repeated demand of the liberation narrative: "Let my people go that they may worship me" (cf. 5:1; 7:16; 8:1, 20; 9:1, 13; 10:3). On the other hand, and in a very different way, this careful preparation anticipates the detailed enterprise of "sanctification" in Exodus 25–31 and 35–40, whereby a meeting is made possible for Israel.

The fact that this narrative is cast in liturgical categories permits the narrator to hold together two different aspects of Israel's meeting with God. On the one hand, this is a dangerous, once-for-all event, never to be repeated. On the other hand, this is a model meeting that serves as a paradigm for all future covenantal confrontations.

Second, while the meeting is "at the mountain," there is a great deal of movement up and down the mountain. Thus Moses goes up (v. 3) and comes down (v. 14), while the people stand at the foot of the mountain (v. 17). Yahweh descends (vv. 18, 20), and Moses goes up (v. 20) and comes down (v. 25) as commanded in vv. 21, 24. Thomas Dozeman has proposed that movement up and down the mountain in the several literary sources articulates different "geographies of power" among the several parts of this community.[94] Thus the movements up and down are at least scene changes, and likely intend to portray power relations concerning who has access and who stands over whom.

Third, the cast of characters is also complicated. God and Moses are clearly the central protagonists. In addition "the people" are given direct access to God. The elders (v. 7), Aaron (v. 24), and the priests (v. 24) are also specified in their several roles. These various references may indicate, as Dozeman suggests, that in different sources, the distribution of power is differently portrayed; "the people" indicates a broadly based democratic shape of power, "the elders" indicates authorized lay leadership, and the "priests" (Aaron) are a sacerdotal alternative to lay leadership.

19:1-2. These two verses provide a narrative setting of time and place for the meeting to follow. Israel arrives at Rephadim in 17:1 (cf. 17:8), but 18:5 has a narrative episode at the mountain. These verses thus place the meeting at Sinai in the context of the wilderness sojourn. Moreover, the "third full moon" suggests that for this narrative, the events of 15:22–18:27 do not take very long. In any case, the purpose of these verses is to make the mountain the context for what follows. It is futile to try to identify the mountain geographically. More important is the affirmation that the mountain is the place where earth touches heaven, where the human realm makes contact with the abode of God (or the gods). The place thus is laden with holy presence.

19:3-6. God speaks to Moses, abruptly and with sovereign power. This speech is likely the most

programmatic for Israelite faith that we have in the entire tradition of Moses. It divides into two parts.

First, v. 4 is an indicative statement recalling the entire narrative of liberation. It affirms that Egypt is now past tense to Israel and that unambiguously the initiative of God has changed Israel's destiny. This verse fully and completely summarizes the memory of the exodus, which is the ground of all that follows. Israel has witnessed God's decisive combat against and triumph over Egypt. Moreover, Yahweh, with enormous power, has taken Israel up, out of Egypt and bondage. Remarkably, the "flight out of Egypt" has not had as its destination the mountain, the land, or any other place, but "to me." That is, the goal of the exodus is presented as a flight from Pharaoh to Yahweh, from one master to a new one.

The metaphor of an eagle for Yahweh's rescue of Israel from bondage is compelling. According to Deut 32:11-14, the eagle (Yahweh) is a nurturing, protective agent who carries, guides, feeds, and protects (cf. Exod 15:4-10, 13-17). The predominant note concerning the eagle here, however, is one of majestic, devastating power (cf. Deut 28:49; Jer 48:40; 49:27). Thus the image holds together majestic power and protective nurturing. The exodus required both power to override the grip of Egypt and nurturing to sustain when there was no other sustenance. Later on, the same image is used in Isa 40:31 very differently, for now Israel itself is like a powerful eagle that does not grow weary or faint (cf. Ps 103:5). That eagle, however, derives its strength from attentiveness to Yahweh, the one who creates and authorizes soaring eagles (cf. Job 39:27).

This extraordinary memory (v. 4) now turns to anticipation of life in devotion to Yahweh (vv. 5-6). Two facts of this anticipation interest us. First, the future of Israel is governed by an "if" and by a powerful infinitive absolute; Israel's future is conditional. Everything depends on Israel's readiness to listen (שמע *šmʿ*; cf. 15:26) and to keep covenant. This strong conditional surprises us after the indicative of v. 4. It is as though the generous God of exodus has abruptly become the demanding God of Sinai; and so it is. While Yahweh's initial rescue is unconditional and without reservation, a sustained relation with Yahweh is one of rigorous demand for covenant. Indeed,

94. Dozeman, *God on the Mountain.*

the long Sinai text that follows is a statement of condition whereby this rescued people can be a community of ongoing covenant.

The second element of the statement is a promise of Israel's special status. On the one hand, Israel (assuming the conditions are met) is Yahweh's especially prized, peculiar possession. One can see in this verse the faith of Israel, struggling with the tension between universal claim ("all the earth is mine") and the special election of Israel. Indeed, these verses may indicate that Yahweh's own life is a struggle over this tension. Yahweh is indeed the creator who possesses and governs all creation, all peoples. Yahweh also, however, has a special, intimate relation with Israel.

On the other hand, Israel (assuming the conditions are met) is to occupy a position in the world that partakes both of sacral significance and political authority. The two nouns used are specifically political references, *kingdom* and *nation*. Their modifiers, however, move in a sacerdotal direction, *priestly* and *holy*. Israel is to be a community in which worldly power and holy purpose converge.[95] Israel thus has an unparalleled vocation, and Sinai is the meeting whereby that vocation is to be given and accepted.

Verses 5-6 are extraordinary, because they manage in a single utterance to voice both an unthinkable purpose that foresees a people the like of which has never existed, and an unaccommodating condition affirming that Israel's peculiar status is endlessly derivative and never possessed. Israel's holy distinctiveness depends on moment-by-moment listening to the God who commands and authorizes. Whenever Israel ceases to listen and to keep covenant, and presumes upon its "status," it forfeits its claim in that moment.

These three verses, as James Muilenburg has shown, provide the primary themes and the elemental structure for "Mosaic faith."[96] In the long, sacerdotal section beginning in Exodus 25, this link between promise and demand is not forgotten. Israel is to be holy and priestly; obedience to commands is pivotal even in the sacerdotal tradition, which takes such a high view of Israel (cf. 25:16, 22).

19:7-8. As the go-between, Moses carries Yahweh's message of vv. 4-6 to the waiting community. While the narrative introduction identifies "the elders" as the addressees of Moses, it is "the people" who answer. Israel's answer is a vow and pledge of loyalty to the commands of Yahweh. Israel has sworn to "really listen" and to "keep covenant" (cf. v. 5). Israel has agreed to its identity and status as subject and vassal of Yahweh, in the full expectation that it will become a new kind of kingdom and a new kind of nation, one marked by priestly, holy marks. This pledge not only binds Israel unequivocally to Yahweh, but also sets Israel apart from all other peoples.

The oracle of Yahweh, voicing saving memory (v. 4), command (v. 5a), and promise (vv. 5b-6), is matched by the oath of Israel (v. 8). Together the oracle and the oath constitute the foundational acts of Israel's existence. In this moment, a new people is born into the world. Never before has such an offer been tendered to any people; never before has such an oath been taken. It is on the basis of this oracle and oath that preparations for the meeting now begin.

19:9-15. When Yahweh has the oath reported in Yahweh's own ears by Moses, Yahweh announces a stunning resolve: Yahweh will "come to you" (v. 9). The statement is direct and unconditional. We can see that this initial promise of presence, in the final form of the text, looks ahead to Exodus 25–31, which is preoccupied with the presence of God. Even in this direct statement, however, the intervention of Yahweh is immediately hedged about by "a dense cloud." Even God's direct presence will be shrouded in mystery and shadow. The most that is intended is that God will speak and Israel will hear. No possibility of Yahweh's being seen is offered.

The intent of Yahweh's direct speech to Israel is not to secure obedience. Yahweh's speech is offered, remarkably enough, only as a way to certify and legitimate Moses, so that Israel may "trust" Moses' words. This text thus has one eye on the authority of Moses and the enduring "office of Moses." The problem of believing Moses has been present in the narrative very early (4:1-9), but seemed resolved in 14:31. The subsequent protests against Moses (16:2-3; 17:2) suggest that because his requirements are so rigorous, issues of authority inevitably recur. This verse makes

---

95. See Buber, *Moses* 101-9.
96. James Muilenburg, "The Form and Structure of the Covenantal Formulation," *VT* 9 (1959) 347-65.

clear that Moses' radical vision is indeed Yahweh's vision.

Yahweh's resolve to "come to you" is a guarded one, protected by "a dense cloud." As Yahweh takes such precaution that Yahweh's own holiness should not be trivialized, so Israel must make adequate, careful ritual preparation for this spectacular meeting (vv. 10-15). This is not a spontaneous, intrusive, surprising confrontation, but a paced meeting that will be carefully choreographed. On the one hand, such intentionality suggests that the narrator's imagination is under the influence of regular worship, so that every meeting with God, including this one, is imagined in this form. On the other hand, this preparation is so that the initial Sinai meeting can be replicated and reenacted, much as Passover replicates exodus or as Eucharist replicates the "last supper."

The work of preparation is to become "holy"— qualified to be in the presence of the holy God (vv. 10, 14). The prescribed preparation consists primarily in ritual cleansing. (On such washing, see 30:17-21. The act of ritual washing has become essential as a dramatic enactment to separate the sphere of worship from all other spheres, to assert that this meeting is different and one must be different to be there.) One can detect here the beginning of the distinctions of "clean and unclean" and "holy and profane," which will come to dominate later sacerdotal thought in Israel (cf. Lev 10:10; Ezek 22:26). One cannot approach this meeting carelessly, as though it were continuous with the rest of one's life.

Around the central preparation of washing, we may observe three other facets on "sanctification." First, the reference to "the third day" likely means as soon as all things are ready and is not to be taken as an exact number. The reference to the third day is perhaps taken up by Hos 6:2, which in turn is influential in the gospel narrative concerning the resurrection of Jesus on the third day. Indeed, "the meeting" of Easter is not unlike a replication of the meeting of Sinai, whereby life begins anew.

Second, the dire warning culminating in "shall surely die" (מות יומת *môt yûmāt*, v. 12) underscores the danger of the meeting and the otherness of God's holiness. Not only is God's "person" dangerous but even the mountain as God's habitat constitutes a great risk for Israel as well. Contact with Yahweh's holiness can be pursued only under intense discipline.

Third, in addition to the general notion of cleanness, the final line of v. 15 gives a powerful masculine tilt to the narrative, for contact with a woman will either profane, weaken, or render them impure. While we can only abhor the sexist reference in this text, which treats women as troublesome and men as "proper worshipers," even this rigorous tradition notices the odd and freighted connection between religion and sexuality; a connection that still operates powerfully among us. That inescapable connection is worth notice here, even though we might propose a very different adjudication of the issue.

19:16-25. Yahweh does what Yahweh says. Yahweh had announced an appearance to Israel (v. 9), and now that meeting happens on the third day as Moses had promised.

What an arrival it is, beyond anything Israel has ever experienced (vv. 16-20). There has been preparation, but the coming seems to override and disregard it. The narrative strains to find language to portray the disruptive, cataclysmic upheaval caused by the entry of God's own holiness. There are hints here of a storm God, causing thunder and lightning. There is evidence of a cultic rendition with the blast of trumpets. The "thick cloud" seems to join these other two accents. All of these images together are enough to cause the camp to tremble (v. 16), to make the entire mountain shake violently (v. 18). There is now set loose sources of energy, power, and authority so enormous and so fearful that the intended "containers" of God's presence are unable to contain.

The coming of the holy one is unutterable. There are no adequate words, yet all we have left from the meeting is a text. The narrator wants us to see so much. In that hidden holiness, however, as words fail to utter, so vision fails to show, and all that is given is fire, smoke, violent movement, and a trumpet louder and louder. Yahweh is an alien presence, a foreboding, threatening, and de-stabilizing otherness. The narrator wants to take us up in awe and terror, in the presence of the holy one who is beyond all portrayal.

One more time, echoing vv. 12-13a, Yahweh warns Moses about the danger (vv. 21-25). The warning may be pictured in three concentric circles. First, the whole of the mountain is kept (or made) holy (v. 23). Second, the people are warned not to look (v. 21; vv. 12-13 warn them not to touch). It is not denied that God has a visible form. To see that form, however, is enormously dangerous (cf. 33:22-23)! Third, even the priests, the ones who confidently operate in the zone of God's holiness, are warned to be careful. They must not be complacent or comfortable in the presence of this God. Twice the term "break out" (פרץ *pāraṣ*) is used (v. 22, 24), as though Yahweh is a contained poison, almost substantive, that will break out to contaminate, destroy, and kill. One is struck in by the tumbling out of words and phrases in these verses, without a coherent picture or presentation. As the speech is untamed, so the God who comes in Israel is untamed, and on the loose.

REFLECTIONS

1. The mountain is no ordinary place (vv. 1-2). It is the dangerous environment of holiness, the place where the ordinariness of human, earthly life has contact with the holy that destabilizes and consequently transforms. We have trivialized "mountaintop experiences" as though they are romantic opportunities for religious self-indulgence. This account, against any such domestication, portrays the mountain of holiness as a dangerous meeting place that will leave nothing unchanged. In his study of theophany, Jörg Jeremias has identified two constant factors in theophanic narrative: a cataclysmic coming and a decisive after-effect of transformation.[97] Care must be taken not to reduce, trivialize, or routinize theophany, which here attests to God's terrible confrontation with Israel.

2. Israel's life begins in an oracle of God that is abrupt and without any antecedents (vv. 4-6). Israel is formed by the sovereign speech of Yahweh. This God is as majestic as an eagle, terrible in power, protective of its own treasured people. We are left with the wondrous image of being carried safely (albeit dangling dangerously) out of the reach of bondage.

The gospel premise of v. 4 is matched by a massive gospel demand of v. 5*a*. The "if" of v. 5 looms large in Mosaic faith. It is easy to treat the promise of v. 4 and the demand of v. 5 as a dialectic of gospel and law. The imposition of these categories, however, can be distorting. It is enough to see that Mosaic faith, i.e., the canonical core of the Bible, is vigorous in its requirement. The powerful verb "really *listen*" ("obey"; שמע *šāmaʿ*), perhaps with an allusion to the tradition of Deuteronomy (cf. Deut 6:4-9), insists that biblical faith focuses on ethical reality. Communion with "the eagle God" takes the form of adherence to the powerful purpose of God, soon to be specified at Sinai but already evidenced in the exodus.

The memory and the demand lead to the promise of vv. 5*b*-6. As the mountain is not ordinary and this God is not ordinary, so this people is destined not to be ordinary. The community of faith (synagogue, church) is given a vocation to be a distinct presence in the world on behalf of the world. Specifically, the priestly vocation of this community is to ponder and mediate the presence of the holy God in the midst of the nations, acting to resist any profanation of life that dismisses and banishes the powerful inconvenience of God.

The language of this promise is taken up in 1 Pet 2:9-10, in an attempt to characterize the early church.

3. Israel's response is an appropriate answer to the oracle (vv. 7-8). Israel must decide to accept its odd identity and destiny in the world, and that decision is for complete obedience. The oracle and responsive oath seem to be something like the initial questions asked the bride and groom prior to taking their vows, when each party states the intention and resolve for

---

97. Jörg Jeremias, *Theophanie: Die Geschichte einer alttestamentlichen Gattung,* WMANT 10 (Neukirchen-Vluyn: Neukirchener Verlag, 1965).

the relation. In these verses, Yahweh and Israel make an initial commitment to each other that is to be explicated in what follows.

4. The preparation of vv. 9-15 is ordered and severe. Our conventional trivializations of God make God in practice too available, too easy, and too immediate. We drop to our knees or bow our heads, and we imagine that God is eagerly awaiting attention. Or we drop in casually for worship, assuming that God is always there. Most of our worship takes place well short of the mountain, where we can seize and maintain the initiative, imagining God at our beck and call.

This meeting with Yahweh is clearly not one between "buddies." It is more like a meeting with an inscrutable, remote sovereign in which there is a scheduled preparation, a schooling in required steps, and an ordered ushering from chamber to chamber as the awe intensifies.

As the monarch enters the room only after everyone else is appropriately in place and waiting, so Yahweh comes only where disciplined readiness is evident. The text asserts that the holy God of Sinai will not come into the midst of our casual indifference. Some other god might, but it will not be this powerful God of liberation who rescues, demands, and promises.

5. The meeting (vv. 16-25) is cast as a theophany, a cataclysmic confrontation that destabilizes all conventional certitudes. In a society "explained" by the commonalities of the social sciences and received in the assurances of the "therapeutic," theophany is so raw and ragged that we scarcely have access to it. Theophany is by definition disruptive. As an alternative mode of discourse, it employs dramatic images in order to say what cannot be said and to witness what cannot be portrayed.

This raw, pre-rational mode of discourse is crucial for what is uttered in Scripture. First, the pivot points of the Bible are narratives of theophany that witness to the utter holiness of God. Note, for example, the great prophetic encounters with God (Elijah, Isaiah, Ezekiel), the pivot points in the life of Jesus (birth, baptism, transfiguration, crucifixion, and resurrection), and the break points in the life of the church (Pentecost, apocalyptic vision). Our reading of the Bible is often poverty-stricken, either because we exclude these texts as beyond our "realism," or because we trivialize their discourse with our banal exposition. These texts propose that our lives should also be structured by these pre-rational, dangerous comings of God, which lie beyond our capacity for explanation and control.

Second, theophany belongs to a faith-ordered human life. Our lives are not to be lived on a flat plane of bourgeois control. We are visited by the holy in both disruptive and healing ways. What Abraham Maslow too easily calls "peak experiences" are indeed definitional for human life. Persons flattened by modernity require a daring mode of discourse and a more venturesome field of images, whereby intrusions of the holy can be accepted as belonging to our human life. Theophanic texts provide access to experiences in the ongoing life of God to which we have no access without such speech. Israel's sense of humanness does not arise simply from political liberation but from this theophanic incursion that reorders its life.

In the end, however, theophanic discourse primarily serves neither a liturgic agenda nor notions of human personhood. Theophanic discourse is required in order to speak adequately about the character of this holy God who intrudes dangerously and disruptively in order to transform. This God lives neither in easy intimacy with us nor in remote sovereignty over us, but in odd ways comes and goes, seizing initiative and redefining reality.

In this dramatic narrative, Yahweh seizes initiative to establish the relation. This text concerns the freedom of God utterly untamed and undomesticated. In the face of all of Israel's preparations, God is loosed in a sovereignty that evokes trembling. There is something here of Barth's "otherness," an other who is decisively present and who insists that all else must be ordered and reoriented around this coming.

This text seems odd in the bourgeois context of Western Christianity. It witnesses to an extraordinary mountain, an extraordinary God, and an extraordinary people. It invites a reconsideration of our profanation of life whereby we manage and control and leave for religion only innocuous fringes. It models an endangered community that is willing to entertain holiness at its center. The narrative is so dramatic that we may miss its uncommon affirmation. In v. 27, the people "meet God." In vv. 18 and 20, God "comes down." This is an entry of heaven into earth, and earth is never again the same. This is an entry of holiness into Israel, and Israel is never again the same. The unloosing (breaking out) of holiness is so odd for us; the only thing odder is that in chapter 20 this holiness is fully mobilized around succinct and measured demand. The God of Sinai is a revolutionary sovereign who invites this prepared people to come under the discipline of the revolution (cf. Luke 1:17).

EXODUS 20:1-17, THE TEN COMMANDMENTS

OVERVIEW

The terrible, holy God of Sinai is always at the brink of "breaking out" against Israel and spilling over in self-aggrandizing destructiveness (19:22, 24). We are, in the light of that danger, hardly prepared for the proclamation of the Ten Commandments in this next unit. The God who threatens to break out in inexplicable rage instead breaks out in magisterial command. The relation of *theophany* to *law* is an odd one. The juxtaposition of the two genres, however, is definitional for what happens to Israel at Sinai. Command is rooted in theophany. The juxtaposition of theophany and command asserts that, for Israel, there is nothing more elemental or fundamental (even primordial) than the commands that intend to shape and order the world according to the radical and distinctive vision of the God of the exodus.

The Decalogue itself is likely a distinct literary entity that originally was not connected to this theophany. There is, moreover, serious critical question about the date and provenance of the decalogue and, therefore, about its Mosaic authorship. These commands may, like much of the legal material of the OT, have some linkages to already established legal materials of the ancient Near East. None of that, however, takes us very far in interpreting the commands as we have them.

We must, even with all of these critical uncertainties, try to take the corpus of commands as they are given. This means, first, that they are given in the context of the Sinai covenant. They constitute the substantive vision around which the

God-Israel relation is ordered. Sinai binds Israel to this vision of social possibility and places Israel under this particular obedience. Second, the commands are given with the authority of Moses. They are in some sense an authentic articulation of what Mosaic faith in its core is all about. Third, even if these two traditions originated separately, the connection of exodus and command in 19:4-6 (and 20:1) binds the Sinai commands to the liberation passion of the exodus narrative. The commands are a decisive way in which Israel (and Yahweh) intend to sustain and institutionalize the revolutionary social possibility that is asserted and enacted in the exodus narrative.

The commands are commonly understood as divided into two "tablets": one concerning relations to God (vv. 1-11), and one concerning the neighbor (vv. 12-17). The relation between the two tablets is of crucial importance to biblical faith. It is self-evident that the second tablet is the more readily available, practical, and pertinent to us. It is risky, however (especially among "theological liberals"), to take the second tablet by itself, as positive law concerning human relations. But such a view misses the primary covenantal point that these "neighbor demands" have their warrant, impetus, and urgency in the character of this particular God. The second tablet is not just a set of good moral ideas. It contains conditions of viable human life, non-negotiable conditions rooted in God's own life and God's ordering of the world. Thus it is important to "get it right" about Yahweh, in order to "get it right" about neighbor. Karl Marx has seen this most clearly and programmatically: "The criticism of heaven is thus transformed into the criticism of earth, the criticism of religion into the criticism of law, and the criticism of theology into the criticism of politics."[98]

Marx means that "God talk" always implicitly asserts neighbor relations and that every mode of neighbor relations inevitably bootlegs some powerful (even if hidden) notion of God. Thus it is not the case simply that Israel must attend both to God and to neighbor, but that the way of attending to God determines our ways of attending to neighbor and vice versa. It is precisely the worship of the God of the exodus that provides the elemental insistence and passionate imagination to reshape human relations in healing (cf. 15:26), liberating ways.

Norman Gottwald is correct in saying that in its recital of liberation and especially in the actions at Sinai, Israel initiates a revolutionary social experiment in the world, to see whether non-exploitative modes of social relationship can be sustained in the world.[99] In commenting upon the first commandment, Pixley comments:

The problem is not, of course, whether to call the rain God Yahweh or Baal. Behind the conflict of these gods is the social reality of a class struggle. . . . The polemical formulation of the commandment to worship Yahweh, then, has its explanation in the long struggle of the peasantry to rid itself of the domination of a long series of kings . . . who resurrected the old forms of class domination. . . . An Israelite had no choice but to reject any form of loyalty to any god who had not saved the slaves of Egypt.[100]

Thus the Decalogue stands as a critical principle of protest against every kind of exploitative social relation (public and interpersonal, capitalist and socialist) and as a social vision of possibility that every social relation (public and interpersonal, economic and political) can be transformed and made into a liberating relation.

98. David McLellan, *The Thought of Karl Marx: An Introduction* (London: Macmillan, 1971) 22.

99. Norman K. Gottwald, *The Tribes of Yahweh: A Sociology of the Religion of Liberated Israel, 1250–1050 B.C.* (Maryknoll, N.Y.: Orbis, 1979) 200-226 and *passim*.

100. George V. Pixley, *On Exodus: A Liberation Perspective* (Maryknoll, N.Y.: Orbis, 1987) 129.

Exodus 20:1-7, "No Other Gods Before Me"

NIV

20 And God spoke all these words:

2"I am the LORD your God, who brought you out of Egypt, out of the land of slavery.
3"You shall have no other gods before[a] me.
4"You shall not make for yourself an idol in the form of anything in heaven above or on the earth beneath or in the waters below. 5You shall not bow down to them or worship them; for I, the LORD your God, am a jealous God, punishing the children for the sin of the fathers to the third and fourth generation of those who hate me, 6but showing love to a thousand ⌊generations⌋ of those who love me and keep my commandments.
7"You shall not misuse the name of the LORD your God, for the LORD will not hold anyone guiltless who misuses his name.

a3 Or *besides*

NRSV

20 Then God spoke all these words:
2I am the LORD your God, who brought you out of the land of Egypt, out of the house of slavery; 3you shall have no other gods before[a] me.

4You shall not make for yourself an idol, whether in the form of anything that is in heaven above, or that is on the earth beneath, or that is in the water under the earth. 5You shall not bow down to them or worship them; for I the LORD your God am a jealous God, punishing children for the iniquity of parents, to the third and the fourth generation of those who reject me, 6but showing steadfast love to the thousandth generation[b] of those who love me and keep my commandments.

7You shall not make wrongful use of the name of the LORD your God, for the LORD will not acquit anyone who misuses his name.

a Or *besides*   b Or *to thousands*

COMMENTARY

Israel's destiny under command is rooted in the self-disclosure of God. These commands might be taken not as a series of rules, but as a proclamation in God's own mouth of who God is and how God shall be "practiced" by this community of liberated slaves. The speech of God itself is abrupt in its beginning. Except for vv. 5-6, which are quite general, chapter 19 gives no hint that commands are to follow from the theophany. In Israel, however, God's self-giving is in the form of command. Thus the tradition holds closely together "a god so near" and "a torah so righteous" (Deut 4:7-8). God is known in torah; nearness is expressed as righteousness.

20:1-2. The self-disclosure of God begins with a succinct reference to and summary of the recital of liberation (v. 2). The first utterance is, "I am Yahweh." Thus God speaks the same powerful formula that has been reiterated throughout the exodus narrative (cf. 7:5), in which the formula is designed to reassure Israel and to challenge Pharaoh. Here the formula serves to impose a claim upon Israel. The event of the exodus provides the authority for the commands as well as the material claim of those commands.[101]

20:3. This verse (conventionally the first commandment) is programmatic for all Israelite reflection on obedience. Walther Zimmerli and Werner H. Schmidt have taken this command (together with the second command of vv. 4-6) as the essential command, for which all other law is exegesis, and as the *leitmotif* of OT theology.[102] We may identify four related themes.

First, the command requires Israel to mobilize all of its life, in every sphere, around one single loyalty. In the contemporary world, as in the ancient world, we practice a kind of henotheism, which lets different gods have their play in different spheres. This command insists on the integrity, coherence, and unity of all of life. Israel is a community destined to "will one thing."

Second, it is not likely that this command makes any claim about monotheism in any formal sense. That is, it does not insist that there are no

other gods.[103] It insists only that other gods must receive none of Israel's loyalty or allegiance. This command thus is in keeping with Deut 6:4, which also allows for the existence of other gods, but denies them "air time."[104]

Third, the last phrase, "before me," may also be read, "before my face." Because *face* in reference to God often means "sanctuary" or "altar," the command may mean "in my presence"—"in my shrine." On this reading, the command pertains precisely to the practice of worship and asserts that the liturgic life of Israel must be under stringent discipline in order to avoid compromise.

Fourth, H. Graf Reventlow has offered an alternative reading of this command that has considerable merit.[105] Reventlow observes that the formulation of this command is not "Thou shalt not," but rather "there will not be to you." He proposes that the statement is not an imperative command, but an indicative, whereby Yahweh in light of the exodus declares the banishment of all other gods (cf. Psalm 82 for the same motif). On this reading, the statement is a declaration of theological emancipation, whereby Israel can freely and gladly serve Yahweh, without any distracting compromise. One does not need to obey this command but only to hear and trust the good news of triumph and banishment.

20:4-6. The second command (vv. 4-6), often linked to the first, further asserts Yahweh's distinctiveness, which is to be enacted in Israel. The command, in fact, is a series of three prohibitions followed by an extended motivational clause. The three prohibitions are: You shall not make. . . . You shall not bow down. . . . You shall not serve. . . . This threefold prohibition serves as a counterpart to the formula of banishment in v. 3.

Two understandings of the commandment are

---

101. See Zimmerli, *I Am Yahweh*, 1-28.

102. Walther Zimmerli, *Old Testament Theology in Outline* (Atlanta: John Knox, 1978) 109-40; Werner H. Schmidt, *The Faith of the Old Testament* (Philadelphia: Westminster, 1983) 53-88.

103. On the emergence of monotheism in ancient Israel, see Bernhard Lang, *Monotheism and the Prophetic Minority* (Sheffield: Almond, 1983) 13-59. James A. Sanders, "Adaptable for Life: The Nature and Function of Canon," in *Magnalia Dei: The Mighty Acts of God, Essays on the Bible and Archaeology in Memory of G. Ernest Wright*, eds. Frank Moore Cross et al. (Garden City, N.Y.: Doubleday, 1976) 541-52, nicely speaks of the "monotheizing tendency" in early Israel.

104. On Deut 6:4 in relation to the commandments, see J. G. Janzen, "On the Most Important Word in the Shema," *VT* 37 (1987) 280-300; and S. Dean McBride, "The Yoke of the Kingdom: An Exposition of Deuteronomy 6:4-5," *Int* 27 (1973) 273-306.

105. H. Graf Reventlow, *Gebot und Predigt im Dekalogue* (Gütersloh: G. Mohn, 1962) 25-28.

possible. In the NRSV and NIV renderings, the command precludes "idols," the assignment of theological significance to any element of creation, the investment of ultimacy in what is not ultimate. Clearly, if "no other god" has any real power and, therefore, any real, substantive existence, it is grossly inappropriate that Israel should invest such an object with ultimacy.

The word פסל (*pesel*), however, need not be rendered "idol." It is more properly rendered "image," a visible representation of Yahweh. The temptation, then, is not the creation of a rival that detracts from Yahweh, but an attempt to locate and thereby domesticate Yahweh in a visible, controlled object. This latter reading, which is the more probable, is also more subtle. It does not fear a rival but a distortion of Yahweh's free character by an attempt to locate Yahweh and so diminish something of Yahweh's terrible freedom.

The motivational clause begins in v. 5*b*, introduced by כי (*kî,* "for"). The reason for the prohibition is Yahweh's very own character; Yahweh is a "jealous God" who will operate in uncompromised and uncontested freedom. Yahweh's jealousy is evidenced in two ways in a formula that is more fully stated in Exod 34:6-7. Negatively, this jealous God is one of deep moral seriousness who takes affront at violations of commands, so that the cost of the affront endures over the generations (34:7*b*). Positively, this jealous God is one who practices massive fidelity (חסד *ḥesed*) to those who are willing to live in covenant (34:6-7*a*). The two motivational phrases are in fact more symmetrical than the NRSV suggests, for "reject me" is in fact "hate" (שׂנא *śānē*'), as the NIV translates, thus contrasting precisely those who "love" and those who "hate" Yahweh.

Thus the idol (as rival and alternative) or the image (as localization and domestication) is an attempt to tone down Yahweh's jealousy. There are two reasons for toning down God's jealousy: resistance to God's deep moral seriousness or discomfort with God's massive fidelity. Yahweh's character, to which this command witnesses, holds to both moral seriousness and covenantal fidelity. The measure of both "punishment" and "showing steadfast love" is adherence to the command. The temptation of Israel, here precluded, is to tone down the primacy of command. Israel in covenant must trust itself to the terrible freedom of the God who will be obeyed.

20:7. The third command continues the line of the disclosure of God from the first two commands. This command is often misunderstood and misused, when it is taken to refer to "bad" or vulgar language. While "right speech" is indeed at issue, more is at stake than not cursing or using obscenities. What must be understood is that the "name" of Yahweh bespeaks God's powerful presence and purpose. The utterance of the name is the mobilization of the presence and power of God, an assumption that is still evident in prayers offered "in the name of Jesus." To make "wrongful use of the name," or as Walter Harrelson suggests, the use of the name "for mischief,"[106] means to invoke through utterance the power and purpose of Yahweh in the service of some purpose that is extraneous to Yahweh's own person. That is, the violation is to make Yahweh (who is an ultimate end) into a means for some other end. Such a practice may be done in quite pious ways (without anything like "curse") with an instrumental view of God. This command thus follows well from the first two, because all three concern seductive ways in which the God of the exodus is diminished or trivialized.

The sanction (threat) of this command is ominous indeed: Yahweh will not "acquit" those who seek to use God for their own purposes but will hold such persons guilty to perpetuity. The severity of this threat is congruent with the motivational clause of v. 5.

---

106. Harrelson, *The Ten Commandments and Human Rights,* 72-76.

REFLECTIONS

These first three commandments are preoccupied with the awesome claims of God's person. God insists, in the light of the exodus, upon being accepted, affirmed, and fully obeyed.

1. It is not always helpful in teaching and preaching the commandments to go through them one rule at a time, as though using a check list. To be sure, there is some need for specificity of interpretation. That, however, is only preliminary to the main interpretive task, which is to voice the large and demanding vision of God that defines biblical faith.

The truth of the matter is that the biblical God is not "user friendly." The theological crisis present in all our modern situations of proclamation and interpretation is that we are all "children of Feuerbach." In the nineteenth century, Ludwig Feuerbach fully articulated the hidden assumption of the Enlightenment, that God is in the end a projection of our best humanness. That Feuerbachian "betrayal" takes more than one form. The "liberal temptation" is to diminish the role of God, either to remove God from public spheres of life and leave God for interpersonal matters, or to make God an object of adoration rather than a subject who can do anything. One signal of such reductionism is the slogan that "God has no hands but ours." The reactive "conservative temptation" is the projection of a settled, sovereign God who in fact is not operative as a political character (as in the drama of the exodus) but is only a set of fixed propositions that give certitude and stability. Either way, in our shared theological failure of nerve, we end with a God very unlike the one who makes a self-disclosure here.

2. Exposition of these commandments has as its topic the voicing of the holy, jealous God of the Bible who saves and commands; a God who is an active, decisive presence in our common public life, but who in holiness is beyond all our most pious efforts at control and manipulation.[107]

There are no analogues, no parallels, no antecedents, no adequate replications or explanations for this God who confronts us in and through the narrative of liberation. It is the majestic act of "getting glory over Pharaoh" (14:4, 17) that bestows upon Yahweh the right to speak and to command. The exodus shows that Yahweh has now displaced every other loyalty, has driven from the field all rivals, and now claims full attention and full devotion from Israel. This people would not have entered history except for Yahweh's demanding solidarity against Pharaoh. The question of this faith in the modern world is whether there is a people, a concrete community, that can embrace and practice this demanding loyalty. Most of the people with whom we preach and teach are (like us) both yearning and reluctant, both ready and hesitant, to embrace these commandments that bespeak a lifetime of ceding over authority.

How, indeed, can a "mystery" be demanding? We expect a mystery to be amorphous and transcendental; we expect a demand to be coercive, visible, and political. In these three utterances, however, Yahweh is indeed holy mystery who, in the very utterance of mystery, enunciates demand.

3. This uncompromising demand is properly voiced in a world of unacknowledged polytheism. We have always lived in a world of options, alternative choices, and gods who make powerful, competing appeals. It does us no good to pretend that there are no other offers of well-being, joy, and security. In pursuit of joy, we may choose Bacchus; in pursuit of security, we may choose Mars; in pursuit of genuine love, we may choose Eros. It is clear that these choices are not Yahweh, that these are not gods who have ever wrought an Exodus or offered a covenant.

In the Christian tradition, baptism is the dramatic form of making a God choice, in which receiving a new name and making promises is choosing this liberating-covenantal faith against any other shape of life. Thus in the Christian tradition, appropriating and living out baptism means living by a single loyalty among a mass of options.

4. The second commandment, in its prohibition, inventories the heavens above, the earth beneath, and the waters under the earth (v. 4; cf. Deut 4:17-18). The triad, of course, refers to all of creation (cf. Gen 1:28). The command asserts that nothing in creation is usable in making God visible or available. God's sovereign mystery is discontinuous from everything and anything in creation. The propensity to encapsulate God in creation leads to an attempt to

---

107. See Emil Fackenheim, *God's Presence in History: Jewish Affirmations and Philosophical Reflections* (New York: Harper & Row, 1972) 8-19.

retain for ourselves control over some piece of creation. The clearest, most extensive treatment of this confusion in the Bible is Rom 1:20-25. To imagine that anything in creation could possibly embody the creator God is a result of "futile thinking" and "senseless darkened minds" (Rom 1:21). The outcome is false worship based on a lie instead of the truth (v. 20).

In contemporary church discussions, this powerful, polemical, doxological statement has often been side-tracked and related only to issues of homosexuality. The confusion of creator-creation, however, is much more profound and ominous than an argument about sexuality. Attempts to "image God" by taking creation in our own hands are much more evident in technological abuse of creation and in military exploitation, by which "God as power" comes into play without any restraining awareness that "God as power" is also "God as Holy Mystery." It may in the end be the case that the "shameless acts" men commit with men (cf. Rom 1:27-28) are not sexual as much as they are military and technological. The Mosaic prohibition against idols and images has profound sociopolitical implications, for the practice of worshiping idols is never simply a theological or liturgical matter but always spills over into social, ideological, and political practice, inevitably with the intent of partisan advantage. Carlos M. N. Eire has shown how the prohibition on idols became a driving power for Calvinism as a sociopolitical force.[108] Where the church is soft on idols, it becomes muted on social criticism.

5. The third commandment asserts that God cannot be put to use and is never a means toward an end (v. 7). The notion that the ultimate human purpose is to "glorify and enjoy God" means that God is pure end and never means. Using God's name mischievously however, is an enormous temptation, because the holy God is vulnerable to being made into an ideological tool.

108. Carlos M. N. Eire, *War Against the Idols: The Reformation of Worship from Erasmus to Calvin* (Cambridge: Cambridge University Press, 1986) esp. 276-310.

Exodus 20:8-11, "You Shall Not Do Any Work"

NIV

8"Remember the Sabbath day by keeping it holy. 9Six days you shall labor and do all your work, 10but the seventh day is a Sabbath to the LORD your God. On it you shall not do any work, neither you, nor your son or daughter, nor your manservant or maidservant, nor your animals, nor the alien within your gates. 11For in six days the LORD made the heavens and the earth, the sea, and all that is in them, but he rested on the seventh day. Therefore the LORD blessed the Sabbath day and made it holy.

NRSV

8Remember the sabbath day, and keep it holy. 9Six days you shall labor and do all your work. 10But the seventh day is a sabbath to the LORD your God; you shall not do any work—you, your son or your daughter, your male or female slave, your livestock, or the alien resident in your towns. 11For in six days the LORD made heaven and earth, the sea, and all that is in them, but rested the seventh day; therefore the LORD blessed the sabbath day and consecrated it.

COMMENTARY

The fourth commandment is conventionally included in the first tablet. However, because the sabbath command occupies such a prominent and decisive position in the Decalogue, and because it enjoins rest for humanity as well as honoring God the creator, I take it as a command that stands between and connects to both tablets.[109]

Unlike most of the other commands (see also

109. Here I follow Patrick D. Miller, *Deuteronomy, Interpretation* (Louisville: Westminster/John Knox, 1990) 79-84.

v. 12), this one is not a prohibition; rather, it enjoins Israel to positive action. Israel is to remember (זכר *zākar*). The act of remembering here, as in the remembering of the Eucharist, means to appropriate actively as a present reality. The seventh day is to be marked as "holy time"—i.e., as time completely devoted to Yahweh.

The initial command of v. 8 is explicated in three parts. There is first an acknowledgment of six legitimate days of work. Then comes the command for a day of rest for the one addressed, ostensibly a land-owning man, who will provide rest for all creation under his dominion (vv. 9-10). Finally there is a motivational clause (v. 11).

The positive command itself indicates that sabbath remembrance is in fact a complete and comprehensive work stoppage. There is no mention of worship. The way in which this day is to be acknowledged as holy—i.e., different and special—is to separate it from all days of required activity, productivity, coercive performance, self-securing, or service to other human agents. Moreover, this covenantal work stoppage is not a special privilege of the male believer. The entire society that makes up the family, village, or clan is to share publicly in this act.

How is it that a covenantal work stoppage bears witness to this self-disclosing God? The answer is given in the motivational clause: Israel rests because God rests. This God is not a workaholic; Yahweh has no need to be more secure, more sufficient, more in control, or more noticed. It is ordained in the very fabric of creation that the world is not a place of endless productivity, ambition, or anxiety. Fretheim has made the case that exodus liberation is aimed at the full restoration of peaceable creation.[110] There is no more powerful hint of that connection than in this commandment.

While the motivational clause links this teaching explicitly to creation, the preamble of v. 2 links the command to the exodus as well. Such a connection between the command and the preamble hints at a connection made much more explicit in Deut 5:12-15, where the motivation of creation has been subordinated to that of the exodus. In this text the purpose of the covenantal work stoppage is to remember and reenact the exodus. Moreover, Hans Walter Wolff has observed that the phrase "as you" in Deut 5:14 makes the sabbath a great day of equalization in which all social distinctions are overcome, and all rest alike.[111] To be sure, that nice phrase is not present in our version of the command, but it is in any case implicit. The implicit act of equalization in sabbath witnesses to the intention of the creator that creation should be a community of well-being, in which all creatures stand together, equally and in shared rest.

110. This is a main thesis of his commentary; see Fretheim, *Exodus.* See more specifically Terence E. Fretheim, "The Plagues as Ecological Signs of Historical Disaster," *JBL* 110 (1991) 385-96.

111. Hans Walter Wolff, *Anthropology of the Old Testament* (Philadelphia: Fortress, 1974) 139-40. See the helpful exposition of sabbath by Marva J. Dawn, *Keeping the Sabbath Wholly: Ceasing, Resting, Embracing, Feasting* (Grand Rapids: Eerdmans 1989).

REFLECTIONS

1. This sabbath commandment stands at mid-point between two other extended expositions of sabbath in the book of Exodus, both of which are important for explicating the command (16:5, 22-26; 31:12-17). The story of manna (16:5, 22-26) indicates that rest is possible because God gives enough food, and all who gather either little or much have equally enough. The command of 31:12-17 indicates that God needs to be "refreshed," and therefore that those made in God's image also need to have life (נפש *nepeš*) restored (cf. Pss 19:7; 23:3). Sabbath is necessary because of God's own vulnerability. Thus in sabbath, Israel relies on God's generosity and participates in God's vulnerability.

2. The sabbath command is given its foundation in the creation narrative of Gen 1:1–2:4*a*. That text, commonly taken to be exilic, is part of the development whereby Israel in exile comes to rely on sabbath as one of the two major distinguishing marks of Judaism. (The other is circumcision.) The cruciality of sabbath is further evident in Lev 26:1-2, where it is paired with making images as the preliminary to the great recital of blessings and curses. (Notice that these two verses have a double use of the formula "I am Yahweh.") In Isa 56:4, 6, moreover, sabbath is reckoned as the key mark of keeping covenant in the community after the exile.

Sabbath looms so large in exilic and post-exilic Judaism because the Jews are now politically marginal and vulnerable. They are endlessly at the behest of someone else. Sabbath becomes a way, in the midst of such vulnerability, to assert the distinctiveness of this community by a theological announcement of loyalty to Yahweh. It is also a political assertion of disengagement from the economic system of productivity that never has enough. Thus Judaism in its covenantal work stoppage practices disengagement from the socioeconomic political enterprise that in its endless productivity offers safe, secure rest and well-being.

3. Contemporary practice of sabbath is not concerned to devise a system of restrictions and "blue laws." Rather, sabbath concerns the periodic, disciplined, regular disengagement from the systems of productivity whereby the world uses people up to exhaustion. That disengagement refers also to culture-produced expectations for frantic leisure, frantic consumptions, or frantic exercise.

The pastoral issue for many persons is to develop habits and disciplines that break those patterns of behavior. Sabbath practice is not to be added on to everything else, but requires the intentional breaking of requirements that seem almost ordained in our busy life. Sabbath thus may entail the termination of routines, the disengagement from some social conventions, or even the lowering of one's standard of living. The very concreteness of sabbath is a sacrament witnessing to the reality of exodus and to the governance of the creator who has broken the restless penchant for productive activity. The healing of creation, and of our lives as creatures of God, requires a disengagement from the dominant systems of power and wealth. Sabbath is the daring recognition that with the change of sovereigns wrought in the exodus, such unrewarding expenditure of labor is no longer required. It is only a bad habit we continue in our disbelieving foolishness (cf. Luke 12:16-20).

4. This fourth commandment is commonly placed in the first tablet, honoring the majesty of God. It belongs in the sequence concerning God's sovereignty (first commandment), God's freedom (second commandment), God's holy name (third commandment), and now God's holy time (fourth commandment). It is clear, however, that the neighbor concerns of the second tablet begin here to intrude upon the first tablet. The affirmation about God's rest leads to a command about human rest. In this latter accent, sabbath serves to acknowledge and enact the peculiar worth and dignity of all creatures, and especially of human creatures. Consequently there are limits to the use of human persons, and of all creatures, as instrumental means to other ends. Sabbath is a day of special dignity, when God's creatures can luxuriate in being honored ends and not mobilized means to anything beyond themselves. In the commandments that follow, we shall see that this limit to the "usefulness" of human creatures introduced in the fourth commandment now becomes a *leitmotif* for the second tablet.

Exodus 20:12-17, Neighbor Relations

NIV	NRSV
12"Honor your father and your mother, so that you may live long in the land the LORD your God is giving you.	12Honor your father and your mother, so that your days may be long in the land that the LORD your God is giving you.
13"You shall not murder.	13You shall not murder.[a]
14"You shall not commit adultery.	14You shall not commit adultery.
15"You shall not steal.	15You shall not steal.
	a Or kill

NIV

16"You shall not give false testimony against your neighbor.

17"You shall not covet your neighbor's house. You shall not covet your neighbor's wife, or his manservant or maidservant, his ox or donkey, or anything that belongs to your neighbor."

NRSV

16You shall not bear false witness against your neighbor.

17You shall not covet your neighbor's house; you shall not covet your neighbor's wife, or male or female slave, or ox, or donkey, or anything that belongs to your neighbor.

COMMENTARY

This set of six commands includes one positive command (v. 12), followed by five prohibitions. Calvin offers that charity "contains the sum of the second tablet."[112]

20:12. God enjoins Israel at the mountain to "honor" father and mother. The command consists in an imperative followed by a motivational clause. The command concerns the problematic relationships between one generation and the next. We have seen that the Exodus narrative is understood as a tale told to ensure that the children and the children's children will know and embrace the memory of liberation (10:1-2). The book of Genesis is preoccupied with the safe transmission of blessing and promise from one generation to the next. Moreover, Michael Fishbane has suggested that the urgent command of Deut 6:4-9 evidences that the children were resistant and recalcitrant to the core teaching of Israel (cf. Ps 78:5-8).[113] And Deut 21:15-17 attests to the fact that Israel struggled with the continuity of generations and the valuing of the life-world of the parents by the children. It may be that every society struggles with this issue, but the children's loyalty is peculiarly urgent in a community whose faith works only by remembering unrepeatable events.

The command is to "honor." The Hebrew term כבד (kābēd) includes among its meanings "be heavy," suggesting the sense of "give weight to." The negative warning of 21:17 forms a suggestive counterpoint to this command, because the term curse (קלל qll) may also be rendered "to treat lightly." Such a nuance is important, because the

command does not advocate obeying or being subordinate but treating parents with appropriate seriousness. Childs concludes that it was "a command which protected parents from being driven out of the home or abused after they could no longer work."[114] (Cf. Prov 19:26.) Calvin shrewdly notes that in Eph 6:1, the commandment is quantified, "in the Lord," so that "the power of a father is so limited as that God, on whom all relationships depend, shall have the rule over fathers as well as children . . . Paul . . . indicates, that if a father enjoins anything unrighteous, obedience is freely to be denied him."[115]

The motivational clause concerns keeping the land, which is God's gift. This is the only command of the Decalogue that includes land as a motivation. Several possible connections might be made concerning this command and its motivation. First, the connection may be a quite general one, that distorted relations between the generations lead to a forfeiture of shared well-being. Second, the connection may be a quasi-legal one, suggesting that the capacity to retain the inheritance (נחלה naḥălâ) of land depends on embracing the promises of father and mother. Third, if the land is understood as a result of withdrawing from the slave economy for the sake of a covenantal, egalitarian community, then the land will be held only as long as the covenantal vision is held with passion. In any case, socioeconomic security depends on the right ordering of interpersonal relations between the generations, perhaps between the generation of power and that of vulnerability.

20:13. The command against murder is terse and unadorned. While scholars continue to sort

112. Calvin, *Commentaries*, 6-7.

113. Michael Fishbane, *Text and Texture: Close Readings of Selected Biblical Texts* (New York: Schocken, 1979) 79-83.

114. Childs, *Exodus*, 418.

115. Calvin, *Commentaries*, 8.

out the exact intent of the term *murder* (רצח *rāṣaḥ*), the main point is clear: Human life belongs to God and must be respected. Walter Harrelson (following Barth) takes a maximal view of the prohibition and interprets it broadly as "reverence for life"—i.e., all human life.[116] H. Graf Reventlow suggests that the term *murder* originally referred to blood feuds and epidemics of killings that grew out of an insatiable thirst for vengeance between clans and families.[117] Still other interpretations of this command suggest that murder is precluded within the community of covenant but that the prohibition does not apply outside of one's own community of covenant. It is entirely possible that all such distinctions, in a kind of casuistry, make too fine a point. Appeal to Gen 9:6 suggests that biblical faith has drawn an uncompromising line against the taking of another life, period. Human life is intrinsically of value and may not be ultimately violated.

20:14. The prohibition against adultery concerns distorted sexual relations, or more broadly, distorted human relations. Again, the command is so terse as to invite and require interpretation. Most narrowly construed, "adultery" consists in the violation of the wife of another man. Such a patriarchal reading understands the woman to be the property and trust of a man. For ample reason, of course, the command has been much more broadly understood in Jewish and Christian communities. Most comprehensively, the prohibition points to the recognition that sexuality is enormously wondrous and enormously dangerous. The wonder of sexuality is available in a community only if it is practiced respectfully and under discipline. The danger of sexuality is that it is capable of evoking desires that are destructive of persons and of communal relations. It is inevitable that such a command will be subject to ongoing dispute, because around the subject of freedom and discipline in sexuality we deal with the most intense and elemental mystery of human existence. There is in this command neither license for permissiveness nor a puritanical restrictiveness. Everything else is left to the interpretive community.

20:15. The eighth command on stealing is characteristically terse. On the face of it, the commandment concerns respect for the property of another. It does not probe behind the social

fact of "property" to notice, as Marx has done so poignantly, the probability that private property arises regularly from violence. It is enough that what is possessed by another must not be seized.

On the basis of Exod 21:16 and Deut 24:7, Albrecht Alt has proposed that the original form of the prohibition was "Thou shalt not steal a person."[118] The gain of such an interpretation is that it focuses on the cruciality of the human and is not drawn away toward lesser "objects." It is, perhaps, neither necessary nor wise to choose between a more conventional focus on property and Alt's focus. The materiality of Israel's faith recognizes that selfhood includes the necessary "goods" to make a life of dignity possible. That, of course, leaves the vexed question of relation between the essential goods of the "have nots" and the extravagant goods of the "haves." This command cannot be used as a defense of "private property" without reference to the kinds of sharing that are required for available human community. Harrelson concludes: "The commandment not to steal means, in effect, that persons are not to whittle down, eat away at, the selfhood of individuals or of families or of communities."[119]

20:16. The ninth commandment (v. 16) is not a general command against "lying" but concerns courtroom practice. The prohibition understands that a free, independent, and healthy judiciary system is indispensable for a viable community. The courtroom must be a place where the truth is told and where social reality is not distorted through devious manipulation or ideological perversion. It is remarkable in this list of prohibitions that concern the sanctity of human life, the mystery of sexuality, and the maintenance of property, that courts should be so prominent. The prohibition, however, is a recognition that community life is not possible unless there is an arena in which there is public confidence that social reality will be reliably described and reported.

The sphere of this command is narrowly circumscribed. Truth-telling concerns "your neighbor"—i.e., a fellow member of the covenant

---

116. Harrelson, *The Ten Commandments and Human Rights,* 109-10.
117. Reventlow, *Gebot und Predigt,* 71-77.

118. See the summary review by Robert Karl Gnuse, *You Shall Not Steal: Community and Property in the Biblical Tradition* (Maryknoll, N.Y.: Orbis, 1985). While Alt has been credited with this reading of the command, in fact the interpretation of "kidnapping" was already proposed in early rabbinic interpretation. See M. H. Gottstein, "Du sollst nicht stehlen," *TZ* 9 (1953) 394-95; and Jacob J. Petuchowski, "A Note on W. Kessler's Problematik des Dekalogs," *VT* 7 (1957) 397-98.
119. Harrelson, *The Ten Commandments and Human Rights,* 42.

community. The neighbor is not to be "used" by lying in order to enhance one's own interest. Community requires drawing a line against private interest in order to make social relations workable.

20:17. The tenth commandment, on coveting, is somewhat different from the other elements of the second tablet. It concerns the destructive power of desire. It is not helpful, however, to interpret "desire" as a vague, undifferentiated attitude. Rather, it here concerns desire acted upon publicly, whereby one reaches for that which is not properly one's own. Such reaching inevitably destroys community. The text knows that humans are indeed driven by desire. The commandment regards desire in and of itself as no good or bad thing; its quality depends on its object. The tale of Genesis 3 is the tale of desire misdirected (cf. v. 3).

Notice that desire in ancient Israel is characteristically not directed toward sexual objects (as we might expect) but pertains primarily to eco-nomics. Its concern is to curb the drive to acquisitiveness. Thus the object of desire may be silver and gold (Deut 7:25; Josh 7:21) or land (Exod 34:24; Mic 2:2).

The supreme and legitimate "desire" of Israel is to do the will and purpose of Yahweh.

In this prohibition, the primary object of desire is the neighbor's house. That "house," however, includex wife (reckoned in a patriarchal society as property), slaves, and working animals. The command expects that within a community of genuine covenanting, the drive of desire will be displaced by the honoring of neighbor, by the sharing of goods, and by the acceptance of one's own possessions as adequate. This commandment, placed in final position in the Decalogue, is perhaps intended as the climactic statement of the whole, referring to Yahweh's claims at the beginning (v. 1). Yahweh's victory over the Egyptian gods in the same action defeated the spiritual power of coveting.

REFLECTIONS

This second tablet, anticipated in the fourth commandment, indicates that the holiness of God puts God beyond the reach of Israel, and *mutatis mutandis,* the intrinsic worth of human persons as creatures of God puts humans beyond the reach of abuse and exploitation.

The second tablet is a magisterial assertion that human life is situated in a community of rights and responsibilities that is willed by God. Within that community, human life in all its ambiguity and inscrutability is endlessly precious and must not be violated. This affirmation seems so obvious that we are reluctant to voice it. It is now clear that in the obduracy of totalitarian society and in the rapaciousness of market economy, a humane life of shared rights and responsibilities is exceedingly fragile. The interpretive task is to show that this fragile bonding in covenant that guarantees dignity and well-being is a live possibility among us. The second tablet is indeed an articulation of a more excellent way; it is a way in which human life is intrinsically worthy of respect, in which human persons are honored ends rather than abused means, and in which rapacious desire is properly curbed for the sake of viable community.

1. The fifth commandment concerns the struggle between the generations, a struggle that is inherently filled with tension (v. 12). On the one hand, there can be a kind of traditionalism that submits excessively to "the way we were." On the other hand, there can be a one-generation narcissism that imagines nothing important happened until "us." That intergenerational tension requires a seriousness that does not simply capitulate but that honors in freedom and response. In the angel's announcement to Zechariah, a remarkable transposition of the relation of the generations is anticipated: "With the spirit and power of Elijah he will go before him, to turn the hearts of parents to their children, and the disobedient to the wisdom of the righteous, to make ready a people prepared for the Lord" (Luke 1:17 NRSV).

Here it is not the children who submit to the parents, but the parents who are "turned" to the children. This assertion of the angel does not override Moses' command. Rather, the two statements are in tension, and adjudication requires that both parties, parents and children, must be engaged in the process. The commandment precludes a new generation that disregards the parents and does not give them due weight. The angel's poem precludes a blind, mechanical submissiveness of children to parents.[120] "Honor" is a more delicate, transactive maneuver, whereby both parties grow in dignity through the process.

2. The prohibition on killing asserts that human life is valuable to God, and under God's protective custody (v. 13). No doubt distinctions and differentiations are to be made in enacting this command. The most obvious of these now before us concern capital punishment, war, euthanasia, and abortion. The interpretive community is of no single mind on these great questions, and no consensus is in prospect. The commandment itself states a non-negotiable principle and nothing more. That, however, is a great deal in a society where life is cheap, where technology is impersonal, where economic greed is unbridled, where bombs are "smart," and where ideology is powerful. The murder that makes the newspapers signifies a breakdown of the human infrastructure, which legitimates brutality. The murder behind the headlines—i.e., the killing that happens a little at a time, mostly unnoticed and unacknowledged—is kept ideologically obscure. Such slow, unnoticed destruction diminishes human life among those not powerful enough to defend themselves. The interpretive issue may be this: If human life is precious, what public policies are required in order to enhance and protect it? The old-fashioned responses of employment, housing, and health care are not remote from this command. Calvin counts on the positive application of this command, "that we should not only live at peace with men . . . but also should aid, as far as we can, the miserable who are unjustly oppressed, and should endeavor to resist the wicked, lest they should injure men."[121]

Jesus intensified the command to include anger (Matt 5:21-26; cf. 1 John 3:15). One wonders whether in our society Jesus might have focused not on anger but on cynical indifference that is sanctified by a greedy, uncaring individualism that is in its own way killing.

3. The prohibition against adultery concerns the primal mystery of human existence and viable human relationships (v. 14). Our interpretive concern, of course, moves beyond the patriarchal assumption that operates with a double standard. Fidelity should be the guiding theme of interpretation of this command, as distinct from legal arrangements that bespeak old property practices and rights. Formal, legal relations of marriage provide the most durable context and basis for such fidelity. They do not, however, in and of themselves amount to fidelity. Our social context has few models or norms for fidelity of a genuine conventional kind. (It is for that reason that the relation of Yahweh-Israel or Christ-church have become such powerful models and metaphors, though these metaphors are beset with enormous problems in their patriarchal articulation.)

Continuing reflection on this commandment, which concerns genuine fidelity, may go in two directions. On the one hand, there is a struggle with legally constituted relations (marriage), which are not always relations of fidelity because of abusive behavior and a lack of authentic mutuality. On the other hand, there is a struggle concerning the possibility of a genuine relation of fidelity that is outside the conventional sanctions of legal marriage. It is clear on both counts that interpretive issues are not simple and one-dimensional.

In its fullest interpretation, the command against adultery envisions covenantal relations of mutuality that are genuinely life-giving, nurturing, enhancing, and respectful. Such a notion of long-term trust is treated as almost passé in a narcissistic society, preoccupied with individual freedom and satisfaction.

---

120. Alice Miller, *Thou Shalt Not Be Aware: Society's Betrayal of the Child* (New York: New American Library, 1986), has suggested that the command to honor parents has functioned programatically as a warrant for the abuse of children by parents. Thus the corrective proposed, that the parents turn to the children, counters such a potentially abusive misreading.

121. Calvin, *Commentaries,* 21.

4. There are many ways to "steal a self" (v. 15). Such a focus in the eighth commandment raises important issues regarding what it takes to make a self socially viable. We are, of course, aware of theft and household burglary. We are increasingly aware of white-collar crime whereby large sums of money and property are seized in seemingly "victimless" crimes. Serious covenantal relations preclude such activity.

We must take care, however, that our interpretation of this commandment is not a mere defense of private property and the status quo as a justification for the unjust distribution of goods. Faithful interpretation requires us to probe even the subtle forms of "theft" that rob persons of their future. Here are three facets of theft to which the commandment may point.

First, the terrible inequity of haves and have nots in our society (as in many others) means that babies born into acute poverty are at the outset denied any realistic chance of surviving in a market economy. Because we believe in the goodness of God's creation, we believe such children are intended by God to have what is necessary for an abundant life. Very often, however, they do not—because they have been robbed of their future. They are not robbed by "bad people"; they are robbed by power arrangements and structures that have long since relegated them to the permanent underclass. Over such arrangements and structures, the command speaks out: "Thou shalt not steal!"

Second, a like theft continues to occur between developed and developing nations, whereby a long-term pattern of deathly dependence is fostered. For a long time Third World countries have been treated only as colonies, natural resources, or markets, kept in a dependency relation, so that nearly all benefits of the relation go to the developed economy and its colonial agents. Patterns of military control and credit arrangements guarantee not only long-term dependency but a predictable cycle of poverty, hunger, and endless destabilization. There is no doubt that we in the West are the primary beneficiaries of such practice.

Third, in interpersonal relations that lack mutuality, characteristically there is an aggressor and a victim. In that unequal relation, which is carried on by invisible but brutal power, the "self" of the victim is endlessly stolen and diminished. The radical vision of Moses is that covenantal practice does not permit these modes of destructive power in relations, public or interpersonal.

5. The three commands on killing, adultery, and stealing together constitute something of a special group. Not only are they the most tersely expressed commands, but also they all address the ways in which vulnerable persons in community are assaulted, diminished, and destroyed. Such actions, condemned in these commands, are all acts of uncurbed power, which fails to recognize that the perpetrator and the victim share a commonality and a solidarity that preclude destructiveness. Contemporary interpretation need not get bogged down in casuistry about this or that command, but can focus on the shared solidarity that precludes destructiveness, either in the transactions of public (economic) power or in the intimacy of interpersonal relations.

6. Viable human community depends on truth telling (v. 16). This commandment is not concerned with "white lies," but the public portrayal of reality that is not excessively skewed by self-interest or party ideology. The primary point of reference is the court, where witnesses speak and testimony is given. The commandment insists that courts must resist every distortion of reality, every collusion with vested interest (cf. 18:21; Pss 15:2; 24:4), which makes such truth telling prerequisite to worship.

More broadly construed, the commandment enjoins members of the covenant community not to distort reality to each other. The major pertinence of the prohibition in our society is the collapse of truth into propaganda in the service of ideology.[122] That is, public versions of truth are not

---

122. See the critical analysis of propaganda as deception by Jacques Ellul, *Propaganda: The Formation of Men's Attitudes* (New York: Knopf, 1965). See also Neil Postman, *Amusing Ourselves to Death: Public Discourse in the Age of Show Business* (New York: Penguin, 1986).

---

committed to a portrayal of reality, but to a rendering that serves a partisan interest. Such a practice may take many forms. Among the more blatant practices of "false witness" in recent times has been the use of propaganda through which defeat has been described as military victory or reporting has simply been silenced, so that no truth need be told at all.[123] Such a public tendency is not new. Isaiah 5:20 already addresses those who distorted reality (self-)deception.

Moreover, Jeremiah understood that religious leadership is equally tempted to deception, which both advances institutional interests and seeks to give credence to theological claims (see Jer 6:13-14; 8:10-11). The commandment continues to expect that there is a viable alternative to this deceptiveness in public life.

7. The final commandment on coveting does not address general envy (v. 17), but concerns a kind of acquisitiveness that destabilizes the property and, therefore, the life of another. Marvin Chaney has shown that the oracle of Mic 2:1-5 is, in fact, an exposition of the command.[124] That is, the command concerns primarily land and the development of large estates at the expense of vulnerable neighbors.

The propensity to covet in our society is enacted through an unbridled consumerism that believes that the main activity of human life is to accumulate, use, and enjoy more and more of the available resources of the earth. An undisciplined individualism has taught us that we are entitled to whatever we may want no matter who else may be hurt. Such individualism, however, is driven by a market ideology based on an elemental assumption of scarcity. If there is a scarcity of goods needed for life, then energy and passion are generated to gather and accumulate all that one can (cf. 16:19-21). M. Douglas Meeks has shown that the ideology of scarcity, which drives our economy, is, in the end, an act of theological doubt that does not believe that God's providential generosity is finally reliable.[125] This commandment summons the faithful to break with the practice of acquisitive individualism and to reject the ideology of scarcity upon which it is based. Thus the commandment requires a massive repentance that is theological in substance, but that is manifested economically.

This commandment functions as a crucial conclusion to the entire Decalogue. We may note two important connections to the preceding commands. First, this command is related to the command on sabbath. Whereas coveting is an activity of untrusting restlessness, sabbath resists such anxious activity.

Second, the decision to cease coveting relates to the first commandment. Giving up such a fearful ideological pursuit cannot be accomplished by an act of will. Rather, it may grow out of an affirmation that the powers of coveting and greedy consumption have been defeated. Such powers, then, need have no control over us. In Col 3:5 (NRSV), the first and tenth commandments are nicely joined: "Put to death, therefore, whatever in you is earthly . . . greed (which is idolatry)." Violating the tenth command derives from a violation of the first.

8. In interpreting any of the commandments, it is important to discern clearly the position they occupy in biblical faith. It is possible to conclude simply that these are the most foundational absolutes of God's purpose in the world. That is, the commandments occupy a peculiar and decisive claim, articulated in the categories of revelation. They disclose the non-negotiable will of God.

Alongside that claim, George Mendenhall's political understanding of the Decalogue may be

123. See David Halberstam, *The Best and the Brightest* (New York: Random House, 1972); Neil Sheeham, *A Bright Shining Lie: John Paul Vann and America in Vietnam* (New York: Random House, 1988).

124. Marvin L. Chaney, "You Shall Not Covet Your Neighbor's House," *Pacific Theological Review* 15 (Winter 1982) 3-13. See also D. N. Premnath, "Latifundialization and Isaiah 5:8-10," *JSOT* 40 (1988) 49-60.

125. M. Douglas Meeks, *God the Economist: The Doctrine of God and Political Economy* (Minneapolis: Fortress, 1989) 170-77 and *passim.*

useful. Mendenhall has proposed that these ten commands are "policy" statements.[126] They are not in themselves guidelines for specific action, but provide the ground and framework from which specifics may be drawn. Taking them as policies links the commands quite clearly to the concrete community Moses formed. This means that, rather than contextless absolutes, they are proposals that counter other kinds of policies. Such an understanding invites adherents to this covenant to recognize that they have made, and are making, peculiar and distinctive ethical decisions related to a core decision about covenantal existence.

There are important ecclesiological implications in such a recognition. In fact, in some older Christian liturgies, the commandments are recited at baptism. In baptism, the believer pledges allegiance to a vision of social reality that is rooted in God's wonders and deeply at odds with the dominant assumptions of an acquisitive, individualistic society. The community of faith in our time urgently needs to recover the programmatic intentionality of these commands.

9. In Matt 19:16-22, Mark 10:17-22, and Luke 18:18-30, Jesus alludes to the commandments, though he does not cite them all. Two matters strike us in reading those narratives. First, the reference to specific commandments is kept selective. Harrelson observes that Jesus uses only those commands that pertain to the rich—i.e., the one to whom he speaks.[127] Second, the commandments are, for Jesus, a first-level demand, preparatory to the more rigorous demand, "Go, sell, give, come follow." In these narratives, the commands are not considered unattainable modes of conduct; they are, rather, the threshold to more serious discipleship and a step on the demanding way to "eternal life"!

126. George E. Mendenhall, *Law and Covenant in Israel and the Ancient Near East,* 5-6. See his fuller explication of the decisive difference made by these "policies" in Mendenhall, "The Conflict Between Value Systems and Social Control," in *Unity and Diversity: Essays in the History, Literature, and Religion of the Ancient Near East,* eds. Hans Goedicke and J. J. M. Roberts (Baltimore: Johns Hopkins University Press, 1975) 169-80.

127. Harrelson, *The Ten Commandments and Human Rights,* 162-64.

EXODUS 20:18-21, MOSES AS MEDIATOR

NIV	NRSV
18When the people saw the thunder and lightning and heard the trumpet and saw the mountain in smoke, they trembled with fear. They stayed at a distance 19and said to Moses, "Speak to us yourself and we will listen. But do not have God speak to us or we will die." 20Moses said to the people, "Do not be afraid. God has come to test you, so that the fear of God will be with you to keep you from sinning." 21The people remained at a distance, while Moses approached the thick darkness where God was.	18When all the people witnessed the thunder and lightning, the sound of the trumpet, and the mountain smoking, they were afraid[a] and trembled and stood at a distance, 19and said to Moses, "You speak to us, and we will listen; but do not let God speak to us, or we will die." 20Moses said to the people, "Do not be afraid; for God has come only to test you and to put the fear of him upon you so that you do not sin." 21Then the people stood at a distance, while Moses drew near to the thick darkness where God was. a Sam Gk Syr Vg: MT *they saw*

COMMENTARY

This transitional section consists of a brief narrative about the response of the people to the theophanic coming of Yahweh (19:16-19). While these verses may assume the giving of the commands in 20:1-17, there is no mention of that. For this reason, critical scholarship has often judged this unit to be displaced from the end of chapter 19, before the Decalogue.[128] The fact that it comes *after* the Decalogue serves to enhance the Ten Commandments as words from God's own mouth. In 19:16-19, Israel witnesses thunder, lightning, trumpets, and a smoking mountain, and these items are now reiterated. The people's response is that they see, they tremble, and they keep their distance.

In their fear, the people move to secure protection from Yahweh in the person of Moses (v. 19); they ask Moses to be the go-between. Perhaps, this proposal fulfills God's resolve to Moses in 19:9. Now Israel will "trust" Moses (cf. 14:31). His response to Israel's request is indirect; Moses, in effect, assures Israel that God will not destroy them, but only wants to find out whether their faith is serious (cf. 14:13-14). (According to source analysis, this testing of Israel is parallel to the testing of Abraham in Gen 22:1-14.) While the narrative does not explicitly say that Moses has agreed to be a mediator, v. 21 confirms the fact. Moses is near, and Israel is distant. Israel will not again be exposed to the direct presence of God.

Two matters are important in this narrative unit. First, the office of the mediator is authorized. Hans-Joachim Kraus has made the case that this authorization is not only for the person of Moses, but for a continuing office of mediator, likely

occupied subsequently by many persons.[129] The "presence," from now on, will be ordered, formal, and to some extent institutionalized. In the ongoing life of the biblical community, "presence" is characteristically channeled through a recognized instrument. While this led to christology in the Christian tradition, in the Jewish tradition that mediation is through the authority of torah or, in the Priestly tradition, through the priesthood.[130]

Second, an unspoken outcome of the sequence of theophany (19:16-25), commands (20:1-17), and mediation (20:18-21) is the fact that the Decalogue receives a stunningly distinctive place in the tradition. Before this proclamation, there was no formal command. After this, there was command only through mediation (as in 21:1–23:33). Consequently, 20:1-17 stands alone as the only direct, unmediated address of command from Yahweh to Israel. This is the only speech heard directly by Israel. The "ten words" thus are unique as "direct revelation." All the rest is exegesis. Commandments given subsequently by the mediator will be important, but cannot rival in authority this direct address, which constitutes the core of Yahweh's intent and charter for Israel's covenantal existence.

128. See Childs, *Exodus,* 351-60.

129. Hans-Joachim Kraus, *Die prophetische Verkündigung des Rechts in Israel,* Theologische Studien 51 (Zollikon: Evangelischer Verlag, 1957). See James Muilenburg, "The 'Office' of the Prophet in Ancient Israel," in *The Bible in Modern Scholarship,* ed. J. Philip Hyatt (Nashville: Abingdon, 1965) 74-97.

130. See James A. Sanders, "Torah and Christ," *Int* 29 (1975) 372-90.

REFLECTIONS

1. The narrative of theophany in 19:16-25 suggests that encounter with the Holy One of Israel is ominous and dreadful. The response to the theophany in 20:18-19 affirms the awesome reality of God, which is often trivialized in our "therapeutic" propensity.

2. The characteristic mode of meeting as mediated regularly precludes immediacy with God. This motif may give us pause, given the easy religiosity now evident in our society. Many folk imagine an easily available God who may be readily "experienced." Mediation, by contrast, suggests something like an audience gained with a person of majesty, before whom extra care must be taken.

3. The office of mediator, one who will willingly stand at risk between God and the community, provides a category for the Christian claim concerning Jesus. Jesus is, in a variety of theological modes, understood as the mediator who "opens a way" to the presence of God (see Heb 7:26; 10:20). The argument in Hebrews asserts both the cruciality of the mediator and the direct access Jesus provides to God. A proper theology, of course, handles this tension by the affirmation that this mediator is ultimate and decisive and has dispelled the need for any other mediator. As Moses gives Israel assurance in v. 20, so Jesus offers such assurance with a world-transforming, "Do not be afraid."

EXODUS 20:22–23:19, THE COVENANT CODE

NIV

²²Then the LORD said to Moses, "Tell the Israelites this: 'You have seen for yourselves that I have spoken to you from heaven: ²³Do not make any gods to be alongside me; do not make for yourselves gods of silver or gods of gold.

²⁴" 'Make an altar of earth for me and sacrifice on it your burnt offerings and fellowship offerings,ᵃ your sheep and goats and your cattle. Wherever I cause my name to be honored, I will come to you and bless you. ²⁵If you make an altar of stones for me, do not build it with dressed stones, for you will defile it if you use a tool on it. ²⁶And do not go up to my altar on steps, lest your nakedness be exposed on it.'

21 "These are the laws you are to set before them:

²"If you buy a Hebrew servant, he is to serve you for six years. But in the seventh year, he shall go free, without paying anything. ³If he comes alone, he is to go free alone; but if he has a wife when he comes, she is to go with him. ⁴If his master gives him a wife and she bears him sons or daughters, the woman and her children shall belong to her master, and only the man shall go free.

⁵"But if the servant declares, 'I love my master and my wife and children and do not want to go free,' ⁶then his master must take him before the judges.ᵇ He shall take him to the door or the doorpost and pierce his ear with an awl. Then he will be his servant for life.

⁷"If a man sells his daughter as a servant, she is not to go free as menservants do. ⁸If she does not please the master who has selected her for himself,ᶜ he must let her be redeemed. He has no right to sell her to foreigners, because he has

ᵃ24 Traditionally *peace offerings*   ᵇ6 Or *before God*
ᶜ8 Or *master so that he does not choose her*

NRSV

22The LORD said to Moses: Thus you shall say to the Israelites: "You have seen for yourselves that I spoke with you from heaven. ²³You shall not make gods of silver alongside me, nor shall you make for yourselves gods of gold. ²⁴You need make for me only an altar of earth and sacrifice on it your burnt offerings and your offerings of well-being, your sheep and your oxen; in every place where I cause my name to be remembered I will come to you and bless you. ²⁵But if you make for me an altar of stone, do not build it of hewn stones; for if you use a chisel upon it you profane it. ²⁶You shall not go up by steps to my altar, so that your nakedness may not be exposed on it."

21 These are the ordinances that you shall set before them:

2When you buy a male Hebrew slave, he shall serve six years, but in the seventh he shall go out a free person, without debt. ³If he comes in single, he shall go out single; if he comes in married, then his wife shall go out with him. ⁴If his master gives him a wife and she bears him sons or daughters, the wife and her children shall be her master's and he shall go out alone. ⁵But if the slave declares, "I love my master, my wife, and my children; I will not go out a free person," ⁶then his master shall bring him before God.ᵃ He shall be brought to the door or the doorpost; and his master shall pierce his ear with an awl; and he shall serve him for life.

7When a man sells his daughter as a slave, she shall not go out as the male slaves do. ⁸If she does not please her master, who designated her for himself, then he shall let her be redeemed; he shall have no right to sell her to a foreign people, since he has dealt unfairly with her. ⁹If he designates her for his son, he shall deal with her as

ᵃ Or *to the judges*

NIV

broken faith with her. ⁹If he selects her for his son, he must grant her the rights of a daughter. ¹⁰If he marries another woman, he must not deprive the first one of her food, clothing and marital rights. ¹¹If he does not provide her with these three things, she is to go free, without any payment of money.

¹²"Anyone who strikes a man and kills him shall surely be put to death. ¹³However, if he does not do it intentionally, but God lets it happen, he is to flee to a place I will designate. ¹⁴But if a man schemes and kills another man deliberately, take him away from my altar and put him to death.

¹⁵"Anyone who attacks*a* his father or his mother must be put to death.

¹⁶"Anyone who kidnaps another and either sells him or still has him when he is caught must be put to death.

¹⁷"Anyone who curses his father or mother must be put to death.

¹⁸"If men quarrel and one hits the other with a stone or with his fist*b* and he does not die but is confined to bed, ¹⁹the one who struck the blow will not be held responsible if the other gets up and walks around outside with his staff; however, he must pay the injured man for the loss of his time and see that he is completely healed.

²⁰"If a man beats his male or female slave with a rod and the slave dies as a direct result, he must be punished, ²¹but he is not to be punished if the slave gets up after a day or two, since the slave is his property.

²²"If men who are fighting hit a pregnant woman and she gives birth prematurely*c* but there is no serious injury, the offender must be fined whatever the woman's husband demands and the court allows. ²³But if there is serious injury, you are to take life for life, ²⁴eye for eye, tooth for tooth, hand for hand, foot for foot, ²⁵burn for burn, wound for wound, bruise for bruise.

²⁶"If a man hits a manservant or maidservant in the eye and destroys it, he must let the servant go free to compensate for the eye. ²⁷And if he knocks out the tooth of a manservant or maidservant, he must let the servant go free to compensate for the tooth.

²⁸"If a bull gores a man or a woman to death,

NRSV

with a daughter. ¹⁰If he takes another wife to himself, he shall not diminish the food, clothing, or marital rights of the first wife.*a* ¹¹And if he does not do these three things for her, she shall go out without debt, without payment of money.

12Whoever strikes a person mortally shall be put to death. ¹³If it was not premeditated, but came about by an act of God, then I will appoint for you a place to which the killer may flee. ¹⁴But if someone willfully attacks and kills another by treachery, you shall take the killer from my altar for execution.

15Whoever strikes father or mother shall be put to death.

16Whoever kidnaps a person, whether that person has been sold or is still held in possession, shall be put to death.

17Whoever curses father or mother shall be put to death.

18When individuals quarrel and one strikes the other with a stone or fist so that the injured party, though not dead, is confined to bed, ¹⁹but recovers and walks around outside with the help of a staff, then the assailant shall be free of liability, except to pay for the loss of time, and to arrange for full recovery.

20When a slaveowner strikes a male or female slave with a rod and the slave dies immediately, the owner shall be punished. ²¹But if the slave survives a day or two, there is no punishment; for the slave is the owner's property.

22When people who are fighting injure a pregnant woman so that there is a miscarriage, and yet no further harm follows, the one responsible shall be fined what the woman's husband demands, paying as much as the judges determine. ²³If any harm follows, then you shall give life for life, ²⁴eye for eye, tooth for tooth, hand for hand, foot for foot, ²⁵burn for burn, wound for wound, stripe for stripe.

26When a slaveowner strikes the eye of a male or female slave, destroying it, the owner shall let the slave go, a free person, to compensate for the eye. ²⁷If the owner knocks out a tooth of a male or female slave, the slave shall be let go, a free person, to compensate for the tooth.

28When an ox gores a man or a woman to

a15 Or kills *b18 Or with a tool* *c22 Or she has a miscarriage*

a Heb of her

NIV

the bull must be stoned to death, and its meat must not be eaten. But the owner of the bull will not be held responsible. ²⁹If, however, the bull has had the habit of goring and the owner has been warned but has not kept it penned up and it kills a man or woman, the bull must be stoned and the owner also must be put to death. ³⁰However, if payment is demanded of him, he may redeem his life by paying whatever is demanded. ³¹This law also applies if the bull gores a son or daughter. ³²If the bull gores a male or female slave, the owner must pay thirty shekels*a* of silver to the master of the slave, and the bull must be stoned.

³³"If a man uncovers a pit or digs one and fails to cover it and an ox or a donkey falls into it, ³⁴the owner of the pit must pay for the loss; he must pay its owner, and the dead animal will be his.

³⁵"If a man's bull injures the bull of another and it dies, they are to sell the live one and divide both the money and the dead animal equally. ³⁶However, if it was known that the bull had the habit of goring, yet the owner did not keep it penned up, the owner must pay, animal for animal, and the dead animal will be his.

22 "If a man steals an ox or a sheep and slaughters it or sells it, he must pay back five head of cattle for the ox and four sheep for the sheep.

²"If a thief is caught breaking in and is struck so that he dies, the defender is not guilty of bloodshed; ³but if it happens*b* after sunrise, he is guilty of bloodshed.

"A thief must certainly make restitution, but if he has nothing, he must be sold to pay for his theft.

⁴"If the stolen animal is found alive in his possession—whether ox or donkey or sheep—he must pay back double.

⁵"If a man grazes his livestock in a field or vineyard and lets them stray and they graze in another man's field, he must make restitution from the best of his own field or vineyard.

⁶"If a fire breaks out and spreads into thornbushes so that it burns shocks of grain or standing grain or the whole field, the one who started the fire must make restitution.

a32 That is, about 12 ounces (about 0.3 kilogram) b3 Or if he strikes him

NRSV

death, the ox shall be stoned, and its flesh shall not be eaten; but the owner of the ox shall not be liable. ²⁹If the ox has been accustomed to gore in the past, and its owner has been warned but has not restrained it, and it kills a man or a woman, the ox shall be stoned, and its owner also shall be put to death. ³⁰If a ransom is imposed on the owner, then the owner shall pay whatever is imposed for the redemption of the victim's life. ³¹If it gores a boy or a girl, the owner shall be dealt with according to this same rule. ³²If the ox gores a male or female slave, the owner shall pay to the slaveowner thirty shekels of silver, and the ox shall be stoned.

33If someone leaves a pit open, or digs a pit and does not cover it, and an ox or a donkey falls into it, ³⁴the owner of the pit shall make restitution, giving money to its owner, but keeping the dead animal.

35If someone's ox hurts the ox of another, so that it dies, then they shall sell the live ox and divide the price of it; and the dead animal they shall also divide. ³⁶But if it was known that the ox was accustomed to gore in the past, and its owner has not restrained it, the owner shall restore ox for ox, but keep the dead animal.

22 *a*When someone steals an ox or a sheep, and slaughters it or sells it, the thief shall pay five oxen for an ox, and four sheep for a sheep.*b* The thief shall make restitution, but if unable to do so, shall be sold for the theft. ⁴When the animal, whether ox or donkey or sheep, is found alive in the thief's possession, the thief shall pay double.

2ᶜIf a thief is found breaking in, and is beaten to death, no bloodguilt is incurred; ³but if it happens after sunrise, bloodguilt is incurred.

5When someone causes a field or vineyard to be grazed over, or lets livestock loose to graze in someone else's field, restitution shall be made from the best in the owner's field or vineyard.

6When fire breaks out and catches in thorns so that the stacked grain or the standing grain or the field is consumed, the one who started the fire shall make full restitution.

7When someone delivers to a neighbor money

a Ch 21.37 in Heb b Verses 2, 3, and 4 rearranged thus: 3b, 4, 2, 3a c Ch 22.1 in Heb

NIV

7"If a man gives his neighbor silver or goods for safekeeping and they are stolen from the neighbor's house, the thief, if he is caught, must pay back double. 8But if the thief is not found, the owner of the house must appear before the judges[a] to determine whether he has laid his hands on the other man's property. 9In all cases of illegal possession of an ox, a donkey, a sheep, a garment, or any other lost property about which somebody says, 'This is mine,' both parties are to bring their cases before the judges. The one whom the judges declare[b] guilty must pay back double to his neighbor.

10"If a man gives a donkey, an ox, a sheep or any other animal to his neighbor for safekeeping and it dies or is injured or is taken away while no one is looking, 11the issue between them will be settled by the taking of an oath before the Lord that the neighbor did not lay hands on the other person's property. The owner is to accept this, and no restitution is required. 12But if the animal was stolen from the neighbor, he must make restitution to the owner. 13If it was torn to pieces by a wild animal, he shall bring in the remains as evidence and he will not be required to pay for the torn animal.

14"If a man borrows an animal from his neighbor and it is injured or dies while the owner is not present, he must make restitution. 15But if the owner is with the animal, the borrower will not have to pay. If the animal was hired, the money paid for the hire covers the loss.

16"If a man seduces a virgin who is not pledged to be married and sleeps with her, he must pay the bride-price, and she shall be his wife. 17If her father absolutely refuses to give her to him, he must still pay the bride-price for virgins.

18"Do not allow a sorceress to live.

19"Anyone who has sexual relations with an animal must be put to death.

20"Whoever sacrifices to any god other than the Lord must be destroyed.[c]

21"Do not mistreat an alien or oppress him, for you were aliens in Egypt.

22"Do not take advantage of a widow or an orphan. 23If you do and they cry out to me, I will

a8 Or before God; also in verse 9   b9 Or whom God declares
c20 The Hebrew term refers to the irrevocable giving over of things or persons to the Lord, often by totally destroying them.

NRSV

or goods for safekeeping, and they are stolen from the neighbor's house, then the thief, if caught, shall pay double. 8If the thief is not caught, the owner of the house shall be brought before God,[a] to determine whether or not the owner had laid hands on the neighbor's goods.

9In any case of disputed ownership involving ox, donkey, sheep, clothing, or any other loss, of which one party says, "This is mine," the case of both parties shall come before God;[a] the one whom God condemns[b] shall pay double to the other.

10When someone delivers to another a donkey, ox, sheep, or any other animal for safekeeping, and it dies or is injured or is carried off, without anyone seeing it, 11an oath before the Lord shall decide between the two of them that the one has not laid hands on the property of the other; the owner shall accept the oath, and no restitution shall be made. 12But if it was stolen, restitution shall be made to its owner. 13If it was mangled by beasts, let it be brought as evidence; restitution shall not be made for the mangled remains.

14When someone borrows an animal from another and it is injured or dies, the owner not being present, full restitution shall be made. 15If the owner was present, there shall be no restitution; if it was hired, only the hiring fee is due.

16When a man seduces a virgin who is not engaged to be married, and lies with her, he shall give the bride-price for her and make her his wife. 17But if her father refuses to give her to him, he shall pay an amount equal to the bride-price for virgins.

18You shall not permit a female sorcerer to live.

19Whoever lies with an animal shall be put to death.

20Whoever sacrifices to any god, other than the Lord alone, shall be devoted to destruction.

21You shall not wrong or oppress a resident alien, for you were aliens in the land of Egypt. 22You shall not abuse any widow or orphan. 23If you do abuse them, when they cry out to me, I will surely heed their cry; 24my wrath will burn, and I will kill you with the sword, and your wives shall become widows and your children orphans.

a Or before the judges   b Or the judges condemn

NIV

certainly hear their cry. ²⁴My anger will be aroused, and I will kill you with the sword; your wives will become widows and your children fatherless.

²⁵"If you lend money to one of my people among you who is needy, do not be like a moneylender; charge him no interest.ᵃ ²⁶If you take your neighbor's cloak as a pledge, return it to him by sunset, ²⁷because his cloak is the only covering he has for his body. What else will he sleep in? When he cries out to me, I will hear, for I am compassionate.

²⁸"Do not blaspheme Godᵇ or curse the ruler of your people.

²⁹"Do not hold back offerings from your granaries or your vats.ᶜ

"You must give me the firstborn of your sons. ³⁰Do the same with your cattle and your sheep. Let them stay with their mothers for seven days, but give them to me on the eighth day.

³¹"You are to be my holy people. So do not eat the meat of an animal torn by wild beasts; throw it to the dogs.

23 "Do not spread false reports. Do not help a wicked man by being a malicious witness.

²"Do not follow the crowd in doing wrong. When you give testimony in a lawsuit, do not pervert justice by siding with the crowd, ³and do not show favoritism to a poor man in his lawsuit.

⁴"If you come across your enemy's ox or donkey wandering off, be sure to take it back to him. ⁵If you see the donkey of someone who hates you fallen down under its load, do not leave it there; be sure you help him with it.

⁶"Do not deny justice to your poor people in their lawsuits. ⁷Have nothing to do with a false charge and do not put an innocent or honest person to death, for I will not acquit the guilty.

⁸"Do not accept a bribe, for a bribe blinds those who see and twists the words of the righteous.

⁹"Do not oppress an alien; you yourselves know how it feels to be aliens, because you were aliens in Egypt.

¹⁰"For six years you are to sow your fields and harvest the crops, ¹¹but during the seventh year let

ᵃ25 Or excessive interest   ᵇ28 Or Do not revile the judges
ᶜ29 The meaning of the Hebrew for this phrase is uncertain.

NRSV

25If you lend money to my people, to the poor among you, you shall not deal with them as a creditor; you shall not exact interest from them. 26If you take your neighbor's cloak in pawn, you shall restore it before the sun goes down; 27for it may be your neighbor's only clothing to use as cover; in what else shall that person sleep? And if your neighbor cries out to me, I will listen, for I am compassionate.

28You shall not revile God, or curse a leader of your people.

29You shall not delay to make offerings from the fullness of your harvest and from the outflow of your presses.ᵃ

The firstborn of your sons you shall give to me. 30You shall do the same with your oxen and with your sheep: seven days it shall remain with its mother; on the eighth day you shall give it to me.

31You shall be people consecrated to me; therefore you shall not eat any meat that is mangled by beasts in the field; you shall throw it to the dogs.

23 You shall not spread a false report. You shall not join hands with the wicked to act as a malicious witness. 2You shall not follow a majority in wrongdoing; when you bear witness in a lawsuit, you shall not side with the majority so as to pervert justice; 3nor shall you be partial to the poor in a lawsuit.

4When you come upon your enemy's ox or donkey going astray, you shall bring it back.

5When you see the donkey of one who hates you lying under its burden and you would hold back from setting it free, you must help to set it free.ᵃ

6You shall not pervert the justice due to your poor in their lawsuits. 7Keep far from a false charge, and do not kill the innocent and those in the right, for I will not acquit the guilty. 8You shall take no bribe, for a bribe blinds the officials, and subverts the cause of those who are in the right.

9You shall not oppress a resident alien; you know the heart of an alien, for you were aliens in the land of Egypt.

10For six years you shall sow your land and gather in its yield; 11but the seventh year you shall

ᵃ Meaning of Heb uncertain

NIV

the land lie unplowed and unused. Then the poor among your people may get food from it, and the wild animals may eat what they leave. Do the same with your vineyard and your olive grove.

[12]"Six days do your work, but on the seventh day do not work, so that your ox and your donkey may rest and the slave born in your household, and the alien as well, may be refreshed.

[13]"Be careful to do everything I have said to you. Do not invoke the names of other gods; do not let them be heard on your lips.

[14]"Three times a year you are to celebrate a festival to me.

[15]"Celebrate the Feast of Unleavened Bread; for seven days eat bread made without yeast, as I commanded you. Do this at the appointed time in the month of Abib, for in that month you came out of Egypt.

"No one is to appear before me empty-handed.

[16]"Celebrate the Feast of Harvest with the firstfruits of the crops you sow in your field.

"Celebrate the Feast of Ingathering at the end of the year, when you gather in your crops from the field.

[17]"Three times a year all the men are to appear before the Sovereign Lord.

[18]"Do not offer the blood of a sacrifice to me along with anything containing yeast.

"The fat of my festival offerings must not be kept until morning.

[19]"Bring the best of the firstfruits of your soil to the house of the Lord your God.

"Do not cook a young goat in its mother's milk.

NRSV

let it rest and lie fallow, so that the poor of your people may eat; and what they leave the wild animals may eat. You shall do the same with your vineyard, and with your olive orchard.

[12]Six days you shall do your work, but on the seventh day you shall rest, so that your ox and your donkey may have relief, and your homeborn slave and the resident alien may be refreshed. [13]Be attentive to all that I have said to you. Do not invoke the names of other gods; do not let them be heard on your lips.

[14]Three times in the year you shall hold a festival for me. [15]You shall observe the festival of unleavened bread; as I commanded you, you shall eat unleavened bread for seven days at the appointed time in the month of Abib, for in it you came out of Egypt.

No one shall appear before me empty-handed.

[16]You shall observe the festival of harvest, of the first fruits of your labor, of what you sow in the field. You shall observe the festival of ingathering at the end of the year, when you gather in from the field the fruit of your labor. [17]Three times in the year all your males shall appear before the Lord God.

[18]You shall not offer the blood of my sacrifice with anything leavened, or let the fat of my festival remain until the morning.

[19]The choicest of the first fruits of your ground you shall bring into the house of the Lord your God.

You shall not boil a kid in its mother's milk.

COMMENTARY

This long corpus of laws is regarded as a very old collection, perhaps the oldest legal material in the OT. It probably existed first of all on its own, without reference to the context of the Sinai covenant. It is a miscellaneous collection, no doubt including materials from the general cultural deposit of the Near East, as well as materials that are distinctly Israelite.

It is not possible to identify a coherent structure, pattern, or order for the material. Paul Hanson has proposed that there are competing tendencies, reflecting respectively more exclusive and inclusive tendencies.[131] Hanson's suggestion has merit, as long as those tendencies are seen as simply thematic stresses. If, however, they are viewed as distinct and rival documents, then the argument is quite speculative. Ludger Schwienhorst-Schönberger believes that a subtle

131. Paul D. Hanson, "The Theological Significance of Contradiction Within the Book of the Covenant," in *Canon and Authority: Essays in Old Testament Religion and Theology,* eds. George W. Coats and Burke O. Long (Philadelphia: Fortress, 1977) 110-31.

and complicated pattern of organization is at work in the material.[132] While there is no doubt that there are sub-collections in the material that have been joined together with some intentionality, his specific hypothesis is highly speculative and unconvincing. In any case, this miscellaneous collection has now been placed in the center of the Sinai pericope and is made to serve as a series of stipulations specifying the conditions for the covenant between Israel and Yahweh.

In 24:7 the narrative refers to the "Book of the Covenant" as a document for the treaty to which Israel now agrees. On the basis of that reference, chaps. 21–23 have come to be referred to as the Covenant Code, or Book of Covenant.[133] It is not necessary that the reference in 24:7 is to these materials. It is enough that this material be brought into an intentional relation to the covenant. Set in that context, this already extant material now becomes a way whereby Israel thinks and speaks about Yahweh's sovereign intention for its life. The focus on sovereign intention shows that for every part of its life (cultic, ethical, public, personal, economic, and sexual) Yahweh is known to be the governor who intends obedient conduct. This material is, in fact, a series of probes, explorations, and attempts in the community to discern the mind and will of Yahweh. But then, that is often the nature of biblical "law." It is not "relativistic" but manifestly open to revision as Israel more fully discerns the will of Yahweh.

20:22-26. This extended body of laws begins with guidelines for worship. The unit is introduced by a formula that echoes 19:4. In that verse, what is seen is the triumph of the exodus; here what is "seen" is the speech of God at Mt. Sinai.

There are five commands, of which only the third is a positive assertion. The first two commands are arranged chiastically, assuming and reiterating the two commandments of vv. 3-6. In Hebrew the order of the sentences is:

132. Ludger Schwienhorst-Schönberger, *Das Bundesbuch (Ex. 20, 22-23, 33), Studien zu seiner Entstehung und Theologie,* BZAW 188 (Berlin: De Gruyter, 1990).

133. See Dale Patrick, *Old Testament Law* (Atlanta: John Knox, 1985) 63-96.

You shall not make alongside me
gods of silver
and gods of gold
you shall not make for yourselves.

The command prohibits other gods as in v. 3, and it prohibits visible forms of a god, as in vv. 4-6.

Then follow three laws concerning a proper altar. While these commands seem less weighty than the preceding two, they are, in fact, of a piece with them. The *character* of God (v. 23) and the *worship* of God (vv. 24-26) are intimately connected. How God is worshiped depends on who God is.

First, an altar of earth (אדמה *'ădāmâ*) is authorized (v. 24). Apparently this altar is simply a mound of dirt, sufficient to support the activity of animal slaughter and sacrifice. The provision intends that the place of sacrifice should be modest and simple. The last part of the verse has greatly figured in the classical (Wellhausenian) construction of the history of Israel's religion. The "remembrance of the name" of God is a device (used by the Deuteronomists) to guard against claims of a crass, material presence of God in the shrine. The formula "in every place" has suggested to scholars that altars might be erected and legitimated in many places. This has been taken by scholars to reflect an early form of worship, not yet centralized or carefully administered as in Deut 12:1-7. The picture of worship thus suggested is a widespread, more or less free and spontaneous practice, not yet cramped by hierarchy or complicated procedure.

Second (perhaps as an addendum), it is authorized that the altar may be made of stone, rather than of earth (v. 25). This may reflect subsequent development to a more sophisticated and stylized form of worship. The purpose of the command, however, is not to authorize a stone altar but to preclude the use of hewn stones. Thus a concession to stone is made, but the statement resists excessive craftsmanship or aesthetic concern. We are not told why crafted stone work would profane the altar. The sentence seems to identify simplicity and holiness.

Third, the prohibition warns against having an elevated altar whereby the "nakedness" of the priest would be revealed (v. 26). Concern about nakedness reflects a rigorous concern of the priestly tradition for propriety and discipline. Reference to "profane" in v. 25, along with this reference, suggests an intense priestly agenda and, perhaps, a recognition that worship, especially if undertaken with aesthetic finesse, lives close to the energy and danger of sexuality. We will see this connection brought to full expression in Exodus 32.

21:1-11. The introduction to the main body of material identifies what follows as "ordinances" (מִשְׁפָּטִים *mišpāṭîm*) (v. 1). The term suggests secular rulings concerned with mundane issues of daily life. Because the text admits of no obvious or compelling coherence, it seems necessary to take up the several ordinances *seriatim*, which in the end leaves us with a lot of fragments, but no systematic interpretive picture.

The corpus begins with two laws concerning debt slaves. It is telling indeed that these laws are placed first. Assuming that this text is old, the community of this text can poignantly remember the exodus and the abuse of debt slaves (cf. Gen 47:13-21). Thus the just treatment of slaves is definitional for the larger practice of justice in ancient Israel. Because of unpaid debts, some eventually become owned by others. The burden of these laws is to affirm that, even in such a sorry situation of debt, these slaves nonetheless have certain rights that must be respected.

The first law concerns a male slave (vv. 2-6) and is structured around a basic principle (v. 2), followed by three contingencies (vv. 3-6). The basic principle, echoed in Deut 15:1, is that a debt slave can be held in servitude for only six years. No matter how great the debt, or how slow the pay-back, or how large the residue of debt at the end of six years, neither servitude nor debt can be sustained more than six years. In this principle, the Mosaic covenant has established the priority of persons over money and has set limits on the ways in which economic reversal can impinge on human well-being.

This principle is clarified (or qualified) in three ways. First, the marital status of the slave is respected (v. 3). Second, a family acquired in bondage is not emancipated with the slave (v. 4). Presumably, the wife given by the slave owner is reckoned still to belong to the owner and not to the slave-husband. Third, the slave may at the end of six years prefer bonded status and forego freedom (v. 6; apparently deriving from v. 4). That is, a slave who acquires a wife in bondage may retain her (and children) in bondage, or he may have freedom without her.

This law reflects the difficult tension between the requirements of the economy and the truth of human dignity. In principle, Israel is willing to curb the demands of the economy (v. 1), but in concrete practice, it does not do so in an unambiguous manner.

The second law concerns a female slave (vv. 7-11), and this time a principle is enunciated (v. 7), followed by four qualifying comments. The principle is that a female slave is to be treated differently and is not subject to the preceding rule on slaves. The case concerns an indebted man who offers his daughter for the debt, presumably in place of himself. It is clear in the qualifying comments that the female slave is regarded as no person in her own right, as her fate is linked in each case to a man.

In the first instance, she is assigned to the slave owner—to the one who holds the debt (v. 8). But there are limits to his power over her. If the intended marriage is not to his choosing, he may reject her; but he then loses control over her. In the second case, the owner who holds the debt may "assign" her to his son, and the same provision applies (v. 9). In the third case, if the master rejects her and takes a second wife, her rights will be guaranteed (v. 10). In the fourth case, if she is not protected adequately, she shall be freed, without having to buy back her freedom (v. 11).

The careful, if not tortured, reasoning of these laws indicates that Israel cautiously and uncertainly explored a troubled area of public life. Clearly the law wants to set limits to the practice of debt bondage. But it is equally clear that it goes about the problem in a cowardly way, submitting the claims of human dignity to the realities of the economy. The position taken is "reformist," desiring to make debt slavery more palatable and humane, but reluctant to criticize or assault the practice directly and in principle. Patrick is no doubt correct in his conclusion: "The very act of enunciating slave rights laid the foundation for a more radical critique of the institution in later law."[134] The outcome is that a female slave's options are quite narrow. Moreover, in a patriarchal society a daughter-slave is largely at the behest of powerful men. Guarantees are offered her, but they are of a quite circumscribed range.

134. Ibid., 72.

21:12-17. The next unit consists in four laws that lead to a death penalty, each introduced by an impersonal participle. These laws, unlike the case laws of vv. 1-11, articulate general principles of public policy.

Of the four laws, only the first receives comment and qualification (vv. 12-14). The first law simply provides retaliation for murder: "a life for a life" (v. 12). As in all such provisions concerning capital punishment, however, issues promptly arise that require interpretation and evoke ambiguity. The double "if" of vv. 13-14 inquires about motive: Was the killing intentional, premeditated, willful, and treacherous? If the killing is accidental, an "act of God," the perpetrator can flee to a city of refuge (see Deut 4:41-43; 19:1-10). If the killing is intentional, the perpetrator will receive no protection, not even at God's altar, but shall be executed. Thus the text recognizes options in the law. It does not comment on the enormous difficulties in adjudicating the subtle issue of motive.

The second provision appears to be only a special case of the first (v. 15). The third provision uses the verb for "steal" (גּנב *gānab*, v. 16). The earlier commentary on 20:15 suggests that the commandment may relate to "stealing a person." The law is concerned with the prospect that it was profitable to kidnap persons and sell them into slavery. Clearly, such an act of depriving one of full life is nearly as serious as killing.

The fourth provision (v. 17) parallels that of v. 15. This time, however, the destructive action is not forceful violence but only destructive speech. In our comment on 20:12, we have contrasted "honor" (כבד *kābēd*) with "trivialize" (קלל *qll*). This is a severe provision for upholding that commandment.

These harsh laws of capital punishment are offered in defense of human life, to preclude actions that would destabilize community. They seek to make killing, kidnapping, or cursing too costly. Whether the emphasis is on punishment or deterrence, Israel takes the maintenance of human life and human dignity seriously.

21:18-27. Four laws concern violent assault by one member of the community upon another.

The first concerns a physical altercation between two men, one of whom injures the other (vv. 18-19). This law is the counterpart of 21:12,

where the attacked person dies and a life is required in return. In this law, the attacked person is hurt but recovers. The accent of the law is that the attacker shall be free of liability (נקה *niqqâ*). Restitution is required for only lost time and full recovery (רפא ירפא *rapō' yĕrapē'* is an absolute infinitive). The term for "loss of time" is שׁבת (*šebet*), i.e., his enforced sabbath rest. The theme of restitution is not, however, the major accent of the law. Rather, it aims to minimize the quarrel. The settlement is to be complete, but not beyond actual damage. No litigious society here!

The second case concerns brutality against one's own slave, male or female (vv. 20-21). While the law indicates there was enough of such brutality to require a ruling, it also indicates that the community pondered the human worth of a slave. This emancipated community is not so far from its liberation that it forgets the emergency created by brutality to slaves. The law makes a distinction between death occurring immediately to a beaten slave, literally "under his hand," and death that occurs sometime later. Noth suggests that the distinction may be between intentional and accidental death, but it may well reflect the severity of a beating.[135] In the case of an immediate death, the slave who dies will "surely be avenged" (infinitive absolute) against the master who killed. The measure of punishment or who inflicts it is not indicated. But the verb for "avenge" is strong, perhaps suggesting a *quid pro quo*—the death of the master for the death of the slave. Although the measure of punishment is unspecified in the Hebrew text, the Samaritan text has "shall surely die" (מות יומת *môt yûmāt*), the same harsh formula we have seen in vv. 12-17. If the Samaritan variant is an interpretation of the MT, then v. 20 suggests that a murdered slave is treated like any other murdered person. This is a remarkable law in a cultural context where slaves characteristically have no such protection, but it is exactly what one might expect from this community of erstwhile slaves.

What v. 20 gives by way of dignity to slaves, v. 21 seems immediately to contradict. In an alternative case where the slave does not immediately die, the brutalizing owner is not punished, and the dead slave is not vindicated. (Again the

---

135. Noth, *Exodus*, 181.

Samaritan tradition has *yûmāt* for "avenge," נקם *nāqam*.) The rather anemic justification for this ruling is "for he is his property." The term rendered "property" is כסף (*kesep*, "silver"). The slave is the owner's money, and he can do what he wants with it. This latter ruling reflects hard-nosed economic thinking without regard to the humanity of the slave. One can either be amazed at the venturesome ruling of v. 20 or dismayed at the conventional relapse of v. 21. The community obviously ponders the value of a "person" who is not fully a person.

The third law in this group concerns bodily harm to a pregnant woman resulting from a quarrel (vv. 22-25). The premise of the case is that a miscarriage is caused. It is important that this constitutes in Mosaic Israel a special case worthy of a ruling.

As in the previous case, distinctions are drawn. On the one hand, a ruling follows if there is "no further harm" (v. 22 NRSV; "no serious injury," NIV). The phrasing seems a bit crass, as though enough harm has not already been done in the miscarriage. The other uses of the term for "harm" (אסון *'āsôn*) (see Gen 42:4, 38; 44:29, concerning risk to the beloved Benjamin) indicate that harm is bodily injury resulting in death, here death to the injured mother. Thus the first ruling applies to the mother. If she is not bodily injured, a fine must be paid, as much as the husband requires. The imposition of a fine is an attempt at reparations as an alternative to retaliation. The loss of the pregnancy in and of itself is not judged serious enough to evoke retaliation. The fine constitutes punishment and an attempt at solace, a feeble attempt indeed.

On the other hand, "if harm follows"—if the mother does sustain injury—severe and exact retaliation is required. This is the most complete and extreme statement of retaliation in the Bible, suggesting that punishment for the one who hurts the mother must be exact and point for point. The case permits no misunderstanding as it lists eight illustrative equivalences: life, eye, tooth, hand, foot, burn, wound, and stripe. Childs (following Finkelstein) regards this extensive program of retaliation as a device to ensure equality of treatment for members of the community with unfavorable social standing. The eye, hand, and tooth of any member are protected and valued.[136]

---

136. Childs, *Exodus,* 472. See also Pixley, *On Exodus,* 173-74.

In this ruling, one can see the community adjudicating satisfaction to offended parties with the maintenance of a functioning public order. The community moves between honoring wounds and keeping a lid on vengeance.

The fourth law in this group concerns damage done to a slave (vv. 26-27). This law relates to that of vv. 20-21. It is placed here, perhaps, because it addresses the loss of an eye or a tooth and so picks up the language and theme of v. 24. Again the law reflects a context in which the beating of a slave is not uncommon and is a cause for concern in the community.

This ruling concerns permanent damage, the loss of an eye or a tooth. In the ruling of vv. 23-24 there is exact retribution. In this law the loss of an eye or a tooth leads to the slave's emancipation. If the slave is a debt slave (cf. 21:2), this entails the cancellation of the debt. It may be argued that this is less than exact retribution, for no eye or tooth is required of the brutalizing master. In the context of the exodus, however, the assurance of liberation is greater in value than is retaliation. The cost of an eye or a tooth to the master might deter brutality, but emancipation changes fundamental social relations.

In all of these laws, the community sorts out the tricky and unclear relation between economic value and the elemental, non-negotiable claims of humanness. The economic dimension is evident in payment (vv. 19, 22) and in the power of the slave owner (vv. 21, 26-27). The claims of humaneness are evident in the implied protection of slaves, pregnant women, and injured parties, all of whom are persons at risk. The adjudication of economic and human claims is not clear or unambiguous. It is evident, nonetheless, that the tension between the two is well recognized in Israel and is not easily disposed of.

21:28–22:4. Four laws are voiced concerning either the behavior or the value of livestock. In an agricultural economy, concern for possession, management, control, and disposal of animals is clearly important for the well-being of the community. In the context of covenant, every aspect of daily life pertains to the covenantal rule of Yahweh.

The first law concerns death caused by an ox

that gores (vv. 28-32). A farm animal left unattended can do acute damage, and the law reflects upon the resolution of such a problem under several circumstances. Because an agricultural economy is not likely to be litigious, the working principle seems to be to handle damages as simply and directly as possible, so that the disruption of social relations is as minimal as possible.

The primary ruling concerning an ox that gores is stated in v. 28: An ox that kills must be promptly destroyed.(The verb *stone* is an infinitive absolute.) The important point is that the owner is not held liable. Everyone familiar with animals knows that such damage can happen under the best management.

Four qualifying remarks follow that adjust the primary ruling. First, it is clear that the ruling of v. 28 applies only to first offenders (v. 29). If the animal is a "repeat offender" (which implies that the initial ruling was not implemented), the owner is indeed held accountable. In that event not only is the animal killed, as in v. 28, but the owner is also at fault and may be executed. The community will not endure the continued maintenance of a dangerous animal. Second, in this latter case, the owner may pay a fine instead of execution (v. 30). The terms for "ransom" (כפר *kōper*) and "redemption" (פדין *pidyōn*) here are used in their proper economic sense. Third, the death of a child is as serious, therefore as costly, as the death of an adult (v. 31). Fourth, the death of a slave also requires reparation (v. 32), but here the cost of retribution is limited (30 shekels), while it is left open-ended in the other cases. Further, the reparation is paid to the slave's owner rather than to the slave's family. Economic reality continues to intrude upon human settlements.

While the law does indeed concern the behavior of an ox, and so introduces this series of laws on animals, the subject matter of the law also links it to the preceding section, which concerns assault and death. Thus we are able to detect a certain logic to the present arrangement of the text.

The second law concerns the loss of an animal through human negligence (vv. 33-34). Domestic animals are enormously valuable, and their loss is ominous, particularly to those who own small plots of land. The principle practiced here is restitution, expressed in the verb שלם (*šālam*).

Like the noun *shalom*, this verb concerns action that restores balance, harmony, and well-being. Its content is to pay back, correct a wrong, and recover equity. One must pay for one's negligence. The ruling adds that the negligent party, with the payment of restitution, may keep the dead animal. The dead animal, of course, is of small worth compared with a live animal, but its meat is valuable enough to matter in the process of adjudication. This latter concern suggests that the laws reflect a small agrarian economy.

The third law (vv. 35-36) parallels the first (vv. 28-32). Here, however, the injured party is not a human being but another ox, which is property of another owner. If the offending ox is a first-time offender, then the two owners will share the cost; no fault is assigned. If the offending ox is a repeat offender, then its owner is liable and must restore the damaged ox of the other owner. Again, the one who pays may retain the dead animal.

The fourth law concerns the theft of an ox or a sheep (22:1-4). (The NRSV has rearranged the text of these verses. That rearrangement is helpful, though it rests on no textual basis.) It is impossible to maintain watch over the animals, which are exceedingly valuable. Consequently, the owner's well-being is at risk, and sanctions are severe.

Four principles are enunciated to govern such a case: (1) Extensive restitution is exacted of the thief who has disposed of a stolen animal, by either selling or butchering, so that the animal is not recoverable (v. 1). The price of restitution is fivefold for an ox and fourfold for a sheep, indicating their relative worth to the farmer. (2) If the thief still possesses the stolen animal, then restitution is double. (The extent of penalty indicates a harsh treatment of an adversary, whereas the loss of an ox in 21:33-34, 35-36 is accidental and occurs between friendly neighbors.) (3) If the thief is unable to make restitution, he may be sold into debt slavery. As the text is arranged, this severe penalty applies only to the fivefold or fourfold payment, and not the twofold payment. We may, however, surmise that it applies there as well. (4) Exodus 22:2-3 reflects a social situation in which a farmer is prepared to defend his own property. The farmer is serious, and a potential thief must beware. Again, the ruling makes an important distinction. If the thief comes in the dark of the night, he may be killed, and the farmer is not held accountable. During the daylight, however, the farmer is not free to kill the thief. If the thief is killed in the daylight, it may be assumed that the farmer could have taken less severe measures, and so is guilty of murder. The daytime provision thus provides protection for a thief, even when caught in the act.

This series of laws, two on a dangerous animal (vv. 28-32, 35-36) and two on the loss of a valuable animal (vv. 33-34; 22:1-4), reflects a patient struggle with most mundane matters. In precisely such mundane matters, however, the health and well-being of a community is gained or lost.

22:5-17. The dominant theme of the next section, restitution (*šālam*), makes clear that the aim of the laws is to guard against excessive or unfair loss of property, which would disrupt the stability of the community. Such an agenda may suggest a cautious defense of private property, but it also affirms the cruciality of the community and its right ordering, over against personal and private interests. There is here no unbridled individualism in which individual operators may view the community as an arena for ambitious exploitation. Rather, the individual prospers only by maintaining a stable, communal equilibrium.

The first law concerns the violation of someone else's field or vineyard (v. 5). The term rendered "graze" (בער *bi'ēr*) by both the NRSV and the NIV is not used elsewhere for "graze," but regularly means "burn," as in v. 6. In any case, a neighbor's field or vineyard must not be violated. Notice that the law is not concerned with animals that accidentally intrude but with the intentional intrusion of one farmer upon the field of another. There is no severe penalty, but only the return of equilibrium.

The second law concerns the burning of a neighbor's field (v. 6). Here the same verb (*bā'ar*) is used, this time in its normal meaning. A farmer's fire on his own land can get out of hand and spread to the field of another. Again, restitution is required, this time expressed with an infinitive absolute. This suggests a peculiarly serious matter, perhaps because fire can cause much more serious and immediate damage than can grazing.

The third law concerns the loss of goods entrusted to the care of a neighbor (vv. 7-8). In v. 7 the law assumes that the neighbor is not at fault, but that a thief is responsible for the loss. Whereas vv. 5 and 6 require restitution only of equivalence, with a thief the restitution is double (cf. v. 1). Verse 8 adds a proviso: If the thief is not caught, it is possible there was no thief. In that case, the neighbor who has had the goods in his care is brought to trial to adjudicate his guilt or innocence. The case is brought "before God," i.e., before the tribunal, which enacts and administers covenantal law. In 18:19-22, Moses established a system of courts, presided over by those who "hate dishonest gain." If the neighbor is convicted as the thief, then he must, of course, pay double. If he is acquitted, there is no suggestion that he is liable for the loss.

The fourth case concerns a property dispute (v. 9). In an agrarian community, disputes may arise over such items, particularly in the probation of estates (cf. Luke 12:13). The disputants are not left on their own, but are commended to the court. The court can "condemn" (רשע *rāša'*, i.e., declare guilty) or "acquit" (צדק *ṣādaq*, i.e., declare innocent). (On such language, see Isa 50:7-8 and Rom 8:31-34.) The court's verdict is absolute. The one whose claim is denied must pay reparation to the other party, perhaps to compensate for inconvenience and embarrassment. Again, the cost of a false claim is double payment (cf. vv. 1, 7).

The fifth case, like the third (vv. 7-8), concerns one neighbor having custody of another's goods (vv. 10-13). If there are witnesses to the loss, then the case can be resolved. The difficult cases occur, however, when there are no witnesses. In such a circumstance, the court must decide on the basis of what is not obvious or publicly available.

The case will be decided on the basis of an oath made by the keeper of the goods. This is a specific case of the ninth commandment, concerning false witnesses. In a society that regards taking an oath a high-risk venture, an oath is enough and functions like a lie-detector test. If one asserts innocence in the matter, there is no restitution.

The ruling then adds two other conditional clauses. First, "if it was in fact stolen . . . " (with an infinitive absolute), and if the custodian cannot swear innocence, then he must make restitution. Even in the case of such theft by a neighbor, however, no more than restitution is required. Finally, the ruling notes one other possibility (v. 13): If the goods have been "mangled" (טרף *ṭārap*), i.e., torn by a wild animal, again there is no restitution. The law is willing to allow the caprice of an animal beyond the control of the custodian. Thus the ruling entertains a variety of ways in which goods may be lost—stolen, mangled, killed, injured, or carried off. Only in the case of theft is restitution required.

The sixth case again concerns property damage (vv. 14-15). Presumably the law concerns a work animal that is injured or killed while borrowed. The owner may be "borrowed" along with the animal. If the owner is not present with the animal, then the borrower is responsible for its loss and must repay. If, however, the owner accompanies the animal, then he is responsible and the borrower is without liability. The last line of v. 15 is not very clear, but it seems to make a distinction between borrowing and hiring. An arrangement of paid hire apparently limits liability for the hirer.

The seventh case, concerning a "bride price" (מהר *mōhar*), is very different from the six preceding cases (vv. 16-17). I group it with the others because it does have as its subject the matter of reparations, though the familiar term *šālam* is not used. The case concerns the seduction and violation (rape) of a virgin. The act of violation is not in doubt. Something must be done to the violator, even though in this patriarchal scenario the violation is not against the woman but against her father. In any case, the violator must pay a "bride price" to the father, an unspecified amount of money for the use/abuse of the young woman. For that price, he may receive her as his wife.

But it is the father who has all the options. He may, in response to the payment, make his daughter the man's wife. Or he may refuse the marriage, perhaps finding the man unsuitable, but he still receives the same amount of money. Because the daughter is not engaged, the violation is not a capital crime—i.e., not a serious threat to the community. For that reason, the penalty would seem to protect the family's honor. The law pays no attention to the violated woman herself, and, in that regard, the settlement with the father is not unlike the other cases of retribution for "the owner."

In all seven cases in this group, "property" that belongs to someone is in some way damaged by another: (a) a field is damaged (by grazing?), (b) a field is burned, (c) goods are lost, (d) an animal is wrongly claimed, (e) an animal is lost, (f) an animal is damaged, (g) a young woman is violated.

In each case, restitution must be paid unless exceptional circumstances vindicate the allegedly guilty party. In the last case, the payment is of a "bride price" rather than restitution, but the principle is the same. The practice of restitution, evident in all of these cases, intends to provide guidelines and checks on the abuse of one neighbor by another. The intent is to maintain a community in which all may live in harmony.

22:18-31. Chapter 22 concludes with a series of miscellaneous laws. I am unable to detect any pattern to these commands, for they vary in both form and subject matter. Grouping them together is largely a matter of convenience.

Israel is forbidden to host a female sorcerer (v. 18). It is not specifically clear what a sorcerer does, but it is enough to recognize that sorcery is an attempt to manage and manipulate power that truly belongs only to God. Sorcery is regularly treated as a technique used by foreign peoples who compete with, jeopardize, and seduce Israel away from its proper trust in Yahweh (cf. Deut 18:9-13). Note that in 7:11, sorcerers joined the Egyptian opposition to Moses and Aaron.

Sexual relations with an animal embody a distortion of God's proper ordering of life (v. 19). The commandment concerns a severely distorted and distorting cultural practice (cf. Lev 18:23; 20:15). If the seventh commandment is broadly construed to concern all distorted sexual relations, then this becomes an extreme case in point. Such practices mock the intention of the creator for a rightly ordered, life-giving creation.

The prohibition of sacrifice to the gods is a strong reiteration of the first commandment (v. 20). The punishment of being "devoted to destruction" utilizes the notion of חרם (*ḥērem*), wherein anything that detracts from Yahweh is to be consumed in fire. There is no doubt that the practice of *ḥērem* is a matter of extreme ideological rigor that refuses any compromise at all (cf. Deut 20:16-18; 1 Sam 15:10-33).

Israel's protective affirmation of the socially marginal is rooted in its exodus memory and imagination (vv. 21-24). The paragraph consists in two negative commands (vv. 21-22), followed by interpretive commentary. The first command protects resident aliens—i.e., permanent residents in the community who have no rights of citizenship and, therefore, are vulnerable to all kinds of social pressure. The second command protects widows and orphans, those in the community who have lost their male advocate and protector and so are exposed to endless social threat. The two commands together show that early Israelite law was especially aware of the socially marginated and vulnerable, making it a principle of law that they must be fully guaranteed.

The two commands are supported by two motivational comments. The first, concerning the sojourners, appeals to the exodus tradition. As Israel was protected in its time of marginality, so it is to be the protector of the marginal (cf. Deut 10:19). Cynthia Ozick has observed the way in which the exodus memory has become a powerful metaphor for ethics in ongoing Jewish life.[137]

The second command is supported by a more extended and ominous comment (vv. 23-24). In a less direct way, this command also alludes to the exodus, for it knows that oppressed widows and orphans will cry out as Israel in slavery cried out. Verse 23 is of special interest because it is so emphatic, featuring three absolute infinitives in succession: "If you *truly oppress* . . . if they *truly cry out* . . . I will *truly hear.*" This sequence makes the most decisive appeal Israel can muster for obedience to covenantal ethics. The theological pivot of the exodus narrative is the conviction that God hears and is moved by such cries (cf. 2:23-25; 3:7-8). As the cry of Israel against Egypt mobilized Yahweh against the oppressive Egyptians, so now the cry of widows and orphans will mobilize Yahweh against oppressive Israel. This theological reality posits a God passionately against oppression, no matter where it is found, even in Israel.

The upshot of such a mobilization of God is that when widows and orphans cry out in pain and need, God will destroy husbands and fathers, leaving Israel as helpless as the present vulnerable ones. Thus the punishment fits the crime.[138] The truth is that oppressive societies have more than their share of violence. And when such violence eventually and inevitably leads to military action, fathers and husbands are killed, producing widows and orphans. This law understands, for all its theological language, exactly the dynamic of social oppression and its outcome. Abuse of the vulnerable has enormous social costs for the abusers that cannot be avoided or denied.

The next group of commands, linked to the preceding by reference to the "poor" (עני 'ānî; cf. vv. 22-23 on the abuse of ענה 'ānâ), consists in three commands set up as a protasis-apodosis (condition-consequence), plus a twofold motivational clause (vv. 25-27): "you shall not deal with them as a creditor; you shall not exact interest from them" (v. 25); "you shall restore it before the sun goes down" (v. 26).

These brief commands are enormously radical. They insist that the workings of the economy must be submitted to the principle of community solidarity. Israelites, in their economic dealings, are not to be conventional bankers and business people. They are to act differently for the sake of the community. Pixley comments: "We are told that basic human rights arise from basic human needs. Misery is not to be trafficked in. The right to life takes precedence over the right to poverty."[139] Specifically, the poor are to have money grants without interest, i.e., without creating economic leverage that will make the poor endlessly indebted and dependent. The law does not argue about the economic viability of such a practice. It simply requires the need for care in concrete ways, and it expects the community to work out the practical details.

The third command cites a quite primitive practice as a case in point. A poor man who has no property may put up his only coat as collateral for the loan. While such collateral may be taken, it may be kept only during the day. It must be returned to the debtor every night. The provision invites a ludicrous scene of the creditor each night going to the house of the poor man to drop off the coat, and returning each morning to pick it up. Since collateral that is held only part-time is no real collateral at all, the practical outcome of

---

137. Ozick, *Metaphor and Memory,* 265-83.

138. On this general principle in biblical ethics, see Patrick D. Miller, Jr., *Sin and Judgment in the Prophets: A Stylistic and Theological Analysis* (Chico, Calif.: Scholars Press, 1982).

139. Pixley, *On Exodus,* 179.

such a proposal is to operate without collateral from the poor.

The motivational clause of v. 27 appeals first to a very practical matter. The poor man must not be taken advantage of, for he will be cold in the night. If the retention of his coat is difficult, much more problematic is the charging of interest that deprives the poor of even more than a coat. This pastoral motivation is further supported by a theological affirmation, echoing vv. 23-24. The God who gives these commands does indeed hear on behalf of the weak and against the abusive strong. God is compassionate (חָנַן *ḥānan*), willing to act gratuitously (cf. 34:6). God's compassion, however, is only the positive side of God's vengeance.[140] Indeed, Israel has known this about Yahweh since its own origin in the pain of slavery. Now this law daringly applies the lessons of the exodus to ongoing public policy and practice.

Speech is dangerous and power-laden, and must be undertaken prudently (v. 28). In close parallelism, this law prohibits speech that trivializes (קלל *qll;* cf. 21:17) God or that curses a leader. Both verbs, *revile* (NIV, "blaspheme") and *curse* mean to pronounce words capable of diminishing, delegitimating, or damaging their object. No person of power or influence can survive speeches that are derogatory, for they will eventually erode claims of authority. The provision concerning God is related to the first commandment. Clearly one is not permitted to delegitimate the God who has liberated Israel and defeated all the other gods. It is worth noting that the urging of Job's wife (Job 2:9) cannot risk, according to the narrator, the statement "curse God," but must use a euphemism, "bless God." One dare not risk a word of terrible power against the God who commands all power.

The second line of this law shows the clever way in which human, political power is "wrapped in a flag," so that the human leader is placed parallel and in close proximity to God (cf. 1 Kgs 21:10). Thus the two are protected in the same instant by the same prohibition. The term for "leader" (נָשִׂיא *nāśî'*) is generic, but likely reflects a pre-monarchical, and thus informal, office.

The command in v. 29*a* is vague and problem-

atic. The NRSV and the NIV have provided an imaginative, and perhaps correct, extrapolation. The Hebrew text includes only four words: "Your fullness and your flow you shall not delay." The notion that this is an offering to Yahweh may be appropriated from vv. 29*b*-30, but it is not in the text itself. If the command does concern the firstfruits of crops, then its purpose is to acknowledge that the land belongs to Yahweh.

The law of the firstborn consists in two quite distinct parts (vv. 29*b*-30). The first line is an apodictic statement (v. 29*b*). It explains nothing and requires nothing—except the firstborn. It may be that the assertion has a conscious connection to the liberation narrative, where Israel is Yahweh's firstborn son (4:22). In reparation for Israel, Yahweh violently claims the firstborn of Egypt (11:5, 12:29). When the claim of the firstborn is reduced to a cultic regulation, provision is made for the "redemption" of the firstborn son (13:11-16). Thus while the formula of 22:29*b* makes an important point about God's utter sovereignty and Israel's complete subordination, it is not likely that the statement intends a direct sacrifice of the firstborn. Indeed, v. 29*b* seems to be a premise for the claim of v. 30. That is, the claim of the firstborn applies concretely to oxen and sheep, not humans. Even so, the requirement is an expensive one, especially in a modest agrarian economy that worries about reparations for one damaged ox.

The final provision in this unit concerns a specific dietary restriction (v. 31). Domestic animals that have been attacked and torn in the field by wild animals are not to be eaten. This quite specific prohibition derives from the very large premise that Israel is a people holy to Yahweh. The text tells us nothing about the relation between the large premise and the specific restriction. (See the same linkage in Deut 14:1-21.) The reason may be hygienic, or it may be that eating such meat is simply beneath the dignity of this people.

23:1-9. Chapter 23 begins with a series of apodictic laws intended to safeguard the well-being of the community through the practice of justice.

A series of five apodictic assertions, four introduced by the negative לֹא (*lō'*) and one by the negative אַל (*'al*), provide guidelines for behavior in court that will enhance or diminish equity.

---

140. See George Mendenhall, "The 'Vengeance' of Yahweh," *The Tenth Generation: The Origins of the Biblical Tradition* (Baltimore: Johns Hopkins University Press, 1973) 69-104.

While these five assertions are all concerned with false witness, the more general concern is the perversion of justice. These regulations are first aware that false witness can be socially destructive (v. 1) and that following majority opinion can greatly miscarry justice (v. 2).

Two textual questions are of special interest here. In v. 2 the term *justice* is absent in the Hebrew, though is supplied in the Greek. In v. 3, the phrase "partial to the poor" (דל *dāl*) is clear enough in the text, but the reading is odd, because the context does not worry about favoritism to the poor and because such a warning seems superfluous. On the basis of the parallel in Lev 19:15, many scholars read גדל (*gādōl*) for *dāl,* thus, "you shall not be partial to the powerful." If the Hebrew reading is retained, then the text suggests that in its own context even the poor are subject to the demands of justice.

In any case, these laws express Israel's awareness that the life of the entire community is at risk in the practice of injustice. Injustice, which may indeed be the will of the majority, is an enormous seduction, which the covenanted community must intentionally resist.

Two laws are given that reflect an intimate, face-to-face agrarian community (vv. 4-5). In such communities, as in any community, there are "enemies" (v. 4) and those whom one hates (v. 5). One is not inclined to help or enhance the life of one's adversaries. Nonetheless, in an agrarian economy the loss of one's working animals is a most serious matter. Thus even an enemy's stray animal must be returned, and if it has fallen from too heavy a load, then it is to be assisted. These two commands indicate that for the sake of the neighbor, i.e., for the health of the community, one has obligations that override one's emotional propensity. Calvin suggests that believers "should testify their forgiveness of their enemies by being merciful to their animals."[141] The basis of this command is not some romantic "do-gooder" sense, but the practical awareness that the community depends on neighborly acts that enhance the life of all.

The section concludes with four apodictic requirements and one positive imperative, paralleling the concerns of vv. 1-3 (vv. 6-9). The five

rules are: (1) Do not pervert justice due the poor. (2) Keep far from a false charge. (3) Do not kill the innocent or the righteous. (4) Do not take a bribe. (5) Do not oppress a resident alien.

The first, second, and fourth of these pertain directly to courtroom conduct. It is plausible that "murder" in the third law and "oppress" in the fifth are also concerned with court cases. That is, "murder" might include capital execution of the innocent, or less dramatic laws that deny power and access to some.

These five statements intend to maintain the courts as an arena for the true practice of justice, in which manipulation of the law for advantage and private interest is curbed by a genuine commitment to the rights of all the aggrieved. The programmatic phrase "pervert justice" is likely paralleled in v. 2, though the text seems incomplete. (It is also a central concern of the prophet Amos; 5:7-15; 8:4-6.) Justice is the commitment of the covenant community to maintaining the viability and integrity of all its members, in this case especially the poor, resident aliens, and those in the right. The text knows that bribery is a powerful tool for distorting the vision of justice (cf. 18:21), tending to serve the powerful, who are most able to provide a bribe.

The last three regulations are supported by powerful motivational clauses. In v. 7, those who damage the innocent are in jeopardy for their guilt; in v. 8 bribery subverts; and in v. 9 the exodus memory is given as impetus for obedience.

The entire section of vv. 1-9 portrays a passionate commitment to the maintenance of a community in which all members are safe and respected, in which due process is guaranteed, and in which selfish interest is curbed for the sake of the weaker, more vulnerable members of society. This section powerfully reflects, in legal form, the ongoing passion of the community of liberation.

23:10-19. The Book of Covenant concludes with a series of provisions that are rooted in cultic regulations and practices.

Although not properly cultic, vv. 10-11 are included in this section because of their sabbatical connection to v. 12. While vv. 10-11 do concern regularity of time, they might equally well have been included in the preceding group of laws concerning civil justice. The pattern of seven years may indeed derive from old cultic procedure, but

141. Calvin, *Commentaries,* 57.

here the law simply concerns crop rotation and the practice of letting the land lie fallow every seventh year. The motivation for such rotation is noteworthy. It is not said that such "rest" is good for the land—which it is. Rather, the fallow land, which will continue to produce some useful volunteer growth, is for the benefit of those who have no property of their own. Thus fields, vineyards, and orchards are, in the "off year," fair territory for the poor and for wild animals. The law resists any practice of "enclosure" that draws too tightly the bounds of private property.[142] Even private property must be managed to keep it sometimes open to the needs and requirements of the community.

The keeping of the seventh day (v. 12) is another form of the sabbath command of 20:8-11. The rhythm of agrarian life requires such a day of rest. The rest is clearly egalitarian, applying to animals and resident aliens. (On the odd term *refreshed,* see 31:17.)

It is curious that v. 13 adds three imperatives of a quite general kind, echoing the first commandment. The present text suggests that other gods will jeopardize sabbath—i.e., lure Israel out of its confident rest—and that sabbath is a way to maintain loyalty to Yahweh.

Finally, this legal corpus concludes with a rather inexact festal calendar (vv. 14-19). Three festivals are specified: (1) Festival of Unleavened Bread (vv. 15, 18), on which see Exodus 12–13; (2) Festival of Harvest, when the firstfruits of the land are brought to Yahweh (vv. 16*a*, 19); and (3) Festival of Ingathering at the end of the harvest season (v. 16*b*).

This festival pattern is likely very old in Israel. While v. 15 connects unleavened bread to the exodus, for the most part the laws reflect the life of an agrarian community. The festivals are not primarily oriented to the memory of liberation but to the patterns of agricultural life. In the festivals, Yahweh is acknowledged as the owner of the land and the giver of crops, i.e., a God of fertility who gives life to all of creation.[143]

Two specific requirements are made for this pattern of festivals. First, no one shall come empty-handed (v. 15*b*). All shall bring an offering, thus acknowledging gratitude and dependence. Second, all males—i.e., all heads of households— shall come to the shrine three times a year, thus regularly enacting their membership in the covenant community as adherents to the covenantal claims of Yahweh (v. 17).

The addendum of v. 19*b* is enigmatic (cf. Deut 14:21*b*). Apparently the prohibited practice is something done in Canaanite ritual. While there is nothing intrinsically evil about the practice, it is known and recognized as an act of devotion to Canaanite gods, so Israel must desist.

The festival ritual is a regular, disciplined demonstration of loyalty to Yahweh, acknowledging that life comes from Yahweh alone and is given back to Yahweh. The memory of the exodus is only marginally important in this pattern for worship. What counts here is land ownership and allegiance, precisely what one expects in an agrarian community. The God of this festal calendar is indeed the creator who "satisfied the desire of everything" (Ps 145:16).

142. Karl Polanyi, *The Great Transformation* (Boston: Beacon, 1957), notes the decisive and devastating socioeconomic consequences of practices of enclosure.

143. See Walter Harrelson, *From Fertility Cult to Worship* (Garden City, N.Y.: Doubleday, 1969).

REFLECTIONS

Contemporary interpretation will need to handle these legal provisions with some interpretive distance and freedom. That is, the laws do not "apply" as commandments simply to be acted out by an obedient community, remote from their social context. An ancient law is not precisely and automatically pertinent to new and massively transformed social circumstance.

This does not suggest, however, that there is nothing of value for contemporary interpretation and proclamation in this material. I suggest three avenues of approach to this material. First, one can seek to identify the assumptions and principles that lie behind the concrete laws. For example, the requirement of saving the ox or donkey of one's enemy (23:4-5) recognizes that neighbors who do not like each other are nonetheless bound together in a common good. The principle behind the laws on restitution is that a stable, healthy community requires the maintenance of and respect for property that prevents excessive or catastrophic loss.

Second, law is not a matter of settled conclusion. It is an ongoing process of adjudication to see what will work, what is required, and what is acceptable. In these ancient laws, we are able to observe the processes by which a community does the difficult, ongoing work of adjudicating competing claims and interests. Thus, for example, in the laws of release (21:1-11) the claims and interests of human freedom and dignity are in profound tension with the property rights of slave owners. Quite clearly, these laws do not entertain the notion of abolishing the practice of debt slavery. At best, the laws are reformist, seeking to make a troublesome social practice as humane as possible. One does not need to claim that these legal settlements are right, or that they will not be subject to revision. On the whole, law is not an effort to fix eternal principles but to adjudicate some question at hand. If we understand these laws in relation to the specific case in question, then interpretive practice might allow the church in its moral bewilderment to lower its strident voice and address the human questions before it.

Just as the church has been, in my judgment, excessively busy in recent times stating "absolutes," so also conversation about civil law has fallen into an advocacy of strict constructionism that pretends that law has a once-for-all meaning and intention. These texts are a model for the power of law as a continuing dynamic process. Such a process leaves the community short of absolutes but better able to meet the crises of the day.

Third, because the laws reflect a simple, face-to-face agrarian society, they are not directly applicable to a more complex, urban, technological, and post-industrial society. The temptation is to let the laws pertain to neighbor relations while refusing to interpret them in relation to greater social complexity. These laws require a careful social criticism in order to see how these modes of covenant in a face-to-face community might operate in a complex society. Fretheim suggests that "one is invited by the law to go beyond the law."[144] Thus bond slavery may apply not to a male Hebrew but to a permanent underclass. Thus charging interest may apply not "to the poor among you" but to debtor nations whose economies are rendered hopelessly dependent by creditors. Thus "boiling a kid" may apply not to Canaanite practice but to participation in an extravagantly consumeristic society.

When one exercises interpretive freedom, as well as interpretive responsibility, consideration of these texts can open conversation concerning how the covenantal intention of Yahweh pertains to shared human life. Such consideration might invite the church to ethical reflection in new modes, consisting not in arguments about absolute principles but in provisional decisions to get through the day faithfully, humanely, and covenantally.

Theological conviction eventuates in concrete, ethical reflection. There is no easy, obvious, one-to-one match between them. But the one does necessarily result in the other. On the one hand, theological reflection must come down to concrete decisions concerning worship, economics, and sexuality, for these are the hazardous arenas of loyalty and responsibility. Such a text as the present one undermines the dictum that the church should not mix religion with politics and economics. Politics and economics are what these laws are all about. Allegiance to the Lord of the exodus concerns liberation for slaves, humane rates of interest, restitution for crippled oxen, and reparations for a raped woman. Yahweh's exodus sovereignty is daily and concrete, and concerns the ordinariness of life, where covenant becomes visible.

On the other hand, it is equally clear that concrete ethics always lag behind theological conviction. The wondrous claims of liberation that are now available to Israel do not fully function in daily practice. Thus slaves are still "money" (21:21), and women are still property (22:16-17). The ethics of the community is always playing "catch-up" with the theological

144. Fretheim, *Exodus,* 248.

passions that identify it. The community is always engaged in counting costs, running risks, protecting interests, to see how far it will go with its exodus imagination.

We may now consider in turn the several sections into which the material is divided to see what interpretive possibilities are available:

1. A right understanding of God is closely connected to a right worship of God. I have suggested that the provision for altars is free of hierarchical protocols and concerned for simplicity and modesty as modes of holiness. Altars can be free and spontaneous, yet holy in their simplicity. The God who is worshiped, reflected, and "enacted" in such worship likewise partakes of a holiness free of pretense, extravagance, and grandeur. (We shall see that this mode of worship is in deep tension with the worship proposals of chaps. 25–31.)

2. These two laws on bond servants and their release in 21:1-11 show that the community is aware of the tension between human rights and economic power. In such an economy, slaves represent considerable financial investment. This community, haunted by the exodus, knows that a fettered person can have no full self. It is not willing to forego all economic interest for the sake of full humanness, but it understands the urgency of the question. Such a reformist position is a long way from proclaiming that there is "no longer slave or free" (Gal 3:28), but even Paul was far behind his own lyrical dictum, as demonstrated in Philemon. The interpretive points concern the ways in which persons are held in bondage in economic structures, the costs of liberation, and the high price of keeping persons bonded.

3. The four laws in 21:12-17 are held together by the formula "shall be put to death." They concern any practice of physical or verbal violence in the community. All such violence diminishes persons and thereby destroys community. Thus interpretation might focus on the full human functioning of life in which freedom, dignity, respect, and safety are prized goods.

The means to curb violence is itself an act of violence (capital punishment), albeit an ordered, sanctioned violence. Such a law should not be used to sanction capital punishment in our time and place. Rather, it should help us to consider how a community may be able to maintain human life, human freedom, and human dignity against life-robbing violence.

4. The four laws in 21:18-27 concern violence that does not lead to death. (In two cases, concerning a slave [v. 20] and a miscarried pregnancy [v. 22], a life is terminated. But in neither case is this termination the point of the law.) In all four cases, the community metes out punishment that is equitable without vengeance. The community sets a limit on vengeance and thereby seeks to control violence. We live in an inordinately violent society. In our fearfulness, we seek private oases of security, but we do not want to expend the money or energy on the public infrastructure, which has largely disintegrated. No doubt violence begets violence. These laws take the threat of violence seriously, but they characteristically propose a minimal penalty. Thus the laws seek to de-escalate the violence and have it over and done with.

5. The four laws in 21:28–22:4 concern damage done by an ox or to an ox. These laws suggest that one must control one's "means of production" (oxen) in order to guard the well-being of one's neighbor. The danger to which the law points is a disregard of the neighbor because one is preoccupied with one's own interests.

It requires no great imagination to see that, in a post-industrial society, preoccupation with one's own well-being and profit can lead to neglect of the neighbor's well-being. Thus the "ox that gored" might be understood as water rights, careless chemical pollution, or the introduction of technical "advances" (i.e., smarter oxen) that endanger the environment and destroy another person's context for a good life. "A man and his ox"—that is, a person and his or her possessions—do not exist in a vacuum. We cannot conduct our lives in disregard of our neighbors.

6. Exodus 22:5-17 has to do with restitution. There will be no "communal wholeness" (שׁלוֹם

šālôm) until "reparations" are made (שׁלם *šillēm*). *Shalom* refers to a harmonious equilibrium. But such social equilibrium is not possible in a community that is strongly at odds and in which some are denied what is rightfully and necessarily theirs. Whereas *shalom* characterizes a state of existence, *šillēm* is a very powerful, active intervention to right a wrong.

In these laws, the interventions are domestic and the repayments are modest. They do nonetheless evidence a principle of concrete payment to compensate for an unjust loss. The concreteness of restitution here invites reflection upon the *principle* of reparation and the active work of social redress. In a society that currently resists "affirmative action"—action that compensates for a long, habituated social wrong—the notion of reparations is worth pursuing. The difficulty is in recognizing that those to whom reparations are owed have so long ago lost their ox that we scarcely notice the need to restore it. In a society that dreams of *shalom*, or one that prattles ideologically about *shalom*, those old needs for compensation must be recovered. Thus reparations are due to women from men, to blacks from whites, to the Third World from the first, and to all of those who by the political manipulations of the economy have lost their "ox" without any restitution.

7. In the miscellaneous collection of 22:18-31, attention might most usefully be given to the two provisions in 22:21-24 and 25-27. In both cases, the powerful are warned against exploiting the weak, and the motivation for the instruction is theological. God is wrathful (v. 24), and God is compassionate (v. 27). God's attentive concern extends into the economy. In the second of these laws, it is argued that genuine human concern impinges upon economic transactions. Michael Polanyi has chronicled the way in which the European economy (and by extrapolation the economy of the United States) progressively separated market exchanges from the human fabric.[145] The end result is a market that operates "autonomously," without reference to human costs. The covenantal community will not tolerate such a separation and will insist that economic power be subordinated to the human realities of pain, need, and hope.

These two laws on valuing the needy of the community are framed by laws that insist on singular devotion to Yahweh (vv. 20, 28, 29*a*, 29*b*-30, 31). The two accents are, of course, deeply intertwined. That *Yahweh rules* makes unavoidable that the *poor neighbor counts* (cf. Jer 22:15-16). Israel cannot make the first affirmation without making the derivative ethical commitment.

8. The laws in 23:1-9 rigorously and consistently voice the Mosaic commitment to justice as the norm for the community. In vv. 1-3 and 6-9 that concern focuses primarily on the courts, on honest testimony without distortions to protect vested interest. In vv. 4-5, the practice of justice concerns concrete acts of neighborliness. In neither case, however, is such action mere charity. Rather, it is a discipline that defines the identity of this community. The double use of the word *poor* (vv. 3, 6; cf. v. 9) indicates that the law is not unaware of social differentiations; there is no insidious pretense of classlessness. They know very well that money "talks" in court and wherever power is shaped. The laws dare to insist, nonetheless, that voices other than those of money (voices of need, of pain, and of memory) might prevail.

9. Finally, the laws culminate with a festival calendar urging that Israel should "take time to be holy," take time to be whole (23:10-19). This group of laws focuses on the three-festival agricultural cycle, introduced by a seven-year cycle for the land (vv. 10-11) and a seven-day cycle for the economy (vv. 12-13).

The three-festival calendar is explicitly oriented to Yahweh. In it, the crucial times of the agricultural economy become times at which Yahweh's sovereignty is enacted. The two "laws of seven" have a very different orientation, being primarily concerned for God's creation (for the poor and wild animals, for the ox and donkey, for the slave, and for the resident alien).

---

145. Polanyi, *The Great Transformation*. See Meeks's comments, *God the Economist*, 37-40, 52-55.

These laws themselves do not say much about Yahweh, aside from the motivational addendum of v. 13. Thus vv. 10-12 (13) concern creaturely well-being, and vv. 14-19 concern the creator who owns the land.

Concerning both creaturely well-being and acknowledgment of the creator, the covenant community practices a rhythm of observations not unlike the church year. The community is enjoined to treat time as holy, both in order to value creation and to honor the creator. (In Gen 2:1-4*a*, *time* is the first element of creation that God makes holy.) All of these times, the festivals of seven and the threefold festival, intend to break the conventional economic practice of working, getting, and spending, or ingathering and harvest. The festivals are an act of faith because they make an ordered acknowledgment that prevents human business from degenerating into an endless effort at management, success, and self-security.

10. It is not clear that this corpus has any intentional shape, though Schwienhorst-Schönberger argues that it does.[146] The corpus begins with the vexed question of human freedom and dignity (21:1-11), and after a powerful accent on justice (23:1-9), it concludes with a pattern for worship and acknowledgment of God's generous sovereignty (23:10-19). If we dare imagine the two units as beginning and end, there is then a move from *human freedom* (21:1-11) to acknowledging *God's governance of creation* (23:10-19). A text that may illuminate this connection is Matt 5:23-24: "So when you are offering your gift at the altar, if you remember that your brother or sister has something against you, leave your gift there before the altar and go; first be reconciled to your brother or sister, and then come and offer your gift" (NRSV).

In this corpus, Israel wants in the end to offer its gift at the altar (23:16, 19). It cannot do so, however, until it has been reconciled to brother and sister, in this case a male slave (21:1-6) and a female slave (21:7-11). The commands of Moses never permit the separation of God and neighbor, or of worship and human justice.

146. Schwienhorst-Schönberger, *Das Bundesbuch* 22-37 and esp. the summary on 23.

EXODUS 23:20-33, CONQUEST OF CANAAN PROMISED

NIV

20"See, I am sending an angel ahead of you to guard you along the way and to bring you to the place I have prepared. 21Pay attention to him and listen to what he says. Do not rebel against him; he will not forgive your rebellion, since my Name is in him. 22If you listen carefully to what he says and do all that I say, I will be an enemy to your enemies and will oppose those who oppose you. 23My angel will go ahead of you and bring you into the land of the Amorites, Hittites, Perizzites, Canaanites, Hivites and Jebusites, and I will wipe them out. 24Do not bow down before their gods or worship them or follow their practices. You must demolish them and break their sacred stones to pieces. 25Worship the LORD your God, and his

NRSV

20I am going to send an angel in front of you, to guard you on the way and to bring you to the place that I have prepared. 21Be attentive to him and listen to his voice; do not rebel against him, for he will not pardon your transgression; for my name is in him.

22But if you listen attentively to his voice and do all that I say, then I will be an enemy to your enemies and a foe to your foes.

23When my angel goes in front of you, and brings you to the Amorites, the Hittites, the Perizzites, the Canaanites, the Hivites, and the Jebusites, and I blot them out, 24you shall not bow down to their gods, or worship them, or follow

NIV

blessing will be on your food and water. I will take away sickness from among you, ²⁶and none will miscarry or be barren in your land. I will give you a full life span.

²⁷"I will send my terror ahead of you and throw into confusion every nation you encounter. I will make all your enemies turn their backs and run. ²⁸I will send the hornet ahead of you to drive the Hivites, Canaanites and Hittites out of your way. ²⁹But I will not drive them out in a single year, because the land would become desolate and the wild animals too numerous for you. ³⁰Little by little I will drive them out before you, until you have increased enough to take possession of the land.

³¹"I will establish your borders from the Red Sea*a* to the Sea of the Philistines,*b* and from the desert to the River.*c* I will hand over to you the people who live in the land and you will drive them out before you. ³²Do not make a covenant with them or with their gods. ³³Do not let them live in your land, or they will cause you to sin against me, because the worship of their gods will certainly be a snare to you."

a31 Hebrew *Yam Suph*; that is, Sea of Reeds   *b31* That is, the Mediterranean   *c31* That is, the Euphrates

NRSV

their practices, but you shall utterly demolish them and break their pillars in pieces. ²⁵You shall worship the LORD your God, and I*a* will bless your bread and your water; and I will take sickness away from among you. ²⁶No one shall miscarry or be barren in your land; I will fulfill the number of your days. ²⁷I will send my terror in front of you, and will throw into confusion all the people against whom you shall come, and I will make all your enemies turn their backs to you. ²⁸And I will send the pestilence*b* in front of you, which shall drive out the Hivites, the Canaanites, and the Hittites from before you. ²⁹I will not drive them out from before you in one year, or the land would become desolate and the wild animals would multiply against you. ³⁰Little by little I will drive them out from before you, until you have increased and possess the land. ³¹I will set your borders from the Red Sea*c* to the sea of the Philistines, and from the wilderness to the Euphrates; for I will hand over to you the inhabitants of the land, and you shall drive them out before you. ³²You shall make no covenant with them and their gods. ³³They shall not live in your land, or they will make you sin against me; for if you worship their gods, it will surely be a snare to you.

a Gk Vg: Heb *he*   *b* Or *hornets*: Meaning of Heb uncertain   *c* Or *Sea of Reeds*

COMMENTARY

Moses' presentation of God's commandments ends abruptly in 23:19. Now God speaks an enormous promise to Israel, matched by an insistent requirement. Two themes intertwine in this speech: God is going to give land, blessing, and well-being; and Israel must worship Yahweh alone.

God's way of being present in this dangerous journey is in three "sendings": (a) God will send an "angel" (messenger) (v. 20); (b) God will send "my terror" (v. 27); and (c) God will send "the pestilence" (v. 28).

The angel will protect Israel along the way and will guide Israel safely into the land of promise. We have seen the angel in 3:2 as the forerunner of God's holiness and in 14:19 as a protective presence. Clearly the "angel" is a way of speaking

about God's own work on behalf of Israel. (Note that in 34:11, a parallel passage, the angel is not mentioned but it is "I" who will do what the angel does in this passage.) The language likely reflects a polytheistic image in terms of a high God with obedient heavenly servants and functionaries. Thus, as in Ps 91:11-12, God is a guardian to keep Israel safe, but the work is done through an angel.

The angel is also the voice of the God who commands, and Israel must listen (i.e., obey). In v. 22, the verb for "hear" is reiterated with an infinitive absolute, as in 19:5. Hearing is made the condition of protection. The God who protects is the God who commands; there will be no protection without obedience.

The purpose of the protected journey, as already anticipated in 3:8 and 17, and as set forth programmatically in 15:13-17, is to situate the former slaves in a productive, secure land. Three affirmations are made about the land in vv. 23-26. First, the land is presently occupied by other, hostile peoples who must be displaced. The list of six peoples in v. 23 is conventional and stylized, although such a list characteristically includes seven nations. Without blinking, God will "blot out" the present occupants of the land. Second, the new land will be a place of rigorous theological decision. Israel must eliminate all the signs, symbols, and seductions of other faith options, must hew to the first commandment, to worship "only Yahweh." Third, the elimination of enemies and the practice of pure loyalty will eventuate in a land that is finally blessed by Yahweh; it will be safe, productive, and fertile. Verses 25-26 cite examples of what a blessed life will be like: good bread and good water, i.e., adequate sustenance (unlike the jeopardy of the wilderness); no sickness (cf. 15:26); and no miscarriages or barrenness. The land will be saturated with God's good power for life. The rhetoric of vv. 20-26 holds promise and demand in splendid relation.

The speech of God then turns to the strategy whereby the land will be taken. There will be two more "sendings": terror and pestilence, which, unlike the angel, are Yahweh's agents, sent to afflict the enemy. It is not at all clear, however, in what these agents consist. "Terror" (אימה *'êmâ*) is also used in Exod 15:16 and Josh 2:9 concerning the taking of the land; it suggests that Israel's appearance is so formidable that the other peoples will be fearful and retreat. The second term, "pestilence," is equally uncertain. The NRSV also renders it "pestilence" (צרעה *ṣir'â*) in Deut 7:20, but in Josh 24:12 (and here in the NIV), it is rendered "hornet" (both instances are in the context of land seizure). In many other places (including 4:6) the term is rendered "lep-

rosy." It is enough for our purposes that God will cause panic and destabilization, which will cause retreat and withdrawal, making the land available.

Two other motifs appear in this promise of the land. First, vv. 29-30 assert that the displacement of the other peoples will be gradual. The reason given is that in the transition the land will be unoccupied, left to become an unmanageable wilderness; but in the book of Judges three other, very different, reasons for delay are given. The larger attention in Judges is given to the first (and most theological) reason (Judg 2:2-3, 20-23): God is angry at disobedient Israel and will not clear the land. A second, derivative reason is that Israelites inexperienced in war must be given opportunity to learn (Judg 3:1-2). A third, more practical, military reason is that Israel cannot compete against chariots of iron (Judg 1:19; cf. vv. 21, 27-33). It is likely that our verses reflect a situation in which the established population was not easily dislodged, whether the reason is understood theologically, pedagogically, or militarily. The same reasons would pertain, even if the "conquest" is a social revolution of peasants.

Second, the rhetoric concerning the new land is massively escalated (v. 31). Here the narrative envisions a "greater Israel" of the Solomonic Empire. The theological claim is the same (promise and demand), but the dream of Israel has now expanded, and it still drives the ideological claims of many in the contemporary state of Israel.

After discoursing about the wondrous land of promise (vv. 23-31), God's speech returns one more time to a covenantal accent (vv. 32-33). The Mosaic tradition is acutely aware of the theological threat posed by cultural-religious alternatives. It understands that any benign hosting of other peoples, their symbolizations of reality (cf. v. 24; Deut 12:1-7), and their gods will endanger the identity and destiny of Israel.

REFLECTIONS

1. This text, like much of the OT, insists that biblical faith is profoundly materialistic in its intention. This faith is not a "good idea" or a "spiritual relation," but it is about a communal existence of well-being, security, productivity, and prosperity. Israel's faith inherently spills over into politics and economics, thereby raising issues of power. This God intends for this people a good life in a fully bodied existence. A great deal of work on this point is needed in the church in the United States, where there is a large temptation to gnostic-spiritualizing tendencies (e.g., the popular work of Joseph Campbell). This interpretive tendency, not surprisingly, seems to increase commensurate with the affluence of religious practitioners.

2. This sort of text is problematic because it is so savagely hostile and intolerant of other peoples. We are rightly nervous about any such ideology/dream of displacement. Without denying the problem, the best I know to do is to offer a sociocritical comment that issues in a theological claim. The sociocritical discernment of which I am persuaded (as offered by Norman Gottwald) is that Israel's ideology is formed by a revolutionary cadre of Levites to support a peasant uprising against an exploitative city-state system of economics and politics.[147] (On the Levite connection, see 2:1; 6:16-25; and 32:25-29.) That is, the displacement proposed is not of one ethnic community by another but of a hated class of exploiters by those who are too long abused. This peasant community, so the argument runs, intends a "social experiment" to see whether public power can be organized in covenantal ways. The destruction to be wrought for the purpose of the revolution, then, is not to kill Canaanites at random but to destroy the "system," its practices, its symbols, and inevitably its functionaries.

The Israelite system of covenant is totally incompatible with Canaanite modes of exploitative power, and the rhetoric of the text serves the revolutionary cause by making the contrast unbridgeable. It is inevitable, then, that the program of Moses is not only uncompromising, but intolerant. Such a view of Israel's faith may be unpalatable to us. It is, however, more likely to be unpalatable to affluent, established believers who themselves have compromised with dominant power. This is not to excuse the intolerance, but to suggest that our own social location matters enormously in our assessment of this tradition and its rhetoric.

3. The good land now given is conditional. It depends on worship of Yahweh alone (vv. 21, 24-25, 32). Christianity has for so long represented itself as a religion of free grace, that we flinch from the thought that God's gifts are conditional. Mosaic faith, however, is realistically grounded in a comprehensive "if" (v. 22; cf. 19:5). This is not because God is calculating or bargaining but because the gift of a productive, secure land cannot be held carelessly or through patterns of exploitation. Under such practices, the land will soon succumb to self-serving economics that will void any prospect of peace, security, or justice. The "if" is a realistic understanding that social practice determines social destiny. I will cite three cases in which this conditionality of the good land seems clear enough.

The technological capacity to exploit, distort, and destroy our natural environment is unmistakable. The worship of the gods of military security and unfettered profit does cause a forfeiture of the good land. This is evident in the production of acid rain, and in the environment-threatening residue of modern warfare.

In our day, a variety of obdurate, small tyrants have learned too late that power to govern is not unconditional. When their exploitative system pays no attention to social *conditions*, the land is lost. Super powers, of course, imagine they are immune to such threats. But the turns in the fortunes of the former Soviet Union put even super powers on notice that the conditional quality of the good land in the end has no exceptions, not even for uncommon and unrivalled power.

In the great cities of the United States, the limitless drive of greed and selfishness and the unwillingness to pay taxes in order to sustain the public good have destroyed the infrastructure. As a result, these cities have been overrun with violence. The city cannot be sustained unconditionally. The condition of good life in the good land is adherence to covenantal practices. Israel is always on its way to exile, having learned too slowly. Our own learning is not noticeably swift.

---

147. It is a primary methodical insistence of Norman K. Gottwald, *The Tribes of Yahweh*, that Yahwism is deeply enmeshed in and shaped by social relationships in ancient Israel. See esp. 591-621, 700-702.

EXODUS 24:1-18, THE COVENANT CEREMONY

24 Then he said to Moses, "Come up to the LORD, you and Aaron, Nadab and Abihu, and seventy of the elders of Israel. You are to worship at a distance, [2]but Moses alone is to approach the LORD; the others must not come near. And the people may not come up with him."

[3]When Moses went and told the people all the LORD's words and laws, they responded with one voice, "Everything the LORD has said we will do." [4]Moses then wrote down everything the LORD had said.

He got up early the next morning and built an altar at the foot of the mountain and set up twelve stone pillars representing the twelve tribes of Israel. [5]Then he sent young Israelite men, and they offered burnt offerings and sacrificed young bulls as fellowship offerings[a] to the LORD. [6]Moses took half of the blood and put it in bowls, and the other half he sprinkled on the altar. [7]Then he took the Book of the Covenant and read it to the people. They responded, "We will do everything the LORD has said; we will obey."

[8]Moses then took the blood, sprinkled it on the people and said, "This is the blood of the covenant that the LORD has made with you in accordance with all these words."

[9]Moses and Aaron, Nadab and Abihu, and the seventy elders of Israel went up [10]and saw the God of Israel. Under his feet was something like a pavement made of sapphire,[b] clear as the sky itself. [11]But God did not raise his hand against these leaders of the Israelites; they saw God, and they ate and drank.

[12]The LORD said to Moses, "Come up to me on the mountain and stay here, and I will give you the tablets of stone, with the law and commands I have written for their instruction."

[13]Then Moses set out with Joshua his aide, and Moses went up on the mountain of God. [14]He said to the elders, "Wait here for us until we come back to you. Aaron and Hur are with you, and anyone involved in a dispute can go to them."

[15]When Moses went up on the mountain, the cloud covered it, [16]and the glory of the LORD settled on Mount Sinai. For six days the cloud

24 Then he said to Moses, "Come up to the LORD, you and Aaron, Nadab, and Abihu, and seventy of the elders of Israel, and worship at a distance. [2]Moses alone shall come near the LORD; but the others shall not come near, and the people shall not come up with him."

3Moses came and told the people all the words of the LORD and all the ordinances; and all the people answered with one voice, and said, "All the words that the LORD has spoken we will do." [4]And Moses wrote down all the words of the LORD. He rose early in the morning, and built an altar at the foot of the mountain, and set up twelve pillars, corresponding to the twelve tribes of Israel. [5]He sent young men of the people of Israel, who offered burnt offerings and sacrificed oxen as offerings of well-being to the LORD. [6]Moses took half of the blood and put it in basins, and half of the blood he dashed against the altar. [7]Then he took the book of the covenant, and read it in the hearing of the people; and they said, "All that the LORD has spoken we will do, and we will be obedient." [8]Moses took the blood and dashed it on the people, and said, "See the blood of the covenant that the LORD has made with you in accordance with all these words."

9Then Moses and Aaron, Nadab, and Abihu, and seventy of the elders of Israel went up, [10]and they saw the God of Israel. Under his feet there was something like a pavement of sapphire stone, like the very heaven for clearness. [11]God[a] did not lay his hand on the chief men of the people of Israel; also they beheld God, and they ate and drank.

12The LORD said to Moses, "Come up to me on the mountain, and wait there; and I will give you the tablets of stone, with the law and the commandment, which I have written for their instruction." [13]So Moses set out with his assistant Joshua, and Moses went up into the mountain of God. [14]To the elders he had said, "Wait here for us, until we come to you again; for Aaron and Hur are with you; whoever has a dispute may go to them."

15Then Moses went up on the mountain, and

---

a5 Traditionally *peace offerings*   b10 Or *lapis lazuli*

a Heb *He*

covered the mountain, and on the seventh day the LORD called to Moses from within the cloud. [17]To the Israelites the glory of the LORD looked like a consuming fire on top of the mountain. [18]Then Moses entered the cloud as he went on up the mountain. And he stayed on the mountain forty days and forty nights.

the cloud covered the mountain. [16]The glory of the LORD settled on Mount Sinai, and the cloud covered it for six days; on the seventh day he called to Moses out of the cloud. [17]Now the appearance of the glory of the LORD was like a devouring fire on the top of the mountain in the sight of the people of Israel. [18]Moses entered the cloud, and went up on the mountain. Moses was on the mountain for forty days and forty nights.

COMMENTARY

This chapter concludes the covenant-making process at Sinai (chaps. 19–24), and resumes the themes of theophany, confrontation, and presence, featured in chapter 19. Chapters 19 and 24 thus form a frame that brackets the presentation of law in 20:1-17 and 21:1–23:19.

This chapter holds together two themes, one vertical and one horizontal. The first theme is *communion in the presence of God*, which entails receiving the tablets of commands from God (vv. 1-2, 9-18). The second theme is *covenant making*, whereby Moses dramatically and liturgically binds Israel to Yahweh. These two themes are not, of course, mutually exclusive. But they are expressed in very different forms and rhetoric. According to conventional source analysis, the themes roughly divide into P material (communion) and JE material (covenant making).

24:1-2. God invites Moses to go back up the mountain. According to the analysis of Thomas Dozeman, the movements up and down the mountain not only provide location patterns but also indicate relations of power and influence.[148] In this brief text we are able to see three levels of approach to the presence of God. At the lowest level are "the people," who do not come up. Second are the priests Aaron, Nadab, and Abihu, and seventy elders. Aaron no doubt signifies a particular priestly interest in the narrative. This priestly company is permitted to "come up" further than the people, but they still must worship "at a distance" (v. 1). Third, Moses is permitted to "come near" (v. 2). Thus the narrative once again enhances the singular authority of Moses

and prepares the way for the subsequent polemic against and dismissal of the Aaronides in chap. 32. (This threefold pattern is perhaps distantly echoed in the Gospel narrative of Gethsemane, in which three disciples go part way with Jesus into his ordeal [see Matt 26:36-39; Mark 14:32-35].)

24:3-8. In these verses, however, Moses is not on the mountain but with the people. These verses do not logically follow after vv. 1-2 but seem more appropriate after 20:17 or 20:21. In any case, Moses is now preoccupied with binding Israel in fidelity to the rule of God. There is nothing here of "presence," but only of sovereign will. At the outset, the community swears full allegiance (v. 3). Indeed, this oath seems almost a blank check. Israel swears to obey everything God has said, even that which Moses may yet tell them. Anticipated in 19:8, and reiterated in 24:7, the moment of oath taking is the moment of Israel's constitution as a people unlike any other; they are a people not constituted by blood, language, or territory but only by its singular hearing. Its resolve to "hear" is an acknowledgment that Israel is not self-made, self-invented, or autonomous, but is formed by the power, and for the pleasure, of the Holy One.

Three acts of Moses consummate the relation with Yahweh. First, an altar is built (cf. 20:24-26) on which burnt offerings and whole offerings are given, commensurate with the twelve-tribe structure of Israel (vv. 4-5). Second, there is the "book of the covenant," apparently a literary deposit of the commands given by God to Moses (cf. Deut 31:9-13). While it may be constituted by the Decalogue, scholars are inclined to relate this

148. See Dozeman, *God on the Mountain*.

reference to the corpus of 21:1–23:19. Third, in a ritual act, Moses sprinkles blood from the sacrifice upon both the altar (v. 6) and the people (v. 8). The "blood of the covenant" thus creates solidarity between the two parties. This dramatic act is not rationally explicable, but no doubt arises from the recognition that "blood" is the distinctive element that makes life possible. (See the comparable actions of Gen 15:9-11; Jer 34:18-19.) Thus Israel now begins a new life of obedience, signified by sacrifice, the "book of the covenant," and the "blood of the covenant."

24:9-11. As the narrative advances, we return to the scene at the mountain, as in vv. 1-2. The characters are the same as in vv. 1-2: Moses, Aaron, Nadab, Abihu, and the seventy elders. This is the authorized leadership of the community. In the Priestly tradition, we are at an awesome moment of peculiar and dreadful encounter. A. Henton Davies describes these verses as "some of the most astonishing and inexplicable verses in the Old Testament."[149]

The narrative is abrupt: "They saw God!" (v. 10). There God was, fully visible in concrete form. In v. 11, the theme intensifies: "They beheld God," or better, "They gazed upon God." The scene suggests a stunned, astonished silence. They look and are mesmerized. They do not speak; they do not move. Ernest Nicholson quotes Rabbi Hoshoia: "They fixed gloating eyes upon the Divine Presence."[150] This is indeed a foundational moment, not to be repeated in Israel's life.

Then the narrative adds three notes. First, it attempts to say what they see (v. 10) in words that are, as might be expected, stammering and inadequate. The "description" is governed by the double use of "like" ($k\ddot{e}$), for the scene will not admit of direct reportage. What is seen is unutterable and can only be narrated by indirection. It is not "a pavement of sapphire stone," but it is "like" that. It is not "heavenly clearness," but it is "like" that, even as it is beyond it and unutterable. The most remarkable parallel to this report is Ezekiel's vision, in which "like" is used repeatedly (Ezek 1:13, 16, 22, 24 [three times], 26 [four times], 27 [three times], 28 [two times]). The

narrator wants to characterize what is real and visible and tangible. What is given in the meeting, however, is holy and unapproachable.

Second, the narrative reports God's astonishing deference to Israel (v. 11). Ordinarily one may not see God; certainly one may not see God and live (Judg 6:22-23). This is not because God is invisible, but because God is dangerously holy (33:22-23). Thus these priests and elders are at great risk. But God does not lay a hand upon them, and they are safe. Presumably it is a moment of God's generous self-giving, not repeatable, but very real.

Third, they eat and drink (v. 11). It is conventional to say that here Israel participates with God in a meal of covenantal solidarity, thus sealing the relation. Harold Bloom, in what may be a slight trivialization, calls this "a picnic."[151] But we are not told the meal was light or celebrative. It may as well have been solemn, ominous, and dreadful.

The narrative intends to leave us stunned, bewildered, and awestruck. And it does! We do not know what happened, for here earth entered into face-to-face contact with the Holy One around the most elemental activity of eating (cf. Luke 24:35). It is entirely plausible that in Priestly rhetoric "seeing God" and "eating with God" are understood as cultic actions (cf. Ps 17:15; Isa 6:1). Such recognition, however, explains nothing and diminishes nothing, but only locates the moment of awe. More likely, the narrator invites us to an irreducible moment that allows no useful probing. The outcome is that Israel is even more stunned by the holiness; the leadership is freshly authorized, but, we may imagine, shaken to its respective toes by this Reality so utterly present and so completely, unutterably beyond them.

24:12-14. Then Moses goes farther up the mountain. He is now alone—except for Joshua. The reference to Joshua is odd, for it is "Moses alone" in v. 2. In fact, Joshua plays no role here at all (previously we have him only in 17:14). The narrator is perhaps looking forward to the time when Joshua must be legitimated as Moses' successor. With that peculiar and inconsequential exception, it is "Moses alone." Aaron (and Hur) are left behind. Thus the narrator prepares the

149. G. Henton Davies, *Exodus: An Introduction and Commentary* (London: SCM, 1967) 193.
150. Ernest Nicholson, "The Interpretation of Exodus XXIV 9–11," *VT* 24 (1974) 89-90.

151. Harold Bloom, "From J to K, or The Uncanniness of the Yahwist," in *The Bible and the Narrative Tradition,* ed. Frank McConnell (New York: Oxford University Press, 1986) 35.

way for the crisis of chap. 32. Later, Joshua and Aaron will come to represent conflicting trajectories of Israel's life and faith. There is, moreover, no doubt where the narrator's sympathies lie.

24:15-18. Finally, Moses is alone, now without even Joshua, exposed, at risk, on the mountain, into the cloud. Here, he is to wait in complete obedience to be addressed and to receive.

The counterpoint to Moses in this meeting is not the God who is seen. It is "the glory of the LORD," which is "like" a devouring fire: alive, dangerous, and visible. We have seen the glory of Yahweh arise from combat with Pharaoh (14:4, 17), and we have been surprised to find the glory inhabiting, of all places, the wilderness (16:10). Now, however, the glory is in its natural habitat, high above, inaccessible, in the midst of the cloud.

And "Moses entered the cloud." What a statement! He goes where no one has ever gone. He leaves the zone of humanness and enters the very sphere of God. And there he stays, forty days and forty nights—i.e., a very long time. No one, not Aaron or Israel or the narrator, knows whether he will ever come out again. The rootage of Israel's worship (now to be authorized in chaps. 25–31 and to be actualized in 40:34-38) is not a human device, but a holy gift that comes from God's own awesome intentionality. God wants God's glory to abide, "to tabernacle" (שׁכן *šākan*) in the realm of the human, in the very life of Israel. But for God to come here, Moses must go there!

REFLECTIONS

This chapter, perhaps by juxtaposing P and JE materials, holds together *awesome presence* and *covenantal demand.* Faithful interpretation must take both seriously, and must perhaps accent the theme that in each context is the more difficult. In a context focused on rigorous obedience, the awesome glory warrants attention; in a context fascinated with glorious presence, the demand of covenant deserves attention.

1. The oath of loyalty (vv. 3-8), together with its dramatic bonding through book and blood, creates a new community in the world. Kutsch has argued strongly that "covenant" (ברית *běrît*) is in fact not a "relationship" (*Bund*) but an "obligation" (*Verpflichtung*).[152] Israel's distinctive life in the world is due to its sworn allegiance to this God alone. Such a hard-nosed claim is exceedingly difficult in a culture that is so fearful of authority, so bent on the therapeutic, and so committed to individual freedom and self-fulfillment. That, of course, has made Israel (and the "New Israel"?) endlessly odd and problematic. The oath of allegiance is access to a radical ecclesiology.

Moreover, that community is finally constituted not forensically but sacramentally. Israel comes into being not primarily by an act of its own will, but by liturgic action taken upon it by God, which bestows upon it a solidarity, a destiny, and an identity that it could not choose for itself. The reference to blood is a witness to profound solidarity, wrought by the initiative of God (cf. Heb 9:18-21). In this self-giving, Yahweh is fully pledged to Israel, as Israel is sworn to Yahweh. See the more formal and symmetrical assertion of this solidarity in 6:7.

2. "Gazing upon God" leads our reflection in a very different direction. At the center of the Sinai tradition is an act of contemplation, an awed, silent, respectful look at God. This tradition is in deep tension with the oath of loyalty and obedience, but it is powerfully present, nonetheless, in the text. Samuel Terrien has poignantly juxtaposed the "ethical ear" and the "contemplative eye" in his study of the presence of God in the OT.[153] The "beholding of God" curtails all the listening and is overwhelmed by the vision. As I write this, a British hostage

---

152. E. Kutsch, *Verheissung und Gesetz. Untersuchungen zum Sogenannten "Bund" im Alten Testament,* BZAW 131 (Berlin: De Gruyter, 1973). See the critical summary of his work by Ernest Nicholson, *God and His People,* 89-117.
153. Samuel Terrien, *The Elusive Presence: Towards a New Biblical Theology,* Religious Perspectives (San Francisco: Harper & Row, 1978). On this passage, see 134-36.

has just been released from five years of captivity in Lebanon. He reports that after four years of confinement, he and his cohorts were given a bowl of red cherries, the first fruit and the first color they had seen in four years. Despite their eagerness to taste the fruit, he reports, they waited a day, simply to gaze upon the cherries in wonder and gratitude. This mundane report may hint at what the priests and elders did at Sinai: They gazed before they ate.

3. The stammering speech of the narrator is crucial to the telling. The biblical tradition is, of course, eloquent and articulate. It does, however, reach the point of the unutterable. Karl Barth has said of this faith: "As ministers we ought to speak of God. We are human, however, and so cannot speak of God."[154]

This text has perhaps its closest NT counterpart in the narrative of the transfiguration of Jesus, in which the narrator also stammers: "His face shone like the sun, and his clothes became dazzling white" (Matt 17:2 NRSV); "His clothes became dazzling white, such as no one on earth could bleach them" (Mark 9:3 NRSV). Luke then writes, "They saw his glory" and "they were terrified as they entered the cloud" (Luke 9:32, 34 NRSV). Here also there is glory; here also the cloud overwhelms; and here also, finally, a massive, terrifying voice is heard. The narrative of the transfiguration is no ordinary story. It tells of the faithful disciples' being given an intimate glimpse into the reality of God's holiness. This holiness is embodied in Jesus who echoes and replicates the oddity of Sinai.

At the core of Christian faith is an overpowering, unutterable disclosure that gives access to the awesome holiness and moves in the direction of contemplation, wonderment, and grateful awe. Conventional Protestantism, with its moral passion, has been reluctant to probe or consider these matters, being frightened of anything that smacks of mysticism. No doubt such an accent is just now problematic, given the rage of gnostic spirituality. But neglect of this dimension of faith may be equally hazardous. This vision provides the legitimation and energy for Moses and for all who draw life from this vision.

4. The vision of God is inescapably transformative. Martin Smith takes the expression "No one can see God and live" to mean "No one could see God and remain unchanged."[155] The power of God's appearing changes those who see (see 1 John 3:2-3). Those who see become "more like God." But then, seeing God has transformative power, which leads to more dangerous obedience. The presence of God and communion with God are "the real thing" in and of themselves. Nonetheless, they have profound transformative effect on those who "enter the cloud."

154. Karl Barth, *The Word of God and the Word of Man* (New York: Harper and Bros., 1957) 186.
155. Martin Smith, *The Word Is Very Near You: A Guide to Praying with Scripture* (London: Darton, Longman and Todd, 1989) 131.

EXODUS 25:1–31:18

THE PATTERN OF THE TABERNACLE

OVERVIEW

These seven chapters, consisting in seven speeches by Yahweh to Moses, purport to be instructions given on Mt. Sinai (cf. 24:15-18). They are instructions to Moses about how to build a suitable place in which Yahweh will dwell (שכן šākan) in the midst of Israel (25:8). The consensus of critical scholarship is that these chapters are an exilic or post-exilic piece of the Priestly tradition that describes a notion of a sanctuary suitable to the post-exilic situation of a displaced people.[156]

The noun *tabernacle* (משכן *miškān*) derives from the verb *šākan*, which means "to dwell" or "to sojourn." The verb suggests full presence, but it is not a stable guarantee of a permanent presence. The God who dwells here does so with freedom to leave. The tabernacle is a "portable temple," which is appropriate for a displaced people who are no longer in Jerusalem and are, therefore, in transit. Thus the proposed tabernacle guarantees a combination of presence and mobility.

Recent scholars, however, have not been content to leave this as a descriptive text. With more interpretive imagination, they have asked how this allegedly descriptive account functions in and serves the larger Priestly theology. Joseph Blenkinsopp has proposed that this text is a quite deliberate complement to the creation narrative of Gen 1:1–2:4*a*, both in terms of the rhetoric of "command and performance" and with the affirmation of 39:32 and 40:33 that the work of the tabernacle is "finished" (cf. Gen 2:1).[157] Blenkinsopp proposes that the creation of the tabernacle parallels the creation of the world in P theology. (He also suggests a third parallel in the distribution of the land in Joshua 18–24.) Thus for P, the completion of the tabernacle to house God's glory is as momentous as the creation of the world.

This text can be seen as a theological statement about God's willingness to be present in the midst of the community of Israel, under the custodial auspices of the priests. Frank H. Gorman, Jr., has helpfully shown how liturgic interests are indeed an important public agenda for a community that wants to order its life in intentional ways.[158] Thus the interpreter is invited to think with these texts about how the power and goodness of God are present in the world. The answer to that wonderment given here is that the presence of God is available through a cultic apparatus authorized and designed by God's own self-disclosure, and implemented through skilled, obedient human authority.

Beyond a concern for source analysis and religious history, but also beyond a particular theological strand in the Pentateuch (P), we must at last ask what it means to have a *canonical text* that talks seriously about these matters. As a canonical text, it is no longer an actual description, or even a sixth-century theological strategy, but a revealing, authorizing text for all the generations. As readers of the text, we are not making a tabernacle and have no particular interest in one, per se. So then, what do we do when we read this text?

In the end, the exodus scenario is not only a transformative "event," but also a settled, reliable, sustained "pattern" for God's presence. This text, then, is an act of daring imagination that invites erstwhile slaves to imagine a world in which God is palpably, visibly, wondrously present.

Imagining the presence is an invitation to a certain kind of theological sensitivity that is marked by extravagance and aesthetic yearning.

---

156. See the important alternative proposal on the dating of the Priestly material by Jacob Milgrom, *Leviticus 1–16: A New Translation with Introduction and Commentary,* AB 3 (New York: Doubleday, 1991).

157. Joseph Blenkinsopp, "The Structure of P," *CBQ* 38 (1976) 275-92. See also P. J. Kearney, "Creation and Liturgy: The P Redaction of Ex 25–40," *ZAW* 89 (1977) 375-87.

158. Frank H. Gorman, Jr., *The Ideology of Ritual: Space, Time and Status in the Priestly Theology,* JSOTSup 91 (Sheffield: Sheffield Academic, 1990).

This act of imagination is crucial in our own time for two reasons. On the one hand, mainline Christianity in the United States has been preoccupied with either moral or doctrinal matters, giving far less energy to sacramental imagination. In the tradition of the Reformation in particular, an actual cherishing of the presence in and for itself is largely avoided. Such a shunning of the mystery of presence has permitted much faith to become blatant ideology practiced in a tone and posture of coercion. Imagination about the presence may tone down such hard-nosed certitude to permit a less triumphalistic sureness.

On the other hand, a society of technological secularism is increasingly a profaned society, having banished mystery and largely emptied the world of any meaning beyond the small significances we ourselves devise. In such a world, brutality is possible and increasingly palatable, both informally and as official public practice and policy. The mystery of presence does indeed function as a counter to the threat of profanation so powerful among us. This text requires us to think and believe in trajectories largely neglected in most popular religion as well as in most cavalier rejections of religion. This text asserts, against both ideological religious certitude and against confident secularism, that there is a sacramental foundation that makes life possible, that defines life in certain ways, and that precludes the destructiveness and despair that seem so potent among us.

EXODUS 25:1-40, TABERNACLE FURNISHINGS

NIV

25 The LORD said to Moses, [2]"Tell the Israelites to bring me an offering. You are to receive the offering for me from each man whose heart prompts him to give. [3]These are the offerings you are to receive from them: gold, silver and bronze; [4]blue, purple and scarlet yarn and fine linen; goat hair; [5]ram skins dyed red and hides of sea cows*a*; acacia wood; [6]olive oil for the light; spices for the anointing oil and for the fragrant incense; [7]and onyx stones and other gems to be mounted on the ephod and breastpiece.

[8]"Then have them make a sanctuary for me, and I will dwell among them. [9]Make this tabernacle and all its furnishings exactly like the pattern I will show you.

[10]"Have them make a chest of acacia wood—two and a half cubits long, a cubit and a half wide, and a cubit and a half high.*b* [11]Overlay it with pure gold, both inside and out, and make a gold molding around it. [12]Cast four gold rings for it and fasten them to its four feet, with two rings on one side and two rings on the other. [13]Then make poles of acacia wood and overlay them with gold. [14]Insert the poles into the rings on the sides of the chest to carry it. [15]The poles are to remain

a5 That is, dugongs   b10 That is, about 3 3/4 feet (about 1.1 meters) long and 2 1/4 feet (about 0.7 meter) wide and high

NRSV

25 The LORD said to Moses: [2]Tell the Israelites to take for me an offering; from all whose hearts prompt them to give you shall receive the offering for me. [3]This is the offering that you shall receive from them: gold, silver, and bronze, [4]blue, purple, and crimson yarns and fine linen, goats' hair, [5]tanned rams' skins, fine leather,*a* acacia wood, [6]oil for the lamps, spices for the anointing oil and for the fragrant incense, [7]onyx stones and gems to be set in the ephod and for the breastpiece. [8]And have them make me a sanctuary, so that I may dwell among them. [9]In accordance with all that I show you concerning the pattern of the tabernacle and of all its furniture, so you shall make it.

10They shall make an ark of acacia wood; it shall be two and a half cubits long, a cubit and a half wide, and a cubit and a half high. [11]You shall overlay it with pure gold, inside and outside you shall overlay it, and you shall make a molding of gold upon it all around. [12]You shall cast four rings of gold for it and put them on its four feet, two rings on the one side of it, and two rings on the other side. [13]You shall make poles of acacia wood, and overlay them with gold. [14]And you shall put the poles into the rings on the sides of

a Meaning of Heb uncertain

in the rings of this ark; they are not to be removed. [16]Then put in the ark the Testimony, which I will give you.

[17]"Make an atonement cover[a] of pure gold—two and a half cubits long and a cubit and a half wide.[b] [18]And make two cherubim out of hammered gold at the ends of the cover. [19]Make one cherub on one end and the second cherub on the other; make the cherubim of one piece with the cover, at the two ends. [20]The cherubim are to have their wings spread upward, overshadowing the cover with them. The cherubim are to face each other, looking toward the cover. [21]Place the cover on top of the ark and put in the ark the Testimony, which I will give you. [22]There, above the cover between the two cherubim that are over the ark of the Testimony, I will meet with you and give you all my commands for the Israelites.

[23]"Make a table of acacia wood—two cubits long, a cubit wide and a cubit and a half high.[d] [24]Overlay it with pure gold and make a gold molding around it. [25]Also make around it a rim a handbreadth[c] wide and put a gold molding on the rim. [26]Make four gold rings for the table and fasten them to the four corners, where the four legs are. [27]The rings are to be close to the rim to hold the poles used in carrying the table. [28]Make the poles of acacia wood, overlay them with gold and carry the table with them. [29]And make its plates and dishes of pure gold, as well as its pitchers and bowls for the pouring out of offerings. [30]Put the bread of the Presence on this table to be before me at all times.

[31]"Make a lampstand of pure gold and hammer it out, base and shaft; its flowerlike cups, buds and blossoms shall be of one piece with it. [32]Six branches are to extend from the sides of the lampstand—three on one side and three on the other. [33]Three cups shaped like almond flowers with buds and blossoms are to be on one branch, three on the next branch, and the same for all six branches extending from the lampstand. [34]And on the lampstand there are to be four cups shaped like almond flowers with buds and blossoms.

[a]17 Traditionally *a mercy seat*   [b]17 That is, about 3 3/4 feet (about 1.1 meters) long and 2 1/4 feet (about 0.7 meter) wide
[c]23 That is, about 3 feet (about 0.9 meter) long and 1 1/2 feet (about 0.5 meter) wide and 2 1/4 feet (about 0.7 meter) high
[d]25 That is, about 3 inches (about 8 centimeters)

the ark, by which to carry the ark. [15]The poles shall remain in the rings of the ark; they shall not be taken from it. [16]You shall put into the ark the covenant[a] that I shall give you.

17Then you shall make a mercy seat[b] of pure gold; two cubits and a half shall be its length, and a cubit and a half its width. [18]You shall make two cherubim of gold; you shall make them of hammered work, at the two ends of the mercy seat.[b] [19]Make one cherub at the one end, and one cherub at the other; of one piece with the mercy seat[b] you shall make the cherubim at its two ends. [20]The cherubim shall spread out their wings above, overshadowing the mercy seat[b] with their wings. They shall face one to another; the faces of the cherubim shall be turned toward the mercy seat.[b] [21]You shall put the mercy seat[b] on the top of the ark; and in the ark you shall put the covenant[a] that I shall give you. [22]There I will meet with you, and from above the mercy seat,[b] from between the two cherubim that are on the ark of the covenant,[a] I will deliver to you all my commands for the Israelites.

23You shall make a table of acacia wood, two cubits long, one cubit wide, and a cubit and a half high. [24]You shall overlay it with pure gold, and make a molding of gold around it. [25]You shall make around it a rim a handbreadth wide, and a molding of gold around the rim. [26]You shall make for it four rings of gold, and fasten the rings to the four corners at its four legs. [27]The rings that hold the poles used for carrying the table shall be close to the rim. [28]You shall make the poles of acacia wood, and overlay them with gold, and the table shall be carried with these. [29]You shall make its plates and dishes for incense, and its flagons and bowls with which to pour drink offerings; you shall make them of pure gold. [30]And you shall set the bread of the Presence on the table before me always.

31You shall make a lampstand of pure gold. The base and the shaft of the lampstand shall be made of hammered work; its cups, its calyxes, and its petals shall be of one piece with it; [32]and there shall be six branches going out of its sides, three branches of the lampstand out of one side of it and three branches of the lampstand out of

[a]Or *treaty,* or *testimony;* Heb *eduth*   [b]Or *a cover*

35One bud shall be under the first pair of branches extending from the lampstand, a second bud under the second pair, and a third bud under the third pair—six branches in all. 36The buds and branches shall all be of one piece with the lampstand, hammered out of pure gold.

37"Then make its seven lamps and set them up on it so that they light the space in front of it. 38Its wick trimmers and trays are to be of pure gold. 39A talent*a* of pure gold is to be used for the lampstand and all these accessories. 40See that you make them according to the pattern shown you on the mountain.

a39 That is, about 75 pounds (about 34 kilograms)

the other side of it; 33three cups shaped like almond blossoms, each with calyx and petals, on one branch, and three cups shaped like almond blossoms, each with calyx and petals, on the other branch—so for the six branches going out of the lampstand. 34On the lampstand itself there shall be four cups shaped like almond blossoms, each with its calyxes and petals. 35There shall be a calyx of one piece with it under the first pair of branches, a calyx of one piece with it under the next pair of branches, and a calyx of one piece with it under the last pair of branches—so for the six branches that go out of the lampstand. 36Their calyxes and their branches shall be of one piece with it, the whole of it one hammered piece of pure gold. 37You shall make the seven lamps for it; and the lamps shall be set up so as to give light on the space in front of it. 38Its snuffers and trays shall be of pure gold. 39It, and all these utensils, shall be made from a talent of pure gold. 40And see that you make them according to the pattern for them, which is being shown you on the mountain.

COMMENTARY

Moses enters the cloud and is in the inscrutable presence for forty days and forty nights (24:18). What happens during that time is hidden from us. We only know that Yahweh speaks and Moses listens. Kearney has observed that the extended address to Moses is divided into seven discreet speeches.[159] By far the longest of these is the first, 25:1–31:11. Since that speech is so long, however, I have chosen to follow conventional chapter divisions, because the discussion will be easier to follow, and because in teaching and/or preaching, the conventional chapter divisions are most likely to be employed. It is important to remember, however, that these chapters do indeed form one long speech.

Two obvious preliminary points merit careful attention. First, these long speeches are dominated by God, the same God who has worked wonders against Egypt (chaps. 1–15) on behalf of Israel (chaps. 16–17). This is also the God who has met with Moses and Israel at Sinai (chaps. 19–24). In that meeting, God has asserted sovereignty over the future of this liberated people, and has bound Israel to a rigorous obedience.

In the process of covenant making at Sinai, however, this God has also been bound to a new loyalty. The bonding of Sinai is a two-way affair, and God has been decisively impinged upon by Israel. Nothing of God's sovereignty has been diminished, but that sovereignty is now differently deployed. The God who has been ferocious and resolute about victory and deliverance is now the God who speaks to an attentive, responsive Moses. The mood of this speech is one of acceptance between friends, albeit friends who live at a respectful distance.

Second, we take special note of what this newly bound, newly impinged upon God does. God *speaks.* God announces God's will and thereby reveals something of God's own self. God discloses a generous provision for how the holiness

159. Kearney, "Creation and Liturgy."

of God can be hosted in a community that is not easily God's habitat. Thus the speech of God, even cast as an imperative, is an act of inordinant generosity.

25:1-8. God's self-disclosing, generous command is to be initiated through an offering (תרומה *tĕrûmâ*) of the materials out of which the modes of communion will be constructed. The entire program of constructing a fitting place for God's presence begins in an offering from Israel. God does not unilaterally bestow or impose a habitat. Constructing an adequate place for the holiness of God is indeed human work, wrought in generosity. The term *offering* (*tĕrûmâ*) refers to what is "raised, lifted," here reinforced by the phrase "whose hearts prompt them." The term *prompt* (נדב *nādab*) refers to those who are compelled or motivated gladly to make an offering. The materials to be used are those freely given, without coercion or requirement. These are people who genuinely want communion with God.

The materials of the offering provide an inventory of the kinds of wealth required for what follows and the kinds of wealth available in this economy. We are surprised to learn that this community now possesses all these goods. Perhaps the list here has a counterpart in 3:21-22; 11:3; and 12:35-36, in which Israel is "empty-handed" and able only to take what is needed. Israel is now indeed to "give of its best." Such a requirement means that the development of an adequate place for holiness concerns the center of the economy. While the list of requirements is more than a little obscure, we may note that gold and silver stand at the top of the list (no doubt also first in value) as well as oil for both lamps and anointing. We shall see in what follows that a provision for light will be important, and the "oil for anointing" suggests a concern not only for God's presence, but also for human agents in worship. In this list of things to be produced, the mention of "ephod" and "breast plate" anticipates the dress and, therefore, the centrality of the priestly office. From the outset, this speech focuses on priesthood as the necessary means of communion.

The purpose of the offering (and of this long speech) is indicated in vv. 7-8, with particular attention to three terms. First, this is to be a "sanctuary" (מקדש *miqdāš*). This is a noun formed

from the term for "holy" (קדש *qādaš*). Second, and perhaps most important, God uses the phrase "that I may dwell among you"—the governing intention of this long speech. God intends to be among the people, in the midst of, at the center of Israel's life.

The verb *dwell* (*šākan*) is peculiarly important and delicate. On the one hand, it signifies an abiding presence. That is, God now intends to be "at home" in the midst of Israel. On the other hand, the verb *šākan* implies much less than "to sit permanently" (ישב *yāšab*). It suggests a settling in, but with freedom and capacity to move on at will, i.e., to bivouac.

The use of this term is part of an ongoing, unresolved tension in the OT about the presence of God, a tension that this speech exploits to the full. Thus we may suggest a continuum concerning God's presence:

come/go . . . . . sojourn . . . . . inhabit permanently
בוא (*bô'*)   שכן (*šākan*)   ישב (*yāšab*).

There are texts to support each of these views. Our text takes up the middle position, wanting to assure presence, but also carefully avoiding the more crass assumption that God is a permanent occupant. Our text seeks to respect and take seriously the freedom of God, who is committed to Israel but who will not be domesticated by cultic practice.

The third term, *tabernacle* (משכן *miškān*), derives from *šākan*. The term appears to be simply the conversion of a verb into a noun that specifies the place wherein God will bivouac. This term shows the tradition struggling to work out a theory and understanding of God's presence that both honors the freedom of God and takes seriously the need for regularity and reliability of God's presence in the community.

25:9. Finally in v. 9, God says, "I will cause you to see concerning the pattern (תבנית *tabnît*). . . . " This is a remarkable statement in two regards. First, the text that started in speech that Moses can *hear* ends in showing that Moses *sees*. While this statement is presented to us as a speech of God, in fact it is a drawing or picturing by God. In this text, the book of Exodus moves a *recital* of narrative to an *exhibit* of blueprints, and Israel's mode of faith is transformed from conversation to observation. The move negatively suggests a static quality of faith, an attempt to "freeze" the presence. Positively, it introduces, alongside ethical concerns for justice and liberation, aesthetic concerns for symmetry, beauty, and loveliness. Prior to this, Israel had seen what the mighty liberating hand of God did to Egypt. Now what Moses sees is an abiding portrayal that gives durability to the prospect of communion.

This emphasis on "see" is reinforced by the term *pattern* (*tabnît*), a noun from the verb for "build" (בנה *bānâ*). The expression "show the pattern" is important because it suggests that there is an overall plan fully conceived in God's mind as a habitat within the community. The plan is God's own vision of what is required and what is possible. Just as God has seen ahead of time, and as Moses is now permitted to see, so also the community of this text is invited to see what is intended in beauty and symmetry.

Second, the architect charges the engineer: "You do it." The habitat for communion is a human responsibility and a human possibility, but it is a human enterprise undertaken in obedience to a grand, God-given design of proportion.

The remainder of this chapter describes four aspects of the tabernacle, each of which is to serve and enhance presence and communion: the ark (vv. 10-16), the mercy seat (vv. 17-22), a table of acacia wood (vv. 23-30), and a lampstand (vv. 31-40). All four of these pieces of equipment are specified in two ways. First, there is great precision in their construction. Second, nothing is to be spared in extravagant materials. In both precision and extravagance, the making of these objects is an urgent matter that is undertaken gladly by the community in order to enhance the promise of presence.

25:10-16. One can trace through the OT varied and, no doubt, rival understandings of the function and purpose of the ark, though here no interpretation is given. It is plausible that the ark was a dramatic paladin for war. In other uses, it was a throne upon which sat the invisible God, so that a notion of royal presence may have displaced military dynamism. While these two functions can be distinguished, they are not discontinuous. Both attest to the real action and sovereign presence of God.

A third view of the ark, one that seeks to minimize the notion of "presence," is that the ark is a container for the tablets of the command-

ments (Deut 4:7-8 may suggest holding these two accents together, as it places in parallel "a God so near" and "a torah so righteous.") First Kgs 8:1-13 closely relates to our text. The text seems to have a high view of presence connected to the ark, referring to some of the same features as in our text, and yet also asserts that "the two tablets of stone" were in it (1 Kgs 8:9 NRSV). The fact that such different interpretations of the ark exist side by side indicates that Israel never arrived at a consensus view.

In our text, v. 16 makes a comment not unlike that of 1 Kgs 8:9, suggesting that the ark is essentially a container for "the covenant" (עדת *'ēdūt*). The term *'ēdūt* is elsewhere rendered "testimony," and seems to refer to actual, physical tablets of commands, which endure and testify to and remind Israel of its solemn oath to Yahweh. Thus in this paragraph describing sanctuary furniture, the climactic statement concerns membership in covenant.

25:17-22. The second element in the tabernacle is the "mercy seat" (כפרת *kapōret*). Again we are given the precise shape and measurements, and this second object is again overlaid with gold. The term for "mercy seat" is once more a noun (*kapōret*), from the verb כפר (*kāpar*), which means to "cover." While the term itself may only mean a covering or a place of covering, the verb here means to cover over the power and danger of sin, so that the mercy seat is the place where the power of sin is covered over and neutralized. The cruciality of the term is evidenced by its recurrence in the book of Leviticus at the end of each sacrifice to be enacted by a priest. The noun is a special theological term created by this tradition, and it represents a remarkably imaginative achievement, whereby a verb has been visualized as an identifiable object. The operation of "covering" at the mercy seat is like putting a sealer over a contaminated substance so that it can no longer infect or threaten. Thus "mercy seat" is a place or an object that functions to overcome the danger from sin, wherein sin is treated almost as a material, physical threat. There is a considerable theological development from the primitive, substantive notion of "cover" to the relational notion of conciliation, but they are held together in the term *atone*. The meaning of the cult object depends on interpretive decision, because the text tells us nothing about the function of the tabernacle. In Lev 16:2-16, however, the term is used exactly to describe the liturgic process whereby the power of guilt is overcome in *Yom Kippur*, the day of "covering," i.e., the Day of Atonement.

The mercy seat is encompassed by two "cherubim," perhaps a carving of two winged creatures hovering over the mercy seat. The cherubim are members of the court of the holy God (not innocent, overweight children as in artistic portrayals of cherubs) who function to signify the presence, sovereignty, and protection of God. The visual portrayal of cherubim witnesses to a "peopled" place that mediates a God who is distantly transcendent but palpably available.

The description culminates again in an interpretive-promissory comment (vv. 21-22). Again, there is reference to the "testimony" (*'ēdût*) in the ark. The mercy seat, however, is the place where God will meet (יעד *yā'ad*) Moses. More than a place of deposit, the purpose of the ark and the mercy seat is "meeting"! Perhaps even more astonishing than the prospect of the meeting is its purpose. While the language of "mercy seat" might suggest a covering of guilt and the gift of forgiveness, the purpose of the meeting is "I will command you to the Israelites" (v. 22)—i.e., the purpose is to issue commandments.

This remarkable interpretation of the "meeting" suggests two things. First, the cult tradition believes that obedience is indeed possible; this tradition is not mired down in a heavy preoccupation with guilt. Second, there is no ground for separating the cultic and the ethical. The purpose of the cult is mediation of torah, to assure that the community of Moses will be a torah-keeping community. The "mercy seat" is concerned with the giving of the torah, itself a profound act of mercy in Israel!

25:23-30. The third piece of furniture in the tabernacle is a table made of acacia wood. Again, we are told not only of its exact measurements, but also about the vessels that are to sit upon it—plates, dishes, flagons, and bowls, all of which are to be gold plated.

Yet a third time (as in vv. 16, 22), the paragraph that contains specifications of measurement and luxurious construction culminates in a statement that gives a theological twist to the provision (v. 30). The purpose of the table is for "the bread of presence," i.e., the bread of faces. The text tells us nothing about this bread. It takes no great imagination to see that the bread is in some sense sacramental, but we are not told more than that. Most plausibly, it is bread that the human community eats (with God) as "table fellowship." Or it may be bread that the people provide for the "care and feeding" of God. Either way, it bespeaks presence and, perhaps, solidarity between God and Israel.

25:31-40. The fourth piece of furniture is a lampstand. It is described in enormous detail, more than the preceding three objects. It is, indeed, an elaborate object, and it as well is to be decorated with pure gold. We are not told much of its precise function, but that perhaps may be taken as obvious. The concluding statement is that it should "give light" (v. 37). It is plausible that the light is understood to have liturgical, sacramental significance, but nothing is said of that. More likely, in a context where there are no other lights and where the darkness is peopled and enormously threatening, the practical function of light and its sacramental significance cannot be easily divided. The light creates a safe place in a world of threat. The light witnesses to and presents a place that God has carved out of the dangerous darkness, where God's good rule is fully established, and where Israel may be fully at ease in well-being.

The final verse of the chapter pertains not only to the last paragraph concerning the lampstand, but to all four items named and described (v. 40). For all four objects, there is a pattern: a visible, precise intention that Moses and the community are permitted to see or imagine. Thus the articulation of these four items is an act of hope and a promise of how the worship and the world of Israel will be when a proper context for community is established.

REFLECTIONS

For many readers, entry into the second half of Exodus is rather like stepping into a dark, dank archive. The texts at first glance appear remote and opaque, without discernible windows of interpretation. This impression may be acutely strong among Christians who imagine that such old texts have been overcome in the Christian gospel, and especially among Protestants who are in any case suspicious of ritual punctiliousness and precision.

The problem of engaging these texts is larger, however, than simply Christian supersessionism or Protestant negativity toward cult. The problem is rooted in modernity's impatience with any notion of holy mystery, or with any offer of holy mystery and holy presence that requires discipline, order, and planning. Or, said another way, modernity is restless with any offer of transcendent meaning and power that must be mediated when, in fact, this text is all about the possibility and the problem of such mediation.

It may be nearly impossible to do so, but the interpreter should attempt to hear these texts as though for the first time (as indeed they will be for many readers)! Imagine that in the context of covenant at Mt. Sinai God should take care to think through, speak about, and propose modes and procedures whereby Israel can count upon with certitude a rendezvous with the Holy One. There is, in our own time and place, a deep hunger and yearning for reliable contact with the holy mystery of God. This text invites the community to imagine that meeting and to receive the offer of presence given in the text.

The text makes two fundamental affirmations. First, such a meeting is possible. Second, such presence is not "immediately" available, but is mediated through the regularized disciplines of the community. Such an articulation does not deny that there may be immediate meetings, but no textual procedure can produce, assure, or generate that possibility. This is presence for "ordinary times" when there is no crisis, but simply the deep, abiding hunger for that which can satisfy and give rest to the restless. This text affirms that there is in God a counterpart to human restlessness—a willingness to meet.

1. As the interpreter moves from liberation to presence, from recital to blueprint, it is worth asking whether there are any counterpoints between the two parts of the text and between cultic offer and contemporary need. I suggest the following possibilities for the four cultic objects listed in this chapter.

The purpose of the **ark** is to provide a place for the "testimonies" (*'ēdût*) that give Israel its membership in a community with God. The "testimonies" may be commandments or other tokens of identity, but in any case they witness to and voice a peculiar identity as the people of Yahweh.[160] Such a witness needs care and special housing. This special people with this visible membership is what came into being at Sinai, when the slave community was taken as "my treasured possession out of all the peoples," "a priestly kingdom and a holy nation" (19:5-6). That special identity depended on and still depends on hearing and obeying (19:5).

Prior to the hearing, prior to the belonging, there was no special people, no priestly kingdom, no holy nation. Prior to Sinai this was at best a "community of Hebrews." The phrase is almost an oxymoron, for at best to be "Hebrew" meant to have no social identity and no membership except as "surplus" population. Or at worst, this people was a "mixed crowd" (12:38), without identity of any kind. Thus the ark contains the "testimonies" that give membership through which Israel resists being merely a nondescript, powerless, vulnerable "mixed crowd."

The ark of membership (testimony) is *still* an offer in God's fidelity to lost, isolated people who not only want a larger belonging, but who must have a larger belonging in order for their humanness not to shrivel. The ark articulates signs, assurances, and reminders of belonging to a community in a mass of displaced persons.

The **mercy seat** has as its explicit purpose a meeting to receive commandments. It has as its implicit purpose covering—i.e., activity that makes possible reconciliation and forgiveness. In its two functions in relation to *obedience* and *communion*, the mercy seat offers life to this people that is peculiarly congenial to Yahweh, who both commands and treasures.

---

160. See Frank Moore Cross, *Canaanite Myth and Hebrew Epic: Essays in the History of the Religion of Israel* (Cambridge: Harvard University Press, 1973) 311-14.

The Hebrews in Pharaoh's brickyards were exactly a pre-mercy-seat people. Instead of the offer of reconciliation and communion made possible through the mercy seat, the pre-liberated slaves were destined for a life of alienation, not only from their overlords, but, according to 2:13-15, from each other as well.

The Hebrew slave people had no religious vehicles of their own, no symbolic apparatus with which to break the vicious cycles of abuse and self-hatred. Of course, it is the work of the slave owner to keep the symbolic life of the slaves thin and poverty-stricken, so that there can never be an act of sacramental imagination to let folks begin again. In the mercy seat, Israel now has a vehicle, given in God's graciousness, for periodically beginning again, not only in life with God but in the community of economic reality. (On the economic dimension of כפר [kāpar], see Lev 6:1-7.)

The mercy seat is *still* an offer in God's graciousness for life to begin again, out beyond the vicious cycles of dehumanization so visible and powerful among us. "Modern" folk tend to be fated folk, because we believe there is no new thing yet to be enacted. New beginnings cannot be willed; they must arise from great initiatives and gestures of holy otherness. Having eliminated holiness in our modernist narcissism, we cannot imagine how that newness can come. Here, however, provision is made precisely for newness that arises from God's inscrutable, palpable, self-giving presence.

The **table** has on it perpetually the **Bread of Presence.** Whether an offer of bread to God or an invitation to eat in the presence of God, this community has at the center of its symbolic life an enduring sign, offer, and promise of nourishment. In this symbolization, Israel moves from the planned, enforced scarcity of Pharaoh to the guaranteed plenty of Yahweh.

In the completed form of the text, it may be that this table looks back especially to the gift of "bread from heaven" in chapter 16, bread gathered and eaten so that there need never be hunger again. It is a long leap, and the text gives no hint of any intended connection between the two. The reiterated focus on bread nonetheless lets one ponder the two texts simultaneously. Entry into the liturgic presence of Yahweh is a sure offer of nourishment that the world (of Pharaoh) cannot give.

The table of the Bread of the Presence needs to be seen, held up (blessed and broken), in order to remind the community that it is always enough, with seven or twelve baskets left over.

As a community, we are in the grip of an ideology of scarcity. We are either short on bread, or we have plenty of bread but are short on joy and freedom. Our scarcity leads us to do brutal things to each other. The bread of the table, and the Christian extrapolation from the table to Eucharist, are about an abundance that breaks our parsimonious fears.

The **lampstand** is in order that there will be "light in the space in front of it." While illuminating the sanctuary, such light is never mere illumination. It is a reference laden with surplus significance, inevitably alluding to God's power to push back darkness and to defeat the death-threatening force of chaos, which is all around in the darkness.

The Israelites who make this lampstand for the tabernacle are no strangers to the crisis of light and darkness. No doubt they remember the "wonder of darkness" (10:21-29) and recall with delight that "all the Israelites had light where they lived" (10:23). The "darkness," in the exodus narrative, and the wonder of light for the Israelites, concerns the power of God to create a safe place for life in a body of death. The God of this text can "form light and create darkness" (Isa 45:7 NRSV). Around the lampstand, with its glow of well-being, Israel can remember the darkness and the Egyptians who disappeared in it.

The lampstand is *still* an offer of the light-giving God to "people who walk in darkness." The metaphor of darkness bespeaks the endless procession of fears, hurts, hates, enslavements, and despairs that beset us. Already in this text, there is a "light of the world" (cf. John 9:5). There need be no bewildering, terrifying lostness, and no terror before the power of death.

The world, in the scope of this light, is redefined as a safe place. The lamp of God gives light that culminates in *shalom*.

2. As the text stands in the book of Exodus, this speech of Yahweh "shows the pattern," anticipating chaps. 35–40, wherein Moses will implement the commands for the tabernacle of presence. The prospective power of this "showing" is not, however, completed or exhausted in these chapters. It continues to operate well beyond the book of Exodus in a way we may call eschatological. Israel and the church continue to wait for the time when the full worship imagined by God will be actualized.

This powerful text thus is generative of intensive anticipation, which comes to its fullest, most lyrical expression in the book of Revelation. This community looks with confidence to the time when the full worship of God will be perfectly established, and all the faithful will share in the joy and in the presence. Thus the whole of this literature is cast in a doxological frame. Revelation 4:1-6 offers a vision of "what must take place after this," which is a vision of the throne of God and "seven burning torches" (lamps, Rev 4:5). In 11:19, the ark is in the temple of God, which is in the heavens. The tent (tabernacle) is in heaven, where the temple is filled with glory (15:5-8). And in the final lyrical vision of "the end," God's own self has become the light (21:24; 22:5), and God's dwelling place (tabernacle) is in the midst of the human community (cf. 21:3-6a).

In relation to the book of Exodus, it is instructive that in Rev 11:19 and 15:5 the temple is the source of plagues, which suggests a way in that the two parts of the book of Exodus are held together. Just as chaps. 1–15 are dominated by *plagues*, so also chaps. 25–31 are dominated by *presence*. Both are manifestations of God's sovereign power and God's utter commitment to this people.

The book of Revelation thus relies heavily on the theology of presence in the Priestly tradition of Exodus. It anticipates that the full, perfect, joyous, lyrical goal of humanity is to be in the unending liturgy of praise and celebration, very close to the throne and in intimate contact with the holy Presence. This accent on worship as the quintessence of existence in God's creation is precisely what Exodus 25 intends to evoke and implement.

3. This powerful eschatological anticipation of the "not yet" of worship in the book of Revelation is claimed as "already" in the epistle to the Hebrews, which asserts that in the person of Jesus, the new, full worship of God has already come into existence. Hebrews 9:1-12 makes a powerful claim for the decisiveness and distinctiveness of Jesus in the worship of the holy God. That claim depends for its articulation precisely on the cultic functions of Exodus 25, although it moves in a different order: lampstand, table, bread of presence, tent (tabernacle), cherubim, and mercy seat. These are all attempts at disclosing the way into the holy of holies. This worship arrangement, however, "cannot perfect the conscience of the worshiper" (Heb 9:9 NRSV), but in Christ "a greater and perfect tent" has been offered that is a "new covenant" in "his own blood" (see Heb 9:11-15).

There are, of course, serious problems concerning "supersessionism" pervading the letter to the Hebrews. The point to stress, however, is that liturgy becomes both a way of speaking about the significance of Christ and a metaphor for the fullness and joy of human life. The letter to the Hebrews wants to show forth the inadequacy of the tabernacle arrangement; yet, it cannot speak of the new adequacy of Jesus except in those very same categories.

In both the "not yet" of Revelation and the "already" of Hebrews, it is insisted that worship is what human life is all about and that communion with God is the fulfillment of all human longing. Such a notion of *homo liturgicus* is a polemical alternative to contemporary notions of the human person as maker, as player, as consumer, and as fighter.

EXODUS 26:1-37, TABERNACLE CURTAINS AND FRAME

NIV

26 "Make the tabernacle with ten curtains of finely twisted linen and blue, purple and scarlet yarn, with cherubim worked into them by a skilled craftsman. [2]All the curtains are to be the same size—twenty-eight cubits long and four cubits wide.[a] [3]Join five of the curtains together, and do the same with the other five. [4]Make loops of blue material along the edge of the end curtain in one set, and do the same with the end curtain in the other set. [5]Make fifty loops on one curtain and fifty loops on the end curtain of the other set, with the loops opposite each other. [6]Then make fifty gold clasps and use them to fasten the curtains together so that the tabernacle is a unit.

[7]"Make curtains of goat hair for the tent over the tabernacle—eleven altogether. [8]All eleven curtains are to be the same size—thirty cubits long and four cubits wide.[b] [9]Join five of the curtains together into one set and the other six into another set. Fold the sixth curtain double at the front of the tent. [10]Make fifty loops along the edge of the end curtain in one set and also along the edge of the end curtain in the other set. [11]Then make fifty bronze clasps and put them in the loops to fasten the tent together as a unit. [12]As for the additional length of the tent curtains, the half curtain that is left over is to hang down at the rear of the tabernacle. [13]The tent curtains will be a cubit[c] longer on both sides; what is left will hang over the sides of the tabernacle so as to cover it. [14]Make for the tent a covering of ram skins dyed red, and over that a covering of hides of sea cows.[d]

[15]"Make upright frames of acacia wood for the tabernacle. [16]Each frame is to be ten cubits long and a cubit and a half wide,[e] [17]with two projections set parallel to each other. Make all the frames of the tabernacle in this way. [18]Make twenty frames for the south side of the tabernacle [19]and make forty silver bases to go under them—

---

a2 That is, about 42 feet (about 12.5 meters) long and 6 feet (about 1.8 meters) wide   b8 That is, about 45 feet (about 13.5 meters) long and 6 feet (about 1.8 meters) wide   c13 That is, about 1 1/2 feet (about 0.5 meter)   d14 That is, dugongs   e16 That is, about 15 feet (about 4.5 meters) long and 2 1/4 feet (about 0.7 meter) wide

NRSV

26 Moreover you shall make the tabernacle with ten curtains of fine twisted linen, and blue, purple, and crimson yarns; you shall make them with cherubim skillfully worked into them. [2]The length of each curtain shall be twenty-eight cubits, and the width of each curtain four cubits; all the curtains shall be of the same size. [3]Five curtains shall be joined to one another; and the other five curtains shall be joined to one another. [4]You shall make loops of blue on the edge of the outermost curtain in the first set; and likewise you shall make loops on the edge of the outermost curtain in the second set. [5]You shall make fifty loops on the one curtain, and you shall make fifty loops on the edge of the curtain that is in the second set; the loops shall be opposite one another. [6]You shall make fifty clasps of gold, and join the curtains to one another with the clasps, so that the tabernacle may be one whole.

7You shall also make curtains of goats' hair for a tent over the tabernacle; you shall make eleven curtains. [8]The length of each curtain shall be thirty cubits, and the width of each curtain four cubits; the eleven curtains shall be of the same size. [9]You shall join five curtains by themselves, and six curtains by themselves, and the sixth curtain you shall double over at the front of the tent. [10]You shall make fifty loops on the edge of the curtain that is outermost in one set, and fifty loops on the edge of the curtain that is outermost in the second set.

11You shall make fifty clasps of bronze, and put the clasps into the loops, and join the tent together, so that it may be one whole. [12]The part that remains of the curtains of the tent, the half curtain that remains, shall hang over the back of the tabernacle. [13]The cubit on the one side, and the cubit on the other side, of what remains in the length of the curtains of the tent, shall hang over the sides of the tabernacle, on this side and that side, to cover it. [14]You shall make for the tent a covering of tanned rams' skins and an outer covering of fine leather.[a]

---

a Meaning of Heb uncertain

two bases for each frame, one under each projection. ²⁰For the other side, the north side of the tabernacle, make twenty frames ²¹and forty silver bases—two under each frame. ²²Make six frames for the far end, that is, the west end of the tabernacle, ²³and make two frames for the corners at the far end. ²⁴At these two corners they must be double from the bottom all the way to the top, and fitted into a single ring; both shall be like that. ²⁵So there will be eight frames and sixteen silver bases—two under each frame.

²⁶"Also make crossbars of acacia wood: five for the frames on one side of the tabernacle, ²⁷five for those on the other side, and five for the frames on the west, at the far end of the tabernacle. ²⁸The center crossbar is to extend from end to end at the middle of the frames. ²⁹Overlay the frames with gold and make gold rings to hold the crossbars. Also overlay the crossbars with gold.

³⁰"Set up the tabernacle according to the plan shown you on the mountain.

³¹"Make a curtain of blue, purple and scarlet yarn and finely twisted linen, with cherubim worked into it by a skilled craftsman. ³²Hang it with gold hooks on four posts of acacia wood overlaid with gold and standing on four silver bases. ³³Hang the curtain from the clasps and place the ark of the Testimony behind the curtain. The curtain will separate the Holy Place from the Most Holy Place. ³⁴Put the atonement cover on the ark of the Testimony in the Most Holy Place. ³⁵Place the table outside the curtain on the north side of the tabernacle and put the lampstand opposite it on the south side.

³⁶"For the entrance to the tent make a curtain of blue, purple and scarlet yarn and finely twisted linen—the work of an embroiderer. ³⁷Make gold hooks for this curtain and five posts of acacia wood overlaid with gold. And cast five bronze bases for them.

15You shall make upright frames of acacia wood for the tabernacle. ¹⁶Ten cubits shall be the length of a frame, and a cubit and a half the width of each frame. ¹⁷There shall be two pegs in each frame to fit the frames together; you shall make these for all the frames of the tabernacle. ¹⁸You shall make the frames for the tabernacle: twenty frames for the south side; ¹⁹and you shall make forty bases of silver under the twenty frames, two bases under the first frame for its two pegs, and two bases under the next frame for its two pegs; ²⁰and for the second side of the tabernacle, on the north side twenty frames, ²¹and their forty bases of silver, two bases under the first frame, and two bases under the next frame; ²²and for the rear of the tabernacle westward you shall make six frames. ²³You shall make two frames for corners of the tabernacle in the rear; ²⁴they shall be separate beneath, but joined at the top, at the first ring; it shall be the same with both of them; they shall form the two corners. ²⁵And so there shall be eight frames, with their bases of silver, sixteen bases; two bases under the first frame, and two bases under the next frame.

26You shall make bars of acacia wood, five for the frames of the one side of the tabernacle, ²⁷and five bars for the frames of the other side of the tabernacle, and five bars for the frames of the side of the tabernacle at the rear westward. ²⁸The middle bar, halfway up the frames, shall pass through from end to end. ²⁹You shall overlay the frames with gold, and shall make their rings of gold to hold the bars; and you shall overlay the bars with gold. ³⁰Then you shall erect the tabernacle according to the plan for it that you were shown on the mountain.

31You shall make a curtain of blue, purple, and crimson yarns, and of fine twisted linen; it shall be made with cherubim skillfully worked into it. ³²You shall hang it on four pillars of acacia overlaid with gold, which have hooks of gold and rest on four bases of silver. ³³You shall hang the curtain under the clasps, and bring the ark of the covenant ᵃ in there, within the curtain; and the curtain shall separate for you the holy place from the most holy. ³⁴You shall put the mercy seat ᵇ on the ark of the covenant ᵃ in the most holy place. ³⁵You

ᵃ Or *treaty*, or *testimony*; Heb *eduth*   ᵇ Or *the cover*

NRSV

shall set the table outside the curtain, and the lampstand on the south side of the tabernacle opposite the table; and you shall put the table on the north side.

36You shall make a screen for the entrance of the tent, of blue, purple, and crimson yarns, and of fine twisted linen, embroidered with needlework. [37] You shall make for the screen five pillars of acacia, and overlay them with gold; their hooks shall be of gold, and you shall cast five bases of bronze for them.

COMMENTARY

Yahweh's initial speech to Moses continues to "show the pattern" (cf. 25:8, 40). After the more specific furnishings listed in 25:10-39, the speech now returns to the main subject: the tabernacle (cf. 25:8-9). What is called a "pattern" in 25:9 and 40 is here referred to as a "plan" (משפט *mišpāṭ*, 26:30), but the intention is the same.

This chapter contains exceedingly technical and sometimes quite obscure instructions about the proper design and construction of the cultic apparatus.[161] Two dimensions are clear. First, there is care and precision in detail, so that its builders will have no misgivings about what is to be done or how the parts relate to each other. For this concern, the "blueprint" employs vocabulary of curtains, loops, clasps, frames, pegs, bases, bars, and pillars. Not much is to be learned from an analysis of that special vocabulary.

Second, the design intends that the tabernacle should embody the wealth, treasure, and luxury of the community (cf. 25:3-7). For that concern, an unusual vocabulary is also employed with particular reference to colors.[162] These terms for colors (blue, purple, crimson) are rarely used elsewhere in the OT. We may note, however, that their use is characteristically poignant where it is used. Thus see Judg 8:26, wherein Gideon collects the wealth of Israel, but promptly uses it for self-aggrandizement, so that "all Israel prostituted themselves"

(Judg 8:27 NRSV). And in Jer 10:9, the same vocabulary issues as a vigorous polemic against false idols, well-decorated images that are in fact powerless and false.

As color terms are used in religious polemic, so they are also employed in political critique. Thus the king of Tyre is criticized for his arrogant extravagance and pride in making himself and his realm beautiful (Ezek 27:7; cf. also v. 16). In both religious and political criticism, this extravagance is seen to be not only unseemly, but also religiously unacceptable.

In the narrative of Esther, however, we can see a more delicate and complex use of the terminology. In Esth 1:2-8, the king in Susa is critically described as extravagant and cynically self-serving. In this case, however, the narrative goes on to dramatize an inversion of political power, whereby the persecuted Jews come to well-being and prosperity. Mordecai, faithful Jew, is then extravagantly clothed in all the finery previously possessed by the condemned Haman (Esth 8:15-16). Thus the text is able to affirm that what may be seductive and destructive, when properly and faithfully appropriated, is not only acceptable but is a celebrative and legitimate way to express honor.

Thus the pattern given to Moses intends that God's sanctuary be outfitted in the most luxurious way possible, because the sanctuary becomes the promise and embodiment of the new world of abundant blessing and well-being. There is nothing too good or too costly for the Holy One.

The tradition of Moses is rightly known among

---

161. On the technical matters, see Menahem Haran, "The Priestly Image of the Tabernacle," *HUCA* 36 (1965) 191-226.

162. See Athalya Brenner, *Colour Terms in the Old Testament*, JSOTSup 21 (Sheffield: JSOT, 1982).

us as a tradition of ethical rigor. Here we are able to see that, in its completed form, it is one of great aesthetic concern and sensitivity as well. This part of the tradition does not focus on the "ear of obedience," but on the "eye of loveliness."[163]

In the midst of artistic attentiveness and aesthetic extravagance, we may note especially the prescribed curtain (פרכת *pārōket*), which is different from the more numerous curtains (יריעה *yĕrî'ōt*)

163. Samuel Terrien, *The Elusive Presence: Toward a New Biblical Theology,* Religious Perspectives (San Francisco: Harper & Row, 1978), has made the tension between "ear" and "eye" definitional for his understanding of biblical theology. The same contrast is evident in the contrast David Tracy makes between "proclamation" and "manifestation," behind which stands the distinction of Paul Ricoeur concerning a "hermeneutics of suspicion" and a "hermeneutics of retrieval."

earlier listed (vv. 33 34). This curtain (*pārōket*) provides for a separation between "the holy place" and "the most holy place" (i.e., the holy of holiness), wherein are housed the ark and the mercy seat. While we may detect in this design gradations of holiness that inevitably lead to elitism and special priestly privilege, none of that danger is noted here. Rather, what is intended is the creation of the most protected, awesome place to host and entertain properly the very self-giving of God. No doubt the screen was proposed with only the best of liturgical intentions, and it seems first of all to be appreciated for that intention.

REFLECTIONS

1. Worship, the hosting of the holy, requires order, discipline, planning, and forethought. To be sure, there are dangers in excessive preoccupation with liturgical niceties, a danger well and regularly noted in both the prophets and the tradition of the Reformation. While that danger is real, this text invites reflection in the opposite direction. The tradition of the priests, while no doubt aware of prophetic strictures against excessive preoccupation with worship details, nonetheless wants to guard against casual, slovenly, easy access to the holy.

Of course, how one assesses this text depends not only on one's context, but also on one's view of God. If we take God to be a royal sovereign who is to be approached with awe, then care must be taken. The notion of entering into an awesome throne room is, to be sure, not the only imagery of the Bible for worship, but it is an image that carries considerable importance, both for the text and in relation to human yearning.

2. Worship is an exercise in extravagance that depends on the willing generosity of the community and that, as an act of hope, lives in tension with what may have been the leanness of the community in its actual ordering of everyday life. All of us are aware of the abuses of a self-indulgent church that has built great golden edifices out of the bitter sweat of peasant offerings. The text, however, does not focus on the ethics of care for the poor. Rather, it engages in an act of hope that believes the world "in here," in the sanctuary, must be luxurious in contrast to the world "out there," which is mean, thin, and hopeless. Such a liturgic strategy may, of course, be escapist; but it may also function as an antidote to despair, keeping alive a vision of the "other world" of God in which we are welcomed as beloved members.

Such "misdirected extravagance" calls to mind the interaction of Jesus with the woman who anointed him with precious oil (Mark 14:3-9). The woman extravagantly uses the oil to anoint Jesus, presumably for his death. The disciples protest that the money is better used in the service of the poor. Jesus, however, remonstrates his disciples. Something similar operates in this tabernacle provision, which asks for opulence in the celebration of God's holy presence.

3. Attention to the aesthetic dimension of the tabernacle (design, symmetry, color, luxurious materials) invites reflection on worship as a practice of the "beauty of holiness." Our technological, consumeristic society inclines to turn everything (even art objects) into commodities with utilitarian values. As part of that tendency, self-indulgent religion turns God into a commodity and worship into a calculating utilitarianism. The "beauty of holiness" by contrast enacts the truth that God is not a useful commodity. Rather, worship is an end in itself.

Hans-Georg Gadamar underscores three dimensions of the artistic that pertain to our subject.[164] (1) Art is the play and practice of *excess*, the human activity of moving beyond what is managed, to what is inscrutably surplus and transcendent. (2) Art is the act of making oneself "*at home* in the world," where one is largely and deeply homeless. (3) Art is a festival that draws isolated individuals into *unity*.

The tabernacle in the wilderness (exile?) serves such purposes. The design is clearly a *proposal for excess*. Because it is mobile in the wilderness, it is also a *home for displaced persons* who have no other place to belong. And no doubt by offering itself as the core home for exiles, it intends to draw all the scattered, conflicted elements of the exiled community together *into a unity*. In all three ways, the activity and function of the tabernacle propose an alternative existence.

These three points from Gadamar provide contact with the pastoral realities of our own situation of faith. Worship can be an invitation and practice of an "otherness" *beyond fearful utilitarianism*. Worship can be a place of overriding *belonging at home*, even in the face of our powerful and insistent homelessness. Worship can be *a post-rational embrace of oneness* in a world where we are so deeply and angrily divided. Worship that is to enact such transformative possibility must indeed be aesthetically rich.

4. The reference to the "curtain" (פרכת *pārōket*, LXX καταπέτασμα *katapetasma*) that partitions the holy place and the holy of holies (vv. 33-35) directs our attention to Matt 27:51 and Hebrews 10:20.

In Matt 27:51, the cosmic upheaval evoked by the crucifixion of Jesus causes the tearing of "the curtain" (*katapetasma*) of the Temple. There is no doubt that this text directly refers to Exod 26:33-35. The original use of the "curtain" is to make the holy of holies the locus of the core of God's holiness in all the world—the epicenter of cosmic reality. This curtain, never intended to be a barrier, is now destroyed in order to permit access again to God's holiness. In the process of destroying the curtain, the whole of the "system of holiness" is brutally dismantled.

In Heb 10:19-23, the same claim as Matt 27:51 is made for the person of Jesus, who made possible "the new and living way that he opened for us through the curtain" (Heb 10:20). This use serves the larger argument of the letter to the Hebrews that Jesus has displaced the system of worship in the Levitical system.

The way in which Matthew 27 and Hebrews 10 play against Exodus 26 lets us see that Jesus' death is understood in the early church as a largely subversive act, deeply in touch with the institutional context of established religion. Without this reference in Exodus 26, the Gospel portrayal makes little sense. More broadly, the connection of these texts suggests the way in which well-intended religious devices become distorted in their function. The gospel exercises a profound critical function against even our best enhancements of God, which often turn out to be domestications and manipulations.

164. Hans-Georg Gadamar, *The Relevance of the Beautiful and Other Essays* (Cambridge: Cambridge University Press, 1987).

EXODUS 27:1-21, ALTAR, COURT, LAMP

NIV	NRSV
27 "Build an altar of acacia wood, three cubits[a] high; it is to be square, five cubits long and five cubits wide.[b] ²Make a horn at each of the four corners, so that the horns and the altar	**27** You shall make the altar of acacia wood, five cubits long and five cubits wide; the altar shall be square, and it shall be three cubits high. ²You shall make horns for it on its four corners; its horns shall be of one piece with it, and you shall overlay it with bronze. ³You shall

a1 That is, about 4 1/2 feet (about 1.3 meters)   b1 That is, about 7 1/2 feet (about 2.3 meters) long and wide

NIV

are of one piece, and overlay the altar with bronze. ³Make all its utensils of bronze—its pots to remove the ashes, and its shovels, sprinkling bowls, meat forks and firepans. ⁴Make a grating for it, a bronze network, and make a bronze ring at each of the four corners of the network. ⁵Put it under the ledge of the altar so that it is halfway up the altar. ⁶Make poles of acacia wood for the altar and overlay them with bronze. ⁷The poles are to be inserted into the rings so they will be on two sides of the altar when it is carried. ⁸Make the altar hollow, out of boards. It is to be made just as you were shown on the mountain.

⁹"Make a courtyard for the tabernacle. The south side shall be a hundred cubits^a long and is to have curtains of finely twisted linen, ¹⁰with twenty posts and twenty bronze bases and with silver hooks and bands on the posts. ¹¹The north side shall also be a hundred cubits long and is to have curtains, with twenty posts and twenty bronze bases and with silver hooks and bands on the posts.

¹²"The west end of the courtyard shall be fifty cubits^b wide and have curtains, with ten posts and ten bases. ¹³On the east end, toward the sunrise, the courtyard shall also be fifty cubits wide. ¹⁴Curtains fifteen cubits^c long are to be on one side of the entrance, with three posts and three bases, ¹⁵and curtains fifteen cubits long are to be on the other side, with three posts and three bases.

¹⁶"For the entrance to the courtyard, provide a curtain twenty cubits^d long, of blue, purple and scarlet yarn and finely twisted linen—the work of an embroiderer—with four posts and four bases. ¹⁷All the posts around the courtyard are to have silver bands and hooks, and bronze bases. ¹⁸The courtyard shall be a hundred cubits long and fifty cubits wide,^e with curtains of finely twisted linen five cubits^f high, and with bronze bases. ¹⁹All the other articles used in the service of the tabernacle, whatever their function, including all the tent pegs for it and those for the courtyard, are to be of bronze.

---

^a9 That is, about 150 feet (about 46 meters); also in verse 11
^b12 That is, about 75 feet (about 23 meters); also in verse 13
^c14 That is, about 22 1/2 feet (about 6.9 meters); also in verse 15
^d16 That is, about 30 feet (about 9 meters)
^e18 That is, about 150 feet (about 46 meters) long and 75 feet (about 23 meters) wide   ^f18 That is, about 7 1/2 feet (about 2.3 meters)

NRSV

make pots for it to receive its ashes, and shovels and basins and forks and firepans; you shall make all its utensils of bronze. ⁴You shall also make for it a grating, a network of bronze; and on the net you shall make four bronze rings at its four corners. ⁵You shall set it under the ledge of the altar so that the net shall extend halfway down the altar. ⁶You shall make poles for the altar, poles of acacia wood, and overlay them with bronze; ⁷the poles shall be put through the rings, so that the poles shall be on the two sides of the altar when it is carried. ⁸You shall make it hollow, with boards. They shall be made just as you were shown on the mountain.

9You shall make the court of the tabernacle. On the south side the court shall have hangings of fine twisted linen one hundred cubits long for that side; ¹⁰its twenty pillars and their twenty bases shall be of bronze, but the hooks of the pillars and their bands shall be of silver. ¹¹Likewise for its length on the north side there shall be hangings one hundred cubits long, their pillars twenty and their bases twenty, of bronze, but the hooks of the pillars and their bands shall be of silver. ¹²For the width of the court on the west side there shall be fifty cubits of hangings, with ten pillars and ten bases. ¹³The width of the court on the front to the east shall be fifty cubits. ¹⁴There shall be fifteen cubits of hangings on the one side, with three pillars and three bases. ¹⁵There shall be fifteen cubits of hangings on the other side, with three pillars and three bases. ¹⁶For the gate of the court there shall be a screen twenty cubits long, of blue, purple, and crimson yarns, and of fine twisted linen, embroidered with needlework; it shall have four pillars and with them four bases. ¹⁷All the pillars around the court shall be banded with silver; their hooks shall be of silver, and their bases of bronze. ¹⁸The length of the court shall be one hundred cubits, the width fifty, and the height five cubits, with hangings of fine twisted linen and bases of bronze. ¹⁹All the utensils of the tabernacle for every use, and all its pegs and all the pegs of the court, shall be of bronze.

20You shall further command the Israelites to bring you pure oil of beaten olives for the light, so that a lamp may be set up to burn regularly.

NIV

²⁰"Command the Israelites to bring you clear oil of pressed olives for the light so that the lamps may be kept burning. ²¹In the Tent of Meeting, outside the curtain that is in front of the Testimony, Aaron and his sons are to keep the lamps burning before the LORD from evening till morning. This is to be a lasting ordinance among the Israelites for the generations to come.

NRSV

²¹In the tent of meeting, outside the curtain that is before the covenant,^a Aaron and his sons shalltend it from evening to morning before the LORD. It shall be a perpetual ordinance to be observed throughout their generations by the Israelites.

^a Or *treaty*, or *testimony*; Heb *eduth*

COMMENTARY

God's speech to Moses continues to show Moses the "pattern" for right worship. In this chapter, three further provisions are made for worship: an altar (vv. 1-8), a court for the tabernacle (vv. 9-19), and a lamp, which will be kept burning for all time (vv. 20-21).

27:1-8. The altar of the tabernacle is now mentioned for the first time, as a part of the larger pattern from the mountain (v. 8). This altar is quite in contrast to that authorized by the earlier tradition of 20:24-26, which was to be plain and simple. While its horns were likely ornamental, or serve a symbolic function now lost to us, they come to provide a place of political refuge (cf. 1 Kgs 2:28).

The altar is to be fully equipped with everything necessary for a place of sacrifice, though once again nothing is said about its proper function. (In 30:27-28, a distinction is made between the "altar of incense," described in 30:1-10, and an "altar of burnt offering." While burnt offerings are not mentioned in our passage, presumably this is the altar referred to there.) The design is careful and precise. We may notice that the overlay is of bronze and not of gold, as are most of the other objects in the tabernacle. This suggests that there is a gradation of values whereby the altar is not as important as the other objects covered with gold.

This terse "blueprint" gives us little room or warrant for the theological purpose of the altar. It will become evident in Leviticus 1–7 that the altar is for sacrifices. Moreover, the sacrifices seem to serve two functions: to acknowledge sovereignty ("to glorify God") and to enjoy communion ("enjoy God forever"). But nothing is made here of these characteristic actions.

The inventory of utensils in v. 3 calls attention to two other texts that connect our text to more specific social contexts. In 1 Kgs 7:40-45 (cf. vv. 46-51), a closely paralleled list belongs to the construction and equipment of the Jerusalem Temple. Two things are evident. First, all of this equipment is linked to and evidence for Solomon's enormous opulence. Second, the production of all of these vessels is done by Hiram of Tyre, reflecting Solomon's international connections and likely attesting as well his religious syncretism.

The second telling reference to these utensils is in 2 Kgs 25:13-17 (cf. Jer 52:17-23). It is reported that the Babylonians carry away everything portable from the Temple in Jerusalem. Moreover, Ezra 1:7-11 reports that under Cyrus, the vessels are restored to the reestablished place in Jerusalem. The removal of the vessels signifies not only avarice on the part of Babylon but also ritual humiliation of Yahweh, whose own "treasures" are now confiscated and taken up by a more powerful god. Further, as Peter Ackroyd has seen, the fact that the text reports in detail the return of the vessels to Jerusalem indicates that the Temple utensils function as more than ornaments or equipment.[165] They are, in fact, theological symbols of continuity for a community facing severe discontinuity and tokens of God's resilient fidelity in a time of enormous danger and displacement.

Taken together, 1 Kgs 7:40-45 and 2 Kgs 25:13-17 show that the Temple vessels play a pivotal symbolic role at the beginning of the royal period (the time of Solomon) and at the end of the royal period (exile), articulating, respectively, both the origin and termination of legitimated worship. When read in the light of these texts, moreover, it is evident that our text carries sym-

165. Peter R. Ackroyd, "The Temple Vessels: A Continuity Theme," in *Studies in the Religion of Ancient Israel,* ed. by the Board of the Quarterly VTSup 23 (1972) 166-81.

bolic significance that is enormously vulnerable to historical-political vagaries.

27:9-19. The building of the court of the tabernacle again focuses on structure and design and not at all on its function. Again we note the symmetry and detail of the design, and the fact that it is all of bronze (not gold). In v. 16 we note two special features of the court. First, it is to have a screen (מסך *māsāk*), which again suggests the protectedness of the space and, perhaps, gradation of access and privilege. Second, only the screen is detailed with color through fine needlework. Artistic sensibility is much less evident here than in the preceding chapter on the tabernacle.

27:20-21. The third provision of this chapter is the maintenance of "the light," not to be confused with the lampstand (25:31-39). This particular instruction is a departure from the mode of discourse thus far in chaps. 25–27, for it moves away from design to speak about maintenance. The introduction of questions of maintenance necessarily entails delineation of personnel for the first time. Thus in these two verses there is a significant change of subject. Maintenance involves two functions. On the one hand, the people are to provide pure olive oil for the light; pure olive oil is the offer of one's best, and it likely assured the clearest, most reliable light.

On the other hand, "Aaron and his sons," no doubt a priestly order, are for the first time marked as the ones who will maintain the lamp. This mention of Aaron does not concern a person or a brother of Moses, but a priestly order and office. If this mention grants to "Aaron" special privilege in cultic function, then one may see how this text serves to enhance the authority that "Aaron" claims as distinct from and perhaps in conflict with other priestly orders (on which see chap. 32).[166]

As with the altar and the court, we are told nothing here of a function or intention for the lamp. It is plausible, however, to suggest three related dimensions to the lamp. First, the light is practical. Second, however, because the light is to be kept burning regularly (תמיד *tāmîd*, "constantly"), it is clear that this light is more than functional. Its symbolism is to provide a safe, reliable place in a world filled with ominous threat. Moreover, if we follow the suggestion of Kearney and Blenkinsopp, the perpetual light signifies the order, safety, and well-being of creation.[167] The tabernacle is the "dry land" in the flood of chaos. Third, the light bespeaks the very presence of God, a bespeaking made possible by the attentiveness of the priests. It is the cooperation of the lay community and the priestly office that does the human work of signifying, actualizing, and assuring the presence of God.

166. On the priestly rivalries, see Frank Moore Cross, *Canaanite Myth and Hebrew Epic*, 195-215, and more broadly Aelred Cody, *A History of Old Testament Priesthood* (Rome: Pontifical Biblical Institute, 1969).
167. See esp. Kearney, "Creation and Liturgy," 375.

REFLECTIONS

1. The altar is essential to the public life of this liberated, covenanted community. Israel must have a place where it regularly submits in gratitude to the sovereignty of God. As in all of these instructions, Israel has long known that *the actual practice* of the presence in and through these objects is essential. It will not do to "think" the presence or intend it; it must be done in bodily engagement.

2. The references to the Temple utensils in 1 Kings 7 and 2 Kings 25, and by extrapolation the entire cultic apparatus, invites reflection upon the ways in which Temple furniture, which arises in concrete circumstance, takes on transcendent power and authority. The theological issue to be explored is the way concrete religious experience acquires or receives transcendental authority, so that a functional arrangement becomes a non-negotiable presence. That theological principle is never confronted in the abstract. It meets us in the concreteness of an altar Bible, a pew hymnal, a picture of Jesus, or a memorial piano.

These texts might permit us to see both the value and the danger in such an unavoidable human process. The value of investing the ordinary with transcendent significance is essential to the development of culture, especially religious culture. The process protects life from becoming finally utilitarian or cheaply relativistic. The danger of such absolutizing, which I infer from 1 Kings 7 and 2 Kings 25, is that a community can take these objects with such seriousness that it assigns ultimate meaning to what is not ultimate. I imagine that the adjudication of symbolizing and criticism, of valuing and seeing the danger, is an endless human process. No doubt in the circumstance of a jeopardized exilic community, exactly a "hermeneutic of retrieval" is urgent. It is precisely the retrieval of symbol that mediates to this community a clear sense of presence.

3. The light is a liturgic gesture of safety and well-being in a world under threat. While the light assures God's presence and God's governance, there is a strand of spirituality in the Bible that insists not only that the light witnesses to God but that, in the end, God is the light. In the Fourth Gospel, the theme of light recurs (see, e.g., John 1:8-9; 8:12). Other NT texts (e.g. 1 John 1:5; Rev 22:5) push even beyond such christological claims, echoing the doxological affirmation of Ps 27:1 that God "is my light and my salvation" (NRSV).

Revelation 21:23-24 plays with the duality of "light" and "lamp" (as we have seen that duality already in Exod 27:20): "And the city has no need of sun or moon to shine on it, for the glory of God is its light, and its lamp is the Lamb. The nations will walk by its light, and the kings of the earth will bring their glory into it" (NRSV).

This text manages to make an affirmation about God as light, yet it uses the same imagery to express a distinct christological claim. This lyrical affirmation anticipates that the power of chaos and evil (in the form of darkness) finally will be banished when God's light prevails everywhere. Thus the light in the Temple is a harbinger of the new creation. That light, so well maintained, anticipates that God's light will move out from the tabernacle, so that the presence will pervade the entire earth.

EXODUS 28:1-43, PRIESTLY VESTMENTS

NIV

28 "Have Aaron your brother brought to you from among the Israelites, along with his sons Nadab and Abihu, Eleazar and Ithamar, so they may serve me as priests. ²Make sacred garments for your brother Aaron, to give him dignity and honor. ³Tell all the skilled men to whom I have given wisdom in such matters that they are to make garments for Aaron, for his consecration, so he may serve me as priest. ⁴These are the garments they are to make: a breastpiece, an ephod, a robe, a woven tunic, a turban and a sash. They are to make these sacred garments for your brother Aaron and his sons, so they may serve me as priests. ⁵Have them use gold, and blue, purple and scarlet yarn, and fine linen.

⁶"Make the ephod of gold, and of blue, purple and scarlet yarn, and of finely twisted linen—the work of a skilled craftsman. ⁷It is to have two shoulder pieces attached to two of its corners, so it can be fastened. ⁸Its skillfully woven waistband

NRSV

28 Then bring near to you your brother Aaron, and his sons with him, from among the Israelites, to serve me as priests—Aaron and Aaron's sons, Nadab and Abihu, Eleazar and Ithamar. ²You shall make sacred vestments for the glorious adornment of your brother Aaron. ³And you shall speak to all who have ability, whom I have endowed with skill, that they make Aaron's vestments to consecrate him for my priesthood. ⁴These are the vestments that they shall make: a breastpiece, an ephod, a robe, a checkered tunic, a turban, and a sash. When they make these sacred vestments for your brother Aaron and his sons to serve me as priests, ⁵they shall use gold, blue, purple, and crimson yarns, and fine linen.

6They shall make the ephod of gold, of blue, purple, and crimson yarns, and of fine twisted linen, skillfully worked. ⁷It shall have two shoulder-pieces attached to its two edges, so that it may be joined together. ⁸The decorated band on

NIV

is to be like it—of one piece with the ephod and made with gold, and with blue, purple and scarlet yarn, and with finely twisted linen.

⁹"Take two onyx stones and engrave on them the names of the sons of Israel ¹⁰in the order of their birth—six names on one stone and the remaining six on the other. ¹¹Engrave the names of the sons of Israel on the two stones the way a gem cutter engraves a seal. Then mount the stones in gold filigree settings ¹²and fasten them on the shoulder pieces of the ephod as memorial stones for the sons of Israel. Aaron is to bear the names on his shoulders as a memorial before the LORD. ¹³Make gold filigree settings ¹⁴and two braided chains of pure gold, like a rope, and attach the chains to the settings.

¹⁵"Fashion a breastpiece for making decisions—the work of a skilled craftsman. Make it like the ephod: of gold, and of blue, purple and scarlet yarn, and of finely twisted linen. ¹⁶It is to be square—a span[a] long and a span wide—and folded double. ¹⁷Then mount four rows of precious stones on it. In the first row there shall be a ruby, a topaz and a beryl; ¹⁸in the second row a turquoise, a sapphire[b] and an emerald; ¹⁹in the third row a jacinth, an agate and an amethyst; ²⁰in the fourth row a chrysolite, an onyx and a jasper.[c] Mount them in gold filigree settings. ²¹There are to be twelve stones, one for each of the names of the sons of Israel, each engraved like a seal with the name of one of the twelve tribes.

²²"For the breastpiece make braided chains of pure gold, like a rope. ²³Make two gold rings for it and fasten them to two corners of the breastpiece. ²⁴Fasten the two gold chains to the rings at the corners of the breastpiece, ²⁵and the other ends of the chains to the two settings, attaching them to the shoulder pieces of the ephod at the front. ²⁶Make two gold rings and attach them to the other two corners of the breastpiece on the inside edge next to the ephod. ²⁷Make two more gold rings and attach them to the bottom of the shoulder pieces on the front of the ephod, close to the seam just above the waistband of the ephod. ²⁸The rings of the breastpiece are to be

a16 That is, about 9 inches (about 22 centimeters)
b18 Or *lapis lazuli*   *c20* The precise identification of some of these precious stones is uncertain.

NRSV

it shall be of the same workmanship and materials, of gold, of blue, purple, and crimson yarns, and of fine twisted linen. ⁹You shall take two onyx stones, and engrave on them the names of the sons of Israel, ¹⁰six of their names on the one stone, and the names of the remaining six on the other stone, in the order of their birth. ¹¹As a gem-cutter engraves signets, so you shall engrave the two stones with the names of the sons of Israel; you shall mount them in settings of gold filigree. ¹²You shall set the two stones on the shoulder-pieces of the ephod, as stones of remembrance for the sons of Israel; and Aaron shall bear their names before the LORD on his two shoulders for remembrance. ¹³You shall make settings of gold filigree, ¹⁴and two chains of pure gold, twisted like cords; and you shall attach the corded chains to the settings.

15You shall make a breastpiece of judgment, in skilled work; you shall make it in the style of the ephod; of gold, of blue and purple and crimson yarns, and of fine twisted linen you shall make it. ¹⁶It shall be square and doubled, a span in length and a span in width. ¹⁷You shall set in it four rows of stones. A row of carnelian,[a] chrysolite, and emerald shall be the first row; ¹⁸and the second row a turquoise, a sapphire[b] and a moonstone; ¹⁹and the third row a jacinth, an agate, and an amethyst; ²⁰and the fourth row a beryl, an onyx, and a jasper; they shall be set in gold filigree. ²¹There shall be twelve stones with names corresponding to the names of the sons of Israel; they shall be like signets, each engraved with its name, for the twelve tribes. ²²You shall make for the breastpiece chains of pure gold, twisted like cords; ²³and you shall make for the breastpiece two rings of gold, and put the two rings on the two edges of the breastpiece. ²⁴You shall put the two cords of gold in the two rings at the edges of the breastpiece; ²⁵the two ends of the two cords you shall attach to the two settings, and so attach it in front to the shoulder-pieces of the ephod. ²⁶You shall make two rings of gold, and put them at the two ends of the breastpiece, on its inside edge next to the ephod. ²⁷You shall make two rings of gold, and attach them in front to the lower part of the two shoulder-pieces of the

a The identity of several of these stones is uncertain   *b* Or *lapis lazuli*

NIV

tied to the rings of the ephod with blue cord, connecting it to the waistband, so that the breastpiece will not swing out from the ephod.

²⁹"Whenever Aaron enters the Holy Place, he will bear the names of the sons of Israel over his heart on the breastpiece of decision as a continuing memorial before the LORD. ³⁰Also put the Urim and the Thummim in the breastpiece, so they may be over Aaron's heart whenever he enters the presence of the LORD. Thus Aaron will always bear the means of making decisions for the Israelites over his heart before the LORD.

³¹"Make the robe of the ephod entirely of blue cloth, ³²with an opening for the head in its center. There shall be a woven edge like a collarᵃ around this opening, so that it will not tear. ³³Make pomegranates of blue, purple and scarlet yarn around the hem of the robe, with gold bells between them. ³⁴The gold bells and the pomegranates are to alternate around the hem of the robe. ³⁵Aaron must wear it when he ministers. The sound of the bells will be heard when he enters the Holy Place before the LORD and when he comes out, so that he will not die.

³⁶"Make a plate of pure gold and engrave on it as on a seal: holy to the LORD. ³⁷Fasten a blue cord to it to attach it to the turban; it is to be on the front of the turban. ³⁸It will be on Aaron's forehead, and he will bear the guilt involved in the sacred gifts the Israelites consecrate, whatever their gifts may be. It will be on Aaron's forehead continually so that they will be acceptable to the LORD.

³⁹"Weave the tunic of fine linen and make the turban of fine linen. The sash is to be the work of an embroiderer. ⁴⁰Make tunics, sashes and headbands for Aaron's sons, to give them dignity and honor. ⁴¹After you put these clothes on your brother Aaron and his sons, anoint and ordain them. Consecrate them so they may serve me as priests.

⁴²"Make linen undergarments as a covering for the body, reaching from the waist to the thigh. ⁴³Aaron and his sons must wear them whenever they enter the Tent of Meeting or approach the altar to minister in the Holy Place, so that they will not incur guilt and die.

"This is to be a lasting ordinance for Aaron and his descendants.

ᵃ32 The meaning of the Hebrew for this word is uncertain.

NRSV

ephod, at its joining above the decorated band of the ephod. ²⁸The breastpiece shall be bound by its rings to the rings of the ephod with a blue cord, so that it may lie on the decorated band of the ephod, and so that the breastpiece shall not come loose from the ephod. ²⁹So Aaron shall bear the names of the sons of Israel in the breastpiece of judgment on his heart when he goes into the holy place, for a continual remembrance before the LORD. ³⁰In the breastpiece of judgment you shall put the Urim and the Thummim, and they shall be on Aaron's heart when he goes in before the LORD; thus Aaron shall bear the judgment of the Israelites on his heart before the LORD continually.

31You shall make the robe of the ephod all of blue. ³²It shall have an opening for the head in the middle of it, with a woven binding around the opening, like the opening in a coat of mail,ᵃ so that it may not be torn. ³³On its lower hem you shall make pomegranates of blue, purple, and crimson yarns, all around the lower hem, with bells of gold between them all around—³⁴a golden bell and a pomegranate alternating all around the lower hem of the robe. ³⁵Aaron shall wear it when he ministers, and its sound shall be heard when he goes into the holy place before the LORD, and when he comes out, so that he may not die.

36You shall make a rosette of pure gold, and engrave on it, like the engraving of a signet, "Holy to the LORD." ³⁷You shall fasten it on the turban with a blue cord; it shall be on the front of the turban. ³⁸It shall be on Aaron's forehead, and Aaron shall take on himself any guilt incurred in the holy offering that the Israelites consecrate as their sacred donations; it shall always be on his forehead, in order that they may find favor before the LORD.

39You shall make the checkered tunic of fine linen, and you shall make a turban of fine linen, and you shall make a sash embroidered with needlework.

40For Aaron's sons you shall make tunics and sashes and headdresses; you shall make them for their glorious adornment. ⁴¹You shall put them on your brother Aaron, and on his sons with him, and shall anoint them and ordain them and consecrate them, so that they may serve me as priests. ⁴²You shall make for them linen undergarments

ᵃ Meaning of Heb uncertain

NIV

to cover their naked flesh; they shall reach from the hips to the thighs; ⁴³Aaron and his sons shall wear them when they go into the tent of meeting, or when they come near the altar to minister in the holy place; or they will bring guilt on themselves and die. This shall be a perpetual ordinance for him and for his descendants after him.

COMMENTARY

The mention of Aaron and his sons in 27:21 changes the subject of Yahweh's instruction to Moses. The central concern is no longer the objects for worship but the priesthood. This long chapter is primarily preoccupied with the proper appearance of the priests and only incidentally with their function. Taken critically, this text appears to be a self-serving method of enhancing priestly prestige, wealth, and power. Taken theologically, the priest is the one who shall enter into the holy presence of God, an awesome and dreadful undertaking.

The chapter begins with a summary about equipping Aaron for his office (vv. 1-5) and concludes with a like statement concerning the sons of Aaron (vv. 40-43). The material between these two sections deals in close detail with priestly garb: ephod (vv. 6-14), breastplate (vv. 15-30), robe (vv. 31-35), rosette (vv. 36-38), tunic, and turban (v. 39). The way in which these paragraphs grow progressively shorter may be evidence that the priestly inventory received *ad hoc* additions as time went on, as the expectations of priestly garb continued to develop in more ambitious and punctilious ways.

28:1-5. Aaron, with his sons, is to serve Yahweh as priest. It is decisive that in this speech of Yahweh, they are called to "serve me." That is, the priestly office is not concerned first of all with Israel; the priests exist for the sake of Yahweh.

Unlike the early period, Israel in the later period of the OT, with its profound sense of dislocation, works overtime to be sure that legitimating genealogies are clear and in order. This concern is likely related to the crisis of legitimacy alluded to in chapter 27. No genealogy is provided

for Aaron in this text, because in 6:14-25, Aaron is already fully connected to Levi, and his authority here can be assumed. The four sons of Aaron, who are named in 6:23, reappear here.

In other narratives related to the sons of Aaron, we may distinguish two pairs of sons. On the one hand, Nadab and Abihu are quickly disposed of in Lev 10:1-5, for what appears to be an unauthorized priestly act (cf. Num 3:4). We may imagine this narrative of execution is reflective of struggles between priestly orders concerning authority and power.

On the other hand, Ithamar and, especially, Eleazar continue to be important for the function and history of the priesthood. In 1 Chr 24:1-6 these two sons are assigned considerable priestly power and are said to be the progenitors of the later (so far as this text stands) priesthood of Zadok and Abiathar. In particular, Eleazar is the successor to Aaron (cf. Num 20:25-28), who functions along with Moses (Num 26:1, 3, 63) and Joshua (Num 27:18-23).

The other element in this introduction is a concern that Aaron as priest should be properly clothed. The elliptical language of v. 3 (not fully reflected in English translations) suggests that the proper vestments contributed to the holiness that is acknowledged in consecration. The comprehensive catalogue of vv. 3-5 suggests that the dress of the great priest is carefully arranged in every detail, and that only the very best, most extravagant materials may be used. It is a matter of serious concern to the community that Aaron be made into the most impressive, attractive official possible, one who is "glorious in adornment" (v. 2).

The body of the chapter now consists for the

most part in characterizing in detail elements of the inventory of v. 4. Very little is said about the function of these pieces of dress; the appearance itself counts. Five elements are named, with most of the attention given to the first two.

28:6-14 The Ephod. Nobody knows what an ephod is. Apparently it is a priestly garment, but the specificity of the apparel is known only from biblical texts that are notoriously unclear and often contradictory. It is enough for us that the ephod was worn to announce and enhance the authority of Aaron and the Aaronides. We may observe two important matters in its description. First, it is exotically decorated in gold, precious stones, and rich coloring. Second, inscribed upon it are the names of the "twelve sons of Israel"—i.e., the twelve tribes (cf. 1:1-5). Moreover, the inscribed stones are said to be "stones of remembrance." In its intention, the ephod serves to bring Israel, with all its generations gathered in a moment, into the holy presence of God, where Israel can be reconciled, basking in light that it can find nowhere else.

28:15-30 The Breastplate. This priestly garment again is exceedingly odd in its design, and is known only here and in Lev 8:6-9, where Moses finally gives Aaron all these authorized insignia of office and authority. Again we meet with the two features we have come to expect in description: precision of design and extravagance of ornamentation.

Having become accustomed by now to extravagant decoration, this particular object is nonetheless relatively excessive. The text proposes that here the community must mobilize all its wealth and the best of its imagination. All the best materials and all the most dramatic colors are to be used. What is most striking, however, is the symmetrical list of twelve precious stones, all contained in gold.

The vocabulary of these stones is exceedingly obscure, with many of the terms unknown in the OT beyond this cluster of texts. We may refer to three other places in the Bible where mention is made of some of these stones. A like list occurs in Ezek 27:16 to characterize the rich commerce of Tyre. The list is used to state the huge economic success of Tyre and to condemn it as arrogance. In Job 28:16-19 is a list of precious stones used as a foil to assert that wisdom from

God is of more value than any of these stones. In Cant 5:10-16, such language is used as a way to express the loveliness and beauty of "my beloved." In all three usages, the terms voice the extreme case—extreme arrogance, extreme value of wisdom, extreme loveliness. Aaron is to be clothed in the extremes of pride, value, and loveliness. Israel has at its disposal no better language with which to make that point.

Now we may rightly ask, How could this language be used for this community, either by the tradition in the wilderness, where the text places itself, or in the exile, where it is placed by critical scholarship? In either canonical or critical reading, the community is in a situation of little wealth and surplus. If this community of erstwhile slaves (or of subsequently marginated people) has no such wealth, then the cultic extravagance, or rhetoric about alleged cultic extravagance, is an act of hope whereby Israel, in its worship and imagination, takes on a splendor that the world will nowhere else permit it. This community, permitted so little, endows its priest with "glorious adornment" (v. 2) as a vigorous, hopeful protest against its concrete context.

As we have come to expect, we are told little about the breastplate's liturgic function. The only hint of function we have is the mention of Urim and Thummim, which will be the work and trust of Aaron (v. 30). While the meaning of Urim and Thummim is enigmatic, it probably refers to lots (dice) that are used to determine the will of God. In Deut 33:8-9, the Urim and Thummim are entrusted to Levi, so that in our text it is the Aaronide line of the house of Levi that claims and administers the lots.

This priesthood has enormous power, because it is entrusted to make known the will of God, discerned precisely through this priestly mechanism.[168] The breastplate is apparently garb that makes the lots visible and enhances their authority. As the ephod is to bring all of Israel into the presence of God, so the breastplate, filled with all the names, brings the purpose of God fully into the company of Israel.

28:31-35 The Robe. The priest is to be dressed in a way worthy of entering into the awesome presence of the holy God. Verse 35 adds a note

168. Pixley, *On Exodus*, 200, speaks of the "hegemonic function" of priestly religion.

that is odd and enigmatic. In a descriptive account that accents the visual, the "sound" (קוֹל *qôl*, "voice") of the robe is emphasized. Presumably the bells are to sound according to the priest's movement, with the sound indicating his coming and going. Such sounds will at least signal that the priest is moving about, doing his work. Perhaps the sound related to coming and going is concerned with access to the holy for the people.

The statement becomes even more enigmatic in the last clause, which takes us completely by surprise: "that he may not die." This suggests that the work of the priest is a dangerous, life-and-death matter. We do not know whether his dysfunction means he will be struck down by God or destroyed by the people. One way or the other, the priests had better get it right with the bells.

28:36-38 The Rosette. This reference is to a blossom or shining object, some kind of golden ornament worn on the priest's forehead (turban). The insignia on it, "Holy to Yahweh," identifies the unambiguous, unqualified loyalty and devotion of the priest. The phrase suggests that "Aaron" is not a priest to the people but is concerned only for the glory of Yahweh.

Every contact within the holiness of Yahweh, however, is freighted with risk and dangers. The risk of "Aaron" is that if the offering is not suitable, the priest, and not the people, is at fault. The purpose of the priest's activity, and therefore of this insignia, is to ensure that the offering "finds favor" (רָצוֹן *rāṣôn*), that it is ritually proper and, therefore, acceptable. Otherwise, the priest must be prepared to suffer the consequences.

28:39 The Tunic and Turban. The purpose of the turban is to carry the rosette. It also is to be made of fine material artistically adorned.

28:40-43. This chapter culminates in a general statement about the sons of Aaron that corresponds to vv. 1-5 concerning Aaron. We may note two triads of terms that speak about the authority and function of priesthood. The authority of Aaron and his sons is expressed in three verbs in v. 41: *anoint* (מָשַׁח *māšaḥ*) *ordain,* (מִלֵּא *mālē'* i.e.,"fill the hand"), and *consecrate* (קִדֵּשׁ *qādaš*). These are roughly synonymous terms that concern investing the priests with holy power and authority. The actual ordination of Aaron and his sons is delayed until Leviticus 8–9; attention should be paid to Lev 8:6-9, which is a quite specific and intentional enactment of the commands of Exodus 28.

The future of Aaron and his sons is also expressed in a triad (v. 43). The priests are to function at "the tent of meeting, the altar, and the holy place." These are three distinct elements of the apparatus that is to ensure the real presence of God. Of the three, the most interesting is the tent. This phrase reflects a tradition different from, and likely older than, that of "tabernacle." It specifies an actual face-to-face meeting to which only priests have access, and in which they participate on behalf of the people. Moreover, in the tent of meeting, according to the older traditions, God does not reside there but comes specifically for the meeting. Thus it accents the freedom of God, who only comes to meet as God chooses. Reference to the risk of death is made again, suggesting that this is an urgent, dreadful activity, important to the community and risky for the priest (v. 43).

REFLECTIONS

1. The polity and liturgical practice centered around Aaron tends to order rather than to dynamism, to stability rather than change, to symmetrical structure rather than to liberating transformation. Thus the office of the priest is to enact, embody, and guarantee orderliness of life with God. This text is ostensibly placed in the wilderness and is taken critically to be located in exile. Both wilderness and exile are situations of extreme disorder, i.e., of chaotic conditions. One might imagine that liturgical communities in such contexts would take great care to enact order that overrides the palpable disorder of life.

Moreover, if life is to be ordered in a way that dramatically triumphs over disorder within the sphere of the cult, then the beauty, loveliness, and elegance of this lavish portrayal intend to assert the good rule of God against the meanness, ugliness, and social experience wherein life is cheap and thin. The patient, almost tedious directions for ephod, breastplate, robe, and rosette are the patient, trustful preparation for a glorious moment of epiphany when life is reconfigured in a splendor not otherwise available.

The beauty and order of the priest, moreover, are fully subsumed by the holiness of God. While Israel may be grateful for holy presence, there is here no hint of intimacy or coziness. Therefore, what Israel must have—access to the holy through the offer of beauty and order—comes only at high risk.

2. The majestic splendor and richness of the religious establishment is rarely simply liturgical and aesthetic, but it characteristically spills over into commodity fetishism, in which the risk and dread of the priestly function is overridden by the power and grandeur of the office.

Conversely, splendid adornment becomes offensive as an end in itself when the community no longer understands itself in wilderness or exile. What is not offensive in "churches of poverty" becomes offensive in "churches of affluence."

To be sure, there is no explicit word of criticism in this text. One may wonder, however, if the text is so completely without irony that one so well appointed could be under threat of death. If there is no irony here, then at least in a canonical arrangement that moves from chaps. 25–31 to chap. 32 (admittedly a different textual tradition), it is clear that "Aaron" is indeed seduced by his own "glorious adornment." Thus the full affirmation and the devastating critique of Aaron live close together. The affirmation, the temptation, and the critique belong intrinsically to the office of priesthood and to any handler of holy things.

3. The priestly genealogy—the sense that holiness is an inherited prerogative—is here handled innocently. While the text unqualifiedly speaks of Aaron's four sons (v. 1), we know in Lev 10:1-3 that two "dropped out of ministry" for their presumptuousness. There is no inherited privilege in being holy.

4. The administration of Urim and Thummin (v. 30) suggests that the priestly office is to probe the mind of God in ways that give guidance to the people. This notation warns against two dangers. On the one hand, there is danger in assuming that there is no more to covenantal responsibility than good common sense or the "reason of this age." The priest is called to a different mode of knowledge to which only the priest has access. This is odd knowledge, indeed!

On the other hand, the device of Urim and Thummin may ensure that such priestly teaching really comes from God, and is not simply a reflection of the passions or interests of the priest. There is no complete, sure safeguard against this latter distortion, but the tradition understands the problem. For that reason, the "will of God" is mediated in ways outside mere priestly articulation.

5. The purpose of priesthood is "meeting" (v. 43). This text believes that, done well and carefully, meeting is possible. Such a way of understanding guards against both worship that is moralistic, didactic, and instructive and worship that is excessively therapeutic and narcissistic. Both didactic and therapeutic tendencies tend to *talk about* the meeting, rather than to *enact* such a meeting with this one who is profoundly holy and yet genuinely present.

6. The letter to the Hebrews finds the imagery of this priesthood poignant for articulating the claims of Jesus Christ (Heb 10:11-25). It is there insisted that Jesus did decisively, "once for all" what the priests of the old order could never fully accomplish. There is, to be sure, an inevitable dimension of supersessionism in this claim. However, the accent in Hebrews is not on displacing the old priestly provisions. Rather, the point is to affirm and celebrate the completeness and adequacy of Jesus in continuity with the old order. Jesus has taken the guilt of the community and made it an acceptable sacrifice (cf. Exod 28:38; Heb 10:22).

7. To some extent, this chapter affirms that "clothes make the priest." In Zech 3:4-5, the high priest Joshua is said to be guilty of violating his priestly office. But his "filthy clothes" are removed, and he is "clothed with festal apparel."

The notion of taking off "filthy clothes" and putting on new clothes and thereby being made new is taken up in powerful, metaphorical ways in Ps 132:9, 16, 18 (cf. 2 Chr 6:41). The imagery may be used positively in celebration of newness, as in Isa 61:10. Or the same imagery may be used negatively concerning judgment, as in Ezek 26:16.

This imagery is also used eschatologically for a vision of the blessed end, when the saints of God are clothed in pure, white linen (see Rev 3:5, 18; 4:4; 7:9; 15:6; 19:14). Note, moreover, how it relates to the transformation wrought in baptism: "You were taught to put away your former way of life, your old self, corrupt and deluded by its lusts, and to be renewed in the spirit of your minds, and to clothe yourselves with the new self, created according to the likeness of God in true righteousness and holiness" (Eph 4:22-24 NRSV).

The process of faith is the process of being "reclothed," as were the priests, as was the man summoned to sanity in Mark 5:1-20, and as are all the faithful. It continues to be a crucial pastoral issue that very many yearn to be "reclothed" in righteousness and salvation, and many yearn to be reinscribed with a new "belonging."

EXODUS 29:1-46, ORDINATION OF PRIESTS

NIV

29 "This is what you are to do to consecrate them, so they may serve me as priests: Take a young bull and two rams without defect. [2]And from fine wheat flour, without yeast, make bread, and cakes mixed with oil, and wafers spread with oil. [3]Put them in a basket and present them in it—along with the bull and the two rams. [4]Then bring Aaron and his sons to the entrance to the Tent of Meeting and wash them with water. [5]Take the garments and dress Aaron with the tunic, the robe of the ephod, the ephod itself and the breastpiece. Fasten the ephod on him by its skillfully woven waistband. [6]Put the turban on his head and attach the sacred diadem to the turban. [7]Take the anointing oil and anoint him by pouring it on his head. [8]Bring his sons and dress them in tunics [9]and put headbands on them. Then tie sashes on Aaron and his sons.[a] The priesthood is theirs by a lasting ordinance. In this way you shall ordain Aaron and his sons.

[10]"Bring the bull to the front of the Tent of Meeting, and Aaron and his sons shall lay their hands on its head. [11]Slaughter it in the LORD's presence at the entrance to the Tent of Meeting. [12]Take some of the bull's blood and put it on the horns of the altar with your finger, and pour out the rest of it at the base of the altar. [13]Then take

[a]40 That is, probably about 2 quarts (about 2 liters)

NRSV

29 Now this is what you shall do to them to consecrate them, so that they may serve me as priests. Take one young bull and two rams without blemish, [2]and unleavened bread, unleavened cakes mixed with oil, and unleavened wafers spread with oil. You shall make them of choice wheat flour. [3]You shall put them in one basket and bring them in the basket, and bring the bull and the two rams. [4]You shall bring Aaron and his sons to the entrance of the tent of meeting, and wash them with water. [5]Then you shall take the vestments, and put on Aaron the tunic and the robe of the ephod, and the ephod, and the breastpiece, and gird him with the decorated band of the ephod; [6]and you shall set the turban on his head, and put the holy diadem on the turban. [7]You shall take the anointing oil, and pour it on his head and anoint him. [8]Then you shall bring his sons, and put tunics on them, [9]and you shall gird them with sashes[a] and tie headdresses on them; and the priesthood shall be theirs by a perpetual ordinance. You shall then ordain Aaron and his sons.

[10]You shall bring the bull in front of the tent of meeting. Aaron and his sons shall lay their hands on the head of the bull, [11]and you shall slaughter the bull before the LORD, at the entrance

[a] Gk: Heb *sashes, Aaron and his sons*

all the fat around the inner parts, the covering of the liver, and both kidneys with the fat on them, and burn them on the altar. [14]But burn the bull's flesh and its hide and its offal outside the camp. It is a sin offering.

[15]"Take one of the rams, and Aaron and his sons shall lay their hands on its head. [16]Slaughter it and take the blood and sprinkle it against the altar on all sides. [17]Cut the ram into pieces and wash the inner parts and the legs, putting them with the head and the other pieces. [18]Then burn the entire ram on the altar. It is a burnt offering to the LORD, a pleasing aroma, an offering made to the LORD by fire.

[19]"Take the other ram, and Aaron and his sons shall lay their hands on its head. [20]Slaughter it, take some of its blood and put it on the lobes of the right ears of Aaron and his sons, on the thumbs of their right hands, and on the big toes of their right feet. Then sprinkle blood against the altar on all sides. [21]And take some of the blood on the altar and some of the anointing oil and sprinkle it on Aaron and his garments and on his sons and their garments. Then he and his sons and their garments will be consecrated.

[22]"Take from this ram the fat, the fat tail, the fat around the inner parts, the covering of the liver, both kidneys with the fat on them, and the right thigh. (This is the ram for the ordination.) [23]From the basket of bread made without yeast, which is before the LORD, take a loaf, and a cake made with oil, and a wafer. [24]Put all these in the hands of Aaron and his sons and wave them before the LORD as a wave offering. [25]Then take them from their hands and burn them on the altar along with the burnt offering for a pleasing aroma to the LORD, an offering made to the LORD by fire. [26]After you take the breast of the ram for Aaron's ordination, wave it before the LORD as a wave offering, and it will be your share.

[27]"Consecrate those parts of the ordination ram that belong to Aaron and his sons: the breast that was waved and the thigh that was presented. [28]This is always to be the regular share from the Israelites for Aaron and his sons. It is the contribution the Israelites are to make to the LORD from their fellowship offerings.[a]

[a]40 That is, probably about 1 quart (about 1 liter)

of the tent of meeting, [12]and shall take some of the blood of the bull and put it on the horns of the altar with your finger, and all the rest of the blood you shall pour out at the base of the altar. [13]You shall take all the fat that covers the entrails, and the appendage of the liver, and the two kidneys with the fat that is on them, and turn them into smoke on the altar. [14]But the flesh of the bull, and its skin, and its dung, you shall burn with fire outside the camp; it is a sin offering.

15Then you shall take one of the rams, and Aaron and his sons shall lay their hands on the head of the ram, [16]and you shall slaughter the ram, and shall take its blood and dash it against all sides of the altar. [17]Then you shall cut the ram into its parts, and wash its entrails and its legs, and put them with its parts and its head, [18]and turn the whole ram into smoke on the altar; it is a burnt offering to the LORD; it is a pleasing odor, an offering by fire to the LORD.

19You shall take the other ram; and Aaron and his sons shall lay their hands on the head of the ram, [20]and you shall slaughter the ram, and take some of its blood and put it on the lobe of Aaron's right ear and on the lobes of the right ears of his sons, and on the thumbs of their right hands, and on the big toes of their right feet, and dash the rest of the blood against all sides of the altar. [21]Then you shall take some of the blood that is on the altar, and some of the anointing oil, and sprinkle it on Aaron and his vestments and on his sons and his sons' vestments with him; then he and his vestments shall be holy, as well as his sons and his sons' vestments.

22You shall also take the fat of the ram, the fat tail, the fat that covers the entrails, the appendage of the liver, the two kidneys with the fat that is on them, and the right thigh (for it is a ram of ordination), [23]and one loaf of bread, one cake of bread made with oil, and one wafer, out of the basket of unleavened bread that is before the LORD; [24]and you shall place all these on the palms of Aaron and on the palms of his sons, and raise them as an elevation offering before the LORD. [25]Then you shall take them from their hands, and turn them into smoke on the altar on top of the burnt offering of pleasing odor before the LORD; it is an offering by fire to the LORD.

NIV

29"Aaron's sacred garments will belong to his descendants so that they can be anointed and ordained in them. 30The son who succeeds him as priest and comes to the Tent of Meeting to minister in the Holy Place is to wear them seven days.

31"Take the ram for the ordination and cook the meat in a sacred place. 32At the entrance to the Tent of Meeting, Aaron and his sons are to eat the meat of the ram and the bread that is in the basket. 33They are to eat these offerings by which atonement was made for their ordination and consecration. But no one else may eat them, because they are sacred. 34And if any of the meat of the ordination ram or any bread is left over till morning, burn it up. It must not be eaten, because it is sacred.

35"Do for Aaron and his sons everything I have commanded you, taking seven days to ordain them. 36Sacrifice a bull each day as a sin offering to make atonement. Purify the altar by making atonement for it, and anoint it to consecrate it. 37For seven days make atonement for the altar and consecrate it. Then the altar will be most holy, and whatever touches it will be holy.

38"This is what you are to offer on the altar regularly each day: two lambs a year old. 39Offer one in the morning and the other at twilight. 40With the first lamb offer a tenth of an ephah[a] of fine flour mixed with a quarter of a hin[b] of oil from pressed olives, and a quarter of a hin of wine as a drink offering. 41Sacrifice the other lamb at twilight with the same grain offering and its drink offering as in the morning—a pleasing aroma, an offering made to the LORD by fire.

42"For the generations to come this burnt offering is to be made regularly at the entrance to the Tent of Meeting before the LORD. There I will meet you and speak to you; 43there also I will meet with the Israelites, and the place will be consecrated by my glory.

44"So I will consecrate the Tent of Meeting and the altar and will consecrate Aaron and his sons to serve me as priests. 45Then I will dwell among the Israelites and be their God. 46They will know that I am the LORD their God, who brought them

a9 Hebrew; Septuagint *on them*   b28 Traditionally *peace offerings*

NRSV

26You shall take the breast of the ram of Aaron's ordination and raise it as an elevation offering before the LORD; and it shall be your portion. 27You shall consecrate the breast that was raised as an elevation offering and the thigh that was raised as an elevation offering from the ram of ordination, from that which belonged to Aaron and his sons. 28These things shall be a perpetual ordinance for Aaron and his sons from the Israelites, for this is an offering; and it shall be an offering by the Israelites from their sacrifice of offerings of well-being, their offering to the LORD.

29The sacred vestments of Aaron shall be passed on to his sons after him; they shall be anointed in them and ordained in them. 30The son who is priest in his place shall wear them seven days, when he comes into the tent of meeting to minister in the holy place.

31You shall take the ram of ordination, and boil its flesh in a holy place; 32and Aaron and his sons shall eat the flesh of the ram and the bread that is in the basket, at the entrance of the tent of meeting. 33They themselves shall eat the food by which atonement is made, to ordain and consecrate them, but no one else shall eat of them, because they are holy. 34If any of the flesh for the ordination, or of the bread, remains until the morning, then you shall burn the remainder with fire; it shall not be eaten, because it is holy.

35Thus you shall do to Aaron and to his sons, just as I have commanded you; through seven days you shall ordain them. 36Also every day you shall offer a bull as a sin offering for atonement. Also you shall offer a sin offering for the altar, when you make atonement for it, and shall anoint it, to consecrate it. 37Seven days you shall make atonement for the altar, and consecrate it, and the altar shall be most holy; whatever touches the altar shall become holy.

38Now this is what you shall offer on the altar: two lambs a year old regularly each day. 39One lamb you shall offer in the morning, and the other lamb you shall offer in the evening; 40and with the first lamb one-tenth of a measure of choice flour mixed with one-fourth of a hin of beaten oil, and one-fourth of a hin of wine for a drink offering. 41And the other lamb you shall offer in the evening, and shall offer with it a grain offering

NIV

out of Egypt so that I might dwell among them. I am the LORD their God.

NRSV

and its drink offering, as in the morning, for a pleasing odor, an offering by fire to the LORD. ⁴²It shall be a regular burnt offering throughout your generations at the entrance of the tent of meeting before the LORD, where I will meet with you, to speak to you there. ⁴³I will meet with the Israelites there, and it shall be sanctified by my glory; ⁴⁴I will consecrate the tent of meeting and the altar; Aaron also and his sons I will consecrate, to serve me as priests. ⁴⁵I will dwell among the Israelites, and I will be their God. ⁴⁶And they shall know that I am the LORD their God, who brought them out of the land of Egypt that I might dwell among them; I am the LORD their God.

COMMENTARY

Chapter 28 has been concerned with the proper dress and appearance of the priesthood of Aaron. Chapter 29 continues with specifics about ordination, consecration, and authorization. The chapter is a technical manual that appears to consist in directives given for officials who must conduct the specific rituals of ordination. We are given concrete directives on performance but almost no interpretive hint of the significance of the acts prescribed. Matters of significance are perhaps passed on orally, or taken for granted in that small community of privilege and expertise.

The chapter begins with authorization from God to proceed with the ordination (v. 1), and it concludes with a theological crescendo concerned with presence (vv. 43-46). Between is a series of obscure ritual activities that seem to be organized around a series of quite specific offerings. Moses is to "make priests" of the family of Aaron (v. 1). Thus the ultimate authority of Moses is preserved, from whom the priests derive their authority (cf. 7:1-2).

29:1-3. Then follows a series of consecrating acts. The materials needed for the consecration include a young bull and two rams who are "perfect" (תמים tāmîm), unleavened bread, cakes with oil, and wafers. The repeated reference to "unleavened," of course, recalls the festival provisions of chaps. 12–13, and anticipates v. 46, concerning the exodus.

29:4-9. The candidates for priesthood are to be washed (purified) and clothed. The inventory of clothing derives from chap. 28, though here the "rosette" of 28:36 is a "diadem" (v. 6; נזר nēzer). The candidate is then anointed with oil, i.e., peculiarly and distinctively designated.

29:10-14. The procedure requires the altar and the blood of the bull. The altar has been authorized in 27:1-10 (not to be confused with the one authorized in 30:1-10). The offering that is given from the residue of the bull is termed a "sin offering" (v. 14).

29:15-18. The blood of one of the rams is also used for the altar. The residue of the ram is given as a burnt offering, an "offering by fire" (v. 18), which is said to yield a smell that is offered up to Yahweh (cf. Lev 1:9).

29:19-21. The blood of the second ram is used on the priestly candidates. The person—the very body—of the priest is being ordained. That is, the priesthood is concerned not so much with what a priest *does*, but who he *is*. Accent is ontological rather than functional, a very "high" view of priesthood. The outcome of this act, which presumably has overlooked nothing of the priest, is that the priest "shall be holy." The formula קדש הוא (qādaš hû'), as Gerhard von Rad has shown, is a liturgical verdict, in which the subject is "reckoned" or declared to be of this status.[169] Thus the priest is *made* holy by these human, authorized actions.

29:22-28. The second ram is used in two ways. Part of the residue of this ram is mixed with the bread, cake of bread, and wafer (vv. 22-25; cf. v. 2). It is held by the priestly candidate and offered as an "elevated offering." The verb used to describe this offering is נוף (*nwp*), which apparently means there was a rhythmic gesture preliminary to this sacrifice. The other part of the second ram, the breast and thigh, which have been held back from the fire, are now offered as a "peace offering" (vv. 26-28). This offering belongs especially and peculiarly to the priestly candidate.

29:29-30. Provision is made for the sons of Aaron to receive the vestments and insignia as an inheritance from Aaron. Clearly the tradition is concerned to assure genealogical legitimacy and continuity in office.

29:31-37. The meat of the second ram is to be eaten by the priestly candidate. No one else shall eat of it, and none shall be left over. This section of the text is dominated by the threefold use of כפר (*kāpar*, "atonement"), the same term from which "mercy seat" in 25:17-22 derives. The eating of the food and the offering of a sacrifice do the work of atonement.

29:38-42. Finally, provision is made for a daily sacrifice. It is not clear how this provision relates to the preceding material. We are told in v. 35 that seven days are required for the process of ordination. This provision may intend that two lambs are offered for each of the seven days of the ritual of ordination. In any case, this offering, morning and night, is a grain offering and a drink offering (v. 41).

It is clear that this primitive ritual activity (primitive because it seems so elemental and pre-rational, and because we do not understand it) is the process whereby *holiness is created* in the community, holiness that authorizes and qualifies a few, select persons to go to the very core of God's holiness on behalf of the people. Thus the text refers regularly to the "tent of meeting" (vv. 10-11, 30, 32, 42). In the developing theory of presence, the "tent of meeting" performs a very different function from the tabernacle. In the tabernacle, God "dwells" (שׁכֵן *šākan*). In the "tent of meeting," God comes for specific engagements. One is struck by the odd juxtaposition of such an ambitious religious intention and the daily specifics whereby that intention is actualized. That meeting with the holy God is wrought through rams and bulls and blood and kidney and liver and flour and wafers! The transcendent holy is mediated in and through the stuff of daily life. Moreover, the accent is on the physical practice and not on thoughts or ideas or "knowledge." Holiness is made by proper doing.

The middle section of this chapter appears to be a report on a series of ritual activities (vv. 10-42). However, it may also be that this material is, in fact, organized to give formal, systematic structure to the range of different sacrifices belonging to the priestly office. These include sin offering (vv. 14, 36), burnt (whole) offering (vv. 18, 25, 42), elevation offering (v. 24), peace offering (v. 28), grain offering (v. 41), and drink offering (v. 41).

These same offerings are more systematically presented in Leviticus 1–7.[170] The priestly office is portrayed here as very well developed with technical specificity that we can no longer explicate. It also seems clear that the offerings have a series of intentions that likely cover the gamut of human suffering, joy, need, and gratitude.

29:43-45. The chapter concludes with the first hint of theological intentionality that we have encountered in a long while. At the center of this conclusion is an affirmation of priesthood, which makes all else possible (v. 44). On the basis of this properly established priesthood, the text can declare the full presence of God. This includes three affirmations concerning (1) the availability of God's glory (v. 43); (2) the promise "I will dwell [*šākan*] among the Israelites" (v. 45; cf. 25:8); and (3) a promise, "I will be their God" (v. 45). This latter statement echoes and reiterates the covenant formula of 6:7, but here is stated only the one side of the relation. This is God's

---

169. Gerhard von Rad, "Faith Reckoned as Righteousness," *The Problem of the Hexateuch and Other Essays* (New York: McGraw-Hill, 1966) 125-30. He regards such categorizing as a priestly verdict that determines the status of the object assessed by priestly expertise.

170. Older studies of the sacrificial system of the priests from which one can still learn include, H. H. Rowley, *Worship in Ancient Israel: Its Forms and Meanings* (Philadelphia: Fortress, 1967) 111-43; Hans-Joachim Kraus, *Worship in Israel: A Cultic History of the Old Testament* (Richmond: John Knox, 1966); and George Buchanan Gray, *Sacrifice in the Old Testament* (Oxford: Clarendon, 1925). These and all other studies are now displaced, however, by the magisterial work of Jacob Milgrom, *Leviticus 1–16.*

resolve to take up a new habitation, fully present in sovereign, life-giving power even without consideration of Israel's readiness or responsiveness.

29:46. The final statement of the chapter is especially remarkable. It not only refers to the exodus, but also reasserts the formula of acknowledgment. Then, remarkably, the old liberation formulas are joined to an affirmation concerning the abiding, dwelling presence of God. By bringing together "brought out" (יצא *yāṣāʾ*) and "know" (ידע *yādaʿ*) with "dwell" (*šākan*), this verse joins together liberation with presence and historical event with ritual stability. It holds together the "recital" and the "pattern," and in a canonical mode joins chaps. 1–15 and 25–31. This juxtaposition is made possible by a rightly performed ordination.

REFLECTIONS

1. These human actions of Moses, at God's command, are about the work of "making holiness," of generating holy reality. Religious communities, synagogues and churches, are always in the process of "making holy"—meals, persons, buildings, times, and places. "Making holy" is a daring, awesome enterprise that imagines ways in which the mystery of God in all its inscrutable power may be available to us.

Two dangers are present, however. On the one hand, there is the easy, ready distortion of taking the process of "making holy" as automatic. Then it becomes a tool for control and manipulation. This is the temptation to be "at ease in Zion," a temptation faced in every religious establishment and to which there is regular, predictable yielding. The other danger is an urbane attitude that believes such primitivism is beneath us and that life can be better ordered around morality and reasonableness. With this attitude, life is emptied of surplus power and significance and reduced to one horizontal plane.

2. The process of "making holy" requires an ongoing and complex action of self-giving. We may be dazzled by or impatient with the rich vocabulary for offerings, thinking it pretentious or overly scrupulous, especially since we do not know enough to decode the vocabulary. We may, however, ponder what it means to have such a rich variety of vocabulary and practice.

Any community has a rich, refined, and carefully nuanced vocabulary for what matters most to it. Thus apple growers in the Northwest of the United States have a legion of words for "apple," making necessary distinctions that outsiders cannot master. Israel, in the same way, is a community whose preoccupation is with "offerings" in all seasons of life. At least in this text, Israel's life is shaped and defined by the richness of "offering business." It is clear that the capacity to "make holy" depends on the fullness of giving. Where there is no rich offering, there will be very little "making holy." In a community that is unable or unwilling to give or to yield, the outcome can only be profanation, whereby neighborhood, environment, and finally self become mere objects, commodities for exploitation.

3. The letter to the Hebrews asserts that the work of Jesus Christ displaces all older patterns of priesthood. In Hebrews 7:11-14, the "order of Aaron" is explicitly mentioned. It is affirmed of Jesus Christ: "Unlike the other high priests, he has no need to offer sacrifices day after day, first for his own sins, and then for those of the people; this he did once for all when he offered himself" (Heb 7:27 NRSV).

While this is a christological claim that dispenses with the old order of Aaron, we shall not understand the argument about the new priesthood of Jesus Christ without attending to the details of the old text. Jesus Christ does not override the categories of priesthood, nor does he dismiss them as old fashioned or superstitious. Rather, these requirements for a genuinely holy priest are honored, enacted, and fulfilled. In our society of enormous isolation, many persons seek a priest who can be with them and for them in the dangerous zones of holiness or in the terrible profanation of life where holiness is lost. This yearning is for more than a counselor or an intercessor. It is a yearning for "atonement." The work of the priest is to reach behind all the issues that are more easily available and back to the core issue of presence, wherein rests the inscrutable gift of our humanness. The priest is the one who can take our offered selves and let them be the material through which God's own holiness is known.

EXODUS 30:1-10, THE INCENSE ALTAR

NIV

30 "Make an altar of acacia wood for burning incense. ²It is to be square, a cubit long and a cubit wide, and two cubits high*a*—its horns of one piece with it. ³Overlay the top and all the sides and the horns with pure gold, and make a gold molding around it. ⁴Make two gold rings for the altar below the molding—two on opposite sides—to hold the poles used to carry it. ⁵Make the poles of acacia wood and overlay them with gold. ⁶Put the altar in front of the curtain that is before the ark of the Testimony—before the atonement cover that is over the Testimony—where I will meet with you.

⁷"Aaron must burn fragrant incense on the altar every morning when he tends the lamps. ⁸He must burn incense again when he lights the lamps at twilight so incense will burn regularly before the LORD for the generations to come. ⁹Do not offer on this altar any other incense or any burnt offering or grain offering, and do not pour a drink offering on it. ¹⁰Once a year Aaron shall make atonement on its horns. This annual atonement must be made with the blood of the atoning sin offering for the generations to come. It is most holy to the LORD."

a2 That is, about 1 1/2 feet (about 0.5 meter) long and wide and about 3 feet (about 0.9 meter) high

NRSV

30 You shall make an altar on which to offer incense; you shall make it of acacia wood. ²It shall be one cubit long, and one cubit wide; it shall be square, and shall be two cubits high; its horns shall be of one piece with it. ³You shall overlay it with pure gold, its top, and its sides all around and its horns; and you shall make for it a molding of gold all around. ⁴And you shall make two golden rings for it; under its molding on two opposite sides of it you shall make them, and they shall hold the poles with which to carry it. ⁵You shall make the poles of acacia wood, and overlay them with gold. ⁶You shall place it in front of the curtain that is above the ark of the covenant,*a* in front of the mercy seat*b* that is over the covenant,*c* where I will meet with you. ⁷Aaron shall offer fragrant incense on it; every morning when he dresses the lamps he shall offer it, ⁸and when Aaron sets up the lamps in the evening, he shall offer it, a regular incense offering before the LORD throughout your generations. ⁹You shall not offer unholy incense on it, or a burnt offering, or a grain offering; and you shall not pour a drink offering on it. ¹⁰Once a year Aaron shall perform the rite of atonement on its horns. Throughout your generations he shall perform the atonement for it once a year with the blood of the atoning sin offering. It is most holy to the LORD.

a Or treaty, or testimony; Heb eduth   b Or the cover   c Or treaty, or testimony; Heb eduth

COMMENTARY

This section concerning the incense altar concludes Yahweh's first, most extended speech to Moses. In 27:1-8, we have already had authorization of an altar, presumably the altar of burnt offerings (cf. 30:28). The altar in this text is different in every way from that one. It is different in its measurements. It is to be overlaid with gold instead of bronze, indicating its greater importance, and it is specifically for the purpose of offering incense to God.

We may observe three items about this particular altar. First, it is carefully placed in relation to our cultic furniture (v. 6), which the text tradition delights in naming and reviewing. Second, the offering of incense is to be made regularly, twice a day, to perpetuity (v. 7). No reason is given for this regularity. The offer of incense is perhaps derivative of royal courts, in which the most exotic spices are to be used to create a most pleasing environment for the sovereign. Again, notice how this aesthetic tradition attends to all of the senses.

Third, in a belated thought, not fully integral to its context, v. 10 provides special priestly opportunity and responsibility, once each year on the Day of Atonement (*Yom Kippur*). On that day, "Aaron" shall do the peculiar work of atonement through blood. This is the most holy and most crucial priestly activity (cf. Leviticus 16).

REFLECTIONS

1. The priestly responsibility of offering fragrant incense morning and night to perpetuity suggests a rigorous, uncompromising discipline, sustained through thick and thin. The priestly tradition understands that "the practice of the presence" is not an *ad hoc* affair and does not take place in fits and starts. It requires regular, sustained, ordered, intentional efforts. Moreover, those efforts are promised no specific pay-outs or results. They are simply what must be done. Such discipline is required of any who would enter the presence of the Holy One.

2. The offer of fragrance involves the expenditure of resources in order to create a pleasing environment for one who is important and warrants special deference. Thus the offer itself is a dramatic enactment of honor and deference, the bestowal of prestige. The incense to make God's place pleasant is not unlike expensive preparation for the coming of a VIP, who must be protected from the sordidness of daily life. A Christian tradition speaks of prayer as a suitable "aroma" to God, indicating how this practice of incense can be taken metaphorically. Such a practice can be taken as appropriate "court action" that pays homage to one who peculiarly warrants such deference.

3. The priest has the capacity and responsibility once a year to perform the dangerous, crucial act of atonement. The writer of Hebrews is familiar with the language of the Exodus text concerning the Aaronides. On the one hand, the priest is said to enter the Holy Place "year after year" (Heb 9:25). On the other hand, "every priest stands day after day" (Heb 10:11 NRSV). What we have affirmed as regular discipline and repeated activity is interpreted in Hebrews as a recognition that none of these priestly acts is ever sufficient or adequate.

In contrast to that need for repetition, so runs the argument, the priestly offering of Jesus—his own blood—is not so inadequate or incomplete that it must be repeated again and again. Instead, this offering is done "once for all," never to be done again (see Heb 7:27; 9:25-28; 10:11-14). The accent on "once for all" is pervasive and is sharply polemical against the Aaronide provision.

The second contrast made to Aaron is that the priest offers blood that is not his own for atonement (cf. Heb 9:25), but from bulls and goats that cannot be effective (cf. Heb 10:4). By contrast, the blood (i.e., life) of Jesus is his own; therefore, it has sure efficacy.

One does not need to probe the intention of the manipulation of blood, nor does one need to engage in militant supersessionism, to appropriate this teaching. The point of the argument is that the offer of Jesus' own life for the sin of the world is sufficient and complete for all time. The letter to the Hebrews provides the ground for sure celebration of a most evangelical kind, a certitude that intends to counter the anxious practice of having to do atonement all over, again and again.

Moreover, if the imagery of adequate atonement is transferred to our "Age of Anxiety," it is enormously reassuring to affirm "once for all" that everything needed, everything hoped for, and everything required has been resolved by this beloved person. Therefore, there need be no anxiety, no restlessness, no tentativeness, no fear, no uncertainty. (Neither was the action of "once a year" in Exodus perceived as a terrible thing to repeat but a wondrous assurance of being able to deal with the problem of sin.)

The claim of Heb 10:21-23 does not need to be aimed at Judaism in a mood of supersessionism. Its critical relevance in our time is in relation to the anxiety of profane secularization that leaves the core of our humanness endlessly unresolved and perpetually at risk. In the face of our obsessive, repetitious, unsatisfying rituals of secularism, this decisive priestly claim has an urgent pertinence.

EXODUS 30:11–31:11, OTHER PRIESTLY MATTERS

This portion of text includes the middle five of Yahweh's seven addresses to Moses, each of which specifies an element in the general Aaronide arrangement for Presence.

Exodus 30:11-16, The Atonement Money

NIV

¹¹Then the LORD said to Moses, ¹²"When you take a census of the Israelites to count them, each one must pay the LORD a ransom for his life at the time he is counted. Then no plague will come on them when you number them. ¹³Each one who crosses over to those already counted is to give a half shekel,ᵃ according to the sanctuary shekel, which weighs twenty gerahs. This half shekel is an offering to the LORD. ¹⁴All who cross over, those twenty years old or more, are to give an offering to the LORD. ¹⁵The rich are not to give more than a half shekel and the poor are not to give less when you make the offering to the LORD to atone for your lives. ¹⁶Receive the atonement money from the Israelites and use it for the service of the Tent of Meeting. It will be a memorial for the Israelites before the LORD, making atonement for your lives."

ᵃ13 That is, about 1/5 ounce (about 6 grams); also in verse 15

NRSV

11The LORD spoke to Moses: ¹²When you take a census of the Israelites to register them, at registration all of them shall give a ransom for their lives to the LORD, so that no plague may come upon them for being registered. ¹³This is what each one who is registered shall give: half a shekel according to the shekel of the sanctuary (the shekel is twenty gerahs), half a shekel as an offering to the LORD. ¹⁴Each one who is registered, from twenty years old and upward, shall give the LORD's offering. ¹⁵The rich shall not give more, and the poor shall not give less, than the half shekel, when you bring this offering to the LORD to make atonement for your lives. ¹⁶You shall take the atonement money from the Israelites and shall designate it for the service of the tent of meeting; before the LORD it will be a reminder to the Israelites of the ransom given for your lives.

COMMENTARY

Maintaining the structures of presence costs money. This speech gives the "stewardship" angle.

This is a rather odd speech in context, containing almost none of the usual references to the cultic apparatus. It provides that all Israelites will be "signed up" (counted and registered in the census) as belonging to the community of the redeemed. However, membership costs. Every adult must pay a set fee, one half shekel, to maintain the machinery of presence. Moreover, the very payment itself is an act of remembering where one belongs, who one is, and what one owes. Each time the money is given, the giver will recall that he or she has been "ransomed" (כפר *kāpar*). This concrete act of payment will recall and make available the whole mystery of faith. This is, indeed, a sacramental use of money.

REFLECTIONS

This provision is stated in careful, rather archaic language. The intent of the instruction, however, is not difficult or obscure. Maintenance of cultic practice costs money. There is ground here for stewardship, which holds together very well the particularity of the "service of the tent of meeting" and the large action of God, which is to be remembered. One may observe that the taxing arrangement of v. 15 is regressive; rich and poor pay the same. Perhaps this regressive arrangement reflects the indifference of this tradition to matters of justice, since the provision for equal payment contrasts sharply with the notice of 16:16-18.

Exodus 30:17-21, The Basin for Washing

NIV

[17]Then the LORD said to Moses, [18]"Make a bronze basin, with its bronze stand, for washing. Place it between the Tent of Meeting and the altar, and put water in it. [19]Aaron and his sons are to wash their hands and feet with water from it. [20]Whenever they enter the Tent of Meeting, they shall wash with water so that they will not die. Also, when they approach the altar to minister by presenting an offering made to the LORD by fire, [21]they shall wash their hands and feet so that they will not die. This is to be a lasting ordinance for Aaron and his descendants for the generations to come."

NRSV

17The LORD spoke to Moses: [18]You shall make a bronze basin with a bronze stand for washing. You shall put it between the tent of meeting and the altar, and you shall put water in it; [19]with the water[a] Aaron and his sons shall wash their hands and their feet. [20]When they go into the tent of meeting, or when they come near the altar to minister, to make an offering by fire to the LORD, they shall wash with water, so that they may not die. [21]They shall wash their hands and their feet, so that they may not die: it shall be a perpetual ordinance for them, for him and for his descendants throughout their generations.

[a] Heb *it*

COMMENTARY

Yahweh's third speech provides for yet another cultic instrument. Its purpose is the ritual cleansing of the priesthood, in order that the priests should enter the zone of holiness clean and pure. The seriousness of the provision is underscored by the double warning, "that they may not die" (vv. 20-21; cf. 28:35, 43). The ritual provision again makes clear the ominous nature of approaching the holy and the high risk in which the priest operates. The text appears to be related to 1 Kgs 7:23-39, in which the "basin" is described as part of the Solomonic establishment.

REFLECTIONS

God cannot be approached carelessly or casually. It may be that a heavy emphasis on "free grace" in much recent theology, rooted in a particular reading of Paul, has suggested that disciplines of purity are not important for communion.

"Washing" concerns being well qualified for the holy. In the cultic traditions of the OT, one must have "clean hands" in order to enter the shrine (Ps 24:4). In Pss 26:6 and 73:13, there is a "washing in innocence." While the phrase may have become metaphorical, it is plausible that such a washing was a specific ritual act (see also Ps 51:2; Isa 1:16). More generally, attention may be given to the significance of baptism (see Acts 22:16; 1 Cor 6:11; Titus 3:5; Heb 10:22; Rev 1:5), and reference might be made to the washing by Jesus in John 13:1-11. Jesus' severe warning "Unless I wash you, you have no share with me" (John 13:8) does not seem remote from our text.

Exodus 30:22-38, Anointing Oil and Incense

NIV

22Then the LORD said to Moses, 23"Take the following fine spices: 500 shekels[a] of liquid myrrh, half as much (that is, 250 shekels) of fragrant cinnamon, 250 shekels of fragrant cane, 24500 shekels of cassia—all according to the sanctuary shekel—and a hin[b] of olive oil. 25Make these into a sacred anointing oil, a fragrant blend, the work of a perfumer. It will be the sacred anointing oil. 26Then use it to anoint the Tent of Meeting, the ark of the Testimony, 27the table and all its articles, the lampstand and its accessories, the altar of incense, 28the altar of burnt offering and all its utensils, and the basin with its stand. 29You shall consecrate them so they will be most holy, and whatever touches them will be holy.

30"Anoint Aaron and his sons and consecrate them so they may serve me as priests. 31Say to the Israelites, 'This is to be my sacred anointing oil for the generations to come. 32Do not pour it on men's bodies and do not make any oil with the same formula. It is sacred, and you are to consider it sacred. 33Whoever makes perfume like it and whoever puts it on anyone other than a priest must be cut off from his people.'"

34Then the LORD said to Moses, "Take fragrant spices—gum resin, onycha and galbanum—and pure frankincense, all in equal amounts, 35and make a fragrant blend of incense, the work of a perfumer. It is to be salted and pure and sacred.

a23 That is, about 12 1/2 pounds (about 6 kilograms)   b24 That is, probably about 4 quarts (about 4 liters)

NRSV

22The LORD spoke to Moses: 23Take the finest spices: of liquid myrrh five hundred shekels, and of sweet-smelling cinnamon half as much, that is, two hundred fifty, and two hundred fifty of aromatic cane, 24and five hundred of cassia—measured by the sanctuary shekel—and a hin of olive oil; 25and you shall make of these a sacred anointing oil blended as by the perfumer; it shall be a holy anointing oil. 26With it you shall anoint the tent of meeting and the ark of the covenant,[a] 27and the table and all its utensils, and the lampstand and its utensils, and the altar of incense, 28and the altar of burnt offering with all its utensils, and the basin with its stand; 29you shall consecrate them, so that they may be most holy; whatever touches them will become holy. 30You shall anoint Aaron and his sons, and consecrate them, in order that they may serve me as priests. 31You shall say to the Israelites, "This shall be my holy anointing oil throughout your generations. 32It shall not be used in any ordinary anointing of the body, and you shall make no other like it in composition; it is holy, and it shall be holy to you. 33Whoever compounds any like it or whoever puts any of it on an unqualified person shall be cut off from the people."

34The LORD said to Moses: Take sweet spices, stacte, and onycha, and galbanum, sweet spices with pure frankincense (an equal part of each),

a Or treaty, or testimony; Heb eduth

NIV

³⁶Grind some of it to powder and place it in front of the Testimony in the Tent of Meeting, where I will meet with you. It shall be most holy to you. ³⁷Do not make any incense with this formula for yourselves; consider it holy to the LORD. ³⁸Whoever makes any like it to enjoy its fragrance must be cut off from his people."

NRSV

³⁵and make an incense blended as by the perfumer, seasoned with salt, pure and holy; ³⁶and you shall beat some of it into powder, and put part of it before the covenant^a in the tent of meeting where I shall meet with you; it shall be for you most holy. ³⁷When you make incense according to this composition, you shall not make it for yourselves; it shall be regarded by you as holy to the LORD. ³⁸Whoever makes any like it to use as perfume shall be cut off from the people.

^a Or *treaty*, or *testimony*, Heb *eduth*

COMMENTARY

The fourth (vv. 22-33) and fifth (vv. 34-38) speeches of Yahweh to Moses share a common concern: the preparation and use of precious spices in order to produce perfumes for anointing the holy apparatus. The action of anointing the holy furniture with pleasing smells is an act of ritual adornment bespeaking deference and perhaps purification. The richly endowed, carefully prepared oil is to be used on all the temple furniture and upon the priests. Verses 32-33 and 37-38 suggest how serious is the act of anointing. This particular oil, especially prepared for Yahweh's habitat, cannot be otherwise used, on pain of excommunication.

REFLECTIONS

The practice of holiness mobilizes all of life and attends to all the senses. Thus the practice of holiness "smells good." (Notice the contrast to the "bad odor" in the liberation narrative [7:21; 8:14].) The OT is aware that a "good smell" in worship may cause worship to degenerate into bribery and manipulation. See the prophetic strictures of Isa 1:11-15 and Amos 4:4-5. The relentless critique of the sacrificial system in Heb 10:5-6 explicitly quotes the prophetic strictures. Thus the polemic in Hebrews against "acceptable sacrifice" joins cause with the prophetic strictures, but it intends to make a very different point, one that is christological rather than ethical.

In utilizing such critiques, one must be careful not to fall into a "knee-jerk Protestantism" that condemns worship in principle. Old Testament scholars agree that the prophetic critique of worship is aimed at distortion of ritual practice and not at sacrifice per se.

The reference to myrrh (v. 23) and frankincense (v. 34), moreover, suggests Matt 2:11, concerning the "adoration of the magi." The other two obvious OT practices to which Matthew may refer concern the use of spices by royalty (see Esth 2:12; Ps 45:8) and by lovers (Cant 3:6; 4:6, 17; 5:1, 5). All of these uses of precious spices—in relation to royalty, love, and holiness—concern deference, allegiance, extravagance, and devotion. If the Matthew text can be brought into the sphere of our text, then the wise ones knew they were entering into the zone of the holy in approaching the child. Such imagery concerning the sphere of the holy is not primary in Matthew, but it could not fail to be on the horizon of the Jewish listener to that story.

Exodus 31:1-11, Two Skilled Artisans

NIV

31 Then the LORD said to Moses, ²"See, I have chosen Bezalel son of Uri, the son of Hur, of the tribe of Judah, ³and I have filled him with the Spirit of God, with skill, ability and knowledge in all kinds of crafts— ⁴to make artistic designs for work in gold, silver and bronze, ⁵to cut and set stones, to work in wood, and to engage in all kinds of craftsmanship. ⁶Moreover, I have appointed Oholiab son of Ahisamach, of the tribe of Dan, to help him. Also I have given skill to all the craftsmen to make everything I have commanded you: ⁷the Tent of Meeting, the ark of the Testimony with the atonement cover on it, and all the other furnishings of the tent— ⁸the table and its articles, the pure gold lampstand and all its accessories, the altar of incense, ⁹the altar of burnt offering and all its utensils, the basin with its stand— ¹⁰and also the woven garments, both the sacred garments for Aaron the priest and the garments for his sons when they serve as priests, ¹¹and the anointing oil and fragrant incense for the Holy Place. They are to make them just as I commanded you."

NRSV

31 The LORD spoke to Moses: ²See, I have called by name Bezalel son of Uri son of Hur, of the tribe of Judah: ³and I have filled him with divine spirit,ᵃ with ability, intelligence, and knowledge in every kind of craft, ⁴to devise artistic designs, to work in gold, silver, and bronze, ⁵in cutting stones for setting, and in carving wood, in every kind of craft. ⁶Moreover, I have appointed with him Oholiab son of Ahisamach, of the tribe of Dan; and I have given skill to all the skillful, so that they may make all that I have commanded you: ⁷the tent of meeting, and the ark of the covenant,ᵇ and the mercy seatᶜ that is on it, and all the furnishings of the tent, ⁸the table and its utensils, and the pure lampstand with all its utensils, and the altar of incense, ⁹and the altar of burnt offering with all its utensils, and the basin with its stand, ¹⁰and the finely worked vestments, the holy vestments for the priest Aaron and the vestments of his sons, for their service as priests, ¹¹and the anointing oil and the fragrant incense for the holy place. They shall do just as I have commanded you.

ᵃ Or *with the spirit of God*   ᵇ Or *treaty*, or *testimony*; Heb *eduth*
ᶜ Or *the cover*

COMMENTARY

Yahweh's sixth speech to Moses concerns the pertinent, practical question of how the actual work on the tabernacle will be completed. This text thus parallels 30:11-16 in that it is about the practical implementation of the pattern.

The work has been entrusted to two skilled artisans, Bezalel and Oholiab. Beyond their pedigrees and competence, nothing is known of them. It is remarkable that with the complete domination of the text by Moses (and to a lesser extent by Aaron) the names of the senior craftsmen have not been lost. Three items are worth noting. First, this text forms something of a summary and a conclusion to the longer speech, because it names

and reiterates the long list of authorized elements for the tabernacle (vv. 7-11), all of which are the responsibility of these two artisans.

Second, these men are consummately skilled to work in every medium required (vv. 4-5). They are endowed with wisdom, discernment, and knowledge. It is worth noticing that "wisdom" here is quite practical. Consistent with the aesthetic sensibility of this text, wisdom is not excessively cerebral. It takes wisdom to create a place for God's holiness that is visually adequate and pleasing to smell. Third, the workmen are filled with God's Spirit, energized and authorized to use their enormous skill in ways befitting the holy (v. 3).

REFLECTIONS

The text explicitly states what is everywhere assumed in God's address to Moses: Creating a home for holiness is *human work.* That human effort, however, is powered and driven by the wind of God. If Fretheim is correct in relating these texts to creation, then this action entrusted to Bezalel and Oholiab is indeed a new creation fitted for holiness, generated by God's wind, which was the initial agent of creation (Gen 1:2). This text suggests that artistry is a creative act. These artists are, in a proper sense, "in-spired" to do this awesome work.

It is important that the triad of "artists-wisdom-Spirit" converge precisely in this text, which we might have expected to be parochial and confined to a narrower range of cultic interests and perceptions. Very recent secularization notwithstanding, the religious community since ancient times has been the central context and habitat for genuinely creative artistry. The work of the Spirit is evident not only in dramatic acts of liberation but in the awesome work of making a new world possible, gathered about God's holiness. With reference to literature, George Steiner has argued that certain kinds of art depend on the reality and presence of the Holy One.[171] In this text, likewise, the connection between genuinely creative art and the power of God's Spirit is decisive for making the earth a suitable place for God's presence. An inadequate doctrine of creation, a failure to value creativity as a gift of God, has caused the church to fail to appreciate or appropriate art as a gift of the Spirit. These artisans are indeed agents of God's powerful Spirit, which makes new life possible.

171. George Steiner, *Real Presences* (Chicago: University of Chicago Press, 1989). More broadly, see Ralph Harper, *On Presence: Variations and Reflections* (Philadelphia: Trinity Press International, 1991).

EXODUS 31:12-18, THE SABBATH

NIV

[12]Then the LORD said to Moses, [13]"Say to the Israelites, 'You must observe my Sabbaths. This will be a sign between me and you for the generations to come, so you may know that I am the LORD, who makes you holy.[a]

[14]"'Observe the Sabbath, because it is holy to you. Anyone who desecrates it must be put to death; whoever does any work on that day must be cut off from his people. [15]For six days, work is to be done, but the seventh day is a Sabbath of rest, holy to the LORD. Whoever does any work on the Sabbath day must be put to death. [16]The Israelites are to observe the Sabbath, celebrating it for the generations to come as a lasting covenant. [17]It will be a sign between me and the Israelites forever, for in six days the LORD made the heavens and the earth, and on the seventh day he abstained from work and rested.'"

a13 Or who sanctifies you; or who sets you apart as holy

NRSV

12The LORD said to Moses: [13]You yourself are to speak to the Israelites: "You shall keep my sabbaths, for this is a sign between me and you throughout your generations, given in order that you may know that I, the LORD, sanctify you. [14]You shall keep the sabbath, because it is holy for you; everyone who profanes it shall be put to death; whoever does any work on it shall be cut off from among the people. [15]Six days shall work be done, but the seventh day is a sabbath of solemn rest, holy to the LORD; whoever does any work on the sabbath day shall be put to death. [16]Therefore the Israelites shall keep the sabbath, observing the sabbath throughout their generations, as a perpetual covenant. [17]It is a sign forever between me and the people of Israel that in six days the LORD made heaven and earth, and on the seventh day he rested, and was refreshed."

18When God[a] finished speaking with Moses on

a Heb he

NIV

NRSV

18When the LORD finished speaking to Moses on Mount Sinai, he gave him the two tablets of the Testimony, the tablets of stone inscribed by the finger of God.

Mount Sinai, he gave him the two tablets of the covenant,a tablets of stone, written with the finger of God.

a Or *treaty,* or *testimony;* Heb *eduth*

COMMENTARY

This is God's seventh and final speech to Moses from the mountain, and it is quite unlike the preceding six in its concern and in its vocabulary. It has no interest in things liturgical or priestly, nor is it preoccupied with presence. It is, rather, concerned with sabbath as rest (and not as worship), a concern that touches primarily the public, economic sphere of Israel's life.

The speech consists in a series of imperatives followed by motivational clauses introduced by the particle כִּי (*kî*). This speech is roughly chiastic:

A Keep sabbath as a sign (v. 13).
   B Keep sabbath, for violators will be executed (v. 14).
   B′ Keep sabbath, for violators will be executed (v. 15).
A′ Keep sabbath as a sign (vv. 16-17a).
Conclusion: Yahweh rested (v. 17b).

31:12-13. The work stoppage on sabbath, the breaking of the vicious cycle of production and consumption, is a sign for all the world to see. What will be known through this freighted gesture is that Yahweh "makes Israel holy" (sanctifies) (cf. 19:6). This is an extraordinary claim; it asserts that Israel is fitted and qualified to enter the realm beyond realms, to participate in the joy, well-being, and power of God's own life. It is noteworthy in this text that entry into God's holiness does not depend on particular cultic scruples of clean and unclean, as we might expect (cf. 30:17-21), but only on a willing, obedient work stoppage.

31:14. The sabbath is "holy," freighted with the power for life. This requirement of holy rest in Israel is so urgent that violators shall "surely die." We have seen this formula מוֹת יוּמָת (*môt yûmāt*) in the legal series of 21:15-17. The phrasing is an ominous, formal, legal death sentence that is reserved in Israel as punishment for the most dangerous and objectionable affronts. The formula of excommunication at the end of v. 14, "cut off from among the people," may be an

attempt to back off from and tone down the severe threat of the death penalty.

We may nevertheless ponder why such a seemingly innocent matter as sabbath carries such a severe sentence. The answer, of course, is that violation of the sabbath is not as innocuous as it seems. This text is still powerfully infused by the exodus narrative. The kingdom of Pharaoh still represents the quintessence of a life lived for productivity (see 5:13-14; 16:19-21). This text evidences anxiety that any violation of sabbath as obedient work stoppage means being seduced by the production values and rewards of Pharaoh, which will predictably end in slavery. Thus "profaning" the sabbath means jeopardizing all that is most precious and definitional about Israel's existence in the world and its loyalty to Yahweh.

31:15. In reverse order, vv. 15-17a reiterate the command and warning of vv. 13-14. Verse 15 again evokes the death sentence, *môt yûmāt*, though this time the following formula of excommunication is absent. Abraham Heschel has seen that in Gen 2:1-4a, the very first thing God "hallows" (makes holy), is time—not a place (shrine) or a person (priest). The hallowing of time permits Israel in the end to confess "My times [all of them] are in your hand" (Ps 31:15 NRSV).[172]

Violating sabbath is to withhold for self that which rightly belongs to God. Clearly the reason for withholding for self is in order to have joy, well-being, and security on one's own terms and without reference to or reliance upon God. Violation of sabbath as a gesture of self-sufficiency means in the end to overthrow all that is crucial and definitional in Israel's faith (cf. Deut 8:17-20).

31:16-17a. Thus Israel's refusal of such self-sufficiency, shunning such profanation, and resisting

172. See Abraham Heschel, *The Sabbath: Its Meaning for Modern Man* (New York: Farrar, Straus, and Young, 1951).

the seductiveness of productivity, endlessly reenacts this sign. The sign is "forever."

Both Israel's destiny and Israel's danger are forever. The notion of a perpetual covenant as the reference point of sabbath is a relation for all time that cannot be disrupted. This affirmation of perpetual covenant is made in a limited number of texts, all of which appear to be dated to the exile. Thus in Gen 9:8-17 God's promise after the flood is that there will be no more jeopardy to the relation. It is remarkable that in the acute disruption and discontinuity of exile Israel's faith affirms the durability and reliability of covenant!(See Isa 54:9-10; 55:3; Jer 31:35-37; 33:20-25; Ezek 16:60-62; 34:25-31; 37:24-28. See also Gen 17:2-21; Lev 26:40-45; Pss 89:3-4, 33-34; 105:8, 10.)

31:17b. The last part of v. 17 contains a remarkable affirmation. On the one hand, as expected, rest is linked to God's own rest on the seventh day of creation (Gen 2:1-4a). Rest is not recuperation for the next day's work, but is the goal and climactic event of all creation, the point of it all. This quite explicit reference to the Genesis text supports the hypothesis that Exodus 25–31 is consciously and deliberately related to the seven days of creation, which culminate in rest. It supports the hypothesis both in its sequence of seven speeches like seven days and in the larger substantive claim that the goal of creation is God's palpable glory in the midst of Israel.

On the other hand, this text, perhaps inadvertently, makes an affirmation that is quite unexpected and has no counterpart in the Genesis text: Yahweh "was refreshed." The term translated "refreshed" is נפש (*nepeš*); as a noun it means "life/self" or in older translations, "soul." As a verb, it means to be "lifed, selfed, souled," to be given more of one's *nepeš*. The form in our text is *niphʿal*, which could be translated passively as in the NRSV, "was refreshed," though the agent of refreshment is implied and not named; or it could be rendered in the reflexive, "refreshed self." The verb of *nepeš* occurs in only two other places. In 23:12, as here, it is used in relation to sabbath rest, so that an ox, donkey, homeborn slave, or resident alien may be "refreshed." In 2 Sam 16:14, as David flees Absalom, he "refreshed himself in the Jordan."

What is utterly astonishing about v. 17 is that the sabbath is for God to be refreshed, *nepheshed*,

given back God's own, diminished self. With either a passive or a reflexive translation, the point is still the same. The inescapable inference is that in six days of creation God worked very hard, and God's own self had been diminished through that exertion. This usage is all the more astonishing in the Priestly tradition, which tends to present God primarily in terms of majestic transcendence. For a moment here, the text lets the reader see God from the other side, the side of frailty and vulnerability.

This point about God and sabbath is quite in tension with the notion that God rests in supreme confidence and assurance about the reliability of creation. Verse 17 thus provides a wondrous juxtaposition concerning God. At the same time, this is the God whose magnificent and serene power made heaven and earth, and yet who is exhausted and needs to recuperate. The sabbath is a sign that Israel is linked to perpetuity with this majestic, vulnerable God. Nobody can be an endless agent of productivity without a break—nobody, not even Yahweh. Israel trusts in and is utterly devoted to this glorious One who overrides Pharaoh's production schedule and who authorizes joyous rest as definitional to the life and destiny of creation.

31:18. God's long speech, which begins in 25:1, now comes to an end. It is finished! The whole pattern has been disclosed. The blueprint is complete. Moses and Israel now know everything that needs to be known about living with the holiness of God.

When God finishes, however, a remarkable outcome is reported. The whole, long speech is not written down for formal transmission. What is written down is only the two tablets (לחת העדת *lūḥōt haʿēdūt*) which are placed in the ark (cf. 25:16). That is all, and that is everything. In the very moment of utterance, the tradition asserts that the other commands (20:1-17), not the ones now being uttered, are primary. They are the ones given in stone for all time.

This verse creates something of a "canon within the canon," instructing the community in what counts the most. And what counts the most, so that it is formalized and transmitted in writing, is not tabernacle provisions but the commandments.

Moreover, the elevation and priority of the two tablets are made as dramatic and unambiguous as possible by the affirmation that the two tablets are written with "the finger of God" (cf. Deut 9:10).

Only twice in the tradition of Exodus is the "finger of God" mobilized. Here the "finger of God" is to bring Israel to a new, covenantal obedience. In 8:19, the "finger of God" dispatches the gnats and defeats the pretense of the empire (cf. Luke 11:20). The two uses are, in fact, intimately related, and together they witness to the unity of intention in the book of Exodus. Both in sending gnats (the story of liberation) and in giving the Torah (the rules for new community) Yahweh acts powerfully and decisively to make new, liberated, covenantal life possible for Israel.

REFLECTIONS

1. In our contemporary situation, sabbath is an urgent check on the *ideology of productivity*, which in turn is rooted in a myth of scarcity used to justify the great surpluses of the empire (cf. 1:11; Gen 47:7-20). The state acts as though there is not enough; therefore, the supreme virtue is in producing and accumulating more.

The ideology of productivity is subtle in its force and variegated in its presence. The most obvious manifestation is the work ethic, whereby one must work harder to achieve more in order to prove one's worth. But, of course, there are other ways to gain "more" besides the "old-fashioned way" of earning it. There is a leisure culture of more games, more expensive shoes, more victories, more entertainment, and more sex. There is a cult of gracious living that specializes in better stereo equipment, better wines, more vacations, a nicer home or better neighborhood, and a better school for the children. And there is a narcissistic cult of more jogged miles and more eating disorders, which is only another mode of a brick quota.

These several self-indulgences are not much removed from the "fool" in Luke 12:16-20 who was in his own ideology of productivity and who could not entertain the thought of sabbath. That story, as with our text, understands that a life that cannot imitate the creator in rest is in the end self-destructive. If the goal of life is, as in chaps. 25–31, the presence of God, then it is clear that a life committed to endless productivity is empty of the promise of God and cut off from the power of holiness. Such a life abandons the exodus narrative and, in the end, violates the very fabric of creation.

2. The main point about sabbath is not worship but the stoppage of work. That fact is noteworthy, especially in this larger text (chaps. 25–31), which is consumed by worship. Such an awareness invites us to rethink the meaning of worship. In this context, worship is God's creation engaged in joyous rest. It may give pause that it is largely the communities at the social margin who maintain restful, playful delight in the act of worship. The reason why worship is such a delight in these contexts is that it is a genuine sabbath, such a contrast to zones dominated by Pharaoh's production schedules. Too much worship has become too heavy, too didactic, too insistent, and too promotional to be a genuine sabbath. As proposed here, worship is a place in which to "enjoy God."

3. Consideration of sabbath provides a context for raising issues about the ultimate purpose of life. In a production-oriented life, we do not reflect much on an ultimate goal or destiny, being too busy with the next quota or assignment. Commitment to production programmatically screens out questions of ultimate goal or destiny, and one is fated to live a penultimate existence. Conversely, a practice of peaceful "at homeness" with God brings us close to an ultimate "at homeness" with God (cf. Heb 3:1–4:11). The fact that this passage on sabbath is placed last in God's speech to Moses suggests that sabbath belongs as the final question of faith and as the final goal of existence. That is, its literary placement bespeaks its eschatological significance.

4. Our text is more than moral instruction about work stoppage. It affirms the very structure and fabric of creation, as willed and practiced by the creator. Rest is not just a Mosaic idea or an outcome of the exodus, as might be suggested in Deut 5:12-15, but belongs to the core and structure of reality. God is not anxious about the world and not worried that it will fall apart. On the seventh day, God is not indispensable, for creation has enough momentum, viability, and coherence that it can, for one day, work on its own. And just as the creator has much confidence in the viability of creation, so also Israel is invited to trust that no human agent is indispensable for creation.

A "market ideology" has given many of us a powerfully atheistic notion of creation. We view all of creation as open to commodity manipulation. All of creation is for sale, for use, or for hoarding. But creation belongs to God and is not reducible to our management, coercion, or purchase. Thus sabbath is an act whereby we may restore and reaccept our proper relation to creator and to creation. Creation is not an object to administer but is a fabric and network of life-giving resources, functioning on its own before us and without us, generous in its sustenance, reliable for us if we will trust and receive (cf. Ps 104:27-28 as a confident conclusion to vv. 1-26). All of this God had to trust in God's own moment of being "refreshed." God trusts creation, and God is restored. We need not do otherwise.

5. Finally, the difficult question posed by this text is whether sabbath is a viable, practical undertaking in our busy, driven world. The hard fact is that sabbath cannot be added on to an ideology of production. There will never be enough time or energy or will or leisure or peaceableness for sabbath, as long as one is in pursuit of one more achievement, one more sale, one more commodity, one more party, or one more advance. The issue of sabbath, while it has practical economic outcomes, is first of all an eminently pastoral, spiritual one. It concerns being weaned away from the deep disorder of distrust, anxiety, and self-sufficiency that haunts all modern people.

M. Tsevat affirms that sabbath is a day to renounce autonomy and to give one's life back to God in gratitude and trust.[173] Freedom to do that requires life in a community intent upon liberation and covenant, a community that is confident that coveting is inappropriate in a world where "your heavenly father knows all you need" (see Luke 12:30).

This teaching on sabbath is oddly juxtaposed to the extensive provisions for tabernacle and priesthood (25:1–31:11). The logic of this juxtaposition is in the awareness that right living (sabbath) and right worship (tabernacle) go together. When one can trust enough in the holy power of Yahweh, one may be eligible for entry into the presence of the glory, utterly at home even in exile. The *practice of sabbath* and the *embrace of the holy* likely do not come in sequence, but are practices common to life with Yahweh.

---

173. Matitiahu Tsevat, "The Basic Meaning of the Biblical Sabbath," in *The Meaning of Job and Other Biblical Studies: Essays on the Literature and Religion of the Hebrew Bible* (New York: KTAV, 1980) 39-52, esp. 48.

EXODUS 32:1–34:35

SIN AND RESTORATION

OVERVIEW

These three chapters are crucially and peculiarly placed in the book of Exodus. According to scholarly consensus, they belong to the early sources of the book (JE), and so are a continuation of chaps. 19–24. Indeed, in the usual reading informed by critical scholarship, one reads directly from 24:18 to 32:11, skipping over the intervening materials of 25–31.

With a more recent accent on canonical reading, we must ask about chapters 32–34 in their immediate context, even when a conventional source analysis is accepted. Before chaps. 32–34 come 25–31, with the command for building the tabernacle. After chaps. 32–34 come 35–40, with the implementation of that command. Thus chaps. 32–34 disrupt the expected sequence of command (25–31) and performance (35–40). The sequence of command-disruption-implementation is likely an important and intentional theological arrangement.

Formally, the disruption of God's command is like the sequence of Genesis 1–2 (creation), 3–8 (sin), and 9:1-17 (new covenant). Exodus 32 is something like a paradigmatic break in the world intended by God for Israel. That formal sequence of creation, sin, and new covenant, however, may be further illuminated if one considers closely the relation between chaps. 25–31 and chap. 32. The most striking commonality is the figure of Aaron, who is authorized as the singular priest (chaps. 28–29), but who perverts Israel's faith in chap. 32. Thus it is possible that chaps. 32–34 present a polemic against the very Aaron so celebrated in 28–29, in favor of Moses' faith and leadership.

When we turn to 32–34 itself, we see again that an intentional design has been wrought in the material (helpfully discussed by Moberly).[174] These three chapters are likely made up of quite distinct materials. While chap. 32 concerns the offense of the calf, it has no particular relation to chap. 33. In like manner, the theophanic disclosure of 34:6-7, the resolve to make covenant (v. 10), and the proclamation of covenant law (vv. 11-26), likely reflect an old practice of covenant making that has no connection to broken covenant.

These materials have now been formed, as Moberly shows, into a new configuration around a pattern of sin (32), dialogue and negotiation (33), and new covenant (34). When arranged in this way, the materials are not simply concerned with a moment of crisis in Israel's past, but make a remarkable theological statement that has continuing force and significance. Yahweh has a will, capacity, and yearning for the restoration of broken covenant with Israel. This new beginning, which is enacted in chap. 34, is made possible (or necessary) because of the fierce insistence of Moses. In the assertion of 33:19, in the self-disclosure of 34:6-7a, and in the answer to the petition in 34:10, Israel receives an articulation of God's fierce, unwarranted graciousness, in the face of a profound act of disobedience. This is precisely the theological conclusion that would be most important to the exilic makers of canon. Put another way, the exile is exactly such a context of violation and brokenness that requires a fresh gift of Yahweh's mercy.[175]

In the end, we can appropriate this assertion of Yahweh's unfettered graciousness in two ways. If read critically, i.e., according to source analysis, the relation of Sinai is reconstituted on a firmer basis. If read canonically (as the book stands), even Aaron's waywardness does not preclude the miracle of fidelity and presence. Either way, the final form of the text shows that Israel's future depends on Yahweh's inordinant fidelity.

---

174. R. W. L. Moberly, *At the Mountain of God: Story and Theology in Exodus 32–34,* JSOTSup 22 (Sheffield: *JSOT,* 1983).

175. See Walter Brueggemann, "A Shattered Transcendence? Exile and Restoration," in *Problems and Prospects in Biblical Theology,* eds. Ben C. Ollenburger et al. (Nashville: Abingdon, FORTHCOMING).

EXODUS 32:1-35, THE GOLDEN CALF

32 When the people saw that Moses was so long in coming down from the mountain, they gathered around Aaron and said, "Come, make us gods[a] who will go before us. As for this fellow Moses who brought us up out of Egypt, we don't know what has happened to him."

[2]Aaron answered them, "Take off the gold earrings that your wives, your sons and your daughters are wearing, and bring them to me." [3]So all the people took off their earrings and brought them to Aaron. [4]He took what they handed him and made it into an idol cast in the shape of a calf, fashioning it with a tool. Then they said, "These are your gods,[b] O Israel, who brought you up out of Egypt."

[5]When Aaron saw this, he built an altar in front of the calf and announced, "Tomorrow there will be a festival to the LORD." [6]So the next day the people rose early and sacrificed burnt offerings and presented fellowship offerings.[c] Afterward they sat down to eat and drink and got up to indulge in revelry.

[7]Then the LORD said to Moses, "Go down, because your people, whom you brought up out of Egypt, have become corrupt. [8]They have been quick to turn away from what I commanded them and have made themselves an idol cast in the shape of a calf. They have bowed down to it and sacrificed to it and have said, 'These are your gods, O Israel, who brought you up out of Egypt.'

[9]"I have seen these people," the LORD said to Moses, "and they are a stiff-necked people. [10]Now leave me alone so that my anger may burn against them and that I may destroy them. Then I will make you into a great nation."

[11]But Moses sought the favor of the LORD his God. "O LORD," he said, "why should your anger burn against your people, whom you brought out of Egypt with great power and a mighty hand? [12]Why should the Egyptians say, 'It was with evil intent that he brought them out, to kill them in the mountains and to wipe them off the face of the earth'? Turn from your fierce anger; relent and do not bring disaster on your people. [13]Re-

32 When the people saw that Moses delayed to come down from the mountain, the people gathered around Aaron, and said to him, "Come, make gods for us, who shall go before us; as for this Moses, the man who brought us up out of the land of Egypt, we do not know what has become of him." [2]Aaron said to them, "Take off the gold rings that are on the ears of your wives, your sons, and your daughters, and bring them to me." [3]So all the people took off the gold rings from their ears, and brought them to Aaron. [4]He took the gold from them, formed it in a mold,[a] and cast an image of a calf; and they said, "These are your gods, O Israel, who brought you up out of the land of Egypt!" [5]When Aaron saw this, he built an altar before it; and Aaron made proclamation and said, "Tomorrow shall be a festival to the LORD." [6]They rose early the next day, and offered burnt offerings and brought sacrifices of well-being; and the people sat down to eat and drink, and rose up to revel.

[7]The LORD said to Moses, "Go down at once! Your people, whom you brought up out of the land of Egypt, have acted perversely; [8]they have been quick to turn aside from the way that I commanded them; they have cast for themselves an image of a calf, and have worshiped it and sacrificed to it, and said, 'These are your gods, O Israel, who brought you up out of the land of Egypt!'" [9]The LORD said to Moses, "I have seen this people, how stiff-necked they are. [10]Now let me alone, so that my wrath may burn hot against them and I may consume them; and of you I will make a great nation."

[11]But Moses implored the LORD his God, and said, "O LORD, why does your wrath burn hot against your people, whom you brought out of the land of Egypt with great power and with a mighty hand? [12]Why should the Egyptians say, 'It was with evil intent that he brought them out to kill them in the mountains, and to consume them from the face of the earth'? Turn from your fierce wrath; change your mind and do not bring disaster on your people. [13]Remember Abraham, Isaac,

a1 Or *a god*; also in verses 23 and 31   b4 Or *This is your god*; also in verse 8   c6 Traditionally *peace offerings*

a Or *fashioned it with a graving tool*; Meaning of Heb uncertain

member your servants Abraham, Isaac and Israel, to whom you swore by your own self: 'I will make your descendants as numerous as the stars in the sky and I will give your descendants all this land I promised them, and it will be their inheritance forever.'" [14]Then the LORD relented and did not bring on his people the disaster he had threatened.

[15]Moses turned and went down the mountain with the two tablets of the Testimony in his hands. They were inscribed on both sides, front and back. [16]The tablets were the work of God; the writing was the writing of God, engraved on the tablets.

[17]When Joshua heard the noise of the people shouting, he said to Moses, "There is the sound of war in the camp."

[18]Moses replied:

"It is not the sound of victory,
  it is not the sound of defeat;
  it is the sound of singing that I hear."

[19]When Moses approached the camp and saw the calf and the dancing, his anger burned and he threw the tablets out of his hands, breaking them to pieces at the foot of the mountain. [20]And he took the calf they had made and burned it in the fire; then he ground it to powder, scattered it on the water and made the Israelites drink it.

[21]He said to Aaron, "What did these people do to you, that you led them into such great sin?"

[22]"Do not be angry, my lord," Aaron answered. "You know how prone these people are to evil. [23]They said to me, 'Make us gods who will go before us. As for this fellow Moses who brought us up out of Egypt, we don't know what has happened to him.' [24]So I told them, 'Whoever has any gold jewelry, take it off.' Then they gave me the gold, and I threw it into the fire, and out came this calf!"

[25]Moses saw that the people were running wild and that Aaron had let them get out of control and so become a laughingstock to their enemies. [26]So he stood at the entrance to the camp and said, "Whoever is for the LORD, come to me." And all the Levites rallied to him.

[27]Then he said to them, "This is what the LORD, the God of Israel, says: 'Each man strap a sword to his side. Go back and forth through the camp

and Israel, your servants, how you swore to them by your own self, saying to them, "I will multiply your descendants like the stars of heaven, and all this land that I have promised I will give to your descendants, and they shall inherit it forever.'" [14]And the LORD changed his mind about the disaster that he planned to bring on his people.

15Then Moses turned and went down from the mountain, carrying the two tablets of the covenant[a] in his hands, tablets that were written on both sides, written on the front and on the back. [16]The tablets were the work of God, and the writing was the writing of God, engraved upon the tablets. [17]When Joshua heard the noise of the people as they shouted, he said to Moses, "There is a noise of war in the camp." [18]But he said,

"It is not the sound made by victors,
  or the sound made by losers;
  it is the sound of revelers that I hear."

[19]As soon as he came near the camp and saw the calf and the dancing, Moses' anger burned hot, and he threw the tablets from his hands and broke them at the foot of the mountain. [20]He took the calf that they had made, burned it with fire, ground it to powder, scattered it on the water, and made the Israelites drink it.

21Moses said to Aaron, "What did this people do to you that you have brought so great a sin upon them?" [22]And Aaron said, "Do not let the anger of my lord burn hot; you know the people, that they are bent on evil. [23]They said to me, "Make us gods, who shall go before us; as for this Moses, the man who brought us up out of the land of Egypt, we do not know what has become of him.' [24]So I said to them, "Whoever has gold, take it off'; so they gave it to me, and I threw it into the fire, and out came this calf!"

25When Moses saw that the people were running wild (for Aaron had let them run wild, to the derision of their enemies), [26]then Moses stood in the gate of the camp, and said, "Who is on the LORD's side? Come to me!" And all the sons of Levi gathered around him. [27]He said to them, "Thus says the LORD, the God of Israel, "Put your sword on your side, each of you! Go back and forth from gate to gate throughout the camp, and

[a] Or treaty, or testimony; Heb eduth

NIV

from one end to the other, each killing his brother and friend and neighbor.'" [28]The Levites did as Moses commanded, and that day about three thousand of the people died. [29]Then Moses said, "You have been set apart to the LORD today, for you were against your own sons and brothers, and he has blessed you this day."

[30]The next day Moses said to the people, "You have committed a great sin. But now I will go up to the LORD; perhaps I can make atonement for your sin."

[31]So Moses went back to the LORD and said, "Oh, what a great sin these people have committed! They have made themselves gods of gold. [32]But now, please forgive their sin—but if not, then blot me out of the book you have written."

[33]The LORD replied to Moses, "Whoever has sinned against me I will blot out of my book. [34]Now go, lead the people to the place I spoke of, and my angel will go before you. However, when the time comes for me to punish, I will punish them for their sin."

[35]And the LORD struck the people with a plague because of what they did with the calf Aaron had made.

NRSV

each of you kill your brother, your friend, and your neighbor.'" [28]The sons of Levi did as Moses commanded, and about three thousand of the people fell on that day. [29]Moses said, "Today you have ordained yourselves[a] for the service of the LORD, each one at the cost of a son or a brother, and so have brought a blessing on yourselves this day."

[30]On the next day Moses said to the people, "You have sinned a great sin. But now I will go up to the LORD; perhaps I can make atonement for your sin." [31]So Moses returned to the LORD and said, "Alas, this people has sinned a great sin; they have made for themselves gods of gold. [32]But now, if you will only forgive their sin—but if not, blot me out of the book that you have written." [33]But the LORD said to Moses, "Whoever has sinned against me I will blot out of my book. [34]But now go, lead the people to the place about which I have spoken to you; see, my angel shall go in front of you. Nevertheless, when the day comes for punishment, I will punish them for their sin."

[35]Then the LORD sent a plague on the people, because they made the calf—the one that Aaron made.

[a] Gk Vg Compare Tg: Heb *Today ordain yourselves*

COMMENTARY

According to conventional source analysis, 32:1 resumes the narrative of 24:14 (or 24:18). Even without such a critical distinction, however, 32:1 follows appropriately as a narrative account after 24:14, for the intervening material (24:15–31:18) takes place on the mountain between God and Moses.

32:1-6. For forty days and nights, Israel is without Moses and without access to God. Indeed, they are so anxious for Moses' return that they seize an initiative of their own to have access to God, without reference to Moses or his demanding scruples (32:1).

The next best source of theological authority (after Moses) is Aaron, thus they appeal to him (v. 1). According to the narrative, Aaron is Moses' brother and aide. As the story develops, however, Aaron becomes Moses' competitor and the pro-

genitor of a priestly line and style that are in principle deeply at odds with Mosaic faith.

In vv. 1-6, Moses is absent, still on the mountain. The only players in the immediate drama are "the people" and Aaron. The people are intensely religious, awaiting an alternative to Moses. They appeal to Aaron: "Make for us gods!" The appeal is a crude and frontal assault on the first and second commandments (20:1-6). In the interest of religious survival, Israel proposes to have gods who are the products of their own invention.

Aaron obliges. He takes an offering of the wealth and jewelry of Israel (cf. 25:1-7; 35:5-9; 36:3-7). The difference of this offering from that of Moses, of course, is in its intent. Moses acts to make the presence of Yahweh possible, according to the promise and command of Yahweh

(25:3 8), whereas Aaron acts on his own hook, thus anticipating a rival to Yahweh.

While the people instigate the action, Aaron takes the important initiatives and authorizes the religious adventure. He casts the image of a calf (on which see Exod 20:4). The god Israel makes for itself is a calf. Nowhere in the OT are we given any clarity about the calf, which in this narrative stands almost as an empty cipher for idolatry. It is plausible that it was no more a departure from Yahwism than was the ark, but was simply one more object upon which the invisible God sat or rode. In 1 Kings 12, in his break with Jerusalem and with the Davidic house, Jeroboam chooses a calf as a symbol of presence, an alternative to the ark. His choice of a calf may be innocent (cf. 1 Kgs 12:27-30). Notice that Aaron's dummy formula (32:4) is precisely paralleled by Jeroboam (1 Kgs 12:28). Our narrative, however, if understood in terms of that religious-political controversy, may be a polemic against the northern rivalry to Jerusalem. It may also be that the calf (i.e., bull) is a powerful symbol of some form of Canaanite fertility religion (cf. Hos 13:2). In that case, the calf symbolizes a way to secure one's own existence, to govern fertility, without recourse to the commands of Yahweh. Either way, the calf invites sharp polemic from the Mosaic purists in Israel.

The people immediately respond to the calf with the affirmation "These are your gods" of the exodus, who "brought you up out of the land of Egypt" (v. 4). Aaron then consolidates this new theological arrangement by building an altar, proclaiming a festival, and receiving offerings (vv. 5-6). That is, Aaron authorizes and constitutes a full alternative liturgical practice. His lame excuse is that Moses, who is clearly still on the mountain with Yahweh (i.e., at risk), is forgotten: "We do not know what has become of him" (v. 1). Short memory!

The elements of this new liturgic practice around these newly cast gods is not incongruent with the intention of the earlier text. In terms of form, Aaron does what Moses has authorized: An altar has been authorized (20:24), and burnt offerings and offerings of well-being are permitted, exactly the ones offered here (20:24). The festival (גח *hag*) has been the aim of the liberation from the beginning, and the celebration in eating and drinking seems to replicate the awesome act at the mountain (24:11).

The failure of Aaron, upon which the narrative does not yet comment, is that this newly authorized worship is distorted at its very core, because the God of the exodus cannot be "produced," by either the whim of the people or the inventiveness of the priest. The true God of the exodus is a lively subject and not a manipulatable object. Thus a deep contrast may perhaps be signaled in the final word of v. 6: They "rose up to revel" (צחק *ṣaḥēq*). The term *revel* may indicate self-indulgence. This sentence reiterates "eat and drink" from 24:10, but to very different effect. In place of the expression "gaze upon God" in 24:10, we have "rose up to revel." Whereas 24:10 is fully directed to God, 32:6 is an act of self-reference and, we may imagine, self-indulgence.

32:7-14. The narrative moves abruptly from Aaron's initiative to the conversation between God and Moses on the mountain. God speaks first (vv. 7-10). God knows fully what Aaron has done. The speech of Yahweh is in the form of a prophetic lawsuit. First, there is an indictment, indicating the violation of commandment by Israel (vv. 7-8). Yahweh's speech is terse. Yahweh's decisive role in the life of Israel has been disregarded. Israel has accepted an *ersatz* god, completely misconstruing the exodus. They are no longer "my people," but "your people" (v. 7).

Second, Yahweh proposes to burn Israel with wrath, to nullify the covenant and to eradicate Israel (vv. 9-10). The covenant from the outset has been conditional. Yahweh here expresses no restraint or reservation and is not excessively committed to Israel. Moreover, God proposes that for Moses alone there will be a "great nation." God is prepared to scuttle Israel as the promised "great nation," and to reassign and redeploy the great Abrahamic promise of Gen 12:2 to Moses. The lawsuit speech portrays Israel as the deep adversary of Yahweh, who is prepared to terminate Israel and begin again with Moses.

Moses responds at length to Yahweh's speech (vv. 11-13), acting as a daring intercessor on behalf of Israel for the first time. The cause would seem hopeless in light of Yahweh's rage. At great risk to himself, Moses throws himself against the wrath of Yahweh. Moses' speech is in two parts. The first part, in the form of two questions, is a motivation to persuade Yahweh to have a change of heart (vv. 11-12a). Moses identifies Israel as "your people" (v. 11, contra v. 7), appeals to the exodus, and warns that the proposed destruction of Israel will create an impression among the watching Egyptians that the exodus was a bad scheme on Yahweh's part (cf. Num 14:13-16).

Second, on the basis of that appeal to Yahweh's pride and vanity, Moses issues three demanding imperatives to God: Turn (שׁוב *šûb*) from your anger, change (נחם *niḥam*) your mind, and remember (זכר *zākar*) your promises (vv. 12*b*-13). Moses seeks to contextualize the present crisis for God by situating Israel in the midst of the old promises of Genesis. To that end, Moses quotes a classic unconditional promise from Gen 15:5. This is a telling appeal, because it is precisely on the basis of these old memories and promises that the exodus was at first undertaken at all (cf. 2:24; 3:6, 16; 6:8).

The exchange thus features two speeches with two parts each: God in a lawsuit speech: indictment and sentence; Moses in intercession: motivation and petition.

The narrator adds tersely that, on the basis of Moses' appeal, Yahweh has a change of mind (*nḥm*, v. 14). Moses' petition is effective and moves Yahweh away from the harsh resolve of the lawsuit speech. Such freedom on God's part is, of course, a problem for scholastic theology, which wants an immutable God, but such a God stands in deep tension with the biblical presentation of God.[176]

32:15-29. The terrible theological distortion enacted by Aaron (vv. 1-6) has in fact been overcome by the daring intervention of Moses (vv. 7-14). Now Moses must come to see for himself what Yahweh has already seen (vv. 15-29). Moses' response to the sorry situation of compromised Israel is twofold.

32:15-20. First, Moses, alone except for Joshua (cf. 24:2, 13), sees and responds all alone. Here the narrative is at pains to describe with precision the two tablets of the covenant, which are in fact the main issue in the narrative. They are not the work of Moses (but see 34:27). The tablets are "the work of God," the writing of God (v. 16). They provide an angle of vision for Moses and a deep contrast to the Aaronide accomplishment. The sounds coming from the camp at the foot of the mountain are no longer the singing of Miriam

---

176. See Terence E. Fretheim, *The Suffering of God: An Old Testament Perspective*, OBT (Philadelphia: Fortress, 1984); and Francis I. Andersen and David Noel Freedman, *Amos: A New Translation with Introduction and Commentary*, AB 24A (New York: Doubleday, 1989) 638-79.

(cf. 15:20-21) but of those who eat and drink and dance and revel (vv. 18-19; cf. v. 6).

Now Moses' "anger burned hot" (v. 19). Ironically, the phrase is the same as in v. 11. In his innocence, Moses has talked Yahweh out of the rage. But now Moses, upon witnessing the scene, reacts with the same rage as that of Yahweh. In his anger, Moses breaks both religious symbols, the tablets he carries and the calf he despises (vv. 19-20). The breaking of the tablets shows that the commandment-based covenant with Yahweh is abrogated. The breaking of the calf with the powerful, violent verbs *burn, grind*, and *scatter* is to make Israel choke on its own perversion. Moses' action indicates that Israel's relation with Yahweh, so carefully wrought at Sinai, has been quickly and completely nullified.

32:21-24. Moses' second response of Moses involves his confrontation with Aaron, his brother turned competitor and nemesis. Moses speaks to Aaron only briefly (v. 21). He asks a question, but the question is also a heavy accusation. Aaron is permitted the longer speech (vv. 22-24), but speeches of self-justification are characteristically long.

First, Aaron chides his brother, trying to talk him out of his massive anger as Moses has talked Yahweh out of anger. Now a third time, the phrase is used, "anger burns hot" (יחר־אף *yiḥar-'ap*). Aaron suggests Moses' anger is somewhat overwrought and inappropriate. "You know," says Aaron (as do I), "that this people Israel is inclined to evil." Aaron deftly "triangles" with Moses against Israel, seeking Moses as his ally, skillfully exempting himself from the crisis. It is as though Aaron is not at all involved in the trouble.

Aaron continues in v. 23, saying that, given the demand of Israel, Aaron is only marginally involved, and Moses is inappropriately upset with him. Aaron's account of what happened is reliable, until he comes to his own role. In his version he is scarcely involved at all! Aaron's single act, so his report goes, is to collect gold and cast it into the fire; that is all. Aaron's last line (he is permitted to speak no more) is a marvelous act of abdication, "Out came this calf!" (v. 24). The calf itself is the subject of the verb. Nobody did it, certainly not Aaron!

Aaron's shrewd speech seeks to exonerate himself at the expense of the people. His argument, lacking any conviction, is not unlike that of the

man and the woman in Gen 3:12-13: Everyone else, but not me. Fretheim asserts, "It is Genesis 3 all over again."[177]

32:25-29. Moses' third response, after the ini-tial reaction with Joshua (vv. 19-20) and after the confrontation with Aaron (vv. 21-24), is a quite public response that seeks to deal with the public damage of the treasonable act. Moses observes the scene. The problem is that the people are "without restraint" (פרע *pārûa'*), which is a cause of mockery among the observing nations (cf. v. 12). The same term is used, ironically enough, in 5:4, wherein Pharaoh describes Israel, who has not kept at its work (cf. Prov 29:18). It is clear to Moses that such "running wild" must be stopped. It is incongruous with the character of Israel and the God with whom Israel is allied. The intention of the liberation of the exodus was not to create a people "on the loose."

Moses' strategic response to a people out of control is to summon those who will to stand with Yahweh against the Aaronide travesty (v. 26). Notice that Moses does not summon folk to his side but to Yahweh's cause. That is, Moses preempts Yahweh (as he characteristically does), so that his enemies are the enemies of God (cf. 23:22).

Those who respond to Moses' summons are "the sons of Levi," a priestly order linked to Mosaic authority (cf. 2:1; 6:16-25). There can be little doubt that in a late period, they were rivals to the powerful Zadokite priesthood, which claims Aaronide rootage.[178] In the earlier period, it may be that the Levites were a "revolutionary cadre" who provided the will and theological legitimacy for the Mosaic revolution.[179] They were the ones with a radical social vision rooted in a radical discernment of Yahweh. If that is who the Levites were, then it is not surprising that they rally here to the summons of Moses to act for the purity

and fidelity of Israel against a perverse, compromising tendency. Thus a deep and fundamental theological issue concerning the nature of Yahweh and the faith of Israel is overlaid with a vigorous rivalry between priestly orders.

As is characteristic when Moses is involved, Israel is once again embroiled in a staggering, costly "either/or." Either one is with Yahweh (and Moses), or one is under threat. The Levites here demonstrate their singular devotion to a Mosaic vision of faith by their readiness to execute the distorters—3,000 of them, including their own relatives. The Levites, through this act, are "ordained" and receive a blessing from Moses (cf. 12:33 and 40:43 on Moses as a giver of blessing). This becomes the foundational authorization for this priestly order. Thanks to the unlimited and unhesitating fidelity of the Levites, Israel is purged of the aberration wrought by Aaron and is placed in a position to be reconstituted as a covenant people. The courage of the Levites gives Israel a future.

32:30-35. There is, however, unfinished business for Moses and for Yahweh. Moses' concern is with a "great sin." The phrase occurs in v. 21, and now is the *leitmotif* of vv. 30-31. The "great sin" is unfinished business. Moses first of all indicts the people for this action (v. 30). He is in no way romantic or "therapeutic" about the guilt of Israel nor about the jeopardy in which it has placed itself. Moses will seek to "make atonement" (כפר *kāpar*), a task assigned in the later source to Aaron (cf. 29:36-37). Moses' effort at atonement is not the performance of a priestly act, but a conversation in which he seeks to persuade God away from God's great anger (vv. 31-32). Moses begins his address to God, nonetheless, with a full acknowledgment of Israel's sin (v. 31).

Moses' central appeal is telling, for both the force of its rhetoric and Moses' inability to speak a full sentence (v. 32). It is structured as a double "if": "if . . . if not." However, the structure fails with the first "if." We expect a protasis and an apodosis, "if . . . then." But Moses can think of nothing to say that will balance the possibility of the first "if." He might have said, "If . . . then you will be honored," or "If . . . then we will be obedient," or "If . . . then the nations will see you vindicated." But the sentence is incomplete, and the thought is broken off. Moses cannot utter it.

177. Fretheim, *Exodus*, 279. It is instructive that in this great exposition of sin in the OT, Karl Barth, *Church Dogmatics* IV (Edinburgh: T. & T. Clark, 1956) 358-513, sets the text of Exodus 32 alongside Genesis 3 (as well as 1 Samuel 8 and 1 Kings 21).

178. See the hypothetical reconstruction of this rivalry by Cross, *Canaanite Myth and Hebrew Epic*, 195-215. See as well the way in which Hanson, *The Dawn of Apocalyptic*, has taken this struggle as a way to understand the recurring tensions concerning the nature of Judaism.

179. The phrase is used by Gottwald, *The Tribes of Yahweh*, 496, cf. 688. Behind Gottwald lies the explication of Max Weber, *Ancient Judaism* (Glencoe, Ill.: Free Press, 1952) 169-93, concerning the pivotal importance of the Levites for the revolutionary strain in Israelite faith. Hans Walter Wolff, "Hoseas Geistige Heimat," *TLZ* 81 (1956) 83-94, has proposed that Hosea as well as Deuteronomy reflects that radical commitment of the Levitical tradition.

He cannot think of a gain to be made by the sheer forgiveness of Yahweh.

The rhetoric then shifts to a second "if" in which Moses entertains a negative from God. It is on this second "if" that the force of the rhetoric falls. In an almost Job-like challenge to God, Moses wants, if God will not forgive, to be blotted out (מחה *māḥâ*) along with all the other Israelites. Moses stands in complete solidarity with recalcitrant Israel. He does not wish to be exempted from the wrath, as God has proposed in v. 10. Moses does not want to go on with Yahweh in the absence of Israel. Perhaps Moses plays "brinkmanship" with God, rather like threatening to resign from the government if he does not get his way. His speech is at least enormously daring, and perhaps noble as well.

God, however, will not be intimidated, nor will God be blackmailed, even by Moses (vv. 33-34). God will give nothing of what Moses asks. God will neither "forgive their sin" nor "blot out" Moses. God is perfectly capable of making distinctions in judgment, the very distinctions Moses wishes to forestall. God's punishment of Israel is no business of Moses, and he may not interfere with divine judgment. Thus God will "blot out" (*māḥâ*) (v. 33).

However, God has other work for Moses to do. Moses is to go to "the place"—the land of promise. Moses will be led and protected by an angel, and Moses is to get on with God's resolve (cf. 23:20, 23). Then God's speech adds a heavy conclusion: nevertheless, "I will punish" (פקד *pāqad*). Its effect is twofold. First, it reminds us that Yahweh's initial burning wrath (v. 10) is unassuaged. Second, it separates the positive function of Moses from the unfinished negativity of Yahweh.

This awesome confrontation between Yahweh and Moses is skillfully narrated, showing God working massive judgment. Even while the "great sinners" stand under judgment, the Mosaic community (including the Levites) is still the carrier of the promise. Neither the judgment nor the promise is permitted to crowd out each other. God has preserved God's sovereign capacity to adjudicate and to make distinctions. In the end, the calfmakers, the Aaron crowd, get their plague (v. 35). There is a "blotting out." The commandment will not be broken with impunity, and the God of the commandments will not be mocked. The commandments persist, and the Moses community stands ready to obey them.

REFLECTIONS

1. The narrative concerning Aaron introduces us to Israel's primordial (original?) sin. This narrative not only reports an episode, but presents to us a paradigm of Israel's most foundational waywardness. The "great sin" (vv. 21, 30-31) is to substitute an available, produced God for the sovereign one who is not immediately available and who is not made with hands. The first and second commandments require receiving, accepting, and obeying this God. The reality of this God causes Israel to live in endless jeopardy.

Israel, however, cannot tolerate the risk of faith (exemplified by the absence of Moses), so it incessantly seeks to reduce that risk by domesticating God to manageable proportion. The people who seek to reduce faith to palpable certitude are intensely religious, hungry for god(s) (v. 1). Their hunger, however, fails to deal with the reality of this God, and so the very community in partnership with this God becomes a factory for the production of more available, palpable gods.

2. The text stands by itself as a model of sin, punishment, intercession, and forgiveness. Its rich themes present a recurrent drama in the life of faith. We may enter the drama of the text more intensely, however, if we take it in the larger context of the book of Exodus. On the one hand, following critical source analysis, this text (together with 33–34) follows promptly after 19–24. On that reading, Israel's first act after its covenant oath of 24:3, 7 is a deep violation of covenant. Thus we are left, as was Israel, with the following questions: Is this the end? Will covenant be restored? The delicate, mixed ending of the episode in vv. 33-35 shows Israel struggling with this unresolved question.

On the other hand, if we take the final form of the text, chap. 32 comes after chaps. 28–29, which accent the enormous power, prestige, splendor, and wealth of the Aaronide office, perhaps suggesting that Aaron succumbs to the temptations of his office. It is possible to read the conflict as Moses vs. Aaron, Levites vs. Zadokites, or torah priests vs. temple priests. In more simple fashion, it may be enough to see the power of distorted desire among those who benefit too well from holy things, who lose critical self-awareness, and who begin to think they are the producers of the holy. The narrative suggests that this dreadful God "blots out" those who take unto themselves the production of holiness.

3. Insofar as this text is theological, i.e., concerned with God's life and self-presentation, we can see how the easy "both/and" of Aaron and the hard "either/or" of Moses exhibit the profound tension in God's own life. The tension is not simply the work of the narrator, nor is it only a quarrel between Moses and Aaron kicked upstairs. This tension of mercy that forgives and sovereignty that will not be mocked is an endless adjudication for the God of the Bible, who permits no final or systematic resolve. It is a tension we all know in our most intimate and treasured relations. In Exodus the crisis is kept raw, alive, and unresolved. It must be kept so for Moses and for Israel, as it is even for God's own life. This tension is what makes Moses' intercession so dangerous, so urgent, and so future-producing.

EXODUS 33:1-23, MOSES SEEKS ASSURANCE

NIV

33 Then the LORD said to Moses, "Leave this place, you and the people you brought up out of Egypt, and go up to the land I promised on oath to Abraham, Isaac and Jacob, saying, 'I will give it to your descendants.' [2]I will send an angel before you and drive out the Canaanites, Amorites, Hittites, Perizzites, Hivites and Jebusites. [3]Go up to the land flowing with milk and honey. But I will not go with you, because you are a stiff-necked people and I might destroy you on the way."

[4]When the people heard these distressing words, they began to mourn and no one put on any ornaments. [5]For the LORD had said to Moses, "Tell the Israelites, 'You are a stiff-necked people. If I were to go with you even for a moment, I might destroy you. Now take off your ornaments and I will decide what to do with you.'" [6]So the Israelites stripped off their ornaments at Mount Horeb.

[7]Now Moses used to take a tent and pitch it outside the camp some distance away, calling it the "tent of meeting." Anyone inquiring of the LORD would go to the tent of meeting outside the camp. [8]And whenever Moses went out to the tent, all the people rose and stood at the entrances

NRSV

33 The LORD said to Moses, "Go, leave this place, you and the people whom you have brought up out of the land of Egypt, and go to the land of which I swore to Abraham, Isaac, and Jacob, saying, 'To your descendants I will give it.' [2]I will send an angel before you, and I will drive out the Canaanites, the Amorites, the Hittites, the Perizzites, the Hivites, and the Jebusites. [3]Go up to a land flowing with milk and honey; but I will not go up among you, or I would consume you on the way, for you are a stiff-necked people."

[4]When the people heard these harsh words, they mourned, and no one put on ornaments. [5]For the LORD had said to Moses, "Say to the Israelites, 'You are a stiff-necked people; if for a single moment I should go up among you, I would consume you. So now take off your ornaments, and I will decide what to do to you.'" [6]Therefore the Israelites stripped themselves of their ornaments, from Mount Horeb onward.

[7]Now Moses used to take the tent and pitch it outside the camp, far off from the camp; he called it the tent of meeting. And everyone who sought the LORD would go out to the tent of meeting, which was outside the camp. [8]Whenever Moses went out to the tent, all the people would

NIV

to their tents, watching Moses until he entered the tent. [9]As Moses went into the tent, the pillar of cloud would come down and stay at the entrance, while the LORD spoke with Moses. [10]Whenever the people saw the pillar of cloud standing at the entrance fo the tent, they all stood and worshiped, each at the entrance to his tent. [11]The LORD would speak to Moses face to face, as a man speaks with his friend. Then Moses would return to the camp, but his young aide Joshua son of Nun did not leave the tent.

[12]Moses said to the LORD, "You have been telling me, 'Lead these people,' but you have not let me know whom you will send with me. You have said, "I know you by name and you have found favor with me.' [13]If you are pleased with me, teach me your ways so I may know you and continue to find favor with you. Remember that this nation is your people."

[14]The LORD replied, "My Presence will go with you, and I will give you rest."

[15]Then Moses said to him, "If your Presence does not go with us, do not send us up from here. [16]How will anyone know that you are pleased with me and with your people unless you go with us? What else will distinguish me and your people from all the other people on the face of the earth?"

[17]And the LORD said to Moses, "I will do the very thing you have asked, because I am pleased with you and I know you by name."

[18]Then Moses said, "Now show me your glory."

[19]And the LORD said, "I will cause all my goodness to pass in front of you, and I will proclaim my name, the LORD, in your presence. I will have mercy on whom I will have mercy, and I will have compassion on whom I will have compassion. [20]But," he said, "you cannot see my face, for no one may see me and live."

[21]Then the LORD said, "There is a place near me where you may stand on a rock. [22]When my glory passes by, I will put you in a cleft in the rock and cover you with my hand until I have passed by. [23]Then I will remove my hand and you will see my back; but my face must not be seen."

NRSV

rise and stand, each of them, at the entrance of their tents and watch Moses until he had gone into the tent. [9]When Moses entered the tent, the pillar of cloud would descend and stand at the entrance of the tent, and the LORD would speak with Moses. [10]When all the people saw the pillar of cloud standing at the entrance of the tent, all the people would rise and bow down, all of them, at the entrance of their tent. [11]Thus the LORD used to speak to Moses face to face, as one speaks to a friend. Then he would return to the camp; but his young assistant, Joshua son of Nun, would not leave the tent.

[12]Moses said to the LORD, "See, you have said to me, 'Bring up this people'; but you have not let me know whom you will send with me. Yet you have said, 'I know you by name, and you have also found favor in my sight.' [13]Now if I have found favor in your sight, show me your ways, so that I may know you and find favor in your sight. Consider too that this nation is your people." [14]He said, "My presence will go with you, and I will give you rest." [15]And he said to him, "If your presence will not go, do not carry us up from here. [16]For how shall it be known that I have found favor in your sight, I and your people, unless you go with us? In this way, we shall be distinct, I and your people, from every people on the face of the earth."

[17]The LORD said to Moses, "I will do the very thing that you have asked; for you have found favor in my sight, and I know you by name." [18]Moses said, "Show me your glory, I pray." [19]And he said, "I will make all my goodness pass before you, and will proclaim before you the name, 'The LORD';[a] and I will be gracious to whom I will be gracious, and will show mercy on whom I will show mercy. [20]But," he said, "you cannot see my face; for no one shall see me and live." [21]And the LORD continued, "See, there is a place by me where you shall stand on the rock; [22]and while my glory passes by I will put you in a cleft of the rock, and I will cover you with my hand until I have passed by; [23]then I will take away my hand, and you shall see my back; but my face shall not be seen."

[a] Heb YHWH; see note at 3.15

COMMENTARY

The conclusion of chap. 32 leaves Israel in acute crisis, under assault from Yahweh. Chapter 33 is a narrative concerning "next steps." Those next steps are fragile and tentative; Israel under Moses is in a precarious position. The crisis concerns the plausibility and continuation of Israel's existence as a people. Because Israel is formed from "no people" into a people of the covenant, the abrogation of the covenant implies the termination of Israel. The stakes are very high, because this "people" may become again "no people," exactly what the prophet Hosea envisions (Hos 1:8; cf. 2:23).

That crisis of continued existence, however, is transposed in this chapter into a crisis of God's presence. Only upon the condition of *God's presence* is *Israel's existence* viable. This chapter is the most thorough and sustained struggle with the problem of presence in the entire OT. It is made up of three rhetorical elements. First, vv. 1-6 constitute something of a conclusion to chap. 32, juxtaposing the promise and the danger of Yahweh's presence. Second, vv. 7-11 report on a most elemental and direct mode of confrontation between Yahweh and Moses. Third, vv. 12-23 report on a dramatic encounter between Yahweh and Moses, culminating in a promised theophany (concluded in chap. 34). In all three episodes, one can sense a profound tension concerning Yahweh's way with Israel. Through the episode of the calf, that relationship has lost whatever innocence it may have had. Now Yahweh's will for the relationship is characteristically qualified by the awareness that Israel has betrayed Yahweh. That is an irreversible reality that will endlessly haunt both parties.

33:1-6. The first move beyond the disaster of chap. 32 consists of an oracle of Yahweh to Moses (vv. 1-3) and a narrative response to the oracle that reiterates something of Yahweh's speech (vv. 4-6). The oracle itself is a stunning act of God's graciousness (vv. 1-3). Yahweh might have kept silent, and therefore been absent to Israel. But Yahweh still intends a future for Israel and still expects to be obeyed. The imperative "go" (לך *lēk*), remarkably, is the same verb initially addressed to Abram in Gen 12:1. The speech is dominated, moreover, by the exodus verb for "go up" (עלה *'ālâ*). The NRSV renders the verb in its first use as "leave." Thus Israel is to "go up" from Sinai as Yahweh "brought up" (*'ālâ*) Israel from Egypt. Verse 1 in fact gathers together the whole of Israel's faith tradition, including the liberation of Exodus and the promise of Genesis. Moreover, in vv. 2-3*a*, the two great memories of promise and liberation are powered by a reference to the future in the land. As in 23:23, the angel is promised and the enemies are named who are to be overcome. The land to be given is richly described in a reminiscence of the promises of 3:8, 17. Thus in vv. 1-3*a* the oracle of Yahweh asserts that the entire tradition in all its power and authority is still operative. The calf episode has not disrupted Yahweh's intentionality for Israel. Yahweh's resolve has endured past the moment of rage (cf. Isa 54:7-10).[180]

Such a resounding affirmation, however, is poignantly qualified in v. 3*b*. One more time, Yahweh uses the exodus verb: "I will not go up" (v. 3). Yahweh will not be on the way with Israel. The reason is that Israel is "stiff-necked"—stubborn and resistant. Were Yahweh to be directly involved with this people, Yahweh would consume and exterminate them. Yahweh's anger over the calf is enough in check to permit this new declaration of fidelity, but just barely. There will be an exodus; Israel will "go up." But Israel must go alone. Its obduracy has cost the full presence of God.

In providing a mode of presence, the narrative has distinguished between "an angel" and "I." In 23:22-23, "the angel" becomes, as the rhetoric moves on, Yahweh's own person. Here, however, the distinction is maintained. Israel is assured of a great deal, but not of everything. Israel has enough on which to go, but it does not have Yahweh's own personal accompaniment. The angel does not here become "I," because "I" am not going.

The people's response (vv. 4-6) has at its center a reiteration of part of the oracle just uttered (v. 5). Again the threat of Yahweh's presence is affirmed. Also, an act of obedience is voiced in v. 5 that was not in the original oracle of vv. 1-3. Israel must "remove its ornaments" (vv. 5-6), which seems to refer to gold rings like those in

---

180. On this text, see Brueggemann, "A Shattered Transcendence?" and "This Is Like . . . " *Pulpit Digest* (May/June, 1991) 5-8.

32:2-3, out of which the calf was made. Moreover, the verb translated "stripped themselves" (נצל *nāṣal*) is the same verb used in 3:22 and 12:36 for the seizure of Egyptian valuables. Israel, now possessing wealth and ostentation, is to free itself of such decorations; Israel is to do to itself what it has done to Egypt. Quite clearly, the narrative perceives the ornaments as a seduction and, therefore, a threat.

Three connections may be made concerning the removal of the ornaments. First, there is no doubt a reference here to the materials used for the calf. In this post-calf situation, reconstituted Israel, constituted by God's mercy and in spite of God's rage, is to unburden itself of such provocative possessions. The calf episode lurks for a perfectly possible reenactment. Second, the uses of the verb *nāṣal* suggest that the narrative intends to contrast the empty-handed circumstance of the slaves, who are free to take from their masters (3:22; 12:36), with the full-handed community of Sinai, which now stands under the seduction and danger known by the Egyptians. Third, less directly, this imperative may contain a critique of the priestly portrayal of Aaron as exotic in garb and appearance (chap. 29). Moses, by contrast, always represents lean, stripped-down obedience.

Because Yahweh speaks, Israel has a post-calf possibility. But it must forego the commodities that seduce and distort. Israel willingly obeys (vv. 4-6), as it did in Gen 35:1-4. In v. 5, this unburdening becomes the precondition of Yahweh's next act: "I will decide what to do to you." This entire paragraph displays a people in severe jeopardy. God has now laid down stringent requirements for the future, and Israel accepts those requirements.

33:7-11. These verses stand in stark contrast to the threat and demand of vv. 1-6. They tell about a most primitive, characteristic, and recurring mode of God's presence. It is noteworthy that these verses do not tell of a particular meeting, but a reliable, regularly operative mode of presence. While the narrative accent of "the tent" is straightforward, we are told very little about it.

The tent is commonly regarded as perhaps the most primitive and elemental cultic device Israel has for God's presence. A device that both makes God available and allows for God's freedom, it is not to be confused with the more sophisticated and developed "tabernacle" (25:1), which seems

to derive in part from the tent. We may observe the following features in this paragraph.

The tent is thoroughly and exclusively a Mosaic enterprise. It serves, embodies, and enhances Moses' authority. Most likely, the mention of Joshua in v. 11 (as in 32:17) serves to prepare us for his coming authority after Moses.

The tent is a place to which Yahweh really does come to speak to Moses, face to face. The mode of Yahweh's coming, however, is a visible "pillar of cloud." As is characteristic in the tradition, this text struggles to affirm full presence but also to make sure that God is not impinged upon or presumed upon.

There is a real meeting (v. 11); Moses speaks to God face to face. Indeed, the text suggests an intimate conversation between friends. Thus the text moves between intimate conversation and regal formality (cf. Gen 18:17; Isa 41:8). Through the person of Moses, there is genuine access to Yahweh. Moreover, this access has not been diminished by the calf episode. We are not told what transpires in that access and conversation, but the context permits us to believe that the conversation includes the sovereign affirmation of promise, the sovereign insistence upon command, and the daring intercession of Moses. In the hiddenness of this transaction, full communion between God and Israel is enacted.

The people play a minimal, secondary role in the meeting. They are only observers, not participants. If a person has a petition, it can be taken to the tent (v. 7). Presumably the function of the people is to watch in awe, wonder, and amazement, for in this meeting between the cloud-hidden God and God's friend, their destiny is resolved. There is nothing here of the threatening disruption that the meeting causes at Sinai (19:16-25).

33:12-23. The reference to the tent (vv. 7-11) is almost a pause to relieve the pressure of the narrative. As we have seen, the possibility of Israel's future survival and well-being depends on Yahweh's promise and presence. The reference to the tent might have given assurance on this point. Nonetheless in v. 12, Moses takes up the conversation as though neither the promise of an angel (v. 2) nor the regularity of the tent (vv. 7-11) is operative. This narrative is divided into two parts, an exchange about presence (vv. 12-16) and a final resolution by God to grant a less than complete self-disclosure (vv. 17-23). (The precise breaking point of the material into these two parts is somewhat uncertain, but it does divide in two sections, one dominated by Moses and the other by Yahweh.[181])

33:12-16. We are given two speeches by Moses, with only one brief utterance by Yahweh in v. 14. In Moses' first speech (vv. 12-13), the verb translated "know" (ידע *yāda'*) is used three times:[182]

> You have not let me know.
> You said, "I know."
> Show me (הודעני *hôdi'ēnî*),
> that I may know.

Moses wants to know, to have certitude. He can only know if God lets him know, for only God knows (cf. the rhetoric of Jer 11:18). What Moses wants to know is "whom you will send." Moses wants to know about the future and the mode of God's presence with Israel. The text obviously is unrelated to vv. 1-3, where the one to be sent is an angel. We are dealing here with a distinct voicing of Israel's crisis of presence.

The verb for "see" is used twice as an envelope for the speech: "See" (v. 12) and "consider" (v. 13). The last phrase is a motivational clause. Moses asks that God let him know because this is "your people" (contra 32:7). As in Num 11:11-15, Moses is clear and insistent that Israel belongs to Yahweh, and that Yahweh cannot escape responsibility.

This intense petition does, indeed, evoke a response from Yahweh (v. 14). It is a terse response consisting of only four words, but it contains everything needed. It is an assurance that "my face" will go—i.e., Yahweh's own self. Childs observes that God's promise in v. 14 is given only to Moses, "to you" (singular).[183] Moses' continuing prayer is to include Israel in the assurance. Thus in v. 16, he prays, "I and your people." The promise is for a much more intense and immediate presence than either the angel of v. 2 or the cloud of v. 9. The promise of "rest" is an allusion to the land (cf. vv. 2-3*a*). Thus Yahweh seems to give Moses everything for which he asks.

The mood of Moses' second speech (vv. 15-16) is not obvious. On the one hand, his response

seems like a second sharp insistence, as though Moses has not yet gotten satisfaction and must insist one more time. On the other hand, Moses' insistence may be a statement back to Yahweh, receiving the promise and underscoring how indispensably important God's presence is. In either case, Moses affirms that the "face" is crucial. Again, the exodus verb "go up" (*'ālâ*) is used. Moses asserts that the "going up" from Sinai should not be undertaken if Yahweh has no intention of following through into the wilderness.

The reason for Moses' resistance is that without the evidence of continued presence, Israel will appear to be on its own, abandoned. Moses' leadership will be fragile and ineffective. Finally, in v. 16, Moses utters his decisive confessional statement. It is only Yahweh's presence that marks Israel as distinct! Notice that in this last exclamation, the word *face* is used in a different way: "face of the earth." And Moses once more identifies Israel as "your people." The primary point, however, is that Israel's only claim to uniqueness is Yahweh's accompaniment. Moses' verdict may be an insistence, or it may be yet an acknowledgment in gratitude of the assurance of v. 14. I am inclined to think it is an insistence. Moses in this passage always wants more from God, and what he has by way of presence is never enough.

33:17-23. The dialogue continues. Yahweh responds once more to Moses and seems to give over to Moses all that has been asked. In v. 12, Yahweh had assured Moses that he had "found favor." In v. 16, Moses asks for a sign that he has "found favor." Now in v. 17, Yahweh asserts yet again that Moses has "found favor." The point is established! Yahweh is fully committed to Moses and to the future Moses will give to Israel. This assurance is heightened by Yahweh's final utterance in v. 17, once more using the verb *know*. Moses is fully known by Yahweh. Yahweh knows Moses' name! Notice that the use of the verb has been inverted. Moses wants to know, but now he is "known."

Moses, one more time, is relentless (v. 18). He has now received assurance of "face," "rest," and "favor." Now he asks one more request: "Show me [i.e., cause me to see] your glory." The verb *see* is used yet a third time, introducing another mode of God's presence. "Glory" bespeaks God's awesome, shrouded, magisterial presence, some-

181. See Walter Brueggemann, "The Crisis and Promise of Presence in Israel," *HBT* 1 (1979) 47-86.

182. See James Muilenburg, "The Intercession of the Covenant Mediator (Ex. 33:1*a*, 12-17)," in *Words and Meanings*, eds. Peter R. Ackroyd and Barnabas Lindars (Cambridge: Cambridge University Press, 1968) 159-81.

183. Childs, *Exodus*, 594-95.

thing like an overpowering light. It is in this passage as though the request for glory is to draw even closer, more dangerously, more intimately, to the very core of God's own self.

In his request, Moses has reached the limit of what even he may ask in his venturesome courage. Yahweh takes Moses' petition seriously, but will not grant the request. God will not let even Moses crowd into the hidden core of God's own life.

Yahweh's response to Moses' request consists in four powerful affirmations, with a massive negative at the end (vv. 19-23). The four affirmations are assertions of what God will do:

I will make all my goodness pass before you.
I will proclaim before you, my name, "Yahweh."
I will be gracious to whom I will be gracious.
I will show mercy upon whom I will show mercy.

The four statements voice an astonishingly generous, yet guarded, commitment to Moses. The first resolve concerns God's "goodness" (מוב *ṭôb*), i.e., Yahweh's generous, friendly power for life. The term *goodness* can be used as a synonym for *shalom*, and thus refers to the material blessings of creation. In our context, this promise parallels the concerns of vv. 3 and 14. In response to Moses' request to see glory, this is a manifestation of God's good gifts but not Yahweh's own self.

The second promise concerns God's name and embodies the full disclosure of Yahweh's sovereign character. This phrasing perhaps looks back to 3:14 and 6:2 and anticipates 34:6-7. The third affirmation concerns the completely unfettered capacity of Yahweh to be generous. The term translated "gracious" (חן *ḥēn*) is the same word rendered "favor" in vv. 12, 16, and 17. It generally concerns God's capacity to be unconditionally generous but most specifically refers to Yahweh's resolve to be generous to Moses. The fourth affirmation concerning "mercy" is parallel in structure and content to the third, and it again asserts Yahweh's capacity to act positively as Yahweh chooses. Jack R. Lundbom has shown that the literary structure of these last two promises, as in 3:14, is a rhetorical device used to terminate a conversation abruptly.[184]

To be sure, these four affirmations do not explicitly concern Israel, but they do seem to reassure Moses on the future attentiveness of Yahweh toward Israel in its hazardous journey.

Life goes on for Israel only because Yahweh is free, gracious, and merciful.

The negative of v. 20, which comes upon us abruptly, is an exceedingly odd statement. Moses had asked to see the "glory." Yahweh refuses to show the "face." To be sure, both "glory" and "face" concern presence and access to Yahweh. "Glory," however, is less direct, seeming to honor Yahweh's majestic hiddenness. Thus Moses asks to glimpse God in God's transcendent splendor, but Yahweh's refusal is as though Moses has been more disrespectful than he had in fact been. Perhaps Yahweh ups the ante and attributes more to Moses than Moses had dared, only to make the refutation more credible. In this last utterance, God draws a protective cover around the inscrutable mystery of God. The motivational clause of v. 20 suggests that God's refusal to be seen is because such "seeing" is too dangerous. This conclusion in v. 20 is in profound tension with 24:10-11, where the mountain party "gazed upon" God. Clearly the tradition is not concerned to harmonize all these assertions. It is enough to notice that the struggle for and with God's presence is complicated and hard fought. It admits of and requires a diversity of articulations, none of which can alone say all that must be said.

After the negative qualification of v. 20, Yahweh finally goes far in letting Moses stand in the presence (vv. 21-23). This final response seems not to be concerned for the hiddenness of Yahweh but for the safety of Moses. Yahweh's offer to Moses is indeed gentle and protective. Yahweh finds for Moses a safe place to stand and watch "with me." This statement is filled with specific phrasing about the physical presence of Yahweh: "my glory, my hand, my back, my face." It is as though God plays peek-a-boo with Moses. Moses is permitted to look, just as the face of glory is past, and what Moses is permitted to see is the back side, the rear end of God—but not the face! The only thing he is denied is that for which he has never asked, the "face." It is worth noting that all we have is a promise of a distinctive disclosure to Moses. Nowhere are we ever told that the encounter does take place (cf. 34:5-6). The passing of God's glory seems always to be in prospect.[185]

184. Jack R. Lundbom, "God's Use of the *idem per idem* to Terminate Debate," *HTR* 71 (1978) 193-201.

185. Hans Urs von Balthasar, *The Glory of the Lord I: Seeing the Form* (New York: Crossroad, 1982) 317-31, concludes that "the Biblical experience of God is always proleptic."

REFLECTIONS

1. Life goes on, even after the calf episode! In these verses, the text reasserts the power of the old promise and the validity of the exodus (v. 1). It reiterates the enduring promise of the land. God's whole life with Israel from the beginning continues to operate, the calf notwithstanding. The sin of Aaron has not disrupted the power of God's intentionality, any more than the flood disrupts God's fidelity to Noah (Gen 8:20-22; 9:1-17), any more than the exile interrupts Israel's covenant (Isa 49:14-15; 54:7-10; Jer 31:31-34).

The amazing response of God to the events of chap. 32 is at the heart of biblical faith. The voicing of God's continued faithful resolve is first of all as an imperative: "go." Because God continues in fidelity, Israel, even after the calf, must continue in obedience.

2. The primary condition for a resumed relation with Yahweh in this chapter is the "stripping of ornaments" (vv. 4, 6). Chapters 32–33 are deeply aware of the destructive power of "commodity fetishes," of endless fascination with natural objects that are mistakenly supposed to enhance worth. It may be in our interpretative context that the "ornaments" that seduce are not material but psychological, moral, intellectual, or dialogical. Perhaps so, but we must not move too far from commodities, particularly in a consumer society wherein greed generates brutality and skewed neighbor relations. In these chapters, Israel is indeed "rich in things and poor in soul." The requirement for resumed covenant is divestment and unburdening of the accoutrements of self-sufficiency, which impede and finally preclude a "hearing" relationship. In his encounter with the "rich young ruler" (Mark 10:17-22), Jesus' comments on riches (vv. 2-27) are not far removed from this stern demand of Yahweh for divestment.

3. The primary agenda of this entire chapter revolves around the awareness that *survival* depends on *presence. Survival* means exactly the durability of a cultural system that can provide a "home" for individual persons. *Presence* means the holy source of covenantal life in our very midst. The juxtaposition suggests that the survival of a durable cultural system depends on the known, acknowledged power of holiness in its midst. In *Real Presences*, George Steiner persuasively argues that where God is not present, certain kinds of literature and art become impossible.[186] One may extrapolate from Steiner's argument that without God, certain kinds of social relationships are precluded.

The two great modern social experiments of Eastern communism and Western capitalism have struggled in different ways with this juxtaposition. It is now relatively easy to see that in the communism of Eastern Europe (perhaps most visible in Romania, Albania, and the former Soviet Union), where the holy dimension of covenant was denied, social relationships became increasingly brutal and empty. As a consequence, fear became pervasive, human dignity diminished, and creation as a life-giving system was nearly destroyed.

It is not so easy to see, or palatable to notice, that a Western free-market system in a different way evidences the same risks. "Presence" is little more evoked in a consumer economy than in a statist system. In the end, the results are not so different, wherein human dignity fails and life becomes paralyzing and empty. A market society devalues persons who have no productive capacity and relates rapaciously to the environment.

4. The calm, almost flat episode of the tent suggests that in this community of post-calf, stiff-necked people, meeting is nonetheless possible (vv. 7-11). We may imagine that in our secularized society, such a notion is too odd to entertain. But that community, like ours, had little inclination for such a meeting. It was, however, prepared to offer its petitions and to

---

186. Steiner, *Real Presences*, 70, suggests that a refusal to face "presence" leads to "a misreading of man's place in the natural world." While Steiner refers to the objectivism rooted in Descartes and Kant, his insight is not far removed from the struggle for presence in our text, and for a right reading of reality.

watch in awe and amazement. The meeting is not a big public meeting, when it happens. The meeting depends on the daring of one person who is prepared on behalf of the community to risk God's holiness and to treat the terror of holiness face to face, as "best friend."

5. In v. 16, Moses actualizes a crucial principle of community. He understands that even this Israelite community, in and of itself, possesses no marks of specialness. Moses would refuse to brood about the "marks of the church," and would opt for the radical principle that the church's only claim is its close solidarity to the God who invites camaraderie. The temptation for any community is to imagine that its specialness is its own peculiar property. The point applies first of all to religious communities. Derivatively, it applies as well to national states and every other kind of group that imagines itself to be special.

6. Moses' performance in vv. 12-18 is a model for daring, insistent prayer. He prays with enormous *hutzpah*, and is prepared to crowd God in insistent ways. First, he asks to know *God's ways*. Then he insists on the *face as accompaniment*. Finally, he asks to see the *glory*. Moses refuses to let God determine the limits of asking. This model of Jewish prayer offers much to learn for Christians, whose piety is characteristically too deferential.[187]

We may note two other features of this prayer. It is intensely theological, concerned with the person and presence of God. Moses' mind does not wander onto other agendas, but stays fixed on presence as the crucial issue for his people. Second, Moses knows when to stop, for after vv. 21-23 he goes no further. Moses is a model for prayer, because he takes into full and knowing account the one with whom he must do business. He acknowledges not only the sovereignty of God but also his own considerable freedom in prayer.

7. The God who responds to Moses is genuinely self-giving. We might not have expected this in the light of chap. 32. This God, however, is fully attentive to the insistent petitions of Moses. God does grant to Moses that God's own face will be present on the journey. God agrees to show goodness to Moses. Most of all, God, in uncompromised freedom, is utterly gracious and utterly merciful. This is not cheap grace; neither is it a blanket offer for any and all. The text suggests, nonetheless, that the God of Moses extends God's self in extreme ways, in order to meet the needs and yearnings of Israel.

8. Only in the final moment is there a limit to presence. The limit on accessibility and intimacy is the limit of God's own inscrutable holiness. This accent is, of course, in tension with God's self-giving. God holds in non-negotiable and unending tension self-giving and the self-reserve that makes self-giving possible. God is endlessly at work in this tension, upon which the vitality of biblical faith depends.

Derivatively, there is in this tension a model for humanness. The keeping or holding of self belongs in tension with the giving of self. To fall out on either side is to destroy the prospect of a serious relation. We are most "God-like" when this tension is kept visible and operative. Too much traditional Christianity has one-sidedly urged self-giving. As a counterpart, secular ideology urges the complete keeping of self. This text suggests that neither posture by itself will bring us to full humanness. We are called to imitate the God who is shown in this text, the God who both holds and gives away.

9. The culmination of this chapter is a vision of God (vv. 22-23). It is, however, a vision that embodies exactly the tension and juxtaposition we have seen all through the chapter. Moses does get to see God—but not God's face. Moses' *"seeing"* is honored—but not fully.

---

187. On the legitimacy and cruciality of such prayer, see Claus Westermann, "The Role of the Lament in the Theology of the Old Testament," *Int* 28 (1974) 20-38; and Moshe Greenberg, *Biblical Prose Prayer as a Window to the Popular Religion of Ancient Israel* (Berkeley: University of California Press, 1983) esp. 11-14. On the efficacy of such prayer, see Harold Fisch, *Poetry with a Purpose: Biblical Poetics and Interpretation* (Bloomington: Indiana University Press, 1990) 108-14.

Moses anticipates Paul: "For now we see in a mirror, dimly, but then we will see face to face" (1 Cor 13:12 NRSV).

The experience of seeing God might have been given peculiarly to Moses (33:11), but Paul knows such communion is not given to us. Moses' *knowing* is honored—but not fully. Moses here again anticipates Paul: "For we know only in part, and we prophesy only in part; but when the complete comes, the partial will come to an end. . . . Now I know only in part; then I will know fully, even as I have been fully known" (1 Cor 13:9-10, 12 NRSV). The seeing is "dimly"; the knowing is "in part." But "dimly" and "in part" are enough.

EXODUS 34:1-28, RENEWAL OF THE COVENANT

NIV

34 The LORD said to Moses, "Chisel out two stone tablets like the first ones, and I will write on them the words that were on the first tablets, which you broke. [2]Be ready in the morning, and then come up on Mount Sinai. Present yourself to me there on top of the mountain. [3]No one is to come with you or be seen anywhere on the mountain; not even the flocks and herds may graze in front of the mountain."

[4]So Moses chiseled out two stone tablets like the first ones and went up Mount Sinai early in the morning, as the LORD had commanded him; and he carried the two stone tablets in his hands. [5]Then the LORD came down in the cloud and stood there with him and proclaimed his name, the LORD. [6]And he passed in front of Moses, proclaiming, "The LORD, the LORD, the compassionate and gracious God, slow to anger, abounding in love and faithfulness, [7]maintaining love to thousands, and forgiving wickedness, rebellion and sin. Yet he does not leave the guilty unpunished; he punishes the children and their children for the sin of the fathers to the third and fourth generation."

[8]Moses bowed to the ground at once and worshiped. [9]"O Lord, if I have found favor in your eyes," he said, "then let the Lord go with us. Although this is a stiff-necked people, forgive our wickedness and our sin, and take us as your inheritance."

[10]Then the LORD said: "I am making a covenant with you. Before all your people I will do wonders never before done in any nation in all the world. The people you live among will see how awesome is the work that I, the LORD, will do for you. [11]Obey what I command you today. I will drive

NRSV

34 The LORD said to Moses, "Cut two tablets of stone like the former ones, and I will write on the tablets the words that were on the former tablets, which you broke. [2]Be ready in the morning, and come up in the morning to Mount Sinai and present yourself there to me, on the top of the mountain. [3]No one shall come up with you, and do not let anyone be seen throughout all the mountain; and do not let flocks or herds graze in front of that mountain." [4]So Moses cut two tablets of stone like the former ones; and he rose early in the morning and went up on Mount Sinai, as the LORD had commanded him, and took in his hand the two tablets of stone. [5]The LORD descended in the cloud and stood with him there, and proclaimed the name, "The LORD."[a] [6]The LORD passed before him, and proclaimed,

"The LORD, the LORD,
a God merciful and gracious,
slow to anger,
and abounding in steadfast love and
    faithfulness,
[7] keeping steadfast love for the thousandth
    generation,[b]
forgiving iniquity and transgression and sin,
yet by no means clearing the guilty,
but visiting the iniquity of the parents
upon the children
and the children's children,
to the third and the fourth generation."

[8]And Moses quickly bowed his head toward the earth, and worshiped. [9]He said, "If now I have found favor in your sight, O Lord, I pray, let the

a Heb *YHWH;* see note at 3.15   b Or *for thousands*

out before you the Amorites, Canaanites, Hittites, Perizzites, Hivites and Jebusites. [12]Be careful not to make a treaty with those who live in the land where you are going, or they will be a snare among you. [13]Break down their altars, smash their sacred stones and cut down their Asherah poles.[a] [14]Do not worship any other god, for the LORD, whose name is Jealous, is a jealous God.

[15]"Be careful not to make a treaty with those who live in the land; for when they prostitute themselves to their gods and sacrifice to them, they will invite you and you will eat their sacrifices. [16]And when you choose some of their daughters as wives for your sons and those daughters prostitute themselves to their gods, they will lead your sons to do the same.

[17]"Do not make cast idols.

[18]"Celebrate the Feast of Unleavened Bread. For seven days eat bread made without yeast, as I commanded you. Do this at the appointed time in the month of Abib, for in that month you came out of Egypt.

[19]"The first offspring of every womb belongs to me, including all the firstborn males of your livestock, whether from herd or flock. [20]Redeem the firstborn donkey with a lamb, but if you do not redeem it, break its neck. Redeem all your firstborn sons.

"No one is to appear before me empty-handed.

[21]"Six days you shall labor, but on the seventh day you shall rest; even during the plowing season and harvest you must rest.

[22]"Celebrate the Feast of Weeks with the firstfruits of the wheat harvest, and the Feast of Ingathering at the turn of the year.[b] [23]Three times a year all your men are to appear before the Sovereign LORD, the God of Israel. [24]I will drive out nations before you and enlarge your territory, and no one will covet your land when you go up three times each year to appear before the LORD your God.

[25]"Do not offer the blood of a sacrifice to me along with anything containing yeast, and do not let any of the sacrifice from the Passover Feast remain until morning.

a13 That is, symbols of the goddess Asherah   b22 That is, in the fall

Lord go with us. Although this is a stiff-necked people, pardon our iniquity and our sin, and take us for your inheritance."

[10]He said: I hereby make a covenant. Before all your people I will perform marvels, such as have not been performed in all the earth or in any nation; and all the people among whom you live shall see the work of the LORD; for it is an awesome thing that I will do with you.

[11]Observe what I command you today. See, I will drive out before you the Amorites, the Canaanites, the Hittites, the Perizzites, the Hivites, and the Jebusites. [12]Take care not to make a covenant with the inhabitants of the land to which you are going, or it will become a snare among you. [13]You shall tear down their altars, break their pillars, and cut down their sacred poles[a] [14](for you shall worship no other god, because the LORD, whose name is Jealous, is a jealous God). [15]You shall not make a covenant with the inhabitants of the land, for when they prostitute themselves to their gods and sacrifice to their gods, someone among them will invite you, and you will eat of the sacrifice. [16]And you will take wives from among their daughters for your sons, and their daughters who prostitute themselves to their gods will make your sons also prostitute themselves to their gods.

[17]You shall not make cast idols.

[18]You shall keep the festival of unleavened bread. Seven days you shall eat unleavened bread, as I commanded you, at the time appointed in the month of Abib; for in the month of Abib you came out from Egypt.

[19]All that first opens the womb is mine, all your male[b] livestock, the firstborn of cow and sheep. [20]The firstborn of a donkey you shall redeem with a lamb, or if you will not redeem it you shall break its neck. All the firstborn of your sons you shall redeem.

No one shall appear before me empty-handed.

[21]Six days you shall work, but on the seventh day you shall rest; even in plowing time and in harvest time you shall rest. [22]You shall observe the festival of weeks, the first fruits of wheat harvest, and the festival of ingathering at the turn of the year. [23]Three times in the year all your

a Heb Asherim   b Gk Theodotion Vg Tg: Meaning of Heb uncertain

NIV

26"Bring the best of the firstfruits of your soil to the house of the Lord your God.

"Do not cook a young goat in its mother's milk."

27Then the Lord said to Moses, "Write down these words, for in accordance with these words I have made a covenant with you and with Israel." 28Moses was there with the Lord forty days and forty nights without eating bread or drinking water. And he wrote on the tablets the words of the covenant—the Ten Commandments.

NRSV

males shall appear before the Lord God, the God of Israel. 24For I will cast out nations before you, and enlarge your borders; no one shall covet your land when you go up to appear before the Lord your God three times in the year.

25You shall not offer the blood of my sacrifice with leaven, and the sacrifice of the festival of the passover shall not be left until the morning.

26The best of the first fruits of your ground you shall bring to the house of the Lord your God.

You shall not boil a kid in its mother's milk.

27The Lord said to Moses: Write these words; in accordance with these words I have made a covenant with you and with Israel. 28He was there with the Lord forty days and forty nights; he neither ate bread nor drank water. And he wrote on the tablets the words of the covenant, the ten commandments.ᵃ

ᵃ Heb words

COMMENTARY

This chapter forms the conclusion to the great triad of chaps. 32–34. Together they express a great dramatic moment in Israel's life with Yahweh: 32, broken covenant; 33, intercession and the crisis of presence; 34, renewed, restored covenant.

Chapter 34 provides the dramatic moment whereby Israel, by the graciousness and mercy of Yahweh (cf. 33:19), and by the office of Moses, is restored to be God's covenant partner. The text may be divided into three parts, though such a division fails to deal with the detail and complexity of the several elements: (1) initial theophany and petition preparatory to renewed covenant (vv. 1-10), (2) divine decree concerning covenant stipulations (vv. 11-26), (3) conclusion of the covenant, which preserves the stipulations of covenant for generations to come (vv. 27-28).

34:1-10. The main business of this encounter is to make possible the survival of Israel into the future as the people of Yahweh. The personal interaction of Yahweh and Moses intends to serve the larger purpose of forgiveness, reconciliation, and restoration of the relation with Israel that had been broken by the calf episode.

That drama of restoration has the sternness of command at its center. In vv. 1-3, Yahweh issues to Moses a decree of three items concerning the renegotiation of covenant. The first item is "the two tablets" for the commands of Yahweh (v. 1). Heretofore the tablets had been mentioned in two connections. In 24:12, Yahweh gives Moses the two tablets of command. In 32:15-20, the tablets are destroyed in anger, symbolizing the destruction of this relation based in command and obedience. Now the tablets are reissued. This time Moses must supply the blank tablets upon which Yahweh will write the commands that are at the core of the covenant.

The second item of the initial decree is that entry into the sphere of the holy requires ritual preparation (v. 2). These requirements closely parallel the initial provisions of 19:10-11. This time, however, the instruction applies only to Moses, for only Moses will approach the mountain.

The third item is that Moses alone will conduct this encounter (v. 3). The contrast with the first meeting is clear. This time there are no elders, no people, no priests, not even Aaron. Moses has gained a monopoly in the narrative, perhaps through his daring and singular obedience in chap.

32 or perhaps through his relentless insistence in chap. 33.

Moses then presents himself for the theophany to which he alone has been summoned (vv. 4-7). Moses is obedient. He goes alone, with the tablets. (The ritual preparation is not mentioned.) Primary attention is given, rather, to the descent and speech of Yahweh (vv. 5-7). Yahweh's descent seems to allude to the promise of God's passing presence in 33:22-23, a theophany that has been promised but never, so far as we are told, enacted. This report, however, of a "passing" provides no detail to match the expectations of 33:22-23. The only parallel between the two texts is the reuse of the verb for "pass before" (עבר *ābar*).

This text, in contrast to 33:22-23, is not interested in any visual encounter, but only in the speech of Yahweh, as indicated by the double use of the verb *proclaim* (קרא *qārā'*). The first use utters the awesome name of God, without any commentary or delineation, as in 33:19. All else is commentary on the unutterable name, now uttered in Moses' ear. (The awesomeness of the name here is reminiscent of 3:14 and perhaps also recalls the warning of 20:7.)

The second use of the verb, in v. 6, introduces one of the most remarkable and important utterances in the OT. It is not unambiguously clear that Yahweh (and not Moses) speaks. I shall accept the more common assumption that Yahweh is the speaker. Thus the speech of vv. 6-7 is Yahweh's self-disclosure, revealing to Moses the fullness of God's character and intentionality. Nowhere before this speech has anyone been privileged to hear directly a disclosure of what is most powerful and definitional for God's own life.

The proclamation begins with a double utterance, "Yahweh, Yahweh," in which the name is even more starkly and poignantly put than in 33:19 or 34:5. This double utterance enunciates and makes powerfully present the majestic, inscrutable sovereignty of Yahweh in the life of Israel. Verses 6-7, then, are an exegesis of the content of that name, which divides into two parts.

On the one hand, Yahweh is wondrously generous and forgiving (vv. 6-7*a*). This affirmation is profoundly important in this context, for it is exactly and only Yahweh's generosity that will restore Israel to covenant. The declaration employs seven terms to make this assertion. These seven elements provide

the core vocabulary of the OT for the affirmation of God's awesome graciousness:

Merciful (רחום *raḥûm*). Phyllis Trible has effectively made the case that this term is related to the noun *womb* (רחם *reḥem*), and thus speaks of the kind of positive inclination a mother has toward her child, a "womb-like mother-love."[188]

Gracious (חנון *ḥannûn*). This term refers to completely gratuitous positive inclination, given without cause or warrant, unmerited favor. It is used in 33:12, 16-17 in reference to the "favor" Moses receives from God.

Slow to Anger (ארך אפים *'erek 'apayim*). The phrase literally is "long-nosed." It apparently suggests that whatever "heat of rage" there was in Yahweh's anger has a chance to cool off, as it must be breathed out the long nostril. This phrasing is crucial in the light of 32:10 and 12, where the phrase is literally "heat of my nostrils." Thus the heat of 32:10, 12, which destroys, is here seen to have a cooling mechanism.

Abounding in Steadfast Love (רב-חסד *rab-ḥesed*). Katharine Sakenfeld has shown that *ḥesed* refers to sustained covenantal solidarity.[189] This formula affirms that Yahweh has a great capacity and resolve to remain loyal in covenantal commitment to Israel. In this context, the phrase suggests that Yahweh will "put up with" a great deal because of Yahweh's own powerful resolve to sustain covenant, even when the partner reneges. (In Isa 54:8-10, even exile does not disrupt God's abiding *ḥesed*.)

Faithfulness (אמת *'ĕmet*). This term is frequently used in a pair with *ḥesed* and is a close synonym. It witnesses to Yahweh's complete reliability. The phrase *"ḥesed we'ĕmet"* occurs frequently and is echoed in the christological formula "grace and truth," in John 1:14, 17.

Keeping Steadfast Love (*ḥesed*), for the thousandth generation. This formula reiterates the term *ḥesed* and assures that God's *ḥesed* continues to operate for a long time, and for a host of subjects.

Forgiving (נשא *nāśā'*). The verb literally means "lift," which here means to relieve covenant violators of the burden of their violation. The verb here governs Israel's primary vocabulary for sin, including the three most common words for

188. Phyllis Trible, *God and the Rhetoric of Sexuality*, OBT (Philadelphia: Fortress, 1978) chap. 2.

189. Katherine Doob Sakenfeld, *The Meaning of Hesed in the Hebrew Bible* (Missoula, Mont.: Scholars Press, 1978).

covenant violation, *iniquity, transgression,* and *sin.*

The use of the seven terms has cumulative impact. It is not possible or necessary to delineate precisely the meaning of each term by itself, for the effect of the whole is to assure Moses (and Israel) that God is deeply committed to sustaining covenant with Israel, even when the other party is careless and unresponsive, as Israel had been in chap. 32. It is crucial and precisely characteristic of this God that the statement of self-disclosure is given in the moment when God is most deeply offended and Israel is most profoundly in jeopardy.

On the other hand, this same God who is so generous and forgiving also responds in sovereign ferocity to affront (v. 7*b*). This time there are only two terms, two negatives as over against seven positives. They are, however, weighty and severe. God will not acquit (נקה *nqh*). This takes the form of an infinitive absolute. God will *really* not pardon! God will not overlook or ignore violations of covenant. Second, God will "visit" (פקד *pāqad*) covenant sanctions upon the community for generations to come. God will not be mocked, and grace is not cheap. Moreover, God has a long and powerful memory for being wronged. The travesty of Aaron in chap. 32 is a serious matter that continues to have decisive impact on the relation Yahweh will have with Israel.

This is an astonishing disclosure of God, which tells Moses (and us) as much about the God of the Bible as any verse can. We may observe four matters about this formulation. First, this is no doubt a highly stylized liturgical formula reflecting Israel's mature and disciplined theological reflection. Fretheim observes that it echoes, in inverted order, the assertion of 20:5. Taking it, as we do, as God's self-disclosure, this formulation is not exhausted in its particular use after the calf episode, but provides an enduring reference point in Israel's life with God. This characterization of God is always and everywhere about God *in relation.* No "attribute" of God is given here concerning God's own character in itself—e.g., omnipotence, omniscience—because Israel characteristically is unconcerned with such categories. God is by character and definition in Israel a God who always stands in relation toward the people.

Second, structurally and at the heart of this formulation is a profound, unacknowledged, and

unresolved contradiction. It is explicit in the double use of the term *iniquity* (עון *'āwōn*), which is "lifted" (*nāśā'*) and "visited upon" (*pāqad*). That is, God *forgives* iniquity, and God *punishes* iniquity. The contradiction, however, is not confined to this one double usage but is reflected all through the rhetoric. God does deal with violators of covenant in two very different ways that cannot be logically or in practice harmonized. Moreover, the formula itself gives no hint of how to work out this contradiction.

It is inadmissible to resolve the tension programmatically or systematically. Israel has discerned that there is in the very core existence of Yahweh a profound and durable incongruity: God inclines to be utterly *for the other,* and God characteristically is for *God's own self.*[190] That twofold inclination most marks the God of the Bible, over against more lyrical, more benign, more romantic, and more domesticated gods.

That contradiction makes the God of the Bible interesting, credible, and dangerous. This God is interesting, because one does not know ahead of time who God will be or how God will act. This God is credible, because this contradiction corresponds fully to the way we find our own life with others being enacted. This God is dangerous, because just when almost "deciphered" and made predictable, this God surprises us and keeps us off balance. Serious biblical faith requires a readiness to live precisely with and in the midst of this terrible, double-minded danger, which leaves God's partners always exposed and at risk.

Third, while this contradictory self-disclosure of God has a more general significance, here it pertains to the immediate crisis of Israel. It is in that post-calf situation that Yahweh is generous and severe. Even in that crisis, or especially in that crisis, the narrative provides no hint of adjudication of Yahweh's options. Moses knows only that the conversation requires him to face fully the possibility and risk of Yahweh, for Israel has no other ground for its future.

Fourth, Phyllis Trible, David Noel Freedman, and a host of other scholars have shown that this stylized creed-like formulation forms the basis of much of Israel's subsequent reflection upon the

190. See Walter Brueggemann, "A Shape for Old Testament Theology I: Structure Legitimation," *CBQ* 47 (1985) 28-46; "A Shape for Old Testament Theology II: Embrace of Pain," *CBQ* 47 (1985) 395-415.

character of God.[191] Thus, for example, in Num 14:18-19 Moses prays back to Yahweh Yahweh's own self-disclosure, and he holds Yahweh to the terms of that self-disclosure. Yahweh nonetheless inclines to act ferociously toward the offenders (vv. 21-23). Thus, even where God's generosity prevails, Yahweh is unsettled and yearns in continuing ways to act differently.

In other texts, it is clear that the contradiction has been resolved by choosing a side as a theological affirmation. Thus in Ps 145:8-9, the doxology of Israel voices only the generosity of Yahweh, whereas in Nah 1:2-3, the affirmation stresses God's severity (cf. Joel 3:21). In Jonah 4:2, the creed is stated in its positive force, but it is an affirmation that the narrator, in deep irony, has the speaker reject. This remarkable self-disclosure of Yahweh is inordinately supple and open to various theological tilts and uses.

For Moses at the mountain, it is not at all clear how the statement will play for Israel's future. It may be, taken dramatically, that Yahweh also is not yet clear on this future. While the options are stated, the specific implementation for this case at the mountain is yet to be determined. In this determination, Moses in his boldness has a role to play.

On the basis of God's rich self-disclosure, Moses now makes a petition (vv. 8-9) to which Yahweh responds (v. 10). Moses' petition is that Yahweh should choose the first option (generosity) instead of the second (severity), though the latter is fully available to God and perhaps warranted in light of chap. 32. Moses' petition relates to three themes of the preceding narrative. First, the premise of the petition is that Moses has found "favor" with Yahweh. Although Moses prays on a conditional "if," he has already been told that he has favor with Yahweh (33:12, 16-17). Thus Moses has a legitimate and credible place from which to address Yahweh. Second, Moses prays yet again for presence. It is Yahweh's willingness to be engaged with Israel on the way that will make or break Israel's future. Third, Moses acknowledges that Israel is "stiffnecked" (cf. 32:9; 33:5). In so doing, he prepares the way for Yahweh to enact the second half of the self-disclosure: "visiting iniquity."

Only now, with these three notes sounded,

does Moses allude to the possibility of newness, just disclosed in vv. 6-7a. And even here, Moses does not use the exact language of the self-disclosure. He appeals to the offer that Yahweh will "forgive" (lift), but he uses a new, powerful term: *pardon* (סלח *sālaḥ*). (See the same term in a parallel usage in Num 14:19.) In effect, Moses petitions Yahweh to enact generosity, to act in mercy, graciousness, steadfast love, and faithfulness toward this stiff-necked people who deserve only punishment. Moreover, Moses prays against the clear warning of 23:21 that God "will not pardon" (*nāśā'*). Moses' appeal to God's generosity is with the full awareness that God's severity is appropriate and warranted.

The petition is intensified at the end of v. 9 with an appeal to the larger tradition of the promise of the land: "inherit us"—i.e., regard us as your special and beloved possession (cf. Jer 12:7-13, in which God abandons God's very own "inheritance"). Everything now hangs in the balance for Israel. Moses has uttered his best, most passionate appeal. In the instant between vv. 9 and 10, Yahweh must decide.

Yahweh's response is like a salvation oracle uttered in response to a petition, as in 14:13-14. It is long and exaggerated, but it is the resolve of Yahweh that opens for Israel a new future. Yahweh has accepted Moses' petition. In this moment of utterance, Yahweh has put aside the calf episode and is prepared to move on afresh from this point. Moses has won from Yahweh precisely the generosity necessary for Israel to have any future.

The promise of Yahweh, as a way to implement a renewed covenant, is to perform "wonders" that have not yet been "created" (ברא *bārā'*). Yahweh will do before Israel and for Israel what no people has ever seen. The hyperbolic language is reminiscent of the plague rhetoric of 9:18 and 10:14. The text does not identify what these "wonders" will be. In the larger tradition, they may refer either to miracles in the wilderness or power for the entry into the land. In either case, these occurrences will make clear to Israel, and to the watching nations, that the holy power of Yahweh has been fully and passionately mobilized for the sake of this people.

The last phrase of v. 10 is a reprise, reiterating the promise of the verse. The rhetoric invites Israel to be astonished, and even suggests that Yahweh is rather overwhelmed with the resolve

191. Trible, *God and the Rhetoric of Sexuality*, chap. 1; David Noel Freedman, "God Compassionate and Gracious," *Western Watch* 6 (1955) 6-24.

just announced. As Israel's life was initiated by the wonders of Egypt, so Israel's life now renewed will again be marked by wonders. Thus v. 10 voices a decisive turning point in the larger narrative. The severity of chap. 32 and the unresolved question of presence in chap. 33 have now been fully overcome and wondrously resolved.

This new beginning is rooted in Yahweh's mercy—and in nothing else. It is accomplished, however, through Moses' courage and tenacity.

34:11-26. The act of sovereign generosity promptly becomes a summons to singular obedience. The God who will make covenant (v. 10) is a jealous God (v. 14) who will not tolerate any positive inclination toward any competing God. This list of commands may well be a very old, complete collection existing independently and functioning in some part of the community as a code alternative to the Decalogue.

In the completed form of the Sinai tradition, of course, no question arose that this collection could ever rival the Ten Commandments. Thus in this collection, what we have is another, perhaps well-known collection that is no rival to the Decalogue, but is placed in a secondary position to reiterate some elements of the covenantal command. It may be that this collection aims at the particular temptations evident in the calf episode.

This collection is based on the promise that God is about to displace other peoples to give the land to Israel (v. 11). This motif is already present in 3:8 and 17, in the covenantal conclusion of 23:23-33, and may indeed be the point of the "wonders" in 34:10. In any case, this collection of laws concerns exactly a decision to order the new land differently, in obedience to Yahweh.

If the conquest of the land is seen as a "peasant revolt," it is plausible that this text reflects competing and conflicting notions of land management. Against the more usual, exploitative land practices of the established economy, the community of Moses holds to a radical egalitarian vision. This legal collection is devoted to a defense and authorization of those alternative land practices, which reflect God's intention for covenant.

Two general points are worth considering. First, the claims of Yahweh are deeply linked to socio-economic practice. Thus faith in Yahweh is not merely a religious exercise but a decision about social values, commitments, and practices. Sec-

ond, this radical alternative vision of land practice admits of no compromise. The covenant insists on a clear "either/or" concerning the land. Any attempt to work a compromise will eventuate in distortion and finally abandonment of a covenantal possibility. Pixley observes, "To enter into pacts with the rulers of Canaan would be to renounce the whole movement that began in Egypt with the exodus and the victory over Pharaoh."[192] Just as the possibility of covenant concerns social practice, so also does the risk of violating covenant. That is, the "snare" of an alternative is not a supernatural threat (v. 12), but the danger of compromise on equitable social practice.

The covenant with Yahweh precludes alliances with those who do not adhere to Yahwism (vv. 12-16). "Yahweh is jealous"; Yahweh has a socio-economic intention that admits of no halfway measures. This teaching holds together the danger of alternative religious symbolism (v. 13) and the power of other gods (vv. 15-16), along with cooperation with other peoples in their agricultural practices (vv. 12-15). Other ways of handling the land and ordering social power will have a costly theological outcome.

Verse 17 is perhaps a succinct closure to the long instruction of vv. 12-16. The "casting of idols" is exactly what Aaron had done, and it led Israel away from Yahweh and away from a faith focused on commands.

After this passionate and general urging to avoid entangling alliances with gods or human neighbors (vv. 12-16), the text now proceeds to voice a series of five ritual activities that are to give formal, public expression of allegiance to Yahweh as the true Lord of the land (vv. 17-26). Moberly suggests that these verses give specificity to the general claims of vv. 11-16.[193] To enact and confess Yahweh as Lord of the land is a polemic against Baalism as a religious claim; it is also a polemic against all other systems of political security and economic productivity.

The Festival of Unleavened Bread recalls the exodus (v. 18). The community to be settled in the land is to recall regularly its rootage in the miracle of liberation and especially its hurried departure from bondage.

The offer of the firstborn of livestock—cows,

192. Pixley, *On Exodus*, 158.
193. Moberly, *At the Mountain of God*, 98.

sheep, and donkeys—affirms Yahweh as Lord of the land (vv. 19-20). The provision exempting (through "redemption") the firstborn son from the demand indicates that this is clearly an agricultural requirement and no longer entertains any primitive thought concerning human sacrifice (cf. 13:13). Thus while rooted in the exodus demand of the firstborn (cf. 4:22, 11:5), this provision has moved a long way toward concrete agricultural practice.

The practice of work stoppage on the sabbath is a sacramental assertion that human beings exist neither from nor for productivity, but for well-being in the land (v. 21; cf. 20:8-11).

The festivals of Weeks, First Fruits, and Ingathering are observances of harvest (v. 22). They affirm quite concretely that Yahweh is the giver of crops that sustain the life of Israel.

The offering of First Fruits, like that of the firstborn in vv. 19-20, bespeaks the debt owed to Yahweh, which is acknowledged in ritual performance (v. 26).

These laws all govern ritual practice. But they all have agricultural-economic dimensions and function in a polemical way to fend off alternative economic practices that contain temptations to manipulative self-sufficiency. (On v. 26 as a polemical prohibition, see 23:19*b*.)

The theoretical intention of this set of commands is most evident in vv. 23-24. Israel shall act out its Yahwistic commitments in a public way three times a year. It may be that "three times" came to reflect a stable festival calendar, or perhaps it reflects the decisive times in the rhythms of agricultural life. In a less structured way, it may be that "three times" means "regularly and periodically." In any case, the agricultural community is always under severe temptation to imagine that the land is not subject to the concerns of liberation and covenant, and that other, less costly economic practices might work as well.

Verse 24 adds a curious and powerful notice. It makes two assertions. First, it promises that the zone of land managed covenantally will continue to expand. Such a claim might relate to military success. It might also be a promise that covenantal land and neighbor practices will be economically effective, so that more and more land (and land owners) will want to share in these practices. Second, it affirms that Yahwistically managed land

will not be threatened by ("coveted") other economic systems while its owners are in pilgrimage to Yahweh. Those who do not submit their land to the destructive pressures of credit, interest, and profit will not be subject to land seizures that are the inevitable outcome of coveting.

What emerges from this list is a daring social proposal: (a) that the land can indeed be ordered in different, covenantal ways; and (b) that different land ordering must be given explicit symbolic, liturgical expression. Aaron's abortive theological coup was in fact a seductive *commodity fetishism* that is inherently a partner of *economic coveting*. The requirements of vv. 11-26 are designed to guard against such a preoccupation with commodities. The required sacramental acts are to symbolize and mediate a very different system of values and practices that make covenantal life possible and effective.

34:27-28. The conclusion of making covenant and the conclusion of Moses' long stay on the mountain (cf. 24:18, 32:1) concern writing.[194] God instructs Moses to write down "the things" (words) that are the substance of covenant. Moberly has argued well that there is an insoluble tension between vv. 27 and 28.[195] In v. 27, it is apparently the commands of vv. 11-26 that are to be written, but in v. 28, the "ten words" refer to the Decalogue.

What may matter is not the harmonization of these two verses, but that the covenant consists in written commands that persist and endure from generation to generation. In both written forms of covenantal requirement, the materials of vv. 11-26 in v. 27 and the Decalogue in v. 28, what is crucial is the magisterial "either/or" of Yahweh's will. Thus the culmination of covenant shows that Israel's life has now begun again by a God who generously moves beyond the crisis of the calf, but who jealously insists on complete obedience. The writing commanded by Yahweh is so that this massive contrast between Israel and its cultural, agricultural context may be always again available for Israel in time to come.

194. See the subtle argument of Carol Kern Stockhausen, *Moses' Veil and the Glory of the New Covenant: The Exegetical Substructure of II Cor. 3:1-4, 6*, Analecta Bibleca 116 (Rome: Pontifical Biblical Institute, 1989) 106-7.

195. Moberly, *At the Mountain of God*, 101-6.

REFLECTIONS

This chapter concerns an astonishing renewal of covenant. It is a renewal made exclusively from God's side in the face of Israel's profound "stiff-necked" character. The interpretive center of the passage may be "beginning again." In Christian proclamation, this theme is often flatly taken simply as a statement of grace. This chapter makes clear that the prospect of beginning again is marked at the outset by risk, uncertainty, and ambivalence, and it is marked at the end by rigorous, uncompromising demand.

1. Verses 6-7 witness to the profoundly personal reality of Yahweh's presence to Israel. That reality is marked by an open-ended, unresolved two-sidedness. This God is at the same time capable of inordinate generosity (mercy, graciousness, steadfast love, faithfulness) and an assaulting severity (visiting iniquities).

For many people, such an unresolved quality in God is deeply distressing. On the one hand, conventional orthodoxy prefers a settled God, with these matters neatly harmonized in a logical fashion. On the other hand, a liberal tendency will easily imagine that God's generosity has "evolved" past and superseded God's severity. Both are forms of reductionism, seeking to domesticate God and deny God's continued capacity for choosing more than one way in the world. Moreover, we are no more honest or better off if we imagine that these tensions have all been overcome in Christian supersessionism, for honest Christian faith must continue to struggle with the oddness of this God. To seek to resolve in programmatic fashion the intentional uncertainty of vv. 6-7 is to miss out on the main point: Moses and Israel must come to terms with God's surprising, magisterial freedom. The reductionism so convenient to us ends either in a strict retributionism that confines God to a set of moral statements, or in an easy affirmation that makes God endlessly accepting and forgiving. If God should be distorted in either of these more comfortable directions, then we are continuing the work of Aaron and producing a God more to our liking. As Fretheim concludes: "There is no predictability or inevitability about the divine grace. This serves as a reminder that the community of faith ought not live close to the margins of God's patience (cf. Rom 6:1)."[196]

2. The ground of the new covenant is rigorous demand. The covenant requires that Israel undertake complete loyalty to God in a social context where attractive alternatives exist. In that ancient world, the attractive alternative was the established religion of the inhabitants of the land, with all its altars, pillars, and sacred poles—its technology to ensure productivity. In our own Western context, *mutatis mutandis*, the attractive alternatives to covenanted faith are likely to be the techniques of consumerism, which provide "the good life" without rigorous demand or cost and without the covenantal requirement of the neighbor. Then, as now, the jealous God calls for a decision against that easy alternative.

The sketch of the practical "either/or" here given Israel is concerned with two dimensions of public life. On the one hand, the "either/or" is to be practiced liturgically. This is evident from the festal calendar authorized in this set of commands. The text provides a steady sequence of liturgical acts in order to give sustained, visible sacramental embodiment to the "either/or."

On the other hand, these several liturgical gestures are in fact public assertions that the blessings of the land come from Yahweh and belong to Yahweh. In that folk society, the liturgical gestures point to economic realities. In this sequence of religious acts, Israel refuses Canaanite perceptions of the land and insists that ownership, management, and governance of the land are all under the rule of Yahweh.

It is possible, through this bifocal acknowledgment of liturgy and land, that the land

196. Fretheim, *Exodus*, 307.

(i.e., the economy) might be kept free of the rapacious, competitive practice (vv. 23-24) that destroys the possibility of community. In this text, Moses is doing the difficult interpretive work of transposing the covenant of the wilderness mountain to an agricultural economy.

I suggest that our comparable work is to transpose the covenant of the God of an agrarian economy to the governance of a post-industrial society. That work, like the interpretive work of Moses, will need to be liturgically inventive and economically critical. In a North American context, Wendell Berry has, in a series of novels, imagined that the land could indeed be part of a different social fabric.[197] Thus the deep "either/or" of the covenant is not simply a rigorous religious act, but is a mandate to organize differently the practice of property (land, economics) and the symbols that justify and legitimate those practices (liturgy).

3. The concluding act of writing (done by Moses in vv. 27-28 and by Yahweh in v. 1) gives body, continuity, and visible shape to Israel's new possibility. Writing solidifies the claims of covenant and makes them enduringly available to ongoing generations. It amounts at least to the production of a powerful tradition and perhaps to the production of an authorized canon that shapes communal imagination in normative ways.

In our current theological context, there is a kind of romantic attraction to what is new and spontaneous, which has the effect of scuttling tradition. Some of this scuttling is not done from hostility or resistance as much as from ignorance. Many persons do not know that biblical faith (and the communities that practice it) is an ongoing struggle with a body of explicit teaching. Biblical faith is not a series of isolated events or of momentary inclinations, but is a corpus of teaching that has continuing authority. The written corpus requires and permits endless liberated interpretation, so that there is no ethical scholasticism here. This community, receiver of God's radical graciousness, is addressed in a resounding and unending "either/or." This "people of the book" is destined by the decree of this jealous God to struggle with this "either/or," both in terms of its symbolic expressions (liturgy) and in its economic practice (land).

197. See Berry, *The Memory of Old Jack* (New York: Harcourt, Brace, Jovanovich, 1975); *Nathan Coulter* (San Francisco: North Point, 1985); *The Wild Birds: Six Stories of the Port William Membership* (San Francisco: North Point, 1986).

EXODUS 34:29-35, MOSES' SHINING FACE

NIV

[29]When Moses came down from Mount Sinai with the two tablets of the Testimony in his hands, he was not aware that his face was radiant because he had spoken with the LORD. [30]When Aaron and all the Israelites saw Moses, his face was radiant, and they were afraid to come near him. [31]But Moses called to them; so Aaron and all the leaders of the community came back to him, and he spoke to them. [32]Afterward all the Israelites came near him, and he gave them all the commands the LORD had given him on Mount Sinai.

[33]When Moses finished speaking to them, he put a veil over his face. [34]But whenever he entered the LORD's presence to speak with him, he

NRSV

[29]Moses came down from Mount Sinai. As he came down from the mountain with the two tablets of the covenant[a] in his hand, Moses did not know that the skin of his face shone because he had been talking with God. [30]When Aaron and all the Israelites saw Moses, the skin of his face was shining, and they were afraid to come near him. [31]But Moses called to them; and Aaron and all the leaders of the congregation returned to him, and Moses spoke with them. [32]Afterward all the Israelites came near, and he gave them in commandment all that the LORD had spoken with him on Mount Sinai. [33]When Moses had finished speaking with them, he put a veil on his face;

a Or *treaty*, or *testimony*; Heb *eduth*

NIV

removed the veil until he came out. And when he came out and told the Israelites what he had been commanded, [35]they saw that his face was radiant. Then Moses would put the veil back over his face until he went in to speak with the LORD.

NRSV

[34]but whenever Moses went in before the LORD to speak with him, he would take the veil off, until he came out; and when he came out, and told the Israelites what he had been commanded, [35]the Israelites would see the face of Moses, that the skin of his face was shining; and Moses would put the veil on his face again, until he went in to speak with him.

COMMENTARY

The second meeting at the mountain is now completed. Moses had "gone up" in 34:4, and now "comes down." During that time, the impossible is wrought: A renewed covenant is established with this stiff-necked people. There remains now the difficult work of Moses' reentry into Israel's life after his extraordinary rendezvous at the mountain. After this meeting, Moses is no ordinary person, for he has entered deeply into God's own life. He has seen the back side of God's glory (33:22-23). He comes down with face shining, reflecting the awesome presence. In this difficult passage, two motifs are at work that are not easily reconciled.

On the one hand, Moses is the go-between for Yahweh and Israel, as authorized in 20:18-21. He regularly speaks with God (33:11), and he regularly reports to Israel. The tradition treats the subject as though no further explanation is required. Moreover, even in the older tradition, that function is given a workable institutional form (33:7-11).

On the other hand, this paragraph makes clear that there is an exotic dimension to Moses' mediatorial function. This is no ordinary matter. One cannot lightly or routinely move back and forth between an audience in God's glory and communication in Israel. Thus the text describes a device used by Moses as an acknowledgment of this stunning movement. We are told that his face "shone" (קרן *qāran;* v. 29) and that a "veil" (מסוה *masweh;* v. 33) was used to dim the glow.

We are told neither the problem with the shining face nor why the glow has to be toned down. It may be that the veil is a protection for the Israelites. Or it may be that the glow of God needs protection from common contact, which would cheapen or trivialize it.

Against either possibility, however, the routine is that the veil is removed for purposes of communication with both God and Israel and is worn only between such times of communication. Thus it is exceedingly difficult to determine its purpose or function. It appears that the urgency of communication (word) takes priority over the danger of exposure (light).

The problems intensify when we consider two crucial words in this odd practice. First, *shine* (*qāran*) seems clear enough, except that no other uses of the term in the OT have this meaning. The conventional meaning in many places is "horn," which is the basis for Michelangelo's famous presentation of Moses with horns. If the verb translated "shine" derives from that for "horn," this may suggest a shaft of light not unlike a horn, but the usage is in any case most peculiar. (The rendering "shine" is already taken up in the LXX.)

In like manner, the term *veil* (*masweh*) is nowhere else used in the OT, although the context would seem to require this meaning. As indicated above, however, we cannot determine its purpose.

We may do better with this enigmatic narrative by focusing on its larger concern in relation to the book of Exodus. Two matters seem important.

First, the glory of God, the pure, dazzling light of presence is the way in which Yahweh is disclosed to Israel. (Note well that this is quite in contrast to an announcement of commands. While the commands depend on speaking and listening, this is a visual contact that has no identifiable or expressed content.) Earlier, it was in triumph over Pharaoh that Yahweh "got glory" (14:4, 17). In the second half of the book of Exodus, the text is concerned with glory as an institutional form of presence, whereby Yahweh can lead, govern, and instruct Israel (24:15-18; 40:34-38). We do not need to labor over the precise meaning of "shine" and "veil" to see that the text is concerned with the power, significance, authority, and danger of God's glory, without which Israel will not be Israel.

Our text stands midway between two other texts concerning God's glory in Israel's life that seem to figure in a Priestly theory of presence. This text looks back to 24:15-18, where Moses enters the cloud and communes with the glory. This paragraph provides a transition from the covenant making of chaps. 19–24 to the theme of cultic presence in 25–31. Moses goes deeply into the mystery of God with all of its danger, and receives guidance for the ways in which presence can be mediated and made available.

At the same time 34:29-35 looks forward to 40:34-38, the culmination of the text concerning glory as presence. The inscrutable glory of God comes to inhabit the tabernacle, which God authorizes in chaps. 25–31 and Moses instigates in 36–40. Now the glory as presence is no longer at the mountain, but is in the mobile shrine, always with Israel. Thus our text belongs to a self-conscious theory of glory that moves in dramatic narrative stages from mountain to tabernacle via Moses:

24:15-18	34:29-35	40:34-38
glory at the	glory brought	glory in the
mountain	via *Moses*	*tabernacle*

Moses' descent from the mountain is a device for the awesome coming of heavenly glory to dwell in the midst of Israel.

Second, in this text, especially as it is located between 24:15-18 and 40:34-38, Moses is strategically indispensable for God's gift of glory to Israel. As a result, all others, including Aaron and the priests (v. 30), are only passive recipients of what Moses has accomplished. Moses is the one who does not flinch in his insistence before God and who wants to see the glory (33:18). Moses is the one protected by God while the glory passes by (33:22; 34:6-8). Moses, a human agent, is the one who makes possible the glory of God in the midst of Israel.

That glory threatens Israel, and it enlivens Israel. It is not necessary, finally, to decipher completely the problematic verb *shine* and the difficult noun *veil*. We can see enough in this text to know that in the person (body, face) of Moses, a new contact between heaven and earth, between Yahweh and Israel, has come about. Israel is rightly frightened, but Israel is also able to receive its life as God inscrutably gives it.

REFLECTIONS

This is the key text in making "glory" pivotal for God's way in Israel. The term *glory* is elusive, but nonetheless saturates the primal language of the church. Thus the church sings and prays: "Glory be to the Father and to the Son and to the Holy Ghost; as it was in the beginning, is now, and ever shall be, world without end. Amen." And "For thine is the kingdom and the power and the glory, forever and ever. Amen."

Moreover, in the core events of the life of Jesus (birth, resurrection), the church has insisted that the glory of God was visible. The pivotal events in the biblical story, and in the story of Christian faith, concern the awesome entry of heavenly, holy mystery, into human experience. The Bible struggles to find ways to speak about this awesome entry, and one of its preferred, most effective ways is "glory."

1. Imagine a life context in which the glory of God has been completely nullified. The result would be a completely one-dimensional, flattened, profane existence. The outcome of such a profane existence is sure to be brutality, in which any affront against the neighbor is possible and permitted. Such brutality inevitably ends in despair, because there is no "surplus power" to generate any alternative. In handling this text, the interpreter must be aware that many people live at the brink of such a profane existence in which there is no ray of "glory," no power beyond self, and no opening to hopefulness. This text is precisely for such hopelessness.

The news of this text is that in spite of stiff-necked resistance, the glory of God is not necessarily withheld. In Israel's discernment, human life is kept open to the presence, the power, and the possibility of God.

2. The narrative of the transfiguration of Jesus (Matt 17:1-8; Mark 9:2-8; Luke 9:28-36) is marked by the appearance of dazzling glory. As Moses is the one through whom God's glory comes to earth, so now Jesus is the mediatorial figure who brings God's splendid authority into the midst of the disciples. Everything pivots, so the Gospels confess, on this one visited, transformed man!

3. Paul has taken up this narrative of Moses in order to make a statement about the priority, superiority, and cruciality of Jesus in 2 Cor 3:7-18.[198] In making this claim for Jesus, Paul uses our text's themes, but turns the text against Moses. Whereas the veil seems to be a protective device in our text, for Paul it is a blocking mechanism for Jews "whenever Moses is read" (2 Cor 3:15), so that the covenant is inevitably misread. As Richard B. Hays has shown, Paul's strategy is to make a contrast between the glory shown in Moses and a "greater glory" (3:10-11). But that contrast, according to Paul, is already known to Moses, who anticipates the full glory in Christ. Thus Moses becomes "a symbol of unveiling as well as of veiling. Moses prefigures Christian experience, but he is not a Christian. He is both the paradigm for the Christian's direct experience of the spirit and the symbol for the old covenant to which that experience is set in antithesis."[199]

Derivatively, Paul makes a different use of the notion of "veil" and "glory" in 2 Cor 4:3. Here also Paul takes the veil as a block to seeing the glory of the gospel. Only this time the subject is not Jesus but "unbelievers," whose minds are blinded "to keep them from seeing the light of the gospel of the glory of Christ, who is the image of God" (2 Cor 4:4 NRSV). In this text, Paul connects the light of the gospel with the creator's command for light in the world (Gen 1:3). In the end, it is "in the face of Jesus Christ" that one sees the "glory of God." While Paul's interpretive methods may strike us as unduly polemical, the positive point from the text should not be missed. He shares with the Exodus text the claim that the glory of God has become available on earth. To be sure, he locates it not in Moses' face but in the face of Jesus, but his claim moves in the very same categories as the Exodus text.

4. Less directly, the Fourth Gospel dares to speak as well of the glory of Jesus: "We have seen his glory, the glory as of a father's only son, full of grace and truth" (John 1:14 NRSV); "Father, glorify your name. Then a voice came from heaven, 'I have glorified it, and I will glorify it again' " (John 12:28 NRSV).

The words are so familiar to us that we miss their daring claim, a claim as daring as our text makes about the Sinai experience. The text claims to "gaze upon the glory of Jesus!" The Fourth Gospel not only reassigns the glory of God to the person of Jesus, but it also locates the glory of Jesus precisely in the cross (John 12:23). In the shame and shattering of crucifixion, Jesus' sovereign splendor is manifest. Here we are at the core claim of Christian faith, and we do well not to misunderstand. It is not urged that the cross is a step along the way to glory, as an instrumental achievement anticipating the resurrection. Rather, in the crucified one the glory of God is shattered and transposed, so that the vocation of suffering for others is made into the presence of God's power.

5. This appearance of God's splendor in human affairs is not an easy theme to interpret or proclaim. Moses in any case had it right (33:16): The presence of God makes Israel's life distinctive. Indeed, God's presence makes all creation different.

---

198. On Paul's use of this text, see Stockhausen, *Moses' Veil and the Glory of the New Covenant;* and Richard B. Hays, *Echoes of Scripture in the Letters of Paul* (New Haven: Yale University Press, 1989) 122-53.

199. Hays, *Echoes of Scripture in the Letters of Paul,* 142, 144.

Without this One of holy, dangerous splendor, life may indeed be reduced to banal control and self-indulgence, to the management of technique, the trivialization of human dignity, and the self-serving devouring of the earth. In our memory and in our own time, the most extreme cases of such disregard of glory include the diabolical drama of Auschwitz, the savagery of Hiroshima, and the heinous abuse of the Soviet gulags, where life is cheap, humanity is diminished, and where winds of life chill, and then cease.

The steadfast witness of the synagogue and the church, of Moses and Jesus, is that Auschwitz, Hiroshima, and the gulags are not the true or decisive narrative of creation. The glory will descend in its unbearable brightness and make all things new. That glory from God is carried in the faces and persons of odd, strange human models—Moses and Jesus. This is not a summons that all should be "carriers," for those carriers are chosen only in God's inscrutable power and freedom. It is, rather, an invitation to Aaron, to the Israelites, and to all who "behold" to notice the glory of God in the faces of those who refuse the golden calf, who stand in the breach to see the glory, and who bring the tablets and let life begin again. God's glory is never far from God's command, which authorizes the revamping of all of life. There is dread in the coming of this glory, but there is also inordinate, practical possibility. For all of his shining, Moses' work is on earth, with this people.

ISRAEL'S OBEDIENT WORK

OVERVIEW

These chapters of dutiful obedience match the commands of chaps. 25–31. Like 25–31, they are judged to be a Priestly characterization of a shrine that will host God's glory. They show Israel (and Moses) fully obedient to Yahweh's command. Read in canonical sequence, they show that after the sin of chap. 32 and the new beginning of chap. 34, Israel must again do its obedient work. This section concludes with the full coming of God's glory (40:34-38). The fullness of creation has now been enacted. The erstwhile slaves now can live anew in the presence of the gracious, awesome One who wills to be with this people. In this final act of God's coming in the midst of Israel, the circumstance of bondage is now completely reversed. Israel can, at the end of Exodus, continue its journey to the land of promise.

EXODUS 35:1–36:7, MATERIALS FOR THE TABERNACLE

NIV

35 Moses assembled the whole Israelite community and said to them, "These are the things the LORD has commanded you to do: ²For six days, work is to be done, but the seventh day shall be your holy day, a Sabbath of rest to the LORD. Whoever does any work on it must be put to death. ³Do not light a fire in any of your dwellings on the Sabbath day."

⁴Moses said to the whole Israelite community, "This is what the LORD has commanded: ⁵From what you have, take an offering for the LORD. Everyone who is willing is to bring to the LORD an offering of gold, silver and bronze; ⁶blue, purple and scarlet yarn and fine linen; goat hair; ⁷ram skins dyed red and hides of sea cows*; acacia wood; ⁸olive oil for the light; spices for the anointing oil and for the fragrant incense; ⁹and onyx stones and other gems to be mounted on the ephod and breastpiece.

¹⁰"All who are skilled among you are to come and make everything the LORD has commanded:

7 That is, dugongs; also in verse 23

NRSV

35 Moses assembled all the congregation of the Israelites and said to them: These are the things that the LORD has commanded you to do:

2Six days shall work be done, but on the seventh day you shall have a holy sabbath of solemn rest to the LORD; whoever does any work on it shall be put to death. ³You shall kindle no fire in all your dwellings on the sabbath day.

4Moses said to all the congregation of the Israelites: This is the thing that the LORD has commanded: ⁵Take from among you an offering to the LORD; let whoever is of a generous heart bring the LORD's offering: gold, silver, and bronze; ⁶blue, purple, and crimson yarns, and fine linen; goats' hair, ⁷tanned rams' skins, and fine leather;* acacia wood, ⁸oil for the light, spices for the anointing oil and for the fragrant incense, ⁹and onyx stones and gems to be set in the ephod and the breastpiece.

10All who are skillful among you shall come

a Meaning of Heb uncertain

¹¹the tabernacle with its tent and its covering, clasps, frames, crossbars, posts and bases; ¹²the ark with its poles and the atonement cover and the curtain that shields it; ¹³the table with its poles and all its articles and the bread of the Presence; ¹⁴the lampstand that is for light with its accessories, lamps and oil for the light; ¹⁵the altar of incense with its poles, the anointing oil and the fragrant incense; the curtain for the doorway at the entrance to the tabernacle; ¹⁶the altar of burnt offering with its bronze grating, its poles and all its utensils; the bronze basin with its stand; ¹⁷the curtains of the courtyard with its posts and bases, and the curtain for the entrance to the courtyard; ¹⁸the tent pegs for the tabernacle and for the courtyard, and their ropes; ¹⁹the woven garments worn for ministering in the sanctuary—both the sacred garments for Aaron the priest and the garments for his sons when they serve as priests."

²⁰Then the whole Israelite community withdrew from Moses' presence, ²¹and everyone who was willing and whose heart moved him came and brought an offering to the LORD for the work on the Tent of Meeting, for all its service, and for the sacred garments. ²²All who were willing, men and women alike, came and brought gold jewelry of all kinds: brooches, earrings, rings and ornaments. They all presented their gold as a wave offering to the LORD. ²³Everyone who had blue, purple or scarlet yarn or fine linen, or goat hair, ram skins dyed red or hides of sea cows brought them. ²⁴Those presenting an offering of silver or bronze brought it as an offering to the LORD, and everyone who had acacia wood for any part of the work brought it. ²⁵Every skilled woman spun with her hands and brought what she had spun—blue, purple or scarlet yarn or fine linen. ²⁶And all the women who were willing and had the skill spun the goat hair. ²⁷The leaders brought onyx stones and other gems to be mounted on the ephod and breastpiece. ²⁸They also brought spices and olive oil for the light and for the anointing oil and for the fragrant incense. ²⁹All the Israelite men and women who were willing brought to the LORD freewill offerings for all the work the LORD through Moses had commanded them to do.

³⁰Then Moses said to the Israelites, "See, the LORD has chosen Bezalel son of Uri, the son of

and make all that the LORD has commanded: the tabernacle, ¹¹its tent and its covering, its clasps and its frames, its bars, its pillars, and its bases; ¹²the ark with its poles, the mercy seat,ᵃ and the curtain for the screen; ¹³the table with its poles and all its utensils, and the bread of the Presence; ¹⁴the lampstand also for the light, with its utensils and its lamps, and the oil for the light; ¹⁵and the altar of incense, with its poles, and the anointing oil and the fragrant incense, and the screen for the entrance, the entrance of the tabernacle; ¹⁶the altar of burnt offering, with its grating of bronze, its poles, and all its utensils, the basin with its stand; ¹⁷the hangings of the court, its pillars and its bases, and the screen for the gate of the court; ¹⁸the pegs of the tabernacle and the pegs of the court, and their cords; ¹⁹the finely worked vestments for ministering in the holy place, the holy vestments for the priest Aaron, and the vestments of his sons, for their service as priests.

20Then all the congregation of the Israelites withdrew from the presence of Moses. ²¹And they came, everyone whose heart was stirred, and everyone whose spirit was willing, and brought the LORD's offering to be used for the tent of meeting, and for all its service, and for the sacred vestments. ²²So they came, both men and women; all who were of a willing heart brought brooches and earrings and signet rings and pendants, all sorts of gold objects, everyone bringing an offering of gold to the LORD. ²³And everyone who possessed blue or purple or crimson yarn or fine linen or goats' hair or tanned rams' skins or fine leather,ᵇ brought them. ²⁴Everyone who could make an offering of silver or bronze brought it as the LORD's offering; and everyone who possessed acacia wood of any use in the work, brought it. ²⁵All the skillful women spun with their hands, and brought what they had spun in blue and purple and crimson yarns and fine linen; ²⁶all the women whose hearts moved them to use their skill spun the goats' hair. ²⁷And the leaders brought onyx stones and gems to be set in the ephod and the breastpiece, ²⁸and spices and oil for the light, and for the anointing oil, and for the fragrant incense. ²⁹All the Israelite men and women whose hearts made them willing to bring

ᵃ Or the cover   ᵇ Meaning of Heb uncertain

NIV

Hur, of the tribe of Judah, [31]and he has filled him with the Spirit of God, with skill, ability and knowledge in all kinds of crafts— [32]to make artistic designs for work in gold, silver and bronze, [33]to cut and set stones, to work in wood and to engage in all kinds of artistic craftsmanship. [34]And he has given both him and Oholiab son of Ahisamach, of the tribe of Dan, the ability to teach others. [35]He has filled them with skill to do all kinds of work as craftsmen, designers, embroiderers in blue, purple and scarlet yarn and fine linen, and weavers—all of them master craftsmen and designers.

36 [1]So Bezalel, Oholiab and every skilled person to whom the LORD has given skill and ability to know how to carry out all the work of constructing the sanctuary are to do the work just as the LORD has commanded."

[2]Then Moses summoned Bezalel and Oholiab and every skilled person to whom the LORD had given ability and who was willing to come and do the work. [3]They received from Moses all the offerings the Israelites had brought to carry out the work of constructing the sanctuary. And the people continued to bring freewill offerings morning after morning. [4]So all the skilled craftsmen who were doing all the work on the sanctuary left their work [5]and said to Moses, "The people are bringing more than enough for doing the work the LORD commanded to be done."

[6]Then Moses gave an order and they sent this word throughout the camp: "No man or woman is to make anything else as an offering for the sanctuary." And so the people were restrained from bringing more, [7]because what they already had was more than enough to do all the work.

NRSV

anything for the work that the LORD had commanded by Moses to be done, brought it as a freewill offering to the LORD.

[30]Then Moses said to the Israelites: See, the LORD has called by name Bezalel son of Uri son of Hur, of the tribe of Judah; [31]he has filled him with divine spirit,[a] with skill, intelligence, and knowledge in every kind of craft, [32]to devise artistic designs, to work in gold, silver, and bronze, [33]in cutting stones for setting, and in carving wood, in every kind of craft. [34]And he has inspired him to teach, both him and Oholiab son of Ahisamach, of the tribe of Dan. [35]He has filled them with skill to do every kind of work done by an artisan or by a designer or by an embroiderer in blue, purple, and crimson yarns, and in fine linen, or by a weaver—by any sort of artisan or skilled designer.

36 Bezalel and Oholiab and every skillful one to whom the LORD has given skill and understanding to know how to do any work in the construction of the sanctuary shall work in accordance with all that the LORD has commanded.

[2]Moses then called Bezalel and Oholiab and every skillful one to whom the LORD had given skill, everyone whose heart was stirred to come to do the work; [3]and they received from Moses all the freewill offerings that the Israelites had brought for doing the work on the sanctuary. They still kept bringing him freewill offerings every morning, [4]so that all the artisans who were doing every sort of task on the sanctuary came, each from the task being performed, [5]and said to Moses, "The people are bringing much more than enough for doing the work that the LORD has commanded us to do." [6]So Moses gave command, and word was proclaimed throughout the camp: "No man or woman is to make anything else as an offering for the sanctuary." So the people were restrained from bringing; [7]for what they had already brought was more than enough to do all the work.

[a]Or *the spirit of God*

COMMENTARY

In the last chapters of the book of Exodus, the text is preoccupied with the problem and possibility of hosting the holy. The plan for providing a viable home for the holy is God's own plan given to Moses on the mountain (chaps. 25–31). The actual construction of the vehicle for presence, however, is human work, to be done on earth, after Moses descends from the mountain (35–40). The actual implementation is orderly and intentional. It must begin with the mustering of adequate materials and personnel (the concern of our present unit). The offering for the necessary materials is narrated in three sections: the command (vv. 4-9), the offering itself (vv. 20-29), and the cessation of the offering (36:3-7). The countertheme of personnel is given in two parts, as recruitment (vv. 10-19) and response (35:30–36:2).

35:1-3. In v. 1, Moses assembles the congregation of Israel. The reference, both as a verb (*assemble*) and as a noun (*assembly*), is thoroughly ecclesiological. This is a religious body, without reference to any state official. The purpose of the assemblage is to perform the commands of chaps. 25–31. Israel, as convened by Moses, exists for obedience (cf. 19:8; 24:3, 7). This Israel is quite contrasted with Israel in chap. 32, a community of radical disobedience.

It is odd and remarkable that the first command after the sin and renewal of chaps. 32–34 concerns sabbath (vv. 2-3). In the corresponding section of chaps. 25–31, sabbath is the final concern (31:12-17). Thus sabbath is the last command (31:12-17) and now the first reiteration (35:2-3). Said another way, sabbath concerns bracket the material of chaps. 32–34. This community is preoccupied with sabbath as the quintessential mark of obedience, for in sabbath, life is willingly handed back to Yahweh in grateful rest (cf. chap. 16).

35:4-9. Moses' first act after coming down from the mountain is to authorize an offering, to gather materials for the tabernacle. The specifics of the offering are precisely those of 25:3-7. The tabernacle is to be made out of the best that Israel can provide. The offering is to be brought by those of "generous heart" (cf. 25:2). The term translated "generous" (נדיב *nĕdîb*) refers to an offering that is spontaneous and unrequired. It is not a much-used term, but regularly refers to generosity for the sake of the temple. The most important parallel to our passage is 1 Chronicles 28–29, where David collects the materials with which his son Solomon will construct the Temple. The people respond generously to David's appeal (29:5-9). His prayer in 29:10-19 acknowledges to Yahweh the people's generous offering and affirms that the offering is not commensurate with Yahweh's own generosity to Israel.

Thus the language as well as the generosity and intensity of leader and people is closely paralleled between Moses and David, tabernacle and Temple. God will be adequately housed only when the people give generously and abundantly. This is Moses' program for the materials.

35:10-19. Moses' second need is to assemble competent personnel to do the required work. Because the tabernacle is to be a work of beauty, the work must be done by skilled and gifted craftspersons. Those required are said to be "wise" (i.e., "skillful"; חכם *ḥākām*). This passage reiterates the inventory of the main features of the tabernacle from the commands of Yahweh: the tabernacle itself (v. 10; cf. 25:9; 26:1-6), the tent (v. 11; cf. 26:7-14), the ark (v. 12; cf. 25:10-16); the mercy seat (v. 12; cf. 25:17-22) the table (v. 13; cf. 25:23-30); the lampstand (v. 14; cf. 25:31-40); the altar of incense (v. 15; cf. 30:1-10); the altar of burnt offerings (v. 16; cf. 27:1-8), the court (v. 17; cf. 27:9-19), and the priestly vestments (v. 19; cf. 28:1-43).

35:20-29. The offering authorized in vv. 4-9 is now received. Two rhetorical features dominate this report of unprecedented generosity. First, it is clear that behind the financial transaction of the offering, which is a considerable matter in and of itself, is a deeply felt religious motivation. Thus the paragraph is saturated with phrases of religious motivation: "heart stirred," i.e., lifted (v. 21); "spirit willing" (v. 21); "willing heart" (v. 22); "hearts moved," i.e., lifted (v. 26); "hearts willing" (v. 29).

The picture presented is a community so convinced of its covenantal affirmations and so taken up in its conviction of the truth of its liberation narrative that it acts completely beyond the usual calculations of prudence and caution.

The second rhetorical feature pervasive in this paragraph is the word *all* (כל *kōl*), suggesting that the offering and its intent are utterly comprehensive. On the one hand, the word is used to describe the participation of all the people (vv. 20-26, 29). The contributors include men and women, leaders and people, and each gives at the point of personal strength, those who have goods and those who have skill. On the other hand, *all* is used for the totality of materials and the totality of the work to be done as well (vv. 22, 24, 29).

The use of the phrases concerning religious motivation and the recurring "all" of comprehensiveness yield a picture of a community alive, bestirred, and energized to act well outside itself and well beyond any conventional practice. This is indeed a once-in-a-lifetime effort for a once-for-all-time theological purpose. The text is enormously restrained, providing no clues as to the cause or driving power of this economic gesture. Aside from the ground of the act in God's own stirring, we may suggest four reference points for such uncalculating generosity.

First is the promise and expectation that the offering will provide a tabernacle in which the very presence of God will dwell. That in itself is sufficient reason for generosity. The Israelites are convinced that their offerings will let the gifts and guarantees of heaven come among them.

Second, as a sequel to chap. 32, Israel has now come face to face with God's incredible graciousness and willingness to begin again with this stiff-necked people. Moreover, this offering poignantly contrasts the disastrous offerings brought to Aaron (32:2-3). In this gesture, Israel has a chance to redress that terrible deed of disobedience.

Third, reading across the book of Exodus and the journey from liberation to presence (cf. 29:43-45), this offering is a response to the wonder of liberation. The people who in their destitute condition had to seize silver and gold from the Egyptians (cf. 3:21-22; 11:2-3; 12:35-36) are now able to give from their abundance. This Israel, unlike the desperate slave community, knows that it is much better to give than to receive.

Fourth, taken critically, the opportunity to con-

struct a home for the holy means that Israel has a chance to put behind it the terrible season of absence called "exile." In the post-exilic period when this text was put into its final form, Israel is indeed beginning again, after "the absence," with the glorious God who has now promised to be present (cf. Ezekiel 40–48). Thus Israel's new beginning is an act of profound generosity by the God who has been so generous in liberation (1–15), in covenant making (19–24), and in forgiveness (32–34). Israel is about the happy work of completing a transaction in which both parties, God and Israel, practice uncommon generosity.

35:30–36:2. As the need for money in 35:4-9 is resolved in 35:20-29, so the requirement of trained personnel in 35:10-19 is now resolved in 35:30–36:2. In 31:1-11, God specifies Bezalel and Oholiab as the key workmen, and they are now authorized. One is struck by the practical, commonsense approach to the construction project. Just as the project requires real financial resources, so also it requires trained and skilled artisans. Moses and Aaron are not builders of tabernacles! This is not work for the religious leaders but requires a very different kind of ministry.

The most striking feature of vv. 30-35 is that Yahweh is the subject of the section, while Bezalel and Oholiab are only objects and recipients of Yahweh's actions: Yahweh has called by name (v. 30); Yahweh has filled (vv. 31, 35); and Yahweh has given heart ("inspired," v. 34).

It is all Yahweh's doing! Yahweh has called, authorized, equipped, and inspired. As a result, the workmen are peculiarly competent for the work. The rhetoric of the chapter, in order to make a proper account, uses an extended series of words to characterize these workmen. Thus in v. 31, four words are used for competence: *spirit, skill, intelligence,* and *knowledge.* In v. 32, a series of materials is enunciated, and in v. 35 a more comprehensive list is given. Moreover, these workmen are equipped to teach others (v. 34), no doubt those who will work under their supervision. In this entire arrangement of adequate personnel, Moses plays a subordinate role. These are competent laypersons, authorized directly by Yahweh. Their commitment and skill correspond in personnel to the generosity of the money. The program is both well financed and well staffed.

Chapter 36:1-2 provides summary statements

on the leadership of Bezalel and Oholiab and a host of other craftspersons. Two points are stressed: They are uncommonly skilled, and they are keenly motivated. Moreover, both their skill and their motivation are the work and gift of Yahweh.

36:3-7. However, concerning the careful preparations, which are both precise and prudent, one unforeseen factor causes Moses' speech to pause momentarily in its march toward obedient construction (36:3-7). Until this point, this portion of the text has developed two themes symmetrically: (1) concerning material offering—command (35:4-9) and response (35:20-29); (2) concerning skilled personnel—command (35:10-19) and response (35:30–36:2). In this fifth element of the unit, however, the text breaks beyond this symmetrical pattern. Beyond command and response, there is now a third, very odd element concerning the offering: The artisans are overwhelmed by too much material! This is generosity run rampant.

The workmen report to Moses an overwhelming supply of goods, and Moses must order a cessation of offerings. Three rhetorical elements express the intensity of the offerings. First, the Israelites bring offerings "morning by morning" (v. 3; see what is perhaps a parody of this in Amos 4:4). Second, twice the adverb עוד (ʿôd) is used (vv. 3, 6). It is rendered "still kept" and "anything else," suggesting repeated, reiterated action. Third, twice the term די (dê) is used, rendered "much more than enough" (v. 5) and "more than enough" (v. 7). In v. 7 the term is matched with הותר (hôtēr), so that the Hebrew construction is "enough and some left over" (cf. Mark 6:43; 8:8). The term dê regularly means "sufficient, all that is needed," and suggests "overflowing blessing" (cf. Mal 3:10).

We are not told why there was such an overflow of commitment and generosity on the part of Israel. Clearly this is an extraordinary moment in Israel's liturgic life, in which generosity toward God and God's promised presence is unprecedented. The only explicit comment in the text concerning motivation is that the people have "generous hearts and willing spirits." The construction of the tabernacle in chaps. 36–39, at the command of chaps. 25–31, begins, not in calculated obedience, but in unfettered, undisciplined, extravagant devotion. Israel's response is indeed commensurate with the awesome self-giving of Yahweh.

REFLECTIONS

This text portrays a stewardship dream come true, in which the motivation for giving is pure and untroubled and in which the generosity of Israel is staggering. The text may be a model for giving when a community stands, on the one hand, reflecting on God's forgiving generosity, and on the other hand, in anticipation of God's full presence.

1. The assumption of the chapter is that Israel has a "generous heart" and a "willing spirit." The text does not reflect on the psychological aspects of such disposition. Perhaps the best commentary on this generous inclination is voiced in Ps 51:10-17. In this prayer of supplication, the speaker invokes the language of creation, asking God to begin again, to give the Spirit (wind [רוח rûaḥ]) that makes one as new as on the first day of creation. The speaker prays that his heart (organ of loyalty [לב lēb]) and spirit (capacity for energy [rûaḥ]), which had become disaffected from Yahweh, might again be renewed, restored, and engaged for Yahweh. All of this is accomplished through forgiveness. From that restored heart and spirit will come acceptable sacrifice and offerings for rebuilding (vv. 17-19).

In Num 14:24, Caleb has a "different spirit," and in Ezek 36:26-27 Israel in exile will be given "a new heart and a new spirit," suited for obedience. All of these uses concern beginning again out of exile, out of alienation. These texts perhaps illuminate for us the ground of generosity in our chapter. Either directly from the glory of Sinai (Exod 24:15-18; 25:1–31:17; with a source reading), or directly from the mercy of chaps. 33–34 (with a canonical reading), Israel is at a moment of new beginning, as new and fresh as new creation. (Recall that in 34:10, the verb create [ברא bārāʾ] is used for God's powerful, wondrous new beginning.) In that moment, nothing impedes generosity, nothing qualifies extravagance. The only compelling motivation for generous stewardship is a theological awareness that life is a pure gift and that gratitude is the only fitting posture for life.

2. The text is characteristically realistic in its recognition that the chance of hosting God's holiness requires a concrete strategy that must be financed. Religion that is significant and sustaining costs money, and Moses does not hesitate to commandeer Israel's wealth.

The narrative and prayer of David in 1 Chronicles 28–29 concerning the gathering of materials for the Temple are likely related to our text, and they provide the best exposition. In his prayer, David speaks Israel's most programmatic statement concerning astonishment that he and his people could offer worthy, acceptable offerings. David then acknowledges that the offering is a return of God's own gifts (cf. v. 14). Thus David asserts, "All this abundance . . . comes from your hand and is all your own" (1 Chr 29:16 NRSV).

In response to the prayer, finally, the people offer to Yahweh "a thousand bulls, a thousand rams, and a thousand lambs . . . and sacrifices in abundance for all Israel" (1 Chr 29:21; cf. Mic 6:6-7). No wonder "they ate and drank before the LORD on that day with great joy" (v. 22 NRSV; cf. Exod 19:10-11)!

This remarkable act of stewardship is a dramatic assertion against every notion of self-sufficiency. The psychology and economics of autonomy, of being "self-made," are enormously powerful among us and constitute the fundamental ideology of modern consumerism. That psychology teaches that humans are isolated individuals capable of self-sufficiency. Commensurately, that economics teaches that each is entitled to all that can be acquired. The result of such ideology is a grudging, thin capacity for giving, sharing, or sacrifice.

The strategy of these texts is not to coerce or manipulate or to "nickel and dime" in order to get enough money. Rather, both Moses and David directly counter the fundamental assumptions of autonomy and self-sufficiency. Once it is established that life itself is pure gift, then generosity and gratitude flow easily and readily. These texts (Exod 36:3-7 and 1 Chr 29:6-22) are a powerful alternative to the kind of self-deceiving amnesia reflected in Deut 8:17: "Do not say to yourself, 'My power and the might of my own hand have gotten me this wealth' " (NRSV). A habitat for God's holiness will never be constructed by self-made persons but only by those who are continually moved by the extraordinary gift of new life.

3. A series of NT texts come to mind around this theological theme of evangelical generosity: In his instruction to his disciples, Jesus urges: "You received without payment; give without payment" (Matt 10:8 NRSV). In urging would-be disciples to consider seriously the cost of commitment, Jesus uses an analogy: "For which of you, intending to build a tower, does not first sit down and estimate the cost, to see whether he has enough to complete it?" (Luke 14:28 NRSV). Paul utilizes the metaphor of building for growth in faith: "For we are God's servants, working together; you are God's field, God's building" (1 Cor 3:9 NRSV). In commenting on the work of a steward and warning against autonomy, Paul uses rhetoric reminiscent of 1 Chr 29:14: "What do you have that you did not receive?" (1 Cor 4:7 NRSV) In his great appeal for the "collection" with a reference to exodus manna and a christological reference, Paul appeals for generosity: "So we want you to excel also in this generous undertaking" (2 Cor 8:7 NRSV). Before the writer of Ephesians moves to the imperatives of the Christian life, he ends with a lyrical affirmation of God's inordinate generosity: "Now to him who by the power at work within us is able to accomplish abundantly far more than all we can ask or imagine, to him be glory in the church and in Christ Jesus to all generations, forever and ever. Amen" (Eph 3:20-21 NRSV).

These texts (and many others) suggest that theological foundations lead the community of faith to share its wealth with liberality. Those theological foundations serve to counter the ideology of the world, which moves from fear and ends in selfishness. In the place of fear, faith invites gratitude. In the place of selfishness, faith ends in extravagant generosity.

4. This text knows that the stewardship required for the tabernacle includes "time and talents." "Hosting the Holy" requires many skills, gifts, and competencies that are not "religious." Along with the two master-artisans, Moses seeks out "all who are skillful" (35:10; 36:2). Moreover, the skill is a gift from God (36:2), which may be energized and motivated by God's stirring. Thus, long before the Reformers, this text understands the cruciality of "secular vocation." This is even more important, since it occurs in a Priestly text wherein priests are regarded as the key players in the life of Israel. Here it is clear that the priestly corps fully depends on secular workers who understand their work in terms of the claims of God.

Because the tabernacle is a thing of beauty and artistic sensitivity, one may find in this text a warrant for a community of artists who work to make available "expressions of surplus" that witness to the holy dimension of all of life. That is, the tabernacle is more than something "churchy." It is a sign and vehicle that the community is inhabited by holiness. The religious leaders in this text have profound respect, as well as need, for artisans who are their indispensable allies. The work of this alliance is to make sure that Israel need not live in "real absence," in a profane existence devoid of awe, amazement, and God-given vitality.

EXODUS 36:8–39:43, THE WORK OF CONSTRUCTION

NIV

[8]All the skilled men among the workmen made the tabernacle with ten curtains of finely twisted linen and blue, purple and scarlet yarn, with cherubim worked into them by a skilled craftsman. [9]All the curtains were the same size—twenty-eight cubits long and four cubits wide.[a] [10]They joined five of the curtains together and did the same with the other five. [11]Then they made loops of blue material along the edge of the end curtain in one set, and the same was done with the end curtain in the other set. [12]They also made fifty loops on one curtain and fifty loops on the end curtain of the other set, with the loops opposite each other. [13]Then they made fifty gold clasps and used them to fasten the two sets of curtains together so that the tabernacle was a unit.

[14]They made curtains of goat hair for the tent over the tabernacle—eleven altogether. [15]All eleven curtains were the same size—thirty cubits long and four cubits wide.[b] [16]They joined five of the curtains into one set and the other six into another set. [17]Then they made fifty loops along the edge of the end curtain in one set and also along the edge of the end curtain in the other set. [18]They made fifty bronze clasps to fasten the tent

[a]9 That is, about 42 feet (about 12.5 meters) long and 6 feet (about 1.8 meters) wide   [b]15 That is, about 45 feet (about 13.5 meters) long and 6 feet (about 1.8 meters) wide

NRSV

[8]All those with skill among the workers made the tabernacle with ten curtains; they were made of fine twisted linen, and blue, purple, and crimson yarns, with cherubim skillfully worked into them. [9]The length of each curtain was twenty-eight cubits, and the width of each curtain four cubits; all the curtains were of the same size.

[10]He joined five curtains to one another, and the other five curtains he joined to one another. [11]He made loops of blue on the edge of the outermost curtain of the first set; likewise he made them on the edge of the outermost curtain of the second set; [12]he made fifty loops on the one curtain, and he made fifty loops on the edge of the curtain that was in the second set; the loops were opposite one another. [13]And he made fifty clasps of gold, and joined the curtains one to the other with clasps; so the tabernacle was one whole.

[14]He also made curtains of goats' hair for a tent over the tabernacle; he made eleven curtains. [15]The length of each curtain was thirty cubits, and the width of each curtain four cubits; the eleven curtains were of the same size. [16]He joined five curtains by themselves, and six curtains by themselves. [17]He made fifty loops on the edge of the outermost curtain of the one set, and fifty loops

NIV

together as a unit. ¹⁹Then they made for the tent a covering of ram skins dyed red, and over that a covering of hides of sea cows.ᵃ

²⁰They made upright frames of acacia wood for the tabernacle. ²¹Each frame was ten cubits long and a cubit and a half wide,ᵇ ²²with two projections set parallel to each other. They made all the frames of the tabernacle in this way. ²³They made twenty frames for the south side of the tabernacle ²⁴and made forty silver bases to go under them—two bases for each frame, one under each projection. ²⁵For the other side, the north side of the tabernacle, they made twenty frames ²⁶and forty silver bases—two under each frame. ²⁷They made six frames for the far end, that is, the west end of the tabernacle, ²⁸and two frames were made for the corners of the tabernacle at the far end. ²⁹At these two corners the frames were double from the bottom all the way to the top and fitted into a single ring; both were made alike. ³⁰So there were eight frames and sixteen silver bases—two under each frame.

³¹They also made crossbars of acacia wood: five for the frames on one side of the tabernacle, ³²five for those on the other side, and five for the frames on the west, at the far end of the tabernacle. ³³They made the center crossbar so that it extended from end to end at the middle of the frames. ³⁴They overlaid the frames with gold and made gold rings to hold the crossbars. They also overlaid the crossbars with gold.

³⁵They made the curtain of blue, purple and scarlet yarn and finely twisted linen, with cherubim worked into it by a skilled craftsman. ³⁶They made four posts of acacia wood for it and overlaid them with gold. They made gold hooks for them and cast their four silver bases. ³⁷For the entrance to the tent they made a curtain of blue, purple and scarlet yarn and finely twisted linen—the work of an embroiderer; ³⁸and they made five posts with hooks for them. They overlaid the tops of the posts and their bands with gold and made their five bases of bronze.

37 Bezalel made the ark of acacia wood—two and a half cubits long, a cubit and a half wide, and a cubit and a half high.ᶜ ²He overlaid

ᵃ19 That is, dugongs   ᵇ21 That is, about 15 feet (about 4.5 meters) long and 2 1/4 feet (about 0.7 meter) wide   ᶜ1 That is, about 3 3/4 feet (about 1.1 meters) long and 2 1/4 feet (about 0.7 meter) wide and high

NRSV

on the edge of the other connecting curtain. ¹⁸He made fifty clasps of bronze to join the tent together so that it might be one whole. ¹⁹And he made for the tent a covering of tanned rams' skins and an outer covering of fine leather.ᵃ

²⁰Then he made the upright frames for the tabernacle of acacia wood. ²¹Ten cubits was the length of a frame, and a cubit and a half the width of each frame. ²²Each frame had two pegs for fitting together; he did this for all the frames of the tabernacle. ²³The frames for the tabernacle he made in this way: twenty frames for the south side; ²⁴and he made forty bases of silver under the twenty frames, two bases under the first frame for its two pegs, and two bases under the next frame for its two pegs. ²⁵For the second side of the tabernacle, on the north side, he made twenty frames ²⁶and their forty bases of silver, two bases under the first frame and two bases under the next frame. ²⁷For the rear of the tabernacle westward he made six frames. ²⁸He made two frames for corners of the tabernacle in the rear. ²⁹They were separate beneath, but joined at the top, at the first ring; he made two of them in this way, for the two corners. ³⁰There were eight frames with their bases of silver: sixteen bases, under every frame two bases.

³¹He made bars of acacia wood, five for the frames of the one side of the tabernacle, ³²and five bars for the frames of the other side of the tabernacle, and five bars for the frames of the tabernacle at the rear westward. ³³He made the middle bar to pass through from end to end halfway up the frames. ³⁴And he overlaid the frames with gold, and made rings of gold for them to hold the bars, and overlaid the bars with gold.

³⁵He made the curtain of blue, purple, and crimson yarns, and fine twisted linen, with cherubim skillfully worked into it. ³⁶For it he made four pillars of acacia, and overlaid them with gold; their hooks were of gold, and he cast for them four bases of silver. ³⁷He also made a screen for the entrance to the tent, of blue, purple, and crimson yarns, and fine twisted linen, embroidered with needlework; ³⁸and its five pillars with their hooks. He overlaid their capitals and their bases with gold, but their five bases were of bronze.

ᵃ Meaning of Heb uncertain

it with pure gold, both inside and out, and made a gold molding around it. ³He cast four gold rings for it and fastened them to its four feet, with two rings on one side and two rings on the other. ⁴Then he made poles of acacia wood and overlaid them with gold. ⁵And he inserted the poles into the rings on the sides of the ark to carry it.

⁶He made the atonement cover of pure gold—two and a half cubits long and a cubit and a half wide.ᵃ ⁷Then he made two cherubim out of hammered gold at the ends of the cover. ⁸He made one cherub on one end and the second cherub on the other; at the two ends he made them of one piece with the cover. ⁹The cherubim had their wings spread upward, overshadowing the cover with them. The cherubim faced each other, looking toward the cover.

¹⁰Theyᵇ made the table of acacia wood—two cubits long, a cubit wide, and a cubit and a half high.ᶜ ¹¹Then they overlaid it with pure gold and made a gold molding around it. ¹²They also made around it a rim a handbreadthᵈ wide and put a gold molding on the rim. ¹³They cast four gold rings for the table and fastened them to the four corners, where the four legs were. ¹⁴The rings were put close to the rim to hold the poles used in carrying the table. ¹⁵The poles for carrying the table were made of acacia wood and were overlaid with gold. ¹⁶And they made from pure gold the articles for the table—its plates and dishes and bowls and its pitchers for the pouring out of drink offerings.

¹⁷They made the lampstand of pure gold and hammered it out, base and shaft; its flowerlike cups, buds and blossoms were of one piece with it. ¹⁸Six branches extended from the sides of the lampstand—three on one side and three on the other. ¹⁹Three cups shaped like almond flowers with buds and blossoms were on one branch, three on the next branch and the same for all six branches extending from the lampstand. ²⁰And on the lampstand were four cups shaped like almond flowers with buds and blossoms. ²¹One bud was under the first pair of branches extending from

ᵃ6 That is, about 3 3/4 feet (about 1.1 meters) long and 2 1/4 feet (about 0.7 meter) wide   ᵇ10 Or *He;* also in verses 11-29
ᶜ10 That is, about 3 feet (about 0.9 meter) long, 1 1/2 feet (about 0.5 meter) wide, and 2 1/4 feet (about 0.7 meter) high   ᵈ12 That is, about 3 inches (about 8 centimeters)

37 Bezalel made the ark of acacia wood; it was two and a half cubits long, a cubit and a half wide, and a cubit and a half high. ²He overlaid it with pure gold inside and outside, and made a molding of gold around it. ³He cast for it four rings of gold for its four feet, two rings on its one side and two rings on its other side. ⁴He made poles of acacia wood, and overlaid them with gold, ⁵and put the poles into the rings on the sides of the ark, to carry the ark. ⁶He made a mercy seatᵃ of pure gold; two cubits and a half was its length, and a cubit and a half its width. ⁷He made two cherubim of hammered gold; at the two ends of the mercy seatᵃ he made them, ⁸one cherub at the one end, and one cherub at the other end; of one piece with the mercy seatᵃ he made the cherubim at its two ends. ⁹The cherubim spread out their wings above, overshadowing the mercy seatᵃ with their wings. They faced one another; the faces of the cherubim were turned toward the mercy seat.ᵃ

10He also made the table of acacia wood, two cubits long, one cubit wide, and a cubit and a half high. ¹¹He overlaid it with pure gold, and made a molding of gold around it. ¹²He made around it a rim a handbreadth wide, and made a molding of gold around the rim. ¹³He cast for it four rings of gold, and fastened the rings to the four corners at its four legs. ¹⁴The rings that held the poles used for carrying the table were close to the rim. ¹⁵He made the poles of acacia wood to carry the table, and overlaid them with gold. ¹⁶And he made the vessels of pure gold that were to be on the table, its plates and dishes for incense, and its bowls and flagons with which to pour drink offerings.

17He also made the lampstand of pure gold. The base and the shaft of the lampstand were made of hammered work; its cups, its calyxes, and its petals were of one piece with it. ¹⁸There were six branches going out of its sides, three branches of the lampstand out of one side of it and three branches of the lampstand out of the other side of it; ¹⁹three cups shaped like almond blossoms, each with calyx and petals, on one branch, and three cups shaped like almond blossoms, each with calyx and petals, on the other

ᵃ Or *a cover*

NIV

the lampstand, a second bud under the second pair, and a third bud under the third pair—six branches in all. ²²The buds and the branches were all of one piece with the lampstand, hammered out of pure gold.

²³They made its seven lamps, as well as its wick trimmers and trays, of pure gold. ²⁴They made the lampstand and all its accessories from one talent[a] of pure gold.

²⁵They made the altar of incense out of acacia wood. It was square, a cubit long and a cubit wide, and two cubits high[b]—its horns of one piece with it. ²⁶They overlaid the top and all the sides and the horns with pure gold, and made a gold molding around it. ²⁷They made two gold rings below the molding—two on opposite sides—to hold the poles used to carry it. ²⁸They made the poles of acacia wood and overlaid them with gold.

²⁹They also made the sacred anointing oil and the pure, fragrant incense—the work of a perfumer.

38 They[c] built the altar of burnt offering of acacia wood, three cubits[d] high; it was square, five cubits long and five cubits wide.[e] ²They made a horn at each of the four corners, so that the horns and the altar were of one piece, and they overlaid the altar with bronze. ³They made all its utensils of bronze—its pots, shovels, sprinkling bowls, meat forks and firepans. ⁴They made a grating for the altar, a bronze network, to be under its ledge, halfway up the altar. ⁵They cast bronze rings to hold the poles for the four corners of the bronze grating. ⁶They made the poles of acacia wood and overlaid them with bronze. ⁷They inserted the poles into the rings so they would be on the sides of the altar for carrying it. They made it hollow, out of boards.

⁸They made the bronze basin and its bronze stand from the mirrors of the women who served at the entrance to the Tent of Meeting.

⁹Next they made the courtyard. The south side was a hundred cubits[f] long and had curtains of

---

a24 That is, about 75 pounds (about 34 kilograms)   b25 That is, about 1 1/2 feet (about 0.5 meter) long and wide, and about 3 feet (about 0.9 meter) high   c1 Or He; also in verses 2-9   d1 That is, about 4 1/2 feet (about 1.3 meters)   e1 That is, about 7 1/2 feet (about 2.3 meters) long and wide   f 9 That is, about 150 feet (about 46 meters)

NRSV

branch—so for the six branches going out of the lampstand. ²⁰On the lampstand itself there were four cups shaped like almond blossoms, each with its calyxes and petals. ²¹There was a calyx of one piece with it under the first pair of branches, a calyx of one piece with it under the next pair of branches, and a calyx of one piece with it under the last pair of branches. ²²Their calyxes and their branches were of one piece with it, the whole of it one hammered piece of pure gold. ²³He made its seven lamps and its snuffers and its trays of pure gold. ²⁴He made it and all its utensils of a talent of pure gold.

25He made the altar of incense of acacia wood, one cubit long, and one cubit wide; it was square, and was two cubits high; its horns were of one piece with it. ²⁶He overlaid it with pure gold, its top, and its sides all around, and its horns; and he made for it a molding of gold all around, ²⁷and made two golden rings for it under its molding, on two opposite sides of it, to hold the poles with which to carry it. ²⁸And he made the poles of acacia wood, and overlaid them with gold.

29He made the holy anointing oil also, and the pure fragrant incense, blended as by the perfumer.

38 He made the altar of burnt offering also of acacia wood; it was five cubits long, and five cubits wide; it was square, and three cubits high. ²He made horns for it on its four corners; its horns were of one piece with it, and he overlaid it with bronze. ³He made all the utensils of the altar, the pots, the shovels, the basins, the forks, and the firepans: all its utensils he made of bronze. ⁴He made for the altar a grating, a network of bronze, under its ledge, extending halfway down. ⁵He cast four rings on the four corners of the bronze grating to hold the poles; ⁶he made the poles of acacia wood, and overlaid them with bronze. ⁷And he put the poles through the rings on the sides of the altar, to carry it with them; he made it hollow, with boards.

8He made the basin of bronze with its stand of bronze, from the mirrors of the women who served at the entrance to the tent of meeting.

9He made the court; for the south side the hangings of the court were of fine twisted linen, one hundred cubits long; ¹⁰its twenty pillars and their twenty bases were of bronze, but the hooks

NIV

finely twisted linen, [10]with twenty posts and twenty bronze bases, and with silver hooks and bands on the posts. [11]The north side was also a hundred cubits long and had twenty posts and twenty bronze bases, with silver hooks and bands on the posts.

[12]The west end was fifty cubits[a] wide and had curtains, with ten posts and ten bases, with silver hooks and bands on the posts. [13]The east end, toward the sunrise, was also fifty cubits wide. [14]Curtains fifteen cubits[b] long were on one side of the entrance, with three posts and three bases, [15]and curtains fifteen cubits long were on the other side of the entrance to the courtyard, with three posts and three bases. [16]All the curtains around the courtyard were of finely twisted linen. [17]The bases for the posts were bronze. The hooks and bands on the posts were silver, and their tops were overlaid with silver; so all the posts of the courtyard had silver bands.

[18]The curtain for the entrance to the courtyard was of blue, purple and scarlet yarn and finely twisted linen—the work of an embroiderer. It was twenty cubits[c] long and, like the curtains of the courtyard, five cubits[d] high, [19]with four posts and four bronze bases. Their hooks and bands were silver, and their tops were overlaid with silver. [20]All the tent pegs of the tabernacle and of the surrounding courtyard were bronze.

[21]These are the amounts of the materials used for the tabernacle, the tabernacle of the Testimony, which were recorded at Moses' command by the Levites under the direction of Ithamar son of Aaron, the priest. [22](Bezalel son of Uri, the son of Hur, of the tribe of Judah, made everything the LORD commanded Moses; [23]with him was Oholiab son of Ahisamach, of the tribe of Dan—a craftsman and designer, and an embroiderer in blue, purple and scarlet yarn and fine linen.) [24]The total amount of the gold from the wave offering used for all the work on the sanctuary was 29 talents and 730 shekels,[e] according to the sanctuary shekel.

[25]The silver obtained from those of the commu-

a12 That is, about 75 feet (about 23 meters)   b14 That is, about 22 1/2 feet (about 6.9 meters)   c18 That is, about 30 feet (about 9 meters)   d18 That is, about 7 1/2 feet (about 2.3 meters) e24 The weight of the gold was a little over one ton (about 1 metric ton).

NRSV

of the pillars and their bands were of silver. [11]For the north side there were hangings one hundred cubits long; its twenty pillars and their twenty bases were of bronze, but the hooks of the pillars and their bands were of silver. [12]For the west side there were hangings fifty cubits long, with ten pillars and ten bases; the hooks of the pillars and their bands were of silver. [13]And for the front to the east, fifty cubits. [14]The hangings for one side of the gate were fifteen cubits, with three pillars and three bases. [15]And so for the other side; on each side of the gate of the court were hangings of fifteen cubits, with three pillars and three bases. [16]All the hangings around the court were of fine twisted linen. [17]The bases for the pillars were of bronze, but the hooks of the pillars and their bands were of silver; the overlaying of their capitals was also of silver, and all the pillars of the court were banded with silver. [18]The screen for the entrance to the court was embroidered with needlework in blue, purple, and crimson yarns and fine twisted linen. It was twenty cubits long and, along the width of it, five cubits high, corresponding to the hangings of the court. [19]There were four pillars; their four bases were of bronze, their hooks of silver, and the overlaying of their capitals and their bands of silver. [20]All the pegs for the tabernacle and for the court all around were of bronze.

[21]These are the records of the tabernacle, the tabernacle of the covenant,[a] which were drawn up at the commandment of Moses, the work of the Levites being under the direction of Ithamar son of the priest Aaron. [22]Bezalel son of Uri son of Hur, of the tribe of Judah, made all that the LORD commanded Moses; [23]and with him was Oholiab son of Ahisamach, of the tribe of Dan, engraver, designer, and embroiderer in blue, purple, and crimson yarns, and in fine linen.

[24]All the gold that was used for the work, in all the construction of the sanctuary, the gold from the offering, was twenty-nine talents and seven hundred thirty shekels, measured by the sanctuary shekel. [25]The silver from those of the congregation who were counted was one hundred talents and one thousand seven hundred seventy-five shekels, measured by the sanctuary shekel; [26]a beka a head

a Or treaty, or testimony; Heb eduth

NIV

nity who were counted in the census was 100 talents and 1,775 shekels,[a] according to the sanctuary shekel— [26]one beka per person, that is, half a shekel,[b] according to the sanctuary shekel, from everyone who had crossed over to those counted, twenty years old or more, a total of 603,550 men. [27]The 100 talents[c] of silver were used to cast the bases for the sanctuary and for the curtain—100 bases from the 100 talents, one talent for each base. [28]They used the 1,775 shekels[d] to make the hooks for the posts, to overlay the tops of the posts, and to make their bands.

[29]The bronze from the wave offering was 70 talents and 2,400 shekels.[e] [30]They used it to make the bases for the entrance to the Tent of Meeting, the bronze altar with its bronze grating and all its utensils, [31]the bases for the surrounding courtyard and those for its entrance and all the tent pegs for the tabernacle and those for the surrounding courtyard.

39 From the blue, purple and scarlet yarn they made woven garments for ministering in the sanctuary. They also made sacred garments for Aaron, as the Lord commanded Moses.

[2]They[f] made the ephod of gold, and of blue, purple and scarlet yarn, and of finely twisted linen. [3]They hammered out thin sheets of gold and cut strands to be worked into the blue, purple and scarlet yarn and fine linen—the work of a skilled craftsman. [4]They made shoulder pieces for the ephod, which were attached to two of its corners, so it could be fastened. [5]Its skillfully woven waistband was like it—of one piece with the ephod and made with gold, and with blue, purple and scarlet yarn, and with finely twisted linen, as the Lord commanded Moses.

[6]They mounted the onyx stones in gold filigree settings and engraved them like a seal with the names of the sons of Israel. [7]Then they fastened them on the shoulder pieces of the ephod as memorial stones for the sons of Israel, as the Lord commanded Moses.

[8]They fashioned the breastpiece—the work of

a25 The weight of the silver was a little over 3 3/4 tons (about 3.4 metric tons).   b26 That is, about 1/5 ounce (about 5.5 grams)   c27 That is, about 3 3/4 tons (about 3.4 metric tons)   d28 That is, about 45 pounds (about 20 kilograms)   e29 The weight of the bronze was about 2 1/2 tons (about 2.4 metric tons).   f2 Or He; also in verses 7, 8 and 22

NRSV

(that is, half a shekel, measured by the sanctuary shekel), for everyone who was counted in the census, from twenty years old and upward, for six hundred three thousand, five hundred fifty men. [27]The hundred talents of silver were for casting the bases of the sanctuary, and the bases of the curtain; one hundred bases for the hundred talents, a talent for a base. [28]Of the thousand seven hundred seventy-five shekels he made hooks for the pillars, and overlaid their capitals and made bands for them. [29]The bronze that was contributed was seventy talents, and two thousand four hundred shekels; [30]with it he made the bases for the entrance of the tent of meeting, the bronze altar and the bronze grating for it and all the utensils of the altar, [31]the bases all around the court, and the bases of the gate of the court, all the pegs of the tabernacle, and all the pegs around the court.

39 Of the blue, purple, and crimson yarns they made finely worked vestments, for ministering in the holy place; they made the sacred vestments for Aaron; as the Lord had commanded Moses.

[2]He made the ephod of gold, of blue, purple, and crimson yarns, and of fine twisted linen. [3]Gold leaf was hammered out and cut into threads to work into the blue, purple, and crimson yarns and into the fine twisted linen, in skilled design. [4]They made for the ephod shoulder-pieces, joined to it at its two edges. [5]The decorated band on it was of the same materials and workmanship, of gold, of blue, purple, and crimson yarns, and of fine twisted linen; as the Lord had commanded Moses.

[6]The onyx stones were prepared, enclosed in settings of gold filigree and engraved like the engravings of a signet, according to the names of the sons of Israel. [7]He set them on the shoulder-pieces of the ephod, to be stones of remembrance for the sons of Israel; as the Lord had commanded Moses.

[8]He made the breastpiece, in skilled work, like the work of the ephod, of gold, of blue, purple, and crimson yarns, and of fine twisted linen. [9]It was square; the breastpiece was made double, a span in length and a span in width when doubled. [10]They set in it four rows of stones. A row of

a skilled craftsman. They made it like the ephod: of gold, and of blue, purple and scarlet yarn, and of finely twisted linen. ⁹It was square—a span*a* long and a span wide—and folded double. ¹⁰Then they mounted four rows of precious stones on it. In the first row there was a ruby, a topaz and a beryl; ¹¹in the second row a turquoise, a sapphire*b* and an emerald; ¹²in the third row a jacinth, an agate and an amethyst; ¹³in the fourth row a chrysolite, an onyx and a jasper.*c* They were mounted in gold filigree settings. ¹⁴There were twelve stones, one for each of the names of the sons of Israel, each engraved like a seal with the name of one of the twelve tribes.

¹⁵For the breastpiece they made braided chains of pure gold, like a rope. ¹⁶They made two gold filigree settings and two gold rings, and fastened the rings to two of the corners of the breastpiece. ¹⁷They fastened the two gold chains to the rings at the corners of the breastpiece, ¹⁸and the other ends of the chains to the two settings, attaching them to the shoulder pieces of the ephod at the front. ¹⁹They made two gold rings and attached them to the other two corners of the breastpiece on the inside edge next to the ephod. ²⁰Then they made two more gold rings and attached them to the bottom of the shoulder pieces on the front of the ephod, close to the seam just above the waistband of the ephod. ²¹They tied the rings of the breastpiece to the rings of the ephod with blue cord, connecting it to the waistband so that the breastpiece would not swing out from the ephod—as the Lord commanded Moses.

²²They made the robe of the ephod entirely of blue cloth—the work of a weaver— ²³with an opening in the center of the robe like the opening of a collar,*d* and a band around this opening, so that it would not tear. ²⁴They made pomegranates of blue, purple and scarlet yarn and finely twisted linen around the hem of the robe. ²⁵And they made bells of pure gold and attached them around the hem between the pomegranates. ²⁶The bells and pomegranates alternated around the hem of the robe to be worn for ministering, as the Lord commanded Moses.

a9 That is, about 9 inches (about 22 centimeters)   *b11* Or *lapis lazuli*   *c13* The precise identification of some of these precious stones is uncertain.   *d23* The meaning of the Hebrew for this word is uncertain.

carnelian,*a* chrysolite, and emerald was the first row; ¹¹and the second row, a turquoise, a sapphire,*b* and a moonstone; ¹²and the third row, a jacinth, an agate, and an amethyst; ¹³and the fourth row, a beryl, an onyx, and a jasper; they were enclosed in settings of gold filigree. ¹⁴There were twelve stones with names corresponding to the names of the sons of Israel; they were like signets, each engraved with its name, for the twelve tribes. ¹⁵They made on the breastpiece chains of pure gold, twisted like cords; ¹⁶and they made two settings of gold filigree and two gold rings, and put the two rings on the two edges of the breastpiece; ¹⁷and they put the two cords of gold in the two rings at the edges of the breastpiece. ¹⁸Two ends of the two cords they had attached to the two settings of filigree; in this way they attached it in front to the shoulder-pieces of the ephod. ¹⁹Then they made two rings of gold, and put them at the two ends of the breastpiece, on its inside edge next to the ephod. ²⁰They made two rings of gold, and attached them in front to the lower part of the two shoulder-pieces of the ephod, at its joining above the decorated band of the ephod. ²¹They bound the breastpiece by its rings to the rings of the ephod with a blue cord, so that it should lie on the decorated band of the ephod, and that the breastpiece should not come loose from the ephod; as the Lord had commanded Moses.

22He also made the robe of the ephod woven all of blue yarn; ²³and the opening of the robe in the middle of it was like the opening in a coat of mail,*c* with a binding around the opening, so that it might not be torn. ²⁴On the lower hem of the robe they made pomegranates of blue, purple, and crimson yarns, and of fine twisted linen. ²⁵They also made bells of pure gold, and put the bells between the pomegranates on the lower hem of the robe all around, between the pomegranates; ²⁶a bell and a pomegranate, a bell and a pomegranate all around on the lower hem of the robe for ministering; as the Lord had commanded Moses.

27They also made the tunics, woven of fine linen, for Aaron and his sons, ²⁸and the turban of

a The identification of several of these stones is uncertain
b Or *lapis lazuli*   *c* Meaning of Heb uncertain

NIV

²⁷For Aaron and his sons, they made tunics of fine linen—the work of a weaver— ²⁸and the turban of fine linen, the linen headbands and the undergarments of finely twisted linen. ²⁹The sash was of finely twisted linen and blue, purple and scarlet yarn—the work of an embroiderer—as the LORD commanded Moses.

³⁰They made the plate, the sacred diadem, out of pure gold and engraved on it, like an inscription on a seal: HOLY TO THE LORD. ³¹Then they fastened a blue cord to it to attach it to the turban, as the LORD commanded Moses.

³²So all the work on the tabernacle, the Tent of Meeting, was completed. The Israelites did everything just as the LORD commanded Moses. ³³Then they brought the tabernacle to Moses: the tent and all its furnishings, its clasps, frames, crossbars, posts and bases; ³⁴the covering of ram skins dyed red, the covering of hides of sea cows*ᵃ* and the shielding curtain; ³⁵the ark of the Testimony with its poles and the atonement cover; ³⁶the table with all its articles and the bread of the Presence; ³⁷the pure gold lampstand with its row of lamps and all its accessories, and the oil for the light; ³⁸the gold altar, the anointing oil, the fragrant incense, and the curtain for the entrance to the tent; ³⁹the bronze altar with its bronze grating, its poles and all its utensils; the basin with its stand; ⁴⁰the curtains of the courtyard with its posts and bases, and the curtain for the entrance to the courtyard; the ropes and tent pegs for the courtyard; all the furnishings for the tabernacle, the Tent of Meeting; ⁴¹and the woven garments worn for ministering in the sanctuary, both the sacred garments for Aaron the priest and the garments for his sons when serving as priests.

⁴²The Israelites had done all the work just as the LORD had commanded Moses. ⁴³Moses inspected the work and saw that they had done it just as the LORD had commanded. So Moses blessed them.

ᵃ34 That is, dugongs

NRSV

fine linen, and the headdresses of fine linen, and the linen undergarments of fine twisted linen, ²⁹and the sash of fine twisted linen, and of blue, purple, and crimson yarns, embroidered with needlework; as the LORD had commanded Moses.

30They made the rosette of the holy diadem of pure gold, and wrote on it an inscription, like the engraving of a signet, "Holy to the LORD." ³¹They tied to it a blue cord, to fasten it on the turban above; as the LORD had commanded Moses.

32In this way all the work of the tabernacle of the tent of meeting was finished; the Israelites had done everything just as the LORD had commanded Moses. ³³Then they brought the tabernacle to Moses, the tent and all its utensils, its hooks, its frames, its bars, its pillars, and its bases; ³⁴the covering of tanned rams' skins and the covering of fine leather,*ᵃ* and the curtain for the screen; ³⁵the ark of the covenant*ᵇ* with its poles and the mercy seat;*ᶜ* ³⁶the table with all its utensils, and the bread of the Presence; ³⁷the pure lampstand with its lamps set on it and all its utensils, and the oil for the light; ³⁸the golden altar, the anointing oil and the fragrant incense, and the screen for the entrance of the tent; ³⁹the bronze altar, and its grating of bronze, its poles, and all its utensils; the basin with its stand; ⁴⁰the hangings of the court, its pillars, and its bases, and the screen for the gate of the court, its cords, and its pegs; and all the utensils for the service of the tabernacle, for the tent of meeting; ⁴¹the finely worked vestments for ministering in the holy place, the sacred vestments for the priest Aaron, and the vestments of his sons to serve as priests. ⁴²The Israelites had done all of the work just as the LORD had commanded Moses. ⁴³When Moses saw that they had done all the work just as the LORD had commanded, he blessed them.

ᵃ Meaning of Heb uncertain   ᵇ Or treaty, or testimony; Heb eduth   ᶜ Or the cover

COMMENTARY

With adequate resources (35:4-9, 20-29; 36:3-7) and personnel (35:10-19; 35:30–36:2), the actual work on the tabernacle can now proceed. These texts are closely connected to the commands given earlier (chaps. 25–31). Commentaries rightly handle these texts by referring to the corresponding command. Not much more needs to be said or can be said about these texts. We may make four general observations.

First, the texts closely correlate to the commands of Yahweh. The construction of the tabernacle is a sustained act of obedience. Israel characteristically affirms that as command is issued by the God of glory, so observance is human work done on earth. Obedience is indeed a mode of communion between holy God and responding people.

Second, this is nitty-gritty human work. Not much is made of that fact in this text, but we must keep it in mind. Thus we may imagine the real cutting of lumber, real measuring of frames, real decisions about design and technique, informal conferences and tactical decisions along the way. Tabernacle construction is human work.

Third, in this long sequence of texts, Moses is for the most part absent. To be sure, there are some third-person singular pronouns for which the antecedent is unclear. With the authorization of work in 35:30–36:3, however, it is more probable that Moses stayed out of the actual work. The construction is done by those who have the skill to do it.

Fourth, the actual work of construction moves toward the culminating drama of presence in chap. 40, wherein Moses again becomes decisive. The workers are marked with an awesome religious intentionality: They are making possible the presence.

The text is divided into four sections: the construction of the tabernacle (36:8–38:20), an audit of expenditures (38:21-31), the preparation of priestly attire (39:1-31), and a concluding summary statement (39:32-43).

36:8–38:20. In large measure, the commands of chaps. 25–27 and parts of 30 are implemented: 36:8-38, concerning the tabernacle, refers to 26:1-37; 37:1-5, concerning the ark, refers to 25:10-14; 37:6-9, concerning the mercy seat, refers to 25:17-20; 37:10-16, concerning the table, refers to 25:23-29; 37:17-24, concerning the lampstand, refers to 25:31-39; 37:25-28, concerning the altar of incense, refers to 30:1-5; 37:29, concerning oil and incense, refers to 30:22-25; 38:1-7, concerning the altar of burnt offering, refers to 27:1-8*a;* 38:8, concerning the bronze basin, refers to 30:17-18; and 38:9-20, concerning the court, refers to 27:9-19.

To be sure, there are some small departures from the texts of command, by way of omission, reordering, and in a few cases by addition. (The priority of the tabernacle in 36 before the furnishings in 37–38 seems logically preferable to the sequence in 25–27.) On the whole, however, the variations in content and order do not need to concern us. The most important and consistent omissions are comments about the theological function of items. However, these omissions make good sense, because this is a report on construction and not a building manual. Except in details that for our purposes are insignificant, the tabernacle is built according to specifications.

38:21-31. These verses present something like a formal, final, and complete audit of the finances, divided into two parts. First, the three responsible officers are identified (vv. 21-23). It is as though they are the signatories to the final contract. The inclusion of Ithamar surprises us in this context. While we have encountered his name elsewhere (6:23; 28:1), we have had no clue that he is involved in the construction of the tabernacle. His name keeps the project securely related to the priestly houses and their influence.

The second part of this report concerns the expenditure of funds (vv. 24-31). This passage is especially interesting when set in juxtaposition with the texts concerning the offerings in 35:4-9, 20-29 and 36:3-7. While the community may give freely, lavishly, and spontaneously, those responsible for the project must be precise, in order to both cover actual costs and give account of their management.

The formal audit is in three parts, concerning three previous materials used. First, gold is the most precious and most sparingly used metal (v. 24). The second metal reported is silver (vv. 25-28). This must have been the normative material because it receives the most attention in the text. Two matters are noticed. First, the amounts used relate to an actual census tax (on which, see 30:11-16). This procedure for raising money contrasts with the freewill offering mentioned earlier. This text suggests that the project is so ambitious that it requires institutional discipline to raise the money, even beyond uncommon generosity. In any case, the text does not acknowledge any tension between the two modes of finance. The second element related to silver is a detailed accounting of the uses made of it, as though the leadership wants to be clear on where every penny is spent. The third metal, bronze, is used for lesser objects (vv. 29-31).

This audit suggests a report with no questions outstanding and no bills left unpaid. The report evidences care, precision, and comprehensiveness.

39:1-31. The preparation of attire for the Aaronide priesthood is again closely guided by the commands given to Moses and again with some variations: 39:2-7 constructs the ephod, authorized by 28:6-14; 39:8-21 constructs the breastplate, authorized by 28:15-28; 39:22-26 constructs the robe, authorized by 28:31-34; 39:27-29 constructs the tunic, authorized by 28:39; 39:30-31 constructs the rosette, authorized by 28:36-37.

Seven times (39:1, 5, 7, 21, 26, 29, 31) it is asserted, "As the Lord had commanded Moses." This formula is absent in chaps. 36–38 concerning the tabernacle, but it is used with reference to Aaron. Perhaps its repeated usage serves to subordinate the priesthood of Aaron to the tradition of Moses, a recurrent accent of Exodus. Conversely, the formula may also function to give strong legitimacy to the house of Aaron.

39:32-43. This unit reports the completed construction of the tabernacle and all its equipment. The main body of the text provides an inventory of the fixtures (vv. 33-41). Although this list is somewhat more detailed it corresponds to the list in 35:10-19. The two lists together form an envelope for the long text on construction (chaps. 35–39). Moreover, this list of fixtures roughly corresponds to the general outline, of chaps. 25–31 and 36–39. Everything needed is supplied to make the presence possible in Israel.

Primary interest in this passage will be carefully focused on the beginning and end (vv. 32-33*a*, 42-43). The beginning statement, which clearly draws to a close the general statement on construction, contains three interesting features. First, the work is "finished" (כלה *kālâ*). This is not in any way an exceptional word. It is of interest here, however, because the same word is used in a similar formula for the completion of the Temple (see 1 Kgs 6:9, 14, 38; 9:1, 25; 1 Chr 28:20;

2 Chr 8:16). Our text clearly intends the tabernacle to be an anticipation of the Temple.

Second, the introductory formula asserts that all is done "just as the Lord had commanded Moses." This tabernacle is in full compliance and should make presence possible.

Third, the tabernacle is "brought" to Moses. This suggests that Moses has indeed stayed out of the construction. The presentation to him is a formal one, not unlike the legal process of a contractor's handing over a new building to the owner. At this moment, Moses accepts responsibility for the building. Correspondingly, Bazalel, Oholiab, and Ithamar (cf. 38:21-23) disappear from the text. Mosaic activity is screened out of construction (36:9–39:31), just as the workmen have no part in the subsequent Mosaic work of legitimation in 40:1-33.

The conclusion of this passage contains corresponding themes (vv. 42-43). First, though the term *finish* is not used, the formula of completion parallels v. 32: "had done all of the work." Second, the formula "just as the Lord had commanded Moses" is twice repeated. Third, the unit ends with the succinct but freighted statement, "Moses blessed them"—i.e., the Israelites who had done the work. This refers to a powerful gesture of well-being, which Moses is fully authorized to pronounce. This act indicates that he approves the work. Moreover, the act of blessing may mark for Israel a transition to chap. 40 and a commendation to the presence.

We may note one other matter concerning the conclusion. Only two other uses of *bless* in Exodus pertain to Moses. In 12:32, Pharaoh in his anguish petitions Moses, "Bring a blessing on me too!" Moses ignores the petition, and Pharaoh remains unblessed. Here the Israelites do not ask or seek a blessing from Moses, but they nonetheless receive one. The connection to 12:32 once again dramatically contrasts Egypt in the absence of blessing, with Israel, the people where the power for life is given.

The other usage is in 32:29, where Moses acknowledges that the Levites are blessed. They, like the workmen on the Temple, are models of tenacious faithfulness.

REFLECTIONS

While commanded by Yahweh, the work of constructing a house for the holy is human work, and it must be done well. The specificity and concreteness of the work protest against any tendency to make communion with God easy or "spiritual." This God needs *a place* that is reserved precisely for this holiness. The creation of such a place, moreover, requires a combination of passion, generosity, competence, and devotion.

We may identify two other notes about this building project: (1) There is a careful audit and accounting of funds. This fact attests once again to the unembarrassed materiality of the project. (2) The building is "finished," but the conclusion of this chapter is still penultimate. The building is an act of hope and expectation. This can be a people prepared (cf. Luke 1:17) and a place prepared, but all the preparation finally leaves Israel waiting. The place for God's holiness is not finally readied for presence until God readies it.

EXODUS 40:1-33, MOSES FINISHES THE WORK

NIV

40 Then the LORD said to Moses: [2]"Set up the tabernacle, the Tent of Meeting, on the first day of the first month. [3]Place the ark of the Testimony in it and shield the ark with the curtain. [4]Bring in the table and set out what belongs on it. Then bring in the lampstand and set up its lamps. [5]Place the gold altar of incense in front of the ark of the Testimony and put the curtain at the entrance to the tabernacle.

[6]"Place the altar of burnt offering in front of the entrance to the tabernacle, the Tent of Meeting; [7]place the basin between the Tent of Meeting and the altar and put water in it. [8]Set up the courtyard around it and put the curtain at the entrance to the courtyard.

[9]"Take the anointing oil and anoint the tabernacle and everything in it; consecrate it and all its furnishings, and it will be holy. [10]Then anoint the altar of burnt offering and all its utensils; consecrate the altar, and it will be most holy. [11]Anoint the basin and its stand and consecrate them.

[12]"Bring Aaron and his sons to the entrance to the Tent of Meeting and wash them with water. [13]Then dress Aaron in the sacred garments, anoint him and consecrate him so he may serve me as priest. [14]Bring his sons and dress them in tunics. [15]Anoint them just as you anointed their father, so they may serve me as priests. Their anointing will be to a priesthood that will continue for all

NRSV

40 The LORD spoke to Moses: [2]On the first day of the first month you shall set up the tabernacle of the tent of meeting. [3]You shall put in it the ark of the covenant,[a] and you shall screen the ark with the curtain. [4]You shall bring in the table, and arrange its setting; and you shall bring in the lampstand, and set up its lamps. [5]You shall put the golden altar for incense before the ark of the covenant,[b] and set up the screen for the entrance of the tabernacle. [6]You shall set the altar of burnt offering before the entrance of the tabernacle of the tent of meeting, [7]and place the basin between the tent of meeting and the altar, and put water in it. [8]You shall set up the court all around, and hang up the screen for the gate of the court. [9]Then you shall take the anointing oil, and anoint the tabernacle and all that is in it, and consecrate it and all its furniture, so that it shall become holy. [10]You shall also anoint the altar of burnt offering and all its utensils, and consecrate the altar, so that the altar shall be most holy. [11]You shall also anoint the basin with its stand, and consecrate it. [12]Then you shall bring Aaron and his sons to the entrance of the tent of meeting, and shall wash them with water, [13]and put on Aaron the sacred vestments, and you shall anoint him and consecrate him, so that he may serve me as priest. [14]You shall bring his sons also

[a] Or *treaty*, or *testimony*; Heb *eduth*   [b] Or *treaty*, or *testimony*; Heb *eduth*

NIV

generations to come." [16]Moses did everything just as the LORD commanded him.

[17]So the tabernacle was set up on the first day of the first month in the second year. [18]When Moses set up the tabernacle, he put the bases in place, erected the frames, inserted the crossbars and set up the posts. [19]Then he spread the tent over the tabernacle and put the covering over the tent, as the LORD commanded him.

[20]He took the Testimony and placed it in the ark, attached the poles to the ark and put the atonement cover over it. [21]Then he brought the ark into the tabernacle and hung the shielding curtain and shielded the ark of the Testimony, as the LORD commanded him.

[22]Moses placed the table in the Tent of Meeting on the north side of the tabernacle outside the curtain [23]and set out the bread on it before the LORD, as the LORD commanded him.

[24]He placed the lampstand in the Tent of Meeting opposite the table on the south side of the tabernacle [25]and set up the lamps before the LORD, as the LORD commanded him.

[26]Moses placed the gold altar in the Tent of Meeting in front of the curtain [27]and burned fragrant incense on it, as the LORD commanded him. [28]Then he put up the curtain at the entrance to the tabernacle.

[29]He set the altar of burnt offering near the entrance to the tabernacle, the Tent of Meeting, and offered on it burnt offerings and grain offerings, as the LORD commanded him.

[30]He placed the basin between the Tent of Meeting and the altar and put water in it for washing, [31]and Moses and Aaron and his sons used it to wash their hands and feet. [32]They washed whenever they entered the Tent of Meeting or approached the altar, as the LORD commanded Moses.

[33]Then Moses set up the courtyard around the tabernacle and altar and put up the curtain at the entrance to the courtyard. And so Moses finished the work.

NRSV

and put tunics on them, [15]and anoint them, as you anointed their father, that they may serve me as priests: and their anointing shall admit them to a perpetual priesthood throughout all generations to come.

16Moses did everything just as the LORD had commanded him. [17]In the first month in the second year, on the first day of the month, the tabernacle was set up. [18]Moses set up the tabernacle; he laid its bases, and set up its frames, and put in its poles, and raised up its pillars; [19]and he spread the tent over the tabernacle, and put the covering of the tent over it; as the LORD had commanded Moses. [20]He took the covenant[a] and put it into the ark, and put the poles on the ark, and set the mercy seat[b] above the ark; [21]and he brought the ark into the tabernacle, and set up the curtain for screening, and screened the ark of the covenant;[a] as the LORD had commanded Moses. [22]He put the table in the tent of meeting, on the north side of the tabernacle, outside the curtain, [23]and set the bread in order on it before the LORD; as the LORD had commanded Moses. [24]He put the lampstand in the tent of meeting, opposite the table on the south side of the tabernacle, [25]and set up the lamps before the LORD; as the LORD had commanded Moses. [26]He put the golden altar in the tent of meeting before the curtain, [27]and offered fragrant incense on it; as the LORD had commanded Moses. [28]He also put in place the screen for the entrance of the tabernacle. [29]He set the altar of burnt offering at the entrance of the tabernacle of the tent of meeting, and offered on it the burnt offering and the grain offering as the LORD had commanded Moses. [30]He set the basin between the tent of meeting and the altar, and put water in it for washing, [31]with which Moses and Aaron and his sons washed their hands and their feet. [32]When they went into the tent of meeting, and when they approached the altar, they washed; as the LORD had commanded Moses. [33]He set up the court around the tabernacle and the altar, and put up the screen at the gate of the court. So Moses finished the work.

a Or *treaty,* or *testimony;* Heb *eduth*   *b* Or *the cover*

COMMENTARY

Now Moses reappears in his full power. Since 35:6, the project (and the text) have been turned over to the artisans who construct the holy place. The tabernacle is "finished" (39:32), except that it is not in fact finished until Moses finishes it. The construction of 36:8–39:31 has been the work of the laity. That action must now be matched and done again by Moses, before it is done effectively. These verses are constructed as command (vv. 1-15) and performance (vv. 16-33); thus they repeat in miniature the same pattern of command and performance in chaps. 25–31 and 35–39.

Yahweh speaks to Moses (vv. 1-15), this time to issue the decisive commands concerning the tabernacle. In this speech, Moses is the subject of a long series of imperative verbs that now finally put in place the tabernacle and all its furnishings. This series of verbs serves as a technique for reiterating (yet one more time) all the elements of the tabernacle that have been authorized in chaps. 25–31, summarized in 35:10-19, implemented in 36:8–39:31, and summarized again in 39:32-41. All of these lists vary in detail, but they refer to the same pattern and plan. Moses is instructed to take action on the "first of the first," a new year, at the beginning (v. 2).

Perhaps the most important matter of these commands is the series of pivotal verbs addressed to Moses: *anoint, consecrate,* and *wash.* Moses is to mark with oil (משׁח *māšaḥ*; vv. 9-11, 13, 15). Through the anointing, Moses is to "make holy" (קדשׁ *qādaš*, vv. 9-11, 13). Moses is to wash Aaron and his sons, and so purify the priesthood. The most intense outcome of the three verbs is that the altar of burnt offering will become "most holy," i.e., "holy of holies" (v. 10). Moses must transpose the visible objects that have been constructed into something they have not been, and could not be, without his authority.

Even the priesthood of Aaron comes to its existence only through Moses and derives its very life from Moses. Indeed, it is startling and telling that in this extended Priestly sequence of chaps. 25–40 (which does not include 32), Aaron, the paradigmatic priest, is only a passive recipient of God's action through Moses. (And in chap. 32, the only text in which Aaron acts, he does less

than well!) The priestly office of Aaron is legitimate and important to Israel, but it belongs on a plane of authority quite secondary to, and derived from, the unrivaled, elemental, and personal power of Moses.

Once more, the text reviews the complete inventory of all that is to house the holy. Three matters in the course of this recital of obedience may interest us. First, Moses does act on the "first day." In the constitutive mystery of liturgy, this is something of a primordial event, whereby Israel begins again. So Joseph Blenkinsopp draws a compelling parallel between creation, which is "finished" (Gen 2:1), and tabernacle, which is "finished."[200]

Second, it is striking that of the three crucial verbs we have cited in God's command, only one is present. Nowhere in this text of obedience is the verb *anoint* (*māšaḥ*) or *consecrate* (*qādaš*) used. The third verb, *wash,* occurs twice. In its second usage (v. 31), Moses is not, as the Hebrew text has it, even the single subject of the verb, for Aaron and his sons now join in the washing. Thus Moses' action seems to be greatly reduced.

But, third, the most striking rhetorical feature is that Moses "did as Yahweh commanded." After this general statement in v. 16, the formula occurs seven times in a subordinate position (vv. 19, 21, 23, 25, 27, 29, 32). Seven times may bespeak total, complete obedience. It may also reflect the shape of "new creation," which takes place in seven acts. Moses has done all, and everything is "finished."

The verb rendered "finished" has already been used in 39:32, where the workmen have finished. Now, however, Moses finishes with theological authorization (v. 33). The verb for "finish" (*kālâ*) here is the one used in Gen 2:1 to conclude the work of creation. In this cultic action of Moses, however, this is a new "finishing." A new world begins in a new time. The new creation is not yet visible in the world. It is offered to Israel only in worship. What now happens in worship, therefore, is more than the completion of creation begun in Gen 1:1–2:4*a*. It is the initiation of a new creation wherein the power and presence of God are fully present in the earth.

200. Blenkinsopp, "The Structure of P," 275-92.

REFLECTIONS

Moses has initiated, at the behest of God, a mode and means whereby God's very self can now be present in the world. This text does not lend itself to the notion that holy acts can be undertaken or replicated by any among us. In this text, we are permitted a glimpse into the awesome, inscrutable moment of authorization, in which an enduring and reliable religious practice is made possible. Having this text is like being present at the institution of a sacrament. Israel expresses a conviction that, in this irrepeatable moment, a way has been opened whereby the holy God becomes present, palpable, and visible in the earth. God who has bestowed upon us sacraments as "visible means" of "invisible grace."

1. Moses' inimitable act is one of full, comprehensive, and massive obedience. Moses neither initiates nor imagines the tabernacle. It is all given through the magisterial speech of God.

2. The fact that Moses' obedience is voiced seven times, and the fact that this is the "first day," suggests that this is a new act of creation in which the world begins again. In this text, we are "present at creation." (This text in its final form is dated closely to the time of Isa 43:18-19, when another poetic figure in Israel sang lyrically about a "new thing" wrought by God.) This text obviously accepts that what is done in the cultic apparatus is indeed real work that affects everything decisively.

3. In a profane, self-sufficient society like ours, interpretation will usefully dwell on the specificity of religious symbolism that powerfully transforms reality. Against both profanation and universalizing religion, the symbolization completed by Moses is specific. Moses is seen to be the one who "makes holy" at a time and place, and thereby institutes a fresh possibility in a world that has become flat and hopeless. Without denigrating morality, piety, social policy, or doctrine, this text affirms that holy acts by holy persons in holy places give access to the liberating, healing, forgiving power of the holy God.

4. The work is finished! Everything has been done that can be done. This cultic horizon is now kept open eschatologically. Everything is now completed and in readiness, awaiting God's assured coming. But even now, Moses and Israel engage only in an act of hope.

This text has powerful echoes in the Fourth Gospel. In John 19:30, the declaration from the cross, "It is finished" (τετέλεσται *tetelestai*) is a triumphant cry asserting that God's purpose has been fully accomplished. In John 4:34, 5:36, and 17:4, Jesus asserts that he will finish God's work. These fundamental religious figures (Moses and Jesus), who defy our explanation, do indeed accomplish something transformative and irreversibly intended by God.

This daring statement of completion, which still waits for the presence, invites us to reflect on God's continuing work of "finishing" our lives as creatures.

Biblical hope, for both Jews and Christians, is always the celebration of what is finished and the waiting for that yet to be finished. In this text, the accent is on what is finished. Nonetheless, there is waiting, for Moses' splendid, perfectly constituted "holy place" still awaits its awesome Inhabitant. It is always like that with our human ways of hosting the holy—keeping all in readiness, waiting for the One whom we invite to "come be our guest" (cf. Matt 25:1-13).

EXODUS 40:34-38, THE GLORY OF THE LORD

NIV

³⁴Then the cloud covered the Tent of Meeting, and the glory of the LORD filled the tabernacle. ³⁵Moses could not enter the Tent of Meeting because the cloud had settled upon it, and the glory of the LORD filled the tabernacle.

³⁶In all the travels of the Israelites, whenever the cloud lifted from above the tabernacle, they would set out; ³⁷but if the cloud did not lift, they did not set out—until the day it lifted. ³⁸So the cloud of the LORD was over the tabernacle by day, and fire was in the cloud by night, in the sight of all the house of Israel during all their travels.

NRSV

34Then the cloud covered the tent of meeting, and the glory of the LORD filled the tabernacle. ³⁵Moses was not able to enter the tent of meeting because the cloud settled upon it, and the glory of the LORD filled the tabernacle. ³⁶Whenever the cloud was taken up from the tabernacle, the Israelites would set out on each stage of their journey; ³⁷but if the cloud was not taken up, then they did not set out until the day that it was taken up. ³⁸For the cloud of the LORD was on the tabernacle by day, and fire was in the cloudᵃ by night, before the eyes of all the house of Israel at each stage of their journey.

ᵃ Heb *it*

COMMENTARY

The work on the tabernacle was finished (כלה *kālâ;* 39:32). Moses' work of legitimating the tabernacle is also finished (*kālâ;* 40:33). Everything that could be done by human agents is now complete. What remains unfinished is that which only Yahweh can do. Yahweh had promised, "Have them make me a sanctuary, so that I may dwell [שכן *šākan*] among them" (25:8 NRSV). Now the sanctuary is complete, and Israel awaits the Dweller for whom the tabernacle is constructed.

This is obviously the literary conclusion of the book of Exodus. It is also the theological conclusion of a priestly theory of presence and the liturgical culmination of the work commanded in chaps. 25–31 and enacted in 36:8–40:33. Indeed, for the book of Exodus, it is for this moment and this event of presence that all of creation has been preparation. Creation is God's work with the goal of God's full and glorious presence. The tabernacle is the vehicle through which the glory of God sojourns with Israel. It is also the means by which the glory of God can be present in sovereign ways in the midst of the whole earth.

This brief text explicates two quite distinctive but related themes: presence (vv. 34-35) and guidance (vv. 36-38). In the first, God is static, settled, and stationary. In the second, God is on the move and under way. Each theme is important to the completed tradition of Israel and to the faith of Israel.

40:34-35. The affirmation of presence is expressed in two devices: cloud and glory. The "cloud" does not refer to an overcast sky, but is a standard device to signify presence and at the same time to keep God hidden, remote, and inaccessible. The cloud "covers"—i.e., surrounds—the tabernacle and "settles" (*šākan*) upon the tent of meeting. The "glory," in contrast, is a bright light that is nearly physical in its power and appearance. It "fills" the tabernacle, so forcefully that even Moses cannot enter the place.

The intent and effect of "cloud" and "glory" are to assert that the cult Moses has authorized does indeed host the real presence of God, which has faithfully, specifically, visibly, and powerfully come. This presence-filled place becomes the center and focus of Israel's life. This company of erstwhile slaves now becomes the caretakers, custodians, and "possessors" of the very place and device where the glory of God has chosen to dwell on earth. God has taken up habitation, not in the world's grand palaces, but among a slave band in the wilderness. In 24:15-18, a closely related text, the cloud and the glory are at the mountain. The process of 25:1–40:33 has transferred the cloud and the glory from the mountain to the tabernacle, thus making the presence mobile.

40:36-38. The process of making the cloud and the glory mobile prepares us for a very different theme. Now the verbs are active: "take up" (עלה ʿālâ) and "journey" (נסע nāsaʿ). The tabernacle is the locus of cloud and glory, but the cloud would "lift up and go." In this second part of the paragraph, the "glory" is not mentioned, but now the cloud is paired with "the fire." This pairing looks back to 13:20-22; cloud and fire are devices for protection and guidance for sojourning Israel, both day and night. These concealing forms of presence accompany and lead Israel in its dangerous travels. Gerhard von Rad has suggested that "glory" is a vehicle for presence that has displaced the more primitive and material (and, therefore, awkward) presence in the ark.[201] Given that possibility, reference should be made to Num 10:33-36. In that text, the cloud is over Israel, but it is the ark that sits, acts, and rests in order to guide

---

201. von Rad, *Studies in Deuteronomy*, 37-44. For a more recent and comprehensive review of the problem, see T. N. D. Mettinger, *The Dethronement of Sabbath: Studies in the Shem and Kabod Theologies* (Land: CWK Gleerup, 1982).

---

and protect Israel. One can see that, in the collage of ark-cloud-fire-glory, Israel struggles to articulate presence that is powerfully known and confidently trusted but that has not been made directly available for administration.

This passage accomplishes for Israel two important gains. First, it has provided a centering place of reliable, abiding presence. Second, because of the presence, this community cannot stay centered in a place but must be on the move. This is a profound tension both in the character of God and in the destiny of Israel. God yearns to be in an available place for Israel, but this God is always on the move (cf. 2 Sam 7:6-7). Israel wants a safe place, but must be on the way, powered by a promise yet unfulfilled.

This tension is well accomplished in this paragraph, so that vv. 34-35 address the need for a place, and vv. 36-38 address the need for a traveling presence. This shrewd theological tradition speaks about and affirms both.

REFLECTIONS

1. There is an assurance in this text that the very presence of God abides, continually, reliably, enduringly. Moreover, that abiding presence is not just a good idea or a personal experience. Rather, it is a visible, identifiable, liturgic enactment to which the community has recourse and in which the community may have confidence. The visible, institutional place of worship is a place of real presence.

To be sure, the Reformed tradition is uneasy and nervous about such claims, and there have no doubt been overstatements and abuses of the gift of presence, often in the interest of elitism and priestly advantage. Nonetheless, the claim of presence, championed as we might expect by a Priestly tradition, is a powerful insistence that zeal for "reform" does not lead the community to live in the "real absence." God is willing to be present with God's people.

The tabernacle establishment and its claim of presence do indeed curb God's freedom to come and go at will. But it is God's own command that has authorized this liturgic arrangement. Whatever limitation on God's freedom is required by sustained cultic presence, it is a limitation growing out of God's own resolve and commitment. This conviction of centered, cultic presence is crucial to the wilderness community. It is likewise crucial to a community of faith that makes its way in a world of emptied, one-dimensional profanation.

2. The God who stays is the God who goes, travels with, and keeps safe. God's people are not sent out alone in the world, for alone they lack resources for survival. Already in the ancestral stories of Genesis, the recurrent promise is, "I will be with you" (Gen 28:15; 46:4; cf. Exod 33:14). Our text seeks to express in concrete, visible ways the willingness and capacity of Yahweh to travel with this people. This willingness distinguishes the God of the Bible from other kinds of gods bound to a place.

The conviction of God's "traveling mercies" is evident in a variety of texts. Among the more familiar are Pss 23:4a, 91:9-13; and 121:5-7. Israel knows that in every dangerous circumstance, its path is transformed because of this accompanying presence.

3. This particular text has managed to join two themes that are not easily related. The ideas of a place of presence and a traveling guidance are in tension. This text uses "glory" for the notion of a placed presence, "fire" for traveling presence, and "cloud" for both. The imaginative quality of the affirmation is not unlike the later, daring affirmation of the Trinity in the early church, a liturgical formulation for holding together what is in profound tension. The connection of *faithful abiding* and *powerful accompaniment* is exactly what we experience in our most treasured, intimate human relations. It is no less so for the God of Israel.

4. The Priestly presentation of these claims of presence may strike us as somewhat crude, primitive, and mechanical. The Bible makes no apology for that, and neither should we. I suggest two reasons for refusing such a critique. First, if such a notion of abiding presence and powerful accompaniment seems awkward, then consider the alternative of a profane world without presence. Indeed, the brutalizing world of technological consumerism is a world of "real absence." In that world, there is no ordering center to which one may refer, but only endless, fleeting reference points. Life with a "real absence" is a world likely to be fraught with anxiety and to end in exhaustion and despair. This is not a special pleading for faith but a recognition that humans are indeed marked by fragility, vulnerability, and mortality. For such persons, the reality of presence matters enormously, even though we have poor ways in which to speak about it. In the end, one may not mumble somewhere between real presence and real absence. One must face that it is a stark either/or. Israel has cast its lot and voiced its text in a conviction of presence. Israel has concluded that "absence" is for fools (cf. Pss 10:4; 14:1; Luke 12:20-21).

Second, this crude, elemental notion of presence is characteristic of the biblical "scandal of particularity." It may be that "God is everywhere." But this God who is everywhere has chosen and designated times and places. Israel's faith does not operate with generalities and generic claims but is always concrete. Thus it is congruent with Israel's way in the world to confess that in this construct of the tabernacle, the omnipresent God has taken up residence, and Israel has guarded crucial access to holiness.

5. These two themes of presence are in the NT transposed into christological affirmations, where Jesus has become the mode and place of real presence.

The theme of *abiding presence* is taken up particularly in the Fourth Gospel. Jesus promises those who keep the word that he will "make a home with them" (14:23). The Fourth Gospel witnesses to Jesus' assured presence in the church. He is the One who "abides."

The theme of *traveling fidelity*, on the other hand, is more fully reflected in the synoptic portrayal of Jesus. He is "on the way" with his disciples, instructing and guiding them (cf. Mark 10:32). Indeed, much of his ministry with his disciples is "conversation on the way." The conclusion of Matthew's Gospel is a summons to put the church on the way: "Go" (Matt 28:19). It is precisely to that company of travelers that Jesus promised, "I am with you always" (Matt. 28:20).

Thus in both modes the presence is reassigned to Jesus. The affirmation that is enacted by Moses and embodied by Jesus is that in staying and in going, the faithful do not live in a world of absence but before a Presence whose glory and splendor transforms everything.

6. The ultimate promise of the gospel, already given as the "gospel beforehand" by Moses, is that God's presence will be fully known on earth. Thus it is promised concerning the new heaven and new earth:

The tabernacle of God is among mortals.
He will tabernacle with them as their God;
they will be his people,
and God himself will be with them.
(Rev 21:3, author's translation)

The noun and verb translated "tabernacle" echo the noun משכן *miškān* ("tabernacle") and the verb שכן (*šākan,* "to sojourn"). What Moses has made possible locally will in the end be true cosmically. The earth shall be filled with the glory of God, and all creation shall be fully inhabited by God's glory. All of that is already present inchoately in our text. It is taken as a promise from Moses that God's healing presence and God's protective accompaniment are intended for all the earth. And when that presence and accompaniment are fully actualized, it is no wonder that heaven and earth break out in wondrous doxology.

In the meantime, until the full coming of presence, the daily pastoral word is much more concrete and immediate. But it is the same word. God intends not only that slaves be rescued but that rescued slaves be transformed in, by, for, and with divine presence.

We are at the finish of Exodus. The workmen finished (39:32). Then Moses finished (40:33). And now God has finished (40:34-38). The seer of Revelation also anticipates a "finish" (Rev 21:3). In our candid self-knowledge, we pray hungrily that God should "finish" for our good. Our prayer for this presence, however, is not a desperate prayer. It is urgent, but it is also confident and bold. Such confidence is grounded in, and informed by, the sacramental enactment by Moses in this text before our very eyes. We dare also say, "It is finished." That lyrical affirmation is part celebration and part anticipation, all grateful, joyous, and confident.

THE BOOK OF LEVITICUS

INTRODUCTION, COMMENTARY, AND REFLECTIONS
BY
WALTER C. KAISER, JR.

THE BOOK OF
LEVITICUS

INTRODUCTION

F ew books of the Bible challenge modern readers like Leviticus. In fact, even the most venturesome individuals, who aspire to read through the whole Bible, usually run out of enthusiasm as they begin to read this third book of the Bible. However, such initial discouragement may be mitigated when we realize that Leviticus discloses the character of God in important ways. One central concern involves the oft-repeated injunction: "Be holy, for I am holy" (11:44-45; 19:2; 20:26). (The Hebrew root for "holy" [קדשׁ *qōdeš*] occurs as a verb, noun, or adjective 150 times in Leviticus.) Moreover, this book calls upon both priests and people constantly to "distinguish between the holy and the profane [common], between the unclean and the clean" (10:10).

THE NAME LEVITICUS

The Greek translators called this third book of the Bible *Leuitikon*, "the Levitical book." Our English title derives from the Greek one, but through the Latin translation. Oddly, the Levites, as such, are mentioned only in 25:32-34, even though all Israelite priests were members of the tribe of Levi.

Leviticus belongs to the section of the Bible that Jewish tradition designated as the *Torah*, "law" or "instruction." This sense of תורה (*tôrâ*)—an extension of that noun in passages such as Deut 1:5; 4:8; 17:18-20; 33:4—applies to everything from Genesis to Deuteronomy. Eventually this same corpus of material came to be known (since 160 CE) by the Greek term *Pentateuch*, the "five-sectioned" work.

As with most works in antiquity, this third book of the Torah is identified by its opening word ויקרא (*wayyiqrā'*, "And he [the LORD] called"). The rabbinic name for this book is *tôrat kōhănîm*, a title that can be translated "instruction *for* the priests" (hence, rules and regulations by which priests will conduct their services) or "instruction *of* [or *by*] the priests" (hence, teaching and guidance offered to the people by the priests). This double dimension of the rabbinic title allows us to understand the dual focus of Leviticus: The priesthood is instructed in proper rules for officiating, observing purification, and administering at the sanctuary; but the priests also teach the people what God requires of all Israelites.

THE CONTENT OF LEVITICUS

Except for the brief historical narratives in 10:1-7 and 24:10-16, the book of Leviticus focuses initially on instructions, many of which involve worship of the most holy God as well as the purity of the people. Oversight of such worship is given over to Aaron and his sons, that part of the tribe of Levi designated for the task of officiating at the altar.

The first seven chapters present the laws of sacrifice. Chapters 1–3 articulate the spontaneously motivated sacrifices (burnt, grain, and peace), chaps. 4–5 deal with sacrifices required for expiation of sin (sin and guilt), and chaps. 6–7 rehearse these same five sacrifices, with special emphasis on directions for the priests.

The second main section (chaps. 8–10) concentrates on the priesthood. After their installation (chap. 8), the priests begin to officiate (chap. 9). However, improper officiating could lead to death, as in the case of Aaron's two sons, Nadab and Abihu (chap. 10).

The focus changes to matters of purity in chaps. 11–15. Chapter 11 lists the marks and the names of clean and unclean animals. But impurity of various sorts may also arise from childbirth (chap. 12), from skin diseases and various infections in houses and clothing (chaps. 13–14), and from aspects relating to the sexual life (chap. 15).

Chapter 16 appears central to the life of the worshiping community. One of the best known of all the sections in Leviticus, it is read in the synagogue on Yom Kippur. On this day, according to the ancient prescriptions, the high priest entered the innermost sanctum of the sanctuary with the blood of a goat that had been sacrificed as a sin offering. Afterward, a second goat was released, never to be seen again in the camp.

With chaps. 1–16 as the first major block, chaps. 17–27 constitute the second division, most of which is often termed the Holiness Code. It opens with a prologue (chap. 17) and ends with an epilogue (26:3-46). Chapters 18–20 deal with holiness in the family, especially its sexual activity. Chapters 21–25 return to the ritual life of the community with regulations for the priests, Israelite marriages, mourning rites, and the holy days and feasts. Probably no biblical chapter is quoted or alluded to more in prophetic literature than Leviticus 26. It portrays the alternative prospects for either reward or punishment, depending on Israel's obedience or disobedience.

Most scholars consider chap. 27 to be an appendix. It speaks to the matters of redemption of persons, animals, or lands dedicated to the Lord by vow. Its closing formula (v. 34) is almost a repetition of 26:46.

The content of Leviticus exhibits a plan and a reasonably clear structure. Basically, chaps. 1–16 are addressed to the priests, while chaps. 17–27 focus on priestly instructions for the people. The first division provides directions concerning acts of officiating and purifying directed to the priests, while the second division emphasizes holiness among all Israelites. Despite this basic distinction, chap. 11 fits better in the holiness section (chaps. 17–27), since it provides the first reference to the theme of holiness (11:44-45). Indeed, 11:46-47 ("These are the regulations [tōrâ] concerning animals. . . . You must distinguish between the unclean and the clean") may have originally been part of the holiness law, but it may have been moved forward since it stipulates a basic duty of the priests—namely, to "distinguish between the holy and the profane, between the unclean and the clean" (10:10).[1]

LITERARY FORM OF LEVITICUS

The formula "the LORD said to Moses" (or a similar one) occurs fifty-six times. (In three of these fifty-six formulations, Aaron is named along with Moses [11:1; 14:33; 15:1], and once Aaron is addressed alone [10:8].) Seventeen of the twenty-seven chapters begin with the formula "And the LORD said. . . ." Leviticus, more than any other OT book, claims to be a divine word for humanity.

Even though the Greek and Latin origins for the name of this book would tend to limit it as a manual for priests from the tribe of Levi, who indeed are mentioned nearly two hundred times, approximately half of the divine address formulas specifically involve all the people. For example, 1:2 states, "Speak to the Israelites and say to them."

Only in the epilogue to the Holiness Code (26:3-46) does a prose composition appear. Two other narratives make brief appearances: the tragic death of Aaron's sons Nadab and Abihu (10:1-7), and the incarceration and stoning of the blasphemer (24:10-16).

Aside from these brief narratives, Leviticus is a book of rituals and laws. The style we encounter here is very similar to what we would expect in legal documents. Leviticus is filled with specialized terminology, technical vocabulary, and repeated formulaic statements. Even words used frequently in other parts of Scripture are often highly nuanced in their usages in this book.[2]

To summarize: Leviticus is a book that offers rituals and prescriptions for officiating priests and a purified people.

THE PURPOSE OF LEVITICUS

The book is given to Israel so that the people might live holy lives in fellowship with a holy God. But that intent does not tell the whole story, for a greater purpose is also served

1. Baruch A. Levine, *The JPS Torah Commentary: Leviticus* (Philadelphia: Jewish Publication Society, 1989) xvi-xvii.
2. As Levine (*JPS Torah Commentary* xviii-xix) has shown by citing three such formulas.

in furnishing Israel with laws that secure their well-being: They are to be a blessing to the nations. As expressed in the covenant with Abraham (see Gen 12:2-3), these beneficiaries of God's covenant are to be mediators of blessing to the nations at large. Seen in this light, the Levitical laws are intended to train, teach, and prepare the people to be God's instruments of grace to others. Consequently, one of the key purposes for the law of Leviticus is to prepare Israel for its world mission. What Israel communicates most immediately to the nations is the character of God, especially the deity's unapproachable holiness. Israel's disclosure of God's holiness to the nations is visible primarily through the sacrificial system. All can see that any sin, no matter what the status or rank of the individual, is an offense against a holy God.

The importance of God's holiness is also evident in the severity of the penalties attached to some of the laws in Leviticus. Although we mortals are often tempted to play down the seriousness of sin, God's holiness demands intolerance of sin and impurity.

However, God's holiness also involves a positive side: "The LORD, the LORD, the compassionate and gracious God, slow to anger, abounding in love and faithfulness, maintaining love to thousands, and forgiving wickedness, rebellion and sin" (Exod 34:6-7 NIV). What the austere law demands, and what mortals find themselves unable to do, a loving and forgiving Lord provides in the same law that upholds so high a standard. Mercy and remission of sins are available for all who turn to God with a repentant heart.

One of the most frequently repeated terms in Leviticus is *atonement;* it occurs almost fifty times. In connection with the sacrifices, the members of the Israelite community heard the reassuring words repeatedly offered: "The priest will make atonement for [that person's] sin, and [that one] will be forgiven" (e.g., 4:20, 26, 31, 35).

Leviticus 17:11, 14 provides a key statement regarding atonement: "Because the life of a creature [literally life of the flesh] is in the blood." Blood outside the flesh is equivalent to death; however, blood in all creatures makes possible life. Somehow, according to the prevailing belief among ancient Israelites, animal blood could affect mortal sin. Some have suggested that a sacrifice was effective because of an accompanying divine word.

Some Christian readers think the Levitical law was intended to be typical and prophetic of Messiah and his work of redemption. Perhaps some such thought pattern prepared John the Baptist for his sudden declaration when he met Jesus of Nazareth for the first time: "Look, the Lamb of God, who takes away the sin of the world!" (John 1:29*b* NIV).

One more purpose for Leviticus must be noted: to teach Israel and all subsequent readers how to worship God. True worship can best be expressed by joining the visible forms of the religious life with holiness of the worshiper's life. The external forms are important, but they do not suffice to denote the proper worth and value that a person is attempting to express to God. Although persons must not divorce the sacred from the secular, since God is Lord over all, they must be able to distinguish between what is holy and what is common or profane, between the clean and the unclean. But the holiness of God dictates that any approach to God must acknowledge the yawning gulf between the character of

God and the character of all humans. Thus the distinctions between the holy and the ordinary help mortals to realize that God is unapproachably different from humans.

THE MEANING OF SACRIFICE

Whereas the word *sacrifice* in today's common usage means something of value that a person gives up for the sake of some greater value, it did not have that connotation in the ancient world of Israel and its neighbors. For the ancients, *sacrifice* meant a religious rite, something someone offered to some deity or power.

Our English word *sacrifice* comes from a Latin word meaning "to make something sacred, [or] holy." As the object is offered, it passes from the common or mundane world to the sacred realm; it is consecrated. The heart of the sacrificial act, then, is the transference of property from the profane to the sacred realm. The most common Hebrew equivalent for "sacrifice" is קרבן (*qorbān*), meaning "something [that is] brought near [to the altar]." Thus the connection of sacrifice with the altar and meeting place with God is evident in the OT. But what is brought must be a מתנה (*mattānâ*, a "gift"). That probably explains why game and fish were unacceptable as sacrifices, since, as David declared, "I will not sacrifice to the LORD my God burnt offerings that cost me nothing" (2 Sam 24:24 NIV).

In the last century, a huge literature has developed on both the *origin* and the *significance* of sacrifice in the OT and the ancient Near East.[3] Of the two, the question of origin has been the most exasperating, since neither the OT nor the cultures of the ancient Near East provide clear evidence about the subject. Scholars have propounded a number of theories, but no theory has ever commanded anything approaching a consensus. Some have suggested that sacrifices originally belonged either to totemic practices or to ancestor worship.[4] But such speculative theories have now been abandoned.

Generally, researchers in comparative religions have identified four purposes for sacrifice: (1) to provide food for the deity; (2) to assimilate the life force of the sacrificial animal; (3) to effect a union with the deity; and (4) to persuade the deity to give the offerer help as a result of the gift.[5] Some think the first three purposes are not found in Israel and the fourth is in evidence only to a lesser degree than elsewhere in the Near East.

"The feature which distinguishes Israelite and Canaanite rituals from those of other Semitic peoples is that, when an animal is sacrificed, the victim, or at least a part of it, is burnt upon the altar. This rite did not exist in Mesopotamia or in Arabia, but it did exist among the Moabites and the Ammonites, according to allusions in the Bible [1 Kgs 11:8;

---

3. For analysis of the earlier discussion, see D. Davies, "An Interpretation of Sacrifice in Leviticus," *ZAW* 89 (1977) 387-99.

4. One of the standard books is Roland de Vaux's *Ancient Israel: Its Life and Institutions,* trans. John McHugh (New York: McGraw-Hill, 1961); see chap. 12, "The Origin of Israelite Ritual," 433-46. De Vaux's work continues a line of study set forth in J. Pedersen, *Israel, Its Life and Culture* (Copenhagen: V. Pio-P. Branner, 1926) vols. 1 and 2 (Copenhagen: Branner og Korch, 1940) vols. 3 and 4.

5. As set forth by Jacob Milgrom, *Leviticus 1-16,* AB (New York: Doubleday, 1991) 440.

1 Kings 18; 2 Kgs 5:17; 10:18-27; Jer 7:9; 11:12, 13, 17; 32:29]."[6] Clearly, there are strong affinities in the terms and practices for sacrifice between the west Semitic peoples.

Our knowledge of west Semitic peoples comes from three sources: (1) allusions to or condemnations of the ritual practices in Moab, Ammon, and Edom found in the Bible; (2) inscriptions from Phoenicia or its colonies to its cultic practice; and (3) the terms for sacrifice used in the texts from Ras Shamra, i.e., ancient Ugarit. De Vaux provides evidence for the first source in the quotation above. Evidence for the second can be found in the Phoenician and Punic inscriptions. The most important of these are the Carthage price list and the price list of Marseilles, a stone taken from North Africa. These lists fix the amount of money to be paid for each type of sacrifice, including the portion of the sacrifice that is given to the priest and the part that is given to the person making the sacrifice. The four sacrifices mentioned are the *minḥâ*, the *kālîl*, the *sewaʿat*, and the *šelem kalil*. In the *kālîl*, almost everything is burned on the altar except for a small portion given to the priest. In the *sewaʿat*, the breast and the leg are given to the priest and the rest to the person making the sacrifice. At Ras Shamra, archaeologists have discovered texts dating from the fourteenth century BCE with a number of similar terms to those used in Israel's sacrificial vocabulary. They include *dbh*, "sacrifice" (cf. Hebrew זבח *zebaḥ*); *šlmm*, "peace offering" (cf. Hebrew שלמים *šelāmîm*); *šrp*, "burnt offering"; and perhaps *ʾtm*, "guilt offering(?)" (cf. Hebrew אשם *ʾāšām*).

Accordingly, whether through close contact with each other or through other means as yet unnoticed, there were some very strong connections with at least the sacrificial terms, and in some cases with some of the practices, in the west Semitic world of the first and second millennia BCE.

But if the origin of sacrifice in Israel and the ancient Near East remains elusive, what may we say about the religious significance of sacrifice? Some anthropologists and historians of religion offer explanations based on cross-cultural comparisons and emphasize the social function of such rituals.[7] These judgments may be based on slim analogies. Also, some Christian readers have moved beyond the evidence by using NT sacrificial concepts to explain the meaning of the OT sacrificial system. Both parties can err by reading into the situation outside materials before the text itself is given a chance to speak.

Some scholars have argued that sacrifice symbolically expresses the interior feelings of the person making the offering. But, as such, it can be an act with many aspects: It is a gift to God, but it is more; it is a means of achieving union with God, but it is more; it is a means of expiating sin, but it is more. Often all three aspects are present, including a response of a conscience motivated by a desire to obey God.

As a *gift*, the act of sacrifice acknowledges that everything a person has comes from God (see 1 Chron 29:14). And just as a contract between men is often sealed by sharing a meal together (cf. Gen 26:28-30; 31:44-54), so also *communion* and *union with God* are

6. De Vaux, *Ancient Israel*, 440, see also 438.

7. For an excellent recent example, see G. Anderson, "Sacrifice and Sacrificial Offerings (OT)," *The Anchor Bible Dictionary* 5:871-86.

often achieved by sharing a sacrificial meal together. Moreover, since the life of the sacrificial animal is symbolized by its blood (Lev 17:11), sacrifice also carries *expiatory* value.

Some scholars have focused on the polemics of the prophets against sacrifices as an indication that they condemned outright the practice of sacrifice (e.g., Isa 1:11-17; Jer 7:21-22; Hos 6:6; Amos 5:21-27; Mic 6:6-8). But such a conclusion misunderstands the prophets. Never did they intend their words to be taken as an unconditional condemnation of the cult and its sacrifices. Instead, theirs was a qualified negation in which they said in effect, "What is the use of *this* [offering sacrifices] without *that* [a proper heart relationship as the basis for offering sacrifices to God]?" Or to put the proverb in another form: "Not this, but that," which is another way of saying, "Not so much this as that." The prophets were opposed to formalism and the mere external practice of religion without corresponding interior affections or repentance of the heart (e.g., 1 Sam 15:22; Isa 29:13).

No less concerned were the wisdom writers who verbalize the same message: "The LORD detests the sacrifice of the wicked,/but the prayer of the upright pleases him" (Prov 15:8 NIV); or "The sacrifice of the wicked is detestable—/how much more so when brought with evil intent" (Prov 21:27 NIV); and "To do what is right and just/is more acceptable to the LORD than sacrifice" (Prov 21:3 NIV).

As a result of such evidence, the older thesis that the pre-exilic prophets repudiated rituals, especially sacrifice, has now been abandoned.[8] It was the abuse, not the practice, of the cult itself that the prophets so thoroughly condemned. For them, ritual activity had no efficacy or value if it was not preceded and motivated by genuine repentance and a proper intention.

However, two texts have continued to haunt biblical scholars since they seem to claim that Israel did not offer sacrifices in the wilderness and was not commanded to do so. The two texts are found in Jeremiah and Amos:

> This is what the LORD Almighty, the God of Israel, says: Go ahead, add your burnt offerings to your other sacrifices and eat the meat yourselves! For when I brought your forefathers out of Egypt and spoke to them, I did not just give them commands about burnt offerings and sacrifices, but I gave them this command: Obey me, and I will be your God and you will be my people.
>
> (Jer 7:21-23*a* NIV)

> Even though you bring me burnt offerings and grain offerings,
> I will not accept them . . . .
> Did you bring me sacrifices and offerings
> forty years in the desert, O house of Israel? (Amos 5:22, 25 NIV)

The NIV has added "just" to Jer 7:22, but this is of little help in rendering the על־דבר (*'al-dĕbār*, NRSV "concerning"; NIV "about"). The dilemma posed by Jeremiah's text, which appears to disclaim any command or knowledge of a practice of sacrifice in the wilderness, is solved by translating *'al-dĕbār* as "for the sake of." This meaning for *'al-dĕbār* is clearly

---

8. For a convenient listing of these scholars dating from 1885 with Julius Wellhausen to P. Volz in 1937, see Milgrom, *Leviticus 1-16,* 482. The thesis of this group of scholars "has been unanimously and convincingly rejected by its successor," argues Milgrom, by scholars such as H. H. Rowley, Y. Kaufmann, R. Rendtorff, and R. de Vaux.

attested in passages such as Gen 20:11, 18; and Ps 79:9. Jeremiah announced that God had not spoken "for the sake of" sacrifices and offerings, i.e., for sacrifices in and of themselves. Jeremiah (chaps. 7–10) provided a strong denunciation of the people's penchant for carrying out external religion without any corresponding interior intentions and desires. Indeed, the very sacrifices named by Jeremiah, the עלה (*ʿōlâ*) and the זבח (*zebaḥ*), could apply only to those voluntarily brought by individuals and not to those of the community as a whole.

The solution for the Amos text is different. His question drips with sarcasm and hyperbole. Did Israel indeed bring sacrifices and offerings to the Lord during those forty years in the wilderness? Amos inquired with more than a slight touch of sarcasm. The implication of Amos's pointed barb seems to be that Israel had lifted their sacrifices up to the idols they had made for themselves. Once again the priority of the heart and the intentions is asserted over the mere external performance of the cult.

But this whole discussion raises a further point: What counts for righteous behavior in the OT? Is it the act itself, or does it also involve the disposition and the intent of the sacrificer? Even though many have tried to make the case for the former, attributing most, if not all, of OT cultic and moral practice to the mere carrying out of perfunctory acts, forms, and rituals, the case for intentionality as a major factor in OT cult cannot be avoided. Proverbs 21:27 denounces bringing sacrifices with evil intent (בזמה *bĕzimmâ*). Sanctification begins with a declaration that someone intends to sacrifice and then continues with an announcement that the individual intends to follow through with it. One story in Scripture reports how a mother attempted to dedicate stolen money to the Lord by making an oral declaration (see Judg 17:3).

At times, scholars have offered rationalistic explanations for the sacrificial system in the OT. Moses Maimonides (1135–1204 CE) develops such an approach to the sacrificial legislation when he describes it as a concession to human frailty. As this line of thinking goes, the Israelites could not imagine a religion without sacrifice, such as they had witnessed while in Egypt. Thus sacrifices to Yahweh were permitted to wean the Israelites away from making sacrifices to other deities. In this view, sacrifices were a temporary expedient due to the pressure of idolatry. However, Maimonides draws no such conclusion but goes on to affirm that when Messiah returns, the sacrificial rites must again be ready and the Temple must be rebuilt for Messiah's use.[9]

The sacrificial cult came to an end when the Romans burned the Temple in 70 CE and ordered that it not be rebuilt. Another institution, the synagogue, had arisen during the years of the Babylonian captivity. It was a place of prayer and study, but it made no provision for sacrifices.

---

9. Nachmanides did not agree with the explanation that sacrifices were merely to protect Israel from falling into idolatry. He argued that Abel and Noah brought sacrifices at a time when idolatry had not yet appeared.

THE HOLINESS CODE

Leviticus 18–23 and 25–26 were first identified as an independent corpus in 1866 by K. Graf.[10] Graf also proposed Ezekiel as the author of this corpus, for Graf found many linguistic ties with the book of Ezekiel. In 1874, A. Kayser accepted Graf's thesis and noted other linguistic characteristics that he had observed, while adding, most significantly, Leviticus 17.[11] Then in 1877, A. Klostermann gave the corpus, Leviticus 17–26, its name—the Holiness Code—and explored its ties with Ezekiel.[12] However, Julius Wellhausen ensured that this hypothesis would have a permanent berth in the scholarly literature.[13] Wellhausen maintained that Leviticus 17–26 occupied a singularly distinct position within the Priestly (P) document, which he dated to the last years of the exile.

In the late nineteenth and early twentieth centuries the debate about Leviticus 17–26 continued. In 1894 and 1899, L. Paton published several articles in which he sought to identify three primary strata in this code: the original holiness material, a pre-Priestly corpus that was built on the deuteronomistic program for centralization, and a work by a Priestly redactor.[14] In 1912, B. D. Eerdmans attacked the concept of an independent Holiness Code, for in his view no basic structure held the whole corpus together. He complained that other texts in the Pentateuch issued calls for holiness (e.g., Exod 19:6; 22:30 [31]; Lev 11:44-45; Deut 7:6; 14:2, 21; 26:19; 28:9), so holiness could not be limited to this section.[15] Moreover, the alleged distinctive vocabulary of the Holiness Code occurred in other OT texts. S. Küchler supported Eerdmans's position,[16] but scholars, in the main, were not persuaded by Eerdmans's and Küchler's objections.

G. von Rad's *Studies in Deuteronomy* (1947 [German]; 1953 [English ed.]) marked a dramatic change in the direction of research on the Holiness Code.[17] Von Rad emphasized that this material ought to be attributed to the Yahwist, since the deity's role as speaker was emphasized by the repeated formula "I am Yahweh." With this argument, von Rad started a trend that focused on the growth and development of the sections within the Holiness Code.

In 1961, H. G. Reventlow completed a comprehensive study on the code in which he argued that this corpus evolved at the ancient yearly covenant festival, including traditions

---

10. K. Graf, *Die geschichtlichen Bücher des Alten Testaments: Zwei historische-kritische Untersuchungen* (Leipzig: T. O. Weigel, 1866).

11. A. Kayser, *Das vorexilischen Büch der Urgeschichte Israels und seine Erweiterungen: Ein Beitrag zur Pentateuch-kritik* (Strassburg: C. F. Schmidt's Universitäts-Buchhandlung, 1874).

12. August Klostermann used the term *Holiness Code* for the first time in "Beiträge zur Entstehungsgeschichte des Pentateuchs," *Zeitschrift für Lutherische Theologie für die gesamte Lutherische Theologie und Kirche* 38 (1877) 416. Later he incorporated the term in *Der Pentateuch: Beiträge zu seinem Verständis und seiner Entstehungsgeschichte* (Leipzig: U. Deichert'sche Verlagsbuchhandlung, 1893) 368-69. See also Klostermann's "Ezechiel und das Heiligkeitsgesetz" in the same volume, 419-47.

13. Julius Wellhausen, *Die Composition des Hexateuchs und der historischen Bücher des Alten Testaments* (Berlin: Georg Reimer, 1889) 152-54.

14. For a comprehensive analysis of the positions and bibliography in this discussion of the Holiness Code, see H. T. C. Sun, "An Investigation into the Compositional Integrity of the So-Called Holiness Code (Leviticus 17-26)" (Ph.D. diss., Claremont, 1990).

15. B. D. Eerdmans, *Alttestamentliche Studien 4: Das Buch Leviticus* (Giessen: Töpelmann, 1912).

16. S. Küchler, *Das Heiligkeitsgesetz Lev 17-26: Eine literarkritische Untersuchung* (Königsberg: Kümmel, 1929).

17. G. von Rad, *Studies in Deuteronomy,* trans. D. Stalker (London: SCM, 1953).

from Israel's arrival at Mount Sinai.[18] Older materials came from the wilderness period but were supplemented by later elements. The preacher who delivered the sermons found in this code was probably Moses' successor.

R. Kilian returned to the source-critical approach in 1963 as a means for identifying two major redactions in the basic code.[19] And again, in 1964, C. Feucht promoted the independent existence of the Holiness Code, declaring that it was made up of two collections.[20] But in 1966, K. Elliger published his commentary on Leviticus with a denial that the Holiness Code ever had an independent existence.[21] He theorized that the material was grafted onto the Priestly materials in two stages, each with a supplement, thereby leaving us with four identifiable layers in Leviticus 17–26. In 1976, A. Cholewiński concluded that the Holiness Code had not gone through a major Priestly redaction; instead, Leviticus 17–26 was composed by members of a priesthood who belonged to the deuteronomistic circle.[22]

Most recently, H. T. C. Sun has analyzed both the history of the discussion and the compositional history of the Holiness Code.[23] In his view, the Holiness Code had no existence prior to its present location in the text. His conclusion was based on three arguments: (a) The texts in the Holiness Code appear to be of widely varying ages; (b) there is no conclusive evidence that a compositional layer extends throughout the entire corpus; and (c) some texts appear to have been composed as supplements for other materials in the corpus. Therefore, even though blocks of material appear to stand together (e.g., 18–20, 21–22, 23 and 25), no overall structure unites all of Leviticus 17–26.

Consistent with Sun's work, some scholars express doubts about the Holiness Code as a self-contained, independent document. As a result, some conclude that the holiness corpus was composed in its present position in Leviticus as a continuation of the concerns for ritual purity found in chaps. 11–15.[24]

These chapters, more than any others in the book, emphasize the holiness of God and the fact that Israel is also called to be holy. One command is repeated: "Be holy because I, the LORD your God, am holy" (19:2; 20:7, 26; 21:6, 8), along with a similar declaration: "I am the LORD, who makes them holy" (21:15, 23; 22:9, 16, 32).

The book consistently reminds the reader, "I am the LORD." This refrain, or the expanded one listed below, appears more than thirty times in this latter section (e.g., 18:5; 19:14; 21:12; 22:2; 26:2). Or again: "I am the LORD your God" (e.g., 18:4; 19:3; 20:7; 24:22;

18. H. G. Reventlow, *Das Heiligkeitsgesetz: Formgeschichtlich untersucht* (Neukirchen: Neukirchener Verlag, 1961).

19. R. Kilian, *Literarkritische und formgeschichtliche Untersuchung des Heiligkeitsgesetzes* (Bonn: Peter Hanstein, 1963).

20. C. Feucht, *Untersuchungen zum Heiligkeitsgesetz,* Theologische Arbeiten 20 (Berlin: Evangelische Verlagsanstalt, 1964).

21. K. Elliger, *Leviticus,* HAT (Tübingen: Mohr, 1966).

22. A. Cholewiński, *Heiligkeitsgesetz und Deuteronomium: Eine vergleichende Studie,* AnBib 66 (Rome: Biblical Institute Press, 1976).

23. See note 14 above.

24. This is the conclusion of John E. Hartley, *Leviticus,* WBC (Dallas: Word, 1992) 259-60.

26:1). Finally, this holiness section in Leviticus repeatedly admonishes the reader, "You must obey my laws and be careful to follow my decrees" (e.g., 18:4; 19:3; 20:8; 22:31; 25:18; and throughout chap. 26).

Although these chapters have a distinctive style and content, the absence of any introductory formula in 17:1 would seem to work against the hypothesis that they constitute a volume of laws inserted into Leviticus. Moreover, scholars have been unable to discern an overarching organization, which, if present, would indicate that the chapters had a life of their own outside the book.

Readers may find it difficult to locate chap. 17 in the Holiness Code. It could just as easily be grouped with the preceding chapters with their emphasis on directions for the priests. Yet, though it does not specifically mention the concept of holiness, chap. 17 contains some of the other terminology typical of the holiness section. Chapter 17 may be best regarded as a transitional chapter between the two major sections of the book.

To summarize: Leviticus 17–26 does not appear to be a single, systematic, and consistently ordered document; instead, it is a collection of materials grounded in the affirmation of God's holiness. Chapter 17 functions as a hinge chapter between the first major division, addressed mainly to the priests, and this second major division, which concerns itself with the conduct of the general public.

UNITY, AUTHORSHIP, AND DATE OF LEVITICUS

The colophon at the conclusion of the book places the site for its composition at Sinai at the time when Israel stopped during the first year of the exodus from Egypt: "These are the commands the LORD gave Moses on Mount Sinai for the Israelites" (27:34). This sentiment, of course, stands in contrast with Num 36:13, which has a similar colophon but locates the place for the composition of the materials "on the plains of Moab by the Jordan across from Jericho" (NIV).

Much in Leviticus is consistent with the claim that Israel was still in the wilderness wanderings at the time that most of these laws were promulgated, e.g., the people were dwelling "in the camp" (4:12; 9:11; 10:4-5; 14:3; 17:3; 24:10). Their sanctuary is routinely referred to as the "tent of meeting." Outside the camp lies "the desert" (16:21-22). And entrance into the land of Canaan lies in the future (14:34; 18:3; 19:23; 20:22; 25:2).

The aforementioned references, along with the prominent formula "The LORD said to Moses," help explain why both the synagogue and the church held to the essential unity of this book and to a Mosaic authorship until well into medieval times. The internal claims of the book, in their present shape, argue for the beginning of the forty years of wandering as the canonical setting for Leviticus, with Moses, Aaron, and the Israelites of that generation as the ones who are addressed.

This traditional view stood as the scholarly consensus, with very few exceptions, until the rise of the critical method in the sixteenth and seventeenth centuries. Today, most biblical scholars think that Leviticus (and parts of Genesis, Exodus, and Numbers) originated during post-exilic times in conjunction with the Priestly source, often designated as "P." Julius Wellhausen provided one important formulation of that position.[25]

In Wellhausen's view, the earliest days of Israel's worship were simple, spontaneous, and fairly unstructured. Accordingly, whereas it seemed possible to sacrifice wherever one chose in the days of Samuel (see 1 Sam 16:2), King Josiah, during the 621 BCE revival, made a strong case for limiting sacrifice to the Temple in Jerusalem (see 2 Kings 23). As a result, many scholars have argued that Leviticus reflects this notion of worship at a central shrine. Moreover, with the collapse of the institutions of the kingdom and the Davidic monarchy, the priestly guild in Israel had its first real opportunity to assert its point of view—especially after the Babylonian exile.

Another argument often used on behalf of a late dating for P, and therefore of Leviticus, depends on differences between the books of Kings and Chronicles. Since most scholars agree that Chronicles is post-exilic, and since Chronicles has much to say about worship, whereas Kings has very little to offer on the subject, the similarities between P and Chronicles, especially emphasis on ritual matters, suggest that most of the materials in Leviticus derive from the same period as Chronicles—namely, the post-exilic era.

More recently, Yehezkel Kaufmann, among others, has put forth a third and mediating position. Taking aim at the central thesis of Wellhausen, Kaufmann observes that "fixity in times and rites and absence of 'natural spontaneity' characterize the festivals of ancient Babylonia, Egypt, and all known civilizations. Annual purifications are likewise ubiquitous. . . . That these elements are found in P rather than in JE or D is, in itself, no indication of lateness."[26]

Kaufmann argues that P is pre-exilic but not Mosaic. His reasons are: (a) the laws, institutions, and the terminology of P do not fit in with the post-exilic books of Chronicles, Ezra, and Nehemiah; (b) Deuteronomy and Joshua quote Leviticus along with other P passages, suggesting that P comes before, not after, D;[27] and (c) the rules for war and certain other rituals more closely approximate those mentioned in Judges and Samuel than any other period of time. Scholars who follow this mediating position tend to date P to the early seventh century BCE.

For those who have watched the accumulation of the epigraphic materials gathered from the archaeological discoveries of this century, it comes as little surprise that substantial material in Leviticus appears similar to ancient Near Eastern materials from the second millennium BCE.[28]

25. Julius Wellhausen, *Prolegomena to the History of Israel,* trans. W. Robertson Smith (New York: Meridian, 1957). Originally published in 1878.

26. Yehezkel Kaufmann, *The Religion of Israel,* trans. and abr. M. Greenberg (Chicago: University of Chicago Press, 1960) 178.

27. See, for instance, Milgrom, *Leviticus 1-16,* 9-10. Milgrom follows this discussion with fifteen other arguments for P's antiquity.

28. For example, see E. A. Speiser, "Leviticus and the Critics," in *Yehezkel Kaufmann Jubilee Volume,* ed. M. Haran (Jerusalem: Magnes, 1960) 29-45. Also see William W. Hallo, "Leviticus and Ancient Near Eastern History," in *The Torah: A Modern Commentary,* ed. W. Gunther PLant (New York: Union of American Hebrew Congregations, 1981) 740-48.

Still, it is too early to call for a conclusion to this debate between the traditional, critical, and mediating positions on the date and authorship of Leviticus. If we were to emphasize comparisons with ancient Near Eastern texts, some might discern a tendency for dating Leviticus to the pre-exilic period. Scholars who focus primarily on the internal data will tend to side with the critical resolution, i.e., a post-exilic date, to this question. Pentateuchal studies remain in flux, as the recent studies of Blenkinsopp, Cross, Moberly, and Rendtorff, among others, demonstrate.[29] It is now abundantly clear that there is no sole, higher-critical position; rather, there are a number of quite diverse ways by means of which to understand the origins of the Pentateuch and, hence, Leviticus.

THE THEOLOGY OF LEVITICUS

The keynote to the book of Leviticus is holiness to the Lord, a phrase occurring some 152 times. Leviticus 20:26 exemplifies this concept: "You are to be holy to me because I, the LORD, am holy, and I have set you apart from the nations to be my own."[30]

Leading the way and serving as a model for all other aspects of holiness is the holiness of the deity. In its basic ideology, holiness involves a double separation: distinct *from* and separate *unto/to* someone or something. Thus, God as creator is separate from all creatures. This is the so-called *ontological* gulf that separates beings. God is immortal, omnipotent, omniscient, and totally different from all creatures. But there is another gulf: a *moral* gap between humanity and God because of human sinfulness.

This latter emphasis appears in the second major division of Leviticus (chaps. 17–26). Here individuals are called to act, think, and live holy lives patterned after the norm established by the character of God. The accent is, normally, on the moral rather than the ceremonial and ritual aspects of life.

The first major division of Leviticus treats primarily the sacrificial order and the distinctions between the unclean and the clean. Although the theme of holiness is mentioned directly only once (11:44-45), behind both the sacrificial instructions and the concerns over defilements is the overriding concern for the holiness of God. A holy God graciously provides these rituals to make it possible for mere mortals, who are also sinners, to walk in fellowship with one who is pure. Israel is taught, both in word and in deed, what the holiness of God entails.

The laws of holiness are addressed not to selected individuals but to the entire community of Israel. Instead of attempting to produce a selected group of pure individuals, the laws aim at producing a holy people, a holy nation, who collectively will be a royal priesthood, a rich treasure belonging to God (see Exod 19:5-6). The demonstration of this

---

29. See J. Blenkinsopp, *The Pentateuch: An Introduction to the First Five Books of the Bible,* ABRL (New York: Doubleday, 1992); F. Cross, *Canaanite Myth and Hebrew Epic* (Cambridge, Mass.: Harvard University Press, 1973); R. Moberly, *The Old Testament of the Old Testament: Patriarchal Narratives and Mosaic Yahwism* (Minneapolis: Fortress, 1992); and R. Rendtorff, *The Problem of the Process of the Transmission of the Pentateuch,* trans. J. Schullion, JSOTSup 89 (Sheffield: JSOT, 1990).

30. See John G. Gammie, *Holiness in Israel,* OBT (Philadelphia: Fortress, 1989).

consecration to God is to be displayed by the whole nation in every walk and area of life: family life, community affairs, farming, commerce, and worship of God. Among the ethical duties entailed in this life of holiness by the total community, the book singles out sexual holiness for special emphasis. Even in this most intimate area, holiness of life demands control and regard for the sanctity of life (and not ascetic abstinence).

Holiness has more dimensions than just the vertical aspect of our relations with the divine and the interior dimension of basic self-integrity. There is also the horizontal relationship with others, which comes to full expression in 19:18*b* (often termed the Golden Rule): "Love your neighbor as yourself." Hillel used this verse to summarize the entire Torah: "What is hateful to you, do not do to your fellow."[31] Likewise, Jesus declared that this commandment is second in importance only to the command to "love the LORD your God with all your heart and with all your soul and with all your mind and with all your strength" (Mark 12:28-31 NIV; quoting Deut 6:4-5).

Many have suggested that the "neighbor" in 19:18*b* is a fellow Israelite, but lest some think that this observation limits the scope of this injunction, 19:34 requires this same love to be shown to the resident alien in their midst. And the love extended to such non-Israelites is to be the same sort of love with which Israelites love each other (v. 34*b*).

For those who fail to measure up to the standard of God's holiness, this same Lord has provided a number of reconciling sacrifices. Leviticus describes five major sacrifices. These Israelite sacrifices are unique (even though the institution of sacrifices is common throughout the ancient Near East, many with some of the same names for the sacrifice and often specifying some of the same parts of the animal in the ritual) in their treatment of blood, especially in the expiatory sacrifices.[32]

The word for and notion of "atonement" become important at this point; it occurs forty-five times in this book. The verb כפר (*kipper*, "to atone") used to be understood as cognate with the Arabic root that means "to cover."[33] Thus it was said that the sins in the OT were covered over by the blood of the animals (and in Christian terms, until the final and all-sufficient sacrifice of Christ). However, the meaning "cover" does not adequately convey the meaning of this term in Leviticus. The Hebrew verb is used in causative stem (the *piel*) and as such probably is a denominative verb taken from the noun *kōper*, which means "a ransom." Consequently, the verb carries the meaning "to pay a ransom" or "to ransom, deliver by a substitute."

The related noun *kappōret* is used as the name for the lid on the ark, variously translated as the "mercy seat" or "atonement cover." The same lid is labeled in Greek the ἱλαστήριον

31. Rabbi Hillel, *Sabb.* 31a.

32. See R. J. Daly, *The Origins of the Christian Doctrine of Sacrifice* (Philadelphia: Fortress, 1979) 30: "Comparative religion has been unable to find a highly illuminating parallel for the OT blood rites." Also, D. J. McCarthy, "The Symbolism of Blood Sacrifice," *JBL* 95 (1969) 167-76; and Leon Morris, *The Apostolic Preaching of the Cross* (Grand Rapids: Eerdmans, 1956) 110-11, 122-24.

33. See J. Hermann, "*kipper* and *koper*," in *Theological Dictionary of the New Testament,* trans. G. Bromiley (Grand Rapids: Eerdmans, 1965) 3:303-10. Hermann concluded by saying, "It would be useless to deny that the idea of substitution is present to some degree" (310).

(*hilastērion*), a word directly applied to Christ's atoning work in Rom 3:25: "God presented him [Jesus] as a sacrifice of atonement" (NIV).

This concept of delivering and ransoming from sin by means of a substitute is most forcefully expressed in Leviticus 16 and the great Day of Atonement, Yom Kippur. In part it is a ritual of purification for the sanctuary itself and its furniture. It does involve that, to be sure; but three times the text refers explicitly to the atonement made "on behalf of" (literal translation of בעד *baʿad*; "make atonement *on behalf of*" the high priest and his family [16:11]; "make atonement *on behalf of*" all the congregation of Israel [16:17, 24]), whereas this combination of prepositions is not used with reference to the tabernacle. The uncleanness of the sanctuary and its furniture is due to ("because of," מן *min*, literally "from" [16:16, 19]) the uncleanness and sinfulness of the Israelites.

The one sin offering on the great Day of Atonement is divided into two parts, as the presence of the two goats attests. The first goat is slain and its blood is taken into the holy of holies, behind the veil, where the high priest dares to enter only on this one day every year. The blood of the first goat is placed on the lid of the ark of the covenant, called here the "atonement cover" (16:14-15). After Aaron emerges from the tent of meeting, he is to lay his hands on the head of the second goat, confess all the sins of all Israel, and send the goat away into the desert. In graphic and concrete terms, the rite symbolizes two aspects in the remission of sins: Sins are *forgiven* on the basis of a substitute that gives its life so the people can go free, and sins are *forgotten* and removed, as the psalmist says, "As far as the east is from the west,/so far has he removed our transgressions from us" (Ps 103:12 NIV).

This does not, of course, exhaust all possible meanings of the various sacrifices. In addition to the expiatory sacrifices, mainly in the sin and guilt offerings, the sacrifices bring the believer closer to God through communion, dedication, service, worship, and thanksgiving. However, foundational to all of the offerings is the atonement for sin by blood, i.e., through the life of a victim, which serves as a substitute for the offerer.

Leviticus has as one of its main purposes to teach Israel how to distinguish "between the holy and the common, and between the unclean and the clean" (10:10). No less significant is the theology of cleanness in this book, for the word *unclean* occurs 132 times and the word *clean* appears 74 times!

Just as the sacrificial laws and the theology of atonement are provided to promote ethical holiness as separation from sin, so also the laws on the clean and the unclean are given to promote ritual holiness as a separation from defilements that come as barriers in the worship of God. Thus holiness has both an ethical and a ritual side. Being unclean does not mean the same thing as being dirty, just as being pure means more than being physically clean. "Cleanliness is next to godliness" is not the operating adage for chaps. 11–15. Instead, what is profane (literally what is distant or outside the Temple) and unclean temporarily disqualifies a person from coming into the presence of God. On the other hand, to be holy or clean indicates one who is fit or qualified to enter into the presence of God. It is not always possible to identify what makes something common/profane or unclean. Therefore, from the standpoint of many worshipers, some of the items in the lists of clean/unclean appear to have an arbitrary quality, just as the line drawn around Mount Sinai when Moses ascended it to receive the Ten Commandments was an aribtrary line that neither people nor beasts were to cross on penalty of death. When an individual comes into the presence of a holy God, a line of demarcation must be drawn; otherwise, the worshiper's entrance may trivialize what is absolutely set apart from all of life. And when the profane is blended into the sacred, there is always a loss of the absolute otherness and transcendence of God. Thus some of the boundaries drawn here may seem arbitrary, but drawing the line remains necessary.

When the Almighty confronts Moses at the burning bush (see Exod 3:1-6), the Almighty tells Moses to take off his sandals because the ground he is standing on is holy. It is conceivable to imagine that Moses might well have protested, "But why?" But Moses is informed it is imperative that he do so because the ground on which he is standing is holy ground. Again, Moses might have responded, "But, Lord, what do you mean this is holy ground? Didn't sheep and goats pass over this same spot as recently as this very day? How could such ordinary, common ground be holy?" And the answer is simply this: The presence of God at the burning bush demands that Moses worship God—visibly, concretely, bodily, as well as with his inner spirit. That episode helps us understand both a certain arbitrariness in distinguishing the sacred from the secular and the radical difference between God and everything else in creation.

Recently, Mary Douglas has argued that cleanness is a matter of wholeness or normality. Using anthropological categories, she presses the case that animals are clean when they conform wholly to the class to which they belong. Animals that split the hoof and chew the cud are "normal," but those who lack one of these characteristics are "unclean" according to this scheme: They do not wholly conform to their class.[34] However, it remains difficult to define what is normal or clean. All creatures, as they came from the hand of the Creator, were pronounced "good"; therefore, it is difficult to see why only the clean animals, for example, should be regarded as normal. There are many imponderables here that almost all interpreters frankly confess are baffling. But on the central point there can be little room for doubt: A holy God demands that we draw the line between the sacred and the secular, the clean and the unclean, the holy and the common.

THE PRESENT-DAY USE OF LEVITICUS

The question most contemporary readers of this book raise is this: Of what use can the book of Leviticus be for us today? The answer, of course, must not be contrived or involve a manipulation of the text, as some have done by allegorizing and reducing the book to

34. Mary Douglas, *Purity and Danger,* rev. ed. (London: Routledge & Kegan Paul, 1978) 53.

a series of symbols with modern values and meanings. Philo, some of the early church fathers, and Cabalistic interpreters have already traversed this route—with minimal results!

First and foremost, in all attempts of modern persons to worship God, the fact of God's absolute otherness and transcendence must influence all initial thoughts about approaching or entering into the divine presence. However, that sense of divine transcendence must also signal the divine separateness from sin and help create the call for followers of God to be holy. God's mercy is available to those who are penitent, as exemplified in this book.

But if the age and strange features of these rituals cause a stumbling block, let us realize that, although the Aaronic priesthood and blood sacrifices have disappeared, the spiritual truth they signal remains constant. Some would say that what Leviticus depicts in a specific ritual points to a later type that would fulfill in the abstract what had earlier been put in a more figurative form.

In addition to ritual prescriptions, Leviticus includes civil laws. Nowhere are modern readers encouraged to attempt to reintroduce the theocracy of Israelite days to our generation. But just as contemporary legal experts read old legal cases to discern the abiding principles, so also readers of Leviticus can use the civil laws contained here in the same way. In so doing, we will find that impartiality in the administration of justice, fairness in the treatment of the poor, provision for unemployed persons, and scrupulous honesty in all business dealings are demanded as the minimal standard for people who are called to be holy as their Lord is holy.

Finally, for those who have difficulty understanding the abstract and theological language of the NT concerning the forgiveness of sins and atonement, the book of Leviticus could serve as an introduction, a primer with big pictures and big print. In it everything is put in the concrete rather than in abstract, philosophical, or theological terms. In the NT, the book of Hebrews capitalizes on this advantage and brilliantly argues its case about salvation and atonement.

In short, Leviticus helps present an overarching view of God, humans, and the physical world. We need only note that the eschatological picture of how history concludes involves a reference to God's holiness. For, on that day, even the bells on the horses and the inscriptions on the pots and pans will have emblazoned on them: "HOLY TO THE LORD" (Zech 14:20 NIV). Leviticus is the book par excellence about this holiness. God remains the quintessence of holiness; and the deity's creatures can hardly offer to be less in their aspirations and in their everyday conduct.

BIBLIOGRAPHY

Bamberger, Bernard J. *The Torah: A Modern Commentary: Leviticus*. New York: Union of American Hebrew Congregations, 1981. A reissue and a slight expansion of a significant work that appeared seventeen years earlier.

Bush, George. *Notes, Critical and Practical on the Book of Leviticus*. New York: Newman and Ivison, 1852 (reprinted, Minneapolis: James & Klock, 1976). A classic evangelical exegetical and theological commentary.

Calvin, John. *Commentary on the Four Last Books of Moses.* Grand Rapids: Eerdmans, reprint of 1852 translation. This is the best representative of pre-critical Reformed thinking and theology.

Gammie, John G. *Holiness in Israel* OBT. Philadelphia: Fortress, 1989. The most thorough treatment of the concept of holiness available in English.

Harris, R. Laird. *The Expositor's Bible Commentary.* 12 vols. Grand Rapids: Zondervan, 1990. 2:500-654. This commentary includes detailed word studies and outlines the implications of Leviticus for biblical theology.

Harrison, Roland K. *Leviticus: An Introduction and Commentary.* Downers Grove, Ill.: InterVarsity, 1980. Insightful for college-level lay Bible study groups and for brief overviews of the text in personal Bible study.

Hartley, John E. *Word Biblical Commentary: Leviticus.* Dallas: Word, 1992. This commentary provides a comprehensive bibliography on each section of Leviticus along with detailed exegetical notes from a conservative point of view. It includes an essay on the history of the exposition of Leviticus.

Keil, C. F., and Franz Delitzsch. *Biblical Commentary on the Old Testament.* Vol. 2, *The Pentateuch.* Translated by J. Martin. Grand Rapids: Eerdmans, 1956. This book, though dated on historical and archaeological matters, still holds interest because of its influence in conservative theological circles.

Kellogg, S. H. *The Book of Leviticus.* The Expositor's Bible. 3rd ed. Minneapolis: Klock & Klock, 1978 (reprint of 1899 edition published by A. C. Armstrong). A classic that is readable and theologically stimulating.

Levine, Baruch A. *The JPS Torah Commentary: Leviticus.* Philadelphia: JPS, 1989. A masterful exegetical commentary that is fully informed by recent linguistic and archaeological advances.

Micklem, Nathaniel. *The Interpreter's Bible.* 12 vols. Nashville: Abingdon-Cokesbury, 1953. 2:1-134. An excellent representative of mid-twentieth century scholarship, written for an ecumenical Christian readership.

Milgrom, Jacob. *The Anchor Bible: Leviticus 1-16.* New York: Doubleday, 1991. The first of a projected two-volume commentary that will probably be the benchmark for all studies on Leviticus in the foreseeable future.

Noordtzij, A. *Bible Student's Commentary: Leviticus.* Translated by Raymond Togtman. Grand Rapids: Zondervan, 1982 (originally published in Dutch by J. H Kok, B. V. Kampen, 1950). An excellent example of continental evangelical thought and exegesis in 1950, one that interacts with historical-critical studies.

Noth, Martin. *Leviticus: A Commentary.* Old Testament Library. Philadelphia: Westminster, 1965. A standard historical-critical commentary.

Wenham, Gordon J. *The New International Commentary on the Old Testament: The Book of Leviticus.* Grand Rapids: Eerdmans, 1979. The most recent evangelical contribution, which examines rhetorical features of the text as a basis for discerning structure and NT theological parallels.

OUTLINE

I. 1:1–7:38   The Laws of Sacrifice

1:1–6:7   The Laws of the Five Major Offerings
    1:1–3:17   The Three Voluntary Offerings
        1:1-17   The Whole Burnt Offering
        2:1-16   The Grain Offering
        3:1-17   The Peace Offering
    4:1–6:7   Two New Atoning Offerings
        4:1–5:13   The Sin Offering
        5:14–6:7   The Guilt Offering
6:8–7:38   Instructions for the Priests
    6:8-13   The Perpetual Burnt offering
    6:14-18   The Daily Grain Offering
    6:19-23   The Priests' Daily Grain Offering
    6:24-30   The Sin Offering
    7:1-10   The Guilt Offering
    7:11-21   The Peace Offering
    7:22-27   The Prohibition on Eating Fat/Blood
    7:28-36   The Priests' Portion of the Peace Offering
    7:37-38   The Summary

II. 8:1–10:20   The Inauguration of Worship at the Tabernacle

8:1-36   The Consecration of Aaron and His Sons
9:1-24   The Inauguration of the Tabernacle Service
10:1-20   The Death of Nadab and Abihu

III. 11:1–15:33   The Regulations on Clean and Unclean

11:1-47   The Clean and the Unclean
12:1-8   The Uncleanness of Childbirth
13:1–14:57   The Uncleanness of Skin and Fungus Diseases
15:1-33   The Uncleanness of Genital Discharges

IV. 16:1-34   The Great Day of Atonement

V. 17:1–26:46   The Holiness Code

17:1-16   The Prologue: Holiness in Eating
18:1-30   Holiness in Sexual Behavior

LEVITICUS 1:1–7:38

THE LAWS OF SACRIFICE

LEVITICUS 1:1–6:7, LAWS FOR THE FIVE MAJOR OFFERINGS

OVERVIEW

So foreign to our day is the whole institution of sacrifice that even the word itself raises totally different expectations and connotations. We tend to think of a sacrifice as a loss we have suffered or something we have deprived ourselves of for one reason or another. Thus we make sacrifices during Lent or during a national emergency.

But these concepts are not to be equated with the sacrifices mentioned in Leviticus. Instead of regarding a sacrifice in a negative way as something that someone must give up for some greater good, it signifies the joyous dedication of something valuable to one's Lord.

Indeed, the word *sacrifice* comes from a Latin word meaning "to make something holy." As such, sacrificing is fully in accord with the main theme of holiness stressed in Leviticus.

The most common Hebrew equivalent for our English word *sacrifice* is קרבן (*qorbān*), meaning "[that which is] brought near [to the altar or presence of God]."

Nowhere in the Bible is there any indication as to how sacrifices got started. The scholarly literature is replete with various theories, but none can be demonstrated as the correct solution. The most that can be said is that the institution of sacrifice can be attested all over the ancient Near East. Even though many of the same terms and parts of the ritual seem to be shared, Israelite sacrifices exhibit some unique features. One is the part that blood plays in the ritual. We will say more on this later (also see the "Introduction"). From a canonical standpoint, God had accepted sacrifices from the time of Cain and Abel (see Gen 4:1-16). Noah offered burnt offerings as he emerged from the ark (see Gen 8:20). Moreover, Abraham offered sacrifices (see Gen 22:9), as did Jacob (see Gen 46:1) and the congregation of Israel (see Exod 10:25). But, then, so did the Midianite Jethro, Moses' father-in-law, offer (or participate in offering) sacrifices before he joined up with the Israelites exiting from Egypt (see Exod 18:12).

Chapters 1–7 make up the first main section of the book of Leviticus. But there are clearly defined subsections within these seven chapters.

Chapters 1–3 take up three types of offerings that are voluntarily brought to the altar. A separate chapter is given to each: the whole burnt offering; the grain offering; and the peace offering. An introductory formula is provided for these three chapters in 1:1-2*a*, but there is no closing formula. The only possible candidate for such a closing formula, 3:16*b*-17 appears to be little more than a restatement of the thought already announced in chap. 3.

Chapter 4, chap. 5 and the first part of chap. 6 form a second subsection. They deal with two more sacrifices that are given for the expiation of sins: the sin offering (4:1–5:13) and the guilt offering (5:14–6:7). There is an introductory formula in 4:1-2*a*, but as with the previous three chapters, there is no closing formula.

The next subsection (6:8–7:21) in some ways repeats the instructions given for the five offerings, but the emphasis this time is on regulations to Aaron and his sons. This third subsection is further divided in half by the repeated "The LORD said to Moses" (6:8, 19), both of which are further divided by the repeated "These are the regulations . . . " (6:8*b*, 25; 7:1, 11).

The law on the sacrifices closes with a fourth and final section (7:22-36). The first portion is directed to all the congregation of Israel wherein the eating of fat and blood is strictly forbidden (7:22-27). The second portion spells out the share of the offerings to be given to the priests (7:28-36).

A concluding formula in 7:37-38 wraps up the total package of legislation given in chaps. 1–7.

Leviticus 1:1–3:17, The Three Voluntary Offerings

OVERVIEW

Chapters 1–3 outline the three principal types of sacrifices regularly offered by individual Israelites, by their families, kings, and leaders, or often by the entire congregation. Since they could be offered as stand-alone sacrifices, or as part of a variety of other celebrations, they tended to serve multiple functions in the community.

Leviticus 1:1-17, The Whole Burnt Offering

NIV

1 The LORD called to Moses and spoke to him from the Tent of Meeting. He said, ²"Speak to the Israelites and say to them: 'When any of you brings an offering to the LORD, bring as your offering an animal from either the herd or the flock.

³"'If the offering is a burnt offering from the herd, he is to offer a male without defect. He must present it at the entrance to the Tent of Meeting so that it*a* will be acceptable to the LORD. ⁴He is to lay his hand on the head of the burnt offering, and it will be accepted on his behalf to make atonement for him. ⁵He is to slaughter the young bull before the LORD, and then Aaron's sons the priests shall bring the blood and sprinkle it against the altar on all sides at the entrance to the Tent of Meeting. ⁶He is to skin the burnt offering and cut it into pieces. ⁷The sons of Aaron the priest are to put fire on the altar and arrange wood on the fire. ⁸Then Aaron's sons the priests shall arrange the pieces, including the head and the fat, on the burning wood that is on the altar. ⁹He is to wash the inner parts and the legs with water, and the priest is to burn all of it on the altar. It is a burnt offering, an offering made by fire, an aroma pleasing to the LORD.

¹⁰"If the offering is a burnt offering from the flock, from either the sheep or the goats, he is to

a3 Or he

NRSV

1 The LORD summoned Moses and spoke to him from the tent of meeting, saying: ²Speak to the people of Israel and say to them: When any of you bring an offering of livestock to the LORD, you shall bring your offering from the herd or from the flock.

3If the offering is a burnt offering from the herd, you shall offer a male without blemish; you shall bring it to the entrance of the tent of meeting, for acceptance in your behalf before the LORD. ⁴You shall lay your hand on the head of the burnt offering, and it shall be acceptable in your behalf as atonement for you. ⁵The bull shall be slaughtered before the LORD; and Aaron's sons the priests shall offer the blood, dashing the blood against all sides of the altar that is at the entrance of the tent of meeting. ⁶The burnt offering shall be flayed and cut up into its parts. ⁷The sons of the priest Aaron shall put fire on the altar and arrange wood on the fire. ⁸Aaron's sons the priests shall arrange the parts, with the head and the suet, on the wood that is on the fire on the altar; ⁹but its entrails and its legs shall be washed with water. Then the priest shall turn the whole into smoke on the altar as a burnt offering, an offering by fire of pleasing odor to the LORD.

10If your gift for a burnt offering is from the flock, from the sheep or goats, your offering shall be a male without blemish. ¹¹It shall be slaughtered on the north side of the altar before the

NIV

offer a male without defect. ¹¹He is to slaughter it at the north side of the altar before the Lᴏʀᴅ, and Aaron's sons the priests shall sprinkle its blood against the altar on all sides. ¹²He is to cut it into pieces, and the priest shall arrange them, including the head and the fat, on the burning wood that is on the altar. ¹³He is to wash the inner parts and the legs with water, and the priest is to bring all of it and burn it on the altar. It is a burnt offering, an offering made by fire, an aroma pleasing to the Lᴏʀᴅ.

¹⁴" 'If the offering to the Lᴏʀᴅ is a burnt offering of birds, he is to offer a dove or a young pigeon. ¹⁵The priest shall bring it to the altar, wring off the head and burn it on the altar; its blood shall be drained out on the side of the altar. ¹⁶He is to remove the crop with its contents*ᵃ* and throw it to the east side of the altar, where the ashes are. ¹⁷He shall tear it open by the wings, not severing it completely, and then the priest shall burn it on the wood that is on the fire on the altar. It is a burnt offering, an offering made by fire, an aroma pleasing to the Lᴏʀᴅ.

ᵃ16 Or crop and the feathers; the meaning of the Hebrew for this word is uncertain.

NRSV

Lᴏʀᴅ, and Aaron's sons the priests shall dash its blood against all sides of the altar. ¹²It shall be cut up into its parts, with its head and its suet, and the priest shall arrange them on the wood that is on the fire on the altar; ¹³but the entrails and the legs shall be washed with water. Then the priest shall offer the whole and turn it into smoke on the altar; it is a burnt offering, an offering by fire of pleasing odor to the Lᴏʀᴅ.

14If your offering to the Lᴏʀᴅ is a burnt offering of birds, you shall choose your offering from turtledoves or pigeons. ¹⁵The priest shall bring it to the altar and wring off its head, and turn it into smoke on the altar; and its blood shall be drained out against the side of the altar. ¹⁶He shall remove its crop with its contents*ᵃ* and throw it at the east side of the altar, in the place for ashes. ¹⁷He shall tear it open by its wings without severing it. Then the priest shall turn it into smoke on the altar, on the wood that is on the fire; it is a burnt offering, an offering by fire of pleasing odor to the Lᴏʀᴅ.

ᵃ Meaning of Heb uncertain

COMMENTARY

The introduction to the whole burnt offering has a somewhat unusual expression. Generally, in the OT, the Lord "speaks" or "says" rather than "calls." In fact, the word *Lord* is inserted in our translations of the first clause (literally "And he called"), even though it occurs in the second clause. The Jerusalem *Targum* renders it, "And the Word of God called." However, it is clear that Leviticus is a sequel to the erection of the tabernacle in Exodus. The unusual Hebrew syntax suggests, as many commentators have observed, that this opening verse of Lev 1:1 begins where Exod 40:34-35 leaves off.

As the cloud of glory fills the recently completed tabernacle and prevents all access to its interior, the Lord calls to Moses, who now stands outside the tabernacle, from the midst of the Shekinah ("the divine presence") glory residing over the ark of the covenant.

The voice of God, which had boomed out from Sinai, now calls out from the tent of meeting. No longer does God speak with a loud thundering voice, as upon Mount Sinai, but presumably in kinder and gentler tones. But the first words from the tent of meeting are words of grace, concerned about maintaining fellowship with God through sacrifice and atonement for sin. Even the name for the tabernacle, the tent of meeting, implies a coming together of two parties by previous appointment. Having taken possession of the tent of meeting (a name that first appears in Exod 27:21), the Lord speaks "from" or "out of " the place where the deity has come to reside (the same place is called God's "dwelling place" in Lev 15:31; 26:11) among Israel, in contrast to the previous speech from the clouds. Thus, by gracious provision, God has condescended to appoint a place to "dwell" among the people in a special way and manifest the divine will to them. *Tabernacle* has become the more standard term for this place, based on the Latin term *tabernaculum,* meaning "tent" or "wooden hut." The word *meeting* derives from the Hebrew verb meaning "gather" or "come together" (See Josh 11:5; Neh 6:2) in the niphal stem. The same Hebrew verb, יעד (*yāʿad*), can also mean to meet with someone with the purpose "to reveal" something when the term is used of the Lord (see Exod 25:22; 30:6; Num 17:4); thus the tabernacle likewise is a tent of revelation. As mediator and people meet before

the Lord, the Lord will reveal the holy will from the tent of meeting.

This is only the third time that the Lord "called" to Moses; the first was at the burning bush (see Exod 3:4), and the second was on Mount Sinai (see Exod 19:3). Leviticus is part of the ongoing historical narrative, for the laws about the sacrifices and ceremonies are given to describe what Aaron and his sons will do now that they have been ordained to the office of priest (chaps. 8–9). Accordingly, Leviticus stands at the center not only of the Pentateuch but also of Israel's story of the move to nationhood, with the exodus from Egypt and the entry into the land of promise on either side.

Nevertheless, the laws in Leviticus contain a sort of built-in obsolescence, for they are given to Moses after the pattern of what God had shown him on the mount (see Exod 25:8, 40). These

MAJOR INDIVIDUAL SACRIFICES PRESCRIBED BY LEVITICUS

Requirements (in order of presentation):

Reason for Offering	Atoning Sacrifices		Burnt Offering	Grain Offering
	Guilt Offering	Sin Offering		
For violations of the Lord's holy things (5:14-19)	A ram without defect Value of profaned item plus 20%			
For violations of human property rights (6:1-7)	A ram without defect Full restitution plus 20%			
For lepers (14:4f.) when cleansed	A male lamb and a log of oil (as a wave offering) and	A male lamb and	A ewe lamb a year old and	3/10 ephah, mixed with oil
or if poor	A male lamb and	A turtledove or a pigeon and	A turtledove or a pigeon and	1/10 ephah, a log of oil
Inadvertent Sins (4:3–5:10):				
for Priests		A young bull		
for Congregation		A young bull		
for Ruler		A male goat		
for Individuals		A female goat or lamb		
if poor		A turtledove or a pigeon and	A turtledove or a pigeon or	1/10 ephah, no oil or incense
For purification after childbirth (12:6)		A pigeon or a turtledove and	A year-old lamb	
or if poor		A turtledove or a pigeon and	A turtledove or a pigeon	
For discharges (15:1-33)		A turtledove or a pigeon and	A dove or a pigeon	
Voluntary (1:3-17)			A male animal from the herd or flock or or a turtledove or pigeon	Fine flour, oil incense, and salt If cooked, no yeast or honey
Peace Offerings (3:1-17) Thank Offerings (7:12-15) Votive Offerings (7:16-18) Freewill Offerings			A male or female from the herd and or flock	Bread, no yeast, made with oil Wafers, no yeast spread with oil Cakes, mixed with oil

laws, then, are only copies or types: The real or actual ones remain with the living Lord. The laws are designed to mold Israel into being a "holy nation" (Exod 19:6), according to the model of God, whose own self is "holy." What remains unchanging through all the ages is the holiness of God; however, the expressions of that holiness are subject to change. What Moses receives, he is to "speak to the Israelites." Thus he will be a prophet of God and act as the Lord's mediator to the nation (see Deut 18:15-22; Ps 105:15; Hos 12:13) and an intercessor to God when they sin (see Exodus 32–34; Num 12:6-15).

Before proceeding with specific directions about the various sacrifices, 1:2 gives a general case that applies to all offerings. In fact, v. 2 uses the standard legal form that introduces general cases: כִּי (*kî*, "when," "if"). Individual legal cases are introduced with a separate word: אִם (*'im*, "if"; see 1:3, 10, 14; 3:1). Even the word קָרְבָּן (*qorbān*, "offering") is the general term that applies to all offerings. *Qorbān* is related to the verbal stem "to draw near," "to approach," and it is used for bringing something to God, whether it be a sacrifice or a gift made to the Lord (cf. Num 7:3, 10; Neh 10:35). Therefore, it is something that one "brings near to" God, and as a consequence, the person enjoys God's nearness (see Ps 73:28). The term *qorbān* occurs in Mark 7:11 in a negative context, because some Pharisees claimed that the gifts they had dedicated to God prevented them from supporting their parents. Any gift, therefore, brought to the altar and dedicated to God is given this general name of offering. Indeed, the very wood used to burn the sacrifices on the altar is called *qorbān* in Neh 10:34 because it too is "brought near to" the Lord.

One further general instruction is given before the specific details for each sacrifice are taken up. Only five kinds of living creatures are acceptable for sacrifices—namely, of animals: cattle, i.e., beef or horned domestic animals and sheep and goats from the flock, including the young of each kind eight days of age and older (22:27); and of fowl: turtledoves and pigeons (1:14; 5:7; 12:6, 8; 14:22, 30; 15:14, 29). Wild animals, or hunted game, are not allowed as sacrifices for several reasons: (a) They are not taken from one's possessions; (b) only perfect animals can serve as sacrificial offerings; (c) only tame, gentle, and harmless animals can be sacrifices because of their serviceability to humanity; and (d) only what costs the offerer something can be given, for David declared, "I will not sacrifice to the LORD my God burnt offerings that cost me nothing" (2 Sam 24:24 NIV). The prophet Malachi rhetorically asked his audience in a later day, " 'When you bring injured, crippled, or diseased animals and offer them as sacrifices, should I accept them from your hand?' says the LORD" (Mal 1:13 NIV).

Notice that no "must" or demand is indicated here; the message is addressed to those who, in covenant relation with God and out of a heart filled with gratitude, desire to express that appreciation before God. What gives the offering its greatest value, from the human side of the act, is its voluntariness and its spontaneity.

Before taking up the six parts of the whole burnt offering, the name, antiquity, and function of this offering must be considered. This offering may well have been known as the "whole offering" (Hebrew כָּלִיל *kālîl*), for that term formed part of the name for this offering in 1 Sam 7:9 ("Then Samuel took a suckling lamb and offered it up as a whole burnt offering [עוֹלָה כָּלִיל *'ôlâ kālîl*] to the LORD" [NIV]). Moreover, the root *kll* occurs in Ugaritic (a Canaanite alphabetic script whose language is very close to Hebrew) and Punic, meaning "whole."

However, it appears that another name, "that which ascends" (Hebrew עלה *'ōlâ*), replaced the name for "whole" *(kālîl)*, perhaps at a time when the skin of the burnt offering was given to the officiating priest (Lev 7:8). Thus the name "whole" may have seemed inaccurate and misleading. Nevertheless, the term *'ōlâ* indicates that, except for the skin, the whole animal is burned. It "goes up" to God or in smoke, and none of it is eaten by priest or worshiper.

The law of the whole burnt offering comes first, even though it is not first in the order of ritual: That spot belongs to the sin offering, and the burnt offering follows in second place. Why, then, is it placed first here? Probably because it is the most ancient of the offerings and it is the one in the most constant use. Noah and Abraham brought burnt offerings and peace offerings, but there is no notice of sin or guilt offerings until Leviticus. Moreover, a burnt offering is offered each morning and evening. On every one of the feast days, except the Day of Atonement, where the sin offering is the central act, the burnt offering is the most important sacrifice.

The purpose or function of the burnt offering is a little more complicated than it may seem at first glance. The explicit purpose assigned in 1:4 is "to make atonement for [the individual]"; therefore, it has both propitiatory (to avoid the deserved wrath of God against sin) and expiatory (to appease and cleanse from sin) functions. As Rabbi Ibn Ezra observed, this expression in v. 4 may well be an abbreviation of the full formula in Exod 30:12, to serve as "a ransom for [a] life" (NIV). Accordingly, the favorable acceptance of the burnt offering signals God's willingness to be approached; it also serves as a substitute ransom that averts the deserved wrath of God. Three times Leviticus assigns this expiatory role to the burnt offering but always in connection with the sacrifice of the sin offering (9:7; 14:20; 16:24). Ezekiel also seems to attribute this same expiatory role to the burnt offerings (see Exek 45:15, 17) but, again, in connection with other offerings.

But other functions are assigned to the burnt offering. Saul appears to connect it with his desperate need to entreat God: " 'I have not sought the LORD's favor.' So I felt compelled to offer the burnt offering" (1 Sam 13:12 NIV). Does this mean that Saul's purpose is to appease God, or is it to render God homage or thanksgiving? Or is he hoping for expiation of his sins? However, in other texts, such as Lev 22:17-19 and Num 15:3, burnt offerings are joyful acts of fulfilling vows and making freewill offerings to God. In the binding of Isaac to be a burnt offering (see Genesis 22), it is an act of obedience and a dedication of everything back to God in thanksgiving for all that God had first given Abraham. Thanksgiving is not out of place when persons offer this sacrifice after childbirth, healing, and release from bodily pollution (Lev 12:6; 14:13, 19; 15:30). Thus the range of purposes for the burnt offering is quite broad.

Where a combination of sacrifices is observed, the burnt offering frequently appears as the first sacrifice in the ritual. This may seem to favor the suggestion that it is the inviting offering; i.e., it is employed to attract the favor of God. Thus it desires a response from God as much as it pledges the entirety of one's being to God by giving of this totally offered substitute.

The ritual for sacrifices of all types involves six identifiable parts: (1) the presentation of the victim, (2) the laying on of the hand(s), (3) the slaughtering of the victim, (4) the sprinkling of the blood, (5) the sacrificial burning, and (6) the sacrificial meal. Although some differences appear in the various sacrifices, each will exhibit all, or most, of these six parts of the offering ritual.

First comes the presentation of the victim in the whole burnt offering. While the final three parts of the ritual are done by the priest for the offerer, the first three parts are usually reserved for the one drawing near with a gift to God. The offerer must bring the victim.

The place of presentation is prescribed as being "at the entrance to the tent of meeting" (1:3). This restriction to the entrance to the tabernacle takes direct aim at the ever present tendency in Israel toward idolatry. By so specifying, the worship of God is set apart from all worship of false gods. And all forms of self-will in worship are also prohibited. The mode and conditions for the worship of God cannot be other than what God appoints. To think and act otherwise are to offer nonacceptable worship to God.

The acceptance of the sacrifice means that the one making the offering can also find acceptance with God. When God accepts the sacrifice, that is good enough indication that God also accepts the offerer. The zone in which this is to be accomplished is "before the LORD" (literal rendering of 1:3c). By this second reminder, the law specifically limits sacrifice to a particular area by the altar in the sanctuary courtyard to the interior of the tent of meeting.

The concept that sacrifices are pleasing to God is further raised by the oft-repeated phrase "an aroma pleasing to the LORD" (1:9, 13, 17). This phrase is used forty-three times in the OT and only in this expression. The word *pleasing* comes from the same root as the word *rest,* implying that the sacrifice brings peace between God and the worshiper. If the picture is an anthropomorphic one depicting God like a human being smelling the odor from the sacrifices, it is problematic for those who see Leviticus as P material, since P is supposed to minimize anthropomorphisms. To make matters even more complicated for the P thesis, Ezekiel and later literature avoid this expression and the verb for "smelling" that often goes with it. However, instead of being an anthropomorphic figure of speech here, it may be little more than a stock phrase of the language that endures long after the conception of God as literally smelling something.

One other consideration must be made about the nature of this sacrifice. Is the victim offered as an "offering made by fire" (1:9)? It is clear that it is immolated as a holocaust, but the Hebrew term אשׁה ('iššeh) is probably to be connected not with אשׁ ('ēš), "fire," but with the Ugaritic root itt, "gift." Surprisingly enough, such sacrifices are described in 21:6 as "the bread of their God" (KJV). Therefore, the priests are not to defile themselves, since "they present the offerings made to the LORD by fire [or as gifts of/to the LORD], the food of their God, they are to be holy" (21:6; cf. 3:11, 16; 21:21). If the translation of "offering made by fire" is correct, it cannot be used as it is for the portions that the priests eat (2:3, 10; 7:31, 35) and for the bread of presence (24:7, 9). The addition of the word for "bread" alongside this term of uncertain translation may add some force to translating it "food offering" as NEB and GNB favor.

The second act of the ceremony of the burnt offering is the laying on of the hand(s). At first it appears that nothing more is indicated than declaring that it is the offerer's property, whose right it is to give it back to God. But that would leave this question: Why is this ceremony confined to bloody sacrifices? Certainly nonbloody sacrifices are just as much the property of the offerer, who has the right to give.

The laying on of the hand(s) may originally have been a legal and juridical procedure. When Moses appointed Joshua leader over Israel, he laid his hands on him (see Num 27:18-23; Deut 34:9). The people laid their hands on the Levites (see Num 8:10) and thereby formally substituted the Levites for each firstborn in Israel. Likewise, when they laid hands on the one convicted of blasphemy (see Lev 24:10-16), they transferred the obligation from their heads to the blasphemer. But the fullest symbolic expression of what the imposition of hands means is to be found in the ceremony of the Day of Atonement. There Aaron was ordered to lay his hands on the head of one of the goats of the sin offering (Lev 16:21) and "confess over it all the wickedness and rebellion of the Israelites—all their sins—and put them on

the goat's head." Members of the early church laid hands on Paul and Barnabas as they designated them for special service (see Acts 13:2-3).

But even more than the idea of substitution is meant here. This symbolic act, which in later Hebrew would be known as semikhah for the verb "to lay," means to lean heavily on the victim, not to lightly rest the hand on it. The force of the verb סמך (sāmak, "to rest heavily on [something or someone]") is illustrated in Ps 88:7L: "Your wrath lies heavily upon me" (NIV). The offerer is heavily resting on the fact that the victim is procuring from God the needed atonement and acceptance. When the hands are laid on the victim, the one making the offering has to take it by faith that the victim will, in God's merciful provision, symbolically express what the offerer deserves but is now excused by virtue of another who substitutes life for life.

Sometimes the question is raised, Was this part of the ceremony done with one or two hands? Leviticus 16:21 clearly specifies both hands. But that is why others have seen a distinction between that function on the Day of Atonement and what is specified here. However, the Mishnah, tractate Menahoth 93a, notes that two hands are everywhere required. The Hebrew consonantal text in 1:4 merely reads ידו (ydw), which the MT invariably vocalizes as singular (yādô) but which is equally possible to render as a dual form (yādāw), for both words are written the same way in the ancient unvocalized text.

The conclusion to this evidence is persuasive: The purpose of the laying on of hands is to transfer the spiritual qualities (in this case one's sin and impurities) from the one doing the ceremony to the one offered as a sacrifice. The idea of substitution, however, is more all-encompassing than the idea of transference of sin, identification of the offerer with the animal, or ownership of the animal. The laying on of hands makes it clear that when the life of the sacrifice is poured out in death, it is just as if the person who brings the offering dies.

The promise that follows is that the sacrifice "will be accepted on [that person's] behalf to make atonement for [that one]" (1:4c). Atonement is a key word in Leviticus, for it appears here almost fifty times (along with almost another fifty times in the rest of the OT), usually in association with the priest making atonement by means of a sacrifice.

The word does not mean "to cover," even though a verb in a different Hebrew stem (the Qal) using the same consonants appears in Gen 6:14 meaning "to smear with pitch," "to caulk" or in that sense, "to cover." Rather than resorting to this single usage of the verb in Gen 6:14 as the root meaning of this word, Hebrew grammar is better served by deriving this verb from the noun of the same consonants meaning "a ransom" (see Num 35:31; Isa 43:3). Since the verb "to atone" is used only in the intensive stem (the Hebrew piel), it is better to understand it as a denominative verb meaning "to give a ransom" or "to deliver or atone by a substitute." Even the lid to the ark of the covenant, called the "mercy seat" in the KJV, is literally "a place of atonement."

The slaughter of the victim is the third part of the ceremony and the last act performed by the offerer (1:5). But it may well be that the third-person singular form of the verb, "he is to slaughter," is used here in an impersonal sense, "one is to slaughter," a usage seen often in the Hebrew text of Leviticus.[35] This would explain the apparent contradiction between the thought in Leviticus that the offerer must slaughter the victim and the claim in Ezek 44:10-11 that the Levites are authorized to do so in the eschatological times. Both the LXX and the Samaritan Pentateuch render the verb as plural, thereby allowing for either or both the offerer and the priests to participate. This does not necessarily mean that the Greek and Samaritan versions had a different text before them, for it again is only a matter of vocalizing the same consonantal text.

Our text uses the technical term for ritual slaughter, which involves slitting the throat of the animal. So drastic is the penalty for the offerer's sin that it demands death. The wages of sin is death; but in this case, it means death for the sacrificial victim.

The tendency seemed to be to turn over the duties of slaughtering the animals to the Levites or priests as 1 Chr 23:31 notes. In the days of King Hezekiah, the skinning of the animals was performed by the priests, who being too few in number required the help of the Levites (see 2 Chr 29:34). And whenever the offerers were

35. See George Bush, *Notes, Critical and Practical, on the Book of Leviticus* (New York: Newman & Ivison, 1852; reprint, Minneapolis, James & Klock, 1976) 15, 44, *passim*.

not ceremonially clean, the Levites had to step in again to kill the sacrifice in the days of Hezekiah (see 2 Chr 30:17). Later, in the days of King Josiah, the Levites slaughtered all the Passover lambs (see 2 Chr 35:6).

The sprinkling of the blood follows. Since only the priests are allowed to ascend the altar (see 1 Sam 2:28), they have to perform the rest of the ritual. The directions to the priest on the use of the blood from the sacrifice vary in each offering. For example, in the sin offering the blood assumes a central role, but here in the burnt offering it is not as dominant. However, the idea of atonement by the blood is not absent even in the burnt offering; therefore, the sprinkling of the blood cannot be omitted, even it if takes a lesser role.

Leviticus 1:5*b* reads, "Then Aaron's sons the priests shall bring the blood and sprinkle it against the altar on all sides at the entrance to the Tent of Meeting." It is difficult to say precisely how the blood was handled since quite a bit of blood was involved and different verbs are used with a range of meaning from "sprinkling" with one's finger or with a bunch of hyssop (14:7) to "dashing," "throwing," or "pouring" (1:5, 11; 3:2, 8, 13; 9:18). However, in Num 19:18-21 both verbs of "sprinkling" and "throwing" are used as synonyms. The NT understood the concept as one of sprinkling as well (cf. the use of Exod 24:8 in Heb 9:19).

Whether the blood was thrown "against" the altar or poured "on" it is another question. Again, the preposition can have either meaning. Because the fire was no doubt very hot, it was necessary to stand back some distance. Nevertheless, the blood was part of the sacrifice, and so we conclude that part of it was thrown "on" the altar "round about" or "on all sides." To argue that the blood was not part of the offering because it was the life of the animal (17:10-14) and must therefore be returned to God by placing it alongside the altar lest the offerer be considered a murderer is to avoid the symbolism of substitution and the wholeness and completeness of the burnt offering.

The atoning work is completed in the sprinkling of the blood. In this act of presenting and sprinkling the blood on the altar, the life of the innocent victim is presented to God as a ransom and a substitute for the sinner. All of this is done at the altar, the designated place where God promised to meet persons bringing an offering.

The use of the blood is the prerogative of the priest alone. The offerer must leave to the priests the presentation of the blood toward God. The pouring out or sprinkling of the blood, the very life of the victim, constitutes the real virtue of the sacrifice. No doubt, it is deliberately calculated to remind the offerer that each person deserves to have one's own blood shed for sins. Thus, without the shedding of blood, there is no hope of having any sins remitted.

The sacrificial burning is the fifth part of the ritual. First, the animal has to be "skinned" or "flayed" (1:6a). Only the skin (which is to be given to the priests; see 7:8), the crop of a bird, and the animial's viscera are exempted from the whole burnt offering; everything else is burned on the altar: That is the distinctive aspect of the whole burnt offering. To prepare the animal for this total holocaust, it has to be "cut up into its parts" (1:6b). Before the pieces are carefully arranged on the altar (1:8), the priests are to "put fire on the altar" (literally "shall give fire" 1:7). This probably means to stir up the fire or to stoke it, for the divine command is that the fire is to be kept burning continually (6:12). The carefully arranged wood also is intended to stoke up the fire for the burnt offering about to be offered.

To prevent any pollution of this sacred offering, 1:9 advises that the internal portion of the animal and its legs must be washed with water. Nothing extraneous or corrupt must come into contact with what has been set aside to be presented to God. The viscera of the animal (made unclean by the presence of undigested food) and the legs (possibly contaminated by contact with excreta or with the ground) are to be washed with water.

Now the total offering is to be burned on the altar (1:9b). However, the writer does not use the usual word for consuming something with fire. The verb appears to be derived from the noun for "smoke." Furthermore, since in Hebrew and several of the Semitic languages the word for "incense" appears to be derived from the word for "smoke," it is safe to say that the burned parts of the sacrifice rise in smoke as if they are a perfume or an incense to God.

Thus the holocaust, or the whole burnt offering, with the exception of the skin of the animal or the crop of a bird and the viscera, is entirely dedicated to the Lord and ascends heavenward as a sweet-smelling aroma to the Lord.

Those who are not as wealthy, who cannot offer one of the large domestic horned cattle, can bring a sheep or a goat (1:10-13) from the flock. It too has to be a "male without defect" (1:10). Whereas v. 5 does not specify, v. 11 orders that the animal from the flock be slaughtered on "the north side of the altar," just as the text specifies for the sin offering (4:24, 29, 33; 6:25), the guilt offering (7:2), and offerings performed for ceremonial cleansing (14:13).

As a further concession to the poor people of the land, either a dove or a pigeon can be brought as a whole burnt offering. Thus Mary, the mother of our Lord, brought such an offering (see Luke 2:22-24).

The ritual for sacrificing the dove or pigeon has several unique features. The expression in 1:15, "wring off the head," is probably overtranslated in the NIV, for one need only twist or yank the head to disjoin it from the top of the vertebrae. That would be sufficient to kill the bird; thus the head need not be completely severed. The removal of "the crop with its contents" (1:16) is an uncertain translation. Instead, it has recently been suggested that the word translated "crop" actually was the bird's tail, which directs its flight. If so, we are being given instructions on how to clean a bird. Jacob Milgrom argues that the rare word in v. 16 should be rendered "crissum." The crissum is made up of the loose fatty material that can be removed by cutting through the bird's tail wing: "The anus is removed along with the tail. However, the anus separates from the intestines when it is removed. This leaves a portion of the intestines exposed. By pulling on these, the rest of the intestines can be pulled from the abdomen like a string attached to the gizzard."[36]

Only later in the Second Temple times was the decision made to add the requirement that the gizzard of the bird should be removed as well as its intestines. But the crop contains no excrement, as do the lower intestines; therefore, Scripture does not require this addition. The bird is offered with all of its feathers except for the tail, contrary to some translations.

36. Milgrom, *Leviticus 1-16*, 171, quoting his student S. Pfann.

The "ashes" (literally "fatness"); 1:16c are created mainly from the suet. These ashes are placed on the east side of the altar. There does not appear to be an apparent reason for choosing this side of the altar.

In all three types of victims, whether from the cattle, flock, or two types of birds, everything is given up to God in its entirety (with the exceptions of the skin and viscera). The only missing aspect of the six-part ceremony is the sacrificial meal. Since everything is dedicated wholly to the Lord, there is no provision for sharing a portion with the priests or in a communal meal. The whole is burned on the altar.

REFLECTIONS

The details for the ritual of the whole burnt offering appear so exotic and foreign to our experience that little, if anything, is expected by way of contemporary relevance. However, the reverse is the case. For those who have difficulty understanding and appreciating all the abstract forms used in NT theology to explain Christian concepts of redemption, concepts that often seem to relate more to Greek philosophical thought than to modern concerns, Leviticus offers a real breakthrough. The concepts are not abstract in Leviticus; rather, they are brutally concrete. The pictures are large and terribly real. In Leviticus, abstract thinking and theologizing are reduced to a huge primer.

1. Though sometimes the OT sacrificial system is understood in harsh and legalistic terms, in the NT, Jesus was critical of abuses of the concept of sacrifices.

At their best and in their own context, the sacrifices described in Leviticus are offerings made to God flowing freely from grateful hearts. As the commentary notes, there is no "must" or demand about the sacrifices; sacrifices grow out of a covenant relationship with God.

So, far more than sheep, goats, or birds, the offerings described in Leviticus are signs of our deeper and richer desire to make an offering of ourselves to God. At the conclusion of his masterful *The Denial of Death,* Ernest Becker states, "Who knows what form the forward momentum of life will take in the time ahead or what use it will make of our searching. The most anyone of us can seem to do is to fashion something—an object or ourselves—and drop it into the confusion, make an offering of it, so to speak."[37] At the core of Leviticus is a conviction that human life is most rich, beautiful, and free when, amid the confusion of life, people fashion themselves into offerings to God.

2. The proper mode for worshiping God is not left to human invention; it is by divinely revealed instruction. All self-will in worship is prohibited; the offerer must come on the terms of faith, trusting God and bringing only what God has indicated will be acceptable. The human temptation to add or delete terms or requirements as to the mode and condition for presenting oneself to God is ever present, but this impulse must be firmly resisted.

3. What worshipers offer to God must be the best, most perfect of its kind, and it must cost something. To give to God what costs little or nothing is to invite divine displeasure against the work of our own hands, as the audience of Malachi's day learned (see Malachi 1). Just as King David refused to accept as a gift something that he could in turn offer to God, since he would be giving what cost him nothing (see 2 Sam 24:24), so modern persons should resist the temptation to send to the house of God whatever we could just as well do without or whatever we are trying to get rid of. Almost every community has its share of stories about the person who saved the used tea bags to send to the missionaries, or persons who boxed up all the unsold clothes from the garage sale to send them to homeless people near or far. Is this not a modern variation on the ancient malpractice of offering to God sacrificial animals

37. Ernest Becker, *The Denial of Death* (New York: Free Press, 1973) 285.

that were injured, crippled, or diseased (see Mal 1:13)? The widow "put in more than all the others" (Luke 21:3*b* NIV) who were placing their offerings in the Temple treasury as Jesus and his disciples watched, because she gave herself first, and then out of the poverty of what she had to live on, she gave the best she had. That is costly giving, and so it was commanded and taught in bold relief in the whole burnt offering.

4. The whole burnt offering depicts in type what Christ our Savior did on our behalf when he wholly surrendered to the will of the Father. Just as the innocent sacrificial victim submissively yielded its life on behalf of the offerer, "so also through the obedience of the one man [Christ] the many will be made righteous" (Rom 5:19 NIV). Christ "being found in appearance as a man,/ he humbled himself/ and became obedient to death—/ even death on a cross!" (Phil 2:8 NIV).

5. As the burnt offering was "an aroma pleasing to the LORD" (Lev. 1:17), so Christ became exactly the same for all who believe on him. The apostle Paul was making that very point when he urged in Eph 5:1-2, "Be imitators of God, therefore, as dearly loved children and live a life of love, just as Christ loved us and gave himself up for us as a fragrant offering and sacrifice to God" (NIV). The death of Christ, like that of the sacrificial animal, was like perfume that pleased God.

6. The sacrifices are not called the "food" of God (Lev 21:6) because they are in any sense something that the deity needs to be sustained. Psalm 50:8-15 sharply rebukes that idea. After all, argues the psalmist, God owns "the cattle on a thousand hills" (Ps 50:10 NIV); "the world" and "all that is in it" (Ps 50:12 NIV) belong to God. The concept of the food of God must not be understood here in any material sense. Rather, it symbolizes the thanksgiving, loyalty, commitment, and desire for nearness that the sacrifices express. That is the food of God.

7. The whole burnt offering of Leviticus 1 is reflected in the Pauline admonition in Rom 12:1: "Therefore, I urge you, brothers [meaning also 'and sisters'], in view of God's mercy, to offer your bodies as living sacrifices, holy and pleasing to God—this is your spiritual act of worship" (NIV). Nowhere is the call to total commitment of one's life put in a more graphic way. Just as the whole burnt offering was consumed on the altar, in a similar manner Paul exhorted believers to place their whole selves at the disposal of the living God. Such self-giving would be as "living sacrifices" rather than as dead victims. Such an act of consecration is something pleasing to God, even as the aroma of the sacrificial smoke was said to be perfume to the Lord.

Leviticus 2:1-16, The Grain Offering

NIV

2 " 'When someone brings a grain offering to the LORD, his offering is to be of fine flour. He is to pour oil on it, put incense on it ²and take it to Aaron's sons the priests. The priest shall take a handful of the fine flour and oil, together with all the incense, and burn this as a memorial portion on the altar, an offering made by fire, an aroma pleasing to the LORD. ³The rest of the grain offering belongs to Aaron and his sons; it is a most holy part of the offerings made to the LORD by fire.

⁴" 'If you bring a grain offering baked in an

NRSV

2 When anyone presents a grain offering to the LORD, the offering shall be of choice flour; the worshiper shall pour oil on it, and put frankincense on it, ²and bring it to Aaron's sons the priests. After taking from it a handful of the choice flour and oil, with all its frankincense, the priest shall turn this token portion into smoke on the altar, an offering by fire of pleasing odor to the LORD. ³And what is left of the grain offering shall be for Aaron and his sons, a most holy part of the offerings by fire to the LORD.

4When you present a grain offering baked in

NIV

oven, it is to consist of fine flour: cakes made without yeast and mixed with oil, or[a] wafers made without yeast and spread with oil. [5]If your grain offering is prepared on a griddle, it is to be made of fine flour mixed with oil, and without yeast. [6]Crumble it and pour oil on it; it is a grain offering. [7]If your grain offering is cooked in a pan, it is to be made of fine flour and oil. [8]Bring the grain offering made of these things to the LORD; present it to the priest, who shall take it to the altar. [9]He shall take out the memorial portion from the grain offering and burn it on the altar as an offering made by fire, an aroma pleasing to the LORD. [10]The rest of the grain offering belongs to Aaron and his sons; it is a most holy part of the offerings made to the LORD by fire.

[11]" 'Every grain offering you bring to the LORD must be made without yeast, for you are not to burn any yeast or honey in an offering made to the LORD by fire. [12]You may bring them to the LORD as an offering of the firstfruits, but they are not to be offered on the altar as a pleasing aroma. [13]Season all your grain offerings with salt. Do not leave the salt of the covenant of your God out of your grain offerings; add salt to all your offerings.

[14]" 'If you bring a grain offering of firstfruits to the LORD, offer crushed heads of new grain roasted in the fire. [15]Put oil and incense on it; it is a grain offering. [16]The priest shall burn the memorial portion of the crushed grain and the oil, together with all the incense, as an offering made to the LORD by fire.

a4 Or and

NRSV

the oven, it shall be of choice flour: unleavened cakes mixed with oil, or unleavened wafers spread with oil. [5]If your offering is grain prepared on a griddle, it shall be of choice flour mixed with oil, unleavened; [6]break it in pieces, and pour oil on it; it is a grain offering. [7]If your offering is grain prepared in a pan, it shall be made of choice flour in oil. [8]You shall bring to the LORD the grain offering that is prepared in any of these ways; and when it is presented to the priest, he shall take it to the altar. [9]The priest shall remove from the grain offering its token portion and turn this into smoke on the altar, an offering by fire of pleasing odor to the LORD. [10]And what is left of the grain offering shall be for Aaron and his sons; it is a most holy part of the offerings by fire to the LORD.

[11]No grain offering that you bring to the LORD shall be made with leaven, for you must not turn any leaven or honey into smoke as an offering by fire to the LORD. [12]You may bring them to the LORD as an offering of choice products, but they shall not be offered on the altar for a pleasing odor. [13]You shall not omit from your grain offerings the salt of the covenant with your God; with all your offerings you shall offer salt.

[14]If you bring a grain offering of first fruits to the LORD, you shall bring as the grain offering of your first fruits coarse new grain from fresh ears, parched with fire. [15]You shall add oil to it and lay frankincense on it; it is a grain offering. [16]And the priest shall turn a token portion of it into smoke— some of the coarse grain and oil with all its frankincense; it is an offering by fire to the LORD.

COMMENTARY

Scripture preserves two types of grain offerings: one that accompanies animal sacrifices, and an independent offering. This offering is regularly prescribed as an accompanying sacrifice with the burnt offering and the peace offering. Its auxiliary function is well attested in the historical books of the OT (e.g., Josh 22:23, 29; Judg 13:19, 23; 1 Sam 1:24; 2:29; 3:14; 10:3; 1 Kgs 8:64; 2 Kgs 16:13, 15). This fact probably accounts for its being introduced second in the order of the sacrifices in Leviticus. The grain offering is also one

of the three sacrifices (along with the burnt offering and the peace offering) that produces "an aroma pleasing to the LORD" (1:9, 17; 2:2, 9, 12; 3:5, 16).

The precise connotation for the name of this offering is difficult to determine (since its meaning is never explicitly stated), even though the Hebrew name for it (מנחה *minḥâ*) is well known and exhibits a number of meanings. For example, it can mean a "gift" or a "present," such as Jacob sent to his brother, Esau (see Gen 32:13), or as he later sent to Joseph in Egypt (see Gen 43:11). It can also refer to both an animal and a grain offering, as a sort of generic term for any type of offering, as with Cain's and Abel's offerings (see Gen 4:3, 5). In nonreligious usages, it meant "tribute," the money paid by a vassal king to his overlord (see 2 Sam 8:6; 1 Kgs 4:21). It is likely, then, that the *minḥâ* is a present or gift made to God. The worshiper brings the sacrifice as a gift in recognition of God's supreme authority and in the hope of gaining God's favor and blessing.

The KJV calls this a "meal offering," meaning in the English of that day "food-offering." Other translations come closer to the mark by calling it a "cereal offering," even though it specifies the choicest part of the wheat grain rather than any of the other grains. This criticism, of course, must also be made of the label "grain offering."

This offering is made of semolina, the inner kernels of the wheat grain. Leviticus 2:1 says that the offering is to "be of fine flour" (סלח *sōlet*). In Exod 29:2, *sōlet* is identified as "semolina of wheat." This semolina is identified with grits, for in rabbinic tradition, "A sieve lets through the flour but retains the *sōlet*" ('Abot 5:15).

Although it is made to God by fire, the grain offering never implies that a life is being given to God, as is true of the burnt offering. Also, the grain offering does not require the laying on of hands, as the burnt offering does, for there is no idea of transfer or substitution. The dominant idea is that this is a gift to God from the produce of the soil—namely, the inner kernels of the wheat grain.

Not only must the grain offering be a product of the soil, but it must be grown by cultivation. In this way it represents the result of human labor. In addition to human labor in growing it, there is the work of grinding, sifting, and, in some cases, cooking it that further emphasizes the investment of labor. Therefore, just as an aspect of the whole burnt offering emphasizes the consecration of the person to God, so the grain offering represents a similar consecration of the results of one's labors to God.

Three kinds of grain offerings are described here: (1) grain offerings of uncooked grain (Lev 2:1-3); (2) cooked grain offerings and general requirements for this offering (Lev 2:4-13); and (3) grain offerings of firstfruits (Lev 2:14-16). Some have supposed that the various implements used, such as the oven, the baking pan, or the frying pan, represent what different classes of people were likely to have owned. The poorer classes ate parched grain since they usually could not afford an oven or a baking pan. Regardless of the individual means, God is willing to accept all at whatever economic level they come. The size or the status of the gift, as indicated by the mixtures and the method of cooking, is not to keep the worshiper from presenting the grain offering.

Wheat was the most highly prized of all the grains. In offering the inner kernels of wheat, the best of the grains, one is offering the best to God. It also represents what is the most labor-intensive to produce, given the grinding and sifting required to produce this special form of wheat grits.

After the offerer brings the semolina wheat grits to the altar, Aaron's sons take a portion of the offering and add oil to it. Oil is applied in five different ways: pouring (v. 1), mixing (v. 4), spreading (v. 4*b*), frying (v. 7), and adding (v. 15). The oil is the ubiquitous olive oil of that part of the world. Olive oil also represents the intense labor of the offerer, for the olives had to be crushed—i.e., put into heavy presses with enormous beams used as levers weighted with heavy stones—and ground up. The same olive oil is used to anoint the leaders, priests, and Levites for their offices. Indeed, that oil comes on a gravity feed from the two olive trees into the seven-branched lampstand or menorah in Zech 4:1-3. There it is explained to the two symbolic olive trees, the high priest Joshua and the Davidic governor Zerubbabel, that it is " 'not by might nor by power, but by my Spirit,' says the LORD Almighty" (Zech 4:6 NIV). Thus the grain offering, when kneaded with the olive oil, in whatever form, teaches Israel that in all the work offered as a gift to God, the in-working and enabling agent is the Spirit of God. Elsewhere oil is associated with the Spirit of God (see 1 Sam 10:1; 9-11). But oil is also associated with joy (see Ps 45:7; Prov 27:9; Isa 61:3).

A pinch of incense is also usually added to the grain offering (Lev 2:2, 15-16). It is not a late addition to the grain offering, as some have suggested, for incense burners have been discovered from periods of Israelite occupation much earlier than the time of Jeremiah.[38]

---

38. A point made by Gordon J. Wenham, *The New International Commentary on the Old Testament: Leviticus* (Grand Rapids: Eerdmans, 1979) 68 n. 1, citing as evidence Ruth Amiran, *Ancient Pottery of the Holy Land* (Jerusalem: Massada, 1969) 302-6.

The incense mentioned in 2:2 is actually frankincense. Frankincense is a fragrant gum resin that comes from three different species of *Boswellia* trees, native to southern Arabia and Somaliland on the African coast.

Instead of conjecturing that the frankincense or incense is to cover up the odors of the whole burnt offerings, which are said to be an aroma pleasing to God, it is better to note with the text that the frankincense is a "memorial"[39] to God (2:2). Even though the rest of the grain offering is to go to the priests, the frankincense is to be given totally to God as a memorial. In that it ascends totally to God, it may symbolize the prayers and praise of God's people. Because Psalms 38 and 70 use a similar form in their title lines as the word translated "memorial" in Lev 2:2, some have speculated that these two psalms were recited as "petitions" with the offering of the grain offering. The same word used in the titles to these two psalms occurs in 1 Chr 16:4, meaning "to make petition" or "to bring to remembrance." The portion that the priests take out of the grain offering, then, is a "memorial," or in "remembrance" of God's supreme dominion over all. It put the priests in mind of the divine promise in the covenant to accept the services the people render to God. As Ps 20:3 enjoins, "May [God] *remember* all your sacrifices/and accept your burnt offerings" (emphasis added, NIV). This is similar to what an angel told the Roman centurion Cornelius in Acts 10:4: "Your prayers and gifts to the poor have come up as a *memorial gift* before God" (emphasis added, NIV).

The sin offering (Lev 5:11) and the jealousy offerings (Num 5:15) specifically say that no oil or incense is to be mixed with them. These offerings bring iniquity and sin to mind rather than

all that Israel holds and enjoys because of the gracious provision of the sovereign covenant-maker. Both the sin and the jealousy offerings are devoid of the elements that make the whole burnt offering and the grain offering an aroma pleasing to the Lord.

The prohibition of yeast (or, as it is called in many versions, "leaven") and honey from the grain offerings is of special interest. Yeast was forbidden at the time of the exodus and the first Passover (see Exod 12:15; 13:3, 7) because Israel was to leave in haste; there was no time to wait around for the yeast to rise (see Exod 12:39). However, we must be careful of claiming that all leaven symbolizes decay and corruption and thus refers to evil in every instance where it appears in Scripture. That is not so: The loaves of the firstfruits were made with yeast (see Lev 23:17, 20), and even honey was introduced into the firstfruits offered in Hezekiah's time (see 2 Chr 31:5). Nevertheless, in the context of the grain offering, it still seems fair to conclude that yeast and honey may be excluded to avoid all suggestions of wickedness, malice, moral decay, and spiritual corruption.

Even though Israel was to be brought to a "land of milk and honey," the widespread use of honey in the pagan cults must have brought this strong aversion to its use in Israelite sacrifices. In the Ugaritic myths of the Canaanite religion, the hero Keret offers honey to the chief Canaanite god, El. Instances could be multiplied from Akkadian cuneiform sources in Mesopotamia and ancient Syria. Accordingly, the offerings made to God must be absolutely free of everything corrupt among God's people.

In 2:13, one other requisite is added to the grain offering: salt. Salt is just the opposite of honey and yeast in that it symbolizes preservation from corruption. It is found in every sacrifice. The best clue to its meaning is in the phrase "the salt of the covenant of your God" (2:13). Often, covenants, in that day and this, were sealed and confirmed by a formal meal in which the parties partook of salt together, thus concluding the pact. Therefore, solemn covenants are described in Scripture as "[covenants] of salt" (see Num 18:19; 2 Chr 13:5). The effect of this concept is to render the expression "the salt of the covenant of your God" as a "covenant made binding by salt." Salt

---

39. The precise meaning of this Hebrew word, *'azkārātāh*, is uncertain. If it is understood as an *Afel* form, it would mean "that which calls to mind," or "a memorial portion," coming from the verb *zākar*, "to remember." Another way to view it would be to take it from the noun *zeker*, meaning "a commemorative object." In that case, the word in Lev 2:2, 9, 16; 5:12; 6:15 (Heb. 6:8); 24:7; Num 5:26 would mean "a token portion." The Akkadian vocabulary has *zikru*, "an effigy," "a double." This would strengthen the position for the second option; however, we still think the first meaning of "memorial" is preferable. Actually, both concepts say nearly the same thing: The grain offering, in both views, would be a sign that the worshiper has been taught and reminded of the fact that everything is owed to God, but God is pleased to accept a portion of the sacrifice as a "token" of it, while releasing the rest of the offering for consumption by the priests. Thus this offering is a "tribute" or "a gift that fulfills the covenant," while reminding the offerer that God deserves to have everything that we are and have.

cannot be destroyed by fire or the passing of time. The addition of salt is a deliberate act to remind the offerer that the covenant relationship the act symbolizes is an eternal and binding relationship. God will never forsake the worshiper—and the one bringing the offering has a duty to remember to do all that the covenant teaches.

The grain offering is unique in specifying that a portion goes to Aaron and his sons: "It is a most holy part of the offerings made to the LORD by fire" (2:3b). Only a small part of the grain offering is offered by the priest to the Lord as a "memorial"; the larger portion is given to Aaron and his sons. And most surprisingly of all, that portion is called "a most holy part"! The Hebrew expression used here is the standard way of expressing the superlative degree: "holiness of holinesses," or "most holy." The expression occurs only with the grain, sin, and guilt offerings (2:3; 6:17[cf. Heb 6:10], 25 [cf. Heb 6:18]; 7:6) in distinction to the rest of the sacrifices, which are designated as "sacred" (the peace offering, firstfruits of the harvest, firstfruits of the animals, and all that is devoted, i.e., part of the חרם *ḥērem* to the Lord [see Num 18:12-19]). These designations of the "sacred" and the "most holy" are always used with the portions to be eaten. That is why the burnt offering is left off the list of "most holy," since no one is to eat any of it.

This distinction, then, between things that are *lighter in holiness* and things that are *most holy* is fairly common among the Jewish communities and in the Egyptian and Hittite cultic texts.[40] "The lighter holy things" may be eaten by persons who are not priests in any place in the encampment, or within Jerusalem, so long as they are ceremonially clean. They include all peace offerings made by particular individuals, the paschal lamb, the tithes, and the firstlings of cattle. But "the most holy things" are to be eaten by no one, or by none except Aaron and his sons, in the sanctuary (6:16-26). Included in this category are all burnt offerings, all sin offerings, and all peace offerings made for the whole community. The grain offering is put into this category of "most holy" as well. A particular sacredness is attached to it because of its use of the inner kernels of the wheat and because of its being set aside for the priests to be eaten in the sanctuary.

This distinction between the sacred and the most holy among the sacrificial instructions supports the argument for a similar distinction within the whole law of God. Many moderns have great difficulty seeing any distinction between the moral law of God and the civil and ceremonial aspects of that same law. However, by Christian times the rabbis were distinguishing between the light and the heavy aspects of the law, just as Jesus referred to the "weightier matters of the law" (Matt 23:23 NRSV). The separation between the "sacred," or lighter holy things, and the "most holy" things helps us to see that such distinctions were not late fictions concocted by apologists who were hard pressed to find any contemporary relevance for certain legal portions of Scripture.

Three types of cooked grain offerings are mentioned in vv. 4-10. Verse 4 mentions the one baked in an "oven." The oven was partially embedded in the ground in a circular pit, usually four to five feet deep and three feet in diameter, with plastered walls, or it was cylindrical, a three-foot-high unglazed earthen vessel with an opening about fifteen inches wide in diameter at the top that gradually widened toward the bottom, where a hole was placed to remove the ashes conveniently. In both models, the bread was baked by heating the oven to glowing embers in the bottom. Then large oval or round cakes, not thicker than pancakes, were thrown against the sides of the oven. The cake was not turned since it was thin and could, in most cases, be removed in three minutes. If it were not removed in time from the sides of the oven after its moisture had been removed, it would fall into the fire and be wasted. The bread thus produced was usually soft and flexible, and it could be rolled up like paper, a type of falafel. If it stayed in the oven too long, it could become crisp and hard.

Verse 5 speaks of another type of cooking instrument: a "griddle." The griddle was made of either clay [41] or iron (see Ezek 4:3). The latter form is a convex plate of iron (copper often still being in use for some) placed about nine inches from the ground by supporting stones. With a slow fire beneath it, it produces cakes very similar to those stuck to the sides of the oven, but it is a much slower process.

---

40. See Jacob Milgrom, *Cult and Conscience: The Asham and the Priestly Doctrine of Repentance* (Leiden: Brill, 1976) 41-43.

41. Milgrom mentions some clay griddles found at Gezer (*Leviticus 1-16*, 185) and described and illustrated in *IDB*, vol. 1 (Nashville: Abingdon, 1962) 1:462, fig. 48.

The last cooking instrument mentioned is a "pan" in v. 7. Apparently, the main difference between the griddle and the pan was that the pan had a lid. Originally, they were shallow earthen vessels resembling our frying pans, then other metal forms appeared.

The prescriptions in this chapter conclude with the third type of grain offering: the grain offering of the firstfruits to the Lord (2:14-16). The firstfruits of all the harvest are to be brought each year to the Lord as the real owner of all the land and what it produced. In this line of thinking, the Israelites have the status of tenants (see Exod 22:29; 23:19; 34:26; Lev 23:9; Deut 26:1-2).

The ears of grain are to be brought to the Lord in the form in which they are to be eaten: roasted first in the fire so as to dry out the moisture, and then ground in a mill, usually between two stones. Whether these grains could be barley as well as wheat is unknown. The term *firstfruits* is applied to barley in 2 Kgs 4:42 but to wheat in Num 28:26. To this day, Arabs roast barley as described here, but not wheat, due to its flat taste.

This offering, like all the cooked grain offerings, is mixed with oil and presented with incense. Once again, the priest takes a handful and burns that portion to the Lord mixed with the oil and all the incense. The remainder, as in the other grain offerings, belongs to the priests, though that is not explicitly stated this time. Since the priests are given no land among the tribal inheritances, they depend on this provision from the Lord and the people for their daily bread.

The crushing or bruising of the "firstfruits" will play a large role in the typology of both the OT and the NT. Christians identify the resurrection of Christ as the "firstfruits of those who have fallen asleep" (1 Cor 15:20 NIV). They see this typology also in the fact that Christ sanctified himself, "that they too may be truly sanctified" (John 17:19 NIV). Thus, to sanctify the first part of the harvest is to sanctify the whole harvest.

REFLECTIONS

The grain offering symbolized the dedication of a person's life, and especially one's labor, to God. This central thesis is illustrated in the following applications to our contemporary lives.

1. If the whole burnt offering required that the entire animal be burned on the altar (except the skin and viscera) to signify the consecration of the whole life to God, why was such a small part of the grain offering placed on the altar since it too indicated a total surrender of the person to God? The answer is readily available: All of the grain offering was presented to God, even if only a small portion was placed in the fire on the altar. Thus the Lord accepted the entire grain offering. The limited portion of the grain offering that was burned was offered as a "memorial," thereby signifying that the offerer served the Lord in all thoughts and labors in life. In the grain offering, Israel and all subsequent generations are reminded that God's claim upon us for full consecration covers everything, even the very food that we eat. Thus, as Paul directed, "So whether you eat or drink or whatever you do, do it all for the glory of God" (1 Cor 10:31 NIV).

2. The idea that the grain offering was a "memorial" (2:2; cf. NRSV) also signifies that one purpose of an offering is to jog memories. We often think of an offering only in the task-oriented sense; that is, we put money in the offering plate to pay for the church expenses, to feed hungry people, to send the youth choir to choir camp, and so on. In other words, we tend to think of offerings as means to get things done. To be sure, getting things done is a worthy reason to make an offering, but Leviticus suggests that one of the most basic reasons we make offerings is not so that something will get done but so that something will be brought to mind.

First, an offering brings to our minds the blessings of God in our lives. At Christmas, we give a necktie to Uncle Joe, not because he really needs another tie, but because the very act of giving a gift brings our loving relationship to the surface. In the same way, we make offerings to God, not because God needs what we offer, but because we need to have our relationship with God continually brought to mind. Making an offering, in this sense, is like participating in the Lord's Supper; we do so "in remembrance" of God's merciful acts.

Second, and more radical, Leviticus suggests that offerings are made to jog God's memory! As noted in the commentary, Ps 20:3 states, "May [God] remember all your sacrifices/ and accept your burnt offerings" (NIV). This is picture language, of course; there is no notion here that God is forgetful, a divine absent-minded professor who needs to be reminded of things. The claim, rather, is that by making an offering, we become present to God. An offering, then, is a form of prayer. It is a way of making active, visible, and concrete what is always tacitly true: our communion with God. In this sense, offerings "bring us to God's mind."

3. The grain offering was one main source of income for the priesthood. The laity were responsible to their ministers to care properly for them. The responsibility to provide for those in ministry still rests with the people of God, even though the ancient grain offerings have ceased to be required or encouraged. (Paul made that point abundantly clear in 1 Cor 9:13-14.) In every dispensation, God has prescribed a demonstrated concern toward those who have devoted themselves to the ministry of "most holy things." To avoid participating in this responsibility, or to do so in a shabby manner that forces economic pressures on those who should be busy about the things of God, is ultimately to demean both the Lord, whom worshipers say they wish to serve, and the service roles God has given. In the long run it reflects on the claims of the laity. How can such miserly pittances be an expression of the lordship of their sovereign Lord? Those who are called and who faithfully labor in the Word and the holy things of God are to be competently and adequately supported.

4. The tendency to import into our worship of God such negative leavening influences as are found in the wickedness and corruption of our day is all too tempting. But we must maintain constant vigilance to make sure that our worship does not imitate pagan practices or exhibit the leaven of hypocrisy.

5. In accord with the usage of leaven in this text, there are other instances where leaven/yeast symbolizes wickedness in its various forms. For example, Paul warns in 1 Cor 5:7, "Get rid of the old yeast that you may be a new batch without yeast—as you really are. For Christ, our Passover lamb, has been sacrificed" (NIV). Paul goes on to warn in v. 8, "Therefore, let us keep the Festival, not with the old yeast, the yeast of malice and wickedness, but with bread without yeast, the bread of sincerity and truth" (NIV).

6. All promises and covenants with God should be seasoned with "salt," for our word and our practice should be as permanent and binding as the sacrifices where salt indicated the same reality. The apostle Paul must have had the same metaphor in mind when he urged in Col 4:6 that our life-style should always be marked by graciousness; in fact, it ought to be "seasoned with salt." Likewise, Jesus taught in Mark 9:49*b*-50, "Every sacrifice will be salted with salt. Salt is good; but if salt has lost its saltiness, how can you season it? Have salt in yourselves, and be at peace with one another" (NRSV).[42] Rather than exhibiting decay, corruption, hypocrisy, and negativism, the call is for a purifying and preserving effect on all of life by each individual. Salt is the symbol of our friendship with our Lord and a pledge of our faithfulness to the holiness God has called us to display.

7. The distinctions between what is sacred and what is most holy remind us that distinctions within the one law of God were not only possible but required. Such fences around portions of the law appear to make it arbitrary to a certain extent; yet, in other ways they teach us that God is so totally different from us (both in being and in behavior) that it is crass

---

42. The sentence "every sacrifice will be salted with salt" is omitted from the primary NRSV text but is reported in a textual note as included by some ancient authorities.

presumption for worshipers to lunge headlong into worship practices that fail to remind us of this distinction. All that God made is good and may be employed for the good of humanity, but how, where, and why these things are used must also be a consideration, especially when we mortals seek to worship the holy God.

8. The One to whom the "firstfruits" pointed was Christ, who was "bruised" (or "crushed") for our iniquities (see Isa 53:5). Christ is the "Firstfruit" par excellence (see 1 Cor 15:20) because his resurrection signaled the possibility of the resurrection of others.

9. Christ is also the "bread of God . . . who comes down from heaven and gives life to the world" (John 6:33 NIV). Regarded in this manner, the grain offering was a type of Christ who is to come, the One symbolized in the Lord's Supper. As the grain was bruised and crushed to make the sacrifice for the ancient Israelite, so the living Bread was bruised and crushed for all who would believe.

Leviticus 3:1-17, The Peace Offering

NIV

3 " 'If someone's offering is a fellowship offering,[a] and he offers an animal from the herd, whether male or female, he is to present before the LORD an animal without defect. ²He is to lay his hand on the head of his offering and slaughter it at the entrance to the Tent of Meeting. Then Aaron's sons the priests shall sprinkle the blood against the altar on all sides. ³From the fellowship offering he is to bring a sacrifice made to the LORD by fire: all the fat that covers the inner parts or is connected to them, ⁴both kidneys with the fat on them near the loins, and the covering of the liver, which he will remove with the kidneys. ⁵Then Aaron's sons are to burn it on the altar on top of the burnt offering that is on the burning wood, as an offering made by fire, an aroma pleasing to the LORD.

⁶" 'If he offers an animal from the flock as a fellowship offering to the LORD, he is to offer a male or female without defect. ⁷If he offers a lamb, he is to present it before the LORD. ⁸He is to lay his hand on the head of his offering and slaughter it in front of the Tent of Meeting. Then Aaron's sons shall sprinkle its blood against the altar on all sides. ⁹From the fellowship offering he is to bring a sacrifice made to the LORD by fire: its fat, the entire fat tail cut off close to the backbone, all the fat that covers the inner parts or is connected to them, ¹⁰both kidneys with the fat on them near the loins, and the covering of

a] Traditionally *peace offering*, also in verses 3, 6 and 9

NRSV

3 If the offering is a sacrifice of well-being, if you offer an animal of the herd, whether male or female, you shall offer one without blemish before the LORD. ²You shall lay your hand on the head of the offering and slaughter it at the entrance of the tent of meeting; and Aaron's sons the priests shall dash the blood against all sides of the altar. ³You shall offer from the sacrifice of well-being, as an offering by fire to the LORD, the fat that covers the entrails and all the fat that is around the entrails; ⁴the two kidneys with the fat that is on them at the loins, and the appendage of the liver, which he shall remove with the kidneys. ⁵Then Aaron's sons shall turn these into smoke on the altar, with the burnt offering that is on the wood on the fire, as an offering by fire of pleasing odor to the LORD.

6If your offering for a sacrifice of well-being to the LORD is from the flock, male or female, you shall offer one without blemish. ⁷If you present a sheep as your offering, you shall bring it before the LORD ⁸and lay your hand on the head of the offering. It shall be slaughtered before the tent of meeting, and Aaron's sons shall dash its blood against all sides of the altar. ⁹You shall present its fat from the sacrifice of well-being, as an offering by fire to the LORD: the whole broad tail, which shall be removed close to the backbone, the fat that covers the entrails, and all the fat that is around the entrails; ¹⁰the two kidneys with the fat that is on them at the loins, and the appendage

NIV

the liver, which he will remove with the kidneys. [11]The priest shall burn them on the altar as food, an offering made to the LORD by fire.

[12]"'If his offering is a goat, he is to present it before the LORD. [13]He is to lay his hand on its head and slaughter it in front of the Tent of Meeting. Then Aaron's sons shall sprinkle its blood against the altar on all sides. [14]From what he offers he is to make this offering to the LORD by fire: all the fat that covers the inner parts or is connected to them, [15]both kidneys with the fat on them near the loins, and the covering of the liver, which he will remove with the kidneys. [16]The priest shall burn them on the altar as food, an offering made by fire, a pleasing aroma. All the fat is the LORD's.

[17]"'This is a lasting ordinance for the generations to come, wherever you live: You must not eat any fat or any blood.'"

NRSV

of the liver, which you shall remove with the kidneys. [11]Then the priest shall turn these into smoke on the altar as a food offering by fire to the LORD.

12If your offering is a goat, you shall bring it before the LORD [13]and lay your hand on its head; it shall be slaughtered before the tent of meeting; and the sons of Aaron shall dash its blood against all sides of the altar. [14]You shall present as your offering from it, as an offering by fire to the LORD, the fat that covers the entrails, and all the fat that is around the entrails; [15]the two kidneys with the fat that is on them at the loins, and the appendage of the liver, which you shall remove with the kidneys. [16]Then the priest shall turn these into smoke on the altar as a food offering by fire for a pleasing odor.

All fat is the LORD's. [17]It shall be a perpetual statute throughout your generations, in all your settlements: you must not eat any fat or any blood.

COMMENTARY

According to a later section in the laws of the sacrifices, 7:11-16, the peace offerings are of three kinds: sacrifices of thanksgiving, of vows, and of freewill offerings.

The name for this offering has puzzled commentators from earliest days. The traditional rendering of the Hebrew שלמים (šĕlāmîm) as "peace offerings" (assuming that it derives from שלום šālôm, "peace") reflects a rendering borrowed from the Vg's *pacificus* and the LXX εἰρηνικός *eirēnikos* (although the LXX uses no less than three terms to render this one Hebrew term). Both mean "that which relates to peace." Accordingly, the idea is that this sacrifice signifies a peaceful, harmonious relationship between the worshiper and God.

More recent interpreters have favored other renderings as the name for this sacrifice: (a) "the well-being offering" (NRSV) (taken from שלם šālēm, "whole," "sound," "harmonious"); (b) "the shared offering" or "the fellowship offering" (NIV) (taken from the fact that it always involves God, the donor, and the donor's friends and

family, and the priests); (c) "the gift of greeting offering" (taken from the Ugaritic epic of Keret who offers a "tribute," "gift of greeting" to an attacking commander, called a *šalamūna*); and (d) "the recompense offering" (based on *šillēm*, "repayment," "recompense"). Since all of these are based solely on etymologies, they are no more than mere educated guesses. It is clear, however, that the idea of "peace" (*shalom*) includes the concepts of wholeness, health, and well-being and the cessation of hostilities.

The peace offering, like the whole burnt offering and the grain offering, is represented from a canonical standpoint as being in use prior to the days of its codification in Leviticus. It appears in Gen 31:54, related to the covenant formed between Jacob and Laban. In Exod 18:12, Jethro, Moses' father-in-law, joined Aaron and all the elders in sharing a peace offering. There is even an instance of an improper use of this offering by Israel as part of the golden calf episode (see Exod 32:6).

One of the most detailed illustrations of the ceremony of the peace offering is in 1 Samuel 9.

The "invited guests" partake of what has been first blessed (the fat portions, which are then offered up to the Lord on the altar), and the remainder is boiled in pots and served to the guests in rooms nearby. The main function of the peace offering is to express friendship, fellowship, and peace with God. To conclude that its only purpose is to provide meat for the table is to assume a minimalist view of what is happening in this offering.

To say that no thoughts of expiation or of atonement are connected with this offering is going too far. This is true only to a limited degree, for 3:5 carefully requires that the peace offering must be burned "on the altar *on top of the burnt offering that is on the burning wood*" (emphasis added). The connection between the two offerings cannot be stated more clearly: The burnt offering is foundational in sequence and logically prior to the ritual and the significance of the peace offering. Furthermore, all six parts of the ritual mentioned in our discussion of chap. 1 are present in chap. 3, namely, (1) the presentation, (2) the laying on of hands, (3) the slaughter of the victim, (4) the sprinkling of the blood, (5) the sacrificial burning, and (especially here) (6) the sacrificial meal. The first four parts, though the text does not dwell on them in 3:1-2, still carry the symbolic and typical significance they carry in the other blood offerings. There still is the innocent victim. The offerer must still present the victim by faith. The blood of the slain victim must still be shed in the place appointed by God and applied to the altar, thereby indicating the vertical dimension of the sacrifice. The basis of the communion and fellowship shared in the peace offering rests, therefore, on the atonement signified in the animal sacrifice. No single offering can set forth all the facets that needed to be taught to Israel through the whole sacrificial system. All five types of sacrifice were needed before the whole picture of what was involved in the process of restoring and maintaining humans in fellowship with God could be gained.

The plan for chap. 3 is fairly straightforward and falls into three paragraphs, just as chaps. 1–2 do. The three divisions are (1) peace offerings of cattle (3:1-5); (2) peace offerings of sheep (3:6-11); and (3) peace offerings of goats, (3:12-17). Each of the three paragraphs ends with a different

remark that the offering is "an aroma pleasing to the LORD" (v. 5), "an offering made to the LORD by fire" (v. 11), or "an offering made by fire (but see our discussion on 1:9), a pleasing aroma" (v. 16). Some would make a separate fourth paragraph for vv. 16c and 17, entitling it the law of suet and blood. But since it is so brief, and since it applies to all of the prescriptions for all the peace offerings, it is better to regard it as a closing colophon to the whole chapter.

The fact that there is a sacrificial meal in connection with this sacrifice has attracted unfair comparisons with similar meals in the ancient Near Eastern world. But the peace offering does not exhibit any mystical union with the deity or any other expression of a sensuous-magical form. These suggestions can be categorically rejected for several reasons: (a) The all-consuming holiness of God sets the peace offering apart from pagan sacrificial meals, where thoughts of a relationship of a blood kinship linkage were present; (b) the initiative for the presence of God rests with God and not with any mystical participation in the divine; and (c) the sacrifice is eaten "before the LORD" (see Deut 27:7), not "with the LORD"—thus humans are not entertaining God at a feast, but God is banqueting mortals. This last point is most important. Here is one of the most instructive contrasts and striking distinctions between all other sacrificial meals in the ancient Near East and Scripture. The host is the deity, not mortals! The meal has to be eaten at God's house, not at a place of the offerer's choosing. Invited guests, along with the donor and the priests, all sit down at the table of the Lord. Although the offerer brings the victim, which also serves as the food for the banquet, the ownership of the victim has already changed hands when it is offered to God, similar to the other blood offerings. From that moment onward, the victim is no longer the property of the offerer, the priest, or the community; it belongs to God! Having received the victim, God now directs how it is to be used.

First, the Lord directs that a portion of it is to be burned on the altar: only the fat, as we shall see. Then, God instructs that the priests, servants who minister at the altar, must receive the specified pieces after the fat has been burned on the altar (and not before that, as the sons of Eli did so wickedly in 1 Sam 2:12-17). The remaining portion, which is by far the largest part, is given as a feast for the worshiper, family, and friends. Had there been any hint of any mystic participation in the life of the divine, surely the order of the service would have been reversed, and God would have demanded more than the fat; certainly there would have been some eating of the meat together, at the very minimum. But none of that appears here. The regulations used for selecting the animals to be offered are different in several respects from those of the materials specified for the whole burnt offering. The most noticeable change is that doves and pigeons are not permitted in the peace offering. This is not to discriminate against poor people; instead, due to the birds' smallness, they would not provide ample food for a meal.

The second most noticeable feature is that a female is permitted as well as a male animal (3:6; and possibly v. 12, though the text is not completely clear; עֵז 'ēz sometimes, however, refers only to a female, a nanny goat). This in no way indicates that it is a second-class sacrifice or one of a lesser status. Instead, it provides for greater liberty of choice, especially since the purpose of this sacrifice is to conclude with a sacrificial meal shared by the offerer with family and friends.

To emphasize the point of greater liberty of choice in the animal, a third exception to the rules for materials used in the whole burnt offering can be observed. It is, perhaps, even more striking than the other two exceptions. Even though the general rule for the peace offering is the same as for the burnt offering, i.e., "an animal without defect" (3:1), in the case of the freewill offerings, 22:23 allows even greater freedom by providing that one might offer a cow or sheep that "is deformed or stunted"! This could not be done, however, in connection with any other type of peace offering. The latitude permitted in this one case is explained because the chief aspect of this form of peace offering is to be the offerer's spontaneous expression of love and joy for God. It does not have a particular occasion as the basis for the act; it is completely impulsive, instinctive, and automatically done almost as a spur-of-the-moment deed. This is not to deny what has already been affirmed, i.e., that the ideas of representation, substitution, propitiation and expiation have a place in peace offerings, as indeed they do

have in all offerings involving blood, but that is not the chief intent here. Moreover, since the leeway of offering the less expensive birds does not exist in this offering, a concession is made, no doubt, to help the poorer worshipers in acts of participation.

The ritual itself, as has been noted, is identical to the burnt offering through the first four parts: (1) the presentation of the victim, (2) the laying on of hands, (3) the slaughter of the sacrifice, and (4) the sprinkling of the blood against the altar (3:1-2). From that point the ceremony is distinctive, for the burning of the sacrifice and the sacrificial meal (parts five and six of the sacrificial ritual) are markedly different from the burnt offering.

Whereas the whole animal (except the skin and viscera) is burned in the whole burnt offering, in the peace offering only the fat is placed on the altar as an offering to God. The fat referred to here is not the ordinary fat entwined in the musculature of an animal, called שׁוּמָן (šûmān) in rabbinic Hebrew, but the fat that covers or surrounds the kidneys, the liver, and the entrails (3:3), called חֵלֶב (ḥēleb) in Hebrew. This fat protects the vital parts of the body and functions as an energy reserve in maintaining the life of the animal. The kidneys, in the eastern Mediterranean world, were thought to be the seat of the emotions, feelings, and conscience. Often, the kidneys are linked with the heart in representing this idea (see Pss 7:9; 26:2; Jer 17:10; 20:12—"kidneys" translated as "mind" in the NIV).

When a sheep is used, "its fat [אַלְיָה 'alyâ], the entire fat tail cut off close to the backbone" (3:9), is an additional requirement. The reference here is to a special breed of sheep still found in the Near East known as the fat- or broad-tailed sheep (*Ovis laticaudata*). The tail grows several feet and generally weighs about fifteen pounds; however, some have been known to reach fifty and even eighty pounds! Sometimes shepherds used low platforms on wheels to support the tails and to prevent them from dragging on the ground and breaking out in sores.

No symbolism is directly assigned to the fat, as with most of these sacrifices. However, from the culture, times, and Scripture, it is possible to conclude that fatness represents the richest and the best part of the animal. Leviticus 3:16 concludes this chapter with the affirmation that "all the fat is the LORD's"; thus the theology of the action is firmly established. The idea that fat is valuable perplexes many readers in today's Western culture, who are trying to reduce their weight by not eating fat. But our culture does not need to add fat to our diet. Since we get it from so many sources we can afford to be selective and choosy. The ancients never ate this fat alone, but mixed it into many of their dishes with lean meat. They also used it as a substitute for butter and oil. It was especially palatable in boiled rice; the oil from the fat of this sheep's tail made the rice into an outstanding dish. It is interesting to read stories of those who went through severe shortages of food in Eastern Europe during World War II and during the Russian occupation of those lands. What was sought more than anything else was some lard or fat to nourish their vitamin-starved bodies. Only in extreme cases such as these, when fat is absent altogether, do we begin to realize the vital function that fat performs in our bodies.

The other distinctive feature of the peace offering is the sacrificial meal. After the priests burn the specified fat on the altar as the portion that is the Lord's, the breast is given for all the priests and the right shoulder to the priest who officiates (7:30-34). The greatest part by far is left for the offerer and family and friends, i.e., all who are ceremonially clean. If the peace offering is for thanksgiving, all of it has to be eaten on the same day it is offered. If it is a vow or freewill offering, i.e., a voluntary offering, part of it may be eaten on the day it is offered and part of it on the next day; however, if any remains on the third day, that part cannot be eaten but must be burned with fire (7:16-18; 19:5-8).

The meal has three specifications that are to be closely followed. First, it is to be a feast that is an occasion of great joy to the Lord, representing the labors of the donor's hands. Second, the meal is to be eaten by the donor before the Lord at the sanctuary and not at the donor's home. And third, the meal is to include all members of the donor's family and any Levite or priest who might be passing through the neighborhood.

The ancient Near East offered many examples of similar sacrificial meals. Isaiah 65:11 notes that some idolatrous Israelites "spread a table for [the god] Fortune/and [filled] bowls of mixed wine for [the goddess] Destiny" (NIV). When the participants ate and drank in the feasts set for pagan deities, they expressed the same desire that Israel did for friendship, communion, and closeness to their gods. That is the thought behind such biblical sentiments as "You prepare a table before me/ in the presence of my enemies" (Ps 23:5 NIV), the parable of the great banquet (see Luke 14:15-24), the homecoming of the prodigal son for whom the father killed the fatted calf (see Luke 15:23), and the parable of the wedding banquet (see Matt 22:1-14).

At first, the emphasis in the description of the peace offering is on offering up the fat pieces to the Lord. Later on, the spotlight will fall on the meal itself as the grand culmination of this offering. In this later aspect of the sacrifice, the startling factor is that the victim that symbolizes, as it does in all offerings of blood, the satisfaction and substitution for the donor's sin becomes the food on the table for the same offending donor.

Leviticus 3:17 concludes with a stern prohibition on eating blood or fat. "This is a lasting ordinance for the generations to come," warns v. 17, a sentence that occurs seventeen times in Leviticus. The same ban on blood and fat does not appear in Deut 12:15-16, 21-24 because these verses relate to a separate set of ceremonial circumstances. The reason for the ban on blood, however, is that blood in the flesh is life itself, something that only God owns and has control over. In a similar way, the ban on fat is in effect because it surrounds the organs thought to be at the center of a person's being. It also represents the best, and as such it too belongs to God.

REFLECTIONS

We humans can have peace with God but not peace without a price. The peace offering must be understood as it so often appeared in practice: linked with the whole burnt offering. It was placed on top of the fire for the whole burnt offering. Therefore, we are never far away from the redemptive concepts shared in all the sacrifices that involved blood. But this sacrifice sets forth several unique contributions, again in concretely graphic terms.

1. All peace offerings, whether presented as a thanksgiving, supplication, or vow, were to be offered on top of the burnt offering on the altar, thus indicating that the sacrifices of praise, petition, or vow were grounded on the atonement. Many Christian readers understand this to suggest that no matter what service or praise the offerer presents to God, the only way such worship can be made acceptable is on the basis of the atonement of Christ. The only possible way mortals can ever find acceptance and be able to offer to God fitting worship is through the access Christ provided in his obedience and death on a cross.

2. Peace offerings gather up the many meanings of peace: not only the end of warfare and hostility but also mental, physical, and spiritual health. In our culture, there is a gradual reawakening to the fact that illness is more than an isolated, clinically treatable condition. Illness involves the whole self; a brokenness anywhere in our lives affects us everywhere, and the popularity of alternative forms of healing today testifies to people's hunger to treat the spiritual side of illness as well as the clinical. One meaning of the peace offering is that our hopes for wholeness rest finally in God. To be ill becomes, then, not just a concern of physicians and a matter for antibiotics; it becomes a concern of God and a matter for prayer.

3. Whereas in pagan ritual humans gave a feast for God, in the biblical prescription of the peace offering that is reversed: God hosted mortals at the banquet. As soon as the sacrifice was presented to God, it was no longer the property of the offerer or the community. The victim belonged to God. The host of the meal was not the donor but the Lord. That is why the animal had to be eaten at God's house and not at the donor's house or anywhere else in town. All of this strikes at the heart of a popular religious notion: that mortals can make God their friend by doing something or giving something to the deity. That is certainly excluded here. Instead, God does the inviting and provides the occasion for joy. Once the possibility exists for God and humans to enjoy the state of being at one with another (our word *atonement,* the state of being "at one" [with God]), a fellowship is possible that restores the disruption that sin introduced.

4. The prohibition against eating any fat or blood will be explained in the supplemental materials on the law of the peace offering (7:22-27) and in the central declaration (17:11-16). The fat referred to, of course, was limited to the fat specified for the sacrifices; there the law was absolute. To use any portions of the fat specifically set aside for offering to God on the altar in the peace offering, the sin offering, or the guilt offering was to steal what had been appropriated for God. But the prohibition on blood covered all situations since "the life of the flesh is in the blood" (17:11; literal rendering). As such, all life belonged to God. Thus, in these two prohibitions, Israel was reminded of two important facts: (1) God's claim on humans is for their "best," and (2) only life is valuable enough to depict the grounds of atonement with God, as a life was spilled out and the blood yielded up in death on behalf of another.

To treat the "blood of the covenant" as a common or "unholy thing" is offensive, the writer of Hebrews warns (10:26-29 NIV). Such an offense exposes the perpetrators to a much more severe punishment than what came upon those who "rejected the law of Moses" and therefore died without mercy. It is tantamount to "[insulting] the Spirit of grace" (Heb 10:29 NIV). In fact, continues the writer of Hebrews, "It is a dreadful thing to fall into the hands of the living God" (v. 31 NIV). Modern believers must be careful not to undervalue or to despise and regard as something uncouth the sanctity of the blood of the sacrifices, especially the sacrifice of the One to which these offerings pointed.

5. A later regulation concerning the peace offering ordered that none of the peace offering was to remain until the third day presumably to prevent decay. But this provision would one day remind Israel of the Antitype who was to come. Psalm 16:10 affirms that God would not let the "Holy One see decay" (NIV) for he too was raised on the third day from the grave.

Is this the source for the Pauline affirmation that Christ "was raised on the third day *according to the Scriptures*" (1 Cor 15:4; emphasis added, NIV)? This certainly is a more convincing source than the text traditionally pointed to in Hos 6:2: "After two days he will revive us;/on the third day he will restore us" (NIV).

Leviticus 4:1– 6:7, Two New Atoning Offerings

OVERVIEW

The last two of the five major offerings differ from the first three in several ways. The assumption in the first three offerings seems to be that most were acquainted with the burnt offering, grain offering, and peace offering because of previous experience with them. But in the two offerings that are now to be described, the sin offering and guilt offering, a more detailed description of the meaning and purpose of each is necessary.

Neither offering appears in the narratives of the present canonical order of texts prior to Mosaic times; in fact, Job offers whole burnt offerings where technically, based on what is taught here, he should have offered sin offerings (see Job 1:5; 42:8). But if Job is located, as some believe, in the patriarchal times, the situation agrees with what has been observed elsewhere.

In the view of the older historical-critical school, as best summarized by Julius Wellhausen, these two offerings did not appear until the seventh or, better still, the sixth and fifth centuries BCE, when they presumably took the place of monetary penalties, such as are mentioned in 2 Kgs 12:16. But this line of reasoning appears to reverse what one would normally expect. Usually, the concrete act of the ceremony would later be replaced by the abstract payment of goods or money. And if the allusion to the priests "[feeding] on the *sins* of my people" (Hos 4:8, emphasis added, NIV) is a direct reference to the provision made in the sin offering for the priests to eat a portion of the sacrifice (the Hebrew word

for "sins" is the same word used for the "sin offering"), this is a clear eighth-century BCE reference to the regulation in Lev 6:25-26. The prophets Micah (6:7) and Ezekiel (40:39; 42:13; 43:19; 44:27, 29; 45:17; 46:20) treat the sin offering as if it had been in existence prior to their times as well. One of the most difficult arguments for the classical Wellhausian thesis to handle, in this regard, is the failure of Leviticus to make any provision for the sin of the "king"! Provision is made for the forgiveness of the sin of the "leader," but not a word about the "king." This suggests that the text could reflect a time prior to the first king in Israel, i.e., prior to c. 1000 BCE.

There is a second major difference between the two offerings described in chaps. 4–6 and the ones in chaps. 1–3. The first group of offerings are usually voluntary. But for the sin and guilt offerings, a specific offense makes their presentation necessary (4:1, 13, 22, 27; 5:1, 14; 6:2 [MT 5:21]).

The distinctions between the sin and guilt offerings are sometimes very difficult to draw. Provisions for both of them are very similar (7:7: "the same law applies to both the sin offering and the guilt offering"), and the Hebrew word אשׁם ('āšām) has two distinct connotations, both used in this section: (1) a "guilt offering" (e.g., 5:15-16) and (2) a "penalty" (e.g., 5:5-6). Failure to observe this distinction has led some (e.g., the KJV) to designate 5:1-13 as a section on the guilt offering, even though vv. 11-12 specifically call it a "sin offering."

Leviticus 4:1–5:13, The Sin Offering

NIV	NRSV
4 The LORD said to Moses, ²"Say to the Israelites: 'When anyone sins unintention-	**4** The LORD spoke to Moses, saying, ²Speak to the people of Israel, saying: When anyone sins unintentionally in any of the LORD's

ally and does what is forbidden in any of the Lord's commands—

3"'If the anointed priest sins, bringing guilt on the people, he must bring to the Lord a young bull without defect as a sin offering for the sin he has committed. [4]He is to present the bull at the entrance to the Tent of Meeting before the Lord. He is to lay his hand on its head and slaughter it before the Lord. [5]Then the anointed priest shall take some of the bull's blood and carry it into the Tent of Meeting. [6]He is to dip his finger into the blood and sprinkle some of it seven times before the Lord, in front of the curtain of the sanctuary. [7]The priest shall then put some of the blood on the horns of the altar of fragrant incense that is before the Lord in the Tent of Meeting. The rest of the bull's blood he shall pour out at the base of the altar of burnt offering at the entrance to the Tent of Meeting. [8]He shall remove all the fat from the bull of the sin offering—the fat that covers the inner parts or is connected to them, [9]both kidneys with the fat on them near the loins, and the covering of the liver, which he will remove with the kidneys— [10]just as the fat is removed from the ox[a] sacrificed as a fellowship offering.[b] Then the priest shall burn them on the altar of burnt offering. [11]But the hide of the bull and all its flesh, as well as the head and legs, the inner parts and offal— [12]that is, all the rest of the bull—he must take outside the camp to a place ceremonially clean, where the ashes are thrown, and burn it in a wood fire on the ash heap.

13"'If the whole Israelite community sins unintentionally and does what is forbidden in any of the Lord's commands, even though the community is unaware of the matter, they are guilty. [14]When they become aware of the sin they committed, the assembly must bring a young bull as a sin offering and present it before the Tent of Meeting. [15]The elders of the community are to lay their hands on the bull's head before the Lord, and the bull shall be slaughtered before the Lord. [16]Then the anointed priest is to take some of the bull's blood into the Tent of Meeting. [17]He shall dip his finger into the blood and sprinkle it before

a10 The Hebrew word can include both male and female.
b10 Traditionally *peace offering*; also in verses 26, 31 and 35
c11 That is, probably about 2 quarts (about 2 liters)

commandments about things not to be done, and does any one of them:

3If it is the anointed priest who sins, thus bringing guilt on the people, he shall offer for the sin that he has committed a bull of the herd without blemish as a sin offering to the Lord. [4]He shall bring the bull to the entrance of the tent of meeting before the Lord and lay his hand on the head of the bull; the bull shall be slaughtered before the Lord. [5]The anointed priest shall take some of the blood of the bull and bring it into the tent of meeting. [6]The priest shall dip his finger in the blood and sprinkle some of the blood seven times before the Lord in front of the curtain of the sanctuary. [7]The priest shall put some of the blood on the horns of the altar of fragrant incense that is in the tent of meeting before the Lord; and the rest of the blood of the bull he shall pour out at the base of the altar of burnt offering, which is at the entrance of the tent of meeting. [8]He shall remove all the fat from the bull of sin offering: the fat that covers the entrails and all the fat that is around the entrails; [9]the two kidneys with the fat that is on them at the loins; and the appendage of the liver, which he shall remove with the kidneys, [10]just as these are removed from the ox of the sacrifice of well-being. The priest shall turn them into smoke upon the altar of burnt offering. [11]But the skin of the bull and all its flesh, as well as its head, its legs, its entrails, and its dung— [12]all the rest of the bull—he shall carry out to a clean place outside the camp, to the ash heap, and shall burn it on a wood fire; at the ash heap it shall be burned.

13If the whole congregation of Israel errs unintentionally and the matter escapes the notice of the assembly, and they do any one of the things that by the Lord's commandments ought not to be done and incur guilt; [14]when the sin that they have committed becomes known, the assembly shall offer a bull of the herd for a sin offering and bring it before the tent of meeting. [15]The elders of the congregation shall lay their hands on the head of the bull before the Lord, and the bull shall be slaughtered before the Lord. [16]The anointed priest shall bring some of the blood of the bull into the tent of meeting, [17]and the priest shall dip his finger in the blood and sprinkle it the LORD seven times in front of the curtain. [18]He is to put some of the blood on the horns of the altar that is before the LORD in the Tent of Meeting. The rest of the blood he shall pour out at the base of the altar of burnt offering at the entrance to the Tent of Meeting. [19]He shall remove all the fat from it and burn it on the altar, [20]and do with this bull just as he did with the bull for the sin offering. In this way the priest will make atonement for them, and they will be forgiven. [21]Then he shall take the bull outside the camp and burn it as he burned the first bull. This is the sin offering for the community.

[22]"'When a leader sins unintentionally and does what is forbidden in any of the commands of the LORD his God, he is guilty. [23]When he is made aware of the sin he committed, he must bring as his offering a male goat without defect. [24]He is to lay his hand on the goat's head and slaughter it at the place where the burnt offering is slaughtered before the LORD. It is a sin offering. [25]Then the priest shall take some of the blood of the sin offering with his finger and put it on the horns of the altar of burnt offering and pour out the rest of the blood at the base of the altar. [26]He shall burn all the fat on the altar as he burned the fat of the fellowship offering. In this way the priest will make atonement for the man's sin, and he will be forgiven.

[27]"'If a member of the community sins unintentionally and does what is forbidden in any of the LORD's commands, he is guilty. [28]When he is made aware of the sin he committed, he must bring as his offering for the sin he committed a female goat without defect. [29]He is to lay his hand on the head of the sin offering and slaughter it at the place of the burnt offering. [30]Then the priest is to take some of the blood with his finger and put it on the horns of the altar of burnt offering and pour out the rest of the blood at the base of the altar. [31]He shall remove all the fat, just as the fat is removed from the fellowship offering, and the priest shall burn it on the altar as an aroma pleasing to the LORD. In this way the priest will make atonement for him, and he will be forgiven.

[32]"'If he brings a lamb as his sin offering, he is to bring a female without defect. [33]He is to lay

seven times before the LORD, in front of the curtain. [18]He shall put some of the blood on the horns of the altar that is before the LORD in the tent of meeting; and the rest of the blood he shall pour out at the base of the altar of burnt offering that is at the entrance of the tent of meeting. [19]He shall remove all its fat and turn it into smoke on the altar. [20]He shall do with the bull just as is done with the bull of sin offering; he shall do the same with this. The priest shall make atonement for them, and they shall be forgiven. [21]He shall carry the bull outside the camp, and burn it as he burned the first bull; it is the sin offering for the assembly.

[22]When a ruler sins, doing unintentionally any one of all the things that by commandments of the LORD his God ought not to be done and incurs guilt, [23]once the sin that he has committed is made known to him, he shall bring as his offering a male goat without blemish. [24]He shall lay his hand on the head of the goat; it shall be slaughtered at the spot where the burnt offering is slaughtered before the LORD; it is a sin offering. [25]The priest shall take some of the blood of the sin offering with his finger and put it on the horns of the altar of burnt offering, and pour out the rest of its blood at the base of the altar of burnt offering. [26]All its fat he shall turn into smoke on the altar, like the fat of the sacrifice of well-being. Thus the priest shall make atonement on his behalf for his sin, and he shall be forgiven.

[27]If anyone of the ordinary people among you sins unintentionally in doing any one of the things that by the LORD's commandments ought not to be done and incurs guilt, [28]when the sin that you have committed is made known to you, you shall bring a female goat without blemish as your offering, for the sin that you have committed. [29]You shall lay your hand on the head of the sin offering; and the sin offering shall be slaughtered at the place of the burnt offering. [30]The priest shall take some of its blood with his finger and put it on the horns of the altar of burnt offering, and he shall pour out the rest of its blood at the base of the altar. [31]He shall remove all its fat, as the fat is removed from the offering of well-being, and the priest shall turn it into smoke on the altar for a pleasing odor to the LORD. Thus the priest shall

his hand on its head and slaughter it for a sin offering at the place where the burnt offering is slaughtered. [34]Then the priest shall take some of the blood of the sin offering with his finger and put it on the horns of the altar of burnt offering and pour out the rest of the blood at the base of the altar. [35]He shall remove all the fat, just as the fat is removed from the lamb of the fellowship offering, and the priest shall burn it on the altar on top of the offerings made to the LORD by fire. In this way the priest will make atonement for him for the sin he has committed, and he will be forgiven.

5 " 'If a person sins because he does not speak up when he hears a public charge to testify regarding something he has seen or learned about, he will be held responsible.

[2]" 'Or if a person touches anything ceremonially unclean—whether the carcasses of unclean wild animals or of unclean livestock or of unclean creatures that move along the ground—even though he is unaware of it, he has become unclean and is guilty.

[3]" 'Or if he touches human uncleanness—anything that would make him unclean—even though he is unaware of it, when he learns of it he will be guilty.

[4]" 'Or if a person thoughtlessly takes an oath to do anything, whether good or evil—in any matter one might carelessly swear about—even though he is unaware of it, in any case when he learns of it he will be guilty.

[5]" 'When anyone is guilty in any of these ways, he must confess in what way he has sinned [6]and, as a penalty for the sin he has committed, he must bring to the LORD a female lamb or goat from the flock as a sin offering; and the priest shall make atonement for him for his sin.

[7]" 'If he cannot afford a lamb, he is to bring two doves or two young pigeons to the LORD as a penalty for his sin—one for a sin offering and the other for a burnt offering. [8]He is to bring them to the priest, who shall first offer the one for the sin offering. He is to wring its head from its neck, not severing it completely, [9]and is to sprinkle some of the blood of the sin offering against the side of the altar; the rest of the blood must be drained out at the base of the altar. It is a sin

make atonement on your behalf, and you shall be forgiven.

[32]If the offering you bring as a sin offering is a sheep, you shall bring a female without blemish. [33]You shall lay your hand on the head of the sin offering; and it shall be slaughtered as a sin offering at the spot where the burnt offering is slaughtered. [34]The priest shall take some of the blood of the sin offering with his finger and put it on the horns of the altar of burnt offering, and pour out the rest of its blood at the base of the altar. [35]You shall remove all its fat, as the fat of the sheep is removed from the sacrifice of well-being, and the priest shall turn it into smoke on the altar, with the offerings by fire to the LORD. Thus the priest shall make atonement on your behalf for the sin that you have committed, and you shall be forgiven.

5 When any of you sin in that you have heard a public adjuration to testify and—though able to testify as one who has seen or learned of the matter—does not speak up, you are subject to punishment. [2]Or when any of you touch any unclean thing—whether the carcass of an unclean beast or the carcass of unclean livestock or the carcass of an unclean swarming thing—and are unaware of it, you have become unclean, and are guilty. [3]Or when you touch human uncleanness—any uncleanness by which one can become unclean—and are unaware of it, when you come to know it, you shall be guilty. [4]Or when any of you utter aloud a rash oath for a bad or a good purpose, whatever people utter in an oath, and are unaware of it, when you come to know it, you shall in any of these be guilty. [5]When you realize your guilt in any of these, you shall confess the sin that you have committed. [6]And you shall bring to the LORD, as your penalty for the sin that you have committed, a female from the flock, a sheep or a goat, as a sin offering; and the priest shall make atonement on your behalf for your sin.

[7]But if you cannot afford a sheep, you shall bring to the LORD, as your penalty for the sin that you have committed, two turtledoves or two pigeons, one for a sin offering and the other for a burnt offering. [8]You shall bring them to the priest, who shall offer first the one for the sin

offering. ¹⁰The priest shall then offer the other as a burnt offering in the prescribed way and make atonement for him for the sin he has committed, and he will be forgiven.

¹¹"'If, however, he cannot afford two doves or two young pigeons, he is to bring as an offering for his sin a tenth of an ephah*a* of fine flour for a sin offering. He must not put oil or incense on it, because it is a sin offering. ¹²He is to bring it to the priest, who shall take a handful of it as a memorial portion and burn it on the altar on top of the offerings made to the LORD by fire. It is a sin offering. ¹³In this way the priest will make atonement for him for any of these sins he has committed, and he will be forgiven. The rest of the offering will belong to the priest, as in the case of the grain offering.'"

a11 That is, probably about 2 quarts (about 2 liters

offering, wringing its head at the nape without severing it. ⁹He shall sprinkle some of the blood of the sin offering on the side of the altar, while the rest of the blood shall be drained out at the base of the altar; it is a sin offering. ¹⁰And the second he shall offer for a burnt offering according to the regulation. Thus the priest shall make atonement on your behalf for the sin that you have committed, and you shall be forgiven.

11But if you cannot afford two turtledoves or two pigeons, you shall bring as your offering for the sin that you have committed one-tenth of an ephah of choice flour for a sin offering; you shall not put oil on it or lay frankincense on it, for it is a sin offering. ¹²You shall bring it to the priest, and the priest shall scoop up a handful of it as its memorial portion, and turn this into smoke on the altar, with the offerings by fire to the LORD; it is a sin offering. ¹³Thus the priest shall make atonement on your behalf for whichever of these sins you have committed, and you shall be forgiven. Like the grain offering, the rest shall be for the priest.

COMMENTARY

The law of the sin offering is divided into four sections with an unusual sliding scale of responsibility for each worshiper. The four sections are (1) the sin offering for the high priest (4:3-12); (2) the sin offering for the congregation (4:13-21); (3) the sin offering for the leader (4:22-26); and (4) the sin offering for the individual (4:27-35). Added to these four distinct sections is 5:1-13, where special instructions are given for other circumstances in the use of the sin offering.

4:1-2. A general introduction serves as the opening rubric with the expression, "When [כִּי *kî*] anyone [נֶפֶשׁ *nepeš*] sins." This same idiom appears again in 5:1, 15. The subsections are likewise clearly demarcated; however, rather than use the conditional word *kî* ("when," "if") they use the word אִם (*'im*, "if"; 4:3, 13, 27, 32; 5:7, 11; also see 5:14, 17 in the guilt offering). Many of the sections close with the formula of absolution, "The priest will make atonement for him for the sin he has committed, and he will be forgiven"

(4:35; 5:13; and in the guilt offering 5:18, 26 [MT 6:7]). The only exception to this use of a separate word *'im*, "if," for the subordinate sections is the unusual and rare usage of the word אֲשֶׁר (*'ăšer*, "if," "whoever") in 4:22 in regard to the ruler or tribal leader. The reason for this departure from the norm is not altogether clear.

The name of this offering presents a problem, just as the name of the other offerings proves difficult. All ancient and modern translations name it the sin offering. However, many modern commentators vehemently protest this rendering as being inaccurate on all grounds: etymological, morphological, and contextual!

The grammatical grounds for this objection are somewhat technical. The noun, it is argued, does not derive from the basic stem (called the qal by Hebrew grammarians), which indeed means "to sin," "to do wrong"; instead, the noun comes from the intensive form of the verb (called the piel by grammarians), which means "to cleanse," "expurgate," or "to decontaminate." Therefore, it is argued, this offering should be called the purification offering, not the sin offering.

Added to this objection is the contextual argument. This offering is also used by women recovering from childbirth or from a hemorrhage (12:6, 8; 15:25-30), by those completing a Nazirite vow (Num 6:13-14), and when a newly constructed altar is dedicated (8:15). Naturally, there can be no question of sinning in these cases.

However, in 4:2, 3, 22, 27 the verb "to sin" appears in the very chapter that uses the debated cognate term as a noun. Therefore, this offering deals with sin and its consequences in many, if not most, situations. But the impression is left that this is the only offering that deals with sin and its consequences; that, of course, is incorrect. The other sacrifices involving blood also speak to this point or rest on the fact that it has been accomplished in an accompanying offering.

The chief argument for changing the traditional name of the sin offering to the purification offering or the offering of purgation is the reason given in 16:16-20 on the Yom Kippur ritual, where this offering plays a central role. The sacrifice, made from the first goat of the two specially chosen on the day for this offering, which for the moment we will leave unnamed here, is to be slain and taken into the holy of holies this one time each year. The high priest is to sprinkle the blood of this sacrifice on the top of the ark of the covenant and in front of it. This is done, comments 16:16, to "make atonement for the Most Holy Place because of the uncleanness and rebellion of the Israelites, whatever their sins have been." It is further contended that blood of this sacrifice (or of any other, for that matter) is never applied to any person; it is put on the "horns [the projections of the four corners] of the altar" (the altar of incense in the holy place in front of the curtain that divided the two main sections of the sanctuary, on the Day of Atonement; or in other cases on the horns of the altar in the open courtyard of the sanctuary), against the sides of the altar, or at the base of the altar (e.g., 8:15). Since nowhere else does the text indicate any other purpose for this offering, it is assumed that the purpose of purging the sanctuary is the correct one.

Admittedly, the conclusion is an extrapolation from one piece of data in 16:16 retrojected over the whole range of sin offerings. Furthermore, 16:16 may be a form of synecdoche, where the part, the most holy place, is said to be infected and stained by the sins of the whole nation. If it is this figure of speech, the conclusion that this purges only the sanctuary is too minimalist in its view of the effects and results of this sacrifice.

A much broader view of the purpose of the sin offering is to regard it as providing a way of atonement for specific sins done by representative leaders, by individuals, or by all the people. Moreover, its purpose also provides for graded levels of responsibility for all sin. If the question about the major difference between the sin offering and the guilt offering remains, the answer is: It is in the nature of the sin. The sin offering covers a number of general sins, while the guilt offering deals with sins involving injury to other persons or those that detract from the worship of God. Thus, in the guilt offering, provision is made for restitution and a fine along with the usual pardon and forgiveness.

The most amazing part of the discussion on the sin offering is the massive confusion on the expression to sin "unintentionally" (4:2; בִּשְׁגָגָה *bišĕgāgâ*). It has been all too traditional by commentators of all theological stripes to describe this term as limiting the effectiveness of these offerings to sins committed inadvertently or unknowingly. The problem with this rendering, however, is that the root שׁגג (*šāgag*) means "to err," "go astray," "to wander." Never is the idea of intent part of the meaning. That aspect has been added to the noun form that regularly means "error" or "mistake."

The same expression is translated as sinning "unintentionally" in the guilt offering (5:15-18), yet the sins listed in 6:2-3 are clearly overt acts of rebellion against the law of God: stealing, lying, cheating, extorting, and false swearing. And surely the high priest cannot be excused of any culpability on the grounds of ignorance of the law!

At the center of this storm over the proper meaning of this term, traditionally translated "unintentional," is Numbers 15:22-31. But once again the contrast is not between sinning in ignorance of the law and sinning deliberately. The issue in Num 15:30 is one of defiance, sinning "with a high hand," as the Hebrew put it. This evokes the ancient sign of the upraised, cocked arm with the clenched fist waved menacingly against heaven and its occupant. Num 15:30-31 deliberately says that this person "blasphemes the LORD" and "[despises] the LORD's word" (NIV). This is the closest parallel in the OT for the NT's unpardonable sin against the Holy Spirit.

As R. Laird Harris correctly contends, "The sense of the verb *šāgag* will be adequately caught if in all the verses concerned here in Leviticus 4–5, the phrase 'sins unintentionally' is rendered [instead] by 'goes astray in sin' or 'does wrong' or the like."[43] The same would be true for the passages in Num 15:22-29; they sinned "wrongly" or "in error" rather than "unintentionally." Even in the manslaughter passages (see Num 35:11-22; Josh 20:3-5), it is best to say that it was "by mistake."

The sin offering is unique in distinguishing between the rank and the status of the offenders and in specifying whether the blood is applied to the outer altar or to the altar of incense inside the sanctuary. Each of these may now be considered in turn.

4:3-12. The sin of the "anointed priest" is given first position for consideration. The expression "anointed priest" (4:3; see also 6:22 [MT 6:15]) is somewhat unusual since Aaron and his sons were anointed. But based on 16:32 and 21:10 (cf. Exod 29:29), it is clear that the title refers to Aaron, or the current presiding high priest, since the two titles are synonymous in these contexts.

This offering begins the same way as the other sacrifices: The worshiper brings the animal to the entrance of the tent of meeting, lays his hand(s) on its head, probably states why the sacrifice has been brought, and then slaughters it by himself or with the help of the priest. From this point the ceremony is unique. Whereas the blood of the burnt and peace offerings is splashed against the side of the altar, in the sin offering the blood is caught in a basin and used in a variety of ways according to the office, status, and responsibility of the person making the offering. Part of the blood is poured out at the base of the altar, but the rest is either sprinkled seven times in front of the curtain that divided the holy of holies from the holy place or put on the four horns of the

incense altar. (For the sin offering of a tribal leader or a member of the community, the blood is applied to the four horns of the large altar in the open court of the tabernacle.)

The high priest, then, is to bring a bull calf (פר *par*, a "calf"; not to be confused with שׁור *šôr*, an "ox" that served as the victim in the peace offering) without any defect as his sin offering (4:3). The choice of the sacrificial victim is determined by two considerations: the rank or position of the person who sins, and the ability of the person to provide a more costly sacrifice. Thus, the higher a person stands in the theocratic order of governing and ministry, the more costly the offering required. Also, the guilt of any sin is proportional to the rank and position of the offender. One conclusion must be drawn immediately: The guilt of sins committed by those in positions of religious authority is heaviest of all. The reason for this law of graded responsibility is set forth in 4:3—the high priest brings guilt on all the people.

Although individual responsibility is stressed, especially in the latter prophets such as Jeremiah and Ezekiel (e.g., Ezek 18:4: "The soul who sins is the one who will die" [NIV]), an equal emphasis is placed on the collective or corporate effects of sin on a community. Persons in such high positions can bring enormous effects, for good or ill, upon a group, a city, a region, or a whole country. This effect may take place in several ways. In some cases, the people may be tempted to indulge in sins they ordinarily would never think to try until they hear or see the public example of their spiritual leader doing the same or some similar outlandish sin. In other cases, the priest may involve the people in the very act that God condemns, by teaching or permitting it. In still other cases, the mere failure to carry out faithfully the high calling of one's own holy walk with God may leave a vacuum that opens up the nation to moral and spiritual decline. In all cases, however, the priests are to be teachers of the people (see Deut 33:10; Mal 2:6) and lead pure, holy, exemplary lives for others to follow. When the high priest falls into sin, not only is he guilty before God, but so is the whole nation tainted and placed under God's judgment.

The imposition of hands once again is to denote that the victim is the donor's substitute. The blood

---

43. R. Laird Harris, "Leviticus," in *The Expositor's Bible Commentary,* ed. Frank E. Gaebelein, 12 vols. (Grand Rapids: Zondervan, 1990) 2:547-48.

is sprinkled seven times in front of the curtain, behind which the Shekinah ("the divine presence") glory resides, where the presence of God remains in the camp. Then the blood is applied to four horns, or projections, on the altar of incense, intimating that there is no acceptance of the offender's prayers and intercessions to God (the smoke of the incense is often likened to prayers ascending to God) until that one is absolved by the life of an intervening victim and the blood is applied to the altar.

What remains so strikingly significant about the sin offering of the high priest is that no part of the animal comes near the altar except portions of the blood (already described) and the fat portions said to belong to God (see the earlier discussion of the peace offering). None of the sacrifice is shared with either priest or people. Instead, the bull calf is carried outside the camp, skin and all, to be burned by fire on the ground. Surely, this act, more than many of the other parts of the ritual, must have driven home in the minds of all thoughtful Israelites that the state of the guilt of sin is so great that it forces one to be excluded from one's own people until being reconciled by some substitute. The loneliness and the shame of being left to burn on the outskirts of the camp are enough to depict the shame and the reproach that sin brings into the life of the offender. No altar is used for burning the offering outside the camp; the sacrifice is placed on the wood on the ground where the ash pile is (4:12). This absence of an altar only adds to the reproach already attached to this sacrifice because of the sin it deals with.

4:13-21. The sin offering for the whole congregation follows the same order of ceremony, except in this instance the elders bring the bull calf. Some have been perplexed over whether there is a difference between the "community" (עדה *'ēdâ;* vv. 13, 15) and the "assembly" (קהל *qāhāl;* vv. 13, 14). Among some Jewish commentators, the word here translated "community" is taken to mean the supreme court of justice in ancient Israel, i.e., the Sanhedrin. However, the word as used in the OT has a much broader meaning; the two terms are often used interchangeably (see Exod 12:6; Num 14:5), as is probably the case here.

The whole community has sinned by breaking some commandment and thus has fallen into error, begins v. 13. However, the fault "is hidden from the assembly," or "the matter is hidden from the eyes of the assembly" (v. 13), i.e., it is not brought out in the open before the worshiping congregation. It is clear, however, that the people have done "what is forbidden in [one or more] of the LORD's commandments" (v. 13). Who actually broke the silence and how it was made known is not disclosed here. It may have come through prophecy, a vision, or the Urim and Thummim. The point is that the congregation now has this sin out in the open (v. 14). The sin offering has to be brought by the elders on behalf of all the people. The elders, acting as representatives for all the people, place their hands on the head of the bull (v. 15). The rest of the ritual follows exactly what is spelled out for the high priest's ritual. This is how the priest "will make atonement for them" (v. 20).

4:22-26. The sin offering for a tribal leader (נשׂיא *nāśî'*) is not as serious as that of the high priest or the whole congregation. He is required to bring only a male goat, and the blood is not taken into the tent of meeting but is sprinkled on the altar of burnt offering in the open court of the sanctuary. Thus the victim is of lesser value than that for the high priest and whole congregation, but it is more valuable than that for a private individual. The civil leader is also held accountable to God and not just to the people (or in our day, the electorate) for the execution of the trust of that office. God holds civil leaders, then, to a higher standard than that of individual persons. This refers to all official acts of the office and all private actions. No distinction is raised in this text between sin resulting from some act in office or in one's private life: both are culpable and carry the same requirement of the more expensive sacrifice. High office gives no immunity to sin or to the need for divine forgiveness.

4:27-35. The sin offering of the common people is taken up last in this descending order of four sin offerings; it can be either a female goat (4:28) or a female lamb (4:32). If the previous three sin offerings teach that no persons are high in position or office as to be above the need for God's cleansing, so here we are taught that no persons are so lowly and poor in their station in life that their sins are not worth the trouble of forgiving or that they should be overlooked. If anything, this section on the common folk bulks larger than the previous sections to make sure that no one is left out of the means of grace simply for lack of enough of this world's goods to make a sacrifice.

The unusual addition is found in v. 31. When the portion of fat is burned on the altar for the ordinary person, as is required in all the sin offerings that involve bloody sacrifices, it is declared to be "an aroma pleasing to the LORD." It may be inferred that this is true of all the sin offerings, just as it is declared in the peace offerings. But the point remains that only with regard to the ordinary person is this portion said to be an aroma pleasing to God. If it is meant to be distinctive in this situation, this word must be intended as special comfort to the lowest class of people: They too share in the same hope, mercy, and grace of God, even though their sacrifices are less costly, glamorous, and flamboyant in comparison to all the others listed in this chapter.

5:1-13. Leviticus 5:1-4 specifies some sins for which a sin offering is necessary. The first instance is the duty and obligation of a witness to come forward regarding something seen or heard that, if left unreported, will offend the interests of truth or justice (5:1). Truth and justice cannot and will not be served when the populace refuses to become involved. It is a sin to assume the attitude that individuals are responsible only for themselves and their loved ones.

Having contact with anything ceremonially unclean, even if the person is at first unaware of the fact, requires a sin offering (5:2-3). This is not just in the interest of public health; uncleanness also brings temporary disqualification from worship of the living Lord and the accompanying guilt of sin.

A false oath is displeasing to the Lord (5:4).

Once again, not being fully aware of the falsity of what is said does not constitute an excuse. A person must atone with a sin offering.

An individual who is unable to offer either a female goat or a female lamb must bring two birds (two doves or two pigeons) as an offering (5:7-10): one as a sin offering and the other as a whole burnt offering (v. 7c). The order of these two sacrifices is deliberate: First, peace with God is to be won by means of the sin offering, and then the gift of the whole burnt offering can be accepted.

But the provision of God reaches to the poorest of the poor. If the price of two doves or two pigeons, which were just as plentiful in the cities of that day as they are in ours, is beyond the humble means of the offerer, two quarts of fine flour will be acceptable (5:11-13). The point is that *some* type of offering must be made, even when the prescribed one is unattainable due to economic pressures. However, unlike the offering of oil in the grain offering, the fine flour is to be given without any olive oil or incense added. This is a sin offering; it has to demonstrate the awfulness and loathsomeness of sin.

While the principle remains that without blood there is no atonement, here is another case of an understood *ceteris paribus*, "all other things being equal," in that it permits flour to be used in what is basically a blood offering. However, in this instance there is no equality in the economic levels; therefore, the principle does not apply to each level of society. This one exception tends to prove the rule, but an exception it surely is, mercifully provided by a loving Lord. Nevertheless, a distinction is made with the grain offering so that there is no adorning sin with frankincense and olive oil.

REFLECTIONS

The most prominent feature of the sin offerings is the expiation of guilt by the sacrifice of a substituted victim. But the most astounding provision is the sliding scale of graded responsibility. From these two central truths we can legitimately make a number of observations.

1. The guilt of sin in God's sight is proportional to the rank, office, and responsibilities of the offender. At the head of this sliding scale must come those who are in religious authority. The NT restates this principle in several ways: "From everyone who has been given much, much will be demanded; and from the one who has been entrusted with much, much more will be asked" (Luke 12:48 NIV). That is the reason, no doubt, why the half-brother of our

Lord, James, taught "not many of you should presume to be teachers, my brothers, because you know that we who teach will be judged more strictly" (Jas 3:1 NIV).

2. This law of the sin offering also teaches that religion is not just a personal or an individual matter. Responsibility is attached also to the associations of individuals in their collective groups as nations, cities, communities, corporations, societies, and religious affiliations. While there is individual sin, there also is such a thing as the sin of the whole community or congregation. Associations can be held just as responsible for sin of a whole group as they can be held accountable for the sin of a private person. In modern Western democratic societies, it seems taken for granted that religion is a matter of concern only to the individual and to no one else. We assume that there is no way in which we can be implicated in the guilt of the sin of the whole group by virtue of our association with that group, and that we therefore bear no responsibility for relief, confession, or petition for the removal of any judgment that hangs over us. But this text makes all such opinions a delusion. It further urges our involvement in the corporate whole.

3. The sin of noninvolvement in the cause of justice and truth is strikingly set forth as a crime against God and society. This text demands involvement. The recent rash of cases of persons' being beaten and brutalized in our cities while numerous people watch but refuse to come to the aid of the victims, either during the attack or during the court trial, is a blight on the honor and reputation of any city or society and on the cause of truth and justice. But all too frequently, the norm for the actions of modern men and women has fallen far short of God's standards.

4. The law of God that required atonement by the shedding of blood—i.e., by the death of a substitute—is set aside in the exceptional case where the person is unable to bring an offering of either animals or birds. This provision should go a long way in relieving the charges of a harsh legalism in the Levitical law, for it shows that whatever is said often has a suppressed "if" or "unless" with it. This exception seems not to be in operation only when the law is based on the character of God. God cannot change; hence, there is not a chance that the moral law based on the nature and character of God will be modified. But in instances where moral law is illustrated by setting forth ceremonial or civil provisions, each provision of the law is subject to the rule "all other things being equal." Only in this manner can God be said to be immutable and yet graciously responsive to the needs of the people.

Leviticus 5:14–6:7, The Guilt Offering

NIV

[14]The LORD said to Moses: [15]"When a person commits a violation and sins unintentionally in regard to any of the LORD's holy things, he is to bring to the LORD as a penalty a ram from the flock, one without defect and of the proper value in silver, according to the sanctuary shekel.[a] It is a guilt offering. [16]He must make restitution for what he has failed to do in regard to the holy things, add a fifth of the value to that and give it all to the priest, who will make atonement for him with the ram as a guilt offering, and he will be forgiven.

[a]*15 That is, about 2/5 ounce (about 11.5 grams)*

NRSV

14The LORD spoke to Moses, saying: [15]When any of you commit a trespass and sins unintentionally in any of the holy things of the LORD, you shall bring, as your guilt offering to the LORD, a ram without blemish from the flock, convertible into silver by the sanctuary shekel; it is a guilt offering. [16]And you shall make restitution for the holy thing in which you were remiss, and shall add one-fifth to it and give it to the priest. The priest shall make atonement on your behalf with the ram of the guilt offering, and you shall be forgiven.

NIV

17"If a person sins and does what is forbidden in any of the Lord's commands, even though he does not know it, he is guilty and will be held responsible. 18He is to bring to the priest as a guilt offering a ram from the flock, one without defect and of the proper value. In this way the priest will make atonement for him for the wrong he has committed unintentionally, and he will be forgiven. 19It is a guilt offering; he has been guilty of*a* wrongdoing against the Lord."

6 The Lord said to Moses: 2"If anyone sins and is unfaithful to the Lord by deceiving his neighbor about something entrusted to him or left in his care or stolen, or if he cheats him, 3or if he finds lost property and lies about it, or if he swears falsely, or if he commits any such sin that people may do— 4when he thus sins and becomes guilty, he must return what he has stolen or taken by extortion, or what was entrusted to him, or the lost property he found, 5or whatever it was he swore falsely about. He must make restitution in full, add a fifth of the value to it and give it all to the owner on the day he presents his guilt offering. 6And as a penalty he must bring to the priest, that is, to the Lord, his guilt offering, a ram from the flock, one without defect and of the proper value. 7In this way the priest will make atonement for him before the Lord, and he will be forgiven for any of these things he did that made him guilty."

a19 Or has made full expiation for his

NRSV

17If any of you sin without knowing it, doing any of the things that by the Lord's commandments ought not to be done, you have incurred guilt, and are subject to punishment. 18You shall bring to the priest a ram without blemish from the flock, or the equivalent, as a guilt offering; and the priest shall make atonement on your behalf for the error that you committed unintentionally, and you shall be forgiven. 19It is a guilt offering; you have incurred guilt before the Lord.

6 *a*The Lord spoke to Moses, saying: 2When any of you sin and commit a trespass against the Lord by deceiving a neighbor in a matter of a deposit or a pledge, or by robbery, or if you have defrauded a neighbor, 3or have found something lost and lied about it—if you swear falsely regarding any of the various things that one may do and sin thereby— 4when you have sinned and realize your guilt, and would restore what you took by robbery or by fraud or the deposit that was committed to you, or the lost thing that you found, 5or anything else about which you have sworn falsely, you shall repay the principal amount and shall add one-fifth to it. You shall pay it to its owner when you realize your guilt. 6And you shall bring to the priest, as your guilt offering to the Lord, a ram without blemish from the flock, or its equivalent, for a guilt offering. 7The priest shall make atonement on your behalf before the Lord, and you shall be forgiven for any of the things that one may do and incur guilt thereby.

a Ch 5.20 in Heb

COMMENTARY

The fifth and final offering in chaps. 1–6 is the guilt offering. As with each of the previous four offerings, there is debate on its precise name.

The KJV renders it as the "trespass offering," but that name fails to communicate that among the central issues in this offering is the problem of lying, or dealing fraudulently, especially in religious matters. The case for its use by the KJV is that "trespass" usually denotes an invasion of the rights of others, of either their property or their service. But the KJV uses the opening terms in 5:15 (תמעל מעל *tim'ōl*

ma'al; literally "trespass a trespass"; cf. NIV) as the basis for naming this offering.

The current preference for the name (אשם *'āšām*) of this offering seems to be reparation offering, since its provisions place so much emphasis on redressing the wrong that is committed.[44] The meanings of the verbal form of this offering are twofold: (a) "to incur liability [to someone]" (when it is followed by the preposition *to* or *for* with a

44. See the lengthy discussion by Milgrom, *Leviticus 1-16*, 339-61.

personal object), and (b) "to feel guilt" (without a personal object). The meanings of the noun form are also dual: (a) the reparation, i.e., the money paid for redressing a wrong, and (b) the reparation or guilt offering. The case made by Jacob Milgrom is that even though the verb ʾāšam means "is guilty" and its noun ʾāšām means "guilt," these meanings are attested only in noncultic texts. This same verb and noun, as used in cultic texts, argues Milgrom, have one of the four consequential meanings mentioned already. One needs to add to this discussion the findings of Leon Morris in favor of the rendering "guilt" even in these cultic texts.[45]

Actually, the two sides (guilt offering and reparation offering) are not all that far apart. The former stresses the cause, and the latter stresses the need to redress the incurred guilt. Thus, to reduce the amount of exotic-appearing terms, we have decided to stay with guilt offering. However, if it is insisted that reparation offering is more technically correct since the verb from which this name probably derives is what is known in Hebrew grammar as a stative verb, we will not dissent.

The arrangement of the law of the guilt offering is fairly simple. There are two sections: Lev 5:14-19 deals with the violation of any of "The LORD's holy things" (v. 15), and Lev 6:1-7 (MT 5:20-26) deals with violations of human property rights.

5:14-19. The expression "sins unintentionally" appears in 5:14, 18 in several versions, just as we observed in Lev 4:2, 13, 22, 27 and also in Num 15:25, 27, 28. But the comment made in Leviticus 4 must be made here as well: The Hebrew term does not include the idea of intentionality. An adequate translation in all these cases will be to define this as a sin committed "mistakenly" or "in error." The contrast in Num 15:25-28 is not between sins that are unknown and sins that are known. The traditional teaching that concludes that forgiveness is available for the sins about which we are ignorant while no forgiveness is available for known sins is faulty. It rests on a misinterpretation of Numbers 15. The contrast in Numbers 15, however, is between sins of error and sins of defiance. The expression in Num 15:30, to sin "with a high hand" (literal translation), is explained in context as a defiant and blasphemous attack on God. Therefore, the expres-

sion in our text deliberately speaks to those whose sins are committed "in error" or "mistakenly" but not with an attempt to mock God or, as it were, to take on heaven in a frontal attack, thereby blaspheming God.

The guilt offering, as already remarked in the discussion of the sin offering, is very similar to that sacrifice. But some major differences exist. Whereas the sin offering emphasizes the idea of expiation of sin, the guilt offering represents the same atonement with God by stressing the reparation that has to be paid for the wrong committed. Just as the whole burnt offering symbolizes the total consecration of the person and the peace offering symbolizes fellowship with God, so the guilt offering (with the sin offering) offers reinstatement of the offerer to full covenantal relationship with God.

Uniquely, the guilt offering is never offered by the congregation; it is used only by individuals. The situations the guilt offering describes are scarcely attributable to the whole congregation.

Another distinctive feature of this offering is the restriction imposed on the animal used. Only one animal is acceptable: "A ram from the flock, one without defect and of the proper value in silver, according to the sanctuary shekel" (5:15). There is no distinction between the rich or the poor, the high or the lowly. The debt incurred, along with the resulting guilt, is such that a valuable offering must be brought. Fortunately, the text does not demand a bull, which would have put it hopelessly out of the reach of many. Nevertheless, it holds the standard high and demands that all meet it.

This offering has one other most unusual feature. The priest has to appraise the male sheep (as appears from Lev 27:8, 12) to make sure that it does not fall below a certain standard. This whole phrase ("proper value") is an old technical term, as the fossilized Hebrew ending of ךָ (-kā, "by you") attests (and as a result, the ending is not to be translated). It appears in the vows (Lev 27:2) and in Num 18:16. Ephraim Speiser concludes that the appearance of such antique terms in Leviticus argues for an early date of this legislation.[46] The "shekel" must be of full weight and on the standard set by God, not mortals: "the sanctuary shekel" (v. 15). Human

---

45. Leon Morris, "ʾāshām," EvQ, 30 (1958) 196-210.

46. Ephraim A. Speiser, *Oriental and Biblical Studies* (Philadelphia: University of Pennsylvania Press, 1967) 124-28.

standards do not measure up to the high standards of God in this case.

The guilty person is not allowed to gain even a temporary advantage in the use of goods or services thus falsely appropriated, for v. 16 demands that along with the offering of a ram, the offender must add "a fifth of the value to [what has been taken]." This would counter any interim disadvantage suffered by the one wronged. It would also prevent those who would wish to take advantage of another by merely restoring what had been taken without making any reparations for its loss during the time it was gone and presumably being used free of charge.

No other offering makes it as clear as this one that sin is treated as a debt. Among many ancient peoples—including the Hebrews, Arabs, and later, the Romans—sheep, but particularly rams, were used as a means of payment for debts and tribute. Thus Mesha, king of Moab, annually gave the king of Israel one hundred thousand lambs, and the wool of one hundred thousand rams (see 2 Kgs 3:4) as his tribute money. Isaiah intoned in a later passage, "Send lambs as tribute to the ruler of the land" (16:1 NIV). This fact reinforces the concept that the guilt offering is given because sin places the offender under debt.

The designation "the LORD's holy things" points to all that is the property of the Lord in a special sense. To mistakenly appropriate the parts of the sacrifice that belong to the Lord or to use the tithe or some other things vowed or dedicated to the Lord is to violate this category and to place oneself in need of making a guilt offering. In the singular, this word is translated as "holiness" or "sanctuary." But in the plural form, used in this designation, it appears to refer to all the things specially dedicated by mortals to God.

Leviticus 5:17-19 takes up a second type of trespass for which the guilt offering is provided to give relief. It deals with instances where the conscience troubles the individual, but for some reason, the offender cannot say precisely why. Leviticus 5:17 specifically says the person cannot tell why this guilt occurs. Since the person has done "what is forbidden in [one or more] of the LORD's commands" (v. 17), it hardly appears to be a case of ignorance of the law. Nor is it a matter of subsequent knowledge of the law. Instead, it appears to be a sensitized conscience suddenly

convicting the individual so that one begins to sense guilt and to feel responsible for what has been done. As R. Laird Harris comments, "Guilt in the biblical sense is not just a feeling but a condition. There may be known transgressions that bring feelings of guilt, but there is also a condition of guilt before God, caused by sins known or unknown."[47] However, even though vv. 17-18 repeat the disclaimer that the offender "does not know" it is a transgression, the point is made that ignorance of the law was no excuse for not observing it. Ignorance cannot affect the fact of the condition of guilt or of the necessity of making subsequent satisfaction to be restored to one's covenantal relationship with God.

The law of this offering is given in more detail in 7:1-7. Only a ram is accepted. It is brought by the guilty person along with a confession of the fault. Next, the priest slays the animal, but the blood is not applied this time, as it is in the sin offering, to the horns of the altar. Instead, the blood is sprinkled against the altar in the courtyard on all sides. The reason for this difference in the application of the blood is that the guilt offering represents the need for *satisfaction* for the trespass committed; expiation is symbolized more fully in the sin offering.

As it is with the sin offering, where only the fat parts are placed on the altar, so it is with the guilt offering. The fat tail, the fat that covers the inner parts of the ram, the two kidneys with the fat on them, and the covering of the liver are all burned on the altar. Then, similar to the sin offering, the rest is to be eaten only in the holy place by the priests.

6:1-7. The second section of the guilt offering deals with the trespasses against one's fellow human beings. Just as the previous section focuses on trespasses against God and requires full restitution with the added compensation of 20 percent along with a ram as a guilt offering, so also the law requires the same in the five illustrations of sins against one's neighbor.

The first case (6:2) takes up the matter of leaving something on deposit with others only to learn that it has been kept, sold, or used unlawfully as if it had been one's own. Aspects of this law are announced in the civil code of Exod 22:9-11.

47. Harris, "Leviticus" 2:551.

The second point treats all cases of fraud (v. 2c). The expression used here appears only once: "the placement in [or of] the hand" (author's trans.; cf. NIV). This seems to refer to stipulations made in partnerships where a bargain is struck and hands are shaken on the deal. Thus this sin seems to include all acts of misrepresentation of goods and services to obtain a better price than what one should get for the goods and services delivered, or a failure to deliver what was agreed upon in the handshake.

The third sin is robbery. It is something taken by force or under the duress and threat of force: otherwise known as extortion. Exodus 22:7, 15 deals with cases where the theft can be proven; but what is one to do when there are no witnesses? That is the problem in Lev 6:2c. The NIV rendering of "or stolen" is a little too tame for the vigor of this expression.

Oppression is fourth on this list of sins. It is a matter of fraudulently taking advantage of an employee, buyer, or seller. When the tax collector Zacchaeus came to the Lord, he had to acknowledge this sin and make it right. He imposed a fourfold restitution to all persons he had wronged (see Luke 19:8).

The fifth and final instance of sinning against one's neighbors is in assuming that "finders, keepers" legitimizes "losers, weepers." However, under biblical law, a person who finds something is obligated to search for its rightful owner, for retaining the found item defrauds and injures the proper owner.

The reference to swearing falsely in v. 5 does not apply to the last named sin, as if it is only a matter of finders vehemently denying that they have found what they now declare to be their own. No, it applies equally to all five cases mentioned in vv. 2-4. The temptation is always present for individuals to lie and swear falsely to gain a financial edge over their neighbors. With the false oath, the appeal is made not only to mortals to believe their false words but to God to act as a witness of the truthfulness of the false words! That makes a bad thing even worse.

But the very act of swearing falsely raises this dilemma: How can the guilt offering provide forgiveness and satisfaction for an oath that Exod 20:7 and Deut 5:11 state is such a misuse of God's holy name that it will not be a matter on which one will be held guiltless? However, when the guilty party comes forward and confesses this sin (as another version of this law has it in Num 5:5-7), it too will be forgiven. Exodus 22:1, 7, 9 makes it clear that when a person is guilty of any of the offenses noted here and is convicted by witnesses in court before the person voluntarily confesses, a double, fourfold, or fivefold restitution is required for the damages done to one's neighbors. On the other hand, the voluntary acknowledgment mollifies the penalty so that only a fifth part, or 20 percent, needs to be added to the offering of the male sheep.

Of course, the five sins specified here are merely examples. If all instances of possible sins were raised at this point, or at any other, Leviticus would be filled with lists of sins. The law of Num 5:5-10 goes beyond the law of Lev 6:1-7 in that it touches on what is to be done if the victim against whom the crimes listed here has, in the meantime, died.

The description of the guilt offering ends in Lev 6:7, much as the repeated sentence in the sin offering: "The priest will make atonement . . . before the Lord, and [that one] will be forgiven for any of these things . . . that made [that one] guilty." Once again, the purpose of the sacrifice is to effect a reinstatement into the favor and blessing of God. The most beautiful word comes at the conclusion of the sin and guilt offerings: *forgiven*. Everything depends, at this point, solely on the words spoken by the priest and grounded in the authority of the One in whose name he pronounced these words of relief.

REFLECTIONS

1. Over and over again, sin is portrayed in Scripture as a debt. That is why we are taught in the Lord's Prayer to pray, "Forgive us our debts" or, as another reading has it, our "trespasses." Twice in the parables Jesus depicts the sinner as a debtor to God: the parable of the unmerciful servant, who being forgiven much seizes another who owes a much smaller debt and throws him into prison until he has paid all (see Matt 18:21-35), and the parable about the moneylender, who forgives one huge and another minor debt (see Luke 7:41-42). So connected was this thought of debt with our sin that our present English word *ought* is the old preterit form of *owe*, as demonstrated in Tyndale's NT, where he translated Luke 7:41, "There was a certain lender, which *ought* him five hundred pence" (emphasis added). Clearly, all mortals are debtors to God, unable to pay back even a fraction of what we owe. Yet, God is an easy creditor, who personally provides the reparation we are unable to pay.

2. God claims from all persons certain rights of property. Nothing, not even our forgetfulness or inadvertence, will exonerate us from this obligation. The charge made in Malachi's day must be recalled every time this principle is raised: "Will a [person] rob God? Yet you rob me. But you ask, 'How do we rob you?' In tithes and offerings" (Mal 3:8 NIV). Thus taking what rightfully belongs to God, whether it is tithes, offerings, vows, time, talents, or gifts, is tantamount to robbing God. For this reason the apostle Paul teaches in 2 Cor 8:7 that believers are to "excel in this grace of giving" (NIV) just as we abound in the other graces and gifts from the Lord.

3. Humans also have rights, just as God has rights. When these rights are violated, it is a matter for divine justice, even though the act is against mere mortals. Human rights cannot be grounded in certain implied or observed values that are said to be actually or potentially present in one's fellow creatures. Human rights are grounded in the divine declarations of truth and justice and in the fact that men and women are made in the image of God.

4. In a most amazing statement, Isa 53:10 asserts that God made the life of the suffering servant "a guilt offering" (NIV). The very same word is used in Lev 5:14–6:7 for the ritual of the guilt offering. Thus Isaiah declares that the Servant of the Lord, the Messiah, gave up his life in death as a guilt offering on behalf of sinners who were too heavy in debt to help themselves. In this way, the death of Christ became a perfect reparation offering, for just as the ram of the guilt offering was appraised "according to the sanctuary shekel," so Jesus was assessed and given a divine verdict in Matt 3:17: "With him I am well pleased" (NIV).

5. The sin offering represents the passive aspect of the death of Christ in that he met the demands of the law by dying in the place of sinners. But the guilt offering represents the active aspect of the work of Christ in that he carried out the will of God completely by an act of voluntary obedience. This is hardly a moral influence theory of the death of Christ; it is payment of a debt to render satisfaction plus reparation for the wrong committed, thus making reinstatement to the covenant family possible.

LEVITICUS 6:8–7:38, INSTRUCTIONS FOR THE PRIESTS

OVERVIEW

To complete the directions for the offerings, 6:8–7:38 goes over much of the same material as in the first five sacrifices described in 1:1–6:7. At first glance, the repetition seems to the modern reader superfluous. Various modern explanations give one reason or another for this apparent redundancy, but the best clue is found in the text itself. Leviticus 1:2 and 4:2 introduce the materials in their sections under the rubric "Speak/Say to the Israelites." Over against this heading for the contents of 1:1–6:7 is the new rubric in 6:9 (MT 6:2) and 6:25 (MT 6:18): "Give Aaron and his sons this command: 'These are the regulations'" (תורת *tôrat*).[48] In fact, in this second section of 6:7 –7:38 the people are addressed in only three paragraphs (7:11, 22, 28).

The difference, then, between the two sections is a difference in emphasis. Leviticus 1–6:7 concerns mainly the worshiper, but Lev 6:8–7:38 focuses on the officiating priest(s). This generalization is not without certain crossovers, for some items primarily addressed to the people by their very nature also affected the officiating priest.

Within the sections the order of the sacrifices also differs. In the opening chapters of Leviticus the order is burnt, grain, peace, sin, and guilt offerings. In the last two chapters of this first major section of the book the order is burnt, grain, the high priest's daily grain, sin, guilt, and peace offerings.

Leviticus 6:8–7:38 can be subdivided into the following nine paragraphs: the perpetual burnt offering (6:8-10); the daily grain offering (6:14-18); the priests' daily grain offering (6:19-23); the sin offering (6:24-30); the guilt offering (7:1-10); the peace offering (7:11-21); the prohibition on eating

48. Hebrew *tôrâ* is incorrectly rendered "law" in these contexts. Instead, Torah is now viewed as being derived from the stem *y-r-h,* "to cast," "to shoot," as one would shoot an arrow, for instance. In the hiphil stem of the Hebrew verb, *hôrâ* would mean "to aim, or direct toward something"; therefore, "to point out the way," "to instruct." The conclusion is that "instruction" is the best rendering for the word *torah.*

fat or blood (7:22-27); the priests' portion of the peace offering (7:28-36); and summary (7:37-38).

Each of these paragraphs opens with either "The LORD said to Moses" (6:19; 7:22, 28) or "This is the instruction for the . . . offering" (literal translation; 6:14; 7:1, 11, 37). Twice the two rubrics come together in the same opening line (6:8-9, 24-25). A colophon ends the first major section of Leviticus (7:37-38), just as concluding summaries exist elsewhere in the book (11:46-47; 13:59; 14:54-57; 15:32-33).

The colophon in 7:37-38 summarizes the whole legislative section on the sacrifices: "These, then, are the regulations for the burnt offering, the grain offering, the sin offering, the guilt offering, the ordination offering and the fellowship offering, which the LORD gave Moses on Mount Sinai on the day he commanded the Israelites to bring their offerings to the LORD, in the Desert of Sinai." The fact that 1:1 is revealed in the tabernacle, while 7:38 places it at Mount Sinai, has led some to attribute the rubric of 1:1 as a heading just for 1:2– 6:7. Thus the colophon refers, in this view, only to 6:8–7:38. The thought is that Lev 6:8–7:38 was revealed at the same time that Exodus 29 was given, while Moses was on Sinai; Lev 1:1– 6:7, in this view, would have come later. While this solution is possible, it cannot be demonstrated as certain.

Leviticus 6:8-13, The Perpetual Burnt Offering

NIV

[8]The LORD said to Moses: [9]"Give Aaron and his sons this command: 'These are the regulations for the burnt offering: The burnt offering is to remain on the altar hearth throughout the night, till morning, and the fire must be kept burning on the altar. [10]The priest shall then put on his linen clothes, with linen undergarments next to his body, and shall remove the ashes of the burnt offering that the fire has consumed on the altar and place them beside the altar. [11]Then he is to take off these clothes and put on others, and carry the ashes outside the camp to a place that is

NRSV

[8][a]The LORD spoke to Moses, saying: [9]Command Aaron and his sons, saying: This is the ritual of the burnt offering. The burnt offering itself shall remain on the hearth upon the altar all night until the morning, while the fire on the altar shall be kept burning. [10]The priest shall put on his linen vestments after putting on his linen undergarments next to his body; and he shall take up the ashes to which the fire has reduced the burnt offering on the altar, and place them beside the altar. [11]Then he shall take off his vestments and

a Ch 6.1 in Heb

NIV

ceremonially clean. [12]The fire on the altar must be kept burning; it must not go out. Every morning the priest is to add firewood and arrange the burnt offering on the fire and burn the fat of the fellowship offerings[a] on it. [13]The fire must be kept burning on the altar continuously; it must not go out.

[a]12 Traditionally *peace offerings*

NRSV

put on other garments, and carry the ashes out to a clean place outside the camp. [12]The fire on the altar shall be kept burning; it shall not go out. Every morning the priest shall add wood to it, lay out the burnt offering on it, and turn into smoke the fat pieces of the offerings of well-being. [13]A perpetual fire shall be kept burning on the altar; it shall not go out.

COMMENTARY

Five times in this paragraph the burden of this instruction for the priests is stressed: The fire on the altar in the courtyard of the sanctuary is not to go out (6:9*b*, 12, 13*b*). It is to be kept going day and night.

These verses are informed by the law of the "continual" or "perpetual" offering (תמיד *tāmîd*) in Exod 29:38–46, where we are told that two yearling lambs are to be sacrificed, one each morning and the other each evening (cf. Num 28:3-8; see also 2 Kgs 16:15; Ezek 46:13-15). The whole burnt offering sacrificed each morning and evening forms the foundation for all the other sacrifices. Since no other offering is placed on the altar after the evening sacrifice of the whole burnt offering, the fire has to be tended all night to make sure it does not go out. The whole burnt offering makes atonement each evening for the sins of that day; but come the next morning, it is necessary to atone for the sins of the preceding night. Thus the perpetual whole burnt offering

reminds Israel of its need for continual repentance, cleansing, prayer, and thanksgiving to God.

The priest's instructions also include what he is to wear as he removes the ashes from the altar of the burnt offering. To indicate the sacredness of even the ashes, his directions specify that he wear his linen garment, a linen, incidentally, that is made not of the common flax but of the type imported from Egypt. The ashes are deposited beside the altar until the priest once again completely changes his garments, for otherwise the people might be sanctified (see Ezek 44:17, 19) if he were to go outside the sanctuary wearing them; the linen garments are to be used exclusively in the sanctuary. Then the ashes are removed to a clean place outside the camp.

One of the main reasons for maintaining the fire on the altar is to signify that the altar, originally lit by fire from heaven (Lev 9:24), is the divinely approved means for receiving atonement and for expressing uninterrupted worship of Yahweh.

REFLECTIONS

1. One emphasis of this passage is on the ceaseless quality of service to God. The fire on the altar must always be kept burning as a sign that the dedication and consecration the Lord desires from us are not to be occasional but continuous, perpetual, and habitual.

This ceaseless service is to be understood not as exhausting but as hopeful. The worship of God never ends. Even when the night comes and the sanctuary candles are extinguished, somewhere in the world the sun is rising and the morning praises of God are beginning. Even when we are asleep, the God of Israel never slumbers, and God's watchful eye is ever vigilant (see Ps 121:3).

2. With the beginning of each new day there ought to arise a new resolve to dedicate ourselves to God. And before we retire each evening, the ardor of our devotion should be stirred up, not extinguished.

Leviticus 6:14-18, The Daily Grain Offering

NIV

14" 'These are the regulations for the grain offering: Aaron's sons are to bring it before the LORD, in front of the altar. 15The priest is to take a handful of fine flour and oil, together with all the incense on the grain offering, and burn the memorial portion on the altar as an aroma pleasing to the LORD. 16Aaron and his sons shall eat the rest of it, but it is to be eaten without yeast in a holy place; they are to eat it in the courtyard of the Tent of Meeting. 17It must not be baked with yeast; I have given it as their share of the offerings made to me by fire. Like the sin offering and the guilt offering, it is most holy. 18Any male descendant of Aaron may eat it. It is his regular share of the offerings made to the LORD by fire for the generations to come. Whatever touches them will become holy.ᵃ' "

ᵃ18 Or *Whoever touches them must be holy*; similarly in verse 27

NRSV

14This is the ritual of the grain offering: The sons of Aaron shall offer it before the LORD, in front of the altar. 15They shall take from it a handful of the choice flour and oil of the grain offering, with all the frankincense that is on the offering, and they shall turn its memorial portion into smoke on the altar as a pleasing odor to the LORD. 16Aaron and his sons shall eat what is left of it; it shall be eaten as unleavened cakes in a holy place; in the court of the tent of meeting they shall eat it. 17It shall not be baked with leaven. I have given it as their portion of my offerings by fire; it is most holy, like the sin offering and the guilt offering. 18Every male among the descendants of Aaron shall eat of it, as their perpetual due throughout your generations, from the LORD's offerings by fire; anything that touches them shall become holy.

COMMENTARY

The grain offering appears in the same sequence here as in the earlier section of Leviticus. This offering, unlike the one described in chap. 2, is not brought by the ordinary Israelite; instead, this daily grain offering is part of the continual or perpetual burnt offering.

First the priest takes a handful of fine flour mixed with oil and together with incense burns it on the altar as a "memorial portion" (see the discussion of this term in 2:2). The remainder of the offering is considered "most holy" (2:3; 6:17). The grain offering, the sin offering, and the guilt offering are said to be "most holy" (6:17, 25; 7:6); that is, only Aaron, his sons, and their descendants can eat any part of these offerings, and then only within the holy place of the tabernacle courtyard.

The expression in 6:18c and 27a, "Whatever touches it [or the flesh] will become holy," is problematic. But in line with the principles of 7:19-20, it would be better if the expression were translated "*Who*ever touches it will become holy," since the Hebrew simply says, "All

who touch it." This question must have concerned Israel much, for we find it still being raised in Hag 2:12-13. Apparently, according to Haggai, holiness was not as contagious as uncleanness was. Nevertheless, a warning still had to be issued about touching the most holy sacrifices. What the text means by "become holy" is not certain, even though similar expressions occur elsewhere (see Exod 29:37; 30:29; Deut 22:9). It may imply that by touching or eating a portion designated "most holy," laypersons expose themselves to the potential wrath of God unless they undergo an act of purification.[49]

Once again, we meet this distinction between the common and the holy (see the discussion on this matter in 2:10). Notice that when the altar is consecrated in Exod 29:37 and its furniture in Exod 30:29, they are said to be "most holy" with the result that everything put on the altar or the tabernacle furniture also is said to be holy.

Having said all of that, the solution may rest in a proper understanding of the Hebrew verb

49. Ellinger, *Leviticus*, 97, as cited by Wenham, *Leviticus*, 121.

יקדש (*yiqdāš*), which has usually been translated "will become holy" (presumably as a result of contacting sanctified objects or substances). But the problem of a contagious holiness still remained on this basis. While the verb קדש (*qādaš*) may connote a resultant holiness, here it seems to refer to what occurred prior to its contact with the sacred. There-fore, with Baruch A. Levine, it is proposed that a better translation is "must be in a holy state" if it is to touch the altar or any of these dedicated things.[50] Incidentally, such a view also makes the answer of Haggai more understandable.

50. Levine, *JPS Torah Commentary,* 37-38.

REFLECTIONS

1. Holiness is not something that acts like a contagious disease. Sin can be caught and is easily transmitted, but holiness does not work that way.

2. The daily offering of fine flour to God signifies Israel's daily consecration and dedication to the Lord.

3. Since God created all things, both the common and the holy must be received as gifts from above and not divorced from each other. But the common must be distinguished from the holy due to the presence of sin in the world, which God originally created "good."

Leviticus 6:19-23, The Priests' Daily Grain Offering

NIV

[19]The LORD also said to Moses, [20]"This is the offering Aaron and his sons are to bring to the LORD on the day he[a] is anointed: a tenth of an ephah[b] of fine flour as a regular grain offering, half of it in the morning and half in the evening. [21]Prepare it with oil on a griddle; bring it well-mixed and present the grain offering broken[c] in pieces as an aroma pleasing to the LORD. [22]The son who is to succeed him as anointed priest shall prepare it. It is the LORD's regular share and is to be burned completely. [23]Every grain offering of a priest shall be burned completely; it must not be eaten."

a20 Or *each*   *b20* That is, probably about 2 quarts (about 2 liters) *c21* The meaning of the Hebrew for this word is uncertain.

NRSV

19The LORD spoke to Moses, saying: [20]This is the offering that Aaron and his sons shall offer to the LORD on the day when he is anointed: one-tenth of an ephah of choice flour as a regular offering, half of it in the morning and half in the evening. [21]It shall be made with oil on a griddle; you shall bring it well soaked, as a grain offering of baked[a] pieces, and you shall present it as a pleasing odor to the LORD. [22]And so the priest, anointed from among Aaron's descendants as a successor, shall prepare it; it is the LORD's—a perpetual due—to be turned entirely into smoke. [23]Every grain offering of a priest shall be wholly burned; it shall not be eaten.

a Meaning of Heb uncertain

COMMENTARY

This offering is not mentioned in the list of the five major ones; therefore, along with the continual or perpetual burnt offering and the daily grain offering, we are being given new instructions.

The chief difference between the high priest's grain offering and the daily grain offering, or even the regular grain offering, is that it must be completely burned on the altar; none of it is to be eaten (v. 23). This same principle is enunciated in the sin offering; if the priest brings the sin offering, the entire animal has to be burned without any of it being eaten (4:3-12). Since the offering is for the high priest, he in no way can at one and the same time be a partaker and a mediator of what he brings out of his own need for atonement and dedication to God.

Verse 20 refers to this as a "regular" (תמיד *tāmîd*) grain offering. Accordingly, it is not limited to the time when the high priest is installed into his office as an initiation offering. The expression in v. 20, "on the day he is anointed," may point to the fact that when Aaron, or any high priest, was anointed, his sons brought this offering from that day onward. How the anointing of the priests in general differed from the anointing of the high priest is not known. But the offerings specified in connection with the anointing of the high priest do not seem to include the daily grain offering. Leviticus 8:26 refers to a basket of bread made without yeast and another made with oil and a wafer, but no mention is made of this grain offering. Since v. 20 specifically directs this instruction to "Aaron and his sons," this solution seems to resolve most of the difficulties. This solution understands the pronominal suffix on the direct object marker in v. 20 in a distributive sense so that it reads, "On the day each [of all the priests] is anointed."[51]

51. As suggested by A. Noordtzij, *Bible Student's Commentary: Leviticus,* trans. Raymond Togtman (Grand Rapids: Zondervan, 1982) 77.

REFLECTIONS

1. The priest's offering must be totally burned since he symbolically bears the sins of the people in his office as a mediator. However, no one figuratively bears his or her own sins, nor can one bear them oneself. That is another reason why the system of sacrifices reveals its weaknesses and its anticipation of a sacrifice that can overcome these imperfections.

2. Hebrews 7:27 uses this loophole to show how Christ's priesthood was superior to that of Aaron's priesthood: "Unlike the other high priests, he does not need to offer sacrifices day after day, first for his own sins, and then for the sins of the people. He sacrificed for their sins once for all when he offered himself " (NIV). Verse 28 goes on to clinch the point: "For the law appoints as high priests men who are weak; but the oath, which came after the law, appointed the Son, who has been made perfect forever" (NIV).

Leviticus 6:24-30, The Sin Offering

NIV	NRSV
[24]The LORD said to Moses, [25]"Say to Aaron and his sons: "These are the regulations for the sin offering: The sin offering is to be slaughtered before the LORD in the place the burnt offering is slaughtered; it is most holy. [26]The priest who offers it shall eat it; it is to be eaten in a holy place, in the courtyard of the Tent of Meeting. [27]Whatever touches any of the flesh will become holy, and if any of the blood is spattered on a garment, you must wash it in a holy place. [28]The clay pot the meat is cooked in must be broken; but if it is cooked in a bronze pot, the pot is to be scoured and rinsed with water. [29]Any male in a priest's family may eat it; it is most holy. [30]But any sin offering whose blood is brought into the Tent of Meeting to make atonement in the Holy Place must not be eaten; it must be burned.	24The LORD spoke to Moses, saying: [25]Speak to Aaron and his sons, saying: This is the ritual of the sin offering. The sin offering shall be slaughtered before the LORD at the spot where the burnt offering is slaughtered; it is most holy. [26]The priest who offers it as a sin offering shall eat of it; it shall be eaten in a holy place, in the court of the tent of meeting. [27]Whatever touches its flesh shall become holy; and when any of its blood is spattered on a garment, you shall wash the bespattered part in a holy place. [28]An earthen vessel in which it was boiled shall be broken; but if it is boiled in a bronze vessel, that shall be scoured and rinsed in water. [29]Every male among the priests shall eat of it; it is most holy. [30]But no sin offering shall be eaten from which any blood is brought into the tent of meeting for atonement in the holy place; it shall be burned with fire.

COMMENTARY

Leviticus 6:24–7:34 takes up offerings that have already been discussed in 3:1–6:7. These now concern the people at large, whereas the preceding group in 6:8-23 deals mainly with the priests.

The sin offering is included in the category of "most holy" (see the discussion of this term at 6:17). Also, on the improbable translation of "Whatever [or whoever] touches any of the flesh will become holy," a better rendering (as already indicated 6:18) is this: "Everything that touches any of the flesh [now that it has been brought into the courtyard of the tent of meeting] must [itself] be in a holy state." That is why garments that have been accidentally splattered with blood during the ceremony of the sin offering must be washed in the holy place. If washing is impossible, say in the case of a clay pot in which the meat was cooked and thus had penetrated the clay, it has to be destroyed (v. 28). The distinction between the holy and the common is thereby maintained once again.

While the priests can eat the sin offering in the holy place, they cannot eat it if the priest himself brings it (v. 30). It has to be totally burned just as the previous offering specifies, and for the same reason.

REFLECTIONS

1. Only persons consecrated to God could touch any part of this sacrifice once it was devoted to God. That was especially true of the blood of the offering, for should any of it fall on the garment of even a priest who stood nearby, it had to be thoroughly cleansed. The gulf between what was common/ordinary and what was holy was huge, and mortals disregarded it to their own hurt.

2. The NT teaches that Christ was made to be sin for us so that we might be redeemed. It is not without significance, then, that such reverential and holy treatment was given to the dedicated sacrifice and all its parts. Such an example suggests the type of deferential attitude that believers should show to the mysteries of our redemption in Christ.

Leviticus 7:1-10, The Guilt Offering

NIV

7 "'These are the regulations for the guilt offering, which is most holy: ²The guilt offering is to be slaughtered in the place where the burnt offering is slaughtered, and its blood is to be sprinkled against the altar on all sides. ³All its fat shall be offered: the fat tail and the fat that covers the inner parts, ⁴both kidneys with the fat on them near the loins, and the covering of the liver, which is to be removed with the kidneys. ⁵The priest shall burn them on the altar as an offering made to the LORD by fire. It is a guilt offering. ⁶Any male in a priest's family may eat it, but it must be eaten in a holy place; it is most holy.

⁷"'The same law applies to both the sin offering and the guilt offering: They belong to the priest who makes atonement with them. ⁸The priest

NRSV

7 This is the ritual of the guilt offering. It is most holy; ²at the spot where the burnt offering is slaughtered, they shall slaughter the guilt offering, and its blood shall be dashed against all sides of the altar. ³All its fat shall be offered: the broad tail, the fat that covers the entrails, ⁴the two kidneys with the fat that is on them at the loins, and the appendage of the liver, which shall be removed with the kidneys. ⁵The priest shall turn them into smoke on the altar as an offering by fire to the LORD; it is a guilt offering. ⁶Every male among the priests shall eat of it; it shall be eaten in a holy place; it is most holy.

7The guilt offering is like the sin offering, there is the same ritual for them; the priest who makes atonement with it shall have it. ⁸So, too, the priest

NIV	NRSV
who offers a burnt offering for anyone may keep its hide for himself. ⁹Every grain offering baked in an oven or cooked in a pan or on a griddle belongs to the priest who offers it, ¹⁰and every grain offering, whether mixed with oil or dry, belongs equally to all the sons of Aaron.	who offers anyone's burnt offering shall keep the skin of the burnt offering that he has offered. ⁹And every grain offering baked in the oven, and all that is prepared in a pan or on a griddle, shall belong to the priest who offers it. ¹⁰But every other grain offering, mixed with oil or dry, shall belong to all the sons of Aaron equally.

COMMENTARY

The close connection of the guilt offering with the sin offering is made explicit in v. 7—both are regarded as "most holy" (v. 6c). Once again, their consumption is strictly limited to the Aaronic priesthood (v. 6a).

This offering is to be slaughtered at the same site where the burnt offering is (1:11; 7:2). The rites for the guilt offering are the same as those for the sin offering, except for the way in which the blood is disposed. The blood of the guilt offering is sprinkled around the altar, whereas the blood of the sin offering is put on the horns of the altar (cf. 4:34; 7:2b).

The fatty tissues are to be burned on the altar as a reparation sacrifice, corresponding to the instructions given for the peace offering (3:9-10). The remainder of the offering, then, belongs to the priests; however, its consumption is restricted to male members of the priesthood, who may eat it only in the precincts of the sanctuary.

No mention is made of the laying on of hands as appears in the sin offering (4:4), but since these two offerings are treated as having the same law (7:7), presuming its presence here as well is reasonable.

The officiating priest is also given all the grain offering that had been cooked, whether in an oven or a pan or on a griddle (7:9). The same rule applies to the hide of the guilt offering; it too belongs to the officiating priest.

REFLECTIONS

1. These provisions for the priests enunciate the distinct principle that those who minister at the altar are to share in the sacrificial offerings. This theme will again be announced in 1 Cor 9:13 and 10:18.

2. A corollary of the first reflection is that it is the responsibility of the Lord's people to support those who minister the gospel (see 1 Tim 5:17-18), lest they be distracted from their primary task and be forced to give less of themselves and their time to the primary call of God. Although it was not specifically mentioned previously in connection with this offering, the priest was allowed to keep the animal hide for himself. It must have been valuable, since animal hides were often used as mattresses by night and as carpets to sit on by day.

3. The hide may well have acquired a special significance, through the laying on of hands, in that the guilt of the person was transferred to the animal. When the offerer left behind the skin of the animal, the symbolism may well have been that the offerer left his guilt behind and departed from the sanctuary in a purified state. Thus sins were forgiven through the atoning sacrifice, but they were also forsaken and removed, which was pictured in abandoning the hide to the care of the priest.

Leviticus 7:11-21, The Peace Offering

NIV

11 " 'These are the regulations for the fellowship offering[a] a person may present to the LORD:

12 " 'If he offers it as an expression of thankfulness, then along with this thank offering he is to offer cakes of bread made without yeast and mixed with oil, wafers made without yeast and spread with oil, and cakes of fine flour well-kneaded and mixed with oil. 13Along with his fellowship offering of thanksgiving he is to present an offering with cakes of bread made with yeast. 14He is to bring one of each kind as an offering, a contribution to the LORD; it belongs to the priest who sprinkles the blood of the fellowship offerings. 15The meat of his fellowship offering of thanksgiving must be eaten on the day it is offered; he must leave none of it till morning.

16 " 'If, however, his offering is the result of a vow or is a freewill offering, the sacrifice shall be eaten on the day he offers it, but anything left over may be eaten on the next day. 17Any meat of the sacrifice left over till the third day must be burned up. 18If any meat of the fellowship offering is eaten on the third day, it will not be accepted. It will not be credited to the one who offered it, for it is impure; the person who eats any of it will be held responsible.

19 " 'Meat that touches anything ceremonially unclean must not be eaten; it must be burned up. As for other meat, anyone ceremonially clean may eat it. 20But if anyone who is unclean eats any meat of the fellowship offering belonging to the LORD, that person must be cut off from his people. 21If anyone touches something unclean—whether human uncleanness or an unclean animal or any unclean, detestable thing—and then eats any of the meat of the fellowship offering belonging to the LORD, that person must be cut off from his people.' "

a11 Traditionally peace offering; also in verses 13-37

NRSV

11This is the ritual of the sacrifice of the offering of well-being that one may offer to the LORD. 12If you offer it for thanksgiving, you shall offer with the thank offering unleavened cakes mixed with oil, unleavened wafers spread with oil, and cakes of choice flour well soaked in oil. 13With your thanksgiving sacrifice of well-being you shall bring your offering with cakes of leavened bread. 14From this you shall offer one cake from each offering, as a gift to the LORD; it shall belong to the priest who dashes the blood of the offering of well-being. 15And the flesh of your thanksgiving sacrifice of well-being shall be eaten on the day it is offered; you shall not leave any of it until morning. 16But if the sacrifice you offer is a votive offering or a freewill offering, it shall be eaten on the day that you offer your sacrifice, and what is left of it shall be eaten the next day; 17but what is left of the flesh of the sacrifice shall be burned up on the third day. 18If any of the flesh of your sacrifice of well-being is eaten on the third day, it shall not be acceptable, nor shall it be credited to the one who offers it; it shall be an abomination, and the one who eats of it shall incur guilt.

19Flesh that touches any unclean thing shall not be eaten; it shall be burned up. As for other flesh, all who are clean may eat such flesh. 20But those who eat flesh from the LORD's sacrifice of well-being while in a state of uncleanness shall be cut off from their kin. 21When any one of you touches any unclean thing—human uncleanness or an unclean animal or any unclean creature—and then eats flesh from the LORD's sacrifice of well-being, you shall be cut off from your kin.

COMMENTARY

The ritual of the peace offering has already been discussed in chap. 3, but now more specific orders are given to the priests on how this offering is to be observed.

The *peace offering* is actually a collective term for three types of offerings: the eucharistic or thank offering (v. 12), the votive offering (v. 16), and the freewill or voluntary offering (v. 16). The peace offering also is the only one that the laity are allowed to eat.

The eucharistic, or thanksgiving, offering is given on occasions of praise, thanksgiving, or confession. The word תּוֹדָה (tôdâ, "thanksgiving") covers the ideas of thankfulness and confession of sin (see Josh 7:19; Ezra 10:11). As urged in Psalm 107, this sacrifice is to be offered as a token of gratitude for a number of mercies and favors received, such as recovery from sickness, preservation on a journey, deliverance at sea, and rescue from captivity (see Ps 107:22). The writer of Hebrews had this sacrifice in mind when he wrote, "Through Jesus, therefore, let us continually offer to God a sacrifice of praise—the fruit of lips that confess his name" (13:15 NIV; an allusion to Hos 14:2d). The same offering is mentioned in Pss 56:12-13; 116:17; Jer 17: 26; 33:11; Amos 4:5. Indeed, the liturgical formula used with this offering may appear in Jer 33:11: "Give thanks to the LORD Almighty,/ for the LORD is good;/ his love endures forever" (NIV; cf. Pss 100:4-5; 106:1; 107:1; 118:1; 136:1). The occasion, then, is some moment recalled from the past when God intervened and thus provided an opportunity for the offerer to be grateful and to rejoice in the goodness of the Lord.

The oblations required for this peace offering, along with the usual bull, goat, or sheep, include pancakes mixed with pure oil, but unleavened, inasmuch as part of them is to be offered up to God on the altar with the fatty pieces. Leaven, however, is not prohibited from another part of the offering, i.e., the bread given to the priests, which is not burned on the altar.

All thanksgiving offerings are to be eaten on the same day they are offered, whereas the other peace offerings may be eaten on the second day but never on the third day. For this reason the thanksgiving offering stands first among the class of peace offerings. This rule may also be required to make sure that the thanksgiving offerings are shared with poor people (v. 15). Poor people are invited on the condition that they are ceremonially clean (see 1 Sam 20:24-26; 21:5; cf. Ps 22:25-26). Since the sacrifice belongs to God, who in turn graciously grants it to be shared with the offerer's friends and poorer neighbors, no part of it is to be left around to be diverted to any other use or to putrefy.

The other two types of peace offerings, the votive and the freewill, are often mentioned together in Scripture as they are here in v. 16 (see Lev 22:21; Num 15:3; Deut 12:6, 17). The votive offering is made to fulfill a vow made during an emergency of life (see Gen 28:20; Judg 11:30-31; 1 Sam 1:11; 2 Sam 15:8). Israelites are not required to make vows, but if they make them, they must to keep them (see Eccl 5:4-6). The freewill offering comes as a spontaneous impulse of the heart in gratitude to God (see 2 Chr 31:14; 35:8-9; Ps 54:6). The unusual aspect of the freewill offering is that it is not subject to the same stringent rules applied to the other sacrifices. It can be from an animal that is "deformed and stunted" (Lev 22:23b). Here is the single exception to the rule that all animals offered for sacrifice have to be perfect and without blemish. The passage that grants this single exception warns the offerer that this exception will not be accepted even for the companion votive offering, for returning to God anything less than perfect will reflect on the perfection of God's most gracious gifts to the people.

Leviticus 7:20-21 warns that all who participate in eating the sacrificial meal must be ritually clean. Should someone violate this rule, "that person must be cut off from his people" (v. 21). This penalty appears some twenty-five times, usually with regard to a ceremonial violation. It is associated with capital crimes only three times (Exod 31:14; Lev 17:14; 18:29). This phrase appears to be used in various ways, often meaning some kind of excommunication rather than capital punishment. For many sins of even greater magnitude, provision is made for removal of the sin by God's atonement. Furthermore, since 17:10 and 20:3-6 are clear that it is a divine rather than a human punishment, it would be best to understand it as God cutting off the offenders from their kin instead of a premature death.[52]

---

52. See the discussion by Milgrom, "Karet," in Leviticus 1-16, 457-60. Milgrom lists nineteen cases in the Torah of karet. He concludes that either extirpation (of a person's line of descendants) or premature death is to be seen in these cases of "cutting off."

REFLECTIONS

1. The peace offerings stress that God values more than the mere word of praise and thankfulness. The tangible response of the sacrifice has the effect of backing up the verbal profession of gratitude

and appreciation for all that God has done on behalf of the worshiper. Similarly, 1 John 3:18 encourages believers to love, not just in word or speech, but in deed and in truth.

2. The motivating force behind the peace offerings is the desire to express appreciation and gratitude. Accordingly, Christians are still being urged to make their petitions known to God with thanksgiving (see Phil 4:6) and to continue in prayer with thanksgiving (see Col 4:2), giving thanks in everything, always, to God (see Eph 5:20).

Leviticus 7:22-27, The Prohibition on Eating Fat or Blood

NIV

²²The LORD said to Moses, ²³"Say to the Israelites: 'Do not eat any of the fat of cattle, sheep or goats. ²⁴The fat of an animal found dead or torn by wild animals may be used for any other purpose, but you must not eat it. ²⁵Anyone who eats the fat of an animal from which an offering by fire may be^a made to the LORD must be cut off from his people. ²⁶And wherever you live, you must not eat the blood of any bird or animal. ²⁷If anyone eats blood, that person must be cut off from his people.'"

^a25 Or *fire is*

NRSV

22The LORD spoke to Moses, saying: ²³Speak to the people of Israel, saying: You shall eat no fat of ox or sheep or goat. ²⁴The fat of an animal thatdied or was torn by wild animals may be put to any use, but you must not eat it. ²⁵If any one of you eats the fat from an animal of which an offering by fire may be made to the LORD, you who eat it shall be cut off from your kin. ²⁶You must not eat any blood whatever, either of bird or of animal, in any of your settlements. ²⁷Any one of you who eats any blood shall be cut off from your kin.

COMMENTARY

Whereas the previous material in chaps. 6–7 is directed to the priests, these verses address the people.

The prohibition on eating fat is not an absolute injunction; it applies only to the fat of beasts offered in sacrifice. The rule also applies to clean animals that have died a natural death or have been killed by wild animals. In both additional cases the animal is made unclean because its death may have come due to disease or contact with unclean wildlife; the resulting uncleanness makes it unsuitable for food. The main principle, however, is that the fat belongs to the Lord (3:16).

The prohibition on the use of blood as food, however, is absolutely universal. Whether the blood comes on the occasion of the sacrificial feasts or some other setting makes no difference. The reason is given in 17:11-12: "For the life of a creature is in the blood, and I have given it to you to make atonement for yourselves on the altar; it is the blood that makes atonement for one's life. Therefore I say to the Israelites, 'None of you may eat blood, nor may an alien living among you eat blood'" (cf. Lev 3:17; Deut 12:16; 15:23).

REFLECTIONS

While nothing may seem more remote from the modern believer than these two prohibitions, two most important principles underlie these directions. These principles state how sinful beings can enter into fellowship with a reconciling God.

1. The first principle is that happy communion with God rests on the willing consecration of the best fruit of our lives to God. Just as the peace offering, the sin offering, and the guilt offering required that all the fat be laid on the altar in dedication to God, so we are reminded that we owe God our best.

2. The second principle recognizes the supreme sanctity of the sacrificial blood of the Lamb of God on our behalf. It is a tacit acceptance of the fact that the death of a substitute in our place, as symbolized by the loss of blood from the flesh of the animal sacrifice, is the only grounds for our acceptance into fellowship with God.

Leviticus 7:28-36, The Priests' Portion of the Peace Offering

28The LORD said to Moses, 29"Say to the Israelites: 'Anyone who brings a fellowship offering to the LORD is to bring part of it as his sacrifice to the LORD. 30With his own hands he is to bring the offering made to the LORD by fire; he is to bring the fat, together with the breast, and wave the breast before the LORD as a wave offering. 31The priest shall burn the fat on the altar, but the breast belongs to Aaron and his sons. 32You are to give the right thigh of your fellowship offerings to the priest as a contribution. 33The son of Aaron who offers the blood and the fat of the fellowship offering shall have the right thigh as his share. 34From the fellowship offerings of the Israelites, I have taken the breast that is waved and the thigh that is presented and have given them to Aaron the priest and his sons as their regular share from the Israelites.' "

35This is the portion of the offerings made to the LORD by fire that were allotted to Aaron and his sons on the day they were presented to serve the LORD as priests. 36On the day they were anointed, the LORD commanded that the Israelites give this to them as their regular share for the generations to come.

28The LORD spoke to Moses, saying: 29Speak to the people of Israel, saying: Any one of you who would offer to the LORD your sacrifice of well-being must yourself bring to the LORD your offering from your sacrifice of well-being. 30Your own hands shall bring the LORD's offering by fire; you shall bring the fat with the breast, so that the breast may be raised as an elevation offering before the LORD. 31The priest shall turn the fat into smoke on the altar, but the breast shall belong to Aaron and his sons. 32And the right thigh from your sacrifices of well-being you shall give to the priest as an offering; 33the one among the sons of Aaron who offers the blood and fat of the offering of well-being shall have the right thigh for a portion. 34For I have taken the breast of the elevation offering, and the thigh that is offered, from the people of Israel, from their sacrifices of well-being, and have given them to Aaron the priest and to his sons, as a perpetual due from the people of Israel. 35This is the portion allotted to Aaron and to his sons from the offerings made by fire to the LORD, once they have been brought forward to serve the LORD as priests; 36these the LORD commanded to be given them, when he anointed them, as a perpetual due from the people of Israel throughout their generations.

COMMENTARY

All the people are addressed in these verses, which form a supplement to the peace offering regulations in vv. 11-21. The special emphasis is on the fact that offerers are to bring the peace offering with their own hands (v. 30) so as to prevent anyone's thinking that coercion is involved (cf. 8:27-28).

The priests are entitled to a portion of the peace offering (v. 35). They are assigned two parts: the breast (v. 30) and the right thigh (v. 33).

The right thigh probably indicates the right hindquarter, even though Deut 18:3 and Philo[53] are occasionally incorrectly used to argue that "the

53. *Laws* 1.145.

thigh of the right [side]" (literal translation) means the right shoulder. What further contributed to the shoulder interpretation was the archaeological excavation of a Lachish Canaanite temple (destroyed about 1220 BCE) that uncovered the right forelegs of a number of species found near an altar, mostly untouched by fire.[54] But the choicest part of the animal was the hindquarter; therefore, this is the preferred interpretation. Moreover, whenever the same Hebrew term is applied to humans in Scripture, the leg, not the arm, is signified.

The breast is said to constitute a "wave offering" (תנופה *těnûpâ*), which seems to mean moving the arms back and forth in a horizontal motion (v. 30). The right thigh is, according to the AV, offered as a "heave offering" (תרומה *těrûmâ;* v. 32), presumably because of its being related to the Hebrew verb "to exalt," "to raise," or "to lift." The NIV does not translate the term this way; instead, it has "as a contribution." The NRSV has "as an offering," and the TNK has "as a gift."

The wave offering, according to the several translators of the English Bible and the works of Jewish commentators, was toward the sanctuary, while the so-called heave offering was a vertical motion toward heaven and thus dedicated to the Lord. However, based on an Egyptian relief from Karnak, Jacob Milgrom argues persuasively that the so-called wave offering should now be understood as an elevation offering, a ritual of elevating and lifting the offering in dedication to God.[55]

The so-called heave offering may now be understood as "gift," coming from the verb *rûm*, meaning "to give a gift."[56] This is further collaborated by the fact that in every instance where *těrûmâ* is used, it is always "to the LORD," never "before the LORD"—as happens when *těnûpâ* appears. Thus the breast is said to be a "dedication" (*těnûpâ*) before the Lord, first, and then it along with the leg is to be a "contribution" or "gift" (*těrûmâ*) to the officiating priest. If a difference be sought between these two terms, it is that only certain items underwent a ritual ceremony of "dedication" in the sanctuary itself, while a "contribution" may have represented only the first stage in giving anything to God according to Jacob Milgrom. However, finality on these matters must await the further results of study in lexicography.

---

54. See G. Ernest Wright, *Biblical Archaeology* (Philadelphia: Westminster, 1960) 15.

55. Milgrom, "The *Tenûpâ*," in *Leviticus 1-16*, 461-72.
56. Milgrom, "The *Sôq Hatterûmâ*," in *Leviticus 1-16*, 473-81.

REFLECTIONS

1. In the act of elevating the breast, the priests both dedicate this portion to their Lord and acknowledge their dependence on God as the supplier of their food.

2. Both the dedication and the contribution teach us that it is the will of God that those who give up secular occupations to devote themselves to the ministry of the house of God are to be supported with the offerings of God's people. This would hardly need to be said today, except that some small groups deny this privilege to the clergy and its responsibility to the laity. The apostle Paul came to the same conclusion in 1 Cor 9:13-14; for him the principle had not been set aside, but still held.

Leviticus 7:37-38, Summary

NIV	NRSV
[37]These, then, are the regulations for the burnt offering, the grain offering, the sin offering, the guilt offering, the ordination offering and the fellowship offering, [38]which the LORD gave Moses on Mount Sinai on the day he commanded the Israelites to bring their offerings to the LORD, in the Desert of Sinai.	37This is the ritual of the burnt offering, the grain offering, the sin offering, the guilt offering, the offering of ordination, and the sacrifice of well-being, [38]which the LORD commanded Moses on Mount Sinai, when he commanded the people of Israel to bring their offerings to the LORD, in the wilderness of Sinai.

COMMENTARY

These last two verses are written in the style of a colophon, which normally gives the title or designation of the contents, date when it was written, name of the owner, and the scribe who wrote the materials.

The case is sometimes made that the legislation of the section just concluded or certain parts of it were not given "from the tent of meeting" (1:1), but were uniquely given "on Mount Sinai" (7:38). But the case is not beset with dualities or contradictions as may be at first supposed, for while it is true that the expression "on/in Mount Sinai" (בהר *běhar* may mean "in/on/at Mount [Sinai]") usually refers to the peak itself, it may also be true that some of these instructions had indeed been given for the first time while Moses was still on the mount. It may also be true that these instructions were given "in [the area] of Mount Sinai." Thus, already in the wilderness of Sinai, Israel had worshiped God with these same sacrifices.

THE INAUGURATION OF WORSHIP AT THE TABERNACLE

OVERVIEW

E ven though most tend to think of the book of Leviticus as a book of laws, it is actually the continuation of the story of Israel's history, providing the setting for the laws on worship. Nothing strengthens this judgment more than the section of Leviticus that is before us, chaps. 8–10.

This second section of Leviticus is a narrative account of the consecration of the tabernacle and of Aaron and his sons as the priests of that tent of meeting (chap. 8), of the induction of the Aaronic priesthood into the duties of their offices (chap. 9), and of the awesome judgment that falls on two of Aaron's sons who violated an instruction with regard to carrying out the duties of their offices (chap. 10). Therefore, the style is more descriptive than in the previous seven chapters, and it carries on the story of Israel, which was begun earlier.

One of the most noticeable features of chaps. 8–10 is the remarkable frequency with which the statement "Moses did as the LORD commanded him" (or its equivalent) appears. This statement (or ones similar to it) appears sixteen times in these three chapters alone (8:4, 5, 9, 13, 17, 21, 29, 34, 36; 9:6, 7, 10, 21; 10:7, 13, 15). Fidelity to the Word of God given in the blueprint God laid out on Mount Sinai is stressed repeatedly, especially with the instructions given for the ordination of Aaron and his sons in Exodus 28–29.

In fact, so careful was Moses to follow the directions given to him on the mount that practically every verse in chap. 8 is a quotation or an adaptation of the commands given in Exodus 29–30. We may see this in the following list of parallel passages[57]:

Exodus 29–30	Leviticus 8
29:1-3	8:2
29:4-6	8:6-8
29:7	8:12
30:26-29	8:10-11
29:8-9	8:13
29:10-14	8:14-17
29:15-18	8:18-21
29:19-20	8:22-24
29:22-25	8:25-28
29:26	8:29
29:21	8:30
29:31-32	8:31
29:34	8:32
29:35-37	8:33-35

Moses' strict adherence to the revealed will of God could not be demonstrated more elaborately than by means of this close paralleling of the instructions given in Exodus. All of these sacred instructions were fulfilled in accordance with the aim stated in Exod 29:43-46 and Lev 9:23—i.e., so that "the glory of the LORD [would appear] to all the people" and "dwell among the Israelites."

One other remarkable feature in these texts deserves special mention. After God had given the instructions for the installation of the priests in Exodus 29, the story of Israel's sin at the golden calf (see Exodus 32–34) interrupted the continuation of plans for the design and erection of the tabernacle, its services, and its officiants. One willing participant in the whole fiasco was Aaron, the man marked out to be the future high priest. Even though Moses intervened and saved the people from certain destruction, there was no assurance that Aaron would be named high priest. Indeed, the garments for Aaron had been completed, but he played no part in the services of

57. This list appears in Wenham, *Leviticus,* 131 n. 1.

Exodus 40. Would Aaron be named, or would he be by-passed and permanently debarred from the office?

We are surprised by the grace and forgiveness of God when Leviticus 8 makes it clear that Aaron will be named high priest, serving along with his sons. After failing as a leader, he is reinstated. This turn of events makes the lapse of Nadab and Abihu (chap. 10) all the more startling. Was their sin any more grievous than that of their father? We are left pondering this question and the remarkable uniqueness of the holiness of God.

The precise chronology for the events of these chapters cannot be fixed with certainty. What is known is that Moses had set up the tabernacle on the first day of the first month in the second year after the exodus (see Exod 40:2, 17). And according to Leviticus 8–9, the consecration of Aaron and his sons lasted seven days (8:33). The only suggestion that can be made is that the "eighth day" mentioned in Lev 9:1 may be the same as the first day of the first month of the second year after the exodus mentioned in Exod 40:17. But then there is the problem of the twelve days mentioned in Numbers 7, when each of the chieftains of the twelve tribes brought gifts for twelve days after Moses had finished setting up the tent of meeting. The Talmud felt obliged to harmonize the data; therefore, it concluded that the dedication program began on the twenty-third day of the twelfth month. Moses officiated for the last seven days of the month; the eighth day of Lev 9:1 came on the first day of the first month, as noted in Exod 40:2, 17, when Aaron assumed the priestly duties from that point onward. That was the same day that Moses "finished setting up the tabernacle" (Num 7:1 NIV) and discharged his responsibilities to the priests. Then the first of the princes came on that first day of the priestly leadership (see Num 7:12). All of this is possible, but the text gives us no assurance that the harmonization is secure.

LEVITICUS 8:1-36, CONSECRATION OF AARON AND HIS SONS

NIV

8 The Lord said to Moses, [2]"Bring Aaron and his sons, their garments, the anointing oil, the bull for the sin offering, the two rams and the basket containing bread made without yeast, [3]and gather the entire assembly at the entrance to the Tent of Meeting." [4]Moses did as the Lord commanded him, and the assembly gathered at the entrance to the Tent of Meeting.

[5]Moses said to the assembly, "This is what the Lord has commanded to be done." [6]Then Moses brought Aaron and his sons forward and washed them with water. [7]He put the tunic on Aaron, tied the sash around him, clothed him with the robe and put the ephod on him. He also tied the ephod to him by its skillfully woven waistband; so it was fastened on him. [8]He placed the breastpiece on him and put the Urim and Thummim in the breastpiece. [9]Then he placed the turban on Aaron's head and set the gold plate, the sacred diadem, on the front of it, as the Lord commanded Moses.

NRSV

8 The Lord spoke to Moses, saying: [2]Take Aaron and his sons with him, the vestments, the anointing oil, the bull of sin offering, the two rams, and the basket of unleavened bread; [3]and assemble the whole congregation at the entrance of the tent of meeting. [4]And Moses did as the Lord commanded him. When the congregation was assembled at the entrance of the tent of meeting, [5]Moses said to the congregation, "This is what the Lord has commanded to be done."

6Then Moses brought Aaron and his sons forward, and washed them with water. [7]He put the tunic on him, fastened the sash around him, clothed him with the robe, and put the ephod on him. He then put the decorated band of the ephod around him, tying the ephod to him with it. [8]He placed the breastpiece on him, and in the breastpiece he put the Urim and the Thummim. [9]And he set the turban on his head, and on the turban, in front, he set the golden ornament, the holy crown, as the Lord commanded Moses.

NIV

¹⁰Then Moses took the anointing oil and anointed the tabernacle and everything in it, and so consecrated them. ¹¹He sprinkled some of the oil on the altar seven times, anointing the altar and all its utensils and the basin with its stand, to consecrate them. ¹²He poured some of the anointing oil on Aaron's head and anointed him to consecrate him. ¹³Then he brought Aaron's sons forward, put tunics on them, tied sashes around them and put headbands on them, as the LORD commanded Moses.

¹⁴He then presented the bull for the sin offering, and Aaron and his sons laid their hands on its head. ¹⁵Moses slaughtered the bull and took some of the blood, and with his finger he put it on all the horns of the altar to purify the altar. He poured out the rest of the blood at the base of the altar. So he consecrated it to make atonement for it. ¹⁶Moses also took all the fat around the inner parts, the covering of the liver, and both kidneys and their fat, and burned it on the altar. ¹⁷But the bull with its hide and its flesh and its offal he burned up outside the camp, as the LORD commanded Moses.

¹⁸He then presented the ram for the burnt offering, and Aaron and his sons laid their hands on its head. ¹⁹Then Moses slaughtered the ram and sprinkled the blood against the altar on all sides. ²⁰He cut the ram into pieces and burned the head, the pieces and the fat. ²¹He washed the inner parts and the legs with water and burned the whole ram on the altar as a burnt offering, a pleasing aroma, an offering made to the LORD by fire, as the LORD commanded Moses.

²²He then presented the other ram, the ram for the ordination, and Aaron and his sons laid their hands on its head. ²³Moses slaughtered the ram and took some of its blood and put it on the lobe of Aaron's right ear, on the thumb of his right hand and on the big toe of his right foot. ²⁴Moses also brought Aaron's sons forward and put some of the blood on the lobes of their right ears, on the thumbs of their right hands and on the big toes of their right feet. Then he sprinkled blood against the altar on all sides. ²⁵He took the fat, the fat tail, all the fat around the inner parts, the covering of the liver, both kidneys and their fat and the right thigh. ²⁶Then from the basket of

NRSV

10Then Moses took the anointing oil and anointed the tabernacle and all that was in it, and consecrated them. ¹¹He sprinkled some of it on the altar seven times, and anointed the altar and all its utensils, and the basin and its base, to consecrate them. ¹²He poured some of the anointing oil on Aaron's head and anointed him, to consecrate him. ¹³And Moses brought forward Aaron's sons, and clothed them with tunics, and fastened sashes around them, and tied headdresses on them, as the LORD commanded Moses.

14He led forward the bull of sin offering; and Aaron and his sons laid their hands upon the head of the bull of sin offering, ¹⁵and it was slaughtered. Moses took the blood and with his finger put some on each of the horns of the altar, purifying the altar; then he poured out the blood at the base of the altar. Thus he consecrated it, to make atonement for it. ¹⁶Moses took all the fat that was around the entrails, and the appendage of the liver, and the two kidneys with their fat, and turned them into smoke on the altar. ¹⁷But the bull itself, its skin and flesh and its dung, he burned with fire outside the camp, as the LORD commanded Moses.

18Then he brought forward the ram of burnt offering. Aaron and his sons laid their hands on the head of the ram, ¹⁹and it was slaughtered. Moses dashed the blood against all sides of the altar. ²⁰The ram was cut into its parts, and Moses turned into smoke the head and the parts and the suet. ²¹And after the entrails and the legs were washed with water, Moses turned into smoke the whole ram on the altar; it was a burnt offering for a pleasing odor, an offering by fire to the LORD, as the LORD commanded Moses.

22Then he brought forward the second ram, the ram of ordination. Aaron and his sons laid their hands on the head of the ram, ²³and it was slaughtered. Moses took some of its blood and put it on the lobe of Aaron's right ear and on the thumb of his right hand and on the big toe of his right foot. ²⁴After Aaron's sons were brought forward, Moses put some of the blood on the lobes of their right ears and on the thumbs of their right hands and on the big toes of their right feet; and Moses dashed the rest of the blood against all sides of the altar. ²⁵He took the fat—the broad

NIV

bread made without yeast, which was before the LORD, he took a cake of bread, and one made with oil, and a wafer; he put these on the fat portions and on the right thigh. ²⁷He put all these in the hands of Aaron and his sons and waved them before the LORD as a wave offering. ²⁸Then Moses took them from their hands and burned them on the altar on top of the burnt offering as an ordination offering, a pleasing aroma, an offering made to the LORD by fire. ²⁹He also took the breast—Moses' share of the ordination ram—and waved it before the LORD as a wave offering, as the LORD commanded Moses.

³⁰Then Moses took some of the anointing oil and some of the blood from the altar and sprinkled them on Aaron and his garments and on his sons and their garments. So he consecrated Aaron and his garments and his sons and their garments.

³¹Moses then said to Aaron and his sons, "Cook the meat at the entrance to the Tent of Meeting and eat it there with the bread from the basket of ordination offerings, as I commanded, saying,ᵃ 'Aaron and his sons are to eat it.' ³²Then burn up the rest of the meat and the bread. ³³Do not leave the entrance to the Tent of Meeting for seven days, until the days of your ordination are completed, for your ordination will last seven days. ³⁴What has been done today was commanded by the LORD to make atonement for you. ³⁵You must stay at the entrance to the Tent of Meeting day and night for seven days and do what the LORD requires, so you will not die; for that is what I have been commanded." ³⁶So Aaron and his sons did everything the LORD commanded through Moses.

ᵃ31 Or *I was commanded:*

NRSV

tail, all the fat that was around the entrails, the appendage of the liver, and the two kidneys with their fat—and the right thigh. ²⁶From the basket of unleavened bread that was before the LORD, he took one cake of unleavened bread, one cake of bread with oil, and one wafer, and placed them on the fat and on the right thigh. ²⁷He placed all these on the palms of Aaron and on the palms of his sons, and raised them as an elevation offering before the LORD. ²⁸Then Moses took them from their hands and turned them into smoke on the altar with the burnt offering. This was an ordination offering for a pleasing odor, an offering by fire to the LORD. ²⁹Moses took the breast and raised it as an elevation offering before the LORD; it was Moses' portion of the ram of ordination, as the LORD commanded Moses.

30Then Moses took some of the anointing oil and some of the blood that was on the altar and sprinkled them on Aaron and his vestments, and also on his sons and their vestments. Thus he consecrated Aaron and his vestments, and also his sons and their vestments.

31And Moses said to Aaron and his sons, "Boil the flesh at the entrance of the tent of meeting, and eat it there with the bread that is in the basket of ordination offerings, as I was commanded, 'Aaron and his sons shall eat it'; ³²and what remains of the flesh and the bread you shall burn with fire. ³³You shall not go outside the entrance of the tent of meeting for seven days, until the day when your period of ordination is completed. For it will take seven days to ordain you; ³⁴as has been done today, the LORD has commanded to be done to make atonement for you. ³⁵You shall remain at the entrance of the tent of meeting day and night for seven days, keeping the LORD's charge so that you do not die; for so I am commanded." ³⁶Aaron and his sons did all the things that the LORD commanded through Moses.

COMMENTARY

8:1-5. Before the services of worship can begin, the consecration of the tabernacle and the priests who will serve in it is necessary. But such consecration presupposes the call of God on the lives of those who will serve. Thus the installation of Aaron and his sons begins with the command of God, "Take Aaron and his sons . . ." (literal translation; v. 1).

Aaron's family had been selected to be the line through which the priests of Israel would come, even though all the other Levites, to which Aaron and his family also belonged, would carry all the other related duties of the sanctuary. No one might intrude into that perpetual appointment; it was to remain in Aaron's family.

Aaron was indeed succeeded by Eleazar, his oldest living son, after the death of Nadab and Abihu. Eleazar's line was traced for at least seven generations until the death of Eli in the days of Samuel. On Eli's death, the line was removed from Eli's sons, because of their wickedness, to the descendants of Ithamar, Aaron's other son. However, in the time of Solomon the line returned again to Eleazar's descendants and continued until the Babylonian captivity. Joshua, the high priest after the return from the Babylonian exile, was also from this line, but after his time the appointments became irregular and uncertain. In fact, under Roman occupation, no attention was paid to the original instructions for succession in this office, as it often was sold to the highest bidder, whether that bidder was from Aaron's family or not.

From its inception, however, priesthood was not from human beings, but from God. The high priest could act only under divine appointment.

Moses is instructed to gather all the nation together at the door of the tent of meeting (v. 3). Naturally, such a feat, if literally understood, was a logistical impossibility. Moreover, to hold that many people for all seven days of the consecration would stretch the limits of accommodations in the area of the tabernacle. Perhaps it is best to understand this command as an illustration of the figure of speech called synecdoche, where the whole is put for a part—or as it was in this case, all the congregation is put for the elders and principal people of Israel who represented the entire group, as Lev 9:1 seems to confirm.

The consecration ceremonies involve four main parts: the washing (v. 6), the investiture (vv. 7-9), the anointing (vv. 10-13), and the sacrifices (vv. 14-32). Moses acts as the mediator who represents God throughout, since no ordained priest has preceded Aaron in this office. Nowhere is Moses' distinctive role in these ceremonies brought out more clearly than in the sacrifices. Portions that normally would be eaten by the priests are either totally burned on the altar,

thereby being given to God, or are given to Moses (see the discussion of the sin offering above).

8:6. This verse records the washing ceremony. The ceremonial washing signifies the inward purification of the spirit. Often the OT requires washings and ablutions, as it does for the one cured of "leprosy" (Lev 14:8-9) or the one who experienced bodily discharges (Leviticus 15). The same word is used for washing away "the filth of the women of Zion" (Isa 4:4 NIV). Washing is a means of restoring persons and things to a state of being made clean (see Num 31:23-24). The symbolism points to cleansing from the defilements of sin that acted as impediments to carrying out the office of the priesthood. Scripture also frequently links the concepts of "clean hands" and a "pure heart" (see Pss 24:4; 73:13; Isa 1:16).

By NT times, washing would be linked with the "washing with water through the word [of God]" (Eph 5:26 NIV), the "washing of rebirth and renewal" (Titus 3:5 NIV), and having "our hearts sprinkled to cleanse us from a guilty conscience and having our bodies washed with pure water" (Heb 10:22 NIV).

Later specifications would determine that this washing was done behind a linen sheet and involved washing the priests' entire bodies. After this, whenever the priests went into the sanctuary, they were required to wash only their hands and feet (see Exod 30:19-21; 40:30-31).

8:7-9. These verses describe the investiture. Eight pieces are assigned to the official uniform of the priests—four are shared with all priests, and four are distinctive to the office of high priest. The garments reflect the office and not the individual. There is no mention of sandals, for the priests probably ministered in their bare feet, just as Moses and Joshua were instructed in their encounter with the living God (see Exod 3:5; Josh 5:15).

The first garment (assuming that the priest is already wearing linen breeches) is a "tunic," or undergarment. It is worn against the naked body, extends to the knees and has short sleeves (cf. Exod 20:26; 28:42). The tunic is held in place by a "sash." Over this is placed a purple "robe," woven into one piece (cf. Exod 28:31-35), reaching to the knees, and adorned with cloth pomegranates made of three different colors of yarn, each pomegranate alternated with a golden bell, all attached to the bottom of this garment. A shoulder garment, an "ephod," forms a type of vest held in place by a waistband. This ephod supports a "breastpiece," a square piece of cloth measuring about ten inches square and made of the same cloth as the ephod. This breastpiece is studded with jewels,[58] symbolizing each of the twelve tribes, and is folded in half so as to form a pouch to hold the "Urim" and "Thummim." The meaning of these two terms remains elusive, though "Lights" and "Perfections," respectively, are the two most frequent suggestions. In form they probably resembled flat stones, similar to the פורים (pûrîm), i.e., the dice used for casting lots in the book of Esther. First Samuel 14:41-43 attaches the verb "to cast" or "to throw down" in connection with the use of these two objects. Thus they were probably something like a pair of dice used by the priest to receive a yes, no, or neutral reply to questions put to the Lord by the priest.

On Aaron's head is placed a "turban," a headdress that differs both in name and in design from that worn by the other priests. Attached to it is a gold plate, a sacred diadem, inscribed with the words "HOLY TO THE LORD" (see Exod 28:36).

8:10-13. Before the priests are anointed to their service, the tabernacle and all that pertains to it must be anointed with oil. The anointing oil is a unique combination of four choice spices, which is not to be duplicated under any circumstances (cf. Exod 25:6; 30:22-33): myrrh, cinnamon, cane, and cassia.

The purpose of the anointing is to set the person or object apart for the service of the Lord. The anointing, not the oil, signals something or someone who has been chosen by the Lord. Only when the priests are on the verge of commencing their work can they and the sanctuary be anointed.

Scripture often connects the act of anointing with the receiving of God's Spirit. This is the case for Saul (see 1 Sam 10:1-10) and for David (see 1 Sam 16:13). The connection is clearly seen in Isa 61:1 where the servant of the Lord announces, "The Spirit of the Sovereign LORD is on me,/ because the LORD has anointed me" (NIV). Jesus applies this verse to himself in Luke 4:18.

58. See Walter C. Kaiser, Jr., "Exodus," in *The Expositor's Bible Commentary,* 467, for further discussion on Exodus 28–29. On the identity of the jewels, see A. Paul Davis and E. L. Gilmore, *Lapidary Journal* (Dec. 1968) 1124-28, 1130-34.

The apostle Peter declares much later that God "anointed Jesus of Nazareth with the Holy Spirit" (Acts 10:38 NIV), for that indeed is what the name Messiah means, "Anointed [One]."

Ordinary priests have small quantities of anointing oil applied to them with the finger, but the oil is "poured" on Aaron's head. It runs down on his beard and the robe of the ephod (see Ps 133:2).

8:14-32. This passage describes the sacrifices connected with the investiture. Three of the main sacrifices are part of the consecration ceremony: first the sin offering, then the burnt offering, and finally the peace offering.

8:14-17. The sin offering symbolizes the further need for cleansing. The washing of Aaron cannot effectively deal with his need for expiation of the guilt of his sins. Apparently, the ablution can care only for defilements of nature, by bringing renewal and regeneration through the Word of God and the Holy Spirit; but there remains the need for dealing with the removal of objective guilt and the need for forgiveness for the sin that caused the guilt.

The animal of choice for this occasion is the most costly of all: a bull, the same animal ordered for the sin offering of the anointed priest in chap. 4. Aaron and his sons lay their hands on the victim to clearly indicate that it is their substitute.

The ceremony takes place as described in 4:3-12, except that the blood is not taken into the holy place to be smeared on the horns of the altar of incense; instead, it is put on the altar of burnt offering in the courtyard to sanctify the altar and to prepare it for the next offering Aaron is to make. Moreover, Aaron and his sons have not yet been inducted into their offices, so they cannot enter the holy place yet. Another major difference between this consecration ceremony's sin offering and any other sin offering is that neither Aaron nor his sons are to eat any of this sin offering. The one for whom the sin offering is made must not eat of its flesh; it is to be burned outside the camp after the requisite parts have been offered on the altar (vv. 8:16-17). In this way, "atonement" is also made "for [the altar]" (v. 15). Even the impurities of the altar itself have to be removed.

8:18-21. Now that reconciliation has been effected through the sin offering, the priest offers the burnt offering. This offering signals the complete dedication of the lives of the priests in accordance with the directions of Lev 1:10-13 and Exod 29:15-18.

Once again, the major difference in this offering is that the priests being installed take the part of ordinary worshipers, while Moses performs the priestly aspects of the sacrifice.

8:22-30. The ceremony culminates in a special aspect of the peace offerings described in chap. 3. As in the previous sacrifices, Moses takes the part of the officiating priest. This is especially clear in that the breast of the animal, normally given to the officiating priest, is given to Moses. And the right thigh, normally also assigned to the officiant, is added to the portions burned on the altar, which all belong to God. This strengthens the idea that the ordination of Aaron is carried out jointly by God and Moses.

The sacrificial animal for this peace offering is a "ram" or, to be more specific, "the ram for the ordination" (v. 22). The Hebrew term for "ordination" is מלאים (*millu'îm*), i.e., "fillings." The fuller form of this expression is "to fill the hands." The significance of this phrase comes out immediately in vv. 25-27. Moses places the fat, the fat tail, and all the fat around the inner parts of the ram along with the right thigh of the ram on three differently made pieces of bread, all of which he puts into the hands of Aaron and his sons as a sign of their priestly office. Thus Aaron and his sons have their hands filled. Apparently, Moses next slides his hands under theirs and waves the contents of what fills the hands of those being dedicated back and forth in dedication to God.

Since the right thigh normally belongs to the priests (7:32), in these rites of dedication they are surrendering a portion that is theirs to God. Thus only when the priests are of service to others can they in any way benefit from it. When it is offered on their own behalf, it is improper for them to benefit from any of the sacrifice.

Later on, in the dedication of the Levites (see Num 8:9-14), the men themselves are waved before the Lord as a wave offering. The conclusion is the same: As the priests give what fills their hands, or even as they dedicate themselves, they just as surely devote themselves to God for service as their gift to God.

An even more remarkable feature about this peace offering is the way the blood is used (v. 23). It is applied to the tip of Aaron's right

ear, the thumb of his right hand, and his right big toe instead of being thrown against the altar, as is usual for this offering (3:2, 8, 13). Having previously anointed Aaron with oil, Moses now consecrates him with blood.

This act is surely another instance of the part standing for the whole—in this case, the entirety of his body; he is to be totally consecrated to the service of God in the tabernacle. But the rest of the symbolism is just as clear: Aaron's ear must ever be attentive to the word of the Lord; his hand ever ready to do the work of God; and his feet ever alert to run in the service of the One who called him. Therefore, just as the blood ratifies the covenant at Sinai with all of Israel (see Exod 24:8), and as the same ceremony involving smearing the right ear, thumb, and toe of the cleansed leper signals his being restored to communion with God (Lev 14:14), so also the blood designates Aaron as God's person for the office he is being called to fill (Lev 8:30).

The repetition of the ritual in v. 30 appears at first to be out of place and in conflict with Exod 29:21. However, it is similar to the rite with the leper in Lev 14:10-20, where the remaining oil is poured on the leper's head after the sin offerings have been completed; it is an exact replica of the provisions mentioned here. This is a better solution than suspecting the presence of "later hands" inserting dissonant material into the text.

8:31-32. The ordination ceremony of dedication and consecration is now followed with a meal. This meal also confirms the covenant made between God and the house of Aaron. Given the seriousness of this meal, however, everything that is left over has to be burned and not left until the next day as in certain of the peace offerings. In this regard, the holiness of the act of ordaining is stressed; this act, no doubt, belongs to the category of the things treated as "most holy" (6:25, 29).

8:33-36. These verses treat one more aspect of the ordination services. To avoid any possible contamination or defilement, Aaron and his sons are to remain in the sanctuary precincts for seven days. It would appear from Exod 29:35, 37 that a bull is to be offered on each of the seven days, perhaps accompanied by a burnt offering. The duties for these priests will not begin until the eighth day after the mediators of the old covenant are themselves sanctified.

REFLECTIONS

1. The ordination of Aaron is but one of many biblical examples of God's calling flawed and broken people to places of leadership. We can think of Jacob the trickster, David the adulterer, Paul the persecutor, Peter the one who denied Jesus, and many others. Hebrews 7:28 makes the identical point we have just made: "For the law appoints as high priests men who are weak; but the oath, which came after the law, appointed the Son, who has been made perfect forever" (NIV). The contrast between previous high priests and the Savior as our high priest could not have been any greater. The amazing thing is that God will still use persons with infirmities; God does not demand perfection to permit the services ordained to be rendered.

2. Originally, all Israel was called to be a "kingdom of priests" (Exod 19:6 NIV), but the sin at the golden calf prevented that from happening. However, that original call for all laity to be a royal priesthood never was forgotten. It was repeated for believers after the resurrection of Christ (see Rev 1:6; 5:10). Contemporary believers have been made kings and priests unto God; indeed, they have been given "an altar from which those who minister at the tabernacle [had] no right to eat" (Heb 13:10 NIV).

3. Just as the Urim and Thummim were used to ascertain the will of God, some have pointed to Ps 19:7-8 (Hebrew vv. 8-9) as a modern equivalent for guidance today, where the same two words may be weakly reflected: "The law of the LORD is perfect" (תמימה *těmîmâ*; the same root as Thummim); and "The commands of the LORD are radiant,/ giving light (מאירת *mě'îrat*; the same root as Urim] to the eyes" (NIV). Perhaps, but the words are related only in their root forms and any assumed connection is not immediately clear.

4. What is most immediately necessary for service to the living God is cleansing. We must be cleansed and washed to be used in the service of God. Today this washing comes by means of the Holy Spirit's using the Word of God (see John 13:10; Eph 5:26; Titus 3:5; Heb 10:22).

LEVITICUS 9:1-24, THE INAUGURATION OF THE TABERNACLE SERVICE

NIV

9 On the eighth day Moses summoned Aaron and his sons and the elders of Israel. ²He said to Aaron, "Take a bull calf for your sin offering and a ram for your burnt offering, both without defect, and present them before the LORD. ³Then say to the Israelites: 'Take a male goat for a sin offering, a calf and a lamb—both a year old and without defect—for a burnt offering, ⁴and an ox[a] and a ram for a fellowship offering[b] to sacrifice before the LORD, together with a grain offering mixed with oil. For today the LORD will appear to you.' "

[a]4 The Hebrew word can include both male and female; also in verses 18 and 19.   [b]4 Traditionally *peace offering*, also in verses 18 and 22

NRSV

9 On the eighth day Moses summoned Aaron and his sons and the elders of Israel. ²He said to Aaron, "Take a bull calf for a sin offering and a ram for a burnt offering, without blemish, and offer them before the LORD. ³And say to the people of Israel, 'Take a male goat for a sin offering; a calf and a lamb, yearlings without blemish, for a burnt offering; ⁴and an ox and a ram for an offering of well-being to sacrifice before the LORD; and a grain offering mixed with oil. For today the LORD will appear to you.' " ⁵They brought what Moses commanded to the front of the tent of meeting; and the whole congregation

NIV

⁵They took the things Moses commanded to the front of the Tent of Meeting, and the entire assembly came near and stood before the LORD. ⁶Then Moses said, "This is what the LORD has commanded you to do, so that the glory of the LORD may appear to you."

⁷Moses said to Aaron, "Come to the altar and sacrifice your sin offering and your burnt offering and make atonement for yourself and the people; sacrifice the offering that is for the people and make atonement for them, as the LORD has commanded."

⁸So Aaron came to the altar and slaughtered the calf as a sin offering for himself. ⁹His sons brought the blood to him, and he dipped his finger into the blood and put it on the horns of the altar; the rest of the blood he poured out at the base of the altar. ¹⁰On the altar he burned the fat, the kidneys and the covering of the liver from the sin offering, as the LORD commanded Moses; ¹¹the flesh and the hide he burned up outside the camp.

¹²Then he slaughtered the burnt offering. His sons handed him the blood, and he sprinkled it against the altar on all sides. ¹³They handed him the burnt offering piece by piece, including the head, and he burned them on the altar. ¹⁴He washed the inner parts and the legs and burned them on top of the burnt offering on the altar.

¹⁵Aaron then brought the offering that was for the people. He took the goat for the people's sin offering and slaughtered it and offered it for a sin offering as he did with the first one.

¹⁶He brought the burnt offering and offered it in the prescribed way. ¹⁷He also brought the grain offering, took a handful of it and burned it on the altar in addition to the morning's burnt offering.

¹⁸He slaughtered the ox and the ram as the fellowship offering for the people. His sons handed him the blood, and he sprinkled it against the altar on all sides. ¹⁹But the fat portions of the ox and the ram—the fat tail, the layer of fat, the kidneys and the covering of the liver— ²⁰these they laid on the breasts, and then Aaron burned the fat on the altar. ²¹Aaron waved the breasts and the right thigh before the LORD as a wave offering, as Moses commanded.

²²Then Aaron lifted his hands toward the people and blessed them. And having sacrificed the sin

NRSV

drew near and stood before the LORD. ⁶And Moses said, "This is the thing that the LORD commanded you to do, so that the glory of the LORD may appear to you." ⁷Then Moses said to Aaron, "Draw near to the altar and sacrifice your sin offering and your burnt offering, and make atonement for yourself and for the people; and sacrifice the offering of the people, and make atonement for them; as the LORD has commanded."

8Aaron drew near to the altar, and slaughtered the calf of the sin offering, which was for himself. ⁹The sons of Aaron presented the blood to him, and he dipped his finger in the blood and put it on the horns of the altar; and the rest of the blood he poured out at the base of the altar. ¹⁰But the fat, the kidneys, and the appendage of the liver from the sin offering he turned into smoke on the altar, as the LORD commanded Moses; ¹¹and the flesh and the skin he burned with fire outside the camp.

12Then he slaughtered the burnt offering. Aaron's sons brought him the blood, and he dashed it against all sides of the altar. ¹³And they brought him the burnt offering piece by piece, and the head, which he turned into smoke on the altar. ¹⁴He washed the entrails and the legs and, with the burnt offering, turned them into smoke on the altar.

15Next he presented the people's offering. He took the goat of the sin offering that was for the people, and slaughtered it, and presented it as a sin offering like the first one. ¹⁶He presented the burnt offering, and sacrificed it according to regulation. ¹⁷He presented the grain offering, and, taking a handful of it, he turned it into smoke on the altar, in addition to the burnt offering of the morning.

18He slaughtered the ox and the ram as a sacrifice of well-being for the people. Aaron's sons brought him the blood, which he dashed against all sides of the altar, ¹⁹and the fat of the ox and of the ram—the broad tail, the fat that covers the entrails, the two kidneys and the fat on them,ᵃ and the appendage of the liver. ²⁰They first laid the fat on the breasts, and the fat was turned into smoke on the altar; ²¹and the breasts and the right

ᵃGk: Heb the broad tail, and that which covers, and the kidneys

NIV

offering, the burnt offering and the fellowship offering, he stepped down.

²³Moses and Aaron then went into the Tent of Meeting. When they came out, they blessed the people; and the glory of the LORD appeared to all the people. ²⁴Fire came out from the presence of the LORD and consumed the burnt offering and the fat portions on the altar. And when all the people saw it, they shouted for joy and fell facedown.

NRSV

thigh Aaron raised as an elevation offering before the LORD, as Moses had commanded.

22Aaron lifted his hands toward the people and blessed them; and he came down after sacrificing the sin offering, the burnt offering, and the offering of well-being. ²³Moses and Aaron entered the tent of meeting, and then came out and blessed the people; and the glory of the LORD appeared to all the people. ²⁴Fire came out from the LORD and consumed the burnt offering and the fat on the altar; and when all the people saw it, they shouted and fell on their faces.

COMMENTARY

After a whole week dedicated to the ordination services, Aaron is now ready to commence his ministry as the fully installed high priest. Significantly enough, his work commences not on the seventh day but on the eighth day—the first day of the week. Surely, this is something more than mere happenstance, for repeatedly the eighth day of the week, i.e., "the first day" or "the day after the Sabbath," will be specified in the list of the feasts given in Leviticus 23 (e.g., 7, 11, 15, 16, 35, 36, 39). To what degree this is symbolic or a type of the change in the day of worship that is to come must await our discussion of the Feast of Firstfruits and the Feast of Tabernacles in connection with chap. 23.

The first day of worship at the tabernacle begins with Moses summoning Aaron and his sons along with the "elders of Israel," acting, no doubt, as the representatives of the people (v. 1). Five times in this chapter Moses issues commands, or Aaron and his sons act on the basis of the commands (vv. 2, 5, 6, 7).

Once again, Aaron is instructed to offer a sin offering and a burnt offering, just as he has been doing for the past seven days. If anything emphasizes the sheer tedium and the repetitious nature of the sacrificial system, by now the point must have impressed itself on Aaron. A more perfect sacrifice and a more perfect officiant are needed. But the repetition on this eighth day is probably necessary, since Aaron must also publicly acknowledge that he too is a sinner in need of God's

forgiveness. Even though Aaron has been lifted to the office of high priest, he needs atonement just as much as anyone else. The closer one follows the Lord in obedience and service, the more conscious that person becomes of how short each individual falls from the holy standard of God. So it is with Aaron; hence the need for further sacrifices!

Aaron may have been astonished when Moses ordered him to bring a bull calf (vv. 2-3). This is the only time in the sacrificial instructions where a calf is prescribed for an offering. Was the point of such a command, as many Jewish writers have supposed, to call back to his memory his sin of involvement with the golden calf? (See Exodus 32.) And since we are speculating about that matter, was the requirement of a "ram" for his burnt offering another attempt to help him recall that Abraham had sacrificed a ram, rather than his son Isaac? (See Genesis 22.) These two questions merely introduce intriguing connections and analogies to other parts of the canonical witness.

Meanwhile the people are to prepare themselves for a series of offerings, but only in their proper order: The sin offering is to come first, then the burnt offering, followed by the peace offering with the grain offering.

The purpose for all these offerings is clearly stated twice: "For today the LORD will appear to you" (v. 4c) and "So that the glory of the LORD may appear to you" (v. 6b). That is described in Exod 24:16-17. But in each of these statements, the emphasis falls on the theological concept of "the glory of the LORD."

The glory of the Lord is more than just the visible manifestation of God in fiery displays and effulgences of glory. It signals the very presence of God in the sheer weight of the divine person and the fact that God is immediately present.

Probably the cloudy pillar by day, which became a pillar of fire by night, was the visible manifestation of the fact of God's presence. The same glory that had settled on Mount Sinai when Moses was on the mount, and had led them in the wilderness thus far, is now the glory that will always be present in the tabernacle. Prior to this, it appears, God's glory had already descended on the finished tabernacle (see Exod 40:34), but now that same glory will ratify the ministry about to be undertaken at this place. With the evidence of divine glory, all worship, liturgy, and sacrifices will now be meaningful. Without that glory, worship, no matter how exact, will be worthless.

As the congregation draws near, especially in the persons of the elders who now act as leaders, Aaron begins by slaughtering the calf as his sin offering (v. 8). Then, in ritual details we rarely see in other passages, Aaron's sons assist him by collecting the blood in a basin; it is clear that these sons enter into the ministry with Aaron on the very same day he begins to serve. The blood is brought to Aaron; he, in turn, dips his finger into the blood and puts the blood on the horns of the altar in the courtyard. In that regard, the details once again differ slightly from those given in 4:3-12 (see the comment on 8:15). The rest of the blood is poured out at the base of the altar where the fat, the kidneys, and the covering of the liver are being totally burned as a sin offering to God. The remaining flesh and hide of the calf are to be burned up outside the camp (v. 11). This, then, is the high priest's public admission of his sinfulness and his desire to receive God's expiation for his sins.

As a sign of Aaron's complete self-surrender to God, he next offers a whole burnt offering (vv. 12-14). First his sons hand him the blood (which Aaron sprinkles against the altar on all sides), then they pass him the ram "piece by piece" (although Aaron first washes the unclean portions, such as the inner parts and the legs), and then they hand him the head—all of which

are to be totally consumed on the altar to indicate his complete dedication to God.

Now that Aaron and his sons are in a right relationship with the Lord, they can begin to make atonement for the people. Four sacrifices are brought on behalf of the people: a goat as a sin offering to cleanse the altar (vv. 3, 15), a calf and a lamb for a whole burnt offering (vv. 3, 16), a grain offering (vv. 4, 17), and a cow and a ram as a peace offering (vv. 4, 18).

What is new and of importance in the discussion of these sacrifices is the *order* in which they are presented here: always first the sin offering, then the burnt offering with its grain offering, and last, as always, the peace offering. The sin offering provides the grounds for all the other offerings in that it offers both propitiation and expiation from all sin by the shedding of the blood of a substitute. The burnt offering symbolizes the offerer's full surrender to God just as the victim is totally given back to God as a whole burnt offering. Likewise, the grain offering symbolizes the consecration of the fruits of one's labors to God as a total dedication for God's use. Only then is it possible to announce that fellowship in the joy, peace, and life with God is now possible as God and mortals commune around the table of the shared sacrifice of the peace offering. The order of the sacrifices, then, is determined by a law of the spiritual life: Perfect fellowship with God in peace, joy, and life is possible only after one has fully consecrated to God all that one is and produces; but one is unable to consecrate anything to God until one's sin has been forgiven and the wrath of God against all unrighteousness has been satisfied.

This first day of divine services at the tabernacle ends with a double blessing from Aaron. In a motion characteristic of prayer directed toward God, Aaron raises his hands and blesses the people. Whether the words of the famous benediction that now appear in Num 6:24-26 were in use at that time is impossible to say. But the solemnity and joy of granting a blessing on the people are particularly detailed as a part of the priestly office in Deut 10:8. Not only is the tribe of Levi to carry the ark of the covenant and to stand before God to minister, but the Levites are "to pronounce blessings in [God's] name" as well.

To conclude the day, Moses takes Aaron into the tabernacle for the first time. Moses goes with

Aaron, in all likelihood, to instruct him on how he is to burn incense on the golden altar, light the lamps, and set the bread of presence in order.

As both men emerge from the tabernacle, they once again bless the waiting congregation. Then the "glory of the LORD appeared to all the people" (v. 23), and "fire came out from the presence of the LORD and consumed the burnt offering and the fat portions on the altar" (v. 24). This act stamps God's approval on the proceedings of the day and all that led up to it through the past week. No doubt, the sacrifices that Aaron has placed on the large altar are still burning and are not as yet completely consumed. But in an instant they are consumed by a divine fire, perhaps from the holy of holies where now God has taken up permanent residence. Such a fiery display must have made a most memorable impression on the minds of all who saw it: The burning of sacrifices symbolized the acceptance and response of the Lord, who had commanded that the offerings be brought.

Scripture frequently employs fire as the symbol of God's presence and work (see Deut 4:24; Ps 18:8-14; Ezek 1:4). That fiery presence can depict Messiah's coming in judgment (see Mal 3:2; Matt 3:11; Luke 3:16) or it can be the occasion of great joy, thanksgiving, surprise, and relief, as it is here in Lev 9:24. So overwhelmed with joy and adoration are the people that they let out a shout, even though they simultaneously fall face down in awesome respect and fear at the awfulness of God's mighty presence (cf. Judg 6:21; 1 Kgs 18:38; 1 Chr 21:26; 2 Chr 7:1).

Only on three other occasions has God shown approval and acceptance by sending fire in the OT: at the birth of Samson (see Judg 13:15-21), at the dedication of Solomon's Temple (see 2 Chr 7:1), and at the Elijah's Mount Carmel contest with the prophets of Baal (see 1 Kgs 18:38). This is certainly a great conclusion to a most significant day in the life of Israel.

REFLECTIONS

Apart from all its pomp and ceremony, the purpose of this worship ritual rings so clear that it remains the key teaching point of the whole chapter: Worship that does not function in the light of the presence of God is worthless, empty, and vain. To miss the glory, i.e., the presence of God, is to miss everything in worship. The glory of God transforms ordinary ritual into divine worship. This leads to several other considerations.

1. Worship at its most profound level is communion with God, the experience of God's intense presence, what Leviticus calls "the glory of the LORD." Sometimes, however, we miss the glory of God in worship because we are looking for something too exalted. We want the sermon to move us to tears, the music to carry us to the heights, the prayers to reveal the secrets of our hearts. Occasionally, such profound experiences do happen in worship, but most of the time God is present to us in smaller, quieter, less-dramatic ways. A prayer phrase here, the face of a child over there, the curious way the hymn we least like nonetheless compels our attention—sometimes these are the vessels God chooses to convey glory.

2. Full consecration of persons and their works must precede fellowship with God. All too many worshipers have aimed at fellowship within the group as the primary purpose of worship without first counting the cost of loving self-surrender to God as a prerequisite for any and all fellowship—whether it be with God or with one another.

3. A cleansed conscience that has received God's atonement must precede a full consecration of the person and service for God. It is possible to give of oneself in numerous acts of self-devotion and sacrifice with an aim of exhibiting the love of God to others, yet such altruism may remain empty and hollow if it does not spring out of a heart motivated with the realization of the expiation and forgiveness that come from the One "who had no sin [but was made] to be sin for us" (2 Cor 5:21 NIV).

4. Aaron's concluding benediction is reminiscent of another high priest's conclusion to his ministry. When Christ had finished his earthly ministry, he too lifted up his hands and blessed his disciples as he ascended into heaven (see Luke 24:50).

LEVITICUS 10:1-20, THE DEATH OF NADAB AND ABIHU

NIV

10Aaron's sons Nadab and Abihu took their censers, put fire in them and added incense; and they offered unauthorized fire before the LORD, contrary to his command. ²So fire came out from the presence of the LORD and consumed them, and they died before the LORD. ³Moses then said to Aaron, "This is what the LORD spoke of when he said:

"'Among those who approach me
 I will show myself holy;
in the sight of all the people
 I will be honored.'"
Aaron remained silent.

⁴Moses summoned Mishael and Elzaphan, sons of Aaron's uncle Uzziel, and said to them, "Come here; carry your cousins outside the camp, away from the front of the sanctuary." ⁵So they came and carried them, still in their tunics, outside the camp, as Moses ordered.

⁶Then Moses said to Aaron and his sons Eleazar and Ithamar, "Do not let your hair become unkempt,ᵃ and do not tear your clothes, or you will die and the LORD will be angry with the whole community. But your relatives, all the house of Israel, may mourn for those the LORD has destroyed by fire. ⁷Do not leave the entrance to the Tent of Meeting or you will die, because the LORD's anointing oil is on you." So they did as Moses said.

⁸Then the LORD said to Aaron, ⁹"You and your sons are not to drink wine or other fermented drink whenever you go into the Tent of Meeting, or you will die. This is a lasting ordinance for the generations to come. ¹⁰You must distinguish between the holy and the common, between the unclean and the clean, ¹¹and you must teach the Israelites all the decrees the LORD has given them through Moses."

ₐ6 Or *Do not uncover your heads*

NRSV

10Now Aaron's sons, Nadab and Abihu, each took his censer, put fire in it, and laid incense on it; and they offered unholy fire before the LORD, such as he had not commanded them. ²And fire came out from the presence of the LORD and consumed them, and they died before the LORD. ³Then Moses said to Aaron, "This is what the LORD meant when he said,

"Through those who are near me
 I will show myself holy,
and before all the people
 I will be glorified.'"
And Aaron was silent.

4Moses summoned Mishael and Elzaphan, sons of Uzziel the uncle of Aaron, and said to them, "Come forward, and carry your kinsmen away from the front of the sanctuary to a place outside the camp." ⁵They came forward and carried them by their tunics out of the camp, as Moses had ordered. ⁶And Moses said to Aaron and to his sons Eleazar and Ithamar, "Do not dishevel your hair, and do not tear your vestments, or you will die and wrath will strike all the congregation; but your kindred, the whole house of Israel, may mourn the burning that the LORD has sent. ⁷You shall not go outside the entrance of the tent of meeting, or you will die; for the anointing oil of the LORD is on you." And they did as Moses had ordered.

8And the LORD spoke to Aaron: ⁹Drink no wine or strong drink, neither you nor your sons, when you enter the tent of meeting, that you may not die; it is a statute forever throughout your generations. ¹⁰You are to distinguish between the holy and the common, and between the unclean and the clean; ¹¹and you are to teach the people of Israel all the statutes that the LORD has spoken to them through Moses.

12Moses spoke to Aaron and to his remaining

NIV

¹²Moses said to Aaron and his remaining sons, Eleazar and Ithamar, "Take the grain offering left over from the offerings made to the LORD by fire and eat it prepared without yeast beside the altar, for it is most holy. ¹³Eat it in a holy place, because it is your share and your sons' share of the offerings made to the LORD by fire; for so I have been commanded. ¹⁴But you and your sons and your daughters may eat the breast that was waved and the thigh that was presented. Eat them in a ceremonially clean place; they have been given to you and your children as your share of the Israelites' fellowship offerings.ᵃ ¹⁵The thigh that was presented and the breast that was waved must be brought with the fat portions of the offerings made by fire, to be waved before the LORD as a wave offering. This will be the regular share for you and your children, as the LORD has commanded."

¹⁶When Moses inquired about the goat of the sin offering and found that it had been burned up, he was angry with Eleazar and Ithamar, Aaron's remaining sons, and asked, ¹⁷"Why didn't you eat the sin offering in the sanctuary area? It is most holy; it was given to you to take away the guilt of the community by making atonement for them before the LORD. ¹⁸Since its blood was not taken into the Holy Place, you should have eaten the goat in the sanctuary area, as I commanded."

¹⁹Aaron replied to Moses, "Today they sacrificed their sin offering and their burnt offering before the LORD, but such things as this have happened to me. Would the LORD have been pleased if I had eaten the sin offering today?" ²⁰When Moses heard this, he was satisfied.

ᵃ14 Traditionally *peace offerings*

NRSV

sons, Eleazar and Ithamar: Take the grain offering that is left from the LORD's offerings by fire, and eat it unleavened beside the altar, for it is most holy; ¹³you shall eat it in a holy place, because it is your due and your sons' due, from the offerings by fire to the LORD; for so I am commanded. ¹⁴But the breast that is elevated and the thigh that is raised, you and your sons and daughters as well may eat in any clean place; for they have been assigned to you and your children from the sacrifices of the offerings of well-being of the people of Israel. ¹⁵The thigh that is raised and the breast that is elevated they shall bring, together with the offerings by fire of the fat, to raise for an elevation offering before the LORD; they are to be your due and that of your children forever, as the LORD has commanded.

16Then Moses made inquiry about the goat of the sin offering, and—it had already been burned! He was angry with Eleazar and Ithamar, Aaron's remaining sons, and said, ¹⁷"Why did you not eat the sin offering in the sacred area? For it is most holy, and Godᵃ has given it to you that you may remove the guilt of the congregation, to make atonement on their behalf before the LORD. ¹⁸Its blood was not brought into the inner part of the sanctuary. You should certainly have eaten it in the sanctuary, as I commanded." ¹⁹And Aaron spoke to Moses, "See, today they offered their sin offering and their burnt offering before the LORD; and yet such things as these have befallen me! If I had eaten the sin offering today, would it have been agreeable to the LORD?" ²⁰And when Moses heard that, he agreed.

ᵃ Heb *he*

COMMENTARY

10:1-7. While it is still the eighth day of the installation and inaugural ceremonies of the tabernacle services, the events of 10:1 unfold. Suddenly, for what reasons we do not know, the two eldest of Aaron's four sons, Nadab and Abihu, "took their censers, put fire in them and added incense; and they offered unauthorized fire before the LORD" (v. 1). In the midst of the most solemn

and impressive set of ceremonies, on what might well have been one of the happiest days for Aaron and his family, all is tragically turned into a moment of deep loss and judgment.

We are unable to ascertain what precisely happened from the texts before us. Many suggestions have been posed. Some attach the blame to the *manner* in which the two sons lighted their firepans. The "unauthorized fire" or "strange fire" (אֵשׁ זָרָה 'ēš zārâ) is understood, in this view, to mean they used hot coals that did not come from the altar in the sanctuary courtyard. It is true, of course, that Moses was careful to warn Aaron on the Day of Atonement to take "coals from the altar before the LORD" (Lev 16:12), just as he instructed Aaron to do on another occasion of the Korah, Dathan, and Abiram uprising (see Num 16:46).

Others suggest the problem may have been that Nadab and Abihu offered this fire at the wrong *time*. Moses' instructions were very specific with regard to the order of the sacrifices, but nothing here suggests that was the problem plaguing the two men. The event mentioned here no doubt took place toward the evening of that eighth day. Accordingly, the two men may have performed some ceremony that belonged to another part of the day.

Others have suggested that the *place* was incorrect. Perhaps they wanted to offer their incense on the golden altar, thereby usurping Aaron's sole privilege and designated task. Or perhaps they wished to go inside the veil to the holy of holies where only the high priest was allowed to go once a year.

The connection with strong drink and the possibility of *intoxication* cannot be ruled out, given its otherwise unexplained proximity and discussion in this very same context (10:8-11). This may have impeded the ability of the two brothers to think and act responsibly in a situation that called for their highest degree of alertness, caution, and sensitivity.

The more one studies this text, the greater the impression arises that the situation may have involved a combination of some or all of the above suggestions. One thing is certain: The offense is by no means accidental. There is a sudden reversal of everything that has been taught on the day to all of Israel. What is most holy and sacred to the Lord is suddenly trivialized in some unexplained way so as to make what has been set apart for God now common, trite, and secular.

Exodus 30:9 warns that no "strange incense" (KJV using the same adjective זָרָה zārâ, "alien," "strange") is to be offered on the altar before the Lord. Perhaps from this warning it should have been enough of an obvious inference that the same would apply to "strange/alien fire" offered to God.

The phrase at the end of v. 1, "which he did

not command them" (literal translation), is the figure of speech known as *meiosis;* that is, a negative expression is stated when the opposite affirmation is emphatically implied (cf. Ps 78:50; Prov 12:3; 17:21). Thus, even though we may not be able to point to the precept that Nadab and Abihu expressly violate, what they do is clearly "contrary to [God's] command" (1*d*).

What takes place, however, is certain and decisive. Fire comes out from the presence of God and consumes Nadab and Abihu. What has moments before been a sign of divine approval, acceptance, and approbation (as the fire falls on the sacrifice) is swiftly turned into an expression of divine disfavor and wrath. While still serving in their priestly tunics, the men are struck down. But the fire does not consume their tunics, for v. 5 notes that they are still in this priestly garb when they are carried outside the camp by Mishael and Elzaphan, the two sons of Aaron's uncle, Uzziel.

Moses uses this occasion to teach a powerful lesson on the holiness and worship of God (v. 3). Moses refers to something the Lord said at an earlier occasion, but a statement that is not an explicit part of the canonical record we now possess. Some think that the principle cited here may have been alluded to in Exod 19:22: "The priests, who approach the LORD, must consecrate themselves, or the LORD will break out against them" (NIV). Others suppose that the allusion is to Exod 29:43: "I will meet with the Israelites, and the place will be consecrated by my glory" (NIV). But these texts preserve only a certain tenor of the principle raised in Lev 10:3. Maybe that is all Moses means by his statement that the Lord spoke the following words.

The point is that those who by virtue of their office are called to draw near to God constantly place themselves in a perilous, as well as a privileged, position. Whatever they do or fail to do, they must bear in mind that God is absolutely unique above all other creatures. Any act, or failure thereof, that may detract from the deity's absolute holiness, and thus tend to treat God in a light, trite, or unthinking manner, would immediately expose those who draw near to possible danger. If God is not sanctified by those who are supposed to know best, by virtue of their constant opportunity to draw near in acts of serving the people for God, God will be sanctified in the eyes of the people by swift judgment and wrath upon all trivalizers of the ministry.

Aaron's two remaining sons, Eleazar and Ithamar, are not allowed to handle the dead bodies of their two fallen older brothers, even though contact with the corpse of a close relative does not, in general, defile members of the priesthood (21:1-2). The reason for this prohibition, then, is not that they are on the threshold of commencing their ministries; instead, it is due to the fact that they are about to eat the "most holy" sacrificial meals of the offerings made that day (10:12-14).

Not only are they to refrain from carrying out the corpses, but Aaron and his sons are told not to "uncover" their heads or tear their garments in grief over what has happened (v. 6). The Hebrew root for "uncover," variously rendered as to "become unkempt" (NIV), "to dishevel" (NRSV), or to "bare" (TNK) their heads, is the word פרע (*pāra'*). Its primary meaning is "to make free" or "to uncover"; accordingly, it must connote something like letting one's hair become disarrayed or disheveled while mourning for the dead.[59] Thus none of the usual signs of grief and mourning for the dead are to be seen among them as they minister at the altar. Failure to heed this command could have resulted in death to Aaron and his remaining sons as well as wrath on the whole congregation of Israel. Once again, the significance of corporate solidarity is illustrated in the way that the sins of the leaders could have a negative impact on the people, even though they have not personally done anything to provoke the negative response.

These priests are to continue on even in the midst of this dire emergency in their families because "the LORD's anointing oil [is] on [them]" (v. 7). This anointing signifies that the call to the service of God takes precedence over every other earthly affection. This injunction later on becomes law, as Lev 21:10, 12 demonstrates.

10:8-11. Immediately, the text plunges into a warning to Aaron and his sons about the evils of intoxication while ministering in the house of God. Surely, some link is present, or vv. 8-11 are left dangling with no context or setting. Even if one posits editorial insertions, they are extremely clumsy ones. No wonder, then, that older Jewish commentators thought there was a connection, and Nadab and Abihu had drunk wine to excess. In their view (and ours), this circumstance provides the occasion for the warning found here in vv. 8-11.

Even though the biblical text says that wine is given to humanity to cheer their hearts (see Ps 104:15; cf. Judg 9:13), it also contains some stern warnings against drunkenness. The text condemns drinking to excess and the resulting ugly, degrading, and foolish behavior (see Gen 9:20-27; Prov 23:29-35; 31:4-7; Isa 5:11-12; Amos 2:8).

But vv. 8-11 do not take up all these issues; they merely forbid priests to drink intoxicants while performing sacred tasks.

A question arises whether Israel knew about "strong drink" (שכר *šēkār*) at this time. The term may refer to any kind of intoxicating drink, whether made from corn, apples, honey, dates, or other fruit. Islamic peoples in many parts of the world refer to one of the four prohibited drinks as *Sakar*, meaning an intoxicating beverage. We also know that the ancient Egyptians made liquor from fermented barley.[60] So we can conclude that the technology for making strong or fermented drink was available at this time.

The reason given for this prohibition against wine and intoxicating drinks is that the priests are serving in the sanctuary. Intoxicants would cloud the mind and darken the understanding in such a way that priests would not be able to distinguish "between the holy and the common, between the unclean and the clean." Even though all things were created good by God, not everything is equally holy and equally dedicated to God. Some things have been "removed from the Temple" (the literal meaning of *profane*) and, therefore, are for common use. By maintaining this distinction between the two, the priests would continually remind themselves and their congregants of the

---

59. Milgrom notes the Akkadian root *pertu* actually denotes "the hair of the head" (*Leviticus 1-16*, 608). Thus the Hebrew cognate *pr'* has something to do with the hair of the head. But what it is cannot be defined exactly because of the wide range of meanings for this root—from figurative contexts such as Exod 32:25 where the people were "out of control" (NIV; Hebrew *paru'*) to legal texts such as Lev 13:45; Num 5:18; 6:5.

60. This is reported by Herodotus 27.7. A similar claim, though extended throughout the ancient Near East, is made by Diosorus Siculus in book 1 of *Osirus*. The Greek and Latin forms of *Sheker* and *Sikera* or *Sicera* may be the origins for English *cider*, a term used for fermented juice from apples. Eventually, the word *sugar* may have had its origins here as well.

wide gulf that yawned between a holy God and a sinning people.

10:12-15. The instructions given previously concerning the use of the grain offerings (6:18) and the peace offerings (7:30-34) are repeated. It would appear that Moses wants to remind Aaron and his sons anew about these matters in light of the events of the day. The emphasis falls on who might eat which portions of these sacrifices and where they must be eaten. But all of this has been stated previously. The oft-repeated category of "most holy" (v. 12) and the identity of the courtyard of the sanctuary as "a holy place" (v. 13) underscore the constant care taken to distinguish between the holy and the common, the clean and the unclean.

10:16-20. A misunderstanding erupts between Moses and Aaron's two sons, Eleazar and Ithamar, over the disposal of the goat of the sin offering. When Moses learns that this goat has been burned up rather than eaten in the holy place by the priests, he becomes angry. Since it is a sin offering, it is "most holy" (v. 17); it should have been eaten in the sanctuary. Furthermore, its blood is not taken into the sanctuary (v. 18), as 4:16-18 requires. How can the guilt of the community be taken away (v. 17) when violations of what God commanded are allowed to take place? Verse 17 lays down an enormously important theological principle when it states that God had given the portion of the sin offering to be eaten in the sanctuary "to bear the iniquity of the congregation" (KJV). "To bear" is from the verb נשא (*nāśā᾽*, "to lift up," "to bear away"). These sins are in some sense transferred to the priests on behalf of the people. It was to this role that the early church appealed in understanding Jesus Christ as the ultimate mediator who would come to bear our sins in his own body (see 1 Pet 2:24), the "Lamb of God, who *takes away* [bears away] the sin of the world" (John 1:29, emphasis added, NIV).

Apparently, Aaron had ordered his sons to burn the whole offering, so he seems to step in and take responsibility for any deviation from the command. But in Aaron's view, he has no other choice than to do what he has done. First, Aaron refers obliquely to the events of the day by saying, "Such things as . . . have happened to me" (v. 19). He deliberately avoids referring to his sons Nadab and Abihu by name.

But then Aaron conscientiously resists eating the sin offering in the holy place with his two youngest sons because he is not absolutely sure whether he and his sons will be permitted to do so on a day when God's wrath is revealed against his family. By saying this, he implies that he shared in the sinfulness of his two oldest sons when they sinned. Accordingly, even though Aaron and his two youngest sons have not personally sinned, their consciences are so awakened to the holiness of God, and to their tendency to sinfulness, that they hesitate to venture into areas where they have no explicit directions.

Moses also is unable to give an immediate answer to this query; therefore, he withdraws his accusations and remains silent. Where God has not spoken, God's servants do best to remain silent. A new principle is set forth, therefore, that would be appealed to on other occasions: Sometimes the circumstances alter what is often perceived at face value to be an unalterable law. Later on, David would have his men eat of the bread of presence when they were hungry and without any provisions, even though the law strictly limited that bread to be eaten only by the priests (see 1 Sam 21:1-9). Hezekiah would also make a temporary change in the rules for the time for eating the Passover due to extenuating circumstances (see 2 Chr 30:18-20).

Some have held that Aaron was uncertain about eating the portions of the sacrifice because he and his sons were in mourning. It is possible to infer from Deut 26:14 that mourners were not allowed to partake of devoted foods. Had this rule also been in effect at this time, perhaps Aaron had extrapolated an application of the same principle to his own situation. However, he and his sons had been warned against any outward sign of mourning, so it is doubtful that this explanation helps.

REFLECTIONS

1. One principle highlighted in this account about Nadab and Abihu's sin is that intentions, no matter how earnest and goodwilled they are, cannot be a substitute for genuine piety of the heart and obedience to the declared will of God.

2. Those who, by virtue of their office and ordination, are privileged constantly to approach God's presence are also exposed to danger when God is not honored through their ministries. That special sense of nearness to God is an opportunity that must not be defrauded in the worship experience, lest times of corporate worship by the group end up being mere will-worship, with God being created in the image of humans. The will and needs of mortals must not be substituted for a high view of God. The primary focus must be on the nature, works, and being of God, which must be central in all true worship.

3. The effect that disciplining Nadab and Abihu had on Aaron and his sons is the same result that the apostle Paul expected discipline would have on the members of the church at Corinth. In 2 Cor 7:11, Paul was pleased that godly sorrow experienced by the members there had led to earnest care, indignation against all sin, an alarm against evil, a genuine concern, and a desire to see that justice was done. In such instances, by the grace of God, that kind of godly sorrow leads to repentance without regrets.

4. If the penalty here seems to be unduly harsh, the response is that ministers, like the Aaronic priests, should be above all reproach (see 1 Tim 3:3, 8). Moreover, as stated in Luke 12:48, "To whom much has been given, much will be required" (NRSV). That is why James invoked the double indemnity rule for those who teach, for they are responsible not only for themselves, but also for those they teach (3:1).

5. The priests were to be good examples of distinguishing between the holy and the common. If they were not models in this most important area, the whole law of God would be made a mockery, and a holy God would quickly have been devalued into an ordinary person who "belonged to this age" (i.e., the literal meaning of *secular*). So significant were these words that the Lord spoke them directly to Aaron rather than going, as usual, through Moses.

THE REGULATIONS ON CLEAN AND UNCLEAN

OVERVIEW

The third major section in the book of Leviticus deals with the issue of clean and unclean and defilement by dead bodies. Few chapters in the Bible present more difficulties for the application of biblical materials to the modern day for the contemporary reader than Leviticus 11–15. But the religion espoused in this book is not limited to the spheres of the spirit and inner person; rather, faith is carried over into every mundane sphere of life.

Chapters 11–15 consider various types of uncleanness and how persons might be cleansed from their defiling and contaminating effects. The distinctions between the clean and the unclean are set forth under four headings: the clean and unclean foods (chap. 11); the uncleanness of childbirth (chap. 12); the uncleanness of skin and fungus diseases (chaps. 13–14); and the uncleanness of genital discharges (chap. 15).

But how do these chapters fit into the argument and plan of the book of Leviticus as it has come down to us in its present canonical form? Gordon J. Wenham[61] suggests that these five chapters had two vital links in their canonical context: one that looked back to 10:10, and the other that looked forward in anticipation of the ceremonies on the Day of Atonement in chap. 16, especially 16:16. The backward-looking text called for a distinction to be made between the holy and the common, between the clean and the unclean. But no less connected was the text in 16:16 declaring that the ceremonies on the Day of Atonement were necessary "because of the uncleanness . . . of the Israelites." Without the background explanation of chaps. 11–15, much of the significance of chap. 16 would be missed.

61. Wenham, *Leviticus*, 161.

The narrative literary form in chaps. 8–10 and chap. 16 frames the intervening section of the laws, for the story of the Torah continues to be an ongoing narration that acts as the framing device for the whole. To argue that the laws provide the grid on which the narrative hangs is to reverse the logic; it is to run counter to the reality of the nation of Israel and its history.

In chaps. 11–15 we move from the sanctuary, which occupies the center of attention in chaps. 1–10, to the sphere of everyday mundane life of an Israelite. Immediately, we are struck by the emphasis on the concept of being clean or unclean. But neither notion originates in the physical realm or even the ethical sphere. In other words, being unclean has nothing to do with being dirty or being in need of a shower. Instead, these terms focus on the cultic and ritual sphere; they deal with being personally qualified and ready to meet God in worship.

Simply put, being clean makes a person fit and suitable for entering into the worship of God. Cleanness is not the same thing as holiness, though clean and holy are intimately linked. In fact, without cleanness, there can be no holiness. Thus, to be holy, one has to first experience the condition of ritual and ceremonial cleanness by means of washing, fasting, and abstaining from certain foods or sexual unions (see Exod 19:10; Num 11:18; Josh 3:5; 1 Sam 16:5).

Holiness, as we will discover in the Holiness Code of Leviticus 17–26, cannot be contrived, manipulated, or induced externally as if it is magical or a substance-like essence that one can put on to wear. On the contrary, holiness circumscribes a person as totally set apart for God's use. It marks a person, a community, or even an object as belonging entirely to the Lord. These holy persons are subject to God's will and are bound by the specific demands that God makes on each person so dedicated.

Another clue to the meaning of these terms can be found in the close relationship observed between uncleanness and sin. A person is rendered unclean by being involved in the following sins: being in contact with the worship of foreign gods (Jer 2:7, 23; 3:2; 7:30; Hos 6:10); consulting mediums or spiritists (Lev 20:6); using mourning rites borrowed from foreign cults (Lev 19:27-28; Deut 14:1); or engaging in religious prostitution (Lev 19:29). Other sources of uncleanness are related to various sexual phenomena and functions: discharges, menstruation, or copulation (Leviticus 15).

Given the understanding of God as a living person, additional forms of uncleanness involve coming into contact with a corpse (Lev 21:1-4, 11; Num 6:6-7; 19:11-16), a carcass (Lev 11:8, 11, 24-40), a grave (Num 19:16), or any skin or fungus disease (Leviticus 13–14). Each involvement temporarily disqualifies a person from entering into the presence of God for worship.

Although the emphasis on the external qualifications carries the potential danger that Israelite religion might be thought of only in terms of an externalization of faith, it is not meant to be left there. It has as its main thrust the attempt to call the community to a holistic concept of worship—one that involves the body, the soul, and the spirit. This linking of clean hands and a pure heart is evident in Psalms 15 and 24:4.

Leviticus 11:44 plainly states that the people are to be holy because the Lord is holy. Accordingly, the people are not to make themselves unclean by eating unclean things, such as creatures that crawl along the ground. But that text, helpful as it is in supplying the main rationale for the long list of foods included, does not explain why the unclean foods have a defiling effect.

This vacuum, as usually happens when this sort of phenomenon appears, has touched off a search for the principle behind the approval of some animals and foods and the disapproval of others.

The earliest explanation was a moralistic one given by Philo of Alexandria; his conclusion was that the laws were given to teach *self-denial.* To discourage excessive indulgence, certain foods were to be avoided. A thousand years later Maimonides, in partial agreement, made a similar case for *self-control.*

Others argued that the connection was a *mystical* one between the body and the soul. That thesis was perpetuated by an overly literal LXX translation of Lev 11:44 as, "You shall not defile your *souls."* But the Hebrew original text often used "soul" (נפש *nepeš*) as another way of saying the personal pronoun "you" or, as it appeared with a pronominal suffix here, "yourselves."

Some tried to take refuge in an *allegorical* interpretation of the animals mentioned here. Therefore, it was argued that the behavior and habits of some of the animals exercised certain influences on the character of those who ate them as food. Thus the revengeful character of the camel tended to impart a vindictive propensity in its eater. And the hog's predilections, it was claimed, rendered its eaters gross and sensual. But none of that could be demonstrated, and it usually struck most observers as being extremely fanciful. For instance, what can be said, given this view, of an unclean animal, such as a lion, being used as the symbol of our Lord?

Another approach has been to champion the view that the distinctions are purely *arbitrary.* God is the only One who knows the rationale behind these rules. The most we can say is that they were given to test our obedience.

In more recent times, many readers of Scripture favor another reason for the distinctions between clean and unclean; they argue that the underlying principle was *hygienic.* The divine mind knew of the dangers of tapeworm, trichina in pork, tularemia in rabbits, and infection and spoiling in shellfish, and therefore restricted all potentially dangerous foods for the sake of the health of Israel. That is why, so the argument goes, Jewish people tend to live longer than their fellow citizens, even when they live under sanitary conditions that are worse than those of their compatriots. Now all of this may be very close to some of the truth on this matter, but observing salutary *results* is not necessarily the same as discerning the *intent* for issuing these dietary restrictions.

The most celebrated solution offered to this problem in recent times has come from Mary

Douglas.[62] Using the field of social anthropology, she suggests that uncleanness has a *symbolic* significance. When the social background is kept in mind, argues Douglas, certain natural groupings emerged. For those who shepherded sheep and goats, it was natural to regard those animals as clean. The animals in that class appeared to conform to the similar norms desired in humans. The holiness desired in mortals had as its corollary standards of cleanness desired in animals. The division between clean and unclean corresponded to the division between holy Israel and the Gentile world. Thus, for Douglas, the notion of wholeness or normality was the key to determining the distinctions in the animal realm: Those animals, birds, and fish that conform wholly to the class to which they belong are those that are "clean." Any deviation from normality within a particular class (such as insects walking on all fours, thereby creating confusion with other realms) rendered that member unclean. She illustrates this by saying that the dietary code "rejects creatures which are anomalous, whether living between two spheres, or having defining features of members of another sphere, or lacking defining features."[63] Only the clean species have all the criteria of their class. Douglas's view emphasizes the similarities between clean animals and righteous Israelites. However, Douglas's category of "normality" seems to run opposite to the creation account, where all creatures that came from God's hand were called "good." Even some of the animals that conformed to their own class were not called clean. Interesting and detailed as Douglas's proposal is, it does not answer many of these key questions.[64]

What are we left with? If none of these attempted explanations can supply us with the principle behind these rather esoteric laws, how can any contemporary application be made from directions so foreign to our own culture and times?

The answer may be simpler than all those that have been given thus far. It may well be that in addition to any hygienic *results*, which may have been attached as secondary reasons for these distinctive laws, their main purpose was to forever mark Israel off from all the other nations. The purpose, then, was to demonstrate Israel's *separateness*.

Nothing becomes more cumbersome and immediately marks one as set apart as the request for certain unique foods when it comes time to sit down around a table. The difference such dietary restrictions cause would always be present on almost every possible social contact that could be made with any other people in the ordinary course of daily events. Israel would be marked for all time by the oddities of diet and thus would ever be both an unwilling and a willing witness to a unique attachment to God. It was part of Israel's call to be separate and distinct from all the other nations. It was one more mark of that distinctiveness, both in calling and in mission for the nation.

Jacob Milgrom comes to a similar conclusion.[65] He calls attention to the three divine covenants, which he arranges in three concentric circles: the Noachic covenant made with all humankind (see Gen 9:1-11), the outermost circle; the covenant made with Israel (see Gen 17:2; Lev 26:42), the next circle; and the covenant of a lasting priesthood (see Num 25:12-15; Jer 33:17-22), the innermost circle of the three. These three circles, Milgrom advises, were matched by another set of three circles that divided up the animals: (a) all animals are permitted for all humankind, except their blood (see Gen 9:3-5); (b) the edible few are given to Israel (see Leviticus 11); and (c) from this edible group, only the domesticated and perfect specimens could qualify as sacrifices to the Lord (see Lev 22:17-25). Thus there was a congruency between the two concentric circles: all animals—humankind; few animals—Israel; and sacrificial animals—priests. This bond between the choice of Israel and the choice of Israel's food is made explicit in Deuteronomy 14 where the chapter begins (v. 2) and ends (v. 21) in an inclusio that

---

62. Mary Douglas, *Purity and Danger,* 53. Douglas follows the thesis set forth by the Emile Durkheim school, which contends that the customs and rituals of any society reflect its values. Therefore, the way a society's taxonomy works will afford us an insight into how that society's values work. Douglas applies Durkheim's theory to Leviticus 11, using her own theory of dirt, which is matter out of place. "Order" is fine; "disorder" is dirt. Douglas discovered that the Lele tribe of Africa had a very complex set of dietary regulations. This started her inquiry into Leviticus 11. Incidentally, A. S. Meigs, in the article "A Papuan Perspective on Pollution," *Man* 13 (1978) 304-18, gave a stinging criticism of Douglas's theory of dirt, arguing that many things may be out of place, but only a few pollute.

63. Mary Douglas, *Implicit Meanings: Essays in Anthropology* (Boston: Routledge & Kegan, 1975) 266.

64. For a critique of Mary Douglas's thesis, see Harris, "Leviticus," 2:526-30.

65. Milgrom, "[Excursus] E. The Ethical Foundations of the Dietary System: 3. The Prohibited Animals," in *Leviticus 1-16,* 718-36.

frames the proper foods with the theology that Israel is to be "a holy people." Moreover, this emphasis on separation appears four times in the scope of two and a half verses in Lev 20:24*b*-26. And specifically included in that description of holiness is the call for Israel to be separate from the nations and selective in diet.

The identical approach can be found as early as the *Letter of Aristeas,* written by a first-century BCE Egyptian Jew. It declared:

An additional signification [of the diet laws] is that we are *set apart* from all men. For most of the rest of mankind defile themselves by their promiscuous unions, working great unrighteousness, and whole countries and cities pride themselves on these vices. Not only do they have intercourse with males, but they even defile mothers and daughters. But we have kept apart from these things.[66]

We believe this explanation of separateness is the most meaningful explanation for these laws.

66. *Letter of Aristeas* 151-52.

LEVITICUS 11:1-47, THE CLEAN AND THE UNCLEAN

NIV

11 The LORD said to Moses and Aaron, [2]"Say to the Israelites: 'Of all the animals that live on land, these are the ones you may eat: [3]You may eat any animal that has a split hoof completely divided and that chews the cud.

[4]" 'There are some that only chew the cud or only have a split hoof, but you must not eat them. The camel, though it chews the cud, does not have a split hoof; it is ceremonially unclean for you. [5]The coney,[a] though it chews the cud, does not have a split hoof; it is unclean for you. [6]The rabbit, though it chews the cud, does not have a split hoof; it is unclean for you. [7]And the pig, though it has a split hoof completely divided, does not chew the cud; it is unclean for you. [8]You must not eat their meat or touch their carcasses; they are unclean for you.

[9]" 'Of all the creatures living in the water of the seas and the streams, you may eat any that have fins and scales. [10]But all creatures in the seas or streams that do not have fins and scales— whether among all the swarming things or among all the other living creatures in the water—you are to detest. [11]And since you are to detest them, you must not eat their meat and you must detest their carcasses. [12]Anything living in the water that does not have fins and scales is to be detestable to you.

[13]" 'These are the birds you are to detest and

*a*5 That is, the hyrax or rock badger

NRSV

11 The LORD spoke to Moses and Aaron, saying to them: [2]Speak to the people of Israel, saying:

From among all the land animals, these are the creatures that you may eat. [3]Any animal that has divided hoofs and is cleft-footed and chews the cud—such you may eat. [4]But among those that chew the cud or have divided hoofs, you shall not eat the following: the camel, for even though it chews the cud, it does not have divided hoofs; it is unclean for you. [5]The rock badger, for even though it chews the cud, it does not have divided hoofs; it is unclean for you. [6]The hare, for even though it chews the cud, it does not have divided hoofs; it is unclean for you. [7]The pig, for even though it has divided hoofs and is cleft-footed, it does not chew the cud; it is unclean for you. [8]Of their flesh you shall not eat, and their carcasses you shall not touch; they are unclean for you.

[9]These you may eat, of all that are in the waters. Everything in the waters that has fins and scales, whether in the seas or in the streams— such you may eat. [10]But anything in the seas or the streams that does not have fins and scales, of the swarming creatures in the waters and among all the other living creatures that are in the waters—they are detestable to you [11]and detestable they shall remain. Of their flesh you shall not eat, and their carcasses you shall regard as detestable. [12]Everything in the waters that does not have fins and scales is detestable to you.

NIV

not eat because they are detestable: the eagle, the vulture, the black vulture, ¹⁴the red kite, any kind of black kite, ¹⁵any kind of raven, ¹⁶the horned owl, the screech owl, the gull, any kind of hawk, ¹⁷the little owl, the cormorant, the great owl, ¹⁸the white owl, the desert owl, the osprey, ¹⁹the stork, any kind of heron, the hoopoe and the bat.ᵃ

²⁰" 'All flying insects that walk on all fours are to be detestable to you. ²¹There are, however, some winged creatures that walk on all fours that you may eat: those that have jointed legs for hopping on the ground. ²²Of these you may eat any kind of locust, katydid, cricket or grasshopper. ²³But all other winged creatures that have four legs you are to detest.

²⁴" 'You will make yourselves unclean by these; whoever touches their carcasses will be unclean till evening. ²⁵Whoever picks up one of their carcasses must wash his clothes, and he will be unclean till evening.

²⁶" 'Every animal that has a split hoof not completely divided or that does not chew the cud is unclean for you; whoever touches ⌊the carcass of⌋ any of them will be unclean. ²⁷Of all the animals that walk on all fours, those that walk on their paws are unclean for you; whoever touches their carcasses will be unclean till evening. ²⁸Anyone who picks up their carcasses must wash his clothes, and he will be unclean till evening. They are unclean for you.

²⁹" 'Of the animals that move about on the ground, these are unclean for you: the weasel, the rat, any kind of great lizard, ³⁰the gecko, the monitor lizard, the wall lizard, the skink and the chameleon. ³¹Of all those that move along the ground, these are unclean for you. Whoever touches them when they are dead will be unclean till evening. ³²When one of them dies and falls on something, that article, whatever its use, will be unclean, whether it is made of wood, cloth, hide or sackcloth. Put it in water; it will be unclean till evening, and then it will be clean. ³³If one of them falls into a clay pot, everything in it will be unclean, and you must break the pot. ³⁴Any food that could be eaten but has water on it from such a pot is unclean, and any liquid that

ᵃ19 The precise identification of some of the birds, insects and animals in this chapter is uncertain.

NRSV

13These you shall regard as detestable among the birds. They shall not be eaten; they are an abomination: the eagle, the vulture, the osprey, ¹⁴the buzzard, the kite of any kind; ¹⁵every raven of any kind; ¹⁶the ostrich, the nighthawk, the sea gull, the hawk of any kind; ¹⁷the little owl, the cormorant, the great owl, ¹⁸the water hen, the desert owl,ᵃ the carrion vulture, ¹⁹the stork, the heron of any kind, the hoopoe, and the bat.ᵇ

20All winged insects that walk upon all fours are detestable to you. ²¹But among the winged insects that walk on all fours you may eat those that have jointed legs above their feet, with which to leap on the ground. ²²Of them you may eat: the locust according to its kind, the bald locust according to its kind, the cricket according to its kind, and the grasshopper according to its kind. ²³But all other winged insects that have four feet are detestable to you.

24By these you shall become unclean; whoever touches the carcass of any of them shall be unclean until the evening, ²⁵and whoever carries any part of the carcass of any of them shall wash his clothes and be unclean until the evening. ²⁶Every animal that has divided hoofs but is not cleft-footed or does not chew the cud is unclean for you; everyone who touches one of them shall be unclean. ²⁷All that walk on their paws, among the animals that walk on all fours, are unclean for you; whoever touches the carcass of any of them shall be unclean until the evening, ²⁸and the one who carries the carcass shall wash his clothes and be unclean until the evening; they are unclean for you.

29These are unclean for you among the creatures that swarm upon the earth: the weasel, the mouse, the great lizard according to its kind, ³⁰the gecko, the land crocodile, the lizard, the sand lizard, and the chameleon. ³¹These are unclean for you among all that swarm; whoever touches one of them when they are dead shall be unclean until the evening. ³²And anything upon which any of them falls when they are dead shall be unclean, whether an article of wood or cloth or skin or sacking, any article that is used for any purpose; it shall be dipped into water, and it shall be

ᵃ Or pelican   ᵇ Identification of several of the birds in verses 13-19 is uncertain

NIV

could be drunk from it is unclean. ³⁵Anything that one of their carcasses falls on becomes unclean; an oven or cooking pot must be broken up. They are unclean, and you are to regard them as unclean. ³⁶A spring, however, or a cistern for collecting water remains clean, but anyone who touches one of these carcasses is unclean. ³⁷If a carcass falls on any seeds that are to be planted, they remain clean. ³⁸But if water has been put on the seed and a carcass falls on it, it is unclean for you.

³⁹" 'If an animal that you are allowed to eat dies, anyone who touches the carcass will be unclean till evening. ⁴⁰Anyone who eats some of the carcass must wash his clothes, and he will be unclean till evening. Anyone who picks up the carcass must wash his clothes, and he will be unclean till evening.

⁴¹" 'Every creature that moves about on the ground is detestable; it is not to be eaten. ⁴²You are not to eat any creature that moves about on the ground, whether it moves on its belly or walks on all fours or on many feet; it is detestable. ⁴³Do not defile yourselves by any of these creatures. Do not make yourselves unclean by means of them or be made unclean by them. ⁴⁴I am the LORD your God; consecrate yourselves and be holy, because I am holy. Do not make yourselves unclean by any creature that moves about on the ground. ⁴⁵I am the LORD who brought you up out of Egypt to be your God; therefore be holy, because I am holy.

⁴⁶" 'These are the regulations concerning animals, birds, every living thing that moves in the water and every creature that moves about on the ground. ⁴⁷You must distinguish between the unclean and the clean, between living creatures that may be eaten and those that may not be eaten.' "

NRSV

unclean until the evening, and then it shall be clean. ³³And if any of them falls into any earthen vessel, all that is in it shall be unclean, and you shall break the vessel. ³⁴Any food that could be eaten shall be unclean if water from any such vessel comes upon it; and any liquid that could be drunk shall be unclean if it was in any such vessel. ³⁵Everything on which any part of the carcass falls shall be unclean; whether an oven or stove, it shall be broken in pieces; they are unclean, and shall remain unclean for you. ³⁶But a spring or a cistern holding water shall be clean, while whatever touches the carcass in it shall be unclean. ³⁷If any part of their carcass falls upon any seed set aside for sowing, it is clean; ³⁸but if water is put on the seed and any part of their carcass falls on it, it is unclean for you.

39If an animal of which you may eat dies, anyone who touches its carcass shall be unclean until the evening. ⁴⁰Those who eat of its carcass shall wash their clothes and be unclean until the evening; and those who carry the carcass shall wash their clothes and be unclean until the evening.

41All creatures that swarm upon the earth are detestable; they shall not be eaten. ⁴²Whatever moves on its belly, and whatever moves on all fours, or whatever has many feet, all the creatures that swarm upon the earth, you shall not eat; for they are detestable. ⁴³You shall not make yourselves detestable with any creature that swarms; you shall not defile yourselves with them, and so become unclean. ⁴⁴For I am the LORD your God; sanctify yourselves therefore, and be holy, for I am holy. You shall not defile yourselves with any swarming creature that moves on the earth. ⁴⁵For I am the LORD who brought you up from the land of Egypt, to be your God; you shall be holy, for I am holy.

46This is the law pertaining to land animal and bird and every living creature that moves through the waters and every creature that swarms upon the earth, ⁴⁷to make a distinction between the unclean and the clean, and between the living creature that may be eaten and the living creature that may not be eaten.

COMMENTARY

The Torah contains two lists of clean and unclean animals: Leviticus 11 and Deut 14:3-20. The similarities between these two chapters constitute one of the greatest blocks of shared texts in the Pentateuch.

Naturally, this raises questions about which list came first and why two lists were needed. The prevailing view, following the late-nineteenth-century school of Wellhausen, is to treat Deuteronomy 14 as the more ancient of the two lists.

But is the prevailing view convincing? A better case can be made for giving Leviticus 11 the nod for priority. Several reasons in support of a reversal of the conventional wisdom on this point should be noted: (a) Leviticus 11:2-3 merely specifies quadrupeds, while Deut 14:4-5 proceeds to name ten such clean animals; (b) Lev 11:20-23 limits the edibles in one category to four types of flying insects, but Deut 14:20 opens it up to "any winged creature that is clean you may eat" (NIV); (c) Lev 11:4-6 constantly repeats the reason why certain animals may not be eaten, but Deut 14:7 feels no need to give such reasons (perhaps assuming that such information was already in hand); and (d) Leviticus 11 addresses only the Israelite, but Deut 14:21 must now reckon with the additional presence of the the "resident alien," (גר *gēr*), who dwells in their midst.[67] This alien is one to whom the carcass can be given or sold. There would have been no need for including such a provision when the Israelites were journeying in the wilderness in Leviticus, but as they come into residential life in Deuteronomy, the need is obviously present. We can even see a revision of an older provision found in Lev 11:39-40 that permitted Israelites to eat meat from dead animals that were clean, so long as they washed themselves after eating. But by the time Deut 14:21 was written, it had become an absolutely forbidden act; thus Deuteronomy must reflect a time after Leviticus was given a

different type of cultural setting. Regardless of when the final form of Leviticus was fixed, it seems clear that the author of Deuteronomy 14 had a text of Leviticus 11, which he used.

The structure of Leviticus 11 falls into six divisions marked out in the Hebrew text by זה (*zeh*, "this" [masculine]), זאת (*zō't*, "this" [feminine]) and אלה (*'ēlleh*, "these"), in vv. 2, 9, 13, 24, 29, and 46. The resulting outline is clean and unclean land animals (vv. 1-8); clean and unclean aquatic creatures (vv. 9-12); clean and unclean flying creatures (vv. 13-23); pollution from land animals (vv. 24-28); pollution from swarming creatures (vv. 29-45); and summary (vv. 46-47).

11:1-8. Surprisingly, both Moses and Aaron are addressed together as the chapter begins. Perhaps Aaron is included here (and in 13:1; 14:33; and 15:1) because the priests are particularly charged with "[distinguishing] . . . between the unclean and the clean" and with the task of "[instructing] the Israelites" (10:10-11).

The edible land animals are listed first in vv. 2-3. The hoof of these animals must be split, and they must be ruminants. These include the ox, the sheep, and the goat (see Deut 14:4); later, Deut 14:5 adds seven wild animals to this category.

Four other animals do not meet these criteria: the camel, the coney or rock badger, the hare or rabbit, and the pig. Some split the hoof (e.g., the pig) but do not "chew the cud" while others meet the reverse criteria. The ones chewing the cud, but without split hoofs, are the camel (the single-humped dromedary is intended here), the Syrian coney, and the hare. Of course, "chew the cud" does not mean a ruminant that possesses four stomachs. When Hebrew uses this term, it means the crosswise moving of the jaw while chewing, rather than any elaborate theory of multiple stomachs that allowed regurgitation and rechewing of the cud before it was swallowed and digested.

Were the four animals listed as unclean placed there because of hygienic reasons as potential disease carriers, as William Foxwell Albright proposes,[68] or were they excluded from the list of clean animals because, as Mary

---

67. This list is from Noordtzij, *Bible Student's Commentary,* 119-20. More recently, Milgrom concludes his "Excursus B. Deut 14:4-21, An Abridgment of Lev 11" by saying, "The cumulative evidence of this investigation [698-704] points, without exception, in one direction. All the additions, omissions, protuberances, inconcinnities, and inconsistencies that mark off Deut 14:4-21 from Lev 11 can be explained by one premise: D had the entire MT of Lev 11 before him, which he copied, altered, and above all abridged to suit his ideological stance and literary style" (*Leviticus 1-16,* 704).

Douglas claims, they fail to meet the criteria of their taxonomy? Jacob Milgrom argues that neither of these two explanations fits since, in Albright's theory, these would merely be samples of other animals that would be unfit for the table, and in Douglas's theory, if they are listed because they do not fit the criteria, the list must be complete. However, Milgrom finds that only six animals fall into the lists of vv. 4-8: The four listed in vv. 4-8 and two others. One of the two not listed is the llama, which is a ruminant, but its hoofs are not split. It is indigenous to South America (along with its relatives, the alpaca and the guanaco). The other is the hippopotamus, which is split-hoofed but is a nonruminant, existing in the marshy areas of the Philistine coast (perhaps discussed in Job 40:15-24). Milgrom concludes that the criteria came first and then the animals were disqualified. But in the case of the pig, he thinks that it was so abominated that the revulsion came first and then the criteria were made deliberately to disqualify it.[69]

Israel's diet, then, is to be limited to three domesticated species: cattle (the ox and the cow), sheep, and goats. These same three animal groups are also allowed in the innermost circle as sacrifices by the priests. Because Israel occupies the second of Milgrom's three concentric circles, seven additional wild animals are allowed. It is not always possible to identify all of the animals in the lists of Leviticus 11 and Deuteronomy 14, since, according to one expert, as many as 60 percent of the Hebrew terms for the creatures in these lists are unknown or are of dubious identification.[70] From the list of seven wild animals in Deut 14:5, the first three may be confidently identified: the roe deer, the gazelle, and the fallow deer. They are not to be used as sacrifices on the altar (although the faunal remains at an archaeological excavation of an altar room from the eleventh to eighth centuries BCE at Tel Dor revealed bone fragments of twenty-eight deer).[71] Both types of deer are also listed among the

68. William Foxwell Albright, *Yahweh and the Gods of Canaan* (Garden City, N.Y.: Doubleday, 1968) 175-81.

69. Milgrom, *Leviticus 1-16*, 728.

70. As cited by Wenham, *Leviticus*, 164 n. 2, quoting F. S. Bodenheimer in G. Bare, *Plants and Animals of the Bible* (London: United Bible Societies, 1969) iii.

71. As reported by Milgrom, *Leviticus 1-16*, 723, citing P. Wapnish and B. Hesse.

Ugaritic sacrificial animals at the Canaanite site of Ugarit.

11:9-12. The criteria for distinguishing which water creatures are clean or unclean are limited to whether they have fins and scales. Fish that possess both are free swimming and may be eaten (v. 9); but those without fins or scales may not (vv. 10-12). Those in the latter category are more likely to be scavengers that dwell in the mud bottoms; consequently, they might carry parasites.

11:13-23. No principle is set forth in vv. 13-19 for distinguishing the birds that are clean. Although many of the modern equivalents for many of the creatures in this whole chapter are uncertain, based on the current state of our lexicographical knowledge, it is easy to see that the birds listed here are all birds of prey. They feed on carrion, or garbage, and nest and roost in ruins or desert places. Because they eat flesh with blood in it, Mary Douglas points out that they break the covenant law that they, along with mortals, were expected to keep and are therefore unclean.[72]

A distinguishing mark is set forth for all the noxious pests that fly and "walk on all fours" (v. 20). They too are said to be "detestable," just as the fish without fins and scales are (v. 12). The pesky insects included here are flies, mosquitoes, and cockroaches. The term שרץ (*šeres*) broadly includes all sorts of vermin: rodents, reptiles, worms, insects, and the like.

Only four locusts or grasshoppers are declared to be clean. Although we cannot give their modern equivalents, the added distinguishing feature that they possess over those that, like them, go on all fours is that they have "jointed legs for hopping" (v. 21). The key illustration of one who lived on locusts was John the Baptist (see Mark 1:6). No one in the OT is known to have eaten locusts.

11:24-47. At this point in the chapter, a change is apparent. Thus far the discussion has been about what is clean or unclean. But other types of questions come to mind as well. What happens if someone accidentally touches something unclean? What is one to do about dead things? And on and on go the questions.

Three sources of uncleanness that help answer some of the remaining questions are now listed:

72. Douglas, *Purity and Danger*, 56.

contacting carcasses of unclean land animals (vv. 26-28), contacting carcasses of animals that "move along the ground" (vv. 29-38), and contacting carcasses of clean animals (vv. 39-40). All dead animals are unclean, and they will pollute anyone who comes into contact with them. Unless an animal has been slaughtered in the prescribed manner, it will contaminate all who come into contact with it. This is true even for an animal that would otherwise be described as clean (v. 39). This pollution is temporary, lasting only until evening of the day it is contacted (vv. 24, 25, 27, 28, 31, 32, 39, 40).

Verse 32 presents a new situation. Any object used in one's everyday existence that comes into contact with the carcass of one of these animals itself becomes unclean. Articles made of wood, cloth, hide, or sackcloth are to be washed, but the easily replaced clay pottery has to be smashed and replaced (v. 33). Likewise, pottery kilns or ovens and cooking pots made of pottery are to be smashed for the same reason.

If, however, food is present in the pot when it is contaminated by a carcass, it would depend on whether the food is dry or wet. If it is dry, it remains clean; but if it is food prepared with water, it is unclean (v. 34). The same logic is used on seed; if the seed is wet and a carcass falls on it, it is defiled (vv. 37-38). The exception comes when running water is present, such as in a spring or a cistern; they are not polluted by such contact (v. 36).

What if a clean animal dies a natural death or is killed by other animals (vv. 39-40)? Contacting such carcasses does make one unclean; whoever eats of it or picks it up has to wash the clothes and remain unclean until evening. Leviticus 17:15 increases the stringency of this rule further by requiring the person to bathe as well. Later rabbinical thinking directed that it was only the flesh that defiled; but the hide, bones, and horns were exempt from this injunction. However, Lev 7:24 exempts only the fat for use from clean animals found dead or torn by wild animals. Even the fat is not to be eaten but used only for other purposes.

This chapter concludes with one rule, apparently returning to the cases mentioned in vv. 20-23 and 29-38 (especially v. 31): "Every creature that moves about on the ground is detestable" (v. 41). Here is the summary of the whole case in this complicated chapter. Israel is to be different because it has been called to be holy (v. 44). This call to holiness is stressed by its repetition in the space of two verses (44-45). It will appear in this direct form of "be holy, because I am holy" three more times in this book (Lev 19:2; 20:7, 26). Indeed, here is the sole purpose for all of the distinctions between the clean and the unclean. God called Israel to be separate and distinct from everything else so that Israel might carry out the mission given in the Abrahamic covenant: "In you all the families of the earth shall be blessed" (Gen 12:3*b* NRSV).

REFLECTIONS

1. The Levitical food laws were the physical expressions of the call for holiness in the totality of Israel's life. The laws were meant to make Israelites sensitive to the need to distinguish between the sacred and the secular in every area of their lives. Holiness could not be practiced merely in the religious realm, with all other areas free and open only to the common. God looked for wholeness, completion, and separateness in every aspect of one's life-style.

The distinction between clean and unclean reminded Israel of its election to be a holy people called for a holy purpose. Similarly, in the NT believers are called to be part of a holy people, a chosen race, a royal priesthood, and a holy nation (see 1 Pet 2:9). Just as Israel was reminded of this fact in the very mundane act of eating, so Christians are to put their minds "on things that are above, not on things that are on earth" (Col 3:2 NRSV). Holiness of life must penetrate the secular, as well as the sacred, realm of existence.

2. The NT teaches that these food laws, as was true of all of the ceremonial law, are no longer binding on Christians. Since observance of these laws marked one as a faithful member of the Jewish nation, the Gentiles did not share in this mark of identification. This is not to say that no abiding principles remained valid for all times and peoples; it merely removed the necessity of rigid observance of all its details.

In Mark 7:19, Jesus "declared all foods clean" (NRSV). By so saying, Jesus abrogated the distinction that had held up to this time between clean and unclean foods. The apostle Peter was surprised to learn this same principle in his contact with the Gentile Cornelius (see Acts 10:11-16). Peter had to be told three times that he was not to call common or unclean what God had cleansed. It finally dawned on Peter that, while it had been previously unlawful for a Jew to associate with or to visit anyone of another nationality, "God [had now] shown [him] that [he] should not call any man impure or unclean" (Acts 10:28 NIV).

The apostle Paul enlarges on the theology of clean and unclean when he affirms, "As one who is in the Lord Jesus, I am fully convinced that no food is unclean in itself. But if anyone regards something as unclean, then for him it is unclean" (Rom 14:14 NIV); and "Food does not bring us near to God; we are no worse if we do not eat, and no better if we do" (1 Cor 8:8 NIV). Paul's grand conclusion is: "So whether you eat or drink or whatever you do, do it all for the glory of God" (1 Cor 10:31 NIV). The call for holiness and promoting the glory of God has not lessened between the OT and the NT; only the means we use to demonstrate it. The call for holiness affects all of life, even though there is no longer a specified list of clean or unclean foods that we must honor.

LEVITICUS 12:1-8, THE UNCLEANNESS OF CHILDBIRTH

NIV

12 The LORD said to Moses, ²"Say to the Israelites: "A woman who becomes pregnant and gives birth to a son will be ceremonially unclean for seven days, just as she is unclean during her monthly period. ³On the eighth day the boy is to be circumcised. ⁴Then the woman must wait thirty-three days to be purified from her bleeding. She must not touch anything sacred or go to the sanctuary until the days of her purification are over. ⁵If she gives birth to a daughter, for two weeks the woman will be unclean, as during her period. Then she must wait sixty-six days to be purified from her bleeding.

⁶"'When the days of her purification for a son or daughter are over, she is to bring to the priest at the entrance to the Tent of Meeting a year-old lamb for a burnt offering and a young pigeon or a dove for a sin offering. ⁷He shall offer them before the LORD to make atonement for her, and then she will be ceremonially clean from her flow of blood.

"'These are the regulations for the woman who gives birth to a boy or a girl. ⁸If she cannot afford a lamb, she is to bring two doves or two young

NRSV

12 The LORD spoke to Moses, saying: ²Speak to the people of Israel, saying:

If a woman conceives and bears a male child, she shall be ceremonially unclean seven days; as at the time of her menstruation, she shall be unclean. ³On the eighth day the flesh of his foreskin shall be circumcised. ⁴Her time of blood purification shall be thirty-three days; she shall not touch any holy thing, or come into the sanctuary, until the days of her purification are completed. ⁵If she bears a female child, she shall be unclean two weeks, as in her menstruation; her time of blood purification shall be sixty-six days.

⁶When the days of her purification are completed, whether for a son or for a daughter, she shall bring to the priest at the entrance of the tent of meeting a lamb in its first year for a burnt offering, and a pigeon or a turtledove for a sin offering. ⁷He shall offer it before the LORD, and make atonement on her behalf; then she shall be clean from her flow of blood. This is the law for her who bears a child, male or female. ⁸If she cannot afford a sheep, she shall take two turtledoves or two pigeons, one for a burnt offering

pigeons, one for a burnt offering and the other for a sin offering. In this way the priest will make atonement for her, and she will be clean.'"

and the other for a sin offering; and the priest shall make atonement on her behalf, and she shall be clean.

COMMENTARY

While chap. 11 deals with uncleanness that is outside humans in the external world, chaps. 12–15 deal more with uncleanness found within the human constitution itself and not in the outside environment. The problem of cleanness for a holy people is not merely one of contact with the external world, but also pollution that comes from within. This double-edged confrontation with the demands of holiness also teaches Israel to be aware of the two sources from which sin might arise: both within and outside the person.

The structure of this brief chapter is as follows: command to Moses (v. 1); uncleanness due to childbirth (vv. 2-5), including birth of a son (vv. 2-4) and birth of a daughter (v. 5); sacrifices after the time of purification (vv. 6-7); and alternative sacrifices for the poor (v. 8).

This brief law prescribes the period of purification after a woman has given birth and the sacrifices she is to offer at the completion of these days.

The law begins by using the resultative form of the Hebrew verb "to sow seed." In the niphal stem of this verb, it usually means "to become pregnant" or "to conceive" (cf. NIV). But in the resultative form (as it appears in Gen 1:11-12, "plants bearing seed" [NIV]), it denotes something like "produces offspring" or, in the stative form of the resultative, "comes to the completion of her pregnancy" and gives birth to a son.

This law continues with the provision that the mother who delivers a son remains unclean for seven days, similar to her condition after her monthly period. This connection with her monthly menses is made in vv. 2 and 5. That law is given in greater detail in 15:19-24.

In the week following the birth of a male, the woman is not only unclean in herself, but anyone or anything that touches her is unclean as well. She is not allowed, either, to touch any hallowed thing or to come into the sanctuary. Presumably, she is

not allowed marital relations with her husband or contact with persons in her household.

On the eighth day the son is circumcised. Even though the mother must not enter the sanctuary or contact any sacred things for another thirty-three days, she can reestablish normal relations with persons in her household. The circumcision of her son cuts her days of purification in half.

Circumcision, of course, had been given as a sign of God's covenant in Gen 17:10-14. The rite of circumcision, as such, was not unknown in the ancient world. According to Jer 9:25-26, it was known among the Egyptians, Edomites, Ammonites, Moabites, and Arabs. In Hellenistic times in Egypt, it was limited to the priests. Everywhere else, outside Israel, it appeared to have functioned as a puberty rite that prepared a man for marriage. Thus Ishmael was circumcised at age thirteen (see Gen 17:25). This may have been the situation in Israel prior to the covenant made with Abraham, for Hebrew philology tends to support that thesis. In Hebrew a "son-in-law," or a "daughter's husband," literally means "one who undergoes circumcision" (חתן ḥātān), while "father-in-law," or "wife's father," is literally "circumciser" (ḥōtēn). Apparently, then, God took a ceremony already known and reconstituted it as a new symbol of a special relationship with Israel and as a mark of the covenant.

If the newborn is a daughter, both periods of time are doubled; the seven days are stretched to fourteen, and the remaining thirty-three are increased to sixty-six. This doubling of the time has been an occasion for much speculation. We must be careful not to think that a greater sinfulness is attached to a female than to a male. If that is so, why are the sacrifices specified at the end of the period the same for both a male and a female? Furthermore, the fact of childbirth itself involves no sin offering. Rather, contrary to the normal order, a whole burnt offering is made first, and then a sin offering is given on the forty-first or eighty-first day, depending on whether the baby is male or female.

Those who flee to Leviticus 27 to argue that the valuation of males as opposed to females is two to one make the mistake of confusing the value of female *services* at the sanctuary in comparison to male services. But the text gives no support to those who try to establish intrinsic worth of the sexes based on the values established there. This passage does not prove that women are inferior to men.

Nevertheless, the real reason for the doubling of the time for purification escapes modern interpreters. *Jubilees* 3:8-14 and the Mishnah give an etiological explanation for the difference: Adam was created at the end of the first week of creation and entered Eden on the forty-first day, while Eve was created at the end of the second week and was finally admitted to the Garden of Eden on the eighty-first day.

Occasionally, some of the rabbis have attempted a biological explanation: The male embryo is completely formed in forty-one days but the female in eighty-one. Aristotle said the male was formed in forty days but the female in three months; Hippocrates answered with thirty days for the male and forty-two days for the female.

Whatever the reason, a great deal of comparative material could be cited to indicate that the parturient undergoes a longer period for a girl than for a boy.[73] But it must be stressed once again: A longer period of time for purification is not necessarily a sign of lesser social standing or worth. This is jumping categories and assuming that we know the reasons for the differences in time duration—which we do not know!

Certainly, we must not conclude that there is anything unclean or sinful in bearing children. Has not the Creator approved and blessed this function (see Gen 1:28)? The difficulty that this passage, and others like it in Leviticus 15, raises is that acts that are both blessed and approved are also said in this context to bring defilement. The point must be a symbolic or typological one rather than a condemnation of either the act of sexual union or the children who are born from it. What this

text does say—in fact, it emphasizes three times in vv. 4, 5, and 7—is that it is the blood of the woman's discharge that makes her unclean. That is vastly different from saying that the sexual union, or the child who was born, makes her unclean. In any case, we must not confuse ritual impurity with sinfulness or moral worth.

Many cultures preserve the same views about the postpartum state. The best explanation to date is the one that equates all bodily discharges, regardless of their cause, with death. The acts of begetting and giving birth present the very moments in time when life and death come together. Since the loss of blood can sometimes lead to death, the threat is always present in childbirth. And any discharge is always a reminder of what could be seen in decaying corpses: Discharges can cause corruption. Hence the connection here with the loss of blood, even though blood, on the other hand, is also the most effective means for reconciling the sinner with God. Therein lies the mystery of this book.

Two offerings are prescribed at the completion of the mother's purification—a burnt offering and a sin offering. It is surprising that a burnt offering is placed first when the usual order prescribed in these offerings is to deal with the sin question first (see our discussion on 9:2-4). The reversal of that pattern here adds further evidence to the point that childbearing in itself is not sinful. The whole burnt offering is one of dedication to God and gratefulness for God's goodness during the delivery and God's protection of the child during the critical days of infancy.

The second offering is a sin offering to "make atonement for her" (vv. 7-8). Is this to bring her back into fellowship with the living God after she has been absent for forty to eighty days? One thing for sure, the external cessation of the flow of blood is somehow connected with her being declared ceremonially clean after the sacrifice of the sin offering. Perhaps the lesson to be learned is not that the act of conception is sinful, but that all who conceive are also at one and the same time sinners; even those born cannot escape the sinful human condition (see Ps 51:5).

Provision is made for those who, like Mary in Luke 2:21-24, are too poor to offer the expensive offering of a year-old lamb. Two

73. See Milgrom for additional sources and examples (*Leviticus 1-16*, 750). In this century, a physician has attempted to give a medical reason for the postnatal discharge being longer for the delivery of females than males, but nothing there justifies a doubling of the time. See D. I. Macht, "A Scientific Appreciation of Leviticus 12:1-5," *JBL* 52 (1933) 253-60.

doves or two young pigeons can be substituted, one for the burnt offering and one for the sin offering. How graciously God continues to look out for persons who are destitute and have very little of this world's goods.

REFLECTIONS

1. The male baby was circumcised on the eighth day; but why that day? We would have guessed that the seventh day would have been chosen, for even though it is the Sabbath, babies will still be circumcised if that is when the eighth day comes. The suggestion here is that since circumcision had a spiritual impact by means of the associated idea of a circumcision of the heart (see Deut 10:16; Jer 4:4; Rom 2:29), so eight was a number symbolic of the new creation on the first day of the week. So frequently in the feast days do we see not only the seventh day but also the eighth day being described as a day holy to the Lord. There may be a typological anticipation of the new covenant, with its pointing to the first day of the week when Christ arose from the dead, he who is called the Firstfruits of all who will one day likewise be raised by him from the dead.

2. Love, marriage, and human sexuality are never described in the Bible as dirty, unclean, or sinful. The discussion in this chapter on the discharge of blood does not challenge the testimony of Scripture elsewhere that sexual love is a good gift to be cherished.

3. An estimate of the low status of women in the OT receives a bad rap when passages like this one or Leviticus 27 are used. Proverbs 31, with its poem of the "woman of valor," demonstrates that the ancient Israelite woman wielded power in the home equal to that exercised by her husband. Those who cite the tenth commandment (see Exod 20:17; Deut 5:21) to demonstrate that a wife was merely a husband's "chattel" or possession overlook the fact that the wife is listed first, not as part of the possessions of the husband, but because she is the first-named member of the household. This point is confirmed by the fact that a wife could never be sold, even if she was a captive in war (see Deut 21:14).

LEVITICUS 13:1–14:57, THE UNCLEANNESS OF SKIN AND FUNGUS DISEASES

NIV

13 The LORD said to Moses and Aaron, [2]"When anyone has a swelling or a rash or a bright spot on his skin that may become an infectious skin disease,[a] he must be brought to Aaron the priest or to one of his sons[b] who is a priest. [3]The priest is to examine the sore on his skin, and if the hair in the sore has turned white and the sore appears to be more than skin deep,[c] it is an infectious skin disease. When the priest examines him, he shall pronounce him ceremoni-

[a]2 Traditionally *leprosy*; the Hebrew word was used for various diseases affecting the skin—not necessarily leprosy; also elsewhere in this chapter. [b]2 Or *descendants* [c]3 Or *be lower than the rest of the skin*; also elsewhere in this chapter

NRSV

13 The LORD spoke to Moses and Aaron, saying:

[2]When a person has on the skin of his body a swelling or an eruption or a spot, and it turns into a leprous[a] disease on the skin of his body, he shall be brought to Aaron the priest or to one of his sons the priests. [3]The priest shall examine the disease on the skin of his body, and if the hair in the diseased area has turned white and the disease appears to be deeper than the skin of his body, it is a leprous[a] disease; after the priest has examined

[a] A term for several skin diseases; precise meaning uncertainclean. [4]But if the spot is white in the skin of his

ally unclean. [4]If the spot on his skin is white but does not appear to be more than skin deep and the hair in it has not turned white, the priest is to put the infected person in isolation for seven days. [5]On the seventh day the priest is to examine him, and if he sees that the sore is unchanged and has not spread in the skin, he is to keep him in isolation another seven days. [6]On the seventh day the priest is to examine him again, and if the sore has faded and has not spread in the skin, the priest shall pronounce him clean; it is only a rash. The man must wash his clothes, and he will be clean. [7]But if the rash does spread in his skin after he has shown himself to the priest to be pronounced clean, he must appear before the priest again. [8]The priest is to examine him, and if the rash has spread in the skin, he shall pronounce him unclean; it is an infectious disease.

[9]"When anyone has an infectious skin disease, he must be brought to the priest. [10]The priest is to examine him, and if there is a white swelling in the skin that has turned the hair white and if there is raw flesh in the swelling, [11]it is a chronic skin disease and the priest shall pronounce him unclean. He is not to put him in isolation, because he is already unclean.

[12]"If the disease breaks out all over his skin and, so far as the priest can see, it covers all the skin of the infected person from head to foot, [13]the priest is to examine him, and if the disease has covered his whole body, he shall pronounce that person clean. Since it has all turned white, he is clean. [14]But whenever raw flesh appears on him, he will be unclean. [15]When the priest sees the raw flesh, he shall pronounce him unclean. The raw flesh is unclean; he has an infectious disease. [16]Should the raw flesh change and turn white, he must go to the priest. [17]The priest is to examine him, and if the sores have turned white, the priest shall pronounce the infected person clean; then he will be clean.

[18]"When someone has a boil on his skin and it heals, [19]and in the place where the boil was, a white swelling or reddish-white spot appears, he must present himself to the priest. [20]The priest is to examine it, and if it appears to be more than skin deep and the hair in it has turned white, the priest shall pronounce him unclean. It is an infec-

him he shall pronounce him ceremonially unbody, and appears no deeper than the skin, and the hair in it has not turned white, the priest shall confine the diseased person for seven days. [5]The priest shall examine him on the seventh day, and if he sees that the disease is checked and the disease has not spread in the skin, then the priest shall confine him seven days more. [6]The priest shall examine him again on the seventh day, and if the disease has abated and the disease has not spread in the skin, the priest shall pronounce him clean; it is only an eruption; and he shall wash his clothes, and be clean. [7]But if the eruption spreads in the skin after he has shown himself to the priest for his cleansing, he shall appear again before the priest. [8]The priest shall make an examination, and if the eruption has spread in the skin, the priest shall pronounce him unclean; it is a leprous[a] disease.

[9]When a person contracts a leprous[a] disease, he shall be brought to the priest. [10]The priest shall make an examination, and if there is a white swelling in the skin that has turned the hair white, and there is quick raw flesh in the swelling, [11]it is a chronic leprous[a] disease in the skin of his body. The priest shall pronounce him unclean; he shall not confine him, for he is unclean. [12]But if the disease breaks out in the skin, so that it covers all the skin of the diseased person from head to foot, so far as the priest can see, [13]then the priest shall make an examination, and if the disease has covered all his body, he shall pronounce him clean of the disease; since it has all turned white, he is clean. [14]But if raw flesh ever appears on him, he shall be unclean; [15]the priest shall examine the raw flesh and pronounce him unclean. Raw flesh is unclean, for it is a leprous[a] disease. [16]But if the raw flesh again turns white, he shall come to the priest; [17]the priest shall examine him, and if the disease has turned white, the priest shall pronounce the diseased person clean. He is clean.

[18]When there is on the skin of one's body a boil that has healed, [19]and in the place of the boil there appears a white swelling or a reddish-white spot, it shall be shown to the priest. [20]The priest shall make an examination, and if it appears deeper than the skin and its hair has turned white,

[a] A term for several skin diseases; precise meaning uncertain

tious skin disease that has broken out where the boil was. ²¹But if, when the priest examines it, there is no white hair in it and it is not more than skin deep and has faded, then the priest is to put him in isolation for seven days. ²²If it is spreading in the skin, the priest shall pronounce him unclean; it is infectious. ²³But if the spot is unchanged and has not spread, it is only a scar from the boil, and the priest shall pronounce him clean.

²⁴"When someone has a burn on his skin and a reddish-white or white spot appears in the raw flesh of the burn, ²⁵the priest is to examine the spot, and if the hair in it has turned white, and it appears to be more than skin deep, it is an infectious disease that has broken out in the burn. The priest shall pronounce him unclean; it is an infectious skin disease. ²⁶But if the priest examines it and there is no white hair in the spot and if it is not more than skin deep and has faded, then the priest is to put him in isolation for seven days. ²⁷On the seventh day the priest is to examine him, and if it is spreading in the skin, the priest shall pronounce him unclean; it is an infectious skin disease. ²⁸If, however, the spot is unchanged and has not spread in the skin but has faded, it is a swelling from the burn, and the priest shall pronounce him clean; it is only a scar from the burn.

²⁹"If a man or woman has a sore on the head or on the chin, ³⁰the priest is to examine the sore, and if it appears to be more than skin deep and the hair in it is yellow and thin, the priest shall pronounce that person unclean; it is an itch, an infectious disease of the head or chin. ³¹But if, when the priest examines this kind of sore, it does not seem to be more than skin deep and there is no black hair in it, then the priest is to put the infected person in isolation for seven days. ³²On the seventh day the priest is to examine the sore, and if the itch has not spread and there is no yellow hair in it and it does not appear to be more than skin deep, ³³he must be shaved except for the diseased area, and the priest is to keep him in isolation another seven days. ³⁴On the seventh day the priest is to examine the itch, and if it has not spread in the skin and appears to be no more than skin deep, the priest shall pronounce him clean. He must wash his clothes, and he will be

the priest shall pronounce him unclean; this is a leprous*a* disease, broken out in the boil. ²¹But if the priest examines it and the hair on it is not white, nor is it deeper than the skin but has abated, the priest shall confine him seven days. ²²If it spreads in the skin, the priest shall pronounce him unclean; it is diseased. ²³But if the spot remains in one place and does not spread, it is the scar of the boil; the priest shall pronounce him clean.

24Or, when the body has a burn on the skin and the raw flesh of the burn becomes a spot, reddish-white or white, ²⁵the priest shall examine it. If the hair in the spot has turned white and it appears deeper than the skin, it is a leprous*a* disease; it has broken out in the burn, and the priest shall pronounce him unclean. This is a leprous*a* disease. ²⁶But if the priest examines it and the hair in the spot is not white, and it is no deeper than the skin but has abated, the priest shall confine him seven days. ²⁷The priest shall examine him the seventh day; if it is spreading in the skin, the priest shall pronounce him unclean. This is a leprous*a* disease. ²⁸But if the spot remains in one place and does not spread in the skin but has abated, it is a swelling from the burn, and the priest shall pronounce him clean; for it is the scar of the burn.

29When a man or woman has a disease on the head or in the beard, ³⁰the priest shall examine the disease. If it appears deeper than the skin and the hair in it is yellow and thin, the priest shall pronounce him unclean; it is an itch, a leprous*a* disease of the head or the beard. ³¹If the priest examines the itching disease, and it appears no deeper than the skin and there is no black hair in it, the priest shall confine the person with the itching disease for seven days. ³²On the seventh day the priest shall examine the itch; if the itch has not spread, and there is no yellow hair in it, and the itch appears to be no deeper than the skin, ³³he shall shave, but the itch he shall not shave. The priest shall confine the person with the itch for seven days more. ³⁴On the seventh day the priest shall examine the itch; if the itch has not spread in the skin and it appears to be no deeper than the skin, the priest shall pro-

a A term for several skin diseases; precise meaning uncertain

clean. [35]But if the itch does spread in the skin after he is pronounced clean, [36]the priest is to examine him, and if the itch has spread in the skin, the priest does not need to look for yellow hair; the person is unclean. [37]If, however, in his judgment it is unchanged and black hair has grown in it, the itch is healed. He is clean, and the priest shall pronounce him clean.

[38]"When a man or woman has white spots on the skin, [39]the priest is to examine them, and if the spots are dull white, it is a harmless rash that has broken out on the skin; that person is clean.

[40]"When a man has lost his hair and is bald, he is clean. [41]If he has lost his hair from the front of his scalp and has a bald forehead, he is clean. [42]But if he has a reddish-white sore on his bald head or forehead, it is an infectious disease breaking out on his head or forehead. [43]The priest is to examine him, and if the swollen sore on his head or forehead is reddish-white like an infectious skin disease, [44]the man is diseased and is unclean. The priest shall pronounce him unclean because of the sore on his head.

[45]"The person with such an infectious disease must wear torn clothes, let his hair be unkempt,[a] cover the lower part of his face and cry out, 'Unclean! Unclean!' [46]As long as he has the infection he remains unclean. He must live alone; he must live outside the camp.

[47]"If any clothing is contaminated with mildew—any woolen or linen clothing, [48]any woven or knitted material of linen or wool, any leather or anything made of leather— [49]and if the contamination in the clothing, or leather, or woven or knitted material, or any leather article, is greenish or reddish, it is a spreading mildew and must be shown to the priest. [50]The priest is to examine the mildew and isolate the affected article for seven days. [51]On the seventh day he is to examine it, and if the mildew has spread in the clothing, or the woven or knitted material, or the leather, whatever its use, it is a destructive mildew; the article is unclean. [52]He must burn up the clothing, or the woven or knitted material of wool or linen, or any leather article that has the contamination in it, because the mildew is destructive; the article must be burned up.

[a]45 Or clothes, uncover his head

nounce him clean. He shall wash his clothes and be clean. [35]But if the itch spreads in the skin after he was pronounced clean, [36]the priest shall examine him. If the itch has spread in the skin, the priest need not seek for the yellow hair; he is unclean. [37]But if in his eyes the itch is checked, and black hair has grown in it, the itch is healed, he is clean; and the priest shall pronounce him clean.

[38]When a man or a woman has spots on the skin of the body, white spots, [39]the priest shall make an examination, and if the spots on the skin of the body are of a dull white, it is a rash that has broken out on the skin; he is clean.

[40]If anyone loses the hair from his head, he is bald but he is clean. [41]If he loses the hair from his forehead and temples, he has baldness of the forehead but he is clean. [42]But if there is on the bald head or the bald forehead a reddish-white diseased spot, it is a leprous[a] disease breaking out on his bald head or his bald forehead. [43]The priest shall examine him; if the diseased swelling is reddish-white on his bald head or on his bald forehead, which resembles a leprous[a] disease in the skin of the body, [44]he is leprous,[a] he is unclean. The priest shall pronounce him unclean; the disease is on his head.

[45]The person who has the leprous[a] disease shall wear torn clothes and let the hair of his head be disheveled; and he shall cover his upper lip and cry out, "Unclean, unclean." [46]He shall remain unclean as long as he has the disease; he is unclean. He shall live alone; his dwelling shall be outside the camp.

[47]Concerning clothing: when a leprous[a] disease appears in it, in woolen or linen cloth, [48]in warp or woof of linen or wool, or in a skin or in anything made of skin, [49]if the disease shows greenish or reddish in the garment, whether in warp or woof or in skin or in anything made of skin, it is a leprous[a] disease and shall be shown to the priest. [50]The priest shall examine the disease, and put the diseased article aside for seven days. [51]He shall examine the disease on the seventh day. If the disease has spread in the cloth, in warp or woof, or in the skin, whatever be the use of the skin, this is a spreading leprous[a] disease;

[a]A term for several skin diseases; precise meaning uncertain

53"But if, when the priest examines it, the mildew has not spread in the clothing, or the woven or knitted material, or the leather article, 54he shall order that the contaminated article be washed. Then he is to isolate it for another seven days. 55After the affected article has been washed, the priest is to examine it, and if the mildew has not changed its appearance, even though it has not spread, it is unclean. Burn it with fire, whether the mildew has affected one side or the other. 56If, when the priest examines it, the mildew has faded after the article has been washed, he is to tear the contaminated part out of the clothing, or the leather, or the woven or knitted material. 57But if it reappears in the clothing, or in the woven or knitted material, or in the leather article, it is spreading, and whatever has the mildew must be burned with fire. 58The clothing, or the woven or knitted material, or any leather article that has been washed and is rid of the mildew, must be washed again, and it will be clean."

59These are the regulations concerning contamination by mildew in woolen or linen clothing, woven or knitted material, or any leather article, for pronouncing them clean or unclean.

14 The LORD said to Moses, 2"These are the regulations for the diseased person at the time of his ceremonial cleansing, when he is brought to the priest: 3The priest is to go outside the camp and examine him. If the person has been healed of his infectious skin disease,[a] 4the priest shall order that two live clean birds and some cedar wood, scarlet yarn and hyssop be brought for the one to be cleansed. 5Then the priest shall order that one of the birds be killed over fresh water in a clay pot. 6He is then to take the live bird and dip it, together with the cedar wood, the scarlet yarn and the hyssop, into the blood of the bird that was killed over the fresh water. 7Seven times he shall sprinkle the one to be cleansed of the infectious disease and pronounce him clean. Then he is to release the live bird in the open fields.

8"The person to be cleansed must wash his clothes, shave off all his hair and bathe with

a3 Traditionally *leprosy;* the Hebrew word was used for various diseases affecting the skin—not necessarily leprosy; also elsewhere in this chapter.

it is unclean. 52He shall burn the clothing, whether diseased in warp or woof, woolen or linen, or anything of skin, for it is a spreading leprous[a] disease; it shall be burned in fire.

53If the priest makes an examination, and the disease has not spread in the clothing, in warp or woof or in anything of skin, 54the priest shall command them to wash the article in which the disease appears, and he shall put it aside seven days more. 55The priest shall examine the diseased article after it has been washed. If the diseased spot has not changed color, though the disease has not spread, it is unclean; you shall burn it in fire, whether the leprous[a] spot is on the inside or on the outside.

56If the priest makes an examination, and the disease has abated after it is washed, he shall tear the spot out of the cloth, in warp or woof, or out of skin. 57If it appears again in the garment, in warp or woof, or in anything of skin, it is spreading; you shall burn with fire that in which the disease appears. 58But the cloth, warp or woof, or anything of skin from which the disease disappears when you have washed it, shall then be washed a second time, and it shall be clean.

59This is the ritual for a leprous[a] disease in a cloth of wool or linen, either in warp or woof, or in anything of skin, to decide whether it is clean or unclean.

14 The LORD spoke to Moses, saying: 2This shall be the ritual for the leprous[a] person at the time of his cleansing:

He shall be brought to the priest; 3the priest shall go out of the camp, and the priest shall make an examination. If the disease is healed in the leprous[a] person, 4the priest shall command that two living clean birds and cedarwood and crimson yarn and hyssop be brought for the one who is to be cleansed. 5The priest shall command that one of the birds be slaughtered over fresh water in an earthen vessel. 6He shall take the living bird with the cedarwood and the crimson yarn and the hyssop, and dip them and the living bird in the blood of the bird that was slaughtered over the fresh water. 7He shall sprinkle it seven times upon the one who is to be cleansed of the leprous[a] disease; then he shall pronounce him clean, and

a A term for several skin diseases; precise meaning uncertain

water; then he will be ceremonially clean. After this he may come into the camp, but he must stay outside his tent for seven days. [9]On the seventh day he must shave off all his hair; he must shave his head, his beard, his eyebrows and the rest of his hair. He must wash his clothes and bathe himself with water, and he will be clean.

[10]"On the eighth day he must bring two male lambs and one ewe lamb a year old, each without defect, along with three-tenths of an ephah[a] of fine flour mixed with oil for a grain offering, and one log[b] of oil. [11]The priest who pronounces him clean shall present both the one to be cleansed and his offerings before the LORD at the entrance to the Tent of Meeting.

[12]"Then the priest is to take one of the male lambs and offer it as a guilt offering, along with the log of oil; he shall wave them before the LORD as a wave offering. [13]He is to slaughter the lamb in the holy place where the sin offering and the burnt offering are slaughtered. Like the sin offering, the guilt offering belongs to the priest; it is most holy. [14]The priest is to take some of the blood of the guilt offering and put it on the lobe of the right ear of the one to be cleansed, on the thumb of his right hand and on the big toe of his right foot. [15]The priest shall then take some of the log of oil, pour it in the palm of his own left hand, [16]dip his right forefinger into the oil in his palm, and with his finger sprinkle some of it before the LORD seven times. [17]The priest is to put some of the oil remaining in his palm on the lobe of the right ear of the one to be cleansed, on the thumb of his right hand and on the big toe of his right foot, on top of the blood of the guilt offering. [18]The rest of the oil in his palm the priest shall put on the head of the one to be cleansed and make atonement for him before the LORD.

[19]"Then the priest is to sacrifice the sin offering and make atonement for the one to be cleansed from his uncleanness. After that, the priest shall slaughter the burnt offering [20]and offer it on the altar, together with the grain offering, and make atonement for him, and he will be clean.

[21]"If, however, he is poor and cannot afford these, he must take one male lamb as a guilt

he shall let the living bird go into the open field. [8]The one who is to be cleansed shall wash his clothes, and shave off all his hair, and bathe himself in water, and he shall be clean. After that he shall come into the camp, but shall live outside his tent seven days. [9]On the seventh day he shall shave all his hair: of head, beard, eyebrows; he shall shave all his hair. Then he shall wash his clothes, and bathe his body in water, and he shall be clean.

10On the eighth day he shall take two male lambs without blemish, and one ewe lamb in its first year without blemish, and a grain offering of three-tenths of an ephah of choice flour mixed with oil, and one log[a] of oil. [11]The priest who cleanses shall set the person to be cleansed, along with these things, before the LORD, at the entrance of the tent of meeting. [12]The priest shall take one of the lambs, and offer it as a guilt offering, along with the log[a] of oil, and raise them as an elevation offering before the LORD. [13]He shall slaughter the lamb in the place where the sin offering and the burnt offering are slaughtered in the holy place; for the guilt offering, like the sin offering, belongs to the priest: it is most holy. [14]The priest shall take some of the blood of the guilt offering and put it on the lobe of the right ear of the one to be cleansed, and on the thumb of the right hand, and on the big toe of the right foot. [15]The priest shall take some of the log[b] of oil and pour it into the palm of his own left hand, [16]and dip his right finger in the oil that is in his left hand and sprinkle some oil with his finger seven times before the LORD. [17]Some of the oil that remains in his hand the priest shall put on the lobe of the right ear of the one to be cleansed, and on the thumb of the right hand, and on the big toe of the right foot, on top of the blood of the guilt offering. [18]The rest of the oil that is in the priest's hand he shall put on the head of the one to be cleansed. Then the priest shall make atonement on his behalf before the LORD: [19]the priest shall offer the sin offering, to make atonement for the one to be cleansed from his uncleanness. Afterward he shall slaughter the burnt offering; [20]and the priest shall offer the burnt offering and the grain offering on

NIV

offering to be waved to make atonement for him, together with a tenth of an ephah[a] of fine flour mixed with oil for a grain offering, a log of oil, [22]and two doves or two young pigeons, which he can afford, one for a sin offering and the other for a burnt offering.

[23]"On the eighth day he must bring them for his cleansing to the priest at the entrance to the Tent of Meeting, before the LORD. [24]The priest is to take the lamb for the guilt offering, together with the log of oil, and wave them before the LORD as a wave offering. [25]He shall slaughter the lamb for the guilt offering and take some of its blood and put it on the lobe of the right ear of the one to be cleansed, on the thumb of his right hand and on the big toe of his right foot. [26]The priest is to pour some of the oil into the palm of his own left hand, [27]and with his right forefinger sprinkle some of the oil from his palm seven times before the LORD. [28]Some of the oil in his palm he is to put on the same places he put the blood of the guilt offering—on the lobe of the right ear of the one to be cleansed, on the thumb of his right hand and on the big toe of his right foot. [29]The rest of the oil in his palm the priest shall put on the head of the one to be cleansed, to make atonement for him before the LORD. [30]Then he shall sacrifice the doves or the young pigeons, which the person can afford, [31]one[b] as a sin offering and the other as a burnt offering, together with the grain offering. In this way the priest will make atonement before the LORD on behalf of the one to be cleansed."

[32]These are the regulations for anyone who has an infectious skin disease and who cannot afford the regular offerings for his cleansing.

[33]The LORD said to Moses and Aaron, [34]"When you enter the land of Canaan, which I am giving you as your possession, and I put a spreading mildew in a house in that land, [35]the owner of the house must go and tell the priest, 'I have seen something that looks like mildew in my house.' [36]The priest is to order the house to be emptied before he goes in to examine the mildew, so that nothing in the house will be pronounced unclean. After this the priest is to go in and inspect the house. [37]He is to examine the mildew on the walls, and if it has greenish or

[a]21 That is, probably about 2 quarts (about 2 liters)
[a]31 Septuagint and Syriac; Hebrew *31such as the person can afford, one*

NRSV

the altar. Thus the priest shall make atonement on his behalf and he shall be clean.

[21]But if he is poor and cannot afford so much, he shall take one male lamb for a guilt offering to be elevated, to make atonement on his behalf, and one-tenth of an ephah of choice flour mixed with oil for a grain offering and a log[a] of oil; [22]also two turtledoves or two pigeons, such as he can afford, one for a sin offering and the other for a burnt offering. [23]On the eighth day he shall bring them for his cleansing to the priest, to the entrance of the tent of meeting, before the LORD; [24]and the priest shall take the lamb of the guilt offering and the log[a] of oil, and the priest shall raise them as an elevation offering before the LORD. [25]The priest shall slaughter the lamb of the guilt offering and shall take some of the blood of the guilt offering, and put it on the lobe of the right ear of the one to be cleansed, and on the thumb of the right hand, and on the big toe of the right foot. [26]The priest shall pour some of the oil into the palm of his own left hand, [27]and shall sprinkle with his right finger some of the oil that is in his left hand seven times before the LORD. [28]The priest shall put some of the oil that is in his hand on the lobe of the right ear of the one to be cleansed, and on the thumb of the right hand, and the big toe of the right foot, where the blood of the guilt offering was placed. [29]The rest of the oil that is in the priest's hand he shall put on the head of the one to be cleansed, to make atonement on his behalf before the LORD. [30]And he shall offer, of the turtledoves or pigeons such as he can afford, [31]one[b] for a sin offering and the other for a burnt offering, along with a grain offering; and the priest shall make atonement before the LORD on behalf of the one being cleansed. [32]This is the ritual for the one who has a leprous[b] disease, who cannot afford the offerings for his cleansing.

[33]The LORD spoke to Moses and Aaron, saying:

[34]When you come into the land of Canaan, which I give you for a possession, and I put a leprous[b] disease in a house in the land of your possession, [35]the owner of the house shall come and tell the priest, saying, "There seems to me to be some sort of disease in my house." [36]The priest

[a] A liquid measure
[a] Gk Syr: Heb *afford,* 31such as he can afford, one

reddish depressions that appear to be deeper than the surface of the wall, ³⁸the priest shall go out the doorway of the house and close it up for seven days. ³⁹On the seventh day the priest shall return to inspect the house. If the mildew has spread on the walls, ⁴⁰he is to order that the contaminated stones be torn out and thrown into an unclean place outside the town. ⁴¹He must have all the inside walls of the house scraped and the material that is scraped off dumped into an unclean place outside the town. ⁴²Then they are to take other stones to replace these and take new clay and plaster the house.

⁴³"If the mildew reappears in the house after the stones have been torn out and the house scraped and plastered, ⁴⁴the priest is to go and examine it and, if the mildew has spread in the house, it is a destructive mildew; the house is unclean. ⁴⁵It must be torn down—its stones, timbers and all the plaster—and taken out of the town to an unclean place.

⁴⁶"Anyone who goes into the house while it is closed up will be unclean till evening. ⁴⁷Anyone who sleeps or eats in the house must wash his clothes.

⁴⁸"But if the priest comes to examine it and the mildew has not spread after the house has been plastered, he shall pronounce the house clean, because the mildew is gone. ⁴⁹To purify the house he is to take two birds and some cedar wood, scarlet yarn and hyssop. ⁵⁰He shall kill one of the birds over fresh water in a clay pot. ⁵¹Then he is to take the cedar wood, the hyssop, the scarlet yarn and the live bird, dip them into the blood of the dead bird and the fresh water, and sprinkle the house seven times. ⁵²He shall purify the house with the bird's blood, the fresh water, the live bird, the cedar wood, the hyssop and the scarlet yarn. ⁵³Then he is to release the live bird in the open fields outside the town. In this way he will make atonement for the house, and it will be clean."

⁵⁴These are the regulations for any infectious skin disease, for an itch, ⁵⁵for mildew in clothing or in a house, ⁵⁶and for a swelling, a rash or a bright spot, ⁵⁷to determine when something is clean or unclean.

These are the regulations for infectious skin diseases and mildew.

shall command that they empty the house before the priest goes to examine the disease, or all that is in the house will become unclean; and afterward the priest shall go in to inspect the house. ³⁷He shall examine the disease; if the disease is in the walls of the house with greenish or reddish spots, and if it appears to be deeper than the surface, ³⁸the priest shall go outside to the door of the house and shut up the house seven days. ³⁹The priest shall come again on the seventh day and make an inspection; if the disease has spread in the walls of the house, ⁴⁰the priest shall command that the stones in which the disease appears be taken out and thrown into an unclean place outside the city. ⁴¹He shall have the inside of the house scraped thoroughly, and the plaster that is scraped off shall be dumped in an unclean place outside the city. ⁴²They shall take other stones and put them in the place of those stones, and take other plaster and plaster the house.

43If the disease breaks out again in the house, after he has taken out the stones and scraped the house and plastered it, ⁴⁴the priest shall go and make inspection; if the disease has spread in the house, it is a spreading leprous*ᵃ* disease in the house; it is unclean. ⁴⁵He shall have the house torn down, its stones and timber and all the plaster of the house, and taken outside the city to an unclean place. ⁴⁶All who enter the house while it is shut up shall be unclean until the evening; ⁴⁷and all who sleep in the house shall wash their clothes; and all who eat in the house shall wash their clothes.

48If the priest comes and makes an inspection, and the disease has not spread in the house after the house was plastered, the priest shall pronounce the house clean; the disease is healed. ⁴⁹For the cleansing of the house he shall take two birds, with cedarwood and crimson yarn and hyssop, ⁵⁰and shall slaughter one of the birds over fresh water in an earthen vessel, ⁵¹and shall take the cedarwood and the hyssop and the crimson yarn, along with the living bird, and dip them in the blood of the slaughtered bird and the fresh water, and sprinkle the house seven times. ⁵²Thus he shall cleanse the house with the blood of the

ᵇA term for several skin diseases; precise meaning uncertain

NRSV

bird, and with the fresh water, and with the living bird, and with the cedarwood and hyssop and crimson yarn; [53]and he shall let the living bird go out of the city into the open field; so he shall make atonement for the house, and it shall be clean.

[54]This is the ritual for any leprous[a] disease: for an itch, [55]for leprous[a] diseases in clothing and houses, [56]and for a swelling or an eruption or a spot, [57]to determine when it is unclean and when it is clean. This is the ritual for leprous[a] diseases.

[a] A term for several skin diseases; precise meaning uncertain

COMMENTARY

Leviticus 13–14 takes up various pathological phenomena referred to by the Hebrew term צרעת (ṣāraʿat), originally understood as a "stroke," from an alleged verbal root that implies someone is "struck [by God]." This etymology, however, remains elusive. The Greek translators rendered the Hebrew term as λέπρα (lepra), meaning "a scaly condition," which in turn was introduced into the Vg. Apparently, during the Middle Ages lepra was identified with the disease we now call leprosy. Formerly, the Greeks referred to this same disease as elephantiasis Graecorum or elephas.

A nineteenth-century Norwegian physician named Hansen identified the microorganism (Mycobacterium leprae) that causes the real leprosy (1871), so it has been customary to refer to that disease as Hansen's Disease, or Hansenitis. Under most circumstances, Hansen's disease is not contagious. It develops slowly and exhibits distinctive characteristics. It changes color; It develops growths on the skin; and most uniquely of all, the affected parts experience a loss of sensitivity to pain. In extreme cases, the extremities, the nose, the eyes, and the hair rot and fall away.

Hansen's disease is known in only two principal types. The nodular or lepromatous form is characterized by the appearance of soft, spongy lumps on the skin and a general thickening of the skin tissues. Often these lumps will develop into painless ulcers that secrete pus if they are left unattended. Meanwhile, the mucous membranes of the nose and throat begin to degener-

ate, affecting, in the disease's advanced stages, other internal organs. The other form of Hansen's disease is the anesthetic or tuberculoid variety. This form is less severe, but its main telltale sign is a degeneration of nerves in the skin. This results in a discoloration of patches of skin that no longer have any sensation. Frequently, ulcers develop on these affected patches. In severe cases the extremities fall off. Often this disease lasts as long as thirty years. The favored medication for Hansen's disease is chaulmoogra oil, a derivative from the seed of an Indian shrub. Today various antibiotics have been used and some unusual results have come from the use of thalidomide.[74]

Clinical leprosy has been around for a long time. Some have supposed its existence in India and China in 4000 BCE. The disease is attested in Mesopotamia in the third millennium BCE, and there is at least one case of it in an Egyptian mummy.

The most difficult question for the exegete is whether the Hebrew term ṣāraʿat is to be equated with Hansen's disease. Interestingly enough, even though everyone will agree that ṣāraʿat is of uncertain etymology, almost all modern commentators are adamant on the point that it cannot mean leprosy. Why there is such intransigence on this one aspect of the argument is baffling unless

74. See the following discussions of leprosy and skin diseases in the Bible: S. G. Browne, Leprosy in the Bible (London: Christian Medical Fellowship, 1970); E. V. Hulse, "The Nature of Biblical 'Leprosy' and the Use of Alternative Medical Terms in Modern Translations of the Bible," PEQ 107 (1975) 87-105.

it is to protect modern sufferers of this malady from the stigma of being under the judgment of God.

Ṣāraʿat surely includes many more ailments than Hansen's disease, but it would appear that Hansen's disease is one of them. In the Greek world *lepra* was a generic term for multiple skin diseases, just as the word *cancer* is used today as a generic term to describe any type of malignant growths. But there are numerous types of cancer, some that respond to treatment and some that do not. Therefore, *ṣāraʿat* is probably also a general term for a wide class of skin diseases, one of which no doubt includes leprosy.

Most render *ṣāraʿat* as "scales" or a "scaly [affliction]." Medical personnel who have studied these chapters have come up with a variety of suggestions for the plethora of diseases described under the general term *ṣāraʿat*. Among the suggestions have been eczema, psoriasis, impetigo, favus, and vitiligo. Yet no one of these identifications has commanded the agreement of the rest of the scholarly community. For example, some complain that such chronic skin diseases as these will not disappear or even change within a one- or two-week period when the priest examines those suffering from these so-called scaly conditions in chap. 13. Therefore, Jacob Milgrom settles simply for "scale disease" as his translation for the Hebrew *ṣāraʿat*.[75] We are in general agreement with this conclusion, except that Milgrom is too certain, on very slim grounds, that one manifestation of this scale disease was not leprosy.[76] But this conclusion is too confident in an area where all must admit a great deal of puzzlement. Others, such as J. Preuss,[77] are not that confident and do not hesitate to include leprosy in this category.

There are several reasons for equating *ṣāraʿat* with leprosy, at least in some of the biblical texts. First, except for Lev 13:9-11, only the earliest stages of the disease are described; therefore, some of its distinctive features that come at the end of the disease are not yet present. Second, since it was desirable to get the earliest possible identification of leprosy, other forms of skin disease were noted and acted upon promptly; not everything described here is leprosy. Third, the objection that

highly contagious persons like the assumed leprous Naaman and Gehazi would not be left to walk around in society is countered by the fact that modern medical opinion is not at all sure that leprosy is that contagious.

The conditions exhibited in other parts of Scripture seem to indicate something more serious than a mere case of psoriasis. Aaron's words to Moses are almost incomprehensible if Miriam was not struck with leprosy, for he pleaded, "Do not let her be like a stillborn infant coming from its mother's womb with its flesh half eaten away" (Num 12:12 NIV). Surely these words answer the objection that the use of the Hebrew word *ṣāra-ʿat* (see Num 12:10*b*) is never connected with rotting or mutilation of the body. Psoriasis is bad enough, but it never caused half the flesh to be eaten away. Healing a case of leprosy, complained the king of Israel when a letter arrived asking him to heal the foreign enemy leader Naaman of his "leprosy" (2 Kgs 5:1), was equated with being "God . . . [with the ability to] kill and bring back to life" (2 Kgs 5:7 NIV). No doubt Naaman had exhausted all the regular avenues for help in Syria, and he remained uncured. His attitude indicated that his problem was something more serious than a scaly skin condition.

We conclude that leprosy is mentioned in this chapter, especially where the person is declared to be "unclean," but a vast number of other skin conditions is also represented by the one Hebrew term *ṣāraʿat*.

Leviticus 13:1-59 provides a description of various scaly diseases: discoloration (vv. 2-8); swellings (vv. 9-17); ulcers (vv. 18-23); burns (vv. 24-28); ringworm (vv. 29-37); rashes (vv. 38-39); baldness (vv. 40-44); life-styles of certified carriers (vv. 45-46); and scaly disease in clothing (vv. 47-58).

Chapter 14 rehearses cleansing rituals for scaly diseases, particularly cleansing ritual after healing (vv. 2-31) and cleansing ritual for houses (vv. 34-53).

13:1-59. 13:1. The descriptions of the diseases that follow in chaps. 13–14 are not to be judged by the state of ancient learning at that time or as the product of folklore and pagan therapeutic practices. Leviticus 13:1 decisively affirms that the Lord reveals these matters to both Moses and Aaron. This material is not to be compared to the Greek temples and the god Asclepius, the deity of healing. The role of Aaron and his sons in these

---

75. Milgrom, *Leviticus 1-16,* 817.
76. Ibid., 816.
77. As noted by Milgrom, *Leviticus 1-16,* 816. J. Preuss, *Biblisch-talmüdische Medizin,* trans. F. Rosner (New York: KTAV; reprint, New York: Sanhedrin, 1978). The original edition came from Berlin (S. Karger, 1911).

matters is entirely ritualistic; there is no attempt at giving medical treatment or cures. Thus chaps. 13–14 do not present a combination of a religious observance along with a center for medical treatment. The concern, as in this whole section of chaps. 11–15, is to present all persons in such a condition as to make them qualified and fit to enter into the worship of God as holy persons.

13:2-8. The first type of scaly disease is that of discoloration. As soon as an area of skin on the body changes its appearance, appearing to be different from the skin around it, especially if the hair in the area turns white, the person is placed under quarantine for a week (v. 4). Both forms of Hansen's disease start with a pink or white discoloration of the skin; that appears to be what is suspected here. If at the end of that first week the symptoms are inconclusive, the person must be isolated for yet another week before being examined by the priest and declared to be clean. If subsequent to the person's being pronounced clean the infection begins to spread, the person must go to the priest again and be pronounced unclean. This first test applied by the priest, then, turns on two criteria: Has the hair turned white? Is the affected area deeper than the skin? The person who is pronounced clean may have had no more than a rash or an allergic reaction. Once pronounced clean, a person can resume a normal life after washing all the clothing.

13:9-17. The second type of scaly disease involves swelling. In this case, the diagnosis involves sores on the skin that are abnormally white mixed in with some patches of normal color. In this situation, the whitened membranous cavity has also turned the hair white, and there is a lesion exhibiting ulcerating tissue.

This is a "chronic skin disease" (v. 11) and may be a documented case of Hansen's disease. Typically in Hansen's disease, the hairs growing on the affected area break off, split, or become depigmented. Also, in that disease, the shiny white vesicles rupture and discharge a white substance. This is probably the nodular or lepromatous form of leprosy (vv. 9-11).

But if the skin condition covers a person's whole body from head to foot (vv. 12-17)—yet no swellings, sores, lesions, or ulcerations are connected with it—it is probably something like vitiligo (*acquired leucoderma*), a condition where the skin loses its normal color and becomes white. Since it is only a condition where the skin loses its pigmentation, this individual can be pronounced clean. But should sores and lesions break out subsequently, that person's status would be changed from clean to unclean.

The constant emphases of chaps. 13–14 are on being clean and being unclean. In these two chapters alone, variations of "clean" (טהר *ṭāhēr*) appear thirty-six times while forms of "unclean" (טמא *ṭāmēʾ*) occur thirty times. Only four times does the word נרפא (*nirpāʾ*, "be healed") occur.[78] Accordingly, we are involved in ritual questions here and not medical ones.

13:18-23. Another condition involves a boil or an ulcer on the person's skin that has healed and then suddenly erupted where the ulcer had been. If there is discoloration of the hair, it is treated as being very serious and once again could have been a clinical form of leprosy. But if the swelling is pale, not deep, and without any white hairs, it is a minor inflammation of old scar tissue. It might be no more than staphylococci or another skin disease known as carbuncle. In this case the priest may pronounce the person clean.

13:24-28. Similar provisions are made for suspicious symptoms following a burn. When a burn produces a pustule, it presents a potentially unclean condition, especially when the hair changes color and the infection penetrates deep into the layer of skin that carries the nerves. The quarantine procedures are the same once again: seven days in isolation with an examination by the priest. If the infection has spread, that one is pronounced unclean; however, if there is no change in the affected area and it has not spread, the priest is to pronounce the person clean (v. 28).

13:29-37. Still another type of skin disease involves an "itch" on the scalp, and also in the beard for men. This condition is serious enough to be called a נגע (*negaʿ*, "a plague"; v. 29 KJV; cf. NIV). In v. 30 it is called a נתק (*neteq*), from the root meaning "to tear off"; in this context it means any tearing off of scabs by scratching. Some have rendered it "scall," meaning any scaly or scabby disease of the skin, even though the word technically refers to the condition of the hair

78. Milgrom, *Leviticus 1-16*, 817, quoting the statistical work of Wright and Jones.

follicles. It is a situation where the hair follicles are being "torn" from the scalp after "splitting."

The critical telltale sign in this instance is the presence of yellow hair, a condition characteristic of favus. Favus belongs to the ringworm group of afflictions (*tinea tonsurans* or *tinea favosus*). Ringworm is usually found among children and is contracted by a fungus found around animals. Normally, this ringworm invades the scalp, penetrating the skin and forming yellow saucer-like crusts. It is an infectious disease that requires treatment.[79] Others, less convincingly, have suggested that it is a severe case of acne.

Verse 31 is problematic, for as it stands it does not represent the opposite of v. 30, as we would expect. If v. 30 has recessed lesions and yellow hair in the affected area, the reverse of this would be no recessed lesions and no yellow hair in v. 31. However, v. 31 has no recessed lesions and no black hair. C. F. Keil suggests emending the Hebrew text from שׁחר (*ṣāḥōr*, "black") to צהר (*ṣāḥōr*, "yellow").[80] But such a change would be unnecessary since it fails to understand the progressive stages of moving into the state of being declared clean. Verse 30 records two symptoms, but in v. 31 it has been reduced to only one symptom: the absence of normal black hair, a condition that equals the presence of yellow hair, even though the other symptom has now left the person. Since a final determination cannot be made as yet, the quarantine is continued.

13:38-39. These verses raise another case. Patches of skin, in this example, go completely white. In Hebrew it is termed בהק (*bōhaq*, "brightness"). Here the hair is not discolored, and it is only skin deep. The RSV uses the obsolete English word *tetter* for the set of skin disorders represented here. They would include eczema, impetigo, acne, and perhaps herpes simplex. The person is pronounced clean.

13:40-44. While ordinary baldness is not equated with anything unclean, another type of baldness evidences reddish-white membranous cavities on the scalp. If the sore begins to ooze, it probably is serious and belongs to the types of skin diseases that make a person unclean. The rest of the procedure is the same as for all the other cases.

13:45-46. When the diagnoses of these skin diseases find that they are defiling, sufferers must rip up their clothes, let their hair become unkempt, and, while covering their lips, cry, "Unclean! Unclean!" to anyone who approaches them. Moreover, they have to live alone outside the camp in isolation from the congregation. All three of these actions—tearing the clothes (cf. Gen 37:34; 2 Sam 1:11), messing up the hair, and covering the lower part of the face (cf. Ezek 24:17, 22; Mic 3:7)—are signs of mourning for the dead. So serious is the state of uncleanness that it is similar to the state of death. Living outside the camp is not equivalent to our modern idea of "getting away from it all," as Gordon Wenham reminds us, but is living in the place most removed from the presence of God, a place to which the sinner and the impure were banished (Lev 10:4-5; Num 5:1-4; 12:14-15; 31:19-24).[81]

13:47-58. The discussion moves from skin diseases to types of mold that affect clothing and other household articles. However, the same word that has been used for the "scaly diseases" (צרעת *ṣāraʿat*) of the skin is used for abnormal surface conditions that show fungoid or sporoid infections. The operating principle is that disease, like all forms of uncleanness, is transmitted by contact (cf. Lev 11:24-40).

The presence of a greenish or reddish mold in the warp and woof of the fibers of a garment, in an animal skin garment, in a household article, or in the walls of a dwelling was enough to place it under suspicion of the regular seven-day quarantine. The reference to "the warp and woof" (vv. 48-49, 51-53, 56-59) seems strange here since it cannot refer to two different types of yarn, in that Israelites were forbidden to mix yarns and material in garments (see Deut 22:11). But the reference to the warp is to the vertical, drawn threads on the loom, and the woof designates the threads woven in by means of the shuttle, going across horizontally. The mold or mildew, then, is not just a surface matter; it has penetrated into the very fabric itself.

The process for declaring an article clean or unclean is once again invoked. After the examination of the garment or article, each is shut up

---

79. I am indebted to R. K. Harrison, *Leviticus: An Introduction and Commentary* (Downers Grove, Ill.: InterVarsity, 1980) 144-45, for his clear discussion on this point and on several other key points in this chapter. His discussion of Leviticus 13 is one of the best I have seen.

80. C. F. Keil, *The Pentateuch* (Grand Rapids: Eerdmans, 1950) 2:381.

81. Wenham, *Leviticus,* 200-201.

for a week. If at the end of that time the mold has spread, the article is declared unclean and has to be burned (v. 52). But if the mildew or mold has not spread, the priest orders it to be washed and isolated for another seven days. And if after another week's wait there is no improvement or the damage has spread, it is destroyed.

13:59. The concluding verse of this chapter reiterates the theme of this section: These are the regulations on clean and unclean. Clearly, the law of cleanness does not focus solely on the spiritual aspect of cleanness; rather, it puts both physical well-being and spiritual vitality together and demonstrates that men and women worship God holistically. It is impossible in this view, either to be holy or to worship a holy God without meeting the conditions for holiness by being made clean.

14:1-32. It would be a serious blow to the picture of God's gracious character if chap. 13 were to stand by itself with no hope for restoration and cleansing once someone is found to be unclean. Chapter 14 provides the companion piece to chap. 13. It deals with the ceremonies for the restoration of the healed leper or fellow sufferer of scaly diseases.

The ceremonies for the restoration of these former sufferers are staged in two parts. The first takes place outside the camp. The second takes place inside the camp on the eighth day following the first ceremony. This latter ceremony consists of offering every major type of sacrifice except the peace offering. After being anointed, the newly declared clean worshiper is once more a full member of the covenant of God with all its rights and responsibilities.

14:2-9. First comes the ritual outside the camp. Since the individual is still unclean in the sight of the law, it is impossible, to go to the priest or to the sanctuary inside the camp. Instead, one has to summon the priest to come outside the camp and examine the skin.

If the priest is convinced that the person is cured, two live clean birds are brought to the priest along with some cedar wood, scarlet yarn, and hyssop. Then the priest orders that one bird be killed over a clay pot filled with fresh water taken from a stream or spring that is flowing. The blood of the slain bird is received in this clay pot with fresh water. Next, the other bird, the cedar wood, the scarlet yarn, and the hyssop are all dipped into the clay pot with the blood of the slain bird. The priest then takes the hyssop, perhaps bound with the cedar and the scarlet yarn, and sprinkles blood from the clay pot seven times on the one newly pronounced clean. Then the bird stained with the blood of the slain bird is released and set free to return to its nest. The person for whom the ceremony has been performed washes the clothes, shaves off all the hair, bathes in water, and finally comes home to the camp. But this is just the beginning of the restoration process.

On the seventh day, the individual shaves again and undergoes another ritual bath for cleansing to be fit to enter the tabernacle courts on the eighth day (v. 9).

The exact meaning of the symbolism here is not altogether clear. Even the identity of the hyssop is not secure since there are several varieties: thyme, sage, or the gray-green marjoram plant (*Origanum maru*). The last-named variety appears to be correct, since it is used in Samaritan Passover celebrations.

The slaying of one bird and the releasing of the other are certainly also filled with symbolism. But of what? The two clean birds are characteristic of the holy nation. The bird's blood sprinkled on the individual undergoing this rite identifies that one as once again restored to the fellowship of the congregation. Thus a death makes possible the restoration.

The release of the other bird probably symbolizes the new life that the cured person has been given. Accordingly, it is not by means of death alone but also by the release of life that new life can now be experienced. Many see the same pattern here in the two birds as is evident in the two goats on the Day of Atonement—especially in the release of the scapegoat (16:21-22), i.e., sins forgiven on the basis of a substitute and sins forgotten as the led-away goat is removed, never to return to the camp.

14:10-20. On the eighth day (vv. 10-11), a concept that is becoming familiar to us by now, the once unclean person appears before Yahweh in the tent of meeting with a male lamb for a guilt offering, a male lamb for a sin offering, a ewe lamb for a burnt offering, and about one-third of a bushel (about 6 quarts or 6.5 liters) of fine flour ("three-tenths of an ephah") for a grain offering along with about two-thirds of a pint of oil.

The oil and the lamb for the guilt offering are

consecrated to the Lord by lifting them up as an elevation offering. (On the issue of a wave offering, see our comments on 7:28-36.) It is most unusual to hear that the whole lamb is elevated in dedication to God. Then the male lamb is slain as prescribed in the guilt offering.

What follows in vv. 14-20 is most astonishing! As is true in the ordination ceremony of the high priest, where Moses uses the blood of the sacrifice with specially dedicated oil (see comments on 8:22-24), so here the blood of the guilt offering is used with ordinary oil, which the cleansed Israelite brings. The priest anoints the person's right ear, the thumb on the right hand, and the big toe of the right foot, first with the blood of the offering and then with the oil. The significance is the same for the cleansed person as it is for the priest: God sets apart ears to hear God's voice, hands to perform the works of righteousness, and feet to walk in the way of the Lord.

Just as the priest is anointed with holy oil, so also the cleansed person is anointed with oil; however, it is ordinary oil. The officiating priest would pour some of the oil in the palm of his hand, and then with his right forefinger, he would sprinkle some of the oil seven times before the Lord (v. 27). With the remaining oil in his hand, the priest would put the oil on the same places where he had smeared the blood: the offerer's right ear, right thumb, and right big toe (v. 28). What is left of the oil in the palm of his hand the priest applies to the head of the one who is to be cleansed in order "to make atonement" (v. 29) for the person.

14:21-32. The prominence given to the guilt offering can be seen not only in the special use of the blood, as already described, but also in the fact that no diminution is allowed for bringing the lamb as a guilt offering even though all the other offerings can be diminished because of a person's poverty (vv. 21-22). Some may question why the guilt offering should receive such prominence. Two answers are generally given. First, the guilt offering serves as a reparation and satisfaction for the person's long absence from the service of God while he or she was in an unclean state. (But why is this not required after a lengthy illness [cf. Luke 8:43]?) Second, the guilt offering is necessary because the seriousness of this illness may suggest that it is the result of some sin the person com-

mitted. (But the thesis that all illness or suffering is the result of sin is too reductionistic and was condemned by Jesus [see John 9:2-3].) Neither answer is completely satisfactory, though if preference is to be given, the first is better than the second. A good response to the first objection, however, might be that it is not the duration of the absence from the sanctuary worship services that is in question, but the nature of the ailment from which deliverance is gained; it is like a dead person's being brought back to life. No doubt more of a renewed consecration of life is being symbolized, for note that this guilt offering deviates slightly from the standard guilt offering in that both the lamb and the two-thirds of a pint of oil are treated as an elevation offering, thereby signifying the person's self-surrender to God.

The sin offering that comes next signifies purification and the purging of uncleanness. Then come the whole burnt offering and the grain offering, both of which indicate the offerer's total dedication to do the will of God and thankfulness and gratitude for being healed.

As with the cleansing of the woman after childbirth (chap. 12), so special concessions are made on the other three offerings (sin, burnt, and grain) for persons who are unable to afford the standard offerings. While the guilt offering standard remains the same, a dove or a young pigeon can be substituted for each of the sin and burnt offerings. Also the grain offering is reduced to one-tenth of an ephah (about two quarts, or approximately two liters) of fine flour along with the two-thirds of a pint of oil.

14:33-53. A final section in chap. 14 deals with some sort of mold, blight, rot, or fungal growth that produced discoloration or recessed lesions in the plaster or mud used to cover the stones forming the walls of buildings.

14:34-42. The symptoms are the same as they are for צרעת (ṣāraʿat) in humans and those affecting leather and fabrics. The situation has the potential for being something like the plague of God (v. 34; literally "I will afflict an eruptive plague upon a house") and it was treated as contagious and dangerous.

When a homeowner reports this condition to the priest, the priest orders that the building be emptied of its contents before he inspects it. It is a precautionary move, since everything must be declared unclean if the house comes under quarantine. The priest then inspects the place. If he detects greenish or reddish lesions on the plaster-facing of any of the stones, either inside or outside the building, he imposes a quarantine for seven days.

At the end of the seven days, he makes a second inspection. If the affected area has enlarged, the priest orders the removal of the infected stones with their plaster to an unclean place outside the camp reserved for such materials, and new stones and plaster are to be put in their stead.

14:43-47. Now if after all these precautions the plague persists and breaks out once more, the building or house is leveled—all its wood, stones, mud, and plaster are taken outside the camp or city. It is unclean! What is more, all who have entered the building in the meantime, have slept there, or have eaten there during its period of quarantine are to launder their clothes.

14:48-53. Alternatively, if the priest has not noticed any enlargement of the infected area, the dwelling is pronounced clean and the owner can proceed with the ritual of purification. These rites conform to those performed for a person who has recovered from leprosy or a scaly disease (14:1-7).

Two live birds are brought to the priest. One is slain over an earthen vessel containing fresh water. Then the other bird, the cedar wood, the scarlet yarn, and the hyssop are dipped in the vessel containing the fresh water and the blood of the slain bird. The priest then sprinkles the dwelling with the blood and water mixture seven times to purify it with the bird's blood (vv. 51-52). Finally, the live bird is released in the open fields outside town.

The paralleling of this rite of purification with the purification of humans is almost exact. The only difference is that instead of shaving the hair, as humans must do, it is paralleled by scraping the plaster from the building stones. And instead of applying blood and oil to the building, which is done for humans, blood and water are combined to be applied to the dwelling.

14:54-57. These verses summarize the range of chaps. 13–14. Enveloped in these two chapters are the "regulations" (תורת *tôrāt*) given by God (vv. 54, 57). Nothing in these chapters even approaches anything like magic, folklore, or the lore about the gods in pagan literature. It is fair, reasonable, rational, and cautious in its approach to preserving the physical health of the community.

REFLECTIONS

1. Leviticus 14 is unique in being the only section in the Law where hyssop is used in connection with cleansing. The psalmist made a reference to such cleansing with his prayer "Cleanse me with hyssop, and I will be clean;/ wash me, and I will be whiter than snow" (Ps 51:7 NIV). Just as the person once afflicted with leprosy or some other scaly disease would go to the priest after recovering and was pronounced clean when blood and water were applied by a hyssop branch, so the psalmist sought a cleansing touch.

2. God is concerned not only about our souls but also about the welfare of our bodies. We are to remember that same inclusive ministry when it comes to deciding what indeed is the mission of the church. A concerned approach that does not lose perspective on either the spiritual or the physical aspects of human life is in keeping with the expressed will and ways of God.

3. Although leprosy was sometimes imposed as a punishment from God (see Miriam's case in Num 12:10; Gehaz's case in 2 Kgs 5:27), it was by no means the indication par excellence of sin. Biblical authors had better metaphors for sin, such as blindness, stiff-neckedness or obduracy of the will, and hardness of heart. The real tragedy of the severe cases of skin disease, like leprosy, was the person's isolation from fellowship with God and from the people of God. The force of the application to be made in these two chapters, then, is that any and all types of uncleanness separate us from God. The holiness to which this book constantly calls its audience is that of separation *to* God, avoiding what separates us *from* God.

4. The cleansing ritual for the leper, or other sufferers of seriously affected skin diseases, took place outside the camp. Thus, just as the priest had to go outside the camp in pronouncing the person clean, so also Christ went to the cross outside the city walls to atone for human sin (see Heb 13:12).

5. The bird that was killed and the bird that was released alive are graphic illustrations of the double affirmations of Paul that Jesus was put to death for our trespasses but was raised from the dead for our justification (see Rom 4:25). The sprinkling of blood on the leper was a sign that one's life was cleansed through a life vicariously offered up on one's behalf. That offering was accepted in trust by the person needing to be cleansed. But the releasing of the live bird indicated that new life was given, as if one had just come back from the dead.

6. In the two-bird ritual, the blood represented the basis for one's justification, while the anointing oil, in addition to the sprinkled blood, indicated the sustaining presence of God's Holy Spirit. Thus the cleansing of the sufferer argued against a life of selfish pursuit of one's own goals apart from God; the cleansing enabled the one who had been unclean to live in righteousness and holiness with God.

7. The act of smearing the blood on the right ear, right thumb, and right big toe was done to reflect an inclusive claim on a person's total body. It indicated that every area of one's life was affected by the atonement.

LEVITICUS 15:1-33, THE UNCLEANNESS OF GENITAL DISCHARGES

NIV

15 The LORD said to Moses and Aaron, [2]"Speak to the Israelites and say to them: 'When any man has a bodily discharge, the discharge is unclean. [3]Whether it continues flowing from his body or is blocked, it will make him unclean. This is how his discharge will bring about uncleanness:

[4]"'Any bed the man with a discharge lies on will be unclean, and anything he sits on will be unclean. [5]Anyone who touches his bed must wash his clothes and bathe with water, and he will be unclean till evening. [6]Whoever sits on anything that the man with a discharge sat on must wash his clothes and bathe with water, and he will be unclean till evening.

[7]"'Whoever touches the man who has a discharge must wash his clothes and bathe with water, and he will be unclean till evening.

[8]"'If the man with the discharge spits on someone who is clean, that person must wash his

NRSV

15 The LORD spoke to Moses and Aaron, saying: [2]Speak to the people of Israel and say to them:

When any man has a discharge from his member,[a] his discharge makes him ceremonially unclean. [3]The uncleanness of his discharge is this: whether his member[a] flows with his discharge, or his member[a] is stopped from discharging, it is uncleanness for him. [4]Every bed on which the one with the discharge lies shall be unclean; and everything on which he sits shall be unclean. [5]Anyone who touches his bed shall wash his clothes, and bathe in water, and be unclean until the evening. [6]All who sit on anything on which the one with the discharge has sat shall wash their clothes, and bathe in water, and be unclean until the evening. [7]All who touch the body of the one with the discharge shall wash their clothes, and bathe in water, and be unclean until the evening.

[a]Heb *flesh*

NIV

clothes and bathe with water, and he will be unclean till evening.

9" 'Everything the man sits on when riding will be unclean, 10and whoever touches any of the things that were under him will be unclean till evening; whoever picks up those things must wash his clothes and bathe with water, and he will be unclean till evening.

11" "Anyone the man with a discharge touches without rinsing his hands with water must wash his clothes and bathe with water, and he will be unclean till evening.

12" "A clay pot that the man touches must be broken, and any wooden article is to be rinsed with water.

13" 'When a man is cleansed from his discharge, he is to count off seven days for his ceremonial cleansing; he must wash his clothes and bathe himself with fresh water, and he will be clean. 14On the eighth day he must take two doves or two young pigeons and come before the LORD to the entrance to the Tent of Meeting and give them to the priest. 15The priest is to sacrifice them, the one for a sin offering and the other for a burnt offering. In this way he will make atonement before the LORD for the man because of his discharge.

16" 'When a man has an emission of semen, he must bathe his whole body with water, and he will be unclean till evening. 17Any clothing or leather that has semen on it must be washed with water, and it will be unclean till evening. 18When a man lies with a woman and there is an emission of semen, both must bathe with water, and they will be unclean till evening.

19" 'When a woman has her regular flow of blood, the impurity of her monthly period will last seven days, and anyone who touches her will be unclean till evening.

20" 'Anything she lies on during her period will be unclean, and anything she sits on will be unclean. 21Whoever touches her bed must wash his clothes and bathe with water, and he will be unclean till evening. 22Whoever touches anything she sits on must wash his clothes and bathe with water, and he will be unclean till evening. 23Whether it is the bed or anything she was sitting

NRSV

8If the one with the discharge spits on persons who are clean, then they shall wash their clothes, and bathe in water, and be unclean until the evening. 9Any saddle on which the one with the discharge rides shall be unclean. 10All who touch anything that was under him shall be unclean until the evening, and all who carry such a thing shall wash their clothes, and bathe in water, and be unclean until the evening. 11All those whom the one with the discharge touches without his having rinsed his hands in water shall wash their clothes, and bathe in water, and be unclean until the evening. 12Any earthen vessel that the one with the discharge touches shall be broken; and every vessel of wood shall be rinsed in water.

13When the one with a discharge is cleansed of his discharge, he shall count seven days for his cleansing; he shall wash his clothes and bathe his body in fresh water, and he shall be clean. 14On the eighth day he shall take two turtledoves or two pigeons and come before the LORD to the entrance of the tent of meeting and give them to the priest. 15The priest shall offer them, one for a sin offering and the other for a burnt offering; and the priest shall make atonement on his behalf before the LORD for his discharge.

16If a man has an emission of semen, he shall bathe his whole body in water, and be unclean until the evening. 17Everything made of cloth or of skin on which the semen falls shall be washed with water, and be unclean until the evening. 18If a man lies with a woman and has an emission of semen, both of them shall bathe in water, and be unclean until the evening.

19When a woman has a discharge of blood that is her regular discharge from her body, she shall be in her impurity for seven days, and whoever touches her shall be unclean until the evening. 20Everything upon which she lies during her impurity shall be unclean; everything also upon which she sits shall be unclean. 21Whoever touches her bed shall wash his clothes, and bathe in water, and be unclean until the evening. 22Whoever touches anything upon which she sits shall wash his clothes, and bathe in water, and be unclean until the evening; 23whether it is the bed or anything upon which she sits, when he touches it he shall be unclean until the evening.

NIV

on, when anyone touches it, he will be unclean till evening.

²⁴" 'If a man lies with her and her monthly flow touches him, he will be unclean for seven days; any bed he lies on will be unclean.

²⁵" 'When a woman has a discharge of blood for many days at a time other than her monthly period or has a discharge that continues beyond her period, she will be unclean as long as she has the discharge, just as in the days of her period. ²⁶Any bed she lies on while her discharge continues will be unclean, as is her bed during her monthly period, and anything she sits on will be unclean, as during her period. ²⁷Whoever touches them will be unclean; he must wash his clothes and bathe with water, and he will be unclean till evening.

²⁸" 'When she is cleansed from her discharge, she must count off seven days, and after that she will be ceremonially clean. ²⁹On the eighth day she must take two doves or two young pigeons and bring them to the priest at the entrance to the Tent of Meeting. ³⁰The priest is to sacrifice one for a sin offering and the other for a burnt offering. In this way he will make atonement for her before the LORD for the uncleanness of her discharge.

³¹" 'You must keep the Israelites separate from things that make them unclean, so they will not die in their uncleanness for defiling my dwelling place,ᵃ which is among them.' "

³²These are the regulations for a man with a discharge, for anyone made unclean by an emission of semen, ³³for a woman in her monthly period, for a man or a woman with a discharge, and for a man who lies with a woman who is ceremonially unclean.

ᵃ31 Or my tabernacle

NRSV

²⁴If any man lies with her, and her impurity falls on him, he shall be unclean seven days; and every bed on which he lies shall be unclean.

²⁵If a woman has a discharge of blood for many days, not at the time of her impurity, or if she has a discharge beyond the time of her impurity, all the days of the discharge she shall continue in uncleanness; as in the days of her impurity, she shall be unclean. ²⁶Every bed on which she lies during all the days of her discharge shall be treated as the bed of her impurity; and everything on which she sits shall be unclean, as in the uncleanness of her impurity. ²⁷Whoever touches these things shall be unclean, and shall wash his clothes, and bathe in water, and be unclean until the evening. ²⁸If she is cleansed of her discharge, she shall count seven days, and after that she shall be clean. ²⁹On the eighth day she shall take two turtledoves or two pigeons and bring them to the priest to the entrance of the tent of meeting. ³⁰The priest shall offer one for a sin offering and the other for a burnt offering; and the priest shall make atonement on her behalf before the LORD for her unclean discharge.

³¹Thus you shall keep the people of Israel separate from their uncleanness, so that they do not die in their uncleanness by defiling my tabernacle that is in their midst.

³²This is the ritual for those who have a discharge: for him who has an emission of semen, becoming unclean thereby, ³³for her who is in the infirmity of her period, for anyone, male or female, who has a discharge, and for the man who lies with a woman who is unclean.

COMMENTARY

Let it be said immediately that coition and the legitimate use of one's sexuality are meant as gifts to creatures from the Creator for their enjoyment. But this chapter does not address the question of the legitimacy of sex or its satisfaction; rather, it

deals more narrowly with certain qualifications, or lack thereof, for entering into the presence of God in corporate worship.

Some have thought that chap. 15 would be placed more accurately just prior to chap. 12—thereby grouping the uncleanness that comes from genital discharges with the uncleanness that comes from childbirth. This suggested relocation of the chapter only indicates that the organizing principle for this section has not yet been discovered.

The organizational principle may instead be that the various uncleanness laws were arranged, as Gordon Wenham suggests, according to the length of time that the affected person was unclean.[82] Chapter 11 deals with food laws that can bring permanent uncleanness. Chapter 12 limits the uncleanness of childbirth to a maximum of eighty days. Chapters 13–14 specify that the uncleanness lasts as long as the skin disease persists, but the maximum time for uncleanness with genital discharges (chap. 15) is merely one week.

Whatever the real explanation is, chaps. 11–15 are preparatory to the central event in the book, the Day of Atonement. Leviticus 16:16 makes clear that the basic purpose of these laws of clean and unclean is to teach Israel a sensitivity to uncleanness and sin, in whatever form they manifest themselves. Moreover, the Israelites are to be careful about defiling the tabernacle by entering it in an unclean condition.

The outline for this chapter is a beautiful example of symmetry and balance. It treats ritual uncleanness in men first (vv. 2-17) and then ceremonial uncleanness in women second (vv. 19-30). In both cases, it takes up forms that are chronic and sporadic; however, the pattern is reversed in the women's section from the way it appears in the men's section, thereby giving a chiasmic pattern (a literary device where A, B appears B, A in the parallel situation). The final touch of artistic balance can be seen in the verse that joins the male/female sections; v. 18 mentions coition of male and female in the act of oneness as originally designed by the Creator in Gen 2:24.

15:1-18. This chapter deals with a number of different discharges from the sexual organs. The word בשׂר (bāśār, meaning "flesh," "meat," "body," or even "man") probably is used in this context as a euphemism for the male sex organ, a sense it carries in Gen 17:13 and Ezek 16:26 (literally Ezekiel says, "The Egyptians, your neighbors, [the ones] big of flesh" גדלי בשׂר gidlê bāśār]; cf. Ezek 23:20).

The word for "emission" (זוב zôb) is rare with

this nuance of meaning, for it appears with this sense of emission only in Leviticus. Its meaning is clarified in v. 3 by another rare word רר (rār) from the noun ריר (rîr), meaning "slimy juice" or "saliva" (see 1 Sam 21:14 [English 13]; Job 6:6); thus a male discharge runs from his "flesh" periodically.

It is almost impossible to say precisely what this emission is. Some are unhappy with the attachment of these meanings to the sexual organs only, preferring that the text would have used the word זרע (zera', "seed" or "sperm") in this immediate context if that is the meaning. But the disorder does not appear to come from any intestinal malfunction or related areas of the body; therefore, all suggestions that the emission comes from hemorrhoids, diverticulitis, or the like are probably incorrect. Instead, it is either a milder form of gonorrhea or a discharge of mucus from inflammation in the urinary tract.

Additional reasons why this cannot be a case of hemorrhoids are: (a) there is no mention of any loss of blood, a factor that would hardly have escaped some comment in a context such as the book of Leviticus; and (b) v. 19 uses "flesh" (bāśār) for a woman's vagina—thus the use of "flesh" for a man's penis seems to be required in this context.

The reference to a "stopped" or "blocked" discharge (v. 3) can mean only that the emission has ceased. If it means that the male urethra is blocked, this male is in a lot more trouble than anything these laws consider.

The presence of this discharge, though not as serious as the other forms of uncleanness spoken of in Leviticus 11–14, makes a person unclean (v. 3). Anything that the affected male sits on (a chair in v. 6 or a saddle in v. 9) is just as unclean as the bed he sleeps on (vv. 4-5), and therefore is as unclean as the flowing male himself is unclean. And whoever touches any of the affected things is also unclean, for direct contact transmits uncleanness (v. 7). The unclean person has to be careful to wash his hands, for that is another way to convey the ritual impurity (v. 11). Spittle from an unclean male (v. 8) pollutes just as much as the cooking vessels are affected when he touches them (v. 12).

The solution for this state of ritual uncleanness is not as complicated as in the cases previously discussed. The unclean man has to wait only seven days, wash himself, and on the eighth day bring two

82. Wenham, *Leviticus*, 216.

doves or two young pigeons, the least expensive of all the sacrifices, to the priest for a sin offering and a burnt offering (vv. 13-15). This solution indicates that these disorders are nowhere near the level of seriousness associated with the scaly skin diseases in chaps. 13–14.

The more intermittent or spasmodic emissions come from the emission of semen (vv. 16-17). This seems to be what Deut 23:10 refers to as a nocturnal emission, an involuntary discharge of semen that indicates no abnormality of the sex organ. While ejaculated semen is judged enough of a pollutant to make a person ceremonially unclean (just as it was likewise regarded by other Semitic peoples, the Egyptians, the Greeks, and the Romans), it does not require any sacrifices for purification. The man has only to wash himself and any affected clothing; he is unclean until evening comes. The purpose, then, seems only to prevent what is a legitimate, but ceremonially unclean, act from encroaching upon what is holy.

At the center of this chapter on discharges from sexual organs is v. 18, which deals with intercourse between a husband and a wife. It is not entirely clear why sexual intercourse should make the partners unclean, since it would seem to be the fulfillment of the divine command given in Gen 1:28. Perhaps these discharges were viewed as defiling because they were thought to contain dead matter. What the text actually provides is the mere declaration that both partners are judged to be ceremonially impure after coition. It is merely a ritual uncleanness in which both are temporarily disqualified until sundown from approaching God's holiness. Both have to bathe after engaging in the sex act. That is why sexual intercourse is not permitted before a person performs religious duties or participates in God's wars (sometimes called "holy wars"). This same idea is found elsewhere in the OT (see Exod 19:15; 1 Sam 21:5-6; 2 Sam 11:11).

15:19-30. This section deals with female discharges. A woman's uncleanness comes from her monthly period (a thought already raised in Lev 12:2, 5), called in the Hebrew her נדה (niddâ), a root that is to be compared to the cognate Akkadian term nadû, "to cast," "to hurl," or "to throw." Thus the status of a woman during menstruation is that she is unclean (cf. Gen 31:35).

Even though the niddâ lasts, as a rule, only four days, her period of uncleanness is for seven days (12:2). She remains isolated during this time.

Should a man touch her during this time, much less have sexual relations with her, each is liable to divine punishment (Lev 18:19; 20:18; Ezek 18:6; 22:10). Should her period begin while she is having intercourse with her husband, he too will be unclean for seven days.

At face value it would seem that every female beyond the age of puberty spent one week a month out of contact with the rest of society. But some have argued that a monthly menstrual cycle is a fairly recent phenomenon, due more to the change in modern Western society than a change in female physiology. In earlier times, three things kept the monthly cycle from happening as frequently as it does today: (a) Most persons married shortly after puberty, (b) children were not weaned until they were two or three years old, and (c) most persons desired large families, so the children tended to come one after another.[83]

This law is given not to demean women but, as Bernard J. Bamberger comments, to protect women from the importunities of their husbands at a time when they are physically and emotionally not ready for coitus.[84] Perhaps, more than any other sign, this demonstrates that a husband does not have sovereignty over his wife or her body; that she owes only to God.[85]

More chronic female discharges are discussed in vv. 25-30. If a flow of blood continues beyond the menstrual cycle or there is another abnormal discharge, the time of uncleanness is extended for as long as the condition lasts. That was the situation with the woman mentioned in the Gospels, who had suffered from the aggravation for twelve years (see Matt 9:20-21; Mark 5:25-33; Luke 8:43-48). It is remarkable that Jesus did not rebuke her for making him unclean. In desperation the woman acted contrary to the Levitical laws and moved into society in one last desperate attempt simply to touch the Master, hoping thereby to be healed.

Identifying all the possible sources of the bleeding mentioned in this section on chronic female discharges is impossible. Again it has been suggested that gonorrhea is one of the diseases, but no evidence makes this suggestion secure.

As soon as the woman's complaint clears up, she

---

83. Wenham, *Leviticus*, 223-24.
84. Bernard J. Bamberger, "Leviticus," in *The Torah: A Modern Commentary*, 850.
85. See the extended argument in Walter C. Kaiser, Jr., *Toward Old Testament Ethics* (Grand Rapids: Zondervan, 1983) 198-99.

waits seven days and then offers one bird as a sin offering and another as a burnt offering (note the order of the offerings). Since the problem lasts more than a week, sacrifices are required just as they are for the defiling matters raised in 12:1–15:12.

15:31. The laws on genital discharges conclude with a purpose statement. One of the most unusual forms of the verb for "to separate" is placed in command form (הזיר *hizzîr*) from the root נזר (*nāzar,* "to cause to avoid," "to be separate from"). From this form we also get our word *Nazirite.* The only other place where this verb occurs, naturally, is in the Nazirite law, which also stresses the idea of separation (see Num 6:2, 3, 5-6, 12). The Samaritan Pentateuch and the Syriac Version read in this place הזהיר (*hizhîr,* "to warn") instead of "to separate." But the form seems to be well established in its Numbers 6 setting as a separation "to the LORD" and a separation "from" the things Nazirites pledged not to involve them-selves in (Num 6:3 NIV). These laws are to call Israelites away from uncleanness so that when they go to the tabernacle, they will not defile it and as a result die in their uncleanness. They are simultaneously called to be separated unto their God. All of these laws on the clean and unclean are directed at securing a proper degree of reverence for the person and presence of God. Since the tabernacle is the place where God chose to be gloriously manifest, nothing is allowed to come into its precincts that will lower its general esteem and significance. A God who is holy demands a corresponding preparatory cleansing for all who draw near.

15:32-33. There are few, if any, real parallels in the ancient Near East with the provisions given in this closing formula, except in the case of leprosy. The holiness of God could not have been set forth in a more dramatic way. If God is to dwell in the midst of this people, the purity of the community, and especially the purity of God's sanctuary, must be safeguarded.

REFLECTIONS

1. A list of prohibitions in the area of human sexuality should not be misinterpreted to mean that sex is somehow wrong and merely tolerated by God because that is the only way the human race can multiply. Rather, these ritualistic regulations must be balanced against other divine regulations God gave about the sexual side of life.

2. God never intended that a husband should exercise tyrannous power over his wife and her body; therefore, the mandate provided a time of respite for the woman during her menstrual cycle to remind the husband that God, not the mate, was Lord over her life.

3. The change signaled within the NT regarding clean and unclean distinctions is brought out once again in the story of the woman who had a hemorrhage for twelve years but who dared to touch Jesus. She was not the only unclean person Jesus touched. He touched the dead daughter of Jairus (see Mark 5:41) and a leper (see Matt 8:3), and he allowed a sinner to wipe his feet (see Luke 7:36-39). Surely a new age had dawned with the coming of the Messiah. Jesus took the same view toward the laws about bodily uncleanness that he took toward the food laws; he pronounced all things clean. Such teaching led Jesus into direct conflict with the Pharisees (see Mark 7). Jesus emphasized that more was at stake in the matter than an external act; internal preparation and the consent of the heart and mind were also important considerations. This internal feature was already present in the OT, but it tended to be overlooked with all the stress on performance of the act itself.[86]

4. While the main reason for giving these laws on genital discharges was to maintain ritual cleanness, many of the same laws had relevance elsewhere and were not restricted in their application to a single area of life. For example, the law on menstrual uncleanness is found in a ceremonial context in Leviticus 15, but it occurs again in Lev 18:19 among laws that have a broader and much more universal significance. Thus, there may have been accompanying moral principles, or hygienic reasons, that undergirded what appeared to be limited to a ritual observance.

86. See the argument that Old Testament ethics are internal in Kaiser, *Toward Old Testament Ethics,* 7-10.

THE GREAT DAY OF ATONEMENT

NIV

16 The LORD spoke to Moses after the death of the two sons of Aaron who died when they approached the LORD. ²The LORD said to Moses: "Tell your brother Aaron not to come whenever he chooses into the Most Holy Place behind the curtain in front of the atonement cover on the ark, or else he will die, because I appear in the cloud over the atonement cover.

³"This is how Aaron is to enter the sanctuary area: with a young bull for a sin offering and a ram for a burnt offering. ⁴He is to put on the sacred linen tunic, with linen undergarments next to his body; he is to tie the linen sash around him and put on the linen turban. These are sacred garments; so he must bathe himself with water before he puts them on. ⁵From the Israelite community he is to take two male goats for a sin offering and a ram for a burnt offering.

⁶"Aaron is to offer the bull for his own sin offering to make atonement for himself and his household. ⁷Then he is to take the two goats and present them before the LORD at the entrance to the Tent of Meeting. ⁸He is to cast lots for the two goats—one lot for the LORD and the other for the scapegoat.ᵃ ⁹Aaron shall bring the goat whose lot falls to the LORD and sacrifice it for a sin offering. ¹⁰But the goat chosen by lot as the scapegoat shall be presented alive before the LORD to be used for making atonement by sending it into the desert as a scapegoat.

¹¹"Aaron shall bring the bull for his own sin offering to make atonement for himself and his household, and he is to slaughter the bull for his own sin offering. ¹²He is to take a censer full of burning coals from the altar before the LORD and two handfuls of finely ground fragrant incense and take them behind the curtain. ¹³He is to put the incense on the fire before the LORD, and the smoke of the incense will conceal the atonement cover above the Testimony, so that he will not die. ¹⁴He

ᵃ8 That is, the goat of removal; Hebrew *azazel*; also in verses 10 and 26

NRSV

16 The LORD spoke to Moses after the death of the two sons of Aaron, when they drew near before the LORD and died. ²The LORD said to Moses:

Tell your brother Aaron not to come just at any time into the sanctuary inside the curtain before the mercy seatᵃ that is upon the ark, or he will die; for I appear in the cloud upon the mercy seat.ᵃ ³Thus shall Aaron come into the holy place: with a young bull for a sin offering and a ram for a burnt offering. ⁴He shall put on the holy linen tunic, and shall have the linen undergarments next to his body, fasten the linen sash, and wear the linen turban; these are the holy vestments. He shall bathe his body in water, and then put them on. ⁵He shall take from the congregation of the people of Israel two male goats for a sin offering, and one ram for a burnt offering.

6Aaron shall offer the bull as a sin offering for himself, and shall make atonement for himself and for his house. ⁷He shall take the two goats and set them before the LORD at the entrance of the tent of meeting; ⁸and Aaron shall cast lots on the two goats, one lot for the LORD and the other lot for Azazel.ᵇ ⁹Aaron shall present the goat on which the lot fell for the LORD, and offer it as a sin offering; ¹⁰but the goat on which the lot fell for Azazelᵇ shall be presented alive before the LORD to make atonement over it, that it may be sent away into the wilderness to Azazel.ᵇ

11Aaron shall present the bull as a sin offering for himself, and shall make atonement for himself and for his house; he shall slaughter the bull as a sin offering for himself. ¹²He shall take a censer full of coals of fire from the altar before the LORD, and two handfuls of crushed sweet incense, and he shall bring it inside the curtain ¹³and put the incense on the fire before the LORD, that the cloud of the incense may cover the mercy seatᵃ that is upon the covenant,ᶜ or he will die. ¹⁴He shall take

ᵃ Or *the cover*   ᵇ Traditionally rendered *a scapegoat*
ᶜ Or *treaty*, or *testament*; Heb *eduth*

NIV

is to take some of the bull's blood and with his finger sprinkle it on the front of the atonement cover; then he shall sprinkle some of it with his finger seven times before the atonement cover.

[15] "He shall then slaughter the goat for the sin offering for the people and take its blood behind the curtain and do with it as he did with the bull's blood: He shall sprinkle it on the atonement cover and in front of it. [16]In this way he will make atonement for the Most Holy Place because of the uncleanness and rebellion of the Israelites, whatever their sins have been. He is to do the same for the Tent of Meeting, which is among them in the midst of their uncleanness. [17]No one is to be in the Tent of Meeting from the time Aaron goes in to make atonement in the Most Holy Place until he comes out, having made atonement for himself, his household and the whole community of Israel.

[18]"Then he shall come out to the altar that is before the LORD and make atonement for it. He shall take some of the bull's blood and some of the goat's blood and put it on all the horns of the altar. [19]He shall sprinkle some of the blood on it with his finger seven times to cleanse it and to consecrate it from the uncleanness of the Israelites.

[20]"When Aaron has finished making atonement for the Most Holy Place, the Tent of Meeting and the altar, he shall bring forward the live goat. [21]He is to lay both hands on the head of the live goat and confess over it all the wickedness and rebellion of the Israelites—all their sins—and put them on the goat's head. He shall send the goat away into the desert in the care of a man appointed for the task. [22]The goat will carry on itself all their sins to a solitary place; and the man shall release it in the desert.

[23]"Then Aaron is to go into the Tent of Meeting and take off the linen garments he put on before he entered the Most Holy Place, and he is to leave them there. [24]He shall bathe himself with water in a holy place and put on his regular garments. Then he shall come out and sacrifice the burnt offering for himself and the burnt offering for the people, to make atonement for himself and for the people. [25]He shall also burn the fat of the sin offering on the altar.

NRSV

some of the blood of the bull, and sprinkle it with his finger on the front of the mercy seat,[a] and before the mercy seat[a] he shall sprinkle the blood with his finger seven times.

15He shall slaughter the goat of the sin offering that is for the people and bring its blood inside the curtain, and do with its blood as he did with the blood of the bull, sprinkling it upon the mercy seat[a] and before the mercy seat.[a] 16Thus he shall make atonement for the sanctuary, because of the uncleannesses of the people of Israel, and because of their transgressions, all their sins; and so he shall do for the tent of meeting, which remains with them in the midst of their uncleannesses. 17No one shall be in the tent of meeting from the time he enters to make atonement in the sanctuary until he comes out and has made atonement for himself and for his house and for all the assembly of Israel. 18Then he shall go out to the altar that is before the LORD and make atonement on its behalf, and shall take some of the blood of the bull and of the blood of the goat, and put it on each of the horns of the altar. 19He shall sprinkle some of the blood on it with his finger seven times, and cleanse it and hallow it from the uncleannesses of the people of Israel.

20When he has finished atoning for the holy place and the tent of meeting and the altar, he shall present the live goat. 21Then Aaron shall lay both his hands on the head of the live goat, and confess over it all the iniquities of the people of Israel, and all their transgressions, all their sins, putting them on the head of the goat, and sending it away into the wilderness by means of someone designated for the task.[b] 22The goat shall bear on itself all their iniquities to a barren region; and the goat shall be set free in the wilderness.

23Then Aaron shall enter the tent of meeting, and shall take off the linen vestments that he put on when he went into the holy place, and shall leave them there. 24He shall bathe his body in water in a holy place, and put on his vestments; then he shall come out and offer his burnt offering and the burnt offering of the people, making atonement for himself and for the people. 25The fat of the sin offering he shall turn into smoke on the altar. 26The one who sets the goat free for

a Or the cover   b Meaning of Heb uncertain

NIV

²⁶"The man who releases the goat as a scape-goat must wash his clothes and bathe himself with water; afterward he may come into the camp. ²⁷The bull and the goat for the sin offerings, whose blood was brought into the Most Holy Place to make atonement, must be taken outside the camp; their hides, flesh and offal are to be burned up. ²⁸The man who burns them must wash his clothes and bathe himself with water; afterward he may come into the camp.

²⁹"This is to be a lasting ordinance for you: On the tenth day of the seventh month you must deny yourselvesᵃ and not do any work—whether native-born or an alien living among you— ³⁰be-cause on this day atonement will be made for you, to cleanse you. Then, before the Lᴏʀᴅ, you will be clean from all your sins. ³¹It is a sabbath of rest, and you must deny yourselves; it is a lasting ordinance. ³²The priest who is anointed and ordained to succeed his father as high priest is to make atonement. He is to put on the sacred linen garments ³³and make atonement for the Most Holy Place, for the Tent of Meeting and the altar, and for the priests and all the people of the community.

³⁴"This is to be a lasting ordinance for you: Atonement is to be made once a year for all the sins of the Israelites."

And it was done, as the Lᴏʀᴅ commanded Moses.

ᵃ29 Or *must fast*; also in verse 31

NRSV

Azazelᵃ shall wash his clothes and bathe his body in water, and afterward may come into the camp. ²⁷The bull of the sin offering and the goat of the sin offering, whose blood was brought in to make atonement in the holy place, shall be taken out-side the camp; their skin and their flesh and their dung shall be consumed in fire. ²⁸The one who burns them shall wash his clothes and bathe his body in water, and afterward may come into the camp.

29This shall be a statute to you forever: In the seventh month, on the tenth day of the month, you shall deny yourselves,ᵇ and shall do no work, neither the citizen nor the alien who resides among you. ³⁰For on this day atonement shall be made for you, to cleanse you; from all your sins you shall be clean before the Lᴏʀᴅ. ³¹It is a sabbath of complete rest to you, and you shall deny yourselves;ᵇ it is a statute forever. ³²The priest who is anointed and consecrated as priest in his father's place shall make atonement, wearing the linen vestments, the holy vestments. ³³He shall make atonement for the sanctuary, and he shall make atonement for the tent of meeting and for the altar, and he shall make atonement for the priests and for all the people of the assembly. ³⁴This shall be an everlasting statute for you, to make atonement for the people of Israel once in the year for all their sins. And Moses did as the Lᴏʀᴅ had commanded him.

ᵃ Traditionally rendered *a scapegoat*   ᵇ Or *shall fast*

COMMENTARY

Chapter 16 represents the climactic and pivotal point of the whole book. The event it describes would be known later on in Israel as *Yom Kippur,* a shortened form from the sacred writer's יום הכפרים (*yôm hakkippūrîm*). Here, then, is the single most important day, and most characteristic ritual, in all of the legislation of the Pentateuch. Such a central place did this day hold in the sacred calendar of events that the rabbis referred to it simply as *Yoma;* it was *"the* day."

The reason this day was esteemed so highly was that it depicted the sacrificial expiation for *all* sin, except blasphemy against God (see Numbers 15:30; there called the "sin with a high hand"), as well as the consequent removal of the guilt and remembrance of sins against individuals. For devout Jews, it remains to this day the climax, indeed the crowning event, of the religious year. One of the best-known melodies to be associated with this day is that of *Kol Nidre.* All over the world on this day, which comes on the Gregorian calendar somewhere at the end of September or the beginning of October, Leviticus 16 is read in celebrating synagogues. Reform Judaism, how-ever, has replaced Leviticus 16 with Leviticus 19 in the morning reading for Yom Kippur, focusing on the ethical rather than the ritual requirements of repentance. Reform Judaism has, however, retained the traditional *haftarah* (the parallel reading from the Prophets in the synagogue service following the lesson from the Torah) of Isa 57:14–58:14, which declares that fasting and rote prayers are valueless unless they are accompanied with inward regeneration and unless they lead to works of service for poor and helpless persons.

Leviticus 16:1-2 begins with a reference to the events of 10:1-2. This has exasperated some who believe that chap. 16 should have been placed right after chap. 10—just for that reason. However, such a relocation would be a major mistake, for the lesson embodied in the death of Nadab and Abihu in chap. 10 would have been wasted. Any approach to God demands extreme care, self-examination, and the ability to meet the qualifications for coming into God's presence. That necessitates the intervening five chapters. Chapters 11–15 dramatize the point that all mortals are exposed to the liability of being disqualified from meeting with God due to contacting uncleanness in foods, decay, death, disease, and sex.

Rarely are we given such a graphic description of what God has done for humanity as we are treated to on the Day of Atonement. Once every year a substitutionary atonement provides for all the sins of all the people. Some have seen the main purpose of the events of this day to be limited to making atonement for the holy of holies (v. 16). But if that were the only purpose for the events of this day, it would miss the clear statements that there is to be a sacrifice "for" (בעד *bĕʿad*) Aaron himself, for Aaron's household (v. 6), and "because of" (מן *min*, "by reason of") the uncleanness [chaps. 11–15] and rebellion of the Israelites" (v. 16; cf. vv. 33-34).

The structure of chap. 16 is not as clear as the structure of other chapters. There are a number of recurring phrases and statements, such as "to make atonement" (vv. 6, 11, 17, 24, 33, 34) and "This/it is to be a lasting ordinance for you" (vv. 29, 31, 34). The chapter is slightly confusing because it uses a typical Hebrew pattern of outlining the ritual first and then it returns to describe it in greater detail. We can discern the following elements: introduction (vv. 1-2); the sacrificial animals and priestly garb (vv. 3-5); an outline of the ceremonies (vv. 6-10); the ritual of the Day

of Atonement (vv. 11-28), which includes preparations of the high priest (vv. 11-14), the forgiveness of sin (vv. 15-19), the removal of sin (vv. 20-22), the washing of the participants (vv. 23-28); and the spiritual preparation of the people (vv. 29-34).

16:1-2. We are startled to learn that this day is revealed not to Aaron, the high priest, but to Moses. Clearly, Moses retained his function as spokesperson for God and the receiver of revelation, even after the installation of Aaron as high priest.

The first injunction that Moses gives to Aaron, in light of the death of Aaron's two sons, is (literally) "not to go at any time into the Most Holy Place behind the curtain" (v. 2). This is not to be taken as a total prohibition, but it exhibits a characteristic Oriental negative that seems at first to be all-encompassing, only to have its qualifiers follow immediately (e.g., Deut 1:35, but see vv. 36, 38; Josh 11:22*a*, but see v. 22*b*; 1 Cor 1:14*a*, but see vv. 14*b* and 16). The point is that Aaron alone is to enter the most holy place in the tabernacle only this one day of each year.

16:3-5. Even though Aaron is to conduct the ritual, he too is a sinner, just like the people for whom he is offering the sacrifices. Thus he has to bring a bull as his own sin offering and a ram as a burnt offering (v. 3). The people bring two male goats for their sin offering (note that both goats form one sin offering) and a ram for their burnt offering (v. 5).

As the ceremony begins, Aaron must divest himself of the richly ornamented robes of his office and clothe himself, instead, with the white linen garments of an ordinary priest. Of the eight garments worn by the priests, four are of linen (shirt, shorts, sash, and turban) and are called the white garments (see Exod 39:27-29), while the other four are called the golden garments because of the rich gold embroidered on them (see Exod 28:4-5).

This divestiture is more than pageantry; it is an eloquent symbol of the servant role that the high priest must assume on this day as he takes upon himself the form of an ordinary mortal while retaining in his person all the powers of his high priestly office.

Accordingly, the Day of Atonement is a day of sorrow, repentance, and humiliation over the sins committed. Even the high priest clothes himself in the simple and unspectacular garments of the other priests to demonstrate his humility. Only at the end of the day is he to resume his dress in the extraordinary robes of his office (vv. 23-24).

16:6, 11-14. After Aaron offers the bull as a sin offering for himself and his sons, he is to take some of the blood of the bull and sprinkle it not outside the curtain leading to the most holy place, as in the sin offering of the priest in 4:3-12, but right inside the most holy place, at or toward the mercy seat. However, to go into this innermost sanctum of the tabernacle, he must prepare a censer full of hot coals from the altar of burnt offering. Taking this censer and two handfuls of fine incense, he enters the most holy place. At that point he drops the incense into the censer to create smoke and conceal the presence of God, who is closely connected with the כפרת (*kappōret*), variously translated as the "mercy seat" or "lid/cover of the ark."

Obviously, *kappōret* is derived from the verb כפר (*kipper*), meaning "to purify" or "to ransom by means of a substitute" (see the discussions of this word at 1:4). On top of the ark (there is no word here for "lid" or "cover" in Hebrew unless one incorrectly understands *kipper* to mean "to cover") were two cherubs facing each other and extending out to the width of the room (see Exod 25:17-22). The LXX renders *kappōret* in the Greek ἱλαστήριον (*hilastērion*, "instrument of propitiation"). Because of what was transacted at this spot every year on the Day of Atonement, it became known as God's seat of mercy from which atonement was granted. The notion that it formed a footstool for God's feet comes from Ps 99:1, which extolls the Lord who reigns and who "sits enthroned upon the cherubim" (NRSV). Whether the Lord is seated or not may be answered by the fact that this is an exalted figure of speech to portray that the Lord was really present in the tent of meeting and was currently reigning on earth.

But there can be no doubt about the propitiatory nature of what takes place in this most holy place, the innermost sanctum of the tabernacle. Aaron then sprinkles the blood of the bull, slain for himself and his family, seven times, either upon or toward the mercy seat. The high priest must enter behind the veil alone without anyone else in the tabernacle. In the mystery of the silence and the loneliness of his work, he ministers on behalf of his soul, and on behalf of all Israel (v. 17).

16:7-10. The second part of the ceremony involves the two goats. They form *one* sin offering for all the sins of all Israelites who truly "afflict your souls" (vv. 29, 31 KJV), i.e., were repentant and sorrowed over their sins. More will be said about this point when we come to discuss those verses.

When the two goats are seen as one sin offering, only one conclusion can be reached with regard to their connection with each other. The one goat makes possible the expiation of the sins laid on it, and thus it is the *means* of expiating and propitiating Israel's sins, while the other goat exhibits the *effects* of that expiation.[87] The role each goat will play is decided by casting lots.

The Mishnaic tractate *Yoma* fills in the details on this part of the ceremony, along with an elaborate description of the other portions. In the simplest outline of events, as the two goats stand before the high priest, he uses the Urim and Thummim to determine which will be the sacrificial goat and which will be sent away, or he puts two lots into a jar: one saying "to the LORD," and the other "to Azazel." If the latter system is used, Aaron places his hand on one goat as he draws one lot and on the other goat as he draws the other lot.

16:15-19. The first goat is to be sacrificed as a sin offering for all the sins of all the people. The blood of this animal is also taken, this one time each year, behind the veil that separated the two rooms in the tabernacle, and is sprinkled seven times on or toward the mercy seat. The means of forgiveness could not have been stated more strongly. The goat becomes the substitute for the people. Nevertheless, it still is an animal and not a person. And what really makes the ceremony effective is not some magical ingredient in the blood or the ritual itself; it is the declaration of

---

87. As used here, *expiation* is the act of atoning for an offense while *propitiation* is the act of satisfying the person who has been offended. It is possible for a person to be expiated without being propitiated, especially when one is implacable and demands more than what is rightfully his or hers. Contrari wise, it is possible for a person to be propitiated without being expiated if one is too easily satisfied. The sin offering mentioned here involved both expiation and propitiation.

forgiveness by the high priest, based on the authority of the God who promises forgiveness.

16:20-22. Next, the second goat is led away from the camp so that it can be lost in the wilderness. Having made atonement for himself, his family (in his first trip into the holy of holies), and the people of Israel (now in this second trip into the holy of holies), Aaron comes out of the tabernacle once again into the courtyard. He places his hands (the Hebrew ceremony of *Semikhah*, discussed in 1:4) on the head of the live goat as he confesses over it "all the wickedness and rebellion of the Israelites—all their sins—and [puts] them on the goat's head" (v. 21).

The ceremony of the imposition of hands is conclusive on the point that it pictures a transfer of sin to the head of another. Even though what we see is true only in a typical fashion, it nevertheless effectively demonstrates that expiation and propitiation are taking place. Yet so real is this transfer of wickedness, sin, and rebellion on the head of this substitute that the man who takes the goat into the wilderness, as he leads it away, is himself said to become polluted and made unclean because of his contact with the sin-laden goat.

This one sin offering comes in two parts, since the first goat that dies cannot be brought back to life to transact the second part of the ritual. It clearly sets forth the teaching that sins are *forgiven* on the basis of a substitute (the first goat), and sins are *forgotten* and removed from us, as the psalmist said, "as far as the east is from the west,/ so far has he removed our/ transgressions from us" (Ps 103:12 NIV). The first animal pictures the *means* used for atonement—i.e., the shedding of the blood of an innocent substitute—and the second animal pictures the *effect*, the removal of the guilt.

The most difficult question in this chapter concerns the meaning of the statement that the goat is "for/to Azazel" (לעזאזל *laʿăzāʾzēl*) in vv. 8, 10, and 26. The meaning of this term has proven to be most difficult, and the solutions are legion. Several older rabbinical writers and Targumists took Azazel to be the name of *the place* to which the goat was led. It was supposed that it was a rough and rocky place with a precipice from which the goat was thrown down. That is found, for example, in *Tg. Neb.* in v. 10. The Arabic version favored this solution, for they substitute

for *laʿăzāʾzēl*, "to the Mount Azaz," or to the rough mountain (which roughness Azaz depicts).

Others have argued that if this second goat is presented alive "to/for Yahweh" in v. 10, the parallel phrase must be understood as a name as well, "for Azazel." But who is Azazel? It is supposed that he (?) must be a *desert demon* capable of feeding on an animal laden with the sins of the entire nation. This view is generally the one most frequently adopted today. Josephus apparently adopted something close to this view, for he employed the LXX translation of this term as ἀποτροπίασμος (*apotropiasmos*, "the Averter") and said, "The goat is sent away into a remote desert *as an Averter of ills*" (*apotropiasmos*).[88] Some of the early Church Fathers such as Origen, attempted to show that Azazel was the devil. In later Jewish literature, Azalel (*sic*) appears as a demon (*Enoch* 8:1; 9:6). The difficulty with this view is that the very next chapter of Leviticus warns against offering any sacrifices to demons (17:7). Therefore, most who hold this view attempt to show that the goat is in no way an offering to the demon. But the disclaimer is difficult to maintain if the reason for adopting this view is that it is parallel to the expression used "for Yahweh," which does function as a single sin offering!

A simpler view is to see Azazel as a compound word made up of עז (*ʿēz*, "goat") and אזל (*ʾāzal*, from the verb "to go away" or "to lead away"). Thus, the second goat is the "goat of going/leading away," named in older English the "Scapegoat" (by which they meant in that day what we would mean by Escape-goat). New evidence reveals that Ugaritic (an early Canaanite language that is cognate to Hebrew) did exhibit such compound nouns. *Escape-goat* is a better term than the older Scapegoat, (a word that apparently was coined by William Tyndale, the sixteenth-century English Bible translator) since in today's parlance a scapegoat is one who gets stuck with doing jobs others do not wish to do, and therefore, it would have been more appropriately applied to the first goat. In Num 29:11, this Escape-goat is called "the sin offering for atonement."

16:23-28. Having made atonement for himself, his fellow priests, the sanctuary, and the people, the high priest enters the tabernacle one more time. He removes his white linen attire in which

88. Josephus *Antiquities of the Jews* 50.3.10.

he has performed the ceremonies up to this point. He then washes himself thoroughly "in a holy place" (v. 24), presumably somewhere in the sanctuary itself. Now that he has completed the work of atonement, it is appropriate for him to take up the beautiful robes and the splendor of his office once more. When he emerges from the tent of meeting in his splendor, he offers burnt offerings for himself and for the people (v. 24), along with the fat of the sin offering (v. 25). He and the people are able to approach the Lord once more with their sacrificial gifts.

16:29-34. Very little, if anything, has been said so far about the people's responsibilities or duties in this whole ceremony. Even though what Aaron has accomplished focuses mainly on the people, they do not play a major part in this event. However, vv. 29, 31, and 34 make it clear that what is being done is to be a permanent rule for the future. It is all the more striking, then, that this Day of Atonement is not mentioned elsewhere in the OT. The three so-called pilgrimage festivals of Passover, Weeks, and Tabernacles, where all the men of Israel journeyed to Jerusalem for these days, are often mentioned but never this day! The day of purification mentioned in Ezek 45:18-20 comes on the first day of the seventh month. Zechariah 3:9 does not refer to this day either. The only explicit references to the Day of Atonement are in Heb 9:7 and the apocryphal work of Sirach 50. If the suggested solution to this unexplainable silence on the Day of Atonement is to say that the Day of Atonement was a late invention of the post-exilic period, as the school of Julius Wellhausen was fond of saying, the question will be this: Where is the ark of the covenant with its mercy seat, a feature so essential to the ceremonies of this day? That piece of furniture was only a memory by the post-exilic period, for it appears nowhere in the later years before the exile, and Jer 3:16 says it will not come to anyone's mind anymore.

The Day of Atonement is to be held "on the tenth day of the seventh month" (v. 29; see also 23:26-32; 25:9). This date is six months after the celebration of Passover. The seventh month was known in post-exilic times as Tishri (September-October). It was autumn by then, and the early rains had begun to fall. Plowing and sowing would not begin until the next month.

But the most important duty for the people is reserved almost to the last in these instructions that otherwise are given mainly for Aaron and his sons. The people are to "deny [themselves]" (vv. 29, 31) or "afflict [their] souls" (KJV). The expression ענה נפש (ʿnh npš) involves the verbal root from the word ענה (ʿānâ) which in the piel form means "to humble oneself." It appears frequently in the instructions for the Day of Atonement (Lev 16:29, 31; 23:27, 32; Num 29:7). The only other places where this expression occurs are in Ps 35:13-14 and in Isa 58:3, 5 (hence the reason for reading this selection from the Prophets on the Day of Atonement in the synagogues). For the psalmist, the humbling of oneself is defined by its association with fasting: "I put on sackcloth/and humbled myself with fasting./ . . . I went about mourning." Likewise in Isaiah 58, it is connected with fasting.

The principle, then, is one of contriteness and godly sorrow for the sins committed during the year. While all sins, including all wickedness and even outright rebellion against God (v. 21) are forgivable, there is no mechanical or purely rote manner in which carte blanche is given to all persons, regardless of their inner disposition. The heart attitude has to accompany the request for forgiveness. This aspect of fasting and humbling oneself can be seen on days of national repentance (see Judg 20:26; 1 Sam 7:6; Esth 4:16). At these times people mourn over their sins (see 1 Sam 31:13; 2 Sam 3:35) and through self-denial call out to God for forgiveness and deliverance.

So significant is this day that it is called a "sabbath of rest" (v. 31). That expression is used of the sabbath itself (see Exod 31:15; 35:2; Lev 23:3) and of the sabbatical year (see Lev 25:4). But here and in Lev 23:32 it is used of the Day of Atonement. On such a day there is to be a complete cessation of all nonessential activities and work. This holiday from all forms of normal activities applies to everyone, including the native-born and the alien living in Israel's midst.

The chapter closes in v. 34 with another reminder that this event is to be an annual affair. It also makes explicit that all that is done has as its main reason to make "atonement . . . for all the sins of the Israelites." One more postscript is added: Moses carried out all that the Lord had told him to do on this day.

REFLECTIONS

1. Here on the holiest of days, the Day of Atonement, Aaron is to exchange his high priestly clothes for the vestments of an ordinary priest. At the moment when his duties are the most urgent, his garments are the most humble, pointing to the fact that leadership in the community of faith is, at its heart, servant leadership.

All acts of ministry—whether they are performed by ordained clergy or laypeople, whether they are preaching a sermon, officiating at a Eucharist, handing a bowl of soup to a homeless person, teaching a child in church school, listening to a worried friend, or standing up for the right in a difficult situation—are acts of service done by people who know what it means to suffer, to fail, to struggle, to live as less than perfect people. Deeds of mercy are done, in the words of Henri Nouwen, by "wounded healers."

2. The putting off of the glorious robes of the high priestly office and the donning of the white linen garments of an ordinary priest picture what Christ did when he temporarily set aside the glory he had with the Father to take upon himself the form of a man, even that of a servant, in his incarnation (see Phil 2:5-11). This same humble mind-set, argues the apostle Paul in Phil 2:5, ought to characterize the believing community today.

3. Aaron had to proceed carefully behind the veil or curtain that divided the holy place from the most holy place, but that veil was split from top to bottom when Christ gave the final sacrifice at God's mercy seat (see Matt 27:51; Mark 15:38). This rending of the veil was interpreted by the author of Hebrews as God's announcement of human freedom now to enter into the divine presence, the way being opened by our Lord's death on the cross (see Heb 10:19-22).

4. Although traditional theology has insisted that the only sins that could have been forgiven under the old law of Moses were sins of ignorance and sins of inadvertence, this text boldly decries such a meager view by announcing that "all sin," even "transgressions" can be forgiven. Since the term פשׁע (*peša'* v. 21) means not only "transgression" but also "revolt" and "rebellion," it is clear that the forgiveness of God encompasses every sin except blasphemy or sinning against the Holy Spirit (see Num 15:27-31; cf. Heb 10:26-31). God will forgive sin and will remember it against us no more (see Ps 103:12; Mic 7:19; 1 John 1:7, 9).

5. Aaron, also a sinner, had to make atonement for himself first before making atonement for the people. But Christ, being pure and sinless, did not need to offer a sacrifice for himself (see Heb 7:26-28). Thus, mortals, even in the office of high priest, are weak; but how fortunate we are to have One, in the person of Jesus of Nazareth, who is not so afflicted!

6. The annual nature of the Day of Atonement with its repetition of the sacrificial ritual is in strong contrast to our Lord's once-for-all sacrifice (see Heb 9:24). By one act of giving his life in death for all mortals, he has permanently secured forgiveness of sin for all who will claim it.

7. Some are willing to accept divine forgiveness, but they say neither they nor God can ever forget what they have done. If ever there was a text in Scripture that released men and women from the act of sin, its consequences, and the objective reality of the guilt that results, this is the text. Sins were forgiven on the basis of a substitute; sins were forgotten and removed from being a consideration in that one and same sin offering.

LEVITICUS 17:1–26:46

THE HOLINESS CODE

OVERVIEW

Chapters 17–26 constitute a distinctive unit, dealing with the theme of holiness. Ever since the days of A. Klostermann in 1877,[89] it has been traditional to refer to these chapters as the Holiness Code. In 1889, Julius Wellhausen attempted to show that within the Priestly document, these chapters form a unique source of their own, with their own distinctive vocabulary and style, yet bearing some points of contact with the Book of the Covenant in Exodus 20–23, and some parts of Deuteronomy and Ezekiel.[90]

There is no question that these chapters exhibit a uniqueness rarely observed in other chapters. Most noticeable are the constant reference to holiness and the constant exhortation to "be holy because I, the LORD your God, am holy" (NIV 19:2; 20:7, 26; 21:6, 8). There is also the repeated declaration that "I am the LORD your God" (18:4, 30; 19:3, 4, 10, 25, 31, 34; 20:7; 23:22, 43; 24:22; 25:17, 55; 26:1). So there is no question that this is a very unified and unique set of materials. To some, this continues to imply a separate origin from the rest of Leviticus.

But many recent scholars believe that the evidence does not justify the conclusion that these chapters constituted a separate volume of laws that had been inserted into the framework of Leviticus. First of all, there is no evidence in the introduction to chap. 17 that there has been a switch in sources. In fact, the introductory formula of 17:1 is very much like that of previous chapters (cf. 1:1; 4:1; 6:1). Second, a fair amount of material in these chapters has links with what has appeared in chaps. 1–16. For example, 17:10-15 recapitulates matters already taken up in 7:26-27, and 17:15-16 links up with 11:39-40. Third, this section has hardly anything to say about the place of priests in the sacrifices—as if it assumes that that matter has already been described elsewhere and is granted as undergirding the holiness section. And finally, internal clues within these chapters support claims that the author of the first division (chaps. 1–16) uses the same format in the second (chaps. 17–27).

There is one major difference between the two divisions, however. Whereas the first one pictures Moses addressing mainly Aaron the high priest along with his sons, this second division focuses almost entirely on the Israelite people. Almost every chapter opens with a directive to speak to the people themselves; very little is said in chaps. 17–26 directly to the priests, except for the one block of text beginning in chapter 21.

Leviticus 19:2 sounds the theme of the holiness section: "Be holy because I, the LORD your God, am holy." The areas of life in which holiness is required may be seen in the following structural elements: in eating (17:1-16); in sexual behavior (18:1-30); in social ethics (19:1-37); in worship (20:1-8, 27); in family relations (20:9-26); in the priesthood (21:1–22:16); in sacrifical offerings (22:17-33); in observing the festivals (23:1-44); as contrasted (24:1-23); in land ownership (25:1-55); and the alternatives: blessing or curse (26:1-46).

89. Klostermann, *Zeitschrift für Lutherische Theologie*, 401ff.
90. Wellhausen, *Die Composition des Hexateuchs*, 152ff.

LEVITICUS 17:1-16, THE PROLOGUE: HOLINESS IN EATING

NIV

17 The LORD said to Moses, ²"Speak to Aaron and his sons and to all the Israelites and say to them: 'This is what the LORD has commanded: ³Any Israelite who sacrifices an ox,^a a lamb or a goat in the camp or outside of it ⁴instead of bringing it to the entrance to the Tent of Meeting to present it as an offering to the LORD in front of the tabernacle of the LORD—that man shall be considered guilty of bloodshed; he has shed blood and must be cut off from his people. ⁵This is so the Israelites will bring to the LORD the sacrifices they are now making in the open fields. They must bring them to the priest, that is, to the LORD, at the entrance to the Tent of Meeting and sacrifice them as fellowship offerings.^b ⁶The priest is to sprinkle the blood against the altar of the LORD at the entrance to the Tent of Meeting and burn the fat as an aroma pleasing to the LORD. ⁷They must no longer offer any of their sacrifices to the goat idols^c to whom they prostitute themselves. This is to be a lasting ordinance for them and for the generations to come.'

⁸"Say to them: 'Any Israelite or any alien living among them who offers a burnt offering or sacrifice ⁹and does not bring it to the entrance to the Tent of Meeting to sacrifice it to the LORD—that man must be cut off from his people.

¹⁰" 'Any Israelite or any alien living among them who eats any blood—I will set my face against that person who eats blood and will cut him off from his people. ¹¹For the life of a creature is in the blood, and I have given it to you to make atonement for yourselves on the altar; it is the blood that makes atonement for one's life. ¹²Therefore I say to the Israelites, "None of you may eat blood, nor may an alien living among you eat blood."

¹³" 'Any Israelite or any alien living among you who hunts any animal or bird that may be eaten must drain out the blood and cover it with earth, ¹⁴because the life of every creature is its blood. That is why I have said to the Israelites, "You must not eat the blood of any creature, because

^a3 The Hebrew word can include both male and female.
^b5 Traditionally *peace offerings*   ^c7 Or *demons*

NRSV

17 The LORD spoke to Moses: 2Speak to Aaron and his sons and to all the people of Israel and say to them: This is what the LORD has commanded. ³If anyone of the house of Israel slaughters an ox or a lamb or a goat in the camp, or slaughters it outside the camp, ⁴and does not bring it to the entrance of the tent of meeting, to present it as an offering to the LORD before the tabernacle of the LORD, he shall be held guilty of bloodshed; he has shed blood, and he shall be cut off from the people. ⁵This is in order that the people of Israel may bring their sacrifices that they offer in the open field, that they may bring them to the LORD, to the priest at the entrance of the tent of meeting, and offer them as sacrifices of well-being to the LORD. ⁶The priest shall dash the blood against the altar of the LORD at the entrance of the tent of meeting, and turn the fat into smoke as a pleasing odor to the LORD, ⁷so that they may no longer offer their sacrifices for goat-demons, to whom they prostitute themselves. This shall be a statute forever to them throughout their generations.

8And say to them further: Anyone of the house of Israel or of the aliens who reside among them who offers a burnt offering or sacrifice, ⁹and does not bring it to the entrance of the tent of meeting, to sacrifice it to the LORD, shall be cut off from the people.

10If anyone of the house of Israel or of the aliens who reside among them eats any blood, I will set my face against that person who eats blood, and will cut that person off from the people. ¹¹For the life of the flesh is in the blood; and I have given it to you for making atonement for your lives on the altar; for, as life, it is the blood that makes atonement. ¹²Therefore I have said to the people of Israel: No person among you shall eat blood, nor shall any alien who resides among you eat blood. ¹³And anyone of the people of Israel, or of the aliens who reside among them, who hunts down an animal or bird that may be eaten shall pour out its blood and cover it with earth.

14For the life of every creature—its blood is

the life of every creature is its blood; anyone who eats it must be cut off."

¹⁵"'Anyone, whether native-born or alien, who eats anything found dead or torn by wild animals must wash his clothes and bathe with water, and he will be ceremonially unclean till evening; then he will be clean. ¹⁶But if he does not wash his clothes and bathe himself, he will be held responsible.' "

its life; therefore I have said to the people of Israel: You shall not eat the blood of any creature, for the life of every creature is its blood; whoever eats it shall be cut off. ¹⁵All persons, citizens or aliens, who eat what dies of itself or what has been torn by wild animals, shall wash their clothes, and bathe themselves in water, and be unclean until the evening; then they shall be clean. ¹⁶But if they do not wash themselves or bathe their body, they shall bear their guilt.

COMMENTARY

Classifying this opening chapter of the Holiness Code is difficult, for it has very strong affinities with several of the teachings in chaps. 1–16. Some have even doubted that this chapter should be attached to the holiness section that follows because (1) it does not mention once the concept of holiness, a theme that is so distinctive of most of the chapters included in 17–26; (b) it contains no moral injunctions so characteristic of this section; and (c) it forms no natural connection with what follows in chaps 18–26.

But this appraisal may be a bit hasty. There are some phrases that chap. 17 shares in common with the rest of the section. But perhaps the best way to view this chapter is to conclude that it acts as a bridge chapter linking itself especially to chap. 16 and linking the two major divisions of the book, viz. chaps. 1–16 and 18–26. In some ways this chapter could stand alone, much as chap. 16 stands alone. Yet chap. 16 summarizes chaps. 1–15. In a similar way, chap. 17 sets the tone for what is to come in chaps. 18–26.

If it is difficult to locate chap. 17 in its sectional context, it is fairly simple to discern the chapter's internal structure. After an introductory formula, as usual for this book, four paragraphs present four concerns about the eating of meat. Each paragraph is introduced with this formula: "If a man from the house of Israel or from a resident alien sojourning among you . . ." (literal translation). This formula is found in vv. 8, 10, and 13; however, a shortened form of it occurs (without reference to the resident alien) in v. 3. This, then, allows us to identify several elements: introductory for-

mula (vv. 1-2); prohibition of clandestine sacrificial slaughter (vv. 3-7); prohibition of sacrifices outside the tabernacle (vv. 8-9); prohibition of eating blood (vv. 10-12); and rules on eating wild game (vv. 13-16).

17:1-2. Instead of commanding Moses to speak only to Aaron, or to Aaron and his sons, this introductory formula adds for the first time, "And to all the Israelites." This section will concentrate on laypersons and the possible mistakes that they may make if they do not pay attention to these injunctions. The community is to take heed, for "this is what the LORD has commanded" (v. 2). The same phraseology is used in 8:5 and 9:6.

17:3-7. The first paragraph immediately plunges us into a problem of interpretation. Verses 3-4 warn that no one is to slaughter any meat except in front of the tent of meeting. But Deut 12:20-25 allows those who are too far from the tabernacle/temple site in Jerusalem to butcher their own meat where they live without going through the sacrificial formalities—just so long as they eat only what is clean and they thoroughly drain the blood from it.

Even this difference would be no problem, for it appears that the law in Deuteronomy assumes a settled state in the land; therefore, it really spoke to issues that would be effective only after Israel was in the land. Thus the law in Leviticus 17 came first, since it seems to reflect those times when Israel was still in the wilderness. The problem is v. 7, which concludes this first paragraph by saying, "This is to be a lasting ordinance for them and for the generations to come." If "this" refers to the whole paragraph of vv. 3-7, there is a major problem.

Several responses can be made to this problem. First, this law applied to the animals typically used in sacrifices: the ox/cow (i.e., male or female of that bovine species), sheep, or goats. That restricts the law on one side.

Then there is the word for "kill" (שחט *šāhat*). Seven different words for various forms of killing appear in the OT, but this one is used in an overwhelming number of cases for killing animals for sacrifice. Only when it refers to the "slaughter" of a people does it evidence a major deviation from this general rule. So settled were the translators of the NIV on this meaning that they translated the word as "to sacrifice."[91] That this interpretation is secure may be gathered from v. 5 where in a parallel text to this verb, the word זבח (*zābah*), "to sacrifice," appears. Therefore, the law did not command that no meat could be butchered anywhere in the land except in front of the tabernacle. What it restricted was butchering those domestic animals that were used for sacrifices anywhere but at the sanctuary. The law was aimed at preventing the possibility of sacrificing at other altar installations, which always raised the horror of idolatry and pagan worship in the midst of Israel.

This law, we conclude, was given specifically to bring a halt to laity offering sacrificial animals in the open fields (v. 5). There could be no rival to the living God or to the worship Israel was to bring to God. In fact, in v. 7 the verb זנה (*zānâ*, "to commit harlotry," "to go astray," "to prostitute [oneself]") is used. This verb proved to be correct in both a literal and a figurative sense, for as Israel built the competing altars with the one in the courtyard of the tabernacle (and the one later on at the Temple), they began to fall into ritual prostitution at the pagan sites and prohibited altars. The prophets of Israel used no term more frequently for the people's apostasy, in both a literal and a figurative sense, than this word for harlotry.

But what about the fact that this law was to be for all time? Given the interpretation offered here, this would be the rule: It was part and parcel of the centralized worship concept so strong in Deuteronomy. Another possibility, though not strongly favored here, is that the antecedent to the "this" of v. 7*b* is the command given in v. 7*a*—Israel was no longer to offer any sacrifices to the goat idols.

But before we discuss what these "goats" were, notice the penalty for disobedience of this command. The individual would be considered "guilty of bloodshed" and "must be cut off from his people." The offense was as serious as murder! Whether all the cases of "cutting off" involved capital punishment is difficult to say. Occasionally, it may have involved excommunication from the people of God, when the offense was not moral, but ceremonial. But this division of the question is modern, and a firm basis for such mercy cannot be identified in the text.

Originally, the word translated "goat-gods/demons" (שעירם *šĕ'îrîm*) signified "hairy ones," or "rough, shaggy, or rugged" creatures. Subsequently, it was applied to male goats and then to mythical creatures in half-human and half-goat form.

Lower Egypt had a flourishing worship of goats. It gave rise to the worship of the god Pan in Greek and Roman times, one similar to Christian popular depictions of the devil: a goat form with a tail, horns, and cloven hoofs. So frightening were these depictions of this pagan god that our word for terror comes from the god Pan, i.e., *panic*. It can now be seen why the threat of cutting off is given in v. 7*b*. That had been the warning of Exod 22:19; any Israelite who sacrificed to any other god would be cut off.

The reference here must be to some kind of goat worship, probably not unlike what appeared in Lower Egypt. Joshua 24:14 alluded to the fact that the forefathers of the Israelites had worshiped other gods before Abraham came from Ur of the Chaldees ("worshiped beyond the River") and had also indulged in false worship "in Egypt." A goat worship did flourish in the delta region, which involved, in part, goats copulating with women votaries.

17:8-9. The second regulation prohibits other types of sacrifices people might wish to offer somewhere other than in the tabernacle area. The wisdom of such a restriction can be quickly gathered from reading the subsequent history of the

91. See Victor P. Hamilton's discussion of this Hebrew root in *Theological Wordbook of the Old Testament*, eds. R. Laird Harris, Gleason L. Archer, Jr., and Bruce K. Waltke, 2 vols. (Chicago: Moody, 1980) 915-16.

nation of Israel. Disobedience to injunctions, such as these, led to idolatry on practically every high hill in Judah and Israel. It was the snare that finally destroyed both the northern and the southern kingdoms.

This prohibition applies to the resident alien as much as it does to any Israelite. The reason for this rule is the same as for Israel: to discourage the aliens from sacrificing to pagan gods.

Even more serious is offering a whole "burnt offering" to anyone other than the Lord (v. 8). Total dedication, which this offering symbolizes, is owed only to Yahweh. There is no question of eating some of the meat in a sacrificial meal when "burnt offering" is used; thus, not even the excuse that one needed to butcher some meat for personal use could be used with this offering. It is offered up *totally* on the altar.

17:10-12. The third paragraph deals with the prohibition on eating blood. Again, the resident alien is as much obligated to keep this law as is the Israelite.

This rule had been in force ever since God allowed Noah to eat meat; it was on the condition that he would thoroughly drain the animal's blood before eating it (see Gen 9:4). This is not the only place where this law reappear (see Lev 7:26-27; Deut 12:16, 23; 15:23; 1 Sam 14:32-34).

Why is there so strong a prohibition? Two explanations are given in this text. The first is "For the life of a creature is in the blood." The word translated "life" is נפש (*nepeš*), which has a wide assortment of meanings, such as "throat," "soul," "appetite," "life," and "person." The word translated "creature" is בשר (*bāśār*), which also has a wide range of meanings, including "flesh," "body," "the male reproductive organ," and "creature."

What is v. 11 claiming, then? It is claiming that creatures are living and vital, so long as their blood is in their flesh; but when their blood is separated from the *bāśār*, the creatures are no longer alive! The vitality of the creature is directly linked with its blood. Since there is such a strong link, those who obey and refuse to eat the blood of the animal honor the life of the animal. To honor this injunction is to honor life; to despise this injunction is to despise life.

But a second reason is given for this prohibition on blood in v. 11. The blood has been given not

for eating but for making "atonement for yourselves on the altar; it is the blood that makes atonement for one's life." The understanding of this explanation will literally determine one's whole approach to the book of Leviticus and the sacrificial institution as a whole. It is the most explicit statement on the role and meaning of the blood in the sacrificial system.

Basic to the whole theory of sacrifice in the OT is the concept of substitution. The life of the victim is substituted for the individual human life in such a way that the offender averts the necessity of forfeiting his or her own life, which God could have demanded because of the offense committed. Had not the life of the substituted victim intervened, exposure to the divine wrath would mean certain death to the offender. But the blood, symbolizing the lifeblood of the victim yielded up in death, comes between the offender and the wrath of God to rescue the offender from the just penalty for the sin.

This would also explain the meaning of the formula "to make atonement for yourselves." The sacrifice literally serves as "a ransom" for the lives of those under the threat of death. Therefore, God graciously chooses to accept the blood of the sacrifices in lieu of the lives of humans, i.e., the blood of humans. It is not that the blood atones for sin by setting the life of the animal free, a view that is held by writers like Roland de Vaux,[92] but the blood delivers or ransoms by means of a substitute; it ransoms by delivering the payment of life itself! Instead of requiring that the offender pay a monetary sum (as was permitted in Exod 21:30 for an owner of a bull who had been known to gore people and who killed a man or a woman), the life of the animal is substituted for the offender's life.

Another case that demonstrates the same point of substitution is the commission of a murder by an unknown perpetrator in the open fields (see Deut 21:1-9). Measurements are to be made to determine which town is the closest to where the corpse lay. The elders of the closest town are to bring a young heifer and lead it down to a stream. There they are to break its neck so that the blood pours back into the earth, apparently since the

---

92. Roland de Vaux, "Les sacrifices de porcs en Palestine et dans l'Ancient Orient," BZAW 77 (1958) 250-65; also *idem, Ancient Israel,* 448-49.

very ground cries out against this outrageous assault on human life, as it did when the blood of Abel fell on the ground (see Gen 4:10-13)—until Cain was punished for what he had done. The elders then wash their hands with water over the slain heifer and declare, "Our hands did not shed this blood, nor did our eyes see it done" (Deut 21:7 NIV). The heifer's blood is accepted as a substitute for the lives of all who live in the town closest to the corpse, and it is accepted as an "atonement" (Deut 21:8 NIV). Thus, the people are not held guilty for the blood-life of this innocent slain person.

The blood, therefore, effects deliverance from the exposure to death by exchanging one life for another. The preposition בְּ (*bĕ*) has been understood as an instrumental *bet* ("the *bet* of means," i.e., ransomed *by means of* blood) or the *bet* of price, which usually occurs in legal texts (i.e., ransomed *in the place of* [the offender's] life). The parallel between Exod 21:23 נֶפֶשׁ תַּחַת נֶפֶשׁ (*nepeš taḥat nāpeš*, "a life in place of a life") is restated as *nepeš bĕ-nepeš*, "a life in exchange for a life," showing that the one is taken as the price for the other or is exchanged for the other. Each understanding of the preposition is very close to the other in meaning, and makes a strong case for substitution. The instrumental use of *bet* is usually preferred slightly over the *bet* of price.[93]

Blood is efficacious because it represents life when it is in the flesh or body of a being. But when the blood is separated from the flesh or the body, that is a sure sign of death. And when that death is directly associated, not with something in the victim, but with something in the one laying hands on it and marking it as being in some way one with that person, one life is being given up so that another life can go free.

17:13-16. The fourth and final paragraph sets forth rules about eating wild game killed in hunting. The previous rules in 17:2-10 deal only with domestic animals such as the bovine class.

Wild animals can be killed away from the tabernacle, but the blood prohibition still applies. Wild animals are not subject to being considered for sacrifices at the altar; therefore, it does not matter where they are butchered. However, they must be thoroughly drained of all blood because the reasons cited in v. 11 still hold. One reason is repeated in v. 14—"because the life of every creature is its blood" (occuring twice in this verse).

Anything that is found dead, is killed by another animal, or expires naturally is not to be eaten, since its blood would have coagulated in its veins and arteries and the one who ate that meat would be guilty of violating life itself. Only strangers and resident aliens are allowed to eat such meat (see Deut 14:21), but Israelites and proselytes are to refrain from doing so. This rule does not contradict the rule in Leviticus but adds a provision not mentioned in Leviticus. Both texts agree that Israelites should not eat any meat in the category mentioned here.

Should people innocently eat what they did not know had not been properly drained of blood because it fell in one of these above cases of wild game, it is their duty to bathe and to launder their garments in order to be qualified to worship God again. They remain unclean until the evening of the same day (v. 15).

Every clean wild animal killed in the field is to be bled completely, and then its spilled blood is to be covered over with earth (v. 13).

93. See Levine, *JPS Torah Commentary,* 115-16.

REFLECTIONS

1. The principle of a vicarious substitutionary atonement observed in this passage receives its highest expression in the death of Jesus Christ on the cross at Golgotha. It is possible for those who have offended God, and who are thus worthy of death, to receive atonement and reconciliation with God because of the lifeblood of Christ offered on our behalf as a reconciling means (see Rom 5:9-11). So strong is the proposition that the blood makes atonement that Heb 9:22 lays it down as immutable: "Without the shedding of blood there is no forgiveness" (NIV). Thus, in the NT view, the sacrificial system anticipated and foreshadowed the one and only perfect sacrifice that was to come in the death of Christ. While all agree that his death and resurrection are central to Christian theology in some significant way, the issue of the blood, and what it means, has continued to be one of the most hotly contested issues in modern ecclesiastical history.

2. The prohibition on drinking blood is one of the few ritual obligations passed down to the early church at the Jerusalem Council. Although Gentile believers were not required to observe the ceremonial law, they were enjoined to "abstain from food sacrificed to idols, from blood, from the meat of strangled animals and from sexual immorality" (Acts 15:29 NIV). Two of the four "requirements" came from Leviticus 17—abstaining from eating an animal that had been killed by strangulation, since its blood would not have been properly drained out, and abstaining from eating blood.

Are these two requirements permanent and binding on Christians today? Certainly, no one can make a case for unchastity as being the biblical norm today, so that provision still remains. And Paul also discussed the freedom of the believer to eat meat offered to the idols. Only if eating such meat would wound one's weak conscience or would be misinterpreted by pagans observing Christians doing so would Paul refrain from partaking of meat previously offered to idols (see 1 Corinthians 8; 10:23-33). Paul may have held the same judgment about eating things strangled and eating blood, but this is difficult to say. Certainly, the apostle did not wish to offend any Jewish believers; he would have tended, therefore, to have kept these two principles from Leviticus 17, even where the conditions mentioned in 1 Corinthians 8 and 10 were absent and thus might have permitted him to participate. The question of the continuing force of abstaining from blood and things strangled is more difficult than the other two items in the Jerusalem Council's list of four, since the other two rules involved theological reasons for their prohibition. That is what makes the question of permanence more difficult. It is doubtful that an appeal to eating Christ's body and drinking his blood signals a reversal of the ancient prohibition, for that would be a confusion of the figurative for the literal. While the figure used by our Lord is striking (especially in light of the revealed rule in Leviticus), if it were taken literally, its interpreters would be just as misguided as were those who thought Christ attacked the Temple itself when he claimed he would raise up his temple in three days after it was destroyed!

3. Even though there is nothing wrong in itself with killing an animal in one place rather than another, we are taught a principle of unusual importance: Holiness demands that we abstain from what is in itself wrong and immoral, and that we must keep ourselves from doing lawful and necessary things in ways and in circumstances that may outwardly compromise our otherwise clear testimony as Christians.

4. It is not enough that we as believers abstain from things that are prohibited by God (e.g., in Israel's day it was certain foods), but we must also use what is permitted in such a way that will be well pleasing to God, avoiding even the appearance of evil.

5. All that is connected with God and with the worship of God is to be treated with reverence. Modernity has often lost the sense of the sacredness of everything associated with the divine. The trite, flippant, and irreverent way in which many sacred things are treated today is a public disgrace. Treating irreverently things that are associated with God or with the worship of God can be a mockery of God. Believers must exercise greater caution. If what this text teaches about domestic animals that are connected with the sacrificial order of the altar is true, surely the same principle that denies crossing over the lines of the sacred and the secular applies for all other things connected with the living God.

LEVITICUS 18:1-30, HOLINESS IN SEXUAL BEHAVIOR

18 The LORD said to Moses, [2]"Speak to the Israelites and say to them: 'I am the LORD your God. [3]You must not do as they do in Egypt, where you used to live, and you must not do as they do in the land of Canaan, where I am bringing you. Do not follow their practices. [4]You must obey my laws and be careful to follow my decrees. I am the LORD your God. [5]Keep my decrees and laws, for the man who obeys them will live by them. I am the LORD.

[6]"'No one is to approach any close relative to have sexual relations. I am the LORD.

[7]"'Do not dishonor your father by having sexual relations with your mother. She is your mother; do not have relations with her.

[8]"'Do not have sexual relations with your father's wife; that would dishonor your father.

[9]"'Do not have sexual relations with your sister, either your father's daughter or your mother's daughter, whether she was born in the same home or elsewhere.

[10]"'Do not have sexual relations with your son's daughter or your daughter's daughter; that would dishonor you.

[11]"'Do not have sexual relations with the daughter of your father's wife, born to your father; she is your sister.

[12]"'Do not have sexual relations with your father's sister; she is your father's close relative.

[13]"'Do not have sexual relations with your mother's sister, because she is your mother's close relative.

[14]"'Do not dishonor your father's brother by approaching his wife to have sexual relations; she is your aunt.

[15]"'Do not have sexual relations with your daughter-in-law. She is your son's wife; do not have relations with her.

[16]"'Do not have sexual relations with your brother's wife; that would dishonor your brother.

[17]"'Do not have sexual relations with both a woman and her daughter. Do not have sexual relations with either her son's daughter or her

18 The LORD spoke to Moses, saying: [2]Speak to the people of Israel and say to them: I am the LORD your God. [3]You shall not do as they do in the land of Egypt, where you lived, and you shall not do as they do in the land of Canaan, to which I am bringing you. You shall not follow their statutes. [4]My ordinances you shall observe and my statutes you shall keep, following them: I am the LORD your God. [5]You shall keep my statutes and my ordinances; by doing so one shall live: I am the LORD.

[6]None of you shall approach anyone near of kin to uncover nakedness: I am the LORD. [7]You shall not uncover the nakedness of your father, which is the nakedness of your mother; she is your mother, you shall not uncover her nakedness. [8]You shall not uncover the nakedness of your father's wife; it is the nakedness of your father. [9]You shall not uncover the nakedness of your sister, your father's daughter or your mother's daughter, whether born at home or born abroad. [10]You shall not uncover the nakedness of your son's daughter or of your daughter's daughter, for their nakedness is your own nakedness. [11]You shall not uncover the nakedness of your father's wife's daughter, begotten by your father, since she is your sister. [12]You shall not uncover the nakedness of your father's sister; she is your father's flesh. [13]You shall not uncover the nakedness of your mother's sister, for she is your mother's flesh. [14]You shall not uncover the nakedness of your father's brother, that is, you shall not approach his wife; she is your aunt. [15]You shall not uncover the nakedness of your daughter-in-law: she is your son's wife; you shall not uncover her nakedness. [16]You shall not uncover the nakedness of your brother's wife; it is your brother's nakedness. [17]You shall not uncover the nakedness of a woman and her daughter, and you shall not take[a] her son's daughter or her daughter's daughter to uncover her nakedness; they are your[b] flesh; it is depravity. [18]And you shall not take[a] a woman

[a] Or marry   [b] Gk: Heb lacks your

NIV

daughter's daughter; they are her close relatives. That is wickedness.

18 " 'Do not take your wife's sister as a rival wife and have sexual relations with her while your wife is living.

19 " 'Do not approach a woman to have sexual relations during the uncleanness of her monthly period.

20 " 'Do not have sexual relations with your neighbor's wife and defile yourself with her.

21 " 'Do not give any of your children to be sacrificed[a] to Molech, for you must not profane the name of your God. I am the LORD.

22 " 'Do not lie with a man as one lies with a woman; that is detestable.

23 " 'Do not have sexual relations with an animal and defile yourself with it. A woman must not present herself to an animal to have sexual relations with it; that is a perversion.

24 " 'Do not defile yourselves in any of these ways, because this is how the nations that I am going to drive out before you became defiled. 25 Even the land was defiled; so I punished it for its sin, and the land vomited out its inhabitants. 26 But you must keep my decrees and my laws. The native-born and the aliens living among you must not do any of these detestable things, 27 for all these things were done by the people who lived in the land before you, and the land became defiled. 28 And if you defile the land, it will vomit you out as it vomited out the nations that were before you.

29 " 'Everyone who does any of these detestable things—such persons must be cut off from their people. 30 Keep my requirements and do not follow any of the detestable customs that were practiced before you came and do not defile yourselves with them. I am the LORD your God.' "

a21 Or to be passed through ‿the fire‿

NRSV

as a rival to her sister, uncovering her nakedness while her sister is still alive.

19 You shall not approach a woman to uncover her nakedness while she is in her menstrual uncleanness. 20 You shall not have sexual relations with your kinsman's wife, and defile yourself with her. 21 You shall not give any of your offspring to sacrifice them[a] to Molech, and so profane the name of your God: I am the LORD. 22 You shall not lie with a male as with a woman; it is an abomination. 23 You shall not have sexual relations with any animal and defile yourself with it, nor shall any woman give herself to an animal to have sexual relations with it: it is perversion.

24 Do not defile yourselves in any of these ways, for by all these practices the nations I am casting out before you have defiled themselves. 25 Thus the land became defiled; and I punished it for its iniquity, and the land vomited out its inhabitants. 26 But you shall keep my statutes and my ordinances and commit none of these abominations, either the citizen or the alien who resides among you 27 (for the inhabitants of the land, who were before you, committed all of these abominations, and the land became defiled); 28 otherwise the land will vomit you out for defiling it, as it vomited out the nation that was before you. 29 For whoever commits any of these abominations shall be cut off from their people. 30 So keep my charge not to commit any of these abominations that were done before you, and not to defile yourselves by them: I am the LORD your God.

a Heb to pass them over

COMMENTARY

Chapters 18 –20 form a distinct section within the Holiness Code of chaps. 17–26. It begins with a formal introduction in 18:1-5 and concludes with a formal closing in 20:22-26.

Four areas where holiness must be exemplified

are set forth in these three chapters, including sexual behavior (18:1-30), social ethics (19:1-37), worship (20:1-8, 27), and family relations (20:9-26). Chapters 18 –19 mainly contain moral prohibitions, but chap. 20 has more penal sanctions.

In addition to the prominence given to the theme of the holiness of God as the basis for holiness in the lives of all persons ("Be holy because I, the LORD your God, am holy" [19:2; 20:7, 26; 21:8; and twice previously in 11:44-45]), there is the constant repetition of the formula "I am the LORD your God." Beginning with 18:2, this declaration appears almost fifty times in these three chapters. This affirmation is almost identical to the one that introduces the Ten Commandments in Exod 20:2 and Deut 5:6. It is an assertion of the absolute supremacy and sovereignty of God found in the frequent reminder that "I am the LORD." It also is an obvious allusion to the episodes in Exod 3:15 and 6:2-4 where Yahweh discloses the divine self to Moses and the nation of Israel by this name for the first time.[94]

Chapters 18–20 are unique in the history of morals and ethics, both in grounding their ethical injunctions in the repeated formula of divine self-asserveration and in the way that the institutions of marriage and the family are made the hallmarks and foundations for building morality. None have put it more succinctly than J. H. Hertz. His view is that these chapters set forth

the foundation principles of social morality. The first place among these is given to the institution of marriage . . . the cornerstone of all human society. . . . Any violation of the sacred character of marriage is deemed a heinous offence, calling down the punishment of Heaven both upon the offender and the society that condones the offence.[95]

Chapter 18 is divided into four sections containing four warnings: against the customs of pagan nations (vv. 1-5); against incestuous and illicit sexual unions (vv. 6-20); against Canaanite sexual deviations (vv. 21-23); and about the consequences of neglecting these rules (vv. 24-30).

Chapter 18 is one of the most systematic and complete collections of laws in the Torah on the subject of incest and forbidden sexual unions. More than any other text, it outlines which unions are permissible and which are forbidden.

The biblical family is organized along patrilineal lines with the father being the head of the family. The nuclear family is founded on six relatives,

who are "flesh relations": father, mother, son, daughter, brother, and sister. This definition can be indirectly determined by noting that, according to 21:2-3, any of the priests are permitted to attend the funeral of any one of these six relatives, even though contact with a corpse normally defiles a priest.

Two key principles shape the definition of what is considered incest in this law on sexual behaviors: (1) שאר (šĕʾēr, "flesh relations") also known as blood relations or as consanguine relations; and (2) לגלות ערוה (legallôt ʿerwâ, "to uncover the nakedness") a euphemism for "having sexual relations with [someone]," hence a principle of sexuality. The šĕʾēr relatives are in a different category from the members of the family related by virtue of marriage. The only exception to the ʿerwâ prohibition is the levirate marriage, which according to Deut 25:5-10 allows, if not requires, a man to raise up a male heir with his brother's widow. With the interaction of these two principles of "flesh relations" and "sexual relations," all sexual unions in chap. 18 are defined as either legitimate or illegitimate.

The prohibitions noted in chap. 18 are in no way meant to be an exhaustive list of all possible combinations of unions. In dealing with the more obvious violations against normative chastity, it sets patterns for inferring principles of interpretation not directly addressed.

18:1-5. The scope of the whole chapter is set out in v. 3. The emphasis on "doing" can best be captured in a literal translation: "According to the *doings* of the land of Egypt, where you used to live, you shall not *do:* and according to the *doings* of the land of Canaan, where I am bringing you, you shall not *do:* neither shall you live by their statutes." Instead, Israel is *to do* God's decrees and statutes, and to keep them in mind while going about the business of living (v. 5). The accent falls on an approved life-style as opposed to forms of living that Israel had seen in Egypt and, apparently, would soon see demonstrated in Canaan.

Israel had been called to be a holy nation, a royal priesthood, or a kingdom of priests (see Exod 19:5-6). Any and all trifling with the customs observed among the pagan nations of Egypt or Canaan would mock the call to holiness that had been issued to the nation. It was common for the royal line in Egypt to intermarry brothers and sisters. Even a pharaoh like Rameses II claimed

---

94. See the altogether unique argument of Moberly, *The Old Testament of the Old Testament,* 21-35.

95. J. H. Hertz, *Leviticus* (London: Oxford University Press, 1932) 172.

he was sired by the relations his mother had with the goat-god Ptah. The Canaanites were no more exemplary models of sexual behavior, for the Canaanite Ugaritic texts were lewd in their references to the gods and goddesses and their unrestrained copulation with one another and with animals. The warning was not prudish in the least; it was extremely realistic caution about the surrounding sensate societies of those days.

Men and women will fare much better if they will follow God's laws. This chapter is addressed to those who claim the Lord as their God. In fact, that affirmation literally frames this chapter in vv. 2 and 30. Only those who already have this Lord as their God are commanded to walk in God's ways so that they might live (v. 5). Keeping the law will not lead to eternal life, as some have mistakenly thought this verse teaches, but it will lead to an abundant life.[96] The phrase "will live by them" means that life will be lived in accordance with God's laws and commandments. The subsequent history of interpretation finds both Christian and Jewish commentators attempting to have this phrase reinterpreted to say, "[A person] shall perform, so that [as a result] he or she may acquire life by keeping them." But this result, as one can see, is contrived both in its understanding of "life" and in its unusual construal of the syntax.

18:6-20. This section deals with all types of incestuous and illicit sexual relations. The section begins in v. 6 with a general statement that underlies all prohibitions on the various kinds of incestuous and wrong sexual relations, insisting that its rules apply to everyone. The Hebrew has איש איש ('îš 'îš), meaning literally "man, man," but idiomatically "no one," i.e., "none of you," perhaps implying not only Israelites, but all humans, whether Hebrew or Gentile: "No one is to approach [a euphemism for 'to have sexual intercourse with'; cf. Gen 20:4 or Isa 8:3] any close relative [literally 'to all (any) remainder of his flesh' אל־כל־שאר בשרו 'el-kol-šĕ 'ēr bĕśārô] to have sexual relations." For the fourth time in the first six verses of this chapter, this principle is sealed, as it were, with a signature that underscores the significance of what has just been said: "I am the

LORD." To act differently from this rule's directions would be to make common cause with the customs of the Egyptians and the Canaanites. Such unnatural alliances were sanctioned with some frequency in Egypt between a man and his sister or half-sister. Another form of the same injunction against incest is Paul's rebuke to a man who had committed incest with his mother (see 1 Cor 5:1).

If v. 6 deals with the principle of relatives who are related by virtue of blood relations in the šĕ 'ēr, "flesh," v. 7 announces a similar principle but from the standpoint of affinity by virtue of sexual relations ('erwâ). Verse 7 forbids sexual relations with one's natural mother. Literally the Hebrew text reads: "The nakedness of your father, that is [ו wĕ] the nakedness of your mother, you shall not uncover; she is your mother—you shall not uncover her nakedness." Because the husband and the wife "become one flesh" (Gen 2:24 NIV), to "uncover the nakedness of" (i.e., "to have sexual relations with") one partner is equivalent to exposing the other partner. The husband and the wife are so identified in marriage that they are no longer two. Only sexual relations with the mother is intended in this example even though the father is just as much implicated since he alone should have access to his wife's sexuality. Deuteronomy 27:20 underscores the same thought by saying, "Cursed is the man who sleeps with his father's wife, for he dishonors his father's bed" (NIV). In a similar manner, the nakedness of a brother's wife is exclusively the brother's nakedness (Lev 18:16). The married partners truly are "one flesh."

Incest is forbidden with one's mother (v. 7), stepmother (v. 8; in that a man and his wife are one flesh even if he should die or divorce her), sister (v. 9), granddaughter (v. 10), half-sister on the father's side (v. 11), paternal aunt (v. 12), maternal aunt (v. 13), paternal uncle's wife (v. 14), daughter-in-law (v. 15), brother's wife (v. 16), stepdaughter or granddaughter (v. 17), or wife's sister while the wife is still living (v. 18). These various prohibitions embrace six relationships of consanguinity—i.e., blood relations (vv. 7, 9-13)—and eight cases of affinity (by virtue of sexual relations) in marriage (vv. 8, 14-18).

There is some question about v. 9 with its clause "whether she was born into the household

---

96. For a full discussion of this issue, see Walter C. Kaiser, Jr., *"Leviticus 18:5 and Paul: 'Do This and You Shall Live (Eternally?),"* JETS 14 (1971) 19-28; also *idem , Toward an Old Testament Theology* (Grand Rapids: Zondervan, 1978) 110 -13.

or outside" (literal translation). It may well be that the meaning is one who is one's father's daughter, and thus born into that household, or one who is born outside that household, when the mother is not part of that household. In effect, then, it would distinguish between one who is born from one's father by another woman or one who is born from one's mother by another man.

It is clear, then, that biblical law forbids unions between close blood relatives and, in certain cases, between persons who are connected by marriage. Some relationships that are not present may strike us as being strange, e.g., there is no prohibition of a union between a father and a daughter. However, this is to be inferred from the prohibition on the union between grandfather and granddaughter (v. 10). There is no warning against a union between an uncle and a niece, but that too is to be inferred because a union between a nephew and an aunt is mentioned in v. 14.

Polygamous marriages within a family, apparently, are discouraged by the prohibition on a man marrying his wife's sister during the lifetime of the wife (v. 18). This not only bars polygamous marriages of two sisters; it also bars marriage to the sister of a divorced wife. A widower, apparently, may marry his late wife's sister.[97]

Adultery is considered in v. 20. It consists of a married or an engaged woman having sexual relations with someone who is not her husband. It was traditionally argued that a married man having intercourse with a single woman was judged to be sinful but such action did not constitute adultery and warrant the accompanying death penalty (vv. 24-30). The law here deals only with the violation of another's marriage, and to do so renders one unclean, a matter regarded as most serious by the Holiness Code (vv. 24-30).

18:21-23. The third section warns against the indulgences of the Canaanites. However, grouped with these aberrations are the issues of profaning the name of God (v. 21b), homosexual acts (v. 22), and bestiality (v. 23).

Why Molech worship (v. 21) should suddenly intrude into this discussion of sexual relations cannot be determined exactly, since we still do not know exactly what this cult involved.

The conventional wisdom on this matter usually declares that Molech was a heathen god to whom infants were sacrificed. His worshipers called him מלך (Melek, "king"), but the biblical writers could not abide this offense, so they took the vowels from the word בשת (bōšet, "shame") and substituted them into melek to get mōlek, or as English has it Molech.

Human sacrifice was known in the ancient Near East, for the Moabite king Mesha sacrificed his oldest son at a time of national crisis (see 2 Kgs 3:27), but to whom he sacrificed his son we do not know. First Kings 11:7 also links Molech with the Ammonites, but elsewhere the Ammonite god is called Milcom. No one has ever found a god named Melek in any extrabiblical source.

It is also true that the Canaanites burned their children (see Deut 12:31) as offerings to the gods, but the sacrifice is never linked directly with Molech; nor does the name of a god appear in a similar passage (see Deut 18:10). Only this passage in Lev 18:21 and Jer 32:35 speaks of children being offered to Molech; but there is not a word about fire in these two contexts. The only passage where Molech and fire are connected is in 2 Kgs 23:10. Some say the children were only made to walk between two fires as a symbol of dedication to Molech, while others tell stories of children being tossed back and forth over a fire until they were burned. Others think that Molech was shaped like a huge potbelly stove in which a roaring fire was placed. Children offered to him were placed on the image's outstretched arms; then they rolled down the arms and fell through the image's mouth into the hot fire.[98]

Traces of this form of infanticide have been found in Carthage, North Africa, a known outpost for the late Phoenician-Canaanite society.[99] Evidence has now come from a Late Bronze Age temple in Amman, Jordan, ancient Rabbath-Ammon, capital of the Ammonites. It is also known that during the reigns of Manasseh and Amon, kings of Judah, Molech worship was practiced just outside Jerusalem at Topheth, in the valley of Hinnom. Manasseh even sacrificed his children to this god! (See 2 Chr 36:6.) So disgusting was the practice

97. For further discussion on this important v. 18, see Kaiser, *Toward Old Testament Ethics,* 116, and the arguments of S. E. Dwight, *The Hebrew Wife or the Law of Marriage* (New York: Leavitt, 1836) 105-27.

98. For documentation, see the *Talmud, Sanh.* 64b. and Diodorus *History,* 20.14, and *IDB* 4:154a. Also see N. H. Snaith, "The Cult of Molech," *VT* 16 (1966) 123ff.

99. See Roland de Vaux, *Studies in Old Testament Sacrifice* (Cardiff: University of Wales Press, 1964) 56-90.

that King Josiah, Manasseh's grandson, ordered the Molech installation razed to the ground, and the place was subsequently renamed Gehenna, the awful symbol of hell.[100]

Giving children to Molech is here said to lead to the profanation of the name of God (v. 21b).[101] The direct opposite of holiness is חל (hōl, "profane" or "common"), or what has been taken away from the Temple. Thus, in one word, "to profane" a holy God and to profane a people is to place two opposite principles in mortal combat with each other. And in this case, the "name" of God stands for God's person, character, teaching, and qualities. To make any of these aspects of God common or cheap is to attack the very person of God.

Homosexual behavior carries strong disapproval (v. 22), perhaps because it too is connected with Canaanite practices or because it is an act considered contrary to human nature. This verse labels it an "abomination," and it is included in the abominations condemned in vv. 26-30. The root from which *abomination* comes means "to hate" or "to abhor." The practice itself, not the person, is despised or hated. The practice is considered by many to be condemned throughout Scripture (see Gen 19:1-38; Lev 20:13; Judg 19:22-23; Rom 1:27; and 1 Cor 6:9). Others would argue that many of these texts imply sexual activity that is exploitive, violent, lustful, or connected with pagan cults and thus cannot be used to condemn homosexual behavior as such. This text, however, does not allow for permissible homosexual activity, but the context may suggest such activity implied Canaanite practice to Israel.

It has been argued that this law on homosexual behavior has been removed in Christian times, since it appears in the ceremonial law. Thus, it is argued, forbidding homosexual acts would be like forbidding unclean foods today. But this challenge forgets that this law is in the Holiness Code with its vigorous moral emphasis; therefore, others would argue that its content is still binding on us

today. It is just as normative today as are the laws of blood relations, laws of affinity, laws on incest, laws on adultery, and laws against unjust weights and measures.

Homosexual behavior, until recently, has been regarded as an unnatural, perverted, or degenerate form of sexual relations by most Jewish-Christian morality. Many would argue that this reflects limited Israelite understandings and social context (similar to attitudes on women and slaves) and texts like Lev 18:22 are not to be considered eternally binding. These issues cannot be resolved in the discussion of this text alone. For that reason the rigid condemnation and description of homosexual acts found in v. 22 will anger many modern readers who have become more tolerant of homosexual practices than they have of any critiques of it. The subject arouses violent emotions on both sides of the issue, but there can be no doubt about this text's position on the matter. The Holiness Code does not consider homosexual activity between men (women are not considered) acceptable and judges it an abomination.

No less reprehensible is another practice found among the nations of antiquity: bestiality. Sexual congress between humans and animals is unconditionally forbidden (see Exod 22:19; Lev 18:23; 20:15-16; Deut 27:21). To cross over boundaries set by God is to introduce confusion and mixtures that are condemned as being unnatural from the divine point of view. This theme, however, is a frequent one in the myths. Usually, a woman couples with a beast or a god in the guise of a beast. It too stands under the divine indictment of a God who had no female consort and who had no congress with any animals, as did the gods of antiquity.

18:24-30. This chapter on sexual behavior concludes with a set of warnings. To avoid being "vomited out" (vv. 25, 28) of the holy land that God would give to Israel, men and women would do well to observe all the commandments of God. For just as the Canaanites had been expelled from the very same territory prior to the coming of Israel for disobeying the very same moral principles of a holy God, so it would happen to Israel for the same reasons.

100. A. R. W. Green, *The Role of Human Sacrifice in the Ancient Near East* (Missoula: Scholars Press, 1975).

101. For a fuller study of the meaning of "name," see Walter C. Kaiser, Jr., "Name," in the *Zondervan Pictorial Encyclopedia of the Bible,* ed. M. C. Tenney, 5 vols. (Grand Rapids: Zondervan, 1975) 4:360-70.

REFLECTIONS

1. Sexual purity is only one part of the larger morality that is mandatory for all who would live a godly and righteous life before a holy God. However, sexual holiness may be the first line of practical defense for all who are on the road to living a holy life devoted to God. To give free course to our passions, appetites, and hungers in this area is ultimately to turn loose the controls over every other area of our lives.

2. It is surprising to be asked today if the rules of consanguinity and affinity are still of permanent authority in our contemporary world, for the reasons given are just as valid and foundational now as they were then. The theology of "one flesh" and the relation of blood between members of the same family hold now just as they did then.

3. Important to the well-being of a society is the relation of a man and a woman in the building of a family. While not always able to control and set civil law in modern democratic societies, the church must refuse to compromise where civil law ignores or runs directly counter to the will of God. What contravenes the law of God must be labeled an attack on God's call for mortals to be holy.

On the other hand, a warning must also be issued against the opposite tendency, i.e., to lay heavier burdens on the conscience of the populace than God has first placed there in Scripture. While we resist the tendency to license on the one hand, fairness and truthfulness demand that we proceed with extreme caution when this list of prohibitions in the sexual area is extended by extremely slender grounds of analogy and unfair inference. While trying too hard to avert falling into the ditch on one side of the road, one may fall into the ditch on the other side.

4. When a nation continues to flout the moral standards set by God, that nation can expect the same terrible conclusion to its sovereignty and existence that has come upon every other society in history thus far. This principle was turned into a key warning in Jer 18:7-10. Let the nations beware, because God is not mocked. Whatever a nation sows by way of moral travesty, it will certainly reap—whether there is agreement with the divine morality in the present consensus or not.

LEVITICUS 19:1-37, HOLINESS IN SOCIAL ETHICS

NIV

19 The LORD said to Moses, [2]"Speak to the entire assembly of Israel and say to them: 'Be holy because I, the LORD your God, am holy.

[3] "'Each of you must respect his mother and father, and you must observe my Sabbaths. I am the LORD your God.

[4] "'Do not turn to idols or make gods of cast metal for yourselves. I am the LORD your God.

[5] "'When you sacrifice a fellowship offering[a] to the LORD, sacrifice it in such a way that it will be accepted on your behalf. [6]It shall be eaten on the

[a]5 Traditionally *peace offering*

NRSV

19 The LORD spoke to Moses, saying:
[2]Speak to all the congregation of the people of Israel and say to them: You shall be holy, for I the LORD your God am holy. [3]You shall each revere your mother and father, and you shall keep my sabbaths: I am the LORD your God. [4]Do not turn to idols or make cast images for yourselves: I am the LORD your God.

[5]When you offer a sacrifice of well-being to the LORD, offer it in such a way that it is acceptable on your behalf. [6]It shall be eaten on the same day you offer it, or on the next day; and anything left

NIV

day you sacrifice it or on the next day; anything left over until the third day must be burned up. [7]If any of it is eaten on the third day, it is impure and will not be accepted. [8]Whoever eats it will be held responsible because he has desecrated what is holy to the LORD; that person must be cut off from his people.

[9]"'When you reap the harvest of your land, do not reap to the very edges of your field or gather the gleanings of your harvest. [10]Do not go over your vineyard a second time or pick up the grapes that have fallen. Leave them for the poor and the alien. I am the LORD your God.

[11]"'Do not steal.

"'Do not lie.

"'Do not deceive one another.

[12]"'Do not swear falsely by my name and so profane the name of your God. I am the LORD.

[13]"'Do not defraud your neighbor or rob him.

"'Do not hold back the wages of a hired man overnight.

[14]"'Do not curse the deaf or put a stumbling block in front of the blind, but fear your God. I am the LORD.

[15]"'Do not pervert justice; do not show partiality to the poor or favoritism to the great, but judge your neighbor fairly.

[16]"'Do not go about spreading slander among your people.

"'Do not do anything that endangers your neighbor's life. I am the LORD.

[17]"'Do not hate your brother in your heart. Rebuke your neighbor frankly so you will not share in his guilt.

[18]"'Do not seek revenge or bear a grudge against one of your people, but love your neighbor as yourself. I am the LORD.

[19]"'Keep my decrees.

"'Do not mate different kinds of animals.

"'Do not plant your field with two kinds of seed.

"'Do not wear clothing woven of two kinds of material.

[20]"'If a man sleeps with a woman who is a slave girl promised to another man but who has not been ransomed or given her freedom, there must be due punishment. Yet they are not to be put to death, because she had not been freed.

NRSV

over until the third day shall be consumed in fire. [7]If it is eaten at all on the third day, it is an abomination; it will not be acceptable. [8]All who eat it shall be subject to punishment, because they have profaned what is holy to the LORD; and any such person shall be cut off from the people.

[9]When you reap the harvest of your land, you shall not reap to the very edges of your field, or gather the gleanings of your harvest. [10]You shall not strip your vineyard bare, or gather the fallen grapes of your vineyard; you shall leave them for the poor and the alien: I am the LORD your God.

[11]You shall not steal; you shall not deal falsely; and you shall not lie to one another. [12]And you shall not swear falsely by my name, profaning the name of your God: I am the LORD.

[13]You shall not defraud your neighbor; you shall not steal; and you shall not keep for yourself the wages of a laborer until morning. [14]You shall not revile the deaf or put a stumbling block before the blind; you shall fear your God: I am the LORD.

[15]You shall not render an unjust judgment; you shall not be partial to the poor or defer to the great: with justice you shall judge your neighbor. [16]You shall not go around as a slanderer[a] among your people, and you shall not profit by the blood[b] of your neighbor: I am the LORD.

[17]You shall not hate in your heart anyone of your kin; you shall reprove your neighbor, or you will incur guilt yourself. [18]You shall not take vengeance or bear a grudge against any of your people, but you shall love your neighbor as yourself: I am the LORD.

[19]You shall keep my statutes. You shall not let your animals breed with a different kind; you shall not sow your field with two kinds of seed; nor shall you put on a garment made of two different materials.

[20]If a man has sexual relations with a woman who is a slave, designated for another man but not ransomed or given her freedom, an inquiry shall be held. They shall not be put to death, since she has not been freed; [21]but he shall bring a guilt offering for himself to the LORD, at the entrance of the tent of meeting, a ram as guilt offering. [22]And the priest shall make atonement for him with the ram of guilt offering before the LORD for

[a]Meaning of Heb uncertain   [b]Heb stand against the blood

²¹The man, however, must bring a ram to the entrance to the Tent of Meeting for a guilt offering to the LORD. ²²With the ram of the guilt offering the priest is to make atonement for him before the LORD for the sin he has committed, and his sin will be forgiven.

²³ "When you enter the land and plant any kind of fruit tree, regard its fruit as forbidden.ᵃ For three years you are to consider it forbiddenᵃ; it must not be eaten. ²⁴In the fourth year all its fruit will be holy, an offering of praise to the LORD. ²⁵But in the fifth year you may eat its fruit. In this way your harvest will be increased. I am the LORD your God.

²⁶ "Do not eat any meat with the blood still in it.

"'Do not practice divination or sorcery.

²⁷ "Do not cut the hair at the sides of your head or clip off the edges of your beard.

²⁸ "Do not cut your bodies for the dead or put tattoo marks on yourselves. I am the LORD.

²⁹ "Do not degrade your daughter by making her a prostitute, or the land will turn to prostitution and be filled with wickedness.

³⁰ "Observe my Sabbaths and have reverence for my sanctuary. I am the LORD.

³¹ "Do not turn to mediums or seek out spiritists, for you will be defiled by them. I am the LORD your God.

³² "Rise in the presence of the aged, show respect for the elderly and revere your God. I am the LORD.

³³ "When an alien lives with you in your land, do not mistreat him. ³⁴The alien living with you must be treated as one of your native-born. Love him as yourself, for you were aliens in Egypt. I am the LORD your God.

³⁵ "Do not use dishonest standards when measuring length, weight or quantity. ³⁶Use honest scales and honest weights, an honest ephahᵇ and an honest hin.ᶜ I am the LORD your God, who brought you out of Egypt.

³⁷ "Keep all my decrees and all my laws and follow them. I am the LORD.'"

ᵃ23 Hebrew *uncircumcised*   ᵇ36 An ephah was a dry measure.
ᶜ36 A hin was a liquid measure.

his sin that he committed; and the sin he committed shall be forgiven him.

23When you come into the land and plant all kinds of trees for food, then you shall regard their fruit as forbidden;ᵃ three years it shall be forbiddenᵇ to you, it must not be eaten. ²⁴In the fourth year all their fruit shall be set apart for rejoicing in the LORD. ²⁵But in the fifth year you may eat of their fruit, that their yield may be increased for you: I am the LORD your God.

26You shall not eat anything with its blood. You shall not practice augury or witchcraft. ²⁷You shall not round off the hair on your temples or mar the edges of your beard. ²⁸You shall not make any gashes in your flesh for the dead or tattoo any marks upon you: I am the LORD.

29Do not profane your daughter by making her a prostitute, that the land not become prostituted and full of depravity. ³⁰You shall keep my sabbaths and reverence my sanctuary: I am the LORD.

31Do not turn to mediums or wizards; do not seek them out, to be defiled by them: I am the LORD your God.

32You shall rise before the aged, and defer to the old; and you shall fear your God: I am the LORD.

33When an alien resides with you in your land, you shall not oppress the alien. ³⁴The alien who resides with you shall be to you as the citizen among you; you shall love the alien as yourself, for you were aliens in the land of Egypt: I am the LORD your God.

35You shall not cheat in measuring length, weight, or quantity. ³⁶You shall have honest balances, honest weights, an honest ephah, and an honest hin: I am the LORD your God, who brought you out of the land of Egypt. ³⁷You shall keep all my statutes and all my ordinances, and observe them: I am the LORD.

ᵃ Heb *as their uncircumcision*   ᵇ Heb *uncircumcision*

COMMENTARY

Leviticus 19 is one of the grand chapters of the whole book of Leviticus. In American Reform Judaism it is one of the most quoted and most often read chapters, especially since it is assigned as the Torah reading for Yom Kippur afternoon in that tradition.

The masthead for this chapter is v. 2 "Be holy because I, the LORD your God, am holy." To illustrate just how all-embracing this standard is, a list of examples is given in chap. 19 from almost every area of life. So representative and so wide is the range of the laws and commandments found in this chapter that it might be characterized as a brief Torah. Moreover, the refrain that is repeated no less than fifteen times is: "I am the LORD [your God]," which marks the end of almost every one of the sixteen paragraphs (the full formula appears in vv. 3, 4, 10, 25, 31, 34, and 36; the shorter form, "I am the LORD," appears in vv. 12, 14, 16, 18, 28, 30, 32, and 37).

This chapter may appear somewhat arbitrary and heterogeneous in that it appears to mix up moral, civil, and religious injunctions. But we need only note how foundational the Ten Commandments are to these laws to realize that they illustrate deeper ethical principles. The fact that the Ten Commandments are the formative principles can be seen from the following list of parallels:

Ten Commandments	Leviticus 19
1 and 2	v. 4
3	v. 12
4 and 5	v. 3
6	v. 16
7	v. 29
8 and 9	vv. 11, 16
10	v. 18

This is not to imply that Leviticus 19 is a revision of the Decalogue; on the contrary, chap. 19 is a further reinforcement and a practical illustration of it.

The structure of chap. 19 is easily divided into three main sections with a number of subsections, each usually set off by the refrain, "I am the LORD [your God]." The first section (vv. 3-8) deals with two fundamental duties of life; to honor parents (v. 3) and to reverence God (vv. 4-8). The second section (vv. 9-18) explores holiness in neighborliness, specifically regard for the poor (vv. 9-10), regard for the truth (vv. 11-12), regard for the employee and the helpless (vv. 13-14), regard for the rich (vv. 15-16), and regard for one's neighbor (vv. 17-18). The third section (vv. 19-36) examines further holiness in all areas of life, including against certain mixtures (v. 19), regulating slavery and concubinage (vv. 20-22), regulating firstfruits (vv. 23-25), prohibition of eating blood (v. 26a), prohibition on divination (v. 26b), prohibition on sorcery (v. 26c), prohibition on pagan mourning rites (v. 27), prohibition on tattooing for the dead (v. 28), prohibition on sacred prostitution (v. 29), reverence for God's sabbath and sanctuary (v. 30), prohibition on necromancy (v. 31), respect for the elderly (v. 32), respect for the alien (vv. 33-34), and honesty in trading (vv. 35-36).

The constant theme in chaps. 18–26 is holiness.[102] This theme, which has already appeared in 11:44-45, is the motto and central emphasis of the book of Leviticus. The level of ethical performance expected of all persons was that of an imitation of the very character of God: "Be holy because I, the LORD your God, am holy." Holiness is the essential nature of God, as Isa 6:3 announces: "Holy, holy, holy is the LORD of hosts!" (NRSV). In fact, Isaiah is the very same prophet who calls God קְדוֹשׁ יִשְׂרָאֵל (qĕdôš Yiśrāʾēl, "the Holy One of Israel" [Isa 1:4]).

Holiness stands as the foundational principle in the long list of precepts set forth in this chapter. Holiness is the object of all of the moral and ceremonial law. But since God sets the norm and defines just what holiness does and does not include, God's holiness acts both as model and as motivating force in the development and maintenance of a holy character. To make sure that the point is not lost, fifteen times the sixteen subsections end with the reminder that "I am the LORD [your God]."

The concept of holiness has exercised a major influence in recent generations of scholars, if for no other reason because of the book *The Idea of the Holy* by the Protestant theologian Rudolf

---

102. See Gammie, *Holiness in Israel,* especially chap. 1, 1-70.

Otto.[103] Religion, Otto argues, cannot be reduced to ethics, as was the tendency of the reigning liberal theology of that day. Human nature has a religious aspect that responds to the mysterious and the awesome, a reality that can be embraced only in the word *holy* or the experience of the "numinous." But for Otto, holiness is an affective experience, not one anchored to the character of God.

Otto makes no mention, strangely enough, of Leviticus 19, the key chapter in the Bible on holiness. In his zeal to assert a unique character for religion, he ends up making the ethical aspect of holiness a mere "extra." But Leviticus 19 insists that faith and ethics are necessary aspects of the same coin, though they are by no means identical. Faith must demonstrate its authenticity by the way it operates in the ordinary affairs of life. The religious life of faith must have ethical outcomes if it makes a claim to authenticity.

The character of God stands behind the moral duties for humanity. Other ancient religions did not appeal to the person, nature, and actions of their deities as the basis for moral thinking and acting (cf. Psalm 82). Often the pagan deities were more sensual and debased in their actions and character than the mortals who strove to worship them. Not so with Yahweh, who is holiness itself and a model for all.

19:3-8. The first division of the law of holiness sets forth two fundamental duties for the social and religious life: to honor one's parents (v. 3) and to reverence God (vv. 4-8).

Pride of place in the law of holiness goes to honoring one's parents. This precept is first announced in the fifth commandment (see Exod 20:12). But it should not surprise us that honoring one's parents is placed at the head of this list of precepts, especially since parents function in a very real sense to introduce a child to God during the early years. Notice that the mother is mentioned first, and then the father, reversing the order given in the Ten Commandments. Here, then, is the foundation of all holiness as it is worked out in the sphere of relationships with others.

The second foundational principle is to be found in reverence for God; however, it is not to be taught by direct precept. Instead, three injunctions set forth this reverence for God: Keep the sabbath (v. 3*b*), avoid idolatry (v. 4), and observe the peace offering (vv. 5-8).

But why are these three commands selected from all the possible ones that could have been selected? Perhaps it is because Israel is more liable to fail in these three areas than in any others in the law.

The sabbath law appears frequently: fifteen times in Exodus, twenty-four times in Leviticus, three times in Numbers, three times in Deuteronomy, and sixty-one times in the rest of the books of the OT. The sabbaths could refer to the annual feasts, the sabbatical year, and the weekly sabbath. Yet for all the emphasis in the text, this law seems more like positive law (i.e., a law that depends for its authority on the mere command of God) than like moral law (i.e., a law that depends for its authority on the character and nature of God).

God is Lord of time and, therefore, worthy of a designated portion of time for the worship, service, and honoring of God's name. However, the sabbath is simply positive law in that it specifies the seventh day and grounds its observance in the example of God's action in creation and in the work of delivering Israel from Egypt. But when the law of sabbath worship and rest came into conflict with humanity's love for gain, pleasure, recognition, and haste to become wealthy, a form of idolatry was immediately introduced. Unfortunately, an insatiable greed has generally stamped out the designation of regular times to be set aside in reverence for God (cf. Amos 8:5).

Just as pervasive in the OT are the references to proscribing all forms of idolatry. The second of the Ten Commandments warned Israel against this ever-present danger, but to little avail. Lest the point be lost on modern generations, the nature of idolatry did not reside simply in erecting a physical icon and in offering worship to that icon; instead, it was to be found in making any goal, person, institution, or allegiance equal to, or above, one's commitment to the living God. In that sense the danger of idolatry is still rampant today.

It is much more difficult to see how failure to observe the peace offerings would have a detrimental influence on reverencing God in one's heart—at least, it does not seem, at first, to be on the same level as the previous two injunctions in this set of three. But the offerer is liable to

103. Rudolf Otto, *The Idea of the Holy*, trans. J. W. Harvey (New York: Oxford University Press, 1958).

disobey the provisions of the peace offering (the most frequently offered of all the sacrifices, since it is a shared fellowship meal with many). In an attempt to economize, be thrifty, and be careful to save, Israel would be tempted to retain the food that remained until the third day, even when God had commanded them not to do so (cf. Lev 7:15-18). Disobedience and reverence for God do not go hand in hand. Reverence for God demands that service to God be performed in the prescribed manner. This is the order of holiness—everything else is only self-will.

19:9-18. The second division of this chapter on social ethics and practical holiness embraces five precepts in five paragraphs, all relating to the duties of persons to other persons. Each closes with the characteristic refrain of this law of holiness, "I am the LORD." Five pentads illustrate the law of holiness as it applies to neighborliness.

The first pentad (vv. 9-10) seeks to help poor people by legislating that the three chief products of agriculture—the grain, the product of the vine, and the fruit of the trees—are not to be harvested entirely; some is to be left for poor to glean. Holiness must manifest itself in regard for poor people. As we shall see in 25:23, the Lord is the ultimate owner of everything; thus the land is a gift from the Lord. If the landowners are only stewards of the land and all that it produces, there is no reason to be selfish and stingy. Holiness begins with one's treatment of poor people; but grasping, covetous, and stingy personalities are not holy persons.

The rights of poor people at harvesttime appear again in Lev 23:22 and Deut 24:19-22. Disadvantaged members of the society have a right to harvest the edges of the fields; they are not to depend on voluntary gifts alone.

If the first pentad condemns stinginess, the second relates to outright stealing, lying, and fraud (v. 11). Further, such blatant theft and deception cannot be covered by false swearing in God's name (v. 12) for that is a profanation. Holiness demands the honoring of others' possessions and integrity in dealings with one another. Holy persons refuse to steal (eighth commandment), to lie (ninth commandment), or to fortify their prevarications by a vain use of God's name (third commandment).

The use of fraud to oppress the wage earner or helpless persons is opposed in this third pentad (vv. 13-14). The Deuteronomic law takes up the same cause (see Deut 24:15), and the prophets lash out against such blatant injustice (see Isa 3:14; Jer 22:3). The principle is no less important in our own day: No one is to take advantage of another person's vulnerability in order to get work done at lower wages or to call in mortgages for the slightest legal loophole or momentary lapse in the payments. Just as reprehensible is the practice of retaining someone's daily wages when the person is depending on them to purchase food to assuage hunger that very day (see Deut 24:15; Jas 5:1, 4).

The same principle carries over into all acts of vilifying, defaming and treating with contempt persons who are deaf or blind (v. 14). This law prohibits ridiculing these disabilities; but it is just as concerned about someone taking advantage of the vulnerability of those who are so exposed. To care for deaf and blind persons is related here to the fear of God, and their care is related to the character of God: I am the Lord.

To stop the wrong inference that God is only the God of the poor, the helpless, and the disadvantaged persons of society, this pentad (vv. 15-16) stresses regard for rich people, showing that partiality can go both ways! The rights of rich people are not to be violated, nor are they to be slandered any more than those of poor people are to be.

The last pentad in this section on holiness in neighborliness (vv. 17-18) is itself the culmination of this climactic chapter in Leviticus. Verse 18, "Love your neighbor as yourself," has been called the Golden Rule (though we do not know who coined that name). This rule is the summary of this whole section on holiness, which expresses itself in neighborliness. So comprehensive are these simple and familiar words that they embrace all morality and fair dealing with all other mortals. This injunction goes right to the core of the matter and declares that the state of one's heart toward one's neighbor is the determining factor in being as holy toward the neighbor as God is holy. No one is to hate a brother in the heart (v. 17). It would be better to openly rebuke a brother rather than brood over a matter. Wise persons profit from such rebukes, but fools reject them (see Prov 9:8; 15:12; 19:25; 27:5). Offering a rebuke is not just a matter of doing one's civic duty or acting out of self-interest; it is also done out of concern for the whole community—that it too will not ultimately have to share in the guilt as the fruit of some of the actions deserving rebuke come home to rest on the community.

Each of the five paragraphs on neighborliness closes with the motive clause "I am the LORD" (vv. 10, 12, 14, 16, 18). They climax, however, in v. 18. There is also a build-up of words for one's neighbor in these pentads, for vv. 17-18 use four different words to describe that individual: *brother*, *fellow citizen*, *people*, and *neighbor*.

19:19-36. The third main section of chap. 19 covers fourteen areas of life, all grouped under the general heading of "keep my decrees" (v. 19).

The first decree warns against mixing cattle, seed, or materials in garments. Thus the crossbreeding of animals, the sowing of two different seeds in the same field in a type of hybridization, and the weaving of two different fabrics into a single article of clothing are deemed to be unnatural associations. But why? The second and third examples are mentioned again in Deut 22:9, 11 with another unnatural association intervening there in v. 10—the prohibition of yoking an ox and a donkey to the same plow. This last example is fairly easy to explain: Too great an expectation would be placed on the weaker donkey in such an arrangement. But what of the other associations and mixtures? What principle lies behind their prohibition?

The reason may have been to maintain the created orders "according to its kind." However, mules were used in Israel from the time of David (see 2 Sam 13:29; 18:9; 1 Kgs 1:33; 18:5), and that would require us to see this as a very early regulation. The perspective of Leviticus often seems motivated by a concern for what seems "natural," and this extends to matters that modern perspectives would consider inconsequential and of little moral significance.

The law of vv. 20-22 deals with the act of sexual intercourse between a master and a slave woman who is promised to another but who has not yet been ransomed or given her freedom. The case is similar to the one mentioned in Exod 21:7-8. If the same act is committed with a free woman, and both are guilty, both are liable to capital punishment (see Deut 22:23-24). Instead of dealing with the issue of slavery or concubinage, the law focuses solely on the issue of inflicting harm on someone else's property. Since the slave woman in question has already been promised to a free man, a guilt offering of a ram

must be sacrificed at the tent of meeting. It is a sin. But since sexual intercourse does not take place with a betrothed free woman, the death penalty is not imposed. The "due punishment" spoken of in v. 20 is the Hebrew בקרת (*biqqōret*), probably meaning "indemnity," for the Akkadian verb *baqāru* meant "to make good on a claim," "to indemnify." This is the only time this word occurs in the HB. Some sort of payment must be imposed to be paid to the one who suffers the loss along with the necessary guilt offering.

S. H. Kellogg's comment again is most incisive and thoughtful:

By thus appointing herein a penalty for both the guilty parties such as the public conscience would approve, God taught the Hebrew the fundamental lesson that a slave-girl is not regarded by God as a mere chattel: and that if, because of the hardness of their hearts, concubinage was tolerated for a time, still the slave-girl must not be treated as a thing, but as a person, and indiscriminate license could not be permitted.[104]

Although this command grants some recognition of humanity and rights to slaves, it does not address the institution of slavery itself. Here we can only recognize the moral limitations of Israel even as it struggles to discern and embody God's will in the social order.

The third law (vv. 23-25) restricts eating fruit from a fruit tree during the first three years when the fruit has not yet reached its full form, is tart, and can be considered undeveloped. That fruit is to be regarded as "forbidden" (literally "uncircumcised"). The Hebrew word here is ערל (*'ārēl*), the same stem as the noun ערלה (*'orlâ*), usually translated "foreskin." Literally the clause in v. 23 reads "You shall trim its foreskin as foreskin." The trees, then, are seen as having foreskins that have not yet been circumcised and dedicated to the Lord.

What grows on the fruit trees in the fourth year is called "holy, an offering of praise to the LORD" (v. 24; cf. Isa 62:9). The increase of the yield will be as a result of the blessing of God (v. 25).

For the fourth time in this book (3:17; 7:27; 17:10-14), the Israelites are forbidden to eat anything with blood still in it (v. 26*a*). Given the context here, this law warns about the pagan practice of such eating, where eating things with blood in it was a regular occurrence (cf 1 Sam 14:24; Ezek 33:25).

104 S. H. Kellogg, *The Book of Leviticus*, 3rd ed. (Minneapolis: Klock & Klock, 1978; reprint of A. C. Armstrong & Son, 1899) 405-6.

The next four laws prohibit divination (v. 26*b*), sorcery (v. 26*c*), mourning rites of the pagans (v. 27), and bodily lacerations on behalf of the dead (v. 28). The word for "divination" reflects a denominative verb based on the noun for "snake," since snakes were used in charms and incantations. Sorcery, on the other hand, was a form of soothsaying, where omens were read from the clouds, since the verb was associated with the Hebrew noun for "cloud." Thus the forms, movements, and positions of the clouds, along with other heavenly bodies, were believed to give information and omens about the future. But God's people have been given a revelation, so they have no need to consult the occult world. In fact, they are warned not to do so (see Deut 18:9-14).

Verse 27 prohibits the shaving of hair off the head or beard as a sign of mourning (see also Deut 14:1; Jer 16:6; Ezek 44:20; Amos 8:10), since these practices were known to exist in the Astarte-Tammuz cult of Syria and Arabia. The mourning is not discouraged—only its identification with the pagan rites carrying idolatrous connotations.

The cutting of one's body on behalf of a dead person (v. 28), presumably to appease the demons from tormenting the corpse when they saw the blood shed, is equally reprehensible. Such practices were attested in Israel (see Jer 16:6; 41:5). But any thought that an offering of human blood would procure the favor of the pagan deity was not part of Israel's faith.

The two Hebrew words usually translated "tattoo marks" appear only here in the OT. But since they occur with the word meaning "to write," the sense seems to be clear even if final certainty eludes us. According to 3 Macc 2:21, though much later in time, an ivy leaf was tattooed on the bodies of the adherents of Dionysus. Once again, another pagan practice is prohibited because of Israel's call to holiness.

Another area of life in the ancient Near East that needed regulation was that of religious prostitution (הזונתה *hazenôtāh*, v. 29). Canaanite teaching asserted that the fertility of the land, its animals, and its people depended on "consecrated women," more frequently called in Hebrew קדשה (*qĕdēšâ*, Gen 38:21, Deut 23:18, Hos 4:14), or a cult prostitute, giving their bodies in acts of sacred prostitution. In fact, in this one word *qĕdēšâ* (prostitute), everything "sacred" (קדוש *qādôš*) is brought into mortal combat with everything opposed to God—all within the scope of words both coming from the same Hebrew roots!

The context for v. 30 seems strange and intrusive until we realize that this verse appears again verbatim in 26:2. There it is directed against pagan practices. This intent would explain its appearance at this point as well. Rather than going to the pagan installations to practice their sorcery, divination, mutilations, and bloodletting acts, the Israelites should express reverence and fear in the observance of the day of worship to Yahweh at the place where the sanctuary is set up. Few restraints on immorality and unholiness are equal to the frequent remembrance of God in the sanctuary.

Attempts to consult the dead spirits by way of necromancy are prohibited (v. 31). Allegedly, the supposed spirit of the dead person (אב *'ōb*, translated here "medium" since allegedly the spirit of the dead could later enter a person and become a "medium" through whom control could be exercised over the spirit) was able to give communications to the living (see 1 Sam 28:7-11; Isa 8:19). But such methods of obtaining information are strictly forbidden. Seeking out such spirits leads to uncleanness, which in turn leads to exclusion from worship of the one true living God.

Respect for aged and elderly persons is enjoined in v. 32. Age, according to Prov 16:31 and 20:29, is a "crown of splendor" (NIV). Due to the experience that the years bring, such persons often stand in the same relation to younger persons that parents stand to children. And to show respect for aged persons is simultaneously to walk in the fear of God.

Another member of Israel's society is the resident alien (vv. 33-34). Harassment of aliens is likewise prohibited in this call to holiness, for nothing must be done to an alien that is disallowed to a citizen of Israel (see Exod 22:21; Lev 25:14, 17; Jer 22:3; Ezek 18:7, 16). Noordtzij calculates that the OT warns "no fewer than thirty-six times of Israel's obligation to aliens, widows, and orphans.[105] Most important here, Israel's obligation is to be motivated by the memory that they had been aliens in Egypt. Since God delivered Israel, they are to see this as moral motive for just treatment of aliens.

This list of precepts for the expression of holiness concludes with vv. 35-36 urging honesty in trading. God also is concerned about honest weights and measurements. Holiness does not allow for dishonesty in the marketplace either (see

---

105. Noordtzij, *Bible Student's Commentary: Leviticus,* 207.

Deut 25:13-16; Prov 11:1; 20:23). But in the days of the prophet Amos, the merchants made "the ephah small/ and the shekel great" (Amos 8:5 NRSV; cf. Mic 6:10-11). Here too the memory of the exodus from Egypt is invoked, though it is unclear why it is specially connected to honest weights and measures.

The chapter closes with one final exhortation: "Keep all my decrees and all my laws and follow them. I am the LORD" (v. 37). The authority of the Lawgiver is evident one more time in this chapter literally peppered with direct reminders of the same fact.

REFLECTIONS

1. Holiness cannot be regarded as an optional luxury of a believer's life-style. If Lev 19:2 sets the mark high at "be holy because I, the LORD your God, am holy," the NT sets it just as high: "Be perfect, therefore, as your heavenly Father is perfect" (Matt 5:43 NIV). The standard is not abstract or philosophical but personal and concrete; it represents the very character and nature of the Lord. When Jesus urged Christians to be perfect, he was making the same demands for holiness as those found here in Leviticus 19.

2. In Leviticus, the people of God are called to be holy, not because holiness is an arbitrary religion game that God wants played, but because God is holy. Because God is holy, God's people are to be holy by being like God in the world. We can, therefore, do away with all the cartoon pictures of the sanctimonious holy person wearing a halo and a prudish glare. To be holy is not to be narrow-minded and primly pious; it is, rather, to imitate God. To be holy is to roll up one's sleeves and to join in with whatever God is doing in the world.

That is why, in this great chapter on moral holiness, the emphasis falls on social justice. Produce should be left in the fields for poor people to glean. Neighbors should be dealt with honestly. Wages should be paid promptly. Disputes should be settled with equity and fairness. In Leviticus, if you want to be holy, don't pass out a tract; love your neighbor, show hospitality to the stranger, and be a person of justice.

3. Holiness is so essential to the whole process of believing that the writer of Hebrews could say, "without holiness no one will see the Lord" (12:14*b* NIV). Thus, the *spirit* of all the laws listed in Leviticus 19 remains unchanged, even though the formal expression of some of these same principles will, and often does, change. At every step in life, the call to holiness confronts us: in the field, at home, in business, with friends, with aliens and foreigners, in acts of worship, and in the family.

4. So formative was Leviticus 19 in the life of the early church that some have convincingly argued that the book of James in the NT is a sermon or series of abstracts from sermons based on Lev 19:12-18.[106] Most have seen that Jas 2:8 uses the "royal law" found in Lev 19:18: "Love your neighbor as yourself." But what has been missed is the fact that every verse in that section of Leviticus 19 is commented on except v. 14. An outline of the similarities between the two shows this:

Leviticus 19:	James
12	5:12
13	5:4
[14]	[0]
15	2:1, 8
16	4:11
17*b*	5:20
18*a*	5:9
18*b*	2:8

106. Luke T. Johnson, "The Use of Leviticus 19 in the Letter of James," *JBL* 101 (1982) 391-401; Walter C. Kaiser, Jr., "Applying the Principles of the Ceremonial Law: Leviticus 19; James," in *The Uses of the Old Testament in the New* (Chicago: Moody, 1985), 221-24; *idem,* "James's View of the Law," *Mishkan* 8/9 (1988) 9-12.

LEVITICUS 20:1-8, 27, HOLINESS IN WORSHIP

NIV

20 The LORD said to Moses, ²"Say to the Israelites: "Any Israelite or any alien living in Israel who gives*ª* any of his children to Molech must be put to death. The people of the community are to stone him. ³I will set my face against that man and I will cut him off from his people; for by giving his children to Molech, he has defiled my sanctuary and profaned my holy name. ⁴If the people of the community close their eyes when that man gives one of his children to Molech and they fail to put him to death, ⁵I will set my face against that man and his family and will cut off from their people both him and all who follow him in prostituting themselves to Molech.

⁶"'I will set my face against the person who turns to mediums and spiritists to prostitute himself by following them, and I will cut him off from his people.

⁷"'Consecrate yourselves and be holy, because I am the LORD your God. ⁸Keep my decrees and follow them. I am the LORD, who makes you holy.*ᵇ*. . .

²⁷"'A man or woman who is a medium or spiritist among you must be put to death. You are to stone them; their blood will be on their own heads.'"

a2 Or sacrifices; also in verses 3 and 4   b8 Or who sanctifies you; or who sets you apart as holy

NRSV

20 The LORD spoke to Moses, saying: ²Say further to the people of Israel:

Any of the people of Israel, or of the aliens who reside in Israel, who give any of their offspring to Molech shall be put to death; the people of the land shall stone them to death. ³I myself will set my face against them, and will cut them off from the people, because they have given of their offspring to Molech, defiling my sanctuary and profaning my holy name. ⁴And if the people of the land should ever close their eyes to them, when they give of their offspring to Molech, and do not put them to death, ⁵I myself will set my face against them and against their family, and will cut them off from among their people, them and all who follow them in prostituting themselves to Molech.

6If any turn to mediums and wizards, prostituting themselves to them, I will set my face against them, and will cut them off from the people. ⁷Consecrate yourselves therefore, and be holy; for I am the LORD your God. ⁸Keep my statutes, and observe them; I am the LORD; I sanctify you. . . .

27A man or a woman who is a medium or a wizard shall be put to death; they shall be stoned to death, their blood is upon them.

COMMENTARY

Chapter 20 acts as a natural sequel to chaps. 18–19 in that it specifies the punishments attached to disobedience of the laws given in the preceding statements on holiness. Chapter 20, then, is mainly a penal code. It can be divided into two sections: the penalty for worshiping Molech and going to mediums and spiritists (vv. 1-8, 27), and penalties for sinning against the family (vv. 9-26). Both sections open with the same formula, "If a man . . ."; include strong exhortations calling for holiness of life (vv. 7-8; 22-26); and end with exhortations to holiness.

There is one major difference between chaps. 18–19 and chap. 20. The laws in the previous two chapters are apodictic[107] in form (meaning they are similar in form to the Ten Commandments, with its formula of "you shall . . ."); the laws in chap. 20, on the other hand, are casuistic in form (meaning they are in the form of case laws that begin with, "If a man . . ." or "When . . ."), and the laws of chap. 20

107. This distinction between apodictic and casuistic laws was first pointed out by Albrecht Alt, *Essays on Old Testament History and Religion,* trans R. A. Wilson (Oxford: Blackwell, 1966) 81-132.

also state what the penalties will be for persons who break the apodictic laws of chaps. 18–19.

The brief reference to Molech[108] worship in 18:21 (see the discussion there for more detail) is here expanded, both in what will come to those who worship Molech and in what will happen to the community that fails to carry out the sentence prescribed.

To halt the spread of pagan worship, this law threatens all Israelites and aliens living in Israel who might be tempted to indulge in such practices. The technical expression in v. 4 that describes the legislative body is "people of the land" or "people of the community" (עם הארץ 'am hā'āreṣ). This body, then, is charged with carrying out the sentence of death by stoning if the law is disobeyed. There is some evidence that the expression "people of the land" may have referred originally to the indigenous inhabitants of Canaan (cf. Gen 23:7; 42:6; Num 13:28). But by now, it is employed as the term for the legislative or authoritative body instead of restricting it to the native population, or to the male landowners, as others have tried to limit it.

Death by stoning is the Hebrew form of execution. It is prescribed for blasphemy (see Lev 24:16), idolatry (see Deut 13:6-10), failure to observe the sabbath (see Num 15:32-36), incorrigible children (see Deut 21:18-21), adulterous wives (see Deut 22:21, 24), and involvement in occultism (Lev 20:27). In each of these cases, the witnesses for the prosecution are ordered to cast the first stones. The fact that they are called witnesses (as described in Deut 17:1-7) suggests that a trial under the control of a judge preceded the execution. Never does the text explain exactly why stoning is appropriate punishment, but the inference seems to be that it is the community's way of rejecting the same sins (see Deut 17:7) and refusing to acquiesce to the same sins in their midst. They do not want the community also to be held guilty by tacitly approving these sins.

As noted above, the first reference to Molech in the Torah occurs in Lev 18:21. The verbs generally used in connection with this cult are "to hand over," "to give," "to devote," and "to [make the children] pass through fire" (Deut 18:10, NRSV). King Ahaz is reported to have "burnt his children in the fire" (2 Chr 28:3 KJV), although a simple textual emendation renders "made his sons pass through fire" (NRSV; עבר 'ābar instead of בער bā'ar, the same verb used in Deut 16:10). Second Kings 23:10 reports that King Josiah puts an end to child sacrifice, which used "the fire to Molech" (NIV).

Is the expression "pass through fire" equivalent to "burn in the fire"? Morton Smith demonstrates that the two are indeed equivalent.[109] The proof is in Num 31:22-23, for in this text, the expression "passed through fire" (NRSV) is used of gold, silver, bronze, iron, tin, and lead, which must be put into the fire to be refined. Thus, to pass one's child through the fire, the child had to be submerged, or put into the fire, in the same way that these metals had to be "passed." Accordingly, despite much scholarly controversy about whether the children really were made to pass through the fire in the OT, the conclusion is that they were the objects of child sacrifice. The prophets Jeremiah and Ezekiel were more than justified in their abhorrence of such outrageous activities among the people of God (see Jer 7:31; 32:35; Ezek 20:26, 31). Moreover, two of the Judahite kings in the seventh century BCE (Manasseh and Amon) sponsored the cult of burning children as sacrifices. Cultures that turn away from God soon begin to manifest the irrationality of such a decision, often in violent and dehumanizing forms. One needs only to witness the declination of human rights in the Third Reich of Germany to illustrate that point!

God's name is profaned (see 19:12) when worship is offered to something or someone other than to God. It also simultaneously renders God's sanctuary defiled and impure (20:3). This will be true if the cult is introduced into, near, or even apart from that sanctuary by one professing allegiance to Yahweh and claiming to be part of the people of God. Moreover, such profanation arouses God's wrath.

God and the sanctuary are defiled whenever God is worshiped in any other place or in any other manner than has been commanded. The word meaning to "profane" God's name (v. 3) is

108. See Levine, "Excursus 7: The Cult of Molech in Biblical Israel," in JPS Torah Commentary, 258-60, for a good discussion on this topic. Levine sides with de Vaux, Studies in Old Testament Sacrifice, 52-90, against Moshe Weinfeld, "On Burning Babies," Ugarit-Forschungen 4 (1972) 133-54. Weinfeld argues that the Molech cult did not actually involve child sacrifice in Israel.

109. Morton Smith, "A Note on Burning Babies," JAOS 95 (1975) 477-79.

the same word used in 19:29: "Do not prostitute your daughter" (literal translation). Thus, while honor or reverence is due to God alone, God is profaned, desecrated, made abominable, and prostituted whenever that honor or reverence is lavished on ancient or modern idols. God will never share glory with another (see Isa 42:8).

Verses 4-5 deal with the effect of non-involvement on this same problem. Should Israel merely close its eyes to child sacrifice by not prosecuting such cases, divine judgment will intervene. The family, clan, tribe, or nation that thinks it can help such a person escape judgment by taking a "hands-off" policy will itself be exposed to divine judgment! The inference, of course, is that the whole nation, or larger group, is indeed the brother's keeper. Negligence, in this case, will lead to drastic results.

Another form of infidelity to Yahweh is treated in vv. 6 and 27. This sin has already been alluded to in 19:31. Consulting mediums and spiritists in the hopes or belief that they possess supernatural powers is another form of stealing glory from God and robbing God of the worship that belongs exclusively to the deity. King Saul exhibited the dreadful outcome of the warning given here (see 1 Chr 10:13-14). It is another form of profaning and prostituting the worship of God.

Thus the sections end with an exhortation. Verse 7 is a repetition of 11:44a. The consecration enjoined here on the people of God is one in which they are to separate themselves from all corrupt and idolatrous practices in the nations around them. To substitute child sacrifice, necromancy, and a number of other outrageous abominations for the rightful worship of Yahweh is not only a profane desecration of the holy name and sanctuary of God, but it is a deadly game as well. It leads to severe judgment from God. God wants personal and corporate holiness, not the abominations of the nations.

REFLECTIONS

1. The Hebrew theology of holiness incorporated the twin notions of separation and purity. When applied to worship, holiness dictated that worship had to be separate from any worship given to any other deity, idol, or supernatural being. To involve oneself with any other form or loyalty would also bring uncleanness and disqualification for approaching the house of God.

2. False worship of competing idolatries and religions also had the effect of prostituting and profaning the reputation, honor, character, and person of Yahweh. There is a sense in which contemporary forms of pluralism that urge an eclectic or syncretistic response to the God of Abraham, Isaac, and Jacob will also come under the same indictment this passage makes for those who worshiped Molech and similar substitutes for the living God.

3. Western Christians may find it hard to believe that what they do, or do not do, has an effect on the whole group, but that is what is taught here. In our democratized and individualized Western society, the philosophy is "live and let live." But God's call for holiness will not let Westerners off the hook so easily. Rampant social and moral evil, left unchecked by any group that ought to act, will be laid at the doorstep of the house of God first and then on the steps of the whole nation. One need only to consult history's final verdict on the Third Reich in Germany for the truthfulness of this judgment.

LEVITICUS 20:9-26, HOLINESS IN FAMILY RELATIONS

NIV	NRSV
9"'If anyone curses his father or mother, he must be put to death. He has cursed his father or	9All who curse father or mother shall be put to death; having cursed father or mother, their blood is upon them.

NIV

his mother, and his blood will be on his own head.

¹⁰ "If a man commits adultery with another man's wife—with the wife of his neighbor—both the adulterer and the adulteress must be put to death.

¹¹ "If a man sleeps with his father's wife, he has dishonored his father. Both the man and the woman must be put to death; their blood will be on their own heads.

¹² "If a man sleeps with his daughter-in-law, both of them must be put to death. What they have done is a perversion; their blood will be on their own heads.

¹³ "If a man lies with a man as one lies with a woman, both of them have done what is detestable. They must be put to death; their blood will be on their own heads.

¹⁴ "If a man marries both a woman and her mother, it is wicked. Both he and they must be burned in the fire, so that no wickedness will be among you.

¹⁵ "If a man has sexual relations with an animal, he must be put to death, and you must kill the animal.

¹⁶ "If a woman approaches an animal to have sexual relations with it, kill both the woman and the animal. They must be put to death; their blood will be on their own heads.

¹⁷ "If a man marries his sister, the daughter of either his father or his mother, and they have sexual relations, it is a disgrace. They must be cut off before the eyes of their people. He has dishonored his sister and will be held responsible.

¹⁸ "If a man lies with a woman during her monthly period and has sexual relations with her, he has exposed the source of her flow, and she has also uncovered it. Both of them must be cut off from their people.

¹⁹ "Do not have sexual relations with the sister of either your mother or your father, for that would dishonor a close relative; both of you would be held responsible.

²⁰ "If a man sleeps with his aunt, he has dishonored his uncle. They will be held responsible; they will die childless.

²¹ "If a man marries his brother's wife, it is an

NRSV

10If a man commits adultery with the wife of[a] his neighbor, both the adulterer and the adulteress shall be put to death. ¹¹The man who lies with his father's wife has uncovered his father's nakedness; both of them shall be put to death; their blood is upon them. ¹²If a man lies with his daughter-in-law, both of them shall be put to death; they have committed perversion, their blood is upon them. ¹³If a man lies with a male as with a woman, both of them have committed an abomination; they shall be put to death; their blood is upon them. ¹⁴If a man takes a wife and her mother also, it is depravity; they shall be burned to death, both he and they, that there may be no depravity among you. ¹⁵If a man has sexual relations with an animal, he shall be put to death; and you shall kill the animal. ¹⁶If a woman approaches any animal and has sexual relations with it, you shall kill the woman and the animal; they shall be put to death, their blood is upon them.

17If a man takes his sister, a daughter of his father or a daughter of his mother, and sees her nakedness, and she sees his nakedness, it is a disgrace, and they shall be cut off in the sight of their people; he has uncovered his sister's nakedness, he shall be subject to punishment. ¹⁸If a man lies with a woman having her sickness and uncovers her nakedness, he has laid bare her flow and she has laid bare her flow of blood; both of them shall be cut off from their people. ¹⁹You shall not uncover the nakedness of your mother's sister or of your father's sister, for that is to lay bare one's own flesh; they shall be subject to punishment. ²⁰If a man lies with his uncle's wife, he has uncovered his uncle's nakedness; they shall be subject to punishment; they shall die childless. ²¹If a man takes his brother's wife, it is impurity; he has uncovered his brother's nakedness; they shall be childless.

22You shall keep all my statutes and all my ordinances, and observe them, so that the land to which I bring you to settle in may not vomit you out. ²³You shall not follow the practices of the nation that I am driving out before you. Because they did all these things, I abhorred them. ²⁴But I have said to you: You shall inherit their land, and I will give it to you to possess, a land flowing

---

a Heb repeats *if a man commits adultery with the wife of*

NIV

act of impurity; he has dishonored his brother. They will be childless.

²²" 'Keep all my decrees and laws and follow them, so that the land where I am bringing you to live may not vomit you out. ²³You must not live according to the customs of the nations I am going to drive out before you. Because they did all these things, I abhorred them. ²⁴But I said to you, "You will possess their land; I will give it to you as an inheritance, a land flowing with milk and honey." I am the LORD your God, who has set you apart from the nations.

²⁵" 'You must therefore make a distinction between clean and unclean animals and between unclean and clean birds. Do not defile yourselves by any animal or bird or anything that moves along the ground—those which I have set apart as unclean for you. ²⁶You are to be holy to meᵃ because I, the LORD, am holy, and I have set you apart from the nations to be my own.

ᵃ26 Or be my holy ones

NRSV

with milk and honey. I am the LORD your God; I have separated you from the peoples. ²⁵You shall therefore make a distinction between the clean animal and the unclean, and between the unclean bird and the clean; you shall not bring abomination on yourselves by animal or by bird or by anything with which the ground teems, which I have set apart for you to hold unclean. ²⁶You shall be holy to me; for I the LORD am holy, and I have separated you from the other peoples to be mine.

COMMENTARY

With the exception of v. 9, vv. 9-21 deal exclusively with sexual sins that have already been discussed in chap. 18. Sins against the family are as much a concern of holiness as are other areas of life.

But why was v. 9 placed among this set of precepts and sanctions dealing with sexual sins—and at the head of this list? Could it be that this law, which repeats the command of the fifth commandment, was the all-embracing principle on matters of the family? If it were, as we suspect it was, the examples that followed were viewed as an attack on the basic command to honor the various relationships found in families, of which honoring one's father and mother was the most foundational.

Verse 9 is also quoted in Matt 15:4 and Mark 7:10. In the worlds of the OT and the NT, parents symbolize God's surrogate authority on earth. Whereas the fifth commandment calls for honoring these surrogates, the sin here involves cursing parents. "To honor" in Hebrew is literally "to make heavy," "to make glorious"; but "to curse" in Hebrew means literally "to make light

of," "to lessen [someone in the eyes of others]." The two form a pair of antonyms: heavy/light, bless/curse. Thus all that has the effect of tearing down the esteem, place of honor, respect, and authority of the most basic unit of the family. Ultimately, it has the effect of destroying the fiber of society itself.

So significant is the offense against one's parents that it calls for the death penalty. But this is not the only offense sharing that sanction. The death penalty is also prescribed as the proper sanction in Israel's theocracy for adultery (v. 10), incest with a mother, stepmother, daughter-in-law, or mother-in-law (vv. 11-12, 14), homosexual behavior and sodomy (v. 13), and bestiality (vv. 15-16). Whether incest with a half-sister or a full sister (v. 17) and relations with a woman in her monthly cycle (v. 18) are placed in the same category depends on the interpretation of the phrase "must be cut off."

Many offenses listed in the "cutting off" contexts are also listed as sins punishable by the death penalty. But "cutting off" is contrasted with judicial execution in 20:2-5, in that the one who escapes stoning must be "cut off." Could this signify something different from capital punishment? Some have argued convincingly for some of these contexts where the expression "cut off" occurs that it means excommunication from the community of God. The situation is far from being clear to those of us who are removed so many centuries from the vocabulary nuances and practices of that day. Surely in most of the cases, there appears to be a threat of punishment from God in the form of some kind of premature death.

Nevertheless, the death penalty might also merely indicate the seriousness of the crime without calling for its actual implementation in every case. In fact, there is very little evidence that many of these sanctions were ever actually used in ancient Israel. In only one case is no commutation of the sanction ever allowed; that is in first-degree murder. The law strictly warns, "Do not accept a *ransom* for the life of a murderer, who deserves to die. He must surely be put to death (Num 35:31 NIV, emphasis added). The word emphasized is כפר (*kōper*), a "deliverance or a ransom by means of a substitute."

Traditional wisdom, both in the Jewish and in the Christian communities commenting on this verse, interpreted it to mean that in the fourteen to nineteen other cases (the count is variously given) calling for capital punishment in the OT, it was possible to have the sentence of death commuted by some appropriate *kōper* that a judge would determine. Thus the death penalty showed how serious the crime was, and the provision of a substitute, either of money or of some other reparation, allowed the individual's life to be spared in every case, except where that individual had not spared someone else's life by malice and forethought, i.e., in first-degree murder.

Each of the crimes listed in vv. 10-21 already appears in Leviticus and has been discussed in our commentary on chap. 18.

A few unique expressions occur in vv. 10-21 that do not appear in chap. 18. For example, vv. 9, 11-13, 16, and 27 add to the sanction of the death penalty this provision: "Their [his] blood will be on their [his] own head[s]." The meaning is that the offenders are justly punished and have no one else to blame but themselves for the consequences that ensue. Revenge cannot be taken on those who bring such persons to trial; the offenders have to bear full responsibility for their acts.

In vv. 20-21 there is the statement, "They will die childless." The Hebrew word translated here "childless" is literally "unfruitful." It cannot mean that God will send some miracle to prevent procreation of children or introduce barrenness into the womb, for the expression is used of one who already had five sons in Jer 22:30. But since that king's five sons were made eunuchs (see Isa 39:7), they did not receive the inheritance of the Davidic throne, and in that sense, therefore, the king was left "childless and unfruitful." That would seem to be its meaning in this text as well.

Another interesting idiom is found in the Hebrew word for "marries" in vv. 14 and 17. It is from the verb לקח (*lāqaḥ*, "to take"), an expression found in Hos 1:2. However, in these contexts, the couples lived together without the benefit of a public wedding; thus it was a secondary use of the term in this context, since in the eyes of God it was not a proper marriage.

Another anomaly occurs in v. 14. If a man had sexual relations with a mother and her daughter concurrently, all three "must be burned in the fire, so that no wickedness will be among you." Usually, the incineration was preceded by stoning (see Josh 7:25). We may presume the same here unless other evidence is forthcoming.

But the most unusual word appears in v. 17. The Hebrew word חסד (*ḥesed*), usually translated "lovingkindness," "mercy," "steadfast love," or "grace," has here the meaning of "disgrace." The only other time this word has such an antonymic meaning is in Prov 14:34: "But sin is a *disgrace* to any people" (NIV, emphasis added). Could the word have been chosen to make the point that what should have been a legitimate union, bringing the covenantal love God intended, had been distorted into mere passion and lust? It would appear that was exactly what the writer intended in this ironic use of the word that otherwise would have meant "grace."

This section calling for holiness in the family closes with another exhortation to holiness (vv. 22-26). Israel is again reminded to avoid the customs of the nations, the very point made in chap. 18. In fact, since the same holiness is required of all, even if they are not part of the promised people of God, that is why the Canaanites, and other offending nations like them, are vomited forth from the countries they once inhabited.

Israel will possess their inheritance, which is called fourteen times in the Pentateuch "a land flowing with milk and honey" (only five more uses of this expression appear in the rest of the OT). So green and fertile will the hills of the land of Canaan be that the cattle grazing on them will produce an abundance of milk and the bees will manufacture honey (the only form of sweetener used in that day), so that the inhabitants can eat their fill.

Oddly enough, in the midst of these moral precepts and warnings against pagan affections in the religious realm, is a reminder about the laws of cleanness (v. 25). But what appears to be out of place here (and belongs instead to chap. 11) is attached to what has been considered out of place there (when 11:44-45 quotes the holiness injunction that most judge to be more at home in 19:2 and its contexts). The point, however, is that the writer of Leviticus did not wish the two to be separated; cleanness and holiness are twin concepts. One cannot stand without the other.

REFLECTIONS

1. One of the most impressive commentaries on this situation was made by S. H. Kellogg in 1899. Although his day was almost a century away from the contemporary issues we face in our time, Kellogg's words turn out to be almost prophetic:

The maintenance of the family in its integrity and purity is nothing less than essential to the conservation of society and the stability of good government. . . . The Church must come to the full recognition of the principles which underlie this Levitical code; especially of the fact that marriage and the family are not merely civil arrangements, but Divine institutions; so that God has not left it to the caprice of the majority to settle what shall be lawful in these matters. Where God has declared certain alliances and connections to be criminal, we shall permit or condone them at our peril. God rules, whether modern majorities will it or not; and we must adopt the moral standards of the kingdom of God in our legislation, or we shall suffer. God has declared that not merely the material well-being of [a person], but *holiness,* is the moral end of government and of life; and He will find ways to enforce His will in this respect. "The nation that will not serve Him shall perish." All this is not theology, merely, or ethics, but history. All history witnesses that moral corruption and relaxed legislation, especially in matters affecting the relations of the sexes, bring in their train sure retribution, not in Hades, but here on earth. Let us not miss of taking the lesson by imagining that this law was for Israel, but not for other peoples. The contrary is affirmed in this very chapter (vv. 23, 24), where we are reminded that God visited His heavy judgments upon the Canaanitish nations precisely for this very thing, their doing of these things which are in this law of holiness forbidden. Hence "the land spued them out." Our modern democracies, English, American, French, German, or whatever they be, would do well to pause in their progressive repudiation of the law of God in many social questions, and heed this solemn warning. For despite the unbelief of multitudes, the Holy One still governs the world, and it is certain that He will never abdicate His throne of righteousness to submit any of His laws to the sanction of a popular vote.[110]

2. The NT position on the penalties of this section has not always been easy to describe. On the one hand, Christ seems to endorse the death penalty for cursing one's parent (see Matt 15:4; Mark 7:10). Yet, on the other hand, our Lord did not insist on the death penalty for the woman taken in adultery (see John 7:53–8:11). It is true, of course, that the legal case against the woman taken in adultery broke down since the witnesses all fled. Jesus knew the woman was guilty, for when he forgave her, he told her to go and sin no more. But had the witnesses returned, even though she had been divinely forgiven, the consequences and penalty

---

110. Kellogg, *Leviticus,* 430-31.

of her sin might still have had to be enforced. Even the apostle Paul concludes his list of similar sins in Rom 1:18-32 with "those who do such things deserve death" (NIV).

What, then, can be the purpose of such punishments as listed in these biblical laws? Deuteronomy 19:19b-20 explains, "You must purge the evil from among you. The rest of the people will hear of this and be afraid, and never again will such an evil thing be done among you" (NIV). Gordon Wenham, in discussing this text, finds five principles here for contemporary application:[111] (1) The offender must receive the legal desert. (2) Purging evil from one's midst cannot refer to the offense itself, which could not be undone, but to the guilt that rested on the land and its inhabitants. (3) Punishment is meant to deter others from committing the offense (see Deut 13:11; 17:13; 21:21). (4) Punishment allows the offender to make atonement and to be reconciled with society. (5) The punishment allows the offender to recompense the injured party rather than try to repay the state.

111. Wenham, "Excursus I: 'Principles of Punishment in the Pentateuch,' " in *Leviticus*, 281-86.

LEVITICUS 21:1–22:16, HOLINESS IN THE PRIESTHOOD

NIV

21 The Lord said to Moses, "Speak to the priests, the sons of Aaron, and say to them: 'A priest must not make himself ceremonially unclean for any of his people who die, ²except for a close relative, such as his mother or father, his son or daughter, his brother, ³or an unmarried sister who is dependent on him since she has no husband—for her he may make himself unclean. ⁴He must not make himself unclean for people related to him by marriage,[a] and so defile himself.

⁵" 'Priests must not shave their heads or shave off the edges of their beards or cut their bodies. ⁶They must be holy to their God and must not profane the name of their God. Because they present the offerings made to the Lord by fire, the food of their God, they are to be holy.

⁷" 'They must not marry women defiled by prostitution or divorced from their husbands, because priests are holy to their God. ⁸Regard them as holy, because they offer up the food of your God. Consider them holy, because I the Lord am holy—I who make you holy.[b]

⁹" 'If a priest's daughter defiles herself by becoming a prostitute, she disgraces her father; she must be burned in the fire.

¹⁰" 'The high priest, the one among his brothers

a4 Or *unclean as a leader among his people*
b8 Or *who sanctify you*, or *who set you apart as holy*

NRSV

21 The Lord said to Moses: Speak to the priests, the sons of Aaron, and say to them: No one shall defile himself for a dead person among his relatives, ²except for his nearest kin: his mother, his father, his son, his daughter, his brother; ³likewise, for a virgin sister, close to him because she has had no husband, he may defile himself for her. ⁴But he shall not defile himself as a husband among his people and so profane himself. ⁵They shall not make bald spots upon their heads, or shave off the edges of their beards, or make any gashes in their flesh. ⁶They shall be holy to their God, and not profane the name of their God; for they offer the Lord's offerings by fire, the food of their God; therefore they shall be holy. ⁷They shall not marry a prostitute or a woman who has been defiled; neither shall they marry a woman divorced from her husband. For they are holy to their God, ⁸and you shall treat them as holy, since they offer the food of your God; they shall be holy to you, for I the Lord, I who sanctify you, am holy. ⁹When the daughter of a priest profanes herself through prostitution, she profanes her father; she shall be burned to death.

10The priest who is exalted above his fellows, on whose head the anointing oil has been poured and who has been consecrated to wear the vestments, shall not dishevel his hair, nor tear his

NIV

who has had the anointing oil poured on his head and who has been ordained to wear the priestly garments, must not let his hair become unkempt[a] or tear his clothes. [11]He must not enter a place where there is a dead body. He must not make himself unclean, even for his father or mother, [12]nor leave the sanctuary of his God or desecrate it, because he has been dedicated by the anointing oil of his God. I am the LORD.

[13]" 'The woman he marries must be a virgin. [14]He must not marry a widow, a divorced woman, or a woman defiled by prostitution, but only a virgin from his own people, [15]so he will not defile his offspring among his people. I am the LORD, who makes him holy.[b]' "

[16]The LORD said to Moses, [17]"Say to Aaron: 'For the generations to come none of your descendants who has a defect may come near to offer the food of his God. [18]No man who has any defect may come near: no man who is blind or lame, disfigured or deformed; [19]no man with a crippled foot or hand, [20]or who is hunchbacked or dwarfed, or who has any eye defect, or who has festering or running sores or damaged testicles. [21]No descendant of Aaron the priest who has any defect is to come near to present the offerings made to the LORD by fire. He has a defect; he must not come near to offer the food of his God. [22]He may eat the most holy food of his God, as well as the holy food; [23]yet because of his defect, he must not go near the curtain or approach the altar, and so desecrate my sanctuary. I am the LORD, who makes them holy.[c]' "

[24]So Moses told this to Aaron and his sons and to all the Israelites.

22 The LORD said to Moses, [2]"Tell Aaron and his sons to treat with respect the sacred offerings the Israelites consecrate to me, so they will not profane my holy name. I am the LORD.

[3]"Say to them: 'For the generations to come, if any of your descendants is ceremonially unclean and yet comes near the sacred offerings that the Israelites consecrate to the LORD, that person must be cut off from my presence. I am the LORD.

[4]" 'If a descendant of Aaron has an infectious skin disease[d] or a bodily discharge, he may not

a10 Or not uncover his head   b15 Or who sanctifies him; or who sets him apart as holy   c23 Or who sanctifies them; or who sets them apart as holy   d4 Traditionally leprosy; the Hebrew word was used for various diseases affecting the skin—not necessarily leprosy.

NIV

vestments. [11]He shall not go where there is a dead body; he shall not defile himself even for his father or mother. [12]He shall not go outside the sanctuary and thus profane the sanctuary of his God; for the consecration of the anointing oil of his God is upon him: I am the LORD. [13]He shall marry only a woman who is a virgin. [14]A widow, or a divorced woman, or a woman who has been defiled, a prostitute, these he shall not marry. He shall marry a virgin of his own kin, [15]that he may not profane his offspring among his kin; for I am the LORD; I sanctify him.

[16]The LORD spoke to Moses, saying: [17]Speak to Aaron and say: No one of your offspring throughout their generations who has a blemish may approach to offer the food of his God. [18]For no one who has a blemish shall draw near, one who is blind or lame, or one who has a mutilated face or a limb too long, [19]or one who has a broken foot or a broken hand, [20]or a hunchback, or a dwarf, or a man with a blemish in his eyes or an itching disease or scabs or crushed testicles. [21]No descendant of Aaron the priest who has a blemish shall come near to offer the LORD's offerings by fire; since he has a blemish, he shall not come near to offer the food of his God. [22]He may eat the food of his God, of the most holy as well as of the holy. [23]But he shall not come near the curtain or approach the altar, because he has a blemish, that he may not profane my sanctuaries; for I am the LORD; I sanctify them. [24]Thus Moses spoke to Aaron and to his sons and to all the people of Israel.

22 The LORD spoke to Moses, saying: [2]Direct Aaron and his sons to deal carefully with the sacred donations of the people of Israel, which they dedicate to me, so that they may not profane my holy name; I am the LORD. [3]Say to them: If anyone among all your offspring throughout your generations comes near the sacred donations, which the people of Israel dedicate to the LORD, while he is in a state of uncleanness, that person shall be cut off from my presence: I am the LORD. [4]No one of Aaron's offspring who has a leprous[a] disease or suffers a discharge may eat of the sacred donations until he is clean. Whoever touches anything made unclean by a corpse or a man who

a A term for several skin diseases; precise meaning uncertain

NIV

eat the sacred offerings until he is cleansed. He will also be unclean if he touches something defiled by a corpse or by anyone who has an emission of semen, ⁵or if he touches any crawling thing that makes him unclean, or any person who makes him unclean, whatever the uncleanness may be. ⁶The one who touches any such thing will be unclean till evening. He must not eat any of the sacred offerings unless he has bathed himself with water. ⁷When the sun goes down, he will be clean, and after that he may eat the sacred offerings, for they are his food. ⁸He must not eat anything found dead or torn by wild animals, and so become unclean through it. I am the LORD.

⁹" 'The priests are to keep my requirements so that they do not become guilty and die for treating them with contempt. I am the LORD, who makes them holy.ᵃ

¹⁰" 'No one outside a priest's family may eat the sacred offering, nor may the guest of a priest or his hired worker eat it. ¹¹But if a priest buys a slave with money, or if a slave is born in his household, that slave may eat his food. ¹²If a priest's daughter marries anyone other than a priest, she may not eat any of the sacred contributions. ¹³But if a priest's daughter becomes a widow or is divorced, yet has no children, and she returns to live in her father's house as in her youth, she may eat of her father's food. No unauthorized person, however, may eat any of it.

¹⁴" 'If anyone eats a sacred offering by mistake, he must make restitution to the priest for the offering and add a fifth of the value to it. ¹⁵The priests must not desecrate the sacred offerings the Israelites present to the LORD ¹⁶by allowing them to eat the sacred offerings and so bring upon them guilt requiring payment. I am the LORD, who makes them holy.' "

ᵃ9 Or *who sanctifies them;* or *who sets them apart as holy;* also in verse 16

NRSV

has had an emission of semen, ⁵and whoever touches any swarming thing by which he may be made unclean or any human being by whom he may be made unclean—whatever his uncleanness may be— ⁶the person who touches any such shall be unclean until evening and shall not eat of the sacred donations unless he has washed his body in water. ⁷When the sun sets he shall be clean; and afterward he may eat of the sacred donations, for they are his food. ⁸That which died or was torn by wild animals he shall not eat, becoming unclean by it: I am the LORD. ⁹They shall keep my charge, so that they may not incur guilt and die in the sanctuaryᵃ for having profaned it: I am the LORD; I sanctify them.

10No lay person shall eat of the sacred donations. No bound or hired servant of the priest shall eat of the sacred donations; ¹¹but if a priest acquires anyone by purchase, the person may eat of them; and those that are born in his house may eat of his food. ¹²If a priest's daughter marries a layman, she shall not eat of the offering of the sacred donations; ¹³but if a priest's daughter is widowed or divorced, without offspring, and returns to her father's house, as in her youth, she may eat of her father's food. No lay person shall eat of it. ¹⁴If a man eats of the sacred donation unintentionally, he shall add one-fifth of its value to it, and give the sacred donation to the priest. ¹⁵No one shall profane the sacred donations of the people of Israel, which they offer to the LORD, ¹⁶causing them to bear guilt requiring a guilt offering, by eating their sacred donations: for I am the LORD; I sanctify them.

ᵃ Vg: Heb *incur guilt for it and die in it*

COMMENTARY

The holiness law moves from a consideration of what is expected of ordinary laypersons (chaps. 18–20, to the expectations and manifestations of holiness in religious leaders, the priests (21:1–

22:16). The standards for the priests are obviously higher than those for the laity.

The rhetorical markers in chaps. 21–22 are clear and regular. Six times the formula "I am the

LORD, who makes him [them] holy" appears as a colophon. This formula acts as a divider of the various subjects, and it appears at 21:8, 15, 23; 22:9, 16, and 32. The last paragraph of 22:17-32 is separated from the rest of these two chapters, even though it has the same closing formula, because the opening rubric in 22:17 is addressed to all Israel along with Aaron and his sons. The opening line of address in 21:1 does not include Israel but is made only to "the priests, the sons of Aaron." Therefore, it seems best to block off the last paragraph and deal only with the first five addressed to the priests as a separate division.

The five sections are rules for mourning and marriage of ordinary priests (21:1- 8); rules for mourning and marriage of the high priest (21:9-15); physical impediments to the ministry of the office of the priesthood (21:16-24); impediments to eating food reserved for the office of the priesthood (22:1-9); and restrictions on entitlement to eat the portions reserved for the priesthood (22:10-16).

Even though all the nation is called to be holy to the Lord, there appear to be degrees of successively higher holiness, just as there is a threefold division in the sanctuary and a threefold increase in the degree of holiness in the outer court, the holy place, and the holy of holies. In the outworking in the nation of Israel, the three divisions are the people, the priesthood, and the high priest himself. On the forehead of the high priest an inscription is placed that reads, "HOLY TO THE LORD" (Exod 39:30). These two chapters, then, will move the discussion of holiness from the laity in general (covered in the preceding chapters) first to demands laid on the priests and second to those laid on the high priest. The principle observed here will be an abiding one that special privilege and honor place those on whom they are conferred under special obligations to a higher level of holiness of life.

21:1-8. Holiness of life among the regular priesthood may be observed in two additional requirements not imposed on the ordinary laity: rites of mourning for the dead (21:1-6), and rites of marriage (21:7-8).

With regard to the first, ordinary priests are not to defile themselves by coming into contact with a corpse, for dead bodies are judged to be unclean (see Num 5:1-4; 19:11-13). Thus the only funerals that a priest can attend are those of "close [rela-tives]" (v. 2). The meaning here is the same as is discussed in 18:6. To make sure that there is no confusion, they are listed in vv. 2-3 as one's mother, father, son, daughter, brother, and un-married sister. The same six relatives are listed in Ezek 44:25, but along with the LXX, the Syriac Peshitta, and the Samaritan reading of the present text in 21:2, "father" is listed before "mother," rather than the reverse order in the present text of 21:2! The only surprising feature here is the absence of the priest's wife from this list. The rabbinic view was that she was tacitly included among the "close relatives." An appeal to Ezek 24:15-18 would not help at this point, since the priestly prophet was forbidden to mourn the death of his wife as the public had expected him to do. But given where the general public's knowledge and practice of God's law were at that time, this is certainly no guide as to what was normative. If the wife were included, it will have to be purely an inference that a wife is always regarded as nearer her husband than one's own father and mother. The validity of the inference must be grounded in the fact that the wife is called "one flesh" with her husband.

A curious note appears in 21:4. Literally, the text reads "He must not make himself unclean, being *a leader* [or chief man] among his people" (emphasis added). The Hebrew word for "leader" or "chief" is the infamous בעל (*ba'al*, "Baal"). Nowhere else in the Bible does this word have the meaning of "leader" or "chief" as it must have in this text. The rest of the verse appears to anticipate 21:7, which warns priests not to join themselves in marriage to a woman of doubtful character. Others, however, believe the verse refers to defilement by means of attending a funeral of someone who is related to the priest only through marriage (an in-law) and not through blood. The former interpretation, first proposed by Keil, seems preferable.[112]

Further restrictions are added for funerals that the priest is allowed to attend among his blood relatives. He must not shave his head or the edges of his beard because the custom was observed in pagan mourning rites (vv. 5-6; cf. Lev 19:27-28; Deut 14:1). Nothing that could be interpreted as profaning the name of God is allowed, for each

112. Keil, *The Pentateuch*, 2:430.

priest is to be holy to the Lord. After all, they are the ones who are to officiate at the sacrifices and to present the "food of their God" (v. 6b).

Certain women are also excluded from consideration for marriage to a priest (vv. 7-8). Women who are defiled by virtue of prostitution or divorce are barred from marrying a priest. No matter how innocent the divorcee, she cannot marry a priest. The law of holiness jealously guards against even the appearance of impurity. Therefore, holiness demands that there be a visible separation from death as well as a separation from every possible sign of the operation and presence of sin and uncleanness. The word *holy* occurs four times in v. 8. Surely, that is emphasized.

21:9-15. This passage treats the claims of holiness on the life and character of the high priest. The closing refrains in vv. 8 and 15 give us some objective data for grouping the subject matter in this way. However, v. 9 appears to float between the two sections. Perhaps it is placed after the colophon in v. 8 to make the point that what is said about the life of the family applies to the ordinary priests and to the high priest. Holiness in the priesthood must be evidenced in the life and activities of the priest's family. If a daughter of a priest makes her livelihood by practicing prostitution, her sin is to be punished. But since she has been exposed to greater privilege, and presumably has greater knowledge than most, her punishment is all the heavier. Presumably, she is to be stoned after being tried and proven guilty beyond any shadow of a doubt (see the discussion on 20:14), and then her body is to be burned.

Even tighter standards are required for the high priest. Because he is anointed with oil and ordained to wear the garments of his office, he is forbidden to exhibit the normal expressions of grief (such as letting his hair appear disheveled and tearing his clothes; v. 10), enter a place where there is a dead body (v. 11), or marry anyone except a virgin (v. 13). To do any of these things is to defile and profane his being set apart to God, and it desecrates the sanctuary of God. Although ordinary priests are allowed to attend the funeral of six blood relatives (v. 2), the high priest must not attend even the funeral of his father and mother (v. 11). In fact, the high priest is not to leave the sanctuary (v. 12). Since no living quarters are provided in the tabernacle or its courts,

it is doubtful that the high priest is forced to be a lifetime prisoner, as it were, in the house of God. Rather, the expression must mean that this job is one in which he is on call around the clock; no other commitment must draw him away. Yahweh's claim on him takes precedence over every other natural tie in life.

The anointing oil is literally called a "crown [נזר *nēzer*] of anointing oil" (v. 12b). This can be understood in either of two ways: The golden plate, called a "crown" in Exod 29:6, is anointed while it is on his head as the high priest is being installed, or the anointing oil appears as an appositional phrase that explains the crown. The LXX understands it in this latter fashion, since it has no word in the Greek for crown, apart from the reference to the anointing oil.

The high priest must marry one who is a "virgin" (בתולה *bĕtûlâ*), from the verbal root *bātal*, "to separate," "to set apart," "to seclude." As applied to a virgin, it means one who has been separated and secluded from intercourse with men. In this way, there can be no possible defilement of the offspring of the priesthood (v. 15).

21:16-24. The presence of any physical defect on the bodies of the priests is an impediment to their ministering at the sanctuary. The principle is given in v. 17 that "none of [Aaron's] descendants who has a defect may come near to offer the food of his God." In vv. 18-20, a list of various bodily deformities is given to illustrate this law. A proviso, however, is attached immediately in vv. 21-23, allowing those who have been debarred because of such physical maladies to eat of the priestly portions, whether they are of the "holy" things or of the "most holy" portions assigned to the priests. The only requisite is that the priests should be ceremonially clean when they share these portions.

The twelve defects listed here are not all identified with certainty. Being blind and being lame are clear, but "disfigured" and "deformed" are not clear (v. 18). The "disfigured" (חרם *ḥārum*) is likely a "split nose" (cf. KJV), with the corresponding deformation of the palate causing a distortion in the voice. The reference to "crippled foot or hand" is probably related to the inability to always reset properly broken legs and arms because of the state of the practice of medicine in that day. The word גבן (*gibbēn*), which occurs only in

v. 20, is taken to mean "hunchback" in the Vg and the LXX, but the older Jewish tradition translated it as "misshapen[ed] eyebrows." The word for "dwarfed" is the same one used of the "gaunt" and "thin" cows and grain in Pharaoh's dream (see Gen 41:3-4) or of the incense in Lev 16:12. In that case, it may be consumption, but others think it may be a type of eye problem. The "eye defect" in v. 20 may be "running eye" or "eye discharge." Two more terms in v. 20 appear to point to skin diseases followed by a reference to "damaged testicles," which is probably a case of hernia.

Holiness is not restricted to concerns about the interior being of a person; it is a concern for one's total wholeness and complete separation to God with purity. Mercy and compassion are shown to persons with deformities in that they too can eat with the other priests the portion assigned to them; nevertheless, the standard of wholeness is vividly illustrated by excluding from priestly service persons who evidenced any of these twelve maladies.

22:1-9. The fourth section in these instructions for the priests deals with possible impediments that would keep the priests from eating their portions. Priests in all categories, whether officiating or not, are warned in this paragraph not to partake of the priestly portions assigned to them when they are unclean, whether it is a skin disease (cf. chaps. 13–14), a discharge (cf. chap. 15), or contact with a dead body (cf. 11:39). In all these cases, they are temporarily disqualified from eating the priestly food on pain of being "cut off" (v. 3). Failure to abstain from eating under these conditions is failure to "respect the sacred offerings" (v. 2). The translation "to treat with respect" (NIV), or "to deal carefully with" (NRSV; נזר nzr, "to separate," from which comes our word *Nazirite*), is to be preferred over to "separate themselves" (KJV) or "to keep away" (RSV). At all costs, the priests are to avoid "[profaning God's] holy name" (v. 2). Thus God's character and person and the sanctuary itself will be profaned when the holy things attached either to God's name or to the sanctuary are defiled, i.e., when they are offered or eaten by persons who are unclean and who are, therefore, temporarily disqualified from meeting with God or from appearing in the holy presence.

The possibility of being contaminated merely by touching something unclean (vv. 4-8) is reminiscent of the question that the prophet Haggai brings up on this same issue (see Hag 2:10-19). The illustrations of unclean things contacted are some types of skin diseases or leprosy, a corpse, an emission of semen, or some forbidden creature. The individuals will be unclean until they bathe and "the sun [goes] down."

22:10-16. The final set of instructions for the priests responds to two questions: Of all the people attached to a priest's family, such as a guest or a hired worker, who is entitled to partake of the priestly portions (vv. 10-13)? And what if someone who is not entitled to eat of the sacrificial portions assigned to the priests accidentally eats some of them (vv. 14-16)?

The answer to the first question is that even though the "guest" and the "alien" are both non-Israelite in origin, only the resident alien who resides with the priestly family can partake of priestly food. The guest and the "hired worker" are considered to be outside the family, for they are only temporarily attached to the family. A daughter married to someone other than another priest is judged to be outside the family by virtue of her marriage. However, if the daughter's marriage comes to an end through the death of her husband or through divorce, and there are no children in that union, she can return to her father's priestly household and eat of the portions assigned to them. Also, a slave born to the priestly home can eat of the portions of the family, for that person is a permanent member of the family.

In the event that a disqualified person accidentally (בשגגה *bišgāgâ*) eats some of the priestly portion (vv. 14-16), the offender must provide a full restitution of what is eaten plus a fifth more as a penalty. Accidental deeds are not to be treated as deliberate violations of the law of God; nevertheless, they are desecrations of what God has set apart as holy, hence the restitution and the attached penalty.

REFLECTIONS

1. Although the law was abolished as to its letter, the principles embodied in its spirit are still to be recommended to contemporaries. For example, spiritual privilege and honor carry with them special obligations for holiness of life. Thus it is not enough, in evaluating believers for high positions of service in the body of Christ, to compare them with the best of persons in this world, or even in the church, as graded on the average; a higher level of dedication, holiness, and spiritual achievement must be evidenced if they are to occupy positions with such dignity as teachers or rulers of God's flock. A more stringent obligation to holiness in life-style is laid on these leaders than is laid on the laity.

2. The holy character of the leader must be reflected in the leader's family. Especially leaders in the church should possess a good character (see Acts 6:3; 1 Tim 3; Titus 1:5-11), and their spouses (see 1 Tim 3:11) and their children (see 1 Tim 3:4; Titus 1:6) should also be models for the community to observe and follow.

3. The priests, both in their persons and in their work, were types or models of Christ, who would come as the Lamb without blemish and without spot, holy, undefiled, and separate from sinners (see Eph 5:27; Rev 19:7-8; 21:2). Christ is specially called that Great Priest in Heb 4:14. He is not only the perfect High Priest (see Heb 7:26), but he is also the one who gave himself for the world in his priestly role (see Heb 9:14; 1 Pet 1:19; 2:22).

LEVITICUS 22:17-33, HOLINESS IN SACRIFICIAL OFFERINGS

NIV

[17]The LORD said to Moses, [18]"Speak to Aaron and his sons and to all the Israelites and say to them: 'If any of you—either an Israelite or an alien living in Israel—presents a gift for a burnt offering to the LORD, either to fulfill a vow or as a freewill offering, [19]you must present a male without defect from the cattle, sheep or goats in order that it may be accepted on your behalf. [20]Do not bring anything with a defect, because it will not be accepted on your behalf. [21]When anyone brings from the herd or flock a fellowship offering[a] to the LORD to fulfill a special vow or as a freewill offering, it must be without defect or blemish to be acceptable. [22]Do not offer to the LORD the blind, the injured or the maimed, or anything with warts or festering or running sores. Do not place any of these on the altar as an offering made to the LORD by fire. [23]You may, however, present as a freewill

a21 Traditionally *peace offering*

NRSV

17The LORD spoke to Moses, saying: [18]Speak to Aaron and his sons and all the people of Israel and say to them: When anyone of the house of Israel or of the aliens residing in Israel presents an offering, whether in payment of a vow or as a freewill offering that is offered to the LORD as a burnt offering, [19]to be acceptable in your behalf it shall be a male without blemish, of the cattle or the sheep or the goats. [20]You shall not offer anything that has a blemish, for it will not be acceptable in your behalf.

21When anyone offers a sacrifice of well-being to the LORD, in fulfillment of a vow or as a freewill offering, from the herd or from the flock, to be acceptable it must be perfect; there shall be no blemish in it. [22]Anything blind, or injured, or maimed, or having a discharge or an itch or scabs—these you shall not offer to the LORD or put any of them on the altar as offerings by fire to the LORD. [23]An ox or a lamb that has a limb

NIV

offering an ox[a] or a sheep that is deformed or stunted, but it will not be accepted in fulfillment of a vow. [24]You must not offer to the LORD an animal whose testicles are bruised, crushed, torn or cut. You must not do this in your own land, [25]and you must not accept such animals from the hand of a foreigner and offer them as the food of your God. They will not be accepted on your behalf, because they are deformed and have defects.'"

[26]The LORD said to Moses, [27]"When a calf, a lamb or a goat is born, it is to remain with its mother for seven days. From the eighth day on, it will be acceptable as an offering made to the LORD by fire. [28]Do not slaughter a cow or a sheep and its young on the same day.

[29]"When you sacrifice a thank offering to the LORD, sacrifice it in such a way that it will be accepted on your behalf. [30]It must be eaten that same day; leave none of it till morning. I am the LORD.

[31]"Keep my commands and follow them. I am the LORD. [32]Do not profane my holy name. I must be acknowledged as holy by the Israelites. I am the LORD, who makes[b] you holy[c] [33]and who brought you out of Egypt to be your God. I am the LORD."

[a]23 The Hebrew word can include both male and female.
[b]32 Or made   [c]32 Or who sanctifies you, or who sets you apart as holy

NRSV

too long or too short you may present for a freewill offering; but it will not be accepted for a vow. [24]Any animal that has its testicles bruised or crushed or torn or cut, you shall not offer to the LORD; such you shall not do within your land, [25]nor shall you accept any such animals from a foreigner to offer as food to your God; since they are mutilated, with a blemish in them, they shall not be accepted in your behalf.

26The LORD spoke to Moses, saying: [27]When an ox or a sheep or a goat is born, it shall remain seven days with its mother, and from the eighth day on it shall be acceptable as the LORD's offering by fire. [28]But you shall not slaughter, from the herd or the flock, an animal with its young on the same day. [29]When you sacrifice a thanksgiving offering to the LORD, you shall sacrifice it so that it may be acceptable in your behalf. [30]It shall be eaten on the same day; you shall not leave any of it until morning: I am the LORD.

31Thus you shall keep my commandments and observe them: I am the LORD. [32]You shall not profane my holy name, that I may be sanctified among the people of Israel: I am the LORD; I sanctify you, [33]I who brought you out of the land of Egypt to be your God: I am the LORD.

COMMENTARY

While there is some connection between this section and the preceding five sections in 21:1–22:16 in that all six sections conclude with the closing formula, or colophon, "I am the LORD, who makes you/him/them holy," this sixth section is addressed to all Israel (22:17-18a) and the priests, whereas the previous five are addressed exclusively to the priests (21:1). Therefore, treating it separately is best.

The concern in this section is for a jealous maintenance of the holiness of God in the quality of the offerings brought to God's house. The first requirement is that they are to be "without de-

fect" (vv. 19-21; see 1:3, 10; 3:1, 6; 4:3, 23, 28; cf. Mal 1:8, 13). Only for a freewill offering is an exception to this rule allowed: An animal can be brought that is not altogether perfect but is "deformed or stunted" (v. 23). But such an imperfect victim is not acceptable in making a vow to God. The prophet Malachi alludes to this very exclusion for the vow offerings when he sharply denounces the "cheats" who have an acceptable male in their flocks and who vow to give it to the Lord, "but then [sacrifice] a blemished animal to the LORD" (Mal 1:14 NIV). Can this be the way a great king ought to be treated? asks Malachi.

This unblemished animal has to be a male (see 1:3). It has to come from the cattle, sheep, or goats, not from the wild animals, which belong to no single offerer in particular. There can be no defect in the animals, such as "warts or festering or running sores" (v. 22). The sacrificial animal cannot be a gelding, i.e., castrated in any one of the four ways mentioned in v. 24: bruised, crushed, broken, or cut. Some have taken the clause here in v. 24 to mean that one was not to castrate any animal in the land for any purpose, but our versions are probably correct in taking it to apply only to sacrificial animals.

The second requirement is that this law about not offering blemished animals must be enforced when foreigners make sacrifices to the Lord (v. 25). Offering discount bargains where the holiness of God is involved is to be strictly forbidden; otherwise the offering will not be accepted by the Lord.

The third requirement sets a minimal limit on the age of a sacrificial animal. It has to be no less than eight days old (v. 27), and the mother and its young are not to be slaughtered for sacrifice on the same day (v. 28). One reason why the eighth day is chosen is that an animal is not fit for eating before the eighth day, hence its inappropriateness for sacrifice.

This section closes (vv. 29-30) by repeating the command already given in 7:15 that the meat of the thank offering is to be eaten on the same day in which it is offered.

A concluding admonition is given in vv. 31-33. Israel is urged, once again, to keep God's commands and to obey them. Doing anything less amounts to profaning the name of the Lord. The word חלל (ḥillēl [piel]) means to "demean," "degrade the sacred to the level of the חל (ḥōl), the profane, or secular." Over against the human tendency to degrade God stand God's holiness, lordship, and gracious act of redeeming Israel from Egypt.

REFLECTIONS

1. Offering God the leftovers and scraps of our time, energies, funds, and talents is akin to vowing to give to God our best and then coming with whatever we can spare.

2. The ceremonial law has been repealed in its outward form, since the final and perfect sacrifice of Christ has been offered, yet it abides in its spirit and intention in that we profane the name or sanctuary of God by unholy lives or by lawless worship that fails to acknowledge that God is a great king, priest, and prophet after the orders of David, Aaron-Melchizedek, and Moses, respectively.

LEVITICUS 23:1-44, HOLINESS IN OBSERVING THE FESTIVALS

NIV

23 The LORD said to Moses, [2]"Speak to the Israelites and say to them: 'These are my appointed feasts, the appointed feasts of the LORD, which you are to proclaim as sacred assemblies.

[3]"'There are six days when you may work, but the seventh day is a Sabbath of rest, a day of sacred assembly. You are not to do any work; wherever you live, it is a Sabbath to the LORD.

[4]"'These are the LORD's appointed feasts, the sacred assemblies you are to proclaim at their

NRSV

23 The LORD spoke to Moses, saying: [2]Speak to the people of Israel and say to them: These are the appointed festivals of the LORD that you shall proclaim as holy convocations, my appointed festivals.

[3]Six days shall work be done; but the seventh day is a sabbath of complete rest, a holy convocation; you shall do no work: it is a sabbath to the LORD throughout your settlements.

[4]These are the appointed festivals of the LORD,

NIV

appointed times: [5]The Lord's Passover begins at twilight on the fourteenth day of the first month. [6]On the fifteenth day of that month the Lord's Feast of Unleavened Bread begins; for seven days you must eat bread made without yeast. [7]On the first day hold a sacred assembly and do no regular work. [8]For seven days present an offering made to the Lord by fire. And on the seventh day hold a sacred assembly and do no regular work.' "

[9]The Lord said to Moses, [10]"Speak to the Israelites and say to them: 'When you enter the land I am going to give you and you reap its harvest, bring to the priest a sheaf of the first grain you harvest. [11]He is to wave the sheaf before the Lord so it will be accepted on your behalf; the priest is to wave it on the day after the Sabbath. [12]On the day you wave the sheaf, you must sacrifice as a burnt offering to the Lord a lamb a year old without defect, [13]together with its grain offering of two-tenths of an ephah[a] of fine flour mixed with oil—an offering made to the Lord by fire, a pleasing aroma—and its drink offering of a quarter of a hin[b] of wine. [14]You must not eat any bread, or roasted or new grain, until the very day you bring this offering to your God. This is to be a lasting ordinance for the generations to come, wherever you live.

[15]" 'From the day after the Sabbath, the day you brought the sheaf of the wave offering, count off seven full weeks. [16]Count off fifty days up to the day after the seventh Sabbath, and then present an offering of new grain to the Lord. [17]From wherever you live, bring two loaves made of two-tenths of an ephah of fine flour, baked with yeast, as a wave offering of firstfruits to the Lord. [18]Present with this bread seven male lambs, each a year old and without defect, one young bull and two rams. They will be a burnt offering to the Lord, together with their grain offerings and drink offerings—an offering made by fire, an aroma pleasing to the Lord. [19]Then sacrifice one male goat for a sin offering and two lambs, each a year old, for a fellowship offering.[c] [20]The priest is to wave the two lambs before the Lord as a wave offering, together with the bread of the firstfruits. They are a sacred offering to the Lord for the

[a]13 That is, probably about 4 quarts (about 4.5 liters); also in verse 17   [b]13 That is, probably about 1 quart (about 1 liter)   [c]19 Traditionally peace offering

NIV

the holy convocations, which you shall celebrate at the time appointed for them. [5]In the first month, on the fourteenth day of the month, at twilight,[a] there shall be a passover offering to the Lord, [6]and on the fifteenth day of the same month is the festival of unleavened bread to the Lord; seven days you shall eat unleavened bread. [7]On the first day you shall have a holy convocation; you shall not work at your occupations. [8]For seven days you shall present the Lord's offerings by fire; on the seventh day there shall be a holy convocation: you shall not work at your occupations.

[9]The Lord spoke to Moses: [10]Speak to the people of Israel and say to them: When you enter the land that I am giving you and you reap its harvest, you shall bring the sheaf of the first fruits of your harvest to the priest. [11]He shall raise the sheaf before the Lord, that you may find acceptance; on the day after the sabbath the priest shall raise it. [12]On the day when you raise the sheaf, you shall offer a lamb a year old, without blemish, as a burnt offering to the Lord. [13]And the grain offering with it shall be two-tenths of an ephah of choice flour mixed with oil, an offering by fire of pleasing odor to the Lord; and the drink offering with it shall be of wine, one-fourth of a hin. [14]You shall eat no bread or parched grain or fresh ears until that very day, until you have brought the offering of your God: it is a statute forever throughout your generations in all your settlements.

[15]And from the day after the sabbath, from the day on which you bring the sheaf of the elevation offering, you shall count off seven weeks; they shall be complete. [16]You shall count until the day after the seventh sabbath, fifty days; then you shall present an offering of new grain to the Lord. [17]You shall bring from your settlements two loaves of bread as an elevation offering, each made of two-tenths of an ephah; they shall be of choice flour, baked with leaven, as first fruits to the Lord. [18]You shall present with the bread seven lambs a year old without blemish, one young bull, and two rams; they shall be a burnt offering to the Lord, along with their grain offering and their drink offerings, an offering by fire of pleasing odor to the Lord. [19]You shall also offer one male goat

[a] Heb between the two evenings

NIV

priest. ²¹On that same day you are to proclaim a sacred assembly and do no regular work. This is to be a lasting ordinance for the generations to come, wherever you live.

²²"'When you reap the harvest of your land, do not reap to the very edges of your field or gather the gleanings of your harvest. Leave them for the poor and the alien. I am the LORD your God.'"

²³The LORD said to Moses, ²⁴"Say to the Israelites: 'On the first day of the seventh month you are to have a day of rest, a sacred assembly commemorated with trumpet blasts. ²⁵Do no regular work, but present an offering made to the LORD by fire.'"

²⁶The LORD said to Moses, ²⁷"The tenth day of this seventh month is the Day of Atonement. Hold a sacred assembly and deny yourselves,ᵃ and present an offering made to the LORD by fire. ²⁸Do no work on that day, because it is the Day of Atonement, when atonement is made for you before the LORD your God. ²⁹Anyone who does not deny himself on that day must be cut off from his people. ³⁰I will destroy from among his people anyone who does any work on that day. ³¹You shall do no work at all. This is to be a lasting ordinance for the generations to come, wherever you live. ³²It is a sabbath of rest for you, and you must deny yourselves. From the evening of the ninth day of the month until the following evening you are to observe your sabbath."

³³The LORD said to Moses, ³⁴"Say to the Israelites: 'On the fifteenth day of the seventh month the LORD's Feast of Tabernacles begins, and it lasts for seven days. ³⁵The first day is a sacred assembly; do no regular work. ³⁶For seven days present offerings made to the LORD by fire, and on the eighth day hold a sacred assembly and present an offering made to the LORD by fire. It is the closing assembly; do no regular work.

³⁷("'These are the LORD's appointed feasts, which you are to proclaim as sacred assemblies for bringing offerings made to the LORD by fire—the burnt offerings and grain offerings, sacrifices and drink offerings required for each day. ³⁸These offerings are in addition to those for the LORD's

ᵃ27 Or and fast; also in verses 29 and 32

NRSV

for a sin offering, and two male lambs a year old as a sacrifice of well-being. ²⁰The priest shall raise them with the bread of the first fruits as an elevation offering before the LORD, together with the two lambs; they shall be holy to the LORD for the priest. ²¹On that same day you shall make proclamation; you shall hold a holy convocation; you shall not work at your occupations. This is a statute forever in all your settlements throughout your generations.

22When you reap the harvest of your land, you shall not reap to the very edges of your field, or gather the gleanings of your harvest; you shall leave them for the poor and for the alien: I am the LORD your God.

23The LORD spoke to Moses, saying: ²⁴Speak to the people of Israel, saying: In the seventh month, on the first day of the month, you shall observe a day of complete rest, a holy convocation commemorated with trumpet blasts. ²⁵You shall not work at your occupations; and you shall present the LORD's offering by fire.

26The LORD spoke to Moses, saying: ²⁷Now, the tenth day of this seventh month is the day of atonement; it shall be a holy convocation for you: you shall deny yourselvesᵃ and present the LORD's offering by fire; ²⁸and you shall do no work during that entire day; for it is a day of atonement, to make atonement on your behalf before the LORD your God. ²⁹For anyone who does not practice self-denialᵇ during that entire day shall be cut off from the people. ³⁰And anyone who does any work during that entire day, such a one I will destroy from the midst of the people. ³¹You shall do no work: it is a statute forever throughout your generations in all your settlements. ³²It shall be to you a sabbath of complete rest, and you shall deny yourselves;ᶜ on the ninth day of the month at evening, from evening to evening you shall keep your sabbath.

33The LORD spoke to Moses, saying: ³⁴Speak to the people of Israel, saying: On the fifteenth day of this seventh month, and lasting seven days, there shall be the festival of boothsᵈ to the LORD. ³⁵The first day shall be a holy convocation; you shall not work at your occupations. ³⁶Seven days

ᵃ Or shall fast   ᵇ Or does not fast   ᶜ Or shall fast
ᵈ Or tabernacles. Heb succoth

NIV

Sabbaths and[a] in addition to your gifts and whatever you have vowed and all the freewill offerings you give to the LORD.)

³⁹" 'So beginning with the fifteenth day of the seventh month, after you have gathered the crops of the land, celebrate the festival to the LORD for seven days; the first day is a day of rest, and the eighth day also is a day of rest. ⁴⁰On the first day you are to take choice fruit from the trees, and palm fronds, leafy branches and poplars, and rejoice before the LORD your God for seven days. ⁴¹Celebrate this as a festival to the LORD for seven days each year. This is to be a lasting ordinance for the generations to come; celebrate it in the seventh month. ⁴²Live in booths for seven days: All native-born Israelites are to live in booths ⁴³so your descendants will know that I had the Israelites live in booths when I brought them out of Egypt. I am the LORD your God.' "

⁴⁴So Moses announced to the Israelites the appointed feasts of the LORD.

ᵃ38 Or *These feasts are in addition to the* LORD'*s Sabbaths, and these offerings are*

NRSV

you shall present the LORD's offerings by fire; on the eighth day you shall observe a holy convocation and present the LORD's offerings by fire; it is a solemn assembly; you shall not work at your occupations.

37These are the appointed festivals of the LORD, which you shall celebrate as times of holy convocation, for presenting to the LORD offerings by fire—burnt offerings and grain offerings, sacrifices and drink offerings, each on its proper day— 38apart from the sabbaths of the LORD, and apart from your gifts, and apart from all your votive offerings, and apart from all your freewill offerings, which you give to the LORD.

39Now, the fifteenth day of the seventh month, when you have gathered in the produce of the land, you shall keep the festival of the LORD, lasting seven days; a complete rest on the first day, and a complete rest on the eighth day. ⁴⁰On the first day you shall take the fruit of majestic[a] trees, branches of palm trees, boughs of leafy trees, and willows of the brook; and you shall rejoice before the LORD your God for seven days. ⁴¹You shall keep it as a festival to the LORD seven days in the year; you shall keep it in the seventh month as a statute forever throughout your generations. ⁴²You shall live in booths for seven days; all that are citizens in Israel shall live in booths, ⁴³so that your generations may know that I made the people of Israel live in booths when I brought them out of the land of Egypt: I am the LORD your God.

44Thus Moses declared to the people of Israel the appointed festivals of the LORD.

ᵃ Meaning of Heb uncertain

COMMENTARY

Holiness, thus far, has been related to holy persons, holy things, and holy places. But now in chap. 23 it is extended to holy times. The laws relating to the annual fast, the Feast of Trumpets, and the three annual festivals are brought together into one place and put into their chronological order along with the law of the sabbath.

Just as chaps. 18–19 use the formula "I am the LORD your God" to act as a colophon and a divider

between subsections, so also chap. 23 is divided into two main divisions by the appearance of this same formula in vv. 22 and 43, giving the spring festivals in the first division (vv. 1-22) and the autumn festivals in the second division (vv. 23-43).

These two main divisions are divided again by another subset of closing colophons that use another repeated formula: "This is to be a lasting ordinance for the generations to come, wherever you live" (vv. 14, 21, 31, 41). Several other formulas occur, but they do not appear to govern the structure. They include "the appointed feasts of the LORD" or "the LORD's appointed feasts" (vv. 2, 4, 37, 44); "sacred assemblies" or "holy convocations" (vv. 2, 3, 4, 7, 8, 21, 24, 27, 35, 36, 37); and "do no regular work," "do not work on that day," or "do no work at all" (vv. 7, 8, 21, 25, 30, 31, 36).

The resulting outline suggested by these structural guides is this: introduction (vv. 1-2); the sabbath (v. 3); the spring festivals (vv. 4-22), which include Passover and Unleavened Bread (vv. 5-8), Firstfruits (vv. 9-14), and Feast of Weeks (vv. 15-22); the autumn festivals (vv. 23-44), which include the Feast of Trumpets (vv. 23-25), the Day of Atonement (vv. 26-32), and the Feast of Tabernacles (vv. 33-44).

23:1-2. Eleven times in this chapter the phrase "sacred assembly" occurs either in the singular or in the plural. The Hebrew מקראי קדש (*miqrā'ê qōdeš*) is a somewhat ambiguous expression in the Holiness Code, though it also occurs six times in Numbers 28–29 and twice in Exod 12:16 but nowhere else. The verbal root of the first of these two words is קרא (*qārā'*), meaning "to summon," "to invite," or "to proclaim." Thus the word for "assembly" might also be translated as "convocation" or "convention." The second word, of course, is the repeated word in Leviticus for "holy." Accordingly, it is an occasion when the community is summoned for common worship and celebration—in holy or sacred assembly.

The other expression used in the introduction is the "appointed feasts of the LORD." The Hebrew word מועד (*mô'ēd*) is derived from a verb meaning "to fix" or "to appoint." These are "set" times when the community is to meet to worship and to rejoice in the Lord. This calendar of holy convocations or sacred assemblies is meant primarily for the laity rather than the priests.

The Torah preserves three lists of the festivals and holy days to the Lord: one in the Book of the Covenant, this one in the Holiness Code, and one in Deuteronomy. Each has a distinctive emphasis and often a unique name for each of these celebrations. Exodus 23:12-19, as part of the Book of the Covenant, lists the sabbath and the three pilgrimage festivals (the Festival of Unleavened Bread, the Spring Harvest Festival, and the Festival of Ingathering). Deuteronomy 16:1-17 names Passover, the Festival of Weeks in the late spring, and the Festival of Tabernacles in the autumn. Numbers 28–29 also has a calendrical listing of these feasts including the sabbath, new moon, and all the festivals and holy days, but its emphasis is on the proper offerings that go with each of these occasions. Another brief listing is given in Exod 34:17-26, which is related to the same content given in Exod 23:12-19.

The purpose of the section in Leviticus is set forth in the first verse: It is to give a catalog of "the appointed feasts of the LORD." Only three celebratory events are left out: new moons, the sabbatical year, and the jubilee. But the ones mentioned are listed as sacred times or seasons of worship. These are to be "sacred assemblies." This phrase cannot always refer to the summons of the people to the central sanctuary, for in Exod 34:23 Israel was summoned to the tabernacle only for the feasts of Passover and Weeks and the Day of Atonement. Therefore, this must be a call for local gatherings for worship, such as would take place later at the synagogues.

23:3. The first of this series of appointed times is the sabbath (v. 3). Many have found the inauguration of the list with the sabbath to be most natural, for the whole series of sacred times is based on the sabbatical principle in the number seven. For example, the weekly sabbath comes on the seventh day. There are seven festivals in the year: Passover, Unleavened Bread, Weeks, the day of rest, the Day of Atonement, Tabernacles, and the day after Tabernacles. The duration of each of the great festivals of Unleavened Bread and Tabernacles is seven days. The Feast of Firstfruits, or of Weeks, comes at the end of seven weeks on the fiftieth day. The seventh month is especially holy to the Lord, for it contains three annual times of sacred assembly: the Feast of Trumpets on the first day, the great Day of Atonement on the tenth day, and the Feast of Tabernacles or Ingathering, which lasts for seven days, from the fifteenth day. The sabbatical year comes in the seventh year; but at the end of seven sevens of years, the seventh sabbatical year is the great year of jubilee, the great year of rest, restoration, and release. Thus the number seven has a special place in the order of worship for Israel.

The holiness of the sabbath day is emphasized in the strongest terms possible. It is a שַׁבַּת שַׁבָּתוֹן (šabbat šabbātôn, a "sabbath of sabbatism," [author's trans.]) or to render this Hebrew superlative form another way, it is "the most restful cessation" (v. 3, author's trans.). The sabbath is to be observed by abstaining from all daily tasks. The fact that the sabbatical year is also called a "sabbath of sabbaths" (25:4, author's trans.) is an indication that the prohibition against work is not to be understood as an absolute, for some minor tasks, such as caring for the animals and the like, must always be carried out. The principle, however, stands. Regular work is to come to a halt in favor of a day of rest for humanity and for the worship of the Lord God.

The Hebrew term šabbat, ("sabbath") literally means "to cease," "to stop," "to desist," "to be idle." The Creator gave the day to allow a person to "catch one's breath" (cf. the Hebrew word וַיִּנָּפַשׁ wayyinnāpaš, Exod 23:12, 31:17). This day is intended to be a time of relief, respite, and up-building of all who have labored for the preceding six days.

At one time it was popular among scholars to say that the Hebrew sabbath was derived from the Babylonian abattû, even though the names were not etymologically related. The Babylonian celebration came on the seventh, fourteenth, nineteenth, twenty-first, and twenty-eighth days. In the Babylonian sphere, those days were the concern mainly of the king, soothsayer, and sorcerer since the special dangers created on those days by the activity of demons made it advisable to refrain from doing any official acts. Instead of claiming that they were days of rest, relaxation, and restoration as the OT teaches, the Babylonians viewed their set of times listed above as "evil day(s)" or times when it was unlucky to work.[113]

The sabbath is ever to be valued as the grandest solemnity in the worship of God. Since it is not to be eclipsed or supplanted in the future, it is given pride of place in the list of sacred assemblies.

23:4-8. Verses 4-22 introduce the spring festivals of Passover and Unleavened Bread, and the Feast of Weeks. The most detailed laws on the Passover and Unleavened Bread are given in Exodus 12–13. The Leviticus list offers a simple reminder of these celebrations (vv. 5-8). The reference to the Passover is the briefest of all in v. 5, which asserts that it is to begin "at twilight on the fourteenth day of the first month." The Hebrew expression בֵּין הָעַרְבַּיִם (bên hā'arbāyim, "between the evenings") has given rise to two explanations: (1) between sunset and dark (Aben-Ezer, Qaraites, Samaritans, Keil, and Delitzsch) or (2) between the decline of the sun (three to five o'clock) and sunset (Josephus, Mishnah, and modern practice in Judaism). With Deut 16:6, the time should be fixed as the time "when the sun goes down," i.e., the same time set for lighting the lamps in the tabernacle (see Exod 30:8) and offering the daily evening sacrifice (see Exod 29:39). The first month in which this celebration took place was called Nisan (March-April), when the barley harvest was ready to begin.

The Passover commemorates Israel's deliverance from Egypt by the mighty hand of God.[114] It also marks the establishment of the nation of Israel. On the day following Passover, the Feast of Unleavened Bread begins. It lasts for seven days and is one of the three pilgrimage celebrations (along with the Feast of Pentecost, i.e., "weeks," and the Feast of Tabernacles) in which all adult males in Israel go to the central sanctuary for its observance (see a fuller description in Num 28:16-25; Deut 16:1-8). While all references to the slaying of the paschal lamb are omitted in this context, vv. 6 and 8 mention the eating of the "bread made without yeast" (the round yellow cakes or "matzos") and the sacrifices made by fire to the Lord. Thus the paschal lamb was probably slain on the fourteenth day of the month, and the blood was applied to the doorposts and lintels, indicating that the death angel could "pass over" the household that was under the redemptive coverage of a substituted life. In the Feast of Unleavened Bread the first and seventh days are declared to be days for sacred assemblies to the Lord in which no work is to be done (vv. 7-8).

23:9-14. On the eighth day following Passover,

113. See the attempt made by Stephen Langdon to derive the Jewish sabbath from the Assyrian and Babylonian unlucky days (*Babylonian Menologies and the Semitic Calendars* [London: Oxford University Press, 1935]). This work followed the line of argumentation that had been set by Friedrich Delitzsch in *Die grosse Täuschung* 1 (1920) 99f.

114. For a detailed study of the etymology and meaning of the word *Passover*, see J. B. Segal, *The Hebrew Passover* (New York: Oxford University Press, 1963) 95-100. For a detailed commentary on the Passover and the Feast of Unleavened Bread, see Kaiser, "Exodus," 371-84.

and the seven days of Unleavened Bread ("on the day after the sabbath"; vv. 11, 15), it is decreed that "a sheaf of the first grain you harvest" (v. 10) is to be brought to the Lord to be consecrated by the priest in a ceremony of waving or (as we have argued earlier) elevating it before the Lord. The reference is to a sheaf of barley, which is the first to ripen in the spring. In this celebration of the Feast of Firstfruits, the elevation offering of the sheaf of barley is accompanied by a burnt offering of a year-old lamb (v. 12), a grain offering of approximately four quarts of fine flour mixed with oil (v. 13) and a drink offering of approximately one quart of wine (v. 13). This drink offering is mentioned in Exod 29:38-42, but this is the first time it is mentioned in Leviticus.

Verses 9-14 seem to many commentators to describe a rite similar in purpose to the Feast of Unleavened Bread (v. 14) but with quite a different ceremony. The day for the ceremony is an ambiguously specified "sabbath." This may reflect an originally separate observance in early Israel (or in a particular sanctuary), but in its present context it appears that the intent is to assimilate it into the Feast of Unleavened Bread.

In consecrating the first part of this harvest to the Lord, the whole harvest is thereby dedicated to the Lord. Now the barley can be eaten by all, since Israel receives it as a gift from God. But more is implied than the ethical lesson that God is the bountiful giver of all the harvest. Israel is declared to be God's "firstborn" in Exod 4:22. That is true of God's work in redeeming the nation out of Egypt, and it is to be the NT pattern for all of soteriology, "first for the Jew, then for the Gentile" (Rom 1:16 NIV). The nation, then, just as the harvest, symbolically signifies the consecration of all the nations in that a part of the nations is called to be God's "firstborn."

But even the dedication of the harvest and the dedication of the nation do not exhaust the type. It is specifically declared that following the Passover, on "the day after the sabbath," the first day of the week, the sheaf[115] of firstfruits is to be

<hr>

115. The Hebrew term usually translated here as "sheaf" is contradicted by rabbinic exegesis and Jewish tradition (*Menahoth* 66a, 68b). Both the Septuagint and the Mishnah, which devotes a separate tractate called *Hallah* to this matter, speak of dough and cakes made from the grain in regard to both barley and wheat. Numbers 15:20 speaks of the *ʿōmer* of firstfruits in the form of cakes as well; thus it is difficult to say for certain which translation is correct.

presented to Yahweh. Some debate has centered on what "sabbath" is meant here in vv. 11 and 15. If it is the regular Saturday sabbath, the sheaf is always waved or elevated before the Lord on Sunday, regardless of the date of Passover. Others, however, argue that the "sabbath" referred to is the Passover, which means that the sheaf is waved on the fifteenth of Nisan. The first view is to be preferred, since the Feast of Weeks comes exactly fifty days later and is also said to be on the "day after the seventh sabbath" (v. 16).

23:15-22. The Feast of Weeks (so called because it is celebrated after a week of weeks, or seven weeks after Firstfruits) is called the Feast of Harvest in Exod 23:16 and the "firstfruits of the wheat harvest" in Exod 34:22 (NIV; cf. Num 28:26). Since it follows Passover and Unleavened Bread by fifty days, it came to be known as "pentecost," or "fiftieth," from the Greek πεντηκοστη (*pentēkostē*). It is a one-day celebration (see Deut 16:9-12) of rejoicing over the abundant gifts of food that God has given in the harvest.

The Feast of Firstfruits marks the *beginning* of the harvest with the presentation of the first sheaf of barley to the Lord (v. 10), but now the Feast of Pentecost, or Weeks, celebrates the *completion* of the wheat harvest, which generally lasted from the end of April well into the month of June, depending on the location in Israel, the soil, and the slowness of the season. The firstfruits of barley come from the field, but the "offering of new grain [of wheat]" (v. 16) comes as prepared food. Both the firstfruits and the new grain offerings, however, are unlike the grain offering of chap. 2, for both represent the ordinary food of the people.

The new grain offering is accompanied by seven male lambs, one young bull, and two rams. These are to be offered as a burnt offering to the Lord along with the grain and drink offerings. Another male goat is to be offered as a sin offering, and two yearling lambs are to be sacrificed as a peace offering. The two lambs are to be "waved" or, as argued earlier, "elevated" to the Lord in dedication (v. 20).

This festival, as all others in this sabbatical series, is celebrated with a complete cessation of all regular labors, thus picturing the great sabbath that will follow the harvest that comes at the "end of the age" (Matt 13:39 NIV). In the Feast of Pentecost, God is celebrated as the sustainer of

Israel and provider of daily food. Israel, in turn, expresses full consecration and fellowship with Yahweh in the offerings lifted up on that day.

In the NT "Firstfruits" came to symbolize for early Jewish Christians that Christ "our Passover" would be raised from the dead and be the earnest or promise of the resurrection of all others who hoped to be raised from the grave. The presentation of the new grain at the Feast of Pentecost came to symbolize the raising up of "the church of the firstborn" (Heb 12:23 NIV; cf. Jas 1:18) as constituent parts of a unified body on that sacred day (cf. later on the great event of Pentecost where three thousand were added to the church by the work of the Holy Spirit in Acts 2). Yet, this work cannot be the final work of God for the people, for the two loaves of bread are "baked with yeast" (v. 17), indicating the imperfection of the attainment of the loaves that must also await God's final work of redemption. Because the loaves are made with yeast, i.e., leaven, just like the daily bread of the Israelites, they are not placed on the altar (2:11) but are elevated before the Lord in dedication.

The spring festivals conclude (v. 22) with the reminder already noted in 19:9 (cf. Deut 24:19) that the edges of the field are not to be harvested but are to be left for poor people to harvest.

The autumn festivals begin in the busy seventh month and include the Feast of Trumpets and the Feast of Tabernacles with the solemn Day of Atonement between the two (23:23-44).

23:23-25. The Feast of Trumpets inaugurates this most sacred month of all. The first day of this sabbatical month is sanctified in accordance with the principle already observed: The consecration of a portion of anything signifies the consecration of the whole. Thus, if the first day is holy to the Lord, so is the whole month.

In later times, especially from the Seleucids onward, this day would be known as New Year's Day (ראש השנה *rōʾš haššānâ*). Trumpets were blown on several occasions in Israel, though not always the same type of trumpets, but on this occasion people throughout the land joined in as they were able from sunrise to sunset. It was not the same as the traditional noise-making that has come to be associated with New Year's Day in the rest of the world when the fortunes of the coming year are very much in the forefront of

most thinking; it was to be a festival of celebration to the Lord and of commemorating it with praise to God.

23:26-32. The Day of Atonement comes on the tenth day of the seventh month. It is the only day divinely announced as a fast in the whole OT, even though tradition added several other days of fasting (see Zech 7:2-5; 8:19). This day has already been described in chap. 16, but here it is placed in its relationship to the other annual events of celebration to the Lord.

The emphasis in this paragraph is on the necessity of denying oneself (vv. 27, 29, 32). The same call to inspect one's interior motivations and sorrow over one's sin is the concluding note in the discussion of this same day in chap. 16 (vv. 29, 31). Here, once again, Israel is being warned that the forgiveness of sin on this day is not an automatic carte blanche type of an affair; it has to be accompanied by real repentance or, as the idiom literally says, by "afflicting oneself." This day also is a day sacred to the Lord in which no work is to be done (vv. 28, 31). On this day, the high priest makes atonement for the sins of the people; thus it is a solemn day rather than a day of festivities.

23:33-44. The final event in this septenary series is the Feast of Tabernacles (vv. 33-44). It begins on the fifteenth day of the seventh month and lasts for seven days (v. 34). It is also known as the Feast of Booths and Feast of Ingathering. The historical occasion that it celebrates is the end of the harvest season. During this festival, Israel again lives in booths made of branches of palms, willows, and other trees, as a reminder of the time the Israelites spent in the wilderness wanderings after the exodus. As the harvest is gathered in, it becomes a time of great joy and thanksgiving to God.

As with the other week-long festivals, the first and the last days are to be observed as sabbaths to the Lord. No work or labor is to be carried out on these days. Once again, however, the eighth day following these days is to be a "sacred assembly" (v. 36a); it is "the closing assembly" (v. 36b). The unique term used only here in this chapter is עצרת (*ʿǎṣeret*), meaning "to shut up," "to close," hence the closing day or concluding day of the Feast of Tabernacles. The same term is applied to the concluding day of the Feast of Unleavened Bread in Deut 16:8. Josephus noted that the concluding day of the Feast of Pentecost was called *asartha*, apparently from the Greek word that attempted to reproduce the Hebrew word for "to close."

This "last" day of the feast or, as the Gospel of John later calls it, "the great day" of the feast (John 7:37 NRSV), is so labeled because of the great solemnity of the assembly.

The Sadducees understood that the branches were to be used for making temporary booths or shelters, but the Pharisees, and most adherents of modern Judaism, tie one branch of palm, three branches of myrtle, and one branch of willow together. These they carry in the right hand, but in the left hand they carry a branch of citron, with its fruit left on it. With these they form a procession to their synagogues on each of the seven days, marching around their reading desks as Joshua did around the walls of Jericho and singing "Hosannah." On the last day of the feast, which the rabbis called "the great Hosannah," they process seven times around the same areas, as their ancestors did around Jericho.

Another ceremony on this occasion is the pouring out of water. One of the priests takes a golden pitcher to the pool of Siloam or Bethesda and, after filling it with water from that place, returns by the gate on the south side of the Temple, which became known from this event as the Water Gate. Silver trumpets sound to announce the priest's arrival. He advances directly to the top of the altar, where two basins stand, one with wine for the ordinary drink offering and the other for the water that he brings. The priest pours the water into the empty basin, then mixes the water and wine together, and pours out both as a libation. Nothing in the Mosaic laws reflects this practice, but authority for it is usually traced to Isa 12:3: "With joy you will draw water/ from the wells of salvation" (NIV). It is to this event that Jesus probably refers in the Gospel of John report: "On the last and greatest day of the Feast, Jesus stood and said in a loud voice, 'If anyone is thirsty, let him come to me and drink. Whoever believes in me, as the Scripture has said, streams of living water will flow from within him' " (7:37-38 NIV).

This feast depicts the completion of the physical and the spiritual harvests. Most beautifully, the joy, rejoicing, and happiness of the reunion of everyone, after all the arduous hours of labor have been completed, lie at the heart of this festival. The typical significance of this feast is discussed in Zechariah 14. There is coming a day when the Lord will be king over the whole earth, the Lord will be one (with no more rivals from pagan idols or competing loyalties from the people), and the divine name will be the only name (vv. 5, 9, 16). Then, all the nations will keep the Feast of Tabernacles, and the words "HOLY TO THE LORD" will be written on everything, even the most ordinary utensils (v. 20). Thus the Feast of Tabernacles signifies the completion of the great world harvest at the end of the age.

REFLECTIONS

1. In Israel, holiness was not confined to people and objects but also extended to times and seasons. Life was not an unbroken highway leading endlessly to more of the same. Here and there along the way there were holy oases of refreshment, celebration, and commemoration—sabbaths, festivals, and special days of awe and praise.

The special times of holiness aimed to disclose what was true of all time, that it belongs to God. The purpose of a sabbath, for example, was not to be the one and only holy day in the week. Instead, the sabbath brought to visibility the holiness of all days. A sabbath or a festival was like a kiss between lovers. It gathered into a special moment what is always true. Just so, a Tuesday was as holy as a sabbath, but it took the "kiss" of the sabbath to make that clear.

2. The case for anticipating a change from the seventh day to the first day of the week as the new sabbath is found in chap. 23 with its frequent references to the "day after the sabbath" (vv. 11, 16), to the "eighth day" (vv. 36, 39), or to the "first day" (vv. 7, 35) as being days of sacred assembly when no work is to be done. But even more impressive are the references to the Firstfruit that was to come on the eighth day and to Pentecost also coming on the eighth day (vv. 11, 16). Often in this series of annual events, both the seventh day and the eighth day are called most holy days equally set aside to God as sacred and devoid of all labor.

3. The typical meaning of the feasts and sacred seasons discussed in Leviticus 23 has already received mention in the commentary, but it is well to collect the comments here in one place. The Passover and the Unleavened Bread pointed forward to Christ, our Passover, who was slain for the sins of the world. Pentecost pointed forward to the spiritual ingathering of the firstfruits of the world harvest that was to come, some fifty days after the presentation of the barley sheaf that symbolized the resurrection from the dead of the One who himself was the firstfruits of all who had died. The Feast of Tabernacles signified the completion of the harvest begun at Pentecost; it marked the new age when the fruits of all labors would be enjoyed, just as the harvest of ingathering at the end of the year signified.

4. The religious life depicted here, as elsewhere in the Bible, is not one of gloom and doom but of joy. Just as Neh 8:10 proclaimed, "The joy of the LORD is your strength" (NIV), so all the set times of sabbatical rest were to be times of joy and celebration. Instead of the sabbath and its associated festivals being days of stern repression with negative rules and prohibitions on work, "There remains, then, a Sabbath-rest for the people of God" (Heb 4:9 NIV). Every temporal celebration was intended to point toward the eternal joy that was to come when the final sabbath rest came to the people of God.

5. It is little wonder, then, that the apostle Paul seized on this crucial point of "firstfruits" in the Feast of Weeks in 1 Cor 15:20 and declared the resurrection of Christ on Easter Day to be "the firstfruits of those who have fallen asleep" (NIV). When Christ rose from the dead on the first day after the sabbath, he became the firstfruits of the harvest of all those who had died in faith and who were awaiting the resurrection of their bodies from the dead. The NT writers frequently employed this figure of "firstfruit(s)" (see Rom 8:23; 11:16; 16:5; Jas 1:18; Rev 14:4).

LEVITICUS 24:1-23, HOLINESS CONTRASTED

NIV

24 The LORD said to Moses, 2"Command the Israelites to bring you clear oil of pressed olives for the light so that the lamps may be kept burning continually. 3Outside the curtain of the Testimony in the Tent of Meeting, Aaron is to tend the lamps before the LORD from evening till morning, continually. This is to be a lasting ordinance for the generations to come. 4The lamps on the pure gold lampstand before the LORD must be tended continually.

5"Take fine flour and bake twelve loaves of bread, using two-tenths of an ephah[a] for each loaf. 6Set them in two rows, six in each row, on the table of pure gold before the LORD. 7Along each row put some pure incense as a memorial portion

a5 That is, probably about 4 quarts (about 4.5 liters)

NRSV

24 The LORD spoke to Moses, saying: 2Command the people of Israel to bring you pure oil of beaten olives for the lamp, that a light may be kept burning regularly. 3Aaron shall set it up in the tent of meeting, outside the curtain of the covenant,[a] to burn from evening to morning before the LORD regularly; it shall be a statute forever throughout your generations. 4He shall set up the lamps on the lampstand of pure gold[b] before the LORD regularly.

5You shall take choice flour, and bake twelve loaves of it; two-tenths of an ephah shall be in each loaf. 6You shall place them in two rows, six in a row, on the table of pure gold.[c] 7You shall

a Or treaty, or testament; Heb eduth   b Heb pure lampstand
c Heb pure table

NIV

to represent the bread and to be an offering made to the LORD by fire. ⁸This bread is to be set out before the LORD regularly, Sabbath after Sabbath, on behalf of the Israelites, as a lasting covenant. ⁹It belongs to Aaron and his sons, who are to eat it in a holy place, because it is a most holy part of their regular share of the offerings made to the LORD by fire."

¹⁰Now the son of an Israelite mother and an Egyptian father went out among the Israelites, and a fight broke out in the camp between him and an Israelite. ¹¹The son of the Israelite woman blasphemed the Name with a curse; so they brought him to Moses. (His mother's name was Shelomith, the daughter of Dibri the Danite.) ¹²They put him in custody until the will of the LORD should be made clear to them.

¹³Then the LORD said to Moses: ¹⁴"Take the blasphemer outside the camp. All those who heard him are to lay their hands on his head, and the entire assembly is to stone him. ¹⁵Say to the Israelites: 'If anyone curses his God, he will be held responsible; ¹⁶anyone who blasphemes the name of the LORD must be put to death. The entire assembly must stone him. Whether an alien or native-born, when he blasphemes the Name, he must be put to death.

¹⁷" 'If anyone takes the life of a human being, he must be put to death. ¹⁸Anyone who takes the life of someone's animal must make restitution— life for life. ¹⁹If anyone injures his neighbor, whatever he has done must be done to him: ²⁰fracture for fracture, eye for eye, tooth for tooth. As he has injured the other, so he is to be injured. ²¹Whoever kills an animal must make restitution, but whoever kills a man must be put to death. ²²You are to have the same law for the alien and the native-born. I am the LORD your God.' "

²³Then Moses spoke to the Israelites, and they took the blasphemer outside the camp and stoned him. The Israelites did as the LORD commanded Moses.

NRSV

put pure frankincense with each row, to be a token offering for the bread, as an offering by fire to the LORD. ⁸Every sabbath day Aaron shall set them in order before the LORD regularly as a commitment of the people of Israel, as a covenant forever. ⁹They shall be for Aaron and his descendants, who shall eat them in a holy place, for they are most holy portions for him from the offerings by fire to the LORD, a perpetual due.

¹⁰A man whose mother was an Israelite and whose father was an Egyptian came out among the people of Israel; and the Israelite woman's son and a certain Israelite began fighting in the camp. ¹¹The Israelite woman's son blasphemed the Name in a curse. And they brought him to Moses—now his mother's name was Shelomith, daughter of Dibri, of the tribe of Dan— ¹²and they put him in custody, until the decision of the LORD should be made clear to them.

¹³The LORD said to Moses, saying: ¹⁴Take the blasphemer outside the camp; and let all who were within hearing lay their hands on his head, and let the whole congregation stone him. ¹⁵And speak to the people of Israel, saying: Anyone who curses God shall bear the sin. ¹⁶One who blasphemes the name of the LORD shall be put to death; the whole congregation shall stone the blasphemer. Aliens as well as citizens, when they blaspheme the Name, shall be put to death. ¹⁷Anyone who kills a human being shall be put to death. ¹⁸Anyone who kills an animal shall make restitution for it, life for life. ¹⁹Anyone who maims another shall suffer the same injury in return: ²⁰fracture for fracture, eye for eye, tooth for tooth; the injury inflicted is the injury to be suffered. ²¹One who kills an animal shall make restitution for it; but one who kills a human being shall be put to death. ²²You shall have one law for the alien and for the citizen: for I am the LORD your God. ²³Moses spoke thus to the people of Israel; and they took the blasphemer outside the camp, and stoned him to death. The people of Israel did as the LORD had commanded Moses.

COMMENTARY

A number of puzzles confront the interpreter of chap. 24. The greatest enigma is the connection of this chapter with what has preceded it in chap. 23 and with what follows in chap. 25. Another is the principle of organization that mixes the two topics of rules regulating the holy place with the sudden intrusion of the case of the blasphemer. The final puzzle is the lack of clear structural markers in the repeated clauses and phrases that have been present in many of the surrounding chapters.

The problem of the connection with what has preceded chap. 24 in chap. 23 can be eased somewhat by noting that the completed ingathering of the harvest's grain and fruit in the previous chapter is now to have a portion of it used in the sanctuary as olive oil for lighting the seven-branched lampstand (vv. 1-4), and another portion will be used as grain to produce the twelve loaves placed each week on the table of presence (vv. 5-9).

The story of the blasphemer is probably brought to the fore because of the need to know if the law for native-born persons must also be applied to foreigners. The answer is that it does, as v. 22 plainly attests.

The mixture of the story of the blasphemer (vv. 10-23) with instructions for the lampstand and the table of the bread of presence may be that this problem of blasphemy arose right after Moses had given his directions for the festivals that appear in chap. 23, or after Moses had given his instructions for the two rituals in the tabernacle that appear first in this chapter. But it may also have been occasioned by an inquiry that came about this time as to whether these laws also applied to foreigners. It is difficult to suggest any other plausible connections for such an abrupt change of topics.

The only structural clues appear in v. 22, "I am the LORD your God" (a colophon that appears repeatedly in chap. 19); v. 3, "This is to be a lasting ordinance for the generations to come" (cf. 3:17; 10:9; 16:29; 17:7; 23:14, 21, 31, 41); and v. 9, a "regular share" (cf. 6:11 [English 18]; 7:34; 10:15). But these three clues are enough, along with the distinctive change in subject matter, to indicate that there are three main divisions in this chapter: vv. 2-4, 5-9, and 10-23.

24:2-4. These verses repeat the regulations for the lampstand previously given in Exod 27:20-21 with slight changes. In them, directions are given for the light that is to burn in the holy place from evening until morning. The people are to furnish the oil for the seven-branched lampstand in the

holy place on the south, or lefthand side, as one faced into the tabernacle.

The oil is to be "clear oil of pressed olives" (v. 2). This oil is extracted from unripened olives beaten and pounded in a mortar rather than crushed in a mill. The pulpy mass is then placed in a basket, and the oil, without mixture of other parts of the olive, drips through the basket, giving a clear, pure oil that burns with little or no smoke.

The oil is given by the people so that, though the holy place is attended by the high priest, the light illuminating it is a gift from all the people. In that sense, here is a service that all the people of Israel render in their devotion to God.

Night after night the seven-branched lampstand is tended so that the light will burn throughout the dark hours. There is to be no intermission.

The significance of the olive oil and the burning of the lamps before the Lord in front of the veil that separated the holy place from the holy of holies can best be found in Zech 4:1-14. There the seven-branched lampstand symbolized Israel as God's congregation, who in turn was to give the light of life to the world. In Zechariah's vision, the oil flowed to the golden lampstand through two golden pipes from two olive trees on either side of the lampstand. The explanation that Zechariah was given about this oil was, " 'Not by might nor by power, but by my Spirit,' says the LORD Almighty" (4:6 NIV). Thus the nation's ability to share this light with the world depended on the supply that came from the Spirit of God and the ministry of the high priest in the holy place. Thus the identification of the lampstand with the people, with the dynamic for sharing their light with the nations of the world as coming from the Holy Spirit, does not appear to be inconsistent with the analogy of other Scripture.

24:5-9. The next illustration of holiness is the ordinance of the preparation and presentation of the bread of the presence. It is placed in two rows of six each on the specially designated table made of pure gold on the north side of the tabernacle, or the right side as one faced into the tabernacle. Thus, just as the lampstand is of "pure gold" (v. 4), so the table is of "pure gold" (v. 6). The themes of purity and holiness are never far from view in this book.

Each sabbath day a new set of twelve loaves is placed before the Lord because the priests eat the previous set at the end of the week. Along with the loaves some "pure incense" (v. 7) is placed, perhaps in golden spoons or cups (cf. Exod 37:16). The incense has first been burned as a "memorial portion . . . to be an offering made to the LORD by fire" (v. 7*b*).

Because incense is a symbol of prayer (see Ps 141:2), there may also be the intimation that both our physical and our spiritual food are to be received and sanctified by prayer. Surely, it is God who supplies our daily bread; the weekly dedication of the twelve loaves, representing the twelve tribes of Israel, acknowledges the same truth in a most concrete, but graphic, way.

24:10-23. If the preceding two ordinances depict how holiness is observed, the story of the blasphemer certainly shows how holiness is defiled. The chapter, then, must deliberately present a stark contrast of the two attitudes toward holiness.

Israel is commanded in Exod 22:28, "Do not blaspheme God" (NIV). But here, in one of the rare narrative passages in Leviticus, a case is offered where someone actually blasphemed the "Name." No one knew what to do, for the problem seems not to have arisen before. Therefore, the offender was placed in penal incarceration until God would reveal to Moses what should be done to the individual.

To make matters worse, the blasphemer was of mixed parentage. His mother was an Israelite, but his father was an Egyptian. Apparently, the blasphemer's father was a proselyte to the Jewish faith along with the "many other people" (Exod 12:38 NIV) who went up out of Egypt along with Israel when they left. If the guilty person was somewhere between twelve and twenty years old, the conversion of this Egyptian father must have come some years prior to the Exodus, for these events take place within a year or two of Israel's exodus from Egypt.

At any rate, a physical fight broke out between a full-fledged Israelite and the man of mixed parentage. In the heat of the fight, the man of mixed parentage blasphemed "the Name [of the LORD]." The verb used for "blasphemed" is ויקב (*wayyiqqōb*), coming from the root that means "to pierce," "to bore," or "to strike through" or, by extension, "to specify," "to pronounce explicitly," or "to identify," a type of "striking through or wounding" with the tongue. But when this verb is placed with the second verb in this passage, ויקלל (*wayĕqallēl*, "to curse"), the second verb is made into a sort of adverbial phrase: "He pronounced by cursing blasphemously."

The result would be death for the blasphemer. The story of Naboth (see 1 Kgs 21:10-13) demonstrates that the death penalty for blasphemy was not a dead law without any teeth for implementation. In fact, Job's wife urged her husband to "curse God" (Job 2:9 NIV) and thus end his suffering and his life quickly! The ultimate charges that were brought against Jesus and Stephen were charges of blasphemy, for which both were judged worthy of capital punishment (see Matt 26:65-66; Acts 6:11-15).

The genealogy of the blasphemer's Israelite mother is of more than passing interest. She was from the tribe of Dan, the tribe that would eventually move to the far north and set up the calf at the temple of Dan (along with the parallel one at Bethel, for the ten northern tribes that broke away from Judah and Benjamin after the death of Solomon). In their view, the Temple at Jerusalem had become illegitimate.

The blasphemer cursed "the Name," which of course meant the name of God (v. 11). This verse and v. 16 are of special interest to the Jewish people, for on them they have based the well-known belief that it is unlawful to pronounce the name of "Yahweh," substituting, instead, the name *Adōnay,* "Lord," (אדני) which the LXX also represented by κύριος *kurios.* This is why almost all English versions now render "Yahweh" by "LORD" in capital and small capital letters to distinguish it from the regular appearance of *Adōnay,* which is rendered in upper and lower case as "Lord."

Reviling "the Name" (השם *haššēm*), even in the heat of passion, is not something that God will treat as a rather small infraction. "The Name" expresses who God is par excellence. It stands for God's own self, character, nature (see Ps 20:1; Luke 24:47; John 1:12); doctrine (see Ps 22:22; John 17:6, 26); and ethical teachings (see Mic 4:5).[116]

Thus the offender was placed "in custody" (במשמר *bammišmār,* "in the guardhouse") until the Lord would reveal what to do. This is one of four episodes in the Torah where Moses has to make a

---

116. For a validation of this extended meaning of the "name," see Kaiser, "Name," in *The Zondervan Pictorial Encyclopedia of the Bible,* 4:360-66. Also see Kaiser, *Toward Old Testament Ethics,* 87-88, 132-33.

special inquiry of God about what to do prior to his rendering a legal decision (see Num 9:6-14; 15:32-36; 27:1-11). These four passages are discussed at length by Philo and the rabbis, who were troubled because Moses was unable to handle these cases on his own. However, they also clearly show Moses' dependence on God's revelation. He acted under divine orders, and not on his own!

The divine instruction is that the blasphemer is to be taken outside the camp, where all capital punishments were executed, and there he is to be stoned. First, all who heard him blaspheme are to act as witnesses by placing their hands on the head of the accused man. Hearing, as well as seeing, is a form of witnessing in the biblical law. The entire congregation is to participate in the stoning, for all have been adversely affected by the act of the single individual. Such an affront awakens the anger of God against the whole community—until they deal with it. The imposition of hands symbolizes the transfer of responsibility of guilt from the people to the offender; in this case, the offender turns victim, just as much as it does when their hands are laid on a sacrificial animal (1:4; 16:21).

This incident of blasphemy, then, provides a further occasion for spelling out some other related principles of biblical law in vv. 16-22. In all of the cases discussed here, the penalty is to be the same for the resident alien as for the full-fledged Israel (vv. 16, 22). The six laws in this section are arranged in a careful chiasmus.[117] They appear as follows:

A. Whether an alien or native-born (v. 16)
  B. takes the life of a human being (v. 17)
    C. takes the life of someone's animal (v. 18)
      D. whatever he has done
        must be done to him (v. 19)
      D'. As he has injured the other,
        so he is to be injured (v. 20)
    C'. Whoever kills an animal (v. 21a)
  B'. whoever kills a man (v. 21b)
A'. the same law for the alien and the native born (v. 22)

These laws are announced in Gen 9:6; in Exod 21:12-14, 18-25, 35-36; and later in Deut 19:21. The repetition of these laws in this context indicates that they apply equally to aliens and to full-fledged Israelites.

---

117. Wenham calls this feature "a concentric pattern [named] a palistrophe" (*Leviticus*, 311-12).

The law code of Num 35:9-34 stipulates exceptions to the rule of capital punishment when it is an accidental manslaughter case. Moreover, there is strong reason to suspect that these laws do not require literal retaliation, as the famous "eye for eye," or as it was known in Roman jurisprudence, the *lex talionis*, seems to advocate. Only in the case of deliberate and premeditated murder does Num 35:31 exclude any type of "ransom" or "substitute" being used as compensation, since men and women are made in the image of God. But this one instance where no exclusion is permitted means, as the rabbis and older commentators opined, that all other cases calling for the death penalty can be compensated by some type of "ransom."

The rabbis correctly argued that v. 18 uses the formula "life for life" (נפש תחת נפש *nepeš taḥat nāpeš*), which means that a live animal can be substituted for the one that has been slain, or its equal. Thus the guilty party can offer either an animal in place of the one killed or its equivalent value. If that is so, the identical formula that appears in the *lex talionis*, i.e., "x" *taḥat* "x" (as in "eye for eye, tooth for tooth"), must mean compensation is likewise possible rather than some form of bodily mutilation or personal retaliation against the offending party. In fact, v. 21 reinforces this interpretation by ordering restitution in the case of an animal.

However, some were dissatisfied with this solution because its main proof centers on animals, not humans. The response to this objection has been to call attention to Deut 22:29, where a man who rapes a virgin is instructed to give a compensation of silver to her father (תחת אשר ענה *taḥat ʾăšer ʿinnāh*, literally "in lieu of having forced her"). Accordingly, just as *taḥat* ("in place of" or "instead of") in that case indicates compensation, so *taḥat* in the law of Lev 24:20 ("eye" *taḥat* "eye") indicates possible compensation rather than personal mutilation and retaliation of the offender. This principle was originally given to the judges in the Covenant Code (see Exod 21:1, 6; 22:8); the principle was not given to the general public as wholesale permission to vindicate oneself of whatever injustice one felt had occurred. The rule of "eye for eye" meant nothing more to the judges in Israel than "make the punishment fit the crime," or in modern parlance, "bumper for bumper," "fender for fender" in automobile accidents; do not try to make a major capital gains out of an accident one has suffered by inventing other subsidiary (and often, imaginary!) ailments that must be compensated for at outrageous prices!

The case of the blasphemer ends, however, with the threatened judgment being carried out by the whole congregation (v. 23). Apparently, the blasphemer did not repent or offer compensation.

REFLECTIONS

1. Both the lampstand and the table of consecrated bread are mentioned in Heb 9:2. No special meaning is given to them in that verse, but Jesus mentions the bread of presence (see Matt 12:1-8 and its parallels in Mark 2:23-28 and Luke 6:1-5). In each instance, Jesus uses the action of the high priest, who shared the bread of presence with David and his hungry men, as an example of the fact that positive rules (such as this one that limits the eating of this bread to the priests alone, and the requirement that no work be done on the sabbath) are meant not to place mortals in bondage but to serve human good. The day is meant to be for the good of humans and not to obligate and enslave humans to the rule.

2. The lampstand functioned as a symbol of the people as a light to the nations, spreading the gospel through the energizing power of the Holy Spirit. Zechariah 4:1-14 completes this symbolism in a very explicit way, as does Rev 1:12-13, 20. Surely, whether it is Israel or the church, the principle is the same: "'Not by might nor by power, but by my Spirit,' says the LORD Almighty" (Zech 4:6 NIV).

3. In this sense, Israel was exactly what Jesus declared all believers to be: "You are the light of the world" (Matt 5:14, 16 NIV). Therefore, all must so let their light shine that all might see it and glorify their Father who is in heaven. In a similar way in Rev 1:12-13, Christ appears (in a vision to John the evangelist) to be walking in the midst of seven lampstands, caring for and watching over their burning. The seven lampstands are expressly said to be the seven churches in Asia (see Rev 1:20).

4. The bread of presence was the consecration to God of the labor and work of the Israelites' hands, just as the grain offering symbolized (chap. 2). However, rather than this being an offering from an individual, as in chap. 2, here it is the collective and organized capacity of the whole people and the total fruits of their labors.

5. In our day when swearing and cursing in the name of the Lord have become so common, the law against the blasphemer comes as startling news. Our culture, be it pagan, Christian, or whatever, needs to be warned that God will not hold anyone guiltless who persists in using the divine name, character, doctrines, or teachings as the basis for selfish expressions of wonderment, oaths, or demands.

LEVITICUS 25:1-55, HOLINESS IN LAND OWNERSHIP

NIV	NRSV
25 The LORD said to Moses on Mount Sinai, ²"Speak to the Israelites and say to them: 'When you enter the land I am going to give you,	**25** The LORD spoke to Moses on Mount Sinai, saying: ²Speak to the people of Israel and say to them: When you enter the land that I am

NIV

the land itself must observe a sabbath to the LORD. ³For six years sow your fields, and for six years prune your vineyards and gather their crops. ⁴But in the seventh year the land is to have a sabbath of rest, a sabbath to the LORD. Do not sow your fields or prune your vineyards. ⁵Do not reap what grows of itself or harvest the grapes of your untended vines. The land is to have a year of rest. ⁶Whatever the land yields during the sabbath year will be food for you—for yourself, your manservant and maidservant, and the hired worker and temporary resident who live among you, ⁷as well as for your livestock and the wild animals in your land. Whatever the land produces may be eaten.

⁸" 'Count off seven sabbaths of years—seven times seven years—so that the seven sabbaths of years amount to a period of forty-nine years. ⁹Then have the trumpet sounded everywhere on the tenth day of the seventh month; on the Day of Atonement sound the trumpet throughout your land. ¹⁰Consecrate the fiftieth year and proclaim liberty throughout the land to all its inhabitants. It shall be a jubilee for you; each one of you is to return to his family property and each to his own clan. ¹¹The fiftieth year shall be a jubilee for you; do not sow and do not reap what grows of itself or harvest the untended vines. ¹²For it is a jubilee and is to be holy for you; eat only what is taken directly from the fields.

¹³" 'In this Year of Jubilee everyone is to return to his own property.

¹⁴" 'If you sell land to one of your countrymen or buy any from him, do not take advantage of each other. ¹⁵You are to buy from your countryman on the basis of the number of years since the Jubilee. And he is to sell to you on the basis of the number of years left for harvesting crops. ¹⁶When the years are many, you are to increase the price, and when the years are few, you are to decrease the price, because what he is really selling you is the number of crops. ¹⁷Do not take advantage of each other, but fear your God. I am the LORD your God.

¹⁸" 'Follow my decrees and be careful to obey my laws, and you will live safely in the land. ¹⁹Then the land will yield its fruit, and you will eat your fill and live there in safety. ²⁰You may ask, "What will we eat in the seventh year if we

NRSV

giving you, the land shall observe a sabbath for the LORD. ³Six years you shall sow your field, and six years you shall prune your vineyard, and gather in their yield; ⁴but in the seventh year there shall be a sabbath of complete rest for the land, a sabbath for the LORD: you shall not sow your field or prune your vineyard. ⁵You shall not reap the aftergrowth of your harvest or gather the grapes of your unpruned vine: it shall be a year of complete rest for the land. ⁶You may eat what the land yields during its sabbath—you, your male and female slaves, your hired and your bound laborers who live with you; ⁷for your livestock also, and for the wild animals in your land all its yield shall be for food.

⁸You shall count off seven weeksᵃ of years, seven times seven years, so that the period of seven weeks of years gives forty-nine years. ⁹Then you shall have the trumpet sounded loud; on the tenth day of the seventh month—on the day of atonement—you shall have the trumpet sounded throughout all your land. ¹⁰And you shall hallow the fiftieth year and you shall proclaim liberty throughout the land to all its inhabitants. It shall be a jubilee for you: you shall return, every one of you, to your property and every one of you to your family. ¹¹That fiftieth year shall be a jubilee for you: you shall not sow, or reap the aftergrowth, or harvest the unpruned vines. ¹²For it is a jubilee; it shall be holy to you: you shall eat only what the field itself produces.

¹³In this year of jubilee you shall return, every one of you, to your property. ¹⁴When you make a sale to your neighbor or buy from your neighbor, you shall not cheat one another. ¹⁵When you buy from your neighbor, you shall pay only for the number of years since the jubilee; the seller shall charge you only for the remaining crop years. ¹⁶If the years are more, you shall increase the price, and if the years are fewer, you shall diminish the price; for it is a certain number of harvests that are being sold to you. ¹⁷You shall not cheat one another, but you shall fear your God; for I am the LORD your God.

¹⁸You shall observe my statutes and faithfully keep my ordinances, so that you may live on the land securely. ¹⁹The land will yield its fruit, and

ᵃ Or sabbaths

NIV

do not plant or harvest our crops?" ²¹I will send you such a blessing in the sixth year that the land will yield enough for three years. ²²While you plant during the eighth year, you will eat from the old crop and will continue to eat from it until the harvest of the ninth year comes in.

²³"'The land must not be sold permanently, because the land is mine and you are but aliens and my tenants. ²⁴Throughout the country that you hold as a possession, you must provide for the redemption of the land.

²⁵"'If one of your countrymen becomes poor and sells some of his property, his nearest relative is to come and redeem what his countryman has sold. ²⁶If, however, a man has no one to redeem it for him but he himself prospers and acquires sufficient means to redeem it, ²⁷he is to determine the value for the years since he sold it and refund the balance to the man to whom he sold it; he can then go back to his own property. ²⁸But if he does not acquire the means to repay him, what he sold will remain in the possession of the buyer until the Year of Jubilee. It will be returned in the Jubilee, and he can then go back to his property.

²⁹"'If a man sells a house in a walled city, he retains the right of redemption a full year after its sale. During that time he may redeem it. ³⁰If it is not redeemed before a full year has passed, the house in the walled city shall belong permanently to the buyer and his descendants. It is not to be returned in the Jubilee. ³¹But houses in villages without walls around them are to be considered as open country. They can be redeemed, and they are to be returned in the Jubilee.

³²"'The Levites always have the right to redeem their houses in the Levitical towns, which they possess. ³³So the property of the Levites is redeemable—that is, a house sold in any town they hold—and is to be returned in the Jubilee, because the houses in the towns of the Levites are their property among the Israelites. ³⁴But the pastureland belonging to their towns must not be sold; it is their permanent possession.

³⁵"'If one of your countrymen becomes poor and is unable to support himself among you, help him as you would an alien or a temporary resident, so he can continue to live among you. ³⁶Do

NRSV

you will eat your fill and live on it securely. ²⁰Should you ask, What shall we eat in the seventh year, if we may not sow or gather in our crop? ²¹I will order my blessing for you in the sixth year, so that it will yield a crop for three years. ²²When you sow in the eighth year, you will be eating from the old crop; until the ninth year, when its produce comes in, you shall eat the old. ²³The land shall not be sold in perpetuity, for the land is mine; with me you are but aliens and tenants. ²⁴Throughout the land that you hold, you shall provide for the redemption of the land.

25If anyone of your kin falls into difficulty and sells a piece of property, then the next of kin shall come and redeem what the relative has sold. ²⁶If the person has no one to redeem it, but then prospers and finds sufficient means to do so, ²⁷the years since its sale shall be computed and the difference shall be refunded to the person to whom it was sold, and the property shall be returned. ²⁸But if there is not sufficient means to recover it, what was sold shall remain with the purchaser until the year of jubilee; in the jubilee it shall be released, and the property shall be returned.

29If anyone sells a dwelling house in a walled city, it may be redeemed until a year has elapsed since its sale; the right of redemption shall be one year. ³⁰If it is not redeemed before a full year has elapsed, a house that is in a walled city shall pass in perpetuity to the purchaser, throughout the generations; it shall not be released in the jubilee. ³¹But houses in villages that have no walls around them shall be classed as open country; they may be redeemed, and they shall be released in the jubilee. ³²As for the cities of the Levites, the Levites shall forever have the right of redemption of the houses in the cities belonging to them. ³³Such property as may be redeemed from the Levites—houses sold in a city belonging to them—shall be released in the jubilee; because the houses in the cities of the Levites are their possession among the people of Israel. ³⁴But the open land around their cities may not be sold; for that is their possession for all time.

35If any of your kin fall into difficulty and become dependent on you,ᵃ you shall support

ᵃ Meaning of Heb uncertain

NIV

not take interest of any kind[a] from him, but fear your God, so that your countryman may continue to live among you. ³⁷You must not lend him money at interest or sell him food at a profit. ³⁸I am the LORD your God, who brought you out of Egypt to give you the land of Canaan and to be your God.

³⁹" 'If one of your countrymen becomes poor among you and sells himself to you, do not make him work as a slave. ⁴⁰He is to be treated as a hired worker or a temporary resident among you; he is to work for you until the Year of Jubilee. ⁴¹Then he and his children are to be released, and he will go back to his own clan and to the property of his forefathers. ⁴²Because the Israelites are my servants, whom I brought out of Egypt, they must not be sold as slaves. ⁴³Do not rule over them ruthlessly, but fear your God.

⁴⁴" 'Your male and female slaves are to come from the nations around you; from them you may buy slaves. ⁴⁵You may also buy some of the temporary residents living among you and members of their clans born in your country, and they will become your property. ⁴⁶You can will them to your children as inherited property and can make them slaves for life, but you must not rule over your fellow Israelites ruthlessly.

⁴⁷" 'If an alien or a temporary resident among you becomes rich and one of your countrymen becomes poor and sells himself to the alien living among you or to a member of the alien's clan, ⁴⁸he retains the right of redemption after he has sold himself. One of his relatives may redeem him: ⁴⁹An uncle or a cousin or any blood relative in his clan may redeem him. Or if he prospers, he may redeem himself. ⁵⁰He and his buyer are to count the time from the year he sold himself up to the Year of Jubilee. The price for his release is to be based on the rate paid to a hired man for that number of years. ⁵¹If many years remain, he must pay for his redemption a larger share of the price paid for him. ⁵²If only a few years remain until the Year of Jubilee, he is to compute that and pay for his redemption accordingly. ⁵³He is to be treated as a man hired from year to year; you must see to it that his owner does not rule over him ruthlessly.

a36 Or *take excessive interest*; similarly in verse 37

NRSV

them; they shall live with you as though resident aliens. ³⁶Do not take interest in advance or otherwise make a profit from them, but fear your God; let them live with you. ³⁷You shall not lend them your money at interest taken in advance, or provide them food at a profit. ³⁸I am the LORD your God, who brought you out of the land of Egypt, to give you the land of Canaan, to be your God.

39If any who are dependent on you become so impoverished that they sell themselves to you, you shall not make them serve as slaves. ⁴⁰They shall remain with you as hired or bound laborers. They shall serve with you until the year of the jubilee. ⁴¹Then they and their children with them shall be free from your authority; they shall go back to their own family and return to their ancestral property. ⁴²For they are my servants, whom I brought out of the land of Egypt; they shall not be sold as slaves are sold. ⁴³You shall not rule over them with harshness, but shall fear your God. ⁴⁴As for the male and female slaves whom you may have, it is from the nations around you that you may acquire male and female slaves. ⁴⁵You may also acquire them from among the aliens residing with you, and from their families that are with you, who have been born in your land; and they may be your property. ⁴⁶You may keep them as a possession for your children after you, for them to inherit as property. These you may treat as slaves, but as for your fellow Israelites, no one shall rule over the other with harshness.

47If resident aliens among you prosper, and if any of your kin fall into difficulty with one of them and sell themselves to an alien, or to a branch of the alien's family, ⁴⁸after they have sold themselves they shall have the right of redemption; one of their brothers may redeem them, ⁴⁹or their uncle or their uncle's son may redeem them, or anyone of their family who is of their own flesh may redeem them; or if they prosper they may redeem themselves. ⁵⁰They shall compute with the purchaser the total from the year when they sold themselves to the alien until the jubilee year; the price of the sale shall be applied to the number of years: the time they were with the owner shall be rated as the time of a hired laborer. ⁵¹If many

NIV

54" 'Even if he is not redeemed in any of these ways, he and his children are to be released in the Year of Jubilee, 55for the Israelites belong to me as servants. They are my servants, whom I brought out of Egypt. I am the LORD your God.

NRSV

years remain, they shall pay for their redemption in proportion to the purchase price; 52and if few years remain until the jubilee year, they shall compute thus: according to the years involved they shall make payment for their redemption. 53As a laborer hired by the year they shall be under the alien's authority, who shall not, however, rule with harshness over them in your sight. 54And if they have not been redeemed in any of these ways, they and their children with them shall go free in the jubilee year. 55For to me the people of Israel are servants; they are my servants whom I brought out from the land of Egypt: I am the LORD your God.

COMMENTARY

In many ways, chap. 25 continues the sabbatical cycle observed in chap. 23. The principle of the weekly sabbath is now extended to a sabbatical rest set for every seven years for the land and for what it produces. And that principle is extended once again to seven seven-year cycles, after which is to be the jubilee year.

The structure of this chapter is marked by the key rhetorical device seen in chap. 19, i.e., "I am the LORD your God" (vv. 17, 38, 55). Not only does each of these formulas signify the close of a section (or as we have previously labeled them, colophons), but also they are joined to a rather extended closing theological exhortation. Thus chap. 25 can be divided into three major sections: a sabbath jubilee for the land (vv. 1-22); the redemption of property in the jubilee (vv. 23-38); and the redemption of a slave in the jubilee (vv. 39-55).

Leviticus 25 is indeed unique among all the chapters of the Torah, for it is the only chapter that deals with the subject of land tenure in ancient Israel. Two other complementary passages on the same subject appear briefly in the Torah: Exod 23:10-11, which specifies that every seventh year (without calling it a sabbatical year) the land is to be left fallow, and Deut 15:1-6, which imposes a moratorium on all debts every seventh year.

The Wellhausian school incorrectly regarded the year of jubilee as a priestly invention exhibit-

ing utopian fantasies that dated from the time of the exile. But to argue that case, one had to disregard the many points of contact between Leviticus 25 and the agricultural regulations of many other ancient peoples. Israel's law, of course, never was limited to the socioeconomic motivations that the other nations demonstrated, for Israel's motivations were also clearly religious, as v. 23 affirms. But there was another hurdle that the Wellhausian thesis had to overcome. If Leviticus 25 came *after* Deut 15:1-6, its legislation would represent a retrogression and an undoing of the benefits that Deut 15:1-6 extended, for Deuteronomy endorsed the year of agricultural release and also added further economic relief to poor persons and extended the principle to the area of debts. It is best, then, from the point of view of theological development to see the Covenant Code's Exod 23:10-11 as coming first, followed by Leviticus 25, and ending in the Torah with Deut 15:1-6, instead of placing Leviticus 25 last as this theory proposed.

A "sabbath of the land" was probably observed during the pre-exilic period, even though we have no direct evidence from the time of the first Temple. But there is ample evidence of such an observance from the period just before the common era. First Maccabees 6:49, 53 reports that the city of Beth-zur had to surrender to the Syrians; the city lacked adequate provisions to endure the siege because the attack came in a sabbatical year. The historian Josephus also reports this incident along with other similar examples.[118] But even if the argument is that there is no evidence that Israel ever observed this law of the sabbatical year and the year of the jubilee during the pre-exilic period, the incident of a sabbatical release of slaves followed by taking them back into slavery, which is rebuked by Jeremiah (34:14), shows that the sabbatical and jubilee laws are known even if disregarded.

25:1-22. The introduction in v. 1 notes that this legislation came to Moses while he was on Mount Sinai. Israel had remained for one year at Sinai and did not move on until the twentieth day of the second month of the second year after their exodus from Egypt (see Num 10:11-12). All that is related here in Leviticus probably took place in the first month of the second year, immediately after the setting up of the tabernacle (see Exod 40:17).

Even though their entry into Canaan will not be for another thirty-eight years, as far as Moses knows at this point it is imminent. Therefore, he instructs them that when they enter the land that the Lord their God is giving to them, the "land itself must observe a sabbath to the Lord" (v. 2). Every seventh year, even the soil is to be given a year of rest, just as God's creatures and the persons made in God's image are given a rest every seven days. This rest is to be a "sabbath of sabbatism" (v. 4), a phrase we have commented on as it appears in 16:31 and 23:3, 32. The superlative form of the expression indicates the intensity of its import and the fact that it is to be a complete cessation of work and a complete rest.

During this seventh year, when the land lies fallow, no landowner is to lay exclusive claim to anything that happens to sprout on its own from the seed that has fallen into the ground from the previous year's harvest; everyone can eat of the land regardless of whose property it grows on. Even the vineyards are to be left "unpruned" (v. 5), a word derived from the same root from which the word *Nazirite* comes. Just as a Nazarite is one who is "separated" unto God and who, therefore, lets his hair grow without shaving it, so the vineyards are consecrated and separated unto the Lord and left untouched by the pruning hook and knife.

The sabbatical year is to be observed by both the "hired worker" (שָׂכִיר *śākîr*) and the "temporary resident" (תּוֹשָׁב *tôšāb*) "who live among" the Israelites (v. 6). The second term is rather unusual, but it refers to the practice of billeting employees on the land of their employers, especially when these workers are from foreign lands. Some have suggested the meaning of "bound laborer"[119] for this second term, since v. 35 refers to an Israelite "holding" the person as one would "hold" a resident alien.

To demonstrate that God is the ultimate owner of everything, nothing is to be harvested in the seventh year. The natural produce of the land is to feed poor people (see Exod 23:11). The wildlife is to be given a chance to repopulate itself. Moreover, enough food is promised in the sixth year to carry the people through this sabbatical year. And during this sabbatical year, the law is to be read to the people at the Feast of Tabernacles (see Deut 31:10-13).

After seven sabbatical years, totaling an interim of forty-nine years, a ram's horn is to be sounded (v. 9) on the tenth day of the Day of Atonement throughout the land to mark the commencement of the year of jubilee (vv. 9-11) in the fiftieth year. Thus it would appear that two holy years came back to back—the forty-ninth and fiftieth years. However, having two fallow years in a row would not appear to be very practical. This problem has been relieved in the book of *Jubilees* (written about 200 BCE) by making the jubilee year fall on the sabbatical year, i.e., the forty-ninth year. Apparently, one is not to begin counting the forty-nine years in v. 8 *after* a certain date, but the fifty years are to be counted just as the fifty days in 23:15-16 are reckoned from Sunday to Sunday inclusive. This would mean that the sabbatical year on which the counting begins is the first of the fifty years (i.e., the last year of the previous seven years); thus the seventh sabbatical year is the fiftieth year counted.[120]

The septenary system reaches its pinnacle in this fiftieth year. The name of this year is probably taken from the Hebrew word יוֹבֵל (*yôbēl*), meaning a "ram" in Arabic, because the year is signaled with

118. *Antiquities of the Jews* 11.8.6; 13.8.1; 14.10.6.

119. Levine, *JPS Torah Commentary,* 170-71.
120. So argues Noordtzij, *Bible Student's Commentary,* 251. Also, in part, Harris, "Leviticus," 2:635. See also S. B. Hoenig, "Sabbatical Years and the Year of Jubilee," *JQR* 59 (1969) 222-36, for similar conclusions but from a different standpoint.

the blowing of the ram's horn or the שפר (*šôpār*), as it is also called in v. 9.[121]

The jubilee year is to be hallowed or consecrated (v. 10), just as the sabbath day is set apart to the Lord. In this year, "liberty" or "freedom" (דרור *děrôr*) is to be proclaimed throughout the land (v. 10). This, of course, is the source of the famous inscription on the Liberty Bell in Independence Hall in Philadelphia, Pennsylvania.

Very similar to the Hebrew term is the Akkadian concept of *andurāru*, which was an edict of release proclaimed by the Old Babylonian kings and on into the later periods. In the edicts, the kings declared a moratorium on all debts and bondage. In a similar way, Jer 34:15 records a time when King Zedekiah proclaimed a *děrôr*, "a release" of all slaves as the Babylonians drew near to the city of Jerusalem. In Isa 61:1 a *děrôr*, "release," is proclaimed for prisoners. Jesus read from this same text in Isa 61:1-2*a* in the synagogue and then commented that it was being fulfilled right in front of the people's eyes that very day (see Luke 4:16-21).

The liberty proclaimed is threefold. First, it means liberty for the man who has become dispossessed from his family inheritance of the land and who can now return to it. Second, it means liberty for every Hebrew slave who can become a free person once again. And third, it means liberty or release from the toil of cultivating the land, for the land is to lay fallow all year long and produce only what comes up on its own without any sowing, cultivation, fertilization, or harvesting.

The regulations for the year of jubilee are probably equivalent to those for the "year of freedom" mentioned in Ezek 46:17. Liberty means that the Hebrew slaves can leave the service of their masters and return to the possessions, lands, and homes that they had to abandon. Even those who have had their ears pierced with an awl (see Exod 21:2, 6) as a sign that they would serve their masters forever are free to leave, for the "ever" in the terms of their agreement is superseded by the year of jubilee. All previous leases on the land are terminated, for the

property in this year reverts to the original owners. The sale of the fields is nothing more than the sale of a certain number of harvests until the year of freedom and release comes in the fiftieth year (vv. 13-18, 23-28). Purchases of any farmland are to be on the basis of the number of years remaining until the next jubilee.

Repeatedly, the Israelites are warned "not [to] take advantage of each other" (vv. 14, 17). The reason is simple: "I am the Lord your God" (v. 17); therefore, "fear your God" (v. 17; cf. vv. 36, 43). Once again, a key characteristic of the Holiness Code is this appeal to the fear of God. What follows is an exhortation to obey God's laws and commandments (vv. 18-22). The promise is that if Israel will live as if all transactions take place under the eyes of God, they will find security and a reward for living obedient and God-fearing lives. Those who question, "What will we eat in the seventh year if we do not plant or harvest our crops?" (v. 20) are answered that the Lord will provide so abundantly in the sixth year that it will last into the seventh year. And even while they are planting in the eighth year, they will be eating from the super harvest of year six, given by the Lord. In fact, the old crop from the sixth year will be their supply in the ninth year, since the ground may have become rock hard from not being farmed in the seventh year, and thus the harvest might be slightly off even in the eighth year (vv. 21-22).

25:23-38. The central theology of this section, however, is found in vv. 23-24. The Lord declares that "the land is mine." Thus the land and the crops belong to the Lord. For this reason the land cannot be sold forever. Jezebel failed to comprehend this fact, which Ahab conveniently forgot to tell her. Naboth could not sell, trade, or substitute his land at any price or inducement (see 1 Kings 21), for the ultimate owner of the land forbade such practices. What is true of Israel, in a larger sense, is true of all lands, for Ps 24:1 teaches that the earth is the Lord's and all that is within the earth.

God gave the land to the people in a rather miraculous way. Therefore, they are viewed as God's tenants, and the land is not to be sold in perpetuity. If it does become necessary for someone to temporarily give up the land, there is always the right of redemption of the land in the interim before the year of jubilee. The owner, or a near relative, can pay off the years of crops

---

121. Bush, *Notes on the Book of Leviticus,* 253-54, suggests a number of other, but less likely, derivations for jubilee, including Jubal, the inventor of music in Gen 4:21; the Hiphil form of the verb יבל *ybl,* meaning "to recall," "to bring back," or "to restore" as in restoring liberty to the slaves; or the peculiar sound made by the instrument itself.

remaining until the jubilee, and thus the land will be redeemed. This close relative who redeems the land is known by the famous term גֹּאֵל *gō 'ēl,* the "kinsman-redeemer" (NIV; cf. the famous picture, using the same term, of Boaz in Ruth 3:12–4:6).

The situation is different for persons who live in houses in a walled city (vv. 29-31). Houses in walled cities are more the fruit of the people's labor than the land in the country is; that land is the immediate gift of God. The sale of a house in the city is final if at the end of the first year following the sale the seller does not exercise his option to buy it back. The rules of reversion to the original owner in the year of jubilee do not apply to these situations. Apparently, this provision is made to encourage strangers and proselytes to settle among the people. Even though they cannot purchase land in Canaan, they can purchase and own houses in the walled cities so that they can live and trade among the Israelites. The same permissions do not apply to villages without walls in the country; there the perpetual ownership of the land by the Lord applies, and God gave that land only to Israel. The rules of the year of jubilee apply to the unwalled villages just as they apply to all the farmland in the country.

Leviticus 25:32-34 examines the case of the Levites. The homes in the forty-eight Levitical towns are given to them in perpetuity. They can never be alienated from them. God wants to show favor and watch-care over those who minister in that special service. These same principles continue in many countries to this day with special housing allowances being made for the clergy.

Provision is also made for the one who is "unable to support himself" (vv. 35-38). The Hebrew for this expression is literally "his hand wavers." Relief is to be extended to a native Israelite just as much as to a resident alien or a temporary resident in their midst. But on no account is any "interest" (v. 36) to be charged for such help. Interest in those days could run 30 percent and higher.[122] The word for "interest" in v. 36 is נֶשֶׁךְ (*nešek,* "to bite," as a serpent bites). Some have argued that this interest charge for the loan was "bitten off" before the rest of the principal was granted. Thus, on a one-hundred-shekel loan, a debtor might get only seventy shekels since the

122. See the discussion of this complex subject in Kaiser, "The Question of Interest and Usury," in *Toward Old Testament Ethics,* 212-17.

30 percent was taken right off the top at the start. But whatever the meaning, no one is to take advantage of another person's calamity to profit from it and to seize the moment to advance oneself over one's neighbors. Such cruel exactions are nipped in the bud, and the Israelites are reminded that the Lord God brought them up out of slavery free of charge (v. 38). After all, "I am the LORD your God" (v. 38). In this context no one is allowed to escape the duty of showing love and a helping hand to others. All this is to be done without any interest charges being made.

25:39-55. A second case of need is that of persons who have indentured themselves to pay off a debt (vv. 39-43). Numerous circumstances could bring people to such desperate straits. Persons reduced to extreme need might have no other choice than to sell themselves to another to pay off that debt. Parents might sell a child for a stipulated sum and for a specified number of years to help finance a shortfall for whatever reasons. Someone found guilty of theft, but unable to make restitution, might be sold among the Jewish people by the judicial process. Such individuals are not to be sold as bondservants in a public manner but are to be treated in a private and honorable way. Neither are they to be "[ruled] over . . . ruthlessly" (v. 43) as Pharaoh's taskmasters treated Israel (the same term appears in Exod 1:13 of the Egyptians' cruelty). Inhumanity to one another is forbidden and is not to be permitted under any circumstance.

Verse 42 states why no Israelite can ever be anyone else's slave: "Because the Israelites are my servants." Even this thought may sound offensive to us moderns who prefer to think of God as our Father and of ourselves as sons and daughters. But the Israelites thought of God as Lord and themselves as servants of the Lord. Though they were servants in name only, the point was that they were never to sell their bodies to anyone else; only their service and labor could be sold. In the year of jubilee, if not redeemed prior to that time, all Israelites were to go free, regardless of the terms of their servitude.

The Israelites can own male and female slaves (vv. 44-46) from the non-Israelite residents of Canaan or from the neighboring nations. Nevertheless, kidnapping, the method by which much of the modern abuse in slavery is realized, is a capital offense (see Exod 21:16). The law also carefully guards violence and tyranny of the master over these non-Israelite slaves, even granting the slaves immediate release from the indenture if any type of mark, scar, or physical impairment is seen on the body as a result of the master's abusive treatment (see Exod 21:20-21, 26-27).[123]

The final situation dealt with in this chapter is that of Israelites who indenture themselves to aliens (vv. 47-55). The owners of the enslaved Israelites must, however, recognize the right of redemption and the year of release in the jubilee. Every effort must be made to redeem the Israelites

out of the hands of non-Israelites and to make the servitude as brief as possible. The price and the monetary equivalent of the release must be calculated as the time remaining until the next year of jubilee, minus the labor already rendered, deducted from the price for which the people sold themselves into bondage. In the meantime, the owners of the Israelites must "not rule over [them] ruthlessly" (v. 53).

The law of chap. 25 ends with a reminder that individual Israelites, as well as Israel as a whole, belong to the Lord as servants. As such, they are God's possessions, for the Lord their God brought them out of the land of Egypt.

123. See the discussion of these passages in Kaiser, *Toward Old Testament Ethics*, 101-5, and *idem*, "Exodus," 432-34.

REFLECTIONS

Robert North neatly organizes the four lessons that might be learned from Leviticus 25.[124] They include social justice, social worship, personal virtues, and Messianic typology.

1. According to North, the jubilee was intended to prevent the accumulation of all the wealth of the nation in the hands of a few. Under the jubilee law, every Israelite's freedom and legal right to family land were guaranteed. Once in the lifetime of every generation (every fifty years), what might have been lost through debts could be recovered in the jubilee year. Therefore, this law prevented all monopolies that might come from an unfettered capitalism as well as a total communism that placed all property in the hands of the state. Land belonged to God, who in turn placed it on permanent lease in the hands of families. Thus the unity of the economy was found in the family rather than in an artificial organization created by the state or a corporation.

2. The jubilee, as one of the sabbatical years, was an extension of the sabbath day. It was the joining together of the concerns of religion and the concerns for society. Men and women could not be satisfied merely with performing religious duties, for they had to carry out the effects of their religion by helping those who had fallen into debt and had lost their lands. Moreover, this day of jubilee began with the Day of Atonement when worshipers were remorseful and contrite before God. That was the impetus for the threefold repetition of the command to "fear God" in this chapter. Mercy is as much a desideratum as is sacrifice (see Hos 6:6; Matt 9:13; 12:7).

3. Love and mercy toward one's neighbor lay at the heart of the jubilee legislation. If all Israel were but "aliens and [God's] tenants" (v. 23), the transitory nature of all mortals on this earth and the habitations we occupy must be acknowledged. The same point is made about Christians in Heb 11:10 —we are but strangers and pilgrims here as we look forward to another city, whose builder and maker is God. If God cares for sparrows, and promised to provide more than enough in the sixth year to carry Israel through the sabbatical year, can God not also care for us in the same way? No wonder we are urged to cast all our cares on God (see 1 Pet 5:7). Moreover, persons who place their priorities right by seeking first God's kingdom and righteousness will find all the other cares managed by their Lord (see Matt 6:33).

4. In the messianic typology, North points to Jesus' use of the word *release* from Lev 25:10

124. Robert North, *Sociology of the Biblical Jubilee* (Rome: Pontifical Biblical Institute, 1954) 213-31.

in Isa 61:1 as he read from the Isaiah scroll in the synagogue (Luke 4:16 21 NIV). The reference to the "year of the LORD's favor" in that same Isaianic passage is probably an allusion to the jubilee year principle. The messianic age will bring release to captives and liberty to all the oppressed. This age began when Christ appeared the first time, but it will be completed when he returns the second time and "[restores] everything" in a new heaven and a new earth (Acts 3:21 NIV; 2 Pet 3:13).

5. John Bright summarizes the theology of this passage as one that:

> seeks to tell us that the land is God's and that we live on this earth as aliens and sojourners, holding all that we have as it were on loan from him (vs 23); that God narrowly superintends every business transaction and expects that we conduct our affairs in the fear of him (vss 17, 36, 43) dealing graciously with the less fortunate brother in the recollection that we have all been recipients of grace (vss 38, 42). And that is normative ethics![125]

125. John Bright, *The Authority of the Old Testament* (Nashville: Abingdon, 1967) 153. See also the discussion of three other attempts to treat the problem of contemporary application of the jubilee law in Kaiser, *Toward Old Testament Ethics,* 217-21.

LEVITICUS 26:1-46, THE ALTERNATIVES: BLESSING OR CURSE

26 "'Do not make idols or set up an image or a sacred stone for yourselves, and do not place a carved stone in your land to bow down before it. I am the LORD your God. [2]"'Observe my Sabbaths and have reverence for my sanctuary. I am the LORD.

[3]"'If you follow my decrees and are careful to obey my commands, [4]I will send you rain in its season, and the ground will yield its crops and the trees of the field their fruit. [5]Your threshing will continue until grape harvest and the grape harvest will continue until planting, and you will eat all the food you want and live in safety in your land.

[6]"'I will grant peace in the land, and you will lie down and no one will make you afraid. I will remove savage beasts from the land, and the sword will not pass through your country. [7]You will pursue your enemies, and they will fall by the sword before you. [8]Five of you will chase a hundred, and a hundred of you will chase ten thousand, and your enemies will fall by the sword before you.

[9]"'I will look on you with favor and make you fruitful and increase your numbers, and I will keep my covenant with you. [10]You will still be eating last year's harvest when you will have to move

26 You shall make for yourselves no idols and erect no carved images or pillars, and you shall not place figured stones in your land, to worship at them; for I am the LORD your God. [2]You shall keep my sabbaths and reverence my sanctuary: I am the LORD.

3If you follow my statutes and keep my commandments and observe them faithfully, [4]I will give you your rains in their season, and the land shall yield its produce, and the trees of the field shall yield their fruit. [5]Your threshing shall overtake the vintage, and the vintage shall overtake the sowing; you shall eat your bread to the full, and live securely in your land. [6]And I will grant peace in the land, and you shall lie down, and no one shall make you afraid; I will remove dangerous animals from the land, and no sword shall go through your land. [7]You shall give chase to your enemies, and they shall fall before you by the sword. [8]Five of you shall give chase to a hundred, and a hundred of you shall give chase to ten thousand; your enemies shall fall before you by the sword. [9]I will look with favor upon you and make you fruitful and multiply you; and I will maintain my covenant with you. [10]You shall eat old grain long stored, and you shall have to clear out the old to make way for the new. [11]I

it out to make room for the new. [11]I will put my dwelling place[a] among you, and I will not abhor you. [12]I will walk among you and be your God, and you will be my people. [13]I am the LORD your God, who brought you out of Egypt so that you would no longer be slaves to the Egyptians; I broke the bars of your yoke and enabled you to walk with heads held high.

[14] "'But if you will not listen to me and carry out all these commands, [15]and if you reject my decrees and abhor my laws and fail to carry out all my commands and so violate my covenant, [16]then I will do this to you: I will bring upon you sudden terror, wasting diseases and fever that will destroy your sight and drain away your life. You will plant seed in vain, because your enemies will eat it. [17]I will set my face against you so that you will be defeated by your enemies; those who hate you will rule over you, and you will flee even when no one is pursuing you.

[18] "'If after all this you will not listen to me, I will punish you for your sins seven times over. [19]I will break down your stubborn pride and make the sky above you like iron and the ground beneath you like bronze. [20]Your strength will be spent in vain, because your soil will not yield its crops, nor will the trees of the land yield their fruit.

[21] "'If you remain hostile toward me and refuse to listen to me, I will multiply your afflictions seven times over, as your sins deserve. [22]I will send wild animals against you, and they will rob you of your children, destroy your cattle and make you so few in number that your roads will be deserted.

[23] "'If in spite of these things you do not accept my correction but continue to be hostile toward me, [24]I myself will be hostile toward you and will afflict you for your sins seven times over. [25]And I will bring the sword upon you to avenge the breaking of the covenant. When you withdraw into your cities, I will send a plague among you, and you will be given into enemy hands. [26]When I cut off your supply of bread, ten women will be able to bake your bread in one oven, and they will dole out the bread by weight. You will eat, but you will not be satisfied.

[a]11 Or my tabernacle

will place my dwelling in your midst, and I shall not abhor you. [12]And I will walk among you, and will be your God, and you shall be my people. [13]I am the LORD your God who brought you out of the land of Egypt, to be their slaves no more; I have broken the bars of your yoke and made you walk erect.

[14]But if you will not obey me, and do not observe all these commandments, [15]if you spurn my statutes, and abhor my ordinances, so that you will not observe all my commandments, and you break my covenant, [16]I in turn will do this to you: I will bring terror on you; consumption and fever that waste the eyes and cause life to pine away. You shall sow your seed in vain, for your enemies shall eat it. [17]I will set my face against you, and you shall be struck down by your enemies; your foes shall rule over you, and you shall flee though no one pursues you. [18]And if in spite of this you will not obey me, I will continue to punish you sevenfold for your sins. [19]I will break your proud glory, and I will make your sky like iron and your earth like copper. [20]Your strength shall be spent to no purpose: your land shall not yield its produce, and the trees of the land shall not yield their fruit.

[21]If you continue hostile to me, and will not obey me, I will continue to plague you sevenfold for your sins. [22]I will let loose wild animals against you, and they shall bereave you of your children and destroy your livestock; they shall make you few in number, and your roads shall be deserted.

[23]If in spite of these punishments you have not turned back to me, but continue hostile to me, [24]then I too will continue hostile to you: I myself will strike you sevenfold for your sins. [25]I will bring the sword against you, executing vengeance for the covenant; and if you withdraw within your cities, I will send pestilence among you, and you shall be delivered into enemy hands. [26]When I break your staff of bread, ten women shall bake your bread in a single oven, and they shall dole out your bread by weight; and though you eat, you shall not be satisfied.

[27]But if, despite this, you disobey me, and continue hostile to me, [28]I will continue hostile to you in fury; I in turn will punish you myself sevenfold for your sins. [29]You shall eat the flesh

NIV

27"'If in spite of this you still do not listen to me but continue to be hostile toward me, 28then in my anger I will be hostile toward you, and I myself will punish you for your sins seven times over. 29You will eat the flesh of your sons and the flesh of your daughters. 30I will destroy your high places, cut down your incense altars and pile your dead bodies on the lifeless forms of your idols, and I will abhor you. 31I will turn your cities into ruins and lay waste your sanctuaries, and I will take no delight in the pleasing aroma of your offerings. 32I will lay waste the land, so that your enemies who live there will be appalled. 33I will scatter you among the nations and will draw out my sword and pursue you. Your land will be laid waste, and your cities will lie in ruins. 34Then the land will enjoy its sabbath years all the time that it lies desolate and you are in the country of your enemies; then the land will rest and enjoy its sabbaths. 35All the time that it lies desolate, the land will have the rest it did not have during the sabbaths you lived in it.

36"'As for those of you who are left, I will make their hearts so fearful in the lands of their enemies that the sound of a windblown leaf will put them to flight. They will run as though fleeing from the sword, and they will fall, even though no one is pursuing them. 37They will stumble over one another as though fleeing from the sword, even though no one is pursuing them. So you will not be able to stand before your enemies. 38You will perish among the nations; the land of your enemies will devour you. 39Those of you who are left will waste away in the lands of their enemies because of their sins; also because of their fathers' sins they will waste away.

40"'But if they will confess their sins and the sins of their fathers—their treachery against me and their hostility toward me, 41which made me hostile toward them so that I sent them into the land of their enemies—then when their uncircumcised hearts are humbled and they pay for their sin, 42I will remember my covenant with Jacob and my covenant with Isaac and my covenant with Abraham, and I will remember the land. 43For the land will be deserted by them and will enjoy its sabbaths while it lies desolate without them. They will pay for their sins because they

NRSV

of your sons, and you shall eat the flesh of your daughters. 30I will destroy your high places and cut down your incense altars; I will heap your carcasses on the carcasses of your idols. I will abhor you. 31I will lay your cities waste, will make your sanctuaries desolate, and I will not smell your pleasing odors. 32I will devastate the land, so that your enemies who come to settle in it shall be appalled at it. 33And you I will scatter among the nations, and I will unsheathe the sword against you; your land shall be a desolation, and your cities a waste.

34Then the land shall enjoy[a] its sabbath years as long as it lies desolate, while you are in the land of your enemies; then the land shall rest, and enjoy[a] its sabbath years. 35As long as it lies desolate, it shall have the rest it did not have on your sabbaths when you were living on it. 36And as for those of you who survive, I will send faintness into their hearts in the lands of their enemies; the sound of a driven leaf shall put them to flight, and they shall flee as one flees from the sword, and they shall fall though no one pursues. 37They shall stumble over one another, as if to escape a sword, though no one pursues; and you shall have no power to stand against your enemies. 38You shall perish among the nations, and the land of your enemies shall devour you. 39And those of you who survive shall languish in the land of your enemies because of their iniquities; also they shall languish because of the iniquities of their ancestors.

40But if they confess their iniquity and the iniquity of their ancestors, in that they committed treachery against me and, moreover, that they continued hostile to me— 41so that I, in turn, continued hostile to them and brought them into the land of their enemies; if then their uncircumcised heart is humbled and they make amends for their iniquity, 42then will I remember my covenant with Jacob; I will remember also my covenant with Isaac and also my covenant with Abraham, and I will remember the land. 43For the land shall be deserted by them, and enjoy[a] its sabbath years by lying desolate without them, while they shall make amends for their iniquity, because they dared to spurn my ordinances, and they abhorred

[a]Or make up for

rejected my laws and abhorred my decrees. ⁴⁴Yet in spite of this, when they are in the land of their enemies, I will not reject them or abhor them so as to destroy them completely, breaking my covenant with them. I am the L<small>ORD</small> their God. ⁴⁵But for their sake I will remember the covenant with their ancestors whom I brought out of Egypt in the sight of the nations to be their God. I am the L<small>ORD</small>' "

⁴⁶These are the decrees, the laws and the regulations that the L<small>ORD</small> established on Mount Sinai between himself and the Israelites through Moses.

my statutes. ⁴⁴Yet for all that, when they are in the land of their enemies, I will not spurn them, or abhor them so as to destroy them utterly and break my covenant with them; for I am the L<small>ORD</small> their God; ⁴⁵but I will remember in their favor the covenant with their ancestors whom I brought out of the land of Egypt in the sight of the nations, to be their God: I am the L<small>ORD</small>.

46These are the statutes and ordinances and laws that the L<small>ORD</small> established between himself and the people of Israel on Mount Sinai through Moses.

COMMENTARY

Leviticus 26 and Deuteronomy 28–30 constitute some of the most important and moving chapters in the whole of the Pentateuch. These chapters were quoted or alluded to literally hundreds of times by the four major and twelve minor prophets. But these chapters are also emotionally tender chapters, for the Lord laments the prospect of having to chastise the people as they rebel and become ungrateful.

Chapter 26 is structured very carefully. The key formula, used in several previous chapters of this Holiness Code, now appears once again: "I am the L<small>ORD</small> your God" (vv. 1, 2, 13, 44, 45). As in chap. 19, here again we have a double formula at the beginning (vv. 1-2) and at the end (vv. 44-45) of the chapter. Verse 13, then, forms the middle divider between the blessings section and the curses that follow it.

The largest section, by far, is that on the curses (vv. 14-39). The curses divide themselves into six parts, usually with the introductory clause of "If [after all this] you will not listen to me . . ." (vv. 14, 18, 21, 23, 27), and the accompanying threat of "I will punish you for your sins seven times over" (vv. 16, 18, 21, 24, 28). This adding of judgments and increasing the tempo and severity of the visitations from God is also used in Amos 4:6-12. There the prophet Amos concluded after each announced judgment, "'Yet you have not returned to me,' declares the L<small>ORD</small>" (vv. 6, 8, 9, 10, 11 NIV). Consequently, the northern

ten tribes had better be "[prepared] to meet [their] God" (v. 12 NIV). It was as if the prophet and the Lord were counting with each judgment, 1-2-3-4-5, much as a referee would count for a wrestler whose shoulders were pinned to a mat. And then the referee rendered his verdict, only in this case he said, in effect, "Enough! Get ready for the destruction of the country!"

Based on these phrases, the following components can be identified: four foundational commandments (vv. 1-2), six blessings for obedience (vv. 3-13), six threatened curses for disobedience (vv. 14-39), promise of future restoration (vv. 40-45), and summary (v. 46).

26:1-2. The opening verses summarize the first four commandments of the Decalogue and, therefore, rehearse in a nutshell a person's whole duty to God. Verse 1 prohibits all forms of idolatry because the Lord is God. The Hebrew word for "idols" in this first verse is אֱלִילִם ('ĕlîlîm), which technically means "nothings," "zeroes." Surely, the term alone is enough to drown the concept of any rivals to the living God with contempt. This summarizes the first two commandments of the Ten Commandments.

The next verse calls for observing God's sabbaths (the fourth of the Ten Commandments) and reverencing God's sanctuary, which covered in principle the ground of the third commandment, which focuses on the name of God. The sabbath included not just the weekly sabbath day, but all the days of holy convocation in the total sabbatical system treated in chaps. 23 and 25. Raising the sabbath and the sabbatical principle at this point is especially appropriate, since the weekly sabbath in particular is a sign of God's covenant with Israel (see Exod 31:12-17). And God's sanctuary is the continuing visible sign of God's presence in the midst of Israel.

26:3-13. There follow, then, the six blessings. Everything depends on Israel's obedience in following the decrees and commands of the Lord (v. 3). The promises mentioned here are of a temporal sort and apply primarily to Israel, but they are sufficiently uniform in nature to describe God's special providence for all individuals who make up all the nations on earth.

The first is the promise of rain (v. 4), introduced with the verb "I will give" (as in vv. 6, 11). The rain will come "in its season," meaning the seasonal former and latter rains. The rains, when they came, were concentrated in the months of October through April. For as the abundance of rain falls only during the rainy season, so the crops are able to grow and to mature during the dry season. The threshing will continue, promises this text, until the time of harvesting the grapes (approximately from early June until September), and the grape harvest will continue until time for planting rolls around again. These conditions are almost Edenic, or at least idyllic enough to fit eschatological times, for Amos promised the same thing in the coming age:

"The days are coming," declares the LORD,
"when the reaper will be overtaken by the plowman and the planter by the one treading grapes."
(Amos 9:13 NIV)

The second blessing that obedience will bring is "peace in the land" (v. 6). Nothing will remain to terrorize, frighten, or trouble the thoughts of those who will walk with God in perfect obedience. On the other hand, immorality, reckless living, and unrighteous governing, thinking, and worshiping will invite both civil and foreign disturbance of the peace.

Third, God promises to remove the savage beasts from the land. In the earlier days, lions and bears still inhabited the land of Canaan and continued to be sources of potential danger at times when the supply of food got scarce or when they wandered into the settled areas of habitation (see Exod 23:29; Judg 14:5; 2 Kgs 2:24). But if Israel obeys, God will increase the number of the people, and the rule of the wild beasts will be restricted and contained.

Fourth, Israel will be successful when enemies come against it, for five Israelites will chase a hundred enemy soldiers and a hundred Israelites will take on ten thousand hostile opponents (vv. 7-8). Obedient believers will act as a united force; that is why they can, with the Lord's help, achieve such outstanding feats of victory against such overwhelming odds. Joshua enlarged on this promise by saying, "One of you routs a thousand, because the LORD your God fights for you, just as he promised" (23:10 NIV). Thus it happened that two of David's thirty valiant men experienced this kind of help as one slew 800 men and the other killed 300 men at one time (see 2 Sam 23:8, 18; 1 Chr 11:11). Gideon's band of 300 men experienced the same kind of deliverance when they routed 135,000 Midianites (see Judg 7:1– 8:12).

The fifth promise of God to the obedient people is the increase of their numbers and fruitfulness of their crops and cattle (vv. 9-10). The terminology used here verges on being legal language, for God's promise declares, "I will keep my covenant," or as it is in the Hebrew, "I will cause to rise up [or cause to stand] my covenant." God will have respect for the people, i.e., God will turn toward them with favor. When God's face is toward the people, they prosper (see Num 6:24-27; Ps 67:1-7), but when God turns away from them (see Hos 5:15), they experience misery and shame.

The sixth and final blessing promised (vv. 11-13) is the indwelling presence of God in their midst. God's tabernacle will be set up in the midst of the people, and there God will condescend to take up residence among the people. Both promises of indwelling, whether in the Shekinah glory that resided in the pillar of cloud by day and the pillar of fire by night, which also abode in the tabernacle and went before Israel as they journeyed, are the hallmarks of the presence of God. The immortal deity promises to "walk among" Israel (v. 12) and be their God, and they will be called the people of God.

The combination of these three promises form the oft-repeated (approximately fifty times) tripartite formula of the promise theme found in the OT and the NT: "I will be your God, you shall be my people, and I will dwell in the midst of you." This God set Israel free from bondage in Egypt (v. 13) and enabled Israel to walk without despondency and without the yoke of the heavy burdens of making bricks.

26:14-39. Suddenly, the text changes in v. 14 from the six blessings to the extended discussion of six curses that will be visited on Israel with increasing intensity to punish any disobedience. These threatened punishments are very similar to the ones listed in Deut 28:15-68; 29:18-28. Israel's rejection will not be an abstract abandonment of formal rules and regulations. It will be a turning away from the Lord, for these are the Lord's decrees, laws, commands, and covenant. They are not Israel's laws or laws of some human.

The first curse will come in the form of "sudden terror." The Hebrew root is בהל (bhl, "to be terrified" or "to be confused"). A state of confusion, perplexity, and terror about what is going on is the result of being disoriented from God. Physical ailments will follow in the train of this confusion and fear: "wasting diseases" (such as consumption, dysentery, cholera, typhoid fever, typhus, malaria, tuberculosis, and various types of cancer), and a "fever" that results in the loss of eyesight (v. 16; perhaps something like acute purulent conjunctivitis that spreads rapidly from eye to eye and person to person). Now, instead of five chasing one hundred, Israelites will flee when no one is pursuing them (v. 17).

A second set of curses is set forth in vv. 18-20 —all conditioned on the fact that the disobedience continues and that no response has been given to the first set of curses that God sends to turn them back. The judgment of God will be turned up "seven times" higher (v. 18; see also 21, 24, 28). The number seven is a definite number for an indefinite amount of increase in the severity of the judgments. The number seven is also chosen, no doubt, as a reminder of the whole religion in which the number seven and the sabbatical principle function so frequently, e.g., the seventh day, the seventh month, the seventh year. By reason of Israel's continued provocation of God, its troubles will also become more aggravated, not as a retaliatory device on God's part, but as a further stimulus to capture Israel's attention. If Israel had obeyed simply by hearing the word of God, there would have been no need to capture its attention through the

events of history. Alas, the text predicts that Israel will often turn tone-deaf to the proclaimed word, and so the same love of God that sent the word of the prophets will now send a message of love in the tragedies of life, hoping that the nation will be forced by desperation to cry out to God for forgiveness and love once again. The whole exercise is solely to capture the hearts of faith so that Israel can live by a faith that expresses itself in obedience once again.

In this second series of curses, it will be as if the sky is sealed up and the rain is unable to break through. What has previously been promised about the rain coming in its season when Israel walks in obedience with God (v. 3) is now withdrawn because of disobedience. The heavens will seem to be turned into iron, and the ground will become as hard as bronze from the sun beating down unmercifully on the dry land. Trying to work the soil will be a fruitless task (v. 20), for it will only be a waste of strength. Neither will the trees yield their fruit. It will all be a hopeless cause. Israel is warned not to attempt to wander away from the Lord in disobedience, for the results predicted here will be awesome and mind-boggling.

The third curse will result in wild animals being let loose in their towns and countryside (vv. 21-22). This is the reverse of the blessing promised in v. 6b, where God promises that the beasts will be held in check and be removed far from the populated and farmed areas in deference to Israel's obedience. Ezekiel knew the reality of this threat, for he too warned about the presence of wild animals for a disobedient nation (see Ezek 5:17; 14:15, 21). Once again, the heat is turned up "seven times over" (v. 21). So desperate will conditions become that the beasts will no longer find food in the fields; therefore, the savage brutes will roam into the settled areas preying on livestock, children, and even adults (cf. 2 Kgs 17:25-26).

The fourth curse is the threat of war (vv. 23-26). The fact that all this is coming personally from the Lord is stressed in the text by the reduplication of the personal pronoun "I, [yes] I" (v. 24; cf. vv. 16, 28, 32 in the Hebrew text; NIV and NRSV render some of these repetitions of the pronoun "I" as "I myself").

The previous three curses are intended to lead the people to repent; alas, they have only made the people more adamant and resolute in their sin and disobedience.

This threat of war carries with it the accompanying cousins of plague, captivity, enslavement, and possible famine. The "sword" will fall upon the people "to avenge the breaking of the covenant" (v. 25). There is no way the Israelites can back out of the covenant, for the sword of their enemies will rise up by way of judgment against them. As the people flee from the sword into the walled cities, the crowding together will lead to an outbreak of pestilence that will kill both humans and animals (cf. Amos 4:10). Eventually, the city walls will be breached, the women will probably be violated, and the populace will be forced to go into internment in exile. In the meantime, as the besieged city awaits the inevitable, bread itself will become so scarce that one oven will be more than adequate for ten women to bake in, and the bread will be so little in volume that it will need to be doled out by weight (v. 26; cf. Hos 4:10; Mic 6:14).

If repentance still is not forthcoming, in this future day when Israel abandons the Lord and the covenant, a fifth curse will be imposed on top of the other judgments (vv. 27-33). As Israel's hostility toward the Lord grows, so does the Lord's "anger" or "fury" (v. 28). The famine will lead to the most horrible spectacle of any imaginable, for parents, out of desperation, will eat the flesh of their children (v. 29). Unfortunately, this prophecy was no mere idle threat, for as Deut 28:53-57 also warned, cannibalism did occur in some of Israel's most critical hours, especially during the Babylonian siege of Jerusalem (see 2 Kgs 6:28-29; Jer 19:9; Lam 2:20; 4:10; Ezek 5:10).[126]

Furthermore, the spectacle of the idols erected to Baal and Astoreth will need to be destroyed once and for all. The word used for the "idols," (גלולים gillûlîm), is the worst word imaginable in Hebrew. Ezekiel used this word thirty-nine times as he drew a parallel between human excrement and the form of the idol images. It is the most contemptuous term possible in the Hebrew language. So much for the biblical writer's estimate of what the idols were all about!

The cities will be laid waste, it is further warned, along with "your sanctuaries" (v. 31);

apparently, the plural reference is to all the pagan installations, as opposed to "my sanctuary" in v. 2! No more will the delightful aromas of the sacrificial offerings be the bases for God's pleasure; they will be things of the past.

So desolate will the land become that even Israel's enemies will be appalled. In the meantime, those who survive all of this will be scattered among the nations, and the Diaspora will be on (vv. 31-33). This will be the sixth, and final, curse. While the nation is in exile, the land will enjoy the sabbatical years that Israel failed to observe (v. 34). Based on the 70 years of Babylonian exile, it appears that the nation went 490 years without observing what Leviticus 25 urges (see Jer 25:11). This would be a period from approximately King Saul's time (c. 1100 BCE) until the fall of Jerusalem in 587 BCE. There is no need, however, to work out any exact number of years, for it appears to be a round number dealing with a rather extended period when Israel forgot God.

Meanwhile, those who are left in the land (vv. 36-37), who once lived in "stubborn pride" (v. 19), will now be reduced to frightened cowards, whose hearts are made so "fearful" (מרך mōrek, from the verb meaning "to be soft," "to be tender") that a falling leaf will send them into panic. Moreover, those who go into exile will see their numbers diminish steadily, and they will "waste away" in the land of their captivity (vv. 38-39).

26:40-46. But God will not totally abandon the covenant or forget the obligation to complete what has been promised. This third and final section of the chapter has as its central promise that God will "remember" the covenant with Jacob, Isaac, and Abraham and will "remember the land" as well (v. 42). Actually, there is no Hebrew word to represent the word *with* before each of the patriarchs. Thus the translation should place the emphasis on God's covenant; and Abraham, Isaac, and Jacob may merely be addressed in the vocative here: "I will remember my covenant, O Jacob; my covenant, O Isaac; my covenant, O Abraham."

But in the biblical context, remembering is more than a cognitive activity; remembering is equivalent to doing. Thus the Lord remembers the covenant with the patriarchs when observing the vigor with which the Egyptians pressed the Israelites into making bricks in Egypt (see Exod 6:5-

126. See also Josephus *War* 6.15-32 [3-4].

6). When the Lord "remembered" Hannah (see 1 Sam 1:19), it was more than a sudden recollection of what she had been asking for in prayer in the preceding years; instead, she became pregnant as God acted on the request she had been making in prayer for a son. In a similar way, the Lord remembered the "holy covenant" with Abraham and the house of David (Luke 1:72 NIV), and as a result, Jesus was born. Therefore, God would likewise remember the promise made with Israel about the land, for God's covenants and promises are "irrevocable" (Rom 11:28-29 NIV).

What the people of Israel need to do is to "confess their sins and the sins of their fathers" (v. 40). The principle of the unity of the generations and the corporate solidarity of the nation is repeatedly appealed to in the OT.[127] Although Deut 24:16 makes it clear that children must not be put to death for the sins of the fathers (as does Ezekiel 18), there is another sense in which what the individual does has such an effect on the whole group that its benefits or judgments are shared with the whole group. Thus, when Abraham was blessed, so were his descendants (see Gen 26:2-5); when Achan sinned, all "Israel . . . sinned" (Josh 7:11 NIV). Just as one traitor can have devastating effects on the survival of the whole battalion, so one sinner (or one saint) can affect the whole group. Confession, then, must be more than a request for forgiveness for one's personal sins; it must also be for the group and nation that one is part of. If there is no acknowl-edgment of the sin that has led to the dispersion of the nation, Hosea represents God as promising not to return to the nation "until they acknowledge their guilt" (Hos 5:15 NRSV). For the nation had committed "treachery" (מעל ma'al), i.e., they had betrayed and attacked what had belonged to God (Lev 26:40; a concept also found in Ezek 17:20; 18:24; 39:23; cf. Lev 5:14-16), and they had provoked an encounter ("made me hostile") between themselves and God (Lev. 26:41).

What is needed is repentance by Israel. More than a physical circumcision, they need a "circumcision of the heart" (a concept found in Deut 10:16; 30:6; Jer 4:4; 9:25-26; Acts 7:51; Rom 2:29). Actually, God's law never emphasizes merely the external practice of religion; it all begins in the heart, or it is not at all real.[128] Human beings might look on the outward appearances, but the Lord looks on the heart (see 1 Sam 16:7). The Israelites need to humble themselves first, as illustrated by the humble and corporate prayer of Daniel (see 9:4-19). They also need to "pay for their sin" (v. 41). And pay they will, for Isa 40:1-2 had to comfort the people in the Babylonian exile who had paid "double for all her sins" (NIV).

"Yet in spite of [all] this" (v. 44), God will never totally abandon or reject the people forever. God can never completely destroy them after all that has been promised and done for them. To deny what has been promised to Israel would require a denial of God's own self. Therefore, a day will come when "all Israel will be saved" (Rom 11:26, 29 NIV). As late as 518 BCE, much later than the return from Babylon in 536 BCE, the prophet Zechariah still held out the same hope that Lev 26:44-45 promised:

I will restore them
    because I have compassion on them. . . .
I will signal for them
    and gather them in.
Surely I will redeem them;
    they will be as numerous as before.
Though I scatter them among the peoples,
    yet in distant lands they will remember me.
They and their children will survive,
    and they will return. . . .
and there will not be room enough for them" (Zech 10:6-10 NIV)

God is the Lord (v. 45) and will act on the basis of the covenant.

The chapter concludes with a summary (v. 46), reminding all that these are the decrees, laws, and regulations that the Lord established on Mount Sinai with the Israelites through the Lord's servant Moses.

---

127. See the discussion "Corporate Solidarity," in Kaiser, *Toward Old Testament Ethics*, 67-70.

128. On the case for Old Testament ethics as internal, see Kaiser, *Toward Old Testament Ethics*, 7-10.

REFLECTIONS

1. The significance of singling out the sabbath and the sanctuary may be exactly as Andrew Bonar concluded: "All declension and decay may be said to be begun whenever we see these two ordinances despised—the *Sabbath* and the *Sanctuary.* They are the *outward* fence around the *inward love* commanded in ver. 1."[129]

2. The promises and blessings of God do not exempt God's people from obedience. Instead, they were meant to be encouragements to keep on believing and remain obedient to God's expressed will. In the same way, these blessings and promises were not meant to exempt the people of God from praying for what might be realized; rather, they were given to instruct them and us as to what we should pray for, lest we pray in error and thereby miss the intended proofs of God's love.

3. The judgments and curses of God were never visited on mortals in a vindictive way, but ever and always as another proof that God loved and cared so much that if the people refused to hear the word that had been sent, God would speak to them out of the events of life, so that erring believers might all the more quickly be restored to favor.

4. It would be the height of inconsistency to affirm that God would forgive Israel's sin when the people confessed their sin and the sin of their fathers, but then deny the second half of the promise that God would restore Israel to their land once again (vv. 42, 44-45). To affirm one part of the promise is to affirm the other part about the land. In a similar way, Jesus implied that when "the times of the Gentiles are fulfilled" (Luke 21:24 NIV), and Jerusalem is no longer trodden down under the feet of the Gentiles, the city and the land will be restored to Israel again.

5. The call to "remember" the Lord, even as it is given in the invitation in the celebration of the sacrament or ordinance of the Eucharist, is an invitation to do more than to go through a cerebral exercise. Instead, it calls for the accompanying deeds that are in conformity with the gracious works of this One who has done so much for us. In a like manner, all calls to remember the Lord in the OT text are invitations to action and life-styles that evidence our gratitude and appreciation for all that has been done for us.

6. There are corporate aspects to sin that our Western individualism quickly casts aside. But the fact remains that believers are their nation's keepers. Therefore, what affects the poor, the disenfranchised, the weak, the despised, the immoral, the hateful, and wrathful persons in our society also affects the whole group sooner or later—both for ill and for good. There is no way in which children of God can claim that these matters are of no concern to them. Rather, they must be occasions for acts of compassion, deeds of mercy, and prayers of forgiveness for the whole group, whether they are part of the believing community or not. Otherwise, where will God find persons to stand in the gap and be among that remnant for whom the majority might still experience divine love and mercy?

7. The promise that God would come and dwell in the tabernacle would receive a new impetus when the living Word would become flesh and would "tabernacle in the midst of us" (John 1:14, author's trans.). But even the incarnate Messiah who walked on earth among mortals for thirty years would pale in comparison with the final epiphany of Christ (see Rev 21:3), who would one day forever come to dwell among the people of God.

129. Andrew A. Bonar, *A Commentary on Leviticus* (London: Banner of Truth Trust, 1966) 473 [originally published in 1846]. Emphases belong to Bonar.

EPILOGUE: ENTIRE DEDICATION TO THE LORD

NIV

27 The LORD said to Moses, ²"Speak to the Israelites and say to them: 'If anyone makes a special vow to dedicate persons to the LORD by giving equivalent values, ³set the value of a male between the ages of twenty and sixty at fifty shekels*ᵃ* of silver, according to the sanctuary shekel*ᵇ*; ⁴and if it is a female, set her value at thirty shekels.*ᶜ* ⁵If it is a person between the ages of five and twenty, set the value of a male at twenty shekels*ᵈ* and of a female at ten shekels.*ᵉ* ⁶If it is a person between one month and five years, set the value of a male at five shekels*ᶠ* of silver and that of a female at three shekels*ᵍ* of silver. ⁷If it is a person sixty years old or more, set the value of a male at fifteen shekels*ʰ* and of a female at ten shekels. ⁸If anyone making the vow is too poor to pay the specified amount, he is to present the person to the priest, who will set the value for him according to what the man making the vow can afford.

⁹" 'If what he vowed is an animal that is acceptable as an offering to the LORD, such an animal given to the LORD becomes holy. ¹⁰He must not exchange it or substitute a good one for a bad one, or a bad one for a good one; if he should substitute one animal for another, both it and the substitute become holy. ¹¹If what he vowed is a ceremonially unclean animal—one that is not acceptable as an offering to the LORD—the animal must be presented to the priest, ¹²who will judge its quality as good or bad. Whatever value the priest then sets, that is what it will be. ¹³If the

ᵃ3 That is, about 1 1/4 pounds (about 0.6 kilogram); also in verse 16
ᵇ3 That is, about 2/5 ounce (about 11.5 grams); also in verse 25
ᶜ4 That is, about 12 ounces (about 0.3 kilogram)   ᵈ5 That is, about 8 ounces (about 0.2 kilogram)   ᵉ5 That is, about 4 ounces (about 110 grams); also in verse 7   ᶠ6 That is, about 2 ounces (about 55 grams)   ᵍ6 That is, about 1 1/4 ounces (about 35 grams)
ʰ7 That is, about 6 ounces (about 170 grams)

NRSV

27 The LORD spoke to Moses, saying: ²Speak to the people of Israel and say to them: When a person makes an explicit vow to the LORD concerning the equivalent for a human being, ³the equivalent for a male shall be: from twenty to sixty years of age the equivalent shall be fifty shekels of silver by the sanctuary shekel. ⁴If the person is a female, the equivalent is thirty shekels. ⁵If the age is from five to twenty years of age, the equivalent is twenty shekels for a male and ten shekels for a female. ⁶If the age is from one month to five years, the equivalent for a male is five shekels of silver, and for a female the equivalent is three shekels of silver. ⁷And if the person is sixty years old or over, then the equivalent for a male is fifteen shekels, and for a female ten shekels. ⁸If any cannot afford the equivalent, they shall be brought before the priest and the priest shall assess them; the priest shall assess them according to what each one making a vow can afford.

9If it concerns an animal that may be brought as an offering to the LORD, any such that may be given to the LORD shall be holy. ¹⁰Another shall not be exchanged or substituted for it, either good for bad or bad for good; and if one animal is substituted for another, both that one and its substitute shall be holy. ¹¹If it concerns any unclean animal that may not be brought as an offering to the LORD, the animal shall be presented before the priest. ¹²The priest shall assess it: whether good or bad, according to the assessment of the priest, so it shall be. ¹³But if it is to be redeemed, one-fifth must be added to the assessment.

14If a person consecrates a house to the LORD, the priest shall assess it: whether good or bad, as the priest assesses it, so it shall stand. ¹⁵And if the

NIV

owner wishes to redeem the animal, he must add a fifth to its value.

¹⁴"'If a man dedicates his house as something holy to the LORD, the priest will judge its quality as good or bad. Whatever value the priest then sets, so it will remain. ¹⁵If the man who dedicates his house redeems it, he must add a fifth to its value, and the house will again become his.

¹⁶"'If a man dedicates to the LORD part of his family land, its value is to be set according to the amount of seed required for it—fifty shekels of silver to a homer[a] of barley seed. ¹⁷If he dedicates his field during the Year of Jubilee, the value that has been set remains. ¹⁸But if he dedicates his field after the Jubilee, the priest will determine the value according to the number of years that remain until the next Year of Jubilee, and its set value will be reduced. ¹⁹If the man who dedicates the field wishes to redeem it, he must add a fifth to its value, and the field will again become his. ²⁰If, however, he does not redeem the field, or if he has sold it to someone else, it can never be redeemed. ²¹When the field is released in the Jubilee, it will become holy, like a field devoted to the LORD; it will become the property of the priests.[b]

²²"'If a man dedicates to the LORD a field he has bought, which is not part of his family land, ²³the priest will determine its value up to the Year of Jubilee, and the man must pay its value on that day as something holy to the LORD. ²⁴In the Year of Jubilee the field will revert to the person from whom he bought it, the one whose land it was. ²⁵Every value is to be set according to the sanctuary shekel, twenty gerahs to the shekel.

²⁶"'No one, however, may dedicate the first-born of an animal, since the firstborn already belongs to the LORD; whether an ox[c] or a sheep, it is the LORD's. ²⁷If it is one of the unclean animals, he may buy it back at its set value, adding a fifth of the value to it. If he does not redeem it, it is to be sold at its set value.

²⁸"'But nothing that a man owns and devotes[d] to the LORD—whether man or animal or family

NRSV

one who consecrates the house wishes to redeem it, one-fifth shall be added to its assessed value, and it shall revert to the original owner.

16If a person consecrates to the LORD any inherited landholding, its assessment shall be in accordance with its seed requirements: fifty shekels of silver to a homer of barley seed. 17If the person consecrates the field as of the year of jubilee, that assessment shall stand; 18but if the field is consecrated after the jubilee, the priest shall compute the price for it according to the years that remain until the year of jubilee, and the assessment shall be reduced. 19And if the one who consecrates the field wishes to redeem it, then one-fifth shall be added to its assessed value, and it shall revert to the original owner; 20but if the field is not redeemed, or if it has been sold to someone else, it shall no longer be redeemable. 21But when the field is released in the jubilee, it shall be holy to the LORD as a devoted field; it becomes the priest's holding. 22If someone consecrates to the LORD a field that has been purchased, which is not a part of the inherited landholding, 23the priest shall compute for it the proportionate assessment up to the year of jubilee, and the assessment shall be paid as of that day, a sacred donation to the LORD. 24In the year of jubilee the field shall return to the one from whom it was bought, whose holding the land is. 25All assessments shall be by the sanctuary shekel: twenty gerahs shall make a shekel.

26A firstling of animals, however, which as a firstling belongs to the LORD, cannot be consecrated by anyone; whether ox or sheep, it is the LORD's. 27If it is an unclean animal, it shall be ransomed at its assessment, with one-fifth added; if it is not redeemed, it shall be sold at its assessment.

28Nothing that a person owns that has been devoted to destruction for the LORD, be it human or animal, or inherited landholding, may be sold or redeemed; every devoted thing is most holy to the LORD. 29No human beings who have been devoted to destruction can be ransomed; they shall be put to death.

30All tithes from the land, whether the seed from the ground or the fruit from the tree, are the LORD's; they are holy to the LORD. 31If persons

NIV

land—may be sold or redeemed; everything so devoted is most holy to the LORD.

²⁹" 'No person devoted to destruction*ᵃ may be ransomed; he must be put to death.

³⁰" 'A tithe of everything from the land, whether grain from the soil or fruit from the trees, belongs to the LORD; it is holy to the LORD. ³¹If a man redeems any of his tithe, he must add a fifth of the value to it. ³²The entire tithe of the herd and flock—every tenth animal that passes under the shepherd's rod—will be holy to the LORD. ³³He must not pick out the good from the bad or make any substitution. If he does make a substitution, both the animal and its substitute become holy and cannot be redeemed.' "

³⁴These are the commands the LORD gave Moses on Mount Sinai for the Israelites.

*ᵃ29 The Hebrew term refers to the irrevocable giving over of things or persons to the LORD, often by totally destroying them.

NRSV

wish to redeem any of their tithes, they must add one-fifth to them. ³²All tithes of herd and flock, every tenth one that passes under the shepherd's staff, shall be holy to the LORD. ³³Let no one inquire whether it is good or bad, or make substitution for it; if one makes substitution for it, then both it and the substitute shall be holy and cannot be redeemed.

34These are the commandments that the LORD gave to Moses for the people of Israel on Mount Sinai.

COMMENTARY

Almost everyone has noticed how chap. 27 appears to be somewhat anticlimactic, for the previous chapter, with its alternative prospect of blessings or curses, depending on how people have responded to God's covenant, surely makes an appropriate conclusion to the book. But it is not necessary to suppose that chap. 27 is mislocated or even that it is a later addition to the book.

A fairly straightforward explanation might well be that what has preceded in chaps. 1–26 has all been by way of obligatory duties mandated by Israel's Lord; what follows in chap. 27 is of an optional nature. Indeed, the special vows listed in chap. 27 are not to be required of anyone, for Deut 23:22 expressly teaches, "But if you refrain from making a vow, you will not be guilty" (NIV). Accordingly, the threats and promises of chap. 26 could not apply; that is why this chapter is not placed within the scope and compass of the earlier chapters. In that sense, then, the placement of this material at the end of the book is exactly where it should be.

Nevertheless, the instinct to make vows to God,

even though they are not mandated, and even though there is no sin in refraining from doing so, has always been part of the human heart. Three impulses lead persons to offer vows: (a) the desire to procure something from God in exchange for making a vow, (b) the desire to thank God for some special favor God granted, and (c) the urge to spontaneously express love to the Lord.

The biblical text often refers to vows. Jacob offered vows to God while he was at Bethel (see Gen 28:20-22); Jephthah made his foolish vow as he went off to battle (see Judg 11:30-31); Hannah made her vow to God in the sanctuary at Shiloh, if God would grant her a son (see 1 Sam 1:11); and Absalom offered his vow at Geshur, if the Lord would allow him to return to Jerusalem (see 2 Sam 15:8). Many other vows are made or commented on (see Deut 23:22-24; Pss 22:25; 61:5, 8; 65:1; 66:13-14; 76:11; 116:14; Prov 20:25; Eccl 5:3-4; Isa 19:21; Jonah 1:16; Nah 1:15; Mal 1:14).

Since there will always be occasions for making some kind of vow to God, a series of questions arises in connection with the practice. First, what objects, beings, or possessions can one properly offer to God? Second, what if, after the stress or impulse of the moment has passed, someone who has vowed something suddenly feels that it has been a mistake and wants to be free to recall it? Third, if one can recall a vow, what are the conditions and what are the penalties?

This chapter seeks to settle these types of questions, among other matters. Two of the three sections of this chapter are marked off by clear formulas that function as rhetorical devices for such divisions of the text. The first two sections begin with "if anyone" (אִישׁ כִּי 'iš kî) in vv. 2 and 14. The subsidiary cases are introduced by "and if" (וְאִם we'im) in vv. 4, 5, 6, 7, 8, 9, 11, and 13 in the first section dealing with persons and animals and in vv. 16, 17, 18, 19, 20, and 22 in the second section dealing with the dedication of houses and lands. No such formulas or rhetorical devices can be observed in the third section; it appears to be more of a potpourri of items collected in one place for the sake of convenience.

The resulting structural components derived from the rhetorical devices already noted are as follows: introduction (v. 1); dedication of persons and animals (vv. 2-13), including vowing persons (vv. 2-8), vowing clean animals (vv. 9-10), vowing unclean animals (vv. 11-13); dedication of houses and lands (vv. 14-24), including vowing houses (vv. 14-15), vowing lands (vv. 16-24); assorted rules on other types of vows (vv. 25-33), including the sanctuary shekel value (v. 25), restrictions on vows (vv. 26-33).

Chapter 27, then, rules that persons may vow to God persons, beasts belonging to them, their dwelling places, or the right to some part of their lands. On the other hand, "the firstborn of an animal" (vv. 26-27), anything "devoted to destruction" (vv. 28-29), and the "tithe" (vv. 30-33) may not be used as special vows to God because they already belong to God and are naturally due to God by way of a previous dedication.

27:2-13. The first law is the law of vowing persons (vv. 2-8). It is the most basic kind of vow. In it persons dedicate themselves or their children to the service of God. Thus a person would be attached to the sanctuary as a servant to carry out duties in connection with its elaborate sets of jobs. In this manner, young Samuel was vowed to the

Lord by his mother, and he remained there in the service of the sanctuary (see 1 Samuel 1–2).

Normally, however, the tribe of Levi provided more than enough labor power to carry out the various duties. In this case, the "equivalent value" (v. 2) of the service would be donated to the sanctuary in silver. One key source for understanding this system of equivalents is 2 Kgs 12:4-5, where King Jehoash of Judah needed funds to carry out the repair of the Temple. Jehoash said to the priests, "Collect all the money [silver] that is brought as sacred offerings to the temple of the LORD—the money collected in the census, the money received from personal vows כֶּסֶף נַפְשׁוֹת עֶרְכּוֹ kesep napšôt 'erkô, "silver equivalent of persons"] and the money brought voluntarily to the temple" (NIV). The term עֵרֶךְ ('ērek, "equivalent") is the identical term used in Lev 27:2-5. This allows us to see that most did, as a matter of fact, commute their dedicated service into silver, which was then donated to the sanctuary for such needs as those indicated in Jehoash's renovation of the Temple.

The translation of v. 2 has not always been agreed upon by all for the verb יַפְלִא (yapli'), with the final aleph, presumably a variant for the final heh in the root פלה (pālâ, meaning "to set apart"). But it also reflected the verb פלא (pālā', "to do difficult things, in a wondrous or glorious manner"). Thus the NIV has rendered it "to make a special vow." The noun for "vow" is נֵדֶר (nēder), which refers to the substance of what is vowed, not the act of vowing itself or its pronouncement.

The following estimation of values for votive offerings was operative:

Age	Male	Female
20 to 60 years	50 shekels	30 shekels
5 to 20 years	20 shekels	10 shekels
Over 60 years	15 shekels	10 shekels
1 month to 5 years	5 shekels	3 shekels

The highest value goes to the male who is in the prime of life and whose ability to carry out the work connected with the sanctuary is at its peak. The lower valuation of females has nothing to do with any perceived notion of worth or alleged negative attitudes toward women. The differentiation in estimates of value is not tied to personal worth, dignity, or esteem; instead, it has to do with the fact that much of the work involves such heavy labor as carrying the weight of heavy beasts offered as sacrifices, which normally men are able to assume more readily than most women. Thus the chart of values represents *labor value*, not personal value. The same factor can be seen in persons over sixty years of age, for their strength also would have subsided; thus their valuation is lowered. But this does not indicate that the society considers older people of less worth than younger people.

These valuations are large, for an average person earned only one shekel per month.[130] Apparently, the values are deliberately set high to restrain persons from easily vowing themselves or their children in the heat and passion of the moment.

It is also possible to vow animals to the Lord for the sanctuary (vv. 9-13). If the vowed animal can be used for a sacrifice, in that it is one of the clean animals, the vow is unalterable and irrevocable. Should persons making the vow change their minds and think that, for some reason, the vow is a mistake or too generous and attempt to substitute an inferior animal (see Mal 1:8), both animals, the vowed one and the substitute, are considered holy, and both are therefore forfeited to the sanctuary.

Bargaining is not permitted. The decision and the value set by the priest are final (v. 12). If the vowed animal is an unclean animal, the priest then sets a price value on it, presumably for which it will then be sold, and the proceeds will go to the sanctuary.

Persons who wish to redeem an unclean animal that has been vowed can do so by adding another 20 percent value to its price before buying it back. This provision appears to be included to extricate persons from what they later consider to be rash vows.

27:14-24. A house can be vowed to the Lord (vv. 14-15). However, if the one vowing the house wishes to redeem it, the person has to pay a fifth more in price into the treasury of the sanctuary to do so. The houses referred in this case, however, appear to be ones inside the walled cities that can be bought and sold (cf. 25:29-31); houses that are part of the family estate cannot be bought and sold in perpetuity, as chap. 25 advises.

Consecration of land for a vow is much more complicated (vv. 16-24), since in the year of jubilee it reverts to its owner. Two cases are treated here. The first case (vv. 16-21) involves a field that belongs to an Israelite by inheritance, and the second case (vv. 22-24) of a field that has come to someone by a purchase. What is clear is that the land itself is not consecrated but the crops that it may produce until the year the land is due to be returned to its original owners.

In evaluating the land, the priest is to set its value according to the amount of seed it requires to obtain a certain yield (v. 16). The formula used here is the extent of the area required to sow a field with a homer of seed. The term חמר (*hōmer*) usually indicated a dry measure equal to the load a donkey (hence its derivation from חמור *ḥămôr*) could carry, estimated to be from 3.8 to 6.5 bushels. In Ezek 45:11, a homer equals ten ephahs (approximately 134 to 241 liters or 29 to 53 gallons).[131] The point is that the value of the field is the value of the amount of seed it took to sow it.

Verse 16*b* is somewhat ambiguous, depending on the reference of the word *seed*. Does it refer to the "harvest [seed]" of the land, or does it refer to the "seed [that was sown]" in the field? Wenham and Roland de Vaux argue in their commentaries for the crop or harvest as the meaning, but most others take it the way we have argued for here—the amount of seed needed to sow a field.[132]

The situation in vv. 20-21 is ambiguous. One view is that the man who vowed a field turned around and sold the same field to another man, which would result in a penalty, such as v. 21 mentions. That shady dealer would lose everything, including the return of the field when the year of jubilee rolled around again. Another view is that the man gave the land to the tabernacle without redeeming it; in that case it was an irrevocable gift. Or it was likewise an irrevocable gift if he sold the land for use until the jubilee; at that time, of course, it must still revert to the sanctuary in the year of jubilee. This later case would make it similar to our modern future bequests. A third view is that the man dedicated

---

130. See de Vaux, *Ancient Israel,* 76. De Vaux obtained this figure of one shekel per month from the Code of Hammurabi. Since slaves generally went for thirty to fifty shekels each, it would appear that in the legal limit of six years for Hebrew slaves, an indentured person would pay off approximately twice his value during the seventy-two months at one shekel per month.

131. See de Vaux, *Ancient Israel,* 202. Wenham, *Leviticus,* 340, mentioned that in Mesopotamia the standard price for barley was one shekel per homer. This would make the annual valuation of one shekel per a year for a field of one homer to be quite appropriate in this context of Leviticus 27.

132. Wenham, *Leviticus,* 340 and n. 8; De Vaux, *Ancient Israel,* 168.

the land to the sanctuary, but the priests did not have time to work the land. Therefore, the one making the vow worked the land for them, paying the redemption money while keeping the produce for himself. But if that person decided to lease the field to another person, the field did not revert to the one making the vow in the year of jubilee; it went instead to the sanctuary.

It is impossible to say which of these three views is the correct one, for the passage is so brief. It is clear, however, that the provision is meant to be penal, for the field during the time of the vow belonged to the Lord in a special sense.

A somewhat different case is taken up in vv. 22-24. A person purchases land that does not belong to his paternal inheritance and then dedicates it to the Lord. In the year of jubilee, that land goes back to its original owners according to the law of Lev 25:28. However, the man must pay the full estimated value of the crops that land would produce up to the year of jubilee, for if the owner exercised his right of redemption in the interim, the vow would go unfulfilled. To avoid having any liens against the land and to protect the original owner's right to redeem the land at any time, the instruction is that the vow is to be paid up front in full.

27:25-33. The remaining verses deal with three classes of property, which are excluded from being dedicated by vows to the Lord. First, the value of the "sanctuary shekel" is set at "twenty gerahs to the shekel [or twenty grains of silver]" (v. 25). A shekel weighed a half ounce (twelve grams), but there was lot of variation, depending on local standards. All disputes, however, were to be settled by weighing against the sanctuary shekel, which functioned as a sort of bureau of weights and measure.

The first of the three cases discussed here is the "firstborn of an animal" (vv. 26-27). The firstborn of a clean animal already belongs to the Lord (see Exod 13:2, 15; 34:19); therefore, it cannot be given back to the Lord a second time. If the vow involves an unclean animal—e.g., a donkey—it can be redeemed by paying a fifth more, according to the value usually set on it by the priests. If the one making the vow does not choose to redeem it, however, the animal will be sold according to its value and the money given to the sanctuary.

The second case involves the exclusion of vowing things already "devoted to destruction" (vv. 28-29). The law of חרם (*herem*)[133] seems the strangest of all the laws to Western readers, who have no analogies with which to compare it. But just as there is a positive consecration of persons and things to God, so there is a negative setting apart of some persons and things for destruction. To be sure, this is not something that was done often or precipitously. Only after a long period of chasing men and women with goodness and kindness did God dedicate something for destruction, as in the case where certain cities were marked off (e.g., in the conquest, the city of Jericho), or persons and things in those proscribed places were marked off for final and total annihilation. Historically, this practice of *herem* was associated with wars. This practice of *herem* was also recorded as being in vogue among Israel's neighbors in ancient times, for King Mesha of Moab (a contemporary of King Ahab; see 2 Kgs 3:4) devoted to his god Chemosh the towns he conquered for destruction. This he recorded, with the use of the equivalent cognate Moabite word to the Hebrew *herem*, in his famous Moabite Stone.

In the biblical context, *herem* is carried out as a punishment. To take some of the souvenirs of war from a site placed under this "ban," or under "devotion to destruction," as Achan took from the Jericho military theater (see Josh 7), and then try to dedicate them to the Lord as a part of a vow is to take something that already is dedicated and offer it, as it were, a second time. It already belongs to the Lord!

There are also judicial dedications to destruction, when certain of the Lord's commandments are violated (see Exod 22:20; Lev 20:2; Deut 13:13-16).

Verse 28 presents to both ancient and modern interpreters a serious difficulty, for one would not ordinarily speak of personally and voluntarily proscribing one's possessions or a field, much less someone else's things. Normally, such a serious matter was imposed from a divine source or by those in judicial or leadership positions. The rabbis gave two closely related explanations to the same problem: (a) Verse 28 may be speaking of a person who vowed to devote his property, or

---

133. For a fuller explanation of all that was involved in this "ban," see Kaiser, *Toward Old Testament Ethics,* 74-75.

(b) it may be speaking of one who took an oath on some other matter, but who failed to carry out that oath; consequently, that person's property was forfeited as *ḥerem*. In both cases the oath was a binding obligation; no longer could it be thought of as a voluntary act.

Finally, there is the matter of tithes (vv. 30-33). Two types are discussed: a tenth of all the produce of the field, and a tenth of the flocks and herds. Here, then, is the third and last of the exclusions to what can be vowed to the Lord. Since the tithe is already owed, as it were, to the Lord, it cannot be made the object of a special vow. It is impossible to give away what already belongs to another; that is the case of the tithe. Numbers 18:21 affirms the same principle: A tenth of all that a person earned was to be given to the Levites for the service of the tabernacle.

The Wellhausian school objected that since Deuteronomy did not mention any other tithe than the produce of the field, the reference to the tithe of the flock was an indication that its inclusion in our present book of Leviticus depended on a late Priestly source from the post-exilic period. But it is possible to urge the exact opposite from the same evidence: that we have here in Leviticus the earliest form of the law on the tithe. Furthermore, Jacob promised a tenth of all that God had given him (see Gen 28:22). Surely that included a tenth of all the increase of his flocks, since he specialized in tending animals at the time. Even earlier than the time of Jacob, Abraham promised to give tithes to Melchizedek (see Gen 14:20).

The book of Leviticus ends with the closing formula of v. 34, referring to all the commands that God had given on Mount Sinai. This colophon refers not only to the opening verse of chap. 25 but also to the total legislation that covered the contents of Leviticus.

REFLECTIONS

1. Do the vows mentioned here, or any others similar to them, have a place in NT ethics and the life of faith? This is an important question, for a great deal of theology hangs on it in many circles. Note, however, that nowhere in the OT are vows represented as anything other than personal, *voluntary* promises made to God. Nowhere in either the OT or the NT do we find the practice of vowing urged, recommended, or mandated. Nevertheless, given the religious impulse of persons to make vows, the writer of Leviticus used the occasion as an opportunity to educate individuals in the legitimate bounds within which vows might be used. Thus Deut 23:22 reminds us that persons are not sinning if they refuse to make a vow. The regulations given in Scripture are meant more as a check against entering into consecrations rashly than as a recommendation for using such devices.

Ecclesiastes 5:5-6 summarizes these points best when it teaches, "It is better not to vow than to make a vow and not fulfill it. Do not let your mouth lead you into sin. And do not protest to the temple messenger, 'My vow was a mistake.' Why should God be angry at what you say and destroy the work of your hands?" (NIV). Thus while vows are nowhere forbidden, there is little, if anything, to say that they are approved. Our Lord's condemnation of the Pharisee's abuse of the vow to justify neglect of one's parents does not imply the propriety of vows in the present era. Nor can we find a permanent example in the apostle Paul's vows (See Acts 18:18; 21:24-26), for they are illustrations of what Paul did without any normative teaching for the church. We conclude, therefore, that nothing urges us to make vows to God, but a great deal is said to warn and caution persons who do make vows and who fail to carry through on them.

2. A most practical question emerges as to the Christian's continued obligation to give a tithe, or one-tenth, of all that is earned. Nothing is mentioned about a specific amount for the tithe in the NT or in the first century of the church. In the fourth century of the church, Jerome, Augustine, and others began to advocate the law of the tenth, or a tithe, for the church. This system passed down through the medieval and Reformed churches. But now that the church in Canada and the United States is not tied to the state, the urgency for some form of steady support has become all the more important.

Two elements must be distinguished in the matter of the tithe: One is moral, and the other is legal. The moral aspect is that believers are urged to set aside to God a fixed proportion of their income. The legal aspect is the precise amount of one-tenth. The moral principle is best stated in 1 Cor 16:2, where Paul urges, "On the first day of every week, each one of you should set aside a sum of money in keeping with [one's] income" (NIV). In that the exact amount is not specified, this principle should not lead to impulsive or capricious giving. Instead, there is to be an orderly, clearly thought-out method of regular giving. But how much? The average minimal giving in the OT was a tenth, but the NT answers with another formula: "See that you also excel in this grace of giving. . . . For you know the grace of our Lord Jesus Christ, that though he was rich, yet for your sakes he became poor, so that you through his poverty might become rich" (2 Cor 8:7, 9 NIV). Our conclusion must be that if a tenth was the minimal amount under the law, how can Christians do any less? Perhaps we should consider not how little but how much we can give, seeing how richly blessed we are in Christ.

3. The book of Leviticus has as its supreme lesson the fact that holiness consists of a full and total consecration of one's whole person to the Lord. It is likewise a call to separate oneself from all that defiles and separates one from being as holy as the Lord God is holy. Leviticus also teaches that the only way to attain this high ideal of holiness, both in its initial inception and in its daily renewal, is through the atoning sacrifice and sole mediation of the High Priest appointed by God. Thus it stands written, "Be holy because I, the LORD your God, am holy" (19:2*b*).

TRANSLITERATION SCHEMA

HEBREW AND ARAMAIC TRANSLITERATION

Consonants:

א	=	'	ט	=	ṭ	פ or ף	=	p
ב	=	b	י	=	y	צ or ץ	=	ṣ
ג	=	g	כ or ך	=	k	ק	=	q
ד	=	d	ל	=	l	ר	=	r
ה	=	h	מ or ם	=	m	שׂ	=	ś
ו	=	w	נ or ן	=	n	שׁ	=	š
ז	=	z	ס	=	s	ת	=	t
ח	=	ḥ	ע	=	'			

Masoretic Pointing:

	Pure-long			Tone-long			Short			Composite	
הָ	=	â		=	ā		=	a		=	ă
ִי	=	ê		=	ē		=	e	or	=	ĕ
or	=	î					=	i			
or ֹו	=	ô		=	ō		=	o		=	ŏ
or ֹו	=	û					=	u			

GREEK TRANSLITERATION

α	=	a	ι	=	i	ρ	=	r
β	=	b	κ	=	k	σ or ς	=	s
γ	=	g	λ	=	l	τ	=	t
δ	=	d	μ	=	m	υ	=	y
ε	=	e	ν	=	n	φ	=	ph
ζ	=	z	ξ	=	x	χ	=	ch
η	=	ē	ο	=	o	ψ	=	ps
θ	=	th	π	=	p	ω	=	ō

INDEX OF MAPS, CHARTS, AND ILLUSTRATIONS

ABBREVIATIONS

General

BCE	Before the Common Era	MT	Masoretic Text
CE	Common Era	NT	New Testament
c.	circa	OG	Old Greek
cent.	century	OL	Old Latin
cf.	compare	OT	Old Testament
chap.	chapter	SP	Samaritan Pentateuch
HB	Hebrew Bible	v(v).	verse(s)
LXX	Septuagint	Vg	Vulgate
MS(S)	manuscript(s)		

Names of Bible Translations

CEV	Contemporary English Version	NIV	New International Version
CSB	Catholic Study Bible	NJB	New Jerusalem Bible
GNB	Good News Bible	NRSV	New Revised Standard Version
JB	Jerusalem Bible	REB	Revised English Bible
KJV	King James Version	RSV	Revised Standard Version
NAB	New American Bible	TNK	Tanakh
NEB	New English Bible		

Names of Biblical Books (with the Apocrypha)

Gen	Nah	1–4 Kgdms	John
Exod	Hab	Add Esth	Acts
Lev	Zeph	Bar	Rom
Num	Hag	Bel	1–2 Cor
Deut	Zech	1–2 Esdr	Gal
Josh	Mal	4 Ezra	Eph
Judg	Ps (Pss)	Jdt	Phil
1–2 Sam	Job	Ep Jer	Col
1–2 Kgs	Prov	1–4 Macc	1–2 Thess
Isa	Ruth	Pr Azar	1–2 Tim
Jer	Cant	Pr Man	Titus
Ezek	Eccl	Sir	Phlm
Hos	Lam	Sus	Heb
Joel	Esth	Tob	Jas
Amos	Dan	Wis	1–2 Pet
Obad	Ezra	Matt	1–3 John
Jonah	Neh	Mark	Jude
Mic	1–2 Chr	Luke	Rev

Names of Pseudepigraphical and Early Patristic Books

Barn.	*Barnabas*	*Sib. Or.*	*Sibylline Oracles*
1–3 Enoch	Ethiopic, Slavonic, Hebrew *Enoch*		

Names of Dead Sea Scrolls and Related Texts

CD	Cairo (Genizah text of the) *Damascus (Document)*
DSS	Dead Sea Scrolls
8Hev XIIgr	Greek Scroll of the Minor Prophets from Nahal Hever
Q	Qumran
1Q, 2Q, etc.	Numbered caves of Qumran, yielding written material; followed by abbreviation of biblical or apocryphal book
4QMMT	*Miqsat Ma'aseh Torah* from Qumran Cave 4
11QtgJob	*Targum of Job* from Qumran Cave 11
4Q246	Aramaic Apocalypse (pseudo-Daniel) from Qumran cave 4
4QpaleoDeutr	Copy of Deuteronomy in paleo-Hebrew script from Qumran cave 4
4QpaleoExod	Copy of Exodus in paleo-Hebrew script from Qumran cave 4

Targumic Material

Tg. Neb.   *Targum of the Prophets*

Orders and Tractates in Mishnaic and Related Literature

'Abot	*'Abot*	*Sabb.*	*Sabbat*
B. Bat.	*Baba Batra*	*Sanh.*	*Sanhedrin*
Ber.	*Berakot*	*Ta'an.*	*Ta'anit*
Dem.	*Demai*	*Yad.*	*Yadayim*
Meg.	*Megilla*		

Other Rabbinic Works

Pesiq. R.	*Pesiqta Rabbati*	*Sipra*	*Sipra*

Commonly Used Periodicals, Reference Works, and Serials

AB	Anchor Bible
ABD	*Anchor Bible Dictionary*
ABRL	Anchor Bible Reference Library
AnBib	Analecta biblica
ANET	J. B. Pritchard (ed.), *Ancient Near Eastern Texts*
ANF	The Ante-Nicene Fathers
BAGD	W. Bauer, W. F. Arndt, F. W. Gingrich, and F. W. Danker, *Greek-English Lexicon of the NT*
BASOR	*Bulletin of the American Schools of Oriental Research*
BDB	F. Brown, S. R. Driver, and C. A. Briggs, *Hebrew and English Lexicon of the Old Testament*
BZAW	Beihefte zur *ZAW*
CBQ	*Catholic Biblical Quarterly*
CBQMS	Catholic Biblical Quarterly—Monograph Series
CTM	*Concordia Theological Monthly*
EvQ	*Evangelical Quarterly*
HAT	Handbuch zum Alten Testament
HBT	*Horizons in Biblical Theology*
HSM	Harvard Semitic Monographs
HTR	*Harvard Theological Review*
HUCA	*Hebrew Union College Annual*
IB	*Interpreter's Bible*
IDB	*Interpreter's Dictionary of the Bible*
IDBSup	Supplementary volume to *IDB*
Int	*Interpretation*
IRT	Issues in Religion and Theology
JAAR	*Journal of the American Academy of Religion*
JAOS	*Journal of the American Oriental Society*
JBL	*Journal of Biblical Literature*
JETS	*Journal of the Evangelical Theological Society*
JPS	Jewish Publication Society
JPSV	Jewish Publication Society Version
JQR	*Jewish Quarterly Review*
JSOT	*Journal for the Study of the Old Testament*
JSOTSup	Journal for the Study of the Old Testament—Supplement Series
JTS	*Journal of Theological Studies*
LTQ	*Lexington Theological Journal*
NICOT	*New International Commentary on the Old Testament*
OBT	Overtures to Biblical Theology
OTL	Old Testament Library
PEQ	*Palestine Exploration Quarterly*
SBL	Society of Biblical Literature
SBLDS	SBL Dissertation Series
SBLMS	SBL Monograph Series
SBT	Studies in Biblical Theology
SJT	*Scottish Journal of Theology*
TD	*Theology Digest*
TLZ	*Theologische Literaturzeitung*
TToday	*Theology Today*
TZ	Theologische Zeitschrift
USQR	*Union Seminary Quarterly Review*
VT	*Vetus Testamentum*
VTSup	Vetus Testamentum, Supplements
WA	M. Luther, Kritische Gesamtausgabe (= "Weimar" edition)
WBC	Word Biblical Commentary
WMANT	Wissenschaftliche Monographien zum Alten und Neuen Testament
ZAW	*Zeitschrift für die alttestamentliche Wissenschaft*
ZTK	*Zeitschrift für Theologie und Kirche*